A CRITICAL LEXICON AND CONCORDANCE TO THE ENGLISH AND GREEK NEW TESTAMENT

Also by E. W. Bullinger

The Book of Job
Commentary on Revelation
The Companion Bible (notes and appendixes)
Great Cloud of Witnesses
How to Enjoy the Bible
Number in Scripture
Ten Sermons on the Second Advent
The Witness of the Stars
Word Studies in the Holy Spirit

A CRITICAL LEXICON AND CONCORDANCE TO THE ENGLISH AND GREEK NEW TESTAMENT

E. W. BULLINGER

Kregel Publications

Grand Rapids, MI 49501

A Critical Lexicon and Concordance to the English and Greek New Testament

Originally published in 1908.

Published in 1999 by Kregel Publications, a division of Kregel, Inc., P.O. Box 2607, Grand Rapids, MI 49501.

ISBN 978-0-8254-2096-2

Printed in the United States of America

6 7 8 9 10 / 15 14 13 12 11

Contents

Originally published in 1877, with later editions in 1886, 1892, and 1908, this enduring work combines a dictionary and concordance in one handy reference volume.

Giving every English word in alphabetical order, Bullinger provides the Greek word or words behind each English word. In addition, there is a list of passages in which each English word occurs with a reference to the Greek word used in each passage. Thus, at one glance, the Greek word with its literal and derivative meanings may be found for every word in the English New Testament.

The English text followed is Bagster's CRITICAL NEW TESTAMENT, a printing of the 1611 King James Version. However, the alterations made in 1683 and 1769 in the King James Version are noted. The Greek text is an eclectic one, based not only on the Textus Receptus (the text behind the KJV) but also on the work of Griesbach, Lachmann, Tischendorf, Tregelles, and Alford, well-known textual scholars of the nineteenth century.

The value of this work is enhanced by a Greek-English index, which lists all Greek words in the New Testament in alphabetical order, together with the English words used to translate them. Also included is a concise Greek grammar.

ADDITIONAL FEATURES

- Vocabulary of New Testament Greek
- Concordance of proper names
- Appendix of biblical references to common pronouns, particles, and conjunctions
- Concordance of variant readings

Preface

"Not unto us, O Lord, not unto us; but unto thy name give glory." Such were the words that filled the author's heart on bringing to a close the labors of nine years, begun amidst the duties of a London parish and continued in various parts of the Master's vineyard; it is the fruit of time redeemed from less noble recreations, and devoted to the Master's service.

The need of such a work arose from the study of certain words of more or less importance, for his own edification and that of certain friends; when the thought occurred that it might be useful to himself and to many others if the work were made complete and rendered accessible to all students of God's Word.

With this view a certain portion was done and submitted to the judgment of some who are renowned for their biblical knowledge and criticism. Their kind expressions of opinion encouraged the author in the prosecution of his design.

It is obvious that such a work could not be designed in a day, and the consequence was, that as it grew, the earlier portions (A, B, and C) were written and rewritten, until the design became complete.

There are but few who will really appreciate the nature and character of the labor demanded by the work, and consequently, the daily need of strength, health, courage, and prayer, to persevere unto the end: "thy God hath commanded thy strength" has indeed been verified by experience, and so has the prayer, "Strengthen, O God, that which thou hast wrought for us."

THE DESIGN OF THE WORK

The design of this work is to give every English word in alphabetical order, and under each, the Greek word or words so translated, with a list of the passages in which the English word occurs, showing by a reference figure which is the Greek word used in each particular passage. Thus, at one view, the Greek word with its literal and derivative meanings may be found for every word in the English New Testament.

The great importance of this will be seen at once, when it is stated

that the same English word is used in the translation of several Greek words. For example, if the word "come" may, in thirty-two passages, be represented by as many Greek words, it surely is most important for the Bible student to know which is the particular word in any given passage, and what is its meaning. It is clear that many useless arguments would be saved if it were known precisely what was the exact meaning and force of the words. The Christian would not confuse his "standing" with his "state" if he knew that in Ephesians 1:6, the word "accepted" denoted that which God has made us by grace, *lovely and acceptable,* and that in 2 Corinthians 5:9, "We labour, that, . . . we may be *accepted* of him," denoted simply *well-pleasing*. He would see at once that we do not and need not labor to *become accepted,* but that we labor to *please* Him *well* because we *are* accepted.

When it is further stated that such an important word as "ordain" is used as the representative of ten different Greek words, "destroy" of ten, "condemn" of five, "to minister" of eight, "holiness" of five, "receive" of eighteen, "say" of eight, "know" of six, "judgment" of nine, and "judge" of six, it will be seen at once how necessary it becomes that we should know exactly the shade of meaning to be given to the word in any particular place.

It is by no means asserted that the meaning given to any word in the lexical portion of the work could, or is to be substituted for that in the English translation, but this is affirmed, that in each case a shade, a tint, or a color will be given to what was before only an outline.

THE GREEK TEXT AND VARIOUS READINGS.

In carrying out the design of this work a difficulty soon arose. The assertion that a certain English word was the translation of a certain Greek word was of course true, but only in part. It was the translation of the Greek word now found in the *Textus Receptus,* i.e. in that Greek Text, used by our translators in their great and important work, and afterwards printed. The *Received Text* of the Greek Testament is the second edition published by the Elzevirs at Leyden in 1633. The first Elzevir edition (Leyden 1624) varies very slightly from the second, and the second was a collation of the first, with Robert Stephens' third edition 1550. The Text of our Authorized version however agrees more nearly with Beza's fifth edition (1598) than with any other. In eighty places it agrees with Beza's fifth, when it disagrees with Stephens' third, and while it agrees with Stephens' third in only about forty places, where it disagrees with Beza's fifth, it differs from both editions in about half a dozen places.*D Little is known of the MSS used in preparing

* The Elzevirs edition differs from Stephens' third edition in about 150 places

these various editions, but it is certain that they were neither many, nor ancient, nor of much weight as to their critical authority.†

There being no reason therefore why Stephens' Text should be exalted by Protestants into a similar position as that of the Clementine Vulgate by the Council of Trent, various revisions have been made from time to time by persons who have made the subject the study of their lives.

In saying that a certain English word is the translation of a certain Greek word, was only saying that that Greek word had the authority of Robert Stephens. It appeared therefore to be a matter of the first necessity to add the results of biblical research in this department since 1624, and to give every variation from Stephens' Text which modern editors have for various reasons thought to be necessary.

But in order that the student may be able to come to some conclusion in the matter for himself, when he sees that certain editors prefer a certain word, and that others do not, it is necessary to give here a brief account of those editors and the principles on which they formed their various Texts.

I. — GRIESBACH (1796-1806) based his Text on a *theory of Three Recensions* of the Greek Text (which he thought were apparent in different groups and classes of MSS) regarding the collective witnesses of each recension as one; so that a reading having the authority of all three recensions, or of two out of the three, is regarded by him as genuine. His theory has certainly a foundation of truth, but it is a theory and has many defects; nevertheless his judgment has and always will retain a value peculiarly its own.

II. — LACHMANN (1831-1850) professed to give *the Text as it was received in the East in the fourth Century*, taking into account the Latin and African authorities only when the Eastern disagree. Accordingly he cites entirely the most ancient MSS, to the utter neglect of the other uncial MSS and all the cursive MSS. He professed also to exclude all internal evidence as well as private opinion, and he has done this even where the reading is a palpable error, simply on the ground that it was *the best attested in the fourth century*.

III. — TISCHENDORF (1841-1864), like Lachmann, professed to follow the *most ancient MSS but not to the neglect of the evidence furnished by the ancient versions and Fathers*. In his 8th edition, however, he professes to approach more nearly to the principles of Lachmann.

IV. — TREGELLES (1844-1872). His principle is substantially the same as Lachmann's, but it differs from his in allowing the evidence of

† For further particulars on this subject, see Dr. Tregelles on *the Printed Text of the Greek Testament*. London: Bagster.

uncial MSS down to the seventh century, and by a careful testing of what was a wider circle of authorities. The chief value of his Text arises from its scrupulous fidelity and accuracy, and it is probably the most exact representation of the ancient plenary inspired Text of the Greek Testament ever published. When any of the other editors are cited as agreeing with him, his reading may be taken as being absolutely to be relied on as correct and genuine.

V. — ALFORD (1849-1874) constructed his Text "by following inall ordinary cases the united or preponderating evidence of the most ancient authorities." Where these disagree he takes into account, to a very large extent, *later evidence*. Where, however, evidence is divided, he endeavors *to discover the causes of the variation*. His principles differ from all the other editors by giving a greater prominence to *internal probability*, and a greater weight, in some cases, to his own *judgment*, than to the actual MS authority. He says that that reading has been adopted "which on the whole *seemed most likely to have stood* in the original Text. Such judgments are of course open to be questioned, etc." Consequently, he is often found preferring a word for some reason which he thinks accounts for the various reading, and this in the face of *all the ancient MSS (e.g.* Mark 12:43, for). A word is retained because, he says, it is "more usual," or because its omission appeared to have been a "grammatical correction," or it is rejected because it appears to have been inserted "carelessly from memory," or as a "mechanical repetition." In most cases he seems to feel it necessary to discover the cause of, and to account for, the variation. This necessarily deprives his Text of much weight, and places it far below that of Lachmann, Tischendorf, or Tregelles.

VI. — . This is the Codex Sinaiticus, found by Tischendorf in the Convent of St. Catherine, at the foot of Mount Sinai, in 1844 and 1859, and printed at St. Petersburg in 1862, and at Leipsic in 1863 and 1870. It is considered by Tischendorf and Tregelles to be the work of the fourth century, and therefore is of very high authority, being perhaps the most ancient MS of the Greek Testament in existence. It is given here as a separate authority, because it was not known to Griesbach and Lachmann when they prepared their texts.

In giving the various readings it was not thought necessary to notice those which merely affected the *form* or *spelling* of the Greek words, and not the *meaning*. In other respects this department of the work may be regarded as complete.

With regard to the English words, the English Bibles differ among themselves to a certain extent, and most modern editions differ from the Authorized Version as published in 1611, in italics, references, marginal readings, spelling, and also chapter headings and punctuation. The

chief alterations were made in 1683, and afterwards in 1769, by Dr. Blayney, under the sanction of the Oxford delegates of the Press.* Most of these variations have been noted, with the date (where known) at which they were made.

The English text followed has been Bagster's *Critical New Testament,* which retains the italics of the edition of 1611.

This work could scarcely have been undertaken but for the material assistance afforded by *The Englishman's Greek Concordance,* which, indeed, made it possible; but Hastings' *Critical Greek and English Concordance,* by Hudson & Abbot, Boston, 1871-1875, has been found still more useful.

DIRECTIONS FOR USE.

The English words have been given in their alphabetical order, and when two or more are used in the translation of one Greek word, they will be found in order in each case at the foot of the first body of references, where, if not too numerous, they are referred to.

The order of the Greek words has been determined generally by the frequency with which they have been so translated.

Nouns have been given (with a few exceptions) in the singular number, and verbs in the present tense. Therefore the student must look under COME for came, under DRAW for drew, under GO for went, under TAKE for took, etc. The verb "TO BE" is an exception, and for the convenience of the student, and for the sake of simplicity, this has been, at great labor, divided into its various tenses, AM, ARE, BE, IS, WAS, WERE, WERT, etc.

In reading any passage. — The student desiring to know the exact force of a particular word, should first look for that word in its alphabetical place, and then to the body of references below it for the book, chapter, and verse where the word occurs. The figure prefixed to it will be the Greek word, with its literal meaning. It is obvious that the same information will be gained even though he know nothing of Greek.

Should the passage not be found in the list of references, he must reflect whether it forms part of a phrase, in which case he will find that combination or phrase in its alphabetical order, below.

EXAMPLES.

(1). — He is reading John 5:39, and wishes to know the meaning of the word "search." He turns to that word, finds the reference, which

*See Turton's *Text of the English Bible,* 1833.

shows him that No. 1a is the word so translated, and he learns that he is *commanded* to *trace* or *track* the Scriptures, as a dog does in hunting game; or he is reading Acts 17:11, and refers to this word, where he finds that when the Bereans "searched" the Scriptures they *estimated carefully* the apostles' teaching and *judged of it* by the Word of God.

(2). — He is reading John 8:12, "I am the Light of the World," and by reference, he learns that Jesus speaks of Himself as absolute and underived light; while in John 5:35, speaking of the Baptist as "a light," the word means a hand lamp, fed by oil, burning for a time and then going out.

(3). — He is reading John 13:10, "He that is washed, needeth not, save to wash his feet, but is clean every whit," and by reference he finds that the word wash is represented by two different Greek words; the first, meaning *to bathe*, the second, *to wash a part of the body*; and he learns that as a person who has been bathed needs only the washing of his feet, so the believer being justified by the sacrifice of the brazen altar, needs only the daily cleansing of the brazen laver, i.e. the cleansing of his walk and his ways with the washing of water by the word.

For the special use of the *Index* in connection with further searching out the use of the Greek words, the reader is referred to the Preface prefixed to it.

The foregoing examples (which might be multiplied indefinitely) will be sufficient to show the importance and usefulness of this work; and it is now submitted to all Bible students with the earnest prayer that the result with them will be the same as with the author; and that together, they will be filled with a holy reverence for the words inspired by the Holy Ghost, and exclaim together, "Oh! how I love thy law." "Thy words were found and I did eat them, and thy word was unto me the joy and rejoicing of my heart."

Explanation of Abbreviations, etc.

CASES.

Nom.	... Nominative.	*Dat.*	... Dative.
Gen.	... Genitive.	*Acc.*	... Accusative.

NUMBER.

Sing.	... Singular.	*Pl.*	... Plural.

GENDER.

Masc.	... Masculine.	*Neut.*	... Neuter.
Fem.	... Feminine.	*Pers.*	... Person.

VOICES.

Act.	... Active.	*Pass.*	... Passive.
Mid.	... Middle.		

MOODS.

Ind.	... Indicative.	*Opt.*	... Optative.
Imperat.	Imperative.	*Inf.*	... Infinitive.
Subj.	... Subjunctive.		

TENSES.

Pres.	... Present.	*Perf.*	... Perfect.
Imp.	... Imperfect.	*Plup.*	... Pluperfect.
Aor.	... Aorist.	*Fut.*	... Future.

PARTS OF SPEECH, etc.

Adj.	... Adjective.	*Def.*	... Definite.
Art.	... Article.	*Indef.*	... Indefinite.
Pron.	... Pronoun.	*Rel.*	... Relative.
Part.	... Participle.	*Neg.*	... Negative.

LANGUAGES.

Sanscr.	... Sanscit.	*Heb.*	... Hebrew.
Eng.	... English.	lxx.	... The Greek translation of the Old Test.
Lat.	... Latin.		
Germ.	... German.		

TEXTUAL.

G denotes Griesbach, edition of 1805.

- G⇉ ,, a probable omission by Griesbach, which he did not, however, remove from the text.
- G→ ,, a less probable omission.
- G↚ ,, an addition of some slight probability.
- G≈ ,, a reading of great value, but which Griesbach did not add to the text.
- G∼ ,, a reading of less value, considered by Griesbach as inferior to the text.
- L ,, Lachmann, edition 1842-50.
- T ,, Tischendorf, 7th edition to the word "FAITH," from thence his 8th edition.
- Tr ,, Tregelles.
- A ,, Alford, Four Gospels, 6th edition to the word "FOR," 7th edition, from thence; Acts to 2 Cor., 6th edition; Gal. to Philem., 5th edition; Heb. to Rev., 4th edition.
- A* ,, a reading which Alford regarded as of equal authority with the text.
- א ,, the Codex Sinaiticus, discovered 1859, printed 1862.
- א* ,, an omission in א with the context, in which case it fails to be an authority as to the particular word in question.
- m ,, a reading placed in the margin by the editor after whose initial it is placed, (*e.g.* Trm denotes a reading in the margin of Tregelles.)
- b ,, a reading placed in brackets in the text by the editor after whose initial it is placed; (*e.g.* Ab denotes that Alford placed the reading within brackets.)
- mb ,, a reading placed in the margin, and also within brackets, by the editor; (*e.g.* Trmb.)
- AV. denotes the Authorized Version of 1611. The date of any subsequent year denotes a later edition.
- St ,, the edition of R. Stephens, printed in 1624, as the text from which the AV. had been translated. Hence often called the "Textus Receptus."
- B ,, the edition of Beza, 1565.
- E ,, the edition of the Elzevirs, 1624.
- (ap.) ,, that the word in question is affected by a various reading which concerns a whole clause, verse, or paragraph, etc., which will be found in its place in Appendix *A*.
- *om.* ,, that the word is omitted by such of the textual critics or editors whose initials are placed after it, (but retained by those whose initials are not given).
- Al ,, that all the editors mentioned above concur in their opinion as to any word; viz., G L T Tr A and א.

(When a Greek word, etc., occurs before the above initials, it denotes that that word is preferred by them to the one designated by a figure.)

MISCELLANEOUS.

- *absol.* denotes absolutely.
- *appl.* ,, applied.
- *cf.* ,, the Lat. confer, *i.e.* compare; sometimes put comp.
- *comp.* ,, comparative.
- *ed.* ,, edition.
- *e.g.* ,, for example.
- *emph.* ,, emphatic, or emphasis.
- *esp.* ,, especially.
- *gen.* ,, generally.
- *lit.* ,, literally.
- *marg.* ,, margin; *i.e.* a marginal reading in the English Bible.
- *met.* or *metaph.* ,, metaphorically.
- *obs.* ,, obsolete.
- *occ.* ,, occur, (*i.e.* that the word in question *occurs* only in those passages).
- *non occ.* ,, that the word does *not occur* elsewhere.
- *obj.* ,, objective.
- *opp.* ,, opposed or opposite.
- *part.* ,, particularly.
- *pers.* ,, person.
- *prob.* ,, probably.
- *superl.* ,, superlative.
- *sig.* ,, signifies, or signification.
- *sub.* ,, subjective.
- 1st / 2nd ,, that the English word occurs more than once in the verse, and the 1st or 2nd, as the case may be, is the one that is so translated (though the Greek may be in a reverse order).
- twice ,, that the word occurs twice in that verse.
- A,B,C,etc.,, the capital letter after the word "see," stands for the word in question; *e.g.* under "COME," see "C to pass," denotes see "COME to PASS;" under "PRAYER," "see P (make long)" denotes see "PRAYER (make long)" etc.

A CRITICAL LEXICON AND CONCORDANCE TO THE ENGLISH AND GREEK NEW TESTAMENT

A Critical and Complete Lexicon and Concordance

to the

English and Greek New Testament

A

A or AN.

The indefinite article generally indicates *the absence* of the article in the Greek. (In many passages however the Greek *definite* article, ὁ, ἡ, τό, is translated *indefinitely;* and other passages, which are *indefinite* in the Greek, are *definite* in English. Lists of these will be found in the Appendix.)

A or An is sometimes the representative of other words, *e.g.:*

1. ὁ, ἡ, τό, *the Greek definite article* the. *The article is the symbol of what was uppermost in the writer's mind, either already mentioned, or about to become the object of an assertion. It is strictly anticipative, though with the aid of its predicate it may be retrospective.*

2. εἷς, *the numeral* one.

3. εἰς, *prep.*, into, with a view to; *also, denoting equivalence,* as.

4. τις, *indef. pron.*, some, a certain.

A

1. Matt. i. 23, a virgin.
1. —— iv. 5, a pinnacle.
1. ——— 21, a ship.
1. —— v. 1, a mountain.
1. ——— 15, a bushel.
1. ———— a candlestick
2. ——— 41, a mile.
1. —— vii. 17, a corrupt.
1. ——— 24, a rock.
1. —— viii. 28, a ship (*om.* L Tr A.)
1. ——— 32, a steep.
1. —— ix. 1, a ship (*om.* L Tr.)
1. —— x. 12, a house.
1. —— xii. 35, a good man
1. ———— an evil man.
1. ——— 43, a man.
1. —— xiii. 2, a ship (*om.* L Tr A.)
1. ——— 3, a sower.
1. —— xiv. 23, a mountain
1. —— xv. 20, a man.
1. —— xviii. 17, a heathen
1. ———— a publican
2. —— xxi. 19, a fig tree.
1. —— xxiii. 24, a gnat.
1. ———— a camel.
1. —— xxiv. 32, a parable
1. —— xxv. 32, a shepherd
1. —— xxvi. 51, a servant
2. ——— 69, a damsel.
2. —— xxvii. 14, a word.
2. ——— 15, a prisoner.
1. —— xxviii. 16, a mountain.
1. Mark iii. 13, a mountain
1. ——— 27, a strong man
1. —— iv. 1, a ship (*om.* Tr.)
1. ——— 3, a sower (*om.* L Tr^b.)
1. ——— 21, a candle.
1. ———— a bushel.
1. Mark iv. 21, a bed.
1. ———— a candlestick.
1. ——— 38, a pillow.
1. —— v. 13, a steep place
1. —— vi. 46, a mountain
1. —— vii. 15, a man.
1. —— viii. 10, a ship.
1. —— xi. 4, a place.
1. —— xiii. 28, a parable.
1. —— xiv. 47, a sword.
2. ——— 51, a certain (*om.* L Tr ℵ.)
1. Luke ii. 7, a manger.
1. ——— 12, a sign.
1. ——— 16, a manger (*om.* G→ L Tr.)
1. —— iv. 9, a pinnacle.
1. —— v. 15, a fame.
1. —— vi. 12, a mountain
1. ——— 48, a rock.
1. —— viii. 5, a sower.
1. ——— 6, a rock.
1. —— ix. 28, a mountain
1. —— xi. 21, a strong man.
1. ——— 22, a stronger (*om.* L Tr A.)
1. ——— 33, a bushel.
1. ———— a candlestick.
1. —— xii. 40, an hour.
1. ——— 54, a cloud (*om.* L Tr.)
2 and 1. — xv. 15, a citizen (lit. '*one of the citizens.*')
1. —— xvi. 2, an account.
4. —— xviii. 2, a city.
4. ———— a judge.
1. ——— 13, a sinner.
1. —— xxiii. 31, a green tree (Tr^b.)
1. John iii. 10, a master.
1. —— v. 5, an infirmity.

1. John v. 35, a burning.
1. ——— a shining.
1. — vi. 3, a mountain.
1. ——— 4, a feast.
4. ——— 7, a little (*om.* Lᵇ Tr.)
2. ——— 9, a lad (*om.* G→ Lᵇ Tr ℵ.)
1. ——— 15, a mountain.
1. ——— 17, a ship (*om.* Tr.)
1. — viii. 7, a stone (*ap.*)
1. ——— 44, a lie.
1. — xi. 54, a country.
1. — xii. 24, a corn.
1. — xiii. 5, a bason.
1. ——— 26, a sop.
1. — xvi. 21, a woman.
1. — xviii. 3, a band.
2. — xx. 7, a place.
1. — xxi. 3, a ship.
1. ——— 8, a little ship.
1. Acts i. 13, an upper.
1. — v. 16, a multitude.
4. ——— 34, a little space.
1. — ix. 7, a voice.
1. — xi. 13, an angel.
4. — xvi. 9, a man.
4. — xviii. 14, a matter.
1. — xx. 9, a window.
1. — xxi. 26, an offering.
1. — xxiii. 27, an army.
1. — xxiv. 23, a centurion.
4. — xxvii. 8, a place.
1. Rom. i. 25, a lie.
1. — v. 7, a good.
1. — vii. 1, a man.
1. ——— 21, a law.
1. — ix. 27, a remnant.
1. — xv. 12, a root.
1. — xvi. 23, a brother.
1. 1 Cor. ii. 11, a man.
2. — vi. 5, a wise man.
1. — vii. 15, a brother.
1. ——— — a sister.
1. ——— 28, a virgin (Lᵇ Aᵇ.)
1. ——— 34, a wife.
1. ——— a virgin.
1. 1 Cor. x. 13, a way.
3. — xv. 45, a living soul.
3. ——— a quickening
4. — xvi. 7, a while.
3. 2 Cor. vi. 18, a father.
1. — vii. 8, a letter.
1. — viii. 11, a readiness.
1. ——— a performance.
1. ——— 12, a willing.
4. — xi. 16, a little.
1. — xii. 12, an apostle.
1. ——— 18, a brother.
1. Gal. iv. 22, a bondmaid.
1. ——— a free-woman.
1. ——— 27, an husband.
4. — vi. 1, a fault.
1. Eph. v. 27, a glorious.
1. — vi. 21, a beloved.
1. Phil. i. 23, a desire.
1. — iv. 17, a gift.
1. Col. iv. 9, a faithful.
1. 2 Thes. ii. 3, a falling-away.
1. ——— a lie.
1. 1 Tim. vi. 12, a good.
1. 2 Tim. iv. 7, a good fight.
1. ——— 8, a crown.
1. Titus 7, a bishop.
4. Heb. ii. 7, a little.
4. ——— 9, a little.
1. — vii. 24, an unchangeable.
1. — xi. 8, a place.
1. ——— 23, a proper.
1. James iii. 13, a good.
2. — iv. 13, a year (*om.* L Tr ℵ.)
1. 1 Pet. v. 4, a crown.
1. ——— 12, a faithful.
1. 2 Pet. i. 19, a more sure.
1. 1 John ii. 22, a liar.
1. 2 John 7, a deceiver.
1. ——— an antichrist.
1. Rev. ii. 10, a crown.
2. — viii. 13, an angel.
2. — ix. 13, a voice.
1. — xi. 12, a cloud.
2. — xviii. 21, a mighty.
2. Rev. xix. 17, an angel (*om.* G→); (ἄλλος, *another*, ℵ.)

ABASE.

(-ED, -ING.)

ταπεινόω, to make *or* bring low, to humble.

Matt. xxiii. 12.
Luke xiv. 11.
Luke xviii. 14.
2 Cor. xi. 7.
Phil. iv. 12.

ABBA.

ἀββᾶ, father. *The pronunciation in our Saviour's time of the Hebrew* אב father, *or Chaldee* אבא.

Mark xiv. 36.
Rom. viii. 15.
Gal. iv. 6.

ABHOR.

(-EST.)

1. ἀποστυγέω, to shudder from, (*from* ἀπό, from, *and* στυγέω, to shudder with horror, hate.)
2. βδελύσσομαι, to turn away through loathing *or* disgust. *Properly from an ill smell through voiding of the stomach.*

2. Rom. ii. 22.
1. Rom. xii. 9.

ABIDE.

(-ETH, -ING, ABODE.)

1. μένω, *intransitive*, to remain, abide, dwell; *transitive*, to wait for.
2. ἐπιμένω, to remain upon, *or* at; to continue on.
3. καταμένω, to remain down, to abide continually.
4. παραμένω, to remain beside *or* along with.
5. ὑπομένω, to remain under, stay behind, to endure.
6. διατρίβω, to wear through *by rubbing* to consume or wear away; *e.g. time.*
7. ἀναστρέφω, to turn again, return; overturn.
   (*a*) *In Mid.* to turn one's self round, move about in a place, *i.e.*, sojourn, *and hence, gen.*, to conduct one's self.
8. αὐλίζομαι, to lodge in the αὐλή (an open court or fold), to take up one's night's lodging.
9. ἵστημι, *transitive*, to stand, to stop; *intransitive*, to set, to place.
10. ποιέω, to make, to do; *and hence*, to work, to spend *or* pass *time or life.*

1. Matt. x. 11.
7a. — xvii. 22 (συστρέφω, *collect together*, L Tr ℵ.)
1. Mark vi. 10.
1. Luke i. 56.
— — ii. 8, see A in the field.
1. — viii. 27.
1. — ix. 4.
1. — xix. 5.
8. — xxi. 37.
1. — xxiv. 29.
1. John i. 32, 39.
1. — i. 39, margin (text, *dwell.*)
1. — iii. 36.
1. — iv. 40.
1. — v. 38.
1. — vii. 9.
9. — viii. 44.
1. — viii. 35 twice.
1. — x. 40.
1. — xi. 6.
1. John xii. 24, 34, 46.
1. — xiv. 16 (εἰμί, *be*, L T Tr A ℵ.)
1. — xv. 4 3 times, 5, 6, 10 twice.
3. Acts i. 13 (with εἰμί.)
6 — xiv. 3.
6. ——— 28.
2. — xv. 34 (*ap.*)
6. — xvi. 12.
1. — xvi. 15.
5. — xvii. 14.
1. — xviii. 3.
10. — xx. 3.
1. ——— 23 (marg. *wait for.*)
1. — xxi. 7, 8.
1. — xxvii. 31.
— Rom. xi. 23, see A still.
4. 1 Cor. xvi. 6.
2. Gal. i. 18.
— Phil. i. 24, see A in.
— 1 Tim. i. 3, see A still.

ABIDE IN.

2. Phil. i. 24 (with ἐν, *in*, om. ℵ.)

ABIDE IN THE FIELD.

ἀγραυλέω, to lodge in the fold in the field. (*From* ἀγρός a field, *and* αὐλή a fold; *whence*, αὐλίζομαι, *see No.* 8.)

Luke ii. 8.

ABIDE STILL.

1. προσμένω, to remain towards, wait still longer; to continue.
2. ἐπιμένω, *see above, No.* 2.

2. Rom. xi. 23. | 1. 1 Tim. i. 3

ABILITY.

1. δύναμις, capability, power, (*regarded as inherent and moral.*)
2. ἰσχύς, strength (physical), force, vigour (*regarded as an endowment.*)
3. εὐπορέομαι, to prosper, abound in, to possess abundance; *hence*, to be able to afford.

1. Matt. xxv. 15. | 3. Acts xi. 29.
2. 1 Pet. iv. 11.

ABLE [verb.]

1. δύναμαι, to be able, to have (inherent and moral) power.
2. ἰσχύω, to be strong, to have (physical) ability. (*More emphatic than No.* 1.)
3. ἐξισχύω, to have strength enough, to be thoroughly *and* perfectly able. (*More emphatic than No.* 2.)
4. ἱκανόω, to make sufficient *or* fit, to make competent, to qualify.
5. ἔχω, to have *or* to hold; *of temporary holding and of lasting possession.*

1. Luke i. 20.
2. —— xiii. 24.
2. —— xiv. 29.
2. ———— 30.
2. John xxi. 6.
2. Acts vi. 10.
2. Acts xv. 10.
1. Rom. xv. 14.
— 2 Cor. iii. 6, see A (make.)
3. Eph. iii. 18.
1. 2 Tim. iii. 7.
5. 2 Pet. i. 15.

ABLE (MAKE.)

4. 2 Cor. iii. 6.

ABLE [noun.]

1. δυνατός, *in an active sense* strong, having (inherent and moral) power. *In a passive sense*, possible, capable of being done.
2. ἱκανός, coming to, reaching to, *and hence*, sufficient; *of things*, enough; *of persons*, competent.

Luke xiv. 31.
Acts xxv. 5.
Rom. iv. 21.
—— xi. 23.
—— xiv. 4 (δυνατέω*, *be able*, G∾ L T Tr A ℵ.)
1. 2 Cor. ix. 8 (δυνατέω*, *be able*, L Tr A ℵ.)
1. 1 Tim. i. 12.
2. 2 Tim. ii. 2.
1. Titus i. 9. [*able*, L.)
1. Heb. xi. 19 (δυνατέω*, *be*
1. Jas. iii. 2.

* With emphasis on 'able' instead of on 'is' (as in the text, δυνατὸς εστιν.)

ABLE (as ye are) [margin.]

ἔνειμι, to be in *or* within; *part. with art.*, *as here*, what there is in *your vessel;* the things within.

Luke xi. 41 (text, *such things as ye have.*)

ABOARD (GO.)

ἐπιβαίνω, to go upon, (*from* ἐπί, upon, *and* βαίνω, to go), *hence* to go, walk, *or* tread on; to go on *ship-board.*

Acts xxi. 2.

ABODE [verb.]

See, ABIDE.

ABODE [noun.]

μονή, an abiding place, a mansion, a habitation.

John xiv. 2 John xiv. 23

ABOLISH.

(-ED.)

καταργέω, to render *or* make useless, *or* unprofitable.

2 Cor. iii. 13. | Eph. ii. 15.
2 Tim. i. 10.

ABOMINABLE.

1. ἀθέμιτος, unlawful, criminal.
2. βδελυκτός, disgusting, extremely hateful. *See No.* 3.
3. βδελύσσομαι, to turn away through loathing *or* disgust. *Properly from an ill smell through voiding of the stomach.*

2. Titus i. 16. | 1. 1 Pet. iv. 3.
3. Rev. xxi. 8.

ABOMINATION.

βδέλυγμα, an object of disgust. *See* "ABOMINABLE," *No.* 3.

Matt. xxiv. 15.
Mark xiii. 14.
Luke xvi. 15.
Rev. xvii. 4, 5.
Rev. xxi. 27.

ABORTIVE (an) [margin.]

ἔκτρωμα, a child untimely born, *(from root,* to miscarry.)

1 Cor. xv. 8 (text, *one born out of due time.*)

ABOUND.

(-ED, -ETH, -ING.)

1. *περισσεύω*, *intransitive*, to be over and above, more than enough; *transitive*, to make *or* cause to abound.
2. *ὑπερπερισσεύω*, to superabound, to abound exceedingly.
3. *πλεονάζω*, to become more, to increase, *(from πλέον,* more.)
4. *πληθύνομαι*, to be multiplied, *(from πλῆθος,* a multitude.)

4. Matt. xxiv. 12.
— Rom. iii. 7, see A (more.)
1. —— v. 15.
3. —— 20, 1st.
3. —— 2nd.
— —— 3rd, see A (much more.)
3. —— vi. 1.
1. —— xv. 13.
1. 1 Cor. xv. 58.
1. 2 Cor. i. 5, twice.
1. —— viii. 2.
1. —— 7 twice.
— 2 Cor. ix. 8, see A (make.)
1. —— 2nd.
1. Eph. i. 8.
1. Phil. i. 9.
1. —— iv. 12 twice.
3. —— 17.
1. —— 18.
1. Col. ii. 7.
— 1 Thes. iii. 12, see A (make.)
1. —— iv. 1 (with *μᾶλλον*—A, *more and more.*)
3. 2 Thes. i. 3.
3. 2 Pet. i. 8.

ABOUND (MAKE.)

1. 2 Cor. ix. 8. | 1. 1 Thes. iii. 12.

ABOUND (MORE.)

1. Rom. iii. 7.

ABOUND (MUCH MORE.)

2. Rom. v. 20.

ABOUT.

1. *ἐν*, in; *with plural* amongst. *Indicating a space within the limits of which something is situated.*
2. *ἐπί*, upon. *Superposition.*
   (a) *with Gen. (as springing from)* over, in the presence *or* time of.
   (b) *with Dat. (as resting on)*, in addition to, on account of.
   (c) *with Acc. (motion with a view to superposition)* up to *used of place, number, and aim;* over *of time, place, extent.*
3. *κατά*, down, *(down upon, down from.)*
   (a) *with Acc. (down towards)* according to, throughout, during.
4. *περί*, around *(encircling and inclosing.)*
   (a) *with Gen.* about, concerning, on behalf of.
   (b) *with Acc.* about, round about.
5. *πρός*, towards *(propinquity.)*
   (a) *with Dat.* at, close by.
   (b) *with Acc.* towards, in reference to.
6. *κυκλόθεν*, from all sides, round about.
7. *πού*, somewhere; *with numerals*, nearly.
8. *ὡς*, as, so as; *with numerals*, about.
9. *ὡσεί*, as if, as though, something like.

— Matt. i. 11 (see A the time.)
4b. —— iii. 4.
4b. —— viii. 18.
9. —— xiv. 21.
2c. —— xviii. 6.
4b. —— xx. 3, 5, 6, 9.
4b. —— xxvii. 46.
5b. Mark ii. 2.
4b. —— i. 6.
4b. —— iii. 8, 32.
4b. —— iii. 34 (*om.* G→.)
4b. —— iv. 10 (*with art.*)
8. —— v. 13.
9. —— vi. 44 (*om.* G L T Tr A.) (No. 8, ℵ.)
4b. —— vi. 48.
8. —— viii. 9.
4b. —— ix. 14, 42.
2a. —— xiv. 51.
9. Luke i. 56 (No. 8, L Tr S.)
8. —— ii. 37 (*ἕως, until,* L T Tr A ℵ.)
1. —— 49.
9. —— iii. 23.
8. —— viii. 42.
9. —— ix. 14.
9. —— 28.
4b. —— x. 40, 41.
4b. —— xiii. 8.
4b. —— xvii. 2.
9. —— xxii. 41.
4b. —— xxii. 49 (*with art.*)
9. —— 59.
9. —— xxiii. 44.
8. John i. 39.
4a. —— iii. 25.
9. —— iv. 6 (No. 8, L T Tr A ℵ.)
9. —— vi. 10 (No. 8, Tr ℵ.)
8. —— 19 (No. 9, L.)
8. John xi. 18.
9. —— xix. 14 (No. 8, G∼ L T Tr A ℵ.)
9. —— 39 (No. 8, All.)
2a. —— xx. 7.
8. Acts i. 15.
3a. —— ii. 10.
9. —— 41.
— —— iii. 3, see A (be.)
9. —— iv. 4 (No. 8, L[b] A[b].) (*om.* T ℵ.)
8. —— v. 7.
9. —— 36 (No. 8, L T A.)
9. —— x. 3.
4b. —— x. 9.
2b. —— xi. 19 (2a G ⇄ L.)
3a. —— xii. 1.
8. —— xiii. 18.
8. —— 20 (*ap.*)
4a. —— xv. 2.
— —— xviii. 14, see A, TO (be.)
9. Acts xix. 7.
4a. —— 23.
8. —— 34.
— —— xx. 3, see A (be.)
4b. —— xxii. 6 twice.
4a. —— xxv. 15.
4a. —— 24
3a. —— xxvii. 27.
— —— 30, see A (be.)
7. Rom. iv. 19.
4b. 1 Tim. vi. 4.
— Heb. viii. 5, see A (be.)
4b. Jude 7.
4a. —— 9.
5a. Rev. i. 13.
6. —— iv. 8.
8. —— viii. 1.
— —— x. 4, see A (be.)
8. —— xvi. 21.

ABOUT (BE.)

1. μέλλω, to delay; *with an infinitive following*, to be about to *do anything (immediate or remote.)*
2. ζητέω, to seek.

1. Acts iii. 3.
1. —— xviii. 14.
1. —— xx. 3.
2. Acts xxvii. 30.
1. Heb. viii. 5.
1. Rev. x. 4.

ABOUT THE TIME.

2a. Matt. i. 11.

See also, BEAR, BOUND; CARRY, CAST, COME, COMPASS, COUNTRY; DWELL; GIRD, GO; HANG, HEDGE; LAW, LEAD, LOOK; MIDST, MINISTER; PUT; REGION, ROUND; SET, SHINE, STRIVE, STAND; TURN; WALK, WANDER.

ABOVE.

1. ἐπί, upon *(superposition.)*
   (a) *with Gen. (as springing from)* over, in the presence *or* time of.
   (b) *with Dat. (as resting on)* in addition to, on account of.
   (c) *with Acc.* up to *(used of place, number or aim;)* over, *(of time, place, extent.)*
2. παρά, beside *(juxtaposition.)*
   (a) *with Acc.* to *or* along side of; compared with *(so as to be shown* beyond *or* contrary to, *or* instead of.)
3. περί, around *(encircling and inclosing.)*
   (a) *with Gen.* about, concerning, on behalf of.
4. πρό, before *(whether of time or place.)*
5. ὑπέρ, over,
   (a) *with Acc. (as here)* beyond.
6. ἄνω, above; up, upwards.
   (a) *with the article*—that which is above *e.g. heaven above, or heavenly things.*
7. ἀνώτερον, higher.
8. ἐπάνω, above, superior to.
9. πλείων, more.

5a. Matt. x. 24 twice.
1b. Luke iii. 20.
5a. —— vi. 40.
2a. —— xiii. 2, 4.
— John iii. 31, see A (from.)
8. —————— 2nd.
8. —————— 3rd (*ap.*)
6a. —— viii. 23.
— —— xix. 11, see A (from.)
6. Acts ii. 19.
9. —— iv. 22.
5a. —— xxvi. 13.
2a. Rom. xiv. 5.
5a. 1. Cor. iv. 6.
5a. ——— x. 13.
8. ——— xv. 6.
5a. 2 Cor. i. 8.
— ——— xii. 2, see A...[ago.
5a. 2 Cor. xii. 6.
5a. Gal. i. 14.
6a. —— iv. 26.
5a. Eph. iii. 20.
1a. —— iv. 6.
1b. —— vi. 16 (ἐν, *in*, L Tr ℵ.)
5a. Phil. ii. 9.
6a. Col. iii. 1, 2.
1b. ——— 14.
1c. 2 Thes. ii. 4.
5a. Philem. 16.
2. Heb. i. 9.
7. —— x. 8
— Jas. i. 17 } see A
— —— iii. 15, 17 } (from.)
4. —— v. 12.
4. 1 Pet. iv. 8.
3a. 3 John 2.

ABOVE (FROM.)

ἄνωθεν, from above, from the first.

John iii. 3, margin (text, *again.*)
——— 7, margin (text, *again.*)
John iii. 31.
—— xix. 11.
Jas. i. 17.
—— iii. 15, 17.

ABOVE...AGO.

4. 2 Cor. xii. 2 (often misprinted *about.*)

See also, ABUNDANTLY, EXALT, FAR, MEASURE, REMAIN.

ABSENCE.

ἀπουσία, absence.

Phil. ii. 12.

ABSENCE OF (IN THE.)

ἄτερ, without, not with, *either* not having *or* in the absence of.

Luke xxii. 6 (margin *without.*)

ABSENT, and ABSENT (BE.)

1. ἄπειμι, to be away from, absent.
2. ἐκδημέω, to be away from one's people; *hence,* absent from any one.

1. 1 Cor. v. 3.
2. 2 Cor. v. 6, 8, 9.
1. —— x. 1.
1. 2 Cor. x. 11.
1. ———xiii. 2, 10.
1. Phil. i. 27.
1. Col. ii. 5.

ABSTAIN.

ἀπέχομαι, to hold back one's self from, refrain.

Acts xv. 20, 29.
1 Thes. iv. 3.
1 Thes. v. 22.
1 Tim. iv. 3.
1 Pet. ii. 11.

ABSTINENCE.

ἀσιτία, abstinence from *or* neglect of food.

Acts xxvii. 21.

ABUNDANCE.

1. ἁδρότης, abundance *(in the sense of maturity or ripeness reached from full growth.)*.
2. δύναμις, capability, power *(regarded as moral and inherent.)*
3. περισσεία, abundance, superfluity.
4. περίσσευμα that which remains over.
5. περισσεύω, to remain over and above, more than enough.
6. ὑπερβολή, a passing over, excess, surpassing *(in number or degree.)*

4. Matt. xii. 34.
— — xiii. 12, see A (have more.)
— — xxv. 29, see A (have.)
5. Mark xii. 44.
4. Luke vi. 45.
5. Luke xii. 15.
5. — xxi. 4.
3. Rom. v. 17.
3. 2 Cor. viii. 2.
4. — 14 twice.
1. — 20.
6. — xii. 7.
2. Rev. xviii. 3.

ABUNDANCE (HAVE.)

5. Matt. xxv. 29.

ABUNDANCE (HAVE MORE.)

5. Matt. xiii. 12.

ABUNDANT.

1. περισσεύω, to remain over and above, more than enough.
2. πλεονάζω, to become more, to increase, *(from* πλέον, more.)
3. πολύς, many *(this adjective denotes that the noun is numerous, or exists in a great or high degree.)*

— 1 Cor. xii. 23, 24, see A (more.)
2. 2 Cor. iv. 15.
— — vii. 15, see A (more.)
1. — ix. 12.
— 2 Cor. xi. 23, see A (more).
— Phil. i. 26, see A (be more.)
— 1 Tim. i. 14, see A (be exceeding.)
3. 1 Pet. i. 3.

ABUNDANT (BE EXCEEDING.)

ὑπερπλεονάζω, to abound exceedingly.

1 Tim. i. 14.

ABUNDANT (BE MORE.)

περισσεύω, *see* "ABUNDANT," *No.* 1.

Phil. i. 26.

ABUNDANT (MORE.)

1. περισσότερος, more than above the ordinary measure.
2. περισσοτέρως, more abundantly.

1. 1 Cor. xii. 23 twice, 24. | 2. 2 Cor. vii. 15.
2. 2 Cor. xi. 23.

ABUNDANTLY.

1. { εἰς, into, with a view to, to, unto, περισσεία, abundance, superfluity, } a falling into abundance.
2. πλουσίως, richly.

— John x. 10, see A (more.)
— 1 Cor. xv. 10, see A (more.)
— 2 Cor. i. 12, see A (more.)
— — ii. 4, see A (more.)
1. — x. 15.
— — xii. 15, see A (more.)
— Eph. iii. 20, see A (above.)
— 1 Thes. ii. 17, see A (more.)
2. Titus iii. 6.
— Heb. vi. 17, see A (more.)
2. 2 Pet. i. 11.

ABUNDANTLY (MORE *or* THE MORE.)

1. περισσός, above the ordinary measure.
2. περισσότερος, more than above the ordinary measure.
3. περισσοτέρως, more abundantly.

1. John x. 10.
2. 1 Cor. xv. 10.
3. 2 Cor. i. 12.
3. 2 Cor. ii. 4.
3. — xii. 15.
3. 1 Thes. ii. 17.
2. Heb. vi. 17.

ABUNDANTLY ABOVE (EXCEEDING.)

{ ὑπὲρ, over; *with Gen.* [*as here*] above.
ἐκ, from, out of.
περισσός, above the ordinary measure. }

Eph. iii. 20.

See also, WEEP.

ABUSE (-ING.)

καταχράομαι, to use overmuch; *hence,* to abuse.

1 Cor. vii. 31. | 1 Cor. ix. 18.

ABUSERS OF THEMSELVES WITH MANKIND.

ἀρσενοκοίτης, *(from* ἄρσην, a male; *and* κοίτη, a bed.)

1 Cor. vi. 9.

ACCEPT.

(-ED, -EST, -ETH, -ING.)

1. δέχομαι, to take, accept, receive *that which is offered. (It implies that a decision of the will has taken place, and that the result of this is manifest.)*
2. ἀποδεχομαι, to receive any one kindly *or* heartily, to welcome.
3. προσδέχομαι, to accept, to receive to one's presence: *hence, of things future,* to wait for, expect; *with a negative (as here)* to reject.
4. λαμβάνω, to take, take hold of, to receive *as from another: with* πρόσωπον *(as here)* to respect the person *of any one.*

4. Luke xx. 21.
2. Acts xxiv. 3.
1. 2 Cor. viii. 17.
1. 2 Cor. xi. 4.
4. Gal. ii. 6.
3. Heb. xi. 35.

ACCEPTABLE.

1. δεκτός, elected; acceptable *(of one regarding whom there is, or has been a favourable decision of the will.)*
2. εὐπρόσδεκτος, *a very strong affirmation of No.* 1(δεκτός) favourably accepted, well received.
3. ἀπόδεκτος, acceptable, pleasing, welcome.
4. εὐάρεστος, well-pleasing
5. χάρις, grace. *Objectively it denotes* personal gracefulness, a pleasing work, beauty of speech, etc. *Subjectively, it means* an inclining towards, courteous *or* gracious disposition. *On the part of the giver*—kindness, favour; *on the part of the receiver*—thanks, respect, homage.

1. Luke iv. 19.
4. Rom. xii. 1, 2.
4. —— xiv. 18.
2. —— xv. 16.
4. Eph. v. 10.
1. Phil. iv. 18.
3. 1 Tim. ii. 3.
3. ——— v. 4.
2. 1 Pet. ii. 5. [*thank.*)
5. ——— 20 (margin

ACCEPTABLY.

εὐαρέστως, so as to please, acceptably.

Heb. xii. 28.

ACCEPTATION.

ἀποδοχή, worthy to be received with approbation, acceptation, reception.

1 Tim. i. 15. | 1 Tim. iv. 9.

ACCEPTED.

1. δεκτός, to decide favourably, elected, acceptable *(of one regarding whom there is, or has been a favourable decision of the will.)*
2. εὐπρόσδεκτος, *a very strong affirmation of* δεκτός, *(No.* 1*)* favourably accepted, well received.
3. εὐάρεστος, well-pleasing.
4. χαριτόω, to make lovely *or* acceptable.

1. Luke iv. 24.
1. Acts x. 35.
2. Rom. xv. 31.
3. 2 Cor. v. 9.
1. ——— vi. 2 1st.
2. ——— 2 2nd.
2. 2 Cor. viii. 12.

ACCEPTED (MAKE.)

4. Eph. i. 6.

ACCEPTED (GRACIOUSLY) [margin.]

4. Luke i. 28 (text *highly favoured.*)

ACCESS.

προσαγωγή, a leading *or* bringing to the presence of anyone; freedom of access.

Rom. v. 2. | Eph. ii. 18.
Eph. iii. 12.

ACCOMPANY.

(-IED.)

1. ἔχω, to have *or* hold; *(of temporary holding and of lasting possession.)*
2. προπέμπω, to send forward, to conduct, escort.
3. συνέπομαι, to follow, attend.
4. συνερχομαι, to come *or* go along with, *or together.*
5. { ἔρχομαι, to come *or* go, / σύν, with, } to come *or* go with.

4. Acts x. 23.
5. —— xi. 12.
3. Acts xx. 4.
2. ——— 38.
1. Heb. vi. 9 (mid.)

ACCOMPLISH.

(-ED, -ING.)

1. ἐξαρτίζω, to complete entirely, to furnish *or* fit completely.

2. πλήθω, to be *or* become full, to be fulfilled, completed, ended.

3. πληρόω, to fill, make full, pervade, perform fully.

4. τελέω, to make an end *or* accomplishment; *not merely to end it, but* to bring it to perfection; *generally* to carry out a thing, *to give the finishing stroke.*

5. ἐπιτελέω, to finish, to perfect.

2. Luke i. 23.
2. —— ii. 6, 21, 22.
3. —— ix. 31.
4. —— xii. 50.
4. —— xviii. 31.
4. Luke xxii. 37.
4. John xix. 28.
1. Acts xxi. 5 (with γίνομαι, *to become.*)
5. Heb. ix. 6.
5. 1 Pet. v. 9.

ACCOMPLISHMENT.

ἐκπλήρωσις, entire fulfilment.

Acts xxi. 26.

ACCORD (OF ONE.)

σύμψυχος, joined together in soul *or* sentiment; unity of life in love.

Phil. ii. 2.

ACCORD (OF...OWN.)

1. αὐθαίρετος, choosing *or* willing of himself.

2. αὐτόματος, spontaneous, self-moving, self-acting.

2. Acts xii. 10.
1. 2 Cor. viii. 17.

ACCORD (WITH ONE.)

ὁμοθυμαδόν, with one mind, unanimously, *(from* ὁμός, alike, *and* θυμός, mind.)

Acts i. 14.
—— ii. 1 (ὁμοῦ, *together,* L T A ℵ.)
—— ii. 46.
—— iv. 24.
—— v. 12.
Acts vii. 57.
—— viii. 6.
—— xii. 20.
—— xv. 25.
—— xviii. 12.
—— xix. 29.

ACCORDING AS

1. καθότι, *(adv.)* as, according as, because that, for.

2. καθώς, *(adv.)* according as, even as; like as *(comparison.)*

3. κατά, *(prep.)* down.

(a) *with Gen. (down from)* against, *(the reverse of* ὑπέρ.)

(b) *with Acc. (down towards, denoting object, and intention: and tropically, accordance, conformity, proportion)* according to, *in reference to some standard of comparison stated or implied.*

4. ὡς, *in comparative sentences,* as; *in objective,* that; *in final,* in order to; *in causal,* for, on the ground that.

1. Acts iv. 35.
2. Rom. xi. 8.
4. —— xii. 3.
2. 1 Cor. i. 31.
3b. 2 Cor. iv. 13.
2. 2 Cor. ix. 7.
2. Eph. i. 4.
4. 2 Pet. i. 3.
4. Rev. xxii. 12.

ACCORDING TO.

1. καθώς, *see above, (No.* 2.)

2. κατά, *see above, (No. 3b.)*

3. πρός, towards, *(propinquity).*

(a) *with Gen. (hitherwards)* in favour of, conducive to.

(b) *with Dat. (resting in a direction towards)* near, close *or* hard by.

(c) *with Acc. (hitherwards of actual motion, or mere direction) conformity to a rule or standard; hence, comparison* in consideration of, in accordance with.

2. Matt. ii. 16.
2. —— ix. 29.
2. —— xvi. 27.
2. —— xxv. 15.
2. Mark vii. 5.
2. Luke i. 9, 38.
2. —— ii. 22, 24, 29, 39.
3c. Luke xii. 47.
2. —— xxiii. 56.
2. John vii. 24.
2. —— xviii. 31.
2. Acts ii. 30 (*ap.*)
2. —— vii. 44.
1. —— xi. 29.
2. —— xiii. 23.
2. —— xxii. 3, 12.
2. —— xxiv. 6 (*ap.*)
2. Rom. i. 3, 4.
2. —— ii. 2, 6, 16.
2. —— iv. 18.
2. —— v. 6, margin (text *in due.*)
2. —— viii. 27, 28.
2. —— ix. 3, 11.
2. —— x. 2.
2. —— xi. 5.
2. —— xii. 6 twice.
2. —— xv. 5 (margin *after the example of.*)
2. —— xvi. 25 twice, 26.
2. 1 Cor. iii. 8, 10.
2. —— xv. 3, 4.
2. 2 Cor. i. 17.
3c. —— v. 10.
— —— viii. 12 twice, see A. T. that.
2. —— x. 2, 13, 15.
2. 2 Cor. xi. 15.
2. —— xiii. 10
2. Gal. i. 4.
3c. —— ii. 14.
2. —— iii. 29.
2. Eph. i. 5, 7, 9, 11, 19.
2. —— ii. 2 twice.
2. —— iii. 7, 11, 16, 20.
2. —— iv. 7, 16, 22.
2. —— vi. 5.
2. Phil. i. 20.
2. —— iii. 21.
2. —— iv. 19.
2. Col. i. 11, 25, 29.
2. —— iii. 22.
2. 2 Thes. i. 12.
2. 1 Tim. i. 11, 18.
2. —— vi. 3.
2. 2 Tim. i. 1, 8, 9 twice.
2. —— ii. 8.
2. —— iv. 14.
2. Titus i. 1, 3.
2. —— iii. 5, 7.
2. Heb. ii. 4.
2. —— vii. 5.
2. —— viii. 4, 5, 9.
2. —— ix. 19.
2. Jas. ii. 8.
2. 1 Pet. i. 2, 3, 17.
2. —— iii. 7.
2. —— iv. 6 twice, 19.
2. 2 Pet. iii, 13 (καί, *and,* [L.)
2. —— iii. 15.
2. 1 John v. 14.
2. Rev. ii. 23.
2. —— xviii. 6.
2. —— xx. 12, 13.

ACCORDING TO THAT.

καθό, as, according as.

2 Cor. viii. 12 1st. (with *ἐαν*, *if*.)
——— 12. 2nd.

See also, FASHION.

ACCOUNT [verb.]

(-ING.)

1. *ἡγέομαι*, to go before, lead the way, guide. To deem, think, regard.
2. *λογίζομαι*, to put together an account; to reckon, count, value, esteem; to account, consider, *(from* λόγος, an account, *and* λέγω, to put together.)

2. Heb. xi. 19. | 1. 2 Pet. iii. 15.

ACCOUNT OF.

2. 1 Cor. iv. 1.

See also, PUT...ON, WORTHY.

ACCOUNTED (BE.)

1. *δοκέω*, *intransitive*, to appear, to have the appearance, *transitive*, to be of opinion, to think.
2. *λογίζομαι*, see "ACCOUNT."

1. Mark x. 42 (margin *think good*.)
1. Luke xxii. 24.
2. Rom. viii. 36.
2. Gal. iii. 6 (margin *impute*.)

ACCOUNT [noun.]

λόγος, the word, (*spoken, not written.*) *In a formal sense*, a word *as forming part of what is spoken; as* the expression *which serves for the occasion: as a means or instrument (not as a product)* the speaking. *In a material sense*, the word *as that which is spoken*, an exposition *or* account *which one gives. For further development of* λόγος, *see under* "WORD."

Matt. xii. 36
—— xviii. 23.
Rom. ix 28 margin (text, *work*), (*ap.*)
—— xiv. 12.
Phil. iv. 17.
Luke xvi. 2.
Acts xix. 40.
Heb. xiii. 17.
1 Pet. iv. 5.

ACCURSED.

ἀνάθεμα, an offering; a thing devoted to destruction or given up to the curse.

Romans ix. 3 (margin *separated*.)
1 Cor. xii. 3 (margin *anathema*.)
Gal. i. 8, 9.

ACCUSATION.

1. *αἰτία*, affair, matter, charge *(whether true or false) not necessarily fault or accusation.*
2. *κατηγορία*, a speaking against; an accusation.
3. *κρίσις*, separation, sundering, judgment. *Then, of a definite* accusation, *guilt of some sort being presupposed leading on to* condemnation. *Then, the judgment pronounced*, the sentence.

1. Matt. xxvii. 37.
1. Mark xv. 26.
2. Luke vi. 7 (*κατηγορέω*, *to speak against*, Tr A.)
— Luke xix. 8, see A (take by false.)
2. John xviii. 29.
1. Acts xxv. 18.
2. 1 Tim. v. 19.
3. 2 Pet. ii. 11.
3. Jude 9.

ACCUSATION (TAKE BY FALSE.)

συκοφαντέω, to inform against those who exported figs, *(from σῦκον*, a fig, *and* φαίνω, to show, declare.) *A primitive Athenian law, forbad in time of dearth, the exportation of figs, and not being repealed when a plentiful harvest rendered it unnecessary, occasion was given to illnatured and malicious persons to accuse those who transgressed the letter of the law. Hence the verb means*, to wrong any one by false *or* frivolous accusation, *or* to oppress him under pretence of law.

Luke xix. 8.

ACCUSE.

(-ED, -ETH, -ING.)

1. *κατηγορέω*, to speak against; *before judges*, to accuse. *(Occ.* Acts xxiv. 19.)
2. *ἐγκαλέω*, to call into, to summon into *a court. Pass.* to be called to a judicial account, to be accused.

3. { ἐν, in, κατηγορία, a speaking against, an accusation } in *or* under an accusation.

1. Matt. xii. 10.
1. —— xxvii. 12.
1. Mark iii. 2.
1. —— xv. 3.
— Lu iii. 14, see A (falsely)
1. — xi. 54 (*ap.*)
1. — xxiii. 14 (with κατα.)
1. — xxiii. 2, 10.
1. John viii. 6 (*ap.*)
1. —— v. 45 twice.
2. Acts xxiii. 28, 29.
1. —— xxvi. 2, 7.
1. —— xxii. 30.
1. —— xxiv. 2, 8, 13.
1. —— xxv. 5, 11, 16.
1. —— xxviii. 19.
1. Rom. ii. 15.
3. Titus i. 6.
— 1 Pet. iii. 16, see A (falsely)
1. Rev. xii. 10.

ACCUSE (FALSELY.)

1. ἐπηρεάζω, to injure, harrass, insult; *as it would seem for the pleasure of insulting.*

2. συκοφαντέω, *see* "ACCUSATION (TAKE BY FALSE.)"

2. Luke iii. 14. | 1. 1 Pet. iii. 16.

ACCUSED (BE.)

διαβάλλομαι, to be struck *or* darted through, *hence,* to be struck *or* stabbed with an accusation; to be accused.

Luke xvi. 1.

ACCUSER (-S.)

κατήγορος, an accuser, a speaker against.

John viii. 10 (*ap.*) | Acts xxiv. 8 (*ap.*)
Acts xxiii. 30 35. | —— xxv. 16, 18.
Rev. xii. 10 (κατήγωρ. The Rabbinical form of the word, G L T Tr A.)

ACCUSERS (FALSE-.)

[*margin* makebates.]

διάβολος, a slanderer, an adversary, an accuser, the Devil *(Diabolus) because he was a slanderer of God from the beginning.*

2 Tim. iii. 3. | Titus ii. 3.

ACHAIA.

'Αχαΐα.

In all places, except

Romans xvi. 5 ('Ασία, *Asia*, G L T Tr A ℵ.)

ACKNOWLEDGE (-ED.)

ἐπιγινώσκω, to give heed, notice attentively, to take a view of, to recognise. *Then generally* to know, to understand.

Rom. 1. 28, margin (text, *to retain in knowledge*) (with ἔχω ἐν *to have..in.*)
1 Cor. xiv. 37. | 1 Cor. xvi. 18,
2 Cor. i. 13 twice, 14.

ACKNOWLEDGING.

ἐπίγνωσις, knowledge, clear and exact knowledge; a knowledge *that lays claim to personal sympathy, and exerts an influence upon the person.*

2 Tim. ii. 25. | Titus i. 1.
Philem. 6.

ACKNOWLEDGMENT.

ἐπίγνωσις, *see above* "ACKNOWLEDGING."

Ephes. i. 17, margin (text, *knowledge.*)
Col. ii. 2.

ACQUAINTANCE.

γνωστός, known, *with the underlying idea —capable of being known,* knowable.

Luke ii. 44 (with art.) | Luke xxiii. 49 (with art.)

ACQUAINTANCE (HIS-.)

ἴδιος, one's own, peculiar to one, proper for one.

Acts xxiv. 23.

ACT (IN THE VERY-.)

ἐπαυτοφώρω, in the very theft. *Then applied to any flagrant wickedness, particularly adultery.*

John viii. 4 (*ap.*)

ADD.

(-ED.)

1. προστίθημι, to set, place *or* lay towards *or* in addition to; to put one thing to another, to add.

2. ἐπιτίθημι, to set, place *or* lay upon.

3. προσανατίθημι, to lay anything additional on *one; Mid.* to take such burthen on oneself, *but also* to lay *on another* something additional of one's own. *In N.T. only 2nd Aorist Mid.,* to lay before in addition, to impart *or* communicate further; *by way of consultation,* to take counsel with *one.*

4. ἐπιφέρω, to bring upon, to bring against.

5. *ἐπιχορηγέω, lit.*, to supply the cost of leading the chorus or of theatrical entertainments; *hence*, to furnish *or* supply besides *or* abundantly.

6. *ἐπιδιατάσσομαι*, to appoint *or* order anything beside, to superadd.

7. *δίδωμι*, to give, yield, deliver, supply.

1. Matt. vi. 27, 33.
1. Luke iii. 20.
1. — xii. 25, 31.
1. — xix. 11.
1. Acts ii. 41, 47.
1. — v. 14.
1. — xi. 24.
— Gal. ii. 6, see A in conference.
— Gal. iii. 15, see A thereto
1. Gal. iii. 19 (G∾) (*τίθημι, to set, place*, G.)
4. Phil. i. 16 (*ἐγείρω, to raise up*, G∾ L T Tr
5. 2 Pet. i. 5. [A ℵ.)
7. Rev. viii. 3, margin (text, *offer*.)
— Rev. xxii. 18 twice, see A unto.

ADD IN CONFERENCE.

3. Gal. ii. 6 (mid.)

ADD THERETO.

6. Gal. iii. 15.

ADD UNTO.

2. Rev. xxii. 18 twice.

ADDICT. (-ED.)

τάσσω, to order, set in a certain order, to appoint.

1 Cor. xvi. 15.

ADJURE.

1. *ὁρκίζω*, to cause to swear, to lay under the obligation of an oath, to beseech, conjure, (*from ὅρκος* an oath, *which again may be deduced from the Heb.* ירך the thigh, *see Gen. xxiv.* 2, 9; *xlvii.* 29.)

2. *ἐξορκίζω, the above with ἐξ, intensive.*

2. Matt. xxvi. 63. | 1. Mark v. 7.
1. Acts xix. 13.
1. 1 Thes. v. 27, margin (text, *charge*), (*ἐνορκίζωμαι, to make one swear*, L T Tr A.)

ADMINISTERED (BE-.)

διακονέω, to serve, to wait upon; *in its narrowest sense* to wait at table. *Generally* to do any one a service, to minister.

2 Cor. viii. 19, 20.

ADMINISTRATION.

διακονία, serviceable labour, service. *Every business, every labour, as far as its labour benefits others is a διακονία.*

1 Cor. xii. 5. | 2 Cor. ix. 12.

ADMIRATION.

θαῦμα, a wonderful thing; wonder, astonishment.

Rev. xvii. 6.

ADMIRATION (HAVE IN-.)

θαυμάζω, to wonder, marvel, be astonished; to regard with wonder and reverence, to honour.

Jude 16.

ADMIRED (BE.)

θαυμάζω, see above.

2 Thes. i. 10.

ADMONISH (-ING.)

1. *νουθετέω*, to put in mind, (*from νοῦς* the mind, *τίθημι*, to put) to instruct, warn.

2. *παραινέω*, to recommend, advise; *esp.* to advise publicly.

2. Acts xxvii. 9. | 1. Col. iii. 16.
1. Rom. xv. 14. | 1. 1 Thes. v. 12.
1. 2 Thes. iii. 15.

ADMONISHED OF GOD (BE.)

χρηματίζω, (*from χρῆμα*, an affair, business, *which again is from χράομαι*, to use.) To do *or* carry on business. *Then* to be called *or* named, *since names were imposed on men from their business or office.* To speak to *or* treat with *another about some* business. To utter oracles, give divine directions *or* instructions.

Heb. viii. 5.

ADMONITION.

νουθεσία, a putting into the mind, instruction; an admonition.

1 Cor. x. 11. | Eph. vi. 4.
Titus iii. 10.

ADO (MAKE AN.)

θορυβέομαι, to make a noise *or* disturbance, (*from θόρυβος*, a tumult *or* tumultuous assembly.)

Mark v. 39.

ADOPTION.

υἱοθεσία, the making *or* constituting of a son; adoption; receiving into the relation of a son, (*from* υἱός, a son, *and* θέσις, a setting *or* placing.)

Rom. viii. 15. | Rom. ix. 4.
——— 23. | Gal. iv. 5, see A of sons
Eph. i. 5, see A of children.

ADOPTION OF SONS.

Gal. iv. 5

ADOPTION OF CHILDREN.

Eph. i. 5.

ADORN.

(-ED.)

κοσμέω, to order, set in order; to adorn, garnish; to prepare.

Luke xxi. 5. | Titus ii. 10.
1 Tim. ii. 9. | 1 Pet. iii. 5.
Rev. xxi. 2.

ADORNING [noun.]

κόσμος, (*root*, to polish) an ornament; order; (*for further development of this word see under* "WORLD.")

1 Pet. iii. 3.

ADULTERER (-S.)

μοιχός, an adulterer.

Luke xviii. 11. | Heb. xiii. 4.
1 Cor. vi. 9. | Jas. iv. 4.

ADULTERESS (-ES.)

μοιχαλίς, an adulteress.

Rom. vii. 3 twice. | Jas. iv. 4.

ADULTEROUS.

μοιχαλίς, an adulteress, *applied as an adjective to the Jewish people who had transferred their affections from God.*

Matt. xii. 39. | Matt. xvi. 4.
Mark viii. 38.

ADULTERY (-IES.)

1. μοιχεία, adultery.
2. μοιχαλίς, an adulteress.

1. Matt. xv. 19. | 1. John viii. 3 (*ap.*)
1. Mark vii. 21. | 1. Gal. v. 19 (om. All.)
2. 2 Pet. ii. 14.

ADULTERY.

(IN.)

μοιχεύω, to commit adultery with.

John viii. 4 (*ap.*)

ADULTERY and ADULTERY WITH.*

(COMMIT -ETH.)

1. μοιχεύω, to commit adultery with.
2. μοιχάομαι, to commit adultery, to be guilty of adultery by causing another to commit it.

1. Matt. v. 27, 28.*
2. —— v. 32 1st (No. 1, L Tr א)
2. —— v. 32 2nd.
2. —— xix. 9.
1. —— xix. 18.
2. Mark x. 11, 12.
1. Mark x. 19.
1. Luke xvi. 18 twice.
1. —— xviii. 20.
1. Rom. ii. 22 twice.
1. —— xiii. 9.
1. James ii. 11 twice.
. Rev. ii. 22.

ADVANTAGE [noun.]

1. περισσός, very much, exceedingly; what is over and above.
2. ὠφέλεια, profit, advantage, gain.

1. Rom. iii. 1. | 2. Jude 16.

ADVANTAGED.

(BE.)

1. ὠφελέω, to profit, advantage, benefit, help.
2. ὄφελος, profit, advantage, (*from* ὀφέλλω to heap up, increase.)

1. Luke ix. 25.
2. 1 Cor. xv. 32 (lit. *what to me the profit.*)

ADVANTAGE.

(GET AN.)

πλεονεκτέω, to have more *or* a greater share than others, (*whether of good or evil. In N.T. only in a bad sense.*) *Transitively*, to make a prey of, to defraud; to get the better, *as an enemy by force or fraud.*

2 Cor. ii. 11.

ADVENTURE [verb.]

δίδωμι, to give, give up, deliver.

Acts xix. 31.

ADVERSARY.

(-IES.)

1. *ἀντίδικος*, an adversary *or* opponent in a lawsuit, *any enemy or accuser. (from ἀντί*, against, *and δίκη*, a cause *or* suit at law.)
2. *ἀντίκειμαι*, to be placed against *or* in opposition; *to be* opposite, to oppose, to be an adversary to, *(from ἀντί* against, *and κεῖμαι*, to be placed, to lie.)
3. *ὑπεναντίος*, contrary, adverse. *Plural,* adversaries, enemies.

1. Matt. v. 25 twice.
1. Luke xii. 58.
2. —— xiii. 17.
1. —— xviii 3.
2. —— xxi. 15.
2. 1 Cor. xvi. 9.
2. Phil. i. 28.
2. 1 Tim. v. 14.
3. Heb. x. 27.
1. 1 Pet. v. 8.

ADVERSITY (SUFFER.)

κακουχούμενος, ill treated, harassed, *(from κακόν*, ill, *and ἔχω*, to have.)

Heb. xiii. 3.

ADVICE.

γνώμη, an opinion, sentence, *(from γινώσκω, see under* "ACKNOWLEDGE.")

2 Cor. viii. 10.

ADVISE.

(-ED.)

{ *βουλή*, counsel, *τίθημι*, to place, lay, lay down, } to give advice *or* counsel.

Acts xxvii. 12.

ADVOCATE.

παράκλητος (a verbal adj.) he who has been *or* may be called to help; a pleader *who comes forward in favour of and as the representative of another.*

1 John ii. 1.

AFFAIR (-S.)

1. *πραγματεία*, a handling any matter; an affair; business.
2. *τὰ κατὰ*, *lit.* the things with, *or* respecting [*me or you.*]
3. *τὰ περὶ*, *lit.* the things concerning [*us.*]

2. Eph. vi. 21.
3. —— 22.
3. Phil. i. 27.
1. 2 Tim. ii. 4.

AFAR OFF.

1. *μακρόθεν*, *(from μακρός*, far, *and θεν*, *a syllabic adjective denoting* from *or* at), from far, at a distance.
2. { *ἀπὸ*, *(prep.)* from. *μακρόθεν*, *see No.* 1. }
3. *μακράν*, *(the Acc. of μακρός*, far, *ὁδὸς*, a way, *being understood)*, a long way off. *With article (as here)* that which is afar off.
4. *πόῤῥωθεν*, further, from afar, far off.

2. Matt. xxvi. 58.
2. —— xxvii. 55.
2. Mark v. 6 (No. 1, G→.)
1. —— xi. 13 (No. 2, G⇉ L T Tr A ℵ.).
2. —— xiv. 54.
2. —— xv. 40.
2. Luke xvi. 23.
4. —— xvii. 12.
1. Luke xviii. 13.
1. —— xxii. 54.
1. —— xxiii. 49 (No. 2, L ℵ.)
3. Acts ii. 39.
3. Eph. ii. 17.
4. Heb. xi. 13.
2. Rev. xviii. 10, 15.
2. —— xviii. 17.

AFFECT.

(-ED.)

ζηλόω, to desire zealously, to be jealous over, to envy.

Acts xiv. 2, see A (make evil.)
Gal. iv. 17 1st, see A (zealously.)
—— iv. 17, 2nd.
—— iv. 18, see A (zealously.)

AFFECT (ZEALOUSLY.)

(-ED.)

Gal. iv. 17. | Gal. iv. 18.

AFFECTED (MAKE EVIL.)

κακόω, to evil intreat, abuse, hurt, to disaffect, make disaffected *or* ill-affected.

Acts xiv. 2.

AFFECTION (-S.)

1. *πάθημα*, *(from πάσχω*, to suffer.)
   (a) a suffering, affliction.
   (b) a passion, an affection.
2. *πάθος*, *(from πάσχω.)*
   (a) pain, suffering *or* misfortune.
   (b) a passion, affection, lust, concupiscence.
3. *σπλάγχνα*, the bowels; tender affections, *whether of love, pity, mercy, or compassion.*

2b. Rom. i. 26.
— —— 31, see A (without natural.)
— 2 Cor. vii. 15, see A (inward.)
1. Gal. v. 24, (margin *passion*)
— Col. iii. 2, see A on (set.)
— Col. iii. 5, see A (inordinate.)
2b. 2 Tim. iii. 3, see A (without natural.)

AFFECTION (INORDINATE.)

2b. Col. iii. 5.

AFFECTION (INWARD.)

3. 2 Cor. vii. 15.

AFFECTION ON (SET THE.)

φρονέω, *intransitive*, to think, be of opinion, *(from* φρήν, the membrane about the heart, *hence of* the mind and understanding.) *Transitive* to mind; *an operation of the mind which includes both the* understanding *and the* will.

Col. iii. 2.

AFFECTION (WITHOUT NATURAL.)

ἄστοργος, void of natural affection, *particularly of* that love *and* affection *which parents ought to bear to children and children to parents, and which animals have by natural instinct, and some of them in a remarkable degree, particularly* the stork, *whose English name seems to be of the same origin as the Greek* στοργή, storgē.)

Rom. i. 31. | 2 Tim. iii. 3.

AFFECTIONATELY DESIROUS (BEING.)

ἱμείρομαι, to long for, yearn after, desire.

1 Thes. ii. 8 (G∾), (ὁμείρομαι, same meaning, G L T ℵ.)

AFFECTIONED (BE KINDLY.)

φιλόστοργος, loving with that στοργή *or* tender affection which is natural between parents and children. See "A (WITHOUT NATURAL.")

Rom. xii. 10.

AFFIRM.

(-ED.)

1. φάσκω *(frequentative of No.* 2, φημί) to assert, affirm, to boast.
2. φημί, to say; *(where the speaking or explaining is a development of the primary notion of enlightening, showing.)*
3. διαβεβαιόομαι, to assert strongly *or* constantly, *(from* διά *emphatic, and* βεβαιόω, to confirm.)
3. διϊσχυρίζομαι, to affirm *or* assert strongly *or* vehemently, *(from* δία, *emphatic, and* ἰσχυρίζομαι, to corroborate, *which again is from* ἰσχυρός strong.)

— Luke xxii. 59, see A (confidently.)
— Acts xii. 15, see A (constantly.)
1. Acts xxv. 19.
2. Rom. iii. 8.
3. 1 Tim. i. 7.
— Titus iii. 8, see A (constantly.)

AFFIRM (CONFIDENTLY.)

4. Luke xxii. 59.

AFFIRM (CONSTANTLY.)

4. Acts xii. 15. | 3. Titus iii. 8.

AFFLICTED (BE.)

1. θλίβω, to press, squeeze, throng, crowd; to oppress, afflict.
2. θλίψις, pressure, affliction.
3. ταλαιπωρέω, to labour severely, be worn by labour; to be touched *or* affected with a sense of misery.
4. κακοπαθέω, to suffer evil, to endure *or* sustain afflictions.

2 Matt. xxiv. 9.
1. 2 Cor. i. 6.
1. Heb. xi. 37.
3. Jas. iv. 9.
4. Jas. v. 13.

AFFLICTED (THE.)

Participle of No. 1 above.

1 Tim. v. 10.

AFFLICTION (-S.)

1. θλίψις, pressure, affliction.
2. πάθημα, (a) a suffering, an affliction. (b) a passion, an affection.
3. κάκωσις, ill-treatment, vexation, affliction.

1. Matt. xxiv. 9 (with εἰς, unto.)
1. Mark iv. 17.
1. —— xiii. 19.
1. Acts vii. 10, 11.
3. —— vii. 34.
1. —— xx. 23.
2. 2 Cor. ii. 4.

2. 2 Cor. iv. 17.
2. —— vi. 4.
2. —— viii. 2.
— 2 Tim. i. 8, see A (partaker.)
2. 2 Tim. iii. 11.
— 2 Tim. iv. 5, see A (endure.)
1. Col. i. 24.
1. 1 Thes. i. 6.
1. 1 Thes. iii. 3, 7.
1. Phil. i. 16.
1. —— iv. 14.
2a. Heb. x. 32.
1. —— x. 33.
— —— xi. 25, see A with (suffer.)
1. Jas. i. 27.
— —— v. 10, see A (suffer)
2a. 1 Peter v. 9.

AFFLICTIONS (ENDURE.)

κακοπαθέω, to suffer evil *or* afflictions, to endure *or* sustain afflictions.

2 Tim iv. 5.

AFFLICTIONS (PARTAKER OF THE.)

συγκακοπαθέω, to suffer evil *or* affliction, together with.

2 Tim. i. 8.

AFFLICTION (SUFFERING.)

κακοπάθεια, a suffering of evil, a bearing of affliction.

Jas. v. 10.

AFFLICTION WITH (SUFFER.)

συγκακουχέομαι, to be treated ill *or* afflicted together with.

Heb. xi 25.

AFFRIGHTED.

ἔμφοβος, in fear, afraid, terrified.

Luke xxiv. 37. | Rev. xi. 13.

AFFRIGHTED (BE.)

ἐκθαμβέομαι, to amaze, astonish exceedingly, *(from ἐκ out, or intensive, and θαμβέω*, to amaze, astonish.)

Mark xvi. 5, 6.

AFOOT.

πεζῇ, on foot, afoot *(an adv. but properly the Dat. case fem. of the adj. πεζός*, performed on foot, *from πεζά*, the sole of the foot, *which is from πούς*, the foot.)

Mark vi. 33.

AFOOT (GO.)

πεζεύω, to go *or* travel on foot *or* by land, *(from πεζός which see under πεζῇ*, "AFOOT.")

Acts xx. 13.

AFORE.

See, PREPARE, PROMISE, WRITE.

AFOREHAND.

See, COME.

AFORETIME.

ποτέ, at some time or other, once.

John ix. 13.

AFORETIME (WRITE.)

See, WRITE.

AFRAID.

ἔμφοβος, in fear, afraid, affrighted, *(from ἐν, in, and φόβος*, fear, *see below.)*

Luke xxiv. 5.
Mark ix. 6, see A (sore.)
Acts x. 4.
—— xxii. 9 (*om*. G ≓ L Tr ℵ)

AFRAID (SORE.)

ἔκφοβος, exceedingly afraid, terrified, *(from ἐκ, intensive, or* out from, *and φόβος* fear, *see below.)*

Mark ix. 6.

AFRAID (BE),* and AFRAID OF (BE.)

1. *φοβέομαι*, *intransitive*, to be terrified, affrighted; *transitive*, to fear, to reverence.

2. *δειλιάω*, to shrink for fear, to be timid, *or* a coward.

3. *τρέμω*, to tremble, tremble for fear.

1. Matt. ii. 22.
1. —— xiv. 27, 30.
1. —— xvii. 6, 7.
1. —— xxv. 25.
1. —— xxviii. 10.
1. Mark v. 15, 36.
1. —— vi. 50.
1. —— ix. 32.
1. —— x. 32.
1. —— xvi. 8.
— Luke ii. 9, see A (be sore)
1. —— ii. 9.
1. Luke viii. 25, 35.
1. —— xii. 4.
1. John vi. 19, 20.
2. —— xiv. 27.
1. —— xix. 8.
1. Acts ix. 26.*
1. —— xviii. 9.
1. —— xxii. 29.
1. Rom. xiii. 3,* 4.
1. Gal. iv. 11.*
1. Heb. xi. 23.
1. 1 Pet. iii. 6, 14.*
3. 2 Pet. ii. 10.

AFRAID (BE SORE.)

φοβέομαι, to be terrified. *See above.*
φόβος, *(from φέβομαι*, to run away from, flee), a fleeing *or* running away from through fear, fear, terror.
μέγας, great.

Lit., to fear a great fear.

Luke ii. 9.

AFRESH.

See, CRUCIFY.

AFTER.

1. *μετά*, with, *(in association with [locally] distinguished from σύν, which implies co-operation.)*
   (a) *with Gen. (whence)* together with, among; with and from, *or separable connexion.*
   (b) *with Acc. (whither)* after.
2. *κατά*, down.
   (a) *with Gen. (whence)* down from, against.
   (b) *with Acc. (whither)* down towards, according to.
3. *ἐπί*, upon, *(superposition.)*
   (a) *with Gen. (whence)* upon *as springing from;* over, in the presence *or* time of.
   (b) *with Dat. (where)* upon *as resting on:* in addition to, on account of.
   (c) *with Acc. (whither)* upon *by direction towards;* up to *(of place, number, aim)*, over *(of time, place, extent.)*
4. *ἐν*, in *(denoting inclusion, distinguished from σύν which denotes conjunction)*, in, *of time, place, or element.*
5. *δία*, through, *(from the notion of separation, disjunction.)*
   (a) *with Gen. (whence)* through *as proceeding from; in reference to time it marks the passage through an interval:* during, after the lapse of.
   (b) *with Acc. (whither)* through *or tending towards;* on account of.
6. *ἑξῆς*, to be next *or* immediately following in time, subsequence, succession, order.
7. *καθεξῆς*, in order, following, succeeding *(from κατά,* according to, *and ἑξῆς,* order.)
8. *ὀπίσω*, behind; after, *of place or time.*
9. *ὄπισθεν*, from behind.
10. *ὅτε*, *(an adv. of time)* when; *used with the indicative as relating to an actual event, usually of time past, but sometimes future.*
11. *ὡς*, as. *In comparative sentences it means,* as; *in objective,* that; *in final,* in order to; *in causal,* for, on the ground that.
12. *μέλλω*, to delay; *with an infinitive following,* to be about to do anything *immediate or remote.*
13. *διαγίνομαι*, to pass, pass through *of time, (from διά,* through, *and γίνομαι,* to be *or* become.)
14. *πληρόω*, to fill, make full, fulfil, complete.
15. *ὑπάρχω*, to begin, give a beginning to, to be.
16. *περιέχω*, to surround, to contain *as a writing, (from περί,* about, *and ἔχω,* to have, hold.)

All passages in which the word after *occurs as a preposition, or conjunction, except where it forms part of a verb.*

1b. Matt. i. 12.
8. —— iii. 11.
8. —— x. 38.
9. —— xv. 23.
8. —— xvi. 24.
1b. —— xvii. 1.
2b. —— xxiii. 3.
1b. —— xxiv. 29.
1b. —— xxv. 19.
1b. —— xxvi. 2, 32, 73.
— —— xxvii. 31, see A [that.
1b. ———— 53, 63,
8. Mark i. 7.
1b. ——— 14.
8. ——— 17, 20.
5a. —— ii. 1.
— —— iv. 28, see A that.
— —— viii. 25, see A that.
1b. ——— 31.
8. ——— 34.
1b. —— ix. 2.
— —— xii. 34, see A that.
1b. —— xiii. 24.
1b. —— xiv. 1, 28, 70.
1b. —— xvi. 12 (*ap.*), 19 [(*ap.*)
1b. Luke i. 24.
3b. ——— 59.
2b. —— ii. 27, 42.
1b. ——— 46.
1b. —— v. 27.
6. ——— vii. 11 (lit. *the* [[day] *after.*)
8. —— ix 23.
1b. ——— 28.
1b. —— x. 1.
1b. —— xii. 4, 5.
— —— xiii. 9, see A that.
8. —— xiv. 27.
3c. —— xv. 4.
1b. ——— 13.
8. —— xix. 14.
— —— xx. 40, see A that ..not.
8. —— xxi. 8.
1b. —— xxii. 20, 58.
9. —— xxiii. 26.
8. John i. 15, 27, 30.
— ——— 35, see A (next day.)
— John ii. 6, see A the manner of.
1b. ——— 12.
1b. —— iii. 22.
1b. —— iv. 43.
1b. —— v. 1.
1b. ——— 4, with art (*ap.*)
1b. —— vi. 1.
1b. —— vii. 1.
2b. —— viii. 15.
1b. —— xi. 7, 11.
8. —— xii. 19.
— —— xiii. 5, see A that.
10. ——— 12.
1b. ——— 27.
1b. —— xix. 28, 38.
1b. —— xx. 26.
1b. —— xxi. 1.
1b. Acts i. 3.
7. —— iii. 24 (lit. with art., *those that follow after.*)
1b. —— v. 37 1st.
8. ——— 37 2nd.
1b. —— vii. 5, 7.
— —— ix. 23, see A that.
1b. —— x. 37, 41.
1b. —— xii. 4.
1b. —— xiii. 15.
1b. ——— 20 (*ap.*)
2b. ——— 22.
1b. ——— 25.
1b. —— xv. 13, 16, 36.
11. —— xvi. 10.
1b. —— xviii. 1.
1b. —— xix. 4.
11. ——— 21 1st.
1b. ——— 21 2nd.
1b. —— xx. 1, 6, 29.
8. ——— 30.
— —— xxi. 1, see A (that.)
1b. ——— 15.
2b. —— xxiii. 3.
16. ——— 25 (*ἔχω, to have,* L Tr ℵ.)
1b. —— xxiv. 1.
2b. ——— 14.
5a. ——— 17.
1b. ——— 24.
14. ——— 27.

1b. Acts xxv. 1.
13. ———— 13.
2b. —— xxvi. 5.
15. —— xxvii. 21.
1b. —— xxviii. 11, 13, 17.
2b. Rom. ii. 5.
3b. —— v. 14.
2b. —— vii. 22.
2b. —— viii. 1, twice (*ap.*)
2b. ———— 4, 5 twice, 12, [13.
— 1 Cor. i. 21, see A that.
2b. ———— 26.
2b. ———— vii. 40.
2b. ———— x. 18.
— ———— xi. 25, see A the same manner.
— ———— xii. 28, see A that.
— ———— xv. 6, 7, see A [that.
— 1 Cor. xv. 32, see A the manner of.
2b. 2 Cor. v. 16 twice.
2b. ———— vii. 9, 11.
2b. ———— x. 3, 7.
2b. ———— xi. 17, 18.
2b. Gal. i. 11.
1b. ———— 18.
5b. —— ii. 1.
— —— iii. 14, see A the manner of.
— ———— 15, see A the manner of.
1b. ———— 17.
2b. —— iv. 23.
2b. ———— 29 twice.
2b. Eph. i. 11.
2b. —— iv. 24.
2b. Col. ii. 8 3 times.
2b. ———— 22.
2b. Col. iii. 10.
2b. 2 Thes. ii. 9.
2b. ———— iii. 6
8. 1 Tim. v. 15.
2b. 2 Tim. iv. 3.
2b. Titus i. 1, 4.
— ———— iii. 4, see A that.
1b. ———— 10.
1b. Heb. iv. 7.
4. ———— 11.
2b. —— v. 6, 10.
2b. —— vi. 20.
— —— vii. 2, see A that.
2b. ———— 11 twice, 15, 16 twice.
2b. ———— 21 (*ap.*)
1b. —— viii. 10.
1b. —— ix. 3, 27.
1b. —— x. 15, 16, 26.
— ———— xi. 8, see A (should.)
2b. —— xii. 10.
2b. Jas. iii. 9.
1b. 2 Pet. i. 15.
— ———— ii. 6, see A should (that.)
8. ———— 10.
2b. ———— iii. 3.
2b. 2 John 6.
8. Jude 7.
2b. —— 16, 18.
1b. Rev. iv. 1.
1b. —— vii. 1, 9.
1b. —— xi. 11.
8. —— xii. 15.
8. —— xiii. 3.
1b. —— xv. 5.
1b. —— xviii. 1.
1b. —— xix. 1.
1b. —— xx. 3.

AFTER THAT.

1. *εἶτα*, then, afterwards.
2. *ἔπειτα*, thereupon, then, *(from ἐπί*, upon *or* at, *and εἶτα*, then.)
3. *ἔτι*, any more, any longer, yet, still, even.
4. *οὐκέτι*, no longer, no more.
5. *ὡς*, *see* "AFTER," *No.* 11.
6. *ὅτε*, *see* "AFTER," *No.* 10.
7. *ἐπειδή*, when truly, after that indeed, *(from ἐπεί*, when, *and δή*, truly.)
8. *μέλλω*, *see above*, *No.* 12.
9. *μετὰ ταῦτα*, after these things.

6. Matt. xxvii. 31.
1. Mark iv. 28.
1. ———— viii. 25.
4. ———— xii. 34.
8. Luke xiii. 9.
— —— xx. 40, see A that..not.
1. John xiii. 5.
5. Acts ix. 23.
9. —— xiii. 20 (*ap.*)
— Acts xxi. 1, see A (that.)
7. 1 Cor. i. 21.
2. ———— xii. 28.
2. 1 Cor. xv. 6, 7.
6. Titus iii. 4.
2. Heb. vii. 2.

AFTER THAT...NOT.

4. Luke xx. 40.

AFTER THE MANNER OF.

κατά, down.

(a) *with Gen. (whence)* down from, against.

(b) *with Acc. (whither)* down towards, according to.

b. John ii. 6. | b. Gal. iii. 15. | b. 1 Cor. xv. 32.

AFTER THE MANNER OF GENTILES.

ἐθνικῶς, belonging *or* peculiar to a nation. *In N.T.—to live in a non-Israelitish manner.*

Gal. ii. 14.

AFTER THE SAME MANNER.

ὡσαύτως, likewise, in the same *or* like manner.

1 Cor. xi. 25.

AFTER (SHOULD.)

μέλλω, *see under* "AFTER," *No.* 12.

Heb. xi. 8.

AFTER (THAT.)

ὡς, *see under* "AFTER," *No.* 11.

Acts xxi. 1.

AFTER SHOULD (THAT.)

μέλλω, *see under* "AFTER," *No.* 12.

2 Pet. ii. 6.

AFTER (THE NEXT DAY.)

ἐπαύριον, to-morrow; on the morrow *or* next day.

John i. 35 (with art.)

See also, ASK, COME, COVET, DAY, FEEL, FOLLOW, GODLY, LONG, LOOKING, LUST, MORROW, MANNER, NEXT, SEEK, SPOKEN.

AFTERWARD.

(-s.)

1. ὕστερον, after, afterwards, at length.
2. { μετά, after, *see* "AFTER," No. 1, ταῦτα, these *things*, } after these things.
3. εἶτα, then afterwards.
4. ἔπειτα, thereupon, then.
5. μετέπειτα, afterwards, *(from* μετά, after, *and* ἔπειτα, then.)
6. καθεξῆς, in order, following, *(from* κατά, according to, *and* ἑξῆς, order.)
7. δεύτερος, the second, *of time or place, (from* δεύω, to fail, fall short, *properly spoken of* those who are second *in a trial of skill, etc.)*

1. Matt. iv. 2.
1. —— xxi. 29, 32.
1. —— xxv. 11.
3. Mark iv. 17.
1. —— xvi. 14 (*ap.*)
1. Luke iv. 2 (*om.* G⇉ L T Tr A ℵ.)
6. —— viii. 1.
2. —— xvii. 8.
2. —— xviii. 4.
2. John v. 14.
1. —— xiii. 36.
— Acts xiii. 21, see A (and)
4. Gal. i. 21.
4. 1 Cor. xv. 23, 46.
2. Heb. iv. 8.
1. —— xii. 11.
5, —— 17.
7. Jude 5.

AFTERWARD (AND.)

κἀκεῖθεν, and then, and from that time *(of time;)* and thence *or* from thence *(of place.)*

Acts xiii. 21.

AGAIN.

1. πάλιν, again, back, *of place or time; a particle of continuation,* again, once again, further; *of antithesis,* on the other hand.
2. ἄνωθεν, *adv. of place or time, (from* ἄνω, above, *and* θεν, *denoting* from. *Local*—from above; *temporal*—from of old, from the beginning.)
3. { πάλιν, *see No.* 1. ἄνωθεν, *see No.* 2. } again anew.
4. δεύτερος, the second, *of time or place.*
5. δίς, twice, two times.

The following are all the passages, except where "AGAIN" *forms part of a verb.*

1. Matt. iv. 7, 8.
1. —— v. 33.
1. —— xiii. 44 (*om.* Lb T Tr A ℵ.)
1. Matt. xiii. 45, 47.
1. —— xviii. 19 (ἀμήν, *verily,* L) (add ἀμήν, G→ T Tr A.)
1. —— xix. 24.
1. Matt. xx. 5.
1. —— xxi. 30.
1. —— xxii. 1, 4.
1. —— xxvi. 42, 43, 44, 72.
1. —— xxvii. 50.
1. Mark ii. 1, 13.
1. —— iii. 1, 20.
1. —— iv. 1.
1. —— v. 21.
1. —— vii. 31.
1. —— viii. 13, 25.
1. —— x. 1 twice, 10, 24, 32.
1. —— xi. 27.
1. —— xii. 4.
1. —— 5 (*om.* All.)
1. —— xiv. 39.
1. —— 40 (*ap.*)
1. —— 61, 69, 70 twice.
1. —— xv. 4, 12, 13.
1. Luke xiii. 20.
1 —— xxiii. 20.
1. John i. 35.
2. —— iii. 3. } marg. *from*
2. —— 7. } *above.*
1. —— iv. 3 (*om.* G→ T.)
1. —— 13, 46, 54.
1. —— vi. 15 (*om.* G→ A.)
1. —— viii. 2 (*ap.*), 8 (*ap.*), 12, 21.
1. —— ix. 15, 17.
4. —— 24.
1. —— 26 (*om.* L T Tr A ℵ.)
1. —— 27.
1. —— x. 7, 17, 18, 19, 31, 39, 40.
1. —— xi. 7, 8, 38.
1. —— xii. 22 (ἔρχεται, *cometh,* for καί πάλιν, *and again.*)
1. —— 28, 30.
1. —— xiii. 12.
1. —— xiv. 3.
1. —— xvi. 16, 17, 19, 22, 28.
1. —— xviii. 7, 27, 33, 38, 40
1. —— xix. 4, 9, 37.
1. John xx. 10, 21, 26.
1. —— xxi. 1, 16.
1. Acts x. 15.
1. —— 16 (εὐθύς, *immediately,* L T Tr A ℵ), (*om.* πάλιν, G⇉.)
4. —— xi. 9, 10.
1. —— xvii. 32.
1. —— xviii. 21.
1. —— xxvii. 28.
1. Rom. viii. 15.
1. —— xi. 23.
1. —— xv. 10, 11, 12.
1. 1 Cor. iii. 20.
1. —— vii. 5.
1. —— xii. 21.
1. 2 Cor. i. 16.
1. —— ii. 1.
1. —— iii. 1.
1. —— v. 12.
1. —— x. 7.
1. —— xi. 16.
1. —— xii. 19 (πάλαι, *long ago,* L T Tr A ℵ.)
1. —— 21.
1. —— xiii. 2 (with εἰς [τὸ.)
1. Gal. i. 9, 17.
1. —— ii. 1, 18.
1. —— iv. 9 1st, marg. *back*
3. —— 9 2nd.
1. —— 19.
1. Gal. v. 1, 3.
1. Phil. i. 26.
1. —— ii. 28.
1. —— iv. 4.
5. —— 16.
5. 1 Thes. ii. 18.
1. Heb. i. 5, 6.
1. —— ii. 13 twice.
1. —— iv. 5, 7.
1. —— v. 12.
1. —— vi. 1, 6.
1. —— x. 30.
1. Jas. v. 18.
1. 2 Pet. ii. 20.
1. 1 John ii. 8.
1. Rev. x. 8, 11.

See also, ALIVE, ANSWER, ASK; BEGET, BID, BORN, BRING, BUILD; COME; DELIVER; FLOURISH, FOAM; GIVE, GO; HOPE; LIVE; MEASURE; PUT; RAISE, RAISE TO LIFE, RECEIVE, RECOMPENSE, REMEMBRANCE, RESTORE, RETURN, REVILE, RISE, RISING; SEND, SET AT ONE, SHEW; THAT, TURN; WORD (BRING.)

AGAINST.

1. κατά, down.
   (a) *with Gen. (whence)* down from, against.
   (b) *with Acc. (whither)* down towards, according to.
2. ἐπί, upon *(superposition.)*
   (a) *with Gen. (where)* upon; *as proceeding from;* over, *in the presence or time of.*
   (b) *with Dat. (where)* upon, *as resting on;* in addition to, on account of.

(c) *with Acc. (whither)* upon, *by direction towards;* to, *implying an intention* (for, against.)

3. εἰς, *(motion to the interior)* into, to; unto; towards, *sometimes implying mere reference* in regard to, *sometimes hostility*, against.

4. πρός, towards *(propinquity.)*

(a) *with Gen. (whence)* hitherwards.

(b) *with Dat. (where) resting in a direction towards*, near, hard by.

(c) *with Acc. (whither)* to *of literal direction; of mental direction*, towards, against. *From this mental direction comes* (i) *that of estimation*, in consideration of, *and* (ii) *that of intention*, in order to.

5. μετά, with, *in association with [locally] distinguished from σύν, which implies co-operation.*

(a) *with Gen. (whence)* with, together with.

(b) *with Acc. (whither)* after.

6. παρά, beside *(juxtaposition.)*

(a) *with Gen. (whence) beside and proceeding from;* from *(used of persons, while ἀπό is used of places.)*

(b) *with Dat. (where) beside, out at;* with, near.

(c) *with Acc. (whither) to or along the side of; beside (as not coinciding with, hence* contrary to; beside *with the notion of comparison, superiority*, above, *ὑπέρ affirms superiority, παρά institutes the comparison, and leaves the reader to infer superiority.)*

7. περί, around,

(a) *with Gen. (whence) around and separate from*, about, concerning.

(b) *with Acc. (whither) around and towards*, around, about.

8. ἐν, in, *of time, place or element*,

9. ἐναντίος, opposite, over-against; contrary.

10. ἔμπροσθεν, before *(as opposed to behind;)* before, in the presence of.

4c. Matt. iv. 6.
1a. —— v. 11, 23.
2c. —— x. 21.
1a. ——— 35 3 times.
1a. —— xii. 14. 25 twice.
2c. Matt. xii. 26.
1a. ——— 30, 32 twice.
3. —— xviii. 15 (*om.* L ℵ.)
3. ——— 21.
1a. —— xx. 11.
7a. Matt. xx. 24.
10. —— xxiii. 13.
2c. —— xxiv. 7 twice.
2c. —— xxvi. 55.
1a. ——— 59.
1a. —— xxvii. 1.
1a. Mark iii. 6.
2c. ——— 24, 25, 26.
3. ——— 29.
4c. —— vi. 45, marg. (text, *unto.*)
1a. —— ix. 40.
2c. —— x. 11.
1a. —— xi. 25.
4c. —— xii. 12.
2c. —— xiii. 8 twice, 12.
2c. —— xiv. 48.
1a. ——— 55, 56, 57.
4c. Luke iv. 11.,
4c. —— v. 30.
3. —— vii. 30, marg. *within.*
2c. —— ix. 5 (*ap.*)
1a. ——— 50.
2c. —— xi. 17 twice, 18.
1a. ——— 23.
3. —— xii. 10 twice.
2a. ——— 52 twice.
2b. ——— 53 1st, 2nd, 3rd & 4th.
2c. ——— 53 5th & 6th.
2c. —— xiv. 31 2nd.
3. —— xv. 18, 21,
3. —— xvii. 3 (*om.* G ⇉ L T Tr A ℵ.)
3. ——— 4.
4c. —— xx. 19.
2c. —— xxi. 10 twice.
2c. —— xxii. 52, 53.
3. ——— 65.
3. John xii. 7.
2c. —— xiii. 18.
3. ——— 29.
1a. —— xviii. 29.
1a. —— xix. 11.
1a. Acts iv. 26 twice.
2c. ——— 27.
4c. —— vi. 1.
3. ——— 11.
1a. ——— 13.
2c. —— viii. 1.
3. —— ix. 1.
4c. ——— 5, 29.
2c. —— xiii. 50, 51.
1a. —— xiv. 2.
1a. Acts xvi. 22.
1a. —— xix. 16.
4c. ——— 38.
1a. —— xxi. 28.
4c. —— xxiii. 30.
1a. —— xxiv. 1.
4c. ——— 19.
1a. —— xxv. 2. 3.
1a. ——— 7 (*ap.*)
3. ——— 8 3 times.
1a. ——— 15.
7a. ——— 18.
4c. ——— 19.
1a. ——— 27.
4c. —— xxvi. 14.
1a. —— xxvii. 14.
9. —— xxviii. 17.
2c. Rom. i. 18.
6c. ——— 26.
2c. —— ii. 2.
3. ——— 5.
6c. —— iv. 18.
3. —— viii. 7.
1a. ——— 31.
1a. —— xi. 2.
1a. 1 Cor. iv. 6.
4c. —— vi. 1.
3. ——— 18.
3. —— viii. 12 twice.
2c. 2 Cor. x. 2.
1a. ——— 5.
1a. —— xiii. 8.
1a. Gal. iii. 21.
1a. —— v. 17 twice, 23.
4c. Eph. vi. 11, 12 5 times.
1a. Col. ii. 14.
4c. —— iii. 13, 19.
1a. 1 Tim. v. 19.
3. —— vi. 19.
3. 2 Tim. i. 12.
3. Heb. xii. 3.
4c. ——— 4.
1a. Jas. iii. 14.
1a. —— v. 9.
1a. 1 Pet. ii. 11. [*upon*
2c. —— iii. 12, margin
1a. 2 Pet. ii. 11.
3. —— iii. 7.
1a. Jude 15.
1a. Rev. ii. 4, 14, 20.
5a. ——— 16.
5a. —— xi. 7.
1a. —— xii. 7 (No. 5a, All.)
4c. —— xiii. 6.
5a. —— xix. 19 twice.

See also, BEAT, BOAST, BRING; CRIME, CRY; DASH; FIGHT; INSURRECTION; JUDGE; MAD, MURMUR; OVER; PRATE, PREVAIL; QUARREL; REJOICE, REPLY, RISE UP; SAY, SPEAK, SPOKEN, STRIVE; WANTON, WAR, WILL, WITNESS.

AGE.

1. ἡλικία, time of life, adultness, maturity *of life, mind or person.*

2. ἡμέρα, the day *in distinction from the night, and as a division of time, also used of a longer* space of time.

3. γενεά, birth, race, descent; a generation, an age.

2. Luke ii. 36.
1. ——— 52, marg. (text, *stature.*)
— John ix. 21, 23, see A (be of.)
3. Acts xiii. 36, marg. (text, *generation.*)
1. Eph. iv. 13, marg. (text, *stature.*)
— Heb. v. 14, see A (of full)
1. Heb. xi. 11.

AGE (BE OF.)

{ ἡλικία, *see* "AGE," *No* 1, / ἔχω, to have, } to have maturity.

John ix. 21, 23.

AGE (OF FULL.)

τέλειος, complete, perfect, *(from* τέλος, an end.)

Heb. v. 14, margin *perfect.*

See also, AGES, FLOWER, GREAT, OLD, PASS.

AGED.

1. πρεσβύτης, old, aged, an old man, *(from* πρέσβυς, old, *which again* is *from* προεισβῆναι, to be far entered into *or* advanced in.)

Philem. 9.

AGED MAN.

Titus ii. 2.

AGED WOMAN.

πρεσβῦτις, an old *or* aged woman *(same root as above.)*

Titus ii. 3.

AGES.

1. αἰών, *(from* ἄω, ἄημι, blow, breathe), the life *which hastes away in the breathing of our breath,* life *as transitory; then,* course of life, time of life, life *in its temporal form; then the* space *of human life,* an age, *or generation* (*αἰών looks at a generation from the point of view of duration, while* γενεά [*No.* 2] *does from that of race*), *αἰών always includes a reference to* life, *filling time or a space of time. Accordingly*—the unbounded time, *in which the history or life of the world is accomplished; and hence,* the world *as filling the unmeasurable contents of immeasurable time.*

2. γενεά, progeny, offspring, a generation *or* descent *of men living at the same time;* the time in which such a race lives, *thence generclly* an age *or* period.

1. Eph. ii. 7.
2. —— iii. 5.
2. Eph. iii. 21.
1. Col. i. 26.

AGO.

1. ἀπὸ, from *(the exterior) separation in space with the idea of motion;* from *marking the distance.*
2. πρό, before, *whether of time or place.*
3. πάλαι, long ago, long, *(referring either to long or short spaces of past time, according to the context.)*
4. πέρυσι, *(with* ἀπό) the past year, last year *(from* περάω to pass, pass through.)

— Matt. xi. 21, see A (long)
— Luke x. 13, see A (a great while.)
1. Acts x. 30.
1. —— xv. 7.
1. 2 Cor. viii. 10, see A (a year.)
1. —— ix. 2, see A (a year.)
2. —— xii. 2.

AGO (A GREAT WHILE.)

3. Luke x. 13.

AGO (A YEAR.)

1 & 4. 2 Cor. viii. 10; ix. 2.

AGO (LONG.)

3. Matt. xi. 21.

AGONY.

ἀγωνία, bodily strife, struggle *or* contest; violent struggle *or* agony *both of body and mind, (from* ἄγω, to bring, carry, remove, drag.)

Luke xxii. 44 *(ap.)*

AGREE (-D.)

1. συμφωνέω, to speak a thing together with another, *to agree,* (σύν, with, *implying co-operation, and* φωνέω, to speak.)

2. *συντίθημι*, to put together, agree upon, settle.

3. *εἰμί*, to be, *with*

4. { *εἰμί*, to be, / *ἴσος*, equal, *(in quality, quantity or dignity,)* } to be equal.

5. *εὐνοέω*, to be well affected *or* well minded towards *another, to be* friends with him, *(from εὖ,* well, *and νόος,* the mind.)

6. *πείθω*, *active;* to persuade, to win by words, to influence. *Medial Passive:* suffer one's self to be persuaded *or* convinced.

7. { *ποιέω*, to make, to do, / *εἷς, (μία)*, one *(the numeral,)* / *γνώμη*, an opinion, sentence *(from γινώσκω,* to know,) } to do one mind.

5. Matt. v. 25.
1. —— xviii. 19.
1. —— xx. 2, 13.
4. Mark xiv. 56, 59.
— —— 70, see A thereto.
— Luke v. 36, see A with.
3. John ix. 22.
— Acts v. 9, see A together.
6. —— 40.
1. —— xv. 15.
2. —— xxiii. 20. [not.
— —— xxviii. 25, see A
3. 1 John v. 8.
7. Rev. xvii. 17.

AGREE THERETO.

ὁμοιάζω, to be like.

Mark xiv. 70.

AGREE TOGETHER.

συμφωνέω, *see* "AGREE," *No.* 1.

Acts v. 9.

AGREE NOT.

ἀσύμφωνος, disagreeing in speech.

Acts xxviii. 25.

AGREE WITH.

συμφωνέω, *see* "AGREE," *No.* 1.

Matt. xx. 13. | Luke v. 36.

AGREEMENT.

συγκατάθεσις, consent, agreement, *(from συγκατατίθημι*, to put down together with, *borrowed from those who being of the same opinion* put *their ballots* together *into the urn; hence* to vote with, assent to.)

2. Cor. vi. 16.

AGROUND.

See, RUN.

AH.

οὐά, ah, aha, *(an interjection, or natural exclamation of* derision *or* insult.)

Mark xv. 29.

AIM AT (not) [margin.]

ἀστοχέω, miss the mark, fail.

1 Tim. i. 6 (text, *swerve.*)

AIR.

1. *ἀήρ*, the air, *the celestial fluid above the earth.*

2. *οὐρανός*, heaven, (1) *physically; the over-arching and all embracing* heaven, *excluding the earth beneath and all that is therein.* (2) the dwelling-place of God.

2. Matt. vi. 26.
2. —— viii. 20.
2. —— xiii. 32.
2. Mark iv. 4 (*om.* G L T Tr A ℵ)
2. —— 32.
2. Luke viii. 5.
2. —— ix. 58.
2. —— xiii. 19.
2. Acts x. 12.
2. Acts xi. 6.
1. —— xxii. 23 (*οὐρανός, heaven*, G∾.)
1. 1 Cor. ix. 26.
1. —— xiv. 9.
1. Eph. ii. 2.
1. 1 Thes. iv. 17.
1. Rev. ix. 2.
1. —— xvi. 17.

ALABASTER BOX.

ἀλάβαστρον, a vessel to hold ointment *or* perfume; *(so called because commonly made from the alabaster stone, and afterwards any vessel used for ointment.)*

Matt. xxvi. 7. | Mark xiv. 3. | Luke vii. 37.

ALAS.

οὐαί, woe, alas, *(an interjection of* grief *or* concern); *also used as a noun,* a woe.

Rev. xviii. 10 twice, 16 twice, 19 twice.

ALBEIT.

ἵνα, that, to the end that.

Philem. 19.

ALBEIT...NOT.

{ *ἵνα*, that to the end that, / *μή*, not, lest, } that not, lest.

Philem. 19.

ALIEN.

(-S.)

ἀλλότριος, belonging to others, foreign *or* strange to oneself.

Heb. xi. 34.

ALIENS (BE.)

ἀπαλλοτριόω, to alienate, to estrange.

Eph. ii. 12.

ALIENATE.

(-ED.)

ἀπαλλοτριόω, to alienate, to estrange.

Eph. iv. 18. | Col. i. 21 (with *εἰμί, to be.*)

ALIVE.

Part. of ζάω, *for which see* "ALIVE (BE.)"

Acts i. 3.
—— ix. 41.
—— xx. 12.
Acts xxv. 19.
Rom. vi. 11.
Rev. i. 18.
Rev. xix. 20.

ALIVE (BE.)

ζάω, to live *(physically; opposite of* αποθανεῖν, to die); to live *in the highest sense*, to possess *spiritual and eternal* life.

Matt. xxvii. 63.
Mark xvi. 11 (*ap.*)
Luke xxiv. 23.
Acts xxv. 19.
Rom. vi. 13.
—— vii. 9.
1 Thes. iv. 15, 17.
Rev. ii. 8.

ALIVE AGAIN (BE.)

ἀναζάω, *(the above with* ἀνά, again, *prefixed)*, to live again.

Luke xv. 24, 32 (*ζάω, to live,* T Tr A ℵ.)

ALIVE (MAKE.)

ζωοποιέω, to make alive, vivify, cause to live.

(a) *pass.*, to be quickened, made alive.

a. 1 Cor. xv. 22.

ALL.

1. πᾶς, all; *of one only*, all of him; *of one in a number*, any; *of several*, every; *in pl.*, all.

(a) *Singular, without the article, signifies* every; *with the article*, the whole of the object it qualifies. Thus πᾶσα πόλις, every city; πᾶσα ἡ πόλις—the whole of the city; πάντα πειρασμόν—every *form* of temptation. (Luke iv. 13.)

(b) *Plural, generally has the article when the substantive is expressed (except when it is* ἄνθρωποι, men.) *But generally omits it when the substantive is implied (except where the idea is collective.)* Thus πάντες—all men; πάντα—all things, severally (see Phil. iv. 13.) τὰ πάντα—all things, *as constituting a whole.* (See Col. i. 16.)

* *with* ὅς, who, which; † *with* ὅστις, who- which- whatsoever; ‡ *with* ὅσος, *see No.* 4, *below.*

2. ὅλος, the whole, all. *Generally used with the article, e.g.*, ὅλος ὁ κόσμος—the whole world (Rom. i. 8.) *Sometimes the noun and article precede, which adds emphasis to* ὅλος, ὁ κόσμος ὅλος—the world, *yea* the whole *of it.* (Matt. xvi. 26.)

(a) *Without the article.*

3. ἅπας, quite all, all together, all, *(No.* 1 *strengthened by* ἅμα, at once, at the same time.)

4. ὅσος, how much, how great; *of time*, how long, as long as; *of quantity or number*, how much, how many.

1b. Matt. i. 17.
2. ———— 22.
1a. —— ii. 3.
1b. ———— 4, 16 twice.
1a. —— iii. 5 twice, 15.
1b. —— iv. 8, 9.
2. ———— 23 1st.
— ———— 23, 2nd & 3rd, see A manner of.
2. ———— 24 1st.
1b. ———— 24 2nd.
1b. —— v. 15, 18.
— ———— 34, see A (at.)
1a. —— vi. 29.
1b. ———— 32 1st.
3. ———— 32 2nd.
1b. ———— 33.
— —— vii. 12, see A things
1b. —— viii. 16.
2. —— ix. 26, 31.
1b. ———— 35.
— —— x. 1, see A manner of.
— ———— 22, see A men
1b. ———— 30.
1b. —— xi. 13.
— ———— 27, see A things
1b. ———— 28.
1b. —— xii. 15, 23.
— ———— 31, see A manner of.
1b. Matt. xiii. 32, 34.
— ———— 41, see A things.
1b. ———— 44‡, 46‡, 51, 56 twice.
1b. —— xiv. 20.
2. ———— 35 1st.
1b. ———— 35 2nd.
1b. —— xv. 37.
— —— xvii. 11, see A things.
1b. —— xviii. 25‡, 26.
1b. ———— 29 (*om.* G → L[b] T Tr A ℵ.)
1b. ———— 31.
1a. ———— 32, 34.
— —— xix. 11, see A men.
1b. ———— 20.
— ———— 26, see A things.
1b. ———— 27.
2. —— xx. 6.
2. —— xxi. 4 (*om.* G ⇉ L Tr A ℵ.)
1a. ———— 10.
1b. ———— 12.
— ———— 22 } see A
— —— xxii. 4 } things.
1b. ———— 10‡.
1b. ———— 27, 28.

2. Matt xxii. 37 3 times, 40.
1b. —— xxiii. 3‡, 5, 8.
— ———— 20, see A things.
1a. ———— 27, 35.
1b. ———— 36.
1b. —— xxiv. 2
1b. ———— 6 (om. G→ L Tr ℵ.)
1b. ———— 8, 9.
2. ———— 14 1st.
1b. ———— 14 2nd, 30, 33, 34.
3. ———— 39.
1b. ———— 47.
1b. —— xxv. 5, 7, 31, 32.
2. —— xxvi. 1, 27, 31.
— ———— 33, see A men
1b. ———— 35, 52.
2. ———— 56 1st.
1b. ———— 56 2nd.
2. ———— 59.
1b. ———— 70.
1b. —— xxvii. 1, 22.
1a. ———— 25, 45.
3. —— xxviii. 11.
1a. ———— 18.
1b. ———— 19.
— ———— 20, see A things.
1a. Mark i. 5 1st.
1b. ——— 5 2nd.
1b. ——— 27 (No. 3, T Tr A ℵ.)
2. ——— 28.
1b. ——— 32.
2. ——— 33.
— ——— 37, see A men.
2. ——— 39.
1b. —— ii. 12 twice.
1a. ——— 13.
1b. —— iii. 28.
— —— iv. 11, see A these things.
1b. ——— 13, 31, 32.
— ——— 34, see A things
1b. —— v. 12 (om. G Lb Tr A ℵ.)
— ——— 20, see A men.
1b. ——— 26.
1a. ——— 33.
3. ——— 40 (No. 1, G L T Tr A ℵ.)
— —— vi. 30, see A things
1b. ——— 33, 39, 41, 42, 50.
1b. —— vii. 3.
1a. —— vii. 14 (πάλιν, again, G∾ L T Tr A ℵ.)
1b. ——— 19, 23.
— ——— 37, see A things
— —— ix. 12, see A things
1a. ——— 15.
— ——— 23, see A things
1b. ——— 35 twice.
1b. —— x. 20.
— ——— 27, see A things
1b. ——— 28, 44.
— —— xi. 11, see A things
1b. ——— 17.
1a. ——— 18.
3. —— xi. 32 (No. 1, L ℵ.)
1b. —— xii. 22, 28, 29 (ap.)
2. ——— 30 4 times, 33 1st & 2nd.
2. ——— 33 3rd (ap.)
2. ——— 33 4th.
1b. ——— 33 5th, 43, 44 1st.
1b. ——— 44 2nd‡.
2. ——— 44 3rd.
1b. —— xiii. 4, 10.
— ——— 13, see A men.
— ——— 23, see A things
1b. ——— 30, 37.
1b. —— xiv. 23, 27, 29, 31.
— ——— 36, see A things
1b. ——— 50, 53.
2. ——— 55.
2. —— xiv. 64.
3. —— xvi. 15 (ap.)

— Luke i. 3, see A things.
1b. ——— 6, 48, 63, 65 1st & 2nd.
2. ——— 65 3rd.
1b. ——— 66, 71, 75.
1a. —— ii. 1.
1b. ——— 3.
1a. ——— 10.
1b. ——— 18, 19.
— ——— 20, see A things.
1b. ——— 31, 38.
— ——— 39, see A things.
1b. ——— 47, 51.
1a. —— iii. 3, 6.
1b. ——— 15.
3. ——— 16.
1b. ——— 19, 20.
3. ——— 21.
1b. —— iv. 5.
3. ——— 6.
1b. ——— 7 (No. 1a, G L T Tr A ℵ.)
1a. ——— 13.
2. ——— 14.
1b ——— 15, 20, 22.
1a. ——— 25.
1b. ——— 28, 36, 40‡.
2. —— v. 5.
1b. ——— 9.
3. ——— 11 (No. 1b, L Tr ℵ.)
3. ——— 26.
3. ——— 28 (No. 1b, L Tr A.)
1b. —— vi. 10.
— ——— 12, see A night (continued.)
1a. ——— 17.
1b. ——— 19, 26 (om. G.)
1b. —— vii. 1.
3. ——— 16 (No. 1b, G Tr A.)
2. ——— 17 1st.
1a. ——— 17 2nd.
1b. ——— 18.
1a. ——— 29.
1b. ——— 35 (om. G→.)
1b. —— viii. 40.
2. ——— 43.
1b. ——— 45.
1a. ——— 47.
1b. ——— 52, 54 (ap.)
1b. —— ix. 1, 7.
— ——— 10, see A that.
1a. ——— 13.
3. ——— 15.
1b. ——— 17, 23.
1b. —— ix. 43 1st.
— ——— 43 2nd, see A things
1b. ——— 48.
1a. —— x. 19.
— ——— 22, see A things.
2. ——— 27 4 times.
— —— xi. 22, see A his armour.
— ——— 41, see A things.
1b. ——— 50.
— —— xii. 1, see A (first of.)
1b. ——— 7, 18.
1a. ——— 27.
1b. ——— 30.
1b. ——— 31 (om. G⇄ Lb T Tr A ℵ.)
1b. ——— 41, 44.
1b. —— xiii. 2, 3, 4, 5, 17 1st.
1a. ——— 17 2nd.
1b. ——— 17 3rd, 27, 28.
— —— xiv. 17, see A things
1b. ——— 18, 29, 33.
1b. —— xv. 1.
3. ——— 13 (No. 1b, L Tr.)
1b. ——— 14, 31.
1b. —— xvi. 14, 26.
1b. —— xvii. 10.
3. ——— 27 (No. 1b, L Tr.)
3. ——— 29 (No. 1b, L Tr.)
1b. —— xviii. 12‡, 21, 22‡.
1. ——— 28 (τὰ ἴδια, *our own things*, G∾ L T Tr A.)

— Luke xviii. 31, see A things.
1a. ——— 43.
3. —— xix. 7 (No. 1b, L T Tr A ℵ.)
1b. ——— 37.
3. ——— 48.
1. —— xx. 6 (No. 3, Lm T Tr A ℵ.)
1b. ——— 32 (om. G→ L T Tr A ℵ.)
1b. ——— 38.
1a. ——— 45.
1b. —— xxi. 3.
3. ——— 4, 12.
1b. ——— 15 (No. 3, T Tr A)
— ——— 17, see A men.
— ——— 22, see A things.
1b. ——— 24, 29, 32, 35, 36
1a. ——— 38.
1b. —— xxii. 70.
2. —— xxiii. 5.
— ——— 18, see A at once.
2. ——— 44
1b —— xxiii. 48, 49,
1b. —— xxiv. 9 twice, 14.
1a. ——— 19.
1b. ——— 21, 25, 27 twice.
— ——— 44, see A things.
1b. ——— 47.
— John i. 3, see A things.
— ——— 7, see A men.
1b. ——— 16.
1b. —— ii. 15.
— ——— 24, see A men.
— —— iii. 26, see A men.
1b. ——— 31 1st, 31 2nd (ap)
— ——— 35, see A things.
— —— iv. 25, 29, see A things.
1b. ——— 39‡.
— ——— 45 } see A things
— —— v. 20 }
1a. ——— 22.
— ——— 23, see A men.
1b. ——— 28.
1a. —— vi. 37, 39.
1b. ——— 45.
1b. —— vii. 21.
1a. —— viii. 2 (ap.)
1b. —— x. 8‡, 29.
— ——— 41, see A things.
— —— xi. 48, see A men.
— ——— 49, see A (nothing at.)
1b. —— xiii. 10, 11, 18.
1b. —— xv. 21.
1a. —— xvi. 13.
1a. —— xvii. 2.
1b. ——— 10, 21.
1b. —— xviii. 40.
— —— xxi. 11, see A there were (for.)
1b. Acts i. 1.
1a. ——— 8.
1b. ——— 14, 18, 19.
1a. ——— 21.
3. —— ii. 1 (om. ℵ), (No. 1b, L T Tr A.)
2. ——— 2.
3. ——— 4 (No. 1b, T Tr ℵ)
1b. ——— 7 1st (om. G→ L T Trb A.)
1b. ——— 7 2nd (No. 3, L T A ℵ.)
1b. ——— 12.
3. ——— 14 (No. 1b, L Tr ℵ.)
1a. ——— 17.
1b. ——— 32.
1a. ——— 36.
1b. ——— 39.
1b. ——— 44 1st.
— ——— 44 2nd, see A things.
— ——— 45, see A men.
1a. —— iii. 9, 11.
1b. ——— 16, 18.
— ——— 21 1st, see A things
1b. ——— 21 2nd (G∾), (om. G L T Tr A ℵ.)

— Acts iii. 22, see A things
1b. ——— 24, 25.
1b. —— iv. 10 twice, 16.
— ——— 18, see A (at.)
— ——— 21, see A men.
— ——— 23, see A that.
1b. ——— 28.
1a. ——— 22.
3. ——— 31.
— ——— 32, see A things.
1b. ——— 33.
2. —— v. 5.
2. ——— 11.
3. ——— 12 (No. 1b, L Tr.)
1b. ——— 17, 20.
1a. ——— 21.
1b. ——— 23.
1a. ——— 34.
1b. ——— 36‡.
1b. ——— 37‡.
3. —— vi. 15 (No. 1b, L Tr ℵ.)
1b. —— vii. 10 1st.
2. ——— 10 2nd, 11.
1a. ——— 14, 22.
1b. ——— 50.
1b. —— viii. 1.
1b. ——— 10 (om. G→ T.)
1a. ——— 27.
2. ——— 37 (ap.)
1b. ——— 40.
1b. —— ix. 14, 21, 26.
2. ——— 31.
— ——— 32, see A quarters (throughout.)
1b. ——— 35, 39, 40.
2. ——— 42.
1a. —— x. 2.
3. ——— 8.
— ——— 12, see A manner of.
2. ——— 22.
1b. ——— 33 1st.
— ——— 33 2nd, see A things.
1b. ——— 36.
2. ——— 37.
1b. ——— 38.
— ——— 39, see A things.
1b. —— x. 43, 44.
3. —— xi. 10.
1a. ——— 14.
1b. ——— 23.
2. ——— 28.
1a. —— xii. 11.
1a. —— xiii. 10 3 times.
1b. ——— 22.
1a. ——— 24.
3. ——— 29 (No. 1b, G L T Tr A ℵ.)
1a. ——— 39 1st.
— ——— 39 2nd, see A things.
2. ——— 49.
— —— xiv. 15, see A things
1b. ——— 16.
— ——— 27, see A that.
1b. —— xv. 3.
— ——— 4, see A things that.
1a. ——— 12.
1. ——— 17 1st, 17 2nd (ap.), 18 (ap.)
3. —— xvi. 3 (No. 1b, L.)
1b. ——— 26.
3. ——— 28.
1b. ——— 32, 33.
— ——— 34, see A in house (with.)
1b. —— xvii. 7.
1a. ——— 11.
— ——— 15, see A speed (with.)
1b. ——— 21.
— ——— 22, 24, see A things.
— ——— 25 1st.
— ——— 25 2nd, see A things.
1a. ——— 26 twice.

1b. Acts xvii. 30, 31.
1b. —— xviii. 2.
2. —— 8.
1b. —— 17.
— —— 21, see A means [(by.)
1b. —— 23.
1b. —— xix. 7, 10, 17 twice.
— —— 19, see A men.
1a. —— 26.
2. —— 27.
1b. —— 34.
1a. —— xx. 18, 19.
1b. —— 25, 26.
1a. —— 27, 28.
1b. —— 32.
— —— 35, see A things.
1b. —— 36, 37.
— —— 38, see A (most of.)
1b. —— xxi. 5, 18, 20.
1b. —— 21 (om. G→ L Trb.)
1b. —— 24.
1a. —— 27.
— —— 28, see A men.
2. —— 30.
2a. —— 31.
1b. —— xxii. 3.
1a. —— 5.
— —— 10, see A things.
1b. —— 12, 15.
2. —— 30 (No. 1a, G L T Tr A ℵ.)
1a. —— xxiii. 1.
— —— xxiv. 3 1st, see A places (in.)
1a. —— 3 2nd.
1b. —— 5, 8.
— —— 14, see A things.
— —— xxv. 8, see A (anything at.)
1b. —— 24 1st.
1. —— 24 2nd (No. 3, L T Tr ℵ.)
— —— xxvi. 2, see A things
1b. —— 3, 4, 14.
1a. —— 20.
1b. —— 29.
1a. —— xxvii. 20.
1b. —— 24.
3. —— 33.
1b. —— 35, 36, 37, 44.
1b. —— xxviii. 30.
1a. —— 31.
1b. Rom. i. 5, 7, 8.
1a. —— 18, 29.
1b. —— iii. 9. 12.
1a. —— 19.
1b. —— 22 1st, 22 2nd (ap), 23.
1b. —— iv. 11.
1a. —— 16 1st.
1b. —— 16 2nd.
1b. —— v. 12 twice, 18 twice.
— —— vii. 8, see A manner of.
— —— viii. 28, see A things
1b. —— 32 1st.
— —— 32 2nd, see A things.
— —— 36, see A..long.
1b. —— 37.
1b. —— ix. 5, 6, 7.
1a. —— 17.
1b. —— x. 12 twice, 16.
1a. —— 18.
— —— 21, see A..long.
1a. —— xi. 26.
1b. —— 32 twice.
— —— xi. 36, see A things.
1b. —— xii. 4.
1b. —— 17 (om. L.)
1b. —— 18.
1b. —— xiii. 7.
— —— xiv. 2, see A things
1b. —— 10.
— —— 20, see A things.
1b. —— xv. 11 twice.

1a. Rom. xv. 13, 14.
1b. —— 33.
1b. —— xvi. 4, 15.
— —— 19, see A men.
1b. —— 24 (ap.), 26.
1a. 1 Cor. i. 5 twice.
1b. —— 10.
— —— ii. 10, 15, } see A
— —— iii. 21, } things
1b. —— 22.
— —— iv. 13, see A things
— —— vi. 12 3 times, see A things.
1b. —— vii. 7, 17.
1b. —— viii. 1.
— —— 6 twice, } see A
— —— ix. 12, } things
— —— 19 1st, see A [men.
1b. —— 19 2nd.
— —— 22 1st, see A things.
— —— 22 2nd, see A men.
— —— 22 3rd, A means (by.)
1b. —— 24.
— —— 25, see A things
1b. —— x. 1 twice, 2, 3, 4.
1b. —— 11 (om. Lb T Tr Ab.)
1b. —— 17.
— —— 23 4 times, see A things.
1b. —— 31.
— —— 33 1st, see A men.
— —— 33 2nd, } see A
— —— xi. 2, 12, } things
— —— 18, see A (first of.)
1b. —— xii. 6 twice, 11, 12, 13 twice, 19, 26 twice.
1b. —— 29 4 times, 30 3 times.
1b. —— xiii. 2 1st.
1a. —— 2 2nd & 3rd.
1b. —— 3.
— —— 7 4 times, see A things.
1b. —— xiv. 5, 18.
— —— 21, see A that (for.)
1b. —— 23, 24 3 times.
— —— 26, see A things
1b. —— 31 3 times, 33.
— —— 40, see A things
1b. —— xv. 7, 8, 10, 19, 22.
1a. —— 24 twice.
1b. —— 25.
— —— 27 3 times, 28 1st & 2nd, see A things.
1b. —— 28 3rd & 4th.
— —— 29, see A (at.)
1a. —— 39.
1b. —— 51.
— —— xvi. 12, see A (at.)
— —— 14, see A things
1b. —— 20, 24.
1a. 2 Cor. i. 1 1st.
2. —— 1 2nd.
1a. —— 3, 4.
4. —— 20.
1b. —— ii. 3 twice, 5.
— —— 9, see A things
1b. —— iii. 2, 18.
— —— iv. 15, see A things
1b. —— v. 10, 14 twice, 15.
— —— 17, 18, } see A
— —— vi. 10, } things
1a. —— vii. 1, 4.
1b. —— 13, 15.
— —— 14, see A things
1a. —— viii. 7.
1b. —— 18.
1a. —— ix. 8 1st & 2nd.
— —— 8 3rd, see A things.
1a. —— 11.

— 2 Cor. ix. 13, see A men.
1a. —— x. 6.
— —— xi. 6, see A things.
1b. —— 28.
1a. —— xii. 12.
— —— 19, see A things
1b. —— xiii. 2, 13, 14.
1b. Gal. i. 2.
1b. —— ii. 14.
1b. —— iii. 8.
— —— 10, see A things
1b. —— 22, 26, 28.
1b. —— iv. 1. [Tr A ℵ.)
1b. —— 26 (om. G Lb T
1a. —— v. 14.
1b. —— vi. 6.
— —— 10, see A men.
1a. Eph. i. 3, 8. [men.
— —— 10, 11, see A
1b. —— 15.
1a. —— 21. [men.
— —— 22 twice, see A
1b. —— 23 twice.
1b. —— ii. 3.
1a. —— 21.
1b. —— iii. 8.
— —— 9 1st, see A men
— —— 9 2nd, see A
1b. —— 18. [things.
1a. —— 19.
1b. —— 20, 21.
1a. —— iv. 2.
1b. —— 6 4 times, 10 1st.
— —— 10 2nd, see A things.
1b. —— 13.
— —— 15, see A things
1a. —— 19, 31 twice.
1a. —— v. 3, 9. [things.
— —— 13, 20, see A
3. —— vi. 13.
1b. —— 16.
1a. —— 18 1st & 2nd.
1b. —— 18 3rd.
— —— 21, see A things
1b. —— 24.
1b. Phil. i. 1, 4, 7 twice, 8.
1a. —— 9.
2. —— 13 1st.
1b. —— 13 2nd.
1a. —— 20.
1b. —— 25.
— —— ii. 14, see A things.
1b. —— 17, 21, 26.
1a. —— 29. [things.
— —— iii. 8 twice, 21, see A
1b. —— iv. 5.
1a. —— 7. [things.
— —— 12, 13, see A
1b. —— 18.
1a. —— 19.
1b. —— 22.
1b. —— 23 (τοῦ πνεύματος *your spirit*, L T Tr A ℵ.)
1b. Col. i. 4.
1a. —— 6, 9, 10, 11 twice.
— —— 16 twice, 17 twice, see A things.
1b. —— 18, margin (text, *all things*.)
1b. —— 19.
— —— 20, see A things.
1a. —— 28.
1a. —— ii. 2.
1b. —— 3.
1a. —— 9, 10.
1b. —— 13.
1a. —— 19.
1b. —— 22.
1b. —— iii. 8, 11 twice, 14.
1a. —— 16.
1b. —— 17.
— —— 20, 22, see A things
1b. —— iv. 7.
— —— 9, see A things.
1a. —— 12.
1b. 1 Thes. i. 2, 7.

1b. 1 Thes. ii. 15.
1a. —— iii. 7, 9.
— —— 12, see A men.
1b. —— 13.
1b. —— iv. 6, 10 1st.
2. —— 10 2nd.
1b. —— v. 5.
— —— 14, 15, see A men.
— —— 21, see A things.
1a. —— 22.
1b. —— 26, 27.
1b. 2 Thes. i. 3, 4, 10.
1a. —— 11.
1a. —— ii. 4, 9, 10. [A ℵ.)
1b. —— 12 (No. 3, Lm Tr
— —— iii. 2, see A men.
1a. —— 16.
1b. —— 18.
1a. 1 Tim. i. 15. [A ℵ.)
1a. —— 16 (No. 3, L T Tr
1b. —— ii. 1 twice, 2 1st.
1a. —— 2 2nd.
1b. —— 4, 6.
1a. —— 11.
1a. —— iii. 4.
— —— 11, } see A
— —— iv. 8, } things.
1a. —— 9. [things.
1b. —— 10, 15, margin *all*
1a. —— v. 2.
1b. —— 20.
1a. —— vi. 1.
1b —— 10.
— —— 13, 17, see A things.
1b. 2 Tim. i. 15.
— —— ii. 7, 10, see A things.
— —— 24, see A men.
1b. —— iii. 9, 11, 12.
1a. —— 16, 17.
1a. —— iv. 2.
— —— 5, see A things.
11. —— 8 (om. G→.)
— —— 16, see A men.
1b. —— 17, 21.
— Titus i. 15, see A things.
— —— ii. 7, 9.
1a. —— 10 1st. [things.
— —— 10 2nd, see A
1b. —— 11.
1a. —— 14, 15.
1a. —— iii. 2 1st.
1b. —— 2 2nd, 15 twice.
1b. Philem. 5.
— Heb. i. 2, 3, see A things.
1b. —— 6, 11, 14.
— —— ii. 8 1st, see A things
1b. —— 8 2nd. [A things.
— —— 8 3rd, 10 twice, see
1b. —— 11.
1a. —— 15.
— —— 17, see A things.
2. —— iii. 2.
— —— 4, see A things.
1b. —— 16.
1b. —— iv. 4.
— —— 13, see A things.
— —— 15, see A points (in.)
1b. —— v. 9.
1a. —— vi. 16.
1b. —— vii. 2.
1a. —— 7.
— —— viii. 5, see A things
1b. —— 11. [at.)
— —— ix. 17, see A (no..
1a. —— 19 twice.
1b. —— 21.
— —— 22, see A things.
— —— x. 10, see A (once
1b. —— xi. 13, 39. [for.)
1b. —— xii. 8.
— —— 14, see A things.
1b. —— 23.
1b. —— xiii. 4.
— —— 18, see A things.
1b. —— 24 twice, 25.
1a. Jas. i. 2.
— —— 5, see A things.

1b. Jas. i. 8.
1a. —— 21.
1b. —— ii. 10.
3. —— iii. 2.
1a. —— iv. 6.
— —— v. 12, see A things.
— 1 Pet. i. 15, see A manner of.
1a. —— 24 twice.
1a. —— ii. 1 1st.
1b. —— 1 2nd.
1a. —— 1 3rd.
— —— 17, see A men.
1a. —— 18.
1b. —— iii. 8.
— —— iv. 7, 8, 11, see A things.
1b. —— v. 5.
1a. —— 7, 10.
1b. —— 14.
— 2 Pet. i. 3, see A things.
1a. —— 5.
— —— iii. 4, see A things.
1b. —— 9, 11, 16.
1a. 1 John i. 7, 9.
1a. —— ii. 16.
1b. —— 19.
— —— 27, } see A
— —— iii. 20, } things.
1a. —— v. 17.
1b. 2 John 1.
— 3 John 2, see A things.
1b. —— 12.
1a. Jude 3.
1b. —— 15 4 times.
— Rev. i. 2, see A things [that.
1b. —— 7.
1b. —— 23.
2. —— iii. 10.
— Rev. iv. 11, see A things.
1a. —— v. 6.
1b. —— 13.
1a. —— vii. 4, 9.
1b. —— 11.
1a. —— 17.
1b. —— viii. 3.
1a. —— 7.
1a. —— xi. 6.
1b. —— xii. 15.
2. —— xiii. 3.
1a. —— 7.
1b. —— 8.
1a. —— 12.
1b. —— 16.
1b. —— xiv. 8.
1b. —— xv. 4.
— —— xviii. 3.
1a. —— 12 1st.
— —— 14 2nd & 3rd, see A manner of.
— —— 14 1st, see A things
— —— 14 2nd, see A (at)
1a. —— 17.
1b. —— 19.
— —— 21, 22 twice, 23 1st & 2nd, see A (no..at.)
— —— 23 3rd, 24.
1b. —— xix. 5, 17.
— —— 18, see A men.
1b. —— 21.
1a. —— xxi. 4.
— —— 7, see A things.
1b. —— 8.
— —— 19, see A manner of.
— —— 25, see A (not at)
1b. —— xxii. 21.

ALL AT ONCE.

παμπληθεί, *(adv.)* with all their multitude, all together.

Luke xxiii. 18.

ALL HIS ARMOUR.

πανοπλία, complete armour, a complete suit of armour *offensive and defensive (from* πᾶς, all; *and* ὅπλον, armour.)

Luke xi. 22.

ALL...LONG.

ὅλος, *see* "ALL," *No.* 2.

Rom. viii. 36. | Rom. x. 21.

ALL MANNER.

πᾶς, *see* "ALL," *No.* 1.

Rev. xviii. 12 twice.

ALL MANNER OF.

πᾶς, *see* "ALL," *No.* 1.

1a. Matt. iv. 23 twice.
1a. —— v. 11.
1a. —— x. 1 twice.
1a. —— xii. 31.
1a. Luke xi. 42.
1b. Acts x. 12.
1a. Rom. vii. 8.
1a. 1 Pet. i. 15.
Rev. xxi. 19.

ALL MEN.

πᾶς, *see* "ALL," *No.* 1.

Except where the two words are separate, in which case see under each.

1. Matt. x. 22.
1b. —— xix. 11.
1b. —— xxvi. 33.
1b. Mark i. 37.
1b. —— v. 20.
1b. —— xiii. 13.
1b. Luke xxi. 17.
1b. John i. 7.
1b. —— ii. 24.
1b. —— iii. 26.
1b. —— v. 23.
1b. —— xi. 48.
1b. —— xii. 32.
1b. —— xiii. 35.
1b. Acts i. 24.
1b. —— ii. 45.
1b. —— iv. 21.
1b. Acts xix. 19.
1b. —— xxi. 28.
1b. Rom. xvi. 19.
1b. 1 Cor. ix. 19, 22.
1b. —— x. 33.
1b. 2 Cor. ix. 13.
1b. Gal. vi. 10.
1b. Eph. iii. 9 (om. Lb ℵ.)
1b. 1 Thes. iii. 12.
1b. —— v. 14, 15.
1b. 2 Thes. iii. 2.
1b. 2 Tim. ii. 24.
1b. —— iv. 16.
1b. Heb. xii. 14.
1b. Jas. i. 5.
1b. 1 Pet. ii. 17.
1b. Rev. xix. 18.

ALL THAT.

ὅσος, *see* "ALL," *No.* 4.

Luke ix. 10. | Acts iv. 23.
Acts xiv. 27.

ALL THESE THINGS.

τὰ πάντα, *see* "ALL," *No.* 1b, all things *as constituting a whole.*

Mark iv. 11.

ALL THINGS.

1. πᾶς, *see* "ALL," *No.* 1b.

2. ἅπας, *see* "ALL," *No.* 3.

1. Matt. vii. 21‡.
1. —— xi. 27.
1. —— xiii. 41.
1. —— xvii. 11.
1. —— xix. 26.
1. —— xxi. 22‡.
1. —— xxii. 4.
1. —— xxiii. 20.
1. —— xxviii. 20‡.
1. Mark iv. 34.
1. —— vi. 30.
1. —— vii. 37.
1. —— ix. 12. 23.
1. —— x. 27 (ap.)
1. —— xi. 11.
1. —— xiii. 23.
1. —— xiv. 36.
1. Luke i. 3.
1. —— ii. 20.
2. —— 39 (No. 1, Tr A.)
1. —— ix. 43.
1. —— x. 22.
1. —— xi. 41. (ℵ.)
1. —— xiv. 17 (om. Lb Trb
1. —— xviii. 31.
1. —— xxi. 22.
1. —— xxiv. 44.
1. John i. 3.
1. —— iii. 35. [A ℵ.)
1. —— iv. 25 (No. 3, T Tr
1. —— 29‡.
1. —— 45*.
1. —— v. 20*.
1. —— x. 41‡.
1. —— xiii. 3.
1. —— xiv. 26 1st, 26 2nd*.
1. John xv. 15*.
1. —— xvi. 15‡, 30.
1. —— xvii. 7‡.
1. —— xviii. 4.
1. —— xix. 28.
1. —— xxi. 17.
2. Acts ii. 44.
1. —— iii. 21*.
1. —— 22‡.
2. —— iv. 32 (No. 1, L.)
2. —— x. 8.
1. —— 33, 39*.
1. —— xiii. 39*.
1. —— xiv. 15.
1. —— xvii. 22, 24, 25.
1. —— xx. 35.
1. —— xxii. 10.
1. —— xxiv. 14.
1. —— xxvi. 2*.
1. Rom. viii. 28, 32.
1. —— xi. 36.
1. —— xiv. 2, 20.
1. 1 Cor. ii. 10, 15.
1. —— iii. 21.
1. —— iv. 13.
1. —— vi. 12, 3 times.
1. —— viii. 6 twice.
1. —— ix. 12, 22, 25.
1. —— x. 23 4 times, 33.
1. —— xi. 2, 12.
1. —— xiii. 7 4 times.
1. —— xiv. 26, 40.
1. —— xv. 27 3 times, 28 twice.
1. —— xvi. 14.
1. 2 Cor. ii. 9.

1. 2 Cor. iv. 15. [ℵ.)
1. —— v. 17 (*om.* G → L A
1. ——— 18.
1. —— vi. 10.
1. —— vii. 14 (πάντοτε, *always*, Lm.)
1. —— ix. 8.
1. —— xi. 6.
1. —— xii. 19.
1. Gal. iii. 10.
1. Eph. i. 10, 11, 22 twice.
1. —— iii. 9.
1. —— iv. 10, 15.
1. —— v. 13, 20.
1. —— vi. 21.
1. Phil. ii. 14.
1. —— iii. 8 twice, 21.
1. —— iv. 12, 13.
1. Col. i. 16 twice, 17 twice.
1. ——— 18, margin *all.*
1. ——— 20.
1. —— iii. 20, 22.
1. —— iv. 9.
1. 1 Thes. v. 21.
1. Rev. xxi. 5.
1. 1 Tim. iii. 11.
1. —— iv. 8. [*all.*)
1. ——— 15, margin (text,
1. —— vi. 13, 17.
1. 2Tim. ii. 7, 10.
1. —— iv. 5.
1. Titus i. 15.
1. —— ii. 7, 9, 10.
1. Heb. i. 2, 3. [17.
1. —— ii. 8 twice, 10 twice,
1. —— iii. 4.
1. —— iv. 13.
1. —— viii. 5.
1. —— ix. 22.
1. —— xiii. 18.
1. Jas. v. 12.
1. 1 Pet. iv. 7, 8, 11.
1. 2 Pet. i. 3.
1. —— iii. 4.
1. 1 John ii. 20, 27.
1. ——iii. 20.
1. 3 John 2.
1. Rev. iv. 11.
1. —— xviii. 14.
1. Rev. xxi. 7, (ταῦτα, *these things*, G L T Tr A ℵ.)

ALL THINGS THAT.

ὅσος, *see* "ALL," *No.* 4.

Acts xv. 4. | Rev. i. 2.

ALL...HOUSE (WITH.)

πανοικί, with all one's house *or* family.

Acts xvi. 34.

ALL MEANS (BY.)

πάντως, wholly, entirely; in every way, by all means, assuredly, certainly.

Acts xviii. 21. | 1 Cor. ix. 22.

ALL NIGHT (CONTINUE.)

διανυκτερεύω, to pass the whole night through, (*from* διά, through, *and* νυκτερεύω, to pass the night, *from* νύξ, night.)

Luke vi. 12.

ALL PLACES (IN.)

πανταχοῦ, (*adv.*) everywhere.

Acts xxiv. 3.

ALL POINTS (IN.)

{ κατά, *with Acc. as here*, according to, throughout.
{ πάντα, (*neut. pl. of* "ALL," *No.* 1), all (*things.*)

Heb. iv. 15.

ALL QUARTERS (THROUGHOUT.)

{ διά, through (*as proceeding from*) *with Gen. as here.*
{ πάντων, (*Gen. pl. of* "ALL," *No.* 1), all.

Acts ix. 32.

ALL SPEED (WITH.)

{ ὡς, as, } with the ut-
{ τάχιστα, most speedily, } most speed.

Acts xvii. 15.

ALL THAT (FOR.)

οὕτω, thus, even so, in this wise.

1 Cor. xiv. 21.

ALL THERE WERE (FOR.)

ὤν, (*pres. part. of* εἰμί, to be), being.

John xxi. 11.

ALL (ANYTHING AT.)

τίς, any one, some one, a certain one; anything.

Acts xxv. 8.

ALL (AT.)

1. πάντως, wholly, entirely; in every way, by all means, assuredly, certainly.
2. καθόλου, entirely.
   (a) *with* μή—not at all.
3. { οὐ, not, *denying a thing itself.* / μή, not, *denying the thought or intention of it.* } *an emphatic negative*, in no wise, by no means.
4. ὅλως, wholly, altogether, (*adv. of* "ALL," *No.* 2.)
   (a) *with negative preceding*, not at all.

4a. Matt. v. 34.
2a. Acts iv. 18.
4a. 1 Cor. xv. 29.
1. ——— xvi. 12.
3. Rev. xviii. 14.

ALL (FIRST OF.)

πρῶτον, first, *in time, place or order*, (*superlative of* πρό, before.)

Luke xii. 1. | 1 Cor. xi. 18.

ALL (MOST OF.)

μάλιστα, most of all, especially, *(superlative of* μάλα, very.)

Acts xx. 38.

ALL (NO...AT.)

1. μήποτε, *(conjunction)*, lest at any time, lest, lest perhaps.
   (a) *adverb*, no longer.
2. { οὐ, μή, } see under "A (AT)," *No.* 3.
3. οὐδέποτε, not ever, never.

3. John xviii. 38. | 2. Rev. xviii. 21.
1a. Heb. ix. 17. | 2. —— 22 twice.
2. Rev. xviii. 23 twice.

ALL (NOT AT.)

1. μηδείς, not one, *either person or thing.*
2. { οὐ, μή, } *see* "A (AT)," *No.* 3.

1. 2 Thes. iii. 11. | 2. Rev. xxi. 25.

ALL (NOTHING AT.)

οὐ, no, not, *denying the thing itself.*

John xi. 49.

ALL (ONCE FOR.)

ἐφάπαξ, once for all, once, at once.

Heb. x. 10.

ALL.

See also, CONTINUE, FIRST, GO, HAIL, HOLY, HOUSE, LAST, MEANS, MOST, NO, NOT, ONCE, ONE, PLACES, SPEED.

ALLEGE.

παρατίθημι, to place near *or* by the side of *as food;* to set *or* lay before, *as instruction;* to set clearly before one by argument, and especially to prove *by citations from writers.*

Acts xvii. 3.

ALLEGORY (BE AN.)

ἀλληγορέω, *(from* ἄλλος, other, *and* ἀγορεύω, to speak in *or* to an assembly of men), to speak *so that* one thing is spoken, and somewhat different is meant, *of which the thing spoken is the* emblem *or* representative.) *Compare the word* "PARABLE."

Gal. iv. 24 (pass. participle), (lit. suggesting another meaning.)

ALLELUIA.

ἀλληλούϊα, Alleluia, *Heb.* הללו־יה Praise ye Jah *or* Jehovah, *(retained untranslated in the Septuagint.)*

Rev. xix. 1, 3, 4, 6.

ALLOW.

(-ETH -ED.)

1. δοκιμάζω, to prove, assay, *as refiners do metals by fire,* to try, examine, try the fitness, *or* goodness of; *hence,* to have experience of by trial, to approve.
2. γινώσκω, to perceive, to observe, to obtain a knowledge of *or* insight into, to know; γινώσκω *frequently denotes a personal relation between the person knowing and the object known; equivalent to,* to be influenced by our knowledge of the object, *and hence,* to allow oneself to be determined by one's knowledge.
3. προσδέχομαι, to accept, to receive; to expect, wait for.
4. συνευδοκέω, to think well together with, to consent to, approve of, be well pleased with, take complacency in.

4. Luke xi. 48. | 2. Rom. vii. 15, margin [know.
3. Acts xxiv. 15. | 1. —— xiv. 22.
1. 1 Thes. ii. 4.

ALLOWANCE [margin.]

ὀψώνιον, whatever is bought to be eaten with bread, a relish. *Then, because hired soldiers were at first partly paid in meat, grain, or fruit, etc.*, a stipend, allowance, *and generally,* wages.

Luke iii. 14 (text, *wages.*)

ALLURE.

δελεάζω, to take *or* catch, *properly with* a bait, *as birds or fishes are caught, (from* δέλεαρ, a bait.)

2 Pet. ii. 18.

ALMIGHTY.

παντοκράτωρ, *(from* πᾶς, all, *and* κράτος, strength), almighty, omnipotent. (occ. Rev. xix. 6.)

2 Cor. vi. 18 ; Rev. i. 8 ; iv. 8 ; xi. 17 ; xv. 3 ; xvi. 7, 14 ; xix. 15 ; xxi. 22.

ALMOST.

1. σχεδόν, nearly, almost, *(from root,* to be near.)

2. { ἐν, in, ὀλίγος, small, *or* little *in number place or quantity or magnitude.* } in a little, *i.e. in a short compass, in a brief narrative of facts, or* in a few words, see Eph. iii. 3.

1. Acts xiii. 44.
1. —— xix. 26.
— Acts xxi. 27, see A (be.)
2. —— xxvi. 28, 29.
1. Heb. ix. 22.

ALMOST (BE.)

μέλλω, to delay ; *with an infinitive following,* to be about to *do anything (immediate or remote.)*

Acts xxi. 27.

ALMS.

ἐλεημοσύνη, pity, compassion; a work of mercy, *particularly* almsgiving; *then by putting the effect for the cause,* the alms *itself or* money given to *the poor.* (occ. Acts ix. 36.)

Matt. vi. 1 (δικαιοσύνη, *righteousness,* G L T Tr A ℵ.)
—— 2, 3, 4.
Luke xi. 41.
—— xii. 33.
Acts iii. 2, 3, 10.
—— x. 2, 4, 31.
—— xxiv. 17.

ALMSDEEDS.

Acts ix. 36.

ALOES.

ἀλόη, the aloe, *(the* xylo-aloes *whose resinous and aromatic qualities rendered it very proper for embalming dead bodies.)*

John xix. 39.

ALONE.

1. μόνος, alone, only, single; without company, solitary.

2. μόνον, *(neuter of No.* 1, *used adverbially),* only, exclusively.

3. καταμόνας, apart, in private. (κατά μόνας, L T Tr.)

1. Matt. iv. 4.
1. —— xiv. 23.
— —— xv. 14, see A (let.)
1. —— xviii. 15.
— Mark i. 24, see A (let.)
3. —— iv. 10.
— —— 34, see A (when they were.)
1. —— vi. 47.
— —— xiv. 6, see A (let.)
— —— xv. 36, see A (let.)
1. Luke iv. 4.
— —— 34, see A (let.)
1. —— v. 21.
1. —— vi. 4.
3. —— ix. 18.
1. —— 36.
1. Luke x. 40.
— —— xiii. 8, see A (let.)
1. John vi. 15, 22.
1. —— viii 9. (*ap.*), 16, 29.
— —— xi. 48, see A (let.)
— —— xii. 7, see A (let.)
1. —— 24.
1. —— xvi. 32 twice.
2. —— xvii. 20.
— Acts v. 38, see A (let.)
2. —— xix. 26.
2. Rom. iv. 23.
1. —— xi. 3.
— Jas. ii. 17, see A (being.)
1. Gal. vi. 4.
1. 1 Thes. iii. 1.
1. Heb. ix. 7.

ALONE (BEING.)

{ κατά, according to *or* by, ἑαυτοῦ. himself, herself, itself, } by itself.

Jas. ii. 17.

ALONE (LET.)

1. ἀφίημι, to send away, dismiss, *(hence* to divorce ;) to set free, *(hence* to forgive.) *In general* to leave *anything,* to leave behind *(as at death;)* to let alone.

2. ἐάω, to permit, to suffer.

3. ἔα, *an interjection denoting* indignation *or* grief *(like* ah ! *or* hah !) *It may however be the imperfect of No.* 2, *but the former seems preferable.*

1. Matt. xv. 14.
3. Mark i. 24 (*om.* G → L Tr [A ℵ.)
1. —— xiv. 6.
1. —— xv. 36.
3. Luke iv. 34, marg. *away.*
1. —— xiii. 8.
1. John xi. 48.
1. —— xii. 7.
2. Acts v. 38 (No. 1, G ∾ L S.)

ALONE (WHEN THEY WERE.)

{ κατά, according to, ἴδιος, one's own, proper; what belongs to one, private, separate, } κατ' ἰδίαν, in a private *place,* (χώραν, place *being understood.)*

Mark iv. 34.

ALOUD (CRY.)

ἀναβοάω, to cry out aloud, to exclaim, *(from* ἀνά *emphatic, and* βοάω, to cry out.)

Mark xv. 8 (ἀναβαίνω, *having gone up,** L T Tr A ℵ.)

* i.e. to the governor's house.

ALPHA.

A, (ἄλφα, L T Tr A) alpha, *the first of the Greek letters corresponding in name, order, and power to the Hebrew* א aleph, *and in form developed from it. Popularly however* Alpha *being the* first *letter of the* alphabet, *is applied to what is* first, *whether in time or rank.*

Rev. i. 8 (*ap.*)
—— 11.
Rev. xxi. 6.
—— xxii. 13.

ALREADY.

ἤδη, *an adverb of time*, now, at *or* by this time. Already, *i.e. without mentioning or insisting upon anything further.*

Matt. v. 28.
—— xvii. 12.
Mark xv. 44.
Luke xii. 49.
John iii. 18.
—— iv. 35.
—— ix. 22, 27
John xi. 17 (*om.* T)
—— xix. 33
1 Cor. v. 3.
Phil. iii. 12 twice.
2 Thes. ii. 7.
1 Tim. v 15.
2 Tim ii 18.
1 John iv 3.

ALREADY ATTAINED.

φθάνω, to come *or* do before *another*, to be beforehand with, overtake, outstrip.

Phil. iii. 16 (the word "*others*" being understood.)

ALREADY (NOW.)

{ καί, and, also.
{ ἤδη, *see* "ALREADY."

Acts xxvii. 9

ALREADY (SINNED.)

προαμαρτάνω, to sin before.

2 Cor. xii. 21.

ALSO.

1. καί, and, also, even. καί, *a conjunction of annexation differing from* τε, (No. 2), *by uniting things strictly co-ordinate, while* τε *annexes something which does not directly or necessarily follow.* [καί, as meaning *also*, always immediately precedes the word which is emphatic. For example John ix. 40, "Are WE also blind?" (not "Are we BLIND also?"); Rom. v. 2, "By whom we have ACCESS also," (not "By whom also we have access.")]

* *with* αὐτός, he, she, it; † *with a comparative*; ‡ δὲ καί, καὶ...*or* δέ τε καί, (*the* δέ, *assuming what has been said, and passing on to something more*), moreover.

2. τε, *only annexes, often with implied relation or distinction*, and, also.

3. { ἀλλα, but.
{ καί, *see No.* 1.

4. μέντοι, *conjunc.*, yet truly, certainly, nevertheless, however.

5. ἅμα, *adverb*, at the same time, with *or* together with.

6. δή, *a particle indicating* certainty *or* reality, *and so augmenting the vivacity of a sentence;* truly, indeed, by all means.

7. ἔτι, *adverb*, any more, any longer, yet still, even; *implying accession*, besides.

1. Matt. iii. 10 (*om.* G→ L T Tr A S.)
1. —— v. 39, 40.
1. —— vi. 14, 21.
1. —— x. 4.
6. —— xiii. 23.
1. ——— 26.
1. —— xv. 3, 16.
1. —— xvii. 12.
1. —— xviii. 33.
1. —— xix. 28.
1. —— xx. 4, 7.
— —— xxi. 21, see A if.
1. —— xxii. 26, 27.
1. —— xxiii. 26.
1. —— xxiv. 27 (*om.* G⇉ L T Tr A.) [A ℵ.)
1. ——— 37 (*om.* L T Tr
1. ——— 39 (*om.* L T Tr
1. ——— 44. [A.)
1. —— xxv. 11. [T Tr ℵ.)
1. ——— 17* (*om.* G→ L
1. ——— 22‡, 41, 44.
1. —— xxvi. 13. [Tr A.)
1. ——— 35‡ (*om.* δέ, G⇎
1. ——— 69, 71, 73.
1. —— xxvii. 41‡ (*om.* Lb ℵ) (*om.* δέ, Trb.)
1. ——— 44, 57.
1. Mark i. 19.
1. ——— 38.
1. —— ii. 26, 28.
1. —— iii. 19.
1. —— iv. 36.
1. —— vii. 18.
1. —— viii. 7, 38.
1. —— xi. 25.
1. —— xii. 6, 22.
1. —— xiv. 9, 31‡.
1. —— xv. 31‡, 40, 41, 43‡.
1. Luke i. 35, 36*.
1. —— ii. 4.
1. —— iii. 9‡, 12‡.
1. —— iv. 23, 43.
1. —— v. 10, 36.
1. —— vi. 4 (*om.* L Tr A.)
1. ——— 5.
1. ——— 6 (*om.* L Tr ℵ.)
1. ——— 13, 14. [ℵ.)
1. ——— 16 (*om.* L T Tr A
1. ——— 29 twice, 31, 32.
— ——— 33, see A even.
1. Luke vi. 34.
1. ——— 36 (*om.* Lb Trb ℵ)
1. —— vii. 8, 49. [Tr ℵ.)
1. —— viii. 36 (*om.* G⇉ L
1. —— ix. 61.
1. —— x. 1 (*om.* Trb.)
1. ——— 39.
1. —— xi. 1, 4*, 30, 34 twice, 40, 45, 46, 49.
1. —— xii. 8, 34, 40, 54.
1. —— xiii. 8.
1. —— xiv. 12‡ 1st, 12* 2nd
7. ——— 26. [22, 28.
1. —— xvi. 1, 10 twice, 14,
1. —— xvii. 26, 28.
1. —— xviii. 15.
1. —— xix. 9*, 19.
1. —— xx. 12, 31.
1. ——— 32‡ (*om.* δέ, G⇉ L T Tr A ℵ.) [Tr ℵ.)
1. —— xxi. 2 (*om.* G→ Lb
1. —— xxii. 20, 24, 39, 56,
1. —— xxiii. 7. [58, 59, 68.
1. ——— 27 (*om.* G→ L Tr
1. ——— 32, 35, 36. [ℵ.)
1. ——— 51 (*om.* G∾ L Tr A ℵ.) [A ℵ.)
1. ——— 55 (*om.* G⇉ L Tr
1. —— xxiv. 23.
1. John iii. 23.
1. —— iv. 45*.
1. —— v. 18, 19, 27.
1. —— vi. 36, 37.
1. —— vii. 3, 10*, 47, 52.
1. —— viii. 17‡, 19.
1. —— ix. 15, 27, 40.
1. —— xi. 16, 52.
1. —— xii. 9, 10, 18, 26, 32.
4. ——— 42.
1. —— xiii. 9, 14, 32, 34.
1. —— xiv. 3, 7, 19.
1. —— xv. 20 twice, 23.
1. —— xvii. 1 (*om.* G⇉ L T Tr A ℵ.)
1. ——— 19*, 20, 21*.
1. —— xviii. 2, 5, 17, 25.
1. —— xix. 39.
1. —— xx. 8.
1. —— xxi. 3, 20, 25.
1. Acts i. 3, 11. [Tr A ℵ.)
1. —— ii. 22* (*om.* G⇉ L T
1. ——— 26.

1. Acts iii. 17.
1. —— v. 2, 16.
1. —— vii. 45.
1. —— viii. 13*.
1. —— ix. 32.
1. —— x. 45.
1. —— xi. 1, 18, 30.
1. —— xii. 3.
1. —— xiii. 5, 9, 22, 33, 35.
1. —— xiv. 15.
1. —— xv. 27.
1. ——— 32*, 35.
1. —— xvii. 6. 28 twice.
1. —— xix. 21, 27.
1. —— xx. 30.
1. —— xxi. 13, 16, 24*, 28.
1. —— xxii. 5 twice, 20*.
1. —— xxiii. 11, 30, 33, 35.
1. —— xxiv. 6, 9, 15*.
5. &1. —— 26.
1. —— xxv. 22*.
1. —— xxvi. 10, 26, 29.
1. —— xxvii. 10.
1. —— xxviii. 9, 10.
1 Rom. i. 6, 13, 15.
1. ——— 24 (om. G⇉ L Tr Ab ℵ.)
1. ——— 27.
1. —— ii. 12. (All.)
1. —— iii. 29‡ 1st (om. δέ, 21. 24.
1. ——— 29 2nd.
— —— iv. 6, 9, 11*, 12, 16.
— —— v. 2, 3, 11, 15.
3. —— vi. 5.
1. ——— 8, 11.
1. —— vii. 4. [26‡, 29.
1. —— viii. 11, 17, 21*, 23,
— ——— 30 3 times, 32, 34.
1. —— ix. 10, 24, 25.
1. —— xi. 1, 16.
— ——— 21, see A..not.
1. ——— 22, 31 1st, 31* 2nd.
1. —— xiii. 5, 6. [27.
1. —— xv. 7, 14 3 times, 22,
1. —— xvi. 4, 7.
1. 1 Cor. i. 8, 16.
1. —— ii. 13.
1. —— iv. 8. [A.
1. —— v. 12 (om. G⇉ L Tr
1. —— vii. 3, 4. [ℵ.
1. ——— 22 (om. L T Tr A
1. ——— 34 (om. St G.)
1. —— ix. 8. [Tr A ℵ.)
1. —— x. 9 (om. G⇉ L T
1. ——— 10 (om. G⇉ L T
1. ——— 13. [Tr A ℵ.)
1. —— xi. 6, 19, 23, 25.
1. —— xii. 12.
1. —— xiii. 12.
1. —— xiv. 15 twice, 19, 34.
1. —— xv. 1, 2, 3, 14, 18, 21.
1. ——— 28 (om. Lb Tr Ab.)
1. ——— 42, 48, 49.
1. —— xvi. 10.
1. 2 Cor. i. 5, 6, 7, 11, 14 twice, 22.
1. —— ii. 9, 10.
1. —— iii. 6.
1. —— iv. 10, 11, 13, 14.
1. —— v. 5 (om. G⇉ L Tr
1. ——— 11. [A ℵ.)
1. —— vi. 13. [11, 14, 19.
1. —— viii. 6 twice, 7, 10,
1. —— ix. 12.
1. —— x. 11, 14
1. —— xi. 15.
1. 2 Cor. xiii. 4, 9.
1. Gal. ii. 1, 10, 13, 17*.
1. —— v. 21, 25.
1. —— vi. 1, 7.
1. Eph. i. 11, 13 twice, 21.
1. —— ii. 3, 22.
1. —— iv. 9, 10.
1. —— v. 2, 25.
1. —— vi. 9 (καὶ αὐτῶν, *both their* [ἑαυτῶν, *their own*, ℵ] καὶ ὑμῶν, *and your*; instead of καὶ ὑμῶν αὐτῶν, *your..also* AVm G∾ L T Tr A ℵ)
1. ——— 21.
1. Phil. i. 15, 20, 29.
1. —— ii. 4, 5, 9, 18, 24*, [27.
1. —— iii. 4, 12, 20.
1. —— iv. 3, 10, 15.
1. Col. i. 6. [Tr A ℵ.)
1. ——— 7 (om. G⇉ L T
1. ——— 8, 9, 29.
1. —— ii. 11, 12.
1. —— iii. 4, 7, 8, 13, 15.
1. —— iv. i. 3 twice, 16.
1. 1 Thes. i. 5. [Tr A ℵ.)
1. ——— 8 (om. G⇉ L T
1. —— ii. 8, 13 twice, 14.
1. —— iii. 6.
1. —— iv. 6.
1. ——— 8 (om. L Tr Ab.)
1. —— v. 11, 24.
1. 2 Thes. i. 5, 11.
1. 1 Tim. ii. 9 (om. L Trb ℵ)
1. —— v. 13, 20, 25.
1. 2 Tim. i. 5, 12. [20.
1. —— ii. 2, 5, 10*, 11, 12,
1. —— iii. 8, 9.
1. —— iv. 8, 15.
1. Titus iii. 3, 14.
1. Philem. 9, 21, 22.
1. Heb. i. 2.
1. —— ii. 14*.
1. —— iii. 2.
1. —— iv. 10*.
1. —— v. 2*, 3. 5, 6.
1. —— vii. 2 twice, 12, 25.
1. —— viii. 3†, 6.
1. —— ix. 1.
1. —— x. 15.
1. —— xi. 11, 19.
2. ——— 32.
1. —— xii. 1, 26.
1. —— xiii. 3*, 12.
1. Jas. i. 11.
1. —— ii. 2, 11, 19, 25‡.
1. —— iii. 4.
1. —— v. 8.
1. 1 Pet. ii. 5, 8, 18, 21.
1. —— iii. 1, 5, 18, 19, 21.
1. —— iv. 6, 13.
1. —— v. 1.
1. 2 Pet. ii. 1.
1. —— iii. 15, 16 twice.
1. 1 John i. 3.
1. —— ii. 2, 6*, 24.
1. —— iii. 4.
1. —— iv. 11, 21.
1. —— v. 1 (om. Lb Trb.)
1. 2 John i.
4 & 1. Jude 8‡.
1. ——— 14.
1. Rev. ii. 15.
1. —— vi. 11.
1. —— xi. 8.

ALSO EVEN.

1. Luke vi. 33.

ALSO IF.

κἄν *(for* καὶ ἐάν), and if, even if, but at least.

Matt. xxi. 21.

ALSO...NOT.

οὐδέ, *(from* οὐ, not, *and* δέ, *a copulative conj.), a disjunctive negative*, neither, nor, not, not even. (οὐ *denies a matter of fact, while* μή *denies a matter of thought or supposition.)*

Rom. xi. 21.

See, AND, AND SO, BEAR WITNESS, EVEN, HE, I, ME, THERE, THENCE, YEA. ELDER.

ALTAR.

1. θυσιαστήριον, an altar, *(from* θυσιάζω, to sacrifice), *whether of burnt offerings or incense.*
2. βωμός, the altar structure, *(properly* a raised place, *Heb.)*

1. Matt. v. 23, 24.
1. —— xxiii. 18, 19, 20, 35.
1. Luke i. 11.
1. —— xi. 51.
2. Acts xvii. 23.
1. Rom. xi. 3.
1. 1 Cor. ix. 13 twice.
1. ——— x. 18.
1. Heb. vii. 13.
1. —— xiii. 10.
1. Jas. ii. 21.
1. Rev. vi. 9.
1. —— viii. 3 twice, 5.
1. —— ix. 13.
1. —— xi. 1.
1. —— xiv. 18.
1. Rev. xvi. 7.

ALTERED.

ἕτερος, another, *(distributive pronoun,)* another *in kind (while* ἄλλος *denotes* another *individual, see* "ANOTHER.")

Luke ix. 29.

ALTHOUGH.

1. { καί, and, also. / εὐ, in case.
2. καίτοι, nevertheless, though, indeed.
3. { ἐάν, in case. / καί, and, also.

1. Mark xiv. 29 (εἰ καί, Tr A ℵ)
3. Gal. vi. 1.
2. Heb. iv. 3.

ALTOGETHER.

1. ὅλος, all, the whole.
2. πάντως, wholly, entirely, in every way.
3. { ἐν, in, / πολύς, much, great in number, *pl.* many, } in much, *i.e. in long comparison, in elaborate argument.*

1. John ix. 34.
3. Acts xxvi. 29 (ἐν, *in*, μέγας, *great*, G→ L T Tr A ℵ)
2. 1 Cor. v. 10.
2. ——— ix. 10.

ALTOGETHER WITHOUT HELP, OR *MEANS* [margin.]

ἐξαπορέομαι, to be utterly at a loss *or* a stand, to be in the utmost perplexity. (occ. 2 Cor. i. 8.)

2 Cor. iv. 8 (**text,** ***in despair.***)

ALWAY (-S.)

1. πάντοτε, always, ever, constantly, *(from* πᾶς, all, *and* τότε, there.)
2. ἀεί, always, *of continuous time,* unceasingly; *of successive intervals,* from time to time, on every occasion.
3. διαπαντός, through all *(the)* time, always. *(No.* 6 *in one word.)*
4. ἑκάστοτε, *(adv. of* time, *from* ἕκαστος. each, *and* ὅτε, when), each time, every time.
5. πάντη, in every way.
6. { διά, through, πᾶς, all, the whole, every one, } through all (time *understood),* continually *(No.* 3 *in two words.)*
7. { ἐν, in, πᾶς, all, every, καιρός, *the right measure and relation, esp. as regards place and time; hence* the right time, a definite or fixed time, a season. } in every season at every opportunity.
8. { πᾶς, all, ὁ, the, ἡμέρα, day, } *plural,* all the days.

6. Matt. xviii. 10 (No. 3, G.)
1. —— xxvi. 11 twice.
8. —— xxviii. 20.
3. Mark v. 5 (No. 6, L T.)
1. —— xiv. 7 twice.
1. Luke xviii. 1.
7. —— xxi. 36.
1. John viii. 29.
1. —— xi. 42.
1. —— xii. 8 twice.
1. —— xviii. 20 (G ∾), (πάντες, All, G L T Tr ℵ.)
6. Acts ii. 25 (No. 3, G.)
2. —— vii. 51.
8. —— x. 2 (No. 6, L T Tr.)
5. —— xxiv. 3.
3. —— 16 (No. 6, L T Tr.)
1. Rom. i. 9.
3. —— xi. 10 (No. 6, L T Tr.)
1. 1 Cor. i. 4.
1. —— xv. 58.
1. 2 Cor. ii. 14.
1. —— iv. 10.
2. 2 Cor. iv. 11.
1. —— v. 6.
2. —— vi. 10.
1. —— ix. 8.
1. Gal. iv. 18.
1. Eph. v. 20.
7. —— vi. 18.
1. Phil. i. 4, 20.
1. —— ii. 12.
1. Col. i. 3.
1. —— iv. 12.
1. 1 Thes. i. 2.
1. —— iii. 6.
— 2 Thes. i. 3, 11.
1. —— ii. 13.
6. —— iii. 16 (No. 3, G.)
2. Titus i. 12.
1. Philem. 4.
2. Heb. iii. 10.
8. —— ix. 6 (No. 6, L T Tr.)
2. 1 Pet. iii. 15.
2. 2 Pet. i. 12.
4. —— 15.

AM (I) AND I AM.

When this is not part of another word, it is the translation of

εἰμί, I am. *When this is rendered by the personal pronoun* (ἐγώ, I,) *an asterisk is affixed.*

Matt. iii. 11; viii. 8, 9*; xi. 29; xviii. 20*; xx. 15*; xxii. 32*; xxiv. 5*; xxvii. 24, 43; xxviii. 20; Mark i. 7; xiii. 6*; xiv. 62*; Luke i. 18*, 19*; iii. 16; v. 8; vii. 6, 8; xv. 19, 21; xviii. 11; xxi. 8*; xxii. 27*, 33, 58, 70*; John i. 20*, 21, 27*; iii. 28 1st, 28 2nd; iv. 26*; vi. 35*, 41*, 48*, 51*; vii. 28 1st, 29, 33, 34*, 36*; viii. 12*, 16, 18*, 23 twice, 24*, 28*, 58*; ix. 5 (subj.), 9*; x. 7*, 9*, 11*, 14*, 36; xi. 25*; xii. 26*; xiii. 13, 19*, 33; xiv. 3*, 6*; xv. 1*, 5*; xvi. 32; xvii. 11, 14, 16, 24*; xviii. 5*, 6*, 8*, 17, 25, 35*, 37*; xix. 21; Acts ix. 5*; x. 21*, 26*; xiii. 25* 1st, 25 2nd; xviii. 10*; xxi. 39*; xxii. 3*, 8*; xxiii. 6*; xxvi. 15*, 29*; xxvii. 23; Rom. i. 14; vii. 14*; xi. 1*, 13*; 1 Cor. i. 12*; iii. 4*; ix. 1 twice, 2; xii. 15 twice, 16 twice; xiii. 2; xv. 9* 1st, 9 2nd, 10 twice; 2 Cor. xii. 10; Phil. iv. 11; Col. ii. 5; 1 Tim. i. 15*; 1 Pet. i. 16* (*om.* εἰμί, L T A ℵ); 2 Pet. i. 13; Rev. i. 8*, 11* (*ap.*), 17*, 18; ii. 23*; iii. 17; xviii. 7; xix. 10; xxi. 6* (*om.* εἰμί, G ∾ Ab ℵ); xxii. 9, 13* (*om.* εἰμί, AV) 16*.

AM (THAT...I.)

"That" *being a conjunction, not a pronoun,*

εἶναι, to be, *the infinitive of* εἰμί, I am, *(with the Acc. of the pronoun* με, me, *and infinitive of verb, means,* that... I am.)

Matt. xvi. 13 (*om.* pron. Lb T Tr A), 15; Mark viii. 27, 29; Luke ix. 18 (*om.* pron. T Tr), 20; John xviii. 37; Acts xiii. 25.

AM (WHICH.)

ὤν, οὖσα, ὄν *(participle of* εἰμί), being.

John iv. 9.

AMAZED (BE.)

1. ἐξίστημι, *transitive,* to change *from one condition to another, denoting the state of mind caused by inexplicable occurrences, (from* ἐξ, out, *and* ἵστημι, to stand, place.)
2. ἐκπλήσσω, to be exceedingly struck in mind, *(from* ἐκ *intensive, and* πλήσσω, to strike.)
3. { λαμβάνω, to take, take hold of ἔκστασις, *transitive,* removal; *intransitive,* remoteness, *then the state of a man* carried out of *his senses, lunacy. In N.T. the weaker sense of* bewilderment, fear, amazement; a trance, the state of rapture. } taken *or* seized with astonishment

4. { ἔχω, to have,
ἔκστασις, *see No.* 3, *above.*

5. θαμβέω, to be awed, astonished, *either with wonder or fear.*

1. Matt. xii. 23.
1. —— xix. 25.
5. Mark i. 27.
1. —— ii. 12.
1. —— vi. 51.
— —— ix. 15, see A (be greatly.)
5. —— x. 32.
— Mark xiv. 33, see A (be sore.)
4. Mark xvi. 8.
2. Luke ii. 48.
— —— iv. 36, see amazed.
3. —— v. 26.
2. —— ix. 43.
1. Acts ii. 7, 12.
1. Acts ix. 21.

AMAZED.

θάμβος, awe, surprise *at a strange or unusual deed or expression;* amazement.

Luke iv. 36.

AMAZED (BE GREATLY.)

ἐκθαμβέομαι, to be amazed, astonished exceedingly, *(from* ἐκ, out *or intensive, and* θαμβέω, *No.* 5, *above.)*

Mark ix. 15.

AMAZED (BE SORE.)

ἐκθαμβέομαι, *see above.*

Mark xiv. 33.

AMAZEMENT.

1. ἔκστασις, *see* "AMAZED," *No.* 3.
2. πτόησις, terror, consternation; a being affrighted, *(from* πτοέω, to terrify.)

1. Acts iii. 10. | 2. 1 Pet. iii. 6.

AMBASSADOR (BE AN.)

πρεσβεύω, to be the elder *or* eldest; *to rank* before, take precedence of *others.* To be an ambassador *or* go as one; to treat *or* negotiate as one.

2. Cor. v. 20. | Eph. vi. 20.

AMBASSAGE.

πρεσβεία, age, eldership; rank, dignity, respect; an embassy *(this sense arose from* elders *being chosen as ambassadors.)*

Luke xiv. 32.

AMEN.

ἀμήν, *a Hebrew word* אמן, *a verbal adjective;* firm; *metaph.,* faithful; *adverb,* verily, truly, certainly, *(from* אמן, to prop, stay, support.) *Intransitive,* to be durable, lasting, permanent, such as one can lean upon; *hence* to be faithful, trustworthy, sure, certain, true.

Matt. vi. 13 (*ap.*)
—— xxviii. 20 (*om.* All.)
Luke xxiv. 53 (*om.* G L^b T Tr A ℵ.)
John xxi. 25 (*om.* All.)
Rom. i. 25.
—— ix. 5.
—— xi. 36.
—— xv. 33 (*om.* G → L^b Tr^b)
—— xvi. 20 (*om.* S^t G L T Tr A ℵ.)
———— 24 (*ap.*)
———— 27.
1 Cor. xiv. 16.
—— xvi. 24 (*om.* G ⇉ L^b T Tr A^b.)
2 Cor. i. 20.
—— xiii. 14 (*om.* All.)
Gal. i. 5.
—— vi. 18.
Eph. iii. 21.
—— vi. 24 (AV. 1617 & subsequent editions), (*om.* AV. 1611 & All.)
Phil. iv. 20.
———— 23 (*om.* G ⇉ L^b T Tr A.
Col. iv. 18 (*om.* All.)
1 Thes. v. 28 (*om.* G L T Tr A.)
2 Thes. iii. 18 (*om.* G ⇉ T Tr A ℵ.)
1 Tim. i. 17.
—— vi. 16.
———— 21 (*om.* All.)
2 Tim. iv. 18.
———— 22 (*om.* All.)
Titus iii. 15 (*om.* G L^b T Tr A ℵ.)
Philem. 25 (*om.* G L T Tr A)
Heb. xiii. 21.
———— 25 (*om.* G → ℵ.)
2 John 13 (*om.* All.)
Jude 25.
Rev. i. 6, 7.
———— 18 (*om.* All.)
—— iii. 14.
—— v. 14.
—— vii. 12 1st.
———— 2nd (*om.* L T Tr^b A.)
—— xix. 4.
—— xxii. 20.
———— 21 (*om.* G L T Tr^b A ℵ.)

AMEND (BEGAN TO.)

{ ἔχω, to have, κομψότερον, more elegantly, better in health, } had *himself* better, *i.e. was better, (the medical term for one recovering from a fever.)*

John iv. 52.

AMENDMENT OF LIFE [margin.]

μετάνοια, *for meaning see under* "REPENTANCE."

Matt. iii. 8 (text, *repentance.*)

AMETHYST.

ἀμέθυστος, (1) *in classical Greek,* not drunken, without drunkenness, *(Plutarch.)*

(2) *a substantive.* (i) a remedy against drunkenness, *(a kind of herb.)* (ii) *the precious stone,* amethyst, *supposed to have this power.*

Pliny says, "The reason assigned for its name is because though it approaches to the colour of wine, it falls short of it *and stops at a violet colour," from* ἀ, *negative, and* μέθυ, wine.

Rev. xxi. 20.

AMISS.

1. *ἄτοπος*, out of place, out of the way; inconvenient, unsuitable, improper.
2. *κακῶς*, (*adverb, from κακός*, bad), ill, wickedly, wrongly.

1. Luke xxiii. 41. | 2. Jas. iv. 3.

AMONG, AMONGST.

1. ἐν, in, *of time, place, or element;* among.
2. πρός, towards (*in the direction of.*)
   (a) *with Gen.* in favour of.
   (b) *with Dat.* at, close by.
   (c) *with Acc.* (*hitherwards*) to; *after the substantive verb,* with; *of mental direction,* towards, against; *hence* in consideration of, in order to, with regard to.
3. εἰς, (*motion to the interior*), into, to, unto, with a view to.
4. μετά, with (*in association, not co-operation.*)
   (a) *with Gen.* together with, among.
   (b) *with Acc.* after.
5. ἐκ, from, out of.
6. ἐπί, upon (*superposition.*)
   (a) *with Gen.* upon, (*as springing from;*) over.
   (b) *with Dat.* upon, (*as resting on;*) in addition to, on account of.
   (c) *with Acc.* upon, (*by direction towards*) up to (*of place, number, aim;*) over (*of time, place, extent.*)
7. παρά (*juxtaposition*) beside.
   (a) *with Gen.* (*from beside*) from.
   (b) *with Dat.* (*at the side of*) near, with (*of persons only.*)
   (c) *with Acc.* (*to or along the side of*) beside, by, near.
8. κατά, down.
   (a) *with Gen.* (*down from*) down, against.
   (b) *with Acc.* (*down towards*) down (*upon*), throughout, over against, *then,* according to, (*in reference to some standard of comparison, stated or implied.*)
9. ὑπό, under.
   (a) *with Gen.* (*beneath and separate from*) by, (*marking the agent or efficient cause.*)
   (b) *with Acc.* under, (*figuratively or locally*) in the power of, close upon (*of time.*)
10. μέσος, the middle, midst (*of time or place.*)
11. { ἐν, in.
    { μέσος, the middle *or* midst.
12. διά, through.
    (a) *with Gen.* through, by means of.
    (b) *with Acc.* on account of *or* owing to.
13. ἐντός, inside, in the midst, among.

1. Matt. ii. 6.
1. —— iv. 23.
1. —— ix. 35 (*om. among the people,* All).
1. —— xi. 11.
5. —— xii. 11.
6c. —— xiii. 7.
3. —— 22.
10. —— 25, 49.
1. —— xvi. 7, 8.
1. —— xx. 26 twice, 27.
1. —— xxi. 38.
1. —— xxvi. 5.
1. —— xxvii. 56.
7b. —— xxviii. 15.
2c. Mark i. 27.
3. —— iv. 7 (No. 6c, Lm.)
3. —— 18.
1. —— v. 3.
1. —— vi. 4.
2c. —— viii. 16.
3. —— 19, 20.
2c. —— ix. 16, margin (text, *with.*)
2c. —— 33 (*om.* G⇌ L Tr A ℵ.)
2c. —— 34.
2c. —— x. 26.
1. —— 43 twice.
2c. —— xii. 7.
3. —— xiii. 10.
2c. —— xv. 31.
1. —— 40.
2c. —— xvi. 3.
1. Luke i. 1, 25.
1. —— i. 28 (*ap.*)
1. —— 42.
1. —— ii. 44 1st.
1. —— 44 2nd (*om.* All.)
2c. —— iv. 36.
1. —— vii. 16, 28.
11. —— viii. 7.
3. —— 14.
1. —— ix. 46, 48.
11. —— x. 3.
— —— 30, see fall A.
3. —— 36.
1. —— xvi. 15.
13. —— xvii. 21, margin (text, *within.*)
2c. —— xx. 14.
2. —— xxii. 23.
1. —— 24, 26.
11. —— 27.
4a. —— 37.
11. —— 55.
4a. —— xxiv. 5.
3. —— 47.
1. John i. 14.
10. —— 26.
3. —— vi. 9.
4a. —— 43.
2c. —— 52.
1. —— vii. 12, 43.
2c. —— 35 1st.
— —— 35 2nd, the translation of Gen. case of the *Gentiles.*
1. John ix. 16.
1 —— x. 19.
1. —— xi. 54.
4a. —— 56.
2c. —— xii. 19.
5. —— 20, 42.
1. —— xv. 24.
2c. —— xvi. 17.
4a. —— 19.
2c. —— xix. 24 1st.
— —— 24 2nd, the translation of the Dat. case *for themselves.*
3. —— xxi. 23.
6c. Acts i. 21.
3. —— ii. 22.
— —— iii. 23, see A (from.)
1. —— iv. 12.
2c. —— 15.
3. —— 17.
1. —— 34.
1. —— v. 12.
5. —— vi. 3.
1. —— 8.
9a. —— x. 22.
1. —— xii. 18.
1. —— xiii. 26.
— —— xiv. 14 see A (in.)
1. —— xv. 7, 12, 22.
10. —— xvii. 33.
1. —— 34.
1. —— xviii. 11.
1. —— xx. 25.
— —— 29, see A (in.)
1. —— 32.
1. —— xxi. 19.
8b. —— 21.
1. —— 34.
10. —— xxiii. 10.
1. —— xxiv. 21.
1. —— xxv. 5, 6.
8b. —— xxvi. 3.
1. —— 4, 18.
5. —— xxvii. 22.
2c. —— xxviii. 4.
2c. —— 25.
1. —— 29 (*ap.*)
1. Rom. i. 5, 6.
1. —— 13 1st, marg. *in.*
1. —— 13 2nd.
1. —— ii. 24.
1. —— viii. 29.
1. —— xi. 17, marg. *for.*
1. —— xii. 3.
1. —— xv. 9.
1. —— xvi. 7.
1. 1 Cor. i. 10, 11.
1. —— ii. 2, 6.
1. —— iii. 3, 18.
1. —— v. 1 twice.
1. —— 2.
— —— 13, see A (from)
1. —— vi. 5.
1. —— 7 (*om.* All.)
1. —— xi. 18, 19 twice, 30
1. —— xv. 12.
1. 2 Cor. i. 19.
10. —— vi. 17.

1. 2 Cor. x. 1.
——— 12, see compare A
3. ——— xi. 6.
1. ——— 26.
1. ——— xii. 12.
2c. ——— 21.
1. Gal. i. 16.
1. —— ii. 2.
1. —— iii. 1 (*om.* G ⇉ L Tr ℵ.)
1. ——— 5.
1. Eph. ii. 3.
1. —— iii. 8 (*om.* L Tr ℵ.)
1. —— v. 3.
1. Phil. ii. 15.
1. Col. i. 18, 27, margin (text, *in.*)
7b. —— iv. 16.
1. 1 Thes. i. 5.
11. ——— ii. 7.
1. 1 Thes v. 12, 13.
3. ——— v. 15.
6c. 2 Thes. i. 10.
1. ——— iii. 7, 11.
12. 2 Tim. ii. 2, margin *by*.
5. Heb. v. 1.
1. Jas. i. 26 (G ~), (*om. among you*, All.)
1. —— iii. 6, 13.
1. —— iv. 1.
1. —— v. 13, 14.
1. 1 Pet. ii. 12.
3. ——— iv. 8.
1. ——— v. 2, margin *as much as in you is* (τὸ ἐν ὑμῖν.)
1. 2 Pet. ii. 1 twice, 8.
7b. Rev. ii. 13.
6c. —— vii. 15.

AMONG (FROM.)

5. Acts iii. 23. | 5. 1 Cor. v. 13. | 5. Heb. v. 1.

AMONG (IN.)

3. Acts xiv. 14. | 3. Acts xx. 29.

See also, COMPARE, DWELL, FALL, OUT, PUBLICAN, SPEAK.

ANATHEMA.

ἀνάθεμα, an offering, *a thing* devoted to destruction *or* given up to the curse.

1 Cor. xii. 3, margin (text, *accursed*) ; xvi. 22.

ANCHOR (-s.)

ἄγκυρα, an anchor, *(from its* curve *form.)*

Acts xxvii. 29, 30, 40. | Heb. vi. 19.

ANCLE BONE.

σφυρόν, the ancle bone, *(from* σφῦρα, a hammer, *the head of which this bone somewhat resembles.)*

Acts iii. 7.

AND.

1. καί, *the conjunction of annexation, uniting things strictly co-ordinate,* and, also, even, *(*καί *connects thoughts;* δέ, *No.* 3, *introduces them.)*

2. τε, *a conj. of annexation, annexing with implied relation or distinction,* and, also, *(annexing something added)* *(*τε *denotes an internal, co-equal relation;* καί *an external relation.)*

3. δέ, *conj. of antithesis, less emphatic than* ἀλλά, *No.* 4. *It is to be carefully distinguished from* καί, *No.* 1, *and* τε, *No.* 2, but, *with an adversative force, and sometimes concealed antithesis; frequently rendered in N.T. by* and, then, now, so.

4. ἀλλά, but, *(emphatic as contrasted with* δέ, *No.* 3; *it is used to mark opposition, interruption, transition.)*

5. οὖν, *the particle of formal inference,* therefore.

6. { μέν, *an antithetic particle,* truly, indeed, οὖν, *the particle of inference,* therefore. } therefore indeed, moreover.

7. γάρ, *the demonstrative causal conj. is a contraction of* γὲ ἄρα, verily then; *hence,* in fact; *and, when the fact is given as a reason or explanation,* for.

8. ἤ, *a disjunctive particle,* or; *(after a comparative,* than.)

9. δή, certainly, now, *a particle of emphasis.*

10. ἅμα, *adverb,* at the same time, with *or* together with.

11. ἀνά, *preposition,* up in *or* up by, upon *(also used distributively.)*

12. μετά, together with, among.
 (b) *with Acc.* after.

13. ὅστις, *compound relative,* who- which- what- soever.

No. 1 *is the general word for* "AND" *when* not at the beginning *of the English sentence.*

No. 3 *is generally the word translated* "AND," *when* "AND" *occurs* at the beginning *of a sentence.*

Their occurrence is too frequent for quotation.

The following are the exceptions.

1. Matt. x. 18 3 times.
— —— xv. 18, see A they.
1. —— xvi. 18 3 times, see A also.
5. —— xviii. 29 1st.
1. —— xx. 4 3 times, see A ..them.
2. —— xxiii. 6 1st (No. 3, L T Tr A ℵ.)
— ——— 23, see A the other. [Trbm A ℵ.)
1. —— xxv. 17 (*om.* Lb
2. —— xxvii. 48 3rd.
2. —— xxviii. 12 2nd.
1. Mark iv. 24 twice (*ap.*)
— ——— 36 twice, see A also.
— Mark v. 38, see A..A.
8. —— vi. 11, 2nd (*ap.*)
— —— x. 1 1st, see A from
1. —— xii. 4 1st. [thence.
— ——— 4 2nd, see A him.
— ——— 4 3rd (translation of part.)
1. ——— 4 4th.
1. ——— 5 1st.
— ——— 5 2nd, see A him.
1. ——— 5 3rd.
3. ——— 5 4th.
1. —— xiv. 67 1st.
— ——— 67 2nd, see A ..also.
2. —— xv. 36 2nd (*om.* L Tr A ℵ.)

— Mark xvi. 11 1st } see A
— ——— 13 1st } they.
— ——— 18, see A if.
1. Luke ii. 16 1st & 2nd.
— ——— 16 3rd & 4th, see [A..A.
6. —— iii. 18.
— —— iv. 41, see A also.
— —— v. 35, see A then.
11.—— x. 1 2nd.
1. ——— 8 1st.
— —— xi. 7 1st, see A he.
— ——— 7 4th, translation of inf. to give.
— ———42, see A the other.
— —— xii. 45 3rd & 4th, see A..A.
— —— xiii. 9, see A if.
— —— xiv. 26, see A also.
— —— xvii. 8 1st, see A rather.
3. & 1.— xviii. 9 (om. 1 G→ Lb.) [them.
— ——— 19, see A
1. —— xx. 30 1st (ap.)
2. —— xxi. 11 1st & 4th.
— —— xxii. 12, see A he.
1. —— xxiii. 54 1st (om. G⇉.)
2. —— xxiv. 20 1st.
4. ——— 21.
12. John iii. 25.
— —— iv. 35 1st, see A then.
7. ——— 37 1st.
2. ——— 42 1st.
2. —— vi. 18.
5. ———62.
— —— vii. 29, see A he.
1. —— x. 22 2nd (om. G→ T A ℵ.)
— —— xv. 27, see A also.
— John xix. 35, see A he.
5. —— xx. 11 1st.
1. ——— 12 1st.
2. Acts ii. 3 2nd, 9 4th, 10 1st, 33 1st, 37 1st, 40 1st, 43 2nd, 46 1st & 2nd.
2. —— iii. 10 1st (No. 3, L Tr A ℵ.)
2. —— iv. 13 3rd, 33 2nd.
2. —— v. 19 1st.
— ——— 32, see A..A also or A so also.
2. ——— 35.
— ——— 36, see A they.
6. ——— 41.
2. ——— 42 1st.
2. —— vi. 7 3rd, 12 1st, 13 1st.
— —— vii. 4, see A from thence.
2. ——— 26 1st (G∾) (No. 3, G.)
2. —— viii. 1 3rd (No. 3, L T Tr A) (om. ℵ.)
2. ——— 3 1st.
2. ——— 6 1st (No. 3, L T Tr A ℵ.)
2. ——— 13 2nd.
6. ——— 25 1st.
2. ——— 31 2nd, 35 3rd.
7. ——— 39 2nd.
2. —— ix. 6 1st (ap.)
2. ——— 15 2nd, 18 2nd.
2. ——— 24 1st (δέ καί, *and also*, L T Tr A ℵ.)
13. ——— 35 2nd.
2. —— x. 22 3rd, 28, 33, 48.
2. —— xi. 13 1st (No. 3, L Tr ℵ.)
2. ——— 21 1st, 26 4th.
2. —— xii. 6 2nd.
2. ——— 8 1st (No. 3, L Tr.)
2. ——— 12.
2. —— xiii. 1 3rd.

2. Acts xiii. 4.
1. ——— 20 twice (ap.)
2. —— xiv. 12 1st, 21 1st.
— ——— 26, see A from thence.
6. —— xv. 3 1st.
2. ——— 4 3rd, 5.
9. ——— 36 2nd.
5. ——— 39 1st (No. 3, L T Tr A ℵ.)
2. ——— 39 2nd.
— —— xvi. 5, see A so.
2. ——— 11.
2. ——— 12 1st, κἀκεῖθεν, *and thence*, for ἐκεῖθέν τε, *and from thence*, L Tr A ℵ.)
2. ——— 13 1st, 23.
2. ——— 26 2nd (No. 3, L Tr A ℵ.)
2. ——— 34 1st.
2. —— xvii. 4 2nd & 3rd, 5 3rd, 19 1st, 26 1st.
6. ——— 30.
2. —— xviii. 4 2nd.
2. ——— 11 1st (No. 3, L Tr A ℵ.)
2. ——— 26 1st.
2. —— xix. 3 1st, 6 2nd, 11, 12 2nd, 18 1st.
2. ——— 27 (No. 3, St.)
2. ——— 29 2nd.
2. —— xx. 3 1st, 7 2nd.
2. ——— 11 3rd (om. L T ℵ.)
— ——— 15, see A from thence.
2. ——— 35.
— Acts xxi. 1, see A from thence.
2. ——— 11 2nd (om. G⇉ L T Tr A ℵ.)
2. ——— 18 2nd, 20 2nd, 28 3rd, 30 1st, 37.
2. —— xxii. 7 1st.
2. ——— 8 2nd (No. 3, L ℵ), (om. T.)
2. ——— 28 1st.
— ——— 29, see A also
2. —— xxiii. 10 3rd.
— ——— 14, see A they
2. ——— 24 1st, 35.
2. —— xxiv. 5 2nd.
2. ——— 23 1st & 2nd (om. 1st, G⇉ L T Tr A ℵ.)
2. ——— 27.
5. —— xxv. 23 1st.
2. —— xxvi. 10 2nd, 11 3rd 16 2nd.
— ——— 20, see A..A
2. ——— 30 3rd.
2. —— xxvii. 3 1st.
— ——— 4, see A from thence.
2. ——— 5, 8, 17, 20, 21 3rd.
— ——— 36, see A also
10. ——— 40 2nd.
2. ——— 43 1st.
6. —— xxviii. 5 1st.
— ——— 15, see A from thence.
2. Rom. i. 27 (No. 3, G⇉ L T.)
2. —— ii. 19.
— —— xi. 23, see A also.
2. —— xiv. 8.
— ——— 2, see A..also.
2. ——— 26.
2. 1 Cor. i. 30 1st.
— —— ii. 2, see A..A.
2. —— iv. 21.
— —— vi. 14, see A also.
8. —— xi. 27 1st (No. 1, Lm.)
— —— xiv. 7, see A even
— ——— 27, see A that

2. Eph. iii. 19.
1. Col. ii. 2 (ap.)
1. ——iii. 17 2nd (om. G→ L T Tr ℵ.)
— 1 Tim. iii. 10, see A also
7. 2 Tim. ii. 7.
1. —— iv. 18 1st (om. G→ L T Tr A ℵ.)
2. Heb. i. 3 2nd.
— —— iv. 12, see A..A.
2. —— vi. 2 1st & 2nd, 4 1st, 5 2nd.
2. —— ix. 1.

2. Heb. xi. 32 1st.
2. —— xii 2 2nd.
— ——— 20, see A if so much.
— Jas. iii. 2, see A..also.
— ——— 7, see A..A.
— ——— v. 15, see A if.
8. 1 Pet. i. 18.
— 1 John i. 3, see A truly.
2. Jude 6.
2. Rev. i. 2 2nd.
— —— xvii. 8, see A yet.
2. —— xxi. 12 1st (om. All.)

AND AFTERWARD.

κἀκεῖθεν, and thence, and from thence, *of place;* and from that time.

Acts xiii. 21.

AND...ALSO.

1. καί, *see* "AND," *No.* 1.
2. { καί, *see* "AND," *No.* 1. / δέ, *see* "AND," *No.* 3.
3. καί...καί.

2. Matt. xvi. 18. [ℵ.)
2. Mark iv. 36 (om. δέ, L Tr
1. —— xiv. 67.
2. Luke iv. 41.
2. —— xiv. 26.
1. John xv. 27.
2. Acts v. 32 (om. δέ, G→ L Tr Ab ℵ.)

2. Acts xxii. 29.
1. —— xxvii. 36.
2. Rom. xi. 23.
3. —— xvi. 2.
1. 1 Cor. vi. 14.
2. 1 Tim. iii. 10.
1. Jas. iii. 2.

AND...AND.

1. τε...καί, both...and; not only...but.
2. καί...καί, and...also; both...and.

1. Mark v. 38 (om. 1st, St G→.)
2. Luke ii. 16.
2. —— xii. 45.

2. Acts xxvi. 20.
1. Col. ii. 2 (ap.)
2. Heb. iv. 12.
2. Jas. iii. 7.

AND...AND ALSO.

καί...καί...δέ.

Acts v. 32 (om. δέ, G→ L Ab ℵ.)

AND EVEN.

ὅμως, yet, nevertheless.

1 Cor. xiv. 7.

AND...FROM THENCE.

κἀκεῖθεν, and from thence, *of place* (καί, *and* ἐκεῖθέν, from thence.)

Mark x. 1 (καὶ ἐκεῖθέν, L Tr A ℵ.)
Acts vii. 4.

Acts xxi. 1.
—— xxvii. 4.

AND HE (HIM, THEM, THEY, etc.)

Sometimes this is the conjunction, *and part of the* verb. *Sometimes it is the* conjunction, *with the* pronoun, *for this see* "HE." *In a few places it is*

1. κἀκεῖνος, and he, she, it, *(from* καί *and* ἐκεῖνος *an emphatic demonstrative pronoun,* that.*)*

2. ὅστις, who- which- what- soever.

1. Matt. xv. 18.
1. —— xx. 4.
1. Mark xii. 4, 5.
1. —— xvi. 11 (*ap.*)
1. Mark xvi. 13 (*ap.*)
1. Luke xi. 7.
1. —— xviii. 19.
1. Luke xxii. 12.
1. John vii. 29.
1. —— xix. 35 (καὶ ἐκεῖνος, L.)
2. Acts v. 16.
1. —— xviii. 19.
2. —— xxiii. 14.

AND I.

When not the conjunction and part of the verb; and not the conjunction *and the* pronoun, *(for which see* "I"*) it is*

κἀγώ, *(for* καὶ ἐγω*)*, and I.

Matt. xi. 28.
—— xxvi. 15.
Luke ii. 48.
—— xi. 9.
—— xvi. 9 (καὶ ἐγώ, T Tr A ℵ.)
—— xxii. 29.
John i. 31, 33, 34.
—— v. 17.
—— vi. 56, 57.
—— viii. 26.
—— x. 27, 28, 38.
—— xii. 32.
John xiv. 20.
—— xv. 15.
—— xvii. 21, 26.
—— xx. 15.
Acts xxii. 13, 19.
Rom. xi. 3.
1 Cor. ii. 1.
2 Cor. vi. 17.
—— xii. 20.
Gal. vi. 14.
Phil. ii. 28.
Heb. viii. 9.
Jas. ii. 18 twice.

AND IF.

When not the separate conjunctions, and *and* if *(for which see* "IF"*) it is*

κἄν, and if, even if, but, at least, although, *(for* καὶ ἐάν.*)*

Mark xvi. 18 (*ap.*) | Luke xiii. 9.
Jas. v. 15.

AND IF SO MUCH AS.

κἄν, *see* "AND IF."

Heb. xii. 20.

AND RATHER.

ἀλλά, *see* "AND," *No.* 4.

Luke xvii. 8.

AND SO.

οὖν, *see* "AND," *No.* 5.

Acts xvi. 5.

AND SO ALSO.

καί δέ, *see* "AND," *Nos.* 1 *and* 3.

Acts v. 32 (*om.* δέ G→ L A^b ℵ.)

AND THAT.

καί, *see* "AND," *No.* 1.

1 Cor. xiv. 27.

AND THE OTHER.

κἀκεῖνος, *see* "AND HE," *No.* 1.

Matt. xxiii. 23. | Luke xi. 42.

AND THEN.

1. καί, *see* "AND," *No.* 1.

2. τότε, *demons. adv.*, then.

2. Luke v. 35. | 1. John iv. 35.

AND THENCE.

κἀκεῖθεν, *see* "AND FROM THENCE."

Acts xiv. 26; xx. 15.

AND THERE.

κἀκεῖ, and there, thither, *(for* καί, and, *conj.*, ἐκεῖ, there, *adv.)*

In all passages it is the conj. *and the* adv., *two separate words (which see), except*

Matt. v. 23 (καὶ ἐκεῖ, T.)
—— x. 11.
—— xxviii. 10.
Mark i. 35 (καὶ ἐκεῖ, L.)
John xi. 54.
Acts xiv. 7.
—— xxii. 10.
—— xxv. 20.
Acts xxvii. 6.

AND YET.

καίπερ, although.

Rev. xvii. 8 (καὶ πάρεσται, *and shall be present,* for καίπερ ἐστίν, *and yet is,* G L T Tr A), (καὶ πάλιν πάρεσται, *and shall again be present,* ℵ.)

ANGEL (-s.)

ἄγγελος, messenger, *(from* ἀγγέλλω, to tell *or* deliver a message), one who is sent *in order to announce, teach, or perform anything. It is a question whether the angels of the Seven Churches probably may not be the Sheliach Tzibbūr, or the heads of the Jewish Synagogue (congregations of the faithful remnant in the latter day.)* (i) *because of the entire absence*

of any proof that Ministers of the Christian Church were ever so called (ii) *because the internal evidence seems to point to the Jewish character of the Seven Churches. See "Synagogue,"* Rev. ii. 9; iii. 9. *"Jews,"* Rev. ii. 9, *and all the figures, illustrations, and promises.* (iii) *because the whole scene of these Churches seems to be laid in the latter day, see* Rev. i. 10, *"I became, in spirit, on the Lord's day," (see "day");* Rev. ii. 13 *and* xiii. 2 *and* xvi. 10, *"Satan's seat";* Rev. ii. 10; iii. 10, *special persecutions; and the peculiar personal manifestation of Satan,* ii. 10, 13, 24; iii. 9.

Matt. i. 20, 24.
—— ii. 13, 19.
—— iv. 6, 11.
—— xiii. 39, 41, 49.
—— xvi. 27.
—— xviii. 10.
—— xxii. 30.
—— xxiv. 31, 36.
—— xxv. 31, 41.
—— xxvi. 53.
—— xxviii. 2, 5.
Mark i. 13.
—— viii. 38.
—— xii. 25.
—— xiii. 27, 32.
Luke i. 11, 13, 18, 19, 26.
———— 28 (*om.* T Tr^b A.)
———— 30, 34, 35, 38.
—— ii. 9, 10, 13, 15, 21.
—— iv. 10.
—— ix. 26.
—— xii. 8, 9.
—— xv. 10.
—— xvi. 22.
—— xx. 36, see A (equal unto the.)
—— xxii. 43 (*ap.*)
—— xxiv. 23.
John i. 51.
—— v. 4 (*ap.*)
—— xii. 29.
—— xx. 12.
Acts v. 19.
—— vi. 15.
—— vii. 30, 35, 38, 53.
—— viii. 26.
—— x. 3, 7, 22.
—— xi. 13.
—— xii. 7, 8, 9, 10, 11, 15, 23.
—— xxiii. 8, 9.
—— xxvii. 23.
Rom. viii. 38.
1 Cor. iv. 9.
—— vi. 3.
—— xi. 10.
—— xiii. 1.
2 Cor. xi. 14.
Gal. i. 8.
—— iii. 19.
—— iv. 14.
Col. ii. 18.
2 Thes. i. 7.
1 Tim. iii. 16.
———— v. 21.
Heb. i. 4, 5, 6, 7 twice, 13.
—— ii. 2, 5, 7, 9, 16.
—— xii. 22.
—— xiii. 2.
1 Pet. i. 12.
—— iii. 22.
2 Pet. ii. 4, 11.
Jude 6.
Rev. i. 1, 20.
—— ii. 1, 8, 12, 18.
—— iii. 1, 5, 7, 14.
—— v. 2, 11.
—— vii. 1, 2 twice, 11.
—— viii. 2, 3, 4, 5, 6.
———— 7, (*om.* All.)
———— 8, 10, 12.
———— 13 1st (ἀετός, *eagle* [All.)
———— 13 2nd.
—— ix. 1, 11, 13, 14 twice, [15.
—— x. 1, 5, 7, 8, 9, 10.
—— xi. 1 (*ap.*)
———— 15.
—— xii. 7 twice, 9.
—— xiv. 6, 8, 9, 10, 15, 17, [18, 19.
—— xv. 1, 6, 7, 8.
—— xvi. 1. [A ℵ.
———— 3 (*om.* G⇉ L T Tr
———— 4 (*om.* All.)
———— 5.
———— 8 (*om.* All.)
———— 10 (*om.* All.)
———— 12 (*om.* All.)
———— 17 (*om.* All.)
—— xvii. 1, 7.
—— xviii. 1, 21.
—— xix. 17.
—— xx. 1.
—— xxi. 9.
———— 12 (*ap.*)
———— 17.
—— xxii. 6, 8, 16.

ANGELS (EQUAL UNTO THE.)

ἰσάγγελος, *(the above with* ἴσος, equal, *prefixed.)* Equal to the angels.

Luke xx. 36.

ANGER [noun.]

ὀργή, anger, *together with* the desire of revenge, *(from Heb.,* הרג, to kill, and all the tumults of passion which terminate in killing. *This is traced in German* kreig, *war; French,* orgueil, *and Eng.,* rage), *the idea of* sanguinary revenge *belongs etymologically to* ὀργή, *(while* θυμός *is from* חמה, *and is* the animus, the working and fermenting of the mind, the demonstration of strong passion, *which may issue in anger or revenge, though it does not necessarily include it.)*

Mark iii. 5. | Eph. iv. 31. | Col. iii. 8.

ANGER [verb.]

παροργίζω, to provoke to ὀργή, *(see above)* by *or* along with *some other act or thing.*

Rom. x. 19.

ANGRY (BE.)

1. ὀργίζομαι, to be provoked to ὀργή, *(see "ANGER")* to be *or* become angry.
2. χολάω, to be full of black bile, *(from* χολή, gall, bile), to rage with jealous anger *or* resentment.

1. Matt. v. 22.
1. Luke xiv. 21.
1. —— xv. 28.
2. John vii. 23.
1. Eph. iv. 26.
1. Rev. xi. 18.

ANGRY (SOON.)

ὀργίλος, prone to ὀργή, *(see "ANGER")* revengeful.

Titus i. 7.

ANGUISH.

1. θλῖψις, pressure, oppression, affliction.
2. στενοχωρία, narrowness of space, straits, difficulty.
3. συνοχή, a meeting *or* joining, distress, conflicts, *anguish.*

1. John xvi. 21. | 2. Rom. ii. 9.
3. 2 Cor. ii. 4.

ANISE.

ἄνηθον, dill, anise, *(perhaps from* ἀνά, up, *and* θεῖν, to run, *from the running up of the stalk), used for food and pickling.*

Matt. xxiii. 23.

ANOINT (-ED.)

1. ἀλείφω, to anoint with oil *or* ointment. *(Indicates the anointing for festal purposes, health or embalmment.)*
2. χρίω, to touch the surface of a body slightly, graze; to rub over, anoint. *(This word denotes the* official *anointing as of a king or priest, hence* χριστός, Christ.)
3. ἐγχρίω, to rub in.
4. ἐπιχρίω, to rub on, besmear, anoint; lay on ointment.
   (a) *followed by ἐπί,* upon.
5. μυρίζω, to rub with ointment; anoint with aromatic ointment.

1. Matt. vi. 17.
1. Mark vi. 13.
5. —— xiv. 8.
1. —— xvi. 1.
2. Luke iv. 18.
1. —— vii. 38, 46 twice.
4a. John ix. 6, margin *spread upon.*
4. John ix. 11.
1. —— xi. 2.
1. —— xii. 3.
2. Acts iv. 27.
2. —— x. 38,
2. 2 Cor. i. 21.
2. Heb. i. 9.
1. Jas. v. 14.
3. Rev. iii. 18.

ANOINTING.

χρῖσμα, anything smeared on *or* rubbed in, *(referring to the O.T. practice and reminding of the calling or rank)* the anointing, *which was emblematic of the Spirit descending and abiding upon, as was afterwards the laying on of hands.*

1 John ii. 27 twice.

ANON.

1. εὐθύς, straight; *metaph.*, right, true; *adverb of time,* straight, *i.e.,* immediately, forthwith.
2. εὐθέως, *(adverb of above)* immediately, soon, speedily.

1. Matt. xiii. 20.
2. Mark i. 30 (No. 1, L T Tr A ℵ.)

ANOTHER.

1. ἄλλος, other, not the same, *i.e., one besides what has been mentioned; denoting numerical distinction, see No.* 2.
   (a) *with art.*, the other.
2. ἕτερος, *denotes generic distinction,* the other (different) one of two; *a stronger expression therefore than No.* 1. *This distinction is generally observed and is important.* (Compare Gal. i. 6, 7, *"to another (No. 2) Gospel, which is not another" (No. 1) i.e., there may be many so-called Gospels, but there is really no other than that preached by the Apostle.)*
3. { ἄλλος, *see above,* τις, any one, a certain, } some other, any other, a certain other.

1. Matt. ii. 12.
1. —— viii. 9.
2. —— 21.
1a. —— x. 23 (No. 2, G ⇎ L Tr ℵ.)
2. —— xi. 3.
1. —— xiii. 24, 31, 33.
1. —— xix. 9.
1. —— xxi. 33.
1. —— xxvi. 71.
1. Mark x. 11, 12.
1. —— xii. 4, 5.
1. —— xiv. 19 (*ap.*)
1. —— 58.
2. —— xvi. 12 (*ap.*)
2. Luke vi. 6.
1. —— vii. 8.
1. —— 19 (No. 2, Tr ℵ.)
1. —— 20.
2. —— ix. 56, 59, 61.
2. —— xiv. 19, 20, 31.
2. —— xvi. 7, 18.
2 —— xix. 20.
2. —— xx. 11.
2. —— xxii. 58.
3. —— 59.
1. John v. 7, 32, 43.
1. —— xiv. 16.
1a. —— xviii. 15 (*om.* art. G ⇉ L Tr b.)
2. —— xix. 37.
1. —— xxi. 18.
2. Acts i. 20.
2. —— vii. 18.
2. —— xii. 17.
2. —— xiii. 35.
2. —— xvii. 7.
2. Rom. ii. 1, 21.
2. —— vii. 3 twice, 4, 23.
2. —— xiii. 8 2nd.
2. 1 Cor. iii. 4.
1. —— 10.
2. —— iv. 6.
2. —— vi. 1.
2. —— x. 24.
1. —— xii. 8.
2. —— 9 1st.
1. —— 9 2nd, 10 1st, 2nd & 3rd times.
2. —— 10 4th time.
1. —— 10 5th time.
1. —— xiv. 30.
1. —— xv. 39 3 times.
2. —— 40.
1. —— 41 twice.
1. 2 Cor. xi. 4 1st.
2. —— 4 2nd & 3rd
2. Gal. i. 6.
1. —— 7.
2. —— vi. 4.
1. Heb. iv. 8.
2. —— v. 6.
2. —— vii. 11, 13, 15.
2. Jas. ii. 25.
2. —— iv. 12 (πλησίον, *a neighbour,* G ∾ L T Tr A ℵ.)
1. Rev. vi. 4.
1. —— vii. 2.
1. —— viii. 3.
1. —— x. 1 (*om.* G →.)
1. —— xii. 3.
1. —— xiii. 11.
1. —— xiv. 6 (*om.* G ⇉ A b ℵ.)
1. —— 8, 15, 17, 18.
1. —— xv. 1.
1. —— xvi. 7 (*om.* All.)
1. —— xviii. 1, 4.
1. —— xx, 12.

ANOTHER MAN'S.

1. ἄλλος, another, *see above.*
2. ἀλλότριος, of *or* belonging to another (ἄλλος), *opp. to* ἴδιος, *q.v.*

2. Luke xvi. 12.
2. Rom. xiv. 4.
2. Rom. xv. 20.
1. 1 Cor. x. 29.
2. 2 Cor. x. 16.

ANOTHER NATION (ONE OF.)

ἀλλόφυλος, of another tribe, foreign, strange.

Acts x. 28.

See, COMPASSION, ONE, OTHER, PREFERRING.

ANSWER [noun.]

(-s.)

1. **ἀπόκρισις**, a separating from, *(from* ἀπό, from, κρίσις, separation, judgment), *hence* a decision, an answer.
2. **ἀπόκριμα**, a judicial sentence, condemnation.
3. **ἀπολογία**, a defence, speech in defence.
4. **ἐπερώτημα**, a question, an asking; enquiry after, seeking by enquiry.

1. Luke ii. 47.
1. —— xx. 26.
1. John i. 22.
1. —— xix. 9.
3. 1 Cor. ix. 3.
2. 2 Cor. i. 9, margin (text, *sentence.*)
3. 2 Tim. iv. 16.
3. 1 Pet. iii. 15.
4. ——— 21.

ANSWER OF GOD.

χρηματισμός, a doing of business, *commercial or public, esp.*, a negotiation, a giving evidence to ambassadors; *also, of an oracle*, a response; *hence* a divine answer.

Rom. xi. 4.

ANSWER [verb.]

(-ING, -ED.)

1. **ἀποκρίνομαι**, *(in N.T. in Mid. only,)* to give a judicial answer, *and hence gen.*, to answer, respond, to reply to *a question; esp.*, to answer charges.
2. **ἀπολογέομαι**, to talk one's self out of *a difficulty;* to speak one's self off, *i.e.*, to plead for one's self, to defend one's self *before a tribunal, or elsewhere.*
3. **εἶπον**, to utter with the mouth, to say, speak, *(relating to* the words, *rather than* the sentiment, *which is* λέγω.)
4. **ὑπολαμβάνω**, to take under *any person or thing, i.e.*, to take up *by placing oneself* underneath, to take up *the discourse, continue it, i.e.*, to reply.

1. Matt. iii. 15.
1. —— iv. 4.
1. —— viii. 8.
1. —— xi. 4, 25.
1. —— xii. 38, 39, 48.
1. —— xiii. 11, 37.
1. —— xiv. 28.
1. —— xv. 3, 13, 15, 23, 24, 26, 28.
1. —— xvi. 2, 16, 17.
1. —— xvii. 4, 11, 17.
1. —— xix. 4, 27.
1. —— xx. 13, 22. [30.
1. —— xxi. 21, 24, 27, 29,
1. Matt. xxii. 1, 29, 46.
1. —— xxiv. 4.
1. —— xxv. 9, 12, 26, 37, 40, 44, 45.
1. —— xxvi. 23, 25, 33, 62.
1. ——— 63 (*om.* Tr ℵ.)
1. ——— 66.
1. —— xxvii. 12, 14, 21, 25.
1. —— xxviii. 5.
1. Mark iii. 33.
1. —— v. 9 (G∼), (*om.* All.)
1. —— vi. 37.
1. —— vii. 6 (*om.* T Tr A [ℵ.)
1. ——— 28.
1. Mark viii. 4.
1. ——— 28 (No. 3, T A ℵ.)
1. ——— 29.
1. —— ix. 5, 12, 17, 19.
1. ——— 38 (φημί, *said*, T Tr A ℵ.)
1. —— x. 3, 5 (*om.* Tr A ℵ.)
1. ——— 20, 24.
1. ——— 29 (*om.* T A ℵ.)
1. ——— 51.
1. —— xi. 14, 22.
1. ——— 29 1st (*om.* T Tr A
1. ——— 29 2nd. [ℵ.)
1. ——— 30, 33 1st.
1. ——— 33 2nd (Trmb Lb), (*om.* T Tr ℵ.)
1. —— xii. 17.
1. ——— 24 (*om.* T Tr A ℵ.)
1. ——— 28, 29, 34, 35.
1. —— xiii. 2 (*om.* T Tr A [ℵ.)
1. ——— 5 (*om.* T Tr A ℵ.)
1. —— xiv. 20 (*om.* G→ L T Tr A ℵ.)
1. ——— 40, 48, 60, 61.
1. —— xv. 2, 4, 5, 9, 12.
1. Luke i. 19, 35, 60.
1. —— iii. 11, 16.
1. —— iv. 4, 8, 12.
1. —— v. 5.
1. ——— 22 (*om.* L Trb.)
1. ——— 31.
1. —— vi. 3.
1. —— vii. 22, 40, 43.
1. —— viii. 21, 50.
1. —— ix. 19, 20, 41, 49.
1. —— x. 27, 28.
4. ——— 30.
1. ——— 41.
1. —— xi. 7, 45.
2. —— xii. 11.
1. —— xiii. 2, 8, 14, 15, 25.
1. —— xiv. 3.
1. ——— 5 (*om.* G⇉ L Tr.)
— ——— 6, see A again.
1. —— xv. 29.
1. —— xvii. 17, 20, 37.
1. —— xix. 40.
1. —— xx. 3 1st.
3. ——— 3 2nd.
1. ——— 7, 24. [ℵ.)
1. ——— 34 (*om.* L T Tr A
1. Luke xx. 39.
2. —— xxi. 14.
1. —— xxii. 51, 68.
1. —— xxiii. 3, 9, 40.
1. —— xxiv. 18.
1. John i. 21, 26, 48, 49, 50.
1. —— ii. 18, 19.
1. —— iii. 3, 5, 9, 10, 27.
1. —— iv. 10, 13, 17.
1. —— v. 7, 11, 17, 19.
1. —— vi. 7, 26, 29, 43, 68, 70. [47, 52.
1. —— vii. 16, 20, 21, 46,
1. —— viii. 14, 19, 33, 34, 39, 48, 49, 54.
1. —— ix. 3, 11, 20, 25, 27, 30, 34, 36.
1. —— x. 25, 32, 33, 34.
1. —— xi. 9.
1. —— xii. 23, 30, 34.
1. —— xiii. 7, 8, 26, 36, 38.
1. —— xiv. 23.
1. —— xvi. 31.
1. —— xviii. 5, 8, 20, 22, 23, 30, 34, 35, 36, 37.
1. —— xix. 7, 11, 15, 22.
1. —— xx. 28.
1. —— xxi. 5.
1. Acts iii. 12.
1. —— iv. 19.
1. —— v. 8, 29.
1. —— viii. 24, 34.
1. ——— 37 (*ap.*)
1. —— ix. 13.
1. —— x. 46.
1. —— xi. 9.
1. —— xv. 13.
1. —— xix. 15.
1. —— xxi. 13.
1. —— xxii. 8, 28.
1. —— xxiv. 10 1st.
2. ——— 10 2nd.
1. ——— 25.
1. —— xxv. 4.
— ——— 8, see A for...self.
1. ——— 9, 12 1st.
— ——— 16 2nd } see A for
— —— xxvi. 1, 2 } ..self.
— Gal. iv. 25, see A to.
1. Col. iv. 6.
— Titus ii. 9, see A again.
Rev. vii. 13.

ANSWER AGAIN.

1. **ἀνταποκρίνομαι**, to do *No.* 1, *(above)* again; to answer again, *or* to reply against, contradict.
2. **ἀντιλέγω**, to speak against.

1. Luke xiv. 6.
1. Rom. ix. 20, margin (text, *repliest against.*)
2. Titus ii. 9, margin *gainsay.*

ANSWER FOR...SELF.

1. **ἀπολογέομαι**, *see* "ANSWER," *No.* 2.
2. **ἀπολογια**, a defence, speech in defence *(Eng. apology.)*

1. Acts xxv. 8.
2. Acts xxv. 16.
1. Acts xxvi. 1, 2.

ANSWER TO (-ETH.)

συστοιχέω, to stand in the same row *or* line with, correspond to.

Gal. iv. 25, margin *be in the same rank with.*

ANTICHRIST (-s.)

ἀντίχριστος, opponent of Christ; *that which sets itself in the place of Christ, which appears as Christ in opposition to Christ, (as distinct from ψευδόχριστος, which means rather a false hypocritical representative of Christ than an opponent of Him.) The many Antichrists must be regarded not only as forerunners of the actual Antichrist, but as attempts to realize it.*

1 John ii. 18 twice, 22. 2 John 7. 1 John iv. 3.

ANY.

1. τις, any one, some one.
2. πᾶς, all; *of one only,* all of him; *of one in a number,* any; *of several,* every; *in pl.,* all.
3. οὐδείς, not one, no one, none, nothing, *(with another negative which in Greek makes the negation stronger.)*
4. μή, not.
5. μηδείς, not one, no one.
6. μήτις, *interrog. pron.,* has *or* is any one?
7. εἷς, *card. num.,* one.

— Matt. xi. 27, } see A man
— —— xii. 19, }
— —— xiii. 19, see A one.
2. —— xviii. 19.
— —— xxi. 3, } see A man
— —— xxii. 16, 46 1st }
— ——— 46 2nd, see A more
— —— xxiv. 17, see A thing
— ——— 23, } see A man.
— Mark i. 44, }
— —— v. 4, see A man (neither.)
— ——— 35, see A further
1. —— viii. 26.
— —— ix. 8, see A more.
— ——— 30, } see A man.
— —— xi. 3, }
— ——— 13, see A thing.
— ——— 16, see A man.
1. ——— 25.
— —— xiii. 5, see A man.
— ——— 15, see A thing.
— ——— 21, see A man.
— —— xiv. 63, see A more.
— —— xvi. 8 1st, see A thing
— ——— 8 2nd, see A man.
1. ——— 18 (*ap.*)
3. Luke viii. 43.
3. —— ix. 36.
— —— xiv. 8, see A man.
— —— xix. 8 1st, see A thing. [man.
— ——— 8 2nd, 31, see A
4. —— xx. 27.
— ——— 28, see A man.
— ——— 36, see A more.
— ——— 40, see A question at all.

— Luke xxii. 16, see A more
— ——— 35, see A thing.
— ——— 71, see A further.
1. —— xxiv. 41.
— John i. 3, see A thing.
1. ——— 46.
1. —— ii. 25.
— —— iv. 33, } see A man.
— —— vi. 46, 51, }
— —— vii. 4, see A thing.
— ——— 17, 37, see A man.
4 & 1. —— 48.
— —— viii. 33, see A man (never.)
— —— ix. 22, 31, 32, see A man.
— —— x. 9, 28, } see A man
— —— xi. 9, 57, }
— —— xii. 26 twice, 47 }
— —— xiv. 14, see A thing
— —— xvi. 30, } see A man.
— —— xviii. 31, }
6. —— xxi. 5.
3. Acts iv. 12 (*ap.*)
7. ——— 32.
1. ——— 34.
1. —— ix. 2.
— —— x. 14, see A thing.
— ——— 28, see A (not.)
— ——— 47, see A man.
— —— xvii. 25, see A thing.
— —— xix. 38, see A man.
— ——— 39, see A thing.
— —— xxiv. 12, see A man
— —— xxv. 8, see A thing at all.
— ——— 11, see A thing.
1. ——— 16.

— Acts xxv. 17, see A (without.)
— ——— 24, see A longer.
— —— xxvii. 22, see A more (no..)
— ——— 34, see A (not.)
1. ——— 42.
1. —— xxviii. 21 twice.
— Rom. vi. 2, see A longer.
— —— viii. 9, see A man.
1. ——— 39.
1. —— ix. 11.
— —— xiii. 8, see A thing.
— —— xiv. 13, see A more (not.)
— ——— 14, see A thing.
1. —— xv. 18.
2. 1 Cor. i. 15.
— —— ii. 2, } see A thing
— —— iii. 7, }
— —— v. 11, see A man.
1. —— vi. 1.
1. ——— 12.
— —— vii. 18 1st, see A man.
1. ——— 18 2nd.
— —— viii. 2, see A thing.
— ——— 10, } see A man
— —— ix. 15, }
— —— x. 19 twice, see A thing.
— ——— 28, see A man.
— —— xiv. 27, see A man.
— ——— 35, see A thing.
2. 2 Cor. i. 4.
— —— ii. 10, } see A thing.
— —— iii. 5, }
1. —— xi. 21.
— —— xii. 6, see A man.
1. ——— 17.
— Gal. v. 6, } see A thing.
— —— vi. 15, }
— Eph. ii. 9, see A man.
1. —— v. 27.

— Eph. vi. 8, } see A man
— Col. ii. 4, 8, }
1. ——— 23.
— —— iii. 13 1st, see A man
1. ——— 13 2nd.
— 1 Thes. i. 8, see A thing.
1. —— ii. 9.
1. —— iv. 6 (G ∾) (No. 8, G L T Tr A) margin *the.*
1. —— v. 15.
5. 2 Thes. ii. 3.
1. —— iii. 8.
1. Heb. iii. 12, 13.
1. —— iv. 1.
— ——— 11, see A man.
2. ——— 12.
— —— xii. 15 1st, see A man.
1. ——— 15 2nd, 16.
— ——— 19, see A more (speak to.)
— Jas. i. 7, see A thing.
— ——— 13, see A man (neither.)
1. —— v. 12, 13 twice, 14, 19
5. 1 Pet. iii. 6.
1. 2 Pet. iii. 9.
— 1 John ii. 1, 15, 27, see A man.
— —— v. 14, see A thing.
— ——— 16, } see A man.
— Rev. iii. 20, }
2. —— vii. 1 (No. 1, G ∾ L T Tr Ab.)
— ——— 16 1st, see A more.
2. ——— 16 2nd.
2. —— ix. 4 twice.
— —— xii. 8, } see A more.
— —— xviii. 11, }
— ——— 22, see A more (no.)
— —— xxi. 4, see A more.
— ——— 27, see A thing.
— —— xxii. 18, 19, see A man.

ANY (NOT.)

1. οὐδείς, *see* "ANY," *No.* 3.
2. μηδείς, not one, no one.
   (a) *with another negative.*

2a. Acts x. 28. | 1. Acts xxvii. 34.

ANY AT ALL (NOT.)

οὐδείς, *see* "ANY," No. 3.

Luke xx. 40.

ANY (WITHOUT.)

μηδείς, not one, no one, no person *or* thing, nothing.

Acts xxv. 17.

ANY FURTHER.

ἔτι, any more, any longer, yet, still, even.

Mark v. 35. | Mark xiv. 63. Luke xxii. 71.

ANY LONGER.

1. ἔτι, *see above.*
2. μηκέτι, no more, no longer, lest further.

2. Acts xxv. 24. | 1. Rom. vi. 2.

ANY MAN.

1. τις, any one, some one.
2. οὐδείς, not one, no one.
3. μηδείς, not one, no one.
4. μήτις. *interrog. pron.*, has *or* is any one?
5. ἕκαστος, each one, every one.

All the places, except where the equivalent is two separate words, (which see.)

1. Matt. xi. 27.
1. —— xii. 19.
1. —— xxi. 3.
2. —— xxii. 16,
1. —— —— 46.
1. —— xxiv. 23.
3. Mark i. 44.
— —— v. 4, see A M (neither.)
1. —— ix. 30.
1. —— xi. 3, 16.
1. —— xiii. 5, 21.
2. —— xvi. 8.
1. Luke xiv. 8.
1. —— xix. 8, 31.
1. —— xx. 28.
4. John iv. 33.
1. —— vi. 46, 51.
1. —— vii. 17, 37.
— —— viii. 33, see A M (never.)
1. —— ix. 22, 31, 32.
1. —— x. 9, 57.
1. —— xii. 26 twice, 47.
1. —— xvi. 30.
2. —— xviii. 31.
1. Acts x. 47.
1. —— xix. 38.
1. Acts xxiv. 12.
— —— xxvii. 22, see A M (no..)
1. Rom. viii. 9.
1. 1 Cor. v. 11.
1. —— vii. 18.
1. —— viii. 10.
1. —— ix. 15 (No. 2, for ἵνα τις, *that any man*, L Tr.)
1. —— x. 28.
1. —— xiv. 27.
1. 2 Cor. xii. 6.
1. Eph. ii. 9.
5. —— vi. 8.
1. Col. ii. 4 (No. 3, for μή τις, *lest any man*, L T Tr A ℵ.)
1. —— —— 8.
1. —— iii. 13.
1. 2 Thes. iii. 8.
1. Heb. iv. 11.
1. —— xii. 15.
— Jas. i. 13, see A M (neither.)
1. 1 John ii. 1, 15, 27.
1. —— v. 16.
1. Rev. iii. 20.
1. —— xxii. 18, 19.

ANY MAN (NEITHER.)

οὐδείς, not one, no one, *(without another negative.)*

Mark v. 4. | Jas. i. 13.

ANY MAN (NEVER.)

οὐδείς, not one, no one, *(without another negative.)*

John viii. 33.

ANY MAN (NO.)

οὐδείς, not one, no one, *(without another negative.)*

Acts xxvii. 22.

ANY MAN (NOTHING.)

μηδείς, not one, no one, *(with another negative.)*

Mark i. 44.

ANY MEANS (BY.)

οὐ μή, *double negative.*

Luke x. 19.

ANY MORE.

1. ἔτι, any more, any longer, yet, still, even.
2. οὐκέτι, no further, no more, no longer.
3. οὐ μή, *double negative.*

2. Matt. xxii. 46.
2. Mark ix. 8.
1. Luke xx. 36.
2. —— xxii. 16 (*om.* L[b] Tr[b] A ℵ.)
1. Rev. vii. 16.
1. —— xii. 8.
2. —— xviii. 11.
1. —— —— 22.
1. —— xxi. 4.

ANY MORE (NO....)

οὐ μή ἔτι, not...no more.

Rev. xviii. 22.

ANY MORE (NOT.)

1. οὐκέτι, no further, no more, no longer.
2. μηκέτι, no more, no longer, lest further.

1. Luke xxii. 16. | 2. Rom. xiv. 13.

ANY MORE (SPEAK TO.)

προστίθημι, to place near *or* by the side of, to add to.

Heb. xii. 19 (lit. should not *be added* to them.)

ANY ONE.

πᾶς, all, every one, *see* "ANY," *No.* 1.

Matt. xiii. 19.

ANY QUESTION AT ALL.

οὐδείς, not one, no one, nothing.

(a) *with another negative.*

a. Luke xx. 40.

ANY THING.

1. τις, any one, some one *person or thing.*

2. *πᾶς*, all, every, *see under* "ALL," *No.* 1.

3. *οὐδείς*, not one, no one, nothing.
  (a) *with another negative.*

4. *μηδείς*, not one, no one, nothing.
  (a) *with another negative.*

5. *εἷς*, one.

1. Matt. xxiv. 17 (*τά, the things*, G L T Tr A) (*τό, the thing*, ℵ.)
1. Mark xi. 13.
1. —— xiii. 15.
3a. —— xvi. 8.
1. Luke xix. 8.
1. —— xxii. 35.
5. John i. 3.
1. —— vii. 4.
1. —— xiv. 14.
2. Acts x. 14.
1. —— xvii. 25.
1. —— xix. 39.
2. —— xxi. 27.
1. —— xxv. 11.
4a. Rom. xiii. 8.
1. —— xiv. 14.
1. 1 Cor. ii. 2.
1. —— iii. 7.
1. —— viii. 2.
1. —— x. 19 1st (*ap.*)
1. ———— 19 2nd.
1. —— xiv. 35.
1. 2 Cor. ii. 10.
1. —— iii. 5.
4a. —— vi. 3.
1. Gal. v. 6.
1. —— vi. 15.
1. 1 Thes. i. 8.
1. Jas. i. 7.
1. 1 John v. 14.

ANY THING (NO....)

μηδείς, not one, no one, nothing.

2 Cor. vi. 3.

ANY THING AT ALL.

τις, any one, some thing, some one.

Acts xxv. 8.

ANY WISE (NOT IN.)

οὐ μή, *double negative.*

Mark xiv. 31.

See also, BY, FURTHER, IF, LEST, LONGER, MEANS, NEVER, NEITHER, NOT, TIME, WHETHER, WHILE.

APART.

{ *κατά*, according to, } *adverbially*, *κατ' ἰδίαν*, privately.
{ *ἴδιος*, one's own, }

Matt. xiv. 13, 23; xvii. 1, 19; xx. 17; Mark vi. 31; ix. 2.

APART (LAY.)

ἀποτίθημι, to put away, lay aside.

Jas. i. 21.

APIECE.

ἀνά, up to *or* up by, *with numerals or measures of quantity or value*, apiece.

Luke ix. 3. | John ii. 6.

APOSTLE (-S.)

ἀπόστολος, *primarily an adj.*, sent forth. *Then a subst.*, one sent, messenger, ambassador, envoy, *Apostle*, *(from ἀποστέλλω*, to send off *or* send away from.) (occ. John xiii. 16; 2 Cor. viii. 23; Phil. ii. 25.)

Matt. x. 2.
Mark vi. 30.
Luke vi. 13.
—— ix. 10.
—— xi. 49.
—— xvii. 5.
—— xxii. 14.
—— xxiv. 10.
Acts i. 2, 26.
—— ii. 37, 42, 43.
—— iv. 33, 35, 36, 37.
—— v. 2, 12, 18, 29.
———— 34 (*ἄνθρωπος, a man*, G∾ L T Tr A ℵ.)
———— 40.
—— vi. 6.
—— viii. i. 14, 18.
—— ix. 27.
—— xi. 1.
—— xiv. 4, 14.
—— xv. 2, 4, 6, 22, 23.
———— 33 (G∾) (*ἀποστείλαντας αὐτούς, those who sent them*, G L T Tr A ℵ*.)
—— xvi. 4.
Rom. i. 1.
—— xi. 13.
—— xvi. 7.
1 Cor. i. 1.
—— iv. 9.
—— ix. 1, 2, 5.
—— xii. 28, 29.
—— xv. 7, 9 twice.
2 Cor. i. 1.
—— xi. 5.
———— 13 1st, see A(false.)
———— 13 2nd.
—— xii. 11, 12.
Gal. i. 1, 17, 19.
Eph. i. 1.
—— ii. 20.
—— iii. 5.
—— iv. 11.
Col. i. 1.
1 Thes. ii. 6.
1 Tim. i. 1.
—— ii. 7.
2 Tim. i. 1, 11.
Titus i. 1.
Heb. iii. 1.
1 Pet. i. 1.
2 Pet. i. 1.
—— iii. 2.
Jude 17.
Rev. ii. 2.
—— xviii. 20.
—— xxi. 14.

* ℵ originally had *ἑαυτούς*, but the *ε* has been erased.

APOSTLES (FALSE.)

ψευδαπόστολοι, *the above (in pl.) with ψεῦδος*, false, *affixed*, *(non. occ.)*

2 Cor. xi. 13.

APOSTLESHIP.

ἀποστολή, a sending off *or* away, a mission; *then*, the office of an apostle, *(non. occ.)*

Acts i. 25.
Rom. i. 5.
1 Cor. ix. 2.
Gal. ii. 8.

APPAREL.

1. *ἐσθής*, a robe, garment, apparel, *generally applied to what is ornate and splendid.*

2. *ἱμάτιον*, a garment, raiment *generally; also an* outer garment *(a blanket, a cloak, loose garment as opposed to χιτών*, the inner vest, Matt. v. 40.)

3. *ἱματισμός*, clothing, apparel.

4. *καταστολή*, equipment, dress, *properly* a long garment *or* robe reaching

down to the feet, *(from* καταστέλλω, to send *or* let down.)

1. Acts i. 10.
1. —— xii. 21.
3. —— xx. 33.
4. 1 Tim. ii. 9.
1. Jas. ii. 2.
2. 1 Pet. iii. 3.

APPARELLED.

{ ἐν, in.
{ ἱματισμός, clothing, apparel.

Luke vii. 25.

APPEAL.

ἐπικαλέομαι, to call to, to call on, *(not towards or hither)*, to call on *any one (by turning towards and crying to him.) Mid.* to appeal *to any one.*

Acts xxv. 21.

APPEAL TO.

Acts xxv. 25.

APPEAL UNTO.

Acts xxv. 11, 12. | Acts xxvi. 32.
Acts xxviii. 19.

APPEAR (-ED, -ETH.)

1. φαίνω, *trans.*, to make light, let shine, throw light upon. *In N.T. only intrans.*, to appear, *expressive of how a matter phenominally shows and presents itself, with no necessary assumption of any beholder at all. This "phenomenon" may represent a reality, or a mere show.*
2. ὄπτομαι, to see, *(from* ὄψ *or* ὤψ, the eye), to look, to see *an object appearing; pass.* to be seen. *It refers to the thing seen, whether in itself (objectively) or in regard to its impression on the mind (subjectively) different from* βλέπω *which denotes* the act of seeing *and is referred to the organ.)*
3. φανερόω, to make manifest, make apparent, show forth.
4. ἐπιφαίνω, to shine forth, display; appear upon; to come into light.
5. ἐμφανίζω, to show plainly *or* clearly; *passive,* to be manifested, appear plainly.
6. ἀναφαίνομαι, to make to give light, blaze up; *pass. (as here),* to come to light *or* into sight, to be shown forth.
7. ἔρχομαι, to come *or* go, *see* "COME."
8. { εἰμί, to be, φανερός, visible, manifest, open to sight, } be visible, open to sight, etc.

1. Matt. i. 20.
1. —— ii. 7, 13, 19.
1. —— vi. 16, 18.
1. —— xiii. 26.
2. —— xvii. 3.
1. —— xxiii. 27, 28.
1. —— xxiv. 30.
5. —— xxvii. 53.
2. Mark ix. 4.
1. —— xvi. 9 (*ap.*)
3. —— 12 (*ap.*), 14(*ap.*)
2. Luke i. 11.
1. —— ix. 8.
2. —— 31.
— —— xi. 44, see A not.
6. —— xix. 11.
2. —— xxii. 43 (*ap.*)
2. —— xxiv. 34.
2. Acts ii. 3.
2. —— vii. 2, 30, 35.
2. —— ix. 17.
2. —— xvi. 9.
7. —— xxii. 30 (συνέρχομαι, *come together,* G L T Tr A.)
2 Acts xxvi. 16 twice.
4. —— xxvii. 20.
1. Rom. vii. 13.
3. 2 Cor. v. 10.
3. —— vii. 12.
1. —— xiii. 7.
3. Col iii. 4 twice.
8. 1 Tim. iv. 15.
4. Titus ii. 11.
4. —— iii. 4.
5. Heb. ix. 24.
3. —— 26.
2. —— 28.
— —— xi. 3, see A (things which do.)
1. Jas. iv. 14.
1. 1 Pet. iv. 18.
3. —— v. 4.
3. 1 John ii. 28.
3. —— iii. 2 twice.
3. Rev. iii. 18.
2. —— xii. 1, 3.

APPEAR NOT.

ἄδηλος, not seen *or* known; not apparent, concealed.

Luke xi. 44.

APPEAR (THINGS WHICH DO.)

{ τά, the.
{ φαινόμενα, things seen *(from No.* 1.)

Heb. xi. 3.

APPEARANCE.

1. εἶδος, that which is seen, form, shape, figure; appearance *that may or may not have any basis in reality.*
2. πρόσωπον, a face, visage, countenance, *later,* the front *of anything;* one's look, countenance; a person, *(from* πρός, to, *and* ὤψ, the eye, *properly therefore* that part of anything which is presented or turned to the eye.)
3. ὄψις, *objective,* a sight, *i.e.,* an appearance, figure, form; outward appearance; *subjective,* the power of sight, *or* seeing, eyesight; a viewing, view, sight.

3. John vii. 24.
2. 2 Cor. v. 12 margin Greek, *the face.*
— 2 Cor. x. 7, see A (outward.)
1. 1 Thes. v. 22.

APPEARANCE (OUTWARD.)

2. 2 Cor. x. 1, margin (text, *presence*), 7.

APPEARING.

1. *ἐπιφάνεια*, the appearance, manifestation; *lit.*, the shining upon.
2. *ἀποκάλυψις*, an uncovering, an unveiling; disclosure, revelation. *When used of a person it always denotes the appearance of the person. See* Rom. viii. 19; 1 Cor. i. 7; 2 Thes. i. 7; 1 Pet. i. 7, 13; iv. 13.

1. 1 Tim. vi. 14.
1. 2 Tim. i. 10.
1. 2 Tim. iv. 1, 8.
1. Titus ii. 13.
2. 1 Pet. i. 7.

APPEASE (-ED.)

καταστέλλω, *properly* to put *or* let down, *hence* to quell, appease, pacify, quiet.

Acts xix. 35.

APPOINT (-ED.)

1. *τίθημι*, to put, set, place; *then generally* to bring *a thing* into a place; *and so*, to bring into a situation, to bring about, cause, *metaph.* to put in a certain place or condition; *hence*, to appoint.
   (a) *middle*, to cause to put *or* put for one's self; to assign, determine.
2. *διατίθημι*, to place separately, arrange, put *things* in their places. *Middle διατίθεμαι, as here and in N.T. only*, to arrange as one likes, dispose of.
3. *τάσσω*, (a) to arrange, put in order, *especially in military sense, to* draw up *soldiers*, array; (b) *mid.* to appoint *or* order *any thing* to be done.
4. *διατάσσω*, to arrange throughout, to dispose in order; *then*, to set fully in order, arrange, (a) *in mid.* appoint, ordain.
5. *συντάσσω*, to arrange in order with others; *generally* to arrange, order, *as parts of a whole;* institute, appoint.
6. *ἵστημι*, (a) *trans.*, to place; (b) *intrans.*, to stand.
7. *καθίστημι*, (a) *trans.*, to set down, set, set in order *as soldiers; set as guards; then to ordain, appoint*, (b) *intrans.* to be set, set one's self down, settle.
8. *ἀναδείκνυμι*, to lift up and shew, shew forth; make public, declare, notify; to consecrate, dedicate.
9. *ἀπόκειμαι*, to be laid away; to be laid up in store, be in reserve. *Impers.* it is in store *for one.*
10. *ποιέω*, to make, produce, create.

1. Matt. xxiv. 51.
5. —— xxvi. 19.
5. —— xxvii. 10.
3b.—— xxviii. 16.
4. Luke iii. 13.
8. —— x. 1.
1. —— xii. 46.
2. —— xxii. 29 twice.
6a. Acts i. 23.
7b.—— vi. 3.
4a.—— vii. 44.
— —— xvii. 26, see A (before.)
6a.———— 31.
4. Acts xx. 13 (pass. with *εἰμί, to be.*)
3. —— xxii. 10.
3b.—— xxviii. 23. [death.
— 1 Cor. iv. 9, see A to
— Gal. iv. 2, see A (time.)
— 1 Thes. iii. 3, see A (be)
1b.——— v. 9.
1. 2 Tim. i. 11.
4. Titus i. 5.
1. Heb. i. 2.
10.—— iii. 2.
9. —— ix. 27.
1. 1 Pet. ii. 8.

APPOINTED (BE.)

κεῖμαι, to be laid *(used as a passive to τίθημι, No.*1*)*, to be set *or appointed.*

1 Thes. iii. 3.

APPOINTED (BEFORE.)

προτάσσω, *to place or post in front*, to arrange *one person* before *another (so as to defend him), pass.*, to take the lead, go first; *generally* to appoint *or* determine beforehand.

Acts xvii. 26 (G ~) (*προστάσσω, appointed*, G L[b] T Tr A ℵ.)

APPOINTED (TIME.)

προθεσμία, a before appointed *day or time;* a fixed *or* limited time *within which money was to be paid, actions brought, etc.*

Gal. iv. 2.

APPOINTED TO DEATH.

ἐπιθανάτιος, condemned *or* appointed to death.

1 Cor. iv. 9 (in A.V. 1611, error *approved to death.*)

APPREHEND. (-ED.)

1. *καταλαμβάνω*, to seize upon, lay hold of; to hold down, keep under; catch, overtake, come up with.
2. *πιάζω*, to press by laying one's hand upon, to lay hold *or* hands on; *to catch, apprehend in a violent or hostile manner.*

2. Acts xii. 4.
2. 2 Cor. xi. 32.
1. Phil. iii. 12 twice, 13

APPROACH.

(- ETH, - ING.)

ἐγγίζω, to bring near, bring up to; *intransitive*, to be near, come near, approach; *also* to draw nigh, be at hand.

Luke xii. 33. | Heb. x. 25.

APPROACH UNTO (WHICH NO MAN CAN.)

ἀπρόσιτος, unapproachable, unaccessible.

1 Tim. vi. 16.

APPROVE.

(- ED, - ETH, - ING.)

1. δοκιμάζω, to assay, examine, prove *or* test *metals, to see if they be pure; hence generally* to scrutinize, examine, *then as the consequence of such trial* to approve, sanction, hold good *after trial.*
2. συνίστημι, (a) *intrans.* to place *or* set together with, *hence* to bring forward *for the sake of commending;* (b) *trans.* to commend *to esteem and confidence.*
3. ἀποδείκνυμι, to lift up and show, shew forth; make public, declare wholly.

3. Acts ii. 22.
1. Rom. ii. 18 marg. *try.*
1. 1 Cor. xvi. 3.
2b. 2 Cor. vi. 4, margin, Greek *commend.*
2b. —— vii. 11.
1. Phil. i. 10 margin, *try.*

APPROVED.

δόκιμος, assayed, examined, tested; *hence generally of persons,* approved, esteemed.

Rom. xiv. 18.
—— xvi. 10.
1 Cor. xi. 19, see A (which is.)
2 Cor. x 18.
—— xiii. 7.
2 Tim. ii. 15.

APPROVED (WHICH IS.)

1 Cor. xi. 19.

APRON.

σιμικίνθιον, an apron *or* handkerchief.

Acts xix. 12.

APT TO TEACH.

διδακτικός, apt at teaching, willing, able and fit to teach; capable of teaching.

1 Tim. iii. 2. | 2 Tim. ii. 24.

ARCHANGEL.

ἀρχάγγελος, first *or* highest angel.

1 Thes. iv. 16. | Jude 9.

ARE (WE, YE, THEY, SEEING, INASMUCH, THAT, WHO.)

Sometimes this word is in italics, *and then there is no corresponding word in the Greek.*

Sometimes it is the translation of the article *with a* noun, adjective *or* numeral, *and is translated* "they that are," *etc.; or of the* article *with an* adverb *or* preposition, "they that are," *etc. Sometimes also, after nouns with defining words following, the* article *is repeated, and is then commonly translated* "who are," *etc.*

Sometimes it is only part of another verb.

When it is not any of these, then it is the translation of one of these following

1. εἰμί, I am, *the ordinary state of existence, (for the difference between this and No. 2, see* Heb. xi. 6, *etc.)*
   (a) ἐστί *or* ἐστίν, (3 *pers. sing. pres.)* he, she, *or* it is. *When used with plural noun marked with* (*) *as* 1a*.
   (b) ἐσμέν, we...are; are we. *When the personal pronoun* ἡμεῖς, we *is prefixed, marked with* (*) *as* 1b*.
   (c) ἐστέ, ye...are, are ye. *When the pers. pron.* ὑμεῖς, you *or* ye, *is prefixed, marked* *.
   (d) εἰσί *or* εἰσίν, they are; are they.
   (e) εἶναι, *inf.*, to be. * *with the Acc. preceding*—that...is, are, *etc.* † *with* εἰς τὸ, the ... being, to the end ... might be.
   (f) ὤν, οὖσα, ὄν, *participle*, being; *with art.*, he who is, they who are, *etc.*
2. γίνομαι, *implying origin*, to come into being, to become; *or result*, to take place, happen, *and in this sense* to be.
3. ὑπάρχω, to begin, to start; to begin to be, *(referring to original state or existence.)*
4. ἔχω, to have.
5. ἐκ, *prep.*, out of, of.

6. *μέλλω*, to be on the point to do *anything*, (*gen.* with the *inf. of another verb*); to be about to do, to intend *or* purpose doing.

1a. Matt. ii. 18.
1c. —— v. 11.
1c*. ———13, 14.
1d. —— vii. 15.
1c. —— viii. 26.
1a*. —— x. 2.
1d. ———30.
1d. —— xi. 8.
1d. —— xii. 5, 48.
1d. —— xiii. 38 twice, 39, [56.
1c*. —— xv. 16.
1a*. ——— 20.
1d. —— xvii. 26.
1d. —— xviii. 20.
1d. —— xix. 6, 12 twice.
1a*. ——— 26 (*om.* All)
1d. —— xxii. 14 1st (2nd not in Greek.)
1d. ——— 30 2nd.
1c*. —— xxiii. 8.
1c. ——— 28, 31.
1d. Mark iv. 15, 16.
1d. ———18 1st (*om* G⇉)
1d. —— iv. 20 1st.
1d. ———40.
1b. —— v. 9.
1d. —— vi. 3.
1a*. —— vii. 15.
1c*. ——— 18.
1d. —— x. 8.
1a*. ———27 (*ap.*)
1d. —— xii. 25 2nd.
1c. Luke vi. 22.
1d. —— vii. 25 2nd, 31, 32.
1d. —— viii. 12, 14 1st, 15, [21.
1b. —— ix. 12.
1c. ——— 55 (*ap.*)
1d. —— xi. 7.
1a*. ——— 21, 41.
1c. ——— 44 1st.
1d. —— xii. 38.
1d. —— xiii. 14.
1c. ——— 25, 27.
1d ——— 30 twice.
1a*. —— xiv. 17.
1d. —— xvi. 8.
1c*. ——— 15.
1b. —— xvii. 10 2nd.
1a*. —— xviii. 27 2nd.
1c. —— xx. 36 twice.
1c. —— xxii. 28.
1c. —— xxiv. 17 2nd (*ἐστάθεσαν, they stood still or came to a stand*, Tr A ℵ)
1c. ——— 38.
1c*. ——— 48 (*om.* T Trb [A.)
1a*. John iii. 21.
1a. —— iv. 35 1st.
1d. ———35 2nd.
1d. —— v. 39.
1a*. —— vi. 9.
1a*. ———63 twice.
1a*. —— vii. 7.
1d. ———49.
1d. —— viii. 10 (*ap.*)
1c*. ——— 23 1st.
1c. ——— 23 2nd, 31, 37, 44, 47.
1b. —— ix. 28.
1b*. ———40.
1d. —— x. 8.
1d. ———12 (No. 1a, L Tr A ℵ.)
1a*. ———16.
1a*. ———21.
1c. ———26.
1b. ———30.
1c. ———34.
1d. —— xi. 9.
1c. —— xiii. 10, 11, 17.
1c. ——— 35.
1d. John xiv. 2.
1c*. —— xv. 3, 14.
1c. ——— 19.
1a*. —— xvi. 15.
1a*. —— xvii. 7 (No. 1d, T Tr A ℵ.)
1d. ——— 9.
1a*. ——— 10 1st (2nd not in Greek.)
1d. ——— 11 1st (2nd not in Greek.)
1d. ——— 14, 16.
1b*. ——— 22 (*om.* T Tr [A ℵ.)
1a*. —— xx. 30.
1a*. —— xxi. 25.
1d. Acts ii. 7, 13.
1b*. ——— 32.
1b*. —— iii. 15.
1c*. ———25.
1d. —— v. 25.
1b*. ———32.
4. —— vii. 1.
1c*. ——— 26.
1b*. —— x. 39 (*om.* All.)
4. —— xii. 15.
1d. —— xiii. 31.
1b*. —— xiv. 15 1st (2nd not in Greek.)
1a*. —— xv. 18 (*ap.*)
1d. —— xvi. 17.
1b. ——— 28.
1b. —— xvii. 28.
3. ——— 29.
1c*. —— xix. 15.
1d. ——— 38 2nd.
1d. —— xxi. 20 1st.
3. ——— 20 2nd.
1a*. ——— 24.
1c*. —— xxii. 3.
1b*. —— xxiii. 15.
1d. ——— 21.
1d. —— xxiv. 11.
1c. Rom. i. 6.
1c†. ———20 3rd margin
1d. ——— 32. [*may be.*
5. —— ii. 8 (lit. "of contention.")
1d. ——— 14.
1e*. —— iii. 9 2nd.
1c. —— vi. 14.
1b. ——— 15.
1c. ——— 16.
1f. —— viii. 5 twice, that A.
1f. ——— 8, that A.
1c. ——— 9.
1b. ——— 12.
1d. ——— 14 2nd.
1b. ——— 16.
1f. ——— 28, who..are.
1d. —— ix. 4, 7.
1b. —— xii. 5.
1d. —— xiii. 1, 3, 6.
1b. —— xiv. 8.
1c. —— xv. 14.
1d. ——— 27.
1d. —— xvi. 7.
1f. ——— 11.
1d. 1 Cor. i. 11.
1f. ——— 28 2nd & 3rd, who are.
1c*. ——— 30.
1a*. —— ii. 14 1st.
1c. —— iii. 3 twice, 4.
1d. ——— 8.
1b. ——— 9 1st.
1c. ——— 9 2nd & 3rd, 16.
1c*. ——— 17.
1d. ——— 20.
1a*. ——— 21.
1a*. ——— 22 (*om.* G⇉ L T Tr A ℵ.)
1c. 1 Cor. v. 2, 7.
1c. —— vi. 2.
1a*. ——— 15.
1c. ——— 19.
1a*. ——— 20 2nd (*ap.*)
1a*. —— vii. 14.
1c*. —— ix. 1, 2.
1b —— x. 17 1st.
1d. ——— 18.
1b. ——— 22.
1d. —— xii. 4. 5, 6.
1a*. ——— 12, 22.
1c*. ——— 27.
1a*. —— xiv. 10 (No. 1d, L T Tr A ℵ.)
1c. ——— 12.
1d. ——— 22.
1d. ——— 37 (No. 1a, L T Tr A ℵ.)
1c. —— xv. 17.
1b. ——— 19.
1f. 2 Cor. i. 1.
1c. ——— 7.
1b. ——— 14, 24.
1b. —— ii. 15 1st, 17.
1c. —— iii. 2.
1c* ——— 3.
1b. ——— 5.
1f. —— v. 4, who are.
1c*. —— vi. 16 (*ἡμεῖς .. ἐσμέν, we are* instead of *ὑμεῖς..ἐστέ, ye are*, [L Tr ℵ.)
1c. —— vii. 3.
1b. —— x. 11 1st.
1f. —— xi. 19, seeing..are.
1d. ——— 22 3 times, 23.
1b*. —— xiii. 6.
1d. ——— 9 3rd.
1c. Gal. iii. 8 1st.
1d. ——— 7 2nd, 10 1st & [2nd.
1b. ——— 25.
1c. ——— 26.
1c*. ——— 28.
1c. ——— 29.
1c. —— iv. 6.
1f. ——— 8, who are.
1a*. ——— 24 1st.
1d. ——— 24 2nd.
1b*. ——— 28 (*ὑμεῖς... ἐστέ, ye are*, instead of *ἡμεῖς..ἐσμέν, we are*, L [T Tr A.)
1b. ——— 31.
1c. —— v. 18.
1a*. ———19 twice.
1f. Eph. i. 1.
1c. —— ii. 5, 8.
1b. ——— 10.
1c. ——— 19.
1b. —— iv. 25.
1d. —— v. 16.
1b. ——— 30.
1f. Phil. i. 1, who are.
1f. ——— 7, inasmuch as..are.
2. ——— 13.
1b*. —— iii. 3.
1a*. —— iv. 8.
1d. Col. ii. 3.
1c. ——— 10.
1a*. ———17, 22.
1f. 1 Thes. ii. 14, who A.
1c*. ——— 20.
1c. —— iv. 9.
1c. —— v. 4.
1c*. ——— 5 1st.
1b. ——— 5 2nd.
1f. ——— 8, who are.
1f. 1 Tim. ii. 2, who are.
1d. 1 Tim. v. 24.
1a*. ———25 1st (*om.* L T Tr A ℵ.)
4 ———25 2nd.
1d. —— vi. 1.
1d. ——— 2 twice.
1f. 2 Tim. ii 19, who are.
1a*. ——— 20.
1d. —— iii. 6.
1d. Titus i. 10.
1a*. —— iii. 8.
1d. ———9.
1d. Heb. i. 10, 14.
1b*. —— iii. 6.
2. —— v. 11.
1f. —— viii. 4, seeing that there are.
1b. —— x. 10.
1b*. ——— 39.
1. —— xii. 8 1st.
1c. ——— 8 2nd.
2. Jas. v. 2 2nd.
2. 1 Pet. iii. 6 1st.
1f. 2 Pet. ii. 11, who are.
1d. ——— 17 1st.
3. ——— 19.
1d. —— iii. 7 2nd.
1a*. ——— 16 1st.
1b. 1 John ii. 5.
1c. ——— 14.
2. ——— 18.
1b. —— iii. 2.
1a*. ——— 10.
1b. ——— 19.
1a*. —— iv. 1 1st.
1d. ——— 4.
1d. ——— 5.
1b*. ———6, 17.
1d. —— v. 3.
1d. ——— 7 1st.
1d. ——— 7 2nd.
1d. ——— 8 (*ap.*)
1b. ——— 19, 20.
1d. Jude 12, 16.
— Rev. i. 4 1st, not in Greek.
1a*. ——— 4 2nd (*om.* G⇉ L T Tr A ℵ.)
— ——— 11 (*om. ταῖς ἐν Ἀσίᾳ, which are in Asia*, All.)
1d. ——— 19, 20 twice.
1d. —— ii. 2 2nd.
1e. ———2 3rd.
1e. ———9 1st.
1d. ———9 2nd.
1d. —— iii. 4.
1e. ———9 1st.
1d. ———9 2nd.
1d. —— iv. 5 (*ἃ ἐστίν, which is*, instead of *αἵ εἰσιν, which are*, T) (*om.* ℵc.)
1d. ———11 (*ἦσαν, they were*, All.)
1d. —— v. 6, 8.
1a*. ———13 1st.
1d. —— vii. 13, 14, 15.
6. —— viii. 13, are yet.
1d. —— xi. 4.
1d. —— xiv. 4 1st & 2nd.
1d. ——— 4 3rd (*om. are they*, G→L T Trb A ℵ.)
1d. ——— 5.
1d. —— xvi. 6, 14.
1d. —— xvii. 9, 10 1st, 12, [15.
1d. —— xix. 9 2nd.
1d. —— xxi. 5.
1a*. ——— 12.
1a ——— 16, 22.

ARISE (-ETH, AROSE.)

1. *ἀνίστημι*, *trans.*, to make to stand up, raise up, set up; *intrans.*, to stand up, rise.

2. ἐγείρω, to awaken, to wake up; *pass.* awakened, to wake, *used primarily of sleepers*, to wake them up; *pass.*, to wake up. *Then of the sick and needy*, to help them; *pass.*, recover, rise from bed. *Especially however of the dead*, to rise to life; *pass.*, to rise again.

3. διεγείρω, to wake quite up, *pass.*, *as here*, woke up.

4. γίνομαι, *implying origin*, to come into being, to become; *or result*, to take place, happen, *and in this sense*, to be.

5. ἀναβαίνω, to go up, ascend, *in whatever manner;* rise up.

6. εἰσέρχομαι, to go in, *or* into, enter.

7. ἀνατέλλω, to make rise up; *intrans.*, to rise up, come to light, rise, *esp. of heavenly bodies.*

8. βάλλω, to throw at *or* hit, *(strictly opposed to* striking, τύπτειν) to throw, to cast, to put.

2. Matt. ii. 13, 14, 20, 21.
2. —— viii. 15.
4. ——— 24.
2. ——— 26. [Tr A ℵ.)
2. —— ix. 5 (act. G∾ L T
2. ——— 6 (act. L Tr.)
2. ——— 7.
1. ——— 9.
2. ——— 19, 25.
4. —— xiii. 21.
2. —— xvii. 7.
2. —— xxiv. 24.
2. —— xxv. 7.
1. —— xxvi. 62.
2. —— xxvii. 52. [ℵ.)
2. Mark ii. 9 (act. G L T A
2. ———11 (act. G L T
2. ———12. [Tr A ℵ.)
1. ———14.
4. —— iv. 17, 37.
3. ———39. [A ℵ.)
2. —— v. 41 (act. G L T Tr
1. ———42.
1. —— vii. 24.
1. —— ix. 27.
1. —— x. 1.
1. —— xiv. 57.
1. Luke i. 39.
1. —— iv. 38, 39. [ℵ.)
2. —— v. 24 (act. G L T A
1. —— vi. 8.
4. ———48.
2. —— vii. 14. [A ℵ.)
2. —— viii. 24 (No. 3, T Tr
2. ———54 (act. L.)
1. ———55.
6. Luke ix. 46.
4. —— xv. 14.
1. ——— 18, 20.
1. —— xvii. 19.
1. —— xxiii. 1.
1. —— xxiv. 12 (*ap.*)
5. ———38.
4. John iii. 25.
3. —— vi. 18.
2. —— vii. 52.
2. —— xi. 29.
2. —— xiv. 31.
1. Acts v. 6.
4. —— vi. 1.
1. ——— 9.
1. —— vii. 18.
1. —— viii. 26, 27.
1. —— ix. 6.
2. ——— 8. [39, 40.
1. ——— 11, 18, 34 twice,
1. —— x. 20,
1. —— xi. 7.
4. ——— 19.
— —— xii. 7, see A up.
4. —— xix. 23.
1. —— xx. 30.
1. —— xxii. 10, 16.
4. —— xxiii. 7, 9 1st.
1. ——— 9 2nd.
4. ——— 10.
8. —— xxvii. 14, margin *beat.*
1. Eph. v. 14.
1. Heb. vii. 15.
7. 2 Pet. i. 19.
5. Rev. ix. 2.

ARISE UP.

1. Acts xii. 7.

ARK.

κιβωτός, a wooden box, chest; a hollow vessel.

Matt. xxiv. 38.
Luke xvii. 27.
Heb. ix. 4.
Heb. xi. 7.
1 Pet. iii. 20.
Rev. xi. 19.

ARM [noun.]

βραχίων, *prop.*, the *shorter* part of the arm from the shoulder to the elbow. The arm *in general, and because the arm of man is his principal organ of strength, hence,* the strength *or* power *of God.*

Luke i. 51.
John xii. 38.
Acts xiii. 17.

ARMS.

1. ἄγκαλαι, the bent arms; the arms *considered as* bent, *or* crooked *to receive anything, (from Heb.* עקל, to be crooked.)

2. ὅπλον, a tool, implement, *in pl.*, implements of war, arms.

1. Luke ii. 28.
2. Rom. vi. 13, margin (text, *instruments.*)

ARMS (TAKE IN)* and (TAKE UP IN.)†

ἐναγκαλίζομαι, to take in *or* embrace in the arms.

* Mark ix. 36.
† Mark x. 16.

ARM [verb.]

καθοπλίζομαι, to be equipped; armed well *or* all over.

Luke xi. 21.

ARM...SELF.

ὁπλίζομαι, to make or get ready; *pass.*, to be made ready; *hence,* to arm, *and in* middle *as here*, to arm one's self.

1 Pet. iv. 1.

ARMOUR.

ὅπλα, *in sing.*, a tool, implement; *hence, in pl., as here*, implements of war, *all that goes to fit out a soldier*, arms, *esp. offensive arms, but also* armour; *then* the large shields *and* heavy arms.

Rom. xiii. 12 (ἔργα, *works*, Lm.)
2. Cor. vi. 7.

ARMOUR (ALL...)

πανοπλία, *(the above with* πᾶς, all, *prefixed)* complete armour, a complete suit of armour; *properly such as was used by* the heavy-armed infantry.

Luke xi. 22.

ARMOUR (WHOLE.)

πανοπλία, *see above.*

Eph. vi. 11, 13.

ARMY.

1. στράτευμα, an armament, army, host.
2. στρατόπεδον, *strictly,* the ground on which soldiers are encamped; *hence,* a camp, encampment, encamped army.
3. παρεμβολή, insertion besides, between *or* among *others; then* a putting in *or* distributing *men through an army; also a* body so drawn up; *hence* any fortified camp.

1. Matt. xxii. 7.	3. Heb. xi. 34.
2. Luke xxi. 20 (non. occ.)	1. Rev. ix. 16.
1. Acts xxiii. 27.	1. —— xix. 14.

1. Rev. xix. 19.

ARRAY [noun.]

ἱματισμός, clothing, apparel; outer raiment.

1 Tim. ii. 9.

ARRAY IN [verb.]

περιβάλλω, to throw round about *or* over; put on; to clothe.

Luke xxiii. 11.

ARRAYED (BE.)

1. ἐνδύω, to go in *or* under, *also* to put on; clothe; invest, *used of bodily raiment, Christian virtues, gifts of the Spirit, etc.*
2. περιβάλλω, *see* "ARRAY IN."

2. Matt. vi. 29.	— Rev. vii. 13, see A in (be.)
2. Luke xii. 27.	—— xix. 8, see A in [(be.)
1. Acts xii. 21.	

ARRIVE.

1. παραβάλλω, to throw beside *or* by, to throw to; *hence* to bring to the side of *or* to *or* near, *especially as a naval term;* to bring to, put to land.
2. καταπλέω, to sail down; *i.e.,* to sail from the high sea to the shore, sail to land, put in.

2. Luke viii. 26. | 1. Acts xx. 15.

ART [noun.]

τέχνη, an art, handicraft, trade, *especially a metal-worker's art;* art, skill.

Acts xvii. 29.

ART (THOU) AND ART THOU.

When in italics, there is no Greek equivalent.

When not part of another verb it is the translation of εἶ, *the second person singular of* εἰμί, to be. *Where the personal pronoun* σύ, thou, *precedes, an asterisk is affixed.*

Matt. ii. 6*; v. 25; xi. 3*; xiv. 33; xvi. 16*, 17, 18, 23; xxii. 16; xxv. 24; xxvi. 73*; xxvii. 11*; Mark i. 11*, 24; iii. 11*; viii. 29*; xii. 14, 34; xiv. 61*, 70 twice; xv. 2*; Luke iii. 22*; iv. 34, 41*; vii. 19*, 20*; xv. 31; xix. 21; xxii. 58*, 67*, 70*; xxiii. 3*, 40; John i. 19*, 21 twice*, 22, 42*, 49 twice*; iii. 10*; iv. 12*, 19*; vi. 69*; vii. 52*; viii. 25*, 48*, 53*; ix. 28*; xi. 27*; xviii. 17*, 25*, 33*, 37*; xix. 9*, 12; xxi. 12*; Acts ix. 5; xiii. 33*; xxi. 38*; xxii. 8, 27*; xxvi. 15; Rom. ii. 1 1st; ix. 20*; xiv. 4*; Gal. iv. 7; Heb. i. 5*, 12*; v. 5*; Jas. iv. 11, 12*; Rev. ii. 9; iii. 1, 15, 16, 17; iv. 11; v. 9; xi. 17 2nd (see "COME"); xvi. 5 1st.

ART (THAT THOU.)

εἶναι, to be, *with Acc. of pronoun, as here, means,* that...thou art.

Acts viii. 23 2nd (part.)* | Rom. ii. 19*.

ART (WHICH.)

ὁ ὤν, the *one* who *(essentially)* is.

Rev. xi. 17 1st. | Rev. xvi. 5 2nd.

ART......OLD.

ἔχω, to have.

John viii. 57 (lit. "hast not yet fifty years.")

ARTS (USED CURIOUS.)

περίεργον, working all round, overdoing, doing with care and pains what is not worth the pains; *then,* busy about other folks' affairs, meddling, curious, a busy-body; *in neuter plural as here,* magic, curious arts *or* works; *so called because of being* over curious *by searching into things above and below.*

Acts xix. 19.

AS.

1. ὡς, as. *In comparative sentences,* as; *in objective,* that; *in final,* in order to; in *causal,* for the ground that.
2. καθώς, like as, according as, even as.
3. ὥσπερ, *(No. 1 strengthened by* περ); *adv.,* wholly as, just as.
4. ὅσος, *rel. pron. of quantity,* how much, how great; *of time,* how long; *of quantity,* how many.
5. καθάπερ, *adv.,* even as, truly as.
6. κατά, *prep.,* down.
   (a) *with Gen. (whence)* down from, against.
   (b) *with Acc. (whither)* down towards, according to, *etc.*
7. ἐν, in, *of time, place, or element, with the infinitive following, as here,* "in *his teaching,*" "in *his sowing,*" *etc.*
8. ὡσεί, *adv.,* as if, as though, as, about.
9. οἷος, *rel. pron. of quality,* of what kind *or* sort.
10. { ὅς, *rel. pron.* who, which, what; τρόπος, a turn, way *or* direction; *hence metaph.* way, manner, fashion, } what manner, *etc.*
11. ὅστις, *indef. rel. pron.* whoever, whatever, whatsoever.
    (b) *with* ἄν, *expressing* conditionality, contingency.
12. ὥστε, *conj.* so that, *marking the result. With the infinitive it expresses the result as the natural and logical consequence of what has been previously done or said; while with the indicative, it states it simply as a fact which occurs or has occurred.*
13. καθότι, *adv.* as, according as, because that, for.
14. καθό, *adv. (for* καθ' ὅ, according to what) as, according as.
15. καθά, *adv. (for* καθ' ἅ, according to which) according as.
16. ὡσπερεί, *adv.* just as if, as it were.
17. οὕτω *or* οὕτως, *adv.* thus, in this wise, so.
18. εἰς, *(motion to the interior)* into, to, with a view to.
19. γάρ, *(a contraction for* γέ ἄρα, verily therefore) *hence,* in fact, *and when the fact is given as a reason or explanation,* for; *but it is more extensive in meaning than the English* for, *since it expresses the cause, reason, motive, principle, occasion, inducement of what has been previously affirmed or implied.*
20. καθ' ὅσον, according to so much, inasmuch as.

19. Matt. i. 18.
1. —— 24.
— —— v. 48, see even A.
3. —— vi. 2.
3. —— 5 (No. 1, L Tr
3. —— 7. [A ℵ.)
1. —— 10, 12.
3. —— 16 (No. 1, L Tr
1. —— vii. 29 twice. [A ℵ.)
1. —— viii. 13.
— —— ix. 15, see A long as.
8. —— 36 (No. 1, Tr.)
— —— x. 16 3 times, 25 twice.
3. —— xii. 40.
3. —— xiii. 40.
1. —— 43.
1. —— xiv. 5.
— —— 36, see A many
12. —— xv. 33. [as.
1. —— xvii. 2 twice, 20.
1. —— xviii. 3, 4.
3. —— 17.
— —— 19, see A touch-
1. —— 33. [ing.
1. —— xix. 19.
1. —— xx. 14.
— —— 28, see even A.
2. —— xxi. 6.
1. —— 26.
— —— xxii. 9, } see A
— —— 10, } many as.
1. —— 30.
· —— 31, see A touch-
1. —— 39. [ing.
— —— xxiii. 37, see even A. [A.
— —— xxiv. 21, see such
3. —— 27, 37.
3. —— 38 (No. 1, L T Tr A ℵ.)
3. —— xxv. 14, 32.
— —— 40, } see Inas-
— —— 45, } much as.
1. —— xxvi. 19.
2. —— 24.
1. —— 39, 55.
15. —— xxvii. 10.
8. —— xxviii. 3 (No. 1, L Tr A ℵ.)
8. —— 4 (No. 1, L T
2. —— 6. [Tr A ℵ.)
1. —— 9 (*ap.*), 15.
1. Mark i. 2 (No. 2, T Tr ℵ), 22 twice.
7. —— ii. 15 (*om.* Tr[b] ℵ.)
— —— 19, see A long as.
1. —— iii. 5 (*om.* All.)
— —— 10, see A many as.
7. —— iv. 4.
— —— 20, see such A.
1. —— 26.
2. —— 33.
— —— v. 36, see A soon
1. —— vi. 15, 34. [as.
— —— 56, see A many
1. —— vii. 6. [as.
1. —— viii. 24.
1. Mark ix. 3 1st (*om.* ὡς χιών, *as snow,* G⇉ T Tr A ℵ.)
— —— 3 2nd, see so A.
2. —— 13.
8. —— 26.
1. —— x. 1, 15.
— —— xi. 2, see A soon as.
— —— 6, see even as.
1. —— xii. 25, 31, 33.
— —— 26, see A touching. [A.
— —— xiii. 19, see such
1. —— 34.
2. —— xiv. 16, 21.
1. —— 48.
2. —— xv. 8.
2. —— xvi. 7.
— Luke i. 2, see even A.
2. —— 55, 70.
1. —— ii. 15.
2. —— 20, 23.
7. —— 43.
1. —— iii. 4, 23.
— —— iv. 16, see A .. was.
7. —— v. 1.
2. —— 14.
1. —— vi. 10 (*ap.*)
1. —— 22.
2. —— 31.
— —— 34, see A much.
2. —— 36.
1. —— 40.
7. —— viii. 5, 42.
7. —— ix. 18.
7. —— 29 (γίνομαι ἐν, *it came to pass in.*)
7. —— 33, 34.
1. —— 54 (*ap.*)
1. —— x. 3, 18, 27.
7. —— 38.
7. —— xi. 1 1st.
2. —— 1 2nd.
1. —— 2 (*ap.*)
— —— 8, see A many as.
7. —— 27.
2. —— 30.
1. —— 36.
7. —— 37.
1. —— 44.
10. —— xiii. 34.
7. —— xiv. 1.
1. —— 22.
1. —— xv. 19, 25.
— —— 30, see A soon as.
1. —— xvii. 6.
7. —— 11, 14.
3. —— 24.
2. —— 26.
1. —— 28 (No. 2, instead of καὶ ὡς, *also as,* Tr ℵ.)
— —— xviii. 9 (margin) see
3. —— 11 1st. [A being.
1. —— 11 2nd, 17.
7. —— 35.
— —— xix. 9, see forasmuch A.
— —— 32, see even A.
1. —— xxi. 35.
2. —— xxii. 13.

6b. Luke xxii. 22.
1. —— 26 twice, 27.
2. —— 29.
1. —— 31.
6b. —— 39.
— —— 44, see A it were.
1. —— 52.
1. —— xxiii. 14, 26.
7. —— xxiv. 4.
8. —— 11.
— —— 24, see even A.
7. —— 30.
2. —— 39.
— —— 50, see A far as.
— John i. 12, see A many
1. —— 14. [as.
2. —— 23.
2. —— iii. 14.
3. —— v. 21.
— —— 23, see even A.
3. —— 26, 30.
— —— vi. 11, see A much
2. —— 31, 57, 58. [as.
2. —— vii. 38.
2. —— viii. 28.
— —— ix. 5, see A long as
2. —— x. 15.
2. —— 26 (ap.)
2. —— xii. 14.
— —— 50, see even A.
2. —— xiii. 15, 33, 34.
2. —— xiv. 31.
2. —— xv. 4.
1. —— 6.
2. —— 9.
— —— 10, see even A.
2. —— 12.
— —— xvi. 21, see A soon
2. —— xvii. 2 1st. [as.
— —— 2 2nd, see A many
2. —— 11. [as.
— —— 14, } see even A.
— —— 16, }
2. —— 18, 21.
— —— 22, see even A.
2. —— 23.
2. —— xix. 40.
— —— xx. 9, see A yet..
1. —— 11. [not
2. —— 21.
— Acts i. 19, see insomuch
3. —— ii. 2. [A.
— —— 3, see like A.
2. —— 4.
1. —— 15.
2. —— 22.
— —— 39, see A many as.
13. —— 45.
1. —— iii. 12.
3. —— 17.
— —— 24, } see A many
— —— iv. 6, } as.
— —— 34, }
— —— 35, see according
A. [ing.
— —— v. 35, see A touch-
— —— 36, } see A many
— —— 37, } as.
— —— vi. 15, see A it had
10. —— vii. 28. [been.
1. —— 37, margin (text
2. —— 42. [—*like.*)
2. —— 44, 48.
1. —— 51 (No. 2, L.)
— —— viii. 16, see A yet.
1. —— 32, 36.
7. —— ix. 3.
— —— 18, see A it had
1. —— x. 25. [been.
— —— 45, see A many
as. [as.
2. —— 47, see A well
7. —— xi. 15 1st.
3. —— 15 2nd.
— —— 17 1st, see foras-
1. —— 17 2nd. [much A.
— —— 19, } see A far
— —— 22, } as.

1. Acts xiii. 25, 33.
— —— 34, see A con-
cerning. [as.
— —— 43, see A many
2. —— xv. 8. [A.
10. —— 11, but see even
2. —— 15. [A.
— —— 24, see forasmuch
1. —— xvi. 4.
— —— xvii. 2, see A..was.
— —— 14, see A it were.
— —— 23 (the trans. of
the part.)
1. —— 28.
— —— xxi. 25, see A touch-
2. —— xxii. 3. [ing.
1. —— 5, 25.
1. —— xxiii. 11, 15, 20.
6b. —— 31.
1. —— xxv. 10.
10. —— xxvii. 25, but see
1. —— 30. [even A.
— —— xxviii. 15, see A far
2. Rom. i. 13. [as.
— —— 15, see A much
2. —— 17. [as.
1. —— 21.
— —— 28, see even A.
— —— ii. 12 twice, see A
2. —— 24. [many as.
2. —— iii. 4.
6b. —— 5.
1. —— 7.
2. —— 8 twice, 10.
— —— iv. 1, see A pertaining to.
— —— 6, see even as.
2. —— 17 1st.
1. —— 17 2nd.
3. —— v. 12.
1. —— 15, 16, 18.
3. —— 19, 21. [A.
— —— vi. 3, see so many
— —— 4, see like A.
1. —— 13 (No. 8, L Tr
A ℵ.)
— —— vii. 1, see A long as.
— —— viii. 14, see A many
14. —— 26. [as.
2. —— 36 1st.
1. —— 36 2nd. [ning.
— —— ix. 5, see A concer-
9. —— 6 (with ὅτι,—*as*
2. —— 13. [*though.*)
1. —— 27.
2. —— 29 1st.
1. —— 29 2nd.
2. —— 33.
2. —— x. 15. [A.
— —— xi. 8, see according
— —— 13, see inasmuch
2. —— 26 [A.
— —— 28 1st, see A con-
cerning. [touching.
— —— 28 2nd, see A
— —— xii. 3, see according
5. —— 4. [A.
— —— 18, see A much as
1. —— xiii. 9, 13.
2. —— xv 3, 7, 9.
1. —— 15.
2. —— 21. [eth.
— —— xvi. 2, see A becom-
— 1 Cor. i. 6, see even A.
— —— 31, see according
2. —— ii 9. [A.
1. —— iii. 1 3 times.
6b. —— 3.
1. —— 10, 15.
1. —— iv. 1, 7, 13, 14.
2. —— 17.
1. —— 18.
— —— v. 1, see such as.
1. —— 3 twice.
2. —— 7.
1. —— vii. 7, 8, 17 twice,
25, 29, 30 3 times, 31.
— —— 39, see A long as.

— 1 Cor. viii. 1, see A
2. —— 2. [touching.
— —— 4, see A concern-
3. —— 5. [ing.
1. —— 7.
6b. —— ix. 8.
1. —— 20 twice, 21.
1. —— 22 (*om* Lb T Tr
1. —— 26 twice. [A ℵ.
2. —— x. 6, 7 1st.
1. —— 7 2nd (No. 3, G∾
L T Tr A ℵ.)
2. —— 8, 9, 10.
1. —— 15.
— —— 33, } see even
— —— xi. 1, } A.
2. —— 2.
— —— 5, see A if (even
3. —— 12. [all one.)
— —— 25, see A oft as.
— —— 26, see A often
2. —— xii. 11. [as.
5. —— 12.
2. —— 18.
1. —— xiii. 11 3 times.
— —— 12, see even A.
— —— xiv. 12, forasmuch
1. —— 33. [A.
2. —— 34.
16. —— xv. 8.
3. —— 22.
2. —— 38.
9. —— 48 twice.
2. —— 49.
3. —— xvi. 1.
11b. —— 2.
1. —— 10.
2. 2 Cor. i. 5.
3. —— 7 (No. 1, L T Tr
2. —— 14 1st. [A ℵ.)
— —— 14 2nd, see even
A. [(not.)
— —— 23, see A yet
1. —— ii. 17 3 times.
1. —— iii. 1, 5.
5. —— 13.
— —— 18, see behold
as in a glass.
— —— 18, see even A.
2. —— iv. 1.
— —— 13, see accord-
1. —— v. 20. [ing A.
1. —— vi. 4, 8, 9 3 times,
10 3 times, 13.
2. —— 16.
1. —— vii. 14.
2. —— viii. 5, 6.
3. —— 7.
5. —— 11.
2. —— 15.
— —— ix 1, see A touch-
2. —— 3. [ing.
1. —— 5 1st.
3. —— 5 2nd (No. 1, All.)
— —— 7, see according
2. —— 9. [A.
1. —— x. 2, 14.
2. —— 7.
— —— 11, see such A.
— —— 14, see A far as
1. —— xi. 3. [to.
2. —— 12.
1. —— 15, 16. [cerning.
— —— 21, see A con-
— —— xii. 20 twice, see such
1. —— xiii. 2, 7. [A.
1. Gal. i. 9.
2. —— ii. 7. [Jews.
— —— 14, see A do the
— —— iii. 6, see even A.
— —— 10, see A many as.
1. —— 16 twice.
— —— 27, see A many as.
— —— iv. 1, see A long as.
1. —— 12 twice, 14 twice.
6b. —— 28.
3. —— 29.
1. —— v. 14.

2. Gal. v. 21.
1. —— vi. 10.
— —— 12, } see A many
— —— 16, } as.
— Eph. i. 4, see according
1. —— ii. 3. [A.
2. —— iii. 3.
1. —— 5.
— —— iv. 4, see even A.
2. —— 17, 21.
2. —— 32.
1. —— v. 1.
2. —— 2, 3. [28.
1. —— 8, 15 twice, 22, 23,
3. —— 24 (No. 1, L T Tr
2. —— 25, 29. [A ℵ.)
1. —— vi. 5, 6 twice.
1. —— 7 (*om.* St.)
1. —— 20.
— Phil. i. 7 1st, see even A
— —— 7 2nd (trans. of
1. —— 20. [part.)
— —— 27, see A becometh
1. —— ii. 8.
2. —— 12 1st.
1. —— 12 2nd, 15, 22.
— —— iii. 5, see A touching
— —— 12, see A though.
— —— 15, see A many as.
2. —— 17. [cerning.
— —— iv. 15, see A con-
2. Col. i. 6 twice, 7.
— —— ii. 1, see A many as.
1. —— 6.
2. —— 7.
1. —— 20.
1. —— iii. 12.
2. —— 13.
1. —— 18, 22, 23.
1. —— iv. 4.
2. 1 Thes. i. 5.
2. —— ii. 2, 4 1st.
1. —— 4 2nd.
2. —— 5.
1. —— 7.
5. —— 11 1st.
1. —— 11 2nd.
1. —— 13 1st (*om.* St E
G L T Tr A ℵ), (Beza, has
οὐχ ὡς, *not as*, for οὐ,
2. —— 13 2nd, 14. [*not.*)
2. —— iii. 4.
5. —— 6.
— —— 12, see even A.
2. —— iv. 1.
— —— 5, see even A.
2. —— 6.
— —— 9, see A touch-
2. —— 11, 13. [ing.
1. —— v. 2, 4, 6.
— —— 11, see even A.
2. 2 Thes. i. 3.
1. —— ii. 2 twice.
1. —— 4 (*om.* All.)
2. —— iii. 1.
1. —— 15 twice.
2. 1 Tim. i. 3.
1. —— v. 1 twice, 2 twice.
— —— vi. 1, A many as.
1. 2 Tim. ii. 3, 9, 17.
10. —— iii. 8.
1. —— 9.
1. Titus i. 5, 7.
6b. —— 9
— —— ii. 3, see A becometh
1. Philem. 9, 16, 17.
4. Heb. i. 4.
1. —— 11.
8. —— 12. [much A.
— —— ii. 14, see foras-
1. —— iii. 2, 5, 6, 8, 15.
— —— 3, see inasmuch
2. —— 7. [A.
— —— iv. 2, see A well as.
2. —— 3 1st.
1. —— 3 2nd.
2. —— 7.
3. —— 10.

— Heb. iv. 15, see like A.
2. —— v. 3.
5. ——— 4 (No. 2, L) (*καθώσπερ, as indeed*, T Tr A ℵ.)
2. ——— 6.
1. —— vi. 19.
1. —— vii. 9.
— ——— 20, see inasmuch
3. ——— 27. [A.
2. —— viii. 5.
— —— ix. 9, see A pertain-
3. ——— 25. [ing to.
20. ——— 27.
2. —— x. 25 1st.
4. ——— 25 2nd.
1. —— xi. 9.
2. ——— 12 1st.
8. ——— 12 2nd (No. 1, All)
1. ——— 27, 29.
1. —— xii. 5, 7, 16, 27.
1. —— xiii. 3 twice, 17.
1. Jas. i. 10.
1. —— ii. 8, 9, 12.
3. ——— 26.
1. —— v. 3. [ℵ.)
1. ——— 5 (*om.* L T Tr A
1. 1 Pet. i. 14.
6b. ——— 15.
1. ——— 19.
1. ——— 24 1st (*om.* L) (No. 8, ℵ.)
1. ——— 24 2nd.
1. —— ii. 2, 5, 11, 12, 14, 16 twice, 25.
1. —— iii. 7 twice, 16 (*ap.*)
2. —— iv. 10 1st. [12.
1. ——— 10 2nd, 11 twice,
— ——— 13, see inasmuch A.
1. ——— 15 twice, 16.
1. ——— 19 (*om.* L A ℵ.)
1. —— v. 3, 8, 12. [A.
— 2 Pet. i. 3, see according
— ——— 13, see A long
2. ——— 14. [A.
1. ——— 10.
1. —— ii. 1, 19.
1 —— iii. 8 twice, 9, 10.
17. ——— 14 (with No. 1 denotes *as they were*.)
2. ——— 15.
1. ——— 16 twice.
1. 1 John i. 7.
2. —— ii. 6, 18.
1. ——— 27 1st.
— 1 John ii. 27 2nd, see even
2. —— iii. 2. [A.
— ——— 3, } see even
— ——— 7, } A.
2. ——— 12.
2. ——— 23.
2. —— iv. 17.
2. 2 John 4.
1. ——— 5.
2. ——— 6.
— 3 John 2, } see even A.
— ——— 3, }
1. Jude 10.
1. Rev. i. 10, 14 twice, 15 twice, 16, 17. [as.
— —— ii. 24 1st, see A many
1. ——— 24, 27 twice.
— —— iii. 3.
— ——— 19, see A many
1. ——— 21. [as.
1. —— iv. 1.
1. ——— 7 (G ∾) (Ab)
1. —— v. 6. [(*om.* G.)
1. —— vi. 11, 12 twice, 13, 14.
— —— viii. 12, see so A.
1. —— ix. 2, 3, 5, 7, 8 twice,
1. —— x. 1. [9, 17.
— ——— 3, see A when.
1. ——— 7, 9, 10 1st.
— ——— 10 2nd, see A soon as. [as.
— —— xi. 6, see A often
1. —— xii. 15.
1. —— xiii. 2 twice, 11.
— ——— 15, see A many
1. —— xiv. 2 twice. [as.
— ——— 3, see A it were.
1. —— xvi. 3, 15.
— ——— 18, see such as.
— —— xvii. 12 1st, see no [..A yet.
1. ——— 12 2nd.
1. —— xviii. 6.
— ——— 17, see A many
1. —— xix. 6 1st. [as.
1. ——— 6 2nd (*om.* L.)
1. ——— 12 (*om.* G ⇉ T
1. —— xx. 8. [Ab ℵ.)
1. —— xxi. 2.
— ——— 11, see crystal (clear A.)
— ——— 16 1st, see As
4. ——— 16 2nd. [large.
1. —— xxii. 1. [ing A.
— ——— 12, see accord-

AS BECOMETH.

ἀξίως, worthily, suitably *(from ἄξιος, q.v.)*

Rom. xvi. 2. | Phil. i. 27.

AS BECOMETH HOLINESS.

ἱεροπρεπής, such as becometh a holy person, place *or* matter, venerable *(non occ.)*

Titus ii. 3, margin *as becometh holy women.*

AS BEING [margin.]

{ ὅτι, that, seeing that, because.
{ εἰσὶ, they were.

Luke xviii. 9 (text, *that they were.*)

AS CONCERNING.

1. κατά, *see* "AS," *No.* 6*b*.
2. περί, around.
   (a) *with Gen.* about, concerning.
   (b) *with Acc.* about, round about.
3. { εἰς, into, to, unto, with a view to, λόγον, the word *(spoken or written)*; *formally*, a word *or* expression; *materially*, the word, *as that which is spoken*, an exposition *or* account *which one gives.* } *lit.* for an account.

1. Rom. ix. 5. | 1. 1 Cor. viii. 4.
1. —— xi. 28. | 1. 2 Cor. xi. 21.
3. Phil. iv. 15.

AS CONCERNING THAT.

ὅτι, that. *It points in general to some existing fact, something which lies before us, and hence answers to* that, *as well as* because.

Acts xiii. 34.

AS DO THE JEWS.

Ἰουδαϊκῶς, Jewishly, after the manner of the Jews. *(Nationally, as distinguished from Gentiles.) (non. occ.)*

Gal. ii. 14.

AS FAR AS.

1. ἄχρι, unto, even unto *(of time or place.)*
2. ἕως, till, until *(of time)*; up to, as far as *(of place.)*

2. Luke xxiv. 50. | 2. Acts xi. 22.
2. Acts xi. 19. | 1. —— xxviii. 15.

AS FAR AS TO.

1. 2 Cor. x. 14.

AS IT HAD BEEN.

1. ὡς, as, *see* "AS," *No.* 1.
2. ὡσεί, as if, *see* "AS," *No.* 8.

2. Acts vi. 15. | 1. Acts x. 11.
2. —— ix. 18 (*ap.*) | 1. —— xi. 5.

AS IT WERE.

1. ὡς, as, *see* "AS," *No.* 1.
2. ὡσεί, as if, *see* "AS," *No.* 8.

2. Luke xxii. 44 (*ap.*)
1. John vii. 10.
1. —— xxi. 8.
1. Acts xvii. 14 (ἕως, as far as, L Tr ℵ.)
1. Rom. ix. 32.
1. 1 Cor. iv. 9.
1. 2 Cor. xi. 17.
1. Philem. 14.
1. Jas. v. 3.
1. Rev. iv. 1.
1. —— vi. 1.
1. —— viii. 8, 10.
1. —— ix. 7, 9.
1. —— x. 1.
1. —— xiii. 3.
1. —— xiv. 3 (*om.* G T A^b ℵ.)
1. —— xv. 2.
1. —— xxi. 21.

AS LARGE.

τοσοῦτος, *demons. pron.* so great, so much, so long; *pl.* so many.

Rev. xxi. 16 (*om.* all.)

AS LONG AS.

1. ὅσος, *see* "AS," *No.* 4.
2. { ἐπί, upon, *with Acc. as here,* up to (*of place, number, or aim*), over (*of time, place, extent,*) ὅσος, how long, *see above.* } for as long as.
3. ὅταν, whensoever, as long as.

2. Matt. ix. 15.
1. Mark ii. 19.
1. —— vi. 56.
3. John ix. 5.
1. Rom. vii. 1.
2. 1 Cor. vii. 39.
1. Gal. iv. 1.
1. 2 Pet. i. 13.

AS MANY AS.

1. ὅσος, *see* "AS," *No.* 4.
2. { πᾶς, all, ὅς, who *or* which, } πᾶν ὅ, all which.

1. Matt. xiv. 36.
1. —— xxii. 10.
1. Mark iii. 10.
1. Luke xi. 8.
1. John i. 12.
2. —— xvii. 2.
1. Acts ii. 39.
1. —— iii. 24.
1. —— iv. 6, 34.
1. —— v. 36, 37.
1. —— x. 45 (ὅι, *who,* L.)
1. Acts xiii. 48.
1. Rom. ii. 12 twice.
1. —— viii. 14.
1. Gal. iii. 10, 27.
1. —— vi. 12, 16.
1. Phil. iii. 15.
1. Col. ii. 1.
1. 1 Tim. vi. 1.
1. Rev. ii. 24.
1. —— iii. 19.
1. —— xviii. 17.

AS MUCH.

ἴσος, equal to, the same as (*in appearance, size, strength, or number.*)

Luke vi. 34.

AS MUCH AS.

ὅσος, *see* "AS," *No.* 4.

John vi. 11.

AS MUCH AS IN ME IS.

{ ὁ, the, κατά, according to, ἐγώ, I, myself, } τὸ κατ' ἐμὲ, as far as in me is. *Eras. Beza. Pisc.;* as much as in me lieth, *Alf.; the eagerness* on my part, *Rotherham.*

Rom. i. 15.

AS MUCH AS LIETH IN YOU.

{ ὁ, the, ἐξ, out of, σύ, thou, you, } τὸ ἐξ ὑμῶν, as much as depends upon you, *Ellicott, Alford, Rotherham;* according to your ability, *Stuart.*

Rom. xii. 18.

AS OFT *or* OFTEN AS.

ὁσάκις, as many times as.

1 Cor. xi. 25, 26. | Rev. xi. 6.

AS PERTAINING TO.

κατά, *see* "AS," *No.* 6*b.*

Rom. iv. 1. | Heb. ix. 9.

AS SOON AS.

1. ὡς, *see* "AS," *No.* 1.
   (a) *with* ἄν.
2. εὐθέως, immediately, instantly, (*adv. from* εὐθύς, straight, direct.)
3. ὅτε, when, *of a thing actually gone before.*
4. ὅταν, whenever, as long as *or* as soon as, *implying a possible contingency, present or future.*

2. Mark v. 36 (*om.* G⇉ L^b [Tr ℵ.)
2. —— xi. 2.
1. Luke i. 23, 44.
3. —— xv. 30.
1. —— xxii. 66.
1. John xi. 20, 29.
4. John xvi. 21.
1. —— xviii. 6.
1. —— xxi. 9.
1a. Phil. ii. 23.
3. Rev. x. 10.
4. —— xii. 4.

AS THOUGH.

(*Where not two words in Greek.*)

ὅτι, that, *see* "AS CONCERNING THAT."

Phil. iii. 12.

AS TOUCHING.

1. ἐπί, upon.
   (a) *with Gen.* up to, *(of place, number, or aim.)*
   (b) *with Acc.* over, *(of time, place, or extent.)*
2. περί, around.
   (a) *with Gen.* about, concerning, on behalf of.
   (b) *with Acc.* about, round about.
3. κατά, *see* "AS," *No.* 6*b*.

2a. Matt. xviii. 19.
2a. —— xxii. 31.
2a. Mark xii. 26.
1b. Acts v. 35.
2a. —— xxi. 25.
3. Rom. xi. 28.
2a. 1 Cor. viii. 1.
2a. —— xvi. 12.
2a. 2 Cor. ix. 1.
3. Phil. iii. 5.
2a. 1 Thes. iv. 9.

AS...WAS.

κατά, *see* "AS," *No.* 6*b*.

Luke iv. 16. | Acts xvii. 2.
(lit. *according to* his custom, etc.)

AS WELL AS.

1. καθάπερ, even as, truly as.
2. { ὡς, as, / καί, and, also, } as also.
3. { καθώς, according as, / καί, and, also, } even as also, *etc.*

3. Acts x. 47 (No. 2, L T Tr A ℵ.)
2. 1 Cor. ix. 5.
1. Heb. iv. 2.

AS WHEN.

ὥσπερ, wholly as, just as.

Rev. x. 3.

AS YET.

οὔπω, not yet, *(opp. to* οὐκέτι, no more.*)*

Acts viii. 16 (οὐδέπω, *and not yet*, G ~ L T Tr A ℵ.)
2 Cor. i. 23, see not..as yet.
Rev. xvii. 12, see no..as yet.

AS YET...NOT.

οὐδέπω, and not yet, not as yet.

John xx. 9.

See also, ACCORDING, BECOMETH, BEHOLD, CONCERNING, CRYSTAL, CUSTOM, EVEN, FORASMUCH, HAVE, INASMUCH, INSOMUCH, LIKE, MAKE, MAN, MANNER, MANY, MEN, MUCH, NO, NOT, PERTAINING, SET, SO, SUCH, TOUCHING, WONT.

ASCEND* AND ASCEND UP†.

(-ED, -ETH, -ING.)

ἀναβαίνω, to go up, climb, mount.

Luke xix. 28†; John i. 52*; iii. 13†; vi. 62†; xx. 17 twice*; Acts ii. 34*; xxv. 1*; Rom. x. 6*; Eph. iv. 8†, 9*, 10†; Rev. vii. 2*; viii. 4†; xi. 7*, 12†; xiv. 11†; xvii. 8*.

ASHAMED (BE.)

1. αἰσχύνομαι, to be ashamed, feel shame, *(to have the feeling which attends the performance of a dishonourable deed, or the feeling which deters a man from bad conduct through fear of shame.)*
2. ἐπαισχύνομαι, to be ashamed of *or* at. *In N.T. only in Mid.* to shame one's self upon, in *or* at.
3. καταισχύνω, to disgrace, dishonour, put to shame.
   (a) *Pass. and Mid.*, to feel shame before another.
4. ἐντρέπομαι, to turn towards, give heed to, pay regard to; to be turned upon one's self on account *or* from reverential awe of, *(to have an innate moral repugnance to the doing of a dishonourable act.)*

3a. Luke xiii. 17.
1. —— xvi. 3.
— Rom. v. 5, see A (make)
3a. —— ix. 33, margin *be confounded.*
3a. —— x. 11.
3a. 2 Cor. vii. 14.
3a. —— ix. 4.
1. —— x. 8.
1. Phil. i. 20.
4. 2 Thes. iii. 14.
2. 2 Tim. i. 12.
— —— ii. 15, see A (need not be.)
4. Titus ii. 8.
2. Heb. ii. 11.
2. —— xi. 16.
3a. 1 Pet. iii. 16.
1. —— iv. 16.
1. 1 John ii. 28.

ASHAMED OF (BE.)

2. Mark viii. 38 twice.
2. Luke ix. 26 twice.
2. Rom. i. 16.
2. Rom. vi. 21 (with ἐπί, *upon* or *at.*)
2. 2 Tim. i. 8, 16.

ASHAMED (MAKE.)

3. Rom. v. 5.

ASHAMED (NEED NOT BE.)

ἀνεπαίσχυντος, *(from a, neg. and No. 2 above)* not ashamed, having no cause for shame.

2. Tim. ii. 15.

ASHES.

σποδός, wood-ashes, embers; *gen.* ashes.

Matt. xi. 21. | Heb. ix. 13.
Luke x. 13. | 2 Pet. ii. 6, see A (turn into.)

ASHES (TURN INTO.)

τεφρόω, to make into ashes, reduce to ashes, *(from τέφρα,* ashes, *as of the funeral pile.)*

2 Pet. ii. 6.

ASIA.

'Ασία, Asia.

In all places, except

Acts vi. 9 (*om.* L.)
Rev. i. 11 (*om.* ταῖς ἐν 'Ασίᾳ, *which are in Asia, om.* All.)

ASIDE.

κατά, according to, ἴδιος, one's own, distinct from all else } κατ' ἰδίαν, *lit.* according to one's own, *i.e.* privately.

Mark vii. 33.

ASIDE (GO.)

1. ἀναχωρέω, to go back, depart, withdraw, retire.
2. ὑποχωρέω, to go back; retire, recoil.

2 Luke ix. 10. | 1 Acts xxiii. 19.
1. Acts xxvi. 31.

ASIDE (LAY.)

1. ἀποτίθημι, to put away, to lay off; to put by for one's self, stow away.
2. ἀφίημι, to send away, dismiss, set free; *gen.* to leave *anything,* to free one's self *therefrom,* to let lie.

2. Mark vii. 8. | 1. Heb. xii. 1.
1. 1 Pet. ii. 1.

ASIDE (TURN.)

1. ἀναχωρέω, to go back, depart, withdraw, retire.
2. ἐκτρέπομαι, to turn out of *or* from the course, to turn aside.

1. Matt. ii. 22. | 2. 1 Tim. i. 6.
2. 1 Tim. v. 15.

ASK.

(-ED, -EST, -ETH, -ING.)

1. αἰτέω, to entreat, beg, supplicate; *implies a distinction in position and circumstances between the parties, and expresses a petition from an inferior to a superior. Never used by Christ to the Father, but No. 2 invariably.*
2. ἐρωτάω, to ask *for information,* to question *as well as supplicate; implies familiarity if not equality. Never used of our prayers to the Father, see* John xvi. 23, and 1 John v. 16.
3. ἐπερωτάω, *(No. 2 with ἐπί prefixed, intensive),* to consult, inquire of, question; to ask about *a thing.*
4. πυνθάνομαι, to ask *for information,* to inquire; to learn by asking *or* inquiry; to hear, learn, understand.
5. ἐξετάζω, to examine well *or* closely, to scrutinize, review *of persons, hence,* to question; *of things,* to inquire into *or* sift.
6. λέγω, to lay, to lay together, to collect, to read, *hence,* to speak *or* say. *(λέγω is never used for λαλέω, which means simply* to speak, *to employ the organ of utterance; while λέγω is referred to the* sentiment *of what is spoken. λέγω therefore is always rational and* intelligent, *while λαλέω may be mere sound, either of the sane or insane.)*

1. Matt. v. 42.
1. —— vi. 8.
1. —— vii. 7, 8, 9, 10, 11.
3. —— xii. 10.
1. —— xiv. 7.
2. —— xvi. 13.
3. —— xvii. 10.
1. —— xviii. 19.
1. —— xx. 22.
1. —— xxi. 22.
2. ———— 24.
3. —— xxii. 23.
— ———— 35, see A a question.
3. ———— 41, 46.
3. —— xxvii. 11.
1. ———— 20.
2. Mark iv. 10.
3. —— v. 9.
1. —— vi. 22, 23, 24, 25.
3. —— vii. 5, 17. [A N.)
3. —— viii. 5 (No. 2, T Tr
3. Mark viii. 23, 27.
3. —— ix. 11, 16, 21, 28, 32, 33.
3. —— x. 2, 10, 17.
1. ———— 38.
3. —— xii. 18, 28, 34.
3. —— xiii. 3.
3. —— xiv. 60, 61.
3. —— xv. 2, 4, 44.
1. Luke i. 63.
— —— ii. 46, see A questions.
3. —— iii. 10.
3. —— vi. 9.
1. ———— 30 1st.
— ———— 30 2nd, see A again
3. —— viii. 9, 30.
3. —— ix. 18.
2. ———— 45 (No. 3, L.)
1. —— xi. 9, 10, 11 1st & 3rd*
1. —— xii. 48. [12, 13.
4. —— xv. 26.
3. —— xviii. 18.

* 2nd not in Greek.

4. Luke xviii. 36.
3. —— 40.
2. —— xix. 31.
2. —— xx. 3
3. —— 21, 27, 40.
3. —— xxi. 7.
3. —— xxii. 64.
2. —— 68.
3. —— xxiii. 3 (No. 2, T Tr A ℵ.)
3. —— 6.
2. John i. 19, 21, 25.
1. —— iv. 9, 10.
2. —— v. 12.
2. —— viii. 7 (*ap.*)
2. —— ix. 2, 15, 19, 21, 23.
1. —— xi. 22.
4. —— xiii. 24 (*ap.*)
1. —— xiv. 13, 14.
1. —— xv. 7, 16.
2. —— xvi. 5, 19, 23 1st.
1. —— 23 2nd, 24 twice, 26.
2. —— 30.
3. John xviii. 7.
2. —— 19.
3. —— 21 twice (No. 2, L T Tr A ℵ.)
5. —— xxi. 12.
1. Acts iii. 2.
2. —— 3.
4. —— iv. 7.
3. —— v. 27.
4. —— x. 18, 29.
4. —— xxiii. 19.
3. —— 34.
6. —— xxv. 20.
— Rom. x. 20, see A after.
— 1 Cor. x. 25, } see A
— —— 27, } question
3. —— xiv. 35.
1. Eph. iii. 20.
1. Jas. i. 5, 6.
1. —— iv 2, 3 twice.
1. 1 Pet. iii. 15.
1. 1 John iii. 22.
1. —— v. 14, 15, 16.

ASK AFTER.

3. Rom. x. 20.

ASK AGAIN.

ἐπαιτέω, (*No.* 1 *with* ἐπί, upon, *prefixed),* to ask besides, to beg as a mendicant.

Luke vi. 30.

ASK A QUESTION.

ἐπερωτάω, *see* "ASK," *No.* 3.

Matt. xxii. 35.

ASK QUESTIONS.

1. ἐπερωτάω, *see* "ASK," *No.* 3.
2. ἀνακρίνω, to examine well *or* closely, to question, sift.

1. Luke ii. 46. | 2. 1 Cor. x. 25, 27.

ASK WHO WAS THERE [margin.]

ὑπακούω, to hearken to and obey, *(from* ὑπό, under, *and* ἀκούω, to hear), *with the idea of stealth, stillness or with attention, in order to answer.*

Acts xii. 13 (text, *hearken.*)

ASLEEP.

καθεύδω, to lie down to sleep, to sleep; *metaph.*, to rest, be at rest, still, quiet.

Mat. xxvi. 40, 43. | Mark iv. 38. | Mark xiv. 40.

See also, SLEEP.

ASLEEP (BE.)

1. καθεύδω, to lie down to sleep, to sleep, *metaph.*, to rest, be at rest, still, quiet.
2. κοιμάομαι, to be laid down to sleep, to be *or* fall asleep *in death*, to sleep the sleep of death; *used thus by the Ancients, though in connection with such words as exclude the hope of "waking" or resurrection, e.g., "eternal," "unawakened," "everlasting," "brazen sleep," "iron sleep," etc.*

1. Matt. viii. 24. | 2. 1 Thes. iv. 13, 15.

ASLEEP (FALL.)

1. ἀφυπνόω, to cease to sleep, to awake from sleep, *(from* ἀπό, from, *and* ὕπνος, sleep), *in N.T. and later writers* to sleep away, *i.e.* to fall into a deep and prolonged sleep.
2. κοιμάομαι, *see* "ASLEEP," *No.* 2.

1. Luke viii. 23.
2. Acts vii. 60.
2. 1 Cor. xv. 6, 18.
2. 2 Pet. iii. 4.

ASP.

ἀσπίς, an asp, a kind of viper. *(The* coluber naja *of Egypt.)*

Rom. iii. 13.

ASS.

1. ὄνος, an ass, *male or female, (prob. from* ὀνίνημι, to help, *as Latin jumentum, an ass, from juvo,* to help, *because it helps or assists man in his labours.)*
2. ὑποζύγιον, an animal subject to the yoke, *particularly* an ass, *(from* ὑπό, under, *and* ζυγός, a yoke.)

1. Matt. xxi. 2.
1. —— 5 1st.
2. —— 5 2nd.
1. —— 7.
1. Luke xiii. 15.
1. Luke xiv. 5 (υἱός, *a son,* G ~ L T Tr A.)
— John xii. 14, see A [(young.)
— —— 15.
2. 2 Pet. ii. 16.

ASS (YOUNG.)

ὀνάριον, *(the diminutive of No.* 1 *above)* a young ass *or* ass's colt.

John xii. 14.

ASSAULT [verb.]

ἐφίστημι, *trans.* to set *or* place upon; *intrans.* to stand upon; *in hostile signif.* to stand against, to come upon by surprise.

Acts xvii. 5.

ASSAULT [noun.]

ὁρμή, any violent pressure onwards, an assault, attack; *esp.* the first shock, onset *in war.* (*Lat.* impetus.)

Acts xiv. 5.

ASSAY (-ED, -ING.)

1. *πειράω*, (*from πείρω,* to perforate, pierce through, *by which trial is made of things)* to attempt, undertake, endeavour, try; *then* to put to the proof.
2. *πειράζω*, to make proof *or* trial, to make an attempt.
3. { *λαμβάνω*, to take, to take hold of, to apprehend, *πεῖρα*, a trial, attempt, } *πεῖραν λαμβάνειν*, to make an attempt.

1. Acts ix. 26. | 2. Acts xvi. 7.
3. Heb. xi. 29.

ASSEMBLED (-BE.)

1. *συνάγω*, to bring together, lead together, *hence*, to lead *or* take *with one's self into one's house, to receive to one's hospitality.*
2. *γίνομαι*, to become.

— Matt. xxvi. 3, see A together.
1. ——— 57.
1. —— xxviii. 12.
— Mark xiv. 53, see A (with...)
1. John xx. 19 (—G → L T Tr A ℵ.)
— Acts i. 4, see A together (be.)
— —— iv. 31, see A together (be.)
— —— xi. 26, see A..selves.
2. —— xv. 25 (lit. *causing to be of one accord.*)

ASSEMBLE...SELVES.

συνάγω, *see above.*

Acts xi. 26.

ASSEMBLE TOGETHER.

συνάγω, *see above.*

Matt. xxvi. 3.

ASSEMBLED (WITH...)

συνέρχομαι, to come *or* go together; *abs.* to come together, meet, assemble.

Mark xiv. 53.

ASSEMBLED TOGETHER (BE.)

1. *συνάγω*, *see* "A (BE)," *No.* 1.
2. *συναλίζομαι*, to make throng together, to be assembled, met, gathered together.

2. Acts i. 4. | 1. Acts iv. 31.

ASSEMBLING TOGETHER [noun.]

ἐπισυναγωγή, a gathering together to *a place or person.*

Heb. x. 25.

ASSEMBLY.

1. *ἐκκλησία*, *the common term for a meeting of the ἔκκλητοι, assembled to discuss the affairs af a Free State. The body of citizens summoned by the crier* (*κῆρυξ*), *hence, the* popular assembly. *Transferred by the LXX to designate* the assembly of the people of Israel, *whether summoned for a definite purpose, or considered as the representative of the whole nation. In N.T. applied to the community of the people of Israel,* Acts vii. 38; *but elsewhere to* "the Church." *This ἐκκλησία is constituted by the old terms "calling" (καλεῖν) and "preaching" (κηρύσσειν), but inspired with a new force. Hence it denotes* the N.T. redeemed community *in its twofold aspect.* (i) The entire community of all who are called by and to Christ. (ii) The N.T. Churches as confined to particular places; every church in which the character of the church as a whole is repeated. *Its being* summoned *is expressed by the latter part of the word* (*καλεῖν*), *and its being summoned* out of *the whole population is expressed by the first part* (*ἐκ.*) (*See "Cremer."*)
2. *συναγωγή*, a bringing together, a gathering *of persons or things. No.* 1 *may be expressed by* convocation, *this by* congregation. *The former*

is aggregative, *the latter* congregative. *The former calls, invites, and summons men from the whole world to become its members; the latter brought together the members of an existing society, excluding all others. The former is attributed to the Christian Church, the latter to the Jewish synagogue.*

See under "CHURCH."

1. Acts xix. 32, 39. | — Heb. xii. 23, see A (general.)
1. ——— 41. |
2. Jas. ii. 2, margin, Greek *synagogue.*

ASSEMBLY (GENERAL.)

πανήγυρις, an assembly of a whole nation *for a public festival such as the Olympic games:* a high festival, a solemn assembly on such festival. (πανηγυρικὸς λόγος *is a speech or eulogy pronounced on any one at a public assembly, hence, the English word,* panegyric, *etc.)*

Heb. xii. 23.

ASSENT (-ED) [verb.]

1. συντίθημι, to place *or* put together, agree upon, settle.
2. ἐπικρίνω, to decide, determine, adjudge.

2. Luke xxiii. 24, margin (text, *give sentence.*)
1. Acts xxiv. 9(*συνεπιθημι, joined in setting upon him,* All)

ASSIST.

παρίστημι, (a) *trans.* to place by *or* beside; (b) *intrans.* to stand by *or* near *so as to defend or help.*

b. Rom. xvi. 2.

ASSURANCE.

1. πίστις, faith, the trust *which one entertains or puts in a person or thing. Parallel to this is the meaning of* conviction; *a conviction based upon trust, not upon knowledge; a persuasion fortified by faith.* A firmly relying confidence. *A confidence cherished by firm conviction.*
2. πληροφορία, full conviction, perfect certitude, *(from* πληροφορέω, to bring in full measure, complete an act), *not an effect of the logical faculty, but produced by the inner working of the Holy Ghost.*

1. Acts xvii. 31, marg. *faith.* | 2. 1 Thes. i. 5.
— Col. ii. 2, see A (full) | — Heb. vi. 11, see A (full)
— Heb. x. 22, see A (full.)

ASSURANCE (FULL.)

2. Col. ii. 2. | 2. Heb. vi. 11.
2. Heb. x. 22.

ASSURE.

πείθω, *intrans. as here,* to persuade, to win by words, to influence.

1 John iii. 19, margin Greek *persuade.*

ASSURED (be fully) [margin.]

πληροφορέω, to bear *or* bring fully, *hence,* to give full assurance.

(a) *Pass.* to have full satisfaction, to be fully assured.

(a.) Rom. xiv. 5 (text, *fully persuaded.*)

ASSURED OF (BE.)

πιστόω, *in pass. as here,* to guarantee *or* give bail for one's self, to become security for; *or* to be made faithful; to put trust in, confide.

2 Tim. iii. 14.

ASSUREDLY.

ἀσφαλῶς, safely, certainly, *(from* ἀσφαλής, that cannot be tripped up *or* thrown down.)

Acts ii. 36.

ASSUREDLY GATHERING.

συμβιβάζομαι, to cause to be put together, *metaph.* to examine closely, to conclude from laying circumstances together.

Acts xvi. 10.

ASTONISHED (BE.)

1. ἐκπλήσσομαι, *to be driven out of one's senses* by a sudden shock, to be exceedingly struck *in mind.*
2. ἐξίστημι, (a) *trans.* to change *from one condition to another,* to put out of its place, *metaph.* to drive *one* out of *his senses;* (b) *intrans.* to stand aside from, go away from, yield; to be out of one's wits.

3. *θαμβέομαι*, to be astonied, astounded, amazed, *(from θάμβος)*, (a) *the active.*

4. { *θάμβος*, astonishment, amazement.
περιέχω, to encompass, surround, embrace.

Lit. amazement, encompassed him.

1. Matt. vii. 28.
1. —— xiii. 54.
1. —— xxii. 33.
1. Mark i 22.
2b. —— v. 42.
1. —— vi. 2.
1. —— vii. 37.
3. —— x. 24.
1. ———— 26.
1. —— xi. 18.
2b. Luke ii. 47.
1. —— iv. 32.
4. —— v. 9.
2b. —— viii. 56.
— —— xxiv. 22, see A (make.)
3a. Acts ix. 6 (*ap.*)
2b. —— x. 45.
2b. —— xii. 16.
1. —— xiii. 12.

ASTONISHED MAKE.

2. Luke xxiv. 22.

ASTONISHMENT.

ἔκστασις, *any* displacement *or* removal *from the proper place. Metaph. of the mind*, distraction, astonishment, entrancement.

Mark v. 42.

ASTRAY (GO, WENT, etc.)

πλανάομαι, to wander, roam about. *Metaph.* to be misled, to err, be mistaken.

Matt. xviii. 12 twice, 13. 1 Pet. ii. 25.
2 Pet. ii 15.

ASUNDER.

See, BURST, CUT, DEPART, DIVIDING, PLUCK, PUT, SAW.

AT.

1. *ἐν*, in, *of time, place, or element;* among.
2. *ἐπί*, *(superposition)* upon.
   - (a) *with Gen.* upon, *(as springing from)* over, in the presence *or* time of.
   - (b) *with Dat.* upon, *(as resting on)* in addition to, on account of.
   - (c) *with Acc.* up to, *(of place, number, aim);* over, *(of time, place, extent.)*
3. *εἰς*, *(motion to the interior)* into, to, unto, with a view to, *(opp. of No.11.)*
4. *παρά*, *(juxtaposition)* beside.
   - (a) *with Gen.* beside *and proceeding* from, *(used of persons as No.6 is of places.)*
   - (b) *with Dat.* beside *and* at; near, with, *(of persons only, except* John xix. 25.*)*
   - (c) *with Acc. (to or along the side of)* beside, compared with, *i.e. so as to be shown contrary or superior to.*
5. *πρός*, *(in the direction of)* towards.
   - (a) *with Gen.* hitherwards, *(whence)* in favour of, *(occ.* Acts xxvii. 34.*)*
   - (b) *with Dat. (resting in a direction towards)* at, close by.
   - (c) *with Acc.* hitherwards, *(whither)* towards, in reference to.
6. *ἀπό*, *(motion from the exterior)* from, away from.
7. *κατά*, down.
   - (a) *with Gen. (down from)* against.
   - (b) *with Acc. (down towards)* according to, throughout; *in reference to time*, at *or* in, *i.e.* at the period of, correspondent with, *etc.*
8. *περί*, around.
   - (a) *with Gen. (around and separate from)* about, concerning.
   - (b) *with Acc. (around and towards)* around, about, *(of time, or any object of thought.)*
9. *διά*, through, *(from the notion of separation, disjunction.)*
   - (a) *with Gen. (through as proceeding from)* through, by means of, *(denoting instrument of an action.)*
   - (b) *with Acc. (through, as tending towards)* on account of, *(denoting ground of the action.)*
10. *ἐκ*, from, out of, *(motion from the interior, opp. of No.* 3.*)*
11. *ἔμπροσθεν*, *of place*, before, in front; *of time*, before, earlier, *etc.*

9a. Matt. vii. 18.
2b. ——— 28.
1. —— viii. 6.
2c. —— ix. 9.
1. —— xi. 22, 25.
1. —— xii. 1.
8. ———— 41.
1. —— xiii. 49.
1. —— xiv. 1.
4c —— xv. 30.
1. —— xviii. 1.
8. ———— 29 (*om.* G L [Tr ℵ.)
6. —— xix. 4.
2b. Matt. xxii. 33.
1. —— xxiii. 6.
2b. —— xxiv. 33.
1. ———— 41.
5c —— xxvi. 18 2nd.
7b. —— xxvii. 15.
2b. Mark i. 22.
5c. ———— 33.
5c. —— v. 22.
1. —— vi. 3.
5c. —— vii. 25.
2b. —— x. 22, 24.
5c. —— xi. 1.

2b. Mark xi. 18.
2b. —— xii 17.
1. ——— 39.
2b. ——xiii. 20.
5c. —— xiv. 54.
7b. —— xv 6.
2b. Luke i. 14.
2b. ——— 29 (om G∾.)
8a. —— ii. 8.
2b. ——— 33, 47.
1 —— iv. 18.
2b. ——— 22, 32.
2b. —— v. 5, 9.
2c. ——— 27.
4c. —— vii 38.
3. —— viii 26.
4c. ——— 35, 41.
1. —— ix. 31.
2b. ——— 43 twice.
3. ——— 61 2nd.
1 —— x. 14.
7b. ——— 32.
4c. ——— 39 (No. 5c, Lm T Tr A ℵ)
3. —— xi 32.
1. —— xii. 46.
1. —— xiii. 1.
8a ——— 24.
1. —— xiv. 14.
5c —— xvi. 20.
4c. —— xvii. 16.
1. —— xix 5.
5c. ——— 29.
5b. ——— 37.
1. —— xx om L T Tr A ℵ)
2b. ——— 26.
2a. ——— 37.
1. ——— 46.
2c. —— xxii. 30, 40.
1. —— xxiii. 7 twice, 12.
7b. ——— 17 (ap.)
2c. —— xxiv. 22.
6. ——— 27, 47.
1. John iv. 21, 45 twice 46.
1. ——— 53 (om. Trb ℵ)
7b —— v. 4 (ap.)
2a. —— vi 21
1 ——— 39 (om Tr A)
8a. ——— 41, 61.
1. —— vii. 11.
3 ——— 26.
1. ——— 29
2b. —— viii. 7 (ap.)
6. ——— 9 (ap.)
2c ——— 59.
1. —— x. 22.
1. —— xi 24
3 ——— 32.
1. —— xii. 20.
1. —— xiv 20.
10. —— xvi. 4
1 ——— 26.
5b. —— xviii. 16.
1. ——— 39.
5b —— xx. 11 (No. 5b, G L T Tr A) (No. 1, ℵ)
5b. ——— 12 twice.
3. ——— 14 15
2a. —— xxi 1.
1. ——— 20.
1. Acts i. 6.
1. —— ii. 5.
2b. —— iii 1.
5c ——— 2
2b. ——— 10 twice, 12
3. —— iv. 6 (No. 1, G∾L T Tr A)
4c. ———39, 37.
4c. ——v. 2.
2b. ———9.
4c. ———10 (No. 5c. L T Tr. A ℵ.)

1. Acts vii. 13, 29.
4c. ——— 58.
1. —— viii. 1, 14.
6. ——— 35.
3 ——— 40.
1. —— ix. 10, 13. 19 23, 27.
1. ——— 28 [εἰς, into, G∾L T Tr A ℵ)
1 ——— 36.
2c. —— x 25.
1. —— xi. 15
1. —— xiii. 1 5.
2b. ——— 12.
1. ——— 27.
1 —— xiv. 8.
1. —— xvi. 2, 4.
7b. ——— 25.
1. —— xvii. 13, 16.
3. —— xviii. 22.
1. —— xix. 5.
1 ——— 14.
1. ——— 15 1st (ap.)
3 ——— 15 2nd, 16.
3 —— xxi. 3.
1 ——— 11.
3 ——— 13.
4c. —— xxii. 3.
3 —— xxiii 11.
6 ——— 23.
1. —— xxv. 4 (εἰς into, G∾L T Tr A ℵ.)
2a. ——— 10
3. ——— 15.
1 ——— 24.
6 —— xxvi 4 1st.
1. ——— 4 2nd.
3. —— xxvii. 3.
3. —— xxviii. 12.
1. Rom. i. 15.
3. —— iv. 20.
1. —— viii. 34.
7b. —— ix. 9.
1. —— xi. 5.
1. —— xv. 26.
1. —— xvi. 1.
1. 1 Cor. i. 2.
1. —— xi. 34.
2b. —— xiv. 16.
1 ——— 35.
1. —— xv 23, 32, 52.
1. —— xvi. 8.
1. 2 Cor. i. 1.
1. —— vii. 14
1. Eph i 1 (om ἐν Ἐφέσῳ, in Ephesus, Tb Ab ℵ.)
1. —— ii. 12 (om. G∾L T
1 —— ii. 13. [Tr A ℵ.)
1. Phil. i. 1.
1. —— ii. 10.
1. Col i. 2
1. —— ii. 1.
1 1 Thes. ii. 2. 19.
1. —— iii. 1. 13.
1. 1 Tim. i. 3.
1. 2 Tim. i. 18
3. —— ii. 26.
1. —— iii. 11 3 times.
7b —— iv. 1 (καί, both [by], G∾L T Tr A ℵ.)
1 ——— 8 13 16. 20 twice.
1 Heb xii. 2.
10. Jas iii 11.
1. 1 Pet. i. 7, 13.
3 —— iv. 17 twice.
1. —— v. 13.
1. 1 John ii 28.
5c Rev. i. 17.
2c. —— iii. 20.
2c. —— viii 3 (No. 2a, G∾ T Tr A ℵ.)
10. —— xix 2.
11. ——— 10.
2b —— xxi 12 (ap.)

See, ALL, ANY, ATTENDANCE, BEGINNING, CHARGES, COME, DEATH, DWELL, DWELLER, FALL, FIRST, HAND, HOME, LAST, LAW, LEAST, LENGTH, LOOK, MARVEL, MOST, NOT, NOUGHT, ONCE, ONE, PIETY, SET, SIT, STRAIN, STUMBLE, TIME, WAIT, WINK, WONDER.

ATHIRST (AND BE.)

διψάω, to thirst; *and of the ground* to be dry, parched; *fig.* to desire ardently.

Matt. xxv. 44 | Rev. xxi. 6. | Rev. xxii. 17.

ATONEMENT.

καταλλαγή, the exchange effected; *then* the reconciliation, *(for which* διαλλαγή *and* συναλλαγή *are generally used.)* *"It denotes the* result *of the divine salvation, i.e. the new moulding of the relation in which the world stands to God, so far as it no longer remains the object of His wrath,"—Cremer. (Occ.* Rom. xi. 15; 2 Cor. v. 18, 19.)

Rom. v. 11.

ATTAIN.

1. λαμβάνω, to take, take hold of, apprehend.
2. καταλαμβάνω, to seize upon, lay hold of, apprehend.
3. φθάνω, to come *or* do before *another*, to be beforehand with, *to* overtake, outstrip; to come first.
4. καταντάω, to come, arrive; to result, happen.
5. παρακολουθέω, to accompany beside *or* near, follow close *or* on the heels; *metaph.* to follow close with one's thoughts, *i.e.* to understand.

4. Acts xxvii. 12.
— Rom. ix. 30, see A to.
3. ——— 31.
4. Phil. iii. 11.
1. ——— 12. (ready.)
— ——— 16, see A (already.)
5. 1 Tim. iv. 6.

ATTAIN ALREADY.

3. Phil. iii. 16 (aorist.)

ATTAIN TO.

2. Rom. ix. 30.

(In other cases the word "TO" is represented by another Greek word.)

ATTEND.

εὐπρόσεδρος, one who constantly sits to *or* applies to *anything*.

1 Cor. vii. 35 (εὐπάρεδρος, same sense, All.)

ATTEND CONTINUALLY UPON.

προσκαρτερέω, to persist in *a thing*, apply diligently *to it;* persevere.

Rom. xiii. 6.

ATTEND UNTO.

προσέχω, to hold to, bring to *or* near; to turn one's mind, thoughts, attention *to a thing;* to attach one's self *to a thing*, cleave unto *it*.

Acts xvi. 14.

ATTENDANCE AT (GIVE.)*
ATTENDANCE TO (GIVE.)†

προσέχω, *see* "ATTEND UNTO."

†1 Tim. iv. 13. | * Heb. vii. 13.

ATTENTIVE (BE VERY.)

ἐκκρέμαμαι, to hang from, be suspended; to depend upon *(non. occ.)*

Luke xix. 48, margin *hang on*.

AUDIENCE.

ἀκοή, hearing; the sense of hearing, *and so* the ear; a hearing, listening to; the thing heard, report, saying, fame.

Luke vii. 1.

AUDIENCE (GIVE.)

ἀκούω, to hear, give ear, listen.

Acts xiii. 16. | Acts xv. 12. | Acts xxii. 22.

AUDIENCE OF (IN THE.)

ἀκούω, *see above.*

Luke xx. 45.

AUGHT *or* OUGHT.

1. τις, any *one or thing*.
2. οὐδείς, not one, nothing.

1. Matt. v. 23.
1. —— xxi. 3.
2. Mark vii. 12 (with another negative.)
1. Acts iv. 32.
1. —— xxviii. 19.
1. Philem. 18.

AUGHT IF.

{ εἴ, if,
{ τις, any *one or thing*.

Mark viii. 23. | Mark xi. 25. | Acts xxiv. 19.

AUGHT TO EAT.

φαγεῖν, to eat.

John iv. 33.

AUGUSTUS'.

Σεβαστός, reverenced, venerable; *the imperial name* Augustus *was rendered by this word.*

Acts xxvii. 1.

AUSTERE.

αὐστηρός, making the tongue dry *and* rough, harsh; *metaph.* harsh, crabbed.

Luke xix. 21, 22.

AUTHOR.

1. αἴτιος, causing, occasioning, *with art.* the originator.
2. ἀρχηγός, beginning, originating, *with art.* the leader, founder, princely-leader.

2. Acts iii. 15, margin.
1. Heb. v. 9.
2. Heb. xii. 2, margin *beginner*.

AUTHORITY.

1. ἐξουσία, power *(delegated)*, authority *to do anything;* permission, license.
2. ἐπιταγή, injunction, command.
3. ὑπεροχή, a projecting *or* standing forth, a projection, prominent; *metaph.* a surpassing, superiority, power, dignity.

1. Matt. vii. 29.
1. —— viii. 9.
1. —— xxi. 23 twice, 24, 27.
1. Mark i. 22, 27.
1. —— xi. 28 twice, 29, 33.
1. —— xiii 34.
1. Luke iv. 36.
1. —— vii. 8.
1. —— ix. 1.
1. —— xix. 17.
1. Luke xx. 2 twice, *8, 20.
1. John v. 27.
1. Acts ix. 14.
1. —— xxvi. 10, 12.
1. 1 Cor. xv. 24.
1. 2 Cor. x. 8.
3. 1 Tim. ii. 2, margin *eminent place.*
2. Titus ii. 15.
1. 1 Pet. iii. 22.
1. Rev. xiii. 2.

AUTHORITY UPON (EXERCISE.)

1. ἐξουσιάζω, to use authority, to have authority over *any one or thing.*

2. *κατεξουσιάζω*, to exercise *or* use excessive *or* arbitrary authority.

2. Matt. xx. 25. | 2. Mark x. 42. 1. Luke xxii. 25.

AUTHORITY (OF GREAT.)

δυνάστης, a lord, master, ruler.

Acts viii. 27.

AUTHORITY (USE) [margin.]

{ *ἐν*, in.
βάρει, the pressure of a weight.
εἶναι, to be.

1 Thes. ii. 6 (text, *be burdensome.*)

AUTHORITY OVER (USURP.)

αὐθεντέω, to use or exercise power over, to domineer, *(from αὐθέντης*, one acting by his own authority; *in Old Greek, a* self-murderer.

1 Tim. ii. 12.

AVAIL (-ETH.)

ἰσχύω, to be strong *in body;* to be mighty, powerful; to prevail.

Gal. v. 6. | Gal. vi. 15 (*εἰμί, is*, All.) | Jas. v. 16.

AVENGE.

1. *ἐκδικέω*, to avenge, revenge, punish.

2. { *ποιέω*, to make, to do.
ἐκδίκησις, a revenging, vengeance.

3. { *κρίνω*, to divide, to separate, *hence*, to select. *Then* to come to a decision, to judge,
κρίμα, *(the result or issue of κρίνω)*, the decision arrived at, decrees, determinate judgment, } to judge judgment.

1. Luke xviii. 3, 5.
2. —— 7, 8.
2. Acts vii. 24.
1. Rom. xii. 19.
1. Rev. vi. 10.
3. —— xviii. 20.
1. Rev. xix. 2.

AVENGER.

ἔκδικος, carrying out *or* maintaining the right, avenging, *with art.* an avenger, *occ.* Rom. xiii. 4.

1 Thes. iv. 6.

AVOID (-ING.)

1. *διά*, through, *(from the notion of separation, disjunction.)*

(a) *with Gen.* (through, *as proceeding from)* through, by means of, *(denoting the instrument of the action.)*

(b) *with Acc.* (through, *as tending towards)* on account of, *(denoting the ground of the action.)*

2. *ἐκκλίνω*, to bend out of *the regular line*, bent outwards *or* away; to turn away from, shun.

3. *ἐκτρέπομαι*, *(in Mid. as here)*, to turn off *or* aside, to get out of the way, avoid.

4. *παραιτέομαι*, to beg of *or* from *another;* to obtain by prayer; to avert by entreaty, deprecate; to decline, beg to be excused.

5. *περιΐστημι*, (a) *trans.* to put, place, set, lay, round *a thing, etc.*

(b) *Pass., Mid., and intrans.*, to stand round about; *to step* aside out of the way, shun, beware of.

6. *στέλλω*, to set, place, *esp.* to set in order, arrange, get ready, *then* (a) *Mid.* to put on, arrange *as robes;* (b) *Pass.* to fit one's self out, get ready.

2. Rom. xvi. 17.
1b. 1 Cor. vii. 2 (italics.)
6a. 2 Cor. viii. 20.
3. 1 Tim. vi. 20.
4. 2 Tim. ii. 23.
5b. Titus iii. 9.

AWAIT (LAYING.)

ἐπιβουλή, a plan against *another*, a plot.

Acts ix. 24.

AWAKE (BE.)

διαγρηγορέω, to awake thoroughly.

Luke ix. 32.

AWAKE (-ING.)

1. *ἐγείρω*, (a) *Active*, to awaken, wake up, rouse, stir; (b) *Pass.* to wake, rouse, stir *one's self.*

2. *διεγείρω*, to wake quite up.

3. ἐκνήφω, to awake sober, out of a drunken sleep, *applied spiritually in N.T.*

1a. Matt. viii. 25.
2. Mark iv. 38 (No. 1, Tr [A ℵ.)
3. Luke viii. 24.
1b. Rom. xiii. 11.
3. 1 Cor. xv. 34.
1b. Eph. v. 14 (No. 1a, All)

AWAKE OUT OF SLEEP.

1. ἐξυπνίζω, to rouse another out of sleep.
2. { γίνομαι, to become. ἔξυπνος, roused out of sleep.

1. John xi. 11. | 2. Acts xvi. 27.

AWARE (BE.)

1. γινώσκω, to perceive, observe, obtain a knowledge of, *hence*, to know, be acquainted with, *(as contrasted with No. 2, which denotes I learn, and expresses subjective knowledge.)*
2. οἶδα, *(perf. of obs. root* εἴδω), I have seen, *implies knowledge from without, (obj.)* to have knowledge of, *(No. 2 denotes* not to forget, *No.* 1, to notice.)

2. Luke xi. 44. | 1. Luke xii. 46.

AWARE OF (BE.)

1. Matt. xxiv. 50,

AWAY.

1. ἔξω, without, on the outside, out of doors.
2. ἔα, *imper. of* ἐάω, to let, suffer, permit.

1. Matt. xiii. 48.
2. Luke iv. 34 margin (text, *let alone.*)

AWAY WITH.

αἴρω, to seize, lift up, take away, *imp.* αἶρε, αἶρον,—away with, *i.e. to execution.*

Luke xxiii. 18.
John xix. 15 twice.
Acts xxi. 36.
—— xxii. 22.

See also, CARRY, CARRYING, CAST, CASTING, CATCH, CONVEY, DO, DONE, DRAW, FADE, FADETH, FALL, FALLING, FLEE, FLOOD, GO, LEAD, MOVE, PASS, PINE, PUT, PUTTING, ROLL, SAIL, SEND, TAKE, TAKEN, THRUST, TURN, UNTAKEN, VANISH, WASH, WEAR, WIPE, WITHER.

AXE.

ἀξίνη, an axe, *(from* ἄγω, *fut.* ἄξω, to break.)

Matt. iii. 10. | Luke iii. 9.

B

BABBLER.

σπερμολόγος, *(from* σπέρμα, a seed, *and* λέλογα, *perf. mid. of* λέγω, a small bird, *so called from picking up seeds. Applied by Athenians to idle fellows who lived on* collecting the refuse *of the market-places, hence, because these were talkative and noisy, applied to* babbling, chattering fellows.

Acts xvii. 18, margin *base fellow.*

BABE.

1. βρέφος, a child while yet in the womb (ἔμβρυον), the new-born babe.
2. νήπιος, a babe *without the power of speech*, an infant, a minor.

2. Matt. xi. 25.
2. —— xxi. 16.
1. Luke i. 41, 44.
1. —— ii. 12, 16.
2. Luke x. 21.
2. Rom. ii. 20.
2. 1 Cor. iii. 1.
2. Heb. v. 13.
1. 1 Pet. ii. 2.

BACK [noun.]

νῶτος, the back *of a man.*

Rom. xi. 10 (non occ.)

BACK [adv.]

ὀπίσω, *of place,* behind, backwards ; *of time,* hereafter, *since the future is uncertain, and therefore* behind *us.*

Matt. xxiv. 18.

See also, DRAW, DRIVE, FRAUD, KEEP, RETURN, ROLL, TURN.

BACKBITER.

κατάλαλος, a speaker against *another*, a detractor.

Rom. i. 30.

BACKBITING

καταλαλία, a speaking against, open evil speaking *as opposed to* ψιθυρισμός, *see* "WHISPER."

2 Cor. xii. 20.

BACKSIDE (ON THE.)

ὄπισθεν, *of place*, behind, at the back; *of time*, after, in future, hereafter.

Rev. v. 1 (ἔξωθεν, *the outside*, G ∾.)

BACKWARD.

{ εἰς, unto, ὁ, the, ὀπίσω, behind, } εἰς τὰ ὀπίσω, backward.

John xviii. 6.

BAD.

1. κακός, bad, (*opp. to* ἀγαθός, good.) *It expresses the lack of those qualities which constitute a person or thing what it claims to be.* Incapable, useless, bad, *generically, including every form of evil, physical and moral.*
2. πονηρός, (*connected with* πόνος, labour, pains), troublesome, bad, evil. *It expresses the more active form of evil,* malignant, *and describes the quality according to its nature, as No.* 1 *does according to its effects.*
3. σαπρός, bad, *in the sense of* putrid, rotten, (*from* σήπω, to rot.)

3. Matt. xiii. 48. | 2. Matt. xxii. 10.
1. 2 Cor. v. 10 (φαῦλος *worthless*, G ∾ T Tr ℵ.)

BAG.

1. γλωσσόκομον, a case to keep the tongues of wind instruments in, *then used for any small* case, purse *or* bag.
2. βαλάντιον, (βαλλάντιον, L T Tr A ℵ) a bag *or* purse, *into which money or other valuables are* cast *or* put, (*from* βάλλω, to cast.)

2. Luke xii. 33. | 1. John xii. 6.
1. John xiii. 29.

BALANCES (PAIR OF.)

ζυγός, any thing that joins two *bodies*; the yoke *or* cross-bar *tied to the end of the pole, and having collars at each end for the animals, then the* beams of a balance, *etc.*

Rev. vi. 5.

BAND [noun.]

1. σπεῖρα, any thing round, wrapped round *or* upon a thing, a twisted rope, a body of men-at-arms, *used to translate the Roman* manipulus—2 centuries, *also a larger body*, a cohort.
2. δεσμός, a band, bound, fetter, any thing for tying *or* fastening.
   (a) *in pl.*, bonds, imprisonment.
3. ζευκτηρία, fit for *or* belonging to joining, yoking, *etc.*
4. σύνδεσμος, that which binds together, a band *or* bond, that which is bound together, a bundle.

1. Matt. xxvii. 27.
1. Mark xv. 16.
2a. Luke viii. 29.
1. John xviii. 12.
1. Acts x. 1 1st.
2a. Acts xvi. 26.
1. —— xxi. 31.
2. —— xxii. 30 (*om.* All.)
1. —— xxvii. 1.
3. —— 40.
4. Col. ii. 19.

BAND OF MEN.

1. John xviii. 3.

BAND (Italian.)

Ἰταλικός, Italian.

Acts x. 1 2nd (italics.)

BAND TOGETHER.

{ ποιέω, to make, to do. συστροφή, a rolling up together, *then* any dense mass, *a body of* men, a crowd, a seditious meeting. }

Acts xxiii. 12.

BANK.

τράπεζα, a table, *esp.* a dining table, *then* a money changer's table *or* counter, a bank.

Luke xix. 23.

BANQUETING.

πότος, a drinking, *esp.* a drinking bout, carousal, *(non. occ.)*

1 Pet. iv. 3.

BAPTISM.

1. βάπτισμα, an immersion *or* washing with water, *(washing unto purification from sin), used in N.T. for the rite of* baptism.

2. βαπτισμός, the washing. *It denotes the act as a fact, as No.* 1 *does the result of the act.*

1. Matt. iii. 7.
1. —— xx. 22 (*ap.*), 23 (*ap.*)
1. —— xxi. 25.
1. Mark i. 4.
1. —— x. 38, 39.
1. —— xi. 30.
1. Luke iii. 3.
1. —— vii. 29.
1. —— xii. 50.
1. —— xx. 4.
1. Acts i. 22.
1. —— x. 37.
1. —— xiii. 24.
1. —— xviii. 25.
1. —— xix. 3, 4.
1. Rom. vi. 4.
1. Eph. iv. 5.
1. Col. ii. 12 (No. 2, Lm.)
2. Heb. vi. 2.
1. 1 Pet. iii. 21.

BAPTIST.

1. βαπτιστής, the Baptist, *the name of John suggested by the function committed to and exercised by him.*

2. βαπτίζω, to immerse, baptize. *(See below.)*

(a) *part. with article denotes* he who baptizes.

1. Matt. iii. 1.
1. —— xi. 11, 12.
1. —— xiv. 2, 8.
1. —— xvi. 14.
1. —— xvii. 13.
2a. Mark vi. 14. [A ℵ.)
1. ——— 24 (No. 2, T Tr
1. Mark vi. 25.
1. —— viii. 28.
1. Luke vii. 20.
1. ——— 28 (*om.* G→ T Tr A ℵ.)
1. ——— 33.
1. —— ix. 19.

BAPTIZE.

βαπτίζω, *(in form a frequentative or factitive of* βάπτω, dip *or* dye.) βαπτίζω *to make a thing* dipped *or dyed.* To immerse *for a religious purpose, may be traced back to the Levitical washings, see* Lev. xiv. 8, 9; *etc., (out of which arose the baptism of proselytes), which were connected with the purification which followed on and completed the expiation from sin. What was unusual in John's baptism was, that he performed the* βαπτίζειν *on others, whereas under the law each one accomplished it for himself. Baptism of John was the Baptism of repentance, see* Mark i. 4; Luke iii. 3; Acts xiii. 24; xix. 4, *and Christian Baptism is Baptism of Faith, see* Acts xix. 4, 5. *The difference lies not in the Baptism, but in the relation thereof to Jesus Christ. By Baptism therefore we must understand* an immersion, whose design *like that of the Levitical washings and purifications was united with the washing away of sin. (See "Cremer.")*

Matt. iii. 6, 11 twice, 13, 14, 16. [23 twice (*ap.*)
—— xx. 22 twice (*ap.*),
—— xxviii. 19.
Mark i. 4, 5, 8 twice, 9.
—— x. 38 twice, 39 twice.
—— xvi. 16 (*ap.*)
Luke iii. 7, 12, 16 twice, [21 twice.
—— vii. 29, 30.
—— xii. 50. [33 twice.
John i. 25, 26, 28, 31,
—— iii. 22, 23 twice, 26.
—— iv. 1, 2.
—— x. 40.
Acts i. 5 twice.
—— ii. 38, 41.
—— viii. 12, 13, 16, 38.
—— ix. 18.
—— x. 47, 48.
—— xi. 16 twice.
—— xvi. 15, 33.
—— xviii. 8.
—— xix. 3, 4, 5.
Rom. vi. 3 twice.
1 Cor. i. 13, 14, 15, 16 twice, [17.
—— xii. 13.
—— xv. 29 twice.
Gal. iii. 27.

BAPTIZED (BE.)

Mid. and pass. aor. of above.

Acts xxii. 16. | 1 Cor. x. 2.

BAR.

βάρ, *Heb.* בַּר, a son, *see* Mark x. 46; John i. 42; xxi. 15, 16, 17; Acts xiii. 6.

Matt. xvi. 17 (joined with Ἰωνᾶ, *Jonas*, by L T A.)

BARBARIAN.

βάρβαρος, a man who speaks a foreign *or* strange language. Barbarous, *i.e.*, not Greek, strange to Greek manners and language. *The Egyptians had a like term for all foreigners as the Chinese and Hebrews have now. After the Persian war, the word took the contemptuous sense of* outlandish, brutal, rude. *The Romans even called themselves Barbarians, until the Greek language and literature became naturalized at Rome (prob. an onomatopoetic to express the sound of a foreign tongue.)*

Acts xxviii. 4.
Rom. i. 14,
1 Cor. xiv. 11 twice.
Col. iii. 11.

BARBAROUS.

βάρβαρος, *see* "BARBARIAN."

Acts xxviii. 2.

BARE.

γυμνός, naked.

1 Cor. xv. 37.

BARLEY [noun.]

κριθή, barley.

Rev. vi. 6.

BARLEY [adj.]

κρίθινος, made of *or* from barley.

John vi. 9, 13.

BARN.

ἀποθήκη, any place wherein to lay up *a thing*, a storehouse.

Matt. vi. 26. | Matt. xiii. 30. | Luke xii. 18, 24.

BARNABAS.

Βαρνάβας, son of consolation, *surname of Joses, a Levite of Cyprus.*

In all places, except

Acts xi. 25 (*om.* G⇶ L T Tr A ℵ.)

BARREN.

1. ἀργός, not working, *esp.* not working the ground, living without labour, *hence*, idle; *of money, etc.*, lying idle, yielding no return.
2. στεῖρος, barren, not bearing children.

2. Luke i. 7, 36.
2. —— xxiii. 29.
2. Gal. iv. 27.
1. 2 Pet. i. 8.

BASE.

ταπεινός, low, *of place*, lying low, *of condition*, brought down, humbled, lowly, *of style*, low, poor.

2 Cor. x. 1.

BASE FELLOW [margin.]

See "BABBLER."

BASE THINGS.

ἀγενής, unborn, uncreated, *of* no family, low born; *hence*, low, vile.

1 Cor. i. 28.

BASER SORT (OF THE.)

ἀγοραῖος, loose fellows spending their time idly in the market place.

Acts xvii. 5.

BASKET.

1. κόφινος, a wicker basket, the Jewish travelling basket, *(prop. of a certain measure or capacity.)*
2. σπυρίς, a basket of a larger kind, a large hamper, *(used for storage, and capacious enough to contain a man.)*
3. σαργάνη, a twisted rope, a rope basket, a wicker basket *made of twigs* entwined *with each other.*

1. Matt. xiv. 20.
2. —— xv. 37.
1. —— xvi. 9.
2. ———— 10.
1. Mark vi. 43.
2. —— viii. 8.
1. Mark viii. 19.
2. ———— 20.
1. Luke ix. 17.
1. John vi. 13.
2. Acts ix. 25.
3. 2 Cor. xi. 33.

BASON *or* BASIN.

νιπτήρ, a large ewer *or* vessel *for washing the feet.*

John xiii. 5.

BASTARD.

νόθος, a bastard, *(non. occ.)*

Heb. xii. 8.

BATTLE.

πόλεμος, a battle, a fight.

1 Cor. xiv. 8; Rev. ix. 7, 9; xvi. 14; xx. 8.

BE.

IT MAY BE, LET BE, MAY BE, MIGHT BE, SHALL BE, SHOULD BE, THAT MAY BE, THAT MIGHT BE, THAT SHOULD BE, THAT WOULD BE, THOUGH...BE, TO BE, WILL BE.

When this word is in italics, there is no corresponding word in the Greek.

Sometimes it is only part of another verb, or of a phrase for which there is no exact equivalent.

When it is an independent word, it is the translation of one of these following.

1. εἰμί, I am, *the ordinary state of existence, (for the difference between this word and No. 2 see* Heb. xi. 6.)

Present:

(a) εἶ, thou art, (2 *pers. sing. pres. ind.)* * *with pron.* συ, thou.

(b) ἐστί *or* ἐστίν, he, she, it is, (3 *pers. sing. pres. ind.)*

(c) ἐσμεν, we are, (*1 pers. pl. pres. ind.*)

(d) ἐστέ, ye are, (*2 pers. pl. pres. ind.*)

(e) εἰσί, they are, (*3 pers. pl. pres. ind.*)

(f) *Subj.*, ὦ, I may be, ᾖς, thou may'st be, ᾖ, he, she, it, may be; ὦμεν, we may be, ἦτε, ye may be, ὦσιν, they may be.

(g) *Opt.*, εἴην, I might be, εἴης, thou might'st be, εἴη, he, she, it might be; εἴημεν, we might be, εἴητε, ye might be, εἴησαν, they might be.

(h) ἴσθι, be thou, (*2 pers. sing. imp*)

(i) ἔστω (*or* ἤτω), *and* ἔστωσαν, (*imp.*) be he *or* let him be, *and* be ye.

(k) εἶναι, to be, (*infin.*) * *with Acc. of the noun before it denotes* that...am is, was, were, *etc.* † *with* εἰς, unto, to, *and the art. denotes* with a view to, to the end that.

(l) ὤν οὖσα ὄν, being, (*part.*) * *with Acc. of noun before it denotes* that ...am, art, *etc.*, *or* who...am, art.

Imperfect:

(m) ἦν, he was, (*3 pers. sing.*)

(n) ἤμην, I was, (*1 pers. sing.*)

Future:

(o) ἔσομαι, (*indic.*) I shall be, ἔσῃ, thou shalt be, ἔσται, he shall be; ἐσόμεθα, we shall be, ἔσεσθε, ye shall be, ἔσονται, they shall be.

(p) ἔσεσθαι, (*inf.*) to be about to be, *then with* μέλλειν, to be about to do *anything; which, followed by an infin. as here,* to be about to *do a thing*, to be on the point of *doing it.*

(q) ἐσόμενος, (*part.*) about to be.

2. γίνομαι, *implying origin*, to come into being, to become, *or result*, to take place, happen.

3. ὑπάρχω, to begin, to start, to begin to be, (*referring to original state and continued existence.*)

4. φέρω, to bear.

(a) *pass.*, to be borne *or* carried from *a place.*

5. εἰς, (*motion to the interior*) into, to, unto, with a view to.

6. εἰ, if, since, though. τυγχάνω, to hit, *esp.* to hit a mark *with an arrow; then* to happen, be by chance.

7. τυχόν, by chance, perhaps, (*Acc. of the part. neut. aor. 2 of* τυγχάνω, *above.*)

1h. Matt. ii. 13, B thou.
1a. —— iv. 3, 6.
1o. —— v. 21, shall B, 22 3 times.
1i. —— 37, let be (ἔσται, *shall be*, L A.)
2. —— 45, may B,
1o. —— 48.
1f. —— vi. 4, may B.
1o. —— 5, will B.
2. —— 16, 21, shall B.
1f. —— 22 1st.
1o. —— 22 2nd, } shall
1f. —— 23 1st, } B
1o. —— 23 2nd, shall B.
1b. —— 23 3rd.
1e. —— vii. 13, 14.
1o. —— viii. 12, shall F.
2. —— ix. 29.
1f. —— x. 13 twice.
1o. —— 15, shall B.
2. —— 16.
1o. —— 22, shall B.
2. —— 25.
1o. —— xi. 22, 24, shall B.
1o. —— xii. 11, shall B (*om.* T Tr A.) [B.
1o. —— 27, 40, 45, shall
1o. —— xiii. 40, 42, 49, 50, shall B.
1a*. —— xiv. 28.
1e. —— xv. 14.
2. —— 28.
1o. —— xvi. 19 twice } shall
1o. —— 22, } B.
1e. —— 28.
1k. —— xvii. 4, to B.
1o. —— 17, shall B.
2. —— xviii. 13.
1i. —— 17, } shall
1o. —— 18 twice, } B.
1o. —— xix. 5, shall B.
1b. —— 10.
1e. —— 12.
1k. —— 21.
1o. —— 30, shall B.
1o. —— xx. 16 1st, shall B.
1e. —— 16 2nd.
1o. —— 26 1st, shall B (No. 1b, L Tr.)
2. —— 26 2nd.
1i. —— 26 3rd, let .. B (No. 1o, G ∾ L Tr ℵ.)
1k. —— 27 1st.
1i. —— 27 2nd, let .. B (No. 1o, G ∾ L Tr ℵ.)
1o. —— xxii. 13, 28, shall B.
1o. —— xxiii. 11, shall B.
2. —— 26, may B.
1o. —— xxiv. 3, 7, 9, shall
2. —— 20. [B.
1o. —— 21 1st, shall B.
2. —— 21 2nd, shall R.
1o. —— 27, 37, 39, 40,
2. —— 44. [shall B.
1o. —— 51, shall R.
1o. —— xxv. 30, shall B.
2. —— xxvi. 5.
1b. —— 39.
2. —— 54.
1a*. —— 63.
1a. —— xxvii. 40.
1b. —— 42.
1o. —— 64, shall B.
1f. Mark iii. 14, should B.
1f. —— v. 18, might B.
1h. Mark v. 34.
1o. —— vi. 11, (*ap.*) shall
1b. —— vii. 4. [B.
1e. —— ix. 1.
1k. —— 5, to B.
1o. —— 19, shall R.
1k. —— 35 1st, to B.
1o. —— 35 2nd, shall B.
1o. —— x. 8, 31, shall B.
1o. —— 43 1st (No. 1 b, L T Tr A ℵ.)
2. —— 43 2nd, will B.
1o. —— 43 3rd, shall B.
2. —— 44 1st (No. 1 k, L Tr A ℵ.)
1o. —— 44 2nd, shall B.
1o. —— xii. 7, 23, } shall
1o. —— xiii. 4. } B.
2. —— 7.
1o. —— 8 twice, shall B.
1o. —— 13, shall B.
2. —— 18.
1o. —— 19 1st.
2. —— 19 2nd.
1o. —— xiv. 2.
1k. —— 64, to B.
1o. Luke i. 15, 20, shall B.
1g. —— 29, should B.
1o. —— 32, 33, 34, shall
2. —— 38. [B.
1o. —— 45, 66, } shall
1o. —— ii. 10, } B.
1k. —— 49.
— —— iii. 23, see B (be-
1a. —— iv. 3. [gan to)
1o. —— 7, shall B.
1a. —— 9. [B.
1o. —— vi. 35 twice, shall
2. —— 36.
1o. —— 40, shall B.
1g. —— viii. 9, might R.
1k*. —— 38 that..might
1e. —— ix. 27. [B.
1k. —— 33, to B.
1o. —— 41, shall B.
1g. —— 46, should B.
1o. —— 48, shall B (No. 1b, G ∾ L T Tr A ℵ.)
1f. —— x. 6.
1o. —— 12, 14, } shall
1o. —— xi. 19, 30, } B.
1b. —— 35.
1o. —— 36, } shall
1o. —— xii. 20, } B.
1o. —— 34, will B.
1i. —— 35, let .. B.
2. —— 40.
1o. —— 52, shall B.
1o. —— 55, will B.
1o. —— xiii. 28, 30 twice, shall B.
1f. —— xiv. 8.
1o. —— 14, shall B.
1k. —— 26, 27.
1b. —— 31.
1k. —— 33 2nd.
1o. —— xv. 7, shall R.
1o. —— xvii. 24, 26, 30, 31, 34, 35, shall B.
1o. —— 36 (*ap.*)
2. —— xix. 19.
2. —— xx. 14, may B (No. 1o, Lm.)
1o. —— xxi. 7, 11 twice, 17, shall B.
1e. —— 22 1st. [R.
1o. —— 23, 24, 25, shall

2. Luke xxii. 26, let..B.
2. —— xxiii. 24.
1b. —— 35.
1a*. —— 37, 39.
1o. —— 43, shall B.
1a*. John i. 25.
1f. —— iii. 2.
2. —— 9.
1f. —— 27.
2. —— iv. 14, } shall B.
1o. —— vi. 45, }
1k. —— vii. 4, to B.
1b. —— 17.
1c. —— viii. 33.
1o. —— 36, 55, shall B.
2. —— ix. 22, should B.
1b. —— 25.
2. —— 27.
1f. —— 31.
2. —— x. 16.
1a*. —— 24.
1o. —— xii. 26, shall B.
2. —— 36, may B.
2. —— 42, should B.
1g. —— xiii. 24 (*ap.*)
1f. —— xiv. 3, may B.
1o. —— 17, shall B (No. 1b, L Tr.)
2. —— xv. 8, shall B.
1f. —— xvi. 24, } may B.
1f. —— xvii. 11, }
1f. —— 19, might B.
1f. —— 21 twice, 22, 23, may B.
1f. —— 24.
1f. —— 26, may B.
1o. —— xix. 24, shall B.
2. —— xx. 27.
1o. Acts i. 8, shall B.
2. —— 20, let B.
— —— 22, see B ordained to be.
1i. —— ii. 14.
1i. —— iv. 10.
1b. —— 19
1k. —— v. 36.
1f. —— 38.
1b. —— 39.
1p. —— xi. 28, that there should B.
1o. —— xiii. 11, shall B.
5. —— 22.
1i. —— 38.
5. —— 47, to B.
1h*. —— 47 2nd, that.. should'st B.
1k. —— xvi. 15, to B.
1k. —— xvii. 18, to B.
3. —— 27.
1b. —— xviii. 15 1st
1k. —— 15 2nd, will B.
1e. —— xix. 26.
3. —— 36, to B.
2. —— xx. 16, to B.
1o. —— xxii. 15, shall B.
1p. —— xxiv. 15, that there shall B.
1e. —— xxvi. 3, to B.
2. —— 28, to B (ποιέω, *to make*, L Tr A ℵ.)
1p. —— xxvii. 10, that.. will B.
1o. —— 22 2nd, 25 2nd, shall B.
1i. —— xxviii. 28.
1i. Rom. i. 7.
1k. —— 22, to B.
1f. —— ii. 25.
2. —— iii. 4. [B.
1kt. —— 26, that might
1kt. —— iv. 11 1st, that might B.
1k*. —— 13, that should B. [B.
1kt. —— 16, that might
1o. —— 18, shall B.
1o. —— vi. 5, shall B.
1k. —— 11, to B.
1kt. Rom. viii. 29 2nd, that might B.
1f. —— ix. 27.
1f. —— xi. 25, should B.
2. —— xii. 16.
1k. —— xiv. 14, to B.
1kt. —— xv. 16, that.. should B.
2. —— 16, might B.
2. —— 31.
— —— xvi. 11, see "householder."
1f. 1 Cor. i. 10 twice.
1k. —— iii. 18, to B.
2. —— 18, may B.
2. —— iv. 16.
1f. —— v. 7, may B.
1f. —— 11 (ἤ, *or*, St.)
1o. —— vi. 16, shall B.
2. —— vii. 23.
1k. —— 25, 26, to B.
1f. —— 29.
1f. —— 34, may B.
1e. —— viii. 5 twice.
1. —— ix. 2.
1l. —— 19, though..B.
2. —— 23.
2. —— 27, should B.
2. —— x. 7.
2. —— xi. 1.
1k. —— 16, to B.
3. —— 18.
1k. —— 19.
1o. —— 27, shall B.
3. —— xii. 22, to B.
1k. —— 23, to B.
1f. —— 25, should B.
6. —— xiv. 10, it may B.
1o. —— 11, shall B.
2. —— 20 1st & 3rd.
1f. —— 28.
1k. —— 37.
1o. —— xv. 12, shall B.
1f. —— 28, may B.
2. —— 37, that shall B.
2. —— 58.
2. —— xvi. 2.
1f. —— 4.
7. —— 6, it may B.
2. —— 10, may B.
1i. —— 22, let..B.
1f. 2 Cor. i. 17, should B.
1d. —— ii. 9.
1d. —— iii. 3, to B (*ital.*) (ὅτι ἐστὲ, *that ye are.*)
1o. —— 8, shall B.
1f. —— iv. 7, may B.
1k*. —— v. 9, that..may B.
2. —— vi. 14.
1o. —— 16, will B.
1o. —— 16, shall B.
1o. —— 18, will B.
1o. —— 18, shall B.
1k. —— vii. 11, to B.
2. —— viii. 14, may B twice.
1f. —— ix. 3, may B
1k*. —— 5, that might B.
1o. —— xi. 15 2nd, shall B.
1o. —— xii. 6, shall B.
1d. —— xiii. 5 twice.
1f. —— 7.
1o. —— 11, shall B.
1e. Gal. i. 7.
1i. —— 8, 9, let B.
1n. —— 10.
1k. —— ii. 6. 9, to B.
1l. —— iv. 1, though..B.
2. —— 12.
1k. —— 21.
1f. —— v. 10 2nd.
2. —— 26, let B.
1k. —— vi. 3, to B.
1k*. Eph. i. 4, } that
1kt. —— 12, } should B.
1k*. —— iii. 6, }
1f. —— iv. 14.
2. —— 32.
2. —— v. 1, 7, 17.
1f. Eph. v. 27, should B.
1o. —— 31 2nd, shall B.
2. —— vi. 3, } may B.
1f. Phil. i. 10, }
1k. —— 23, } to B.
1k. —— ii. 6. }
2. —— 15, may B (No. 1f, L.)
2. —— 17.
1f. —— 28.
2. —— iii. 21 (*ap.*)
1o. —— iv. 9, shall B.
1k. —— 11, to B.
2. Col. iii. 15.
2. 1 Thes. iii. 5.
1o. —— iv. 17, shall B.
1k. 1 Tim. i. 7, } to B.
1k. —— ii. 12, }
1k. —— iii. 2.
1i. —— 12, let B.
1o. —— iv. 6, shall B.
2. —— 12.
1f. —— v. 7, may B.
1o. 2 Tim. ii. 2, 21, shall B.
1k. —— 24.
1o. —— iii. 2, 9, shall B.
1f. —— 17, may B.
1k. Titus i. 7.
1f. —— 9, may B.
1k. —— ii. 2, that..B.
1k. —— iii. 1 2nd, 2, to B.
1f. —— 14.
1f. Philem. 14, should B.
1o. Heb. i. 5, will B.
1o. —— 5, shall B.
2. —— ii. 17, might B.
1k. —— v. 12, to B.
2. —— vi. 12.
1. —— viii. 4.
1o. —— 10, will B.
1o. —— 10, shall B.
1o. —— 12, will B.
4. —— ix. 16, marg. *be brought in.*
1d. —— xii. 8.
1k. —— 11.
1f. Jas. i. 4, may B.
1kt. —— 18, that should B.
1i. —— 19, let B.
2. —— 22.
1o. Jas. i. 25, shall B.
1k. —— 26, to B.
3. —— ii. 15.
2. —— iii. 1.
1l. —— 4, though..B.
2. —— 10.
1k. —— iv. 4.
1o. —— v. 3, shall B.
1i. —— 12, let B.
2. —— 15.
2. —— 16 (No. 1o, G∾ L T Tr A ℵ.)
1k. 1 Pet. i. 21, that might B (with ὥστε, *so that.*)
1i. —— iii. 3, let B.
2. —— 13.
2. 2 Pet. i. 4.
3. —— 8 1st, if..B (πάρειμι, *to be present*, L.)
1o. —— ii. 1, shall B.
3. —— iii. 11, to B.
1f. 1 John i. 4, may B.
1o. —— iii. 2, shall B twice.
1o. 2 John 2, shall B.
1o. —— 3.
1f. —— 12, may B.
2. 3 John 8, might B.
1o. Jude 18, should B (ἐλεύσονται, *shall come*, G∾.)
2. Rev. i. 19.
2. —— ii. 10 2nd.
2. —— iii. 2.
2. —— iv. 1.
1o. —— x. 6, should B.
1o. —— 9, shall B.
— —— xvi. 5 (with art.) which shalt B (no Greek authority whatever) (ὅσιος, *holy*, or *the holy one*, All.)
1o. —— xx. 6, shall B.
1o. —— xxi. 3 twice, 4 twice, shall B.
1o. —— 7, will B
1o. —— 7, 25, shall B.
1o. —— xxii. 3 twice, 4 twice, 5, shall B.
1o. —— 12, shall B (No. 1b, L T Tr A) (om. G→.)

BE ORDAINED TO BE

2. Acts i. 22.

BEAM.

δοκός, (*from* δέχομαι, to receive, *because in building, beams are* received *at their ends into other pieces of timber)* a beam *or* rafter. *In N.T. metaph.* a great fault *or* vice, *according to a Jewish proverb.*

Matt. vii. 3, 4, 5. | Luke vi. 41, 42 twice.

BEAR [noun.]

ἄρκτος, (ἄρκος, *All)* the bear *(non. occ.)*

Rev. xiii. 2.

BEAR [verb.]

(BARE, BORNE, BAREST, -ETH, -ING.)

1. βαστάζω, to lift, *(properly* a heavy burden), lift up, carry; carry off.

2. φέρω, to bear, *hence*, to produce *fruit*, to carry *as a burden;* to bear, endure, suffer *pain, etc.;* to sustain, support; to bring forward *(as charges.)*

3. ἀναφέρω, to bring *or* carry up; *hence*, to offer *sacrifices, i.e.* to bring *them* up *on the altar,* and hence again*, to bear *sins by imputation really, as those sacrifices did typically.*

4. ἐκφέρω, to bring *or* carry out of *or* away; *of the ground* to bring forth *or* produce.

5. ὑποφέρω, to bear up under; *hence*, to suffer,† endure.

6. αἴρω, to raise, lift up; *(applied to the mind)* to suspend, keep in suspense; carry, remove, take away.

7. ποιέω, to make, *i.e.* to form, bring about; *of trees, etc.*, to germinate, produce.

8. φορέω, *strictly implies a constant repetition of No.* 2, *and therefore signifies* to wear, *as well as* to bear; to bear about.

9. γεννάω, to beget, bring forth, bear; *gen.* generate, produce, occasion.

10. στέγω, to cover closely, *esp. so as to keep out wet; gen.* to keep off, fend off; to cover over, shelter, protect; *gen.* to sustain, support.

11. τίκτω, to bring into the world; *of the father*, to beget; *of the mother*, to bring forth.

12. τροφοφορέω, to bring one nourishment, sustain; *or*, to carry about like a nurse *(from* τροφός, a feeder *or* nurse, *and* φορέω, to carry about, *see No.* 8.)

*In Heb. the victim is called עולה (from עלה, *to ascend.*) In lxx., ἀναφορά, Ps. l. 20.

† Compare Lat. suffero. (sub, *under;* fero, *to bear*) and Eng. *suffer*.

1. Matt. iii. 11.
— —— iv. 6, see B up.
1. —— viii. 17.
1. —— xx. 12.
6. —— xxvii. 32.
6. Mark i. 3.
1. —— xiv. 13.
6 —— xv. 21.
9. Luke i. 13.
— —— iv. 11, see B up.
1. —— vii. 14.
7. —— viii. 8.
1. —— xi. 27.
7. —— xiii. 9.
1. Luke xiv. 27.
— —— xviii. 7, see B long.
1. —— xxii. 10.
2. —— xxiii. 26.
9. —— 29. *(take away.)*
6. John i. 29, marg. (text,
2. —— ii. 8 twice.
1. —— xii. 6.
2. —— xv. 2 twice, 4, 8.
1. —— xvi. 12.
1. —— xix. 17.
1. —— xx. 15.
1. Acts ix. 15.
12. Acts xiii. 18, marg. (G L T A) (text—τροποφορέω, *to bear with the manners of others*, Tr ℵ.)
1. —— xv. 10.
1 —— xxi. 35.
— —— xxvii. 15, see B up into.
1. Rom. xi. 18.
8. —— xiii. 4.
1. —— xv. 1.
5. 1 Cor. x. 13.
10. —— xiii. 7.
8. —— xv. 49 twice.
— 2 Cor. iv. 10, see B about.
— —— xi. 1 twice, 4, see B (with.
11. Gal. iv. 27.
1. —— v. 10.
1. —— vi. 2, 5, 17.
— Heb. v. 2, marg. see B (with.
4. —— vi. 8.
3. —— ix. 28.
2. —— xiii. 13.
7. Jas. iii. 12.
3. 1 Pet. ii. 24.
1. Rev. ii. 2, 3.
7. —— xxii. 2.

BEAR ABOUT.

περιφέρω, to carry round, to carry about *with one, hence*, to publish, make known

2 Cor. iv. 10.

BEAR LONG.

μακροθυμέω, to suffer long, to endure *or* wait patiently, *hence*, to delay.

Luke xviii. 7.

BEAR UP.

αἴρω, *see* "BEAR," *No.* 6.

Matt. iv. 6. | Luke iv. 11.

BEAR UP INTO.

ἀντοφθαλμέω, to direct the eye against *another who looks at one*, to look in the face; *app. to a ship*, to look the storm in the face, *as it were*, to bear up against it.

Acts xxvii. 15.

BEAR WITH.

ἀνέχομαι, to hold up *against a thing; hence*, to bear with.

2 Cor. xi. 1 twice. | 2 Cor. xi. 4.

BEAR WITH (reasonably) [margin.]

μετριοπαθέω, to moderate one's anger towards, to treat with mildness *or* moderation.

Heb. v. 2 (text, *have compassion on.*)

See, CHILDREN, FRUIT, HOSTILE, RECORD, WITNESS.

BEAST (-s.)

1. *θηρίον*, a wild beast, a beast of prey, *esp. such as are hunted;* a savage beast.

2. *ζῶον*, a living being, an animal, *on account of* life, *which is its main feature. The appearance of the four in Rev. represents the concentration of all created life in this world. They are distinct from the angels, and symbolical throughout the Scriptures of the future new creation (see, for further development, under "cherubim.")*

3. *κτῆνος*, property *in general; then,* property *in* herds *or* flocks; *hence,* a beast of burden, *and in pl.*, cattle, *for slaughter.*

— Mark i. 13, see B (wild.)
3. Luke x. 34.
— Acts x. 12 2nd, see B (wild.)
3. —— xxiii. 24.
— —— xxviii. 4, see B (venomous.)
1. ——— 5.
3. 1 Cor. xv. 39.
1. Titus i. 12.
1. Heb. xii. 20.
2. —— xiii. 11.
1. Jas. iii. 7.
2. 2 Pet. ii. 12.
2. Jude 10.
2. Rev. iv. 6, 7 4 times.
2. ——— 8, 9.
2. —— v. 6, 8, 11, 14.
2. Rev. vi. 1, 3, 5, 6, 7.
1. ——— 8.
2. —— vii. 11.
1. —— xi. 7.
1. —— xiii. 1, 2, 3, 4 3 times, 11, 12 twice, 14 twice, 15 3 times, 17, 18.
2. —— xiv. 3.
2. ——— 9, 11.
1. —— xv. 2.
2. ——— 7.
1. —— xvi. 2, 10, 13.
1. —— xvii. 3, 7, 8 twice, 11, 12, 13, 16, 17.
3. —— xviii. 13.
2. —— xix. 4.
1. ——— 19, 20 twice.
1. —— xx. 4, 10.

BEAST (VENOMOUS.)

1. Acts xxviii. 4.

BEAST (WILD.)

1. Mark i. 13.
1. Acts x. 12 2nd (*om.* G⇶ L T Tr A ℵ.)
1. Acts xi. 6.

See, FIGHT WITH, FOUR-FOOTED, SLAIN.

BEAT (-EN, -ETH, -ING.)

1. *δέρω*, to skin, flay *of animals; then (like the slang words* to tan *or* hide*)* to cudgel, thrash.

2. *τύπτω*, to strike, smite, beat, *strictly with a stick.*

3. *βάλλω*, to throw at *or* hit *with any kind of missile; strictly opposed to striking, (No. 2.) In a ment. sense,* to rush, *as a wind.*

4. *ῥαβδίζω*, to beat with a rod *or* stick, cudgel.

— Matt. vii. 25, 27, see B upon.
1. —— xxi. 35.
— Mark iv. 37, see B into.
1. —— xii. 3, 5.
1. —— xiii. 9.
— Luke vi. 48, see B vehemently upon.
— ——— 49, see B vehemently (against.)
2. —— xii. 45.
1. ——— 47, 48.
1. Luke xx. 10, 11.
1. Acts v. 40.
4. —— xvi. 22.
1. ——— 37.
2. —— xviii. 17.
2. —— xxi. 32.
1. —— xxii. 19
3. —— xxvii. 14, margin (text, *arise.*)
1. 1 Cor. ix. 26.
— 2 Cor. xi. 25, see B with rods.

BEAT INTO.

ἐπιβάλλω, to throw *or* cast upon.

Mark iv. 37 (with *εἰς*, *into.*)

BEAT UPON.

1. *προσκόπτω*, to strike against, *esp. with the foot; hence,* to stumble, *etc.*

2. *προσπίπτω*, to fall upon *or* before, to rush against.

2. Matt. vii. 25 (*προσπαίω*, same sense, Lm.)
1. ——— 27 (*προσρήγνυμι*, *to dash* or *break against* as a flood, Lm.)

BEAT VEHEMENTLY UPON.

προσρήγνυμι, to break *or* dash against *as a flood.*

Luke vi. 48.

BEAT VEHEMENTLY (AGAINST...)

προσρήγνυμι, *see above.*

Luke vi. 49.

BEAT WITH RODS.

ῥαβδίζω, *see* "BEAT," *No.* 4.

2 Cor. xi. 25.

BEAUTIFUL.

ὡραῖος, produced *or* ripened at the fit season, *(from ὥρα,* season *of the year),* seasonable *as used of ripe* fruits, *and as they are most beautiful when ripe, it comes to signify* beautiful.

Matt. xxiii. 27; Acts iii. 2, 10; Rom. x. 15.

BECAUSE.

1. *ὅτι*, that. *It points in general to some existing fact, something which lies*

before us, and hence answers to that *as well as* because. *In obj. sentences it is equivalent to Acc. with infin.; and as a particle of explanation* for that, seeing that, because.

2. διά, through.

(a) *with Gen.* through *as proceeding from*, by means of; *(denoting the instrument of an action.)*

(b) *with Acc.* through *as tending towards*, on account of; *(denoting the ground or reason of an action.)*

3. διότι, for this reason—that, wherefore, on this account.

4. καθότι, in what manner, so far as; inasmuch as.

5. ἐπεί, since, since if so, since if otherwise.

6. ἐπειδή, since truly, after that indeed, for truly.

7. γάρ, *(compounded of* γέ, verily, *and* ἄρα, therefore, *hence*, the fact is, in fact; *and when the fact is given as a reason or explanation*, for.

8. ἕνεκα, on account of, for the sake of; *originally signifying* to please *or* gratify one, as a favour to one, *and next used* of the motive *or* object of *a thing;* that which has brought on a consequence, *(with* οὗ, where, whither.)

9. ἵνα, *a final particle indicating purpose*, to the end that, in order that *(with the emphasis on the result.)*

10. ὅπως, *a final particle denoting not only end or purpose, but is also a simple conjunction (correlative to* πῶς how?) *denoting the way or manner.* In order that *(with the emphasis on the method.)*

11. { ἀντί, over against, *containing the notion of opposition; as an equivalent*, instead of for, in return for, ὧν, *neut. rel. pl.*, which things, } ἀνθ᾽ ὧν, in return for which things, *i.e.* because.

1. Matt. ii. 18.
1. —— v. 36.
1. —— vii. 14, marg. *how* (G∾) (τί, *why or how?* A Vm G L Tr.)
1. —— ix. 36
1. —— xi. 20, 25.
1. —— xii. 41.
2b. Matt. xiii. 5, 6.
1. ——— 11, 13.
— ——— 21, 58, see B of.
1. —— xiv. 5.
1. —— xv. 32.
1. —— xvi. 7, 8.
— —— xvii. 20, see B of.
5. —— xviii. 32.
1. Matt. xx. 7, 15.
9. ——— 31.
6. —— xxi. 46 (No. 5. Tr [A ℵ.)
1. —— xxiii. 29.
2b.—— xxiv. 12.
5. —— xxvii. 6.
— ——— 19, see B of.
1. Mark i. 34, marg. *that.*
— —— iii. 9, see B of.
1. ——— 30.
2b.—— iv. 5, 6.
1. ——— 29.
2b.—— v. 4.
— —— vi. 6, see B of.
1. ——— 34.
1. —— vii. 19.
1. —— viii. 2, 16, 17.
1. —— ix. 38 (*ap*), 41.
1. —— xi. 18 (No. 7, T Tr [A ℵ.)
5. —— xv. 42.
1. —— xvi. 14 (*ap.*)
11. Luke i. 20.
2b.—— ii. 4.
3. ——— 7.
8. —— iv. 18.
— —— v. 19, see B of.
2b.—— viii. 6.
1. ——— 30.
2b.—— ix. 7.
1. ——— 49, 53.
2b.—— xi. 8 1st.
— ——— 8 2nd, see B of.
1. ——— 18.
1. —— xii. 17.
1. —— xiii. 2, 14.
1. —— xv. 27.
1. —— xvi. 8.
1. —— xvii. 9.
2b.—— xviii. 5.
1. —— xix. 3.
2b.——— 11 1st.
1. ——— 11 2nd, 17, 21, 31.
11.——— 44.
2b.—— xxiii. 8.
1. John i. 50.
2b.—— ii. 24.
1. —— iii. 18.
7. ——— 19.
1. ——— 23.
— ——— 29, } see B
— —— iv. 41, 42, } of.
1. —— v. 16, 18, 27, 30.
1. —— vi. 2, 26 twice, 41.
1. —— vii. 1, 7, 22. 23, 30,
— ——— 43, see B of. [39.
1. —— viii. 22, 37, 43, 44,
1. —— ix. 16, 22. [45, 47.
1. —— x. 13, 17.
7. ——— 26.
1. ——— 33, 36.
1. —— xi. 9, 10.
— ——— 42, see B of.
1. —— xii. 6, 11.
— ——— 30, see B of.
1. ——— 39.
— ——— 42, see B of.
5. —— xiii. 29.
1. —— xiv. 12, 17, 19, 28.
1. —— xv. 19, 21, 27.
1. —— xvi. 3,4,6,9,10,11.
1. ——— 16 (*ap.*)
1. ——— 17, 21, 27, 32.
1. —— xvii. 14.
1. —— xix. 7.
5. ——— 31.
— ——— 42, see B of.
1. —— xx. 13, 29.
1. —— xxi. 17.
1. Acts ii. 6.
4. ——— 24.
1. ——— 27.
— —— iv. 21, see B of.
1. —— vi. 1.
1. —— viii. 20.
— —— x. 45, see B that.
2b.—— xii. 20.
11.——— 23.
6. —— xiv. 12.
— Acts xvi. 3, see B of.
1. —— xvii. 18 (*ap.*)
3. ——— 31 (No. 4, G∾ L T Tr A ℵ.)
2b.—— xviii. 3.
10.—— xx. 16.
1. —— xxii. 29.
2b.—— xxvii. 4, 9.
—— xxviii. 2, see B of.
2b.——— 18.
3. Rom. i. 19.
7. —— iv. 15.
1. —— v. 5.
1. —— vi. 15.
— ——— 19, see B of.
3. —— viii. 7.
— ——— 10, see B of.
1. ——— 21.
1. ——— 27, marg. *that.*
1. —— ix. 7, 28 (*ap*), 32.
1. —— xiv. 23.
— —— xv. 15, see B of.
1. 1 Cor. i. 25.
1. —— ii. 14.
1. —— iii. 13.
1. —— vi. 7.
— —— xi. 10, see B of.
1. —— xii. 15, 16.
3. —— xv. 9.
1. ——— 15.
1. 2 Cor. vii. 13.
1. —— xi. 7, 11.
— Gal. ii. 4, see B of.
1. ——— 11.
1. —— iv. 6.
— Eph. iv. 18, }
— —— v. 6, } see B of.
1. ——— 16, }
2b. Phil. i. 7.
1. —— ii. 30.
1. —— iv. 17.
3. 1 Thes. ii. 8.
1. ——— 13.
— 2 Thes. i. 3, see B that.
1. ——— 10.
11.—— ii. 10.
1. ——— 13.
1. —— iii. 9.
— —— iv. 6, see B that.
1. 1 Tim. i. 13.
1. —— iv. 10.
1. —— v. 12.
1. —— vi. 2 twice.
1. Philem. 7.
5. Heb. vi. 13.
2b.—— vii. 24.
1. —— viii. 9.
2b.—— x. 2.
3. —— xi. 5.
5. ——— 11.
3. ——— 23.
1. Jas. i. 10.
2b.—— iv. 2.
3. ——— 3.
3. 1 Pet. i. 16.
1. —— ii. 21.
1. —— v. 8 (*ap.*)
1. 1 John ii. 8.
— ——— 11, see B that.
1. ——— 12.
1. ——— 13 3 times, 14 twice, 21 twice. [22.
1. —— iii. 1, 9, 12, 14, 16,
1. —— iv. 1, 4.
— ——— 9, see B that.
1. ——— 13, 17, 18, 19.
1. —— v. 6, 10.
1. Rev. ii. 4.
1. ——— 14 (*om.* L T Trb.)
1 ——— 20.
1. —— iii. 10, 16.
1. —— v. 4.
1. —— viii. 11.
1. —— xi. 10, 17.
1. —— xiv. 8 (ἥ, *who*, L T Tr A) (*om.* G⇉ ℵ*.)
1. —— xvi. 5.

* ℵ omits the whole verse.

BECAUSE OF.

1. διά, *see* "BECAUSE," *No.* 2*b*.
2. ἀπό, *motion from the exterior*, away from; from, of, *of origin, derivation*; from, on account of, *of cause or occasion*.
3. ἐκ, *motion* from *the interior*, out of; from, of, *of origin, etc.*, *hence*, the occasion *and* the reason *as the source* out of *which a result flows*.
4. ἐν, in.
5. ἐπί, upon.
   (a) *with Gen.* upon, *(as proceeding from)* over, *etc.*
   (b) *with Dat.* upon, *(as resting upon)* on account of.
   (c) *with Acc.* upon, *(by direction towards)* towards, *as the direction of thought, feeling, speech.*
6. πρός, towards, *(in the direction of.)*
   (a) *with Gen.* hitherwards, in favour of.
   (b) *with Dat.* towards *(as resting in a direction towards)* at, close by.
   (c) *with Acc.* hitherwards, *(of literal direction;) of mental direction*, towards; *then from the general notion of mental direction comes* (i) *that of estimation or proportion*, in consideration of, *and* (ii) *that of intention*, in order to.
7. χάριν, *(Acc. of* χάρις, favour, grace, *used adverbially)* in *any one's* favour, for *his* pleasure; for the sake of *a person or thing*, on account of.

1. Matt. xiii. 21, 58.
1. —— xvii. 20.
2. —— xviii. 7.
6c. —— xix. 8.
4. —— xxvi. 31, 33.
1. —— xxvii. 19.
1. Mark iii. 9.
1. —— vi. 6.
4. —— xiv. 27 (*om.* ἐν ἐμοι, *in me*, G⇉ T Tr A ℵ.)
1. Luke v. 19.
1. —— xi. 8.
1 John iii. 29.
1 —— iv. 41, 42.
1 —— vii. 43.
1 —— xi. 42.
1 —— xii. 30, 42
1. —— xix. 42.
1. Acts iv. 21.
1. —— xvi. 3.
1. —— xxviii. 2.
1. Rom. vi. 19.
1. —— viii. 10 twice.
1. ——— 11, margin (text, *by*.)
1. —— xv. 15.
1. 1 Cor. xi. 10.
1. Gal. ii. 4.
7. —— iii. 19.
1. Eph. iv. 18.
1. —— v. 6.
1. Heb. iii. 19.
1. —— iv. 6.
7. Jude 16.
5c. Rev. i. 7.
3. —— xvi. 11, 21.

BECAUSE THAT.

1. γάρ, *see* "BECAUSE," *No.* 7.
2. διά, *see* "BECAUSE," *No.* 2*b*.
3. διότι, *see* "BECAUSE," *No.* 3.
4. ὅτι, *see* "BECAUSE," *No.* 1.
5. καθότι, *see* "BECAUSE," *No.* 4.

5. Luke i. 7.
2. Acts viii. 11.
4. —— x. 45.
2. —— xviii. 2.
1. —— xxviii. 20,
3. Rom. i. 21.
3. Phil. ii. 26.
3. 1 Thes. iv. 6.
4. 2 Thes. i. 3.
4. 1 John ii. 11.
4. —— iv. 9.
1. 3 John 7.
1 & 4. Rom. iii. 2 (*om* No. 1, (γάρ) G∾ L Tr A[b].)

BECAUSE...WOULD.

πρός, *see* "BECAUSE OF," *No.* 6*c*.

1 Thes. ii. 9.

BECAUSE HE WOULD NOT.

{ ὅπως, in order that.
{ μὴ γένηται, it should not happen.
{ αὐτῷ, to him.

Acts xx. 16.

BECKON (-ED, -ING.)

1. κατασείω, to move downwards, *to move the hand to another, as a sign for him to be silent.*
2. νεύω, to incline in any direction, to nod *or* beckon *as a sign*; to nod *or* bow in token of assent.
3. διανεύω, to intimate *or* signify by nodding *or* beckoning.

3. Luke i. 22 (with εἰμί, *to be.*)
— —— v. 7, see B unto.
2. John xiii. 24.
1. Acts xii. 17.
1. Acts xiii. 16.
1. —— xix. 33.
1. —— xxi. 40.
2. —— xxiv. 10.

BECKON UNTO.

κατανεύω, to nod, *esp.* to nod assent; *(properly by inclining the head.)*

Luke v. 7.

BECOME (-ETH, -ING, BECAME.)

γίνομαι, *denoting origin*, to come into being, to be born, to become; *or result*, to take place, to happen, **followed by* εἰς, *denoting equivalence*, to become for *or* as.

Matt. xiii. 22, 32.
—— xviii. 3.
—— xxi. 42*.
—— xxviii. 4.
Mark i. 17.
—— iv. 19, 32.
—— ix. 3.
—— xii. 10*.
Luke xx. 17*.
John i. 12.
Acts iv. 11*.
—— vii. 40.
—— x. 10.
—— xii. 18.
Rom. iii. 19.
—— iv. 18.
—— vii. 13.
1 Cor. iii. 18.

1 Cor. viii. 9.
—— ix. 20, 22
—— xiii. 1, 11.
—— xv. 20 (*om.* All.)
2 Cor. v. 17.
—— xii. 11.
Gal. iv. 16.
Phil. ii. 8.
1 Thes. i. 6.
—— ii. 14.
Philem. 6.
Heb. v. 9, 12.
—— x. 33.
—— xi. 7.
Jas. ii. 4, 11.
Rev. vi. 12 twice.
—— viii. 8, 11.*
—— xi. 15.
—— xvi. 3, 4.
—— xviii. 2.

See also DEAD, EFFECT, FOOL, POOR, SERVANT, UNCIRCUMCISED, UNPROFITABLE, VAIN.

BECOME (*to be fitting.*)

(-ETH, BECAME.)

πρέπω, (a) to be conspicuous *among a number*, to be distinguished in *or* by *a thing*; (*properly of impressions on the senses*) to become, beseem, suit.

(b) *Impersonal*, it is fitting, it beseems, it suits.

b. Eph. v. 3.
a. 1 Tim. ii. 10.
a. Titus ii. 1.
a. Heb. vii. 26.

BECOMETH (IT.)

b. Matt. iii. 15.
b. Heb. ii. 10.

BECOMETH AS.

ἀξίως, (*adv. from* ἄξιος, weighing as much, of equal value), worthily, deservedly

Rom. xvi. 2.
Phil. i. 27.

BECOMETH HOLINESS (AS.)

ἱεροπρεπής, beseeming a sacred place, person, *or matter*.

Titus ii. 3, margin, *as becometh holy women.*

BED.

1. κράββατος, (κράβαττος, L T Tr A ℵ), κράβακτος, ℵ.) *It denotes a* mean kind of bed, *such as the Ancients used to recline on at noon*, (*Latin* grabatus) a mattress *for the poor*.

2. κλίνη, that on which one lies, a couch for meals, *or* a bed to sleep on, *used by the rich*.

3. κοίτη, a lying; *hence*, a place of repose, bed, *esp.* the marriage bed.

2. Matt. ix. 2, 6.
1. Mark ii. 4, 9, 11, 12.
2. —— iv. 21.
1. —— vi. 55.
2. —— vii. 30, marg. (text, *table*.)
2. —— —— 30.
2. Luke v. 18.
2. —— viii. 16.
3. Luke xi. 7.
2. —— xvii. 34.
1. John v. 8, 9, 10; 11.
1. —— —— 12 (*om.* T Tr[b] A ℵ)
2. Acts v. 15 (κλινάριον, *a small bed*, G~ L T Tr A ℵ)
1. —— ix. 33.
3. Heb. xiii. 4.
2. Rev. ii. 22.

BED (MAKE...)

στρωννύω, to spread, spread *or* stretch out, strew; to spread *or* make up *a bed*.

Acts ix. 34.

BEEN.

(HAD, HATH, HAST, HADST, HAVE (SHOULD), HAVE (TO), HAD (THAT), HAST (THAT), HAVE B., WITH, HAVING.)

When this word is not part of another verb or phrase it is the translation of one of these following.

1. εἰμί, I am, (*the ordinary state of existence.*)
   (a) ἐστί, he, she, it is, (3 *pers. sin. pres. ind.*)
   (b) ἐστέ, ye...are, (2 *pers pl. pres. ind.*)
   (c) εἶναι, to be, (*infinitive*) **with the Acc. of the noun*, that...been.
   (d) ὤν οὖσα ὄν, being (*participle*).
   (e) ἦν, *etc.*, he, she, it, was, *etc.* (*imperf.*)
2. γίνομαι, *denoting origin*, to come into being, to become; *or result* to take place, to happen.
3. διατρίβω, to wear away *or* consume by rubbing; *hence*, to spend, *or* pass away time, *live*.
4. ποιέω, to make, to do; *with idea of time*, to spend *time on anything*, to make *the time long*.
5. προσμένω, to remain with, to wait still longer.

1e. Matt. xxiii. 30, had B (ἤμεθα, same meaning All).
1e. —— —— 30, should have B (with ἄν) (ἤμεθα, All)
1e. —— xxv. 21, } hast B
1e. —— —— 23. }
1e. —— xxvii. 54, had B.
1c. Mark vi. 49 that had B
5. —— viii. 2, B with (have).
2. —— xvi. 10, had B (*ap*)
1c. Luke ii. 44, to have B.
1e. —— iv. 16, } had B.
1e. —— viii. 2, }
2. Luke xvi. 11, 12, } have B
2. —— xix. 17. }
1a. —— xxiv. 21.
1e. John ix. 18[1st], had B.
1e. —— xi. 21, 32, hadst B.
1b. —— xv. 27, have B.
1e. Acts iv. 13, had B.
2. —— vii. 52, have B.
1e. —— xiv. 26, } had B
2. —— xv. 7 }
2 —— xix. 21, } have B
2. —— xx. 18. }
1d. —— xxiv. 10, that hast B.

3. Acts xxv. 14, had B.
2. Rom. vi. 5, have B.
2. —— ix. 29, had B.
2. —— xi. 34, } hath B.
2. —— xvi. 2, }
4. 2 Cor. xi. 25, } have B.
1e. Gal. iii. 21 2nd }
2. Col. iv. 11, } have B.
1c. 1 Thes. ii 6, }
2. 1 Tim. v. 9, having B.
1e. Heb. viii. 7, }
1e. 2 Pet. ii. 21, } had B.
1e. 1 John ii. 19, }

BEFALL (-ELL.)

1. **γίνομαι**, to come into being, to be born, to become, to arise, to happen.
2. **συμβαίνω**, to stand with the feet together; come together, *meet; of events,* to come to pass, fall out, happen.

1. Mark v. 16. | 2. Acts xx. 19

BEFALL (THE THINGS WHICH SHALL.)

τὰ, the *things,* (*neut. pl. of art.*)
συναντήσοντα, (*part of* συναντάω, to come to meet together, *i.e.,* to fall in with *or* meet one another.)
} the things which shall happen.

Acts xx. 22.

BEFALLEN TO (WHAT WAS.)

τά, the *things,* (*neut. pl. of art.*)

Matt. viii. 33, lit, *the things* of the, or relating to the demonized [men.]

BEFORE.

1. **πρό**, in front of, before *of place, time, or superiority.*
2. **ἔμπροσθεν**, *of place,* before, (*as opp. to behind*), in front of; *of time,* earlier, of old.
3. **ἐνώπιον**, being in sight; in one's presence, face to face.
4. **κατενώπιον**, (*No.* 3 *with* κατά, (*No.* 10), against, *prefixed*), right over against, right opposite.
5. **ἐναντίον**, over against, opposite, fronting; *in hostile signification,* against.
6. **ἐπί**, upon.
   (a) *with Gen.* upon and proceeding from (*e.g. a pillar;*) over, in the presence of, *hence,* before; *fig. on the basis of,* upon *or* before.
   (b) *with Dat.* upon and resting upon; over *of superintendence, etc.;* in addition to, on account of; on *or* at, *etc., as the ground-work of any fact or circumstance.*
   (c) *with Acc.* upon, *by direction towards,* (*motion being implied*); to, *implying an intention* for, against.
7. **εἰς**, (*motion to the interior*) into, to, unto.
8. **παρά**, beside (*of juxtaposition.*)
   (a) *with Gen.* beside, *as proceeding from,* from beside.
   (b) *with Dat.* beside and at; with, *in the estimation of.*
   (c) *with Acc.* beside, *as alongside of; so as to be compared with, as* contrary *or* superior *to, etc.*
9. **ἐν**, in, *of time, place, or element;* among.
10. **κατά**, down.
   (a) *with Gen.* down from, against.
   (b) *with Acc.* down towards, down upon *or* along, throughout, *in ref. to time* at *or* in, *i.e.,* correspondent with, at the period of, over against.
11. **πρός**, towards (*in the direction of.*)
   (a) *with Gen.* in favour of.
   (b) *with Dat.* at, close by.
   (c) *with Acc.* towards, in reference to.
12. **ἀπό**, from, (*motion from the exterior*) away from, *hence, sometimes denoting cause or occasion,* from, on account of.
13. **ἔναντι**, in against, opposite, over against.
14. **ἀπέναντι**, (*No.* 13 *with* ἀπό, (*No.* 10) *prefixed*), opposite, over against, in the presence of.
15 **κατέναντι**, down over against, *i.e.,* in the sight and estimation of.
16. **πρῶτος**, (*a superl. from* πρό, *No.* 1), the first, foremost, *of place, rank, or time.*
17. **πρῶτον**, (*neut. sing. of No.* 16, *used as adv.*) first *of time, whether in a superl. sense or compart.,* before *of order or dignity.*
18. **πρότερον**, before *others, of place, time or rank;* formerly.
   (a) *with art.* the former *time, etc.*
   (b) *with* ἐάν μή, except, unless.

19. { πρό, before, *see No.* 1, πρόσωπον, face, countenance ; a person, } before *the* face.

20. { εἰς, into, unto, *see No.* 7, πρόσωπον, a face, a person, *see No.* 19, } to *the* face.

21. { ἐν, in, τῷ, the, μέσος, middle, in the middle, in the midst, } in the midst.

22. πρίν, before, formerly, erst, one time.

(a) *with* ἤ, before that, sooner than.

22a. Matt. i. 18.
1. —— v. 12.
2. ——— 16, 24.
2. —— vi. 1, 2
1. ——— 8.
2 —— vii. 6.
1. —— viii. 29.
6c. —— x. 13.
2. ——— 32 twice, 33 twice.
1. —— xi. 10 1st.
2. ——— 10 2nd.
21. —— xiv. 6.
2. —— xvii. 2.
1. —— xxiv. 38 (*om.* G→ [T A.)
2. —— xxv. 32.
22 —— xxvi. 34.
2. ——— 70.
22. ——— 75.
2. —— xxvii. 11.
14. ——— 24 (No.15, L Tr.)
2. ——— 29.
1. Mark i. 2 1st.
2. ——— 2 2nd (*om.* All.)
5. —— ii. 12.
2. —— ix. 2.
6a. —— xiii. 9.
22a. ——xiv. 30.
22. ——— 72.
3. Luke i. 6 (No.5, Tr A ℵ.)
13. ——— 8 (No.5, G~ ℵ.)
3. ——— 17, 75.
1. ——— 76.
1. —— ii. 21.
22a. ——— 26.
10b. ——— 31.
3. —— v. 18.
2. ——— 19.
3. ——— 25.
1. —— vii. 27 1st
2. ——— 27 2nd.
— —— viii. 47 1st, see fall down B
3. ——— 47 2nd.
1. —— ix. 52.
1. —— x. 1.
1. —— xi. 38.
3. —— xii. 6.
2. ——— 8 twice.
3. ——— 9 1st (No.2, L ℵ.)
3. ——— 9 2nd.
2. —— xiv. 2.
3. —— xv. 18.
3. —— xvi. 15.
2. —— xix. 4, 27, 28.
5. —— xx. 26.
1. —— xxi. 12 1st.
6c. ——— 12 2nd.
2. ——— 36.
1. —— xxii. 15.
— ——— 34, see B that.
22. ——— 61.
— —— xxiii. 12, see B (be.)
3. ——— 14.
5. —— xxiv. 19.
3. ——— 43.
2. John i. 15 1st.
16. ——— 15 2nd.
2. ——— 27 (*ap.*)
2. ——— 30 1st.
16. ——— 30 2nd.
1. ——— 48.
2. —— iii. 28.
1. —— v. 7.
18a. ——vi. 62.
18b ——vii. 51 (No.17, with ἐὰν μή, *except*, G~L T Tr A ℵ.)
22. —— viii. 58.
18a. —— ix. 8.
2. —— x. 4.
1. ——— 8.
1. —— xi. 55.
1. —— xii. 1.
3. ——— 37.
1. —— xiii. 1.
1. ——— 19.
22. —— xiv. 29.
17 —— xv. 18.
1. —— xvii. 5, 24.
22a. Acts ii. 20 (*om.* ἤ, G→ [L Tr ℵ.)
3. ——— 25.
3. —— iv. 10.
1. —— v. 23 (No. 6a, L T [Tr A ℵ)
9. ——— 27.
1. ——— 36.
3. —— vi. 6.
22a. ——vii. 2.
12. ——— 45.
3. ——— 46.
5. —— viii. 32.
3. —— ix. 15.
3 —— x. 4 (No.2, L T Tr [A ℵ.)
6c. ——— 17.
3. ——— 30, 33.
1. —— xii. 6, 14.
19. —— xiii. 24.
1. —— xiv. 13.
2. —— xviii. 17.
3. —— xix. 9, 19.
1. —— xxi. 38.
7. —— xxii. 30.
6a. —— xxiii. 30.
6a. —— xxiv. 19, 20.
6a —— xxv. 9.
— ——— 16, see B that.
6a. ——— 26 twice.
6a. —— xxvi. 2.
11c. ——— 26.
8b. Rom. ii. 13.
14. —— iii. 18
11c. ——iv. 2.
15. ——— 17, margin *like* [*unto.*
1. —— xvi. 7.
1. 1 Cor. ii. 7.
1. —— iv. 5.
6a. —— vi. 1 twice, 6.
18. 2 Cor. i. 15.
2. —— v. 10.
6a. —— vii. 14.
20. —— viii. 24.
4. 2 Cor. xii. 19 (No.15, G~ L Tr A ℵ.)
1. Gal. i. 17.
3. ——— 20.
1. —— ii. 12.
2. ——— 14.
10b. ——iii. 1.
1. ——— 23 1st.
1. Eph. i. 4 1st.
4. ——— 4 2nd.
2. Phil. iii. 13.
1. Col. i. 17.
2. 1 Thes. iii. 9, 13.
18a. 1 Tim. i. 13.
3. —— v. 4.
6a. ——— 19, marg. *under.*
3. ——— 20, 21 1st.
— ——— 21 2nd, see prefer [B.
3. —— vi. 12.
6a. ——— 13.
1. 2 Tim. i. 9.
3. —— ii. 14.
3. —— iv. 1.
1. ——— 21.
1. Titus i. 2.
1. Heb. xi. 5.
8b. Jas. i. 27.
7. —— ii. 6.
1. Jas. v. 9.
1. 1 Pet. i. 20.
8b. 2 Pet. ii. 11 (*om.* "before the Lord," G ⇄ L [T Tr b.)
12. 1 John ii. 28.
2. —— iii. 19.
3. 3 John 6.
3. Rev. i. 4.
3. —— ii. 14.
3. —— iii. 2, 5 twice, 8, 9.
3. —— iv. 5, 6 1st.
2. ——— 6 2nd.
3. ——— 10 twice.
3. —— v. 8.
3 —— vii. 9 twice, 11, 15.
3. —— viii. 2, 3, 4.
3. —— ix. 13.
6b. —— x. 11.
3. —— xi. 4, 16.
3. —— xii. 4, 10.
3. —— xiii. 12.
3. —— xiv. 3 twice.
3. ——— 5 (*ap.*)
3. —— xv. 4.
3. —— xvi. 19.
3. —— xix. 20.
3. —— xx. 12.
2. —— xxii. 8.

BEFORE (BE.)

προϋπάρχω, to be before *or* beforehand *in a thing; intrans.*, to exist before, to be formerly.

Luke xxiii. 12.

BEFORE THAT.

22a. Luke xxii. 34 (ἕως, *until*, L T Tr A ℵ.)
22a. Acts xxv. 16.

See also, APPOINT, BEGIN, BROUGHT, CHOOSE, CONFIRM, DAY, DETERMINE, FALL, GO, GOSPEL, HEAR, INSTRUCT, KNOW, MEDITATE, NEVER, NOTICE, ORDAIN, PREACH, PREFERRING, PRESENCE, PROVE, RUN, SABBATH, SAY, SEE, SET, SHOW, SPEAK, SPOKEN, STAND, SUFFER, TAKE, TELL, WORLD.

BEFOREHAND.

See, MAKE, MANIFEST, OPEN, TESTIFY, THOUGHT.

BEFORETIME (BE.)

προϋπάρχω, to be before *or* beforehand *in a thing, intrans.* to exist before, to be formerly.

Acts viii. 9.

BEG.

1. αἰτέω, to entreat, beg, supplicate ; *it implies a distinction in position and circumstances between the parties*

and expresses a petition from an inferior to a superior, see under "pray" and "ask."

2. προσαιτέω, to ask besides, to demand more; to continue asking, *and so* to beg, ask an alms of *one*; to beg hard.

3. ἐπαιτέω, to ask besides, to beg as a mendicant.

1. Matt. xxvii. 58.
2. Mark x. 46 (προσαίτης, *a beggar*, T Tr A ℵ.)
3. Luke xvi. 3.
2. Luke xviii. 35 (No. 3, L T Tr A ℵ.)
1. —— xxiii. 52.
2. John ix. 8.

BEGET.

1. γεννάω, to beget; *of the mother*, to bear, bring forth. *Met.* an influence *excited on some one moulding his life.*

2. ἀποκυέω, to bring forth; to beget *when spoken of the male.*

1. Matt. i. 2 3 times, 3 3 times, 4 3 times, 5 3 times, 6 twice, 7 3 times, 8 3 times, 9 3 times, 10 3 times, 11, 12 twice, 13 3 times, 14 3 times, 15 3 times, 16.
1. Acts vii. 8, 29.
1. Acts xiii. 33.
1. 1 Cor. iv. 15.
1. Philem. 10.
1. Heb. i. 5.
1. —— v. 5.
2. Jas. i. 18.
1. 1 John v. 1 twice, 18.

BEGET AGAIN.

ἀναγεννάω, to beget again, to bear again. (occ. 1 Pet. i. 23.)

1 Pet. i. 3.

BEGGAR.

πτωχός, one who crouches *or* cringes, *hence as a subst.*, a beggar.

Luke xvi. 20, 22.

BEGGARLY.

πτωχός, *see* "BEGGAR."

Gal. iv. 9.

BEGIN.

1. ἄρχομαι, *(in Mid.)* to be first, *and that in point of time*, to begin, make a beginning *(both Act. and Mid. as here.)*

2. ἐνάρχομαι, to make a beginning of.

3. προενάρχομαι, to begin before *or* already, to begin in.

4. { ἐπιβάλλω, to throw *or* cast upon, to lay on, *etc.*, χείρ, the hand, } to lay hands on *or* to thrust forth *his* hands.

5. μέλλω, to be on the point to *do anything*, to be about to do.

1. Matt. iv. 17.
1. —— xi. 7, 20.
1. —— xii. 1.
1. —— xiv. 30.
1. —— xvi. 21, 22.
1. —— xviii. 24.
1. —— xx. 8.
1. —— xxiv. 49.
1. —— xxvi. 22, 37, 74.
1. Mark i. 45.
1. —— ii. 23.
1. —— iv. 1.
1. —— v. 17, 20.
1. —— vi. 2, 7, 34, 55.
1. —— viii. 11, 31, 32.
1. —— x. 28, 32, 41, 47.
1. —— xi. 15.
1. —— xii. 1.
1. —— xiii. 5.
1. —— xiv. 19, 33, 65, 69, 71.
1. —— xv. 8, 18.
1. Luke iii. 8.
1. —— 23, with εἰμί, *to be* (lit, *was—when beginning.*)
1. —— iv. 21.
1. —— v. 21.
1. —— vii. 15, 24, 38, 49.
1. Luke ix. 12.
1. —— xi. 29, 53.
1. —— xii. 1, 45.
1. —— xiii. 25, 26.
1. —— xiv. 9, 18, 29, 30.
1. —— xv. 14, 24.
1. —— xix. 37, 45.
1. —— xx. 9.
1. —— xxi. 28.
1. —— xxii. 23.
1. —— xxiii. 2, 5, 30.
1. —— xxiv. 27, 47.
1. John viii. 9 (*ap.*)
1. —— xiii. 5.
1. Acts i. 1, 22.
1. —— ii. 4.
1. —— viii. 35.
1. —— x. 37.
1. —— xi. 15.
4 —— xii. 1, marg. (text, *stretch forth.*)
1. —— xviii. 26
1. —— xxiv. 2.
1. —— xxvii. 35.
1. 2 Cor. iii. 1.
3. —— viii. 6.
2. Gal. iii. 3.
1. 1 Pet. iv. 17.
5. Rev. x. 7.

BEGIN AT THE FIRST.

{ λαμβάνω, to take *or* receive, ἀρχή, beginning, origin, } receive a beginning.

Heb. ii. 3.

BEGIN BEFORE.

3. 2 Cor. viii. 10.

BEGIN FIRST.

πρῶτον, first, in the first place.

1 Pet. iv. 17.

BEGIN TO BE.

εἰμί, I am, *the verb of ordinary existence.*

Luke iii. 23 (with αρχόμαι, lit, *was—when beginning.*)

See also, AMEND, DAWN, SINK, WANTON, WORLD.

BEGINNER [margin.]

ἀρχηγός, beginning, originating; *as subs.* a leader, founder, first father, prince *or* chief.

Heb. xii. 2 (text, *author.*)

BEGINNING.

1. ἀρχή, beginning, origin.
2. πρῶτος, the first, foremost *of place, rank or time.*

1. Matt. xix. 4. 8.
1. —— xxiv. 8, 21.
1. Mark i. 1.
1. —— x. 6.
1. —— xiii 8, 19.
1. Luke i. 2.
1. John i. 1, 2.
1. —— ii. 11.
1. —— vi. 64.
1. —— viii. 25, 44.
1. —— xv. 27.
1. —— xvi. 4.
1. Acts xi. 15.
1. Phil. iv. 15.
1. Col. i. 18.
1. 2 Thes. ii. 13 (ἀπαρχήν, *an offering of first-fruits,* instead of ἀπ' ἀρχῆς, *from the beginning,* L.)
1. Heb. i. 10.
1. —— iii. 14.
1. —— vi. 1, marg. (text, *principles.*)
1. —— vii. 3.
2. 2 Pet. ii. 20.
1. —— iii. 4.
1. 1 John i. 1.
1. —— ii. 7 1st, 13, 14, 24 twice.
1. —— 7 2nd (*om.* G ⇌ L T Tr A ℵ.)
1. —— iii. 8, 11.
1. 2 John 5, 6.
1. Rev. i. 8 (*om.* G L T Tr A.)
1. —— iii. 14.
1. —— xxi. 6.
1. —— xxii. 13.

BEGINNING (AT THE.)

πρῶτον, first, at the first.

John ii. 10.

BEGINNING (FROM THE.)

ἄνωθεν, *of place,* from above; *of time,* from the beginning.

Acts xxvi. 5.

See also, REHEARSE, WORLD.

BEGOTTEN (ONLY.)

μονογενής, only begotten; *used to denote the relation of Christ to the Father.*

John i. 14, 18; iii. 16, 18; 1 John iv. 9.

BEGOTTEN SON (ONLY.)

Heb. xi. 17.

See, FIRST-BEGOTTEN.

BEGUILE.

1. δελεάζω, to entice *or* catch by a bait.
2. ἐξαπατάω, to cheat, deceive, beguile thoroughly.
3. παραλογίζομαι, to reckon wrong, miscount; to reason falsely; *then,* to cheat *or* delude by false reasoning.

2. 2 Cor. xi. 3.
3. Col. ii. 4.
3. Col. ii. 18, see reward.
1. 2 Pet. ii. 14.

BEHALF.

μέρος, a part, share; one's portion *or* lot.

2 Cor. ix. 3.
1 Pet. iv. 16 (ὄνομα, *name,* G ∾ L T Tr A ℵ.)

BEHALF OF (IN.)

ὑπέρ, over.

(a) *with Gen. (over and separate from)* on behalf of, for *(as though bending over to protect.)* ὑπέρ *may thus denote* instead of, *but does not determine the way in which the service is performed. It only affirms it.* ἀντί *on the other hand is strictly definite.*

(b) *with Acc. (over and towards)* beyond, above.

a. Phil. i. 29.

BEHALF (ON.)

1. ὑπέρ, *see* "BEHALF OF (IN)" (a.)
2. ἐπί, upon.
   (a) *with Gen. (as springing from)* over, in the presence *or* time of.
   (b) *with Dat. (as resting on)* in addition to, on account of.
   (c) *with Acc. (upon, by direction towards)* up to, over *of time, place, or extent.*
3. περί, around.
   (a) *with Gen.* about, concerning, *as the object of thought, emotion, etc.*
   (b) *with Acc.* about, round about, *of place or time.*

2b. Rom. xvi. 19 (τὸ ἐφ' ὑμιν, *om.* art, G → L T Tr A ℵ, denote *over you.*)
3a. 1 Cor. i. 4.
1. 2 Cor. i. 11.
1. —— v. 12.
1. —— viii. 24.

BEHAVE...SELF.

1. ἀναστρέφω, to turn upside down.
   (a) *Pass. or Mid., hence,* to turn one's self around, to move about in *a place, hence,* to sojourn, dwell; *then of the manner of this dwelling,* to behave, conduct one's self.
2. γίνομαι, to begin to be, come into existence, *(implying origin, result, or change of state.)*

2. 1 Thes. ii. 10.
1a. 1 Tim. iii. 15.

See also, DISORDERLY, UNCOMELY, UNSEEMLY.

BEHAVIOUR.

καταστημα, the condition *or* constitution *of anything; spoken of external circumstances or deportment.*

Titus ii. 3.

BEHAVIOUR (OF GOOD.)

κόσμιος, well ordered, *of persons*, orderly, well behaved, discreet, *etc.*

1 Tim. iii. 2, marg. *modest.*

BEHEAD.

1. ἀποκεφαλίζω, to cut off the head.
2. πελεκίζω, to cut with an axe, *hence*, to behead, (πέλεκυς, an axe.)

1. Matt. xiv. 10.
1. Mark vi. 16, 27.
1. Luke ix. 9.
2. Rev. xx. 4.

BEHIND.

1. ὄπισθεν, *of place*, from behind, at the back; *of time*, after, in future, hereafter.
2. ὀπίσω, *of place*, behind, backwards.

1. Matt. ix. 20.
2. —— xvi. 23.
1. Mark v. 27.
2. —— viii. 33.
2. Luke iv. 8 (*ap.*)
2. —— vii. 38.
1. —— viii. 44.
2. Rev. i. 10.
1. Rev. iv. 6.

BEHIND (BE.)

ὑστερέω, to be behind *or* later; *of place or time* to come after, *metaph.* to fall short of; *in pass. esp.* to be in want of, to lack, miss.

2 Cor. xi. 5; xii. 11.

BEHIND (COME.)

ὑστερέω, *see above.*

1 Cor. i. 7.

BEHIND.

(THOSE THINGS WHICH ARE.)

{ τὰ, the *things.*
{ ὀπίσω, behind.

Phil. iii. 13.

BEHIND (WHICH IS.)

ὑστέρημα, a coming short, deficiency, want

Col. i. 24, plural.

See also, TARRY.

BEHOLD.

(-EST, -ING,- BEHELD.)

1. ὁράω, to see, *is used of bodily sight, and is referred to the thing seen, whether in itself (objectively), or in regard to its impression on the mind (subjectively;) see No.* 7.
2. εἶδον, *(from root* εἴδω, *used as aor. act. for No.* 1*)* to see, *same signification as No.* 1.
3. ἰδού, *(imperat. aor. mid. of above)* behold! *calling attention to what may be seen, heard, or apprehended in any way, see No.* 1.
4. ἴδε, *(imperat. of above) used as interjection, see No.* 1.
5. ἐπεῖδον, *(No.* 2, *with* ἐπί, upon, *prefixed)* to look upon, regard.
   (a) *with* ἐπί, upon.
6. ἐποπτεύω, *(deriv. of No.* 1, *with* ἐπί*)*, to look over, overlook, watch; to to be an eye-witness of.
7. βλέπω, *denotes* the act of seeing, *and is referred to the organ (as No.* 1 *is to the thing seen.) Both this and No.* 1 *are applied to mental vision, but No.* 7 *implies greater vividness, to express a more intent, earnest spiritual contemplation.*
8. ἐμβλέπω, *(No.* 7 *with* ἐν, in *or* on *prefixed)*, to look upon, view *with steadfastness and attention.*
   (a) *with* εἰς, unto, *denotes* look unto, *etc.*
9. θεωρέω, to look at, gaze upon, *akin to No.* 7, *but when used of bodily vision it always assumes that the object is actually present.*
10. ἀναθεωρέω, *(No.* 9 *with* ἀνά *emphatic prefixed)*, to look at purposely, to gaze upon, consider *attentively.*
11. θεάομαι, to fix the eyes upon an object; *(it is referred to the subject, as*

No. 9 is to the object), to look at *intently*, contemplate, observe.

12. κατανοέω, to perceive, to observe; *it is the mental correlative of sensational perception, conscious* action of the mind, to understand, apprehend, learn, know, *referring to the object of knowledge rather than the fact of knowing* (*cf.* γινώσκω.)

3. Matt. i. 20, 23.
3. —— ii. 1, 13, 19.
3. —— iv. 11.
3a.—— vi. 26.
7. —— vii. 3.
3. ———— 4.
3. —— viii. 2, 24, 29, 32, 34. [32.
3. —— ix. 2, 3, 10, 18, 20.
3. —— x. 16.
3. —— xi. 8, 10, 19.
3. —— xii. 2, 10, 18, 41, 42, [46, 47, 49.
3. —— xiii. 3.
3. —— xv. 22.
3. —— xvii. 3, 5 twice.
7. —— xviii. 10.
3. —— xix. 16.
8. ———— 26.
3. ———— 27.
3. —— xx. 18, 30.
3. —— xxi. 5.
3. —— xxii. 4
3. —— xxiii. 34, 38.
3. —— xxiv. 25, 26 twice.
3. —— xxv. 6.
4. ———— 20, 22.
3. —— xxvi. 45, 46, 51.
4. ———— 65.
3. —— xxvii. 51.
9. ———— 55.
3. —— xxviii. 2, 7, 9, 11.
3. Mark i. 2.
4. —— ii. 24.
3. —— iii. 32.
4. ———— 34 (No. 3, L.)
3. —— iv. 3.
3. —— v. 22 (om. G⇉ L[b] T [Tr A ℵ.)
2 —— ix. 15.
8. —— x. 21.
3. ———— 33.
4. —— xi. 21.
9. —— xii. 41.
3. —— xiii. 23 (om. L[b] T [Tr A)
3. —— xiv. 41.
4. —— xv. 4.
3. ———— 35 (No. 4. T Tr [A ℵ.)
9. ———— 47.
4. —— xvi. 6.
3. Luke i. 20, 31, 36, 38, 48.
3. —— ii. 10, 25, 34, 48.
3. —— v. 12, 18.
3. —— vi. 23.
7. ———— 41, 42
3. —— vii. 12, 25, 27, 34, 37.
3. —— viii. 41.
3. —— ix. 30, 38.
3. —— x. 3.
0 ———— 18.
3. ———— 19, 25.
3. —— xi. 31, 32, 41.
3. —— xiii. 7, 11, 30, 32, 35.
3. —— xiv. 2.
9. ———— 29.
3. —— xvii. 21.
3. —— xviii. 31.
3. —— xix. 2, 8, 20.
2. ———— 41.
8. —— xx. 17.
9. —— xxi. 6.
2. ———— 29. [47.
3. —— xxii. 10, 21, 31, 38,
3. —— xxiii. 14, 29.
9. Luke xxiii. 45, 48.
1. ———— 49.
3. ———— 50.
11.———— 55.
3. —— xxiv. 4.
7. ———— 12 (ap.)
3. ———— 13.
2. ———— 39.
3. ———— 49.
11. John i. 14.
4. ———— 29, 36.
8. ———— 42.
4. ———— 47.
4. —— iii. 26.
3. —— iv. 35.
3. —— xii. 15.
3. —— xvi. 32.
3. —— xix. 26 (G∼) (No. 4, G L T Tr A.)
3. ———— 27 (No. 4, L T Tr A) (No. 2, ℵ.)
7. Acts i. 9.
3. ———— 10.
3. —— ii. 7.
7. —— iv. 14.
5a.———— 29.
3. —— v. 9, 25, 28.
12.—— vii. 31, 32.
3. ———— 56.
9. —— viii. 13.
3. ———— 27.
3. —— ix. 10, 11.
3. —— x. 17, 19, 21, 30.
3. —— xi. 11.
3. —— xii. 7.
3. —— xiii. 11, 25.
2. ———— 41.
3. —— xvi. 1.
10.—— xvii. 23.
9. ———— 24.
3. —— xx. 22, 25.
4. Rom. ii. 17 (εἰ δέ, but if, [All.)
3. —— ix. 33.
2. —— xi. 22.
7. 1 Cor. x. 18.
3. —— xv. 51.
— 2 Cor. iii. 18, see B as in a glass.
3. —— v. 17.
3. —— vi. 2 twice, 9.
3. —— vii. 11.
3. —— xii. 14.
3. Gal. i. 20.
4. —— v. 2.
7. Col. ii. 5.
3. Heb. ii. 13.
8. —— viii. 8.
12. Jas. i. 23, 24.
3. —— iii. 3 (No. 4, G) (εἰ δέ, but if, G ∼ L T Tr A) (ειδε γαρ, for behold, ℵ; om. γαρ, for, ℵ[c].)
3. ———— 4, 5.
3. —— v. 4, 7, 9, 11.
3. 1 Pet. ii. 6.
6. ———— 12.
6. —— iii. 2.
2. 1 John iii. 1.
3. Jude 14.
3. Rev. i. 7, 18.
3. —— ii. 10, 22.
3. —— iii. 8. 9 twice.
3. Rev. iii. 11 (om. All.)
3. ———— 20.
3. —— iv. 1, 2.
3. —— v. 5.
2. ———— 6, 11.
3. —— vi. 2.
2. ———— 5 (om. G∻.)
3. ———— 8
5. ———— 12.
2. —— vii. 9.
2. —— viii. 13.
3. —— ix. 12.
0. Rev. xi. 12.
3. ———— 14.
3. —— xii. 3.
2. —— xiii. 11.
3. —— xiv. 14.
3. —— xv. 5 (om. All.)
3. —— xvi. 15.
7. —— xvii. 8.
3. —— xix. 11.
3. —— xxi. 3, 5.
3. —— xxii. 7, 12.

BEHOLD AS IN A GLASS.

κατοπτρίζομαι, (*mid., from* κάτοπτρον a mirror, *which again is from* κατά, against, *and* ὄπτομαι, to look, *a tense of No. 1 above*), *hence*, to behold one's self in a mirror. *Inasmuch as ancient mirrors were made of metal highly polished* (Ex. xxxviii. 22), *the person who looked on his image in them would necessarily have his face illuminated by the reflected rays* (*compare* Ex. xxxiv. 29, 30, *and* 2 Cor. iii. 7.)

2 Cor. iii. 18.

See also, EARNESTLY, STEADFASTLY.

BEHOVE (-ED.)

δεῖ, (*impers. of* δέω, to bind, tie; to have need, want, lack.)

(a) *with Acc.* it is binding on *one to do*, it behoves *one to do*, one must, one ought.

(b) *with Gen.* there is need of.

(c) *with Dat.* there is need for *one to do, etc.*

a. Luke xxiv. 46 (om. G→ L[b] T Tr A ℵ.)

BEHOVETH ONE (IT.)

ὀφείλω, to owe, have to pay *or* account for.

(a) *pass.* to be due, *in wider signif.* to be under an obligation.

a. Heb. ii. 17.

BEING

When not part of another verb (generally the participle), or part of a phrase it is the translation of one of these following.

1. ὤν, οὖσα, ὄν, being, (*part. of εἰμί, the verb of ordinary existence.*)
2. γίνομαι, to come into being, to become, to arise, to happen, (*denoting origin or result.*)
3. ὑπάρχω, to begin, to start, to begin to be, (*referring to original state of existence*)

1. Matt. i. 19.
1. —— vii. 11.
1. —— xii. 34.
1. Mark viii. 1.
2. —— ix. 33.
1. —— xiv. 3.
1. Luke ii. 5.
1. —— iii. 23.
3. —— xi. 13.
1. —— xiii. 16.
3. —— xvi. 23.
1. —— xx. 36.
1. —— xxii. 3.
2. ———— 44 (*ap.*)
1. John iv. 9.
1. —— vi. 71 (*om.* G ⇉ L [Tr A.)
1. —— vii. 50.
1. —— x. 33.
1. —— xi. 49, 51.
1. —— xviii. 26.
1. —— xix. 38.
3. Acts vii. 55.
3. —— xiv. 8 (*om* All.)
1. —— xv. 32.
3. —— xvi. 20.
1. ———— 21.
3. Acts xvi. 37.
— —— xvii. 28, see B (have our.)
3. —— xix. 40.
1. —— xxvii. 2.
1. Rom. xi. 17.
1. 1 Cor. viii. 7.
1. —— ix. 21.
1. —— xii. 12.
3. 2 Cor. viii. 17.
3. —— xii. 16.
3. Gal. i. 14.
1. —— ii. 3.
3. ———— 14.
1. Eph. ii. 20.
1. —— iv. 18.
3. Phil. ii. 6.
1. Col. ii. 13.
1. 1 Tim. iii. 10.
1. Titus i. 16.
1. —— iii. 11.
1. Philem. 9.
1. Heb. i. 3.
1. —— xiii. 3.
2. Jas. i. 25.
2. 1 Pet. v. 3 2nd.

BEING (WE HAVE OUR.)

ἐσμέν, we are. Acts xvii. 28.

BELIEF.

πίστις, the trust *which I entertain or put in a person or thing*, the persuasion *which I have*, the conviction *which I cherish. It implies a conviction which is based upon trust, not upon knowledge*, (*see under* "FAITH.")

2 Thes. ii. 13.

BELIEVE.

(-ED, -EST, -ETH, -ING.)

1. πιστεύω, be persuaded, to rely upon, to trust; (*not used in the Classics religiously, but* νομιζω.) *The N. T. conception of faith is* (i) *a fully convinced acknowledgment*, (ii) *a self-surrendering fellowship*, (iii) *a fully assured and unswerving confidence.*
   (a) *with* εἰς, unto or into, *implying direction towards the object of faith, to give one's self up to.*
   (b) *with* ἐν, in *referring to the foundation of the faith*, put confidence in.
   (c) *with* ἐπί, upon, *implying repose, rest and reliance, or with a view to that reliance.*
   (d) with the simple dative, to give credit to one, trust to his fidelity.
2. πείθω, *in mid. and pass. as here*, to suffer one's self to be persuaded *or* convinced *by any fair means, but esp. by words*, to be won over, prevailed upon.
3. πιστός, (*a verbal adj. from No.* 2) to obey, *hence* obedient, faithful; to trust, *hence*, trusting. *From this meaning arises the so-called pass. sig.* true, *one whom we may trust*, trusty *of persons*, trustworthy *of things.*
4. πίστις, *see under* "BELIEF."

1. Matt. viii. 13.
1. —— ix. 28.
1a. —— xviii. 6.
1. —— xxi. 22, 25, 32 3 times.
1. —— xxiv. 23, 26.
1. —— xxvii. 42.
1b. Mark i. 15.
1. —— v. 36. [Tr Ab ℵ.)
1. —— ix. 23 1st. (*om.* G → T
1. ———— 23 2nd.
1. ———— 24.
1a. ———— 42 (πίστιν ἔχω, *to have faith*, T A.)
1. —— xi. 23, 24, 31.
1. —— xiii. 21.
1. —— xv. 32.
1. —— xvi. 13 (*ap*), 14 (*ap*), 16 1st (*ap.*)
— ———— 16 2nd, see B not
1. ———— 17 (*ap.*)
1. Luke i. 1, see B (most surely).
1. ———— 20, 45.
1. —— viii. 12, 13, 50.
1. —— xx. 5.
1. —— xxii. 67.
1c. —— xxiv. 25.
1. John i. 7a, 12, 50.
1. —— ii. 11a, 22a, 23.
1. —— iii. 12 twice a, 15a, 16a 1st, 18 3 times a, 36.
1. —— iv. 21a, 39, 41, 42, 49, 50, 53.
1. —— v. 24d, 38, 44d, 46 twice, 47 twice.
1. —— vi. 29a, 30a, 35, 36, 40a, 47a, 64 twice, 69.
1a. —— vii. 5, 31, 38, 39, 48.
1. —— viii. 24a, 30d, 31, 45d, 46.
1. —— ix. 18a, 35a, 36, 38.
1. —— x. 25, 26, 37, 38 1st & 2nd.
1. ———— 38 3rd (γνῶτε καὶ γινώσκητε, *perceive* (the introductory act) *and know* (the abiding state), instead of γνῶτε καὶ πιστεύατε, *know and believe*, L T Tr A).
1a. ———— 42.
1. —— xi. 15a, 25a 1st, 26 twice, 27, 40, 42, 45, 48.
1. —— xii. 11a, 36a, 37a, 38, 39a, 42a, 44 twice a, 46.
1. ———— 47 (φυλάσσω, *guard or keep* G ≈ L T Tr A ℵ).
1. —— xiii. 19.
1. —— xiv. 1a twice, 10, 11 twice, 12, 29.
1. —— xvi 9a, 27, 30, 31.
1. —— xvii. 8a, 20, 21.
1. —— xix. 35.
1. —— xx. 8, 25.
3. ———— 27.
1. ———— 29 twice, 31 twice.
1. Acts ii. 44.
1. Acts iv. 4, 32. [obe .)
2. —— v. 36, marg. (text,
1. —— viii. 12, 13, 37 twice
1. —— ix. 26, 42c. [(ap.)
1a. —— x. 43.
3. ———— 45, which B.
1. —— xi. 17c, 21.
1. —— xiii. 12, 30, 41, 48.
1. —— xiv. 1a, 23.
1. —— xv. 5, 7, 11.
3. —— xvi. 1, which .. B
1. ———— 31c, 34d.
2. —— xvii. 4.
1. ———— 12, 34.
1. —— xviii. 8d 1st, 8 2nd, 27
1. —— xix. 2a, 4, 18.
1. —— xxi. 20, 25.
1c. —— xxii. 19.
1. —— xxiv. 14.
1. —— xxvi. 27 twice.
2. —— xxvii. 11.
1. ———— 25.
2. —— xxviii. 4 1st.
— ———— 24 2nd, see B not
1. Rom. i. 16.
1. —— iii. 22.
4. ———— 26, with art., denotes he which B.
1. —— iv. 3c, 5, 11, 17, 18, [24c.
1. —— vi. 8.
1c. —— ix. 33.
1. —— x. 4, 9, 10c, 11, 14a 1st, 14 2nd, 16.
1. —— xiii. 11
1. —— xiv. 2.
1. 1 Cor. i. 21.
1. —— iii. 5.
1. —— xi. 18.
1. —— xiii. 7.
1. —— xiv. 22 twice.
1. —— xv. 2, 11.
1. 2 Cor. iv. 13 twice.
3. —— vi. 15, that B.
1a. Gal. ii. 16.
1. —— iii. 6, 22.
1. Eph. i. 13, 19.
1a. Phil. i. 29.
1. 1 Thes. i. 7.
1. —— ii. 10. 13.
1. —— iv. 14.
1. 2 Thes. i. 10 twice.
1. —— ii. 11, 12.
1c. 1 Tim. i. 16.
1. —— iii. 16.
3. —— iv. 3, which B.
3. ———— 10, that B.
3. —— v. 16.
3. —— vi. 2.
1. 2 Tim. i. 12, marg. *trust*
1. Titus iii. 8.
1. Heb. iv. 3.
4. —— x. 39, gen. (denotes *of them that B.*)
1. —— xi. 6.
1. Jas. ii. 19 twice, 23.
1. 1 Pet. i. 8.
1a. ———— 21 (No. 3, L T Tr [A.
1. —— ii. 6, 7.
1d. 1 John iii. 23.
1. —— iv. 1, 16.

1. 1 John v. 1, 5.
1a. ——— 10 1st.
1. ——— 10 2nd & 3rd.
1a. 1 John v. 13 1st (ap.)
1a. ——— 13 2nd.
1. Jude 5.

BELIEVE NOT.

(Where not two separate words in the Greek. For which, see under "BELIEVE" *and* "NOT.")

1. ἀπιστέω, to put no confidence in.
2. ἀπειθέω, to be disobedient, *(opp. of* πείθομαι, *see* "BELIEVE," *No.* 2.)
3. ἄπιστος, not worthy of confidence, untrustworthy; not confident, mistrustful, faithless, *(opp. of* πιστός, see "BELIEVE," *No.* 3.)

1. Mark xvi. 11 (*ap*), 16 2nd (*ap.*)
1. —— xxiv. 11, 41.
2. John iii. 36.
2. Acts xvii. 5 (*om.* G L Tr A ℵ.)
2. —— xix. 9.
1. —— xxviii. 24.
1. Rom. iii. 3.
2. —— xi. 30.
2. ———31, marg. *obey not.*
2. Rom. xv. 31, marg. *be disobedient.*
3. 1 Cor. vii. 12, 13, see that B not.
3. —— x. 27, that B not.
3. —— xiv. 22 twice, 24, that B not.
3. 2 Cor. iv. 4, which B not.
1. 2 Tim. ii. 13.
2. Heb. iii. 18.
2. —— xi. 31, marg. *be disobedient.*

BELIEVED (THOSE THINGS WHICH ARE MOST SURELY.)

πληροφορέω, *prop.* to make full; fulfil; *used of measures and weights, etc.; in pass. as here, of persons,* to have full satisfaction, to be fully assured, *of things,* to be fully believed *or* fully proved *and* confirmed.

Luke i. 1 (pass. part. with art.)

BELIEVER (-s.)

1. πιστεύω, *see* "BELIEVE," *No.* 1.
2. πιστός, *see* "BELIEVE," *No.* 3.

1. Acts v. 14. | 2. 1 Tim. iv. 12

BELIEVING [noun.]

πιστεύω, *see* "BELIEVE," *No.* 1.

Rom. xv. 13.

BELIEVING [adj.]

πιστός, *see* "BELIEVE," *No.* 3.

John xx. 27. | 1 Tim. vi. 2.
1 Tim. vi. 2, marg. (text, *faithful.*)

BELLY (-IES.)

1. κοιλία, the hollow of the belly; the belly; *then* the contents of the belly, the inward parts.
2. γαστήρ, *the belly; often used of the belly as craving food, hence,* pleasure in eating, gluttony.

1. Matt. xii. 40.
1. —— xv. 17.
1. Mark vii. 19.
1. Luke xv. 16.
1. John vii. 38.
1. Rom. xvi. 18.
1. 1 Cor. vi. 13 twice.
1. Phil. iii. 19.
2. Titus i. 12.
1. Rev. x. 9, 10.

BELONG TO* *or* UNTO†.

(-ED, -ETH.)

1. ἐστί, it is, (3 *pers. sing. pres. of* εἰμί, to be.)
   (a) *with* ἐκ, from, out of.
2. ἐστέ, ye are, (2 *pers. pl. pres. of* εἰμί, to be.)

2. Mark ix. 41* (with Gen.) | 1a. Luke xxiii. 7†.
1. Heb. v. 14.

BELONG TO *or* UNTO (THE THINGS THAT *or* WHICH.)

1. τά, the *things, (neut. pl. of art.) with Gen. following,* the things of.
2. { τὰ, the *things (see No.* 1.) / πρός, towards, in reference to.

2 Luke xix. 42. | 1 Cor. vii. 32.

BELOVED.

1. ἀγαπητός, beloved, *(from* ἀγαπάω, *No.* 2 *with force of perf. pass. part.)*
2. ἀγαπάω, to love, *it denotes the deliberative exercise of the judgment; the giving of a decided preference to one object or person out of many. It frequently implies* regard *and* satisfaction, *rather than affection. A higher word therefore than* φιλέω, *which denotes greater strength of feeling, as between brethren in blood.*

1. Matt. iii. 17.
1. —— xii. 18.
1. —— xvii. 5.
1. Mark i. 11.
1. —— ix. 7.
1. —— xii. 6, see B (well.)
1. Luke iii. 22.
1. —— ix. 35 (ἐκλελεγμένος, *chosen for one's self,* G ∼
1. ——xx. 13. [Lm T Tr A ℵ)
1. Acts xv. 25.
1. Rom. i. 7.
2. —— ix. 25 twice.
1. —— xi. 28.
— —— xii. 19, see B (dearly)
— —— xvi. 5, see B (well.)
1. ——— 8, 9, 12 (*ap.*)
1. 1 Cor. iv. 14, 17.
— —— x. 14, see B (dearly)
1. —— xv. 58.
— 2 Cor. vii. 1, } see B
— —— xii. 19, } (dearly)
2. Eph. i. 6.
1. —— vi. 21.
1. Phil. ii. 12.
— —— iv. 1 twice, see B (dearly.)
2. Col. iii. 12.
1. —— iv. 7, 9, 14.
2. 1 Thes. i. 4.
2. 2 Thes. ii. 13.
1. 1 Tim. vi. 2.
— 2 Tim. i. 2, } see B
— Philem. 1, } (dearly.)
1. ——— 2 (ἀδελφή, *sister,* G ∼ L Tr A ℵ.)
1. ——— 16.
1. Heb. vi. 9.
1. Jas. i. 16, 19.
1. —— ii. 5.

— 1 Pet. ii. 11, see B (dearly)
1. —— iv. 12.
1. 2 Pet. i. 17.
1. —— iii. 1, 8, 14, 15, 17.
1. 1 John iii. 2, 21.
1. 1 John iv. 1, 7, 11.
— 3 John 1, see B (well.)
1. —— 2, 5, 11.
1. Jude 3, 17, 20.
2. Rev. xx. 9.

BELOVED (DEARLY.)

1. Rom. xii. 19.
1. 1 Cor. x. 14.
1. 2 Cor. vii. 1.
1. —— xii. 19.
1. Phil. iv. 1 twice.
1. 2 Tim. i. 2.
1. Philem. 1.
1. 1 Pet. ii. 11.

BELOVED (WELL.)

1. Mark xii. 6. | 1. Rom. xvi. 5.
1. 3 John 1.

BENEATH.

κάτω, *(adv. of place, from* κατά, down) down, downwards; beneath, below.

Mark xiv. 66. | Acts ii. 19.

BENEFACTOR (-s.)

εὐεργέτης, a well doer, *esp. to others,* a benefactor.

Luke xxii. 25.

BENEFIT.

1. ἀγαθός, good, *in its kind, (opp. of* κακός, *which is bad of its kind.)*
2. εὐεργεσία, well doing, good service.
3. χάρις, free favour, grace; *objectively it denotes* personal gracefulness, *a* pleasing work; *subjectively* an inclining towards, gracious disposition; *on the part of the giver it denotes* kindness, favour; *on the part of the receiver,* thanks, respect, homage.

3. 2 Cor. i. 15, marg. *grace.* | 2. 1 Tim. vi. 2.
1. Philem. 14.

BENEVOLENCE.

εὔνοια, good will, favour, kindness.

1 Cor. vii. 3 (ὀφειλή, *a debt, duty,* All.)

BERRY.

See, OLIVE.

BERYL.

βήρυλλος, a jewel of sea green colour, *(prob. from Heb.* בר, pure, bright, *and* הלל, to shine, *hence English,* brilliant.)

Rev. xxi. 20.

BESEECH (-ING, BESOUGHT.)

1. παρακαλέω, to call to one's side, *hence,* to call to aid; *every kind of* calling to *which is meant to produce a particular effect, whether of admonishing, exhorting, cheering, helping, etc.*
2. ἐρωτάω, to ask *something* of *one;* to ask *specifically,* to ask about, *hence* to question.
3. δέομαι, to be in want *or* need, *hence,* to beseech, supplicate.
4. προσκυνέω, to kiss the hand to *another as a mark of respect,* to do obeisance, *etc. to another, esp. of the Oriental fashion by* prostration, *hence* to worship.

1. Matt. viii. 5, 31, 34.
1. —— xiv. 36.
2. —— xv. 23.
4. —— xviii. 26, margin (text, *worship.*)
1. —— 29.
1. Mark i. 40.
1. —— v. 10, 12, 23.
1. —— vi. 56.
2. —— vii. 26.
1. —— 32.
1. —— viii. 22.
2. Luke iv. 38.
3. —— v. 12.
2. —— vii. 3.
3. —— viii. 28.
1. —— 31, 32, 41.
2. —— 37.
3. —— 38.
3. —— ix. 38, 40.
2. —— xi. 37.
3. —— xxi. 39.
3. —— xxvi. 3.
2. John iv. 40, 47.
2. —— xix. 31, 38.
1. Acts xiii. 42.
1. —— xvi. 15, 39.
1. —— xxi. 12.
3. —— 39.
1. Acts xxv. 2.
3. —— xxvi. 3.
1. —— xxvii. 33.
1. Rom. xii. 1.
1. —— xv. 30.
1. —— xvi. 17.
1. 1 Cor. i. 10.
1. —— iv. 16.
1. —— xvi. 15.
1. 2 Cor. ii. 8.
1. —— v. 20.
1. —— vi. 1.
1. —— x. 1.
3. —— 2.
1. —— xii. 8.
3. Gal. iv. 12.
1. Eph. iv. 1.
1. Phil. iv. 2 twice.
2. 1 Thes. iv. 1, marg. *request.*
1. —— 10.
2. —— v. 12.
1. —— 14, marg. (text, *exhort.*)
2. 2 Thes. ii. 1.
1. 1 Tim. i. 3.
1. Philem. 9, 10.
1. Heb. xiii. 19, 22.
1. 1 Pet. ii. 11.
2. 2 John 5.

BESET.

(WHICH DOTH SO EASILY.)

εὐπερίστατος, standing well around, well *or* easily surrounding *or* encompassing; well circumstanced, *of a temptation or sin, which has every advantage in favour of its prevailing, (non occ.)*

Heb. xii. 1.

BESIDE (-s.)

1. ἐπί, upon.
   (a) *with Gen.* upon, *as springing from,* over, *etc.*
   (b) *with Dat.* upon, *as resting on,* in addition to.

(c) *with Acc.* upon, *by direction towards*, up to, *etc.*

2. σύν, *conjunction*, with, *(union of co-operation)* together with.

3. χωρίς, separately, by itself, apart from, exclusive of.

4. λοιπόν, for the rest, further.

3. Matt. xiv. 21.
3. —— xv. 38.
1b. —— xxv. 20. [א.]
1b. —— 22 (*om.* G → L Tr
1b. Luke xvi. 26 (ἐν, *in*, Lm
2. —— xxiv. 21. [א.]
4. 1 Cor. i. 16.
3. 2 Cor. xi. 28.
Philem. 19, *see* OWE.

BESIDE (-s) THIS.

(Where "this" is not a separate word.)

καὶ αὐτὸ τοῦτο δέ, yea moreover for this very thing, but for this very reason also.

2 Pet. i. 5.

BESIDE ONE'S SELF (BE.)

1. ἐξίστημι, to put out of its place, to change *from one condition into another*; *metaph.* to drive *one* out of *his senses.*

(a) *intrans.* (2 *aor.*, *and Mid.*) to step aside, go away, yield; to be confused, perplexed.

2. μαίνομαι, to rage, be furious; *used of prophetic frenzy;* to be mad.

2. Mark iii. 21. | 2. Acts xxvi. 24.
1. 2 Cor. v. 13.

See, OWE.

BEST.

1. κρείσσων, stronger, more powerful, *comparative of* κρατός, power, *in effect*, strength, *as exerted.*

2. πρῶτος, the first, *of place or rank.*

2. Luke xv. 22.
1. 1 Cor. xii. 31 (μείζων, *greater*, (in ref. to size and importance) (L T Tr A א.)

BESTOWED (-ED.)

1. δίδωμι, to give, present, *(with implied notion of* giving freely, *and* enforced.)

2. συνάγω, to lead together, to gather together.

2. Luke xii. 17, 18.
— John iv. 38, } see B
— Rom. xvi. 6, } labour.
— 1 Cor. xii. 23, *see* B upon.
— 1 Cor. xiii. 3, *see* B to feed.
1. 2 Cor. viii. 1.
— Gal. iv. 11, *see* B labour.
1. 1 John iii. 1.

BESTOW LABOUR (ON.)*

κοπιάω, to be tired, grow weary, fatigued, spent *with labour.*

* John iv. 38. | Rom. xvi. 6. | Gal. iv. 11.

BESTOW TO FEED.

ψωμίζω, to feed by putting little bits into the mouth *as nurses do children; then gen.* to feed, fatten.

1 Cor. xiii. 3.

BESTOW UPON.

περιτίθημι, to place round about, put round *or* on, *hence*, to bestow, confer upon.

1 Cor. xii. 23, marg. *put on.*

BETRAY (-ED, -EST, -ETH.)

παραδίδωμι, to give *or* hand over to another *(as a torch in a torch race, one's son to a tutor, a purchase to a buyer, etc.) then* to deliver up, surrender; to give *a city or person, etc.* into another's hands.

Matt. x. 4.
—— xvii. 22.
—— xx. 18.
—— xxiv. 10.
—— xxvi. 2, 16, 21, 23, 24, 25, 45, 46, 48.
—— xxvii. 3, 4.
Mark iii. 19.
—— xiii. 12.
Mark xiv. 10, 11, 18, 21, 41, 42, 44.
Luke xxi. 16.
—— xxii. 4, 6, 21, 22, 48.
John vi. 64, 71.
—— xii. 4.
—— xiii. 2, 11, 21.
—— xviii. 2, 5.
—— xxi. 20.
1 Cor. xi. 23.

BETRAYERS.

προδότης, a betrayer, a traitor *(from* προδίδωμι, to give up to the enemy.)

Acts vii. 52.

BETTER.

1. κρείσσων, stronger, more powerful *(comp. of* κρατός, power, *in effect;* strength *as exerted.)*

(a) *neut. used as adv.* better.

2. καλός, beautiful, fair, honourable; *it contains the notion of* giving pleasure.

(a) *with* μᾶλλον, more, rather.

3. χρηστότερός, *(comp. of* χρηστός, good *of its kind)* better.

4. ὑπερέχω, to hold up *or* on high; to have above; *metaph.* to be above *others*, be superior.

2. Matt. xviii. 8, 9.
2a. Mark ix. 42.
2. ——— 43, 45, 47.
3. Luke v 39 (Positive, T [Tr A ℵ.)
1. 1 Cor. vii. 9.
1a. ——— 38.
2a. —— ix. 15.
1. —— xi. 17.
1. Phil. i. 23.
4. —— ii. 3.
1. Heb. i. 4.
— Heb. vi. 9, see B thing.
1. —— vii. 7, 19, 22.
1. —— viii. 6 twice.
1. —— ix. 23.
1. —— x. 34.
— —— xi. 16, see B country
1. ——— 35.
— ——— 40, } see B thing.
— —— xii. 24, } see B thing.
1. 1 Pet. iii. 17.
1. 2 Pet. ii. 21.

BETTER (BE.)

1. διαφέρω, to carry over *or* across, to bear abroad, carry different ways; *hence,* (a) *intrans.* to differ, *to be* different from, to be other than, *gen. in a good sense, but sometimes inferior (but not in N.T.)*

2. συμφέρω, to bear *or* bring together.
   (a) *intrans. and imp.* to contribute to, conduce to, *to be* profitable to.

3. προέχομαι, to hold before one's self, to have before *or* in preference to others; *in running,* to have the start, have the advantage of.

4. λυσιτελέω, to indemnify for expenses incurred; *hence,* to be useful *or* advantageous to.
   (a) *impers.* it profits, it is better for.

1a. Matt. vi. 26.
1. —— xii. 12.
2a. —— xviii. 6.
1a. Luke xii. 24.
4a. Luke xvii. 2.
3. Rom. iii. 9.
— 1 Cor. viii. 8, see B (be the.)

BETTER (BE THE.)

περισσεύω, to be over and above *the number;* to be more than enough, remain over; to be preëminent *or* superior.

1 Cor. viii. 8, marg. *have the more.*

BETTER COUNTRY.

κρείσσων, *see* "BETTER," *No.* 1.

Heb. xi. 16.

BETTER THING.

κρείσσων, *see* "BETTER," *No.* 1 *(neut.)*

Heb. vi. 9; xi. 40; xii. 24.

BETTERED (BE.)

ὠφελέω, to help, aid, assist, succour; *gen.* to be of service *to any one.*

(a) *mid. or pass.* to be helped, *i.e.* to receive help, aid *or* succour; to derive profit *or* advantage.

Mark v. 26.

BETWEEN.

1. μεταξύ, in the midst, *hence, of place,* betwixt, between; *of time,* between whiles, meanwhile.

2. πρός, in the direction of.
   (a) *with Gen. (hitherwards)* in favour *of.*
   (b) *with Dat. (resting in a direction towards)* near, hard by.
   (c) *with Acc. (hitherwards) of literal direction,* to; *of mental direction,* towards, against, in reference to.

3. ἐν, in, *of time, place, or element; among, with plurals, etc.*

4. { ἀνὰ, up to, up by, *has a special meaning in this and other phrases,* μέσον, middle, *of time or place; gen. in phrases,* among, } in the midst.

1. Matt. xviii. 15.
1. —— xxiii. 35.
1. Luke xi. 51.
1. —— xvi. 26.
2c. —— xxiii. 12.
— John iii. 25, see B some of.
1. John iv, 31, marg. (text, *meanwhile.*)
1. Acts xii. 6.
1. —— xiii. 42, marg. (text, [*next.*)
1. —— xv. 9.
2c. —— xxvi. 31.
3. Rom. i. 24.
4. 1 Cor. vi. 5.

BETWEEN MEATS (discern or put a difference) [margin.]

διακρίνω, to separate one from another; to distinguish; to settle, decide *as* judges.
   (a) *mid.* to doubt, hesitate *(cf.* Matt. xxi. 21; Jas. i. 6.)

Rom. xiv. 23 (text, *doubt.*)

BETWEEN SOME OF...AND.

{ ἐκ, out of, } *some* of [*John's disciples*],
{ μετά, with, } with [*the Jews.*]

John iii. 25.

See also, DIFFERENCE, WALL.

BETWIXT.

ἐκ, *(motion from the interior)* from, out of, *locally ; or as originating* from ; *or as the source, cause, or occasion,* by.

Phil. i. 23 (lit., constrained *by.*)

BEWAIL.

1. κόπτω, to beat *or* cut *as by a blow.*
   (a) *mid.* to strike one's self, *esp. one's breast, etc. through grief ; hence,* to mourn for, *with striking the breast.*
2. κλαίω, to wail, *not only with the expression of* tears, *but also with every external expression of grief* (δακρύω *is* to shed tears, John xi. 35 ; θρήνω *is* to shriek, *etc.*
3. πενθέω, to lament, mourn for, *esp. one dead ; absol.* to mourn, go into mourning.

1a. Luke viii. 52.	3. 2 Cor. xii. 21.
1a. —— xxiii. 27.	2. Rev. xviii. 9.

BEWARE.

1. βλέπω, to see, *denotes* the act of seeing. *It is also applied to mental vision,* to consider, contemplate.
2. προσέχω, to hold to, bring near to ; to turn one's mind, thoughts, attention to *a thing.*
   (a) *with pron.* to give heed to one's self.
3. φυλάσσω, (a) *intrans.* to watch, be sleepless ; to keep watch, guard.
   (b) *trans.* to watch, guard, defend. *Metaph.* to preserve, maintain.
   (c) *in mid.* to heed, take heed *or* care, to be on one's guard.

2. Matt. vii. 15.	2a. Luke xii. 1.
3. —— x. 17.	3. —————— 15.
2. —— xvi. 6, 11, 12.	2. —— xx. 46.
1. Mark viii. 15.	1. Acts xiii. 40.
1. —— xii. 38.	1. Col. ii. 8.

3. 2 Pet. iii. 17.

BEWARE OF.

3. 2 Tim. iv. 15.	1. Phil. iii. 2 3 times.

BEWITCH (-ED.)

1. βασκαίνω, to prate, *esp. about any one. Then* to prate to *any one,* to mislead *by pretences as if by magic arts,* to fascinate.
2. ἐξίστημι, (a) *trans.* to change *from one condition to another,* to drive *any one* out of his mind, to confuse, (b) *intrans.* to step aside, go away, yield ; to be confused, perplexed.

2a. Acts viii. 9, 11.	1. Gal. iii. 1.

BEWRAY (-ETH.)

{ ποιέω, to make, to do, δῆλος, visible, clear ; manifest, evident, } *lit.* makes thee manifest.

Matt. xxvi. 73.

BEYOND.

2. πέραν, on the other side, across ; *usually with notion of* water *lying between ;* beyond in a place, *without reference to motion.*
2. ἐπέκεινα, on yonder side of, beyond ; *the part beyond the far side of.*
3. ὑπέρ, over.
   (a) *with Gen. (over and separate from)* on behalf of, for.
   (b) *with Acc. (over and towards)* beyond, above, *used in comparison.*

1. Matt. iv. 15, 25.	1. John x. 40.
1. —— xix. 1.	2. Acts vii. 43.
1. Mark iii. 8.	3b. 2 Cor. viii. 3 (παρά,* *beside* or *beyond,* L T Tr A ℵ.)
1. John i. 28.	
1. —— iii. 26.	

* ὑπέρ, *affirms* superiority ; παρά, institutes the comparison and leaves the reader to *infer* superiority.

See also, GO, MEASURE, REGIONS, STRETCH.

BID (-EN, BADE.)

1. καλέω, to call ; *then,* to summon *or* invite, to call by name.
2. λέγω, to lay, to lay together, to collect, to read ; *then,* to speak, to say, λέγω *always refers to the* sentiment *of what is spoken, as No.* 3 *does to* the words.
3. εἶπον, to speak, to say ; to order, to command.
4. κελεύω, to urge *or* drive on ; *of superiors,* to exhort, command ; *of inferiors,* to urge, intreat.

5. προστάσσω, to place *or* post at *a place;* to enjoin, give as a command.

5. Matt. i. 24.
4. —— xiv. 28.
3. —— xvi. 12.
1. —— xxii. 3, 4, 8, 9.
3. —— xxiii. 3.
1. Luke vii. 39.
— —— ix. 61, see B farewell.
3. —— x. 40.
1. Luke xiv. 7, 8 twice, 9, 10 twice, 12 1st, (2nd B again) 17, 24.
3. Acts xi. 12.
— —— xviii. 21, see B farewell.
3. —— xxii. 24.
1. 1 Cor. x. 27.
2. 2 John 10, 11.

BID AGAIN.

ἀντικαλέω, to call *or* invite back *or* in return.

Luke xiv. 12 2nd.

BID FAREWELL.

ἀποτάσσομαι, *in mid.* to bid adieu *to a person or thing (from act. sig.* to set apart, assign specially.)

Luke ix. 61. | Acts xviii. 21.

BIER.

σορός, a bier *on which dead bodies were* carried *to burial (doubtless from Eng. verb* to bear, *as* feretrum *is from* fero, *Lat.* to bear.)

Luke vii. 14, marg. *coffin.*

BILL.

1. βιβλίον, a roll, scroll, billet *(dim. of* βίβλος, a roll *or* book.)
2. γράμμα, a stroke in writing, a line; *then,* a letter; *then,* anything committed to writing.

1. Mark x. 4. | 2. Luke xvi. 6, 7.

BIND (-ING, BOUND.)

1. δέω, to bind, tie, fasten.
2. δεσμεύω, to fetter, put in chains, *(non occ.)*
3. δεσμέω, *same meaning as No.* 2, *(non occ.)*
4. προτείνω, to stretch out before, to stretch out, *(non occ.)*

1. Matt. xii. 29.
1. —— xiii. 30.
1. —— xiv. 3.
1. —— xvi. 19 twice.
1. —— xviii. 18 twice.
1. —— xxii. 13.
2. —— xxiii. 4.
1. —— xxvii. 2.
1. Mark iii. 27.
1. —— v. 3, 4.
1. —— vi. 17.
1. Mark xv. 1, 7.
3. Luke viii. 29.
1. —— xiii. 16.
1. John xi. 44.
1. —— xviii. 12, 24.
1. Acts ix. 2, 14, 21.
1. —— xii. 6.
1. —— xx. 22.
1. —— xxi. 11 twice, 13, 33.
2. —— xxii. 4.
1. ———— 5.
4. Acts xxii. 25.
1. ———— 29.
1. —— xxiv. 27.
1. Rom. vii. 2.
1. 1 Cor. vii. 27, 39.
1. 2 Tim. ii. 9.
1. Rev. ix. 14.
1. —— xx. 2.

BIND ABOUT.

περιδέω, *(No.* 1 *with* περί, about, *prefixed)* to bind *or* tie round *or* on.

John xi. 44.

BIND ON.

ὑποδέω, to bind *or* tie under *(No.* 1, *with* ὑπό, under.)

(a) *in mid.* to bind under one's feet, put on *shoes (occ.* Mark vi. 9; Eph. vi. 15.)

a. Acts xii. 8.

BIND UP.

καταδέω, *(No.* 1, *with* κατά, down) to bind on *or* to, bind fast; to tie down, stop, check, *(non occ.)*

Luke x. 34.

BIND WITH.

συνδέω, *(No.* 1, *with* σύν, with) to bind together, *(implying* association,) *(non occ.)*

Heb xiii. 3.

See also, CURSE, EXECRATION, OATH.

BIRD.

1. πετεινόν, able to fly, winged; *the general epithet of birds.*
2. ὄρνεον, a bird, *both wild and domestic* (ὁ ὄρνις, *denotes* the cock.)
3. πτηνόν, feathered, winged, *(non occ.)*

1. Matt. viii. 20.
1. —— xiii. 32.
1. Luke ix. 58.
1. Rom. i. 23.
3. 1 Cor. xv. 39.
1. Jas. iii. 7.
2. Rev. xviii. 2.

BIRTH.

1. γέννησις, an engendering, producing, *(non occ.)*

2. γενετή, the hour of birth, a being born, *(non occ.)*

1. Matt. i. 18 (G ∾) (γένεσις G L T Tr A ℵ.) | 1. Luke i. 14 (γένεσις, G L T Tr A ℵ.) | 2. John ix. 1.

See also, TRAVAIL IN BIRTH.

BIRTHDAY.

γενέσια, *in pl.* the festivities of a birthday, a birthday, *(non occ.)*

Matt. xiv. 6. | Mark vi. 21.

BIRTHRIGHT.

πρωτοτόκια, the rights of the first-born. *Among the Hebrews it included the double portion,* Deut. xxi. 17; xlviii. 22; 1 Chron. v. 1, 2; *preeminence and authority,* Gen. xxvii. 29; xlix. 3. *The pro-genitorship also of the Messiah was connected with it, (non occ.)*

Heb. xii. 16.

BISHOP.

ἐπίσκοπος, watching over, taking care of. *It was the name given in Athens to the men sent into subdued states to conduct their affiairs. In the N.T. used of* πρεσβύτεροι, elders, *denoting the watchful care pertaining to them.* πρεσβύτερος, *seems to denote the* dignity *of the office; while* ἐπίσκοπος, *denotes its* duties *(occ.* Acts xx. 28.)

Phil. i. 1. | Titus i. 7.
1 Tim. iii. 2. | 1 Pet. ii. 25.

BISHOP (OFFICE OF A.)

ἐπισκοπή, *(belongs to Ecclesiastical Greek. In Classics, it denotes* visit. *The common word in Classics and* lxx. *is* ἐπίσκεψις, inspection, inquiry, visitation.) *It seems to have a twofold sense of* inspection *or* oversight, *and* guardianship; *and hence, the office or duty of an* ἐπίσκοπος.

1 Tim. iii. 1.

BISHOPRIC.

ἐπισκοπή, *see* "BISHOP (OFFICE OF.)"

Acts i. 20, marg. *office* or *charge.*

BIT.

χαλινός, a bridle *or* rein, *esp.* the bit of a bridle, *(occ.* Rev. xiv. 20.)

Jas. iii. 3.

BITE.

δάκνω, to bite, *esp. of dogs; metaph.* molest, irritate, *(non occ.)*

Gal. v. 15.

BITTER.

πικρός, pointed, sharp, keen; *hence, gen.* piercing, pungent *to the senses of taste, smell, feeling, hearing. Gen.* painful, cruel, *(non occ.)*

Jas. iii. 11, 14.

BITTER (BE.)

πικραίνω, to make sharp, keen *or* bitter, *esp. to the taste; metaph.* to embitter, irritate.

(a) *passive,* to grow angry, to foster bitter feelings.

a. Col. iii. 19. | a. Rev. x. 10.

BITTER (MAKE.)

πικραίνω, *see above. (Active.)*

Rev. viii. 11; x. 9.

BITTERLY.

πικρῶς, *adv. of* πικρός. *See* "BITTER," *(non occ.)*

Matt. xxvi. 75. | Luke xxii. 62.

BITTERNESS.

πικρία, bitterness, *of taste; of temper,* bitterness, venom, spleen.

Acts viii. 23. | Eph. iv. 31.
Rom. iii. 14. | Heb. xii. 15.

BLACK.

μέλας, black.

Matt. v. 36. | Rev. vi. 5, 12.

BLACKNESS.

1. γνόφος, a *kind of* storm, a dense cloud, darkness.

2. ζόφος, the gloom of the nether world, nether darkness.

1. Heb. xii. 18. | 2. Jude 13.

BLADE.

χόρτος, an enclosed place, *but always with the notion of* a feeding place, *then, gen.* any feeding ground. *The word soon passed from its original signification into that of* food, fodder, *esp. for cattle,* grass, hay *(from this comes Lat.* hortus, *a garden, and Eng.* gard-en; *also akin to* χορός, court.)

Matt. xiii. 26. | Mark iv. 28.

BLAME (WITHOUT.)

ἄμωμος, without blame, ridicule *or* disgrace; without blemish of sin *in himself.*

Eph. i. 4.

BLAME (-ED) [verb.]

μωμάομαι, to find fault with, to criticise *(in a bad sense.)*

2 Cor. vi. 3; viii. 20.

BLAMED (TO BE.)

καταγινώσκω, to remark, discover, *esp.* to one's prejudice, *hence,* to judge *something* of *a person,* lay *something* to his charge.

(a) *pass. part.* accused, charged, *hence,* blameworthy, *(occ.* 1 John iii. 20, 21.)

a. Gal. ii. 11.

BLAMELESS.

1. ἀνέγκλητος, not accused, with nothing laid to one's charge, *(occ.* Col. i. 22,) *(as the result of public investigation)* though blamed yet undeserving of blame.
2. ἄμεμπτος, not blamed, without reproach, *(occ.* 1 Tim. iii. 13; Heb. viii. 7.)
3. ἀμέμπτως, so as to merit no blame, so that nothing can be said against, *(occ.* 1 Thes. ii. 10.)
4. ἀμώμητος, not open to censure *or* adverse criticism.
5. ἀναίτιος, without reason *or* motive, groundless; *of persons,* guiltless, not the cause *or* fault of *a thing.*
6. ἀνεπίληπτος, not to be caught *anywhere by an antagonist (used in wrestling of a man defended and prepared at all points); hence,* one in whom there was no just cause for blame.

5. Matt. xii. 5.
2. Luke i. 6.
1. 1 Cor. i. 8.
2. Phil. ii. 15.
2. —— iii. 6.
3. 1 Thes. v. 23.
6. 1 Tim. iii. 2.
1. ——— 10.
6. —— v. 7.
1. Titus i. 6, 7.
4. 2 Pet. iii. 14 (ἄμωμος, without stain or spot of defilement, G~.)

BLASPHEME (-ED, -EST, -ING.)

βλασφημέω, to drop evil *or* profane words, revile, calumniate; *esp. to* revile God *or* divine things.

Matt. ix. 3; Mark iii. 28, 29; Luke xii. 10 (*om.* G→); John x. 36; Acts xiii. 45; xviii. 6; xxvi. 11; Rom. ii. 24; 1 Tim. i. 20; vi. 1; Titus ii. 5; Jas. ii, 7; Rev. xiii. 6; xvi. 9, 11, 21.

BLASPHEMER (-S.)

1. βλασφημέω, *see above; here the participle.*
2. βλάσφημος, abusive, reviling, destroying one's good name.

1. Acts xix. 37. | 2. 1 Tim. i. 13.
2. 2 Tim. iii. 2.

BLASPHEMOUS.

βλάσφημος, *see* "BLASPHEMER," *No.* 2.

Acts vi. 11. | Acts vi. 13 (*om.* All.)

BLASPHEMOUSLY.

βλασφημέω, *see* "BLASPHEME;" *here the participle.*

Luke xxii. 65.

BLASPHEMY.

βλασφημία, calumniation, abuse. *It seems to denote the very worst kind of slander.*

In all passages, except.

Mark ii. 7 (βλασφημέω, see under "Blaspheme," L T Tr A ℵ.) | Rev. xiii. 5 (βλάσφημος, see "Blasphemer," No. 2, G~ L Tr A.)

BLASPHEMY (SPEAK.)

βλασφημέω, *see under* "BLASPHEME."

Matt. xxvi. 65.

BLAZE ABROAD.

διαφημίζω, to make known, spread abroad.

Mark i. 45.

BLEMISH.

μῶμος, blame, shame, stain, disgrace *visibly attached to anything (prob. from Heb.* מום, a spot.) *(Personified,* Momus, *was the Critic God,) (non occ.)*

2 Pet. ii. 13.

BLEMISH (WITHOUT.)

ἄμωμος, *the above with* a, *negative prefixed.*

Eph. v. 27. | 1 Pet. i. 19.

BLESS (-ED, -ETH, -ING.)

εὐλογέω, to speak well of, praise, *as men towards God; of men toward men, etc.,* to bless, *prop. to invoke God's blessing on; of God towards men to* bless, *i.e. to distinguish with favour, confer happiness.*

Matt. v. 44 (*ap.*)
—— xiv. 19.
—— xxi. 9.
—— xxiii. 39.
—— xxv. 34.
—— xxvi. 26 (εὐχαριστέω *to give thanks,* Rec^m
Mark vi. 41. [G ∾.)
—— viii. 7.
—— x. 16 (κατευλογέω, *to bless much,* T Tr A ℵ.)
—— xi. 9, 10.
—— xiv. 22.
Luke i. 28 (*ap.*)
—— ii. 28, 34.
—— vi. 28.
—— ix. 16.
Luke xiii. 35.
—— xix. 38.
—— xxiv. 30, 50, 51.
—— 53 (*ap.*)
John xii. 13.
Acts iii. 26.
Rom. xii. 14 twice.
1 Cor. iv. 12.
—— x. 16.
—— xiv. 16.
Gal. iii. 9.
Eph. i. 3.
Heb. vi. 14 twice.
—— vii. 1, 6, 7.
—— xi. 20, 21.
Jas. iii. 9.
1 Pet. iii. 9.

BLESSED.

1. μακάριος, happy, *applied to men; but in* 1 Tim. i. 11 *and* vi. 15 *applied to God to exalt the glory of the gospel, as shewing His mercy in this dispensation.*
2. εὐλογητός, *(verbal adj. of* ευλογέω, *see* "BLESS,") blessed, *applied to God only, never to man.*

1. Matt. v. 3, 4, 5, 6, 7, 8, 9, 10, 11.
1. —— xi. 6.
1. —— xiii. 16.
1. —— xvi. 17.
1. —— xxiv. 46.
2. Mark xiv. 61.
1. Luke i. 45.
2. —— 68.
1. —— vi. 20, 21 twice, 22.
1. —— vii. 23.
1. —— xi. 27, 28.
1. —— xii. 37, 38, 43.
1. —— xiv. 14, 15.
1. —— xxiii. 29.
1. John xx. 29.
1. Acts xx. 35.
2. Rom. i. 25.
1. —— iv. 7, 8.
2. —— ix. 5.
2. 2 Cor. i. 3.
2. —— xi. 31.
2. Eph. i. 3.
1. 1 Tim. i. 11.
1. —— vi. 15.
1. Titus ii. 13.
1. Jas. i. 12, 25.
2. 1 Pet. i. 3.
1. Rev. i. 3.
1. —— xiv. 13.
1. —— xvi. 15.
1. —— xix. 9.
1. —— xx. 6.
1. —— xxii. 7, 14.

BLESSED (BE.)

ἐνευλογέομαι, to be blessed in *or* by.

Acts iii. 25. | Gal. iii. 8.

BLESSED (CALL.)

μακαρίζω, to call happy.

Luke i. 48.

BLESSEDNESS.

μακαρισμός, a pronouncing happy, felicitation.

Rom. iv. 6, 9. Gal. iv. 15.

BLESSING.

εὐλογία, good speaking, praise; *then,* thanksgiving *(from which our "eulogy.")*

Rom. xv. 29; 1 Cor. x. 16; 2 Cor. ix. 5, marg. (text, *bounty*); Gal. iii. 14; Eph. i. 3; Heb. vi. 7; xii. 17; Jas. iii. 10; 1 Pet. iii. 9; Rev. v. 12, 13; vii. 12.

BLIND [adj.]

τυφλός, blind, *naturally or spiritually* (*strictly* smoky, misty, darkened.)

Matt. xi. 5.
—— xii. 22 1st. [A ℵ.)
—— 22 2nd (*om.* L T Tr
—— xv. 14 4 times, 30, 31.
—— xxi. 14
—— xxiii. 16, 17, 19, 24, [26.
Mark x. 46.
Luke iv. 18.
—— vi. 39 twice.
—— vii. 22.
—— xiv. 13, 21.
John v. 3.
—— ix. 1, 2, 18, 19, 20, 24, 25, 32, 39, 39, 40, 41.
—— 8 (προσαίτης, *the beggar,* G L T Tr A ℵ.)
—— x. 21.
—— xi. 37.
Acts xiii. 11.
Rom. ii. 19.
2 Pet. i. 9.
Rev. iii. 17.

BLIND MAN.

Matt. ix. 27, 28.
—— xx. 30.
Mark viii. 22, 23.
Mark x. 49, 51.
Luke xviii. 35. [A ℵ.)
John ix. 6 (*om.* G→ L^b Tr
John ix. 17.

BLIND (HE THAT WAS.)

Luke vii. 21 (with art.) | John ix. 13 (with art.)

BLIND [verb.]

1. τυφλόω, to blind, make blind; *met.* to dull, baffle, *(non occ.)*
2. πωρόω, to petrify; to cause a hardening; *metaph.* to harden the heart, blunt the feelings.

1. John xii. 40.
2. Rom. xi. 7, marg. *harden.*
2. 2 Cor. iii. 14.
1. 1 John ii. 11.

BLINDFOLD (-ED.)

περικαλύπτω, to cover all round, cover quite.

Luke xxii. 64.

BLINDNESS

πώρωσις, the process by which the extremities of fractured bones are reunited by a callus; *metaph.* a hardening, hardness.

Rom. xi. 25, margin *hardness.*
Eph. iv. 18, margin *hardness.*

BLOCK.

See, STUMBLING.

BLOOD.

αἷμα, blood, (*prob. from* αἴθω, to be hot, *or from* ἄω, to breathe, *because it requires constant refrigeration from the external air.*)

Matt. ix. 20, see B (issue of)
— xvi. 17.
— xxiii. 30, 35 3 times.
— xxvi. 28.
— xxvii. 4, 6, 8, 24, 25.
Mark v. 25, 29.
— xiv. 24.
Luke viii. 43, 44.
— xi. 50, 51 twice.
— xiii. 1.
— xxii. 20, 44 (*ap.*)
John i. 13.
— vi. 53, 54, 55, 56.
— xix. 34.
Acts i. 19.
— ii. 19, 20.
— v. 28.
— xv. 20, 29.
— xvii. 26 (*om.* G→ L Tr Ab ℵ.)
— xviii. 6.
— xx. 26, 28.
— xxi. 25.
— xxii. 20.
Rom. iii. 15, 25.
— v. 9.
1 Cor. x. 16.
— xi. 25, 27.
— xv. 50.
Gal. i. 16.
Eph. i. 7.
— ii. 13.
— vi. 12.
Col. i. 14 (*ap*), 20.
Heb. ii. 14.
— ix. 7, 12 twice, 13, 14, 18, 19, 20, 21, 22 1st, 22 2nd, see B (shedding of), 25.
— x. 4, 19, 29.
— xi. 28.
— xii. 4. 24.
— xiii. 11, 12, 20.
1. Pet. i. 2, 19.
1. John i. 7.
— v. 6 twice, 8.
Rev. i. 5.
— v. 9.
— vi. 10, 12.
— vii. 14.
— viii. 7, 8.
— xi. 6.
— xii. 11.
— xiv. 20.
— xvi. 3, 4, 6 twice.
— xvii. 6 twice.
— xviii. 24.
— xix. 2, 13.

BLOOD (DISEASED WITH AN ISSUE OF.)

αἱμοῤῥοέω, (αἷμα, blood, *and* ῥόος, (*from* ῥέω, to flow,) a flux), to have *or* labour under a flow of blood, (*non occ.*)

Matt. ix. 20.

BLOOD (SHEDDING OF.)

αἱματεκχυσία, (αἷμα, blood, *and* ἐκχέω, to pour out), a pouring out *or* shedding of blood, *blood shedding*, (*non occ.*)

Heb. ix. 22.

BLOODY.

See, FLUX.

BLOT OUT (-ED, -ING.)

ἐξαλείφω, to anoint *or* smear completely, to plaster over; to wipe out, obliterate.

Acts iii. 19. | Col. ii. 14.
Rev. iii. 5.

BLOW (-ETH, BLEW.)

1. πνέω, to blow, to breathe.
2. ἐπιγίνομαι, to become after, to happen after, (*non occ.*)

1. Matt. vii. 25, 27.
1. Luke xii. 55.
1. John iii 8.
1. John vi. 18.
2. Acts xxviii. 13.
1. Rev. vii. 1.

BLOW SOFTLY.

ὑποπνέω, to breathe gently *or* softly, (*No.* 1 *with* ὑπό, *denoting* repression) (*non occ.*)

Acts xxvii. 13.

BOARD.

σανίς, a board, a plank, *or anything made of it*, (*non occ.*)

Acts xxvii. 44.

BOAST (-ED, -ETH, -ING) [verb.]

1. καυχάομαι, to speak loud, be loud tongued; to boast *or* vaunt one's self, boast of.
2. κατακαυχάομαι, to boast against *one*, exult over *him*.
3. λέγω, to lay together, collect, read; speak *or* say.

3. Acts v. 36.
2. Rom. xi. 18 2nd.
1. 2 Cor. vii. 14.
1. — ix. 2.
1. 2 Cor. x. 8.
1. — 13 (*om.* G→.)
1. — 15, 16.
1. Eph. ii. 9.

BOAST AGAINST.

1. Rom. xi. 18 1st.

BOAST GREAT THINGS.

μεγαλαυχέω, to boast highly, talk big.

Jas. iii. 5.

BOAST ONE'S SELF.

1. 2 Cor. xi. 16.

BOAST (MAKE ONE'S.)

1. Rom. ii. 17, 23.

BOASTER (-s.)

ἀλαζών, a wanderer about the country, vagabond *(the Scottish* landlouper,) *hence,* a false pretender, imposter, quack, *(non occ.)*

Rom. i. 30. | 2 Tim. iii. 2.

BOASTING [noun.]

1. καύχησις, a boasting, reason to boast, *denoting the* act.
2. καύχημα, a vaunt *or* boast; a subject of boasting.
3. ἀλαζονεία, the character of an ἀλαζών, *(see* "BOASTER,") false pretension, imposture, quackery.

1. Rom. iii. 27. | 2. 2 Cor. ix. 3.
1. 2 Cor. vii. 14. | 1. —— 4 *(om.* All.)
1. —— viii. 24. | 1. —— xi. 10, 17
3. Jas. iv. 16.

BOAT (-s.)

1. πλοιάριον, a skiff *or* boat, *(dim. of* πλοῖον, *which means strictly* a floating vessel, *hence,* a ship *or* vessel *in the most general sense.)*
2. σκάφη, any thing dug *or* scooped out *as* a trough, tub *or* basin; *hence,* a light boat *or* skiff, *(non occ.)*

1. John vi. 22 1st. | 1. John vi. 23.
1. —— 22 2nd (πλοῖον, see above, G L T Tr ℵ.) | 2. Acts xxvii. 16, 30, 32.

BODILY.

1. σῶμα, the body *as a whole, whether of men or animals, see* "BODY."
2. σωματικός, bodily, of *or* for the body, corporeally, *(adj. of No.* 1.)
3. σωματικῶς, corporeally, *(adv. of No.* 1.)

2. Luke iii. 22. | 3. Col. ii. 9.
1. 2 Cor. x. 10 (Gen.) | 2. 1 Tim. iv. 8.

BODY.

1. σῶμα, the body *as a whole, whether of man or animals, dead or alive. The necessary constituent part and organic basis of human nature; the necessary medium for the possession and manifestation of life.*
2. χρώς, the surface of any body; *esp. of the human body,* the skin *or* the flesh, *as opp. to bone; then, gen.* one's body *or* frame.

1. Matt. v. 29, 30.
1. —— vi. 22 twice, 23, 25 twice.
1. —— x. 28 twice.
1. —— xiv. 12 (πτῶμα, *a fall;* then, *that which is fallen* or *killed, a corpse,* G∾ L Tr ℵ.)
1. —— xxvi. 12, 26.
1. —— xxvii. 52, 58 1st.
1. —— 58 2nd *(om.* Trb ℵ.)
1. —— 59.
1. Mark v. 29.
1. —— xiv. 8, 22.
1. —— xv. 43.
1. —— 45 (πτῶμα, see above, Matt. xiv. 12, L T Tr A ℵ.)
1. Luke xi. 34 3 times, 36.
1. —— xii. 4, 22, 23.
1. —— xvii. 37.
1. —— xxii. 19.
1. —— xxiii. 52, 55.
1. —— xxiv. 3, 23.
1. John ii. 21.
1. —— xix. 31, 38 twice, 40.
1. —— xx. 12.
1. Acts ix. 40.
2. —— xix. 12.
1. Rom. i. 24.
1. —— iv. 19.
1. —— vi. 6, 12.
1. —— vii. 4, 24.
1. —— viii. 10, 11, 13, 23.
1. —— xii. 1, 4, 5.
1. 1 Cor. v. 3.
1. 1 Cor. vi. 13 twice, 15, 16, 18 twice, 19, 20.
1. —— vii. 4 twice, 34.
1. —— ix. 27.
1. —— x. 16, 17.
1. —— xi. 24, 27, 29.
1. —— xii. 12 3 times, 13, 14, 15 twice, 16 twice, 17, 18, 19, 20, 22, 23, 24, 25, 27.
1. —— xiii. 3.
1. —— xv. 35, 37, 38 twice, 40 twice.
1. —— 44 1st, 2nd, & 3rd.
1. —— 44 4th *(om.* G→ L T Tr A ℵ.)
1. 2 Cor. iv. 10 twice.
1. —— v. 6, 8, 10.
1. —— xii. 2 twice, 3 twice.
1. Gal. vi. 17.
1. Eph. i. 23.
1. —— ii. 16.
1. —— iv. 4, 12, 16 twice.
1. —— v. 23, 28, 30.
1. Phil. i. 20.
1. —— iii. 21 twice.
1. Col. i. 18, 22, 24.
1. —— ii. 11, 17, 19, 23.
1. —— iii. 15.
1. 1 Thes. v. 23.
1. Heb. x. 5, 10, 22.
1. —— xiii. 3, 11.
1. Jas. ii. 16, 26.
1. —— iii. 2, 3, 6.
1. 1 Pet. ii. 24.
1. Jude 9.
1. Rev. xviii. 13, margin (text, *slave.*)

BODY (DEAD.)

πτῶμα, a fall, *then* that which is fallen, a corpse.

Rev. xi. 8, 9 twice.

BODY (OF THE SAME.)

σύσσωμος, together with the same body, united in the same body, *(non occ.)*

Eph. iii. 6.

BOISTEROUS.

ἰσχυρός, strong, mighty, powerful, *(adj. from* ἰσχύω, *see* "ABLE."

Matt. xiv. 30, marg. *strong.*

BOLD (BE.)

1. τολμάω, to undertake, take heart *either* to do *or* bear *anything terrible or difficult;* to dare, to venture, to have courage.
2. παῤῥησιάζομαι, to speak freely, openly, boldly, with fearless candour.

3. θαρρέω, *(from* θέρω, to be warm, *and because persons of a warm temper are naturally* confident *and* courageous *it denotes* to be of good cheer, to be full of hope *and* confidence.

3. 2 Cor. x. 1.	1. 2 Cor. xi. 21 twice.
3. —— 2 1st.	1. Phil. i. 14.
1. —— 2 2nd.	2. 1 Thes. ii. 2.

BOLD (BE MUCH.)

ἔχω, to have,
πολλὴν, much,
παῤῥησίαν, freedom *or* frankness of speaking; *a frankness that sometimes amounts to* boldness *and* intrepidity; fearless candour.

Philem. 8.

BOLD (BE VERY.)

ἀποτολμάω, to make a bold venture, to dare very much, *(non occ.)*

Rom. x. 20.

BOLD (WAX.)

παῤῥησιάζομαι, to speak freely, openly, boldly.

Acts xiii. 46.

BOLDLY.

1. παῤῥησία, the speaking all one thinks, freedom *or* frankness of speaking; *a frankness that under some circumstances amounts to* boldness *and* intrepidity; fearless candour.
   (a) *with* ἐν, in.
   (b) *with* μετά, with.
2. παῤῥησιάζομαι, to speak freely *or* with fearless candour.
3. θαρρέω, *see* "BOLD," *No.* 3.
4. τολμάω, *see* "BOLD," *No.* 1.

4. Mark xv. 43	2. 1 Thes. ii. 2.
1. John vii. 26 (Dat.)	1b. Heb. iv. 16.
1a. Eph. vi. 19.	3. —— xiii. 6.

BOLDLY (PREACH.)

2. Acts ix. 27.

BOLDLY (SPEAK.)

2. Acts xiv. 3.	2. Acts xix. 8.
2. —— xviii. 26.	2. Eph. vi. 20.

BOLDLY (THE MORE.)

τολμηρότερον, *(comp. of* τολμηρός,) more daring, more boldly *or* freely, *(non occ.)*

Rom. xv. 15.

BOLDNESS.

παῤῥησία, *see* "BOLDLY," *No.* 1.

Acts iv. 13, 29, 31.	1. Tim. iii. 13.
Eph. iii. 12.	Heb. x. 19, marg. *liberty.*
Phil. i. 20.	1. John iv. 17.

BOLDNESS OF SPEECH.

2 Cor. iii. 12, marg. (text, *plainness of speech.*)
—— vii. 4.

BOND (-s) [noun.]

1. δεσμός, a band, bond *or* fetter; *gen.* anything for tying or fastening; bonds, imprisonment.
   * *denotes neut. pl.*
2. σύνδεσμος, that which binds together, a band *or* bond; that which is bound together, a bundle.
3. ἅλυσις, a chain, *esp. a woman's ornament (from* a, *negative, and* λύω, to loose.)

1. Luke xiii. 16.	2. Col. iii. 14.
2. Acts viii. 23.	1. —— iv. 18.
1*. —— xx. 23.	1. 2 Tim. ii. 9.
1. —— xxiii. 29.	1. Philem. 10, 13.
1. —— xxvi. 29, 31.	1. Heb. x. 34 (δέσμιος, *those in bonds,* instead of δεσμοῖς μοῦ, G L T Tr [A.)
2. Eph. iv. 3.	1. —— xi. 36.
3. —— vi. 20, marg. *chain.*	
1. Phil. i. 7, 13, 14, 16.	

BONDS (IN.)

δέσμιος, a binding, one bound.

Acts xxv. 14.

BONDS (BE IN.)

δέω, to bind, tie, fasten, fetter.

Col. iv. 3 (perf. pass.)

BONDS (THAT IS IN.)

δέσμιος, a binding, one bound.

Heb. xiii. 3.

BOND. [adj.]

δοῦλος, a slave; *the lowest word in the scale of servitude, (see under* "SERVANT,") *strictly* one born a slave.

1 Cor xii. 13.
Gal. iii. 28.
Eph. vi. 8.
Col. iii. 11.
Rev. xiii. 16.
—— xix. 18.

BONDAGE.

δουλεία, servitude, slavery.

Rom. viii. 15, 21.
Gal. iv. 24.
Gal. v. 1.
Heb. ii. 15.

BONDAGE (BE IN.)

δουλεύω, to serve *as a slave;* to be a slave, *(diff. from* δουλόω, to enslave.)

John viii. 33.
Acts vii. 7.
Gal. iv. 9, 25.

BONDAGE (BE UNDER.)

δουλόω, to make a slave of.

(a) *pass.* to be enslaved.

a. 1 Cor. vii. 15.

BONDAGE (BRING INTO)* *or* (BRING IN.)†

δουλόω, to make a slave of.

(a) *pass.* to be enslaved.

Acts vii. 6*.
a. 2 Pet. ii. 19†.

BONDAGE (IN.)

a. Gal. iv. 3.

BONDMAID.

παιδίσκη, a young girl, a maiden; a young female slave.

Gal. iv. 22.

BONDMAN.

δοῦλος, a slave; *the lowest word in the scale of servitude (cf.* "SERVANT,") *strictly* one born a slave.

Rev. vi. 15.

BONDWOMAN.

παιδίσκη, *see* "BONDMAID."

Gal. iv. 23, 30 twice, 31.

BONE (-s.)

ὀστέον, a bone, *(prob. from* עָז, strength, *or* עֵץ, firmness, *so Latin* os.)

Matt. xxiii. 27.
Luke xxiv. 39.
John xix. 36.
Eph. v. 30 (*ap.*)
Heb. xi. 22.

See also, ANCLE.

BOOK (-s.)

1. *βίβλος*, the inner part of the papyrus (*βύβλος*); *gen.* bark, *then* the paper made of this bark *(first in Egypt)*, a paper, a written book, roll *or* volume.

2. *βιβλίον*, *(dim. of No.* 1), a paper, a letter; a book.

1. Matt. i. 1.
1. Mark xii. 26.
1. Luke iii. 4.
2. —— iv. 17 twice, 20.
1. —— xx. 42.
2. John xx. 30.
2. —— xxi. 25.
1. Acts i. 20.
1. —— vii 42.
1. —— xix. 19.
2. Gal. iii. 10.
1. Phil. iv. 3.
2. 2 Tim. iv. 13.
2. Heb. ix. 19.
2. —— x. 7.
2. Rev. i. 11.
1. —— iii. 5.
2. Rev. v. 1, 2, 3, 4, 5.
2. —— 7 (*om.* G⇉ L T Tr A ℵ.)
2. —— 8, 9.
1. —— xiii. 8 (No. 2, G L T Tr A.)
2. —— xvii. 8.
2. —— xx. 12 3 times.
1. —— 15.
2. —— xxi. 27.
2. —— xxii. 7, 9, 10, 18 twice.
1. —— 19 1st (No. 2, G L T Tr A ℵ.)
1. —— 19 2nd (*ξύλον*, *tree*, G L T Tr A ℵ.),
2. —— 19 3rd.

BOOK (LITTLE.)

βιβλαρίδιον, *(a dim. of No.* 1), a little book.

Rev. x. 2 (No. 2, G∾.)
—— x. 8 (No. 2, L Tr) (*βιβλιδάριον*, *a small cord of* [*βιβλος*, T.)
—— x. 9, 10.

BORDER (-s.)

1. *κράσπεδον*, the edge, border, margin, hem *of a thing, esp. of cloth; met.* the edge *of a country.*

2. *μεθόριος*, lying between as a boundary; the frontier,

3. *ὅριον*, a bound, goal, limit, *in pl.* the borders *of a place, hence,* districts, territory.

3. Matt. iv. 13.
1. —— xxiii. 5.
1. Mark vi. 56.
2. Mark vii. 24 (No. 3, L Tr ℵ.)
1. Luke viii. 44.

BORN AT ALEXANDRIA.

{ *Ἀλεξανδρεὺς*, an Alexandrian,
{ *τῷ γένει*, by birth.

Acts xviii. 24.

BORN IN PONTUS.

{ *Ποντικὸς*, a Pontic,
{ *τῷ γένει*, by birth,

Acts xviii. 2.

BORN (BE.)

1. γεννάω, to beget, *of the father;* to bring forth, *of the mother.*

   (a) *pass.* be born.

2. τίκτω, to bring into the world; *of the father,* to beget; *of the mother,* to bring forth.

   (a) *passive.*

1a. Matt. i. 16.
1a. —— ii. 1.
2a. —— 2.
1a. —— 4.
1a. —— xix. 12.
1a. —— xxvi. 24.
1a. Mark xiv. 21.
1a. Luke i. 35.
2a. —— ii. 11.
1a. John i. 13.
1a. —— iii. 3, 4 twice, 5, 6, 7, 8.
1a. —— viii. 41.
1a. —— ix. 2, 19, 20, 32, 34.
1a. John xvi. 21.
1a. —— xviii. 37.
1a. Acts ii. 8.
1a. —— vii. 20.
1a. —— xxii. 3, 28.
1a. Rom. ix. 11.
1a. Gal. iv. 23, 29.
1a. Heb. xi. 23.
1a. 1 John ii. 29.
1a. —— iii. 9 twice.
1a. —— iv. 7.
1a. —— v. 1, 4, 18.
2. Rev. xii. 4.

BORN AGAIN (BE.)

ἀναγεννάω, to beget again, to bear again. *It is used of the redeeming act of God; a new beginning of personal life.*

(a) *passive.*

a. 1 Pet. i. 23.

BORN OUT OF DUE TIME (ONE.)

ἔκτρωμα, a child untimely born, an abortion.

1 Cor. xv. 8, marg. *an abortive.*

BORN (THAT IS.)

γεννητός, begotten, *(non occ.)*

Matt. xi. 11. | Luke vii. 28.

See also, FIRST, NEW.

BORNE.

See, GRIEVOUS.

BORROW.

δανείζω, to put out money at usury, to lend.

(a) *mid.* to have lent to one, to borrow.

(b) *pass. of the money,* to be lent out. *(occ.* Luke vi. 34, 35.)

a. Matt. v. 42.

BOSOM.

κόλπος, the bosom, the chest; *any bosom-like hollow, esp.* that between the waves; a bay *or* gulph, *etc.*

Luke vi. 38.
—— xvi. 22, 23.
John i. 18.
—— xiii. 23.

BOTH.

1. καί, *(conj.) the conjunction of annexation, uniting things strictly co-ordinate,* and, also, even. *When translated* both *is always followed by another* καί, *which is translated* and, (καί unites; τε annexes.)

2. τε, *a conj. of annexation, annexing with an implied relation or distinction* and, also, *(annexing something added)* τε *denotes an internal, logical relation;* καί, *(No.* 1*) an external relation. When translated* both, *it is followed*

   (a) *either by* καί, and,

   (b) *or by another* τε,

   (c) *or by* δέ, *a conj. of antithesis,* and *or* but.

3. ἀμφότερος, *(adj.)* both, *of two.*

4. δύο, two *(so in all kindred languages, Lat.* duo; *Sans.* dwi; *Old Germ.* zwo, zwei.)

5. ἕκαστος, each one, every one.

3. Matt. ix. 17.
1. —— x. 28.
1. —— xii. 22.
3. —— xiii. 30.
3. —— xv. 14.
2a. —— xxii. 10.
1. Mark vi. 30 (*om.* G⇉L Tr A ℵ.)
1. —— vii. 37.
3. Luke i. 6, 7.
1. —— ii. 46.
3. —— v. 7.
1. —— 36.
3. —— 38 (*om.* G→T Trb A ℵ.)
3. —— vi. 39.
3. —— vii. 42.
1. —— xxii. 33.
1. John iv. 36.
1. —— vii. 28.
1. —— xi. 48.
1. —— 57 (*om.* L T Tr A ℵ.)
1. —— xii. 28.
1. —— xv. 24.
4. —— xx. 4.
2a. Acts i. 1, 8, 13.
1. —— ii. 29.
2a. —— iv. 27.
2c. —— v. 14.
3 2a. —— viii. 12.
3. —— 38 1st.
2a. —— 38 2nd.
2a. —— x. 39.
2a. —— xiv. 1, 5.
2a. —— xix. 10.
2a. Acts xx. 21.
2a. —— xxi. 12.
2a. —— xxii. 4.
3. —— xxiii. 8.
2a. —— xxiv. 15.
2a. —— xxv. 24.
2b. —— xxvi. 16.
1. —— 29.
2a. —— xxviii. 23.
2a. Rom. i. 12, 14 twice.
2a. —— iii. 9.
1. —— xi. 33.
1. —— xiv. 9 twice.
2a. 1 Cor. i. 2, 24.
1. —— iv. 11.
1. —— vi. 13.
1. —— 14, B..and also.
1. —— vii. 34.
2a. Eph. i. 10 (*om.* All.)
3. —— ii. 14, 16, 18.
2a. Phil. i. 7.
1. —— ii. 13.
1. —— iv. 9 1st.
1. —— 12 (δέ, St.)
1. —— 12 2nd & 3rd.
1. 1 Thes. ii. 15.
1. —— v. 15 (*om.* G⇉L Tr ℵ.)
1. 2 Thes. iii. 4.
1. 1 Tim. iv. 10 (*om.* G→L Tr Ab ℵ.)
1. —— 16.
1. Titus i. 9.
1. Philem. 16.
2a. Heb. ii. 4, 11.
2a. —— v. 1, 14.

2a. Heb. vi. 19.
2a. —— ix. 9, 19.
2a. —— x. 33.
5. —— xi. 21.
1. 2 Pet. iii. 18.
1. 2 John 9.
1. Rev. xiii. 15.
4. —— xix. 20.

BOTTLE (-s.)

ἀσκός, a leathern bag, *mostly of goatskin;* a wine skin.

Matt. ix. 17 4 times.
Mark ii. 22 3 times (*ap.*)
Luke v. 37 3 times.
—— 38.

BOTTOM.

κάτω, down, downwards.

Matt. xxvii. 51.

BOTTOMLESS.

ἄβυσσος, bottomless, unfathomed, *gen.* boundless, *exhaustless, as a noun,* the deep, the abyss, *(occ.* Luke viii. 31; Rom. x. 7; *"deep.")*

Rev. ix. 1, 2 (*ap.*)

BOTTOMLESS PIT.

Rev. ix. 11.
—— xi. 7.
Rev. xvii. 8.
—— xx. 1, 3.

BOUND (-s) [noun.]

ὁροθεσία, the fixing of a boundary, a boundary set, *(non occ.)*

Acts xvii. 26.

BOUND (BE.)

ὀφείλω, to owe, have to pay *or* account for; *gen.* to be in debt; *in wider sig.* to be under an obligation, to be bound.

Matt. xxiii. 18, marg (text, *be guilty.*)
2 Thes. i. 3.
—— ii. 13.

BOUND WITH (BE.)

περίκειμαι, to lie round about; to have round one, wear.

Acts xxviii. 20.

See, BIND.

BOUNTIFULLY.

εὐλογία, good speaking, good language, commendation, *in a good sense, "eulogy;"* adulation, *in a bad sense. Then* blessing, the blessing which the gospel secures, bounty.

2 Cor. ix. 6 twice (pl. with ἐπί, *upon.*)

BOUNTIFULNESS.

ἁπλότης, simplicity, sincerity of mind, freedom from sinister design; *then, that which springs from such a mind,* liberality, bountifulness.

2 Cor. ix. 11.

BOUNTY.

εὐλογία, *see* "BOUNTIFULLY."

2 Cor. ix. 5 1st (marg. *Gr. blessing.*)

BOUNTY (MATTER OF.)

2 Cor. ix 5 2nd.

BOW [noun.]

τόξον, a bow, *(non occ.)*

Rev. vi. 2.

BOW [verb.]

1. κάμπτω, to bend, to curve, *used of the knee in worship or prayer, (non occ.)*
2. κλίνω, to make to bend, *to bow in reverence or in death.*
3. τίθημι, to put, set, place; *then, gen.* to bring *a thing* into a place, *and so* to bring into a situation, to bring about, cause.

3. Mark xv. 19.
2. John xix. 30.
1. Rom. xi. 4.
1. Rom. xiv. 11.
1. Eph. iii. 14.
1. Phil. ii. 10.

BOW DOWN.

1. συγκάμπτω, to bend together, bend *the knee-joint; metaph.* to bow down, humble, *(non occ.)*
2. κλίνω, *see No.* 2, *above.*

2. Luke xxiv. 5.
1. Rom. xi. 10.

BOWED TOGETHER (BE.)

συγκύπτω, to bend forwards towards each other, *(non occ.)*

Luke xiii. 11.

See also, KNEE.

BOWELS.

σπλάγχνα, the inward parts, *esp. the nobler parts of them; metaph. like Eng.* heart, the seat of the feelings, affections.

Luke i. 78, marg. (text, *tender.*)
Acts i. 18.
2 Cor. vi. 12.
—— vii. 15, marg. (text, *inward affection.*)
Phil. i. 8.
—— ii. 1.
Col. iii. 12.
Philem. 7, 12, 20.

BOWELS OF COMPASSION.

1 John iii. 17.

BOX.

See, ALABASTER.

BRAMBLE BUSH.

βάτος, a bramble bush.

Luke vi. 44.

BRANCH.

1. *κλάδος*, a young slip *or* shoot *of a tree, such as is broken off for grafting; gen.* a young branch *or* shoot *of any tree, but esp. the olive, (non occ.)*
2. *κλῆμα*, a slip, a cutting, *esp.* a vine twig, *(non occ.)*
3. *στοιβάς*, a kind of bed *composed of* boughs *of trees*, leaves *or the like* trampled *or* crammed together *(from στείβω,* to tread upon); *in pl.* the branches themselves.
4. *βαΐον*, a branch of the palm tree.
5. *ἀνατολή*, a rising, *as of the sun or moon (or of a river or teeth), or of plants*, a shoot, *cf.* Zech. vi. 12.

1. Matt. xiii. 32.
1. —— xxi. 8.
1. —— xxiv. 32.
1. Mark iv. 32.
3. —— xi. 8.
1. —— xiii. 28.
5. Luke i. 78, marg. (text, *day-spring.*)
1. —— xiii. 19.
4. John xii. 13.
2. —— xv. 2, 4, 5, 6.
1. Rom. xi. 16,17,18,19,21.

BRASS.

χαλκός, copper, *(the first metal which men learned to smelt and work), hence used for metals in general, but later applied to* bronze, a mixture of copper and tin, *(our brass, which is a mixture of copper and zinc, is said to have been quite unknown to the Ancients.) Used also of any thing* made of brass *or* metal, *as* arms, vessels *or* coins.

Matt. x. 9. | 1 Cor. xiii. 1. | Rev. xviii. 12.

BRASS (FINE.)

χαλκολίβανον, white *or* shining copper, *(from χαλκός,* copper, *and* לבן, white.) *Some, however, think it to be* frankincense of a gold colour *(from λίβανος,* frankincense, *and χαλκός,* copper.)

Rev. i. 15; ii. 18.

BRASS (OF.)

χάλκεος, adj. of copper *or* bronze.

Rev. ix. 20.

BRAWLER (NO)* (NOT A).†

ἄμαχος, without battle; *and so,* with whom no one fights; disinclined to fight, peaceful.

† 1 Tim. iii. 3. | * Titus iii. 2.

BRAWLING [margin.]

μάχη, battle, fight, combat; a quarrel, strife, wrangling.

Jas. iv. 1 (text, *fighting.*)

BRAZEN VESSEL (-s.)

χαλκίον, a copper utensil, vessel, *etc.*

Mark vii. 4.

BREAD.

ἄρτος, bread, a loaf, *esp.* of wheat *(barley-bread denotes μᾶζα) (prob. from Sans. root* AR, the earth, *from which a large number of words in various languages are derived, all connected with the earth, e.g. ἄρατρον,* a plough, *Lat.* aratrum; *so ἄρτος,* bread, *it being the most important product of the earth.)*

Matt. iv. 3, 4.
—— vi. 11.
—— vii. 9.
—— xv. 2, 26, 33.
—— xvi. 5, 7, 8, 11.
—— 12 (*om.* T ℵ.)
—— xxvi. 26.
Mark iii. 20.
—— vi. 8.
—— 36 (*om.* G ∾ L[b] Tr) (*βρῶμα, that which is eaten, food,* ℵ.)
—— 37.
—— vii. 2, 5, 27.
—— viii. 4, 14, 16, 17.
—— xiv. 22.
Luke iv. 3, 4.
—— vii. 33 (*om.* G→.)
—— ix. 3.
Luke xi. 3, 11.
—— xiv. 1.
—— 15 (*ἄριστον*, the morning *meal*, G∾ℵ[c].)
—— xv. 17.
—— xxii. 19.
—— xxiv. 30, 35.
John vi. 5, 7, 23, 31, 32 twice, 33, 34, 35, 41, 48, 50, 51 3 times, 58 twice.
—— xiii. 18.
—— xxi. 9, 13.
Acts ii. 42, 46.
—— xx. 7, 11.
—— xxvii. 35.
1 Cor. x. 16, 17 twice.
—— xi. 23, 26, 27, 28.
2 Cor. ix. 10.
2 Thes. iii. 8, 12.

BREAD (SHEW.)

1. { ἄρτοι, loaves,
   τῆς, of the,
   προθέσεως, setting before.

2. { πρόθεσις, the setting before,
   τῶν ἄρτων, of the loaves.

1. Matt. xii. 4.
1. Mark ii. 26.
1. Luke vi. 4.
2. Heb. ix. 2.

BREAD (UNLEAVENED.)

ἄζυμος, without process of fermentation; *of bread*, unleavened, *with art. it denotes* the feast of unleavened bread; *metaph.* uncorrupted, sincere, (*occ.* 1 Cor. v. 7.)

Matt. xxvi. 17.
Mark xiv. 1, 12.
Luke xxii. 1, 7.
Acts xii. 3.
—— xx. 6.
1 Cor. v. 8.

See also, DAILY.

BREADTH.

πλάτος, breadth, width.

Eph. iii. 18.
Rev. xxi. 16 twice.
Rev. xx. 9.

BREAK [noun.]

See, DAY.

BREAK (-AKE, -ING, -OKEN) [verb.]

1. κλάω, to break, break off *or* in pieces.
2. κατακλάω, to break down, break short, snap off.
3. λύω, to loose; loosen, unbind, unfasten.
4. συντρίβω, to rub together; shatter, shiver, break in pieces *by crushing*.
5. ῥήγνυμι, to break *or* burst; to tear, rend *as garments, a line of soldiers, etc.*
6. διαῤῥήγνυμι, to break *or* burst through, burst asunder; rend *or* cleave *in various ways*.
7. κατάγνυμι, to break in pieces, break.
8. συνθλάω, to crush together.
9. συνθρύπτω, to break small, weaken, enfeeble.
10. σχίζω, to split, cleave; *gen.* to part asunder, separate; rend, tear.

3. Matt. v. 19.
— —— vi. 19, 20, see B through.
5. —— ix. 17.
7. —— xii. 20.
1. —— xiv. 19.
1. —— xv. 36.
8. —— xxi. 44 (*ap.*)
— —— xxiv. 43, see B up.
1. —— xxvi. 26.
— Mark ii. 4, see B up.
— —— v. 4, see B in pieces.
2. —— vi. 41.
1. —— viii. 6, 19.
4. —— xiv. 3.
1. ———— 22.
6. Luke v. 6.
6. —— viii. 29.
2. —— ix. 16.
— —— xii. 39, see B through
8. —— xx. 18.
1. —— xxii. 19.
1. Luke xxiv. 30.
3. John v. 18.
3. —— vii. 23.
3. —— x. 35.
7. —— xix. 31, 32, 33.
4. ———— 36.
10. —— xxi. 11.
1. Acts ii. 46.
— —— xiii. 43, see B up.
1. —— xx. 7, 11.
9. —— xxi. 13.
1. —— xxvii. 35.
3. ———— 41.
— Rom. xi. 17, 19, 20, see B off.
1. 1 Cor. x. 16.
1. —— xi. 24 twice (*om.* 2nd L T Tr A ℵ.)
— Gal. iv. 27, see B forth.
3. Eph. ii. 14.
— Rev. ii. 27, see B to shivers.

BREAK FORTH.

5. Gal. iv. 27.

BREAK IN PIECES.

4. Mark v. 4.

BREAK OFF.

ἐκκλάω, (*or* ἐκκλάζω,) to break off, (*No.* 1 *with* ἐκ, from.)

Rom. xi. 17, 19, 20 (No. 1, L Tr.)

BREAK THROUGH.

διορύσσω, to dig through; *metaph.* to undermine, ruin.

Matt. vi. 19, 20.
Luke xii. 39.

BREAK TO SHIVERS.

4. Rev. ii. 27.

BREAK UP.

1. λύω, *see* "BREAK," *No.* 3.
2. διορύσσω, to dig through.
3. ἐξορύσσω, to dig out *or* through, force up, to pluck out *the eyes*.

2. Matt. xxiv. 43.
1. Acts xiii. 43.
3. Mark ii. 4.

See also, BROKEN.

BREAKER (-s.)

παραβάτης, one who goes beside, *as the combatant with the charioteer; one who* passes by the side of, a transgressor.

Rom. ii. 25.

See also, COVENANT, TRUCE.

BREAKING [noun.]

1. κλάσις, a breaking, fracture; a breaking off.
2. παράβασις, a going aside, deviation; an overstepping, transgression.

1. Luke xxiv. 35. | 1. Acts ii. 42.
2. Rom. ii. 23.

BREAST.

στῆθος, the breast, *of both sexes, also of animals; metaph.* the breast as the seat of feeling, passion, *and* thought *(non occ.)*

Luke xviii. 13. | John xiii. 25.
—— xxiii. 48. | —— xxi. 20.
Rev. xv. 6.

BREASTPLATE.

θώραξ, a breastplate, cuirass, *(non occ.)*

Eph. vi. 14. | 1 Thes. v. 8.
Rev. ix. 9 twice, 17.

BREATH.

1. πνοή, a blowing, wind, blast, air; *of animals,* a breathing hard, fetching breath; *then, gen. the breath, (occ.* Acts ii. 2.*)*
2. πνευμα, wind, air; the air we breathe, breath; life; a Spirit; a Spiritual Being.

1. Acts xvii. 25.
2. Rev. xiii 15, marg. (text, *life.*)

BREATHE ON.

ἐμφυσάω, to breathe upon, blow upon, *(non occ.)*

John xx. 22.

BREATHE OUT.

ἐμπνέω, to blow *or* breathe on *or* in, *(non occ.)*

Acts ix. 1.

BRETHREN.

See, BROTHER.

BRIDE.

νύμφη, a bride *or* young wife *(prob. from* nubo, to veil, *because led* veiled *from her home to the bridegroom's;) hence,* a daughter-in-law.

John iii. 29. | Rev. xxi. 2, 9 (*om.* G∾.)
Rev. xviii. 23. | —— xxii. 17.

BRIDECHAMBER.

νυμφών, a bridal chamber, *(non occ.)*

Matt. ix. 15. | Mark ii. 19.
Luke v. 34.

BRIDEGROOM.

νυμφίος, of marriageable age; *with art.* a bridegroom.

Matt. ix. 15 twice. | Luke v. 34, 35.
—— xxv. 1, 5, 6, 10. | John ii. 9.
Mark ii. 19 1st (*ap.*) | —— iii. 29 3 times.
—— 19 2nd, 20. | Rev. xviii. 23.

BRIDLE [noun.]

χαλινός, a bridle *or* rein, *esp.* the bit of a bridle, *(occ.* Jas. iii. 3.)

Rev. xiv. 20.

BRIDLE (-ETH) [verb.]

χαλιναγωγέω, to lead, guide with *or* as with a bridle, *(non occ.)*

Jas. i. 26; iii. 2.

BRIEFLY.

{ δι', by means of, in, / ὀλιγων, few, } in few [*words.*]

1 Pet. v. 12.

See also, COMPREHEND.

BRIER (-s.)

τρίβολος, three pointed, three pronged; *from the likeness of shape,* a prickly water-plant; *also a like* plant on land, *which was apt to stick in sheep's wool, (occ.* Matt. vii. 16.)

Heb. vi. 8.

BRIGHT.

1. λαμπρός, bright, brilliant, radiant.
2. φωτεινός, shining, bright, *(opp. to σκοτεινός, dark.)*

2. Matt. xvii. 5 (G ~) (φωτος *of light*, G.) | — Luke xi. 36, see shining | 1. Acts x. 30. 1. Rev. xxii. 16.

BRIGHTNESS.

1. ἀπαύγασμα, what is radiated, reflected light, reflection, *(non occ.)*
2. ἐπιφάνεια, the appearance, manifestation; *esp. the second coming of Christ.*
3. λαμπρότης, brilliancy, splendour, *(non occ.)*

3. Acts xxvi. 13. | 1. Heb. i. 3. | 2. 2 Thes. ii. 8.

BRIM (UP TO THE.)

ἕως, up to, as far as, ἄνω, up, above, *with art. deno es* that which is above, } up to the higher parts *or* brim.

John ii. 7.

BRIMSTONE.

θεῖον, fire from heaven, *(places touched by lightning were called θεῖα,) as lightning leaves a sulphureous smell, and sulphur was used in heathen purifications, it got the name of θεῖον.* Brimstone *(from* brienne *or* brin, *i.e.* burn *and* stone.) *From heathen uses in their religions God made it an instrument of His vengeance in the heathen*; *(cf.* Gen. xix. 24; Job. xviii. 15; Ps. xi. 6; Deut. xxix. 23; Is. xxx. 33; xxxiv. 9; Jude 7.)

Luke xvii. 29. | Rev. xix. 20.
Rev. ix. 17 2nd. | —— xx. 10.
—— xiv. 10. | —— xxi. 8.

BRIMSTONE (OF.)

θειώδης, *(from θεῖον, above)* of brimstone, brimstone-like.

Rev. ix. 17 1st.

BRING.

(-EST, -ETH, -ING; BROUGHT, but see also, BROUGHT (BE).)

1. φέρω, to bear, *(Lat.* fero, *Sans.* bhri, *Pers.* ber, *Germ.* bahren, fahren, *Eng.* bear) to bear *or* carry a *load (with idea of motion;)* to bear *as fruit,* to endure, bear with.
2. ἀποφέρω, *(No.* 1, *with* ἀπό, from, *prefixed)* to carry off *or* away; to carry *or* bring back.
3. ἐπιφέρω, *(No.* 1, *with* ἐπί, upon) to bring, put, *or* lay upon; to bring *(i.e.* to confer *or* impose) upon, *in a good or bad sense,* to charge upon *one.*
4. προσφέρω, *(No.* 1, *with* πρός, towards) to bring to *or* towards; to bring in addition to, contribute.
5. ἄγω, to lead, lead along, take with one *(used of persons, as No.* 1 *is of things),* to lead *as a General,* to guide *as the gods.*
6. ἀνάγω, *(No.* 5, *with* ἀνά, up) to lead up, *from a lower place to a higher.*
7. ἀπάγω, *(No.* 5, *with* ἀπό, from) to lead away, take off.
8. κατάγω, *(No.* 5, *with* κατά, down) to lead down, *gen.* to lead *or* carry to a place.
9. προσάγω, *(No.* 5, *with* πρός, towards) *trans.* to lead to *or* towards, to bring near, *intrans.* to come to, to approach.
10. λαμβάνω, *orig. signif. twofold one (more active)* to take, *the other (more passive)* to receive; to take, take hold of, grasp, seize, *as with the hand: hence,* to receive, obtain.
11. κομίζω, to take care of, provide for; to carry away, *so as to preserve;* to carry, convey, bear; bring to.
12. παρέχω, to hold beside *or* near, hold in readiness; *then,* to offer, furnish, supply.

— Matt. i. 21, 23, 25, see B forth. | — Matt. vii. 17twice, 18twice, 19, see B forth.
— —— iii 8, 10, see B forth. | — —— viii. 16, see B unto.
— —— iv. 24, see B unto. | — —— ix. 2, 32, see B to.
— —— v. 23, see B to. | 5. —— x. 18.

— Matt. xi. 23, see B down.
— —— xii. 22, see B unto.
— ——— 35 twice, see B forth.
— —— xiii. 8, 23, 26, 52, see B forth.
1. —— xiv. 11 twice, 18.
— ——— 35, see B unto.
10. —— xvi. 8 (ἔχετε, ye have, L ℵ.)
— —— xvii. 1, see B up.
— ——— 16, see B to.
1. ——— 17.
— —— xviii. 24, } see B
— —— xix. 13, } unto.
5. —— xxi. 2, 7.
— ——— 43, see B forth.
— —— xxii. 19, see B unto
4. —— xxv. 20.
— —— xxvii. 3, see B again
1. Mark i. 32.
1. —— ii. 3.
— —— iv. 8, see B forth.
— ——— 20, 28, see fruit.
1. —— vi. 27, 28.
1. —— vii. 32.
1. —— viii. 22.
1. —— ix. 17, 19, 20.
— —— x. 13 1st, see B to.
4. ——— 13 2nd (αὐτοῖς, them, for τοῖς προσφέρουσιν, Lm ℵ.)
5. —— xi. 2 (No. 1, G∾ T Tr A ℵ.)
5. ——— 7 (No. 1, G∾ T
1. —— xii. 15, 16. [Tr A.)
1. —— xv. 22.
— Luke i. 31, 57, } see B
— —— ii. 7, } forth.
6. ——— 22.
— ——— 27, see B in.
— —— iii. 8, 9, see B forth.
5. —— iv. 9.
— ——— 16, see B up.
5. ——— 40.
8. —— v. 11.
1. ——— 18 1st.
— ——— 18 2nd, 19, see B in.
— —— vi. 43 twice, 45 twice, see B forth.
11. —— vii. 37.
— —— viii. 15, see fruit.
9. —— ix. 41.
5. —— x. 34.
— —— xii. 11, see B unto.
— ——— 16, see B forth abundantly.
— —— xiv. 21, see B in.
— —— xv. 22, see B forth
1. ——— 23.
— —— xviii. 15, see B unto.
5. ——— 40.
5. —— xix. 27, 30, 35.
5. —— xxi. 12 (No. 7, T Tr A ℵ.)
— —— xxii. 54, see B into.
— —— xxiii. 14, see B unto.
1. —— xxiv. 1.
5. John i. 42.
1. —— iv. 33.
5. —— vii. 45.
5. —— viii. 3 (ap.)
5. —— ix. 13.
5. —— x. 16.
— —— xii. 24, see B forth.
— —— xv. 2, 5, 16, see B forth.
— —— xviii. 16, see B in.
1. ——— 29.
5. —— xix. 4, 13.
1. ——— 39.
1. —— xxi. 10.
1. Acts iv. 34, 37.
1. —— v. 2.
— ——— 15, see B forth.
1. ——— 16.
— ——— 19, see B forth.
5. ——— 21, 26, 27.
— Acts v. 28, see B upon.
5. —— vi. 12.
— —— vii. 36, 40, see B out
— ——— 45, see B in.
5. —— ix. 2.
— ——— 8, see B into.
5. ——— 21, 27.
— ——— 30, see B down.
6. ——— 39.
5. —— xi. 26.
— —— xii. 4, 6, see B forth
— ——— 17, } see B
— —— xii. 17, } out.
1. —— xiv. 13.
— —— xv. 3, see B on
12. —— xvi. 16. [one's way.
9. ——— 20.
— ——— 30, see B out.
6. ——— 34.
— ——— 39, see B out.
5. —— xvii. 5 (προάγω, to lead forth, L Tr A ℵ.)
5. ——— 15, 19.
— ——— 20, see B to.
5. —— xviii. 12.
3. —— xix. 12 (No. 2, G∾ L T Tr A ℵ.)
— ——— 19, see B together
5. ——— 37.
5. —— xx. 12.
— —— xxi. 5, see B on
5. ——— 16. [one's way.
— ——— 28, 29, see B into.
— —— xxii. 3, see B up.
5. ——— 5.
5. ——— 24 (εἰσάγω, to lead in or into, All.)
— ——— 30, see B down.
5. —— xxiii. 10.
— ——— 15, see B down.
7. ——— 17.
5. ——— 18 twice.
— ——— 20, see B down.
— ——— 28, see B forth.
5. ——— 31.
5. —— xxv. 6.
— ——— 17, see B forth.
3. ——— 18 (No. 1, G∾ L T Tr A ℵ.)
— ——— 23, } see B
— ——— 26, } forth.
— Rom. vii. 4, 5, see fruit.
— —— x. 6, see B down.
— ——— 7, see B up.
— —— xv. 24, see B on one's way.
2. 1 Cor. xvi. 3.
— ——— 6, see B on one's journey.
— 2 Cor. i. 16, see B on one's way.
— Eph. vi. 4, see B up.
5. 1 Thes. iv. 14.
— 1 Tim. vi. 7, see B in
5. 2 Tim. iv. 11. [upon.
1. ——— 13.
— Titus iii. 13, see B on one's journey.
— Heb. i. 6, see B in.
5. —— ii. 10.
— —— vi. 7, see B forth.
— —— xiii. 11, see B in upon.
— ——— 20, see B again.
— Jas. i. 15 twice, } see B
— —— v. 18, } forth.
9. 1 Pet. iii. 18. [privily.
— 2 Pet. ii. 1 1st, see B in
— ——— 1 2nd, see B upon.
— ——— 5.
1. ——— 11.
1. 2 John 10.
— 3 John 6, see B forward on one's journey.
— Jude 9, see B against.
— Rev. xii. 5, 13, see B forth.
1. —— xxi. 24, 26.

BRING AGAIN.

1. ἀνάγω, *see* "BRING," *No.* 6.
2. ἀποστρέφω, to turn back, to turn away from.

2. Matt. xxvii. 3 (στρέφω, *to turn*, T Tr A ℵ.)
1. Heb. xiii. 20.

BRING AGAINST.

ἐπιφέρω, *see* "BRING," *No.* 3.

Jude 9.

BRING DOWN.

1. κατάγω, *see* "BRING," *No.* 8.
2. καταβιβάζω, to make to go down, to bring down lower.

2. Matt. xi. 23 (καταβαίνω, (pass) *to step down*, L T Tr A.)
1. Acts ix. 30.
1. Acts xxii. 30.
1. ——— 15, 20.
1. Rom. x. 6.

BRING FORTH.

1. ἄγω, *see* "BRING," *No.* 5.
2. ἀνάγω, *see* "BRING," *No.* 6.
3. ἐξάγω, to lead out, lead away; to bring forth, produce.
4. κατάγω, *see* "BRING," *No.* 8.
5. προάγω, to lead forth, lead before, lead on *or* onward.
6. φέρω, *see* "BRING," *No.* 1.
7. ἐκφέρω, to carry out of, carry away *or* off.
8. προφέρω, to bring before *one*, bring to, give, present; bring forward, *(non occ.)*
9. βλαστάνω, to bud, sprout, grow, *strictly of plants; of children*, to be born; *trans.* to bring forth, bring up.
10. δίδωμι, to give, present *(with notion of* giving freely, unforced.)
11. ποιέω, to make, *(i.e.* to form, bring about) *strictly of something external to one's self;* to do *(with notion of a continued rather than of a complete action,)* to be doing.
12. ἐκβάλλω, to throw *or* cast out of, to strike out of.
13. γεννάω, to beget, *of the father;* to bring forth, bear, *of the mother.*

14. *τίκτω*, to bring into the world; *of the father*, to beget; *of the mother*, to bring forth; *metaph.* to produce, bring about.

15. *ἀποκυέω*, to bear young, bring forth.

14. Matt. i. 21, 23, 25.
11. —— iii. 8, 10.
11. —— vii. 17 twice, 18 twice, [19.
12. —— xii. 35 twice.
10. —— xiii. 8.
11. ——— 23, 26.
12. ——— 52.
11. —— xxi. 43.
6. Mark iv. 8.
14. Luke i. 31.
13. ——— 57.
14. —— ii. 7.
11. —— iii. 8, 9.
11. —— vi. 43 twice.
8. ——— 45 twice (non occ.)
7. Luke xv. 22.
6. John xii. 24.
6. —— xv. 2, 5, 16.
7. Acts v. 15.
3. ——— 19.
2. —— xii. 4.
5. ——— 6.
4. —— xxiii. 28.
1. —— xxv. 17, 23.
5. ——— 26.
14. Heb. vi. 7.
14. Jas. i. 15 1st.
15. ——— 15 2nd.
9. —— v. 18.
14. Rev. xii. 5, 13.

BRING FORTH PLENTIFULLY.

εὐφορέω, to bear well, be productive, *(non occ.)*

Luke xii. 16.

BRING ON ONE'S JOURNEY.

προπέμπω, to send forth; send before *or* beforehand.

1 Cor. xvi. 6 | Titus iii. 13.

BRING FORWARD ON ONE'S JOURNEY.

προπέμπω, *see above.*

3 John 6.

BRING IN.

1. *εἰσάγω*, to lead in *or* into; *esp.* to lead into one's dwelling.
2. *εἰσφέρω*, to carry in *or* into; to bring in, contribute; introduce.

1. Luke ii. 27.
2. —— v. 18, 19.
1. —— xiv. 21.
1. John xviii. 16.
1. Acts vii. 45.
1. Heb. i. 6.

BRING IN PRIVILY.

παρεισάγω, (*No.* 1 *with* *παρά*, beside,) to lead in by one's side; introduce secretly.

2 Pet. ii. 1.

BRING IN UPON.

ἐπάγω, to bring upon; *so* to charge with *and* make answerable for.

2 Pet. ii. 5.

BRING INTO.

1. *εἰσάγω*, *see* "BRING IN," *No.* 1.
2. *εἰσφέρω*, *see* "BRING IN," *No.* 2.

1. Luke xxii. 54.
1. Acts ix. 8.
1. Acts xxi. 28, 29.
2. 1 Tim. vi. 7.
2. Heb. xiii. 11.

BRING ON ONE'S WAY.

προπέμπω, to send forth; send before *or* beforehand.

Acts xv. 3.
—— xxi. 5.
Rom. xv. 24.
2 Cor. i. 16.

BRING OUT.

1. *ἐξάγω*, *see* "BRING FORTH," *No.* 3.
2. *προάγω*, *see* "BRING FORTH," *No.* 5.

1. Acts vii. 36, 40.
1. —— xii. 17.
1. Acts xiii. 17.
2. —— xvi. 30.
1. Acts xvi. 39.

BRING TO.

1. *εἰσφέρω*, to carry in *or* into, bring in, contribute, introduce.
2. *προσφέρω*, to bring to *or* towards; to bring in addition to, contribute.

2. Matt. v. 23 (with *ἐπί*, *upon.*)
2. —— ix. 2, 32.
2. Matt. xvii. 16.
2. Mark x. 13.
1. Acts xvii. 20.

BRING TOGETHER.

συμφέρω, to bring together, bring with *(implying association;)* collect, conduce to.

Acts xix. 19.

BRING UNTO.

προσφέρω, to bring to *or* towards, to bring in addition to, contribute.

Matt. iv. 24.
—— viii. 16.
—— xii. 22.
—— xiv. 35.
—— xviii. 24 (*προσάγω*, *to lead to* or *towards*, L T Tr A.)
Luke xix. 13.
—— xxii. 19.
Luke xii. 11 (*φέρω*, *to bear* or *carry*, T A) (*εισφέρω* *to carry into*, Tr ℵ.)
—— xviii. 15.
—— xxiii. 14.

BRING UP.

1. *ἀναφέρω*, to bring *or* carry up; bring *or* carry back.
2. *τρέφω*, to make firm, thick *or* solid; *hence*, to make fat, fatten, nourish, feed, make to grow *or* increase, nurse, bring up.

3. ἀνατρέφω, to bring up, nurse, cherish, educate.

4. ἐκτρέφω, to bring up from childhood, rear up, (*occ.* Eph. v. 29.)

1. Matt. xvii. 1.
2. Luke iv. 16.
3. Acts xxii 3.
4. Eph. vi. 4.

BRING UP AGAIN.

ἀνάγω, to lead up *from a lower place to a higher.*

Rom. x. 7.

BRING UPON.

ἐπάγω, to bring upon; *so,* to charge with, and make answerable for, (*occ.* 2 Pet. ii. 5.)

Acts v. 28. | 2 Pet. ii. 1 2nd.

See also, BONDAGE, BROUGHT (BE), CAPTIVITY, CHILD, DESOLATION, LIGHT, LOW, NOTHING, NOUGHT, PERFECTION, POWER, REMEMBRANCE, SAFE, SALVATION, SUBJECTION, TIDINGS, WORD.

BRINGING IN.

ἐπεισαγωγή, a bringing in besides *or* over; introduction, (*non occ.*)

Heb. vii. 19.

BROAD.

εὐρύχωρος, with broad places, roomy, spacious. (*non occ.*)

Matt. vii. 13.

BROAD (MAKE.)

πλατύνω, to make broad, wider, extend, (*occ.* 2 Cor. vi. 11, 13.)

Matt. xxiii. 5.

BROIDED HAIR.

(*Sometimes wrongly printed as* BROIDERED *or* BRAIDED.)

πλέγμα, anything twined *or* plaited, (*non occ.*)

1 Tim. ii. 9, marg. *plaited.*

BROILED.

ὀπτός, roasted, broiled; *also,* baked; *gen.* prepared by fire, (*non occ.*)

Luke xxiv. 42.

BROKEN MEAT.

κλάσμα, that which is broken off, a fragment, morsel.

Matt. xv. 37, pl. | Mark viii. 8, pl.

See also, PIECE.

BROKEN HEARTED.

{ συντετριμμένους, rubbed together, shattered.
{ τὴν καρδίαν, the heart.

Luke iv. 18 (*ap.*)

BROOD.

νοσσιά, a nest of young birds, a nest; *then* the brood, (*non occ.*)

Luke xiii. 34.

BROOK.

χείμαῤῥος, winter-flowing; a stream which runs only in the winter *or* when swollen with rains, (*non occ.*)

John xviii. 1.

BROTHER, BRETHREN.

1. ἀδελφός, brother, *or gen.* near kinsman; *then, in pl.* a vital community based on identity of origin, *i.e.* life; *then, out of this* community of life *springs also the necessary idea of* a community of love. *In pl.* brethren.

2. ἀδελφότης *denotes* a brotherly relation; *then it is transferred to* the community in which this relation is realized; brotherhood, (*occ.* 1 Pet. ii. 17.)

1. Matt. i. 2, 11.
1. —— iv. 18 twice, 21 twice.
1. —— v. 22 twice, 23, 24.
1. ——47 (φίλος, *a friend* [G∾.)
1. —— vii. 3, 4, 5.
1. —— x. 2 twice, 21 twice.
1. Matt. xii. 46, 47, 48, 49, [50.
1. —— xiii. 55.
1. —— xiv. 3.
1. —— xvii. 1.
1. —— xviii. 15 twice, 21, 35.
1. —— xix. 29.

1. Matt. xx. 24.
1. —— xxii. 24 twice, 25 twice
1. —— xxiii. 8.
1. —— xxv. 40 (Lb.)
1. —— xxviii. 10.
1. Mark i. 16, 19.
1. —— iii. 17, 31, 32, 33,
1. —— v. 37. [34, 35.
1. —— vi. 3, 17, 18.
1. —— x. 29, 30.
1. —— xii. 19 3 times, 20.
1. —— xiii. 12 twice.
1. Luke iii. 1, 19.
1. —— vi. 14, 41, 42 3 times.
1. —— viii. 19, 20, 21.
1. —— xii. 13.
1. —— xiv. 12, 26.
1. —— xv. 27, 32.
1. —— xvi. 28.
1. —— xvii. 3.
1. —— xviii. 29.
1. —— xx. 28 3 times, 29.
1. —— xxi. 16.
1. —— xxii. 32.
1. John i. 40, 41.
1. —— ii. 12.
1. —— vi. 8.
1. —— vii. 3, 5, 10.
1. —— xi. 2, 19, 21, 23, 32.
1. —— xx. 17.
1. —— xxi. 23.
1. Acts i. 14, 16.
1. —— ii. 29, 37.
1. —— iii. 17, 22.
1. —— vi. 3 (*om.* L.)
1. —— vii. 2, 13, 23, 25,
1. —— ix. 17, 30. [26, 37.
1. —— x. 23.
1. —— xi. 1, 12, 29.
1. —— xii. 2, 17.
1. —— xiii. 15, 26, 38.
1. —— xiv. 2.
1. —— xv. 1, 3, 7, 13, 22, 23 twice, 32, 33, 36, 40.
1. —— xvi. 2, 40.
1. —— xvii. 6, 10, 14.
1. —— xviii. 18, 27.
1. —— xx. 32 (*om.* G→ L T Tr A ℵ.)
1. —— xxi. 7, 17, 20.
1. —— xxii. 1, 5, 13.
1. —— xxiii. 1, 5, 6.
1. —— xxviii. 14, 15, 17, 21.
1. Rom. i. 13.
1. —— vii. 1, 4.
1. —— viii. 12, 29.
1. —— ix. 3.
1. —— x. 1.
1. —— xi. 25.
1. —— xii. 1.
1. —— xiv. 10 twice, 13, 15,
1. —— xv. 14. [21.
1. ——— 15 (*om.* L Tr Ab ℵ)
1. ——— 30 (*om.* T Ab.)
1. —— xvi. 14, 17, 23.
1. 1 Cor. i. 1, 10, 11, 26.
1. —— ii. 1.
1. —— iii. 1.
1. —— iv. 6.
1. —— v. 11.
1. —— vi. 5, 6, 8.
1. —— vii. 12, 15, 24, 29.
1. —— viii. 11, 12, 13 twice
1. —— ix. 5.
1. —— x. 1.
1. —— xi. 2 (*om.* L Tr A ℵ)
1. 1 Cor. xi. 33.
1. —— xii. 1.
1. —— xiv. 6, 20, 26, 39.
1. —— xv. 1, 6, 50, 58.
1. —— xvi. 11, 12 twice, 15.
1. 2 Cor. i. 1, 8. [20.
1. —— ii. 13.
1. —— viii. 1, 18, 22, 23.
1. —— ix. 3, 5.
1. —— xi. 9.
— ——— 26, see B (false.)
1. —— xii. 18.
1. —— xiii. 11.
1. Gal. i 2, 11, 19.
— —— ii. 4, see B (false.)
1. —— iii. 15.
1. —— iv. 12, 28, 31.
1. —— v. 11, 13.
1. —— vi 1, 18.
1. Eph. vi. 10 (*om.* G→ L T
1. ——— 21, 23. [Tr A ℵ.)
1. Phil. i. 12, 14.
1. —— ii. 25.
1. —— iii. 1, 13, 17.
1. —— iv. 1, 8, 21.
1. Col. i. 1, 2.
1. —— iv. 7, 9, 15.
1. 1 Thes. i. 4.
1. —— ii. 1, 9, 14, 17.
1. —— iii. 2, 7.
1. —— iv. 1, 6.
— ——— 9, see B (love of.)
1. ——— 10 twice, 13.
1. —— v. 1, 4, 12, 14, 25,
1. 2 Thes. i. 3. [26, 27.
1. —— ii. 1, 13, 15.
1. —— iii. 1, 6 twice, 13, 15.
1. 1 Tim. iv. 6.
1. —— v. 1.
1. —— vi. 2.
1. 2 Tim. iv. 21.
1. Philem. 1, 7, 16, 20.
1. Heb. ii. 11, 12, 17.
1. —— iii. 1, 12.
1. —— vii. 5.
1. —— viii. 11.
1. —— x. 19.
1. —— xiii. 22, 23.
1. Jas. i. 2, 9, 16, 19.
1. —— ii. 1, 5, 14, 15.
1. —— iii. 1, 10, 12.
1. —— iv. 11 3 times.
1. —— v. 7, 9, 10, 12, 19.
— 1 Pet. i. 22, see B (love of)
— ——— iii. 8, see B (love as.)
— ——— 8, see B (loving to the), margin.
2. —— v. 9.
1. ——— 12.
1. 2 Pet. i 10.
1. —— iii. 15.
1. 1 John ii. 7 (ἀγαπητός, *beloved*, G L T Tr A ℵ.)
1. ——— 9, 10, 11. [14 1st.
1. —— iii. 10, 12 twice, 13,
1. ——— 14 2nd (*om.* LTℵ.)
1. ——— 15, 16, 17.
1. —— iv. 20 twice, 21.
1. —— v. 16.
1. 3 John 3, 5, 10.
1. Jude 1.
1. Rev. i. 9.
1. —— vi. 11.
1. —— xii. 10.
1. —— xix. 10.
1. —— xxii. 9.

BRETHREN (FALSE.)

ψευδάδελφος, a false brother, a pretended Christian, *(in pl. with εἰμί,* to be.)

2 Cor. xi. 26. | Gal. ii. 4.

BRETHREN (LOVE AS.)

φιλάδελφος, fond of one's brethren.

1 Pet. iii. 8, marg. *loving to the brethren.*

BRETHREN (LOVE OF.)

φιλαδελφία, brotherly love.

Rom. xii. 10, marg. (text, *brotherly love.*)
1 Pet. i. 22.

BRETHREN (loving to) [margin.]

φιλάδελφος, fond of one's brethren.

1 Pet. iii. 8, text, *love as brethren.*

BROTHERHOOD.

ἀδελφότης, a brotherly relation, *then it is transferred to the community in which this relation is realized,* brotherhood, *(occ.* 1 Pet. v. 9.)

1 Pet. ii. 17.

BROTHERLY KINDNESS.

φιλαδελφία, brotherly love, love of the brethren.

2 Pet. i. 7 twice.

BROTHERLY LOVE.

Rom. xii. 10, marg. *love of the brethren.* | 1 Thes. iv. 9. Heb. xiii. 1.

BROUGHT (BE.)

(See also BRING.)

1. ἔρχομαι, to come *or* go.
2. ἵστημι, (a) *trans.* to make to stand, set.
   (b) *intrans.* to stand, be set *or* placed.
3. γίνομαι, to come into being, to be born, to become, to arrive, to happen.

1. Mark iv. 21. | 2b. Mark xiii. 9.
3. Acts v. 36.

BROUGHT TO (AFTER THEY WERE.)

μετοικεσία, change of abode, removal, migration.

Matt. i. 12 (lit. the Babylonian *migration.*)

BROUGHT (BE TO BE.)

φέρω, to bear, carry.

1 Pet. i. 13 (pass.)

BROUGHT BEFORE (BE.)

παρίστημι, (a) *trans.* to place by *or* beside.

(b) *intrans.* to stand by beside *or* near.

Acts xxvii. 24.

BROUGHT FORTH (BE.)

παραδίδωμι, to give *or* hand over *to another;* yield *or* deliver up.

Mark iv. 29, marg. *be ripe.*

BROUGHT IN (be) [margin.]

φέρω, to bear, carry.

Heb. ix. 16, pass. (text, *be.*)

BROUGHT IN UNAWARES.

παρείσακτος, brought in beside, introduced privately.

Gal. ii. 4.

BROUGHT TO PASS (BE.)

γίνομαι, see "BROUGHT (BE)," *No.* 3.

1 Cor. xv. 54.

BROUGHT UP WITH (WHICH HAD BEEN.)

σύντροφος, brought up together with; *gen.* living with.

Acts xiii. 1, marg. *foster-brother.*

See also, BRING.

BROW.

ὀφρύς, the eye-brow; *hence, from likeness of shape*, the brow of a hill, a ridge with overhanging bank.

Luke iv. 29, marg. *edge.*

BRUISE (-ED, -ING) [verb.]

1. *συντρίβω*, to rub together, to shatter, shiver; *metaph.* to be in perplexity, affliction, anguish.

2. *θραύω*, to break, break in pieces, to break down, *(non occ.)*

1. Matt. xii. 20.
2. Luke iv. 18.
1. Luke ix. 39. [*tread.*
1. Rom. xvi. 20, marg.

BRUTE [adj.]

ἄλογος, without *λόγος*, *i.e.* without speech, speechless; *hence*, unreasoning, irrational, *(occ.* Acts xxv. 27.)

2 Pet. ii. 12.
Jude 10.

BUD (-ED) [verb.]

βλαστάνω, to bud, sprout, grow.

Heb. ix. 4.

BUFFET.

κολαφίζω, to strike with the hands, the fingers being clenched, to buffet with the fist, *(non occ.)*

Matt. xxvi. 67.
Mark xiv. 65.
1 Cor. iv. 11.
2 Cor. xii. 7.
1 Pet. ii. 20.

BUILD (-ED, -EST, -ING, BUILT.)

1. *οἰκοδομέω*, to build a house; *then gen.* to build; *metaph.* to edify *(which is simply the Latin for οἰκοδομέω.)*

2. *κατασκευάζω*, to prepare, to furnish, to adorn fully *with a thing*, to get ready.

1. Matt. vii. 24, 26.
1. —— xvi. 18.
1. —— xxi. 33.
1. —— xxiii. 29.
1. —— xxvi. 61.
1. —— xxvii. 40.
1. Mark xii. 1.
1. —— xiv. 58.
1. —— xv. 29.
1. Luke iv. 29.
1. —— vi. 48, 49.
1. —— vii. 5.
1. —— xi. 47, 48.
1. —— xii. 18.
1. —— xiv. 28, 30.
1. —— xvii. 28.
1. Acts vii. 47, 49.
— Acts xv. 16, see B again.
— —— xx. 32, see B up.
1. Rom. xv. 20.
— 1 Cor. iii. 10 1st, see B thereon.
— ——— 10 2nd, see B thereupon.
— ——— 12, see B upon.
— ——— 14, see B thereupon.
1. Gal. ii. 18.
— Eph. ii. 20, see B upon.
— ——— 22, see B together
— Col. ii. 7, see B up.
2. Heb. iii. 3, 4 twice.
— 1 Pet. ii. 5, see B up.
— Jude 20, see B up on.

BUILD AGAIN.

ἀνοικοδομέω, *(No.* 1 *with ἀνά,* again,) *denotes* to build a house again, *(non occ.)*

Acts xv. 16 twice.

BUILD THEREON.

ἐποικοδομέω, *(No.* 1 *with ἐπί,* upon,) *denotes* to build a house upon.

1 Cor. iii. 10 1st.

BUILD THEREUPON.

1 Cor. iii. 10 2nd, 14.

BUILD TOGETHER.

συνοικοδομέω, *(No.* 1 *with* σύν, together, *implying association,)* to build together.

Eph. ii. 22.

BUILD UP.

1. οἰκοδομέω, *see* "BUILD," *No.* 1.
2. ἐποικοδομέω, *see* "BUILD THEREON."

2 Acts xx. 32 (No. 1, G ∾ L Tr A ℵ.) | 2. Col. ii. 7. | 1. 1 Pet. ii. 5.

BUILD UPON.

ἐποικοδομέω, to build upon, *see* "BUILD THEREON."

1 Cor. iii. 12 (with ἐπί, *upon*); Eph. ii. 20.

BUILD UP ON.

Jude 20.

BUILDER.

1. οἰκοδομέω, *see* "BUILD," *No.* 1. *Here art. with part.* he *etc.* who builds.
2. τεχνίτης, an artificer; *esp.* one who does *or* handles *a thing* by the rules of art.

1. Matt. xxi. 42. | 1. Mark xii. 10. | 1. Luke xx. 17. | 1. Acts iv. 11 (οικοδόμος, *building a house, a house-builder*, G ∾ L T Tr A ℵ.) | 2. Heb. xi. 10; 1. 1 Pet. ii. 7.

See also, MASTER.

BUILDING [noun.]

1. οἰκοδομή, *prop.* the act of building a a house; a building, an edifice; *metaph.* edification, spiritual profit *or* advancement.
2. ἐνδόμησις, a thing built in, structure, *(non occ.)*
3. κτίσις, a founding, settling, foundation; a making, creating, *esp.* the creation *of the universe; then,* that which is created, the universe, the creation.

1. Matt. xxiv. 1. | 1. Mark xiii. 1, 2. | 1. 1 Cor. iii. 9. | 1. 2 Cor. v. 1. | 1. Eph. ii. 21. | 3. Heb. ix. 11. | 2. Rev. xxi. 18.

BUILDING (BE IN.)

οἰκοδομέω, *see* "BUILD," *No.* 1.

John ii. 20, pass.

BULL.

ταῦρος, a bull, a beeve.

Heb. ix. 13; x. 4.

BUNDLE.

1. δέσμη, *(from* δέω, to bind,) a bundle; *(which Eng. word is from the verb* to bind.)
2. πλῆθος, a great number.

1. Matt. xiii. 30. | 2. Acts xxviii. 3.

BURDEN [noun.]

1. βάρος, weight; *it denotes the pressure of a weight which may be relieved or transferred; met.* the heavy weight of trial *or* temptation, *while*
2. φορτίον, *is a specific* load; the freight *or* lading *that has to be borne, (non occ.)*
3. γόμος, a ship's freight, *(occ.* Rev. xviii. 11, 12.)

2. Matt. xi. 30. | 1. —— xx. 12. | 2. —— xxiii. 4. | 2. Luke xi. 46 twice. | 1. Acts xv. 28. | 3. —— xxi. 3. | 1. Gal. vi. 2. | 2. —— 5. | 1. Rev. ii. 24.

See also, GREATER.

BURDEN (-ED) [verb.]

καταβαρέω, to weigh down, overload, *(non occ.)*

2 Cor. xii. 16.

BURDENED.

θλῖψις, pressure; *metaph.* oppression, affliction.

2 Cor. viii. 13.

BURDENED (BE.)

βαρέομαι, to be weighed down *as with affliction or calamity,* be oppressed.

2 Cor. v. 4.

BURDENSOME (BE.)

ἐν, in, βάρει, weight, burden, εἶναι, to be,	we might have been a charge; *Alf.* when we might have stood on our dignity; *Roth.* we had power to be burdensome.

1 Thes. ii. 6 marg. *use authority.*

BURDENSOME TO (BE.)

καταναρκάω, to be numbed *or* torpid; to grow quite stiff; *(cf.* νάρκη, the torpedo *or* cramp-fish,) to be idle to another's damage, to incommode *or* lie heavy upon, *like a torpid or useless limb*, *(occ.* 2 Cor. xi. 8.)

2 Cor. xii. 13, 14.

BURDENSOME (FROM BEING.)

ἀβαρής, without weight; not burdensome, *(non occ.)*

2 Cor. xi. 9.

BURIAL (MY.)

τὸ, the, ενταφιάσαι, to prepare *a corpse* for burial, με, me,	to the preparing me for burial.

Matt. xxvi. 12.

BURN.

1. καίω, to light, kindle.
   (a) *in pass.* to be lighted, to burn.
2. κατακαίω, to burn down, *esp. of sacrifices.*
   (a) *in pass.* to be burned down *or* out.
3. ἐκκαίω, to burn out; to light up, set on fire.
   (a) *pass.* to be kindled, burn up, *(non occ.)*
4. πυρόομαι, to glow with heat *as in a furnace; metaph.* to burn *or* be fired *as it were, with grief or zeal, etc.*
5. καυματίζω, to scorch with excessive heat.

— Matt. iii. 12, see B up.
2. —— xiii. 30.
2. —— 40 (No. 1, G T Tr A.)
2. Luke iii. 17.
1a. —— xii. 35.
1a. —— xxiv. 32 (with εἰμί, be.)
1a. John v. 35.
— —— xv. 6, see B (be.)
2. Acts xix. 19.
3. Rom. i. 27 (non occ.)
2. 1 Cor. iii. 15.
4. —— vii. 9.
— 1 Cor. xiii. 3, see B (be.)
4. 2 Cor. xi. 29.
— Heb. vi. 8, see B (be.)
1a. —— xii. 18.
2. —— xiii. 11.
— 2 Pet. iii. 10, see B up.
4. Rev. i. 15.
1a. —— iv. 5.
— Rev. viii. 7 twice, see B up
1a. —— 8, 10.
5. —— xvi. 9, marg. (text, *scorch.*)
2. —— xvii. 16.
— —— xviii. 8, see B utterly.
1a. —— xix. 20.
1a. Rev. xxi. 8.

BURN UP.

2. Matt. iii. 12. | 2. 2 Pet. iii. 10. | 2. Rev. viii. 7 twice.

BURN UTTERLY.

2. Rev. xviii. 8.

BURNED (BE.)

1. καίω, see "BURN," *No.* 1*a*.
2. καῦσις, a burning; *(here preceded by* εἰς, unto, with a view to.)

1. John xv. 6. | 1. 1 Cor. xiii. 3. | 2. Heb. vi. 8.

See also, INCENSE.

BURNING.

πύρωσις, a burning, lighting, kindling, *(occ.* 1 Pet. iv. 12.)

Rev. xviii. 9, 18.

See also, HEAT.

BURNT-OFFERING.

ὁλοκαύτωμα, *(from* ὁλοκαυτόω, to burn the whole, *spoken of sacrifices; and this, from* ὅλος, the whole, *and* καίω, to burn.) A burnt-offering, the whole of which was burnt on the altar, *and no part eaten by the priests. (In the lxx. the word answers to* עלה, *which is from* עלה, to ascend, *because it* ascended *in flame and smoke towards heaven, see* Ex. x. 25; xxiv. 5, *etc.)*

Heb. x. 6, 8.

BURNT-OFFERING (WHOLE.)

Mark xii. 33.

BURST.

ῥήγνυμι, to break, to break *or* burst through; to break asunder *or* in pieces.

Mark ii. 22. | Luke v. 37.

BURST ASUNDER.

λάσκω, to sound, *of things which* ring *when struck;* to break with a crash; burst with a noise, break with a loud report, *(non occ.)*

Acts i. 18.

BURY (-ED.)

1. θάπτω, to pay the last dues to a corpse, to honour with funeral rites.
2. ἐνταφιάζω, to prepare *a corpse* for the burial.

1. Matt. viii. 21, 22.
1. —— xiv. 12.
— —— xxvii. 7, see B in (to.)
1. Luke ix. 59, 60.
1. —— xvi. 22.
2. John xix. 40.
1. Acts ii. 29.
1. —— v. 6, 9, 10.
— Rom. vi. 4, see B with.
1 1 Cor. xv. 4
— Col. ii. 12, see B with.

BURY IN (TO.)

ταφή, burial; *here with* εἰς, unto, with a view to burial.

Matt. xxvii. 7.

BURY WITH.

συνθάπτω, *(No.* 1 *with* σύν, with, *prefixed,)* to bury with *or* together.

Rom. vi. 4. | Col. ii. 12.

BURYING.

ἐνταφιασμός, a preparation *of a corpse* for burial, *as by anointing, etc., (non occ.)*

Mark xiv. 8. | John xii. 7.

BUSH.

βάτος, a bramble bush.

Mark xii. 26 (τοῦ βάτου, *concerning the bush, i.e.* in that part of the Book of Moses concerning it, G L T Tr A ℵ.)
Luke xx. 37.
Acts vii. 30, 35.

BUSH (BRAMBLE.)

Luke vi. 44.

BUSHEL.

μόδιος, *(from Heb.* מד, to measure, *whence also Eng.* mete, made, moderate, *and Lat.* modus.) A dry measure of capacity, *containing about a peck, (non occ.)*

Matt. v. 15. | Mark iv. 21.
Luke xi. 33.

BUSINESS.

1. πρᾶγμα, that which has been done, a deed; *then gen.* a thing done, a matter, an affair.
2. σπουδή, haste, speed, readiness; *hence,* zeal, pains, trouble; an earnest, serious purpose.
3. χρεία, use; *as a property,* use, advantage, service; *in plural,* uses, services *received; as an action,* using, use.
4. ὁ, *(the def. article) here, neut. pl.* the things; *lit.* the things of my Father.

4. Luke ii. 49.
3. Acts vi. 3.
2. Rom. xii. 11.
1. —— xvi. 2.

BUSINESS (ONE'S OWN.)

τὰ ἴδια, *neut. pl.* one's own *things.*

1 Thes. iv. 11.

BUSY-BODY.

περίεργος, careful overmuch, taking needless trouble; meddling, curious.

1 Tim. v. 13.

BUSY-BODY (BE A.)

περιεργάζομαι, to take more pains than enough about *a thing; hence,* to waste one's labour; to meddle *or* interfere with other folk's affairs, *(non occ.)*

2 Thes. iii. 11.

BUSY-BODY IN OTHER MEN'S MATTERS.

ἀλλοτριοεπίσκοπος, an inspector *or* observer of other people's affairs; prying into the affairs of others, *(non occ.)*

1 Pet. iv. 15.

BUT.

1. *When "*BUT*" introduces a sentence, it is generally the translation of* δέ, *which is an adversative conjunction, carefully to be distinguished from* καί *or* τέ *(see under "*AND*" or "*BOTH*");* δέ, *generally marks a contrast, and an otherwise concealed antithesis; cf.* Matt. xxi. 3; Acts xxiv. 17; Rom. iv. 3. *(It occurs too often to admit of quotation.)*

2. ἀλλά, but, *more emphatic than* δέ *(No. 1,) and is used to mark opposition, interruption, or transition; (cf.* Matt. v. 17; Rom. iii. 31.)

3. { εἰ, if, since, though, / μή, not, } unless, except.

4. πλήν, more than, over, beyond; *hence,* except.

5. οὖν, then, *denoting the* sequence *of one clause upon another; and also always denoting the* consequence and logical inference *of what has been said before,* therefore *(cf.* Matt. iii. 8, "therefore;" Gal. ii. 21, "then.")

   (a) *with* μέν, truly, indeed.

6. γάρ *is a contraction of* γὲ ἄρα, verily then; *hence,* in fact; *and when the fact is given as a reason or explanation,* for.

7. μή, not.

8. { ἐὰν, *(for* εἰ ἄν*)* if, / μή, not, } except, unless.

9. { ἐκτός, without, outside, besides, / εἰ, if, since, though, / μή, not, } nevertheless, except.

10. ἤ, or.

11. ἀλλ' ἤ, other than, except.

12. μέντοι, yet truly, certainly, nevertheless, however.

13. μόνον, only.

14. καί, and, also, *see* "AND."

No. 1 in all passages, except

2. Matt. iv. 4.
3. —— v. 13 2nd.
3. —— 15, 17, 39.
2. —— vi. 13, 18.
2. —— vii. 21.
2. —— viii. 4, 8.
2. Matt. ix. 12 2nd, 13 2nd [17, 18.
13. —— 21.
4. —— 22.
2. —— 24.
2. —— x. 20, 34.
2. —— xi. 8, 9.
4. Matt. xi. 22, 24.
3. —— 27.
3. —— xii. 24, 39.
2. —— xiii. 21.
3. —— xiv. 17.
2. —— xv. 11.
3. —— 24 2nd.
3. —— xvi. 4.
2. —— 12, 17, 23 2nd.
2. —— xvii. 12.
3. —— 21 (*ap.*)
4. —— xviii. 7.
2. —— 22, 30.
2. —— xix. 6.
3. —— 17 1st (*ap.*)
2. —— xx. 23 2nd, 26 2nd, [28.
3. —— xxi. 19.
2. —— 21.
2. —— xxii. 30, 32.
2. —— xxiv. 6.
3. —— 36 2nd.
— —— 48, see B and if.
2. —— xxvi. 39.
2. —— xxvii. 24.
2. Mark i. 44, 45 2nd.
3. —— ii. 7.
2. —— 17 twice, 22 (*ap.*)
3. —— 26.
2. —— iii. 26, 29 2nd.
2. —— iv. 17, 22.
2. —— v. 19, 26.
— —— 28, see B (if.)
2. —— 39.
3. —— vi. 4.
2. —— 9.
— —— 56, see B (if.)
2. —— vii. 5, 15, 19.
2. —— viii. 33.
2. —— ix. 13, 22.
3. —— 29.
2 —— 37.
2. —— x. 8.
3. —— 18.
2. —— 27.
3. —— 30.
2. —— 40 2nd, 43 3rd, 45.
3. —— xi. 13.
2. —— 23, 32.
2. —— xii. 14, 25, 27,
4. —— 32.
2. —— xiii. 7, 11 twice, 20, [24.
3. —— 32 2nd.
2. —— xiv. 28, 49.
2. —— xvi. 7.
2. Luke i. 60.
2. —— iv. 4 (*ap.*)
2. —— v. 14.
3. —— 21.
2. —— 31, 32, 38
3. —— vi. 4.
4. —— 24, 35.
2. —— 27.
2. —— vii. 7, 25, 26.
2. —— viii. 16, 27, 52 2nd.
— —— ix. 13 2nd, see B (no more.)
2. —— 56 (*ap.*)
4. —— x. 14.
3. —— 22 twice.
2. —— xi. 4 (*ap.*)
3. —— 29.
2. —— 33.
— —— 41, see B rather.
2. —— 42.
2. —— xii. 7.
— —— 31, see B rather.
— —— 45, see B and if.
— —— 51, see B rather.
2. —— xiii. 3, 5.
2. —— xiv. 10, 13.
2. —— xvi. 30.
— —— xvii. 1 1st, see B [that.
2. —— xviii. 13.
4. —— xix. 27.
— —— xx. 6, see B and if.
2. —— 21, 38.
5. —— xxi. 7 (with πότε, [when.)
2. —— 9 2nd.
4. Luke xxii. 21, 22.
2. —— 26 2nd, 36, 42, 53.
4. —— xxiii. 28 2nd.
2. —— xxiv. 6.
2. John i. 8, 13, 31, 33.
2. —— iii. 8.
3. —— 13.
2. —— 15 (*ap*), 16, 17, 28, 36.
2. —— iv. 14 2nd (*ap*), 23.
2. —— v. 18.
3. —— 19.
2. —— 22, 24, 30, 34 2nd, 42.
2. —— vi. 9, 22, 26, 27, 32, 36, 38, 39, 64.
2. —— vii. 10 2nd, 12, 16, 22, 24, 28, 44, 49.
5. —— viii. 5 (*ap.*)
4. —— 10 (*ap.*)
2. —— 12, 16, 26, 28, 37, 42, 49, 55 2nd.
2. —— ix. 3.
5. —— 18.
2. —— 31.
2. —— x. 1, 5, 8.
3. —— 10.
2. —— 18, 26, 33.
2. —— xi. 4, 11.
2. —— 22 (*om.* Lb Tr ℵ.)
2. —— 30, 42, 51, 52, 54.
2. —— xii. 6, 9, 16, 27, 30, 42, 44, 47, 49.
2. —— xiii. 9, 10 twice, 18.
3. —— xiv. 6.
2. —— 24, 31.
2. —— xv. 16, 19 2nd, 21, 25. [20 2nd.
2. —— xvi. 4, 6, 12, 13,
2. —— 25 1st (*om.* G Lb T Tr A ℵ.)
2. —— 25 2nd, 33.
2. —— xvii. 9.
3. —— 12.
2. —— 15, 20.
2. —— xviii. 28, 40.
3. —— xix. 15.
2. —— 21, 24, 34.
2. —— xx. 7, 27.
12. —— xxi. 4 2nd.
2. —— 8, 23.
2. Acts i. 4, 8.
2. —— ii. 16.
2. —— iv. 17.
7. —— 20.
2. —— 32.
2. —— v. 4, 13.
2. —— vii. 39.
2. —— x. 35, 41.
3. —— xi. 19.
2. —— xiii. 25.
2. —— xv. 11, 20.
2. —— xvi. 37 2nd.
— —— xvii. 21, see B either
— —— 30, see B now.
2. —— xviii. 9, 21 1st.
2. —— xix. 26, 27.
7. —— xx. 20.
2. —— 24.
2. —— xxi. 13, 24.
5. —— xxiii. 21.
— —— xxiv. 11, see B (yet.)
5a. —— xxv. 4.
2. —— xxvi. 16, 20, 25 2nd, 29.
2. —— xxvii. 10.
4. —— 22.
2. Rom. i. 21, 32.
2. —— ii. 13, 29 twice.
2. —— iii. 27.
2. —— iv. 2, 4, 10, 12, 13, 16, 20, 24.
2. —— v. 3, 11, 15.
2. —— vi. 13, 14, 15.
3. —— vii. 7.
2. —— 13, 15, 17, 19, 20.
2. —— viii. 1 (*ap*), 4, 9 2nd, 15, 20, 23, 26, 32.

2. Rom. ix. 7, 8, 10, 11, 16, 20, see B (nay.)
2. ——— 24, 32.
2. —— x. 2, 8, 16, 18, 19.
2. —— xi. 4, 11.
3. ——— 15.
2. ——— 18 2nd, 20.
2. —— xii. 2, 3, 16, 19, 21.
3. —— xiii. 1.
2. ——— 3, 5.
3. ——— 8.
2. ——— 14.
2. —— xiv. 13.
3. ——— 14.
2. ——— 17, 20.
3. —— xv. 3, 21.
2. —— xvi. 4, 18.
3. 1 Cor. i. 14.
2. ——— 17, 27.
2. —— ii. 4, 5, 7, 9.
3. ——— 11.
2. ——— 12, 13.
2. —— iii. 1.
2. ——— 5 (*om.* G L Tr A [ℵ.)
2. ——— 6, 7.
2. —— iv. 14, 19 2nd, 20.
2. —— v. 8.
2. —— vi. 6, 11 3 times, 12 twice, 13 2nd.
2. —— vii. 4 twice, 7, 10.
3. ——— 17.
2. ——— 19.
2. ——— 21, see B if.
2. ——— 35
3. —— viii. 4.
2. ——— 6 (Lb.)
2. —— ix. 12, 21, 27.
2. —— x. 5.
3. ——— 13 1st.
2. ——— 13 3rd, 20, 23 twice, 24, 29, 33.
2. —— xi. 8, 9, 17.
3. —— xii. 3.
2. ——— 14, 24, 25.
2. —— xiv. 2, 17, 22 twice, 33, 34.
2. —— xv. 10 2nd & 3rd, 35, 37, 39, 40, 46.
2. 2 Cor. i. 9 twice, 12, 19, 24.
3. —— ii. 2.
2. ——— 4, 5 2nd, 13, 17 twice.
2. —— iii. 3 twice, 5, 6 1st, 14, 15.
2. —— iv. 2 twice.
— ——— 3, see B if.
2. ——— 5, 8, 9 twice.
— ——— 16, see B though
— ——— 17, see moment.
2. ——— 18 1st.
2. —— v. 4, 12, 15.
2. —— vi. 4.
2. —— vii. 5, 7, 9, 12, 14.
2. —— viii. 5, 8, 10, 14, 19, 21
2. —— ix. 12.
2. —— x. 4, 12, 13 2nd, 18.
— —— xi. 6 1st, see B though
2. ——— 6 2nd.
3. —— xii. 5.
2. ——— 14 twice.
2. —— xiii. 3, 4, 7, 8.
2. Gal. i. 1.
3. ——— 7.
2. ——— 8, 12, 17.
2. —— ii. 3, 7, 14.
3. ——— 16.
2. —— iii. 12.
— ——— 15, see B (though it be.)
2. ——— 16, 22.
2. —— iv. 2, 7, 14, 23 1st, 29, 31.
2. —— v. 6, 13.
2. —— vi. 13, 15.
2. Eph. i. 21.
2. —— ii. 19.
3. —— iv. 9.
2. Eph. iv. 29.
2. —— v. 4, 15, 17, 18, 27, 29.
2. —— vi. 4, 6, 12.
2. Phil. i. 20, 29.
2. —— ii. 3, 4, 7, 12, 27 twice.
2. —— iii. 7, 9.
2. —— iv. 6.
3. ——— 15.
2. ——— 17.
2. Col. iii. 11, 22.
2. 1 Thes. i. 5, 8.
2. —— ii. 2, 4 twice, 7, 8, 13.
2. —— iv. 7, 8.
2. —— v. 6, 9, 15.
2. 2 Thes. ii. 12.
2. —— iii. 8, 9, 11, 15.
2. 1 Tim. i. 13.
2. —— ii. 10, 12 2nd.
2. —— iii. 8.
2. —— iv. 12.
2. —— v. 1, 13.
9. ——— 19.
2. ——— 23.
2. —— vi. 2, 4, 17.
2. 2 Tim. i. 7, 8, 9, 17.
2. —— ii. 9, 20 2nd, 24.
2. —— iii. 9.
2. —— iv. 3, 8, 16.
2. Titus i. 8, 15 2nd.
2. —— ii. 10.
2. —— iii. 5.
2. Philem. 14 2nd, 16 1st.
2. Heb. ii. 16.
2. —— iii. 13.
3. ——— 18.
2. —— iv. 2.
2. —— v. 4, 5.
2. —— vii. 16.
2. —— ix. 24.
2. —— x. 3, 25, 39 2nd.
2. —— xi. 13.
2. —— xii. 11, 22, 26 2nd.
2. —— xiii. 14.
2. Jas. i. 25 2nd, 26.
2. —— iii. 15.
2. —— iv. 11 2nd.
2. 1 Pet. i. 15, 19, 23.
2. —— ii. 16, 18, 20, 25.
2. —— iii. 4.
— ——— 14, see B and if.
2. ——— 21.
2. —— iv. 2, 13.
6. ——— 15.
2. —— v. 2 twice, 8.
6. 2 Pet. i. 9.
2. ——— 16, 21.
2. —— ii. 4, 5.
2. —— iii. 9 twice.
2. 1 John ii. 2, 7, 16, 19 twice, 21.
3. ——— 22.
14. ——— 27 1st.
2. ——— 27 2nd.
2. —— iii. 18.
2. —— iv. 1, 10, 18.
3. —— v. 5.
2. ——— 6, 18.
2. 2 John 1, 5, 8.
2. ——— 12 (G ∾), (No. 4, G L.)
3. 3 John 9, 11 1st, 13.
2. Jude 6, 9.
— ——— 10 2nd, see B what.
2. Rev. ii. 6, 9, 14.
4. ——— 25.
2. —— iii. 9.
3. —— ix. 4.
2. ——— 5.
2. —— x. 7, 9.
3. —— xiv. 3.
2. —— xvii. 12.
3. —— xix. 12.
2. —— xx. 6.
3. —— xxi. 27.

BUT AND IF.

1. { ἐὰν, if, / δὲ, and *or* but, *see No.* 1, } but if.

2. { ἀλλα, but, *see No.* 2, / εἰ, if, / καὶ, and, } but and if *or* but if also.

1. Matt. xxiv. 48.
1. Luke xii. 45.
1. Luke xx. 6.
2. 1 Pet. iii. 14.

BUT EITHER.

ἤ, or,

Acts xviii. 21.

BUT IF.

1. { εἰ, if, / δὲ, but, *see No.* 1, / καὶ, and, } but and if *or* and if also.

2. { ἀλλα, but, *see No.* 2, / εἰ, if, / καὶ, and, } but and if *or* but if also.

2. 1 Cor. vii. 21.
1. 2 Cor. iv. 3.

BUT NOW.

ταν͂υν, (*for* τὰ νῦν, the things that now are,) now *or* in present circumstances.

Acts xvii. 30.

BUT RATHER.

1. { ἀλλα, but, *see No.* 2, / ἤ, or, } other than, except.

2. πλήν, *see* "BUT," *No.* 4.

2. Luke xi. 41.
2. Luke xii. 31.
1. Luke xii. 51.

BUT THAT.

μή, not.

Luke xvii. 1.

BUT THOUGH.

1. { εἰ, if, since, / δὲ, but, / καὶ, and, also, } but and if *or* but if also.

2. { εἰ, if, / καὶ, and, also, } and if if also.

3. 2 Cor. iv. 16.
1. 2 Cor. xi. 6.

BUT WHAT.

{ δὲ, however, / ὅσα, as many things.

Jude 10.

BUT (IF.)

κἄν, and if, even if, at least, although.

Mark v. 28; vi. 56.

BUT (NAY.)

μενοῦνγε, yea rather, yea truly.

Rom. ix. 20 (*om.* G →.)

BUT (NO MORE.)

{ οὐ, not, πλείων, more, ἤ, or; *after comp.* than, } not more than.

Luke ix. 13.

BUT (THOUGH IT BE.)

ὅμως, yet, nevertheless.

Gal. iii. 15.

BUT (YET.)

See "BUT (NO MORE.)"

Acts xxiv. 11 (*om.* ἤ, or, All.)

See also, MOMENT, TIME, WHEN.

BUY (-ETH, BOUGHT.)

1. ἀγοράζω, to be in the ἀγορά (the market-place), to attend it, have free use of it; *hence*, to do business there, buy *or* sell.
2. ὠνέομαι, to buy, purchase, *(opp.* to sell.)
3. τιμάω, to deem *or* hold worthy; *of things* to value, to estimate *or* value at *a certain price.*

1. Matt. xiii. 44, 46.
1. —— xiv. 15.
1. —— xxi. 12.
1. —— xxv. 9, 10.
1. —— xxvii. 7.
3. —— 9, marg. (text, *value.*)
1. Mark vi. 36, 37.
1. —— xi. 15.
1. —— xv. 46.
1. —— xvi. 1.
1. Luke ix. 13.
1. —— xiv. 18, 19.
1. Luke xvii. 28.
1. —— xix. 45 (*ap.*)
1. —— xxii. 36.
1. John iv. 8.
1. —— vi. 5.
1. —— xiii. 29.
2. Acts vii. 16.
1. 1 Cor. vi. 20.
1. —— vii. 23, 30.
1. 2 Pet. ii. 1.
1. Rev. iii. 18.
1. —— xiii. 17.
1. —— xviii. 11.

BUY AND SELL.

ἐμπορεύομαι, to go *or* travel in *or* to; *absol.* to be on a journey; *then,* to travel for traffic *or* business; *hence,* to be a merchant, to trade, traffic.

Jas. iv. 13.

BY.

1. By *is often expressed simply by the Dative case of the noun, without any preposition; and then indicates* the instrument *by which a thing is done.*
2. διά, through, *from the notion of separation, disjunction.*
   (a) *with Gen.* through, *as proceeding from;* by means of, *denoting the instrument of an action.*
   (b) *with Acc.* through, *as tending towards;* on account of, owing to, *denoting the ground and reason of an action, (cf.* Heb. xi. 10; Rom. xii. 3 *with* xv. 15; 1 Cor. xi. 9 *with* 12.)
3. ἐν, in; *of place,* within, upon, at; *with pl.* among; *of investiture,* in *or* with; *of power,* by.
4. ἐκ, from, out of, *implying motion from the interior; originating in, as the source, cause, or occasion,* from, by; *the material from which anything is made,* of.
5. ὑπό, under.
   (a) *with Gen.* beneath and separate from. *It marks that from which a fact, event, or action springs, i.e. the agent; hence, its meaning,* by.
   (b) *with Acc.* under and towards, close upon *(i.e.* under, *as e.g.* under a wall, hill,) *see* Acts v. 21, "close upon the dawn."
6. ἀπό, from, *implying motion from the exterior (while the governed noun denotes the point of departure;) hence esp.* the cause *or* occasion, from, on account of.
7. κατά, down.
   (a) *with Gen.* down from; *of place,* down upon; against, in opposition to; *(opp. of No.* 12); *in asservations,* by, (Heb. vi. 13-16; 1 Cor. xv. 15.)
   (b) *with Acc.* down towards; throughout; over against; according to, *in reference to some standard of comparison stated or implied.*

8. παρά, beside, *of juxtaposition.*

(a) *with Gen.* beside and proceeding from; *with persons only,* from, *gen. with notion of something imparted.*

(b) *with Dat.* beside and at; with, near, *of persons only (except* John xix. 25;) with, *in the estimation or power of.*

(c) *with Acc.* to, *or* along the side of; by, near; beside, *as not coinciding, hence,* contrary to; beside, above, *(instituting a comparison and leaving the superiority to be inferred, while* ὑπέρ *affirms the superiority.)*

9. ἐπί, upon, *of superposition.*

(a) *with Gen.* upon and proceeding from, *(e.g. as a pillar upon the ground,)* over, *in the presence or time of.*

(b) *with Dat.* upon and resting upon; over, *of superintendence;* in addition to, on account of; on *or* at, *as the groundwork of any fact or circumstance.*

(c) *with Acc.* upon, *by direction towards (motion being implied)* to, *(implying an intention)* for, against.

10. πρός, towards, in the direction of.

(a) *with Gen.* hitherwards, conducive to.

(b) *with Dat.* resting in a direction towards; near, hard by.

(c) *with Acc.* hitherwards, *(of literal direction,)* to, towards.

11. εἰς, into, *implying motion to the interior;* to, unto, with a view to; *(opp. of No.* 4.)

12. ὑπέρ, over.

(a) *with Gen.* over and separate from; on behalf of, *as though bending over to protect, (opp. of No.* 7;) *of things* for their sake, *in various ways.*

(b) *with Acc.* over and towards; beyond, above, *used in comparison.*

The agent *is expressed by No.* 5.

The instrument *by No.* 1.

The minister of another's will *by No.* 2a.

The motive *or* cause *by No.* 2b.

The occasion *by No.* 6.

No. 1 *in all passages, except where it forms part of a verb, and the following.*

2a. Matt. i. 22.
2a. —— ii. 5, 15.
5a. —— 17 (No. 2a, G∾ L T Tr.)
2a. —— 23.
5a. —— iii. 3 (No. 2a, G∾ L T Tr A ℵ.)
9b. —— iv. 4 1st.
9b. —— 4 2nd (No. 3, G∾ L T Tr A.)
2a. —— 14.
8c. —— 18.
3. —— v. 34.
3. —— 35 1st.
11. —— 35 2nd.
3. —— 36.
6. —— vii. 16.
6, —— 20 (No. 4, L.)
2a. —— viii. 17, 28.
2a. —— xii. 17.
3. —— 24, 27 twice, 28.
4. —— 33, 37 twice.
— —— xiii. 1, 4, 19, see B side.
— —— 21, see B and B.
2a —— 35.
3. —— xiv. 13
2b. —— xv. 3.
4. —— 5.
2b. —— 6.
3. —— xvii. 21 (*ap.*)
2a. —— xviii. 7.
— —— xx. 30, see B..side.
2a. —— xxi. 4.
3. —— 23, 24, 27.
3. —— xxii. 1.
5a. —— 31.
3. —— xxiii. 16 twice, 18 twice, 20 3 times, 22 3 times.
2a. —— xxiv. 15.
2a. —— xxvi. 24.
7a. —— 63.
2a. —— xxvii. 9.
5a. —— 35 (*ap.*)
8c. Mark i. 16.
— —— ii. 13, see B..side.
3. —— iii. 22.
— —— iv. 1 1st, see B..side.
10c. —— 1 2nd.
3. —— 2.
— —— 4, 15, see B..side.
5a. —— v. 4.
3. —— 21.
2a. —— vi 2.
— —— 25, see B and B.
— —— 40, see "Hundreds" and "Fifties."
4. —— vii. 11.
3. —— viii. 3, 27.
— —— ix. 2, see B themselves.
3. —— 29 twice, 33.
3. —— 34 (*om.* Lb)
2a. —— x. 1 (καί *and,* instead of διὰ τοῦ, *by the,* L T Tr A ℵ.)
— —— 46, see B..side.
10c. —— xi. 4.
3. —— 28, 29, 33.
3. —— xii. 1, 36.
5a. —— xiii. 14 (*ap.*)
3. —— xiv. 1.
— —— 19, see one Bone.
2a. —— 21.
3. Luke i. 17, marg. (text, to.)
2a. —— 70.
3. —— 77, marg. *for.*
5a. —— ii. 18, 26.
3. —— 27.
5a. Luke iii. 19.
3. —— iv. 1.
9b. —— 4 twice (*ap.*)
8c. —— v. 1, 2.
5a. —— 15 (*om.* "by Him," G⇉ L T Tr A
2a. —— 19 (*om.* All) [ℵ)
4. —— vi. 44.
2a. —— viii. 4.
— —— 5, 12, see B..side
5a. —— ix. 7 (*om.* "by Him" G⇉ Lb T Tr A ℵ.)
— —— 14, see "Fifties."
8b. —— 47.
7b. —— x. 4, 31 1st.
3. —— xi. 19 twice.
5a. —— xiii. 17.
5a. —— xvi. 22.
— —— xvii. 7, see B and B.
2a. —— xviii. 31.
— —— 35, see B side.
3. —— xx. 2, 8.
— —— xxi. 9, see B and B
5a. —— 16.
2a —— xxii. 22.
10c. —— 56.
5a. —— xxiii. 8.
— —— xxiv. 12, see B themselves.
3. —— 32.
2a. John i. 3, 10, 17 twice.
4. —— iii. 34.
9. —— v. 2.
2b. —— vi. 57 twice.
— —— viii. 9 1st (*ap.*)
— —— 9 2nd, see one by one (*ap.*)
2a. —— x. 1, 2.
7b. —— 3.
2a. —— 9.
3. —— xiii. 35.
2a. —— xiv. 6.
3. —— xvi. 30.
7b. —— xix. 7.
8b. —— 25.
— —— xx. 7, see B itself.
3. Acts i. 3.
2a. —— 16. [43.
2a. —— ii. 16, 22 2nd, 23 2nd, 43.
2a. —— iii. 16, 18, 21.
3. —— iv. 7 twice, 10 twice.
2a. —— 16, 25.
3. —— 30 1st.
2a. —— 30 2nd.
5a. —— 36.
10c. —— v. 10.
2a. —— 12, 19.
2a. —— vii. 25.
3. —— 35 (σύν, *with,* G∾ L T Tr A.)
11. —— 53.
6. —— ix. 13.
2a. —— 25 2nd.
— —— x. 6, see B..side.
5a. —— 22.
— —— 32, see B..side.
2a. —— 36.
2a. —— xi. 28, 30.
2a. —— xii. 9 (No. 5a, T.)
6. —— 20.
5a. —— xiii. 4
3. —— 39 twice.
5a. —— 45.
2a. —— xiv. 3.
5a. —— xv. 3.
2a. —— 7, 12, 23, 27.
5a. —— 40.
5a. —— xvi. 2.
— —— 13, see B..side.

2a. Acts xvii. 10.
3. ——— 31.
2a. —— xviii. 9, 28.
2a. —— xix. 11.
4. ——— 25.
3. —— xx. 19.
2a. —— xxi. 19.
2a. —— xxiii. 31.
2a. —— xxiv. 2 twice.
5a. ——— 21 (No. 9a, L T Tr A.)
5a. —— xxv. 14.
7b. —— xxvii. 2.
5a. ——— 11.
7b. —— xxviii. 16.
2a. ——— 25.
2a. Rom. i. 2.
4. ——— 4.
2a. ——— 5.
3. ——— 10.
2a. ——— 12.
4. ——— 17.
7b. —— ii. 7.
2a. ——— 12, 16.
4. ——— 27 1st.
2a. ——— 27 2nd.
4. —— iii. 20 1st.
2a. ——— 20 2nd.
5a. ——— 21.
2a. ——— 22, 27 twice.
4. ——— 30.
4. —— iv. 2.
7b. ——— 16.
4. —— v. 1.
2a. ——— 2.
2a. ——— 5.
3. ——— 9.
2a. ——— 10 1st.
3. ——— 10 2nd.
2a. ——— 11, 12 twice.
3. ——— 15.
2a. ——— 16 1st.
4. ——— 16 2nd.
2a. ——— 17 twice, 18 twice, 19 twice, 21.
2a. —— vi. 4 twice.
2a. —— vii. 4, 5, 7, 8, 11 twice, 13 twice.
2b. —— viii. 11 twice, marg. *because of.*
4. —— ix. 10 1st, 32 twice.
3. —— x. 5.
4. ——— 17 1st.
2a. ——— 17 2nd.
9. ——— 19 twice.
7b. —— xi. 24.
2a. —— xii. 1.
3. —— xiv. 14.
3. —— xv. 16.
2a. ——— 18 1st.
3. ——— 19.
5a ——— 24 (No. 6, L T A)
2a. ——— 28, 32.
2a. —— xvi. 18, 26.
3. 1 Cor. i. 4, 5.
2a. ——— 9, 10.
5a. ——— 11.
2a. ——— 21 twice.
2a. —— ii. 10.
2a. —— iii. 5.
3. ——— 13.
2a. ——— 15.
3. —— vi. 2, 11.
2a. ——— 14.
7b. —— vii. 6.
3. ——— 14 twice.
2a. —— viii. 6 twice.
2a. —— xi. 12.
3. —— xii. 3 twice.
2a. ——— 8 1st.
7b. ——— 8 2nd.
3. ——— 9 twice, 13.
3. —— xiv. 6 4 times.
2a. ——— 9.
7b. ——— 27.
— ——— 31, see one by [one.
2a. —— xv. 2, 21 twice.
2b. —— xvi. 2.

2a. 1 Cor. xvi. 3.
3. ——— 7.
2a. 2 Cor. i. 1, 4, 5, 11 3rd.
3. ——— 12.
2a. ——— 16, 19 twice, 20.
4. —— ii. 2.
2a. ——— 14.
5a. —— iii. 3.
6. ——— 18, marg. *of.*
2a. —— iv. 14 (σύν, *with.* G ∾ L T Tr A ℵ.)
2a. —— v. 7 twice, 18, 20.
3. —— vi. 6 6 times, 7 1st & 2nd.
2a. ——— 7 3rd, 8 twice.
3. —— vii. 6, 7 twice.
4. ——— 9.
6. ——— 13.
2a. —— viii. 5.
7b. ——— 8.
4. ——— 14.
5a. ——— 19, 20.
2a. —— ix. 12, 13.
2a. —— x. 1, 9, 11.
3. ——— 12.
3. ——— 15, marg. *in.*
4. —— xi. 26 twice.
2a. ——— 33.
2a. —— xii. 17.
4. —— xiii. 4 twice.
2a. Gal. i. 1 twice, 12, 15.
7b. —— ii. 2 1st.
4. ——— 16 1st.
2a. ——— 16 2nd.
4. ——— 16 3rd, 4th & 5th.
3. ——— 17, 20.
2a. ——— 21.
4. —— iii. 2 twice, 5 twice.
3. ——— 11 1st.
4. ——— 11 2nd.
2a. ——— 18, 19.
4. ——— 21, 22, 24.
2a. ——— 26.
4. —— iv. 22 twice.
2a. ——— 23.
3. —— v. 4.
4. ——— 5.
2a. ——— 6, 13.
2a. —— vi. 14 (δι' οὗ, *by whom*, marg. *whereby.*)
2a. Eph. i. 1, 5.
5a. —— ii. 11 1st.
3. ——— 13.
2a. ——— 16.
3. ——— 18.
7b. —— iii. 3.
3. ——— 5.
2a. ——— 6.
7b. ——— 7.
2a. ——— 9 (*ap*), 10, 12, [16, 17.
3. ——— 21.
3. —— iv. 14 twice.
2a. ——— 16.
3. ——— 21.
5a. —— v. 13.
3. ——— 26.
2a. Phil. i. 11, 20 twice, 26.
5a. ——— 28.
9. —— iii. 9.
3. —— iv. 19.
2a. Col. i. 1.
3. ——— 16 1st.
2a. ——— 16 2nd.
3. ——— 17.
3. ——— 20 1st.
2a. ——— 20 2nd (*om.* "by Him," G → L Tr.)
3. ——— 21 (marg. *in.*)
3. —— ii. 11.
5a. ——— 18.
2a. ——— 19.
2a. —— iii. 17.
3. 1 Thes. iii. 3.
2a. ——— 7.
3. —— iv. 1.
2a. ——— 2.
3. ——— 15.
2a. —— v. 9.
12a. 2 Thes. ii. 1.

2a. 2 Thes ii. 2 3 times.
7b. ——— 3.
2a. ——— 14, 15 (2nd not translated, lit. *by our Epistle.*).
2a. —— iii. 12 (No. 3, G ∾ L T Tr A ℵ.)
3. ——— 16.
7b. 1 Tim. i. 1.
3. ——— 18.
2a. —— iv. 5, 14.
7b. —— v. 21.
2a. 2 Tim. i. 1, 6, 10, 14.
2a. —— ii. 2, marg. (text, *among.*)
5a. ——— 26.
2a. —— iv. 17.
3. Titus i. 9.
4. —— iii. 5 1st.
2a. ——— 5 2nd.
3. Philem. 6.
2a. ——— 7.
3. Heb. i. 1, 2 1st.
2a. ——— 2 2nd.
3a. ——— 3 2nd (*om.* "by Himself," L Tr A ℵ.)
2a. —— ii. 2, 3 1st.
5a. ——— 3 2nd.
2a. ——— 10.
5a. —— iii. 4.
2a. ——— 16.
6. —— v. 8.
2b. —— vi. 7, marg. *for.*
7a. ——— 13 twice, 16.
2a. ——— 18.
2a. —— vii. 11, 19, 21.
7b. ——— 22.
2a. ——— 25.
2a. —— ix. 11, 12 twice.
7b. ——— 22.
2a ——— 26.
— —— x. 1, see year.
7b. ——— 8.
3. ——— 10, 19.
4. ——— 38.
3. —— xi. 2.
2a. ——— 4 twice, 7 2nd.

7b. Heb. xi. 7 3rd.
8c. ——— 12.
2a. ——— 29.
2a. —— xiii. 11, 15.
2a. Jas. ii. 12.
— ——— 17, marg. see B itself.
4. ——— 18, marg. (text, *without*, χωρίς, without All.)
4. ——— 18, 21, 22, 24 twice, [25.
2a. 1 Pet. i. 3.
3. ——— 5.
2a. ——— 12, 21, 23.
2a. —— ii. 5.
4. ——— 12.
2a. ——— 14.
2a. —— iii. 1.
3. ——— 19.
2a. ——— 20, 21.
3. —— v. 10.
2a. ——— 12.
2a. 2 Pet. i. 4.
3. ——— 13.
5a. ——— 21.
— —— iii. 1, see B many [of.
5a. ——— 2.
4. 1 John iii. 24.
3. —— v. 2.
2a. ——— 6 1st.
3. ——— 6 2nd & 3rd.
7b. 3 John 14.
3. Jude 1.
6. —— 23.
2a. Rev. i. 1.
3. —— v. 9.
5a. —— ix. 18 1st (No. 6, All.) [G ∾.)
4. ——— 18 2nd (No. 6,
4. ——— 18 3rd & 4th (*om.* All.)
3. ——— 20.
3. —— x. 6.
2b. —— xii. 11 twice.
2b. —— xiii. 14.
6. —— xviii. 15.
3. ——— 23.

BY AND BY.

1. ἐξαυτῆς, at the very point of time, at once.
2. εὐθύς, straight, direct; *of time*, straight *i.e.* immediately, straightway.
3. εὐθέως, immediately, forthwith.

2. Matt. xiii. 21. | 1. Mark. vi. 25.
3. Luke xvii. 7 : xxi. 9.

BY ITSELF.

1. χωρίς, separately, apart ; without, separate from.
2. { κατά, according to, / ἑαυτοῦ, him-, her-, it-self, } by itself.

1. John xx. 7.
2. Jas. ii. 17, marg. (text, *alone.*)

BY THEMSELVES.

μόνος, alone, left alone, solitary.

Mark ix. 2. | Luke xxiv. 12 (*ap.*)

BY...SIDE.

παρά, with Dat. see "BY," *No.* 8.

Matt. xiii. 1, 4, 19.
—— xx. 30.
Mark ii. 13.
—— iv. 1, 4, 15.
—— x. 46.
Luke viii. 5.
—— 12 (with art. *those by the side.*)
—— xviii. 35.
Acts x. 6, 32.
—— xvi. 13.

BY WAY OF.

ἐν, see "BY," *No.* 3.

2 Pet. iii. 1.

BY.

See also, CALLED, CLOSE, COME, COMPANY, CONSTRAINT, COURSE, DIVIDE, FIFTIES, FORCE, FRAUD, HAND, HEREOF, HIGHWAY, HOLD, HUNDREDS, INHERITANCE, INTERPRETATION, KNOW, LEST, MEANS, ONE, ORDER, PASS, PROTEST, REASON, SAIL, SIDE, SIT, SOOTHSAYING, SPACE, STAND, TAKE, TRADE, WAY, YEAR.

C

CÆSAR.

Καῖσαρ, Cæsar, *a title applied to the Roman Emperors after Julius.*

In all passages, except

Acts xi. 28 (*om.* All.)

CÆSAR'S COURT [margin.]

πραιτώριον, (from the Lat. prætor) the public hall in the Governor's house; the quarters of the prætorian army *in Rome.*

Phil. i. 13 (text, *palace.*)

CAGE.

φυλακή, a watching *or* guarding; *of persons,* a watch *or* guard; *of place,* a watch, station, post; *of time,* a watch, *e.g. of the night; lastly,* a place for keeping *others in,* a ward, a prison.

Rev. xviii. 2.

CALF.

μόσχος, any thing young, *used of plants, animals, etc.; esp. of the young of kine,* a calf, *but also* a young bull; a heifer, a young cow, *(non occ.)*

Luke xv. 23, 27, 30. | Heb. ix. 12, 19.
Rev. iv. 7.

CALF (MAKE A.)

μοσχοποιέω, to make a calf, *(said of the Israelites in imitation of the Egyptian worship of Apis), (non occ.)*

Acts vii. 41.

CALL.

(-ED, -EST, -ETH, -ING.)

1. *καλέω,* to call; *with personal object,* to call any one, invite, summon; *with impersonal object,* to call the name; *hence,* to name; *then in pass.* to bear the name, be called *anything, (καλέω, thus has the two ideas of* vocation *and* designation; *see* Rom. ix. 25, 26, *and the context, etc. must determine which.)*

2. *προσκαλέω, (No.* 1, *with πρός,* towards, *prefixed)* to call hither; *in N.T. as also in* lxx. *only the mid.* to call to one's self; *but also* to call any one *to* a work; to call before *a court; hence,* to accuse.

3. *ἐπικαλέω, (No.* 1, *with ἐπί,* upon, *prefixed)* to call on, to call to, *(denoting the object, not the subject, as No.* 2) to call on *any one (by turning towards and crying to him); in N.T. mid. implying interest and advantage,* to appeal; to call out *something to some one, i.e.* to name, designate.

4. *μετακαλέω, (No.* 1, *with μετά,* with, *prefixed; denoting* participation *or* change) to call away *or* to another place; to call back, re-call; to invite to one's self, *(only in mid. in N.T.)*

5. *φωνέω,* to produce a sound *or* tone, to sound; *esp. of men,* to speak loud *or* clearly; to call out, cry out to.

6. λέγω, to lay *asleep; then,* to lay in order, arrange, *and so* to collect; to lay among, *and so* to recount, tell, relate; *then gen.* to say, tell, utter in words; *used of all kinds of* oral *communications.* (*λέγω differs from λαλέω, in that it always implies rational and intelligent utterance, and denotes the sentiment.*

7. ἐπιλέγω, (*No.* 6 *with* ἐπί, upon, *prefixed,*) to say in addition, to add to *what has been said,* to call *or* name. (*Implying that a thing has another name.*)

8. ὄνομα, the name *by which a person or thing is called. In phrases* "called Simon," *it is lit.* by name Simon.

3. ὀνομάζω, to name *or* speak of by name, to call one *something;* to name *or* mention; to name, impose a name.

10. ἐπονομάζω, (*No.* 9 *with* ἐπί, upon, *prefixed,*) to give another name to.
(a) *in pass.* to be named, *esp.* to be surnamed.

11. χρηματίζω, to do *or* carry on business, have dealings, *esp. in money matters; hence, since names were imposed on men from their* business *or* office, *it signifies* to be named *or* called, (*cf. the Eng.* Smith, Taylor, Carpenter, *etc., etc.*)

12. προσαγορεύω, to speak to in the ἀγορά (the market-place *or* assembly,) *hence,* to address, accost; *but also,* to proclaim, (*non occ.*)

13. εἶπον, to speak, say; *also,* to call *one so and so,* to say *that.*

14. ἐρῶ, to say, to speak; to call, to name.

15. ἐστί, he, she *or* it is.

6. Matt. i. 16.
1. —— 21, 23, 25.
1. —— ii. 7, 15.
6. —— 23 1st.
1. —— 23 2nd.
6. —— iv. 18.
1. —— 21.
1. —— v. 9, 19 twice.
1. —— ix. 13.
— —— x. 1, see C unto one.
6. —— 2.
1. —— 25 (No. 3, All.)
6. —— xiii. 55.
2. —— xv. 10.
— —— 32, see C unto one.
— —— xviii. 2, see C unto one.
2. —— 32,
6. —— xix. 17 (*ap.*)
1. —— xx. 8.
— —— 25, see C unto one.
5. Matt. xx. 32.
1. —— xxi. 13.
1. —— xxii. 3, 43, 45.
1. —— xxiii. 7, 8, 9, 10.
1. —— xxv. 14.
6. —— xxvi. 3, 14, 36.
— —— xxvii. 8.
6. —— 16, 17, 22, 33.
— —— 47, see C for.
1. Mark i. 20.
1. —— ii. 17.
—— iii. 13, } see C.
—— 28, } unto one.
5. —— 31 (No. 1, L T Tr A ℵ) (*om.* G →.)
— —— vi. 7, } see C
— —— vii. 14, } unto
— —— viii. 1, 34, } one.
5. —— ix. 35.
6. —— x. 18.
— Mark x. 42, see C to one
5. —— 49 3 times.
1. —— xi. 17.
6. —— xii. 37.
— —— 43, see C unto one.
6. —— xv. 12 (*om.* whom ye call, L Tr.)
15. —— 16 1st.
— —— 16 2nd, see C together.
5. —— 35.
— —— 44, see C unto one.
1. Luke i. 13, 31, 32, 35, 36, 59, 60, 61, 62, 76.
1. —— ii. 4, 21, 23.
1. —— v. 32.
— —— vi. 13, see C unto one.
1. —— 15, 46.
1. —— vii. 11.
— —— 19, see C unto one.
— —— 32, see C to.
1. —— viii. 2.
5. —— 54.
— —— ix. 1, see C together.
1. —— 10.
1. —— x. 39.
— —— xiii. 12, see C to one.
5. —— xiv. 12.
1. —— 13.
— —— xv. 6, 9, see C together.
1. —— 19, 21.
2. —— 26.
5. —— xvi. 2.
— —— 5, } see C
— —— xviii. 16, } unto one
6. —— 19.
1. —— xix. 13.
5. —— 15.
1. —— 29.
6. —— xx. 37.
1. —— 44.
1. —— xxi. 37.
6. —— xxii. 1.
1. —— 25.
6. —— 47.
— —— xxiii. 13, see C together.
1. —— 33.
8. —— xxiv. 13.
1. John i. 42.
5. —— 48.
1. —— ii. 2.
5. —— 9.
6. —— iv. 5.
5. —— 16.
6. —— 25.
7. —— v. 2.
6. —— ix. 11.
5. —— 18, 24.
1. —— x. 3 (No. 5, G ∾ L T Tr A ℵ.)
13. —— 35.
6. —— xi. 16.
5. —— 28 1st.
— —— 28 2nd, see C for.
6. —— 54.
5. —— xii. 17.
5. —— xiii. 13.
6. —— xv. 15 1st.
13. —— 15 2nd.
5. —— xviii. 33.
6. —— xix. 13, 17 twice.
6. —— xx. 24.
6. —— xxi. 2.
1. Acts i. 12, 19, 23.
— —— ii. 21, see C on.
2. —— 39.
6. —— iii. 2.
1. —— 11.
1. —— iv. 18.
— —— v. 21, see C together
2. —— 40.
— —— vi. 2, see C unto one.
6. —— 9.
— —— vii. 14, see C to one's self.
— —— 59, see C upon.
8. —— viii. 9.
1. —— ix. 11 1st.
8. —— 11 2nd.
— Acts ix. 14, 21, see C on.
6. —— 36.
5. —— 41.
1. —— x. 1 1st.
8. —— 1 2nd.
— —— 5, see C for.
5. —— 7, 18.
— —— 23, see C in.
— —— 24, see C together
6. —— 28.
— —— 32, see C hither.
— —— xi. 13, see C for.
11. —— 26.
1. —— xiii. 1.
— —— 2, see C whereunto
— —— 7, see C for.
1. —— xiv. 12.
2. —— xvi. 10.
— —— 29, see C for.
9. —— xix. 13.
— —— 25, see C together
— —— 40, see C in question.
— —— xx. 1, see C unto one.
4. —— 17.
— —— xxii. 16, see C on.
— —— xxiii. 6, see C in question.
— —— 17, 18, 23, see C unto one.
— —— xxiv. 2, see C forth.
6. —— 14.
— —— 21, see C in question.
— —— 25, see C for.
1 —— xxvii. 8, 14, 16.
1. —— xxviii. 1.
— —— 17, see C together.
— —— 20, see C for.
10. Rom. ii. 17.
1. —— iv. 17.
11. —— vii. 3.
1. —— viii. 30 twice.
1. —— ix. 7, 11, 24, 25, 26.
— —— x. 12, 13, see C upon.
— —— 14, see C on.
— 1 Cor. i. 1, see called.
— —— 2 2nd, see C upon.
1. —— 9.
9. —— v. 11.
1. —— vii. 15, 17, 18 twice, 20, 21, 22 twice, 24.
6. —— viii. 5.
6. —— xii. 3 (with λαλέω to speak.)
1. —— xv. 9.
3. 2 Cor. i. 23.
1. Gal. i. 6, 15.
1. —— v. 8, 13.
6. Eph. ii. 11 twice.
1. —— iv. 1, 4.
1. Col. iii. 15.
6. —— iv. 11.
1. 1 Thes. ii. 12.
1. —— iv. 7.
1. —— v. 24.
1. 2 Thes. ii. 4.
1. —— 14.
1. 1 Tim. vi. 12.
— 2 Tim. i. 5, see C to.
1. —— 9.
— —— ii. 22, see C on.
1. Heb. ii. 11.
1. —— iii. 13.
1. —— v. 4.
12. —— 10.
6. —— vii. 11.
6. —— ix. 2, 3.
1. —— 15.
1. —— xi. 8, 18.
6. —— 24.
1. Jas. ii. 23.
— —— v. 14, see C for.
1. 1 Pet. i. 15.
— —— 17, see C on.
1. —— ii. 9, 21.
1. —— iii. 6, 9.
1. —— v. 10.
1. 2 Pet. i. 3.
1. 1 John iii. 1.

1. Rev. i. 9.
6. — ii. 20.
1. — xi. 8.
1. Rev. xii. 9.
1. — xvi. 16.
1. — xix. 9, 11, 13.

CALL FOR.

1. *αἰτέω*, to ask *for something*, to beg *or* crave *something*, to ask *a person* for *a thing.*
2. *μετακαλέω*, *see* "CALL," *No.* 4.
3. *παρακαλέω*, to call to *or* beside *one; every kind of* calling to *which is meant to produce a particular effect; hence*, to beseech, exhort, comfort, *etc.*
4. *προσκαλέω*, *see* "CALL," *No.* 2.
5. *φωνέω*, *see* "CALL," *No.* 5.
6. *μεταπέμπω*, to send *one* after another, to send for, summon.

5. Matt. xxvii. 47.
5. John xi. 28.
6. Acts x. 5.
6. — xi. 13.
4. Acts xiii. 7.
1. — xvi. 29.
2. — xxiv 25.
3. — xxviii. 20.
4. Jas. v. 14.

CALL FORTH.

καλέω, *see* "CALL, *No.* 1.

Acts xxiv. 2.

CALL HITHER.

μετακαλέω, *see* "CALL," *No.* 4.

Acts x. 32.

CALL IN.

εἰσκαλέω, to call *or* invite in, *(non occ.)*

Acts x. 23.

CALL IN QUESTION.

1. *ἐγκαλέω*, to call in *as a debt; then gen.*, to demand *as one's due*, to bring a charge *or* accusation against *a person.*
2. *κρίνω*, to separate, part, put asunder; to enquire *or* search into, investigate; *hence*, to form an estimate of, to come to a decision, to judge, *(not necessarily to condemn.) In profane Greek*, to call any one to account, to begin a lawsuit.

1. Acts xix. 40.
2. Acts xxiii. 6.
2. Acts xxiv. 21.

CALL ON.

ἐπικαλέω, *see* "CALL," *No.* 3.

Acts ii. 21.
— ix. 14, 21.
— xxii. 16.
Rom. x. 14.
2 Tim. ii. 22.
1 Pet. i. 17.

CALL TO.

1. *προσφωνέω*, to call *or* shout to *any one*, to cry aloud, to call to one's self.
2. *λαμβάνω*, to take, *as in the hand, hence*, to receive. *In paraphrastic expressions*, to take *a beginning, i.e.* to begin *so*, to take *remembrance*, take *experience of*, *etc.*

1. Luke vii. 32.
2. 2 Tim. i. 5.

CALL TO ONE.

1. *προσκαλέω*, *see* "CALL," *No.* 2.
2. *προσφωνέω*, *see* "CALL TO," *No.* 1.
3. *μετακαλέω*, *see* "CALL," *No.* 4.

1. Mark x. 42.
2. Luke xiii. 12.
3. Acts vii. 14.

CALL TOGETHER.

1. *συγκαλέω*, to call *or* summon together; call a council.
   (a) *Mid.* to call *or* collect together to *one's self.*
2. *συναθροίζω*, to throng *or* crowd together.

1. Mark xv. 16.
1a. Luke ix. 1.
1a. — xv. 6, 9.
1a. — xxiii. 13.
1. Acts v. 21.
1a. — x. 24.
2. — xix. 25.
1a. — xxviii. 17.

CALL UNTO.

προσφωνέω, *see* "CALL TO," *No.* 1.

Matt. xi. 16.

CALL UNTO ONE.

1. *προσκαλέω*, *see* "CALL," *No.* 2.
2. *προσφωνέω*, *see* "CALL TO," *No.* 1.

1. Matt. x. 1.
1. — xv. 32.
1. — xviii. 2.
1. — xx. 25.
1. Mark iii. 13, 23.
1. — vi. 7.
1. — vii 14.
1. — viii. 1, 34.
1. Mark xii. 43.
1. — xv. 44.
2. Luke vi. 13.
1. — vii. 19.
1. — xvi. 5.
1. — xviii 16.
1. Acts vi. 2.
1. — xx. 1.
1. Acts xxiii. 17, 18, 23.

CALL UPON.

ἐπικαλέω, *see* "CALL," *No.* 3.

Acts vii. 59. | Rom. x. 12, 13. | 1 Cor. i. 2.

CALL WHEREUNTO.

προσκαλέω, *see* "CALL," *No.* 2, *with* ὅ.

Acts xiii. 2.

See also, BLESSED, COMMON, MIND, REMEMBRANCE.

CALLED.

1. κλητός, called, invited; welcome, chosen.
2. ὄνομα, the name *by which a person or thing is called*, by name.
3. { ὅ, which, ἐστι, is.

1. Matt. xx. 16 (*ap.*)
1. —— xxii. 14.
3. Mark xv. 16 1st.
2. Luke xxiv. 13.
2. Acts viii. 9.
— —— ix. 11 1st, see C.
2. —— 11 2nd.
2. —— x. 1.
— —— xv. 17, see C upon (be.)
1. Rom. i. 1, 6, 7.
1. —— viii. 28.
1. 1 Cor. i. 1 (*om.* G→ Lb Ab.)
1. —— 2.
— —— 24, see C (which is.)
— Heb. xi 16, see C (be.)
— Jas. ii. 7, see C by (be.)
1. Jude 1.
1. Rev. xvii. 14.

CALLED (BE.)

ἐπικαλέω, *see* "CALL," *No.* 3.

Heb. xi. 16 (pass.)

CALLED BY (BE.)

Jas. ii. 7 (with ἐπί, *upon.*)

CALLED UPON (BE.)

Acts xv. 17 (with ἐπί, *upon.*)

CALLED (WHICH IS.)

κλητός, *see* "CALLED," *No.* 1.

1 Cor. i. 24.

See also, FALSELY.

CALLING.

κλῆσις, a calling, summons, invitation; *used in N.T. for that* calling *whose origin, nature, and goal are heavenly, see* Heb. iii. 1, *(occ.* Eph. iv. 1, *denotes* vocation.)

Rom. xi. 29.
1 Cor. i. 26.
—— vii. 20.
Eph. i. 18.
—— iv. 4.
Phil. iii. 14.
2 Thes. i. 11.
2 Tim. i. 9.
Heb. iii. 1.
2 Pet. i. 10.

CALM.

γαλήνη, stillness of the sea, calmness, gentleness, *(from* γελάω, to smile, *so Ovid, "The storm is hushed, and dimpled ocean* smiles," *(non occ.)*

Matt. viii. 26. | Mark iv. 39. | Luke viii. 24.

CALVARY.

κρανίον, a skull, *(Lat.* Calvaria, a skull.)

Luke xxiii. 33.

CAME.

See, COME.

CAMEL.

κάμηλος, a camel, *(from Heb.* גמל, bearer, carrier,) *(non occ.)*

Matt. iii. 4.
—— xix. 24.
—— xxiii. 24.
Mark i. 6.
—— x. 25.
Luke xviii. 25.

CAMP.

παρεμβολή, insertion beside, between *or* among *others;* a parenthesis; a putting in *or* distributing *men through an army*, a drawing up in battle order; *and then* a camp; *hence*, any fortified place.

Heb. xiii. 11, 13. | Rev. xx. 9.

CAN, COULD (-ST,) CANNOT, &c., (with a negative.)

When not part of another word it is one of these following:

1. δύναμαι, to be able, capable, strong enough. *It denotes moral power (while* ἰσχύω, *No.* 2 *denotes* physical ability.) *It is from* δύνος, *which is equivalent to* divine, good; *and the idea is* I make myself good, am strong enough, equal, able.

2. ἰσχύω, to be strong *in body or physical health,* strong *in mental power,* have efficiency, prevail; *used of* physical strength and mental validity; *more emphatic than No.* 1.

3. ἔχω, to have in the hands; *hence, to* possess *anything.*

4. γινώσκω, to learn to know, to perceive, mark, *and in past tenses, sometimes,* to know. *It implies* the possession of a knowledge which produces some emotion and affection of the mind; to be influenced by our knowledge; to know how.

5. οἶδα, *(perf. of* εἴδω, to see,) I have seen *and therefore* know.

6. ἐστί, (3 *pers. sing. pres. of* εἰμί, I am,) he, she *or* it is.

1. Matt. v. 14, 36.
1. —— vi. 24 twice, 27.
1. —— vii. 18.
1. —— viii. 2.
1. —— ix. 15.
1. —— xii. 29, 34.
4. —— xvi. 3 1st.
1. —— —— 3 2nd.
1. —— xvii. 16, 19.
1. —— xix. 25.
— —— xxi. 27, see C tell.
2. —— xxvi. 40.
1. —— —— 53.
1. —— xxvii. 42.
5. —— —— 65.
1. Mark i. 40, 45.
1. —— ii. 4, 7, 19 1st.
1. —— —— 19 2nd (ap.)
1. —— iii. 20, 23, 24, 25, 26, 27.
1. —— v. 3.
2. —— —— 4.
1. —— vi. 5, 19.
1. —— vii. 15, 18, 24.
1. —— viii. 4.
1. —— ix 3.
2. —— —— 18.
— —— —— 22, see C do.
1. —— —— 23, 28, 29, 39.
1. —— x. 26, 38, 39.
— —— xi. 33, see C tell.
3. —— xiv. 8.
2. —— —— 37.
1. Luke i. 22.
1. —— v. 12, 21, 34.
1. —— vi. 39, 42.
2. —— —— 48.
1. —— viii. 19.
2. —— —— 43.
1. —— ix. 40.
1. —— xi. 7.
1. —— xii. 25.
5. —— —— 56.
1. —— xiii. 11.
— —— —— 33, see cannot be (it.)
2. —— xiv. 6.
3. —— —— 14.
1. —— —— 20, 26, 27, 33.
2. —— xvi 3.
1. —— —— 13 twice, 26 1st.
1. —— xviii. 26.
1. —— xix. 3.
— —— xx. 7, see C tell.
2. —— —— 26.
1. —— —— 36.

1. John i. 46.
1. —— iii. 2, 3, 4 twice, 5.
— —— —— 8, see C tell.
1. —— —— 9, 27.
1. —— v. 19, 30, 44.
1. —— vi. 44, 52, 60, 65.
1. —— vii. 7, 34, 36.
— —— viii. 14, see C tell.
1. —— —— 21, 22, 43.
1. —— ix. 4, 16, 33.
1. —— x. 21, 35.
1. —— xi 37.
1. —— xii. 39.
1. —— xiii. 33, 36, 37.
1. —— xiv. 5 (*om.* G∼ L T Tr A.)
1. —— —— 17.
1. —— xv. 4 1st, 5.
1. —— xvi. 12.
— —— —— 18, see C tell.
— —— xix. 11, see C have.
3. Acts iv. 14.
1. —— —— 16, 20.
1. —— v. 39.
1. —— viii. 31.
1. —— x. 47.
— —— xi. 17, see could.
1. —— xiii. 39.
1. —— xv. 1.
1. —— xxi. 34.
1. —— xxiv. 13.
2. —— xxv. 7.
1. —— xxvii. 15, 31, 43.
— Rom. viii. 3, see could.
1. —— —— 7, 8.
1. 1 Cor. ii. 14.
1. —— iii. 1, 11.
1. —— x. 21 twice.
6. —— xi. 20, marg. (text [is.)
1. —— xii. 3, 21.
1. —— xv. 50.
1. 2 Cor. iii. 7.
— —— xii. 2 twice, see C [tell.
— —— —— 3, see C tell.
— —— xiii. 8, see C do.
1. Gal. iii. 21.
— Phil. iv. 13, see C do.
1. 1 Thes. iii. 9.
1. 1 Tim v. 25.
1. —— vi. 7, 16 2nd.
1. 2 Tim. ii. 13.
1. Heb. iii. 19.
1. —— iv. 15.
1. —— v. 2.
3. —— vi. 13.
6. —— ix. 5.

1. Heb. ix. 9.
1. —— x. 1, 11.
1. Jas. ii. 14.
1. —— iii. 8, 11.
1. —— iv. 2.
1. 1 John iii. 9.
1. 1 John iv. 20.
1. Rev. ii. 2.
1. —— iii. 8.
1. —— vii. 9.
1. —— ix. 20.
1. —— xiv. 3.

CAN NOT BE (IT.)

ἐνδέχομαι, to take upon one's self; to accept, admit, allow of. *Impers.* it may be, it is possible, *(here, with negative.)*

Luke xiii. 33.

CAN DO.

1. δύναμαι, *see* "CAN," *No.* 1.
2. ἰσχύω, *see* "CAN," *No.* 2.

1. Mark ix. 22.
2. Phil. iv. 13.
1. 2 Cor. xiii. 8.

CAN HAVE.

ἔχω, *see* "CAN," *No.* 3.

John xix. 11.

CAN TELL.

οἶδα, *see* "CAN," *No.* 5.

Matt. xxi. 27.
Mark xi. 33.
Luke xx. 7.
John iii. 8.
John viii. 14.
—— xvi. 18.
2 Cor. xii. 2 twice.
—— —— 3 (*om.* L.)

See also, APPROACH, CEASE, CONDEMN, CONTAIN, COULD, DO, ESCAPE, FIND, FORBEAR, GREEK, HAVE, LIE, MOVE, PASS, RECEIVE, REMOVE, SEE, SPEAK, SPOKEN, TEMPT, UTTER, WISH.

CANDLE.

λύχνος, a lamp, *(it must be distinguished from* φῶς, light, λυχνία, a lampstand, λαμπάς, a torch, (Matt. xxv. 1,) φέγγος, light in its splendour, radiance, φωστήρ, luminary,) a hand lamp fed with oil.

Matt. v. 15.
Mark iv. 21.
Luke viii. 16.
Rev. xxii. 5.
Luke xi. 33, 36.
—— xv. 8.
Rev. xviii. 23.

CANDLESTICK.

λυχνία, a lamp-stand, *see above.*

Matt. v. 15.
Mark iv. 21.
Luke viii. 16.
—— xi. 33.
Heb. ix. 2.
Rev. i. 12, 13, 20 twice.
—— ii. 1, 5.
—— xi. 4.

CANKER [noun.]

γάγγραινα, a gangrene *or* mortification *which spreads and* eats away *or* consumes *by putrefaction* the neighbouring parts, *(from* γράω, to eat, consume.)

2 Tim. ii. 17, marg. *gangrene.*

CANKER [verb.]

κατίωμαι, to be rusted *or* tarnished with rust, *(non occ.)*

Jas. v. 3.

CANNOT.

See, CAN.

CAPTAIN.

1. χιλίαρχος, the commander of a thousand men. *It was the word used by the Greeks to translate the Persian* vizer, *and the Roman* tribunus militum *or* military tribune.
2. στρατηγός, the leader *or* commander of an army, a general. *Applied in Athens to the war department at home, hence also,* a civil officer who had any command in chief.
3. ἀρχηγός, *(from* ἀρχή, beginning, origin, *and* ἄγω, to lead,) beginning, originating; *as subst.,* a leader, founder, first-father; *so,* a prince *or* chief; first-cause, author.

2. Luke xxii. 4, 52.	2. Acts v. 24, 26.
1. John xviii. 12.	3. Heb. ii. 10.
2. Acts iv. 1, marg. *ruler.*	1. Rev. xix. 18.

CAPTAIN (CHIEF.)

1. Acts xxi. 31, 32, 33, 37.	1. Acts xxiv. 7 *(ap),* 22.
1. —— xxii. 24, 26, 27, 28, 29.	1. —— xxv. 23.
1. —— xxiii. 10, 15, 17, 18, 19, 22.	1. Rev. vi. 15.

CAPTAIN (HIGH.)

1. Mark vi. 21.

CAPTAIN OF THE GUARD.

στρατοπεδάρχης, a general officer; *the Lat.* tribunus legionis, *properly* the commander of a camp *or of the Roman Emperor's guards, i.e.* the prætorian cohorts, *(non occ.)*

Acts xxviii. 16 *(ap.)*

CAPTIVE.

αἰχμάλωτος, taken by the spear *or* in war, a prisoner of war.

Luke iv. 18.

CAPTIVE (LEAD.)

αἰχμαλωτεύω, (a) to be a prisoner of war, *governing Dat.;* (b) to make a prisoner of war, *governing Acc., as here.*

b. Eph. iv. 8. [All.)
b. 2 Tim. iii. 6 (αἰχμαλιτίζω, *to make prisoners of war,*

CAPTIVE (LEAD AWAY.)

αἰχμαλωτίζω, to make prisoners of war.

Luke xxi. 24.

CAPTIVE (TAKE.)

ζωγρέω, to take alive, take prisoner *instead of killing.*

2 Tim. ii. 26, marg. Greek, *take alive.*

CAPTIVES (multitude of) [margin.]

αἰχμαλωσία, a being prisoner of war; a body of captives; those who suffer captivity.

Eph. iv. 8 (text, *captivity.*)

CAPTIVITY.

αἰχμαλωσία, *see above.*

Eph. iv. 8, marg *multitude of captives.* | Rev. xiii. 10 twice.

CAPTIVITY (BRING INTO.)

αἰχμαλωτίζω, to make prisoners of war.

Rom. vii. 23. | 2 Cor. x. 5.

CARCASE.

1. κῶλον, a limb, member *of a body; gen.* of the extremities. *This word in* Heb. iii. 17, *where only it occurs, sets before us, the unburied* limbs *and* bones *of those who fell in the wilderness. (Used by lxx. for Heb.* פגרים, carcases, Lev. xxvi. 30; Num. xiv. 29, 32, 33, *etc.)*
2. πτῶμα, a fall; *hence,* a misfortune, calamity; then that which is fallen *or* killed, a corpse, carcase.

2. Matt. xxiv. 28. | 1. Heb. iii. 17.

CARE [noun.]

1. *μέριμνα*, dividing *or* distracting the mind; *then, that which does so, as* care, thought, *esp.* anxious care, trouble, *(non occ.)*
2. *σπουδή*, haste, speed, readiness; zeal, pains, trouble; an earnest, serious purpose.
3. *φρονέω*, *the verb which expresses the* action of the *φρήν*, (mind), *as well as the heart and will, hence,* to think, *i.e. either* to think *or* be minded to do *a thing, or simply,* to think, consider, reflect.
4. *ἀγών*, a gathering, assembly, *esp.* an assembly *of the Greeks* at their great national games, *hence,* the contest for a prize *at their games; gen.* any struggle, trial, *or* danger.

In No. 1 *we have* anxiety, *in No.* 2 earnestness, *in No.* 3 solicitude; *see also* "CARE OF (TAKE.)"

1. Matt. xiii. 22.
1. Mark iv. 19.
1. Luke viii. 14.
— —— x. 34, 35, see C of (take.)
1. —— xxi. 34.
— 1 Cor. ix. 9, see C (take)
— —— xii. 25, see C (have)
2. 2 Cor. vii. 12.
— —— viii. 16, see C (earnest.)
1. —— xi. 28.
3. Phil. iv. 10. [*conflict.*)
4. Col. ii. 1, marg. (text,
— 1 Tim. iii. 5, see C of (take.)
1. 1 Pet. v. 7.

CARE (EARNEST.)

2. 2 Cor. viii. 16.

CARE (HAVE.)

μεριμνάω, to be anxious about, distracted about; think earnestly upon.

1 Cor. xii. 25.

CARE (TAKE.)

μέλω, to be an object of care *or* interest. *Imp. with Dat. as here,* it is a care to me, an object of thought, anxiety *or* interest.

1 Cor. ix. 9.

CARE OF (TAKE.)

ἐπιμελέομαι, to take care of, have the management of; solicitude expressed in forethought *or* the employment of means for a desired result.

Luke x. 34, 35. | 1 Tim. iii. 5.

CARE (-ED, -EST, -ETH) [verb.]

1. *μεριμνάω*, to be anxious about, to have anxious *or* distracting care.
2. *μέλω*, to be an object of care *or* interest; *imp. with Dat. as here,* it is a care to me, an object of thought. *This verb implies* forethought. *as No.* 1 *does* anxiety.

2. Matt. xxii. 16.
2. Mark iv. 38.
2. —— xii. 14.
2. Luke x. 40.
2. John x. 13.
2. John xii. 6.
2. Acts xviii. 17.
2. 1 Cor. vii. 21.
1. —— 32, 33, 34 twice.
1. Phil. ii. 20.
2. 1 Pet. v. 7.

CAREFUL (BE.)

1. *μεριμνάω*, to be anxious about, to have anxious *or* distracting care.
2. *φρονέω*, *see* "CARE" (noun), *No.* 3.
3. *φροντίζω*, to think, consider, reflect; to take thought for; be thoughtful, *(non occ.)*

1. Luke x. 41.
1. Phil. iv. 6.
2. Phil. iv. 10.
3. Titus iii. 8.

See also, SUSPENSE.

CAREFULLY (THE MORE.)

σπουδαιοτέρον, *comp. of σπουδή, see* "CARE" (noun), *No.* 2.

Phil. ii. 28.

See also, SEEK.

CAREFULNESS.

σπουδή, *see* "CARE" (noun), *No.* 2.

2 Cor. vii. 11.

CAREFULNESS (WITHOUT.)

ἀμέριμνος, free from anxiety.

1 Cor. vii. 32.

CARNAL.

1. *σάρξ*, flesh; *then,* corporeity according to its material side, *(which as an organic whole is called σῶμα,* body,) *σάρξ denotes* human nature and all that is peculiar to it, in and according to its corporeal embodiment, *and hence,* sinfully conditioned human nature.

(a) *Genitive*, of flesh, fleshly, *etc.*

2. σαρκικός, fleshly, distinctive of the flesh, what attaches to the flesh as corporeity; *more abstract, and not so gross in its idea as the various reading* σάρκινος, *which denotes* of flesh, fleshy.

2. Rom. vii. 14 (*σάρκινος, of flesh, fleshy,* All.)
1a. —— viii. 7.
— —— xv. 27.
2. 1 Cor. iii. 1 (*σάρκινος, of flesh, fleshy,* All)
2. —— 3 1st (*σάρκινος, of flesh, fleshy,* G∼.)
2. 1 Cor. iii. 3 2nd.
2. —— 4 (*ἄνθρωπος, men,* L T Tr A ℵ.)
— —— ix. 11.
2. 2 Cor. x. 4.
2. Heb. vii. 16 (G∼) (*σάρκινος, of flesh, fleshy,* All.)
1a. Heb. ix. 10.

CARNAL THINGS.

τὰ, the,
σάρκικα, fleshly *things, see* "CARNAL," *No.* 2.

Rom. xv. 27 | 1 Cor. ix. 11.

CARNALLY.

σάρξ, *see* "CARNAL," *No.* 1a.

Rom. viii. 6, marg. Greek, *of the flesh.*

CARPENTER.

τέκτων, any worker, craftsman, *or* workman; *but esp.* a worker in wood, *i.e.* a carpenter *or* builder, *(non occ.)*

Matt. xiii. 55. | Mark vi. 3.

CARRIAGE.

See, TAKE.

CARRIED.

See, FLOOD.

CARRY (-IED, -IETH.)

1. φέρω, to bear *or* carry *a load,* to bear *with idea of* motion; bring, produce.

2. ἀποφέρω, to carry away from, carry off *from one place to another.*

3. αἴρω, to raise *or* lift up; to take up *to carry, and so,* to carry; to lift up and take away; *and so gen.,* to take away.

4. ἄγω, to lead, lead along, take with one, *(usually of persons, as No.* 1 *is of things,)* to lead towards *a point.*

5. βαστάζω, to raise upon a basis, to support; to take up and hold, to bear; to bear *or* carry about *as attached to one's person; hence sometimes,* to wear.

6. ἐλαύνω, to drive, drive on, set in motion, *esp. of driving flocks, but very frequently of horses, chariots, ships, etc.*

7. συγκομίζω, to take up and bear together; *of several persons* to bear away together, *as the harvest, or a dead body for burial.*

— Matt. i. 11, see C away to.
— —— 17, see carrying.
— Mark vi. 55, see C about.
— —— xi 16, see C through
— —— xv. 1, see C away.
— Luke vii. 12, see C out.
5. —— x. 4.
2. —— xvi. 22.
— —— xxiv. 51, see C up.
3. John v. 10.
1. —— xxi. 18.
5. Acts iii. 2.
— —— v. 6, 9, see C out.
— —— 10, see C forth.
— —— vii. 16, see C over.
— Acts vii. 43, see C away.
7. —— viii. 2.
4. —— xxi. 34.
— 1 Cor. xii. 2, see C away.
— Gal. ii. 13, see C away with.
— Eph. iv. 14, see C about.
— 1 Tim. vi. 7, see C out.
— Heb xiii. 9, see C about.
6. 2 Pet. ii. 17.
— Jude 12, see C about.
— Rev. xii. 15, see flood.
— —— xvii. 3, see C away.
5. —— 7.
— —— xxi. 10, see C away

CARRY ABOUT.

περιφέρω, to carry round, carry about, *(No.* 1 *with* περί, around, *prefixed.)*

Mark vi. 55.
Eph. iv. 14.
Heb. xiii. 9. [*along,* All.)
Jude 12 (*παραφέρω, bear*

CARRY AWAY.

1. ἀποφέρω, to bear *or* carry away *from one person or place to another.*

2. ἀπάγω, to lead away, conduct away.

3. μετοικίζω, to cause to change one's abode, to cause to remove *or* migrate.

1. Mark xv. 1.
3. Acts vii. 43.
2. 1 Cor. xii. 2.
1. Rev. xvii. 3.
1. Rev. xxi. 10.

CARRY AWAY TO (THE TIME THEY WERE) (-IED.)

μετοικεσία, change of abode, migration.

Matt. i. 11 (lit. *the Babylonian migration.*)

CARRY AWAY WITH.

συναπάγω, to lead off *or* away with *any one; gen. in a bad sense, but also in a good sense, (cf.* 2 Pet. iii. 17 *and* Rom. xii. 16.)

Gal. ii. 13.

CARRY FORTH.

ἐκφέρω, to bear out, carry out; to bring forth.

Acts v. 10.

CARRY OUT.

1. ἐκφέρω, *see above.*
2. ἐκκομίζω, to carry *or* take out (to a place of safety); *esp.* to carry out a corpse, *(non occ.)*

2. Luke vii. 12. | 1. Acts v. 6, 9.
1. 1 Tim. vi. 7.

CARRY OVER.

μετατίθημι, to place among, put in another place; *hence,* to transport, to transfer.

Acts vii. 16.

CARRY THROUGH.

διαφέρω, to bear *or* carry through *(a place)*, bear asunder, carry different ways.

Mark xi. 16 (with διά, *through.*)

CARRY UP.

ἀναφέρω, to bear upwards, carry up *(from a lower to a higher place.)*

Luke xxiv. 51 (*ap.*)

CARRYING AWAY INTO.

μετοικεσία, change of abode, migration.

Matt. i. 17 twice (lit. *the Babylonian migration.*)

CASE.

αἰτία, a cause; *esp.* the occasion (of something bad); *then,* a charge, accusation, *or* a ground of accusation; *then, in the sense of* affair, matter, case.

Matt. xix. 10.

CASE (BE IN THAT.)

ἔχω, to have *or* hold.

John v. 6.

CASE (IN NO.)

{ οὐ, not, } *an intensive neg.*, in no wise,
{ μή, lest, } by no means.

Matt. v. 20.

CAST [noun.]

βολή, a throwing, (λίθου βολή, a stone's throw.)

Luke xxii. 41.

CAST (-ING) [verb.]

When not part of another verb, it is one of these following:

1. βάλλω, *trans,* to throw at *or* hit, *with any kind of missile, strictly opposed to striking, intrans.* to fall, tumble.
2. ἐκβάλλω, *(No. 1 with* ἐκ, out of *or* from, *prefixed,)* to throw *or* cast out of.
3. ῥίπτω, to throw *or* cast, *with a sudden motion,* to hurl, jerk; to cast forth, throw apart, scatter.

1. Matt. iii. 10.
1. —— iv. 6, 18.
1. —— v. 13, 25, 29 twice, 30 1st.
1. —— 30 2nd (ἀπέρχομαι *to go away,* L T Tr A ℵ)
1. —— vi. 30.
1. —— vii. 6, 19.
1. —— xiii. 42, 47, 48, 50.
1. —— xv. 26.
1. —— xvii. 27.
1. —— xviii. 8 twice, 9 twice, 30.
1. —— xxi. 21.
2. —— xxii. 13.
2. —— xxv. 30.
1. —— xxvii. 35 1st.
1. —— 35 2nd (*ap.*)
1. Mark i. 16 (ἀμφιβάλλω, *to throw* or *put around, throw to and fro,* All.)
1. —— iv. 26.
1. —— vii. 27.
1. —— ix. 22, 42, 45, 47.
1. —— xi. 23.
1. —— xii. 41 twice, 43 twice, 44 twice.
1. Mark xv. 24.
1. Luke iii. 9.
1. —— iv. 9.
1. —— xii. 28, 58.
1. —— xiii. 19.
1. —— xiv. 35.
3. —— xvii. 2.
1. —— xxi. 1, 2, 3, 4 twice.
1. —— xxiii. 19, 25, 34.
1. John iii. 24.
1. —— viii. 7 (*ap*), 59.
1. —— xv. 6 twice.
1. —— xix. 24.
1. —— xxi. 6 twice, 7.
1. Acts xvi. 23, 37.
3. —— xxvii. 29.
1 Rev. ii. 10, 14, 22.
1. —— iv 10.
1. —— vi. 13.
1. —— viii. 5, 7, 8.
1. —— xii. 4, 13, 15, 16.
1. —— xiv. 19.
1. —— xviii. 19, 21.
1. —— xix. 20.
1. —— xx. 3, 10, 14, 15.

CAST (BE.)

ἐκπίπτω, to fall out of, to fall from *or* off; *spoken of things which* fall out of *or* from *their places; of sea-faring men* to be thrown ashore.

Acts xxvii. 26.

CAST ABOUT.

περιβάλλω, *(No. 1 with* περί, about, around,) to cast *or* throw around, to put around *any person or thing.*

(a) ***Mid. and pass.*** to put on *one's own garments,* to clothe one's self.

Luke xix. 43.

CAST ABOUT (HAVE...)

a. Mark xiv. 51.

CAST AWAY.

1. ἀποβάλλω, *(No.* 1 *with* ἀπό, from, *prefixed,)* to throw off from, to throw away.
2. ἀπωθέω, to thrust away, drive away. *In N.T. only in Mid.* to thrust from one's self, *hence,* to banish, reject, disdain.

1. Mark x. 50. | 1. Heb. x. 35. | 2. Rom. xi. 1, 2.

CAST AWAY (BE.)

ζημιόω, to cause loss *or* do damage to *any one, hence,* to punish, *esp.* to fine, mulct.

(a) *pass. or Mid.* to be fined *or* amerced, *gen.* to suffer loss.

a. Luke ix. 25.

CAST DOWN.

1. καταβάλλω, *(No.* 1 *with* κατά, down, *prefixed,)* to throw *or* cast down, overthrow, to strike down, kill, *esp. with missiles.)*
2. ῥίπτω, *see* "CAST," *No.* 3.
3. καθαιρέω, to take down, *(as from a higher place,) with the idea of force* to pull down, demolish.

2. Matt. xv. 30.
2. —— xxvii. 5.
1. 2 Cor. iv. 9.
3. 2 Cor. x. 5.
1. Rev. xii 10 (βάλλω, see cast, No. 1, G∾L T Tr A ℵ.)

CAST DOWN HEADLONG.

κατακρημνίζω, to cast down from a precipice, *gen.* to throw headlong down, *(non occ.)*

Luke iv. 29.

See also, HELL.

CAST FORTH.

ἐκβάλλω, *see* "CAST," *No.* 2.

Mark vii. 26.

CAST IN ONE'S MIND.

διαλογίζομαι, to reckon through, *i.e.* to balance accounts; *hence,* to take account of, consider, think over.

Luke i. 29.

CAST IN ONE'S TEETH.

ὀνειδίζω, to defame, *i.e.* to disparage, reproach; *then,* to rail at, reproach with *any thing.*

Matt. xxvii. 44.

CAST INTO.

ἐμβάλλω, *(No.* 1 *with* ἐν, in, *prefixed,)* to cast in, throw in.

Luke xii. 5 (with εἰς, *into.*)

CAST INTO PRISON.

παραδίδωμι, to give near, with, to *any one,* to hand over *to another,* to deliver up, surrender, *in a good or bad sense, i.e.* to deliver over *to suffer any thing, or to the charge or care of any one.*

Matt. iv. 12, marg. *deliver up.*

CAST OFF.

1. ἀθετέω, to displace, to set aside, disregard *a treaty, oath, promise, etc.*
2. ἀποτίθημι, to put off, lay aside. *In N.T. only in Mid.* to put off from one's self.
3. ῥιπτέω, *(frequentative of* "CAST," *No.* 3,) to throw *or* cast repeatedly, to throw *or* toss about, *(non occ.)*

3. Acts xxii. 23. | 1. 1 Tim. v. 12. | 2. Rom. xiii. 12.

CAST ON.

ἐπιβάλλω, ("CAST," *No.* 1 *with* ἐπί, upon, *prefixed,)* to cast *or* throw upon.

Mark xi. 7.

CAST ONE'S SELF.

ἀποῤῥίπτω, to cast off, throw aside. *In N.T. with reflex. pron. implied,* throwing *or* letting themselves off, *i.e. from the ship into the water, (non occ.)*

Acts xxvii. 43.

CAST OUT.

1. βάλλω, *see* "CAST," *No.* 1.
2. ἐκβάλλω, *see* "CAST," *No.* 2.
3. ῥίπτω, *see* "CAST," *No.* 3.
4. ἐκτίθημι, to place out, expose, *esp. of a new-born child,*
5. ἐκτείνω, to stretch out, to extend, put forth, reach out.
6. { ποιέω, to make, / ἔκθετος, exposed, *esp. of an infant,* } cause to be exposed.

No: 2 in all passages, except

2. Matt. xxi. 39 (*with* ἔξω, *without.*)
2. Mark xvi. 17 (*ap.*)
2. John ix. 34, marg. *excommunicate.*
6. Acts vii. 19.
4. Acts vii. 21.
3. —— xxvii. 19.
5. —— 30.
1. 1 John iv. 18.
2. Rev. xi. 2, marg. (text, *leave out.*)
1. Rev. xii. 9 3 times.

CAST OUT OF.

ἐκβάλλω, *see* "CAST," *No.* 2.

(a) *with* ἀπό, from.
(b) *with* ἐκ, out of.
(c) *with* ἔξω, out, without.

c. Mark xii. 8.
a. Mark xvi. 9 (*ap.*)
c. Luke xx. 15.
c. Acts vii. 58.
b. 3 John 10.

CAST UPON.

1. ἐπιβάλλω, *see* "CAST ON."
2. ἐπιῤῥίπτω, ("CAST," *No.* 3 *with* ἐπί, upon, *prefixed,*) to throw *or* cast upon.
   (a) *with* ἐπί, upon, *added.*

2a. Luke xix. 35.
1. 1 Cor. vii. 35.
2a. 1 Pet. v. 7.

See also, LOT, STONE.

CAST DOWN [adj.]

ταπεινός, low, not high; low, humble, poor; lowly, humble, modest; depressed.

2 Cor. vii. 6.

CASTAWAY.

ἀδόκιμος, unapproved, spurious, that will not stand proof, *gen. spoken of metals, (cf.* Sept., Prov. xxv. 4; Is. i. 22,) *(occ.* Rom. i. 28; 2 Cor. xiii. 5, 6, 7; 2 Tim. iii. 8; Tit. i. 16; Heb. vi. 8.)

1 Cor. ix. 27.

CASTING AWAY.

ἀποβολή, a casting off *or* from; rejection, loss, deprivation.

Rom. xi. 15.

CASTLE.

παρεμβολή, insertion beside, between *or* among *others;* parenthesis; a putting in *or* distributing *men through an army;* a drawing up in battle order (juxta-army); *also,* a body so drawn up; *in later usage,* a camp *(i.e. juxta-arrangement in a camp;) hence, spoken of* a standing camp, quarters, barracks, *viz., the quarters of the Roman soldiers in Jerusalem in the fortress Antonia, which was adjacent to the temple, and commanded it, (occ.* Heb. xi. 34; xiii. 11, 13; Rev. xx. 4.)

Acts xxi. 34, 37.
Acts xxii. 24.
Acts xxiii. 10, 16, 32.

CATCH (-ETH, CAUGHT.)

1. ἁρπάζω, to snatch away, to carry off *(suddenly and by force,) esp. of wild beasts.*
2. συναρπάζω, to snatch and carry with *one,* carry clean away, *also of a mob seizing individuals.*
3. λαμβάνω, *actively,* to take; *passively,* to receive; to take *as with the hand,* to lay hold of, grasp.
4. ἐπιλαμβάνω, to take hold upon, to take *or* get besides; *in N.T. only in Mid.* to hold one's self *on* by, lay hold of, *with or without violence,*
5. συλλαμβάνω, to take together *(prop.* to enclose in the hands,) to comprehend, embrace; to bring together *esp. scattered hopes,* to take hold with *another,* to arrest.
6. ἀγρεύω, to hunt, take by hunting, catch; *metaph.* to hunt after.
7. θηρεύω, to hunt wild beasts, to take *or* catch wild beasts in hunting.

8. *πιάζω*, to press *by laying one's hand upon, hence,* to lay hold of; *of persons,* to take by the hand *(with or without violence;) of animals,* to take *or* catch *(as fish.)*

9. *ζωγρέω*, to take alive, to take prisoner *instead of killing.*

— Matt. xiii. 19, see C away
4. —— xiv. 31.
3. —— xxi. 39.
3. Mark xii. 3.
6. —— 13.
9. Luke v. 10 (with *εἰμί, to be,*) lit. *be a catcher.*
2. —— viii. 29.
7. —— xi. 54.
1. John x. 12.
8. —— xxi. 3, 10.
2. Acts vi. 12.
— —— viii. 39, see C away
4. —— xvi. 19.
2. —— xix. 29.
5. —— xxvi. 21.
2. —— xxvii. 15.
— 2 Cor. xii. 2, 4, see C up.
3. —— xii. 16.
— 1 Thes. iv. 17, } see C up.
— Rev. xii. 5, }

CATCH AWAY.

1. Matt. xiii. 19. | 1. Acts viii. 39.

CATCH UP.

1. 2 Cor. xii. 2, 4. | 1. 1 Thes. iv. 17.
1. Rev. xii. 5.

CATTLE.

θρέμμα, that which is fed, bred, reared *or* tended, a nurseling; *mostly of tame animals, hence,* cattle, flocks, herds.

John iv. 12 (pl.)

CATTLE (FEED.)

ποιμαίνω, to exercise the care of a *ποιμήν* (shepherd), (Acts xx. 28), to tend *as shepherds do their flocks, hence,* to rule, govern, (Matt. ii. 6; Rev. ii. 27.)

Luke xvii. 7.

CAUSE [noun.]

1. *αἰτία*, a cause, origin, ground, *(from αἰτέω,* to ask, require, *because* an accusation, *etc. is that for which any one is* required *to appear before judges and be* questioned;) *esp.* the occasion of something bad, a fault, a charge, accusation.

2. *αἴτιον*, causative of; a cause, reason, *esp. of punishment.*

3. *λόγος*, the (spoken) word; a word *as forming part of what is spoken;* a word *as that which is spoken, whether* doctrine, prophecy, question, saying, command, teaching, rumour, argument, charge *or* accusation; *then,* the reason, *as demanded or assigned, i.e.* reckoning, account.

3. Matt. v. 32.
1. —— xix. 3.
1. Luke viii. 47.
2. —— xxiii. 22.
1. Acts x. 21.
1. Acts xiii. 28.
2. —— xix. 40.
1. —— xxiii. 28.
1. —— xxviii. 18, 20.
1. 2 Tim. i. 12.
1. Heb. ii. 11.

CAUSE (FOR THE SAME.)

αὐτός, *pron.*, he, she, it; *prop. demons.*, self, very; *with the article, as here,* the same, *(lit.* as to the same thing.)

Phil. ii. 18.

CAUSE (FOR THIS.)

1. *ἀντὶ τοῦτου*, instead of this, for this cause; *denoting the principle or motive.*

2. *διὰ τοῦτου*, on account of this; *denoting the ground or reason.*

3. *εἰς τοῦτου*, unto this, with respect to this, with a view to this; *denoting the object.*

4. *ἕνεκεν τοῦτου*, for the sake of this.

4. Matt. xix. 5.
4. Mark x. 7.
2. John xii. 18, 27.
3. —— xviii. 37.
2. Rom. i. 26.
2. —— xiii. 6.
2. —— xv. 9.
2. 1 Cor. iv. 17.
2. 1 Cor. xi. 10, 30.
1. Eph. v. 31.
2. Col. i. 9.
2. 1 Thes. ii. 13.
2. —— iii. 5.
2. 2 Thes. ii. 11.
2. 1 Tim. i. 16.
2. Heb. ix. 15.
3. 1 Pet. iv. 6.

CAUSE (FOR WHICH.)

διό, on which account, wherefore, (*διά*, on account of, *and ὅ*, which.)

Rom. xv. 22. | 2 Cor. iv. 16.

CAUSE (WITHOUT A.)

1. *δωρεάν*, as a free gift, freely, for nothing; *hence,* without a cause.

2. *εἰκῆ*, *(from εἴκω,* to yield,) rashly, heedlessly, *(i.e.* yielding *to one's mind or passion;)* without plan *or* purpose, to no purpose *(i.e.* yielding *to opposition or difficulty.)*

2. Matt. v. 22 (*om.* L T Tr[b] ℵ) | 1. John xv. 25.

CAUSE (PAUL'S.)

{ τὰ, the things,
κατὰ, relating to,
τὸν Παῦλον, Paul.

Acts xxv. 14.

See also, FOR.

CAUSE (-ED, -ETH) [verb.]

1. ποιέω, to make, produce; to make, to cause, be the means of *a thing;* to do *with notion of continued rather than completed action.*

2. κατεργάζομαι, to effect, accomplish, achieve; to work out, *i.e.* to bring about; work done, *i.e.* make an end of.

1. Matt. v. 32.
— — vi. 2, see *C a trumpet to be sounded.*
1. John xi. 37.
1. Acts xv. 3.
1. Rom. xvi. 17.
2. 2 Cor. ix. 11.
1. Col. iv. 16.
— Rev. xii. 15, see C to be.
1. — xiii. 12, 15, 16.

CAUSE TO BE.

1. Rev. xii. 15.

CAUSE A TRUMPET TO BE SOUNDED [margin.]

σαλπίζω, to sound the trumpet.

Matt. vi. 2, text, *sound a trumpet.*

See also, DEATH, GRIEF, OFFEND, TRIUMPH, TRUMPET.

CAVE.

1. ὀπή, an opening, a hole, such as a fissure in the earth, rocks, *etc.*, *(occ* Jas. iii. 11.)

2. σπήλαιον, a grotto, cave, cavern, den.

2. John xi. 38. | 1. Heb. xi. 38.

CEASE (-ED, -ETH, -ING.)

1. παύω, to make an end *or* cease, to stop; *in pass. and Mid.* to come to an end, take one's rest, cease, rest, *gen. the Mid. denotes willing, and the pass. forced cessation. In N.T. only in Mid.*

2. καταπαύω, to quiet down.

(a) *trans.* to cause to cease, to make desist, *and so* to restrain; to cause to rest, give rest.

(b) *intrans.* to cease from, rest from.

3. διαλείπω, to leave between, *i.e.* to leave an interval, *as of space or time; hence,* to intermit, desist, cease, *(non occ.)*

4. ἡσυχάζω, to be still, sedate *or* quiet, to be quiet from speaking, silent.

5. καταργέω, to leave unemployed *or* idle; to make useless, void, abolish; *thus,* to cause to cease, to cease from.

6. κοπάζω, to cease through extreme fatigue *or* being spent with labour; *gen.* to abate.

6. Matt. xiv. 32.
6. Mark iv. 39.
6. — vi. 51.
3. Luke vii. 45.
1. — viii. 24.
1. — xi. 1.
— — xxiv. 31, see *C to be seen.*
1. Acts v. 42.
1. — vi. 13.
1. — xiii. 10.
1. Acts xx. 1, 31.
4. — xxi. 14.
1. 1 Cor. xiii. 8.
5. Gal. v. 11.
1. Eph. i. 16.
1. Col. i. 9.
2. Heb. iv. 10.
1. — x. 2.
1. 1 Pet. iv. 1.
— 2 Pet. ii. 14, see C (that cannot.)

CEASE (THAT CANNOT.)

ἀκατάπαυστος, not to be set at rest, incessant; that cannot be restrained from *anything, (non occ.)*

2 Pet. ii. 14 (ἀκατάπαστος, *unfed, hungry,* L.)

CEASE TO BE SEEN [margin.]

{ ἄφαντος, made invisible, not seen,
γίνομαι, to become, } *lit.* to become invisible.

Luke xxiv. 31, text, *vanish out of sight.*

CEASING (WITHOUT.)

1. ἀδιάλειπτος, not leaving an interval between, unintermitting, incessant.

2. ἀδιαλείπτως, unceasingly, without intermission, *i.e.* assiduously, *(non occ.)*

3. ἐκτενής, stretched out, extended; *hence,* earnest, intent, fervent.

3. Acts xii. 5, marg. *instant and earnest* (ἐκτενῶς, adv. of No. 3, L Tr A [ℵ].)
2. Rom. i. 9.
2. 1 Thes. i. 3.
2. — ii. 13.
2. — v. 17.
1. 2 Tim. i. 3.

CELESTIAL.

ἐπουράνιος, upon *or* above the heavens, *i.e.* in heaven, heavenly.

1 Cor. xv. 40 twice.

CENSER.

1. θυμιατήριον, a vessel *or* instrument for burning incense, a censer, *(occ.* 2 Chron. xxvi. 19; Ezek. viii. 11,) *(non occ.)*

2. λιβανωτός, frankincense, the gum of the tree λίβανος, *used to burn* at sacrifices, *(so* 1 Chron. ix. 29, *for Heb.* לבונה.) *In N.T. however it is used for* a vessel to burn the incense in.

1. Heb. ix. 4. | 2. Rev. viii. 3, 5.

CENSURE [margin.]

ἐπιτιμία, the condition of an ἐπίτιμος, (a person who possesses all civil rights and franchises.) *In N.T. spoken of* the estimate fixed upon a wrong by a Judge, a judicial infliction; *hence*, rebuke, punishment.

2 Cor. ii. 6 (text, *punishment.*)

CENTURION.

1. ἑκατόνταρχος, a military officer commanding a hundred men; a centurion.

2. ἑκατοντάρχης, *same as No.* 1. *(The Sept. very frequently used th. word for* Captains of hundreds.)

3. κεντυρίων, *(Lat.)* a Roman military officer who commanded a hundred men, *(from* centum, a hundred, *which again is from* ἑκατόν, a hundred, *from which Nos.* 1 *and* 2 *are derived.)*

1. Matt. viii. 5, 8.
1. —— 13 (No. 2, All.)
1. —— xxvii. 54.
3. Mark xv. 39, 44, 45.
1. Luke vii. 2, 6.
1. —— xxiii. 47 (No. 2, Tr ℵ)
2. Acts x. 1, 22.
1. —— xxi. 32 (No. 2, L T Tr A ℵ.)
1. —— xxii. 25.
1. —— 26 (No. 2, L T ℵ.)
1. Acts xxiii. 17, 23.
2. —— xxiv. 23.
2. —— xxvii. 1.
1 —— 6 (No. 2, L T Tr A ℵ.)
1. —— 11 (No. 2, G ∾ L T Tr A ℵ.)
2. —— 31.
1. —— 43 (No. 2, L T Tr A ℵ.)
1. Acts xxviii. 16 (*ap.*)

CEREMONY [margin.]

δικαίωμα, an act of right, any thing justly *or* rightly done; *strictly*, an amendment of a wrong; *hence*, justification, acquitted, *or* condemnation *implying punishment*; *gen.* a decree *as defining what is right and just*, *i.e.* a law, ordinance, precept.

Heb. ix. 1, (text, *ordinance*); 10, (text, *ordinance.*)

CERTAIN [adj.]

1. ἀσφαλής, not liable to fall, firm, fast, steadfast; unfailing, sure, trusty.

2. δῆλος, visible, clear; manifest, evident.

1. Acts xxv. 26; 2. 1 Tim. vi. 7 (*om*, G→L Tr A ℵ.)

CERTAIN (A) *and* CERTAIN [indef. pron.]

1. τίς, any one, any thing; one, someone, a certain one.

2. ἄνθρωπος, a man, a member of the human family (homo), *(diff. from* ἀνήρ, a man in sex and age (vir).)

3. εἷς, *the numeral* one.

3. Matt. viii. 19.
1. —— ix. 3.
1. —— xii. 38. (a.)
— —— xx. 20, see A thing
1 & 2. — xxi. 33 (*om.* No. 1, [All.
1. Mark ii. 6.
1. —— v. 25 (*om.* G ⇉ L Tr [ℵ.)
1. —— vii. 1.
1. —— xi. 5.
1. —— xii. 13.
3. —— 42.
1. —— xiv. 51, 57.
1. Luke i. 5.
3. —— v. 12, 17.
1. —— vi. 2.
1. —— vii. 2, 41.
1. —— viii. 2.
3. —— 22.
1. —— 27.
— —— ix. 57, see C man (a.)
1. —— x. 25.
— —— 30, see C man (a.)
1. —— 31, 33, 38 twice.
1. —— xi. 1, 27.
1. —— 37 (*om.* T Tr A ℵ.)
1. —— xii. 16.
— —— xiii. 6, see C man [(a.)
1. —— 31.
1. —— xiv. 2, 16.
1. —— xv. 11.
1. —— xvi. 1, 19 20.
1. —— xvii. 12.
1. —— xviii. 9, 18.
2. —— 23.
1. —— 35.
1. —— xix. 12.
1. —— xx. 9 (*om.* All.)
1. —— 27, 39.
1. —— xxi. 2.
2. —— xxii. 2.
1. Luke xxii. 56.
1. —— xxiii. 19.
— —— xxiv. 1, see C others.
1. —— 22, 24.
1. John iv. 46.
1. —— v. 5.
— —— xi. 1, see C man (a.)
1. —— xii. 20.
1. Acts iii. 2.
1. —— v. 1, 2.
1. —— vi. 9.
1. —— viii. 9, 36.
1. —— ix. 10, 19, 33, 36.
1. —— x. 1. 11, 23, 48.
1. —— xi. 5.
1. —— xii. 1. [Tr A ℵ.)
1. —— xiii. 1 (*om.* G ⇉ L T
1. —— 6.
1. —— xiv. 8.
1. —— xv. 1, 2, 5, 24.
1. —— xvi. 1 1st.
1. —— 1 2nd (*om.* All.)
1. —— 12, 14, 16
1. —— xvii. 5, 6, 18, 20,
1. —— xviii. 2. [28, 34.
— —— 7, see C man (a.)
1. —— 24.
1. —— xix. 1, 13, 31.
1. —— xx. 9.
1. —— xxi. 10.
1. —— xxiii. 12 (*om.* All.)
— —— 17, see C thing (a)
1. —— xxiv. 1, 18; 24.
1. —— xxv. 13, 14, 19.
1. —— xxvii. 1, 16, 26, 39.
1. Rom. xv. 26.
1. Gal. ii. 12.
1. Heb. iv. 7.
1. —— x. 27.
— Jude 4, see C man.

CERTAIN MAN (A)

1. Luke ix. 57.
1. —— x. 30.
1. —— xiii. 6.
1. John xi. 1.
1. Acts xviii. 7.
1. —— xix. 24.

Jude 4 (pl.)

CERTAIN OTHERS.

1. Luke xxiv. 1 (*ap.*)

CERTAIN THING.

1. Matt. xx. 20. | 1. Acts xxiii. 17.

See also, PLACE, SEASON.

CERTAINLY.

ὄντως, really, actually, verily, (*adv. part. from* εἰμί, to be.)

Luke xxiii. 47.

CERTAINTY.

1. ἀσφαλής, not liable to fall, firm, fast; unfailing, sure, trusty.
2. ἀσφάλεια, steadfastness, firmness, stability.

2. Luke i. 4. | 1. Acts xxi. 34 (with art.)
1. Acts xxii. 30 (with art.)

CERTIFY.

γνωρίζω, to make known, point out, explain.

Gal. i. 11.

CHAFF.

ἄχυρον, chaff, bran, husks *left after threshing or grinding.*

Matt. iii. 12. | Luke iii. 17.

CHAIN (-S.)

1. ἅλυσις, a bond, a chain, (*from* ἀ, *neg. and* λύω, to loose.)
2. δεσμός, a band, bond, fetter; *gen.* any thing for tying *or* fastening, (*from* δέω, to bind.)
3. σειρά, a cord, rope, string, band.

1. Mark v 3, 4 twice.
1. Luke viii 29
1. Acts xii. 6, 7.
1. —— xxi. 33
1. —— xxviii. 20 [*bonds.*)
1. Eph. vi. 20, marg. (text,
1. 2 Tim i. 16
3 2 Pet. ii. 4 (σειρός, *a pit, a cavern*, L Tr A ℵ)
2 Jude 6.
1. Rev. xx. 1.

CHALCEDONY.

χαλκηδών, the name of a gem including several varieties, one of which is like a cornelian.

Rev. xxi. 19 (χαρκηδών, *carbuncle*, G∼.)

CHAMBER (SECRET.)

ταμεῖον, a store-chamber, store-house; *hence, gen.* any place of privacy.

Matt. xxiv. 26.

CHAMBER (UPPER.)

ὑπερῷον, the upper part of the house, the upper story *or* upper rooms *where the women resided.*

Acts ix. 37, 39; xx. 8.

See also, BRIDE, GUEST.

CHAMBERING.

κοίτη, a place to lie down in, a bed, couch, *esp.* the marriage bed.

Rom. xiii. 13 (pl.)

CHAMBERLAIN.

1. { ἐπί, upon *or* over, κοιτών, a bed-chamber, } (*non occ.*)
2. οἰκονόμος, a person who manages the domestic affairs of a family, a steward, *gen.* a manager.

1. Acts xii. 20, marg. *over the bedchamber.*
2. Rom. xvi. 23.

CHANCE [noun.]

συγκυρία, a meeting together with, a concurrence *or* coincidence of circumstances, a happening, (*non occ.*)

Luke x. 31.

CHANCE (IT MAY.)

{ εἰ, if, τύχοι, it may be so, perchance, } if it may fall out, if it may happen.

1 Cor. xv. 37.

CHANGE [noun.]

μετάθεσις, transposition, a being transferred from one place to another, (*occ.* Heb. xi. 5; xii. 27.)

Heb. vii. 12.

CHANGE (-ED) [verb.]

1. *ἀλλάττω*, to make other than it is, to alter, transform; *then*, to change *one thing for another*, exchange.
2. *μεταλλάττω*, to change one thing for *or* into another, to transmute.
3. *μετασχηματίζω*, to change the form *or* appearance *of a thing*, transform.
4. *μετατίθημι*, to place among, to place differently; *hence*, to change, alter.

1. Acts vi. 14.
1. Rom. i. 23.
2. —— 25, 26.
1. 1 Cor. xv. 51, 52.
1. Gal. iv. 20.
3. Phil. iii. 21.
1. Heb. i. 12.
4. —— vii. 12.

CHANGE ONE'S MIND.

1. *μεταβάλλω*, to throw round, *esp.* to turn quickly *or* suddenly; to turn about, change, alter.
   (a) *in Mid.* to change what is one's own, *(yet rather by chance than of set purpose,)* to change one's mind *or* purpose.
2. *μετάνοια*, after-thought, a change of mind *affecting the whole life, hence, involving* reformation, *(more than μεταμέλομαι, which is only* change of feeling, to regret.)

1a. Acts xxviii. 6.
2. Heb. xii. 17, marg. (text, *repentance.*)

CHANGED (BE.)

μεταμορφόω, to transform, transfigure.
(a) *in Mid.* to change one's form, be transfigured, *(occ.* Matt. xvii. 2; Mark ix. 2; Rom. xii. 2.)

a. 2 Cor. iii. 18.

CHANGER (-S.)

κολλυβιστής, a money-changer *(from κόλλυβος*, a small coin, change.)

John ii. 15.

See also, MONEY.

CHARGE [noun.]

1. *παραγγελία*, a proclamation, public notice, command, *esp. as a military term*, a general order.
2. *διακονία*, serviceable labour, service. *Every business, every calling, so far as its labour benefits others.* Any ministerial office in the Church with reference to the labour pertaining thereto.
3. *ἐπισκοπή*, the office of *ἐπίσκοπος*, (one who inspects); the act of visiting *or* being visited: visitation, the duty of visiting, *i.e.* charge, office.

— Matt. iv. 6, } see C
— Luke iv. 10, } (give.)
3. Acts i. 20, marg. (text, *bishopric.*)
— —— vii. 60, see C (lay to one's.)
— —— viii. 27, see C of (have the.)
2. —— xii. 25, marg. (text *ministry.*)
1. —— xvi. 24.
— —— xxi. 24, see Cs (be at.)
— Acts xxiii. 29, see C (lay to one's.)
— Rom. viii. 33, see C of (lay to the.)
— 1 Cor. ix. 7, see Cs.
— —— 18, see C (without.
1. 1 Tim. i. 18.
— —— v. 7, see C (give in)
— —— vi. 13, see C (give)
— 2 Tim. iv. 16, see C (lay to one's)

CHARGE (GIVE.)

1. *ἐντέλλομαι*, to enjoin upon, to charge with, to command.
2. *παραγγέλλω*, to announce beside, *i.e.* to hand on an announcement from one to another; *esp. as a military term* to give the watchword, *which was* passed *from man to man; then,* to give the word, *and so gen.*, to order, recommend.

1. Matt. iv. 6.
1. Luke iv. 10.
2. 1 Tim. vi. 13.

CHARGE (GIVE IN.)

παραγγέλλω, see above.

1. Tim. v. 7.

CHARGE OF (HAVE THE.)

{ *εἰμί*, to be,
{ *ἐπί*, over.

Acts viii. 27.

CHARGE (LAY TO ONE'S.)

1. *ἔγκλημα*, an accusation, charge, complaint; a bill of indictment.
2. *ἵστημι*, (a) *trans.* to make to stand, set, place, put in the balance, weigh.
   (b) *intrans.* to stand still *or* firm, be set *or* placed.

3. *λογίζομαι*, to count, reckon, calculate, *(esp. of numerical calculation;)* to take into account.

2a. Acts vii. 60. | 1. Acts xxiii. 29.
3. 2 Tim. iv. 16.

CHARGE OF (LAY TO THE.)

ἐγκαλέω, to call in *as a debt*, to demand as one's due; to bring a charge *or* accusation against *a person*.
κατά, against.

Rom. viii. 33.

CHARGE (WITHOUT.)

ἀδάπανος, without expense, *and so* costing nothing.

1 Cor. ix. 18.

CHARGES.

οψώνιον, whatever is bought to be eaten with bread, provisions, *esp.* supplies for an army; *gen.* wages, recompense.

1 Cor. ix. 7 (pl.)

CHARGES (BE AT.)

δαπανάω, to spend, to be at the expense of *any thing.*

Acts xxi. 24.

CHARGE (-ED, -ING) [verb.]

1. *παραγγέλλω*, *see* "CHARGE (GIVE)," *No.* 2
2. *διαστέλλομαι*, to give a decision, determine; to command, give orders.
3. *ἐπιτιμάω*, to put further honours upon; *of things*, to set a further value upon, to estimate higher, *e.g. in price;* to adjudge, confirm by a judgment. *In N.T. spoken of an estimate or judgment put upon what is wrong, and hence,* to admonish, reprove; admonish strongly with urgency, authority, *i.e.* to enjoin upon, charge strictly, *the idea of rebuke or censure being employed.*
4. *μαρτυρέω*, to be a witness, to bear witness.
   (a) *in Mid.* to call to witness, to invoke as a witness; to make a solemn appeal *either* by protest or by exhortation.
   (b) *Pass.* to be *or* become a witness.
5. *διαμαρτύρομαι*, *(Mid.)* to call throughout to witness, *(viz., God, men, and all beings.* To testify through and through, *i.e.* to bear solemn and complete witness, *hence,* to admonish solemnly, charge earnestly, testify *or* declare fully.
6. *ἐντέλλομαι*, to enjoin upon, to charge with, to command.
7. *ὁρκίζω*, to make *one* swear, tender an oath to a person.
8. *ἐπιτάσσω*, to set over, put in command; put upon *one* as a duty, to enjoin, command.

— Matt. ix. 30, see C (straitly.)
3. —— xii. 16.
2. —— xvi. 20 (No. 3, G ∾ L.)
6. —— xvii. 9.
— Mark i. 43, see C (straitly)
3. —— iii. 12.
2. —— v. 43.
2. —— vii. 36 twice.
2. —— viii. 15.
3. ——— 30.
2. —— ix. 9.
8. ——— 25.
3. —— x. 48.
1. Luke v. 14.
1. Luke viii. 56.
— —— ix. 21, see C (straitly)
1. Acts xvi. 23.
1. —— xxiii. 22.
— Rom. iii. 9, see C before
4a. 1 Thes. ii. 11 (No. 4b, L Tr A ℵ.)
7. —— v. 27, marg. *adjure* (*ἐνορκίζω, to swear in, adjure,* L T Tr A.)
1. 1 Tim. i. 3.
— —— v. 16, see C (bo.)
5. ——— 21.
1. —— vi. 17.
5. 2 Tim. ii. 14.
5. —— iv. 1.

CHARGE BEFORE.

προαιτιάομαι, to accuse beforehand.
(a) *Aor.* 1, to have already accused, to have already brought a charge, *(non occ.)*

a. Rom. iii. 9.

CHARGE (STRAITLY.)

1. *ἐμβριμάομαι*, to snort in, *of horses; of men,* to fret, to be deeply *or* painfully moved; *then,* to express indignation against *any one, hence,* to admonish urgently, rebuke.
2. *ἐπιτιμάω*, *see* "CHARGE," *No.* 3.

1. Matt. ix. 30. 1. Mark i. 43.
2. Luke ix. 21.

See also, STRAITLY.

CHARGED (BE.)

βαρέω, to weigh down.

(a) *pass.* to be heavy, to be weighed down, to be oppressed.

a. 1 Tim. v. 16

CHARGEABLE TO (BE.)

1. ἐπιβαρέω, to weigh upon, press heavily upon, *(occ.* 2 Cor. ii. 5.)
2. καταναρκάω, to become torpid against, *i.e. to the detriment of any one,* to be burdensome to *any one, (occ.* 2 Cor. xii. 13, 14.)

2. 2 Cor xi. 9. | 1. 2 Thes. iii. 8.

CHARGEABLE UNTO (BE.)

1. 1 Thes. ii. 9.

CHARGER.

πίναξ, a board, plank; *hence, various things made of wood,* a drawing *or* writing tablet, a wooden trencher *or* plate, *etc.*

Matt. xiv. 8, 11. | Mark vi. 25, 28.

CHARIOT (-S.)

1. ἅρμα, a chariot, *esp.* a chariot of war, car, *with two wheels.*
2. ῥέδα, (*Lat.* rheda), a waggon *with four wheels, for travelling.*

1. Acts viii. 28, 29, 38. | 1. Rev. ix. 9.
2. Rev. xviii. 13.

CHARITABLY.

{ κατά, according to,
{ ἀγάπη, love.

Rom. xiv. 15, marg. *according to charity.*

CHARITY.

ἀγάπη, love, *(a word not found in Greek writers, nor in Philo, Josephus, in Acts, Mark, or James; apparently coined by the lxx.)* Love *that is self-denying and compassionately devoted to its object; the highest word among the Greeks was* φιλανθρωπία (philanthropy), *but this does not denote love to man as such, but rather justice, giving him who was entitled to it his full rights; it even falls short of the* φιλαδελφία (brotherly love) of *the N.T.* ἀγάπη *therefore designates a love unknown to writers outside of the N.T.)* Love it its fullest conceivable form; *first exhibited by Christ* (1 John iii. 16), *expressive of God's relation to us* (1 John iv. 9), *and the relation between the Father and the Son* (John xv. 10, xvii. 26, Col. i. 13). *Lastly it is* the distinctive character of the christian life *in relation to the brethren and to all.*

1 Cor. viii. 1
——xiii. 1, 2, 3, 4 (3 times), 8, 13 (twice)
——xiv. 1
——xvi. 14.
Col. iii. 14.
1 Thes. iii. 6.
2 Thes. i. 3.
1 Tim. i. 5.
1 Tim. ii. 15
——iv. 12.
2 Tim. ii. 22.
——iii. 10
Titus ii. 2.
1 Pet. iv. 8 (twice)
——v. 14.
2 Pet. i. 7.
3 John 6.
Rev. ii. 19.

CHARITY (FEAST OF.)

Jude 12.

CHASE OUT [margin.]

ἐκδιώκω, to chase out, drive out of *or* from *a place, (from* ἐκ, out of, *and* διώκω, to make run, set in quick motion, *(occ.* Luke xi. 49.)

1 Thes. ii. 15 (text, *persecute.*)

CHASTE.

ἁγνός, impressed with ἅγος (religious awe), *esp. of places, etc. sacred to the gods, hence,* holy, sacred; *then of the gods,* undefiled, unsullied, chaste; *esp. of* virgin chastity, *the idea lying at the basis is* untouched.

2 Cor. xi. 2. | Titus ii. 5.
1 Pet. iii. 2.

CHASTEN (-ED, -ETH.)

παιδεύω, to bring up *or* rear a child, *(the opposite of* τρέφω, to nurse,) to train and educate; *hence, because to learn is to suffer, (see numerous Greek proverbs in Wetstein and Bleek, and compare* Prov. xix. 18, *and* Heb. v. 8,) to chasten *or* correct.

1 Cor. xi. 32.
2 Cor. vi. 9.
Heb. xii. 6, 7, 10.
Rev. iii. 19.

CHASTENING.

παιδεία, the bringing up of a child, *esp.* its training, teaching, and education, *(opp. to, τροφή*, nourishment,) *hence*, discipline, correction.

Heb. xii. 5, 7, 11.

CHASTISE.

παιδεύω, see "CHASTEN."

Luke xxiii. 16, 22.

CHASTISEMENT.

παιδεία, see "CHASTENING."

Heb. xii. 8.

CHEEK.

σιαγών, the jaw-bone, jaw. *In N.T. gen.* the cheek.

Matt. v. 39. | Luke vi. 29.

CHEER (OF GOOD.)

εὔθυμος, well-minded, *i.e.* well-disposed, benign; of good cheer, cheerful.

Acts xxvii. 36.

CHEER (BE OF GOOD.)

1. *θαρσέω*, to be of good courage, take courage, cheer up.
2. *εὐθυμέω*, to be of a cheerful mind, to be in good spirits.

1. Matt. ix. 2.
1. —— xiv 27.
1. Mark vi. 50.
1. John xvi. 33.
1. Acts xxiii. 11.
2. —— xxvii. 22, 25.

CHEERFUL.

ἱλαρός, cheerful, gay, joyous, *(non occ.,) prob. from* הל, to shine, and אור, the light. *The lxx. in* Psalm civ. 15, *render the Heb.* הצהיל, to cause to shine, *by the verb ἱλαρῦναι, so that ἱλαρός would denote* one whose countenance shineth *as it were* with joy and satisfaction, *and so* cheerful.

2 Cor. ix. 7.

CHEERFULLY (MORE.)

εὐθυμότερον, comp. of εὔθυμος, see "CHEER (BE OF GOOD,)" *(non occ.)*

Acts xxiv. 10 (*εὐθύμως, cheerfully*, G ~ L T Tr A ℵ.

CHEERFULNESS.

ἱλαρότης, gaiety, hilarity, *see under* "CHEERFUL," *(non occ.)*

Rom. xii. 8.

CHERISH (-ETH.)

θάλπω, to heat, soften by heat; to warm, make warm *by incubation, hence,* to cherish, to nourish, *(non occ.)*

Eph. v. 29. | 1 Thes. ii. 7.

CHERUBIMS.

χερουβίμ, (*χερουβείν*, L T Tr), (*χερουβίν*, A ℵ.) The Cherubim; *their form is twice given*, Ezek. i. 5-14; x. 20; *and* Rev. iv. 6-9.

[*Significance.*

I. *Negatively.*

1. Not the *Trinity.*
   (a) God *forbade* any likeness, Deut. iv. 15, 16, *etc.*
   (b) the Godhead is presented *at the same time* with them, and uses them as the basis of His throne.
   (c) they are never worshipped, but offer worship, Is. vi. 3; Rev. iv. 8, 9.
2. Not the *angels.*
   (a) there is no reason, evidence, *or* connection.
   (b) they are distinguished from the angels in Rev. v. 8, 11, and vii. 11. First they, and then the angels worship, and angels in Rev. v. would scarcely be represented emblematically and literally in the same verse.
   (c) they are never dismissed on any errand as angels are, but are ever attached to the throne.
3. Not the *Church.*
   (a) they are distinguished from the Church in Rev. v. 9, 10. See the critical readings, where in ver. 9 the word "us" should be omitted (G ~ L T A), and in ver. 10 the words "us" and "we" should be "them" and "they" (G L T Tr A ℵ), (see *Ap.)*
   (b) also distinguished in Rev. vii. 9-11.
4. Not the *Four Gospels.*

(a) not in keeping with their presence in Eden, Tabernacle, and Temple.

(b) they are ministers of wrath, call for plagues, give vials, see Rev. vi. and xv. 7.

(c) not books, but living creatures (ζῶον, not θηρίον) giving worship.

II. *Positively:* they are not symbols,* but representatives.

1. Derivation: the word כ־רבים may de note *as the great ones* or *as multitudes;* or, according to Fuerst and perhaps Eichorn, the root may be found in כרב, *to grasp, to seize, to hold,* (corresponding to a similar Persian root.) We have the three letters of this root, g, r, p, appearing in Eng. words of kindred meaning, *grasp, grip, grab, gripe;* hence the word would denote (in a passive sense) *the seized, possessed,* or perhaps *reclaimed ones.* So in Ezek. x. 1, and Rev. iv. 6, and Ps. xcix. 1, etc. the throne is *held* or possessed by the Cherubim; the material figures are *held* to the mercy-seat, and then by their posture are, as it were, *held* entranced, (but see below.)

2. Meaning: they represent *the future glorified animate creation;* the pledge from Eden to the Apocalypse that the "curse" will one day be removed, and the "vanity" to which it is made subject be taken away.

(a) their number, four, is the number of *creation, e.g.* four winds; four corners; four elements; four divisions, (heaven, earth, under-the-earth, and sea, Rev. v. 13, xiv. 7); four designations, (tribe, tongue, people, nation, Rev. v. 9, vii. 9, x. 11, xi. 9, xiii. 7, xiv. 6, xvii. 15; Gen. x. 5, 20, 31); four great world-powers, Dan. vii.

(b) they are the heads of *animate creation;* lion, of wild beasts; ox, of tame beasts; eagle, of birds; man, of all.

(c) they are beneath the throne, for the *earth* is the Lord's footstool.

* Symbols are always explained, see Rev. iv. 5; v. 6, 8, etc.

(d) Their song is of *creation* (Rev. iv. 11); and whenever they speak it is in connection with the *earth.* When they sing of *redemption* (v. 9), it is a "new" song relating to others.

(e) In Gen. iii. when *creation* was brought under the curse, they were placed (*i.e.* "placed in a tabernacle" where the Divine presence was manifested, see Gen. iv. 3, 4, 14, 16), at the east of Eden to keep (*i.e.* to preserve, *cf.* Gen. ii. 15, same word), the way of the Tree of Life, and thus prevent the curse being perpetuated, and keep (כרב) the hope of *re-genesis* alive.

(f) When figures of them were afterwards placed in the tabernacle (Ex. xxv. 18, 23) over the mercy-seat, and made out of the same piece of gold, the hope of creation was shown to be *bound up* (כרב) with "the blood," *i.e.* redemption—the Lamb slain (Rev. v. 6, 9; Col. i. 19, 20.) And indicate God's purpose to redeem "all things." The God of Eden is thus shown to be the God of Israel.

(g) their position there also indicates that the hope of *creation* was henceforth *bound up* (כרב) with "Israel" (see Acts iii. 19-21, where, instead of "preached unto," read "prepared for," G L T Tr A א.)

(h) the Cherubim are a golden thread that links the books of the Bible together. Introduced in Gen. iii. 24; in tabernacle, Exod. xxv. 18; the supporters of God's throne, 1 Sam. iv. 4; 2 Sam. vi. 2; 2 Kings xix. 15; 1 Chron. xiii. 6; Is. xxxvii. 16; Ps. lxxx. 1; xcix. 1 ("Thou that sittest between the Cherubims"); and so through Ezek. and Rev. connected with the "glory of God."]

Heb. ix. 5.

CHICKEN.

νοσσίον, a young bird, nestling, chick, (*non occ. except* Luke xiii. 34, *where* L *prefers it in pl. to* νοσσία, *a* brood.)

Matt. xxiii. 37.

CHIEF.

1. *πρῶτος*, the first, foremost, *of time or place.*

2. *ἄρχων*, a ruler, commander, chief, *(from ἄρχω*, to be first.)

3. *ἡγέομαι*, to go before, to lead the way, *hence*, to preside, rule, be the chief *or* principal.

1. Matt. xx. 27.
— Mark vi. 21, see C estate.
2. Luke xi. 15.
2. —— xiv. 1.
1. —— xix. 47.
— —— xxii. 26, see C (be)
— Acts xiii 50, see C man.
3. —— xv 22
1. Acts xvi. 12, marg. *first*
1. —— xvii. 4.
— —— xix. 31, see C of Asia.
1. —— xxv. 2
— —— xxviii. 7, see C man.
1. —— 17.
1. 1 Tim. i. 15.

CHIEF (BE.)

3. Luke xxii. 26.

CHIEF ESTATE.

1. Mark vi. 21

CHIEF MAN.

1 Acts xiii. 50. | 1 Acts xxviii. 7.

CHIEF OF ASIA.

Ἀσιάρχης, an Asiarch, the highest religious official under the Romans in the province of Asia.

Acts xix. 31.

See also, CAPTAIN, CORNER, PRIEST, PUBLICAN, ROOM, RULER, SEAT, SHEPHERD, SPEAKER, SYNAGOGUE.

CHIEFEST.

πρῶτος, the first, foremost, *of place or time.*

Mark x. 44.

CHIEFEST (VERY.)

{ *ὑπέρ*, *(lit.* over and towards) beyond, above, *affirming superiority (not merely inferring it as παρά does.)*
λίαν, very, exceedingly, very much. }

ὑπερλίαν, (G L T A) over-much, very exceedingly, super-eminently; *with art. as here*, the most eminent.

2 Cor. xi 5 | 2 Cor. xii. 11.

CHIEFLY.

1. *μάλιστα*, *(superl. of μάλα*, very, very much, exceedingly,) most, most of all, especially.

2. *πρῶτον*, first, in the first place.

2. Rom. iii. 2. | 1. 2 Pet ii. 10. | 1. Phil. iv. 22.

CHILD, CHILDREN

1. *τέκνον*, that which is born *(from τίκτω*, to bear; *like Ang. Sax.* bearn, *Scot.* bairn, *from* beran, to bear,) a child, *whether son or daughter;* a child *by natural descent.*

2 *υἱός*, a son, a male child, *strictly spoken only of man, (for fuller meaning see under* "SON.")

3. *παῖς*, *in relation to descent*, a child, *whether* son *or* daughter; *in relation to age*, a boy *or* girl; *in relation to condition (like Lat.* puer), a slave, servant, maid *(as the French use* garcon, *and we say* "*post*-boy.")

4. *παιδίον*, a little *or* young child, *(dim. of No.* 3), an infant.

5. *παιδάριον*, a lad, a little boy *or* girl, *(dim. of No.* 3.)

6. *νήπιος*, not speaking, *and so precisely the Lat.* infans, our infant, a babe, without the power of speech; *also*, a minor.

7. *βρέφος*, the child while yet in the womb, *(denotes ἔμβρυον)*; the new born babe.

— Matt. i. 18, } see C (be
— —— 23, } with.)
— —— ii. 8, 9, 11, 13 twice, 14, see C young.
3. —— 16.
1. —— 18.
— —— 20 twice, 21, see C (young.)
1. —— iii. 9.
2. —— v. 9, 45.
1. —— vii. 11.
2. —— viii. 12.
2. —— ix. 15.
1. —— x. 21 twice.
5. —— xi. 16 (No. 4, All.)
1 —— 19 (*ἔργων, works*, Tr ℵ.)
2. —— xii. 27.
2. —— xiii. 38 twice.
4. —— xiv. 21.
1. —— xv. 26.
4. —— 38.
3. —— xvii. 18.
2. —— 25, 26.
— —— xviii. 2, 3, 4, 5, see C (little.)
1. —— 25.
— —— xix. 13, 14, see C (little.)
1. Matt. xix. 29.
2. —— xx. 20.
3. —— xxi. 15.
1. —— xxii. 24.
2. —— xxiii. 15, 31.
1. —— 37.
— —— xxiv. 19, see C (be with.)
2. —— xxvii. 9.
1. —— 25.
2. —— 56.
2. Mark ii. 19.
1. —— vii. 27 twice.
4. —— 28.
— —— ix. 21, see C (of a.)
4. —— 24, 36, 37.
— —— x. 13, see C (young)
— —— 14, 15, see C (little)
1. —— 24 (*τεκνίον, a little child* (dim. of No. 1), L.)
1. —— 29, 30.
1. —— xii. 19.
1. —— xiii. 12.
— —— 17, see C (be with)
1. Luke i. 7.
2. —— i. 16.

1. Luke i. 17.
4. —— 59, 66, 76, 80.
— —— ii. 5, see C (great with.)
4. —— 17.
4. —— 21 (*αὐτός*, *him*, [All.)
4. —— 27, 40.
3. —— 43.
1. —— iii. 8.
2. —— v. 34.
2. —— vi. 35.
4. —— vii. 32.
1. —— 35
— —— ix. 38, see C (only.)
3. —— 42.
4. —— 47, 48.
4. —— xi. 7.
1. —— 13.
1. —— xiii. 34.
1. —— xiv. 26.
2. —— xvi 8 twice.
— —— xviii. 16, 17, see C (little.)
1. —— 29.
1. —— xix. 44.
— —— xx. 28, 29, see C (without.)
1. —— 31.
2. —— 34, 36 twice.
— —— xxi. 23, see C (be with.)
1. —— xxiii. 28.
2. John iv. 12.
4. —— 49.
1. —— viii. 39.
1. —— xi. 52.
2. —— xii. 36.
— —— xiii. 33, see C (little.)
4. —— xvi. 21.
4. —— xxi. 5, marg. *sirs.*
1. Acts ii. 39.
2. —— iii. 25.
3. —— iv. 27, 30.
2. —— v. 21.
1. —— vii. 5.
— —— 19, see C (young)
2 —— 23, 27.
2. —— ix. 15.
2. —— x. 36.
2. —— xiii. 10.
— —— 18, see *C* (*bear.*)
2. —— 26.
1. —— 33.
1. —— xxi. 5, 21.
1. Rom. viii. 16, 17, 21.
1. —— ix. 7, 8 3 times.
2 —— 26, 27.
1 1 Cor. vii. 14.
5. 1 Cor. xiii. 11 4 times.
4. —— xiv. 20 1st.
— —— 20 2nd, see C (be a.)
2. 2 Cor. iii. 7, 13.
1. —— vi. 13.
1. —— xii. 14 twice.
2. Gal. iii. 7, 26.
6. —— iv. 1, 3.
— —— 19, see C (little.)
1. —— 25, 27, 28, 31.
— Eph. i. 5, see C (adoption of.)
2. —— ii. 2.
1. —— 3.
6. —— iv. 14.
2. —— v. 6.
1. —— 8.
1. —— vi. 1, 4.
2. Col. iii. 6 (*ap.*)
1. —— 20, 21.
1. 1 Thes. ii. 7, 11.
— —— v. 3, see C (be with.)
2. —— 5 twice.
1. 1 Tim. iii 4, 12.
1. —— v. 4.
— —— 10, see C (bring up.)
— —— 14, see C (bear)
7. 2 Tim iii. 15.
1. Titus i. 6.
— —— ii. 4, see C (love one's.)
4. Heb. ii. 13, 14.
2. —— xi. 22.
4. —— 23.
2. —— xii. 5.
1. 1 Pet. i. 14.
1. 2 Pet. ii. 14.
— 1 John ii. 1, 12, 13, 18, 28, see C (little)
— —— iii. 7, see C (little)
1. —— 10 twice.
— 1 John iii. 18, } see C
— —— iv. 4, } (little.)
1. —— v. 2.
— —— 21, see C (little.)
1. 2 John i. 4, 13.
1. 3 John 4.
2. Rev. ii. 14.
1. —— 23.
2. —— vii. 4.
— —— xii. 2, see C (be with.)
1. —— 4.
2. —— 5 1st.
1. —— 5 2nd.
2. —— xxi. 12

CHILD (BE A.)

νηπιάζω, to be, play *or* act the *νήπιος*, *for which see* "CHILD," *No.* 6.

1 Cor. xiv. 20.

CHILD (bear or feed, as a nurse beareth or feedeth her) [margin.]

τροφοφορέω, to bear as a nurse, to carry in the arms, *as a nurse her nurseling*, *hence*, to cherish, care for.

Acts xiii. 18 (Stm G L T A) (text, *τροποφορέω*, *to bear with the turn* of any one, i.e., *with his disposition* or *manners*, G~ Tr ℵ.)

CHILD (BE WITH.)

ἐν, in, } to be with child.
γαστήρ, the belly, }
ἔχω, to have, }

Matt. i. 18, 23.
—— xxiv. 19.
Mark xiii. 17.
Luke xxi. 23.
1 Thes. v. 3.
Rev. xii. 2.

CHILD (GREAT WITH.)

ἔγκυος, *(from* *ἐν*, in, *and* *κύω*, to hold, contain,) *used of females*, *(non occ.)*

Luke ii. 5.

CHILD (LITTLE.)

1. *παιδίον*, *see* "CHILD," *No.* 4.

2. *τεκνίον*, *dim. of* "CHILD," *No.* 1, *(non occ.)*

1. Matt. xviii. 2, 3, 4, 5
1. —— xix. 13, 14.
1. Mark x. 14, 15.
1. Luke xviii. 16, 17.
2. John xiii. 33.
2. Gal. iv. 19 (*τέκνον*, see C, No. 1, L ℵ.)
2 1 John ii. 1, 12.
1. —— 13, 18.
2. —— 28.
2. —— iii. 7, 18.
2 —— iv. 4.
2. —— v. 21.

CHILD (OF A.)

παιδιόθεν, *(from* *παιδίον*, *see* "CHILD," *No.* 4, *and* *θεν*, *denoting* from a place *or* time,) from a child, from infancy.

Mark ix. 21.

CHILD (ONLY.)

μονογενής, only born, only-begotten, *i.e.* only child, *(involving the idea of preciousness and attachment.)*

Luke ix. 38.

CHILD (YOUNG.)

1. *παιδίον*, *see* "CHILD," *No.* 4.

2. *βρέφος*, *see* "CHILD," *No.* 7.

1. Matt. ii. 8, 9, 11, 13 twice, 14, 20 twice, 21.
1. Mark x. 13.
2. Acts vii. 19

CHILDREN (ADOPTION OF.)

υἱοθεσία, the placing as a son, adoption, the receiving into the relationship of a child.

Eph. i. 5.

CHILDREN (BEAR.)

τεκνογονέω, to bear children, to be the mother of a family, *and so by implication, including all the duties of the maternal relation, (non occ.)*

1 Tim. v. 14.

CHILDREN (BRING UP.)

τεκνοτροφέω, to nourish, rear *or* bring up children, *(non occ.)*

1 Tim. v. 10.

CHILDREN (LOVE ONE'S.)

φιλότεκνος, loving one's children, *(non occ.)*

Titus ii. 4.

CHILDREN (WITHOUT.)

ἄτεκνος, without children, *(occ.* Luke xx. 30), *see* "CHILD," *No.* 1.

Luke xx. 28, 29.

CHILD-BEARING.

τεκνογονία, the begetting *or* bearing of children, *and so by implication including all the duties of the maternal relation, (non occ.)*

1 Tim. ii. 15.

CHILDISH.

νήπιος, *see* "CHILD," *No.* 6.

1 Cor. xiii. 11 (Gen.)

CHILDLESS.

ἄτεκνος, without children, *see* "CHILD," *No.* 1.

Luke xx. 30 (ap.)

CHOICE (MAKE.)

ἐκλέγομαι, *(Mid.)* to lay out together, to pick out for one's self, choose out, select, *not implying the rejection of that which is not chosen, but like the choosing of Levi from the twelve tribes;* to choose out, *with the accessory idea of kindness, favour, love.*

Acts xv. 7.

CHOKE (-ED.)

1. πνίγω, to stifle, choke, seize by the throat, throttle, *pass.* to be choked, *etc.*, to be drowned, *(occ.* Matt. xviii. 28.)

2. ἀποπνίγω, *(No.* 1, *with* ἀπό, *prefixed, denoting* completeness,) to strangle, suffocate, *pass.* to be choked *or* suffocated, *(non occ.)*

3. συμπνίγω, *(No.* 1, *with* σύν, *prefixed, denoting* association *or* compression,) to choke together, to suffocate by crowding; to choke up, *(occ.* Luke viii. 42.)

2. Matt. xiii. 7.
3. ——— 22.
3. Mark iv. 7, 19.
1. Mark v. 13.
2. Luke viii. 7.
3. ——— 14.
2. Luke viii. 33.

CHOOSE (-ING, -OSE, -OSEN.)

1. ἐκλέγω, to lay out together, pick out, select, choose.

   (a) *Mid.* to pick out for one's self, choose out, *from preference, favour, or love, see* "CHOICE."

2. ἐπιλέγω, to say upon, *hence,* to name *or* call.

   (a) *Mid.* to choose upon, *i.e.* in addition to *or* succession *to another.*

3. αἱρέομαι, *(Mid.)* to take, take for one's self, to choose; to separate *rather by the act of* taking *than by showing preference, favour, or love, (see No.* 1), *(non occ.)*

4. αἱρετίζω, *(from same root as No.* 3, *viz., Sans.* hri, *from which we have* χείρ *(old Lat.* hir), the hand, ἀγρέω, to lay hold of, ἁρπάζω, seize, take off, αἱρέω *(No.* 3), to take with the hand, αἴρω, to raise, raise up, *and* ἄγρα, a catching, the chase, that which is taken; *and also our Eng. word* grip;) *hence,* αἱρετίζω, *(from* αἱρετός, *verbal adj. of No.* 3, that may be taken,) to take, *and by implication, to separate* by taking, to take that which is adapted *or* eligible for being taken. *(It only occurs in* Matt. xii. 18, *where it is the Septuagint translation of* תמך, to take hold of; hold up, support.)

5 *προχειρίζομαι*, to make any person *or* thing to be at hand, ready *to do or be any thing*, (*occ.* Acts xxvi. 16.)

6. *χειροτονέω*, to stretch out the hand, *esp. for the purpose of giving one's vote in the Athenian ἐκκλησία* ; to choose by vote *or* suffrage ; also to appoint by laying on the hands, (*occ.* Acts xiv. 23.)

4. Matt. xii. 18.
1a. Mark xiii. 20
1a. Luke vi. 13.
1a. —— x. 42
1a. —— xiv. 7.
1a. John vi. 70.
1a. —— xiii. 18.
1a. —— xv. 16 twice, 19.
1a. Acts i. 2, 24.
1a. —— vi. 5.
— —— x. 41, see C before.
1a. —— xiii. 17
— —— xv 7, see C (make.)
1. Acts xv. 22, 25
2a. —— 40
5. —— xxii. 14.
1a. 1 Cor. i. 27 1st, 27 2nd (*ap*), [28.
6. 2 Cor. viii. 19.
1a. Eph. i. 4.
3. Phil. i. 22.
8. 2 Thes. ii. 13.
— 1 Tim. v. 9, marg. see C *into the number*
— 2 Tim. ii. 4, see C..to be a soldier.
3. Heb. xi. 25.
1a. Jas. ii. 5.

CHOOSE BEFORE (-OSEN.)

προχειροτονέω, (*No.* 6 *with πρό*, before, *prefixed,*) (*non occ.*)

Acts x. 41.

CHOOSE INTO THE NUMBER [margin.]

καταλέγω, to lay down, *e.g. apart from others, hence*, to select ; *or among others, hence*, to reckon under *or* to a number, to enrol, (*non occ.*)

1 Tim. v. 9, text; *take*, etc.

CHOOSE...TO BE A SOLDIER.

στρατολογέω, to collect an army, enlist soldiers, *part. with art. as here*, one who does this, *i.e.* a commander, a general.

2 Tim. ii. 4.

CHOSEN.

1. *ἐκλεκτός*, chosen out, preferred, selected.

2. *ἐκλογή*, a picking out, selection; *then*, selection made, that which is chosen (*hence the word* eclogue.)

1. Matt. xx. 16 (*ap.*)
1. —— xxii. 14.
1. Luke xxiii. 35.
2. Acts ix. 15.
1. Rom. xvi. 13.
1. 1 Pet. ii. 4, 9.
1. Rev. xvii. 14.

CHRIST.

Χριστός, anointed ; *Septuagint for* משיח, Messiah, *a term applied to every one anointed with the holy oil*, chiefly to the High Priest, Lev. iv. 3, 5, 16, vi. 15. *On the ground of* Dan. ix. 25, *and* Ps. ii. 2, *it is used in the Targums to designate* the expected Saviour, *as* the anointed of God, *to be the King and Redeemer of His people*, (Luke xxiii. 2, 35, 37); (*βασιλεύς*, king, *denotes His relation to the people and sphere of dominion*, *Χριστός expresses the source of this relationship as one of divine ordination.*)

* ὁ *Χριστός*, (*with the article.*) In the Gospels and Acts : the Anointed, the Christ, the Messiah. *The article in Greek is not simply definite, but also objective and emphatic. As a rule, the subject (or thing spoken of) has the article, the predicate (or that which is spoken of it) has it not. In the Church Epistles it often denotes* Christ spiritual: Christ as the head of the one body.

*** Most interesting and valuable suggestions will arise in connection with the use and omission of the article here. It is worthy of the patient attention of the student.

Matt. i. 1, 16, 17*, 18*, see [Jesus.
—— ii. 4*.
—— xi. 2*.
—— xvi. 16*, 20*.
—— xxii. 42*.
—— xxiii. 8* (*om.* All.)
—— xxiv. 5*, 23*.
—— 24, see C (false.)
—— xxvi. 63*, 68.
—— xxvii. 17, 22
Mark i. 1.
—— viii. 29*.
—— ix. 41 (Gen.)
—— xii. 35*.
—— xiii. 21*.
—— 22, see C (false.)
—— xiv. 61*.
—— xv. 32*.
Luke ii. 11, 26*
—— iii. 15*.
—— iv. 41* 1st (*om.* All.)
—— 41* 2nd.
—— ix. 20*.
—— xx. 41*.
—— xxii. 67*
—— xxiii. 2, 35*, 39*
—— xxiv. 26*, 46*.
John i. 17, 20*, 25*.
—— 41* (*om.* art. G L T Tr A ℵ) (marg. *anointed.*)
John iii. 28*.
—— iv. 25, 29*.
—— 42* (*om.* G ∸ L T Tr A ℵ.)
—— v. 69* (*ap.*)
—— vii. 26*, 27, 31*, 41* twice, 42*.
—— ix. 22.
—— x. 24*.
—— xi. 27*.
—— xii. 34*.
—— xvii. 3.
—— xx. 31*.
Acts ii. 30* (*ap*), 31*, 36, 38.
—— iii. 6, 18*, 20.
—— iv. 10, 26*.
—— v. 42*.
—— viii. 5*, 12, 37 (*ap.*)
—— ix. 20* (Ἰησοῦς, *Jesus*, G L T Tr A ℵ.)
—— 22*.
—— 34* (*om.* art. L Tr ℵ)
—— x. 36.
—— xi. 17.
—— xv. 11 (*om.* G T Tr A ℵ.)
—— 26.
—— xvi. 18. [ℵ.)
—— 31 (*om.* L T Tr A

Acts xvii. 3* 1st.
—— 3* 2nd (om. art. L ℵ)
—— xviii. 5*, 28*.
—— xix. 4* (om. All.)
—— xx. 21 (om. L T Tr^b A.)
—— xxiv. 24 (add, Ἰησοῦς, *Jesus*, L ℵ.)
—— xxvi. 23*.
—— xxviii. 31.
Rom. i. 1, 3, 6, 7, 8.
—— 16* (om. All.)
—— ii. 16.
—— iii. 22, 24.
—— v. 1, 6, 8, 11, 15, 17, 21.
—— vi. 3, 4, 8, 9, 11, 23.
—— vii. 4*, 25.
—— viii. 1, 2, 9, 11* (om. art. L T Tr A ℵ) (add Ἰησοῦς, *Jesus*, L^b ℵ.)
—— 17, 34 (add Ιησοῦς, *Jesus*, L^b ℵ), 35*, 39
—— ix. 1, 3*, 5*.
—— x. 4, 6, 7.
—— xii. 5.
—— xiii. 14.
—— xiv. 9.
—— 10* (ὁ Θεός, *God*, G∼ L T Tr A ℵ.)
—— 15.
—— 18* (om. art. L Tr^b)
—— xv. 3*, 5, 6, 7*, 8, 16, 17, 18, 19*, 20.
—— 29* (om. τοῦ εὐαγγελίου τοῦ, *of the gospel of the* L T Tr A ℵ.)
—— 30.
—— xvi. 3, 5, 7.
—— 9 (Κύριος, *Lord*, L)
—— 10, 16*, 18, 20, 24 (ap), 25, 27.
1 Cor. i. 1, 2 twice, 3, 4, 6*, 7, 8, 9, 10, 12, 13*, 17 1st (add art. L), 17* 2nd, 23, 24, 30.
—— ii. 2.
—— 16 (Κύριος, *Lord*, L)
—— iii. 1, 11* (om. art. G Tr A ℵ) (Χριστός Ιησοῦς, *Christ Jesus*, instead of Ιησοῦς ὁ Χριστός, *Jesus the Christ*, L T.)
—— 23 twice.
—— iv. 1, 10 twice, 15 twice.
—— 17 (add Ἰησοῦς, *Jesus*, L ℵ.)
—— v. 4 1st (om. L T Tr A)
—— 4 2nd (om. L T Tr A
—— 7. [ℵ.)
—— vi. 15 1st, 15* 2nd.
—— vii. 22.
—— viii. 6, 11, 12.
—— ix. 1 (om. L T Tr A ℵ)
—— 12*.
—— 18* (om. G⇄ L T Tr A ℵ.)
—— x. 4*.
—— 9* (ὁ Κύριος, G∼ L T Tr A ℵ.)
—— 16* twice.
—— xi. 1, 3 1st*.
—— 3 2nd (add art., L^b T Tr A ℵ.)
—— xii. 12*, 27.
—— xv. 3, 12, 13, 14, 15*, 16, 17, 18, 19, 20, 22*, 23 1st, 23 2nd (add art., B G L T Tr A ℵ), 31, 57.
—— xvi. 22 (om. G⇄ L T Tr A ℵ.)

1 Cor. xvi. 23 (om. T Tr A ℵ)
—— 24.
2 Cor. i. 1, 2, 3, 5* 1st.
—— 5 2nd (add art., G L T Tr A ℵ.)
—— 19, 21.
—— ii. 10, 14*, 15, 17.
—— iii. 3, 4*, 14.
—— iv. 4*, 5, 6.
—— v. 10*, 14*, 16, 17, 18, 19, 20 twice.
—— vi. 15 (Χριστοῦ, *of Christ*, L T Tr A ℵ.)
—— viii. 9, 23.
—— ix. 13*.
—— x. 1*, 5*, 7 1st.
—— 7 2nd (om. G T Tr A ℵ.)
—— 14*.
—— xi. 2*, 3*, 10, 13, 23.
—— 31 (om. L T Tr A ℵ)
—— xii. 2, 9*, 10, 19.
—— xiii. 3, 5, 14.
Gal. i. 1, 3.
—— 6 (om. G→.)
—— 7*, 10, 12, 22.
—— ii. 4, 16 3 times, 17 twice 20 twice, 21.
—— iii. 1, 13, 14, 16.
—— 17 (om. G⇄ L T Tr A ℵ.)
—— 22, 24, 26, 27, 28, 29.
—— iv. 7 (ap), 14, 19.
—— v. 1, 2.
—— 4* (om. art., G⇄ L Tr A^b ℵ.)
—— 6.
—— 24* (add Ἰησοῦς, *Jesus*, L^b T Tr A ℵ.)
—— vi. 2*, 12*, 14, 15 (ap), 18.
Eph. i. 1 twice, 2, 3* 1st, 3 2nd, 5, 10*, 12*, 17, 20*.
—— ii. 5*, 6, 7, 10, 12, 13 1st, 13* 2nd, 20.
—— iii. 1*, 4*.
—— 6* (om. art., L T T Tr A ℵ) (add Ἰησοῦς *Jesus*, L T Tr A ℵ.)
—— 8*, 9 (ap.)
—— 11 (add art., L T Tr A ℵ.) [21.
—— 14 (ap), 17*, 19*,
—— iv. 7*, 12*, 13*, 15* (om. art., G→ L T Tr A ℵ), 20*, 32.
—— v. 2*, 5*, 14*, 20, 23*, 24*, 25*, 32.
—— vi. 5*, 6* (om. art., G⇄ L T Tr A ℵ), 23, 24.
Phil. i. 1 twice, 2, 6, 8, 10, 11, 13, 15*, 16* (om. art. L^b Tr^b A^b ℵ†), 18, 19, 20, 21 (χρηστός, *profitable*, G∼), 23, 26, 27*, 29.
—— ii. 1, 5, 11, 16, 21* (om. art. G L T Tr A ℵ), 30* (om. G→ T A) (om. art. L Tr) (Κύριος, *Lord*, ℵ.)
—— iii. 3, 7*, 8 1st (add art. L), 8 2nd, 9, 12* (om. art. G L T Tr A ℵ), 14, 18*, 20.
—— iv. 7, 13 (om. G L T Tr A ℵ), 19, 21, 23.
Col. i. 1, 2 1st (add, Ιησοῦς, *Jesus*, L Tr), 2 2nd (ap) 3, 4, 7*, 24*, 27, 28.
—— ii. 2* (ap), 5, 6*, 8, 11*, 17* (om. art. G T), 20* (om. art. G L T Tr A ℵ.)

† marks for erasure have been placed in ℵ but removed.

Col. iii. 1* twice, 3*, 4*, 11, 13* (ὁ Κύριος, *Lord*, L Tr A), (Θεός, *God*, ℵ), 16*, 24.
—— iv. 3*.
—— 12 (add, Ἰησοῦς, *Jesus*, L T Tr A ℵ.)
1 Thes. i. 1 1st, 1 2nd (ap), 3.
—— ii. 6, 14.
—— 19 (om. G⇄ L T Tr A ℵ.)
—— iii. 2*.
—— 11 (om. L T Tr A ℵ)
—— 13 (om. G⇄ L T Tr A ℵ.)
—— iv. 16.
—— v. 9, 18, 23, 28.
2 Thes. i. 1, 2, 8 (om. L^b T Tr A), 12 1st (om. L^b T Tr A ℵ), 12 2nd.
—— ii. 1, 2* (ὁ Κύριος, *the Lord*, G L T Tr A ℵ), 14, 16.
—— iii. 5*, 6, 12, 18.
1 Tim. i. 1 twice, 2, 12, 14, 15, 16.
—— ii. 5.
—— 7 (om. ἐν Χριστῷ, *in Christ*, G L T Tr A†)
—— iii. 13.
—— iv. 6.
—— v. 11*, 21.
—— vi. 3, 13, 14.
2 Tim. i. 1 twice, 2, 9, 10, [13.
—— ii. 1, 3, 8, 10.
—— 19 (Κύριος, *the Lord* G L T Tr A ℵ.)
Titus i. 1, 4.
—— ii. 13.
—— iii. 6.
Philem. 1, 3, 6, 8, 9, 23, 25.
Heb. iii. 1 (om. G L T Tr A ℵ.)

Heb. iii. 6, 14*.
—— v. 5*.
—— vi. 1*.
—— ix. 11, 14*.
—— 24* (om. art. L Tr A ℵ), 28*.
—— x. 10.
—— xi. 26*.
—— xiii. 8, 21.
Jas. i. 1.
—— ii. 1.
1 Pet. i. 1, 2, 3 twice, 7, 11 twice, 13, 19.
—— ii. 5, 21.
—— iii. 16, 18, 21.
—— iv. 1, 11, 13*, 14.
—— v. 1*, 10, 14.
2 Pet. i. 1 twice, 8, 11, 14, 16.
—— ii. 20.
—— iii. 18.
1 John i. 3.
—— 7 (om. L T Tr A ℵ)
—— ii. 1, 22*.
—— iii. 23.
—— iv. 2, 3 (ap.)
—— v. 1*, 6* (om. art. G⇄ T Tr A ℵ), 20 (om. G→)
2 John 3, 7, 9* 1st.
—— 9* 2nd (om. G→ L T Tr A ℵ.)
Jude 1 twice, 4, 17, 21.
Rev. i. 1, 2, 5.
—— 9 1st (om. L T Tr A ℵ.)
—— 9 2nd (om. G⇄ L T Tr A ℵ.)
—— xi. 15*.
—— xii. 10*.
—— 17 (om. G L T Tr A ℵ.)
—— xx. 4, 6*.
—— xxii. 21 (om. L T Tr A ℵ.)

† ℵ *omits*, ℵ³ *inserts*.

CHRISTS (FALSE.)

ψευδόχριστοι, false Christs, pretended Messiahs, *(opp. to that which is true,) to be distinguished from* ἀντίχριστος, opponent of Christ.

Matt. xxiv. 24. Mark xiii. 22 (om. T A.)

CHRISTIAN (-s.)

χριστιανός, Christian, *(a word formed not after the Greek but after the Roman manner, denoting* attachment to *or* adherents of Christ. *Only occurs as used by others of them, not by Christians of themselves. Tacitus* (A.D. 96) *says* (Annals xv. 44), *"The vulgar call them Christians. The author or origin of this denomination, Christus, had, in the reign of Tiberius been executed by the procurator, Pontius Pilate,") (non occ.)*

Acts xi. 26. Acts xxvi. 28.
1 Pet. iv. 16.

CHRYSOLITE.

χρυσόλιθος, *(from* χρυσός, gold, *and* λιθός, a stone,) the chrysolith *or* gold stone; a precious stone of a gold colour; *now called* a topaz, *(occ.* Ex. xxviii. 30 *and* Ezek. xxviii. 13,) *(non occ.)*

Rev. xxi. 20.

CHRYSOPRASUS.

χρυσόπρασος, a chrysoprase, *(from* χρυσός, gold, *and* πράσον, a leek.) *Pliny reckons it among the* beryls, *the best of which he says are of a* green *colour; and others resemble the juice of* a leek.

Rev. xxi. 20.

CHURCH.

ἐκκλησία, *the common term for* a meeting of the ἔκκλητοι (those summoned) *to discuss the affairs of a Free State;* the body of citizens summoned together by a herald (κῆρυξ.) *The lxx. transfer the term to* the assembly of the people of Israel, *whether summoned or met for a definite purpose* (1 Kings viii. 65), *or considered as* the representative of the entire nation. *In N.T. it denotes* the redeemed community *in its two-fold aspect.* (i) The entire community of all who are called by and to Christ out of the world, the Church universal, (ii) every Church in which the character of the Church as a whole is seen in miniature. *The* summoning *is expressed by the latter part of the word* (καλεῖν), *and* out of *by the first part* (ἐκ.) *It does not occur in Mark, Luke, John,* 1 *and* 2 *John,* 2 *Timothy, Titus, Jude, (occ.* Acts xix. 32, 39, 41.)

Matt. xvi. 18.
—— xviii. 17 twice.
Acts ii. 47 (om. L T* Tr A [ℵ.)
—— v. 11.
—— vii. 38.
—— viii. 1, 3.
—— ix. 31.
—— xi. 22, 26.
—— xii. 1, 5.
—— xiii. 1.
—— xiv. 23, 27.
—— xv. 3, 4, 22, 41.
—— xvi. 5.
—— xviii. 22.
—— xix. 37, see Robber.
—— xx. 17, 28.
Rom. xvi. 1, 4, 5, 16, 23.
1 Cor. i. 2.
—— iv. 17.
—— vi. 4.
—— vii. 17.
—— x. 32.
—— xi. 16, 18, 22.
—— xii. 28.
—— xiv. 4, 5, 12, 19, 23, 28, 33, 34, 35.
—— xv. 9.
—— xvi. 1, 19 twice.
2 Cor. i. 1.
—— viii. 1, 18, 19, 23, 24.
—— xi. 8, 28.
—— xii. 13.

* eighth edition.

Gal. i. 2, 13, 22.
Eph. i. 22.
—— iii. 10, 21.
—— v. 23, 24, 25, 27, 29, 32.
Phil. iii. 6.
—— iv. 15.
Col. i. 18, 24.
—— iv. 15, 16.
1 Thes. i. 1.
—— ii. 14.
2 Thes. i. 1, 4.
1 Tim. iii. 5, 15.
—— v. 16.
Philem. 2.
Heb. ii. 12.
—— xii. 23.
Jas. v. 14.
3 John 6, 9, 10.
Rev. i. 4, 11, 20 twice.
—— ii. 1, 7, 8, 11, 12, 17, 18, 23, 29.
—— iii. 1, 6, 7, 13, 14, 22.
—— xxii. 16.

CINNAMON.

κινάμωμον, (κιννάμωμον, L T Tr A ℵ.) *From an Arabic verb,* to emit a smell, Cinnamon. *It is not certain whether it is the same as our Cinnamon. In* Ex. xxx. 23, *it is* an ingredient in the holy oil for anointing, and occurs in Prov. vii. 17, *and* Cant. iv. 14; *what is now so named is a second and inward bark of an aromatic tree, called* canella zeylanica.

Rev. xviii. 13 (*add,* καὶ ἄμωμον, *and* amomum, (a precious ointment made from an Asiatic shrub, and used for the hair) G L T Tr A ℵ.)

CIRCUMCISE (-ED, -ING.)

περιτέμνω, to cut around, to circumcise.

Luke i. 59.
John vii. 22.
Acts vii. 8.
—— xv. 1, 5, 24 (ap.)
—— xvi. 3.
—— xxi. 21. [not.)
Rom. iv. 11, see C (though
1 Cor. vii. 18 twice.
Gal. ii. 3.
—— v. 2, 3.
—— vi. 12, 13 1st.
—— 13 2nd, see C (have..)
Phil. iii. 5, see circumcised.
Col. ii. 11.

CIRCUMCISED.

περιτομή, a cutting all round, circumcision, *Dat. as here,* in circumcision.

Phil. iii. 5.

CIRCUMCISED (HAVE...)

περιτέμνω, *in pass. as here,* to be getting circumcised.

Gal. vi. 13 2nd.

CIRCUMCISED (THOUGH...NOT.)

διά, throughout, (διά, *with Gen. has the local sense of* passing through, *including that of* proceeding from *and* passing out,)
ἀκροβυστία, the foreskin, uncircumcision; *then used, either of* the state of being uncircumcised *or* an uncircumcised man *or* men.

Rom. iv. 11 (lit. throughout uncircumcision.)

CIRCUMCISING.

Infinitive of περιτέμνω, *(see* "CIRCUMCISED (HAVE...)"), the circumcising, *lit.* "the to-circumcise."

Luke ii. 21

CIRCUMCISION

περιτομή, a cutting all round, circumcision.

John vii. 22, 23.
Acts vii. 8
—— x. 45
—— xi. 2.
Rom. ii. 25 twice, 26, 27, 28, 29.
—— iii. 1, 30.
—— iv. 9, 10 twice 11, 12 twice
—— xv 8
1 Cor. vii. 19.
Gal. ii. 7, 8, 9, 12
—— v. 6, 11.
—— vi. 15
Eph. ii. 11
Phil. iii. 3.
Col. ii. 11 twice
—— iii. 11
—— iv. 11
Titus i. 10

CIRCUMSPECTLY

ἀκριβῶς, *(adv. of* ἀκριβής, *derived by some from* εἰς ἄκρον βῆναι, going up to the top *or* summit ; *and as this requires* great pains, care, *and* diligence, *it means* accurate, exact, perfect *in its kind. of argument,* close, subtle; *of thoughts,* clear, definite ; *of persons,* exact, strict ;) *adv.* to a nicety, precisely.

Eph v 15

CITIZEN

πολίτης, a member of a city *or* state, citizen, freeman, *gen.* belonging to, connected with one's city *or* country.

Luke xv 15
Acts xxi 3
Luke xix. 14.

CITIZEN (FELLOW.)

συμπολίτης, *(the above with* σύν, *prefixed, implying* union *or* co-operation,) fellow citizen.

Eph. ii. 19.

CITY

πόλις, a city *or* town, *(Lat.* urbs,) *properly* a town enclosed with a wall.

Matt. ii. 23
—— iv. 5
—— v. 14, 35
—— viii 33, 34
—— ix. 1, 35
—— x. 5, 11, 14, 15, 23 twice.
—— xi 1. 20
—— xii 25
Matt. xiv. 13
—— xxi. 10. 17, 18
—— xxii. 7
—— xxiii. 34 twice.
—— xxvi. 18.
—— xxvii. 53.
—— xxviii. 11.
Mark i. 33, 45
Mark v. 14.
—— vi. 11 (*ap*), 33, 56
—— xi. 19.
—— xiv. 13, 16
Luke i. 26. 39.
—— ii. 3, 4 twice, 11, 39
—— iv. 29 twice, 31, 43.
—— v. 12.
—— vii. 11, 12 twice, 37
—— viii. 27, 34, 39.
—— ix. 5, 10.
—— x. 1, 8, 10, 11. 12
—— xiii. 22.
—— xiv. 21.
—— xviii. 2, 3.
—— xix. 17, 19, 41
—— xxii. 10.
—— xxiii. 19, 51
—— xxiv. 49.
John i. 44.
—— iv. 5, 8, 28, 30. 39
—— xi. 54.
—— xix 20
Acts v. 16.
—— vii. 58
—— viii. 5. 8. 9. 40
—— ix. 6
—— x. 9.
—— xi. 5
—— xii. 10.
—— xiii. 44, 50.
—— xiv. 4, 6, 13, 19, 20, 21.
—— xv. 36.
—— xvi. 4, 12 twice.
Acts xvi. 13 (πύλη, *the gate,* G ⇉ L T Tr A ℵ.)
—— —— 14, 20, 39.
—— xvii. 5.
—— —— 6, 8, see ruler.
—— —— 16.
—— xviii. 10.
—— xix. 29, 35
—— xxi. 5, 29 30. 39.
—— xxii. 3.
—— xxiv. 12
—— xxv. 23.
—— xxvi. 11
—— xxvii. 8
Rom. xvi. 23
2 Cor. xi. 26, 32
Heb. xi. 10, 16
—— xii. 22
—— xiii 14
Jas. iv. 13.
2 Pet. ii. 6
Jude 7.
Rev. iii. 12
—— xi. 2, 8, 13
—— xiv. 8 (*om.* All.)
—— —— 20.
—— xvi. 19 twice
—— xvii. 18.
—— xviii. 10 twice, 16, 18, 19, 21.
—— xx. 9.
—— xxi. 2, 10, 14, 15. 16 twice, 18, 19, 21, 23
—— xxii. 14, 19.

See also, RULER.

CLAMOUR.

κραυγή, a crying out, screaming, shouting ; cry, *of public information ;* clamour, *of tumult or controversy,* wailing, *of sorrow, (occ.* Matt. xxv. 5 ; Acts xxiii. 9 ; Heb. v. 7 ; Rev. xxi. 4.)

Eph. iv. 31.

CLAY

πηλός, clay, earth, *esp. such as was used by the mason or potter ; metaph.* the clay *or* matter from which things and especially man are made, *(non occ.)*

John ix. 6 twice, 11, 14, 15.
Rom. ix. 21

CLEAN [adj. *and* adv.]

1. καθαρός, clean, free from impure admixture, without blemish in its kind, spotless, *see* "CLEAR."
2. ὄντως, *(adv. part. from* εἰμί, to be,) really, actually, verily.

— Matt. viii. 2, see C (make)
— —— 3, see C (be.)
— —— xxiii. 25, see C (make)
1. —— 26.
1. —— xxvii. 59.
— Mark i. 40, see C (make)
— —— 41, see C (be.)
— Luke v. 12, see C (make)
—— 13, see C (be.)
— Luke xi. 39, see C (make)
1. —— 41.
1. John xiii. 10 twice, 11.
1. —— xv. 3.
1. Acts xviii. 6.
2, 2 Pet. ii. 18 (ὀλίγως, *scarcely, hardly,* AVm G L T Tr A ℵc) (marg. *for a little* or *a little*)
1. Rev. xix. 8, 14.

CLEAN (BE.)

καθαρίζω, to make *καθαρός*, (clean, *see* "CLEAR.")

(a) *pass.* to be clean.

a. Matt. viii. 3. | a. Mark i. 41.
a. Luke v. 13.

CLEAN (MAKE.)

Matt. viii. 2. | Mark i. 40.
—— xxiii. 25. | Luke v. 12
Luke xi. 39.

CLEANSE.

καθαρίζω, *see* "CLEAN (BE.)"

Matt. viii. 3. | Luke xvii. 14, 17.
—— x. 8. | Acts x. 15.
—— xi. 5. | —— xi. 9.
—— xxiii. 26. | 2 Cor. vii. 1.
Mark i. 42. | Eph. v. 26.
Luke iv. 27. | Jas. iv. 8.
—— vii. 22. | 1 John 1, 7, 9.

CLEANSING.

καθαρισμος, cleansing, *(denoting the action of the verb proceeding from the subject, i.e. the action and its result.)*

Mark i. 44. Luke v. 14

CLEAR.

1. *ἁγνός*, pure, clean, *(in a ceremonial sense); properly* an outward cleanliness of body, *and then* inward purity; pure from every defilement of mind.
2. *καθαρος*, clean, free from impure admixture. *(It has a more extensive meaning than No. 1. A thing is No. 2 in which there is no foreign admixture whether it be itself good or evil; No. 1 is that which is not contaminated by anything in itself really evil. That which is ἁγνός is necessarily καθαρός, but many things that are καθαροί are free from being ἁγνοί.)*
3. *λαμπρός*, shining, bright, radiant

1. — 2 Cor. vii. 11 1st, see C of [one's self. | — Rev. xxi. 11, see crystal
1. —— 11 2nd. | 2. —— 18.
3. Rev. xxii. 1.

CLEARING OF ONE'S SELF.

ἀπολογία, a defence, speech in defence, verbal defence, *hence Eng.* apology.

2 Cor. vii. 11 1st.

CLEARLY.

τηλαυγῶς, *(adv. of τηλαυγής*, far-shining, far-beaming; *gen.* far-seen, conspicuous,) brilliantly, conspicuously.

Mark viii. 25.

See also, SEE.

CLEAVE (-ETH, CLAVE.)

κολλάω, to glue, cement, *to join one metal to another; gen.* to join fast together. *In N.T. only in Mid.* to adhere, cleave unto.

Luke x. 11. | Acts xvii. 34.
Acts xi. 23, see C unto. | Rom. xii. 9.

CLEAVE UNTO.

προσμένω, to remain towards, wait still longer; to continue.

Acts xi. 23.

CLEAVE [margin.]

σχίζω, to split, *(esp. of wood,)* to rend asunder, separate, part asunder.

Mark i. 10 (text, *open.*)

CLEMENCY.

ἐπιείκεια, a yielding disposition, *(contrasted with* justice, *and approximating to* kindness,) a tempering of strict justice, correcting its inaccuracies, and supplying its defects with the gentleness and firmness of equity; sweet reasonableness, *(occ.* 2 Cor. x. 1.)

Acts xxiv. 4.

CLERK.

See, TOWN.

CLIMB UP (-ED, -ETH.)

ἀναβαίνω, to go up, climb, mount, ascend, *see* "COME," *No.* 13.

Luke xix. 4, with *ἐπί*, *upon*; John x. 1.

CLOAK.

1, *ἐπικάλυμμα*, a covering, a veil, a means of hiding.

2. *ἱμάτιον*, raiment *generally*, the outer garment *as opposed to χιτών*, the vest.

3. *πρόφασις*, that which is shown *or* appears before *any one ; and so*, that which is alleged to cover, either a deeper existent cause, *or* the true cause ; *hence*, pretext *or* ostensible pretence.

4. *φαιλόνης*, (*φελόνης*, G L T Tr A ℵ,) *from a passage in Hesychius it appears to be the Cretan word for χιτών*, a tunic *or* inner garment. *Others, without authority have chosen to transpose the ν and λ* (*φαινολης*), *and derive it from the Lat.* pœnula, a great coat *with a hood used chiefly on journies or in the army , but there is no authority for this transposition.*

2. Matt. v. 40.
2. Luke vi. 29.
3. John xv 22, marg excuse.
3. 1 Thes. ii. 5.
4. 2 Tim. iv. 13.
1. 1 Pet. ii. 16.

CLOSE [verb.]

1. *καμμύω*, (*for καταμύω*), to close down, *hence of persons*, to shut the eyes (*The root is μυ, which is pronounced by closing the lips, hence, gen.* to close, be shut.)

2. *πτύσσω*, to fold, double up, *used of garments or scrolls of parchment, etc.*

1. Matt. xiii. 15. | 2. Luke iv 20.
1. Acts xxviii. 27.

CLOSE (KEEP.)

σιγάω, to be silent *or* still, to keep silence ; to cease to speak, *and then gen.* to cease, to rest.

Luke ix. 36.

CLOSE BY.

ἆσσον, *adv.* (*comp. of ἄγχι*,) nearer, (*used mostly with verbs,*) *to draw* near *as friend or foe ;* very nigh.

Acts xxvii. 13.

CLOSET.

ταμεῖον, a store-chamber, store-house, (*from ταμίας*, a steward *and ταμιεύω, his* office,) *hence, gen.* any place of privacy, (*occ.* Matt. xxiv. 26 ; Luke xii. 24.)

Matt. vi. 6. | Luke xii. 3.

CLOTH.

ῥάκος, a ragged, tattered garment ; a piece torn off, a rag.

Matt. ix. 16. | Mark ii. 21.

See also, LINEN.

CLOTHE (-ED.)

1. *περιβάλλω*, to cast *or* throw around *or* about ; *of clothing*, to put on.
   (a) *Mid. or pass.* to put on *one's own garments*, to clothe one's self.

2. *ἀμφιέννυμι*, to put clothes round *or* on ; invest. *Some think it means rather* to ornament.
   (a) *Mid.* to clothe one's self, to put on.

3. *ἱματίζω*, to put on *ἱμάτιον* (raiment *generally, esp.* outer garments.)

3. Matt. vi 30.
— — 31, see C wherewithal (be.)
2. — xi 8.
1 — xxv. 36. 38, 43
— Mark i. 6, see C with (be.)
3. — v. 15.
— — xv. 17, see C with.
— — xvi. 5, see C in (be)
2. Luke vii. 25.
3. — viii 35.
2. — xii. 28 (*ἀμφιάζω, to put round or on,* L T Tr A.)
— — xvi. 19, see C in (be)
— 2 Cor. v. 2, see C upon (be)
— 2 Cor v 3, see C (be.)
— — 4, see C upon (be)
— 1 Pet. v. 5, } see C with (be.)
— Rev. i. 13, }
— — iii. 5, 18, } see C (be)
— — iv 4, }
— — vii. 9, } see C with (be.)
— — x. 1, }
— — xi. 3, see C in (be.)
— — xii. 1, see C with (be.)
— — xv. 6, } see C in (be.)
— — xviii. 16, }
— — xix. 13, see C with (be.)
— — 14, see C in (be.)

CLOTHE (WITH.)

ἐνδύω, to go in, enter into , get into *as clothes.*

Mark xv. 17 (*ἐνδιδύσκω*, same meaning, the ending *σκω* denoting the beginning or progress of the action, L T Tr A ℵ.)

CLOTHED (BE)

1. *ἐνδύω, see* "CLOTHE (WITH.)"

2. *περιβάλλω, see* "CLOTHE," *No.* 1.

1. 2 Cor. v. 3, pass. (*ἐκδύω, to set out of as clothes,* G ∾ T.)
2. Rev. iii 5. 18 (pass.)
2. — iv. 4 (pass.)

CLOTHED IN (BE.)

1. *περιβάλλω, see* "CLOTHE," *No.* 1.

2. *ἐνδύω, see* "CLOTHE WITH."

3. *ἐνδιδύσκω, same meaning as No.* 2, *the termination σκω denoting the beginning or progress of the action.*

1. Mark xvi. 5.
3. Luke xvi 19, mid.
1. Rev. xi. 3.
2. Rev. xv. 6, mid.
1. — xviii. 16.
2. — xix. 14, mid.

CLOTHED UPON (BE.)

ἐπενδύνομαι, to have put on over, *as over one's own garments, (Mid of* ἐνδύω, *see* "CLOTHE (WITH).")

2 Cor. v 2 4.

CLOTHED WHEREWITHAL (BE.)

περιβάλλω, *see* "CLOTHE," *No.* 1.

Matt vi. 31, pass (with τί, with what.)

CLOTHED WITH (BE.)

1. περιβάλλω, *see* "CLOTHE," *No.* 1, *only in Mid. here*
2. ἐνδύω, *see* "CLOTHE WITH," *only in Mid. or pass here.*
3. εγκομβόομαι, to bind a thing on *one's self*, wear it constantly, *(from* ἐν, in, *and* κόμβος, a knot *or* roll of cloth,) to clothe with an outer ornamental garment tied closely upon one with knots.

2. Mark i. 6
3. 1 Pet. v. 5.
2. Rev. i. 13
1 Rev vii. 9.
1 —— x 1.
1. —— xii. 1.
1. Rev xix. 13

CLOTHES.

1. ἱμάτιον, *(pl.)* raiment *generally*, the outer garments.
2. χιτών, the inner vest, strictly a woollen shirt *worn next the body, (perhaps our* cotton *from this,) in pl. sometimes two worn, prob.* of different stuffs for ornament or luxury.

1. Matt. xxi 7.
1. —— xxiv. 18 (singular No. 2, G∾ L Tr A ℵ)
1. —— xxvi. 65.
1. Mark v. 28, 30.
2. —— xiv. 63, pl.
1. Mark xv. 20.
1 Luke xix 36.
1. Acts vii. 58.
1. —— xiv 14.
1. —— xvi 22.
1. —— xxii. 23.

See also, GRAVE, SWADDLING.

CLOTHING.

1. ἐσθής, apparel, vesture, *gen. used of that which is* splendid *or* ornate, *(whence Eng.* vest, *etc.)*
2. ἔνδυμα, anything put on, a garment of any kind. *Spoken of the clothing of the ancient prophets in token of their contempt of earthly splendour,* 1 Kings xix. 13, 2 Kings i. 8, Zech. xiii. 4.

2. Matt vii. 15.
— Mark xii. 38, see C[(long.)]
1. Acts x 30.
1. Jas. ii. 3.

CLOTHING (LONG.)

στολή, a fitting out, *(from* στέλλω, to send,) *esp.* equipment in clothes. *In N.T. like Lat.* stola, a long, flowing robe reaching to the feet, *worn by kings* (Jonah iii. 6), *priests* (Ex. xxviii. 2), *and by persons of rank or distinction* (Mark xvi. 5; Luke xv. 22; xx. 46; Rev. vi. 11; vii. 9, 13, 14, *etc.)*

Mark xii. 38.

See also, SOFT.

CLOUD (-S.)

1. νέφος, an indefinite cloudy mass *that covers the heavens, (non occ.)*
2. νεφέλη, a particular distinct cloud, *(non occ.)*

2 Matt. xvii. 5 twice.
2 —— xxiv. 30.
2. —— xxvi 64.
2. Mark ix. 7 twice
2 —— xiii. 26
2. —— xiv. 62.
2. Luke ix. 34 twice, 35.
2. —— xii. 54.
2. —— xxi. 27.
2. Acts i. 9.
2 1 Cor. x. 1, 2.
2. 1 Thes. iv. 17.
1. Heb. xii. 1.
2. 2 Pet. ii. 17 (καὶ ὁμίχλαι, *and mists*, G L T Tr A [ℵ.])
2. Jude 12.
2. Rev. i. 7.
2. —— x. 1
2. —— xi. 12.
2. —— xiv. 14 twice, 15, 16.

CLOVEN.

διαμερίζω, to distribute, divide up, separate, *(referring here not to the tongues but to the apostles amongst whom the flames were* divided out *from one common source.)*

Acts ii. 3 (pass.)

CLUSTER.

βότρυς, a cluster *or* bunch of grapes; *gen.* autumn fruit, *(non occ.)*

Rev. xiv. 18.

COAL (-S.)

ἄνθραξ, live *or* burning charcoal, *(non occ.)*

Rom. xii. 20.

COALS (FIRE OF.)

ἀνθρακία, a heap *or* fire of live charcoal, *(non occ.)*

John xviii. 18 ; xxi. 9.

COASTS.

1 ὅριον, a bound, goal, limit ; *in pl. as here,* the boundaries, the frontier, *(from* ὁρίζω, to bound, limit.)

2. μέρος, a part, share, one's lot ; *in pl. as here,* the parts, region, country, *(from* μείρω, to divide.)

3. τόπος, a place, a spot, *as occupied or filled by any person or thing.*

4. χώρα, space, *which receives, contains, or surrounds anything, and so* place, *where any thing is or takes place; hence, gen.* a country, land, region, territory.

1. Matt. ii. 16.
1. —— viii. 34.
2. —— xv. 21.
1. —— 22, 39.
2. —— xvi. 13.
1. —— xix. 1.
1. Mark v. 17.
1. —— vii. 31 twice.
1. —— x. 1.
1. Acts xiii. 50.
2. —— xix. 1.
4. —— xxvi. 20.
3. Acts xxvii. 2.

See also, SEA.

COAT.

χιτών, a tunic, *i.e.* the inner garment worn next the body mostly with sleeves, and reaching usually to the knees, rarely to the ancles.

Matt. v. 40.
—— x. 10.
Mark vi. 9.
Luke iii. 11.
Luke vi. 29.
—— ix. 3.
John xix. 23 twice.
—— xxi. 7, see C (fisher's.)
Acts ix. 39.

COAT (FISHER'S.)

ἐπενδύτης, a tunic worn over *another*, the upper *or* outer *(i.e. the usual)* tunic, *in distinction from the inner garment* which was called ὑποδύτης.

John xxi. 7.

COCK.

ἀλέκτωρ, a cock, house-cock, *(some derive from* ἄλεκτρος, the sleepless, *but Parkhurst from* הליכת אור, the coming of the light, *for giving notice of which he was among the ancients sacred to the sun.* ἠλέκτωρ, *denotes* the blazing sun, *whence Eng.* electron. *There were two cock-crowings,* one after midnight, and one before *dawn, Mark mentions both* (xiv. 30), *but the other Evangelists only mention the latter, which was emphatically* THE *cock-crowing.*

Matt. xxvi. 34, 74, 75.
Mark xiv. 30.
—— 68 (om. Lb ℵ.)
Mark xiv. 72 twice.
Luke xxii. 34, 60, 61.
John xiii. 38.
John xviii. 27.

COCK-CROWING.

ἀλεκτοροφωνία, the crowing of a cock; *hence,* cock-crow *or* the third watch of the night, *see* "COCK."

Mark xiii. 35.

COFFIN [margin.]

σορός, a vessel for holding *any thing,* a coffer, urn, *esp.* the cinerary urn; *hence,* any receptacle for a dead body, a coffin.

Luke vii. 14, text, *bier.*

COLD.

1. ψῦχος, coldness, *the result or product of the verb* ψύχω, *see* "COLD (WAX.)"

2. ψυχρός, *(adj.)* cold, chill; *also,* cool, fresh, *(denoting the full expression and complete possession of the act of the verb* ψύχω, *see* "COLD (WAX).")

1. John xviii. 18.
1. Acts xxviii. 2.
1. 2 Cor. xi. 27.
2. Rev. iii. 15 twice, 16.

COLD WATER.

ψυχρός, *see* "COLD," *No.* 2.

Matt. x. 42.

COLD (WAX.)

ψύχω, to breathe, blow ; *hence,* to make cool *or* cold.

Matt. xxiv. 12 (pass.)

COLLECTION.

λογία, a gathering *or* collection, *(occ.* 1 Cor. xvi. 2.)

1 Cor. xvi. 1.

COLONY.

κολωνία, *(a Latin word,* colonia,) *i.e.* a Roman colony.

Acts xvi. 12.

COLOUR.

πρόφασις, that which is shown *or* appears before *any one; and so*, that which is alleged to cover, either a deeper co-existent cause *or* the true cause; *hence*, pretext *or* ostensible pretence.

Acts xxvii. 30.

See also, SCARLET.

COLOURED.

See, SCARLET.

COLT.

πῶλος, a foal, whether colt *or* filly; a young animal *esp.* of a domestic kind, *(non occ.) (Lat.* pullus, *Germ.* fohlen, *Eng.* foal.)

Matt. xxi. 2, 5, 7.	Luke xix. 30, 33 twice, 35.
Mark xi. 2, 4, 5, 7.	John xii. 15.

COMB.

See, HONEY.

COME (-EST, -ETH, -ING, CAME.)

1. ἔρχομαι, to come *or* go, *used of persons or of things. It denotes* the act of coming *or* going, *as*, I am coming, *etc., in distinction from No.* 17, *which denotes* the result, *as*, I am come and am here, *(cf.* John viii. 42 *and* Heb. x. 9.) *The verb means* to go, *as well as* come, *and the context must determine which it is. It is combined with a large number of prepositions, for which see below.*

   (a) *In* Rev. vi. 1, 3, 5, 7, *it should be* go, *and the words* and see *should be omitted according to the best authorities, see under* "SEE."

2. ἐξέρχομαι, *(No.* 1 *with* ἐξ, out of, *prefixed,)* to come *or* go out of *any place*, to come *or* go forth.

   (a) *followed by* ἀπό, from, *expressing removal and separation.*

   (b) *followed by* ἐκ, out of.

3. προσέρχομαι, *(No.* 1, *with* πρός, towards, *prefixed,)* to come *or* go near to *any place or person*, to approach.

4. συνέρχομαι, *(No.* 1, *with* σύν, with, *prefixed, implying co-operation,)* to come *or* go with *any one*, to come along with *or* together, to meet, assemble.

5. ἐπέρχομαι, *(No.* 1, *with* ἐπί, upon, *prefixed,)* to come *or* go upon *or* over *any place*, to arrive at. *(In* Eph. ii. 7, *it is* the art, *with* participle (pl.) *for which see* "COMETH (HE THAT).")

6. κατέρχομαι, *(No.* 1, *with* κατά, down, *prefixed,)* to come *or* go down, descend.

7. εἰσέρχομαι, *(No.* 1, *with* εἰς, to, into, *prefixed,)* to come *or* go into.

   (a) *followed by* εἰς, unto, *marking the object and intention, as well as motion or direction.*

8. ἀπέρχομαι, *(No.* 1, *with* ἀπό, from, *prefixed,)* to come *or* go away from *one place to another; hence, gen.* to go away, depart for, set off.

9. παρέρχομαι, *No.* 1 *with* παρά, beside, *prefixed,)* to come near to *or* beside any person *or* thing; to go *or* pass near, pass along by.

10. διέρχομαι, *(No.* 1, *with* διά, through, *prefixed,)* to come *or* go through, to pass through; *here followed by* ἕως, *denoting the limit*, to, as far as.

11. γίνομαι, to begin to be, *(i.e.* to come into existence *or* into any state, *and then also in Aor. and Perf.* to have come into existence, *or simply* to be.) *It implies* origin, *either from natural causes*, to be born *or* made; *or through special agency* result, to take place, happen; *and change of state*, to become; *or change of place*, to come.

12. παραγίνομαι, *(No.* 11 *with* παρά, beside, *prefixed,)* to become near, to become present, *i.e.* to come, to approach, to arrive. *In Aor.* to have come *or* arrived, be present, *in all passages, except* Matt. iii. 1, 13 *and* Mark xiv. 43, *pres.; and* John iii. 23, *imperf.*

13. ἀναβαίνω, to cause to ascend, to go by, climb, mount, ascend, *(from* βαίνω, *used of all motion on the*

ground, go, walk, tread, step, *the direction being determined by a preposition; here by ἀνά*, up *or* back.)

14. ἐπιβαίνω, to go upon, to tread upon; to set foot upon, to come into, to arrive in *a country or province, etc.*, to embark.

15. ἐμβαίνω, to step into, go into, enter, *followed by* εἰς, unto *or* into.

16. ἀποβαίνω, to go away, to depart; to go from, descend from, to disembark.

17. ἥκω, to come, *i.e.* to have come, to be here, *in the sense of a preterite.*

18. δεῦρο, *adv.* hither, here, *with all verbs of motion, used in cheering up or calling to one.* Here! this way! Come on! Come! *always used with a verb sing.*

18a. δεῦτε, *adv. just the same as No.* 18, *except that it is always used with a verb plural, and more generally as an exclamation.*

19. μέλλω, to be on the point *to do or suffer anything (gen. with infin. of another verb,)* to be about to do, to intend *or* purpose doing *(of one's own free will), but often implying necessity, accordance with the nature of things or with the divine appointment, and therefore certain to take place.*

20. καταντάω, *(here only participle,)* to come down against, *i.e.* to come down to, to arrive at *a place; of things*, to tend *to a certain end*, come to such and such an issue; *gen.* to result.

(a) *followed by* εἰς, unto, into.

(b) *followed by* ἀντικρύ, opposite to, over against.

21. ἐκπορεύομαι, to go out *or* forth, march out from *and* to *a place (with the idea of compulsion,)* proceed out of.

(a) *followed by* ἐκ, out of, from.

(b) *followed by* ἀπό, from, away from.

(c) *followed by* ἔσωθεν, from within.

22. ἐπιπορεύομαι, to go *or* come upon, *i.e. to a place or person*, to go, travel, march to, *(non occ.)*

(a) *followed by* πρός, towards.

23. εἰμί, to be *(of ordinary existence,)* to exist, to have existence, Phil. ii. 6, *(whereas No.* 11 *means* to become, Jas. i. 22.)

(a) ἐστί, *(present)* he, she, *or* it is.

(b) ἔσται, *(future)* he, she, *or* it shall be.

(c) εἶναι, *(inf. pres.)* to be.

(d) ἔσεσθαι, *(inf. fut.)* to be about to be; *here* (Acts xxiv. 15), *with* μέλλω *preceding, see No.* 19.)

24. πάρειμι, *(No.* 23, *with* παρά, beside, *prefixed,)* to be beside, near by *or* present; *absol.* to have come.

25. ἐφίστημι, *trans.* to set *or* place upon *or* over. *In N.T. only in trans. and Mid* to place one's self upon; *of persons,* to stand by *or* near; *also implying approach,* to come and stand by, to come to *or* upon *a person or place* (*of a sudden appearance or in a hostile sense.*)

(a) *followed by* ἐπί, upon.

26. παρίστημι, (a) *trans.* to place by *or* beside, to cause to stand near.

(b) *intrans.* to stand by beside *or* near; *hence*, to be at hand.

27. ἐνίστημι, *trans.* to put, set, *or* place in; *intrans.* to stand in *or* on; *absol.* to be at hand, imminent, begin, arise; to stand in the way of, oppose, resist.

28. φθάνω, to come *or* do before *another*, to be beforehand with; *absol.* to come first, precede, anticipate, come sooner than expected; arrive, attain.

29. φέρω, (a) to bear *(with motion implied.)*

(b) *pass.* to be borne *or* carried from *a place, esp.* involuntarily as by waves *or* winds; to produce, furnish.

30. συμπληρόω, (a) to help to fill, fill completely.

(b) *in pass.* to be filled; *of time*, fulfilled, completed.

31. χωρέω, to make room for another, give way, yield.

32. τρέχω, to run, hasten, hurry.

— Matt. i. 18, see C together.
12. — ii. 1.
1. — 2.
2a. — 6.
1. — 8, 9, 11.
1. — 21 (No. 7, L Tr A ℵ.)
1. — 23.
12. — iii. 1.
1. — 7 1st.
19. — 7 2nd.
— — 11, see cometh (he that.)
12. — 13.
1. — 14.
— — iv. 3, see C to.
3. — 11.
1. — 13.
— — v. 1, see C unto.
1. — 17 twice, 24.
— — 26, see C out.
23a. — 37.
1. — vi. 10.
1. — vii. 15, 25, 27.
— — 28, see C to pass
— — viii. 1, see C down
1. — 2 (No. 3, G∾L T Tr A ℵ.)
— — 5, see C unto.
1. — 7.
7. — 8.
1. — 9 twice.
17. — 11.
1. — 14.
11. — 16.
3. — 19.
— — 25, see C to.
1. — 28 1st.
2b. — 28 2nd.
1. — 29.
— — 32, 34, see C out.
1. — ix. 1.
— — 10 1st, see C to pass.
1. — 10 2nd, 13.
— — 14, see C to.
1. — 15.
1. — 18 1st (No. 7, G∾ T A) (No. 3, L ℵ.)
1. — 18 2nd.
3. — 20.
1. — 23.
1. — 28 1st.
— — 28 2nd, see C to.
7a. — x. 12.
1 — 13, 23, 34 twice, 35.
— — xi. 1, see C to pass.
— — 3, see C (he that should.)
— — 14, see C (which was for to.)
1. — 18, 19.
18a. — 28.
28. — xii. 28.
19. — 32.
1. — 42.
— — 44 1st, see C out.
1. — 44 2nd.
1. — xiii. 4.
3. — 10.
1. — 19, 25.
3. — 27.
1. — 32.
— — 36, see C unto.
— — 49, see C forth.
— — 53, see C to pass
1. — 54.
3. — xiv. 12.
— — 15, see C to
11. — 23.
1. — 28, 29 1st.
— — 29 2nd, see C down.
15. — 32 (No. 13, L Tr A ℵ.)
1. — 33, 34.
— — xv 1, see C to.
21a. — 11.
3 — 12.

— Matt. xv. 18, see C forth.
2a. — 22.
3. — 23.
1. — 25, 29.
— — 30, see C unto
1. — 39.
3. — xvi. 1.
1. — 5, 13, 24, 27, 28.
3. — xvii. 7.
— — 9, see C down.
1. — 10, 11, 12, 14 1st.
— — 14 2nd, 19, see C to.
1. — 24 1st.
— — 24 2nd, see C to.
7a. — 25, (ἐλθόντα, *coming;* for ὅτε εἰσῆλθεν, *when he was come*, Tr A.)
— — 27, see C up.
— — xviii. 1, see C unto.
1. — 7, 11 (*ap.*)
— — 21, see C to.
1. — 31.
— — xix. 1 1st, see C to
1a. — 1 2nd.
— — 3, see C unto.
1. — 14.
3. — 16.
18. — 21.
11. — xx. 8.
1. — 9, 10
— — 20, see C to.
1. — 28.
1. — xxi. 1, 5.
— — 9, see cometh (he that.)
7a. — 10.
— — 14, see C to.
1. — 19.
1. — 23 1st.
— — 23 2nd, see C unto.
— — 28, 30, see C to.
1. — 32.
18a. — 38.
1. — 40.
1. — xxii. 3.
18a. — 4.
— — 11, 12, see C in
— — 23, see C to.
1. — xxiii. 35.
17. — 36.
— — 39, see cometh (he that.)
— — xxiv. 1, see C to.
— — 3, see C unto.
1. — 5.
— — 6, see C to pass
17 — 14.
— — 17, see C down
2a. — 27.
1. — 30, 39, 42, 43, 44, 46.
17. — 50.
1. — xxv. 6 (*om.* G⇄ L T Tr A ℵ.)
1. — 10, 11, 13 (*ap*), 19.
3. — 20, 22, 24.
1. — 31.
18a. — 34.
1. — 36, 39.
— — xxvi. 1, see C to pass.
— — 7, see C unto.
— — 17, see C to.
11. — 20.
1. — 36, 40, 43, 45, 47.
— — 49, see C to.
24. — 50 1st.
3. — 50 2nd.
— — 55, see C out.
3. — 60 1st (*ap*), 60 2nd
1. — 64.
— — 69, 73, see C unto.
11. — xxvii. 1.
— — 32, see C out.
1. — 33.
— — 40, 42, see C down.
1. — 49.
2b. — 53.

11. Matt. xxvii. 57 1st.
1. — 57 2nd.
— — 62, see C together.
1. — 64.
1. — xxviii. 1.
3. — 2.
18a. — 6.
3. — 9.
1. — 11, 13.
3. — 18.
1. Mark i. 7.
— — 9 1st, see C to pass.
1. — 9 2nd.
— — 10, see C up.
11. — 11.
1. — 14.
18a. — 17.
1. — 24.
2b. — 25, 26, 29.
3. — 31.
— — 38, see C forth
1. — 40, 45.
1. — ii. 3.
— — 4, see C nigh unto.
— — 15, see C to pass.
1. — 17, 18, 20.
— — 23, see C to pass.
1. — iii. 8.
3. — 13.
— — 22, see C down.
1. — 31.
— — iv. 4 1st, see C to pass.
1. — 4 2nd, 15, 22.
26b. — 29.
11. — 35.
1. — v. 1.
2b. — 2.
32. — 6 (in Editions 1611—1687, probably a misprint.)
2b. — 8.
1. — 15.
15. — 18.
1. — 22, 23, 27, 33, 35, 38.
— — 39, see C in.
1. — vi. 1.
11. — 2, 21.
— — 22, 25, see C in
1 — 29.
18a. — 31 1st.
1. — 31 2nd.
— — 33, see C together.
— — 34, see C out.
— — 35, see C unto.
11. — 47.
1. — 48, 53.
2b. — 54.
— — vii. 1 1st, see C together.
1. — 1 2nd.
21b. — 15.
21a. — 20.
21c. — 23.
1. — 25.
3. — 30.
1. — 31.
17. — viii. 3 (εἰσίν, *were*, T A.)
1. — 10.
— — 11, see C forth
1. — 22.
1. — 34 (ἀκολουθέω, *to follow*, G T Tr A ℵ.)
1. — 38.
1. — ix. 1, 7.
— — 9, see C down.
1. — 11, 12, 13, 14.
11. — 21.
— — 25 1st, see C running together.
2b. — 25 2nd.
— — 26, see C out.
7a. — 28.
— — 29, see C forth
1. — 33.
1. — x. 1.
— — 2, see C to.
1. — 14.
18. — 21.

1. Mark x. 30.
— — 35, see C unto.
1. — 45, 46, 50.
1. — xi. 9, 10.
2. — 12.
1. — 13 twice, 15.
11. — 19.
— — 23, see C to pass.
1. — 27.
17. — xii. 7.
1. — 9, 14, 18.
3. — 28.
1. — 42.
1. — xiii. 6, 26.
— — 29, see C to pass.
1. — 35, 36.
1. — xiv. 3.
— — 8, see C beforehand.
1. — 16, 17, 32, 37, 41 twice.
12. — 43.
1. — 45, 62, 66.
1. — xv. 21.
— — 30, see C down
11. — 33.
1. — 36.
— — 41, see C up with.
11. — 42.
1. — 43.
1. — xvi. 1, 2.
— Luke i. 8, see C to pass.
— — 22, see C out.
— — 23, see C to pass
— — 28, see C in.
— — 35, see C upon
— — 41, see C to pass
1. — 43.
— — 59 1st, see C to pass.
1. — 59 2nd.
11. — 65.
— — ii. 1, see C to pass.
— — 9, see C upon.
— — 15 twice, see C to pass.
1. — 16, 27.
— — 38, see C in.
— — 46, see C to pass.
1. — 51 (*om.* G→.)
11. — iii. 2.
1. — 3.
— — 7 1st, see C forth
19. — 7 2nd.
1. — 12, 16.
— — 21, see C to pass.
11. — 22.
1. — iv. 16.
— — 31, see C down
1. — 34.
2a. — 35 twice.
— — 36, see C out.
2a. — 41.
1. — 42.
— — v. 1, see C to pass.
1. — 7 twice.
— — 12, see C to pass
— — 15, see C together.
— — 17 1st, see C to pass.
1. — 17 2nd (No. 4, L)
1. — 32, 35.
— — vi. 1, 6, 12, see C to pass.
— — 17 1st, see C down.
1. — 17 2nd, 47.
1. — vii. 3.
12. — 4.
1. — 7, 8 twice.
— — 11, see C to pass
3. — 14.
— — 16, see C on.
— — 19, see C (he that should.)
12. — 20 1st.
— — 20 2nd, see C (he that should.)
1. — 33, 34.
— — 45, see C in.
— — viii. 1, see C to pass
22a. — 4.
1. — 12, 17.

12. Luke viii. 19 1st.
— ——— 19 2nd, see C at.
— ——— 22, see C to pass.
— ——— 23, see C down.
— ——— 24, see C to.
2a. ——— 29.
1. ——— 35. [pass.
— ——— 40, see C to
1. ——— 41 1st.
7a. ——— 41 2nd.
3. ——— 44.
1. ——— 47, 49.
7. ——— 51 (No. 1, G L Tr ℵ.)
— ——— 55, see C again.
3. —— ix. 12.
— ——— 18, see C to pass
1. ——— 23, 26.
— ——— 28, 33, see C to pass.
11. ——— 34, 35.
— ——— 37 1st, see C to pass. [down.
— ——— 37 2nd, see C
— ——— 42, see coming (be a.)
— ——— 51 1st, see C to
30b. ——— 51 2nd. [pass.
— ——— 54, see C down
1. ——— 56 (ap.)
— ——— 57, see C to pass
1. —— x. 1 (No. 7, Lm.)
— ——— 31, see C down
1. ——— 32 (om. G → ℵc)
1. ——— 33.
— ——— 35, see C again
— ——— 38, see C to pass.
— ——— 40, see C to.
— —— xi. 1, see C to pass.
1. ——— 2.
12. ——— 6.
— ——— 14, see C to
28. ——— 20. [pass.
— ——— 22, see C upon
— ——— 24, see C out.
1. ——— 25.
— ——— 27, see C to
1. ——— 31. [pass.
— ——— 33, see C in.
1. —— xii. 36, 37 1st.
— ——— 37 2nd, see C forth.
1. ——— 38 1st (om. Tr ℵ)
1. ——— 38 2nd, 39, 40, 43
17. ——— 46.
1. ——— 49.
12. ——— 51.
1. ——— 54.
— ——— 55, see C to pass
1. —— xiii. 6, 7, 14.
17. ——— 29.
3. ——— 31.
17. ——— 35 1st.
1. ——— 35 2nd.
— —— xiv. 1, see C to pass
1. ——— 9, 10, 17, 20
12. ——— 21.
— ——— 23, see C in.
1. ——— 26, 27, 31.
1. —— xv. 6, 17, 20, 25.
17. ——— 27.
— ——— 28, see C out.
1. —— xvi. 21.
— ——— 22, see C to
1. ——— 28. [pass.
1. —— xvii. 1 twice.
7. ——— 7.
— ——— 11, 14, see C to pass.
1. ——— 20 twice, 22, 27.
— ——— 31, see C down.
1. —— xviii. 3, 8, 16.
18. ——— 22.
1. ——— 30.
— ——— 35, see C to pass.
1. —— xix. 5 1st.
— Luke xix. 5 2nd, 6, see C
11. ——— 9. [down.
1 ——— 10, 13.
— ——— 15, see C to
12. ——— 16. [pass.
1. ——— 18, 20.
— ——— 29, see C to pass
— ——— 38, see cometh (that.)
17. ——— 43.
— —— xx. 1 1st, see C to pass.
— ——— 1 2nd, see C upon
18a. ——— 14 (om. G → L T Tr A.)
1. ——— 16.
— ——— 27, see C to.
1. —— xxi. 6.
— ——— 7, see C to pass
1. ——— 8.
— ——— 9, see C to pass.
— ——— 26, see coming on (those things which
1. ——— 27. [are.)
— ——— 28, 31, see C to
25a. ——— 34. [pass.
— ——— 35, see C on.
— ——— 36, see C to
1. —— xxii. 7. [pass.
11. ——— 14.
1. ——— 18.
— ——— 39, see C out.
1. ——— 45.
12. ——— 52 1st.
— ——— 52 2nd, see C out. [gether.
— ——— 66, see C to-
1. —— xxiii. 26.
— ——— 29, see coming (be.) [ℵ.)
8. ——— 33 (No. 1, L Tr
— ——— 36, see C to.
1. ——— 42.
— ——— 48, see C together.
— ——— 55, see C with.
1. —— xxiv. 1.
— ——— 4, 12, 15, 18, see C to pass.
1. ——— 23.
— ——— 30, 51, see C to pass.
1. John i. 7, 9, 11.
— ——— 15, see cometh
11. ——— 17. [(he that.)
— ——— 27, see coming (who.)
1. ——— 29, 30, 31, 39.
23c. —— 46 1st.
1. ——— 46 2nd, 47.
17. —— ii. 4.
1. —— iii. 2 twice, 8.
— ——— 13, see C down.
1. ——— 19, 20, 21, 22.
12. ——— 23.
1. ——— 26 twice.
— ——— 31 twice, see cometh (he that.)
1. —— iv. 5. 7, 15, 16, 21, 23, 25 twice, 27.
18a. —— 29.
1. ——— 30, 35, 40, 45, 46.
17. ——— 47 1st.
— ——— 47 2nd, 49, see C
1. ——— 54. [down.
— —— v. 7, see coming (be)
11. ——— 14.
1. ——— 24.
— ——— 25, 28, see coming (be.)
— ——— 29, see C forth.
1. ——— 40, 43 twice.
1. —— vi. 5.
— ——— 14, see C (that
11. ——— 16. [should.)
1. ——— 17, 23, 24.
11. ——— 25.
— ——— 33, see C down.
1. John vi. 35.
17. ——— 37 1st.
1. ——— 37 2nd.
— ——— 38, 41, 42, see C
1. ——— 44, 45. [down.
— ——— 50, 51, 58, see C
1. ——— 65. [down.
24. —— vii. 6.
1. ——— 27, 28, 30, 31, 34, 36, 37, 41, 42, 45, 50.
12. —— viii. 2 1st (ap.)
1. ——— 2 2nd (ap.)
1. ——— 14 twice, 20, 21, 22.
17. ——— 42 1st.
1. ——— 42 2nd.
1. —— ix. 4, 7, 39.
1. —— x. 8, 10 twice, 12.
11. ——— 35.
1. —— xi. 17, 19.
— ——— 20, see coming (be.)
— ——— 27, see C (which should.)
24. ——— 28.
1. ——— 29, 30, 32.
— ——— 33, see C with.
1. ——— 34, 38.
18. ——— 43.
— ——— 44, see C forth.
1. ——— 45, 48, 56.
1. —— xii. 1, 9, 12 1st.
— ——— 12 2nd, see coming (be.)
— ——— 13, see cometh
1. ——— 15. (that.)
— ——— 20, see C up.
3. ——— 21.
1. ——— 22, 23, 27, 28.
11. ——— 30.
— ——— 35, see C upon.
1. ——— 46, 47.
1. —— xiii. 1.
2. ——— 3.
1. ——— 6.
11. ——— 19 1st.
— ——— 19 2nd, see C to
1. ——— 33. [pass.
1. —— xiv. 3, 6, 18, 23, 28.
— ——— 29 twice, see C to
1. ——— 30. [pass
1. —— xv. 22, 26.
1. —— xvi. 2, 4, 7, 8, 13 twice, 21, 25.
— ——— 27, see C out.
— ——— 28 1st, see C forth
1. ——— 28 2nd.
— ——— 30, see C forth.
1. ——— 32 twice.
1. —— xvii. 1.
— ——— 8, see C out.
1. ——— 11, 13.
1. —— xviii. 3, 4, 37.
2. —— xix. 5.
1. ——— 32, 33. [out.
— ——— 34, see C there-
1. ——— 38, 39 twice.
1. —— xx. 1, 2, 3, 4, 6, 8, 18, 19, 24, 26.
11. —— xxi. 4.
1. ——— 8.
16. ——— 9.
18a. —— 12.
1. ——— 13, 22, 23.
— Acts i. 6, see C together.
— ——— 8, see C upon.
1. ——— 11.
— ——— 13, see C in.
— —— ii. 1, see C (be fully)
11. ——— 2.
— ——— 6, see C together.
— ——— 17, see C to pass.
1 ——— 20.
— ——— 21, see C to pass.
11. ——— 43.
1. —— iii. 19.
— ——— 23, see C to pass.
— —— iv. 1, see C upon.
— ——— 5, see C to pass.
11. Acts v. 5.
— ——— 7, 10, see C in.
11. ——— 11.
4. ——— 16.
12. ——— 21, 22, 25.
— ——— 38, see C to naught.
— —— vi. 12, see C upon.
18. —— vii. 3.
2b. ——— 4.
— ——— 7, see C forth.
1. ——— 11.
13. ——— 23.
11. ——— 31.
— ——— 34 1st, see C down
18. ——— 34 2nd.
— ——— 45, see C after.
— —— viii. 7, see C out of.
— ——— 15, see C down.
— ——— 24, see C upon.
1. ——— 27.
— ——— 31, see C up.
1. ——— 36.
— ——— 39, see C up.
1. ——— 40.
11. —— ix. 3.
— ——— 12, see C in.
1. ——— 17, 21.
12. ——— 26.
— ——— 28, see C in.
— ——— 32 1st, see C to pass.
— ——— 32 2nd, see C down
— ——— 37, see C to pass.
10. ——— 38.
12. ——— 39.
— ——— 43, see C to pass.
— —— x. 3, see C in.
— ——— 4, see C up.
11. ——— 13.
24. ——— 21.
— ——— 25, see C in.
— ——— 27, see C together
— ——— 28, see C unto.
1. ——— 29.
12. ——— 32 (ap), 33.
— ——— 45, see C with.
— —— xi. 2, see C up.
1. ——— 5.
25a. —— 11.
7a. ——— 20 (No. 1, G L T Tr A ℵ.)
12. ——— 23.
— ——— 26, see C to pass.
6. ——— 27.
— ——— 28, see C to pass.
— —— xii. 7, see C upon.
1. ——— 10.
11. ——— 11.
1. ——— 12.
3. ——— 13.
24. ——— 20.
1. —— xiii. 13.
12. ——— 14.
1. ——— 25.
— ——— 31, see C up with.
— ——— 40, see C upon.
— ——— 44, see C together.
1. ——— 51.
— —— xiv. 1, see C to pass.
— ——— 11, see C down.
— ——— 19, see C thither
7a. ——— 20.
1 ——— 24.
12. ——— 27.
— —— xv. 1, see C down.
12. ——— 4.
— ——— 6, see C together
1. ——— 30 (No. 6, G ~ L Tr A ℵ.)
20a. —— xvi. 1.
1. ——— 7.
— ——— 8, see C down.
— ——— 9, see C over.
7a. ——— 15.
— ——— 16, see C to pass.
— ——— 18 1st, see C out.
2. ——— 18 2nd.

11. Acts xvi. 29.
1. ——— 37, 39.
1. —— xvii. 1.
24. ——— 6.
— ——— 10, see C thither
1. ——— 13, 15.
1. —— xviii. 1, 2 1st.
— ——— 2 2nd, see C unto
6. ——— 5.
20a. —— 19.
1. ——— 21 (*ap.*)
20a. —— 24.
12. ——— 27. [pass.
— —— xix. 1 1st, see C to
1. ——— 1 2nd.
— ——— 4, see C (he which
1. ——— 6, 18. [should.)
— ——— 32, see C together.
1. —— xx. 2, 6.
— ——— 7, see C together
— ——— 11, see C up again
1. ——— 14.
20b. —— 15 1st.
1. ——— 15 2nd.
12. ——— 18 1st.
14. ——— 18 2nd.
— —— xxi. 1, see C to pass.
1. ——— 1 2nd.
20a. —— 7.
1. ——— 8.
— ——— 10, see C down.
1. ——— 11.
11. ——— 17.
— ——— 22 1st, see C to-
1. ——— 22 2nd. [gether.
13. ——— 31
11. ——— 35.
— —— xxii. 6, see C to pass
1. ——— 11, 13. [pass.
— ——— 17 1st, see C to
— ——— 17 2nd, see C again
3. ——— 27.
— —— xxiii. 14, see C to.
25. ——— 27.
7a. ——— 33.
12. ——— 35.
9. —— xxiv. 7 (*ap.*)
1 ——— 8 (*ap.*)
12. ——— 17.
— ——— 22, see C down.
— ——— 23, see C unto.
12. ——— 24.
19&23d. —25 (*om.* 23d, G L Tr A ℵ.)
— ——— 27, see C into one's room.
12. —— xxv. 7 1st.
— ——— 7 2nd, see C down
20a. —— 13.
4. ——— 17
1. ——— 23.
20a. —— xxvi. 7.
11. ——— 22.
6. —— xxvii. 5.
11. ——— 7.
1. ——— 8.
— ——— 16, see C by.
11. ——— 27 (ἐπιγίνομαι, *to arise upon*, T.)
— ——— 33, see coming on (be.)
— ——— 44, see C to pass.
2b. —— xxviii. 3 (διεξέρχομαι, *to come out through*, G∾ T A.)
11. ——— 6.
— ——— 8, see C to pass.
3. ——— 9.
20a. —— 13 1st.
1. ——— 13 2nd.
2. ——— 15.
1. ——— 16 (No. 7, L T Tr A ℵ.)
— ——— 17 1st, see C to pass. [gether.
— ——— 17 2nd, see C to-
12. ——— 21. [Tr A ℵ.)
17 ——— 23 (No 1, G∾ L

— Acts xxviii. 30, see C in.
1. Rom. i. 10, 13.
1. —— iii. 8.
— —— v. 14, see C (be to.)
1. —— vii 9. [to.)
— —— viii. 33, see C (thing
1. —— ix. 9.
— ——— 26, see C to pass.
— —— xi. 25, see C in.
17. ——— 26.
1. —— xv. 23, 24 (*ap.*)
8. ——— 28.
1. ——— 29 twice, 32.
— —— xvi. 19, see C abroad
1. 1 Cor. ii. 1 twice.
— —— iii. 22, see C (thing to.)
1. —— iv. 5, 18, 19, 21.
— —— vii. 5, see C together
20a. —— x. 11.
— —— xi. 17, 18, 20, see C together.
1. ——— 26.
— ——— 33, 34 1st, see C together.
1. ——— 34 2nd.
1. —— xiii. 10.
1. —— xiv. 6.
— ——— 23 1st, see C together.
— ——— 23 2nd, 24, see C in.
— ——— 26, see C together
— ——— 36 1st, see C out.
20a. —— 36 2nd.
1. —— xv. 35.
1. —— xvi. 2.
12. ——— 3.
1. ——— 5, 10, 11, 12 3 times.
11. 2 Cor. i. 8.
1. ——— 15, 16, 23.
1. —— ii. 1, 3, 12.
— —— vi. 17, see C out
1. —— vii. 5.
1. —— ix. 4.
28. —— x. 14.
1. —— xi. 4, 9.
— ——— 28, see cometh upon (that which.)
1. —— xii. 1, 14, 20, 21.
— —— xiii. 1, coming (be)
1. ——— 2.
1. Gal. i. 21.
— —— ii. 4, see C in privily.
1. —— ii. 12.
11. —— iii. 14.
1. ——— 19, 23, 25.
1. —— iv. 4.
— Eph. i. 21, see C (be to.)
5. —— ii. 7.
1. ——— 17.
20a. — iv. 13.
1. —— v. 6.
1. Phil. i. 27.
1. —— ii. 24.
24. Col. i. 6.
— —— ii. 17, see C (thing to.)
1. —— iii. 6.
1. —— iv. 10.
11. 1 Thes. i. 5.
1. ——— 10.
28. —— ii. 16.
1. ——— 18.
— —— iii. 4, see C to pass.
1. ——— 6.
1. —— v. 2.
— ——— 3, see C upon.
1. 2 Thes. i. 10.
1. —— ii. 3.
1. 1 Tim. i. 15.
1. —— ii. 4.
1. —— iii. 14.
— —— iv. 8, see C (be to.)
1. ——— 13.
11. —— vi. 4.
— ——— 19, see C (time to)

27. 2 Tim. iii. 1.
1. ——— 7.
11. ——— 11.
23b. — iv. 3.
1. ——— 9, 13, 21.
1. Titus iii. 12.
19. Heb. ii. 5.
2b. —— iii. 16.
— —— iv. 16, see C unto.
19. —— vi. 5.
1. ——— 7.
2b. —— vii. 5.
— ——— 25, see C unto.
1. —— viii. 8.
12. —— ix. 11 1st.
19. ——— 11 2nd (No. 11, L.)
19. —— x. 1.
7a. ——— 5.
17. ——— 7, 9.
— ——— 37 1st, see C (he that shall.)
17 ——— 37 2nd.
— —— xi. 6, see C to.
— ——— 15, see C out.
— ——— 20, see C (thing to.)
11. ——— 24.
— —— xii. 18, 22, see C unto.
19. —— xiii. 14.
1. ——— 23.
— Jas. i. 17, see C down.
7a. —— ii. 2 1st.
— ——— 2 2nd, see C in.
— —— v. 1, see C upon.
8. 1 Pet. ii. 4.
29b. 2 Pet. i. 17, 18, 21.
1. —— iii. 3.
31. ——— 9.
17. ——— 10.
1. 1 John ii. 18.
1. —— iv. 2, 3 1st (*ap*), 3 2nd.
— —— v. 6, see came (he that.)
17. ——— 20.
1. 2 John 7, 10.
1. ——— 12 (No. 11, G∾ L T Tr A ℵ.)
1. 3 John 3, 10.
1. Jude 14.
— Rev. i. 1, see C to pass.
— ——— 4, see C (which is to.)

1. Rev. i. 7.
— ——— 8, see C (which is to.)
1. —— ii. 5, 16.
17. ——— 25.
17. —— iii. 3 twice, 9.
1. ——— 10, 11.
— ——— 12, see C down.
— ——— 20, see C in.
— —— iv. 1, see C up.
— ——— 8, see C (which is to.)
1. —— v. 7.
1a. —— vi. 1, 3, 5, 7
1. ——— 17.
1. —— vii. 13, 14.
1. —— viii. 3.
2b. —— ix. 3.
1. ——— 12.
— —— x. 1, see C down.
— —— xi. 12, see C up.
1. ——— 14.
— ——— 17, see C (which art to.)
11. —— xii. 10.
— ——— 12, see C down.
— —— xiii. 11, see C up.
— ——— 13, see C down.
1. —— xiv. 7
2b. ——— 15 1st.
1. ——— 15 2nd.
2b. ——— 17, 20.
— ——— 18, see C out.
17. —— xv. 4.
2b. ——— 6.
1 —— xvi. 15.
2a. ——— 17.
1. —— xvii. 1 1st.
— ——— 1 2nd, see C hither
1. —— xvii. 10 twice.
— —— xviii. 1, see C down
2b ——— 4.
17. ——— 8.
1. ——— 10.
2b. —— xix. 5.
1. ——— 7.
18a. —— 17.
— —— xx. 1, 9, } see C
— —— xxi. 2, } down.
1. ——— 9 1st.
— ——— 9 2nd, see C hither.
1. —— xxii. 7, 12, 17 3 times, 20 twice.

COME ABROAD.

ἀφικνέομαι, to arrive at, to come to a *person or place, (connected with* "COME," *No.* 17,) to come from one place to another, *(non occ.)*

Rom. xvi. 19.

COME AFOREHAND.

προλαμβάνω, to take beforehand, to take before *or* sooner *than another;* to outstrip, to be beforehand with, anticipate, *(occ.* 1 Cor. xi. 21; Gal. vi. 1.)

Mark xiv. 8.

COME AFTER.

διαδέχομαι, to receive one from another, to take up next; *hence,* to succeed *one,* take his place, *(non occ.)*

Acts vii. 45.

COME AGAIN.

1. *ἐπανέρχομαι*, to come back upon *or* to a place; to return, *(occ.* Luke xix. 15.)
2. *ἐπιστρέφω*, to turn upon, to turn towards, return to.
3. *ὑποστέφω*, to turn behind, *i.e. back*, to turn about.

2. Luke viii. 55. | 1. Luke x. 35.
3. Acts xxii. 17.

COME AT

συντυγχάνω, *of persons*, to fall in with, to meet with, to come to *or* at *any one; of things*, to happen, befall, *(non occ.)*

Luke viii. 19.

COME BY.

περικρατής, strong round about *any thing*, all powerful; having wholly in one's power,
γίνομαι, to become,
} to become master of [*the boat*] *i.e.* to secure it by hoisting it into the ship, *(non occ.)*

Acts xxvii. 16.

COME DOWN.

1. *καταβαίνω*, to come *or* go down, *see* "COME," *No.* 13.
2. *κατέρχομαι*, *see* "COME," *No.* 6.

1 Matt. viii. 1.
1. —— xiv. 29.
1 —— xvii. 9.
1. —— xxiv. 17.
1. —— xxvii. 40, 42.
1. Mark iii. 22.
1. —— ix 9.
1 —— xv. 30.
2 Luke iv. 31.
1. —— vi. 17.
1. —— viii 23.
2. —— ix. 37.
1. ——— 54.
1. —— x. 31
1. —— xvii 31.
1 —— xix 5, 6.
1. John iii. 13.
1. —— iv. 47, 49.
1. John vi. 33, 38, 41, 42, 50, 51, 58.
1. Acts vii. 34.
1 —— viii. 15.
2. —— ix. 32.
1. —— xiv. 11.
2. —— xv. 1.
1. —— xvi. 8.
2. —— xxi. 10.
1. —— xxiv. 22.
1. —— xxv. 7.
1. Jas. i. 17.
1. Rev. iii. 12.
1. —— x. 1.
1. —— xii. 12.
1. —— xiii. 13.
1. —— xviii. 1.
1. —— xx. 1, 9.
1. —— xxi. 2.

COME FORTH.

1. *ἐξέρχομαι*, *see* "COME," *No.* 2.
2. *παρέρχομαι*, *see* "COME," *No.* 9.
3. *ἐκπορεύομαι*, *see* "COME," *No.* 21.

1 Matt. xiii. 49.
1. —— xv. 18.
1. Mark i. 38 (*ἔρχομαι*, see come, No. 1, G ~.)
1. —— viii. 11.
1. —— ix. 29.
3. Luke iii. 7.
2. —— xii. 37.
3. John v. 29.
1. —— xi. 44.
1. —— xvi. 28, 30.
1. Acts vii. 7.

COME HITHER.

δεῦρο, *see* "COME," *No.* 18.

Rev xvii. 1; xxi. 9.

COME IN.

1. *εἰσέρχομαι*, *see* "COME," *No.* 7.
2. *εἰσπορεύομαι*, to go into, to enter; to pass into, *(with the idea of being conveyed or compelled.)*
3. *ἐφίστημι*, *see* "COME," *No.* 25.

1. Matt. xxvi. 11, 12.
1. Mark v. 39
1. —— vi. 22, 25.
1 Luke i 28.
3 —— ii. 38.
1. —— vii 45.
2 —— xi. 33
1 —— xiv 23.
1 Acts i. 13.
1. Acts v. 7, 10.
1. —— ix. 12.
2. ——— 28.
1 —— x. 3, 25.
2. —— xxviii 30.
1. Rom. xi. 25.
1 1 Cor. xiv. 23, 24.
1 Jas. ii. 2.
1 Rev. iii 20.

COME IN PRIVILY.

παρεισέρχομαι, ("COME," *No.* 1, *with* *παρά*, beside *and* *εἰς*, into *prefixed,)* to come *or* go in beside, *so as to be present along with it. The idea of* stealth *being implied.*

Gal. ii. 4.

COME INTO.

See under "COME" *and* "INTO," *when* "COME" *is the translation of* 7, 14, *and* 15; *and* "INTO" *of* *εἰς*.

COME INTO ONE'S ROOM.

{ *λαμβάνω*, to receive,
{ *διάδοχος*, a successor,
} *(non occ.)*

Acts xxiv. 27.

COME NIGH UNTO.

προσεγγίζω, to become, *ἐγγύς*, (near), to any person *or* thing.

Mark ii. 4.

COME ON.

1. **ἐπέρχομαι**, *see* "COME," *No.* 5.

2. **λαμβάνω**, to take, lay hold of.

2. Luke vii. 16. [A ℵ.)
1. —— xxi. 35 (*ἐπεισέρχομαι, to come in upon,* L T T

COME OUT.

ἐξέρχομαι, see "COME," *No.* 2.

Matt. v. 26.
—— viii 32, 34.
—— xii 44.
—— xxvi. 55.
—— xxvii. 32
Mark vi. 34.
—— ix. 26.
Luke i. 22.
—— iv. 36.
—— xi. 24.
Luke xv. 28.
—— xxii. 39.
John xvi. 27.
—— xvii. 8.
Acts xvi. 18.
1 Cor. xiv. 36.
2 Cor. vi. 17.
Heb. xi. 15 (*ἐκβαίνω, to come out* (see under C, No. 13), L T Tr A ℵ.)
Rev. xiv. 18 (*om.* G→ L.)

COME OUT OF.

See under "COME" *and* "OUT OF," *where* "COME" *is the translation of Nos.* 2 *and* 21, *and* "OUT OF," *of ἀπό and ἐκ.*

COME OVER.

διαβαίνω, to pass through, step across, pass over, (*βαίνω used of all motion on the ground* walking, riding, *etc.*, (*occ.* Luke xvi. 26; Heb. xi. 29.)

Acts xvi. 9.

COME OVER AGAINST.

See "COME" *and* "OVER AGAINST."

COME RUNNING TOGETHER.

ἐπισυντρέχω, to run together upon *or* to *the scene of any action, (non occ.)*

Mark ix. 25.

COME THEREOUT.

ἐξέρχομαι, see "COME," *No.* 2.

John xix. 34.

COME THITHER.

1. *ἐπέρχομαι, see* "COME," *No.* 5.

2. *παραγίνομαι, see* "COME," *No.* 12.

1. Acts xiv. 19. | 2. Acts xvii. 10.

COME TO.

Where "TO" *is not the translation of a preposition (πρός or εἰς), for which see under* "COME" *and* "TO".

1. *προσέρχομαι, see* "COME," *No.* 3.

2. *ἐφίστημι, see* "COME," *No.* 25.

1. Matt. iv. 3
1 —— viii. 2?
1. —— ix. 14, 28.
1. —— xiv. 15.
1. —— xv. 1
1. —— xvii. 14, 19, 24.
1 —— xviii. 21.
1. —— xx 20
1. —— xxi. 14, 28, 30.
1. Matt. xxii. 23.
1. —— xxiv. 1
1. —— xxvi. 17, 49.
1. Mark x. 2.
1. Luke viii 24.
2 —— x. 40
1 —— xx. 27
1. —— xxiii 36.
1 Acts xxii. 14.
1. Heb xi. 6.

COME TO NOUGHT.

καταλύω, to loosen down, to dissolve, to disunite the parts of anything, *hence, of buildings, etc.*, to destroy.

Acts v. 38 (pass.).

COME TO PASS.

1. *γίνομαι, see* "COME," *No.* 11.

2. *ἔσται, see* "COME," *No.* 23b.

1. Matt. vii. 28.
1 —— ix. 10.
1. —— xi. 1.
1. —— xiii. 53.
1. —— xix. 1.
1 —— xxiv. 6.
1 —— xxvi. 1
1. Mark i. 9.
1 —— ii 15, 23
1. —— iv. 4.
1. —— xi. 23.
1. —— xiii. 29.
1 Luke i. 8, 23, 41, 59
1. —— ii. 1, 15 twice, 46.
1 —— iii. 21.
1. —— v. 1, 12, 17.
1 —— vi. 1, 6, 12.
1. —— vii. 11.
1. —— viii. 1, 22, 40
1. —— ix. 18, 28, 33, 37, 51.
1. —— 57 (*om.* G∞ T Tr
1. —— x. 38. (A ℵ.)
1. —— xi. 1, 14, 27.
1 —— xii. 55.
1. —— xiv. 1.
1 Luke xvi. 22
1 —— xvii. 11, 14.
1. —— xviii. 35
1 —— xix. 15, 29.
1. —— xx. 1.
1. —— xxi. 7, 9, 28, 31, 36.
1 —— xxiv. 4, 12 (*ap*), 15, 18, 30, 51.
1 John xiii. 19
1 —— xiv. 29 twice.
2 Acts ii. 17, 21.
2 —— iii 23
1. —— iv. 5
1 —— ix. 32, 37, 43
1. —— xi. 26, 28.
1 —— xiv. 1
1. —— xvi. 16.
1. —— xix. 1.
1. —— xxi. 1.
1 —— xxii. 6, 17.
1 —— xxvii. 44.
1. —— xxviii. 8, 17.
2. Rom. ix. 26.
1. 1 Thes. iii. 4.
1. Rev. i. 1.

COME TOGETHER.

1. *συνέρχομαι, see* "COME," *No.* 4.

2. *συνάγω*, to lead *or* bring together, to gather together.

   (a) *in Pass. or Mid.* to be gathered together, be assembled, come together.

3. *συμπαραγίνομαι*, ("COME," *No.* 12, *with σύν, prefixed,*) to become near with *any one; of a multitude,* to come together.

1. Matt. i. 18.
2a. — xxvii. 62
1. Mark iii. 20.
1. — vi. 33 (*ap.*)
2a. — vii. 1.
1. Luke v. 15.
2a. — xxii. 66.
3. — xxiii. 48.
1. Acts i. 6
1. — ii. 6.
1. — x. 27.
2a. — xiii. 44.
2a. Acts xv. 6.
1. — xix. 32
2a. — xx. 7.
1. — xxi. 22.
1. — xxviii. 17.
1. 1 Cor. vii. 5 (ἦτε, *ye may be**, G L T Tr A ℵ.)
1. — xi. 17, 18, 20, 33, 34.
1. — xiv. 23 (ἔρχομαι, see come, No. 1, L.)
1. — 26.

* ἐπὶ τὸ αὐτὸ, together for the same purpose.

COME UNTO.

Where "UNTO" *is not the translation of a preposition* (εἰς *or* ἐπί), *for which see under* "COME" *and* "UNTO."

1. προσέρχομαι, *see* "COME," *No.* 3.

2. προσπορεύομαι, to go *or* come to *any one*, approach, *(non occ.)*

1. Matt. v. 1.
1. — viii. 5.
1. — xiii. 36.
1. — xv. 30
1. — xviii. 1.
1 — xix. 3.
1. — xxi. 23.
1. — xxiv. 3.
1. — xxvi. 7, 69, 73
1. Mark vi. 35.
2. — x. 35.
1. Acts x. 28.
1. — xviii. 2.
1. — xxiv. 23 (*om.* G ⇒ L T Tr A ℵ.)
1 Heb. iv. 16.
1. — vii. 25.
1. — xii. 18, 22.

COME UP.

ἀναβαίνω, *see* "COME," *No.* 13.

Matt xvii. 27.
Mark i 10.
John xii. 20.
Acts viii. 31, 39.
Acts x. 4
— xi. 2
Rev. iv. 1.
— xi. 12.
Rev xiii. 11.

COME UP AGAIN.

ἀναβαίνω, *see* "COME," *No.* 13.

Acts xx. 11.

COME UP WITH.

συναναβαίνω, ("COME," *No.* 13, *with* σύν, with, *implying co-operation prefixed,)* to go *or* come up together with, *(non occ.)*

Mark xv. 41. | Acts xiii. 31.

COME UPON.

Where "UPON" *is not the translation of a preposition* (εἰς), *for which see* "COME," *and* "UPON."

1. ἐπέρχομαι, *see* "COME," *No.* 5.

2. ἐφίστημι, *see* "COME," *No.* 25.

3. καταλαμβάνω, to take, receive, *with idea of eagerness; hence,* to lay hold of, seize.

1. Luke i. 35.
2. — ii. 9.
1. — xi. 22.
2. — xx. 1.
2. — xxi. 34, with ἐπί, [upon.
3. John xii. 35.
1. Acts i. 8, see margin.
2. Acts iv. 1.
2. — vi. 12.
1. — viii. 24.
2. — xii. 7.
1. — xiii. 40.
2. 1 Thes. v. 3.
1. Jas. v. 1.

COME WITH.

συνέρχομαι, *see* "COME," *No.* 4.

Luke xxiii. 55, with εἰμί, *to be.* | John xi. 33.
Acts x. 45.

COME (BE FULLY.)

συμπληρόω, to help to fill, to fill completely, to fill up altogether.

(a) *of time, pass.,* to be fulfilled, completed, *(occ.* Luke viii. 23; ix. 51.)

Acts ii. 1.

COME (BE TO.)

μέλλω, *see* "COME," *No.* 19.

Rom. v. 14. | Eph. i. 21.
1 Tim. iv. 8.

COME (HE THAT SHALL.)

ὁ ἐρχόμενος, *(part. of* "COME," *No.* 1, *with article,)* the one who is coming. *Not merely the one who is* about to come, *but* the coming one—*in whom there is a steadfast and firm belief that* He is coming (Matt. xi. 3; Luke vii. 19.) *The art. with pres. part., denoting not merely that which will immediately happen, but that which is certain to take place.*

Heb. x. 37.

COME (HE THAT SHOULD.)

Matt. xi. 3. | Luke vii. 19, 20.

COME (HE WHICH SHOULD.)

Acts xix. 4.

COME (THAT SHOULD.)

John vi. 14.

COME (THING TO.)

μέλλω, *see* "COME," *No.* 19, *(here only participle.)*

Rom. viii. 38. | Col. ii. 17.
1 Cor. iii. 22. | Heb. xi. 20.

COME (TIME TO.)

1 Tim. vi. 19.

COME (WHICH ART TO.)

ὁ ἐρχόμενος, *see* "COME (HE THAT SHALL.)"

Rev. xi. 17 (*om.* G L T Tr A ℵ.)

COME (WHICH IS TO.)

Rev. i. 4, 8 ; iv. 8.

COME (WHICH SHOULD.)

John xi. 27.

COME (WHICH WAS FOR TO.)

ὁ, μέλλων, the *one* who is on the point to come, *see* "COME," *No.* 19; ἔρχεσθαι, to come, *see* "COME," *No.* 1. — the one who is about to, certain to *or* destined to come.

Matt. xi. 14.

COMETH (HE THAT.)

ὁ ἐρχόμενος, *see* "COME (HE THAT SHALL.)"

Matt. iii. 11. | Matt. xxiii. 39.
— xxi. 9. | John i. 15
John iii. 31 twice.

COMETH (THAT.)

Luke xix. 38. | John xii. 13.

COMETH UPON (THAT WHICH.)

ἡ ἐπισύστασις, the crowd *(of cares, etc.)*

2 Cor. xi. 28 (ἐπίστασις, *the stopping or checking, concourse*, L ℵ.)

COMING (BE.)

ἔρχομαι, *see* "COME," *No.* 1.

Luke xxiii. 29. | John xi. 20.
John v. 7, 25, 28. | — xii. 12.
2 Cor. xiii. 1.

COMING (BE A.)

προσέρχομαι, *see* "COME," *No.* 3.

Luke ix. 42.

COMING (WHO.)

ὁ ἐρχουμενος, *see* "COME (HE THAT SHALL.)"

John i. 27.

COMING ON (BE.)

μέλλω, *see* "COME," *No.* 19, γίνομαι, *see* "COME," *No.* 11, — it was about to become [day.]

Acts xxvii. 33.

COMING ON (THOSE THINGS WHICH ARE.)

τὰ ἐπερχομένα, the things which are coming upon, *(not merely* which are about to, *but* which are certain to come upon.)

Luke xxi. 26.

CAME (HE THAT.)

ὁ ἐλθών, the *one* who came, *(the Aor. part. denoting* a thing *which happened once, a complete act.)*

1 John v. 6.

See also, BEHIND, COMING [noun], EARS, FULL, HITHER, MORNING, NEAR, NEWLY, NIGH, NOUGHT, REMEMBRANCE, ROUND, RUN, SHORT, STRAIGHT, TIDINGS, TIME.

COMELINESS.

εὐσχήμων, elegance of figure and bearing, gracefulness, decorum, *(non occ.)*

1 Cor. xii. 23.

COMELY.

εὐσχήμων, elegant in figure, mien and bearing, graceful; well-fashioned, well-formed, comely; *metaph.* decorus.

1 Cor. xii. 24.

COMELY (BE.)

πρέπω, to be conspicuous *among a number*, to be distinguished in *or* by *a thing, (properly of impressions on the senses,)* to become, beseem, suit.

(a) *impers.* it is fitting, it becomes, it suits.

1 Cor. xi. 13.

COMELY (THAT WHICH IS.)

εὐσχήμων, *see* "COMELY."

1 Cor. vii. 35, with art.

COMER THEREUNTO.

προσέρχομαι, *see* "COME," *No.* 3.

Heb. x. 1.

COMFORT [noun.]

1. παράκλησις, a calling near, a summons to one's side; *hence*, an admonitory, encouraging, *and* consolatory exhortation, invitation *or* entreaty, *(opp. to* παραίνεσις, warning.)
2. παραμυθία, a speaking near *or* with *any one, i.e. kindly, soothingly; implying persuasive power, and expressive of more tenderness than No.* 1. *(The termination of the word marks the action as incomplete and in progress.)*
3. παραμύθιον, a consolation, comfort, solace, *(differing from No.* 2 *only in the termination, which denotes the instrument wherewith the agent acts,* the speaking with which he persuades and soothes.)
4. παρηγορία, an addressing exhortation, a consolation *or* soothing, *(the verbal form of the word is used of medicines which* allay *irritation.)*

1. Acts ix. 31.
1. Rom. xv. 4.
2. 1 Cor. xiv. 3.
1. 2 Cor. i. 3 4.
1. —— vii. 4, 13.
3. Phil. ii. 1.
4. Col. iv. 11.

COMFORT (BE OF GOOD.)

1. θαρσέω, *(in N.T. only in imperative,)* be of good courage! take courage! cheer up! take heart! feel confidence!
2. εὐψυχέω, *(in N.T. only in imperative,)* be in good spirits! be animated!
3. παρακαλέω, to call to *one*, call near, to call for; *every kind of* speaking to, *which is meant to produce a particular effect, e.g., exhortation, encouragement, comfort, etc.*

1. Matt ix. 22.
1. Mark x. 49.
1. Luke viii. 48 (*om.* G→L
3. 2 Cor. xiii. 11. [T TrA א)
2. Phil ii 19.

COMFORT (-ED, -ETH.)

1. παρακαλέω, *see* "COMFORT (BE OF GOOD)," *No.* 3.
2. παραμυθέομαι, to speak near *or* with *any one, (i.e. kindly, soothingly,) hence*, to soothe, pacify, speak persuasively and tenderly.

1. Matt ii. 18.
1. —— v 4.
1. Luke xvi. 25
2. John xi 19, 31.
1. Acts xvi. 40
1. —— xx. 12 [gether (be)
— Rom. i. 12, see C to-
1 1 Cor. xiv. 31.
1. 2 Cor i. 4 3 times, 6.
1. —— ii. 7.
1. 2 Cor vii 6 twice, 7, 13.
1 Eph. vi. 22.
1. Col. ii 2
1. —— v 8.
2. 1 Thes ii 11.
1. —— iii. 2, 7.
1 —— iv. 18
1. —— v 11, marg. *exhort.*
2 —— 14.
1 2 Thes. ii. 17.

COMFORTED TOGETHER (BE.)

συμπαρακαλέω, *(No.* 1 *with* σύν, together, *prefixed,)* to call for *or* invite with, *at the same time. Pass.* to be comforted together with others, *i.e. in the society of men.*

Rom. i. 12.

COMFORTER.

παράκλητος, called to one's aid, *(prop. a verbal adj implying capability or adaptation for giving the aid.) Here as a subs. with article,* he who has been *or* may be called to help, *(esp. in a court of justice,* a legal assistant.) *Used of both the second and third persons in the Holy Trinity. (*1 John ii. 1, *so that there is one paraclete with us that we may not sin, and* 'another' *paraclete with the Father if we do sin.)*

John xiv. 16, 26, xv. 26 · xvi. 7.

COMFORTLESS.

ὀρφανός, orphan, bereaved, *(root prob. Sanscr.* rabh, *Lat.* rapis, *Eng.* reft,) *(occ.* Jas. i. 27.)

John xiv. 18, marg. *orphan.*

COMING [noun.]

1. παρουσία, the being *or* becoming present, *(from* πάρειμι, to be present,) *hence,* presence, arrival; a coming *which includes the idea of* a permanent dwelling from that coming onwards, *(occ.* 2 Cor. x. 10; Phil. ii. 12.

2. ἔλευσις, a coming, advent, *(from* ἔρχουμαι, *see No.* 5.)

3. εἴσοδος, way into *any place,* entrance.

4. ἀποκάλυψις, an uncovering, unveiling, manifestation. *(When used of a person it always denotes* the appearance *of the person.)*

5. ἔρχομαι, to come *or* go, denoting the act of coming *or* going.
   (a) ἔρχεσθαι, *pres. inf.* to come.
   (b) ἐρχόμενος, *pres. part.* coming, *(not merely about to come but actually* coming.)
   (c) ἐλθεῖν, *2nd aor. inf.* to have come.
   (d) ἐλθών, *2nd aor. part.* having come.

1. Matt. xxiv. 3, 27, 37, 39.
5c. —— 48 (*om.* L Tr ℵ.)
5d. —— xxv. 27.
5a. Luke xii. 45.
5b. —— xviii. 5.
5d. —— xix. 23.
2. Acts vii. 52.
3. —— xiii. 24.
5c. Rom. xv. 22.
4. 1 Cor. i. 7.
1. —— xv. 23.
1. 1 Cor. xvi. 17.
1. 2 Cor. vii. 6, 7.
1. Phil. i. 26.
1. 1 Thes. ii. 19.
1. —— iii. 13.
1. —— iv. 15.
1. —— v. 23.
1. 2 Thes. ii. 1, 8, 9.
1. Jas. v. 7, 8.
1. 2 Pet. i. 16.
1. —— iii. 4, 12.
1. 1 John ii. 28.

COMMAND (-ED, -EST, -ETH, -ING.)

1. κελεύω, to urge *or* drive on, incite; order *or* command *something to be done.*

2. παραγγέλλω, to announce beside *or* near to *any one, i.e.* to hand an announcement from one to another, pass it on; *then,* to give the word, give orders, *and so gen.,* to order, recommend, exhort, *(not so strong as No.* 1.)

3. ἐντέλλομαι, *(Mid.)* to enjoin upon, charge with.

4. ἐπιτάσσω, to appoint over, put in command; to put upon *one* as a duty, to enjoin.

5. διατάσσω, to arrange throughout, to dispose in order; *then,* to set fully in order, arrange.
   (a) *Mid.* appoint, ordain, post.

6. προστάσσω, to arrange *or* set in order towards *or* to *any person or thing; hence,* to order towards *or* to *any one,* to give as a command, to prescribe to.

7. εἶπον, to say, to speak, *i.e. to utter definite words, (thus differing from* λαλέω, *which is simply to use the voice,)* and words successively spoken, *(thus differing from* λέγω, *which refers to the sentiment.) Often modified by the context where the sense lays more in the adjuncts than in what is said; hence,* to enquire, answer, call, tell, bid, command.

8. ῥέω, *(an obs. root, furnishing tenses for No.* 7,) to say, *but differing from No.* 7, *and words referred to under it, in that it relates not to the words only but to the mind and will of the speaker,* to enunciate, give forth the thought; *hence, it includes the notion of* denouncing, objecting, affirming, and commanding, *(never means to interrogate.)*

7. Matt. iv. 3.
6. —— viii. 4.
2. —— x. 5.
5. —— xi. 1.
1. —— xiv. 9, 19.
3. —— xv. 4 (No. 7, G ~ L Tr.)
1. —— 35 (No. 2, L Tr ℵ.)
1. —— xviii. 25.
3. —— xix. 7.
6. —— xxi. 6 (συντάσσω, *to arrange* or *set in order together* or *with* any one, *direct,* L T Tr A.)
1. —— xxvii. 58, 64.
3. —— xxviii. 20.
4. Mark i. 27.
6. —— 44.
7. —— v. 43.
2. —— vi. 8.
4. —— 27, 39.
2. —— viii. 6.
7. —— 7.
3. —— x. 3.
7. —— 49.
3. —— xi. 6 (No. 7, G ~ L T Tr A ℵ.)
3. —— xiii. 34.
7. Luke iv. 3.
4. —— 36.
6. —— v. 14.
4. —— viii. 25.
2. —— 29.
4. —— 31.
5. —— 55.
2. —— ix. 21.
7. —— 54.
4. —— xiv. 22.
5. Luke xvii. 9, 10.
1. —— xviii. 40.
7. —— xix. 15.
3. John viii. 5 (*ap.*)
3. —— xv. 14, 17.
2. Acts i. 4.
1. —— iv. 15.
2. —— 18.
2. —— v. 28.
1. —— 34.
2. —— 40.
1. —— viii. 38.
6. —— 33
2. —— 42.
6. —— 48.
1. —— xii. 19.
3. —— xiii. 47.
2. —— xv. 5.
2. —— xvi. 18.
1. —— 22.
2. —— xvii. 30.
5. —— xviii. 2.
1. —— xxi. 33, 34.
1. —— xxii. 24, 30.
4. —— xxiii. 2.
1. —— 3, 10.
5. —— 31.
1. —— 35.
1. —— xxiv. 8 (*ap.*)
5a. —— 23.
1. —— xxv. 6, 17, 21.
1. —— xxvii. 43.
2. 1 Cor. vii. 10.
7. 2 Cor. iv. 6.
2. 1 Thes. iv. 11.
2. 2 Thes. iii. 4, 6, 10, 12.
2. 1 Tim. iv. 11.
— Heb. xii. 20, see commanded (be.)
8. Rev. ix. 4.

COMMANDED (BE.)

διαστέλλω, to put asunder, to set apart, distinguish, *hence*,

(a) *in Mid.* to state distinctly, explain clearly, command expressly.

(b) *Pass.* to be commanded *or* charged.

b. Heb. xii. 20.

COMMANDMENT (-S.)

1. *ἐντολή*, that which has been enjoined, an injunction, charge, precept, a single precept ; *pl.* moral injunctions, prohibitions, *(occ.* Mark x. 5; Heb. ix. 19.)

2. *ἔνταλμα*, the thing enjoined, a commission and command, *(non occ.)*

3. *ἐπιταγή*, *lit.* imposition of tribute ; *hence*, that which has been commanded by supreme authority, express injunction of law, *(occ.* Tit. ii. 15.)

4. *διάταγμα*, the thing imposed by law, an order, *(non occ.)*

5. *παραγγελία*, a proclamation, public notice ; *esp. as a military term*, word of command ; *then*, any annoucement *or* declaration *by authority.*

1. Matt v. 19.
— —— viii.18, see C (give)
1. —— xv. 3.
1. —— 6 (*λόγος*, *word*, L Tr) (*νόμος*, *law*, T A ℵ)
2. —— 9.
1. —— xix. 17.
1. —— xxii. 36, 38, 40.
2. Mark vii. 7.
1. —— 8, 9.
1. —— x. 19.
1. —— xii. 28, 29 (*ap*), 30 (*ap*), 31.
1. Luke i. 6.
1. —— xv. 29.
1. —— xviii. 20.
1. —— xxiii. 56.
1. John x. 18.
1. —— xi. 57.
1. —— xii. 49, 50.
1. —— xiii. 34.
1. —— xiv. 15, 21.
— —— 31, see C (give.)
1. —— xv. 10 twice, 12.
— Acts i. 2, } see C
— —— xv. 24, } (give.)
.. —— xvii. 15.
— —— xxiii. 30, see C (give)
— —— xxv. 23, see C (at one's.)
1. Rom. vii. 8, 9, 10, 11, 12, 13.
1. —— xiii. 9.
3. —— xvi. 26.
3. 1 Cor vii. 6
1. —— 19.
3. —— 25
1. —— xiv. 37 (*om.* T A[b]) (sing. instead of pl. L Tr A[b] ℵ)
3. 2 Cor. viii. 8.
1. Eph. ii. 15.
1. —— vi. 2.
2. Col. ii. 22.
1. —— iv. 10.
5. 1 Thes. iv. 2.
3. 1 Tim. i. 1.
5. —— 5.
1. —— vi. 14.
3. Titus i. 3.
1. —— 14.
1. Heb. vii. 5, 16, 18.
— —— xi. 22, see C (give.)
4. —— 23 (*δόγμα*, *that which seems true to one, a public resolution, decree*, L.)
1. 2 Pet. ii. 21.
1. —— iii. 2.
1. 1 John ii. 3, 4, 7 3 times, 8.
1. —— iii. 22, 23 twice, 24.
1. —— iv. 21.
1. —— v. 2, 3 twice.
1. 2 John 4, 5, 6 twice.
1. Rev. xii. 17.
1. —— xiv. 12.
1. —— xxii. 14 (*ap.*)

COMMANDMENT (AT ONE'S.)

κελεύω, *see* "COMMAND," *No.* 1.

Acts xxv. 23.

COMMANDMENT (GIVE.)

1. *ἐντέλλομαι*, *(Mid.)* to enjoin upon, charge with.

2. *διαστέλλομαι*, *(Mid.)* to state distinctly, explain clearly, command expressly.

3. *κελεύω*, *see* "COMMAND," *No.* 1.

4. *παραγγέλλω*, *see* "COMMAND," *No.* 2.

3. Matt. viii. 18.
1. John xiv. 31 (*ἐντολὴν δίδωμι*, *to give an injunction*, see No. 1 above, L Tr.)
1 Acts i. 2.
2. —— xv. 24.
4. —— xxiii. 30.
1. Heb. xi. 22.

COMMEND (-ED, -ETH, -ING.)

1. *συνίστημι*, (a) *trans.* to place *or* set together ; *of persons*, to introduce *to one's acquaintance and favourable notice*, *hence*, to commend, *to represent as worthy.*

(b) *intrans.* to stand with *or* together, to put together, compose, constitute.

2. *παρίστημι*, (a) *trans.* to place by *or* beside, to place *or* set before *any one*, *hence*, to commend.

(b) *intrans.* to stand by *or* near, to be at hand.

3. *παρατίθημι*, to put *or* place near *any one*, *as food*, *or as a teacher.*

(a) *Mid.* to place with *any one on one's own account*, *i.e.* to commit, to entrust as a deposit.

4. *ἐπαινέω*, *lit.* to praise upon ; to applaud, laud.

4. Luke xvi. 8.
3a. —— xxiii. 46.
3a. Acts xiv. 23.
3a. —— xx. 32.
1a. Rom. iii. 5.
1a. —— v. 8.
1a. —— xvi. 1.
2a. 1 Cor. viii. 5.
1a. 2 Cor. iii. 1.
1a. —— iv. 2.
1a. —— v. 12. (*approve.*)
1a. —— vi. 4, marg. (text, *approve.*)
1a. —— x. 12, 18 twice.
1a. —— xii. 11.

COMMENDATION (OF.)

συστατικός, drawing together, making compact ; introductory, commentary ; *with ἐπιστολή it denotes* a letter of introduction, *(non occ.)*

2 Cor. iii. 1 1st, 1 2nd (*om.* G→ L Tr A ℵ.)

COMMISSION.

ἐπιτροπή, a reference of *a thing* to *another*, *a receiving of* full powers, *(non occ.)*

Acts xxvi. 12.

COMMIT (-ED, -ETH, -ING.)

1. *ποιέω*, to make, *i.e.* to form, bring about, cause; *gen.* to do, *i.e. habitually* to perform, practise, *i.e.* to pursue a course of action.
2. *πράσσω*, to do, to work, *(expressing an action as continued or not yet completed; denoting what one does habitually.)*
3. *τίθημι*, to put, to set, to place.
   (a) *Mid.* to set *or* put for one's self, *i.e.* on one's own part *or* behalf, by one's own order, to assign.
4. *παρατίθημι*, to put *or* place near *any one*.
   (a) *Mid.* to put *or* place with *any one on one's own account, i.e.* to entrust, deposit
5. *δίδωμι*, to give, *(with implied notion of* giving freely, unforced, *and of* one's own accord,) to give into the hands, power *or* possession of any one.
6. *ἐάω*, to let, suffer, allow; to leave to, commit to
7. *ἐργάζομαι*, to work, labour; *used of all kinds of labour; metaph.* to work *good or evil*, to commit, practise.
8. *πορνεύω*, to commit fornication.

1. Mark xv. 7.
1. Luke xii. 48 1st.
4a. —— 48 2nd.
— —— xvi. 11, see C to one's trust.
— John ii. 24, see C unto.
5. —— v. 22.
1. —— viii. 34.
2. Acts xxv. 11, 25.
6. —— xxvii. 40, margin, *leave*.
1. —— xxviii. 17.
2. Rom. i. 32.
2. —— ii. 2.
— —— iii. 2, } see C unto.
— 1 Cor. ix. 17, }
8. —— x. 8 2nd.
5a. 2 Cor. v. 19, marg. *put*.
1. —— xi. 7.
2. —— xii. 21.
— Gal. ii. 7, see C unto.
— 1 Tim. i. 11, see C to my trust (be.)
4a. —— 18.
- —— vi. 20, see C to one's trust (that which is.)
— 2 Tim. i. 12, see C unto him (that which I have.)
— —— 14, see C unto one (that thing which is.)
4a. —— ii. 2.
— Titus i. 3, see C unto (be.)
7. Jas. ii. 9.
1. —— v. 15.
— 1 Pet. iv. 19, see C the keeping of.
1. 1 John iii. 4, 8, 9.

COMMIT THE KEEPING OF.

παρατίθημι, *(Mid.) see* "COMMIT," *No.* 1a.

1 Pet. iv. 19.

COMMIT TO ONE'S TRUST.

πιστεύω, to believe, rely upon, trust, put confidence in.

(a) *with Dat. of person, and Acc. of the thing*, to entrust or confide anything to anyone..

Luke xvi. 11.

COMMIT UNTO.

a. John ii. 24.
a. Rom. iii. 2.
a. 1 Cor. ix. 17.
a. Gal. ii. 7.

COMMITTED TO MY TRUST (BE.)

πιστεύομαι, *(Pass. of above)*, any thing is entrusted to me, *or without an object*, to be committed unto me.

1 Tim. i. 11.

COMMITTED UNTO ME (BE.)

Titus i. 3.

COMMITTED UNTO ONE (THAT THING WHICH IS.)

παρακαταθήκη, any thing deposited with one, *(esp.* of money *or* property entrusted to one's care.)

2 Tim. i. 14 (*παραθήκη, a deposit*, G L T Tr A ℵ.)

COMMITTED UNTO HIM (THAT WHICH I HAVE.)

{ *ἡ*, the, *παραθήκη*, deposit, *μοῦ*, of me, } my deposit.

2 Tim. i. 12.

COMMITTED TO ONE'S TRUST (THAT WHICH IS.)

παρακαταθήκη, any thing deposited with one, *(esp.* of money *or* property entrusted to one's care.)

1 Tim. vi. 20 (G∾) (*παραθήκη, a deposit*, G L T Tr A ℵ.)

See also, ADULTERY, FORNICATION, SACRILEGE, TRUST, UNGODLY.

COMMODIOUS (NOT.)

ἀνεύθετος, not conveniently placed.

Acts xxvii. 12.

COMMON.

1. κοινός, pertaining equally to all, *i.e.* common; *in a Levitical sense*, not bound, not forbidden; *hence*, not sacred, that which is ceremonially unlawful *or* unholy.

2. δημόσιος, belonging to the common people *or* state, public.

3. πολύς, *of number*, many, numerous; *of space*, far, far and wide, wide-stretched.

(a) *with article, (lit.* the wide-stretched multitude, Mark xii. 37.)

— Matt. xxvii. 27, see hall.
1. Mark vii. 2, marg. (text, *defiled.*)
3a. — xii. 37.
1. Acts ii. 44.
1. — iv. 32.
2. — v. 18.
1. — x. 14.
— Acts x. 15, see C (call.)
1. — 28.
1. — xi. 8.
— — 9, see C (call.)
1. Rom. xiv. 14 twice, marg. (text, *unclean.*)
— 1 Cor. x. 13, see man.
1. Titus i. 4.
1. Jude 3.

COMMON (CALL.)

κοινόω, to make κοινόν, *(see No.* 1), carrying out the act which is proper to κοινός, to make common.

Acts x. 15; xi. 9.

COMMONLY.

ὅλως, wholly, altogether; *also*, everywhere, generally.

1 Cor. v. 1.

See also, REPORT.

COMMONWEALTH.

πολιτεία, the relation in which a citizen stands to the state, the condition, rights of a citizen, citizenship; *then*, the civil polity, the condition of a state, *esp.* a well ordered republican government, *(occ.* Acts xxii. 28.)

Eph. ii. 12.

COMMOTION (-S.)

ἀκαταστασία, a being unstable, unsettled; a state of disorder, tumult, confusion.

Luke xxi. 9.

COMMUNE.

διαλαλέω, to speak to and fro, *i.e.* to talk with *any one*, to converse with, *(denoting simply* the using of the organ of *utterance without any reference to the words or the sentiment.)*

Luke vi. 11.

COMMUNE TOGETHER.

ὁμιλέω, to be in a crowd *or* in company with *any one*, to have intercourse with; *hence*, to converse with.

Luke xxiv. 15.

COMMUNE WITH.

1. συλλαλέω, to speak *or* talk with *any one (without reference to the words or sentiment.)*

2. ὁμιλέω, *see* "COMMUNE TOGETHER."

1. Luke xxii. 4. | 2. Acts xxiv. 26.

COMMUNICATE.

1. ἀνατίθεμαι, *(Mid.)* to place before, *i.e.* to delare to *any one*, to make known, *(occ.* Acts xxv. 14.)

2. κοινωνέω, to have *a thing* in common, have a share; *of things*, to partake of; *of persons*, to partake with.

3. κοινωνία, the act of partaking *or* sharing, *i.e.* participation, communion.

1. Gal. ii. 2.
2. — vi. 6.
2. Phil. iv. 15.
3. Heb. xiii. 16.

COMMUNICATE (WILLING TO.)

κοινωνικός, fitted for communication, apt *or* ready to communicate.

1. Tim. vi. 18, marg. *sociable.*

COMMUNICATE WITH.

συγκοινωνέω, to be partaker with others, to share with others in *any thing.*

Phil. iv. 14.

COMMUNICATION.

λόγος, the word *(spoken, not written.) In a formal sense*, a word *as* forming part of what is spoken; *as a*

means or instrument (not as a product *or* result), the speaking; *in a material sense*, the word *as that which is spoken*, an exposition *or* account *which one gives.*

2. κοινωνία, *see* "COMMUNICATE," *No.* 3.
3. ὁμιλία, a being together *or* in company with *any one*, intercourse, (*Eng.* homily), *(non occ.)*

1. Matt. v. 37.
1. Luke xxiv. 17.
3. 1 Cor. xv. 33.
1. Eph. iv. 29.
— Col. iii. 8, see filthy.
2. Philem. 6.

COMMUNION.

κοινωνία, *see* "COMMUNICATE," *No.* 3.

1 Cor. x. 16 twice. | 2 Cor. vi. 14.
2 Cor. xiii. 14.

COMPACTED (BE.)

συμβιβάζω, to make come together, to bring together; to join *or* knit together, to unite.

(a) *Pass.* to be put together.

a. Eph. iv. 16.

COMPANION.

1. κοινωνός, a partner, partaker, companion.
2. συγκοινωνός, a joint-partaker, copartner, companion with.

— Acts xix. 29, see travel.
— Phil. ii. 25, see labour.
1. Heb. x. 33.
2. Rev. i. 9 (No. 1. G∾.)

COMPANY (-IES) [noun.]

1. ὄχλος, a throng of people, an irregular crowd; *esp.* the mob, *(opp. to* δῆμος, the people,) a confused multitude.
2. ὅμιλος, any assembled people, a throng *or* crowd, *(from* ὅμος, at the same *place or time*, together,) *(non occ.)*
3. πλῆθος, fulness, *hence*, a multitude, a great number, *(from* πλήθω, to be *or* become full.)
4. συνοδία, a journeying together, a company of travellers, a caravan.

— Mark vi. 39, see C (by.)
4. Luke ii. 44.
1. — v. 29.
1. — vi. 17.
— Luke ix. 14, see C (in a.)
1. — — 38.
1. — xi. 27.
1. — xii. 13.
3. Luke xxiii. 27.
— — xxiv. 22, see C (our)
1. John vi. 5.
— Acts i. 21, see C with.
— — iv. 23, see C (one's own.)
1. — vi. 7.
— — x. 28, see C (keep.)
— — xiii. 13, see C (Paul and his.)
— Acts xvii. 5, see C (gather a.)
— — xxi. 8, see C (we that were of Paul's.)
— 1 Cor. v. 9, see C with.
— — 11, see C (keep.)
— 2 Thes. iii. 14, see C with (have.)
— Heb. xii. 22, see C (an innumerable.)
2. Rev. xviii. 17 (*ap.*)

COMPANY (AN INNUMERABLE.)

μυριάς, a myriad, *i.e.* ten thousand, often used for an indefinitely large number.

Heb. xii. 22 (pl.)

COMPANY (GATHER A.)

ὀχλοποιέω, to make a crowd *or* riot, raise a mob, *(non occ.)*

Acts xvii. 5.

COMPANY (IN A.)

κλισία, a place for lying down *or* reclining, *hence*, any temporary *or* slight building *as used by shepherds or soldiers. In Acc. pl. as here*, companies *of people* sitting at meals, table parties, *(non occ.)*

Luke ix. 14.

COMPANY (ONE'S OWN.)

ἴδιος, own, one's own, *(as pertaining to a private person, and not to the public.)*

Acts iv. 23 (pl.)

COMPANY (OUR.)

{ ἐκ, of,
{ ἡμῶν, us.

Luke xxiv. 13.

COMPANY (PAUL AND HIS.)

{ οἱ, the *people*, περὶ, around about τον Παῦλον, Paul, } those about Paul, *(including himself)* *i.e.* Paul and his companions.

Acts xiii. 13.

COMPANY (WE THAT WERE OF PAUL'S.)

Acts xxi. 8 (*ap.*)

COMPANIES (BY.)

συμπόσιαν, a drinking together, a drinking party; *hence, any* table-party; *here,* συμπόσια συμπόσια, *(i.e. adverbially and distributively,)* by table-parties—by table-parties, *(non occ.)*

Mark vi. 39.

COMPANY (KEEP) [verb.]

1. κολλάω, to glue together, to make cohere, join fast together.
   (a) *In N.T. Mid.* to adhere cleave to, *of things;* to join one's self unto, *of persons,* to associate with.
2. συναναμίγνυμι, to mix up together.
   (a) *Pass. or Mid.* to mingle together with, have intercourse *or* keep company with.

1a. Acts x. 28. | 2a. 1 Cor. v. 11.

COMPANY WITH.

1. συνέρχομαι, to come *or* go with *any one, i.e.* to accompany; *then,* to come together, to convene, to assemble.
2. συναναμίγνυμι, *see above, No.* 2a.

1. Acts i. 21. | 2a. 1 Cor. v. 9.

COMPANY WITH (HAVE.)

2. 2 Thes. iii. 14.

COMPARE.

παραβάλλω, to throw beside *or* near, to cast before, *as food to animals; then,* to throw *or* place side by side *so as* to compare.

Mark iv. 30 (*τίθημι, to put, set, place,* L T Tr A ℵ.)

COMPARE AMONG.

συγκρίνω, to separate distinct things and then bring them together into one; *hence,* to join together, combine; *later,* to place together and then judge of, *i.e.* to compare, to estimate by comparison.

2 Cor. x. 12.

COMPARE WITH.

1 Cor. ii. 13 | 2 Cor. x. 12.

COMPARED WITH (TO BE.)

πρός, towards.
(a) *with Gen.* hitherwards, belonging to the character of.
(b) *with Dat.* near, hard by, *(resting in a direction towards.)*
(c) *with Acc.* hitherwards, to, *of literal direction; of mental direction,* towards; *then, from general notion of mental direction arises that of estimation or proportion,* in consideration of.

c. Rom. viii. 18.

COMPARISON.

παραβολή, a placing side by side, *hence,* comparison *or* similitude.

Mark iv. 30.

COMPASS (FETCH A.)

περιέρχομαι, to go about, to wander up and down, *used of a ship sailing on an irregular course with unfavourable winds.*

Acts xxviii. 13.

COMPASS (-ED) [verb.]

1. κυκλόω, to make a circle, encircle; move in a circle.
2. περιάγω, to lead about, *intrans.* to go about, go up and down.

2. Matt. xxiii. 15. | 1. Luke xxi. 20.

COMPASS ABOUT.

κυκλόω, *see* "COMPASS," *No.* 1.

Heb. xi. 30.
Rev. xx. 9 (*κυκλεύω, surround,* G ~ L T Tr A.)

COMPASS ROUND.

περικυκλόω, to make a circle round, encircle round about.

Luke xix. 43.

COMPASSED ABOUT WITH (BE.)

περίκειμαι, to lie around, *also,* to be laid around, to have round *one.*

Heb. xii. 1.

COMPASSED WITH (BE.)

Heb. v. 2.

COMPASSION (BE MOVED WITH.)

σπλαγχνίζομαι, to feel the bowels yearn, to have compassion; to pity.

Matt. ix. 36. — xiv. 14. Mark vi. 34. Matt. xviii. 27. Mark i. 41.

COMPASSION (HAVE.)

Matt. xv. 32. — xx. 34. Mark viii. 2. Luke xv. 20. Mark ix. 22. Luke vii. 13. — x. 33.

COMPASSION OF (HAVE.)

1. ἐλεέω, to show mercy, *(more than have compassion)*, to have the desire of relieving the miserable, to show kindness by beneficence *or* help.
2. συμπαθέω, to suffer with another, to be affected in like manner, *(occ.* Heb. iv. 15.)

2. Heb. x. 34. | 1. Jude 22 *(ap.)*

COMPASSION ON (HAVE.)

1. ἐλεέω, *see above, No.* 1.
2. οἰκτείρω, to have merely pity *or* a sense of unhappiness for the ills of others; to have a subjective distress at witnessing misfortune, etc. *(weaker than No.* 1.)
3. μετριοπαθέω, to be moderate in one's passions, *hence*, to be gentle, indulgent *toward any one.*

1. Matt. xviii. 33. 1. Mark v. 19. 2. Rom. ix. 15 twice. | 3. Heb. v. 2, marg. *reasonably bear with.*

COMPASSION ONE OF ANOTHER (HAVING.)

συμπαθής, feeling *or* suffering with another, like-affected, the same in feeling.

1 Pet. iii. 8 (pl.)

See also, BOWELS.

COMPEL (-ED, -EST.)

1. ἀναγκάζω, to necessitate, constrain, *(by persuasion or force.)*
2. ἀγγαρεύω, to despatch as an ἄγγαρος, (a mounted courier *kept at regular stages through Persia, with power of empressment); hence*, to press into service for a journey in the manner of an ἄγγαρος.

— Matt. v. 41, see C to go. 2. — xxvii. 32. 2. Mark xv. 21. 1. Luke xiv. 23. 1. Acts xxvi. 11. 1. 2 Cor. xii. 11. 1. Gal. ii. 3, 14.

COMPEL TO GO.

2. Matt. v. 41.

COMPLAINER (-S.)

μεμψίμοιρος, finding fault with one's lot, *i.e.* discontented, repining.

Jude 16.

COMPLAINT.

1. αἰτίαμα, charge, guilt *imputed.*
2. μομφή, fault found, blame, censure, *i.e.* occasion of complaint.

1. Acts xxv. 7 *(ap.)*
2. Col. iii. 13, marg. (text, *quarrel.)*

COMPLETE.

πληρόω, to make full, fill up.

(a) *Pass.* to be filled full, to be fully furnished.

a. Col. ii. 10.
a. — iv. 12, marg. *filled* (πληροφορέω, *to bear* or *bring fully*, hence, *to give full assurance, persuade fully*, G ∾ L T Tr A ℵ.)

COMPREHEND (-ED.)

καταλαμβάνω, (a) to seize upon, lay hold of, *with the idea of eagerness or suddenness*, to seize *with the mind* to comprehend, *hence*,

(b) *Mid.* to comprehend for one's self, perceive.

a. John i. 5. | b. Eph. iii. 18.

COMPREHENDED (BE BRIEFLY.)

ἀνακεφαλαιόομαι, to comprehend several things under one, to reduce under one head, *(occ.* Eph. i. 10.)

Rom. xiii. 9.

CONCEITS (IN YOUR OWN.)

{ παρά, with, *in the estimation of.*
{ ἑαυτοις, yourselves, your own selves.

Rom. xi. 25 (ἐν, *in, among*, instead of παρά, T Tr A.)
Rom. xii. 16.

CONCEIVE (-ED.)

1. συλλαμβάνω, to take together, *prop.* to enclose in the hands; *(Lat.* comprehendere, *Eng.* to comprehend.) *Spoken of persons, gen.* to take *or* seize altogether, *all around, stronger than* λαμβάνω, *from the idea of* clasping together, grasping with the hands. *Spoken of females,* to conceive.
2. γεννάω, *of men,* to beget; *of women,* to bear, bring forth.
3. { ἔχω, to have, κοίτη, a lying down, place of repose, bed, *esp.* the marriage-bed, } to conceive.
4. { εἰς, unto, καταβολή, a casting down, *of seed,* a casting in, } for conception.
5. τίθημι, to set, put, place, lay.
   (a) *Mid.* to set *or* put for one's self, to fix, *as in the mind.*

2. Matt. i. 20.
1. Luke i. 24, 31, 36.
1. —— ii. 21.
5a. Acts v. 4.
3. Rom. ix. 10.
4. Heb. xi. 11.
1. Jas. i. 15.

CONCERN (THE THINGS WHICH.)

τὰ, the *things; followed by Gen. of noun, lit.* the things of my infirmity.

2 Cor. xi. 30.

CONCERN (THOSE THINGS WHICH.)

{ τὰ, the *things.*
{ περί, about, concerning, *(chiefly as the object of thought, emotion, knowledge, etc.)*

Acts xxviii. 31.

CONCERNING.

1. περί, around.
   (a) *with Gen.* (around and separate from) about, concerning, *chiefly as the object of thought, emotion, knowledge, discourse, etc.*
   (b) *with Acc.* (around and towards) around, *of place;* about, *of time;* about, in reference to, *of any object of thought.*
2. εἰς, into, to, unto, with a view to, *marking the direction of thought or speech.*
3. κατά, down.
   (a) *with Gen.* down from, against.
   (b) *with Acc.* down upon, over against, *hence,* according to, in reference *to some standard of comparison stated or implied.*
4. ὑπέρ, over.
   (a) *with Gen.* over and separate from, on behalf of, *as though bending* over *to protect; then, simply* about, in reference to, with *or* without the idea of benefit.
   (b) *with Acc.* over and towards, beyond.
5. πρός, towards.
   (a) *with Gen.* hitherwards, conducive to.
   (b) *with Dat.* resting in the direction towards, near.
   (c) *with Acc.* to, *of literal direction;* towards, against, *of mental direction; from this mental direction arises estimation,* in consideration of; *and intention,* in order to.

1a. Matt. iv. 6.
1a. —— xi. 7.
1a. —— xvi. 11.
1a. Mark v. 16.
1a. —— vii. 17 (*om.* G ∾ L T Tr A ℵ.)
1a. Luke ii. 17.
1a. —— vii. 24.
— —— xxii. 37, see C (the things.)
1a. —— xxiv. 19.
— ——— 27, see C (the things.)
1a. ——— 44.
1a. John vii. 12, 32.
1a. —— ix. 18.
1a. —— xi. 19.
1a. Acts i. 16.
2. —— ii. 25.
— —— viii. 12, see C (the things.)
— —— xiii. 34, see C that (as.) [things.)
— —— xix. 8, see C (the
1a. ——— 39 (περαιτέρω, *beyond,* instead of περὶ ἑτέρων, *concerning other matters,* L T Tr.)
1a. —— xxi. 24.
1a. —— xxii. 18.
1a. —— xxiii. 15.
1a. —— xxiv. 24.
1a. Acts xxv. 16.
1a. —— xxviii. 21.
— ——— 22, see C (as.)
1a. ——— 23 (with article)
1a. Rom. i. 3.
— —— ix. 5, see C (as.)
4a. ——— 27.
— —— xi. 28, see C (as.)
2. —— xvi. 19.
1a. 1 Cor. vii. 25.
— —— viii. 34, see C that
1a. —— xii. 1. [(as.)
1a. —— xvi. 1.
2. 2 Cor. viii. 23.
— —— xi. 21, see C (as.)
3b. Eph. iv. 22.
2. —— v. 32 1st.
2. ——— 32 2nd (*om.* L Ab)
3b. Phil. iii. 6.
— —— iv. 15, see C (as.)
1a. 1 Thes. iii. 2 (No. 4a, G L T Tr A ℵ.)
1a. —— iv. 13.
2. —— v. 18.
1b. 1 Tim. i. 19.
1b. —— vi. 21.
1b. 2 Tim. ii. 18.
1b. —— iii. 8.
1a. Heb. vii. 14.
1a. —— xi. 20, 22.
1a. 1 John ii. 26. [in.)
5c. —— v. 14, marg. (text,

CONCERNING (AS.)

1. *περί*, *(with Gen.) see* "CONCERNING," *No.* 1*a*.
2. *κατά*, *(with Acc.) see* "CONCERNING," *No.* 3*b*.
3. { *εἰς*, for, / *λογός*, a word *spoken (not written,)* the word *or* account *which one gives*, } for an account.

1. Acts xxviii. 22.
2. Rom. ix. 5.
2. —— xi. 28.
1. 1 Cor. viii. 4.
2. 2 Cor. xi. 21.
3. Phil. iv. 15.

CONCERNING THAT (AS.)

ὅτι, that, because, inasmuch as, seeing that. *It introduces* that which rests on a patent fact.

Acts xiii. 34.

CONCERNING (THE THINGS.)

{ *τὰ*, the *things*.
{ *περί*, concerning, *(see above, No.* 1.*)*

Luke xxii. 37.
—— xxiv. 27.
Acts viii. 12.
—— xix. 8.

CONCISION.

κατατομή, a cutting off, mutilation. *Used contemptuously for the Jewish circumcision in contrast with the true spiritual circumcision, (non occ.)*

Phil. iii. 2.

CONCLUDE (-ED.)

1. *συγκλείω*, to shut up, hem in, enclose; to close up, conclude, *(occ.* Luke v. 6; Gal. iii. 23.)
2. *κρίνω*, to divide, to separate, *hence*, to separate from, select; to come to a decision, to judge, *(not necessarily for condemnation.)*
3. *λογίζομαι*, to occupy one's self with reckonings *or* calculations, *hence*, to reckon, count; value, esteem, *or* take for; to account, conclude, *or* infer.

2. Acts xxi. 25.
3. Rom. iii. 28.
1. Rom. xi. 32, marg. *shut up together.*
1. Gal. iii. 22.

CONCORD.

συμφώνησις, a speaking *a thing* together with another, *hence*, agreement, unison, *(non occ.)*

2 Cor. vi. 15.

CONCOURSE.

συστροφή, a turning *or* winding together, *then*, that which is rolled up together, any dense mass *as of men*, *(occ.* Acts xxiii. 12.)

Acts xix. 40.

CONCUPISCENCE.

ἐπιθυμία, desire, yearning, longing; *denoting* the inward passion of the mind *in a good or bad sense.* The mental desire *(not the object desired.)*

Rom. vii. 7, marg. (text, *lust.*)
—— 8.
Col. iii. 5.
1 Thes. iv. 5.

CONDEMN (-ED, -EST.)

1. *κρίνω*, to separate, to distinguish, to select, to choose out *the good, hence, gen.* to judge, *i.e.* to form *or* give an opinion after separating and considering *the particulars of a case (not necessarily implying condemnation.)*
2. *κατακρίνω*, to give judgment *(as above)* against; *hence*, to condemn, *the crime or punishment being implied, (occ.* Mark xvi. 16 *(ap.)*; Rom. xiv. 23.)
3. { *πρός*, towards, in reference to, / *κατάκρισις*, condemnation, censure, blame.
4. *καταδικάζω*, to exercise *δίκη* (right, order, law) against *any one; with the definite signification*, to pronounce judgment against, to condemn, *(non occ.)*
5. *καταγινώσκω*, to know *or* note against *any one to his disadvantage, hence*, to think ill of, to condemn, *(occ.* Gal. ii. 11.)

4. Matt. xii. 7, 37.
2. —— 41, 42.
2. —— xx. 18.
2. —— xxvii. 3.
2 Mark x. 33.
2. —— xiv. 64.
4. Luke vi. 37 twice.
2. —— xi. 31, 32.
— —— xxiv. 20, see C (to be.)
1. John iii. 17, 18 twice.
2. —— viii. 10 *(ap.)*, 11 *(ap.)*
1. Acts xiii. 27.
2. Rom. ii. 1.
2. —— viii. 3, 34.
1. —— xiv. 22.
2. 1 Cor. xi. 32.
3. 2 Cor. vii. 3.

— Titus ii. 8, see C (that cannot be.)	4. Jas. v. 6.
— — iii. 11, see C of one's self.	2. —— 9 (No. 1, G L T Tr A ℵ.)
2. Heb. xi. 7.	2. 2 Pet. ii. 6.
	5. 1 John iii. 20, 21.

CONDEMNED OF ONE'S SELF.

αὐτοκατάκριτος, self-condemned *(not directly or explicitly, but by* doing in his own case that which he condemns in general), *(non occ.)*

Titus iii. 11.

CONDEMNED (TO BE.)

{ εἰς, into, to, unto, with a view to, *(denoting object)*; in order to, *(denoting purpose)*, κρίμα, a judgment, a sentence, condemnation, } with a view to *or* in order to a sentence.

Luke xxiv. 20.

CONDEMNED (THAT CANNOT BE.)

ἀκατάγνωστος, not worthy of condemnation, *(non occ.)* *See* "CONDEMN," *No.* 5.

Titus ii. 8.

CONDEMNATION.

1. κρίμα, the sentence pronounced, the result *or* product of judgment.
2. κατάκριμα, the sentence pronounced against, condemnation, *(non occ.)*
3. κρίσις, judgment, the process of separation, the act *or* time of judgment.
4. κατάκρισις, judgment against, *(denoting the action incomplete and in progress.)*
5. ὑπόκρισις, *(No. 3 with* ὑπό, *prefixed, implying* concealment,) *hence*, a false *or* feigned pretence, an acting *as it were* under *a mask*, *(whence, Eng.,* hypocrisy.)

1. Luke xxiii. 40.	1. Jas. iii. 1, marg. *judgment.*
3. John iii. 19.	5. —— v. 12 (ὑπὸ κρίσιν, *under judgment*, instead of εἰς ὑπόκρισιν, *unto hypocrisy*, B E G L T Tr A ℵ.)
3. —— v. 24.	1. Jude 4.
2. Rom. v. 16, 18.	
2. —— viii. 1. [*judgment.*	
1. 1 Cor. xi. 34, margin,	
4. 2 Cor. iii. 9.	
1. 1 Tim. iii. 6.	

CONDESCEND.

συναπάγω, to lead off *or* away with *any one. In N.T. only Pass.*, to be led *or* carried away with *any thing; in a bad sense*, to be led astray, (Gal. ii. 13); *in a good sense*, led away. *(In* Rom. xii. 16, τοῖς ταπεινοῖς, *doubtless neuter*, lowly things, *the antithesis of* "the high things.")

Rom. xii. 16.

CONDITIONS OF.

{ τὰ, the *things*,
πρός, *with Acc. as here*, relating to.

Luke xiv. 32.

CONDUCT [verb.]

καθίστημι, to set down, set, to set one down *on a journey, i.e.* to accompany, conduct, *out of respect or for security.*

Acts xvii. 15.

CONDUCT FORTH.

προπέμπω, to send on before, to send forward *on one's journey.*

1 Cor. xvi. 11.

CONFER (-ED.)

1. προσανατίθημι, to lay anything additional on *one. In N.T. only Mid.*, to take such burthen on one's self, *also*, to place before in addition, to impart *or* communicate further, *(i.e. on one's own part)*, *(occ.* Gal. ii. 6.)
2. συλλαλέω, to speak *or* talk with *or* together, *(referring only and merely to the general idea of talking, without reference to the sentiment or subject matter.)*
3. συμβάλλω, to throw *or* strike together, *(as of streams or persons* to come together); *then*, to throw together *as words*, to dispute, discourse *or* consult together.

3. Acts iv. 15. | 2. Acts xxv. 12.
1. Gal. i. 16.

CONFERENCE (ADD IN.)

προσανατίθημι, *see* "CONFER," *No.* 1.

Gal. ii. 6.

CONFESS (-ED, -ETH, -ING.)

1. ὁμολογέω, to speak *or* say the same together *with another*, *i.e.* to speak the same language, to say the same things, *i.e.* to assent, accord, agree with, *hence*, to concede, admit, confess.

   (a) *followed by* ἐν, in, to confess in *one's case*, *i.e.* to profess *or* acknowledge *him*.

2. ἐξομολογέω, *(No.* 1 *with* ἐξ, out of, *prefixed,)* to speak out the same things *with or as another*, confess fully. *Here, only Mid.* to make acknowledgment, *(occ.* Matt. xi. 25; Luke x. 21; xxii. 6.)

2. Matt. iii. 6.
1a. —— x. 32 twice.
2. Mark i. 5.
1a. Luke xii. 8 twice.
1. John i. 20 twice.
1. —— ix 22.
1. —— xii. 42.
2. Acts xix. 18.
1. —— xxiii. 8.
1. —— xxiv. 14.
1. Rom. x. 9.
2. Rom. xiv. 11.
2. —— xv. 9.
2. Phil. ii. 11.
1. Heb. xi. 13.
1. —— xiii.15, marg. (text, *give thanks.*)
2. Jas. v. 16.
1. 1 John i. 9.
1. —— iv. 2, 3, 15.
1. 2 John 7. [T Tr A ℵ.)
2. Rev. iii. 5 (No. 1, act., G L

CONFESSION.

ὁμολογία, assent, accord, agreement; an agreement made, confession, profession.

1 Tim. vi. 13, marg. *profession.*

CONFESSION IS MADE.

ὁμολογέω, *see* "CONFESS," *No.* 1.

Rom. x. 10, pass.

CONFIDENCE.

1. παῤῥησία, the speaking all one thinks, *i.e.* free-spokenness, *as characteristic of a frank and fearless mind, hence*, boldness, openness, frankness, *(perhaps also sometimes implying confidence or assurance.)*

2. πεποίθησις, persuasion, trust, assurance, confidence.

2. ὑπόστασις, a standing under; that which is set *or* stands under, a foundation, origin, beginning, *hence*, spoken of that quality which leads one to stand under, endure *or* undertake anything, *e.g.* firmness, boldness, confidence, *then*, the foundation *or* ground of this confidence, well-founded trust; *(see under* "SUBSTANCE" *and* "PERSON.")

1. Acts xxviii. 31.
2. 2 Cor. i. 15.
— —— ii. 3, } see C
— —— vii. 16, } (have.)
2. —— viii. 22.
2. —— x. 2.
3. —— xi. 17.
— Gal. v. 10, see C (have.)
2. Eph. iii. 12.
— Phil. i. 25, } see C
— —— iii. 3, } (have.)
2. Phil. iii. 4.
— 2 Thes. iii. 4, } see C
— Philem. 21, } (have.)
1. Heb. iii. 6.
3. —— —— 14.
1. —— x. 35.
3. —— xi. 1, marg. (text, *substance.*)
1. 1 John ii. 28.
1. —— iii. 21.
1. —— v. 14.

CONFIDENCE (HAVE.)

1. πείθω, (a) *trans.* to persuade, win by words, influence, *(as opp. to force.)*

   (b) *intrans. Mid.* to suffer one's self to be persuaded *or* convinced.

   (c) *Pass.* to be moved by fair means, *esp.* by words, to be won over, prevailed upon.

2. θαῤῥέω, to be of good cheer, to have good courage, to be full of hope and confidence.

1a. 2 Cor. ii. 3.
2. —— vii. 16.
1a. Gal. v. 10.
1a. Phil. i. 25.
1a. —— iii. 3.
1a. 2 Thes. iii. 4.
1a. Philem. 21.

CONFIDENT.

1. ὑπόστασις, *see* "CONFIDENCE," *No.* 3.

2. θαῤῥέω, *see* "CONFIDENCE (HAVE)," *No.* 2.

2. 2 Cor. v. 6.
1. 2 Cor. ix. 4.

CONFIDENT (BE.)

1. πείθω, *see* "CONFIDENCE (HAVE)," *No.* 1a.

2. θαῤῥέω, *see* "CONFIDENCE (HAVE)," *No.* 2.

1. Rom. ii. 19.
1. Phil. i. 6.
2. 2 Cor. v. 8.

CONFIDENT (WAX.)

πείθω, *see* "CONFIDENCE (HAVE)," *No.* 1a.

Phil. i. 14.

CONFIDENTLY.

See, AFFIRM.

CONFIRM (-ED, -ING.)

1. *βεβαιόω*, to make firm, make steadfast, secure, make good, corroborate, *i.e.* make firm *or* establish *by arguments or proofs.*

2. *ἐπιστηρίζω*, to make to lean on, to strengthen upon, establish, *(occ.* Acts xviii. 23.)

3. *κυρόω*, to make valid, give authority *or* influence, *(non occ.)*

4. *μεσιτεύω*, to be *or* act as a mediator; to come between, interpose, *(non occ.)*

1. Mark xvi. 20 (*ap.*)
2. Acts xiv. 22.
2. —— xv. 32, 41.
1. Rom. xv. 8.
1. 1 Cor. i. 6, 8.
3. 2 Cor. ii. 8.
3. Gal. iii. 15.
— —— 17, see C before.
1. Heb. ii. 3.
4. —— vi. 7, marg. *interpose [one's self.*

CONFIRM BEFORE.

προκυρόω, to do *No.* 3, before *or* previously; establish *or* confirm before, *(non occ.)*

Gal. iii. 17.

CONFIRMATION.

βεβαίωσις, firm establishment, *(non occ.)*

Phil. i. 7. | Heb. vi. 16.

CONFLICT.

ἀγών, a gathering, assembly, *esp.* an assembly to see games, *then*, the assembly *of the Greeks* at their great national games, *and hence*, the contest for a prize *at their games; gen.* any struggle *or* trial *with the accessory idea of peril.*

Phil. i. 30. | Col. ii. 1, marg. *fear* or *care.*

CONFORMABLE UNTO (MAKE.)

συμμορφόω, to make of like form with *another person or thing, (non occ.)*

Phil. iii. 10 (*συμμορφίζω, to be* or *become of like form with*, G∼ L T Tr A ℵ.)

CONFORMED TO.

σύμμορφος, having the like form with *another person or thing, (occ.* Phil. iii. 11.)

Rom. viii. 29.

CONFORMED TO (BE.)

συσχηματίζω, to form, fashion, *or* shape *one thing* after *or* like another. *In N.T. only Mid. or Pass.* to form, fashion, *or* shape one's self after *another*, to be conformed to his example, *(occ.* 1 Pet. i. 14.)

Rom. xii. 2.

CONFOUND (ED.)

1. *καταισχύνω*, to make ashamed, put to shame, bring down shame upon.

2. *συγχέω*, (*or* *συγχύνω*), to pour together, commingle; *of persons*, to confuse, trouble; *of the mind*, to perplex.

2. Acts ii. 6.
2. —— ix. 22.
1. 1 Cor. i. 27 1st (*ap*), 27 2nd.
1. 1 Pet. ii. 6.

CONFOUNDED (be) [margin.]

1. Rom. ix. 33, text, *be ashamed.*

CONFUSE.

συγχέω, *see* "CONFOUND," *No.* 2.

Acts xix. 32.

CONFUSION.

1. *ἀκαταστασία*, a being in a state of disorder *or* instability, *hence*, disorder, anarchy, tumult.

2. *σύγχυσις*, a mixing together; *of persons*, confusion; *of composition*, indistinctness, *(non occ.)*

2. Acts xix. 29.
1. 1 Cor. xiv. 33, marg. *tumult* or *unquietness.*
1. Jas. iii. 16, marg. *tumult* or *unquietness.*

CONGREGATION.

συναγωγή, a bringing together, a gathering *of persons or things, esp.* a Jewish assembly held in the synagogues; *then, of the place itself*, a synagogue, *(whence the Eng. word.)* *(See under* "ASSEMBLY.")

Acts xiii. 43.

CONQUER (-ING.)

νικάω, to have *νίκη* (victory), to be victorious, get the upper hand, prevail.

Rev. vi. 2 twice.

CONQUEROR (BE MORE THAN.)

ὑπερνικάω, to more than conquer, to have victory beyond measure.

Rom. viii. 37.

CONSCIENCE.

συνείδησις, a knowing with one's self, consciousness; the being one's own witness; the testimony to one's own conduct borne by consciousness, *esp.* the consciousness man has of himself in his relation to God, *manifesting itself in the form of a self-testimony. Consequently it is* the effect and result of faith, *for a man's conscience will never condemn that which he believes to be right, and vice versa: hence the only conscience worth having is that which springs from* "a faith unfeigned," *see* 1 Tim. i. 5, *(non occ.)*

John viii. 9 (*ap.*)
Acts xxiii. 1.
—— xxiv. 16.
Rom. ii. 15.
—— ix. 1.
—— xiii. 5.
1. Cor. viii. 7 1st (συνήθεια, *familiarity,* G ~ L Tr A* ℵ.)
—— 7 2nd, 10, 12.
—— x. 25, 27, 28, 29 twice.
2 Cor. i. 12.
2 Cor. iv. 2.
—— v. 11.
1 Tim. i. 5, 19.
—— iii. 9.
—— iv. 2.
2 Tim. i. 3.
Titus i. 15.
Heb. ix. 9, 14.
—— x. 2, 22.
—— xiii. 18.
1 Pet. ii. 19.
—— iii. 16, 21.

CONSECRATE (-ED.)

1. ἐγκαινίζω, to renew; to be, become *or* make new; *hence,* to initiate, consecrate, set forth *something* as new, *(occ.* Heb. ix. 18.)
2. τελειόω, to bring to a full end, to finish, *as a work or a duty; then,* to make complete so that nothing more is wanting, to make perfect.

2. Heb. vii. 28, margin, *perfect.*
1. —— x. 20, margin, *make new.*

CONSENT (WITH.)

{ ἐκ, of, σύμφωνος, symphonious, in unison, *(prop. of sounds,) metaph.* accord, agreement, } by agreement.

1 Cor. vii. 5.

CONSENT (WITH ONE.)

{ ἀπὸ, from, μιᾶς, one, } with one, *(some such word as* consent *being implied.)*

Luke xiv. 18.

CONSENT (-ED, -ING) [verb.]

ἐπινεύω, to nod to, *in token of command, approval, etc.,* to nod assent, *(non occ.)*

Acts xviii. 20.

CONSENT TO.

1. προσέρχομαι, to come *or* go to *or* near *any person or thing;* to come near *in thought or intention, hence,* to assent to, concur in.
2. συγκατατίθημι, to put *or* lay down together with another; to deposit one's vote with others *in the urn, hence,* to assent to, agree with, *(non occ.)*

2. Luke xxiii. 51. | 1. 1 Tim. vi. 3.

CONSENT UNTO.

1. σύμφημι, to speak with, *i.e. in the same manner,* to express agreement with, *(non occ.)*
2. συνευδοκέω, to think well of with *others,* to take pleasure with *others in any thing, hence,* to approve, assent to.

2. Acts viii. 1. | 2. Acts xxii. 20.
1. Rom. vii. 16.

CONSENT WITH [margin.]

συνευδοκέω, *see No.* 2 *above.*

Rom. i. 32, text, *have pleasure in.*

CONSIDER (-ED, -EST, -ING.)

1. νοέω, to perceive, *implying* the perception of the mind *consequent upon sight;* to mark, think about.
2. κατανοέω, to perceive *or* discern distinctly *or* clearly; to understand, consider, observe.
3. θεωρέω, to be a spectator of, to behold an object present, contemplate *with the idea of admiration and wonder,* to look at purposely and attentively, to regard.

4. *ἀναθεωρέω*, (*No.* 3 *with ἀνά*, up, *prefixed*), (*occ.* Acts xvii. 23.)

5. *ἀναλογίζομαι*, to reckon up, compute; to count up again, think over, reflect upon.

6. *διαλογίζομαι*, to reckon through, *i.e.* to complete *or* settle an account, balance accounts, *hence*, to take account of, stop to consider.

7. *εἶδον*, to see, (*referred to the subject, as No.* 3 *is to the object,*) to behold, (*used of the mind of him who sees.*)

8. *συνεῖδον*, to see *or* perceive with one's self (*by the senses*), *i.e.* to be aware, conscious.

9. *καταμανθάνω*, to observe well, learn thoroughly, note accurately, (*non occ.*)

10. *σκοπέω*, to look at *or* upon *a thing*, to watch, behold, regard, (*from σκοπός*, an object set up in the distance at which one looks and aims.)

11. *συνίημι*, to send *or* bring together, *hence*, to bring *or* put together *in mind*, to discern, understand, comprehend.

9. Matt. vi. 28.
2. —— vii. 3.
11. Mark vi. 52.
2. Luke xii. 24, 27.
6. John xi. 50 (*λογίζομαι, to reckon*, G∾L T Tr ℵ.)
2. Acts xi. 6.
8. —— xii. 12.
7. Acts xv. 6.
2. Rom. iv. 19.
10. Gal. vi. 1.
1. 2 Tim. ii. 7.
2. Heb. iii. 1.
3. —— vii. 4.
2. —— x. 24.
5. —— xii. 3.
4. Heb. xiii. 7.

CONSIST (-ETH.)

1. *εἰμί*, to be, *the ordinary verb of existence.*

2. *συνίστημι*, (a) *trans.* to cause to stand with *or* together, to place *or* set together, associate.

(b) *intrans.* to stand with *or* together, to be compact (placed together), to be constituted.

1. Luke xii. 15.
2b. Col. i. 17.
2b. 2 Pet. iii. 5, margin, (text, *stand.*)

CONSOLATION.

παράκλησις, a calling near, a summons to one's side, *hence*, an admonitory, encouraging *and* consolatory exhortation, invitation *or* entreaty, (*opp. to παραίνεσις*, warning.)

Luke ii. 25.
—— vi. 24.
Acts iv. 36.
—— xv. 31.
Rom. xv. 5.
2 Cor. i. 5, 6 twice, 7.
—— vii. 7.
Phil. ii. 1.
2 Thes. ii. 16.
Philem. 7.
Heb. vi. 18.

CONSORT WITH (-ED.)

προσκληρόω, to assign by casting lots. *In Pass. as here*, to cast in one's lot with *another*, (*non occ.*)

Acts xvii. 4.

CONSPIRACY.

συνωμοσία, a swearing together, a being leagued by oath, *hence*, a conspiracy, (*non occ.*)

Acts xxiii. 13.

CONSTANTLY.

See, AFFIRM.

CONSTRAIN (-ED, -ETH.)

1. *ἀναγκάζω*, to necessitate, force, constrain, compel, (*either by force or by entreaty.*)

2. *παραβιάζομαι*, to do *a thing* by force against nature *or* law, to compel, (*as though by overmuch entreaty*), (*non occ.*)

3. *συνέχω*, to hold *or* keep together, confine, secure, *hence*, to constrain, hold fast.

1. Matt. xiv. 22.
1. Mark vi. 45.
2. Luke xxiv. 29.
2. Acts xvi. 15.
1. —— xxviii. 19.
3. 2 Cor. v. 14.
1. Gal. vi. 12.

CONSTRAINT (BY.)

ἀναγκαστῶς, by force, unwillingly.

1 Pet. v. 2.

CONSULT (-ED, -ETH.)

1. *βουλεύομαι*, to take counsel, *i.e.* to consult with one's self, deliberate.

2. *συμβουλεύω*, to take counsel with *any one*, *i.e.* to give him counsel, to advise.

(a) *in Mid. spoken of several*, to counsel *or* consult together, (*e.g. for evil, hence*, to plot.)

2a. Matt. xxvi. 4.
1. Luke xiv. 31.
1. John xii. 10.

CONSULTATION.

συμβούλιον, counsel, advice.

(a) *with ποιέω*, to make *or* hold a consultation.

a. Mark xv. 1.

CONSUME (-ED, -ING.)

1. *ἀναλίσκω*, to use up, spend, *esp. in a bad sense, hence*, to consume; *of persons*, to destroy, *(non occ.)*
2. *καταναλίσκω*, *(No. 1 with κατά prefixed, intensifying it,)* to consume wholly *or* thoroughly *(as fire)*, *(non occ.)*
3. *δαπανάω*, to spend, be at expense, to spend upon *a thing*, *hence*, to waste, exhaust, impoverish.

1. Luke ix. 54. | 2. Heb. xii. 29.
1. Gal. v. 15. | 3. Jas. iv. 3.

CONTAIN (-ING.)

1. *χωρέω*, to give space, make room.

Trans. to have space *or* room for *a thing*, to hold, contain, *esp. of measures.*

John ii. 6.

CONTAIN (CAN.)

1. *χωρέω*, *see above.*
2. *ἐγκρατεύομαι*, to exercise mastery *or* dominion over, *hence*, to exercise self-control.

1. John xxi. 25. | 2. 1 Cor. vii. 9.

CONTAINED (BE.)

περιέχω, to have *or* hold one's self round, *hence*, to encompass, embrace, surround, enclose, to contain *as a* writing.

1 Pet. ii. 6.

CONTAINED IN (THE THINGS.)

τά, the *things.*

Rom. ii. 14.

CONTEMPTIBLE.

ἐξουθενέω, to set out at nought, *i.e.* to despise, contemn.

2 Cor. x. 10, pass. (*ἐξουδενόω, same meaning*, L.)

CONTEND.

διακρίνω, to separate throughout, *i.e.* wholly, completely, *hence*, to distinguish, judge, decide.

(a) *Mid.* to separate one's self from, *as in battle, hence*, to contend with, dispute *or* strive with.

a. Acts xi. 2. | a. Jude 9.

CONTEND EARNESTLY FOR.

ἐπαγωνίζομαι, to contend as a combatant upon (*i.e.* for *or* about) *a thing*, *(non occ.)*

Jude 3.

CONTENT.

1. *ἀρκέω*, to ward off, defend, *hence*, to assist, succour; *then*, to be strong enough, suffice; *in pass.* to be satisfied with a thing, to be contented to *do.*
2. *αὐτάρκης*, sufficient in one's self, self-adequate, needing no aid, *hence*, contented, *(non occ.)*
3. { *τὸ*, the *thing*, / *ἱκανὸν*, coming to, reaching to, *hence*, sufficing, satisfaction, / *ποιέω*, to make, to do, } to do that which gives satisfaction *or* is satisfactory.

3. Mark xv. 15. | 2. Phil. iv. 11.
1. 3 John 10.

CONTENTED (BE.)

ἀρκέομαι, *(Mid. of No. 1 above,)* to suffice one's self with, *i.e.* to be satisfied *or* content with.

Luke iii. 14. | 1 Tim. vi. 8.
Heb. xiii. 5.

CONTENTED WITH (be) [margin.]

συναπάγω, to lead off *or* away with *any one*, *hence*, to be led *or* carried away with *any thing; gen. in a bad sense, i.e.* to be led astray; *but also in a good sense*, to be led away with.

Rom. xii. 16, text, *condescend to.*

CONTENTION (-S.)

1. *ἔρις*, strife, quarrel, *esp.* rivalry, contention, wrangling.

2. ἐριθεία, labour for wages, work for gain, *then,* any work for ambitious purposes, canvassing, intriguing, *hence,* party-spirit, faction.

3. ἀγών, place of assembly *where games were celebrated,* place of contest, *then,* the conflict itself *in the public* games.

4. παροξυσμός, a sharpening, *hence, of* a sharpening of the feeling *or* action, incitement, impulse, paroxysm *of anger,* sharp contention, (*occ.* Heb. x. 24.)

4. Acts xv. 39. | 2. Phil. i. 16.
1. 1 Cor. i. 11. | 3. 1 Thes. ii. 2.
1. Titus iii. 9.

CONTENTIOUS.

φιλόνεικος, loving quarrel, fond of strife, (*non occ.*)

1 Cor. xi. 16.

CONTENTIOUS (THEY THAT ARE.)

3. { οἱ, the *persons,* ἐξ, of, ἐριθεία, *see* "CONTENTION," *No.* 2, } those *who are* of contention.

Rom. ii. 8.

CONTENTMENT.

αὐτάρκεια, self-sufficiency (*in a good sense*), sufficiency within one's self; *spoken of a mind satisfied with its lot,* contentment, (*occ.* 2 Cor. ix. 8.)

1 Tim. vi. 6.

CONTINUAL.

1. ἀδιάλειπτος, not leaving any space between, *hence,* unintermitting, unceasing, (*occ.* 2 Tim. i. 3.)

2. { εἰς, unto, τέλος, the end. }

2. Luke xviii. 5. | 1. Rom. ix. 2.

CONTINUALLY.

1. διαπαντός, through the whole *time, i.e.* continually, always.

2. { εἰς, unto, τό, the, διηνεκής, carried through, extended, protracted, *of time,* continuous, perpetual, } unto *or* for the unbroken continuance, (*occ.* Heb. x. 12, 14.)

1. Luke xxiv. 53. | 2. Heb. x. 1.
2. Heb. vii. 3. | 1. —— xiii. 15.

CONTINUALLY UPON (ATTEND.)

προσκαρτερέω, to be strong *or* firm towards *anything,* to endure *or* persevere in *or* with; *of a work or business,* to be constantly occupied *or* engaged in; *of a person,* to remain near, to wait upon.

Rom. xiii. 6.

CONTINUALLY TO (GIVE ONE'S SELF.)

Acts vi. 4.

CONTINUALLY (WAIT ON.)

Acts x. 7.

CONTINUANCE (PATIENT.)

ὑπομονή, a remaining behind *or* under, *hence,* a bearing up under, patient, persevering endurance.

Rom. ii. 7.

CONTINUE (-ED, -ETH, -ING.)

1. μένω, *intrans.* to remain, abide, (*Lat.* manes;) *trans.* to remain for *any one,* await.

2. ἐπιμένω, to remain upon, *i.e.* in addition, longer; *whence,* to continue.

3. διαμένω, to remain through *or* throughout, *i.e.* permanently; to remain the same, not to change.

4. παραμένω, to remain near by *or* with *any one, hence,* to continue *or* persevere in *anything,* (*occ.* 1 Cor. xvi. 6.)

5. διατρίβω, to rub in pieces, rub continually, *hence,* to wear *or* consume away *by rubbing; spoken of time,* to spend, to pass.

6. ἵστημι, (a) *trans.* to cause to stand, set, place.
   (b) *intrans.* to stand; *metaph.* to stand fast, *hence*, to remain.
7. καθίζω, (a) *trans.* to cause to sit down, to seat.
   (b) *intrans. and Mid.* to seat one's self, sit down, *hence*, to abide, continue.
8. παρατείνω, to stretch out near, by, *or* to; to extend near, *hence*, to extend *or* prolong *as time*, to continue, *(non occ.)*
9. διατελέω, to bring through to a full end, to finish fully, complete; *spoken of time*, to continue through the whole time, continue throughout, *(non occ.)*
10. γίνομαι, to begin to be; *implying* origin, to come into existence; *implying* result, to take place, come to pass; *implying* change *of state*, to become, enter upon any state *or* condition.
11. ποιέω, to make; to do, to work; *with Acc. of time (prop. intrans.)*, to do *or* act for a certain time *or* *(as in vulgar Eng.)* do up a certain time, to spend *or* pass time.

11. Matt. xx. 12, marg. (text, *work*.)
— Luke vi. 12, see C all night.
3. —— xxii. 28.
1. John ii. 12.
2. —— viii. 7 (*ap.*)
1. —— 31.
5. —— xi. 54.
1. —— xv. 9.
— Acts i. 14, see C in.
— —— ii. 42, see C steadfastly in.
— —— 46, see C in.
— —— viii. 13, see C with.
2. —— xii. 16.
— —— xiii. 43, } see C in.
— —— xiv. 22, } see C in.
5. —— xv. 35.
7b.—— xviii. 11, marg. *sit.*
10.—— xix. 10.
8. —— xx. 7.
6b.—— xxvi. 22.
9. —— xxvii. 33.
— Rom. vi. 1, } see C in.
— —— xi. 22, } see C in.
— —— xii. 12, see C instant in.
3. Gal. ii. 5.
— —— iii. 10, } see C in.
— Col. i. 23, } see C in.
— —— iv. 2, } see C in.
1. 1 Tim. ii. 15.
— —— iv. 16, } see C in.
— —— v. 5, } see C in.
1. 2 Tim. iii. 14.
4. Heb. vii. 23.
1. —— 24.
— —— viii. 9, see C in.
1. —— xiii. 1, 14.
4. Jas. i. 25.
11.—— iv. 13.
8. 2 Pet. iii. 4.
1. 1 John ii. 19, 24.
11. Rev. xiii. 5, marg. *make war* (om. G⇉) (add, ὃ θέλει, *to do what he will*, ℵ) (add, πόλεμος, *make war*, Elz. AVm.)

CONTINUE ALL NIGHT.

{ ἦν, was, διανυκτερεύω, to bring the night through, pass the night, } was passing *or* spending the night.

Luke vi. 12.

CONTINUE IN.

1. ἐμμένω, to remain in, *(non occ.)*
2. ἐπιμένω, *see* "CONTINUE," *No.* 2.
3. προσμένω, to remain at *a place* with *a person*, *i.e.* to remain there.
4. προσκαρτερέω, to be strong *or* firm towards *any thing*, to endure *or* persevere in *or* with, to be continually in with *or* near *any person or thing*.

4. Acts i. 14 (with εἰμί, *to be*.)
4. —— ii. 46 (with ἐν, *in*.)
2. —— xiii. 43 (No.3, G L T Tr A ℵ.)
1. —— xiv. 22.
2. Rom. vi. 1.
2. Rom. xi. 22.
1. Gal. iii. 10 (with ἐν, *in*.)
2. Col. i. 23.
4. —— iv. 2.
2. 1 Tim. iv. 16.
3. —— v. 5.
1. Heb. viii. 9.

CONTINUE INSTANT IN.

προσκαρτερέω, *see* "CONTINUE IN," *No.* 4.

Rom. xii. 12.

CONTINUE STEADFASTLY.

Acts ii. 42, with εἰμί, *to be* (with ἐν, Lb.)

CONTINUE WITH.

1. προσκαρτερέω, *see* "CONTINUE," *No.* 4.
2. συμπαραμένω, to remain near with *any one*, *(non occ.)*

1. Acts viii. 13, with εἰμί, *to be*.
2. Phil. i. 25 (παραμένω, *to remain near*, G∾L Tr A ℵ.)

CONTRADICT.

ἀντιλέγω, to speak against *or* in opposition.

Acts xiii. 45.

CONTRADICTION.

ἀντιλογία, a speaking against *or* in opposition to; controversy.

Heb. vii. 7; xii. 3.

CONTRARIWISE.

τοὐναντίον, the opposite. *In N.T. used as adv.* on the contrary, *(non occ.)*

2 Cor. ii. 7. | 1 Pet. iii. 9. | Gal. ii. 7.

CONTRARY.

1. *ἐναντίος*, over-against, opposite.
2. *ὑπεναντίος*, opposed, adverse, *with the idea of* stealth, covertness, clandestineness.

1. Matt. xiv. 24.
1. Mark vi. 48.
— Acts xvii. 7, } see C to.
— —— xviii. 13, } see C to.
1. —— xxvi. 9.
1. —— xxvii. 4.
— Rom. xi. 24, see C to.
— Rom. xvi. 17, see C to,
— Gal. v. 17, see C (be.)
2. Col. ii. 14.
1. 1 Thes. ii. 15.
— 1 Tim. i. 10, see C (be.)
1. Titus ii. 8.

CONTRARY (BE.)

ἀντίκειμαι, to lie opposite; to oppose, be adverse to.

Gal. v. 17. | 1 Tim. i. 10.

CONTRARY TO.

1. *παρά*, beside *(of juxtaposition.)*
   (a) *with Gen.* beside *(as proceeding from.)*
   (b) *with Dat.* beside and at.
   (c) *with Acc.* to *or* alongside of; beside *(as not coinciding with), hence,* contrary to; beside *(with idea of comparison), hence,* inferred superiority, above.
2. *ἀπέναντι*, from over against, opposite to.

2. Acts xvii. 7.
1c. —— xviii. 13.
1c. Rom. xi. 24.
1a. —— xvi. 17.

See also, LAW.

CONTRIBUTION.

κοινωνία, act of partaking, sharing; participation, communion; distribution.

Rom. xv. 26.

CONTROVERSY (WITHOUT.)

ὁμολογουμένως, by consent of all, confessedly, *(non occ.)*

1 Tim. iii. 16.

CONVENIENT.

εὔκαιρος, well-timed, timely, opportune, *(occ.* Heb. iv. 16.)

Mark vi. 21.

CONVENIENT (BE.)

ἀνήκω, to have come up to *any thing,* to extend *or* reach to, *hence,* to pertain to *anything,* to refer to *or* be pertinent to *anything, (occ.* Col. iii. 18.)

Eph. v. 4. | Philem. 8.

CONVENIENT (THOSE THINGS WHICH ARE NOT.)

τὰ, the *things*,
μή, not,
καθήκοντα, befitting, beseeming, meet, fit *or* proper,
} the *things* not seemly.

Rom. i. 28.

CONVENIENT TIME (HAVE.)

εὐκαιρέω, to have good time, *i.e.* to have leisure, opportunity.

1 Cor. xvi. 12.

See also, SEASON.

CONVENIENTLY.

εὐκαίρως, in good time, opportunely, *(occ.* 2 Tim. iv. 2.)

Mark xiv. 11.

CONVERSATION.

1. *ἀναστροφή*, a turning about; life, *as made up of* actions; mode of life, conduct, deportment, *(non occ.)*
2. *τρόπος*, a turning, turn, *hence,* manner, way, mode.
3. *πολίτευμα*, the being *or* the result of being a *πολίτης*, (a member of a free city *or* state); citizenship, life as a citizen, *(non occ.)*

— 2 Cor. i. 12, see C (have one's.)
1. Gal. i. 13.
1. Eph. iv. 22.
— Phil. i. 27, see C is (one's.)
3. —— iii. 20 (see also, is.)
1. 1 Tim. iv. 12.
2. Heb. xiii. 5.
1. —— 7.
1. Jas. iii. 13.
1. 1 Pet. i. 15, 18.
1. —— ii. 12.
1. —— iii. 1, 2, 16.
1. 2 Pet. ii. 7.
1. —— iii. 11.

CONVERSATION (HAVE ONE'S.)

ἀναστρέφω, to turn up, turn back again, *and intrans.* to return.

(a) *Mid.* to turn one's self round, move about among, *hence, gen.* to live, conduct one's self.

a. 2 Cor. i. 12.
a. Eph. ii. 3.

CONVERSATION IS (ONE'S.)

πολιτεύω, to be a πολίτης, (a member of a free city *or* state); to have a certain form of πολιτεία, (government); *hence, trans.* to govern; *intrans.(of the state)* to be governed.

(a) *Mid.* to be a free citizen, and live as such; to conduct one's self according to all the laws and customs of a state, *hence, gen.* to live, order one's life and conduct, *(occ.* Acts xxiii. 1.)

Phil. i. 27.

CONVERSION.

ἐπιστροφή, a turning one's self round *or* towards, a turning about, *(non occ.)*

Acts xv. 3.

CONVERT (-ED, -ETH) [verb.]

ἐπιστρέφω, to turn about, to turn towards.

(a) *trans.* to turn *or* convert to.

(b) *intrans.* to turn one's self unto.

(c) *Mid. and intrans.* to turn one's self round, come to one's self; *also,* to return, retract, *or* repent.

a. Jas. v. 19, 20.

CONVERTED (BE.)

1. ἐπιστρέφω, *see* (b) *and* (c) *above.*
2. στρέφω, to turn.
   (a) *trans.* to turn *into a thing, i.e.* to convert, change.
   (b) *Mid. and intrans.* to turn *in mind,* be converted *or* changed, to become *as it were* another man.

1b. Matt. xiii. 15.
2b. —— xviii. 3.
1b. Mark iv. 12.
1b. Luke xxii. 32.
1c. John xii. 40 (No. 2b, L T Tr A ℵ.)
1b. Acts iii. 19.
1b. —— xxviii. 27.

CONVEY ONE'S SELF AWAY.

ἐκνεύω, to nod from, turn the head aside, turn away *as a horse, hence,* to shun, avoid, turn aside, *(non occ.)*

John v. 13.

CONVICT (-ED.)

ἐλέγχω, to disgrace, shame, *hence, of persons,* to convince, refute, confute, *and so* put to shame.

John viii. 9 (*op.*)

CONVINCE (-ED, -ETH.)

1. ἐλέγχω, *see* "CONVICT."
2. ἐξελέγχω, to do *No.* 1 fully, to show to be wholly wrong, to rebuke sternly, *(non occ.)*
3. διακατελέγχομαι, to confute in disputation, *(non occ.)*

1. John viii. 46.
1. —— xvi. 8, marg.(text, *reprove.*)
3. Acts xviii. 28.
1. 1 Cor. xiv. 24.
1. Titus i. 9.
1. Jas. ii. 9.
2. Jude 15 (No. 1, G∾ L T [Tr A ℵ.)

COOL [verb.]

καταψύχω, to cool down, to refresh by cooling, *(non occ.)*

Luke xvi. 24.

COPPERSMITH.

χαλκεύς, a brazier, coppersmith; *then of any worker in metals,* a smith, *(non occ.)*

2 Tim. iv. 14.

CORBAN.

κορβᾶν, κορβανᾶς, *same as Heb.* קרבן, Corban, *i.e.* a gift, offering, oblation; something devoted to God, *(occ.* Matt. xxvii. 6.)

Mark vii. 11.

CORD (-S) (SMALL.)

σχοινίον, a cord made of bulrushes, *hence,* any small cord *or* rope, *(occ.* Acts xxvii. 32.)

John ii. 15 (pl.)

CORN.

1. σῖτος, wheat, corn; *in pl.* grain.
2. σπόριμος, sown, to be sown, fit for sowing.
   (a) *in pl.* sown fields, fields of grain.
3. κόκκος, a kernel, a grain, seed.

2a. Matt. xii. 1 1st.
— —— 1 2nd, see C (ears of.)
— Mark ii. 23 1st, see C fields.
— —— 23 2nd, see C (ears of.)
1. —— iv. 28.
— Luke vi. st, see C fields.
— —— 1 2nd e C (ears of.)
3. John xii. 24.
1. Acts vii. 12 (pl. *σιτία*, from *σιτίον*, *provision of grain*, G ~ LTTrAℵ)

CORN-FIELDS.

2a. Mark ii. 23. | 2a. Luke vi. 1.

CORN (EARS OF.)

στάχυς, an ear *of grain*.

Matt. xii. 1. | Luke vi. 1. | Mark ii. 23.

See also, TREAD.

CORNER.

1. *γωνία*, (*Eng.* coign,) an angle; *an exterior projecting* corner; *an interior angle, and hence,* a dark corner, (*occ.* Rev. xx. 8.)
2. *ἀρχή*, beginning, *of time, place or dignity;* the first *in time, order or rank; also of place,* the extremity, the corner *as of a sheet.*

1. Matt. vi. 5.
1. —— xxi. 42.
1. Mark xii. 10.
1. Luke xx. 17.
1. Acts iv. 11.
2. —— x. 11.
2. Acts xi. 5.
1. —— xxvi. 26.
— Eph. ii. 20, } see C
— 1 Pet. ii. 6, } (chief.)
1. —— 7.
1. Rev. vii. 1.

CORNER (CHIEF.)

ἀκρογωνιαῖος, at the extreme angle; the corner foundation stone, (*important because of the support given, and the honourable position*), (*non occ.*)

Eph. ii. 20. | 1 Pet. ii. 6.

CORPSE.

πτῶμα, a fall, *then,* anything fallen, *hence,* a body fallen, *i.e.* a dead body, carcase.

Mark vi. 29.

CORRECTED US (WHICH.)

παιδευτής, a teacher, master, *hence,* administrator of discipline, (*occ.* Rom. ii. 20.)

Heb. xii. 9 (pl.)

CORRECTION.

ἐπανόρθωσις, to right up again, set to rights again, to restore; *metaph.* a setting right, correction, (*non occ.*)

2 Tim. iii. 16.

CORRUPT [adj.]

1. *σαπρός*, bad, rotten, putrid, (*properly of vegetable or animal substances*), (*occ.* Matt. xiii. 48.)
2. *διαφθείρω*, to spoil throughout, corrupt utterly.
   (a) *Pass.* to decay wholly, perish.
3. *καταφθείρω*, to destroy, corrupt.
   (a) *pass.* to perish.

1. Matt. vii. 17, 18.
1. —— xii. 33 twice.
1. Luke vi. 43 twice.
1. Eph. iv. 29.
2. 1 Tim. vi. 5.
3a. 2 Tim. iii. 8.

CORRUPT [verb.]

1. *φθείρω*, to spoil, corrupt, destroy, *gen.* to bring into a worse state.
2. *διαφθείρω*, *see No.* 2 *above.*
3. *ἀφανίζω*, to cause to disappear, put out of sight, *hence,* to do away with.
4. *καπηλεύω*, to be a *κάπηλος* (a retailer *or* vintner, *who were notorious for adulterating their commodities*), *hence,* to adulterate, (*non occ.*)
5. *σήπω*, to cause to rot *or* become putrid, (*non occ.*)

3. Matt. vi. 19, 20.
2. Luke xii. 33.
1. 1 Cor. xv. 33.
4. 2 Cor. ii. 17, marg. *deal deceitfully with.*
1. —— vii. 2.
1. —— xi. 3.
— Eph. iv. 22, see C (be.)
5. Jas. v. 2.
— Jude 10, see C one's self.
2. Rev. xi. 18, marg. (text, *destroy.*)
1. —— xix. 2 (No. 2, G ~.)

CORRUPT (BE.)

1. Eph. iv. 22, pass.

CORRUPT ONE'S SELF.

1. Jude 10, middle.

CORRUPTIBLE.

φθαρτός, corruptible, perishable, (*part. of No.* 1 *above.*)

Rom. i. 23.
1 Cor. ix. 25.
1 Cor. xv. 53, 54.
1 Pet. i. 23.

CORRUPTIBLE THINGS.

1 Pet. i. 18 (neut. pl.)

CORRUPTIBLE (NOT.)

ἄφθαρτός, incorruptible ; *of persons*, immortal ; *of things*, imperishable, enduring.

1 Pet. iii. 4.

CORRUPTION.

1. φθορά, a spoiling, corruption, destruction, *gen.* the bringing *or* being brought into a worse state.
2. διαφθορά, a spoiling throughout, thorough corruption, *esp. as arising from* putrescence, *(non occ.)*

2. Acts ii. 27, 31.
2. —— xiii. 34, 35, 36, 37.
1. Rom. viii. 21.
1. 1 Cor. xv. 42, 50.
1. Gal. vi. 8.
1. 2 Pet. i. 4.
1. 2 Pet. ii. 12, 19.

COST.

δαπάνη, expense, expenditure : money spent, *also* money for spending ; extravagance, *(non occ.)*

Luke xiv. 28.

COSTLINESS.

τιμιότης, preciousness, costliness, *(non occ.)*

Rev. xviii. 19.

COSTLY.

πολυτελής, the very end *or* extremity ; *spoken of price*, the very uttermost *or* highest cost, very expensive *or* costly.

1 Tim. ii. 9.

COSTLY (VERY.)

πολύτιμος, of great value, great worth, *(occ.* Matt. xiii. 46.)

John xii. 3.

COUCH.

1. κλινίδιον, a little κλίνη (any thing on which one lies *or* reclines), couch *or* divan, *(non occ.)*
2. κράββατος, a litter *or* mattrass, *used by the poor, which might be carried about.*

1. Luke v. 19, 24.
2. Acts v. 15.

COULD.

See, CAN.

When not part of another verb.

COULD NOT DO (WHAT THE LAW.)

{ τὸ, the thing,
ἀδύνατος, impossible,
τοῦ νόμου, by the law.

Rom. viii. 3.

COULD (THAT I.)

δυνατός, *in an active sense*, strong (having inherent and moral power) ; *in a passive sense*, possible, capable of being done.

Acts xi. 17 (the words "*that I should be*" must be understood.)

COUNCIL.

1. συνέδριον, a sitting together, a council *or* senate ; *Eng.* Sanhedrim. The supreme council of the Jewish nation composed of seventy members, besides the high priest, selected from former high priests and heads of the twenty-four courses.
2. συμβούλιον, a joining in counsel, *hence*, a council, *and then*, counsellors, *i.e.* those who sat in public trials with the governors of a province.

1. Matt. v. 22.
1. —— x. 17.
2. —— xii. 14.
1. —— xxvi. 59.
1. Mark xiii. 9.
1. —— xiv. 55.
1. —— xv. 1.
1. Luke xxii. 66.
1. John xi. 47.
1. Acts iv. 15.
1. —— v. 21, 27, 34, 41.
1. —— vi. 12, 15.
1. —— xxii. 30.
1. —— xxiii. 1, 6, 15, 20, 28.
1. —— xxiv. 20.
2. —— xxv. 12.

COUNSEL (-s) [noun.]

1. βουλή, will, determination, propensity ; purpose, design, plan ; counsel, advice.
2. συμβούλιον, *see* "COUNCIL," *No.* 2.

2. Matt. xxii. 15.
2. —— xxvii. 1, 7.
2. —— xxviii. 12.
2. Mark iii. 6.
1. Luke vii. 30.
1. —— xxiii. 51.
1. John xi. 53, see C together (take.)
— —— xviii. 14, see C (give.)
1. Acts ii. 23.
1. —— iv. 28.
— —— v. 33, see C (take.)
1. —— 38.
— —— ix. 23, see C (take)
1. —— xx. 27
1. —— xxvii. 42.
1. 1 Cor. iv. 5.
1. Eph. i. 11.
1. Heb. vi. 17.

COUNSEL (GIVE.)

συμβουλεύω, to counsel with *any one*, *i.e.* to give him counsel, to advise.

(a) *Mid. spoken of several*, to counsel *or* consult together.

John xviii. 14.

COUNSEL (TAKE.)

1. *βουλεύομαι*, to take counsel, to consult, determine, to deliberate *with one's self or with another in council.*
2. *συμβουλεύω, see* "COUNSEL (GIVE)."

1. Acts v. 33 (*βούλομαι, to will, to be willing,* L Tr.)
2. —— ix. 23.

COUNSEL TOGETHER (TAKE.)

συμβουλεύω, Mid. see "COUNSEL (GIVE)." (a.)

John xi. 53 (*βουλεύομαι*, see C (take), No. 1, L Tr ℵ.)

COUNSEL [verb.]

συμβουλεύω, see "COUNSEL (GIVE)."

Rev. iii. 18.

COUNSELLOR.

1. *βουλευτής*, a counsellor, senator *(spoken of a member of the Jewish Sanhedrim), (non occ.)*
2. *σύμβουλος*, one joined in counsel, *hence*, a counsellor, *(non occ.)*

1. Mark xv. 43. | 1. Luke xxiii. 50.
2. Rom. xi. 34.

COUNT (-ED, -ETH.)

1. *ἡγέομαι*, to lead, *i.e.* to lead the way, go before, *hence*, to be a leader *or* chief; *then*, to lead out *before the mind*, *i.e.* to view, regard *as being so and so*, to esteem, count, reckon.
2. *λογίζομαι*, *strictly of numerical calculation*, to count, calculate, compute, *then*, to take into account, consider.
3. *ἔχω*, to have, to hold, *i.e.* to have and hold, *implying* continued having *or* possession; *hence*, to have *as* in the mind, regard, count.
4. *ψηφίζω*, to count *or* reckon with *ψῆφοι* (small pebbles worn round and smooth by water), to reckon, calculate, *(just like Lat.* calculare, *from* calculus, *(non occ.)*
5. *συμψηφίζω*, *(No. 4 with σύν*, together, *prefixed*, to reckon together, count up, *(non occ.)*

3. Matt. xiv. 5.
3. Mark xi. 32.
4. Luke xiv. 28.
5. Acts xix. 19.
3. —— xx. 24 (*om.* T Tr A ℵ.)
2. Rom. ii. 26.
2. —— iv. 3, 5.
2. —— ix. 8.
1. Phil. iii. 7, 8 twice.
2. Phil. iii. 13.
1. 2 Thes. iii. 15.
1. 1 Tim. i. 12.
1. —— vi. 1.
3. Philem. 17.
1. Heb. x. 29.
1. Jas. i. 2.
1. 2 Pet. ii. 13.
1. —— iii. 9.
4. Rev. xiii. 18.

See also, DESCENT, HAPPY, WORTHY.

COUNTENANCE.

1. *πρόσωπον*, *the part* towards, at, *or* around the eye, *hence*, *gen.* the face, visage, countenance.
2. *ἰδέα* (*εἰδέα*, T Tr), aspect, appearance, *(non occ.)*
3. *ὄψις*, the sight, faculty of seeing, *then*, a sight, appearance, thing seen.

— Matt. vi. 16, see C (of a sad.)
2. —— xxviii. 3.
1. Luke ix. 29.
1. Acts ii. 28.
1. 2 Cor. iii. 7.
3. Rev. i. 16.

COUNTENANCE (OF A SAD.)

σκυθρωπός, of a gloomy, sorrowful countenance. *Used by* lxx. *for* רַע, bad, Gen. xl. 7; *and for* זעף, disturbed, Dan. i. 10; *also in* Ps. xxxv. 14; xxxviii. 6, *for* קדר, to be dark, mournful, *(occ.* Luke xxiv. 17.)

Matt. vi. 16.

COUNTRY (-IES.)

1. *ἀγρός*, a field, *esp.* a cultivated field, *hence*, the country *as distinguished from town.*
2. *χώρα*, space *which receives, contains, or surrounds anything, hence*, place, spot in which one is; *then*, a country, land, region.
3. *πατρίς*, father-land, native country, *hence*, one's own native place, home.
4. *γῆ*, earth, *as opp. to heaven;* land, *as opp. to water; then, used of* a country, region, territory.
5. *γένος*, genus, race, offspring, lineage, kind of people.

2. Matt. ii. 12.
2. —— viii. 28.
4. —— ix. 31.
— —— xiii. 54, 57, see C (one's own.)
— —— xiv. 35, see C round about.
— —— xxi. 33, see C (go into a far.)
— —— xxv. 14, see C (travel into a far.)
2. Mark v. 1, 10.
1. ——— 14.
— —— vi. 1, 4, see C (one's own.)
1. ——— 36, 56.
— —— xii. 1, see C (go into a far.)
1. —— xv. 21.
1. —— xvi. 12 (*ap.*)
2. Luke ii. 8.
— —— iii. 3, see C about.
3. —— iv. 23.
— Luke iv. 24, see C (one's own.)
— ——— 37, see C round about.
2. —— viii. 26.
1. ——— 34.
— ——— 37, see C round about.
1. —— ix. 2.
2. —— xv. 13, 15.
2. —— xix. 12.
— —— xx. 9, see C (go into a far.)
2. —— xxi. 21.
1. —— xxiii. 26.
3. John iv. 44.
2. —— xi. 54, 55.
5. Acts iv. 36.
4. —— vii. 3.
2. —— xii. 20.
2. —— xviii. 23.
2. —— xxvii. 27.
3. Heb. xi. 14.

COUNTRY ABOUT.

περίχωρος, about a place, circumjacent, neighbouring, *hence*, country round about, circumjacent region.

Luke iii. 3.

COUNTRY ROUND ABOUT.

Matt. xiv. 35. | Luke viii. 37. | Luke iv. 37

COUNTRY (GO INTO A FAR.)

ἀποδημέω, to be absent from one's own people, *hence*, to go abroad, travel into foreign countries.

Matt. xxi. 33. | Luke xx. 9. | Mark xii. 1.

COUNTRY (TRAVEL INTO A FAR.)

Matt. xxv. 14.

COUNTRY (ONE'S OWN.)

πατρίς, *see* "COUNTRY," *No.* 3.

Matt. xiii. 54, 57. | Luke iv. 24. | Mark vi. 1, 4.

See also, BETTER, KING.

COUNTRYMAN.

συμφυλέτης, one of the same tribe *or* fraternity, *hence*, a fellow-countryman.

1 Thes. ii. 14.

COUNTRYMEN (ONE'S OWN.)

γένος, genus, race, offspring, lineage, kind of people.

2 Cor. xi. 26.

COURAGE.

θάρσος, cheer, *i.e.* cheerful mind, courage, spirit, *(non occ.)*

Acts xxviii. 15.

COURSE.

1. δρόμος, a running, a race, *gen. of horses; metaph.* a course, career, *(non occ.)*
2. τροχός, a runner, *i.e.* any thing made round for rolling *or* running, *hence*, a wheel; *metaph.* a course *as run by a wheel, hence*, a circuit, *(non occ.)*
3. ἐφημερία, daily service, *(see* 2 Chron. xiii. 10, 11), *hence, in N.T.* a course *or* class, *into which the priests were divided for the daily temple service; each class continuing one week at the time (cf.* 1 Chron. xxiv.; 2 Chron. viii. 14; *and* Josephus, ant. vii. 14, 7), *(non occ.)*
4. πλόος, sailing, navigation, voyage.
5. αἰών, the life that hastes away in the breathing of the breath, life as transitory, course of life, *and gen.* life in its temporal form; *then*, the space of human life, a space of time, time as moving, an age, time so far as history is accomplished in it; an age *or* dispensation.

3. Luke i. 5, 8.
1. Acts xiii. 25.
— —— xvi. 11, see straight.
1. —— xx. 24.
4. —— xxi. 7.
— 1 Cor. xiv. 27, see C (by.)
5. Eph. ii. 2.
— 2 Thes. iii. 1, see C (have.)
1. 2 Tim. iv. 7.
2. Jas. iii. 6.

COURSE (BY.)

{ ἀνά, *a prep. marking* distribution, μέρος, a part, } each in his part *or* portion.

1 Cor. xiv. 27.

COURSE (HAVE.)

τρέχω, to run.

2 Thes. iii. 1, marg. *Gk. run.*

COURT.

1. αὐλή, a yard *or* court; any inclosed space in the open air, *hence*, a sheepfold, the court of an eastern house *or* of the temple.
2. ἀγορά, any place of public resort, *hence*, a market-place *or* forum.

— Luke vii. 25, see king.
2. Acts xvi. 19, marg. (text, *market-place.*)
1. Rev. xi. 2.

COURT of the AREOPAGITES [margin.]

Ἄρειος, of *or* belonging to Mars, *(from* Ἄρης, Mars, *the supposed god of war)*, πάγος, a hill, *(as composed of fixed or solid materials)*, — Mars' hill, *situated in the midst of the city of Athens.*

Acts xvii. 22, text, *Mars' hill.*

COURT (CÆSAR'S) [margin.]

πραιτώριον, *a Latin word denoting* the general's tent in a camp, *then*, the house *or* palace of the governor of a province, *hence*, any large house *or* palace.

Phil. i. 13, text, *palace.*

COURT DAYS [margin.]

ἀγοραῖος, pertaining to the ἀγορά, *(see* "COURT," *No.* 2); days *or* advocates pertaining to the forum, *(here followed by* ἄγω, to hold, *as a court,) lit.* court days are held.

Acts xix. 38, text, *law.*

COURTEOUS.

φιλόφρων, friendly-minded, *(non occ.)*

1 Pet. iii. 8 (ταπεινόφρων, *of lowly mind*, G L T Tr A ℵ.)

COURTEOUSLY.

1. φιλανθρώπως, humanely, *(non occ.)*
2. φιλοφρόνως, friendly-minded manner, courteously, *(non occ.)*

1. Acts xxvii. 3. | 2. Acts xxviii. 7.

COURTIER [margin.]

βασιλικός, belonging to a king; spoken of a person attached to a court; kingly, royal.

John iv. 46, text, *nobleman.*

COUSIN.

συγγενής, born with, connate; of the same stock *or* descent, *hence*, kin, kindred.

Luke i. 36 (συγγενίς, *kinswoman*, L A ℵ.)
—— 58.

COVENANT [noun.]

διαθήκη, a disposition, *esp. of property by will*, a will and testament. *This word is the usual rendering of* בְּרִית, *in the O.T. which certainly means* a covenant *or* agreement, *(from* בָּרָה, to cut *or* divide, *in allusion to the practice of making a covenant*, Gen. xv. 9.) בְּרִית *is used of* the covenant relation into which God enters with Israel *or* of Israel with God, *and then of* the twofold relation. *When it refers to the O.T.*, διαθήκη *must have the meaning of* covenant *or* agreement; *but when it refers to the N.T. (in which* heirship *takes the place of covenant,) it has the meaning of* will *or* testament.

Luke i. 72.
Acts iii. 25.
—— vii. 8.
Rom. i. 31, see C breaker.
—— ix. 4, marg. *testament.*
—— xi. 27.
Gal. iii. 15, marg. *testament.*
—— 17.
Gal. iv. 24, marg. *testament.*
Eph. ii. 12.
Heb. viii. 6, marg. *testament.*
—— 8, 9 twice, 10. [marg. *testament.*]
—— ix. 4 twice.
—— x. 16, 29.
—— xii. 24, } marg.
—— xiii. 20, } *testament.*

COVENANT BREAKER.

ἀσύνθετος, not compounded; bound by no covenant, faithless.

Rom. i. 31.

COVENANT (-ED) [verb.]

συντίθημι, to set *or* put together. *In N.T. only in Mid.* to set together with *another;* to agree *or* covenant together with anyone.

Luke xxii. 5.

COVENANT WITH FOR (-ED.)

ἵστημι, (a) *trans.* to make to stand, to place, *hence*, to place in the balance, weigh.

(b) *intrans.* to stand, be set *or* placed.

a. Matt. xxvi. 15.

COVER (-ED, -ETH.)

1. καλύπτω, to cover with *a thing* (*from* קלף, a covering), to cover, *hence*, to hide.
2. ἐπικαλύπτω, (*No.* 1 *with* ἐπί, upon, *prefixed*,) to cover over, cover up, (*non occ.*)
3. κατακαλύπτω, (*No.* 1 *with* κατά, down, *prefixed*,) to cover *as with a veil that* hangs down. *In N.T. only Pass. or Mid.* to be veiled, wear a veil.
4. περικαλύπτω, (*No.* 1 *with* περί, around, *prefixed*,) to cover around, *e.g. the face*, *hence*, to blind-fold.
5. συγκαλύπτω, (*No.* 1 *with* σύν, together with, *prefixed*,) to cover together, cover wholly, (*non occ.*)

1. Matt. viii. 24.
1. —— x. 26.
4. Mark xiv. 65.
1. Luke viii. 16.
5. —— xii. 2.
1. —— xxiii. 30.
2. Rom. iv. 7.
— 1 Cor. xi. 4, see C (having one's head.)
— ——6, see C (be.)
3. ——7.
1. 1 Pet. iv. 8.

COVERED (BE.)

3. 1 Cor. xi. 6 twice.

COVERED (HAVING ONE'S HEAD.)

{ κατὰ, down from, κεφαλή, the head, ἄχω, to have, } *lit.* having [anything] depending from the head.

1 Cor. xi. 4.

COVERING [noun.]

περιβόλαιον, *something* thrown around, *i.e.* a covering, garment; *of the body*, a mantle; *of the head*, a veil, (*here preceded by* ἀντὶ, instead of.)

1 Cor. xi. 15, marg. *veil*.

COVET (ED.)

1. ἐπιθυμέω, to fix the desire upon, desire earnestly. *It denotes* the affection of the mind, (*compare* ὀρέγομαι, *below*.)
2. ζηλόω, to be zealous towards, (*i.e.* for *or* against *anything*,) to be eager for.

1. Acts xx. 33.
1. Rom. vii. 7.
1. —— xiii. 9.
— 1 Cor. xii. 31, see C earnestly.
2. —— xiv. 39.
— 1 Tim. vi. 10, see C after.

COVET AFTER.

ὀρέγομαι, to stretch one's self, reach after *a thing, with special reference to the thing or object desired*, *hence*, to long after, try to gain.

1 Tim. vi. 10.

COVET EARNESTLY.

ζηλόω *see* "COVET," *No.* 2.

1 Cor. xii. 31.

COVETOUS.

1. πλεονέκτης, one who will have more, a covetous person, a defrauder for gain, (*far worse than No.* 2), (*non occ.*)
2. φιλάργυρος, money-loving.

2. Luke xvi. 14.
1. 1 Cor. v. 10, 11.
1. —— vi. 10.
— Eph. v. 5, see C man.
2. 2 Tim. iii. 2.
— 2 Pet. ii. 14, see C practice.

COVETOUS MAN.

1. Eph. v. 5.

COVETOUS PRACTICE.

πλεονεξία, *see* "COVETOUSNESS."

2 Pet. ii. 14.

COVETOUS (NOT.)

ἀφιλάργυρος, not money-loving, (*occ.* Heb. xiii. 5.)

1 Tim. iii. 3.

COVETOUSNESS.

πλεονεξία, a having more; the will to have more, (*e.g. a larger portion, advantage, superiority.*) *In plural*, covetous thoughts, plans of fraud and extortion.

Mark vii. 22 (pl.)
Luke xii. 15.
Rom. i. 29.
2 Cor. ix. 5.
Eph v. 3.
Col. iii. 5.
1 Thes. ii. 5.
Heb. xiii. 5, see C (without.)
2 Pet. ii. 3.

COVETOUSNESS (WITHOUT.)

ἀφιλάργυρος, not money-loving, *hence*, liberal, generous.

Heb. xiii. 5.

CRAFT.

1. δόλος, a bait, *hence*, fraud, guile, deceit.
2. ἐργασία, work, labour; *metaph.* pains effort; a working, *i.e.* practice.

3. τεχνή, an art, trade *or* craft, *gen.* art, skill.

4. μέρος, a part *of a whole*, a portion.

1. Mark xiv. 1. [the same.)
— Acts xviii. 3, see C (of
2. Acts xix. 25.
4. —— 27.
3. Rev. xviii. 22.

CRAFT (OF THE SAME.)

ὁμότεχνος, (*No.* 3 *with* ὁμοῦ, together,) of the same art *or* craft.

Acts xviii. 3.

CRAFTINESS.

πανουργία, shrewdness, craftiness, *hence,* unscrupulous conduct, (*from* πανοῦργος, *see* "CRAFTY.")

Luke xx. 23. | 2 Cor. iv. 2. | 1 Cor. iii. 19.

CRAFTINESS (CUNNING.)

Eph. iv. 14

CRAFTSMAN.

τεχνίτης, an artificer, artisan, (*from* "CRAFT," *No.* 3), (*occ.* Heb. xi. 10.)

Acts xix. 24, 38. | Rev. xviii. 22.

CRAFTY.

πανοῦργος, doing *or* ready to do everything, *hence,* (*almost always used in a bad sense,*) shrewd, cunning, *or as subst.*, a knave, (*non occ.*)

2 Cor. xii. 16.

CRAVE (-ED.)

αἰτέω, to ask, entreat, supplicate, (*implies a distinction between the parties, and expresses the petition of an inferior towards a superior.*)

Mark xv. 43.

CREATE (-ED.)

κτίζω, to bring under tillage and settlement, (*e.g. land,*) to people *a country*, build houses and cities *in it*, *hence,* to found, set up, establish, produce, bring into being.

Mark xiii. 19.
1 Cor. xi. 9.
Eph. ii. 10.
— iii. 9.
— iv. 24.
Col. i. 16 twice.
— iii. 10.
1 Tim. iv. 3.
Rev. iv. 11 twice.
— x. 6.

CREATION.

κτίσις, a founding, settling, foundation; a making *or* creation, *then,* that which was created, creation, (*denoting the action as incomplete and in progress.*)

Mark x. 6.
— xiii. 19.
Rom. i. 20.
Rom. viii. 22, marg. creature.
2 Pet. iii. 4.
Rev. iii. 14.

CREATOR.

1. κτίζω, *see* "CREATE."

2. κτίστης, a founder, establisher, (*esp. of a city.*) *In N.T. spoken of God as* Creator, (*non occ.*)

1. Rom. i. 25. | 2. 1 Pet. iv. 19.

CREATURE (-S.)

1. κτίσις, *see* "CREATION."

2. κτίσμα, the thing founded, established *or* created, the result *or* product of creation.

1. Mark xvi. 15 (ap.)
1. Rom. i. 25.
1. — viii. 19, 20, 21.
1. —— 22, marg. (text, creation.)
1. —— 39.
1. 2 Cor. v. 17.
1. Gal. vi. 15.
1. Col. i. 15, 23.
2. 1 Tim. iv. 4.
1. Heb. iv. 13.
2. Jas. i. 18.
2. Rev. v. 13.
2. — viii. 9.

CREDITOR.

δανειστής, (δανειστής, T א), a money-lender, *hence,* a creditor, (*non occ.*)

Luke vii. 41.

CREEK.

κόλπος, the bosom, the front of the body between the arms.) *Used of a hollow place in the shore, as a* bay, gulf *or* inlet.

Acts xxvii. 39.

CREEP IN UNAWARES.

παρεισδύνω, to get in by the side, to slip in, insinuate one's self, to go *or* come in by stealth, (*non occ.*)

Jude 4.

CREEP INTO.

{ ἐνδύνω, to go *or* enter in, } (*non occ.*)
{ εἰς, into *or* unto. }

2 Tim. iii. 6.

CREEPING THINGS.

ἑρπετόν, (*neut. of* ἑρπετός, creeping, *from* ἕρπω), a creeping animal, reptile, (*occ.* Jas. iii. 7.)

Acts x. 12. | Acts xi. 6.
Rom. i. 23.

CRIME.

αἰτία, a cause, ground; *esp.* the occasion of some charge, *not necessarily fault or accusation, but* a charge *whether true or false.*

Acts xxv. 27.

CRIME LAID AGAINST.

ἔγκλημα, a charge *or* accusation; the formal indictment, (*occ.* Acts xxiii. 29.)

Acts xxv. 16.

CRIPPLE (BEING A.)

χωλός, lame *in the feet,* halting, limping.

Acts xiv. 8.

CROOKED.

σκολιός, crooked, bent, *esp.* bent sideways *from dryness. In N.T. used of a way,* crooked, not straightforward, *or of persons,* perverse, untoward.

Luke iii. 5. | Phil. ii. 15.

CROSS.

σταυρός, an upright pale *or* stake; *i.e.* a stake on which malefactors were nailed for execution *or* crucified, (*non occ.*) *See under* "TREE."

Matt. x. 38.
— xvi. 24.
— xxvii. 32, 40, 42.
Mark viii. 34.
— x. 21 (*om.* G⇉ L^b Tr [ℵ.)
— xv. 21, 30, 32.
Luke ix. 23 (*ap.*)
— xiv. 27.
— xxiii. 26.
John xix. 17, 19, 25, 31.
1 Cor. i. 17, 18.
Gal. v. 11.
— vi. 12, 14.
Eph. ii. 16.
Phil. ii. 8.
— iii. 18.
Col. i. 20.
— ii. 14.
Heb. xii. 2.

CROW [verb.]

φωνέω, to produce a sound *or* tone, utter a sound; *of men,* to speak, call out, to cry to; *of animals,* to utter their various cries; *of instruments,* to sound.

Matt. xxvi. 34, 74, 75.
Mark xiv. 30.
— 68 (*om.* L^b ℵ.)
Mark xiv. 72 twice.
Luke xxii. 34, 60, 61.
John xiii. 38.
John xviii. 27.

CROWN [noun.]

1. **στέφανος,** that which surrounds *or* encompasses, a circlet *or* chaplet worn on the head; *of kings,* a crown; *of victors in games,* a wreath, (*non occ.*)

2. **διάδημα,** (*from* διαδέω, to bind quite round,) a band *or* fillet, *esp.* that worn by the king, *hence,* the diadem, (*non occ.*)

1. Matt. xxvii. 29.
1. — xv. 17.
1. John xix. 2, 5.
1. 1 Cor. ix. 25.
1. Phil. iv. 1.
1. 1 Thes. ii. 19.
1. 2 Tim. iv. 8.
1. Jas. i. 12.
1. 1 Pet. v. 4.
1. Rev. ii. 10.
1. — iii. 11.
1. — iv. 4, 10.
1. — vi. 2.
1. — ix. 7.
1. — xii. 1.
2. — 3.
2. — xiii. 1.
1. — xiv. 14.
2. Rev. xix. 12.

CROWN (-ED, -EST.)

στεφανόω, to put round, *hence,* to crown, (*non occ.*)

2 Tim. ii. 5. | Heb. ii. 7, 9.

CRUCIFY (-IED.)

1. **σταυρόω,** to stake, drive stakes; *later and in N.T.* to nail to a stake, (*non occ.*). *See under* "TREE."

2. **προσπήγνυμι,** to fix *or* fasten to *anything,* to affix, (*non occ.*)

1. Matt. xx. 19.
1. — xxiii. 34.
1. — xxvi. 2.
1. — xxvii. 22, 23, 26, 31, 35, 38.
— — 44, see C with.
1. — xxviii. 5.
1. Mark xv. 13, 14, 15, 20, 24, 25, 27.
— — 32, see C with.
1. — xvi. 6.
1. Luke xxiii. 21 twice, 23, [33.
1. — xxiv. 7, 20.
1. John xix. 6 3 times, 10, 15 twice, 16, 18, 20, 23.
— John xix. 32, see C with.
1. — 41.
2. Acts ii. 23.
1. — 36.
1. — iv. 10.
— Rom. vi. 6, see C with.
1. 1 Cor. i. 13, 23.
1. — ii. 2, 8.
1. 2 Cor. xiii. 4.
— Gal. ii. 20, see C with.
1. — iii. 1.
1. — v. 24.
1. — vi. 14.
— Heb. vi. 6, see C afresh.
1. Rev. xi. 8.

CRUCIFY AFRESH.

ἀνασταυρόω, to raise up and fix upon the cross *or* to crucify again, (*No.* 1 *with* ἀνά, up *or* again, *prefixed*), (*non occ.*)

Heb. vi. 6.

CRUCIFY WITH.

συσταυρόω, to crucify with *any one*, (*No.* 1 *with σύν*, together with, *prefixed*), (*non occ.*)

Matt. xxvii 44.
Mark xv. 32.
John xix. 32.
Rom. vi. 6.
Gal. ii. 20.

CRUMB (-s.)

ψιχίον, (*dim. of ψίξ*, a bit *or* crumb), a little bit *or* crumb, *as of bread or meat, etc.* (*occ. only in N.T.*), (*non occ.*)

Matt. xv. 27.
Mark vii. 28.
Luke xvi. 21 (*om.* L^{b} T Tr^{b} A ℵ.)

CRY (-IES) [noun.]

1. *κραυγή*, a crying out, *from sorrow or pain.*
2. *βοή*, (*a word formed from the sound* boē, like bellow, moo, *and Lat.* boare) *hence*, a cry, *esp.* for help, (*non occ.*)

1. Matt. xxv. 6.
1. Acts xxiii. 9.
2. Jas. v. 4.
1. Rev. xiv. 18 (*φωνή*, *a voice*, L Tr ℵ.)

CRY (-IED, -ETH, -ING) [verb].

1. *κράζω*, (*a word that imitates the hoarse cry of the raven, Germ.* krächzen,) *hence, gen.* to cry, cry out; *used of* inarticulate cries *from fear or pain, etc.*
2. *βοάω*, (*like Lat.* boare,) to cry aloud, to shout, (*a word formed from the sound, like* bellow, moo *in Eng.*) *esp.* to cry *for help, etc.* (*non occ.*)
3. *ἀναβοάω*, (*No.* 2 *with ἀνά*, up *or* again, *prefixed*,) to lift up the voice, exclaim.
4. *ἐπιβοάω*, (*No.* 2 *with ἐπί*, upon, *prefixed*,) to cry out upon, exclaim vehemently, (*non occ.*)
5. *φωνέω*, to sound, utter a sound; *of animals*, to make the noise peculiar to them; *of persons*, to call out; *of instruments*, to sound.
6. *ἐπιφωνέω*, (*No.* 5 *with ἐπί*, upon, *prefixed*,) to cry out upon, *i.e.* thereupon, in acclamation *or* against.
7. *κραυγάζω*, to make a clamour *or* outcry.
8. *ἀφίημι*, to send forth *or* away, to let go from *one's self*, to dismiss, *hence*, to send forth *a loud* cry.

2. Matt. iii. 3.
— —— viii. 29, see C out.
1. —— ix. 27.
7. —— xii. 19.
— —— xiv. 26, see C out.
1. ——— 30.
7. —— xv. 22 (No. 1, L Tr ℵ.)
1. ——— 23.
— —— xx. 30.
1. ——— 31.
1. —— xxi. 9, 15.
— —— xxvii. 23, see C out.
3. ——— 46 (No. 2, L^{m} Tr.)
1. ——— 50.
2. Mark i. 3.
— ——— 23, see C out.
1. ——— 26 (No. 5, T Tr A ℵ.)
1. —— iii. 11.
1. —— v. 5, 7.
— —— vi. 49, } see C
— —— ix. 24, } out.
1. ——— 26.
— —— x. 47, see C out
1. ——— 48.
1. —— xi. 9.
— —— xv. 8, see C aloud
— ——— 13, 14, see C out
2. ——— 34.
8. ——— 37.
— ——— 39, see C out.
2. Luke iii. 4.
— —— iv. 33, 41, see C out.
5. —— viii. 8.
— ——— 28.
— —— ix. 38, 39, see C out.
5. —— xvi. 24.
2. —— xviii. 7, 38.
1. ——— 39.
— —— xix. 40, } see C
— —— xxiii. 18, } out.
6. ——— 21.
5. Luke xxiii. 46.
1. John i. 15.
2. ——— 23.
1. —— vii. 28, 37.
7. —— xi. 43.
1. —— xii. 13 (No. 7, L T Tr A ℵ.)
1. ——— 44.
7. —— xviii. 40.
— —— xix. 6, 12, 15, } see C
— Acts vii. 57, } out.
1. ——— 60.
2. —— viii. 7.
— —— xiv. 14, see C out.
1. —— xvi. 17.
5. ——— 28.
2. —— xvii. 6.
— —— xix. 28, see C out.
1. ——— 32.
— ——— 34, see C out.
— —— xxi. 28, see C out.
2. ——— 34 (No. 6 G∾L T Tr A ℵ.)
1. ——— 36.
— —— xxii. 23, see C out.
— ——— 24, see C against.
— —— xxiii. 6, see C out.
1. —— xxiv. 21 (*ἐκκράζω*, *to cry out*, T Tr A ℵ.)
4. —— xxv. 24 (No. 2, L Tr ℵ.), [*ἐπί*] *βοάω*, A.)
1. Rom. viii. 15.
1. —— ix. 27.
1. Gal. iv. 6.
2. ——— 27.
1. Jas. v. 4.
1. Rev. vi. 10.
1. —— vii. 2, 10.
1. —— x. 3.
1. —— xii. 2.
1. —— xiv. 15.
5. ——— 18.
1. —— xviii. 2, 18, 19.
1. Rev. xix. 17.

CRY AGAINST.

6. Acts xxii. 24.

CRY ALOUD.

3. Mark xv. 8 (*ἀναβαίνω*, *having gone up*, *L T Tr A ℵ.)
* *i.e.* to the governor's house.

CRY OUT.

1. *κράζω*, *see* "CRY," *No.* 1.
2. *ἀνακράζω*, (*No.* 1 *with ἀνά*, up *or* again, *prefixed*,) to lift up the voice, cry out.
3. *ἀναβοάω*, *see* "CRY," *No.* 3.
4. *κραυγάζω*, *see* "CRY," *No.* 7.

1. Matt. viii. 29.
1. —— xiv. 26.
1. —— xx. 30.
1. —— xxvii. 23.
2. Mark i. 23.
2. —— vi. 49.
1. —— ix. 24.
1. —— x. 47.
1. —— xv. 13, 14.
1. ——— 39 (*om.* Tr^{b} A ℵ.)
2. Luke iv. 33.
1. ——— 41 (No. 4, L T A.)
2. —— viii. 28.
3. —— ix. 38 (*βοάω*, see cry, No. 2, L Tr ℵ.)
1. ——— 39.
1. —— xix. 40.
2. —— xxiii. 18.
4. John xix. 6. (*om.* ℵ.)
1. ——— 12 (No. 4, L T Tr)

4. John xix. 15.
1. Acts vii. 57.
1. —— xiv. 14.
1. Acts xix. 28, 34.
1. —— xxi. 28.
4. —— xxii. 23.
1. Acts xxiii. 6.

CRYING [noun.]

κραυγή, a crying out, *from sorrow or pain.*

Heb. v. 7. | Rev. xxi. 4.

CRYSTAL.

κρύσταλλος, clear ice, water concreted by cold, *hence*, anything congealed and pellucid, *then*, crystal, *from its resemblance to ice*, (*non occ.*)

Rev. iv. 6. | Rev. xxii. 3.

CRYSTAL (CLEAR AS.)

κρυςταλλίζω, to be like crystal, *i.e.* clear and sparkling.

Rev. xxi. 11.

CUBIT (-S.)

πῆχυς, the fore-arm *from the wrist to the elbow. In N.T.* a cubit, *the common ancient measure of length, equal in distance from the elbow to the tip of the middle finger, or about twenty-four or twenty-five inches*, (*non. occ.*)

Matt. vi. 27.
Luke xii. 25.
John xxi. 8.
Rev. xxi. 17.

CUMBER (-ED, -ETH.)

1. περισπάω, to draw from around *any one*, to draw off *or* away. *In N.T. Pass.* to be drawn about *in mind*, *hence*, to be distracted, over-occupied *with cares or business*, (*non occ.*)

2. καταργέω, to render inactive, idle, useless; *prop. of land*, to spoil; *hence*, *metaph.* to make without effect, to make vain, void *or* fruitless.

1. Luke x. 40. | 2. Luke xiii. 7.

CUMI.

κοῦμι, (κοῦμ, T Tr A ℵ.) *The Heb. imperat. fem.* קוּמִי, arise, *expressed in Greek letters*, (*non occ.*)

Mark v. 41.

CUMMIN.

κύμινον, cumin, (*the* cuminum sativum *of modern botany; Heb.* כַּמֹּן; *Germ.* kümmel,) an umbelliferous plant with aromatic seeds, used as a condiment, (*non occ.*)

Matt. xxiii. 23.

CUNNING.

See, CRAFTINESS.

CUNNINGLY.

See, DEVISE.

CUP.

ποτήριον, a drinking vessel, a cup. *Metaph. from the Heb.* lot *or* portion, *under the emblem of a cup which God presents to be drank either for good or evil*, (Ps. xxiii. 5 and xi. 6.)

Matt. x. 42.
—— xx. 22, 23.
—— xxiii. 25, 26.
—— xxvi. 27, 39.
—— 42 (om. G⇉L T Tr A ℵ.)
Mark vii. 4, 8 (ap.)
—— ix. 41.
—— x. 38, 39.
—— xiv. 23, 36.
Luke xi. 39.
—— xxii. 17, 20 twice, 42.
John xviii. 11.
1 Cor. x. 16, 21 twice.
—— xi. 25 twice, 26, 27, 28.
Rev. xiv. 10.
—— xvi. 19.
—— xvii. 4.
—— xviii. 6.

CURE (-S) [noun.]

ἴασις, healing, cure.

Luke xiii. 32.

CURE [verb.]

θεραπεύω, to wait upon, to minister unto, *i.e.* to render voluntary service and attendance; to take care of *the* sick, *hence*, *in N.T.* to relieve, heal, cure.

Matt. xvii. 16, 18.
Luke vii. 21.
Luke ix. 1.
John v. 10.

CURIOUS ARTS (USED.)

See, ARTS.

CURSE (noun.)

1. κατάρα, imprecation against, *hence*, cursing, *of men*, accursed, *of land*, barren.

2. *καταναθεμα*, a great curse, a most cursed thing *or* person.

1. Gal. iii. 10, 13 twice.
2. Rev. xxii. 3 (*κατάθεμα, a curse*, G L T Tr ℵ°) (*κάταγμα, breakage, fracture*, ℵ.)

CURSE (BIND UNDER A.)

ἀναθεματίζω, to declare one to be *ἀνάθεμα*, *(i.e.* devoted to destruction, accursed), to bind by a curse.

Acts xxiii. 12, marg. *bind with an oath of execration.*

CURSE (BIND UNDER A GREAT.)

{ *ἀνάθεμα*, devoted to destruction, accursed, *ἀναθεματίζω*, *see above*, } to bind with a great *or* heavy curse.

Acts xxiii. 14.

CURSE (-ED, -EDST, -ETH, -ING) [verb.]

1. *καταράομαι*, to wish *or* pray against *any one, i.e.* to wish evil to, *hence*, to curse.

2. *ἀναθεματίζω*, to declare one to be *ἀνάθεμα*, *(i.e.* devoted to destruction, accursed,) to bind by a curse.

3. *καταναθεματίζω*, *(No. 2 with κατά*, against, *prefixed,)* to utter curses against, *(stronger than No. 2.)*

4. *κακολογέω*, to speak evil of, revile.

1. Matt. v. 44 (*ap.*)
4. —— xv. 4.
3. —— xxvi. 74 (*καταθεματίζω, to curse*, G L T
4. Mark vii. 10. [Tr A ℵ.)
1. Mark xi. 21
2. —— xiv. 71.
1. Luke vi. 28.
1. Rom. xii. 14.
1. Jas. iii. 9.

CURSED.

1. *κατάρα*, imprecation against, *hence*, cursing *of men*, accursed.

2. *ἐπικατάρατος*, one upon whom a curse rests; devoted to the curse, doomed to punishment, *(non occ.)*

2. John vii. 49 (*ἐπάρατος, laid under a curse*, L T Tr A ℵ.)
2. Gal. iii. 10, 13.
1. 2 Pet. ii. 14 (Gen.)

CURSED (BE.)

καταράομαι, *see* "CURSE," *No.* 1.

Matt. xxv. 41.

CURSING.

1. *ἀρά*, prayer, *i.e.* supplication. *In N.T.* imprecation, *(non occ.)*

2. *κατάρα*, imprecation, against.

1. Rom. iii. 14.
2. Jas. iii. 10.
2. Heb. vi. 8.

CUSTOM (-S.)

1. *ἔθος*, a custom, usage, manner, *whether established by law or otherwise.*

2. *ἐθίζω*, to accustom, use.

   (a) *Pass.* to be accustomed; *and of things*, to be customary, *(non occ.)*

3. *συνήθεια*, a dwelling *or* living together, a being wonted together, familiarity. *In N.T.* a usage, custom, *(non occ.)*

4. *τέλος*, an end *or* termination, *in respect to time; then*, what is paid for public ends, a toll, tax, custom.

— Matt. ix. 9, see C (receipt of.)
4. —— xvii. 25.
— Mark ii. 14, see C receipt of.)
1. Luke i. 9.
2. —— ii. 27.
1. —— 42.
— —— iv. 16, see C was (as his.)
— Luke v. 27, see C (receipt of.)
3. John xviii. 39.
1. Acts vi. 14, marg. *rite.*
1. —— xvi. 21.
1. —— xxi. 21.
1. —— xxvi. 3.
1. —— xxviii. 17.
4. Rom. xiii. 7 twice.
3. 1 Cor. xi. 16.

CUSTOM (RECEIPT OF.)

τελώνιον, a toll-house, custom-house, collector's-office.

Matt. ix. 9.
Mark ii. 14, marg. *place where C was received.*
Luke v. 27.

CUSTOM WAS RECEIVED (place where) [margin.]

τελώνιον, *see above.*

Luke v. 27, text, *receipt of custom.*

CUSTOM WAS (AS HIS.)

{ *κατὰ*, according to, *τὸ*, the, *εἰωθὸς*, custom, *αὐτῷ*, His, } according to His custom, as He was wont.

Luke iv. 16.

CUT (-ING.)

1. κατακόπτω, to hew or cut down, to cut in pieces. *In N.T.* to beat, cut, wound.

2. περιαιρέω, to take away what is round about, *hence*, to take away wholly.

1. Mark v. 5.
2. Acts xxvii. 40, marg. (text, *take up*.)

CUT ASUNDER.

διχοτομέω, to cut in two; *a cruel punishment inflicted by ancient nations.*

Matt. xxiv. 51, marg. *cut off.*

CUT IN SUNDER.

Luke xii. 46, marg. *cut off.*

CUT DOWN.

1. κόπτω, to cut by a blow, e.g., branches of trees, to cut off or down.

2. ἐκκόπτω, to cut off, strike or cut out.

1. Matt. xxi. 8. | 1. Mark xi. 8.
2. Luke xiii. 7, 9.

CUT OFF.

1. ἀποκόπτω, to cut off from, amputate.

(a) *Mid.* to cut off *their own* (*part usually circumcised*), (*non occ.*)

2. ἐκκόπτω, to cut off or out of.

---

3. διχοτομέω, see "CUT ASUNDER."

4. ἀφαιρέω, to take away, remove from.

2. Matt. v. 30. | 4. Luke xxii. 50.
2. — xviii. 8. [C asunder | 1. John xviii. 10, 26.
3. — xxiv. 51.marg.(text | 1. Acts xxvii. 32.
1. Mark ix. 43, 45. | 2. Rom. xi. 22.
4. — xiv. 47. | 2. 2 Cor. xi. 12.
3. Luke xii. 46, marg. | 1a. Gal. v. 12.
(text, *C in sunder.*)

CUT OUT.

ἐκκόπτω, to cut off or out of.

Rom. xi. 24.

CUT SHORT.

συντέμνω, to cut together, i.e. to contract by cutting.

Rom. ix. 28 (ap.)

CUT (BE.)

διαπρίω, to saw through or asunder, *as with the teeth. In N.T. only in Mid.* to be enraged, moved with anger.

Acts vii. 54.

CUT TO THE HEART (BE).

Acts v. 33.

CYMBAL.

κύμβαλον, a cymbal, (*so called from its shape*, κύμβος, a hollow bason.)

1 Cor. xiii. 1.

D

DAILY.

1. κατὰ, (with Acc.) down upon; *of a period or time* down upon which (i.e. in, at or during which) *any thing takes place; of place or time, from the idea of pervading all the parts of a whole, distributively, from one to another,* ἡμέρα, a day, — throughout the day or from day to day.

2. πᾶσα, all or every, ἡμέρα, a day, — every day.

3. κατὰ, see above, ἕκαστος, each, ἡμέρα, a day, — on each day.

4. κατὰ, see above, πᾶσα, all or every, ἡμέρα, a day, — through every day.

5. ἐφήμερος, for the day, i.e. *English,* ephemeral; hence, daily (*non occ.*)

6. καθημερινός, day by day (*non occ.*)

7. ἐπιούσιος (*a word coined by our Lord, and found only as below*), coming upon or over one, *here qualifying the word* "bread," *not* "daily." *It*

refers to the bread "*which cometh down from heaven,*" *and is compared and contrasted with the manna,* John vi. 32, 33. *This bread* came *down* upon them, *and came in a daily supply; hence it is here coupled with the word* (σήμερον), "this day," *but separated from it by the words* (δὸς ἡμῖν), "give to us." (*It cannot be derived from* ἐπί, upon, *and* εἰμί, to be, *because the participle would in that case be* ἐπούσα; *but it is from* ἐπί, upon, *and* εἶμι, to go *or* come, *with participle* ἐπιόύσα.) *Lit.* "our bread, coming upon *us*, give us this day" *or* "our bread for our going upon (*or* journeying, give us this day."

7. Matt. vi. 11.
1. —— xxvi. 55.
1. Mark xiv. 49.
1. Luke ix. 23 (*ap.*)
7. —— xi. 3.
1. —— xix. 47.
1. —— xxii. 53.
1. Acts ii. 46, 47.
1. —— iii. 2.
2. —— v. 42.
6. Acts vi. 1.
1. —— xvi. 5.
1. —— xvii. 11.
4. —— 17.
1. —— xix. 9.
1. 1 Cor. xv. 31.
1. 2 Cor. xi. 28.
3. Heb. iii. 13.
1. —— vii. 27.
1. —— x. 11.
5. Jas. ii. 15.

DAINTY.

λιπαρός, fatty, oily, shiny with oil, anointed therewith; *of things, esp. as belonging to ornament or luxury,* shining, sumptuous.

Rev. xviii. 14.

DAMAGE.

ζημία, loss, (*opp. to* κέρδος, gain,) damage.

Acts xxvii. 10.

DAMAGE (RECEIVE.)

ζημιόω, to bring loss upon *any one. In N.T. only Pass. or Mid.* to suffer loss, receive detriment.

2 Cor. vii. 9.

DAMNABLE.

ἀπώλεια, *transitively*, the losing *or* loss; *intransitively*, perdition, ruin. *In N.T. of the state after death, wherein man, instead of becoming what he might have been, is* lost *and* ruined.

2 Pet. ii. 1.

DAMNATION.

1. ἀπώλεια, *see* "DAMNABLE."
2. κρίμα, the result *or* issue of κρίνω, (to separate, *hence*, to judge), the decision arrived at, decree, determination; *then*, the decision of a judge, judgment.
3. κρίσις, the act of separation, sundering; judgment; *esp.* of judicial process, judgment directed against the guilty and leading on to condemnation.

2. Matt. xxiii. 14.
3. —— 33.
3. Mark iii. 29 (ἁμάρτημα, *a sin*, G∾L T Tr A ℵ), (ἁμαρτία, *sin* [generically], G∾.)
2. —— xii. 40.
2. Luke xx. 47.
3. John v. 29.
2. Rom. iii. 8.
2. —— xiii. 2.
2. 1 Cor. xi. 29, marg. *judgment.*
2. 1 Tim. v. 12.
1. 2 Pet. ii. 1.

DAMNED (BE.)

1. κρίνω, to divide, to separate, make a distinction, come to a decision; *hence*, to judge.
2. κατακρίνω, to give judgment against, pronounce condemnation against *any one*.

2. Mark xvi. 16 (*ap.*) pass.
2. Rom. xiv. 23, pass.
1. 2 Thes. ii. 12, pass.

DAMSEL.

1. κοράσιον, (*dim. of* κόρη,) a little girl, maiden, *a word only used in familiar discourse.*
2. παιδίον, a young child, *male or female,* (*dim. of* παῖς.)
3. παιδίσκη, a young girl, a female slave.

1. Matt. xiv. 11.
3. —— xxvi. 69.
2. Mark v. 39, 40 twice.
2. —— 41 1st.
1. Mark v. 41 2nd, 42.
1. —— vi. 22, 28 twice.
3. John xviii. 17.
3. Acts xii. 13.
3. Acts xvi. 16.

DANCE (-ED.)

ὀρχέω, to take *or* lift up, *as the feet, hence, Mid.* to leap *as by rule*, to dance, (*non. occ.*)

Matt. xi. 17.
—— xiv. 6.
Mark vi. 22.
Luke vii. 32.

DANCING.

χορός, a dance in a ring, a round dance, *gen.* dancing *as connected with music and song, esp. on festive occasions,* (*non. occ.*)

Luke xv. 25.

DANGER (BE IN.)

κινδυνεύω, to be daring, face danger, run a risk; *intrans.* to be hazarded *or* endangered.

Acts xix. 27, 40.

DANGER OF (IN.)

ἔνοχος, held in, contained in, fastened in *or* on *any thing*, *hence*, liable, subject to.

Matt. v. 21, 22 3 times. | Mark iii. 29.

DANGEROUS.

ἐπισφαλής, near upon falling, *i.e.* ready to fall, *hence*, insecure, dangerous, (*non occ.*)

Acts xxvii. 9.

DANIEL.

Δανιήλ, Daniel.

Matt. xxiv. 15. | Mark xiii. 14 (*ap.*)

DARE.

τολμάω, to have *τόλμη* (daring); to take heart *either* to do *or* bear *anything terrible or difficult*; to venture, dare.

Matt. xxii. 46.
Mark xii. 34.
Luke xx. 40.
John xxi. 12.
Acts v. 13.
Acts vii. 32.
Rom. v. 7.
—— xv. 18.
1 Cor. vi. 1.
2 Cor. x. 12.
Jude 9.

DARK.

1. *σκοτία*, darkness, absence of light.
2. *σκοτεινός*, dark, without light.
3. *αὐχμηρός*, (*from αὐχμός*, drought by too much heat,) *hence*, dry, dusty, murky, (*non occ.*)

2. Luke xi. 36.
1. John vi. 17.
1. John xx. 1.
3. 2 Pet. i. 19.

DARKEN (-ED.)

σκοτίζω, to make dark, deprive of light. *In N.T. only Pass.* to be darkened.

Matt. xxiv. 29.
Mark xiii. 24.
Luke xxiii. 45.
Rom. i. 21.
—— xi. 10.
Eph. iv. 18 (*σκοτόω*, *to darken, cover with darkness*, L T Tr A ℵ.)
Rev. viii. 12. [L T A.)
—— ix. 2 (*σκοτόω*, see above

DARKLY.

{ *ἐν*, in, *αἴνιγμα*, an enigma, (*from αἰνίσσομαι*, to hint obscurely,) } obscurely, (*non occ.*)

1 Cor. xiii. 12, marg. *in a riddle.*

DARKNESS.

1. *σκότος*, darkness, absence of light. (a) *masc.* (b) *neuter.*
2. *σκοτία*, *used by later writers for No.* 1. *Same meaning.*
3. *ζόφος*, the gloom of the nether world, nether darkness, murkiness, thick gloom.

1b. Matt. iv. 16 (No. 2, L T Tr A.)
— —— vi. 23 1st, see D (full of.)
1b. —— 23 2nd & 3rd.
1b. —— viii. 12.
2. —— x. 27.
1b. —— xxii. 13.
1b. —— xxv. 30.
1b. —— xxvii. 45.
1b. Mark xv. 33.
1b. Luke i. 79.
— —— xi. 34, see D (full of.)
1b. —— 35.
2. —— xii. 3.
1b. —— xxii. 53.
1b. —— xxiii. 44.
2. John i. 5 twice.
1b. —— iii. 19.
2. —— viii. 12.
2. —— xii. 35 twice, 46.
1b. Acts ii. 20.
1b. —— xiii. 11.
1b. Acts xxvi. 18.
1b. Rom. ii. 19.
1b. —— xiii. 12.
1b. 1 Cor. iv. 5.
1b. 2 Cor. iv. 6.
1b. —— vi. 14.
1b. Eph. v. 8, 11.
1b. —— vi. 12.
1b. Col. i. 13.
1b. 1 Thes. v. 4, 5.
1a. Heb. xii. 18 (No. 3, G∾ L T Tr A ℵ.)
1b. 1 Pet. ii. 9.
3. 2 Pet. ii. 4.
1b. —— 17.
2. 1 John i. 5.
1b. —— 6.
2. —— ii. 8, 9, 11 3 times
3. Jude 6.
1b. —— 13.
— Rev. xvi. 10, see D (be full of.)

DARKNESS (FULL OF.)

σκοτεινός, dark, without light.

Matt. vi. 23. | Luke xi. 34.

DARKNESS (BE FULL OF.)

σκοτόω, to darken, cover with darkness. *In N.T. only in Pass.*

Rev. xvi. 10.

DART (-S.)

1. *βέλος*, a missile, weapon, *e.g.* a dart, arrow *or* javelin; *sometimes fitted with combustibles*, (*non occ.*)
2. *βολίς*, something thrown, *as the lead in sounding*, *hence*, a missile weapon, (*non occ.*)

1. Eph. vi. 16. | 2. Heb xii. 20 (*ap.*)

DASH.

1. προσκόπτω, to beat towards, *i.e.* upon *any thing*, to strike against; *esp. of the foot*, to stumble, (*here followed by* πρός, towards *or* against.)
2. ῥήγνυμι, to rend, tear, break, burst.

1. Matt. iv. 6.
2. Mark ix. 18, marg. (text, *tear.*)
1. Luke iv. 11.

DAUGHTER (s.)

1. θυγάτηρ, a daughter.
2. τέκνον, a child by natural descent, *whether male or female, son or daughter.*

1. Matt. ix. 18, 22.
1. —— x. 35, 37.
1. —— xiv. 6.
1. —— xv. 22, 28.
1. —— xxi. 5.
— Mark v.23, see D(little.)
1. ——— 34, 35.
1. —— vi. 22.
1. ——vii.25,seeD(young)
1. ——— 26, 29.
1. ——— 30 (παιδίον, *a little child*, L T Tr A ℵ.)
1. Luke i. 5.
1. —— ii. 36.
1. —— viii. 42, 48, 49.
1. —— xii. 53.
1. —— xiii. 16.
1. —— xxiii. 28.
1. John xii. 15.
1. Acts ii. 17.
1. —— vii. 21.
1. —— xxi. 9.
1. 2 Cor. vi. 18.
1. Heb. xi. 24.
2. 1 Pet. iii. 6, marg. *child.*

DAUGHTER (LITTLE.)

θυγάτριον, *dim. of No.* 1 *above.*

Mark v. 23.

DAUGHTER (YOUNG.)

Mark vii. 25.

DAUGHTER IN LAW.

νύμφη, a bride, spouse, *newly married*, (*from Lat.* nubo, to veil.) *As opposed to* πενθερά, mother in law, *it is put for* daughter in law.

Matt. x. 35. | Luke xii. 53 twice.

DAWN [verb.]

διαυγάζω, to shine through, *i.e. spoken of daylight*, to break forth, dawn, (*non occ.*)

2 Pet. i. 19.

DAWN (BEGIN TO.)

ἐπιφώσκω, to grow light upon, to dawn upon, (*occ.* Luke xxiii. 54.)

Matt. xxviii. 1.

DAY (-s.)

ἡμέρα, day, *i.e.* the time from one sunrise or sunset to another; *also*, day, *i.e.* day-light from sunrise to sunset; *then, sometimes*, time in general; *in sing.* a period *or* point of time; *in plur.* days, *i.e.* time.

Matt. ii. 1.
—— iii. 1.
—— iv. 2.
—— vi. 11, see D (this.)
——— 34.
—— vii. 22.
—— ix. 15.
—— x. 15.
—— xi. 12, 22.
——— 23, see D (this.)
——— 24.
—— xii. 36, 40 twice.
—— xiii. 1.
—— xv. 32.
—— xvi. 21.
—— xvii. 1, 23.
—— xx. 2, 6, 12, 19.
—— xxii. 23, 46.
—— xxiii. 30.
—— xxiv. 19, 22 twice, 29, 36, 37, 38 twice, 50.
—— xxv. 13.
—— xxvi. 2, 29, 61.
—— xxvii. 8, 19, see D (this.)
——— 40, 63, 64.
—— xxviii.15,seeD(this)
Mark i. 9, 13.
——— 35, see D (a great while before.)
—— ii. 4, 20 twice.
—— 26, see days of (in the.)
—— iv. 27, 35.
—— v. 5.
—— vi. 11 (*ap.*) 21.
——— 35, see D was far spent (when the.)
—— viii. 1, 2, 31.
—— ix. 2, 31.
—— x. 34.
—— xiii. 17, 19, 20 twice, 24, 32.
—— xiv. 1, 12, 25.
——— 30, see D (this.)
——— 58.
—— xv. 29.
Luke i. 5, 20, 23, 24, 25, 39, 59, 75, 80.
—— ii. 1, 6.
——— 11, see D (this.)
——— 21, 22, 37, 43, 44, 46.
—— iv. 2 twice, 16.
——— 21, see D (this.)
——— 25, 42.
——v.17,seeD(acertain.)
——— 35 twice.
—— vi. 12, 13, 23.
—— viii, 22, see D (a certain.)
—— ix. 12, 22, 28, 36, 37.
—— x. 12.
—— xi. 3, see D by D, or D (*for the.*)
—— xii. 46.
—— xiii. 14 twice, 16.
——— 31 (ὥρα, *hour*, G∾ T ℵ.)
—— xiv. 5.
—— xv. 13.
——xvi. 19.
—— xvii. 4 1st.
——— 4 2nd (*om.* L T Tr A ℵ.)
Luke xvii. 22 twice, 24 (*ap*), 26 twice, 27, 28, 29, 30, 31.
—— xviii. 7, 33.
—— xix. 9, see D (this.)
——— 42, 43.
—— xx. 1.
—— xxi. 6, 22, 23, 34.
—— xxii. 7.
——— 34, see D (this.)
——— 66.
—— xxiii. 12, 29, 54.
—— xxiv. 7, 13, 18, 21, 29, 46.
John i. 39.
—— ii. 1, 12, 19, 20.
—— iv. 40, 43.
—— v. 9.
—— vi. 39, 40, 44, 54.
—— vii. 37.
—— viii. 56.
—— ix. 4.
—— xi. 6, 9 twice, 17, 24.
——— 39, see D (four.)
——— 53.
—— xii. 1, 7, 48.
—— xiv. 20.
—— xvi. 23, 26.
—— xix. 31.
—— xx. 19, 26.
Acts i. 2, 3.
——— 5, see days hence (many.)
——— 15, 22.
—— ii. 1, 15, 17, 18, 20, 29, 41.
—— iii. 24.
—— iv. 9, see D (this.)
—— v. 36, 37.
—— vi. 1.
—— vii. 8, 26, 41, 45.
—— ix. 9, 19, 23, 24, 37, 43.
—— x. 3, 30, 40, 48.
—— xi. 27.
——— 28, see days of (in the.)
—— xii. 3, 18, 21.
—— xiii. 14, 31.
——— 33, see D (this.)
——— 41.
—— xv. 36.
—— xvi. 12, 18, 35.
—— xvii. 31.
—— xix. 40, see D (this.)
—— xx. 6 3 times.
———11,seeD(breakof.)
——— 16, 18.
——— 26, see D (this.)
——— 31.
—— xxi. 4, 5, 7, 10, 15, 26 twice, 27, 38.
—— xxii. 3, see D (this.)
—— xxiii. 1, 12.
—— xxiv. 1, 11.
——— 21, see D (this.)
——— 24.
—— xxv. 1, 6, 13, 14.
—— xxvi. 2, see D (this.)
——— 7, 22.
——— 29, see D (this.)
—— xxvii. 7, 20, 29, 33 1st.
——— 33 2nd, see D(this.)
——— 33 3rd, 39.
—— xxviii. 7, 12, 13, 14, 17, 23.

Rom. ii. 5, 16.
— viii. 36.
— x. 21.
— xi. 8, see D (unto this.)
— xiii. 12, 13.
— xiv. 5 twice.
— 6 1st.
— 6 2nd (ap.)
1 Cor. i. 8.
— iii. 13. [this.)
— iv. 13, see D (unto
— v. 5.
— x. 8.
— xv. 4.
2 Cor. i. 14.
— iii. 14, 15, see D (this.)
— iv. 16, see D by D.
— vi. 2 twice.
— xi. 25, see night and [a D.
Gal. i. 18.
— iv. 10.
Eph. iv. 30.
— v. 16.
— vi. 13.
Phil. i. 5, 6, 10.
— ii. 16.
Col. i. 6, 9.
1 Thes. ii. 9.
— iii. 10.
— v. 2, 4, 5, 8.
2 Thes. 1, 10.
— ii. 2.
— iii. 8.
1 Tim. v. 5.
2 Tim. i. 3, 12, 18.
2 Tim. iii. 1.
— iv. 8.
Heb. i. 2.
— 5, see D (this.)
— iii. 8.
— iv. 4, 7, 8.
— v. 7.
— vii. 3.
— viii. 8, 9, 10.
— x. 16, 25, 32.
— xi. 30.
— xii. 10.
Jas. v. 3, 5.
1 Pet. ii. 12.
— iii. 10, 20.
2 Pet. i. 19.
— ii. 8, see D to D (from.)
— 9, 13.
— iii. 3, 7, 8 twice 10, 12.
1 John iv. 17.
Jude 6.
Rev. i. 10, see D (Lord's.)
— ii. 10, 13.
— iv. 8.
— vi. 17.
— vii. 15.
— viii. 12.
— ix. 6, 15.
— x. 7.
— xi. 3, 6, 9, 11.
— xii. 6, 10.
— xiv. 11.
— xvi. 14.
— xviii. 8.
— xx. 10.
— xxi. 25.

DAY BY DAY.

1. { ἡμέρα, day, καὶ, and, also, ἡμέρα, day } day by day.

2. { κατὰ, *see* "DAILY," *No.* 1, ἡμέρα, day, } throughout the day, *or* from day to day.

2. Luke xi. 3, marg. *for the day.*
1. 2 Cor. iv. 16.

DAY (A CERTAIN.)

{ μιᾶ, one
τῶν ἡμερῶν, of the days.

Luke v. 17; viii. 22.

DAY (A GREAT WHILE BEFORE.)

{ ἔννυχον, (ἔνυχα, *acc. pl. neut.* G∾L TTrA℞), in the night, by night, λίαν, very, exceedingly, } very early, yet in the night, (*non occ.*)

Mark i. 35.

DAY (BREAK OF.)

αὐγή, light, brightness, *spoken* of the light of day, the sun, etc., *hence*, the dawn, (*non occ.*)

Acts xx. 11.

DAY (*for the*) [margin.]

{ κατὰ ἡμέρα } *see* "DAY BY DAY," *No.* 2.

Luke xi. 3, text, *day by day.*

DAY TO DAY (FROM.)

{ ἡμέρα, day, ἐξ, out of, from, ἡμέρα, day, } day by day.

2 Pet. ii. 8.

DAY (THE LORD'S.)

{ ἡ, the, κυριακῆ, pertaining to the Lord, (*occ.* 1 Cor. xi. 20), ἡμέρα, day, } the Lord's day.

Rev. i. 10.

[It is submitted that the term, "The Lord's Day," denotes not the Christian Sunday, but "The Day of the Lord," *i.e.* the Day of the Lord's judgment *or* of His coming, for the following reasons:—

a. It is a pure assumption that the earliest use of the term can have a meaning which subsequent usage alone makes intelligible.

b. Sunday is in the N.T. invariably called "The first day of the week," *see* Matt. xxviii. 1; Mark xvi. 2, 9; Luke xxiv. 1; Acts xx. 7; 1 Cor. xvi. 2; and even in John's Gospel, written after the Apocalypse. John xx. 1, 19.

c. We have the similar expressions, "ἡμέραι τοῦ υἱοῦ τοῦ ἀνθρώπου," *days of the Son of Man*, Luke xvii. 22; and, "ανθρωπίνη ἡμέρα," *man's day*, 1 Cor. iv. 3. Why not ἡμέρα τοῦ κυριοῦ, *day of the Lord;* and κυριακῆ ἡμέρα, *Lord's Day?*

d. ἀνθρωπίνη ἡμέρα, *man's day*, in 1 Cor. iv. 3, means *man's judgment*, the time or period in which man judges. So the corresponding expression in Rev. i. 10, κυριακῆ ἡμέρα, denotes *the Lord's judgment*, and the book is a history of the events which will take place during the time or period in which the Lord will judge the earth.

e. The use of the adjective throws the emphasis on to the word DAY; whereas the use of the Genitive case of the noun instead, (by the figure of *Enallage*) places the emphasis on the word LORD'S. See the only other occurrence of the adjective in 1 Cor. xi. 20, where it is "κυριακόν δεῖπνον," *Lord's SUPPER*, not "δεῖπνον τοῦ κυριοῦ," *Supper of THE LORD.*

f. The day in Rev. i. 7, has all the marks of the day as described by Zech. xii. 12-14.

g. It is the fact that the term "Lord" was applied to the *Sun* by most of the ancient nations, and that the sun was worshipped on the first day of the week. Among the Pagan Romans, the first day was called "dies Dominus Sol," *day of the Lord Sun*, and so now the ecclesiastical term, "dies dominica." In transferring this term in Rev. i. 10, to "the first day of the week," the early Christians were acting on the principle of replacing *heathen* days and festivals by those which were *Christian*. (See Bingham Ant. xx. § 5. In chap. xx. § 2, he mentions the fact that the early Christians were charged with being worshippers of the sun. Is not this accounted for by the fact stated above?)]

DAY (THIS.)

σήμερον, to-day.

Matt. vi. 11.
— xi. 23.
— xxvii. 8, 19.
— xxviii. 15.
Mark xiv. 30.
Luke ii. 11.
— iv. 21.
— xix. 9.
— xxii. 34.
Acts iv. 9.
— xiii. 33.
— xix. 40.
— xx. 26.
— xxii. 3.
— xxiv. 21.
— xxvi. 2, 29.
— xxvii. 33.
2 Cor. iii. 14, 15.
Heb. i. 5.

DAY (UNTO THIS.)

1. { ἕως, until, unto, / ἄρτι, now, just now, } until even now.

2. { ἕως, until, unto, / ἡ ἡμέρα, the day, / σήμερον, to-day, } until this very day.

2 Rom. xi. 8. | 1. 1 Cor. iv. 13.

DAY WAS FAR SPENT (WHEN THE.)

{ ὥρας, hours, / πολλῆς, many, / γενόμενης, becoming } many hours having passed, *or* late hour having arrived.

Mark vi. 35.

DAYS (FOUR.)

When not two separate words.

τεταρταῖος, *an adj. marking a succession of days, used adverbially*, on the fourth day.

John xi. 39.

DAYS HENCE (NOT MANY).

{ οὐ, not, / μετὰ, after, / πολλὰς, many, / ταύτας, these, / ἡμέρας, days, } after not many of these days.'

Acts i. 5.

DAYS OF (IN THE.)

ἐπί, (*with Gen.*) upon; in the presence *or* time of.

Mark ii. 26. | Acts xi. 28.

See also, AFTER, COURT, EIGHTH, FEAST, FIRST, FOLLOWING, MID, NEXT, NIGHT, SABBATH, THIRD, TO-DAY.

DAY-SPRING.

ἀνατολή, an up-rising, *esp. of the sun or moon, hence*, the rising sun *or* the quarter of sun-rise, the east; *but also*, a growing, *hence*, a shoot, *as* lxx. *for* צמח, Jer. xxiii. 15; Zech. iii. 8; vi. 12.

Luke i. 78, marg. *sunrising* or *branch*.

DAY-STAR.

φωσφόρος, light-bearing. *In N.T. as subst.* the light bringer; (*Lat.* lucifer,) the morning star. (*The title of* Star is applied to Christ under various aspects, Rev. xxii. 16, and Num. xxiv. 17. It cannot here refer to the conversion of the sinner, for prophecy is not given as a light until this takes place!), (*non occ.*)

2 Pet. i. 19.

DAY-TIME (IN THE.)

τὰς ἡμέρας, the days.

Luke xxi. 37.

DEACON.

διάκονος, a servant, attendant, waiter at table. (*Derivation uncertain, but prob. from* διήκω, to run to serve.) *The main thought in the word is* service rendered to another, the servant of him whom the labour benefits; *as an officer in Primitive times it denoted orig.* one who had charge of the alms, etc., of the Assembly, Acts vi. 1-6; *but those chosen for this work may have been qualified to stand by and assist the Apostles in higher acts of ministry; see* Acts vi. 8-10; viii. 5-8; *of a female*, one who had charge of sick and poor, Rom. xvi. 1.

Phil. i. 1.
1 Tim. iii. 8.
1 Tim. iii. 10, 13, see D (use
—— 12. [the office of.)

DEACON (USE THE OFFICE OF.)

διακονέω, to serve, render service, to wait upon; *in its narrowest sense*, to wait at table, *but gen.* to do any one a service, to care for one's need, (*there is a special reference to* the service rendered, *as distinct from* to serve *or* to be subject to, *though both may co-exist*), *hence*, to do the duties of a διάκονος.

1 Tim. iii. 10, 13, marg. *minister*.

DEAD [adj.* *and* noun.]

1. νεκρός, dead, *as subst. and adj.* prop. only of persons or in allusion to them; as subst.* one dead, a dead person; *as adj.** dead. (*The Scrip. element in the conception of death is* a judicial sentence on account of sin, νεκρός *is therefore used of one* given over to death *even during life; not merely of* religious inactivity *or so-called* spiritual death.)

2. νεκρόω, to make νεκρός (*No.* 1), *hence*, to put to death; *Pass. as here*, to be dead, lifeless.

3. θνήσκω, to die, (*as the primitive sentence of God upon or account of sin.*) *In N.T. only in perf.* to have died, *i.e.* to be dead *in a present sense.*

4. ἀποθνήσκω, (*No.* 3, *with* ἀπό, *prefixed, rendering the verb more vivid and intense, and representing the action of the simple verb* (*No.* 3) *as consummated and finished*,) to die out, to expire, to become quite dead.

— Matt. ii. 19, 20, see D (be.)
1. —— viii. 22 twice.
— —— ix. 18, 24, see D (be.)
1. —— x. 8 (*om.* G → T.)
1. —— xi. 5.
1. —— xiv. 2.
1. —— xvii. 9.
1. —— xxii. 31, 32.
— —— xxiii. 27, see D man.
1. —— xxvii. 64.
— —— xxviii. 4, see D man.
1. —— 7.
— Mark v. 35, 39, see D (be.)
1. —— vi. 14.
1. —— 16 (*om.* T Tr[b] A ℵ.)
1. —— ix. 9, 10.
— —— 26, see D (be.)
1. —— xii. 25, 26, 27.
— —— xv. 44 twice, see D (be.)
3. Luke vii. 12 (*om.* L[b].)
— —— 15, see D (he that is.)
1. —— 22.
— —— viii. 49, 52, 53, see D (be.)
1. —— ix. 7, 60 twice.
— —— x. 30, see D (half.)
1. —— xv. 24, 32.
1. —— xvi. 30, 31.
1. —— xx. 35, 37, 38.
1. —— xxiv. 5, 46.
1. John ii. 22.
1. —— v. 21, 25.
— —— vi. 49, 58, see D (be.)
— —— viii. 52, 53 twice, see D (be.)
— —— xi. 14, 25, 39, see D (be.)
3. —— 41 (*ap.*)
— —— 44, } see D
— —— xii. 1 1st, } (be.)
1. —— 1 2nd, 9, 17.
3. —— xix. 33.
1. —— xx. 9.
1. —— xxi. 14.
— Acts ii. 29, see D (be.)
1. —— iii. 15.
1. —— iv. 2, 10.
1*. —— v. 10.
— —— vii. 4, see D (when ..was.)
1. —— x. 41, 42.
1. —— xiii. 30, 34.
— —— xiv. 19, see D (be.)
1. —— xvii. 3, 31, 32.
1*. —— xx. 9.
1 —— xxiii. 6.
1 —— xxiv. 15 (*om.* G ⇉ L T Tr A ℵ.)
1. —— 21.
— —— xxv. 19, see D (be.)
1. —— xxvi. 8, 23.
1*. —— xxviii. 6.
1. Rom. i. 4.
1. —— iv. 17.
2. —— 19.
1. —— 24.
— —— v. 15, } see D
— —— vi. 2, } (be.)
1. Rom. vi. 4.
— —— 7, 8, see D (be.)
1. —— 9.
1*. —— 11.
1. —— 13.
— —— vii. 2, 3, see D (be.)
— —— 4 1st, see D (become.)
1. —— 4 2nd.
— —— 6, see D (be.)
1*. —— 8.
1*. —— viii. 10.
1. —— 11 twice.
1. —— x. 7, 9.
1. —— xi. 15.
1. —— xiv. 9.
— 1 Cor. vii. 39, see D (be.)
1. —— xv. 12 twice, 13, 15, 16, 20, 21, 29 1st & 2nd.
1. —— 29 3rd (αὐτοί, *them*, G L T Tr A ℵ.)
1. —— 32, 35, 42, 52.
1. 2 Cor. i. 9.
— —— v. 14, see D (be.)
1. Gal. i. 1.
— —— ii. 19, 21, see D (be.)
1. Eph. i. 20.
1*. —— ii. 1, 5.
1. —— v. 14.
1. Phil. iii. 11.
1. Col. i. 18.
1. —— ii. 12.
1. —— 13.
— —— 20, see D (be.)
1. 1 Thes. i. 10.
1. —— iv. 16.
— 1 Tim. v. 6. see D (be.)
1. 2 Tim. ii. 8.
— —— 11, see D with (be)
1. —— iv. 1.
1*. Heb. vi. 1.
1. —— 2.
1*. —— ix. 14.
— —— 17, see D (after men are.)
— —— xi. 4, see D (be.)
2. —— 12.
1. —— 19, 35.
1. —— xiii. 20.
1*. Jas. ii. 17.
1*. —— 20 (ἀργός, *idle, without result*, L T Tr A)
1*. —— 26 twice.
1. 1 Pet. i. 3, 21.
— —— ii. 24, see D (be.)
1. —— iv. 5.
— —— 6, see D (he that is.)
4. Jude 12.
1. Rev. i. 5.
1*. —— 17, 18.
1*. —— ii. 8.
1*. —— iii. 1.
1. —— xi. 18.
1. —— xiv. 13.
— —— xvi. 3, see D man.
1. —— xx. 5, 12 twice, 13 twice.

DEAD (AFTER MEN ARE.)

{ ἐπί, upon, *with Dat. as here,* over, νεκροῖς, dead ones, } over dead ones.

Heb. ix. 17.

DEAD (BE.)

1. θνήσκω, *see* "DEAD," *No.* 3.
2. ἀποθνήσκω, *see* "DEAD," *No.* 4.
3. τελευτάω, to end, *i.e.* to finish, complete, *hence,* to end *one's life, (sometimes of a violent death.)*
4. κοιμάω, to lull *or* hush to sleep, put to sleep.
   (a) *Pass.* to lie down to sleep, to fall asleep, *hence,* to die.
5. ἀπογίνομαι, to be away from, have no part in, *hence,* to be absent from *everything,* in death, *(non occ.)*

3. Matt. ii. 19.
1. —— 20.
3. —— ix. 18.
2. —— 24.
2. Mark v. 35, 39.
2. —— ix. 26.
1. —— xv. 44 1st,
2. —— 44 2nd.
1. Luke viii. 49.
1. —— 52, 53.
2. John vi. 49, 58.
2. —— viii. 52, 53 twice.
2. —— xi. 14, 25.
1. —— 39 (No. 3, G ∾ L T Tr A ℵ.)
1. —— 44.
1. —— xii. 1 (*om.* Lb Trb ℵ.)
3. Acts ii. 29.
1. Acts xiv. 19.
1. —— xxv. 19.
2. Rom. v. 15.
2. —— vi. 2, 7, 8.
2. —— vii. 2, 3.
2. —— 6 (ἀποθανόντες, *we having died,* instead of ἀποθανόντος, *that being dead,* AVm G L T Tr A ℵ.)
4. 1 Cor. vii. 39.
2. 2 Cor. v. 14.
2. Gal. ii. 19, 21.
2. Col. ii. 20.
2. —— iii. 3.
1. 1 Tim. v. 6.
2. Heb. xi. 4.
5. 1 Pet. ii. 24.

DEAD WITH (BE.)

συναποθνήσκω, (Dead, *No.* 4, *with* σύν, together with, *prefixed,)* to die with *any one.*

2 Tim. ii. 11, Aor.

DEAD (BECOME.)

θανατόω, to put to death, *(by the intervention of others,) hence,* to cause to be put to death, to deliver over to death.

(a) *Pass.* to become dead, *like the Eng.* to mortify.

a. Rom. vii. 4.

DEAD MAN.

νεκρός, *see* "DEAD," *No.* 1.

Matt. xxiii. 27. | Matt. xxviii. 4.
Rev. xvi. 3.

DEAD (HALF.)

ἡμιθανής, half-dead.

Luke x. 30.

DEAD (HE THAT IS.)

νεκρός, *see* "DEAD," *No.* 1.

Luke vii. 15. | 1 Pet. iv. 6.

DEAD (ONE.)

νεκρός, *see* "DEAD," *No.* 1.

Mark ix. 26.

DEAD (WHEN...WAS.)

{ μετὰ, after, τὸ, the, αποθανεῖν, to die, } after the death *or* after the dying.

Acts vii. 4.

See also, BODY.

DEADLY.

1. θάνατος, death *whether natural or violent,* the natural end of life, *but esp.* death as the punishment pronounced by God upon sin.
2. θανατηφόρος, death bearing *or* death bringing, *hence,* deadly, *(non occ.)*

— Mark xvi. 18, see D thing. | 2 Jas. iii. 8.
1. Rev. xiii. 3, 12.

DEADLY THING.

θανάσιμος, of *or* belonging to death, deadly, *(non occ.)*

Mark xvi. 18 (neut.) (*ap.*)

DEADNESS.

νέκρωσις, a putting to death, *expressive of the action as incomplete and in progress, (occ.* 2 Cor. iv. 10.)

Rom. iv. 19.

DEAF.

κωφός, blunted, dull, *as a weapon. In N.T. metaph.* of the senses and faculties, *esp.* of the tongue *or* hearing.

Matt. xi. 5. | Mark ix. 25.
Mark vii. 32, 37. | Luke vii. 22.

DEAL [noun.]

See, GREAT.

DEAL (-ETH, DEALT.)

μερίζω, to divide into two parts, to part; *then by implication*, to distribute, divide out.

Rom. xii. 3.

DEAL WITH.

1. *ποιέω*, to make, to do, *spoken of any external act obvious to the senses, i.e. completed action;* to do, *expressing an action as continued or repeated, spoken in reference to a person (with Dative)* to do to *or* in respect to *any one, i.e.* for *or* against *him.*
2. *ἐντυγχάνω*, to fall in with, light upon, to meet and talk with, *hence,* to make intercession for *or* against *any one.*
3. *προσφέρω*, to bear *or* bring to *any place or person.*
   (a) *Mid.* to bear one's self towards *any one, i.e.* to conduct towards, to deal with *any one so and so.*

1. Luke i. 25.
1. —— ii. 48.
2. Acts xxv. 24.
3. Heb. xii. 7.

See also, DECEITFULLY, SUBTILELY.

DEALINGS WITH (HAVE.)

συγχράομαι, to use with *another*, to have in common use, *hence*, to have dealings *or* intercourse with *any one, (non occ.)*

John iv. 9.

DEAR.

1. *ἀγάπη*, love, (*see under* "CHARITY,") *here, gen.* of love.
2. *ἀγαπητός*, beloved, dear.
3. *τίμιος*, held worth, estimated; *hence, in a good sense,* esteemed, honoured; valued, prized.
4. *ἔντιμος*, in estimation, in honour, *i.e.* estimable, prized.

4. Luke vii. 2.
3. Acts xx. 24.
2. Eph. v. 1.
— Phil. ii. 20, see *D* (so.)
2. Col. i. 7.
1. —— 13. marg. *of love.*
2. 1 Thes. ii. 8 (Gen.)

DEAR (so) [margin.]

ἰσόψυχος, of equal soul, *i.e.* actuated by the same motives, *(non occ.)*

Phil. ii. 20, text, *like-minded.*

DEARLY.

See, BELOVED.

DEARTH.

λίμος, failure, want, *esp. of food, hence,* hunger, famine.

Acts vii. 11; xi. 28.

DEATH (-S.)

1. *θάνατος*, death, the natural end of life, *esp.* death *as the sentence and punishment of God against sin, not merely an occurrence, but a state,* the state of man *as condemned through sin. (It is doubtful whether it ever has the meaning of* moral *or* spiritual insensibility.)
2. *ἀναίρεσις*, a taking up *or* away, *as of dead bodies for burial; or* a taking away, *as of life, hence,* a putting to death, a destroying, *(non. occ.)*
3. *τελευτή*, an end, limit, *hence,* the end *of life,* death, *(non. occ.)*

3. Matt. ii. 15.
1. —— iv. 16.
1. —— x. 21 1st.
— —— 21 2nd, see D (cause to be put to.)
— —— xiv. 5, see D (when he would have put. .to)
1. —— xv. 4.
1. —— xvi. 28.
1. —— xx. 18.
1. —— xxvi. 38.
— —— 59, see D (put to.)
1. —— 66.
— —— xxvii. 1, see D (put to.)
— Mark v. 23, see D (lie at the point of.)
1. —— vii. 10.
1. —— ix. 1.
1. —— x. 33.
1. —— xiii. 12 1st.
— —— 12 2nd, see D (cause to be put to.)
— —— xiv. 1, see D (put to.)
1. —— 34.
— —— 55, see D (cause to be put to.)
1. —— 64.
1. Luke i. 79.
1. —— ii. 26.
1. —— ix. 27.
— —— xviii. 33, see D (put to.)
— —— xxi. 16, see D (cause to be put to.)
1. —— xxii. 33.
1. —— xxiii. 15, 22.
— Luke xxiii. 32, see D (put to.)
1. —— xxiv. 20.
— John iv. 47, see D (be at the point of.)
1. —— v. 24.
1. —— viii. 51, 52.
1. —— xi. 4, 13.
— —— 53, } see D
— —— xii. 10, } (put to.)
1. —— 33.
— —— xviii. 31, see D (put to.)
1. —— 32.
1. —— xxi. 19.
1. Acts ii. 24 (ᾅδης, G∾.)
2. —— viii. 1.
— —— xii. 19, see D (put to.)
1. —— xiii. 28.
1. —— xxii. 4.
2. —— 20 (*om.* G L T Tr A ℵ.)
1. —— xxiii. 29.
1. —— xxv. 11, 25.
— —— xxvi. 10, see D (put to.)
1. —— 31.
1. —— xxviii. 18.
1. Rom. i. 32.
1. —— v. 10, 12 1st.
1. —— 12 2nd (*om.* G →T) (not 8th edition.)
1. —— 14, 17, 21.
1. —— vi. 3, 4, 5, 9.
1. —— 16 (*om.* G⇉.)
1. —— 21, 23.
1. —— vii. 5, 10, 13 twice, 24.

1. Rom. viii. 2, 6, 38.
1. 1 Cor. iii. 22.
— — iv. 9, see D (appointed to.)
1. — xi. 26.
1. — xv. 21, 26, 54, 55, 56.
1. 2 Cor. i. 9, 10.
1. — ii. 16 twice.
1. — iii. 7.
1. — iv. 11, 12.
1. — vii. 10.
1. — xi. 23.
1. Phil. i. 20.
1. — ii. 8 twice, 27, 30.
1. — iii. 10.
1. Col. i. 22.
1. 2 Tim. i. 10. [15.
1. Heb. ii. 9 twice, 14 twice,
1. — v. 7.
1. Heb. vii. 23.
— — ix. 15, see D (by means of.)
1. — 16.
1. — xi. 5.
1. Jas. i. 15.
1. — v. 20.
— 1 Pet. iii. 18, see D (put to.)
1. John iii. 14 twice.
1. — v. 16 3 times, 17.
1. Rev. i. 18.
1. — ii. 10, 11, 23.
1. — vi. 8.
1. — ix. 6 twice.
1. — xii. 11.
1. — xiii. 3.
1. — xviii. 8.
1. — xx. 6, 13, 14 twice.
1. — xxi. 4, 8.

DEATH (APPOINTED ["APPROVED" error in A.V. 1611] TO.)

ἐπιθάνιτος, condemned *or* appointed to death; death-devoted, (*non. occ.*)

1 Cor. iv. 9.

DEATH (BE AT THE POINT OF.)

{ μέλλω, to be about to, ἀποθνήσκειν, to die out, become quite dead, } about to die.

John iv. 47.

DEATH (BY MEANS OF.)

{ θανάτου, γενομένου, } a death taking place. *See under* TESTAMENT.

Heb. ix. 15.

DEATH (CAUSE TO BE PUT TO.)

θανατόω, to put to death (*esp. by the intervention of others*), *hence*, to cause to be put to death.

Matt. x. 21. | Mark xiii. 12.
Luke xxi. 16.

DEATH (LIE AT THE POINT OF.)

{ ἐσχάτως, extremely, *i.e.* in extremity, ἔχω, to have, } to be in extremity, to be at the last (*gasp*), "in extremis."

Mark v. 23.

DEATH (PUT TO.)

1. θανατόω, to put to death (*esp. by the intervention of others*), *hence*, to cause to be put to death.
2. ἀποκτείνω, to kill outright.
3. ἀναιρέω, to take up, lift up, (*as of bodies for burial*), to take away, (*as of life*), *hence*, to put to death
4. ἀπάγω, to lead away, conduct away, (*chiefly in a judicial sense, either to judgment or to prison or to death.*)

1. Matt. xxvi. 59.
1. — xxvii. 1.
2. Mark xiv. 1.
1. — 55.
2. Luke xviii. 33.
3. — xxiii. 32.
2. John xi. 53.
2. — xii. 10.
2. — xviii. 31.
4. Acts xii. 19.
3. — xxvi. 10.
1. 1 Pet. iii. 18.

DEATH (WHEN HE WOULD HAVE PUT... TO.)

{ θέλω, to will, to wish, (*implying active natural impulse or desire or purpose, thus differing from βούλομαι, which merely expresses* determination (*cf.* Mark xv. 9, 12, *with* 15, ἀποκτεῖναι, to kill outright, } *lit.* desiring to kill.

Matt. xiv. 5.

DEBATE (-S) [noun.]

ἔρις, strife, quarrel, *esp.* rivalry, contention. *After Homer*, *gen.* wrangling, *esp.* wordy-wrangling, disputation.

Rom. i. 29. | 2 Cor. xii. 20.

DEBT (-S.)

1. ὀφείλω, to be indebted, to owe *any thing to any one*, (*with an inf. following*, to be under obligation to.)
2. ὀφείλημα, the debt which one owes. *Sin is called* ὀφείλημα, *because it involves expiation and the payment of it as a debt by punishment and satisfaction*, (*non occ.*)
3. ὀφειλή, indebtedness, *hence*, duty, obligation, (*occ.* Rom. xiii. 7.)
4. δάνειον, a loan, money lent.

2. Matt. vi. 12. | 1. Matt. xviii. 30.
4. — xviii. 27. | 3. — 32.
2. Rom. iv. 4.

DEBTOR (-S.)

1. ὀφειλέτης, the debtor, he who owes any thing *or* is under obligation on any account. *The use of the word involves the idea that the debtor is one who must expiate his guilt.*

2. χρεωφειλέτης, (χρεοφειλέτης, L T Tr A ℵ), a debt-ower, *(No. 1 with* χρέος, debt, *prefixed.)*

1. Matt. vi. 12.
2. Luke vii. 41.
1. —— xiii. 4, marg. (text, *sinner.*)
2. —— xvi. 5.
1. Rom. i. 14.
1. —— viii. 12.
1. —— xv. 27.
1. Gal. v. 3.

DEBTOR (BE A.)

ὀφείλω, *see* "DEBT," *No.* 1.

Matt. xxiii. 16.
—— 18, marg. (text, *be guilty.*)

DECAY [noun] [margin.]

ἥττημα, a being inferior, a worse state *(as compared with any other or former state); hence,* diminution, degradation, (occ. 1 Cor. vi. 7, *and* Is. xxxi. 8, "defeat.")

Rom. xi. 12, text, *diminishing.*

DECAY (-ETH.)

παλαιόω, to let grow old. *In Pass. as here,* to wax old, become old.

Heb. viii. 13.

DECEASE [noun.]

ἔξοδος, way out, exodus, *hence,* journey out, departure; *spoken of* departure *from life,* decease.

Luke ix. 31. | 2 Pet. i. 15.

DECEASE (-ED.)

τελευτάω, to end, *i.e.* to finish, complete, *hence,* to end *one's life,* to die.

Matt. xxii. 25.

DECEIT.

1. δόλος, a bait, *hence, gen.* the adulteration of the truth to catch *or* deceive.
2. ἀπάτη, deceit, *esp.* by false statements.
3. πλάνη, a wandering, *esp. from the truth, hence,* a being led astray, delusion.

1. Mark vii. 22.
1. Rom. i. 29.
— Rom. iii. 13, see D (use.)
2. Col. ii. 8.
3. 1 Thes. ii. 3.

DECEIT (USE.)

δολιόω, to use a bait, to deceive, *(esp. by* adulteration *or* false admixtures), *(non occ.)*

Rom. iii. 13.

DECEITFUL.

1. δόλιος, deceitful, *(adj. of* "DECEIT," *No.* 1), *(non occ.)*
2. ἀπάτη, *see* "DECEIT," *No.* 2, *here Gen. case,* "of deceit."

1. 2 Cor. xi. 13. | 2. Eph. iv. 22.

DECEITFULLY WITH (deal) [marg.]

καπηλεύω, to be a κάπηλος (a retailer, vintner); *and because the* κάπηλοι *were notorious for adulteration, it denoted* to adulterate, corrupt, *(non occ.)*

2 Cor. ii. 17, text, *corrupt.*

DECEITFULLY (HANDLE.)

δολόω, to deceive, *esp.* by a bait, *hence,* to falsify, corrupt, *(non occ.)*

2 Cor. iv. 2.

DECEITFULNESS.

ἀπάτη, deceit, *esp. by false statements,* self deception, *(see* "DECEIT.")

Matt. xiii. 22. | Mark iv. 19.
Heb. iii. 13.

DECEIVABLENESS.

ἀπάτη, *see above.*

2 Thes. ii. 10.

DECEIVE (-ED, -ETH, -ING.)

1. ἀπατάω, to deceive, to delude, *(esp. with false statements, (non occ.)*
2. ἐξαπατάω, *(No. 1 with* ἐξ, out of, *intensive, prefixed,)* to deceive wholly, delude thoroughly.
3. φρεναπατάω, *(No.* 1 *with* φρήν, the mind, *prefixed,)* to deceive the mind *of any one; implying a self-originating and subjective deception, (non occ.)*
4. πλανάω, to make to wander, cause to err, lead astray; *used of religious deceit or doctrinal error.*
5. πλάνη, a wandering, seduction from the truth, *here, the Gen. lit.,* of deceit.
6. παραλογίζομαι, to reckon wrong, misreckon, miscount; *hence,* to draw false conclusions. *Then* to cheat *or* deceive by false reasoning, *hence,* to deceive.

7. ψεύδω, to speak falsely, to lie to *any one.*

(a) *Mid.* to lie, speak false, belie.

4. Matt. xxiv. 4, 5, 11, 24.
4. Mark xiii. 5, 6.
4. Luke xxi. 8.
4. John vii. 12, 47.
7a. Acts v. 3, marg. (text, *to lie to.*)
2. Rom. vii. 11.
2. —— xvi. 18.
2. 1 Cor. iii. 18.
4. —— vi. 9.
4. —— xv. 33.
3. Gal. vi. 3.
4. —— 7.
5. Eph. iv. 14.
1. —— v. 6.
2. 2 Thes. ii. 3.
1. 1 Tim. ii. 14 1st.
1. —— 14 2nd (No. 2, L T Tr A ℵ.)
4. 2 Tim. iii. 13 twice.
4. Titus iii. 3.
6. Jas i. 22.
1. —— 26.
4. 1 John i. 8.
4. —— iii. 7.
4. Rev. xii. 9.
4. —— xiii. 14.
4. —— xviii. 23.
4. —— xix. 20.
4. —— xx. 3, 8, 10.

DECEIVER (-S.)

1. πλάνος, wandering about; *subst.* a wanderer, vagabond, juggler; *hence* deceiving, seducing. *Subst.* a deceiver, *esp.* a religious imposter *or* teacher of error.

2. φρεναπάτης, a mind-deceiver, *i.e.* deceivers of men's minds, *(see* "DECEIVE," *No.* 3.)

1. Matt. xxvii. 63.
1. 2 Cor. vi. 8.
2. Titus i. 10.
1. 2 John 7 twice.

DECEIVING.

ἀπάτη, deceit, *esp.* by false statements.

2 Pet. ii. 13 (ἀγάπη, *love-feasts*, G ~ L Tr.*)

* Alford, on MSS. grounds, prefers the Rec. Text, ἀπάτη; but has "the strongest suspicion that ἀγάπαις, *love-feasts*, is the original reading.")

DECENTLY.

εὐσχημόνως, *(from* εὐ, well, *and* σχήμα, figure, mien, deportment,) gracefully, becomingly, like a gentleman, decorously, with dignity, (occ. 1 Thes. iv. 12.)

Rom. xiii. 13, marg. (text, *honestly.*)
1 Cor. xiv. 40.

DECK (-ED.)

χρυσόω, to gild, deck with gold, *(non occ.)*

Rev. xvii. 4, marg. *gild;* xviii. 16.

DECLARATION.

διήγησις, narration, history, *(from* διηγέομαι, to lead *or* conduct through *to the end, hence,* to recount, *etc.,) (non occ.)*

Luke i. 1.

DECLARE (-ED, -ING.)

1. ἀναγγέλλω, (ἀνά, back, *and* ἀγγέλλω, to bear a message, announce, proclaim,) to report back; *used of the reports brought by persons returning from somewhere. It is then used with a weaker sense of* ἀνά, *and signifies* to send news of, *and gen.* to notify, announce.

2. ἀπαγγέλλω, to announce *or* report from *some place or person; and then gen.* to announce, publish; *and esp.* to publish *something that has happened, been experienced or heard.*

3. διαγγέλλω, to make known through *an intervening space or* throughout, to convey a message *or* tidings. *Then,* to report fully, proclaim far and wide, (occ. Luke ix. 60; Acts xxi. 26.)

4. καταγγέλλω, to bring word down upon *any one, i.e.* to bring it home to him; *hence,* to announce *(as with emphasis.)*

5. παραγγέλλω, to bring *or* send word near to *any one, i.e.* to announce to *any one; used esp. of military commands, also in N.T. of apostolic injunctions (not merely arbitrary enactments),* to strictly enjoin *or* urge *something to be done.*

6. διηγέομαι, to lead *or* conduct through *(to the end), hence,* to go through with, recount, tell, narrate.

7. ἐκδιηγέομαι, *(No.* 6 *with* ἐκ, out from, *prefixed,)* to tell out, relate in full, *(non occ.)*

8. ἐξηγέομαι, to lead *or* bring out, *hence,* to make known, declare, unfold, (occ. Luke xxiv. 35.)

9. γνωρίζω, to make known, point out, explain.

10. δηλόω, to make manifest *or* evident, make visible *or* clear.

11. ἀνατίθεμαι, to place before, *i.e.* to declare to *any one,* to make known, (occ. Gal. ii. 2.)

12. ὁρίζω, to divide *or* separate from, as a border *or* boundary; to mark out boundaries, *hence,* to determine, mark out definitely, *i.e.* constitute.

13. φράζω, to phrase it, *i.e.* to tell *in words, hence,* to explain, interpret.

14. ἔνδειξις, a pointing out, *(prop. with the finger,)* declaration, indication, (occ. 2 Cor. viii. 24; Phil. i. 28.)

(a) *with* εἰς, unto.

13. Matt. xiii. 36 (Trm) διασαφέω, *make quite plain,* L Tr ℵ.)
13. —— xv. 15.
2. Luke viii. 47.
8. John i. 18.
9. —— xvii. 26 twice.
6. Acts viii. 33.
6. —— ix. 27.
8. —— x. 8.
6. —— xii. 17.
— —— xiii. 32, see tidings (D glad.)
7. —— 41.
7. —— xv. 3.
1. —— 4.
8. —— 12, 14.
4. —— xvii. 23.
1. —— xx. 27.
8. Acts xxi. 19.
11. —— xxv. 14.
12. Rom. i. 4.
14a. —— iii. 25, 26.
3. —— ix. 17.
10. 1 Cor. i. 11.
4. —— ii. 1.
10. —— iii. 13.
5. —— xi. 17.
9. —— xv. 1.
— 2 Cor. iii. 3, see D manifestly.
10. Col. i. 8.
9. —— iv. 7.
2. Heb. ii. 12.
— —— xi. 14, see D plainly.
2. 1 John i. 3.
1. —— 5.
— Rev. x. 7, see D to.

DECLARE TO.

εὐαγγελίζω, to bring a joyful message, announce it. *In N.T.* (a) *Mid. (with personal object,)* to proclaim *something (to somebody) as* a divine message of salvation; *(with impersonal object)* to proclaim something as a joyful message, *(without impersonal object)* to proclaim the divine message of salvation.

Rev. x. 7.

DECLARE GLAD TIDINGS UNTO.

a. Acts xiii. 32.

DECLARE MANIFESTLY.

φανερόω, to make apparent, make manifest, show openly.

2 Cor. iii. 3.

DECLARE PLAINLY.

εμφανίζω, to cause to be seen, to shew.

Heb. xi. 14.

DECREASE [verb.]

ἐλαττόω, to make less *or* inferior, *in quality or degree.*

(a) *Pass. or Mid.* to become less.

a. John iii. 30.

DECREE [noun.]

δόγμα, that which seems true to *one,* an opinion, *esp. of philosophic dogmas. Then* such an opinion expressed with authority, *hence,* a decree, edict, ordinance.

Luke ii. 1. | Acts xvii. 7. | Acts xvi. 4.

DECREE [verb.]

κρίνω, to divide, to separate; to make a distinction, *hence,* to come to a decision, to judge.

1 Cor. vii. 37.

DEDICATE.

ἐγκαινίζω, *(a word almost confined to lxx. and N.T. In lxx. it is put for* חדש, renew, 1 Sam. xi. 14, *etc., and* חנך, consecrate,) to do something new with something new; solemnly to set forth something new as such and to give it over to use, to cause it to enter into operation.

Heb. ix. 18, marg. *purify.*

DEDICATION (FEAST OF THE.)

τὰ, the,
ἐγκαίνια, *(derivation of above),* the festival of the consecration of the renovated Temple, *see* 2 Mac. i. 9, 18; x. 1, *etc.*; 1 Mac. iv. 41, *etc.*; Jos. Ant. xii. 7. 6, 7.

John x. 22.

DEED (-s.)

1. ἔργον, work, *i.e.* labour, business, employment, *and then,* work, *i.e.* something done, deed, act, action.

2. πρᾶξις, a doing *(the action being regarded as incomplete and in progress.)*

3. ποίησις, a making *or* doing *(denoting the action and its result), (non occ.)*

1. Luke xi. 48.
— —— xxiii. 41, see D (our.)
2. —— 51.
1. —— xxiv. 19.
1. John iii. 19, 20, 21.
1. —— viii. 41.
— Acts iv. 9, see D done to (good.)
1. —— vii. 22.
2. —— xix. 18.
1. Rom. ii. 6.
1. —— iii. 20, 28.
2. —— viii. 13.
1. —— xv. 18.
1. 1 Cor. v. 2.
— —— 3, see D (do this.)
1. 2 Cor. x. 11.
2. Col. iii. 9.
1. —— 17.
3. Jas. i. 25, marg. *doing.*
1. 2 Pet. ii. 8.
1. 1 John iii. 18.
1. 2 John 11.
1. 3 John 10.
1. Jude 15.
1. Rev. ii. 6, 22.
1. —— xvi. 11.

DEED (DO THIS.)

κατεργάζομαι, to work out *i.e.* bring about, be the cause *or* author of, } perpetrate
τοῦτο, this *thing,* } this thing.

1 Cor. v. 3.

DEED DONE TO (GOOD.)

εὐεργεσία, a good deed, benefit; *gen.* well-doing, (occ. 1 Tim. vi. 2.)

Acts iv. 9.

DEEDS (OUR.)

ἅ, the *things which,*
ἐπραξάμεν, we practised.

Luke xxiii. 41.

See also, MIGHTY, THIS, WORTHY.

DEEM (-ED.)

ὑπονοέω, to suspect, surmise; conjecture, suppose, (occ. Acts xiii. 25; xxv. 18.)

Acts xxvii. 27.

DEEP [noun.]

1. ἄβυσσος, without depth *or* bottom, *(lxx. for* תהום, abyss, *either of the ocean or the underworld.*
2. βάθος, depth, *(used also metaph. to mark greatness or quantity; or secret unrevealed purposes.)*
3. βυθός, depth, the deep, *also* the deepest part, *(non occ.)*

2. Luke v. 4.
1. —— viii. 31.
1. Rom. x. 7.
3. 2 Cor. xi. 25.

DEEP [adj.]

1. βαθύς, deep, profound.
2. βάθος, *see above, No.* 2.

1 John iv. 11.
2. 2 Cor. viii. 2.
1. Acts xx. 9.

DEEP THINGS.

2. 1 Cor. ii. 10 (pl.)

DEEP (DIG.)

βαθύνω, to deepen, make deep, *(non occ.)*

Luke vi. 48.

DEEPLY.

See, SIGH.

DEEPNESS.

βάθος, *see* "DEEP," *No.* 2.

Matt. xiii. 5.

DEFAME (-ED)

βλασφημέω, to drop evil *or* profane words, speak lightly *or* amiss of sacred things; to speak ill *or* to the prejudice of one.

1 Cor. iv. 13 (δυσφημέω, to be δύσφημος (of ill omen), *to use words of ill omen,* G ~ T A ℵ.)

DEFENCE.

ἀπολογία, defence, speech of defence.

Acts xxii. 1. | Phil. i. 7, 17.

DEFENCE (MAKE.)

ἀπολογέομαι, to speak one's self off, to talk one's self out of *a difficulty, hence,* to defend one's self *before a tribunal or elsewhere.*

Acts xix. 33.

DEFEND (-ED.)

ἀμύνομαι, to avert, repel; *then,* to aid, fight for, avenge; *hence,* to aid, assist, defend, *(non occ.)*

Acts vii. 24.

DEFER (-ED.)

ἀναβάλλομαι, *in a forensic sense,* put off *or* over, defer, *(non occ.)*

Acts xxiv. 22.

DEFILE (-ED, -ETH.)

1. κοινόω, to make common, to communicate with *others. In N.T.* to make common *ceremonially, hence,* to render unholy *or* unclean, to defile.
2. μιαίνω, to stain with colour, to tinge, colour, *(as the staining of glass or ivory),* to spot, *but not necessarily* to blot, *which is No.* 3, *(non occ.)*
3. μολύνω, to soil, besmear, *as with mud or filth,* to blot, *(non occ.)*

4. *σπιλόω*, to make a *σπῖλος*, (a stain, mark, freckle, mole; *in pl.* spots *in a moral sense,)* to defile, (occ. Jude 23.)

5. *φθείρω*, to spoil, corrupt, destroy; *gen.* to bring into a worse state; to deprave.

1. Matt. xv. 11 twice, 18, 20 twice.
— Mark vii. 2, see defiled.
1. ——— 15 twice, 18, 20, 23.
2. John xviii. 28.
5. 1 Cor. iii. 17, margin, *destroy.*
3. —— viii. 7.
— 1 Tim. i. 10, see D one's self with mankind.
2. Titus i. 15 twice.
2. Heb. xii. 15.
4. Jas. iii. 6.
2. Jude 8.
3. Rev. iii. 4.
3. —— xiv. 4.
1. —— xxi. 27 (*κοινόν*, *common*, see defiled, G L T Tr A ℵ.)

DEFILE ONE'S SELF WITH MANKIND.

ἀρσενοκοίτης, *(from ἄρσην*, a male, *and κοίτη*, a bed,) (occ. 1 Cor. vi. 9.)

1 Tim. i. 10.

DEFILED.

κοινός, common, in common; *then, from the idea of* coming into contact with everything, *it denotes* that which is opposed to the divine *ἅγιος* (holy), *hence,* unclean *ceremonially.*

Mark vii. 2.

DEFRAUD (-ED.)

1. *ἀποστερέω*, to deprive of, to defraud of.

2. *πλεονεκτέω*, *intrans.*, to have more *than another*, have an advantage. *In N.T. trans.* to take advantage of *any one so as to get more;* circumvent for gain.

1. Mark x. 19.
1. 1 Cor. vi. 7, 8.
1. 1 Cor. vii. 5.
2. 2 Cor. vii. 2.
2. 1 Thes. iv. 6.

DEGREE.

βαθμός, a step *(as of a stair or door.) In N.T.* a step *(as of dignity or standing, (non occ.)*

1 Tim. iii. 13.

See also, LOW.

DELAY [noun]

ἀναβολή, earth thrown up; *hence,* delay *(used in a forensic sense), (non occ.)*

Acts xxv. 17.

DELAY (-ETH) [verb.]

1. *χρονίζω*, to while away time, *i.e.* to linger, be long *in coming or doing,* (occ. Matt. xxv. 5; Luke i. 21; Heb. x. 37.)

2. *ὀκνέω*, to be slow, tardy, *(non occ.)*

1. Matt. xxiv. 48.
1. Luke xii. 45.
2. Acts ix. 38, marg. *be grieved.*

DELICACY (-IES.)

στρῆνος, rudeness, insolence, pride; *hence,* revel, riot, luxury, *(non occ.)*

Rev. xviii. 3.

DELICATELY.

ἐν, in,
τρυφή, delicate living, luxury, *(from θρύπτω* to break,) *as though,* breaking down *the mind and making it effeminate, (non occ,)*
} delicately, luxuriously.

Luke vii. 25.

DELICATELY (live) [margin.]

σπαταλάω, to live "fast," live lewdly, run riot, (occ. Jas. v. 5.)

1 Tim. v. 6, text, *live in pleasure.*

DELICIOUSLY (LIVE.)

στρηνιάω, to live strenuously, rudely, to live "hard," revel, *(non occ.)*

Rev. xviii. 7, 9.

DELIGHT IN.

συνήδομαι, to joy *or* rejoice with *any one,* to delight in *any thing* with *others, (non occ.)*

Rom vii. 22.

DELIVER (-ED, -EDST, -ING.)

1. *δίδωμι*, to give, present, *(with implied notion of* giving freely, unforced, *opp. of No.* 3,) *then,* to give, *as though* to present, commit to, entrust to.

2. *ἀναδίδωμι*, *(No.* 1 *with ἀνά*, up, *prefixed,)* to give up, deliver over, *(non occ.)*

3. **ἀποδίδωμι**, (*No.* 1 *with* ἀπό, from *prefixed*,) to give away from one's self, to give back, restore.

4. **ἐπιδίδωμι**, (*No.* 1 *with* ἐπί, upon, *prefixed*,) to give upon, *i.e.* in addition to, to give forth *as* from *one's self* upon *or* to *another; hence*, to deliver over, *i.e.* to put into one's hands.

5. **παραδίδωμι**, (*No.* 1 *with* παρά, beside, *prefixed*,) to give near, with *or* to *any one*, to give *or* hand over to *another*, to deliver up, surrender.

6. { δίδωμι *see above*, *No.* 1, σωτηρία, safety, deliverance, preservation *from danger or destruction. In the Christian sense*, salvation, } to give deliverance.

7. **ῥύομαι**, to draw *or* snatch to one's self; *hence, gen.* to draw *or* snatch from danger, to rescue, to deliver.

8. **ἐξαιρέω**, to take out of.
   (a) *in Mid.* to take out of for one's self, *hence*, to rescue, deliver.

9. **ἀπαλλάσσω**, to change from, to set free from, release, let go.

10. **ἐλευθερόω**, to free, set at liberty

11. **καταργέω**, to leave unemployed *or* idle; to make useless, void.

12. **χαρίζομαι**, to gratify, to do what is pleasing *or* grateful to any one; *hence, of persons*, to deliver over *so as to gratify them*.

— Matt. iv. 12, see D up.
5. —— v. 25 1st.
5. ——— 25 2nd (*om.* L Trb ℵ.)
7. —— vi. 13.
— —— x. 17, 19, 21, see D up.
5. —— xviii. 34.
5. —— xx. 19.
— —— xxiv. 9, see D up.
5. —— xxv. 14, 20, 22.
5. —— xxvi. 15.
5. —— xxvii. 2, 18, 26.
7. ——— 43.
3. ——— 58.
5. Mark vii. 13
5. —— ix. 31.
5. —— x. 33 twice.
— —— xiii. 9, 11, see D up.
5. —— xv. 1, 10, 15.
5. Luke i. 2.
— ——— 57, 74, } see D (be.)
— —— ii. 6, }
5. —— iv. 6.
4. ——— 17.
1. —— vii. 15 (No. 3. Lm)
— —— ix. 42, see D again.
5. ——— 44.
5. Luke x. 22.
7. —— xi. 4 (*ap.*)
9. —— xii. 58 1st.
5. ——— 58 2nd.
5. —— xviii. 32,
5. —— xx. 20.
5. —— xxi. 12.
5. —— xxiii. 25.
5. —— xxiv. 7, 20.
— John xvi. 21, see D of (be.)
5. —— xviii. 30, 35, 36.
5. —— xix. 11, 16.
— Acts ii. 23, see D (being.)
— —— iii. 13, see D up.
5. —— vi. 14.
8a. —— vii. 10, 34.
6. ——— 35.
5. —— xii. 4.
8a. ——— 11.
4. —— xv. 30.
5. —— xvi. 4.
5. —— xxi. 11.
5. —— xxii. 4.
2. —— xxiii. 33.
12. —— xxv. 11, 16.
8a. —— xxvi. 17.
5. —— xxvii. 1.
5. Acts xxviii. 16 (*ap.*), 17.
5. Rom. iv. 25.
5. —— vi. 17.
11. —— vii. 6.
7. ——— 24.
10. —— viii. 21.
— ——— 32, see D up.
— —— xv. 31, see D (be.)
5. 1 Cor. v. 5.
5. —— xi. 2, 23.
5. —— xv. 3.
— ——— 24, see D up.
7. 2 Cor. i. 10 3 times.
5. —— iv 11.
8a. Gal. i. 4.
7 Col. i. 13.
7. 1 Thes. i. 10.
— 2 Thes. iii. 2, see D (be.)
5. 1 Tim. i. 20.
7. 2 Tim. iii. 11.
— —— iv. 17, see D (be.)
7. ——— 18.
9. Heb. ii. 15.
— —— xi. 11, see D of (be.)
5. 2 Pet. ii. 4.
7. ——— 7, 9.
5. ——— 21.
5. Jude 3.
— Rev. xii. 2, 4, see D (be.)
— —— xx. 13, see D up.

DELIVER AGAIN.

3. Luke ix. 42.

DELIVER UP.

5. Matt. iv. 12, marg. (text, *cast into prison.*)
5. —— x. 17, 19, 21.
5. —— xxiv. 9.
5. Mark xiii. 9, 11.
5. Acts iii. 13.
5. Rom. viii. 32.
5. 1 Cor. xv. 24.
1. Rev. xx. 13.

DELIVERED (BE.)

1. **ῥύομαι**, *see* "DELIVER," *No.* 7. ***Aorist.***

2. **τίκτω**, to bring forth, to bear *as offspring*.

2. Luke i. 57.
1. ——— 74.
2. —— ii. 6.
1. Rom. xv. 31.
1. 2 Thes. iii. 2.
1. 2 Tim. iv. 17.
2. Rev. xii. 2, 4.

DELIVERED OF (BE.)

1. **τίκτω**, *see above*, *No.* 2.

2. **γεννάω**, *spoken of men*, to beget; *of women*, to bear. *Pass.* to be begotten, be born.

2. John xvi. 21.
1. Heb. xi. 11 (G ~ ℵ²) (*om.* All.)

DELIVERED (BEING.)

ἔκδοτος, given *or* delivered out of *or* up.

Acts ii. 23.

DELIVERANCE.

1. **ἀπολύτρωσις**, a ransoming; deliverance *on account of a ransom paid*, (*non occ.*)

2. **ἄφεσις**, a letting go, a sending forth; dismission, a setting free *as from captivity*, or *as from sins, hence*, remission, pardon.

2. Luke iv. 18.
1. Heb. xi. 35.

DELIVERER.

1. *λυτρωτής*, a redeemer, a ransomer.

2. ὁ, the, ῥυόμενος, delivering one, *(from ῥύομαι, to draw or snatch for one's self, (as from danger,)* — the Deliverer.

1. Acts vii. 35. | 2. Rom. xi. 26.

DELUSION.

πλάνη, a wandering, seduction *from the truth*, error.

2 Thes. ii. 11.

DEMAND (-ED.)

1. *πυνθάνομαι*, to ask, enquire, learn by asking *or* inquiring, to ask for information.

2. *ἐπερωτάω*, to ask at *or* of *any one*, to question, ask *specifically*.

1. Matt. ii. 4. | 2. Luke xvii. 20.
1. Acts xxi. 33.

DEMAND OF.

2. Luke iii. 14.

DEMONSTRATION.

ἀπόδειξις, a pointing out, a showing *as by argument*, a demonstration, proof, *(non occ.)*

1 Cor. ii. 4.

DEN (-s.)

σπήλαιον, a cave, cavern, den, *(Latin*, spelunca,) (occ. John xi. 38.)

Matt. xxi. 13. | Luke xix. 46.
Mark xi. 17. | Heb. xi. 38.
Rev. vi. 15.

DENY (-ED, -ETH, -ING.)

1. *ἀρνέομαι*, to deny, disown; to say no, refuse, decline, (occ. Acts vii. 35; Heb. xi. 24.)

2. *ἀπαρνέομαι*, *(No.* 1 with *ἀπό*, from, *prefixed,)* to deny utterly, abjure.

   (a) *with μή*, not.

3. *ἀντιλέγω*, to speak against, to contradict.

   (a) *followed by μή*, not, *as here*, to deny.

1. Matt. x. 33 twice.
2. —— xvi. 24.
2. —— xxvi. 24, 35.
1. —— 70, 72.
2. —— 75.
2. Mark viii. 34.
2. —— xiv. 30, 31.
1. —— 68, 70.
2. —— 72.
1. Luke viii. 45.
2. —— ix. 23 (No. 1, G L T Tr A ℵ.)
1. —— xii. 9 1st.
2. —— 9 2nd.
3a. —— xx. 27 (λέγω, *say*, Lm Tr ℵ.)
2. —— xxii. 34 (*om.* μή, L Tr ℵ.)
1. Luke xxii. 57.
2. —— 61.
1. John i. 20.
2. —— xiii. 38 (No. 1, L T Tr A.)
1. —— xviii. 25, 27.
1. Acts iii. 13, 14.
1. —— iv. 16.
1. 1 Tim. v. 8.
1. 2 Tim. ii. 12 twice, 13.
1. —— iii. 5.
1. Titus i. 16.
1. —— ii. 12.
1. 2 Pet. ii. 1.
1. 1 John ii. 22 twice, 23.
1. Jude 4.
1. Rev. ii. 13.
1. —— iii. 8.

DEPART (-ED, -ETH, -ING.)

1. *ἀπέρχομαι*, to come *or* go away from *one place to another; hence, gen.* to go away, depart for, set off.

2. *διέρχομαι*, to come *or* go through, to pass through, *hence*, simply to pass to *a place.*

3. *ἐξέρχομαι*, to come *or* go out of *any place*, to come *or* go forth.

4. *κατέρχομαι*, to come *or* go down, to descend.

5. *πορεύω*, to cause to pass over *by land or water*, transport, *hence, Mid.*, to transport one's self, to betake one's self, *i.e.* to depart from *one place* to *another.*

6. *ἐκπορεύομαι*, *(No.* 5 *with ἐκ*, out of *prefixed,)* to go out of, to go *or* come forth, to proceed out of.

7. *χωρίζω*, to put apart, sever.

   (a) *Mid.* to separate one's self, to depart *as from a place or person.*

8. *ἀποχωρίζω*, *(No.* 7 *with ἀπό*, from, *prefixed,)* to separate off, *i.e.* to designate, appoint.

   (a) *Mid.* to separate one's self from, (occ. Acts xv. 39.)

9. *διαχωρίζω*, *(No.* 7 *with διά*, through, *prefixed,)* to separate throughout, *i.e.* wholly.

   (a) *Mid.* to separate one's self wholly from, *(non occ.)*

10. *ἀναχωρέω*, to go back, recede, *(spoken of those who flee. In N.T. simply* to retire, withdraw, *(from ἀνά*, up *or* back, *and χωρέω*, to make room for, give place to.)

11. ἀποχωρέω, to depart from, go away, withdraw from, *(from* ἀπό, from, *and* χωρέω, to make room for, give place to,) *(non occ.)*

12. ἀνάγω, to lead up, conduct *or* bring up, *as from* a lower to a higher place.

(a) *In N.T. Mid. as a nautical term,* to lead *a ship* up *or* out *as upon the sea, hence,* to put to sea, set sail from *any place.*

13. παράγω, to lead along near, to lead by *or* past, to pass along, pass by.

14. ὑπάγω, to lead *or* bring under *as horses under a yoke. In N.T. and later usage,* to go away *(prop.* under *cover, out of sight, strictly with the idea of stealth, stillness, without noise or notice.)*

15. μεταβαίνω, to pass over *from one place to another,* remove, *(from* βαίνω, *used of all motion on the ground,* go, walk, tread, step, *etc., the direction being determined by the prep. prefixed, here by* μετά, after.)

16 { εἰς, unto, with a view to, / τὸ, the, / ἀναλῦσαι, to return, } *Lit.*, to loosen back again, *and so,* to return, (Luke xii. 36.) See every occurrence in the lxx : Tob. ii. 1; Judith xiii. 1, 1 Esd. iii. 3; Wisd. ii. 1; v. 12; xvi. 14; Ecclus. iii. 15; 2 Macc. viii 25; ix. 1, xii. 7.; xv 28. *See pp.* 739, 740.

17. ἀπολύω, to loose from, set free, release from, to disband *as an army.*

(a) *in Mid.* get free, depart from.

18 μεταίρω to lift away, take away, *from one place to another. In N.T intrans.* to take one's self away, *i.e.* depart, *(non occ.)*

19 ἔξειμι, to go out of *a place,* go away, depart out of.

20 ἀπαλλάσσω, to change from, remove from.

(a) *Mid* to remove one's self from, *or intrans* to leave

5 Matt ii 9.
10 —— 12. 13, 14
10 —— iv 12.
11 —— vii 23
1 Matt viii 18
15 —— 34.
1 —— ix 7
13 —— 27.
8. Matt. ix. 31.
— —— x.14, see D out of.
15. —— xi. 1.
5. —— 7.
15 —— xii. 9.
18. —— xiii. 53
10. —— xiv. 13.
1. —— 16.
10. —— xv. 21.
15. —— 29.
1. —— xvi. 4.
— —— xvii. 18, see D out of.
18. —— xix. 1.
5. —— 15.
6. —— xx. 29
5. —— xxiv. 1.
5. —— xxv. 41.
10. —— xxvii. 5.
1. —— 60.
8. —— xxviii. 8 (No. 1, T Tr A ℵ.)
1. Mark i. 35, 42.
1. —— v. 17, 20.
8. —— vi 10.
6. —— 31.
1. —— 32
14. —— 33
1 —— 46.
3. —— vii. 31.
1. —— viii. 13.
8. —— ix. 30.
1. Luke i. 28, 38.
— —— ii. 29, see D (let.)
— —— 37, } see D
— —— iv. 13, } from.
3. —— 42 1st.
5. —— 42 2nd.
8. —— v. 8.
1. —— 13, 25.
1. —— vii. 24.
8. —— viii. 35.
1. —— 37.
8. —— 38.
8. —— ix. 4, 6.
9a. —— 33 (inf.)
11. —— 39.
1. —— x. 30.
3. —— 35 (om. G ⇉ L Tr ℵ.)
3. —— xii. 59.
— —— xiii. 27, see D from.
5 —— 31.
— —— xxi. 21, see D out.
1 —— xxiv. 12 (ap.)
1 John iv. 3.
3. —— 43.
1 —— v 15
10. John vi. 15.
15. —— vii. 3.
1. —— xii. 36.
15. —— xiii. 1.
6. —— xvi. 7.
7a. Acts i 4.
5. —— v. 41.
1. —— x. 7.
3. —— xi. 25.
— —— xii. 10, see D from.
8. —— 17.
4. —— xiii. 4
11. —— 13.
2. —— 14.
8. —— xiv. 20.
— —— xv. 38, see D from.
— —— 39, see D asunder.
3. —— 40.
3. —— xvi. 36.
— —— 39, see D out of.
3. —— 40.
19. —— xvii. 15.
8. —— 33.
7a. —— xviii. 1, 2.
15. —— 7.
8. —— 23.
—— xix. 9, see D from
20a. —— 12.
8, —— xx. 1.
19. —— 7
8. —— 11
8. —— xxi. 5, 8.
5. —— xxii. 21.
— —— 29, see D from.
— —— xxiii. 22, see D (let.)
6. —— xxv. 4.
12a. — xxvii. 12.
12a. — xxviii. 10, 11.
17a. —— 25.
1. —— 29 (ap.)
7a. 1 Cor. vii. 10, 11 15 twice.
— 2 Cor. xii. 8, see D from.
16. Phil. i. 23.
3. —— iv. 15.
— 1 Tim. iv. 1, } see D
— 2 Tim. ii. 19, } from
5. —— iv. 10.
7a. Philem. 15.
— Heb. iii. 12, see D from.
14. Jas ii. 16.
8a. Rev. vi. 14.
1 —— xviii. 14 1st.
1. —— 14 2nd (ἀπόλλυμι, *to perish,* G L T Tr A ℵ.)

DEPART ASUNDER.

ἀποχωρίζομαι, *see* "DEPART," *No.* 8a.

Acts xv 39

DEPART FROM.

ἀφίστημι, (a) *trans.* to place away from, *i.e.* remove, cause to depart.

(b) *intrans. (Mid.)* to place one's self away from, *i.e.* depart from.

b. Luke ii. 37
a. —— iv. 13.
b. —— xiii. 27.
a Acts xii. 10
a. —— xv 38
a. Acts xix. 9
a. —— xxii. 29
a. 2 Cor xii 8.
b. 1 Tim iv. 1.
a. 2 Tim ii. 19.
a. Heb. iii. 12

DEPART OUT.

ἐκχωρέω, to go out and away, to leave *a country,* emigrate, *(non occ.)*

Luke xxi. 21.

DEPART OUT OF.

ἐξέρχομαι, *see* "DEPART," *No.* 3.

Matt. x. 14.
—— xvii. 18, with ἀπό, *from.*
Acts xvi. 39 (No. 1, with ἀπό, *from,* L T Tr A ℵ.)

DEPART (LET.)

ἀπολύω, *see* "DEPART," *No.* 17.

Luke ii. 29. | Acts xxiii. 22.

DEPARTING.

1. ἄφιξις, an arrival, a coming to *a place or person, hence,* a departure *regarded in the light of its end and object, (non occ.)*
2. ἔξοδος, a way out, exit; *(hence, Eng.* exodus,) journey out, departure.

1. Acts xx. 29. | 2. Heb. xi. 22.

DEPARTURE.

ἀνάλυσις, a loosing, releasing; dissolving, *used of* the breaking up *of a banquet; and also of the body, (whence Eng.* analysis,) *(non occ.)*

2 Tim. iv. 6.

DEPTH.

1. βάθος, depth. *In N.T.* the deep water *as opp. to the shallows near the shore. Metaph.* the depth, *and pl.* the deep things, *i.e.* the secret unrevealed purposes *of any one.*
2. πέλαγος, the high sea, the open sea, (occ. Acts xxviii. 5.)

2. Matt. xviii. 6.
1. Mark iv. 5.
1. Rom. viii. 39.
1. —— xi. 33.
1. Eph. iii. 18.
1. Rev. ii. 24 (βαθύς, *the deep* [*things*], G L T Tr A.)

DEPUTY.

ἀνθύπατος, a pro-consul, *(non occ.)*

Acts xiii. 7, 8, 12; xix. 38.

DEPUTY (BE.)

ἀνθυπατεύω, to be a pro-consul.

Acts xviii. 12 (ἀνθυπάτου ὄντος, *being a pro-consul,* G ~ L T* Tr A ℵ.)
* 7th Edition.

DERIDE (-ED.)

ἐκμυκτηρίζω, to turn up the nose at, deride out and out, *(non occ.)*

Luke xvi. 14; xxiii. 35.

DESCEND (-ED, -ETH, -ING.)

1. καταβαίνω, to go *or* come down, to descend *from a higher to a lower place, (from* βαίνω, *used of all kinds of motion on the ground, as* go, walk, step.)
2. κατέρχομαι, to come *or* go down, *used of the act of coming.*

1. Matt. iii. 16.
1. —— vii. 25, 27.
1. —— xxviii. 2.
1. Mark i. 10.
1. —— xv. 32.
1. Luke iii. 22.
1. John i. 32, 33, 51.
1. Acts x. 11.
1. —— xi. 5.
1. —— xxiv. 1.
1. Rom. x. 7.
1. Eph. iv. 9, 10.
1. 1 Thes. iv. 16.
2. Jas. iii. 15.
1. Rev. xxi. 10.

DESCENT.

κατάβασις, a going down; a way down, descent, *(non occ.)*

Luke xix. 37.

DESCENT IS...COUNTED (ONE'S.)

γενεαλογέομαι, to derive one's pedigree, *(non occ.)*

Heb. vii. 6, marg. *one's pedigree, etc.*

DESCENT (WITHOUT.)

ἀγενεαλόγητος, without genealogy, without pedigree, *(non occ.)*

Heb. vii. 3, marg. *without pedigree.*

DESCRIBE (-ETH.)

1. γράφω, to grave *or* cut in; *prop.* to form letters with a stylus in the ancient manner so that the letters were cut in *or* graven upon the material, *hence,* to write.
2. λέγω, to lay, to lay before, *i.e.* to relate, to recount; *hence,* to say, to speak, to discourse.

2. Rom. iv. 6. | 1. Rom. x. 5.

DESERT [noun.]

1. **ἔρημος**, *adj.*, deserted, desolate, waste, *as subst. with art.* a desert.
2. **ἐρημία**, a solitude; loneliness; an uninhabited tract, a desert.

1. Matt. xxiv. 26.
1. Luke i. 80.
1. John vi. 31.
2. Heb. xi. 38.

DESERT [adj.]

ἔρημος, *adj.*, *see above, No.* 1.

Matt. xiv. 13, 15.
Mark i. 45.
—— vi. 31, 32, 35.
Luke iv. 42.
—— ix. 10 (*ap.*), 12.
Acts viii. 26.

DESIRE [noun.]

1. **ἐπιθυμία**, a desire, yearning, longing; *denoting the inward passion and mental desire, thus differing from* ὄρεξις, which combines the *notion of the outward thing desired.*
2. **εὐδοκία**, a being well pleased, delight *in any person or thing;* good-pleasure.
3. **θέλημα**, will, active volition, the act of willing.

1. Luke xxii. 15 (dative) (marg. *heartily.*)
2. Rom. x. 1.
— —— xv. 23, see D (great)
— 2 Cor. vii. 7, see D (earnest)
— 2 Cor. vii. 11, see D (vehement.)
3. Eph. ii. 3, marg. *will.*
1. Phil. i. 23.
1. 1 Thes. ii. 17.

DESIRE (EARNEST.)

ἐπιπόθησις, a longing for, desire after, earnest desire.

2 Cor. vii. 7.

DESIRE (GREAT.)

ἐπιποθία, earnest desire.

Rom. xv. 23.

DESIRE (VEHEMENT.)

ἐπιπόθησις, *see* "DESIRE (EARNEST)."

2 Cor. vii. 11.

DESIRE (-ED, -ETH, -ING) [verb.]

1. **αἰτέω**, to ask *for something*, require, demand, *(expressive of a petition from an inferior to a superior.)*
2. **ἐξαιτέω**, to ask out and out, desire to have.
   (a) *Mid.* to demand for one's self, *(No.* 1 *with* ἐξ, out of, *prefixed.)*
3. **θέλω**, to will, wish, desire, *implying the active volition and purpose, and expressive of the natural impulse or desire.*
4. **παρακαλέω**, to call hither *or* towards, to speak to; *used of every kind of* speaking to *which is meant to produce a particular effect;* to call some one hither, that *he may do something, or to admonish, encourage, exhort, comfort or persuade him, (appealing to the will rather than to the head or the heart.)*
5. **ἐπιθυμέω**, to fix the desire upon, desire earnestly, long for; *denoting the inward affection of the mind rather than the external object.*
6. **ἐρωτάω**, to ask *as for information*, to question *as well as* supplicate.
7. **ἐπερωτάω**, *(No.* 6 *with* ἐπί, upon, *prefixed,)* to ask at *or* of *any one*, require, demand.
8. **ζητέω**, to seek after, look for, to strive to find.
9. **ἐπιζητέω**, *(No.* 8 *with* ἐπί, upon, *prefixed,)* to seek earnestly *or* continuously.
10. **ἐπιπόθεω**, to desire upon, *i.e.* over and above, besides, to desire earnestly, long for.
11. **ἀξιόω**, deem worthy, regard as suitable, deem proper.
12. **ὀρέγω**, to reach *or* stretch out; *in N.T. only Mid.*, to stretch one's self, *reach after a thing, hence,* long after, try to gain *with special reference to object desired.*
13. **ζηλόω**, to have zeal for, *i.e.* for *or* against *any person or thing;* to be zealous towards *in a good or bad sense.*

8. Matt. xii. 46, 47.
5. —— xiii. 17.
7. —— xvi. 1.
4. —— xviii. 32.
1. —— xx. 20.
8. Mark ix. 35.
1. —— x. 35.
1. —— xi. 24.
1. —— xv. 6, 8.
3. Luke v. 39.
6. Luke vii. 36.
8. —— viii. 20.
8. —— ix. 9.
3. —— x. 24.
6. —— xiv. 32.
5. —— xvi. 21.
5. —— xvii. 22.
3. —— xx. 46.
5. —— xxii. 15.
2a. —— 31.

1. Luke xxiii. 25.
6. John xii. 21.
1. Acts iii. 14.
1. —— vii. 46.
4. —— viii. 31.
1. —— ix. 2.
4. ——— 38.
1. —— xii. 20.
9. —— xiii. 7.
1. ——— 21, 28.
6. —— xvi. 39.
6. —— xviii. 20.
4. —— xix. 31.
6. —— xxiii. 20.
1. —— xxv. 3, 15.
4. —— xxviii. 14.
11. ——— 22.
13. 1 Cor. xiv. 1.
4. —— xvi. 12.
— 2 Cor. v. 2, see D earnestly.
4. —— viii. 6.
3. 2 Cor. xi. 12.
3. 2 Cor. xii. 6.
4. ——— 18.
3. Gal. iv. 9, 20, 21.
3. —— vi. 12, 13.
1. Eph. iii. 13.
9. Phil. iv. 17 twice.
1. Col. i. 9.
— 1 Thes. iii. 6, see D greatly.
3. 1 Tim. i. 7.
4. —— ii. 1, marg. (text, *exhort.*)
12. —— iii. 1 1st.
5. ——— 1 2nd.
— 2 Tim. i. 4, see D greatly.
5. Heb. vi. 11.
12. —— xi. 16.
— Jas. iv. 2, see D to have.
5. 1 Pet. i. 12.
10. —— ii. 2.
1. 1 John v. 15.
5. Rev. ix. 6.

DESIRE EARNESTLY.

10. 2 Cor. v. 2.

DESIRE GREATLY.

10. 1 Thes. iii. 6. | 10. 2 Tim. i. 4.

DESIRE TO HAVE.

13. Jas. iv. 2.

DESIROUS.

θέλω, *see* "DESIRE," *No.* 3.

Luke xxiii. 8. | 2 Cor. xi. 32.

DESIROUS (BE.)

John xvi. 19.

DESIROUS OF (BE AFFECTIONATELY.)

ἱμείρομαι, to have a strong affection for, yearning after.

1 Thes. ii. 8 (G∾) (ὁμείρομαι, same meaning, G L T Tr A ℵ.)

DESIROUS OF VAIN GLORY.

κενόδοξος, vain-glorious, *i.e.* full of empty pride and ambition.

Gal. v. 26.

DESOLATE.

1. ἔρημος, *(adj.)* deserted, desolate, waste.
2. ἐρημόω, to make desolate, lay waste.
3. μονόω, to leave alone.
   (a) *Pass.* to be left alone, *as a widow*, to be solitary, *i.e.* childless.

1. Matt. xxiii. 38 (*om.* L.)
1. Luke xiii. 35 (*om.* G L T Tr A ℵ.)
1. Acts i. 20.
1. Gal. iv. 27.
3a. 1 Tim. v. 5.
2. Rev. xvii. 16.

DESOLATE (MAKE.)

2. Rev. xviii. 19.

DESOLATION.

ἐρήμωσις, a making desolate, a laying waste, *(non occ.)*

Matt. xxiv. 15. | Mark xiii. 14. | Luke xxi. 20.

DESOLATION (BRING TO.)

ἐρημόω, to make desolate, lay waste.

Matt. xii. 25. | Luke xi. 17.

DESPAIR (IN.)

ἐξαπορέομαι, to be wholly without resource, to despair utterly, *(non occ.)*

2 Cor. iv. 8, marg. *altogether without help of means.*

DESPAIR (-ED) [verb.]

2 Cor. i. 8.

DESPISE (-ED, -EST, -ING.)

1. καταφρονέω, to think down upon *or* against *any one; hence,* to think slightly of, *(non occ.)*
2. περιφρονέω, to think round about *a thing*, turn over in the mind, speculate about; *then,* to pass over *or* beyond in thought, *i.e.* to neglect, overlook, *(non occ.)*
3. ἀθετέω, to displace, set aside, disregard.
4. ἐξουθενέω, to set out at nought, treat as contemptible.
5. ἀτιμάζω, not to hold in honour, esteem lightly, dishonour.
6. ὀλιγωρέω, to care little for, careless about.
7. { λογίζομαι, to count, reckon, calculate, consider, εἰς, unto, for, οὐδέν, nothing, } be counted for nothing.

1. Matt. vi. 24.
1. —— xviii. 10.
3. Luke x. 16 4 times.
1. —— xvi. 13.
4. —— xviii. 9.
7. Acts xix. 27.
1. Rom. ii. 4.
4. —— xiv. 3.
4 1 Cor. i. 28.
1. —— xi. 22.
4. —— xvi. 11.
4. Gal. iv. 14.
3. 1 Thes. iv. 8 twice, marg. *reject.*
4. —— v. 20.
1. 1 Tim. iv. 12.
1. —— vi. 2.
2. Titus ii. 15.
3. Heb. x. 28.
1. —— xii. 2.
6. —— 5.
5. Jas. ii. 6.
1. 2 Pet. ii. 10.
3. Jude 8.

DESPISED.

ἄτιμος, without honour.

1 Cor. iv. 10.

DESPISER (-S.)

καταφρονητής, a despiser, contemner, *(from* "DESPISE," *No.* 1,) *(non occ.)*

Acts xiii. 41.

DESPISER (-S) OF THOSE THAT ARE GOOD.

ἀφιλάγαθος, without love to good men, unfriendly, *(non occ.)*

2 Tim. iii. 3.

DESPITE UNTO (DO.)

ἐνυβρίζω, to use wanton insult towards *any one, (non occ.)*

Heb. x. 29.

DESPITEFUL.

ὑβριστής, outrageous in personal insults, a wanton insolent man, (occ. 1 Tim. i. 13.)

Rom. i. 30.

DESPITEFULLY (USE.)

1. ἐπηρεάζω, to use threats, threaten; to treat with insult, (occ. 1 Pet. iii. 6.)
2. ὑβρίζω, to use wanton insult, act with insolence.

1. Matt. v. 44 (*ap.*) | 1. Luke vi. 28.
2. Acts xiv. 5.

DESTITUTE.

1. ἀποστερέω, defraud of, to deprive of.
2. λείπω, to leave, forsake.
   (a) *Pass.* to be left, forsaken of *any thing, i.e.* destitute of.

1. 1 Tim. vi. 5 (pass.) | 2a. Jas. ii. 15 (part.)

DESTITUTE (BE.)

ὑστερέω, to be last, *(of place, dignity or condition, etc.,)* to be behind, *hence,* to lack, fail *of a thing,* come short of.

Heb. xi. 37.

DESTROY (-ED, -EST.)

1. ἀπόλλυμι, to destroy utterly *(stronger form of* ὄλλυμι, to destroy.) *Homer uses it chiefly of death in battle,* to kill; to lose utterly (the subject being the sufferer.) *The fundamental thought is* not annihilation, *but* ruin, loss, *(as* sheep, Matt. x. 6; xv. 24, *etc.;* Luke xv. 4, 6, lost *to the fold and to the shepherd; so the* lost son, Luke xv. 24,) to perish, come to an end *(as* bread, John vi. 27; gold, 1 Pet. i. 7.)
2. λύω, to loose, loosen *(what is fast), i.e.* unbind; to loosen, *i.e.* dissolve, sever, break, demolish.
3. καταλύω, *(No.* 2 *with* κατά, down, *prefixed,)* to loosen down, to dissolve, *i.e.* to disunite the parts of any thing, *spoken of buildings* to throw down, put an end to.
4. καταργέω, to render inactive, idle; *esp. of land* to spoil, make useless, void, abolish, make without effect.
5. ὀλοθρεύω, to destroy, slay, *(non occ.)*
6. ἐξολοθρεύω, *(No.* 5 *with* ἐξ, out of, *prefixed,)* to destroy utterly, slay wholly, *(non occ.)*
7. φθείρω, to spoil, corrupt, to bring into a worse state, deprave, mar.
8. διαφθείρω, *(No.* 7 *with* δία, through, *prefixed,)* to corrupt throughout *or* entirely, decay wholly, perish.
9. πορθέω, to lay waste, ravage, destroy, (occ. Gal. i. 13.)
10. καθαιρέω, to take down *(as from a higher place); then, with the idea of force,* to pull down, overthrow, *hence,* to conquer, cast down *as kings from their thrones.*

1. Matt. ii. 13.
3. —— v. 17 twice.
1. —— x. 28.
1. —— xii. 14.
1. —— xxi. 41.
1. —— xxii. 7.
3. Matt. xxvi. 61.
1. —— xxvii. 20.
3. —— 40.
1. Mark i. 24.
1. —— iii. 6.
1. —— ix. 22.

1. Mark xi. 18.
1. —— xii. 9.
3. —— xiv. 58.
3. —— xv. 29.
1. Luke iv. 34.
1. ——vi. 9(G ~)(*ἀποκτείνω to kill outright*, G.)
1. —— ix. 56 (*ap.*)
1. —— xvii. 27, 29.
1. —— xix. 47.
1. —— xx. 16.
2. John ii. 19.
1. —— x. 10.
6. Acts iii. 23.
3. —— vi. 14.
9. —— ix. 21.
10. —— xiii. 19 (part.)
10. —— xix. 27.
4. Rom. vi. 6.
1. —— xiv. 15.
3. ——— 20.
1. 1 Cor. i. 19.
7. —— iii. 17 1st.
7. ——— 17 2nd, marg. *defile.*
4. —— vi. 13.
— —— x. 9, 10, see D (be)
4. —— xv. 26.
— 2 Cor. iv. 9, see D (be.)
9. Gal. i. 23.
3. —— ii. 18.
4. 2 Thes. ii. 8.
4. Heb. ii. 14.
5. —— xi. 28.
1. Jas. iv. 12.
— 2 Pet. ii. 12, see D (to be.)
2. 1 John iii. 8.
1. Jude 5.
8. Rev. viii. 9.
8. —— xi. 18 1st, 2nd, marg. *corrupt.*

DESTROYED (BE.)

ἀπόλλυμι, *(Mid. of* "DESTROY," *No.* 1, *which see,)* to be destroyed, perish; *of persons*, to be put to death; *of things*, to be lost, ruined.

1 Cor. x. 9, 10. | 2 Cor. iv. 9.

DESTROYED (TO BE.)

{ εἰς, unto, for, φθορά, a spoiling, corruption, the bringing into a worse state, } for a spoiling.

2 Pet. ii. 12.

DESTROYER.

1. ὀλοθρευτής, a destroyer, *(from* "DESTROY," *No.* 5,) *(non occ.)*
2. Ἀπολλύων, *(part. of* "DESTROY," *No.* 1,) the Destroyer, Apollyon, *(non occ.)*

1. 1 Cor. x. 10.
2. Rev. ix. 11, marg. (text, *Apollyon.*)

DESTRUCTION.

1. ἀπώλεια, loss; *of things*, waste, ruin; *of persons*, death, *esp. by violence*, perdition.
2. ὄλεθρος, ruin, death; that which causes death, a ruin *to others*, *(non occ.)*
3. καθαίρεσις, a taking down, a pulling down, demolition, (occ. 2 Cor. x. 4.)
4. σύντριμμα, a breaking together, crushing; *hence*, ruin, destruction, *(non occ.)*

1. Matt. vii. 13.
4. Rom. iii. 16.
1. —— ix. 22.
2. 1 Cor. v. 5.
3. 2 Cor. x. 8.
3. —— xiii. 10.
1. Phil. iii. 19.
2. 1 Thes. v. 3.
2. 2 Thes. i. 9 (ὀλέθριος, *destructive, deadly*, L.)
2. 1 Tim. vi. 9.
1. 2 Pet. ii. 1.
1. 2 Pet. iii. 16.

DETERMINATE.

ὁρίζω, to bound, to make *or* set a boundary; *hence*, to mark out definitely, *i.e.* to determine.

Acts ii. 23 (part.)

DETERMINE (-ED.)

1. κρίνω, to divide, separate; make a distinction, *hence*, select; come to a decision; *hence*, to decide, to judge.
2. ὁρίζω, *see* "DETERMINATE."
3. βουλεύομαι, to resolve in council. *In N.T. only Mid.*, to take counsel, *i.e.* to consult, deliberate *with one's self or with another in council.*
4. ἐπιλύω, to let loose upon *(as dogs)*; *of letters*, to break open thereupon; *then*, to solve, *the idea of* further being implied, (occ. Mark iv. 34.)
5. τάσσω, to order, set in order, arrange *(as soldiers)*; *hence*, to appoint.

2. Luke xxii. 22.
1. Acts iii. 13.
— —— iv. 28, see D before.
2. —— xi 29.
5. —— xv. 2.
3. ——— 37 (βούλομαι, *to be willing*, G ~ L T (8th ed.) Tr A ℵ.)
2. —— xvii. 26.
4. Acts xix. 39.
1. —— xx. 16.
1. —— xxv. 25.
1. —— xxvii. 1.
1. 1 Cor. ii. 2.
1. —— v. 3, marg. (text, *judge.*)
1. 2 Cor. ii. 1.
1. Titus iii. 12.

DETERMINE BEFORE.

προορίζω, to mark out beforehand, to make *or* set a bound before.

Acts iv. 28.

DEVICE (-S.)

1. ἐνθύμησις, consideration, cogitation, supposition.
2. νόημα, thought, *i.e.* that which is thought out, excogitated; *hence*, purpose, project, device.

1. Acts xvii. 29. | 2. 2 Cor. ii. 11.

DEVIL (-S.)

1. δαίμων, *Eng.* demon *or* subordinate divinity, *(non occ.)*

2. *δαιμόνιον, dim. of N.* 1, (occ. Acts xvii 18.)

[In classic Greek, these words were originally the same as θεός, God, but in what sense is not certain. From Homer downwards they answered to the Latin *numen,* and denoted general divine agency, the working of a higher power, and afterwards it came to denote a destructive power. *In the Septuagint,* δαιμόνιον, is used in a bad sense, and in contrast to θεός, God, (Deut. xxxii. 17), and ἄγγελος, angel. *In the New Test.* the word is specially applied to evil spirits, which are viewed in their morally-destructive influence. They appear as special powers of evil in the service of Satan (Matt. xii. 26-28) influencing the physical and psychical life of human beings. Probably they take possession of the place that belongs to the πνεῦμα (spirit), so that the action of the personal life is disturbed and deranged, hence, Plut. and Xen. use the verb διαμονάω, as meaning "to be deranged." Demoniacal violence essentially differs from Satanic influence wherein the man becomes like the demons the instrument of Satan himself.]

3. Διάβολος, Diabolus, the chief of the Demons, who are his angels, slanderous, calumnious, *also as subst.,* calumniator, accuser, traducer, *(from* διάβαλλω, to throw over, *hence,* accuse, malign.) *Hence, the more general term of* the enemy, the enemy of men, because he is the disturber of their connection with God. *The Hebrew* שטן, Σατανᾶς, Satan, *is more generic than the Greek* Διάβολος, *the former describes his character as* the antagonist and opposer of all good; *the latter, describes his relation to* the saints as their accuser and calumniator, (occ. 1 Tim. iii. 11; 2 Tim. iii. 3; Tit. ii. 3.)

3. Matt. iv. 1, 5, 8, 11.
— —— 24, see Ds (be possessed of the.)
2. —— vii. 22.
— —— viii. 16, 28, see Ds (be possessed with.)
1. —— 31. [sessed of the)
— —— 33, see Ds(be pos-
— Matt. ix. 32, see D (be possessed with a.)
2. —— 33, 34 twice.
2. —— x. 8.
2. —— xi. 18.
— —— xii. 22, see D (be possessed with a.)
2. —— 24 twice, 27, 28.
3. Matt. xiii. 39.
— —— xv. 22, see D (be vexed with a.)
2. —— xvii. 18.
3. —— xxv. 41.
— Mark i. 32, see Ds (be possessed with.)
2. —— 34 twice, 39.
2. —— iii. 15, 22 twice.
1. —— v. 12 (om. G ⇉ L T (8th ed.) Tr A ℵ.)
— —— 15, 16, 18, see D (be possessed with a.)
2. —— vi. 13.
2. —— vii. 26, 29, 30.
2. —— ix. 38.
2. —— xvi. 9 (*ap.*), 17(*ap.*)
2. Luke iv. 2, 3.
3. —— 5 (*om.* G ⇉ T Tr A ℵ.)
3. —— 6, 13.
2. —— 33, 35, 41.
2. —— vii. 33.
2. —— viii. 2.
3. —— 12.
1. —— 29 (No. 2, L ℵ.)
2. —— 30, 33, 35.
— —— 36, see Ds (be possessed of the.)
2. —— 38.
2. —— ix. 1, 42, 49.
2. Luke x. 17.
2. —— xi. 14 twice, 15 twice, 18, 19, 20.
2. —— xiii. 32.
3. John vi. 70.
2. —— vii. 20.
3. —— viii. 44.
2. —— 48, 49, 52.
2. —— x. 20, 21.
3. —— xiii. 2.
3. Acts x. 38.
3. —— xiii. 10.
2. 1 Cor. x. 20 twice, 21 twice.
3. Eph. iv. 27.
3. —— vi. 11.
3. 1 Tim. iii. 6, 7.
2. —— iv. 1.
3. 2 Tim. ii. 26.
3. Heb. ii. 14.
2. Jas. ii. 19.
3. 1 Pet. v. 8.
3. 1 John iii. 8 3 times, 10.
3. Jude 9.
3. Rev. ii. 10.
2. —— ix. 20.
3. —— xii. 9, 12.
1. —— xvi. 14 (No. 2, G L T Tr A ℵ.)
1. —— xviii. 2 (No 2, L Tr A ℵ.)
3. —— xx. 2, 10.

DEVIL (BE POSSESSED WITH A.)

δαιμονίζομαι, to be under the power of a δαίμων, *(see* "DEVIL," *No.* 1,) to be possessed by a δαίμων.

Matt. ix. 32; xii. 22. | Mark v. 15, 16, 18.

DEVIL (BE VEXED WITH A.)

Matt. xv. 22.

DEVIL (HE THAT HATH A.)

John x. 21 (part.)

DEVILS (BE POSSESSED OF THE.)

Matt. viii. 33. | Luke viii. 36 (om. G ⇉.)

DEVILS (BE POSSESSED WITH.)

Matt. iv. 24; viii. 16, 28. | Mark i. 32.

DEVILISH.

δαιμονώδης, demon-like *(adj. of* "DEVIL," *No.* 2,) *(non occ.)*

Jas. iii. 15.

DEVISE (-ED) (CUNNINGLY.)

σοφίζω, to make wise, *i.e.* skilful, expert.

(a) *Mid.,* to make wisely, devise skilfully *or* artfully. *In Greek profane writers* to deceive.

a. 2 Pet. i. 16 (part.)

DEVOTION.

σέβασμα, that for which awe is felt, an object of awe *or* worship, (occ. 2 Thes. ii. 4.)

Acts xvii. 23, marg. *god that one worshippeth.*

DEVOUR (-ETH, -ED.)

1. ἐσθίω, *(strengthened form, from obs. root* ἔδω ; *Aor.* 2, ἔφαγον, *from obs. root* φάγω,) to eat, take food; *hence,* consume by eating.
2. κατεσθίω, to eat down, swallow down, devour.
3. καταπίνω, to drink down, swallow down *as by drinking, same as Eng.,* to swallow up.

2. Matt. xiii. 4, see D up.
2. —— xxiii. 14 *(ap.)*
— Mark iv. 4, see D up.
2. —— xii. 40.
2. Luke viii. 5.
2. —— xv. 30.
2. —— xx. 47.
2. 2 Cor. xi. 20.
2. Gal. v. 15.
1. Heb. x. 27.
3. 1 Pet. v. 8.
2. Rev. xi. 5.
2. —— xii. 4.
2. —— xx. 9.

DEVOUR UP.

2. Matt. xiii. 4. | 2. Mark iv. 4.

DEVOUT.

1. εὐλαβής, taking well hold, *i.e.* carefully, circumspectly, *hence,* cautious, careful *as to what is right in religion ;* avoidance through godly fear of doing anything contrary to right, the fulfilling of all the duties of piety and humanity, *(non occ.)*
2. εὐσεβής, reverence for God which shews itself in actions, practical piety of every kind, the energy of piety in the life, *(just as No. 1 is* that piety which governs the soul,) reverence well and rightly directed, (occ. 2 Pet. ii. 9.)
3. σέβομαι, to feel awe *or* fear before God and man *(esp. when about to do wrong, hence,* to feel shame, be ashamed ;) to worship, honour.

1. Luke ii. 25.
1. Acts ii. 5.
1. —— viii. 2.
2. Acts x. 2, 7.
3. —— xiii. 50 (part.)
— —— xvii. 17, see D person
2. Acts xxii. 12 (No. 1, L T Tr A ℵ.)

DEVOUT PERSON.

3. Acts xvii. 17 (part.)

DIE (-ED, -ETH, -ING) [verb.]

1. θνήσκω, to die, be dying *of natural as of violent death.*
2. ἀποθνήσκω, to die out, expire, become quite dead.
3. τελευτάω, to end, *i.e.* to finish, to complete; *hence,* to end *one's life,* to die.
4. ἀπόλλυμι, to destroy wholly, cause to perish, *(see* "DESTROY," *No.* 1.)
   (a) *Mid., of persons,* to be put to death.
5. { εἰς, unto, ἀπώλεια, destruction.

3. Matt. xv. 4
2. —— xxii. 24, 27.
2. —— xxvi. 35.
3. Mark vii. 10.
3. —— ix. 44 *(ap.)*, 46, 48.
2. —— xii. 19, 20, 21, 22.
— —— xiv. 31, see D with.
3. Luke vii. 2.
2. —— xvi. 22 twice.
2. —— xx. 28 1st.
2. —— 28 2nd (ἤ, *be,* L T (8th ed.) Tr ℵc.)
2. —— 29, 30 *(ap.)*, 31, 32, 36.
2. John iv. 49.
2. —— vi. 50.
2. —— viii. 21, 24 twice.
2. —— xi. 16.
1. —— 21 (No. 2, G ∾ L T (8th ed.) Tr ℵ.)
2. —— 26, 32, 37, 50, 51.
2. —— xii. 24 twice, 33.
4. —— xviii. 14 (No. 2, G ∾ L T (8th ed.) Tr ℵ.)
2. —— 32.
2. —— xix. 7.
2. —— xxi. 23 twice.
3. Acts vii. 15.
2. —— ix. 37.
2. Acts xxi. 13.
2. —— xxv. 11.
5. —— 16 *(om.* G L T Tr A ℵ.)
2. Rom. v. 6, 7 twice, 8.
2. —— vi. 9, 10 twice.
2. —— vii. 9.
2. —— viii. 13, 34.
2. —— xiv. 7, 8 3 times, 9, 15.
2. 1 Cor. viii. 11.
2. —— ix. 15.
2. —— xv. 3, 22, 31, 32, 36.
2. 2 Cor. v. 14, 15 twice.
2. —— vi. 9.
— —— vii. 3, see D with.
2. Phil. i. 21.
2. 1 Thes. iv. 14.
2. —— v. 10.
2. Heb. vii. 8.
2. —— ix. 27.
2. —— x. 28.
2. —— xi. 13.
3. —— 22 (part.)
2. Rev. iii. 2 (ἀποβάλλω, *cast away,* G ∾.)
2. —— viii. 9, 11.
2. —— ix. 6.
2. —— xiv. 13.
2. —— xvi. 3.

DIE WITH.

συναποθνήσκω, *(No.* 2 *with* σύν, together with, *prefixed,)* to die with *any one.*

Mark xiv. 31. | 2 Cor. vii. 3.

DIFFER (things that) [margin.]

{ τὰ, the *things,* διαφέροντα, differing, *(from* διαφέρω, *see* "DIFFER (FROM).")

Rom. ii. 18, text, *things that are more excellent.*
Phil. i. 10, text, *things that are excellent.*

DIFFER FROM.

διαφέρω, to bear *or* carry through ; bear asunder, carry different ways, *hence,* to be different from.

1 Cor. xv. 41. | Gal. iv. 1.

DIFFER (MAKE TO.)

διακρίνω, to separate throughout, *i.e.*, wholly, completely, *hence*, to make a distinction, to separate one from another.

1 Cor. iv. 7, marg. *distinguish.*

DIFFERENCE (-S.)

1. *διαίρεσις*, the act of dividing, division, (occ. 1 Cor. xii. 4, 6.)
2. *διαστολή*, a putting *or* drawing asunder, separation, distinction, (occ. 1 Cor. xiv. 7.)

2 Rom. iii. 22; x. 12. | 1. 1 Cor. xii. 5.

DIFFERENCE BETWEEN (BE.)

μερίζω, to part, divide into parts.

(a) *Pass.*, to be divided, *hence*, be distinct.

a. 1 Cor. vii. 34.

DIFFERENCE (MAKE A.)

διακρίνω, to separate throughout *or* one from another, *hence*, to make a distinction.

(a) *Mid. and Pass.* to separate one's self from.

a. Jude 22.

DIFFERENCE (PUT A.)

Acts xv. 9.
a. Rom. xiv. 23, marg. (text, *doubt.*)

DIFFERING.

διάφορος, different, *i.e.* diverse, various.

Rom. xii. 6.

DIG (-ED.)

1. *ὀρύσσω*, to dig, dig up *as soil*, *(non occ.)*
2. *σκάπτω*, to dig, delve *(akin to Eng.* scoop), *(non occ.)*

1. Matt. xxi. 33.
1. —— xxv. 18.
1. Mark xii. 1.
2. Luke vi. 48.
2. —— xiii. 8.
2. —— xvi. 3.

DIG DOWN.

κατασκάπτω, to dig down under, to undermine, *hence*, overthrow.

Rom. xi. 3.

See also, DEEP.

DIGNITY (-IES.)

δόξα, opinion, notion; seeming; reputation, renown *gen. in an honourable sense, then*, appearance, aspect *which commands recognition, equivalent to* splendour, brilliance, glory; manifestation of glory; angelic powers *so far as their appearance is such as to command recognition.*

2. Pet. ii. 10. | Jude 8.

DILIGENCE.

1. *σπουδή*, speed, haste, as manifested in earnestness, diligence, zeal.
2. *ἐργασία*, work, labour; effort, occupation.

2. Luke xii. 58.
1. Rom. xii. 8.
1. 2 Cor. viii. 7.
— 2 Tim. iv. 9, 21, see D(do.)
1. Heb. vi. 11.
1. 2 Pet. i. 5.
— —— 10, see D (give.)
1. Jude 3.

DILIGENCE (DO.)

σπουδάζω, to make haste, *esp. as manifested in diligence, earnestness;* to do the utmost.

2 Tim. iv. 9, 21.

DILIGENCE (GIVE.)

2 Pet. i. 10.

DILIGENT.

σπουδαῖος, speedy, hasty, *esp. as shewn in earnest diligence*, (occ. 2 Cor. viii. 17.)

2 Cor. viii. 22 twice.

DILIGENT (BE.)

σπουδάζω, *see* "DILIGENCE (DO)."

Titus iii. 12. | 2 Pet. iii. 14.

See also, FOLLOWER.

DILIGENTLY.

1. *σπουδαίως*, speedily, *i.e*, earnestly, eagerly, (occ. Titus iii. 13.)
2. *ἀκριβῶς*, accurately, assiduously.
3. *ἐπιμελῶς*, carefully, sedulously, *(non occ.)*

4. πυγμῇ, (*Dat. of* πυγμή,) with the fist, *i.e.* thoroughly, *in opposition to superficial.* (Oft *seems to be a translation of* πυκνῇ), (*non occ.*)

— Matt. ii. 7, see inquire.
2. —— 8.
— —— 16, see inquire.
4. Mark vii. 3, marg. (text, oft.)
3. Luke xv. 8.
2. Acts xviii. 25.
— 2 Tim. i. 17, see D (very.)
1. Titus iii. 13.
— Heb. xi. 6, see seek.
— —— xii. 15, see look.
— 1 Pet. i. 10, see search.

DILIGENTLY (VERY.)

σπουδαιοτέρως, the more speedily (*comp. of No.* 1) with more diligence (*than could have been looked for; or perhaps, because I was in chains.*)

2 Tim. i. 17 (No. 1, L Tr ℵ.)

DIMINISHING.

ἥττημα, a being inferior, a worse state, *as compared with a former or better state; hence,* diminution, (occ. 1 Cor. vi. 7.)

Rom. xi. 12, marg. *decay* or *loss.*

DINE (-ED.)

ἀριστάω, to breakfast, *i.e.* to take any meal before the principal one *or* supper, (*non occ.*)

Luke xi. 37. | John xxi. 12, 15.

DINNER.

ἄριστον, breakfast, *i.e.* a Jewish meal which corresponded sometimes to our breakfast, sometimes to our dinner, *but which was always taken before the principal meal of the day, which was* δεῖπνον, supper, (*non occ.*)

Matt. xxii. 4. | Luke xi. 38.
Luke xiv. 12.

DIP (-ED, -ETH.)

1. βάπτω, to dip, to immerse; *also* to tinge, to dye, (*non occ.*)
2. ἐμβάπτω, (*No.* 1 *with* ἐν, in, *prefixed*) to dip into, (*non occ.*)

2. Matt. xxvi. 23.
2. Mark xiv. 20.
1. Luke xvi. 24.
1. John xiii. 26 1st (part.) (No. 2, L.) [T Tr A ℵ.)
2. —— 26 2nd (No. 1, Lm
1. Rev. xix. 13.

DIRECT [verb.]

κατευθύνω, to guide straight towards *or* upon *any thing; then, gen.* to guide, direct, (occ. Luke i. 79.)

1. Thes. iii. 11. | 2 Thes. iii. 5, marg. *guide.*

DISALLOW.

ἀποδοκιμάζω, to reject on scrutiny *or* trial.

1. Pet. ii. 4, 7.

DISANNUL (-ETH.)

1. ἀθετέω, to displace; *hence,* set aside, *i.e.* abrogate.
2. ἀκυρόω, to deprive of authority, *hence,* to cancel, (occ. Matt. xv. 6; Mark vii. 13.)

1. Gal. iii. 15. | 2. Gal. iii. 17.

DISANNULLING.

ἀθέτησις, a displacement, a setting aside.

Heb. vii. 18.

DISCERN (-ED, -ING.)

1. ἀνακρίνω, to separate *or* divide up, *hence,* to examine carefully, investigate, *then,* to determine, judge of, estimate.
2. διακρίνω, to separate throughout, *i.e.* wholly, completely, *hence,* to distinguish, make a distinction.
   (a) to separate one's self from, *i.e.* to contend with, *then,* to contend with one's self, *i.e.* to hesitate, waver.
3. { πρός, towards, for, διάκρισιν, a distinguishing, discriminating, } for discriminating.
4. δοκιμάζω, to assay, examine, prove *or* test *metals to see if they are pure, hence,* to scrutinize.

2. Matt. xvi. 3.
4. Luke xii. 56 twice.
2a. Rom. xiv. 23, marg. (text, *doubt.*)
1. 1 Cor. ii. 14.
1. —— 15 twice, marg. (text, *judge.*)
2. —— xi. 29.
3. Heb. v. 14.

DISCERNER.

κριτικός, skilled in judging, capable of judging, (*non occ.*)

Heb. iv. 12.

DISCERNING.

διάκρισις, a distinguishing, discerning clearly, discriminating.

1 Cor. xii. 10.

DISCIPLE (-S.)

1. *μαθητής*, a learner, pupil. *In N.T. more than this*, a follower, one who follows both the teacher and the teaching, *(non occ.)*

2. *μαθήτρια*, a female pupil *or* disciple, *(non occ.)*

1. Matt. v. 1.
1. —— viii. 21, 23.
1. ——— 25 (*om.* Lb T (8th ed.) Tr ℵ.)
1. —— ix. 10, 11, 14 twice, 19, 37.
1. —— x. 1, 24, 25, 42.
1. —— xi. 1, 2.
1. —— xii. 1, 2, 49.
1. —— xiii. 10, 36.
1. —— xiv. 12, 15, 19 twice, 22, 26.
1. —— xv. 2, 12, 23, 32, 33, 36 twice.
1. —— xvi. 5, 13, 20, 21, 24.
1. —— xvii. 6, 10, 13, 16,
1. —— xviii. 1. [19.
1. —— xix. 10, 13, 23, 25.
1. —— xx. 17 (*om.* T (8th ed.) Tr ℵ.)
1. —— xxi. 1, 6, 20.
1. —— xxii. 16.
1. —— xxiii. 1.
1. —— xxiv. 1, 3.
1. —— xxvi. 1, 8, 17, 18, 19, 26, 35, 36, 40, 45, 56.
— —— xxvii. 57, see D (be a.)
1. ——— 64.
1. —— xxviii. 7, 8, 9 (*ap*), 13, 16.
— ——— 19, see D (make)
1. Mark ii. 15, 16, 18 3 times,
1. —— iii. 7, 9. [23.
1. —— iv. 34.
1. —— v. 31.
1. —— vi. 1, 29, 35, 41, 45.
1. —— vii. 2, 5, 17.
1. —— viii. 1, 4, 6, 10.
1. ——— 14 (*om.* ℵt E G L T Tr A ℵ.)
1. ——— 27 twice, 33, 34.
1. —— ix. 14, 18, 28, 31.
1. —— x. 10, 13, 23, 24,
1. —— xi. 1, 14. [46.
1. —— xii. 43.
1. —— xiii. 1.
1. —— xiv. 12, 13, 14, 16,
1. —— xvi. 7. [32.
1. Luke v. 30, 33.
1. —— vi. 1, 13, 17, 20, 40.
1. —— vii. 11, 18, 19.
1. —— viii. 9, 22.
1. —— ix. 1 (*om.* G T Tr) (ἀπόστολους, *apostles*, ℵ.)
1. Luke ix. 14, 16, 18, 40, 43, 54.
1. —— x. 23.
1. —— xi. 1 twice.
1. —— xii. 1, 22.
1. —— xiv. 26, 27, 33.
1. —— xvi. 1.
1. —— xvii. 1, 22.
1. —— xviii. 15.
1. —— xix. 29, 37, 39.
1. —— xx. 45 (*ap.*)
1. —— xxii. 11, 39, 45.
1. John i. 35, 37.
1. —— ii. 2, 11, 12, 17, 22.
1. —— iii. 22, 25.
1. —— iv. 1, 2, 8, 27, 31, 33.
1. —— vi. 3, 8, 11 twice (*ap*), 12, 16, 22 1st (*ap*), 22 2nd & 3rd, 24, 60, 61, 66.
1. —— vii. 3.
1. —— viii. 31.
1. —— ix. 2, 27, 28 twice.
1. —— xi. 7, 8.
— ——— 16, see D (fellow)
1. ——— 54.
1. —— xii. 4, 16.
1. —— xiii 5, 22, 23, 35.
1. —— xv. 8.
1. —— xvi. 17, 29.
1. —— xviii. 1 twice, 2, 15 twice, 16, 17, 19, 25.
1. —— xix. 26, 27 twice, 38.
1. —— xx. 2, 3, 4, 8, 10, 18, 19, 20, 25, 26, 30.
1. —— xxi. 1, 2, 4, 7, 8, 12, 14, 20, 23, 24.
1. Acts i. 15 (ἀδέλφοι, *brethren*, G∾ L T Tr A ℵ.)
1. —— vi. 1, 2, 7.
1. —— ix. 1, 10, 19, 25, 26 twice.
2. ——— 36.
1. ——— 38.
1. —— xi. 26, 29.
1. —— xiii. 52.
1. —— xiv. 20, 22, 28.
1. —— xv. 10.
1. —— xvi. 1.
1. —— xviii. 23, 27.
1. —— xix. 1, 9, 30.
1. —— xx. 1.
1. ——— 7 (pl.) (ἡμῶν, *we*, G L T Tr A ℵ.)
1. ——— 30.
1. —— xxi. 4, 16 twice.

DISCIPLE (BE...)

μαθητεύω, (a) *trans. (followed by Acc., and therefore expressing some action implied in or consequent upon the state or quality,)* to make a *μαθητής* (a disciple), (occ. Acts xiv. 21.)

(b) *intrans. and followed by Dat.* to be a *μαθητής* (disciple.)

(b) Matt. xxvii. 57 (passive, *was discipled* to, etc., L T (8th ed.) Tr ℵ.)

DISCIPLES (make) [margin.]

(a) Matt. xxviii. 19 (text, *teach.*)

DISCIPLE (FELLOW.)

συμμαθητής, a disciple together with *another*, *(non occ.)*

John xi. 16.

DISCOURAGED (BE.)

ἀθυμέω, to despond, be disturbed in mind, disheartened, *(non occ.)*

Col. iii. 21.

DISCOVER (-ED.)

1. *ἀναφαίνομαι*, to be shown, *i.e.* to have *any thing* pointed out to *one's self*, (occ. Luke xix. 11.)

2. *κατανοέω*, to perceive distinctly, discern clearly.

3. *ἐλέγχω*, to test, try, search out *in an unfriendly way; then*, to prove *what is disputed*, convince, convict, *hence*, reprimand, blame.

3. John iii. 20, marg. (text, *reprove.*)
1. Acts xxi. 3 (part.)
2. Acts xxvii. 39.
3. Eph. v. 13, marg. (text, *reprove.*)

DISCREET.

σώφρων, of sound mind, *used of one who follows sound reason and restrains his passions, hence*, sober-minded.

Titus ii. 5.

DISCREET (be) [margin.]

σωφρονέω, to be *σώφρων* (of sound mind), to use sound judgment and moderation.

Titus ii. 6, text, *sober-minded (be.)*

DISCREETLY.

νουνεχῶς, understandingly, *(from νουνεχής*, having understanding, *(non occ.)*

Mark xii. 34.

DISEASE (-S.)

1. *νόσος*, disease, sickness; confirmed disease.

2. *νόσημα*, a sickness, a disease, *(non occ.)*

3. *μαλακία*, incipient complaint, softness (*as opp. to καρτερία*, endurance), (*non occ.*)
4. *ἀσθένεια*, want of strength *or* energy, infirmity, feebleness.

3. Matt. iv. 23.
1. —— 24.
3. —— ix. 35.
3. —— x. 1.
1. Mark i. 34.
1. Luke iv. 40.
1. —— vi. 17.
1. —— ix. 1.
2. John v. 4 (*ap.*)
1. Acts xix. 12.
4. Acts xxviii. 9.

DISEASED (BE.)

1. { *ἔχω*, to have, / *κακῶς*, badly, } to be ill *or* in evil case.
2. *ἀσθενέω*, to want strength, be infirm, weak, feeble.

1. Matt. xiv. 35.
1. Mark i. 32.
2 John vi. 2.

See also, BLOOD.

DISFIGURE.

ἀφανίζω, to cause to disappear, to put out of sight, hide.

Matt. vi. 16.

DISH.

τρύβλιον, a dish *or* bowl *for eating or drinking*.

Matt. xxvi. 23. | Mark xiv. 20.

DISHONESTY.

αἰσχύνη, shame, the sense of disgrace, the feeling of shame which attends the performance of a dishonourable deed, *also*, the feeling which deters one from bad conduct through fear of being put to shame.

2 Cor. iv. 2, marg. *shame*.

DISHONOUR [noun.]

ἀτιμία, dishonour, disgrace, insult.

Rom. ix. 21.
1 Cor. xv. 43.
2 Cor. vi. 8.
2 Tim. ii. 20.

DISHONOUR (-EST, -ETH.)

1. *ἀτιμάζω*, to dishonour, esteem lightly, contemn.
2. *καταισχύνω*, to bring down shame upon.

1. John viii. 49.
1. Rom. i. 24 (mid.)
1. Rom. ii. 23.
2. 1 Cor. xi. 4, 5.

DISMISS (-ED.)

ἀπολύω, to let loose from, to let go.

Acts xv. 30 (part); xix. 41.

DISOBEDIENCE.

1. *ἀπείθεια*, unwillingness to be persuaded, wilful unbelief that opposes itself *to the gracious purpose of God*.
2. *παρακοή*, that which has been heard amiss, neglect *or* refusal to hear, *hence*, the sin of omission, carelessness in ascertaining *or* regarding the rule of duty, (*non occ.*)

2. Rom. v. 19.
2. 2 Cor. x. 6.
1. Eph. ii. 2.
1. —— v. 6, marg *unbelief*.
1. Col. iii. 6.
2. Heb. ii. 2.
1. —— iv. 11, marg. (text, *unbelief*.)

DISOBEDIENT.

1. *ἀπειθής*, unwilling to be persuaded, refusing belief and obedience, contumacious, (*non occ.*)
2. *ἀπειθέω*, not to suffer one's self to be persuaded, to refuse belief.
3. *ἀνυπότακτος*, unsubjected, insubordinate, refractory.

1. Luke i. 17.
1. Acts xxvi. 19.
1. Rom. i. 30.
2. —— x. 21 (part.)
3. 1 Tim. i. 9.
1. 2 Tim. iii. 2.
1. Titus i. 16.
1. —— iii. 3.

DISOBEDIENT (BE.)

2. Rom. xv. 31, marg. (text, *believe not*.)
2. Heb. xi. 31.
2. 1 Pet. ii. 7, 8.
2. 1 Pet. iii. 20.

DISORDERLY.

1. *ἄτακτος*, not keeping the ranks *as of soldiers*, not in one's place, out of order; *hence*, neglectful of duties.
2. *ἀτάκτως*, (*adv. of above*,) disorderly.

1. 1 Thes. v. 14, marg. (text, *unruly*.)
2. 2 Thes. iii. 6, 11.

DISORDERLY (BEHAVE ONE'S SELF.)

ἀτακτέω, to leave or break the ranks (*spoken of soldiers*,) to be out of one's place, be undisciplined, disorderly.

2 Thes. iii. 7.

DISPENSATION.

οἰκονομία, administration of a household, *Actively* the administrative activity of the owner *or* the steward; *passively*, that which is administered, *(Eng.* economy,) *i.e.* a disposition *or* arrangement of things, a scheme *or* dispensation, (occ. Luke xvi. 2, 3, 4.)

1 Cor. ix. 17. | Eph. iii. 2.
Eph. i. 10. | Col. i. 25.

DISPERSE (-ED.)

διασκορπίζω, to scatter throughout, *i.e.* abroad; disperse abroad.

Acts v. 37.

DISPERSE (-ED) ABROAD.

σκορπίζω, to scatter, disperse.

2 Cor. ix. 9.

DISPERSED (THE.)

{ ὁ, the, διασπορά, dispersion, (occ. James i. 1, and 1 Pet. i. 1,) } the dispersion *of the Gentiles, i.e. the countries where the Jews lay scattered.*

John vii. 35.

DISPLEASED (BE MUCH.)

ἀγανακτέω, to be much pained *(in body or mind.)*

Mark x. 14, 41.

DISPLEASED (BE SORE.)

Matt. xxi. 15.

DISPLEASED WITH (BE HIGHLY.)

θυμομαχέω, to fight fiercely; have a hot quarrel.

Acts xii. 20 (part.), with εἰμί, *to be* (marg. *bear an hostile mind intending war with.*)

DISPOSED (BE.)

1. βούλομαι, to wish; *denoting the inward predisposition from which the active will proceeds;* to purpose, *after deliberation and consideration of all the circumstances of the case.*

2. θέλω, to will, *denoting the natural active volition or impulse, and indicating a less formal purpose.*

1. Acts xviii. 27 (part.) | 2. 1 Cor. x. 27.

DISPOSITION.

διαταγή, a disposing in order, *as of troops;* arrangement, (occ. Rom. xiii 2.)

Acts vii. 53.

DISPUTATION (-S.)

1. διάκρισις, a distinguishing, a discerning clearly, a deciding.

2. συζήτησις, a joint-inquiry, *and so* a disputation.

2. Acts xv. 2 (*om.* G⇉) (ζήτησις, *a seeking,* G L T Tr A ℵ.)
1. Rom. xiv. 1, marg. (with εἰς, *unto, for,*) *to judge,* (lit. *for a deciding.*)

DISPUTE (-ED, -ING.)

1. διαλέγομαι, to speak to and for, *i.e.* alternately, to converse with; *hence,* discuss, dispute.

2. διαλογίζομαι, to reckon through, complete *or* settle an account, *hence,* to take account of, consider.

3. συζητέω, to seek *or* examine with, at the same time *or* together; to seek jointly, *hence,* dispute.

2. Mark ix. 33. | 1. Acts xvii. 17.
1. —— 34. | 1. —— xix. 8, 9.
— Acts vi. 9, see D with. | 1. —— xxiv. 12.
3. —— ix. 29. | — Rom. ix. 20, see D with.
1. Jude 9.

DISPUTE WITH.

1. συζητέω, *see above, No.* 3.

2. ἀνταποκρίνομαι, to answer again, reply against.

1. Acts vi. 9.
2. Rom. ix. 20, marg. (text, *reply against.*)

DISPUTER.

συζητητής, a joint inquirer; *hence,* disputer, *(non occ.)*

1 Cor. i. 20.

DISPUTING (-S) [noun.]

1. διαλογισμός, balancing *or* adjustment of accounts, computation; *hence,* reflection, cogitation.

2. συζήτησις, a joint inquiry; *hence*, disputation.

1. Acts xv. 7. | 2. Phil. ii. 14.

DISPUTINGS (PERVERSE.)

παραδιατριβάι, useless disputation, idle occupation.

1 Tim. vi. 5, marg. *gallings one of another* (διαπαρατριβή, *incessant quarrellings*, G L T Tr A ℵ.)

DISSEMBLE WITH.

συνυποκρίνομαι, to play the hypocrite with *any one*, *(non occ.)*

Gal. ii. 13.

DISSENSION.

στάσις, a setting up, erection; *hence*, an upstand, uproar; *of a popular commotion*, insurrection; *in a private sense*, controversy *with idea of violence*.

Acts xv. 2; xxiii. 7, 10.

DISSIMULATION.

ὑπόκρισις, answer, response *as of an oracle; gen.* stage-playing, the playing a part, *hence*, *Eng.* hypocrisy.

Gal. ii. 13.

DISSIMULATION (WITHOUT.)

ἀνυπόκριτος, *(the above with ἀ, negative, prefixed,)* unfeigned, without hypocrisy.

Rom. xii. 9.

DISSOLVE (-ED.)

1. λύω, to loose, loosen *what is fast bound;* dissolve, sever; *of buildings*, demolish.
2. καταλύω, to loosen down, disunite *the parts of anything*, destroy.

2. 2 Cor. v. 1. | 1. 2 Pet. iii. 11, 12.

DISTINCTION.

διαστολή, a drawing asunder, separation, distinction, (occ. Rom. iii. 22; x. 12.)

1 Cor. xiv. 7.

DISTRACTION (WITHOUT.)

ἀπερισπάστως, without drawing from around, *hence*, without distraction, *(non occ.)*

1 Cor. vii. 35.

DISTRESS [noun.]

1. ἀνάγκη, force, constraint, necessity.
2. στενοχωρία, a crowding into a narrow place, straitness of place, want of room, *hence*, straits, anguish.
3. συνοχή, a meeting, joining *or* holding together, a shutting up, *hence*, *metaph.* distress, (occ. 2 Cor. ii. 4.)

1. Luke xxi. 23.
3. ——— 25.
2. Rom. viii. 35.
1. 1 Cor. vii. 26, marg. *necessity.*
2. 2 Cor. vi. 4.
2. ——— xii. 10.
1. 1 Thes. iii. 7.

DISTRESS (-ED.)

στενοχωρέω, to crowd into a narrow place, to straiten as to room. *In N.T. Pass.* to be straightened, not able to turn *one's self*, distressed, (occ. 2 Cor. vi. 12.)

2 Cor. iv. 8.

DISTRIBUTE (-ED, -ING.)

1. διαδίδωμι, to give *or* deliver through, *as through various hands, from one to another;* deal out.
2. μεταδίδωμι, to give with *any one*, *i.e.* to share with, communicate.
3. μερίζω, to part, to divide into parts.
4. κοινωνέω, to be partaker of *or* in *any thing* with *any person*, to share in common.

1. Luke xviii. 22 (δίδωμι, *give*, L ℵ.)
1. John vi. 11.
4. Rom. xii. 13.
3. 1 Cor. vii. 17.
3. 2 Cor. x. 13.
2. Eph. iv. 28, marg. (text, *give.*)

DISTRIBUTE (READY TO.)

εὐμετάδοτος, readily imparting *or* sharing, *(non occ)*

1 Tim. vi. 18.

DISTRIBUTION.

1. κοινωνία, act of partaking with *any person;* participation.
2. μερισμός, division, parting, separation.

1. 2 Cor. ix. 13. | 2. Heb. ii. 4, marg. (text, *gift.*)

DISTRIBUTION (MAKE.)

διαδίδωμι, *see* "DISTRIBUTE," *No.* 1.

Acts iv. 35.

DITCH.

βόθυνος, any hole *or* pit dug in the ground, (occ. Matt. xii. 11.)

Matt. xv. 14. | Luke vi. 39.

DIVERS.

1. ποικίλος, variegated, party-coloured. *Metaph.* changing colour, *and hence*, various, divers.
2. τις, one, some one, a certain one.

1. Matt. iv. 24.	1. 2 Tim. iii. 6.
1. Mark i. 34.	1. Titus iii. 3.
2. —— viii. 3.	1. Heb. ii. 4.
1. Luke iv. 40.	1. —— xiii. 9.
2. Acts xix. 9.	1. Jas. i. 2.

DIVERS MANNERS (IN.)

πολυτρόπως, in many ways.

Heb. i. 1.

DIVERS PLACES (IN.)

{ κατά, down, throughout; *used distributively*, from one to another, τόπους, places, } from place to place.

Matt. xxiv. 7. | Mark xiii. 8. | Luke xxi. 11.

DIVERSE.

διάφορος, different, unlike, various.

Heb. ix. 10.

DIVERSITY.

1. διαίρεσις, act of taking apart, division *as into parts, hence*, distribution, (occ. 1 Cor. xii. 5.)
2. γένος, genus, class, sort, *(opp. to* εἶδος, species.)

1. 1 Cor. xii. 4, 6. | 2. 1 Cor. xii. 28, marg. *kind.*

DIVIDE (-ED, -ETH, -ING.)

1. μερίζω, to part, divide into parts.
   (a) *Mid.*, to divide *any thing* with *another*, to share with.
2. διαμερίζω, *(No.* 1 *with* δία, through, *prefixed,)* to divide through, *i.e.*, completely; divide up.
3. διαιρέω, to take apart, to separate; to take *as into* parts, distribute.
4. σχίζω, to split, rend, cleave *as wood;* to divide *with violence.*
5. ἀφορίζω, to set off by bounds, to limit off; to set off apart, separate.
6. διαδίδωμι, to give *or* deliver through *(as through various hands from one to another in succession,) hence,* to deal out.

1. Matt. xii. 25 twice, 26.	— Acts xiii. 19, see D by lot.
5. —— xxv. 32.	4. —— xiv. 4.
1. Mark iii. 24, 25, 26.	4. —— xxiii. 7.
1. —— vi. 41.	1. 1 Cor. i. 13.
2. Luke xi. 17, 18.	3. —— xii. 11.
6. —— 22.	— 2 Tim. ii. 15, see D (rightly.)
1a. —— xii. 13.	— Rev. xvi. 19, see D (be.)
2. —— 52, 53.	
3. —— xv. 12.	
2. —— xxii. 17.	

DIVIDE BY LOT.

κατακληροδοτέω, to give by lot to each.

Acts xiii. 19 (*ap.*), (κατακληρονομέω, *to inherit completely*, G L T Tr A ℵ.)

DIVIDE (RIGHTLY.)

ὀρθοτομέω, to cut straight, to divide right *(as sacrificial victims,* Lev. i. 6,) *(non occ.)*

2 Tim. ii. 15.

DIVIDED (BE.)

γίνομαι, to become.

Rev. xvi. 19.

DIVIDER.

μεριστής, a divider, a distributor, *(non occ.)*

Luke xii. 14.

DIVIDING ASUNDER.

μερισμός, act of partition, division *or* separation, (occ. Heb. ii. 4.)

Heb. iv. 12.

DIVINATION.

πύθων, *Eng.* Python. *In Greek mythology the name of* a serpent or dragon slain by Apollo, *then, transferred to* Apollo himself; *later, spoken of* diviners, soothsayers, *held to be inspired by the pythian Apollo. They*

appear to have been a kind of ventriloquists, *the spirit being supposed to speak from the belly without motion of the lips.*

Acts xvi. 16, marg. *python.*

DIVINE.

θεῖος, divine, what is God's, *esp.* what proceeds from Him, (occ. *with art.*, Acts xvii. 29.)

2 Pet. i. 3, 4.

DIVINE SERVICE.

λατρεία, service, *esp.* the service of God, *and with relation to sacrifice.*

Heb. ix. 1.

DIVISION. (-s.)

1. σχίσμα, that which is cloven *or* parted, a cleft, division, rent. *Eng.* schism.
2. διχοστασία, dissension, discord, (occ. Gal. v. 20.)
3. διαμερισμός, division, disunion, *(non occ.)*

3. Luke xii. 51.
1. John vii. 43.
1. —— ix. 16.
1. —— x. 19.
2. Rom. xvi. 17.
1. 1 Cor. i. 10.
2. 1 Cor. iii. 3, marg. *faction* (*om.* G⇉ L T Tr A ℵ.)
1. —— xi. 18, marg. *schism.*
1. —— xii. 25, marg. (text, *schism.*)

DIVORCE [verb.]

ἀπολύω, to let loose from, let go free.

Matt. v. 32.

DIVORCEMENT.

ἀποστάσιον, defection, desertion, departure from.

Matt. xix. 7. | Mark x. 4.

DIVORCEMENT (WRITING OF.)

Matt. v. 31.

DO (-ST, -TH, -ETH, -ING, DID.)

[See also, DONE (BE.)]

1. ποιέω, to make, *i.e.* to form, produce, *spoken of an external act as manifested in the production of something tangible, completed action; also,* to do, *expressing an action as continued or not yet completed; what one does repeatedly, continually, more like No.* 2.
2. πράσσω, to do, to practice, *esp. expressing it as continued or not completed,* to do *repeatedly, continuedly, habitually.*
3. ἐργάζομαι, to work, to labour; *trans.* to form by labour, perform.
4. κατεργάζομαι, *(No.* 3, *with* κατά, down, *prefixed,)* to work out, bring about, accomplish, effect, be the cause *or* author of.
5. ἐνεργέω, to be in work, *i.e.* to be effective, operative, *(Eng.* energy,) to produce effect, operate.
6. ἐπιτελέω, to bring through to an end, to finish.
7. ἔχω, to have, to hold, *i.e.* to have and hold, *implying continued holding or possession. It is also spoken of what one is said* to have with *himself, i.e. of any condition or circumstances in which one is, etc.*
8. κατατίθημι, to put *or* lay down, deposit; to lay up for future use.
9. προσφέρω, to bear *or* bring to *any place or person;* to bring near, to offer, present to *any one.*
10. πρός, towards.
   (a) *with Gen.* in favour of.
   (b) *with Dat.* at, close by.
   (c) *with Acc.* to, in reference to, in consideration of, with a view to.

1. Matt. i. 24.
1. —— v. 19, 44, 46, 47 twice.
1. —— vi. 1, 2 twice, 3 1st (part.), 3 2nd.
1. —— vii. 12 twice, 21, 22, 24, 26.
1. —— viii. 9 twice.
1. —— ix. 28.
1. —— xii. 2 twice, 3, 12, 50.
1. —— xiii. 28, 41, 58.
1. —— xvii. 12.
1. —— xviii. 35.
1. —— xix. 16.
1. —— xx. 5, 15, 32.
1. —— xxi. 6, 15, 21, 23, 24, 27, 31, 36, 40.
1. —— xxiii. 3 3 times, 5, 23.
1. —— xxiv. 46.
1. —— xxv. 40 twice, 45 twice
1. —— xxvi. 12, 13, 19.
1. —— xxvii. 22, 23.
1. —— xxviii. 15.
1. Mark ii. 24, 25.
1. —— iii. 8, 35.
1. Mark v. 19, 20, 32.
1. —— vi. 5, 20, 30.
1. —— vii. 8 (*ap.*), 12, 13, 37.
1. —— ix. 13, 39.
1. —— x. 17, 35, 36, 51.
1. —— xi. 3 (*ap.*), 5, 28 twice, 29, 33.
1. —— xii. 9.
1. —— xiv. 7, 8, 9.
1. —— xv. 8, 12, 14.
1. Luke i. 49.
1. —— ii. 27.
1. —— iii. 10, 11, 12, 14, 19.
1. —— iv. 23.
1. —— v. 6 (part.)
1. —— vi. 2 1st.
1. —— —— 2 2nd (*om.* L T Tr A.)
1. —— —— 3.
1. —— —— 10 (ἐκτείνω, *stretch forth,* G∼ ℵ.)
1. —— —— 11, 23, 26, 27, 31 twice, 33, 46, 47, 49.

— Luke vii. 4, see D (for.)
1. ——— 8 twice.
1. —— viii. 21, 39 twice.
1. —— ix. 10, 15, 43, 54 (*ap.*)
1. —— x. 25, 28, 37.
1. —— xi. 42.
1. —— xii. 4, 17, 18, 43, 47.
6. —— xiii. 32 (ἀποτελέω, *finish off*, *perfect*, L T Tr A ℵ.)
1. —— xvi. 3, 4, 8.
1. —— xvii. 9, 10 3 times.
1. —— xviii. 18, 41.
1. —— xix. 48.
1. —— xx. 2, 8, 13, 15.
1. —— xxii. 19.
2. ——— 23.
2. —— xxiii. 15.
1. ——— 22, 31, 34 (*ap.*)
2. ——— 41.
1. John ii. 5, 11, 18, 23.
1. —— iii. 2 twice.
2. ——— 20.
1. ——— 21.
1. —— iv. 29, 34, 39, 45, 54.
1. —— v. 16, 19 4 times, 20, 29 1st.
2. ——— 29 2nd.
1. ——— 30, 36.
1. —— vi. 2, 6, 14, 28, 38.
1. —— vii. 3, 4 twice, 17, 21, 31 twice, 51.
1. —— viii. 28, 29, 38, 39, 40, 41, 44.
1. —— ix. 16, 26, 31, 33.
1. —— x. 25, 37, 38, 41.
1. —— xi. 45, 46, 47 twice.
1. —— xii. 16, 18, 37 (part.)
1. —— xiii. 7, 12, 15 twice, 17, 27 twice.
1. —— xiv. 10, 12 3 times, 13, 14, 31.
1. —— xv. 5, 14, 15, 21, 24 twice.
9. —— xvi. 2.
1. ——— 3.
1. —— xvii. 4.
1. —— xviii. 35.
1. —— xix. 24.
1. —— xx. 30.
1. —— xxi. 25.
1. Acts i. 1.
1. —— ii. 22, 37.
2. —— iii. 17.
1. —— iv. 7, 16, 28.
2. —— v. 35.
1. —— vi. 8.
1. —— viii. 6.
1. —— ix. 6 1st (*ap.*), 6 2nd, 13, 36.
1. —— x. 6 (*ap.*), 33, 39.
1. —— xi. 30.
1. —— xii. 8.
1. —— xiv. 11, 15, 27.
1. —— xv. 4, 17.
2. ——— 29.
7. ——— 36.
1. —— xvi. 18.
2. ——— 28.
1. ——— 30.
2. —— xvii. 7.
1. —— xix. 14.
2. ——— 36.
1. —— xxi. 23, 33 (with ἐστί.)
1. —— xxii. 10 twice, 26 (with μέλλω, lit. *about to do.*)
8. —— xxv. 9.
2. —— xxvi. 9.
1. ——— 10.
2. ——— 20, 26, 31.
1. Rom. i. 28, 32 1st.
2. ——— 32 2nd.
2. —— ii. 1, 3 1st.
1. ——— 3 2nd.
4. ——— 9.
1. ——— 14.
1. —— iii. 8, 12.
4. —— vii. 15 1st.
2. ——— 15 2nd.
1. ——— 15 3rd, 16.
4. ——— 17.
1. ——— 19 1st.
2. ——— 19 2nd.
4. ——— 20.
1. ——— 21.
2. —— ix. 11.
1. —— x. 5.
1. —— xii. 20.
1. —— xiii. 3, 4 1st.
2. ——— 4 2nd.
1. 1 Cor. v. 2 (No. 2, G ∾ T Trm ℵ.)
4. ——— 3.
1. 1 Cor. vi. 18.
1. —— vii. 36, 37, 38 twice.
2. —— ix. 17.
1. ——— 23.
1. —— x. 31 twice.
1. —— xi. 24, 25.
— —— xiii. 10, see D away.
1. —— xv. 29.
1. —— xvi. 1.
— 2 Cor. iii. 7, see done away (be.)
— ——— 11, 14, see D away.
2. —— v. 10.
1. —— viii. 10.
10. —— xi. 8.
1. ——— 12.
1. —— xiii. 7 twice.
1. Gal. ii. 10.
1. —— iii. 10, 12.
1. —— v. 3.
— ——— 17, see D (can.)
2. ——— 21.
3. —— vi. 10.
1. Eph. iii 20.
1. —— vi. 6, 8, 9.
4. ——— 13, marg. *overcome.*
2. ——— 21.
5. Phil. ii. 13.
1. ——— 14.
2. —— iv. 9.
— ——— 13, see D (can.)
1. ——— 14.
1. Col. iii. 17, 23 1st.
3. ——— 23 2nd.
1. 1 Thes. iv. 10.
2. ——— 11.
1. —— v. 11, 24.
1. 2 Thes. iii. 4 twice.
1. 1 Tim. i. 18.
1. —— v. 21.
1. 2 Tim. iv. 5.
1. Titus iii. 5.
1. Philem. 14, 21.
— Heb. iv. 3, see D (we have to.)
1. —— vi. 3.
1. —— vii. 27.
1. —— x. 7, 9, 36 (part.)
1. —— xiii. 6, 17, 19, 21.
1. ——— 21, marg. (text, *work.*)
1. Jas. ii. 8, 12, 19.
1. —— iv. 15, 17 twice.
1. 1 Pet. ii. 22.
1. —— iii. 11, 12.
1. 2 Pet. i. 10 (part.), 19.
1. 1 John i. 6.
1. —— ii. 17, 29.
1. —— iii. 7, 10 (*ap.*), 22.
1. 3 John 5 1st.
3. ——— 5 2nd.
1. ——— 6, 10.
1. Rev. ii. 5.
1. —— xiii. 13, 14.
— —— xix. 10, } see D it
— —— xxii. 9, } not (thou)
1. ——— 14 (*ap.*)

DO AWAY.

καταργέω, to render inactive, idle, useless; *then*, to make useless *or* void; *hence*, abolish, do away.

1 Cor. xiii. 10. | 2 Cor. iii. 11, 14.

DO (CAN.)

1. ποιέω, *see* "DO," *No.* 1.
2. ἰσχύω, to be strong, prevail.

1. Gal. v. 17. | 2. Phil. iv. 13.

DO (FOR...)

παρέχω, to hold beside *or* near to *any one*, *i.e.* to present, offer, furnish, supply.

Luke vii. 4.

DO IT NOT (THOU.)

μή, not, *(with Imperative.)*

Rev. xix. 10; xxii. 9.

DO (WE HAVE TO.)

ἡμῖν ὁ λογός, [is] our account.

Heb. iv. 13.

See also, CAN, COULD, DESPITE, DILIGENCE, DONE, EVIL, GOOD, HAVE, MURDER, SACRIFICE, SERVICE, VIOLENCE, WELL, WHAT [interrog.], WIT, WRONG.

DOCTOR (-S.)

διδάσκαλος, a teacher, instructor.

Luke ii. 46.

See also, LAW.

DOCTRINE (-S.)

1. διδαχή, teaching, process of teaching, thing taught; *esp.* the act.
2. διδασκαλία, teaching, *esp.* the substance *or* result of teaching.
3. λόγος, word *spoken*, the speaking *(as a means, not as a product)*; the word *as that which is* spoken, *i.e.*, an exposition *or* account *which one gives.*

1. Matt. vii. 28.
2. —— xv. 9.
1. —— xvi. 12.
1. —— xxii. 33.
1. Mark i. 22, 27.
1. —— iv. 2.
2. —— vii. 7.
1. —— xi. 18.
1. —— xii. 38.
1. Luke iv. 32.
1. John vii. 16, 17.
1. —— xviii. 19.
1. Acts ii. 42.
1. —— v. 28.
1. —— xiii. 12.
1. —— xvii. 19.
1. Rom. vi. 17.
1. —— xvi. 17.
1. 1 Cor. xiv. 6, 26.
2. Eph. iv. 14.
2. Col. ii. 22.
— 1 Tim. i. 3, see teach.
2. —— 10.
2. —— iv. 1.
2. —— 6, 13, 16.
2. —— v. 17.
2. —— vi. 1, 3.
2. 2 Tim. iii. 10, 16.
1. —— iv. 2.
2. —— 3.
2. Titus i. 9.
2. —— ii. 7, 10.
3. Heb. vi. 1, marg. *word.*
1. —— 2.
1. —— xiii. 9.
1. 2 John 9 twice, 10.
2. Rev. ii. 14, 15, 24.

DOER (-S.)

ποιητής, a maker of *any thing (hence, Eng.* poet, *i.e.* maker *of a poem,) then gen.* a doer, (occ. Acts xvii. 28.)

Rom. ii, 13.
Jas. i. 22, 23, 25; iv. 11.

See also, EVIL.

DOG (-S.)

1. κύων, a dog, *pl.* dogs.
2. κυνάριον, *(dim. of No.* 1,) a little dog, a puppy.

1. Matt. vii. 6.
2. —— xv. 26, 27.
2. Mark vii. 27, 28.
1. Luke xvi. 21.
1. Phil. iii. 2.
1. 2 Pet. ii. 22.
1. Rev. xxii. 15.

DOING [noun.]

1. ποιέω, *see* "DO," *No.* 1.
2. ποίησις, a making, a doing.
3. ἔργον, a work; labour, business, employment, deed, act, action.

3. Rom. ii. 7. | 1. 2 Cor. viii. 11 (inf.)
2. Jas. i. 25, marg. (text, *deed.*)

DOING (IN.)

1. Gal. vi. 9 (part.) | 1. 1 Tim. iv. 16.

DOING (BE ONE'S.)

γίνομαι, to begin to be, come into existence, come to pass.

Matt. xxi. 42, Mark xii. 11, } lit. *from the Lord this came to pass.*

See also, EVIL, WELL.

DOMINION.

1. κράτος, strength, power in action, force, superiority.
2. κυριότης, lordship, dominion.

— Matt. xx. 25, see D over (exercise.)
— Rom. vi. 9, 14, see D over (have.)
— —— vii. 1, see D over (have.)
— 2 Cor. i. 24.
2. Eph. i 21.
2. Col. i. 16.
1. 1 Pet. iv. 11.
1. —— v. 11.
2. 2 Pet. ii. 10, marg. (text, *government.*)
2. Jude 8.
1. —— 25.
1. Rev. i. 6.

DOMINION OVER (EXERCISE.)

κατακυριεύω, to lord it against, *i.e.* over *any one.*

Matt. xx. 25.

DOMINION OVER (HAVE.)

κυριεύω, to be lord over *any person or thing.*

Rom. vi. 9, 14; vii. 1. | 2 Cor. i. 24.

DONE (SO BE IT.)

γίνομαι, to begin to be, *implying* origin, *either from natural causes or through special agency;* result *and* change *of state, etc.*

Matt. i. 22.
—— vi. 10.
—— viii. 13.
—— xi. 20, 21, 23 twice.
—— xviii. 19, 31 twice.
—— xxi. 4, 21.
—— xxvi. 42, 56.
—— xxvii. 54.
—— xxviii. 11.
Mark iv. 11.
—— v. 14, 33.
—— xiii. 30.
Luke iv. 23.
—— viii. 34, 35, 56.
—— ix. 7.
—— x. 13 twice.
—— xi. 2 *(ap.)*
—— xiii. 17.
Luke xiv. 22.
—— xxii. 42.
—— xxiii. 8, 31, 47, 48.
—— xxiv. 21.
John i. 28.
—— xv. 7.
—— xix. 36.
Acts ii. 43.
—— iv. 16, 21, 28, 30.
—— v. 7.
—— viii. 13.
—— x. 16.
—— xi. 10.
—— xii. 9.
—— xiii. 12.
—— xiv. 3.
—— xxi. 14.
—— xxiv. 2 (part.)
Acts xxviii. 9 (part.)

DONE AWAY (BE.)

καταργέω, to render inactive, idle, useless; hence, *to spoil.*

(a) *Pass.* to cease, be done away.

a. 2 Cor. iii. 7. 11. 14.

See also, DEED, WELL.

DOOR.

θύρα, door, (*Germ.* thur, *Sans.* Dûar, *Eng.* door,) *whether of a room or a house.* *Metaph.* access, opportunity.

Matt. vi. 6.
—— xxiv. 33.
—— xxv. 10.
—— xxvii. 60.
—— xxviii. 2 (*om.* G → L T Tr A ℵ.)
Mark i. 33.
—— ii. 2.
—— xi. 4.
—— xiii. 29.
—— xv. 46.
—— xvi. 3.
Luke xi. 7.
—— xiii. 25 twice.
John x. 1, 2, 7, 9.
John xviii. 16 1st.
—— 16 2nd, 17, see D (that keepeth.)
—— xx. 19, 26.
Acts v. 9, 19, 23.
—— xii. 6, 13.
—— xiv. 27.
—— xvi. 26, 27.
—— xxi. 30.
1 Cor. xvi. 9.
2 Cor. ii. 12.
Col. iv. 3.
Jas. v. 9.
Rev. iii. 8, 20 twice.
—— iv. 1.

DOOR KEEPER.

θυρωρός, a door keeper, porter, *male or female.*

John xviii. 16, 17, with art.

DOTE.

νοσέω, to be sick, ill, to ail, whether in body or mind, (*non occ.*)

1 Tim. vi. 4 (part.), marg. *sick.*

DOUBLE [adj.]

διπλοῦς, two-fold, double.

1 Tim. v. 17. | Rev. xviii. 6 twice.

DOUBLE [verb.]

διπλόω, to double, to repay two-fold, (*non occ.*)

Rev. xviii. 6.

DOUBLE-MINDED.

δίψυχος, double-minded, two-souled, (*non occ.*)

Jas. i. 8; iv. 8.

DOUBLE-TONGUED.

δίλογος, uttering the same thing twice, repeating, (*non occ.*)

1 Tim. iii. 8.

DOUBT (-ED, -ETH, -ING.)

1. *διακρίνω*, to separate throughout, *i.e.* wholly, completely.

   (a) ***Mid. and Pass.*** **to separate one's self from, *i.e.* contend with, *then,* to be in strife with with one's self, *i.e.* hesitate, waver.**

2. *διστάζω*, to stand *in* two *ways*, be uncertain *as to which to take*, (*French* balancer), (*non occ.*)

3. *ἀπορέομαι*, to be without resource, to know not what to do.

4. *διαπορέω*, (*No.* 3 *with* *δία*, throughout, *prefixed,*) to be entirely without resource, to be in great doubt *or* perplexity.

2. Matt. xiv. 31.
1a. —— xxi. 21.
2. —— xxviii. 17.
1a. Mark xi. 23.
— Luke xi. 20, see D (no.)
— John x. 24, see D (make to.)
3. —— xiii. 22.
— Acts ii. 12, see D (be in.)
4. —— v. 24.
4. —— x. 17.
1a. Acts x. 20.
1a. —— xi. 12 (*om.* G → A.)
3. Acts xxv. 20, marg. *be doubtful.*
— —— xxviii. 4, see D (no.)
1a. Rom. xiv. 23, marg. *discern and put a difference between meats.*
— 1 Cor. ix. 10, see D (no.)
— Gal. iv. 20, see D (stand in.)

DOUBT (BE IN.)

4. Acts ii. 12.

DOUBT (MAKE TO.)

ψυχὴν, the breath, vital breath, (*Lat.* anima,) the principle of life,
αἴρω, to take up, lift up, raise,
} hold up *our* lives.

John x. 24.

DOUBT (NO.)

1. *ἄρα*, still farther, beyond that; *a particle marking a transition, or drawing a conclusion,* therefore.

2. *γάρ*, (*γέ*, verily, *compounded with No.* 1,) the fact is, in fact, *and when the fact is given as the reason or explanation,* for; *more extensive than the Eng.* for, since it expresses the cause, reason, *or* motive of what has been previously affirmed.

3. *πάντως*, wholly, entirely; in every way, by all means.

1. Luke xi. 20. | 3. Acts xxviii. 4.
2. 1 Cor. ix. 10.

DOUBT (STAND IN.)

ἀπορέομαι, *see* "DOUBT," *No.* 3.

Gal. iv. 20, marg. *be perplexed.*

DOUBTFUL.

διαλογισμός, computation, adjustment of accounts; *hence*, consideration, suspense, *i.e.* doubts.

Rom. xiv. 1, marg. *doubtful thoughts.*

DOUBT (be in) [margin.]

ἀπορέομαι, *see* "DOUBT," *No.* 3.

Acts xxv. 20, text, *doubt.*

DOUBTFUL MIND (BE OF.)

μετεωρίζω, to lift up on high, raise in the air. *In N.T. Mid. or Pass.* to be fluctuating *in mind (as if floating in the air,) (non occ.)*

Luke xii. 29, marg. *live in careful suspense.*

DOUBTING.

διαλογισμός, *see* "DOUBTFUL."

1 Tim. ii. 8.

DOUBTLESS.

δή, *denotes the definiteness and certainty of an expression, serving to strengthen or limit the word to which it is attached;* truly, indeed.

2 Cor. xii. 1 (*ap.*)

See also, YEA, YET.

DOVE.

περιστερά, a dove *or* pigeon, (occ. Luke ii. 24.)

Matt. iii. 16.	Mark xi. 15.
—— x. 16.	Luke iii. 22.
—— xxi. 12.	John i. 32.
Mark i. 10.	—— ii. 14, 16.

See also, TURTLE.

DOWN.

1. κατά, *(prep.)* down.
   (a) *with Gen.* down from.
   (b) *with Acc.* down towards.
2. κάτω, *(adv.)* downwards.

2. Matt. iv. 6.	2. Luke iv. 9.
1a. —— viii. 32.	1a. —— viii. 33.
1a. Mark v. 13.	2. John viii. 6 (*ap.*), 8 (*ap.*)

2. Acts xx. 9.

See also, BOW, BRING, CAST, COME, CUT, DIG, DRIVE, FALL, GET, GO, HANG, HEW, KNEEL, LAY, LET, LIE, PRESS, PULL, PULLING, PUT, REAP, RUN, SINK, SIT, STEP, STOOP, TAKE, THROW, THRUST, TREAD, TURN.

DOWN TO.

See, FOOT, HELL.

DRAG (-ING.)

σύρω, to draw, drag, haul, trail along *as a net.*

John xxi. 8.

DRAGON.

δράκων, a dragon, *i.e.* a large kind of serpent, *(so called from his sight which is very acute.) In the N.T. it is used for* "that old serpent," the Devil.

Rev. xii. 3, 4, 7 twice, 9, 13, 16, 17; xiii. 2, 4, 11; xvi. 13; xx. 2.

DRAUGHT.

1. ἀφεδρών, "draught," latrine, *(non occ.)*
2. ἄγρα, a hunting, catching. *In N.T. spoken only of fishing,* a draught, *(non occ.)*

1. Matt. xv. 17. | 1. Mark vii. 19.
2. Luke v. 4, 9.

DRAW (-ETH, -EW, -AWN.)

1. ἑλκύω, } to draw, *esp. implying a certain attraction mentally or morally; also,* to draw *to a certain point.*
2. ἕλκω, } *(older form of same word.)*
3. σύρω, to draw, drag, *or* trail along *as a net; esp. with the notion of force and sometimes with violence.*
4. ἀντλέω, to bale out *bilge water,* bale the ship, *(from* ἄντλος, a hold,) *hence,* draw out *as wine or water.*
5. σπάω, to draw, *i.e* to pull.
   (a) *Mid.* to draw out, pull out, *as a sword.*
6. ἀποσπάω, to draw from, pull away, *as from the scabbard.*

7. ἀναβιβάζω, to cause to ascend, make go up to a higher place; to draw *a ship* up *on* land, *(non occ.)*

8. γίνομαι, to begin to be, to become.

9. προβιβάζω, to cause to go towards, cause to advance out of, urge forward.

7. Matt. xiii. 48.
6. —— xxvi. 51.
— Mark vi. 53, see D to the shore.
5a. —— xiv. 47.
— Luke xxiii. 50, see D on.
— John ii 8, see D out.
4. ——— 9.
4. —— iv. 7.
— ——— 11, see D with.
4. ——— 15.
8. —— vi. 19.
1. ——— 44.
1. —— xii. 32.
1. —— xviii. 10.
1. —— xxi. 6, 11.
— Acts v. 37, see D away.
Acts xi. 10, see D up.
3. —— xiv. 19.
1. —— xvi. 19.
— ——— 27, see D out.
3. —— xvii. 6.
9. —— xix. 33 (συμβιβάζω, *to bear aloft*, L T (8th ed.) Tr A ℵ.)
— —— xx. 30, see D away.
2. —— xxi. 30.
— Heb. x. 38, see D back.
— ——— 39, see D back (of them who.)
— Jas. i. 14, see D away (be.)
2. —— ii. 6.
3. Rev. xii. 4.

DRAW AWAY.

1. ἀποσπάω, *see* "DRAW," *No.* 6.

2. ἀφίστημι, *trans.* to place away from, cause to depart, to make to revolt, move to revolt, *or* detach from *another*.

2. Acts v. 37. | 1. Acts xx. 30.

DRAWN AWAY (BE.)

ἐξέλκομαι, *(No.* 2. *with* ἐκ, out of, *prefixed,)* to be drawn out, hurried away.

Jas. i. 14 (part.)

DRAW BACK.

ὑποστέλλω, to send *or* draw under *or* back. *In N.T. Mid.* to draw one's self back *esp. under cover, out of sight.*

Heb. x. 38.

DRAW BACK (OF THEM WHO.)

ὑποστολή, a shrinking *or* drawing back *under cover, or out of sight.*

Heb. x. 39 (Gen.)

DRAW ON.

ἐπιφώσκω, to grow light upon, to dawn upon, (occ. Matt. xxviii. 1.)

Luke xxiii. 50.

DRAW OUT.

1. ἀντλέω, *see* "DRAW," *No.* 4.

2. σπάω, *see* "DRAW," *No.* 5a.

1. John ii. 8. | 2. Acts xvi. 27.

DRAW TO THE SHORE.

προσορμίζω, to bring a ship to anchor at *or* near *a* place; to cast anchor, land at, *(non occ.)*

Mark vi. 53.

DRAW UP.

ἀνασπάω, *(No.* 5 *with* ἀνά, up, *prefixed,)* to draw up, (occ. Luke xiv. 5.)

Acts xi. 10.

DRAW WITH (TO.)

ἄντλημα, what is drawn. *In N.T.* a bucket, *i.e.* any vessel for drawing water.

See also, NEAR, NIGH.

DREAM (-s) [noun.]

1. ὄναρ, a dream, a vision in sleep *as opp. to a waking vision and esp. a significant or prophetic dream, (non occ.)*

2. ἐνύπνιον, what comes in sleep, *hence,* a dream, a mere dream, *(non occ.)*

1. Matt. i. 20.
1. —— ii. 12, 13, 19, 22.
1. Matt. xxvii. 19.
2. Acts ii. 17.

DREAM [verb.]

ἐνυπνιάζομαι, to dream, *(from No.* 2, *above,)* (occ. Jude 8, *part.)*

Acts ii. 17.

DREAMER (FILTHY.)

ἐνυπνιάζομαι, to dream.

Jude 8 (part.)

DRESSED (BE.)

γεωργέομαι, to be a γεωργός (a farmer), *hence,* to till, cultivate, *(non occ.)*

Heb. vi. 7.

DRESSER.

See, VINEYARD.

DRIED (be) [margin.]

ξηραινόμαι, to be dried up, *hence*, dried *as fruits.*

Rev. xiv. 15, text, *be ripe.*

DRINK [noun.]

1. *πόσις*, a drinking, *(the action being incomplete and in progress,) (non occ.)*
2. *πόμα*, drink, *i.e.* the thing drunk, *(non occ.)*

1. John vi. 55. | 2. 1 Cor. x. 4.
1. Rom. xiv. 17. | 1. Col. ii. 16, marg. *drinking.*
2. Heb. ix. 10.

DRINK (STRONG.)

σίκερα, sikerd, *i.e.* any intoxicating liquor, (lxx. for שֵׁכָר, Lev. x. 9; Deut. xxix. 6; Judges xiii. 4, 7, 14,) *(non occ.)*

Luke i. 15.

DRINK (-ETH, -ING, -ANK, -UNK, -UNKEN.)

πίνω, to drink, *(non occ.)*

Matt. vi. 25 (*om.* G⇉ T (8th ed.) ℵ), 31; xi. 18, 19; xxiv. 38, 49; xxvi. 27, 29 twice, 42; xxvii. 34 twice. Mark ii. 16 (*om.* Lb ℵ); xiv. 23, 25 twice; xv. 23 (*om.* T Tr A ℵ); xvi. 18 (*ap.*). Luke i. 15; v. 30, 33, 39; vii. 33, 34; x. 7; xii. 19, 29, 45; xiii. 26; xvii. 8 twice, 27, 28; xxii. 18, 30. John iv. 7, 9, 10, 12, 13, 14; vi. 53, 54, 56; vii. 37; xviii. 11. Acts ix. 9; xxiii. 12, 21. Rom. xiv. 21. 1 Cor. ix. 4; x. 4 twice, 7, 21, 31; xi. 22, 25, 26, 27, 28, 29 twice; xv. 32. Heb. vi. 7. Rev. xiv. 10; xvi. 6; xviii. 3.

DRINK OF.

Matt. xx. 22 twice, 23. | Mark x. 38 twice, 39 twice.

DRINK WITH.

συμπίνω, to drink together with *another, (non occ.)*

Acts x. 41.

DRINK (GIVE.)

ποτίζω, to let drink, to give to drink.

Matt. xxv. 35, 37, 42. | Rom. xii. 20.

DRINK (GIVE TO.)

Matt. x. 42. | Mark ix. 41.
— xxiii. 48. | — xv. 36.

DRINK (MAKE.)

Rev. xiv. 8.

DRINK (MAKE TO.)

1 Cor. xii. 13.

See also, DRUNK, WATER.

DRINKING [margin.]

πόσις, *see* "DRINK," *No.* 1.

Col. ii. 16, text, *drink.*

DRIVE (-ETH, -EN, -AVE, -OVE.)

1. *ἐκβάλλω*, to throw out, cast out *with the idea of force.*
2. *ἐλαύνω*, to drive, impel, urge on, *as horses, etc.*
3. *ἀπελαύνω*, to drive away from, *(non occ.)*

1. Mark i. 12. | 1. John ii. 15, with *ἐκ*, *out of.*
2. Luke viii. 29. | 3. Acts xviii. 16.
2. Jas. iii. 4.

DRIVE BACK [margin.]

ἀνακόπτω, to beat *or* drive back.

Gal. v. 7, text, *hinder* (*ἐγκόπτω*, *to beat* or *drive on*, G L T Tr A ℵ.)

DRIVE OUT.

ἐξωθέω, to thrust out, expel, (occ. Acts xxvii. 39.)

Acts vii. 45.

DRIVE UP AND DOWN.

διαφέρω, to bear *or* carry through a place, to carry different ways, bear asunder, to be borne hither and thither.

Acts xxvii. 27 (part.)

DRIVE (LET.)

{ *ἐπιδίδωμι*, to give up, *(here, part.)*, *φέρω*, to bear *or* carry, } *lit.* giving [her] up, we were being borne along *(or* before it, *i.e. the wind.)*

Acts xxvii. 15.

DRIVEN (BE.)

φερόμαι, to be borne *or* carried.

Acts xxvii. 17.

See also, WIND.

DROP (-S) (GREAT.)

θρόμβος, a lump *or* piece, a clot *or* gout *of blood, (non occ.)*

Luke xxii. 44 (*ap.*)

DROPSY (WHICH HAD THE.)

ὑδρωπικός, hydropic, dropsical.

Luke xiv. 2.

DROWN (-ED.)

1. βοθίζω, to sink in the deep, *i.e.* to cause to sink.
2. καταπίνω, to drink down, swallow up, *(same as Eng.* to swallow up ;) *of the earth,* to absorb ; *of the sea,* to overwhelm.

1. 1 Tim. vi. 9. | 2. Heb. xi. 29.

DROWNED (BE.)

καταποντίζω, to throw into the sea, *Pass.* to be plunged or drowned therein.

Matt. xviii. 6.

DRUNK or DRUNKEN (BE.)

1. μεθύω, to be drunken with wine, *(from* μέθυ, mulled wine, *hence, Germ.* meth, *Eng.* mead.)
2. μεθύσκω, to grow drunk *(marking the beginning of No.* 1,) *(non occ.)*

1. Matt. xxiv. 49.
2. Luke xii. 45.
1. Acts ii. 15.
1. 1 Cor. xi. 21.
2. Eph. v. 18.
2. 1 Thes. v. 7 1st.
1. —— 7 2nd.
1. Rev. xvii. 6.

DRUNK (BE MADE.)

1. Rev. xvii. 2.

DRUNK (HAVE WELL.)

1. John ii. 10 (Mid.)

DRUNKARD.

μέθυσος, *adj.* drunken with wine, *with art. as subst.* a drunkard, *(non occ.)*

1 Cor. v. 11 ; vi. 10.

DRUNKENNESS.

μέθη, strong drink ; drunkenness ; *(acc. to Pott. from Sans.* mad, to be drunk *or* mad,) *see under* "DRUNK," *(non occ.)*

Luke xxi. 34. | Gal. v. 21. | Rom. xiii. 13.

DRY [adj.]

1. ἄνυδρος, without water.
2. ξηρός, dry, withered, *of trees, as opp. to green ; of land, as opp. to water.*

1. Matt. xii. 43. | 2. Luke xxiii. 31. | 1. Luke xi. 24.

DRY LAND.

2. Heb. xi. 29.

DRY UP.

ξηραίνω, to dry, make dry.

Mark v. 29. | Rev. xvi. 12. | Mark xi. 20.

DUE [noun.]

ὀφειλή, what is due, indebtedness, debt.

Rom. xiii. 7.

DUE [adj.]

1. ἴδιος, own, one's own.
2. ὀφείλω, to owe, be indebted, *esp. in a pecuniary sense.*

2. 1 Cor. vii. 3 (part.) (ὀφειλή, *what is due,* instead of ὀφειλομένην εὔνοιαν, *due benevolence,* G L T Tr A ℵ.)
1. Gal. vi. 9. 1. 1 Tim. ii. 6. 1. Titus i. 3.

DUE (BE.)

2. Matt. xviii. 34.

See also, BORN, REWARD, REASON, TIME.

DULL.

νωθρός, sluggish, slothful, lazy, *esp. physically,* (occ. Heb. vi. 12.)

Heb. v. 11.

See also, HEARING.

DUMB.

1. ἄφωνος, voiceless, *(with reference to the voice.)*
2. ἄλαλος, speechless, *(with reference to the words,) (non occ.)*
3. κωφός, blunted, lame; *as to the tongue,* dumb.
4. σιωπάω, to be silent, still.

3. Matt. ix. 32, 33.
3. —— xii. 22 twice.
3. —— xv. 30, 31.
2. Mark vii. 37.
2. —— ix. 17, 25.
4. Luke i. 20 (part.)
3. —— xi. 14 twice.
1. Acts viii. 32.
1. 1 Cor. xii. 2.
1. 2 Pet. ii. 16.

DUNG [noun.]

σκύβαλον, dregs, refuse, *(prob. from κύσὶ βάλλειν,* to cast to the dogs.)

Phil. iii. 8 (pl.)

DUNG [verb.]

{ βάλλω, to cast, throw.
{ κοπρία, dunghill, dung, manure, (occ. Luke xiv. 35.)

Luke xiii. 8 (κόπριος, *full of dung, filthy,* instead of κοπρία, G L T Tr A ℵ.)

DUNGHILL.

κοπρία, dunghill.

Luke xiv. 35.

DURE.

See, WHILE.

DURST.

See, DARE.

DUST.

1. κονιορτός, dust raised *or* stirred up, a cloud of dust, *(non occ.)*
2. χόος, (χοῦς,) earth, *as dug out and thrown up,* heap of earth, *hence, gen.* loose earth, *(non occ.)*

1. Matt. x. 14.
2. Mark vi. 11.
1. Luke ix. 5.
1. Luke x. 11.
1. Acts xiii. 51.
1. —— xxii. 23.
2. Rev. xviii. 19.

DUTY (BE ONE'S.)

ὀφείλω, to owe, to be indebted, *esp. in a pecuniary sense.*

Luke xvii. 10. | Rom. xv. 27.

DWELL (-EST, -ETH, -LT, -ING.)

1. οἰκέω, to inhabit, hold as one's abode, to house, *(from οἶκος,* a house,) *(non occ.)*
2. κατοικέω, *(No.* 1 *with* κατά, down, *prefixed,)* to settle down in a fixed dwelling; to dwell fixedly in a place.
3. μένω, to remain, stay, abide, *(Lat.* manes.)
4. σκηνόω, to tent, to pitch tent; *hence,* to dwell in tents, to tabernacle.
5. κάθημαι, to sit down, sit.

2. Matt. ii. 23.
2. —— iv. 13.
2. —— xii. 45.
— —— xxiii. 21, see D in.
- Luke i. 65, see D round about.
2. —— xi. 26.
2. —— xiii. 4.
5. —— xxi. 35.
4. John i. 14.
3. —— 39, marg. *abide.*
3. —— 40.
3. —— vi. 56.
3. —— xiv. 10, 17.
2. Acts i. 20 (with εἰμί, *to be.*)
2. —— ii. 5.
— —— 9, see D in.
— —— 14, see D at.
— —— iv. 16, see D in.
2. —— vii. 2, 4 twice, 48.
2. —— ix. 22.
— —— 32, 35, see D at.
2. —— xi. 29.
2. —— xiii. 27.
2. —— xvii. 24, 26.
— —— xix. 10, see D in.
— —— 17, see D at.
2. —— xxii. 12.
3. —— xxviii. 16, 30.
1. Rom. vii. 17, 18. 20.
1. —— viii. 9.
1. Rom. viii. 11 1st.
— —— 11 2nd, see D in.
1. 1 Cor. iii. 16.
1. —— vii. 12, 13.
— 2 Cor. vi. 16, see D in.
2. Eph. iii. 17.
2. Col. i. 19.
2. —— ii. 9.
— —— iii. 16, see D in.
1. 1 Tim. vi. 16.
— 2 Tim. i. 5, 14, see D in.
2. Heb. xi. 9.
2. Jas. iv. 5 (κατοικίζω, *to take up a dwelling,* L Tr A ℵ.)
— 1 Pet. iii. 7, see D with
— 2 Pet. ii. 8, see D among.
3. 1 John iii. 17, 24.
3. —— iv. 12, 13, 15, 16 twice.
3. 2 John 2.
2. Rev. ii. 13 twice.
2. —— iii. 10.
2. —— vi. 10.
4. —— vii. 15.
2. —— xi. 10 twice.
4. —— xii. 12.
4. —— xiii. 6.
2. —— 8, 12, 14 twice.
2. —— xiv. 6 (No. 5, G L T Tr A ℵ.)
2. —— xvii. 8.
4. —— xxi. 3.

DWELL AMONG.

ἐγκατοικέω, *(No.* 2, *with* ἐν, in, *prefixed,)* to dwell fixedly in *or* among.

2 Pet. ii. 8.

DWELL AT.

κατοικέω, *see* "DWELL," *No.* 2.

Acts ii. 14; ix. 32, 35; xix. 17.

DWELL IN.

(When not two separate words.)

1. κατοικέω, *see* "DWELL," *No.* 2.
2. ἐνοικέω, to inhabit, dwell in.

1. Matt. xxiii. 21.
1. Acts ii. 9.
1. —— iv. 16.
1. —— xix. 10.
2. Rom. viii. 11 2nd.
2. 2 Cor. vi. 16.
2. Col. iii. 16.
2. 2 Tim. i. 5. 14.

DWELL ROUND ABOUT.

περιοικέω, to dwell around, *(non occ.)*

Luke i. 65.

DWELL WITH.

συνοικέω, to dwell together with, *(non occ.)*

1 Pet. iii. 7.

See also, STRANGER.

DWELLER AT (-S.)

κατοικέω, *see* "DWELL," *No.* 2.

Acts i. 19 (part.)

DWELLER IN.

Acts ii. 9 (part.)

DWELLING [noun.]

κατοίκησις, a dwelling, habitation, *(non occ.)*

Mark v. 3.

DWELLING PLACE (HAVE NO CERTAIN.)

αστατέω, to be a wanderer, to have no fixed residence, wander without a home, *(non occ.)*

1 Cor. iv. 11.

DYING [noun.]

νέκρωσις, a putting to death, *(expressive of the action as incomplete and in progress,)* (occ. Rom. iv. 19.)

2 Cor. iv. 10.

DYING (BE A.)

ἀποθνήσκω, to die out, expire, become quite dead, *(the termination denoting the beginning or progress of the act.)*

Heb. xi. 21 (part.)

DYING (LIE A.)

Luke viii. 42.

E

EACH.

1. *ἓν*, one, *κατά*, by, *ἓν*, one, *ἀνά*, apiece, severally.
2. *ἕκαστος*, each, every one, *(i.e. of any number separately.)*

2. Acts ii. 3. | 1. Rev. iv. 8 (*ap.*)

EACH ONE.

2. Luke xiii. 15.

See also, OTHER.

EAGLE (-S.)

ἀετός, an eagle, (lxx. for נשר.) *(The eagle feeds only upon fresh or living prey,) (non occ.)*

Matt. xxiv. 28.
Luke xvii. 37. | Rev. iv. 7.
—— xii. 14.

EAR (-S.)

(Part of the body.)

1. *οὖς*, an ear, *in pl.* ears, *(Lat.* auris, *Germ.* ohr, *Eng.* ear.)
2. *ὠτίον*, *(dim. of No.* 1*)* an ear, *esp.* one of the ears.
3. *ἀκοή*, hearing, *(the action of hearing actively or passively,) hence*, that which hears, and that which is heard ; hearing, report.

1. Matt. x. 27.
1. —— xi. 15.
1. —— xiii. 9, 15 twice, 16, 43.
2. —— xxvi. 51.
— —— xxviii. 14, see E (come to one's.)
1. Mark iv. 9, 23.
1. —— vii. 16, 33.
3. —— —— 35.
1. —— viii. 18.
2. —— xiv. 47 (*ὠτάριον, a little ear,* G∾ L T Tr A ℵ.)
1. Luke i. 44.
1. —— iv. 21.
1. —— viii. 8.
1. —— ix. 44.
1. —— xii. 3.
1. Luke xiv. 35.
1. —— xxii. 50.
2. —— —— 51.
2. John xviii. 10 (*ὠτάριον, a little ear,* T Tr A ℵ.)
2. —— —— 26.
1. Acts vii. 51, 57.
1. —— xi. 22.
3. —— xvii. 20.
1. —— xxviii. 27 twice.
1. Rom. xi. 8.
1. 1 Cor. ii. 9.
1. —— xii. 16.
3. 2 Tim. iv. 3, 4.
1. Jas. v. 4.
1. 1 Pet. iii. 12.
1. Rev. ii. 7, 11, 17, 29.
1. —— iii. 6, 13, 22.
1. —— xiii. 9.

EARS (COME TO ONE'S.)

{ ἀκουω, to hear, *pass.* to be heard, ἐπί, upon, } to come to the ears of, *i.e.* come before him officially, be borne witness of before.

Matt. xxviii. 14 (ὑπό, *by*, instead of ἐπί, -(lit., *be heard by*), L Tr.)

See also, ITCHING.

EAR.

(Of corn.)

στάχυς, an ear *of grain.*

Mark iv. 28 twice.

EAR OF CORN.

Matt. xii. 1. | Mark ii. 23.
Luke vi. 1.

EARLY.

1. πρωΐ, early in the day, at morn *(from* πρό, before, *cf. Germ.* fruh, *Sans.* prâh-na, forenoon.)
2. πρώϊος, early, the morning.
3. πρώϊμος, *(a poetic and later form of No.* 2,) early, *spoken of the early rain, (non occ.)*
4. ὄρθριος, at day-break *(from* ὄρθρος, the rising time *of the sun, man, and beast; Lat.* orior, ortor, hortor,*)* *(non occ.)*

1. Mark xvi. 9 (*ap.*)
4. Luke xxiv. 22 (ὀρθρινός, same meaning, L T Tr A ℵ.)
2. John xviii. 28 (No. 1, G L T Tr A ℵ.)
1. —— xx. 1.
3. Jas. v. 7.

See also, MORNING.

EARNEST [noun.]

ἀῤῥαβών, earnest-money, caution-money *deposited in case of purchasers, gen.* a pledge, *(Heb.* ערבון*), (non occ.)*

2 Cor. i. 22; v. 5. | Eph. i. 14.

EARNEST (adj.) [margin.]

ἐκτενής, extended, stretched out, *hence,* earnest, assiduous.

Acts xii. 5, text, *without ceasing* (ἐκτενῶς, adv. of above, L T (8th ed.) Tr A ℵ.)

See also, CARE, DESIRE, EXPECTATION, HEED.

EARNESTLY.

προσευχή, a prayer to *God, (here Dat. lit. with* prayer.)

Jas. v. 17, marg. *in his praying.*

EARNESTLY (BEHOLD.)

ἀτενίζω, to fix the eyes intently upon.

Acts xxiii. 1.

EARNESTLY ON (LOOK.)

Acts iii. 12.

EARNESTLY UPON (LOOK.)

Luke xxii. 56.

EARNESTLY (MORE.)

ἐκτενέστερον, *(comp. of* ἐκτενῶς, intently,) more intently.

Luke xxii. 44.

See also, CONTEND, COVET, DESIRE.

EARTH.

1. γῆ, the earth, land, *(i.e. one of the four elements)*, the earth *as opposed to heaven or to water*, the earth, ground as cultivated.
2. οἰκουμένη, *(pres. part. Pass. of* οἰκέω, to inhabit,) *see under* the earth, *(prop. as inhabited by the Greeks; and later, by Greeks and Romans,) hence,* the Roman Empire, *hence, further,* the whole earth considered as inhabited, *cf.* Heb. i. 6; ii. 5, etc., "WORLD."

1. Matt. v. 5, 13, 18, 35.
1. —— vi. 10, 19.
1. —— ix. 6.
1. —— x. 34.
1. —— xi. 25.
1. —— xii. 40, 42.
1. —— xiii. 5 twice.
1. —— xvi. 19 twice.
1. —— xvii. 25.
1. —— xviii. 18 twice, 19.
1. —— xxiii. 9, 35.
1. —— xxiv. 30, 35.
1. —— xxv. 18, 25.
1. —— xxvii. 51.
1. —— xxviii. 18.
1. Mark ii. 10.
1. —— iv. 5twice, 28, 31 1st, 31 2nd (*ap.*)
1. —— ix. 3.
1. —— xiii. 27, 31.
1. Luke ii. 14.
1. —— v. 24.
1. —— vi. 49.
1. —— x. 21.
1. —— xi. 2 (*ap.*), 31.
1. —— xii. 49, 51, 56.
1. —— xvi. 17.
1. —— xviii. 8.
1. —— xxi. 25.
2. —— —— 26.
1. —— —— 33, 35.
1. —— xxiii. 44, marg. *land*
1. —— xxiv. 5.
1. John iii. 31 twice.
1. —— xii. 32.
1. —— xvii. 4.
1. Acts i. 8.
1. —— ii. 19.
1. —— iii. 25.
1. —— iv. 24, 26.

1. Acts vii. 49.
1. —— viii. 33.
1. —— ix. 4, 8.
1. —— x. 11.
1. —— 12 (om. G→TrA.)
1. —— xi. 6.
1. —— xiii. 47.
1. —— xiv. 15.
1. —— xvii. 24, 26.
1. —— xxii. 22.
1. —— xxvi. 14.
1. Rom. ix. 17, 28.
1. —— x. 18.
1. 1 Cor. viii. 5.
1. —— x. 26, 28 (ap.)
1. —— xv. 47.
1. Eph. i. 10.
1. —— iii. 15.
1. —— iv. 9.
1. —— vi. 3.
— Phil. ii. 10 1st, see E(in.)
— —— 10 2nd, see E (under the.)
1. Col. i. 16, 20.
1. —— iii. 2, 5.
— 2 Tim. ii. 20, see E (of.)
1. Heb. i. 10.
1. —— vi. 7.
1. —— viii. 4.
1. —— xi. 13, 38.
1. —— xii. 25, 26 twice.
1. Jas. v. 5, 7, 12, 17, 18.
1. 2 Pet. iii. 5, 7, 10, 13.
1. 1 John v. 8 (ap.)
1. Rev. i. 5, 7.
1. —— iii. 10.
1. —— v. 3 twice, 6, 10, 13 twice.
1. —— vi. 4, 8 twice, 10, 13, 15.
1. —— vii. 1 3 times, 2, 3.
1. —— viii. 5, 7, 13.
1. —— ix. 1, 3 twice, 4.
1. —— x. 2, 5, 6, 8.
1. —— xi. 4, 6, 10 twice, 18.
1. —— xii. 4, 9, 12, 13, 16 twice.
1. —— xiii. 8, 11, 12, 13, 14 twice.
1. —— xiv. 3, 6, 7, 15, 16 twice, 18, 19 twice.
1. —— xvi. 1, 2.
1. —— 14 (om. G L T Tr A ℵ.)
1. —— 18.
1. —— xvii. 2 twice, 5, 8, 18.
1. —— xviii. 1, 3 twice, 9, 11, 23, 24.
1. —— xix. 2, 19.
1. —— xx. 8, 9, 11.
1. —— xxi. 1 twice, 24.

EARTH (IN.)

ἐπίγειος, upon the earth, extant in the earth.

Phil. ii. 10.

EARTH (OF.)

ὀστράκινος, like earthenware, made of clay, earthen, (occ. 2 Cor. iv. 20.)

2 Tim. ii. 20.

EARTH (UNDER THE.)

καταχθόνιος, *(from* κατά, down, and χθών, the earth, ground, *akin to Lat.* humi,) under-ground, subterraneous.

Phil. ii. 10.

EARTHEN.

ὀστράκινος, like earthenware, made of clay, (occ. 2 Tim. ii. 20.)

2 Cor. iv. 7.

EARTHLY.

1. { ἐκ, of, γῆ, *see* "EARTH," *No.* 1, } of the earth.
2. ἐπίγειος, upon the earth, terrestrial.

1. John iii. 31. | 2 Cor. v. 1.
2. Jas. iii. 15.

EARTHLY THINGS.

2. John iii. 12, } neut. pl. with article.
2. Phil. iii. 19, }

EARTHQUAKE.

σεισμός, motion, shaking, shock, *(from* σείω, to move to and fro *with idea of shock,* concussion, (occ. Matt. viii. 24.)

Matt. xxiv. 7.
—— xxvii. 54.
—— xxviii. 2.
Mark xiii. 8.
Luke xxi. 11.
Acts xvi. 26.
Rev. vi. 12.
—— viii. 5.
—— xi. 13 twice, 19 (om. G→)
—— xvi. 18 twice.

EARTHY.

χοϊκός, *(from* χόος, earth dug *or* thrown up,) of rubbish, of earth *or* clay, *(non occ.)*

1 Cor. xv. 47, 48, 49.

EASE (TAKE.)

ἀναπαύω, to cease *or* desist from labour, *(constantly used in lxx. of resting on the Sabbath.) Here, Mid.* to take this rest, enjoy repose, *(the idea of previous toil and anxiety being prominent.)*

Luke xii. 19.

EASED (BE.)

ἄνεσις, a letting loose, relaxation, *hence,* rest, *(not from labour, but a relaxation of the strain of endurance, etc.)*

2 Cor. viii. 13.

EASIER.

εὐκοπώτερος, *(comp. of* εὖ, well, *and* κόπος, labour,) that which is done by labour more easily, requiring less labour, *(non occ.)*

Matt. ix. 5.
—— xix. 24.
Mark ii. 9.
Mark x. 25.
Luke v. 23.
—— xvi. 17.
Luke xviii. 25.

EASILY.

See, BESET, PROVOKED.

EAST.

ἀνατολή, a rising, *esp.* of the sun, *hence,* the east, *(same as Anglo Saxon, cf.* east, easter, yeast), (occ. Luke i. 78.)

Matt. ii. 1, 2, 9.
—— viii. 11.
—— xxiv. 27.
Luke xiii. 29.
Rev. vii. 2, } with ἡλίου,
—— xvi. 12, } *of the sun.*
Rev. xxi. 13.

EASTER

Πάσχα, *(from Heb.* פסח, a sparing, immunity, *hence,* פסח, to spare, pass over,) the feast of the Passover.

Acts xii. 4.

EASY.

χρηστός, apt for use, useful; *of things,* better for *any* use, good to be done *or* be borne.

Matt. xi. 30.

EAT (-EN, -ETH, -ING, ATE.)

1. φάγω, *(an obsolete root furnishing some tenses for No. 2,)* to eat, devour, *both of men and beasts,* eat up. *This word seems to differ from No. 2 in idea, in that it combines both eating and drinking, while No. 2 is to eat as opp. to drinking, (whence prob. Lat.* fauces, the jaws.)
2. ἐσθίω, to eat, *(as opp. to* πίνω, to drink,) to consume, live upon, *(a strengthened form of* ἔδω, *a root found in nearly all cognate languages, Sanscr.* ad; *Lat.* edo, esse; *Eng.* eat; *Germ.* ess-en, *etc.)*
3. τρώγω, to gnaw, chew; to eat *raw vegetables as opp. to dressed food;* to eat *fruits, nuts, beans, etc., which require cracking, (hence,* τρωγαλια, τρωκτά, fruits, nuts, almonds, *set on as dessert.) In N.T. gen.* to eat, feast, *(non occ.)*
4. γεύομαι, to taste, *hence, metaph.* to experience.
5. βιβρώσκω, to eat, *(akin to* βορά, eatage, food, *and Lat.* voro, to eat up, swallow.)
6. μεταλαμβάνω, to take a part *or* share *of anything* with *others; i.e.* to partake of, share.
7. { νομή, the act of feeding; *metaph.* a feeding, eating, spreading, (occ. John x. 9) ἔχω, to have, } to have pasture.

1. Matt. vi. 25, 31.
2. —— ix. 11.
2. —— xi. 18, 19.
2. —— xii. 1.
1. —— 4 twice.
1. —— xiv. 16, 20.
2. —— 21.
2. —— xv. 2.
1. Matt. xv. 20.
2. —— 27.
1. —— 32, 37.
2. —— 38.
3. —— xxiv. 38.
2. —— 49.
1. —— xxvi. 17.
2. —— 21 (part.)
— Matt. xxvi. 26 1st, see eating (be.)
1. —— 26 2nd.
2. Mark i. 6.
2. —— ii. 16 twice.
1. —— 26 twice.
1. —— iii. 20.
1. —— v. 43.
1. —— vi. 31, 36, 37 twice, 42, 44.
2. —— vii. 2, 3, 4, 5, 28.
1. —— viii. 1, 2, 8.
1. —— 9 (*om.* G ⇉ T Tr[b] A ℵ.)
1. —— xi. 14.
1. —— xiv. 12, 14.
2. —— 18 1st (part.)
2. —— 18 2nd, 22 1st (part)
1. —— 22 2nd (*om.* G L T Tr A ℵ.)
1. Luke iv. 2.
2. —— v. 30, 33.
2. —— vi. 1.
1. —— 4 twice.
2. —— vii. 33, 34.
1. —— 36.
1. —— ix. 13, 17.
2. —— x. 7, 8.
1. —— xii. 19, 22, 29.
2. —— 45.
1. —— xiii. 26.
1. —— xiv. 1, 15.
— —— xv. 2, see E with.
2. —— 16.
1. —— 23.
1. —— xvii. 18 twice.
2. —— 27, 28.
1. —— xxii. 8, 11, 15, 16.
2. —— 30.
1. —— xxiv. 43.
— John ii. 17, see E up.
1. —— iv. 31, 32.
— —— 33, see E (aught to.)
1. —— vi. 5.
5. —— 13.
1. —— 23, 26, 31 twice, 49, 50, 51, 52, 53.
3. —— 54 (part. with art.)
3. —— 56, 57.
1. —— 58 1st.
3. —— 58 2nd.
3. —— xiii. 18.
1. —— xviii. 28.
— Acts i. 4, see *E together with.*
6. Acts ii. 46.
1. —— ix. 9.
4. —— x. 10.
1. —— 13, 14.
— —— 41, } see E with.
— —— xi. 3, }
1. —— 7.
— —— xii. 23, see worms.
4. —— xx. 11 (part.)
4. —— xxiii. 12.
4. —— 14.
1. —— 21.
2. —— xxvii. 35.
— —— 38, see E enough.
1. Rom. xiv. 2 1st.
2. —— 2 2nd, 3 4 times, 6 3 times, 20.
1. —— 21, 23.
— 1 Cor. v. 11, see E with.
— —— viii. 4, see eating.
2. —— 7.
1. —— 8 twice.
2. —— 10.
1. —— 13.
1. —— ix. 4.
2. —— 7 twice.
1. —— x. 3, 7.
2. —— 18, 25, 27, 28, 31.
1. —— xi. 20.
— —— 21, see eating.
2. —— 22.
1. —— 24 (*om.* G L T Tr A ℵ.)
2. —— 26, 27, 28, 29 twice.
1. —— 33.
2. —— 34.
1. —— xv. 32.
— Gal. ii. 12, see E with.
— Col. ii. 16, see eating.
1. 2 Thes. iii. 8.
2. —— 10, 12.
7. 2 Tim. ii. 17.
1. Heb. xiii. 10.
— Jas. v. 2, see moth.
1. —— 3.
1. Rev. ii. 7, 14.
1. —— 17 (*om.* G L T Tr A ℵ.)
1. —— 20.
— —— x. 9, 10 1st, see E up.
1. —— 10 2nd.
1. —— xvii. 16.
1. —— xix. 18.

EAT ENOUGH.

κορέννυμι, to sate, to satisfy *as with food and drink,* (occ. 1 Cor. iv. 8.)

(a) *Pass. or Mid.* to be sated, to be full, *i.e.* to have eaten and drunk enough.

Acts xxvii. 38 (part.)

EAT TOGETHER WITH [margin.]

συναλίζω, to gather together in a heap *(of things.) In N.T. of persons,* to meet together, *(non occ.)*

Acts i. 4, text, *be assembled together.*

EAT UP.

κατεσθίω, *(No. 2, with* κατά, down, *prefixed,)* to eat down, swallow down.

John ii. 17. | Rev. x. 9, 10.

EAT WITH.

συνεσθίω, (*No.* 2 *with* συν, together with, *prefixed,*) to eat with *any one; hence, gen.* to associate with.

Luke xv. 2. | Acts xi. 3.
Acts x. 41. | 1. Cor. v. 11.
Gal. ii. 12.

EAT (AUGHT TO.)

φάγω, *see* "EAT," *No.* 1.

John iv. 33 (Inf.)

EATING (BE.)

ἐσθίω, *see* "EAT," *No.* 2.

Matt. xxvi. 26 (part.)

EATING [noun.]

1. βρῶσις, the act of eating.
2. φάγω, *see* "EAT," *No.* 1.

1. 1 Cor. viii. 4. | 2. 1 Cor. xi. 21 (Inf.)
Col. ii. 16, marg. (text, *meat.*)

EDGE (-S.)

1. στόμα, the mouth.
2. ὀφρύς, the eye-brow; *then, from likeness of shape,* the brow of a hill.

2. Luke iv. 29, marg. (text, *brow.*) | 1. Luke xxi. 24.
1. Heb. xi. 34.

TWO EDGES (WITH.)

δίστομος, double-mouthed.

Rev. ii. 12.

See also, TWO.

EDIFICATION.

οἰκοδομή, the act *or* process of building a house, a building up. *In N.T. only metaphorically.*

Rom. xv. 2. | 2 Cor. x. 8.
1 Cor. xiv. 3. | —— xiii. 10.

EDIFY (-ED, -ETH, -ING.)

1. οἰκοδομέω, to build a house, *and then gen.* to build, construct. *Metaph.* to build up, establish. *(Identical with Lat.* œdes, a house, and fio, to construct.)
2. οἰκοδομή, *see* "EDIFICATION."

1. Acts ix. 31. | 1. 1 Cor. x. 23.
1. 1 Cor. viii. 1. | 1. —— xiv. 4 twice, 17.
1. —— 10, marg. (text, *embolden.*) | 2. Eph. iv. 29, marg. (text, *edifying.*)
1. 1 Thes. v. 11.

EDIFY (THE THINGS WHEREWITH ONE MAY.)

τὰ, the *things,*
τῆς, of the,
οἰκοδομῆς, building up.

Rom. xiv. 19.

EDIFYING.

1. οἰκοδομή, *see* "EDIFICATION."
2. οἰκοδομία, building a house, *(the action incomplete and in progress.) Metaph.* edifying.

1. 1 Cor. xiv. 5, 12, 26. | 2. 1 Tim. i. 4 (so Elzevir, ed. 1624) (οἰκονομία, *management of a household,* S^tGLTTrAℵ)(No. 1G ∾)
1. 2 Cor. xii. 19.
1. Eph. iv. 12, 16.
1. —— 29, marg. *edify.*

EFFECT (BECOME OF NO.)

καταργέω, to leave unemployed *or* idle, make useless, void, abolish. *In Pass.* to be done away.

Gal. v. 4 (pass.)

EFFECT (MAKE OF NONE.)

1. καταργέω, *see above.*
2. ἀκυρόω, to deprive of authority, (occ. Gal. iii. 17.)
3. κενόω, to make empty, vain, fruitless.

2. Matt. xv. 6. | 1. Rom. iv. 14.
2. Mark vii. 13. | 3. 1 Cor. i. 17.
1. Gal. iii. 17.

EFFECT (MAKE WITHOUT.)

1. Rom. iii. 3.

EFFECT (TAKE NONE.)

ἐκπίπτω, to fall out of, *as things from their places. Metaph.* to fail.

Rom. ix. 6.

EFFECTUAL.

ἐνεργής, energic, *i.e.* at work; active working, (occ. Heb. iv. 12.)

1 Cor. xvi. 9. | Philem. 6.

EFFECTUAL (BE.)

ἐνεργέω, to be at work, be in active operation.

(a) *Mid.* to show one's self active, to be active, operate.

2 Cor. i. 6, marg. *be wrought.*

EFFECTUAL FERVENT.

Jas. v. 16 (part.)

EFFECTUAL WORKING.

ἐνέργεια, *Eng.* energy, the being at work; power in action, energetic exercise, effectual operation.

Eph. iii. 7; iv. 16.

EFFECTUALLY.

See, WORK.

EFFEMINATE.

μαλακός, soft, *(Lat.* mollis); soft *to the touch; hence, of things not subject to the touch,* soft, gentle.

1 Cor. vi. 9.

EGG.

ᾠόν, an egg, *(Lat.* ovum; *Germ.* ey; *Anglo Saxon,* aeg), *(non occ.)*

Luke xi. 12.

EIGHT.

ὀκτώ, eight, *(Lat.* octo, *Sancr.* ashten.)

Luke ii. 21.
—— ix. 28.
John v. 5.
John xx. 26.
Acts ix. 33.
1 Pet. iii. 20.

EIGHTEEN.

{ δέκα, ten,
καί, and,
ὀκτώ, eight.

Luke xiii. 4, 11, 16.

EIGHTH.

ὄγδοος, eighth.

Luke i. 59.
Acts vii. 8.
Phil. iii. 5, see E day(the.)
2 Pet. ii. 5.
Rev. xvii. 11.
—— xxi. 20.

EIGHTH DAY (THE.)

ὀκταήμερος, an eighth-day *person or thing.*

Phil. iii. 5.

EITHER.

ἤ, either, *(a disjunctive particle),* or; *interrogative,* whether.

Matt. vi. 24.
—— xii. 33.
Luke vi. 42 (*om.* T Trb A ℵ.)
—— xv. 8.
Luke xvi. 13.
Acts xvii. 21.
1 Cor. xiv. 6.
Phil. iii. 12.
Jas. iii. 12.

EITHER SIDE (ON.)

{ ἐντεῦθεν, hence,
καί, and,
ἐντεῦθεν, hence, } hence and thence, *i.e.* on this side and that side.

John xix. 18.
Rev. xxii. 2 (ἐντεῦθεν, *hence,* καὶ, *and,* ἐκεῖθεν, *thence,* G∾ L T Tr A) (ἔνθεν καί, *and hence,* ℵ.)

ELDER (-s) [noun.]

πρεσβύτερος, *(comp. of* πρέσβυς, old, *which Döderlein derives from* πρέπω, πρέψω, *and so strictly,* one that is conspicuous *or* distinguished,) older, *i.e.* elder. *In pl.* aged men, elders, *just like Anglo Saxon* aldermen, *i.e.* eldermen. *The word always implying dignity and wisdom.*

[Among the Gentiles it was the name of dignity and official position—as Egyptians, Gen. l. 7; Moabites and Midianites, Num. xxii. 7; in Sparta, a political official title.

In the Jewish nation, persons who were apparently the deputies of the tribes and families according to the right of the first-born, 1 Kings viii. 1, 3. From among these, Moses at God's command chose seventy men who were no longer the representatives of the people, but who bore "with him the burden of the people," Num. xi. 16; Deut. xxvii. 1; cf. with Ex. xix. 7, and Josh. viii. 10.

With these is connected (not perhaps in historical continuity) the institution of the Sanhedrim, side by side with the institute of the elders revived throughout Israel in our Lord's time.

In the christian church they were men appointed (*καθιστάναι*, Titus i. 5) or chosen (*χειροτονεῖν*, Acts xiv. 23) everywhere (*κατ' ἐκκλησίαν*, Acts xiv. 23; *κατὰ πόλιν*, Titus i. 5.]

[The twenty-four elders in the Apocalypse are entirely different, in their standing before God, in their relation to Jesus and to John; in their appearance and their disappearance, in the essence and object of their worship, in their history and their destiny. They appear to be "Elders of the Priests." *See* Isa. xxxvii. 2; and Jer. xix. 1. The chief priests of the heavenly courses (for the earthly order of the temple was only a "pattern" of things in the heaven, Heb. viii. 5; ix. 23; 1 Chron. xxviii. 11—13.)

Their number, twenty-four, is the number of the earthly "pattern," 1 Chron. xxiv. 3—5. It was also the *total number*, 1 Chron. xxiii. 3, 4. Also the number of the prophets, 1 Chron. xxv. 31, and the porters of the tribe of Levi, 1 Chron. xxvi. 17—19. It is the number that reigns in the temple, 1 Chron. xxvii. 1—15, 25—31, in its constitution in the hands of God's king, after Eli and his sons were set aside through their failure.

They distinguish themselves from the Church or those redeemed by Christ in Rev. v. 9, 10, (*see* "the critical readings" *in Ap.,*) where, in verse 9, the word "us" should be omitted (G→ L T A), and in verse 10, the words "us" and "we" should be "them" and "they," (G L T Tr A ℵ.) Their robes are white (iv. 4), but not because washed in the blood of the Lamb, (cf. vii. 14.) They are also distinguished from the great multitude which is so washed. They are in heaven, but no mention is made of blood by which alone any can enter, even Christ Himself, Heb. ix. 7, 12, 25; x. 19; xiii. 11. They act as Priests before the great multitude appears (v. 8), but not afterwards. They are seen crowned and on thrones (iv. 4, *θρονοι*) before Jesus and the great multitude are seen, and they are not seen after (xix. 4) when Jesus and the ransomed host leave heaven for earth. We never read of their reigning for ever and ever, for they are *angels*, and "unto angels hath He not put in subjection the world to come," (Heb. ii. 5.)

In the life of our Lord, the earthly elders formed the main body of His adversaries, Matt. xxi. 23, etc. Now, these heavenly elders own the Lamb slain, as their worthy Lord. "Thy will be done on earth as it is in heaven."

The twenty-four elders in the Apocalypse therefore appear to be the heavenly "course" of angelic royal priests, ministering in heaven in relation to earth, (hence *the earth* is prominent in all their utterances, iv. 10, 11; v. 9, 10; xi. 18, 19; and xix. 2—4.) They are seen resigning their office when God's government is about to undergo a change, and others more worthy—a new body of royal priests, *men* redeemed by blood—associated with the man Christ Jesus are to take their place.]

Matt. xv. 2.
—— xvi. 21.
—— xxi. 23.
—— xxvi. 3, 47, 57.
—— 59 (*om.* G⇉ L T (8th ed.) Tr A ℵ.)
—— xxvii. 1, 3, 12, 20, 41.
—— xxviii. 12.
Mark vii. 3, 5.
—— viii. 31.
—— xi. 27.
—— xiv. 43, 53.
—— xv. 1.
Luke vii. 3.
—— ix. 22.
—— xx. 1.
—— xxii. 52.
—— 66, see elders.
Acts iv. 5, 8, 23.
—— vi. 12.
—— xi. 30.
—— xiv. 23.
—— xv. 2, 4, 6, 22, 23.
Acts xvi. 4.
—— xx. 17.
—— xxi. 18.
—— xxii. 5, see E (estate of.)
—— xxiii. 14.
—— xxiv. 1.
—— xxv. 15.
1 Tim. v. 1, 17, 19.
Titus i. 5.
Heb. xi. 2.
Jas. v. 14.
1 Pet. v. 1 1st.
—— 1 2nd, see E (also an.)
2 John 1.
3 John 1.
Rev. iv. 4, 10.
—— v. 5, 6, 8, 11, 14.
—— vii. 11, 13.
—— xi. 16.
—— xiv. 3.
—— xix. 4.

ELDER (ALSO AN.)

συμπρεσβύτερος, a fellow-elder.
1 Pet. v. 1.

ELDERS.

πρεσβυτέριον, an assembly of aged men, a council of elders, senate, (*whence, Eng.* presbytery), (occ. 1 Tim. iv. 14.)
Luke xxii. 66.

ELDERS (ESTATE OF.)

Acts xxii. 5.

ELDER [adj.]

1. πρεσβύτερος, *see* "ELDER (ALSO AN.)"

2. μείζων, *(comp. of* μέγας, great, large,) greater, larger; *of age,* ὁ μείζω, the elder, *(Lat.* major natu.) *In* Rom. ix. 12, *quoted from* Gen. xxv. 23, *where lxx. for* רַב.

1. Luke xv. 25. | 2. Rom. ix. 12, marg. *greater.*
1. 1 Pet. v. 5.

ELDER WOMAN.

1. 1 Tim. v. 2.

ELDEST.

πρεσβύτερος, elder, *(see above.)*

John viii. 9 *(ap.)*

ELECT [adj.]

ἐκλεκτός, chosen out, preferred, selected, (occ. "CHOSEN.")

Matt. xxiv. 22, 24, 31.
Mark xiii. 20, 22, 27.
Luke xviii. 7.
Rom. viii. 33.
Col. iii. 12.
1 Tim. v. 21.
2 Tim. ii. 10.
Titus i. 1.
1 Pet. i. 2.
—— ii. 6.
2 John i. 13.

ELECTED TOGETHER WITH.

συνεκλεκτός, (ἐκλεκτός, *see above, and* σύν, together with,) chosen out, preferred, selected together with, *(non occ.)*

1 Pet. v. 13.

ELECTION.

ἐκλογή, a picking out, selection, then, selection made, that which is chosen, *(hence, Eng.* eclogue,) (occ. Acts ix. 15.)

Rom. ix. 11.
—— xi. 5, 7, 28.
1 Thes. i. 4.
2 Pet. i. 10.

ELEMENT (-s.)

στοιχεῖον, *(dim. of* στοῖχος, a small upright rod, *esp.* the gnomon *of the sundial, or* the shadow *thrown by it, hence, from the degrees of the shawm,* a row *or* a series, *from* στείχω, to go up by steps. *The root is also seen in the Lat.* ve-stig-ium, a footstep.) a first-beginning, first-principle *or* element. *The* στοιχεῖα *were different from written letters, (which are* γράμματα,) *they were* the first and simplest component parts *of the letters, hence,* the primary matter. *Used in this sense in physics and sciences,* (occ. Heb. v. 12.)

Gal. iv. 3.
—— 9, marg. *rudiment.*
Col. ii. 8, 20, marg. (text,
2 Pet. iii. 10, 12. [*rudiment.*)

ELEVEN.

ἕνδεκα, eleven, *(non occ.)*

Matt. xxviii. 16.
Mark xvi. 14 *(ap.)*
Luke xxiv. 9, 33.
Acts i. 26.
Acts ii. 14.

ELEVENTH.

ἑνδέκατος, eleventh, *(non occ.)*

Matt. xx. 6, 9. | Rev. xxi. 20.

ELI.

'Ηλί, *Greek for* אֵלִי, Eli, my God, *(quoted from* Ps. xxii. 2.)

Matt. xxvii. 46 twice.

ELIAS.

'Ηλίας, Elias, *(Heb. for* אֵלִיָּה *and* אֵלִיָּהוּ, Elijah, *i.e.* my God is Jehovah.)

In all passages, except

Luke ix. 54 *(ap.)*

ELOI.

'Ελωΐ, Eloi, *(Aramaic* אֱלָהִי, my God; *quoted from* Ps. xxii. 2, *where the lxx. is* ὁ θεός μου *for Heb.* אֵלִי, *which in* Matt. xxvii. 46, *is* ἠλί), *(non occ.)*

Mark xv. 34 twice.

ELOQUENT.

λόγιος, skilled in words *or* speech; *gen.* learned, *(occurs first in Herodotus, who used the word esp. for* one learned in history, chroniclers *as opp. to Epic Poets.)*

Acts xviii. 24.

ELSE.

1. ἐπεί, since, since if so, otherwise, since if otherwise.

2. { ἐπεί, see *No.* 1, ἄρα, still farther beyond that, *(marking a transition or drawing a conclusion,)* } else by consequence, *or* since otherwise indeed.

3. { εἰ, if, δὲ, but, μή, not, } but if not, otherwise at least; (εἰ μή, *introduces an incredible or untenable hypothesis.)*

4. { εἰ, if, δὲ, but, μήγε, not indeed, } if otherwise indeed *or* otherwise at least indeed.

5. ἕτερος, the other, *(denoting generic distinction,)* the other *(different,)* one of two, *(stronger than* ἄλλος.)

6. καί, and, even.

4. Matt. ix. 17. | 6. Rom. ii. 15.
3. Mark ii. 21, 22. | 2. 1 Cor. vii. 14.
4. Luke v. 37. | 1. —— xiv. 16.
5. Acts xvii. 21. | 1. —— xv. 29.

See also, OR.

EMBOLDENED (BE.)

οἰκοδομέω, to build a house, *and then, gen.* to build up, construct. *Metaph.* edify, establish, confirm.

1 Cor. viii. 10, marg. *edify.*

EMBRACE (-ED, -ING.)

1. ἀσπάζομαι, to draw to one's self, *hence,* to embrace, salute, *spoken of those who meet and separate; of things,* to welcome, embrace.

2. συμπεριλαμβάνω, to take around with *something else, i.e.* to embrace with, comprehend, include, *(non occ.)*

1. Acts xx. 1. | 1. Heb. xi. 13. | 2. Acts xx. 10.

EMERALD.

1. σμαράγδινος, of smaragdus, of emerald, *(non occ.)*

2. σμάραγδος, an emerald, a precious stone of a light green colour, *(non occ.)*

1. Rev. iv. 3. | 2. Rev. xxi. 19.

EMINENT PLACE [margin.]

ὑπεροχή, a prominent place, eminence, *as* a mound, a hill, *etc.; also of authority or station,* excellence, (occ. 1 Cor. ii. 1.)

1 Tim. ii. 2, text, *authority.*

EMPTY [adj.]

1. κενός, empty, *(opp. to* πλήρης, full.) *Metaph.* empty, vain.

2. σχολάζω, to have leisure, be free from labour; *of place,* to be vacant, unoccupied.

2. Matt. xii. 44 (part.) | 1. Luke i. 53.
1. Mark xii. 3. | 1. —— xx. 10, 11.

EMULATION (-S.)

ζῆλος, zeal, fervour; *in a good sense,* ardour; *in a bad sense,* jealousy.

Gal. v. 20.

EMULATION (PROVOKE TO.)

παραζηλόω, to render miszealous, *i.e.,* to make jealous, provoke to jealousy.

Rom. xi. 14.

ENABLE (-ED.)

ἐνδυναμόω, to strengthen in, *i.e.,* to render strong, to impart strength to.

1 Tim. i. 12.

ENCOUNTER (-ED.)

συμβάλλω, to throw together; *of persons,* to throw one's self together with another, *i.e.* to meet with.

Acts xvii. 18.

END [noun.]

1. τέλος, the fulfilment *or* completion of any thing, *(Lat.* effectus,) *i.e.* its end *or* issue, *(not its cessation.) It denotes strictly, not the ending of a departed state, but,* the arrival of a complete *or* perfect one.

2. συντέλεια, a bringing to one end together; the combination of parts to one end, *marking the unity, perfection, and accomplishment of a scheme, (non occ.)*

3. πέρας, end, *i.e.,* extremity. *Metaph. of what comes to an end,* conclusion, termination.

4. ἔκβασις, a going out of, a way out of, *hence,* the issue *or* event *of a matter.*

1. Matt. x. 22.
— —— xi. 1, see E (make an.)
2. —— xiii. 39, 40, 49.
2. —— xxiv. 3.
1. —— 6, 13, 14.
— —— 31, see E to the other (from one.)
1. —— xxvi. 58.
— —— xxviii. 1, see E (in the.)
2. —— 20.
1. Mark iii. 26.
1. —— xiii. 7, 13.
1. Luke i. 33.
— —— xviii. 1, see E that (to this.)
1. —— xxi. 9.
1. —— xxii. 37.
1. John xiii. 1.
— —— xviii. 37, see E (to this.)
— Acts vii. 19, see E (to the.)
— —— xiii. 47, see ends.
— Rom. i. 11, } see E
— —— iv. 16, } (to the.)
1. —— vi. 21, 22.
1. Rom. x. 4.
3. —— 18.
— —— xiv. 9, see E (to this.)
1. 1 Cor. 1, 8.
1. —— x. 11.
1. —— xv. 24.
1. 2 Cor. i. 13.
— —— ii. 9, see E (to this.)
1. —— iii. 13.
1. —— xi. 15.
1. Phil. iii. 19.
— 1 Thes. iii. 13.
1. 1 Tim. i. 5.
1. Heb. iii. 6 (*ap.*), 14.
1. —— vi. 8, 11.
3. —— 16.
1. —— vii. 3.
2. —— ix. 26.
4. —— xiii. 7.
1. Jas. v. 11.
1. 1 Pet. i. 9.
— —— 13, see E (to the.)
1. —— iv. 7, 17.
— 2 Pet. ii. 20, see E (the latter.)
1. Rev. ii. 26.
1. —— xxi. 6.
1. —— xxii. 13.

END (IN THE.)

ὀψέ, late, after a long time, (*Lat.* sero,) late in the day, at evening, (*opp. to* πρωΐ.)

Matt. xxviii. 1.

END (MAKE AN.)

τελέω, to bring about, complete, fulfil, accomplish, (*Lat.* perficere,) execute fully.

Matt. xi. 1.

END (THE LATTER.)

{ τὰ, the *things*, ἔσχατα, the last, extreme, uttermost, (*of place or time,*) } the last state, (occ. Matt. xii. 45, Luke xi. 26.)

2 Pet. ii. 20.

END (TO THE.)

1. { εἰς, unto, τό, the, } (*with an Inf. following,*) with respect to, with a view to, (*marking the object to which an action is directed.*)

2. τελείως, completely, thoroughly, perfectly.

1. Acts vii. 19.
1. Rom. i. 11.
1. —— iv. 16.
1. 1 Thes. iii. 13.
2. 1 Pet. i. 13, marg. *perfectly.*

END (TO THIS.)

{ εἰς, unto, with a view to, τοῦτο, this. }

John xviii. 37. | 2 Cor. ii. 9. | Rom. xiv. 9.

END THAT (TO THIS.)

{ πρὸς, towards, τό, the, } (*with Inf. following,*) respecting, *marking the remote object, the subjective purpose of the agent, and the relation which one object has towards another.*

Luke xviii. 1.

END TO THE OTHER (FROM ONE.)

{ ἀπό, from, ἄκρων, extremities, ἕως, unto, ἄκρων, extremities. }

Matt. xxiv. 31.

ENDS.

ἔσχατος, the last, extreme, uttermost, (*of place or time.*)

Acts xiii. 47.

See also, WORLD.

END (-ED) [verb.]

1. τελέω, to bring about, complete, fulfil, (*Lat.* perficere,) to perform, *not merely* to end, *but, to* complete and perfect.
2. συντελέω, to bring to one end together, bring quite to an end.
3. πληρόω, to make full, fill up, perform fully, accomplish, fulfil.

2. Matt. vii. 28 (No. 1, L T Tr A ℵ.)
1. —— x. 23, marg. (text, *go over.*)
2. Luke iv. 2 (part.)
2. —— 13 (part.)
3. —— vii. 1.
3. Acts xix. 21.
2. Acts xxi. 27.

ENDED (BE.)

γίνομαι, to begin to be, *implying origin;* to take place, *implying result;* to be in progress, *implying change of state or condition.*

John xiii. 2.

ENDEAVOUR (-ED, -ING.)

1. σπουδάζω, to make haste, *as manifested in diligence, earnestness, zeal;* to do the utmost.

2. *ζητέω*, to seek after, look for, to strive to find; to seek to *do*.

3. *φιλοτιμέομαι*, to love honour, to be ambitious of *doing any thing*, to exert one's self, to strive *as from a love and sense of honour*.

2. Acts xvi. 10.
3. 2 Cor. v. 9, marg. (text, *labour*.)
1. Eph. iv. 3.
1. 1 Thes. ii. 17.
1. 2 Pet. i. 15.

ENDING [noun.]

τέλος, *see* "END," *No.* 1.

Rev. i. 8 (*om.* G L T Tr A.)

ENDLESS.

1. *ἀκατάλυτος*, indissoluble, *(non occ.)*

2. *ἀπέραντος*, unlimited, boundless; which is not able to be passed, interminable, *(non occ.)*

1. Heb. vii. 16. | 2. 1 Tim. i. 4.

ENDUED WITH (BE.)

ἐνδύω, to go in, enter in *as a garment*, to cause to go into a garment.

(a) *Pass. or Mid.* to be clothed, to clothe one's self.

a. Luke xxiv. 49. | Jas. iii. 13, see knowledge.

ENDURE (-ED, -ETH, -ING.)

1. *μένω*, stay, stand fast, continue, abide, *(Lat.* manes.)

2. *ὑπομένω*, *(No.* 1 *with ὑπό*, under, *prefixed,)* to remain behind *after others have gone; trans.* to remain under *the approach or presence of any person or thing, i.e.* to await *the onset; then, of persons in conflict,* to keep one's ground, hold out, *(No. 2 is a brave bearing up against sufferings, No. 5 is a more tame and passive sufferance of them.)*

3. *φέρω*, to bear, *(Lat.* fero, *Sans.* bhri, *Pers.* ber, *Germ.* bahren, fahren, *and Eng.* bear,) to bear *or* carry *a load*, to bear *with idea of motion; in Pass.* to bear *pain, misfortune, hardship*.

4. *ὑποφέρω*, *(No.* 3 *with ὑπό*, under, *prefixed,)* to bear *or* carry by being under, to bear up from underneath, support, sustain, (occ. 1 Cor. x. 13.)

5. *ἀνέχομαι*, to hold one's self upright, hold one's self up *against a thing, hence,* hold *or* sustain *an equal mind,* to bear patiently.

6. *καρτερέω*, to be strong, staunch, *or* firm, *(non occ.)*

2. Matt. x. 22.
2. —— xxiv. 13.
— Mark iv. 17, see time.
2. —— xiii. 13.
1. John vi. 27.
3. Rom. ix. 22.
2. 1 Cor. xiii. 7.
— 2 Cor. i. 6, see enduring.
5. 2 Thes. i. 4.
— 2 Tim. ii. 3, see E hardness.
2. —— 10.
4. —— iii. 11.
5. 2 Tim. iv. 3.
— —— 5, see afflictions.
— Heb. vi. 15, see E patiently.
2. —— x. 32.
1. —— 34.
6. —— xi. 27.
2. —— xii. 2, 3, 7.
3. —— 20.
2. Jas. i. 12.
2. —— v. 11.
1. 1 Pet. i. 25.
4. —— ii. 19.

ENDURE HARDNESS.

κακοπαθέω, to suffer evil, *esp. of the evils and hardships of soldiers.*

2 Tim. ii. 3 (*συγκακοπαθέω, suffer hardness with me,* instead of *σὺ οὖν κακοπαθέω, thou therefore endure hardness,* G ∾ L T Tr A ℵ.)

ENDURE PATIENTLY.

μακροθυμέω, to be long-minded, long-suffering, forbearing.

Heb. vi. 15 (part.)

ENDURING.

ὑπομονή, a remaining behind *or* under, endurance, the patience of hope (Rom. viii. 25), *which has faith and hope for its basis. In lxx. used for* מקוה, hope, *because it denotes the peculiar definiteness which hope attains in the economy of grace. (Used for ἐλπίς,* hope, *in* Titus ii. 2, *but ἐλπίς*, 1 Cor. xiii. 13.)

2 Cor. i. 6.

ENEMY (-IES.)

1. *ἐχθρός*, *passively*, hated, odious, object of enmity, *(opp. of ἀγαπητός*, beloved); *actively*, opposite to, hating another and adverse to him; *as subst.* an enemy, adversary, (occ. Matt. x. 36, Acts ii. 35.)

2. { *ἐχθρός*, an enemy, *(see above,)* / *ἄνθρωπος*, a man, } a man [*that is*] an enemy.

1. Matt. v. 43, 44.
1. —— xiii. 25.
2. —— 28.
1. —— 39.
1. —— xxii. 44.
1. Mark xii. 36.
1. Luke i. 71, 74.
1. —— vi. 27, 35.
1. —— x. 19.
1. —— xix. 27, 43.
1. —— xx. 43.
1. Acts xiii. 10.
1. Rom. v. 10.
1. —— xi. 28.
1. —— xii. 20.
1. 1 Cor. xv. 25, 26.
1. Gal. iv. 16.
1. Phil. iii. 18.
1. Col. i. 21.
1. 2 Thes. iii. 15.
1. Heb. i. 13.
1. —— x. 13.
1. Jas. iv. 4.
1. Rev. xi. 5, 12.

ENGRAFTED.

ἔμφυτος, adapted for inward growth *(from* ἐμφύω, to implant; *the termination marking the idea of capability or adaptation both actively and passively, (non occ.)*

Jas. i. 21.

ENGRAVE (-EN.)

ἐντυπόω, to carve in, cut in intaglio, *(opp. to* ἐκτυπόω, in relief,) *(non occ.)*

2 Cor. iii. 7.

ENJOIN.

1. ἐντέλλομαι, to enjoin upon, to charge with, command.
2. ἐπιτάσσω, to set over, put in command; put upon *one* as a duty, to enjoin command.

2. Philem. 8. | 1. Heb. ix. 20.

ENJOY.

1. { εἰς, unto, with a view to, *(marking the immediate purpose,)* ἀπόλαυσις, enjoyment, pleasure, *i.e., the advantage got from a thing,* } for the purpose of getting advantage *or* pleasure.
2. τυγχάνω, to hit, *esp.* to hit a mark *with an arrow; hence, gen.* to hit upon, happen upon; *of persons,* to meet by chance; *of things,* to meet with, reach, gain, obtain *a thing.*

2. Acts xxiv. 2 (part.) | 1. 1 Tim. vi. 17.

ENJOY THE PLEASURES.

{ ἔχω, to have, ἀπόλαυσις, enjoyment, } to be having [sin's] enjoyment.

Heb. xi. 25.

ENLARGE (-ED, -ING.)

1. μεγαλύνω, to make great, magnify.
2. πλατύνω, to make broad, widen, extend, (occ. Matt. xxiii. 5.)

1. Matt. xxiii. 5. | 2. 2 Cor. vi. 11, 13.
1. 2 Cor. x. 15, marg. *magnify.*

ENLIGHTEN (-ING.)

φωτίζω, *trans.* to give light to, shine upon, *intrans.* to give light, to shine.

Eph. i. 18. | Heb. vi. 4.

ENMITY.

ἔχθρα, *(fem. of* ἔχθρος, *see* "ENEMY,") enmity, hatred, (occ. Gal. v. 20.)

Luke xxiii. 12. | Eph. ii. 15, 16.
Rom. viii. 7. | Jas. iv. 4.

ENOUGH.

1. ἀρκετός, sufficient, *(from* ἀρκέω, *see below),* (occ. Matt. vi. 34; 1 Pet. iv. 3.)
2. ἱκανός, coming to, reaching to, *and hence,* sufficing, *i.e.* sufficient; *of things,* enough; *of persons,* competent.

1. Matt. x. 25. | 2. Luke xxii. 38.
— Luke xv. 17, see spare. | — Acts xxvii. 38, see eat.

ENOUGH (BE.)

ἀρκέω, to ward off, keep off, *hence (in N.T.),* to aid, assist; *then, by impl.* to be strong enough and able *to assist any one, hence,* to suffice, be enough, *(Lat.* satis est.)

Matt. xxv. 9.

ENOUGH (IT IS.)

ἀπέχω, to hold off from; to have off *or* out, *i.e.,* to have all *that is one's due so as* to cease from having *any more,* to have received in full.

(a) *impers.* it is sufficient, *(Lat.* sufficit.)

Mark xiv. 41.

ENQUIRE (-ED.)

1. πυνθάνομαι, to ask *for information,* enquire *of or from any one.*
2. ζητέω, to seek after, look for, to strive to find.

3. ἐπιζητέω, *(No. 2 with ἐπί,* upon, *prefixed,)* to seek earnestly *or* continually, enquire after.

4. συζητέω, *(No. 2 with σύν,* together with, *prefixed,)* to seek *any thing* with *another,* to seek together, *i.e. to enquire of one another.*

5. διαγινώσκω, to know throughout, *i.e.* accurately, to obtain an accurate knowledge of *or* insight into, *(with the idea of suffering one's self to be influenced thereby,)* (occ. Acts xxiv. 22.)

6. ἐξετάζω, to verify out, to examine, explore *whether anything is true or not; gen.* to seek out the truth by enquiry.

6. Matt. x. 11. | 2. John xvi. 19.
4. Luke xxii. 23. | 3. Acts xix. 39.
1. John iv. 52. | 5. —— xxiii. 15.
1. Acts xxiii. 20.

ENQUIRE DILIGENTLY.

1. ἀκριβόω, to know *or* do anything accurately; to enquire accurately *or* assiduously.

2. ἐκζητέω, *(No. 2 above, with ἐκ,* out of, *prefixed,)* to seek out, search out, *(as for anything lost.)*

1. Matt. ii. 7, 16. | 2. 1 Pet. i. 10.

ENQUIRE FOR.

ζητέω, *see* "ENQUIRE," *No.* 2.

Acts ix. 11.

ENQUIRE HEREOF (how to) [marg.]

εἰς, as to,
τὴν, the,
περί, concerning,
τούτου, this,
ζήτησιν, enquiry,
} as to the enquiry concerning this (person, *i.e. Jesus or Paul, or this matter.)*

Acts xxv. 20 (εἰς, *as to* (*om.* T (8th ed.) Tr A[b] ℵ).) (τούτων, *these things,* instead of τούτου, *this,* G∾ L T Tr A ℵ) (text, *of such manner of questions.*)

ENQUIRY FOR (MAKE.)

διερωτάω, to enquire through *to the end or till the enquiry is successful, (non occ.)*

Acts x. 17.

ENRICH (-ED.)

πλουτίζω, to make rich, enrich, (occ. 2 Cor. vi. 10.)

1 Cor. i. 5. | 2 Cor. ix. 11.

ENROLLED (be) [margin.]

ἀπογράφω, to write off, *i.e.* to copy; *hence,* to write down, *(lxx. for* כתב, Jude viii. 14,) to inscibe *as in a register.*

Luke ii. 1 pass. (text, *be taxed.*)
Heb. xii. 23, pass. (text, *be written.*)

ENSAMPLE (-S.)

1. τύπος, a blow, that which is produced by a blow, the mark of a blow, impression; the impress *of a seal,* stamp *of a coin, etc.; hence,* that which forms the pattern *or* model after which a thing is made.

2. ὑπόδειγμα, that which is shown, a sign; that which is shown *to any one either for imitation or for warning.*

1. 1 Cor. x. 11, marg. *type* (τυπικῶς, *typically,* L Tr A ℵ.) | 1. 1 Thes. i. 7.
1. Phil. iii. 17. | 1. 2 Thes. iii. 9.
| 1. 1 Pet. v. 3.
| 2. 2 Pet. ii. 6.

ENSUE.

διώκω, to cause to flee, *hence,* to pursue after *as flying enemies, in order to find or overtake.*

1 Pet. iii. 11.

ENTANGLE (-ED, -ETH.)

παγιδεύω, to lay snares for, to trap, *(from* παγίς, anything which fixes *or* holds fast, *hence,* a trap *or* snare.)

Matt. xxii. 15.

ENTANGLE IN.

ἐμπλέκω, to braid in, interweave. *Mid.* to entangle or mix one's self up with, *(non occ.)*

2 Pet. ii. 20.

ENTANGLE ONE'S SELF WITH.

2 Tim. ii. 4 (Mid.)

ENTANGLED WITH (BE.)

ἐνέχω, to have *or* hold in *anything*. *Pass.* to be held in *or* by *anything.*

Gal. v. 1 (Pass.)

ENTER (-ED, -ETH, -ING.)

1. ἔρχομαι, to come *or* go; *it denotes* the act of coming *or* going, *and is used of persons or things.*
2. εἰσέρχομαι, *(No.* 1 *with* εἰς, unto, *prefixed,)* to come *or* go into.
3. παρεισέρχομαι, *(No.* 2 *with* παρά, beside, *prefixed,)* to come *or* go in beside *so as to be present along with, (the idea of stealth being implied,)* (occ. Gal. ii. 4.)
4. εἰσπορεύομαι, to pass into, to convey *or* transport one's self into.
5. ἀναβαίνω, to cause to ascend, to move to a higher place, come up, rise; *spoken of thoughts which* come up into *one's mind,* to spring up.
6. ἐμβαίνω, to go *or* move in; embark.
7. εἴσειμι, to go into, proceed into, enter.
8. εἴσοδος, way into *any place,* entrance; *also,* the act *or* power of entering.

2. Matt. v. 20.
2. —— vi. 6.
— —— vii. 13, see E in.
2. ——— 21.
2. —— viii. 5.
6. ——— 23 (part.)
6. —— ix. 1.
2. —— x. 5, 11.
2. —— xii. 4, 29.
— ——— 45, } see E in.
— —— xv. 17, }
2. —— xviii. 3, 8, 9.
2. —— xix. 17, 23.
2. ——— 24 (*om.* T Tr[b] A ℵ.)
2. —— xxiii. 13.
2. —— xxiv. 38.
2. —— xxv. 21, 23.
2. —— xxvi. 41.
2. Mark i. 21 (*om.* G⇉ T Tr[b] A ℵ.)
1. ——— 29.
2. ——— 45.
2. —— ii. 1.
2. —— iii. 1, 27.
6. —— iv. 1
— ——— 19, see E in.
2. —— v. 12, 13.
— ——— 40, see E in.
2. —— vi. 10.
4. ——— 56.
4. —— vii 15.
2. ——— 17.
4. ——— 18, 19.
2. ——— 24.
6. —— viii. 10, 13.
2. —— ix. 25, 43, 45, 47.
2. —— x. 15, 23, 24, 25.
4. —— xi. 2 (part.)
2. ——— 11.
2. Mark xiii. 15.
2. —— xiv. 38 (No. 1, T A ℵ.)
2. —— xvi. 5 (No.1, T A.)
2. Luke i. 40.
2. —— iv. 38.
6. —— v. 3.
2. —— vi. 6.
2. —— vii. 1, 6, 44.
— —— viii. 16, see E in.
2. ——— 30, 32, 33.
2. —— ix. 4, 34, 52.
2. —— x. 5, 8, 10, 38.
— —— xi. 26, 52 twice, see E in.
— —— xiii. 24 twice, see E in.
2. —— xvii. 12 (part.), 27.
2. —— xviii. 17.
2. ——— 24 (No.4, T Tr A)
2. ——— 25.
2. —— xix. 1.
4. ——— 30 (part.)
2. —— xxi. 21.
2. —— xxii. 3, 10[1st] (part.)
— ——— 10 [2nd], see E in.
2. ——— 40, 46.
— —— xxiv. 3, see E in.
2. ——— 26.
2. John iii. 4, 5.
2. —— iv. 38.
6. —— vi. 17, 22 (*ap.*)
2. —— x. 1.
— ——— 2, 9, see E in.
2. —— xiii. 27.
2. —— xviii. 33.
5. —— xxi. 3 (No. 6, G L T Tr ℵ.)
4. Acts iii. 2.
2. ——— 8.
2. —— v. 21.
4. Acts viii. 3.
2. —— ix. 17.
2. —— x. 24.
2. —— xi. 8, 12.
2. —— xiv. 22.
2. —— xvi. 40.
1. —— xviii. 7 (No. 2, L ℵ)
2. ——— 19.
— —— xix. 30, } see E in.
— —— xx. 29, }
2. —— xxi. 8.
7. ——— 26.
2. —— xxiii. 16.
2. —— xxv. 23 (part.)
— —— xxvii. 2, see E into.
— —— xxviii. 8, see E in.
2. Rom. v. 12.
3. ——— 20.
5. 1 Cor. ii. 9.
— 1 Thes. i. 9, see entering in.
2. Heb. iii. 11, 18.
— ——— 19, see E in.
2. —— iv. 1, 3 twice, 5, 6, 10, 11.
2. —— vi. 19, 20.
— —— ix. 12, see E in.
2. ——— 24, 25.
8. —— x. 19.
2. Jas. v. 4.
2. 2 John 7 (ἐξέρχομαι, *to go out,* G∾ L T Tr A ℵ.)
2. Rev. xi. 11.
2. —— xv. 8.
2. —— xxi. 27.
— —— xxii. 14, see E in.

ENTER IN.

(Where not two separate Greek words.)

2. Matt. vii. 13.
2. —— xii. 45.
4. —— xv. 17.
4. Mark iv. 19.
4. —— v. 40.
4. Luke viii. 16.
2. —— xi. 26 (No. 1, G∾ T A.)
2. ——— 52 twice.
2. —— xiii. 24 twice.
4. Luke xxii. 10.
2. —— xxiv. 3.
2. John x. 2, 9.
2. Acts xix. 30.
2. —— xx. 29.
2. —— xxviii. 8.
2. Heb. iii. 19.
2. —— iv. 6.
2. —— ix. 12.
2. Rev. xxii. 14.

ENTER INTO.

(Where not two separate Greek words.)

ἐπιβαίνω, to go *or* move upon, to go upon *shipboard.*

Acts xxvii. 2.

ENTERING IN.

εἴσοδος, *see* "ENTER," *No.* 8.

1 Thes. i. 9.

ENTERTAIN (-ED.)

ξενίζω, to receive *or* entertain strangers, to receive as a guest.

Heb. xiii. 2 [1st] (2 [2nd], see strangers.)

ENTICE (-ED, -ING.)

δελεάζω, to entice *or* catch by a bait.

Jas. i. 14.

ENTICING.

πειθός, apt for persuading, persuasive, winning.

1 Cor. ii. 4, marg. *persuadible* (πειθώ, *Pitho,* Lat. *Suada, the goddess of persuasion,* G∾.)

ENTICING WORDS.

πιθανολογία, persuasive discourse.

Col. ii. 4.

ENTIRE.

ὁλόκληρος, whole in every part, fixed in all its parts, (occ. 1 Thes. v. 23.)

Jas. i. 4.

ENTRANCE.

εἴσοδος, *see* "ENTER," *No.* 8.

2 Pet. i. 11.

ENTRANCE IN.

1 Thes. ii. 1.

ENTREAT (-ED.)

1. ἐρωτάω, to ask, *i.e.* to interrogate; *also*, to ask, *i.e.* request, beseech, beg, *(implying familiarity if not equality.)*
2. παρακαλέω, to call to *one's side*, call near; *every kind of* calling to *which is meant to produce a particular effect, e.g.* exhortation, help, comfort, *etc.*
3. παραιτέομαι, to ask near *any one, i.e.* at *his hands* to obtain by asking; *also*, to ask aside *or* away, to get rid of by asking, *to* entreat *that something may* not *take place.*
4. χράομαι, to use, make use of, *of things; of persons*, to use *well or ill*, to treat.

— Matt. xxii. 6, see spitefully.
2. Luke xv. 28.
— —— xviii. 32, see spitefully.
— —— xx. 11, see shamefully.
— Acts vii. 6, 19, see evil.
4. Acts xxvii. 3.
2. 1 Cor. iv. 13.
1. Phil iv. 3.
— 1 Thes. ii. 2, see shamefully.
2. 1 Tim. v. 1.
3. Heb. xii. 19.

ENTREATED (EASY TO BE.)

εὐπειθής, easily persuaded, compliant, *(non occ.)*

Jas. iii. 17.

ENTREATY.

παράκλησις, a calling near, a summons to one's side; *hence*, an admonitory, encouraging, *and* consolatory exhortation, invitation, *or* entreaty.

2 Cor. viii. 4.

ENVIOUSLY [margin.]

φθόνος, *see* "ENVY," *No.* 1.

Jas. iv. 5, with πρός, *towards* (text, *envy.*)

ENVY (-IES) [noun.]

1. φθόνος, envy. *The word is always used in a bad sense;* jealousy *of another's success,* depreciation *of his worth,* envy *of his excellence, (associated by sound and sense, with* φόνος (murder), *as* envy *led to the first* murder), (occ. Gal. v. 21.)
2. ζῆλος, zeal; *gen. in a good sense,* ardour, zeal *for the cause of another,* emulation *to imitate superior worth; also, sometimes in a bad sense,* heart-burning, jealousy.

1. Matt. xxvii. 18.
1. Mark xv. 10.
2. Acts v. 17, marg. (text, *indignation.*)
2. —— xiii. 45.
1. Rom. i. 29.
1. Phil. i. 15.
1. 1 Tim. vi. 4.
1. Tit. iii. 3.
1. Jas. iv. 5, with πρός, *towards*(marg. *enviously.*)
1. 1 Pet. ii. 1.

ENVY (BE MOVED WITH.)

ζηλόω, to be zealous towards, *i.e.* for *or* against *any person or thing; gen.* for, and in a good sense.

Acts vii. 9.
—— xvii. 5 (*om.* G T (not 8th ed.))

ENVY (-ETH, -ING) [verb.]

1. φθόνεω, to be φθόνος, *(see* "ENVY," *No.* 1,*) (non occ.)*
2. ζήλόω, *see above.*

2. 1 Cor. xiii. 4. | 1. Gal. v. 26.

ENVYING (-S.)

1. φθόνος, *see* "ENVY." *No.* 1.
2. ζηλόω, *see* "ENVY," *No.* 2.

2. Rom. xiii. 13.
2. 1 Cor. iii. 3.
2. 2 Cor. xii. 20.
1. Gal. v. 21.
2. Jas. iii. 14, 15.

EPHESUS.

Ἔφεσος, Ephesus.

In all passages, except

Eph. i. 1 (*om.* ἐν Ἐφέσῳ, *in Ephesus,* Tr[b] A[b] ℵ.)

EPHESUS (OF.)

Ἐφεσῖνος, Ephesian, of Ephesus.

Rev. ii. 1 (ἐν Ἐφέσῳ, *in Ephesus,* G L T Tr A ℵ.)

EPHPHATHA.

ἐφφαθά, Ephphatha, *an Aramaean imperative,* "be opened," *from Heb.* פתח, to open.

Mark vii. 34.

EPISTLE (-s.)

ἐπιστολή, what is sent to *any one, hence,* a letter.

Acts xv. 30.
— xxiii. 33.
Rom. xvi. 22.
1 Cor. v. 9.
2 Cor. iii. 1, 2, 3.
2 Cor. vii. 8.
Col. iv. 16.
1 Thes. v. 27.
2 Thes. ii. 15.
— iii. 14, 17.
2 Pet. iii. 1, 16.

EQUAL [noun.]

συνηλικιώτης, one of like age, an equal in age, *(non occ.)*

Gal. i. 14, marg. *equal in years.*

EQUAL [adj.]

ἴσος *or* ἶσος, equal to, the same as, *in appearance, size, strength, or number, etc.,* (occ. Acts xi. 17; Luke vi. 34; Mark xiv. 56, 59.)

Matt. xx. 12.
Luke xx. 36, see angels.
John v. 18.
Phil. ii. 6 (neut. pl.)
Rev. xxi. 16.

EQUAL (THAT WHICH IS.)

{ τὸ, the, ἰσότης, equality, *i.e. equal state or proportion,* } what is equitable, equity.

Col. iv. 1.

EQUALITY.

ἰσότης, equality, *i.e. equal state or proportion;* equity.

2 Cor. viii. 14 twice.

ERE.

πρίν, *(adv. of time,)* before, sooner than.

John iv. 49.

ERR (-ED.)

1. πλανάω, to make to wander, cause to err, lead astray, *esp. used of doctrinal error, or religious deceit.*

2. ἀποπλανάω, *(No. 1 with* ἀπό, from, *prefixed,)* to cause to wander away from, lead astray from.

   (a) Pass. to go astray from, swerve from.

3. ἀστοχέω, to miss the mark, to err.

1. Matt. xxii. 29.
1. Mark xii. 24, 27.
2. 1 Tim. vi. 10, marg. *be seduced.*
3. — 21.
3. 2 Tim. ii. 18.
1. Heb. iii. 10.
1. Jas. i. 16.
1. — v. 19.

ERROR (-s.)

1. πλάνη, a wandering, seduction *from the truth.*

2. ἀγνόημα, ignorance, involuntary error, *(lxx. for* משגה, Gen. xliii. 12,) *(non occ.)*

1. Matt. xxvii. 64.
1. Rom. i. 27.
2. Heb. ix. 7.
1. Jas. v. 20.
1. 2 Pet. ii. 18.
1. — iii. 17.
1. 1 John iv. 6.
1. Jude 11.

ESCAPE (-ED.)

1. φεύγω, to flee, take flight, *(Lat.* fuga, fugio.)

2. ἀποφεύγω, *(No. 1 with* ἀπό, away from, *prefixed,)* to flee away from, *(non occ.)*

3. διαφεύγω, *(No. 1 with* διά, through, *prefixed,)* to flee through, escape by flight, *(non occ.)*

4. ἐκφεύγω, *(No, 1 with* ἐκ, out of, *prefixed,)* to flee out of *a place,* escape.

5. ἐξέρχομαι, to go *or* come out of *any place.*

6. διασώζω, to save through, *i.e.* to bring safely through, *as through danger, sickness, etc.*

— Matt. xxiii. 33, see E (can.)
4. Luke xxi. 36.
5. John x. 39.
3. Acts xxvii. 42.
— — 44, see E safe.
6. — xxviii. 1 (part.)
6. — 4 (part.)
4. Rom. ii. 3.
— 1 Cor. x. 13, see E (way to.)
4. 2 Cor. xi. 33.
4. 1 Thes. v. 3.
4. Heb. ii. 3.
1. — xi. 34.
1. — xii. 25 (No. 4, L Tr A ℵ.)
2. 2 Pet. i. 4.
2. — ii. 18, 20 (part.)

ESCAPE (CAN.)

1. Matt. xxiii. 33, with ἀπό, *away from.*

ESCAPE SAFE.

6. Acts xxvii. 44 (pass.)

ESCAPE (WAY TO.)

ἔκβασις, a going out of, way out of, (occ. Heb. xiii. 7.)

1 Cor. x. 13.

ESCHEW.

ἐκκλίνω, to bend out, to turn aside *or* away from.

1 Pet. iii. 11.

ESPECIALLY.

μάλιστα, (*superl. of* μάλα, very, most of all.)

Acts xxvi. 3. | 1 Tim. v. 17.
Gal. vi. 10. | 2 Tim. iv. 13.

ESPOUSE (-ED.)

ἁρμόζομαι, to be fitted *or* joined together, *hence*, to betroth, to be married to, (*non occ.*)

2 Cor. xi. 2.

ESPOUSED (BE.)

μνηστεύω, to ask in marriage, to woo. *In N.T. only in Pass.* to be asked in marriage, *hence*, to be betrothed, affianced.

Matt. i. 18. | Luke i. 27 ; ii. 5.

ESTABLISH (-ED.)

1. στηρίζω, to set fast, make fast, fix firmly.
2. στερεόω, to make stable, strong, to strengthen.
3. ἵστημι, (a) *trans.* to cause to stand, to place, set.
   (b) *intrans.* to stand *as opp. to falling.*
4. βεβαιόω, to make steadfast, make remain in its place, make firm, immoveable, certain, fixed.
5. νομοθετέω, to make *or* give laws, establish as law, legislate, sanction by law.

— Matt. xviii. 16, see E (be.) | — 2 Cor. xiii. 1, see E (be.)
2. Acts xvi. 5. | 1. 1 Thes. iii. 2.
1. Rom. i. 11. | 5. Heb. viii. 6.
3a. —— iii. 31. | 3a. —— x. 9.
3a. —— x. 3. | 4. —— xiii. 9.
1. 2 Pet. i. 12.

ESTABLISHED (BE.)

3b. Matt. xviii. 16. | 3b. 2 Cor. xiii. 1.

ESTATE (YOUR.)

{ τὰ, the *things*, } the things
{ περὶ, concerning, } concerning
{ ὑμῶν, you, } you.

— Mark vi. 21, see chief. | Col. iv. 8 (τὰ περί ἡμῶν, *the things concerning us*, G ∾ L Tr ℵ.)
— Acts xxii. 5, see elders.
— Rom. xii. 16, see low.
— Jude 6, see first.

ESTEEM (-ED, -ETH, -ING.)

1. ἡγέομαι, to lead, *i.e.* go before, go first; *then*, to lead out *before the mind*, *i.e.* to view, regard *as being so and so*, esteem, count, reckon.
2. κρίνω, to divide, to separate, to separate from, select, *hence*, to come to a decision, to judge.
3. λογίζομαι, to occupy one's self with reckonings *or* calculations; to reckon, to count; to take for, value, *or* esteem.
4. τιμάω, to deem *or* hold worthy, *hence*, to esteem, honour, respect; to treat with honour.

2 Rom. xiv. 5 twice. | 1. 1 Thes. v. 13.
3. —— 14. | 1. Heb. xi. 26. [*honour.*)
1. Phil. ii. 3. | 4. 1 Pet. ii. 17, marg. (text,

ESTEEMED (BE LEAST.)

ἐξουθενέω, to set at nought, *i.e.* to despise, contemn.

1 Cor. vi. 4.

See also, HIGHLY.

ETERNAL.

1. αἰών, (*from* ἄω, ἄημι, to blow, breathe,) the life that hastes away in the breathing of our breath, life *as transitory; then*, the course of life, time of life, *and gen.* life in its temporal form; *then*, the space of human life, an age. αἰών *always includes a reference to the* life, *filling time or space of time, hence*, the unbounded time *past and future, in which the life of the world is accomplished;* immeasurable time, (*Gen. pl.* of ages.)
2. αἰώνιος, belonging to the αἰών, (*see No.* 1,) to time in its movement; constant, abiding, eternal.
   (a) *with* ζωή, life.
3. ἀΐδιος, always existing, perpetual, (*adj. from* ἀεί, always), (occ. Jude 6.)

2a. Matt. xix. 16.
2a. —— xxv. 46.
2. Mark iii. 29.
2a. —— x. 17, 30.
2a. Luke x. 25.
2a. —— xviii. 18.
2a. John iii. 15.
2a. —— iv. 36.
2a. —— v. 39.
2a. —— vi. 54, 68.
2a. —— x. 28.
2a. —— xii. 25.
2a. —— xvii. 2, 3.
2a. Acts xiii. 48.
3. Rom. i. 20.
2a. —— ii. 7.
2a. —— v. 21.
2a. —— vi. 23.
2. 2 Cor. iv. 17, 18.
2. 2 Cor. v. 1.
1. Eph. iii. 11 (gen. pl.)
1. 1 Tim. i. 17.
2a. —— vi. 12.
2a. —— 19 (ὄντως, *that which is really*, G L T Tr A ℵ.)
2. 2 Tim. ii. 10.
2a. Titus i. 2.
2a. —— iii. 7.
2. Heb. v. 9.
2. —— vi. 2.
2. —— ix. 12, 14, 15.
2. 1 Pet. v. 10.
2a. 1 John i. 2.
2a. —— ii. 25.
2a. —— iii. 15.
2a. —— v. 11, 13, 20.
2. Jude 7.
2a. —— 21.

EUNUCH (-s.)

εὐνοῦχος, bed-keeper, keeper of the bed-chamber; a eunuch, *and sometimes* a minister of the court, *(non occ.)*

Matt. xix. 12 1st, 2nd & 4th. | Acts viii. 27, 34, 36, 38, 39.

EUNUCH (MAKE.)

εὐνουχίζω, to make a εὐνοῦχος, *(see above.)*

(a) *Pass.* to be made a eunuch.

(b) *Metaph.* to live like a eunuch, *i.e.* in voluntary abstinence, *(non occ.)*

a. Matt. xix. 12 3rd. | b. Matt. xix. 12 5th.

EVANGELIST (-s.)

εὐαγγελιστής, a messenger of glad tidings, a proclaimer of the gospel story, of the facts of redemption, *(as distinct from* προφήτης, *who speaks of the revelation of God, and from* διδάσκαλος, *(who speaks about it,) (non occ.)*

Acts xxi. 8. | 2 Tim. iv. 5. | Eph. iv. 11.

EVEN [noun.]

1. ὀψία, *(fem. of* ὄψιος, late, *as subst.)* late evening, the latter of the two evenings among Hebrews; first being from 3 p.m. to sunset, the latter after sunset. ὀψία appears to be used of both; sometimes perhaps (a) the former, and (b) the latter.
2. ὀψέ, *(adv.)* late, *i.e.* after long time, late in the day, late evening.

1a. Matt. viii. 16.
1b. —— xx. 8.
1b. —— xxvi. 20.
1a. —— xxvii. 57.
1a. Mark iv. 35.
1b. —— vi. 47.
2. —— xi. 19.
1a. —— xv. 42.
1b. John vi. 16.

EVEN (AT.)

2. Mark xiii. 35.

EVEN [adj.]

ὀρθός, upright, erect, *i.e.* straight, right.

Luke xix. 44, see ground.
Heb. xiii. 13, marg. (text, *straight.*)

EVEN

1. καί, *(the conjunction of annexation, uniting things strictly co-ordinate,)* and; *sometimes not merely annexing, but implying increase, addition, something more,* also, *or only emphasis,* even.
2. δέ, *(the conj. of antithesis, to be carefully distinguished from No.* 1,) but, *marking either a contrast to what has gone before; or an addition to it,* moreover.
3. γάρ, *(a contraction of* γὲ ἄρα, verily then,) *hence,* in fact, *and when the fact is given as a reason, or explanation,* for.
4. τε, *(a conj. of annexation, annexing with implied relation or distinction,)* and, also, *annexing something added.*
5. μέν, *(a conj. of antithesis,)* truly, indeed, *(often followed by* δέ, but,) μέν *being* the first thing, δέ the second, *when referring to the different members of a proposition.*
6. ἔτι, *(adv.)* any more, any longer, yet, still, even.
7. οὔτω *or* οὔτως, *(adv.)* thus, in this wise, so.

1. Matt. v. 46, 47.
— —— 48, see E as.
— —— vi. 29, see not.
1. —— vii. 12.
— —— 17, see E so.
1. —— viii. 27.
— —— ix. 18, see now.
— —— xi. 26, see E so.
1. —— xii. 8.
— —— 46, see E so.
1. —— xiii. 12.
— —— xv. 28, see E as.
— —— xviii. 14, see E so.
1. —— 33.
1. —— xx. 14.
— —— 28, see E as.
— —— xxiii. 37, see E as.
1. —— xxv. 29.
— —— xxvi. 38, see unto.
1. Mark i. 27.
1. —— iv. 25.
— —— 36, see E as.
1. —— 41.
1. —— vi. 2.
— —— xi. 6, see E as.
1. —— xiii. 22.
— Mark xiv. 54, see into.
— Luke i. 2, see E as.
6. —— 15.
— —— vi. 33, see E (also.)
1. —— viii. 18, 25.
1. —— ix. 54.
1. —— x. 11.
— —— 21, see E so.
— —— xii. 7, see E very.
1. —— 41, 57.
— —— xvii. 30, see thus.
1. —— xviii. 11.
1. —— xix. 26.
— —— 37, see now.
— —— 32, see E as.
1. —— 42.
1. —— xx. 37.
1. —— xxiv. 24 (*om.* L Tr)
— John iii. 14, see E so.
1. —— v. 21.
— —— 23, see E as.
— —— vi. 57, see E he.
1. —— viii. 25.
— —— x. 15, see E so I.
1. —— xi. 22, 37.
— —— xii. 50, see E as.

— John xiv. 31, see E so.
— —— xv. 10, } see E
— —— xvii. 14, 16, } as.
— ——— 18, see E so I also.
— ——— 22, see E as.
— —— xx. 21, see E so I.
— —— xxi. 25, see not.
1. Acts v. 39.
— —— xi. 5, see to.
— ——— 15, see E so.
1. —— xv. 8.
1. —— xxvi. 11.
7. —— xxvii. 25.
1. Rom. i. 18.
4. ——— 26.
— ——— 28, see E as.
2. —— iii. 22.
— —— iv. 6, see E as.
1. —— v. 7, 14, 18, 21.
1. —— vi. 4.
— ——— 19, see E so.
1. —— viii. 23.
1. ——— 34 (*om.* G→ L[b] T (8th ed.) Tr A[b] ℵ.)
1. —— ix. 24.
2. ——— 30.
1. —— xi. 5.
— ——— 31, see E so.
1. —— xv. 3.
1. ——— 6.
— 1 Cor. i. 6, see E as.
1. —— ii. 11.
1. 1 Cor. iii. 5.
— —— iv. 11, see present.
1. —— vii. 7.
— ——— 8, see E I.
1. —— ix. 14.
— —— x. 33, see E I.
— —— xi. 1, see E I also.
— ——— 5, see me.
1. ——— 12.
— ——— 14, see not.
— —— xii. 2, } see E
— —— xiii. 12, } as.
— —— xiv. 7, see E (and.)
1. ——— 12.
1. —— xv. 22, 24.
1. —— xvi. 1.
1. 2 Cor. i. 3, 8.
1. ——— 13 (*om.* G ⇉ L Tr A ℵ.)
— ——— 14, see E as.
— —— iii. 15, see unto.
— ——— 18, see E as.
1. —— vii. 14.
1. —— x. 7, 13.
1. —— xi. 12.
1. Gal. ii. 16.
— —— iii. 6, see E as.
1. Gal. iv. 3, 29.
1. —— v. 12.
— Eph. i. 10, see E him.
1. —— ii. 3.
1. —— iv. 4, 32,
1. —— v. 12, 23, 29.
— ——— 33, see E as.
— Phil. i. 7, see E as.
1. ——— 15.
2. —— ii. 8.
1. —— iii. 15, 18.
1. —— iv. 16.
1. Col. iii. 13.
— 1 Thes. ii. 4, see E so.
1. ——— 14.
5. ——— 18.
1. ——— 19.
1. —— iii. 4, 12, 13.
1. —— iv. 5, 13, 14.
1. —— v. 11, see E as.
1. 2 Thes. ii. 16 (θεὸς ὁ πατὴρ ἡμῶν, *God our Father*, instead of θεὸς καὶ πατὴρ ἡμῶν, *God even our Father*, G∾ L Tr A ℵ.)
1. —— iii. 1.
— 1 Tim. iii. 11, see E so.
1. Titus i. 15.
1. Philem. 19.
— Heb. iv. 12, see to.
1. —— vii. 4 (*om.* L Tr.)
1. —— xi. 12, 19.
1. Jas. ii. 17.
1. —— iii. 5.
3. —— iv. 14, marg. *for* (*om.* L Tr[b] ℵ.)
— 1 Pet. iii. 6, see E as.
1. 2 Pet. i. 14.
1. —— ii. 1.
— 1 John ii. 6, see E as.
— ——— 9, see now.
1. ——— 18.
— ——— 27, } see E
— —— iii. 3, 7, } as.
— John iv. 3, see E (and.)
— 3 John 2, 3, } see E
— Jude 7, } as.
1. ——— 23.
— Rev. i. 7, see E so.
1. —— ii. 13 (*om.* G⇉ Tr[b] A[b] ℵ.)
— ——— 27, see E I.
— —— iii. 21, see E I also.
— —— xvi. 7, see E so.
1. —— xvii. 11.
1. —— xviii. 6.
— —— xxi. 11, see like.
— —— xxii. 20, see E so.

EVEN ALSO.

(When not two separate Greek words.)

1. 1 Cor. xi. 12.

EVEN AS.

(When not two separate Greek words.)

1. ὡς, as. *In comparative sentences*, as; *in objective*, that; *in final*, in order to; *in causal*, for the ground that.
2. καθώς, like as, according as.
3. ὥσπερ, (*No.* 1 *strengthened by* περ,) wholly as, just as.
4. καθάπερ, even as, truly as.
5. τρόπος, a turning, turn, *hence, gen.* manner, way.

(a) *as adv.* ὃν τρόπον, in what manner.

3. Matt. v. 48 (No. 1, L T (8th ed.) Tr A ℵ.)
1 —— xv. 28.
3. —— xx. 28.
5a. —— xxiii. 37.
1. Mark iv. 36.
2. —— xi. 6.
2. Luke i. 2.
2. —— xix. 32.
2. John v. 23.
2. —— xii. 50.
2. —— xv. 10.
2. —— xvii. 14, 16, 22.
2. Rom. i. 28.
4. —— iv. 6.
2. 1 Cor. i. 6.
2. —— xi. 1.
1. —— xii. 2.
2. —— xiii. 12.
4. 2 Cor. i. 14.
4. —— iii. 18.
2. Gal. iii. 6.
2. Phil. i. 7.
1. Eph. v. 33.
2. 1 Thes. v. 11.
1. 1 Pet. iii. 6.
2. 1 John ii. 6, 27.
2. —— iii. 3, 7.
2. 3 John 2, 3.
1. Jude 7.

EVEN HE.

(When not two Greek words.)

ἐκεῖνος, that, that one there, (*the more remote, connected with the third person.) It is also employed as an emphatic demonstrative*, he, (*and in this case may refer to the nearer, as* οὗτος, this, *may refer to the remoter.)*

John vi. 57.

EVEN HIM.

(When not two Greek words.)

αὐτός, very, self, (*always emphatic when used in the Nom. for the 3rd pers.) not* He *simply, but* He himself.

Eph. i. 10.

EVEN I.

(When not two Greek words.)

κἀγώ, I, (*when used in Nom. for* 1*st pers. is emphatic.)*

1. Cor. vii. 8; x. 33. | Rev. ii. 27.

EVEN I ALSO.

(When not three Greek words.)

1 Cor. xi. 1. | Rev. iii. 21.

EVEN SO.

(When not separate Greek words.)

1. οὕτω, οὕτως, *see* "EVEN," (*adv.) No.* 7.
2. ναί, (*adv.) affirming* yes; yea, *strongly affirming.*
3. ὡσαύτως, in the same way, in like manner as.

1. Matt. vii. 17.
2. —— xi. 26.
1. —— xii. 45.
1. —— xviii. 14.
1. —— xxiii. 28.
2. Luke x. 21.
1. John iii. 14.
1. —— xiv. 31.
1. Acts xii. 15.
1. Rom. vi. 19.
1. —— xi. 31.
1. 1 Cor. xi. 12.
1. 1 Thes. ii. 4.
3. 1 Tim. iii. 11.
2. Rev. i. 7.
2. —— xvi. 7.
2. —— xxii. 20 (*om.* G L T Tr A ℵ.)

EVEN SO I.

(When not separate Greek words.)

κἀγώ, I, *(when used in Nom. for 1st pers. is emphatic.)*

John x. 15 ; xx. 21.

EVEN SO I ALSO.

John xvii. 18.

EVEN VERY.

καί, *see* "EVEN," *(adv.) No.* 1.

Luke xii. 7.

EVEN (ALSO.)

Luke vi. 33.

EVEN (AND.)

1. ὅμως, at the same time, *i.e.* nevertheless, notwithstanding, yet even.
2. καί, *see* "EVEN," *(adv.) No.* 1.

1. 1 Cor. xiv. 7. | 2. 1 John iv. 3.

EVENING.

1. ἑσπέρα, evening, eventide, eve, *(Lat.* vesper), (occ. Acts iv. 3.)
2. ὀψία, *see* "EVEN," [noun] *No.* 1.

2. Matt. xiv. 15, 23.
2. —— xvi. 2.
1. Luke xxiv. 29.
1. Acts xxviii. 23.

EVENING (AT.)

{ οὔσης, being, *(part. of* εἰμί, to be,)
ὀψία, late, } it being late.

John xx. 19.

EVENING (IN THE.)

{ ὀψία, late,
γενομένης, becoming, *(part. of* γίνομαι, to become,) begin to be, } evening, arriving.

Mark xiv. 17.

EVENTIDE.

1. ἑσπέρα, *see* "EVENING," *No.* 1.
2. { ὀψία, late,
ὥρα, the hour, } the hour being late, *(non occ.)*

2. Mark xi. 11. | 1. Acts iv. 3.

EVER.

1. πάντοτε, always, at all times.
2. αἰών, *see* "ETERNAL," *No.* 1.
3. ἀεί, always, *i.e.* ever, continually, *(hence, old Eng. "aye,"* ever.)
4. { εἰς, unto, into,
πάντας, all,
τοὺς, the,
αἰῶνας, ages, } into all the ages.

— Matt. xxiv. 21, see nor.
3. Mark xv. 8.
1. Luke xv. 31.
— John iv. 39, } see that.
— —— x. 8, }
1. —— xviii. 20.
— Acts xxiii. 15, see or.
1. 1 Thes. iv. 17.
1. —— v. 15.
1. 2 Tim. iii. 7.
2. Heb. vii. 24.
1. —— 25.
4. Jude 25.

EVER (FOR.)

1. { εἰς, into, unto,
αἰών, age, *see* "ETERNAL," *No.* 1, } **with the article,* unto the age.
2. αἰώνιος, belonging to the αἰών, *(see* "ETERNAL," *No.* 2.)
3. { εἰς, into, unto,
ἡμέραν, a day,
αἰῶνος, of eternity, } unto [*the*] day of perpetuity.
4. { εἰς, unto, into,
τὸ, the,
διηνεκὲς, carried through, continuous, unbroken, } unto the uninterrupted continuance.

1*. Matt. vi. 13 (pl.) (*ap.*)
1*. —— xxi. 19.
1*. Mark xi. 14.
1*. Luke i. 33 (pl.)
1*. —— 55 (G∾) (ἕως αἰῶνος, *until the age,* G.)
1*. John vi. 51, 58.
1*. —— viii. 35 twice.
1*. —— xii. 34.
1*. —— xiv. 16.
1*. Rom. i. 25 (pl.)
1*. —— ix. 5 (pl.)
1*. —— xi. 36 (pl.)
1*. —— xvi. 27 (pl.)
1*. 2 Cor. ix. 9.
2. Philem. 15.
1*. Heb. v. 6.
1*. —— vi. 20.
1*. —— vii. 17, 21.
4. —— x. 12, 14.
1*. —— xiii. 8 (pl.)
1*. 1 Pet. i. 23 (*om.* G L T Tr A ℵ.)
1*. —— 25.
1. 2 Pet. ii. 17 (*om.* G⇉ L T Tr A ℵ.)
3. —— iii. 18.
1*. 1 John ii. 17.
1*. 2 John 2.
1. Jude 13.

EVER AND EVER (FOR.)

1. { εἰς, unto, into,
τοὺς, the *(pl.)*,
αἰῶνας, ages, *(see* "ETERNAL," *No.* 1),
τῶν, of the *(pl.)*,
αἰώνων, ages.

2. { εἰς, unto, into,
τὸν, the *(sing.)*,
αἰῶνα, age, *(see* "ETERNAL," *No.* 1),
τοῦ, of the *(sing.)*,
αἰῶνος, age.

3. { εἰς, unto, into,
αἰώνας, ages, *(see* "ETERNAL," *No.* 1),
αἰῶνων, of ages.

1. Gal. i. 5.
1. Phil. iv. 20.
1. 1 Tim. i. 17.
1. 2 Tim. iv. 18.
2. Heb. i. 8.
1. —— xiii. 21 *(om.* τῶν αἰῶνων, *of the ages,* G⇉ T.)
1. 1 Pet. iv. 11.
1. —— v. 11 *(om.* τῶν αἰῶνων, *of the ages,* T.)
1. Rev. i. 6 *(om.* τῶν αἰῶνων, *of the ages,* T A ℵ) (ℵ *singular* instead of [plural.)
1. —— iv. 9, 10.
1. —— v. 13, 14 *(ap.)*
1. —— vii. 12.
1. —— x. 6.
1. —— xi. 15.
3. —— xiv. 11.
1. —— xv. 7.
1. —— xix. 3.
1. —— xx. 10.
1. Rev. xxii. 5.

EVERLASTING.

1. αἰώνιος, belonging to the αἰών, *(see* "ETERNAL," *No.* 1.)
   (a) *with* ζωή, life.
2. ἀΐδιος, always existing, perpetual, *(adj. from* ἀεί, always,) (occ. Rom. i. 20.)

1. Matt. xviii. 8.
1a. —— xix. 29.
1. —— xxv. 41, 46.
1. Luke xvi. 9.
1a. —— xviii. 30.
1a. John iii. 16, 36.
1a. —— iv. 14.
1a. —— v. 24.
1a. —— vi. 27, 40, 47.
1a. —— xii. 50.
1a. Acts xiii. 46.
1a. Rom. vi. 22.
1. —— xvi. 26.
1a. Gal. vi. 8.
1. 2 Thes. i. 9.
1. —— ii. 16.
1a. 1 Tim. i. 16.
1. —— vi. 16.
1. Heb. xiii. 20.
1. 2 Pet. i. 11.
2. Jude 6.
1. Rev. xiv. 6.

EVERMORE.

1. πάντοτε, always, at all times.
2. { εἰς, unto, into, τὸ, the, παντελές, very end, } *i.e.* absolutely, perfectly, *(by etymology it refers to* completeness, *but it may refer to* duration *where the context requires it,) (non occ.)*

1. John vi. 34.
1. 1 Thes. v. 16.
2. Heb. vii. 25, marg. (text, *to the uttermost.*)

—

EVERMORE (FOR.)

1. { εἰς, unto, into,
τὸν, the,
αἰῶνα, age, *(see* "ETERNAL," *No.* 1.)

2. { εἰς, unto, into,
τοὺς, the *(pl.)*,
αἰῶνας, ages, *(see* "ETERNAL," *No.* 1),
τῶν, of the *(pl.)*,
αἰῶνων, ages.

1. 2 Cor. xi. 31 (pl.)
1. Heb. vii. 28.
2. Rev. i. 18.

EVERY.

1. πᾶς, *see* "ALL," *No.* 1. *Singular in all passages except those marked* 1b.
2. ἕκαστος, each, every one *of any number separately.*
3. κατά, down.
   (a) *with Gen.* down from.
   (b) *with Acc.* down upon, down along; *of place or time, distributively,* from one to another, *(e.g.* κατ' ἔτος, year by year.)
4. { κατά, from one to another, *(see No.* 3b,) ἕνα, one, ἕκαστος, each, *(see No.* 2,) } from each one[mouth] to another.
5. { εἷς, one, ἕκαστος, each, *(see No.* 2,) } each one.

All passages are included here, except EVERY MAN *and* EVERY ONE; *for which, see below.*

1. Matt. iii. 10.
1. —— iv. 4.
1. —— vii. 17, 19.
— —— viii. 33, see E thing.
1. —— ix. 35 twice.
1. —— xii. 25 twice, 36.
1. —— xiii. 47, 52.
1. —— xv. 13.
1. —— xviii. 16.
1. —— xix. 3.
— Mark i. 45, see E quarter (from.)
1. —— ix. 49 *(ap.)*
1. —— xvi. 15 (ap.)
— —— 20, see E where.
1. Luke ii. 23.
3. —— 41.
1. —— iii. 5 twice, 9.
1. —— iv. 4 *(ap.)*
1. —— 37.
2. —— 40.
1. —— v. 17.
2. —— vi. 44.
— —— viii. 1, see E (throughout.)
— —— 4, see E (out of.)
— —— ix. 6, see E where.
1. —— x. 1.
1. —— xi. 17.
2. —— xvi. 5.
3. —— 19.
— —— xix. 43, see E side (on.)
1. John i. 9.
1. —— ii. 10.
— —— vii. 23, } see E
— —— xiii. 10, } whit.
1. John xv. 2 1st.
1. —— 2 2nd, see E branch.
2. —— xix. 23.
1. Acts ii. 5, 43.
1. —— iii. 23, see E.. which.
— —— v. 42, see E (in.)
— —— viii. 3, see E (into.)
— —— 4, see E where.
1. —— x. 35.
2. —— xiii. 27.
— —— xiv. 23, see E (in.)
— —— xv. 21 1st, see E (in.)
3&1. —— 21 2nd.
1. —— 36.
2. —— xvii. 27.
— —— 30, see E where.
1. —— xviii. 4.
— —— xx. 23, see E (in.)
1. —— 31.
2. —— xxi. 26.
— —— 28, see E where.
— —— xxii. 19, } see E
— —— xxvi. 11, } (in.)
— —— xxviii. 22, see E where.
1. Rom. ii. 9.
1. —— iii. 2, 4, 19.
1. —— viii. 22, marg. (text, *whole.*)
1. —— xiii. 1.
1. —— xiv. 5, 11 twice.
1. 1 Cor. i. 2.
— —— 5, see E thing.
1. —— iv. 17 1st, see E where.
1. —— 17 2nd.
1. —— vi. 18.
— —— vii. 2, see E woman.

1. 1 Cor. xi. 3, 4, 5.
2. —— xii. 13.
1. —— xv. 30.
2. ——— 38.
1. 2 Cor. ii. 14.
1. —— iv. 2.
— ——— 8, see E side(on.)
— —— viii. 7, see E thing.
1. —— ix. 8.
— ——— 11, see E thing.
1. —— x. 5 twice.
1. —— xiii. 1.
1. Gal. v. 3.
1. Eph. i. 21.
2. —— iv. 7.
1. ——— 14, 16 1st.
5. ——— 16 2nd.
— —— v. 24 see E thing.
— ——— 33, see E one in particular.
1. Phil. i. 3, 4, 18.
1. —— ii. 9, 10, 11.
— —— iv. 6, see E thing.
— ——— 12, see E where.
1. ——— 21.
1. Col. i. 10, 15, 28 3 times.
1. 1 Thes. i. 8.
2. —— ii. 11.
— —— v. 18, see E thing.
2. 2 Thes. i. 3.
1. —— ii. 17.
1. —— iii. 6, 17.
— 1 Tim. ii. 8, see E where.
1. —— iv. 4.

1. 1 Tim. v. 10.
1. 2 Tim. ii. 21.
1. —— iv. 18.
— Titus i. 5, see E'(in.)
1. ——— 16.
1. —— iii. 1.
1. Philem. 6.
1. Heb. ii. 2.
1. —— iii. 4.
1. —— v. 1.
1. —— viii. 3.
1. —— ix. 19.
3. ——— 25.
3. —— x. 3.
1. ——— 11.
1. —— xii. 1, 6.
1. —— xiii. 21.
1. Jas. i. 17 twice, 19.
1. —— iii. 7, 16.
1. 1 Pet. ii. 13.
1. 1 John iv. 1, 2, 3.
1. Rev. i. 7.
1. —— v. 9, 13.
1. —— vi. 14, 15 1st.
1. ——— 15 2nd (*om.* G ⇉ L T Tr ℵ.)
1. —— xiv. 6.
1. —— xvi. 3, 20.
1. —— xviii. 2 twice, 17.
— —— xxi. 21, see E several.
4. —— xxii. 2 (*om.* ἕνα, *one*, G L T Tr A ℵ.)

EVERY BRANCH.

(When not separate words in the Greek.)

πᾶς, *see* "ALL," *No.* 1.

John xv. 2.

EVERY MAN.

(When not separate words in the Greek.)

1. πᾶς, *see* "ALL," *No.* 1.
2. ἅπας, quite all, all together, all at once *or* at the same time.
3. ἕκαστος, *see* "EVERY," *No.* 2.
4. { εἷς, ἕκαστος, } *see* "EVERY," *No.* 5.
5. ἀνά, *(prep.* up to *or* up by,) *with numerals or measures of quantity or value,* apiece; *here* ἀνὰ δηνάριον, a denarius apiece.
6. { ἄν, *a particle expressing* uncertainty, conditionality, possibility, τις, any one, } any one *(who might be needing.)*
7. { τίς, who? τί, what? } who...what?

3. Matt. xvi. 27.
5. —— xx. 9, 10.
3. —— xxv. 15.
2. Mark viii. 25.
3. —— xiii. 34.
7. —— xv. 24.

1. Luke vi. 30.
1. —— xvi. 16.
— —— xix. 15, see E M (how much.)
1. John vi. 45.
3. —— vii. 53 (*ap.*)

3. John xvi. 32.
4. Acts ii. 6.
3. ——— 8.
6. ——— 45.
3. —— iv. 35.
3. —— xi. 29.
3. Rom. ii. 6.
1. ——— 10.
1. —— xii. 3 1st.
3. ——— 3 2nd.
3. —— xiv. 5.
3. 1 Cor. iii. 5, 8, 10, 13 twice.
3. —— iv. 5.
3. —— vii. 2, 7, 17, 20, 24.
1b. —— viii. 7.
1. —— ix. 25.
3. —— x. 24 (*om.* G L T Tr A ℵ.)

3. 1 Cor. xii. 7, 11.
3. —— xv. 23.
3. 2 Cor. ix. 7.
3. Gal. vi. 4, 5.
3. Eph. iv. 25.
3. Phil. ii. 4 twice.
4. Col. iv. 6.
1. Heb. ii. 9.
3. —— viii. 11 twice.
3. Jas. i. 14.
3. 1 Pet. i. 17.
1. —— iii. 15.
3. —— iv. 10.
1. 1 John iii. 3.
3. Rev. xx. 13.
3. —— xxii. 12.
1. ——— 18.

EVERY MAN (HOW MUCH.)

{ τίς, who? τί, what? } who...what?

Luke xix. 15 (om. τίς, Tr ℵ.)

EVERY ONE.

(When not separate words in the Greek.)

1. πᾶς, *see* "ALL," *No.* 1.
2. ἅπας, *see* "EVERY MAN," *No.* 2.
3. ἕκαστος, *see* "EVERY," *No.* 5.
4. { κατά, from one to another, *see* "EVERY," *No.* 3b, εἷς, one, } from one to another.

1. Matt. vii. 8, 21, 26.
3. —— xviii. 35.
1. —— xix. 29.
1. —— xxv. 29.
3. —— xxvi. 22.
1. Mark ix. 49.
3. Luke ii. 3.
1. —— vi. 40.
1b. —— ix. 43.
1. —— xi. 4, 10.
1. —— xviii. 14.
1. —— xix. 26.
1. John iii. 8, 20.
3. —— vi. 7.
1. ——— 40.
1. —— xviii. 37.
4. —— xxi. 25.
3. Acts ii. 38.
3. —— iii. 26.
2. —— v. 16.
1b. —— xvi. 26.
1b. —— xxviii. 2.
1. Rom. i. 16.
1. —— x. 4.
4. —— xii. 5.

3. Rom. xiv. 12.
3. —— xv. 2.
3. 1 Cor. i. 12.
3. —— vii. 17.
3. —— xi. 21.
3. —— xiv. 26.
3. —— xvi. 2.
1. ——— 16.
3. 2 Cor. v. 10.
1. Gal. iii. 10, 13.
3. Eph. v. 33.
3. 1 Thes. iv. 4.
1. 2 Tim. ii. 19.
1. Heb. v. 13.
3. —— vi. 11.
1. 1 John ii. 29.
1. —— iv. 7.
1. —— v. 1.
3. Rev. ii. 23.
3. —— v. 8.
3. —— vi. 11 (αὐτοῖς, *unto them*, G T Tr A) (αὐτοῖς ἑκάστῳ, *unto them severally*, L Tr[b] A[b] ℵ)

EVERY ONE IN PARTICULAR.

{ κατά, from one to another, *see* "EVERY," *No.* 3b, ἕνα, one, ἕκαστος, each, *see* "EVERY," *No.* 5. } each one by one, *i.e.* individually.

Eph. v. 33.

EVERY SEVERAL.

ἀνά, *see* "EVERY MAN," *No.* 5, each one separately.
εἷς, one,
ἕκαστος, each, *see* "EVERY," *No.* 5,

Rev. xxi. 21.

EVERY THING.

(When not separate words in the Greek.)

πᾶς, *see* "ALL," *No.* 1.

(a) *singular.*

(b) *plural.*

b. Matt. viii. 33
a. 1 Cor. i. 5.
a. 2 Cor. viii. 7.
a. 2 Cor. ix. 11.
a. Eph. v. 24.
a. Phil. iv. 6.
a. 1 Thes. v. 18.

EVERY WHERE.

(When not separate words in the Greek.)

1. πανταχοῦ, in every place, everywhere.
2. ἐν, in, παντί, every, } in every (way *or* manner *being understood.)*
3. ἐν, in, παντί, every, τόπῳ, place, *locus,* } in every place.

1. Mark xvi. 20 (ap.)
1. Luke ix. 6.
— Acts viii. 4, seego.
1. —— xvii. 30.
1. —— xxi. 28 (πανταχῇ, *in every direction,* G ∾ L T Tr A ℵ.)
1. Acts xxviii. 22.
1. 1 Cor. iv. 17.
2. Phil. iv. 12.
3. 1 Tim. ii. 8.

EVERY WHIT.

ὅλος, *see* "ALL," *No.* 2.

a. John vii. 23; a. xiii. 10.

EVERY WOMAN.

(When not separate words in the Greek.)

ἕκαστος, each, *see* "EVERY," *No.* 5.

1 Cor. vii. 2 (fem.)

EVERY (IN.)

κατά, *see* "EVERY," *No.* 3b.

Acts v. 42.
—— xiv. 23.
—— xv. 21 1st.
Acts xx. 23.
—— xxii. 19.
—— xxvi. 11, with πᾶς (pl.)
Titus i. 5.

EVERY (INTO.)

Acts viii. 3.

EVERY (OUT OF.)

Luke viii. 4.

EVERY (THROUGHOUT.)

Luke viii. 1.

EVERY QUARTER (FROM.)

πανταχόθεν, from all sides.

Mark i. 45 (πάντοθεν, *from every place,* G ∾ L T Tr A.)

EVERY SIDE (ON.)

1. πάντοθεν, from every place, *hence,* on every side.
2. ἐν, in, παντί, every, } in every (way, manner *or* side.)

1. Luke xix. 43. | 2. 2 Cor. iv. 8.

EVIDENCE.

ἔλεγχος, evidence, demonstration, proof, convincing argument, (occ. 2 Tim. iii. 16, ἐλεγμός, conviction, reproof, L T Tr A ℵ.)

Heb. xi. 1.

EVIDENT.

1. δῆλος, plain, manifest, made known.
2. κατάδηλος, most evident, *etc., (No.* 1 *with* κατά, *intensive,) (non occ.)*
3. πρόδηλος, manifest beforehand, *or* manifest before *all,* conspicuous, *(No.* 1 *with* πρό, before, *prefixed.)*

1. Gal. iii. 11.
— Phil. i. 28, see token.
3. Heb. vii. 14.
2. —— 15.

EVIDENTLY.

φανερῶς, openly, *i.e.* clearly, manifestly, (occ. Mark i. 45; John vii. 10.)

Acts x. 3. | Gal. iii. 1, see set forth.

EVIL [noun and adj.]

1. πονηρός, causing *or* having labour, sorrow, pain; *(denoting the more active form of evil,) hence,* evil, malignant.

(a) *with article,* ὁ πονηρός, the Evil one, the active worker out of evil, *with * prefixed denotes the translation by the adj. in English.*

2. κακός, bad, *generically*, embracing every form of evil *whether moral or physical, (hence No.* 3.)

κακόν, *(neut.) as subs., with * prefixed denotes the translation by the adj. in English.*

3. κακία, badness, the evil habit of mind *not restricted to malevolence, but gen.* badness *in its forms of* meanness, cowardice, *etc., but sometimes* malice.

4. κακῶς, *(adv. of No.* 2,) badly, ill, evil *physically or morally.*

5. φαῦλος, light, blown about by every wind, *(with a moral reference opp.* to ἀγαθός, good,) worthless, good for nothing, *(like the old Eng.* naughty *from* nought.)

*With * denotes that it is translated by the English adjective.*

6. { πονηρός, evil, *see No.* 1, ῥῆμα, a word *as uttered by the living voice; not merely the word, but the whole matter to which it relates,* } evil word or matter.

(Every reference is included in this list, except EVIL SPEAKING *and* SPEAK EVIL, *for which see under* SPEAK.)

6. Matt. v. 11 (*om.* ῥῆμα, *word*, L T (8th ed.) Tr א.)
1a.——— 37, 39.
1*.——— 45.
1a.—— vi. 13.
1*.——— 23.
3. ——— 34.
1*.—— vii. 11, 17, 18.
1. —— ix. 4 (pl.)
1*.—— xii. 34, 35 1st & 2nd.
— ——— 35 3rd, see E thing.
1*.——— 39.
1*.—— xv. 19.
1*.—— xx. 15.
2*.—— xxiv. 48.
2. —— xxvii. 23.
— Mark iii. 4, see E (do.)
2*.—— vii. 21.
1*.——— 22.
— ——— 23, see E thing.
2. —— xv. 14.
1. Luke iii. 19.
— —— vi. 9, see E (do.)
1*.——— 22.
1. ——— 35.
1*.——— 45 1st & 2nd.
— ——— 45 3rd, see E (that which is.)
1*.—— vii. 21.
1*.—— viii. 2.
1a.—— xi. 4 (*ap.*)
1*.——— 13, 29, 34.
— —— xvi. 25, see E thing.
2. —— xxiii. 22.
1*. John iii. 19.
5. ——— 20 (pl.)
5. John v. 29 (pl.)
1*.—— vii. 7
— —— xvii. 15, see E (the.)
4. —— xviii. 23 1st.
2. ——— 23 2nd.
— Acts vii. 6, 19, see E entreat.
2. —— ix. 13 (pl.)
— —— xiv. 2, see E affected (make.)
— —— xviii. 14, see E doing.
1*.—— xix. 12, 13, 15, 16.
4. —— xxiii. 5.
2. ——— 9.
— Rom. i. 30, see E thing.
2. —— ii. 9.
2. —— iii. 8 (pl.)
2. —— vii. 19, 21.
2. —— ix. 11 (No. 5, G ~ L T Tr A א.)
— —— xii. 9, see E (that which is.)
2. ——— 17 twice, 21 twice.
2*.—— xiii. 3.
— ——— 4 1st (see E (that which is.)
2. ——— 4 2nd.
2*.—— xiv. 20.
2. —— xvi. 19.
— 1 Cor. x. 6, see E thing.
2. —— xiii. 5.
2*.—— xv. 33.
— 2 Cor. vi. 8, see report.
2. —— xiii. 7.
1*. Gal. i. 4.
1*. Eph. v. 16.
1*.—— vi. 13.
2*. Phil. iii. 2.
2*. Col. iii. 5.
2. 1 Thes. v. 15 twice.
1. ——— 22.
1a. 2 Thes. iii. 3.
1*. 1 Tim. vi. 4.
2. ——— 10 (pl.)
— 2 Tim. ii. 9, see E doer.
1*.—— iii. 13.
2. —— iv. 14 (pl.)
1*.——— 18.
2*. Titus i. 12.
— —— ii. 8, see E thing.
1*. Heb. iii. 12.
2. —— v. 14.
1*.—— x. 22.
2. Jas. i. 13 (pl.) (marg. *evils.*)
1*. Jas. ii. 4.
2. —— iii. 8.
5*.——— 16.
1*.—— iv. 16.
— 1 Pet. ii. 12, 14, see E doer.
2. —— iii. 9 twice, 10, 11, 12 (pl.)
— ——— 16, see E doer.
— ——— 17, see E doing.
— —— iv. 15, see E doer.
1*. 1 John iii. 12.
— 3 John 11 1st, see E (that which is.)
— ——— 11 2nd, see E (do.)
— Rev. ii. 2, see E (they which are.)

EVIL DOING.

1. ἀδίκημα, an injustice, a wrong, a crime.

2. κακοποιέω, ("EVIL," *No.* 2 *prefixed to* ποιέω, to do, to do evil, practice sin.

1. Acts xxiv. 20. | 2. 1 Pet. iii. 17 (part.)

EVIL DOER.

1. κακοῦργος, an evil-worker.

2. κακοποιός, an evil-doer.

1. 2 Tim. ii. 9.
2. 1 Pet. ii. 12, 14.
2. 1 Pet. iii. 16 (*ap.*)
2. —— iv. 15.

EVIL ENTREAT.

κακόω, to affect with κακός, *(see* "EVIL," *No.* 2,) *physically*, to ill use, maltreat, to harm; *morally*, to exasperate.

Acts vii. 6, 19.

EVIL THING (-s.)

1. πονηρός, *see* "EVIL," *No.* 1.

2. κακός, *see* "EVIL," *No.* 2.

3. φαῦλος, *see* "EVIL," *No.* 5.

1. Matt. xii. 35, }
1. Mark vii. 23, } (neut. pl.)
2. Luke xvi. 25, }
2. Rom. i. 30, } (neut.
2. 1 Cor. x. 6, } pl.)
3. Titus ii. 8 (neut.)

EVIL DO.

(Where not two separate words in the Greek.)

κακοποιέω, to do evil, practice sin, ("EVIL," *No.* 2 *with* ποιέω, to do.)

Mark iii. 4. | Luke vi. 9.
3 John 11.

EVIL (THAT WHICH IS.)

1. πονηρός, *see* "EVIL," *No.* 1, } (a) *with*
2. κακός, *see* "EVIL," *No.* 2, } *article.*

1a. Luke vi. 45. | 2a. Rom. xiii. 4.
1a. Rom. xii. 9. | 2a. 3 John 11.

EVIL (THE.)

{ ὁ, the,
{ πονηρός, *see* "EVIL," *No.* 1.

John xvii. 15.

EVIL (THEY WHICH ARE.)

κακός, *see* "EVIL," *No.* 2.

Rev. ii. 2 (pl.)

EVIL AFFECTED (MAKE.)

κακόω, *see* "EVIL ENTREAT."

Acts xiv. 2.

See also, SPEAK and SPEAKING.

EXACT [verb.]

πράσσω, to do, *expressing an action continued, not completed,* to do, *i.e.,* to exercise, practice. *Then in ref. to a person,* to do to *or* in respect to *any one, (in N.T.) only of harm or evil, also, in the sense of* to do *a person, i.e. to get money from any one.*

Luke iii. 13.

EXALT (-ED, -ETH.)

ὑψόω, to raise high, elevate, lift up, *(spoken of the brazen serpent, and of Jesus on the cross.) Metaph.* to elevate, *i.e. to dignity, etc.,* to exalt.

Matt. xi. 23. | Luke xviii. 14 twice.
— xxiii. 12 twice. | Acts ii. 33.
Luke i. 52. | — v. 31.
— x. 15. | — xiii. 17.
— xiv. 11 twice. | 2 Cor. xi. 7.
1 Pet. v. 6.

EXALT HIGHLY.

ὑπερυψόω, to make high above, raise high aloft; *only used metaph.* to highly exalt over all, *(non occ.)*

Phil. ii. 9.

EXALT ONE'S SELF.

1. ἐπαίρω, to take up, raise up *(as a sail or one's hands, etc.)*
   (a) *Mid.* to lift up one's self, raise up *as against any thing. Metaph.* to be lifted up, become elated.
2. ὑπεραίρω, to lift up over *or* above *any thing.*
   (a) *Mid.* to lift up one's self over *others, or* over-much, become conceited, arrogant, *etc.*

1a. 2 Cor. x. 5. | 1a. 2 Cor. xi. 20.
2a. 2 Thes. ii. 4.

EXALTED ABOVE MEASURE (BE.)

2a. 2 Cor. xii. 7 1st, 7 2nd (*ap.*)

EXALTED (IN THAT HE IS.)

{ ἐν, in, } }
{ τῷ, the, } his up- } in his
{ ὕψει, uplifting, } lifting, } uplifting.
{ αὐτοῦ, of him, } }

Jas. i. 9.

EXAMINATION.

ἀνάκρισις, a dividing *or* separating up, *hence,* examination.

Acts xxv. 26.

EXAMINE (-ED, -ING.)

1. ἀνακρίνω, to separate *or* divide up, *hence,* to examine carefully, investigate.
2. ἀνετάζω, to examine thoroughly, inquire strictly, *esp. by scourging or torture,* (ἐτασμός, *is used of* torture *in* 2 Macc. vii. 37,) *(non occ.)*
3. δοκιμάζω, to prove by test, put to the proof, examine; *esp. metals, etc., by fire, and of other things by use;* to examine, judge of, estimate; *hence,* approve by trial.
4. πειράζω, to make trial; *of actions,* to attempt, try; *of persons,* to put to the test, *in a good or bad sense.*

1. Luke xxiii. 14. | 1. Acts xxiv. 8.
1. Acts iv. 9. | 1. — xxviii. 18 (part.)
1. — xii. 19. | 1. 1 Cor. ix. 3.
2. — xxii. 24. | 3. — xi. 28.
2. ——— 29, marg. *torture.* | 4. 2 Cor. xiii. 5.

EXAMPLE.

1. δεῖγμα, that which is shown, a sample, specimen, example, *(non occ.)*
2. ὑπόδειγμα, *(No.* 1 *with* ὑπό, under, *prefixed,)* that which is shown under *or before the eyes, i.e.* plainly.
3. τύπος, anything produced by repeated blows, *hence,* a mark *or* impression *made by a hard substance on one of softer material ; then,* a model, pattern, exemplar *in the widest sense, (Eng.* type.)
4. ὑπογραμμός, a writing-copy, *hence,* a pattern, *etc., for imitation, (non occ.)*

— Matt. i. 19, see E (make a public.)
2. John xiii. 15.
— Rom. xv. 5, see E of (after the.)
3. 1 Cor. x. 6, marg. *figure.*
3. 1 Tim. iv. 12.
2. Heb. iv. 11.
2. —— viii. 5.
2. Jas. v. 10.
4. 1 Pet. ii. 21.
1. Jude 7.

EXAMPLE OF (after the) [margin.]

κατά, down.

(a) *with Gen.* down from.

(b) *with Acc.* down upon, over against, *hence,* according to, *(some standard of comparison being stated or implied.)*

b. Rom. xv. 5, text, *according to.*

EXAMPLE (MAKE A PUBLIC.)

παραδειγματίζω, to make an example of near *or* beside *others, hence,* to expose *to public shame as an* example to others, (occ. Heb. vi. 6.)

Matt. i. 19 (δειγματίζω, *to make an example* (G~ L T Tr A).)

EXCEED.

1. ὑπερβάλλω, to throw *or* cast over *or* beyond, *(i.e.* beyond *a certain limit.) Also* to throw beyond *or* farther than *another,* to surpass *in throwing, hence gen.,* to surpass, excel, exceed.
2. περισσεύω, to be over and above, to be over a certain number *or* measure, *hence,* to abound, exceed.

2. Matt. 7.20 (with πλεῖον, *more.*)
2. 2 Cor. ii. 9.
1. 2 Cor. ix. 14.
1. Eph. i. 19.
1. —— ii. 7.

EXCEEDING.

1. λίαν, much, very, exceedingly.
2. σφόδρα, vehemently, eagerly, very much.
3. { ὁ, the, θέος, God, } *here, Dative case,* to God.
4. { κατά, ὑπερβολή, } exceedingly super-eminently.

2. Matt. ii. 10.
1. —— 16.
1. —— iv. 8.
1. —— viii. 28.
2. —— xvii. 23.
2. —— xxvi. 22.
1. Mark ix. 3.
1. Luke xxiii. 8.
3. Acts vii. 20, marg. *to God.*
4. Rom. vii. 13.
— 2 Cor. iv. 17, see E (far more.)
— 1 Pet. iv. 13, — Jude 24, } see joy.
2. Rev. xvi. 21.

EXCEEDING (FAR MORE.)

{ κατά, according to, ὑπερβολή, a passing beyond, surpassing, εἰς, unto, ὑπερβολή, a surpassing, } in a surpassing manner, still surpassing, *(referring here to the verb* 'working out,' *not to the word* 'eternal,' *which forbids such a qualification ; nor to* 'weight,' *which is separated from it by the adjective.)*

2 Cor. iv. 17.

See also, ABUNDANT, ABUNDANTLY, GLAD, GREAT, JOYFUL, SORROWFUL, SORRY.

EXCEEDINGLY.

1. περισσοτέρως, more abundantly, more, *whether of number or degree.*
2. σφόδρα, vehemently, eagerly, very much, *(neut. pl. of* σφοδρός, eager, vehement.)
3. σφοδρῶς, *(adv.)* vehemently, eagerly, very much.
4. { ὑπὲρ, over ; *with Gen. (as here),* above, ἐκ, from, out of, περισσοῦ, above the ordinary measure, } exceeding abundantly.
5. { φόβον, fear, μέγαν, great, } a great fear.

2. Matt. xix. 25.
5. Mark iv. 41.
— —— xv. 14, see E (the more.)
— Acts xvi. 20, see trouble.
3. Acts xxvii. 18.
1. 2 Cor. vii. 13.
— Gal. i. 14, see E (more.)
4. 1 Thes. iii. 10.
— 2 Thes. i. 3, see grow.
— Heb. xii. 21, see fear.

EXCEEDINGLY (MORE.)

1. Gal. i. 14.

EXCEEDINGLY (THE MORE.)

1. Mark xv. 14 (περισσῶς, *vehemently*, G L T (8th ed.) Tr A ℵ.)

EXCEL (-ETH.)

1. περισσεύω, to be over and above, to excel *in number or measure.*
2. ὑπερβάλλω, to throw *or* cast beyond *a certain limit or goal; also* to throw beyond *or* farther *than another, hence,* to surpass, exceed, excel.

1. 1 Cor. xiv. 12. | 2. 2 Cor. iii. 10.

EXCELLENCY.

1. ὑπερβολή, a throwing *or* casting beyond, *hence,* a surpassing, super-eminence, excellence.
2. ὑπερέχω, (a) *trans.* to hold over.
   (b) *intrans.* to hold one's self over, *i.e.* to be over, jut out over *or* beyond; *also,* to hold one's self above, *i.e.* to be superior, excel.
3. ὑπεροχή, *(from No.* 2,) a prominence, eminence; *of things,* superiority, excellence, (occ. 1 Tim. ii. 2.)

3. 1 Cor. ii. 1. | 1. 2 Cor. iv. 7.
2b. Phil. iii. 8 (part.)

EXCELLENT.

μεγαλοπρεπής, becoming to a great man, magnanimous; *of things,* magnificent, *(non occ.)*

2 Pet. i. 17.

EXCELLENT (MORE.)

1. διαφορώτερος, *(comp. of* διάφορος, diverse, various, distinguished,) more distinguished.
2. πλείων, more, *(the usual comp. of* πολύς, much,) *properly of number, but also of magnitude and in comparison expressed or implied.*
3. { κατά, according to, ὑπερβολή, *see* "EXCELLENCY," *No.*1, } more excellent *or* surpassing.

3. 1 Cor. xii. 31. | 1. Heb. viii. 6.
1. Heb. i. 4. | 2. —— xi. 4.

EXCELLENT (MOST.)

κράτιστος, *(superl. of* κράτος, power *in effect,* force, superiority,) most excellent, most noble, *(used in addressing persons of rank and authority.*

Luke i. 3. | Acts xxiii. 26.

EXCELLENT (THINGS THAT ARE.)

{ τὰ, the *things,* διαφέροντα, different, discrepant, } the things that *are* different.

Phil. i. 10, marg. *differ.*

EXCELLENT (THE THINGS THAT ARE MORE.)

Rom. ii. 8, marg. *differ.*

EXCEPT.

1. { ἐὰν, *(for εἰ ἄν,)* in case, if perhaps *(assuming the hypothesis as a possibility or uncertainty with the prospect of decision),* μή, not, } in case...not *(the condition referring to future time.)* * *followed by the Aorist subj. which may be rendered by the fut. perfect.*

   † *followed by the Subj. pres.*
2. { εἰ, in case, if possibly, *(more decisive and less uncertain than* ἐάν,) μή, not, } in case...not *(assuming an incredible or untenable hypothesis.)*
3. { ἐκτός, without, besides, except, { εἰ, in case, μή, not, } *see No.* 2, } except the case if *or* unless indeed.
4. { εἰ, in case, *(see above,)* ἤ μή, not, τι, some *or* any *respect,* } except perhaps, unless perchance *or* unless in some respect, *(non occ.)*
5. παρεκτός, near by without, *i.e.* on the outside, without.
6. πλήν, more than, over and above, *hence,* besides, except.

1*. Matt. v. 20.	1†. John iii. 2.
1*. —— xii. 29.	1*. —— 3, 5.
1*. —— xviii. 3.	1†. —— 27.
2. —— xix. 9 (ap.)	1*. —— iv. 48.
2. —— xxiv. 22.	1*. —— vi. 44, 53.
1*. —— xxvi. 42.	1†. —— 65.
1*. Mark iii. 27.	1*. —— xii. 24.
1*. —— vii. 3, 4.	1*. —— xv. 4 twice.
— —— xiii. 20, see E that.	2. —— xix. 11.
4. Luke ix. 13.	6. Acts viii. 1.

1*. Acts viii. 31.
1*.—— xv. 1.
—— xxiv. 21, see E it be.
5. —— xxvi. 29.
1*.—— xxvii. 31.
2. Rom. vii. 7.
2. —— ix. 29.
1*.—— x. 15.
4. 1 Cor. vii. 5.
3. —— xiv. 5.
1*.—— 6, 7, 9.
1*.—— xv. 36.
2. 2 Cor. xii. 13.
4. —— xiii. 5.
1*. 2 Thes. ii. 3.
1*. 2 Tim. ii. 5.
1*. Rev. ii. 5, 22.

EXCEPT IT BE.

ἤ, either, or.

Acts xxiv. 21.

EXCEPT THAT.

εἰ μή, *see* "EXCEPT," *No.* 2.

Mark xiii. 20.

EXCEPTED (BE.)

ἐκτός, without, beside, except, *(here lit., there is* an excepting *of the one who, etc.)*

1 Cor. xv. 27.

EXCESS.

1. ἀκρασία, incontinence, intemperance, (occ. 1 Cor. vii. 5.)
2. ἀνάχυσις, a pouring out upon, emptying out, *(non occ.)*
3. ἀσωτία, the life and character of an ἄσωτος (not to be saved, past hope,) profligacy, debauchery, (occ. Tit. i. 6; 1 Pet. iv. 4.)

1. Matt. xxiii. 25 (G∾) (ἀδικία, *injustice*, G.)
2. 1 Pet. iv. 4.
3. Eph. v. 18.
— 1 Pet. iv. 3, see wine.

EXCHANGE (IN.)

ἀντάλλαγμα, that which is exchanged against anything, compensation, equivalent, *hence gen.*, price, *(non occ.)*

Matt. xvi. 26. | Mark viii. 37.

EXCHANGER (-S.)

τραπεζίτης, a tabler, *i.e. one who sat at a table and exchanged money, or received it on deposit, (non occ.)*

Matt. xxv. 27.

EXCLUDE (-ED.)

ἐκκλείω, to shut out, to exclude, *(non occ.)*

Rom. iii. 27 (pass.) | Gal. iv. 17.

EXCOMMUNICATE [margin.]

ἐκβάλλω, to throw *or* cast out; *gen. with the idea of force or impulse.*

John ix. 34 twice (text, *cast out.*)

EXCUSE [noun] [margin.]

πρόφασις, what is shown *or* appears before any one, *i.e.* show, pretence, pretext.

John xv. 22 (text, *cloak.*)

EXCUSE (MAKE.)

παραιτέομαι, to ask near *any one, i.e. at his hands,* to obtain by asking; to entreat *that something may not be done*, to ask aside *or* away, *hence*, to excuse one's self *from an invitation.*

Luke xiv. 18.

EXCUSE (WITHOUT.)

ἀναπολόγητος, without apology *or* defence, (occ. Rom. ii. 1.)

Rom. i. 20.

EXCUSE (-ED, -ING.)

ἀπολογέομαι, to speak one's self off, *i.e.*, to plead for one's self, defend one's self *before a tribunal.*

Rom. ii. 15.

EXCUSE ONE'S SELF.

2 Cor. xii. 19.

EXCUSED (BE.)

παραιτέομαι, *see* "EXCUSE (MAKE.)"

Luke xiv. 18, 19 (pass.)

EXECRATION (bind with an oath of) [margin.]

ἀναθεματίζω, to declare one to be ἀνάθεμα (accursed), to bind by a curse.

Acts xxiii. 12 (text, *bind under a curse.*)

EXECUTE (-ED.)

ποιέω, to make, bring about, effect; to do, execute, practice, *(e.g.* to do judgment, *i.e.* to act as a judge.

John v. 27. | Luke i. 8, see priest.
Jude 15.

EXECUTIONER.

σπεκουλάτωρ, *Lat.* speculator *or* spicula-
tor, *(from* spicula, *a spear,) Eng.* a
pike-man, halberdier. *In Roman
army forming the body-guard and
acting as executioners, (non occ.)*

Mark vi. 27.

EXERCISE [noun.]

γυμνασία, gymnastic exercise, *(so called
because practised nude or nearly so,
see below,) (non occ.)*

1 Tim. iv. 8.

EXERCISE (-ED, -ETH.)

1. γυμνάζω, to practise gymnastic exercises, *(from* γυμνός, naked,) *hence,*
to train, accustom, *(non occ.)*

2. ἀσκέω, to work up with skill, *as raw
materials, hence,* to exercise one's
self in *any thing,* to endeavour,
strive, *(non occ.)*

3. ποιέω, *see "* EXECUTE.*"*

— Matt. xx.25,see author- ity and dominion.	2. Acts xxiv. 16.
— Mark x. 42, see author- ity and lordship.	1. 1 Tim. iv. 7.
— Lukexxii.25,see author- ity and lordship.	1. 1 Heb. v. 14.
	1. —— xii. 11.
	1. 2 Pet. ii. 14.
	3. Rev. xiii. 12.

EXHORT (-ED, -ETH, -ING.)

1. παρακαλέω, to call to *one,* call near,
call for ; *every kind of* speaking to
*which is meant to produce a particu-
lar effect, e.g. exhortation, comfort,
encouragement.*

2. παραινέω, to tell *or* speak of near,
before *or* to *any one ; hence,* to recommend, warn, (occ. Acts xxvii.9.)

3. προτρέπω, to turn forward, *i.e.* to
propel, impel, *morally.*

(a) *Mid.* to cause one to turn himself
forward ; *hence,* to exhort, to
morally impel him onward, *(non
occ.)*

1. Acts ii. 40.	1. 1 Thes.v.14,marg. (text,
1. —— xi. 23.	1. 2 Thes. iii. 12. [beseech.)
1. —— xiv. 22.	1. 1 Tim. ii. 1, marg. de-
1. —— xv. 32.	1. —— vi. 2. [sire.
3a.—— xviii. 27.	1. 2 Tim. iv. 2.
2. —— xxvii. 22.	1. Titus i. 9.
1. Rom. xii. 8.	1. —— ii. 6, 15.
1. 2 Cor. ix. 5.	1. Heb. iii. 13.
1. 1 Thes. ii. 11.	—— x. 25, see E one
1. —— iv. 1.	another.
1. —— v. 11, marg. (text,	1. 1 Pet. v. 1, 12.
comfort.)	1. Jude 3.

EXHORT ONE ANOTHER.

1. Heb. x. 25.

EXHORTATION.

παράκλησις, a calling near, a summons
to one's side ; *hence,* an admonitory
encouraging *and* consolatory exhortation, invitation *or* entreaty,
(opp. to παραίνεσις, warning.)

Luke iii.18,see E (in one's)	2 Cor. viii. 17.
Acts xiii. 15.	1 Thes. ii. 3.
—— xx. 2, see E (give	1 Tim. iv. 13.
Rom. xii. 8. [much.)	Heb. xii. 5.
1 Cor. xiv. 3.	—— xiii. 22.

EXHORTATION (GIVE MUCH.)

⎧ παρακαλέω, *see "* EX- ⎫ e x h o r t i n g
⎪ HORT," *No.* 1, ⎪ [them] with
⎨ λόγῳ, discourse, ⎬ much
⎩ πολλῷ, much, ⎭ d i s c o u r s e .

Acts xx. 2.

EXHORTATION (IN ONE'S.)

παρακαλέω, *see "* EXHORT," *No.* 1.

Luke iii. 18 (part.)

EXORCIST.

ἐξορκιστής, one who uses an oath, *i.e.*
one who by adjuration professes to
expel demons, *(Eng.* exorcist, *non
occ.)*

Acts xix. 13.

EXPECT (-ING.)

1. ἐκδέχομαι, to receive from *another,
hence, of kings,* to succeed. *In N.T.
inactively* to be about to receive
from *another, hence,* to wait for.

2. προσδοκάω, to watch toward *or* for
anything, *hence,* to look for, expect.

2. Acts iii. 5.	1. Heb. x. 13.

EXPECTATION.

προσδοκία, a watching *or* looking for,
expectation, *(in N.T. only of evil,*
occ. Luke xxi. 26.)

Acts xii. 11.

EXPECTATION (BE IN.)

προσδοκάω, *see "* EXPECT," *No.* 2.

Luke iii. 15 (part.) (marg. suspense.)

EXPECTATION (EARNEST.)

ἀποκαραδοκία, a looking away towards *any thing* with the head bent forward, (*from* ἀπό, from, κάρα, the head, *and* δοκεύω, to look.)

Rom. viii. 19. | Phil. i. 20.

EXPEDIENT (BE.)

συμφέρω, to bear *or* bring together, to contribute, to collect; *hence*, to be profitable, expedient, advantageous.

* *Intrans. and Impers.*

John xi. 50.*
—— xvi. 7*.
—— xviii. 14.* [*profitable*.
1 Cor. vi. 12, marg. *be*
1 Cor. x. 23.
2 Cor. viii. 10.*
—— xii. 1.*

EXPEL (-LED.)

ἐκβάλλω, to throw *or* cast out.

Acts xiii. 50.

EXPERIENCE.

δοκιμή, proof, trial; *either the state of being tried*, a trying; *or*, *the state of having been tried*, tried, probity, approved integrity.

Rom. v. 4 twice.

EXPERIMENT.

δοκιμή, *see above.*

2 Cor. ix. 13.

EXPERT.

γνώστης, a knower, *i.e.*, one who knows, (*non occ.*)

Acts xxvi. 3.

EXPIRE (-ED.)

1. πληρόω, to make full, fill up.
2. τελέω, to end, to finish.

1. Acts vii. 30 (part. pass.)
2. Rev. xx. 7 (μετά, *after*, instead of ὅταν τελεσθῇ, *whensoever may be ended*, G ∾.)

EXPOUND (-ED.)

1. ἐκτίθημι, to place out (*as an infant that may perish*, occ. Acts vii. 21, *pass.*)
   (a) *in Mid.* to set forth, to expound, declare.
2. διερμηνεύω, to interpret fully, to thoroughly explain.
3. ἐπιλύω, to let loose upon, solve; explain farther.

3. Mark iv. 34.
2. Luke xxiv. 27.
1a. Acts xi. 4.
1a. —— xviii. 26.
1a. Acts xxviii. 23.

EXPRESS.

See, IMAGE.

EXPRESSLY.

ῥητῶς, in express words, (*adv. of* ῥητός, said *or* expressed in words.)

1 Tim. iv. 1.

EXTORTION.

ἁρπαγή, the act of seizing upon *or* snatching away, plundering, pillage, (occ. Heb. x. 34; Luke xi. 39.)

Matt. xxiii. 25.

EXTORTIONER.

ἅρπαξ, (*adj. of above,*) ravenous, (*spoken of wild beasts*, rapacious, (occ. Matt. vii. 15.)

Luke xviii. 11. | 1 Cor. v. 10, 11.
1 Cor. vi. 10.

EYE (-S.)

1. ὀφθαλμός, the eye, (occ. Acts i. 9, pl.)
2. ὄμμα, sight; the eye, (*No.* 1 *may be applied to the Deity, but No.* 2 *can only be applied with propriety to men.*)
3. τρυμαλιά, a hole, eye *of a needle*, (*from* τρύω, to rub through,) (*non occ.*)
4. τρύπημα, a hole, eye *of a needle*, (*from* τρυπάω, to bore,) (*non occ.*)

1. Matt. v. 29, 38.
1. —— vi. 22 twice, 23.
1. —— vii. 3 twice, 4 twice, 5 twice.
1. —— ix. 29, 30.
1. —— xiii. 15 twice, 16.
1. —— xvii. 8.
1. —— xviii. 9 1st & 3rd.
— ——— 9 2nd, see E (with one.)
4. —— xix. 24.
1. —— xx. 15, 33.
1. ——— 34 1st (No. 2, L T (8th ed.) Tr A.)
1. ——— 34 2nd (*omit*, αὐτῶν οἱ ὀφθαλμοί, *their eyes*, L T(8th ed.) Tr A ℵ.)
1. Matt. xxi. 42.
1. —— xxvi. 43.
1. Mark vii. 22.
1. —— viii. 18.
2. ——— 23.
1. ——— 25.
1. —— ix. 47 1st & 3rd.
— ——— 47 2nd, see E(with one.)
3. —— x. 25.
1. —— xii. 11.
1. —— xiv. 40.
1. Luke ii. 30.
1. —— iv. 20.
1. —— vi. 20, 41 twice, 42 4 times.
1. —— x. 23.
1. —— xi. 34 twice.

1. Luke xvi. 23.
1. —— xviii. 13.
3. —— 25 (τρῆμα, *a hole*, L T Tr A ℵ.)
1. —— xix. 42.
1. —— xxiv. 16, 31.
1. John iv. 35.
1. —— vi. 5.
1. —— ix. 6, 10, 11, 14, 15, 17, 21, 26, 30, 32.
1. —— x. 21.
1. —— xi. 37, 41.
1. —— xii. 40 twice.
1. —— xvii. 1.
— Acts iii. 4, see fasten.
1. —— ix. 8, 18, 40.
— —— xi. 6, see fasten.
— —— xiii. 9, see set.
1. —— xxvi. 18.
1. —— xxviii. 27 twice.
1. Rom. iii. 18.
1. —— xi. 8, 10.
1. 1 Cor. ii. 9.
1. —— xii. 16, 17, 21.
1. —— xv. 52.
1. Gal. iii. 1.
1. —— iv. 15.
1. Eph. i. 18.
1. Heb. iv. 13.
1. 1 Pet. iii. 12.
1. 2 Pet. ii. 14.
1. 1 John i. 1.
1. —— ii. 11, 16.
1. Rev. i. 7, 14.
1. —— ii. 18.
1. —— iii. 18.
1. —— iv. 6, 8.
1. —— v. 6.
1. —— vii. 17.
1. —— xix. 12.
1. Rev. xxi. 4.

EYE (WITH ONE.)

μονόφθαλμος, one-eyed, *having lost an eye.*

Matt. xviii. 9. | Mark ix. 47.

EYE-SALVE.

κολλούριον, (*dim. of* κολλύρα, a coarse bread *or* cake,) a small cake. *In N.T. Eng.* collyrium, eye-salve, *resembling the dough of the* κολλύρα, (*non occ.*)

Rev. iii. 18.

EYE-SERVICE.

ὀφθαλμοδουλεία, eye-service, *i.e. rendered only under or for the master's eye,* (*non occ.*)

Eph. vi. 6. | Col. iii. 22.

EYE-WITNESS.

1. αὐτόπτης, self-beholding, *i.e.* an eye-witness, (*non occ.*)
2. ἐπόπτης, a looker-on, spectator, *hence* eye-witness, (*non occ.*)

1. Luke i. 2. | 2. 2 Pet. i. 16.

F

FABLE.

μῦθος, anything delivered by word of mouth, *and so in its widest sense* word, speech, talk; *then,* the subject of speech *or* talk, a tale, story, legend. *After Pindar, it always denotes* fiction, fable, a mythic tale. *In Attic Greek prose it usually denoted* a legend of the early Greek times before the dawn of history.

1 Tim. i. 4.
—— iv. 7.
2 Tim. iv. 4.
Titus i. 14.
2 Pet. i. 16.

FACE (-s.)

1. πρόσωπον, *the part* towards, at *or* around the eye; *hence, gen.* the face, visage, countenance.
2. ὄψις, the sight, faculty of seeing; *then,* the thing seen, appearance; *hence,* aspect, looks, *i.e.* the face *or* countenance.

1. Matt. vi. 16, 17.
1. —— xi. 10.
1. —— xvi. 3.
1. —— xvii. 2, 6.
1. —— xviii. 10.
1. —— xxvi. 39, 67.
1. Mark i. 2.
1. —— xiv. 65.
1. Luke i. 76.
1. —— ii. 31.
1. —— v. 12.
1. —— vii. 27.
1. —— ix. 51, 52, 53.
1. —— x. 1.
1. —— xii. 56.
1. —— xvii. 16.
1. Luke xxi. 35.
1. —— xxii. 64 (*ap.*)
1. —— xxiv. 5.
2. John xi. 44.
1. Acts vi. 15 twice.
1. —— vii. 45.
1. —— xvii. 26.
1. —— xx. 25, 38.
— —— xxv. 16, see F to F.
1. 1 Cor. xiii. 12 twice.
1. —— xiv. 25.
1. 2 Cor. iii. 7, 13, 18.
1. —— iv. 6.
1. —— xi. 20.
1. Gal. i. 22.
1. —— ii. 11.
1. Col. ii. 1.
1. 1 Thes. ii. 17.
1. —— iii. 10.
1. Jas. i. 23.
1. 1 Pet. iii. 12.
— 2 John 12, } see F to F.
— 3 John 14, }
1. Rev. iv. 7.
1. —— vi. 16.
1. —— vii. 11.
1. —— ix. 7.
1. —— x. 1.
1. —— xi. 16.
1. —— xii. 14.
1. —— xx. 11.
1. —— xxii. 4.

FACE TO FACE.

1. { κατὰ, *used distributively,* / πρόσωπον, *see No.* 1 *above,* } face to face.
2. { στόμα, mouth, / πρὸς, towards, / στόμα, mouth, } mouth to mouth.

1. Acts xxv. 16. | 2. 2 John 12.
2. 3 John 14.

FACTION [margin.]

διχοστασία, a standing apart, dissension, discord.

1 Cor. iii. 3, text, *division* (*om.* G ⇉ L T Tr A ℵ.)

FADE AWAY.

μαραίνω, to put out, to extinguish *(as fire.)*

(a) *Pass.* to go out, expire, die away, decay, *(non occ.)*

a. Jas. i. 11.

FADETH NOT AWAY (THAT.)

1. ἀμάραντος, *(adj. of above)* unfading.
2. ἀμαράντινος, *(adj. of* ἀμάραντος, *the proper name of the* amaranth *or* everlasting flower,) amaranthine.

1. 1 Pet. i. 4. | 2. 1 Pet. v. 4.

FAIL.

1. ἐκλείπω, to leave out of *or* off, *i.e.* to relinquish, desert; to leave off, *i.e.* to fail, to cease, *(non occ.)*
2. ἐπιλείπω, to leave *or* forsake upon, *i.e.* in *or* during *anything; hence,* to fail, not to suffice, *(non occ.)*
3. πίπτω, to fall, fall *to the ground, hence, to become void.*
4. ἐκπίπτω, to fall out of, fall away from, fail.
5. καταργέω, to leave unemployed *or* idle; make useless, void, abolish; put an end to, to lay aside.
6. ὑστερέω, to be last, hindmost; *hence,* to come short of, not to reach, miss.

— Luke xii. 33, see F not (that.)
1. —— xvi. 9.
3. —— 17.
— —— xxi. 16, see F them (men's hearts.)
1. —— xxii. 32.
4. 1 Cor. xiii. 8 1st (No. 3, L Tr A ℵ.)
5. —— 8 2nd.
1. Heb. i. 12.
2. —— xi. 32.
6. —— xii. 15, with ἀπό, *from* (marg. *fall from.*)

FAILING THEM (MEN'S HEARTS.)

ἀποψυχόντοι, swooning, ready to die, *(non occ.)*

οἱ ἀνθρώποι, the men, *(non occ.)*

Luke xxi. 26.

FAILETH NOT (THAT.)

ἀνέκλειπτος, *(No.*1, *with* ἀ, not, *prefixed,)* unfailing.

Luke xii. 33.

FAIN (WOULD.)

ἐπιθυμέω, to fix the desire upon, desire earnestly, long for, *denoting the inward affection of the mind.*

Luke xv. 16.

FAINT (-ED.)

1. ἐκλύω, to loose out of, to set free from; to loosen out, relax, weary. *In N.T. only Pass. or Mid.* to be weary, exhausted, *esp. from failure of power, (non occ.)*
2. ἐκκακέω, to turn out a coward, *i.e.* to lose one's courage. *In N.T. gen.* to be faint-hearted, *esp. in view of trial or difficulty, or from moral weakness.*
3. κάμνω, to work one's self weary, be weary *(or even* sick), *(occ.* Heb. xii. 3; Jas. v. 15.)

1. Matt. ix. 36, with εἰμί, *to be,* marg. *be tired and lay down* (σκύλλω, *to flay, lacerate,* G L T Tr A ℵ.)
1. —— xv. 32.
1. Mark viii. 3.
2. Luke xviii. 1.
2. 2 Cor. iv. 1, 16.
1. Gal. vi. 9.
2. Eph. iii. 13.
2. 2 Thes. iii. 13, marg. (text, *be weary.*)
1. Heb. xii. 3, 5.
3. Rev. ii. 3.

FAIR.

ἀστεῖος, of the town, *(from* ἄστυ, *and so like Lat.* urbanus, *from* urbs,) polite, *opp.* to ἄγροικος, (of the country, a countryman;) *esp.* clever, polished. *Of the external form,* well-made. *(See description of Moses,* Ex. ii. 2; Jos. Ant. ii. 9, 6, 7), *(occ.* Heb. xi. 23.)

Matt. xvi. 2, see weather.
Acts vii. 20.
Rom. xvi. 18, see speeches.
Gal. vi. 12, see show.

FAIR HAVENS (THE.)

{ καλὸς, handsome, beautiful.
{ λιμήν, a haven, harbour, port.

Acts xxvii. 8.

FAITH.

1. πίστις, faith, *i.e.* firm persuasion, the conviction *which is based upon hearing, not upon sight, or knowledge;* a firmly relying confidence *in what we hear from God in His Word.*

2. ἐλπίς, hope, *i.e.* expectation of something future; a dearly cherished and apparently well-grounded expectation and prospect of some desired good.

— Matt. vi. 30, see F (little.)
1. Matt. viii. 10.
— —— 26, see F (of little.)
1. —— ix. 2, 22, 29.
— —— xiv. 31, see F (of little.)
1. —— xv. 28.
— —— xvi. 8, see F (of little.)
1. —— xvii. 20.
1. —— xxi. 21.
1. —— xxiii. 23.
1. Mark ii. 5.
1. —— iv. 40.
1. —— v. 34.
1. —— x. 52.
1. —— xi. 22.
1. Luke v. 20.
1. —— vii. 9, 50.
1. —— viii. 25, 48.
— —— xii. 28, see F (little.)
1. —— xvii. 5, 6, 19.
1. —— xviii. 8, 42.
1. —— xxii. 32.
1. Acts iii. 16 twice.
1. —— vi. 5, 7.
1. —— 8 (χάρις, *grace*, G L T Tr A ℵ.)
1. —— xi. 24
1. —— xiii. 8.
1. —— xiv. 9, 22, 27.
1. —— xv. 9.
1. —— xvi. 5.
1. —— xvii. 31, marg. (text, *assurance*.)
1. —— xx. 21.
1. —— xxiv. 24.
1. —— xxvi. 18.
1. Rom. i. 5, 8, 12, 17 3 times.
1. —— iii. 3, 22, 25, 27, 28, 30 twice, 31.
1. —— iv. 5, 9, 11, 12, 13, 14, 16 twice, 19, 20.
1. —— v. 1.
1. —— 2 (*om.* G→ L[b] Tr[b] A.)
1. —— ix. 30, 32.
1. —— x. 6, 8, 17.
1. —— xi. 20.
1. —— xii. 3, 6.
1. —— xiv. 1, 22, 23 twice.
1. —— xvi. 26.
1. 1 Cor. ii. 5.
1. —— xii. 9.
1. —— xiii. 2, 13.
1. —— xv. 14, 17.
1. —— xvi. 13.
1. 2 Cor. i. 24 twice.
1. —— iv. 13.
1. —— v. 7.
1. —— viii. 7.
1. —— x. 15.
1. 2 Cor. xiii. 5.
1. Gal. i. 23.
1. —— ii. 16 twice, 20.
1. —— iii. 2, 5, 7, 8, 9, 11, 12, 14, 22, 23 twice, 24, 25, 26.
1. —— v. 5, 6, 22.
1. —— vi. 10.
1. Eph. i. 15.
1. —— ii. 8.
1. —— iii. 12, 17.
1. —— iv. 5, 13.
1. —— vi. 16, 23.
1. Phil. i. 25, 27.
1. —— ii. 17.
1. —— iii. 9 twice.
1. Col. i. 4, 23.
1. —— ii. 5, 7, 12.
1. 1 Thes. i. 3, 8.
1. —— iii. 2, 5, 6, 7, 10.
1. —— v. 8.
1. 2 Thes. i. 3, 4, 11.
1. —— iii. 2.
1. 1 Tim. i. 2, 4, 5, 14, 19 twice.
1. —— ii. 7, 15.
— —— iii. 6, marg. see novice.
1. —— 9, 13.
1. —— iv. 1, 6, 12.
1. —— v. 8, 12.
1. —— vi. 10, 11, 12, 21.
1. 2 Tim. i. 5, 13.
1. —— ii. 18, 22.
1. —— iii. 8, 10, 15.
1. —— iv. 7.
1. Titus i. 1, 4, 13.
1. —— ii. 2.
1. —— iii. 15.
1. Philem. 5, 6.
1. Heb. iv. 2.
1. —— vi. 1, 12.
1. —— x. 22.
2. —— 23.
1. —— 38.
1. —— xi. 1, 3, 4, 5, 6, 7 twice, 8, 9, 11, 13, 17, 20, 21, 22, 23, 24, 27, 28, 29, 30, 31, 33, 39.
1. —— xii. 2.
1. —— xiii. 7.
1. Jas. i. 3, 6.
1. —— ii. 1, 5, 14 twice, 17, 18 3 times, 20, 22 twice, 24, 26.
1. —— v. 15.
1. 1 Pet. i. 5, 7, 9, 21.
1. —— v. 9.
1. 2 Pet. i. 1, 5.
1. 1 John v. 4.
1. Jude 3, 20.
1. Rev. ii. 13, 19.
1. —— xiii. 10.
1. —— xiv. 12.

FAITH (OF LITTLE.)

ὀλιγόπιστος, little of faith, *a word used only by our Lord; and by Him only as quoted below, to rebuke four different states of mind, viz., anxiety, fear, doubt, and forgetfulness. See the passages.*

Matt. vi. 30.
—— viii. 26.
Luke xii. 28.
Matt. xiv. 31.
—— xvi. 8.

FAITHFUL.

πιστός, *prob. a verbal adj. from* πείθειν, (to persuade, win by words, influence,) *hence it may be taken either actively or passively, according to the meanings of the verb. Pass.* faithful, trusty, worthy of confidence; *of persons*, one on whom we may rely; *of things*, trustworthy, sure, firm, certain. *Act.* trusting, believing.

Matt. xxiv. 45.
—— xxv. 21 twice, 23 twice.
Luke xii. 42.
—— xvi. 10 twice, 11, 12.
—— xix. 17.
Acts xvi. 15.
1 Cor. i. 9.
—— iv. 2, 17.
—— vii. 25.
—— x. 13.
Gal. iii. 9.
Eph. i. 1.
—— vi. 21.
Col. i. 2, 7.
—— iv. 7, 9.
1 Thes. v. 24.
2 Thes. iii. 3.
1 Tim. i. 12, 15.
—— iii. 11.
1 Tim. iv. 9.
—— vi. 2, marg. *believing.*
2 Tim. ii. 2, 11, 13.
Titus i. 6, 9.
—— iii. 8.
Heb. ii. 17.
—— iii. 2, 5.
—— x. 23.
—— xi. 11.
1 Pet. iv. 19.
—— v. 12.
1 John i. 9.
Rev. i. 5.
—— ii. 10, 13.
—— iii. 14.
—— xvii. 14.
—— xix. 11.
—— xxi. 5.
—— xxii. 6.

FAITHFULLY.

πιστός, *see above.*

3 John 5, neut.

FAITHLESS.

ἄπιστος, (ἀ, *neg. prefixed to* πιστός, *see above,*) not worthy of confidence, untrustworthy; not confident, distrustful. *In N.T. Greek*, faithless, *of one who refuses to receive God's revelation of grace.*

Matt. xvii. 17.
Mark ix. 19.
Luke ix. 41.
John xx. 27.

FALL [noun.]

1. πτῶσις, a fall, downfall. *Metaph.* downfall, ruin, *(non occ.)*

2. παράπτωμα, a falling aside *as from right, truth, or duty;* the particular special act of sin.

1. Matt. vii. 27.
1. Luke ii. 34.
2. Rom. xi. 11, 12.

FALL (-EN, -ETH, -ING, FELL.)

1. πίπτω, to fall, *as from a higher to a lower place*, fall down.

2. ἐκπίπτω, *(No.* 1, *with* ἐκ, out of, *prefixed,)* to fall out of.

3. εμπίπτω, (*No.* 1, *with* ἐν, in, *prefixed,*) to fall in *or* into.

(a) *followed by* εἰς, into.

4. καταπίπτω, (*No.* 1, *with* κατά, down, *prefixed,*) to fall down, *e.g. prostrate or dead.*

5. ἐπιπίπτω, (*No.* 1, *with* ἐπί, upon, *prefixed,*) to fall upon. *In N.T. only of persons,* to throw one's self upon, *either as embracing, or in a hostile sense. Metaph.* to fall upon *or* come over one.

(a) *followed by* ἐπί, upon.

6. γίνομαι, to begin to be, *i.e.* to come into existence *or* into any state; to become, *marking the* result of any agency.

7. καταβαίνω, to come down, (βαίνω, *being used of all kinds of motion.)*

8. καταφέρω, to bear *or* carry down *from a higher to a lower place. In N.T. only Pass.* to be borne down, thrown down, to fall. *Metaph.* to be borne down, oppressed.

9. πταίω, to stumble, to fall.

— Matt. ii. 11, } see F down.
— —— iv. 9, }
1. —— vii. 25, 27.
1. —— x. 29.
3a. —— xii. 11.
1. —— xiii. 4, 5, 7, 8.
1. —— xv. 14, 27.
1. —— xvii. 6, 15.
— —— xviii. 26, 29, see F down.
1. —— xxi. 44 twice (*ap.*)
1. —— xxiv. 29.
1. —— xxvi. 39.
— Mark iii. 11, see F down before.
1. —— iv. 4, 5, 7, 8.
1. —— v. 22.
— —— 33, see F down before.
— —— vii. 25, see F at.
1. —— ix. 20.
2. —— xiii. 25, with εἰμί, *to be* (No. 1, L T Tr A ℵ.)
1. —— xiv. 35.
5a. Luke i. 12.
— —— iv. 7, see *F down before.*
— —— v. 8, see F down at.
1. —— 12.
1. —— vi. 39 (No. 8, L T Tr A.)
1. —— 49 (συμπίπτω, *to fall together,* T Tr A ℵ)
1. —— viii. 5.
1. —— 6 (No. 4, T Tr A)
1. —— 7, 8.
— —— 13, see F away.
1. —— 14.
— —— 23, see asleep.
— —— 28, 47, see F down before.
— —— 41, see F down.
1. —— x. 18.
— Luke x. 30, see F among.
3a. —— 36.
1. —— xi. 17.
1. —— xiii. 4.
3a. —— xiv. 5 (No. 1, L Tr A ℵ.)
— —— xv. 12, see F to.
5a. —— xv. 20.
1. —— xvi. 21.
— —— xvii. 16, see F down.
1. —— xx. 18 twice.
1. —— xxi. 24.
— —— xxii. 44, see F down
1. —— xxiii. 30.
— John xi. 32, see F down
1. —— xii. 24.
1. —— xviii. 6.
6. Acts i. 18, part., see F headlong.
— —— 25, see transgression.
1. —— 26.
— —— v. 5, 10, see F down.
— —— vii. 60, see asleep.
5a. —— viii. 16.
1. —— ix. 4.
— —— 18, see F from.
5a. —— x. 10 (No. 6, G∾L T Tr A ℵ.)
— —— 25, see F down.
5a. —— 44 (No. 1, L.)
5a. —— xi. 15.
— —— xii. 7, see F off.
5a. —— xiii. 11 (No. 1, L T Tr A ℵ.)
— —— 36, see asleep.
— —— xv. 16, see F down.
— —— xvi. 29, see F down before.
5a. —— xix. 17 (No. 1, L Tr.)
— —— 35, see fell down from Jupiter (which.)
8. Acts xx. 9 1st.
— —— 9 2nd, see F down.
5a. —— 37.
1. —— xxii. 7.
4. —— xxvi. 14, part.
2. —— xxvii. 17, 29.
— —— 32, see F off.
1. —— 34 (ἀπόλλυμι, *to perish,* G L T Tr A ℵ)
— —— 41, see F into.
— —— xxviii. 6, see F down.
1. Rom. xi. 11, 22.
1. —— xiv. 4.
5a. —— xv. 3.
1. 1 Cor. x. 8, 12.
— —— xiv. 25, see F down.
— —— xv. 6, 18, see asleep.
— Gal. v. 4, see F from.
— Phil. i. 12, see F out.
2 Thes. ii. 3, see falling away.
3a. 1 Tim. iii. 6, 7.
3a. —— vi. 9.
1. Heb. iii. 17.
1. —— iv. 11.
— —— vi. 6, see F away.
3a. —— x. 31.
— —— xii. 15, see *F from.*
— —— 30.
— 1 Pet. i. 24, see F away.
9. 2 Pet. i. 10.
— 2 Pet. iii. 4, see asleep.
— —— 17, see F from.
— Jas. i. 2, see F into.
2. —— 11.
1. —— v. 12.
— Jude 24, see F (keep from.)
1. Rev. i. 17.
2. —— ii. 5 (No. 1, G L T Tr A ℵ.)
— —— iv. 10, } see F down.
— —— v. 8, 14, }
1. —— vi. 13, 16.
1. —— vii. 11.
1. —— viii. 10 twice.
1. —— ix. 1.
1. —— xi. 11 (No. 5, G∾ L T Tr A.)
1. —— 13, 16.
1. —— xiv. 8 1st.
1. —— 8 2nd (*om.* A^b $ℵ^{2*}$.)
6. —— xvi. 2.
1. —— 19.
7. —— 21.
1. —— xvii. 10.
1. —— xviii. 2 1st.
1. —— 2 2nd (*om.* Tr A^b ℵ.)
— —— xix. 4, see F down.
1. —— 10.
— —— xxii. 8, see F down.

"The following combinations are where these are not separate words in the Greek."

FALL AMONG.

περιπίπτω, to fall around *any one so as to embrace; or* to fall *so as to be surrounded by any thing, (occ.* Acts xxvii. 41; Jas. i. 2.)

Luke x. 30.

FALL AT.

προσπίπτω, to fall towards *any thing,* to strike against. *In N.T. with idea of purpose,* to fall at, rush upon, dash against, (Matt. vii. 25.) *Of persons,* to fall down to *or* before *any one.*

Mark vii. 25.

FALL AWAY.

1. ἐκπίπτω, *see* "FALL," *No.* 2.

2. παραπίπτω, to fall near by *any one, so as to meet with; also,* to fall aside *so as to desert, (non occ.)*

3. ἀφίστημι, (a) *trans.* to place away from, cause to depart.

(b) *intrans.* to separate one's self, depart, forsake.

3b. Luke viii. 13.
2. Heb. vi. 6, part.
1. 1 Pet. i. 24.

FALL DOWN.

1. πίπτω, *see* "FALL," *No.* 1.

2. καταπίπτω, *see* "FALL," *No.* 4, (*occ.* Acts xxvi. 14.)

3. καταβαίνω, *see* "FALL," *No.* 7.

1. Matt. ii. 11.
1. —— iv. 9.
1. —— xviii. 26, 29.
1. Luke viii. 41.
1. —— xvii. 16.
3. —— xxii. 44 (*ap.*)
1. John xi. 32.
1. Acts v. 5, 10.
1. —— x. 25.
1. Acts xv. 16.
1. —— xx. 9.
2. —— xxviii. 6.
1. 1 Cor. xiv. 25.
1. Heb. xi. 30.
1. Rev. iv. 10.
1. —— v. 8, 14.
1. —— xix. 4.
1. —— xxii. 8.

FALL DOWN AT.

προσπίπτω, *see* "FALL AT."

Luke v. 8.

FALL DOWN BEFORE.

1. προσπίπτω, *see* "FALL AT."

2. { προσκυνέω, to kiss towards *any one*, *i.e.* to kiss one's own hand and extend it towards a person, at the same time prostrating one's self, as a mark of respect and homage; *hence*, to worship, adore.
ἐνώπιον, in the presence of, before. }

1. Mark iii. 11.
1. —— v. 33.
2. Luke iv. 7, marg. (text,
1. —— viii. 28, 47. [*worship.*)
1. Acts xvi. 29.

FALL DOWN FROM JUPITER (WHICH.)

Διοπετής, (*from* Διός, *gen. of* Ζεύς, *and* πίπτω, to fall,) fallen from Jupiter, *i.e.* heaven descended.

Acts xix. 35.

FALL FROM.

1. ἐκπίπτω, *see* "FALL," *No.* 2.

2. ἀποπίπτω, to fall from, (*non occ.*)

3. { ὑστερέω, to be last, behind, inferior,
ἀπό, from, } to fall behind from.

2. Acts ix. 18.
1. Gal. v. 4.
1. 2 Pet. iii. 17. [*fail of.*)
3. Heb. xii. 15, marg. (text,

FALL HEADLONG.

{ πρηνής, bending forward, prostrate,
γενόμενος, becoming, (*see* "FALL," *No.* 6,) } falling headlong.

Acts i. 18.

FALL INTO.

(*When not two words in the Greek.*)

περιπίπτω, *see* "FALL AMONG."

Acts xxvii. 41. | Jas. i. 2.

FALL OFF.

ἐκπίπτω, *see* "FALL," *No.* 2.

Acts xii. 7; xxvii. 32.

FALL OUT.

ἔρχομαι, to come *or* go; move *or* pass along.

Phil. i. 12.

FALL TO.

ἐπιβάλλω, to cast upon *or* over. *Impers.* to fall upon *or* to, *i.e.* to pertain *or* belong to *any one; hence, as here,* τὸ ἐπιβάλλον, the portion which falls (*to me*), *i.e. my* due share.

Luke xv. 12.

FALLING AWAY.

{ ἡ, the,
ἀποστασία,
apostacy, } *viz.*, the one foretold by him, 2 Thes. ii. 5, and by our Lord, Matt. xxiv. 10-12.

2 Thes. ii. 3.

FALLING (KEEP FROM.)

{ φυλάσσω, to watch, *not to sleep*, keep watch; *hence*, to guard, to keep,
ἄπταιστος, not stumbling, *prop. of a horse.* }

Jude 24.

FALSE.

ψευδής, false, *as opp. to what is true*, lying, deceiving, (*occ.* Rev. ii. 2; xxi. 8.)

Acts vi. 13.

See also, ACCUSATION, ACCUSER, APOSTLE, BRETHREN, CHRISTS, PROPHET, WITNESS.

FALSELY.

ψεύδω, to speak falsely, to lie to *any one*, deceive by lying.

Matt. v. 11, part. (marg. *lying*) (*om.* G⇌ L Trmb.)
1 Pet. iii. 16, } see accuse.
Luke iii. 14, }

FALSELY SO CALLED.

ψευδώνυμος, falsely named *(whence Eng.* pseudonym.)

1 Tim. vi. 20.

FAME.

1. φήμη, *(whence, Lat.* fama, *and Eng.* fame,) a voice from heaven, an ominous *or* prophetic voice. *Then,* any voice *or* words; rumour, report, *(non occ.)*
2. ἀκοή, hearing, *either the sense or faculty of* hearing; *the instrument of hearing, i.e.* the ears; *or* that which is heard, *as* instruction *or* report.
3. ἦχος, a ringing in the ears, a sound *or* noise *of any sort.*
4. λόγος, a word *as spoken, whether* the act of speaking *or* the thing spoken, *hence,* talk, an account which one gives.

2. Matt. iv. 24.
1. —— ix. 26.
— ——— 31, see F (spread abroad one's.)
2. Matt. xiv. 1.
2. Mark i. 28.
1. Luke iv. 14.
3. ——— 37.
4. Luke v. 15.

FAME (SPREAD ABROAD ONE'S.)

διαφημίζω, to rumour abroad, make known.

Matt. ix. 31.

FAMILY.

πατριά, paternal descent, lineage. *In N.T.* a family, *as* a subdivision of the Jewish tribe, and containing several households, *(occ.* Luke ii. 4; Acts iii. 25.)

Eph. iii. 15.

FAMINE.

λιμός, failure, want *as of food, hence,* hunger, famine.

Matt. xxiv. 7.
Mark xiii. 8.
Luke iv. 25.
Luke xv. 14.
—— xxi. 11.
Rom. viii. 35.
Rev. xviii. 8.

FAN.

πτύον, winnowing shovel *with which grain is thrown up against the wind in order to cleanse it, (non occ.)*

Matt. iii. 12. | Luke iii. 17.

FAR.

1. μακρός, *(adj.)* long; *of space, i.e. from one point to another, and hence,* far, far distant.
2. μακράν, *(adv.) (prop. acc. fem. of No.* 1), *strictly for* μακρὰν ὁδόν, a long way, a great way; far off.
3. πόῤῥω, *(adv.)* forwards, far forwards, *hence,* far off.
4. { πολλῷ, much, μᾶλλον, more, rather, } much rather, by far, far-far.

3. Matt. xv. 8.
— —— xvi. 22, see F from (be it.)
— —— xxi. 33, } see
— —— xxv. 14, } country.
— Mark vi. 35, see day.
3. —— vii. 6.
— —— viii. 3, see F (from.)
— —— xii. 1, see country.
2 —— 34.
— —— xiii. 34, see journey.
2. Luke vii. 6.
1. —— xv. 13.
1. —— xix. 12.
— Luke xx. 9, see country.
— —— xxii. 51, see F thus.
— —— xxiv. 29, see spent.
2. John xxi. 8.
2. Acts xvii. 27.
— —— xxii. 21, see F hence.
— Rom. xiii. 12, see spent.
— 2 Cor. iv. 17, see exceeding.
— Eph. i. 21, see above.
— —— ii. 13, see F off.
— —— iv. 10, see above.
3. Phil. i. 23.
— Heb. vii. 15, see more.

FAR FROM (BE IT.)

{ ἵλεως, *(adj.) of the gods,* appeased, propitious; *of men,* cheerful; *in N.T. of God,* propitious, favourable, σοι, to thee, } *here, God be* propitious, *or* favourable to thee, *[Lord.]*

Matt. xvi. 22.

FAR HENCE.

μακράν, *see* "FAR," *No.* 2.

Acts xxii. 21.

FAR OFF.

Eph. ii. 13.

FAR (FROM.)

μακρόθεν, from far.

Mark viii. 3.

FAR (THUS.)

{ ἕως, unto, as long as, up to, τούτου, this.

Luke xxii. 51.

FARE (-ED.)

εὐφραίνω, to make merry, rejoice, *as connected with feasting.*

Luke xvi. 19.

FAREWELL or FARE YE WELL.

1. ῥώννυμι, to strengthen, make firm. *In N.T. only imperat. pass. as a formula at the end of epistles like Lat.* vale, *i.e.* fare-well, *(non occ.)*
2. χαίρω, to joy, rejoice, be glad. *Impert. (as here) as a word of salutation or greeting,* joy to thee! joy to you! hail!

1. Acts xv. 29.
1. —— xxiii. 30 (*om.* G→ L T Tr A.)
2. 2 Cor. xiii. 11.

FAREWELL (BID.)

ἀποτάσσομαι, to arrange one's self off, separate one's self from, *i.e.* to take leave of, bid farewell to.

Luke ix. 61. | Acts xviii. 21.

FARM.

ἀγρός, a field, *esp.* a cultivated field.

Matt. xxii. 5.

FARTHER SIDE (THE.)

{ τὸ, the, πέραν, beyond, over, on the other side, } that beyond the other side.

Mark x. 1.

FARTHING.

1. ἀσσάριον, assarion, *dim. of Lat.* as, *Heb.* איסר, a small as; a brass coin equal to one-tenth of a denarius *or* δραχμή, *i.e.* to about three farthings, *(non occ.)*
2. κοδράντης, *Lat.* quadrans, the fourth part of an "as" *(No.* 1), *or* one-fifth of a farthing, *(non occ.)*

2. Matt. v. 26.
1. —— x. 29.
2. Mark xii. 42.
1. Luke xii. 6.

FASHION [noun.]

1. σχῆμα, outward figure, shape, mien, *(non occ.)*
2. εἶδος, thing seen, external appearance.
3. πρόσωπον, *the part* towards, at *or* around the eye, *hence, gen.* the face, countenance.
4. τύπος, a type, *i.e. anything caused or produced by blows;* a mark *or* impress *made by a hard substance on a softer material; also,* a model, pattern, exemplar, *in the widest sense.*

— Mark ii. 12, see F (on this.)
2. Luke ix. 29.
4. Acts vii. 44.
1. 1 Cor. vii. 31.
1. Phil. ii. 8.
— —— iii. 21, see F like unto.
— 1 Pet. i. 14, see F one's self.
3. Jas. i. 11.

FASHION (ON THIS.)

οὕτως, thus, on this wise, in this manner.

Mark ii. 12.

FASHION ONE'S SELF ACCORDING TO.

συσχηματίζω, to give the same form with, *(or* outward figure), to conform to *anything. In N.T. only Mid. or Pass.* to conform one's self, to be conformed to *anything, (occ.* Rom. xii. 2.)

1 Pet. i. 14.

FASHIONED LIKE UNTO.

σύμμορφος, having like form with, *(μορφή denoting* form *abstractedly, and σύν, denoting* association.)

Phil. iii. 21.

FAST [noun.]

νηστεία, a fasting, fast, *i.e.* abstinence from food.

Acts xxvii. 9.

FAST (-ED, -EST, -ING.)

νηστεύω, to fast, to abstain from eating, *(from νή, equal to negative* un, *and* ἐσθίω, to eat.)

Matt. iv. 2, part.
—— vi. 16 twice.
—— 17, part., 18.
—— ix. 14 twice, 15.
Mark ii. 18 1st, see F (use to.)
Mark ii. 18 2nd & 3rd, 19 1st.
—— 19 2nd (*ap.*), 20.
Luke v. 33, 34, 35.
—— xviii. 12.
Acts x. 30 (*om.* L T Tr A ℵ.)
—— xiii. 2, 3, part.

FAST (USED TO.)

{ ἦσαν, they were, νηστεύων, fasting. }

Mark ii. 18.

FAST [adj.]

See, HOLD, STAND, STICK.

FAST (MAKE.)

ἀσφαλίζω, to make firm, fixed, immoveable. Acts xvi 24.

FASTEN ON.

καθάπτω, to adapt, to fit down upon *anything, whence,* to bind *or* fasten on, *(non occ.)*

Acts xxviii. 3.

FASTEN ONE'S EYES.

ἀτενίζω, to fix the eyes intently upon, gaze upon intently.

Luke iv. 20 (with *εἰμι, to be.*)
Acts iii. 4 ; xi. 6, part.

FASTING.

1. *νηστεία*, a fasting, fast, *i.e.* abstinence from food, *(occ.* Acts xxvii. 9.)
2. *νῆστις*, not having eaten, fasting, *(non occ.)*
3. *ἄσιτος*, without food.

2. Matt. xv. 32.
1. —— xvii. 21 (*ap.*)
2. Mark viii. 3.
1. —— ix. 29 (*om.* T Trbm ℵ.)
1. Luke ii. 37.
1. Acts xiv. 23.
3. —— xxvii. 33.
1. 1 Cor. vii. 5 (*om.* G L T Tr A ℵ.)
1. 2 Cor. vi. 5.
1. —— xi. 27.

FATHER (-s.)

πατήρ, father, [*prob. to be derived from Heb.* אב, *which is the simplest labial sound of the infant. Consequently it recurs in all the cognate tongues— Sanscr.* pitri, *Lat.* pater, *Germ.* vater, *Eng.* father], *(occ.* Heb. xi. 23.)

* Spoken of God, as Creator, etc., and as distinguishing the first person of the ever-blessed Trinity.

Matt. ii. 22.
—— iii. 9.
—— iv. 21, 22.
—— v. 16*, 45*, 48*.
—— vi. 1*, 4*, 6 twice*, 8*, 9*, 14*, 15*, 18 twice*, 26*, 32*.
—— vii. 11*, 21*.
—— viii. 21.
—— x. 20*, 21, 29*, 32*, 33*, 35, 37.
—— xi. 25*, 26*, 27* 3 times.
—— xii. 50*.
—— xiii. 43*.
—— xv. 4 twice, 5 twice, 13*.
—— xvi. 17*, 27*.
—— xviii. 10*, 14*, 19*, 35*.
—— xix. 5, 19, 29 (*ap.*)
—— xx. 23*.
—— xxi. 31.
—— xxiii. 9 1st, 9* 2nd, 30, 32.
—— xxiv. 36*.
—— xxv. 34*.
—— xxvi. 29*, 39*, 42*, [53*.
—— xxviii. 19*.
Mark i. 20.
—— v. 40.
—— vii. 10 twice, 11, 12.
—— viii. 38*.
—— ix. 21, 24.
—— x. 7, 19, 29.
—— xi. 10, 25*, 26* (*ap.*)
—— xiii. 12, 32*.
—— xiv. 36*.
—— xv. 21.
Luke i. 17, 32, 55, 59, 62, 67, 72, 73.
—— ii. 48, 49*.
—— iii. 8.
—— vi. 23, 26, 36*.
—— viii. 51.
—— ix. 26*, 42, 59.
—— x. 21* twice, 22* 3 times
—— xi. 2*, 11, 13*, 47, 48.
—— xii. 30*, 32*, 53 twice
—— xiv. 26.
—— xv. 12 twice, 17, 18 twice, 20 twice, 21, 22, 27, 28, 29.
—— xvi. 24, 27 twice, 30.
—— xviii. 20.
—— xxii. 29*, 42*.
—— xxiii. 34* (*ap.*), 46*.
Luke xxiv. 49*.
John i. 14*, 18*.
—— ii. 16*.
—— iii. 35*.
—— iv. 12, 20, 21*, 23* twice.
—— v. 17*, 18*, 19*, 20*, 21*, 22*, 23*, 26*, 30*, (*om.* G L T Tr A ℵ), 36* twice, 37*, 43*, 45*.
—— vi. 27*, 31, 32*, 37*, 39*, (*om.* G L T Tr A ℵ), 42, 44*, 45*, 46* twice, 49, 57* twice, 58.
—— vii. 22.
—— viii. 16*, 18*, 19* 3 times, 27*, 28*, 29* (*om.* G⇉ L T Tr A ℵ), 38* 1st, 38 2nd, 39, 41 1st, 41* 2nd, 42*, 44 3 times, 49*, 53, 54*, 56.
—— x. 15* twice, 17*, 18*, 25*, 29* twice, 30*, 32*, 36*, 37*, 38*.
—— xi. 41*.
—— xii. 26*, 27*, 28*, 49*, 50*.
—— xiii. 1*, 3*.
—— xiv. 2*, 6*, 7*, 8*, 9* twice, 10* 3 times, 11* twice, 12*, 13*, 16*, 20*, 21*, 23*, 24*, 26*, 28* twice, 31* twice.
—— xv. 1*, 8*, 9*, 10*, 15*, 16*, 23*, 24*, 26* twice.
—— xvi. 3*, 10*, 15*, 16* (*ap.*), 17*, 23*, 25*, 26*, 27*, 28* twice, 32*.
—— xvii. 1*, 5*, 11*, 21*, 24*, 25*.
—— xviii. 11*.
—— xx. 17* 3 times, 21*.
Acts i. 4*, 7*.
—— ii. 33*.
—— iii. 13*, 22 (*ap.*), 25.
—— v. 30.
—— vii. 2 twice, 4, 11, 12, 14, 15, 19, 20, 32, 38, 39, 44, 45 twice, 51, 52.
—— xiii. 17, 32, 36.
—— xv. 10.
—— xvi. 1, 3.
—— xxii. 1.
—————— 3, see F (of the.)
—————— 14.
—— xxiv. 14, see F (of one's.)
—— xxvi. 6.
—— xxviii. 8.
—————— 17, see F (of one's.)
—————— 25.
Rom. i. 7*.
—— iv. 1 (*προπάτωρ, fore-father,* G∾L T Tr A ℵ)
—————— 11, 12 twice, 16, 17, [18.
—— vi. 4*.
—— viii. 15*.
Rom. ix. 5, 10.
—— xi. 28.
—— xv. 6*, 8.
1 Cor. i. 3*.
—— iv. 15.
—— v. 1.
—— viii. 6*.
—— x. 1.
—— xv. 24*.
2 Cor. i. 2*, 3* twice.
—— vi. 18*.
—— xi. 31*.
Gal. i. 1*, 3*, 4*.
—————— 14, see F (of one's.)
—— iv. 2, 6*.
Eph. i. 2*, 3*, 17*.
—— ii. 18*.
—— iii. 14*.
—— iv. 6*.
—— v. 20*, 31.
—— vi. 2, 4, 23*.
Phil. i. 2*.
—— ii. 11*, 22.
—— iv. 20*.
Col. i. 2*, 3*, 12*.
—— ii. 2* (*ap.*)
—— iii. 17*, 21.
1 Thes. i. 1* 1st, 1* 2nd (*ap*), [3*.
—— ii. 11.
—— iii. 11*, 13*.
2 Thes. i. 1*, 2*.
—— ii. 16*.
1 Tim. i. 2*.
—————— 9, see F (murderer of a.)
—— v. 1.
2 Tim. i. 2*.
Tit. i. 4*.
Philem. 3*.
Heb. i. 1, 5*.
—— iii. 9.
—— vii. 3, see F (without)
—————— 10.
—— viii. 9.
—— xii. 7, 9 1st, 9* 2nd.
Jas. i. 17*, 27*.
—— ii. 21.
—— iii. 9*.
1 Pet. i. 2*, 3*, 17*.
—————— 18, see F (received by tradition from the)
2 Pet. i. 17*.
—— iii. 4.
1 John i. 3*.
—— ii. 1, 13 1st, 13* 2nd, 14, 15*, 16*, 22*, 23*, 24*.
—— iii 1*.
—— iv. 14*.
—— v. 7* (*ap*).
2 John 3* twice, 4*, 9*.
Jude 1*.
Rev. i. 6*.
—— ii. 27*.
—— iii. 5*, 21*.
—— xiv. 1*.

FATHER (MURDERER OF A.)

πατραλῴας, a smiter of his father, *(non occ.)*

1 Tim. i. 9.

FATHER (WITHOUT.)

ἀπάτωρ, without father, *(non occ.)*

Heb. vii. 3.

FATHERS (OF ONE'S)

1. πατρῷος, of a father, coming *or* inherited from him, descending from a father to a son, *as property or fortune.*
2. πατρικός, from one's fathers *or* ancestors, paternal, ancestral; *used chiefly of hereditary friendships or friends, (non occ.)*

[πάτριος is used of what is handed down from one's forefathers as manners and customs, etc.]

1. Acts xxiv. 14. | 2. Gal. i. 14. | 1. Acts xxviii. 17.

FATHERS (OF THE.)

πατρῷος, *see above, No.* 1.

Acts xxii. 3.

FATHERS (RECEIVED BY TRADITION FROM THE.)

πατροπαράδοτος, handed *or* delivered down from one's fathers, *(non occ.)*

1 Pet. i. 18.

FATHER-IN-LAW.

πενθερός, a father-in-law, *(non occ.)*

John xviii. 13.

FATHERLESS.

ὀρφανός, *Eng.* orphan, bereaved *(prob. from Sanscr.* rabh, *Lat.* rapis, *Eng.* reft), *(occ.* John xiv. 18.)

Jas. i. 27.

FATHOM (-s) [noun.]

ὀργυιά, the length of the arms when stretched out, equal to six feet one inch, *an Eng. fathom being six feet, (non occ.)*

Acts xxvii. 28 twice.

FATLING.

σιτιστός, fed up, fatted, *(non occ.)*

Matt. xxii. 4 (neut.)

FATNESS.

πιότης, fatness, fat, *(non occ.)*

Rom. xi. 17.

FATTED.

σιτευτός, fed *(as with grain,)* fatted, *(non occ.)*

Luke xv. 23, 27, 30.

FAULT (-s.)

1. αἰτία, an asking *(from αἰτέω), then,* a ground of accusation, cause; charge, *whether true or false.*
2. αἴτιον, *(neut. with art. of* αἴτιος, causing, occasioning,) the charge, accusation.
3. ἥττημα, a being inferior, in a worse state, *esp.* as compared with a former state, a failure; in lxx. *denotes* defeat, *(occ.* Rom. xi. 12.)
4. παράπτωμα, a misfall, mishap; a falling aside *as from duty, etc., hence,* sin, *but as* the missing of the right, *rather than a transgression of the law, with special reference to the* subjective weakness *of the person, rather than the objective sin.*

— Matt. xviii. 15, see F (tell one's.)
— Mark vii. 2, see F (find)
2. Luke xxiii. 4, 14.
1. John xviii. 38.
1. —— xix. 4, 6.
— Rom. ix. 19.
3. 1 Cor. vi. 7.
4. Gal. vi. 1.
— Heb. viii. 8, see F (find)
— —— ix. 14, see F (without.)
4. Jas. v. 16 (ἁμαρτίας, *sins,* L T Tr A* ℵ.)
— 1 Pet. ii. 20, see F (for your.)
— Rev. xiv. 5, see F (without.)

FAULT (FIND.)

μέμφομαι, to blame, upbraid, find fault with.

Mark vii. 2 (*om.* G L T Tr A ℵ.) | Rom. ix. 19. | Heb. viii. 8.

FAULT (TELL ONE'S.)

ἐλέγχω, to convict, show to be wrong, prove guilty.

Matt. xviii. 15.

FAULT (WITHOUT.)

ἄμωμος, without spot *or* blemish of sin, without blame.

Heb. ix. 14, marg. (text, *without spot.*)
Rev. xiv. 5.

FAULTS (FOR YOUR.)

ἁμαρτάνω, to miss, *as a mark;* err from, *as a way; hence,* to sin.

1 Pet. ii. 20, part.

FAULTLESS.

1. ἄμεμπτος, not blamed, without reproach.
2. ἄμωμος, with spot *or* blemish of sin.

1. Heb. viii. 7. | 2. Jude 24.

FAVOUR [noun.]

χάρις, grace; *objectively it denotes* personal gracefulness, a pleasing work, beauty of speech; *subjectively it denotes* an inclining towards, courteous *or* gracious disposition. *On the part of the giver,* kindness, favour; *on the part of the receiver,* thanks, respect, homage.

Luke i. 30.
—— ii. 52.
Acts ii. 47.
—— vii. 10, 46.
Acts xxv. 3.

FAVOURED (HIGHLY.)

χαριτόω, to make χάρις *(in the subjective sense,)* to grace, *i.e. in Pass. as here,* to be gracious or favoured, *(occ.* Eph. i. 6.)

Luke i. 28, pass. part. (margin, *graciously accepted* or *much graced.*)

FEAR [noun.]

1. φόβος, fear, terror, fright, dismay, *hence,* flight. *It denotes the outward manifestation rather than the sensation of fear. In a bad sense, it is the effect of the spirit of No.* 2; *in a good sense the fear of God.*
2. δειλία, moral cowardice, timidity, *(non occ.)*
3. ἀγών, contest, *esp. with the idea of* peril *or* danger.

1. Matt. xiv. 26.
1. —— xxviii. 4, 8.
1. Luke i. 12, 65.
— —— 74, see F (without.)
— —— iii. 14, see *F (put in.)*
1. —— v. 26.
1. —— vii. 16.
1. —— viii. 37.
1. —— xxi. 26.
1. John vii. 13.
1. —— xix. 38.
1. —— xx. 19.
1. Acts ii. 43.
1. —— v. 5, 11.
1. —— ix. 31.
1. —— xix. 17.
1. Rom. iii. 18.
1. —— viii. 15.
1. —— xiii. 7 twice.
1. 1 Cor. ii. 3.
— —— xvi. 10, see F (without.)
1. 2 Cor. vii. 1, 5, 11, 15.
3. Col. ii. 1, marg. (text, *conflict.*)
1. Eph. v. 21.
1. —— vi. 5.
— Phil. i. 14, see F (without.)
1. —— ii. 12.
2. 2 Tim. i. 7.
1. Heb. ii. 15.
— —— xi. 7, see F (be moved with.)
— —— xii. 28, see F (godly)
1. 1 Pet. i. 17.
— —— ii. 18.
— —— iii. 2.
— —— 15, marg. *reverence.*
1. 1 John iv. 18 3 times.
— Jude 12, see F (without)
1. —— 28.
1. Rev. xi. 11.
1. —— xviii. 10, 15.

FEAR (BE MOVED WITH.)

εὐλαβέομαι, to act with caution, be circumspect, *resulting from salutary fear,* to act with pious fear, *(occ.* Acts xxiii. 10.)

Heb. xi. 7, marg. *be weary.*

FEAR (GODLY.)

εὐλάβεια, caution, circumspection, *then,* cautious, cautious observance from salutary fear, reverence.

Heb. xii. 28.

FEAR (put in) [margin.]

διασείω, to shake throughout *(trans.) i.e.* to cause to shake violently, *hence,* to inspire terror.

Luke iii. 14, text, *do violence to.*

FEAR (WITHOUT.)

ἄφοβος, *(ἀ, privative, and φόβος, see* "FEAR," *No.* 1.)

Luke i. 74.
1 Cor. xvi. 10.
Phil. i. 14.
Jude 12.

FEAR (-ED, -ETH, -ING.)

1. φοβέω, to strike with fear, scare, frighten. *Mid. or Pass. as here,* to be put in fear, take fright, *(see* "FEAR," *No.* 1.)
2. { φόβος, *see* "FEAR," *No.* 1,) ἔχω, to have, } to have fear.
3. εὐλαβέομαι, *see above,* "FEAR (be moved with.)"

1. Matt. i. 20.
1. —— x. 26.
1. —— 28 1st (with ἀπό, *from.*)
1. —— 28 2nd, 31.
1. —— xiv. 5.
1. —— xxi. 26, 46.
1. —— xxvii. 54.
1. —— xxviii. 5.
1. Mark iv. 41.
1. —— v. 33.
1. —— vi. 20.
1. —— xi. 18, 32.
1. —— xii. 12.
1. Luke i. 13, 30, 50.
1. —— ii. 10.
1. —— v. 10.
1. —— viii. 50.
1. —— ix. 34, 45.
1. —— xii. 5 3 times, 7, 32.
1. —— xviii. 2, 4.
1. —— xix. 21.
1. —— xx. 19.
1. —— xxii. 2.
1. —— xxiii. 40.
1. John ix. 22.
1. —— xii. 15.
1. Acts v. 26.
1. Acts x. 2, 22, 35.
1. —— xiii. 16, 26.
1. —— xvi. 38.
3. —— xxiii. 10 (No. 1 G ~ L Tr A* ℵ.)
1. —— xxvii. 17, 24, 29.
1. Rom. xi. 20.
1. 2 Cor. xi. 3.
1. —— xii. 20.
1. Gal. ii. 12.
1. Col. iii. 22.
2. 1 Tim. v. 20.
1. Heb. iv. 1.
— —— v. 7, see F (in that one.)
1. —— xi. 27.
— —— xii. 21, see F (exceedingly.)
1. —— xiii. 6.
1. 1 Pet. ii. 17.
1. 1 John iv. 18.
1. Rev. i. 17.
1. —— ii. 10.
1. —— xi. 18.
1. —— xiv. 7.
1. —— xv. 4.
1. —— xix. 5.

FEAR EXCEEDINGLY.

{ ἔκφοβος, frightened outright *or* out of one's *senses*, εἰμί, to be, } *lit.* "frightened, outright am I."

Heb. xii. 21.

FEARETH (IN THAT ONE.)

{ ἀπὸ, from, ἡ, the ("of him" *understood,*) εὐλαβεία, *see* "FEAR (GODLY)," } *either* "from his fear" (delivered *understood*) *or* "on account of his devoutness."

Heb. v. 7, marg. *for one's piety.*

FEARFUL.

1. δειλός, cowardly, timid, *esp.* the inward sensation of fear.
2. φοβερός, fearful, terrible, frightful, *(adj. of* "FEAR" [noun], *No.* 1.)

1. Matt. viii. 26.
1. Mark iv. 40.
— Luke xxi. 11, see F sight
2. Heb. x. 27.
— —— 31, see F thing.
1. Rev. xxi. 8.

FEARFUL SIGHT.

φόβητρον, something fearful, terrible portent, *(non occ.)*

Luke xxi. 11.

FEARFUL THING.

φοβερός, *neut. of No.* 2 *above.*

Heb. x. 31.

FEAST [noun.]

1. ἑορτή, a feast *or* festival. *Spoken of the Jewish feasts.*
2. δεῖπνον, the chief meal *of the Jews, Greeks, and Romans* taken at *or* towards evening, *hence, gen.* an evening banquet *or* feast *in general.*
3. δοχή, reception, *as of guests, hence,* a banquet, feast.

2. Matt. xxiii. 6.
1. —— xxvi. 5.
1. —— xxvii. 15.
2. Mark xii. 39.
— —— xiv. 2, see F day.
1. —— xv. 6.
1. Luke ii. 41, 42.
3. —— v. 29.
3. —— xiv. 13.
2. —— xx. 46.
1. —— xxii. 1.
1. —— xxiii. 17 (*ap.*)
— John ii. 8, see governor
— —— 9 1st, see ruler.
— —— 9 2nd, see governor
— —— 23, see F day.
1. —— iv. 45 twice.
1. —— v. 1.
1. —— vi. 4.
1. —— vii. 2, 8 twice, 10, 11, 14, 37.
— —— x. 22, see dedication.
1. —— xi. 56.
1. John xii. 12, 20.
1. —— xiii. 1, 29.
1. Acts. xviii. 21 (*ap.*)
— 1 Cor. v. 8, see F (keep the)
— 2 Pet. ii. 13, see F with.
— Jude 12 1st, see charity.
— Jude 12 2nd, see F with.

FEAST-DAY.

1. Mark xiv. 2. | 1. John ii. 23.

FEAST (KEEP THE.)

ἑορτάζω, to keep an ἑορτή, *(see* "FEAST," *No.* 1,) keep a festival, *(non occ.)*

1 Cor. v. 8, marg. *holyday.*

FEAST WITH [verb.]

συνευωχέω, to let be well fed together, to feast several together; *or,* (a) *Mid.* to feast with *any one,* to revel with, *(non occ.)*

a. 2 Pet. ii. 13, part. | a. Jude 12, part.

FEEBLE.

1. ἀσθενής, without strength *or* energy, infirm, feeble.
2. παραλύω, to loosen at *or* from the side *(i.e. of things joined side by side),* to disjoin; *hence,* to relax, enfeeble, *(only in N.T. perf. part. pass.)*

1. 1 Cor. xii. 22. | 2. Heb. xii. 12.

FEEBLE-MINDED.

ὀλιγόψυχος, of little soul, low-spirited, faint-hearted, *(non occ.)*

1 Thes. v. 14.

FEED (-ED, -ETH, -ING, FED.)

1. βόσκω, to pasture, to feed. *The word* βόω, *from which it is derived, contains the universal idea of nourishing, hence, it is applied* to men. *It refers to the special functions* of providing food, *(occ.* Matt. viii. 33.)
2. ποιμαίνω, to exercise the whole office of a ποιμήν (a shepherd), *which involves not merely* the feeding on grass (ποιά, *whence No.* 2), *but the entire* leading, guiding, guarding, and folding of the flock.
3. τρέφω, to make firm, thick, *or* solid, *then,* to make thick *or* fat *by feeding, and hence,* to feed, make to grow *or* increase, nourish, bring up, rear.

4. χορτάζω, to feed *or* fatten in a χόρτος (an enclosed place *or* feeding place, *Lat.* hortus, *Eng.* court, garden), *gen.* to feed, fatten, fill, satisfy.

5. ψωμίζω, to feed by putting little bits into the mouth *as nurses do children*, *hence*, supply with food, (*occ.* 1 Cor. xiii. 3.)

2. Matt. ii. 6, marg. (text, *rule.*)
3. — vi. 26.
1. — viii. 30, mid.
3. — xxv. 37.
1. Mark v. 11, mid.
1. — 14.
1. Luke viii. 32, mid., 34.
3. — xii. 24.
1. — xv. 15.
4. — xvi. 21.
— — xvii. 7, see F cattle.
1. John xxi. 15.
2. John xxi. 16.
1. — 17.
— Acts xiii. 18, marg. see [bear.
2. — xx. 28.
5. Rom. xii. 20.
— 1 Cor. iii. 2, see F with.
2. — ix. 7.
— — 13, see *F of.*
— — xiii. 3, see bestow.
2. 1 Pet. v. 2.
2. Jude 12.
2. Rev. vii. 17.
3. — xii. 6.

FEED CATTLE.

2. Luke xvii. 7.

FEED OF [margin.]

ἐσθίω, to eat, (*as opp. to* πίνω, to drink,) to consume, live upon, (*see* "EAT," *No.* 2.)

1 Cor. ix. 13, text, *live of.*

FEED WITH.

ποτίζω, to give to drink; *of plants*, to water.

1 Cor. iii. 2.

FEEL, FELT.

1. γινώσκω, to perceive, observe, obtain a knowledge of *or* insight into, become aware of.

2. πάσχω, to be affected by *anything from without*, to be acted upon, *either by good or evil; of good*, to experience; *of evil*, to suffer.

1. Mark v. 29. | 2. Acts xxviii. 5.

FEEL AFTER.

ψηλαφάω, to touch, feel after, grope *like a blind man, or as in the dark.*

Acts xvii. 27.

FEELING (BE PAST.)

ἀπαλγέω, to put off the feeling of pain, cease from feeling pain *at anything*, (*non occ.*)

Eph. iv. 19.

FEELING OF (BE TOUCHED WITH THE.)

συμπαθέω, to feel *or* suffer with *another*, to be affected in like manner, (*occ.* Heb. x. 34.)

Heb. iv. 15.

FEIGN.

ὑποκρίνομαι, to be judged under, *i.e.* to represent another person by acting under *a mask*, *hence*, to personate, pretend, feign, (*non occ.*)

Luke xx. 20, part.

FEIGNED.

πλαστός, formed, fashioned, (*as the clay by the potter or marble by statuary,*) well-turned, (*non occ.*)

2 Pet. ii. 3.

FELLOW (-S.)

1. ἀνήρ, a man, *in relation to his sex and age*, *Lat.* vir.

2. ἑταῖρος, a companion, comrade, messmate, (*only used by* Matthew, *occ.* xx. 13; xxii. 12; xxvi. 50.)

3. μέτοχος, partaking. *As Subst.* a partaker, companion, partner, (*occ.* Luke v. 7; Heb. iii. 1, 14; vi. 4; xii. 8.)

2. Matt. xi. 16 (ἕτεροι, *the others*, G~ T Tr ℵ.)
1. Acts xvii. 5.
3. Heb. i. 9.

See also, BASE, CITIZEN, DISCIPLE, HEIR, HELPER, LABOURER, PESTILENT, PRISONER, SERVANT, SOLDIER, SUCH, THIS, WORK, WORKER, YOKE.

FELLOWSHIP.

1. κοινωνία, *act of* partaking, sharing, *i.e.* participation, communion.

2. μετοχή, partnership, fellowship, (*non occ.*)

1. Acts. ii. 42.
1. 1 Cor. i. 9.
— — x. 20, see F with (have.)
2. 2 Cor. vi. 14.
1. — viii. 4.
1. Gal. ii. 9.
1. Eph. iii. 9 (οἰκονομία, *administration*, G L T Tr A ℵ.)
1. Phil. i. 5.
1. — ii. 1.
1. — iii. 10.
1. 1 John 1, 3 twice, 6, 7.
— Eph. v. 11, see F with (have.)

FELLOWSHIP WITH (HAVE.)

1. { κοινωνός, a partaker, partner, γίνομαι, to begin to be, become, } to become a partner.

2. συγκοινωνέω, to be a joint-partaker with *others*, to share with *others* in *anything*, (*occ.* Eph. v. 11; Phil. iv. 14, part.)

1. 1 Cor. x. 20. | 2. Eph. v. 11.

FEMALE.

θῆλυ, female, (*from* θάλλω, to thrive, *which from* θηλή, the teat.)

Matt. xix. 4. | Mark x. 6.
Gal. iii. 28.

FERVENT.

1. ἐκτενής, extended, stretched *or* strained out; *hence*, earnest, assiduous, (*occ.* Acts xii. 5.)
2. ζέω, to boil, to be hot, *of water*; *hence*, to be fervid, fervent, (*non occ.*)

— Acts xviii. 25, see F (be.)
2. Rom. xii. 11, part.
— 2 Cor vii. 7, see F mind.
— Jas. v. 16, see effectual.
1. 1 Pet. iv. 8.
— 2 Pet. iii. 10, 12, see heat

FERVENT (BE.)

2. Acts xviii. 25.

FERVENT MIND.

ζῆλος, zeal, fervour, (*from No.* 2 *above,*) *gen. in a good sense.*

2 Cor. vii. 7.

FERVENTLY.

ἐκτενῶς, intently, earnestly, (*adv. of No.* 1 *above,*) (*non occ.*)

Col. iv. 12, see labourer. | 1 Pet. i. 22.

FETCH.

See, COMPASS.

FETCH OUT.

ἐξάγω, to lead out, conduct out *as out of any place.*

Acts xvi. 37.

FETTER (-S.)

πέδη, a fetter *or* shackle *for the feet*, (*non occ.*)

Mark v. 4 twice. | Luke viii. 29.

FEVER.

πυρετός, fiery heat, *esp.* feverish heat, *hence*, a fever, (*non occ.*)

Matt. viii. 14. see F (sick of.)
——— 15.
Mark. i. 30, see F (sick of.)
Mark i. 31.
Luke iv. 38, 39.
John iv. 52.
Acts xxviii. 8.

FEVER (SICK OF.)

πυρέσσω, to be feverish, be in a fever.

Matt. viii. 14, part. | Mark i. 30, part.

FEW.

ὀλίγος, little, (*as opp. to* πολύς, much), *used of number or quantity. Here, in plural*, few.

Matt. vii. 14.
—— ix. 37.
—— xv. 34.
—— xx. 16 (*ap.*)
—— xxii. 14.
—— xxv. 21, 23, see F things (a.)
Mark vi. 5.
—— viii. 7.
Luke x. 2.
—— xiii. 23.
Luke xii. 48, see F stripes.
Acts xvii. 4, 12.
—— xxiv. 4, see F words (a.)
Eph. iii. 3, see F words (in)
Heb. xii. 10.
—— xiii. 22, see F words (in.)
1 Pet. iii. 20.
Rev. ii. 14, 20, see F things (a.)
—— iii. 4.

FEW STRIPES.

Luke xii. 48.

FEW THINGS (A.)

Matt. xxv. 21, 23, neut. pl. | Rev. ii. 14, 20, neut. pl.

FEW WORDS (A.)

συντόμως, concisely, briefly, (*adv. of* σύντομος [*from* συντέμνω, to cut in pieces,] cut up, cut short), (*non occ.*)

Acts xxiv. 4.

FEW WORDS (IN.)

1. { διὰ, through, by means of, βραχέων, short, (*Lat.* brev-is), *of number*, few, } in few *words*, with brevity, (*non occ.*)

2. { ἐν, in, ὀλίγῳ, little, } in brief *or* briefly.

2. Eph. iii. 3, marg. *a little.*
1. Heb. xiii. 22.

FIDELITY.

πίστις, faith, *(see* "FAITH," *No.* 1.)

Titus ii. 10.

FIELD (-s.)

1. ἀγρος, a field, *esp.* a cultivated field, *then of such fields in the aggregate,* farms, villages, the country.
2. χώρα, space, *which receives, contains, or surrounds anything, and hence,* place, spot, country, land, province. Open country *as opp. to city.*
3. χωρίον, *(dim. of No. 2 in form, but not in sense,)* a particular place, landed property, estate, *like Eng.* "place."

1. Matt. vi. 28, 30.
1. —— xiii. 24, 27, 31, 36, 38, 44 twice.
1. —— xxiv. 18, 40.
1. —— xxvii. 7, 8 twice, 10.
— Mark ii. 23, see corn.
1. —— xiii. 16.
— Luke ii. 8, see abide.
— Luke vi. 1, see corn.
1. —— xii. 28.
1. —— xv. 25.
1. —— xvii. 7, 31.
1. —— 36 *(ap.)*
2. John iv. 35.
3. Acts i. 18, 19 twice.
2. Jas. v. 4.

FIERCE.

1. ἀνήμερος, not tame, wild, savage, *of persons, a country or plants, (non occ.)*
2. σκληρός, dry, hard; *the meaning being decided by the noun; hence, of winds, as here,* violent.
3. χαλεπός, heavy, difficult; *of things,* perilous; *of persons,* fierce, furious, *(occ.* 2 Tim. iii. 1.)

3. Matt. viii. 28.
— Luke xxiii. 5, see F (be the more.)
1. 2 Tim. iii. 3.
2. Jas. iii. 4.

FIERCE (BE THE MORE.)

ἐπισχύω, to strengthen upon, *(i.e.* in addition); *hence,* to be *or* grow stronger, to be more violent *or* fierce, *(non occ.)*

Luke xxiii. 5.

FIERCENESS.

θυμός, the soul, *(from the spirit which we breathe out,)* an intense passion *or* forcible exhalation of the mind, *not necessarily implying passion or revenge.*

Rev. xvi. 19. | Rev. xix. 15.

FIERY.

1. πῦρ, fire, *here, Genit.* of fire, *(low Germ.* für; *high Germ.* feuer; *Eng.* fire.)
2. πυρόομαι, to be set on fire, ignite; *here, part.* τὰ πεπυρωμένα, the ignited....

2. Eph. vi. 16, part. | 1. Heb. x. 27.

FIERY TRIAL.

πύρωσις, a burning, lighting, kindling, *(occ.* Rev. xviii. 9, 18.)

1 Pet. iv. 12.

FIFTEEN.

δεκαπέντε, fifteen, *(non occ.)*

John xi. 18. | Gal. i. 18. | Acts xxvii. 28.

FIFTEEN (THREE SCORE AND.)

{ ἑβδομήκοντα, seventy, / πέντε, five, } seventy-five.

Acts vii. 14.

[NOTE.

This number refers here to "all his kindred" whom Joseph "sent" for and "called."

The numbers in Gen. xlvi. refer similarly to those who are defined by them. Thus:—

Those who "came with Jacob," who "came out of his loins," (v. 26), ("besides Jacob's sons' wives")	66
Then, Jacob, and Joseph, and his two sons who were *in* Egypt (v. 27)	4
Making . . .	70

The nine "besides" who "went down," in Acts vii. 14, are clearly those of the "kindred" who are *excepted* in Gen. xlvi. 26; so that the complete statement would be as follows:—

	Souls.	
"Went down," "out of loins" (Gen. xlvi. 26).	66	
"besides" (Gen. xlvi. 26), *(i.e.* the "kindred" of Acts vii. 14)	9	
Total, "Kindred" (Acts vii. 14)		75
Jacob and the three already in Egypt (Gen. xlvi. 27) .		4
Total, *"Kindred"* and *issue* in Egypt		79

—]

FIFTEENTH.

πεντεκαιδέκατος, the fifteenth, *(non occ.)*

Luke iii. 1.

FIFTH.

πέμπτος, the fifth, *(non occ.)*

Rev. vi. 9.
— ix. 1.
Rev. xvi. 10.
— xxi. 20.

FIFTY.

πεντήκοντα, fifty, *(non occ.)*

Luke vii. 41.
— xvi. 6.
John viii. 57.
John xxi. 11.
Acts xiii. 20 (*ap.*)
— xix. 19, see thousand.

FIFTIES (BY.)

{ *ἀνὰ*, *(distributive)*, *πεντήκοντα*, fifty, } fifty by fifty.

Mark vi. 40 (*κατὰ*, instead of *ἀνά*, *by fifties*, L T Tr A ℵ)
Luke ix. 14.

FIG.

σῦκον, a fig, *(non occ.)*

Matt. vii. 16.
Mark xi. 13.
Luke vi. 44.
Jas. iii. 12.

FIG (UNTIMELY.)

ὄλυνθος, a fig *which grows under the leaves and does not ripen at the proper season but hangs upon the leaves during the winter. Lat.* grossus, *(non occ.)*

Rev. vi. 13, marg. *green fig.*

FIG-TREE.

συκέα or συκῆ, a fig-tree, *(non occ.)*

Matt. xxi. 19 twice, 20, 21.
— xxiv. 32.
Mark xi. 13, 20, 21.
— xiii. 28.
Luke xiii. 6, 7.
— xxi. 29
John i. 49.
Jas. iii. 12.
Rev. vi. 13.

FIGHT [noun.]

1. *ἀγών*, place of assembly *where games were celebrated, hence,* place of contest, *then,* a conflict in the public games, *and after,* any contest.
2. *ἄθλησις*, a contest *or* combat, *esp. of athletes, gen.* a struggle, trial.
3. *πόλεμος*, the agitation and tumult of battle, *hence,* fight, battle, war.

1. 1 Tim. vi. 12.
1. 2 Tim. iv. 7.
2. Heb. x. 32.
3. — xi. 34.

FIGHT (FOUGHT) [verb.]

1. *ἀγωνίζομαι*, to be a combatant *in the public games, then,* to contend *as with an adversary.*
2. *πολεμέω*, to war, make war, fight.
3. *πυκτεύω*, to fist, to box, to fight as a boxer, *(non occ.)*
4. *μάχομαι*, to fight as in war *or* battle, *hence, gen.* to strive, contend, quarrel.

1. John xviii. 36.
— Acts v. 39, } see F against
— — xxiii. 9, } God.
3. 1 Cor. ix. 26.
— — xv. 32, see F with [beasts.
1. 1 Tim. vi. 12.
1. 2 Tim. iv. 7.
4. Jas. iv. 2.
2. Rev. ii. 16.
2. — xii. 7 twice.

FIGHT AGAINST GOD.

1. *θεομαχέω*, to fight *or* contend against God, *(non occ.)*
2. *θεομάχος*, a fighting against God, a contending with God, *(non occ.)*

2. Acts v. 39.
1. — xxiii. 9 (*om.* G L T Tr A ℵ)

FIGHT WITH BEASTS.

θηριομαχέω, to fight with wild beasts *like condemned persons in the public spectacles.*

1 Cor. xv. 32.

FIGHTING.

μάχη, a fight, a battle, *gen.* strife, controversy.

2 Cor. vii. 5.
Jas. iv. 1, marg. *brawling.*

FIGURE.

1. *παραβολή*, a placing side by side *for the purpose of comparison,* representation *or* similitude.
2. *τύπος*, a blow, *then,* that which is produced by the blow, the mark of a blow, impression; *hence,* model, pattern, exemplar *in the widest sense.*
3. *ἀντίτυπος*, resisting a blow *or* impression, *then,* that which receives the mark *or* impress, [*hence,*, *No.* 2 *is* the thing prefiguring, *No.* 3 *is* the thing prefigured, *while ὑποτύπωσις is simply* delineation, outline,] *(occ.* 1 Pet. iii. 21.)

2. Acts vii. 43.
2. Rom. v. 14.
— 1 Cor iv. 6, see transfer.
3. — 1 Pet. iii. 21.
1. Heb. ix. 9.
1. — xi. 19.
3. — — 24.

FILL (-ED, -ETH, -ING.)

1. *πληρόω*, to fill, make full, to fulfil. *Pass.* to be filled *or* full. *Intrans.* to be complete.
   (a) *with Acc.* of the thing filled.
   (b) *with Gen.* of what it is filled with.
   (c) *with Dative* of "FILLER."
   (d) *Acc. with εἰς*, up to.
   (e) *Hebrew Idiom, Acc.* of what it is filled with.
2. *συμπληρόω*, (*No.* 1 *with σύν*, together with, *prefixed*,) to fill up altogether, to fill wholly *or* completely.
3. *πίμπλημι*, to fill, fill up. *Pass.* to become full of, be satisfied, have enough of.
   (b) *with Gen.* of what filled with.
4. *ἐμπίμπλημι*, (*No.* 3 *with ἐν*, in, *prefixed*,) to fill in, *i.e. Eng.* to fill up, make quite full satiate.
5. *χορτάζω*, to feed with grass *or* hay, to fodder, (*prop. used of beasts*,) *gen.* to feed, fill with food.
6. *γεμίζω*, to fill *or* load.
7. *κεράννυμι*, to mix, to mingle *as wine with water, etc.; hence, gen.* to compound *for drinking.*

5. Matt. v. 6.
— —— ix. 16, see F up.
5. —— xiv. 20.
5. —— xv. 33, 37.
— —— xxiii. 32, see F up.
3. —— xxvii. 48.
— Mark ii. 21, see F up.
5. —— vi. 42.
5. —— vii. 27.
5. —— viii. 8.
— —— xv. 36, see F full.
3. Luke i. 15, 41.
4. ——— 53.
3. ——— 67.
1. —— ii. 40.
1. —— iii. 5.
3. —— iv. 28.
3. —— v. 7, 26.
3. —— vi. 11.
5. ——— 21.
2. —— viii. 23.
5. —— ix. 17.
6. —— xiv. 23.
6. —— xv. 16.
6. John ii. 7 twice.
4. —— vi. 12.
6. ——— 13.
5. ——— 26.
1. —— xii. 3.
1. —— xvi. 6.
3. —— xix. 29 (*ap.*)
1. Acts ii. 2.
3. ——— 4.
3. Acts iii. 10.
3. —— iv. 8, 31.
1. —— v. 3.
3. ——— 17.
1. ——— 28.
3. —— ix. 17.
3. —— xiii. 9, 45.
1. ——— 52.
4. —— xiv. 17.
3. —— xix. 29.
1. Rom. i. 29.
1. —— xv. 13, 14.
4. ——— 24.
1. 2 Cor. vii. 4.
1. Eph. iii. 19.
1. —— iv. 10, marg. *fulfil.*
1. —— v. 18.
— Phil. i. 11, see F with (be).
5. —— iv. 12
1. Col. i. 9.
— ——— 24, see F up.
1. —— iv. 12, marg. (text, *complete*) (*πληροφορέω, fully persuaded*, G ~ L T Tr A ℵ.)
— 1 Thes. ii. 16, see F up.
1. 2 Tim. i. 4.
5. Jas. ii. 16.
6. Rev. viii. 5.
— —— xv. 1, see F up.
6. ——— 8.
7. —— xviii. 6. twice.
5. —— xix. 21.

FILL FULL.

6. Mark xv. 36.

FILL UP.

1. *πληρόω, see* "FILL," *No.* 1.
2. *ἀναπληρόω*, (*No.* 1 *with ἀνά*, up, *prefixed*,) to fill up *as a chasm or a measure, etc.*
3. *ἀνταναπληρόω*, (*No.* 2 *with ἀντί*, instead of, *prefixed*,) to fill up instead of, to make good, (*non occ.*)
4. *τελέω*, to bring about, complete, fulfil, accomplish, *hence*, to end, to perfect.

— Matt. ix. 16, see F up (which is put in to.)
1. —— xxiii. 32.
— Mark ii. 21, see F up (piece that.)
3. Col. i. 24.
2. 1 Thes. ii. 16.
4. Rev. xv. 1.

FILL UP (WHICH IS PUT IN TO.)

πλήρωμα, that with which any thing is filled *or* of which it is full, the contents.

Matt. ix. 16.

FILLETH UP (PIECE THAT.)

Mark ii. 21.

FILLED WITH (BE.)

πληρόω, see "FILL," *No.* 1.

Phil. i. 11, pass.

FILTH.

1. *περικάθαρμα*, cleansings, *i.e.* that which is thrown away in cleansing. *Used in pl.* offscourings. [Used in Athens of worthless persons whom in plague or famine or other visitations were reserved to be thrown into the sea in the belief that they would cleanse or wipe off the guilt of the nation,] (*non occ.*)
2. *ῥύπος*, dirt, filth, dirtiness, uncleanness, (*non occ.*)

1. 1 Cor. iv. 13.
2. 1 Pet. iii. 21.

FILTHINESS.

1. *αἰσχρότης*, deformity, ugliness. *In N.T. metaph.* obscenity, whatever is offensive to Christian purity, (*non occ.*)
2. *ἀκαθάρτης*, uncleanness, filth. *Also moral* uncleanness, *i.e.* lewdness, (*non occ.*)

3. μολυσμός, a soiling, *hence*, defilement, stain.

4. ῥυπαρία, dirt, filth, *in the worst sense.*

3. 2 Cor. vii. 1.
1. Eph. v. 4.
4. Jas. i. 21.
2. Rev. xvii. 4 (τὰ ἀκάθαρτα, *the impurities*, G L T Tr A ℵ.)

FILTHY.

1. αἰσχρός, deformed, ugly. *In N.T. metaph.* indecorous, indecent, *(elsewhere,* "SHAME.")

2. ἀσέλγια, excess, immoderation, intemperance *in any thing, (in language or conduct.)*

— Col. iii. 8, see F communication.
— 1 Tim. iii. 3, } see
— Titus i. 7, } lucre.
1. Titus i. 11.
— 1 Pet. v. 2, see lucre.
2. 2 Pet. ii. 7.
— Jude 8, see dreamer.

FILTHY (BE.)

ῥυπόω, to make foul and filthy. *Mid.* pollute one's self.

Rev. xxii. 11 1st, part. (ὁ ῥυπαρός, *the filthy one*, G L^b T Tr A ℵ.)
Rev. xxii. 11 2nd, Imper. (ῥυπαρένομαι, *be filthy*, G L^b) (ῥυπαίνω, *befoul, defile* (mid.) L T Tr A ℵ.)

FILTHY COMMUNICATION.

αἰσχρολογία, the licence of the ungoverned tongue, obscene language, *but not limited to this, (non occ.)*

Col. iii. 8.

FINALLY.

1. λοιπόν, left, remaining.* *With the article*, the rest, *as of time*, henceforth, henceforward. *Also*, as to the rest, finally.

2. τέλος, an end, completion.* *Adverbially with art.* finally, at last.

1. 2 Cor. xiii. 11.
1*. Eph. vi. 10.
1*. Phil. iii. 1.
1*. Phil. iv. 8.
1*. 2 Thes. iii. 1.
2*. 1 Pet. iii. 8.

FIND (-ETH, -ING, FOUND.)

1. εὑρίσκω, to find, *as without seeking*, meet with, light upon. *Also*, to find *as by search, hence*, find out, discover.

2. ἀνευρίσκω, *(No.* 1 *with* ἀνά, up, *prefixed,)* to find out *as by searching, (non occ.)*

3. καταλαμβάνω, to take, receive *as with eagerness. Metaph.* to seize *with the mind, and Mid. as here,* to comprehend for one's self, gather, perceive.

1 Matt. i. 18.
1 — ii. 8.
1 — vii. 7, 8, 14.
1. — viii. 10.
1 — x 39 twice.
1. — xi. 29.
1 — xii. 43, 44.
1. — xiii. 44, part., 46, [part.
1. — xvi. 25.
1 — xvii. 27.
1. — xviii. 13, 28.
1. — xx. 6.
1 — xxi. 2, 19.
1 — xxii. 9, 10.
1 — xxiv. 46
1 — xxvi. 40, 43, 60 1st
1 — — 60 2nd (om G L^b T Tr A ℵ.)
1 — xxvii. 32
1 Mark i. 37, part.
— — vii. 2, see fault.
1 — — 30.
1 — xi. 2, 4, 13 twice
1 — xiii. 36.
1 — xiv. 16, 37, 40, 55
1 Luke i. 30
1 — ii. 12,
2. — — 16.
1. — — 45, part., 46.
1 — iv 17
1. — v. 19, part.
1. — vi. 7.
1. — vii. 9, 10
1. — viii. 35
1. — ix. 36.
1. — xi. 9, 10, 24, 25
1. — xii. 37, 38, 43.
1. — xiii. 6, 7
1. — xv. 4, 5, part., 6, 8, 9 twice, 24, 32,
1. — xvii. 18.
1. — xviii. 8.
1. — xix. 30, 32.
— — — 48, see F (can.)
1 — xxii. 13, 45.
1 — xxiii. 2, 4, 14, 22.
1. — xxiv 2, 3, 23, part. 24, 33.
1. John i. 41 twice, 43, 45, twice.
1. — ii. 14
1 — v 14.
1 — vi. 25, part.
1 — vii 34, 35, 36
1 — ix. 35, part
1 — x. 9.
1. — xi. 17.
1 — xii. 14, part
1. — xviii. 38.
1 John xix. 4, 6.
1 — xxi. 6.
1 Acts iv. 21.
1. — v. 10, 22, 23 twice, 39.
1. — vii. 11, 46 twice.
1. — viii. 40.
1. — ix. 2, 33.
1. — x. 27.
1. — xi. 26, part.
1. — xii. 19.
1. — xiii. 6, 22, 28, part.
1. — xvii. 6, 23, 27
1. — xviii. 2.
1. — xix. 1, 19.
1. — xxi. 2.
2. — — 4.
1. — xxiii. 9.
1. — xxiv 5, 12, 18, 20
3. — xxv 25, part.
1. — xxvii. 6, 28 twice.
1 — xxviii. 14.
1 Rom. iv 1.
1 — vii 10
1 — — 18 (om *G ~ L T Tr A ℵ.)
1 — — 21.
— — ix 19, see fault.
1 — x 20.
— — xi. 33. see F out. (past.)
1. 1 Cor iv 2.
1. — xv 15.
1. 2 Cor. ii. 13.
1. — v. 3.
— — vii. 14, see F (be.
1. — ix. 4.
1. — xi. 12.
1. — xii. 20 twice.
1. Gal. ii. 17.
1. Phil. ii. 8.
1. — iii. 9.
1. 2 Tim. i. 17, 18
1. Heb. iv. 16.
— — viii. 8, see fault
1. — xi. 5.
1 — xii 17
1. 1 Pet. i. 7.
1. — ii. 22.
1. 2 Pet. iii 14
1. 2 John 4.
1. Rev ii. 2
1. — iii 2
1. — v. 4
1. — ix. 6
1. — xii 8.
1. — xiv 5
1 — xvi. 20.
1 — xviii. 14, 21 22, 24.
1. — xx. 11, 15.

*The *how* must be omitted and the word "is" supplied before "not" Thus, "to perform that which is good is not (present.)"

FIND (CAN.)

1. Luke xix. 48.

FOUND (BE.)

γίνομαι, to begin to be, become, became.

2. Cor. vii. 14.

FINDING OUT (PAST.)

ἀνεξιχνίαστος, which cannot be explored. *Metaph.* inscrutable, untraceable, *(occ.* Eph. iii. 8.)

Rom. xi. 33.

FINE.

See, BRASS, FLOUR, LINEN.

FINGER (-S.)

δάκτυλος, a finger, *(from Sans. root,* diç, to show, point out, *hence, Greek,* δείκω *and* δείκνυμι, *and Lat.* digitus, *and* in-dic-are), *(non occ.)*

Matt. xxiii. 4.
Mark vii. 33.
Luke xi. 20, 46.
Luke xvi. 24.
John viii. 6 (*ap.*)
—— xx. 25, 27.

FINISH (-ED.)

1. τελέω, to bring about, complete, fulfil, accomplish; *hence,* to end, to perfect.
2. ἀποτελέω, *(No.* 1 *with* ἀπό, away from *prefixed,)* to finish off, to perfect. *In N.T. pass.* to be perfected, completed, *(non occ.)*
3. ἐκτελέω, *(No.* 1 *with* ἐκ, out of, *prefixed,)* to finish out *or* off, complete fully, *(non occ.)*
4. ἐπιτελέω, *(No.* 1 *with* ἐπί, upon, *prefixed,)* to bring through to an end, finish, perform.
5. συντελέω, *(No.* 1 *with* σύν, together with, *prefixed,)* to bring to one end *or* terminate together; to end altogether, end fully, finish wholly, bring quite to an end.
6. τελειόω, to make perfect, consummate. *(The word is used of* inaugurating as king, to confirm in the kingdom, *and so,* of the consummation of the martyrs and glorification of the saints.)
7. { τὰ, the *things,* πρὸς, towards *or* for, ἀπαρτισμόν, completion, } the *things or resources necessary* for completion *(non occ.)*
8. διανύω, to bring quite through to an end, complete, *(non occ.)*

1. Matt. xiii. 53.
1. —— xix. 1.
1. —— xxvi. 1.
7. Luke xiv. 28 (εἰς, *unto,* instead of τὰ πρὸς, G T Tr A ℵ) (τὰ εἰς, *the things unto,* L G ~.)
3. —— 29, 30.
6. John iv. 34.
6. —— v. 36.
6. —— xvii. 4.
1. —— xix. 30.
1. Acts xx. 24.
8. —— xxi. 7, part.
5. Rom. ix. 28.
4. 2 Cor. viii. 6.
4. Phil. i. 6, marg. (text, *perform.*)
1. 2 Tim. iv. 7.
— Heb. iv. 3, see F (be.)
2. Jas. i. 15, part.
1. Rev. x. 7.
1. —— xi. 7.
1. —— xx. 5.
1. Rev. xx. 7, marg. *to expire.*

FINISHED (BE.)

γίνομαι, to begin to be, to come into existence.

Heb. iv. 3.

FINISHER.

τελειωτής, a completer, a perfecter, who brings one through to the goal so as to win and receive the prize, *(non occ.)*

Heb. xii. 2.

FIRE.

1. πῦρ, fire, *(low Germ.* für; *high Germ.* feuer; *Eng.* fire.)
2. πυρά, any spot where fire is kindled; *esp.* a heap of fuel collected to be set on fire *or* actually burning; *hence,* a fire *in this sense,* a pyre, pyra, *(non occ.)*
3. φῶς, light, *prop.* the light of the sun, *with the idea of shining, brightness, used as below of* fire-light.

1. Matt. iii. 10.
1. —— 11 (*om.* G →.)
1. —— 12.
1. —— v. 22.
1. —— vii. 19.
1. —— xiii. 40, 42, 50.
1. —— xvii. 15.
1. —— xviii. 8, 9.
1. —— xxv. 41.
1. Mark ix. 22, 43 (*ap.*), 44 (*ap.*), 45 (*ap.*), 46 (*ap.*)
1. —— 47 (*om.* G → L T Tr A ℵ.)
1. —— 48, 49.
3. —— xiv. 54.
1. Luke iii. 9, 16, 17.
1. —— ix. 54.
1. —— xii. 49.
1. —— xvii. 29.
1. —— xxii. 55.
3. —— 56.
1. John xv. 6.
— —— xviii. 18, } see
— —— xxi. 9, } coals.
1. Acts ii. 3, 19.
1. —— vii. 30.
2. —— xxviii. 2, 3.
1. —— 5.
1. Rom. xii. 20.
1. 1 Cor. iii. 13 twice, 15.
1. 2 Thes. i. 8.
1. Heb. i. 7.
1. —— xi. 34.
1. —— xii. 18, 29.
1. Jas. iii. 5, 6 1st.
— —— 6 twice, see F (set on.)
1. —— v. 3.
1. 1 Pet. i. 7.
1. 2 Pet. iii. 7.
— —— 12, see F (be on)
1. Jude 7, 23.
1. Rev. i. 14.
1. —— ii. 18.
1. —— iii. 18.
1. —— iv. 5.
1. —— viii. 5, 7.
1. —— 8 (*om.* G ⇄.)
1. —— ix. 17 1st.
— —— 17 2nd, see F (of)
1. —— 18.
1. —— x. 1.
1. —— xi. 5.
1. —— xiii. 13.
1. —— xiv. 10, 18.
1. —— xv. 2.
1. —— xvi. 8.
1. —— xvii. 16.
1. —— xviii. 8.
1. —— xix. 12, 20.
1. —— xx. 9, 10, 14, 15.
1. Rev. xxi. 8.

FIRE (BE ON.)

πυρόομαι, to be set on fire, to be fired.

2 Pet. iii. 12.

FIRE (OF.)

πύρινος, of fire, fiery, *(non occ.)*

Rev. ix. 17.

FIRE (SET ON.)

φλογίζω, to set on blaze, to set in flames, *(non occ.)*

Jas. iii. 6 twice.

See also, HELL.

FIRKIN (-s.)

μετρητής, one who measures *or* values. *Then, like* ἀμφορεύς, *(Lat.* metreta.) *At Athens the usual liquid measure containing* 33½ English quarts *or* 8⅜ English gallons. (Eng "firkin" equal to 9 gallons), *(non occ.)*

John ii. 6.

FIRM.

βέβαιος, steadfast, firm, sure.

Heb. iii. 6 *(ap.)*

FIRST.

1. πρῶτος, *(adj. as though the superlative of* πρό, before,) foremost, *hence,* first, the first, *of place, order, time, or dignity, (like Lat.* primus.)
2. πρῶτον *or* τὸ πρῶτον, *(neut. sing. of No.* 1, *used as adv.)* first, *(like Lat.* primum,) *used of place, order, time, or rank.*
3. πρότερον, *(a comp. without any posit. in use, answering to Lat.* prior, *and No.*1 *being the superl.)* before others, prior.
4. μία, *(fem. of* εἷς), *the numeral* one.
5. ἀρχή, beginning, commencement.

— Matt. i. 25, see F born.
2. —— v. 24.
2. —— vi. 33.
2. —— vii. 5.
2. —— viii. 21.
1. —— x. 2.
2. —— xii. 29.
1. ——— 45.
2. Matt. xiii. 30.
2. —— xvii. 10.
2. ——— 11 (*om.* G ⇉ L T Tr A ℵ.)
1. ——— 27.
1. —— xix. 30 twice.
1. —— xx. 8, 10, 16 twice.
1. —— xxi. 28.
1. Matt. xxi. 31 (ὁ ὕστερος, he *who* afterwards [*repented,* referring to v. 29] L Tr.)
1. ——— 36.
1. —— xxii. 25, 38.
2. —— xxiii. 26.
— —— xxvi. 17, see F day.
1. —— xxvii. 64.
— —— xxviii. 1, see F day.
2. Mark iii. 27.
2. —— iv. 28.
2. —— vii. 27.
2. —— ix. 11, 12.
1. ——— 35.
— —— x. 31 1st, see F (be.)
1. ——— 31 2nd.
1. —— xii. 20, 28, 29, 30 (*ap.*)
2. —— xiii. 10.
1. —— xiv. 12.
— —— xvi. 2, } see F
— —— xvi. 9 1st, } day.
2. ——— 9 2nd (*ap.*)
— Luke i. 3, see F.. (from the very.)
1. —— ii. 2.
— ——— 7, see F born.
— —— vi. 1, see second.
2. ——— 42.
2. —— ix. 59, 61.
2. —— x. 5.
1. —— xi. 26.
2. ——— 38.
— —— xii. 1, see F of all.
1. —— xiii. 30 twice.
1. —— xiv. 18.
2. ——— 28, 31.
1. —— xvi. 5.
2. —— xvii. 25.
1. —— xix. 16.
1. —— xx. 29.
2. —— xxi. 9.
— —— xxiv. 1, see F day.
1. John i. 42 (No. 2, L Tr.)
1. —— v. 4 (*ap.*)
1. —— viii. 7 (*ap.*)
— —— x. 40, see F (at.)
— —— xii. 16, see F (at the.)
2. —— xviii. 13.
1. —— xix. 32.
— ——— 39, see F (at the)
— —— xx. 1, see F day.
1. ——— 4, 8.
— ——— 19, see F day.
2. Acts iii. 26.
2. —— vii. 12.
2. —— xi. 26.
1. —— xii. 10.
— —— xiii. 24, see preach.
2. ——— 46.
— —— xv. 14, see F (at the.)
1. —— xvi. 12, marg. (text, *chief.*)
— —— xx. 7, see F day.
1. ——— 18.
— —— xxvi. 4, see F (at the.)
2. ——— 20.
1. Acts xxvi. 23.
1. —— xxvii. 43.
2. Rom. i. 8.
2. ——— 16 (*om.* Lb.)
3. —— ii. 9, 10.
— —— viii. 23, see F fruits.
— ——— 29, see F born.
1. —— x. 19.
— —— xi. 16, see F fruits.
— ——— 35, see give.
2. —— xv. 24.
— —— xvi. 5, see F fruits.
— 1 Cor. xi. 18, see F of all.
2. —— xii. 28.
1. —— xiv. 30.
— —— xv. 3, see F of all.
— ——— 20, 23, see F fruits.
1. ——— 45, 47.
2. ——— 46.
4. —— xvi. 2.
— ——— 15, see F fruits.
2. 2 Cor. viii. 5.
— ——— 12, see F (be.)
— Gal. iv. 13, see F (at the.)
— Eph. i. 12, see trust.
2. —— iv. 9 (*om.* G L T Tr [A ℵ.)
1. —— vi. 2.
1. Phil. i. 5.
— Col. i. 15, 18, see F born.
2. 1 Thes. iv. 16.
2. 2 Thes. ii. 3.
1. 1 Tim. i. 16.
2. —— ii. 1.
1. ——— 13.
2. —— iii. 10.
2. —— v. 4.
1. ——— 12.
2. 2 Tim. i. 5.
2. —— ii. 6.
1. —— iv. 16.
4. Titus iii. 10.
— Heb. i. 6, see F begotten.
— —— ii. 3, see begin.
3. —— iv. 6.
5. —— v. 12.
2. —— vii. 2.
3. ——— 27.
1. —— viii. 7, 13.
1. —— ix. 1, 2, 6, 8, 15, 18.
1. —— x. 9.
— —— xi. 28, } see F
— —— xii. 23, } born.
— Jas. i. 18, see F fruit.
2. —— iii. 17.
— 1 Pet. iv. 17, see begin.
2. 2 Pet. i. 20.
2. —— iii. 3.
1. 1 John iv. 19.
— Jude 6, see F estate.
— Rev. i. 5, see F begotten.
1. ——— 11 (*ap.*), 17.
1. —— ii. 4, 5, 8, 19.
1. —— iv. 1, 7.
1. —— viii. 7.
1. —— xiii. 12 twice.
— —— xiv. 4, see F fruits.
1. —— xvi. 2.
1. —— xx. 5, 6.
1. —— xxi. 1 twice, 10.
1. —— xxii. 13.

FIRST AT.

2. John x. 40.

FIRST (AT THE.)

2. John xii. 16.
2. —— xix. 39.
2. Acts xv. 14.
5. Acts xxvi. 4, with ἀπό, *from.*
3. Gal. iv. 13.

FIRST (BE.)

1. πρῶτος, *see* "FIRST," *No.* 1.

2. *πρόκειμαι*, to lie before, to be laid *or* set before *any one;* to lie *or* be before *the mind of any one, i.e.* to be present *to him.*

1. Mark x. 31, pl. "are." | 2. 2 Cor. viii. 12.

FIRST DAY.

1. *πρῶτος, see* "FIRST," *No.* 1.
2. *μία, see* "FIRST," *No.* 4.

1. Matt. xxvi. 17. | 1. Mark xvi. 9 (*ap.*)
2. —— xxviii. 1. | 2. Luke xxiv. 1.
2. Mark xvi. 2. | 2. John xx. 1, 19.
2. Acts xx. 7.

FIRST ESTATE.

ἀρχή, see "FIRST," *No.* 5.

Jude 6, marg. *principality.*

FIRST (FROM THE VERY.)

ἄνωθεν, of place, from above; *of time,* from the first, from the beginning.

Luke i. 3.

FIRST OF ALL.

1. *πρῶτον, see* "FIRST," *No.* 2.
2. { *ἐν*, among, *πρώτοις*, first *matters.* }

1. Luke xii. 1. | 1. 1 Cor. xi. 18.
2. 1 Cor. xv. 3.

FIRST BEGOTTEN.

πρωτότοκος, first-born, *(non occ.)*

Heb. i. 6. | Rev. i. 5.

FIRST BORN.

Matt. i. 25 (*om.* L T Tr A [ℵ.]) | Col. i. 15, 18.
Luke ii. 7. | Heb. xi. 28.
Rom. viii. 29. | —— xii. 23.

FIRST FRUIT (-S.)

ἀπαρχή, an offering of first-fruits; *then,* an offering *generally. In N.T. pl.,* the first-fruits which were consecrated to God, *(non occ.)*

Rom. viii. 23. | 1 Cor. xv. 20, 23.
—— xi. 16, sing. | —— xvi. 15.
—— xvi. 5. | Jas. i. 18.
Rev. xiv. 4.

FISH (-ES) [noun.]

1. *ἰχθύς*, a fish, *(from ἴκω,* to go, *and θύω,* to rush impetuously), *(non occ.)*
2. *ὀψάριον*, a little fish, *(dim. of ὄψον,* whatever is eaten with bread, *which later came to be applied particularly to* fish), *(non occ.)*

1. Matt. vii. 10. | 1. Luke xi. 11 twice.
1. —— xiv. 17, 19. | 1. —— xxiv. 42.
— —— xv. 34, see F (little.) | — John vi. 9, see F (small.)
1. —— 36. | 2. —— 11.
1. —— xvii. 27. | 1. —— xxi. 6, 8.
1. Mark vi. 38, 41 twice, 43. | 2. —— 9, 10.
— —— viii. 7, see F (small.) | 1. —— 11.
1. Luke v. 6, 9. | 2. —— 13.
1. —— ix. 13, 16. | 1. 1 Cor. xv. 39.

FISH (LITTLE.)

ἰχθύδιον, dim. of No. 1 *above, in form, but perhaps not in meaning.*

Matt. xv. 34.

FISH (SMALL.)

1. *ἰχθύδιον, see* "FISH (LITTLE.)"
2. *ὀψάριον, see* "FISH," *No.* 2.

1. Mark viii. 7. | 2. John vi. 9.

FISHER (-S.)

ἁλιεύς, a fisher, fisherman, *(from ἅλς,* the sea.)

Matt. iv. 18, 19. | Mark i. 16, 17.
John xxi. 7, see coat.

FISHERMAN (-MEN.)

Luke v. 2.

FISHING (A.)

ἁλιεύω, to fish, catch fish.

John xxi. 3, inf.

FIT [adj.]

1. *εὔθετος*, well-situated, convenient, *(occ.* Heb. vi. 7.)
2. *καθήκω*, to come *or* reach down to. *In N.T. impers.* to suffice, be enough for *a thing,* it is becoming, fit, proper, *(occ.* Rom. i. 28.)

1. Luke ix. 62. | 2. Acts xxii. 22, part.
1. —— xiv. 35. | (ind. G T Tr A ℵ.)

FIT (-ED) [verb.]

καταρτίζω, to make fully ready, to put in full order, to make complete, *esp. of what is broken, hence,* to refit, repair.

Rom. ix. 22, marg. *make up.*
Heb. x. 5, marg. (text, *prepare.*)

FIT (BE.)

ἀνήκω, **to have come up to** *anything*, **to extend to,** *hence*, **to pertain to, to be fit** *or* **becoming,** (*occ.* Eph. v. 4; Philem. 8.)

Col. iii. 18.

FITLY.

See, FRAME, JOIN.

FIVE.

πέντε, five, (*prob. from* πᾶς, παντός, all, *i.e., all the fingers on the hand.*) See under "THREE," *for spiritual signification.*

Matt. xiv. 17, 19.
—— xvi. 9.
—— xxv. 2 twice, 15, 16 twice, 20 4 times.
Mark vi. 38, 41.
—— viii. 19.
Luke i. 24.
—— ix. 13, 16.
—— xii. 6, 52.
—— xvi. 28.
Luke xix. 18, 19.
John iv. 18.
—— v. 2.
—— vi. 9, 13, 19.
Acts iv. 4.
—— xx. 6.
—— xxiv. 1.
1 Cor. xiv. 19.
2 Cor. xi. 24, see F times.
Rev. ix. 5, 10.
Rev. xvii. 10.

FIVE TIMES.

πεντάκις, five times.

2 Cor. xi. 24.

See also, HUNDRED, THOUSAND.

FIX (-ED.)

στηρίζω, to set fast, steadfast, fix firmly.

Luke xvi. 26.

FLAME.

φλόξ, a flame, blaze, any bright blazing fire.

Luke xvi. 24.
Acts vii. 30.
Heb. i. 7.
Rev. i. 14.
—— ii. 18.
—— xix. 12.

FLAMING.

2 Thes. i. 8, genitive.

FLATTERING.

κολακεία, flattery, adulation (*perhaps from* κολλᾶσθαι, to stick to, to hang on *as we say; or, prob. from* חלק, to smooth.)

1 Thes. ii. 5, genitive.

FLAX.

λίνον, flax, *then, what is* made of flax, *as* raiment, *and also*, the wick *of a lamp*, (*Eng.* linen), (*occ.* Rev. xv. 6.)

Matt. xii. 20.

FLEE (-ETH, FLED.)

1. φεύγω, to flee, to fly, to betake one's self to flight, (*Lat.* fuga, fugio; *also Eng.* fugue.)

2. ἐκφεύγω, (*No.* 1 *with* ἐκ, out of, *prefixed,*) to flee out of, escape.

3. καταφεύγω, (*No.* 1 *with* κατά, down, *prefixed,*) to flee down *to any place, hence,* to flee for refuge, (*non occ.*)

1. Matt. ii. 13.
1. —— iii. 7.
1. —— viii. 33.
1. —— x. 23.
1. —— xxiv. 16.
1. —— xxvi. 56.
1. Mark v. 14.
1. —— xiii. 14.
1. —— xiv. 50, 52.
1. —— xvi. 8.
1. Luke iii. 7.
1. —— viii. 34.
1. —— xxi. 21.
1. John x. 5, 12, 13 (*ap.*)
1. Acts vii. 29.
3. —— xiv. 6.
2. —— xvi. 27.
1. —— xvii. 30.
2. —— xix. 16 (with ἐκ, *out of.*)
1. 1 Cor. vi. 18.
1. —— x. 14.
1. 1 Tim. vi. 11.
1. 2 Tim. ii. 22.
— Heb. vi. 18, see F for refuge.
1. Jas. iv. 7.
1. Rev. ix. 6.
1. —— xii. 6.

FLEE AWAY.

1. Rev. xvi. 20.
1. Rev. xx. 11.

FLEE FOR REFUGE.

3. Heb. vi. 18.

FLESH.

1. σάρξ, flesh; *then,* corporeity according to its material side, (σῶμα, *being the organic whole,* the body, *and therefore is to be distinguished from it*); *then,* the outward form of human nature, *and therefore* human nature *in its embodiment. As used by St. Paul, all that is peculiar to human nature in its corporeal embodiment is said to belong to it; and hence, he uses it as the distinct antithesis to* πνεῦμα, (spirit), *to signify* the sinful condition of human nature, (*occ.* Rom. viii. 6, 7; Col. ii. 18; Heb. ix. 10)

2. κρέας, flesh, dead-meat, (*non occ.*)

1. Matt. xvi. 17.
1. —— xix. 5, 6.
1. —— xxiv. 22.
1. —— xxvi. 41.
1. Mark x. 8 twice.
1. —— xiii. 20.
1. —— xiv. 38.
1. Luke iii. 6.
1. —— xxiv. 39.
1. John i. 13, 14.
1. —— iii. 6 twice.
1. —— vi. 51, 52, 53, 54, 55, 56, 63.
1. —— viii. 15.
1. —— xvii. 2.
1. Acts ii. 17, 26, 30 (*ap.*), 31.
1. Rom. i. 3.
1. —— ii. 28.
1. —— iii. 20.
1. —— iv. 1.
1. —— vi. 19.
1. —— vii. 5, 18, 25.
1. —— viii. 1 (*ap.*), 3 3 times, 4, 5 twice, 8, 9, 12 twice, 13.
1. —— ix. 3, 5, 8.
1. —— xi. 14.
1. —— xiii. 14.
2. —— xiv. 21.
1. 1 Cor. i. 26, 29.
1. —— v. 5.
1. —— vi. 16.
1. —— vii. 28.
2. —— viii. 13.

1. 1 Cor. x. 18.
1. —— xv. 39 1st & 2nd.
1. —— 39 3rd (*om.* G L T Tr A ℵ.)
1. —— 39 4th (*om.* G→.)
1. —— 50.
1. 2 Cor. i. 17.
1. —— iv. 11.
1. —— v. 16 twice.
1. —— vii. 1, 5.
1. —— x. 2, 3 twice.
1. —— xi. 18.
1. —— xii. 7.
1. Gal. i. 16.
1. —— ii. 16, 20.
1. —— iii. 3.
1. —— iv. 13, 14, 23, 29.
1. —— v. 13, 16, 17 twice, 19, 24.
1. —— vi. 8 twice, 12, 13.
1. Eph. ii. 3 twice, 11 twice, 15.
1. —— v. 29, 30 (*ap.*), 31.
1. —— vi. 5, 12
1. Phil. i. 22, 24.
1. —— iii. 3, 4 twice.
1. Col. i. 22, 24.
1. —— ii. 1, 5, 11, 13, 23.
1. —— iii. 22.
1. 1 Tim. iii. 16.
1. Philem. 16.
1. Heb. ii. 14.
1. —— v. 7.
1. —— ix. 13.
1. —— x. 20.
1. —— xii. 9.
1. Jas. v. 3.
1. 1 Pet. i. 24.
1. —— iii. 18, 21.
1. —— iv. 1 twice 2. 6.
1. 2 Pet. ii. 10, 18.
1. 1 John ii. 16.
1. —— iv. 2, 3 (*ap.*)
1. 2 John 7.
1. Jude 7, 8, 23.
1. Rev. xvii. 16.
1. —— xix. 18 5 times, 21.

FLESHLY.

1. σάρξ, *(here the Gen. of No.* 1 *above.)*
2. σαρκικός, fleshly, distinctive of the flesh, what attaches to the flesh in its corporeity, *(more abstract, and not so gross in its idea as σάρκινος, which denotes* of flesh, fleshy; *see below.)*

2. 2 Cor. i. 12. | 2. 1 Pet. ii. 11. | 1. Col. ii. 18.

FLESHY.

σάρκινος, of flesh, fleshy, made of the material substance σάρξ. *Our Lord was σάρκινος, "of human flesh subsisting;" but not, σαρκικός, as other men,* subject to fleshly lusts and appetites, *(non occ.)*

2 Cor iii. 3.

FLIGHT.

φυγή, flight, *(hence, Eng.* fugue, fugitive, *Lat.* fuga), *(non occ.)*

Matt. xxiv. 20.
Mark xiii. 18 (*om.* G ≍ L T Tr A ℵ.)
Heb. xi. 34, see turn.

FLOCK.

1. ποίμνη, a flock, *esp. of sheep; but metaph. also of men, (occ.* John x. 16, *where it is wrongly rendered "fold.")*
2. ποίμνιον, *(prob. dim. of No.* 1 *being contraction of* ποιμένιον,) a little flock, *(non occ.)*

1. Matt. xxvi. 31.
1. Luke ii. 8.
2. —— xii. 32.
2. Acts xx. 28, 29.
1. 1 Cor. ix. 7 twice.
2. 1 Pet. v. 2, 3.

FLOOD (-S.)

1. κατακλυσμός, dashing down upon, an inundation, deluge, *spoken of Noah's flood, (non occ.)*
2. πλήμμυρα, flood-tide, the flow of the sea, *as opp. to the ebb; then, by implication* any flood, *(non occ.)*
3. ποταμός, a river, stream, *(from* ποτάζω, to flow.)

3. Matt. vii. 25, 27.
1. —— xxiv. 38, 39.
2. Luke vi. 48.
1. —— xvii. 27.
1. 2 Pet. ii. 5.
3. Rev. xii. 15 1st.
— —— 15 2nd, see below.
3. —— 16.

FLOOD (CARRIED AWAY OF THE.)

ποταμοφόρητος, borne *or* carried away by a river *or* flood, *(non occ.)*

Rev. xii. 15.

FLOOR.

ἅλων, a threshing-floor, *where corn is trodden out, (non occ.)*

Matt. iii. 12. | Luke iii. 17.

FLOUR (FINE.)

σεμίδαλις, the finest wheaten flour; *Lat.* simila, similago, *(non occ.)*

Rev. xviii. 13.

FLOURISH AGAIN.

ἀναθάλλω, to shoot up again, sprout, *(non occ.)*

Phil. iv. 10, marg. *be revived.*

FLOW.

ῥέω, to flow, *(non occ.)*

John vii. 38.

FLOWER.

ἄνθος, a flower, *(non occ.)*

Jas. i. 10, 11. | 1 Pet. i. 24 twice.

FLOWER OF ONE'S AGE (PASS THE.)

{ εἰμί, to be, ὑπέρακμος, beyond the point, } past *or* beyond the bloom of youth *or* flower of life.

1 Cor. vii. 36.

FLUX (BLOODY.)

δυσεντερία, dysentery, *(non occ.)*

Acts xxviii. 8.

FLY (-ING.)

1. πετάομαι, *(a later form of No. 2,)* to spread the wings to fly, *hence, gen.* to fly, *(non occ.)*
2. πέτομαι, *same meaning, (non occ.)*

1. Rev. iv. 7 (No. 2, G L T Tr A ℵ.).
1. —— viii. 13 (No. 2, G L T Tr A ℵ.)
2 Rev. xii. 14.
1. —— xiv. 6 (No. 2, G L T Tr A ℵ.)
1. —— xix. 17 (No. 2, G L T Tr A ℵ.)

FOAL.

υἱός, a son, *(strictly spoken only of man but, also sometimes in a wider sense.*

Matt. xxi. 5.

FOAM (-ETH, -ING.)

ἀφρίζω, to froth, to foam *at the mouth, (non occ.)*

Mark ix. 18, 20.

FOAM OUT.

ἐπαφρίζω, *(the above with* ἐπί, upon, *prefixed,)* to foam upon, to foam out, *(non occ.)*

Jude 13.

FOAMETH AGAIN (THAT ONE.)

{ μετά, with,
{ ἀφροῦ, foam.

Luke ix. 39

FOE (-S.)

ἐχθρός, *(adj.) Pass.* hated, odious, object of enmity. *Act.* inimical, hostile. *As subst. with art.* an enemy, adversary; *(elsewhere,* "enemy.")

Matt. x. 36. | Acts ii 35.

FOLD [noun.]

1. αὐλή, a court, a yard, any enclosed space in the open air, *hence,* the court of an oriental house, *and also,* a sheep-fold.
2. ποίμνη, a flock, *esp. of sheep.*

— John x. 1 see sheep-fold.
1. John x. 16 1st.
2. John x. 16 2nd.

FOLD UP.

ἑλίσσω, to roll up, fold up, *as a garment to be laid away, (occ.* Rev. vi. 14.)

Heb. i. 12.

FOLK.

See, IMPOTENT, SICK.

FOLLOW.

1. ἀκολουθέω, to be an ἀκόλουθος (following, attending, *hence, as subst.* a follower, footman), to follow one, go with *or* after *him. Used esp. of soldiers, servants, and pupils, (occ.* Rev. xviii. 5.)
2. ἐξακολουθέω, *(No.* 1 *with* ἐκ, out of, *prefixed,)* to follow out.
3. ἐπακολουθέω, *(No.* 1 *with* ἐπί, upon, *prefixed,)* to follow upon, attend upon, accompany.
4. κατακολουθέω, *(No.* 1 *with* κατά down, *prefixed,)* to follow down, *i.e.* to follow closely.
5. παρακολουθέω, *(No.* 1 *with* παρά, beside, *prefixed,)* to follow side by side, to accompany, conform to.
6. συνακολουθέω, *(No.* 1 *with* σύν, together with, *prefixed,)* to follow together with *any one,* to follow with.
7. διώκω, to cause to flee, *hence,* to pursue after *as flying enemies,* pursue *in order to find or overtake; metaph.* to follow earnestly after.
8. μιμέομαι, to mimic, *but in a good sense, i.e.* to imitate, follow *as an example.*
9. γίνομαι, to begin to be, come into existence, come to be, become.
10. { δεῦτε, here! *i.e.* come! come hither! / ὀπίσω, behind, after, } come hither after *me.*
11. { εἰμί, to be, / μετά, after, } *lit.* "*which* is after."

10. Matt. iv. 19.
1. —— 20, 22, 25.
1. —— viii. 1, 10, 19, 22, 23.
1. —— ix. 9 twice, 19, 27.
1 —— x. 38.
1. —— xii. 15.
1. —— xiv. 13.
1. —— xvi. 24.
1. —— xix. 2, 21, 27, 28.
1. —— xx. 29, 34.
1. Matt. xxi. 9.
1. —— xxvi. 58.
1. —— xxvii. 55.
11. —— 62.
1. Mark i. 18.
— —— 36, see F after.
1. —— ii. 14 twice, 15.
1. —— iii. 7 (*om.* G→.)
1. —— v. 24.
6. —— 37 (No. 1, L.)

1. Mark vi. 1.
1. —— viii. 34.
1. —— ix. 38 twice (*ap.*)
1. —— x. 21, 28, 32, part., 52.
1. —— xi. 9.
1. —— xiv. 13.
1. ——— 51 (No. 6, G∾ L T Tr A ℵ.)
1. ——— 54.
1. —— xv. 41.
5. —— xvi. 17 (*ap.*)
3. ———— 20 (*ap.*)
1. Luke v. 11, 27, 28.
1. —— vii. 9.
1. —— ix. 11, 23, 49, 57, 59, 61.
— —— xiii. 33, see following.
7. —— xvii. 23.
1. —— xviii. 22, 28, 43.
1. —— xxii. 10, 39.
— ———— 49, see F (that would.)
1. ———— 54.
1. —— xxiii. 27.
6. ——— 49.
— ——— 55, see F after.
1. John i. 37, 38, 40, 43.
1. —— vi. 2.
— ——— 22, see following
1. —— viii. 12.
1. —— x. 4, 5, 27.
1. —— xi. 31.
1. —— xii. 26.
1. —— xiii. 36 twice, 37.
1. John xviii. 15.
1. —— xx. 6.
1. —— xxi. 19, 20, 22.
— Acts iii. 24, see F after.
1. —— xii. 8, 9.
1. —— xiii. 43.
4. —— xvi. 17.
— —— xxi. 1, 18, see following.
1. ———— 36.
— —— xxiii. 11, see following.
— Rom. ix. 30, 31, } see F
— —— xiv. 19, } after.
1. 1 Cor. x. 4, marg. *go with.*
— —— xiv. 1, } see F
— Phil. iii. 12, } after.
7. 1 Thes. v. 15.
8. 2 Thes. iii. 7, 9.
8. 1 Tim. v. 10.
— ——— 24, } see F
— —— vi. 11, } after.
7. 2 Tim. ii. 22.
7. Heb. xii. 14.
8. —— xiii. 7.
— 1 Pet. i. 11, see F (that should.)
3. —— ii. 21.
2. 2 Pet. i. 16, part.
2. —— ii. 2, 15.
8. 3 John 11.
1. Rev. vi. 8.
9. —— viii. 7.
1. —— xiv. 4, 8, 9, 13.
1. —— xix. 14.

FOLLOW AFTER.

1. ἐπακολουθέω, *see* "FOLLOW," *No.* 3.
2. κατακολουθέω, *see* "FOLLOW," *No.* 4.
3. διώκω, *see* "FOLLOW," *No.* 7.
4. καταδιώκω, *(No.* 3 *with* κατά, down, *prefixed,)* to pursue closely, *as an enemy;* follow closely *in order to find, (non occ.)*
5. καθεξῆς, according to the order *or* succession, *i.e.* successively, consecutively, in connected order. * *With art.*

4. Mark i. 36.
2. Luke xxiii. 55.
5. Acts iii. 24.
3. Rom. ix. 30, 31.
3. Rom. xiv. 19.
3. 1 Cor. xiv. 1.
3. Phil. iii. 12.
1. 1 Tim. v. 24.
3. 1 Tim. vi. 11.

FOLLOW (THAT SHOULD.)

{ μετά, after,
{ ταῦτα, these *things.*

1 Pet. i. 11.

FOLLOW (WHAT SHOULD.)

{ τὸ, the *thing,*
{ ἐσόμενον, about to be.

Luke xxii. 49.

FOLLOWER.

μιμητής, an imitator.

1 Cor. iv. 16.
—— xi. 1.
Eph. v. 1.
Phil. iii. 17, see F together
1 Thes. i. 6.
—— ii. 14.
2 Tim. iii. 10, see *F of (be a diligent.)*
Heb. vi. 12.
1 Pet. iii 13 (ζηλωτής, *emulous of,* G∾ L T Tr A ℵ.)

FOLLOWER OF (be a diligent) [margin.]

παρακολουθέω, *see* "FOLLOW," *No.* 5.

2 Tim. iii. 10, text, *know fully.*

FOLLOWER TOGETHER.

συμμιμητής, a co-imitator, joint-imitator.

Phil. iii. 17.

FOLLOWING.

ἐπιών, coming upon *or* over one; *of time,* succeeding.

Acts xxiii. 11.

FOLLOWING (THE DAY.)

1. { τῇ, the, ἐπιών, coming upon, } *with* ἡμέρα, day, *understood,* the succeeding *or* coming day.
2. { τῇ, the, ἐπαύριον, upon the morrow, } the morrow.
3. { τῇ, the, ἑξῆς, in order, next in order, } the *day* next in order.
4. { τῇ, the, ἐχομένῃ, *Mid. part.* near to, next, } the next *day.*

4. Luke xiii. 33.
2. John i. 44.
2. John vi. 22.
3. Acts xxi. 1.
1. Acts xxi. 18.

FOLLY.

1. ἄνοια, without understanding *or* sense (νοῦς), folly, *(occ.* Luke vi. 11.)
2. ἀφροσύνη, without mind (φρήν), destitute of any sound principle, senselessness.

2. 2 Cor. xi. 1.
1. 2 Tim. iii. 9.

FOOD.

1. τροφή, nourishment, sustinence.
2. διατροφή, *(No.* 1 *strengthened by* διά, through,) sustinence, support, *(non occ.)*

3. *βρῶσις*, eating, the act of eating.

1. Acts xiv. 17.
3. 2 Cor. ix. 10.
2. 1 Tim. vi. 8.
1. Jas. ii. 15.

FOOL (-s.)

1. *μωρός*, dull, not acute; *of the mind*, dull, slow, *(Sans.* muhera, fool, *from Root*, muh, to be silly), (lxx. *for* נבל, Deut. xxxii. 6; Is. xxxii. 5, 6; כסיל, Ps. xciv. 8.)

2. *ἄφρων*, without mind (*φρήν*), senseless, destitute of any sound principle.

3. *ἄσοφος*, without wisdom (*σοφός*), *(non occ.)*

4. *ἀνόητος*, unreflecting, never applying the *νοῦς* (mind) *to moral or religious truth.*

1. Matt. v. 22.
1. —— xxiii. 17.
1. ———— 19 (*om.* G→ L[b] T Tr A ℵ.)
2. Luke xi. 40.
2. —— xii. 20.
4. —— xxiv. 25. [come a.)
— Rom. i. 22, see F (be-
1. 1 Cor. iii. 18.
1. —— iv. 10.
2. —— xv. 36.
2. 2 Cor. xi. 16 twice, 19.
— ——— 23, see F (as a.)
2. —— xii. 6, 11.
3. Eph. v. 15.
— 1 Tim. vi. 4, see *F* (*be a.*)

FOOL (AS A.)

παραφρονέω, to be aside from a right mind, deranged, *(non occ.)*

2 Cor. xi. 23, part.

FOOL (be a) [margin.]

τυφόω, to smoke, fume, surround with smoke, becloud.

1 Tim. vi. 4 (pass.) text, *be proud.*

FOOL (BECOME A.)

μωραίνω, to make dull, make foolish.

Rom. i. 22, pass.

FOOLISH.

1. *μωρός*, *see* "FOOL," *No.* 1.
2. *ἀνόητος*, *see* "FOOL," *No.* 4.
3. *ἀσύνετος*, irrational in conduct, stupid.
4. *ἄφρων*, *see* "FOOL," *No.* 2.

1. Matt. vii. 26.
1. —— xxv. 2, 3, 8.
3. Rom. i. 21.
4. —— ii. 20.
3. —— x. 19.
— 1 Cor. i. 27, see F(make)
— ——— 27, see F thing.
2. Gal. iii. 1, 3.
-- Eph. v. 4, see F talking
2. 1 Tim. vi. 9.
1. 2 Tim. ii. 23.
2. Tit. iii. 3.
1. —— — 9.
4. 1 Pet. ii. 15.

FOOLISH (MAKE.)

μωραίνω, to make dull *or* foolish.

1 Cor. i. 20.

FOOLISH TALKING.

μωρολογία, foolish talking, *(non occ.)*

Eph. v. 4.

FOOLISH THING.

μωρός, *see* "FOOL," *No.* 1.

1 Cor. i. 27, neut.

FOOLISHLY.

{ *ἐν*, in, *ἀφροσύνη*, *see* "FOLLY," *No.* 2, } in folly, in imprudence.

2 Cor. xi. 17, 21.

FOOLISHNESS.

1. *μωρός*, *see* "FOOL," *No.* 1.
2. *μωρία*, folly, foolishness, absurdity.
3. *ἀφροσύνη*, *see* "FOLLY," *No.* 2.

3. Mark vii. 22.
2. 1 Cor. i. 18, 21, 23.
2. 1 Cor. i. 25, neut.
2. —— ii. 14.
2. 1 Cor. iii. 19.

FOOT, FEET.

1. *πούς*, the foot *both of men and beasts, strictly* the foot from the ankle downwards. *(Sanscr.* pad; *hence, Lat.* pes, pedis; *Eng.* pad, foot; *Germ.* fuss), *(non occ.)*

2. *βάσις*, a stepping, power to step *or* walk; *then*, that with which one steps, a foot; *also*, that on which one steps; *hence, Eng.* basis, *(non occ.)*

1. Matt. iv. 6.
— —— v. 13, see tread.
1. —— vii. 6.
1. —— x. 14.
— —— xiv. 13, see F (on.)
1. —— xv. 30.
1. —— xviii. 8 twice.
1. —— xviii. 29 (*om.* "at his feet," G L T Tr ℵ.)
1. —— xxii. 13.
1. —— xxviii. 9.
1. Mark v. 22.
1. —— vi. 11.
1. —— vii. 25.
1. —— ix. 45 twice.
1. Luke i. 79.
1. —— iv. 11.
1. —— vii. 38 3 times, 44 twice,
1. ——— 46 (*om.* G→.) [45.
1. Luke viii. 35, 41.
1. —— ix. 5.
1. —— x. 39.
1. —— xv. 22.
1. —— xvii. 16.
1. —— xxiv. 39, 40 (*ap.*)
1. John xi. 2, 32, 44.
1. —— xii. 3 twice.
1. —— xiii. 5, 6, 8, 9.
1. ——— 10 (*om.* G→T ℵ.)
1. ——— 12, 14 twice.
1. —— xx. 12.
2. Acts iii. 7.
1. —— iv. 35, 37.
1. —— v. 2, 9, 10.
1. —— vii. 5, see F on (set one's.)
1. ——— 33, 58.
1. —— x. 25.

1. Acts xiii. 25, 51.	— Heb. x. 29, see tread.
1. —— xiv. 8, 10.	1. —— xii. 13.
1. —— xvi. 24.	— Rev. i. 13, see F (garment down to the.)
1. —— xxi. 11.	1. —— 15, 17.
1. —— xxii. 3.	1. —— ii. 18.
1. —— xxvi. 16.	1. —— iii. 9.
1. Rom. iii. 15.	1. —— x. 1, 2 1st.
1. —— x. 15.	—— 2 2nd, see F (left.)
1. —— xvi. 20.	1. —— xi. 2, see tread.
1. 1 Cor. xii. 15, 21.	1. —— 11.
1. —— xv. 25, 27.	1. —— xii. 1.
1. Eph. i. 22.	1. —— xiii. 2.
1. —— vi. 15.	1. —— xix. 10.
1. 1 Tim. v. 10.	1. —— xxii. 8.
1. Heb. ii. 8.	

FOOT (GARMENT DOWN TO THE.)

ποδήρης, reaching down to and touching the feet, *(from* πούς, ποδός, the foot, *and* ἄρω, to fit.) *Used of the High Priests' garment,* Ex. xxviii. 4, *(non occ.)*

Rev. i. 13.

FOOT (ON.)

πεζῇ, *(dat. fem. of* πεζός, on foot, *used as adv.)*, on foot, *but usually,* by land, *(occ.* Mark vi. 33.)

Matt. xiv. 13.

FOOT ON (TO SET ONE'S)

{ βῆμα, a step, ποδός, of a foot, } a foot-breadth, what the foot can stand on.

Acts vii. 5.

FOOTSTOOL.

1. ὑποπόδιον, under-foot, *hence,* footstool.
2. { ὑποπόδιον, footstool, τῶν, of the, ποδῶν, feet, } a footstool of his feet.

2. Matt. v. 35.	2. Luke xx. 43.
2. —— xxii. 44 (ὑποκάτω, τῶν ποδῶν, *under thy feet,* G~ L T Tr A ℵ.)	2. Acts ii. 35.
2. Mark xii. 36.	2. —— vii. 49.
	2. Heb. i. 13.
	2. —— x. 13.

1. Jas. ii. 3.

FOR.

*(When "*for*" is not the translation of a case of the noun or part of another word, it is one of these following.)*

1. εἰς, into, to, unto, with a view to; *hence, with respect to a certain event,* in order to, for.
2. ὑπέρ, over *and separate from; here only with Gen.* on behalf of, *as though bending* over *to protect, (the opposite of No.* 13); *then, as the service rendered* on behalf of *another may often be* in his stead, *it comes to have this meaning, but is less definite than No.* 8.
3. διά, through, *implying separation, and disjunction.*
   (a) *with Gen.* through, by means of, by, *(marking the instrument of the action.)*
   (b) *with Acc.* on account of, owing to, because of, *(marking the ground or reason of the action.)*
4. περί, around *and separate from, here only with Gen.* about, concerning, *marking the object of the thought or discourse.*
5. ἐπί, upon.
   (a) *with Gen.* upon and proceeding from, *as a pillar upon the ground.*
   (b) *with Dat.* upon and resting upon, *marking the basis or foundation, and also the ethical basis, the occasion or cause of an action or emotion, also the moving principle or suggesting motive,* about, for.
   (c) *with Acc.* upon *(with a view to* superposition), *motion* to *marking the intention,* for, against.
6. πρός, towards, in the direction of.
   (a) *with Gen.* hitherwards, belonging to the character of, conducive to.
   (b) *with Dat.* near, hard by.
   (c) *with Acc.* hitherwards *(of literal direction),* to; *then, of mental direction,* towards, against, in consideration of.
7. ἀπό, from *(from the exterior),* from, on account of, *marking the cause or occasion.*
8. ἀντί, over against *(denoting opposition or equivalent),* instead of, for, in return for, *(in* John i. 16, *it denotes grace* in the place of *grace, i.e.* continually renewed.)
9. ἐν, in *(of time, place, or element.)*
10. ἐκ, out of *(opp. to No.* 1), *used of time,* from, the *future springing out of the present* from, for.
11. ἄχρι, *(adv. as prep.)* unto, as far as, until, during.

12. ἕνεκα, *(prep. adv.)* because of, by reason of, on account of.

13. κατά, down, here only *with Acc.* down upon *or* along, over against, according to, *in reference to some standard of comparison.*

14. ὡς, as, like as, as it were.

15. ὅ, the, *here with the Inf. marking the result or purpose.*

16. γάρ, *(a contraction* of γε, verily, *and* ἄρα, therefore, further,) the fact is, in fact, *(having a more extensive meaning than the Eng.* for, *expressing the reason, cause, motive, principle, etc. of what has been previously said.)*

17. { καὶ, and, also, / γάρ, *see No.* 16, } and...in fact, *or,* in fact...also.

18. ὅτι, *introduces that which rests on a patent fact,* that *(used in objective sentences as equivalent to the acc. with inf. and as a particle of explanation,)* because, inasmuch as, seeing that.

19. διότι, *(contraction for* διὰ τοῦτο, ὅτι) wherefore, on this account.

20. ἐπειδή, since truly, inasmuch as.

21. καί, and, also.

22. δέ, *(an adversative and disjunctive particle),* but, now, moreover, *(marking a contrast or antithesis sometimes otherwise concealed.)*

16. Matt. i. 20, 21.
16.—— ii. 2, 5, 6.
4. ——— 8.
16.——— 13, 20.
16.—— iii. 2, 3, 9, 15.
16.—— iv. 6, 10, 17, 18.
18.—— v. 3, 4, 5, 6, 7, 8, 9
— ——— 10 1st, see F..sake
18.——— 10 2nd.
— ——— 11, see F..sake.
18.——— 12 1st.
16.——— 12 2nd.
1. ——— 13.
16.——— 18, 20, 29, 30.
18.——— 34, 35 twice.
8. ——— 38 twice.
2. ——— 44.
18.——— 45.
16.——— 46.
18.—— vi. 5.
16.——— 7 1st.
9. ——— 7 2nd.
16.——— 8.
18.——— 13 *(ap.)*
16.——— 14, 16, 21, 24.
18.——— 26.
4. ——— 28.
16.——— 32 twice.
1. ——— 34 1st.
16.——— 34 2nd.
16.—— vii. 2, 8, 12.
18.——— 13.
16.——— 25, 29.
1. —— viii. 4.

17. Matt. viii. 9.
16.—— ix. 5, 13, 16, 21, 24.
1. —— x. 10 1st.
16.——— 10 2nd.
16.——— 17.
— ——— 18 1st, see F..sake
1. ——— 18 2nd.
16.——— 19 *(ap.)*, 20.
— ——— 22, see F..sake.
16.——— 23 *(om.* G→.)
16.——— 26, 35.
— ——— 39, see F..sake.
16.—— xi. 10 *(om.* Lb T Trb Ab ℵ.)
16.——— 13, 18.
18.——— 21, 23, 26, 29.
16.——— 30.
16.—— xii. 8, 33, 34, 37, 40
18.——— 42.
16.——— 50.
16.—— xiii. 12, 15.
18.——— 16.
16.——— 17.
— ——— 21, see while.
7. ——— 44.
16.—— xiv. 3 1st.
— ——— 3 2nd, see F..sake
16.——— 4.
— ——— 9, see F..sake.
16.——— 24.
7. ——— 26.
16.—— xv. 2, 4, 19.
18.——— 23.
16.—— xvi. 2, 3.

18. Matt. xvi. 17, 23.
16.——— 25 1st.
— ——— 25 2nd, see F..sake
16.——— 26, 27.
18.—— xvii. 15 1st.
16.——— 15 2nd, 20.
8. ——— 27. [20.
16.—— xviii. 7, 10, 11 *(ap.)*,
13.—— xix. 3.
— ——— 5, see F..cause.
5b.——— 9.
16.——— 12 1st.
— ——— 12 2nd, see F..sake
16.——— 14, 22.
— ——— 29, see F..sake.
16.—— xx. 1.
10.——— 2.
16.——— 16 *(ap.)*
8. ——— 28.
16.—— xxi. 26, 32.
14.——— 46 (No. 1, G∾ L T Tr A), see also take.
16.—— xxii. 14.
4. ——— 16 1st.
16.——— 16 2nd, 28, 30.
16.—— xxiii. 3.
16.——— 4 (No. 22, G∾ L T Tr A ℵ.)
— ——— 5, see F to.
16.——— 8, 9.
16.——— 10 (No. 18, G∾ L T Tr A.)
18.——— 13 1st.
16.——— 13 2nd.
18.——— 14 1st.
18.——— 15.
16.——— 17.
18.——— 15.
16.——— 19.
18.——— 23, 25, 27.
16.——— 39.
16.—— xxiv. 5, 6, 7.
— ——— 9, see F..sake.
1. ——— 14.
16.——— 21.
— ——— 22, see F..sake.
16.——— 24, 27.
16.——— 28 *(om.* G→ L T Tr A ℵ.)
16.——— 38.
18.——— 42, 44.
18.—— xxv. 8, 13.
16.——— 14, 29, 35, 42.
16.—— xxvi. 9, 10, 11, 12 1st
6c.——— 12 2nd.
1. ——— 13.
— ——— 15, see covenant.
16.——— 28 1st.
4. ——— 28 2nd.
1. ——— 28 3rd.
16.——— 31, 43, 52.
17.——— 73.
1. —— xxvii. 10.
16.——— 18 1st.
3b.——— 18 2nd.
16.——— 19, 43.
16.—— xxviii. 2.
7. ——— 4.
16.——— 5, 6.
1. Mark i. 4, marg. *unto.*
16.——— 16, 22.
18.——— 27 *(om.* G∾ Tr A)
16.——— 38.
4. ——— 44 1st.
1. ——— 44 2nd.
8b.—— ii. 4.
16.——— 15.
3b.——— 27 twice.
5b.—— iii. 5.
16.——— 10 1st.
— ——— 10 2nd, see F to.
16.——— 21.
16.——— 35 *(om.* L T Trb A.)
— —— iv. 17, see F..sake
16.——— 22, 25.
16.——— 28 *(om.* L T Tr A ℵ)

16. Mark v. 8.
18.——— 9.
16.——— 28, 42.
1. —— vi. 8, 11.
16.——— 14, 17 1st.
— ——— 17 2nd, see F..sake
18.——— 17 3rd.
16.——— 18, 20.
— ——— 26, see F..sake.
16.——— 31.
16.——— 36 *(om.* G∾ Lb Tr A ℵ.)
16.——— 48, 50, 52 1st.
16.——— 52 2nd (ἀλλά, *but,* T Tr ℵ.)
16.—— vii. 3.
16.——— 8 *(om.* L T Tr A ℵ)
16.——— 10, 21.
16.——— 25 (ἀλλά, *but,* T Tr A ℵ.)
16.——— 27.
3b.——— 29.
16.—— viii. 3 (No. 21, L T Tr A ℵ.)
18.——— 33.
16.——— 35 1st.
— ——— 35 2nd, see F..sake
16.——— 36.
16.—— ix. 6 twice, 31, 34, 39, 40, 41, 49.
6c.—— x. 5.
— ——— 7, see F..cause.
16.——— 14, 22, 27 *(ap.)*
16.——— 45 1st.
8. ——— 45 2nd.
16.—— xi. 13, 18.
16.——— 23 *(om.* L T Trb A ℵ.)
16.——— 32.
4. —— xii. 12 1st.
16.——— 12 2nd, 23, 25.
18.——— 32.
16.——— 36 *(om.* Lb T Trb A ℵ.)
16.——— 44.
16.—— xiii. 6 *(om.* T Trbm A ℵ.)
16.——— 7 *(om.* T Trb A ℵ)
16.——— 8.
16.——— 9 1st *(om.* T Trb A)
— ——— 9 2nd, see F..sake
1. ——— 9 3rd.
16.——— 11.
— ——— 13, see F..sake.
16.——— 19.
— ——— 20, see F..sake.
16.——— 22, 33, 35.
16.—— xiv. 5, 7.
1. ——— 9.
4. ——— 24 (No. 2, L T Tr A ℵ.)
18.——— 27.
16.——— 40, 56.
17.——— 70.
16.—— xv. 10 1st.
3b.——— 10 2nd.
16.—— xvi. 4.
22.——— 8 1st.
16.——— 8 2nd.
19. Luke i. 13.
16.——— 15, 18, 30.
18.——— 37.
16.——— 44 1st.
9. ——— 44 2nd.
18.——— 45, marg. *that.*
18.——— 48 1st.
16.——— 48 2nd.
18.——— 49, 68.
16.——— 76.
9. ——— 77, marg. (text, *by.*)
16.—— ii. 10.
18.——— 11.
5b.——— 20.
15.——— 21.
4. ——— 27.
18.——— 30.
1. ——— 34 twice.

1. Luke iii. 3.
16.——— 8.
4. ——— 19 twice.
18.—— iv. 6.
16.——— 8 (*om.* G L T Tr A ℵ.)
16.——— 10.
11.——— 13.
18.——— 32, 36.
4. ——— 38.
18.——— 41, marg. *that.*
18.——— 43.
1. —— v. 4.
18.——— 8.
16.——— 9.
4. ——— 14 1st.
1. ——— 14 2nd.
16.——— 39.
— —— vi. 4, see do.
18.——— 19, 20, 21 twice.
— ——— 22, see F..sake.
16.——— 23 twice.
18.——— 24, 25 twice.
16.——— 26.
2. ——— 28 (No. 4, T Trm A ℵ.)
17.——— 32, 33.
17.——— 34 (*om.* γάρ, T Trb A ℵ.)
18.——— 35.
16.——— 38, 43, 44 twice, 45, 48 (*ap.*)
16.—— vii. 5, 6.
18.——— 7.
17.——— 8.
16.——— 28 (*om.* T Tr A ℵ.)
16.——— 33.
18.——— 39.
5a.——— 44.
18.——— 47.
6c.—— viii. 13.
16.——— 17, 18.
3b.——— 19.
18.——— 25.
16.——— 29 twice.
18.——— 37.
16.——— 40.
18.——— 42.
16.——— 46.
3b.——— 47.
1. —— ix. 3, 5.
18.——— 12.
1. ——— 13.
16.——— 14, 24 1st.
— ——— 24 2nd, see F..sake.
16.——— 25, 26.
18.——— 38.
16.——— 44, 48, 50 1st.
2. ——— 50 2nd.
16.——— 56 (*ap.*)
1. ——— 62 (*om.* L T Tr A ℵ.)
16.—— x. 7.
18.——— 13, 21.
16.——— 24.
— —— xi. 3, see *day.*
17.——— 4.
20.——— 6.
16.——— 10.
8. ——— 11.
16.——— 30.
18.——— 31, 32, 42, 43, 44, 46, 47, 48, 52.
16.—— xii. 12.
18.——— 15.
1. ——— 19.
18.——— 24.
4. ——— 26.
16.——— 30.
18.——— 32.
16.——— 34.
18.——— 40.
16.——— 52.
5b.—— xiii. 17.
18.——— 24, 31, 33.
18.—— xiv. 11, 14 1st.
16.——— 14 2nd.
18. Luke xiv. 17.
16.——— 24, 28.
1. ——— 35 twice.
16.—— xv. 6, 9.
11.——— 24, 32.
16.—— xvi. 2.
18.——— 3, 8.
16.——— 13.
18.——— 15, 24.
16.——— 28.
16.—— xvii. 21, 24.
5c.—— xviii. 4.
18.——— 14.
16.——— 16, 23, 25.
— ——— 29, see F..sake.
16.——— 32.
7. —— xix. 3.
18.——— 4.
16.——— 5, 10, 21.
16.——— 26 (*om.* Lb Trb A ℵ.)
4. ——— 37.
18.——— 43.
16.——— 48.
16.—— xx. 6, 19, 33, 36, 38.
16.—— xxi. 4, 8, 9.
— ——— 12, see F..sake.
1. ——— 13.
16.——— 15.
— ——— 17, see F..sake.
18.——— 22.
16.——— 23.
7. ——— 26 1st.
16.——— 26 3rd.
19.——— 28.
16.——— 35.
16.—— xxii. 2, 16, 18.
2. ——— 19, 20.
16.——— 27.
4. ——— 32.
16.——— 37 1st.
17.——— 37 2nd (*om.* γάρ, Lb Trb A.)
7. ——— 45.
17.——— 59.
16.——— 71.
16.—— xxiii. 8, 12, 15.
3b.——— 19, 25.
5c.——— 28 3 times.
18.——— 29, 31.
16.——— 34, 41.
18.—— xxiv. 29, 39.
7. ——— 41.
1. John i. 7.
18.——— 15.
8. ——— 16.
18.——— 17, 30.
16.—— ii. 25.
16.—— iii. 2, 16, 17, 20, 24, 34 twice.
16.—— iv. 8, 9, 18.
18.——— 22.
17.——— 23.
18.——— 35.
3b.——— 39.
16.——— 42, 44, 45, 47.
16.—— v. 4 (*ap.*), 13, 19, 20, 21, 22, 26.
18.——— 28.
6c.——— 35.
16.——— 36.
18.——— 38, 39.
16.——— 46 twice.
16.—— vi. 6.
— ——— 27 1st & 2nd, see labour.
16.——— 27 3rd, 33.
18.——— 38.
2. ——— 51.
16.——— 55, 64, 71.
16.—— vii. 1, 4, 5.
18.——— 8.
3b.——— 13.
18.——— 29.
16.——— 39.
18.——— 52.
18.—— viii. 14, 16, 20.
16.——— 24.
18. John viii. 29.
16.——— 42.
18.——— 44.
4. —— ix. 21.
16.——— 22.
1. ——— 39.
18.—— x. 4, 5.
— ——— 10, see F to.
2. ——— 11.
4. ——— 13.
2. ——— 15.
4. ——— 33 twice.
2. —— xi. 4.
— ——— 15, see F..sake.
16.——— 39.
18.——— 47.
2. ——— 50, 51, 52.
— ——— 53, see F to.
4. —— xii. 6.
16.——— 8.
— ——— 9, see F..sake.
— ——— 18 1st, see F that cause.
— ——— 18 2nd, see F that.
— ——— 27, see F this cause.
— ——— 30, see F..sake.
16.——— 43, 47.
18.——— 49.
16.—— xiii. 11, 13, 15, 29.
— ——— 37, 38, } see F..
— —— xiv. 11, } sake.
18.——— 17, 28.
16.——— 30.
18.—— xv. 5.
2. ——— 13.
18.——— 15 twice.
— ——— 21, see F..sake.
4. ——— 22.
16.—— xvi. 7, 13.
18.——— 14.
4. ——— 26.
16.——— 27.
18.—— xvii. 8.
4. ——— 9 1st, 2nd & 3rd.
18.——— 9 4th.
— ——— 19, see F..sake.
4. ——— 20 twice.
18.——— 24.
18.—— xviii. 2.
16.——— 13.
2. ——— 14.
18.——— 18.
— ——— 37, see F..cause.
16.—— xix. 6.
18.——— 20.
4. ——— 24 1st.
5c.——— 24 2nd.
16.——— 31, 36.
18.——— 42.
16.—— xx. 9, 17.
7. —— xxi. 6.
16.——— 7, 8.
— ——— 11, see all.
18. Acts i. 5, 17.
16.——— 20.
16.—— ii. 15, 25 1st.
18.——— 25 2nd.
16.——— 34.
1. ——— 38.
16.——— 39.
6c.—— iii. 10.
16.——— 22 (*ap.*)
16.—— iv. 3, 12, 16, 20.
18.——— 21 1st.
5b.——— 21 2nd.
16.——— 22, 27, 34.
16.—— v. 26, 36.
18.——— 38.
2. ——— 41.
16.—— vi. 14.
1. —— vii. 5, 21.
16.——— 33, 40.
16.—— viii. 7.
4. ——— 15.
16.——— 16, 21, 23.
2. ——— 24.
18.——— 33.
— Acts ix. 11 1st, see enquire.
16.——— 11 2nd.
18.——— 15.
16.——— 16 1st.
— ——— 16 2nd, see F..sake.
1. —— x. 4.
18.——— 14.
19.——— 20 (G∾) (No. 18, G L T Tr A ℵ.)
18.——— 38.
16.——— 46.
18.—— xi. 8, 24.
2. —— xii. 5 (No. 4, G∾ L T Tr A* ℵ.)
7. ——— 14.
1. —— xiii. 2.
16.——— 8.
11.——— 11.
6c.——— 15.
16.——— 27, 36.
18.——— 41.
16.——— 47 1st.
1. ——— 47 2nd.
1. —— xiv. 26.
5b.—— xv. 14 (*om.* G⇄ L T Tr A ℵ.)
16.——— 21.
2. ——— 26.
16.——— 28.
5b.——— 31.
16.—— xvi. 3, 28.
— —— xvii. 15, see F to.
16.——— 20, 23, 28 twice.
16.—— xviii. 3 (*ap.*)
16.——— 15 (*om.* G→ L T Tr A ℵ.)
16.——— 18, 28.
— —— xix. 8, see space.
16.——— 24, 32, 37.
17.——— 40 1st.
4. ——— 40 2nd.
16.—— xx. 10, 13, 16 twice, 27.
16.——— 29 (*om.* G→ L T Tr A ℵ.)
5b.——— 38.
16.—— xxi. 3.
16.——— 13 1st.
2. ——— 13 2nd.
16.——— 22.
2. ——— 26.
16.——— 29.
3b.——— 34, 35.
16.——— 36.
— —— xxii. 5, see F to.
7. ——— 11.
18.——— 15, 21.
16.——— 22, 26.
16.—— xxiii. 5, 8, 11, 17, 21.
1. ——— 30.
16.—— xxiv. 5.
4. ——— 21.
— —— xxv. 8, see answer.
16.——— 11 (οὖν, *therefore,* G∾ L T Tr A ℵ.)
— ——— 16, see answer.
16.——— 27.
2.—— xxvi. 1 1st (No. 4, G∾ L T Tr A ℵ.)
— ——— 1 2nd, see answer.
5b.——— 6.
— ——— 7, see F..sake.
16.——— 16.
— ——— 21, see F..same.
— ——— 24, see speak.
16.——— 26 3 times.
16.—— xxvii. 22, 23, 25, 34 twice.
6a.——— 34.
16.—— xxviii. 2.
— ——— 20 1st, see F...cause.
— ——— 20 2nd, see call.
16.——— 20 3rd (lit. Nos. 12 and 16, "for, on account of.")

16. Acts xxviii. 22, 27.
1. Rom. i. 5 1st, marg. *to the.*
2. ——— 5 2nd.
2. ——— 8 (No. 4, G∾ L T Tr A ℵ.)
16.——— 9, 11, 16 twice, 17, 18, 19, 20.
— ——— 26 1st, see F.. cause.
16. ——— 26 2nd.
16.—— ii. 1 twice, 11, 12, 13, 14, 24, 25.
1. ——— 26.
16.——— 28.
16.—— iii. 3.
— ——— 6, see F then.
16.——— 7, 9, 20, 22, 23.
3b.——— 25.
16.—— iv. 2, 3 1st.
1. ——— 3 2nd, 5.
16. ——— 9 1st.
1. ——— 9 2nd.
16.——— 13, 14.
16.——— 15 (No. 22, G∾ L T Tr A ℵ.)
1. ——— 22.
— ——— 23, see F.. sake.
3b.——— 24, 25 twice.
16.—— v. 6 1st.
2. ——— 6 2nd.
16. ——— 7 1st.
2 ——— 7 2nd & 3rd, 8.
16. ——— 10.
— ——— 12, see F that.
16. ——— 13, 15, 16, 17, 19.
16.—— vi. 5, 7, 10, 14 twice, 19, 20, 21, 23.
16.—— vii. 1, 2, 5, 7, 8, 11.
16.——— 14 (No. 22, Lm.)
16.——— 15 twice, 18 twice, 19, 22.
16.—— viii. 2, 3 1st.
4. ——— 3 2nd, marg. *by a sacrifice for.*
16.——— 5, 6, 7, 13, 14, 15, 18, 19, 20, 22, 24 twice, 26 1st.
— ——— 26 2nd, see pray.
2. ——— 26 3rd (*om.* ὑπὲρ ἡμῶν, *for us*, G→ L T Tr A ℵ.)
2 ——— 27.
1. ——— 28.
18. ——— 29.
2 ——— 31, 32, 34.
— ——— 36 1st, see F.. sake.
16. ——— 38.
16.—— ix. 3 1st.
2 ——— 3 2nd.
16. ——— 6.
1. ——— 8.
16. ——— 9, 11, 15, 17, 19, 28.
16. ——— 32 (*om.* G⇉ L T Tr A ℵ.)
2. —— x. 1.
16. ——— 2, 3, 4 1st.
1. ——— 4 2nd.
16.——— 5, 10, 11, 12 twice, 13, 16.
16.—— xi. 1.
— ——— 11, see F to.
16.——— 13 (No. 22, L T Tr A ℵ.)
16. ——— 15.
9. ——— 17, marg. (text, *among.*)
16.——— 21, 23, 24, 25.
21. ——— 27.
— ——— 28 twice, see F.. sake.
16. ——— 29, 30, 32, 34.
18. ——— 36.
16.—— xii. 3, 4.
8. ——— 17.

16. Rom. xii. 19, 20.
16.—— xiii. 1, 3, 4 1st.
1. ——— 4 2nd.
16. ——— 4 3rd & 4th.
5b. ——— 5 1st.
— — —— 5 2nd, see F.. sake.
16. ——— 6 1st.
— ——— 6 2nd, see F.. cause.
16. ——— 6 3rd, 8, 9, 11.
— ——— 14, see provision.
16.—— xiv. 3, 4, 6, 7, 8, 9, 10, 11.
2. ——— 15.
16. ——— 17, 18.
12. ——— 20.
1. —— xv. 2.
16. ——— 3, 4 1st.
1. ——— 4 2nd.
2. ——— 8, 9 1st.
— ——— 9 2nd, see F.. cause.
16. ——— 18.
16.——— 24 (*om.* G), 26 1st.
1. ——— 26 2nd.
16. ——— 27.
— ——— 30 1st, see F.. sake.
3a. ——— 30 2nd.
2. ——— 30 3rd.
17.—— xvi. 2.
2 ——— 4.
16. ——— 18, 19.
1. ——— 26.
5b. 1 Cor. i. 4.
16.——— 11.
2. ——— 13 (No. 4, L Trm.)
16.——— 17, 18, 19, 21.
20.——— 22.
16. ——— 26.
16.—— ii. 2, 8, 10, 11, 14.
16. ——— 16.
16.—— iii. 2, 3 twice, 4, 9, 11, 13, 17, 19 twice, 21.
16.—— iv. 4.
— ——— 6 1st, see F.. sake.
2. ——— 6 2nd.
16. ——— 7, 9 1st.
18. ——— 9 2nd.
— ——— 10, see F.. sake.
16.——— 15 twice.
— ——— 17, see F cause.
16. ——— 20.
16.—— v. 3.
1. ——— 5.
17. ——— 7 1st.
2. ——— 7 2nd (*om.* ὑπὲρ ἡμῶν, *for us*, G⇉ L T Tr A ℵ.)
— ——— 10, see F then.
16. ——— 12.
16.—— vi. 16, 20.
6c.—— vii. 5 1st.
3b.——— 5 2nd.
16. ——— 7 (No. 22, G∾ L T Tr A ℵ.)
16. ——— 9, 14, 16, 22.
3b. ——— 26.
16. ——— 31.
6c. ——— 35 twice.
17.—— viii. 5.
16.——— 8 (*om.* L T Tr A ℵ.)
16.——— 10.
3b. ——— 11.
16.—— ix. 2, 9.
— ——— 10 twice, see F.. sake.
16. ——— 15, 16 twice, 17, 19.
— ——— 23, see F.. sake.
16.—— x. 4, 5.
6c.——— 11.
18.——— 17 1st.
16.——— 17 2nd, 26.
— ——— 28 1st, see F.. sake.
16. ——— 28 3rd (*om.* A.V. to 1638) (*ap.*)
16.——— 29.
2. ——— 30.

16. 1 Cor. xi. 5, 6, 7, 8.
3b.——— 9 twice.
— ——— 10, see F.. cause.
16.——— 12.
18.——— 15 1st.
8. ——— 15 2nd.
1. ——— 17 twice.
16.——— 18, 19, 21, 23.
2. —— xi. 24.
16. ——— 26, 29.
— ——— 30, see F.. cause.
16. ——— 31 (No. 22, G∾ L T Tr A ℵ.)
16.—— xii. 8, 12.
17.——— 13, 14.
2. ——— 25.
16.—— xiii. 9 (No. 22, G∾.)
16.——— 12 (*om.* G→.)
16.—— xiv. 2 twice.
16.——— 5 (No. 22, L T Tr A ℵ.)
17.——— 8.
16.——— 9.
16. ——— 14 (*om.* Lb Trb.)
16. ——— 17.
— ——— 21, see F all that.
1. ——— 22.
16.——— 31, 33, 34, 35.
16.—— xv. 3 1st.
2. ——— 3 2nd.
16.——— 9, 16, 21, 22, 25, 27.
2. ——— 29 twice.
16. ——— 32, 34, 41, 52, 53.
1. —— xvi. 1.
16.——— 5, 7, 9, 10, 11.
18.——— 17.
16.——— 18.
2. 2 Cor. i. 6 twice.
16.——— 8.
2. ——— 11.
16. ——— 12, 13, 19, 20.
— ——— 24 1st, see F that.
16.——— 24 2nd.
16.—— ii. 2, 4, 9.
17.——— 10 1st.
— ——— 10 2nd, see F.. sake
16.——— 11.
18.——— 15.
6c.——— 16.
16.——— 17.
16.—— iii. 6.
3b.——— 7.
17.——— 10.
16.——— 11, 14.
16.—— iv. 5 1st.
— ——— 5 2nd, see F.. sake.
18.——— 6.
16.——— 11 1st.
— ——— 11 2nd, see F.. sake
16. ——— 15 1st.
— ——— 15 2nd, see F.. sake
16.——— 17 1st.
— ——— 17 2nd, see mo- [ment.
16.——— 18.
16.—— v. 1, 2.
17.——— 4 1st.
— ——— 4 2nd, see F as [that.
1. ——— 5.
16.——— 7, 10.
16.——— 12 (*om.* G⇉ L T Tr A ℵ.)
16.——— 13 1st.
— ——— 13 2nd, see F cause.
16.——— 14 1st.
2. ——— 14 2nd.
2. ——— 15 twice, 20.
16. ——— 21 1st (*om.* G→ L T Tr A ℵ.)
16.—— vi. 2, 14, 16.
16.—— vii. 3.
17.——— 5.
18.——— 8 1st.
16.——— 8 2nd (*om.* Lb Trbm)
6c.——— 8 3rd.
16.——— 9, 10, 11.
— ——— 12 1st & 2nd, see F .. cause.
2. ——— 12 3rd.

5b. 2 Cor. vii. 13.
18.——— 14.
18.—— viii. 3.
16.——— 9 1st.
— ——— 9 2nd, see F.. sake.
16. ——— 10, 12, 13.
1. ——— 14 twice.
2. ——— 16.
18. ——— 17.
16.—— ix. 1, 2, 7.
1. ——— 10.
18.——— 12.
5b.——— 13.
2. ——— 14 1st.
3b.——— 14 2nd.
5b.——— 15.
16.—— x. 3, 4, 8 1st.
1. ——— 8 2nd & 3rd.
18.——— 10.
16.——— 12, 14 twice, 18.
16.—— xi. 2 twice, 4.
16.——— 5 (No. 22, L Trm.)
16.——— 9, 13, 14, 19, 20.
16.—— xii. 6 twice.
2. ——— 8.
16. ——— 9.
— ——— 10 1st, see F.. sake.
16.——— 10 2nd, 11 twice, 13, 14 twice.
2. ——— 15, 19.
16.——— 20.
16.—— xiii. 4 1st.
17.——— 4 2nd.
16.——— 8 1st.
2. ——— 8 2nd.
16.——— 9.
2. Gal. i. 4 (No. 4, G L T Tr A ℵ.)
16.——— 10 1st.
16.——— 10 2nd (*om.* G∾L T Tr A ℵ.)
16.——— 12, 13.
6c.—— ii. 5.
16.——— 8, 12.
19.——— 16 (No. 18, G∾L T Tr A ℵ.)
16.——— 18, 19.
2. ——— 20.
16.——— 21.
1. —— iii. 6.
16.——— 10 twice.
18.——— 11.
2. ——— 13 1st.
16.——— 13 2nd (No. 18, G∾ L T Tr A ℵ.)
16.——— 18, 21, 26, 27, 28.
18.—— iv. 12.
16.——— 15.
18.——— 20.
16.——— 22, 24, 25, 27 1st.
18.——— 27 2nd.
16.——— 30.
16.—— v. 5, 6, 13 1st.
1. ——— 13.
16.——— 14, 17.
16.—— vi. 3, 5, 7.
18.——— 8.
16.——— 13, 15, 17.
2. Eph. i. 16.
9. ——— 17, marg. (text, *in.*)
3b.—— ii. 4.
16.——— 8, 10, 14.
— ——— 15, see F to.
18.——— 18.
1. ——— 22.
— —— iii. 1 1st, see F.. cause.
2. ——— 1 2nd, 13.
— ——— 14, see F.. cause.
6c.—— iv. 12 1st.
1. ——— 12 2nd & 3rd.
18.——— 25.
— ——— 32, see F.. sake.
2. —— v. 2 1st.
1. ——— 2 2nd.
16.——— 5, 6, 8, 9, 12, 13.

2. Eph. v. 20.
18. —— 23.
2. —— 25.
16. —— 29.
18. —— 30.
— —— 31, see F..cause
16. — vi. 1.
18. —— 12.
4. —— 18.
2. —— 19, 20.
1. —— 22.
2. Phil. i. 4.
5b. —— 5.
2. —— 7.
16. —— 8.
1. —— 17.
16. —— 19, 21.
16. —— 23 (No. 22, G L T Tr A ℵ.)
3b. —— 24.
1. —— 25.
9. —— 26.
— —— 27, see strive.
18. —— 29 1st.
— —— 29 2nd, see F.. sake.
16. — ii. 13, 20, 21.
20. —— 26.
16. —— 27.
3b. —— 30.
16. — iii. 3.
3b. —— 7, 8 twice.
5b. —— 12.
5c. —— 14 (No. 1, L T Tr A ℵ.)
16. —— 18, 20.
16. — iv. 11.
18. —— 16.
4. Col. i. 3 (No. 3, G∾L Tr A*.)
3b. —— 5.
2. —— 7.
— —— 9 1st, see F.. cause.
2. —— 9 2nd.
18. —— 16 1st.
1. —— 16 2nd.
18. —— 19.
2. —— 24 1st.
— —— 24 2nd, see F.. sake.
1. —— 25.
16. — ii. 1 1st.
4. —— 1 2nd (No. 2, L T Tr A ℵ.)
16. —— 5.
18. —— 9.
16. — iii. 3.
— —— 6, see F..sake.
16. —— 20.
16. —— 24 (om. G∾L T Tr A ℵ.)
— —— 25, see receive.
4. — iv. 3 1st.
3b. —— 3 2nd
2. —— 12.
16. —— 13 1st.
2. —— 13 2nd.
4. 1 Thes. i. 2.
18. —— 5 1st.
— —— 5 2nd, see F.. sake.
16. —— 8, 9.
16. — ii. 1, 3, 5, 9 1st.
16. —— 9 2nd (om. G L T Tr A ℵ.)
— —— 13, see F..cause
16. —— 14 1st.
18. —— 14 2nd.
6c. —— 17.
16. —— 19, 20
16. — iii. 3, 4.
— —— 5, see F..cause.
18. —— 8.
16. —— 9 1st.
4. —— 9 2nd.
5b. —— 9 3rd.
— —— 9 4th, see F.. sake.
16. 1 Thes. iv. 2, 3, 7, 9, 14, 15.
18. —— 16.
16. — v. 2.
16. —— 3 (No. 22, Lb Trm) (om. G T Tr A ℵ.)
16. —— 7.
18. —— 9.
2. —— 10.
— —— 13, see F..sake.
8. —— 15.
16. —— 18.
4. —— 25.
4. 2 Thes. i. 3.
2. —— 4, 5.
4. —— 11.
18. — ii. 8.
16. —— 7.
— —— 11, see F..cause
4. —— 13.
4. — iii. 1.
16. —— 2, 7 1st.
18. —— 7 2nd.
— —— 8, see nought.
16. —— 10, 11.
— 1 Tim. i. 12, see F that.
— —— 16 1st, see F.. cause.
6c. —— 16 2nd.
2. — ii. 1, 2
16. —— 3 (om. L T Trmb A ℵ.)
16. —— 5.
2. —— 6.
16. —— 13.
16. — iii. 13.
18. — iv. 4.
16. —— 5, 8, 10, 16.
16. — v. 4.
— —— 8, see provide.
9. —— 10.
16. —— 11, 15, 18.
— —— 23, see F..sake.
16. — vi. 7, 10.
16. 2 Tim. i. 7.
3b. —— 12 1st.
16. —— 12 2nd.
18. —— 16.
— — ii. 10, see F..sake.
16. —— 11, 16.
16. — iii. 2, 6, 9.
6c. —— 16 4 times.
16. — iv. 3, 6, 10, 11 1st.
1. —— 11 2nd.
16. —— 15.
— Titus i. 5, see F..cause.
16. —— 10.
— —— 11, see F..sake.
16. — ii. 11.
2. —— 14.
16. — iii. 3, 9, 12.
1. —— 14.
16. Philem. 7.
— —— 9, see F..sake.
4. —— 10.
16. —— 15 1st.
6c. —— 15 2nd.
16. —— 22.
16. Heb. i. 5.
3b. —— 14.
16. — ii. 2, 5, 8.
3b. —— 9 1st, marg. *by*.
2. —— 9 2nd.
16. —— 11 1st.
3b. —— 11 2nd.
16. —— 16, 18.
16. — iii. 3, 4.
1. —— 5.
16. —— 14, 16.
17. — iv. 2.
16. —— 3, 4, 8, 10, 12, 15.
16. — v. 1 1st.
2. —— 1 2nd & 3rd.
— —— 2, see F that.
4. —— 3 1st & 2nd.
2. —— 3 (No. 4, G∾L T Tr A ℵ.)
— —— 7, see *fear*.
17. —— 12 1st.
3b. Heb. v. 12 2nd.
16. —— 13 twice.
16. — vi. 4, 7.
3b. —— 7, marg. (text, *by*.)
16. —— 10, 13, 16 1st.
1. —— 16 2nd.
2. —— 20.
16. — vii. 1, 10, 11, 12, 13, 14.
— —— 15, see F that.
16. —— 17, 18 1st.
3b. —— 18 2nd.
16. —— 19, 21.
2. —— 25.
16. —— 26.
2. —— 27 1st.
16. —— 27 3rd, 28.
16. — viii. 3.
16. —— 4 (οὖν, *therefore*, L T Tr A ℵ.)
16. —— 5, 7, 8.
18. —— 10, 11, 12.
16. — ix. 2.
2. —— 7.
1. —— 9.
16. —— 13.
— —— 15 1st, see F.. cause.
16. —— 15 2nd.
16. —— 16, 17, 19, 24 1st.
2. —— 24 2nd.
— —— 26, see F then.
16. — x. 1.
— —— 2, see F then.
16. —— 4.
4. —— 6, 8.
— —— 10, see once.
2. —— 12.
16. —— 14, 15.
4. —— 18.
16. —— 23, 26 1st.
4. —— 26 2nd.
— —— 27, see looking.
16. —— 30.
17. —— 34.
16. —— 36, 37.
16. — xi. 2, 5, 6.
1. —— 8.
16. —— 10 1st, 14, 16, 26, 27, 32.
4. —— 40.
8. — xii. 2.
16. —— 3, 6, 7, 10 1st.
6c. —— 10 2nd.
5c. —— 10 3rd.
6c. —— 11.
8. —— 16.
16. —— 17 twice, 18, 20, 25.
17. —— 29.
16. — xiii. 2, 5, 9, 11 1st.
4. —— 11 2nd.
16. —— 14, 16, 17 1st.
2. —— 17 2nd.
16. —— 17 3rd.
4. —— 18 1st.
16. —— 18 2nd.
17. —— 22.
16. Jas. i. 6, 7, 11.
18. —— 12.
16. —— 13, 20.
18. —— 23.
16. —— 24.
16. — ii. 2, 10, 11, 13.
1. —— 23.
16. —— 26.
16. — iii. 2, 7, 16.
16. — iv. 14 1st.
17. —— 14, marg. (text, *even*) (om. L Trb ℵ.)
— —— 15, see F that ..ought to say.
5b. — v. 1.
9. —— 3.
5b. —— 7.
18. —— 8.
2. Jas. v. 16.
1. 1 Pet. i. 4.
5c. —— 13.
18. —— 16.
3b. —— 20.
19. —— 24, marg. *for that*.
— — ii. 13, see F..sake.
1. —— 14.
18. —— 15.
14. —— 16.
16. —— 19 1st.
3b. —— 19 2nd.
16. —— 20 1st.
— —— 20 2nd, see faults
16. —— 21 1st.
2. —— 21 2nd.
16. —— 25.
16. — iii. 5.
8. —— 9 twice.
16. —— 10.
18. —— 12.
— —— 14, see F..sake.
16. —— 17.
18. —— 18 1st.
4. —— 18 2nd.
2. —— 18 3rd.
2. — iv. 1 1st (om. ὑπέρ, ἡμῶν, *for us*, G→L T Tr A) (ὑπέρ, ὑμῶν, *for you*, ℵ.)
18. —— 1 2nd.
16. —— 3, 6 1st.
— —— 6 2nd, see F.. cause.
18. —— 8.
9. —— 14 1st.
18. —— 14 2nd, 17.
18. — v. 5, 7 1st.
4. —— 7 2nd.
16. 2 Pet. i. 8, 10, 11, 16, 17, 21.
16. — ii. 4, 8, 18, 19, 20, 21.
16. — iii. 4, 5.
4. 1 John ii. 2 1st & 2nd.
— —— 2 3rd, see sins.
— —— 12, see F..sake.
18. —— 16.
16. —— 19.
18. — iii. 2.
21. —— 4.
18. —— 8, 9, 11.
2. —— 16 twice.
18. —— 20.
18. — iv. 7, 8.
4. —— 10.
16. —— 20.
16. — v. 3.
18. —— 4, 7, 9.
4. —— 16.
— 2 John 2, see F..sake.
18. —— 7.
16. —— 11.
16. 3 John 3.
— —— 7, see F..sake.
— Jude 3, see contend.
16. —— 4.
18. —— 11.
16. Rev. i. 3.
3b. —— 9 1st.
3b. —— 9 2nd (om. G→L Tr Ab.)
3b. — ii. 3.
16. — iii. 2.
18. —— 4, 8.
18. — iv. 11 1st.
3b. —— 11 2nd.
18. — v. 9.
3b. — vi. 9 1st.
3b. —— 9 2nd (om. L Ab.)
18 —— 17.
18. — vii. 17.
1. — ix. 15 1st, marg. *at*.
— —— 15 2nd, see F to
16. —— 19 twice.
18. — xi. 2.
— — xii. 4, see F to.
18. —— 10, 12 twice.

16. Rev. xiii. 18.
16. —— xiv. 4.
16. ———— 5 (om. G ∾ L Trb A ℵ.)
18. —— xv. 1, 4 3 times.
18. —— xvi. 6 1st.
16. ———— 6 2nd (om. G L T Tr A) (ὅπερ, whosoever, [ℵ.)
10. ———— 10.
16. ———— 14.
18. ———— 21.
8. —— xvii. 14.
16. ———— 17.
18. —— xviii. 3, 5, 7, 8.
5b. ———— 9 (No. 5c, T Tr A ℵ.)
3b. ———— 10 1st.
18. ———— 10 2nd, 11.
3b. Rev. xviii. 15.
18. ———— 17, 19, 20, 23 twice.
18. —— xix. 2 twice, 6, 7.
16. ———— 8, 10.
3b. —— xx. 4 twice.
16. —— xxi. 1.
18. ———— 4 (om. L Trb [Ab.)
18. ———— 5.
16. ———— 22, 23, 25.
7. —— xxii. 2.
18. ———— 5.
16. ———— 9 (om. G L T Tr A ℵ.)
18. ———— 10 (No. 16, G ∾ T Tr A ℵ) (om. G.)
16. ———— 18 (ἐγώ, I, G L T Tr A ℵ.)

FOR ALL THAT.

οὕτω, thus, in this wise, so.

1 Cor. xiv. 21.

FOR...CAUSE.

1. { διὰ, through, τοῦτο, this, } on this account, owing to this *(marking the ground or reason.*
2. { εἰς, into, to, unto, τοῦτο, this, } with a view to this, in order to this.
3. { ἀντὶ, *see* "FOR," *No.* 7, τοῦτο, this, } therefore, for this.
4. { τούτου, of this, χάριν, *adverbially used with Gen.* for the sake of, on account of, } for the sake of this, on account of this.
5. ἕνεκα, *see* "FOR," *No.* 12.
6. ὑμῖν, *(Dat.)* for you.

5. Matt. xix. 5.
5. Mark x. 7.
1. John xii. 18, 27.
2. —— xviii. 37.
5. Acts xxvi. 21, with τούτων, *of these.*
1. —— xxviii. 20.
1. Rom. i. 26.
1. —— xiii. 6.
1. —— xv. 9.
1. 1 Cor. iv. 17.
1. —— xi. 10, 30.
6. 2 Cor. v. 13.
5. —— vii. 12 twice.
4. Eph. iii. 1, 14.
3. —— v. 31.
1. Col. i. 9.
1. 1 Thes. ii. 13.
1. —— iii. 5.
1. 2 Thes. ii. 11.
1. 1 Tim. i. 16.
4. Titus i. 5.
1. Heb. ix. 15.
2. 1 Pet. iv. 6.

FOR...SAKE.

1. διά, *see* "FOR," *No.* 3.
   (a) *with Gen. see* "FOR," *No. 3a.*
   (b) *with Acc. see* "FOR," *No. 3b.*
2. { διά, *see* "FOR," *No. 3b,* ἡμᾶς, us, } on account of *or* owing to us.
3. { διά, *see* "FOR," *No. 3b,* ὑμᾶς, you, } on account of *or* owing to you.
4. { διά, *see* "FOR," *No. 3b,* ἐκεῖνον, that one, *emphatic,* } for the sake of him *or* that one.
5. ἕνεκα, *see* "FOR," *No.* 12.
6. ὑπέρ, *see* "FOR," *No.* 2.
7. περί, *see* "FOR," *No.* 4.
8. ἐν, in, *(of time, place, or element.)*
9. χάριν, *(used adverbially,)* for the sake of, on account of.

5. Matt. v. 10, 11.
5. —— x. 18.
1b. ———— 22.
5. ———— 39.
1b. —— xiv. 3, 9.
5. —— xvi. 25.
1b. —— xix. 12.
5. ———— 29.
1b. —— xxiv. 9, 22.
1b. Mark iv. 17.
1b. —— vi. 17, 26.
5. —— viii. 35.
5. —— x. 29.
5. —— xiii. 9.
1b. ———— 13, 20.
5. Luke vi. 22.
5. —— ix. 24.
5. —— xviii. 29.
5. —— xxi. 12.
1b. ———— 17.
3. John xi. 15.
1b. —— xii. 9.
3. ———— 30.
6. —— xiii. 37, 38.
1b. —— xiv. 11.
1b. —— xv. 21.
6. —— xvii. 19.
6. Acts ix. 16.
7. —— xxvi. 7.
1b. Rom. iv. 23.
5. Rom. viii. 36.
3. —— xi. 28 twice.
1b. —— xiii. 5.
1a. —— xv. 30.
3. 1 Cor. iv. 6.
1b. ———— 10.
2. —— ix. 10 twice.
1b. ———— 23.
1b. —— x. 25, 27.
4. ———— 28 1st.
3. 2 Cor. ii. 10.
1b. —— iv. 5, 11.
3. ———— 15.
3. —— viii. 9.
6. —— xii. 10.
9. Eph. iv. 32.
6. Phil. i. 29.
6. Col. i. 24.
1b. —— iii. 6.
3. 1 Thes. i. 5.
3. —— iii. 9.
1b. —— v. 13.
1b. 1 Tim. v. 23.
1b. 2 Tim. ii. 10.
9. Titus i. 11.
1b. Philem. 9.
1b. 1 Pet. ii. 13.
1b. —— iii. 14.
1b. 1 John ii. 12.
1b. 2 John 2.

6. 3 John 7.

FOR THAT.

(Where not two words in the Greek.)

1. ὁτί, *see* "FOR," *No.* 18.
2. διότι, *see* "FOR," *No.* 19.
3. εἰ, if, since, though.
4. ἐπεί, since, because, seeing that.
5. ἐπειδή, since truly, inasmuch as.
6. ἐπί, *see* "FOR," *No. 5b.*

1. John xii. 18.
6. Rom. 5, 12, marg. *in* [*whom.*
1. 2 Cor. i. 24.
5. —— v. 4 (ἐφ' ᾧ, *on which* [*account*] G L T Tr A ℵ.)
1. 1 Tim. i. 12.
4. Heb. v. 2.
3. —— vii. 15.
2. 1 Pet. i. 24, marg. (text, *for.*)

FOR THAT...OUGHT TO SAY.

{ ἀντὶ, instead of, τοῦ λέγειν, saying.

Jas. iv. 15.

FOR THEN.

1. ἐπεί, since, because, seeing that.

2. { ἐπεί, *see No.* 1, / ἄρα, accordingly, *(marking a correspondence in point of fact,)* } else... by consequence.

1. Rom. iii. 6.	1. Heb. ix. 26.
2. 1 Cor. v. 10.	1. —— x. 2.

FOR TO.

1. ἵνα, that, to the end that.
2. εἰς τὸ, *(with Inf.)* unto the.... in order to, for to...
3. πρὸς τό, *(with Inf.)* with a view to.

3. Matt. xxiii. 5.	1. Acts xxii. 5.
1. Mark iii. 10.	2. Rom. xi. 11.
1. John x. 10.	1. Eph. ii. 15.
1. —— xi. 53.	1. Rev. ix. 15.
1. Acts xvii. 15.	1. —— xii. 4.

See also, CALL, CAUSE, EVER, EVERMORE, HOPE, INTENT, LAY, LIE, LITTLE, LOOK, MAKE, PURPOSE, SEASON, SEEK, SEND, TARRY, TIME, WAIT.

FORASMUCH AS.

1. εἰ, if, since, though.
2. ἐπεί, since, because, seeing that.
3. ἐπειδή, since truly, inasmuch as.
4. ἐπειδήπερ, since verily, forasmuch as, *(non occ.)*

4. Luke i. 1.	3. Acts xv. 24.
1. Acts xi. 17.	2. 1 Cor. xiv. 12.

2. Heb. ii. 14.

FORASMUCH AS...WAS.

ὤν, *(part. of* εἰμί, to be,) being.

Acts ix. 38.

FORBEAR (-ING.)

1. ἀνέχομαι, to hold one's self upright, *hence,* to bear up, hold up, hold out, endure; *then,* to bear with.
2. ἀνίημι, to send up *or* forth, to let up, let go, relax, loosen; *hence,* to cease from.
3. φείδομαι, to spare, *i.e.* to abstain from using *or* doing anything.

— 1 Cor. ix. 6, see F working.	2. Eph. vi. 9, marg. *moderate.*
3. 2 Cor. xii. 6.	1. Col. iii. 13.
1. Eph. iv. 2.	— 1 Thes. iii. 1, 5, see F(can.)

FORBEAR WORKING.

{ μή, not, / ἐργάζομαι, to work, labour. }

1 Cor. ix. 6.

FORBEAR (CAN.)

στέγω, to cover, *hence,* conceal, *(here doubtless referring to the Apostle's anxiety.)*

1 Thes. iii. 1 part., 5 part.

FORBEARANCE.

ἀνοχή, a holding back, delay, *hence,* self-restraint, forbearance.

Rom. ii. 4; iii. 25.

FORBEARING [marg.]

ανεξίκακος, enduring under evils and injuries, *(non occ.)*

2 Tim. ii. 24, text, *patient.*

FORBID.

1. κωλύω, to cut off, to weaken, *hence, gen.* to hinder, prevent, restrain.
2. διακωλύω, *(No.* 1 *with* διά, through, *prefixed,)* to hinder throughout, impede utterly, *(non occ.)*

2. Matt. iii. 14.	1. Acts x. 47.
1. —— xix. 14.	1. —— xvi. 6.
1. Mark ix. 38, 39.	1. —— xxiv. 23.
1. —— x. 14.	— —— xxviii. 31, see F (no man.)
— Luke vi. 29, see F to take.	1. 1 Cor. xiv. 39.
1. —— ix. 49, 50.	1. 1 Thes. ii. 16.
1. —— xi. 52, marg. (text, *to hinder.*)	1. 1 Tim. iv. 3.
1. —— xviii. 16.	1. 2 Pet. ii. 16.
1. —— xxiii. 2.	1. 3 John 10.

FORBID (GOD.)

{ μή, not, / γένοιτο, may it be, } may it not be.

Luke xx. 16.	Rom. xi. 1, 11.
Rom. iii. 4, 6, 31.	1 Cor. vi. 15.
—— vi. 2, 15.	Gal. ii. 17.
—— vii. 7, 13.	—— iii. 21.
—— ix. 14.	—— vi. 14.

FORBID TO TAKE.

κωλύω, *see* "FORBID," *No.* 1.

Luke vi. 29.

FORBIDDING (NO MAN.)

ἀκωλύτως, without hindrance, without restraint, *(non occ.)*

Acts xxviii. 31.

FORCE (be gotten by) [margin.]

βιάζομαι, to use force, to force, (*occ.* Luke xvi. 16.)

Matt. xi. 12, text, *suffer violence.*

FORCE (OF.)

βέβαιος, steadfast, firm, sure.

Heb. ix. 17.

FORCE (TAKE BY.)

ἁρπάζω, to seize upon, snatch awa carry off.

Matt. xi. 12. | John vi. 15. | Acts xxiii. 10.

FOREFATHER (-S.)

πρόγονος, earlier born, older. *In pl.* progenitors, ancestors, (*occ.* 1 Tim. v. 4.)

2 Tim. i. 3.

FOREHEAD (-S.)

μέτωπον, the space between the eyes, *hence,* the forehead.

Rev. vii. 3; ix. 4; xiii. 16; xiv. 1, 9; xvii. 5; xx. 4; xxii. 4.

FOREIGNER (-S.)

πάροικος, dwelling near, neighbouring. *In N.T. with art. as subst.* a by-dweller *or* a foreigner *who* lives in a place *without civil rights, but more prop.* sojourner.

Eph. ii. 19.

FOREKNOW (-KNEW.)

προγινώσκω, to know, perceive, learn *or* understand beforehand, to take note of before.

Rom. viii. 29; xi. 2.

FOREKNOWLEDGE.

πρόγνωσις, a perceiving beforehand; *esp. in medicine,* prognosis.

Acts ii. 23. | 1 Pet. i. 2.

FOREORDAIN.

1. προγινώσκω. *see* "FOREKNOW."
2. προτίθημι, to place *or* set before. *In mid.* (*as here,*) to put forth on one's own part, display, set forth.

2. Rom. iii. 25, marg. (text, *set forth.*)
1. 1 Pet. i. 20.

FOREPART.

πρῶρα, the fore-part of a ship, a ship's head, prow, bow, (*occ.* Acts xxvii. 41.)

Acts xxvii. 30.

FORERUNNER.

πρόδρομος, one who comes to a place whither the rest are to follow, (*non occ.*)

Heb. vi. 20.

FORETELL.

1. προεῖπον, to say before, foretell.
2. προκαταγγέλλω, to announce *or* declare beforehand.
3. προλέγω, to tell before *the event,* to forewarn, (*occ.* Gen. v. 21; 1 Thes. iii. 4.)

1. Mark xiii. 23.
2. Acts iii. 24 (καταγέλλω, *to announce,* G L T Tr A ℵ.)
3. 2 Cor. xiii. 2.

FOREWARN (-ED.)

1. προεῖπον, to say before, foretell.
2. ὑποδείκνυμι, to show underhand *or* secretly, give a sight *or* glimpse of, to give to understand.

2. Luke xii. 5. | 1. 1 Thes. iv. 6.

FORGET (-ETH, -ING, -GOTTEN.)

1. ἐπιλανθάνομαι, to forget upon, *i e.,* over, *or in consequence of something else,* (*occ.* Heb. xiii. 2.)
2. ἐκλανθάνομαι, to forget entirely, forget utterly, (*non occ.*)
3. { λήθη, forgetfulness, oblivion, λαμβάνω, to take, } to take a forgetfulness, forget, (*non occ.*)

1. Matt. xvi. 5.
1. Mark viii. 14.
1. Luke xii. 6.
1. Phil. iii. 13.
1. Heb. vi. 10.
2. — xii. 5.
1. — xiii. 16.
1. Jas. i. 24.
3. 2 Pet. i. 9.

FORGETFUL.

ἐπιλησμονή, a forgetting, forgetfulness, (*non occ.*)

Jas. i. 25.

FORGETFUL (BE.)

ἐπιλανθάνομαι, *see* "FORGET," *No.* 1.

Heb. xiii. 2.

FORGIVE (-ETH, -EN, -ING, -GAVE.)

1. ἀφίημι, to send away, dismiss, set free. *With Acc. of person*, to express the discharge *or* acquittal of a defendant, *whether the appellant is nonsuited by verdict or otherwise*, *esp.* to remit the punishment, where the guilty person *is dealt with as if he were innocent.*

2. χαρίζομαι, to do a person a favour, be kind to. *In the N.T. sense of* χάρις, *it denotes*, to be gracious to; *with Acc. of thing*, to give *or* bestow *a thing* willingly *or* graciously; *hence, the meaning peculiar to the N.T.* to graciously remit a person's debt *or* sin; *hence*, to pardon, forgive graciously.

3. ἀπολύω, to let loose from, to loosen, unbind; set at liberty, *e.g. a debtor*, *hence*, overlook, forgive.

1. Matt. vi. 12 twice, 14 twice, 15 twice.
1. —— ix. 2, 5, 6.
1. —— xii. 31 twice, 32 twice.
1. —— xviii. 21, 27, 32, 35.
1. Mark ii. 5, 7, 9, 10.
1. —— iii. 28.
1. —— iv. 12.
1. —— xi. 25 twice, 26 twice, (*ap.*)
1. Luke v. 20, 21, 23, 24.
3. —— vi. 37 twice.
— —— vii. 42, see F (frankly.)
2. —— 43.
1. Luke vii. 47 twice, 48, 49.
1. —— xi. 4 twice.
1. —— xii. 10 twice.
1. —— xvii. 3, 4.
1. —— xxiii. 34 (*ap.*)
1. Acts viii. 22.
1. Rom. iv. 7.
2. 2 Cor. ii. 7, 10 3 times.
2. —— xii. 13.
2. Eph. iv. 32 twice.
2. Col. ii. 13.
2. —— iii. 13 twice.
1. Jas. v. 15.
1. 1 John i. 9.
1. —— ii. 12.

FORGIVE FRANKLY.

2. Luke vii. 42.

FORGIVENESS.

ἄφεσις, discharge, setting free; *hence*, remission, *(mostly in reference to the year of Jubilee)*, remission *of debt or punishment.*

Mark iii. 29.
Acts v. 31.
—— xiii. 38.
Acts xxvi. 18.
Eph. i. 7.
Col. i. 14.

FORM [noun.]

1. μορφή, form, *abstractedly, without reference to any other object, (non occ.)*

2. μόρφωσις, embodiment, form without substance, *(non occ.)*

3. τύπος, a blow, *then*, that which is produced by the blow; the mark of a blow, impression; *hence*, model, pattern, exemplar *in the widest sense;* figure, form, manner.

4. ὑποτύπωσις, delineation, outline, sketch, *(occ.* 1 Tim. i. 16.)

1. Mark xvi. 12 (*ap.*)
2. Rom. ii. 20.
3. —— iv. 17.
1. Phil. ii. 6, 7.
4. 2 Tim. i. 13.
2. —— iii. 5.

FORMED [verb.]

1. μορφόω, to form, give form to; sketch, figure. *Pass.* have shape *or* form, *(non occ.)*

2. πλάσσω, to form, mould, shape, *(Lat.* fingere,) *strictly used of the artist who works in soft substances such as earth, clay, or wax; gen.* to bring into shape *or* form, *(non occ.)*

2. Rom. ix. 20.
1. Gal. iv. 19, pass.
2. 1 Tim. ii. 13.

FORMED (THING.)

πλάσμα, anything formed *or* moulded, *esp. from wax or clay*, an image, figure.

Rom. ix. 20.

FORMER.

1. πρῶτος, the first, foremost, *of place or time.*

2. πρότερος, before *others, of place or time.*

(a) *neut.* πρότερον, *used as adv.* before, sooner, earlier.

1. Acts i. 1.
2. Eph. iv. 22.
1. Rev. xxi. 4
2a. Heb. x. 32.
2a. 1 Pet. i. 14.

FORNICATION.

1. πορνεία, fornication, *(non occ.)*

2. πόρνη, a harlot.

[*Fornication* seems to be used of the sin of Idolatry in the Church in N.T. as *Adultery* is of the same sin with the Jews.]

1. Matt. v. 32.
1. —— xv. 19.
1. —— xix. 9.
1. Mark vii. 21.
1. John viii. 41.
1. Acts xv. 20, 29.
1. —— xxi. 25.
1. Rom. i. 29 (*om.* G L T Tr A ℵ.)
1. 1 Cor. v. 1 twice.
1. —— vi. 13, 18 1st.
— —— 18 2nd, see F (commit.)
1. —— vii. 2.

— 1 Cor. x. 8, see F (commit.)
1. 2 Cor. xii. 21.
1. Gal. v. 19.
1. Eph. v. 3.
1. Col. iii. 5.
1. 1 Thes. iv. 3.
— Jude 7, see F (give one's self over to.)
— Rev. ii. 14, 20, see F
1. —— 21. (commit.)
1. Rev. ix. 21.
1. —— xiv. 8.
— —— xvii. 2 1st, see F (commit.)
1. —— 2 2nd, 4.
2. —— 5, marg. (text, *harlots.*)
1. —— xviii. 3 1st.
— —— 3 2nd, 9, see F (commit.)
1. Rev. xix. 2.

FORNICATION (COMMIT.)

πορνεύω, to commit fornication, to play the harlot.

1 Cor. vi. 18.
—— x. 8.
Rev. ii. 14, 20.
—— xvii. 2.
Rev. xviii. 3, 9.

FORNICATION (GIVE ONE'S SELF OVER TO.)

ἐκπορνεύω, to be wholly given to fornication, *(non occ.)*

Jude 7.

FORNICATOR (-S.)

πόρνος, a fornicator.

1 Cor. v. 9, 10, 11.
1 Cor. vi. 9.
Heb. xii. 16.

FORSAKE (-ETH, -EN, -ING, -SOOK.)

1. **καταλείπω**, to leave behind, *esp. of persons dying or going into a far country;* to forsake, abandon.

2. **ἐγκαταλείπω**, *(No. 1 with ἐν,* in, *prefixed,)* to leave behind in *any place or state,* leave in the lurch, desert.

3. **ἀφίημι**, to send forth, discharge; to let go, dismiss; pass on, pass by; *hence,* to leave, quit, *in various senses.*

4. **ἀποτάσσω**, to arrange off, *i.e.* to assign to different places. *In N.T. only Mid.* to arrange one's self off, *hence,* to separate one's self from.

5. **ἀποστασία**, an apostacy, defection, revolt.

3. Matt. xix. 27, 29.
3. —— xxvi. 56.
2. —— xxvii. 46.
3. Mark i. 18.
3. —— xiv. 50.
2. —— xv. 34.
3. Luke v. 11.
4. —— xiv. 33.
5. Acts xxi. 21, with ἀπὸ, from.
2. 2 Cor. iv. 9.
2. 2 Tim. iv. 10, 16.
2. Heb. x. 25.
1. —— xi. 27.
2. —— xiii. 5.
1. 2 Pet. ii. 15.

FORSOMUCH AS.

καθότι, as, according as, because that, inasmuch as.

Luke xix. 9.

FORSWEAR ONE'S SELF.

ἐπιορκέω, to swear falsely.

Matt. v. 33.

FORTH.

ἔξω, out, without, *(of place,)* out of, forth.

John xi. 43.
—— xv. 6.
John xix. 4 twice, 5, 13.
Acts v. 34.
Acts ix. 40.

See also, BREAK, BRING, BROUGHT, CALL, CARRY, CAST, COME, CONDUCT, FRUIT, GIVE, GO, HOLD, LAUNCH, LET, MANIFEST, ORDER, PASS, PROCEED, PUT, REACH, SEND, SET, SETTER, SHED, SHINE, SHOOT, SHOW, SPEAK, STAND, STRETCH.

FORTHWITH.

1. **εὐθέως**, straightway, immediately.

2. **εὐθύς**, straight, *(of direction); also of time, like No.* 1.

3. **παραχρῆμα**, with the thing itself, *i.e.* at the very moment, on the spot, immediately, *i.e.* directly after something else has taken place.

1. Matt. xiii. 5.
1. —— xxvi. 49.
1. Mark i. 29, 43 (No. 2, L T Tr A ℵ.) [A ℵ.)
1. —— v. 13 (*om.* L[b] Tr
2. John xix. 34.
3. Acts ix. 18 (*om.* G L T Tr A ℵ.)
1. —— xii. 10.
1. —— xxi. 30.

FORTY.

τεσσαράκοντα, forty.

[As a typical number, it is the number of probation, separation, or judgment. Starting from Israel's wilderness life, it was the measure of God's judicial dealings (Ezek. iv. 6; xxix. 11—15), and was to be the measure of man's (Deut. xxv. 3.) Moses' life of three periods of forty years, and his personal wanderings, were anticipatory of his association with Israel. The number as connected with God's judicial dealings is repeated in the Book of Judges

(iii. 11, 30; v. 31; viii. 28; xiii. 1.) The two periods of forty days Moses was in the mount receiving the law are related to that breaking of the law which led to the forty years in the wilderness. Elijah too, the law's fearless asserter, spent forty days in the wilderness. The time of Nineveh's probation was forty days (Jonah iii. 4.) Our Lord's own wilderness temptation was also forty days; but the forty days after the resurrection point forward to the end of judicial dealings in resurrection life with Christ.]

Matt. iv. 2 twice.
Mark i. 13.
Luke iv. 2.
John ii. 20.
Acts i. 3.
— iv. 22. [old.
— vii. 23, see F years
— 30, 36, 42.
— xiii. 18, see F years (of.)
Acts xiii. 21.
— xxiii. 13, 21.
2 Cor. xi. 24.
Heb. iii. 9, 17.
Rev. vii. 4.
— xi. 2.
— xiii. 5.
— xiv. 1, 3.
— xxi. 17.

FORTY YEARS OLD.

{ τεσσαρακονταετής, forty years,
{ χρόνος, time.

Acts vii. 23.

FORTY YEARS (OF.)

τεσσαρακονταετής, forty years.

Acts xiii. 18.

FORWARD.

σπουδαῖος, speedy, hasty, *esp. as shown in earnest diligence*, (occ. 2 Cor. viii. 22.)

2 Cor. viii. 17.

FORWARD (BE.)

1. θέλω, to will, wish, desire, *implying the active volition and purpose, and expressing the natural impulse and desire.*
2. σπουδάζω, to make haste, be zealous to do, *esp. as manifested in diligence, earnestness;* to do the utmost.

— Mark xiv. 35, see go.
— Acts xix. 33, see put.
1. 2 Cor. viii. 10, marg. *be willing.*
2. Gal. ii. 10.
— 3 John 6, see bring.

FORWARDNESS.

σπουδή, speed, haste, *as manifested in earnestness*, diligence, zeal.

2 Cor. viii. 8.

FORWARDNESS OF MIND.

προθυμία, predisposition, alacrity of mind, eagerness, good-will, ready-kindness.

2 Cor. ix. 2.

FOSTER-BROTHER [margin.]

σύντροφος, nourished *or* nursed together.

Acts xiii. 1, text, *which had been brought up with.*

FOUL.

ἀκάθαρτος, *strictly, in a levitical sense,* impurified, *i.e.* unatoned; *then, gen.* impure, unclean.

Matt. xvi. 3, see weather. | Mark ix. 25.
Rev. xviii. 2.

FOUND, past tense of FIND.

See, FIND.

FOUND (-ED.)

θεμελιόω, to lay the foundation of *any thing*, to found.

Matt. vii. 25. | Luke vi. 48 (*ap.*)

FOUNDATION.

1. θεμέλιος, placed *or* laid as a foundation, fundamental. *Hence in N.T. as subst.* foundation.
   (a) *Neut.* τὸ θεμέλιον, *in St. Luke's writings*, foundation, *(non occ.)*
2. καταβολή, a casting down, *hence*, a laying down, the founding, the establishing, *involving a reference to an intended continuation. In N.T. only in the phrase,* κ. τοῦ κόσμου, beginning of the world, *(except* Heb. xi. 11.)

2. Matt. xiii. 35.
2. — xxv. 34.
1a. Luke vi. 48, 49.
2. — xi. 50.
1a. — xiv. 29.
2. John xvii. 24.
1a. Acts xvi. 26.
1. Rom. xv. 20.
1. 1 Cor. iii. 10, 11, 12.
2. Eph. i. 4.
1. — ii. 20.
1. 1 Tim. vi. 19.
— Heb. i. 10, see F of (lay the.)
2. — iv. 3.
1. — vi. 1.
2. — ix. 26.
1. — xi. 10.
2. 1 Pet. i. 20.
2. Rev. xiii. 8.
2. — xvii. 8.
1. — xxi. 14, 19 twice.

FOUNDATION OF (LAY THE.)

θεμελιόω, to lay the foundation of *any thing*, to found.

Heb. i. 10.

FOUNTAIN.

πηγή, a spring, a well, *hence,* fount, source, (occ. John iv. 6 twice, 11; 2 Pet. ii. 17.)

Mark v. 29.
Jas. iii. 11, 12 (*ap.*)
Rev. vii. 17.
Rev. viii. 10.
—— xiv. 7.
—— xvi. 4.
Rev. xxi. 6.

FOUR.

τέσσαρες, four, *(non occ.)*

[As a typical number, it is the number of the world. It is reproduced in everything earthly, (not by chance, but by the Divine constitution of things.) So we have—the four seasons; four points of compass, (Rev. vii. 1; Ezek. xxxvii. 9; Matt. xxiv. 31; Job. ix. 9); four divisions of people, (Rev. v. 9; vii. 9; x. 11; xiv. 6; xiii. 7); sons of Japheth divided (Gen. x. 5); sons of Ham divided (Gen. x. 20); sons of Shem (Gen x. 31); the four great world-powers (Zech. i. 18); the four Gospels; the twelve Apostles divided into three fours, in each list headed respectively by Peter, Philip, and James. The same number reigns in the camp of Israel, in the Tabernacle and Temple so far as they relate to the world. *See under the word* "CHERUBIM."]

Matt. xv. 38, } see
—— xvi. 10, } thousand.
—— xxiv. 31.
Mark ii. 3.
—— viii. 9, 20, see thousand.
—— xiii. 27.
Luke ii. 37.
John iv. 35, see months.
—— xi. 17.
—— —— 39, see F days (hath been dead.)
—— xix. 23.
Acts v. 36, } see
—— vii. 6, } hundred.
—— x. 11.
—— —— 30, see F days ago.
—— xi. 5.
—— xii. 4.
Acts xiii. 20, see hundred.
—— xxi. 9, 23.
—— —— 38, see thousand.
—— xxvii. 29.
Gal. iii. 17, see hundred.
Rev. iv. 4 twice, 6, 8, 10.
—— v. 6, 8 twice, 14 1st.
—— —— 14 2nd, see F and twenty.
—— vi. 1, 6.
—— vii. 1 3 times, 2, 4, 11.
—— ix. 13 (*om.* LTrbAbℵ.)
—— —— 14, 15.
—— xi. 16.
—— xiv. 1, 3 twice.
—— xv. 7.
—— xix. 4 twice.
—— xx. 8.
—— xxi. 17.

FOUR AND TWENTY.

εἰκοσιτέσσαρες, twenty four.

Rev. v. 14 (*om.* G L T Tr A ℵ)

FOURFOLD.

τετραπλόος, fourfold, quadruple, *(non occ.)*

Luke xix. 8.

FOURFOOTED BEAST.

τετράπους, fourfooted, quadruped.

Acts x. 12.
Acts xi. 6.
Rom. i. 23.

FOURSCORE.

ὀγδοήκοντα, eighty, *(non occ.)*

Luke ii. 37.
Luke xvi. 7.

FOURSQUARE.

τετράγωνος, four-cornered, *(non occ.)*

Rev. xxi. 16.

FOURTEEN.

δεκατέσσαρες, fourteen, *(non occ.)*

Matt. i. 17 3 times.
2 Cor. xii. 2.
Gal. ii. 1.

FOURTEENTH.

τεσσαρεσκαιδέκατος, fourteenth, *(non occ.)*

Acts xxvii. 27, 33.

FOURTH.

τέταρτος, the fourth, (occ. Acts x. 30.)

Matt. xiv. 25.
Mark vi. 48.
Rev. iv. 7.
—— vi. 7 twice.
Rev. vi. 8, see F part.
—— viii. 12.
—— xvi. 8.
—— xxi. 19.

FOURTH PART.

Rev. vi. 8.

FOWL (-s.)

1. πετεινόν, able to fly, winged; *the general epithet of birds.*
2. ὄρνεον, a bird, fowl; *generally the carnivorous.*

1. Matt. vi. 26.
1. —— xiii. 4.
1. Mark iv. 4, 32.
1. Luke viii. 5.
1. Luke xii. 24.
1. —— xiii. 19.
1. Acts x. 12.
1. —— xi. 6.
2. Rev. xix. 17, 21.

FOX (-es.)

ἀλώπηξ, a fox.

[*Derived from* ἀλωπός, cunning; *or, by Eustathices and Bochart from* ἀλᾶσθαι, to wander. *Eng. word* fox, *and Germ.* fuchs, *from the verb* foxa, *which in the Icelandic signifies* to deceive.]

Matt. viii. 20.
Luke ix. 58.
Luke xiii. 32.

FRAGMENT (-S.)

κλάσμα, that which is broken off, a fragment, morsel, (occ. *pl.* Matt. xv. 37; Mark iv. 8.)

Matt. xiv. 20. | Mark viii. 19, 20.
Mark vi. 43. | Luke ix. 17.
John vi. 12, 13.

FRAME (-ED.)

καταρτίζω, to adjust *or* put in order again; settle by acting as mediator, to reform, restore; *involving the idea of positive defects which have to be repaired or adjusted. (Referring here, to the* αἰῶνες, ages.)

Heb. xi. 3.

FRAME TOGETHER (FITLY.)

συναρμολογέω, to join together, to fit *or* joint together.

Eph. ii. 21.

FRANKINCENSE.

λίβανος, *(from Heb.* לבנה, *which is from* לבן, white.) Frankincense, olibanum, a resinous substance produced from a tree growing in the east, particularly in Arabia. It is of a whitish colour, and the best kind nearly transparent, *(non occ.)*

Matt. ii. 11. | Rev. xviii. 13.

FRANKLY.

See, FORGIVE.

FRAUD (KEEP BACK BY.)

ἀποστερέω, to rob, despoil, bereave *or* defraud *one* of *a thing.*

Jas. v. 4.

FREE [adj.]

ἐλεύθερος, one who can go where he will, *hence,* free, at liberty.

Matt. xvii. 26.
John viii. 33, 36.
Rom. v. 15, 16, see gift.
—— vi. 20.
—— vii. 3.
1 Cor. vii. 21, 22.
—— ix. 1, 19.
1 Cor. xii. 13.
Gal. iii. 28.
—— iv. 26, 31.
Eph. vi. 8.
Col. iii. 11.
1 Pet. ii. 16.
Rev. xiii. 16.
Rev. xix. 18.

FREE (MAKE.)

ἐλευθερόω, to free, set at liberty, to save from thraldom.

John viii. 32, 36. | Rom. viii. 2.
Rom. vi. 18, 22. | Gal. v. 1.

FREE WOMAN.

ἐλεύθερος, *see* "FREE."

Gal. iv. 22, 23, 30.

FREE (-D) [verb.]

δικαιόω, to bring forth a δίκαιος, (a just *or* righteous man,) to recognize, set forth as righteous, to justify.

Rom. vi. 7, marg. *justify.*

FREEDOM.

πολιτεία, the relation in which a citizen stands to the state, the condition *or* rights of a citizen, citizenship, (occ. Eph. ii. 12.)

Acts xxii. 28.

FREELY.

1. δωρεάν, *(Acc. of* δωρεά, *as adv.)* as a free gift, freely, *Lat.* gratis.
2. παῤῥησιάζομαι, to speak freely, openly *or* boldly.
3. { μετά, with, παῤῥησία, free-spokenness.

1. Matt. x. 8 twice.
3. Acts ii. 29.
2. —— xxvi. 26, part.
1. Rom. iii. 24.
— Rom. viii. 32, see give.
— 1 Cor. ii. 12, see given.
1. 2 Cor. xi. 7.
1. Rev. xxi. 6.
1. Rev. xxii. 17.

FREEMAN.

1. ἐλεύθερος, *see* "FREE."
2. ἀπελεύθερος, an emancipated slave, a freedman, *(non occ.)*

2. 1 Cor. vii. 22, marg. (text, *made free.*)
1. Rev. vi. 15.

FREQUENT (MORE.)

περισσοτέρως, more abundantly.

2 Cor. xi. 23.

FRESH.

γλυκύς, sweet to the taste. *Of water,* fresh, *(as opp. to* πικρός, bitter), (occ. Jas. iii. 11; Rev. x. 9, 10.)

Jas. iii. 12.

FRIEND (-s.)

1. φίλος, loved, beloved, dear. *Soon came to be used as subst. like Lat.* amicus, a loved one, a friend, *(non occ.)*

2. ἑταῖρος, a comrade, associate, companion, *(freq. used as addressed to followers or servants,) more distant than No.* 1, (occ. Matt. xi. 16.)

1. Matt. xi. 19.
2. —— xx. 13.
2. —— xxii. 12.
2. —— xxvi. 50.
— Mark iii. 21, see F (one's.)
— —— v. 19, see F (thy.)
1. Luke vii. 6, 34.
1. —— xi. 5 twice, 6, 8.
1. —— xiv. 10, 12.
1. —— xv. 6.
1. —— 9 (fem. pl.)
1. —— 29.
1. —— xvi. 9.
1. Luke xxi. 16.
1. —— xxiii. 12.
1. John iii. 29.
1. —— xi. 11.
1. —— xv 13, 14, 15.
1. —— xix. 12.
1. Acts x. 24.
— —— xii. 20. see F (make one's.)
1. —— xix. 31.
1. —— xxvii. 3.
1. Jas. ii. 23.
1. —— iv. 4.
— 3 John 14 twice.

FRIEND (MAKE ONE'S.)

πείθω, to persuade, win by words, to influence, *(as opp. to force.)*

Acts xii. 20.

FRIENDS (HIS ONE'S.)

{ οἱ, the [*persons*], παρά, beside, αὐτοῦ, him, } those belonging to him, his relatives.

Mark iii. 21, marg. *kinsmen.*

FRIENDS (THY.)

{ οἱ, the [*persons*], σοί, with thee, } thine own *people.*

Mark v. 19.

FRIENDSHIP.

φιλία, love, affection, friendship, *(non occ.)*

Jas. iv. 4.

FRO.

See, TOSS, TOSSING.

FROG (-s.)

βάτραχος, a frog, *(so called from its harsh croaking, as prob. the Eng. word is.)*

Rev. xvi. 13.

FROM.

(When "FROM" is not the translation of a case of the noun, or part of another word, it is one of these following.)

1. ἀπό, from, away from, *(motion from the exterior.)**

2. ἐκ, from, from among, out of, *(motion from the interior.)**

3. παρά, beside.*
   (a) *with Gen.* from beside, from, *(used of persons, as No.* 1 *is of places.)*

4. ὑπό, under.
   (a) *with Gen.* by, *(used of the agent or efficient cause.)*

5. διά, through.
   (a) *with Gen.* through, *(as proceeding from.)*

6. ἐγγύς, *adv.* near, *used of both place and time.*

7. τοῦ, *with the Inf. of the verb, lit.* the to...*(marking the purpose or design)*; of *or* in...-ing, *(here,* in my purpose of coming.)

* The exact force of these three prepositions may be thus illustrated—

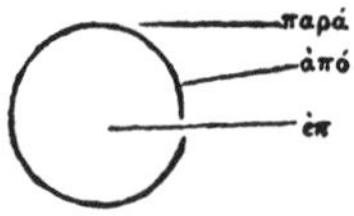

1 Matt. i. 17 3 times, 21, 24.
1. —— ii. 1, 16.
1. —— iii. 7, 13.
2. —— 17.
1. —— iv. 17.
— —— 21, see thence.
1. —— 25.
1. —— v. 18, 29, 30.
— —— 42, see turn.
1. —— vi. 13.
1. —— vii. 23.
1. —— viii. 1, 11, 30.
— —— ix. 9, see thence
1. —— 15, 16, 22.
1. —— xi. 12, 25.
— —— xii. 15, see thence
1. —— 38.
2. —— 42.
— —— 44, see whence.
1. —— xiii. 12.
— —— 27, see whence.
1. —— 35.
2. —— 49, and see F among.
1. —— xiv. 2.
1. —— xv. 8.
2. —— 18.
1. —— 28.
— —— 29, see thence.
2. —— xvi. 1.
— —— 21, see time.
1. —— xvii. 9 1st (No. 2, G L T Tr A ℵ.)
2. —— 9 2nd
1. —— 18.
1. Matt. xviii. 8, 9, 35.
1. —— xix. 1, 8.
2. —— 12.
— —— 20, see F my youth up.
1. —— xx. 8, 29.
1. —— xxi. 8.
2. —— 25 twice
1. —— 43.
1. —— xxii. 46.
1. —— xxiii. 34, 35
1. —— xxiv. 1 (No 2, L.)
1. —— 29.
2. —— 31 1st.
1. —— 31 2nd
1. —— xxv. 28.
1. —— 29.
1. —— 32 twice, 34, 41.
— —— xxvi. 16, see time.
1. —— 39.
1. —— 42 (*om.* ἀπ' ἐμοῦ, *from me,* G ≈ L[b] T Tr A ℵ.)
1. —— 47.
— —— xxvii. 31, see take.
1. —— 40, 42, 45.
— —— 51, see top.
1. —— 55, 64.
2. —— xxviii. 2 1st.
1. —— 2 2nd (*om.* ἀπὸ τῆς θύρας, *from the door,* G → L T Tr A ℵ)
1 —— 7, 8.
1. Mark i. 9.
2. —— 11.
— —— 45, see every

1. Mark ii. 20.
1. —— iii. 7 twice, 8 twice, 22.
1. —— iv. 25.
1. —— v. 35.
— —— vi. 1, see thence.
— ——— 2, see whence.
— ——— 10, see place.
2. ——— 14.
2. ——— 16 (om. ἐκ νεκρῶν, *from the dead*, T Trb A ℵ.)
1. —— vii. 1, 4, 6.
— ——— 15, see without.
1. ——— 17.
— ——— 18, see without.
— ——— 21, 23, see within.
— ——— 24, see thence.
2. ——— 31.
1. ——— 33.
— —— viii. 4, see whence.
1. ——— 11.
1. —— ix. 9 1st (No. 2, L.)
2. ——— 9 2nd, 10.
— —— x. 1, see thence.
1. ——— 6.
2. ——— 20.
1. —— xi. 12.
2. ——— 20, 30, 31.
3a. —— xii. 2.
2. ——— 25.
1. ——— 34.
1. —— xiii. 19.
2. ——— 27.
1. —— xiv. 35, 36.
3a. ——— 43.
1. ——— 52 (om. ἀπ' αὐτῶν, *from them*, G→ Lb T Tr ℵ.)
— —— xv. 20, see take.
1. ——— 30, 32.
— ——— 38, see top.
2. —— xvi. 3 (No. 1, L Tr.)
1. ——— 8.
1. Luke i. 2.
— ——— 3, see first.
2. ——— 15.
4a. ——— 26 (No. 1, L Tr A ℵ)
1. ——— 38.
3a. ——— 45.
— ——— 50, see generation
1. ——— 52.
2. ——— 71 twice, 78, see [high.
3a. —— ii. 1.
1. ——— 4, 15, 36.
1. ——— 37 (om. Tr A) (No. 2, ℵ)
1. —— iii. 7.
2. ——— 22.
1. —— iv. 1.
— ——— 9, see hence.
1. ——— 13, 42.
1. —— v. 3, 8, 13, 35.
1. —— vii. 6.
1. —— viii. 18, 37.
3a. ——— 49 (No. 1, L.)
1. —— ix. 5.
2. ——— 7.
1. ——— 33, 37, 39, 45.
1. ——— 54 (No. 2, L.)
2. —— x. 7, 18.
1. ——— 21, 30, 42.
1. —— xi. 4 (ap.)
— ——— 7, see within.
2. ——— 16, 31.
1. ——— 50, 51.
2. —— xii. 36.
1. ——— 58.
1. —— xiii. 15, 16, 27.
1. ——— 29 (om. G⇄ Lb T Trb Ab)
1. —— xvi. 3.
1. ——— 18 (om. G→.)
1. ——— 21.
— ——— 26, see thence.
— ——— 26, see hence.
1. ——— 30.
2. ——— 31.
2. —— xvii. 7.

1. Luke xvii. 29.
— —— xviii. 21, see F my youth up.
1. ——— 34.
1. —— xix. 24, 26 1st.
1. ——— 26 2nd (om. ἀπ', αὐτοῦ, *from him*, Lb T A ℵ.)
1. ——— 39, 42.
2. —— xx. 4, 5, 35.
1. —— xxi. 11.
1. —— xxii. 41, 42, 43 (ap.), 45.
1. —— xxiii. 5, 49.
2. ——— 55.
1. —— xxiv. 2, 9, 13.
2. ——— 46, 49.
1. ——— 51.
3a. John i. 6.
2. ——— 19, 32.
2. —— ii. 22.
1. —— iii. 2.
— ——— 3, 7, see *above*.
2. ——— 13, 27.
— ——— 31 1st, see above.
2. ——— 31 2nd.
— —— iv. 11, see whence.
2. —— v. 24.
3a. ——— 34, 41, 44.
2. —— vi. 23, 31, 32 twice, 33.
2. ——— 38 (No. 1, L T Tr A.)
2. ——— 41, 42, 50, 51, 58, 64.
— ——— 66, see time.
3a. —— vii. 29.
2. —— viii. 23 twice, 42.
1. ——— 44.
2. —— ix. 1.
— ——— 29, 30, see whence
1. —— x. 5, 18.
2. ——— 32.
1. —— xi. 53.
2. —— xii. 1, 9, 17, 27, 28, 32.
1. ——— 36.
1. —— xiii. 3.
2. ——— 4.
— —— xv. 5, see *severed*.
3a. ——— 26 twice.
1. ——— 27.
1. —— xvi. 22.
3a. ——— 27.
3a. ——— 28 (No. 2, L T Tr A)
1. ——— 30.
3a. —— xvii. 8.
2. ——— 15.
2. —— xviii. 3.
1. ——— 28.
— ——— 36, see hence.
— —— xix. 11, see above.
— ——— 12, see thenceforth.
2. ——— 23.
1. ——— 27.
2. —— xx. 1, 9.
1. —— xxi. 8.
2. ——— 14.
1. Acts i. 4, 11, 12 1st.
6. ——— 12 2nd.
1. ——— 22 twice.
2. ——— 25 (No. 1, L T Tr A ℵ.
2. —— ii. 2.
1. ——— 40.
— ——— 46, see house to house.
2. —— iii. 2, 15.
1. ——— 19.
— ——— 23, see F among.
1. ——— 24, 26.
2. —— iv. 2, 10.
1. —— v. 38, 41.
— —— vii. 4, see thence.
— ——— 39, see thrust.
1. —— viii. 16, 26, 33.
1. —— ix. 3 (No. 2, L T Tr A* ℵ.)
1. ——— 8.
3a. ——— 14.

1. Acts ix. 18.
1. —— x. 17, 21 (ap.), 23, 37.
2. ——— 41.
— —— xi. 4, see rehearse.
2. ——— 5, 9.
1. ——— 11, 27.
2. —— xii. 7.
1. ——— 10, 19.
2. ——— 25.
— —— xiii. 4, see thence.
1. ——— 8, 13 twice, 14, 29.
2. ——— 30.
1. ——— 31.
2. ——— 34.
1. ——— 39.
— ——— 46, see put.
2. —— xiv. 8.
1. ——— 15.
— ——— 17, see heaven.
1. ——— 19.
— ——— 26, see whence.
1. —— xv. 1, 18.
— ——— 19, see F among.
1. ——— 20 (om. L T Tr Ab ℵ.)
2. ——— 24, 29.
1. ——— 33, 38, 39.
1. —— xvi. 11.
— ——— 12, see thence.
2. —— xvii. 3.
1. ——— 27.
2. ——— 31, 33.
— ——— 33, see F among.
2. —— xviii. 1.
1. ——— 2 1st.
2. ——— 2 2nd (No. 1, L T Tr A ℵ.)
1. ——— 5, 6, 16, 21.
1. —— xix. 9, 12 twice.
1. —— xx. 6, 9, 17, 18.
— ——— 20, see house to house.
1. ——— 26.
1. —— xxi. 1 1st.
— ——— 1 2nd, see thence.
1. ——— 7, 10.
3a. —— xxii. 5.
2. ——— 6.
1. ——— 22, 29.
1. ——— 30 (om. ἀπὸ τῶν δεσμῶν, *from his bonds*, G L T Tr A ℵ.)
2. —— xxiii. 10, see among
1. ——— 21.
1. —— xxiv. 18.
1. —— xxv. 1, 7.
2. —— xxvi. 4.
— ——— 5, see beginning.
3a. ——— 10.
3a. ——— 12 (om. G→ L T Tr A ℵ.)
— ——— 13, see heaven.
2. ——— 17.
1. ——— 18.
— —— xxvii. 4, see thence.
1. ——— 21.
2. ——— 34 (No. 1, L T Tr A.)
— ——— 43, see keep.
— —— xxviii. 13, 15, see thence.
2. ——— 17.
1. ——— 23.
1. Rom. i. 7.
2. ——— 17.
1. ——— 18, 20.
2. —— iv. 24.
1. —— v. 9, 14.
2. —— vi. 4.
1. ——— 7.
2. ——— 9, 13, 17.
1. ——— 18, 22.
1. —— vii. 2, 3.
2. ——— 4.
1. ——— 6.
2. ——— 24.

1. Rom. viii. 2.
2. ——— 11 twice.
1. ——— 21, 35, 39.
1. —— ix. 3.
2. —— x. 7, 9.
2. —— xi. 15.
1. ——— 26.
1. —— xv. 19.
7. ——— 22.
1. ——— 31.
1. 1 Cor. i. 3.
2. —— v. 2, see also F among.
— ——— 13, see F among.
1. —— vii. 10, 27.
2. —— ix. 19.
1. —— x. 14.
1. —— xiv. 36.
2. —— xv. 12, 20.
— ——— 41, see differ.
2. ——— 47.
1. 2 Cor. i. 2.
2. ——— 10.
2. —— iii. 1.
1. ——— 18.
2. —— v. 2.
1. ——— 6.
2. ——— 8.
— —— vi. 17, see F among.
1. —— vii. 1.
1. —— xi. 3, 9 1st.
— ——— 9 2nd, see burdensome.
1. —— xii. 8.
2. Gal. i. 1.
1. ——— 3.
2. ——— 4.
1. ——— 6.
2. ——— 8, 15.
1. —— ii. 12.
2. —— iii. 13.
— —— iv. 1, see differ.
1. ——— 24.
1. Eph. i. 2.
2. ——— 20.
1. —— iii. 9, see also world.
2. —— iv. 16.
1. ——— 31.
2. —— v. 14.
2. —— vi. 6.
1. ——— 23.
1. Phil. i. 2, 5.
2. —— iii. 20.
1. —— iv. 15.
3a. ——— 18.
1. Col. i. 2.
2. ——— 13, 18.
1. ——— 23, 26 twice.
2. —— ii. 12, 19.
1. ——— 20.
2. —— iv. 16.
1. 1 Thes. i. 1 (ap.), 8, 9.
2. ——— 10 1st & 2nd.
1. ——— 10 3rd.
1. —— ii. 17.
1. —— iii. 6.
1. —— iv. 3, 16.
1. —— v. 22.
1. 2 Thes. i. 2, 7, 9 twice.
5a. —— ii. 2.
1. ——— 13 (ἀπαρχήν, *first-fruits*, instead of ἀπ' ἀρχῆς, *from the beginning*, L Trm.)
1. —— iii. 2, 3, 6.
1. 1 Tim. i. 2.
— ——— 6, see swerve.
— —— iv. 1, see depart.
— —— v. 13, see house to house.
1. —— vi. 5 (ap.)
1. 2 Tim. i. 2, 3.
— ——— 15, see turn.
2. —— ii. 8.
1. ——— 19, 21.
1. —— iii. 15.
1. —— iv. 4, 18.

1. Titus i. 4
— ——— 14, see turn.
1. —— ii. 14.
1. Philem. 3.
1. Heb. iii. 12.
1. —— iv. 3, 4, 10 twice.
— —— v. 1, see F among.
2. ——— 7.
1. —— vi. 1, 7
1. —— vii. 1.
2. ——— 6.
— ——— 24, see *F one to another.*
1. ——— 26.
1. —— viii. 11.
1. —— ix. 14.
1. —— x. 22.
1. —— xi. 15.
2. ——— 19 1st.
— ——— 19 2nd, see whence.
1. —— xii. 15, marg. (text *of.*)
1. ——— 25.
— Jas. i. 17 1st, see above.
1. ——— 17 2nd, 27.
— —— iii. 15, 17, see above
— —— iv. 1, see whence.
1. ——— 7.
1. —— v. 19.
2. ——— 20 twice.
2. 1 Pet. i. 3.
1. ——— 12.
2. ——— 18, 21.
1. —— iii. 10.
3a. 2 Pet. i. 17 1st.
4a. ——— 17 2nd.
2. ——— 18.
— —— ii. 8, see day to day (from.)
2. ——— 21 (*ap.*)
1. —— iii. 4.
1. 1 John i. 1, 7, 9.
1. —— ii. 7 1st.
1. ——— 7 2nd (*om.* ἀπ' ἀρχῆς, *from the beginning*, G⇉ L T Tr A ℵ.)

1. 1 John ii. 13, 14.
2. ——— 19.
1. ——— 20, 24 twice.
1. —— iii. 8, 11.
2. ——— 14.
1. ——— 17.
1. —— iv. 21.
1. —— v. 21.
3a. 2 John 3 twice, 4.
1. ——— 5, 6.
1. Jude 14.
1. Rev. i. 4 twice, 5 1st.
1. ——— 5 2nd (No. 2, L Tr ℵ.)
— —— ii. 5, see whence.
1. —— iii. 12.
1. —— vi. 4 (No. 2, G L T Tr A ℵ) (ἐκ, *om.* G⇉.)
1. ——— 16 twice.
1. —— vii. 2.
1. ——— 17 (G∾) (No. 2, G L T Tr A.)
2. —— viii. 10.
2. —— ix. 1.
1. ——— 6.
2. ——— 13.
2. —— x. 1, 4, 8.
2. —— xi. 11, 12.
1. —— xii. 14.
1. —— xiii. 8.
2. ——— 13.
2. —— xiv. 2.
1. ——— 3, 4.
2. ——— 13 twice, 18.
2. —— xv. 8 twice.
1. —— xvii. 8.
2. —— xviii. 1, 4.
1. ——— 14 twice.
2. —— xx. 1.
1. ——— 9 (*om.* ἀπὸ τοῦ Θεοῦ, *from God*, G→ L T Trb A ℵ.)
1. ——— 11.
1. —— xxi. 2.
1. ——— 4 (No. 2, L T Tr A ℵ.)
1. ——— 10.
1. —— xxii. 19.

FROM AMONG.

1. ἀπό, *see* "FROM," *No.* 1.
2. ἐκ, *see* "FROM," *No.* 2.
3. { ἐκ, from, μέσου, the midst.

3. Matt. xiii. 49.
2. Acts iii. 23.
1. —— xv. 19.
3. —— xvii. 33.

3. Acts xxiii. 10.
3. 1 Cor. v. 2.
2. ——— 13.
3. 2 Cor. vi. 17.

2. Heb. v. 1.

FROM ONE TO ANOTHER [marg.]

ἀπαραβάτος, not passing from beside, intransmissible, inviolable.

Heb. vii. 24, text, *unchangeable.*

FROM MY YOUTH UP.

1. { ἐκ, *see* "FROM," *No.* 2, νεότης, youth, μου, my, } from my youth.

2. { ἐκ, *see* "FROM," *No.* 2, νεότης, youth. } from youth.

1. Matt. xix. 20 (*om.* G→ L T Tr A. ℵ.)
2. Luke xviii. 21.

See also, FALL, FAR, HENCEFORTH.

FROWARD.

σκολιός, crooked, *metaph.* not straightforward, perverse.

1 Pet. ii. 18.

FRUIT (-s.)

1. καρπός, that which is dry and ripe, fruit, *used of trees but also of the earth; and then gen.* produce, result.
2. γέννημα, that which is born *or* produced; *of men*, offspring; *of trees, etc.*, fruit, produce.

1. Matt. iii. 8.
1. —— vii. 16, 17 twice, 18 twice, 19, 20.
1. —— xii. 33 3 times.
1. —— xiii. 8.
— ——— 23, see F (bear.)
1. ——— 26.
1. —— xxi. 19, 34 twice, 41, 43.
2. —— xxvi. 29.
1. Mark iv. 7, 8.
— ——— 20, 28, see F (bring forth.)
1. ——— 29.
1. —— xi. 14.
1. —— xii. 2.
2. —— xiv. 25.
1. Luke i. 42.
1. —— iii. 8, 9.
1. —— vi. 43 twice, 44.
1. —— viii. 8.
— ——— 14, see perfection
— ——— 15, see F (bring forth.)
1. —— xii. 17.
2. ——— 18 (Trm) (σῖτος, wheat, Tr.)
1. —— xiii. 6, 7, 9.
1. —— xx. 10.
1. John iv. 36.
1. —— xii. 24.

1. John xv. 2 3 times, 4, 5, 8, 16 twice.
1. Acts ii. 30.
1. Rom. i. 13.
1. —— vi. 21, 22.
— —— vii. 4, 5, see F (bring forth.)
— —— viii. 23, see first F.
1. —— xv. 28.
— —— xvi. 5, see first F.
1. 1 Cor. ix. 7.
— —— xv. 20, 23, } see
— —— xvi. 15, } first F.
2. 2 Cor. ix. 10.
1. Gal. v. 22.
1. Eph. v. 9.
1. Phil. i. 11, 22.
1. —— iv. 17.
— Col. i. 6, see F (bring forth.)
1. 2 Tim. ii. 6.
1. Heb. xii. 11.
1. —— xiii. 15.
— Jas. i. 18, see first F.
1. —— iii. 17, 18.
1. —— v. 7, 18.
— Jude 12 1st, see wither.
— ——— 12 2nd, see F (without.)
— Rev. xiv. 4, see first F.
— —— xviii. 14, see fruits
1. —— xxii. 2 twice.

FRUIT (BEAR.)

καρποφορέω, to bear καρπός (fruit.)

(a) *Mid.* to bear fruit to one's self, *i.e.* propagate one's self, increase.

Matt. xiii. 23.

FRUIT (BRING FORTH.)

Mark iv. 20, 28.
Luke viii. 15.

Rom. vii. 4, 5.
a. Col. i. 6, with εἰμί to [be.

FRUIT (WITHOUT.)

ἄκαρπος, unfruitful.

Jude 12.

FRUITS.

ὀπώρα, the part of the year between the rising of Sirius and of Arcturus, *(acc. to the division of the year into seven seasons,) and so, not so much the Lat.* auctumnus, autumn, *as the proper time for field and tree fruits to ripen.* ὀπώρα *also means* the fruit itself, *esp.* tree-fruit.

Rev. xviii. 14.

FRUITFUL.

καρποφόρος, fruitbearing.

Acts xiv. 17.

FRUITFUL (BE.)

καρποφορέω, to bear καρπός (fruit, *see* "FRUIT," *No.* 1.)

Col. i. 10.

FRUSTRATE.

ἀθετέω, to displace, set aside, disregard *as a treaty or oath,* to reject.

Mark vii. 9,
Luke vii. 30, } marg. (text, *reject.*)
Gal. ii. 21

FULFIL (-ED, -ING.)

1. πληρόω, to make full, fill; *then,* to fulfil, perform fully, complete, accomplish.
2. ἀναπληρόω, *(No.* 1 *with* ἀνά, up, *prefixed,)* to fill up, complete, *(stronger than No.* 1.)
3. ἐκπληρόω, *(No.* 1 *with* ἐκ, from, out of, *prefixed,)* to fill out, fill quite up, complete in full, *(non occ.)*
4. τελέω, to bring about, complete, fulfil, accomplish, *not to end a thing or state, but* to bring about a complete and perfect one.
5. συντελέω, *(No.* 4 *with* σύν, together, *prefixed,)* to bring to one end together, bring quite to an end, finish, perfect.
6. τελειόω, to make perfect, consummate, bring to an accomplishment.
7. ποιέω, to make, to do, *(expressing action either as completed or continued.)*
8. πληροφορέω, to bear, or bring fully, to fill up the full measure.

1. Matt i. 22.
1. —— ii. 15, 17, 23
1. —— iii. 15.
1. —— iv. 14.
1. —— v. 17.
— —— 18, see F (be.)
1. —— viii. 17.
1. —— xii. 17.
2. —— xiii. 14.
1. —— xxi. 4.
— —— xxiv. 34, see F (be)
1. —— xxvi. 54, 56.
1. —— xxvii. 9, 35 (*ap.*)
1. Mark i. 15.
5. —— xiii. 4.
1. —— xiv. 49.
1. —— xv. 28 (*ap.*)
1. Luke i. 20, (πίμπλημι, *to fill,* G ∾.)
6. —— ii. 43, part.
1. —— iv. 21.
1. —— xxi. 22 (πίμπλημι, *to fill,* G L T Tr A ℵ.)
1. —— 24.
— —— 32, see F (be.)
1. —— xxii. 16.
1. —— xxiv. 44.
1. John iii. 29.
1. —— xii. 38.
1. —— xiii. 18.
1. —— xv. 25.
1. —— xvii. 12, 13.
1. —— xviii. 9, 32.
1. —— xix. 24.
6. —— 28.
1. John xix. 36.
1. Acts i. 16.
1. —— iii. 18.
1. —— ix. 23.
1. —— xii. 25, part.
7. —— xiii. 22.
1. —— 25, 27
4. —— 29.
3. —— 33.
1. —— xiv. 26.
4. Rom. ii. 27.
1. —— viii. 4.
1. —— xiii. 8.
—— 10, see fulfilling [noun.]
1. 2 Cor. x. 6.
1. Gal. v. 14
4. —— 16
2. —— vi. 2.
7. Eph. ii. 3.
1. —— iv. 10, marg. (text, *fill.*)
1. Phil. ii. 2.
1. Col. i. 25, marg. *preach fully.*
1. —— iv. 17.
1. 2 Thes. i. 11.
8. 2 Tim. iv. 5, marg. (text, *make full proof.*)
4. Jas. ii. 8.
1. —— 23.
1. Rev. vi. 11
4. —— xv. 8.
7. —— xvii. 17 1st
4. —— 17 2nd
1. —— xx. 3.

FULFILLED (BE.)

γίνομαι, to begin to be, *i.e.* to come into any existence *or* state, to become, to enter upon any state *or* condition, to come to pass.

Matt. v. 18; xxiv. 34; Luke xxi. 32.

FULFILLING [noun.]

πλήρωμα, that with which any thing is filled *or* of which it is full, the contents, fulness, filling.

Rom. xiii. 10.

FULL [adj.]

1. πλήρης, full of, filled with; *gen.* full, complete, sufficient.
2. πληρόω, to make πλήρης *(see No.* 1), to fill, *see* "FULFIL," *No.* 1.
3. πλήρωμα, *see* "FULFILLING."
4. μεστός, full, filled *(as with food,)* sated.
5. μεστόω, to make μεστός *(No.* 3,) *here Pass.* to be filled with *or* full of, *(non occ.)*

6. κορέννυμι, to sate, satisfy, fill *one* with *a thing*. *Pass. (as here)* to be sated *or* glutted with *a thing*, have one's fill of *it*.

— Matt. vi. 22, see light.
— ——— 23, see darkness.
— —— xiii. 48, see F (be.)
1. —— xiv 20.
1. —— xv. 37. [of (be.)
— —— xxiii. 25, 27, see F
4. ——— 28.
1. Mark iv. 28.
— ——— 37, see F (be.)
1. —— vi. 43 (No. 3, T Tr A ℵ.)
— —— vii. 9, see well.
1. —— viii. 19.
3. ——— 20.
— —— xv. 36, see fill.
— Luke i. 57, see time.
1. —— iv. 1.
1. —— v. 12.
— —— vi. 25, see F (be.)
— —— xi. 34[1st], see light.
— ———34[2nd], see darkness
— ——— 36[twice], see light
— ——— 39, see F of (be.)
— —— xvi. 20, see sores.
1. John i. 14. [(be.)
— —— vii. 8, see F come
— —— xv. 11, see F (be.)
2. —— xvi. 24, part.
4. —— xix. 29.
4. —— xxi. 11.
5. Acts ii. 13, part.
— ——— 28, see F (make.)

1. Acts vi. 3, 5, 8.
— —— vii. 23, see F (be.)
1. ——— 55.
1. —— ix. 36.
1. —— xi. 24.
1. —— xiii. 10.
— —— xvii. 16, see *idols*.
1. —— xix. 28.
4. Rom. i. 29.
— —— iii. 14, see F of (be)
4. —— xv. 14.
6. 1 Cor. iv. 8, part.
— Phil. ii. 26, see heaviness
— —— iv. 18.
— Col. ii. 2, see assurance.
— 2 Tim. iv. 5, see proof.
— Heb. v. 14, see age.
— —— vi. 11, } see
— —— x. 22, } assurance
4. Jas. iii. 8, 17.
— 1 Pet. i. 8, see glory.
4. 2 Pet. ii. 14.
2. 1 John i. 4, part.
1. 2 John 8.
2. ——— 12, part.
— Rev. iv. 6, see F of.
— ——— 8, see F of (be.)
— —— v. 8, } see F of.
— —— xv. 7, }
— —— xvi. 10, see darkness
— —— xvii. 3, 4, } see
— —— xxi. 9, } F of.

FULL (BE.)

1. πληρόω, *see* "FULFIL," *No.* 1.
   (a) *Pass.*
2. ἐμπίπλημι, to fill in, make full.
   (a) *Pass.* to be filled *(as with food,)* with *any person or thing.*
3. γεμίζω, to fill, load *or* freight.
   (a) *Pass.* to be laden *or* freighted.

1a. Matt. xiii. 48.
3a. Mark iv. 37.
2a. Luke vi. 25.
1a. John xv. 11.
1a. Acts vii. 23.
1a. Phil. iv. 18.

FULL OF.

γέμω, to be full, *(spoken strictly of a ship)* be stuffed with.
(a) *Participle.*

a. Rev. iv. 6.
a. —— v. 8.
a. Rev. xv. 7.
a. —— xvii. 3, 4.
a. Rev. xxi. 9.

FULL OF (BE.)

Matt. xxiii. 25, 27.
Luke xi. 39.
Rom. iii. 14.
Rev. iv. 8.

FULL (MAKE.)

πληρόω, *see* "FULFIL," *No.* 1.

Acts ii. 28.

FULL COME (BE.)

John vii. 8, pass.

FULLER.

γναφεύς, a fuller *(Lat.* fullo,) *i.e.* a cloth carder *or* dresser, a clothes cleaner, *(from* γνάφος, the prickly teasel, *a plant used by fullers to dress or clean cloth, hence,* a carding comb,) *(non occ.)*

Mark ix. 3.

FULLY PREACH.

πληρόω, *see* "FULFIL," *No.* 1.

Rom. xv. 19.
Col. i. 25, marg. (text, *fulfil.*)

FULLY.

See also, ASSURED, COME, KNOW, KNOWN, PERSUADED, RIPE.

FULNESS.

πλήρωμα, that with which any thing is filled *or* of which it is full, the contents, *hence*, fulness, filling.

John i. 16.
Rom. xi. 12, 25.
—— xv. 29.
1 Cor. x. 26, 28 (*ap.*)
Gal. iv. 4.
Eph. i. 10, 23.
—— iii. 19.
—— iv. 13.
Col. i. 19.
—— ii. 9.

FURLONG (-s.)

στάδιος, that which stands fast, *hence*, a fixed standard of length; a stade equal to 606¾ English feet, *(about one eighth of a Roman mile and one tenth of an English mile.) Also* a race-course, *because the most noted (Olympia) was exactly a stade long.* (occ. 1 Cor. ix. 24.)

Luke xxiv. 13.
John vi. 19.
John xi. 18
Rev. xiv. 20.
Rev. xxi. 16.

FURNACE.

κάμινος, an oven, furnace *or* kiln, *(for melting metals or baking earthenware; never a fire or stove for heating rooms,) (prob. from* καίω, to light, *Lat.* caminus. *Eng.* chimney,) *(non occ.)*

Matt. xiii. 42, 50.
Rev. i. 15.
Rev. ix. 2.

FURNISH (-ED.)

1. *στρώννυμι*, to spread, spread out *(as a bed,) of a room,* spread *with furniture; of a table, with food, hence,* furnished.

2. *πίμπλημι*, to fill, make full, be filled *or* full of.

2. Matt. xxii. 10. | 1. Mark xiv. 15. | 1. Luke xxii. 12.
— 2 Tim. iii. 17, see F (throughly.)

FURNISH (THROUGHLY.)

ἐξαρτίζω, to fit out *or* equip fully, to be put in perfect readiness for, complete.

2 Tim. iii. 17, marg. *perfect.*

FURTHER.

1. *ἔτι*, *of the present,* yet, as yet, still; *of the future,* yet longer, still, henceforth; *gen.* yet, further.

2. { *ἔτι*, yet, *see No.* 1. / *πλείων*, more. }

3. *ποῤῥωτέρω*, more forward, far farther.

1. Matt. xxvi. 65.
— Mark v. 35, }
— —— xiv. 63, } see F (any.)
— Luke xxii. 71, }
3. Luke xxiv. 28.
2. Acts iv. 17.
— Acts iv. 21, see threaten
— —— xii. 3, see proceed.
1. —— xxi. 28.
2. —— xxiv. 4.
— —— xxvii. 28, see go.
2. 2 Tim. iii. 9.
1. Heb. vii. 11.

FURTHER (ANY.)

1. Mark v. 35. | 1. Mark xiv. 63.
1. Luke xxii. 71.

FURTHERANCE.

προκοπή, a going forward, progress, advancement, (occ. 1 Tim. iv. 15.)

Phil. i. 12, 25.

FURTHERMORE.

1. *εἶτα*, *of time,* then, next; *of thought,* and so, then, accordingly.

2. { *τὸ*, the, / *λοιπόν*, remaining, } { *used of time.* in future, for the rest, as to what remains. }

2. 1 Thes. iv. 1. | 1. Heb. xii. 9.

G

GADARENES (-s.)

1. *Γαδαρήνος*, a Gadarene, *i.e.* an inhabitant of the city or district of Gadara, (the fortified capital of Peræa, or the region east of the Jordan,) *(non occ.)*

2. *Γερασήνος*, a Gerasene, *i.e.* an inhabitant of the city or district of Gerasa (in the eastern part of Peræa near the Arabian Desert, on the parallel of Samaria, one of the cities of Decapolis.)

[The city must have given its name to a large district, as Jerome says Gilead was then called Gerasa, and Saadias in his Arabic version puts Jerrash (the modern name of Gadarea), for the Heb. Gilead.]

3. *Γεργεσηνός*, a Gergesene, the proper name of one of the ancient tribes of Canaan, destroyed by Joshua, (of which nothing remained but the name,) Gen. xv. 21; Deut. vii. 1; Josh. xxiv. 11.

1. Mark v. 1 (No. 2, G∾ L T Tr ℵ), (No. 3, A.)
1. Luke viii. 26 (No. 2, G∾ L T Tr A), (No. 3, ℵ.)
1. ——— 37 (No. 2, L T Tr A), (No. 3, ℵ.)

GAIN (-s) [noun.]

1. *ἐργασία*, work, daily labour, business.

2. *κέρδος*, gain, profit, advantage.

3. *πορισμός*, a providing, procuring, a source *or* means of making money, gain, *(non occ.)*

1. Acts xvi. 16, 19.
1. —— xix. 24.
— 2 Cor. xii. 17, 18, see G of (make a.)
2. Phil. i. 21.
2. —— iii. 7.
3. 1 Tim. vi. 5, 6.
— Jas. iv. 13, see G (get.)

GAIN (GET.)

κερδαίνω, to derive profit *or* advantage from.

Jas. iv. 13.

GAIN OF (MAKE A.)

πλεονεκτέω, to have *or* claim more *than another*, *esp. in a bad sense*, to claim more than one's due, to be greedy *or* grasping, to over-reach.

2 Cor. xii. 17, 18.

GAIN (-ED) [verb.]

1. κερδαίνω, *see* "GAIN (GET.)"
2. ἐργάζομαι, to work, labour, *(prop. of husbandry, but also of manual labour,)* to work, do, perform, *then* to work out, earn by working, trade, traffic.
3. προσεργάζομαι, *(No.* 2 *with* πρός, towards, *prefixed,)* to work out thereto, to do *something* besides *another*, *hence*, to make *or* earn in addition, *(non occ.)*
4. ποιέω, to make, *i.e.* to form, produce, bring about, cause *(of action completed,) also* to do *(of action incompleted.)*

1. Matt. xvi. 26.
1. —— xviii. 15.
1. —— xxv. 17, 20, 22.
1. Mark viii. 36.
1. Luke ix. 25, part.
— —— xix. 15, see trading
3. Luke xix. 16.
4. —— 18.
1. Acts xxvii. 21.
1. 1 Cor. ix. 19, 20 twice, 21, 22. [*work.*)
2. 2 John 8, marg. (text,

GAINSAY (-ING.)

1. ἀντιλέγω, to contradict, *i.e.* to say against, utter, recount, relate against.
2. ἀντεῖπον, to speak against *or* in answer, gainsay, (occ. Acts iv. 14.)

2. Luke xxi. 15.
1. Rom. x. 21.
1. Titus ii. 9, marg. (text, *answer again.*)
— Jude 11, see gainsaying.

GAINSAYER.

ἀντιλέγω, *see* "GAINSAY," *No.* 1, *here the participle.*

Titus i. 9.

GAINSAYING [noun.]

ἀντιλογία, contradiction.

Jude 11.

GAINSAYING (WITHOUT.)

ἀναντιῤῥήτως, without objection, *(non occ.)*

Acts x. 29.

GALL.

χολή, gall, bile, *gen.* anything extremely bitter, *(used by* lxx. *for* לַעֲנָה, wormwood, Prov. v. 4, *and frequently for* רֹאשׁ, deadly, bitter poison, Jer. viii. 14,) *(non occ.)*

Matt. xxvii. 34. | Acts viii. 23.

GALLINGS ONE OF ANOTHER [margin.]

παραδιατριβή, useless, vain *or* perverse disputings, *(non occ.)*

1 Tim. vi. 5, text, *perverse disputings*, (διαπαρατριβή, continual friction, G L T Tr A ℵ.)

GANGRENE [margin.]

γάγγραινα, a gangrene, an eating sore, ending in mortification *(when it becomes* σφάκελος,) *(non occ.)*

2 Tim. ii. 17, text, *canker.*

GARDEN.

κῆπος, a garden, orchard *or* plantation, *(not a flower-garden,) (non occ.)*

Luke xiii. 19. | John xviii. 1, 26.
John xix. 41 twice.

GARDENER.

κηπουρός, a keeper of a garden, *gen.* a gardener, *(non occ.)*

John xx. 15.

GARLAND (-S.)

στέμμα, materials for crowning, a wreath, garland, chaplet, *(non occ.)*

Acts xiv. 13.

GARMENT.

1. ἱμάτιον, a piece of dress, *esp.* an outer garment *(opp. to No.* 4,) *in pl.* raiment, clothes.
2. ἔνδυμα, anything put on.
3. ἔσθησις, clothing, *(like* ἐσθής, *gen. applied to what is ornate or splendid) (non occ.)*
4. χιτών, the inner vest, a woollen shirt *or* frock *(worn next the body.)*

1. Matt. ix. 16 twice, 20, 21
1. —— xiv. 36.
1. —— xxi. 8.
2. —— xxii. 11, 12.
1. Matt. xxiii. 5 (*om.* G→ L T Tr A ℵ.)
1. —— xxvii. 35 twice (*ap.*)
1. Mark ii. 21.

1. Mark v. 27.
1. —— vi. 56.
1. —— x. 50.
1. —— xi. 7, 8.
1. —— xiii. 16.
1. —— xv. 24.
— —— xvi. 5, see G (long)
1. Luke v. 36 twice.
1. —— viii. 44.
1. —— xix. 35.
1. —— xxii. 36.
3. Luke xxiv. 4.
1. John xiii. 4, 12.
1. —— xix. 23.
1. Acts ix. 39.
1. —— xii. 8.
1. Heb. i. 11.
1. Jas. v. 2.
4. Jude 23.
— Rev. i. 13, see foot.
1. —— iii. 4.
1. —— xvi. 15.

GARMENT (LONG.)

στολή, equipment, fitting out, *esp.* equipment in clothes, dress; *then*, a piece of dress, a robe.

Mark xvi. 5.

GARNER.

ἀποθήκη, any place wherein to lay up *a thing*, a barn, magazine, storehouse.

Matt. iii. 12. | Luke iii. 17.

GARNISH (-ED.)

κοσμέω, to order, set in order, adorn, garnish; prepare.

Matt. xii. 44.
—— xxiii. 29.
Luke xi. 25.
Rev. xxi. 19.

GARRISON (KEEP WITH A.)

φρουρέω, to keep watch *or* guard, to watch.

2 Cor. xi. 32.

GATE (-S.)

1. *πυλών*, a gate, gateway; the gate-tower, gate-house.
2. *πύλη*, one wing of a pair of double gates, *hence usu. in pl.* a gate, the gates *(of a town, as opp. to No.* 3.)
3. *θύρα*, a house-door *or* door of a room, *(Germ.* thur, *Sanscrit* dûar, *Eng.* door.)
4. *προβατικός*, of or belonging to cattle, *(esp. sheep.)*

2. Matt. vii. 13 1st.
2. —— 13 2nd (om. L T^b ℵ)
2. —— 14 (om. L^b.)
2. —— xvi. 18.
2. Luke vii. 12.
1. —— xiii. 24 (G ~), (No. 3, G L T Tr A ℵ.)
1. —— xvi. 20.
4. John v. 2, marg. (text, *sheep market.*)
3. Acts iii. 2.
2. Acts iii. 10.
2. —— ix. 24.
1. —— x. 17.
2. —— xii. 10.
1. —— 13, 14 twice.
1. —— xiv. 13.
2. Heb. xiii. 12.
1. Rev. xxi. 12 1st, 12 2nd, (*ap.*), 13 4 times, 15, 21 twice, 25.
1. —— xxii. 14.

GATHER (-ED, -ETH, -ING.)

1. *συνάγω*, to lead together, gather together, *gen.* to bring together, join in one.
2. *ἐπισυνάγω*, to collect and bring to *a place*, assemble.
3. *συλλέγω*, to collect, gather, *of persons* to call together. *Pass.* to come together, assemble.
4. *τρυγάω*, to gather in ripe fruits, gather in the vintage *or* harvest, *(non occ.)*
5. *συστρέφω*, to twist up together, roll into a mass, *then*, *gen.* to collect, combine, *(non occ.)*

For "GATHER TOGETHER" and "GATHERED TOGETHER (BE)," see below.

1. Matt. ii. 4, part.
1. —— iii. 12.
1. —— vi. 26.
3. —— vii. 16.
1. —— xii. 30.
— —— xiii. 28, 29, see G up
1. —— 30.
3. —— 40, 41.
1. —— 47.
3. —— 48.
2. —— xxiii. 37.
1. —— xxv. 24, 26.
1. —— xxvii. 27.
1. Luke iii. 17.
3. —— vi. 44 1st.
4. Luke vi. 44 2nd.
1. —— xi. 23.
— —— 29, see G thick together (be.)
1. John iv. 36.
— —— vi. 12, see G up.
1. —— xi. 47.
1. —— xv. 6.
— Acts xvi. 10, see assuredly
— —— xvii. 5, see company
5. —— xxviii. 3, part.
— Eph. i. 10, see G together in one.
4. Rev. xiv. 18, 19.
1. —— xvi. 14.

GATHER TOGETHER.

1. *συνάγω*, *see* "GATHER," *No.* 1.
2. *ἐπισυνάγω*, *see* "GATHER," *No.* 2.
3. *συλλέγω*, *see* "GATHER," *No.* 3.
4. *συναθροίζω*, to gather together, assemble, *esp. of soldiers.*

3. Matt. xiii. 30.
1. —— xxii. 10.
2. —— xxiii. 37.
2. —— xxiv. 31.
2. Mark i. 33.
2. —— xiii. 27.
2. Luke xii. 1.
2. —— xiii. 34.
1. —— xv. 13.
4. Luke xxiv. 33, part. (*ἀθροίζω, collected,* L T Tr A ℵ.)
1. John vi. 13.
1. —— xi. 52.
4. Acts xii. 12.
1. —— xiv. 27.
1. —— xv. 30, part.
— Eph. i. 10, see G T in one
1. Rev. xvi. 16.
1. Rev. xx. 8.

GATHER TOGETHER IN ONE.

ανακεφαλαιόομαι, to comprehend several things under one head, to reduce under one head, to reunite for one's self under one head, (occ. Rom. xiii. 9.)

Eph. i. 10.

GATHER UP.

1. *συνάγω*, *see* "GATHER," *No.* 1.
2. *συλλέγω*, *see* "GATHER," *No.* 2.

2. Matt. xiii. 28, 29, part. | 1. John vi. 12.

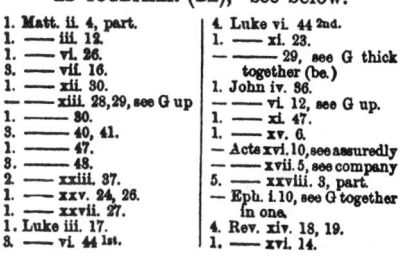

GATHERED TOGETHER (BE.)

1. *συνάγω*, *Pass. or Mid.*, to be gathered together, assembled, be come together.

2. *σύνειμι*, to go *or* come together.

1. Matt. xiii. 2.
1. —— xviii. 20.
1. —— xxii. 41, part.
1. —— xxiv. 28.
1. —— xxvii. 17, part.
1. Mark ii. 2.
2. Luke viii. 4, pres. part.
— Luke xi. 29, see G thick together (be.)
1. —— xvii. 37 (*επισυνάγω*, see gather, No. 2, T Tr [A ℵ.)
1. Acts iv. 6, 27.
1. —— xx. 8.
1. 1 Cor. v. 4, part.
1. Rev. xix. 19.

GATHERED THICK TOGETHER (BE.)

ἐπαθροίζομαι, to collect together to, *or* upon, to crowd together upon, *(non occ.)*

Luke xi. 29, part.

GATHERING (-S) [noun.]

λογία, a collection, *as of money*, (occ. ver. 1.)

1 Cor. xvi. 2.

GATHERING TOGETHER.

ἐπισυναγωγή, a gathering together upon *or* unto, (occ. Heb. x. 25.)

2 Thes. ii. 1.

GAY.

λαμπρός, bright, brilliant, radiant.

Jas. ii. 3.

GAZE (-ING) UP.

ἐμβλέπω, to look upon, view *with steadfastness and attention, (see* "BEHOLD," *Nos.* 7 *and* 8.)

Acts i. 11.

GAZING STOCK (MAKE A.)

θεατρίζω, to be an actor in the theatre; *also*, to bring upon the theatre, to present as a spectacle, *(non occ.)*

Heb. x. 33, part.

GENDER (-ETH.)

γεννάω, to beget, *of men;* to bear, *of women;* bring forth.

Gal. iv. 24. | 2 Tim. ii. 23.

GENEALOGY (-IES.)

γενεαλογία, a tracing of one's genealogy, the making a pedigree, tracing a family. *(Eng.,* genealogy), *(non occ.)*

1 Tim. i. 4. | Titus iii. 9.

GENERAL.

See, ASSEMBLY.

GENERATION (-S.)

1. *γενεά*, birth; race, descent; offspring. *It denotes* an age *or* generation *from the point of view of race, (as αἰών does from that of* duration.)

2. *γέννημα*, that which is produced, *as* a child, fruits *of the earth; hence,* progeny, offspring.

3. *γένεσις*, an origin, source; birth, manner of birth.

4. *γένος*, race, descent; genus; *hence,* a people *or* nation.

3. Matt. i. 1.
1. ——— 17 4 times.
1. —— xi. 16.
2. —— xii. 34.
1. ——— 39, 41, 42, 45.
1. —— xvi. 4.
1. —— xvii. 17.
2. —— xxiii. 33.
1. ——— 36.
1. —— xxiv. 34.
1. Mark viii. 12 twice, 38.
1. —— ix. 19.
1. —— xiii. 30.
1. Luke i. 48.
— Luke i. 50, see G to G (from.)
2. —— iii. 7.
1. —— vii. 31.
1. —— ix. 41. [50, 51.
1. —— xi. 29, 30, 31, 32,
1. —— xvi. 8.
1. —— xvii. 25.
1. —— xxi. 32.
1. Acts ii. 40.
1. —— viii. 33.
1. —— xiii. 36, marg.
1. Col. i. 26.
1. Heb. iii. 10.
4. 1 Pet. ii 9.

GENERATION TO GENERATION (FROM.)

{ *εἰς*, unto,
{ *γενεὰς*, generations,
{ *γενεῶν*, of generations.

Luke i. 50 (*εἰς γενεὰς καὶ γενεὰς*, unto generations and generations, G∾ T Tr A), (*εἰς γενεὰν καὶ γενεὰν*, unto generation and generation, G∾ ℵ.)

GENTILE (-S.)

1. *ἔθνος*, host, multitude, people, *(prob. from ἔθος*, custom, usage, manners, *etc.,)* a number of people living together *bound together by like habits and customs; then gen.* people, tribe, nation, *with reference to the connection with each other rather than the separation from others by descent, language or constitution.*

In the following passages only pl. ἔθνη *or* τὰ ἔθνη, Gentiles. *In the O.T.* those who are not of Israel, *and in the N.T.* those who are neither of Israel nor of the Church, *see* 1 Cor. x. 32. *(The Church being composed of those who are called out of both.)*

[The Gentiles or the nations of the earth stand, in relation to God, in a peculiar position of their own, and their destiny is different from that of the Jew and the Church.]

2. Ἕλλην, Hellen [the proper name of the son of Deucalion, and then of his descendants Ἕλληνες, the early inhabitants of Thessalian Hellas.] *Afterwards a general name for all* the Greeks; *hence, in N.T.* Ἕλλην, a Greek, οἱ Ἕλληνες, the Greeks, *viz. as opp. to* οἱ Βάρβαροι, *(i.e.* all who are not Greeks,) *and as opp. to* οἱ Ἰουδαῖοι (the Jews), all who are not Jews; *and in this sense,* Gentiles.

3. Ἑλληνίς, *(fem. of No.* 2), a female Greek, *(i.e.* not a Jew.)

1. Matt. iv. 15.
1. —— vi. 32.
1. —— x. 5, 18.
1. —— xii. 18, 21.
1. —— xx. 19, 25.
3. Mark vii. 26, marg. (text, *Greek.*)
1. —— x. 33, 42.
1. Luke ii. 32.
1. —— xviii. 32.
1. —— xxi. 24 twice.
1. —— xxii. 25.
2. John vii. 35 1st, marg. *Greek.*
2. —— 35 2nd.
1. Acts iv. 27.
1. —— vii. 45.
1. —— ix. 15.
1. —— x. 45.
1. —— xi. 1, 18.
1. —— xiii. 42 (*om.* G L T Tr A ℵ.)
1. —— 46, 47, 48.
1. —— xiv. 2, 5, 27.
1. —— xv. 3, 7, 12, 14, 17, 19, 23.
1. —— xviii. 6.
1. —— xxi. 11, 19, 21, 25.
1. —— xxii. 21.
1. —— xxvi. 17, 20, 23.
1. —— xxviii. 28.
1. Rom. i. 13.
2. —— ii. 9, } marg.
2. —— 10, } *Greek.*
1. Rom. ii. 14, 24.
2. —— iii. 9.
1. —— 29 twice.
1. —— ix. 24, 30.
1. —— xi. 11, 12, 13 twice, 25
1. —— xv. 9 twice, 10, 11, 12 twice, 16 twice, 18, 27.
1. —— xvi. 4.
1. 1 Cor. v. 1.
1. —— x. 20 (*om.* G∾ L T Trmb A.)
2. —— 32.
1. —— xii. 2.
2. —— 13, marg. *Greek.*
1. Gal. ii. 2, 8, 12.
— —— 14 1st, see G (after the manner of.)
1. —— 14 2nd, 15.
1. —— iii. 14.
1. Eph. ii. 11.
1. —— iii. 1, 6, 8.
1. —— iv. 17.
1. Col. i. 27.
1. 1 Thes. ii. 16.
1. —— iv. 5.
1. 1 Tim. ii. 7.
1. —— iii. 16.
1. 2 Tim. i. 11.
1. —— iv. 17.
1. 1 Pet. ii. 12.
1. —— iv. 3.
1. 3 John 7 (ἐθνικός, *belonging to a nation* or *Gentile,* G∾ L T Tr A ℵ.)
1. Rev. xi. 2.

GENTILES (AFTER THE MANNER OF.)

ἐθνικῶς, in the manner of the Gentiles, *see No.* 1, *(non occ.)*

Gal. ii. 14.

GENTLE.

1. ἐπιεικής, fitting upon, *i.e.* fit, meet, suitable; *hence,* fair, reasonable, *esp. opp. to* δίκαιος (righteous), *i.e.,* not insisting on the letter of the law, considerate, forbearing, kind, fair, (occ. Phil. iv. 5; 1 Tim. iii. 3.)

2. ἤπιος, gentle, mild; soothing, assuaging, *(non occ.)*

2. 1 Thes. ii. 7 (νήπιοι, *child-like,* L ℵ.)
2. Tim. ii. 24.
1. Titus iii. 2.
1. Jas. iii. 17.
1. 1 Pet. ii. 18.

GENTLENESS.

1. ἐπιείκεια, reasonableness, fairness; considerateness, forbearance; the not insisting on just rights.

2. χρηστότης, usefulness *as of persons towards others; hence,* goodness that shows itself in benevolence, kindness.

1. 2 Cor. x. 1.
2. Gal. v. 22.

GERGESENE.

Γεργεσηνός, a Gergesene, *(see* "GADARENE," *No.* 3.)

Matt. viii. 28 (G) (Γερασηνός, see Gadarene, No. 2, G∾ L), (Γαδαρηνός, see Gadarene, No. 1, G∾ T Tr A ℵ), Γαζαρηνός, prob. a mistake for Γαδαρηνός, ℵ.)

GET (GOTTEN.)

1. ἔξειμι, to go *or* come out, *(esp. out of the house,) here,* to get out upon *the land.*

2. εὑρίσκω, to find, find out, discover.

3. κτάομαι, to procure for one's self, acquire.

4. ἐμβαίνω, to step in, go *or* come into, enter.

3. Matt. x. 9, marg. text, *provide.*
— —— xi. 12, see *force.*
4. —— xiv. 22.
4. Mark vi. 45.
2. Luke ix. 12.
1. Acts xxvii. 43.
– 2 Cor. ii. 11, see advantage.
— Jas. iv. 13, see gain.
— Rev. xv. 2, see victory.

GET DOWN.

καταβαίνω, to step down, go *or* come down, descend.

Acts x. 20.

GET THEE.

ὑπάγω, to lead *or* bring under, *(as horses under a yoke,)* to lead *or* bring away

under. *In N.T. and later usage,* to go away *(under cover, strictly with the idea of stealth,) Gen. and Imp.,* go away, depart, begone.

Matt. xvi. 23. | Mark viii. 33.
Luke iv. 8 (*ap.*)

GET THEE HENCE.

Matt. iv. 10.

GET OUT.

ἐξέρχομαι, to come *or* go out *of any place,* to come *or* go forth.

Luke xiii. 31. | Acts vii. 3.
Acts xxii. 18.

GOTTEN FROM (BE.)

ἀποσπάω, to draw from, draw away, *here, Pass. in Mid. sense,* to withdraw one's self, depart, go away.

Acts xxi. 1, part.

GHOST.

[For HOLY GHOST, see HOLY.]

πνεῦμα, the wind, the breath breathed forth, the living principle *(predicated of man and beast,)* breathing *as the sign and condition of life,* breath.

(For fuller meaning see under "SPIRIT."

Matt. xxvii. 50. | John xix. 30.

GHOST (GIVE UP THE.)

1. ἐκπνέω, to breathe out, expire, die, *(non occ.)*
2. ἐκψύχω, to breathe out, to go out, wax cold, become extinct.

1. Mark xv. 37, 39. | 2. Acts v. 5.
1. Luke xxiii. 46. | 2. —— xii. 23.

GHOST (YIELD UP THE.)

2. Acts v. 10.

GIFT (-S.)

1. δῶρον, a gift, a present, an honorary gift; *esp.* a votive offering *to a god; so of* gifts, offerings *dedicated to God or His service,* (occ. Luke xxi. 4.)
2. δωρεά, a free-gift, a present, *(Lat.,* beneficium), *(non occ.)*
3. δώρημα, that which is given, a free-gift.
4. δόμα, a gift, *(non occ.)*
5. δόσις, a giving, the act of giving, (occ. Phil. iv. 15.)
6. χάρισμα, a favour, kindness; that which is freely given, a gift of grace, *gen. the effect of God's gracious working,* the positive blessing *bestowed upon sinners; and also, in a special sense,* a gift of grace *imparted to an individual.* Χάρισμα, *is the gift which requires* χάρις (grace), *that it may be rightly exercised,* (occ. Rom. v. 15, 16.)
7. χάρις, free gift, free favour, *(see* "GRACE," *No.* 1.)
8. μερισμός, a dividing, division, distribution, (occ. Heb. iv. 12.)
9. ἀνάθημα, votive offerings, a thing devoted in honour of God.

1. Matt. ii. 11.
1. —— v. 23, 24 *twice.*
4. —— vii. 11.
1. —— viii. 4.
1. —— xv. 5.
1. —— xxiii. 18, 19 *twice.*
1. Mark vii. 11.
4. Luke xi. 13.
1. —— xxi. 1.
9. —— 5.
2. John iv. 10.
2. Acts ii. 38.
2. —— viii. 20.
2. —— x. 45.
2. —— xi. 17.
6. Rom. i. 11.
— —— v. 15 1st, see G (free)
2. —— 15 2nd.
3. —— 16 1st.
— —— 16 2nd, see G (free)
2. —— 17 (*om.* G→ Lb.)
6. —— vi. 23.
6. —— xi. 29.
6. —— xii. 6.
6. 1 Cor. i. 7.
6. —— vii. 7.
6. —— xii. 4, 9, 28, 30, 31.
— —— xiii. 2, see prophecy
— —— xiv. 1, see spiritual
6. 2 Cor. i. 11.
7. —— viii. 4.
2. —— ix. 15.
1. Eph. ii. 8.
2. —— iii. 7.
2. —— iv. 7.
4. —— 8.
4. Phil. iv. 17.
6. 1 Tim. iv. 14.
6. 2 Tim i. 6. [*bution.*
8. Heb. ii. 4, marg. *distri-*
1. —— v. 1.
2. —— vi. 4.
1. —— viii. 3, 4.
1. —— ix. 9.
1. —— xi. 4.
5. Jas. i. 17.
6. 1 Pet. iv. 10.
1. Rev. xi. 10.

GIFT (FREE.)

6. Rom. v. 15, 16.

GIRD (-ED, -EST, -ING, GIRT.)

1. ζώννυμι *or* ζωννύω, to put on a girdle, to gird round the loins *for conflict or service. Spoken of the long flowing robes of Orientals which are girded up while engaged in any business.*
2. διαζώννυμι, *(No.* 1 *with* διά, through, *prefixed),* to gird throughout *or* quite round, *i.e.,* firmly, (occ. John xxi. 7.)

2. John xiii. 4, 5. | 1. John xxi. 18 *twice.*

GIRD ONE'S SELF.

περιζώννυμι, (*No.* 1 *with περί*, around, *prefixed,*) to gird around. *In N.T. Pass.or Mid.*, to gird one's self around.

John xxi. 7.

GIRD UNTO ONE'S SELF.

διαζώννυμι, see above, No. 2.

John xxi. 7.

GIRD UP.

ἀναζώννυμι, (*No.* 1 *above, with ἀνά*, up, *prefixed*), to gird up *as with a belt or girdle. Here Mid.*, to gird up one's self, (*non occ.*)

1 Pet. i. 13.

GIRT (BE.)

περιζώννυμι, see "GIRD ONE'S SELF."

Rev. i. 13.

GIRT ABOUT (HAVE.)

Eph. vi. 14.

GIRDED ABOUT (BE.)

Luke xii. 35.

GIRDED (HAVE...)

Rev. xv. 6, with *περί, around.*

GIRDLE.

ζώνη, *Eng.* zone *or* belt, girdle, [worn by both sexes among the Jews, often hollow, and served as a purse, as well as to gird up the long flowing dress], (occ. Matt. x. 9; Mark vi. 8.)

Matt. iii. 4. | Acts xxi. 11 twice.
Mark i. 6. | Rev. i. 13.
Rev. xv. 6.

GIRT.

See, GIRD.

GIVE (-EN, -EST, -ETH, -ING, GAVE, GAVEST.)

1. *δίδωμι*, to give, present (*with implied notion of* giving freely unforced; *opp. to No.* 2.) *Hence, in various connections*, to yield, deliver, supply, commit, *etc.*
2. *ἀποδίδωμι*, (*No.* 1 *with ἀπό*, from, *prefixed*), to give away from *one's self; i.e.*, give back, deliver over, yield, restore.
3. *διαδίδωμι*, (*No.* 1 *with διά*, through, *prefixed*), to deliver through *as through various hands, i.e., from one to another in succession*, to give *or* hand over.
4. *ἐπιδίδωμι*, (*No.* 1 *with ἐπί*, upon, *prefixed*), to give upon, *i.e.*, in addition to. To give forth, *i.e., from one's self* upon *or* to another; *or* to give besides *or* in addition.
5. *μεταδίδωμι*, (*No.* 1 *with μετά*, with, *prefixed,*) to give with *or* part of, give a share; to impart, communicate.
6. *παραδίδωμι*, (*No.* 1 *with παρά*, beside, *prefixed,*) to give near, with *or* to *any one*, to give *or* hand over to *another*, deliver over.
7. *χαρίζομαι*, to do a person a favour, to be kind *or* gracious to, to give *or* bestow *a thing* graciously, (*the end in view must be inferred from the context.*)
8. *παρέχω*, to hold near *to any one*, to hold out near *or* towards *any one*, to present, offer.
9. *δωρέω*, to make a gift of.
10. *παρεισφέρω*, to bear *or* bring in therewith *or* thereunto, to bring forward therewith *or* along with.
11. *τίθημι*, to put, set, place, *then gen.*, to bring *a thing* into a place, *hence*, to lay down *and* to give by so doing.
12. *ἀπονέμω*, to apportion, assign, share, (*non occ.*)
13. *μαρτυρέω*, to be a witness, to bear witness, testify, give testimony to, (*hence, Eng.* martyr.)
14. *ποιέω*, to make, form, produce, *as of a completed action;* to do, *expressing an action continued or not completed.*
15. *χορηγέω*, to be chorus leader, to lead out *or* furnish a chorus, *hence*, to furnish, supply, (occ. 2 Cor. ix. 10.)

16. πρός, towards, in the direction of.

(a) *with Gen.*, in favour of, (occ. Acts xxvii. 34.)

(b) *with Dat.*, at, close by.

(c) *with Acc.*, towards, in reference to, with.

1. Matt. iv. 9.
1. —— v. 31, 42.
1. —— vi. 11.
1. —— vii. 6, 7.
4. ——— 9, 10.
1. ——— 11 twice.
1. —— ix. 8.
— ——— 24, see place.
1. —— x. 1, 8, 19 (*ap.*)
— —— xi. 28, see rest.
2. —— xii. 36.
1. ——— 39.
1. —— xiii. 11 twice, 12.
1. —— xiv. 7, 8, 9, 11, 16, 19
1. —— xv. 36.
1. —— xvi. 4, 19, 26.
1. —— xvii. 27.
1. —— xix. 7, 11, 21.
1. —— xx. 4.
2. ——— 8.
1. ——— 14, 23, 28.
1. —— xxi. 23, 43.
1. —— xxii. 17.
1. —— xxiv. 29, 45.
1. —— xxv. 8, 15, 28, 29, 35, 42.
1. —— xxvi. 9, 15, 26, 27, 48
— ——— 53, see G (presently.)
1. —— xxvii. 10, 34.
1. —— xxviii. 12, 18.
1. Mark ii. 26.
1. —— iv. 11.
— ——— 24, see G more.
1. ——— 25.
— —— v. 13, see leave.
1. ——— 43.
1. —— vi. 2, 7, 22, 23, 25, 28 twice, 37 twice, 41.
1. —— viii. 6, 12, 37.
1. —— x. 21, 40, 45.
1. —— xi. 28.
1. —— xii. 9, 14, 15 twice.
1. —— xiii. 11, 24, 34.
1. —— xiv. 5, 11, 22, 23, 44.
1. —— xv. 23.
— ——— 37, 39, see ghost
9. ——— 45.
1. Luke i. 32, 77.
1. —— iv. 6 twice.
— ——— 20, see G again.
1. —— vi. 4, 30, 38 twice.
7. —— vii. 21.
1. ——— 44, 45.
1. —— viii. 10, 18, 55.
1. —— ix. 1, 13, 16.
— —— x. 7, see G (such things as one.)
1. ——— 19, 35.
1. —— xi. 3, 7, 8 twice, 9.
4. ——— 11 twice.
1. ——— 13 twice, 29, 41.
1. —— xii. 32, 33, 42, 48, 51, 58.
1. —— xiv. 9.
1. —— xv. 12, 16, 29.
2. —— xvi. 2.
1. ——— 12.
1. —— xvii. 18.
— —— xviii. 12, see tithes
1. ——— 43.
1. —— xix. 8, 15, 23, 24, 26.
1. —— xx. 2, 10, 16, 22.
1. —— xxi. 15.
1. —— xxii. 5, 19 twice.
1. —— xxiii. 2.
— Luke xxiii. 24, see sentence.
— ——— 46, see ghost.
4. —— xxiv. 30, 42.
1. John i. 12, 17, 22.
1. —— iii. 16, 27, 34, 35.
1. —— iv. 5, 7, 10 twice, 12, 14 1st, 14 2nd (*ap.*), 15.
1. —— v. 26, 27, 36.
1. —— vi. 27, 31, 32 twice, 33, 34, 37, 39, 51 1st, 51 2nd (*ap.*), 52, 65.
1. —— vii. 19, 22.
1. —— ix. 24.
11. —— x. 11.
1. ——— 28, 29.
1. —— xi. 22, 57.
1. —— xii. 5, 49.
1. —— xiii. 3, 15.
4. ——— 26 1st (ᾧ ἐγὼ βαψω το ψωμιον και δώσω (No. 1) αὐτῷ, *for whom I shall dip the sop and give it to him*, instead of, ᾧ ἐγὼ βάψας τὸ ψωμίον ἐπιδώσω (No. 4), *to whom I shall give the sop when I have dipped it*, L Tr A.)
1. ——— 26 2nd, 29, 34.
1. —— xiv. 16, 27 3 times.
1. —— xv. 16.
1. —— xvi. 23.
1. —— xvii. 2 3 times, 4, 6 twice, 7, 8 twice, 9, 11, 12, 14, 22 twice, 24 twice.
1. —— xviii. 9, 11.
— ——— 14, see counsel.
1. —— xix. 9, 11.
— ——— 30, see G up.
— ——— 38, see leave.
1. —— xxi. 13.
— Acts i. 26, see G forth.
1. —— ii. 4. 19.
1. —— iii. 6, 16.
1. —— iv. 12.
2. ——— 33.
— —— v. 5, see ghost.
1. ——— 31, 32.
— —— vi. 4, see continually
1. —— vii. 5 twice, 8, 10, 38
— ——— 42, see G up.
— —— viii. 9, see G out.
1. ——— 18, 19.
1. —— ix. 41.
14. —— x. 2, part.
— ——— 43, see witness.
1. —— xi. 17.
— —— xii. 22, see shout.
1. ——— 23 1st.
— ——— 23 2nd, see ghost.
— —— xiii. 16, see audience
1. ——— 20 (*ap.*), 21.
— ——— 22, see testimony
1. ——— 34.
— —— xiv. 3, see testimony
1. ——— 17.
1. —— xv. 8.
— ——— 12, see audience.
— —— xvii. 16, see idolatry
1. ——— 25, part.
8. ——— 31, marg. *offer.*
2. —— xix. 40 (No. 1 G∾)
— —— xx. 2, see exhortation.
1. ——— 32, 35.
— Acts xxi. 40, part., see license.
— —— xxii. 22, see audience
1. —— xxiv. 26.
— —— xxvi. 10, see G against.
— —— xxvii. 3, see liberty
7. ——— 24.
— Rom. i. 24, 26, see G up
— ——— 28, see G over.
1. —— iv. 20.
1. —— v. 5.
— —— viii. 32, see G freely
1. —— xi. 8.
— ——— 35, see G first.
1. —— xii. 3, 6.
5. ——— 8, marg. *impart.*
— ——— 13, see given to.
1. ——— 19.
1. —— xiv. 12 (No. 2, L Tr Ab.)
1. —— xv. 15.
— 1 Cor. ii. 12, see G (the things that are freely)
— —— iii. 6, 7, see increase
— —— vii. 5, see G one's self to.
— —— x. 32, see offence.
— —— xii. 3, see understand.
6. —— xiii. 3.
— —— xvi. 1, see order.
1. 2 Cor. i. 22.
— —— iii. 6, see life.
1. —— v. 5, 12, 18.
1. —— vi. 3.
1. —— viii. 5, 10.
1. —— ix. 9.
1. —— x. 8.
1. —— xii. 7.
1. —— xiii. 10.
1. Gal. i. 4.
— —— ii. 5, see place.
1. ——— 9 twice.
6. ——— 20.
7. —— iii. 18.
1. ——— 21 1st.
— ——— 21 2nd, see life.
1. ——— 22.
1. —— iv. 15.
1. Eph. i. 17, 22.
1. —— iii. 2, 7, 8.
1. —— iv. 7, 8, 11.
— ——— 19, see G over.
1. ——— 27.
5. ——— 28, marg. *distribute.*
6. —— v. 2, 25.
1. —— vi. 19.
7. Phil. i. 29.
7. —— ii. 9.
— —— iv. 15, see G [noun.]
1. Col. i. 25.
1. 1 Thes. iv. 2, 8.
1. 2 Thes. ii. 16.
1. —— iii. 16.
1. 1 Tim. ii. 6.
— —— iii. 2, see hospitality
— 1 Tim. iii. 3, see wine.
— ——— 8, see given to (be)
— —— iv. 13, see attendance.
1. ——— 14.
— ——— 15, see G thyself wholly to.
1. —— v. 14.
8. —— vi. 17.
1. 2 Tim. i. 7, 9, 16.
1. —— ii. 7, 25.
— —— iii. 16, see inspiration.
2. —— iv. 8.
— Titus i. 7, see lucre.
— —— ii. 3, see given to.
1. ——— 14.
7. Philem. 22.
1. Heb. ii. 13.
— —— iv. 8, see rest.
— —— vii. 2, see part.
1. ——— 4.
— ——— 13, see attendance.
2. —— xiii. 17.
1. 1 Pet. i. 21.
12. —— iii. 7.
16. ——— 15.
2. —— iv. 5.
15. ——— 11.
1. —— v. 5.
9. 2 Pet. i. 3, 4.
10. ——— 5.
— ——— 10, see diligence.
1. —— iii. 15.
1. 1 John iii. 23, 24.
1. —— iv. 13.
13. —— v. 10.
1. ——— 11, 16, 20.
14. Jude 3, mid.
— —— 7, see fornication.
1. Rev. i. 1.
1. —— ii. 7, 10, 17 twice, 21, 23, 26, 28.
1. —— iv. 9.
1. —— vi. 2, 4 twice, 8, 11.
1. —— vii. 2.
1. —— viii. 2, 3.
1. —— ix. 1, 3, 5.
1. —— x. 9.
1. —— xi. 1, 2, 3, 13, 18.
1. —— xii. 14.
1. —— xiii. 2, 4, 5 times, 7 1st (*ap.*), 7 2nd, 15.
1. —— xiv. 7.
1. —— xv. 7.
1. —— xvi. 6, 8, 9, 19.
3. —— xvii. 13 (διδόασιν, *give* (No. 1), instead of διάδιδώσουσιν, *shall give* (No. 3), G L T Tr A ℵ.)
1. ——— 17.
1. —— xviii. 7.
1. —— xix. 7.
1. —— xx. 4.
— ——— 13, see G up.
1. —— xxi. 6.

GIVE AGAIN.

2. Luke iv. 20.

GIVE AGAINST.

καταφέρω, to bear *or* carry down, to bring down as with violence; *also with* ψῆφον, to give a vote, *(implying alacrity or zeal,)* bring against *any one* a vote.

Acts xxvi. 10.

GIVE FIRST.

προδίδωμι, to give beforehand, pay in advance, *(non occ.)*

Rom. xi. 35.

GIVE FORTH.

δίδωμι, *see* "GIVE," *No.* 1.

Acts i. 26.

GIVE FREELY.

χαρίζομαι, *see* "GIVE," *No.* 7.

Rom. viii. 32.

GIVE MORE.

προστίθημι, to put to, to add.

Mark iv. 24 (*ap.*)

GIVE ONE'S SELF TO.

σχολάζω, to have leisure *or* spare time, have nothing to do; have leisure *or* opportunity for *a thing; then*, to devote one's time to *a thing*, (occ. Matt. xii. 44, *part.)*

1 Cor. vii. 5.

GIVE OUT.

λέγω, to say, *see under* "SAY."

Acts viii. 9.

GIVE OVER.

παραδίδωμι, *see* "GIVE," *No.* 6.

Rom. i. 28. | Eph. iv. 19.

GIVE PRESENTLY.

παρίστημι, to place by *or* beside.

Matt. xxvi. 53.

GIVE THYSELF WHOLLY TO.

{ **ἴσθι**, be thou, *(Imp. of* εἰμί, to be.)
{ **ἐν**, in.

1 Tim. iv. 15.

GIVE UP.

1. **δίδωμι**, *see* "GIVE," *No.* 1.
2. **παραδίδωμι**, *see* "GIVE," *No.* 6.

2. John xix. 30.
2. Acts vii. 42.
2. Rom. i. 24, 26.
1. Rev. xx. 13.

GIVETH (SUCH THINGS AS ONE.)

{ **τὰ**, the things, } *lit.*, what [they
{ **παρά**, beside *or* by, } have] by *them.*

Luke x. 7.

See also, CHARGE, COMMANDMENT, DRINK, HEED, LIGHT, MARRIAGE, SUCK, THANKS.

GIVEN TO.

1. **διώκω**, to make run, set in quick motion, pursue.
2. **δουλόω**, to make a slave of, enslave.

— Acts xvii. 16, see Idolatry
1. Rom. xii. 13, part.
— 1 Cor. ii. 12, see Below.
— 1 Tim. iii. 2, see Hospitality.
— 1 Tim. iii. 3, see Wine.
— ——— 8, see G to (be.)
— 2 Tim. iii. 16, see Inspiration.
— Titus i. 7, see Lucre.
2. Titus ii. 3, part.

GIVEN TO (BE.)

προσέχω, to hold to, bring to *or* near, *of a ship; of the mind*, to turn one's thoughts *or* attention to *a thing*, be intent upon it.

1 Tim. iii. 8.

GIVEN (THE THINGS THAT ARE FREELY.)

{ **τὰ**, the *things*, } the things
{ **χαρισθέντα**, *(part. of* χαρίζομαι, "GIVE," *No.* 7,) } given-in-favour.

1 Cor. ii. 12.

GIVER.

δότης, a giver, dispenser, *(non occ.)*

2 Cor. ix. 7.

GIVING [noun.]

δόσις, a giving, a gift, (occ. Jas. i. 17.)

Phil. iv. 15.

See also, LAW, THANKS.

GLAD (BE.)

1. **χαίρω**, to rejoice, be delighted *or* pleased with, *(answering to the*

Germ., gern, to desire; *old high Germ.*, ger; *and Eng.*, eager,) *not used in Greek writers.*

2. ἀγαλλιάω, to leap *or* dance much, *hence,* to rejoice, exult.

— Matt. v. 12, see G (be exceeding.)
1. Mark xiv. 11.
1. Luke xv. 32.
1. —— xxii. 5.
1. —— xxiii. 8.
1. John viii. 56.
1. —— xi. 15.
1. —— xx. 20.
2. Acts ii. 26.
1. —— xi. 23.
1. —— xiii. 48.
1. Rom. xvi. 19.
1. 1 Cor. xvi. 17.
— 2 Cor. ii. 2, see G (make)
1. —— xiii. 9.
1. 1 Pet. iv. 13.
1. Rev. xix. 7.

GLAD (BE EXCEEDING.)

2. Matt. v. 12.

GLAD (MAKE.)

εὐφραίνω, to cheer, delight, gladden.

2 Cor. ii. 2.

See also, TIDINGS.

GLADLY.

1. ἡδέως, sweetly, *i.e. with relish of eating, hence,* with relish, with pleasure.

2. ἀσμένως, gladly, readily, joyfully.

1. Mark vi. 20.
1. —— xii. 37.
— Luke viii. 40, see Receive
2. Acts ii. 41 (*om.* G ⇉ L T Tr A ℵ.)
1. 2 Cor. xi. 19.

GLADLY (MOST.)

ἥδιστα, (*Superl. of* ἡδύς, sweet,) most sweetly, *i.e.* with high relish.

2 Cor. xii. 9.

GLADLY (VERY.)

2 Cor. xii. 15.

GLADNESS.

1. χαρά, joy, delight.

2. ἀγαλλίασις, much leaping, *or* dancing; exultation, rejoicing, (occ. Luke i. 44; Jude 24.)

3. εὐφροσύνη, mirth, merriment, *esp. of a banquet;* good cheer, festivity, *(hence,* Euphrosyné, *one of the graces who presided at festive meetings,)* (occ. Acts ii. 28.)

1. Mark iv. 16.
2. Luke i. 14.
2. Acts ii. 46.
1. Acts xii. 14.
3. —— xiv. 17.
1. Phil. ii. 29.
2. Heb. i. 9.

GLASS.

1. ἔσοπτρον, a mirror, looking-glass, (made usually of polished metal), *(see* Ex. xxxviii. 8 *and* Job xxxvii. 18,) *(non occ.)*

2. ὕαλος, anything transparent like water, *i.e.* any transparent stone *or* gem, *as* crystal, amber, *etc., hence,* a convex lens of crystal; glass. *(This accords with the Greek origin of the word; but it is held by some to be Egyptian, which will agree with the place of its earliest manufacture,) (non occ.)*

1. 1 Cor. xiii. 12.
— 2 Cor. iii. 18, see Behold
1. Jas. i. 23.
2. Rev. xxi. 18, 21.

GLASS (OF.)

ὑάλινος, of *or* made of glass, *(see No.* 2 *above.)*

Rev. iv. 6; xv. 2 twice.

GLISTER (-ING.)

ἐξαστράπτω, to flash as with lighting, *(non occ.)*

Luke ix. 29.

GLORIFY (-ED, -ING.)

δοξάζω, to think, be of opinion, to hold any one for anything; *in later Greek writers* to recognize, honour, praise; *in the* lxx, to invest with dignity, make any one important, to cause him honour by putting him into an honourable position. *Hence, the N.T. meanings* are, (1) to recognize, honour, praise; (2) to bring to honour, make glorious, glorify, *but strictly,* to give any one importance. *(When predicated of Christ it means that His innate glory is made manifest and brought to light.)*

Matt. v. 16.
—— ix. 8.
—— xv. 31.
Mark ii. 12.
Luke ii. 20.
—— iv. 15.
—— v. 25, 26.
—— vii. 16.
—— xiii. 13.
—— xvii. 15.
—— xviii. 43.
—— xxiii. 47.
John vii. 39.
—— xi. 4.
John xii. 16; 23, 28 3 times.
—— xiii. 31 twice, 32 1st (*ap.*), 32 2nd & 3rd.
—— xiv. 13.
—— xv. 8.
—— xvi. 14.
—— xvii. 1 twice, 4, 5, 10.
—— xxi. 19.
Acts iii. 13.
—— iv. 21.
—— xi. 18.
—— xiii. 48.
—— xxi. 20.
Rom. i. 21.

Rom. viii. 17, see G together
——— 30.
—— xv. 6, 9.
1 Cor. vi. 20.
2 Cor. ix. 13, part.
Gal. i. 24.
2 Thes. i. 10, 12, see G (be)
—— iii. 1.
Heb. v. 5.
1 Pet. ii. 12.
—— iv. 11, 14 (*ap.*), 16.
Rev. xv. 4.
Rev. xviii. 7.

GLORIFY (-IED) TOGETHER.

συνδοξάζω, *(the above with* σύν, together with, *prefixed,) (implying* union, co-existence, and association *not necessarily local,) (non occ.)*

Rom. viii. 17.

GLORIFIED (BE.)

ἐνδοξάζομαι, (δοξάζω, *see* "GLORIFY," *with* ἐν, in, *prefixed,)* to cause to be ἐν δόξῃ, (in glory), *i.e.* to appear glorious.

2 Thes. i. 10, 12.

GLORIOUS.

1. δόξης, *(Gen. of* δόξα, *see* "GLORY," *No.* 1,) of glory.

2. { διά, through, *(as proceeding from,)* through, by means of, δόξης, *see No.* 1, } through glory.

3. { ἐν, in, *(the sphere in which the subject dwells or is acting,)* δόξῃ, *see No.* 1, } in glory.

4. ἔνδοξος, recognized, honoured, honourable, distinguished; *(there is no example of the meaning glorious in Greek writers or the* lxx, *but see* "GLORY," *No.* 1, *and* "GLORIFIED (BE),") (occ. 1 Cor. iv. 10.)

4. Luke xiii. 17.
1. Rom. viii. 21.
3. 2 Cor. iii. 7, 8. [made.)
— ——— 10, see G (be
2. ——— 11 1st.
3. ——— 11 2nd.
1. 2 Cor. iv. 4.
1. Phil. iii. 21.
1. Col. i. 11.
4. Eph. v. 27.
1. 1 Tim. i. 11.
1. Titus ii. 13.

GLORIOUS (BE MADE.)

δοξάζομαι, *(Pass. of* δοξάζω, *see* "GLORIFY.")

2 Cor. iii. 10.

GLORY [noun.]

1. δόξα, *from the Trans.*, opinion, notion, *(opp. to* ἐπιστήμη, real knowledge of a matter;) *from the Intrans.*, seeming *(opp. to* ἀλήθεια, what is not concealed, truth;) *in Prof. Gr. it denotes* the recognition *which any one finds, or which belongs to him*, renown (differing from τιμή, honour, *as* recognition *does from* estimation.) *Then from the meaning* seeming *comes* appearance, form, aspect, *viz., that appearance of a person or thing which attracts attention or commands recognition*, looks *like something, equivalent therefore to* splendour, brilliance, glory.

In this sense δόξα *denotes*, the appearance of glory attracting the gaze, manifestation of glory *(not the person or thing itself whose glorious appearance attracts attention, but the appearance which attracts attention)*, splendour, glory, brightness.

The δόξα *of God, is, as explained by Philo*, the unfolded fulness of the divine δυνάμεις (manifested powers); *and coincides with His self-revelation.* (In Ex. xxxiii. 18 *Moses asks*, "show me thy glory," *and God replies*, ver. 19, "I will make all my goodness pass before thee...and will be gracious to whom I will be gracious, and will show mercy," etc., cf. v. 22.) *Hence as it comprises*, all that God is for us for our good, the fulness of all that is good in Him, *so is it* the form in which He reveals Himself in the economy of salvation, and becomes the means (2 Pet. i. 3,) and the goal of the Christian vocation and hope (1 Pet. v. 10; 1 Thes. ii. 12,) for its disclosure belongs to the future and the close of the history of redemption.

2. κλέος, report, rumour; good report, fame, *(in pl.*, the lays *that were sung* of the *achievements of heroes,) (non occ.)*

1. Matt. iv. 8.
— —— vi. 2, see G (have.)
1. ——— 13 (*ap.*), 29.
1. —— xvi. 27.
1. —— xix. 28.
1. —— xxiv. 30.
1. —— xxv. 31 twice.
1. Mark viii. 38.
1. —— x. 37.
1. —— xiii. 26.
1. Luke ii. 9, 14, 32.
1. —— iv. 6.
1. —— ix. 26, 31, 32.
1. —— xii. 27.
1. —— xvii. 18.
1. —— xix. 38.
1. Luke xxi. 27.
1. —— xxiv. 26.
1. John i. 14.
1. —— ii. 11.
1. —— vii. 18 twice.
1. —— viii. 50.
1. —— xi. 4, 40.
1. —— xii. 41.
1. —— xvii. 5, 22, 24.
1. Acts vii. 2, 55.
1. —— xii. 23.
1. —— xxii. 11.
1. Rom. i. 23.
1. —— ii. 7, 10.
1. —— iii. 7, 23.
1. —— iv. 20.

1. Rom. v. 2.
1. —— vi. 4.
1. —— viii. 18.
1. —— ix. 4, 23 twice.
1. —— xi. 36.
1. —— xv. 7.
1. —— xvi. 27.
1. 1 Cor. ii. 7, 8.
1. —— x. 31.
1. —— xi. 7 twice, 15.
1. —— xv. 40, 41 4 times.
1. ——— 43.
1. 2 Cor. i. 20.
1. —— iii. 7, 9 twice.
— ——— 10 1st, see G (have)
1. ——— 10 2nd, 18 3 times.
1. —— iv. 6, 15, 17.
1. —— viii. 19, 23.
1. Gal. i. 5.
— —— v. 26, see G (desirous of vain.)
1. Eph. i. 6, 12, 14, 17, 18.
1. —— iii. 13, 16, 21.
1. Phil. i. 11.
1. —— ii. 11.
1. —— iii. 19.
1. —— iv. 19, 20.
1. Col. i. 27 twice.
1. —— iii. 4.
1. 1 Thes. ii. 6, 12, 20.
1. 2 Thes. i. 9.
1. —— ii. 14.
1. 1 Tim. i. 17.
1. —— iii. 16.
1. 2 Tim. ii. 10.
1. —— iv. 18.
1. Heb. i. 3.
1. —— ii. 7, 9, 10.
1. —— iii. 3.
1. —— ix. 5.
1. —— xiii. 21.
1. Jas. ii. 1.
1. 1 Pet. i. 7.
— ——— 8, see G (full of)
1. ——— 11, pl., 21, 24.
2. —— ii. 20.
1. —— iv. 13, 14.
1. —— v. 1, 4, 10.
1. ——— 11 (*om.* ἡ δόξα καὶ, *glory and*, G → L T Tr A)
1. 2 Pet. i. 3, 17 twice.
1. —— iii. 18.
1. Jude 24, 25.
1. Rev. i. 6.
1. —— iv. 9, 11.
1. —— v. 12, 13.
1. —— vii. 12.
1. —— xi. 13.
1. —— xiv. 7.
1. —— xv. 8.
1. —— xvi. 9.
1. —— xviii. 1.
1. —— xix. 1.
1. —— xxi. 11, 23, 24, 26.

GLORY (DESIROUS OF VAIN.)

κενόδοξος, (κενός, empty, and δόξα, glory,) full of empty pride and ambition, vain-glorious, *(non occ.)*

Gal. v. 26.

GLORY (FULL OF.)

δοξάζομαι, (*Pass. of* δοξάζω, *see* "GLORIFY,") *here, part.*, glorified.

1 Pet. i. 8, part.

GLORY (HAVE.)

Matt. vi. 2. | 2 Cor. iii. 10.

GLORY (-ING) [verb.]

1. καυχάομαι, to speak loud, be loud-tongued, boast *or* vaunt one's self.
2. κατακαυχάομαι, *(No.* 1 *with* κατά, down *or* against, *prefixed,)* to boast against *one*, exult over *him*.
3. καύχημα, a vaunt, a boast, the subject matter of boasting.

3. Rom. iv. 2.
1. —— v. 3.
— —— xv. 17, see G (whereof I may.)
1. 1 Cor. i. 29, 31 twice.
— —— v. 6, } see the
— —— ix. 15, } noun.
— 1 Cor. ix. 16, see G of (nothing to.)
3. 2 Cor. v. 12.
— —— vii. 4, } see the
— —— xii. 11, } noun.
1. Jas. i. 9, } marg. (text,
2. —— ii. 13, } *rejoice.*)
2. Jas. iii. 14.

GLORY OF (NOTHING TO.)

{ οὐ, not,
{ καύχημα, a matter of boasting.

1 Cor. ix. 16.

GLORY (WHEREOF I MAY.)

καύχησις, the act of boasting, a boasting.

Rom. xv. 17.

GLORYING [noun.]

1. καύχημα, the subject matter, *or* theme of boasting.
2. καύχησις, the act of boasting.

1. 1 Cor. v. 6. | 1. 1 Cor. ix. 15.
2. 2 Cor. vii. 4.

GLORYING (IN.)

καυχάομαι, *see* "GLORY," [verb], *No.* 1.

2 Cor. xii. 11, part. (*om.* G L T Tr A ℵ.)

GLUTTONOUS.

φάγος, an eater, a glutton.

Matt. xi. 19. | Luke vii. 34.

GNASH (-ED, -ETH.)

βρύχω, to roar, howl, *esp.*, the death cry *of a wounded hero. (If the common form of the Attic* βρύκω, *then* to bite, gnash, with the teeth,) *(non occ.)*

Acts vii. 54.

GNASH WITH.

τρίζω, *of animals*, to cry sharp and shrilly, squeak; the noise of gnashing *or* grinding of teeth; *of a cart wheel*, to creak, *(non occ.)*

Mark ix. 18.

GNASHING [noun.]

βρυγμός, a biting, a gnashing of the teeth, *(non occ.)*

Matt. viii. 12.
—— xiii. 42, 50.
—— xxii. 13.
Matt. xxiv. 51.
—— xxv. 30.
Luke xiii. 28.

GNAT.

κώνωψ, a gnat *or* mosquito, *Lat.*, culex, *(non occ.)*

Matt. xxiii. 24.

GNAW (-ED.)

μασσάομαι, to chew, gnaw, *(non occ.)*
Rev. xvi. 10.

GO (-EST, -ETH, -ING, GONE, WENT, WENTEST.)

1. πορεύω, to cause to pass over *by land or water*, transport. *In N.T. only Pass.*, to transport one's self, *i.e.*, pass from *one place* to *another*, to pass, to go; *(from* πόρος, a passing, passage, *from* πείρω, to pierce through.)
2. ἐκπορεύομαι, *(No.* 1 *with* ἐκ, out of, *prefixed,)* to pass out of, go *or* come forth.
   (a) *followed by* ἀπό, from, away from.
   (b) *followed by* ἐκ, out of.
   (c) *followed by* ἔξω, outside, without.
3. παραπορεύομαι, *(No.* 1 *with* παρά, beside, *prefixed,)* to pass near *or* by the side of *any one*, pass along by.
   (a) *followed by* διά, through.
4. ἔρχομαι, to come *or* go, *denoting the act as distinguished from the result.*
5. ἀπέρχομαι, *(No.* 4 *with* ἀπό, away from, *prefixed,)* to come *or* go away from *one place to another; hence*, to go away, depart, set off.
6. ἐξέρχομαι, *(No.* 4 *with* ἐκ, out of *prefixed,)* to come *or* go out of any place, come *or* go forth.
   (a) *followed by* ἀπό, from, away from.
   (b) *followed by* ἐκ, out of.
   (c) *followed by* ἔξω, outside, without.
   (d) *followed by* παρά, beside.
7. εἰσέρχομαι, *(No.* 4 *with* εἰς, into, *prefixed,)* to come *or* go into, to enter, enter into *or* among.
   (a) *followed by* διά, through.
   (b) *followed by* εἰς, into.
   (c) *followed by* ἔσω, inside, within.
8. διέρχομαι, *(No.* 4 *with* διά, through, *prefixed,)* to come *or* go through, to pass through; *of water*, to pass over.
   (a) *followed by* διά, through.
   (b) *followed by* κατά, down.
9. προσέρχομαι, *(No.* 4 *with* πρός, towards, in the direction of, *prefixed,)* to come *or* go to *or* near to *any place or person*, to approach, draw near to.
10. παρέρχομαι *(No.* 4 *with* παρά, beside, *prefixed,)* to come *or* go near to *or* beside *any person or thing*, to go *or* pass near, pass along by.
11. ἄγω, to lead, lead along, *(usually of persons*, φέρω, to bear, *being used of things,)* to lead towards *a point; here, only Mid. or reflexive*, to lead on, to go, to depart; *with the pronoun*, let us be leading on.
12. ὑπάγω, *(No.* 11 *with* ὑπό, under, *prefixed,)* to lead *or* bring under, *as horses under a yoke; also*, to lead on *or* away under *cover, with the idea of stealth, without noise or notice, hence, gen.*, to go away, depart *so as to be under cover, out of sight.*
13. ἄπειμι, to go away from, depart, *(non occ.)*
14. εἴσειμι, to go into, enter.
   (a) *followed by* εἰς, into.
15. ἀναβαίνω, to cause to ascend, to go up, climb up, mount, ascend, *(from* βαίνω, *used of all motion on the ground*, go, walk, tread, step, *the direction being determined by the preposition prefixed; here by* ἀνά, up *or* back.)
   (a) *followed by* ἐπί, upon.
16. ἐμβαίνω, *(No.* 15 *with* ἐν, in *prefixed, instead of* ἀνά up), to go in, to enter, *esp. a ship, etc.*, to embark.
   (a) *followed by* εἰς, into.
17. μεταβαίνω, *(No.* 15 *with* μετά in association with, *prefixed, instead of* ἀνά up), to go *or* pass over *from one place to another*, to remove.
18. παραγίνομαι, to become near, become present, *i.e.*, approach, arrive.
19. περιπατέω, to walk round, walk about.
20. χωρέω, to give space, give way, find way, retire, retreat *from.*
21. { ὁδὸν a way, ποιεῖν to make, } to go forward.

1. Matt. ii. 8.
— ——— 9, see G before.
1. ——— 20.
5. ——— 22.
— —— iii. 5, see G out.
— ——— 16, see G up.
— —— iv. 21, see G on.
— ——— 23, see G about.
5. ——— 24.
— —— v. 1, see G up.
— ——— 24, see G one's way.
— ——— 41 1st, see Compel
12. ——— 41 2nd.
— —— vii. 13, see G in.
— —— viii. 4, see G one's way.
1. ——— 9 twice.
— ——— 13, see G one's way.
5. ——— 19, 21.
— ——— 31, see G away.
12. ——— 32 1st.
5. ——— 32 2nd.
— ——— 33, see G one's way.
12. —— ix. 6.
1. ——— 18.
— ——— 25, see G in.
— ——— 26, see G abroad.
— ——— 32, see G out.
— ——— 35, see G about.
5. —— x. 5.
1. ——— 6, 7, part.
— ——— 11, see G thence.
— ——— 23, see G over.
— —— xi. 7, 8, 9, see G out
1. —— xii. 1.
4. ——— 9.
— ——— 14, see G out.
6a. ——— 43.
1. ——— 45.
6a. —— xiii. 1.
16a. ——— 2.
— ——— 3, see G forth.
— ——— 25, see G one's way.
5. ——— 28.
4. ——— 36.
12. ——— 44.
5. ——— 46.
4. —— xiv. 12.
— ——— 14, see G forth.
5. ——— 15.
— ——— 22, see G before.
— ——— 23, see G up.
5. ——— 25 (No. 4, G ~ L T Tr ℵ.)
4. ——— 29.
— ——— 34, see G over.
7b. —— xv. 11.
20. ——— 17.
6. ——— 21.
— ——— 29, see G up.
5. —— xvi. 21.
— —— xvii. 21, see G out.
1. ——— 27.
— —— xviii. 11, see Going (be.)
— ——— 12, 13, see Astray
12. ——— 15.
— ——— 28, see G out.
5. ——— 30.
1. ——— 32.
12. —— xix. 21.
— ——— 22, see G away.
8a. ——— 24 (No. 7, G T Tr A* ℵ)
— —— xx. 1, 3, see G out.
12. ——— 4 1st.
— ——— 4 2nd, see G one's way.
— ——— 5, 6, see G out.
12. ——— 7.
— ——— 14, see G one's way.
— ——— 17, 18, see G up.
1. —— xxi. 2, 6.

— Matt. xxi. 9, see G before
7b. ——— 12.
6c. ——— 17.
12. ——— 28.
5. ——— 29, 30.
— ——— 31, see G before.
— ——— 33, see Country.
— —— xxii. 5, see G one's way.
1. ——— 9.
— ——— 10, see G out.
1. ——— 15.
— ——— 22, see G one's way.
— —— xxiii. 13 twice, see G in.
— —— xxiv. 1, see G out.
— ——— 26, } see G
— —— xxv. 1, } forth.
— ——— 6, } see G out.
— ——— 8, }
1. ——— 9.
5. ——— 10 1st, part.
— ——— 10 2nd, see G in.
1. ——— 16.
5. ——— 18, 25.
— ——— 46, see G away.
1. —— xxvi. 14.
12. ——— 18, 24.
— ——— 30, see G out.
— ——— 32, see G before.
5. ——— 36.
— ——— 39, see G farther.
— ——— 42, 44, see G away
11. ——— 46.
7c. ——— 58.
— ——— 71, 75, see G out.
5. —— xxvii. 5.
7b. ——— 53.
— ——— 58, see G to.
— ——— 65, see G one's way.
1. ——— 66.
1. —— xxviii. 7 1st.
— ——— 7 2nd, see G before
1. ——— 9 (ap.)
12. ——— 10 1st.
5. ——— 10 2nd.
— ——— 16, see G away.
1. ——— 19.
— Mark i. 5, see G out.
— ——— 19, see G farther
5. ——— 20.
— ——— 35, see G out.
11. ——— 38.
— ——— 44, see G one's way.
— ——— 45, see G out.
— —— ii. 11, see G one's way.
— ——— 12, 13, see G forth
3a. ——— 23 1st.
21. ——— 23 2nd.
7b. ——— 26.
— —— iii. 6, see G forth.
— ——— 13, see G up.
4. ——— 19.
— ——— 21, } see G
— —— iv. 3, } out.
— —— v. 13, 14, }
12. ——— 19.
5. ——— 24.
6b. ——— 30.
12. ——— 34.
— —— vi. 1, see G out.
— ——— 6, see G round about.
— ——— 12, see G out.
— ——— 24, see G forth.
5. ——— 27, 36, 37.
— ——— 45, see G before.
— ——— 51, see G up.
— —— vii. 19, see G out.
5. ——— 24.
— ——— 29 1st, see G one's way.
6b. ——— 29 2nd.
— ——— 30, see G out.

7b. Mark viii. 26.
— ——— 27, see G out.
5. —— ix. 43.
— —— x. 17, see G forth.
— ——— 21, see G one's way.
— ——— 22, see G away.
7a. ——— 25 (St G ~ ℵ) (No. 8, G L T Tr A.)
— ——— 32 1st, see G up.
— ——— 32 2nd, see G before
— ——— 33, see G up.
2a. ——— 46, part.
— ——— 52, } see G
— —— xi. 2, 4, } one's way
— ——— 6, see Let.
— ——— 9, see G before.
— ——— 11, see G out.
2a. ——— 19.
— —— xii. 1, see Country.
— ——— 12, see G one's way.
19. ——— 38.
2b. —— xiii. 1, part.
— ——— 15, see G down.
5. —— xiv. 10, 12.
12. ——— 13.
— ——— 14, see G in.
— ——— 16, see G forth.
12. ——— 21.
— ——— 26, see G out.
— ——— 28, see G before.
— ——— 35, see G forward
— ——— 39, see G away.
11. ——— 42.
9. ——— 45.
— ——— 68, see G out.
— —— xv. 43, see G in.
— —— xvi. 7 1st, see G one's way.
— ——— 7 2nd, see G before
— ——— 8, see G out.
1. ——— 10 (ap.), 12, part. (ap.)
5. ——— 13 (ap.)
1. ——— 15 (ap.)
— ——— 20, see G forth.
7b. Luke i. 9.
— ——— 17, see G before.
1. ——— 39.
— ——— 76, see G before.
— —— ii. 1, see G out.
1. ——— 3.
— ——— 4, see G up.
— ——— 15 1st, see G away
8. ——— 15 2nd.
1. ——— 41.
— ——— 42, see G up.
4. ——— 44.
— ——— 51, see G down.
— —— iv. 14, see G out.
7b. ——— 16.
— ——— 30, see G one's way.
— ——— 37, see G out.
1. ——— 42.
— —— v. 2, see G out.
5. ——— 14.
— ——— 15, see G abroad.
15a. ——— 19.
1. ——— 24.
— ——— 27, see G forth.
— —— vi. 1, see G through
7b. ——— 4.
— ——— 12, see G out.
6d. ——— 19.
1. —— vii. 6, 8 twice, 11 1st.
— ——— 11, see G with.
— ——— 17, see G forth.
— ——— 22, see G one's way.
— ——— 24, 25, 26, see G out.
7b. ——— 36.
1. ——— 50.
— —— viii. 1, see G throughout.
6a. ——— 2.

— Luke viii. 5, see G out.
— ——— 14, see G fo[illegible].
16a. ——— 22 1st.
— ——— 22 2nd, see G over
— ——— 27, see G forth.
— ——— 31, see G out.
6a. ——— 33.
5. ——— 34 (om. G L T Tr A ℵ.)
— ——— 35, see G out.
— ——— 37, see G up.
— ——— 39, see G one's way.
12. ——— 42 (ap.)
6a. ——— 46.
1. ——— 48.
— ——— 51, see G in.
6a. —— ix. 5, part.
8b. ——— 6.
— ——— 10, see G aside.
5. ——— 12 (G ~) (No. 1, G L T Tr A ℵ.)
1. ——— 13.
— ——— 28, see G up.
1. ——— 51, 52, 53, part., 56, 57 1st, part.
5. ——— 57 2nd, 59, 60.
— —— x. 3, see G one's way.
17. ——— 7.
— ——— 10, see G out.
— ——— 30, see G down.
— ——— 34, see G to.
1. ——— 37, 38.
1. —— xi. 5.
— ——— 14, see G out.
6a. ——— 24.
1. ——— 26.
— ——— 37, see G in.
12. —— xii. 58.
— —— xiii. 22, see G through.
1. ——— 32.
4. —— xiv. 1.
— ——— 4, see Let.
1. ——— 10 1st.
— ——— 10 2nd, see G up.
6. ——— 18.
1. ——— 19.
— ——— 21, 23, see G out.
— ——— 25, see G with.
1. ——— 31.
1. —— xv. 4, 15, 18.
— ——— 28, see G in.
1. —— xvi. 30.
10. —— xvii. 7.
1. ——— 11, 14 1st.
12. ——— 14 2nd (lit. *in their withdrawing.*)
— ——— 19, see G one's way.
5. ——— 23.
6a. ——— 29.
— —— xviii. 10, see G up.
— ——— 14, see G down.
7a. ——— 25 (No. 8, L Trm.)
— ——— 31, see G up.
— ——— 39, see G before.
7. —— xix. 7.
1. ——— 12, 28.
12. ——— 30.
— ——— 32, see G one's way.
1. ——— 36.
7b. ——— 45.
— —— xx. 9, see Country.
1. —— xxi. 8.
— ——— 37, see G out.
— —— xxii. 4, see G one's way.
1. ——— 8.
5. ——— 13.
1. ——— 22, 33, 39.
— ——— 47, see G before.
— ——— 62, see G out.
— ——— 68, } see Let
— —— xxiii. 22, }
— ——— 52, see G unto.

1. Luke xxiv. 13, part., with εἰμί (lit. *were going.*)
— —— 15, see G with.
5. —— 24.
1. —— 28 twice.
— —— 29, see G in.
— John i. 44, see G forth.
— —— ii. 12, see G down.
— —— 13, see G up.
12. —— iii. 8.
8a. —— iv. 4.
— —— 8, see G away.
12. —— 16.
— —— 28, see G one's way.
6b. —— 30.
5. —— 43.
4. —— 45.
5. —— 47.
— —— 50, see G one's way.
— —— 51, see G down.
— —— v. 1, see G up.
— —— 4, see G down.
5. —— vi. 1.
— —— 3, see G up.
— —— 16, see G down.
4. —— 17.
12. —— 21. [with.
— —— 22 1st, see G into
— —— 22 2nd, see G away
5. —— 66.
— —— 67, see G away.
5. —— 68.
12. —— vii. 3.
— —— 8 twice, 10 twice, 14, see G up.
— —— 19, 20, see G about
12. —— 33.
1. —— 35 twice.
1. —— 53 (*ap.*)
1. —— viii. 1 (*ap.*)
— —— 9, see G out.
1. —— 11 (*ap.*)
12. —— 14 twice.
— —— 21 1st, see G one's way.
12. —— 21 2nd, 22.
6b. —— 59 1st.
8a. —— 59 2nd (*ap.*)
12. —— ix. 7 1st.
— —— 7 2nd, see G one's way.
5. —— 11 1st.
12. —— 11 2nd.
1. —— x. 4.
— —— 9, see G in and G out.
— —— 40, see G away.
11. —— xi. 7.
12. —— 8.
1. —— 11.
11. —— 15, 16.
— —— 20, see Meet.
— —— 28, see G one's way.
— —— 31 1st, see G out.
12. —— 31 2nd, 44.
— —— 46, see G one's way.
5. —— 54.
— —— 55, see G up.
— —— xii. 11, see G away
— —— 13, see G forth.
5. —— 19.
12. —— 35.
12. —— xiii. 3.
— —— 30, 31, see G out
12. —— 33, 36 twice.
1. —— xiv. 2, 3.
12. —— 4, 5.
1. —— 12.
— —— 28 1st, see G away
1. —— 28 2nd.
12. —— xv. 16.
— —— xvi. 5 1st, see G one's way.
12. John xv. 5 2nd.
— —— 7 twice, see G away.
12. —— 10, 16 (*ap.*), 17.
1. —— 28.
— —— xviii. 1, 4, see G forth.
5. —— 6.
— —— 8, see G one's way
— —— 15, see G in with
— —— 16, see G out.
7b. —— 28.
— —— 29, 38, see G out.
— —— xix. 4, see G forth
7b. —— 9.
— —— 12, see Let.
— —— 17, }
— —— xx. 3, } see G forth
— —— 5, see G in.
7b. —— 6.
— —— 8, see G in.
— —— 10, see G away.
1. —— 17.
12. —— xxi. 3 1st.
4. —— 3 2nd.
— —— 3 3rd, see G forth
— —— 11, see G up.
— —— 23, see G abroad
— Acts i. 10, see G up.
1. —— 11.
— —— 13, see G up.
— —— 21, see G in and G out.
1. —— 25.
— —— iii. 1, see G up.
14a. —— 3.
— —— 13, see Let.
— —— iv. 15, see G Aside.
— —— 21, 23 1st, see Let
4. —— 23 2nd.
1. —— v. 20.
5. —— 26, part.
— —— 40, see Let.
— —— vii. 15, see G down
— —— 40, see G before.
— —— viii. 4, see G everywhere.
— —— 5, see G down.
1. —— 26 1st.
— —— 26 2nd, see G down
1. —— 27.
— —— 29, see G near.
1. —— 36.
— —— 38, see G down.
1. —— 39.
— —— ix. 1, see G unto.
7b. —— 6.
1. —— 11.
— —— 15, 17, see G one's way.
— —— 28, see G out.
— —— 29, see G about.
— —— 39, see G with.
— —— x. 9 1st, see Journey
— —— 9 2nd, see G up.
1. —— 20.
— —— 21, see G down.
— —— 23, see G away.
— —— 27, see G in.
— —— 38, see G about.
— —— xi. 3, see G in.
— —— 12, see G with.
8. —— 22 (*om.* L T Tr ℵ)
— —— xii. 9, 10, see G out
1. —— 17.
— —— 19, see G down.
— —— xiii. 6, see G through
— —— 11, see G about.
7b. —— 14.
— —— 42, see G out.
7b. —— xiv. 1.
— —— 25, see G down.
— —— xv. 2, see G up.
— —— 24, see G out.
— —— 33, see Let.
— —— 36, see G again.
— —— 38, see G with.
— —— 41, see G through
— Acts xvi. 3, see G forth
— —— 4, see G through
— —— 6, see G through- [out.
1. —— 7.
6c. —— 13.
1. —— 16, part.
— —— 35, 36 1st, see Let
1. —— 36 2nd.
6b. —— 40.
— —— xvii. 2, see G in.
— —— 9, see Let.
13. —— 10.
1. —— 14.
1. —— xviii. 6.
— —— 22 1st, see G up.
— —— 22 2nd, see G down
— —— 23, see G over all
7b. —— xix. 8.
6a. —— 12 (No. 2, G L T [Tr A ℵ.)
1. —— 21.
1. —— xx. 1.
— —— 2, see G over.
— —— 5, see G before.
— —— 10, see G down.
— —— 13 1st, see G before
— —— 13 2nd, see, Afoot.
1. —— 22.
8. —— 25.
— —— xxi. 2, see Aboard.
— —— 4, see G up.
— —— 5, see G one's way
— —— 12, 15, see G up.
— —— 16, see G with.
— —— 18, see G in.
— —— 31, see G about.
1. —— xxii. 5, 10.
9. —— 26.
— —— xxiii. 10, see G down
13. —— 16.
— —— 19, see G aside.
1. —— 23.
1. —— 32 (No. 5, G∾ L Tr A ℵ.)
— —— xxiv. 6, see G about
— —— 11, see G up.
— —— 25, see G one's way. [with.
— —— xxv. 5, see G down
— —— 6, see G down.
— —— 9, see G up.
1. —— 12, 20.
1. —— xxvi. 12, part.
— —— 21, see G about.
— —— 31, see G aside.
1. —— xxvii. 3.
— —— 28, see G further or Little.
4. —— xxviii. 14.
— —— 18, see Let.
1. —— 26.
— Rom. iii. 12, see G out of the way.
— Rom. x. 3, see G about.
6. —— 18.
1. —— xv. 25.
6b. 1 Cor. v. 10.
— —— vi. 1, 6, 7, see Law
— —— ix. 7, see Warfare.
— —— x. 4, see *G with.*
1. —— 27.
1. —— xvi. 4 twice, 6.
6. 2 Cor. ii. 13.
6. —— viii. 17.
— —— ix. 5, see G before
— Gal. i. 17 1st, see G up.
5. —— 17 2nd.
— —— 18, }
— —— ii. 1, 2, } see G up
— Eph. iv. 26, see G down
— Phil. ii. 23, see G with (how it will.)
— 1 Thes. iv. 6, see G beyond.
1. 1 Tim. i. 3, part.
— —— 18, } see G
— —— v. 24, } before.
— Heb. vi. 1, see G on.
— —— vii. 18, see G before
14a. —— ix. 6.
— —— xi. 8 1st & 2nd, see G out.
4. —— 8 3rd.
— —— xiii. 13, see G forth
— Jas. i. 24, see G one's way.
— —— iv. 13 1st, see G to.
1. —— 13 2nd.
— —— v. 1, see G to.
— 1 Pet. ii. 25, see Astray.
1. —— iii. 19, 22.
— 2 Pet. ii. 15, see Astray.
12. 1 John ii. 11.
— —— 19, }
— —— iv. 1, } see G out.
— 3 John 7, see G forth.
5. Jude 7.
1. —— 11.
2b. Rev. i. 16.
— —— iii. 12, see G out.
— —— vi. 2, see G forth.
— —— 4, see G out.
12. —— x. 8.
5. —— 9.
5. —— xii. 17.
12. —— xiii. 10.
12. —— xiv. 4.
— —— xvi. 1, see G one's way.
5. —— 2.
— —— 14, see G forth.
12. —— xvii. 8, 11.
2b. —— xix. 15.
— —— xx. 8, see G out.
— —— 9, see G up.

The following combinations do not include those which are represented by two or more separate Greek words. For these see under *each* word respectively.

GO ABOUT.

1. διέρχομαι, *see* "GO," *No.* 8.
2. ἐπιχειρέω to lay hands upon, put one's hand to *a work*, set to work at, attempt.
3. ζητέω, to seek, seek for ; search out, enquire into ; to seek *to do.*
4. πειράζω, to make proof *or* trial, make an attempt.

5. πειράω, to attempt, undertake, endeavour; to make an attempt, try to do, (occ. Acts ix. 26.)

6. περιάγω, to lead round, to go about *or* round.

6. Matt. iv. 23.	6. Acts xiii. 11.
6. —— ix. 35.	3. —— xxi. 31, part.
3. John vii. 19, 20.	4. —— xxiv. 6.
2. Acts ix. 29	5. —— xxvi. 21.
1. —— x. 38.	3. Rom. x. 3.

GO ABROAD.

1. ἐξέρχομαι, *see* "GO," *No.* 6.

2. διέρχομαι, *see* "GO," *No.* 8.

1. Matt. ix. 26. | 2. Luke v. 15.
1. John xxi. 23.

GO AGAIN.

ἐπιστρέφω, to turn upon *or* towards, return.

Acts xv. 36.

GO ASIDE.

1. ἀναχωρέω, to go back, recede, *spoken of those who flee*, to go away, depart, *withdraw for privacy.*

2. ὑποχωρέω, to give place covertly, withdraw one's self under *cover, without noise or notice.*

3. ἀπέρχομαι, *see* "GO," *No.* 5.

2. Luke ix. 10.	1. Acts xxiii. 19.
3. Acts iv. 15.	1. —— xxvi. 31, part.

GO AWAY.

1. ἀπέρχομαι, *see* "GO," *No.* 5.

2. ἐξέρχομαι. *see* "GO," *No.* 6.

3. πορεύομαι, *see* "GO," *No.* 1.

4. ὑπάγω, *see* "GO," *No.* 12.

1. Matt. viii. 31, (G∾), (ἀποστέλλω ἡμᾶς, *send us away*, instead of, ἐπίτρεψον ἡμῖν ἀπελθεῖν, *suffer us to go away*, G L T Tr A ℵ)	1. Mark xiv. 39.
1. —— xix. 22.	1. Luke ii. 15.
1. —— xxv. 46.	1. John iv. 8.
1. —— xxvi. 42, 44.	1. —— vi. 22.
3. —— xxviii. 16.	4. —— 67.
1. Mark x. 22.	1. —— x. 40.
	4. —— xii. 11.
	4. —— xiv. 28.
	1. —— xvi. 7 twice.
	1. —— xx. 10.
	2. Acts. x. 23.

GO BEFORE.

1. προάγω, ("GO," *No.* 11, *with* πρό, before, *prefixed,*) to lead forth, *intrans.*, to go before, *of place*, to go in front, *of time*, to go first, precede.

2. προέρχομαι, (*No.* 4 *with* πρό, before, *prefixed,*) to go *or* come before *or* forward, *i.e.*, in front *of place, or* first *of time.*

3. προπορεύομαι, (*No.* 1 *with* πρό, before, *prefixed,*) to pass before, *i.e.*, in front *of place, or* first *of time.*

1. Matt. ii. 9.	2. Luke i. 17.
1. —— xiv. 22.	3. —— 76.
1. —— xxi. 9, 31.	1. —— xviii. 39 (παράγω, to lead along near, Lm.)
1. —— xxvi. 32.	2. —— xxii. 47.
1. —— xxviii. 7.	3. Acts vii. 40.
1. Mark vi. 45.	2. —— xx. 5, 13.
1. —— x. 32, part with ἦν, lit., *was leading on before.*	2. 2 Cor. ix. 5.
1. —— xi. 9.	1. 1 Tim. i. 18.
1. —— xiv. 28.	1. —— v. 24.
1. —— xvi. 7.	1. Heb. vii. 18.

GO BEYOND.

ὑπερβαίνω, to go, walk, tread, step beyond, to overstep, go too far.

1 Thes. iv. 6.

GO DOWN.

1. καταβαίνω, to go, walk, tread *or* step down, descend *from a higher to a lower plac*

2. κατέρχομαι, to go *or* come down, *denoting the act as distinguished from the result.*

3. ἐπίδυω, to sink upon, go down *or* set upon.

(a) *followed by* ἐπί, upon.

1. Mark xiii. 15.	2. Acts viii. 5.
1. Luke ii. 51.	1. —— 26, 38.
1. —— x. 30.	1. —— x. 21.
1. —— xviii. 14.	2. —— xii. 19.
1. John ii. 12.	1. —— xiv. 25.
1. —— iv. 51, part.	1. —— xviii. 22.
1. —— v. 4 (*ap.*)	1. —— xx. 10.
1. —— vi. 16.	1. —— xxiii. 10.
1. Acts vii. 15.	1. —— xxv. 6.

3a. Eph. iv. 26.

GO DOWN WITH.

συνκαταβαίνω, ("GO DOWN," *No.* 1 *with* σύν, together with, *prefixed, implying union or co-operation.*)

Acts xxv. 5.

GO EVERYWHERE.

διέρχομαι, *see* "GO," *No.* 8.

Acts viii. 4.

GO FARTHER.

1. προβαίνω, to go, step, walk forward, advance.

2. προέρχομαι, *see* "GO BEFORE," *No.* 2.

2. Matt. xxvi. 39 (προσέρχομαι, see G, No. 9, G~ T Tr [א.)
1. Mark i. 19, part.

GO FORTH.

1. ἐξέρχομαι, *see* "GO," *No.* 6.

2. πορεύομαι, *see* "GO," *No.* 1.

3. ἐκπορεύομαι, *see* "GO," *No.* 2.

1. Matt. xiii. 3.
1. —— xiv. 14.
1. —— xxiv. 26.
1. —— xxv. 1.
1. Mark ii. 12, 13.
1. —— iii. 6.
1. —— vi. 24.
3. —— x. 17, part.
1. —— xiv. 16.
1. —— xvi. 20 (*ap.*)
1. Luke v. 27.
1. —— vii. 17.
2. Luke viii. 14.
1. —————— 27, part.
1. John i. 44.
1. —— xii. 13.
1. —— xviii. 1, 4.
1. —— xix. 4, 17.
1. —— xx. 3.
1. —— xxi. 3.
1. Acts xvi. 3.
1. Heb. xiii. 13.
1. 3 John 7.
1. Rev. vi. 2.
3. Rev. xvi. 14 (*om.* G→.)

GO FORWARD.

προέρχομαι, *see* "GO BEFORE," *No.* 2.

Mark xiv. 35 (προσέρχομαι, see G, No. 9, G~ Tr.)

GO FURTHER.

διΐστημι, to divide, place asunder, stand at certain distances *or* intervals.

Acts xxviii. 28, part.

GO WITH (HOW IT WILL.)

τά, the *things*,
περὶ, concerning,
ἐμέ, me,
[*the verb* "see" *in this text meaning* "to look away from."]

Phil. ii. 23.

GO IN.

1. εἰσέρχομαι, *see* "GO," *No.* 7.

2. εἴσειμι, *see* "GO," *No.* 14.

1. Matt. vii. 13.
1. —— ix. 25.
1. —— xxiii. 13 twice.
1. —— xxv. 10.
1. Mark xiv. 14.
1. —— xv. 43.
1. Luke viii. 51.
1. —— xi. 37.
1. —— xv. 28.
1. Luke xxiv. 29.
1. John x. 9.
1. —— xx. 5, 8.
1. Acts i. 21.
1. —— ix. 6.
1. —— x. 27.
1. —— xi. 3.
1. —— xvii. 2.
2. —— xxi. 18.

GO IN WITH.

συνεισέρχομαι, ("GO," *No.* 7, *with* σύν, together with, *prefixed, implying* union *and* co-operation.)

John xviii. 15.

GO INTO WITH.

John vi. 22.

GO NEAR.

προσέρχομαι, *see* "GO," *No.* 9.

Acts viii. 29.

GO ON.

1. προβαίνω, *see* "GO FARTHER," *No.* 1.

2. φέρω, to bear *(as a burden,) then*, to bear *with the idea of motion*, bear along.

(a) *Mid.*, to bear one's self along, tend.

1. Matt. iv. 21.
2a. Heb. vi. 1.

GO ONE'S WAY.

1. απέρχομαι, *see* "GO," *No.* 5.

2. ὑπάγω, *see* "GO," *No.* 12.

3. πορεύομαι, *see* "GO," *No.* 1.

2. Matt. v. 24.
2. —— viii. 4, 13.
1. ——— 33.
1. —— xiii. 25.
1. —— xx. 4.
2. ——— 14.
1. —— xxii. 5, 22.
2. —— xxvii. 65.
2. Mark i. 44.
2. —— ii. 11.
2. —— vii. 29.
2. —— x. 21, 52.
2. —— xi. 2.
1. ——— 4.
1. —— xii. 12.
2. —— xvi. 7.
3. Luke iv. 30.
3. —— vii. 22.
1. Luke viii. 39.
2. —— x. 3.
3. —— xvii. 19.
1. —— xix. 32.
1. —— xxii. 4.
1. John iv. 28.
3. ——— 50 twice.
2. —— viii. 21.
1. —— ix. 7.
1. —— xi. 28, 46.
2. —— xvi. 5.
2. —— xviii. 8.
3. Acts ix. 15.
1. ——— 17.
3. —— xxi. 5.
3. —— xxiv. 25.
1. Jas. i. 24.
2. Rev. xvi. 1.

GO OUT.

1. ἐξέρχομαι, *see* "GO," *No.* 6.

2. ἀπέρχομαι, *see* "GO," *No.* 5.

3. ἐκπορεύομαι, *see* "GO," *No.* 2.

4. ἀποβαίνω, to go, step, walk away from.

5. ἔξειμι, to go out of *or* out from among.

6. σβέννυμι, to quench, extinguish *as a light or fire.*

(a) *Pres. Pass.*, to be going out.

3. Matt. iii. 5.
1. —— ix. 32, part.
1. —— xi. 7, 8, 9.
1. —— xii. 14.
3. —— xvii. 21 (*ap.*)
1. —— xviii. 28.
1. —— xx. 1, 3, 5, 6.
1. —— xxii. 10.
1. —— xxiv. 1.
1. —— xxv. 6.
6a. —— 8, marg. *be going out.* [75.
1. —— xxvi. 30, 71, part.,
3. Mark i. 5.
1. ——— 35, 45.
1. —— iii. 21.
1. —— iv. 3.
1. —— v. 13.
1. ——— 14 (ἐρχόμαι, see G, No. 4, G∾ L T Tr A ℵ3.)
1. —— vi. 1, 12.
3. —— vii. 19.
1. ——— 30.
1. —— viii. 27.
1. —— xi. 11.
1. —— xiv. 26, 68.
1. —— xvi. 8.
3. Luke ii. 1.
1. Luke iv. 14.
3. ——— 37.
4. —— v. 2.
1. —— vii. 24, 25, 26.
1. —— viii. 5.
2. ——— 31.
1. ——— 35.
1. —— x. 10.
1. —— xi. 14, part. (ἐκβαλλόμαι, *cast out*, L.)
1. —— xiv. 21, 23.
1. —— xxi. 37.
1. —— xxii. 62.
1. John viii. 9 (*ap.*)
1. —— x. 9.
1. —— xi. 31.
1. —— xiii. 30, 31.
1. —— xviii. 16, 29, 38.
1. Acts i. 21.
3. —— ix. 28.
1. —— xii. 9, 10.
5. —— xiii. 42, part.
1. —— xv. 24.
1. Heb. xi. 8 twice.
1. 1 John ii. 19.
1. —— iv. 1.
1. Rev. iii. 12.
1. —— vi. 4.
1. —— xx. 8.

GO OUT OF THE WAY.

ἐκκλίνω, to bend out, turn aside *or* away.

Rom. iii. 12.

GO OVER.

1. διέρχομαι, *see* "GO," *No.* 8.
2. διαπεράω, to drive right through, to pass right across *or* through *a space*, pass right over.
3. τελέω, to bring about, complete, fulfil, accomplish.
   (a) *Pass.*, to be brought about, bring to an end.

3. Matt. x. 23, marg. *end*, or *finish*.
2. Matt. xiv. 34, part.
1. Luke viii. 22.
1. Acts xx. 2, part.

GO OVER ALL.

διέρχομαι, *see* "GO," *No.* 8.

Acts xviii. 23.

GO ROUND ABOUT.

περιάγω, ("GO," *No.* 11 with περί, around, *prefixed,*) to lead round, lead about.

Mark vi. 6.

GO THENCE.

ἐξέρχομαι, *see* "GO," *No.* 6.

Matt. x. 11.

GO THROUGH.

1. διαπορεύομαι, ("GO," *No.* 1 *with* διά, through, *prefixed,*) to pass through.
2. διέρχομαι, *see* "GO," *No.* 8.

1. Luke vi. 1.
1. —— xiii. 22.
2. Acts xiii. 6, part.
2. —— xv. 41.
1. Acts xvi. 4.

GO THROUGHOUT.

1. διέρχομαι, *see* "GO," *No.* 8.
2. διοδεύω, to travel through, to traverse, (occ. Acts xvii. 1, part.)

2. Luke viii. 1.
1. Acts xvi. 6, part.

GO TO.

1. προσέρχομαι, *see* "GO," *No.* 9.
2. ἄγε, *Imperat. of* "GO," *No.* 11.

1. Matt. xxvii. 58.
1. Luke x. 34.
2. Jas. iv. 13.
2. —— v. 1.

GO UNTO.

προσέρχομαι, *see* "GO," *No.* 9.

Luke xxiii. 52.
Acts ix. 1.

GO UP.

1. ἀναβαίνω, *see* "GO," *No.* 15.
2. ἐμβαίνω, *see* "GO," *No.* 16.
3. προσαναβαίνω, (*No.* 1 *with* πρός, towards, *prefixed,*) to go up towards, (*non occ.*)
4. ἀνέρχομαι, ("GO," *No.* 4 *with* ἀνά, up, *prefixed,*) (*non occ.*)
5. πορεύομαι, *see* "GO," *No.* 1.

1. Matt. iii. 16.
1. —— v. 1.
1. —— xiv. 23.
1. —— xv. 29.
1. —— xx. 17, 18.
1. Mark iii. 13.
1. —— vi. 51.
1. —— x. 32, 33.
1. Luke ii. 4, 42.
3. —— viii. 37.
1. —— ix. 28.
2. —— xiv. 10.
1. —— xviii. 10, 31.
1. John ii. 13.
1. —— v. 1.
4. —— vi. 3.
1. —— vii. 8 twice.
1. ——— 10 twice, 14.
1. —— xi. 55.
1. John xxi. 11.
5. Acts i. 10, part.
1. ——— 13.
1. —— iii. 1.
1. —— x. 9.
1. —— xv. 2.
1. —— xviii. 22.
1. —— xxi. 4 (ἐπιβαίνω, embark, L T Tr A ℵ.)
1. ——— 12, 15.
1. —— xxiv. 11.
1. —— xxv. 9.
4. —— Gal. i. 17 (ἀποέρχομαι see G, No. 5, L Trm A.)
4. ——— 18, marg. return.
1. —— ii. 1, 2.
1. Rev. xx. 9.

GO WITH.

1. συνέρχομαι, ("GO," *No.* 4 *with* σύν, together with, *prefixed.*)
2. συμπορεύομαι, ("GO," *No.* 1 *with* σύν, together with, *prefixed.*)

3. ἀκολουθέω, to go with, accompany, follow.

2. Luke vii. 11.
2. —— xiv. 25.
2. —— xxiv. 15.
1 Acts ix. 39.
1. Acts xi. 12.
1. —— xv. 38.
1. —— xxi. 16.
3. 1 Cor. x. 4, marg. (text, [follow.)

GOING (BE.)

πορεύομαι, *see* "GO," *No.* 1.

Matt. xxviii. 11, part.

GOING OUT (be) [margin.]

σβέννυμι, *see* "GO OUT," *No.* 6.

Matt. xxv. 8, text, *go out.*

GOAT (-s.)

1. ἔριφος, a kid, a young goat, (occ. Luke xv. 29.)
2. ἐρίφιον, *(dim. of No.* 1,) a young kid, *(non occ.)*
3. τράγος, a he-goat, *(non occ.)*

1. Matt. xxv. 32.
2. —————— 33.
3. Heb. ix. 12, 13, 19.
3. —— x. 4.

GOATSKIN (-s.)

{ αἴγειος, of a goat, δέρμα, a skin *of an animal.* } goat-skin hides, *(non occ.)*

Heb. xi. 37, pl.

GOD (-s.)

1. Θεός, God. *A name reclaimed from the heathen, and used in N.T. for* the true God. *Various derivations, ancient and modern, have been proposed, but it is nearly certain that its origin is from the East and comes from the Sanscrit root,* DIU-S (pronounced *dyus,) which means* (1) *masc.,* fire, the sun, (2) *fem.,* a ray of light, day,* (3) *neut.,* the sky, heaven. DIV-S *also means* (1) *as adj.,* brilliant, (2) *as fem. subst.,* sky *or* heaven.

[Wherever the Sun shines in the world he has been or is, worshipped as God, because he gives light to Heaven and life to earth; and heaven was in turn worshipped as the abode of the Sun, but the object of adoration was Light and Life,* or heaven either as the abode of the Sun, or as personified. Then DIAUS was procreating or generative power dwelling in heaven. The Father of light and life. Hence came Lat., DEUS; Doric, ΣΔΕΥΣ, and ΖΕΟΣ; Lacedæmonian, ΣΙΟΣ; Eolic, ΔΕΥΣ, or ΖΕΥΣ; and Attic, ΘΕΥΣ and ΘΕΟΣ. †

Θεός however, having lost the meaning of the one God came to mean "a God" only, one of the many gods. Hence it became necessary in N.T. gen., to distinguish it by the article, ὁ Θεός, the one supreme with whom is the fountain of life and light; and now, to know Him that hath called us out of darkness into His marvellous light, is "life eternal." He is "the fountain of life" and "in His light alone can we see light."

In the Septuagint the sing. Θεός, is (with a very few exceptions) the translation of the pl. אלהים (Elohim) never the pl. Θεοι. It is also used frequently for יהוה Jehovah (see under "LORD.")

אל is from the root אול or איל which means, (1) to be strong, powerful; (2) to take precedence, be first, אל‡ then means (1) a powerful man, (Ezek. xxxi. 11; xxxii. 21), (2) power, strength, (Gen. xxxi. 29), (3) God, as the mighty one, the one above all, the first, combining the idea of inspiring awe and adoration.

אלהים, plural, is used (1) for all gods, (Ex. xii. 12; xviii. 11; 2 Kings xix. 18.) (2) angels, Ps. lxxxii. 1; xcvii. 7), (3) Kings, Princes, etc., (Ps. lxxxii. 1, 6; Ex. xxi. 6), (4) in the

---

* Hence Lat., Dies (fem.) day.

* Hence ὀυρανίος, is from אור־עין, ὀυρ-αιν the "fountain of light and heat."

† Kindred with these is DIES-PITER, or DIU-PITER (Jupiter), i.e., Heaven-father; and from DIV proceeds the adj. DEVAS, Lat. Divus, i.e., one of DIV, (Heaven) traceable in the Eng. DIV-ine. Hence also the old Icelandic TIFI or TIVI a god, and modern Icelandic DIF-IL a devil.

‡ It is also probably the root of Ἥλιος, the Sun, and is to be traced in the Syr., and Sab., AL-OHO; Arab., ILAH; Chald., ELAH; and Samaritan ALAH.

singular sense, the one God, Three in One.]

* In the following references *(distinguished by the asterisk)*, Θεός is used without the article, and denotes the conception of God, as an Infinite and perfect Being, one who is almighty, infinite, etc.

With the article *(i.e. in all passages not so distinguished)* ὁ Θεός *denotes* the God, the revealed God, the God of the Bible, *and according to the context may denote*, this God, our God, etc., *the article marks the word as objective and definite, and also distinguishes the subject from the predicate.*

Other combinations are also distinguished:

(a) Κύριος ὁ Θεός, Lord the God, *(like O.T.* Jehovah-Elohim.)

(b) υἱὸς Θεοῦ, Son, *or* a Son of God.

(c) Θεοῦ υἱός, God's Son, *more emphatic, see* Matt. xxvii. 54, etc.

(d) ὁ υἱὸς τοῦ Θεοῦ, the Son of the (revealed) God, *see* Matt. xvi. 16; Acts xi. 20, etc.

(e) υἱὸς τοῦ Θεοῦ, Son, *or* a Son of the (revealed) God, *(the Deity being recognised, but the relationship not so fully admitted.)*

(f) Θεός, *used of other Gods.*

2. δαιμόνιον, *see* "DEVIL," *No.* 2.

1. Matt. i. 23.
— — ii. 12, 22, see Warned
1. — iii. 9, 16.
1e. — iv. 3.
1*. —— 4.
1e. —— 6.
1a. —— 7, 10.
1. — v. 8.
1b. —— 9.
1. —— 34.
1*. — vi. 24.
1. —— 30, 33 (*om.* L T ℵ)
1e. — viii. 29.
1. — ix. 8.
1. — xii. 4.
1*. —— 28 1st.
1. —— 28 2nd.
1c. — xiv. 33.
1. — xv. 3, 4, 6, 31.
1d. — xvi. 16.
1. —— 23.
1. — xix. 6, 17 (*ap.*)
1. —— 24 (τῶν οὐρανῶν, *of the heavens*, L T Tr A*.)
1*. —— 26.
1. — xxi. 12 (*om.* G→ L Tr ℵ.)
1. —— 31, 43.
1. — xxii. 16.
1*. Matt. xxii. 21 1st.
1. —— 21 2nd, 29.
1. —— 30 (*om.* G→ L Tr) (1* A^b.) [& 4th.
1. —— 31, 32 1st, 2nd, 3rd,
1*. —— 32 5th (*om.* L T Tr A ℵ.)
1a. —— 37.
1. — xxiii. 22.
1. — xxvi. 61, 63 1st.
1d. —— 63 2nd.
1c. — xxvii. 40 (1b, L.)
1. —— 43 1st.
1c. —— 43 2nd.
1*. —— 46 twice.
1c. —— 54 (No. 1b, L Tr A)
1e. Mark i. 1 (No. 1b, L Tr A) (*om.* T ℵ.)
1. —— 14, 15, 24.
1. — ii. 7, 12, 26.
1d. — iii. 11.
1. —— 35.
1. — iv. 11, 26, 30.
1e. — v. 7 1st.
1. —— 7 2nd.
1. — vii. 8, 9, 13.
1. — viii. 33.
1. — ix. 1, 47.
1. — x. 6 (*om.* L^b T Tr A^b ℵ.)
1. Mark x. 9, 14, 15, 18, 23, 24, 25.
1. —— 27 1st (No. 1*, T Tr A ℵ.)
1. —— 27 2nd (*ap.*)
1*. — xi. 22.
1. — xii. 14, 17 twice, 24.
1. —— 26 1st & 2nd.
1. —— 26 3rd & 4th, 27 1st, (No. 1*, L Tr A.)
1*. —— 27 2nd (*om.* G L Tr A) (No. 1, T.)
1. —— 29, 30.
1*. —— 32 (*om.* G L T Tr A ℵ.)
1. —— 34.
1. — xiii. 19.
1. — xiv. 25.
1. — xv. 34 twice.
1b. —— 39.
1. —— 43.
1. — xvi. 19 (*ap.*)
1. Luke i. 6, 8, 16, 19, 26, 30, 32.
1b. —— 35.
1. —— 37, 47, 64.
1a. —— 68.
1*. —— 78.
1. — ii. 13.
1*. —— 14.
1. —— 20, 28.
1*. —— 40, 52.
1*. — iii. 2.
1. —— 6, 8.
1e. —— 38.
1e. — iv. 3.
1*. —— 4 (*ap.*)
1a. —— 8.
1d. —— 9 (No. 1e, G L T Tr A ℵ.)
1a. —— 12.
1. —— 34.
1d. —— 41.
1. —— 43.
1. — v. 1, 21, 25, 26.
1. — vi. 4, 12, 20.
1. — vii. 16 twice, 28, 29, 30.
1. — viii. 1, 10, 11, 21.
1e. —— 28 (*om.* τοῦ Θεοῦ, *of God*, G→.)
1. —— 39.
1. — ix. 2, 11, 20, 27, 43, 60, 62.
1. — x. 9, 11.
1a. —— 27.
1*. — xi. 20 1st.
1. —— 20 2nd.
1. —— 28, 42, 49.
1. — xii. 6, 8, 9.
1. —— 20 (Κύριος, *Lord*, Lm.)
1*. —— 21.
1. —— 24, 28.
1. —— 31 (αὐτοῦ, *of Him or His*, G∾ L T Tr A ℵ.)
1. — xiii. 13, 18, 20, 28, 29.
1. — xiv. 15.
1. — xv. 10.
1*. — xvi. 13.
1. —— 15 twice, 16.
1. — xvii. 15, 18, 20 twice, 21.
1. — xviii. 2, 4, 7, 11, 13, 16, 17, 19, 24, 25, 27, 29, 43 twice.
1. — xix. 11, 37.
— — xx. 16, see Forbid.
1. —— 21, 25 twice.
1. —— 36 (No. 1*, T Tr A ℵ.)
1. —— 37 1st.
1. —— 37 2nd & 3rd (No. 1*, L T Tr A ℵ.)
1*. —— 38.
1. — xxi. 4 (*om.* T Tr^b ℵ.)
1. Luke xxi. 31.
1. — xxii. 16, 18, 69.
1d. —— 70.
1. — xxiii. 35, 40, 47, 51.
1. — xxiv. 19, 53.
1. John i. 1st.
1*. —— 1 2nd.
1. —— 2.
1*. —— 6, 12, 13, 18.
1. —— 29.
1d. —— 34.
1. —— 36.
1d. —— 50.
1. —— 52.
1*. — iii. 2 1st.
1. —— 2 2nd, 3, 5, 16, 17.
1d. —— 18.
1*. —— 21.
1. —— 33, 34 1st & 2nd.
1. —— 34 3rd (*om.* G→ L^b T Tr^b A ℵ.)
1. —— 36.
1. — iv. 10, 24.
1. — v. 18 twice.
1d. —— 25.
1. —— 42.
1. —— 44 (*om.* L^b.)
1. — vi. 27, 28, 29, 33.
1. —— 45 (No. 1*, L T)
1. —— 46.
1d. —— 69 (ὁ ἅγιος τοῦ Θεοῦ, *the holy one of God*, instead of ὁ Χριστὸς ὁ υἱὸς τοῦ Θεοῦ, *the Christ the holy one of God*, L T Tr A ℵ.)
1. — vii. 17.
1. — viii. 40, 41, 42 twice, 47 3 times.
1*. —— 54.
1. — ix. 3, 16, 24, 29, 31 1st
— —— 31 2nd, see Worshipper.
1*. —— 33.
1d. —— 35 (ὁ υἱὸς τοῦ ἀνθρωποῦ, *the Son of man*, G∾ A* ℵ.)
1*. — x. 33.
1f. —— 34, 35 1st.
1. —— 35 2nd.
1e. —— 36.
1. — xi. 4 1st.
1d. —— 4 2nd.
1. —— 22 twice.
1d. —— 27.
1. —— 40, 52.
1. — xii. 43.
1*. — xiii. 3 1st.
1. —— 3 2nd, 31, 32 1st (*ap.*), 32 2nd.
1. — xiv. 1.
1. — xvi. 2.
1. —— 27 (Tr^m)(No. 1*, L) (ὁ πατήρ, *the Father*, Tr A.)
1* —— 30.
1. — xvii. 3.
1b. — xix. 7 (No. 1e, Beza and Elzevir.)
1*. — xx. 17 twice.
1. —— 28.
1d. —— 31.
1. — xxi. 19.
1. Acts i. 3.
1. — ii. 11, 17, 22 twice, 23, 24, 30, 32, 33, 36.
1a. —— 39.
1. —— 47.
1. — iii. 8, 9, 13 twice, 15, 18, 21.
1a. —— 22.
1. —— 25, 26.
1. — iv. 10, 19 twice, 21, 24 1st.
1. —— 24 2nd (*om.* L T Tr A^b ℵ) (*i.e. he that*, instead of *God which hast.*)

1. Acts iv. 31.
1. —— v. 4.
1*. ———— 29.
1. ———— 30, 31, 32.
1*. ———— 39 1st.
— ———— 39 2nd, see Fight
1. —— vi. 2, 7, 11.
1. —— vii. 2, 6, 7, 9, 17.
— ———— 26, see *God* (*to*) or exceeding.
1. ———— 25.
1. ———— 32 twice (*om.* L T Tr A ℵ.)
1. ———— 35, 37.
1f. ———— 40.
1. ———— 42.
1f. ———— 43.
1. ———— 45, 46 1st.
1. ———— 46 2nd (οἶκος, *the house*, L T Trm A* ℵ.)
1*. ———— 55 1st.
1. ———— 55 2nd, 56.
1. —— viii. 10, 12, 14, 20, 21.
1. ———— 22 (Κύριος, the Lord, G∾ L T Tr A ℵ)
1d. ———— 37 (*ap.*)
1d. —— ix. 20.
1. —— x. 2 twice, 3, 4, 15, 22 1st.
— ———— 22 2nd, see Warned.
1. ———— 28, 31, 33 1st.
1. ———— 33 2nd (ἀπὸ τοῦ Κυρίου, *from the Lord*, instead of ὑπὸ τοῦ Θεοῦ *of God*, G∾ L T (ὑπὸ, *by*) Tr A* ℵ.)
1. ———— 34, 38 twice, 40, 41, 42, 46.
1. —— xi. 1, 9, 17 twice, 18 twice, 23.
1. —— xii. 5.
1f. ———— 22.
1. ———— 23, 24.
1. —— xiii. 5, 7, 16, 17, 21, 23, 26, 30, 33, 36, 37, 43.
1. ———— 44 (Κυρίος, *the Lord*, G∾ L T Tr A ℵ.)
1. ———— 46.
1f. —— xiv. 11.
1. ———— 15 (No. 1*, G∾ L T Tr A ℵ.)
1. ———— 22, 26, 27.
1. —— xv. 4, 7.
1*. ———— 8.
1. ———— 10, 12, 14, 18 (*ap.*), 19.
1. ———— 40 (Κυρίου, *the Lord*, G∾ L T Tr A ℵ)
1. —— xvi. 14, 17, 25, 34.
1. —— xvii. 13.
2. ———— 18.
— ———— 23, see *G that one worshippeth.*
1*. ———— 23.
1. ———— 24, 29, 30.
1. —— xviii. 7, 11, 13, 21.
1. ———— 26 (*om.* G⇉.)
1. —— xix. 8, 11.
1. ———— 20 (Κυρίος, *the Lord*, St E G L T Tr A ℵ.)
1f. ———— 26.
1. —— xx. 21 (No. 1*, T Tr A ℵ.)
1. ———— 24.
1. ———— 25 (*om.* G⇉ L T Tr A ℵ.)
1. ———— 27.
1. ———— 28 (G∾)(Κυρίος *the Lord*, G L T Tr A*.)
1. ———— 32.
1. —— xxi. 19.
1. —— xxii. 3, 14.
1. —— xxiii. 1, 3, 4.
— ———— 9, see Fight.

1. Acts xxiv. 14, 15, 16.
1. —— xxvi. 6, 8, 18, 20, 22, 29.
1. —— xxvii. 23, 24, 25, 35
1f. —— xxviii. 6.
1. ———— 15, 23, 28, 31.
1*. Rom. i. 1.
1b. ———— 4.
1*. ———— 7 twice.
1. ———— 8, 9, 10.
1*. ———— 16, 17, 18.
1. ———— 19 twice, 21 1st.
1*. ———— 21 2nd.
1. ———— 23, 24, 25, 26, 28 twice.
— ———— 30, see G (hater of.)
1. ———— 32.
1. —— ii. 2, 3, 4, 5, 11.
1. ———— 13 (*om.* the article; Lb Trmb.)
1. ———— 16, 17, 23, 24, 29.
1. —— iii. 2, 3.
— ———— 4 1st, see Forbid
1. ———— 4 2nd.
1*. ———— 5 1st.
1. ———— 5 2nd.
— ———— 6 1st, see Forbid
1. ———— 6 2nd, 7, 11.
1*. ———— 18.
1. ———— 19.
1*. ———— 21, 22.
1. ———— 23, 25 twice, 29, 30.
— ———— 31, see Forbid.
1. —— iv. 2 (No. 1*, L T Tr A ℵ.)
1. ———— 3, 6.
1*. ———— 17.
1. ———— 20 twice.
1. —— v. 1, 2, 5, 8, 10, 11, 15.
— —— vi. 2, see Forbid.
1. ———— 10, 11, 13 twice.
— ———— 15, see Forbid.
1. ———— 17 (*lit.*, χάρις τῷ Θεῷ, *thanks to God.*)
1. ———— 22, 23.
1. —— vii. 4.
— ———— 7, 13, see Forbid
1. ———— 22, 25 1st.
1*. ———— 25 2nd.
1. —— viii. 3.
1*. ———— 7 1st.
1. ———— 7 2nd.
1*. ———— 8, 9, 14 1st.
1b. ———— 14 2nd.
1*. ———— 16 (with τέκνα, children.)
1*. ———— 17.
1d. ———— 19.
1. ———— 21.
1*. ———— 27.
1. ———— 28, 31.
1*. ———— 33 twice.
1. ———— 34, 39.
1*. —— ix. 5.
1. ———— 6, 8, 11, 14 1st.
— ———— 14 2nd, see Forbid
1. ———— 16, 20, 22.
1b. ———— 26.
1. —— x. 1.
1*. ———— 2.
1. ———— 3 twice, 9.
1*. ———— 17 (Χριστός, *Christ*, L T Tr A ℵ.)
1. —— xi. 1 1st.
— ———— 1 2nd, see Forbid
1. ———— 2 twice.
— ———— 4, see Answer.
1. ———— 8.
— ———— 11, see Forbid.
1. ———— 21.
1*. ———— 22.
1. ———— 23, 29, 30, 32,
1*. ———— 33.
1. —— xii. 1 twice, 2, 3.

1*. Rom. xiii. 1 1st.
1. ———— 1 2nd (No. 1*, L T Tr A ℵ.)
1. ———— 2.
1*. ———— 4 twice, 6.
1. —— xiv. 3.
1. ———— 4 (ὁ Κυρίος, *the Lord*, L T Tr A ℵ.)
1. ———— 6 twice, 11, 12, (Lb), 17, 18, 20, 22.
1. —— xv. 5, 6.
1*. ———— 7 (No. 1, L T Tr A ℵ.)
1*. ———— 8.
1. ———— 9, 13, 15, 16.
1*. ———— 17 (No. 1, L T Tr A ℵ.)
1*. ———— 19 (G∾) (πνεῦμα ἅγιον, *Holy Spirit*, instead of, πνεῦμα Θεοῦ *Spirit of God*, G L T Tr Ab.)
1. ———— 30.
1*. ———— 32 (Κύριος Ἰησοῦς, *the Lord Jesus*, LTrm)(Ἰησοῦς Χρίστος, *Jesus Christ*, ℵ.)
1. ———— 33.
1. —— xvi. 20, 26.
1*. ———— 27.
1*. 1 Cor. i. 1.
1. ———— 2.
1*. ———— 3.
1. ———— 4 twice, 9, 14.
1*. ———— 18.
1. ———— 20, 21 3 times.
1*. ———— 24 twice.
1. ———— 25 twice.
1. ———— 27 1st, 27 2nd (*ap.*), 28.
1*. ———— 30.
1. —— ii. 1.
1*. ———— 5, 7 1st.
1. ———— 7 2nd, 9, 10 twice, 11 twice, 12 twice, 14.
1. —— iii. 6, 7.
1*. ———— 9 3 times.
1. ———— 10.
1*. ———— 16 1st.
1. ———— 16 2nd, 17 3 times
1. ———— 19 (No. 1*, L Ab)
1*. ———— 23.
1*. —— iv. 1.
1. ———— 5.
— ———— 8, see Would.
1. ———— 9, 20.
1. —— v. 13.
1*. —— vi. 9, 10.
1. ———— 11, 13, 14.
— ———— 15, see Forbid.
1*. ———— 19, 20 1st, 20 2nd (*ap.*)
1*. —— vii. 7.
1. ———— 15.
1. ———— 17 (transpose *God* and *Lord*, G L T Tr A ℵ.)
1*. ———— 19.
1. ———— 24 (No. 1*, G L T Tr A ℵ.)
1*. ———— 40.
1. —— viii. 3.
1*. ———— 4.
1f. ———— 5 twice.
1*. ———— 6.
1. ———— 8.
1. —— ix. 9.
1*. ———— 21 (θεοῦ, of God (and χριστοῦ, *of Christ*) G∾ L T Tr A ℵ.)
1. —— x. 5, 13.
1*. ———— 20, 31.
1. ———— 32.
1. —— xi. 3.
1*. ———— 7.
1. ———— 12, 13, 16, 22.
1*. —— xii. 3.
1. ———— 6, 18, 24, 28.

1. 1 Cor. xiv. 2 (No. 1* L T Tr Ab ℵ.)
1. ———— 18, 25 twice, 28, 33, 36.
1. —— xv. 9.
1*. ———— 10 1st.
1. ———— 10 2nd.
1. ———— 15 twice, 24, 28.
1*. ———— 34.
1. ———— 38.
1*. ———— 50.
1. ———— 57.
1*. 2 Cor. i. 1 1st.
1. ———— 1 2nd.
1*. ———— 2.
1. ———— 3 1st.
1*. ———— 3 2nd.
1. ———— 4, 9.
1*. ———— 12 (No. 1, L T Tr A ℵ.)
1. ———— 18.
1c. ———— 19.
1*. ———— 20 1st.
1. ———— 20 2nd.
1*. ———— 21.
1. ———— 23.
1. —— ii. 14, 15.
1. ———— 17 1st.
1*. ———— 17 2nd.
1. ———— 17 3rd (No. 1*, G⇉ L Tr ℵ3.)
1*. —— iii. 3.
1. ———— 4, 5.
1. —— iv. 2 twice.
1f. ———— 4 1st.
1. ———— 4 2nd, 6 1st.
1. ———— 6 2nd (αὐτοῦ, *of Him*, G∾ L.)
1. ———— 7, 15.
1*. —— v. 1, 5, 11, 13.
1. ———— 18.
1*. ———— 19.
1. ———— 20 twice.
1*. ———— 21.
1. —— vi. 1.
1*. ———— 4, 7, 16 1st & 2nd
1. ———— 16 3rd.
1*. ———— 16 4th.
1*. —— vii. 1.
1. ———— 6.
— ———— 9, see *God* (*according to.*)
1. ———— 12.
1. —— viii. 1.
1*. ———— 5.
1. ———— 16.
1. —— ix. 7, 8.
1. ———— 11 (No. 1*, Lb.)
1. ———— 12, 13, 14, 15.
1. —— x. 4, 5, 13.
— —— xi. 1, see Would.
1. ———— 7, 11, 31.
1. —— xii. 2, 3.
1. ———— 19 (No. 1*, L T Tr A ℵ)
1. ———— 21.
1*. —— xiii. 4 twice.
1. ———— 7, 11, 14.
1*. Gal. i. 1, 3.
1. ———— 4, 10, 13.
1. ———— 15, (*om.* G⇉ Lb T Trmb A.)
1. ———— 20, 24.
1*. —— ii. 6.
— ———— 17, see Forbid.
1*. ———— 19.
1d. ———— 20 (Trm)(ὁ Θεός καὶ Χριστός, *God and Christ*, L Tr.)
1. ———— 21.
1. —— iii. 6, 8, 11, 17, 18, 20.
1. ———— 21 1st (Lb.)
— ———— 21 2nd, see Forbid
1b. ———— 26.
1. —— iv. 4, 6.
1*. ———— 7 (*ap.*), 8 1st.
1f. ———— 8 2nd.

1*. Gal. iv. 9 twice, 14.
1. —— v. 21.
1*. —— vi. 7.
— ———— 14, see Forbid.
1. ———— 16.
1*. Eph. i. 1, 2.
1. ———— 3, 17.
1. —— ii. 4.
1*. ———— 8.
1. ———— 10.
— ———— 12, see G (without.)
1. ———— 16, 19, 22.
1. —— iii. 2, 7, 9, 10, 19.
1*. —— iv. 6.
1d. ———— 13.
1. ———— 18.
1*. ———— 24.
1. ———— 30, 32.
1. —— v. 1, 2.
1*. ———— 5.
1. ———— 6, 20.
1*. ———— 21 (Χριστός, *Christ*, G L T Tr A ℵ.)
1. —— vi. 6, 11, 13.
1*. ———— 17, 23.
1*. Phil. i. 2.
1. ———— 3, 8.
1*. ———— 11, 28.
1*. —— ii. 6 twice.
1. ———— 9.
1*. ———— 11.
1. ———— 13 (No. 1*, G ∾ L T Tr A ℵ.)
1*. ———— 15 (with τέκνα, *children.*)
1. ———— 27.
1*. —— iii. 3 (genitive instead of dative, G ∾ L T Tr A ℵ, lit., *by the Spirit of God*, instead of *God in the Spirit.*)
1*. ———— 9.
1. ———— 14, 15, 19.
1. —— iv. 6, 7, 9, 18, 19, 20.
1*. Col. i. 1, 2.
1. ———— 3, 6, 10, 15, 25 twice, 27.
1. —— ii. 2, 12, 19.
1. —— iii. 1, 3, 6.
1. ———— 12 (No. 1*, L.)
1. ———— 15 (Χριστός, *Christ*, G L T Tr A ℵ.)
1. ———— 17.
1. ———— 22 (G ∾)(Κύριος *the Lord*, G L T Tr A ℵ)
1. —— iv. 3, 11, 12.
1*. 1 Thes. i. 1 1st, 1 2nd (*ap.*)
1. ———— 2, 3.
1*. ———— 4.
1. ———— 8, 9 1st.
1*. ———— 9 2nd.
1. —— ii. 2 twice, 4 1st.
1. ———— 4 2nd (No. 1*, Lb T Tr A ℵ.)
1*. ———— 5.
1. ———— 8, 9, 10, 12, 13 1st & 2nd.
1*. ———— 13 3rd.
1. ———— 14.
1*. ———— 15.
1. —— iii. 2, 9 twice, 11, 13
1*. —— iv. 1.
1. ———— 3, 5, 7, 8.
— ———— 9, see Taught.
1. ———— 14.
1*. ———— 16.
1. —— v. 9.
1*. ———— 18.
1. ———— 23.
1*. 2 Thes. i. 1, 2.
1. ———— 3, 4, 5 twice.
1*. ———— 6, 8.
1. ———— 11, 12.
1*. —— ii. 4 1st.
1. ———— 4 2nd.
1*. ———— 4 3rd (*om.* G L T Tr A ℵ.)
1*. 2 Thes. ii. 4 4th.
1. ———— 11, 13.
1. ———— 16 (Lb.)
1. —— iii. 5.
1*. 1 Tim. i. 1, 2, 11, 17.
1*. —— ii. 3, 5 twice.
1*. —— iii. 5, 15 twice.
1*. ———— 16 (ὃς, *who*, G L T Tr A ℵ, being the relative to an omitted though easily recognized antecedent, viz., Christ, Ellicott.)
1. —— iv. 3.
1*. ———— 4, 5, 10.
1. —— v. 4, 5 (Lb), 21.
1. —— vi. 1.
1. ———— 11 (No. 1*, L Tr Ab ℵ.)
1. ———— 13, 17.
1*. 2 Tim. i. 1, 2.
1. ———— 3, 6, 7.
1*. ———— 8.
1. —— ii. 9, 15, 19, 25.
— —— iii. 4, see G (lover of.)
— ———— 16, see Inspiration.
1. ———— 17.
1. —— iv. 1.
1*. Titus i. 1 twice.
1. ———— 2.
1*. ———— 3, 4, 7, 16.
1. —— ii. 5.
1*. ———— 10.
1. ———— 11.
1*. ———— 13.
1*. —— iii. 4.
1. ———— 8 (No. 1*, G→ L T Tr A ℵ.)
1*. Philem. 3.
1. ———— 4.
1. Heb. i. 1.
1*. ———— 6, 8.
1. ———— 9 twice.
1. —— ii. 4.
1*. ———— 9.
1. ———— 13, 17.
1*. —— iii. 4, 12.
1. —— iv. 4, 9, 10, 12.
1d. ———— 14.
1. —— v. 1, 4, 10, 12.
1*. —— vi. 1.
1. ———— 3.
1*. ———— 5.
1d. ———— 6.
1. ———— 7, 10, 13, 17.
1*. ———— 18.
1. —— vii. 1.
1d. ———— 3.
1. ———— 19, 25.
— —— viii. 5, see Admonished.
1*. ———— 10.
1. —— ix. 14 1st.
1*. ———— 14 2nd
1. ———— 20, 24.
1. —— x. 7.
1. ———— 9 (*om.* G L T Tr A ℵ.)
1. ———— 12, 21.
1d. ———— 29.
1*. ———— 31.
1. ———— 36.
1*. —— xi. 3.
1. ———— 4 1st.
1. ———— 4 2nd (Dat. instead of Gen., L.)
1. ———— 5 twice, 6 (art., Trb.)
— ———— 7, see Warned.
1. ———— 10, 16 1st.
1*. ———— 16 2nd.
1. ———— 19, 25, 40.
1. —— xii. 2, 7, 15.
1*. ———— 22, 23.
1. ———— 28, 29.
1. —— xiii. 4, 7, 15, 16, 20.
1*. Jas. i. 1, 5.
1. ———— 13 1st (No. 1*, L T Tr A ℵ.)
1. ———— 13 2nd.
1*. ———— 20.
1. ———— 27 (No. 1*, L.)
1. —— ii. 5, 19, 23 1st.
1*. ———— 23 2nd.
1. —— iii. 9 1st (Κυρίος, *the Lord*, G ∾ L T Tr A ℵ.)
1*. ———— 9 2nd.
1. —— iv. 4 twice, 6, 7, 8.
1*. 1 Pet. i. 2.
1. ———— 3.
1*. ———— 5, 21 twice, 23.
1*. —— ii. 4.
1. ———— 5 (No. 1*, L T Tr A ℵ.)
1*. ———— 10.
1. ———— 12, 15.
1*. ———— 16 (Θεοῦ δοῦλοι, *God's servants*, instead of δοῦλοι θεοῦ, *servants of God*, T Tr A ℵ.)
1. ———— 17.
1*. ———— 19, 20.
1. —— iii. 4.
1. ———— 5 (εἰς Θεον, *in God* instead of ἐπὶ τὸν Θεὸν *upon God*, L T Tr A.)
1. ———— 15 (Χρίστος, *Christ* i.e. *Christ* [as] *Lord*, instead of the *Lord God*, G ∾ L T Tr A ℵ.)
1. ———— 17, 18, 20, 21, 22
1*. —— iv. 2, 6, 10, 11 1st.
1. ———— 11 2nd & 3rd, 14, 16, 17 twice, 19.
1. —— v. 2, 5, 6, 10, 12.
1. 2 Pet. i. 1, 2.
1*. ———— 17, 21 (No. 1, L.)
1. —— ii. 4.
1. —— iii. 5, 12.
1. 1 John i. 5.
1. —— ii. 5, 14, 17.
1*. —— iii. 1, 2, with τέκνα, *children.*
1d. ———— 8.
1. ———— 9 twice, 10 twice.
1. ———— 16 (*om.* 8t G L T Tr A ℵ.)
1. ———— 17, 20, 21.
1. —— iv. 1, 2 twice, 3, 4, 6 3 times, 7 3 times, 8 twice, 9 twice, 10, 11.
1*. ———— 12 1st.
1. ———— 12 2nd.
1d. ———— 15 1st.
1. ———— 15 2nd, 16 4 times, 20 twice, 21.
1. —— v. 1, 2 twice, 3, 4.
1d. ———— 5.
1. ———— 9 twice.
1d. ———— 10 1st.
1. ———— 10 2nd (υἱός, *the Son*, G ∾ L.)
1. ———— 10 3rd, 11.
1d. ———— 12 (*om.* A.V. 1611 to 1629.)
1d. ———— 13 1st (*ap.*)
1d. ———— 13 2nd.
1. ———— 18 twice, 19.
1d. ———— 20 1st.
1. ———— 20 2nd.
1*. 2 John 3, 9.
— ———— 10, 11, see G speed.
1. 3 John 11 twice.
1*. Jude 1.
1. ———— 4 1st.
1*. ———— 4 2nd (*om.* G L T Tr A ℵ.)
1*. Jude 21, 25.
1. Rev. i. 1, 2, 6, 9.
1. —— ii. 7 (*add* μοῦ, my, G T Ab.)
1d. ———— 18.
1. —— iii. 1.
1. ———— 2 (*add.* μοῦ, my, G L T Tr A ℵ.)
1. ———— 12 4 times, 14.
1. —— iv. 5.
1a. ———— 8.
1. —— v. 6, 9.
1. ———— 10 (*om.* τῷ θεῷ ἡμῶν, *unto our God*, A.)
1. —— vi. 9.
1*. —— vii. 2.
1. ———— 3, 10 (*ap.*), 11, 12, 15, 17.
1. —— viii. 2, 4.
1. —— ix. 4 (*om.* G→.)
1. ———— 13.
1. —— x. 7.
1. —— xi. 1.
1. ———— 4 (ὁ *om.* L) Κύριος *the Lord*, G L T Tr A ℵ.)
1. ———— 11, 13, 16 twice.
1a. ———— 17.
1. ———— 19.
1. —— xii. 5, 6, 10 twice, 17.
1. —— xiii. 6.
1. —— xiv. 4, 5 (*ap.*)
1. ———— 7 (Κύριος, *the Lord*, G ∾.)
1. ———— 10, 12, 19.
1. —— xv. 1, 2, 3 1st.
1a. ———— 3 2nd.
1. ———— 7, 8.
1. —— xvi. 1.
1a. ———— 7.
1. ———— 9, 11, 14, 19, 21.
1. —— xvii. 17 twice.
1. —— xviii. 5.
1a. ———— 8 (*om.* Κύριος, Trb Ab.)
1. ———— 20.
1a. —— xix. 1 (τοῦ Θεοῦ, *of our God*, instead of Κυπίῳ τᾶ Θεῳ, *unto the Lord our God*, G L T Tr A ℵ.)
1. ———— 4.
1. ———— 5 (τῷ Θεῷ, *to our God*, instead of τὸν Θεὸν, *our God*, L T Tr A ℵ.)
1a. ———— 6.
1. ———— 9, 10, 13, 15.
1*. ———— 17 (τὸ μέγα τοῦ Θεοῦ, *the great* [*supper*] *of God*, instead of τοῦ μεγάλου θεοῦ, [supper] *of the great God*, G L T Tr A ℵ.)
1. —— xx. 4, 6.
1. ———— 9 (*om.* ἀπὸ τοῦ θεου, *from God*, G→ L T A.)
1. ———— 12 (θρόνος, *the throne*, G L T Tr A ℵ)
1. —— xxi. 2, 3 1st & 2nd.
1*. ———— 3 3rd (*om.* θεὸς αὐτῶν, [and be] their God, G ⇄ T Tr ℵ.)
1. ———— 4 (*om.* G T Tr Ab ℵ.)
1*. ———— 7.
1. ———— 10, 11.
1a. ———— 22.
1. ———— 23.
1. —— xxii. 1, 3.
1a. ———— 5, 6.
1. ———— 9, 18, 19.

GOD (according to) [margin.]

{ κατὰ, according to,
{ Θεόν, God.

2 Cor. vii. 9, (text, *after godly manner*.)

GOD THAT ONE WORSHIPPETH [margin.]

σέβασμα, an object of worship, any thing venerated.

Acts xvii. 23, (text, *Devotion*.)

HATER OF GOD.

θεοστυγής, hating God.

Rom. i. 30.

LOVER OF GOD.

φιλόθεος, loving God; *subst.*, a lover of God.

2 Tim. iii. 4.

GOD SPEED.

χαίρω, to joy, rejoice, be glad. *Inf.*, to wish joy, bid, hail! salute, *like Eng.* to send greeting.

2 John 10, 11, Inf.

GOD (to) [margin.]

Θεῷ, Dat. of Θεός, (*see* "GOD,") to God.

Acts vii. 20, (text, *Exceeding*.)

GOD (WITHOUT.)

ἄθεος, godless, impious.

Eph. ii. 12

GODDESS.

θεά, (*fem. of* Θεός, *see* "GOD," *No.* 1,) a goddess, (*non occ.*)

Acts xix. 27.
——— 35 (*om.* G L T Tr A ℵ.)
——— 37 (Θεός, *God*, G L T Tr A ℵ.)

GODHEAD.

1. { τὸ, the *thing*, θεῖον, pertaining to Θεός, (*see* "GOD," *No.* 1,) what is God's, or proceeds from him; divine, } that *which is* divine.

2. θειότης, divinity, (*the characteristic or property of* Θεός), (*non occ.*)

3. θεότης, deity, the being in whom θειότης, (*No.* 2,) of the highest order resides, (*non occ.*)

1. Acts xvii. 29. | 2. Rom. i. 20.
3. Col. ii. 9.

GODLINESS.

1. εὐσέβεια, godliness. [The opposite of θρησκεία, *religion*. *Eusebeia* relates to real, true, vital, and spiritual relation with God: while *threskeia* relates to the outward acts of religious observances or ceremonies, which can be performed by the flesh. Our Eng. word "religion" was never used in the sense of true godliness. It always meant the outward forms of worship. In 1 Tim. iii. 16, the *Mystery*, or secret connected with true Christianity as distinct from religion. It is the Gen. of relation. (*Occ.* Acts iii. 12.)]

2. θεοσέβεια, the fear of God, God-fearing, (*non occ.*)

1. 1 Tim. ii. 2.
2. ——— 10.
1. ——— iii. 16.
1. ——— iv. 7, 8.
1. 1 Tim. vi. 3, 5, 6, 11.
1. 2 Tim. iii. 5.
1. Titus i. 1.
1. 2 Pet. i. 3, 6, 7.
1. 2 Pet. iii. 11.

GODLY.

1. Θεοῦ, (*Gen. of* Θεός, *see* "GOD," *No.* 1,) of God.

2. { κατὰ, according to, θεόν, God, (*see* "GOD," No. 1.) } according to God.

3. εὐσεβής, that reverence for God which shews itself in actions, (especially in worship,) pious, devout, *used of one who* is ruled in what he does or avoids by reverence and godly fear, (*occ.* Acts x. 2, 7; xxii. 12.)

4. εὐσεβῶς, (*adv. of No.* 3,) piously, religiously, (*non occ.*)

1. 2 Cor. i. 12.
— ——— vii. 9, see G manner (after a.)
2. ——— 10.
— ——— 11, see G sort (after a.)
1. 2 Cor. xi. 2.
1. 1 Tim. i. 4 (*om.* AV. 1611—1660, error.)
4. 2 Tim. iii. 12.
4. Titus ii. 12.
3. 2 Pet. ii. 9.

GODLY MANNER (AFTER A.)

κατὰ Θεόν, according to God.

2 Cor. vii. 9, marg. *according to God.*

GODLY SORT (AFTER A.)

1. κατὰ Θεόν, according to God.

2. { ἀξίως, worthy,
   τοῦ Θεοῦ, of God.

1. 2 Cor. vii. 11. | 2. 3 John 6.

GOLD.

1. χρυσός, gold.

2. χρυσίον, *(dim. of No.* 1,) gold, *prop.*, in small pieces or quantity; *esp.*, as wrought, any thing made of gold; *hence*, gold coin, money.

1. Matt. ii. 11.
1. —— x. 9.
1. —— xxiii. 16, 17 twice.
2. Acts iii. 6.
1. —— xvii. 29.
2. —— xx. 33.
1. 1 Cor. iii. 12.
1. 1 Tim. ii. 9 (No. 2, L.)
— 2 Tim. ii. 20, see G (of.)
2. Heb. ix. 4.
— Jas. ii. 2, see G ring (with a.)
1. —— v. 3.
2. 1 Pet. i. 7, 18.
2. —— iii. 3.
2. Rev. iii. 18.
— —— iv. 4, see G (of.)
1. —— ix. 7 (G ∾) (χρύσεος, *golden*, instead of ὅμοιος χρυσῷ, *like to gold*, G.)
— —— 20, see G (of.)
1. —— xvii. 4 (No. 2, G L Tr A.)
1. —— xviii. 12. [Tr A.)
1. —— 16 (No. 2, G L
2. —— xxi. 18, 21.

GOLD (OF.)

χρυσέος, golden, of gold.

2 Tim. ii. 20. | Rev. iv. 4; ix. 20.

GOLD RING (WITH A.)

χρυσοδακτύλιος, with ring of gold, having gold rings upon the fingers.

Jas. ii. 2.

GOLDEN.

χρυσέος, golden, of gold.

Heb. ix. 4 twice.
Rev. i. 12, 13, 20.
—— ii. 1.
—— v. 8.
—— viii. 3 twice.
Rev. ix. 13.
—— xiv. 14.
—— xv. 6, 7.
—— xvii. 4.
—— xxi. 15.

GOMORRHA.

Γόμοῤῥα, Gomorrha.

Matt. x. 15.
Mark vi. 11 (*ap.*)
Rom. ix. 29.
2 Pet. ii. 6.
Jude 7.

GONE.

See, GO.

GOOD [adj. and noun.]

1. ἀγαθός, worthy of admiration, admirable; *hence*, good, good of its kind. *The original idea of the word is so broad that it denotes in general*, skilled either for good or evil; *e.g.*, as used of thieves, *it means* cunning. *Then it branches in two directions, from ability it passes to serviceableness and means* good *in relation to something else, i.e.* what is of advantage, *or* that which is to advantage. *Then the word was transferred to the moral sphere*, what is morally good; *hence the N.T. meaning*, and its relation to δικαίος, righteous, *(only that in* δικαίος, *the relation to the* δίκη, *or God's revelation is decisive, while)* ἀγαθός *denotes* the inner harmonious perfection, which is its own standard and measure, and which primarily belongs to God.

2. καλός, beautiful, *referring to objects whose appearance has a certain harmonious perfection:* καλός *is to* ἀγαθός, *what the* phenomenal *is to the* essence; *hence*, beautiful, pleasing, *of objects perceived by the senses;* acceptable, agreeable, well-fitted. *Then, of* a perfect inward nature manifesting and demonstrating itself in an outward shape, *i.e., physically*, exquisite, genuine, perfect *in form and nature; morally*, excellent, worthy of recognition, becoming, well-suited, beautiful, *and in this sense*, good. *(As compared with* δικαίος, righteous; δικαίος, *expresses simply a legal judgment, while* καλός, *reflects* the agreeable impression made by the good as it manifests itself.)

3. καλόν, *(neut. of No.* 2,) *it* agrees with, it is good, beneficial. *(This must not be confounded with* καλόν ἐστί, *in the moral sense, denoting*, it is right *or* proper.)

4. καλῶς, *(adv. of No.* 2,) well, fairly, beautifully.

5. χρηστός, useful, profitable, fit; *of persons*, useful *towards others, hence*, well disposed, actively beneficent in spite of ingratitude, good, gentle.

6. χρηστότης, usefulness, *as of persons towards others*, benignity, the goodness of the divine attributes showing itself in benevolence to man.

7. βίος, life *in its manifestations*, the means of living, the good things of life.

8. εὖ, well, (*with* ποιεῖν, Mark xiv. 7, to do good to.)

2. Matt. iii. 10.
— —— v. 13, see G (be).
2. ——— 16.
4. ——— 44 (*ap.*)
1. ——— 45.
1. —— vii. 11 1st.
— ——— 11 2nd, see G thing
1. ——— 17 1st.
2. ——— 17 2nd.
1. ——— 18 1st.
2. ——— 18 2nd, 19.
— —— viii. 30, see Way off
— —— ix. 2, see Cheer.
— ——— 22, see Comfort.
— —— xi. 26, see Seem.
2. —— xii. 33 twice.
— ——— 34, see G thing.
1. ——— 35 1st & 2nd.
— ——— 35 3rd, see G thing
2. —— xiii. 8, 23, 24, 27, 37, 38, 48.
— —— xiv. 27, see Cheer.
2. —— xvii. 4.
— —— xix. 10, see G (be.)
1. ——— 16 1st (om. G ⇉ L T Tr A ℵ.)
— ——— 16 2nd, see G thing
1. ——— 17 twice (*ap.*)
1. —— xx. 15.
1. —— xxii. 10.
1. —— xxv. 21, 23.
2. —— xxvi. 10, 24.
— Mark iii. 4, see G (do.)
2. —— iv. 8, 20.
— —— vi. 50, see Cheer.
2. —— ix. 5, 50.
1. —— x. 17, 18 twice.
— ——— 42, see *Think*.
— ——— 49, see Comfort.
2. —— xiv. 6.
8. ——— 7.
2. ——— 21.
— Luke i. 3, see Seem.
— ——— 53, see G thing.
— —— ii. 10, see Tidings.
— ——— 14, see Will.
2. —— iii. 9 (*om.* Lb.)
— —— vi. 9, see G (do.)
4. ——— 27.
— ——— 33, 35, see G (do.)
2. ——— 38, 43 twice.
1. ——— 45 twice.
1. —— viii. 8.
2. ——— 15 1st.
1. ——— 15 2nd.
— ——— 48, see Comfort.
2. —— ix. 33.
— —— x. 21, see Seem.
1. ——— 42.
1. —— xi. 13.
2. —— xiv. 34.
— —— xvi. 25, see G thing
1. —— xviii. 18, 19 twice.
1. —— xix. 17.
1. —— xxiii. 50.
— John i. 46, see G thing.
2. —— ii. 10 twice.
1. —— v. 29.
1. —— vii. 12.
2. —— x. 11 twice, 14, 32, 33.
— —— xvi. 33, see Cheer.

— Acts iv. 9, see Deed.
1 —— ix. 36.
— —— x. 22, see Report.
— ——— 38, see G (do.)
1. —— xi. 24.
— —— xiv. 17, see G (do.)
— —— xv. 7, see Ago.
— ——— 25, 28, see Seem.
— ——— 38, see Think.
— —— xviii. 18, see While
— —— xxii. 12, see Report
1. —— xxiii. 1.
— ——— 11, see Cheer.
— —— xxvii. 22, 25, 26, see Cheer.
1. Rom. ii. 10.
1. —— iii. 8.
6. ——— 12.
1. —— v. 7.
1 —— vii. 12.
2. ——— 16.
— ——— 18 1st, see G thing
— ——— 18 2nd, see G (that which is.)
1. ——— 19.
3. ——— 21.
1. —— viii. 28.
1. —— ix. 11.
— —— x. 15, see G thing.
— —— xi. 24, see Olive-tree
1. —— xii. 2, 21.
1. —— xiii. 3, 4.
1. —— xiv. 16.
2. ——— 21.
1. —— xv. 2.
— —— xvi. 18, see Words.
2. 1 Cor. v. 6.
2. —— vii. 1, 8, 26 twice.
5. —— xv. 33.
1. 2 Cor. v. 10.
— —— vi. 8, see Report.
1. —— ix. 8.
2. Gal. iv. 18 1st.
— ——— 18 2nd, see G thing
— —— vi. 6, see G thing.
1. ——— 10.
— Eph. i. 5, 9, see Pleasure
1. —— ii. 10.
— —— iv. 28, see G (the thing which is.)
1. ——— 29.
— —— vi. 7, see Will.
— ——— 8, see G thing.
1. Phil. i. 6.
— ——— 15, see Will.
— —— ii. 13, see Pleasure
— ——— 19, see Comfort.
— —— iv. 8, see Report.
1. Col. i. 10.
— 1 Thes. iii. 4, see Think
— ——— 6 1st, see Tidings.
1. ——— 6 2nd.
— —— v. 2, see G (that which is.)
— 2 Thes. i. 11, see Pleasure
1. —— ii. 16, 17.
1. 1 Tim. i. 5.
2. ——— 8, 18.
1. ——— 19.
1. —— ii. 10.
2. —— iii. 1.
— ——— 2, see Behaviour

2. 1 Tim. iii. 7, 13.
2. —— iv. 4, 6 twice.
2. —— v. 4 (*om. Good and*, G L T Tr A ℵ.)
2. ——— 10 1st.
1. ——— 10 2nd.
2. ——— 25.
2. —— vi. 12 twice, 13.
— ——— 18 1st, see G (do.)
2. ——— 18 2nd, 19.
2. 2 Tim. i. 14.
2. —— ii. 3.
1. ——— 21.
— —— iii. 3, see Despiser.
1. ——— 17.
2. —— iv. 7.
— Titus i. 8, see G men (lover of)
1. ———
— —— ii. 3, see G things (teacher of.)
1. ——— 5.
2. ——— 7.
1. ——— 10.
2. ——— 14.
1. —— iii. 1.

2. Titus iii. 8 twice.
2. ——— 14, marg. *honest.*
3. Heb. v. 14.
2. —— vi. 5.
— —— ix. 11, } see G thing
— —— x. 1, }
2. ——— 24.
— —— xi. 2, 39, see Report
— —— xiii. 9, see G thing
— ——— 16, see G (do.)
2. ——— 18.
1. ——— 21.
1. Jas. i. 17.
— —— ii. 3, see G place (in a.)
2. —— iii. 13.
1. ——— 17.
3. —— iv. 17.
2. 1 Pet. ii. 12.
2. ——— 18.
1. —— iii. 10, 11, 16 twice, 21.
2. —— iv. 10.
7. 1 John iii. 17.
— 3 John 11, see G (do.)
— ——— 12, see Report.

GOOD (BE.)

1. ἰσχύω, to be strong, to have physical abilty; *also* to have efficacy, force *or* value; avail.

2. συμφέρω, to bear *or* bring together, collect; *Intrans.*, to bring together for *any one, i.e.*, to contribute, conduce; *here Intrans. and impers.* it is conducive, it is profitable.

1. Matt. v. 13.
2. Matt xix. 10.

GOOD (DO.)

1. ἀγαθοποιέω, to do good, (from ποιέω, to make, to do, to practice, and ἀγαθός, *see* "GOOD," *No.* 1.)

2. ἀγαθοεργέω, to work good, (ἀγαθός *see* "GOOD," *No.* 1, and obsolete ἔργω, to work, labour,) (*non occ.*)

3. εὐεργετέω, to work well, do well *to*, confer benefits, (*non occ.*)

4. εὐποιΐα, well doing, *i.e.* a doing well *to*, beneficence.

1. Mark iii. 4.
1. Luke vi. 9, 33 twice, 35.
3. Acts x. 38.
1. Acts xiv. 17 (No. 2, G ∾ L T Tr A ℵ.)
2. 1 Tim. vi. 18.
4. Heb. xiii. 16.
1. 3 John 11.

GOOD (THAT WHICH IS.)

1. { τὸ, the,
{ ἀγαθόν, good *thing*, (*see* "GOOD," *No.* 1.)

2. { τὸ, the,
{ καλόν, good *thing*, (*see* "GOOD," *No.* 2.)

1. Luke vi. 45.
1. Rom. vii. 13 twice.
2. —— 18.
1. —— xii. 9.
1. —— xiii. 3.
1. Rom. xvi. 19.
1. 1 Thes. v. 15.
2. —— 21.
1. 1 Pet. iii. 13.
1. 3 John 11.

GOOD (THE THING WHICH IS.)

{ τὸ, the,
ἀγαθόν, good *thing,* (*see* "GOOD," *No.* 1.)

Eph. iv. 28.

GOOD PLACE (IN A.)

καλῶς, (*adv. of* καλός, *see* "GOOD," *No.* 2,) handsomely; well, pleasantly.

Jas. ii. 3, marg. *well or seemly.*

GOOD MEN (LOVER OF.)

φιλάγαθος, loving good, (φίλος, loving *or* loved, *and* ἀγαθός, *see* "GOOD," *No.* 1,) loving *what is good,* (*non occ.*)

Titus i. 8, marg. *things.*

GOOD THINGS (TEACHER OF.)

καλοδιδάσκαλος, *adj.*, teaching what is good, (καλός, *see* "GOOD," *No.* 2, *and* διδάσκαλος, a teacher,) *as subst.* teacher of good, (*non occ.*)

Titus ii. 3.

GOOD THING.

1. ἀγαθόν, *neut. of* "GOOD," *No.* 1.
2. καλόν, *neut. of* "GOOD," *No.* 2.

1. Matt. vii. 11.
1. —— xii. 34, 35.
1. —— xix. 16.
1. Luke i. 53.
1. —— xvi. 25.
1. John i. 46.
1. Rom. vii. 18.
1. Rom. x. 15.
2. Gal. iv. 18.
1. —— vi. 6.
1. Eph. vi. 8.
1. Philem. 6.
1. Heb. ix. 11.
1. —— x. 1.
2. Heb. xiii. 9.

GOODLY.

1. καλός, *see* "GOOD," *No.* 2.
2. λαμπρός, shining, bright, radiant; *of clothing,* gay *or* sumptuous.

1. Matt. xiii. 45.
1. Luke xxi. 5.
2. Jas. ii. 2.
2. Rev. xviii. 14.

GOODMAN.

οἰκοδεσπότης, a house-master, head of a family.

Luke xxii. 11.

GOODMAN OF THE HOUSE.

οἰκοδεσπότης, *see above.*

Matt. xx. 11.
—— xxiv. 43.
Mark xiv. 14.
Luke xii. 39.

GOODNESS.

1. ἀγαθωσύνη, goodness *and* kindness, the quality of him who is ruled by and aims at the good, moral worth, and sterling goodness apart from attractiveness.
2. χρηστότης, the goodness of the Divine attributes; *in God,* benevolence to man; *in human agents,* that benevolence and sweetness of disposition which finds its sphere in our inter course with one another, *hence,* goodness in its attractiveness.
3. χρηστός, well disposed, actively beneficent *in spite of ingratitude,* morally good.

2. Rom. ii. 4 1st.
3. —— 4 2nd, neut.
2. —— xi. 22 3 times.
1. Rom. xv. 14.
1. Gal. v. 22.
1. Eph. v. 9.
1. 2 Thes. i. 11.

GOODS.

1. { τὰ, the *things,* ὑπάρχοντα, existing *or* present, } the things present; in hand, *to any one; as* possessions, property, substance.
2. ὕπαρξις, being, existence; *then,* the being to any one, possession, property, *etc.*, (occ. Heb. x. 34.)
3. ἀγαθός, *see* "GOOD," *No.* 1, *here, neut. plural.*
4. οὐσία, (*part. of* εἰμί, to be,) entity, essence; *then,* what is *to any one, i.e. what he has,* as substance, property, (occ. Luke xv. 13.)

1. Matt. xxiv. 47.
1. —— xxv. 14.
— Luke vi. 30, see G (they.)
1. —— xi. 21.
3. —— xii. 18, 19.
4. —— xv. 12.
1. Luke xvi. 1.
1. —— xix. 8.
2. Acts ii. 45.
1. 1 Cor. xiii. 3.
1. Heb. x. 34.
— Rev. iii. 17, see G (be increased with.)

GOODS (BE INCREASED WITH.)

πλουτέω, to be rich, to be rich *in anything,* to abound.

Rev. iii. 17.

GOODS (THY.)

τὰ, the *things*, σά, thy, } thy things *or* possessions.

Luke vi. 30.

GORGEOUS.

λαμπρός, shining, bright, radiant, *hence by implication*, splendid, sumptuous.

Luke xxiii. 11.

GORGEOUSLY APPARELLED (THEY WHICH ARE.)

οἱ, the *persons*,
ἐν, in,
ἱματισμῷ, clothing, raiment,
ἐνδόξῳ, splendid, glorious,
ὑπάρχοντες, being, remaining, living in *any state or place*,
} those who are living in splendid clothing.

Luke vii. 25.

GOSPEL.

εὐαγγέλιον *from Homer to Plutarch*, the reward for a good message. *Later Greek writers use it in the sense simply of* good message. *As* τὸ διδασκάλιον *denoted primarily* what was taught (doctrina), *and then later, in the pl.*, the fees paid for instruction (merces docendi) ; *so reversedly* εὐαγγέλιον *denoted primarily* the reward paid for a good message, *and then* the good message itself. *The* lxx. *use it in the latter sense only (except perhaps* 2 Sam. iv. 10 *and* xviii. 22).

In N.T., good news, *and always in a special sense. As* ἐπαγγελία *denotes* the promise of salvation, *so* εὐαγγέλιον *denotes* the news of the actual fulfilment of the promise of salvation, *i.e.* the news of salvation.

(a) *with* βασιλεία, kingdom.

(b) *with* Θεός, God.

(c) *with* Χριστός, *etc.*, Christ.

(d) *with* εἰρήνη, peace.

(e) *with* σωτηρία, salvation.

(f) *with* χάρις, grace.

a. Matt. iv. 23.
a. —— ix. 35.
—— xi. 5, see G preached to (have the.)
a. Matt. xxiv. 14.
—— xxvi. 13.
c. Mark i. 1.
ab. —— 14.
Mark i. 15.
—— viii. 35.
—— x. 29.
—— xiii. 10.
—— xiv. 9.
—— xvi. 15 (*ap.*)
Luke iv. 18, see G (preach the.)
—— vii. 22, see G is preached to (the.)
—— ix. 6, see G (preach the.)
—— xx. 1, see G (preach the.)
Acts viii. 25, see G in (preach the.)
—— xiv. 7, 21, see G to (preach the.)
—— xv. 7.
—— xvi. 10, see G unto (preach the.)
f. —— xx. 24.
b. Rom. i. 1.
c. —— 9.
—— 15, see G (preach the.)
c. —— 16.
—— ii. 16.
—— x. 15, see G of (preach the.)
—— 16.
—— xi 28.
b. —— xv. 16.
c. —— 19.
—— 20, see G (preach the.)
c. —— 29 (*om.* G L T Tr A ℵ.)
—— xvi. 25.
1 Cor. i. 17, see G (preach the.)
—— iv. 15.
c. —— ix. 12.
—— 14 twice.
—— 16 twice, see G (preach the.)
—— 18 1st, see G (preach the.)
c. —— 18 2nd.
—— 18 3rd, 23.
—— xv. 1.
c. 2 Cor. ii. 12.
2 Cor. iv. 3.
c. —— 4.
—— viii. 18.
c. —— ix. 13.
c. —— x. 14.
—— 16, see G (preach the.)
—— xi. 4.
b. —— 7.
Gal. i. 6.
c. —— 7.
—— 8, 9, see G... (preach.)
—— 11.
—— ii. 2, 5, 7, 14.
—— iii. 8, see G before (preach the.)
—— iv. 13, see G (preach the.)
e. Eph. i. 13.
—— iii. 6.
d. —— vi. 15.
—— 19 (*om.* Lb.)
Phil. i. 5, 7, 12, 17.
c. —— 27 1st.
—— 27 2nd.
—— ii. 22.
—— iv. 3, 15.
Col. i. 5, 23.
1 Thes. i. 5.
b. —— ii. 2.
—— 4.
b. —— 8, 9.
c. —— iii. 2.
c. 2 Thes. i 8.
—— ii. 14.
b. 1 Tim. i. 11.
2 Tim. i. 8, 10.
—— ii. 8.
Philem. 13.
Heb. iv. 2, see G preached unto (the.)
—— 6, see G is preached to (the.)
1 Pet. i. 12, see G unto (preach the.)
—— 25, see G (be preached by the.)
—— iv. 6, see G is preached (the.)
b. —— 17.
Rev. xiv. 6.

GOSPEL BEFORE (PREACH THE.)

προευαγγελίζομαι, to proclaim beforehand a joyful message.

Gal. iii. 8.

GOSPEL (PREACH THE.)

εὐαγγελίζω, *equivalent to* εὐαγγέλια λέγειν, to bring a joyful message, speak good news.

(a) *Mid. with an impersonal object*, to proclaim *something (to somebody) as* a divine message of salvation ; *with a personal object*, to proclaim the divine message of salvation, *with acc. of the person* by proclaiming the message of salvation, to bring some one into relation to it, *i.e.* to evangelize him.

(b) *Pass.*, to be announced, to have the glad tidings announced to one.

a. Luke iv. 8.
a. —— ix. 6.
a. —— xx. 1.
a. Rom. i. 15.
a. —— xv. 20.
a. 1 Cor. i. 17.
a. —— ix. 16 twice.
a. ——— 18 part.
a. 2 Cor. x. 16.
a. Gal. iv. 13.

GOSPEL...(PREACH.)

a. Gal. i. 8, 9.

GOSPEL IN (PREACH THE.)

a. Acts viii. 25.

GOSPEL OF (PREACH THE.)

a. Rom. x. 15, part (*om.* εὐαγγελιζομένων εἰρήνην τῶν, preach the gospel of peace, L T Trm[b] A[b] ℵ.)

GOSPEL TO (PREACH THE.)

a. Acts xiv. 7, with εἰμί, *to be.*
a. ——— 21, part.

GOSPEL UNTO (PREACH THE.)

a. Acts xvi. 10. | a. 1 Pet. i. 12.

GOSPEL (BE PREACHED BY THE.)

b. 1 Pet. i. 25.

GOSPEL IS PREACHED (THE.)

b. 1 Pet. iv. 6.

GOSPEL IS PREACHED TO (THE.)

b. Luke vii. 22.
b. Heb. iv. 6, marg. (text, *it.*)

GOSPEL IS PREACHED UNTO (THE.)

b. Heb. iv. 2, with εἰμί, *to be.*

GOSPEL PREACHED TO (HAVE THE.)

b. Matt. xi. 5.

GOTTEN.

See, GET.

GOVERNMENT (-S.)

1. κυβέρνησις, a steering, piloting, direction, *hence,* a governing. *The idea being that of* guidance *rather than* rule, *(non occ.)*

2. κυριότης, dominion, lordship.

1. 1 Cor. xii. 28.
2. 2 Pet. ii. 10, marg. *dominion.*

GOVERNOR (S-.)

1. ἡγεμών, a leader, guide. *The general word for all* governours *whether* proconsul, legate *or* procurator.

2. ἡγέομαι, to go before, go first, lead the way, *then* to be leader, chief *in war, etc., (here the participle.)*

3. ἐθνάρχης, an ethnarch, *i.e.* ruler of a people, *(non occ.)*

4. εὐθύνω, to make straight, guide straight, *i.e.* to guide *or* steer a ship, *(here, part.,* the steersman,) (occ. John i. 23.)

5. οἰκονόμος, a house-manager; one who had authority over the servants, *etc.,* of a family as to their tasks and payments; also over the sons in respect to pecuniary matters as distinguished from tutors.

2. Matt. ii. 6 part.
1. —— x. 18. [15, 21.
1. —— xxvii. 2, 11 twice, 14,
1. ——— 23 (*om.* Tr A ℵ.)
1. ——— 27.
1. —— xxviii. 14.
— Luke ii. 2, } see G (be.)
— —— iii. 1, }
1. —— xx. 20. [the feast.)
— John ii. 8, 9, see G of
2. Acts vii. 10 part.
1. —— xxiii. 24, 26, 33.
1. ——— 34 (*om.* G L T Tr A ℵ.)
1. —— xxiv. 1, 10.
1. —— xxvi. 30.
8. 2 Cor. xi. 32.
5. Gal iv. 2.
4. Jas. iii. 4, part.
1. 1 Pet. ii. 14.

GOVERNOR (BE.)

ἡγεμονεύω, to go before, to go first; be a leader, chief. *Then* to be a governour, *as of a Roman province.*

Luke ii. 2, part. ; iii. 1, part.

GOVERNOR OF THE FEAST.

ἀρχιτρίκλινος, the master of a feast, *i.e.* the person who had the direction of an entertainment, arranging the guests, *etc.*

John ii. 8, 9.

GOVERNOR'S HOUSE [margin.]

πραιτώριον, the general's tent in a camp, *then* the house *or* palace of a governor of a province.

Matt. xxvii. 27, text, *common hall.*

GRACE.

1. χάρις, a kind, affectionate, pleasing nature and inclining disposition, *either in person or thing. Objectively it denotes*, personal gracefulness, a pleasing work, beauty of speech, *etc.* Subjectively *it means* an inclining towards, courteous *or* gracious disposition, friendly willingness; *on the part of the giver of a favour*, kindness, favour; *on the part of the receiver*, thanks.

[The word denotes specially, God's grace and favour manifested towards mankind or to any individual, which, as a free act is no more hindered by sin than it is conditional upon works. It is the grace of God, because it denotes the relation assumed and maintained by God towards sinful man. It is joined with Christ, because it is manifested in and through Him.]

2. εὐπρέπεια, beauty, gracefulness, *(of outward appearance,)* comeliness, *(non occ.)*

1. Luke ii. 40.
1. John i. 14, 16 twice, 17.
1. Acts iv. 33.
1. —— xi. 23.
1. —— xiii. 43.
1. —— xiv. 3, 26.
1. —— xv. 11, 40.
1. —— xviii 27.
1. —— xx. 24, 32.
1. Rom. i. 5, 7.
1. —— iii. 24.
1. —— iv. 4, 16.
1. —— v. 2, 15 twice, 17, 20, 21.
1. —— vi. 1, 14, 15.
1. —— xi. 5, 6 1st 2nd & 3rd
1. —— 6 4th (ap.)
1. —— xii. 3, 6.
1. —— xv. 15.
1. —— xvi. 20, 24 (ap.)
1. 1 Cor. i. 3, 4.
1. —— iii. 10.
1. —— x. 30, marg. *thanksgiving.*
1. —— xv. 10 3 times.
1. —— xvi. 23.
1. 2 Cor. i. 2, 12.
1. —— 15, marg. (text, *benefit.*)
1. —— iv. 15.
1. —— vi. 1.
1. —— viii. 1, 6, 7, 9, 19.
1. —— ix. 8, 14.
1. —— xii. 9.
1. —— xiii. 14.
1. Gal. i. 3, 6, 15.
1. —— ii. 9, 21.
1. —— v. 4.
1. —— vi. 18.
1. Eph. i. 2, 6, 7.
1. Eph. ii. 5, 7, 8.
1. —— iii. 2, 7, 8.
1. —— iv. 7, 29.
1. —— vi. 24.
1. Phil. i. 2, 7.
1. —— iv. 23.
1. Col. i. 2, 6.
1. —— iii. 16.
1. —— iv. 6, 18.
1. 1 Thes. i. 1.
1. —— v. 28.
1. 2 Thes. i. 2, 12.
1. —— ii. 16.
1. —— iii. 18.
1. 1 Tim. i. 2, 14.
1. —— vi. 21.
1. 2 Tim. i. 2, 9.
1. —— ii. 1.
1. —— iv. 22 (ap.)
1. Titus i. 4.
1. —— ii. 11.
1. —— iii. 7, 15.
1. Philem. 3, 25.
1. Heb. ii. 9.
1. —— iv. 16 twice.
1. —— x. 29.
1. —— xii. 15, 28.
1. —— xiii. 9, 25.
2. Jas. i. 11.
1. —— iv. 6 twice.
1. 1 Pet. i. 2, 10, 13.
1. —— iii. 7.
1. —— iv. 10.
1. —— v. 5, 10, 12.
1. 2 Pet. i. 2.
1. —— iii. 18.
1. 2 John 3.
1. Jude 4.
1. Rev. i. 4.
1. —— xxii. 21.

GRACED (much) [margin.]

χαριτόω, *see* "FAVOURED (HIGHLY.)"

Luke i. 28, text *highly favoured.*

GRACIOUS.

1. χάρις, *here the Gen. of* "GRACE," *No.* 1.
2. χρηστός, useful, *toward others, i.e.,* well-disposed, actively benevolent in spite of ingratitude.

1. Luke iv. 22. | 2. 1 Pet. ii. 3.

GRACIOUSLY [margin.]

See, ACCEPTED.

GRAFF IN.

ἐγκεντρίζω, to prick in, to stick in *as spurs. In N.T.* to ingraft.

Rom. xi. 17, 19, 23 twice.

GRAFF INTO.

Rom. xi. 24 twice.

GRAIN.

κόκκος, a kernel, grain, seed, (occ. John xii. 24.)

Matt. xiii. 31.
—— xvii. 20.
Mark iv. 31.
Luke xiii. 19.
—— xvii. 6.
1 Cor. xv. 37.

GRANDMOTHER.

μάμμη, *strictly,* a child's attempt to articulate mother *(like our* mamma *and similar forms in all languages)* mother: *(also prob. like the Lat.* mamma, the mother's breast) *later,* a grandmother, *(non occ.)*

2. Tim. i. 5.

GRANT (-ED.)

1. δίδωμι, *see* "GIVE," *No.* 1.
2. εἶπον, to say, to speak.
3. χαρίζομαι, *see* "GIVE," *No.* 7.

2. Matt. xx. 21.
1. Mark x. 37.
1. Luke i. 74.
3. Acts iii. 14.
1. —— iv. 29.
1. —— xi. 18.
1. Acts xiv. 3.
1. Rom. xv. 5.
1. Eph. iii. 16.
1. 2 Tim. i. 18.
1. Rev. iii. 21.
1. —— xix. 8.

GRAPE. (-s.)

σταφυλή, a grape, cluster of grapes, *(non occ.)*

Matt. vii. 16 (pl. LTTrAℵ.) | Luke vi. 44.
Rev. xiv. 18 (sing. G∾.)

GRASS.

χόρτος, an enclosed place, *but with the notion of* a feeding place, *then gen.* any feeding ground, *and afterwards,* food, fodder, *esp. for cattle,* hay, grass. *(From the same root comes Lat.* hortus, *and Eng.* garden, court.)

Matt. vi. 30.
— xiv. 19.
Mark vi. 39.
Luke xii. 28.
John vi. 10.
Jas. i. 10, 11.
1 Pet. i. 24 3 times.
Rev. viii. 7.
Rev. ix. 4.

GRAVE [adj.]

σεμνός, venerable, reverend. *In N.T. of things,* honourable, reputable, *of persons,* grave, dignified, (occ. Ph. iv. 8.)

1. Tim. iii. 8, 11. | Titus ii. 2.

GRAVE [noun.]

1. μνημεῖον, a memorial, monument, *hence,* a sepulchral monument, *and then* a tomb, sepulchre.

   [Among the Hebrews, *gen.* caverns, closed by a door or stone often decorated.]

2. μνῆμα, a memorial, remembrance *or* record *of a person or thing, esp.* a memorial of one dead, a monument *in honour of the dead.*

3. ᾅδης, *see* "HELL," *No.* 1.

1. Matt. xxvii. 52, 53.
1. Luke xi. 44.
1. John v. 28.
1. — xi. 17, 31, 38.
1. — xii. 17.
3. 1 Cor. xv. 55, marg. *hell,* (*θάνατος, death,* L T Tr A ℵ.)
2. Rev. xi. 19. [*hell.*)
3. — xx. 13 marg. (text,

GRAVE-CLOTHES.

κειρίαι bands, or bandages *for swathing infants or dead bodies, (non occ.)*

John xi. 44.

GRAVEN.

χάραγμα, something graven, sculptured; a mark *cut in or stamped,* a stamp *or* sign: *also,* sculptured work, *as idols, etc.*

Acts xvii. 29, dat.

GRAVITY.

σεμνότης, venerableness, gravity, dignity, (occ. 1 Tim. ii. 2.)

1. Tim. iii. 4. | Titus ii. 7

GREAT.

1. μέγας, great, large, *of physical magnitude; also, of the measure, number, cost and estimation of things.*

2. πολύς, many, numerous, *of number, quantity, amount.*

   (a) *with the article,* the much, *i.e.* the abundance.

3. ἱκανός, coming to, reaching to, *and hence,* sufficient; *of things,* enough; *of persons,* competent; *of number or magnitude,* abundant, great, much.

1. Matt. ii. 10.
2. — 18
1. — iv. 16.
2. — v. 12.
1. — 19, 35.
— — vi. 23, see G (how.)
1. — vii. 27.
— — viii. 10, see G (so.)
1. — 24, 26.
— — xiii. 46, see Price.
2. — xiv. 14.
1. — xv. 28.
— — 33, see G (so.)
— — xx. 25, see G (they that are.)
1. — 26.
2. — 29.
— — xxi. 8, see G (very.)
1. — xxii. 36, 38.
1. — xxiv. 21, 24.
2. — 30.
1. — 31.
2. — xxvi. 47.
1. — xxvii. 60.
1. — xxviii. 2, 8.
— Mark i. 35, see While.
2. — iii. 7, 8 1st.
— — 8 2nd, see G things (what.)
2. — iv. 1.
1. — 32, 37, 39.
1. — v. 11 (*om.* G →.)
— — 19, 20, see G things (how.)
1. — 42.
— — vii. 36, see G deal (so much the more a.)
— — viii. 1, see G (very)
2. — ix. 14.
— — x. 42, see G ones.
1. — 43.
— — 46, see G number [of.
— — 48, see G deal (the more a.)
1. — xiii. 2.
2. — 26.
2. — xiv. 43 (*om.* L^b T Tr A ℵ.)
1. — xvi. 4.
1. Luke i. 15, 32.
— — 49, see G thing.
— — 58, see G (show.)
— — ii, 5, see Child.
1. — 10.
— — 36, see Age.
1. — iv. 25, 38.
2. — v. 6.
1 — 29 1st.
2. Luke v. 29 2nd.
2. — vi. 17, 23, 35.
1. — 49.
— — vii. 9, see G (so.)
1. — 16.
1. — viii. 37.
— — 39, see G things (how.)
1. — ix. 48.
2. — x. 2.
— — 13, see Ago.
1. — xiii. 19 (*om.* G → L^b Tr A^b ℵ.)
1. — xiv. 16.
— — 32, } see Way off
— — xv. 20, }
1. — xvi. 26.
1. — xxi. 11 twice, 23.
2. — 27.
2. — xxiii. 27.
— — 44, see Drop.
1. — xxiv. 52.
2. John v. 3 (*om.* G ⇉ L^b T Tr A ℵ.)
2. — vi. 2, 5.
1. — 18.
1. — vii. 37.
1. — xxi. 11.
1. Acts ii. 20.
1. — iv. 33 twice.
1. — v. 5, 11.
2. — vi. 7.
1. — 8.
1. — vii. 11.
1. — viii. 1, 2.
1. — 8 (No. 2, L T Tr A .)
— — 9, see Gone (some.)
1. — 10.
— — 27, see Authority
— — ix. 16, see G things (how.)
1. — x. 11.
1. — xi. 5.
2. — 21.
1. — 28.
2. — xiv. 1.
1. — xv. 3.
1. — xvi. 26.
2. — xvii. 4.
1. — xix. 27, 28, 34, 35.
2. — xxi. 40.
3. — xxii. 6.
2. — 28.
1. — xxiii. 9.
2. — 10.
— — 14, see Curse.

2. Acts xxiv. 2, 7 (*ap.*)
2. —— xxv. 23.
1. —— xxvi. 22.
— —— xxviii. 6, see While
2. —— 29 (*ap.*)
1. Rom. ix. 2.
— —— xv. 23, see Desire.
— 1 Cor. ix. 11, see G thing
1. —— xvi. 9.
— 2 Cor. i. 10, see G (so.)
2. —— iii. 12.
2. —— vii. 4 twice.
2. —— viii. 2, 22.
— —— xi. 15, see G thing
— Gal. iii. 4, see G things (so.)
2a. Eph. ii. 4.
1. —— v. 32.
— Col. ii. 1, see G (very.)
2. —— iv. 13.
2. 1 Thes. ii. 17.
2. 1 Tim. iii. 13.
1. —— 16.
1. —— vi. 6.
1. 2 Tim ii. 20.
1. Titus ii. 13.
2 Philem. 7.
— Heb. ii. 3, see G (so.)
1. —— iv. 14.
— —— vii. 4, see G (how.)
2. —— x. 32.
1. —— 35.
— —— xii. 1, see G (so.)
1. —— xiii. 20.
— Jas. iii. 4, see G (so.)
— —— 5 1st, see Boast.
— —— 5 2nd, see G (how)
— 1 Pet. iii. 4, see Price.
— 2 Pet. i. 4, see G (exceeding.)
— 2 Pet. ii. 18, see Swelling
— —— iii. 10, see Noise.
1. Jude 6.
— —— 16, see Swelling.
1. Rev. i. 10.
1. —— ii. 22.
1. —— vi. 4, 12.
— —— 15, see G men.
1. —— 17.
2. —— vii. 9.
1. —— 14.
1. —— viii. 8, 10.
1. —— ix. 2 (*καιομένης, burning*, G∾.)
1. —— 14. [17, 18, 19.
1. —— xi. 8, 11, 12, 13, 15,
1. —— xii. 1, 3, 9, 12, 14.
1. —— xiii. 2.
— —— 5, see G thing.
1. —— 13, 16.
1. —— xiv. 2, 8, 19.
1. —— xv. 1, 3.
1. —— xvi. 1, 9, 12, 14.
1. —— 17 (*om.* G→ L A)
1. —— 18 twice, 19 twice, 21 twice.
1. —— xvii. 1, 5, 6, 18.
1. —— xviii. 1, 2 (*ap.*), 10, 16.
— —— 17, see G (so.)
1. —— 18, 19, 21 twice.
— —— 23, see G men.
1. —— xix. 1, 2, 5.
2. —— 6.
1. —— 17, 18.
1. —— xx. 1, 11, 12.
1. —— xxi. 3, 10 1st.
1. —— 10 2nd (*om.* G L T Tr A ℵ.)
1. —— 12.

(The following combinations are where there is not a Greek equivalent for each English word.)

GREAT DEAL (THE MORE A.)

{ πολλῷ, much,
{ μᾶλλον, more.

Mark x. 48.

GREAT DEAL (SO MUCH THE MORE A.)

{ μᾶλλον, more,
{ περισσότερος, exceeding abundantly.

Mark vii. 36.

GREAT (EXCEEDING.)

μεγίστος, the greatest, *(superl.* of "GREAT," *No.* 1,) *(non occ.)*

2. Pet. i. 4.

GREAT (HOW.)

1. ἡλίκος, *(relative pron.)* how great *of degree*, (occ. Col. ii. 1.)

2. πηλίκος, *(dependent interrogative pron.)* how great *of degree*, (occ. Gal. vi. 11.)

3. πόσος, *(interrogative pron.)* how great, *of quantity.*

3. Matt. vi. 23. | 1. Jas. iii. 5. | 2. Heb. vii. 4.

GREAT THINGS (HOW.)

ὅσος, *(relative pron.)* how great, *of quantity ; here, only in plural.*

Mark v. 19, 20. | Acts ix. 16. | Luke viii. 39 twice.

GREAT MEN.

μεγιστᾶνες, the great, *Lat.* magnates, *i.e.*, chiefs, nobles, princes, (Mark vi. 21.)

Rev. vi. 15 ; xviii. 23.

GREAT NUMBER OF.

ἱκανός, *see* "GREAT," *No.* 3.

Mark x. 46.

GREAT ONE (SOME.)

{ τις, a certain one. }
{ μέγας, great, } some one great.

Acts viii. 9.

GREAT ONES.

{ οἱ, the,
{ μεγάλοι, great, *(masc. pl.)*

Mark x. 42.

GREAT (SHOW.)

μεγαλύνω, to make great, magnify.

Luke i. 58.

GREAT (SO.)

1. τοσοῦτος, *(demonstrative pron.)* so great, *of quantity.*

2. τηλικοῦτος, *(demonstrative pron.)* so great, *of degree*, (occ. Rev. xvi. 18.)

1. Matt. viii. 10.
1. —— xv. 33.
1. Luke vii. 9.
2. 2 Cor. i. 10.
2. Heb. ii. 3.
1. —— xii. 1.
2. Jas. iii. 4.
1. Rev. xviii. 17.

GREAT THINGS (so) [margin.]

τοσοῦτος, *see* "GREAT (SO,)" *No.* 1, *here neut. pl.*

Gal. iii. 4. text, *so many things.*

GREAT (THEY THAT ARE.)

{ οἱ, the,
μεγάλοι, great, *masc pl.*

Matt. xx. 25.

GREAT THING.

1. μέγα, *neut. of* "GREAT," *No.* 1.
2. τὰ μεγαλεῖα, great, glorious, wonderful *things or works,* (occ. Acts ii. 11.)

2. Luke i. 49 (No. 1, L T Tr A* ℵ.)
*1. 1 Cor. ix. 11.
1. 2 Cor. xi. 15.
1. Rev. xiii. 5.

GREAT (VERY.)

1. πάμπολυς, (πᾶς, all and πολύς, much) very much, vast, *(non occ.)*
2. πλεῖστος, *(Superl.* of "GREAT," *No.* 2,) the most, very great *only of number.*
   (a) *with art,* the greatest [*part of the multitude.*]

2a. Matt. xxi. 8.
1. Mark viii. 1 (πάλιν πολλοῦ, *again a great,* instead of πάμπολλου, *very large,* G∾ L T Tr A ℵ.)

GREAT (WHAT.)

ἡλίκος, *see* "GREAT (HOW)," *No.* 1.

Col. ii. 1

GREAT THINGS (WHAT.)

ὅσος, *see* "GREAT THINGS (HOW,)" *here, neut. pl.*

Mark iii. 8 (ἃ the *what* things, L[m].)

GREATER.

1. μείζων, *comparative of* μέγας, *see* "GREAT," *No.* 1.
2. μειζότερος, *(a double comparative of* μέγας,) far greater.
3. πλείων, *(comparative of* πολός, *see* "GREAT," *No.* 2,) more.
   (a) πλέον, *neut.*
4. περισσότερος, *(comparative of* περισσός, over and above,) more abundant, *esp. of number.*

1. Matt. xi. 11 twice.
1. —— xii. 6.
3. —— 41, 42.
4. —— xxiii. 14 (*ap.*)
1. Matt. xxiii. 17, 19.
1. Mark iv. 32.
1. —— xii. 31.
4. —— 40.
1. Luke vii. 28 twice.
3. —— xi. 31, 32.
1. —— xii. 18.
4. —— xx. 47.
1. —— xxii. 27.
— John i. 50, see G thing.
1. —— iv. 12.
1. —— v. 20, 36.
1. —— viii. 53.
1. —— x. 29.
1. —— xiii. 16 twice.
— —— xiv. 12, see G work
1. —— 28.
1. —— xv. 13, 20.
1. —— xix. 11.
3a. Acts xv. 28.
1. Rom. ix. 12, marg. (text, *elder.*)
1. 1 Cor. xiv. 5.
— —— xv. 28, see G part (the.)
1. Heb. vi. 13, 16.
1. —— ix. 11.
1. —— xi. 26.
1. Jas. iii. 1.
1. 2 Pet. ii. 11.
1. 1 John iii. 20.
1. —— iv. 4.
1. —— v. 9.
2. 3 John 4.

GREATER PART (THE.)

{ ὁ, the,
πλείων, majority, *(pl.)*

1. Cor. xv. 6.

GREATER THINGS.

μείζων, *(neut. pl.), (comp. of* "GREAT," *No.* 1.)

John i. 50.

GREATER WORK.

John xiv. 12.

GREATEST.

1. μέγας, *see* "GREAT," *No.* 1.
2. μείζων, *(comp. of* "GREAT," *No.* 1.)

2. Matt. xiii. 32.
2. —— xviii. 1, 4.
2. —— xxiii. 11.
2. Mark ix. 34.
2. Luke ix. 46.
2. —— xxii. 24, 26.
1. Acts viii. 10.
2. 1 Cor. xiii. 13
1. Heb. viii. 11.

GREATLY.

1. λίαν, *adv.* much, very, exceedingly.
2. πολύς, many, much, *of number, quantity or amount.*
3. σφόδρα, *(neut. pl. of adj.* σφοδρός, eager, vehement,) vehemently, greatly, very much.
4. μεγάλως, *(adv. of* μεγάς, *see* "GREAT," *No.* 1,) greatly, much, *(non occ.)*
5. χαρά, joy; *here, dative,* with joy.

1. Matt. xxvii. 14.
3. —— 54.
2. Mark v. 23, 38, pl.
— —— ix. 15, see Amazed.
2. —— xii. 27.
5. John iii. 29.
— Acts iii. 11, see Wondering
3. —— vi. 7.
2. 1 Cor. xvi. 12, pl.
— Phil. i. 8, see Long.
4. —— iv. 10.
— 1 Thes. iii. 6, } see
— 2 Tim. i. 4, } Desire
1. —— iv. 15.
— 1 Pet. i. 6, see Rejoice.
1. 2 John 4.
1. 3 John 3.

GREATNESS.

μέγεθος, greatness, *(non occ.)*

Eph. i. 19.

GRECIAN.

Ἑλληνιστής, a Hellenist, *i.e.* a Jew by birth or religion who speaks Greek.

Acts vi. 1; —— ix. 29.
—— xi. 20, (Ἕλλην, see Gentile, No. 2, G L T Tr A ℵ) (εὐαγγελιστής, envangelists, ℵ.)

GREEDILY.

See, RUN.

GREEDINESS.

πλεονεξία, a having more, *in N.T. prop.* the will to have more; *the active sin of* covetousness.

Eph. iv. 19.

GREEDY.

See, LUCRE.

GREEK.

1. Ἕλλην, Greek, *see* "GENTILE," *No.* 2.
2. Ἑλληνίς, *(fem. of No.* 1,) a female Greek.
3. Ἑλληνικός, *adj.* Greek, Grecian.
4. Ἑλληνιστί, *adv.* in Greek, *i.e.*, in the Greek language.

3. Mark vii. 26, marg. *Gentile.*
1. John vii. 35 1st, marg. (text, *Gentile.*)
1. —— xi. 20.
1. Acts xiv. 1, 3.
1. —— xvii. 4.
2. —— 12.
1. —— xviii. 4.
1. —— 17 (om. G ⇄ L T Tr A ℵ.)
1. —— xix. 10, 17.
1. —— xx. 21.
1. —— xxi. 28.
4. —— 37.
1. Rom. i. 14, 16.
1. Rom. ii. 9, 10, marg. (text, *Gentile.*)
1. —— x. 12.
1. 1 Cor. i. 22.
1. —— .23 (ἔθνος, see Gentile, No. 1, G L T Tr A ℵ.)
1. —— 24.
1. —— x. 32, marg. (text, *Gentile.*)
1. —— xii. 13, marg. (text, *Gentile.*)
1. Gal. ii. 3.
1. —— iii. 28.
1. Col. iii. 11.
3. Rev. ix. 11.

GREEK (IN.)

4. John xix. 20.

GREEK (OF)

3. Luke xxiii. 38 (*ap.*)

GREEN.

1. *χλωρός*, the colour of young grass, *etc., i.e.* pale green, *and then Gen.* pale, (occ. Rev. vi. 8; ix. 4.)
2. *ὑγρός*, wet, moist: *of a tree*, sappy, (as *opp.* to *ξηρός* dry,) *(non occ.)*

1. Mark vi. 39.
2. Luke xxiii. 31.
— Rev. vi. 13, see Fig.
— —— viii. 7.

GREEN THING.

1. Rev. ix. 4, neut.

GREET (-ETH.)

ἀσπάζομαι, to draw *to* one's self. *Hence,* to embrace, salute, *spoken of those who meet and separate.*

Rom. xvi. 3, 6, 8, 11.
1 Cor. xvi. 20 twice.
2 Cor. xiii. 12.
Phil. iv. 21.
Col. iv. 14.
1 Thes. v. 26.
2 Tim. iv. 21
Titus iii. 15.
1 Pet. v. 14.
2 John 13.
3 John 14.

GREETING.

1. *ἀσπασμός*, salutation, greeting, *either oral or by* letter.
2. *χαίρω*, to joy, to rejoice, to be glad, *here, Inf.* to wish joy, to bid hail, *i.e.* to salute.

1. Matt. xxiii. 7.
1. Luke xi. 43.
1. Luke xx. 46.
2. Jas. i. 1.

GREETING (SEND.)

2. Acts xv. 23; xxiii. 26.

GRIEF.

λυπή, grief, sorrow; *also,* cause of grief, grievance.

1. Pet. ii. 19, pl.

GRIEF (CAUSE.)

λυπέω, to grieve, afflict with sorrow.

2. Cor. ii. 5.

GRIEF (WITH.)

στενάζω, to groan, to sigh *(of persons who are in distress.)*

Heb. xiii. 17, part.

GRIEVE (-ED.)

1. λυπέω, *see* "GRIEF (CAUSE.)"

2. συλλυπέω, *(No.* 1. *with* σύν, together with *prefixed,)* to grieve *or* afflict with another, to be grieved or afflicted with a person, *or*, to be grieved at the same time *or* along with some other emotion, *(non occ.)*

3. στενάζω, *see* "GRIEF (WITH.)"

2. Mark iii. 5.
1. 2 Cor. ii. 5.
1. Eph. iv. 30.
3. Jas. v. 9, marg. (text, *grudge.*)

GRIEVED (BE.)

1. λυπέω, *see* "GRIEF (CAUSE.)" *here, Mid. or Pass.*

2. διαπονέω, to labour through, to produce *or* effect with labour. *In N.T. only Mid.* to pain *or* grieve one's self, to be indignant, *(non occ.)*

3. ὀκνέω, to be slow, tardy, to delay, *(non occ.)*

1. Mark x. 22.
1. John xxi. 17.
2. Acts iv. 2.
3. Acts ix. 38, marg. (text, *delay.*)
2. —— xvi. 18.
1. Rom. xiv. 15.
1. 2 Cor. ii. 4.

GRIEVED WITH (BE.)

προσοχθίζω, to be burdened *or* heavy laden with, to be grieved towards *any one*, to be sore vexed with, *implying loathing, (non occ.)*

Heb iii. 10, 17.

GRIEVOUS.

1. βαρύς, heavy, oppressive, hard to be borne; afflictive, violent. *Also*, weighty, *i.e. not to be made light of*, severe.

2. λυπή, grief, sorrow; *here, Gen.*, of sorrow.

3. ὀκνηρός, slow, tardy; *of persons*, slothful; *of things*, tedious, (occ. Matt. xxv. 26; Rom. xii. 11.)

4. πονηρός, causing *or* having labour, sorrow, pain; *hence*, evil, *in its active form*, malignant.

— Matt. xxiii. 4, see G to be borne.
— Luke xi. 46, see G to be borne.
1. Acts xx. 29.
1. Acts xxv. 7.
3. Phil. iii. 1.
2. Heb. xii. 11.
1. 1 John v. 3.
4. Rev. xvi. 2.

GRIEVOUS TO BE BORNE.

δυσβάστακτος, hard to be borne, oppressive, *(non occ.)*

Matt. xxiii. 4 (*om.* G→ T Tr[b] A* ℵ); Luke xi. 46.

GRIEVOUSLY.

1. δεινῶς, greatly, vehemently, (occ. Luke xi. 53.)

2. κακῶς, badly, ill, evil.

1. Matt. viii. 6.
2. Matt. xv. 22.

GRIND (-ING.)

ἀλήθω, to grind *as with a hand-mill, (mostly done by female slaves,) (non occ.)*

Matt. xxiv. 41.
Luke xvii. 35.

GRIND TO POWDER.

λικμάω, to winnow, *as grain, which in the East is done by throwing it with a fork against the wind which scatters the straw and chaff. Hence,* to scatter, disperse; to scatter to the winds, make chaff of anything, *(non occ.)*

Matt. xxi. 44 (*ap.*)
Luke xx. 18.

GROAN.

1. στενάζω, to groan, to sigh, *as of persons in distress.*

2. ἐμβριμάομαι, to be greatly purturbed in mind, deeply moved.

[The classical use of the word (snorting) can hardly be intended. Jesus could hardly have been indignant, or merely repressing what was passing in His own spirit: whatever it was, it was ἐν ἑαυτῷ, in Himself, and doubtless with the sin and death and the power of Satan before Him and knowing the great crisis that would by this act be brought on, Jesus could not have been otherwise than greatly purturbed in Himself, and deeply moved.]

2. John xi. 33, 38.
— Rom. viii. 22, see G together.
1. —— 23.
1. Rom. viii. 23.
1. 2 Cor. v. 2, 4.
1. Jas. v. 9, marg. (text, *grudge.*)

GROAN TOGETHER.

συστενάζω, *(No.* 1 *above with* σύν, together with, *prefixed,) (non occ.)*

Rom. viii. 22.

GROANING.

στεναγμός, a groaning, a sighing, *as of the distressed, (non occ.)*

Acts vii. 34. | Rom. viii. 26.

GROSS (WAX.)

παχύνω, to make fat, *Pass. (as here)* to become fat and thick, *(non occ.)*, [quoted from Is. vi. 10.]

Matt. xiii. 15. | Acts xxviii. 27.

GROUND [noun.]

1. γῆ, the earth *as part of the creation, as given up to man and standing in relation to heaven which is the dwelling place of God. Also*, earth, *or* land *in contrast to water.*
2. ἔδαφος, base, bottom ; *of a ship*, the hold ; *of a room*, the floor : the ground, *(non occ.)*
3. ἑδραίωμα, basis, foundation ; what is fixed, settled, stationary.
4. χώρα, space *which receives, contains, or surrounds anything, and so*, place, spot *in which one is, or where anything takes place ; esp.*, the country, *as opp. to town, and hence* land as cultivated.
5. ὑπόστασις, *see* "SUBSTANCE," *No.* 3.

1. Matt. x. 29 (*om.* G⇉.)
1. —— xiii. 8, 23.
1. —— xv. 35.
– Mark iv. 5, see Stony.
1. ——— 8.
— ——— 16, see Stony.
1. ——— 20, 6.
1. —— viii. 6.
1. —— ix. 20.
1. —— xiv. 35
1. Luke viii. 8 15.
4. —— xii. 16.
1. —— xiii. 7.
— —— xiv. 18, see G (piece of.)
— Luke xix. 44, see G (lay ever with the.)
1. —— xxii. 44 (*ap.*) [of.)
— John iv. 5, see G (parcel
1. —— viii. 6 (*ap.*), 8 (*ap.*)
— —— ix. 6, see G (on the.)
1. —— xii. 24.
— —— xviii. 6, see G (to the)
1. Acts vii. 33.
2. —— xvii. 7.
— Eph. iii. 17, } see
— Col. i. 23, } the verb.
3. 1 Tim. iii. 15, marg. *stay.*
5. Heb. xi. 1, marg. (text, *substance.*)

GROUND (LAY EVEN WITH THE.)

ἐδαφίζω, to beat level and form like a threshing-floor *or* pavement : to level with the earth, *(non. occ.)*

Luke xix. 44.

GROUND (ON THE.)

χαμαί, on the earth, on the ground, *(belonging to same root as Lat.* humi.)

John ix. 6.

GROUND (TO THE.)

John xviii. 6.

GROUND (PARCEL OF.)

χωρίον, place, spot ; *like Eng.* "place," *i.e.* field, farm, possession.

John iv. 5.

GROUND (PIECE OF.)

ἀγρος, a field, *esp.* a cultivated field.

Luke xiv. 18.

GROUNDED [verb.]

θεμελιόω, to lay the foundation *of anything*, to found.

Eph. iii. 17. | Col. i. 23.

GROW (-ETH, GREW, GROWN.)

1. αὐξάνω, to increase, to augment ; *here Pass.*, to receive, increase *i.e.* to grow, grow up.
2. γίνομαι, to begin to be, to become.
3. ἔρχομαι, to come *or* go.

1. Matt. vi. 28. [gether.
— —— xiii. 30, see G to-
1. —— 32.
2. —— xxi. 19. [G up.
— Mark iv. 7, 27, 32, see
3. —— v. 26.
1. Luke i. 80.
1. —— ii. 40.
1. —— xii. 27 (*ap.*)
1. —— xiii. 19.
2. Acts v. 24, opt
1. —— vii. 17.
1. —— xii. 24.
1. —— xiii. 20.
1. Eph. ii. 21.
— —— iv. 15, see G u.
— 2 Thes. i. 3, see G exceedingly.
1. 1 Pet. ii. 2.
1. 2 Pet. iii. 18.

GROW EXCEEDINGLY.

ὑπεραυξάνω, (*No.* 1 *with* ὑπέρ, over, *prefixed*,) to over-grow, *i.e.* to increase exceedingly, *in good sense, (non occ.)*

2 Thes. i. 3.

GROW TOGETHER.

συναυξάνω, *(No.* 1 *with* σύν, together with, *prefixed,)* to grow *or* increase at the same time with anything else, to grow together *in company, (non. occ.)*

Matt. xiii. 30.

GROW UP.

1. αὐξάνω, *see* "GROW," *No.* 1.
2. ἀναβαίνω, to cause to ascend ; *of plants*, to spring up.

3. μηκύνω, to make long, *in N.T. mid.*, to lengthen one's self, *i.e.*, grow up, *spoken of plants.*

2. Mark iv. 7. | 2. Mark iv. 32.
3. ——— 27. | 1. Eph. iv. 15.

GRUDGE (an inward) [margin.]

ἐνέχω, to have in *anything*, to have in one's self, as *a disposition, etc., towards any one. In N.T. unfavourable*, (occ. Luke xi. 53; Gal. v. 1.)

Mark vi. 19, text, *have a quarrel.*

GRUDGE [verb.]

στενάζω, to groan *or* sigh, *of persons in distress, etc., also from impatience, ill-humour, i.e.*, to murmur, *etc.*

Jas. v. 9, marg. *groan or grieve.*

GRUDGING.

γογγυσμός, uttering in a low voice, murmuring, *i.e.*, the expression of sullen discontent.

1 Pet. iv. 9, pl. (sing, G∾ L T Tr A ℵ.)

GRUDGINGLY.

{ ἐκ, out of.
{ λύπης, sorrow.

2 Cor. ix. 7.

GUARD.

See, EXECUTIONER, CAPTAIN.

GUEST.

ἀνάκειμαι, to be laid up, *as offerings or dead bodies; in later usage* to recline *as at table, then*, to be a guest.

Matt. xxii. 10 & 11, part.

GUEST (BE.)

καταλύω, to loosen down, *i.e.*, to unbind; *hence*, of *travellers*, to halt, *for rest*, put up for the night, *and then, gen.*, to lodge, take lodging.

Luke xix. 7, pass.

GUEST-CHAMBER.

κατάλυμα, a place where one puts up, lodging-place. *In the East*, a menzil, khan, caravanserai.

Mark xiv. 14. | Luke xxii. 11.

GUIDE (-s) [noun.]

ὁδηγός, way-leader, *i.e.*, a leader, guide, (occ. Matt. xv. 14.)

Matt. xxiii. 16, 24. | Acts i. 16.
Rom. ii. 19.

GUIDE (be the) [marg.]

ἡγέομαι, to lead, go before, go first, lead the way, *hence*, be chief *or* ruler.

Heb. xiii. 7, 17 twice, text, *have the rule over.*

GUIDE [verb.]

1. ἡγέομαι, *see* "GUIDE (BE THE.)"
2. κατευθύνω, to guide straight towards *or* upon *anything, i.e.*, to guide, direct *on one's way or journey to a place.*
3. ὁδηγέω, to lead the way, *i.e.*, to lead, guide.

2. Luke i. 79. | 2. 2 Thes. iii. 5, marg. (text, *to direct.*)
3. John xvi. 13. | — 1 Tim. v. 14, see House.
3. Acts viii. 31.
1. Heb. xiii. 24, marg. (text, *have the rule over.*)

GUILE.

δόλος, a bait for fish, *hence*, any cunning contrivance for deceiving or catching. *In the abstract*, wile, craft, cunning.

John i. 47. | 1 Pet. ii. 1, 22.
2 Cor. xii. 16. | ——— iii. 10. [L T Tr A ℵ.)
1 Thes. ii. 3. | Rev. xiv. 5 (ψεῦδος, *lie*, G

GUILTLESS.

ἀναίτιος, without accusation of crime, guiltless, (occ. Matt. xii. 5.)

Matt. xii. 7.

GUILTY.

ὑπόδικος, under process, under sentence, *i.e.*, condemned, guilty.

Rom. iii. 19, marg. *subject to judgment.*

GUILTY (BE.)

ὀφείλω, to owe, to be indebted, then, *(from the Aramæan and by impl.)* to fail *in duty*, be delinquent.

Matt. xxiii. 8, marg. *a debtor, or bound.*

GUILTY OF.

ἔνοχος, held in, contained in, bound by, *hence*, liable, subject to.

Matt. xxvi. 66. | 1 Cor. xi. 27.
Mark xiv. 64. | Jas. ii. 10.

GULF.

χάσμα, a chasm.

Luke xvi. 26.

GUSH OUT.

ἐκχύνω, to pour out, pour forth.

Acts i. 18, pass.

H

HABIT [margin.]

ἕξις, a having possession; a being in a certain state, a permanent condition, *esp. as produced by practice*, a habit: skill *as the result of practice and experience*, *(non occ.)*

Heb. v. 14, text *use*.

HABITATION.

1. οἰκητήριον, a dwelling, habitation (occ. 2 Cor. v. 2.)
2. κατοικητήριον, *(No. 1 with κατά, down, prefixed,)* fit for inhabiting; *with art, as subst.*, a dwelling-place, abode, *(implying more permanency than No. 1,)* *(non occ.)*
3. κατοικία, a dwelling, *i.e.*, a settlement, colony, *also*, the foundation of a colony, *(non occ.)*
4. ἔπαυλις, a fold, a stall; *then* a country-dwelling, cottage: *then, gen.*, house, (quoted from Ps. lxix. 26, where lxx. for טירה,) *(non occ.)*
5. σκηνή, any covered *or* shady place, a booth, hut, tent, tabernacle.

5. Luke xvi. 9.
4. Acts i. 20.
3. —— xvii. 26.
2. Eph. ii. 22.
1. Jude 6.
2. Rev. xviii. 2.

HAIL [noun.]

χάλαζα, something let go, let fall; *hence*, hail, *(non occ.)*

Rev. viii. 7; xi. 19; xvi. 21 twice.

HAIL [verb.]

χαίρω, to joy, to rejoice, be glad; *In Imperat. (as here) as a word of salutation or greeting*, joy to thee, joy to you, *i.e.*, hail. *Lat.* salve.

Matt. xxvi. 49.
—— xxvii. 29.
Mark xv. 18.
Luke i. 28.
John xix. 3.

HAIL (ALL.)

Matt. xxviii. 9.

HAIR.

1. θρίξ, the hair, *both of man and beast; of sheep*, wool; *of birds*, feathers, *(non occ.)*
2. κόμη, the hair, hair of the head, *(Lat.* coma), long hair, *(non occ.)*

1. Matt. iii. 4, pl.
1. —— v. 36.
1. —— x. 30.
1. Mark i. 6, pl.
1. Luke vii. 38, 44.
1. —— xii. 7.
1. —— xxi. 18.
1. John xi. 2, pl.
1. —— xii. 3, pl.
1. Acts xxvii. 34.
— 1 Cor. xi. 14, 15 1st, see H (have long.)
2. —— 15 2nd.
— 1 Tim. ii. 9, see Braided.
1. 1 Pet. iii. 3, pl. (om. L.)
1. Rev. i. 14.
— —— vi. 12, see H (of).
1. —— ix. 8 twice, pl.

HAIR (HAVE LONG.)

κομάω, to let the hair grow long, wear long hair, *(non occ.)*

1 Cor. xi. 14, 15.

HAIR (OF.)

τρίχινος, hairy, made of hair, *(non occ.)*

Rev. vi. 12.

HALE (-ING) [verb.]

1. σύρω, to draw, to drag, to haul, *(implying the use of some force.)*
2. κατασύρω, *(No. 1 with κατά, down, prefixed,)* to drag down, force along, *(non occ.)*

2. Luke xii. 58.
1. Acts viii. 3.

HALF.

ἥμισυ, half, *(non occ.)*

Mark vi. 23.
Luke x. 30, see Dead.
—— xix. 8.
Rev. viii. 1, see Hour.
—— xi. 9, 11.
—— xii. 14.

HALL.

αὐλή, the open court before the house, court-yard; *surrounded with buildings (from* ἄημι, to blow, *the* αὐλή

being open to the air.) Afterwards, any court *or* hall; any dwelling, *and later* a country house.

Matt. xv. 16. | Luke xxii. 55.

HALL (COMMON.)

πραιτώριον, the house *or* palace of the governor of a province, *whether a praetor or any other officer.*

Matt. xxvii. 27, marg. *governor's house.*

See also, JUDGMENT.

HALLOW (-ED.)

ἁγιάζω, to make holy, sanctify; *i.e.*, to set something into a state opposed to κοινόν (common); *or, where the something is already* κοινόν, to deliver it from that state *and put it into a state corresponding to the revealed nature of God.*

Matt. vi. 9. | Luke xi. 2.

HALT.

χωλός, lame, crippled *in the feet.*

Matt. xviii. 8.
Mark ix. 45.
Luke xiv. 21.
John v. 3.

HAND (-S.)

χείρ, the hand, *or rather* the hand and arm, (χείρ *is the old Lat. form,* hir. *Prob. the root is to be found in the Sanscr.* hri, to grasp *and akin to* αἱρέω, ἀγρέω, ἁρπάζω; *Eng.* grip, *etc.)*

Matt. iii. 2, see H (be at).
—— 12.
—— iv. 6.
—— 17, see H (be at).
—— v. 30.
—— vi. 3, see Right.
—— viii. 3, 15.
—— ix. 18, 25.
—— x. 7, see H (be at.)
—— xii. 10, 13, 49.
—— xiv. 31.
—— xv. 2, 20.
—— xvii. 22.
—— xviii. 8 twice.
—— 28, see H on (lay.)
—— xix. 13, 15.
—— xxi. 46, see H on (lay.)
—— xxii. 13.
—— xxv. 41, see Left.
—— xxvi. 18, see H (at.)
—— 23.
—— 45 1st, see H (be at.)
—— 45 2nd.
—— 46, see H (be at.)
—— 50, 51.
Matt. xxvi. 67, see Smite.
—— xxvii. 24.
—— 29, see Right.
Mark i. 15, see H (be at.)
—— 31, 41.
—— iii. 1, 3, 5 twice.
—— v. 23, 41.
—— vi. 2, 5.
—— vii. 2, 3, 5, 32.
—— viii. 23 twice, 25.
—— ix. 27, 31, 43 twice.
—— x. 16.
—— 37, 40, see Left.
—— xiv. 41.
—— 42, see H (be at.)
—— 46.
—— 58, see H (made without.)
—— 65, see Strike.
—— xvi. 18 (*ap.*)
Luke i. 1, see H (take in.)
—— 66, 71, 74.
—— iii. 17.
—— iv. 11, 40.
—— v. 13.
Luke vi. 1, 6, 8, 10 twice.
—— viii. 54.
—— ix. 44, 62.
—— xiii. 13.
—— xv. 22.
—— xx. 19.
—— xxi. 12.
—— 30, 31, see Nigh.
—— xxii. 21, 53.
—— xxiii. 46.
—— xxiv. 7, 39, 40 (*ap.*), 50.
John ii. 13, see H (at.)
—— iii. 35.
—— vii 2, see H (at.)
—— 30, 44.
—— viii. 20, see H on (lay.)
—— x. 28, 29, 39.
—— xi. 44.
—— 55, see Nigh.
—— xiii. 3, 9.
—— xviii. 22, see Strike.
—— xix. 3, see Smite.
—— 42, see Nigh.
—— xx. 20, 25 twice, 27 twice.
—— xxi. 18.
Acts ii. 23.
—— 33, see Right.
—— iii. 7.
—— iv. 3, 28, 30.
—— v. 12, 18.
—— 31, see Right.
—— vi. 6.
—— vii. 25, 35, 41.
—— 48, see H (made with.)
—— 50.
—— viii. 17, 18, 19.
—— ix. 8, see H (lead by the.)
—— 12, 17, 41.
—— xi. 21, 30.
—— xii. 1, 7, 11, 17.
—— xiii. 3, 11 1st.
—— 11 2nd, see H (some to lead by the.)
—— 16.
—— xiv. 3.
—— xvii. 24, see H (made with.)
—— 25.
—— xviii. 6, 11, 26, 33.
—— xx. 34.
—— xxi. 3, see Left.
—— 11 twice, 27, 40.
—— xxii. 11, see H (lead by the.)
—— xxiii. 19.
—— xxiv. 7 (*ap.*)
—— xxvi. 1.
—— xxvii. 19, see H (with one's own.)
—— xxviii. 3, 4, 8, 17.
Rom. viii. 34, see Right.
Rom. x. 21.
—— xiii. 12, see H (be at.)
1 Cor. iv. 12.
—— xii. 15, 21.
—— xvi. 21.
2 Cor. v. 1, see H (not made with.)
—— x. 16, see Ready.
—— xi. 33.
Gal. ii. 9, see Right.
—— iii. 19.
—— vi. 11.
Eph. i. 20, see Right.
—— ii. 11, see H (made by.)
—— iv. 28.
Phil iv. 5, see H (at.)
Col. ii. 11, see H (made without.)
—— iii. 1, see Right.
—— iv. 18.
1 Thes. iv. 11.
2 Thes. ii. 2, see H (be at.)
—— iii. 17.
1 Tim. ii. 8.
—— iv. 14.
—— v. 22.
2 Tim. i. 6.
—— iv. 6, see H (be at.)
Philem. 19.
Heb. i. 3, see Right.
—— 10.
—— ii. 7 (*ap.*)
—— vi. 2.
—— viii. 1, see Right.
—— 9.
—— ix. 11, 24, see H (made with.)
—— x. 2, see Right.
—— 31.
—— xii. 2, see Right.
—— 12.
Jas. iv. 8.
1 Pet. iii. 22, see Right.
—— iv. 7, see H (be at.)
—— v. 6.
1 John i. 1.
Rev. i. 3, see H (at.)
—— 16.
—— 17 (*om.* GLTTrAℵ.)
—— 20, } see Right.
—— ii. 1, } see Right.
—— v. 1, 7, } see Right.
—— vi. 5.
—— vii. 9.
—— viii. 4.
—— ix. 20.
—— x. 2, 5, 8, 10.
—— xiii. 16.
—— xiv. 9, 14.
—— xvii. 4.
—— xix. 2.
—— xx. 1, 4.
—— xxii. 10.

HAND (AT.)

ἐγγύς, near, *spoken of place or time, (but more frequently of time;)* nigh at hand.

Matt. xxvi. 18.
John ii. 13.
—— vii. 2.
Phil. iv. 5.
Rev. i. 3.
—— xxii. 10.

HAND (BE AT.)

1. ἐγγίζω, to bring near, cause to approach; *usually intrans.*, to be near, approach.

2. ἐνίστημι, *In N.T. only fut. mid. and perf. act. Intrans.*, to stand in *or* upon, *hence* to stand near, be at hand.

3. ἐφίστημι, *trans.*, to place upon *or* over, to set over. *In N.T. only intrans.*, to place one's self upon *or* near.

1. Matt. iii. 2.
1. —— iv. 17.
1. —— x. 7.
1. —— xxvi. 45, 46.
1. Mark i. 15.
1. Mark xiv. 42.
1. Rom. xiii. 12.
2. 2 Thes. ii. 2.
3. 2 Tim. iv. 6.
1. 1 Pet. iv. 7

HAND (LEAD BY THE.)

χειραγωγέω, to lead by the hand, *(non. occ.)*

Acts ix. 8; xxii. 11.

HAND (SOME TO LEAD BY THE.)

χειραγωγός, a hand-leader, one who leads by the hand, *(non occ.)*

Acts xiii. 11, pl.

HAND (TAKE IN.)

ἐπιχειρέω, to put one's hand to *a work*, set to work at, attempt, make an attempt on.

Luke i. 1.

HAND (WITH ONE'S OWN.)

αὐτόχειρ, doing with one's own hand, *(non occ.)*

Acts xxvii. 19.

HANDS ON (LAY.)

1. κρατέω, to rule, hold sway, *not merely to conquer, but,* to hold the conquered in subjection.

2. πιάζω, to press, to hold fast; *hence,* to lay hold of, seize. *In a judicial sense* to arrest.

1. Matt. xviii. 28.
1. Matt. xxi. 46.
2. John viii. 20.

HANDS (MADE BY.)

χειροποίητος, made with hands; *hence,* artificial, external.

Eph. ii. 11.

HANDS (MADE WITH.)

Acts vii. 48; xvii. 24; Heb. ix. 11, 24.

HANDS (MADE WITHOUT.)

ἀχειροποίητος, not made with hands, *(non occ.)*

Mark xiv. 58.
Col. ii. 11.

HANDS (NOT MADE WITH.)

2 Cor. v. 1.

HANDKERCHIEF (-S.)

σουδάριον, a sweat-cloth, *then,* a napkin *or* handkerchief.

Acts xix. 12.

HANDLE (ED.)

1. ψηλαφάω, to touch, to feel, to handle, *esp.*, to grope, *like a blind man or as in the dark.*

2. θιγγάνω, to touch lightly, just touch. *(The root* θιγ, *answers to the Lat.* te-tig-i, *Eng.* touch, *etc.)*

— Mark xii. 4, see Shamefully.
1 Luke xxiv. 39.
— 2 Cor. iv. 2, see Deceitfully.
2. Col. ii. 21.
1. 1 John i. 1.

HANDMAID.

δούλη, a female slave *or* servant *(esp. of involuntary service,) (non occ.)*

Luke i. 38.

HANDMAIDEN.

Luke i. 48.
Acts ii. 18.

HANDWRITING.

χειρόγραφον, *Eng.* chirography, handwriting; *also* something written by hand.

Col. ii. 14.

HANG (-ED -ETH.)

κρεμάννυμι, to hang, hang up, let hang down.

(a) *Mid.* to be suspended, *(non occ.)*

Matt. xviii. 6.
a. —— xxii. 40.
—— xxvii. 5, see H one's self.
Mark ix. 42, see H about (be.)
Luke xvii. 2, see H about [(be.)
Luke xix. 48, see H on.
—— xxiii. 39.
Acts v. 30.
—— x. 39.
a. —— xxviii. 4
Gal. iii. 13.
Heb. xii. 12, see H down.

HANG DOWN.

παρίημι, to let drop beside *or* at the side, *hence*, to let pass by, pass unnoticed. *Here Pass.*, to be relaxed, slackened, *metaph.* for yielding, giving way, *(non occ.)*

Heb. xii. 12.

HANG ON [marg.]

ἐκκρέμαμαι, to hang from, *esp. of those who listen to a person speaking;* to hang on the lips of *any one.*

Luke xix. 48, text *be very attentive.*

HANG ONE'S SELF.

ἀπάγχομαι, to strangle one's self, *(non occ.)*

Matt. xxvii. 5.

HANGED ABOUT (BE.)

περίκειμαι, to lie around, encompass. *Here Pass.* to be laid *or* put round, *and so*, hung around.

Mark ix. 42. | Luke xvii. 2.

HAPLY (IF.)

1. { εἰ, if, ἄρα, *(cognate with* ἄρω, to fit, marking a correspondence in point of fact) therefore, accordingly, under these circumstances, } if accordingly.

2. { εἰ, if, ἄραγε, by consequence *(more emphatic than* ἄρα, *above,)* } if by consequence

1. Mark xi. 13. | 2. Acts xvii. 27.

HAPLY (LEST.)

1. μήποτε, lest ever, lest once.
2. μήπως, lest in any way, lest by any means.

1. Luke xiv. 29. | 1. Acts v. 39.
2. 2 Cor. ix. 4.

HAPPEN.

1. συμβαίνω, to go with the feet close together, then to come together, *as of things or events*, to happen together, (occ. Acts xx. 19; xxi. 35.)
2. γίνομαι, to begin to be, come into existence, *as implying origin; also, as implying result*, to take place, come to pass, become.

1. Mark x. 32.
1. Luke xxiv. 14.
1. Acts iii. 10.
2. Rom. xi. 25.
1. 1 Cor. x. 11.
— Phil. i. 12, see H unto me (the things which.)
1. 1 Pet. iv. 12.
1. 2 Pet. ii. 22.

HAPPENED UNTO ME (THE THINGS WHICH.)

{ τὰ, the *things*,
κατά, relating to,
ἐμέ, me. }

Phil. i. 12.

HAPPY.

μακάριος, happy, *applied to men; also as applied to God*, blessed, *which it is elsewhere translated.*

John xiii. 17.
Acts xxvi. 2.
Rom. xiv. 22.
1 Cor. vii. 40.
1 Pet. iii. 14.
—— iv. 14.

HAPPY (COUNT.)

μακαρίζω, to call happy, congratulate, (occ. Luke i. 48.)

Jas. v. 11.

HARD.

1. σκληρός, dried up, *i.e.*, dry, stiff, hard; *of voices*, harsh; *of winds*, fierce; *of words*, offensive; *of things done*, grievous.
2. δύσκολος, difficult about one's food, *i.e.*, hard to please, discontented; *then it is applied to anything that is* disagreeable, *noting here the* fastidiousness *with which those who trust in riches receive the humbling truths of the gospel.*

1. Matt. xxv. 24.
2. Mark x. 24.
1. John vi. 60.
1. Acts ix. 5 (*ap.*)
— —— xviii. 7, see Join.
1. Acts xxvi. 14.
— Heb. v. 11, see Uttered.
— 2 Pet. iii. 16, see Understood.
1. Jude 15.

HARDEN (-ED, -ETH.)

1. πωρόω, to make like πῶρος *(a kind of stone), then, gen.*, to make hard, callous.
2. σκληρύνω, to make dry, hard *or* stiff: to make σκληρός, *(see* "HARD," *No.* 1.)

1. Mark vi. 52.
1. —— viii. 17.
1. John xii. 40.
— Acts xix. 9, see H (be.)
2. Rom. ix. 18.
1. Rom. xi. 7, marg. (text *blind.*)
2. Heb. iii. 8.
— —— 13, see H (be.)
2. —— 15.
2. Heb. iv. 7.

HARDENED (BE.)

2. Acts xix. 9, pass. | 2. Heb. iii. 13, pass.

HARDLY.

1. δυσκόλως, *adv. of* HARD, *No.* 2, *(non occ.)*
2. μόγις, with labour, with pain, trouble *or* distress, *(non occ.)*
3. μόλις, with toil *and* moil.

1. Matt. xix. 23.
1. Mark x. 23.
2. Luke ix. 39.
1. —— xviii. 39.
3. Acts xxvii. 8.

HARDNESS.

1. πώρωσις, a hardening, induration, *(denoting the action incomplete and in progress,) (non occ.)*
2. σκληρότης, dryness, hardness resulting from dryness, *(non occ.)*

— Matt. xix. 8, see Heart.
1. Mark iii. 5, marg. *blindness.*
— —— x. 5, see Heart.
— Mark xvi. 14, see Heart.
2. Rom. ii. 5.
1. —— iv. 8, } marg. (text,
1. —— xi. 25, } *blindness.*)
— 2 Tim. ii. 3, see Endure.

HARLOT.

πόρνη, *(fem. of* πόρνος, *from* περνάω, to sell) a harlot, (occ. Rev. xvii. 1, 15, 16; xix. 2.)

Matt. xxi. 31, 32.
Luke xv. 30.
1 Cor. vi. 15, 16.
Heb. xi. 32.
Jas. ii. 25.
Rev. xvii. 5 (πορνεία, *fornication,* A Vm.) marg. *fornication.*

HARM [noun.]

1. κακός, bad, *generically, including every form of evil, moral and physical; in an active sense,* causing evil, *i.e.,* hurtful, baneful, *(elsewhere translated* "EVIL.")
2. πονηρός, causing *or* having labour, sorrow, pain, *denoting the more active form of evil, hence,* evil, malignant, *(elsewhere translated* "EVIL.")
3. ἄτοπος, out of place, *hence,* unusual, strange; *then,* unnatural, disgusting, foul.
4. ὑβρίς, wanton violence *arising from the pride of strength, passion or lust, etc. Used also of* loss by the sea *arising from its violence.*

1. Acts xvi. 28.
4. —— xxvii. 21.
1. Acts xxviii. 5.
3. —— 6.
2. Acts xxviii. 21.

HARM [verb.]

κακόω, to affect with evil, to do evil to any one.

1 Pet. iii. 13.

HARMLESS.

1. ἄκακος, without κακός, *(see* "HARM," *No.* 1), void of evil, (occ. Rom. xvi. 18.)
2. ἀκέραιος, unmixed, pure, guileless, *(non occ.)*

2. Matt. x. 16, marg. *simple*
2. Rom. xvi. 19, marg. (text *sincere.*)
2. Phil. ii. 15, marg. *sincere.*
1. Heb. vii. 26.

HARP [noun.]

κιθάρα, *the Lat.* cithara, *whence Eng.* guitar. *Sept. for* כִּנּוֹר, Gen. xxxi. 27; 1 Chron. ix. 11. *Josephus describes the Heb. word* (κινύρα,) as having ten strings and as struck with a key (Ant. vii. 12, 3), *(non occ.)*

1 Cor. xiv. 7.
Rev. v. 8.
Rev. xiv. 2.
—— xv. 2.

HARP (-ING) [verb.]

κιθαρίζω, to play upon the κιθάρα, *(see above,) (non occ.)*

1 Cor. xiv. 7. | Rev. xiv. 2.

HARPER (-S.)

κιθαρῳδός, one who plays and sings to a κιθάρα, *(see* HARP,) *(non occ.)*

Rev. xiv. 2; xviii. 22.

HARVEST.

θερισμός, harvest, harvesting, (LXX. for קָצִיר, Jer. v. 17,) *(non occ.)*

Matt. ix. 37, 38 twice.
—— xiii. 30 twice, 39.
Mark iv. 29.
Luke x. 2 3 times.
John iv. 35 twice.
Rev. xiv. 15.

HASTE [noun.]

σπουδή, speed, haste, *esp. as manifested in earnestness, diligence, zeal.*

Mark vi. 25. | Luke i. 39.

HASTE (WITH.)

σπεύδω, *trans.* to urge on, to hasten. *In N.T. intrans.* to urge one's self on, to make haste, *having respect simply to time, (thus differing from* σπουδάζω.)

Luke ii. 16, part.

HASTE (-ED, -ING) [verb.]

σπεύδω, *see* "HASTE (WITH.)"

Acts xx. 16.
2 Pet. iii. 12, marg. (text, *haste unto.*)

HASTE (MAKE.)

Luke xix. 5, 6.

HASTE UNTO.

2 Pet. iii. 12, marg. *Haste.*

HASTILY.

ταχέως, quickly, speedily, *(gen. used of speed.)*

John xi. 31.

HATE (-ED, -EST, -ETH, -ING) [verb.]

μισέω, to hate, *usually implying active ill-will in words and conduct, or a persecuting spirit. (In antithesis to* αγαπάω) to love less, not to love, to slight.

Matt. v. 43, 44 (*ap.*)
— vi. 24.
— x. 22.
— xxiv. 9, 10.
Mark xiii. 13.
Luke i. 71.
— vi. 22, 27.
— xiv. 26.
— xvi. 13.
— xix. 14.
— xxi. 17.
John iii. 20.
— vii. 7 twice.
— xii. 25.
— xv. 18 twice, 19, 23, 24, 25.
John xvii. 14.
Rom. vii. 15.
— ix. 13.
Eph. v. 29.
Titus iii. 3.
Heb. i. 9.
1 John ii. 9, 11.
— iii. 13, 15.
— iv. 20.
Jude 23.
Rev. ii. 6 twice.
— 15 (ὁμοίως, *in like manner*, instead of, ὃ μισῶ, *which thing I hate,* G L T Tr A ℵ.)
— xvii. 16.

HATEFUL.

1. μισέω, *see above; here, pass. part.*

2. στυγητός, hated, abominated, horrid; to be hated, hateful, *(a stronger word than No.* 1, *used of hatred shown, not merely felt.)*

2. Titus iii. 3. | 1. Rev. xviii. 2, pass. part.

HATER.

See, GOD.

HATRED.

ἔχθρα, enmity, *(as it is elsewhere translated.)*

Gal. v. 20.

HAVE (-ING, -HAD, -HAST, -HATH.)

When not the auxiliary to other verbs.

1. ἔχω, to have, to hold, *i.e.*, to have and hold, *implying present, continued having, or lasting possession.*
2. ἀπέχω, *(No.* 1, *with* ἀπό, away from, *prefixed)* to hold off from; *also,* to have off *or* out, *i.e.*, to have all that is one's due, *so as* to cease from having *any more;* to have received in full.
3. κατέχω, *(No.* 1, *with* κατά, down, *prefixed)* to have and hold fast, to hold firmly; *Pass. as here,* to be held down.
4. γίνομαι, to begin to be, come into existence, *implying* origin *either from natural causes or special agency,* to be made, arise, come to pass, happen, come to have, become.
5. λαμβάνω, to take *as with the hand;* to receive.
6. μεταλαμβάνω, *(No.* 5, *with* μετά, with, *prefixed)* to take a part *or* share of *anything, prop.* with *others, then, to* obtain.
7. ὑπάρχω, to begin, to be originally, *by birth or by primary and essential condition. (No.* 4, *implies change of state or condition,* while No. 7, calls attention to the original condition), *hence,* to possess.
8. ἀντιβάλλω, to throw in one's turn, *as a weapon, then, referring to words,* to converse, exchange words, *(non occ.)*

9. εἰμί, to be, to exist, to have existence.

(a) ἐστί, *(3rd. pers. sing. pres. tense)* it is.

* *with Dat.* is to me, is *to him, or* for *him.*

† *with Gen.* of *this*...is, etc.

‡ *with* ἐν, in; is in, [*i.e.*, if there is in you any, etc.]

(b) εἰσί, *(3rd pers. pl. pres. tense) with Dat.* there are to *us, i.e.,* we have.

(c) ἦν, *(3rd pers. sing. Imperfect tense)* he, she, or it was.

* *with Dat.* there was, *or* were to *us, or them, i.e.,* they had.

† *with* ἔχων, having *(part. of No.* 1), was having.

(d) ἔσται, etc. *(Future)* he, she, *or* it shall be, shall there be, *or* there shall be to *him, or us, etc.*

* *with Gen.*, shall be *theirs.*

† *with Dat.*, shall be to *him, her, or them.*

(e) οὖσα, *(pres. participle fem.) with* ἐν, in, *being in, i.e.,* having.

1. Matt. iii. 4, 9, 14.
— —— iv. 24, see Palsey.
1. —— v. 23.
— ——— 40, see Let.
1. ——— 46.
1. —— vi. 1.
— ——— 2 1st, see Glory.
2. ——— 2 2nd, 5.
1. ——— 8.
2. ——— 16.
— ——— 32, see Need.
1. —— vii. 29.
1. ——viii. 9, 20 1st & 3rd.
— ——— 29, see H we to do with thee (what.)
1. —— ix. 6.
— ——— 13, see Will.
1. ——— 36.
— —— xi. 5, see Gospel.
1. ——— 15, 18.
— —— xii. 7 2nd, see Will.
1. ——— 10, 11.
1. —— xiii. 5 twice, 6, 9, 12 1st.
— ——— 12 2nd, see Abundance.
1. ——— 12 3rd & 4th, 21, 27, 43, 44, 46.
1. —— xiv. 4, 17.
— ——— 35, see Knowledge
1. —— xv. 30, 32, 34.
1. —— xvii. 20.
1. —— xviii. 8, 9.
4. ——— 12.
1. ———25 1st part, 25 2nd.
— ———26, 29, see Patience
— ——— 33 1st, see Compassion.
— ——— 33 2nd, see Pity.
1. —— xix. 16 (κληρονομήσω, *inherit,* Lm ℵ.)
— ——— 21 1st, see H (that one.)

1. Matt. xix. 21 2nd.
9c†——— 22.
9d†——— 27.
1. —— xxi. 3, 21, 28.
1. —— xxii. 12, 24, 25 2nd, 28.
— —— xxiii. 30 twice, see Been.
— —— xxv. 21, 23, see Been.
1. ——— 25, 28, 29 1st.
— ——— 29 2nd, see Abundance.
1. ——— 29 3rd & 4th.
1. —— xxvi. 7.
— ——— 8, see Indignation
1. ——— 11 twice, 65 2nd.
1. —— xxvii. 16.
— ——— 19, see H thou nothing to do with.
— ——— 24, see Been.
— ——— 43, see Will.
1. ——— 65.
1. Mark i. 22.
— ——— 24, see H we to do with thee (what.)
1. —— ii. 10, 17, 19 (*ap.*), 25.
1. —— iii. 1, 3, 10 2nd, 15, 22, 26, 29, 30.
1. —— iv. 5 twice, 6, 9, 17, 23, 25 3 times, 40.
1. —— v. 3.
— ——— 7, see H I to do with thee (what.)
1. ——— 15 (*om.* G⥵.)
9e. ——— 25.
— ——— 26 3rd, see H (that one.)
2. —— vi. 2, 5, 16.
1. ——— 18 2nd.
— ——— 19 1st, see Quarrel
— ——— 31, see Leisure.

1. Mark vi. 34.
1. ——— 36, (τί φάγωσιν, *something to eat,* instead of ἄρτους τι γὰρ φάγωσιν ουκ ἔχουσιν, *bread, for they have nothing to eat,* G∾ Lb T Tr Aℵ.)
1. ——— 38.
1. —— vii. 16, 25.
— ——— 32, see Impediment.
1. —— viii. 1, 2 3rd, 5, 7, 14 2nd, 16, 17 twice, 18 twice.
1. —— ix. 17 2nd, 43, 45, 47, 50 2nd.
— ——— 50 3rd, see Peace.
1. —— x. 21 twice.
9c†——— 22.
1. ——— 23.
1. —— xi. 3, 13, 22.
9d†——— 23, 24.
1. ——— 25.
1. —— xii. 6.
5. ——— 22 (*om.* ἔλαβον αὐτὴν καὶ, *had her and,* Lb T Tr A ℵ.)
1. ——— 23, 44.
1. —— xiv. 3.
— ——— 4, see Indignation
1. ——— 7 twice.
— ——— 51, see Cast.
— Luke i. 3, see Understanding.
9c*——— 7.
9d†——— 14.
1. —— iii. 8, 11 3 times.
— —— iv. 16, see Been.
1. ——— 33.
— ——— 34, see H we to do with (what.)
1. ——— 40.
1. —— v. 24.
1. —— vi. 8.
9a*——— 32, 33, 34.
1. —— vii. 8, 33, 40.
9c*——— 41.
1. ——— 42, part.
— —— viii. 2, see Been.
1. ——— 8, 13, 18 3 times, 27
— ——— 28, see H I to do with thee (what.)
9c*——— 42.
9e ——— 43.
1. —— ix. 3, 11.
9b ——— 13.
1. ——— 58 1st & 3rd.
9c*—— x. 39.
1. —— xi. 5, 6, 36.
1. —— xii. 4, 5 2nd, 17, 19.
9a*——— 24.
— ——— 30, see Need.
— ——— 33, 44, see H (that one.)
1. ——— 50.
1. —— xiii. 6, 11.
9d†—— xiv. 10.
1. ——— 18, 19.
— ———28, see H sufficient
— ——— 33, see H (that one.)
1. ——— 35.
1. —— xv. 4, 8, 11.
— ——— 17, see Spare.
— ——— 31, see H (that are.)
1. —— xvi. 1, 28, 29.
1. —— xvii. 6, 7.
1. —— xviii. 22 twice, 24.
1. —— xix. 17 (with εἰμί,) 24, 25, 26 3 times, 31, 34
1 —— xx. 24, 28, 33.
1. —— xxi. 4 3rd.
1. —— xxii. 36 twice, 37.
8. —— xxiv. 17.
1. ——— 39 twice, 41.
1. John ii. 3.

— John ii. 4, see H I to do with thee (what.)
— —— iii. 10, see Drunk.
1. ——— 15, 16, 29, 36.
— —— iv. 9, see Dealings.
1. ———11 twice, 17 1st & 3rd, with (have), 18 twice, 32, 44.
1. —— v. 2.
3. ——— 4 (*ap.*)
1. ——— 5 (*with* ἐν *in*), 7, 24, 26 1st & 3rd, 36 1st, 38 1st, 39, 40, 42.
1. —— vi. 9, 40, 47, 53, 54, 68.
1. —— vii. 20.
1. —— viii. 6 (*ap.*), 12, 26 1st.
— ——— 37, see Peace.
1. ——— 41, 48, 49, 52.
— —— ix. 18 1st, see Been.
1. ——— 41.
1. —— x. 10 twice, 16, 18 1st & 2nd, 20.
— ——— 21, see Devil.
1. —— xii. 6, 8 twice, 35, 36, 48.
1. —— xiii. 8, 29 1st & 3rd, 35.
1. —— xiv. 21, 30.
1. —— xv. 13, 22 2nd 3rd & 4th, 34.
1. —— xvi. 12, 15, 21, 22, 33 2nd & 3rd.
1. —— xvii. 5, 13.
1. —— xviii. 10.
9a*——— 39.
1. —— xix. 7, 10 twice.
— ——— 11 1st, see H (can).
1. ——— 11 2nd, 15.
1. —— xx. 31.
1. —— xxi. 5.
1. Acts ii. 44, 45, 47.
7. —— iii. 6 1st.
1. ——— 6 2nd.
— —— iv. 13, see Been.
9c*——— 32.
1. ——— 35.
7. ——— 37.
— —— v.34, see Reputation
— —— vii. 5, see H no (when as yet he).
9c*——— 44 1st.
— ——viii. 11 1st, see Regard
9a*——— 21.
— ——— 27 1st, see Change
— —— ix. 6, see Will.
1. ——— 14, 31.
1. —— xiii. 5.
9a‡——— 15.
1. —— xiv. 9.
— ——— 26, see Been.
4. Acts xv. 2, part.
1. ——— 21.
— —— xvi. 3, see Will.
— —— xvii. 13, see Knowledge.
— ——— 28 1st, see Being.
9a*—— xviii. 10.
1. ——— 18.
1. —— xix. 13.
9a†——— 25.
1. ——— 38.
9c*—— xxi. 9.
9b. ——— 23 1st.
1. ——— 23 2nd.
— —— xxii. 12, see Report
1. —— xxiii. 17, 18, 19, 29
— ——— 30, see Against.
— —— xxiv. 10 2nd, see Been.
1. ——— 15, 16, 19 2nd.
— ——— 22, see Knowledge
1. ——— 23.
6. ——— 25.
1. —— xxv. 16 1st.
5. ——— 16 2nd.
1. ——— 19, 26 1st.

— Acts xxv. 26 2nd, see Bring forth.
— —— 26 3rd, see Had (be).
1. —— 26 4th.
— —— xxvii. 16, see Work
1. —— xxviii. 9, 19, 29 2nd (*ap.*)
— Rom. i. 10, see Journey
— —— 13 1st, see Will.
1. —— 13 2nd.
1. —— ii. 14 twice, 20.
1. —— iv. 2.
1. —— v. 1 (ἔχωμεν, *let us have*, instead of ἔχομεν *we have*, GLmTTrA א.)
1. —— 2, pluperf.
— —— vi. 9, 14, see Dominion.
1. —— 21, 22.
— —— vii. 1, see Dominion
— —— 2, see Husband.
1. —— viii. 9, 23.
9a* —— ix. 2.
9d† —— 9.
1. —— 21.
1. —— x. 2.
1. —— xii. 4 twice, 6.
1. —— xiii. 3.
1. —— xiv. 22 twice.
1. —— xv. 4, 17, 23 twice.
— —— xvi. 2 1st, see Need
1. 1 Cor. ii. 16.
4. —— iv. 5.
1. —— 7.
— —— 11, see Dwelling-place.
1. —— 15.
1. —— v. 1.
1. —— vi. 1, 4, 19.
1. —— vii. 2 twice.
— —— 4 twice, see Power
1. —— 7, 12, 13, 25 1st, 28 3rd, 29 twice, 37 1st & 2nd, 40.
1. —— viii. 1.
— —— 8 1st, marg., see *More.*
— —— 8 2nd, marg., see *Less.*
1. —— 10.
1. —— ix. 4, 5, 6.
9a* —— 16.
1. —— 17.
— —— x. 20, see Fellowship
— —— xi. 3, see Will.
1. —— 4, 10.
— —— 14, 15, see Hair.
1. —— 16, 22 twice.
• — —— xii. 1, see Will.
1. —— 12, 21 twice, 23, 24 1st.
— —— 25, see Care.
1. —— 30.
1. —— xiii. 1, 2 3 times, 3.
1. —— xiv. 26 5 times.
— —— xv. 19, see Hope.
1. —— 31, 34.
— —— xvi. 12, see Convenient.
1. 2 Cor. i. 9.
— —— 12, see Conversation.
1. —— 15.
— —— 24, see Dominion
1. —— ii. 3 1st.
— —— 3 2nd, see Confidence.
1. —— 4, 13.
1. —— iii. 4.
— —— 10, see Glory.
1. —— 12, part.
1. —— iv. 1 1st, part., 7, 13 1st.
1. —— v. 1, 12.
1. —— vi. 10.
1. —— vii. 1, 5.
— —— 16, see Confidence

1. 2 Cor. viii. 11, 12 twice.
— —— 15 1st, not in the Greek.
— —— 15 2nd, see Over.
— —— 15 3rd, not in the Greek.
— —— 15 4th, see Lack.
— —— ix. 5, see Notice.
1. —— 8.
1. —— x. 6, 15.
1. Gal. ii. 4.
— —— iii. 21, see Been.
1. —— iv. 22, 27 2nd.
— —— v. 10, see Confidence
1. —— vi. 4, 10.
— —— 13, see Circumcised.
1. Eph. i. 7.
— —— ii. 3, see Conversation.
1. —— 12, 18.
1. —— iii. 12.
1. —— iv. 28.
1. —— v. 5.
— —— 11, see Fellowship
1. —— 27.
— —— vi. 14 1st, see Gird.
— —— 14 2nd, see H on.
1. Phil. i. 7, 23.
— —— 25, see Confidence
1. —— 30.
1. —— ii. 2, 20, 27 2nd.
— —— iii. 3, see Confidence.
1. —— 4 1st.
— —— 4 2nd, see Trust.
1. —— 9, 17.
2. —— iv. 18 1st, marg. *have received.*
1. Col. i. 14.
— —— 18, see Pre-eminence.
1. —— ii. 1 1st.
— —— 19, see Ministered
1. —— 23 (with εἰμί, *are things having.*)
1. —— iii. 13.
1. —— iv. 1, 13.
1. 1 Thes. i. 9.
1. —— iii. 6.
1. —— iv. 12.
— —— 13 1st, see Will.
1. —— 13 2nd.
1. —— v. 1.
— 2 Thes. ii. 12, see Pleasure
— —— iii. 1, see Course.
— —— 4, see Confidence
1. —— 9.
— —— 14, see Company
— 1 Tim. ii. 4, see Will.
1. —— iii. 4, 7.
1. —— iv. 8.
1. —— v. 4, 12 1st, 16.
1. —— vi. 2, 8, 16 1st.
1. 2 Tim. i. 3.
1. —— ii. 19.
1. —— iii. 5.
— —— iv. 3, see Itching.
1. Titus i. 6.
1. —— ii. 8.
1. Philem. 5, 7.
— —— 20, see Joy.
— —— 21, see Confidence
1. Heb. ii. 14.
1. —— iii. 3 2nd.
— —— iv. 13, see H to do (with whom.)
1. —— 14, part, 15.
1. —— v. 12 1st, 12 2nd, part., 14.
1. —— vi. 18 1st, 19.
1. —— vii. 3, 5, 6, 24, 28.
1. —— viii. 1 2nd, 3.
— —— 7, see Been.
1. —— ix. 1, 4 twice.
1. —— x. 1, 2.
— —— 6, 8, see Pleasure
1. —— 19, 34 2nd, 35, 36 1st.

— Heb. x. 38, see Pleasure
— —— xi. 5 2nd, see Testimony.
1. —— 10, 15 2nd.
— —— 26, see Respect.
5. —— 36.
1. —— xii. 9.
1. —— 28, marg. *hold fast.*
— —— xiii. 5 1st, see H (such things as one.)
— —— 7 1st, see Rule.
1. —— 10 twice, 14.
— —— 17, see Rule.
1. —— 18.
1. Jas. i. 4.
1. —— ii. 1.
— —— 3, see Respect.
1. —— 14 twice, 17, 18 twice
1. —— iii. 14.
1. —— iv. 2 1st.
— —— 2 2nd, see Desire.
1. —— 2 3rd.
— —— v. 7, see Patience.
1. 1 Pet. ii. 12.
1. —— iii. 16.
1. —— iv. 8.
— 2 Pet. i. 15, see Remembrance.
1. —— 19.
1. —— ii. 14 twice.
— —— 21 1st, see Been.
1. 1 John i. 3 2nd, 6, 7, 8.
1. —— ii. 1, 7 1st.
— —— 19, see Been.
1. —— 23 twice (*ap.*), 28.
1. —— iii. 3, 15, 17 twice, 21.
1. —— iv. 16 2nd, 17, 18, 21
1. —— v. 10 1st, 12 4 times, 13 2nd, 14, 15.
1. 2 John 5, 9 twice, 12.

1. 3 John 4.
— —— 9, see Pre-eminence.
— —— 12, see Report.
1. —— 13.
— Jude 16, see Admiration
1. —— 19.
1. Rev. i 16, 18.
1. —— ii. 3 2nd, 4 1st, 6, 7, 10, 11, 12, 14 twice, 15, 17, 18, 20, 24 1st, 25, 29
1. —— iii. 1 twice, 4 1st, 6, 7, 8 2nd, 11, 13, 17, 22.
1. —— iv. 4, *om.* A L T Tr A א.
1. —— 7, 8.
1. —— v. 6, 8 2nd.
1. —— vi. 2, 5 2nd.
1. —— vii. 2.
1. —— viii. 3, 6, 9.
1. —— ix. 3, 4, 8, 9, 10, 11 twice, 14, 17, 19.
1. —— x. 2.
1. —— xi. 6 twice.
1. —— xii. 3, 6, 12 twice, 17
1. —— xiii. 1, 9, 11.
— —— 14 1st, see Power.
1. —— 14 2nd.
— —— 15, see Power.
1. —— 17, 18.
1. —— xiv. 1, 6, 11, 14, 17, 18 twice.
1. —— xv. 1, 2, 6 1st.
— —— 6 2nd, see Gird.
1. —— xvi. 2, 9.
1. —— xvii. 1, 3, 4, 7, 9, 13
1. —— xviii. 1, 19.
1. —— xix. 10, 12, 16.
1. —— xx. 1, 6 twice.
1. —— xxi. 9, 11, 12 twice, 14, 15, 23.
9d* —— xxii. 14.

HAVE (CAN.)

1 John xix. 11.

HAVE ON.

ἐνδύω, to go in, to envelope, to cause to go into a garment, *i.e.*, to clothe, *Mid.*, to clothe one's self, *Pass.*, to be clothed.

Eph. vi. 14, Mid.

HAVE SUFFICIENT.

1. Luke xiv. 28.

HAVE THOU NOTHING TO DO WITH.

{ μηδέν, nothing, σοι, to thee, } *let* nothing *arise or happen* between thee and, *etc.*

Matt. xxvii. 19.

HAVE I TO DO WITH THEE (WHAT.)

τί, what,
ἐμοὶ, to me,
καὶ, and,
σόι, to thee.

Mark v. 7. | John ii. 4. | Luke viii. 28.

HAVE WE TO DO WITH THEE (WHAT.)

τὶ, what,
ὑμῖν, to us,
καὶ, and,
σοι, to thee.

Matt. viii. 29. | Luke iv. 34. | Mark i. 24.

HAVE TO DO (WITH WHOM.)

πρὸς, unto,
ὅν, whom,
ἡμῖν, to us,
ὁ λόγος, the account,
} unto whom *is* our account.

Heb. iv. 13.

HATH (SUCH THINGS AS ONE.)

τὰ, the *things*,
πάροντα, present.

Heb. xiii. 5.

HATH (THAT ONE.)

1. τὰ, the *things*,
ὑπάρχοντα, present, in hand *to any one, i.e.*, possessions, substance.

2. τὰ, the *things*,
παρά, beside and at,
} the things with, *or*, that one has.

3. τὰ, the *things*,
ἐμά, mine,
} my possessions.

1. Matt. xix. 21, with σοῦ, "*thy.*"
2. Mark v. 26, with ἑαυτῆς, "*she herself*" (but αὐτῆς, "*she,*" G L T Tr A.)
1. Luke xii. 33, with ὑμῶν, "*your.*"
1. —— 44, with αὐτοῦ, ["*his.*"
1. —— xiv. 33, with ἑαυτοῦ,
3. —— xv. 31. ["*his own.*"

HAD (BE.)

γίνομαι, *see* "HAVE," *No.* 4.

Acts xxv. 26, part.

HAD NO (WHEN AS YET HE.)

οὐκ, not,
ὄντος, being,
αὐτῷ, to him,
} *there* not being to him, *or*, he not having.

Acts vii. 5.

See also, COMPASSION and MERCY.

HAVEN.

λιμήν, a harbour, haven, creek; a refuge or retreat, *rather than a landing place (equivalent to* ὅρμος), *(non occ.)*

Acts xxvii. 12 twice.

See, FAIR.

HAVOC OF (MAKE.)

λυμαίνομαι, to treat outrageously, *esp. of personal injuries;* ravage *as savage beasts,* destroy *the sheep and* lay waste *the fruits of the earth, (non occ.)*

Acts viii. 3.

HAY.

χόρτος, an enclosed place, *(from the same root comes Lat.*, chors, cohors, *as also* hortus, *and Eng.*, garden, *also akin to* χορός, cour, court.) *Hence always with the notion of* feeding place; *then* food, fodder, *esp. of cattle*, grass, hay.

1 Cor. iii. 12.

HAZARD (-ED.)

παραδίδωμι, to give *or* hand over *to another*, to deliver up.

Acts xv. 26.

HE.

The pronoun "HE" is generally part of the translation of the verb.

Very frequently it is the translation of the prepositive article (ὁ).

(a) before nouns, adjectives, and numerals, "*he that is*," etc., of which there are upwards of 250 instances.

(b) before participles, "*he that*," or, "*he which*," of which there are 1200 instances, or

(c) before adverbs and prepositions, "*he that is*," "*the things which are*," etc., of which there are 279 instances.

When "HE" is not the translation of any of the above, but the equivalent of a separate Greek word, it is emphatic, and is the translation of one of these below.

1. ἐκεῖνος, the person there, that person. *Strictly it refers to what has gone immediately before, but when No.* 2 *and No.* 1 *refer to two things before mentioned, No.* 1 *belongs to the more remote, and is generally connected with the third person. Its use always marks special distinction either of credit or discredit.*

2. οὗτος, this, this person here, *mostly used to refer to the latter of two objects, as being the nearer to the subject, and connected with the second person. It is always emphatic.*

3. αὐτός, very, self, *joined with each of the persons, with the third pers., not simply* he, *but* he himself, he and no other. *Always emphatic.*

4. τίς, any one, a certain one, *when emphatic, it denotes* somebody important, something great.

5. ὅδε, this one, this one here, *marking a closer relation than No.* 2.

3. Matt. i. 21.
— —— iii. 11 1st, H that, see Come.
3. —— 11 2nd.
— —— v. 26, see Have.
3. —— viii. 24.
— —— x. 38, see H that.
3. —— xii. 3 2nd (*om.* G L T Tr A ℵ.)
2. —— xiii. 22 2nd, 23 2nd.
3. —— xiv. 2.
— —— xv. 18, see H (and)
3. —— xvi. 20 2nd.
— —— xx. 4, see H (and.)
3. —— xxi. 27.
— —— xxiii. } see H
— —— xxv. 17 1st, } that.
3. —— 17 2nd (*om.* G→ L T Tr Ab ℵ.)
2. —— xxvii. 58.
3. Mark i. 8.
3. —— ii. 25 1st (*om.* G→ Lb Tr ℵ.)
3. —— 25 3rd.
3. —— iii. 13 2nd.
— —— 29, see H that.
— —— iv. 25 1st & 2nd, see H that.
3. —— 27, 38.
2&3 —— vi. 16 2nd (*om.* No. 3, G Lb T Tr ℵ.)
3. Mark vi. 45 2nd, 47.
3. —— vii. 36 2nd (*om.* L T Tr A ℵ.)
3. —— viii. 29.
— —— ix. 40, see H that.
3. —— xii. 21 (*ap.*)
3. —— xiv. 15.
3. Luke i 17, 22 4th.
2. —— 32.
3. —— ii. 28.
3. —— iii. 15, 16.
3. —— iv. 15, 30.
3. —— v. 1, 14, 16, 17.
3. —— vi. 8 1st, 20, 35.
3. —— vii. 5 2nd.
3. —— viii. 1, 22 1st, 37.
3. —— 41 1st (No. 2, L Tr.)
3. —— 54.
3. —— ix. 51 2nd.
— —— x. 1, see H himself
3. —— 38.
— —— xi. 7, see H (and.)
3. —— 17, 28.
3. —— xv. 14 2nd.
3. —— xvi. 24 1st.
6. —— 25 (ὧδε, *here*, G∾ L T Tr A ℵ.)
3. —— xvii. 11 2nd, 16.
3. —— xviii. 39 2nd.
2. —— xix. 2 (No. 3, L Tr *om.* T ℵ.)
3. Luke xix. 9.
— —— xxii. 12, see H (and)
3. —— 41.
— —— xxiii. 2, see H himself.
3. —— 9 2nd.
2. —— 22 2nd, 35 2nd.
3. —— xxiv, 21, 25, 28 1st, 31.
1. John i. 18.
3. —— 27 (*om.* αὐτός, ἐστιν, *he it is*, G Lb T Tr A ℵ.)
2. —— 42.
3. —— ii. 12 2nd.
1. —— 21.
3. —— 25.
1. —— iii. 30.
1. —— iv. 25 1st.
2. —— 47 1st.
1. —— v. 19 2nd, 35, 38, 46.
— —— vi. 6 2nd, 15, see H himself.
1. —— 29.
2. —— 42 (*om.* G→ Lb Tr A.)
2. —— 46 2nd.
— —— 57 2nd, see H (even.)
2. —— 71 2nd.
— —— vii. 4, see H himself
3. —— 10.
1. —— 11.
— —— 29, see H himself
2. —— 35 1st.
1. —— viii. 42, 44 1st.
1. —— ix. 9 3rd, 11 1st, 12 1st.
3. —— 21 2nd (*om.* T Tr ℵ.)
3. —— 21 3rd.
1. —— 25st, 36st, 37.
3. —— xii. 49.
1. —— xiii. 25, 26 1st, 30
3. —— xiv. 10.
— —— 12 2nd, see H also
1. —— 21 2nd, 26.
1. —— xv. 26.
1. —— xvi. 8 2nd, 13 1st, 14 1st.
3. —— xviii. 1 2nd.
1. —— 17, 25.
2. —— 30.
1. —— xix. 21.
— —— 35 2nd, see H (and.)
— Acts ii. 34, see H himself.
2. —— iii. 10 (No. 3, G L T Tr A ℵ.)
1. —— 13 (No. 3, G∾ Trb Ab.) (*om.* L T ℵ.)
2. —— iv. 9.
4. —— 35.
— —— v. 37, see H also.
3. —— vii. 15.
2. —— 36 1st.
2. —— ix. 15, 20 2nd, 21 1st.
2. —— x. 6 1st, 6 2nd (*ap.*)
2. —— 32 1st, 36.
3. —— 42 2nd (No. 2, G∾ L.)
3. Acts xiv. 12.
3. —— xvi. 33 2nd.
2. —— xvii. 24.
3. —— 25 2nd.
— —— xviii. 19 1st (should be "*They.*")
3. —— 19 2nd.
— —— 19 3rd, see H himself.
2. —— 26.
— —— xix. 22 2nd, see H himself.
3. —— xx. 35.
— —— xxv. 4, 25, see H himself.
3. —— xxviii. 6 2nd.
2. Rom. viii. 9.
— —— 32 1st, see H that
— 1 Cor. ii. 15 2nd, see H himself.
— —— iii. 15 2nd, see H himself.
3. —— vii. 13 (No. 2, G∾ L T Tr A ℵ.)
— 2 Cor. viii. 15 twice, see H that.
3. —— x. 7 2nd.
1. —— 18.
3. Eph. ii. 14.
3. —— iv. 11.
3. —— v. 23, 27.
3. Col. i. 17, 18 twice.
— 2 Tim. ii. 12, see H also
1. —— 13 1st.
3. Heb. i. 5 2nd.
3. —— ii. 14 1st.
— —— 18 1st, see H himself.
3. —— iv. 10 2nd.
— —— v. 2, see H himself
4. —— x. 28.
3. Jas. i. 13 2nd.
2. —— 23.
2. —— 25 1st (*om.* G→ L T Tr A ℵ.)
3. 1 John i. 7.
3. —— ii. 2.
1. —— 6 3rd.
2. —— 22 2nd.
3. —— 25.
1. —— iii. 3, 5, 7 2nd, 16.
3. —— 24 2nd.
3. —— iv. 10, 13 1st, 15.
1. —— 17.
3. —— 19 (ὁ θεός, L.)
2. 2 John 9 2nd.
— 3 John 10 2nd, see H himself.
3. Rev. iii. 20.
— —— xiii. 10 twice, see H that.
3. —— xiv. 17.
3. —— xvii. 11.
— —— xix. 12 2nd, see H himself.
3. —— 15 2nd & 3rd.
3. —— xxi. 7 2nd.

HE ALSO.

κἀκεῖνος, *see* "HE (AND)."

John xiv. 12. | Acts v. 37. | 2 Tim. ii. 12.

HE HIMSELF.

1. αὐτός, *see* "HE," *No.* 3.

2. { αὐτός, *see* "HE," *No.* 3, / οὗτος, this, } this [man] himself.

3. ἑαυτός, one's self, himself, *(reflexive of No.* 1.)

1. Luke x. 1.
3. —— xxiii. 2.
1. John vi. 6, 15.
1. —— vii. 4.
1. Acts ii. 34.
1. —— xviii. 19.
1. —— xix. 22.
3. Acts xxv. 4.
2. ——— 25.
1. 1 Cor. ii. 15.
1. —— iii. 15.
1. Heb. ii. 18.
1. —— v. 2.
1. 3 John 10.
1. Rev. xix. 12.

HE THAT.

This is generally the translation of the *art.* with *preposition.* When it is not it is one of these following.

1. εἴ τις, if any one.
2. ὅς, *rel. pron.*, who, which, he who.
   * *with* ἄν, *a particle expressing* possibility, uncertainty, *or* conditionality.
3. ὅσγε, who even, *marking a greater in ref. to a less, (non occ.)*
4. ὅστις, whosoever.

2. Matt. x. 38.
4. —— xxiii. 12.
2* Mark iii. 29.
2* Mark iv. 25 (*om.* ἄν, L T Tr ℵ.)
2. —— ix. 40.
3. Rom. viii. 32.
1. Rev. xiii. 10 twice.

...HE (AND.)

κἀκεῖνος, *(No.* 1 *with* καί, and, even, also, *prefixed,)* and he (the person there.)

Matt. xv. 18.
—— xx. 4.
Luke xi. 7.
Luke xxii. 12.
John vii. 29.
—— xix. 35 2nd.
Acts xviii. 19.

HE (EVEN.)

John vi. 57.

See also, I, HIM, HIS, WE, YE, THEY, THEM, etc.

HEAD.

κεφαλή, the head *of man or beast*, the head *or* chief part of anything.

Matt. v. 36.
—— vi. 17.
—— viii. 20.
—— x. 30.
—— xiv. 8, 11.
—— xxi. 42.
—— xxvi. 7.
—— xxvii. 29, 30, 37, 39.
Mark vi. 24, 25, 27, 28.
—— xii. 4, see H (wound in the.)
——— 10.
—— xiv. 3.
—— xv. 19, 29.
Luke vii. 38.
——— 44 (*om.* G L T Tr A ℵ.)
——— 46.
—— ix 58.
—— xii. 7.
—— xx. 17.
—— xxi. 18, 28.
John xiii. 9.
—— xix. 2, 30.
—— xx. 7, 12.
Acts iv. 11.
—— xviii. 6, 18.
—— xxi, 24.
—— xxvii. 34.
Rom xii. 20.
1 Cor. xi. 3 3 times, 4 twice, 5 twice, 7, 10.
—— xii. 21.
Eph. i. 22.
—— iv. 15.
—— v. 23 twice.
Col. i. 18.
—— ii. 10, 19.
1 Pet. ii. 7.
Rev. i. 14.
—— iv. 4.
—— ix. 7, 17 twice, 19.
—— x. 1.
—— xii. 1, 3 twice.
—— xiii. 1 twice, 3.
—— xiv. 14.
—— xvii. 3, 7, 9.
—— xviii. 19.
—— xix. 12.

HEAD (WOUND IN THE HEAD.)

κεφαλαιόω, to bring under heads, sum up briefly: *so here* they made short work of it. *The word is nowhere used of wounding in the head, and a new sense should be not affixed without evident necessity, (non occ.)*

Mark xii. 4.

HEADLONG (CAST DOWN.)

κατακρημνίζω, to cast down from a precipice, *(non occ.)*

Luke iv. 29.

HEADLONG (FALL.)

{ πρηνής, bending forward, prostrate,
{ γενόμενος, becoming,
} falling headlong.

Acts i. 18

HEADY.

προπετής, falling forwards, prone, inclining forwards, *in a bad sense,* precipitate, sudden, headlong, hasty, violent, (occ. Acts xix. 36.)

2 Tim. iii. 4.

HEAL (-ED, -ING.)

1. θεραπεύω, to serve as a θεράπων, (an attendant, *higher than* δοῦλος, *as implying free and honourable service;)* to be an attendant, to do, service; *then,* to take care of, *esp. one's person,* to dress, wash, *etc., then, esp.* to take care of the sick, tend them and treat them medically.
2. ἰάομαι, to heal, to cure; *prop. of surgeons;* to cause to live, revive, *or* recover from illness.
3. σώζω, to save, to rescue, to preserve safe *from danger, loss, or destruction.*
4. διασώζω, to bring safely through *danger or sickness.*
5. { εἰς, unto, for,
   { ἴασις, healing.

1. Matt. iv. 23, 24.
1. —— viii. 7.
2. ——— 8, 13.
1. ——— 16.
1. —— ix. 35.
1. —— x. 1, 8.
1. Matt. xii. 10, 15, 22.
2. —— xiii. 15.
1. —— xiv. 14.
1. —— xv. 30.
1. —— xix. 2.
1. —— xxi. 14.

1. Mark i. 34.
1. —— iii. 2, 10.
1. ——— 15 (*om.* T Tr A ℵ)
3. —— v. 23.
2. ——— 29.
1. —— vi. 5, 13.
2. Luke iv. 18 (*ap.*)
1. ——— 23, 40.
1. —— v. 15.
2. ——— 17.
1. —— vi. 7.
2. ——— 17.
1. ——— 18.
2. ——— 19.
4. —— vii. 3.
2. ——— 7.
1. —— viii. 2.
3. ——— 36.
1. ——— 43.
2. ——— 47.
2. —— ix. 2.
1. ——— 6.
2. ——— 11, 42.
1. —— x. 9.
1. —— xiii. 14 twice.
1. Luke xiv. 3.
2. ——— 4.
2. —— xvii. 15.
2. —— xxii. 51.
2. John iv. 47.
2. —— v. 13 (ασθενέω, *to be sick*, G∼T.)
2. —— xii. 40.
2. Acts iii. 11 (αὐτος, *he, instead of*, τοῦ ιαθάντος χωλοῦ, *the lame man which was healed*, G L T Tr A ℵ.)
1. —— iv. 14.
5. ——— 30.
1. —— v. 16.
1. —— viii. 7.
2. —— x. 38.
3. —— xiv. 9.
2. —— xviii. 8, 27.
1. —— xxviii. 9.
2. Heb. xii. 13.
2. Jas. v. 16.
2. 1 Pet. ii. 24.
1. Rev. xiii. 3, 12.

HEALING [noun.]

1. θεραπεία, voluntary service, attendance; care *of the sick, and then, by implication*, relief, healing.
2. ἴαμα, healing, *(the termination denoting the complete act; the result or product of the act, (non occ.)*
3. ἴασις, healing, *(the termination denoting the action as incomplete and in progress.)*

1. Luke ix. 11.
3. Acts iv. 22.
2. 1 Cor. xii. 9, 28, 30.
1. Rev. xxii. 2.

HEALTH.

σωτηρία, safety, deliverance, preservation *from danger or destruction.*

Acts xxvii. 34.

HEALTH (BE IN.)

ὑγιαίνω, to be sound, healthy, *or* in health.

3 John 2.

HEAP.

1. σωρεύω, to heap *one thing on another*, to heap with *something*, (occ. 2 Tim. iii. 6.)
2. ἐπισωρεύω, *(No.* 1 *with* ἐπί, upon, *prefixed,)* to heap up upon, to accumulate, *(non occ.)*

1. Rom. xii. 20.
2. 2 Tim. iv. 3.
— Jas. v. 3, see Treasure.

HEAR (-EST, -ETH, -ING, HEARD.)

1. ἀκούω, to hear, *intrans.*, to have the faculty of hearing; *trans.*, to hear, perceive with the ears; to give ear, listen; to hear, *i.e.*, to learn by hearing, be informed.
2. εἰσακούω, *(No.* 1 *with* εἰς, unto, *prefixed,)* to hear to, listen to. *Also from the Heb.*, to hear favourably, grant, *(non occ.)*
   * *Passive.*
3. διακούω, *(No.* 1 *with* διά, through, *prefixed,)* to hear through *or* throughout, to hear fully, *(non occ.)*
4. ἐπακούω, *(No.* 1 *with* ἐπί, upon, *prefixed,)* to hearken upon, *i.e.*, to hear *anything* at *or* upon *a particular place or occasion, (non occ.)*
5. ἐπακρόαομαι, to listen upon, *or* to, *(non occ.)*

1. Matt. ii. 3 part, 9 part, 18, 22 part.
1. —— iv. 12 part.
1. —— v. 21, 27, 33, 38, 43
2* —— vi. 7.
1. —— vii. 24, 26.
1. —— viii. 10 part.
1. —— ix. 12 part.
1. —— x. 14, 27.
1. —— xi. 2 part, 4, 5, 15 1st (*om.* T Trb A.)
1. ——— 15 2nd.
1. —— xii. 19, 24 part, 42.
1. —— xiii. 9 1st (*om.* T Trb A ℵ.)
1. ——— 9 2nd, 13, 14, 15, 16.
1. ——— 17 3 times, 18, 19 part, 20, 22, 23, 43 1st (*om.* Lb T Trb A ℵ.)
1. ——— 43 2nd.
1. —— xiv. 1, 13 part twice
1. —— xv. 10, 12.
1. —— xvii. 5, 6 part.
1. —— xviii. 15, 16.
— ——— 17 twice, see H (neglect to.)
1. —— xix. 22 part, 25 part
1. —— xx. 24 part, 30 part
1. —— xxi. 16, 33, 45 part
1. —— xxii. 7 part (*om.* ἀκούσας, *when the King heard thereof*, G∾T Tr A ℵ.)
1. ——— 22 part, 33 part, 34 part
1. —— xxiv. 6.
1. —— xxvi. 65.
1. —— xxvii. 13, 47 part.
1. Mark ii. 17 part.
1. —— iii. 8 part, 21 part.
1. —— iv. 9 twice, 12 twice, 15, 16, 18, 20, 23 twice, 24 1st, 24 2nd (*ap.*), 33.
1. —— v. 27.
1. ——— 36 (παρακούω, *but Jesus overhearing*, instead of *as soon as Jesus heard*, T Tr A ℵ)
1. —— vi. 2, 11, 14, 16 part, 20 1st part, 20 2nd, 29 part, 55.
1. Mark vii. 16, 25, 37.
1. —— viii. 18.
1. —— ix. 7.
1. —— x. 41 part, 47 part.
1. —— xi. 14, 18.
1. —— xii. 28, 29, 37.
1. —— xiii. 7.
1. —— xiv. 11 part, 58, 64.
1. —— xv. 35 part.
1. —— xvi. 11 part (*ap.*)
2* Luke i. 13.
1. ——— 41, 58, 66.
1. —— ii. 18, 20, 46, 47.
1. —— iv. 23, 28, part.
1. —— v. 1, 15.
1. —— vi. 17, 27, 47, 49.
1. —— vii. 3 part, 9 part, 22 twice, 29.
1. —— viii. 8 twice, 10, 12, 13, 14 part, 15, 18, 21, 50 part.
1. —— ix. 7, 9, 35.
1. —— x 16 twice, 24 3 times, 39.
1. —— xi. 28, 31.
1. —— xii. 3.
1. —— xiv. 15, 35 twice.
1. —— xv. 1, 25.
1. —— xvi. 2, 14, 29, 31.
1. —— xviii. 6, 22 part, 23 part, 26, 36.
1. —— xix. 11 part, 48.
1. —— xx. 16 part.
1. —— xxi. 9, 38.
1. —— xxii. 71.
1. —— xxiii. 6 part, 8.
— John i. 41, see H one speak.
1. ——— 37, 40.
1. —— iii. 8, 29, 32.
1. —— iv. 1, 42, 47 part.
1. —— v. 24, 25 twice, 28, 30, 37.
1. —— vi. 45, 60 1st part, 6 2nd.
1. —— vii. 32, 40 part, 51
— —— viii. 6, no Greek equivalent.
1. ——— 9 (*ap.*), 26, 40, 43, 47 twice.
1. —— ix. 27 twice, 31 twice, 32, 35, 40.

1. John x. 3, 8, 16, 20, 27.
1. —— xi. 4 part, 6, 20, 29, 41, 42.
1. —— xii. 12 part, 18, 29, 34, 47.
1. —— xiv. 24, 28.
1. —— xv. 15.
1. —— xvi. 13.
1. —— xviii. 21, 37.
1. —— xix. 8, 13 part.
1. —— xxi. 7 part.
1. Acts i. 4.
1. —— ii. 6, 8, 11, 22, 33, 37 part.
1. —— iii. 22, 23.
1. —— iv. 4, 20, 24 part.
1. —— v. 5 twice, 11, 21 part, 24, 32 part.
1. —— vi. 11, 14.
1. —— vii. 12 part, 34.
1. ——- 37 (*om.* αὐτοῦ ἀκούσεσθε, *Him shall ye hear*, G→L T Tr A ℵ.)
1. ——— 54 part.
1. —— viii. 6, 14, 30.
1. —— ix. 4, 7, 13, 21, 38.
1. —— x. 22.
2* ——— 31.
1. ——— 33, 44, 46.
1. —— xi. 1, 7, 18 part.
1. —— xiii. 7, 44, 48 part.
1. —— xiv. 9, 14.
1. —— xv. 7, 24.
1. —— xvi. 14.
5. ——— 25.
1. ——— 38 part.
1. —— xvii. 8 part, 21, 32 1st part, 32 2nd.
1. —— xviii. 8, 26 part.
1. —— xix. 2, 5 part, 10, 26, 28 part.
1. —— xxi. 12, 20 part, 22
1. —— xxii. 1, 2 part, 7, 9, 14, 15, 26 part.
1. —— xxiii. 16 part.
3. ——— 35.
1. —— xxiv. 4.
1. ——— 22 part (G∾), ἀκούσας ταῦτα, *heard these things* (*om.* G L T Tr A ℵ.)
1. ——— 24.
1. —— xxv. 22 twice.
1. —— xxvi. 3, 14, 29.
1. —— xxviii. 15 part, 22, 26, 27, 28.
1. Rom. x. 14 twice, 18.
1. —— xi. 8 inf.
1. —— xv. 21.
1. 1 Cor. ii. 9.
1. —— xi. 18.
2. —— xiv. 21.
4. 2 Cor. vi. 2.
1. —— xii. 4, 6.
1. Gal. i. 13, 23.
1. —— iv. 21 (ἀναγινώσκω, *to know accurately*, Lm)
1. Eph. i. 13 part, 15 part.
1. —— iii. 2.
1. —— iv. 21.
1. Phil. i. 27, 30.
1. —— ii. 26.
1. —— iv. 9.
1. Col. i. 4 part.
— ——— 5, see H before.
1. ——— 6, 9, 23.
— 1 Thes. ii. 13, see H (which…)
1. 2 Thes. iii. 11.
1. 1 Tim. iv. 16.
1. 2. Tim. i. 13.
1. —— ii. 2.
1. —— iv. 17.
1. Philem. 5.
1. Heb. ii. 1, 3.
1. —— iii. 7, 15, 16 part.
1. —— iv. 2, 7.
2* —— v. 7.
1. —— xii. 19.
1. Jas. i. 19.
1. —— v. 11.
1. 2 Pet. i. 18.
1. 1 John i. 1, 3, 5.
1. —— ii. 7, 18, 24 twice.
1. —— iii. 11.
1. —— iv. 3, 5, 6 twice.
1. —— v. 14, 15.
1. 2 John 6.
1. 3 John 4.
1. Rev. i. 3, 10.
1. —— ii. 7, 11, 17, 29.
1. —— iii. 3 (*ap.*), 6, 13, 20, 22.
1. —— iv. 1.
1. —— v. 11, 13.
1. —— vi. 1, 3, 5, 6, 7.
1. —— vii. 4.
1. —— viii. 13.
1. —— ix. 13, 16, 20.
1. —— x. 4, 8.
1. —— xi. 12.
1. —— xii. 10.
1. —— xiii. 9.
1. —— xiv 2 twice, 13.
1. —— xvi. 1, 5, 7.
1. —— xviii. 4, 22 twice, 23
1. —— xix. 1, 6.
1. —— xxi. 3.
1. —— xxii. 8 twice, 17, 18.

HEAR BEFORE.

προακούω, to hear beforehand; *here the Aorist*, to have heard of before, already, *(non occ.)*

Col. i. 5.

HEAR ONE SPEAK.

{ ἀκουω, to hear, παρὰ, from beside, } *lit.* one out of the two who heard from, *or* as he stood beside John and heard him.

John i. 41, part.

HEAR (NEGLECT TO.)

παρακούω, to hear beside, *esp.*, to hear accidentally; *then*, to hear underhand, to overhear *something* from *another; then*, to hear imperfectly, hear wrong, misunderstand; *and lastly*, not to listen to, take no heed of, or pretend not to hear, *(non occ.)*

Matt. xviii. 17 twice.

HEARD (WHICH…)

ἀκοή, hearing, the sense of hearing, *then*, that which is heard.

1 Thes. ii. 13.

HEARER (-S.)

1. ἀκούω, to hear, *see* "HEAR," *No.* 1, *(here participle.)*
2. ἀκροατής, a hearer.

2. Rom. ii. 13.
1. Eph. iv. 29.
1. 2 Tim. ii. 14.
2. Jas. i. 22, 23, 25.

HEARING.

1. ἀκοή, hearing, the sense of hearing, *and also*, the thing heard.
2. διάγνωσις, knowledge throughout, *i.e.* thorough knowledge; *hence*, a distinguishing and deciding.

1. Matt. xiii. 14.
— ——— 15, see H (be dull of.)
2. Acts xxv. 21, marg. *judgment.*
— ——— 23, see H (place of.)
1. —— xxviii. 26.
— Acts xxviii. 27, see H (be dull of.) [*report.*)
1. Rom. x. 16, marg. (text
1. ——— 17 twice.
1. 1 Cor. xii. 17 twice.
1. Gal. iii. 2, 5.
— Heb. iv. 2, see H (of.)
1. —— v. 11.
1. 2 Pet. ii. 8.

HEARING (of) [margin.]

ἀκοῆς, *Gen.* of ἀκοή, *No.* 1.

Heb. iv. 2, text, *preached.*

HEARING (BE DULL OF)

{ βαρέως, heavily, ἀκούω, to hear, } *lit.* heavily they heard, *(quoted from* Isaiah vi. 10, *where* lxx. *for* הכבד to make heavy.)

Matt. xiii. 15. | Acts xxviii. 27.

HEARING (PLACE OF.)

ἀκροατήριον, place of hearing; *among the Greeks,* the lecture room; *among the Romans,* the place of trial, *(non occ.)*

Acts xxv. 23.

HEARKEN (-ED.)

1. ἀκούω, *see* "HEAR," *No.* 1.
2. ὑπακούω, *(No.* 1 *with* ὑπό, under *prefixed, implying* concealment, *or* repression,) to hear *with the idea of stealth,* stillness *or* attention, *used esp. of a porter or doorkeeper.*

1. Mark iv. 3.
1. —— vii. 14.
— Acts ii. 14, see H to.
1 —— iv. 19.
1. —— vii. 2.
2. Acts xii. 13, marg. *ask who was there.*
1. —— xv. 13. [unto.
— —— xxvii. 21, see H
1. Jas. ii. 5.

HEARKEN TO.

ἐνωτίζομαι, to receive in the ear, *i.e.,* to give ear to, *(non occ.)*

Acts ii. 14.

HEARKEN UNTO.

πειθαρχέω, to obey a ruler *or* one in authority; *hence, gen.* to obey, (occ. Acts v. 29, 32; Titus iii. 1.)

Acts xxvii. 21.

HEART (-S.)

1. καρδία, the heart.

[As the corporeal organ of the body, it is the seat of life, which chiefly and finally participates in all its movements. Also as the seat and centre of man's personal life in which the distinctive character of the human manifests itself. Hence the significance of the heart as the starting point of the developments and manifestations of personal life, as well as the organ of their concentration and outgo.]

2. ψυχή, *(from* ψυχω, to breathe,) life *in individual* existence, the breath *or* life which exists in every living thing, *hence,* a living individual, life in distinct individual existence, *and* the whole man himself, *(see under* "SOUL.")

1. Matt. v. 8, 28.
1. —— vi. 21.
1. —— ix. 4.
1. —— xi. 29.
1. —— xii. 34.
1. ——— 35 (*om.* G L T Tr A ℵ.)
1. ——— 40.
1. —— xiii. 15 twice, 19.
1. —— xv. 8, 18, 19.
1. —— xviii. 35.
— —— xix. 8, see H (hardness of.)
1. —— xxii. 37.
1. —— xxiv. 48.
1. Mark ii. 6, 8.
1. —— iii. 5.
1. —— iv. 15 (*ap.*)
1. —— vi. 52.
1. —— vii. 6, 19, 21.
1. —— viii. 17.
— —— x. 5, see H (hardness of.)
1. —— xi. 23.
1. —— xii. 30, 33.
— —— xvi. 14, see H (hardness of.)
1. Luke i. 17, 51, 66.
1. —— ii. 19, 35, 51.
1. —— iii. 15.
1. —— v. 22.
1. —— vi. 45 1st.
1. ——— 45 2nd (*ap.*)
1. ——— 45 3rd.
1. —— viii. 12, 15.
1. —— ix. 47.
1. —— x. 27.
1. —— xii. 34, 45.
1. —— xvi. 15.
— —— xxi. 6, see Fail.
1. ——— 14, 34.
1. —— xxiv. 25, 32, 38.
1. John xii. 40 twice.
1. —— xiii. 2.
1. —— xiv. 1, 27.
1. —— xvi. 6, 22.
— Acts i. 24, see H (which knoweth the.)
1. —— ii. 26, 37, 46.
1. —— iv. 32.
1. —— v. 3, 4.
— ——— 33, see Cut.
1. —— vii. 23, 39, 51, 54.
1. —— viii. 21, 22, 37 (*ap.*)
1. —— xi. 23.
1. —— xiii. 22.
1. —— xiv. 17.
— —— xv. 8, see H (which knoweth the.)
1. ——— 9.
1. Acts xvi. 14.
1. —— xxi. 13.
1. —— xxviii. 27 twice.
1. Rom. i. 21, 24.
1. —— ii. 5, 15, 29.
1. —— v. 5.
1. —— vi. 17.
1. —— viii. 27.
1. —— ix. 2.
1. —— x. 1, 6, 8, 9, 10.
1. —— xvi. 18.
1. 1 Cor. ii. 9.
1. —— iv. 5.
1. —— vii. 37 twice.
1. —— xiv. 25.
1. 2 Cor. i. 22.
1. —— ii. 4.
1. —— iii. 2, 3, 15.
1. —— iv. 6.
1. —— v. 12.
1. —— vi. 11.
1. —— vii. 3.
1. —— viii. 16.
1. —— ix. 7.
1. Gal. iv. 6.
1. Eph. iii. 17.
1. —— iv. 18.
— ——— 32, see Tender.
1. —— v. 19.
1. —— vi. 5.
2. ——— 6.
1. ——— 22.
1. Phil. i. 7.
1. —— iv. 7.
1. Col. ii. 2.
1. —— iii. 15, 16, 22.
1. —— iv. 8.
1. 1 Thes. ii. 4, 17.
1. —— iii. 13.
1. 2 Thes. ii. 17.
1. —— iii. 5.
1. 1 Tim. i. 5.
1. 2 Tim. ii. 22.
1. Heb. iii. 8, 10, 12, 15.
1. —— iv. 7, 12.
1. —— viii. 10.
1. —— x. 16, 22 twice.
1. —— xiii. 9.
1. Jas. i. 26.
1. —— iii. 14.
1. —— iv. 8.
1. —— v. 5, 8.
1. 1 Pet. i. 22.
1. —— iii. 4, 15.
1. 2 Pet. i. 19.
1. —— ii. 14 [21.
1. 1 John iii. 19, 20 twice,
1. Rev. ii. 23.
1. —— xvii. 17.
1. —— xviii. 7.

HEART (HARDNESS OF.)

σκληροκαρδία, hardness of heart, *(not found in Greek Authors,) (non occ.)*

Matt. xix. 8. | Mark x. 5.
Mark xvi. 14 (*ap.*)

HEART (WHICH KNOWETH THE.)

καρδιογνώστης, heart-knower, heart-searcher.

Acts i. 24; xv. 8.

HEARTILY.

1. { ἐκ, out of, ψυχή, *see* "HEART," *No.* 2, } out of the whole man.

2. ἐπιθυμία, what is directed towards anything, desire which attaches itself to (ἐπι-) its object, to covet.

2. Luke xxii. 15, dat. marg. (text, *desire*.)
1. Col. iii. 23.

HEAT.

1. καύσων, burning, heat *(as of the sun)*, *or* a scorching wind, (lxx. in Jer. xviii. 17; Ezek. xvii. 10; Job. xxvii. 21), the heat that burns, (occ. Jas. i. 11.)

2. καῦμα, the burning *or* heat produced, the result of burning.

3. θέρμη, warmth, heat, *as of the summer, or of the fire, (non occ.)*

1. Matt. xx. 12.
1. Luke xii. 55.
3. Acts xxviii. 3.
— Jas. i. 11, see H (burning)
— 2 Pet. iii. 10, 12, see H (with fervent.)
2. Rev. vii. 16.
2. —— xvi. 9.

HEAT (BURNING.)

1. Jas. i. 11.

HEAT (WITH FERVENT.)

καυσόομαι, to be set on fire, to burn.

2 Pet. iii. 10, 12, pass. part.

HEATHEN.

1. ἔθνος, *see* "GENTILE," *No.* 1, *(only plural here.)*

2. { οἱ, the,
ἐθνίκοι, people of the nations, *(other than Jews.)*

2. Matt. vi. 7.
—— xviii. 7, see H man
1. Acts iv. 25.
1. 2 Cor. xi. 26.
1. Gal. i. 16.
1. —— ii. 9.
1. Gal. iii. 8.

HEATHEN MAN.

ἐθνικός, a man of the nations, *(other than the Jews.)*

Matt. xviii. 17.

HEAVEN (-s.)

οὐρανός, heaven, the over-arching and all-embracing heaven beneath which is the earth and all that is therein.

[The plural is used more often than the singular, and there are many conjectures why. We can know nothing of such a matter but what is revealed (John iii. 12, 13.) We read of τρίτον οὐρανοῦ, "the third heaven." Jewish fable cannot explain this, nor have we any need to go beyond the covers of God's word for its explanation.

We read in Gen. i. 1, "In the beginning, God created the heavens and the earth." Peter tells us (2 Pet. iii. 5, 6), that "The *heavens* were of old, *and the earth* standing out of the water and in the water: whereby the world (κόσμος), that then was, being overflowed with water, *perished*."

What succeeded is called (2 Pet. iii. 7), "The heavens and the earth which now are." John calls these (Rev. xxi. 1), "The first heaven and the first earth," *i.e.*, the former, *see* ver. 4. These are "kept in store, reserved unto fire." In the day of the Lord "the heavens shall pass away with a great noise, and the elements shall melt with fervent heat, the earth also and all the works therein shall be burned up." Again, (ver. 12), "The heavens being on fire shall be dissolved."

What shall follow is called (2 Pet. iii. 13), "New heavens and a new earth;" and in Rev. xxi. 1, "A new heaven and a new earth." In Isaiah lxv. 17, God says, "Behold I create new heavens, and a new earth." (See also Isaiah li. 16; lxvi. 22.)

Thus we have *Three heavens.*

(1st) "The heavens were of old and the earth." "The world that then was," 2 Pet. iii. 5, 6.

(2nd) "The heavens and the earth which now are," 2 Pet. iii. 7.

(3rd) "The new heavens and the new earth," Isaiah lxv. 17.

The origin, causes and progress of these changes make up the whole subject matter of the word of God!

*** Paradise was in the *First* heaven and earth, (Gen. ii.) It "perished" with them at the flood, and therefore is absent in the *Second.* It appears again in the *Third*, with its Tree of Life, Rev. ii. 7; xxii. 1,

2, 14. To this "Third heaven" and "Paradise" Paul was *caught away*, 2 Cor. xii. 2, 4, (not "up," see under "CATCH,") in "visions and revelations of the Lord," 2 Cor. xii. 1. One catching away—with a double revelation of the New heaven and the New earth, the whole earth being then a "Paradise."

In the light of this, we must in Luke xxiii. 43, place the comma after the words "to-day," which indeed is required by the absence of ὅτι. (Compare Luke xxii. 34, and Matt. xxi. 28, with Mark xiv. 30; Luke iv. 21; and xix 9.) Thus the promise of Christ to the dying robber is *Future*, (see under "TO-DAY.")

For the expression "Kingdom of Heaven," see under KINGDOM.]

* The plural is rendered by the singular in those passages marked with an asterisk.

Matt. iii. 2*, 16, 17*.
—— iv. 17*.
—— v. 3*, 10*, 12*, 16*, 18.
—— 19* twice, 20*, 34, 45*.
—— 48* (οὐρανίος, *heavenly*, instead of ἐν τοῖς οὐρανοῖς, *which is in heaven*, G∾L T Tr A ℵ.)
—— vi. 1*, 9*, 10, 20.
—— vii. 11*, 21* twice.
—— viii. 11*.
—— x. 7*, 32*, 33*.
—— xi. 11*, 12*, 23, 25.
—— xii. 50*.
—— xiii. 11* (*om.* G→.)
—— 24*, 31*, 33*, 44*, 45*, 47*, 52*.
—— xiv. 19.
—— xvi. 1, 17*, 19* 3 times
—— xviii. 1*, 3*, 4*, 10* twice, 14*, 18* twice, 19*, 23*.
—— xix. 12*, 14*, 21, 23*.
—— xx. 1*.
—— xxi. 25 twice.
—— xxii. 2*, 30.
—— xxiii. 9* (οὐρανίος, *heavenly*, instead of ἐν τοῖς οὐρανοῖς, *which is in heaven*, L T Tr A ℵ.)
—— 13*, 22.
—— xxiv. 29 twice, 30 twice, 31*, 35, 36*.
—— xxv. 1*.
—— xxvi. 64.
—— xxviii. 2, 18.
Mark i. 10, 11*.
—— vi. 41.
—— vii. 34.
—— viii. 11.
—— x. 21.
—— xi. 25*, 26* (*ap.*), 30, 31.
—— xii. 25*.
—— xiii. 25 1st, 25* 2nd, 27, 31, 32.
—— xiv. 62.
—— xvi. 19 (*ap.*)
Luke ii. 15.
—— iii. 21, 22.
—— iv. 25.
—— vi. 23.
—— ix. 16, 54.
—— x. 15, 18, 20*, 21.
—— xi. 2* 1st (*ap.*), 2 2nd (*ap.*), 16.
—— xii. 33.
—— xv. 7, 18, 21.
—— xvi. 17.
—— xvii. 24 twice, 29.
—— xviii. 13, 22.
—— xix. 38.
—— xx. 4, 5.
—— xxi. 11, 26*, 33.
—— xxii. 43 (*ap.*)
—— xxiv. 51 (*ap.*)
John i. 32, 51.
—— iii. 13 1st & 2nd, 13 3rd (*ap.*), 27, 31.
—— vi. 31, 32 twice, 33, 38, 41, 42, 50, 51, 58.
—— xii. 28.
—— xvii. 1.
Acts i. 10, 11 3 times.
—— ii. 2, 5, 19, 34.
—— iii. 21.
—— iv. 12, 24.
—— vii. 42, 49, 55, 56.
—— ix. 3.
—— x. 11, 16.
—— xi. 5, 9, 10.
—— xiv. 15.
—— 17, see H (from.)
—— xvii. 24.
—— xxii. 6.
—— xxvi. 13, see H (from)
Rom. i. 18.
—— x. 6.
1 Cor. viii. 5.
—— xv. 47.
2 Cor. v. 1, 2.
—— xii. 2.
Gal. i. 8.
Eph. i. 10* (marg. *the heavens.*)
—— iii. 15*.
—— iv. 10.
—— vi. 9*.
Phil. ii. 10, see H (in.)
—— iii. 20*.
Col. i. 5*, 16*, 20*, 23.
—— iv. 1*.
1 Thes. i. 10*.
—— iv. 16.
2 Thes. i. 7.
Heb. i. 10.
—— iv. 14.
—— vii. 26.
—— viii. 1.
—— ix. 23, 24.
—— x. 34* (*om.* G→L T Tr A ℵ.)
—— xii. 23*, 25*, 26.
Jas. v. 12, 18.
1 Pet. i. 4*, 12.
—— iii. 22.
2 Pet. i. 18.
—— iii. 5, 7, 10, 12, 13.
1 John v. 7 (*ap.*)
Rev. iii. 12.
—— iv. 1, 2.
—— v. 3, 13.
—— vi. 13, 14.
—— viii. 1, 10.
Rev. viii. 13, see H (midst of)
—— ix. 1.
—— x. 1, 4, 5, 6, 8.
—— xi. 6, 12 twice, 13, 15.
—— 19 (Tr b.)
—— xii. 1, 3, 4, 7, 8, 10, 12
—— xiii. 6, 13.
—— xiv. 2.
—— 6, see H (midst of.)
—— 7, 13, 17.
—— xv. 1, 5.
—— xvi. 11.
—— 17 (*om.* G⇉ L T Tr A), Θεοῦ, *of God*, instead of οὐρανοῦ ἀπὸ τοῦ θρόνου, *of heaven from the throne*, ℵ.)
—— 21.
—— xviii. 1, 4, 5, 20.
—— xix. 1, 11, 14.
—— 17, see H (midst of)
—— xx. 1, 9, 11.
—— xxi. 1 twice, 2.
—— 3 (θρόνος, *the throne*, L T A ℵ.)
—— 10.

HEAVEN (FROM.)

οὐρανόθεν, from οὐρανός, from Heaven, *(non occ.)*

Acts xiv. 17. | Acts xxvi. 13.

HEAVEN (IN.)

ἐπουράνιος, heavenly, what pertains to *or* is in heaven; οἱ ἐπουράνιοι, *here* denotes beings which come within the heavenly order.

Phil. ii. 10.

HEAVEN (MIDST OF.)

μεσουράνημα, mid-heaven, the midst of the heavens.

Rev. viii. 13; xiv. 6; xix. 17.

HEAVENLY.

1. { ἐκ, out of, from, οὐρανός, heaven, *see under* HEAVEN, } of heaven.

2. οὐράνιος, heavenly.

3. ἐπουράνιος, (*No.* 2, *with* ἐπί, upon, in, heavenly, what pertains to, *or* is in heaven.)

2. Matt. vi. 14, 26, 32.
2. —— xv. 13.
3. —— xviii. 35 (No. 2, G∾ L T T A b ℵ.)
2. Luke ii. 13.
1. —— xi. 13.
— John iii. 12, see H things
2. Acts xxvi. 19.
3. 1 Cor. xv 48 1st.
— —— 48 2nd, see H (they that are.)
3. —— 49.
— Eph. i. 3, see H places.
3. —— 20 (No. 2, L.)
— —— iii. 10, } see H
— —— vi. 12, } places.
3. 2 Tim. iv. 18.
3. Heb. iii. 1.
3. —— vi. 4.
— —— viii. 5, } see H
— —— ix. 23, } things.
3. —— xi. 16.
3. —— xii. 22.

HEAVENLY PLACES.

{ οἱ, the *(masc. pl.)*, ἐπουράνιοι, heavenlies, } the heavenly places, the places pertaining to heaven, in the domain of the heavenly. The phrase defines broadly and comprehensively the region and sphere where are our country, Phil. iii. 20; our High Priest; our Treasure, Matt. vi. 20, 21; our Affections, Col. i. 5; our Inheritance reserved, 1 Pet. i. 4, (occ. Eph. i. 20.)

Eph. i. 3, marg. *the things*
—— ii. 6.
Eph. iii. 10. [*high places.*)
—— vi. 12, marg. (text,

HEAVENLY (THEY THAT ARE.)

{ οἱ, the [*persons,*]
ἐπουράνιοι, heavenly, what pertains to heaven.

1 Cor. xv. 48.

HEAVENLY THINGS.

{ τὰ, the *things (neut.)*,
ἐπουράνια, heavenly, *(see above.)*

John iii. 12. [*H places.*)
Eph. i. 3, masc. marg. (text
Heb. viii. 5.
—— ix. 23.

HEAVINESS.

1. λύπη, grief, sorrow.
2. κατήφεια, a casting the eye downward, dejection, *(non occ.)*

1. Rom. ix. 2.
1. 2 Cor. ii. 1.
— Phil. ii. 26, see H (be [full of.)
2. Jas. iv. 9.
— 1 Pet. i. 6, see H (be in.)

HEAVINESS (BE FULL OF.)

ἀδημονέω, to be troubled *or* in anguish; to be in a state of great anxiety, (occ. Matt. xxvi. 37; Mark xiv. 33.)

Phil. ii. 26.

HEAVINESS (BE IN.)

λυπέω, to give pain to, to pain, distress. *Pass. as here,* to be sad, to mourn, grieve.

1 Pet. i. 6, part.

HEAVY.

1. βαρέομαι, to be heavy, weighed down, oppressed.
2. βαρύς, heavy, *as of burdens, hard to be borne.*

— Matt. xi. 28, see Laden.
2. —— xxiii. 4. [very.)
— —— xxvi. 37, see H (be
1. —— 43, part. [very.)
— Mark xiv. 33, see H (be
1 Mk. xiv. 40 (καταβαρύνομαι same as No. 1, but more emphatic, G ∾ L T Tr), (καταβαρέομαι, ℵ.)
1. Luke ix. 32, part.

HEAVY (BE VERY.)

ἀδημονέω, *see* "HEAVINESS (BE FULL OF,") occ. Phil. ii. 26.

Matt. xxvi. 37. | Mark xiv. 33.

HEBREW.

1. Ἑβραῖος, a Hebrew, *from Heb.* עברי passer over, *Prob., the same as* ὑπέρ, over. *In allusion to Abraham's immigration from the other side of the Euphrates, he was called,* "Abram the Hebrew," Gen. xiv. 13. *In* lxx. ὁ περάτης, *from* πέραν, beyond, *i.e., beyond the river. The title* Hebrew *is therefore their title of separation, and is never used without a special reference to them as distinct from other nations, either latent or expressed.*

   [Ἑλληνιστής, is a Hellenist, *i.e.*, a Hebrew who has unlearned his own tongue and speaks Greek, and expresses a distinction within the nation, and not between that nation and any other (see "GRECIAN.") Ἰουδαῖος, is a Jew in his national distinction from Gentile. It came from the prominence of the single tribe of Judah, to be applied to all who returned from the captivity (see "JEW.") Ἰσραηλίτης, is the Israelite as the heir of the Theocratic privileges and the glorious vocation (see "ISRAELITE.") So we speak now of the Hebrew Tongue and the Jewish nation.]

2. Ἑβραΐς, the Hebrew language, *i.e.*, the Hebrew Aramæan or Syro Chaldaic which was probably the vernacular language of the Palestine Jews at the time of Christ.

1. Acts vi. 1.
2. —— xxi. 40.
2. —— xxii. 2.
2. Acts xxvi. 14.
1. 2 Cor. xi. 22.
1. Phil. iii. 5 twice.

HEBREW (IN.)

Ἑβραϊστί, Hebraicè, in Hebrew.

John xix. 20.

HEBREW (IN THE.)

John xix. 13, 17.

HEBREW TONGUE (IN THE.)

John v. 2. | Rev. ix. 11.
Rev. xvi. 16.

HEBREW (OF.)

Ἑβραϊκός, *adj.*, Hebrew.

Luke xxiii. 38 (*ap.*)

HEDGE [noun.]

φραγμός, a shutting up, fencing *or* hedging in, *also*, a hedge *or* fence.

Mark xii. 1. | Luke xiv. 23.

HEDGE ROUND ABOUT [verb.]

{ περιτίθημι, to put around,
{ φραγμός, a fence, *(see above.)*

Matt. xxi. 33.

HEED (TAKE.)

1. βλέπω, to look, see, have the power of sight *applied to mental vision or consideration*, to consider, take to heart, *employed to express* a more intent, earnest, spiritual contemplation *than No.* 2.
2. ὁράω, to see, applied to bodily sight; to see to, look to.
3. προσέχω, to hold to, bring to *or* near; *used of the mind*, to turn one's mind, thought, *or* attention to *a thing*, be intent upon *it*.
4. σκοπέω, to look at *or* after *a thing*, to consider, examine, *(as No.* 1 *refers to* universal contemplation, *so No.* 4 *refers to* particular.)

3. Matt. vi. 1.
2. —— xvi. 6.
2. —— xviii. 10.
1. —— xxiv. 4.
1. Mark iv. 24.
2. —— viii. 15.
1. —— xiii. 5, 23, 33.
1. Luke viii. 18.
4. —— xi. 35.
2. —— xii. 15.
1. Luke xxi. 8.
2. Acts xxii. 26 (*om.* G L T TrAℵ, the sense being, "What art thou going to do?")
1. 1 Cor. iii. 10.
1. —— viii. 9.
1. —— x. 12.
1. Gal. v. 15.
1. Heb. iii. 12.
3. 2 Pet. i. 19.

HEED TO (GIVE.)

3. Acts viii. 10. | 3. 1 Tim. iv. 1.
3. 1 Tim. i. 4. | 3. Titus i. 14.

HEED TO (TAKE.)

1. Mark xiii. 9. | 3. Luke xxi. 34.
3. Luke xvii. 3. | 3. Acts v. 35.
1. Col. iv. 17.

HEED TO (GIVE THE MORE EARNEST.)

{ περισσοτέρως, more abundantly, προσέχω, *see above, No.* 3, } more abundantly to be holding fast unto.

Heb. ii. 1.

HEED UNTO (GIVE.)

1. προσέχω, *see above, No.* 3.
2. ἐπέχω, to have *or* hold upon, to direct upon, *spoken of the mind*, to pay attention to, mark.

2. Acts iii. 5. | 1. Acts viii. 6.

HEED UNTO (TAKE.)

1. προσέχω, *see above.*
2. ἐπέχω, *see above.*

1. Acts xx. 28. | 2. 1 Tim. iv. 16.

HEEL.

πτέρνα, the heel, *(non occ.)*

[Quoted from Ps. xli. 10, where the figure refers to circumventing, supplanting, *see* Gen. xxvii. 36; Jer. ix. 4; Hos. xii. 3.]

John xiii. 18.

HEIFER.

δάμαλις, a heifer *of fit age to be* tamed *to the yoke,* [here referring to the "red heifer" of Num. xix.], *(non occ.)*

Heb. ix. 13.

HEIGHT.

1. ὕψος, height; the top, summit *or* crown.
2. ὕψωμα, high position, elevation.

2. Rom. viii. 39. | 1. Eph. iii. 18.
1. Rev. xxi. 16.

HEIR (-s.)

κληρονόμος, receiving a portion, *esp.*, *f an inheritance; as Subst.*, an heir, one who has a κλῆρος, (a lot), (*not one to whom a κλῆρος is allotted, because it is derived from the active;* but) he who has the inheritance, *the stress being laid on the possession.*

[Spoken emphatically of Christ, who as the Son of ADAM is the heir of universal dominion, Gen. i. 26, 28; Ps. viii. 4—8; Heb. ii. 6—8; as son of ABRAHAM, heir of the land, Gen. xxii. 16—18; Heb. ii. 16; Rom. iv. 13; as Son of DAVID, the heir to the throne, Matt. i. 1, 6; Luke i. 30—33; as Son of GOD the heir of all, Heb. i. 1, 2; Acts x. 36.]

Matt. xxi. 38.
Mark xii. 7.
Luke xx. 14.
Rom. iv. 13, 14.
— viii. 17, and see H (joint.)
Gal. iii. 29.
— iv. 1, 7.
— 30, see H (be)
Eph. iii. 6, see H (fellow.)
Titus iii. 7.
Heb. i. 2.
— 14, see H of (be.)
— vi. 17.
— xi. 7.
— 9, see H with.
Jas. ii. 5.
1 Pet. iii. 7, see H together

HEIR (BE.)

κληρονομέω, to be a κληρονόμος, (*see* HEIR.)

Gal. iv. 30.

HEIR OF (BE.)

Heb. i. 14.

HEIR TOGETHER.

συγκληρονόμος, a heir together with another, (*non occ.*)

1 Pet. iii. 7.

HEIR WITH.

Heb. xi. 9.

HEIR (FELLOW.)

Eph. iii. 6.

HEIR (JOINT.)

Rom. viii. 17.

HELL.

1. γεέννα, Gehenna.

[Greek for גי הנם, Ghi-Hinnom, *or* valley of Hinnom, Josh. xv. 8, where was the scene of the Moloch worship תפת (Tophet, *i.e.*, abomination.) 2 Chron. xxxiii. 6; Jer. ii. 23; vii. 31; xix. 6, etc. Hence desecrated by Josiah, 2 Kings xxiii. 10. The name was not derived from the worship of Moloch, but from the later use of the burning of carrion, by means of ever-burning fire, Jer. xxxi. 40; Is. lxvi. 24. Probably used by our Lord as a symbol, (*cf.* Is. xxx. 33; lxvi. 24; Mal. iv. 1, with Luke xvii. 29, 30; Matt. xiii 40,) for the notion of a devouring judgment fire, which was current prior to the possible employment of Gehenna in this sense, (Lev. x. 2; Num. xvi. 35; 2 Kings i., etc.)]

2. ᾅδης, HADES. [This is a Heathen word and comes down to us surrounded with heathen traditions, which had their origin in Babel, and not in the Bible, and have reached us through Judaism and Romanism.

As *Hades* (a word of human origin) is used in the New Testament, as the equivalent for the Hebrew *Sheōl* (a word of Divine origin) its meaning can be gathered, not from human imagination, but from its *Divine usage* in the Old Testament. If we know this we know all that can be known. We therefore give a complete list of all its *sixty-five* occurrences in the Old Testament. We give the list, complete, from the A.V., with the R.V. variations; calling attention to the fact that the American R.V. does not translate the word at all, but simply transliterates it thus: "Sheol."

To enable the eye to help the understanding, we have given the three renderings in three different types; and have referred to the R.V. text and margin in the notes. In all cases where not otherwise noted, the R.V. text is the same as the A.V.

The variations are indicated as follows:

* R.V. marg., Heb. *Sheol.*
† R.V. pit; marg., Heb. *Sheol.*
‡ R.V. Sheol.
‖ R.V. Sheol; marg., Or, *grave.*
§ R.V. marg., Or, *the grave;* Heb., *Sheol.*
** R.V. hell; marg., Heb. *Sheol.*

All the Occurrences of the Word שאול *Sheōl.*

1. Gen. xxxvii. 35, I will go down into **the grave.**[a]
2. —— xlii. 38,* then shall ye bring down my grey hairs with sorrow to **the grave.**
3. —— xliv. 29,* with sorrow to **the grave.**
4. —— xliv. 31,* with sorrow to **the grave.**
5. Num. xvi. 30,* they go down quick into the PIT.
6. —— xvi. 33,* they went down alive into the PIT.
7. Deut. xxxii. 22,† shall burn unto the lowest *hell.*
8. 1 Sam. ii. 6,* He bringeth down to **the grave.**
9. 2 Sam. xxii. 6,‡ the sorrows (R.V. cords) of *hell* compassed me.
10. 1 Kings ii. 6.* let not his hoar head go down to **the grave** in peace.
11. —— ii. 9,* his hoar head bring thou down to **the grave.**
12. Job vii. 9,‖ he that goeth down to **the grave.**
13. —— xi. 8,‖ deeper than *hell;* what canst thou know?
14. —— xiv. 13,‖ wouldst hide me in **the grave.**
15. —— xvii. 13,‖ **the grave** in my house.
16. —— xvii. 16,‖ they shall go down to the bars of the PIT.
17. —— xxi. 13,‖ in a moment go down to **the grave.**
18. —— xxiv. 19,‖ so doth **the grave** [consume] those that have sinned.
19. —— xxvi. 6,‖ *hell* is naked before him.
20. Ps. vi. 5,‡ in **the grave** who shall give thee thanks?
21. —— ix. 17,* the wicked shall be turned (R.V. returned) into *hell.*
22. —— xvi. 10,‡ thou wilt not leave my soul in *hell.*
23. —— xviii. 5,‡ the sorrows (R.V. cords) of *hell* compassed me.
24. —— xxx. 3,‡ thou hast brought up my soul from **the grave.**
25. —— xxxi. 17,‡ let them be silent in **the grave.**
26. —— xlix. 14,‡ like sheep are they laid in **the grave.**
27. —— xlix. 14,‡ their beauty shall consume in **the grave.**
28. —— xlix. 15,‡ God will redeem my soul from the power of **the grave.**
29. —— lv. 15,† let them go down quick into *hell.* (A.V. marg., **the grave.**)
30. —— lxxxvi. 13,† thou hast delivered my soul from the lowest *hell.* (A.V. marg., **the grave.**)
31. —— lxxxviii. 3,‖ my life draweth nigh unto **the grave.**
32. Ps. lxxxix. 48,‖ shall he deliver his soul from the hand of **the grave.**
33. —— cxvi. 3,‖ the pains of *hell* gat hold upon me.
34. —— cxxxix. 8,‡ if I make my bed in *hell* thou art there.
35. —— cxli. 7,‡ our bones are scattered at **the grave's** mouth.
36. Prov. i. 12,‖ let us swallow them up alive as **the grave.**
37. —— v. 5,‖ her steps take hold on *hell.*
38. —— vii. 27,‖ her house is the way to *hell.*
39. —— ix. 18,‡ her guests are in the depths of *hell.*
40. —— xv. 11,‖ *Hell* and destruction are before the Lord.
41. —— xv. 24,‖ that he may depart from *hell* beneath.
42. —— xxiii. 14,‖ and shalt deliver his soul from *hell.*
43. —— xxvii. 20,‡ *Hell* and destruction are never full.
44. —— xxx. 16,* **the grave;** and the barren womb.
45. Ecc. ix. 10,* no device, nor knowledge in **the grave.**
46. Song viii. 6,§ jealousy is cruel as **the grave.**
47. Isa v. 14,§ *hell* hath enlarged herself.
48. —— xiv. 9,§ *hell* from beneath is moved for thee (A.V. marg., **the grave.**)
49. —— xiv. 11,** thy pomp is brought down to **the grave.**
50. —— xiv. 15,* thou shalt be brought down to *hell.*
51. —— xxviii. 15,* with *hell* are we at agreement.
52. —— xxviii. 18,* your agreement with *hell* shall not stand.
53. —— xxxviii. 10,* I shall go to the gates of **the grave.**
54. —— xxxviii. 14,* **the grave** cannot praise thee.
55. —— lvii. 9,* and didst debase thyself even unto *hell.*
56. Ezek. xxxi. 15,** he went down to **the grave.**
57. —— xxxi. 16,* I cast him down to *hell.*
58. —— xxxi. 17,* they also went down into *hell.*
59. —— xxxii. 21,* shall speak to him out of the midst of *hell.*
60. —— xxxii. 27,* are gone down to *hell* with their weapons.
61. Hos. xiii. 14,* I will ransom them from **the grave.**
62. —— xiii. 14,* **O grave,** I will be thy destruction.
63. Amos ix. 2,* though they dig into *hell.*
64. Jonah ii. 2, out of the belly of *hell* cried I. (A.V. marg., **the grave.**)
65. Hab. ii. 5, who enlargeth his desire as *hell.*

On a careful examination of the above list, a few facts stand out very clearly.

(i.) It will be observed that in a majority of cases *Sheōl* is rendered "the grave." To be exact, 54 per cent.: while "hell" is 41½ per cent.; and "pit" only 4½ per cent.

The grave, therefore, stands out on the face of the above list as the best and commonest rendering.

(ii.) With regard to the word "pit," it will be observed that in each of the three cases where it occurs (Num. xvi. 30, 33; and Job xvii. 16), *the grave* is so evidently meant, that we may at once substitute that word, and banish "pit" from our consideration as a rendering of *Sheōl.*

(iii.) As to the rendering "hell," it does *not* represent *Sheōl*, because both by Dictionary definition and by colloquial usage "hell" means

---

[a] This being the first occurrence of the word *Sheōl*, the R.V. gives a note in the margin, "Heb. *Sheol*, the name of the abode of the dead, answering to the Greek Hades, Acts ii. 27.' This note is altogether wrong. (1) It is *interpretation* and *not translation.* (2) It prejudges the word from the outset, fixing upon it the word "abode," which has a technical meaning applicable only to the living: thus anticipating the conclusion, which cannot be arrived at until we have obtained all the evidence, and have it before us. (3) *Sheol* has nothing in it "answering to the Greek *Hades.*" Hades must have the same meaning as Sheol; and must answer to that. It must have the meaning which the Holy Spirit puts upon it, and not the meaning which the heathen put on it.

the place of future *punishment*. *Sheōl* has no such meaning, but denotes the *present state of death*. "The grave" is, therefore, a far more suitable translation, because it visibly suggests to us what is invisible to the mind, *viz.*, the state of death. It must, necessarily, be misleading to the English reader to see the former put to represent the latter.

(iv.) The student will find that "THE grave," taken literally as well as figuratively, will meet all the requirements of the Hebrew *Sheōl*: not that *Sheōl* means so much specifically A grave, as generically THE grave.

Holy Scripture is all-sufficient to explain the word *Sheōl* to us.

(v.) If we enquire of it in the above list of the occurrences of the word *Sheōl*, it will teach

(a) That as to *direction* it is down.

(b) That as to *place* it is in the earth.

(c) That as to *nature* it is put for *the state of death*. Not the *act* of dying, for which we have no English word, but the *state* or duration of death. The Germans are more fortunate, having the word *sterbend* for the act of dying.

Sheōl therefore means *the state of death;* or *the state of the dead*, of which *the grave* is a tangible evidence. It has to do only with the dead. It may sometimes be personified and represented as speaking, as other inanimate things are. It may be represented by a coined word, Grave-dom, as meaning the dominion or power of *the grave*.

(d) As to *relation* it stands in *contrast* with the state of the living, see Deut. xxx. 15, 19, and 1 Sam. ii. 6-8. It is never once connected with the living, except by contrast.

(e) As to *association*, it is used in connection with
mourning (Gen. xxxvii. 34, 35),
sorrow (Gen. xlii. 38. 2 Sam. xxii. 6. Ps. xviii. 5; cxvi. 3),
fright and terror (Num. xvi. 27, 34),
weeping (Isa. xxxviii. 3, 10, 15, 20),
silence (Ps. xxxi. 17; vi. 5. Ecc. ix. 10),
no knowledge (Ecc. ix. 5, 6, 10),
punishment (Num. xvi. 27, 34. 1 Kings ii. 6, 9. Job xxiv. 19. Ps ix. 17, R.V. RE-turned, as before their resurrection).

(f) And, finally, as to *duration*, the dominion of *Sheōl* or the grave will continue until, and end only with, *resurrection*, which is the only exit from it (see Hos. xiii. 14, etc.; and compare Ps. xvi. 10 with Acts ii. 27, 31; xiii. 35).

If now the *eleven* occurrences of Hades in the New Testament be carefully examined, the following conclusions will be reached:—

α. *Hadēs* is invariably connected with *death;* but *never with life:* always with *dead* people; but never with the *living*. All in *Hadēs* will "NOT LIVE AGAIN," until they are raised from the dead (Rev. xx. 5). If they do not "live again" until after they are raised, it is perfectly clear that they cannot be *alive* now. Otherwise we do away with the doctrine of resurrection altogether.

β. That the English word "hell" by no means represents the Greek *Hadēs;* as we have seen that it does not give a correct idea of its Hebrew equivalent, *Sheōl*.

γ. That *Hades* can mean only and exactly what *Sheōl* means, *viz.*, the place where "corruption" is seen (Acts ii. 31. Compare xiii. 34-37); and from which, *resurrection* is the only exit.

— Matt. v. 22, see H fire.
1. —— 29, 30.
1. —— x. 28.
2. —— xi. 23.
2. —— xvi. 18.
— —— xviii. 9, see H fire.
1. —— xxiii. 15, 33.
1. Mark ix. 43, 45.
— —— ix. 47, see H fire.
2. Luke x. 15.
1. —— xii. 5.
2. Luke xvi. 23, see above, Note (3.)
2. Acts ii. 27, 31.
2. 1 Cor. xv. 55, marg. (text, *grave*.)
1. Jas. iii. 6.
— 2 Pet. ii. 4, see H (cast down to.)
2. Rev. i. 18.
2. —— vi. 8.
2. —— xx. 13, margin, [*grave*.
2. —— 14.

HELL-FIRE.

{ γεέννα, Gehenna (*see* "HELL" *No.* 1,)
τοῦ, of the,
πυρός, of fire, } the Gehenna of fire.

Matt. v. 22. | Matt. xviii. 9.
Mark ix. 47.

HELL (CAST DOWN TO.)

ταρταρόω, to cast into τάρταρος, (*non occ.*)

[τάρταρος is not Sheol or Hades, (*No.* 2) where all men go in death. Nor is it where the wicked are to be consumed and destroyed, which is Gehenna, (*No.* 1.) Not the abode of *men* in any condition. It is used only here, and here only of "the angels that sinned," (*see* Jude 6.) It denotes the bounds or verge of this material world. The extremity of this lower air—of which Satan is "the prince," (Eph. ii. 2,) and of which Scripture speaks as having "the rulers of the darkness of this world" and "wicked spirits in aerial regions." τάρταρος is not only the bounds of this material creation, but is so called from its coldness.]

2 Pet. ii. 4.

HELM.

πηδάλιον, a rudder, (Acts xxvii. 40.)

Jas. iii. 4.

HELMET.

περικεφαλαία, (*subst. from* περικεφάλαιος, around the head,) a covering for the head, helmet, &c., (*non occ.*)

Eph. vi. 17. | 1 Thes. v. 8.

HELP (-s) [noun.]

1. ἀντίληψις, the receiving of a fee; then a laying hold of *with a view to help. In Biblical Greek it has a sense unknown in Classical Greek, viz.* a rendering assistance, help, (*non occ.*)

2. βοήθεια, aid, succour, rescue; *in pl.*, auxiliaries *or* means of help. (Heb. iv. 16.)

3. ἐπικουρία, aid, succour; an auxiliary *or* allied force, (*non occ.*).

3. Acts xxvi. 22.
2. —— xxvii. 17.
1. 1 Cor. xii. 28.
— 2 Cor. iv. 8, see *H* (without.)

HELP (*without*) [margin.]

See DESPAIR.

HELP [verb]

(-ED, -ETH, -ING, HOLPEN.)

1. βοηθέω, to run to help, come to the rescue, to succour.

2. { εἰς, unto,
βοήθεια, *see* "HELP," *No.* 2, above), } for succour.

3. ἀντιλαμβάνομαι, to lay hold of with a view to help, to hold helpingly.

4. συλλαμβάνω, to take *or* lay hold of together, *and so* to help, aid.

5. συναντιλαμβάνω, to lay hold of *a thing* together with a person and so to assist that person.

6. συμβάλλω, to throw, send *or* strike together. *In mid. as here,* to throw together of one's own with others, *i.e.* to confer benefit, to contribute, *and thus* help.

1. Matt. xv. 25.
1. Mark ix. 22, 24.
3. Luke i. 54.
4. —— v. 7, mid.
5. —— x. 40, mid.
1. Acts xvi. 9.
6. —— xviii. 27.
1. —— xxi. 28.
5. Rom. viii. 26, mid.
— 1 Cor. xvi. 16, see H with.
— 2 Cor. i. 11, see H together.
4. Phil. iv. 3, mid.
2. Heb. iv. 16.
1. Rev. xii. 16.

HELP TOGETHER.

συνυπουργέω, to join in serving *or* working under, to serve *or* work with any one as an underworker.

2 Cor. i. 11.

HELP WITH.

συνεργέω, to join or help in work, to co-operate with, to be a co-worker.

1 Cor. xvi. 16.

HELPER (-s.)

1. Βοηθός, succouring, rescuing. *As subst.* a helper, succourer, supporter, rescuer, *(non. occ.)*

2. συνεργός, working together in conjunction with. *As subst.* a fellow-labourer, a co-worker.

2. Rom. xvi. 3, 9. | 2. 2 Cor. i. 24. 1. Heb. xiii. 6.

HELPER (FELLOW.)

2. 2 Cor. viii. 23. | 2. 3 John 8.

HEM.

κράσπεδον, the edge, border, margin *or* hem *of a thing, esp. of cloth,* (elsewhere, BORDER.)

Matt. ix. 20. | Matt. xiv. 36.

HEN.

ὄρνις, a bird, a fowl. *In N. T. only of poultry,* the hen, *(non occ.)*

Matt. xxiii 37. | Luke xiii. 34.

HENCE.

1. ἐντεῦθεν, hence, thence, from this or that place.

2. μετά, (*with Acc. as here,*) after.

— Matt. iv. 10, see Get.
1. — xvii. 20 (ἔνθεν, *there*, or *thither*, L T Tr A ℵ.)
— Luke iv. 9, see H (from.)
1. — xiii. 31.
— — xvi. 26, see H (from.)
1. John ii. 16.
1. — vii. 3.
1. — xiv. 31.
— — xviii. 36, see H (from.)
2. Acts i. 5.
— — xxii. 21, see Far.
1. Jas. iv. 1.

HENCE (FROM.)

1. Luke iv. 9.
1. — xvi. 26, (ἔνθεν, *there* or *thither*, L T Tr A ℵ.)
1. John xviii. 6.

HENCEFORTH (and FROM HENCEFORTH.*)

1. { ἀπό, from. ἄρτι, now, just now.

2. { τὸ, the, λοιπόν, remaining *time*, } in future.

3. μηκέτι, no more, no longer.

4. { ἀπὸ, from, τοῦ, the, νῦν, now, } from the present.

1. Matt. xxiii. 39.
4. Luke i. 48*.
4. — v. 10*.
4. — xii. 52*.
1. John xiii. 19*, marg. (text, *now*.)
— — xv. 15, see H...not.
3. Acts iv. 17.
4. — xviii. 6*.
— Rom. vi. 6, see H...not.
— 2 Cor. v. 15, see H (not.)
4. — 16 1st.
— — 16 2nd, see H no more.
2. Gal. vi. 17*.
— Eph. iv. 14, see H no more.
— — 17, see H...not.
2. Heb. x. 13*.
1. Rev. xiv. 13*.

HENCEFORTH NO MORE.

1. μηκέτι, no more, no longer, no further, (*referring to what is matter of thought or supposition.*)

2. οὐκέτι, no more, no longer, (*referring to what is matter of fact.*)

2. 2 Cor. v. 16. | 1. Eph. iv. 14.

HENCEFORTH...NOT.

1. μηκέτι, (*see above, No.* 1.)

2. οὐκέτι, (*see above, No.* 2.)

2. John xv. 15. | 1. Rom. vi. 6. 1. Eph. iv. 17.

HENCEFORTH (NOT.)

μηκέτι, (*see above, No.* 1.)

2 Cor. v. 15.

HENCEFORWARD (NO...)

μηκέτι, no more, no longer, (*see above, No.* 1.)

Matt. xxi. 19.

HER.

1. αὐτῆς, (*gen. sing. fem.*) herself, *demonstrative and emphatic.*

2. ἑαυτῆς, of one's self, of her own self.

3. ταύτην, (*acc. fem. of* οὗτος,) this.

The word "HER" is generally the translation of *No.* 1, and is of too frequent occurrence to be quoted below.

— Matt. i. 6, see H...the wife.
2. — xxiii. 37, (No. 1, T Tr^b A ℵ.)
1. Luke i. 36, Dat. (*om.* L.)
1. — ii. 22, (αὐτῶν, *of them, their*, G L T Tr A ℵ) (αὐτοῦ, *of his*, G ~.)
2. Luke xiii. 34.
— Acts vii. 21, see H own.
2. 1 Cor. xi. 5 2nd, (No. 1, L T Tr A ℵ.)
— — xiii. 5, see H own.
2. 1 Thes. ii. 7.
3. Rev. xii. 15, (No. 1, G L T Tr A ℵ.)

HER OWN.

2. Acts vii. 21, Dat. | 2. 1 Cor. xiii. 5.

HER...THE WIFE.

ἡ, the, (*lit.* of the [wife] of Uriah.)

Matt. i. 6.

HERBS.

1. λάχανον, a plant tilled in the ground, *i.e.* garden herbs, *as opp. to wild plants*, vegetables, greens, (*non occ.*)
2. βοτάνη, pasturage, *i.e.* herbage, grass, fodder, (*non occ.*)

1. Matt. xiii. 32. | 1. Luke xi. 42.
1. Mark iv. 32. | 1. Rom. xiv. 2.
2. Heb. vi. 7.

HERD.

ἀγέλη, a herd, (*in N. T. only of swine*,) *non* [illegible].

Matt. viii. 30, 31.
—— 32 1st (*om.* G L Tr ℵ.)
Matt. viii. 32 2nd.
Mark v. 11, 13.
Luke viii. 32, 33.

HERE.

1. ὧδε, (*demonst. adv. of place*) hither, here.
2. ἐνθάδε, thither, hither, *more com.* here *or* there; *of time*, here, now, *as opp. to the future.*
3. αὐτοῦ, (*adv. orig. gen. neut. of* αὐτός, self,) just here, *or* just there.

1. Matt. xii. 41, 42.
1. —— xiv. 8, 17.
1. —— xvi. 28.
1. —— xvii. 4 twice.
1. —— xx. 6.
1. —— xxiv. 2, 23.
3. —— xxvi. 36.
1. —— 38.
1. —— xxviii. 6.
1. Mark vi. 3.
1. —— viii. 4.
1. —— ix. 1, 5.
1. —— xiii. 21.
1. —— xiv. 32, 34.
1. —— xvi. 6.
1. Luke iv. 23.
1. —— ix. 12.
1. —— 27, (No. 3, T Tr A ℵ.)
1. —— 33.
1. —— xi. 31, 32.
1. —— xvii. 21, 23.
1. —— xxii. 38.
1. —— xxiv. 6.
2. —— 41.
1. John vi. 9.
1. —— xi. 21, 32.
— Acts iv. 10, see Stand.
1. —— ix. 14.
— —— x. 33, see H present (be.)
2. —— xvi. 28.
— —— xxiv. 19, see H (be)
— —— 20, see H (these same.)
— —— xxv. 24 1st, see H present with (be.)
2. —— 24 2nd.
1. Col. iv. 9.
1. Heb. vii. 8.
1. —— xiii. 14.
1. Jas. ii. 3 1st.
1. —— 3 2nd (*om.* G ⇉ L T Tr A ℵ.)
— 1 Peter i. 17, see Sojourning.)
1. Rev. xiii. 10, 18.
1. —— xiv. 12 1st.
1. —— 12 2nd (*om.* G L T Tr A ℵ.)
1. Rev. xvii. 9.

HERE (BE.)

παρειμι, to be beside, be near by, be present, to have come.

Acts xxiv. 19.

HERE PRESENT (BE.)

πάρειμι (*see above.*)

Acts x. 33.

HERE PRESENT WITH (BE.)

συμπάρειμι, to be beside, in conjunction with any one, to be near by *or* present with *another*.

Acts xxv. 24.

HERE (THESE SAME.)

{ αὐτοὶ, themselves, οὗτοι, these, (*near*,) } these same *or* these themselves.

Acts xxiv. 20.

HEREAFTER.

1. { μετὰ, after, ταῦτα, these things.
2. { ἀπὸ, from, ἄρτι, now, just now.
3. { ἀπὸ, from, τοῦ, the, νυν, now, } from the present.
4. μηκέτι, no more, no longer.

2. Matt. xxvi. 64.
4. Mark xi. 14.
3. Luke xxii. 69.
2. John i. 52 (*om.* G ~ L T Tr A ℵ.)
1. —— xiii. 7.
— John xiv. 30, see H...not.
— 1 Tim. i. 16, see H (should.)
1. Rev. i. 19.
1. —— iv. 1.
1. Rev. ix. 12.

HEREAFTER...NOT.

{ οὐκ, no, not, ἔτι, yet, still, } no longer.

John xiv. 30.

HEREAFTER (SHOULD.)

μέλλω, to be about to, be on the point of.

1 Tim. i. 16.

HEREBY.

1. { ἐν, in, τούτῳ, this, } in this.

2. { ἐκ, out of, from, / τούτου, this, } in consequence of this.

1. 1 Cor. iv. 4.
1. 1 John ii. 3, 5.
1. —— iii. 16, 19, 24.
1. 1 John iv. 2.
2. —— iv. 6.
1. —— 13.

HEREIN.

{ ἐν, in, / τούτῳ, this.

John iv. 37.
—— ix. 30.
—— xv. 8.
Acts xxiv. 16.
2 Cor. viii. 10.
1 John iv. 10, 17.

HEREOF.

αὕτη, (*fem. sing. of* οὗτος, this) this (*viz.* this *report.*)

Matt. ix. 26, marg. *this.* | Acts xxv. 20, see Question.
Heb. v. 3, see Reason.

HERESY (-IES.)

αἵρεσις, a taking, *esp. of a town; then,* a taking *as of* choice, option; a preference, a chosen way *or* plan; later a philosophic principle, *or* set of principles, a sect *or* school, (elsewhere "SECT.")

Acts xxiv. 14.
1 Cor. xi. 19, marg. *sect.*
Gal. v. 20.
2 Pet. ii. 1.

HERETIC.

αἱρετικός, able to choose *or* select; *then,* one who acts from party spirit, a factious person. *Eng.* "heretic," (*non occ.*)

Tit. iii. 10.

HERETOFORE.

See SIN.

HEREUNTO.

{ εἰς, unto, / τοῦτο, this.

1 Pet. ii. 21.

HERITAGE.

κλῆρος, a lot, a casting lots; then, that which is assigned by lot, an allotment *or* portion of land, *hence,* possessions, heritage.

1 Pet. v. 3.

HEROD.

Ἡρώδης, a name of four persons, Idumæans, successively put in power by the Romans over the whole or part of the Jewish nation.

(a) Herod the Great, son of Antipater, procurator of Galilee, B.C. 41, died A.D. 2, aged 70, after 40 years reign.

(b) Herod Antipas (Herod the Tetrarch) son of Herod the Great, and own brother to Archelaus. Married a daughter of Aretas, and dismissed her for Herodias, whom he induced to leave her husband, his brother Philip Herod.

(c) Herod Agrippa, the elder, oft. called only Agrippa, grandson of Herod the Great, died A.D. 44. Acts xii. 21.

(d) Herod Agrippa, the younger son of (c). It was before this one that Paul was brought.

a. Matt. i. 3, 7, 12, 13, 15, 16, 19, 22.
b. —— xiv. 1, 3, 6 twice.
b. Mark vi. 14, 16, 17, 18, 20—22.
b. —— viii. 15.
a. Luke i. 5.
b. —— iii. 1, 19 twice.
b. —— viii. 3.
b. —— ix. 7, 9.
b. —— xiii. 31.
b. Luke xxiii. 7 twice, 8, 11, 12, 15.
b. Acts iv. 27.
c. —— xii. 1, 6, 11, 19.
c. —— 20, (om. G L T Tr A ℵ), 21.
b. —— xiii. 1.
c. —— xxiii. 35.
d. —— xxv. 13, 22—24, 26.
d. —— xxvi. 1, 2, 7, 19, 28, 32.

HERSELF.

1. αὐτή, self, she herself.

2. ἑαυτῆς, of herself, herself.

2. Matt. ix. 21.
2. Luke i. 24.
1. Heb. xi. 11.
2. Rev. ii. 20.
2. —— xviii. 7.
2. —— xix. 7.

HEW, HEWN.

λατομέω, to quarry *or* hew stones, *(non occ.)*

Matt. xxvii. 60. | Mark xv. 46.

HEW DOWN.

ἐκκόπτω, to cut out, (*as a surgeon does*); *of trees* to cut down, fell, *hence.* to cut off, destroy.

Matt. iii. 10. | Matt. vii. 19.
Luke iii. 9.

HEWN IN STONE.

λαξευτος, hewn in stone, (lxx. Deut. iv. 49.)

Luke xxiii. 53.

HIDE (-ETH, -DEN.)

Also HID, HIDDEN, the adjective.

1. κρύπτω, to hide, cover, cloak; conceal, keep secret, to keep covered for purposes of concealment

2. ἀποκρύπτω, (*No.* 1 *with* ἀπὸ, away from, *prefixed*) to hide away from *any one.*

3. ἐγκρύπτω, (*No.* 1 *with* ἐν, in, *prefixed*) to hide in *anything by covering,* (*non occ.*)

4. περικρύπτω, (*No.* 1 *with* περὶ, around, *prefixed*) to hide all around, hide wholly, (*non occ.*)

5. καλύπτω, to cover with *a thing,* to cover over so that no trace of it can be seen, (*thus differing from No.* 1) *esp.* to cover *with a veil,* (*elsewhere,* Cover.)

6. παρακαλύπτω, (*No.* 5 *with* παρὰ, beside, *prefixed*) to cover over *or* hide by putting anything beside *or* near *an object:* to veil, disguise, (*non occ.*)

7. κρυπτός, (*adj. of No.* 1,) covered for purposes of concealment.

8. ἀπόκρυφος, (*adj. of No.* 2,) hidden away from, (*occ.* Mk. iv. 32.)

1. Matt. v. 14.
1. —— viii. 44 twice.
7. —— x. 26.
2. —— xi. 25, (No. 1, L T Tr A ℵ.)
3. —— xiii. 33, (No. 1, G ∾)
2. —— xxv. 18.
1. ——— 25.
7. Mark iv. 22.
— —— vii. 24, see H (be.)
4. Luke i. 24.
8. —— viii. 17.
— ——— 47, see H (be.)
6. —— ix. 45.
2. —— x. 21.
7. —— xii. 2.
3. —— xiii. 21 (No. 1, T Tr A.)
1. —— xviii. 34.
1. Luke xix. 42.
— John viii. 59, } see H one's self.
— —— xii. 36, }
— Acts xxvi. 26, see H (be.)
2. 1 Cor. ii. 7.
— —— iv. 5, } see H thing.
— 2 Cor. iv. 2, }
5. ——— 3 twice.
2. Eph. iii. 9.
2. Col. i. 26.
8. —— ii. 3.
1. —— iii. 3.
1. 1 Tim. v. 25.
1. Heb. xi. 23.
5. Jas. v. 20.
7. 1 Pet. iii. 4.
1. Rev. ii. 17.
1. —— vi. 15, 16.

HIDE ONE'S SELF.

1. John viii. 59, } passive.
1. —— xii. 36, }

HID (BE.)

λανθάνω, to escape notice, be unnoticed.

Mark vii. 24. | Luke viii. 47.
Acts xxvii. 26.

HIDDEN THING.

7. 1 Cor. iv. 5, } neuter.
7. 2 Cor. iv. 2, }

HIGH.

(*See also* PRIEST.)

1. ὑψηλός, high, elevated; on high, towering.

2. μέγας, great, *esp. of bodily size; but also of importance, degree, and power,* etc.

3. ἄνω, up, above, upwards.

1. Matt. iv. 8.
1. —— xvii. 1.
— Mark v. 7, see H (most.)
— —— vi. 21, see Captain.
1. —— ix. 2.
— Luke i. 78, see H (from on.)
1. —— iv. 5 (*ap.*)
— —— viii. 28, see H (most.)
— —— xxiv. 49, see H (from on.)
2. John xix. 31.
— Acts vii. 48, see H (most.)
1. —— xiii. 17.
— —— xvi. 17, see H (most.)
— Rom. xi. 20, see High-minded.
— —— xii. 16, see H things.
— —— xiii. 11, see Time.
— 2 Cor. x. 5, see H things.
— Eph. iv. 8, see H (on.)
— —— vi. 12, see H places.
3. Phil. iii. 14.
— 1 Tim. vi. 17, see High-minded.
— Heb. i. 3, see H (on.)
— —— vii. 1, see H (most.)
1. ——— 26.
2. —— x. 21.
1. Rev. xxi. 10, 12.

HIGH (ON.)

1. { ἐν, in, { ὑψηλοῖς, high, [*pl. prob.* places.]

2. { ἐν, in, { ὕψος, height, } on high.

2 Eph. iv. 8. | 1 Heb. i. 3.

HIGH (FROM ON.)

{ ἐξ, out of, { ὕψους, high, } from on high.

Luke i. 78; xxiv. 49.

HIGH (MOST.)

ὕψιστος, (*superl.*) highest, loftiest, * *applied to God.*

Mark v. 7. | Acts vii. 48.*
Luke viii. 28. | —— xvi. 17.
Heb. vii. 1.

HIGH PLACES.

{ οἱ, the, (*pl.*) / ἐπουρανίοι, } heavenly *places.*

Eph. vi. 12, marg. *heavenly places.*

HIGH THINGS.

1. { τὰ, the *things,* / ὑψηγα, high *things.*
2. ὕψωμα, high position, height.

2 Cor. x. 5.

See also PRIEST (HIGH.)

HIGHER.

1. ἀνώτερον, higher.
2. ὑπερέχω, to hold over *a thing, as being superior and as protecting. Here, part.* superior, *or* protecting.

1. Luke xiv. 10. | 2. Rom. xiii. 1.

HIGHEST.

ὕψιστος, (*superl.*) highest, loftiest.

Luke i. 32, 35, 76. — vi. 35. | Luke xiv. 8, see Room. — xx. 46, see Seat.

HIGHEST (IN THE.)

1. { ἐν, in, / τοῖς, the, / ὑψίστοις, highest, (*pl.*)
2. { ἐν, in, / ὑψίστοις, highest, (*pl.*)

1. Matt. xxi. 9. 1. Mark xi. 10. | 2. Luke ii. 14. 2. — xix. 38.

HIGHLY.

Luke i. 28, see Favoured. — xvi. 15, see H esteemed, (that which is.) | Acts xii. 20, see Displeased. Rom. xii. 3, see Think. Phil. ii. 9, see Exalt.

1 Thes. v. 13, see H (very.)

HIGHLY ESTEEMED (THAT WHICH IS.)

{ τὸ, the, / ὑψηλος, lofty.

Luke xvi. 15.

HIGHLY (VERY.)

{ ὑπὲρ, over, above, beyond, / ἐκ, out of, / περισσοῦ, abundant, remaining over and above. } exceeding abundantly.

HIGH-MINDED (BE.)

1. τυφόω, to be τῦφος, (smoke, vapour,) to be beclouded.
2. ὑψηλοφρονέω, to think lofty things, to be high-minded, haughty, (*non occ.*)

2. Rom. xi. 20. | 2. 1 Tim. vi. 17.

1. 2 Tim. iii. 4.

HIGHWAY (-S.)

1. ὁδός, a way, path, road, highway.
2. { διέξοδοι, ways out through, passages, / τῶν, of the, / ὁδῶν, of roads, } the crossings of the ways, *or,* the crossways of the roads, (*non occ.*)

2. Matt. xxii. 9. 1. ——— 10. | — Mark x. 46, see H side (by the.)

1. Luke xiv. 23.

HIGHWAYSIDE (BY THE.)

1. Mark x. 46.

HILL.

1. ὄρος, a mountain, hill.
2. ὀρεινός, (*adj.*) mountainous, hilly, (*non occ.*)
3. βουνός, a hill, heap, mound, height, (*non occ.*)

1. Matt. v. 14. 2. Luke i. 39, 65. 3. — iii. 5. | 1. Luke iv. 29. 1. — ix. 37. 3. — xxiii. 30.

— Acts xvii. 19, 22, see Mar's Hill.

HIM.

HIM is generally the translation of αὐτός, (very, self, *he,*) in some of its inflections. Sometimes there is no corresponding Greek word. Except in these cases it is the translation of one of these words following, in the passages below.

1. οὗτος, this, (*the nearer person.*) *Here, the accusative, except * the Dative, and † the Gen.*
2. ἑαυτοῦ, himself. *, *the Dat.*
3. ἐκεῖνος, that one *there.*

1. Matt. xxvii. 32.
2. Mark xiv. 33 (ἀυτôυ, L T Tr A ℵ.)
1. Luke ix. 26.
2*.——— 47.
1. —— xii. 5.
1*.—— xix. 19 (to him.)
1. —— xx. 12, 13.
1. John v. 6.
1*.——— 38.
3. ——— 43.
1. —— vi. 27.
1†.—— ix. 31.
1*.—— x. 3, } (tohim)
1*.—— xiii. 24, } (tohim)
3. ——— 27.
1. —— xxi. 21.
1. Acts ii. 23.
1*.—— iv. 10.
1. —— v. 31.
1. Acts x. 40.
1*.——— 43 (to him.)
1. —— xiii. 27.
1*.——— 39.
1. —— xv. 38.
1. —— xvi. 3.
1. —— xvii. 23.
3. Rom. xiv. 14, 15.
1. 1 Cor. ii. 2.
1. —— iii. 17 (ἀυτόν, *him*, G ∾ L.)
2*.—— xvi. 2.
— Eph. i. 10, see H (ever.)
1. Phil. ii. 23.
1. Heb. xi. 12, neut. plur.
1*.—— 1 John ii. 4, 5.
1. Rev. v. 14 (*ap.*)
1†.—— xix. 20 (ἀυτου, *him*, G L T Tr A ℵ.)

HIM (EVEN) (IN.)

{ ἐν, in,
{ αὐτῷ, him and no other, him alone.

Eph. i. 10.

HIMSELF.

1. ἑαυτοῦ, himself, *masc. sing.*
   * *Accusative.*
   † *Dative*

2. αὐτός, very, self, he *and no other*, he alone.
   * *Accusative.*
   † *Genitive.*
   ‡ *Dative.*

2. Matt. vi. 4 (*om.* G → L T Tr A ℵ.)
2. —— viii. 17.
1*.—— xii. 26.
1. ——— 45 twice.
1†.—— xiii. 21.
1*.—— xvi. 24.
1*.—— xviii. 4.
1*.—— xxiii. 12 twice.
1*.—— xxvii. 42.
2. ——— 57.
1*.Mark iii. 26.
1*.—— v. 5.
1†.——— 30.
2. —— vi. 17.
1*.—— viii. 34.
1*.—— xii. 33.
2. ——— 36.
1*.—— xv. 31.
2. Luke iii. 23.
2. —— vi. 3.
1†.—— vii. 39.
1*.—— ix. 23, 25.
— —— x. 1, see H (he.)
1*.——— 29.
1*.—— xi. 18.
1. ——— 26.
1†.—— xii. 17.
1†.——— 21 (for himself.)
1*.—— xiv. 11 twice.
1*.—— xv. 17.
1†.—— xvi. 3.
1†.—— xviii. 4.
1*.——— 11, 14 twice.
1†.—— xix. 12 (for himself.)
2. —— xx. 42.
— Luke xxiii. 2, see H (he)
1*.——— 35.
1*.—— xxiv. 12 (*ap.*)
2. ——— 15.
1. ——— 27 (No. 2, G L T Tr.)
2. ——— 36.
1*.John ii. 24 No. 2*, L T Tr A ℵ.)
2. —— iv. 2, 12, 44, 53.
1* —— v. 18.
1. ——— 19.
2. ——— 20.
1†.——— 26 twice.
2. ——— 37 (ἐκιέινος, that one there, Lm T Tr A ℵ.)
— —— vi. 6, 15, see H (he.)
1†.——— 61.
— —— vii. 4, see H (he.)
1. ——— 18.
1*.—— viii. 22.
1†.—— xi. 38.
1. ——— 51.
1*.—— xiii. 4.
1†.——— 32 (No. 2‡, T Tr)
1. —— xvi. 13.
2. ——— 27.
1*.—— xix. 7.
1*.—— xxi. 1, 7.
1*.Acts i. 3.
— —— ii. 34, see H (he.)
1*.—— v. 36.
1*.—— viii. 9.
2. ——— 13.
1. ——— 34.
1†.—— x. 17.
1†.Acts xii. 11.
1*.—— xiv. 17 (No. 2*, L T Tr ℵ.)
1*.—— xvi. 27.
— —— xviii. 19 } see H (he.)
— —— xix. 22 } see H (he.)
1*.——— 31.
2. —— xx. 13.
— —— xxv. 4, 25, see H (he.)
1*.—— xxviii. 16.
1†.Rom. xiv. 7 twice, (to H)
1. ——— 12.
1*.——— 22.
1†.—— xv. 3.
— 1 Cor. ii. 15 } see H (he.)
— —— iii. 15 } see H (he.)
1*.——— 18.
1*.—— xi. 28.
1†.——— 29 (to H.)
1*.—— xiv. 4.
1†.——— 28 (to H.)
2. —— xv. 28.
1†.2 Cor. v. 18 (to H.)
1†.———19 (unto H.)
1†.—— x. 7 1st.
1. ——— 7 2nd (with ἀπο, *from.*)
1*.——— 18.
2. ——xi. 14.
1*.Gal. i. 4.
1*.—— ii. 12, 20.
1*.—— vi. 3, 4.
2*.Eph. i. 5.
2‡.——— 9.
1†.——ii. 15, (No. 2 ‡ L T Tr A ℵ.)
2‡.——— 16, marg. (text, *thereby.*)
1*.—— v. 2, 25.
1†.Eph. v. 27, (to H.)
1*.——— 33.
1*.Phil. ii. 7, 8.
1†.—— iii. 21, unto H (No. 2‡, L T Tr A ℵ.)
2*.Col. i. 20.
2. 1 Thes. iii. 11.
2. —— iv. 16.
1*.2 Thes. ii. 4.
2. ——— 16.
2. —— iii. 16.
1*.1 Tim. ii. 6.
1*.2 Tim. ii. 13, 21.
1*.Titus ii. 14 1st.
1†.——— 14 2nd (unto H.)
1. Heb. i. 3 (*om.* L T Tr A ℵ.)
— —— ii. 18, } see H (he.)
— —— v. 2, } see H (he.)
1†.——— 3 (No. 2† L.)
1†.——— 4 (unto H.)
1*.——— 5.
1. —— vi. 13.
1*.—— vii. 27.
1. —— ix. 7.
1*.——— 14, 25.
2†.——— 26.
2*.—— xii. 3.
1*. Jas. i. 24, 27.
2. 1 John ii. 6.
1*.—— iii. 3.
1†.—— v. 10 (No. 2‡, T Tr A.)
1*.——— 18, (No. 2* T Tr A.)
— 3 John 10, see H (he.)
— Rev. v. 14 (*ap.*)
— —— xix. 12, see H (he.)
2. —— xxi. 3.

HIMSELF (HE.)

1. αὐτός, very, self, he *alone*, he *and no other.*

2. ἑαυτοῦ, himself.

3. { αὐτοῦ, self, / τούτου, this. } this [*man*] himself.

1. Luke x. 1.
2. —— xxiii. 2.
1. John vi. 6, 15.
1. ——vii. 4.
1. Acts ii. 34.
1. —— xviii. 19.
1. —— xix. 22.
2. Acts xxv. 4.
3. ——— 25.
1. 1 Cor. ii. 15.
1. —— iii. 15.
1. Heb. ii. 18.
1. —— v. 2.
1. 3 John 10.

1. Rev. xix. 12.

HINDER (-ED) [verb.]

1. ἐγκόπτω, to cut in, *hence,* (of an ἐγκοπὴ, a trench cut in the way of an enemy to impede him); to thwart, hinder, (Acts xxiv. 4.)

2. ἀνακόπτω, to beat back, *hence,* to check, restrain, (*non occ.*)

3. ἐκκόπτω, to cut out, (*as a surgeon does*); then, to beat off from *a place;* repulse *of soldiers.*

4. { ἐγκοπή, a cutting in, as a trench in the way of an enemy, δίδωμι, to give, } to give a hindrance.

5. κωλύω, to cut short, to restrain, check, stop, prevent, forbid.

5. Luke xi. 52, marg. *forbid.*
5. Acts viii. 36.
1. Rom. xv. 22.
4. 1 Cor. ix. 12.
2. Gal. v. 7, marg. *drive back,* (No. 1, G L T Tr A ℵ.)
1. 1 Thes. ii. 18.
3. 1 Pet. iii. 7, (No. 1, G L T Tr A ℵ.)

HINDER PART.

πρύμνα, the hindmost part of a ship, the stern, poop, (*lat.*, puppis,) (*occ.* Acts xxvii. 29.)

Acts xxvii. 41.

HINDER PART OF THE SHIP.

Mark iv. 38.

HIRE [noun.]

μισθός, wages, pay, hire; *gen.*, recompense, reward.

Matt. xx. 8. | Luke x. 7.
Jas. v. 4.

HIRE (-ED) [verb.]

μισθόω, to let out for hire, farm out. *In Mid., as here,* to have let to one, to hire, to engage the services *of any one,* contract, (*non occ.*)

Matt. xx. 1, 7.

HIRED HOUSE.

μισθωμα, that which is let out for hire, hired, *as a house,* (*non occ.*)

Acts xxviii. 30.

HIRED SERVANT (-S.)

1. μισθωτός, one who is hired, a hired servant, (*emphasis on* servant,) (*occ.* John x. 12, 13.)

2. μισθιος, (*adj.*) hired, *as subst.*, hired ones, (*emphasis on* hired,) (*non occ.*)

1. Mark i. 20. | 2. Luke xv. 17, 19.

HIRELING.

μισθωτός, (*see above, No.* 1.)

John x. 12, 13.

HIS.

(see HIS OWN, below.)

("His," is generally the translation of αὐτος, *No.* 1. The following are the exceptions.)

1. αὐτὸς, self, he *and no other*, he alone.
2. ἑαυτοῦ, of himself, etc.
3. ἐκεῖνος, that one *there*.
4. ἴδιος, belonging to any one, one's own.
5. ὁ, *the definite article*, the; *here, the Gen.*, τοῦ, of the (*one referred to, i.e.* God,) *hence*, his.

(All passages not quoted are the translation of *No.* 1.)

4. Matt. xxii. 5.
— —— xxv. 15, see H several.
2. Luke xi. 21.
2. —— xii. 47 (No. 1, L T Tr A ℵ.)
2. —— xiii. 19.
2. —— xiv. 26 (No. 1, L T Tr ℵ.)
2. ——xv. 5 (No. 1, T Tr A ℵ.)
2. ——— 20, (No. 1, L T Tr ℵ.)
2. —— xvi. 5.
2. —— xix. 13.
4. John v. 18.
3. ——— 47.
3. —— ix. 28.
— —— xix. 27, see H own home.
5. Acts xvii. 28.
— —— xxiv. 23, see H acquaintance.
2. Rom. v. 8.
— 1 Cor. vii. 7, see H proper.
2. ——— 37.
3. —— x. 28.
2. 2 Cor. iii. 13, (No. 1, L Tr A.)
3. —— viii. 9
2. Gal. vi. 8.
2. Eph. v. 28, 33.
2. 1 Thes. ii. 11, 12.
2. —— iv. 4.
2. 2 Thes. ii. 6.
4. 1 Tim. vi. 15.
3. 2 Tim. ii. 26.
3. Titus iii. 7.
4. Heb. iv. 10 2nd.
— 1 Pet. ii. 24, see H own self.
3. 1 Pet. i. 16.
4. 2 Pet. ii. 16.
2. Rev. x. 7.

HIS OWN.

1. ἴδιος, belonging to one, his own.
   * τὰ ἴδια, *neut. pl., with article,* one's things *or* own possessions.
2. ἑαυτοῦ, of himself.

1. Matt. ix. 1.
1. —— xxv. 14.
1. Mark xv. 20, (αὐτοῦ, *his,* L) (*om.* G →)
1. Luke ii. 3.
1. —— vi. 44.
1. —— x. 34.
2. —— xiv. 26.
1*. John i. 11 1st, neut. pl., lit., *His own possessions.*
1. ——— 11 2nd, masc. pl., lit., *His own people.*
1. ——— 41.
1. —— iv. 44.
1. —— v. 43.
1. —— vii. 18.
1. —— viii. 44.
1. —— x. 3, 4.
1. —— xiii. 1.
1. —— xv. 19.
1*. —— xvi. 32, marg. *his own home.*
— —— xix. 27, see H own home.
1. Acts i. 7, 25.
1. —— ii. 6.
1. —— iv. 32.
1. —— xiii. 36.
1. Acts xx. 28.
1. —— xxv. 19.
1. —— xxviii. 30.
2. Rom. iv. 19.
1. —— viii. 32.
1. —— xiv. 4, 5.
1. 1 Cor. iii. 8 twice.
1. —— vi. 18.
2. —— vii. 2.
1. ——— 4.
1. —— ix. 7.
2. —— x. 24.
1. —— xi. 21.
1. —— xv. 23, 38.
2. Gal. vi. 4.
1. ——— 5.
2. Eph. v. 29.
2. Phil. ii. 4, pl.
1. 1 Tim. iii. 4, 5.
1. —— v. 8.
1. 2 Tim. i. 9.
1. Heb. vii. 27.
1. —— ix. 12.
1. —— xiii. 12.
1. Jas. i. 14.
— 1 Pet. ii. 24, see H own self.
1. 2 Pet. ii. 22.
2. Rev. i. 5.

HIS ACQUAINTANCE.

1. Acts xxiv. 23, pl. masc.

HIS PROPER.

1. 1 Cor. vii. 7.

HIS SEVERAL.

1. Matt. xxv. 15, (with κατὰ.)

HIS OWN HOME.

1*. John xix. 27.

HIS OWN SELF.

ἀυτός, himself and no other, he alone.

1 Pet. ii. 24.

HITHER.

1. ὧδε, (*demonst. adv.*) *of manner*, in this wise, so, thus; *of state*, so, as it is; *of place*, hither, here. (*The old Grammarians deny the usage of place in Homer, and refer it to manner.*)

2. ἐνθάδε, thither, hither; here.

1. Matt. viii. 29.
1. —— xiv. 18.
1. —— xvii. 17.
1. —— xxii. 12.
1. Mark xi. 3.
1. Luke ix. 41 (om. G→)
1. —— xiv. 21.
1. —— xix. 27.
2. John iv. 15, 16.
1. —— vi. 25.
1. John xx. 27 1st
— ——— 27 2nd, see Reach
1. Acts ix. 21.
— —— x. 32, see Call.
2. —— xvii. 6.
2. —— xxv. 17.
1. Rev. iv. 1.
1. —— xi. 12.
— —— xvii. 1, } see
— —— xxi. 9, } Come.

HITHERTO.

1. { ἕως, until, as long as, / ἄρτι, now, even now, } until now.

* [As used of the working of the Father and the Son it refers to the time when Sin broke God's rest, and He became a worker to redeem and deliver man from sin and its consequences.]

2. { ἄχρι, continuedly until, during, until, / τοῦ, the, / δεῦρο, here, *i.e.* to this place or time. } until the present.

1*. John v. 17.
1. —— xvi. 24.
2. Rom. i. 13.
— 1 Cor. iii. 2, see H, not.

HITHERTO...NOT.

οὔπω, not even yet, not yet.

1 Cor. iii. 2.

HOISE UP.

ἐπαίρω, to raise up, *prop. of a sail*, to hoist up.

Acts xxvii. 40.

HOLD [noun.]

1. τήρησις, a watching *or* keeping, *as with the eye;* custody.

2. φυλακή, a watching *or* guarding, *esp. by night; then*, the place for guarding others in.

1. Acts iv. 3. | 2. Rev. xviii. 2.

HOLD (-EN, -ING, HELD) [verb.]

1. κρατέω, to be strong, powerful; to have power *or* rule over; to have and hold in one's power, to be master of, *and so*, to hold, hold fast, to attain and maintain power over.

2. ἔχω, to have and hold, *implying continued holding and lasting possession.*

3. κατέχω, (*No.* 2, *with* κατὰ, down, *prefixed,*) to have and hold down, *hence used in various senses, here,* to have and hold fast, *or* firmly.

4. λαμβάνω, *actively*, to take, *prop. with the hand; passively*, to receive.

5. ποιέω, to make, to form.

6. ἦσαν, (*3rd pers. pl. imperf. of* εἰμὶ, to be,) they were.

— Matt. vi. 24, see H to.
— —— xii. 11, see H on (lay.)
4. ——— 14, marg. *take.*
— —— xiv. 3, see H on (lay.)
— —— xx. 31, see Peace.
2. —— xxi. 26.
— —— xxvi. 48, see H fast.
— ——— 55, 57, see H on (lay.)
— ——— 63, see Peace.
— —— xxviii. 9, see H by.
— Mark i. 25, } see Peace.
— —— iii. 4, }
— ——— 21, see H on (lay.)
— —— vi. 17, see H upon (lay.)
1. —— vii. 3, 48.
— —— ix. 34, } see Peace.
— —— x. 48, }
— —— xii. 12, see H on (lay.)
— —— xiv. 51, see H on (lay.)
— ——— 61, see Peace.
5. —— xv. 1.
— Luke iv. 35, see Peace.
— —— xiv. 4.
— —— xvi. 13, see H to.
— —— xviii. 39, } see
— —— xix. 40, } Peace.
— —— xx. 20, 26 1st, see Take.
— ——— 26 2nd, see Peace.
— —— xxii. 63, see H (man that.)
— —— xxiii. 26, see H upon (lay.)
1. —— xxiv. 16.
— John x. 24, see *Suspense.*
1. Acts ii. 24.
1. —— iii. 11, part.
— Acts xi. 18, } see
— —— xii. 17, } Peace.
6. —— xiv. 4.
— —— xv. 13, } see
— —— xviii. 9, } Peace.
3. Rom. i. 18.
3. —— vii. 6.
— —— xiv. 4, see H up (be.)
— 1 Cor. xiv. 30, see Peace.
— —— xv. 2, see H fast.
— Phil. ii. 16, see H forth.

2. Phil. ii. 29.
1. Col. ii. 19.
— 1 Thes. v. 21, see H fast.
3. 2 Thes. ii. 6, marg. (text, *withhold*.)
1. —— 15.
2. 1 Tim. i. 19
2. —— iii. 9.
— —— vi. 12, 19, see H on (lay.)
— 2 Tim. i. 13, } see H fast.
— Titus i. 9,
— Heb. iii. 6,
3. —— 14.
— Heb. iv. 14, see H fast.
— —— vi. 18, see H upon (lay.)
— —— x. 23, } see H fast.
— —— xii. 28,
1. Rev. ii. 1.
— —— 13, see H fast.
1. —— 14, 15.
— —— 25, } see H fast.
— —— iii. 3, 11,
2. —— vi. 9.
1. —— vii. 1.
— —— xx. 2, see H on (lay.)

HOLD BY.

1. Matt. xxviii. 9.

HOLD FAST.

1. κρατέω, (*see above, No.* 1.)

2. ἔχω, (*see above, No* 2.)

3. κατέχω, (*see above, No.* 3.)

4. ἀντέχομαι, *in N.T. only mid.*, to hold before one against *something*, hold on by, cling to.

5. τηρέω, to watch over, take care of, give heed to, watch narrowly.

1. Matt. xxvi. 48.
3. 1 Cor. xv. 2, marg. (text, *keep in memory*.)
3. 1 Thes. v. 21.
2. 2 Tim i. 13.
4. Tit. i. 9.
3. Heb. iii. 6.
1. Heb. iv. 14.
3. —— x. 23.
2. —— xii. 28, marg. (text, *have*.)
1. Rev. ii. 13, 25.
5. —— iii. 3, (*ap.*)
1. —— 11.

HOLD FORTH.

ἐπέχω, to have *or* hold upon, to hold out towards, to direct upon, to aim at and hit

Phil. ii. 16.

HOLD TO.

ἀντέχομαι, *see* "HOLD FAST," *No.* 4.

Matt. vi. 24. | Luke xvi. 13.

HOLD ON (LAY.)

1. κρατέω, *see* "HOLD," *No.* 1.

2. ἐπιλαμβάνομαι, to take hold upon, *in order to hold or detain to or for oneself.*

1. Matt. xii. 11.
1. —— xiv. 3.
1. —— xxvi. 55, 57.
1. Mark iii. 21.
1. Mark xii. 12.
1. —— xiv. 51.
2. 1 Tim. vi. 12, 19.
1. Rev. xx. 2

HOLD UPON (LAY.)

1. κρατέω, (*see above, No.* 1.)

2. ἐπιλαμβάνομαι, (*see above, No.* 2.)

1. Mark vi. 17. | 2. Luke xxiii. 26.
1 Heb. vi. 18.

HOLDEN UP (BE.)

ἵστημι, (a) *Trans.*, to cause to stand, to set, to place.

(b) *Intrans.*, to stand.

b. Rom. xiv. 4.

HELD (MEN THAT.)

{ οἱ, the *men*,
{ συνέχοντες, holding in constraint.

Luke xxii. 63.

HOLE (-S.)

1. φωλεός, a hole, burrow, lurking place *of animals, (non occ.)*

2. ὀπή, an opening, a fissure in the earth or rocks, (*occ.* Heb. xi. 38.)

1. Matt. viii. 20. | 1. Luke ix. 58.
2. Jas. iii. 11, marg. (text, *place*.)

HOLIEST.

ἅγια, holy, consecrated to God.

Heb. x. 19.

HOLIEST OF ALL.

1. ἅγια, (*see above.*)

2. { ἅγια, holy,
{ ἁγίων, of holies.

2. Heb. ix. 3. | 1. Heb. ix. 8.

HOLILY.

ὁσίως, piously, holily, *i.e.* as being pure from all crime, and religiously observant of every duty.

(Adv. of "HOLY," *No.* 2, *which see.*)

1 Thes. ii. 10.

HOLINESS.

1. ἁγιασμός, sanctification, essential purity; the accomplishment of what is expressed in ἁγιάζω (*see* "H (be)") and the result of this action, in that it is contemplated as effected. (Elsewhere "Sanctification.")

2. ἁγιωσύνη, sanctity, marking the condition, the state or holy frame of mind in which the action of the verb ἁγιάζω, (*see* "H (be)") is evidenced and exemplified, (*non occ.*)

3. ἁγιότης, holiness, *marking the abstract quality*, (*non occ.*)

4. ὁσιότης, holiness, *or* godliness, *as manifested in the discharge of religious and social duties.*

5. εὐσέβεια, piety, the good and careful cherishing of the fear of God, *the distinctive title for* that which embraces all Christian relations. (Elsewhere " Godliness.")

4. Luke i. 75.
5. Acts iii. 12.
2. Rom. i. 4.
1. — vi. 19, 22.
2. 2 Cor. vii. 1.
4. Eph. iv. 24.
2. 1 Thes. iii. 13.
1. — iv. 7.
1. 1 Tim. ii. 15.
— Tit. ii. 3, see H (as becometh.)
3. Heb. xii. 10.
1. Heb. xii. 14.

HOLINESS (AS BECOMETH.)

ἱεροπρεπής, beseeming the sacred, (*see* "HOLY," *No.* 3,) as becoming to women who are consecrated *or* given and devoted to God.

Tit. ii. 3, marg. *as becometh holy women.*

HOLY.

(For HOLY GHOST, etc., *see below.*)

1. ἅγιος, from ἅζομαι, to have veneration and awe. ἅγος *is* reverence and the object of it, *hence* ἅγιος *is* what belongs to the same, *and denotes* holy, sacred. *As that could not be sacred which was polluted*, purity *becomes part of the meaning.* ἅγιος is that which is sacred, *and that only can be sacred which is* not unclean. [Holiness was taught to the Jews by a series of comparisons, in which purity pervaded all the ceremonies of the Law.]

2. ὅσιος, pure from all crime, the condition of one who has committed no crime, but religiously observes every duty and fulfils every obligation. [The τὰ ὅσια Δαβὶδ τὰ πιστὰ, (the sure mercies of David, Acts xiii. 34, Is. lv. 3,) are the religiously performed promises made to David, the faithfully fulfilled obligations.]

3. ἱερός, that which is consecrated *or* sacred, as given and devoted to God, *irrespective of mind or morals*, that which subserves a sacred purpose. (*Hence*, τὸ ἱερόν, *is* the Temple, ἱερεύς, *is* the priest, τὰ ἱερὰ, *are* the sacrifices.)

1. Matt. iv. 5.
1. — vii. 6.
1. — xxiv. 15.
1. — xxv. 31, (*om.* G L T Tr ℵ.)
1. — xxvii. 53.
— Mark i. 24, see H One.
1. — vi. 20.
1. — viii. 38.
— Luke i. 35, see H thing.
1. —— 49, 70, 72.
1. — ii. 23.
— — iv. 34, see H One.
1. — ix. 26.
1. John xvii. 11.
— Acts ii. 27, see H (be.)
— — iii. 14, see H One.
1. — iv. 27, 30.
1. — vi. 13.
1. — vii. 33.
1. — x. 22.
— — xiii. 34, see H thing
— —— 35, see H One.
1. — xxi. 28.
1. Rom. i. 2.
1. — vii. 12 twice.
1. — xi. 16 twice.
1. — xii. 1.
1. — xvi. 16.
1. 1 Cor. iii. 17.
1. — vii. 14, 34.
— — ix. 13, see H thing.
1. — xvi. 20.
1. 2 Cor. xiii. 12.
1. Eph. i. 4.
1. — ii. 21.
1. — iii. 5.
1. — v. 27.
1. Col. i. 22.
1. — iii. 12.
1. 1 Thes. v. 26.
1. —— 27, (*om.* G L T Tr A ℵ.)
2. 1 Tim. ii. 8.
1. 2 Tim. i. 9.
3. — iii. 15.
2. Titus i. 8.
— — ii. 3, see *H women (as becometh.)*
1. Heb. iii. 1.
2. — vii. 26.
— — viii. 2, see H thing
— — ix. 12, 24, 25, see H place.
1. 1 Pet. i. 15 twice, 16 twice.
1. — ii. 5, 9.
1. — iii. 5.
1. 2 Pet. i. 18.
1. —— 21, (ἀπὸ, *from*, T Trm A) lit., *men spake from God.*
1. — ii. 21.
1. — iii. 2, 11.
— 1 John ii. 20, see H one.
1. Jude 20.
1. Rev. iii. 7.
1. — iv. 8, 3 times.
1. — vi. 10.
1. — xi. 2.
1. — xiv. 10 (*om.* G → A.)
2. — xv. 4 (No. 1, G∾.)
1. — xviii. 20.
1. — xx. 6.
1. — xxi. 2, 10.
1. — xxii. 6, (πνευμάτων τῶν, *of the spirits of the*, G L T Tr A ℵ.)
1. —— 11 1st.
— —— 11 2nd, see H (be)
1. —— 19.

HOLY ONE.

1. Mark i. 24.
1. Luke iv. 34.
2. Acts ii. 27.
1. Acts iii. 14.
2. — xiii. 35.
1. 1 John ii. 20.

HOLY PLACE.

1. Heb. ix. 12, neut. pl.
1. Heb. ix. 24, neut. sing.
1. Heb. ix. 25, neut. pl.

HOLY THING (-s.)

1. Luke i. 35, neut. sing.
2. Acts xiii. 34, neut. pl. with art. (τὰ ὅσια), marg. (text, *mercies.*)
3. 1 Cor. ix. 13, neut. pl. with art. (τὰ ἱερά.)
1. Heb. viii. 2, neut. pl., marg. (text, *sanctuary*)

HOLY WOMEN (*as becometh.*) [margin.]

Titus ii. 3, see "HOLINESS."

HOLY (BE.)

ἁγιαζόμαι, to be ἅγιος (see "HOLY," *No.* 1,) to be set into a state opposed to κοινόν (common, unclean,) *or* to be delivered from that state if already κοινόν, and be put into a state corresponding to the nature of God.

Rev. xxii. 11.

HOLY GHOST.

{πνεῦμα, the wind, the breath breathed forth, the element of life, *predicated of man and beast,* (*see under the word* "SPIRIT,") the life-principle springing from God, spirit, ἅγιον, *see* "HOLY," *No.* 1,} The Holy Spirit, God's Spirit, which manifests itself creatively, equipping Christ; and accomplishing God's saving work in man. [Personality belongs to the Spirit in the same manner as to the Son (Matt. xxviii. 19), and the operations of the Spirit (as John xiv. 17, 26; xv. 26; xvi. 13), must be referred to the Holy Spirit, as the agent who accomplishes in and for man the work of divine redemption.]

The article is not used when the reference is to the gifts, operations, or manifestation of the Spirit in men. Nor when "the Spirit" is regarded subjectively. Nor when the disciples are said to be filled with the Spirit, to walk in or to receive the Spirit. (*Exceptions to this are only apparent.*)

* τὸ ἅγιον πνεῦμα, the Holy Spirit, spoken of as Himself, or regarded objectively.

† τὸ πνεῦμα τὸ ἅγιον, the Spirit, the Holy Spirit, (*very emphatic.*)

Matt. i. 18, 20.
—— iii. 11.
—— xii. 32†.
—— xxviii. 19*.
Mark i. 8.
—— iii. 29†.
—— xii. 36†.
—— xiii. 11†.
Luke i. 15, 35, 41, 67.
—— ii. 25, 26†.
—— iii. 16, 22†.
—— iv. 1.
—— xii. 10*, 12*.
John i. 33.
—— vii. 39 (*om.* ἅγιον, *holy,* G ⇉ L T Tr[b] A[b] ℵ.)
—— xiv. 26†.
—— xx. 22.
Acts i. 2, 5, 8*, 16†.
—— ii. 4, 33*, (τοῦ πνεύματος τοῦ ἁγίου, *of the Spirit of the Holy One,* L T Tr A ℵ.)
—— 38*.
—— iv. 8, 31.
—— 31 (*, L T Tr A.)
Acts v. 3†, 32†.
—— vi. 3 (*om.* ἅγιον, *holy,* G L T Tr A ℵ.)
—— 5.
—— vii. 51†, 55.
—— viii. 15, 17.
—— 18† (*om.* τὸ ἅγιον, *the Holy,* L T Tr[b] A ℵ.)
—— 19.
—— ix. 17, 31*.
—— x. 38, 44†, 45*, (πνεύματος τοῦ ἁγίου, *of the Spirit of the Holy One,* L Tr[m].)
—— 47†.
—— xi. 15†, 16, 24.
—— xiii. 2†, 4† (*om.* both articles, L T; *om.* the 2nd, Tr A ℵ.)
—— 9, 52.
—— xv. 8†, 28*.
—— xvi. 6*.
—— xix. 2 twice, 6†.
Acts xx. 23†, 28†.
—— xxi. 11†.
—— xxviii. 25†.
Rom. v. 5.
—— ix. 1.
—— xiv. 17.
—— xv. 13, 16.
1 Cor. ii. 13 (*om.* ἅγιον, *holy,* G L T Tr A ℵ.)
—— vi. 19*.
—— xii. 3.
2 Cor. vi. 6.
—— xiii. 14*.
1 Thes. i. 5, 6.
2 Tim. i. 14.
Tit. iii. 5.
Heb. ii. 4.
—— iii. 7†.
—— vi. 4.
—— ix. 8†.
—— x. 15†.
1 Pet. i. 12.
2 Pet. i. 21.
1 John v. 7* (*ap.*)
Jude 20.

HOLY SPIRIT.

Luke xi. 13.
Eph. i. 13†.
Eph. iv. 30†.
1 Thes. iv. 8†.

HOLYDAY.

ἑορτή, a feast, festival, (lxx. for חַג, Ex. x. 9, Hos. ii. 11, Am. viii. 10; for מוֹעֵד, Lev. xxiii. 2, Num. x. 10.)

1 Col. v. 8, marg., see Feast (keep the.)
Col. ii. 16.

HOME.

1. {εἰς, unto, οἶκον, a house, abode, dwelling, (*with special reference to the inmates*).} unto a *or* the house, *or* home.

2. {εἰς, unto, τὰ, the, ἴδια, one's own *things,*} unto their own (*things or homes.*)

3. {ὁ, the, ἴδιος, one's own, οἶκος, house, dwelling, (*see above, No.* 1),} their own house *or* home.

— Matt. viii. 6, see H (at.)
1. Mark iii. 19, marg. (text, *unto a house.*)
1. —— v. 19.
1. Luke xv. 6.
— John xvi. 32, see *H* (*to his own.*)
— —— xix. 27, see H (unto his own.)
— John xx. 10, see H (unto their own.)
— Acts ii. 46, see *H* (*at.*)
2. —— xxi. 6.
— 1 Cor. xi. 34, } see H
— —— xiv. 35, } (at.)
— 2 Cor. v. 6, see H (be at.)
3. 1 Tim. v. 4.
— Titus ii. 5, see H (keeper at.)

HOME (at.)

1. { ἐν, in, οἰκίᾳ, a house, a dwelling (the dwelling-house, *as distinct from the inmates*, and *from all the property left at a person's death*), } in the house.

2. { ἐν, in, οἴκῳ, a house, a dwelling (*having reference to the inmates*), } in the house *or* home.

3. { κατὰ, down, towards; *in ref. to time*, at *or* in, οἶκον, a house, or dwelling, } at home.

1. Matt. viii. 6.
3. Acts ii. 46, marg. (text, *from house to house.*)
2. 1 Cor. xi. 34. | 2. 1 Cor. xiv. 35.

HOME (be at.)

ἐνδημέω, to be among one's own people.

2 Cor. v. 6, part.

HOME (keeper at.)

οἰκουρός, keeper or guard of a house.

Tit. ii. 5 (οἰκουργός, *one who attends to domestic affairs*, G ∾ L T Tr A ℵ.)

HOME (to his own.)

{ εἰς, unto, τὰ, the, ἴδια, one's own *things*, } unto one's own *place*, etc.

John xvi. 32, marg. (text, *to his own.*)

HOME (unto his own.)

John xix. 27.

HOME (unto their own.)

{ πρός, towards, unto, ἑαυτοὺς, one's self, } towards the [*house*] of one's self.

John xx. 10 (πρός αὐτούς, *unto them*, T Tr ℵ.)

HONEST.

1. καλός, beautiful, comely, noble, (*see* "good," *No.* 2.)

2. σεμνός, revered, august, venerable; grave, dignified, (*occ.* 1 Tim. iii. 8, 11; Tit. ii. 2.)

1. Luke viii. 15.
— Acts vi. 3, see Report.
— Rom. xii. 17, } see H
— 2 Cor. viii. 21, } thing.
2. Phil. iv. 8, marg. *venerable.*
1. Tit. iii. 14, marg. (text, *good.*)
1 Pet. ii. 12.

HONEST THING.

καλόν, *neut. of No.* 1.

Rom. xii. 17. | 2 Cor. viii. 21.

HONESTLY.

1. εὐσχημόνως, elegant in figure, mien, and bearing; graceful, *hence*, with propriety of outward conduct, with seemly deportment, (*occ.* 1 Cor. xiv. 40.)

2. καλῶς, (*adv. of* καλός, *see* "good," *No.* 2.)

1. Rom. xiii. 13, marg. *decently.*
1. 1 Thes. iv. 12.
2. Heb. xiii. 18.

HONESTY.

σεμνότης, claim to be venerated; gravity, dignified seriousness, (*occ.* 1 Tim. iii. 8, 11, Tit. ii. 2.)

1 Tim. ii. 2.

HONEY.

μέλι, honey, (*lat.*, mel,) *metaph. of any thing sweet*, (*non occ.*)

Matt. iii. 4. | Mark i. 6.
Rev. x. 9, 10.

HONEY-COMB.

{ μελίσσιος, of bees, made by κηρίον, a honey-comb, [bees } (*non occ.*)

Luke xxiv. 42, (*ap.*)

HONOUR (-s) [noun.]

1. τιμή, a holding worth, an estimate of the value *or* price of a thing; *hence*, esteem, honour, respect; intrinsic value, (*see No.* 2.)

2. δοξά, *from trans.*, opinion, notion; *from intrans.*, seeming; *denoting* the recognition of worth, *as No.* 1 *does* the estimation of it. That which attracts honour, *rather than* the honour which is given, (*see* "glory," No. 1.)

— Matt. xii. 57, } see H (without.)
— Mark vi. 4,
1. John iv. 44.
2. —— v. 41, 44 twice.
1. Acts xxviii. 10.
1. Rom. ii. 7, 10.
1. —— ix. 21.
1. —— xii. 10.
1. —— xiii. 7.
1. 1 Cor. xii. 23, 24.
2. 2 Cor. vi. 8.
1. Col. ii. 23.
1. 1 Thes. iv. 4.
1. 1 Tim. i. 17.
1. —— v. 17.
1. —— vi. 1, 16.
1. 2 Tim. ii. 20, 21.
1. Heb. ii. 7, 9.
1. —— iii. 3.
1. —— v. 4.
1. 1 Pet. i. 7.
1. —— ii. 7, marg. (text, precious.
1. —— iii. 7.
1. 2 Pet. i. 17.
1. Rev. iv. 9, 11.
1. —— v. 12, 13.
1. —— vii. 12.
1. —— xix. 1, (om. G L T Tr A ℵ.)
2. ——— 7.
1. —— xxi. 24, (om. G ⇉ L T Tr A ℵ.)
1. ——— 26.

HONOUR (WITHOUT.)

ἄτιμος, without τιμή, (*see* "HONOUR," *No.* 1.)

Matt. xiii. 57. | Mark vi. 4.

HONOUR (-ED, -ETH) [verb.]

1. τιμάω, to estimate *or* value at a certain price, to deem or hold worthy; to honour, (*occ.* Matt. xxvii. 9.)

2. δοξάζω, to think, be of opinion, hold any one for anything; *hence,* to recognise, honour, praise; bring to honour, make glorious; *but strictly*, to give anyone importance.

1. Matt. xv. 4, 5, 8.
1. —— xix. 19.
1. Mark vii. 6, 10.
1. —— x. 19.
1. Luke xviii. 20.
1. John v. 23 4 times.
1. —— viii. 49.
2. ——— 54 twice.
1. —— xii. 26.
1. Acts xxviii. 10.
2. 1 Cor. xii. 26.
1. Eph. vi. 2.
— Phil. ii. 29, marg., see Reputation.
1. 1 Tim. v. 3.
1. 1 Pet. ii. 17 1st marg. esteem.
1. ——— 17 2nd.

HONOURABLE.

1. εὐσχήμων, elegant in figure, mien, *or* bearing, decent, becoming; one of good condition *or* of reputable position, (*opp.* of ἀσχήμων.)

2. ἔνδοξος, recognised, honoured, honourable, distinguished, aristocratic, (*opp.* of ἄτιμος,) (*occ.* Lu. xiii. 17, Eph. v. 27.)

3. ἔντιμος, in honour, honoured, prized, (*opp.* of ἔκτιμος.)

4. τίμιος, valued, esteemed worthy, held in honour, of high price.

1. Mark xv. 43.
3. Luke xiv. 8.
1. Acts xiii. 50.
1. Acts xvii. 12.
2. 1 Cor. iv. 10.
— ——— xii. 23, see H (less.)

4. Heb. xiii. 4.

HONOURABLE (LESS.)

ἄτιμος, (*the opp. of No.* 2 *above,*) without honour.

1 Cor. xii. 23.

HOOK.

ἄγκιστρον, a fish-hook, (lxx. 2 K. xix. 28, Hab. i. 15, Ezek. xxxii. 3), (*non occ.*)

Matt. xvii. 27.

HOPE [noun.]

ἐλπίς, hope, *i.e.* expectation of something future. (1.) *Subjective,* a well-grounded expectation *and* a gladly *and* firmly held prospect of a future good. (2.) *Objective,* the expected good, that for which we hope. (lxx. for תקוה, Job. vi. 8, xiv. 7, xvii. 15, Ez. xxxvii. 11; עזרה, Is. xxxi. 2; לבטח, Ps. iv. 9, xvi. 9,) (*occ.* Heb. x. 23.)

Acts ii. 26.
—— xvi. 19.
—— xxiii. 6.
—— xxiv. 15.
—— xxvi. 6, 7.
—— xxvii. 20.
—— xxviii. 20.
Rom. iv. 18 twice.
—— v. 2, 4, 5.
—— viii. 20, 24 3 times.
—— xii. 12.
—— xv. 4, 13 twice.
1 Cor. ix. 10 1st & 2nd.
——— 10 3rd (ap.)
—— xiii. 13.
—— xv. 19, see H (have.)
Gal. v. 5.
Eph. i. 18.
Eph. ii. 12.
—— iv. 4.
Phil. i. 20.
Col. i. 5, 23, 27.
1 Thes. i. 3.
—— ii. 19.
—— iv. 13.
—— v. 8.
2 Thes. ii. 16.
1 Tim. i. 1.
Tit. i. 2.
—— ii. 13.
—— iii. 7.
Heb. iii. 6.
—— vi. 11, 18.
—— vii. 19.
1 Pet. i. 3, 21.
—— iii. 15.

1 John iii. 3.

HOPE (WE HAVE.)

{ ἐσμὲν, we are, [hoping, } we have
{ ἠλπικότες, who have been } been
hoping, (*implying the endurance of the hope through our lives.*)

1 Cor. xv. 19.

HOPE (-ED, -ETH, -ING) [verb.]

1. ἐλπίζω, to expect, to hope *for any thing* (*elsewhere,* "TRUST.")

(a) *with* ἐπί, upon, * *Dat.* resting upon, † *Acc.* upon, by direction towards.

(b) *with* ἐν, in.

(c) *with* εἰς, unto, towards, (to direct hope towards.)

2. προελπίζω, (*No.* 1 *with* πρό, before, *prefixed,*) to hope for before.

1. Luke vi. 34.
— —— 35, see H for again.
1. —— xxiii. 8.
1. Acts xxiv. 26.
1. —— xxvi. 7.
— Rom. viii. 24, 25, see H for.
1. 1 Cor. xiii. 7.
1. 2 Cor. viii. 5.
2. Eph. i. 12, marg. (text, trust.)
1. Phil. ii. 23.
1. 1 Tim. iii. 14.
1. Heb. xi. 1, see H for (thing.)

1st. 1 Pet. i. 13.

HOPE FOR.

Rom. viii. 24, 25.

HOPE FOR AGAIN.

ἀπελπίζω, to hope out, *i.e.* to have done hoping, to despair. [*Here, with* μηδὲν, not despairing, *i.e.* without anxiety as to the result, *or* never despairing *as to requital,*] (*non occ.*)

Luke vi. 35.

HOPED FOR (THINGS.)

ἐλπιζομένοι, (*participle of* "HOPE," *No.* 1.), *lit.* "Faith is of things hoped for—a confidence."

Heb. xi. 1.

HORN (-S.)

κέρας, a horn, *of a beast. From the Heb. the symbol of strength,* (LXX. for קֶרֶן, Jer. xlviii. 25, Ps. lxxv. 11, etc.,) (*non occ.*)

Luke i. 69.
Rev. v. 6.
—— ix. 13.
Rev. xii. 3.
—— xiii. 1 twice, 11.
—— xvii. 3, 7, 12, 16.

HORSE.

ἵππος, a horse, (*non occ.*)

Jas. iii. 3.
Rev. vi. 2, 4, 5, 8.
—— ix. 7, 9, 17 twice.
Rev. xiv. 20.
—— xviii. 13.
—— xix. 11, 14, 18, 19, 21.

HORSEMEN.

1 ἱππεύς, a horseman, (*as opp. to* πεζος, on foot,) *pl.* cavalry, (*non occ.*)

2. ἱππικόν, of a horse, *or* horses, equestrian, (*opp. to* πεζικός, belonging to a walker,) *neut.* τὸ ἱππικόν, *collectively,* the horsemen, cavalry, *as in Eng.* the horse, (*non occ.*)

1. Acts xxiii. 23, 32. | 2. Rev. ix. 16, (No. 1 G ~.)

HOSANNA.

ὡσαννά, *interj.,* Hosanna, *a slight variation of the Heb.* הוֹשִׁיעָה נָּא, save now! succour now! be now propitious! *used in* Ps. cxviii. 25, *which became a common form of wishing* safety and prosperity to, *as though to say,* save and prosper, O Lord. *Very different from the joyful acclamation, Hallelujah,* (*non occ.*)

Matt. xxi. 9 twice, 15. | Mark xi. 9, 10.
John xii. 13.

HOSPITALITY.

φιλοξενία, love to strangers, *hence,* hospitality.

Rom. xii. 13.

HOSPITALITY (GIVEN TO.)

φιλόξενος, loving strangers, *hence,* hospitable.

1 Tim. iii. 2.

HOSPITALITY (LOVER OF

Tit. i. 8.

HOSPITALITY (USE.)

1 Pet. iv. 9.

HOST [*of Guests.*]

1. ξένος, any person in a foreign city, with whom one has a treaty of hospitality for self and heirs confirmed by mutual presents and an appeal to Ζεῦς. *Thus, both parties were* ξένοι, *and hence,* ξένος *denotes, in a pass. sense,* the person who receives, the guest; *and in an active sense,* the host.

2. πανδοχεύς, one who receives all, *hence,* the keeper of an inn, *or* caravanserai, (*see under* "INN,") (*non occ.*)

2. Luke x. 35. | 1. Rom. xvi. 23.

HOST [*of Soldiers.*]

στρατιά, an army, (LXX. for צָבָא, 2 Sam. iii. 23, 1 K. xi. 15,) (*non occ.*)

Luke ii. 13. | Acts vii. 42.

HOSTILE MIND TENDING TO WAR WITH (*bear a*) [margin.]

εἰμί, to be,
θυμομαχῶν, fighting desperately, having a hot quarrel.

Acts xii. 20, marg (text, *be highly displeased with.*)

HOT.

ζεστός, boiled; boiling hot, hot, (*non occ.*)

1 Tim. iv. 2, see Sear. | Rev. iii. 15 twice, 16.

HOUR (-s.)

ὥρα, (*Lat.* hora, *Eng.* hour,) season, time of blossoming, (ὡραῖος, blossoming; ἄωρος, unseasonable.) *It denotes originally* the season of the year, *then*, the time of the day, *and when reckoning by measured hours was practised*, the hour.

A definite and limited time, a specific period, a certain definite space of time, (*thus differing from* καιρός, *which means* the time, the opportune point of time, opportunity; *but see under the words*, "SEASON," "TIME," etc.)

Matt. viii. 13.
— ix. 22.
— x. 19 (*ap.*)
— xv. 28.
— xvii. 18.
— xx. 3, 5.
—— 6 (*om.* G ⇉ L T Tr A ℵ.)
—— 9, 12.
— xxiv. 36.
—— 42 (ἡμέρα, *day*, L T Tr A ℵ.)
—— 44, 50.
— xxv. 13.
— xxvi. 40, 45, 55.
— xxvii. 45 twice, 46.
Mark xiii. 11, 32.
— xiv. 35, 37, 41.
— xv. 25, 33 twice, 34.
Luke vii. 21, see H (in that same.)
— x. 21, see H (in that.)
— xii. 12, see H (in the same.)
—— 39, 40, 46.
— xx. 19, see H (the same.)
— xxii. 14, 53, 59.
—— 59, see H after (the space of one.)
— xxiii. 44 twice.
— xxiv. 33.
John i. 39.
— ii. 4.
— iv. 6, 21, 23, 52 twice, 53
— v. 25, 28.
John vii. 30.
— viii. 20.
— xi. 9.
— xii. 23, 27 twice.
— xiii. 1.
— xvi. 21, 32.
— xvii. 1.
— xix. 14, 27.
Acts ii. 15.
— iii. 1.
— v. 7.
— x. 3, 9, 30 1st.
—— 30 2nd (*om.* G ⇉ L T ℵ.)
— xvi. 18, see H (the same.)
—— 33.
— xix. 34.
— xxii. 13, see H (the same.)
— xxiii. 23.
1 Cor. iv. 11, see H (even unto this present.)
— viii. 7, see H (unto this.)
— xv. 30.
Gal. ii. 5.
Rev. iii 3, 10.
— viii. 1. see H (the space of half an.)
— ix. 15.
— xi. 13 (ἡμέρα, day, G ∾.)
— xiv. 7.
— xvii. 12.
— xviii. 10, 17, 19.

HOUR (IN THAT.)

ἐν, in,
αὐτῇ, self very,
τῇ, the,
ὥρα, hour,
} in this very hour, in the selfsame hour.

Luke x. 21.

HOUR (THE SAME.)

1. ἐν, in, αὐτῇ, self, very, ὥρα, hour, } in the same hour.

2. αὐτῇ, self, very, τῇ, the, ὥρα, hour, } (*in*) this hour, at this very time.

1. Luke xx. 19. | 2. Acts xvi. 18.
2. Acts xxii. 13.

HOUR (IN THE SAME.)

ἐν αὐτῇ τῇ ὥρα, *see* "HOUR (IN THAT.)"

Luke xii. 12.

HOUR (IN THAT SAME.)

Luke vii. 21 (ἐκείνῃ, *that*, instead of αὐτῇ, L^m T Tr A ℵ.)

HOUR (UNTO THIS.)

ἕως, until,
ἄρτι, now, just now,
} until now.

1 Cor. viii. 7.

HOUR (EVEN UNTO THIS PRESENT.)

ἄχρι, continuedly until,
τῆς, the,
ἄρτι, now, just now,
ὥρας, hour,
} until the present hour.

1 Cor. iv. 11.

HOUR AFTER (THE SPACE OF ONE.)

διαστάσης, being placed asunder, separated, departed,
ὥρας, hour,
μιᾶς, one,
} one hour having elapsed.

Luke xxii. 59.

HOUR (THE SPACE OF HALF AN.)

ἡμιώριον, a half an hour, [in Rev. viii. 1, not a period predicted: prob. referring to vv. 3 and 4, and intended to harmonise with the time usually occupied with the silent worship in the Temple, during the burning of the incense,] (*non occ.*)

Rev. viii. 1 (with, ὡς, *about.*)

HOUSE (-s.)

1. οἶκος, a house, a dwelling, *with special reference to the inmates*, the home.

2. οἰκία, a house, a dwelling, *as distinct from the inmates, and from all the property left at a person's death.*

3. οἰκητήριον, a habitation. [Used only of the resurrection bodies of men, (2 Cor. v. 2); and of the spirit-body of angels, (Jude 6.)]

4. δῶμα, the flat roof of a house, (lxx. *for* גג, Josh. ii. 6, 8; 1 Sam. ix. 25, 26; Ps. cxxix. 6; so also Josephus, Ant. xiii. 5, 3, Bell. ii. 21, 5, iv. 1, 4.)

2. Matt. ii. 11.
2. — v. 15.
2. — vii. 24, 25, 26, 27.
2. — viii. 14.
1. — ix. 6, 7.
2. —— 10, 23, 28.
1. — x. 6.
2. —— 12, 13, 14.
— —— 25, see H (master of the.)
1. — xi. 8.
1. — xii. 4.
2. —— 25, 29 twice.
1. —— 44.
2. — xiii. 1, 36, 57.
1. — xv. 24.
2. — xvii. 25.
2. — xix. 29.
— — xx. 11, see H (goodman of the.)
1. — xxi. 13 twice.
2. — xxiii. 14 (*ap.*)
1. —— 38.
2. — xxiv. 17.
— —— 43 1st, see H (goodman of the.)
2. —— 43 2nd.
2. — xxvi. 6.
— —— 18, see Thy.
— — xxvii. 27, see *Governour.*
2. Mark i. 29.
1. — ii. 1, 11.
2. —— 15.
1. —— 26.
1. — iii. 19, marg. *home.*
2. —— 25 twice, 27 twice.
1. — v. 38.
2. — vi. 4, 10.
1. — vii. 17.
2. —— 24.
1. —— 30.
1. — viii. 3, 26.
1. — ix. 28.
2. —— 33.
2. — x. 10, 29, 30.
1. — xi. 17 twice.
2. — xii. 40.
2. — xiii. 15 1st (*om.* εἰς τὴν οἰκίαν, *into the house,* Lb T א.)
2. —— 15 2nd, 34, 35.
2. — xiv. 3.
— —— 14, see H (goodman of the.)
— — xv. 16, see *Pilate.*
1. Luke i. 23, 27, 33, 40, 56, 69.
1. — ii. 4.
2. — iv. 38.
1. — v. 24, 25.
2. —— 29.
1. Luke vi. 4.
2. —— 48 twice, 49 twice.
2. — vii. 6.
1. —— 10. [A א.)
2. —— 36 (No. 1, L T Tr
2. —— 37, 44.
2. — viii. 27.
1. —— 39, 41.
2. —— 51.
2. — ix. 4.
1. —— 61.
2. — x. 5 1st.
1. —— 5 2nd.
2. —— 7 3 times.
1. —— 38.
1. — xi. 17 twice, 24.
— — xii. 39 1st, see H (goodman of the.)
1. —— 39 2nd.
— — xiii. 25, see H (master of the.)
1. —— 35.
1. — xiv. 1.
— —— 21, see H (master of the.)
1. —— 23.
2. — xv. 8, 25.
1. — xvi. 4, 27.
2. — xvii. 31.
1. — xviii. 14.
2. —— 29.
1. — xix. 5, 9, 46 twice.
— — xx. 24, see Store.
2. —— 47.
2. — xxii. 10, 11.
1. —— 54, (No. 2, T Tr A א.)
1. John ii. 16 twice, 17.
2. — iv. 53.
1. — vii. 53 (*ap.*)
2. — viii. 35.
2. — xi. 20.
2. —— 31.
2. — xii. 3.
2. — xiv. 2.
1. Acts ii. 2, 36.
— —— 46, see H to H (from.)
2. — iv. 34.
— — v. 42, see H (in every.)
1. — vii. 10, 20, 42, 47, 49.
— — viii. 3, see H (into every.)
2. — ix. 11, 17.
1. — x. 2.
2. —— 6.
4. —— 9 (since A.D. 1629 "*house-top;*" before then, *house.*)
2. —— 17.
1. Acts x. 22, 30.
2. —— 32.
2. — xi. 11.
1. —— 12, 13, 14.
2. — xii. 12.
1. — xvi. 15, 31.
2. —— 32.
1. —— 34 1st
— —— 34 2nd, see H (with all his.)
2. — xvii. 5.
2. — xviii. 7 twice.
1. —— 8.
1. — xix. 16.
1. — xxi. 8.
— — xxviii. 30, see Hired.
1. Rom. xvi. 5.
— 1 Cor. i. 11, see H (they which are of the.)
2. — xi. 22.
2. — xvi. 15.
1. —— 19.
2. 2 Cor. v. 1 twice.
3. —— 2.
1. Col. iv. 15.
1. 1 Tim. iii. 4, 5, 12, 15.
— —— v. 8, see H (of one's own.)
— —— 13, see H to H (from.)
— —— 14, see H (guide the.)
1. 2 Tim. i. 16.
2. — ii. 20.
2. — iii. 6.
1. Tit. i. 11.
1. Philem. 2.
1. Heb. iii. 2, 3, 4, 5, 6 twice.
1. — viii. 8 twice, 10.
1. — x. 21.
1. — xi. 7.
1. 1 Pet. ii. 5.
1. — iv. 17.
2. John 10.

HOUSE (GOODMAN OF THE.)

οἰκοδεσπότης, the master of a house *or* household, paterfamilias, house-master.

Matt. xx. 11.
— xxiv. 43.
Mark xiv. 14.
Luke xii. 39.

HOUSE (MASTER OF THE.)

Matt. x. 25.
Luke xiv. 21.
Luke xiii. 25.

HOUSE (GUIDE THE.)

οἰκοδεσποτέω, to be master of a house *or* head of a family, to rule and guide a household, (*non occ.*)

1 Tim. v. 14.

HOUSE (OF ONE'S OWN.)

οἰκεῖος, belonging to an οἰκία, (*see* "HOUSE," *No.* 2,) *hence,* family, kindred. friends, and relations.

1 Tim. v. 8, marg. *kindred.*

HOUSE (THEY WHICH ARE OF THE.)

οἱ, the, *masc. pl.*, the [*friends.*]

1 Cor. i. 11.

HOUSE (WITH ALL ONE'S.)

πανοικί, with all one's household, (lxx. for בית, Ex. i. 1.)

Acts xvi. 34.

HOUSE TO HOUSE (FROM.)

1. { τὰς, the,
οἰκίας, houses, (*see* "HOUSE," *No.* 2.)

2. { κατὰ, down towards; *in ref. to time*, at, *or* in, οἶκον, a house *or* dwelling, (*see* "HOUSE," *No.* 1,) } at home.

2. Acts ii. 46, marg. *at home.*
2. Acts xx. 20.
1. 1 Tim. v. 13.

HOUSE (IN EVERY)

2. Acts v. 42.

HOUSE (INTO EVERY)

2. Acts viii. 3, *pl.*

HOUSEHOLD.

1. οἶκος, *see* "HOUSE," *No.* 1.

2. οἰκία, *see* "HOUSE," *No.* 2.

3. θεραπεια, a waiting on, service, attendance, *esp.*, *of medical attendance; then, collectively*, the body of attendants, a suite, retinue, (*occ.* Lu. ix. 11, Rev. xxii. 2.)

— Matt. x. 25, 36, see H (of one's.)
3. —— xxiv. 45, (οἰκετεία, *the household*, L T Tr A,) (No. 2, ℵ.)
3. Luke xii. 42.
— Acts x. 7, see H servant.
1. Acts xvi. 15.
— Rom. xvi. 10, } see H (they which are of.)
— —— 11, }
1. 1 Cor. i. 16.
2. Phil. iv. 22.
1. 2 Tim. iv. 19.

HOUSEHOLD (OF ONE'S)

οἰκιακός, belonging to a house, *or* household affairs, (*non occ.*)

Matt. x. 25, 36.

HOUSEHOLD (OF THE)

οἰκεῖος, belonging to an οἰκία (*see* "HOUSE" *No.* 2).

Eph. ii. 19.

HOUSEHOLD (THEY WHICH ARE OF)

{ οἱ, the, (*persons*,) ἐκ, of, τῶν, the, } those of the [*household.*]

Rom. xvi. 10, 11.

HOUSEHOLD-SERVANT

οἰκέτης, an inmate of one's house, most used of a house-slave, menial (*elsewhere*, "SERVANT.")

Acts x. 7.

HOUSE-HOLDER.

οἰκοδεσπότης, the master of a house *or* household, paterfamilias, housemaster.

Matt. xiii. 27, 52; xx. 1; xxi. 33.

HOUSE TOP.

δῶμα, the flat roof of a house, (lxx. *for* גג, Josh. ii. 6, 8; 1 Sam. ix. 25, 26; Ps. cxxix. 6. So also Josephus, Ant. xiii. 5, 3; Bell. ii. 21 5; iv. 1, 4.)

Matt. x. 27.
—— xxiv. 17.
Mark xiii. 15.
Luke v. 19.
—— xii. 3.
—— xvii. 31.
Acts x. 9 (A.D. 1629: prior to that date, "*house.*")

HOW.

1. πῶς (adv.) how? used in direct and indirect questions with the indicative, (an absolute question,)

*with the subjunctive, expressive of deliberation and doubt,

†with optative, expressive of a wish,

2. ὡς, in what way. *In comparative sentences*, as, as it were, according as, how; *in objective*, that; *in final*, in order to; *in causal*, for.

3. οτι, (*conj. demonstrative, and causal like, Eng.*), that, *used in objective sentences as = the accusative with infinitive, and as a particle of explanation*, because, inasmuch as, seeing that. ὅτι, introduces that which rests on a patent fact,

4. ὅπως, (*rel. adv. of manner*,) in what manner, how; *also* in the manner that, so that,

5. καθώς, according as, *implying manner; in a causal sense*, even as,

6. τίς, τί, who? which? what? why? *or as an exclamation*, how!

— Matt. vi. 23, see H great.
1. —— 28.
3. —— vii. 14, marg. (text, *because*) (G ~) (No. 6, AVm G L Tr.)
1. —— 4.
— —— 11, see H much.
1*. —— x. 19.
— —— 25, see H much.
— —— xii. 2, see H much.
1. —— 4.
— —— 5, see H that.
4. —— 14.
1. —— 26, 29, 34.
— —— xv. 34, } see Many.
— —— xvi. 9, 10, }
— Matt. xvi. 11, see H is it that?
— —— 12, 21, see H that.
— —— xvii. twice, see Long.
6. —— xviii. 12,
— —— 21, see Oft.
1. —— xxi. 20.
1. —— xxii. 12.
4. —— 15.
1. —— 43, 45.
1*. —— xxiii. 33.
— —— 37, see Often.
1*. —— xxvi. 54.
— —— xxvii. 13, see Many things.

— Mark ii. 16, see H is it?
1. —— 26 (om. Tr^b A^b.)
4. —— iii. 6.
1. —— 23.
1. —— iv. 13.
2. —— 27.
— —— 40, see H is it [that?
1. —— v. 16.
— —— 19, 20, see Great.
— —— vi. 38, } see
— —— viii. 5, 19, 20 } Many
— —— 21, see H is it [that?
1. —— ix. 12.
— —— 19 twice, see Long
— —— 21, see Long ago
1. —— x. 23, 24.
1. —— xi. 18.
2. —— xii. 26 (No. 1, T Tr A ℵ.)
1. —— 35, 41.
1*. —— xiv. 1, 11.
— —— xv. 4, see Many [things.
1. Luke i. 34.
3. —— 58.
6. —— 62.
— —— ii. 49, see H is it?
2. —— vi. (No. 1, L Tr^b.)
1. —— 42.
— —— vii. 22, see H that.
1. —— viii. 18.
— —— 39 twice, see [Great.
2. —— 47.
— —— ix. 41, see Long.
1. —— x. 26.
1. —— xi. 18.
— —— 12, 24, see H [much.
1*. —— xii. 11.
1. —— 27, 50.
— —— 56, see H is it that?
— —— xiii. 34, see Often.
1. —— xiv. 7.
— —— xv. 17, see Many.
— —— xvi. 2, see H is it that?
1. —— xviii. 24.
— —— xix. 15, see H much.
1. —— xx. 41, 44.
3. —— xxi. 5.
1*. —— xxii. 2, 4.
2. —— 61.
2. —— xxiii. 55.
2. —— xxiv. 6 (ὅσα, *what things*, L.)
1. —— 20.
2. —— 35.
1. John iii. 4, 9, 12.
3. —— iv. 1.
— —— 9, see H is it that?
1. —— v. 44, 47.
— —— vi. 42, see H is it that?
1. —— 52.
1. —— vii. 15.
1. —— viii. 33.
1. —— ix. 10, 15, 16, 19, 26.
— —— x. 24, see Long.
1. —— xi. 36.
3. —— xii. 19.
1. —— 34.
1. —— xiv. 5, 9.
6. —— 22.
3. —— 28.
1. Acts ii. 8.
1*. —— iv. 21.
— —— v. 9, see H is it?
— —— vii. 25, see H that.
1*. —— viii. 31 (with ἄν.)
— —— ix. 13, see H much.

— Acts ix. 16, see Great.
1. —— 27 twice.
2. —— x. 28, 38.
1. —— xi. 13.
2. —— 16.
1. —— xii. 17.
— —— xiii. 32, see H that.
3. —— xiv. 17.
5. —— xv. 14.
— —— 7, see H that.
1. —— 36.
2. —— xx. 20.
— —— 35 1st, see H that
3. —— 35 2nd.
— —— xxi. 20, see Many.
— —— xxv. 20, see *H to enquire hereof.*
1. Rom. iii. 6.
1. —— iv. 10.
1. —— vi. 2.
— —— vii. 1, see H that.
1. —— viii. 32.
1. —— x. 14 1st & 2nd (No. 1*, L T Tr A ℵ.)
1. —— 14 3rd (ℵ) (No. 1*, L T Tr A ℵ^b.)
1. —— 15 1st (No. 1*, L T Tr A ℵ.)
2. —— 15 2nd.
2. —— xi. 2, 33.
— 1 Cor. i. 26, see H that.
1. —— iii. 10.
— —— vi. 3, see H much more.
6. —— vii. 16.
1. —— 32, } (No. 1*, L
1. —— 33, } T Tr A
1. —— 34, } ℵ.)
— —— x. 1, see H that.
1. —— xiv. 7, 9, 16.
— —— 26, see H is it?
— —— xv. 3, see H that.
1. —— 12, 35.
1. 2 Cor. iii. 8.
2. —— vii. 15.
— —— viii. 2, } see H
— —— xii. 4, 5, } that.
— Gal. i. 13.
1. —— iv. 9.
3. —— 13.
— —— vi. 11, see H large.
— Eph. iii. 3, see H that.
6. —— vi. 21.
2. Phil. i. 8.
— —— ii. 23, see Go.
1. Col. iv. 6.
1. 1 Thes. i. 9.
2. —— ii. 10, 11.
1. —— iv. 1.
— 2 Thes. i. 18, see Many [things.
1. —— iii. 7.
1. 1 Tim. iii. 5, 15.
— Philem. 16, see H much
3. —— 19.
1. Heb. ii. 3.
— —— vii. 4, see H great.
— —— viii. 6, } see H
— —— ix. 14, } much.
— —— x. 29, }
— —— xii. 17, see H that.
3. Jas. ii. 22.
— —— 24, see H that.
— —— iii. 5, see H great.
1. 1 John iii. 17.
1. —— iv. 20 (Tr^m) (οὐ, *not*, L T Tr A ℵ.)
— Jude 5, 18, see H that.
3. Rev. ii. 2.
1. —— iii. 3.
— —— vi. 10, see Long.
— —— xviii. 7, see H much.

HOW GREAT.

1. πόσος, how great, *of magnitude, number, or time.*

2. πηλίκος, how great, how large, *of size*, (*occ.* Gal. vi. 11.)

3. ἡλίκος, how great, *esp. in expressions of wonder*, extraordinarily great. (*occ.* Col. ii. 1.)

1. Matt. vi. 23.
2. Heb. vii. 4.
3. Jas. iii. 5.

HOW IS IT?

τί, *see* "HOW," *No.* 6.

Mark ii. 16 (*om.* T Tr A) (διὰ τί, *wherefore*, ℵ.)
Luke ii. 49.
Acts v. 9.
1 Cor. xiv. 26.

HOW IS IT THAT?

1. πῶς, *see* "HOW," *No.* 1.

2. τί, *see* "HOW," *No.* 6.

1. Matt. xvi. 11.
1. Mark iv. 40 (*ap.*)
1. —— viii. 21.
1. Luke xii. 56.
2. —— xvi. 2.
1. John iv. 9.
1. John vi. 42.

HOW LARGE.

πηλίκος, how great, how large, *of size*. [*Here in Dat. pl.*, "*with what large letters*," either on account of his unpractised hand or on account of his sight. The dim sight being prob. the thorn in the flesh. (Compare Acts ix. 9; xxiii. 1, 5; Gal. iv. 14—16.)]

Gal. vi. 11.

HOW MUCH.

1. ὅσος, how great, how much, how many, *of magnitude, number, or time.*

2. πόσος, how great, (*correl. of No.* 1,) *of magnitude, number, or time.*

3. τίς, τί, *see* "HOW," *No.* 6.

2. Matt. vii. 11.
2. —— x. 25.
2. —— xii. 12.
2. Luke xi. 12, 24.
3. —— xix. 15 (*om.* τίς Tr A ℵ, *lit. what business they had done.*)
1. Acts ix. 13.
2. Philem. 16.
1. Heb. viii. 6.
2. —— ix. 14.
2. —— x. 29.
1. Rev. xviii. 7.

HOW MUCH MORE.

{ μήτις, *adv. interrog.*, is it? *expecting a neg. answer*, γε, at least, indeed, } to say nothing of, or not to say then.

1 Cor. vi. 3.

HOW THAT.

ὅτι, *see* "HOW," *No.* 3.

Matt. xii. 5.
—— xvi. 12, 21.
Luke vii. 22, (*om.* L Tr^b ℵ)
Acts vii. 25.
—— xiii. 32.
—— xv. 7.
—— xx. 35.
Rom. vii. 1.
1 Cor. i. 26.
1 Cor. x. 1.
—— xv. 3.
2 Cor. viii. 2.
—— xii. 4.
—— xiii. 5.
Gal. i. 13.
Eph. iii. 3.
Heb. xii. 17.
Jas. ii. 24.
Jude 5, 18.

HOW TO ENQUIRE HEREOF [margin.]

εἰς, unto, as to, (*om.* T Tr A^b ℵ.)
τὴν, the [*questioning.*]
περὶ, concerning.
τούτου, this [*man,*] (τούτων, these *things,* G ~ L T Tr A ℵ.)

Acts xxv. 20, (text, *of such manner of questions.*)

HOWBEIT.

1. ἀλλά, but, *marking opposition, interruption, or transition.*

2. δέ, *an adversative and distinctive particle,* but, now, *less emphatic than No.* 1, *marking an atithesis even though concealed.*

3. μέντοι, yet, truly, certainly, nevertheless, however.

1 & 2. John vi. 23, (*om.* δέ, T Tr A^b,) (οὖν, *therefore,* ℵ.)
3. —— vii. 13.
1. —— 27.
1. Acts vii. 48.
1. 1 Cor. viii. 7.
1. —— xiv. 20.
1. —— xv. 46.
1. Gal. iv. 8.
1. 1 Tim. i. 16.
1. Heb. iii. 16.

HOWL.

ὀλολύζω, *orig.,* to cry to the gods with a loud voice, *whether in prayer or thanksgiving; then gen.,* to cry out. *An onomatopoetic verb,* ololuzo, *Lat.,* ululare, *Eng.,* howl, *Heb.,* ילל, yālal, *of which it is the translation in the* lxx. Is. xiii. 6; xv. 3; Ezek. xxi. 12; Jer. iv. 8; (*non occ.*)

Jas. v. 1.

HUMBLE, [adj.]

ταπεινός, *of place,* lying low; *of condition,* brought down, humble, low. *Esp. of rank,* of low degree, lowly.

Jas. iv. 6. | 1 Pet. v. 5.

HUMBLE (-ED) [verb.]

ταπεινόω, to depress, lower; to humble, bring low,

(a) *Middle,* to humble one's self, be humbled.

Matt. xviii. 4.
—— xxiii. 12.
Luke xiv. 11.
Luke xviii. 14.
2 Cor. xii. 21.
Phil. ii. 8.

HUMBLE ONE'S SELF.

a. Jas. iv. 10. | a. 1 Pet. v. 6.

HUMBLENESS OF MIND.

ταπεινοφροσύνη, lowliness of mind.

Col. iii. 12.

HUMILIATION.

ταπείνωσις, a lowering, humbling, abasing; lowliness.

Acts viii. 33.

HUMILITY.

ταπεινοφροσύνη, lowliness of mind.

Col. ii. 18, 23. | 1 Pet. v. 5.

HUMILITY OF MIND.

Acts xx. 19.

HUNDRED.

ἑκατόν, a hundred, (*non occ.*)

[Typically, as a round number, it expresses indefinite magnitude, as does every multiple of ten.]

Matt. xviii. 12, 28.
Mark iv. 8, 20.
—— vi. 37, see H (two.)
—— 40, see H (by.)
—— xiv. 5, see H (three.)
Luke vii. 41, see H (five.)
—— xv. 4.
—— xvi. 6, 7.
John vi. 7, see H (two.)
—— xii. 5, see H (three.)
—— xix. 31.
—— xxi. 8, see H (two.)
—— 11.
Acts i. 15.
—— v. 36, see H (four.)
—— vii. 6, see H (four.)
Acts xiii. 20, see H and fifty (four.)
—— xxiii. 23 twice, } see H
—— xxvii. 37, } (two)
Rom. iv. 19, see H years old (an.)
1 Cor. xv. 6, see H (five.)
Gal. iii. 17, see H (four.)
Rev. vii. 4.
—— ix. 16, see Thousand.
—— xi. 3, } see H (two.)
—— xii. 6, }
—— xiii. 18, see H three score and six (six.)
—— xiv. 1, 3.
—— 20, see H (six.)
Rev. xxi. 17.

HUNDRED (TWO.)

διακόσιοι, two hundred, (*non occ.*)

Mark vi. 37.
John vi. 7.
—— xxi. 8.
Acts xxiii. 23 twice.
—— xxvii. 37.
Rev. xi. 3.
Rev. xii. 6.

HUNDRED (THREE.)

τριακόσιοι, three hundred, (*non occ.*)

Mark xiv. 5. | John xii. 5.

HUNDRED (FOUR.)

τετρακόσια, four hundred (*non occ.*)

* [The four hundred years in Acts vii. 6, refers to "*his seed*," *i.e.* Abraham's descendants, and is predicated of the *sojourning* and the *bondage.* It thus agrees with the prophecy, Gen. xv. 13, which refers also to being a *stranger* and *serving*, and is spoken of "thy seed." In Exod. xii. 40, a period of 430 years is mentioned, but this refers to "the *sojourning* of the *Children of Israel*, who dwelt in Egypt," and dates from the *call of Abraham* himself as distinguished from "his seed." The giving of the law was also 430 years from the "*promise*," Gen. xii. 3, and this agrees with Gal. iii. 17.]

Acts. v. 30.
*—— vii. 6.
| Acts xiii. 20, see H and fifty (four.)
* Gal. iii. 17.

HUNDRED AND FIFTY (FOUR.)

τετρακόσια, four hundred,
καὶ, and
πεντήκοντα, fifty.

Acts xiii. 20.

[NOTE.—If to the 450 years of the Judges be added 40 years in the wilderness, 40 for Saul's reign, 40 for David's reign, and 4 for the first four years of Solomon's, we have 574 years. But in 1st Kings vi. 1, it says:—"It came to pass in the 480th year after the children of Israel were come out of Egypt, &c." This is the *crux chronologorum.* To explain this,

(1) Some impugn the accuracy of Paul.
(2) Others impugn the accuracy of 1st Kings vi. 1.
(3) Others read Acts xiii. 19, 20, with critical emendations (see *ap.*), but Alford treats this as an ancient attempt at meeting the difficulty. Moreover, it only increases it in other ways, both grammatically and chronologically. See Alf. *in loco.*

Adhering to Scripture we have—

		Years	
1.	Exodus to Spies (Nu. x. 11—13, and xiii. 17, 20,) Caleb being 40	2	
2.	Spies to division of land (Jos. xiv. 6—10) Caleb being 85	45	
3.	Div. of land to Captivity I. (to make up 450 years)	20	
4.	Capt. I. (Jud. iii. 8) Cushan, Mesopotamia	...	8
5.	Othniel, younger brother of Caleb, Josh. xv. 17 (Judg. iii. 11) ...	40	
6.	Capt. II. (Jud. iii. 14) Eglon, Moab	...	18
7.	Ehud and Shamgar (Jud. iii. 30, 31)	80	
8.	Capt. III. (Jud. iv. 3) Jabin, Canaan	...	20
9.	Deborah and Barak (Jud. v. 31)	40	
10.	Capt. IV. (Jud. vi. 1) Midianites	...	7
11.	Gideon (Jud. viii. 28)	40	
12.	Abimelech (Jud. ix. 22)	3	
13.	Tola (Jud. x. 2)	23	
14.	Jair (Jud. x. 3)	22	
15.	Capt. V. (Jud. x. 8) Philistines and Ammorites ...	...	18
16.	Jephthah (Jud. xii. 7)	6	
17.	Ibzan (Jud. xii. 9)...	7	
18.	Elon (Jud. xii. 11)	10	
19.	Abdon (Jud. xii. 14)	8	
20.	Capt. VI. (Philistines) [Of this, Samson, "in the days of the Philistines," 20] ...	...	40
21.	Eli (1 Sam. iv. 18)...	40	
22.	Capt. VII. (1 Sam. vii. 2) Philistines [Here begin the times of "Samuel the Prophet" (1 Sam. iii. 19, 20)]	...	20
23.	From Victory at Mizpeh to end of Samuel (To make up 480 of 1 Kings vi. 1, Josephus makes 12.) ...	10	
24.	Saul's reign (Acts xiii. 21)	40	
25.	David's reign (1 Kings ii. 11)	40	
26.	Four years of Solomon (1 Kings vi. 37)	4	
27.	Building of Temple (1 Kings vi. 38)	7	
28.	Time of Furnishing it (1 Kings vii. 13—51)	3	
		490	

(Brackets in the margin: The 480 years (dispensational) of 1 Kings vi. 1. — The 450 years of Acts xiii. 19, 20. — The 300 years of Judges xi. 26. — 131 years of Captivity deducted from dispensational reckoning.)

[Temple finished in eighth month of eleventh year, and dedicated in the seventh month. Therefore not the same year. See also 1 Kings ix. 1—10.]

This period of 490 years or 70 hebdomads makes up the *second* period of "70 weeks" of *years.*

[The *first* is reckoned from the birth of Abraham (cf. Gen. xi. 31, and xii. 3, with Acts vii. 2-4.) to the Exodus (deducting the 15 years that Ishmael and "bondage" was in Abraham's house.)

The *third* is reckoned from the Dedication of the Temple to Nehemiah's return, deducting the 70 years' captivity, during which time the land "kept her Sabbaths."

The *fourth* is reckoned from Nehemiah's return (20th year of Artaxerxes, B.C. 455) to the second advent (Dan. ix. 24-27), the crucifixion, or "cutting off of Messiah," being in A.D. 29, the end of the "seven weeks" and the "threescore and two weeks." The present dispensation is therefore to be deducted from the fourth period of 70 hebdomads, during which time Israel is "Lo Ammi." (Is. liv. 7, 8.) The one hebdomad or week of seven years is still awaiting the fulfilment, in its two divisions of 3½ years (or 1,260 days, or 42 months), during which week God again deals dispensationally with Israel. (That the present dispensation is an interval not entering into subject matter of the prophecies, a Divine parenthesis to be deducted, seems to be implied in such passages as Is. xi 4; ix. 16, and Matt. iv. 14-16; Is. lxi. 1, 2, and Lu. iv. 18; Is. xl. 3, 4; Micah v. 2; Jer. xxxi. 10-17; Zech. ix. 9, 10.)]

HUNDRED (FIVE.)

πεντακόσιοι, five hundred (*non occ.*)

Luke vii. 41. | 1 Cor. xv. 6.

HUNDRED (SIX.)

ἑξακόσιοι, six hundred (*non occ.*)

Rev. xiii. 18, see below. | Rev. xiv. 20.

HUNDRED THREESCORE AND SIX (SIX.)

χξς', 666. The number for which these letters stand, *viz.* (χ' = 600), + (ξ' = 60) + (ς' = 6).

Rev. xiii. 18 (ἑξακόσιοι (-αι, א) *six hundred*, ἑξήκοντα, *sixty*, ἕξ, *six*, L A א), (ἑξακόσιοι δεκα, ἕξ, 616, Lm.)

[NOTE.—It is "the number of the beast." It is not a beast, however, but a man, "the number of a man." The spelling out of a name by the numerical value of letters is unsatisfactory, as the number of such names is legion.

The number is clearly emblematic of Trinity—three numbers, and yet one number, that one *a* perfect number, but not *the* perfect one. [Seven is God's perfect number=שָׂבַע, to be or become satisfied, filled; the number that satisfies God's work in nature, as in sound, in colours, and light.] Six (שֵׁשׁ, with an unknown root) is *a* perfect number, the first and the only number that equals the sum of the three figures that will divide it, and these the first three digits, 1, 2, 3. But it just falls short of God's, as does everything human. The oldest man on record attained the age of 969 years—*i.e.*, 90 (100 short of 1000), 60 (10 short of 70) and 9 (1 short of 10). Lamech, his son, through whom was promised blessing and rest, lived to 777 years.

666 is therefore the triple number of imperfection, the perfection of imperfection—"the number of a man"—the number of the things specially hateful to God, and which culminate in the perfection of wickedness, and which seem to peculiarly describe the "man of sin." It is connected with Babylon. "The image of the beast" (Rev. xiii. 14, 15) is mysteriously like the image of Babylon (Dan. iii. 1) in its numerical proportions—"threescore cubits, and the breadth thereof six cubits"—66—foreshadowing the union of the Antichrist and the False Prophet; whilst in the 600 not seen in the image of Nebuchadnezzar we have the Power of Satan assuming the Fatherhood of God. (Thus we have the Trinity of Hell, awful mimicry of the Holy Trinity!). As Nebuchadnezzar meant to deify himself by this image, so it is here; all who refuse to worship the image are in both cases killed, and the children of God suffer persecution. "The man of sin" is to show himself "that he is God," and he assumes the "name of blasphemy." Those who know the number of his name are those who will detect the blasphemy, and those who detect and resist the falsehood and blasphemy are described (Rev. xv. 2) as having "gotten the victory over the *beast* and over his *image*, and over his *mark*, and over the *number of his name*."

Thus the number points out the character and spirit of Antichrist, the future man who will yet be enthroned as God, and received by the world. He who has understanding, is to count this number.]

HUNDREDS (BY.)

{ ἀνὰ, *with numerals, &c.*, apiece, separately, ἑκατόν, a hundred, } by hundreds.

Mark vi. 40, (*κατὰ ἑκατόν, hundred by hundred*, L T Tr A א.)

HUNDRED YEARS OLD.

ἑκατονταέτης, a hundred years old, (lxx. *in* Gen. xvii. 17.)

Rom. iv. 19.

HUNDREDFOLD.

1. ἑκατόν, a hundred,
2. ἑκατονταπλασίων, a hundredfold, centuple.

1. Matt. xiii. 8, 23.
2. —— xix. 29 (πολλαπλασιων, *manifold*, L T Tr A)
2. Mark x. 30.
2. Luke viii. 8.

HUNGER [noun.]

λιμός, hunger, famine.

Luke xv. 17. | 2 Cor. xi. 27.
Rev. vi. 8.

HUNGER (-ED) [verb.]

πεινάω, to be hungry, suffer hunger; to hunger after, long for.

Matt. v. 6.
—— xxi. 18.
Luke iv. 2.
—— vi. 21, 25.
John vi. 35.
Rom. xii. 20.
1 Cor. iv. 11.
—— xi. 34.
Rev. vii. 16.

HUNGERED (BE AN.)

Matt. iv. 2.
—— xii. 1, 3.
Matt. xxv. 35, 37, 42, 44.
Mark ii. 25.
Luke vi. 3.

HUNGRY.

πεινάω, *see above.*

Luke i. 53, part.

HUNGRY (BE.)

Mark xi. 12. | 1 Cor. xi. 21.
Phil. iv. 12.

HUNGRY (VERY.)

πρόσπεινος, hungry, (*non occ. and not found elsewhere.*)

Acts x. 10.

HURT [noun.]

ὕβρις, wanton violence *arising from pride of strength; then,* injury arising from violence, *esp. of loss at sea.*

Acts xxvii. 10, marg. *injury.*

HURT [verb.]

1. *ἀδικέω*, to do wrong, to act unjustly; *trans.*, to do *one* wrong, to wrong, injure, hurt.

2. *βλάπτω*, to disable, hinder; damage, hurt, mar, (*opp. to No.* 1,) (*non occ.*)

3. *κακόω*, to affect with evil, *physically*, to do evil to *anyone*, to treat badly, maltreat, (*of persons.*)

2. Mark xvi. 18 (*ap.*)
2. Luke iv. 35.
1. —— x. 19.
3. Acts xviii. 10.
1. Rev. ii. 11.
1. —— vi. 6.
1. —— vii. 2, 3.
1. —— ix. 4, 10, 19.
1. Rev. xi. 5 twice.

HURTFUL.

βλαβερός, disabling, weakening, impeding; hurtful, noxious, disadvantageous, (*non occ.*)

1 Tim. vi. 9.

HUSBAND.

ἀνήρ, a man, an adult male person, (*Lat.*, vir, *Heb.*, איש,) *spoken of man in various relations, where the context decides the meaning, e.g.* husband, soldier, &c.

Matt. i. 16, 19.
Mark x. 12.
Luke ii. 36.
—— xvi. 18, (*om.* G →)
John iv. 16, 17 twice, 18 twice.
Acts v. 9, 10.
Rom. vii. 2 1st, see H (which hath.)
—— 2 2nd, 3rd, & 4th.
—— 3 twice.
1 Cor. vii. 2, 3 twice, 4 twice, 10, 11 twice, 13, 14 1st.
—— 14 2nd (*ἀδελφος*, *brother*, (L T Tr A ℵ.)
1 Cor. vii. 16, 34, 39 twice.
—— xiv. 35.
2 Cor. xi. 2.
Gal. iv. 27.
Eph. v. 22, 23, 24, 25, 33.
Col. iii. 18, 19.
1 Tim. iii. 2, 12.
Tit. i. 6.
—— ii. 4, see H (love one's.)
—— 5.
1 Pet. iii. 1, 5, 7.
Rev. xxi. 2.

HUSBANDS (LOVE ONE'S.)

{ *φιλανδρους*, a lover of a husband, husband-lover.
{ *εἶναι*, to be.

Tit. ii. 4.

HUSBAND (WHICH HATH.)

ὕπανδρος, under a husband.

Rom. vii. 2.

HUSBANDMAN.

γεωργός, tilling the ground; *as subst.*, a farmer, husbandman, (*non occ.*)

Matt. xxi. 33, 34, 35, 38, 40, 41.
Mark xii. 1, 2 twice, 7, 9.
Luke xx. 9, 10 twice, 14, 16.
John xv. 1.
2 Tim. ii. 6.
Jas. v. 7.

HUSBANDRY.

γεώργιον, a tilled field, a farm: *also* cultivation, (*non occ.*)

1 Cor. iii. 9, *marg.* tillage.

HUSK.

κεράτιον, a little horn; *hence*, the fruit *or* pod of the *κερατέα*, (the carob *or* locust-tree, *Arab.*, kharoob.) [It is still sometimes eaten by the poor, but is usually given to swine to give the pork a sweet flavour. Common to Syria and S. Europe.] (*non occ.*)

Luke xv. 16.

HYMN.

ὕμνος, a song, *in Homer* only used of the music, *but later of the air and words*, a hymn or festive song in praise of God (lxx. Is. xlii. 10; 2 Ch. vii. 6; Ps. xl. 4.) (*non occ.*) *see under* "PSALM."

Eph. v. 19. | Col. iii. 16.

HYMN (SING AN.)

ὑμνέω, to sing, laud, sing of, tell of, praise; (lxx. Is. xii. 4; 2 Ch. xxix. 30.) (*occ.* Acts xvi. 25; Heb. ii. 12.)

Matt. xxvi. 30, part. | Mark xiv. 26, part.

HYPOCRISY.

ὑπόκρισις, a reply, answer, *esp. as spoken in dialogue on the stage; hence*, the playing a part *on the stage*, dissimulation.

Matt. xxiii. 28.
Mark xii. 15.
Luke xii. 1.
1 Tim. iv. 2.
1 Peter ii. 1.

HYPOCRISY (WITHOUT.)

ἀνυπόκριτος, unfeigned (*opp. of above.*)

Jas. iii. 17.

HYPOCRITE.

ὑποκριτης, one who answers, *esp. on the stage, hence,* one who plays a part, a dissembler (*non occ.*)

Matt. vi. 2, 5, 16.
— vii. 5.
— xv. 7.
— xvi. 3 (*om.* ὑποκριταί, *O ye hypocrites*, G ⇉ L T Tr A ℵ*.)
— xxii. 18.
Matt. xxiii. 13, 14 (*ap*), 15, 23, 25, 27, 29.
Mark vii. 6.
Luke vi. 42.
— xi. 44 (*ap.*)
— xii. 56.
— xiii. 15.

HYSSOP.

ὑσσωπος, (Heb., אזוב) Hyssop, *a low plant or shrub, put in contrast with the cedar, as growing out of the wall or rocks.* In *N.T. used of* a stalk or stem of hyssop; *and also of* a bunch of hyssop for sprinkling.

John xix. 29.
Heb. ix. 19.

I

I.

I is generally part of the verb, in Greek; thus, λέγω is I *say*, but if there be added to this the pronoun, thus, ἐγώ λέγω, *I* say, there is an emphasis designed, which is wanting in the former case. In the oblique cases the pronouns are more necessary, and therefore the emphasis is not so marked, but in the nominative they are regularly omitted, unless emphasis is intended.

The following passages are where the pronoun I in English is represented by the pronoun in the Greek as a separate emphatic word. In all passages or cases not cited below the pronoun I is only part of the verb in Greek.

ἐγώ, I, (*the pronoun of the first person,*) *Lat.*, ego; *Germ.*, Ich; *Eng.*, I.) [In no instance is this pronoun used in the Greek where no emphasis is intended to be expressed. Where it is used, it could not have been omitted without affecting the sense. This emphasis may be manifest or latent; or it may be the consequence of antithesis.]

(a) μοῦ, *Genitive*, of me, (*generally to be translated* I, *in consequence of the case being* the result of *government or construction.*)

(b) ἐμοί, *Dative*, to me, (*the result of construction, e.g.* "*there is to me*" = "*I have.*")

* μοί, *another form of the Dative.*

(c) ἐμέ, *Accusative*, me, (*the result of construction, gen., being the Acc. of the noun with inf. of the verb, e.g.* "*me to be*" = "*that I am.*")

* μέ, *another form of the Accusative.*

2. κἀγώ, even I, *or* I also, (*a contraction of* καὶ, and, also *or* even, *and* ἐγώ, I.)

— Matt. ii. 8, see I also.
1. — iii. 11 1st.
1a. — 11 2nd.
1. — 14. [39, 44.
1. — v. 22, 28, 32, 34,
1. — viii. 7, 9 1st.
1. — x. 16.
— — 32, 33, see I also.
1. — xi. 10 (*om.* Lb.)
1. — 28, see And.
1. — xii. 27, 28.
1. — xiv. 27.
1c* — xvi. 13 (*om.* G → Lb T Tr A ℵ.)
1c* — 15.
— — 18 1st, see I also.
1. — xviii. 33 (ὡς κἀγώ, (No. 2,) *as even I*, instead of ὡς καὶ εγω, *even as I*, L T Tr A ℵ.)
1. — xx. 15 2nd, 22 1st, 22 2nd (*ap.*), 23 (*ap.*)
— — xxi. 24 1st, see I also.
— — 24 2nd, see I in likewise.
1. — 27 1st, 30.
1. — xxii. 32.
1. — xxiii. 34.
1. — xxiv. 5.
1. — xxv. 27.
1. — xxvi. 15, see And.
1. — 22, 25.
1c* — 32 1st.
1. — 33.
1c* — 35 1st.
1. — 39.
1. — xxviii. 20 2nd.
1. Mark i. 2 (*om.* L T Tr A.)
1a. — 7 1st.
1. — 8.
— — v. 7 1st, see I to do with thee (what have.)
1. — vi. 16, 50.
1c* — viii. 27, 29.
1. — ix. 25.
1c* — x. 36 (*om.* G ∾ L Tr A ℵ*.)
1. — 38 twice, 39 twice.
— — xi. 29 1st, see I also.
1. — 33 1st.
1. — xii. 26.
1. — xiii. 6.
1. — xiv. 19 1st, 19 2nd (*ap.*)
1c* — 28 1st.
1. — 29.
1c* — 31 1st.
1. — 36, 58 1st, 62.
1. Luke i. 18 2nd, 19.
1. — ii. 48, see And.
1c* — 49.
1. — iii. 16 1st.
1a. — 16 2nd.
1c* — iv. 43 1st.
1. — vii. 8 1st.
1. — 27 (*om.* L T Tr A ℵ.)
— — viii. 28 1st, see I to do with thee (what have.)
1. — 46.
1. — ix. 9 twice.
1c* — 18, 20.

1. Luke x. 3 (*om.* L T Tr A ℵ.)
1. —— 35 1st.
1c* —— 35 2nd.
1. —— xi. 9, see And.
1c* —— 18.
1. —— 19.
1c* —— xiii. 33.
1. —— xv. 17.
— —— 31, see I have (that.)
1. —— xvi. 9, see And.
1c* —— xix. 5.
1. —— 22 2nd, 23.
1c* —— 27.
— —— xx. 3, see I also.
1. —— 8 1st.
1. —— xxi. 8, 15.
1c* —— xxii. 15 2nd.
1. —— 27.
1. —— 29, see And.
1. —— 32.
1a. —— 53.
1. —— 70.
1. —— xxiii. 14.
1. —— xxiv. 39, see I myself.
1. —— 49.
1. John i. 20, 23, 26
1. —— 27 (*om.* G ⇄ Lb Tr A ℵ.)
1. —— 30.
— —— 31 1st, see I (and.)
1. —— 31 2nd.
1. —— 33, 34, see And.
— —— ii. 4, see I to do with thee (what have)
1. —— iii. 28 2nd.
1c. —— 30.
1. —— iv. 14 1st, 26, 32, 38.
1. —— v. 7 2nd.
1. —— 17, see And.
1. —— 30 1st, 31, 34 1st, 36 1st.
1. —— 36 2nd (*om.* L Tr A ℵ.)
1. —— 43, 45.
1. —— vi. 20, 35.
1. —— 40 (*om.* Lb.)
1. —— 41, 44, 48, 51 1st & 2nd.
1. —— 53 (*ap.*), 54.
— —— 56, 57, see I (and)
1. —— 63, 70.
1. —— vii. 7, 8, 17, 29 1st, 34, 36.
1. —— viii. 11 (*ap.*), 12, 14 1st, 15, 16 1st & 3rd, 18, 21 twice, 22, 23 twice, 24 2nd.
1. —— 26 3rd, see And.
1. —— 29, 38 1st, 42 1st, 45, 49 1st, 50, 54, 55 1st, 58 2nd.
1c. —— ix. 4.
1. —— 9, 39.
1. —— x. 7 2nd, 9, 10, 11, 14.
— —— 15 1st, see Even.
1c* —— 16 2nd.
1. —— 17 1st, 18 1st, 25 2nd
1. —— 27, 28, see And.
1. —— 30, 34.
— —— 38 2nd, see I (and)
1. —— xi. 25, 27, 42 1st.
1. —— xii. 26.
1. —— 32 1st, see And.
1. —— 46, 47 1st, 49 1st, 50 2nd.
1. —— xiii. 7, 14, 15 2nd, 18 2nd, 19 2nd.
1. —— 26, and see Give.
1. —— 33.
1. —— xiv. 3 3rd.
1. —— 4 (*om.* Lb.)
1. —— 6, 10 1st & 2nd, 11, 12 2nd & 3rd.
1. —— 14 (τοῦτο, *this* [I will do] Lm.)
1. —— 16, 19, 20 1st.
1. —— 20 2nd, see And.

1. John xiv. 21, 27 3rd, 28 1st.
1a. —— 28 5th.
1. —— xv. 1.
1. —— 4, see And.
1. —— 5 1st.
1. —— 5 2nd, see And.
— —— 9, see I (so.)
1. —— 10, 14, 16, 19, 20, 26
1. —— xvi. 4 2nd, 7 1st & 2nd
— —— 7 3rd (No. 1, G ∾ L Ab.)
1. —— 16 (*ap.*)
1. —— 17 (*om.* L T Tr A ℵ.) (ᾧ, *for which I*, instead of ὅτι ἐγώ, *Because I*, ℵb.), 26, 27, 33.
1. —— xvii. 4 1st, 9 1st, 11 2nd, 12 2nd, 14 twice, 16.
— —— 18, see Even.
1. —— 19 (*om.* Lb T ℵ.)
1. —— 21, see And.
1. —— 22, 23, 24 2nd, 25.
1. —— 26 2nd, see And.
1. —— xviii. 5, 6, 8 2nd, 20 1st & 2nd, 21 2nd, 26, 35
1. —— 37 1st (*om.* T Tr Ab ℵ.)
1. —— 37 2nd (*om.* Lb.)
1. —— 38.
1. —— xix. 6.
1. —— xx. 15, see And.
— —— 21, see Even.
1b* Acts iii. 6 1st.
1. —— vii. 7, 32.
1. —— ix. 5, 10, 16.
1. —— x. 20, 21.
— —— 26, see I myself also.
1. —— xi. 5 1st.
1c* —— 15.
1. —— 17 1st.
1c* —— xiii. 25 1st (1c L T Tr A ℵ.)
1. —— 25 2nd, 33, 41.
1c* —— xvi. 30.
1. —— xvii. 3, 23 3rd.
1. —— xviii. 6 1st, 10 1st.
1b* —— 10 2nd.
1. —— 15.
1c* —— 21 1st (*ap.*)
1c* —— xix. 21 twice.
1. —— xx. 22, 25 1st.
1. —— 26 2nd (εἰμί, *I am*, instead of ἐγώ, I, T Tr A ℵ.)
1. —— 29.
1. —— xxi. 13.
1b. —— 37.
1. —— 39 1st.
1. —— xxii. 3.
1b. —— 6.
1. —— 8 twice.
1. —— 13, see And.
1b* —— 17 1st.
1a. —— 17 2nd.
1c* —— 17 3rd.
1. —— 19 1st, see And.
1. —— 19 2nd, 21, 28 twice
1. —— xxiii. 1, 6 twice.
— —— xxiv. 16, see I myself.
1a. —— 20.
1. —— 21 2nd.
1c* —— xxv. 10 2nd.
1a. —— 15.
1. —— 18, 20 1st.
— —— 22, see I myself.
1. —— 25 1st.
1. —— xxvi. 9 1st, 10 2nd, 15 twice.
2. —— 29 2nd.
1. —— xxviii. 17 1st.
— Rom. iii. 7, see I also.
1. —— vii. 9 twice.
1b* —— 10.
1. —— 14, 17.
1. —— 20 1st (*om.* G ⇄ L Trmb Ab.)

1. Rom. vii. 20 3rd.
1b. —— 21 2nd.
1. —— 24.
1. —— 25, and see I myself.
1b* —— ix. 3.
— —— 3, see I myself.
1. —— x. 19 2nd.
1. —— xi. 1.
1. —— 3, see And.
1. —— 13 2nd, 19.
1. —— xii. 19.
1. —— xiv. 11.
1. —— xv. 14, and see I myself.
1c* —— 16, 19.
1. —— xvi. 4, 22.
1. 1 Cor. i. 12 2nd, 3rd, 4th, & 5th.
1. —— ii. 1 1st, see And.
1. —— 3.
1. —— iii. 1, 4 twice, 6.
1. —— iv. 15.
1a. —— 18.
1. —— v. 3 1st.
1b* —— 12.
1. —— vi. 12.
— —— vii. 7 2nd, see I myself.
1. —— 8 2nd, see Even.
1. —— 10 2nd, 12, 28.
— —— 40 2nd, see I (also.)
1. —— ix. 6, 15 1st.
1b* —— 16 2nd.
1. —— 26 1st.
— —— 27 3rd, see I myself.
1. —— x. 30 1st & 3rd.
— —— 33, see Even.
— —— xi. 1, see Even.
1. —— 23 1st.
1. —— xv. 9 1st, 10 4th, 11.
1. —— xvi. 10.
1. 2 Cor. i. 23 1st.
1. —— ii. 2.
1c* —— 3 1st.
1. —— 10 1st & 2nd.
1c* —— 13 2nd.
1. —— vi. 17, see And.
1c* —— vii. 7.
1. —— x. 1, and see I myself.
2. —— xi. 16 2nd.
— —— 18, 21 3rd, see I also.
— —— 22 3 times, see I (so.)
1. —— 23 2nd, 29 2nd.
1. —— xii. 11 2nd, 13, and see I myself.
1. —— 15 1st, 16 1st.
1. —— 20 5th, see And.
1c* —— 21 1st (No. 1a, L T Tr A ℵ.)
1. Gal. i. 12 1st.

1. Gal. ii. 19 1st, 20 3rd.
1. —— iv. 12 2nd.
2. —— 12 3rd.
1c* —— 18.
1. —— v. 2, 10, 11 1st.
1b. —— vi. 14 1st.
1. —— 14 2nd, see And
1. —— 17.
— Eph. i. 15 1st, see I also.
1. —— iii. 1.
1. —— iv. 1.
1. —— v. 32.
1c* —— vi. 20 3rd.
1c* Phil. i. 7, *marg. me.*
— —— ii. 19 2nd, see I also.
— —— 24 2nd, see I myself.
1. —— 28 2nd, see And.
1. —— iii. 4 twice.
1. —— iv. 11 2nd.
1. Col. i. 23, 25.
1c* —— iv. 4 2nd.
1. 1 Thes. ii. 18.
2. —— iii. 5 1st.
1. 1 Tim. i. 15.
1. —— ii. 7 1st.
1. 2 Tim. i. 11.
— —— 12 5th, see I have committed unto him (that which.)
1. —— iv. 1 (*om.* G L T Tr A ℵ.)
1. —— 6.
1. Tit. i. 5 2nd.
1. Philem. 13, 19 twice.
1. Heb. i. 5 twice.
1. —— ii. 13 twice.
1. —— v. 5.
1a. —— viii. 9 2nd.
1. —— 9 3rd, see And.
1. —— x. 30.
1. —— xii. 26.
1. James ii. 18 twice, see And.
1. 1 Pet. i. 16.
1. 2 Pet. i. 17.
1. 2 John 1 twice.
1. 3 John 1.
1. Rev. i. 8, 9, 11 (*ap.*), 17 3rd.
— —— ii. 6, see I also.
1. —— 22 (*om.* G L T Tr A ℵ.)
1. —— 23 2nd.
1. —— 27, see Even.
1. —— iii. 9 3rd (*om* G ⇄)
— —— 10, see I also.
1. —— 19 1st.
— —— 21 2nd, see Even.
1. —— v. 4.
1. —— xvii. 7.
1. —— xxi. 2 (*om.* G L T Tr A ℵ.)
1. —— 6 1st (*om.* G ∾)
1. —— 6 2nd.
1. —— xxii. 8 1st, 13, 16 twice.

I ALSO

(*when not two separate words in the Greek.*)

κἀγώ, *contraction for* καί, and, also, even, *and* ἐγώ, I.

Matt. ii. 8.
—— x. 32, 33.
—— xvi. 18.
—— xxi. 24.
Mark xi. 29 (*om.* T Tr A.)
Luke xx. 3.

Rom. iii. 7.
2 Cor. xi. 18, 21.
Eph. i. 15.
Phil. ii. 19.
Rev. ii. 6.
—— iii. 10.

I (ALSO.)

1 Cor. vii. 40.

I (so)

John xv. 9. | 2 Cor. xi. 22 3 times.

I (in likewise)

Matt. xxi. 24.

I MYSELF.

1. αὐτός, self no other, alone.
2. { ἐγώ, I (*see* I, *No*. 1) / αὐτός, self, } I and no other, I alone.
3. ἐμαυτοῦ, myself.

2. Luke xxiv. 39.
1. Acts xxiv. 16.
1. —— xxv. 22.
2. Rom. vii. 25.
2. —— ix. 3.
2. Rom. xv. 14.
3. 1 Cor. vii. 7.
1. —— ix. 27.
2. 2 Cor. x. 1.
2. —— xii. 13.
1. Phil. ii. 24.

I MYSELF ALSO.

{ κἀγώ, and, also, *or* even I, / αὐτός, self, } I also myself, I too myself.

I HAVE (that)

{ τὰ, the things, / ἐμα, mine, } my possessions.

Luke xv. 31.

I HAVE COMMITTED UNTO HIM (that which)

{ ἡ, the, / παραθηκη, deposit, / μοῦ, of me, } my deposit.

2 Tim i. 12.

I TO DO WITH THEE (what have)

{ τὶ, what, / ἐμοὶ, to me, / καὶ, and, / σοὶ, to thee. }

Mark v. 7. | John ii. 4. | Luke viii. 28.

IDLE.

ἀργός, not working, *esp*., not working the ground, living without labour; *hence*, doing nothing, idle, (*occ*. Tit. i.12; 2 Pet. i. 8.

Matt. xii. 36.
—— xx. 3. [A ℵ.)
—— 6 1st (*om*. G L T Tr
Matt. xx. 6 2nd.
Luke xxiv. 11, see I tales.
1 Tim. v. 13 twice.

IDLE TALES.

λῆρος, silly talk, nonsense, (*non occ.*)

Luke xxiv. 11.

IDOL (-s.)

εἴδωλον, an image, a phantom; an image in the mind, *and later*, the image of a god, an idol.

Acts vii. 41.
—— xv. 20.
—— 29, see I (meat offered to.)
—— xvii. 16, see I (*full of*)
—— xxi. 25, see I (thing offered to.)
Rom. ii. 22.
1 Cor. viii. 1, see I (things offered unto.)
—— 4 1st, see (things that are offered in Sac. unto.)
—— 4 2nd.
—— 7 1st.
1 Cor. viii. 7 2nd, see I (thing offered unto an.)
—— 10 1st, see Idol's temple.
—— 10 2nd, I (thing which is offered to.)
—— x. 19 1st (*ap*.)
—— 19 2nd, see I (that which is offered in Sac. to.)
—— xii. 2.
2 Cor. vi. 16.
1 Thes. i. 9.
1 John v. 21.
Rev. ii. 14, 20, see below.
Rev. ix. 20.

IDOL'S TEMPLE.

εἰδωλεῖον, an idol-temple, (*occ. only* 1 Macc. i. 47, x. 83.)

1 Cor. viii. 10.

IDOLS (*full of*) [margin.]

κατείδωλος, given up to idols, full of idols.

Acts xvii. 16, (text, *wholly given to idolatry*.)

IDOLS (meat offered to)

εἰδωλόθυτον, idol-sacrifice, anything sacrificed to idols, the flesh of victims offered to idols which remained over, and was eaten or sold.

Acts xv. 29.

IDOLS (offered in sacrifice unto)

1 Cor. x. 28 (ἱερόθυτον, *offered in sacrifice*, G ~ L T Tr A ℵ)

IDOLS (that which is offered in sacrifice to)

1 Cor. x. 19.

IDOLS (thing offered to)

Acts xxi. 25.

IDOL (thing offered unto an)

1 Cor. viii. 7.

IDOLS (THING OFFERED UNTO)

1 Cor. viii. 1.

IDOLS (THING SACRIFICED UNTO)

Rev. ii. 14, 20.

IDOLS (THING THAT IS OFFERED IN SACRIFICE UNTO)

1 Cor. viii. 4.

IDOLS (THING WHICH IS OFFERED TO)

1 Cor. viii. 10.

IDOLATER.

εἰδωλολάτρης, idol-worshipper, (*occ. only in N.T. and Patristic Greek.*)

1 Cor. v. 10, 11.	Eph. v. 5.
—— vi. 9.	Rev. xxi. 8.
—— x. 7.	—— xxii. 15.

IDOLATRY.

εἰδωλολατρεία, idol-worship, (*occ. only in N.T. and Patristic Greek.*)

1 Cor. x. 14.	Col. iii. 5.
Gal. v. 20.	1 Pet. iv. 3.

IDOLATRY (WHOLLY GIVEN TO.)

κατείδωλος, given up to idols, full of idols.

Acts xvii. 16, marg. *full of idols.*

IF.

1. ἐάν, if haply, if it so be that, (*strictly*, εἰ, [*see No.* 4,] if, *and* ἄν, haply, perchance.) [It differs from εἰ, (*No.* 4,) in that εἰ, expresses a condition which is merely hypothetical, *i.e.* a *subjective* possibility, while ἐάν, (*No.* 1,) implies a condition which experience must determine, *i.e.* an *objective* possibility, and refers therefore to something future,]

(a) *followed by the indicative mood*, expressing the condition simply, without reference to whether the event will decide it or not,

(b) *followed by the subjunctive mood.* This expresses a condition of uncertainty, with an assumption of some small amount of contingency or probability, where experience will show whether the thing is really so or not, (John vii. 17.)

* *Present tense,*

† *Aorist tense*, which may be in most cases translated by the future perfect.

2. { ἐάν, if haply, (*see above,*) καί, and, also, } if also, * with *subj. aorist*, (*see above.*)

3. ἐάνπερ, if indeed, if now,
* with *subj. present*, (*see above.*)

4. εἰ, if, *putting the condition simply*, (*for difference between* εἰ *and* ἐάν, *see above*, *No.* 1,)

(a) *with the indicative mood*, (*present tense*,) assumes the hypothesis as an actual fact, the condition being unfulfilled, but no doubt being thrown on the supposition, (1 Cor. xv. 16). With the *past tense*, the hypothesis is expressed as impossible or contrary to fact, (Rom. iv. 2,)

(b) *with the optative mood*, expressing mere assumption or conjecture, without any subordinate idea; an entire uncertainty—a supposed case, (Acts xvii. 27; 1 Pet. iii. 14,)

(c) *with the subjunctive mood*, like ἐάν with the *subj.*, (*No.* 1b,) except that εἰ puts the condition as depending on the event more decisively than ἐάν, (ἐάν representing the condition more doubtful, as depending on some accidental circumstance; "if possibly" or "perhaps," 1 Cor. ix. 11; xiv. 5.)

5. εἴγε, if at least, if indeed.
* *followed by indic.*, and spoken of what is taken for granted,

6. εἴτε, or εἰ τε, whether.

[It will be seen from the above that the two principal words translated "IF" are *Nos.* 1 *and* 4, (the others being a combination of these with other particles.) For an example of the importance of the difference between them, and their use with certain moods, note,

(1) Acts v. 38, 39, "If this counsel

or this work be of men," (*No.* 1b*, *a point which the result will decide.*) "But if it be of God," (*No.* 4a, *a case which I put.*)

(2) John xiii. 17, "If ye know these things," (*No.* 4a, *assuming the case as a fact,*) "happy are ye if ye do them," (*No.* 1b*, *a result which remains to be seen.*)]

4a. Matt. iv. 3, 6.
1b†—— 9.
1b†—— v. 13.
1b*—— 23.
4a.—— 29, 30.
1b†—— 46, 47.
1b†—— vi. 14.
— —— 15, see If not.
1b†—— 22.
1b†—— 23 1st.
4a.—— 23 2nd, 30.
1b†—— vii. 9, } (*om.* L T
1b†—— 10, } Tr A ℵ, and αἰτήσει for αἰτήσῃ, "*whom his son will ask.*")
4a.—— 11.
1b*—— viii. 2.
— —— 10, see If (or.)
4a.—— 31.
1b†—— ix. 21.
1b*—— x. 13 1st.
— —— 13 2nd, see If not
4a.—— 25.
4a.—— xi. 14, 21, 23.
4a —— xii. 7.
1b†—— 11, 26, 27, 28.
4a.—— xiv. 28.
1b*—— xv. 14.
— —— xvi. 24, see If any man.
1b†—— 26.
4a.—— xvii. 4.
1b*—— 20.
4a.—— xviii. 8, 9.
1b†—— 12, 13, 15 twice.
— —— 16, see If not.
1b†—— 17 twice, 19.
— —— 35, see If not.
4a.—— xix. 10, 17, 21.
1b†—— xxi. 3.
1b*—— 21 1st.
— —— 21 2nd, see If (also.)
1b†—— 24, 25, 26.
1b†—— xxii. 24.
4a.—— 45.
4a.—— xxiii. 30.
1b†—— xxiv. 23.
4a.—— 24, see If it were possible.
4a.—— 26, 43.
— —— 48, see If (but and.)
4a.—— xxvi. 24, 39, 42.
4a.—— xxvii. 40.
4a.—— 42 (*om.* G → T Tr A ℵ: lit. "*He is.*")
4a.—— 43.
1b†—— xxviii. 14.
1b* Mark i. 40.
1b†—— iii. 24, 25.
4a.—— 26.
— —— iv. 23, see If any man.
1b†—— 26 (*om.* T Tr A ℵ: lit. "*as a man may cast.*"
— —— v. 28, } see If but.
— —— vi. 56, }
1b†—— vii. 11.
— —— 16, see If any man.

1b† Mark viii. 3.
— —— 23, see If . . . aught.
1b†—— 36 (*om.* and substitute *inf.* for *subj.*, T A ℵ.)
— —— ix. 22, see If anything.
4a.—— 23.
— —— 35, see If any man.
1b*—— 43, 45, 47.
1b†—— 50.
1b†—— x. 12.
1b†—— xi. 3.
4a.—— 13, and see If haply.
— —— 25, see If . . . aught.
4a.—— 26.
1b†—— 31.
1b†—— 32 (*om.* G ∾ L T Tr A ℵ: lit. "*are we to say.*")
1b†—— xii. 19.
1b†—— xiii. 21.
4a.—— 22, and see If it were possible.
4a.—— xiv. 21.
1b*—— 31.
4a.—— 35.
4a.—— xv. 44.
— —— xvi. 18, see I(and)
4a. Luke iv. 3.
1b†—— 7.
4a.—— 9.
1b*—— v. 12.
— —— 36, see If otherwise.
4a.—— vi. 32.
1b*—— 33.
1b*—— 34 (No. 1b†, L T Trm ℵ,) (No. 1a, G ∾ Lm Tr A.)
4a.—— vii. 39.
— —— ix. 23, see If any man.
1b*—— x. 6 1st.
— —— 6 2nd, see If not.
4a.—— 13.
1b†—— xi. 12 (*om.* T Tr Ab ℵ: lit. "*whom his son shall ask.*")
4a.—— 13.
— —— 18, see If also.
4a.—— 19, 20, 36.
4a.—— xii. 26, 28.
1b*—— 38 (κἀν, for καὶ ἐάν, T Tr A ℵ.)
4a.—— 39.
— —— 45, see If (but and.)
4a.—— 49.
— —— xiii. 9 1st, see If (and.)
— —— 9 2nd, see If not (and.)
— —— 26, see If any man.
1b†—— 34.
1b†—— xv. 8.
4a.—— xvi. 11, 12.

1b† Luke xvi. 30.
4a.—— 31.
1b†—— xvii. 3 twice, 4.
4a.—— 6.
— —— xix. 8, see If any man.
1b*—— 31.
1b†—— 40 (No. 1a, fut., L T Tr A ℵ.)
4a.—— 42.
1b†—— xx. 5.
— —— 6, see If (but and.)
1b†—— 28.
4a.—— xxii. 42.
1b†—— 67, 68.
4a.—— xxiii. 31, 35.
4a.—— 37 (*om.* Lb.)
4a.—— 39 (οὐχί, art not [*thou the Christ?*] Lm T Tr A ℵ.)
4a. John i. 25.
4a.—— iii. 12 1st.
1b†—— 12 2nd.
4a.—— iv. 10.
1b*—— v. 31.
1b†—— 43.
4a.—— 47.
1b*—— vi. 51.
— —— 62, see If (and.)
4a.—— vii. 4.
1b†—— 17.
4a.—— 23.
1b*—— 37.
1b*—— viii. 16.
4a.—— 19.
— —— 24, see If not.
1b†—— 31, 36.
4a.—— 39, 42, 46.
1b†—— 51, 52.
1b*—— 54.
1b†—— 55, κἀν for καὶ ἐάν, L T Tr ℵ.)
1b†—— ix. 22.
1b*—— 31.
— —— 33, see If not.
4a.—— 41.
1b†—— x. 9.
4a.—— 24, 35, 37, 38.
1b*—— xi. 9, 10.
4a.—— 12, 21, 32.
1b†—— 40, 48, 57.
1b†—— xii. 24.
1b*—— 26 twice.
1b†—— 32, 47.
— —— xiii. 8, see If not.
4a.—— 14, 17 1st.
1b*—— 17 2nd.
4a.—— 32 (ap.)
1b*—— 35.
— —— xiv. 2, see If not.
1b†—— 3.
4a.—— 7.
1b†—— 14.
1b*—— 15, 23.
4a.—— 28.
— —— xv. 6, see If not.
1b†—— 7, 10.
1b*—— 14.
4a.—— 18, 19, 20 twice.
— —— 22, 24, } see If
— —— xvi. 7 1st, } not.
1b†—— 7 2nd.
4a.—— xviii. 8, 23 twice.
— —— 30, see If not.
4a.—— 36.
1b†—— xix. 12.
4a.—— xx. 15.
1b*—— xxi. 22, 23, 25.
4a. Acts iv. 9.
1b*—— v. 38.
4a.—— 39.
4a.—— viii. 22, and see If perhaps.
4a.—— 37 (*ap.*)
1b†—— ix. 2.
4a.—— xiii. 15.
4a.—— xvi. 15.
4b.—— xvii. 27, and see If haply.

4a. Acts xviii. 14, 15.
4a.—— xix. 38, 39.
4a.—— xx. 16.
4a.—— xxiii. 9.
— —— xxiv. 19, see If . . . aught.
— —— 20, } see If any
— —— xxv. 5, }
4a.—— 11 twice.
1b*—— xxvi. 5.
— —— 32, see If not.
— —— xxvii. 12, see If by any means.
4b.—— 39.
— Rom. i. 10, see If by any means.
1b*—— ii. 25 twice, 26.
4a.—— iii. 3, 5, 7.
4a.—— iv. 2, 14.
4a.—— v. 10, 15, 17.
4a.—— vi. 5, 8.
1b†—— vii. 2, 3 twice.
4a.—— 16, 20.
— —— viii. 9 1st, see If so be that.
— —— 9 2nd, see If any man.
4a.—— 10, 11, 13 twice, 17, 25, 31.
4a.—— ix. 22.
1b†—— x. 9.
4a.—— xi. 6 1st, 6 2nd (*ap.*), 12.
— —— 14, see If by any means.
4a.—— 15, 16 twice.
— —— 17, see If some.
4a.—— 18, 21.
— —— 23, see If not.
4a.—— 24.
4a.—— xii. 18, and see If it be possible.
1b*—— 20 twice.
1b*—— xiii. 4.
— —— 9, see If any.
4a.—— xiv. 15.
1b*—— 23.
1b†—— xv. 24.
4a.—— 27.
— 1 Cor. iii. 12, 14, 15, 17, 18, see If any man.
— —— iv. 7, see If (now.)
1b†—— 19.
1b*—— v. 11.
4a.—— vi. 2.
1b*—— 4.
1b†—— vii. 8.
4a.—— 9.
— —— 11, see If (but and.)
— —— 12, see If any.
4a.—— 15.
— —— 21, see If (but.)
— —— 28 1st, see If (but and.)
1b*—— 28 2nd.
— —— 36 1st, see If any man.
1b*—— 36 2nd.
1b†—— 39, 40.
— —— viii. 2, 3, see If any man.
1b*—— 8 1st.
— —— 8 2nd, see If . . . not.
1b†—— 10.
4a.—— 13.
4a.—— ix. 2, 11 twice, 12.
— —— 16, see If not.
4a.—— 17 twice.
— —— x. 27, see If any.
1b†—— 28.
4a.—— 30.
— —— xi. 5, see If (even all one as.)
4a.—— 6 twice.
1b*—— 14, 15.
— —— 16, see If any man.
— —— 20 5 times.
4a.—— 31.

— 1 Cor. xi. 34, see If any man.
1b† —— xii. 15, 16.
4a. —— 17 twice, 19.
1b† —— xiv. 6, 8.
— —— 11, see If not.
1b* —— 14.
1b† —— 23.
1b* —— 24.
6. —— 27.
— —— 28, see If no.
1b† —— 30.
4a. —— 35.
— —— 37, 38, see If any man.
4a. —— xv. 2, 12, 13, 14.
— —— 15, see If so be that.
4a. —— 16, 17, 19, 29, 32 twice.
1b* —— xvi. 4, 7.
1b† —— 10.
— —— 22, see If any man.
4a. 2 Cor. ii. 2.
— —— 5, 10, see If anything.
4a. —— iii. 7, 9, 11.
— —— iv. 3, see If (but.)
4a. —— 14 (om. G → L T Tr A ℵ.)
— —— vii. 14, see If anything.
4a. —— viii. 12.
1b† —— ix. 4.
— —— x. 7, see If any man.
4a. —— xi. 4.
— —— 15, see If also.
— —— 16, see If otherwise.
4a. —— 30.
1b† —— xiii. 2.
— Gal. i. 9, see If any man.
4a. —— 10.
4a. —— ii. 14, 17, 18, 21.
— —— iii. 4, see If yet.
4a. —— 18, 21, 29.
4a. —— iv. 7.
4a. —— 15, and see If it had been possible.
1b† —— v. 2.
4a. —— 11, 15, 18, 25.
2*. —— vi. 1, marg. *although.*
— —— 3, see If a man.
5. Eph. iii. 2.
— —— iv. 21, see If so be that.
4a. Phil. i. 22.
— —— ii. 1 4 times, see If any.
— —— 17, see If (yea and.)
— —— iii. 11, see If by any means.
— —— 12, see If that.
— —— 15, see If anything.
— —— iv. 4, see If any man.
— —— 8 twice, see If any
5. Col. i. 23.
4a. —— ii. 20.
4a. —— iii. 1.
1b* —— 13.
1b† —— iv. 10.
1b* 1 Thes. iii. 8 (No. 1a, T Tr A ℵ*.)
4a. —— iv 14.
1b* 2 Thes. i. 8.
— —— iii. 10, see If any.
— —— 13, see If any man.
1b* —— 15.
— 1 Tim. i. 10, see If anything.

1b* 1 Tim. ii. 5.
1b† —— 15.
— —— iii. 1, 5, see If a man.
— —— v. 4, 8, see If any.
4a. —— 10 5 times.
— —— 16, } see If any
— —— vi. 3, } man.
4a. 2 Tim. ii. 11, 12 twice, 13.
1b† —— 21.
— —— 25, see If peradventure.
— Titus i. 6, see If any.
4a. Philem. 17, 18.
4a. Heb. ii. 2.
3*. —— iii. 6 (No. 1b*, L^b T Tr A.) (ℵ has κἀν, *and if*, with ε written above κ.)
1b† —— 7.
3*. —— 14.
1b† —— 15.
4a. —— iv. 3, 5.
1b† —— 7.
4a. —— 8.
3*. —— vi. 3.
4a. —— vii. 11.
4a. Heb. viii. 4, 7.
4a. —— ix. 13.
1b* —— x. 38.
4a. —— xi. 15.
4a. —— xii. 7 (εἰς, *unto*, L T Tr A ℵ: lit. "*with a view to discipline are ye enduring, as to sons is God dealing with you.*")
4a. —— 8.
— —— 10, see If so much as (and.)
4a —— 25.
1b* —— xiii. 23.
— James i. 5, 23, see If any.
— —— 26, see If any man.
1b† —— ii. 2.
4a. —— 8, 9, 11.
1b* —— 15.
— —— 17, see If not.
— —— iii. 2, see If any man.
4a. —— 14.
4a. —— iv. 11.
1b† —— 15.
— —— v. 15, see If (and.)
1b† —— 19.
4a. 1 Pet. i. 6, 17.
— —— ii. 3, see If so be.
4a. —— 19, 20 twice.
— —— iii. 1, see If any.
1b† —— 13.
4b. —— 14, 17.
— —— iv. 11 twice, see If any man.
— —— 13, see If (but and.)
4a. —— 14, 16, 17, 18.
4a. 2 Pet. ii. 20.
1b† 1 John i. 6.
1b* —— 7.
1b† —— 8.
1b* —— 9.
1b† —— 10.
1b† —— ii. 1.
1b* —— 3, 15.
4a. —— 19.
1b† —— 24.
1b* —— 29.
4a. —— iii. 13.
1b* —— 20.
— —— 21, see If not.
4a. —— iv. 11.
1b* —— 12.
1b† —— 20.
4a. —— v. 9.

1b* 1 John v. 14, } (ἀν, L.)
1a. —— 15, }
1b† —— 16.
— 2 John 10, see If any.
1b† 3 John 10.
— Rev. iii. 3, see If not.
1b† —— 20.
— —— xi. 5 twice, } see
— —— xiii. 9, } If any
— —— xiv. 9, } more.

1b† Rev. xxii. 18, 19.

The mood after εἰ in the following combinations is *Indicative*, unless otherwise indicated.

IF ALSO.

1. { εἰ, if (*see* "IF," *No.* 4a,) / καὶ, and also, } and if (4a.)

2. { εἰ, if (*see* "IF," *No.* 4,) / δε, but, / καὶ, and also, } but and if.

2. Luke xi. 18. | 1. 2 Cor. xi. 15.

IF ANY.

{ εἰ, if (*see* "IF" *No.* 4a,)
τις, any.

Acts xxiv. 20 (τί, what, G L T Tr A ℵ.)
—— xxv. 5.
Rom. xiii. 9.
1 Cor. vii. 12.
—— x. 27.
2 Cor. ii. 5.
Phil. ii. 1 4 times.
—— iv. 8.
2 Thes. iii. 10.
1 Tim. v. 4, 8.
Tit. i. 6.
Jas. i. 5, 23.
1 Pet. iii. 1.
2 John 10.

IF ANY MAN.

εἰ τις, if any one, *No.* 4a. With* = *No.* 4b. With† = *No.* 4c.

Matt. xvi. 24.
Mark iv. 23.
—— vii. 16.
—— ix. 35.
Luke ix. 23.
—— xiv. 26.
—— xix. 8.
Rom. viii. 9.
1 Cor. iii. 12, 14, 15, 17, 18.
—— vii. 36.
—— viii. 2, 3.
—— xi. 16, 34.
—— xiv. 37, 38.
—— xvi. 22.
2 Cor. v. 17.
—— x. 7.
Gal. i. 9.
Phil. iii. 4.
2 Thes. iii. 14.
1 Tim. v. 16.
—— vi. 3.
Jas. i. 26.
—— iii. 2.
1 Pet. iv. 11 twice.
*Rev. xi. 5 (4a. G L T Tr) (4a. ℵ 1st.)
—— xiii. 9.
—— xiv. 9.

IF A MAN.

2 Cor. xi. 20 5 times. | Gal. vi. 3.
1 Tim. iii. 1, 5.

IF ANY THING.

Mark ix. 22.
2 Cor. ii. 10.
2 Cor. vii. 14.
Phil. iii. 15.
1 Tim. i. 10.

IF . . . AUGHT.

Mark viii. 23. | Mark xi. 25.
† Acts xxiv. 19.

IF BUT.

κἄν, and if, also if.

Mark v. 28. | Mark vi. 56.

IF BY ANY MEANS.

{ *εἰ*, if (*see* "IF," *No.* 4,) / *πῶς*, how, in what way *or* manner, } *,= *No.* 4c. if by any *or* some means (*non occ.*)

* Acts xxvii. 12. Rom. i. 10. | Rom. xi. 14. Phil. iii. 11.

IF HAPLY.

1. { *εἰ*, if (*see No.* 4a.) / *ἄρα*, accordingly, *marking a correspondence in point of fact*, } if accordingly.

2. { *εἰ*, if (*see No.* 4a,) / *ἄραγε* accordingly indeed, } if accordingly indeed.

1. Mark xi. 13. | 2. Acts xvii. 27.

IF IT BE [HAD BEEN *; WERE †] POSSIBLE.

1. { *εἰ*, if, / *δυνατόν*, possible, able.

2. { *εἰ*, if, / *δύναιντο*, they were able (*optative*.)

. Matt. xxiv. 24.* 1. Mark xiii. 22.† 1. Gal. iv. 15*. | 2. Acts xxvii. 39† (No. 1 [G∾) 1. Rom. xii. 18.

IF NOT.

1. { *ἐάν*, if (*see No.* 1,) / *μή*, not (*see* "NO," *No.* 2,) } *=1b*, †=1b†.

2. { *εἰ*, if (*see No.* 4a,) / *δέ*, but, / *μήγε*, not indeed, } but if not indeed.

3. { *εἰ*, if (*see No.* 4a,) / *μή*, not (*see* "NO," *No.* 2,) } if not.

1*. Matt. vi. 15.
1†. —— x. 13.
1*. —— xviii. 16, 35
2. Luke x. 6.
1*. John viii. 24.
3. —— ix. 33.
1*. —— xiii. 8.
2. —— xiv. 2.
1*. —— xv. 6.
3. —— 22, 24.
1*. John xvi. 7.
3. —— xviii. 30.
2. Acts xxvi. 32.
1*. Rom. xi. 23.
1*. 1 Cor. viii. 8.
1*. —— ix. 16.
1†. —— xiv. 11.
1†. Jas. ii. 17.
1†. 1 John iii. 21.
1*. Rev. iii. 3.

IF NO.

1†. 1 Cor. xiv. 28.

IF OTHERWISE.

3. Luke v. 30. | 3. 2 Cor. xi. 16.

IF PERADVENTURE.

μήποτε, lest at some time *or* other, (*followed here by subjunctive.*)

2 Tim. ii. 25.

IF PERHAPS.

{ *εἰ*, if (*see No.* 4a,) / *ἄρα*, accordingly, } whether.

Acts viii. 22.

IF SOME.

{ *εἰ*, if (*see No.* 4a,) / *τις*, some, certain.

Rom. xi. 17, pl.

IF SO BE THAT.

1. { *εἴγε*, if at least, if indeed, / *καί*, and, also, even, } if indeed also.

2. *εἴπερ*, if indeed, if so be, *assuming the supposition as true, whether justly or not.*

3. { *εἴπερ*, (*see above*, *No.* 2,) / *ἄρα*, accordingly, } if indeed after all.

2. Rom. viii. 9, 17. 3. 1 Cor. xv. 15. | 1. 2 Cor. v. 5. 1. Eph. iv. 21.

IF THAT.

{ *εἰ*, if (*see No.* 4c,) / *καί*, and, also, even.

Phil. iii. 12.

IF YET.

{ *εἴγε*, if at least, if indeed, / *καί*, and, also, even.

Gal. iii. 14.

IF (AND)

1. *ἐάν*, if (*see No.* 1b*.

2. *κἄν*, and if.

2. Mark xvi. 18 (ap.) 2. Luke xiii. 9. | 1. John vi. 62. 2. Jas. v. 15.

IF (ALSO)

2. Matt. xxi. 21.

IF (BUT)

1. { ἀλλά, but (*more emphatic than* δὲ,) / εἰ, if (*see* "IF," *No.* 4,) / καὶ, also, even, } but if even.

2. { εἰ, if (*see* "IF," *No.* 4,) / δὲ, but, (*not so emphatic as* ἀλλά,) / καὶ, and, even, also, } but if even.

1. 1 Cor. vii. 21. | 2. 2 Cor. iv. 3.

IF (BUT AND)

1. { ἐάν, if (*see* "IF," *No.* 1b†,) / δὲ, but.

2. { ἐάν, if (*see* "IF," *No.* 1b†,) / δὲ, but, / καὶ, and, also, even.

3. { ἀλλά, but (*more emphatic than* δὲ,) / εἰ, if (*see No.* 4c,) / καὶ, and, also, even.

1. Matt. xxiv. 48. | 1. Luke xx. 6.
1. Luke xii. 45. | 2. 1 Cor. vii. 11, 28.
3. 1 Peter iii. 14.

IF NOT (AND)

{ εἰ, if, (*see No.* 4,) / δε, but, / μήγε, not indeed, not at least.

Luke xiii. 9.

IF (NOW)

{ εἰ, if (*see No.* 4,) / καὶ, and, also, even, } if even.

1 Cor. iv. 7.

IF (OR)

{ καὶ, and, also, even, / ἐάν, if (*see* "IF," *No.* 1b†.)

Matt. vii. 10, Luke xi. 11, } (ἢ καὶ, *or also*, L T Tr A ℵ.)

IF SO MUCH AS (AND)

κἄν, and if, if also.

Heb. xii. 20.

IF (EVEN ALL ONE AS)

{ αὐτός, same, / ἓν, one, / καὶ, and, } one and the same.

1 Cor. xi. 5.

IF (YEA AND)

{ ἀλλά, but, / εἰ, if (*see No.* 4,) / καὶ, and, also, even, } but if even.

Phil. ii. 17.

See also "AS."

IGNORANCE.

1. ἄγνοια, want of perception, (*non occ.*)

2. ἀγνωσία, a not knowing, (*occ.* 1 Cor. xv. 34.)

1. Acts iii. 17. | 1. Eph. iv. 18.
1. —— xvii. 30. | 1. 1 Pet. i. 14.
2. 1 Pet. ii. 15.

IGNORANT.

1. ἀγνοέω, not to perceive *or* know; not to understand *or* comprehend.

2. ἰδιώτης, a private person, one in a private station, not engaged in public affairs; one who has no professional knowledge, (*as we say* a layman *as to law or other subjects, etc.*, i.e. *one who has no knowledge on such a subject as this,*) (*occ.* 1 Cor. xiv. 16, 23; 2 Cor. xi. 6.)

2. Acts iv. 13. | 1. 1 Cor. xii. 1, inf.
1. Rom. i. 13, inf. | 1. Heb. v. 2, part.

IGNORANT (BE)

1. Rom. x. 3. | 1. 1 Cor. xiv. 38 twice.
1. —— xi. 25. | 1. 2 Cor. ii. 11.
1. 1 Cor. x. 1. | 1. 1 Thes. iv. 13.

IGNORANT OF (BE)

λανθάνω, to escape notice, be unknown, unnoticed; to be hid *as to any one, i.e.* from him, to escape his knowledge or notice.

2 Pet. iii. 5, 8.

IGNORANTLY.

ἀγνοέω, *see* "IGNORANT," *No.* 1.

Acts xvii. 23, part. | 1 Tim. i. 13, part.

ILL [noun.]

κακός, bad, (*opp.* to καλός, *see* "GOOD," *No.* 2,) bad, *generically of every form of evil.*

(a) *neuter, as subst.*, evil, ill, *physical and moral.*

a. Rom. xiii. 10.

ILLUMINATE (-ED.)

φωτίζω, to shine, give light, *trans.*, to enlighten, light up, bring to light, throw light upon. *A word of later Greek, found principally in N.T.* and lxx. *The Hellenistic meaning is to enlighten;* and *the* lxx., to instruct, teach.

Heb. x. 32, part.

IMAGE.

εἰκών, (*from* ἔοικα, to be like, resemble, Jas. i. 6, 23,) that which resembles an object, *or which* represents it, hence, image, likeness.

(a) εἰκών, *denotes not merely* the image *but also* the pattern, the original (*in opp. to* σκιά, the shadow,) which sets forth that likeness or resemblance which is meant to be found in the image, *cf.* Wisd. xiii. 13; Hos. xiii. 2; Gen. v. 3. *This supplies the simplest explanation of the passages marked* (a) and Eph. iv. 24 (*non occ.*)

Matt. xxii. 20.
Mark xii. 16.
Luke xx. 24.
Rom. i. 23.
a. —— viii. 29.
1 Cor. xi. 7.
—— xv. 49 twice.
a. 2 Cor. iii. 18.
—— iv. 4.
Col. i. 15.
a. Col. iii. 10.
Heb. i. 3, see I (express.)
a. —— x. 1.
Rev. xiii. 14.
—— 15 3 times.
—— xiv. 9, 11.
—— xv. 2.
—— xvi. 2.
—— xix. 20.
Rev. xx. 4.

IMAGE (EXPRESS)

χαρακτήρ, (from χαράσσω, to tear, cleave, cut in, engrave.) *Actively*, something engraved *or* impressed, *and esp.*, an instrument for marking, *e.g.* a stamp, *but rarely used in this sense; Passively*, a sign, mark, token, *and hence*, distinctive sign, trait, distinctive type *or* form, the image impressed *as corresponding exactly with the original or pattern.* In Heb. i. 3 *this word is chosen instead of* χάραγμα *because it is not so narrow in sense.* χάραγμα, *is* the thing impressed; it *does not denote* the peculiar characteristic, *and always suggests the passive relation of the subject spoken of.* (*See* "MARK," *No.* 1). (*non occ.*)

Heb. i. 3.

IMAGINATION (-S.)

1. λογισμός, reckoning *or* computing, (*esp. of arithmetic,*) then, calculation, (*in the way of reasoning.*)

2. διαλογισμός, (*No.* 1, *with* διά, through, *prefixed,*) a reckoning through, balancing of accounts, calculation, reasoning through.

3. διάνοια, a thinking over, meditation, reflecting; activity of thinking; *esp.*, moral reflection *as the product of the heart.*

3. Luke i. 51.
2. Rom. i. 21.
1. 2 Cor. x. 5, marg. *reasoning.*

IMAGINE.

μελετάω, to care for, to take care for any thing so as to be able to perform it, (*occ.* Mark xiii. 11; 1 Tim. iv. 15.)

Acts iv. 25.

IMMEDIATELY.

1. εὐθύς, straight, direct, (*whether perpendicular or horizontal.*) *Used of time*, straightway,

2. εὐθέως, (*adv. of No.* 1,) immediately, directly, forthwith, at once.

3. παραχρῆμα, with the thing itself, at the very moment, on the spot.

4. ἐξαυτῆς, from this, *e.g. time, i.e.* forthwith.

2. Matt. iv. 22.
2. —— viii. 3.
2. —— xiv. 31.
2. —— xx. 34.
2. —— xxiv. 29.
2. —— xxvi. 74 (No. 1, Tr)
1. Mark i. 12.
1. —— 28 (om. Tr^b ℵ.)
2. —— 31 (om. T Tr A ℵ)
2. —— 42 (No. 1, T Tr A ℵ.)
2. —— ii. 8 (No. 1, L T Tr A ℵ.)
2. —— 12.
2. —— iv. 5 (No. 1, L T Tr A ℵ.)
2. —— 15 (No. 1, T Tr A ℵ.)
2. —— 16 (No. 1, L T Tr A ℵ.)
2. Mark iv. 17 (No. 1, T Tr A ℵ.)
2. —— 29 (No. 1, T Tr A ℵ.)
2. —— v. 2 (No. 1, T Tr^b A ℵ.)
2. —— 30 (No. 1, T Tr A ℵ.)
2. —— vi. 27 (No. 1, T Tr A ℵ.)
2. —— 50 (No. 1, L T Tr A ℵ.)
2. —— x. 52 (No. 1, L T Tr A ℵ.)
2. —— xiv. 43 (No. 1, L T Tr A ℵ.)
3. Luke i. 64.
3. —— iv. 39.
2. —— v. 13.

3. Luke v. 25.
2. —— vi. 49 (No. 1, T Tr A ℵ.)
3. —— viii. 44, 47.
2. —— xii. 36.
3. —— xiii. 13.
3. —— xviii. 43.
3. —— xix. 11.
3. —— xxii. 60.
2. John v. 9.
2. —— vi. 21.
2. —— xiii. 30 (No. 1, L T Tr A ℵ.)
2. —— xviii. 27.
1. John xxi. 3 (*om.* G ⇉ L T Tr A ℵ.)
3. Acts iii. 7.
2. —— ix. 18, 34.
4. —— x. 33.
4. —— xi. 11.
3. —— xii. 23.
3. —— xiii. 11.
2. —— xvi. 10.
3. —— —— 26.
2. —— xvii. 10, 14.
4. —— xxi. 32.
2. Gal. i. 16.
2. Rev. iv. 2.

IMMORTAL.

ἄφθαρτος, not liable to corruption. [A word never joined with the Hebrew or Greek words for "Soul" or "Spirit," etc., in *O. & N.T.*, though they occur 1,644 times, (*viz.* רוּחַ, *spirit*, 400 times; נֶפֶשׁ, *soul*, 752 times; *πνεῦμα*, *spirit*, 385 times, and *ψυχή*, *soul*, 105 times. Predicated of only one Being—God.)] (*occ.* Rom. i. 23; 1 Cor. ix. 25, xv. 52; 1 Pet. i. 4, 23, iii. 4.)

1 Tim. i. 17.

IMMORTALITY.

1. *ἀφθαρσία*, incorruption, immortality. [Not the inalienable possession of the human family since the fall. (see Gen. iii. 22, 23.) Now, it is restricted to those who "by patient continuance in well-doing seek for" it, (Rom. ii. 7), and received by them as a "gift," (Rom. vi. 23). A truth "brought to light" by the Gospel, 2 Tim. i. 10.] (*occ.* 1 Cor. xv. 42, 50, 53, 54; Eph. vi. 24; Titus ii. 7.)

2. *ἀθανασία*, immortality. [Expressly declared to be possessed by God alone, 1 Tim. vi. 16. Not to be "put on" by man until resurrection, when "mortality shall be swallowed up of life," 1 Cor. xv. 53, 54.] (*non occ.*)

1. Rom. ii. 7.
2. 1 Cor. xv. 53, 54.
2. 1 Tim. vi. 16.
1. 2 Tim. i. 10.

IMMUTABILITY.

{ ὁ, the,
{ *ἀμετάθετος*, not to be transposed, unalterable, without mutation *or* change, immovable, (*occ. ver.* 17.)

Heb. vi. 17.

IMMUTABLE.

ἀμετάθετος, *see above.*

Heb. vi. 18.

IMPART (-ED.)

μεταδίδωμι, to share in association with *anyone*, *i.e.* to impart, communicate.

Luke iii. 11.
Rom. i. 11.
Rom. xii. 8, marg. (text, *give.*)
1 Thes. ii. 8.

IMPEDIMENT IN ONE'S SPEECH (HAVE AN)

μογιλάλος, speaking with difficulty, a stammerer, (lxx. for אלם, tongue-tied, Is. xxxv. 6,) *non occ.*

Mark vii. 32.

IMPENITENT.

ἀμετανόητος, without change of mind, impenitent.

Rom. ii. 5.

IMPLACABLE.

ἄσπονδος, without libation, league, *or* compact; without treaty; *then*, without respect for treaties *or* covenants, (*occ.* 2 Tim. iii. 3.)

Rom. i. 31 (*om.* G ⇉ L T Tr A ℵ.)

IMPLEAD.

ἐγκαλέω, to call in, *esp. a debt, and so* to demand *as one's due; hence,* to bring an accusation against anyone, arraign.

Acts xix. 38.

IMPORTUNITY.

ἀναίδεια, shamelessness, want of modesty, impudence, (*non occ.*)

Luke xi. 8.

IMPOSED ON (BE)

ἐπίκειμαι, to lie upon, to be laid upon.

Heb. ix. 10.

IMPOSSIBLE.

1. *ἀδύνατος*, deficient in strength or power; *act.*, infirm, weak, feeble; *neut. and pass.*, impossible, unable.

2. ἀνένδεκτος, what is not able to be done, what cannot be, impossible, (*non occ.*)

— Matt. xvii. 20, see I	2. Luke xvii. 1.
1. —— xix. 26. [(be.)	1. —— xviii. 27.
1. Mark x. 27.	1. Heb. vi. 4, 18.
— Luke i. 37, see I (be.)	1. —— xi. 6.

IMPOSSIBLE (BE)

ἀδυνατέω, to be ἀδύνατος, (*see above, No.* 1,) to want strength, (*non occ.*)

Matt. xvii. 20. | Luke i. 37.

IMPOTENT.

1. ἀδύνατος, *see* "IMPOSSIBLE," *No.* 1.)

2. ἀσθενής, without strength, *esp. in body; hence,* sick, diseased.

2. Acts iv. 9. | 1. Acts xiv. 8.

IMPOTENT MAN.

ἀσθενέω, to want strength *or* health, to be infirm, weak, feeble; *here, the participle.*

John v. 7, part.

IMPOTENT FOLK.

John v. 3, part. pl.

IMPRISON.

φυλακίζω, to put in ward, imprison, throw into prison, (*non occ.*)

Acts xxii. 19.

IMPRISONMENT.

φυλακή, watch, guard; the act of keeping watch; *then, of persons set to watch, and collectively,* guards; *then,* the place where watch is kept, *i.e.* watch-post, station; *then,* imprisonment.

2. Cor. vi. 5. | Heb. xi. 36.

IMPUTE.

1. λογίζομαι, to occupy one's self with reckonings *or* calculations. To reckon *or* count; to reckon anything to a person, to put it to his account, *either in his favour or what he must be answerable for.*

2. ἐλλογέω, to reckon in; *hence,* to charge, (*occ.* Philem. 18.)

1. Rom. iv. 6, 8, 11, 22, 23, 24.	1. 2 Cor. v. 19.
2. —— v. 13.	1. Gal. iii. 6, marg. (text, *account.*)

1. Jas. ii. 23.

IN.

The English word "IN" is frequently the translation of a case of the noun; these occurrences are not quoted below. Sometimes it is part of a verb or a phrase; these are generally indicated by cross references. When "IN" is the translation of a separate Greek preposition it is one of these words following:

1. ἐν, in, a being or remaining within, *with the primary idea of rest* in *any place or thing. Of place,* in, within, among. *Of time,* on, upon.

2. εἰς, into, unto, to, *implying motion to the interior, governing the Accusative.* * Acts ii. 27, 31, (*with Genitive,*) εἰς ᾅδου = unto (*the habitation or power of*) Hades.

3. ἐπί, upon, over.

(a) *with Gen.*, upon, *as springing or proceeding from;* over, in the presence *or* time of.

(b) *with Dat.*, upon, *as resting on;* upon, *i.e.* in addition to.

(c) *with Acc.*, upon, *by direction towards;* with *implied motion,* up to; during, *of time.*

4. κατά, down.

(a) *with Gen.*, down from; *hence,* against, in opposition to.

(b) *with Acc.*, down towards, down upon *or* along; *hence,* throughout. *In ref. to time,* at *or* in, correspondent with, according to, at the period of, over against.

5. διά, through, *from the notion of separation or disjunction.*

(a) *with Gen.*, through, *as proceeding from;* through, by means of. *In ref. to time,* διά *marks the passage* through *an interval,* during, *or* after the lapse of.

(b) *with Acc.*, through, *as tending towards*, on account of, *or* owing to.

6. πρός, towards, in the direction of.

(a) *with Gen.*, in favour of, (*only in* Acts xxvii. 34,)

(b) *with Dat.*, towards, resting in the direction towards,

(c) *with Acc.*, hitherwards, towards, against; *of mental direction*, in consideration of.

7. ἐκ, out of, from out of, *motion from the interior.*

8. μετά, with, in association with, (*union of locality.*)

(a) *with Gen.*, with and from, (*separable connection,*) together with, among.

(b) *with Acc.*, after.

9. ἀπό, from, (*motion from the exterior*), away from; *hence, as marking esp. the cause or occasion*, from, on account of.

10. ἄχρι, *adv. of time, marking duration*, continuedly, during.

11. ἔσω, *adv. of place*, in, within, (*implying motion into a place.*)

12. περί, around.

(a) *with Gen.*, around and separate from, about, concerning, on behalf of.

(b) *with Acc.*, around and towards; in reference to, about, *of any object of thought.*

13. ὑπό, under.

(a) *with Gen.*, beneath and separate from; by, *marking* the agent.

(b) *with Acc.*, under and towards, close upon.

4b. Matt. i. 20 1st.
1. —— 20 2nd.
1. —— ii. 1 twice, 2, 5, 9.
4b.—— 12, 13.
1. —— 16 twice, 18.
4b.—— 19 1st.
1. —— 19 2nd.
3a.—— 22 1st (*om.* G → L T Tr^b A^b ℵ.)
— —— 22 2nd, see Room
4b.—— 22 3rd.
2. —— 23.
1. —— iii. 1 twice, 3, 6, 12, [17.
3a.—— iv. 6.

2. Matt. iv. 13 1st.
1. —— 13 2nd, 16 twice, 21, 23.
1. —— v. 12, 15, 16.
— —— 18, see No.
1. —— 19 twice.
— —— 20, see Case.
— —— 21, 22 3rd, see Danger.
1. —— 25, 28, 45.
1. —— 48 (οὐράνιος, *heavenly, for* ἐν τοῖς οὐρανοῖς, *in the heavens*, (G ∾ L T Tr A ℵ.)

1. Matt. vi. 1, 2 twice, 4 twice, 5 twice, 6 twice, 9.
3a.—— 10 1st.
1. —— 10 2nd.
1. —— 18 twice, 20, 23, 29
1. —— vii. 3 twice, 4, 11.
— —— 13 1st, see Enter.
— —— 13 2nd, see Go.
1. —— 15, 21, 22 1st.
1. —— viii. 10, 11.
1. —— 13 (No. 9, L.)
1. —— 24, 32.
1. —— ix. 4, 10.
— —— 25, see Go.
1. —— 33, 35.
2. —— x. 9.
1. —— 11, 15, 16, 17, 19, 20, 23.
1. —— 27 1st & 2nd.
2. —— 27 3rd.
1. —— 28, 32, 33.
2. —— 41 twice.
2. —— 42 1st.
— —— 42 2nd, see No.
1. —— xi. 1, 2, 6, 8 twice, 11, 16.
1. —— 21 3 times, 23 twice, 24.
— —— 26, see Sight.
1. —— xii. 5 twice.
— —— 6, see Place.
2. —— 18 (No. 1, Tr) (*om.* L T A ℵ.)
1. —— 19.
1. —— 21 (*om.* G L T Tr A ℵ.)
1. —— 32 twice, 36, 40 twice, [41.
1. —— 42.
— —— 45, see Enter.
1. —— 50.
1. —— xiii. 3, 10, 13.
3b.—— 14 (*om.* G L T Tr A ℵ.)
1. —— 19, 21, 24, 27, 30 1st.
2. —— 30 2nd (*om.* G ⇉ Tr^b A.)
1. —— 31, 32.
2. —— 33.
1. —— 34, 35, 40 2nd, 43, 44, 54, 57 3 times.
1. —— xiv. 2, 3.
3b.—— 8.
1. —— 10.
3b.—— 11.
— —— 24, see Midst.
1. —— 33.
— —— xv. 9, see Vain.
— —— 17, see Enter.
1. —— 32, 33.
— —— xvi. 3, see Morning.
1. —— 17, 19 twice.
— —— 26, see Exchange
1. —— 27, 28.
1. —— xvii. 5, 22.
1. —— xviii. 1, 2, 4.
3b.—— 5.
2. —— 6 1st.
1. —— 6 2nd.
1. —— 10 twice, 14.
3a.—— 16.
1. —— 18 twice, 19.
2. —— 20 1st.
1. —— 20 2nd.
1. —— xix. 21, 28 1st.
3a.—— 28 2nd.
— —— xx. 1, see Morning
1. —— 3, 17, 21.
1. —— xxi. 8 twice.
1. —— 9 twice, 12, 14, 15.
— —— 18, see Morning.
3a.—— 19.
1. —— 22, 28, 32, 33, 41, 42 twice.
— —— xxii. 11, 12, see Come.
1. —— 15, 16, 28, 30 1st & 3rd, 36, 43.

3a. Matt. xxiii. 2.
1. —— 6, 7.
1. —— 9 (οὐράνιος, *heavenly*, for ἐν τοῖς οὐρανοῖς, *in the heavens*, L T Tr A ℵ.)
— —— 13 twice, see Go.
1. —— 30 twice, 34, 39.
3b.—— xxiv. 5.
— —— 7, see Divers places.
1. —— 14, 15, 16, 18, 19, 26 twice.
1. —— 30 1st.
3a.—— 30 2nd.
1. —— 38 1st, 40, 45, 48, 50 twice.
1. —— xxv. 4.
— —— 10, see Go.
1. —— 18 (*om.* T Tr A* [ℵ.)
1. —— 25, 31.
— —— 35, see Take.
1. —— 36.
— —— 38, see Take.
1. —— 39.
— —— 43 1st, see Take.
1. —— 43 2nd, 44.
1. —— xxvi. 6 twice, 13, 23, 29, 55 twice.
11.—— 58, and see Go.
5a.—— 61.
3a.—— 64.
2. —— 67, and see Spit.
1. —— 69.
1. —— xxvii. 5 (No. 2, T [Tr ℵ.
4b.—— 19.
3c.—— 29 (No. 1 G ∾ L T Tr A ℵ.)
1. —— 40.
3c.—— 43 (No. 3b, L.)
2. —— 51.
— —— 59, see Wrap.
1. —— 60 twice.
1. —— xxviii. 18 1st.
3a.—— 18 2nd.
2. —— 19.
1. Mark i. 2, 3, 4, 5, 9 1st.
2. —— 9 2nd.
1. —— 11, 13.
— —— 14, see Put.
1. —— 19, 20, 23.
— —— 35, see Morning.
1. —— 39 (No. 2, G L T Tr A ℵ.)
1. —— 45 (No. 3b, T Tr A ℵ.)
2. —— ii. 1 (No. 1, L T Tr ℵ.)
1. —— 6, 8 2nd, 15, 20.
— —— 26, see Days of (in the.)
1. —— iii. 23.
— —— 29, see Danger.
1. —— iv. 1, 2, 11, 15 (*ap.*), 17.
— —— 19, see Enter.
1. —— 28.
— —— 29, see Put.
3a.—— 31 1st, 31 2nd (*ap.*),
1. —— 36.
3b.—— 38 (G ∾) (No. 1, G L T Tr A ℵ.)
1. —— v. 5 twice, 13.
2. —— 14 twice.
— —— 15, see Mind.
1. —— 20, 27, 30 twice.
3b.—— 33 (*om.* L^b T Tr A ℵ.)
2. —— 34.
— —— 39, see Come.
— —— 40, see Enter.
1. —— vi. 2, 4 twice.
2. —— 8.
— —— 10, see Place.
1. —— 11 (*ap.*), 14, 17.
— —— 22, 25 1st, see Come.

3b. Mark vi. 25 2nd.
1. —— 27.
3b. —— 28.
1. —— 29, 47, 48, 51.
3b. —— 55.
1. —— 56.
— —— vii. 7, see Vain.
1. —— viii. 1.
3a. —— 4.
1. —— 14, 26.
— —— 37, see Exchange.
1. —— 38 twice.
1. —— ix. 33, 36 1st.
3b. —— 37, 39.
1. —— 41.
2. —— 42 (om. L T Trmb A ℵ.)
1. —— 50.
1. —— x. 10 (No. 2, G ∾ L T Tr A ℵ.)
1. —— 21.
3b. —— 24.
1. —— 30 twice, 32, 37, 52.
— —— xi. 4, see In a place where two ways meet.
2. —— 8 1st (No. 1, Lm.)
2. —— 8 2nd (ap.)
1. —— 9, 10 1st (ap.),
1. —— 10 2nd, and see Highest.
1. —— 15.
— —— 20, see Morning.
1. —— 23, 25, 26 (ap.), 27.
1. —— xii. 11.
3a. —— 14.
1. —— 23, 25 2nd, 26 1st.
3a. —— 26 2nd.
1. —— 35, 38 3 times, 39.
3b. —— xiii. 6.
— —— 8, see In divers places.
2. —— 9.
1. —— 11, 14.
2. —— 16.
1. —— 24, 25, 26.
— —— 29, see Manner.
1. —— 32.
1. —— xiv. 3 twice.
— —— 14, see Go.
2. —— 20.
1. —— 25.
1. —— 30 (om. L T Tr A ℵ.)
— —— 31, see Any.
1. —— 49.
2. —— 60.
8a. —— 62.
1. —— 66.
3c. —— xv. 1 (om. L T Tr Ab ℵ.)
1. —— 7.
— —— 17, see In at.
1. —— 29 om. L T Tr A.)
2. —— 38.
1. —— 41.
— —— 43, see Go.
— —— 46 1st, see Wrap.
1. —— 46 2nd.
— —— xvi. 2, see Morning.
— —— 5, see Clothed.
1. —— 12 (ap.), 17 (ap.).
— Luke i. 1 2nd, } see
— —— 3, } Order.
1. —— 5, 6, 7, 8.
— —— 15, see Sight.
1. —— 17, 18.
— —— 19, see Presence
2. —— 20.
1. —— 21, 22, 25, 26.
— —— 28, see Come
1. —— 31, 36, 39, 41.
2. —— 44 1st.

1. Luke i. 44 2nd.
3b. —— 47.
1. —— 66, 69, 75, 79, 80.
1. —— ii. 1, 7 2nd & 3rd, 8 1st, 11, 12 2nd.
1. —— 14, and see Highest.
1. —— 16, 19, 21, 23, 24, 25.
— —— 27, see Bring.
2. —— 28.
1. —— 29, 34.
— —— 38 1st, see Coming; and, In that instant.
1. —— 38 2nd (om. G ∾ L T Tr Ab ℵ.) (lit. *redemption of Jerusalem.*)
1. —— 43, 44, 46 twice, 51.
1. —— iii. 1, 2, 4 twice.
— —— 15 1st, see Expectation and *Suspense.*
1. —— 15 2nd.
1. —— 17, 20, 22 2nd.
1. —— iv. 2, 5.
3a. —— 11.
1. —— 14, 15, 20, 21.
1. —— 23 1st (G∾) (No. 2, G L T Tr A ℵ.)
1. —— 23 2nd, 24, 25 twice, 27 1st.
— —— 27 2nd, In the time of.
1. —— 28, 33.
1. —— 44 (No. 2, T Tr A ℵ.)
1. —— v. 7, 12.
3a. —— 18 1st.
— —— 18 2nd, } see
— —— 19, } Bring.
1. —— 22, 29, 35.
2. —— vi. 8.
1. —— 12 twice.
3a. —— 17.
1. —— 23 1st & 2nd.
4b. —— 23 3rd.
1. —— 41 twice, 42 3 times.
2. —— vii. 1.
1. —— 9.
1. —— 21, and see Hour.
1. —— 23, 25 twice, 28, 32.
1. —— 37 twice.
— —— 45, see Come.
2. —— 50.
1. —— viii. 10, 13, 15.
— —— 16, see Enter.
1. —— 27 twice.
2. —— 34 twice.
— —— 35, see Mind.
2. —— 48.
— —— 51, see Go.
1. —— ix. 12, 26 1st, 31, 36.
3b. —— 48, 49.
1. —— 57.
1. —— x. 7, 12, 13 3 times, 20 twice.
1. —— 21 1st, and see Hour.
— —— 21 3rd, see Sight.
1. —— 26.
— —— 34, see Pour.
1. —— xi. 1.
1. —— 2 1st & 2nd (ap.)
3a. —— 2 3rd (ap.)
7. —— 6, marg. (text, *out of.*)
2. —— 7.
1. —— 21.
— —— 26, see Enter.
1. —— 31, 32.
2. —— 33 1st, and see Secret.
— —— 33 2nd, see Come.

1. Luke x. 35.
— —— 37, see Go.
1. —— 43 twice.
— —— 52 twice, see Enter.
1. —— xii. 1, 3 1st & 2nd.
6c. —— 3 3rd.
1. —— 3 4th.
1. —— 12, and see Hour
1. —— 15, 27, 28.
— —— 29, see *Suspense.*
1. —— 33, 38 twice, 42, 45, 46, 52, 58.
1. —— xiii. 4 1st.
1. —— 4 2nd (om. Tr A.)
1. —— 6, 10.
— —— 11, see No.
1. —— 14 twice, 19.
2. —— 21.
— —— 24 twice, see Enter.
— —— 26 1st, see Presence.
1. —— 26 2nd, 28, 29, 35.
2. —— xiv. 8, 10 1st.
— —— 10 2nd, see Presence.
1. —— 15.
— —— 21, see Bring.
— —— 23, see Come.
1. —— xv. 4, 7.
— —— 10, see Presence
4b. —— 14 1st.
— —— 14 2nd, see Want
— —— 21, see Sight.
1. —— 25.
— —— 28, see Go.
2. —— xvi. 8.
1. —— 10 4 times, 11, 12.
— —— 15, see Sight.
1. —— 23 3 times, 24 2nd, 25.
1. —— xvii. 6, 24 (ap.), 26 twice, 28, 31 3 times.
3a. —— 34.
1. —— 36 (ap.)
1. —— xviii. 2, 3.
3b. —— 9.
— —— 17, see No.
1. —— 22, 30 twice.
1. —— xix. 17, 20, 30, 36.
1. —— 38 3 times, 42.
— —— 43, see Keep.
1. —— 44, 47.
1. —— xx. 1.
— —— 31, see Manner.
1. —— 33, 42.
— —— 45, see Audience
1. —— 46 twice.
— —— xxi. 4, see I unto.
1. —— 6.
3b. —— 8.
— —— 11, see In divers places.
2. —— 14 (No. 1, L T Tr A ℵ.)
1. —— 19, 21 3 times, 23 1st
3a. —— 23 2nd.
1. —— 25 1st, 27.
1. —— 37 2nd.
2. —— 37 3rd.
— —— 38 1st, see Morning.
1. —— 38 2nd.
— —— xxii. 6, see Absence.
— —— 10, see Enter.
1. —— 16.
2. —— 19.
1. —— 20, 28, 30, 37.
1. —— 44 (ap.), 53, 55.
1. —— xxiii. 4, 9.
— —— 11, see Array.
1. —— 14, 19, 22, 29, 31 twice, 40, 43.
— —— 45, see Midst.
— —— 53 1st, see Wrap.
1. —— 53 2nd.
— —— 53 3rd, see Hewn.

— Luke xxiv. 1, see Morning.
— —— 3, see Enter.
1. —— 4, 6.
6c. —— 12 (ap.),
1. —— 18 1st (No. 2, G∾) (om. G T Tr A ℵ.)
1. —— 18 2nd, 19, 27.
— —— 29, see Go.
1. —— 35 twice, 36, 38, 44 1st.
3b. —— 47.
1. —— 49, 53.
1. John i. 1, 2, 4, 5, 10.
2. —— 18.
1. —— 23, 28, 45, 47.
1. —— ii. 1, 11, 14.
1. —— 19 (om. Trb), 20 2nd, 23 1st.
1. —— 23 2nd (om. Lb Tr.)
2. —— 23 3rd.
1. —— 25.
1. —— iii. 13 (ap.), 14.
2. —— 15 (No. 1, Lm T Tr A) (3b. L.)
2. —— 16, 18.
1. —— 21, 23.
1. —— iv. 14, 20 twice, 21, 23 1st, 24 1st, 31, 44, 53.
— —— v. 2, see Hebrew.
1. —— 3.
— —— 4, see Step.
— —— 6, see Case.
1. —— 13, 14, 26 twice, 28 twice, 35, 38, 39, 42, 43 twice.
2. —— 45.
1. —— vi. 10 1st, 31.
— —— 37, see No.
1. —— 45, 49, 53, 56 twice, 59 twice, 61.
1. —— vii. 1 twice, 4.
2. —— 5.
1. —— 9, 10, 18, 28, 37.
1. —— viii. 3 twice (ap.)
— —— 4 2nd, see Act.
1. —— 5 (ap.), 9 (ap), 12, 17, 20 twice, 21, 24 twice, 31.
— —— 33, see Bondage.
1. —— 35, 37, 44 twice.
1. —— ix. 3, 5.
2. —— 7.
1. —— 34.
— —— x. 2, 9 1st, see Enter.
— —— 9 2nd, see Go.
1. —— 23 twice.
— —— 24, see *Suspense.*
1. —— 25, 34, 38 twice.
1. —— xi. 6, 9 2nd, 10 twice, 17, 20, 24.
2. —— 25, 26.
1. —— 30, 31, 38.
2. —— 52.
1. —— 56.
1. —— xii. 13, 25, 35.
2. —— 36.
1. —— 46, 48.
1. —— xiii. 1, 31.
1. —— 32 1st (ap.), 32 2nd.
2. —— xiv. 1 twice.
1. —— 2, 10 3 times, 11 twice, 13 twice, 14, 17, 20 3 times, 26, 30.
1. —— xv. 2, 4 4 times, 5 twice, 6, 7 twice, 9, 10 twice, 11, 16, 25.
1. —— xvi. 23 twice, 24, 25 twice, 26, 33 twice.
1. —— xvii. 10, 11 twice.
1. —— 12 1st (om. ἐν τῷ κόσμῳ, *in the world,* G → L T Tr A ℵ.)
1. —— 12 2nd, 13 twice, 21 3 times.
1. —— 23 1st & 2nd.
2. —— 23 3rd.

1. John xvii. 26 twice.
— —— xviii. 15, see Go.
— —— 16, see Bring.
1. —— 20 1st & 2nd.
1. —— 20 3rd, and see Secret.
1. —— 26, 38.
1. —— xix. 4, 6.
3a. —— 13 1st.
2. —— 13 2nd.
— —— 13 3rd, 17, see Hebrew.
— —— 18, see Midst.
— —— 20, see Hebrew.
1. —— 41 twice.
— —— xx. 5 1st, see Look.
— —— 5 2nd, see Go.
2. —— 7.
— —— 8, see Go.
1. —— 12.
2. —— 19.
1. —— 25.
2. —— 26.
— —— 30 1st, see Presence.
1. —— 30 2nd.
1. Acts i. 7, 8 1st.
1. —— 8 2nd (om. L Trb Ab.)
1. —— 10.
— —— 11, see Manner.
— —— 13, see Come.
— —— 14, see Continue
1. —— 15 twice.
— —— 18, see Midst.
1. —— 20.
— —— 21, see Go.
— —— ii. 1, see One.
— —— 9 3 times, see Dwell, or Dwellers.
1. —— 17, 18, 19 1st.
3a. —— 19 2nd.
1. —— 22.
3b. —— 26.
2*. —— 27, 31.
3b. —— 38 (No. 1 L Tr.)
— —— 42 1st, see Continue.
1. —— 46.
1. —— iii. 6.
3b. —— 11.
4b. —— 13.
— —— 16, see Presence.
4b. —— 22.
1. —— 26.
2. —— iv. 3.
1. —— 7, 12 (ap.),
— —— 16, see Dwell.
3b. —— 17, 18.
— —— 19, see Sight.
1. —— 24.
1. —— v. 4 twice.
— —— 7, 10, see Come.
1. —— 12, 18, 20.
13b. —— 21, and see Morning.
1. —— 22, 25 twice.
3b. —— 28.
1. —— 34 1st.
— —— 34 2nd, see Reputation.
1. —— 37.
3b. —— 40.
1. —— 42 1st.
— —— 42 2nd, see In every house.
1. —— vi. 1 twice, 7, 15.
1. —— vii. 2 twice, 4, 5, 6.
— —— 7 1st, see Bondage.
1. —— 7 2nd.
— —— 10, see Sight.
1. —— 12 (No. 2 G ~ L T Tr A ℵ.)
1. —— 16, 17, 20 twice.
— —— 22 1st (supply ἐν, in, T Tr A ℵ.)
1. Acts vii. 22 2nd.
1. —— 22 3rd (om. G ~ L T Tr A ℵ.)
1. —— 29, 30 1st & 2nd, 34, 35, 36 3 times, 38 3 times, 41 twice, 42 twice, 44.
— —— 45, see Bring.
1. —— 48.
1. —— viii. 8, 9.
2. —— 16.
1. —— 21 1st.
— —— 21 2nd, see Sight
2. —— 23 1st.
3a. —— 28.
1. —— 33.
1. —— ix. 10, 11.
1. —— 12 1st (om. ἐν ὁράματι, *in a vision*, L T Trmb A ℵ.)
— —— 12 2nd, see Come.
1. —— 17, 20, 21, 25, 27 twice.
— —— 28, see Come.
1. —— 29, 37 twice.
3c. —— 42.
1. —— 43.
1. —— x. 1, 3 1st.
— —— 3 2nd, see Come.
1. —— 17.
— —— 23, see Call.
— —— 25, see Come.
— —— 27, see Go.
1. —— 30 twice.
— —— 31 1st, see Remembrance.
— —— 31 2nd, see Sight.
1. —— 32, 35, 39 1st.
1. —— 39 2nd (om. Lb Trmb.)
2. —— 43.
1. —— 48.
4b. —— xi. 1.
— —— 3, see Go.
1. —— 5 twice, 13, 22, 26, 27.
— —— 28, see In the days of: *or* Days.
1. —— 29.
2. —— xii. 4.
1. —— 5, 7.
— —— 14, see Run.
— —— 21, see Array.
4b. —— xiii. 1.
1. —— 5, 17, 18, 19.
2. —— 29.
1. —— 33 2nd, 35, 40.
1. —— 41 1st.
— —— 41 2nd, see No.
— —— 43, see Continue
1. —— xiv. 1.
3b. —— 3.
— —— 11 1st, see In the speech of Lycaonia.
— —— 11 2nd, see Likeness.
— —— 14, see In among, *or* Run.
1. —— 16 1st.
— —— 22, see Continue
— —— 23, see In every church.
1. —— 25.
— —— xv. 21 1st, see In every city.
1. —— 21 2nd.
4b. —— 23.
8a. —— 33.
1. —— 35.
4b. —— 36.
1. —— xvi. 3, 6.
5a. —— 9.
1. —— 12, 18.
2. —— 24.
— —— 29, see Spring.
1. —— 32, 36.
— —— xvii. 2, see Go.
1. —— 11 1st.
— —— 11 2nd, see In that they.
1. Acts xvii. 16, 17 twice.
2. —— 21.
1. —— 22 1st.
4b. —— 22 2nd.
1. —— 24, 28, 31 1st & 2nd.
1. —— xviii. 4, 9, 10, 18.
2. —— 21 (ap.)
— —— 23, see Order.
1. —— 24, 26.
2. —— xix. 5.
1. —— 9.
— —— 10, see Dwell.
1. —— 16, 21.
2. —— 22.
— —— 27, see Danger.
— —— 30, see Enter, *or* In unto.
1. —— 39.
— —— 40 1st, see Danger
— —— 40 2nd, see Call.
10. —— xx. 6.
1. —— 8.
3a. —— 9.
1. —— 10.
— —— 13, 14, see Take.
1. —— 16.
— —— 19, see Wait.
— —— 23, see In every city.
— —— 29, see Enter, *or* In among.
— —— xxi. 18, see Go.
1. —— 27, 29.
— —— 31, see Uproar.
1. —— xxii. 3 1st & 3rd.
1. —— 17 twice.
1. —— xxiii. 6 1st.
— —— 6 2nd, see Call.
1. —— 9.
2. —— 11.
— —— 16, 21, see Wait.
1. —— 35.
— —— xxiv. 3, see Place.
1. —— 12 1st & 2nd.
4b. —— 12 3rd.
4b. —— 14 1st, "in the Law."
1. —— 14 2nd, "in the prophets" (in edition of 1762 and some modern eds.) (om. AV. 1611 and L Ab.)
1. —— 18.
1. —— 20 (om. ἐν ἐμοί, *in me*, L T Trb Ab ℵ.)
— —— 21, see Call.
2. —— 24.
4b. —— xxv. 3.
1. —— 5.
3a. —— 6.
— —— 14, see Bonds.
1. —— xxvi. 10 1st.
4b. —— 11, 13.
2. —— 18.
1. —— 21, 26.
3c. —— xxvii. 20.
1. —— 21, 27, 31.
— —— 35, see Presence.
1. —— 37 2nd.
— —— 39, see Thrust.
1. —— xxviii. 7.
— —— 8, see Enter.
1. —— 9, 11 twice, 18, 30 1st.
— —— 30 2nd, see Come.
1. Rom. i. 2, 7, 9 1st.
3a. —— 9 2nd.
1. —— 13, marg. (text, *among*.)
— —— 15, see In me is (as much as.)
1. —— 18.
1. —— 19, marg. *to*.
1. —— 21, 27 twice.
— —— 32, see Pleasure.
1. —— ii. 12.
— —— 14, see Contain.
1. —— 15, 16.
— Rom. ii. 17, see Rest.
1. —— 19, 20, 28, 29 1st.
1. —— iii. 4.
— —— 9, see No.
1. —— 16.
— —— 20, see Sight.
1. —— 24, 25.
1. —— iv. 10 4 times.
3b. —— 18.
3b. —— v. 2.
1. —— 3, 5.
4b. —— 6, marg. *according to*.
— —— 8, see In that.
1. —— 11.
1. —— 13, 17.
— —— vi. 1, see Continue.
— —— 10 twice, see In that.
1. —— 4, 12 1st, 12 2nd (ap.)
1. —— vii. 5 twice, 6 1st, 8, 17, 18 twice, 20.
— —— 22, see Delight.
1. —— 23 twice.
1. —— viii. 1, 2, 3 3 times, 4, 8, 9 3 times, 10.
1. —— 11 twice, and see Dwell.
2. —— 18.
3b. —— 20.
1. —— 37, 39.
1. —— ix. 1 twice, 7, 17, 25, 26, 28 (ap.), 33.
1. —— x. 6, 8 twice, 9.
2. —— 14 1st.
— —— xi. 17, 19, see Graff.
— —— 22, see Continue.
— —— 23 1st, see Abide still.
— —— 23 2nd & 3rd, see Graff.
— —— 25 1st, see Conceits.
— —— 25 2nd, see Part.
— —— 25 3rd, see Come.
2. —— 32.
1. —— xii. 4, 5.
— —— 12 3rd, see Continue.
— —— 17, see Sight.
— —— xiii. 4, see Vain.
1. —— 9, 13 1st.
1. —— xiv. 5, 17, 18, 22.
3b. —— xv. 12.
1. —— 13 twice.
— —— 15 1st, see Some sort.
— —— 15 2nd, see Mind.
1. —— 23, 27, 29, 30, 31.
1. —— xvi. 2 twice, 3.
4b. —— 5.
1. —— 7, 8, 9, 10, 11, 12 1st, 12 2nd (ap.), 13, 22.
1. 1 Cor. i. 2 twice, 5 1st & 2nd, 6, 7, 8, 10 twice.
2. —— 13, 15.
1. —— 21.
— —— 29, see Preserve.
1. —— 30, 31.
1. —— ii. 3 3 times, 4, 5 twice, 7, 11, 13.
1. —— iii. 1, 16, 18, 19, 21.
1. —— iv. 2, 6 2nd, 10, 15 twice, 17 3 times, 20 twice, 21 1st.
1. —— v. 4, 5, 9.
1. —— vi. 4, 11, 19, 20 1st, 20 2nd (ap.).
1. —— vii. 15.
1. —— 15, marg. (text, *to*.)
1. —— 17, 18, 20, 22, 37, 39.
— —— viii. 4 1st, see Sacrifice.

1. 1 Cor. viii. 4 2nd, 5 1st.
3a. —— 5 2nd.
2. —— 6.
1. —— 7, 10.
1. —— ix. 1, 2, 9.
3b. —— 10 twice.
1. —— 18, 24.
1. —— x. 2 twice, 5.
1. —— 8 (om. L Tr A ℵ.)
— —— 19, see Sacrifice.
1. —— 25.
— —— 28, see Sacrifice.
1. —— xi. 11, 13, 18, 21, 22, 23.
2. —— 24, marg. *for.*
1. —— 25 1st.
2. —— 25 2nd.
— —— 34, see Order.
1. —— xii. 6, 18, 25.
— —— 27, see Particular.
1. —— 28.
3b. —— xiii. 6 1st.
— —— 6 2nd, see Rejoice.
— —— 9 twice, 10, see Part.
1. —— xiv. 10, 19 twice, 21.
— —— 23, 24, see Come.
1. —— 25, 28, 33, 34, 35.
4b. —— 40.
— —— xv. 2 1st, see Keep.
— —— 2 2nd, } see Vain
— —— 10, }
1. —— 17, 18, 19 twice, 22 twice, 23, 28, 31, 41, 42 twice, 43 4 times, 52 twice.
2. —— 54.
1. —— 58 1st.
— —— 58 2nd, see Vain.
— —— xvi. 2, see Store.
1. —— 11, 13, 19 1st.
4b. —— 19 2nd.
1. —— 24.
1. 2 Cor. i. 1.
3b. —— 4 1st.
1. —— 4 2nd.
2. —— 5.
1. —— 6, 8, 9 1st.
3b. —— 9 2nd & 3rd.
2. —— 10.
1. —— 12 twice.
9. —— 14 1st.
1. —— 14 2nd, 19, 20 1st, 20 2nd (ap.)
2. —— 21.
1. —— 22.
1. —— ii. 1.
3c. —— 3.
1. —— 10, 14 twice, 15 twice.
— —— 17 1st, see Sight.
1. —— 17 2nd, marg. *of.*
1. —— iii. 2, 3 twice, and see Write.
1. —— 7 (om. G ⇉ L T ℵ.)
1. —— 9 (om. L Tr A ℵ.)
1. —— 10.
3b. —— 14 1st.
1. —— 14 2nd.
1. —— iv. 2 1st.
— —— 2 2nd, see Sight.
1. —— 4, 6 twice, 7.
— —— 8, see Despair.
1. —— 10 twice, 11, 12 twice
1. —— v. 1, 2, 4, 6.
5a. —— 10 (ἴδια, *one's own,* Lm, Trm.)
1. —— 11, 12 1st, 17, 19.
— —— 20, see I . . . stead.
1. —— 21.
— —— vi. 1, see Vain.
1. —— 2 2nd, 3, 4 5 times 5 6 times, 12 twice.
1. 2 Cor. vi. 16 1st.
— —— 16 2nd, see Walk.
1. —— vii. 1, 3.
3b. —— 4, 7.
1. —— 9, 11 2nd.
1. —— 11 3rd (om. G → Lb T Tr A ℵ.)
— —— 12, see Sight.
3b. —— 13.
1. —— 14, 16 twice.
1. —— viii. 2.
2. —— 6.
1. —— 7 1st, 4th, & 5th, 18, 20.
— —— 21 twice, see Sight
1. —— 22 1st.
2. —— 22 2nd.
— —— ix. 3 1st, see Vain.
1. —— 3 2nd, 4, 8, 11.
3b. —— 14.
4b. —— x. 1.
1. —— 3, 6, 14.
2. —— 16 1st.
1. —— 16 2nd, 17.
2. —— xi. 3.
1. —— 6 3rd, 9, 10 twice, 17, 23 4 times, 25, 26 7th, 9th, 11th.
1. —— 27 1st (om. G → L T Tr A ℵ.)
1. —— 27 2nd, 3rd, 4th, & 5th
1. —— 32, 33.
1. —— xii. 2 twice, 3, 5, 9 twice, 10 5 times.
— —— 11 1st, see Glorying.
1. —— 12 1st.
1. —— 12 2nd (om. L T Tr A ℵ)
1. —— 19.
3a. —— xiii. 1.
1. —— 3 twice.
1. —— 4 (σύν, Lm Trm ℵ,) marg. *with.*
1. Gal. i. 13, 14 twice, 16, 22, 24.
— —— ii. 2, see Vain.
— —— 4 1st, see Brought
— —— 4 2nd, see Come.
1. —— 4 3rd.
— —— 6, see Conference.
— —— 8 1st, see Work.
— —— 8 2nd, see Mighty
2. —— 16.
1. —— 20 twice.
— —— 21, see Vain.
— —— iii. 4 twice, see Vain.
1. —— 8.
— —— 10 1st, see Continue.
1. —— 10 2nd.
— —— 11, see Sight.
1. —— 12.
2. —— 17 (om. εἰς Χριστόν, *in Christ,* G ⇉ L T Tr A ℵ.)
1. —— 19, 26, 28.
— —— iv. 3, 9, see Bondage.
— —— 11, see Vain.
1. —— 14, 18, 19 2nd, 25 1st.
— —— 25 2nd, see Bondage.
— —— 25, see *Rank.*
1. —— v. 6.
2. —— 10.
1. —— 14 twice.
— —— 21, see Time.
1. —— vi. 1 twice.
2. —— 4 twice.
1. —— 6 2nd, 12, 13, 14, 15 (ap.), 17.
1. Eph. i. 1, 3 1st, 3 2nd (om. St.)
1. —— 4 twice, 6, 7, 8, 9.
2. —— 10 1st.
— —— 10 2nd, see Gather
1. —— 10 3rd.
1. Eph. i. 10 4th (ἐπὶ, *upon,* L Tr A ℵ.)
1. —— 10 5th, 11, 12, 13 twice, 15.
3a. —— 16.
1. —— 17, marg. *for.*
1. —— 18, 20 twice, 21 twice 23.
1. —— ii. 2 2nd, 3 2nd, 4, 6 twice, 7 twice, 10 twice, 11 2nd & 3rd, 12, 13, 15 3 times, 16.
— —— 16, see *In Himself;* or Thereby.
1. —— 21 twice, 22.
— —— iii. 3 1st, see Few.
1. —— 3 2nd, 4.
1. —— 5 (om. G L T Tr A ℵ.)
1. —— 6, 9, 10, 11, 12, 15.
2. —— 16.
1. —— 17 twice, 20.
1. —— iv. 2, 3, 4, 6.
2. —— 13, marg. *into.*
1. —— 15 1st, 16 twice, 17 twice, 18, 21, 24.
1. —— v. 2, 5, 8, 9.
— —— 12, see Secret.
1. —— 19, 20, 21, 24.
1. —— vi. 1 (om. ἐν Κυρίῳ, *in the Lord,* G → L Trb Ab.)
1. —— 4, 5, 9, 10 twice, 12, 13, 18, 20, 21.
1. —— 24, marg. *with.*
1. Phil. i. 1, 4.
2. —— 5.
1. —— 6, 7 1st & 2nd, 8, 9 1st.
1. —— 13 1st, marg. *for.*
1. —— 13 2nd, 14, 20 twice, 22.
— —— 23, see Strait.
1. —— 24 (om. G ⇉ T ℵ.)
1. —— 26, 27, 28.
— —— 29, see Behalf.
1. —— 30 twice.
1. —— ii. 1, 5 twice, 6, 7.
— —— 10 1st, see Heaven (in.)
— —— 10 2nd, see Earth (in.)
1. —— 12 twice, 13.
1. —— 15 1st (om. G ⇉ L T Tr A ℵ.)
1. —— 15 2nd.
2. —— 16 1st.
— —— 16 2nd & 3rd, see Vain.
1. —— 19.
2. —— 22.
1. —— 24, 29 1st.
— —— 29 2nd, see Reputation.
1. —— iii. 1, 3 2nd & 3rd, 4 twice, 6, 9, 14, 19, 20.
1. —— iv. 1, 2, 3 twice, 4, 6, 9, 10.
— —— 11 1st, see In respect of.
1. —— 11 2nd, 12, 15, 16, 19, 21.
1. Col. i. 2, 4, 5 twice, 6 3 times, 8, 9, 10 1st.
2. —— 10 2nd (G ∾) (τῇ ἐπιγνώσει, *by the full knowledge;* for, εἰς τὴν ἐπίγνωσιν, *unto the full knowledge,* G T Tr A ℵ.)
1. —— 12, 14, 16 1st.
3a. —— 16 2nd.
1. —— 18, marg. *among.*
1. —— 19.
3a. —— 20 1st.
1. —— 20 2nd, 22 1st.
— —— 22 2nd, see Sight.
— —— 23, see Continue.
1. —— 24 twice.
1. Col. i. 27, marg. *amongst.*
1. —— 28 twice, 29.
1. —— ii. 1, 2.
1. —— 3, (ἐν ᾧ, In whom) marg. *wherein.*
2. —— 5 3rd.
1. —— 6, 7 1st.
1. —— 7 2nd, (om. L T Tr Ab.)
1. —— 9, 10, 11 twice, 12.
1. —— (om. G → T Tr ℵ.)
1. —— 15.
1. —— 16 1st & 2nd, marg. *for.*
1. —— 16 3rd.
1. —— 18, 20, 23 twice.
1. —— iii. 3, 4, 7 twice.
2. —— 10.
1. —— 11, 15 twice.
— —— 16 1st, see Dwell.
1. —— 16 2nd & 3rd, 17 twice, 18.
4b. —— 20, 22 1st.
1. —— 22 2nd.
1. —— iv. 1, 2.
— —— 3, see Bonds.
1. —— 5, 7, 12 twice, 13 twice, 15 1st.
4b. —— 15 2nd.
1. —— 16, 17.
1. 1 Thes. i. 1.
3a. —— 2.
— —— 3 2nd, see Sight.
1. —— 5 4 times, 6, 7, 8 twice.
— —— 9, see Entering.
— —— ii. 1 1st, see Entrance.
— —— 1 2nd, see Vain.
1. —— 2, 3, 13, 14 twice.
— —— 19, see Presence.
1. —— iii. 2.
— —— 5, see Vain.
3b. —— 7.
1. —— 8, 13.
1. —— iv. 4, 5, 6, 10.
5a. —— 14.
1. —— 16, 17 1st.
2. —— 17 2nd.
1. —— v. 2, 4, 12, 13, 18 twice.
1. 2 Thes. i. 1, 4 3 times, 8, 10 3 times, 12 twice.
9. —— ii. 2.
2. —— 4.
1. —— 6.
1. —— 10 (τοῖς ἀπολλ. *for those who are perishing;* for ἐν τοῖς ἀπολλ, *in them that perish,* G → L T Tr A ℵ.)
1. —— 12 (om. G → Lb T Tr Ab ℵ.)
1. —— 17.
1. —— iii. 4, 6, 17.
1. 1 Tim. i. 2, 4, 13, 14, 16.
1. —— ii. 2 twice.
— —— 3, see Sight.
1. —— 7 1st (om. ἐν Χριστῷ, *in Christ,* G L T Tr A ℵ.)
1. —— 7 2nd.
— —— 9 1st, see Manner.
1. —— 9 2nd, 11, 12, 14.
5a. —— 15 1st (lit., διὰ τῆς τεκνογονίας, *by means of the child-bearing, i.e., the Incarnation.*)
1. —— 15 2nd.
1. —— iii. 4, 9, 11, 13 twice, 15, 16 3 times.
1. —— iv. 1, 2.
— —— 6 2nd, see Nourish.

3b. 1 Tim. iv. 10.
1. —— 12 1st, 2nd, & 3rd.
1. —— 12 4th (om. ἐν πνεύματι, in Spirit, G L T Tr A ℵ.)
1. —— 12 5th & 6th, 14.
— —— 16 1st, see Continue.
3c. — v. 5 1st.
— —— 5 2nd, see Continue.
— —— 6, see Pleasure.
1. —— 17.
2. — vi. 9.
— —— 13, see Sight.
1. —— 17 1st.
3a. —— 17 2nd.
1. —— 17 3rd, (ἐπὶ θεῷ upon God, instead of ἐν τῷ θεῷ τῷ ζῶντι, in the living God, L T Tr A* ℵ,) (Alf. ἐν τῷ θεῳ.)
1. —— 18.
— —— 19, see Store.
1. 2 Tim. i. 1, 3, 5 3 times, 6 2nd, 9, 13 twice, 14, 15, 17, 18.
1. — ii. 1 twice, 7, 10, 20, 25.
1. — iii. 1, 12, 14, 15, 16.
— — iv. 2, see Reason.
1. —— 5.
3b. Titus i. 2, marg. *for.*
1. —— 5 1st.
— —— 5 2nd, see In every city.
1. —— 5 3rd, 13.
1. — ii. 3.
12b. —— 7 1st.
1. —— 7 2nd, 9, 10, 12.
— — iii. 1, see Mind.
1. —— 3, 15.
4b. Philem. 2.
3a. —— 4.
1. —— 6 1st.
2. —— 6 2nd.
3b. —— 7.
1. —— 8, 10.
— —— 13 1st, see In . . . stead.
1. —— 13 2nd, 16 twice, 20 twice, 23.
— Heb. i. 1 1st, see Time.
— —— 1 2nd, see Manner.
3a. —— 2.
— —— 6, see Bring.
4b. —— 10.
— — ii. 6, see Place.
— —— 8 1st, see Subjection.
1. —— 8 2nd, 12.
3b. —— 13.
4b. —— 17 1st.
1. —— 18.
1. — iii. 2, 5.
1. —— 8 1st.
4b. —— 8 2nd.
1. —— 8 3rd.
1. —— 11, 12 twice, 15, 17
— —— 19, see Enter.
1. — iv. 3.
— —— 4, see Place.
1. —— 5.
— —— 6, see Enter.
1. —— 7.
— —— 13, see Sight.
4b. —— 15, and see All.
— —— 16, see Time.
1. — v. 6, 7 1st.
— —— 7 2nd, see In that he Feared.
1. — vi. 18.
5a. — vii. 9.
1. —— 10.
— —— 19, see Bringing

1. Heb. viii. 1, 5, 9 twice.
3a. —— 10. marg. *upon.*
1. —— 13.
4b. — ix. 9.
3b. —— 10.
— —— 12, see Enter.
— —— 16, see *Brought.*
1. —— 23.
3b. —— 26.
1. — x. 3, 7.
3a. —— 16 (No. 3c., L T Tr A ℵ.)
1. —— 22, 32.
1. —— 34 2nd (om. G L T Tr A ℵ.)
1. —— 34 3rd (om. ἐν οὐρανοῖς, *in the heavens,* G → L T Tr A ℵ.)
1. —— 38.
2. — xi. 9 1st.
1. —— 9 3rd.
4b. —— 13, marg. *according to.*
1. —— 18, 19.
1. —— 26 (G ∾) (Αἰγύπτου, *of Egypt,* instead of ἐν Αἰγύπτῳ, *in Egypt,* G L T Tr A ℵ.)
1. —— 37 (also add ἐν before "goat-skins.")
1. —— 38 1st (No. 3b, L T Tr A ℵ.)
— — xii. 9, see Subjection.)
1. —— 23.
— — xiii. 3 1st, see Bonds
1. —— 3 2nd, 4, 18, 21 1st & 2nd.
— —— 21 3rd, see Sight.
5a. —— 22, and see Few
1. Jas. i. 6, 8.
1. —— 9, and see In that he is exnlted.
1. —— 10, and see In that he is made low.
1. —— 11, 23, 25, 27.
1. — ii. 2 1st.
— —— 2 2nd, see Come.
1. —— 2 3rd, 4, 5, 10, 16.
1. — iii. 2 2nd.
2. —— 3.
— —— 7, see Sea.
1. —— 14, 18.
1. — iv. 1, 5 2nd.
— —— 10, see Sight.
1. —— 16.
— — v. 5 1st, see Pleasure.
1. —— 5 2nd, 14.
1. 1 Pet. i. 4, 5.
— —— 6, see Heaviness.
2. —— 8.
1. —— 11, 14, 15, 17.
3a. —— 20.
2. —— 21 twice.
1. —— 22.
1. — ii. 6 1st (om. L.)
1. —— 6 2nd, 12, 22, 24.
— — iii. 1, see Subjection.
1. —— 4 1st.
— —— 4 2nd, see Sight.
— —— 5 1st, see Old Time.
2. —— 5 2nd (εἰς Θεον, instead of ἐπὶ τον Θ, G ∾ L T Tr A.)
— —— 5 3rd, see Subjection.
1. —— 15 twice, 16, 19, 20.
1. — iv. 1 2nd (om. G ⇉ L T Tr A ℵ.)
1. —— 2, 3, 11.
— —— 15, see Busybody.
1. —— 19.
— — v. 2, see *In you is* (*as much as.*)

1. 1 Pet. v. 6, 9 3rd, 14.
2. 2 Pet. i. 8 2nd.
1. —— 12 2nd, 13 1st.
2. —— 17.
1. —— 18, 19 twice.
— — ii. 1, 5, see Bondage.
1. —— 10, 12, 13, 18.
1. — iii. 1.
3a. —— 3.
5a. —— 5.
— —— 7, see Store.
1. —— 10 1st (om. ἐν νύκτι, *in the night,* G L T Tr A ℵ.)
1. —— 10 2nd, 11, 14, 16 3 times, 18 1st.
1. 1 John i. 5, 6, 7 twice, 8, 10.
— — ii. 4, 5 twice, 6, 8 twice, 9 twice, 10 twice, 11 twice, 14, 15 twice, 16, 24 1st, 2nd, & 3rd.
1. —— 24 4th (om. L.)
1. —— 27 twice, 28.
3b. — iii. 3.
1. —— 5, 6, 9, 10, 14, 15, 17.
— —— 22, see Sight.
1. —— 24 3 times.
1. — iv. 2, 3 1st (ap.), 3 2nd, 4 twice, 9, 12 twice, 13 twice, 15 twice, 16 3 times, 17 twice, 18 twice.
1. — v. 7 (ap.), 8 1st (ap.)
2. —— 8 2nd.
1. —— 10, 11.
6c. —— 14, marg. *concerning.*
1. —— 19, 20 twice.
1. 2 John 1, 2, 3, 4, 6, 7, 9 twice.
1. 3 John 1 (ἐν ἀλήθεια, marg. *truly.*)
1. —— 3 2nd, 4.
— Jude 4, see Creep.
1. —— 10, 12.
1. —— 18 (No. 3a., G ∾ L T Tr A ℵ.)
1. —— 20, 21.
1. Rev. i. 4, 5, 9 1st.
1. —— 9 2nd (om. G L T Tr A ℵ.)
1. —— 9 3rd, 10.
2. —— 11 1st.
1. —— 11 2nd (om. ταῖς ἐν Ἀσιᾳ, *which are in Asia,* G L T Tr A ℵ.)
1. —— 13.
1. —— 15, 16 twice.
3a. —— 20 (No. 1, L.)
1. — ii. 1 twice.
1. —— 7, 12, 13.
3c. —— 17.
1. —— 18, 24.
1. — iii. 1, 4 twice, 5, 7, 12.
7. —— 18.
— —— 20, see Come.
1. —— 21 twice.
1. — iv. 1, 2 twice, 4, 6.
3c. — v. 1.
1. —— 3, 6 twice, 13 1st.
3a. —— 13 2nd.
1. —— 13 3rd.
1. — vi. 5, 6.
2. —— 15 twice.

— Rev. vii. 3.
1. —— 9, 14, 15.
— —— 17, see Midst.
1. — viii. 1, 9.
3b. — ix. 4.
1. —— 6, 10.
— —— 11 1st, see Hebrew.
1. —— 11 2nd, 17, 19 1st, 19 2nd (ap.)
1. — x. 2, 7, 8, 9, 10.
— — xi. 3, see Clothed.
— —— 5, see Manner.
1. —— 6 (τὰς ἡμέρας, *during the days,* instead of ἐν ἡμεραῖς, *in the days,* G L T Tr A ℵ.)
3a. —— 8.
2. —— 9.
1. —— 12, 13, 15, 19 twice.
1. — xii. 1, 3, 7, 8, 10, 12.
2. — xiii. 6 1st.
1. —— 6 1st, 8.
— —— 13, 14, see Sight.
3a. —— 16 1st.
3a. —— 16 2nd (No. 3c, G L T Tr A ℵ.)
3a. — xiv. 1.
1. —— 5, 6.
3a. —— 9 1st.
3c. —— 9 2nd.
— —— 10 twice, see Presence.
1. —— 13, 14, 17.
1. — xv. 1 twice, 5.
— —— 6, see Clothed.
1. — xvi. 3.
— —— 16, see Hebrew.
— —— 19, see Remembrance.
1. — xvii. 3, 4 2nd.
3c. —— 8.
2. —— 17.
1. — xviii. 6, 7, 8.
1. —— 10 (om. G L T Tr A ℵ.)
— —— 16, see Clothed.
3a. —— 17 2nd.
1. —— 19 1st, 22 3 times
1. —— 23 1st (om. L Ab.)
1. —— 23 2nd.
1. —— 24.
1. — xix. 1.
— —— 8, see Array.
1. —— 11, 14 1st.
— —— 14 2nd, see Clothed.
1. —— 17 twice.
3c. — xx. 1, 4.
1. —— 6, 8, 12, 13 twice, 15.
1. — xxi. 8, 10.
1. —— 14 (No. 3a, G L T Tr A ℵ.)
1. —— 23 (om. G L T Tr A ℵ.)
1. —— 24 (No. 5a, G L T Tr A ℵ.)
— —— 27 1st, see No.
1. —— 27 2nd.
1. — xxii. 2, 3.
3a. —— 4.
— —— 14, see Enter.
3b. —— 16 (No. 1, L Trm) (om. G →)
1. —— 18, 19.

IN AMONG.

εἰς, *see* "IN," *No.* 2.

Acts xiv. 14; xx. 29.

IN A PLACE WHERE TWO WAYS MEET.

ἐπὶ, upon,
τοῦ, the,
ἀμφόδου, any road that leads round a place, a road round, a street,
} on the street.

Mark xi. 4.

IN AT.

εἰς, *see* "IN," *No.* 2.

Mark xv. 17.

IN DIVERS PLACES.

κατὰ, (*see No.* 4b,) *used also distributively*, from one to another,
τόπους, (*pl.*) places,
} in various, or different places; place after place.

Matt. xxiv. 7. | Mark xiii. 8. | Luke xxi. 11.

IN EVERY CITY.

κατὰ, (*see above*,)
πόλιν, a city,
} in various *or* different cities; city by city.

Acts xv. 21. | Acts xx. 23. | Tit. i. 5.

IN EVERY CHURCH.

κατ' (*see above*,)
ἐκκλησιαν, *see under* "CHURCH,"
} church by church; *or* in each church, *or* assembly.

Acts xiv. 23.

IN EVERY HOUSE.

κατ', (*see above*,)
οἶκον, house,
} house by house; *or* in each house.

Acts v. 42.

IN HIMSELF [margin.]

ἐν, (*see* "IN," *No.* 1,) in,
αὐτῷ, himself *or* itself,
} on it, *or* by means of it, [*i.e.* the cross, *see* Col. ii. 15.]

Eph. ii. 16, text, *thereby*.

IN ME IS (AS MUCH AS)

τὸ, the [*ability, or eagerness*,]
κατ', according to,
ἐμέ, me,
} the eagerness on my part; according to my ability; *or* according as it depends on me.

Rom. i. 15.

IN RESPECT OF.

κατὰ, (*see* "IN," *No.* 4b,) according to, as to, as regards.

Phil. iv. 11.

IN...STEAD.

ὑπέρ, (*with the Genitive*,) over and separate from, *hence*, on behalf of, (*as though bending* "over" *to assist*;) *then, as a service rendered* on behalf of another *is often* in his stead, *it has this latter meaning*, (*though not so definite as* ἀντί.)

2 Cor. v. 20. | Philem. 13.

IN THAT.

1. ὅ, he (*who* [*died*, &c.])
2. ὅτι, that, because.

— Acts xvii. 11, see In that they. | 2. Rom. v. 8. 1. — vi. 10.

IN THAT THEY.

οἵτινες, who; being such as, etc.

Acts xvii. 11.

IN THAT HE FEARED.

ἀπὸ, from,
τῆς, the,
εὐλαβείας, fear,
} from his fear.

Heb. v. 7, marg. *for one's piety*.

IN THAT HE IS EXALTED.

ἐν, in,
τῷ, the,
ὕψει, uplifting,
αὐτοῦ, of him,
} in his uplifting.

Jas. i. 9.

IN THAT HE IS MADE LOW.

ἐν, in,
τῇ, the,
ταπεινώσει, becoming low,
αὐτοῦ, of him,
} in his becoming low.

Jas. i. 10.

IN THAT INSTANT.

αὐτῇ, in that very,
τῇ, the,
ὥρᾳ, hour,
} in that very hour, at that very season.

Luke ii. 38.

IN THE DAYS OF.

ἐπὶ, *see* "IN," *No.* 3a.

Mark ii. 26. | Acts xi. 28.

IN THE SPEECH OF LYCAONIA.

Λυκαονιστί, *adv. Lycaonicè*, in the Lycaonic dialect.

Acts xiv. 11.

IN THE TIME OF.

ἐπὶ, *see* "IN," *No.* 3a.

Luke iv. 27.

IN UNTO.

εἰς, *see* "IN," *No.* 2.

Luke xxi. 4. | Acts xix. 30.

IN WHOM [margin.]

{ ἐφ', upon, [*the ground of*,]
{ ᾧ, which, } because.

Rom. v. 12 twice, text, *for that.*

IN YOU IS (*as much as*) [margin.]

{ τὸ, the (*flock*),
{ ἐν, in *or* among,
{ ὑμῖν, you, } the [*flock which is*] among you.

1 Pet. v. 2, text, *which is among you.*

INASMUCH AS.

1. καθό, according to what, in so far as.

2. { καθ', according to,
{ ὅσον, as much as, } by as much as.

— Phil. i. 7, *see below.* | 2. Heb. vii. 20.
2. Heb. iii. 3. | 1. 1 Pet. iv. 13.

INASMUCH AS...ARE.

ὄντας, (*part. of* εἰμί, to be,) being.

Phil. i. 7.

INCENSE.

θυμίαμα, that which is burnt as incense, *esp., in religious worship*, (*occ.* Rev. xviii. 13.)

Luke i. 9, see I (burn). | Rev. v. 8, marg. (text, *odour.*)
—— 10, 11. |
Rev. viii. 3, (pl.) 4, (pl.)

INCENSE (BURN)

θυμιάω, to burn so as to produce smoke; *hence, and esp.*, to burn as incense.

Luke i. 9.

INCLOSE.

συγκλείω, to shut up in conjunction with another, enclose together.

Luke v. 6.

INCONTINENCY.

ἀκρασία, the character of an ἀκρατής, (*see below*), *hence*, incontinence (*Lat.*, impotentia,) *occ.* Matt. xxiii. 25.

1 Cor. vii. 5.

INCONTINENT.

ἀκρατής, not having power *or* command over *a thing*, (*Lat.*, impotens,) *esp.*, without power *or* command over *one's self, or one's passions;* unbridled.

2 Tim. iii. 3.

INCORRUPTIBLE.

ἄφθαρτος, incorruptible, immortal.

1 Cor. ix. 25. | 1 Pet. i. 4, 23. | 1 Cor. xv. 52.

INCORRUPTION.

ἀφθαρσία, incorruption, immortality.

1 Cor. xv. 42, 50, 53, 54.
Eph. vi. 24, marg. (text, *sincerity.*)

INCREASE [noun.]

αὔξησις, growth, enlargement, increase, amplification, (*non occ.*)

1 Cor. iii. 6, 7, see I (give the.) | Eph. iv. 16.
| Col. ii. 19.

INCREASE (GIVE THE)

αὐξάνω, (*see* "INCREASE," *No.* 1a.)

1 Cor. iii. 6, 7.

INCREASE (-ED, -ETH, -ING) [verb.]

1. αὐξάνω, to make large, increase (*like Lat.*, augeo,)

 (a) *trans.*, to give increase, cause to grow, to enlarge,

 (b) *intrans.*, to receive increase, to grow, grow up.

2. περισσεύω, to be over and above *the number;* to be more than enough, remain over; abound more and more, *hence*, increase.

3. προκόπτω, to beat *or* drive forwards *as if with* repeated strokes; *hence,* to forward *a work,* to further, push forwards. To make progress in any thing, advance, increase.

4. προστίθημι, to set, put, *or* lay unto *or* with *any person or thing;* to join to, add unto.

1b. Mark iv. 8 (pass. G ~ L T Tr A ℵ.)
3. Luke ii. 52.
4. —— xvii. 5.
1b. John iii. 30.
1b. Acts vi. 7.
— —— ix. 22, see Strength
2. —— xvi. 5.
1a. 2 Cor. ix. 10.
1b. 2 Cor. x. 15, part.
1b. Col. i. 10.
1b. —— ii. 19.
— 1 Thes. iii. 12, see I (make to.)
— —— iv. 10, see I more and more.
3. 2 Tim. ii. 16.
— Rev. iii. 17, see Goods.

INCREASE (MAKE TO)

πλεονάζω, to be more than enough. *Of things,* to be abundant.

(a) *trans.,* to cause to abound, increase.

1 Thes. iii. 12 (optative.)

INCREASE MORE AND MORE.

{ περισσεύω, *see No.* 2, μᾶλλον, more, rather, } to be overflowing, *or* abounding yet more.

1 Thes. iv. 10.

INCREDIBLE (THING)

ἄπιστος, not to be trusted; *of persons,* not trusty; *of things,* incredible.

Acts xxvi. 8.

INDEBTED (BE)

ὀφείλω, to owe, to have to pay an account for; to be indebted.

Luke xi. 4.

INDEED.

1. μέν, truly, indeed. *A conj. implying affirmation or concession.* The old neut. of μεῖς, μία, μέν, one,=the first thing; while δέ, *a shortened form of* δύο, *denoting* the second thing, *is generally placed in opposition to it in an adversative sentence which sometimes has mentally to be supplied. When* μέν *stands by itself it always looks forward to something antithetic or different. When not used with* δέ, *marked* *.

2. ἀληθῶς, truly, really, *i.e.* in truth, in very deed, certainly; *affirming the truth in opp. to falsehood.*

3. ὄντως, really, actually, verily, (from ὄντος, *gen. of* ὤν, *part. of* εἰμί to be) *denoting therefore real existence.*

4. καί, and, also, even.

1. Matt. iii. 11.
1. —— xiii. 32.
1. —— xx. 23.
1. —— xxiii. 27.
1. —— xxvi. 41.
1. Mark i. 8 (*om.* L[b] T Tr A ℵ.)
5. —— ix. 13.
1. —— x. 39 (*om.* T Tr A ℵ.)
3. —— xi. 32.
1. —— xiv. 21.
1. Luke iii. 16.
1. —— xi. 48.
1. —— xxiii. 41.
3. —— xxiv. 34.
2. John i. 47.
2. —— iv. 42.
2. —— vi. 55 twice, (ἀληθής, *true,* G ~ L T Tr A.)
2. John vii. 26.
2. —— viii. 31.
3. —— 36.
1. Acts iv. 16.
1. —— xi. 16.
1. —— xxii. 9.
1. Rom. vi. 11.
— —— viii. 7, see I (neither.)
1*. —— xiv. 20.
1. 1 Cor. xi. 7.
1. 2 Cor. viii. 17.
— —— xi. 1, see I (and.)
1. Phil. i. 15.
— —— ii. 27, see I (for.)
1. —— iii. 1.
1. Col. ii. 23.
— 1 Thes. iv. 10, see I (and.)
3. 1 Tim. v. 3, 5, 16.
1. 1 Pet. ii. 4.

INDEED (AND)

1. { καὶ, and, even, also, γὰρ, truly then, verily then, in fact, for, } and in fact.

2. { ἀλλὰ, but, καὶ, and, even, also, } but indeed.

2. 2 Cor. xi. 1. | 1. 1 Thes. iv. 10.

INDEED (FOR)

{ καὶ, γὰρ, } *see* "INDEED (AND,)" *No.* 1.

Phil. ii. 27.

INDEED (NEITHER)

{ οὐδὲ, neither, γὰρ, in fact. }

Rom. viii. 7.

INDIGNATION.

1. θυμός, life in its activity and excitement. *In a physical sense,* breath, breath of life; *then, of every outgo of life,* spirit, courage, anger, wrath; impulse, longing, the mind as regards the passions, *esp.,* its turbulent commotions.

2. ὀργή, force *or* impulse, excitement of feeling in general, the opposition of an involuntarily roused feeling, *less sudden in its rise than No.* 1, *but more lasting in its nature. No.* 1 *is the affection itself, No.* 2 *its active outgo. No.* 1 *is the heat of the fire, No.* 2 *is the flame bursting forth.*

3. ζῆλος, zeal, fervour. *In a good sense,* ardour, emulation *to imitate superior worth; in a bad sense,* jealousy *of it, heartburning, envy.*

4. ἀγανάκτησις, physical pain and irritation; *hence,* vexation, annoyance, (*non occ.*)

— Matt. xx. 24, see I (be moved with.)
— — xxvi. 8, } see I
— Mark xiv. 4, } (have.)
— Luke xiii. 14, see I (with.)
3. Acts v. 17, marg. *envy.*
1. Rom. ii. 8.
4. 2 Cor. vii. 11.
3. Heb. x. 27.
2. Rev. xiv. 10.

INDIGNATION (BE MOVED WITH)

ἀγανακτέω, *physically,* to feel a violent irritation; *hence, metaph.,* to be irritated, vexed, *or* annoyed.

Matt. xx. 24.

INDIGNATION (HAVE)

Matt. xxvi. 8. | Mark xiv. 4.

INDIGNATION (WITH)

Luke xiii. 14, part.

INEXCUSABLE.

ἀναπολόγητος, indefensible, without excuse *or* defence, (*occ.* Rom. i. 20.)

Rom. ii. 1.

INFALLIBLE.

See PROOF.

INFANT (S.)

βρέφος, a new born babe.

Luke xviii. 15.

INFERIOR (BE)

ἡττάομαι, to be less *or* weaker than *another, hence,* to be unequal *or* inferior to *him.*

2 Cor. xii. 13.

INFERIOR (*make*) [margin.]

ἐλαττόω to make less *or* smaller, to lessen, diminish, damage.

Heb. ii. 7, text, *lower* (*make.*)

INFIDEL.

ἄπιστος, faithless, *used of one who refuses to receive God's revelation of grace,* (*occ.* Luke xii. 46.)

2 Cor. vi. 15. | 1 Tim. v. 8.

INFIRMITY (-IES.)

1. ἀσθένεια, want of strength, weakness; *hence,* feebleness, sickness.

2. ἀσθένημα, a weakness, a sickness. (*non occ.*)

3. νόσος, confirmed disease.

1. Matt. viii. 17.
1. Luke v. 15.
3. — vii. 21.
1. — viii. 2.
1. — xiii. 11, 12.
1. John v. 5.
1. Rom. vi. 19.
1. — viii. 26.
2. Rom. xv. 1.
1. 2 Cor. xi. 30.
1. — xii. 5, 9, 10.
1. Gal. iv. 13.
1. 1 Tim. v. 23.
1. Heb. iv. 15.
1. — v. 2.
1. — vii. 28.

INFORM (-ED.)

1. ἐμφανίζω, to show forth, manifest, make clear *or* plain.

2. κατηχέω, to resound; to sound *a thing* in one's ears, impress it *upon one* by word of mouth.

2. Acts xxi. 21, 24. | 1. Acts xxiv. 1.
1. Acts xxv. 2, 15.

INGRAFTED.

ἔμφυτος, inborn, innate; implanted (*non occ.*)

Jas. i. 21.

INHABITANT (-S.)

κατοικέω, to dwell in, inhabit, *esp.,* to have settled *or* be planted in a new place (*here particip.*)

Rev. xvii. 2, part. (Since Ed. 1762; before then, "Inhabiter of.")

INHABITER (-S.)

κατοικέω (*see above.*)

Rev. viii. 13, part.

INHABITERS OF.

Rev. xii. 12, part (om. G L T Tr A ℵ.) | Rev. xvii. 2, part. (In Editions from 1611 to 1762.)

INHERIT (-ED.)

κληρονομέω, to be a κληρονόμος (receiver of a portion, *esp.*, of an inheritance), to get or obtain by lot; *esp.*, to receive a share of an inheritance, to inherit.

Matt. v. 5.
— xix. 29.
— xxv. 34.
Mark x. 17.
Luke x. 25.
— xviii. 18.
1. Cor. vi. 9, 10.
1. Cor. xv. 50 twice.
Gal. v. 21.
Heb. vi. 12.
— xii. 17.
1 Pet. iii. 9.
Rev. xxi. 7 (δώσω αὐτῷ, *I will give to him*, G∾)

INHERITANCE.

1. κληρονομία, that which constitutes one a κληρονόμος (receiver *or* possessor of a portion), the inheritance.
2. κλῆρος, a lot, a die; *then*, that which is assigned by lot, an allotment *or* portion *of land*, a possession.

1. Matt. xxi. 38.
1. Mark xii. 7.
1. Luke xii. 13.
1. — xx. 14.
1. Acts vii. 5.
1. — xx. 32.
2. — xxvi. 18.
1. Gal. iii. 18.
— Eph. i. 11, see I (obtain an.)
1. Eph. i. 14, 18.
1. — v. 5.
2. Col. i. 12.
1. — iii. 24.
— Heb. i. 4, see I (obtain by.)
1. — ix. 15.
1. — xi. 8.
1. Pet. i. 4.

INHERITANCE (OBTAIN AN)

κληρόω, to choose by lot; *mid.*, to acquire by lot, to obtain, possess.

Eph. i. 11, *mid.*, (καλόμαι, *to be called*, G∾L.)

INHERITANCE (OBTAIN BY)

κληρονομέω, *see* "INHERIT."

Heb. i. 4.

INIQUITY (-IES.)

1. ανομία, violation of law; non-observance *or* transgression of the law, *whether unknown or wilfully violated;* lawlessness.
2. παρανομία, (*No.* 1, *with* παρά, beside, *prefixed*,) a violation aside from law, contrary to law and custom, (*non occ.*)
3. ἀδικία, the doing contrary to right, (*wider in sense than No.* 1,) wrong, injustice; *as done to others it is* injury; any impropriety which is repugnant to δίκαιον, *see* 1 John v. 17.
4. ἀδίκημα, that which is done in ἀδικία, (*No.* 3,) the wrong, injustice, *or* injury that is done.
5. πονηρία, evil-nature, bad state *or* condition, (*implying* the wicked act of the mind delighting in evil,) malignity.

1. Matt. vii. 23.
1. — xiii. 41.
1. — xxiii. 28.
1. — xxiv. 12.
3. Luke xiii. 27.
3. Acts i. 18.
5. — iii. 26.
3. — viii. 23.
1. Rom. iv. 7.
1. — v. 19, twice.
3. 1 Cor. xiii. 6.
1. 2 Thes. ii. 7.
3. 2 Tim. ii. 19.
1. Titus ii. 14.
1. Heb. i. 9.
1. — viii. 12.
1. — x. 17.
3. Jas. iii. 6.
2. 2 Pet. ii. 16.
4. Rev. xviii. 5.

INJURE (-ED.)

ἀδικέω, to do wrong, *lit.*, to be an ἄδικος, and act like one. *In a narrow sense*, to hurt, to injure; to act unjustly *in a sense defined by the context.*

Gal. iv. 12.

INJURIOUS.

ὑβριστής, a violent, overbearing person; a wanton, insolent man; a licentious, ungovernable man, outrageous in personal insults, (*occ.* Rom. i. 30.)

1 Tim. i. 13.

INJURY [margin.]

ὕβρις, wanton violence arising from pride of strength.

Acts xxvii. 10, text, *hurt.*

INK.

μέλαν, anything black, black pigment *used as* ink, (*non occ.*)

2 Cor. iii. 3.
3 John 13.
2 John 12.

INN.

1. καταλυμα, a loosening down, *e.g. the pads and burdens of beasts, and the girdles and sandals of travellers; hence, used of* the place where this was done, that part of the house of the host used for his guests; a lodging place (*occ.* Mark xiv. 14; Luke xxii. 10.)
2. πανδοχεῖον, a place where all are received, *i.e. in the East*, a menzil, khan, *or* caravanserai; a house for the reception of strangers (*non. occ.*)

1. Luke ii. 7.
2. Luke x. 34.

INNER.

1. ἔσω, within, *with art* (*as here*), the within.

2. ἐσώτερος (*comparative from No.* 1), inner, (*occ.* Heb. vi. 19.)

2. Acts xvi. 24. | 1. Eph. iii. 16.

INNOCENT.

ἀθῷος, not deserving punishment, guiltless, without fault, (*non occ.*)

Matt. xxvii. 4 (δίκαιος, *righteous*, G ∾)
—— 24.

INNUMERABLE.

ἀναρίθμητος, without number, innumerable.

Luke xii. 1, see Multitude. | Heb. xi. 12.
Heb. xii. 22, see Company.

INORDINATE.

See, AFFECTION.

INQUIRE.

See, ENQUIRE.

INQUIRY FOR (MAKE)

διερωτάω, to inquire through, *i.e. to the end, or till* the inquiry is successful, (*non occ.*)

Acts x. 17.

INSCRIPTION [margin.]

ἐπιγραφή, a writing upon, superscription.

Matt. xxii. 20, text *superscription.*

INSCRIPTION (WITH THIS)

{ ἐν, in, ᾧ, which, ἐπεγέγραπτο, had been inscribed, } on which was inscribed.

Acts xvii. 23.

INSOMUCH AS.

ὥστε, so that, *expressing result.*

Acts i. 19.

INSOMUCH THAT.

1. ὥστε, *see above.*

2. { εἰς, unto, τό, the, } *with inf.* to the end that; in order that.

1. Matt. viii. 24.
1. —— xii. 22.
1. —— xiii. 54.
1. —— xv. 31.
1. —— xxiv. 24.
1. —— xxvii. 14.
1. Mark i. 27, 45.
1. Mark ii. 2, 12.
1. —— iii. 10.
1. —— ix. 26.
1. Luke xii. 1.
1. Acts v. 15.
1. 2 Cor. i. 8.
2. —— viii. 6.
1. Gal. ii. 13.

INSPIRATION OF GOD (GIVEN BY)

θεόπνευστος, God-breathed, God-inspired.

2 Tim. iii. 16.

INSTANT [noun.]

ὥρα, a time, season, (*see* " HOUR.")

Luke ii. 38.

INSTANT and EARNEST (margin) [adj.]

ἐκτενής, stretched out, extended, (*occ.* 1 Pet. iv. 8.)

Acts xii. 5, text, *without ceasing* (ἐκτενῶς, adv. L Tr A ℵ.)

INSTANT (BE)

1. ἐπίκειμαι, to lie upon, be laid upon; to press upon *as with entreaties*, be urgent.

2. ἐφίστημι, to place upon or over. *In N.T. only intransitive*, to stand upon, stand by *or* near, take one's position.

1. Luke xxiii. 23.
— Rom. xii. 12, see Continue.
2. 2 Tim. iv. 2.

INSTANTLY.

1. σπουδαίως, speedily, hastily, *implying earnestness*, (*occ.* Tit. iii. 13.)

2. { ἐν, in, ἐκτένεια, extension, } incessantly or with intensity, (*non occ.*)

1. Luke vii. 4. | 2. Acts xxvi. 7.

INSTRUCT (-ED, -ING.)

1. κατηχέω, to sound forth towards, *or* against *anyone; hence*, to teach, *esp.*, orally *or* by preaching.

2. μαθητεύω, to be a pupil, to be a disciple of.

3. μυέομαι, to be initiated, in *a thing*, (from μυω, to keep close, shut up); *hence*, to be instructed, (*non occ.*)
4. παιδεύω, to train up a child, implying discipline, education.
5. συμβιβάζω, to unite *or* knit together; *then*, to put together in reasoning, *and hence*, to demonstrate, prove, *and so*, teach *or* instruct.

2. Matt. xiii. 52.
— — xiv. 8, see I before.
1. Luke i. 4.
1. Acts xviii. 25.
1. Rom. ii. 18.
5. 1 Cor. ii. 16.
3. Phil. iv. 12.
4. 2 Tim. ii. 25.

INSTRUCT BEFORE.

προβιβάζω, to put forward, instigate, (*occ.* Acts xix. 33.)

Matt. xiv. 8.

INSTRUCTION.

παιδεία, the training of a child, *including discipline and instruction, admonition, rewards and punishments.*

2 Tim. iii. 16.

INSTRUCTOR.

1. παιδευτής, a trainer of children, *implying a master, teacher, and chastiser.*
2. παιδαγωγός, a leader of a child. [Among the Greeks a servant whose business it was to attend on the boys of a family, watch over their behaviour, and particularly to lead them to and from school, etc. They were generally slaves, imperious and severe. The word is specially distinguished from διδασκαλος (teacher) by Xenophon and Plutarch, (*occ.* Gal. iii. 24, 25.)]

1. Rom. ii. 20. | 2. 1 Cor. iv. 15.

INSTRUMENT (-s.)

ὅπλον, an instrument, implement with which anything is done, *as of an artisan; of war*, weapons, etc.

Rom. vi. 13 1st pl. marg., *arms or weapons.*
Rom. vi. 13 2nd.

INSURRECTION.

στάσις, a setting up, an upstanding; *hence*, a popular commotion.

Mark xv. 7.

INSURRECTION AGAINST (MAKE)

κατεφίστημι, to stand forth against *and by implication in a hostile sense*, to set *or* rush upon, (*non occ.*)

Acts xviii. 12.

INSURRECTION WITH (THAT HAD MADE)

συστασιαστής, a companion in a popular rising, a fellow-insurgent, (*non occ.*)

Mark xv. 7, (στασιαστής, *one who stirs up to sedition*, L T Tr A ℵ.)

INTEND.

1. βουλομαι, to be willing, to be disposed; the inward predisposition and wish, (formed after due deliberation,) from which the active volition proceeds, (*hence, never used of brutes.*)
2. θέλω, to will, have in mind, purpose, (*expressive of the active volition, or natural impulse or desire, apart from all deliberation.*) θέλω, *may have a stronger meaning than* βουλομαι, (*No.* 1,) *just because natural impulses are stronger than reasonable resolves.*
3. μέλλω, to be about to do *anything*, to be on the point of doing *it*.

2. Luke xiv. 28.
1. Acts v. 28.
3. — — 35.
— Acts xii. 20, see *War* or Displeased.
1. Acts xii. 4.
3. Acts xx. 13.

INTENT (-s.)

1. ἔννοια, what is in the mind, idea, notion.
2. λόγος, the word, *as that which is spoken;* the exposition *or* account *which one gives.*

2. Acts x. 29. | 1. Heb. iv. 12.

INTENT (FOR THAT)

{ εἰς, unto, with a view to, τοῦτο, this, } in order that, for this purpose.

Acts ix. 21.

INTENT (FOR WHAT)

{ πρός, in reference to,
{ τί, what

John xiii. 28.

INTENT (TO THE)

ἵνα, that, to the end that, *with the emphasis on the result.*

John xi. 15.

INTENT THAT (TO THE)

ἵνα, (*see above.*)

Eph. iii. 16.

INTENT...SHOULD (TO THE)

{ εἰς, unto, with a view to, } *with inf.*, to
{ τὸ, the, } the end one should.

1 Cor. x. 6.

INTERCESSION (-S.)

ἔντευξις, a falling in with, meeting with, coming together; access, audience, intercourse; a petition; *then*, intercession; requests concerning others and on their behalf, (*occ.* 1 Tim. iv. 5.)

1 Tim. ii. 1.

INTERCESSION (MAKE)

ἐντυγχάνω, to fall in with, meet and talk with, apply to; *esp.*, *in intercession for or against others*, to intercede, (*occ.* Acts xxv. 24.)

Rom. viii. 27, 34. | Rom. xi. 2.
Heb. vii. 25.

INTERCESSION FOR (MAKE)

ὑπερεντυγχάνω, to intercede on behalf of *another*, (*non occ.*)

Rom. viii. 26.

INTERPRET (-ED.)

1. ἑρμηνεύω, to be an ἑρμηνεύς (an interpreter of foreign tongues); to interpret *foreign tongues.*

2. διερμηνεύω, to interpret through, *i.e.* fully; to explain.

3. μεθερμηνεύω, to translate from one language into another.

3. Matt. i. 23.
3. Mark v. 41.
3. —— xv. 22, 34. [A.)
1. John i. 38 (No. 3, L Tr
3. John i. 42.
3. Acts iv. 36.
2. 1 Cor. xii. 30.
2. —— xiv. 5, 13, 27.

INTERPRETATION.

1. ἑρμηνεία, interpretation, explanation, (*non occ.*)
2. ἐπίλυσις, release from, solution, (*non occ.*)

1. 1 Cor. xii. 10 (διερμηνεία, *full interpretation*, L.)
1. 1 Cor. xiv. 26.
2. 2 Pet. i. 20.

INTERPRETATION (BE BY)

1. ἑρμηνευω, *see* "INTERPRET," *No.* 1.
2. μεθερμηνεύω, *see* "INTERPRET," *No.* 3.

1. John i. 42, } pass.
1. —— ix. 7, } pass.
2. Acts xiii. 8, } pass.
1. Heb. vii. 7, } pass.

INTERPRETATION (BY)

διερμηνεύω, *see* "INTERPRET," *No.* 2.

Acts ix. 36, *pass. part.*

INTERPRETER.

διερμηνευτής, a thorough interpreter, (*non occ.*)

1 Cor. xiv. 28 (ἑρμηνευτής, *an interpreter*, L Tr.)

INTO.

1. εἰς, into (*to the interior*), to, unto.
2. ἐν, in (*of time, place, or element*); *with plural*, among.
3. ἐπί, upon, (a) *with Gen.*, upon (*as springing from*), upon and proceeding from.
   (b) *with Dat.*, upon, (*as resting on.*)
   (c) *with Acc.*, upon, (*by direction towards.*)
4. κατά, down, (a) *with Gen.*, down from.
   (b) *with Acc.*, down towards, down upon *or* along.
5. ἔσω, within, (*implying motion into a place.*)
6. ὑπό, under, (a) *with Gen.*, beneath and separate from, by.
   (b) *with Acc.*, under and towards, in the power of, close upon.

7. ἄχρι, to, unto, as far as, (*of place, time, or degree.*)

— Matt. i. 17, see Carrying.
1. —— ii. 11, 12, 13, 14, 20, 21, 22.
1. —— iii. 10, 12.
1. —— iv. 1, 5, 8.
— —— 12 1st, see Cast.
1. —— 12 2nd, 18.
1. —— v. 1, 20, 25, 29, 30.
1. —— vi. 6, 13, 26, 30.
1. —— vii. 19, 21.
1. —— viii. 5, 12, 14, 23, 28, 31, 32 twice, 33.
1. —— ix. 1 twice, 17 twice, 23, 26, 28, 38.
1. —— x. 5 twice, 11, 12, 23.
1. —— xi. 7.
1. —— xii. 4, 9, 11, 29, 44.
1. —— xiii. 2.
3c. —— 8, 20, 23.
1. —— 30, 36, 42, 47, 48, 50, 54.
1. —— xiv. 13, 15, 22, 23, 32.
1. —— 34 (3c. Tr ℵ.)
1. —— 35.
1. —— xv. 11, 14, 17 twice, 21, 29, 39.
1. —— xvi. 13.
1. —— xvii. 1, 15 twice, 22, 25.
1. —— xviii. 3, 8 twice, 9 twice.
3c. —— 12.
1. —— 30.
1. —— xix. 1, 17, 23, 24.
1. —— xx. 1, 2, 4, 7.
1. —— xxi. 2, 10, 12, 17, 18, 21, 23, 31.
— —— 33, see Country.
3c. —— xxii. 9.
1. —— 10, 13.
3c. —— xxiv. 16 (No. 1, L Tr.)
— —— 27, see I (even.)
1. —— 38.
— —— xxv. 14, see Country.
1. —— 21, 23, 30, 41, 46 twice.
1. —— xxvi. 18, 30, 32.
— —— 38, see I (even.)
1. —— 41, 45, 52, 71.
1. —— xxvii. 6, 27, 53.
1. —— xxviii. 7, 10, 11, 16 twice.
1. Mark i. 12, 14.
2. —— 16.
1. —— 21 twice, 29, 35, 38, 45.
1. —— ii. 1, 11, 22 1st, 22 2nd (*ap.*), 26.
1. —— iii. 1, 13, 19.
1. —— 20, marg. *home* (εἰς οἶκον.)
1. —— 27.
1. —— iv. 1.
— —— 12, see Cast.
3b. —— 26.
1. —— 37.
1. —— v. 12 twice, 13 twice, 18.
1. —— vi. 10, 31, 32, 36, 45, 46, 51.
3c. —— 53.
1. —— 56.
1. —— vii. 15, 17, 18, 19 3 times, 24 twice, 33.
1. —— viii. 10 twice.
1. —— 13 (*om.* εἰς τὸ πλοῖον, *into the ship*, G ⇉ T Trb A ℵ.)
1. —— 26, 27.
1. Mark ix. 2, 22 twice, 25, 28, 31, 42, 43 1st, 43 2nd (*ap.*), 45 1st, 45 2nd (*ap.*), 47 twice.
1. —— x. 1, 17, 23, 24, 25.
1. —— xi. 2 twice, 11 twice, 15, 23.
— —— xii. 1, see Country.
1. —— 41, 43.
1. —— xiii. 15 (*om.* εἰς τὴν οἰκίαν, *into the house*, Lb ℵ.)
1. —— xiv. 13, 16, 26, 28, 38, 41.
— —— 54, see I (even.)
1. —— 68.
5. —— xv. 16.
1. —— 41.
1. —— xvi. 5, 7, 12 (*ap.*), 15 (*ap.*), 19 (*ap.*)
1. Luke i. 9, 39 twice, 40, 79.
1. —— ii. 3, 4, 15, 27, 39.
1. —— iii. 3, 9, 17.
1. —— iv. 1 (ἐν τῇ ἐρήμῳ, *in the wilderness*, instead of, εἰς τὴν ἔρημον, *into the wilderness*, G ∾ L T Tr A ℵ.)
1. —— 5 (*ap.*), 14, 16, 37, [38, 42.
1. —— v. 3, 4.
2. —— 16.
1. —— 19, 37, 38.
1. —— vi. 4, 6, 12, 38, 39.
1. —— vii. 1, 11, 24, 36, 44.
1. —— viii. 22, 29, 30, 31, 32, 33 twice, 37, 41, 51.
1. —— ix. 10, 12, 28, 34, 44 twice, 52.
1. —— x. 1, 2, 5, 8, 10 twice, [38 twice.
1. —— xi. 4.
1. —— xii. 5, 28, 58.
1. —— xiii. 19.
1. —— xiv. 1, 5, 21, 23.
1. —— xv. 13, 15.
1. —— xvi. 4, 9, 16, 22, 28.
1. —— xvii. 2, 12, 27.
1. —— xviii. 10, 24, 25.
3c. —— xix. 4.
1. —— 12.
3c. —— 23.
1. —— 30, 45.
— —— xx. 9, see Country.
1. —— xxi. 1, 24.
1. —— xxii. 3, 10 twice, 33, 40, 46, 54, 66.
1. —— xxiii. 19 (No. 2, T Tr A ℵ.)
1. —— 25.
2. —— 42 (No. 1, Lm.)
1. —— 46.
1. —— xxiv. 7, 26, 51 (*ap.*)
1. John i. 9, 43.
1. —— iii. 4, 5, 17, 19, 22, [24.
2. —— 35.
1. —— iv. 3, 14, 28, 38, 43, 45, 46, 47, 54.
2. —— v. 4 (*ap.*)
1. —— 7, 24.
1. —— vi. 3, 14, 15, 17, 21, [22.
1. —— vii. 3, 14.
1. —— viii. 2 (*ap.*)
1. —— ix. 39.
1. —— x. 1, 36, 40.
1. —— xi. 7, 27, 30, 54.
1. —— xii. 24, 46.
1. —— xiii. 2, 3, 5, 27.
1. —— xv. 6.
1. —— xvi. 13 (No. 2, G ∾ T ℵ.)
1. —— 20, 21, 28.
1. —— xvii. 18 twice.
1. —— xviii. 1, 11, 15, 28, 33, 37.
1. John xix. 9, 17.
1. —— xx. 6, 11, 25 twice, [27.
1. —— xxi. 3, 7.
1. Acts i. 11 3 times, 13.
1. —— ii. 20 twice, 34.
1. —— iii. 1, 2, 3, 8.
4b. —— v. 15 (καί εἰς, *also into*, L T Tr ℵ) marg. *in every street.*
1. —— 21.
1. —— vii. 3, 4.
— —— 6, see Bondage.
1. —— 9, 15, 16.
3c. —— 23.
2. —— 45.
1. —— 34, 39, 55.
— —— viii. 3, see I every house.
1. —— 38.
1. —— ix. 6, 8.
3c. —— 11.
1. —— 17, 39.
— —— x. 10, see Fall.
1. —— 16, 22, 24.
1. —— xi. 8, 10, 12.
— —— xii. 4, see Remove.
1. —— 17.
1. —— xiii. 14.
1. —— xiv. 1, 20, 22, 25.
1. —— xvi. 9, 10, 15, 19, 23, 24, 37.
1. —— 40 (πρός, *towards*, or *to* G L T Tr A ℵ.)
1. —— xvii. 10.
1. —— xviii. 7, 18, 19, 27.
1. —— xix. 8, 22, 29, 31.
1. —— xx. 1, 2, 3.
7. —— 4.
1. —— 18.
1. —— xxi. 3, 8, 11, 26, 28, 29, 34, 37, 38.
1. —— xxii. 4, 10, 11, 23, 24.
1. —— xxiii. 10, 16, 20, 28.
1. —— xxv. 23.
1. —— xxvii. 1.
— —— 2, see Enter.
1. —— 6.
— —— 15, see Bear.
1. —— 17, 30, 38, 39, 41.
1. —— xxviii. 5, 17, 23.
2. Rom. i. 23, 25.
1. —— 26.
1. —— v. 2, 12.
1. —— vi. 3 twice, 4.
1. —— viii. 21.
1. —— x. 6, 7, 18, 24 1st.
— —— xi. 24 2nd, see Graff.
1. —— xv. 24, 28.
3c. 1 Cor. ii. 9.
— —— iv. 17, see Remembrance.
— —— ix. 27, see Subjection.
— —— xi. 20, see One.
1. —— xii. 13 1st.
1. —— 13 2nd (*om.* G ∾ L T Tr A ℵ.)
1. 1 Cor. xiv. 9.
— —— 23, see One.
1. 2 Cor. i. 16.
1. —— ii. 13.
1. —— vii. 5.
2. —— viii. 16.
1. 2 Cor. xi. 13, 14.
1. —— xii. 4.
2. Gal. i. 6.
1. —— 17, 21.
1. —— iii. 27.
1. —— iv. 6.
1. Eph. iv. 9, 15.
1. Col. i. 13.
— —— ii. 18, see Intrude.
1. 2 Thes. iii. 5 twice.
1. 1 Tim. i. 3, 12, 15.
1. —— iii. 6, 7.
2. —— 16.
— —— v. 9, see Number.
1. —— vi. 7, 9.
1. 2 Tim. iii. 6.
1. Heb. i. 6.
1. —— iii. 11, 18.
1. —— iv. 1, 3 twice, 5, 10, [11.
1. —— vi. 19.
1. —— viii. 10.
1. —— ix. 6, 7, 12, 24 twice, [25.
1. —— x. 5.
3b. —— 16.
1. —— 19, 31.
1. —— xi. 8.
1 —— xiii. 11.
— Jas. i. 2, see Fall.
1. —— 25.
1. —— iv. 13.
1. —— v. 4.
6b. —— 12 (ὑπό, *under judgment*, instead of εἰς ὑποκρισιν *into dissembling* (St.), G L T Tr A ℵ.)
1. 1 Pet. i. 12.
1. —— ii. 9.
1. —— iii. 22.
1. —— v. 10.
1. 2 Pet. i. 11.
1. 1 John iv. 1, 9.
1. 2 John 7, 10.
1. Jude 4.
1. Rev. ii. 10, 22 twice.
1. —— v. 6.
1. —— viii. 5, 8.
3c. —— xi. 11 (No. 2, G L T A) (ἐις, ℵ) (*om.* ἐπί, Tr.)
1. —— xii. 6, 9, 14 twice.
— —— xiii. 10 1st, see [Lead.
1. —— 10 2nd.
1. —— xiv. 19 twice.
1. —— xv. 8.
1. —— xvi. 16.
1. —— 17 (G ∾) (3c, G L T Tr A ℵ.)
1. —— 19.
1. —— xvii. 3, 8, 11.
1. —— xviii. 21.
1. —— xix. 20.
1. —— xx. 3, 10, 14, 15.
1. —— xxi. 24, 26, 27.
1. —— xxii. 14.

INTO EVERY HOUSE.

{ κατὰ, down upon, throughout, at *or* in, *or distributively* from one to another,
οἶκος, a house, (*see* "HOUSE,") *here pl.* } at different houses, along the houses, into the houses one after another.

Acts viii. 3.

INTO (EVEN)

{ ἕως, as far as,
{ ἔσω, within,
{ εἰς, into.

Mark. xiv. 54.

INTREAT (-ED) AND INTREATY.

See, ENTREAT, etc.

INTRUDE INTO.

ἐμβατεύω, to step in, enter into; *hence,* to frequent, haunt, (*non occ.*)

Col. ii. 18.

INVENTOR (-S.)

ἐφευρετής, an inventor, (*non occ.*)

Rom. i. 30.

INVISIBLE.

ἀόρατος, unseen.

Col. i. 15, 16. | Heb. xi. 27. | 1 Tim. i. 17.

INVISIBLE THINGS (THE)

{ τὰ, the } *neut.*, the unseen
{ ἀόρατα, unseen, } things.

Rom. i. 20.

INWARD.

ἔσω, within, *adv. of place where.*

Mark vi. 19, see Grudge. | Rom. vii. 22.
2 Cor. vii. 15, see Affection.

INWARD MAN (THE)

{ ὁ, the,
{ ἔσωθεν, from within,

2 Cor. iv. 16, (ὁ ἔσω ἡμῶν, *our inner* [man], L T Tr ℵ, ὁ ἔσω(θεν) ἡμῶν, A.)

INWARD PART.

{ ὁ, } *see above.*
{ ἔσωθεν, }

Luke xi. 39.

INWARDLY.

1. ἔσωθεν, from within.

2. { ἐν, in,
{ κρυπτός, secret.

1. Matt. vii. 15. | 2. Rom. ii. 29.

IRON [noun.]

σίδερος, iron, (*non occ.*)

1 Tim. iv. 2, see Sear. | Rev. xviii. 12.

IRON (OF)

σιδήρεος, of iron.

Rev. ii. 27.
— ix. 9. | Rev. xii. 5.
— xix. 15.

IRON [adj.]

σιδήρεος, of iron.

Acts xii. 10.

IS.

(FORASMUCH AS-, HE-, SEEING THAT-, SHE-, IT-, THAT-, THERE-, WHEN-, WHICH-, WHILE-, WHO-.)

Sometimes there is no equivalent in the Greek for this word.

Sometimes it is the translation of the article with a noun, adj. or numeral, *he that is*, etc. Or of the article with a prep. or adv., *that which is*, etc. Sometimes also after nouns with defining words following, the art. is commonly repeated, and is then translated *who is*, etc.

Sometimes it is part of another verb,

When it is not any of these, then it is the translation of one of these following,

1. εἰμί, I am, *the ordinary state of existence,* * *with pronoun* ἐγω, I.

   (a) ἐστί, *or* ἐστίν, (*3rd pers. sing. pres.,*) he, she, *or* it is.

   (b) ἐστέ, ye...are, * *with pronoun* ὑμεῖς, you *or* ye.

   (c) *subjunctive*, may be.

   (d) εἶναι, to be, *Infinitive with Acc.*, that...is.

   * *with* "that" *understood.*

   † *with* δία τό, because of being...

   (e) ὤν, οὖσα, ὄν, being, (*participle,*) * *with Acc. of noun preceding,* that...is; † *with art. preceding,* who is, *the one who* is.

   (f) *Imperfect*, he, she, it was.

2. ἔνεστι, (*impers. of* ἔνειμι, to be in,) there does not exist, *or* there cannot be.

3. γίνομαι, to come into being, to be born, to become, to arise, to happen.

4. ὑπάρχω, to begin, to start, to begin to be, (*referring to original state or existence.*)

5. ἀπέχω, to keep off *or* away from.

6. καθίστημι, to set down, set. *Intrans.*, *as here*, to be set, to be come into a certain state.

7. ἄγω, to lead, lead along; lead towards *a point*, bring on.

8. κειμαι, to be laid.

1a. Matt. i. 20, 23.
1a.—— ii. 2.
1a.—— iii. 3, 11, 17.
1a.—— v. 3, 10, 34, 35 twice, 48.
1a.—— vi. 13 (*ap.*)
1a.——— 21, 22, 25.
1e.——— 30, which I.
1a.—— vii. 9 (*om.* L Tr A.)
1a.——— 12.
1a.—— ix. 5, 15.
1a.—— x. 10 (*om.* L T Tr A ℵ.)
1a.——— 11.
1b*——— 20.
1a.——— 24, 26, 37 twice, 38.
1a.—— xi. 6, 10, 11, 14, 16, 30 2nd.
1a.—— xii. 6, 8, 23.
1e.——— 30 1st.
1a.——— 30 2nd.
3. ——— 45.
1a.——— 48, 50.
1a.—— xiii. 19, 20, 22, 23, 31, 32 twice, 33, 37, 38, 39 twice, 44, 45, 47, 52, 55, 57.
1a.—— xiv. 2, 15, 26.
1*.——— 27.
5. —— xv. 8.
1a.——— 26 (οὐκ ἔξεστι, *it is not lawful*, for οὐκ ἔστι καλόν, *it is not good*, L T A.)
3. —— xvi. 2, when ... I.
1a.—— xvii. 4, 5.
1a.—— xviii. 1, 4, 8, 9, 14 1st.
1a.—— xix. 14, 24, 26.
1a.—— xx. 1.
1c.——— 4.
1c.——— 7 (*ap.*)
1a.——— 15 2nd, 23.
1a.—— xxi. 10, 11, 38, 42 3rd.
1a.—— xxii. 8.
1d.——— 23, that ... I.
1a.——— 32.
1a. ——— 38, 42, 45.
1a.—— xxiii. 8, 9 1st, 10 (*om.* G ∾), 16, 17, 18.
1a.—— xxiv. 6, 26.
1c.——— 28.
3. ——— 32.
1a.——— 33, 45.
3. —— xxvi. 2.
1a.——— 18.
1*.——— 22, 25.
1a.——— 26, 28, 38, 48, 66, 68.
1a. Matt. xxvii. 6 2nd, 33, 37.
1a.—— xxviii. 6.
1a. Mark i. 27 (*ap.*)
1a.—— ii. 9, 19, 28.
1a.—— iii. 17, 29, 33, 35.
1a.—— iv. 21, 26.
1a.——— 31 (No. 1e, L Tr A ℵ.)
1a.——— 41.
1a.—— v. 41.
1a.—— vi. 3, 4, 15 1st.
1a.——— 15 2nd (*om.* Lb T Tr A ℵ.)
1a.——— 16 1st (*om.* G Lb T Tr A ℵ.)
1a.——— 35.
1*.——— 50.
5. —— vii. 6.
1a.——— 15, 27, 34.
1a.—— ix. 5, 7, 21, 39, 40, 42, 43, 45, 47.
1a.—— x. 14, 24, 25, 29, 40.
1a.—— xii. 7, 11.
1d*——— 18, that I.
1a.——— 27.
3. ——— 28 1st.
1a.——— 28 2nd.
1a.——— 29, 31, 32 twice, 33, 35, 37.
1b*—— xiii. 2.
1e.——— 16 that I (*om.* L Tr A ℵ.)
1a.——— 28 2nd.
1a.——— 29, 33.
1a.—— xiv. 14, 22, 24, 34, 44, 69.
1a.—— xv. 22, 34, 42.
1a.—— xvi. 6.
1a. Luke i. 36, 61, 63.
1a.—— ii. 11.
1a.—— iv. 22, 24.
1a.—— v. 21, 23, 34, 39.
1a.—— vi. 5, 20, 35, 36, 40, 47, 48, 49.
1a.—— vii. 23, 27, 28 twice, 39, 49.
1a.—— viii. 11 twice, 17.
1a.——— 25 1st (*om.* L T Tr A ℵ.)
1a.——— 25 2nd.
1a.——— 26, 30.
1a.—— ix. 9, 33, 35, 38.
4. ——— 48, that I.
1a.——— 50 twice, 62.
1a.—— x. 7 (*om.* L T Tr A ℵ.)
1a.——— 22 twice, 29, 42.
1d†—— xi. 8.
1e.——— 23 1st, that I.
1a.——— 23 2nd.
3. Luke xi. 26.
1a.——— 29.
1a.——— 34 1st & 3rd.
1c.——— 34 2nd & 4th.
1a.—— xii. 1, 2, 6, 23.
1e.——— 28, which I.
1a.——— 34, 42.
3. ——— 54.
1a.—— xiii. 18, 19, 21.
1a.—— xiv. 22 2nd.
1e.——— 32, while ... I.
1a.——— 35.
3. —— xv. 10.
1a.——— 31.
1a.—— xvi. 10 3rd & 5th.
1a.——— 15 2nd (*om.* All.)
1a.——— 17.
1a.—— xvii. 1, 21.
1a.—— xviii. 16, 25, 29.
1a.—— xix. 9 2nd.
1a.——— 46 2nd (ἔσται, *shall be*, Lm T Tr A) (*om.* ℵ.)
1a.—— xx. 2, 14, 17 1st.
1d.——— 27, that I.
3. ——— 33.
1a.——— 38.
1d.——— 41, that I (*om.* G ∾.)
1a.——— 44.
1a.—— xxi. 30, 31.
1a.—— xxii. 11, 19, 38, 53, 59, 64.
1d.—— xxiii. 2, that I.
1a.——— 15, 38 (*ap.*)
1a.—— xxiv. 6.
7. ——— 21.
1a ——— 29.
1*.——— 39.
1e* John i. 18, which I.
1a.——— 19.
1a.——— 27 1st (*om.* G Lb T Tr A ℵ.)
1a.——— 30 1st.
1a.——— 33, 34, 42, 47.
1e.—— iii. 4, when ... I.
1a.——— 6 twice.
1a.——— 8.
1e.——— 13, which ... I (*ap.*)
1a.——— 19, 29 1st.
1a.——— 31 1st & 3rd.
1e.——— 31 2nd.
1a.——— 31 4th (*ap.*)
1a.——— 33.
1a.—— iv. 10, 11, 18, 20, 22, 23, 29, 34, 37, 42.
1a.—— v. 2, 10, 12, 25, 27, 30, 31, 32 twice, 45.
1a.—— vi. 9, 14.
1*.——— 20.
1a.——— 29, 31, 33, 39, 40, 42 1st, 45.
1e.——— 46, which I.
1a.——— 50, 51, 55 twice, 58, 60, 63, 70.
1a.—— vii. 6, 11, 12, 16, 18 twice, 22, 25, 27 twice, 28, 36, 40, 41.
1a.—— viii. 13, 14, 16, 17, 19, 26, 29, 34, 39, 44 twice.
1e.——— 47.
1a.——— 50, 54 3 times.
1a.—— ix. 4, 8, 9 twice, 12, 16 1st, 17, 19, 20, 24, 29, 30 twice, 36, 37.
1a.—— x. 1, 2, 13, 29 1st, 34.
1a.—— xi. 4, 10.
1a.—— xii. 14, 31, 34, 35, 50.
1a.—— xiii. 10, 16, 25, 26.
1a.—— xiv. 21.
3. ——— 22.
1a.——— 24, 28.
1a.—— xv. 1, 12, 20.
1a.—— xvi. 17, 18, 32.
1a. John xvii. 3, 17.
1a.—— xviii. 36 twice, 38.
1a.—— xix. 35, 40.
1a.—— xx. 31.
1a.—— xxi. 7, 20, 24 twice.
1a. Acts i. 7, 12,
1a.—— ii. 15, 16, 25, 29, 39.
1a.—— iv. 11, 12 1st (*ap.*), 12 2nd, 36.
1e.—— v. 17, which I.
1a.—— vi. 2.
1a.—— vii. 33, 37, 38.
1a.—— viii. 10, 21, 26.
1d.——— 37, that I (*ap.*)
1a.—— ix. 15, 20, 21, 22.
1a.—— x. 4, 6, 28 1st, 34, 35, 36, 42.
1a.—— xii. 15.
1a.—— xvi. 12.
1a.—— xvii. 3.
1d.——— 7, that I.
4. ——— 24, seeing that ... I.
1a.—— xix. 35 1st.
1e*——— 35 2nd, that I.
1a.—— xx. 10, 35.
1a.—— xxi. 22, 28.
1a.—— xxii. 26.
1d.—— xxiii. 8, that I.
1a.——— 19.
1a.—— xxv. 14, 16.
4. —— xxvii. 34.
1a.—— xxviii. 4.
1a. Rom. i. 9, 12, 16, 19, 25.
1a.—— ii. 2, 11, 28 1st.
1a.—— iii. 8, 10, 11 twice, 12 twice, 18, 22.
1a.—— iv. 15, 16 4th.
1e.—— v. 13, when ... I.
1a.——— 14.
1a.—— vii. 3 1st.
1d.——— 3 2nd, that I.
1a.——— 14.
1a.—— viii. 9, 24, 34.
1e.—— ix. 5, who is (with art.)
1a.—— x. 1 (*ap.*), 8 twice, 12 1st.
3.—— xi. 5.
2. ——— 6 2nd (1st not in Greek.)
1a.——— 6 3rd & 4th (*ap.*)
1a.——— 23.
1a.—— xiii. 1, 4 1st & 3rd.
1a.—— xiv. 4 (δυνατεῖ, *is* POWERFUL, for δυνατός ἐστίν, IS *powerful*, G ∾ L T Tr A ℵ.)
1a.——— 17, 23.
1e.—— xvi. 1 1st, which I.
1a.——— 5 2nd.
1e. 1 Cor. i. 2, which I.
1a.——— 18 twice, 25 twice.
1a.—— iii. 5, 7, 11, 13, 17, 19.
1a.—— iv. 3, 4, 17.
1a.—— vi. 5 (ἔνι, *one*, All.)
1a.——— 7, 16, 17, 18, 19.
1a.—— vii. 8 (*om.* All.)
1a.——— 9, 19 twice, 22 twice.
4. ——— 26.
1a.——— 39, 40.
1e.—— viii. 10, which I.
1a.—— ix. 3, 16, 18.
1a.—— x. 16 twice, 19 1st (*ap.*), 19 3rd, 28.
1a.—— xi. 3, 5.
4. ——— 7 1st, forasmuch as ... I.
1a.——— 7 2nd, 8, 13, 14, 15.
1a.——— 20 (marg. *can*), 24, 25.
1a.—— xii. 6 (*om.* All.)
1a.——— 12, 14, 15, 16.
1a.—— xiv. 14, 15, 25, 26, 33, 35, 58.
1.—— xv. 12, 13, 44 twice,

1a. 1 Cor. xvi. 15.
1e. 2 Cor. i. 1, which I.
1a.——— 12.
1a.—— ii. 2 1st (om. G → L T Tr A ℵ.)
1a.——— 3.
3. —— iii. 15.
1a.——— 17.
1a. —— iv. 3, 4.
1a.—— vii. 15.
1a.—— ix. 1.
1d.—— x. 7, 18.
1a. 2 Cor. xi. 10.
1e.——— 31, which I.
1a.—— xii. 13.
1a.—— xiii. 5 (om. Lb T Tr Ab.)
1a. Gal. i. 7, 11.
1a.—— iii. 12, 16, 20 twice.
1a.—— iv. 1, 2.
1f. ——— 15 (om. G⇉L T Tr A ℵ.)
1a.——— 24, 25, 26 twice.
1a.—— v. 3, 22, 23.
1e.—— vi. 3, when I.
1a. Eph. i. 1, 14, 18, 23.
1e.—— ii. 4, who I.
1a.——— 14.
1a.—— iii. 13.
1a.—— iv. 9, 10, 15.
1e.——— 18, that I.
1a.——— 21.
1a.—— v. 5, 10, 12, 13, 18, 23 1st.
1. ——— 23 3rd (om. G⇉L T Tr A ℵ.)
1a.——— 32.
1a.—— vi. 1, 2, 9 twice, 17.
1a. Phil. i. 7.
1a.——— 8 (om. G→Lb T Tr A ℵ.)
1a.——— 28.
1a.—— ii. 13.
4. —— iii. 20.
1a. Col. i. 7, 15, 17, 18 twice, 24, 27.
1a.—— ii. 10.
1a.—— iii. 5, 14, 20, 25.
1a.—— iv. 9.
1e.——— 11, which I.
1a. 1 Thes. ii. 13.
1a.—— iv. 3.
1a. 2 Thes. i. 3.
1a.—— ii. 4, 9.
1a.—— iii. 3, 17.
1a. 1 Tim. i. 5, 20.
1a.—— iii. 15, 16.
1a.—— iv. 8, 10.
1a.—— v. 4, 8.
1d.—— vi. 5, that I.
1a.——— 6, 10.
1a. 2 Tim. i. 6, 12.
1a.—— ii. 17.
1a.—— iv. 11 twice.
1a. Tit. i. 13.
1a. Heb. ii. 6.
1a.—— iv. 13.
1a.—— v. 13.
1a.—— vii. 2, 15.
3. ——— 18.
1a.—— viii. 6.
1a.—— ix. 15.
2. ——— 22.
1a. Heb. xi. 1.
1a.——— 6 2nd.
3. ——— 6 3rd.
1a.—— xii. 7 (om. L T Tr Ab ℵ.)
3. Jas. i. 12, when.
1a.——— 17 1st.
2. ——— 17 2nd.
1a.——— 27.
3. —— ii. 10.
1a.——— 17, 19, 20, 26 twice.
1a.—— iii. 5.
5. ——— 6.
1a.——— 17.
1a.—— iv. 4 1st
6. ——— 4 2nd.
1a.——— 12 1st.
1a.——— 14 (*ἔσται, it shall be*, G∾) (*ἐστέ, ye are*, L T Tr A) (om. ℵ.)
1a.——— 16, 17.
1a. 1 Pet. i. 25.
1a.—— ii. 15.
1a.—— iii. 4, 22.
1a.—— v. 12.
1a. 2 Pet. i. 9.
1. ——— 17.
3. ——— 20.
3. —— ii. 20.
1a.—— iii. 4.
1a. 1 John i. 5 3 times, 7, 8, 9, 10.
1a.—— ii. 2, 4 twice, 7, 8.
1d*.——— 9 1st.
1a.——— 9 2nd, 10, 11, 15, 16, 18 twice, 21, 22 3 times, 25, 27 twice, 29.
1a.—— iii. 2, 3, 4, 5, 7 twice, 8, 10, 11, 15, 20.
1a.—— iv. 3, 3 3 times, 4, 6, 7, 8, 10, 12, 15, 16, 17, 18, 20.
1a.—— v. 1, 3, 4, 5, 6 3 times, 9 twice, 11 twice, 14, 16, 17 twice, 20.
1a. 2 John 6 twice, 7.
1a. 3 John 11, 12.
1e† Rev. i. 4, which I.
1e†——— 8, which I.
1a.—— ii. 7.
1e†—— iv. 8, which I.
1a.—— v. 2 (om. G⇉L T Tr A ℵ.)
1a.——— 12.
1a.——— 13 (om. G⇉L T Tr A ℵ.)
1a.—— ix. 19 (ap.)
1a.—— xiii. 10, 18 twice.
1a.—— xiv. 12.
1a.—— xvii. 8 1st & 2nd.
1a.——— 8 3rd (*καὶ παρέσται, and shall be present*, for *καίπερ ἐστίν, and yet is*, G L T Tr A) (*καὶ πάλιν πάρεστιν, and again is present*, ℵ.)
1a.——— 10, 11 3 times, 14, 18.
1a.—— xix. 8, 10.
1a.—— xx. 2, 12, 14.
1a.—— xxi. 8, 16 (om. All), [17.
1a.—— xxii. 10.

ISLAND.

1. *νῆσος*, an island, (*prob.* from *νέω*, to float,) (*non occ.*)

2. *νησίον*, (*dim. of No.* 1) a small island, (*non occ.*)

2. Acts xxvii. 16.
1. ——— 26.
1. Acts xxviii. 1, 7, 9.
1. Rev. vi. 14.
1. Rev. xvi. 20.

ISLE.

νῆσος, *see* "ISLAND," *No.* 1.

Acts xiii. 6.
Rev. i. 9.
Acts xxviii. 11.

ISRAEL.

Ἰσραήλ, (Heb., ישׂראל, wrestler with God) the name given to Jacob, Gen. xxxii. 24, etc. In *N.T.* spoken only of his posterity (*see below.*)

In all places, except—

Acts iv. 8 (om. L T Tr Ab ℵ.)
Acts xiii. 17 (om. G.)
Rom. x. 1 (ap.)

ISRAELITE.

Ἰσραηλίτης, a descendant of Israel. The grand title of the Jew as a member of the theocracy and heir of the promises, theocratic privileges and glorious vocation. *Hence as* the most honourable title, *it was the word chosen by the Apostles in order to obtain an hearing*, (*see* Acts ii. 22, iii. 12, xiii. 16; and Rom. ix. 4; Phil. iii. 5; 2 Cor. xi. 22.)

John i. 47.
Rom. ix. 4.
Rom. xi. 1.
2 Cor. xi. 22.

ISSUE [noun.]

1. *ῥύσις*, a flowing, (lxx. for זוב) (*non occ.*)
2. *σπέρμα*, seed; *hence*, children.

— Matt. ix. 20, see Blood.
2. —— xxii. 25.
1. Mark v. 25.
1. Luke viii. 43, 44.

ISSUE (-ED.) [verb.]

ἐκπορεύομαι, to go or come out of.

Rev. ix. 17, 18.

IT.

(When not part of the translation of a phrase, it is one of these following, and is emphatic.)

1. *ἐκεῖνος*, that, that one there (*the more remote or latter of two; always emphatic.*)
2. *οὗτος*, this, this one here (*the nearer or former of two.*)
   (a) *τοῦτο*, *neut. sing., Nom. or Acc.*
   (b) *τούτου*, *Gen. sing., masc. or neut.*
   (c) *ταύτῃ*, *fem. sing., Dative.*
   (d) *ταύτην*, *fem. sing., Acc.*

3. *αὐτός*, he, she, it (*demonst. pron.*), self, very.

4. *τὸ*, the *thing*.

2a. Matt. xx. 11.
2a. Mark v. 43.
2. —— vi. 16 (No. 3. G ∾)
2a.—— xiv. 5.
2a. Luke xviii. 36.
2b. John vi. 61.
3. —— xii. 24.
2d. 1 Cor. vi. 13.
2c. Heb. xi. 2.
2a. —— xiii. 17.
4. 2 Pet. ii. 22.

IT BE BUT (THOUGH)

ὅμως, yet still, nevertheless.

Gal. iii. 15.

ITCHING EARS (HAVE)

κνηθόμενοι, being tickled, itching,
τὴν, the,
ἀκοήν, hearing,
} being tickled (*or* itching) as to the ears (*or* hearing.)

2 Tim. iv. 3.

ITSELF.

1. *αὐτός*, he, she, it, self.
   (a) *αὐτή*, *fem. sing.*, *Nom.*
   (b) *αὐτό*, *neut. sing.*, *Nom. or Acc.*
   (c) *αὐτόν*, *masc. sing. Acc*
   (d) *αὐτῆς*, *fem. sing. Gen.*

2. *ἑαυτοῦ*, of himself, herself, *or* itself, etc.
   (a) *ἑαυτῆς*, *fem. sing. Gen.*
   (b) *ἑαυτήν*, *fem. sing. Acc.*

— Matt. vi. 34, see I (of.)
2a.—— xii. 25 twice.
2b. Mark iii. 24, 25.
2b. Luke xi. 17.
2. John xv. 4.
— —— xx. 7, see By
1a.—— xxi. 25.
1b. Rom. viii. 16.
1a. Rom. viii. 21.
1b.—— 26.
2. —— xiv. 14, (No. 1, G L T Tr ℵ.)
1a. 1 Cor. xi. 14, (om. G→)
— Eph. iv. 16, see I (of.)
1c. Heb. ix. 24.
1d. 3 John 12.

ITSELF (o

2a. Matt. vi. 34. | 2. Eph. iv. 16.

IVORY (OF)

ἐλεφάντινος, made of ivory (*from ἐλέφας*, the elephant.)

Rev. xviii. 12.

J.

JACINTH.

ὑακίνθος, a hyacinth; a flower of deep purple or reddish blue. *Then*, a gem *of like colour*, (*non occ.*)

Rev. xxi. 20.

JACINTH (OF)

ὑάκινθινος, hyacinthine; having the colour of the hyacinth, (*non occ.*)

Rev. ix. 17.

JAILOR.

εσμοφύλαξ, a prison-keeper.

Acts xvi. 23.

JANGLING (VAIN)

ματαιολογία, vain or foolish talk, (*non occ.*)

1 Tim. i. 6.

JASPER.

ἴασπις, jasper. [A stone of various colours, but prob. the colour of fire is intended (Ezek. i. 27; Deut. iv. 24,) being like the sardius, which two stones were the first and last on the High Priest's breastplate (Ex. xxviii. 17, 20),] (*non occ.*)

Rev. iv. 3. | Rev. xxi. 11, 18, 19.

JEALOUS OVER (BE)

ζηλόω, to be zealous towards, *i.e.* for *or* against *any* person or thing; *then*, to be jealous of.

2 Cor. xi. 2.

JEALOUSY.

ζῆλος, any eager vehement passion, *esp.*, jealousy.

2 Cor. xi. 2.

JEALOUSY (PROVOKE TO)

παραζηλόω, to render mis-zealous, *i.e.* to make jealous, provoke to jealousy.

Rom x. 19. | Rom. xi. 11.
1 Cor. x. 22.

JEOPARDY (BE IN)

κινδυνεύω, to be in danger or peril.

Luke viii. 23.

JEOPARDY (STAND IN)

1 Cor. xv. 30.

JERUSALEM.

Ἱερουσαλήμ, *or* **Ἱεροσόλυμα,** Jerusalem. *Heb.*, ירושלם, dwelling of peace.

In all passages, except—
Luke xxiv. 49, (*om.* G L T Tr A ℵ.)

JESTING.

εὐτραπελία, the behaviour of the εὐτράπελος, (easily turning *or* changing, *of apes and persons,*) wit, liveliness; *in a bad sense,* jesting, ribald, tricky, dishonest, time-serving.

Eph. v. 4.

JESUS.

Ἰησοῦς, Jesus. [Heb. יהושע, i.e. *Jehoshua* or *Joshua,* which in the lxx. and *N.T.* is constantly expressed Ἰησοῦς. The Heb. is a compound of יה, *Jah,* (for *Jehovah,*) and הושיע, *to save,* and implies *Jehovah the Saviour.* Hence applied to Christ, as He who was God, and thus able to "save his people from their sins."

[JESUS is the title of His humiliation. Whenever it occurs alone it brings before us the One who "humbled Himself and became obedient unto death, even the death of the cross." It is the personal name of the "Man of Sorrows," who suffered being incarnate, and died being man. "Wherefore, God also hath highly exalted Him, and given Him a name which is above every name." Thus "CHRIST" becomes the name of His changed position, as raised from the dead, and exalted in glory. "Christ," (in the Epistles) as denoting *our* position, blessing, and standing before God., *e.g.* "in Christ," (never, in Jesus). "THE Christ" (with the article gen. in the gospels) as the official designation of the One offered to Israel, for their then, but now, future blessing.) Hence in the *Gospels* (the record of His earthly life) "JESUS" occurs alone, 566 times, while "CHRIST," or "THE Christ," occurs only 36 times. On the other hand, in the *Acts and Epistles* "JESUS" occurs alone, only 29 times (16 of which are in the Acts, as being the transitional testimony to the crucified One), while "Christ" occurs 217 times.]

The combination of "Jesus Christ" *seems to place the emphasis on* Jesus as "the humbled One now glorified"; *while* "Christ Jesus" *marks Him as* "the now glorified One who was once humbled." *The combination with* "Lord" ("the Lord Jesus Christ") *marks His* authority and power. For "God hath made that same Jesus . . . both LORD and CHRIST." Acts ii. 36.]

* Jesus=Joshua, the son of Nun.

Matt. i. 1, 16.
—— 18 (*om.* G → T Tr.)
—— 21, 25.
—— ii. 1.
—— iii. 13, 15, 16.
—— iv. 1, 7, 10. [A ℵ.)
—— 12 (*om.* G ⇉ T Tr
—— 17. [A ℵ.)
—— 18 (*om.* G L T Tr
—— 23 (*om.* L T Tr^b A.)
—— vii. 28. [A ℵ.)
—— viii. 3 (*om.* L T Tr
—— 4. [Tr A ℵ.)
—— 5 (*αὐτός, he,* G L T
—— 7 (*om.* L T Tr^b A ℵ.)
—— 10, 13, 14, 18, 20, 22.
—— 29 (*om.* G L T Tr
—— 34. [A ℵ.)
—— ix, 2, 4, 9, 10.
—— 12 (*om.* L T Tr^b A ℵ.)
—— 15, 19, 22, 23, 27, 28,
—— x. 5. [30, 35.
—— xi. 1, 4, 7, 25.
—— xii. 1, 15.
—— 25 (*om.* L T Tr A
—— xiii. 1, 34. [ℵ.)
—— 36 (*om.* G ⇉ L T Tr A ℵ.)
—— 51 (*ap.*), 53, 57.
—— xiv. 1, 12, 13.
—— 14 (*om.* G ⇉ L T Tr* A ℵ.)
—— 16.
—— 22, } (*om.* G L T
—— 25, } Tr A ℵ.)
—— 27, 29, 31.
—— xv. 1.
—— 16 (*om.* L T Tr A
—— 21, 28, 29. [ℵ.)
—— 30, (*αὐτός, his,* G ∾ L T Tr A ℵ.)
—— 32, 34.
—— xvi. 6, 8, 13, 17.

Matt. xvi. 20 (*om.* G L T
—— 21, 24. [Tr A ℵ.)
—— xvii. 1, 4, 7, 8, 9.
—— 11 (*om.* G ⇉ L T Tr
—— 17, 18, 19. [A ℵ.)
—— 20 (*om.* L T Tr A ℵ.)
—— 22, 25, 26.
—— xviii. 1.
—— 2 (*om.* T Tr A ℵ.)
—— 22. [26, 28.
—— xix. 1, 14, 18, 21, 23,
—— xx. 17, 22, 25, 30, 32, 34
—— xxi. 1, 6, 11, 12, 16, 21, 24, 27, 31, 42.
—— xxii. 1, 18, 29.
—— 37 (*om.* L T Tr A ℵ.)
—— 41.
—— xxiii. 1.
—— xxiv. 1.
—— 2 (ἀποκριθείς, *he answering,* L T Tr
—— 4. [A ℵ.)
—— xxvi. 1, 4, 6, 10, 17, 19, 26, 31, 34, 36, 49, 50 twice, 51, 52, 55, 57, 59, 63, 64, 69, 71, 75.
—— xxvii. 1, 11 twice, 17, 20, 22, 26, 27, 37, 46, 50, 54, 55, 57, 58.
—— xxviii. 5, 9, 10, 16, 18.
Mark i. 1, 9, 14, 17, 24, 25.
—— 41 (*om.* L T Tr A ℵ.)
—— ii. 5, 8, 15, 17, 19.
—— iii. 7.
—— v. 6, 7.
—— 13 (*om.* εὐθέως ὁ Ἰησοῦς, *forthwith Jesus,* G ⇉ L^b T Tr A^b ℵ.)
—— 15.
—— 19 (*om.* G ⇉ L^b T Tr A ℵ.)
—— 20, 21, 27, 30, 36.
—— vi. 4, 30.

Mark vi. 34 (*om.* G Lb T Tr A ℵ.)
— vii. 27 (καὶ ἔλεγεν, *and he said,* instead of ὁ δὲ Ἰησοῦς εἶπεν. *but Jesus said,* L T Tr A ℵ.)
— viii. 1 (*om.* G L T Tr A ℵ.)
—— 17 (*om.* T Trb A.)
—— 27.
— ix. 2, 4, 5, 8, 23, 25, 27, 39.
— x. 5, 14, 18, 21, 23, 24, 27, 29, 32, 38, 39, 42, 47 twice, 49, 50, 51, 52 1st.
—— 52 2nd (αὐτὸς, *Him,* G L T Tr A ℵ.)
— xi. 6, 7.
—— 11 (*om.* G ⇉ L T Tr A ℵ.)
—— 14, } *om.* G L T Tr
—— 15, } A ℵ.)
—— 22, 29, 33 twice.
— xii. 17, 24, 29, 34, 35.
—— 41 (*om.* Lb T Tr A ℵ
— xiii. 2, 5.
— xiv. 6, 18.
—— 22 (*om.* Lb T Trb A ℵ.)
—— 27, 30, 48, 53, 55, 60, 62, 67, 72.
— xv. 1, 5, 15, 34, 37, 43.
— xvi. 6.
Luke i. 31.
— ii. 21, 27, 43, 52.
— iii. 21, 23.
— iv. 1, 4, 8, 12, 14, 34, 35.
— v. 8, 10, 12, 19, 22, 31.
— vi. 3, 9, 11.
— vii. 3, 4, 6, 9, 19.
—— 22 (*om.* Lb T Tr A
—— 40. [ℵ.)
— viii. 28 1st.
—— 28 2nd (*om.* G→)
—— 30, 35 twice.
—— 38 (*om.* G ⇉ Lb T Tr A ℵ.)
—— 39, 40, 41, 45.
—— 46 (*om.* G ⇉)
—— 50.
— ix. 33, 36, 41, 42.
—— 43 (*om.* G ⇉ T Tr A ℵ.)
—— 47, 50, 58.
—— 60 (*om.* G ⇉ Lb T Tr A ℵ.)
—— 62.
— x. 21 (*om.* L Tr A ℵ.)
—— 29, 30, 37.
—— 39 (Κύριος, *the Lord's,* L T Tr A ℵ.)
—— 41 (Κύριος, *the Lord,* Lm T Trm ℵ.)
— xiii. 2 (*om.* Lb T Tr A ℵ.)
—— 12, 14.
— xiv. 3.
— xvii. 13, 17.
— xviii. 16, 19, 22, 24, 37, 38, 40, 42.
— xix. 3, 5, 9, 35 twice.
— xx. 8, 34.
— xxii. 47, 48, 51, 52.
—— 63 (αὐτός, *Him,* G ∾ L T Tr A ℵ.)
— xxiii. 8, 20, 25, 26, 28.
—— 34 (*ap.*), 42.
—— 43 (*om.* T Trb A ℵ.)
—— 46, 52.
— xxiv. 3, 15, 19.
—— 36 (*om.* G L T Tr A ℵ.)
John i. 17, 29, 36, 37, 38, 42.
John i. 43 (*om.* ὁ Ἰησοῦς, after "*following*" and insert it after "*Philip and,*" G L T Tr A ℵ.)
—— 45, 47, 48, 50.
— ii. 1, 2, 3, 4, 7, 11, 13, 19, 22, 24.
— iii. 2 (αὐτός, *Him,* G L T Tr A ℵ.)
—— 3, 5, 10, 22.
— iv. 1, 2, 6, 7, 10, 13.
—— 16 (*om.* Lb T Trb A.)
—— 17, 21, 26, 34, 44.
—— 46 (*om.* G L T Tr A ℵ.)
—— 47, 48, 50 twice, 53, 54.
— v. 1, 6, 8, 13, 14, 15, 16, 17, 19.
— vi. 1, 3, 5, 10, 11.
—— 14 (*om.* T Tr A ℵ.)
—— 15, 17, 19, 22, 24 twice, 26, 29, 32, 35, 42, 43, 53, 61, 64, 67.
—— 70 (*om.* G ⇉)
— vii. 1, 6, 14, 16, 21, 28, 33, 37, 39.
— viii. 1 (*ap.*), 6 (*ap.*), 9 (*ap.*), 10 (*ap.*), 11 (*ap.*), 12, 14, 19.
—— 20 (*om.* G L T Tr A ℵ.)
—— 21 (*om.* G ⇉ L T Tr A ℵ.)
—— 25, 28, 31, 34, 39, 42, 49, 54, 58, 59.
— ix. 3, 11, 14, 35, 37, 39, 41.
— x. 6, 7, 23, 25, 32, 34.
— xi. 4, 5, 9, 13, 14, 17, 20, 21, 23, 25, 30, 32, 33, 35, 38, 39, 40, 41, 44.
—— 45 (*om.* L T Tr A.)
—— 46, 51, 54, 56.
— xii. 1, 3, 7, 9, 11, 12, 14, 16, 21, 22, 23, 30, 35, 36, 44.
— xiii. 1.
—— 3 (*om.* G ⇉ Lb T Tr A ℵ.)
—— 7, 8, 10, 21, 23 twice, 25, 26, 27, 29, 31, 36, 38.
— xiv. 6, 9, 23.
— xvi. 19, 31.
— xvii. 1, 3.
— xviii. 1, 2, 4, 5 1st.
—— 5 2nd (*om.* Tr A.)
—— 7, 8, 11, 12, 15 twice, 19, 20, 22, 23, 28, 32, 33, 34, 36, 37.
— xix. 1, 5, 9 twice, 11, 13, 16 (*ap.*), 18, 19, 20, 23, 25, 26, 28, 30, 33, 38 1st & 2nd.
—— 38 3rd (αὐτοῦ, *his,* L Tr A,) (αὐτόν, *him,* instead of τὸ σῶμα Ἰησοῦ, *the body of Jesus,* T ℵ.)
—— 39 (αὐτός, *him,* L T Tr A.)
—— 40, 42.
— xx. 2, 12, 14 twice, 15, 16, 17, 19.
—— 21 (*om.* T Tr Ab ℵ.)
—— 24, 26, 29, 30, 31.
— xxi. 1, 4 twice.
—— 5 (*om.* Lb.)
—— 7, 10, 12, 13, 14, 15, 17, 20, 21, 22, 23, 25.
Acts i. 1, 11, 14, 16, 21.
— ii. 22, 32, 36, 38.
— iii. 6, 13, 20.
—— 26 (*om.* G L T Tr A ℵ.)
Acts iv. 2, 10, 13, 18, 27, 30.
—— 33 (*add* Χριστός, Lb ℵ.)
— v. 30, 40, 42.
— vi. 14.
— vii. 45*.
—— 55, 59.
— viii. 12, 16, 35, 37 (*ap.*)
— ix. 5, 17 (*om.* G→), 27.
—— 29 (*om.* L T Tr A ℵ.)
—— 34.
— x. 36, 38.
— xi. 17, 20.
— xiii. 26, 33.
— xv. 11, 26.
— xvi. 18, 31.
— xvii. 3, 7, 18 (*ap.*)
— xviii. 5, 28.
— xix. 4, 5.
—— 10 (*om.* G L T Tr A ℵ.)
—— 13 twice, 15, 17.
— xx. 21, 24, 35.
— xxi. 13.
— xxii. 8.
— xxv. 19.
— xxvi. 9, 15.
— xxviii. 23, 31.
Rom. i. 1, 3, 6, 7, 8.
— ii. 16.
— iii. 22, 24.
—— 26 (*om.* G→)
— iv. 24.
— v. 1, 11, 15, 17, 21.
— vi. 3, 11, 23.
— vii. 25.
— viii. 1, 2, 11, 39.
— x. 9.
— xiii. 14.
— xiv. 14.
— xv. 5, 6.
—— 8 (*om.* G ⇉ L T Tr A ℵ.)
—— 16, 17, 30.
— xvi. 3.
—— 18 (*om.* G L T Tr A ℵ.)
—— 20, 24, 25, 27.
1 Cor. i. 1, 2 twice, 3, 4, 7, 8, 9, 10, 30.
— ii. 2.
— iii. 11.
— iv. 15.
— v. 4 twice.
—— 5 (*om.* A), (*add* Χριστοῦ, Lb Trm.)
— vi. 11 (*add* Χριστός, L Tr ℵ), (κύριος ἡμῶν, *our Lord,* Trmb.)
— viii. 6.
— ix. 1.
— xi. 23.
— xii. 3 twice.
— xv. 31, 57.
— xvi. 22 (*om.* Ἰησοῦς Χριστος, *Jesus Christ,* G ⇉ L T Tr A ℵ.)
—— 23, 24.
2 Cor. i. 1, 2, 3, 14, 19.
— iv. 5 twice.
—— 6 (*om.* L T Tr A.)
—— 10 twice., 11 twice, 14 twice.
— v. 18 (*om.* G ⇉ L T Tr A ℵ.)
— viii. 9.
— xi. 4, 31.
— xiii. 5, 14.
Gal. i. 1, 3, 12.
— ii. 4, 16 twice.
— iii. 1, 14, 22, 26, 28.
— iv. 14.
— v. 6.
— vi. 14, 15 (*ap.*), 17, 18.
Eph. i. 1 twice, 2, 3, 5, 15, 17.
— ii. 6, 7, 10, 13, 20.
Eph. iii. 1, 9 (*ap.*), 11, 14 (*ap.*), 21.
— iv. 21.
— v. 20.
— vi. 23, 24.
Phil. i. 1 twice, 2, 6, 8, 11, 19, 26.
— ii. 5, 10, 11, 19, 21.
— iii. 3, 8.
—— 12 (*om.* G L T Tr A ℵ.)
—— 14, 20.
— iv. 7, 19, 21, 23.
Col. i. 1, 2 (*ap.*), 3, 4.
—— 28 (*om.* G L T Tr A ℵ.)
— ii. 6.
— iii. 17.
1 Thes. i. 1 1st, 1 2nd (*ap.*), 3, 10.
— ii. 14, 15, 19.
— iii. 11, 13.
— iv. 1, 2, 14 twice.
— v. 9, 18, 23, 28.
2 Thes. i. 1, 2, 7, 8, 12 twice.
— ii. 1, 14, 16.
— iii. 6, 12, 18.
1 Tim. i. 1 twice, 2, 12, 14, 15, 16.
— ii. 5.
— iii. 13.
— iv. 6.
— v. 21.
— vi. 3, 13, 14.
2 Tim. i. 1 twice, 2, 9, 10, 13.
— ii. 1, 3, 8, 10.
— iii. 12, 15.
— iv. 1.
—— 22 (*om.* Ἰησοῦς Χριστός, *Jesus Christ,* T Tr ℵ.)
Tit. i. 1, 4.
— ii. 13.
— iii. 6.
Philem. 1, 3, 5.
—— 6 (*om.* L T Tr Ab ℵ.)
—— 9, 23, 25.
Heb. ii. 9.
— iii. 1.
— iv. 8* (marg. *Joshua.*)
—— 14.
— vi. 20.
— vii. 22.
— x. 10, 19.
— xii. 2, 24.
— xiii. 8, 12, 20, 21.
Jas. i. 1.
— ii. 1.
1 Pet. i. 1, 2, 3 twice, 7, 13
— ii. 5.
— iii. 21.
— iv. 11.
— v. 10.
—— 14 (*om.* G ⇉ L T Tr A.)
2 Pet. i. 1 twice, 2, 8, 11, 14, 16.
— ii. 20.
— iii. 18.
1 John i. 3, 7.
— ii. 1, 22.
— iii. 23.
— iv. 2, 3, 15.
— v. 1, 5, 6.
—— 20 (*om.* G→)
2 John 3, 7.
Jude 1 twice, 4, 17, 21.
Rev. i. 1, 2, 5.
—— 9 1st (*om.* G∾)
—— 9 2nd.
— xii. 17.
— xiv. 12.
— xvii. 6.
— xix. 10 twice.
— xx. 4.
— xxii. 16, 20, 21.

JEW (-s.)

'Ιουδαῖος, Jewish, (lxx. 'Ιούδας and 'Ιούδα, Judah,) *with art.*, one of the tribe or country of Judah, *later applied to* all the inhabitants of Judæa, Palestine, and their descendants. A Jew in his national distinction from a Gentile. *See under* "HEBREW."

In all passages.

JEWS (AS DO THE)

'Ιουδαϊκῶς, Jewishly, in the Jewish manner, (*non occ.*)

Gal. ii. 14.

JEWS (LIVE AS DO THE)

'Ιουδαΐζω, to live like the Jews, follow their manners, customs, and rites, (*non occ.*)

Gal. ii. 14.

JEW'S RELIGION.

'Ιουδαϊσμος, Judaism, (*non occ.*)

Gal. i. 13, 14.

JEWISH.

'Ιουδαϊκός, Jewish, current among the Jews.

Tit. i. 14.

JEWRY.

'Ιουδαία, Judea, the territory of his tribe, but often employed in a wider sense; the kingdom of Judah. *After the captivity used of* the whole of Palestine.

Luke xxiii. 5. | John vii. 1.

JOHN.

'Ιωάννης, John, (*Heb.*, יוחנן, Johanan, *i.e.* Jehovah given,) *a proper name, used of four persons in the N.T.*

In all passages, except—
Matt. iii. 14, (om. L T Tr[b] A[b] ℵ.)
Mark vi. 16, (om. G⇌)
John i. 29 (om. G L T Tr A ℵ.)
Rev. xxi. 2 (om. G L T Tr A ℵ.)

JOIN FITLY TOGETHER.

συναρμολογέω, to fit *or* frame together, join together parts fitted to each other, (*occ.* Eph. ii. 21.)

Eph. iv. 16.

JOIN HARD TO.

συνομορέω, to border together, be contiguous with, (*non occ.*)

Acts xviii. 7, (with εἰμί, to be.)

JOIN ONE'S SELF.

κολλάω, to glue together. *In N.T. mid. or pass. aor.*, to adhere, cleave to; to become one's servant *or* follower.

Luke xv. 15.
Acts v. 13.
Acts viii. 29.
— ix. 26.

JOIN ONE'S SELF TO.

προσκολλάω, (*the above, with* πρός, towards, *prefixed*,) to glue one thing to another, to become united with anyone.

Acts v. 36 (προσκλίνω, *to incline towards, to favour*, G∾L T Tr A ℵ.)

JOIN TOGETHER.

συζεύγνυμι, to yoke together, *as animals*, (*non occ.*)

Matt. xix. 6. | Mark x. 9.

JOINED (BE)

κολλάω, *see* "JOIN ONE'S SELF."

1 Cor. vi. 16, 17.

JOINED UNTO (BE)

προσκολλάω, *see* "JOIN ONE'S SELF TO."

Eph. v. 31.

JOINED TOGETHER (BE PERFECTLY)

καταρτίζω, to make fully ready, to make complete, *esp. of what is broken*, refit, repair, mend; *of persons*, restore, set right.

1 Cor. i. 10.

JOINT [noun.]

1. ἁρμός, a joint, (*non occ.*)

2. ἁφή, a ligature, *by which the different members of the body are connected*, (*non occ.*)

2. Eph. iv. 16. | 2. Col. ii. 19.
1. Heb. iv. 12.

JOINT [adj.]

See, HEIR.

JONAS, JONA.

Ἰωνᾶς, the father of Peter.

John i. 42, — xxi. 15, 16, 17, } (Ἰωάνης, John, L Tr,) (Ἰωάννης, John, T A ℵ.)

JOSEPH.

Ἰωσήφ, Joseph, (*Heb.*, יוסף, he will add,) a proper name of seven persons in the *N.T.*

In all passages, except—
Luke ii. 33, (G∼) (πατὴρ αὐτοῦ, *his father*, G T Tr A ℵ.)
——— 43, (ap.)

JOSES.

Ἰωσῆς, Joses.

In all passages, except—
Luke iii. 29, (Ἰησοῦς, *Jesus*, L T Tr A ℵ.)
Acts iv. 36, (Ἰωσήφ, *Joseph*, G ∼ L T Tr A ℵ.)

JOT.

ἰῶτα, iota, (*Heb.* yod י) the smallest Hebrew letter, (*non occ.*)

Matt. v. 18.

JOURNEY [noun.]

1. ὁδός, *in respect to place*, a way, road, etc.; *in respect of action*, a being on the way.

2. ὁδοιπορία, way-faring, journeying, (*occ.* 2 Cor. xi. 26.)

1. Matt. x. 10. | 1. Luke ix. 3.
1. Mark vi. 8. | 1. —— xi. 6, marg. *way*.
1. Luke ii. 44. | 2. John iv. 6.
1. Acts i. 12.

JOURNEY (BRING ON ONE'S)

προπέμπω, to send forth, send before *or* beforehand.

1 Cor. xvi. 6. | Titus iii. 13.

JOURNEY (BRING FORWARD ON ONE'S)

προπέμπω, (*see above.*)

3 John 6.

JOURNEY (GO ON ONE'S)

ὁδοιπορέω, to be on the way, to journey, to travel, (*non occ.*)

Acts x. 9, part.

JOURNEY (HAVE A PROSPEROUS)

εὐοδόομαι, to be led in a good way, to have a prosperous journey, (*occ.* 1 Cor. xvi. 2; 3 John 2 twice.)

Rom. i. 10.

JOURNEY (IN ONE'S)

διαπορεύομαι, to go *or* pass through *a place.*

Rom. xv. 24, part.

JOURNEY (MAKE ONE'S)

πορεύω, to cause to pass over *by land or water*, to transport. *In N.T. only mid.*, to transport one's self, to betake one's self, *i.e.* pass from one place to another.

Acts xxii. 6, part.

JOURNEY (TAKE ONE'S)

1. ἀποδημέω, to be absent from one's people *or* country; *hence*, to go abroad, travel into foreign countries.

2. πορεύω, *see* "J (MAKE ONE'S")

1. Matt. xxv. 15. | 1. Luke xv. 13.
2. Rom. xv. 24.

JOURNEY (TAKING A FAR)

ἀπόδημος, gone abroad, absent in foreign countries, (*non occ.*)

Mark xiii. 34.

JOURNEY (-ED, -ING.) [verb.]

1. πορεύω, *see* "J (MAKE ONE'S")

2. { πορεία, a going away, ποιέω, to make, } making [his] journey, (*occ.* Jas. i. 11.)

3. ὁδεύω, to be on the way, to travel.

Luke x. 33, part. | 1. Acts ix. 3.
2. —— xiii. 22. | 1. —— xxvi. 12.

JOURNEY WITH.

συνοδεύω, (*No.* 3 *with* σὺν, together with, *prefixed*) to be on the way with *any one*, (*non occ.*)

Acts ix. 7.

JOURNEYING.

ὁδοιπορία, a journeying, wayfaring, (*occ.* John iv. 6.)

2 Cor. xi. 26.

JOY [noun.]

1. χαρά, delight, joy, gladness, (*from* χαίρω, *see* "JOY," *No.* 1.)
2. ἀγαλλίασις, exultation, great joy, *esp.*, *with song and dance.*
3. εὐφροσύνη, mirth, merriment, *esp.*, *of a banquet*, (*occ.* Acts xiv. 17.)

1. Matt. ii. 10.
1. —— xiii. 20, 44.
1. —— xxv. 21, 23.
1. —— xxviii. 8.
1. Luke i. 14.
2. ——— 44.
1. —— ii. 10.
— —— vi. 23, see Leap.
1. —— viii. 13.
1. —— x. 17.
1. —— xv. 7, 10.
1. —— xxiv. 41, 52.
1. John iii. 29.
1. —— xv. 11 3 times.
1. —— xvi. 20, 21, 22, 24.
1. —— xvii. 13.
3. Acts ii. 28.
1. —— viii. 8.
1. —— xiii. 52.
1. —— xv. 3.
1. —— xx. 24 (om. G⇉L T Tr A ℵ.)
1. Rom. xiv. 17.
1. —— xv. 13, 32.
1. 2 Cor. i. 24.
1. 2 Cor. ii. 3.
1. —— vii. 13.
1. —— viii. 2.
1. Gal. v. 22.
1. Phil. i. 4, 25.
1. —— ii. 2.
1. —— iv. 1.
1. 1 Thes. i. 6.
1. —— ii. 19, 20.
1. —— iii. 9.
1. 2 Tim. i. 4.
1. Philem. 7 (χάρις, *grace*, G∾)
— ——— 20, see J (have)
1. Heb. xii. 2.
1. —— xiii. 17.
1. Jas. i. 2.
1. —— iv. 9.
1. 1 Pet. i. 8.
— —— iv. 13, see J (with exceeding)
1. 1 John i. 4.
1. 2 John 12.
1. 3 John 4.
— Jude 24, see J (exceeding)

JOY (EXCEEDING)

2. Jude 24.

JOY (WITH EXCEEDING)

ἀγαλλιάω, to rejoice exceedingly, *esp.*, *with song and dance.*

1 Peter iv. 13, part.

JOY (HAVE)

ὀνίνημι, *in N.T. only mid.*, to have profit *or* advantage, to enjoy help, to have the delight or advantage of *being or doing so and so.*

Philem. 20.

JOY (-ED, -ING.) [verb.]

1. χαίρω, to be delighted, *like German*, gern, to desire, *old high Germ.*, ger, *i.e.* eager, to rejoice, be pleased with.
2. καυχάομαι, to speak loud, to be loud-tongued; *hence*, to boast one's self of, *or* exult.

2. Rom. v. 11.
1. 2 Cor. vii. 13.
1. Phil. ii. 17, 18.
1. Col. ii. 5.
1. 1 Thes. iii. 9.

JOYFUL (BE EXCEEDING)

{ ὑπερπερισσεύομαι, to super-abound, greatly,
τῇ, with the,
χαρᾷ, delight, *or* joy. }

2 Cor. vii. 4.

JOYFULLY.

1. { μετὰ, with,
χαρᾶς, joy. }
2. χαίρω, *see* "JOY," [verb] *No.* 1.

2. Luke xix. 6, part.
1. Heb. x. 34.

JOYFULNESS.

χαρά, delight, joy, gladness, (*from* χαίρω, *see* "JOY," *No.* 1.)

Col. i. 11.

JOYOUS.

χαρᾶς, (*Gen.*) of joy.

Heb. xii. 11.

JUDGE (-S.) [noun.]

1. κριτής, he who decides, a judge, umpire. The presiding judge; one who decides according to equity and common sense.
2. δικαστής, one who executes δίκη; a judge, *or*, *rather*, a juror, (*lower than*, *No.* 1,) one who decides according to law and justice.

1. Matt. v. 25 twice.
1. —— xii. 27.
1. Luke xi. 19.
2. —— xii. 14 (No. 1, L T Tr A ℵ.)
1. ——— 58 twice.
1. —— xviii. 2, 6.
2. Acts vii. 27, 35.
1. —— x. 42.
1. —— xiii. 20 (*ap.*)
1. —— xviii. 15.
1. 2 Tim. iv. 8.
1. Jas. ii. 4.
1. —— iv. 11.
1. Jas. v. 9.

JUDGE [verb.]

(-ED, -EST, -ETH, -ING.)

1. κρίνω, to divide, to separate (*akin to Lat.*, cerere, to sift), to make a distinction, come to a decision, to judge, to pronounce final judgment. Not merely sentence of condemnation, but also a decision in any one's favour.

2. ἀνακρίνω, (*No.* 1, *with* ἀνά, *intens., prefixed*) to separate or divide up, investigate.

3. διακρίνω, (*No.* 1, *with* διά, through, *prefixed*) to separate throughout, *i.e.* wholly, completely, to distinguish.

4. { εἰς, unto, with a view to,
{ διάκρισις, the act of scrutinising.

5. κριτήριον, tribunal, the instrument *or* place of judgment; *here, diminutive* and *Genitive,* = " of [very small] judgment-seats."

6. ἡγέομαι, to lead out. *Then, to do so before the mind, i.e.* to view, to regard *as being so and so*, to esteem *or* reckon.

1. Matt. vii. 1, 2 twice.
1. —— xix. 28.
1. Luke vi. 37 twice.
1. —— vii. 43.
1. —— xii. 57.
1. —— xix. 22.
1. —— xxii. 30.
1. John v. 22, 30.
1. —— vii. 24 twice, 51.
1. —— viii. 15 twice, 16, 26, 50.
1. —— xii. 47 twice, 48 twice.
1. —— xvi. 11.
1. —— xviii. 31.
1. Acts iv. 19.
1. —— vii. 7.
1. —— xiii. 46.
1. —— xvi. 15.
1. —— xvii. 31.
1. —— xxiii. 3.
1. —— xxiv. 6 (*ap.*)
1. —— xxv. 9, 10, 20.
1. —— xxvi. 6.
1. Rom. ii. 1 3 times, 3, 12, 16, 27.
1. —— iii. 4, 6, 7.
4. —— xiv. 1, marg. (text, *disputation.*)
1. ——— 3, 4, 10, 13 twice.
2. 1 Cor. ii. 15, marg. discern.
2. —— iv. 3 twice, 4.
1. 1 Cor iv. 5.
1. —— v. 3, marg. *determine.*
1. ——— 12 twice, 13.
1. —— vi. 2 1st & 2nd.
5. ——— 2 3rd.
1. ——— 3.
3. ——— 5.
1. —— x. 15, 29.
1. —— xi. 13.
3. ——— 31 1st.
1. ——— 31 2nd.
1. ——— 32, part.
2. —— xiv. 24.
3. ——— 29.
1. 2 Cor. v. 14, part.
1. Col. ii. 16.
— ——— 18, see J *against.*
1. 2 Tim. iv. 1.
1. Heb. x. 30.
6. —— xi. 11.
1. —— xiii. 4.
1. Jas. ii. 12.
1. —— iv. 11 3 times, 12.
1. 1 Pet. i. 17.
1. —— ii. 23.
1. —— iv. 5, 6.
1. Rev. vi. 10.
1. —— xi. 18.
1. —— xvi. 5.
1. —— xviii. 8.
1. —— xix. 2, 11.
1. Rev. xx. 12, 13.

JUDGMENT AGAINST [margin.]

καταβραβεύω, to give the prize against any one.

Col. ii. 18, text, *beguile of one's reward.*

JUDGMENT (-s.)

1. κρίσις, separating, sundering; judgment, *esp.*, of judicial procedure; the act *or* time of pronouncing sentence.

2. κρίμα, the result *or* issue of the verb κρίνω; the decision arrived at, the sentence pronounced, *unfavourable to those concerned.*

3. κριτήριον, the tribunal, the instrument *or* place of judgment.

4. δικαίωμα, the product *or* result of δικαιόω, (*see* "JUSTIFY,") the action by which a δικαίον, (a right and just thing,) is set forth or brought about, *hence,* act of justice, legal statute.

5. δίκη, right, *as established custom or usage;* right, justice, a judicial process.

6. γνώμη, mind, *implying the sense of* accord, assent; *also,* opinion, judgment.

7. αἴσθησις, perception *by the external senses; hence,* power of discerning, (*non occ.*)

8. διάγνωσις, a knowing through, *i.e.* exact knowledge, *in N.T. in a judicial sense, obtained by* examination *or* trial.

9. ἡμέρα, day. [Here, (1 Cor. iv. 3,) "man's day," the day or time of man's judgment, in opposition to "the Lord's day," the day or period of the Lord's judgment. Compare Rev. i. 10, where the words occur describing the future scene into which John was transported by the Spirit, and which he records in the book of "The Revelation of Jesus Christ."]

1. Matt. v. 21, 22.
2. —— vii. 2.
1. —— x. 15.
1. —— xi. 22, 24.
1. —— xii. 18, 20, 36, 41, 42.
1. —— xxiii. 23.
1. Mark vi. 11, (*ap.*)
1. Luke x. 14.
1. —— xi. 31, 32, 42.
1. John v. 22, 27, 30.
1. —— vii. 24.
1. —— viii. 16.
1. —— xii. 31.
1. —— xvi. 8, 11.
— —— xviii. 28 1st, (see J (hall of)
— ——— 28 2nd, } see J
— —— xix. 9, } hall.
1. Acts viii. 33.
— —— xxiii. 35, see J hall.
5. xxv. 15, (*καταδίκη, sentence against,* G ∾ L Tr. ℵ.)
8. ——— 21, marg. (text, *hearing.*)
— Rom. i. 28, see J (*void of*)
4. ——— 32.
2. —— ii. 2, 3.
— ——— 5, see J (righteous)
— —— iii. 19, see J (*subject to*)
2. —— v. 16.
2. —— xi. 33.
6. 1 Cor. i. 10.

9. 1 Cor. iv. 3, marg. *day*.
3. —— vi. 4.
6. —— vii. 25, 40.
1. —— xi. 29 twice, marg. (text, *damnation*.)
2. ——— 34, marg. (text, *condemnation*.
2. Gal. v. 10.
7. Phil. i. 9, marg. *sense*.
1. 2 Thes. i. 5.
2. 1 Tim. iii. 6, marg. (text, *condemnation*.)
1. —— v. 24.
— 2 Tim. iii. 8, see *J* (*of no*)
— Tit. i. 16, see *J* (*void of*)
2. Heb. vi. 2.
1. —— ix. 27.
1. —— x. 27.
1. Jas. ii. 13 twice.
2. 1 Pet. iv. 17.
2. 2 Pet. ii. 3.
1. ——— 4, 9.
1. —— iii. 7.
1. 1 John iv. 17.
1. Jude 6, 15.
1. Rev. xiv. 7.
4. —— xv. 4.
1. —— xvi. 7.
2. —— xvii. 1.
1. —— xviii. 10.
1. —— xix. 2.
2. Rev. xx. 4.

JUDGMENT (HALL OF)

πραιτώριον, *see below*, "J. HALL."

John xviii. 28.

JUDGMENT (*of no*) [margin.]

ἀδόκιμος, unapproved, unworthy; spurious, that will not stand proof.

2 Tim. iii. 8, text, *reprobate*.

JUDGMENT (RIGHTEOUS)

δικαιοκρισία, just judgment, (*non occ.*)

Rom. ii. 5.

JUDGMENT (*subject to*) [margin.]

ὑπόδικος, under judicial process, under sentence, (*non occ.*)

Rom. iii. 19 twice, text, *guilty*.

JUDGMENT (*void of*) [margin.]

ἀδόκιμος, *see* "J. (OF NO)"

Rom. i. 28, Tit. i. 16, } text, *reprobate*.

JUDGMENT HALL.

πραιτώριον, *Lat.*, prætorium, *i.e.* the general's tent in a camp. *Then*, the house or palace of the governor of a province. A prætorian residence.

John xviii. 28, 33. | John xix. 9.
Acts xxiii. 35.

JUDGMENT-SEAT.

βῆμα, a step, a raised place. *Then*, a tribune to speak from in a public assembly. *In the Roman Law-courts there were two, for plaintiff and defendant. Then*, the elevated seat of a judge, (*occ.* Acts vii. 5.)

[The βῆμα, or Tribunal of Christ, must be distinguished from "the throne of His ['the King's'] glory," (Matt. xxv.): and also from the great white Throne of the Father (Rev. xx.). Before the *First*, "we," (2 Cor. v. 10) *i.e.* the Apostle, and all Christians, "appear"—*i.e.* be made manifest; to "receive." We appear there as raised in incorruption and made like the Judge "as He is." Before the *Second*, "all the nations" "shall be gathered," and separated and judged according to what they have rendered unto the "brethren" of Christ, "when the Son of Man shall come in His glory," (the Church or bride coming and sitting with Him, Rev. iii. 20, 21.). Before the *Third*, stand "the dead" raised in the second Resurrection, after the thousand years, "the resurrection of damnation." These are "judged," and "cast into the lake of fire." *See under* "RESURRECTION."]

2. κριτήριον, the instrument *or* place of judgment, the tribunal where sentence is pronounced

1. Matt. xxvii. 19.
1. John xix. 13.
1. Acts xviii. 12, 16, 17.
1. Acts xxv. 6, 10, 17.
1. Rom. xiv. 10.
1. 2 Cor. v. 10.
2 Jas. ii. 6.

JUPITER (WHICH FELL DOWN FROM)

Διοπετής, fallen from Jove, heaven descended, (*non occ.*)

Acts xix. 35.

JURISDICTION.

ἐξουσία, authority.

Luke xxiii. 7.

JUST.

1. δίκαιος, fulfilling all claims which are right and becoming. A right state, (*of which God and His word is the standard*) so that no fault or defect can be charged. (*Used of God it refers to* His doings as answering to the rule which He has established for Himself.)

Hence, of man it is just, conformity to God's revealed will. *Also the act of God establishing a man as* righteous.

2. ἔνδικος, fair, just. *No.* 1, *characterises the person so far as the* δίκη (right) *is internal or inherent, while No.* 2, *so far as he occupies* the due relation to it, (*non occ.*)

1. Matt. i. 19.
1. —— v. 45.
1. —— xiii. 49.
1. —— xxvii. 19.
1. —— 24 (om. G→L[b] T Tr[b] A.)
1. Mark vi. 20.
1. Luke i. 17.
1. —— ii. 25.
1. —— xiv. 14.
1. —— xv. 7.
1. —— xx. 20.
1. —— xxiii. 50.
1. John v. 30.
1. Acts iii. 14.
1. —— vii. 52.
1. —— x. 22.
1. —— xxii. 14.
1. Acts xxiv. 15.
1. Rom. i. 17.
1. —— ii. 13.
2. —— iii. 8.
1. —— 26.
1. —— vii. 2.
1. Gal. iii. 11.
1. Phil. iv. 8.
1. Col. iv. 1.
1. Tit. i. 8.
2. Heb. ii. 2.
1. —— x. 38.
1. —— xii. 23.
1. Jas. v. 6.
1. 1 Pet. iii. 18.
1. 2 Pet. ii. 7.
1. 1 John i. 9.
1. Rev. xv. 3.

JUSTIFICATION.

1. δικαίωμα, the product or result of making right and just. *It is also used for* the deed by which one is set forth as righteous,—the act of justification accomplished in the sinner.

2. δικαίωσις, the action which establishes right, *i.e.* a sentence in law, therefore also justification. The establishment of a man as just, by acquittal from guilt, (*non occ.*)

2. Rom. iv. 25. | 1. Rom. v. 16.

JUSTIFIER.

δικαιόω, *see below. Here, participle.*

Rom. iii. 26, part.

JUSTIFY.

δικαιόω, to set forth as righteous, to justify by a judicial act. By a judicial decision to free a man from his guilt (which stands in the way of his being right) and to represent him as righteous.

Matt. xi. 19.
—— xii. 37.
Luke vii. 29, 35.
—— x. 29.
—— xvi. 15.
—— xviii. 14.
Acts xiii. 39 twice.
Rom. ii. 13.
—— iii. 4, 20, 24, 28, 30.
—— iv. 2, 5.
—— v. 1, 9.
Rom. vi. 7, marg. (text, *free.*)
—— viii. 30 twice, 33.
1 Cor. iv. 4.
—— vi. 11.
Gal. ii. 16 3 times, 17.
—— iii. 8, 11, 24.
—— v. 4.
1 Tim. iii 16.
Tit. iii. 7.
Jas. ii. 21, 24, 25.

JUSTLY.

δικαίως, justly, rightly, with strict justice.

Luke xxiii. 41. | 1 Thes. ii. 10.

K

KEEP (-EST, -ETH, -ING, KEPT.)

1. τηρέω, to watch over, take care of, keep an eye upon, observe attentively.

2. διατηρέω, (*No.* 1, *with* διά, through, *prefixed,*) to have one's eye upon throughout, to watch carefully, keep with care, (*non occ.*)

3. συντηρέω, (*No.* 1, *with* σύν, together with, *prefixed,*) to have one's eye upon in conjunction *or* with *any one,* to watch, keep together with *any one.*

4. φυλάσσω, to watch, be sleepless, *esp.,* to keep watch and ward *by night;* to watch, guard, defend. *Then, metaph.,* to preserve, maintain.

   (a) *Mid.,* to keep one's self from *or* as to *anything,* to be on one's guard, watch one's self.

5. διαφυλάσσω, (*No.* 4, *with* διά, through, *prefixed,*) to guard through, watch over, protect thoroughly, (*non occ.*)

6. φρουρέω, to guard, keep with a military guard, to keep *or* guard *with power, rather than with the eye, as Nos.* 1 & 4.

7. *ποιέω*, to make, *as with any external act;* to do, *expressing an action as continued, hence*, to perform, fulfil.

8. *ἔχω*, to have and hold.

9. *κατέχω*, (*No.* 8, *with κατά*, down, *prefixed,*) to have and hold fast, to hold firmly.

10. *παρέχω*, (*No.* 8, *with παρά*, beside, *prefixed,*) to hold near *or* towards *anything*, to offer.

11. *ἄγω*, to lead, conduct, bring. *Of time*, to pass, to spend, *then*, occur; *of a feast*, to hold, celebrate.

12. *βόσκω*, to pasture, to tend while grazing.

13. { *κατάκειμαι*, to lie down, *ἐπί*, upon, } lie prostrate upon.

14. *κρατέω*, to be strong, mighty, powerful; to hold fast, not to let go.

15. *πράσσω*, to do repeatedly, habitually; *hence*, to practice.

12. Matt. viii. 33.
— —— xiii. 35, see Secret.
11. —— xiv. 6 (*γίνομαι*, to *occur*, G ∾ L T Tr A [ℵ.)
1. —— xix. 17.
4a. ——— 20.
7. —— xxvi. 18.
— Mark iv. 22, see Secret.
3. ——— vi. 20, marg. (text, *observe.*)
1. —— vii. 9 (*ἵστημι*, *stand*, G ∾)
14. —— ix. 10.
4. Luke ii. 8.
3. ——— 19.
2. ——— 51.
5. —— iv. 10.
9. —— viii. 15.
4. ——— 29.
— —— ix. 36, see Close.
4. —— xi. 21, 28.
4a. —— xviii. 21.
8. —— xix. 20.
— ——— 43, see K from.
1. John ii. 10.
7. —— vii. 19.
1. —— viii. 51, 52, 55.
1. —— ix. 16.
1. —— xii. 7.
4. ——— 25.
1. —— xiv. 15, 21, 23, 24.
1. —— xv. 10 twice, 20 twice
1. —— xvii. 6, 11, 12 1st.
4. ——— 12 2nd.
1. ——— 15.
— —— xviii. 16, 17, see Door.
— Acts v. 2, 3, see K back.
4. —— vii. 53.
13. —— ix. 33.
— —— x. 28, see Company.
4. —— xii. 4.
1. Acts xii. 5, 6.
— —— xv. 12, see Silence.
1. ——— 5, 24 (*ap.*)
2. ——— 29, part.
4. —— xvi. 4.
1. ——— 23.
7. —— xviii. 21 (*ap.*)
— —— xix. 38, see K (be)
— —— xx. 20, see K back.
4. —— xxi. 24.
— ——— 25, see K one's [self.
10. —— xxii. 2.
4. ——— 20.
4. —— xxiii. 35.
1. —— xxiv. 23.
1. —— xxv. 4, 21.
— —— xxvii. 43, see K from.
4. —— xxviii. 16.
15. Rom. ii. 25.
4. ——— 26.
— —— xvi. 25, see Secret.
— 1 Cor. v. 8, see Feast.
— ——— 11, see Company.
1. —— vii. 37.
— —— ix. 27, see *court-days.*
9. —— xi. 2.
— —— xiv. 28, 34, see Silence.
— —— xv. 2, see K in memory.
1. 2 Cor. xi. 9 twice.
— ——— 32, see Garrison.
6. Gal. iii. 23.
4. —— vi. 13.
1. Ephes. iv. 3
6. Phil. iv. 7.
4. 2 Thes. iii. 3.
1. 1 Tim. v. 22.
1. —— vi. 14.
4. 1 Tim. vi. 20.
4. 2 Tim. i. 12, 14.
1. —— iv. 7.
— Heb. iv. 9, see Sabbath.
7. —— xi. 28.
1. Jas. i. 27.
1. —— ii. 10.
— —— v. 4, see Fraud.
6. 1 Pet. i. 5.
— 2 Pet. iii. 7, see Store
1. 1 John ii. 3, 4, 5.
4. —— v. 21.
1. 1 John iii. 22, 24.
1. —— v. 2 (No. 7, G ∾ L T Tr A.)
1. ——— 3, 18.
1. Jude 6, 21.
— ——— 24, see Falling.
1. Rev. i. 3.
1. —— ii. 26.
1. —— iii. 8, 10 twice.
1. —— xii. 17.
1. —— xiv. 12.
1. —— xvi. 15.
1. —— xxii. 7, 9.

KEEP BACK.

1. *νοσφίζω*, to put apart. *In N.T. mid.*, to put apart for one's self, embezzle, (*occ.* Tit. ii. 10.)

2. *ὑποστέλλω*, to send *or* draw under; to shrink or draw back; to keep back, suppress, *from timidity, or clandestinely.*

1. Acts v. 2, 3. | 2. Acts xx. 20.

KEEP FROM.

κωλύω, to cut off, weaken, *and hence gen.*, to hinder, prevent, restrain.

Acts xxvii. 43.

KEEP IN.

συνέχω, to hold *or* press together; shut up, *esp., of a city besieged.*

Luke xix. 43.

KEEP IN MEMORY.

κατέχω, (*see above, No.* 9.)

1 Cor. xv. 2, marg. *hold fast.*

KEEP ONE'S SELF.

φυλάσσω, (*see above, No.* 4.)

Acts xxi. 25.

KEEP UNDER.

ὑπωπιάζω, to strike under the eyes, hit and beat the face black and blue, (*Eng.*, give a black eye), (*occ.* Luke xviii. 5.)

1 Cor. ix. 27 (*ὑποπιάζω, to beat under, suppress*, G ∾)

KEEPER.

1. *φύλαξ*, (*noun, from* "KEEP," *No.* 4,) a watcher, keeper, guard, (*non occ.*)

2. τηρέω, (*see* "KEEP," No. 1,) (*here, participle.*)

2. Matt. xxviii. 4.
1. Acts v. 23.
1. —— xii. 6, 19.
— Acts xvi. 27, 36, see Prison.
— Titus ii. 5, see Home.

KEEPING [noun.]

τήρησις, a watching, keeping, (*occ.* Acts iv. 3, v. 18.)

1 Cor. vii. 19. | 1 Pet. iv. 19, see Commit.

KEY (-s.)

κλείς, a key for locking and unlocking, (*non occ.*)

Matt. xvi. 19.
Luke xi. 52.
Rev. i. 18.
Rev. iii. 7.
—— ix. 1.
—— xx. 1.

KICK [verb.]

λακτίζω, to kick with the heel or foot. (*The word used in the proverb common among Greek authors*, to kick *against the pricks*,) (*non occ.*)

Acts ix. 5 (*ap.*) | Acts xxvi. 14.

KID.

ἔριφος, a young goat, (*occ.* Matt. xxv. 32.)

Luke xv. 29.

KILL (-ED, -EST, -ETH, -ING.)

1. ἀποκτεινω, (*stronger form of* κτείνω, to kill, slay), to kill outright. *Of judges*, to condemn to death; *of the executioner*, to put to death; *i.e.* to put an end to life.

2. ἀναιρέω, to take up, take up and carry off; *then*, to make away with; *of men*, to kill.

3. θύω, to sacrifice, to kill and offer in sacrifice, *or* to kill *animals* for a feast.

4. φονεύω, to murder, (*occ.* Matt. xix. 18, xxiii. 35.)

5. θανατόω, to cause to die, put to death.

6. διαχειρίζομαι, to lay hands upon.

7. σφάζω, (or σφαττω), to slay by violence, slaughter, butcher; *used of slaying by cutting the throat.*

4. Matt. v. 21 twice.
1. —— x. 28 twice.
1. —— xvi. 21.
1. —— xvii. 23.
1. —— xxi. 35, 38.
3. —— xxii. 4.
4. —— xxiii. 31.
1. —— 34, 37.
1. —— xxiv. 9.
1. —— xxvi. 4.
1. Mark iii. 4.
1. —— vi. 19.
1. —— viii. 31.
1. —— ix. 31 1st, 31 2nd (part.)
4. —— x. 19 (om. G →)
1. —— 34.
1. —— xii. 5 twice, 7, 8.
3. —— xiv. 12 marg. *sacrifice.*
1. Luke xi. 47, 48.
1. —— xii. 4, 5.
1. —— xiii. 31, 34.
3. —— xv. 23, 27, 30.
4. —— xviii. 20.
1. —— xx. 14, 15.
2. —— xxii. 2.
1. John v. 18.
1. —— vii. 1, 19, 20, 25.
1. John viii. 22, 37, 40.
3. —— x. 10.
1. —— xvi. 2.
1. Acts iii. 15.
2. —— vii. 28 twice.
2. —— ix. 23, 24.
3. —— x. 13.
2. —— xii. 2.
2. —— xvi. 27.
1. —— xxi. 31.
1. —— xxiii. 12.
2. —— 15, 21, 27.
2. —— xxv. 3.
6. —— xxvi. 21.
5. Rom. viii. 36.
1. —— xi. 3.
4. —— xiii. 9.
1. 2 Cor. iii. 6.
5. —— vi. 9.
1. 1 Thes. ii. 15.
4. Jas. ii. 11 twice.
4. —— iv. 2.
4. —— v. 6.
1. Rev. ii. 23.
7. —— vi. 4.
1. —— 8, 11.
1. —— ix. 5, 18, 20.
1. —— xi. 5, 7.
1. —— xiii. 10 twice, 15.

KIN.

συγγενής, born with, *hence*, of the same stock, kindred.

Mark vi. 4 (συγγενεῦσιν, *kinsfolk*, T Tr.)

KIND [noun.]

1. γένος, race, descent; class, sort, genus, (*as opp. to* εἶδος, species.)

2. φύσις, physis, nature; *then*, a nature *as generated or produced*, a kind.

1. Matt. xiii. 47.
1. —— xvii. 21 (*ap.*)
1. Mark ix. 29.
1. 1 Cor. xii. 10.
1. Cor. xii. 28, marg. (text, *diversity.*)
1. —— xiv. 10.
— Jas. i. 18, see K of (A)
2. Jas. iii. 7, marg. *nature.*

KIND OF (A)

τις, one, some, a certain; *with a noun*, a kind of, a sort of.

Jas. i. 18.

KIND [adj.]

χρηστός, good, gentle, benevolent, benign; actively beneficent in spite of ingratitude.

Luke vi. 35. | Eph. iv. 32.

KIND (BE)

χρηστεύομαι, to show one's self χρηστος, (*see above*,) to be gentle, benign, (*non occ.*)

1 Cor. xiii. 4.

KINDLE (-ETH.)

1. ἅπτω, to put one thing to another; *hence, spoken of fire as* applied *to things*, to put fire to.

2. ἀνάπτω, (*No.* 1, *with* ἀνά, up, *prefixed*,) to light up, fire up, kindle, (*non occ.*)

2. Luke xii. 49.
1. — xxii. 55, part, (*περιάπτω, to light a fire all round*, T Tr A ℵ.)
2. Acts xxviii. 2, (No. 1, L Tr A ℵ.)
2. Jas. iii. 5.

KINDLY.

See, AFFECTIONED.

KINDNESS.

1. χρηστότης, benevolence, benignity; that sweetness of disposition, active beneficence in spite of ingratitude.

2. φιλανθρωπία, love of man, philanthropy, (*occ.* Tit. iii. 4.)

3. εὐσεβέω, to be pious towards anyone.

2. Acts xxviii. 2.
1. 2 Cor. vi. 6.
1. Eph. ii. 7.
1. Col. iii. 12.
3. 1 Tim. v. 4, marg. (text, *show piety*.)
1. Tit. iii. 4.
— 2 Pet. i. 7, see Brotherly [K.

KINDRED.

1. φυλή, a union of individuals into a community *or* state, *hence*, a union formed among citizens, a class *or* tribe, (*elsewhere translated* tribe.)

2. συγγένεια, sameness of stock, descent *or* family relationship, kinsfolk.

3. γένος, genus, race, descent, family, kindred.

4. πατριά, paternal descent, lineage; family, (*occ.* Luke ii. 4; Eph. iii. 15.)

5. οἰκεῖος, belonging to the house, domestic.

2. Luke i. 61.
4. Acts iii. 25.
3. — iv. 6.
2. — vii. 3.
3. — 13.
2. — 14.
3. — 19.
5. 1 Tim. v. 8, marg. (text, *of one's own house*.)
1. Rev. i. 7.
1. — v. 9.
1. — vii. 9.
1. — xi. 9.
1. — xiii. 7.
1. Rev. xiv. 6.

KING.

1. βασιλεύς, King, he who rules over the people, and is in possession of a dominion. *Used in the N.T. of kings of the earth.* * When used of God or Christ.

[As Messiah, Jesus is designated βασιλεύς, He was *prophesied* of as K. in the *O.T.*; *promised* as K. in the *N.T.*, Luke i. 32, 33; *came* as K., Matt. ii. 2; *rejected* as K., Luke xix. 14, (*cf.* Gen. xxxvii. 8, and Exod. ii. 14); *died* as K., Matt. xxvii. 37, etc. *Now* the King is ***hidden*** but will soon be ***revealed*** to fulfil the *O.T.* prophecies, and Luke i. 32, 33.]

2. βασιλεύω, to be king, to rule, to have kingship; *here, part.* τῶν βασιλευόντων, of those who are kings.

1. Matt. i. 6 1st.
1. — 6 2nd (*om.* L T Tr A ℵ.)
1. — ii. 1.
1*. — 2.
1. — 3, 9.
1*. — v. 35.
1. — x. 18.
1. — xi. 8 (βασίλειος, *royal*, G ∾)
1. — xiv. 9.
1. — xvii. 25.
1. — xviii. 23.
1*. — xxi. 5.
1. — xxii. 2, 7, 11, 13.
1*. — xxv. 34, 40.
1*. — xxvii. 11, 29, 37, 42.
1. Mark vi. 14, 22, 25, 26, 27.
1. — xiii. 9.
1*. — xv. 2, 9, 12, 18, 26, 32.
1. Luke i. 5.
— — vii. 35, see K.'s court.
1. — x. 24.
1. — xiv. 31 twice.
1*. — xix. 38.
1. — xxi. 12.
1. — xxii. 25.
1*. — xxiii. 2, 3, 37, 38.
1*. John i. 49.
1. — vi. 15.
1*. — xii. 13, 15.
1*. — xviii. 33, 37 twice, 39.
1*. — xix. 3.
1. — 12.
1*. — 14, 15 1st.
1. — 15 2nd.
1*. John xix. 19, 21 twice.
1. Acts iv. 26.
1. — vii. 10, 18.
1. — ix. 15.
1. — xii. 1, 20 1st.
— — 20 2nd, see K.'s country.
1. — xiii. 21, 22.
1*. — xvii. 7.
1. — xxv. 13, 14, 24, 26.
1. — xxvi. 2, 7, 13, 19, 26, 27, 30.
1. 2 Cor. xi. 32.
1*. 1 Tim. i. 17.
1. — ii. 2.
1*. — vi. 15 1st.
2. — 15 2nd.
1. Heb. vii. 1 twice.
1*. — 2 3 times.
1. — xi. 23, 27.
1. 1 Pet. ii. 13, 17.
1. Rev. i. 5.
1. — 6 (βασιλεία, *a kingdom*, instead of βασιλεῖς και, *Kings and* G L T Tr A ℵ.)
1. — v. 10 (βασιλεία, *a kingdom*, G∾L T Tr A ℵ.)
1. — vi. 15.
1. — ix. 11.
1. — x. 11.
1. — xvi. 12, 14.
1*. — xv. 3.
1. — xvii. 2, 10, 12 twice.
1*. — 14 1st.
1. — 14 2nd, 18.
1. — xviii. 3, 9.
1*. — xix. 16 1st.
1. — 16 2nd, 18, 19.
1. — xxi. 24.

KING'S COUNTRY.

βασιλικός, belonging to a king, the king's.

Acts xii. 20.

KING'S COURT.

βασίλειος, royal, belonging to *or* destined and suitable for the king, (*occ.* 1 Pet. ii. 9.)

Luke vii. 25, with art.

KINGDOM (-s.)

βασιλεία, the royal dominion, including the power and form of government, with the territory and the kingdom.

[The following important expressions are to be carefully distinguished:

(a) *βασιλεία τοῦ θεοῦ*, *the kingdom of God*, the sphere of God's rule, as being then present among the Jews in the person of Christ (Luke xi. 20, xvii. 21, marg.). *Then*, the sphere of Christ's workings; *now* the sphere of the Holy Ghost's workings (Rom. xiv. 17, 1 Cor. iv. 20.)

(b) *βασιλεία τῶν οὐρανῶν*, *the kingdom of the heavens*, as being the development of God's purpose. The kingdom to be introduced by the Messiah. The time when God's will shall be "done on earth as *it* is *in* heaven." *Then*, it was at hand; *now* it is in abeyance (Luke xix. 12-15.)

(c) *βασιλεία τοῦ Πατρός*, *the kingdom of the Father*. This seems to be for the heavenly people, while "the kingdom of the Son of Man" is for the earthly (Dan. vii. 13, 14; Matt. xxv. 31-46; Luke xxi. 36), and the two together form the heavenly and earthly aspect of the "world kingdom of our Lord and of His Christ," Rev. xi. 15. The one the sphere of the Father's glory, the other of the Son's rule. Will both cease or change when He "delivers up the kingdom to God, even the Father"? (1 Cor. xv. 24.)

(d) *ἡ βασιλεία τοῦ υἱοῦ τῆς ἀγάπης αὐτοῦ*, *the kingdom of the Son of His love*. The region of blessing of which Christ is the centre, **and into which all who are united to Him by faith are now translated. It involves the thought of position, as (e) does of display.**

(e) *ἡ αἰωνία βασιλεία τοῦ Κυρίου ἡμῶν καὶ σωτῆρος Ἰησοῦ Χριστοῦ*, ***the eternal kingdom of our Lord and Saviour Jesus Christ***, as distinguished from His earthly milenial kingdom. (d) is now present, (e) is still before us, into which they that are Christ's shall have an "abundant entrance."]

b. Matt. iii. 2.
—— iv. 8.
b. —— 17.
—— 23.
b. —— v. 3, 10, 19 twice, 20.
—— vi. 10.
—— 13 (ap.)
a. —— 33.
b. —— vii. 21.
b. —— viii. 11.
—— 12.
—— ix. 35.
b. —— x. 7.
b. —— xi. 11, 12.
—— xii. 25, 26.
a. —— 28.
b. —— xiii. 11.
—— 19.
b. —— 24, 31, 33.
—— 38, 41.
c. —— 43.
b. —— 44, 45, 47, 52.
b. —— xvi. 19.
—— 28.
b. —— xviii. 1, 3, 4, 23.
b. —— xix. 12, 14, 23.
a. —— 24 (b, L T Tr A.)
b. —— xx. 1.
—— 21.
a. —— xxi. 31, 43.
b. —— xxii. 2.
b. —— xxiii. 13.
—— xxiv. 7 twice, 14.
b. —— xxv. 1.
—— 34.
c. —— xxvi. 29.
a. Mark i. 14 (*om. τῆς βασιλείας, of the Kingdom*, G⇄L[b] T Tr A ℵ.)
a. —— 15.
—— iii. 24 twice.
a. —— iv. 11, 26, 30.
—— vi. 23.
a. —— ix. 1, 47.
a. —— x. 14, 15, 23, 24, 25.
—— xi. 10.
a. —— xii. 34.
—— xiii. 8 twice.
a. —— xiv. 25.
a. —— xv. 43.
Luke i. 33.
—— iv. 5.
a. —— 43.
a. Luke vi. 20.
a. —— vii. 28.
a. —— viii. 1, 10.
a. —— ix. 2, 11, 27, 60, 62.
a. —— x. 9, 11.
—— xi. 2, 17, 18.
a. —— 20.
a. —— xii. 31.
—— 32.
a. —— xiii. 18, 20, 28, 29.
a. —— xiv. 15.
a. —— xvi. 16.
a. —— xvii. 20 twice, 21.
a. —— xviii. 16, 17, 24, 25, 29.
a. —— xix. 11.
—— 12, 15.
—— xxi. 10 twice.
a. —— 31.
a. —— xxii. 16, 18.
—— 29, 30.
—— xxiii. 42.
a. —— 51.
a. John iii. 3, 5.
—— xviii. 36 3 times.
a. Acts i. 3.
—— 6.
a. —— viii. 12.
a. —— xiv. 22.
a. —— xix. 8.
a. —— xx. 25.
a. —— xxviii. 23, 31.
a. Rom. xiv. 17.
a. 1 Cor. iv. 20.
a. —— vi. 9, 10.
a. —— xv. 24, 50.
a. Gal. v. 21.
Eph. v. 5.
d. Col. i. 13.
a. —— iv. 11.
1 Thes. ii. 12.
a. 2 Thes. i. 5.
2 Tim. iv. 1, 18.
Heb. i. 8.
—— xi. 33.
—— xii. 28.
Jas. ii. 5.
e. 2 Pet. i. 11.
Rev. i. 9.
—— xi. 15.
a. —— xii. 10.
—— xvi. 10.
—— xvii. 12, 17.

KINSFOLK (-s.)

συγγενής, born with, *hence*, kin, kindred, related; *as subst.*, a kinsman, relative.

Luke ii. 44, pl. | Luke xxi. 16. pl.

KINSMAN, KINSMEN.

συγγενής, see above.

Mark iii. 21, marg. (text, *one's friends.*)
Luke xiv. 12 (*ap.*)
John xviii. 26.
Acts x. 24.
Rom. ix. 3.
Rom. xvi. 7, 11, 21.

KISS [noun.]

φίλημα, a love-token, *esp., as given in salutation, hence*, a kiss, (*non occ.*)

Luke vii. 45.
—— xxii. 48.
Rom. xvi. 16.
1 Cor. xvi. 20.
2 Cor. xiii. 12.
1 Thes. v. 26.
1 Peter v. 14.

KISS (-ED.) [verb.]

1. φιλέω, to love, (*used of the* passion of love), to show one's love, *hence*, to kiss, (*elsewhere*, "LOVE.")

2. καταφιλέω, (*No.* 1, *with* κατά, down, *prefixed*) to love tenderly, *hence*, to kiss warmly, (*stronger than No.* 1) (*non occ.*)

1. Matt. xxvi. 48.
2. —— 49.
1. Mark xiv. 44.
2. —— 45.
2. Luke vii. 38, 35.
2. —— xv. 20.
1. —— xxii. 47.
2. Acts xx. 37.

KNEE.

γόνυ, the knee,

* *quoted from* Isa. xlv. 23.

Matt. xxvii. 29, see K (bow the)
Mark xv. 19.
Luke v. 8.
Rom. xi. 4*.
—— xiv. 11*.
Eph. iii. 14.
Phil. ii. 10*.
Heb. xii. 12.

KNEE (BOW THE)

γονυπετέω, to fall upon one's knees.

Matt. xxvii. 29.

KNEEL.

τίθημι, to place, τὰ, the, γόνατα, knees, } *i.e.* to kneel down.

Matt. xvii. 14, } see K
Mark i. 40, } down to.
—— x. 17, see K to.
Luke xxii. 41.
Acts vii. 60.
—— ix. 40.
—— xx. 36.
—— xxi. 5.

KNEEL DOWN TO.

γονυπετέω, to fall upon one's knees.

Matt. xvii. 14.
Mark i. 40, (*om.* L T Tr[b] A[b].)

KNEEL TO.

γονυπετέω, see above.

Mark x. 17.

KNIT.

δέω, to bind, to bind together *or* to *anything*, to bind around, to fasten.

Acts x. 11 (*om.* G ⇉ L T Tr A[b] א.) *lit.*, "*let down by four cords.*"

KNIT TOGETHER.

συμβιβάζω, to make come together, *i.e.* to join or knit together, unite.

Col. ii. 2, 19.

KNOCK (-ED, -ETH, -ING.)

κρούω, to knock, to rap, *as at a door for entrance*, (*non occ.*)

Matt. vii. 7, 8.
Luke xi. 9, 10.
—— xii. 36.
Luke xiii. 25.
Acts xii. 13, part, 16.
Rev. iii. 20.

KNOW (-EST, -ETH, -ING; KNEW, -EST.)

1. οἶδα, (*perf. of obsolete root* εἴδω, *like Lat.*, video; *Germ.*, wiss-en; *Eng.*, wit *or* wot. The verb ὁράω *is used as present*, εἶδον *serves as aorist, and* οἶδα *as perfect*,) *lit.*, I have perceived, *or* seen, *hence*, to have knowledge of, to know. *No.* 2 *implies an active relation, and self-reference of the knower to the object of knowledge, while No.* 1 *implies that the subject has simply come within the knower's sphere of perception or circle of vision: hence the force of* οὐκ οἶδα ὑμᾶς, (Matt. xxv. 12,) "you stand in no relation to me." *In profane Greek, it denotes* mediate knowledge, *e.g.* from hearsay.

2. γινώσκω, to perceive, observe, obtain a knowledge of *or* insight into. *It denotes* a personal and true relation between the person knowing and the object known, *i.e.* to be influenced by one's knowledge of the object, to suffer one's self to be determined thereby: *hence the force of* οὐδέποτε ἔγνων ὑμᾶς, (Matt. vii. 23,) "I have never had a true and personal connection with you," (*cf.* verses 21, 22.)

3. ἐπιγινώσκω, (*No.* 2, *with* ἐπί, upon, *prefixed*) to know thereupon, *i.e. by looking on as a spectator*, to give heed, to notice attentively, to know fully *or* well. *It implies a more special* recognition *of the thing known than No.* 2.

4. προγινώσκω, (*No.* 2, *with* πρό, before, *prefixed*) to perceive *or* apprehend beforehand, to know previously, to foreknow.

5. { γνωστόν, known, / ἐστίν, it is, / ἡμῖν, to us, } it is known to us.

6. ἐπίσταμαι, to fix one's mind upon, *i.e.* to understand, to know how to do *anything*, to know well, to have knowledge.

2. Matt. i. 25.
2. —— vi. 3.
1. ——— 8, 32.
1. —— vii. 11.
3. ——— 16, 20.
2. ——— 23.
1. —— ix. 6.
2. ——— 30.
2. —— x. 26.
2. —— xi. 27 twice.
2. —— xii. 7, 15, part.
— ——— 16, see Known.
1. ——— 25.
2. ——— 33.
2. —— xiii. 11.
1. —— xv. 12.
3. —— xvii. 12.
1. —— xx. 22, 25.
1. —— xxii. 16, 29.
2. —— xxiv. 32, 33.
1. ——— 36.
2. ——— 39.
1. ——— 42.
2. ——— 43 1st.
1. ——— 43 2nd.
1. —— xxv. 12, 13.
2. ——— 24.
1. ——— 26.
1. —— xxvi. 2, 70, 72, 74.
1. —— xxvii. 18.
1. —— xxviii. 5.
1. Mark i. 24, 34.
1. —— ii. 10.
— —— iii. 12, see Known.
2. —— iv. 11 (*om.* G ⇉ L T Tr A ℵ, lit., "has been granted.")
1. ——— 13 1st.
2. ——— 13 2nd.
1. ——— 27.
3. —— v. 30.
1. ——— 33.
2. ——— 43.
1. —— vi. 20.
3. ——— 33 (No. 1, L Tr A*.)
2. ——— 38, part.
2. —— vii. 24.
2. —— viii. 17.
2. —— ix. 30.
1. —— x. 19, 38, 42.
2. —— xii. 12.
1. ——— 14.
1. ——— 15 (εἶδον, to see, G ~ T ℵ.)
1. ——— 24, part.
2. —— xiii. 28, 29.
1. Mark xiii. 32, 33, 35.
1. —— xiv. 68, 71.
2. —— xv. 10, 45, part.
3. Luke i. 4.
2. ——— 18, 34.
— —— ii. 15, see Known.
— ——— 17, see Known abroad (make)
2. ——— 43.
1. —— iv. 34, 41.
1. —— v. 24.
1. —— vi. 8.
2. ——— 44.
3. —— vii. 37, part.
2. ——— 39.
2. —— viii. 10, 17.
1. ——— 53.
2. —— ix. 11.
1. ——— 33, 55 (*ap.*)
2. —— x. 22.
1. —— xi. 13, 17.
2. —— xii. 2.
1. ——— 30.
2. ——— 39 1st.
1. ——— 39 2nd.
2. ——— 47, 48.
1. —— xiii. 25, 27.
2. —— xvi. 15.
1. —— xviii. 20.
2. ——— 34.
1. —— xix. 22.
1. —— xx. 21.
2. —— xxi. 20, 30, 31.
1. —— xxii. 34, 57, 60.
3. —— xxiii. 7, part.
1. ——— 34 (*ap.*)
3. —— xxiv. 16.
2. ——— 18.
3. ——— 31.
2. ——— 35.
2. John i. 10.
1. ——— 26, 31, 33.
2. ——— 48.
1. —— ii. 9 twice.
2. ——— 24, 25.
1. —— iii. 2.
2. ——— 10.
1. ——— 11.
2. —— iv. 1.
1. ——— 10, 22 twice, 25.
— ——— 32, see K of.
1. ——— 42.
2. ——— 53.
2. —— v. 6.
1. ——— 32.
2. ——— 42.
1. —— vi. 6, 42, 61, part, 64.
1. John vii. 15.
2. ——— 17, 26.
1. ——— 27 1st.
2. ——— 27 2nd.
1. ——— 28 3 times, 29.
2. ——— 49, 51.
1. —— viii. 14, 19 3 times.
2. ——— 28, 32.
1. ——— 37.
2. ——— 52, 55 1st.
1. ——— 55 2nd, 3rd, & 4th.
1. —— ix. 12, 20, 21 twice, 24, 25 twice, 29 twice, 30, 31.
1. —— x. 4, 5.
2. ——— 14 twice, 15 twice, 27, 38.
1. —— xi. 22, 24, 42, 49.
2. ——— 57.
2. —— xii. 9.
1. ——— 35, 50.
1. —— xiii. 1, part, 3, 7 1st.
2. ——— 7 2nd.
1. ——— 11.
2. ——— 12.
1. ——— 17, 18.
2. ——— 28, 35.
1. —— xiv. 4 1st.
1. ——— 4 2nd (*om.* L^b T Tr A ℵ.)
1. ——— 5 twice.
2. ——— 7 1st.
2. ——— 7 2nd (No. 1, Tr A.)
2. ——— 7 3rd, 9, 17 twice, 20, 31.
1. —— xv. 15 1st.
— ——— 15 2nd, see Known (make)
2. ——— 18.
1. ——— 21.
2. —— xvi. 3, 19.
1. ——— 30.
1. —— xvii. 2.
2. ——— 3.
1. ——— 4.
2. ——— 7.
2. ——— 8 (*om.* L^b ℵ.)
1. ——— 21.
2. ——— 23, 25 3 times.
— —— xviii. 15, 16, see Known.
2. —— xix. 4.
1. ——— 10.
1. ——— 28 (εἶδον, *to see*, G.)
1. ——— 35.
1. —— xx. 2, 9, 13, 14.
1. —— xxi. 4, 12, 15, 16, 17 1st.
2. ——— 17 2nd.
1. ——— 24.
2. Acts i. 7.
— ——— 19, see Known.
— ——— 24, see Hearts.
— —— ii. 14, see Known.
1. ——— 22.
— ——— 28, see Known (make)
1. ——— 30.
2. ——— 36.
3. —— iii. 10.
1. ——— 16.
— —— iv. 10, see Known.
1. —— v. 7.
— —— vii. 13 twice, see Known (be made)
1. ——— 18.
2. —— ix. 24.
3. ——— 30.
— ——— 42, see Known.
2. —— x. 28.
1. ——— 37.
1. —— xii. 11.
3. ——— 14 part.
— —— xiii. 27, see K not.
— ——— 38, see Known.
6. —— xv. 7.
— Acts xv. 8, see Hearts.
— ——— 18, see Known.
1. —— xvi. 3.
2. —— xvii. 19, 20.
6. —— xviii. 25.
2. —— xix. 15 1st.
6. ——— 15 2nd.
— ——— 17, see Known.
6. ——— 25.
1. ——— 32.
3. ——— 34, part.
2. ——— 35.
6. —— xx. 18.
1. ——— 22, 25, 29.
2. ——— 34.
2. —— xxi. 24, 34.
2. —— xxii. 14.
6. ——— 19.
3. ——— 24, 29, part.
2. ——— 30.
2. —— xxiii. 28 (No. 3, L T Tr A ℵ.)
6. —— xxiv. 10, part.
— ——— 22, see K to the uttermost.
3. —— xxv. 10.
1. —— xxvi. 3, part, 4.
4. ——— 5 (with ἄνωθεν, *from the first.*)
6. ——— 26.
1. ——— 27.
3. —— xxvii. 39.
3. ——— xxviii. 1.
5. ——— 22.
— ——— 28, see Known.
— Rom. i. 19, see Known (that which may be)
2. ——— 21.
3. ——— 32.
— —— ii. 4, see K not.
2. ——— 18.
2. —— iii. 17.
1. ——— 19.
1. —— v. 3.
— —— vi. 3, see K not.
2. ——— 6.
1. ——— 9, 16.
— —— vii. 1 1st, see K not.
2. ——— 1 2nd, 7 1st.
1. —— 7 2nd, 14, 18.
1. —— viii. 22, 26, 27, 28.
— —— ix. 22, } see Known
— ——— 23, } (make)
2. —— x. 19.
2. —— xi. 34.
1. —— xiii. 11.
1. —— xiv. 14.
— —— xvi. 26, see Known (make)
1. 1 Cor. i. 16.
2. ——— 21.
1. —— ii. 2.
2. ——— 8 twice.
1. ——— 11 1st.
1. ——— 11 2nd (No. 2, G ~ L T Tr A ℵ.)
1. ——— 12.
2. ——— 14, 16.
1. —— iii. 16.
2. ——— 20.
— —— iv. 4, see K by.
2. ——— 19.
1. —— v. 6.
1. —— vi. 2, 3, 9, 15, 16, [19.
1. —— vii. 16 twice.
1. —— viii. 1.
1. ——— 2 1st (No. 2, L T Tr A ℵ.)
2. ——— 2 3rd & 4th, 3.
1. ——— 4.
1. —— ix. 13, 24.
1. —— xi. 3.
1. —— xii. 2.
2. —— xiii. 9, 12 1st.
3. ——— 12 2nd & 3rd.
2. —— xiv. 7, 9.
1. ——— 11.
1. —— xv. 58 part.

1\. 1 Cor. xvi. 15.
1\. 2 Cor. i. 7.
2\. —— ii. 4, 9.
2\. —— iii. 2.
1\. —— iv. 14.
1\. —— v. 1, 6, 11, 16 1st.
2\. ——— 16 2nd & 3rd, 21.
— —— vi. 9, see K well.
2\. —— viii. 9.
1\. —— ix. 2.
1\. —— xi. 11, 31.
1\. —— xii. 2 twice, 3 twice.
3\. —— xiii. 5.
2\. ——— 6.
1\. Gal. ii. 16.
2\. —— iii. 7.
1\. —— iv. 8, part.
2\. ——— 9 1st, part, 9 2nd.
1\. ——— 13.
— Eph. i. 9, see Known (make)
1\. ——— 18.
— —— iii. 3, 5, 9, see Known (make)
2\. ——— 19.
2\. —— v. 5 (*ἴστε γινώσκοντες, ye know—taking note,* instead of *ἐστέ γινώσκοντες, ye are knowing,* G L T Tr A ℵ.)
1\. —— vi. 8, 9.
— ——— 19, see Known (make)
1\. ——— 21 1st.
— ——— 21 2nd, see Known (make)
2\. ——— 21.
1\. Phil. i. 17, 19, 25.
2\. —— ii. 19, part, 22.
2\. —— iii. 10.
2\. —— iv. 5.
— ——— 6, see Known (make)
1\. ——— 12 twice, 15.
3\. Col. i. 6.
— ——— 27, see Known (make)
1\. —— ii. 1.
1\. —— iii. 24.
1\. —— iv. 1, 6.
2\. ——— 8.
— ——— 9, see Known (make)
1\. 1 Thes. i. 4, 5.
1\. —— ii. 1, 2, 5, 11.
1\. —— iii. 3, 4.
2\. ——— 5.
1\. —— iv. 2, 4, 5.
1\. —— v. 2, 12.
1\. 2 Thes. i. 8.
1\. —— ii. 6.
1\. —— iii. 7.
1\. 1 Tim. i. 8, 9.
1\. —— iii. 5, 15.
3\. —— iv. 3.
6\. —— vi. 4.
1\. 2 Tim. i. 12, 15.
2\. ——— 18.
2\. —— ii. 19.
1\. 2 Tim. ii. 23.
2\. —— iii. 1.
— ——— 10, see K fully.
1\. ——— 14, 15.
— —— iv. 17, see Known (be fully)
1\. Titus i. 16.
1\. —— iii. 11.
1\. Philem. 21.
2\. Heb. iii. 10.
2\. —— viii. 11 1st.
1\. ——— 11 2nd.
1\. —— x. 30.
2\. ——— 34.
6\. —— xi. 8.
1\. —— xii. 17.
2\. —— xiii. 23.
2\. Jas. i. 3.
2\. —— ii. 20.
1\. —— iii. 1.
1\. —— iv. 4.
6\. ——— 14.
1\. ——— 17.
2\. —— v. 20.
1\. 1 Pet. i. 18, part.
1\. —— iii. 9 (*ὅτι, because,* instead of *εἰδότες ὅτι, knowing that,* G ⇉ L T Tr A ℵ.)
1\. —— v. 9.
1\. 2 Pet. i. 12, 14.
— ——— 16, see Known (make)
2\. ——— 20.
1\. —— ii. 9.
2\. —— iii. 3.
— ——— 17, see K before.
2\. 1 John ii. 3 twice, 4, 5.
1\. ——— 11.
2\. ——— 13 twice, 14, 18.
1\. ——— 20, 21 twice, 29 1st.
2\. ——— 29 2nd.
2\. —— iii. 1 twice.
1\. ——— 2, 5.
2\. ——— 6.
1\. ——— 14, 15.
2\. ——— 19, 20, 24.
2\. —— iv. 2, 6 twice, 7, 8, 13, 16.
2\. —— v. 2.
1\. ——— 13, 15 twice, 18, 19, 20 1st.
2\. ——— 20 2nd.
2\. 2 John 1.
1\. 3 John 12.
1\. Jude 5, part, 10 1st.
6\. ——— 10 2nd.
1\. Rev. ii. 2, 9, 13.
2\. ——— 17 (No. 1, G L T Tr A ℵ.)
1\. ——— 19.
2\. ——— 23, 24.
1\. —— iii. 1.
2\. ——— 3.
1\. ——— 8.
2\. ——— 9.
1\. ——— 15, 17.
1\. —— vii. 14.
1\. —— xii. 12, part.
1\. —— xix. 12.

KNOW BEFORE.

4\. 2 Pet. iii. 17, part.

KNOW BY.

σύνοιδα, (*No.* 1 *with συν*, together with, *prefixed*) to know with *any one*, to know what others know, *hence*, to be witness, able to testify. *Here*, with *ἑαυτῷ*, to be compelled to testify against one's self.

1 Cor. iv. 4.

KNOW FULLY.

παρακολουθέω, to accompany side by side, to follow closely; *then*, to follow out closely *in mind*, trace out.

2 Tim. iii. 10, marg., *be a diligent follower of.*

KNOW NOT.

ἀγνοέω, not to know, to be unacquainted with, *then*, to be ignorant of, have no discernment *or* understanding of; also, to commit a fault *from want of discernment or knowledge.*

Acts xiii. 27, part.
Rom. ii. 4.
Rom. vi. 3.
—— vii. 1.

KNOW OF.

οἶδα, *see* "KNOW," *No.* 1.

John iv. 32.

KNOW TO THE UTTERMOST.

διαγινώσκω, ("KNOW," *No.* 2, *with διά*, through, *prefixed*) to know throughout, *i.e.* accurately fully, (*occ.* Acts xxiii. 15.)

Acts xxiv. 12.

KNOW WELL.

ἐπιγινώσκω *see* "KNOW," *No.* 3.

2 Cor. vi. 9.

KNOWLEDGE.

1\. *γνῶσις*, knowing, *or* recognition, the knowledge *or* understanding *of a thing*, the insight which manifests itself in the thorough understanding of the subjects with which it meets and in the conduct determined thereby; *γνῶσις differs from σοφία* (wisdom) *inasmuch as it requires existent objects,* (*occ.* 1 Tim. vi. 10.)

2\. *ἐπίγνωσις*, (*No.* 1 *with ἐπί*, upon, *prefixed*) clear and exact knowledge; *more emphatic* than *No.* 1, *because it expresses* a more thorough participation on the part of the knower, with the object of knowledge; a knowledge that has a powerful influence on the knower.

3. σύνεσις, intelligence, insight into *anything*, understanding, cleverness, as shown in quickness of apprehension; acuteness; the intelligent, penetrating consideration which precedes decision and action. σύνεσις *is used of* reflective thought, σοφία, (wisdom) *of* productive thought, (*elsewhere translated* "understanding.")

— Matt. xiv. 35, see K of (have)
1. Luke i. 77.
1. —— xi. 52.
— Acts iv. 13, see K of (take)
—— —— xvii. 22, see K (have)
—— —— xxiv. 8, see K of (take)
—— —— —— 22, see K (have)
2. Rom. i. 28, marg., with *ἔχω ἐν, to acknowledge*, lit., *to hold in knowledge.*)
1. —— ii. 20.
2. —— iii. 20.
2. —— x. 2.
1. —— xi. 33.
1. —— xv. 14.
1. 1 Cor. i. 5.
1. —— viii. 1 twice, 7, 10, 11.
1. —— xii. 8.
1. —— xiii. 2, 8.
1. —— xiv. 6.
—— —— xv. 34, see K (not)
1. 2 Cor. ii. 14.
1. —— iv. 6.
1. —— vi. 6.
1. —— viii. 7.
1. —— x. 5.
1. —— xi. 6.
2. Eph. i. 17, marg., *acknowledgement.*
3. —— iii. 4.
1. —— —— 19.
2. —— iv. 13.
2. Phil. i. 9.
1. —— iii. 8.
2. Col. i. 9, 10.
1. —— ii. 3.
2. —— iii. 10.
2. 1 Tim. ii. 4.
2. 2 Tim. iii. 7.
2. Heb. x. 26.
1. 1 Pet. iii. 7.
2. 2 Pet. i. 2, 3.
1. —— —— 5, 6.
2. —— —— 8.
2. —— ii. 21 twice.
1. —— iii. 18.

KNOWLEDGE (ENDUED WITH)

ἐπιστήμων, (*part.* of "KNOW," *No.* 6,) (*non occ.*)

Jas. iii. 13.

KNOWLEDGE (HAVE)

1. οἶδα, *see* "KNOW," *No.* 1.
2. γινώσκω, *see* "KNOW," *No.* 2.

2. Acts xvii. 13. | 1. Acts xxiv. 22.

KNOWLEDGE OF (HAVE)

ἐπιγινώσκω, *see* "KNOW," *No.* 3.

Matt. xiv. 35, part.

KNOWLEDGE OF (TAKE)

ἐπιγινώσκω, *see* "KNOW," *No.* 3.

Acts iv. 13. | Acts xxiv. 8.

KNOWLEDGE (NOT)

ἀγνωσία, ignorance, *opp. of* γνῶσις ("KNOW," *No.* 1), denoting a moral want *or* fault, wilful ignorance, (*occ.* 1 Pet. ii. 15.)

1 Cor. xv. 34.

KNOWN.

[*for* MAKE KNOWN, *see below.*]

1. γνωστός, known, capable of being known, knowable.
2. φανερός, visible, manifest; *hence*, known.

2. Matt. xii. 16.
2. Mark iii. 12.
— Luke ii. 17, see K abroad (make)
1. John xviii. 15, 16.
1. Acts i. 19.
1. —— ii. 14.
1. —— iv. 10. [(be made)
—— —— vii. 13 twice, see K
1. Acts ix. 42.
1. —— xiii. 38.
1. —— xv. 18 (*ap.*)
1. —— xix. 17.
1. —— xxviii. 28.
— Rom. i. 19, see K (that which may be)
— 2 Tim. iv. 17, see K (be fully)

KNOWN (BE FULLY)

πληροφορέω, to bear *or* bring fully, *hence*, to give full assurance, to be fully assured *or* persuaded.

2 Tim. iv. 17.

KNOWN (BE MADE)

1. ἀναγνωρίζομαι, to make one's self known, (*non occ.*)
2. { φανερός, visible, manifest, known, γίνομαι, to become, } "became" *or* "were made manifest."

1. Acts vii. 13 1st. | 2. Acts vii. 13 2nd.

KNOWN (MAKE)

γνωρίζω, to make known, declare, reveal

Luke ii. 15.
—— 17, see K abroad (make)
John xv. 15.
Acts ii. 28.
Rom. i. 19, see K (that which may be)
—— ix. 22, 23.
Rom. xvi. 26.
Eph. i. 9.
—— iii. 3, 5, 10.
—— vi. 19, 21.
Phil. iv. 6.
Col. i. 27.
—— iv. 9.
2 Pet. i. 16.

KNOWN ABROAD (MAKE)

διαγνωρίζω, (*the above, with* διά, through, *prefixed*), to make known throughout, *i.e.* everywhere.

Luke ii. 17, (γνωρίζω, (see above) L Tr A ℵ.)

KNOWN (THAT WHICH MAY BE)

{ τὸ, the *thing*, that which [is] γνωστός, known, capable of being known, knowable.

Rom. i. 19.

L

LABOUR [noun.]

1. κόπος, a beating; *then, as of the breast*, wailing, grief; *also*, the being beat out, weariness; *hence*, wearisome effort, toilsome labour.
2. ἔργον, work, labour, business, employment.

— John iv. 38 1st, see L on (bestow)
1. —— 38 2nd.
1. 1 Cor. iii. 8.
1. —— xv. 58.
1. 2 Cor. vi. 5.
1. —— x. 15.
1. —— xi. 23.
— Gal. iv. 11, see L (bestow)
2. Phil. i. 22.
— Phil. ii. 25, see L (companion in)
1. 1 Thes. i. 3.
1. —— ii. 9.
1. —— iii. 5.
1. 2 Thes. iii. 8.
1. Heb. vi. 10 (*om.* G L T Tr A ℵ.)
1. Rev. ii. 2.
1. —— xiv. 13.
— Rev. xvi. 6, see L (bestow)

LABOUR (BESTOW)

κοπιάω, (*see* "LABOUR," [verb] *No.* 1.)

Gal. iv. 11. | Rev. xvi. 6.

LABOUR ON (BESTOW)

κοπιάω, (*see* "LABOUR," [verb] *No.* 1.)

John iv. 38.

LABOUR (COMPANION IN)

συνεργός, working together in conjunction with, co-operating; *then*, as *subst.*, a co-worker, fellow-labourer.

Phil. ii. 25.

LABOUR (-ED, -ETH, -ING.) [verb.]

1. κοπιάω, to be beat out, *i.e.* to be weary, faint; *then*, to weary one's self *as with labour*, to toil.
2. ἐργάζομαι, to work, to labour *as at a trade*, to do business.
3. σπουδάζω, to speed, to make haste, *as manifested in diligence, earnestness, or zeal;* to give diligence, be in earnest.
4. φιλοτιμέομαι, to be ambitious *of doing anything*, to exert one's self *from love of honour*, to make it a point of honour *to do anything*.

1. Matt. xi. 28.
1. John iv. 38.
— —— vi. 27, see L for.
1. Acts xx. 35.
1. Rom. xvi. 12 1st, 12 2nd (ap.)
1. 1 Cor. iv. 12.
1. —— xv. 10.
1. —— xvi. 16.
4. 2 Cor. v. 9, marg., *endeavour*.
1. Eph. iv. 28.
1. Phil. ii. 16.
— —— iv. 3, see L with.
1. Col. i. 1, 29.
— —— iv. 12, see L fervently.
2. 1 Thes. ii. 9.
1. —— v. 12.
1. 1 Tim. iv. 10.
1. —— v. 17.
1. 2 Tim. ii. 6.
3. Heb. iv. 11.
1. Rev. ii. 3 (*ap.*)

LABOUR FERVENTLY.

ἀγωνίζομαι, to be a combatant in the public games. *Hence*, to strive, contend *as with a competitor*.

Col. iv. 12, marg., *strive*.

LABOUR FOR.

ἐργάζομαι, (*see* "LABOUR," *No.* 2.)

John vi. 27.

LABOUR WITH.

συναθλέω, to contend along with *any one, i.e. on his side;* to render mutual help in contesting, (*occ.* Phil. i. 27.)

Phil. iv. 3.

LABOURER.

ἐργάτης, a worker, labourer, *as in the fields*.

Matt. ix. 37, 38. | Luke x. 2 twice, 7
—— xx. 1, 2, 8. | 1 Tim. v. 18.
Jas. v. 4.

LABOURER (FELLOW)

συνεργός, a working together with, co-operating; *then, as subst.*, a co-worker.

Phil. iv. 3. | 1. Thes. iii. 2 (*ap.*)
Philem. i. 24.

LABOURER TOGETHER WITH.

συνεργός, *see above*.

1 Cor. iii. 9.

LACK [noun.]

1. *ὑστέρημα*, that which is wanting, *hence*, want, lack.
2. *χρεία*, occasion, use, usage, employment; *then, from the phrase*, "to have occasion," *it signifies* need, *or* necessity.

1. Phil. ii. 30. | 2. 1 Thes. iv. 12.

LACK (HAVE)

ἐλαττονέω, to make less, to diminish; *then, intrans.*, to be less, in respect of quantity, to lack, fall short, (*non occ.*)

2 Cor. viii. 15.

LACK (-ED, -EST, -ETH.) [verb.]

1. *ὑστερέω*, to be last, behind, posterior; *then*, to come short of *or* fail of *anything; hence*, to want, be without.
2. *λείπω*, to leave, forsake; *pass.*, to be left, forsaken *of anything*, *i.e.* to be destitute of.

1. Matt. xix. 20. | 2. Luke xviii. 22.
1. Mark x. 21. | 1. —— xxii. 35.
Phil. iv. 10, see Opportunity.

LACKED (PART WHICH)

1. 1 Cor. xii. 24, part.

LACKETH (THAT)

ἐνδεής, in want, needy, destitute.

Acts iv. 34.

LACKETH (HE THAT)

{ *ᾧ*, he to whom [*these things are*,]
{ *μὴ*, not,
{ *πάρεστι*, present.

2 Pet. i. 9.

LACKING (WHICH IS)

ὑστέρημα, *see* "LACK," *No.* 1.

1 Cor. xvi. 17. | 2 Cor. xi. 9.
1 Thes. iii. 10.

LAD.

παιδάριον, a little boy, (*elsewhere*, "child.")

John vi. 9.

LADE (-ED, -EN.)

1. *σωρεύω*, to heap, heap up; to heap up with *anything*, (*occ.* Rom. xii. 20.)
2. *φορτίζω*, to burden, load, lay a burden upon *anyone*.

2. Luke xi. 46. | 1. 2 Tim. iii. 6.

LADE WITH.

ἐπιτίθημι, to place *or* put upon, lay upon, lade *or* supply with.

Acts xxviii. 10.

LADEN (HEAVY)

φορτίζω, (*see above, No.* 2.)

Matt. xi. 28, pass. part.

LADING.

φόρτος, what is borne, *i.e.* a burden, load, *of a ship*, the freight, cargo, (*non occ.*)

Acts xxvii. 10 (*φορτίον*, (dim. of above), G L T Tr A ℵ.)

LADY.

κυρία, (*fem. of* *κύριος*, lord) lady, *used as an honourable title of address, as in Eng. Also a Greek proper name*, Kuria *or* Cyria, (*non occ.*)

2 John i. 5.

LAID.

See, LAY.

LAKE.

λίμνη, any standing water, pool, lake.

Luke v. 1, 2. | Rev. xix. 20.
—— viii. 22, 23, 33. | —— xx. 10, 14, 15.
Rev. xxi. 8.

LAMA.

λαμά *or* *λαμμᾶ*, lama, *i.e. Heb.*, לָמָּה, why? *or* wherefore?

Matt. xxvii. 46. | Mark xv. 34.

LAMB (-S.)

1. *ἀρήν*, *later* *ἀρνός*, lamb, (*non occ.*)
2. *ἀρνίον*, (*dim. of No.* 1) a little lamb, *or* lamb. [Used in John xxi. 15; but elsewhere, (in the Apocalypse

only) *of Christ*, probably in contrast to θήριον, the (wild) beast. The lamb, (ὡς,) as if slain, the sacrificial scars, telling of the past sufferings, of present worthiness, and life, etc., and pointing to the cause and ground of future vengeance.]

3. ἀμνός, a lamb: *with art.*, the lamb, the well-known lamb, *provided by God*, (Gen. xxii. 8,) *and typified by the Paschal Lamb*, (*non occ.*)

1. Luke x. 3.
3. John i. 29, 36.
2. —— xxi. 15.
3. Acts viii. 32.
3. 1 Pet. i. 19.
2. Rev. v. 6, 8, 12, 13.
2. —— vi. 1, 16.
2. —— vii. 9, 10, 14, 17.
2. Rev. xii. 11.
2. —— xiii. 8, 11.
2. —— xiv. 1. 4 twice, 10.
2. —— xv. 3.
2. —— xvii. 14 twice.
2. —— xix. 7, 9.
2. —— xxi. 9, 14, 22, 23, 27.
2. —— xxii. 1, 3.

LAME.

χωλός, lame, crippled *in the feet.*

Matt. xi. 5.
—— xv. 30, 31.
—— xxi. 14.
Luke vii. 22.
—— xiv. 13.
Acts iii. 2.

LAME MAN.

Acts iii. 11, (αυτοῦ, *he*, instead of τοῦ ἰαθέντος χωλοῦ, *the lame man which was healed*, G L T Tr A ℵ.)

LAME (THAT WHICH IS)

{ τὸ, the *thing*, / χωλός, lame, } the lame member.

Heb. xii. 13.

LAMENT (-ED.)

1. θρηνέω, to weep aloud, wail, mourn.

2. κόπτω, to beat, to cut. *Here, mid.*, to beat *or* cut one's self, *i.e.* the breast, as the expression of grief.

2. Matt. xi. 17.
1. Luke xxiii. 27.
1. John xvi. 20.
2. Rev. xviii. 9.

LAMENTATION.

1. θρῆνος, loud weeping, wailing, (*non occ.*)

2. κοπετός, beating *of the breast; hence*, lamentation, (*non occ.*)

1. Matt. ii. 18 (om. G⇒L T Tr A ℵ.)
2. Acts viii. 2.

LAMP (-s.)

λαμπάς, a torch. *Eastern torches were fed with oil from a little vessel constructed for the purpose*, the ἀγγεῖον of Matt. xxv. 4, (*occ.* John xviii. 3; Acts xx. 8.)

Matt. xxv. 1, 3, 4, 7, 8.
Rev. iv. 5.
—— viii. 10.

LAND (-s.) [noun.]

1. γῆ, earth, land, *in contrast with water and with heaven.*

2. χώρα, space *which receives, contains, or surrounds anything, and so*, place, spot *where one is, or anything takes place;* place, country, (*esp., as opp. to the city.*)

3. χωρίον, (*dim., in form, of No.* 2, *but not in sense*) place, a field, farm, possession.

4. ἀγρός, a field, *esp.*, a cultivated field.

5. ξηρός, dry, *with art.*, the dry land *as opp. to the* sea.

1. Matt. ii. 6, 20, 21.
1. —— iv. 15 twice.
1. —— ix. 26.
1. —— x. 15.
1. —— xi. 24.
1. —— xiv. 34.
4. —— xix. 29.
5. —— xxiii. 15.
1. —— xxvii. 45.
2. Mark i. 5.
1. —— iv. 1.
1. —— vi. 47, 53.
4. —— x. 29, 30.
1. —— xv. 33.
1. Luke iv. 25.
1. —— v. 3, 11.
1. —— viii. 27.
1. —— xiv. 35.
2. —— xv. 14.
1. —— xxi. 23.
1. Luke xxiii. 44, marg. (text, *earth.*)
1. John iii. 22.
1. —— vi. 21.
1. —— xxi. 8, 9, 11.
3. Acts iv. 34.
4. —— 37.
3. —— v. 3, 8.
1. —— vii. 3, 4 twice, 6.
1. —— 11 (om. G ∾ L T Tr A ℵ.)
1. —— 29, 36, 40.
2. —— x. 39.
1. —— xiii. 17, 19 twice.
1. —— xxvii. 39.
1. —— 43, and see L[(get to)
1. —— 44.
1. Heb. viii. 9.
1. —— xi. 9.
— —— 29, see Dry.
1. Jude 5.

LAND (GET TO)

{ ἔξειμι, to get out, / ἐπὶ, upon, / τὴν, the, / γῆν, land. }

Acts xxvii. 43.

LAND (-ED, -ING.) [verb.]

1. κατάγω, to lead down; *as a nautical term*, to bring *a ship* down to land, *then*, to land.

2. κατέρχομαι, to go *or* come down, to descend, *either from a higher to a lower country, or from the high seas down to land.*

2. Acts xviii. 22, part. | 1. Acts xxi. 3 (No. 2, L T Tr A ℵ.)
1. Acts xxviii. 12.

LANE (-s.)

ῥύμη, (*from* ῥύομαι, to draw) a narrow street *or* lane of a city, (*occ.* Matt. vi. 12; Acts ix. 11, xii. 10.)

Luke xiv. 21.

LANGUAGE.

διάλεκτος, speech, manner of speaking peculiar to a particular people or nation, a language *or* dialect (*elsewhere,* "TONGUE.")

Acts ii. 6.

LANTERN (-s.)

φανός, a light, any kind of light, (*non occ.*)

John xviii. 3.

LAODICEAN.

Λαοδικεύς, a Laodicean.

Col. iv. 16.
Rev. iii. 14, (ἐν Λαοδικείᾳ, *in Laodicea*, AVm, G L T Tr A ℵ,) (marg., *in Laodicea.*)

LARGE.

1. μέγας, great, large, *of physical magnitude.*

2. ἱκανός, coming to, reaching to, *and hence,* sufficing, sufficient.

2. Matt. xxviii. 12. | 1. Luke xxii. 12.
1. Mark xiv. 15. | — Gal. vi. 11, see How.
— Rev. xxi. 16, see As.

LASCIVIOUS WAY [marg.]

ἀπώλεια, loss, destruction; *here, heresies* of destruction, *i.e.* destructive *heresies.*

2 Pet. ii. 2, (text, *pernicious way,*) (ἀσέλγεια, *wanton,* Sᵗ G L T Tr A ℵ.)

LASCIVIOUSNESS.

ἀσέλγεια, excess, immoderation *in anything; hence,* licentiousness, wantonness.

Mark vii. 22. | Eph. iv. 19.
2 Cor. xii. 21. | 1 Pet. iv. 3.
Gal. v. 19. | Jude 4.

LAST.

1. ἔσχατος, the last, the extreme, the most remote; *with ref. to time,* that which concludes anything.

2. ὕστερον, at last, afterwards.

— Matt. xii. 45, see L state (the)
1. — xix. 30 twice.
1. — xx. 8, 12, 14, 16 twice.
— — xxi. 37, see L of all.
2. — xxii. 27.
— — xxvi. 60, see L (at the)
1. — xxvii. 64.
1. Mark ix. 35.
1. — x. 31 twice.
1. — xii. 6.
1. — 22 (adv., G ∾ L Tr A ℵ.)
— Luke xi. 26, see L state (the)
1. — xii. 59.
1. — xiii. 30 twice.
2. — xx. 32.
1. John vi. 39, 40, 44, 54.
1. — vii. 37.
1. John viii. 9 (*ap.*)
1. — xi. 24.
1. — xii. 48.
1. Acts ii. 17.
1. 1 Cor. iv. 9.
1. — xv. 8 (adv.), 26, 45, 52.
— Phil. iv. 10, see L (at the)
1. 2 Tim. iii. 1.
1. Heb. i. 2.
1. Jas. v. 3.
1. 1 Pet. i. 5, 20.
1. 2 Pet. iii. 3.
1. 1 John ii. 18 twice.
1. Jude 18.
1. Rev. i. 11 (*ap.*), 17.
1. — ii. 8, 19.
1. — xv. 1.
1. — xxi. 9.
1. — xxii. 13.

LAST (AT THE)

1. ὕστερον, at last, afterwards.

2. ποτέ, when, whenever, at any time.

1. Matt. xxvi. 60. | 2. Phil. iv. 10.

LAST OF ALL.

(*when only one Greek word.*)

ὕστερον, at last, afterwards.

Matt. xxi. 37.

LAST STATE (THE)

{ τὰ, the, ἔσχατα, last *things,* } (*occ.* 2 Pet. ii. 20.)

Matt. xii. 45. | Luke xi. 26.

LATCHET.

ἱμάς, a thong, a strap *of leather, with which the sandal was bound to the foot,* (*occ.* Acts xxii. 25.)

Mark i. 7. | Luke iii. 16.
John i. 27.

LATE (OF)

νῦν, now, just now.

John xi. 8.

LATELY.

προσφάτως, recently, lately, newly, (*non occ.*)

Acts xviii. 2.

LATIN (IN)

Ῥωμαϊστί, in the Roman tongue, (*non occ.*)

John xix. 20.

LATIN (OF)

Ῥωμαϊκός, Roman, (*non occ.*)

Luke xxiii. 38 (*ap.*)

LATTER.

1. ὄψιμος, late, latter, *as opp. to earlier*, (*non occ.*)
2. ὕστερος, latter, last, (*non occ.*)

2. Tim. iv. 1. | 1. Jas. v. 7.
— 2 Pet. ii. 20, see End.

LAUD.

ἐπαινέω, to praise upon, to applaud, repeat the praises *of any one*, (*occ.* 1 Cor. xi. 2, 17, 22; Luke xvi. 8.)

Rom. xv. 11.

LAUGH (-ED.) [verb.]

γελάω, to laugh *as in joy or triumph*, (*non occ.*)

Luke vi. 21, 25.

LAUGH TO SCORN.

καταγελάω, (*the above, with* κατά, down, *prefixed*) to laugh down, to laugh at, deride, (*non occ.*)

Matt. ix. 24. | Mark v. 40.
Luke viii. 53.

LAUGHTER.

γέλως, laughter, *as of joy or triumph*, (*non occ.*)

Jas. iv. 9.

LAUNCH.

ἀνάγω, to lead up; *as a nautical term*, to lead a ship up *or* out, *upon the sea.*

Acts xxi. 1. | Acts xxvii. 2, 4, part.

LAUNCH FORTH.

Luke viii. 22.

LAUNCH OUT.

ἐπανάγω, (*the above, with* ἐπί, upon, *prefixed*) to lead up upon, to lead (*a ship*) up *or* out *upon the sea*, put out to sea.

Luke v. 4.

LAW.

1. νόμος, anything divided out, what one has in use or possession: *hence*, usage, custom, right, ordinance; law *as prescribed by custom or statute; then, in a special sense*, the laws of state and equity committed to writing, (*the* νόμοι *was used of* written laws *as* ἔθη *was of* the unwritten,) *hence*, νόμος *became* the established name for law when set up in a state and recognised as a standard for the administration of justice.

In the Bible, ὁ νόμος (*i.e. with the art.*), signifies the law of the Israelites, the Divine law with its various enactments. *When* νόμος *is used in this sense, without the art., stress is laid, not upon its historical impress or outward form, but upon the conception of law; not upon the law which God gave, but upon* law *as given by God, as the only one that is or can be. For* law *in the true sense, as the expression of the will of God, has but one historical embodiment.*

* *denotes* νόμος, *without the art.*

2. ἀγοραῖος, pertaining to the forum, forensic; *hence, with some word understood*, ἀγόραιοι ἄγοντες, forensic, *or* judicial days are held, *i.e.* there are public trials held in the forum.

1. Matt. v. 17, 18.
— —— 40, see L (sue at the)
1. —— vii. 12.
— —— x. 35, see Daughter and Mother.
1. —— xi. 13.
1. —— xii. 5.
1. —— xxii. 36, 40.
1. —— xxiii. 23.
1. Luke ii. 22.
1*. —— 23, 24.
1. —— 27, 39.
— —— v. 17, see L (doctor of the)
1. —— x. 26.
— —— xii. 53, see Daughter and Mother.
1. Luke xvi. 16, 17.
1. —— xxiv. 44.
1. John i. 17, 45.
1. —— vii. 19 twice, 23, 49, 51.
1. —— viii. 5 (ap.), 17.
1. —— x. 34.
1. —— xii. 34.
1. —— xv. 25.
— —— xviii. 13, see Father.
1. —— 31.
1. —— xix. 7.
— Acts v. 34, see L (doctor of)
1. —— vi. 13.
1. —— vii. 53.
1. —— xiii. 15, 39.

1. Acts xv. 5, 24 (*ap.*)
1. —— xviii. 13, 15.
2. —— xix. 38, marg., *court-days.*
1. —— xxi. 20, 24, 28.
1. —— xxii. 3, 12.
1. —— xxiii. 3 1st.
— ——— 3 2nd, see L (contrary to the)
1. ——— 29.
1. —— xxiv. 6 (*ap.*), 14.
1. —— xxv. 8.
1. —— xxviii. 23.
— Rom. ii. 12 1st & 2nd, see L (without)
1*.——— 12 3rd & 4th.
1. ——— 13 1st (*om. art.* L T Tr A ℵ.)
1. ——— 13 2nd (*om. art.* G ⇉ L T Tr A ℵ.)
1*.——— 14 1st.
1. ——— 14 2nd.
1*.——— 14 3rd & 4th.
1. ——— 15.
1. ——— 17 (*om. art.* G ⇉ L T Tr A ℵ.)
1. ——— 18, 20.
1*.——— 23 1st.
1. ——— 23 2nd.
1*.——— 25 twice.
1. ——— 26, 27 1st.
1*.——— 27 2nd.
1. —— iii. 19 twice.
1*.——— 20 twice, 21 1st.
1. ——— 21 2nd, 27 1st.
1*.——— 27 2nd, 28, 31 twice.
1*.—— iv. 13, 14.
1. ——— 15 1st.
1*.——— 15 2nd.
1. ——— 16.
1*.—— v. 13 twice, 20.
1*.—— vi. 14, 15.
1*.—— vii. 1 1st.
1. ——— 1 2nd.
1*.——— 2 1st.
1. ——— 2 2nd, 3, 4, 5, 6, 7 1st.
1*.——— 7 2nd.
1. ——— 7 3rd.
1*.——— 8, 9.
1. ——— 12, 14, 16, 21, 22.
1*.——— 23 1st.
1. ——— 23 2nd & 3rd.
1*.——— 25 twice.
1. —— viii. 2 twice, 3, and see L, could not do (what), 4, 7.
— —— ix. 4, see L (giving of the)
1*.——— 31 twice.
1. ——— 32 (*om.* ὁ νόμος, *the law,* G ⇉ L T Tr A ℵ, *i.e. works* instead of *the works of the law.*)
1*. Rom. x. 4.
1. Rom. x. 5.
1*.—— xiii. 8, 10.
— 1 Cor. vi. 1, 6, 7, see L (go to)
1*.—— vii. 39 (*om.* νόμῳ, *by the law,* G L T Tr A ℵ.)
1. —— ix. 8, 9.
1*.——— 20 3 times.
— ——— 21 1st, 2nd, & 3rd, see L (without)
— ——— 21 4th, see L (under the)
— ——— 21 5th, see L (without)
1. —— xiv. 21, 34.
1. —— xv. 56.
1*. Gal. ii. 16 3 times, 19, 21.
1*.—— iii. 2, 5, 10 1st.
1. ——— 10 2nd.
1*.——— 11.
1. ——— 12, 13, 17.
1*.——— 18.
1. ——— 19, 21 1st & 2nd.
1*.——— 21 3rd, 23.
1. ——— 24.
1*.—— iv. 4, 5, 21 1st.
1. ——— 21 2nd.
1. —— v. 3.
1*.——— 4.
1. ——— 14.
1*.—— 18, 23.
1. —— vi. 2.
1*.——— 13.
1. Eph. ii. 15.
1*. Phil. iii. 5, 6, 9.
— 1 Tim. i. 7, see L (teacher of the)
1. ——— 8.
1*.——— 9.
— Titus iii. 9, see L (about the)
1. Heb. vii. 5.
— ——— 11, see L (receive the)
1*.——— 12, 16.
1. ——— 19, 28 twice.
1. —— viii. 4.
1*.——— 10.
1*.—— ix. 19 (*insert art.* L Tr A ℵb.)
1. ——— 22.
1. —— x. 1.
1. ——— 8 (*om. art.* G → L T Tr Ab ℵ.)
1. ——— 16.
1*.——— 28.
1*. Jas. i. 25.
1*.—— ii. 8.
1. ——— 9, 10.
1*.——— 11, 12.
1*.—— iv. 11 4 times.
— 1 John iii. 4 1st, see L (transgress the)
— ——— 4 2nd, see L (transgression of the)

LAW (ABOUT THE)

νομικός, pertaining *or* relating to law.

Tit. iii. 9.

LAW (CONTRARY TO THE)

παρανομέω, to act aside from law, (*non occ.*)

Acts xxiii. 3, part.

LAW (DOCTOR OF), (D. O. THE)†

νομοδιδάσκαλος, a law-teacher, *i.e.* a teacher and expounder of the Jewish law, (*occ.* 1 Tim. i. 7.)

† Luke v. 17 | Acts v. 34.

LAW (GIVING OF THE)

νομοθεσία, lawgiving, legislation, the giving of a code of laws, (*non occ.*)

Rom. ix. 4.

LAW (GO TO)

1. κρίνω, to divide, to separate; to make a distinction, come to a decision, to judge. *In prof. Greek,* to call anyone to account, begin a lawsuit. (*Mid. or pass., occ.* Matt. v. 40.)

2. { κρίματα, lawsuits,
{ ἔχω, to have.

1. 1 Cor. vi. 1, 6. | 2. 1 Cor. vi. 7.

LAW (RECEIVE THE)

νομοθετέω, to make *or* give laws, to establish as law. *Hence, in N.T. pass.,* to be legislated for, receive laws.

Heb. vii. 11.

LAW (SUE AT THE)

κρίνω, *see* "L (GO TO)," *No.* 1.

Matt. v. 40.

LAW (TEACHER OF THE)

νομοδιδάσκαλος, *see* "LAW (DOCTOR OF")*.*

1 Tim. i. 7.

LAW (TRANSGRESS THE)

{ ἀνομία, lawlessness.
{ ποιέω, to do.

1 John iii. 4.

LAW (TRANSGRESSION OF THE)

ἀνομία, lawlessness, contempt of law.

1 John iii. 4.

LAW (UNDER THE)

ἔννομος, what is within the range of law, in the law, (*occ.* Acts xix. 39.)

1 Cor. ix. 20 (*followed by* χριστοῦ, *of Christ,* instead of χριστῷ, *to Christ,* G ∾ L T Tr A ℵ.)
——— 21.

LAW (WITHOUT)

1. ἄνομος, without law, lawless.
2. ἀνόμως, (*adv. of above.*)

2. Rom. ii. 12 twice. | 1. 1 Cor. ix. 21 4 times.

LAW COULD NOT DO (WHAT THE)

τὸ, the *thing*,
ἀδύνατος, impossible,
τοῦ, by the,
νόμου, law,
} what was impossible by the law.

Rom. viii. 3.

LAWFUL.

ἔννομος, what is within the range of the law, based upon law, *and* governed and determined according to law, (*occ.* 1 Cor. ix. 21.)

Acts xix. 39, marg., *ordinary*.

LAWFUL (ARE)

ἔξεστι, (*impers. verb*) it is possible, one can, *referring to moral possibility or propriety*; *hence*, it is right, it is permitted, one may.

Acts xvi. 21. | 1 Cor. vi. 12 twice.
1 Cor. x. 23 twice.

LAWFUL (IS)

Matt. xii. 2. | Mark ii. 24, 26.
Luke vi. 2.

LAWFUL (IT IS)

Matt. xii. 10, 12.
—— xiv. 4.
—— xix. 3.
—— xx. 15.
—— xxii. 17.
—— xxvii. 6.
Mark iii. 4.
—— vi. 18.
—— x. 2.
Mark xii. 14.
Luke vi. 4, 9.
—— xiv. 3.
—— xx. 22.
John v. 10.
—— xviii. 31.
Acts xxii. 25.
2 Cor. xii. 4, marg., *it is possible*.

LAWFUL (WAS)

Matt. xii. 4.

LAWFULLY.

νομίμως, lawfully, according to law and custom, (*non occ.*)

1 Tim. i. 8. | 2 Tim. ii. 5.

LAWGIVER.

νομοθέτης, a lawgiver, legislator.

Jas. iv. 12.

LAWLESS.

ἄνομος, without law, lawless.

1 Tim. i. 9.

LAWYER.

νομικός, pertaining *or* relating to law; *of persons*, skilled in the law.

Matt. xxii. 35.
Luke vii. 30.
—— x. 25.
Luke xi. 45, 46, 52.
—— xiv. 3.
Tit. iii. 13.

LAY (-ING, LAID, LAIN.)

1. τίθημι, to set, to place, to lay.
2. κατατίθημι, (*No.* 1, *with* κατά, down, *prefixed*) to set, put, *or* lay down, deposit.
3. βάλλω, to throw, to cast, *the force being modified by the context.*
4. καταβάλλω, (*No.* 3, *with* κατά, down, *prefixed*) to throw *or* cast down. *In mid.*, used of laying down *as a foundation.*
5. κλίνω, to incline, to recline, to bow *or* lay *the head.*
6. ἀνακλίνω, (*No.* 5, *with* ἀνά, up in, *prefixed*) to lay up in, (*esp. upon a triclinium, in order to take a meal.*)
7. φέρω, to bear, *as a burden*; to bear *or* bring *as a charge against anyone.*

— Matt. iii. 10, see L (be)
— —— vi. 19, 20, see L up.
3. —— viii. 14.
5. ——— 20.
— —— xii. 11, } see
— —— xiv. 3, } Hold.
— —— xviii. 18, see Hands.
— —— xix. 15, see L on.
— —— xxi. 46, see Hands.
— —— xxvi. 55, 57, see Hold.
1. —— xxvii. 60.
— Mark iii. 21, see Hold.
— —— v. 23, see L on.
— —— vi. 5, see L upon.
— ——— 17, see Hold.
1. ——— 29, 56.
— —— vii. 8, see L aside.
3. ——— 30.
— —— xii. 12, } see
— —— xiv. 51, } Hold.
2. —— xv. 46 (No. 1, L Tr A ℵ.)
1. ——— 47.
1. —— xvi. 6.
— Luke i. 66, see L up.
6. —— ii. 7.
— —— iii. 9, see L (be)
— —— iv. 40, see L on.
1. —— v. 18.
1. —— vi. 48.
5. —— ix. 58.
— —— xi. 54, see L wait for.
— —— xii. 19, see L up (be)
— Luke xii. 21, see Treasure.
— ——— xiii. 13, see L (on.)
1. —— xiv. 29, part.
3. —— xvi. 20.
— —— xix. 20, see L up (be)
— ——— 21, 22, see L (down.)
— ——— 44, see Ground.
— —— xxiii. 26, see Hold.
1. ——— 53 1st.
1. ——— 53 2nd, see L (be)
1. ——— 55.
— —— xxiv. 12, see L (be)
— John viii. 20, see Hands.
— —— x. 15, 17, 18 twice, see L down.
1. —— xi. 34.
— ——— 41, see L (be)
— —— xiii. 4, see L aside.
— ——— 37, 38, } see L
— —— xv. 13, } down.
1. —— xix. 41, 42.
1. —— xx. 2, 13, 15.
— —— xxi. 9, see L thereon (be)
1. Acts iii. 2.
— —— iv. 3, see L on.
— ——— 35, see L down.
1. ——— 37.
1. —— v. 2, 15.
— —— vi. 6, see L on.
1. —— vii. 16.

— Acts vii. 58, see L down.
— —— 60, see Charge.
— —— viii. 17, 19, see L on.
1. —— ix. 37.
— —— xiii. 3, see L on.
1. —— 29.
— —— 36, see L unto.
— —— xv. 28, } see L upon.
— —— xvi. 23, } see L upon.
— —— xix. 6, } see L upon.
— —— xxiii. 29, see Charge.
— —— 30, see L wait.
7. —— xxv. 7.
— —— xxviii. 3, 8, see L on.
1. Rom. ix. 33.
— —— xvi. 4, see L down.
1. 1 Cor. iii. 10, 11 1st.
— —— 11 2nd, see L (be)
— 1 Cor. ix. 16, see L upon (be)
1. —— xvi. 2.
— 2 Cor. xii. 14.
— Col. i. 5, see L up (be)
— 1 Tim. v. 22, see L on.
— —— vi. 12, see Hold.
— —— 19 1st, see Store.
— —— 19 2nd, see Hold.
— 2 Tim. iv. 8, see L up (be)
— —— 16, see Charge.
— Heb. i. 10, see Foundation.
4. —— Heb. vi. 1, mid.
— —— 18, see Hold.
— —— xii. 1, see L aside.
— Jas. i. 21, see L apart.
— 1 Pet. ii. 1, see L aside.
1. —— 6.
— 1 John iii. 16 twice, see [L down.
— Rev. xx. 2, see Hold.

LAY APART.

ἀποτίθεμαι, to put off from one's self, to lay aside.

Jas. i. 21.

LAY ASIDE.

1. **ἀποτίθεμαι**, (*see above.*)
2. **ἀφίημι**, to send forth *or* away, let go from *one's self: hence,* to neglect, omit.
3. **τίθημι**, to set, place, lay.

2. Mark vii. 8.
3. John xiii. 4.
1. Heb. xii. 1.
1. 1 Pet. ii. 1.

LAY DOWN.

1. **τίθημι**, to set, place, lay.
2. **ὑποτίθημι**, (*No.* 1, *with* ὑπό, under, *prefixed*) to set *or* put under, lay under, *as the neck under the axe of the executioner*, (*occ.* 1 Tim. iv. 6, *mid.*)
3. **ἀποτίθεμαι**, to put off from one's self, lay aside.

1. Luke xix. 21, 22.
1. John x. 15, 17, 18 twice.
1. —— xiii. 37, 38.
1. —— xv. 13.
1. Acts iv. 35.
3. —— vii. 58.
2. Rom. xvi. 4.
1. 1 John iii. 16 twice.

LAY ON.

1. **ἐπιτίθημι**, to set, place, *or* lay upon.
2. **ἐπιβάλλω**, to throw *or* cast upon.

1. Matt. xix. 15.
1. Mark v. 23.
1. Luke iv. 40.
1. —— xiii. 13.
1. —— xxiii. 26.
2. Acts iv. 3.
1. —— vi. 6.
1. —— viii. 17, 19.
1. —— xiii. 3.
1. —— xxviii. 3, 8.
1. 1 Tim. v. 22.

LAY UNTO.

προστίθημι, to set, put, lay unto, towards *or* with *anything.*

Acts xiii. 36.

LAY UP.

1. **τίθημι**, to set, place, lay. *Mid.*, to set *or* put for one's self, on one's own part.
2. **θησαυρίζω**, to treasure up, lay up in store.

2. Matt. vi. 19, 20.
1. Luke i. 66, mid.
2. 2 Cor. xii. 14.

LAY UPON.

ἐπιτίθημι, to set, place, lay upon.

Mark vi. 5.
Acts xv. 28.
Acts xvi. 23, part.
—— xix. 6, part.

LAY WAIT.

{ **ἐπιβουλή**, counsel upon *or* against, plot,
{ **μέλλειν**, to be on the point to,
{ **ἔσεσθαι**, to be about to be.

Acts xxiii. 30, (*om.* ὑπὸ τῶν Ἰουδαίων, L T Tr A ℵ, and *om.* μελλειν, L T Tr A ℵ.) i.e. "*a plot was about to be laid,*" instead of, "*how that the Jews laid wait.*"

LAY WAIT FOR.

ἐνεδρεύω, to lie in ambush for *or* against, (*in war.*)

Luke xi. 54, (*om.* G ⇉)

LAID (BE)

κεῖμαι, to lie, and also to be laid.

Matt. iii. 10.
Luke iii. 9.
—— xxiii. 53.
Luke xxiv. 12 (*ap.*)
John xi. 41 (*ap.*)
1 Cor. iii. 11.

LAID THEREON (BE)

ἐπίκειμαι, (*the above, with* ἐπί, upon, *prefixed,*) to lie upon, to be laid upon.

John xxi. 9.

LAID UP (BE)

1. **κεῖμαι**, to lie, to be laid.
2. **ἀπόκειμαι**, to be laid away, laid up, *for preservation;* to be in store for.

1. Luke xii. 19.
2. —— xix. 20.
2. Col. i. 5.
2. 2 Tim. iv. 8.

LAID UPON (BE)

ἐπίκειμαι, to lie upon, be laid upon.

1 Cor. ix. 16.

LAYING AWAIT.

ἐπιβουλή, counsel upon *or* against, a plot.

Acts ix. 24.

LAYING ON

ἐπίθεσις, a placing upon, laying upon, *as of hands.*

Acts viii. 18. Heb. vi. 2. 1 Tim. iv. 14.

LEAD (-ETH ; LED, -EST.)

1. ἄγω, to lead, conduct, (*used in a variety of modifications which are determined by the context.*)
2. ἀνάγω, (*No.* 1, *with* ἀνά, up to, *prefixed*) to lead up, to conduct up *as from a lower to a higher place.*
3. ἀπάγω, (*No.* 1, *with* ἀπό, away from, *prefixed*) to lead away, conduct away.
4. ὁδηγέω, to lead the way.
5. φέρω, to bear, to bear along, bear *or* bring forth.

3. Matt. vii. 13, 14.
4. —— xv. 14.
1. Mark xiii. 11.
1. Luke iv. 1, 29.
4. —— vi. 39.
— —— xxi. 11, see Hand.
1. —— xxii. 54.
2. —— 66 (No. 3, T Tr A ℵ.)
1. —— xxiii. 1, 32.
1. John xviii. 28.
1. Acts viii. 32.
— —— ix. 8, see Hand.
5. —— xii. 10.
— —— xxii. 11, see Hand.
1. Rom. ii. 4.
1. —— viii. 14.
1. 1 Cor. xii. 2.
1. Gal. v. 18.
— Eph. iv. 8, see Captive.
— 1 Tim. ii. 2, see Life.
— 2 Tim. iii. 6, see Captive.
4. Rev. vii. 17.

LEAD ABOUT.

περιάγω, to lead around *or* about.

1 Cor. ix. 5.

LEAD AWAY.

1. ἄγω, *see* "LEAD," *No.* 1.
2. ἄπαγω, *see* "LEAD," *No.* 3.

2. Matt. xxvi. 57.
2. —— xxvii. 2, 31.
2. Mark xiv. 44, 53.
2. —— xv. 16.
2. Luke xiii. 15, see below.
2. Luke xxiii. 26.
2. John xviii. 13 (No. 1, L T Tr Ab ℵ.)
2. —— xix. 16 (No. 1, G) (om. G → L T Tr A.)
1. 2 Tim. iii. 6.

LEAD AWAY TO WATERING.

{ ἀπαγαγὼν, leading [*it*] away,
{ ποτίζει, giveth [*it*] drink.

Luke xiii. 15.

LEAD AWAY WITH.

συναπάγω, to lead off *or* away with *any one.*

2 Pet. iii. 17.

LEAD INTO.

1. εἰσάγω, to lead into, (*with* εἰς, into.)
2. εἰσφερω, to bear, bear along, (*with* εἰς, into.)
3. συναγω, to lead together with.

1. Matt. vi. 13.
2. Luke xi. 4.
1. Acts xxi. 37.
3. Rev. xiii. 10 (ἀπάγω, *lead away*, G~) (om. L T Tr A ℵ, i.e. "*is for*," instead of ["*leadeth into*."])

LEAD OUT.

ἐξάγω, to lead out, conduct out from.

Mark viii. 23 (ἐκφέρω, *to bring forth*, T Tr A ℵ.)
—— xv. 20 (ἄγω, *to lead*, L.)
Luke xxiv. 50.
John x. 3.
Acts xxi. 38.
Heb. viii. 9.

LEAD UP.

1. ἀνάγω, to lead up, to conduct up.
2. ἀναφέρω, to bear upwards, carry up.

1. Matt. iv. 1. | 2. Mark ix. 2.

LEADER.

ὁδηγός, way-leader, *i.e.* a leader in the way, a guide.

Matt. xv. 14.

LEAF.

φύλλον, a leaf, (*non occ.*)

Matt. xxi. 19.
—— xxiv. 32.
Mark xi. 13 twice.
—— xiii. 28.
Rev. xxii. 2.

LEAN (-ED, -ING.) [verb.]

1. ἀνάκειμαι, to be laid up; to recline *as at table, upon a triclinium, where the one who was next was in the bosom of the other.*
2. ἀναπίπτω, to fall upon *or* towards, *i.e.* to fall down, to lie down.

1. John xiii. 23. | 2. John xxi. 20.

LEAP (-ED, -ING.)

1. ἅλλομαι, to leap, jump, spring, (*occ.* John iv. 14.)
2. σκιρτάω, to spring, bound, *used of horses*, and *the* skip *or* frolic *of goats*, (*occ.* Luke vi. 23.)

2. Luke i. 41, 44.
— —— vi. 23, see L for joy.
— Acts iii. 8 1st, see L up.
1. Acts iii. 8 2nd.
1. —— xiv. 10.
— —— xix. 16, see L on.

LEAP FOR JOY.

2. Luke vi. 23.

LEAP ON.

ἐφάλλομαι, (*with* ἐπὶ) to leap, jump *or* spring upon, (*non occ.*)

Acts xix. 16.

LEAP UP.

ἐξάλλομαι, to leap out of, i.e *from the place where one sat or was.*

Acts iii. 8.

LEARN (-ED, -ING.)

1. μανθάνω, to learn, *intellectually from others*, or *from study and observation*, to be informed, to understand, (*occ.* Acts xxiii. 27.)
2. παιδεύω, to train up a child, and *hence*, *gen*, to educate, discipline, instruct.

1. Matt. ix. 13.
1. —— xi. 29.
1. —— xxiv. 32.
1. Mark xiii. 28.
1. John vi. 45.
1. —— vii. 15.
— Acts vii. 22, see Learned (be)
1. Rom. xvi. 17.
1. 1 Cor. iv. 6.
1. —— xiv. 31, 35.
1. Gal. iii. 2.
1. Eph. iv. 20.
1. Phil. iv. 9, 11.
1. Col. i. 7.
2. 1 Tim. i. 20.
1. —— ii. 11.
1. —— v. 4, 13.
1. 2 Tim. iii. 7, 14 twice.
1. Tit. iii. 14.
1. Heb. v. 8.
1. Rev. xiv. 3.

LEARNED (BE)

2. Acts vii. 22.

LEARNING [noun.]

1. γράμμα, the thing written, i.e. *something written or cut in with the stylus in the ancient manner of writing; hence*, a letter, *as of the alphabet. Here, only plural*, letters; *hence*, learning.
2. διδασκαλία, teaching, instruction.

1. John vii. 15, marg. (text, letters.)
1. Acts xxvi. 24.
2. Rom. xv. 4.

LEAST.

1. ἐλάχιστος, the least, *in magnitude, number, or quality.*
2. μικρός, small, little, (*properly of magnitude.*)

1. Matt. ii. 6.
1. —— v. 19 twice.
1. —— xxv. 40, 45.
1. Luke xvi. 10.
2. Acts viii. 10.
— 1 Cor. vi. 4, see Esteemed.
1. —— xv. 9.
2. Heb. viii. 11.

LEAST (AT)

{ καί, and, / γε, indeed, } truly.

Luke xix. 42, (*om.* Lb Tr Ab ℵ) (*om.* καί, T.)

LEAST (AT THE)

κἄν, *for* καί ἐάν, and if, also if, even if although.

Acts v. 15.

LEAST (LESS THAN THE)

ἐλάχιστοτερος, (*superl. of No.* 1) far less, less than least, (*non occ.*)

Eph. iii. 8.

LEAST (THAT WHICH IS)

ἐλάχιστος, the least.

Luke xvi. 10.

LEAST (THAT THING WHICH IS)

ἐλάχιστος, the least.

Luke xii. 26.

LEATHERN.

δερμάτινος, made of skin, leathern, (*occ.* Mark i. 6.)

Matt. iii. 4.

LEAVE (GIVE) [noun.]

ἐπιτρέπω, to turn upon, direct upon, *but usually*, to commit or entrust to *any one's care*, refer a matter to *a person*, leave it to his arbitration; *hence*, to permit.

Mark v. 13. | John xix. 38.

LEAVE OF (TAKE)

1. ἀποτάσσομαι, (*mid.*) to arrange one's self off, separate one's self from, *i.e.* to take leave of, bid farewell.

2. ἀσπάζομαι, to draw to one's self; *hence*, to embrace, salute, *spoken of those who meet or separate.*

1. Acts xviii. 18, part.
2. —— xxi. 6, part (ἀπασπάζομαι, *to tear one's self away*, L T Tr A ℵ.)
1. 2 Cor. ii. 13.

LEAVE (-ETH, -ING, LEFT.) [verb.]

1. ἀφίημι, to send forth *or* away, to let go from *one's self*, *then*, to let go from *one's further notice, care*, etc., to leave, let alone.

2. ἀνίημι, to send up, *or* forth, to let up, let go, relax, loosen.

3. καταλείπω, to leave down, *to one's heirs*, leave behind *so as* to descend *to them; gen.*, to leave behind, *but prop. at one's death; hence*, to leave, quit wholly, utterly forsake.

4. ἀπολείπω, (*No.* 3, *with* ἀπό, from, instead of κατά, down, *prefixed*) to leave away from *one's self*, to leave behind.

5. ἐγκαταλείπω, (*No.* 3, *with* ἐν, in, *prefixed*) to leave behind in, to leave remaining.

6. ὑπολείπω, (*No.* 3, *with* ὑπό, under, *instead of* κατά, down, *prefixed*) to leave under, to leave behind, *as implying* concealment.

7. παύω, to pause, cease, refrain *from anything.*

8. ἐάω, to let, suffer, allow, permit; *spoken of things*, to let be, leave alone, desist.

9. ὑπολιμπάνω, (*a lengthened form of No.* 6) to leave behind.

1. Matt. iv. 11.
6. —— 13.
1. —— 20, 22.
1. —— v. 24.
1. —— viii. 15.
— —— xv. 37, see L (be)
3. —— xvi. 4.
1. —— xviii. 12.
3. —— xix. 5.
3. —— xxi. 17.
1. —— xxii. 22, 25.
1. —— xxiii. 23, 38.
1. —— xxiv. 2, 40, 41.
1. —— xxvi. 44.
1. Mark i. 20, 31.
— —— viii. 8, see L (that was)
1. —— 13.
3. —— x. 7.
1. —— 28, 29.
1. —— xii. 12.
3. —— 19 1st.
1. —— 19 2nd, 20, 21 (ap.) [22.
1. Mark xiii. 2, 34.
3. —— xiv. 52.
1. Luke iv. 39.
7. —— v. 4.
3. —— 28.
1. —— x. 30.
3. —— 40.
1. —— xi. 42,
1. —— xiii. 35.
3. —— xv. 4.
1. —— xvii. 34, 35, 36 (ap.)
1. —— xviii. 28, 29.
1. —— xix. 44.
3. —— xx. 31.
1. —— xxi. 6.
1. John iv. 3, 28, 52.
3. —— viii. 9 (ap.)
1. —— 29.
1. —— x. 12.
1. —— xiv. 18, 27.
1. —— xvi. 28, 32.
5. Acts ii. 27.
3. —— 31 (No. 5, G~L [T Tr A ℵ.)
3. Acts vi. 2.
3. —— xiii. 19.
1. —— xiv. 17.
3. —— xxi. 3.
7. —— 32.
8. —— xxiii. 32.
3. —— xxiv. 27.
3. —— xxv. 14.
8. —— xxvii. 40, marg. (text, *commit.*)
1. Rom. i. 27.
5. —— ix. 29.
6. —— xi. 3.
1. 1 Cor. vii. 13.
8. Eph. v. 31.
1. 1 Thes. iii. 1.
4. 2 Tim. iv. 13, 20.
3. Tit. i. 5 (No. 4, G~L T Tr A ℵ.)
— —— 5, marg. (see *Un-* [*dona.*)
1. Heb. ii. 8.
3. —— iv. 1.
1. —— vi. 1.
2. —— xiii. 5.
9. 1 Pet. ii. 21.
4. Jude 6.
1. Rev. ii. 4.
— —— xi. 2, see L out.

LEAVE OUT.

ἐκβάλλω, to throw out, cast out.

Rev. xi. 2, marg. *cast out.*

LEFT (BE)

περισσεύω, to be over and above, to exceed *in number or measure.*

Mark xv. 37.

LEFT (THAT WAS)

περίσσευμα, what is more than enough, left over.

Mark viii. 8.

LEAVEN [noun.]

ζύμη, leaven, sour dough. *Hence, as leaven causes to ferment and turn sour, it is used in the sense of* corruption, (*non occ.*)

Matt. xiii. 33.
—— xvi. 6, 11, 12.
Mark viii. 15 twice.
Luke xii. 1.
—— xiii. 21.
1 Cor. v. 6, 7, 8 twice.
Gal. v. 9.

LEAVEN (-ED, -ETH.) [verb.]

ζυμόω, to leaven, to make ferment, *hence*, to corrupt, (*non occ.*)

Matt. xiii. 33.
Luke xiii. 21.
1 Cor. v. 6, (δολόω, to deceive, G ~)
Gal. v. 9.

LEBBÆUS.

Λεββαῖος, Lebbeus *or* Lebbæus, *the name of the Apostle Jude.*)

Matt. x. 3, (*om.* Λεββαῖος ὁ ἐπικληθεὶς, *Lebbeus, whose surname was*, G → L Tr ℵ,) (*om.* ὁ ἐπικληθεὶς Θαδδαῖος, *whose surname was Thaddeus*, T A.)

LEFT [verb.]

See, LEAVE.

LEFT [adj.]

ἀριστερός, the left, (*occ.* 2 Cor. vi. 7.)

Matt. vi. 3. | Luke xxiii. 33.

LEFT FOOT.

εὐώνυμος, of good name, honoured; *hence*, of good omen, *and used in speaking of* the left, *instead of the above, which was a word of ill omen, since all omens on the left were regarded as unfortunate by the ancients.*

Rev. x. 2.

LEFT (ON THE,) *or* (ON ONE'S)

1. ἀριστερός, left,
2. { ἐξ, of, / εὐώνυμων, *see above*, } on the left.

2. Matt. xx. 21, 23. | 2. Matt. xxvii. 38.
2. —— xxv. 33. | 2. Mark xv. 27.
1. 2 Cor. vi. 7.

LEFT HAND (ON THE,) *or* (ON ONE'S)

2. Matt. xxv. 41.
2. Mark x. 37 (ἀριστερός, T Tr.)
2. Mark x. 40.

LEG.

σκέλος, the leg, (*from the hip to the foot.*)

John xix. 31, 32, 33.

LEGION.

λεγεών, legion, *the largest division of troops in the Roman army, varying at different periods from* 3,000 *to* 6,600. *Used for* an indefinitely great number.

Matt. xxvi. 53. | Mark v. 15.
Mark v. 9. | Luke viii. 30.

LEISURE (HAVE)

εὐκαιρέω, to have a good season, have leisure, have opportunity.

Mark vi. 31.

LEND.

1. δανείζω, to lend money, to loan.
2. κίχρημι, (*from* χράω) to furnish what is needful.

1. Luke vi. 34 twice, 35. | 2. Luke xi. 5.

LENGTH.

μῆκος, length, (*non occ.*)

Eph. iii. 18. | Rev. xxi. 16 twice.

LENGTH (AT)

ποτέ, when, whenever, at any time; *future*, one day, at last.

Rom. i. 10.

LEOPARD.

πάρδαλις, a panther, leopard, (*non occ.*)

Rev. xiii. 2.

LEPER (-s.)

λεπρός, scaly, scabby; *hence*, one so diseased, a leper, (*non occ.*)

Matt. viii. 2. | Mark xiv. 3.
—— x. 8. | Luke iv. 27.
—— xi. 5. | —— vii. 22.
Mark i. 40. | —— xvii. 12.

LEPROSY.

λέπρα, leprosy, *in which the skin becomes* scaly, (*non occ.*)

Matt. viii. 3. | Mark i. 42.
Luke v. 12, 13.

LESS.

1. ἐλάσσων, less, minor, *in quality or age.*
2. μικρότερος, smaller, less, *opp.* to μέγας, large, *of magnitude, quantity, number, or time.*

2. Mark iv. 31. | — Eph. iii. 8, see Least.
— 1 Cor. xii. 23, see Honourable. | — Phil. ii. 28, see Sorrowful.
| 1. Heb. vii. 7.

LESS (*have the*) [marg.]

ὑστερέω, to be last, behind; *of dignity*, to be inferior.

1 Cor. viii. 8, (text, *be the worse.*)

LESSER [marg.]

ἐλάσσων, less, minor, *in quality, age, or dignity.*

Rom. ix. 12, (text, *younger.*)

LEST.

1. { ἵνα, that, to the end that, *with the emphasis on result*, / μή, not, } that not.
2. μήποτε, lest ever, lest perhaps, whether indeed, if so be.
3. μή, not; *or elliptically*, lest.
4. μήπως, lest in any way, that in no way.
5. { εἰς, unto, with a view to, / τὸ, the, / μή, not, } in order that... [might] not.

— Matt. iv. 6, } see L at
— — v. 25, } any time.
2. — vii. 6.
— — xiii. 15, see L at
2. — 29. [any time.
2. — xv. 32.
1. — xvii. 27.
2. — xxv. 9.
1. — xxvi. 5.
2. — xxvii. 64.
1. Mark iii. 9. [any time.
— — iv. 12, see L at
3. — xiii. 5, 36.
2. — xiv. 2.
1. — 38.
— Luke iv. 11, see L at any time.
1. — viii. 12.
2. — xii. 58.
2. — xiv. 8, 12.
1. — 29, and see L
1. — xvi. 28. [haply.
1. — xviii. 5.
— — xxi. 34, see L at any time.
1. — xxii. 46.
1. John iii. 20.
1. — v. 14.
1. — xii. 35, 42.
1. — xviii. 28.
1. Acts v. 26 (*om.* *ἵνα*, L Tr A^b ℵ.)
— — 39, see L haply.
3. — xiii. 40.
3. — xxiii. 10.
3. — xxvii. 17.
4. — 29 (*μήπου, lest perchance,* G ∾ T Tr
3. — 42. [A ℵ.)
2. — xxviii. 27.
4. Rom. xi. 21 (*om.* G⇉L T Tr A ℵ, i.e. *neither will He spare, etc.*)
1. — 25.
1. — xv. 20.
1. 1 Cor. i. 15, 17.
— — viii. 9, see L by means.
1. — 13.
1. — ix. 12.
— — 27, see L that by any means.
3. — x. 12.
1. 2 Cor. ii. 3, 11.
— — 7, see L per-
5. — iv. 4. [haps.
1. — ix. 3.
— — 4, see L haply
— — 27.
— — xi. 3, see L by any means.
3. — xii. 6.
1. — 7 1st, 7 2nd (*ap.*)
4. — 20 twice.
3. — 21.
1. — xiii. 10.
— Gal. ii. 2, see L by any means.
4. — iv. 11.
3. — vi. 1.
1. — 12.
1. Eph. ii. 9.
1. Phil. ii. 27.
1. Col. ii. 4.
3. — 8.
1. — iii. 21.
— 1 Thes. iii. 5, see L by some means.
1. 1 Tim. iii. 6, 7.
— Heb. ii. 1, see L at any time.
2. — iii. 12.
1. — 13.
2. — iv. 1.
1. — 11.
1. — xi. 28.
1. — xii. 3, 13.
3. — 15 twice, 16.
1. Jas. v. 9, 12.
1. Rev. xvi. 15.

LEST AT ANY TIME.

2. Matt. iv. 6.
2. — v. 25.
2. — xiii. 15.
2. Mark iv. 12.
2. Luke iv. 11.
2. — xxi. 34.
2. Heb. ii. 1.

LEST BY ANY MEANS.

4. 1 Cor. viii. 9.
4. 2 Cor. xi. 3.
4. Gal. ii. 2.

LEST BY SOME MEANS.

4. 1 Thes. iii. 5.

LEST HAPLY.

1. { *ἵνα*, that, to the end that,
 { *μήποτε*, lest ever, lest perhaps.
2. *μήποτε, see above, No.* 2.
3. *μήπως*, lest in any way, that in no way.

1. Luke xiv. 29.
2. Acts v. 39.
3. 2 Cor. ix. 4.

LEST PERHAPS.

μήπως, see above, No. 3.

2 Cor. ii. 7.

LEST THAT BY ANY MEANS.

μήπως, see above, No. 3.

1 Cor. ix. 27.

LET (-ETH.)

1. *ἀφίημι*, to send forth *or* away, to let go from one's self, to let pass, permit, suffer.
2. *ἐάω*, to let, let be, leave alone; to suffer, allow.
3. *ἔξεστι*, (*impers. of ἔξειμι*) it is possible, one can; *referring to moral possibility or propriety*, it is lawful, it is permitted, one may.
4. *ἐπιτρέπω*, to turn upon, direct upon, turn to *or* towards; to commit *or* entrust to *any one's care*, to rely upon him, to give up; *hence*, to yield, *and so*, permit.
5. *κατέχω*, to have and hold down, to hold firmly, to restrain, repress.

[In 2 Thes. ii. 7. *The restraining power is evidently the presence of the Holy Ghost in and with the Church.* *ὁ κάτεχων*, he who restraineth, *i.e.* "until the one restraining at present may happen to be out of the midst."]

6. *κωλύω*, to hinder, prevent.

1. Matt. vii. 4.
1. — viii. 22.
1. Mark vii. 27.
— Luke ii. 29, see Depart.
1. — vi. 42.
1. — ix. 44, see Sink.
1. — 60.
4. — 61.
1. John xi. 44.
1. John xviii. 8.
3. Acts ii. 21, marg. *may.*
— — xxiii. 22, see Depart.
— — xxvii. 15, see Drive.
2. — 32.
6. Rom. i. 13.
5. 2 Thes. ii. 7.
— Heb. ii. 1, see Slip.

LET ALONE.

1. Matt. xv. 14.
2. Mark i. 24, imperat. (*om.* *ἔα*, *let us alone.* G → L T Tr A ℵ.)
1. — xiv. 6.
1. Mark xv. 36.
2. Luke iv. 34, marg. *away*
1. — xiii. 8.
1. John xi. 48.
1. — xii. 7.
2. Acts v. 38 (No. 1, G ∾ L T Tr A ℵ.)

LET BE.

ἀφίημι, see "LET," *No.* 1.

2. *ἤτω*, (*imperat. of εἰμί*, to be) let him, her, *or* it be, (*non occ.*)

1. Matt. xxvii. 49.
2. 1 Cor. xvi. 22.
2. Jas. v. 12.

LET DOWN.

1. *καθίημι*, to send, *or* let fall, let down, (*non. occ.*)

2. *χαλάω*, to let go, relax, loosen; *hence*, to let down, to lower, (*occ.* Acts xxvii. 17.)

2. Mark ii. 4.	1. Acts x. 11.
2. Luke v. 4, 5.	1. —— xi. 5.
1. —— 19.	2. —— xxvii. 30.
1. Acts ix. 25.	2. 2 Cor. xi. 33.

LET FORTH.

ἐκδίδωμι, to give out, to deliver out, place out, to give out on hire, let out.

Luke xx. 9.

LET GO.

1. *ἀπολύω*, to let loose from, loosen, unbind.

2. *ἀφίημι*, *see* "LET," *No.* 1.

2. Mark xi. 6.	1. Acts iii. 13.
1. Luke xiv. 4.	1. —— iv. 21, 23.
1. —— xxii. 68 (om. *μοί ἤ ἀπολύσητε*, *me, nor let me go*, T Tr[b] A[b] ℵ.)	1. —— v. 40.
1. —— xxiii. 22.	1. —— xv. 33.
1. John xix. 12.	1. —— xvi. 35, 36.
	1. —— xvii. 9.
	1. —— xxviii. 18.

LET (HAVE)

ἀφίημι, *see* "LET," *No.* 1.

Matt. v. 40.

LET OUT.

ἐκδίδωμι, *see* "LET FORTH."

Matt. xxi. 33, 41. | Mark xii. 1.

LETTER (-s.)

1. *γράμμα*, a picture, *lit.*, the written, *i.e.* something written or cut in with the stylus in the ancient manner of writing, a letter *of the alphabet; hence*, anything written, a writing, a bill, bond, note, letter.

2. *ἐπιστολή*, anything sent by a messenger, a message *or* commission, *whether verbal or in writing; most usually*, a letter, epistle.

1. Luke xxiii. 38 (ap.)	1. Rom. vii. 6.
1. John vii. 15, pl. marg. *learning.*	2. 1 Cor. xvi. 3.
2. Acts ix. 2.	1. 2 Cor. iii. 6 twice.
2. —— xxii. 5.	2. —— vii. 8.
2. —— xxiii. 25.	2. —— x. 9, 10, 11.
1. —— xxviii. 21.	1. Gal. vi. 11.
1. Rom. ii. 27, 29.	2. 2 Thes. ii. 2.
	— Heb. xiii. 22, see Write.

LEWD.

πονηρός, causing *or* having labour, sorrow, pain; *hence, gen.*, evil, malignant; bad, vicious.

Acts xvii. 5.

LEWDNESS.

ῥᾳδιούργημα, what is done easily, light-work, levity; *then, in a bad sense*, wickedness, recklessness, (*non occ.*)

Acts xviii. 14.

LIAR (-s.)

1. *ψεύστης*, one false, a deceiver, liar, (*non occ.*)

2. *ψευδής*, false, deceiving, lying, (*occ.* Acts vi. 13.)

1. John viii. 44, 45.	1. 1 John ii. 4, 22.
1. Rom. iii. 4.	1. —— iv. 20.
1. 1 Tim. i. 10.	1. —— v. 10.
1. Tit. i. 12.	2. Rev. ii. 2.
1. 1 John i. 10.	2. —— xxi. 8 (No. 1, L.)

LIBERAL.

ἁπλότης, simplicity, sincerity, candour, unaffectedness, simplicity *without a thought behind.*

2 Cor. ix. 13.

LIBERALITY.

1. *ἁπλότης*, *see above.*

2. *χάρις*, what causes joy; *hence*, a pleasing work, favour, kindness, benevolence.

2. 1 Cor. xvi. 3, marg. *gift.* | 1. 2 Cor. viii. 2.

LIBERALLY.

ἁπλῶς, simply, *i.e.* in simplicity, with a readiness of heart, answering to the need without a second thought; simply, without a thought behind, freely, (*non occ.*)

Rom. xii. 8, *with ἐν in:* marg. *simplicity.*
Jas. i. 5.

LIBERTY.

1. *ἐλευθερία*, freedom to go where one will, liberty, (*non occ.*)

2. *ἄνεσις*, a letting loose, relaxation, *as of chords or strings hitherto tightly drawn or strained; hence*, rest *from labour and anxiety.*

3. *ἄφεσις*, dismission, deliverance; remission, forgiveness.

4. *ἐξουσία*, authority, the power to *do anything*, right, full-power.

5. παῤῥησία, the speaking all one thinks, free-spokenness, *as characteristic of a frank and fearless mind; hence,* frankness, boldness.

3. Luke iv. 18.
2. Acts xxiv. 23.
— —— xxvi. 32, see L (set at)
— —— xxvii. 3, see L (give)
1. Rom. viii. 21.
— 1 Cor. vii. 39, see L (at)
4. —— viii. 9, marg. *power.*
1. —— x. 29.
1. 2 Cor. iii. 17.
1. Gal. ii. 4.
1. —— v. 1, 13 twice.
5. Heb. x. 19, marg. (text, *boldness.*)
— —— xiii. 23, see L (set at)
1. Jas. i. 25.
1. —— ii. 12.
1. 1 Pet. ii. 16.
1. 2 Pet. ii. 19.

LIBERTY (AT)

ἐλεύθερος, one who can go where he will; *hence,* free, at liberty.

1 Cor. vii. 39.

LIBERTY (GIVE)

ἐπιτρέπω, *see* "LET," *No.* 4.

Acts xxvii. 3.

LIBERTY (SET AT)

ἀπολύω, to let loose from, loosen, unbind.

Acts xxvi. 32. | Heb. xiii. 23.

LICENSE.

τόπος, place; *met.,* opportunity, room.

Acts xxv. 16.

LICENSE (GIVE)

ἐπιτρέπω, *see* "LET," *No.* 4.

Acts xxvii. 3.

LICK (-ED.)

ἀπολείχω, to lick off, *i.e.* to lick clean, (*non occ.*)

Luke xvi. 21 (ἐπιλείχω, *to lick over,* L T Tr A ℵ.)

LIE [noun.]

1. ψεῦδος, falsehood, lying, a lie.
2. ψεῦσμα, a being false, falsehood.

1. John viii. 44.
1. Rom. i. 25.
2. —— iii. 7.
1. 2 Thes. ii. 11.
— 1 Tim. iv. 12, see L (speaking.)
1. 1 John ii. 21, 27.
1. Rev. xxi. 27.
1. Rev. xxii. 15.

LIES (SPEAKING)

ψευδολόγος, speaking falsely, lying.

1 Tim. iv. 2.

LIE (-ED.) [to speak falsely.]

ψεύδω, to speak falsely, to lie to *any one,* to deceive.

Acts v. 3, see L to.
—— 4.
Rom. ix. 1.
2 Cor. xi. 31.
Gal. i. 20.
Col. iii. 9.
1 Tim. ii. 7. [cannot)
Tit. i. 2, see L (that
Heb. vi. 18.
Jas. iii. 14.
1 John i. 6.
Rev. iii. 9.

LIE TO.

Acts v. 3.

LIE (THAT CANNOT)

ἀψευδής, incapable of falsehood, (*non occ.*)

Tit. i. 2.

LIE (-ETH, -ING, LAIN, LAY,)

[to rest, lay down.]

1. κεῖμαι, to lie, *and also* to be laid, *esp.,* of a dead body.
2. ἀνάκειμαι, (*No.* 1, *with* ἀνά, up, *prefixed*) to be laid up.
3. κατάκειμαι, (*No.* 1, *with* κατά, down, *prefixed*) to lie down, to lie, to be recumbent, *gen., of the sick.*
4. βάλλω, to throw, to cast. *Here, pass.,* to be cast, to be thrown down, to lie.
5. βλέπω, to use the eyes, to look.
6. ἔχω, to have and hold. *Here, with* ἐν, in, to be in, continue.

4. Matt. viii. 6.
4. —— ix. 2.
— —— 36, see L down.
1. —— xxviii. 6.
3. Mark i. 30.
3. —— ii. 4.
— —— v. 23, see Death.
2. —— 40 (*om.* G Lb T Tr A ℵ.)
1. Luke ii. 12, 16.
3. —— v. 25.
— —— viii. 42, see Dying.
3. John v. 3, 6.
6. —— xi. 17.
— John xi. 38, see L upon.
— —— xiii. 35, see L on.
1. —— xx. 5, 6, 7, 12.
— Acts xiv. 6, see Region.
— —— xxiii. 16, } see L in
— —— 21, } wait for.
5. —— xxvii. 12.
— —— 20, see L on.
3. —— xxviii. 8, see Sick.
— Rom. xii. 28, see Much.
— Eph. iv. 14, see L in wait (whereby one)
1. 1 John v. 19.
1. Rev. xxi. 16.

LIE DOWN [marg.]

ῥίπτω, to throw *or* cast *with a sudden motion,* hurl, jerk; *then,* to cast forth, scatter.

Matt. ix. 36 (text, *scattered abroad.*)

LIETH IN WAIT (WHEREBY ONE)

πρὸς, towards, τὴν, the, μεθοδείαν, method, system, } with a view to systematized [*error.*]

Eph. iv. 14.

LIE IN WAIT FOR.

ἐνεδρεύω, to lie in wait for, *esp. in war;* to lie in ambush against.

Acts xxiii. 16, see Lying. | Acts xxiii. 21.

LIE ON.

1. ἐπίκειμαι, to lie upon, be laid upon.
2. ἐπίπιπτω, to fall upon.

2. John xiii. 25 (ἀναπίπτω, *lean back,* G ∾ L T Tr A ℵ.)
1. Acts xxvii. 20.

LIE UPON.

ἐπίκειμαι, to lie upon, be laid upon.

John xi. 38, with ἐπί.

LIFE (LIVES.)

1. ζωή, life (*akin to* ἄω, ἄημι, to breathe the breath of life) the perfect and abiding antithesis to θάνατος, (death.)

[ζωή, is life in all its manifestations, from the life of God down to the life of the lowest vegetable. It is necessarily active; it cannot be inert. In its essence or nature it is ever the same, and different only in its developments or manifestations. Each living person or thing has that portion of it which is needful for his or its designed position or purpose. Its one only source is God, who is "the living One." We live only in and by His life. He originates and sustains life in all by giving it out of Himself. "In Him we live and move, and have our being."

ζωή, life, must not be confounded with, or defined as "existence." Existence applies to all created things. Life is the property of only some created things to whom it has been communicated. Whatever has life has existence; but many things have existence which have no life.

ζωή also must be distinguished from βιός, (*No.* 3.) In profane and classical literature ζωή is not the nobler word, because the heathen were ignorant of its true connection with sin and death.

ζωή, as used of the future life which we have now in Christ, is "the gift of God," (Rom. vi. 23); by Christ, (John vi. 27, x. 28). "He that hath the Son, hath life; and he that hath not the Son hath not life," (1 John v. 12); now "hid with Christ in God," (Col. iii. 3.)]

2. ψυχή, breath *of animal life;* one manifestation of ζωή, *viz.* that which is manifested in animals; *hence,* life, animal life, the living individual as such. [In one passage (Is. x. 18), 'nephesh,' or ψυχή, is applied to vegetable life.]

3. βίος, life, *i.e.* the life which we live, the life led; *hence,* manner of life, period or duration of life, means of living.

[ζωή is life as the gift of God, and therefore is applied to everything which has life. βίος is applied only to men, who not only live, but lead lives; *hence,* the difference between the words zoology and BIOGRAPHY. βίος is used only of the lower life, and has no such worthy use as *No.* 1.]

4. πνεῦμα, wind, breath breathed forth.

[When not used for "wind," it expresses immateriality, that which cannot be apprehended by our senses, and which is recognized only by its operations or manifestations. It is seen in life, liveliness, the activities of life, whether these activities be mental, moral, or physical. The πνεῦμα of God is the source of life in all its manifestations. The withdrawal of this πνεῦμα leaves θάνατος, (the opposite of ζωή)].

2. Matt. ii. 20.
— — iii. 8, see Amendment.
2. — vi. 25 twice.
1. — vii. 14.
2. — x. 39 twice.
2. — xvi. 25 twice.
1. — xviii. 8, 9.
— — xix. 16, see L (eternal)
1. — — 17.
— — — 29, see L (everlasting)
2. — xx. 28.
— — xxv. 46, see L (eternal)
2. Mark iii. 4.
2. — viii. 35 1st.
2. — — 35 2nd (*om.* G →)
1. — ix. 43, 45.
— — x. 17, 30, see L (eternal)
2. — — 45.
1. Luke i. 75 (*om.* G L T Tr A ℵ) i.e. *all our days*, instead of "*all the days of our life.*"
2. — vi. 9.
3. — viii. 14.
2. — ix. 24 twice, 56 (*ap.*)
— — x. 25, see L (eternal)
1. — xii. 15.
2. — — 22, 23.
2. — xiv. 26.
2. — xvii. 33.
— — xviii. 18, see L (eternal)
— — — 30, see L everlasting.
— — xxi. 34, see L (of this)
1. John i. 4 twice.
— — iii. 15, see L (eternal)
— — — 16, 36 1st, see L (everlasting)
1. — — 36 2nd.
— — iv. 14, see L (everlasting)
— — — 36, see L (eternal)
— — v. 24 1st, see L (everlasting)
1. — — 24 2nd.
— — — 39, see L (eternal)
1. — — 51, 53, 63.
— — vi. 27, 40, 47, see L (everlasting)
— — — 54, 68, see L (eternal)
1. — viii. 12.
1. — x. 10.
2. — — 11, 15, 17.
— — — 28, see L (eternal)
1. — xi. 25.
2. — xii. 25 1st & 2nd.
— — — 25 3rd, see L eternal.
— — — 50, see L everlasting.
2. — xiii. 37, 38.
1. — xiv. 6.
2. — xv. 13.
— — xvii. 2, see L (eternal)
— — — 3, see L eternal.
1. — xx. 31.
1. Acts ii. 28.
1. — iii. 15.
1. — v. 20.
1. — viii. 33.
1. — xi. 18.
— — xiii. 46, see L (everlasting)
— — — 48, see L (eternal)
2. — xv. 26.
1. — xvii. 25.
2. Acts xx. 10, 24.
— — xxvi. 4, see L (manner of)
2. — xxvii. 10, 22.
— Rom. ii. 7, see L (eternal)
1. — v. 10, 17, 18.
— — — 21, see L (eternal)
1. — vi. 4.
— — — 22, see L (everlasting)
— — — 23, see L (eternal)
1. — vii. 10.
1. — viii. 2, 6, 10, 38.
2. — xi. 3.
1. — — 15.
2. — xvi. 4.
1. 1 Cor. iii. 22.
— — vi. 3, see L (things that pertain to this)
— — — 4, see L (of things pertaining to this)
— — xiv. 7, see L (things without)
1. — xv. 19.
— 2 Cor. i. 8, see L (of)
1. — ii 16 twice.
— — iii. 6, see L (give)
1. — iv. 10, 11, 12.
1. — v. 4.
— Gal. ii. 20, see L which (the)
— — iii. 21, see L (give)
— — vi. 8, see L everlasting.
1. Eph. iv. 18.
1. Phil. i. 20.
1. — ii. 16.
2. — — 30.
1. — iv. 3.
1. Col. iii. 3, 4.
— 1 Tim. i. 16, see L everlasting.
— — ii. 2, see L (lead a)
1. — iii. 16 twice.
1. — iv. 8.
— — vi. 12, 19, see L (eternal)
1. 2 Tim. i. 1, 10.
3. — ii. 4.
— — iii. 10, see L (manner of)
— Titus i. 2, — — iii. 7, } see L (eternal)
1. Heb. vii. 3, 16.
— — xi. 35, see Raised.
1. Jas. i. 12.
1. — iv. 14.
1. 1 Pet. iii. 7, 10.
3. — iv. 3 (*om.* τοῦ βίου, *of our life*, G ⇉ L T Tr A ℵ.)
1. 2 Pet. i. 3.
1. 1 John i. 1, 2 1st.
— — — 2 2nd, see L (eternal)
3. — ii. 16.
— — — 25, see L (eternal)
1. — iii. 14.
— — — 15, see L (eternal)
— — v. 11 1st, see L (eternal)
1. — — 11 2nd, 12 twice.
— — — 13, see L (eternal)
1. — — 16.
— — — 20, see L (eternal)
— Jude 20, see L (eternal)
1. Rev. ii. 7, 10.
1. — iii. 5.
2. — viii. 9.
1. — xi. 11.
2. — xii. 11.
1. — xiii. 8.
4. — — 15, marg. *breath.*
1. — xvii. 8.
1. — xx. 12, 15.
1. — xxi. 6, 27.
1. — xxii. 1, 2, 14, 17, 19.

LIFE ETERNAL.

{ ζωή, *see* "LIFE," *No.* 1, αἰώνιος, belonging to the αἰών, constant, abiding, eternal, } life eternal, *or* life everlasting. [This is the gift of God to those who are "in Christ." *See* John x. 10; x. 28, v. 24; vi. 40, 47; xvii. 2; 1 John v. 11, 12.]

Matt. xxv. 46.
John iv. 36.
John xii. 25.
— xvii. 3.

LIFE (ETERNAL)

Matt. xix. 16.
Mark x. 17, 30.
Luke x. 25.
— xviii. 18.
John iii. 15.
— v. 39.
— vi. 54, 68.
— x. 28.
— xvii. 2.
Acts xiii. 48.
Rom. ii. 7.
— v. 21.
Rom. vi. 23.
1 Tim. vi. 12.
— — 19 (ὄντως, *real*, instead of αἰώνιος, *eternal*, G L T Tr A ℵ.)
Tit. i. 2.
— iii. 7.
1 John i. 2.
— ii. 25.
— iii. 15.
— v. 11, 13, 20.
Jude 21.

LIFE EVERLASTING.

Luke xviii. 30.
John xii. 50.
Gal. vi. 8.
1 Tim. i. 16.

LIFE (EVERLASTING)

Matt. xix. 29.
John iii. 16, 36.
— iv. 14.
John v. 24.
— vi. 27, 40, 47
Acts xiii. 46.
Rom. vi. 22.

LIFE (GIVE)

ζωοποιέω, to make alive, to vivify, endue with ζωή, (*see* "LIFE," *No.* 1.)

2. Cor. iii. 6, marg. *quicken* | Gal. iii. 21.

LIFE (LEAD A...)

{ βίος, *see* "LIFE," *No.* 3, διάγω, to lead through, } to lead a life, (*occ.* Tit. iii. 3.)

1 Tim. ii. 2.

LIFE (MANNER OF)

1. ἀγωγή, a leading, guidance; training, education, tending; *and intrans.*, mode of life.
2. βίωσις, way *or* mode of life, manner *or* habit of life.

2. Acts xxvi. 4. | 1. 2 Tim. iii. 10.

LIFE (of)

ζάω, (*akin to ἄω, ἄημι*, to breathe the breath of life) to live, *see* "LIVE," (verb) *No.* 1. *Here, infinitive.*

2 Cor. i. 8.

LIFE (of this)

βιωτικός, fit for life; of *or* pertaining to *βίος*, (*see* "LIFE," *No.* 3) livelihood *or* living.

Luke xxi. 34.

LIFE (of things pertaining to this)

βιωτικός, *see above.*

1 Cor. vi. 4.

LIFE (things that pertain to this)

βιωτικός, *see above.*

1 Cor. vi. 3.

LIFE (things without)

{ τὰ, the *things*,
ἄψυχα, without ψυχή, (*see* "LIFE," *No.* 2.)

1 Cor. xiv. 7.

LIFE WHICH (the,

ὅ, that which, *lit.*, in what respect.

Gal. ii. 20.

LIFE-TIME.

ζωή, (*see* "LIFE," *No.* 1.)

Luke xvi. 25.

LIFETIME (all their)

{ διὰ, through,
παντὸς, all,
τοῦ, the [*of them*,] *i.e.* their,
ζῆν, life, (*see* "LIFE," *No.* 1.)

Heb. ii. 15.

LIFT OUT.

ἐγείρω, to awaken, wake up, *esp.*, of the dead, to raise up; *then*, (*the idea of sleep being dropped*) to cause to rise up, set upright.

Matt. xii. 11.

LIFT UP (-ed, ing)

1. *ἐπαίρω*, to lift up upon, raise up, (*No.* 3, *with* ἐπί, upon, *prefixed.*)
2. *ὑψόω*, to heighten, elevate, exalt.
3. *αἴρω*, to take up, lift up.
4. *ἐγείρω*, *see* "LIFT OUT."
5. *ἀνίστημι*, to cause to stand up.
6. *ἀνορθόω*, to set upright, to erect again.

1. Matt. xvii. 8, part.
4. Mark i. 31.
4. —— ix. 27.
1. Luke vi. 20.
1. —— xi. 27.
— —— xiii. 11, see L up one's self.
1. —— xvi. 23.
3. —— xvii. 13.
1. —— xviii. 13.
1. —— xxi. 28.
1. —— xxiv. 50.
2. John iii. 14 1st & 2nd (om. Lm.)
1. John iv. 35.
1. —— vi. 5, part.
— John viii. 7, 10, see L up one's self.
2. —— 32, 34.
3. —— xi. 41.
1. —— xiii. 18.
1. —— xvii. 1.
1. Acts ii. 14.
4. —— iii. 7.
3. —— iv. 24.
5. —— ix. 41.
1. —— xiv. 11.
1. —— xxii. 22.
1. 1 Tim. ii. 8.
— —— iii. 6, see Pride.
6. Heb. xii. 12.
2. Jas. iv. 10.

3. Rev. x. 5.

LIFT UP ONE'S SELF.

ἀνακύπτω, to raise one's self up, to rise up from a stooping posture, (*occ.* Luke xxi. 28.)

Luke xiii. 11.
John viii. 7 (*ap.*), 10, part (*ap.*)

LIGHT (-s.) [noun.]

1. *φῶς*, light. *The opp. of* σκοτός, darkness. Light underived, absolute; *hence*, the light of the sun *or* day. *Used therefore of* God, *who* "is Light," (1 John i. 5) *and of* Christ, *who is* "the Light of the world," (John i. 4, 5, viii. 12), (*occ.* Mark xiv. 54; Luke xxii. 56.)
2. *φωστήρ*, a light, light-giver, *used only of* the light of the stars *and* reflected light, (*Lat.*, luminaria); lxx. for מארות, light-holders (Gen. i. 14, 16), (*cf.* Wisd. xiii. 2.)

   [In Rev. xxi. 11, it is the light reflected upon and from the Heavenly City by its "light," which was the Lamb, ver. 23,] (*non occ.*)
3. *φωτισμός*, a lighting, illumination, shining.

4. λύχνος, a portable hand lamp fed with oil; (*not a candle.*) [*Hence*, used of men, whose light is kindled by another, burns for a season, and then is extinguished. *See* John v. 35.]

5. φέγγος, φῶς, (light) in its brightness *or* splendour, radiance, (*non occ.*)

6. λαμπάς, a torch, (lxx. Judg. vii. 16, 20.) [Eastern torches were fed with oil from a sort of bottle, (the ἀγγεῖον of Matt. xxv. 4) constructed for the purpose. *See* Elphinstone's *History of India*, vol. i. p. 333. *See* under "LAMP."]

1. Matt. iv. 16 twice.
1. —— v. 14.
— —— 15, see L (give)
1. —— 16.
4. —— vi. 22 1st.
— —— 22 2nd, see L (full of)
1. —— 23.
1. —— x. 27.
1. —— xvii. 2.
5. —— xxiv. 29.
5. Mark xiii. 24.
— Luke i. 79, see L to (give)
1. —— ii. 32.
1. —— viii. 16.
5. —— xi. 33 (No. 1, L Tr A ℵ.)
4. —— 34 1st.
— —— 34 2nd, see L (full of)
1. —— 35.
— —— 36 1st & 2nd, see L (full of)
— —— 36 3rd, see L (give...)
1. —— xii. 3.
4. —— 35.
1. —— xvi. 8.
1. John i. 4, 5.
1. —— iii. 19 twice, 20 twice, 21.
4. —— v. 35 1st.
1. —— 35 2nd.
1. —— viii. 12 twice.
1. —— ix. 5.
1. —— xi. 9, 10.
1. John xii. 35 twice.
1. —— 36 3 times, 46.
1. Acts ix. 3.
1. —— xii. 7.
1. —— xiii. 47.
1. —— xvi. 29.
6. —— xx. 8.
1. —— xxii. 6, 9, 11.
1. —— xxvi. 13, 18, 23.
1. Rom. ii. 19.
1. —— xiii. 12.
— 1 Cor. iv. 5, see L (bring to)
3. 2 Cor. iv. 4.
1. —— 6 1st.
— —— 6 2nd, see L (give)
1. —— vi. 14.
1. —— xi. 14.
1. Eph. v. 8 twice, 13 twice.
— —— 14, see L (give)
2. Phil. ii. 15.
1. Col. i. 12.
1. 1 Thes. v. 5.
1. 1 Tim. vi. 16.
— 2 Tim. i. 10, see L (bring to)
1. Jas. i. 17.
1. 1 Pet. ii. 9.
4. 2 Pet. i. 19.
1. 1 John i. 5, 7 twice.
1. —— ii. 8, 9, 10.
1. Rev. xviii. 23.
2. —— xxi. 11.
4. —— 23.
1. —— 24.
1. —— xxii. 5 1st.

— Rev. xxii. 5 2nd, see L (give)

LIGHT (BRING TO)

φωτίζω, to light, lighten; *intrans.*, to give light, to shine; *trans.*, enlighten, light up; *hence*, bring to light, make known, publish.

1 Cor. iv. 5. | 2 Tim. i. 10.

LIGHT (FULL OF)

φωτεινός, shining, bright, (*occ.* Matt. xvii. 5.)

Matt. vi. 23. | Luke xi. 34, 36 twice.

LIGHT (GIVE)

1. ἐπιφαύω, to shine upon, to appear unto, (*non occ.*)
2. λάμπω, to give *the* light *of a torch*, to shine *as a torch*, shine forth, beam.
3. φωτίζω, *see* "LIGHT (BRING TO)"
4. { πρὸς, towards, with a view to, φωτισμόν, an illumination, } for the shining forth.

2. Matt. v. 15.
3. Luke xi. 36.
4. 2 Cor. iv. 6.
1. Eph. v. 14.
3. Rev. xxii. 5.

LIGHT TO (GIVE)

ἐπιφαίνω, to cause to appear upon *or* to, to show forth *or* before. *In N.T.*, *mid.*, to show one's self upon *or* to, to appear upon *or* to.

Luke i. 79.

LIGHT (-ED.) LIGHTEN,* ENLIGHTEN † (-ED, -ETH.)

1. φωτίζω, *see* "LIGHT (BRING TO)"
2. ἅπτω, to put one thing to another; *spoken of fire as* applied to things, to set fire to, kindle, light.
3. καίω, to burn, make burn.

3. Matt. v. 15.
2. Luke viii. 16, part.
2. —— xi. 33, part.
2. —— xv. 8.
1. John i. 9.
1. Eph. i. 18.†
1. Heb. vi. 4.†
1. Rev. xviii. 1.*
1. Rev. xxi. 23.*

LIGHT (-ING.) [verb.]

1. ἐρχομενος, coming.
2. πίπτω, to fall, fall upon.

1. Matt. iii. 16. | 2. Rev. vii. 16.

LIGHT [adj.]

ἐλαφρός, light, not heavy, easy to bear, (*non occ.*)

Matt. xi. 30. | 2 Cor. iv. 17.

LIGHT OF (MAKE)

ἀμελέω, not to care for, neglect.

Matt. xxii. 5.

LIGHTEN (-ETH.) [verb.]

(*as to light.*)

1. φωτίζω, *see* "LIGHT (BRING TO)"

2. ἀστράπτω, to lighten *as lightning.*

3. { εἰς, unto, with a view to, for, ἀποκαλυψις, an uncovering, unveiling, } for... unveiling.

3. Luke ii. 32.
2. —— xvii. 24.
1. Rev. xviii. 1.
1. —— xxi. 23.

LIGHTEN (-ED.) [verb.]

(as to weight.)

κουφίζω, to lighten, *as a ship, by throwing things overboard,* (*non occ.*)

Acts xxvii. 38.

LIGHTEN THE SHIP.

{ ἐκβολὴ, a casting out, ποιέω, to make, } making an overthrow [*of the cargo,*] (*non occ.*)

Acts xxvii. 18.

LIGHTLY.

ταχύ, quickly, with haste.

Mark ix. 39.

LIGHTNESS.

ἐλαφρία, lightness, (*prop. in weight*) (*non occ.*)

2 Cor. i. 17.

LIGHTNING.

ἀστραπή, lightning, (*occ.* Luke xi. 36.)

Matt. xxiv. 27.
—— xxviii. 3.
Luke x. 18.
—— xvii. 24.
Rev. iv. 5.
—— viii. 5.
—— xi. 19.
—— xvi. 18.

LIKE [adj.]

1. ὅμοιος, like, resembling, (*gen., of external form and appearance.*)

2. ὡς, in which way, in what way, *and hence, gen.,* as, so as.

3. ὡσεί, (ὡς, as, *and* εἰ, if) as if, as though, as it were.

4. ἴσος, equal, (*spoken of measure, quantity, condition, etc.*)

5. { οὕτως, thus, ὡς, as, } thus, as [*this man.*]

3. Matt. iii. 16.
— —— vi. 8, see L (be)
2. —— 29.
1. —— xi. 16.
— —— xii. 13, see L as.
1. —— xiii. 31, 33, 44, 45, 47, 52.
1. —— xx. 1.
— —— xxi. 24, see L wise.
— —— xxii. 2, see L (be)
1. —— 39.
— —— xxiii. 27, see L unto (be)
2. —— xxviii. 3.
3. Mark i. 10 (No. 2, G L T Tr A ℵ.)
2. —— iv. 31.
— —— vii. 8, 13, see L things.
1. —— xii. 31 (*om.* καὶ ὁμοία, T A ℵ, i.e. *the second is this,* instead of, *and the second is like, namely.*)
— —— xiii. 29, see L manner (in)
3. Luke iii. 22 (No. 2, L T Tr A ℵ.)
— —— vi. 23, see Manner.
1. —— 47, 48, 49.
1. —— vii. 31, 32.
2. —— xii. 27.
1. —— 36.
1. —— xiii. 18, 19, 21.
3. John i. 32 (No. 2, G L T Tr A ℵ.)
5. —— vii. 46 (ap.)
1. —— viii. 55.
1. —— ix. 9.
— Acts i. 11, see Manner.
— —— ii. 3, see L as.
— —— iii. 22, } see L
— —— vii. 37, } unto.
2. —— viii. 32.
4. —— xi. 17.
1. —— xvii. 29.
— —— xix. 25, see Occupation.
— Rom. i. 23, see L to (make)
— —— iv. 17, see L unto.
— Rom. vi. 4, see L as.
— —— ix. 29, see L (made)
— 1 Cor. xvi. 13, see Men.
1. Gal. v. 21.
— Phil. iii. 21, see Fashion
— 1 Thes. ii. 14, see L things.
— Heb. ii. 17, see L (made)
— —— iv. 15, see L as.
— —— vii. 3, see L (be made)
— James i. 6, 23, see L (be)
— —— v. 17, see Passions.
— 1 Pet. iii. 21, see Figure.
— 2 Pet. i. 1, see Precious.
1. 1 John iii. 2.
1. Jude 7.
1. Rev. i. 13.
3. —— 14 (No. 2, G L T Tr A ℵ.)
1. —— 15.
— —— ii. 18 1st, see L unto.
1. —— 18 2nd.
1. —— iv. 3 1st.
1. —— 3 2nd (ὁμοίως, *in like manner,* G ∾), (*om.* ℵ.)
1. —— 6, 7 3 times.
1. —— ix. 7 1st.
1. —— 7 2nd (G ∾), (χρύσεος, *golden,* instead of, ὅμοιος χρυσῷ, *like gold,* G.)
1. —— 10, 19.
1. —— xi. 1.
1. —— xiii. 2, 4, 11.
1. —— xiv. 14.
1. —— xvi. 13 (No. 2, G L T Tr A; εἰ ἐώσεί, as if it were, ℵ), (No. 3, ℵ2.)
1. —— xviii. 18.
2. —— 21.
1. —— xxi. 11 1st.
2. —— 11 2nd.
1. —— 18.

LIKE AS.

1. { κατά, according to [*our*], ὁμοιότης, likeness, } *in* Heb. iv. 15, after our similitude, *i.e.* "according to the likeness of the way in which we are tempted."

2. ὡς, *see No.* 2, *above.*

3. ὡσεί, *see No.* 3, *above.*

4. ὥσπερ, wholly as, just as.

2. Matt. xii. 13.
3. Acts ii. 3.
4. Rom. vi. 4.
1. Heb. iv. 15.

LIKE (BE)

1. ὁμοιόω, to make like; *here, pass.,* to be *or* become like, *in form, condition, or circumstances. Also, in comparisons,* to be likened.

2. *εἴκω*, to the image of, (*non occ.*)

1. Matt. vi. 8. | 1. Matt. xxii. 2.
2. Jas. i. 6, 23.

LIKE UNTO (BE)

παρομοιάζω, to be nearly like, to resemble.

Matt. xxiii. 27, (*ὁμοιάζω*, *to be like*, L Tr.)

LIKE (BE MADE)

ἀφομοιόομαι, to liken off, (*not* "made like.") *It is used by Plato of men who* make *error* appear like *truth; and by Aristotle, of* making *the forms of gods* like *men.* It is contrasted with what *precedes by* δὲ, but, *and indicates the likeness of Melchisedec to another* in his characteristics, (*non occ.*)

Heb. vii. 3.

LIKE (EVEN)

ὡς, *see* "LIKE," *No.* 2.

Rev. xxi. 11.

LIKE MANNER (IN)

{ *οὕτω*, thus,
{ *καί*, also.

Mark xiii. 29. | Luke vi. 23, see Manner.
Acts i. 11, see Manner.

LIKE TO (MAKE)

ὁμοίωμα, something made like, a likeness, *in form, shape, or figure.*

Rom. i. 23.

LIKE (MADE)

ὁμοιόω, *see* "L (BE)"

Rom. ix. 29. | Heb. ii. 17.

LIKE THINGS.

1. *ταὐτά*, these *things.*

2. *παρόμοια*, nearly like *things*, similar *things*, (*non occ.*)

2. Mark vii. 8 (ap.), 13.
1. 1 Thes. ii. 14, (*τὰ αὐτά*, *the same things*, ·;· L T Tr A ℵ.)

LIKE UNTO.

1. *ὡς*, *see* "LIKE," *No.* 2.

2. *κατέναντι*, down over against, *i.e.* at *the point* over against; *hence,* before, in the sight of.

1. Acts iii. 22. | 2. Rom. iv. 17, marg.
1. —— vii. 37, marg., *as.* | (text, *before.*)
1. Rev. ii. 18.

LIKE [verb.]

δοκιμάζω, to assay, prove, to try; to make trial of, put to the proof; *then*, in consequence of such trial, to approve, sanction.

Rom. i. 28.

LIKEMINDED.

ἰσόψυχος, of equal soul.

Phil. ii. 20, marg., *so dear unto me.*

LIKEMINDED (BE)

{ *φρονέω*, to mind *or* regard,
{ *τὸ*, the,
{ *αὐτό*, same *thing.*

Rom. xv. 5. | Phil. ii. 2.

LIKEN (-ED.)

ὁμοιόω, to make like; to liken, to make to resemble any other objects of the same kind, compare, *pass.*, to be likened, to be like.

Matt. vii. 24, 26. | Matt. xxv. 1.
—— xi. 16. | Mark iv. 30.
—— xiii. 24. | Luke vii. 31.
—— xviii. 23. | —— xiii. 20.

LIKENESS.

ὁμοίωμα, something made like, a likeness.

Rom. vi. 5. | Rom. viii. 3.
Phil. ii. 7.

LIKENESS OF (IN THE)

ὁμοιόω, *see* "LIKEN." *Here, part. pass.*, made like.

Acts xiv. 11.

LIKEWISE.

1. *ὁμοίως*, in like manner, (from *ὅμοιος*, like, resembling.)

2. ὡσαύτως, in the same way, (ὡς, as, *and* αὔτως, the same.)

3. καὶ, and also.

4. οὕτως, thus, in this manner, on this wise.

5. παραπλησίως, coming alongside of, near to, nigh by, (*non occ.*)

4. Matt. xvii. 12.
3. —— xviii. 35.
2. —— xx. 5.
3. —— —— 10.
— —— xxi. 24, see L (I in)
2. —— —— 30, 36.
1. —— xxii. 26.
3. —— xxiv. 33.
2. —— xxv. 17.
1. —— xxvi. 35.
1. —— xxvii. 41.
1. Mark iv. 16.
2. —— xii. 21.
2. —— xiv. 31.
1. —— xv. 31.
1. Luke iii. 11.
3. —— —— 14, with τε, and ...*also.*
1. —— v. 33.
1. —— vi. 31.
1. —— x. 32, 37.
2. —— xiii. 3 (No. 1, L T Tr ℵ.)
1. —— —— 5 (No. 2, T Tr A ℵ.)
— —— xiv. 33, see L (so)
4. —— xv. 7, 10.
1. —— xvi. 25.
3. Luke xvii. 10.
1. —— —— 28, 31.
3. —— xix. 19.
3. —— xxi. 31.
2. —— xxii. 20.
1. —— —— 36.
1. John v. 19.
1. —— vi. 11.
1. —— xxi. 13.
3. Acts iii. 24.
1. Rom. i. 27.
4. —— vi. 11.
2. —— viii. 26.
1. 1 Cor. vii. 3, 4, 22.
3. —— xiv. 9.
3. Col. iv. 16.
2. 1 Tim. iii. 8.
2. —— v. 25.
2. Tit. ii. 3, 6.
5. Heb. ii. 14.
1. Jas. ii. 25.
1. 1 Pet. iii. 1, 7.
3. —— iv. 1.
1. —— v. 5.
1. Jude 8.
1. Rev. viii. 12.

LIKEWISE (I IN)

{ καὶ, and, also, } I also.
{ ἐγώ, I, }

Matt. xxi. 24.

LIKEWISE (SO)

{ οὕτως, thus, in this manner,
{ οὖν, then, therefore.

Luke xiv. 33.

LILY (-IES.)

κρίνον, a lily, (*non occ.*)

Matt. vi. 28. | Luke xii. 27.

LIMIT (-ETH.) [verb.]

ὁρίζω, to bound, to make *or* set a boundary; *hence,* mark out definitely.

Heb. iv. 7.

LINE.

κανών, a reed, rod, *or* staff; *then,* a measuring-rod; *hence,* a standard *or* rule *of life and doctrine; Eng.,* canon.

2 Cor. x. 13, marg. (text, *rule.*)
—— 16, marg., *rule.*

LINEAGE.

πατριά, paternal descent, lineage.

Luke ii. 4.

LINEN.

1. σινδών, sindon, a fine Indian cloth, muslin; *later, gen,* fine linen.

2. λίνον, flax; *then,* what is made of flax, linen, (*occ.* Matt. xii. 20.)

1. Mark xv. 46. | 1. Luke xxiii. 53.
2. Rev. xv. 6, (λίθος, *a stone,* L.)

LINEN CLOTH.

1. σινδών, *see* "LINEN," *No.* 1. [The young man who wore the linen cloth in Mark xiv. 51, 52, was doubtless Lazarus, for the following reasons:—1. It was expensive, and only used by the wealthy, and Lazarus was rich, (John xii. 1-3.) 2. The nights of the last week were spent by Jesus at Bethany, John xii. 1; Matt. xxi. 17, xxvi. 6. On this night Lazarus would be looking out for His return, and would go as far as the Mount of Olives to look down towards Jerusalem. He would see the torches and hear the tumult in Gethsemane, and go down. 3. The Jews tried to take him because "the chief priests consulted that they might put Lazarus also to death," (John xii. 10.) They would kill Lazarus, though not His disciples. Hence the suppression of the name of Lazarus in the three other Gospels, written during his life, and the mention of him in John, written A.D. 90.]

2. ὀθόνιον, a piece of fine linen, a linen bandage, (*non occ.*)

1. Matt. xxvii. 59. | 2. Luke xxiv. 12 (*ap.*)
1. Mark xiv. 51, 52. | 2. John xix. 40.
2. John xx. 5, 6, 7.

LINEN (FINE)

1. βύσσος, byssus, a fine yellowish flax and the linen made from it, *highly prized by the ancients.*

2. βύσσινος, byssine, made of byssus *or* fine linen, (*non occ.*)

3. *σινδών*, *see* "LINEN," *No.* 1.

3. Mark xv. 46.
1. Luke xvi. 19.
1. Rev. xviii. 12 (No. 2, G L T Tr A ℵ.)
2. Rev. xviii. 16.
2. —— xix. 8[1st].
2. —— 8[2nd], pl.
2. —— 14.

LINGER (-ETH.)

ἀργέω, not to labour, be inactive, be still, *hence*, to linger, (*non occ.*)

2 Pet. ii. 3.

LION.

λέων, a lion.

2 Tim. iv. 17.
Heb. xi. 33.
1 Pet. v. 8.
Rev. iv. 7.
Rev. v. 5.
—— ix. 8, 17.
—— x. 3.
—— xiii. 2.

LIP (-S.)

χεῖλος, a lip, (*occ.* Heb. xi. 12.)

Matt. xv. 8.
Mark vii. 6.
Rom. iii. 13.
1 Cor. xiv. 21.
Heb. xiii. 15.
1 Pet. iii. 10.

LIQUID NARD [marg.]

See, SPIKENARD.

LIST (-ED, -ETH.) [verb.]

1. *θέλω*, to will, to wish, to desire, *implying active volition and purpose.*
2. *βούλομαι*, to will, to be willing, *implying mere passive willingness, or the inward predisposition and bent from which the active volition proceeds. Hence, never used of brutes.*

1. Matt. xvii. 12.
1. Mark ix. 13.
1. John iii. 8.
2. Jas. iii. 4.

LITTLE.

1. *μικρός*, small, little, *opp. of μέγας*, great.
2. *ὀλίγος*, little, *opp. of πολύς*, much.
3. *ὀλιγον*, *neut. of No.* 2, *used as adv.*
4. { *πρός*, for, / *ὀλίγος*, a little, } *i.e.* for some small things, *rather than a little time. It is in contrast with πρὸς πάντα*, for all things.

2. Luke vii. 47[1st].
3. —— 47[2nd].
1. —— xii. 32.
1. —— xix. 3.
1. John vii. 33.
1. —— xii. 35.
1. 1 Cor. v. 6.
2. 2 Cor. viii. 15.
1. Gal. v. 9.
4. 1 Tim. iv. 8.
2. —— v. 23.
1. Jas. iii. 5[1st].
2. —— 5[2nd] (*ἡλίκος, how small a*, L T Tr A ℵ.)
1. Rev. iii. 8.
1. —— vi. 11 (*om.* G T Tr[b].)
1. —— xx. 3.

LITTLE (A)

1. *μικρον*, *neut. of No.* 1, *above, as adv.*
2. *ὀλίγον*, *neut. of No.* 2, *above, as adv.*
3. { *ἐν*, in, / *ὀλίγος*, a little, } in brief, *or* briefly.
4. { *βραχύ*, short, small, / *τι*, one, a certain, } one small piece, *or* a certain small degree, *or* a short space *of* [*time.*
5. *μετρίως*, measuredly, moderately, *i.e.* with moderation. *Here, with οὐ*, not; *i.e.* beyond measure, (*non occ.*)

1. Matt. xxvi. 39.
2. Mark i. 19.
1. —— xiv. 35, 70.
2. Luke v. 3.
4. John vi. 7.
5. Acts xx. 12.
1. 2 Cor. xi. 1, 16.
3. Eph. iii. 3, marg. (text, *in few words.*)
4. Heb. ii. 7, marg., *a little* [*while.*

LITTLE SPACE (A)

βραχύ τι, *see* "LITTLE (A)," *No.* 4.

Acts v. 34.

LITTLE WHILE (A)

1. *μικρόν*, *neut.* of "LITTLE," *No.* 1.
2. { *μικρὸν*, a little while / *ὅσον*, how short, / *ὅσον*, how short.
3. *βραχύς*, short, small, *of time, distance, or quantity.*
4. { *βραχύ*, / *τι*, } *see* "LITTLE," *No.* 4.

3. Luke xxii. 58, neut.
1. John xiii. 33.
1. —— xiv. 19.
1. John xvi. 16[twice], 17[twice], 18, 19[twice].
4. Heb. ii. 7, marg. (text, [*a little.*
2. Heb. x. 37.

LITTLE (for a) or A WHILE. [marg.]

ὀλίγως, but a little, scarcely, all but, just.

2 Pet. ii. 18, text, *clean.*

LITTLE TIME (FOR A)

{ *πρός*, for, / *ὀλίγος*, a little,

1 Tim. iv. 8, marg. (text, *little*), see "LITTLE," No. 4.
Jas. iv. 14.

LITTLE FURTHER (GO)

βραχὺ, short, small,
διΐστημι, to place asunder, separate,
lit., having moved a short distance further.

Acts xxvii. 28.

LITTLE (NO)

οὐ, no,
τυγχάνω, to happen. *Here, part. as adj.;* happening, *as though anywhere or at all times,* i.e. *chance, casual, common; hence, with* οὐ,
no common, no ordinary.

Acts xxviii. 2.

LITTLE ONE.

μικρὸς, *see* "LITTLE," *No.* 1.

Matt. x. 42.
— xviii. 6, 10, 14.
Mark ix. 42.
Luke xvii. 2.

LITTLE (VERY)

ἐλάχιστος, *superl. of the old* ἐλαχύς, but used *as superl. of* μικρός, ("LITTLE," *No.* 1) the least.

Luke xix. 17.

See also, BOOK, CHILD, DAUGHTER, FAITH, FISH, SHIP.

LIVE (-ED, -EST, -ETH, -ING.) [verb.]

1. ζάω, to live (*akin to* ἄω, ἄημι, to breathe), to have ζωή (*see* "LIFE," *No.* 1). *Not "to be happy," but* to have life *in all or any of its manifestations, from the life of God down to the lowest vegetable. Not* "to exist," for *a thing can exist without living.* To live, is to have that peculiar property communicated by God to some parts only of his creation. *He originates and sustains all life by giving it out of Himself.* "In Him we live, and move, and have our being."
2. τὸ, the, ζῆν, to live, — the living, *i.e.* living, (*emphatic.*)
3. ζωογονέω, to bring forth alive; *pass.,* be born alive; to preserve alive, *occ.* Luke xvii. 33.)
4. ἀναστρέφω, to turn up, overturn, *mid.,* to turn one's self round, (Lat., versari), *hence,* to move about, sojourn, live with, pass one's time.
5. βιόω, to lead a life, pass one's life, (*non occ.*)
6. διάγω, to lead *or* bring through; *of time,* to pass or lead a life, (*occ.* 1 Tim. ii. 2.)
7. πολιτεύω, to be a πολίτης, (a citizen *or* free man) live in a free state, to live as a free and good citizen, (*occ.* Phil. i. 27.)
8. ὑπάρχω, to begin, to be present; *with* ἐν, or *Dat., implies* a being *or* living in *any state, place, or condition.*

1. Matt. iv. 4.
1. — ix. 18.
1. — xvi. 16.
1. — xxii. 32.
1. — xxvi. 63.
1. Mark v. 23.
1. — xii. 27.
1. Luke ii. 36.
1. — iv. 4.
8. — vii. 25.
1. — x. 28.
— — xii. 29, see L *in careful suspense.*
1. Luke xx. 38 twice.
1. — xxiv. 5.
1. John iv. 10, 11, 50, 51, [53.
1. — v. 25.
1. — vi. 51 twice, 57 3 times, 58, 69 (*ap.*)
1. — vii. 38.
1. — xi. 25, 26.
1. — xiv. 19 twice.
3. Acts vii. 19, pass.
1. — xiv. 15.
1. — xvii. 28.
1. — xxii. 22.
7. — xxiii. 1.
1. — xxv. 24.
1. — xxvi. 5.
1. — xxviii. 4.
1. Rom. i. 17.
1. — vi. 2.
— — 8, see L with.
1. — 10 twice.
1. — vii. 1, 2, part., 3, part.
1. — viii. 12, 13 twice.
1. — ix. 26.
1. — x. 5.
1. — xii. 1.
— — 18, see Peaceably.
1. — xiv. 7, 8 3 times, 9, [11.
1. 1 Cor. vii. 39.
— — ix. 13, see L of.
1. — 14.
1. — xv. 45.
1. 2 Cor. iii. 3.
1. — iv. 11.
1. — v. 15 twice.
1. — vi. 9, 16.
— — vii. 3, see L with.
1. — xiii. 4 twice
— — 11, see Peace.
1. Gal. ii. 14 1st.
— — 14 2nd, see Jews.
1. — 19, 20 4 times.
1. Gal. iii. 11, 12.
1. — v. 25.
— Eph. vi. 3, see L long.
2. Phil. i. 21.
1. — 22.
1. Col. ii. 20.
1. — iii. 7.
1. 1 Thes. i. 9.
1. — iii. 8.
1. — v. 10.
1. 1 Tim. iii. 15.
1. — iv. 10.
— — v. 6 1st, see Pleasure or *Delicately.*
1. — 6 2nd, part.
1. — vi. 17 (*om.* τῷ *ζῶντι, the living,* G→L T Tr A ℵ.)
— 2 Tim. ii. 11, see L with.
1. — iii. 12.
1. Titus ii. 12.
6. — iii. 3.
1. Heb. iii. 12.
1. — vii. 8, 25, part.
1. — ix. 14, 17.
1. — x. 20, 31, 38.
1. — xii. 9, 22.
4. — xiii. 18.
1. Jas. iv. 15.
1. 1 Pet. i. 23.
1. — ii. 4, 24.
5. — iv. 2.
1. — 6.
— 2 Pet. ii. 6, see Un- [godly.
4. — 18.
1. 1 John iv. 9.
1. Rev. i. 18.
1. — iii. 1.
1. — iv. 9, 10.
1. — v. 14 (*ap.*)
1. — vii. 2.
1. — 17 (*ζωῆς, of life,* G L T Tr A ℵ, *i.e. "fountains of waters of life,"* instead of *"fountains of living waters."*)
1. — x. 6.
1. — xiii. 14.
1. — xv. 7.
1. — xvi. 3 (*ζωῆς, of life,* G L T Tr[b] A, i.e. *soul of life.*)
— — xviii. 7, 9, see Deliciously.
1. — xx. 4.
— — 5, see L again.

LIVE AGAIN.

ἀναζάω, (*No.* 1, *with* ἀνα, up, *or* again, *prefixed.*)

Rev. xx. 5, (No. 1, G L T Tr A.)

LIVE IN CAREFUL SUSPENSE [marg.]

μετεωρίζω, to be floating in the air, *hence*, to be lifted up, buoyed up, *esp.*, *with false hopes.*

Luke xii. 29 twice, text, *be of doubtful mind.*

LIVE LONG.

{ εἰμί, to be,
μακροχρόνιος, long-timed, *i.e.* long-lived.

Eph. vi. 3.

LIVE OF.

ἐσθίω, to eat, take food.

1 Cor. ix. 13, marg., *feed of.*

LIVE WITH.

συζάω, ("LIVE," *No.* 1, *with* σύν, together in conjunction with, *prefixed*) (*non occ.*)

Rom. vi. 8. | 2 Tim. ii. 11. | 2 Cor. vii. 3.

LIVELY.

ζάω, *see* "LIVE," *No.* 1. *Here part.*, *i.e.* living.

Acts vii. 38. | 1 Pet. ii. 5. | 1 Pet. i. 3.

LIVING [noun.]

βίος, life, means of life.

Mark xi. 44.
Luke viii. 43.
Luke xv. 12, 30.
— xxi. 4.

LIVING (WITH RIOTOUS)

{ ζάω, to live, (*see* "LIVE," *No.* 1) ; *here, part.*
ἀσώτως, dissolutely, (*from* ἀσωτία, not saveable, incorrigible, debauchery), } living in debauchery, *or* living in riotous excess.

Luke xv. 13.

LO!

1. ἰδού, (*imperative of aor.*, *mid. of* εἶδον, *to see*) a particle serving to call attention, (elsewhere, "BEHOLD!")

2. ἴδε, (*imperative of* εἶδον, *to see*) *used as an interjection*, lo! behold!

1. Matt. ii. 9.
1. — iii. 16, 17.
1. — xxiv. 23.
2. — xxv. 25.
1. — xxvi. 47.
1. — xxviii. 7, 20.
1. Mark x. 28.
1. — xiii. 21 1st (No. 2, T Tr A ℵ.)
1. — 21 2nd (No. 2, L T Tr A ℵ.)
1. — xiv. 42.
1. Luke i. 44.
1. — ii. 9.
1. — ix. 39.
1. — xiii. 16.
1. Luke xv. 29.
1. — xvii. 21 1st.
1. — 21 2nd (om. T [ℵ.)
1. — xviii. 28.
1. — xxiii. 15.
2. John vii. 26.
2. — xvi. 29.
1. Acts xiii. 46.
1. — xxvii. 24.
1. Heb. x. 7, 9.
1. Rev. v. 6 (om. *καὶ ἰδοὺ, and lo!* G L Tr A . .)
1. — vi. 5.
1. — 12 (om. G L T Tr A ℵ.)
1. — vii. 9 (om. L Trb.)
1. Rev. xiv. 1.

LOAF (LOAVES.)

ἄρτος, *see* "BREAD."

Mark xiv. 17, 19 twice.
— xv. 34, 36.
— xvi. 9, 10.
Mark vi. 38, 41 twice, 44, 52.
Mark viii. 5, 6, 14, 19.
Luke ix. 13, 16.
— xi. 5.
John vi. 9, 11, 13, 26.

LOCUST (-S.)

ἀκρίς, a locust.

Matt. iii. 4. | Rev. ix. 3, 7. | Mark i. 6.

LODGE (-ED, -ETH.)

1. ξενίζω, to receive *or* entertain strangers, to receive as a guest.

 * *Pass.*, to be entertained as a guest.

2. κατασκηνόω, to plant down a tent, *i.e.* to pitch a tent; *hence*, to sojourn. *Of birds*, to haunt, (*occ.* Acts ii. 26.)

3. καταλύω, to loosen down, unbind, *as the burdens from camels. Hence, of travellers*, to halt *for rest or for the night*, to put up for the night.

4. αὐλίζομαι, to pass the time in the αὐλή, (an open court *or* yard) to encamp in the open air, bivouac, *either by night or day*, (*occ.* Luke xxi. 37.)

2. Matt. xiii. 32.
4. — xxi. 17.
2. Mark iv. 32.
3. Luke ix. 12.
2. Luke xiii. 19.
1. Acts x. 6*, 18, 23, 32.
1. — xxi. 16.
1. — xxviii. 7*.

— 1 Tim. v. 10, *see* Stranger.

LODGING.

ξενία, guest-right, alliance of hospitality. *In N.T.*, place for a guest, a lodging, (*non occ.*)

Acts xxviii. 23. | Philem. 22.

LOFT (THIRD)

τρίστεγος, three-roofed, *having* three floors *or* stories; τὸ τρίστεγον, the third floor, third story, (*non occ.*)

Acts xx. 9.

LOINS.

ὀσφύς, the loins, the lower region of the back, the lumbar region, as *opp.* to the shoulders and thighs.

Matt. iii. 4. | Acts ii. 30.
Mark i. 6. | Eph. vi. 14.
Luke xii. 35. | Heb. vii. 5, 10.
1 Pet. i. 13.

LONG [adj.]

See also, ALL, CLOTHING, GARMENT, HAIR, *PATIENT*, *PATIENCE*, ROBE, TIME.

1. πολύς, many, much. *Of time*, much, long.

2. { ἐπὶ, upon, / πλείων, more, } *i.e.* very much at length, further.

3. { οὐκ, not, / ὀλιγός, a little.

1. Matt. xxv. 19. | 3. Acts xiv. 28.
— Luke xxiii. 8, see L season (of a) | 2. —— xx. 9.
1. John v. 6. | — —— 11, see L while [(a)
— —— xiv. 9, see L (so) | 1. —— xxvii. 14.
| 1. —— xxvii. 21.
— Heb. iv. 7, see L (so)

LONG SEASON (OF A)

{ ἐξ, out of, of, / ἱκανοῦ, sufficing, abundant, great, much. } for a long time.

Luke xxiii. 8, ἐξ ἱκανῶν χρόνων, *for a sufficient number of times*, L Tr A ℵ.)

LONG (SO)

τοσοῦτος, so great, so much. *Of time*, so much, so long.

John xiv. 9. | Heb. iv. 7.

LONG WHILE (A)

{ ἐφ', upon, / ἱκανόν, sufficing, } for a sufficient, *or* long time.

Acts xx. 11.

LONG [adv.]

See AGO, AS, BEAR, LIVE, PATIENT, SUFFER.

LONG (HOW)

{ ἕως, until, / πότε, when? at what time?

Matt. xvii. 17 twice. | Luke ix. 41.
Mark ix. 19 twice. | John x. 24.
—— 21, see L ago (how) | Rev. vi. 10.

LONG AGO (HOW)

{ πόσος, how great, how much, / χρόνος, time, } How long a time.

Mark ix. 21.

LONG (-ED.) [verb.]

ἐπιποθέω, to desire upon, *i.e. over and above, besides; hence*, to desire earnestly.

Rom. i. 11.

LONG AFTER.

2 Cor. ix. 14.
Phil. ii. 26, part. with εἰμί, *to be.*

LONG AFTER (GREATLY...)

Phil. i. 8.

LONGED FOR.

ἐπιπόθητος, much desired upon, earnestlv longed for, (*non occ.*)

Phil. iv. 1.

LONGER.

1. ἔτι, yet, still, *implying duration, accession, or addition.*

2. πλείων, more.

1. Luke xvi. 2. | 2. Acts xviii. 20.

LONGER (ANY)

1. ἔτι, *see No.* 1, *above.*

2. μηκέτι, (*No.* 1, *with* μὴ, no, not, *prefixed*) no longer. (*Here, with another negative*, μὴ, *strengthening the affirmative.*)

2. Acts xxv. 24.	1. Rom. vi. 2.

LONGER (NO)

1. μηκέτι, *see above, No.* 2.

2. οὐκέτι, no further, no more, no longer.

[*No.* 1 refers to what is matter of thought or supposition, while *No.* 2 refers to what is matter of fact.]

2. Gal. iii. 25.	1. Tim. v. 23.
1. 1 Thes. iii. 1, 5.	1. 1 Pet. iv. 2.

LONGSUFFERING [noun.]

μακροθυμία, long before being angry, patient endurance, forbearance, (*occ.* Heb. vi. 12; Jas. v. 10.)

Rom. ii. 4.	Col. iii. 12.
—— ix. 22.	1 Tim. i. 16.
2 Cor. vi. 6.	2 Tim. iii. 10.
Gal. v. 22.	—— iv. 2.
Eph. iv. 2.	1 Pet. iii. 20.
Col. i. 11.	2 Pet. iii. 15.

LONGSUFFERING (BE)

μακροθυμέω, to be μακροθυμία, (*see above*) to be long before being angry, to endure *or* wait patiently.

2 Pet. iii. 9.

LOOK (-ED, -ETH, -ING.) [verb.]

(*See below for words used in connection.*)

1. εἶδον, to see; *implying not the mere act of seeing, but* the actual perception of the object, *thus differing from No.* 2, *and referring to* the mind and thought of him who sees, (the subject,) thus differing from *No.* 4.

2. βλέπω, to use the eyes, to see, look; *used of* the act of seeing, *even though nothing is seen;* to observe accurately with desire; *hence,* of *mental vision; implying more contemplation than No.* 4.

3. ἀναβλέπω, (*No.* 2, *with* ἀνά, up, *prefixed*) to look up.

4. ὁράω, to see, perceive with the eyes, look at, to see something, *used of bodily sight, differing from No.* 2 *in the same way as No.* 1 *does; and differing from No.* 1 *in that it refers in thought to the object, while No.* 1 *refers to the subject.*

5. ἀφοραω, (*No.* 4, *with* ἀπὸ, away from, *prefixed*) to look away from one thing so as to see another, look off from one thing unto another, (*occ.* Phil. ii. 23.)

6. παρακύπτω, to stoop down near by *anything,* to bend forward near *in order to look at anything more closely.*

7. προσδοκάω, to watch toward *or* for anything, to look for, expect, wait for.

3. Mark xvi. 4, part.	5. Heb. xii. 2.
2. Luke ix. 62.	6. Jas. i. 25.
1. John vii. 52, imperative.	6. 1 Pet. i. 12.
2. —— xiii. 22.	1. Rev. iv. 1.
3. —— xix. 37.	1. —— vi. 8 (om. G ⇉)
2. Acts iii. 4.	1. —— xiv. 1, 14.
7. —— xxviii. 6, part.	1. —— xv. 5.

LOOK ABOUT ON.

περιβλέπω, (*No.* 2, *above, with* περί, round about, *prefixed.*)

Mark iii. 34, mid.

LOOK AT.

σκοπέω, to look, inspect, reconnoitre, behold, regard.

2 Cor. iv. 18, part.

LOOK DILIGENTLY.

ἐπισκοπέω, (*the above, with* ἐπί, upon, *prefixed*) to look upon, look after, see to, (*occ.* 1 Pet. v. 2.)

Heb. xii. 15.

LOOK EARNESTLY ON.

ἀτενίζω, to fix the eyes intently upon, gaze upon intently.

Acts iii. 12.

LOOK EARNESTLY UPON.

ἀτενίζω, *see above.*

Luke xxii. 56.

LOOK FOR.

1. προσδοκάω, *see* "LOOK," *No.* 7.

2. προσδέχομαι, to receive to *one's self. Of things future,* to wait for, expect.

3. ἐκδέχομαι, (*No.* 2, *with* ἐκ, out of, *or* from, *prefixed, instead of* πρός, to *or* towards) to receive from *any quarter,* to look for (*being about to receive*), expect.

4. ἀπεκδέχομαι, (*No.* 3, *with* ἀπό, from, *prefixed*) to wait out, *i.e.* to wait long and patiently, to await ardently.

1. Matt. xi. 3.
1. —— xxiv. 50.
2. Luke ii. 38.
1. —— vii. 19, 20.
1. —— xii. 46.
2. Acts xxiii. 21.
3. 1 Cor. xvi. 11.
4. Phil. iii. 20.
2. Tit. ii. 13.
4. Heb. ix. 28.
3. —— xi. 10.
1. 2 Pet. iii. 12, 13, 14, [part.
2. Jude 21.

LOOK ON.

1. βλέπω, *see* "LOOK," *No.* 2.

2. εἶδον, *see* "LOOK," *No.* 1.

3. ἐπεῖδον, (*No.* 2, *with* ἐπί, upon, *prefixed.*)

4. ἀτενίζω, to fix the eyes intently upon, gaze upon intently.

5. θεάομαι, to contemplate earnestly, (*with the idea of desire and pleasure*) to see with regard and admiration.

6. θεωρέω, to be a spectator of, to behold *as with attention or wonder,* to look on *or* regard, (*as not being the act of an instant, but for a lengthened period.*)

7 σκοπέω, to look, inspect, reconnoitre, regard.

1. Matt. v. 28.
2. Mark viii. 33.
6. —— xv. 40.
3. Luke i. 25.
2. —— x. 32.
5. John iv. 35.
4. Acts x. 4, part.
1. 2 Cor. x. 7.
7. Phil. ii. 4.
1. Rev. v. 3, 4.

LOOK OUT.

ἐπισκέπτομαι, to look at *as though to select,* to look out, seek out.

Acts vi. 3.

LOOK ROUND ABOUT.

περιβλέπω, (*see* "L. ABOUT ON.") *Here, mid.*

Mark v. 32. | Mark x. 23. | Mark ix. 8.

LOOK ROUND ABOUT ON OR UPON.

περιβλέπω, *see above.*

Matt. iii. 5. | Luke vi. 10. | Mark xi. 11, part.

LOOK STEADFASTLY.

ἀτενίζω, *see* "L. ON," *No.* 4.

Acts i. 10. | 2 Cor. iii. 13. | Acts vi. 15.

LOOK TO.

1. βλέπω, *see* "LOOK," *No.* 2.

2. ὁράω, *see* "LOOK," *No.* 4.

2. Acts xviii. 15. | 1. 2 John 8.

LOOK UPON (TO)

ὅρασις, the sight, *sense of seeing. Then,* aspect, *external form,* in appearance.

Rev. iv. 3.

LOOK UP.

1. ἀναβλέπω, ("LOOK," *No.* 2, *with* ἀνά, up, *prefixed.*)

2. ἀνακύπτω, to raise one's self up, to rise up *from a stooping posture.*

1. Matt. xiv. 19.
1. Mark vi. 41.
1. —— vii. 34.
1. —— viii. 24.
1. —— 25 (διέβλεψεν, *he saw clearly,* instead of ἐποιήσεν αὐτὸν ἀναβλέψαι, *made him look up,* T Tr A ℵ), (*om.* G→)
1. Luke ix. 16.
1. —— xix. 5.
1. —— xxi. 1.
2. —— 28.
1. Acts xxii. 13.

LOOK UP STEADFASTLY.

ἀτενίζω, *see* "L. ON," *No.* 4.

Acts vii. 55.

LOOK UPON.

1. ἐμβλέπω, ("LOOK," *No.* 2, *with* ἐν, in, *prefixed.*)

2. *ἐπιβλέπω*, ("LOOK," *No.* 2, *with ἐπὶ*, upon, *prefixed.*)

3. *θεάομαι*, (*see* "L. ON," *No.* 5.)

1. Mark x. 27.
1. —— xiv. 67.
2. Luke ix. 38.
1. Luke xxii. 61.
1. John i. 36.
3. 1 John i. 1.

LOOK WHEN.

προσδοκάω, (*see* "LOOK," *No.* 7.)

Acts xxviii. 6.

LOOKING AFTER.

προσδοκία, a looking for, expectation.

Luke xxi. 26.

LOOKING FOR.

ἐκδοχή, a reception, a waiting for, (*non occ.*)

Heb. x. 27.

LOOSE (-ED, -ING.) [verb.]

1. *λύω*, to loose, loosen *what is fast bound; hence*, to unbind.

2. *ἀπολύω*, (*No.* 1, *with ἀπὸ*, from, *prefixed*) to let loose from, free from.

3. *ἀνίημι*, to send up *or* forth, let up, let go.

4. *ἀνάγω*, to lead up, conduct *or* bring up. *As a nautical term*, to lead a ship out *to sea*, to put to sea.

5. *αἴρω*, to take up, lift up, raise; *of anchors*, to weigh *anchor and sail away*.

6. *καταργέω*, to render inactive, idle, useless; *hence*, to cause to cease, do away; cease to be connected with.

1. Matt. xvi. 19 twice.
1. —— xviii. 18 twice.
2. —— 27.
1. —— xxi. 2.
1. Mark vii. 35.
1. —— xi. 2, 4, 5.
2. Luke xiii. 12.
1. —— 15, 16.
1. —— xix. 30, 31.
— —— 33 1st, see Loosing (be)
1. —— 33 2nd.
1. John xi. 44.
1. Acts ii. 24.
4. —— xiii. 13, part.
1. Acts xiii. 25.
4. —— xvi. 11.
3. —— 26.
1. —— xxii. 30.
1. —— xxiv. 26 (ap.)
5. —— xxvii. 13.
4. —— 21.
3. —— 40.
6. Rom. vii. 2.
— 1 Cor. vii. 27 1st, see L (to be)
1. —— 27 2nd.
1. Rev. v. 2.
1. —— 5 (om. L T Tr A.)
1. —— ix. 14, 15.
1. Rev. xx. 3, 7.

LOOSING (BE)

Luke xix. 33, part.

LOOSED (TO BE)

λύσις, a loosening, *from any tie or constraint*, (*non occ.*)

1 Cor. vii. 27.

LORD (-S.)

1. *κύριος*, (*an adj., from κῦρος*, might) mighty. *Then, as subst.*, *ὁ κύριος*, lord, principal, ruler. *Distinguished from No.* 2, *as being* He who *assumes and exercises the power, while δεσπότης really possesses it as unlimited.*

[It is used of man* as the possessor, owner, *or* master, e.g. *property. Hence, a title of address, Eng.*, master, sir; *French*, sieur, monsieur; *Germ.*, herr. *See under No.* 3.

As a name for God, it is used as predicated of Him, or when He is addressed *or* spoken of.

As a name for *Christ*, because He stands in the same relation to us as God. But while *κύριος* is used as a translation of יהוה, (Jehovah) the name Jehovah is never applied to Christ. And when *κύριος* is applied to *God* in the *N.T.*, Jehovah is the word quoted or referred to from the *O.T.* Also when *κύριος* is applied to *Christ*, it is specially and directly explained in the *O.T.*, as in Ps. cx. 1, "Jehovah said unto Adonai," "*εἶπεν ὁ κύριος τῷ κυρίῳ μοῦ.*" *cf.* Matt. xxii. 43—45, and Mark xii. 36, 37.

In the Gospels *κύριος* usually signifies *God*, while in the Epistles it generally refers to *Christ*, and denotes His position of Master in relation to His people, as He who has ownership and authority over them. *Hence*, all the social and natural relationships of life are to be regarded and performed as subject to His authority; *e.g.*,

It is the "Lord's Supper," not the supper of Jesus or Christ, because He who says, "Do this," has the right and authority to institute and command. *Again*, marry, etc.,

in *the Lord*, obey in *the Lord*, (not in Jesus or Christ.) *See further under* "JESUS," and "CHRIST."

2. κυριεύω, to be lord over *any person or thing*, to have dominion over. *Here, part.*, ὁ κυριεύων, he who has dominion over, *i.e.* a lord, potentate. *In pl., as here*, those who reign.

3. δεσπότης, one who has absolute dominion, supreme authority, and unlimited power, *arising from ownership;* a master, *as opp. to a servant. No.* 1 *implies greater honour and respect, No.* 3 *greater submission. As denoting the exercise of supreme authority, it is applied* to God,* and also to Christ.†

4. ῥαββονί, *a Hebrew word, like* ῥαββί, (Rabbi) *but of higher honour, meaning* (*with the suffix*) my great master. *A name publicly given to only seven persons, all of the school of Hillel, and of great eminence.*

1. Matt. i. 20, 22, 24.
1. —— ii. 13, 15, 19.
1. —— iii. 3.
1. —— iv. 7, 10.
1. —— v. 33.
1. —— vii. 21 twice, 22 twice.
1. —— viii. 2, 6, 8, 21, 25.
1. —— ix. 28, 38.
1* —— x. 24, 25.
1. —— xi. 25.
1. —— xii. 8.
1. —— xiii. 51 (*om.* G→L T Tr A ℵ.)
1. —— xiv. 28, 30.
1. —— xv. 22, 25, 27.
1. —— xvi. 22.
1. —— xvii. 4, 15.
1. —— xviii. 21.
1*.—— 25.
1*.—— 26 (om. L T Tr A.)
1*.—— 27, 31, 32, 34.
1*.—— xx. 8.
1. —— 30, 31, 33.
1. —— xxi. 3, 9.
1*.—— 40.
— —— 42, see Lord's (the)
1. —— xxii. 37, 43, 44 twice, [45.
1. —— xxiii. 39.
1. —— xxiv. 42.
1*.—— 45, 46, 48, 50.
1*.—— xxv. 11 twice, 18, 19, 20, 21 twice, 22, 23 twice, 24, 26.
1. —— 37, 44.
1. —— xxvi. 22.
1. —— xxvii. 10.
1. —— xxviii. 2.
1. —— 6 (om. T Tr^b A ℵ, i.e. "*where He lay.*")
1. Mark i. 3.
1. —— ii. 28.
1. —— v. 19.
— —— vi. 21, see Lords.
1. —— vii. 28.

1. Mark ix. 24 (*om.* G L T Tr A ℵ.)
4. —— x. 51.
1. —— xi. 3, 9, 10 (*ap.*)
1*.—— xii. 9.
— —— 11, see Lord's (the)
1. —— 29 twice, 30, 36, 37.
1. —— xiii. 20.
1. —— xvi. 19 (*ap.*), 20 (*ap.*)
1. Luke i. 6, 9, 11, 15, 16, 17, 25, 28, 32, 38, 43, 45, 46, 58, 66, 68, 76.
1. —— ii. 9 1st, 9 2nd (*om.* G→), 11, 15, 22, 23 twice, [24, 26.
3*.—— 29.
1. —— 38 (θεός, L T Tr A ℵ.)
1. —— 39.
1. —— iii. 4.
1. —— iv. 8, 12, 18, 19.
1. —— v. 8, 12, 17.
1. —— vi. 5, 46 twice.
1. —— vii. 6, 31 1st, 31 2nd (*ap.*)
1. —— ix. 54.
1. —— 57 (*om.* G→L T Tr^b ℵ.)
1. —— 59, 61.
1. —— x. 1, 2, 17, 21, 27, 40.
1. —— xi. 1, 39.
1*.—— xii. 36, 37.
1. —— 41, 42 1st.
1*.—— 42 2nd, 43, 45, 46, 47.
1*.—— xiii. 8.
1. —— 15, 23, 25 1st.
1. —— 25 2nd (*om.* L^b T Tr A ℵ.)
1. —— 35.
1*.—— xiv. 21, 22, 23.
1*.—— xvi. 3, 5 twice, 8.
1. —— xvii. 5, 6, 37.
1. —— xviii. 6, 41.

1. Luke xix. 8 twice.
1*.—— 16, 18, 20, 25.
1. —— 31, 34, 38.
1*.—— xx. 13, 15.
1. —— 37, 42 twice, 44.
1. —— xxii. 31 (*ap.*), 33, 38, 49, 61 twice.
1. —— xxiii. 42 (*om.* L^b T Tr A ℵ.)
1. —— xxiv. 3, 34.
1. John i. 23.
1. —— iv. 1.
1. —— vi. 23 (*om.* G→), 34, 68.
1. —— viii. 11 (*ap.*)
1. —— ix. 36, 38.
1. —— xi. 2, 3, 12, 21, 27, 32, 34, 39.
1. —— xii. 13, 38 twice.
1. —— xiii. 6, 9, 13, 14.
1*.—— 16.
1. —— 25, 36, 37.
1. —— xiv. 5, 8, 22.
1*.—— xv. 15, 20.
1. —— xx. 2, 13, 18, 20, 25, 28.
1. —— xxi. 7 twice, 12, 15, 16, 17, 20, 21.
1. Acts i. 6, 21, 24.
1. —— ii. 20, 21, 25, 34 twice, 36, 39, 47.
1. —— iii. 19, 22.
3*.—— iv. 24.
1. —— 26, 29, 33.
1. —— v. 9, 14, 19.
1. —— vii. 30 (*om.* Κύριου, *of the Lord*, G→L T Tr A ℵ.)
1. —— 31, 33.
1. —— 37 (*om.* Κύριος, and ὑμῶν, i.e. *God*, instead of *the Lord your God*, G ⇉ L T Tr A ℵ.)
1. —— 49, 59, 60.
1. —— viii. 16, 24, 25, 26, [39.
1. —— ix. 1, 5 1st.
1. —— 5 2nd (*om.* G ⇉ L T Tr A ℵ)
1. —— 6 twice (*ap*), 10 twice, 11, 13, 15, 17, 27, 29, 31, 35, 42.
1. —— x. 4, 14, 38.
1. —— 48 (Ἰησοῦς Χριστος, *Jesus Christ*, G∾L T Tr ℵ.)
1. —— xi. 8, 16, 17, 20, 21 twice, 23, 24.
1. —— xii. 7, 11, 17, 23.
1. —— xiii. 2, 10, 11, 12, 47, 48, 49.
1. —— xiv. 3, 23.
1. —— xv. 11, 17 twice, 26, 35, 36.
1. —— xvi. 10 (θεός, *God*, G∾L T Tr A ℵ.)
1. —— 14, 15, 31, 32.
1. —— xvii. 24.
1. —— 27 (G∾), (θεός, *God*, G L T Tr A ℵ.)
1. —— xviii. 8, 9, 25 1st.
1. —— 25 2nd (Ἰησοῦς, *Jesus*, L T Tr A ℵ.)
1. —— xix. 5, 10, 13, 17.
1. —— xx. 19, 21, 24, 35.
1. —— xxi. 13, 14.
1. —— 20 (θεός, *God*, G L T Tr A ℵ.)
1. —— xxii. 8, 10 twice.
1. —— 16 (αὐτός, *His name*, instead of *the name of the Lord*, G L T Tr A ℵ.)
1. —— 19.
1. —— xxiii. 11.
1*.—— xxv. 15, 20.
1. —— xxvi. 15.
1. —— xxviii. 31.

1. Rom. i. 3, 7.
1. —— iv. 8, 24.
1. —— v. 11, 21.
1. —— vi. 11 (*om.* τοῦ κυρίου ἡμῶν, *our Lord*, G L T Tr A.)
1. —— 23.
1. —— vii. 25.
1. —— viii. 39.
1. —— ix. 28, 29.
1. —— x. 9, 12, 13, 16.
1. —— xi. 3, 34.
1. —— xii. 11 (G∾), (καιρός, *opportunity*, or *occasion*, St. G.)
1. —— 19.
1. —— xiii. 14.
1. —— xiv. 6 1st, 6 2nd (*ap.*), 6 3rd & 4th, 8 3 times, 11, 14.
1. —— xv. 6, 11, 30.
1. —— xvi. 2, 8, 11, 12 1st, 12 2nd (*ap.*), 13, 18, 20, 22, 24 (*ap.*)
1. 1 Cor. i. 2, 3, 7, 8, 9, 10, 31.
1. —— ii. 8, 16.
1. —— iii. 5, 20.
1. —— iv. 4, 5, 17, 19.
1. —— v. 4 twice, 5.
1. —— vi. 11, 13 twice, 14, 17.
1. —— vii. 10, 12.
— —— 17 (θεός, *God*, G L T Tr A ℵ.) [Note, for θεός, at beginning of verse, κυριός, *Lord*, G L T Tr A ℵ.]
— —— 22 twice, 25 twice, 32 twice, 34, 35, 39.
1*.—— viii. 5.
1. —— 6.
1. —— ix. 1 twice, 2, 5, 14.
1. —— x. 21 twice, 22, 26, 28 (*ap.*)
1. —— xi. 11.
— —— 20, see Lord's (the)
1. —— 23 twice, 26, 27 twice.
1. —— 29 (*om.* τοῦ Κυριοῦ, *the Lord's*, L T Tr A ℵ.)
1. —— 32.
1. —— xii. 3, 5.
1. —— xiv. 21, 37.
1. —— xv. 31.
1. —— 47 (*om.* G ⇉ L T Tr A ℵ.)
1. —— 57, 58 twice.
1. —— xvi. 7, 10, 19, 22, 23.
1. 2 Cor. i. 2, 3, 14.
1. —— ii. 12.
1. —— iii. 16, 17 twice, 18 twice.
1. —— iv. 5.
1. —— 10 (*om.* G L T Tr A ℵ.)
1. —— 14.
1. —— v. 6, 8, 11.
1. —— vi. 17, 18.
1. —— viii. 5, 9, 19, 21.
1. —— x. 8, 17, 18.
1. —— xi. 17, 31.
1. —— xii. 1, 8.
1. —— xiii. 10, 14.
1. Gal. i. 3, 19.
1*.—— iv. 1.
1. —— v. 10.
1. —— vi. 14.
1. —— 17 (*om.* G ⇉ L T Tr A.)
1. Eph. i. 2, 3, 15, 17.
1. —— ii. 21.
1. —— iii. 11, 14 (*ap.*)
1. —— iv. 1, 5, 17
1. —— v. 8, 10.

1. Eph. v. 17 (θεός, God, L[m].)
1. —— 19, 20, 22.
1. —— 29 (χριστός, *Christ*, G L T Tr A ℵ.)
1. —— vi. 1 (*om.* ἐν Κυρίῳ, *in the Lord*, G→ L Tr[b] A[b].)
1. —— 4, 7, 8, 10, 21, 23, 24.
1. Phil. i. 2, 14.
1. —— ii. 11.
1. —— 19 (χριστός, *Christ*, L.)
1. —— 24, 29.
1. —— iii. 1, 8, 20.
1. —— iv. 1, 2, 4, 5, 10, 23.
1. Col. i. 2 (*ap.*), 3, 10.
1. —— ii. 6.
1. —— iii. 16 (G∾), (θεός, God, G L T Tr A ℵ.)
1. —— 17 (*om.* G⇉ L.)
— —— 18, 20, 23, 24[twice].
1. —— iv. 7, 17.
1. 1 Thes. i. 1[1st], 1[2nd] (*ap.*), 3, 6, 8.
1. —— ii. 15, 19.
1. —— iii. 8, 11.
1. —— 12 (*om.* G→)
1. —— 13.
1. —— iv. 1, 2, 6, 15[twice], 16, 17[twice].
1. —— v. 2, 9, 12, 23, 27, 28.
1. 2 Thes. i. 1, 2, 7, 8, 9, 12[twice].
1. —— ii. 1, 8, 13, 14, 16.
1. —— iii. 1.
1. —— 3 (θεός, *God*, L.)
1. —— 4, 5, 6, 12, 16[twice], 18.
1. 1 Tim. i. 1 (*om.* G L T Tr A.)
1. —— 2, 12, 14.
1. —— v. 21 (*om.* G⇉ L T Tr A ℵ.)
1. —— vi. 3, 14, 15[1st].
2. —— 15[2nd] (lit. "*those who reign.*")
1. 2 Tim. i. 2, 8, 16, 18[twice].
1. —— ii. 7.
1. —— 14 (θεός, *God*, L[m] T Tr ℵ.)
1. —— 19, 22, 24.
1. —— iii. 11.
1. —— iv. 1 (*om.* G L T Tr A ℵ.)
1. —— 8, 14, 17, 18, 22.
1. Titus i. 4 (*om.* L T Tr A ℵ.)
1. Philem. 3, 5, 16, 20[1st].
1. —— 20[2nd] (χριστός, *Christ*, G L T Tr A ℵ.)
1. Heb. i. 10.
1. —— ii. 3.
1. Heb. vii. 14, 21.
1. —— viii. 2, 8, 9, 10, 11.
1. —— x. 16.
1. —— 30[1st] (*om.* λέγει κυριός, *saith the Lord*, G⇉ T Tr ℵ.)
1. —— 30[2nd].
1. —— xii. 5, 6, 14.
1. —— xiii. 6, 20.
1. Jas. i. 1, 7.
1. —— 12 (*om.* G→ L T Tr A ℵ, *i.e.* substitute "*He.*"
1. —— ii. 1.
1. —— iv. 10, 15.
1. —— v. 4, 7, 8, 10, 11[1st].
1. —— 11[2nd] (*om.* G⇉)
1. —— 14, 15.
1. 1 Pet. i. 3, 25.
1. —— ii. 3, 13.
1*. —— iii. 6.
1. —— 12[twice], 15.
— —— v. 3, see Lords over (be)
1. 2 Pet. i. 2, 8, 11, 14, 16.
3†. —— ii. 1.
1. —— 9.
1. —— 11 (*om.* παρά Κυρίῳ, *before the Lord*, G ⇉ L Tr[b].)
1. —— 20.
1. —— iii. 2, 8, 9, 10, 15, 18.
1. 2 John 3 (*om.* G ⇉ L T Tr A.)
3†. Jude 4[1st].
1. —— 4[2nd].
1. —— 5 Ἰησοῦς, *Jesus*, G ∾ L Tr[mb] A.)
1. —— 9, 14, 17, 21.
1. Rev. i. 8.
— —— 10, see Lord's (the)
1. —— iv. 8, 11.
3*. —— vi. 10.
1. —— vii. 14.
1. —— xi. 8, 15, 17.
1. —— xiv. 13.
1. —— xv. 3.
1. —— 4 (*om.* G →)
1. —— xvi. 5 (*om.* Κυριε, O Lord, G L T Tr A ℵ)
1. —— 7.
1. —— xvii. 14[1st].
1*. —— 14[2nd].
1. —— xviii. 8.
1. —— xix. 1 (τοῦ θεοῦ, *of our God*, instead of, Κυρίῳ τῷ θεῷ, *Unto the Lord our God*, G L T Tr A ℵ.)
1. —— 6, 16[1st].
1*. —— 16[2nd].
1. —— xxi. 22.
1. —— xxii. 5, 6, 20, 21.

LORDS.

μεγιστᾶνες, great ones, *Lat.*, magnates, *i.e.* chiefs, nobles, princes, (*occ.* Rev. vi. 15, xviii. 23.)

Mark vi. 21.

LORD'S (THE)

1. κυριακός, belonging to the lord, (τὸ κυριακόν, *was the* State, *or* fiscal property.) *In N.T.* belonging to Christ as Lord, having special reference to Him.

2.	παρά, from beside, κυριοῦ, the Lord,	from the Lord [*this came to pass.*]

2. Matt. xxi. 42.
2. Mark xii. 11.
1. 1 Cor. xi. 20.
1. Rev. i. 10, and see "Day (the Lord's")

LORD OF (BE)

κυριεύω, *see* "LORD," *No.* 2.

Rom. xiv. 9.

LORDS OVER (BE)

κυριεύω, *see* "LORD," *No.* 2.

1 Pet. v. 3, marg., *overrule*.

LORDSHIP OVER (EXERCISE)

1. κυριεύω, *see* "LORD," *No.* 2.
2. κατακυριεύω, (*No.* 1, *with* κατά, down, *prefixed*) to lord it against *or* over *any one.*

2. Mark x. 42. | 1. Luke xxii. 25.

LOSE (-ETH, LOST.)

1. ἀπόλλυμι, to destroy utterly (*stronger form of* ὄλλυμι, to destroy) to lose utterly, *the subject being the sufferer; the fundamental thought* is, ruin, loss, *what is* lost *to another, as a sheep, lost to the fold and the shepherd.*
2. ζημιόω, to bring loss upon *any one. In N.T. only mid. or pass.*, to suffer loss, to receive detriment. *Here, only mid.*, to bring loss upon one's self, *i.e.* to lose.

— Matt. v. 13, see Savour.
1. —— x. 6, 39[twice], 42.
1. —— xv. 24.
1. —— xvi. 25[twice].
2. —— 26.
1. —— xviii. 11 (*ap.*)
1. Mark viii. 35[twice].
2. —— 36.
1. —— ix. 41.
— —— 50, see Saltness.
1. Luke ix. 24[twice], 25.
— Luke xiv. 34, see Savour
1. —— xv. 4[1st], part, 4[2nd], 6, 8, 9, 24, 32.
1. —— xvii. 33[twice].
— —— xix. 10.
— John vi. 12, see L (be)
1. —— 39.
1. —— xii. 33[twice].
— —— xvii. 12, see L (be)
1. —— xviii. 9.
— 2 Cor. iv. 3, see L (be)

1. 2 John 8.

LOST (BE)

1. John vi. 12. | 1. John xvii. 12.
1. 2 Cor. iv. 3.

LOSS.

1. ζημία, damage, loss, detriment, (*occ.* Acts xxvii. 10.)
2. ἀποβολή, a casting off *or* away from loss, (*occ.* Rom. xi. 15.)

3. ἥττημα, a being inferior, a worse state, *as compared with any other* or *former state*, (*occ.* 1 Cor. vi. 7.)

1. Acts xxvii. 21.
2. —— 22.
3. Rom. xi. 12, marg. (text, *diminishing.*)
— 1 Cor. iii. 15, see Loss (suffer)
1. Phil. iii. 7, 8 1st.
— —— 8 2nd, see Loss of (suffer)

LOSS (SUFFER.)

ζημιόω, *see* "LOSE," *No.* 2.

1 Cor. iii. 15.

LOSS OF (SUFFER)

ζημιόω, *see* "LOSE," *No.* 2.

Phil. iii. 8.

LOT (-S.)

1. κλῆρος, (*prob. from* κλάω, to break, *because twigs or other* κλάσματα, (fragments) *were used for the purpose of casting lots*) a lot, the lot that apportions *or* allots. *Then*, the lot that is allotted *or* apportioned.

Matt. xxvii. 35 (ap.)
Mark xv. 24.
Luke i. 9, see L (be one's)
—— xxiii. 34.
John xix. 24.
—— 34, see L (cast)
Acts i. 16 twice.
—— viii. 21.
Acts xiii. 9, see Divide.

LOT (BE ONE'S)

λαγχάνω, to have fall to one's lot, obtain as one's portion.

Luke i. 9.

LOTS (CAST)

λαγχάνω, *see above.*

John xix. 34.

LOUD.

μέγας, great, large, *prop. of physical magnitude, but also* great *in force and intensity; hence, of the voice,* loud.

Matt. xxvii. 46, 50.
Mark i. 26.
—— v. 7.
—— xv. 34.
—— 37.
Luke i. 42.
—— iv. 33.
—— viii. 28.
—— xvii. 15.
—— xix. 37.
—— xxiii. 23, 46.
John xi. 43.
Acts vii. 57, 60.
—— viii. 7.
—— xiv. 10.
—— xvi. 28.
—— xxvi. 24.
Rev. v. 2, 12.
—— vi. 10.
—— vii. 2, 10.
—— viii. 13.
—— x. 3,
—— xii. 10.
—— xiv. 7, 9, 15, 18.
Rev. xix. 17.

LOVE [noun.]

ἀγάπη, love. [A word not found in the profane writers, nor in Philo and Josephus, nor in Acts, Mark, and James. It is unknown to writers outside of the *N.T.* φιλανθρωπία, philanthropy *was the highest word used by the Greeks*, which is a very different thing to ἀγάπη, and even far lower than φιλαδελφια. φιλανθρωπία *in its full display was only giving to him who was entitled to it his full rights.*] ἀγάπη *denotes* the love *which springs from admiration and veneration, and which chooses its object with decision of will, and devotes a self-denying and compassionate devotion to it.* Love in its fullest conceivable form.

2. φιλανθρωπία, philanthropy, love of man, (*see above.*)

1. Matt. xxiv. 12.
1. Luke xi. 42.
1. John v. 42.
1. —— xiii. 35.
1. —— xv. 9, 10 twice, 13.
1. —— xvii. 26.
1. Rom. v. 5, 8.
1. —— viii. 35, 39.
1. —— xii. 9.
— —— 10, see Brotherly or Brethren.
1. —— xiii. 10 twice.
1. —— xv. 30.
1. 1 Cor. iv. 21.
1. —— xvi. 24.
1. 2 Cor. ii. 4, 8.
1. —— v. 14.
1. —— vi. 6.
1. —— viii. 7, 8, 24.
1. —— xiii. 11, 14.
1. Gal. v. 6, 13, 22.
1. Eph. i. 4.
1. —— 15 (om. L א.)
1. —— ii. 4.
1. —— iii. 17, 19.
1. —— iv. 2, 15, 16.
1. —— v. 2.
1. —— vi. 23.
1. Phil. i. 9, 17.
1. —— ii. 1, 2.
1. Col. i. 4, 8.
1. —— ii. 2.
1. 1 Thes. i. 3.
1. —— iii. 12.
1. —— v. 8, 13.
1. 2 Thes. ii. 10.
1. —— iii. 5.
1. 1 Tim. i. 14.
— —— vi. 10, see Money.
1. —— 11.
1. 2 Tim. i. 7, 13.
2. Titus iii. 4.
1. Philem. 5, 7, 9.
1. Heb. vi. 10.
1. —— x. 24.
— 1 Pet. i. 22, } see
— —— iii. 8, } Brethren.
1. 1 John ii. 5, 15.
1. —— iii. 1, 16, 17.
1. —— iv. 7, 8, 9, 10, 12, 16 3 times, 17, 18 3 times.
1. —— v. 3.
1. 2 John 3, 6.
1. Jude 2, 21.
1. Rev. ii. 4.

LOVE (-ED, -EDST, -EST, -ETH.) [verb.]

1. ἀγαπάω, to regard, (*Lat.*, diligere) esteem, (the principle of internal feeling of delectation and kindliness,) to acquiesce with satisfaction, to cherish with reverence, to love, *considered in reference to the tendency of the will* (*elsewhere translated* beloved.) (*See note, below.*)

2. φιλέω, to kiss, to love (*Lat.*, amare), *used of the more direct demonstration of regard;* (*hence,* φίλος, a friend, *is from* φιλέω, *from* φίω, *or*

from πίλω, to press; φίλος, *is* he whom we embrace, *or* kiss. Again, φιλία *is* friendship *between men, but* love *when between the sexes,*) to love, *considered in reference to a natural inclination, or an emotion,* (*i.e.* the passion of love) (*elsewhere translated* to kiss.) (*See note, below.*)

[NOTE.—These two words are not used indiscriminately. ἀγαπάω, never means *to kiss;* φιλέω, never means *to acquiesce* or *cherish with reverence.* φιλέω denotes *the sense* or *passion of love*, but in ἀγαπάω is implied *the cause of* φιλέω. ἀγαπάω is *to make much of a thing, to admire* for some good and sufficient reason, but φιλέω denotes the love which springs naturally from the thing loved, even where no just cause of love exists. ἀγαπάω is never used of an improper love; φιλέω is. *Hence,* in the *N.T.* φιλέω is never used of *man's love to God,* but ἀγαπάω, always. Both words are used of *God's love to man,* ἀγαπάω, when He is said to "Love the world," (John iii. 16, etc.) and when He wishes men good, and seeks their salvation; and φιλέω is affirmed of His love to His people who please Him, (John xvi. 27, etc.) Again, φιλέω is used of Jesus' love for Lazarus, (John xi. 3, 36); but in verse 5 the word is ἀγαπάω, because there the *sisters* are included, and therefore this word was more correct. Again, we are commanded to *love our enemies,* etc., but here ἀγαπάω is used, never φιλέω; love cannot be required in this case, though kindness and compassion are. Again, in John xxi. 15-17, in the first question Jesus uses ἀγαπάω, but Peter uses the word φιλέω in his reply; this is repeated, and then Jesus uses Peter's word in the third question. Once more, to love (φιλέω) life, from an excessive desire to preserve it, and so to lose sight of the real object of living, is reproved by our Lord, (John xii. 25.) Whereas to love (ἀγαπάω) life, is to consult its real interest. Other examples may be traced out with much profit, *e.g.* Mark x. 21.]

3. θέλω, to will, desire, wish, *implying active volition and purpose.*

1. Matt. v. 43, 44, 46 twice.
2. —— vi. 5.
1. ——— 24.
2. —— x. 37 twice.
1. —— xix. 19.
1. —— xxii. 37, 39.
2. —— xxiii. 6.
1. Mark x. 21.
1. —— xii. 30, 31, 33 twice.
3. ——— 38.
1. Luke vi. 27, 32 4 times, 35.
1. —— vii. 5, 42, 47 twice.
1. —— x. 27.
1. —— xi. 43.
1. —— xvi. 13.
2. —— xx. 46.
1. John iii. 16, 19, 35.
2. —— v. 20 (No. 1, Lm.)
1. —— viii. 42.
1. —— x. 17.
2. —— xi. 3.
1. ——— 5.
2. ——— 36.
2. —— xii. 25.
1. ——— 43.
1. —— xiii. 1 twice, 23, 34 3 times.
1. —— xiv. 15, 21 4 times, 23 twice, 24, 28, 31.
1. —— xv. 9 twice, 12 twice, [17.
2. ——— 19.
2. —— xvi. 27 twice.
1. —— xvii. 23 twice, 24, 26.
1. —— xix. 26.
2. —— xx. 2.
1. —— xxi. 7, 15 1st.
2. ——— 15 2nd.
1. ——— 16 1st.
2. ——— 16 2nd.
2. ——— 17 3 times.
1. ——— 20.
1. Rom. viii. 28, 37.
1. —— ix. 13.
1. —— xiii. 8 twice, 9.
1. 1 Cor. ii. 9.
1. —— viii. 3.
2. —— xvi. 22.
1. 2 Cor. ix. 7.
1. —— xi. 11.
1. —— xii. 15 twice.
1. Gal. ii. 20.
1. —— v. 14.
1. Eph. ii. 4.
1. —— v. 2, 25 twice, 33.
1. —— vi. 24.
1. Col. iii. 19.
1. 1 Thes. iv. 9.
1. 2 Thes. ii. 16.
1. 2 Tim. iv. 8, 10.
— Tit. ii. 4, see Husband or Children.
— —— iii. 4, see Man.
2. ——— 15.
1. Heb. i. 9.
1. —— xii. 6.
1. Jas. i. 12.
1. —— ii. 5, 8.
1. 1 Pet. i. 8, 22.
1. —— ii. 17.
— —— iii. 8, see Brethren.
1. ——— 10.
1. 2 Pet. ii. 15.
1. 1 John ii. 10, 15 twice.
1. —— iii. 10, 11, 14 twice, 18, 23.
1. —— iv. 7 twice, 8, 10 twice, 11 twice, 12, 19 twice, 20 3 times, 21 twice.
1. —— v. 1 twice, 2 twice.
1. 2 John i. 5.
1. 3 John i.
2. ——— 9.
1. Rev. i. 5.
1. —— iii. 9.
2. ——— 19.
1. —— xii. 11.
2. —— xxii. 15.

LOVELY.

προσφιλής, dear to *any one,* (*non occ.*)

Phil. iv. 8.

LOVER.

See, GOD, GOOD, HOSPITALITY, PLEASURE, SELF.

LOVING TO THE BRETHREN.

[marg.]

See, BRETHREN.

LOW (BRING)

ταπεινόω, to make low, *hence,* to humble, abase.

Luke iii. 5.

LOW ESTATE.

ταπείνωσις, a making low, humiliation. *In N.T.*, the being brought low, low estate, humiliation.

Luke i. 48.

LOW ESTATE (MEN OF)

ταπεινός, low, not high; humble *of condition, or mind.*

Rom. xii. 16, pl. with art.

LOW (IN THAT HE IS MADE)

ἐν, in, *τῇ*, the, *ταπεινώσει*, the being brought low, } in his becoming low.

Jas. i. 10.

LOW DEGREE (OF)

ταπεινός, low, not high; humble *of condition, or mind.*

Luke i. 52. | Jas. i. 9.

LOWER [adj.]

κατώτερος, lower down, *i.e.* lower, used for *ᾅδης*, Hades, (*see* "HELL," *No.* 2), (*non occ.*)

Eph. iv. 9.

LOWER (MAKE)

ἐλαττόω, to make less, *e.g.* in dignity, (*occ.* John iii. 30.)

Heb. ii. 7, marg. *make inferior.*
—— 9.

LOWER (-ING.) [verb.]

στυγνάζω, to be *or* become austere *or* gloomy, (*occ.* Mark x. 22.)

Matt. xvi. 3.

LOWEST.

ἔσχατος, the last, extreme, uttermost.

Luke xiv. 9, 10.

LOWLINESS.

ταπεινοφροσύνη, lowliness of mind, humility, modesty of mind *and deportment.*

Eph iv. 2.

LOWLINESS OF MIND.

Phil. ii. 3.

LOWLY.

ταπεινός, low, not high; humble *of condition, or mind.*

Matt. xi. 29.

LUCRE.

κέρδος, gain, profit, advantage; *then,* desire of gain, love of gain, (*occ.* Phil. i. 21, iii. 7.)

Tit. i. 11.

LUCRE (FOR FILTHY)

αἰσχροκερδῶς, for the sake of dishonourable gain, (*non occ.*)

1 Pet. v. 2.

LUCRE (GIVEN TO FILTHY)

αἰσχροκερδής, eager even for dishonourable gain.

Tit. i. 7.

LUCRE (GREEDY OF FILTHY)

αἰσχροκερδής, *see above.*

1 Tim. iii. 3 (*om.* G L T Tr A ℵ.)
—— 8.

LUKEWARM.

χλιαρός, warm, lukewarm, (*non occ.*)

Rev. iii. 16.

LUMP.

φύραμα, a kneaded mass, *e.g.* of potter's clay, or dough, (*non occ.*)

Rom. ix. 21. | 1 Cor. v. 6, 7.
—— xi. 16. | Gal. v. 9.

LUNATIC (BE)

σεληνιάζομαι, to be moon-struck, lunatic, (*non occ.*)

Matt. iv. 24. | Matt. xvii. 15.

LUST [noun.]

1. ἐπιθυμία, what is directed towards any thing, desire which attaches itself to (ἐπί-) *or* upon its object. *It is used exclusively of* sinful desire, *which corresponds to man's depraved nature.* The inward passion of concupiscence.

2. ὄρεξις, a reaching after, the appetite and tendency towards the external object. *No.* 1 *is only* the mental desire, *but No.* 2 *has conjoined with it*, the notion of the thing desired. *No.* 1 *may therefore be used absolutely, as in* Rom. vii. 7, and xiii. 9, *but No.* 2 *never*, (*non occ.*)

3. ἡδονή, pleasure, gratification, enjoyment.

4. πάθος, suffering, passion, (*i.e.* of affection *or* love.)

1. Mark iv. 19.
1. John viii. 44.
1. Rom. i. 24,
2. —— 27.
1. —— vi. 11 (*ap.*)
1. —— vii. 7, marg. *concupiscence.*
1. —— xiii. 14.
1. Gal. v. 16, 24.
1. Eph. ii. 3.
1. —— iv. 22.
4. 1 Thes. iv. 5.
1. 1 Tim. vi. 9.
1. 2 Tim. ii. 22.
1. 2 Tim. iii. 6.
1. —— iv. 3.
1. Tit. ii. 12.
1. —— iii. 3.
1. Jas. i. 14, 15.
3. —— iv. 1 and 3, marg. *pleasure.*
1. 1 Pet. i. 14.
1. —— ii. 11.
1. —— iv. 2, 3.
1. 2 Pet. i. 4.
1. —— ii. 10, 18.
1. —— iii. 3.
1. 1 John ii. 16 twice, 17.
1. Jude 16, 18.

LUST (-ED, -ETH.) [verb.]

1. ἐπιθυμέω, to fix the desire upon, to have the affections directed towards *any thing*, (*of unlawful desires.*)

2. ἐπιποθέω, to desire upon, i.e. *over and above, besides*, to desire earnestly, long for.

— Matt. v. 28, } see L
— 1 Cor. x. 6 1st, } after.
1. —— 6 2nd.
1. Gal. v. 17.
1. Jas. iv. 2.
2. —— 5.

LUSTETH AFTER (THAT...)

επιθυμία, *see* "LUST," *No.* 1 [noun.]

Rev. xviii. 14.

LYING [noun* and adj.†]

ψεῦδος, falsehood, lying, a lie.

* Eph. iv. 25. | † 2 Thes. ii. 9.

LYING IN WAIT.

1. ἔνεδρον, a lying in wait, *prop.*, *in war*, an ambuscade, (*non occ.*)

2. ἐπιβουλή, counsel upon *or* against; *hence*, plot, conspiracy.

2. Acts xx. 19. | 1. Acts xxiii. 16.

LYSIAS.

Λυσίας, Lysias, *i.e.* Claudius Lysias, a Roman Tribune commanding in Jerusalem.

Acts xxiii. 26. | Acts xxiv. 7 (*ap.*), 22.

M

MAD (BE)

μαίνομαι, to rage, to be furious, (*occ.* Acts xxvi. 24.)

John x. 20.
Acts xii. 15.
Acts xxvi. 25.
1 Cor. xiv. 23.

MAD AGAINST (BE)

ἐμμαίνομαι, (*the above, with* ἐν, in, *prefixed*) to rage *or* be furious against *any person or thing*, (*non occ.*)

Acts xxvi. 11.

MAD (MAKE)

περιτρέπω, to turn about, εἰς, unto, μανίαν, madness, — "is turning [*thee*] round unto raving madness."

Acts xxvi. 24.

MADNESS.

1. ἄνοια, without mind *or* understanding, folly; *Sept.*, for אולת, Prov. xxii. 15; Wisd. xv. 18. *Whence, in N.T.*, madness, *or* foolish temerity, (*occ.* 2 Tim. iii. 9.)

2. παραφρονία, the state of being aside from a right mind, folly, (*non occ.*)

1. Luke vi. 11. | 2. 2 Pet. ii. 16.

MADE (BE)

(*See also other words in connection, e.g.*, CONFESSION, DRUNK, HANDS, KNOWN, LIKE, LOW, PAYMENT, RICH, SUBJECT, WEAK.)

1. γίνομαι, to begin to be, *i.e.* to come into existence, *or* into any state, *as implying origin either from natural causes or through special agency; hence*, to become, come to pass.

2. γεννάω, to beget, *of men;* to bear, *of women; pass.*, to be begotten, be born.

3. κεῖμαι, to lie, *and also* to be laid, laid down; *hence*, appointed.

4. εἶναι, (*inf. of* εἰμί, to be) to be.

5. ἔσται, (*3rd pers. sing. future of* εἰμί to be) he, she, *or* it shall be.

1. Matt. iv. 3.
1. —— ix. 16.
1. —— xxiii. 15.
1. —— xxv. 6.
1. —— xxvii. 24.
1. Mark ii. 21, 27.
1. —— xiv. 4.
5. Luke iii. 5 1st [2nd has no equivalent.]
1. —— iv. 3.
1. —— viii. 17.
1. —— xiv. 12, 19.
1. John i. 3 3 times, 10, 14.
1. —— ii. 9.
1. —— v. 4 (*ap.*), 6, 9, 14.
1. —— viii. 33.
1. —— ix. 39.
1. Acts vii. 13.
1. —— xii. 5.
1. —— xiii. 32.
1. —— xiv. 5.
4. —— xvi. 13.
1. —— xix. 26.
1. —— xxi. 40, part.
1. —— xxvi. 6.
1. Rom. i. 3.
— —— 20, see M (thing that is)
1. —— ii. 25.
1. —— vii. 13.
1. —— x. 20.
1. —— xi. 9.
1. 1 Cor. i. 30.
1. —— iii. 13.
1. —— iv. 9, 13.
1. —— vii. 21.
1. —— ix. 22.
1. —— xi. 19.
1. —— xiv. 25.
1. —— xv. 45.
1. 2 Cor. v. 21.
1. Gal. iii. 13.
1. —— iv. 4 twice.
1. Eph. ii. 13.
1. —— iii. 7.
1. Phil. ii. 7.
1. Col. i. 23, 25.
3. 1 Tim. i. 9.
1. Tit. iii. 7.
1. Heb. i. 4.
1. —— iii. 14.
1. —— v. 5.
1. —— vi. 4, 20.
1. —— vii. 12, 16, 21, 22, 26.
1. —— xi. 3.
1. Jas. iii. 9.
1. 1 Pet. ii. 7 (with εἰς, *unto.*)
2. 2 Pet. ii. 12 (No. 1, St. AV. ℵ), (ζῶα γεννημένα φυσικὰ, *irrational animals born naturally*, G L T Tr A.)

MADE (THING THAT IS)

ποίημα, a thing made, (*occ.* Eph. ii. 10.)

Rom. i. 20.

MAGDALENE.

Μαγδαληνή, of Magdala, *a distinctive appellation of one of the Marys, viz.* Mary of Magdala.

Matt. xxvii. 56, 61.
—— xxviii. 1.
Mark xv. 40, 47.
—— xvi. 1, 9 (*ap.*)
Luke viii. 2.
—— xxiv. 10.
John xix. 25.
—— xx. 1, 18.

MAGISTRATE (-S.)

1. στρατηγός, leader of an army, commander, general, etc.

2. ἀρχή, beginning; *spoken of persons*, the first, primus.

3. ἄρχων, one first in power *or* authority; *hence*, a ruler, chief person.

2. Luke xii. 11.
3. —— 58.
1. Acts xvi. 20, 22, 35, 36, 38
— Tit. iii. 1, see Obey.

MAGNIFICENCE.

μεγαλειότης, greatness, majesty.

Acts xix. 27.

MAGNIFY (-ED.)

1. μεγαλύνω, to make great, enlarge, to praise.

2. δοξάζω, to be of opinion, to think, to hold any one for anything, to invest with dignity, make any one important, cause him honour.

1. Luke i. 46.
1. Acts v. 13.
1. —— x. 46.
1. —— xix. 17.
2. Rom. xi. 13.
1. 2 Cor. x. 15, marg. (text, *enlarge.*)
1. Phil. i. 20.

MAID.

1. παῖς, a child, *male or female*, a boy, youth, girl, maiden.

2. παιδίσκη, (*dim. and fem. of No.* 1) a girl, a young maiden.

3. κοράσιον, girl, maiden, (*this word belongs more to familiar discourse, like Germ.*, mädel) *elsewhere translated* "*damsel.*"

3. Matt. ix. 24, 25.
2. Mark xiv. 66, 69.
1. Luke viii. 54.
2. —— xxii. 56.

MAIDEN.

1. παῖς, *see above, No.* 1.

2. παιδίσκη, *see above, No.* 2.

1. Luke viii. 51. | 2. Luke xii. 45.

MAIMED.

1. *κυλλός*, bent, crooked; *hence*, crippled, lame, *esp.*, *in the hands*, (*non occ.*)

2. *ἀνάπηρος*, maimed, *i.e.* deprived of some member, *or* the use of it, (*non occ.*)

1. Matt. xv. 30, 31.	1. Mark ix. 43.
1. —— xviii. 8.	2. Luke xiv. 13, 21.

MAINSAIL.

ἀρτέμων, (*from ἀρτάω*, to hoist) a topsail, supparum; *others*, a jib, dolon, (*non occ.*)

Acts xxvii. 40.

MAINTAIN.

προΐστημι, *trans.*, to cause to stand before. *Here*, *intrans.*, to stand before, to put . . . forward.

Tit. iii. 8.	Tit. iii. 14, marg. *profess.*

MAJESTY.

1. *μεγαλωσύνη*, majesty, *i.e.* the Divine majesty and greatness.

2. *μεγαλειότης*, greatness, magnificence, glory.

1. Heb. i. 3.	2. 2 Pet. i. 16.
1. —— viii. 1.	1. Jude 25.

MAKE (-EST, -ETH, -ING.)

(*See at foot for list of other words in various connections.*)

1. *ποιέω*, to make, *i.e.* to form, produce, to bring about, cause, *spoken of any external act as manifested in the production of something tangible and obvious to the senses, and referring to completed action.*

   (a) *Middle*, is used with only a remote reference to the subject, which sometimes wholly vanishes and makes it like the active.

2. *τίθημι*, to set, to put, to place, to lay.

3. *διατίθημι*, (*No.* 2, *with διά*, through, *prefixed*) to place apart, to set out in order, arrange. *In N.T. only middle*, to arrange in one's own behalf, to appoint.

4. *καθίστημι*, to set down, to set, to place. *In N.T. only in the trans. forms*, to be set; *of persons*, to constitute.

5. *συνίστημι*, (*No.* 4, *with σύν*, together with, *prefixed*, *instead of κατά*, down.)

   (a) *trans.*, to make stand with *or* together, to place with *or* before *any one.*

   (b) *intrans.*, to stand with *or* together.

6. *δίδωμι*, to give, (*with one's own accord and with goodwill.*)

7. *ἐπιτελέω*, to bring through to an end, to finish, to perform.

8. *συντελέω*, (*No.* 7, *with σύν*, together with, *prefixed*, *instead of ἐπί*, upon) to end or terminate together, to accomplish together.

9. *εἰμί*, to be; *here*, *3rd pers. pres. sing.*, *ἐστί*, is.

10. *κατασκευάζω*, to prepare fully, put in readiness.

11. *κτίζω*, to bring under tillage and settlement, *as land*; *of a city*, to found. *Gen.*, to form.

12. *προχειρίζομαι*, to hand forth, to cause to be at hand, ready; to prepare and appoint.

13. *ῥέω*, *obsol.*, to speak, to utter definite words, *and hence*, *implying more than λαλέω.*

14. *συμβάλλω*, to throw one's self together with another, to encounter, [to, *εἰς*, unto, with a view] to meet in encounter with a view to war.

1. Matt. iii. 3.	1. Mark viii. 25 (*διβελέψεν*, *he saw clearly*, instead of *εποιήσεν αὐτὸν ἀναβλέψαι*, *made him look up*, T Tr A ℵ), (*om.* G→)
1. —— iv. 19.	1. —— ix. 5.
1. —— v. 36.	1. —— x. 6.
1. —— xii. 16, 33 twice.	1. —— xi. 17.
1. —— xvii. 4 1st.	2. —— xii. 36.
1. —— xix. 4 2nd (No. 11, Tr.)	9. —— 42.
1. —— xx. 12.	1. Luke iii. 4.
1. —— xxi. 13.	1. —— v. 29.
1. —— xxii. 2.	1a. —— 33.
2. —— 44.	1. —— 34.
1. —— xxiii. 15 twice.	1. —— ix. 33.
1. —— xxv. 16 (*κερδαίνω*, *to gain*, G ∾ L Tr.)	1. —— xi. 40 twice.
1. Mark i. 3, 17.	4. —— xii. 14.
1. —— iii. 12.	
1. —— vi. 21.	
1. —— vii. 37.	

1. Luke xiv. 12, 13, 16.
14.——— 31.
1. —— xv. 19.
1. —— xvi. 9.
1. —— xix. 46.
2. —— xx. 43.
— —— xxiv. 28, see Me as though.
1. John ii. 15 part, 16.
1. —— iv. 1, 46.
1. —— v. 11, 15, 18.
1. —— vi. 10, 15.
1. —— vii. 23.
1. —— viii. 53.
1. —— ix. 6, 11, 14.
1. —— x. 33.
1. —— xii. 2.
1. —— xiv. 23.
1. —— xviii. 18.
1. —— xix. 7, 12, 23.
1a. Acts i. 1.
2. —— ii. 35.
1. ——— 36.
1. —— iii. 1?.
3. ——— 25.
1. —— iv. 24.
4. —— vii. 10, 27, 35.
1. ——— 40, 43, 44, 50.
1a.—— viii. 2.
1. —— ix. 39.
1. —— xiv. 15.
1. —— xvii. 24, 26.
1. —— xix. 24.
2. —— xx. 28.
— —— xxii. 1, see M now (which I)
1. —— xxiii. 13.
12.—— xxvi. 16.
— —— xxvii. 40, see M toward.
1a. Rom. i. 9.
2. —— iv. 17.
4. —— v. 19 twice.
1. —— ix. 20, 21.
— ——— 22, see M *up*.
1. ——— 28.
1a. —— xiii. 14.
— —— xiv. 19, see M for (the things which)
1a. Rom. xv. 26.
1. 1 Cor. vi. 15.
2. —— ix. 18.
1. —— x. 13.
1. 2 Cor. v. 21.
— —— ix. 5, see M up beforehand.
5a. Gal. ii. 18.
13.—— iii. 16.
1a. Eph. i. 16.
1. —— ii. 14.
11.——— 15 1st.
1. ——— 15 2nd.
1a.—— iv. 16.
1a. Phil. i. 4.
1a. 1 Thes. i. 2.
6. 2 Thes. iii. 9.
1. 1 Tim. ii. 2.
1a. Philem. 4.
1. Heb. i. 2, 7.
2. ——— 13.
4. —— vii. 28.
7. —— viii. 5 1st.
1. ——— 5 2nd.
8. ——— 8.
1. ——— 9.
3. ——— 10.
10.—— ix. 2.
2. —— x. 13.
3. ——— 16.
1. —— xii. 13, 27.
1. Jas. iii. 18.
4. 2 Pet. i. 8.
1a.——— 10.
2. ——— 11, 16.
1. 1 John i. 10.
1. —— v. 10.
1. Rev. i. 6.
6. —— iii. 9 1st.
1. ——— 9 2nd, 12.
1. —— v. 10.
1. —— xi. 7.
1. —— xii. 17.
1. —— xiii. 7 (*ap.*), 13 (*om.* [G), 14.
1. —— xiv. 7.
1. —— xvii. 16.
1. —— xix. 19.
1. —— xxi. 5.
1. —— xxii. 15.

MAKE AS THOUGH.

προσποιέω, to make to *or* for *any one*, to make pretension to be *so and so*. *Hence, in N.T., dep. mid.*, to make a show of *being or doing anything*.

Luke xxiv. 28.

MAKE FOR (THE THINGS WHICH)

τὰ, the things.

Rom. xiv. 19.

MAKE TOWARD.

κατέχω, to have and hold fast. *In navigation*, to hold *a ship* firm towards *the land*.

Acts xxvii. 40.

MAKE UP. [marg.]

καταρτίζω, to make fully ready, put in full order, make complete.

Rom. ix. 22, text, *fit*.

MAKE UP BEFOREHAND.

προκαταρτίζω, (*the above, with* πρό, beforehand, *prefixed*), (*non occ.*)

2 Cor. ix. 5.

MAKE NOW (WHICH I)

νῦν, now, *with art, i.e.* "my defence unto you at this time."

Acts xxii. 1.

See also, ABLE, ABOUND, ACCEPTED, ADO, ALIVE, ASHAMED, ASTONISHED, BED, BITTER, BOAST, BROAD, CALF, CHOICE, CLEAN, CONFORMABLE, DEFENCE, DESOLATE, DIFFER, DIFFERENCE, DISTRIBUTION, DOUBT, DRINK, EFFECT, END, EUNUCH, EVIL, EXAMPLE, EXCUSE, FAST, FOOLISH, FREE, FRIEND, FULL, GAIN, GAZINGSTOCK, GLAD, GLORIOUS, HASTE, HAVOC, INCREASE, INFERIOR, INQUIRY, INSURRECTION, INTERCESSION, JOURNEY, KNOWN, LIGHT, LIKE, LOWER, MAD, MADE, MANIFEST, MATTER, MEET, MELODY, MENTION, MERCHANDISE, MERRY, NEW, NOISE, NUMBER, OBEDIENT, OFFEND, OLD, ORATION, PEACE, PERFECT, PRAYER, PROMISE, PROOF, READY, RECONCILIATION, RENT, REPUTATION, REQUEST, RICH, RISE, RULER, SEE, SERVANT, SHIPWRECK, SHOW, SIGNS, SIT, SORRY, STAND, STRAIGHT, STRONG, SURE, UPROAR, VOID, WAR, WHITE, WHOLE, WISE.

MAKEBATE [marg.]

διάβολος, a calumniator, slanderer, accuser; *the name of the Devil*, the constant enemy of God and man, and of all truth.

2 Tim. iii. 3, } text, *false accuser*.
Tit. ii. 3,

MAKER.

δημιουργός, one who works for the public, a handicraftsman, artificer; *then, used by the Greeks as the name for* the Maker of the world, (*non occ.*)

Acts xviii. 3, see Tent. | Heb. xi. 10.

MALE.

ἄρσην, male, *i.e.* of the male sex, (*occ.* Rom. i. 27.)

Matt. xix. 4.
Mark x. 6.
Luke ii. 23.
Gal. iii. 28.

MALEFACTOR (-s.)

1. κακοῦργος, an evil-worker, the worker *or* author of evil, *the action being prominent*, a labourer for evil, (*occ.* 2 Tim. ii. 9.)

2. κακοποιός, an evil-doer, a doer of some particular evil, *the evil being prominent*, an effector of the evil for which he labours.

1. Luke xxiii. 32, 33, 39.
2. John xviii. 30.

MALICE.

κακία, badness, (*nom. of* κακός, bad, *generically including every form of evil, physical and moral.*) κακία is evil habit flowing from πονηρία, (the wicked act of the mind malignity) vice *generally, in all its forms.*

1 Cor. v. 8.
—— xiv. 20.
Eph. iv. 31.
Col. iii. 8.
Tit. iii. 3.
1 Pet. ii. 1.

MALICIOUS.

πονηρός, causing or having labour, sorrow, pain; *hence*, evil *in its more active form*, malignant.

3 John 10.

MALICIOUSNESS.

κακία, *see* "MALICE."

Rom. i. 29.
1 Pet. ii. 16.

MALIGNITY.

κακοήθεια, evil disposedness, the desire of evil to others, spitefulness, (*non occ.*)

Rom. i. 29.

MAMMON.

μαμμωνᾶς, Chald. ממון, that in which one trusts; *hence*, mammon, *i.e.* wealth, riches, (*non occ.*)

Mark vi. 24.
Luke xvi. 9, marg. *riches.*
Luke xvi. 11, marg. *riches.*
—— 13.

MAN.

(*See at foot, for list of other words used in various connections.*)

NOTE.—Sometimes "MAN" is the translation of the masc. of adjectives or nouns, etc.

When it is the translation of a separate Greek word it is one of these following:—

1. ἄνθρωπος, (ἄνω ἀθρεῖν τῇ ὠπί, looking upwards with his countenance, *or from* ἄνω τρέπειν ὦπα, turning his view upwards) man; *Lat.*, homo, *i.e.* an individual of the human race, a man *or* woman, a person, a human being, *the generic name, relatively, to gods and animals. Man was made out "of the dust of the ground," made in the image of Elohim, the second person of the Trinity. See under* "WORD."

   (a) *with* υἱός, Son, the Son of Man, meaning the Lord Jesus Christ, "the word made flesh."

2. ἀνήρ, a man; *Lat.*, vir., *i.e.* an adult male person, a man *in sex and in age, a more honourable title than No.* 1.

3. τις, one, some one, a certain one.

4. ἄρρην, male, *i.e.* of the male sex.

5. ἄρσην, same meaning as *No.* 4, (*No.* 5 being the old Ionic form, *No.* 4 the later Attic form.)

6. τέλειος, what has reached its end, term, object, *or* limit; *hence*, complete, perfect, full, *wanting in nothing*, of persons of full age, full grown.

1. Matt. iv. 4, 19.
1. —— v. 13, 16, 19.
1. —— vi. 1, 2, 5, 14, 15, 16, 18.
1. —— vii. 9, 12.
2. —— 24, 26.
1. —— viii. 9.
1a. —— 20.
1. —— 27.
1a. —— ix. 6.
1. —— 8, 9.
1. —— 32 (*om.* L T Tr[b] A[b] ℵ.)
1. —— x. 17.
1a. —— 23.
1. —— 32, 33, 35, 36.
1. —— xi. 8.
1a. —— 19 1st.
1. Matt. 19 2nd.
1a. —— xii. 8.
1. —— 10, 11, 12, 13, 31 1st.
1. —— 31 2nd (*om.* L T Tr A ℵ.)
1a. —— 32.
1. —— 35 twice.
1a. —— 40.
2. —— 41.
1. —— 43, 45.
1. —— xiii. 24, 25, 31.
1a. —— 37, 41.
1. —— 44, 45, 52.
2. —— xiv. 21, 35.
1. —— xv. 9, 11 twice, 18, 20 twice.
2. —— 38.
1. —— xvi. 13 1st.

1a. Matt. xvi. 13 2nd.
1. ——— 23, 26 twice.
1a. ——— 27, 28.
1a. —— xvii. 9, 12, 14 1st.
1. ——— 14 2nd.
1. —— xviii. 7.
1a. ——— 11 (ap.)
1. ——— 12.
1. —— xix. 3 (om. L T A ℵ.)
1. ——— 5, 6, 12, 26.
1a. ——— 28.
1. —— xx. 1.
1a. ——— 18, 28.
1. —— xxi. 25, 26, 28.
1. —— xxii. 11, 16.
3. ——— 24.
1. —— xxiii. 4, 5, 7, 13, 28.
1a. —— xxiv. 27, 30 twice, 37, 39, 44.
1a. —— xxv. 13 (ap.)
1. ——— 14, 24.
1a. ——— 31.
1a. —— xxvi. 2, 24 1st.
1. ——— 24 2nd.
1a. ——— 24 3rd.
1. ——— 24 4th.
1a. ——— 45, 64.
1. ——— 72, 74.
1. —— xxvii. 32, 57.
1. Mark i. 17, 23.
1a. —— ii. 10.
1. ——— 27 twice.
1a. ——— 28.
1. —— iii. 1, 3, 5, 28.
1. —— iv. 26.
1. —— v. 2, 8.
2. —— vi. 20, 44.
1. —— vii. 7, 8, 11, 15 twice, 18, 20 twice, 21, 23.
3. —— viii. 4.
1. ——— 24, 27.
1a. ——— 31.
1. ——— 33, 36, 37.
1a. ——— 38.
1a. —— ix. 9, 12, 31 1st.
1. ——— 31 2nd.
2. —— x. 2.
1. ——— 7, 9, 27.
1a. ——— 33, 45.
1. —— xi. 2, 30, 32.
1. —— xii. 1, 14.
3. ——— 19.
1a. —— xiii. 26.
1. ——— 34.
1. —— xiv. 13.
1a. ——— 21 1st.
1. ——— 21 2nd.
1a. ——— 21 3rd.
1. ——— 21 4th.
1a. ——— 41, 62.
1. ——— 71.
1. —— xv. 39.
1. Luke i. 25.
2. ——— 27, 34.
1. —— ii. 14, 25 twice, 52.
1. —— iv. 4, 33.
2. —— v. 8.
1. ——— 10.
2. ——— 12, 18 1st.
1. ——— 18 2nd.
1. ——— 20.
1a. ——— 24.
1a. —— vi. 5.
1. ——— 6.
1. ——— 8 (No. 2, G ∾ T Tr A ℵ.)
1. ——— 10 (*αὐτῷ*, *unto him*, G L T Tr A.)
1. ——— 22 1st.
1a. ——— 22 2nd.
1. ——— 26, 31, 45 1st.
1. ——— 45 2nd (om. G ⇄ Lb T Tr A ℵ.)
1. ——— 48, 49.
1. —— vii. 8.
2. ——— 20.
1. ——— 25, 31.
1a. —— vii. 34 1st.
1. Luke vii. 34 2nd.
2. —— viii. 27.
1. ——— 29, 33, 35.
2. ——— 38, 41.
2. —— ix. 14.
1a. ——— 22.
1. ——— 25.
1a. ——— 26.
2. ——— 30, 32, 38.
1a. ——— 44 1st.
1. ——— 44 2nd.
1a. ——— 56 1st (ap.)
1. ——— 56 2nd (ap.)
1a. ——— 58.
1. —— x. 30.
1. —— xi. 24, 26.
1a. ——— 30.
2. ——— 31, 32.
1. ——— 44, 46.
1. —— xii. 8 1st.
1a. ——— 8 2nd.
1. ——— 9.
1a. ——— 10.
1. ——— 14.
3. ——— 15.
1. ——— 16, 36.
1a. ——— 40.
1. —— xiii. 4, 19.
1. —— xiv. 2, 16.
2. ——— 24.
1. ——— 30.
1. —— xv. 4, 11.
1. —— xvi. 1, 15 twice, 19.
2. —— xvii. 12.
1a. ——— 22, 24, 26, 30.
1. —— xviii. 2, 4.
1a. ——— 8.
1. ——— 10, 11, 27.
1a. ——— 30.
2. —— xix. 2, 7.
1a. ——— 10.
1. ——— 21, 22, 30.
1. —— xx. 4, 6, 9.
1. —— xxi. 26.
1a. ——— 27, 36.
1. —— xxii. 10.
1a. ——— 22 1st.
1a. ——— 22 2nd.
1a. ——— 48.
1. ——— 58, 60.
2. ——— 63.
1a. ——— 69.
1. —— xxiii. 4, 6, 14 twice,
2. ——— 50 twice. [47.
2. —— xxiv. 4.
1a. ——— 7 1st.
1. ——— 7 2nd.
1. John i. 4, 6, 9.
2. ——— 13, 30.
1a. ——— 51.
1. —— ii. 10, 25 twice.
1. —— iii. 1.
3. ——— 3.
1. ——— 4.
3. ——— 5.
1a. ——— 13, 14.
1. ——— 19, 27.
1. —— iv. 28, 29, 50.
1. —— v. 5, 7, 9, 12, 15.
1a. ——— 27.
1. ——— 34, 41.
1. —— vi. 10 1st.
2. ——— 10 2nd.
1. ——— 14.
1a. ——— 27.
3. ——— 50.
1a. ——— 53, 62.
1. —— vii. 22, 23 twice, 46 1st, 46 2nd (ap.), 51.
1. —— viii. 17.
1a. ——— 28.
1. ——— 40.
3. ——— 51, 52.
1. —— ix. 1, 11, 16 twice, 24 twice, 30.
1. —— x. 33.
3. —— xi. 10.
1. ——— 47, 50.
1a. John xii. 23, 34 twice.
1. ——— 43.
1a. —— xiii. 31.
3. —— xiv. 23.
3. —— xv. 6, 13.
1. —— xvi. 21.
1. —— xvii. 6.
1. —— xviii. 14, 17, 29.
1. —— xix. 5.
2. Acts i. 10, 11, 16, 21.
2. —— ii. 5, 14, 22 twice, 29, 37.
2. —— iii. 2, 12.
2. —— iv. 4.
1. ——— 9, 12, 13, 14, 16, 17, 22.
2. —— v. 1.
1. ——— 4.
2. ——— 14, 25.
1. ——— 28, 29.
2. ——— 35 1st.
1. ——— 35 2nd.
2. ——— 36.
1. ——— 38 twice.
2. —— vi. 3, 5, 11.
1. ——— 13.
2. —— vii. 2.
1a. ——— 56.
2. —— viii. 2, 3, 9, 12, 27.
2. —— ix. 2, 7, 12, 13.
1. ——— 33.
2. ——— 38 (om. G →)
2. —— x. 1, 5, 17, 19, 21, 22, 28 1st.
1. ——— 28 2nd.
2. ——— 30.
2. —— xi. 3, 11, 12.
2. ——— 13 (om. G L T Tr A ℵ.)
2. ——— 20.
1. ——— 22.
2. ——— 24.
2. —— xiii. 7, 15, 16, 21, 22 (om. G →), 26, 38.
3. ——— 41.
2. —— xiv. 8.
1. ——— 11, 15.
2. —— xv. 7, 13.
1. ——— 17.
2. ——— 22 twice, 25.
1. ——— 26.
2. —— xvi. 9.
1. ——— 17, 20, 35.
2. —— xvii. 12, 22.
1. ——— 25 (*ἀνθρώπινος*, *human*, G ∾ L T Tr A ℵ.)
1. ——— 26, 29, 30.
2. ——— 31, 34.
1. —— xviii. 13.
2. ——— 24.
2. —— xix. 7.
1. ——— 16.
— ——— 29, see M of Macedonia.
2. ——— 35 1st.
1. ——— 35 2nd.
2. ——— 37.
2. —— xx. 30.
2. —— xxi. 11, 23, 26, 28 1st.
1. ——— 28 2nd.
2. ——— 38.
1. ——— 39.
2. —— xxii. 1, 3, 4, 12.
1. ——— 15, 25, 26.
2. —— xxiii. 1, 6.
1. ——— 9.
2. ——— 21, 27, 30.
2. —— xxiv. 5.
1. ——— 16.
2. —— xxv. 5, 14.
1. ——— 16.
2. ——— 17.
1. ——— 22.
2. ——— 23, 24.
1. —— xxvi. 31, 32.
1. —— xxviii. 4.
2. Acts xxviii. 17.
1. Rom. i. 18, 23.
4. ——— 27 1st (No. 5, Tr A ℵ.)
5. ——— 27 2nd & 3rd.
1. —— ii. 1, 3, 9, 16, 29.
1. —— iii. 4.
— ——— 5, see M (as a)
1. ——— 28.
1. —— iv. 6.
2. ——— 8.
1. —— v. 12 twice, 15, 18 twice, 19.
1. —— vi. 6.
1. —— vii. 1.
2. ——— 3 twice.
1. ——— 22, 24.
3. —— viii. 24.
1. —— ix. 20.
1. —— x. 5.
2. —— xi. 4.
1. —— xii. 17, 18.
1. —— xiv. 18, 20.
1. 1 Cor. i. 25 twice.
— —— ii. 4, see Man's.
1. ——— 5, 9, 11 3 times.
— ——— 13, see Man's.
1. ——— 14.
1. —— iii. 21.
1. —— iv. 1.
3. ——— 2.
— ——— 3, see Man's.
1. ——— 9.
1. —— vi. 18.
1. —— vii. 1, 7.
2. ——— 16.
1. ——— 23, 26.
— —— ix. 8, see M (as a)
— —— x. 13, see M (common to)
2. —— xi. 3 twice, 4, 7 twice, 8 twice, 9 twice, 11 twice, 12 twice, 14.
1. ——— 28.
1. —— xiii. 1.
2. ——— 11.
1. —— xiv. 2, 3.
6. ——— 20, marg. *perfect, or of a ripe age.*
1. —— xv. 12, 21 twice, 39, 45 (om. L), 47 twice.
1. 2 Cor. iii. 2.
1. —— iv. 2, 16.
1. —— v. 11.
3. —— viii. 12 (om. G ⇄ L T Tr A ℵ.)
1. ——— 21.
1. —— xii. 2, 3, 4.
1. Gal. i. 1 twice, 10 3 times.
— ——— 11, see M (after)
1. ——— 12.
1. —— ii. 6, 16.
1. —— iii. 12 (om. G L T Tr A ℵ.)
1. ——— 15.
1. —— v. 3.
1. —— vi. 1, 7.
1. Eph. ii. 15.
1. —— iii. 5, 16.
1. —— iv. 8.
2. ——— 13.
1. ——— 14, 22, 24.
1. —— v. 31.
2. ——— 28.
1. —— vi. 7.
1. Phil. ii. 7, 8.
1. —— iv. 5.
1. Col. i. 28 1st, 28 2nd (om. G →), 28 3rd.
1. —— ii. 8, 22.
1. —— iii. 9, 23.
1. 1 Thes. ii. 4, 6, 13, 15.
1. —— iv. 8.
1. 2 Thes. ii. 3.
1. —— iii. 2.
3. 1 Tim. i. 8.
1. —— ii. 1, 4, 5 twice.
2. ——— 8, 12.

1. 1 Tim. iv. 10.
2. —— v. 9.
1. ——— 24.
1. —— vi. 5, 9, 11, 16.
1. 2 Tim. ii. 2.
3. ——— 5, 21.
1. —— iii. 2, 8, 13, 17.
1. Tit. i. 14.
1. —— ii. 11.
1. —— iii. 2.
— ——— 4, see Man (love toward)
1. ——— 8, 10.
1. Heb. ii. 6 1st.
1a. ——— 6 2nd.
1. —— v. 1 twice.
1. —— vi. 16.
1. —— vii. 8, 28.
1. —— viii. 2.
1. —— ix. 27.
1. —— xiii. 6.
1. Jas. i. 7.
2. ——— 8, 12.
1. ——— 19.
2. ——— 20, 23.
2. —— ii. 2.
3. ——— 14, 18.
1. ——— 20, 24.
2. —— iii. 2.
1. ——— 8, 9.
1. —— v. 17.
1. 1 Pet. i. 24 (*om.* G∾) (αὐτῆς, *its* [glory], G L T Tr A), (αὐτόν, *his* [glory] ℵ.)
1. —— ii. 4.
— ——— 13.
3. ——— 19.
1. ——— 15, see M (of)
1. —— iii. 4.
1. —— iv. 2, 6.
1. 2 Pet. i. 21 twice.
1. —— ii. 16.
3. ——— 19.
1. —— iii. 7.
3. 1 John iv. 20.
1. —— v. 9.
1. Jude 4.
1a. Rev. i. 13.
1. —— iv. 7.
1. —— viii. 11.
1. —— ix. 4, 5, 6, 7, 10, 15, 18, 20.
1. —— xi. 13.
4. —— xii. 5.
— ——— 13, see M child.
1. —— xiii. 13, 18.
1. —— xiv. 4.
1a. ——— 14.
1. —— xvi. 2, 8, 9, 18, 21 twice.
1. —— xviii. 13.

1. Rev. xxi. 3, 17.

MAN (AFTER)

{ κατὰ, according to,
{ ἀνθρώπον, man, (*see No.* 1, *above.*)

Gal. i. 11.

MAN (AS A)

{ κατὰ,
{ ἀνθρώπον, } *see above.*

Rom. iii. 5. | 1 Cor. ix. 8.

MAN-CHILD.

ἄρρην, *see above, No.* 4.

Rev. xii. 13 (ἄρσην, A ℵ.)

MAN (COMMON TO)

ἀνθρώπινος, pertaining to man, human.

1 Cor. x. 13, marg. *moderate.*

MAN (LOVE TOWARD)

φιλανθρωπία, love of man, (*see* "LOVE," *No.* 2, and "MAN," *No.* 1.)

Tit. iii. 4, marg. *pity*, etc.

MAN (OF)

ἀνθρώπινος, pertaining to man, human.

1 Pet. ii. 13.

MAN (*pity towards*) [marg.]

See above, "M (LOVE TOWARDS)"

MAN OF MACEDONIA.

Μακεδών, a Macedonian.

Acts xix. 29.

MAN'S.

ἀνθρώπινος, pertaining to man, human.

1 Cor. ii. 4 (*om.* G L T Tr A ℵ.) | 1 Cor. ii. 13.
—— iv. 3.

See also, AGED, ANOTHER, ANY, BLIND, CERTAIN, CHIEF, COVETOUS, DEAD, EVERY, FORBIDDING, HEATHEN, HOLDETH, IMPOTENT, INWARD, LAME, MEN, MIGHTY, NEITHER, NEVER, NEW, NO, OLD, ONE, OTHER, PERSON, POOR, RICH, SOME, SON, STRONG, SUCH, THAT, THIS, UNGODLY, WHAT, WISE, YOUNG, YOUNGER.

MANGER.

φάτνη, a crib, a manger, (*occ.* Luke xiii. 15.)

Luke ii. 7, 12, 16.

MANIFEST. [adj.]

1. φανερός, apparent, visible, conspicuous.

2. ἐμφανής, appearing in *any thing*, apparent, manifest, (*occ.* Acts x. 40.)

3. δῆλος, plain, evident.

4. ἔκδηλος, (*No.* 3, *with* ἐκ, out of, *prefixed*) quite plain, quite evident.

1. Luke viii. 17.
1. Acts iv. 16.
1. Rom. i. 19.
2. —— x. 20.
1. 1 Cor. iii. 13.
1. —— xi. 19.
1. 1 Cor. xiv. 25.
3. —— xv. 27.
1. Gal. v. 19.
1. Phil. i. 13.
— 2 Thes. i. 5, see Token.
4. 2 Tim. iii. 9.

1. 1 John iii. 10.

MANIFEST (BE)

φανερόω, to make apparent, show openly, make manifest *or* known.

1 Tim. iii. 16, }
1 Pet. i. 20, } pass. *or* mid.

MANIFEST (MAKE)

φανερόω, see above.

John i. 31.
—— iii. 21.
—— ix. 3.
Rom. xvi. 26.
1 Cor. iv. 5.
2 Cor. ii. 14.
—— iv. 10, 11.
—— v. 11 twice.
2 Cor. xi. 6.
Eph. v. 13 twice.
Col. i. 26.
—— iv. 4.
2 Tim. i. 10.
Heb. ix. 8.
1 John ii. 19.
Rev. xv. 4.

MANIFEST (THAT IS NOT)

ἀφανής, not apparent, *i.e.* hidden, concealed, secreted.

Heb. iv. 13.

MANIFEST (-ED.) [verb.]

1. *φανερόω*, to make apparent, make manifest, make openly known.
2. *ἐμφανίζω*, to cause to be seen; *pass.*, to appear, to be seen openly.

1. Mark iv. 22.
— John ii. 11, see M forth.
2. —— xiv. 21, 22.
2. —— xvii. 6.
1. Rom. iii. 21.
— 1 Tim. v. 25, see M beforehand.
1. Tit. i. 3.
1. 1 John i. 2 twice.
1. —— iii. 5, 8.
1. —— iv. 9.

MANIFEST BEFOREHAND.

πρόδηλος, manifest beforehand, *or* openly evident

1 Tim. v. 25.

MANIFEST FORTH.

φανερόω, see "MANIFEST," *No.* 1.

John ii. 11.

MANIFESTATION.

1. *φανέρωσις*, a making known, manifesting, (*non occ.*)
2. *ἀποκάλυψις*, an unveiling, uncovering, revealing. *When spoken of a person or persons it always means their* appearing.

2. Rom. viii. 19. | 1. 1 Cor. xii. 7.
1. 2 Cor. iv. 2.

MANIFESTLY.

See, DECLARE.

MANIFOLD.

1. *ποικίλος*, variegated, parti-coloured; *hence*, changing colour, *and so*, changeful, various, manifold; *in a bad sense*, intricate, riddling.
2. *πολυποίκιλος*, (*No.* 1, *with πολύς*, much, *prefixed*) much variegated, very many-coloured; *then*, multifarious, very various, (*non occ.*)

— Luke xviii. 30, see M, more.
2. Eph. iii. 10.
1. 1 Pet. i. 6.
1. 1 Pet. iv. 10.

MANIFOLD MORE.

πολλαπλασίων, many times more, many times as many, (*non occ.*)

Luke xviii. 30.

MANKIND.

{ *φύσις*, physis, nature,
{ *ἀνθρώπινος*, pertaining to man, human.

1 Cor. vi. 9, see Abuser. | 1 Tim. i. 10, see Defile.
Jas. iii. 7, marg. *nature of man.*

MANNA.

μάννα, manna, the miraculous food with which God fed the Israelites for forty years in the wilderness.

[*Heb.*, מָן, a species. In Exod. xvi. 15: "And when the children of Israel saw it, they said one to another, מָן הוּא, *this is a peculiar species*, for they knew not what it was." So Deut. viii. 3: "Who fed thee with אֶת־הַמָּן, *that peculiar thing* which thou knewest not.? The Sept. and Schleusner makes מָן the same as מַן, *what.* Others, מָנָה, *he measured*, or in Peil, *he prepared. See* Exod. xvi. 15, marg.] (*non occ.*)

John vi. 31, 49.
—— 58 (om. G T Tr A ℵ.)
Heb. ix. 4.
Rev. ii. 17.

MANNER (-s.)

(*For various words in connection, see at end of the word.*)

1. *ἔθος*, a custom, usage, manner, *of a people, established by law or otherwise.*
2. *ἦθος*, an accustomed seat; *hence, in pl.*, the haunts *of animals and men; then*, custom, usage, the manners and habits of man, his disposition, character, (*non occ.*)

3. τρόπος, a turning, turn, *direction; hence*, manner, way, mode.

4. τύπος, a mark *or* impress made by a hard substance on a soft; *hence*, model, pattern.

1. John xix. 40. | 1. Acts xxv. 16.
1. Acts xv. 1. | 2. 1 Cor. xv. 33.
4. —— xxiii. 25. | 1. Heb. x. 25.
3. Jude 7.

MANNER OF (AFTER THE)

κατά, *with the Accus.*, down upon *or* along, over against; *then*, according to, *in reference to some standard of comparison stated or implied;* in accordance with.

John ii. 6.

MANNER (AFTER THE SAME)

ὡσαύτως, as thus, in the same way, in like manner.

1 Cor. xi. 25.

MANNER (AFTER THIS)

1. οὕτω, in this manner, on this wise, *i.e.* so, thus.

2. τόδε, this, this here; *pl.*, τάδε, thus, these things, *that follow. After* λέγω, etc., (to say) ταῦτα, this *that precedes*, τάδε, this *that follows.*

1. Matt. vi. 9. | 2. Acts xv. 23 (*om.* L T Tr A ℵ.)
1. 1 Pet. iii. 5.

MANNER (AFTER WHAT)

πῶς, how? in what way *or* manner?

Acts xx. 18.

MANNER WAS (AS HIS)

{ κατά, according to, τὸ, the, εἰωθὸς, custom, τῷ Παυλῳ, to *or* with Paul, } according to the custom with Paul.

Acts xvii. 2.

MANNER (IN LIKE)

1. καί, and, also.

2. ὡσαύτως, as thus, in the same way.

Mark xiii. 29. | 2. Luke xx. 31.
2. 1 Tim. ii. 9.

MANNER AS (IN LIKE)

ὅν, which, τρόπον, a manner, way, } (κατά, according to, *being understood*) according to what manner, after the manner in which, in the same *or* like manner.

Acts i. 11.

MANNER (IN THE LIKE)

{ κατά, according to, ταῦτα, these same things. }

Luke vi. 23.

MANNER (IN THIS)

οὕτω, thus, on this wise.

Rev. xi. 5.

MANNER OF QUESTIONS (OF SUCH)

{ εἰς, as to, (*om.* T Tr A[b] ℵ) τὴν, the. περὶ, concerning, τουτοῦ, this, (τούτων, of these things, G ~ L T Tr A ℵ) ζήτησιν, enquiry, } as to the enquiry concerning this [person, *i.e. Jesus, Paul; or these matters.*]

Acts xxv. 20, marg. *how to enquire hereof.*

MANNERS (IN DIVERS)

πολυτρόπως, in many ways, (*non occ.*)

Heb. i. 1.

MANNERS (SUFFER ONE'S)

τροποφορέω, to bear with the turn *of any one, i.e.* with his disposition or manners.

Acts xiii. 18, (G ~ Tr ℵ) (τροφοφορέω, *to bear as a nurse, to carry in the arms as a nurse her nurseling*, S[tm] AV[m] G L T A,) marg. *bear or feed, as a nurse beareth or feedeth her child.*

See also, GENTILES, GODLY, LIFE, LIKE, MEN, PERFECT, WHAT.

MAN-SERVANT.

παῖς, child; *then*, boy; *hence*, servant; *here, pl.*

Luke xii. 45.

MANSLAYER.

ἀνδροφόνος, a homicide, murderer, (*non occ.*)

1 Tim. i. 9.

MANSION (s.)

μονή, stay *in a place ; hence*, an abiding place, (*occ.* John xiv. 23.)

John xiv. 2.

MANY.

1. πολύς, many, much, *prop., of number, quantity, amount ; here, in plural.*

   * *with art.*, (*as referring to something well known*) the much *or* the many.

2. πλείων, more, (*compar. of No.* 1) *prop., of number, but also of magnitude, and in comparison ; here, pl.*

   * *with art.*, (*emphatic*) the more.

3. ἱκανός, coming to, reaching to, *and hence*, sufficing, *i.e.* sufficient ; *of things*, enough ; *of persons*, adequate, competent ; *of number, in pl., as here*, many, *but always with the idea of the number sufficing.*

1. Matt. iii. 7.
1. —— vii. 13, 22 twice.
1. —— viii. 11, 16, 30.
1. —— ix. 10.
1. —— x. 31.
— —— xiii. 3, see M things.
1. ——— 17, 58.
— —— xiv. 36, see As.
1. —— xv. 30.
— ——— 34, see M (how)
— —— xvi. 9, 10, see M (how)
— ——— 21, see M things.
1. —— xix. 30.
1. —— xx. 16 (*ap.*), 28.
— —— xxii. 10, see As.
1. ——— 14.
1. —— xxiv. 5 twice, 10, 11 twice.
1*. ——— 12.
— —— xxv. 21, 23, see M things.
1. —— xxvi. 28, 60 (*ap.*).
— —— xxvii. 13, see M things (how)
— ——— 19, see M things.
1. ——— 52, 53, 55.
1. Mark i. 34 twice.
1. —— ii. 2, 15 twice.
1. —— iii. 10 1st.
— ——— 10 2nd, see As.
— —— iv. 2, see M things.
1. ——— 33 (*om.* G →)
1. —— v. 9.
— ——— 26 1st, see M things.
1. ——— 26 2nd.
1. —— vi. 2 (1*, G ↔ T Trmb Ab.)
1. Mark vi. 13 twice.
— ——— 20, see M things.
1. ——— 31, 33.
— ——— 34, see M things.
— ——— 38, see M (how)
1. —— vii. 4, 8 (*ap.*), 13.
— —— viii. 5, 19, 20, see M (how)
— ——— 31, } see M
— —— ix. 12, } things.
1. ——— 26.
1. —— x. 31, 45, 48.
1. —— xi. 8.
1. —— xii. 5, 41.
1. —— xiii. 6 twice.
1. —— xiv. 24, 56.
— —— xv. 3, see M things.
— ——— 4, see M things (how)
1. ——— 41.
1. Luke i. 1, 14, 16.
1. —— ii. 34, 35.
1. —— iii. 18.
1. —— iv. 25, 27, 41.
— —— vii. 11, see M of.
1. ——— 21 twice.
1*. ——— 47.
1. —— viii. 3, 30.
3. ——— 32.
— —— ix. 22, see M things
1. —— x. 24.
— ——— 41, see M things.
— —— xi. 8, see As.
— ——— 53, see M things.
1. —— xii. 7, 19.
— ——— 47, see M stripes
1. —— xiii. 24.
1. —— xiv. 16.
1. —— xv. 13.
— ——— 17, see M (how)
— Luke xv. 29, see M (these)
— —— xvii. 25, see M [things.
1. —— xxi. 8.
1. —— xxii. 65.
— —— xxiii. 8, see M [things.
3. ——— 9.
— John i. 12, see As.
1. —— ii. 12, 23.
1. —— iv. 39.
1. ——— 41 (Dat. sing.)
— —— vi. 9, see M (so)
1. ——— 60, 66.
1. —— vii. 31.
1. ——— 40 (*om.* L T Tr A ℵ.)
— —— viii. 26, see M [things.
1. ——— 30.
1. —— x. 20, 32, 41, 42.
1. —— xi. 19, 45, 47, 55.
1. —— xii. 11.
— ——— 37, see M (so)
1. ——— 42.
1. —— xiv. 2.
— —— xvi. 12, see M things.
— —— xvii. 2, see As.
1. —— xix. 20.
1. —— xx. 30.
— —— xxi. 11, see M (so)
1. ——— 25.
1. Acts i. 3, 5.
— —— ii. 39, see As.
2. ——— 40.
1. ——— 43.
— —— iii. 24, see As.
1. —— iv. 4.
— ——— 6, 34, see As.
1. —— v. 12.
— ——— 36, 37, see As.
1. —— viii. 7 twice, 25.
1. —— ix. 13.
3. ——— 23.
1. ——— 42.
3. ——— 43.
1. —— x. 27.
— ——— 45, see As.
3. —— xii. 12.
2. —— xiii. 31.
1. ——— 43.
— ——— 48, see As.
3. —— xiv. 21.
1. —— xv. 32 (sing.)
1. ——— 35.
1. —— xvi. 18, 23.
1. —— xvii. 12.
1. —— xviii. 8.
1. —— xix. 18.
3. ——— 19.
3. —— xx. 8.
1. ——— 19 (*om.* G L T Tr A ℵ.)
2. —— xxi. 10.
— ——— 20, see M (how)
1. —— xxiv. 10.
2. ——— 17.
1. —— xxv. 7.
2. ——— 14.
— —— xxvi. 9, see M [things.
1. ——— 10.
3. —— xxvii. 7.
2. ——— 20.
1. —— xxviii. 10.
2. ——— 23.
— Rom. ii. 12, see As.
1. Rom. iv. 17, 18.
1*. —— v. 15 twice.
1. ——— 16.
1*. ——— 19 twice.
— —— vi. 3, see M as (so)
— —— viii. 14, see As.
1. ——— 29.
1. —— xii. 4.
1*. ——— 5.
— —— xv. 22, see M *ways.*
1. ——— 23.
1. —— xvi. 2.
1. 1 Cor. i. 26 3 times.
1. —— iv. 15.
1. —— viii. 5 twice.
2*. —— x. 5.
1*. ——— 17, 33.
1. —— xi. 30 1st.
3. ——— 30 2nd.
1. —— xii. 12 twice, 14, 20.
— —— xiv. 10, see M (so)
1. —— xvi. 9.
1. 2 Cor. i. 11 twice.
1. —— ii. 4.
2* ——— 6.
1*. ——— 17 (λοιπός, *the rest*, G ∾)
2*. —— iv. 15.
1. —— vi. 10. [things.
— —— viii. 22, see M
— —— ix. 2, see M (very)
1. ——— 12.
1. —— xi. 18.
1. —— xii. 21.
1. Gal. i. 14.
— —— iii. 4, see M things
— ——— 10, see As. [(so)
1. ——— 16.
— ——— 27, see As.
1. —— iv. 27.
— —— vi. 12, 16, see As.
2*. Phil. i. 14.
— —— iii. 15, see As.
1. ——— 18.
— Col. ii. 1, } see As.
— 1 Tim. vi. 1, }
1. ——— 9, 10, 12.
— 2 Tim. i. 18, see M things (how)
1. —— ii. 2.
1. Tit. i. 10.
1. Heb. ii. 10.
1. —— v. 11, sing.
2*. —— vii. 23.
1. —— ix. 28.
1. —— xii. 15 (1*, L T Tr [A ℵ.)
1. Jas. iii. 1.
— ——— 2, see M things.
1. 2 Pet. ii. 2.
1. 1 John ii. 18.
1. —— iv. 1.
1. 2 John 7.
— ——— 12, } see M
— 3 John 13, } things.
1. Rev. i. 15.
— —— ii. 24, } see As.
— —— iii. 19, }
1. —— v. 11.
1. —— viii. 11.
1. —— ix. 9.
1. —— x. 11.
1. —— xiv. 2.
1. —— xvii. 1.
— —— xviii. 17, see As.
1. —— xix. 6, 12.

MANY (HOW)

πόσος, how great? how much? *of magnitude and quantity ; pl., of number*, how many?

Matt. xv. 34.
—— xvi. 9, 10.
Mark vi. 38.
Mark viii. 5, 19, 20.
Luke xv. 17.
Acts xxi. 20.

MANY THINGS (HOW)

1. ὅσος, how great, how much; *in pl.*, how many.
2. πόσος, (*correlat. of No.* 1) *see above.*

2. Matt. xxvii. 13. | 2. Mark xv. 4.
1. 2 Tim. i. 18.

MANY (SO)

τοσοῦτος, so great, so much; *of number*, so many, so numerous, (*here pl.*)

John vi. 9. | John xxi. 11.
— xii. 37. | 1 Cor. xiv. 10.

MANY AS (SO)

ὅσος, how great, how much; *in pl.*, how many.

Rom. vi. 3.

MANY THINGS (SO)

τοσοῦτος, *see* "M (SO)"

Gal. iii. 4, marg. *great.*

MANY (THESE)

τοσοῦτος, *see above.*

Luke xv. 29.

MANY (VERY)

πλεῖων, *see* "MANY," *No.* 2.

2 Cor. ix. 2, *pl., with art.*

MANY OF.

ἱκανός, *see* "MANY," *No.* 3; *here pl.*

Luke vii. 11 (*om.* G →Lb Tr Ab ℵ.)

MANY STRIPES.

πολλοί, *see* "MANY," *No.* 1.

Luke xii. 47.

MANY WAYS [marg.]

πολλοί, *see* "MANY," *No.* 1, *with art.*

Rom. xv. 22 (text, *much.*)

MANY THINGS.

1. πολὺς, *see* "MANY," *No.* 1. *Here, pl.*
2. πλεῖων, *see* "MANY," *No.* 2. *Here, pl.*

1. Matt. xiii. 3.
1. — xvi. 21.
1. — xxv. 21, 23.
1. — xxvii. 19.
1. Mark iv. 2.
1. — v. 26.
1. — vi. 20, 34.
1. — viii. 31.
1. — ix. 12.
1. — xv. 3.
1. Luke ix. 22.
1. Luke x. 41.
2. — xi. 53.
1. — xvii. 25.
1. — xxiii. 8.
1. John viii. 26.
1. — xvi. 12.
1. Acts xxvi. 9.
1. 2 Cor. viii. 22.
1. Jas. iii. 2.
1. 2 John 12.
1. 3 John 13.

MARAN-ATHA.

μαρὰν ἀθα, *the Greek spelling of Hebrew. Chald., or Syr. words,* מרנא אתה.

(מרא *is Chald. for* a sovereign, *or* supreme Lord (Dan. ii. 47, etc.) ן *is the Syr. suffix,* our, אתה, cometh,) the, *or* our Lord cometh. [A solemn watchword, reminding them and us of the nearness of His coming, and the duty of being ready for it.]

1 Cor. xvi. 22.

MARBLE.

μάρμαρος, glittering stone, *or* rock. *Lat.,* marmor, (*non occ.*)

Rev. xviii. 12.

MARK [noun.]

1. χάραγμα, something graven *or* sculptured, a mark cut in, (*occ.* Acts xvii. 29.)
2. στίγμα, the prick *or* mark of a pointed instrument, a mark burnt in, a brand, *esp., of a runaway slave or prisoner. Hence, Eng.,* stigma, (*non occ.*)
3. σκοπός, an object set up in the distance at which one looks and aims; *hence,* a mark *or* goal, (*non occ.*)

2. Gal. vi. 17.
3. Phil. iii. 14.
1. Rev. xiii. 16, 17.
1. — xiv. 9, 11.
1. Rev. xv. 2 (*ap.*)
1. — xvi. 2.
1. — xix. 20.
1. — xx. 4.

MARK (-ED.) [verb.]

1. σκοπέω, to look, watch, reconnoitre; mark, note.
2. ἐπέχω, to have, *or* hold upon; *spoken of the mind,* to fix the mind upon, give heed to.

2. Luke xiv. 7 part. | 1. Rom. xvi. 17.
1. Phil. iii. 17.

MARKET (-s.)

ἀγορά, any place of public resort *in the towns and cities, where people come together*, (*from* ἀγείρω, to collect, convoke.)

Matt. xi. 16.
—— xxiii. 7.
Mark vii. 4.
Luke xi. 43.
—— xx. 46.
Acts xx. 17.

MARKET-PLACE.

Matt. xx. 3.
Mark xii. 38.
Luke vii. 32.
Acts xvi. 19, marg. *court.*

MARRED (BE)

ἀπόλλυμι, to destroy wholly; *mid. or pass., as here,* to be destroyed wholly, perish utterly.

Mark ii. 22.

MARRIAGE.

γάμος, a wedding, nuptials, *i.e.* the nuptial solemnities, *esp.*, the wedding feast, (which continued seven days, Judg. xiv. 12.)

Matt. xxii. 2. 4, 9.
—— xxv. 10.
John ii. 1, 2.
Heb. xiii. 4.
Rev. xix. 7, 9.

MARRIAGE (GIVE IN)

1. **γαμίσκω**, (*from the above*) to marry, to grow *or* become married, *the termination*, (σκω) *marking the beginning or progress of the action.*

2. **ἐκγαμίσκω**, (*No.* 1, *with* ἐκ, out, *prefixed*) to give out in marriage.

3. **γαμίζω**, to marry, (*the termination* marking *the having, being, or becoming what the noun*, γάμος, *denotes.*)

4. **ἐκγαμιζω**, (*No.* 3, *with* ἐκ, out, *prefixed*) to place out in marriage.

4. Matt. xxii. 30 (No. 3, G ~ L T Tr ℵ.)
4. —— xxiv. 38 (No. 1 L) (No. 3, T ℵ.)
1. Mark xii. 25 (No. 3, L T Tr A ℵ.)
4. Luke xvii. 27 (No. 3, L T Tr A ℵ.)
2. Luke xx. 34 (No. 1, L T Tr A ℵ.)
2. —— 35 (No. 3, L T Tr ℵ) (No. 1, A.)
4. 1 Cor. vii. 38 1st (*ap.*)
4. —— 38 2nd (No. 3, G L T Tr ℵ) (No. 4, Ab.)

MARROW.

μυελός, marrow; *Lat.*, medulla, (*non occ.*)

Heb. iv. 12.

MARRY (-IED, -IETH, -ING.)

1. **γαμέω**, to marry; *trans., of men,* to take as a wife, take a wife; *intrans.*, to marry, enter the marriage state, (*non occ.*)

2. **ἐπιγαμβρεύω**, to connect with one's self by marriage, to become related upon marriage, (*non occ.*)

1. Matt. v. 32.
1. —— xix. 9 twice, 10.
2. —— xxii. 24.
1. —— 30.
1. —— xxiv. 38.
1. Mark vi. 17.
1. —— x. 11, 12.
1. Mark xii. 25.
1. Luke xiv. 20.
2. —— xvi. 18 twice.
1. —— xx. 34, 35.
1. 1 Cor. vii. 9 twice, 28 twice, 33, 34, 36, 39.
1. 1 Tim. iv. 3.
1. 1 Tim. v. 11, 14.

MARRY A WIFE.

1. Matt. xxii. 25 part.
1. Luke xvii. 27.

MARRIED.

1. 1 Cor. vii. 10 part.

MARRIED (BE)

γίνομαι, to become; *here,* to become *another man's; hence,* translated marry.

Rom. vii. 3 1st, 2 2nd part., 4.

MAR'S HILL.

{ **ὁ**, the,
Ἄρειον, of *or* belonging to Mars, Mars's,
πάγος, a hill, }
the hill of Mars, *or* Mars's hill, *or*, (*the two words in one*) Areopagus.

Acts xvii. 19, marg. (text, *Areopagus.*)
—— 22, marg. *Court of the Areopagus.*

MARTYR (-s.)

μάρτυς, (*from Sanscr. root* smri, smarami, to remember) (*in the Zend lang.*, mar *signifies* to recollect), a witness, *i.e.* one who has remembrance or knowledge of anything, *and hence,* one who can give information, or bring to light, or confirm any thing. Then, *because so many sealed* the witness *they bore to Christ with their blood, the Greek word became Anglicised, and* a martyr is one who bears witness to the truth and gospel of Christ with his life. (*See under,* "WITNESS.")

Acts xxii. 20.
Rev. ii. 13.
Rev. xvii. 6.

MARVEL [noun.]

θαυμαστός, wondrous, wonderful, marvellous, strange, unwonted, (*relating to the thing admired.*)

2 Cor. xi. 14 (*θαῦμα, whatever one regards with wonder and astonishment*, G ~ L T Tr A ℵ.)

MARVEL (-ED.) [verb.]

θαυμάζω, to wonder, marvel, be astonied, to look on with wonder and amazement, to wonder, marvel at.

Matt. viii. 10, 27.
— ix. 8 (*φοβέομαι, were afraid*, G ~ L T Tr A [ℵ.)
—— 33.
Mark v. 20.
— vi. 6.
— xii. 17.
— xv. 5. 44.
Luke i. 21, 63.
— ii. 33 (*with εἰμί, to be.*)
— vii. 9, see M at.
— xi. 38.
Luke xx. 26.
John iii. 7.
— iv. 27.
— v. 20.
—— 28, see M at.
— vii. 15, 21.
Acts ii. 7.
— iii. 12.
— iv. 13.
2 Cor. xi. 14, see the noun.
Gal. i. 6.
1 John iii. 13.
Rev. xvii. 7.

MARVEL AT.

Luke vii. 9. | John v. 28.

MARVELLOUS.

θαυμαστός, see "MARVEL." [noun.]

Matt. xxi. 42.
Mark xii. 11.
1 Pet. ii. 9.
Rev. xv. 1, 3.

MARVELLOUS THING.

John ix. 30, neut.

MARY.

Μαρία, or *Μαριάμ*, *the Heb. name of* Miriam *in Greek, as* Maria *is the Greek form in English.* Mary,

In all passages, except—
Mark xvi. 9 (ap.)

MASTER (-s.)

1. *διδάσκαλος*, teacher, a master *or* a teacher of scholars *or* disciples. *In the Christian Church, the διδάσκαλοι have a special gift or function, as acquainted with and interpreters of God's salvation*, distinct from the *κῆρυξ* (herald) and the *εὐαγγελιστής* (Evangelist), Eph. iv. 11; 1 Tim. ii. 7. *In addressing Jesus, it probably answered to the* Heb. of *No.* 3. *Every ref. below of No.* 1 *refers to Christ, except* 1*.

2. *κύριος*, lord, principal, ruler. (*No.* 5 *really has the power, while No.* 2 *assumes and exercises it.*) Master, *with reference to wife, children, and servants; or as* Lord *of* subjects. *No.* 2 *implies more honour and respect than No.* 5.

 * Applied to Christ.

3. *ῥαββί, the Greek spelling of the Heb.* רַבִּי, my master, (רַב *is properly*, one great, a chief) a doctor, teacher, *or* master, a title of honour in the Jewish schools *which began to naturalise itself in our Lord's time, but did not come into common use till after the destruction of Jerusalem.*

 In Matt. xxiii. 8, *it is explained by No.* 6; *and in* John i. 38 *by No.* 1. *A title given to the γραμματεῖς* (scribes). *Elsewhere translated* Rabbi.

4. *ἐπιστάτης*, one set over, *as the head of a* company, *or as the employer of workmen.* Master, *as implying authority.* Superintendent, (*non occ.*, and *used only of Christ.*)

5. *δεσπότης*, a master, implying absolute dominion, supreme authority, and unlimited power, *as a master over slaves; hence, Eng.*, Despot. *No.* 5 *implies more* submission *than No.* 2, *while No.* 2 *implies greater* respect, (*elsewhere translated* Lord.)

6. *καθηγητής*, a leader *or* guide in the way, a leader, director.

 * Used of Christ.

7. *κυβερνήτης*, the governor of a ship, *i.e.* the steersman *or* pilot. (*Lat.*, guberno, to govern a ship) (*occ.* Rev. xviii. 17.)

2. Matt. vi. 24.
1. — viii. 19.
1. — ix. 11.
1*. — x. 24, 25 1st.
— —— 25 2nd, see House.
1. — xii. 38.
2. — xv. 27.
1. — xvii. 24.
1. — xix. 16.
1. — xxii. 16, 24, 36.
6*. — xxiii. 8 (No. 1, G ~ L T Tr A.)
6. —— 10 1st.
6*. —— 10 2nd.
1. — xxvi. 18.
3. Matt. xxvi. 25, 49.
1. Mark iv. 38.
1. — v. 35.
3. — ix. 5.
1. —— 17, 38.
1. — x. 17, 20, 35.
3. — xi. 21.
1. — xii. 14, 19, 32.
1. — xiii. 1.
2. —— 35.
1. — xiv. 14.
3. —— 45 1st.
3. —— 45 2nd (*om.* G → L T Tr A ℵ.)
1. Luke iii. 12.

4. Luke v. 5.
1*.—— vi. 40 twice.
1. —— vii. 40.
4. —— viii. 24 twice, 45.
1. ——— 49.
4. —— ix. 33.
1. ——— 38.
4. ——— 49.
1. —— x. 25.
1. —— xi. 45.
1. —— xii. 13.
—— —— xiii. 25, } see
—— —— xiv. 21, } House.
2. —— xvi. 13.
4. —— xvii. 13.
1. —— xviii. 18.
1. —— xix. 39.
1. —— xx. 21, 28, 39.
1. —— xxi. 7.
1. —— xxii. 11.
1. John i. 38.
1*.—— iii. 10.
3. John iv. 31.
1. —— viii. 4 (ap.)
3. —— ix. 2.
3. —— xi. 8.
1. ——— 28.
1. John xiii, 13, 14.
1. —— xx. 16.
2. Acts xvi. 16, 19.
7. —— xxvii. 11.
2. Rom. xiv. 4.
2. Eph. vi. 5, 9 1st.
2*. ——— 9 2nd.
2. Col. iii. 22.
2. —— iv. 1 1st.
2*. ——— 1 2nd.
5. 1 Tim. vi. 1, 2.
5. 2 Tim. ii. 21.
5. Tit. ii. 9.
5. 1 Pet. ii. 18.
1*. Jas. iii. 1.
— Rev. xviii. 17, see Shipmaster.

MASTER BUILDER.

ἀρχιτέκτων, a chief artificer, master builder, director of works, *esp.*, the author *or* contriver, *as disting. from the workman,* (*non occ.*)

1 Cor. iii. 10.

MATTER.

(*For various combinations with other words, see below.*)

1. λόγος, the spoken word, the outward expression of the inward thought; *then,* the exposition *or* account given, a narrative *or* treatise, the subject matter of discourse.
2. πρᾶγμα, the thing done, *or* to be done; matter, business, affair.
3. ὕλη, a wood, forest; *Lat.,* sylva (*non occ.*)

1. Mark i. 45.
1. Acts viii. 21.
1. —— xv. 6.
1. —— xix. 38.
2. 1 Cor. vi. 1.
2. 2 Cor. vii. 11.
— Gal. ii. 6, see M (make [no)
2. 1 Thes. iv. 6.
3. Jas. iii. 5, marg. wood.

MATTER (MAKE NO)

{ διαφέρω, bear *or* carry through, bear asunder, *hence,* make a difference, οὐδέν, none at all, not the least, } to make not the least difference.

Gal. ii. 6.

See also, BOUNTY, BUSYBODY, OTHER, SAME, SUCH, THIS, THESE, UTTERMOST, WEIGHTIER, WRONG.

MAY, MAYEST, MIGHT.

(*For various combinations, see below.*)

1. δύναμαι, to be able; I can, *physically and morally, and as depending either on the disposition or faculties of the mind, the degree of strength or skill, the nature and external circumstances of the case, etc.*
2. ἔξεστι, it is possible, one can, *referring to moral possibility or propriety,* it is lawful, it is permitted, one may.
3. ἰσχύω, to be strong, to have strength, ability, *or* power *both physical and moral,* to be well able.

3. Matt. viii. 28.
1. —— xxvi. 9, 42.
1. Mark iv. 32.
1. —— xiv. 5, 7
1. Luke xvi. 2.
2. Acts ii. 29, marg. (text, *let.*)
2. —— viii. 37.
1. —— xvii. 19.
1. —— xix. 40.
2. Acts xxi. 37.
1. —— xxiv. 8, 11, part.
1. —— xxv. 11.
1. —— xxvi. 32.
1. —— xxvii. 12.
1. 1 Cor. vii. 21.
1. —— xiv. 31.
—— —— xv. 37, see Chance.
1. Eph. iii. 4.
1. 1 Thes. ii. 6, part.
1. Rev. xiii. 17.

MAY, MIGHT (THAT...)

1. { εἰς, unto, with a view to, τὸ, the, *with inf.* } with a view to the... (*denoting purpose, not result.*)
2. ὁ, *with the inf., expressive of result.*

2. Matt. xxi. 2.
1. Luke iv. 29 (ὥστε, *with inf., so as to,* G L T Tr A ℵ.)
2. Luke xxi. 22.
2. ——— 45.
1. Acts iii. 19.
2. —— xxvi. 18.
1. Rom. iii. 26.
1. —— iv. 11 twice, 18.
2. —— vi. 6.
1. —— viii. 29.
2. —— xi. 10.
1. Rom. xii. 2.
1. —— xv. 13.
2. 1 Cor. x. 13.
1. 2 Cor. i. 4.
1. Eph. i. 18.
1. Phil. i. 10.
2. —— ii. 10.
1. ——— 21 (ap.)
1. 1 Thes. iii. 10.
1. 2 Thes. i. 5.
1. —— ii. 6, 10.
1. Heb. xii. 10.
2. Jas. v. 17.

MAY, MIGHT (TO THE END...)

εἰς τὸ, *see above.*

Acts vii. 19.
Rom. i. 11.
Rom. iv. 16.
1 Thes. iii. 13.

MIGHT (THAT SO...)

εἰς τὸ, *see above.*

Luke xx. 20 (ὥστε, *so as to,* L T Tr A ℵ.)

MAY BE.

1\. ὦ, ᾖς, ᾖ, (*subj. of* εἰμί, to be) I, thou, he, she, it, we, ye or they may be, (*asserting conditionally.*)

2\. { εἰς, unto, with a view to, τὸ, the, εἶναι, to be, } to the end [*they*] might be.

1\. Matt. vi. 4.
1\. John xiv. 3.
1\. —— xvi. 24.
1\. —— xvii. 11, 21 twice, 22, 23, 26.
2\. Rom. i. 20, marg. (text, so that...are.)
1\. 1 Cor. v. 7.
1\. —— vii. 34.
1\. —— xv. 28.
1\. 2 Cor. iv. 7.
1\. —— ix. 3.
1\. Phil. i. 10.
1\. —— ii. 28.
1\. 1 Tim. v. 7.
1\. 2 Tim. iii. 17.
1\. Tit. i. 9.
1\. Jas. i. 4.
1\. 1 John i. 4.
1\. 2 John 12.

MIGHT BE.

1\. ὦ, ᾖς, ᾖ, etc., *see No.* 1, *above.*

2\. εἴην, εἴης, εἴη, (*Opt. of* εἰμί, to be) (*expressing a wish.*)

1\. Mark v. 18.
2\. Luke viii. 9.
1\. John xvii. 9.

MAY BE, MIGHT BE, (THAT...)

1\. { ὥστε, so as, so as to, εἶναι, to be, (*inf. of* εἰμί,) } so as to be, (*expressing result and consequence.*)

2\. { εἰς, unto, with a view to, εἶναι, to be, (*inf. of* εἰμί,) } with a view to there being, (*expressing purpose.*)

3\. εἶναι, to be, (*inf. of* εἰμί.)

3\. Luke viii. 38.
2\. Rom. iii. 26.
2\. —— iv. 11.
3\. ——— 13.
2\. ——— 16.
2\. —— viii. 29.
2\. —— xv. 16.
3\. 2 Cor. v. 9.
3\. —— ix. 5.
3\. Eph. i. 4.
2\. ——— 12.
3\. —— iii. 6.
2\. Jas. i. 18.
1\. 1 Pet. i. 21.

MAY BE (IT)

1\. ἴσως, equally, like; fairly, equitably; *hence,* according to appearances, probably, perhaps.

2\. { εἰ, if, τυγχάνω, to fall in with, meet casually, to fall out, happen; *hence,* perchance, } if perchance.

1\. Luke xx. 13.
2\. 1 Cor. xiv. 10.

ME.

1\. ἐγώ, *Nom.,* I.

2\. ἐμοῦ, *Gen.,* of me, my,

3\. μοῦ, *Gen.,* (*another form*), of me,

4\. ἐμοί, *Dat.,* to, unto, *or* for me,

5\. μοί, *Dat.,* (*another form*), to *or* for me,

(*When these cases are translated* ME, *it is because they are governed by some verb, preposition, etc.*)

6\. ἐμέ, *Accus.,* me.

7\. μέ, *Accus.,* (*another form*), me.

8\. ἐμαυτοῦ, of myself.

5\. Matt. ii. 8.
3\. —— iii. 11.
7\. ——— 14.
5\. —— iv. 9.
3\. ——— 19.
— —— vii. 21, see M (unto)
— ——— 22, see M (to)
2\. ——— 23.
7\. —— viii. 2.
8\. ——— 9.
5\. ——— 21, 22.
5\. —— ix. 9.
— —— x. 28, see M (of)
4\. ——— 32.
7\. ——— 33.
6\. ——— 37 1st.
— ——— 37 2nd, see M (of)
6\. ——— 37 3rd.
— ——— 37 4th, see M (of)
6\. ——— 40 1st & 2nd.
7\. ——— 40 3rd.
4\. —— xi. 6.
— ——— 27, see M (unto)
7\. ——— 28.
2\. ——— 29.
2\. —— xii. 30 3 times.
5\. —— xiv. 8.
— ——— 18, see M (to)
7\. ——— 28, 30.
2\. —— xv. 5.
— ——— 8 1st, see M (unto)
7\. ——— 8 2nd.
5\. ——— 8 3rd.
7\. ——— 9.
5\. ——— 15.
7\. ——— 22.
5\. ——— 32.
3\. —— xvi. 23 1st.
— ——— 23 2nd, see M (unto)
3\. ——— 24 1st.
5\. ——— 24 2nd.
— —— xvii. 17, see M (to)
2\. ——— 27.
5\. —— xviii. 5, 6, 21.
4\. ——— 26 (No. 6, Tr.)
5\. ——— 28 (*om.* G ⇉ L T Tr A ℵ.)
4\. ——— 29 (No. 6, L Tr A.)
7\. ——— 32.
7\. —— xix. 14, 17.
5\. ——— 21, 28.
5\. —— xx. 13.
— ——— 15, see M (for)
— —— xxi. 2, see M (unto)
5\. ——— 24.
7\. —— xxii. 18.
5\. ——— 19.
7\. —— xxiii. 39.
— Matt. xxv. 20, 22, see M (unto)
5\. ——— 35 1st.
7\. ——— 35 2nd & 3rd.
7\. ——— 36 3 times.
— ——— 40, see M (unto,
2\. ——— 41.
5\. ——— 42 1st.
7\. ——— 42 2nd, 43 3 times.
— ——— 45, see M (to)
6\. —— xxvi. 10, 11.
5\. ——— 15.
7\. ——— 21.
2\. ——— 23 1st.
7\. ——— 23 2nd
4\. ——— 31.
7\. ——— 34.
2\. ——— 38, 39, 40.
2\. ——— 42 (*om.* ἀπ᾽ ἐμοῦ, *from me,* G ⇉ L[b] T Tr A ℵ.)
7\. ——— 46.
5\. ——— 53.
7\. ——— 55 twice, 75.
5\. —— xxvii. 10.
7\. ——— 46.
7\. —— xxviii. 10.
— ——— 18, see M (unto)
3\. Mark i. 7, 17.
7\. ——— 40.
5\. —— ii. 14.
7\. —— v. 7.
3\. ——— 31.
7\. —— vi. 22.
7\. ——— 23 (*om.* G → ℵ.)
5\. ——— 25.
7\. —— vii. 6 1st
2\. ——— 6 2nd.
7\. ——— 7.
2\. ——— 11.
3\. ——— 14.
5\. —— viii. 2 (*om.* L Tr[b] A.)
3\. ——— 33, 34 1st.
5\. ——— 34 2nd.
7\. ——— 38.
7\. —— ix. 19.
6\. ——— 37 1st, 2nd, & 3rd.
7\. ——— 37 4th, 39.
6\. ——— 42 (*om.* εἰς ἐμὲ, *in me,* T A ℵ.)
7\. —— x. 14, 18.
5\. ——— 21.
7\. ——— 47, 48.
5\. —— xi. 29, 30.
7\. —— xii. 15 1st.
5\. ——— 15 2nd.
6\. —— xiv. 6 (No. 4, G L T Tr A ℵ.)
6\. ——— 7.
2\. ——— 18 1st.
7\. ——— 18 2nd.
2\. ——— 20.

4. Mark xiv. 27 (om. ἐν ἐμοί, because of me, G ⇉ T Tr A ℵ.)
7. ——— 30.
2. ——— 36.
7. ——— 42, 48, 49, 72.
7. —— xv. 34.
— Luke i. 3, see M also (to)
— ——— 25, see M (with)
— ——— 38, see M (unto)
— ——— 43 1st, see M (to)
7. ——— 43 2nd, 48.
— ——— 49, see M (to)
7. —— ii. 49.
— —— iv. 6, see M (unto)
3. ——— 7 (No. 2, L Tr [ℵ.)
3. ——— 8 (ap.)
6. ——— 18 1st.
7. ——— 18 2nd & 3rd.
— ——— 23, see M (unto)
2. —— v. 8.
7. ——— 12.
5. ——— 27.
7. —— vi. 46, 47.
8. —— vii. 8.
4. ——— 23.
5. ——— 45.
7. —— viii. 28.
3. ——— 45 1st, 45 2nd (ap.), 46 1st.
2. ——— 46 2nd.
3. —— ix. 23 1st.
5. ——— 23 2nd.
7. ——— 26.
6. ——— 48 1st & 2nd.
7. ——— 48 3rd.
5. ——— 59, 61.
2. —— x. 16 1st.
6. ——— 16 2nd & 3rd.
7. ——— 16 4th.
— ——— 22, see M (to)
7. ——— 40 1st.
5. ——— 40 2nd.
5. —— xi. 5.
7. ——— 6.
5. ——— 7 1st.
2. ——— 7 2nd.
2. ——— 23 3 times.
4. —— xii. 8.
7. ——— 9.
2. ——— 13.
7. ——— 14.
2. —— xiii. 27.
7. ——— 35.
7. —— xiv. 18, 19, 26.
3. ——— 27.
5. —— xv. 6, 9, 12.
7. ——— 19.
4. ——— 29.
2. ——— 31.
2. —— xvi. 3.
7. ——— 4, 24.
5. —— xvii. 8.
7. —— xviii. 3.
5. ——— 5 1st.
7. ——— 5 2nd.
— ——— 13, see M (to)
7. ——— 16, 19.
5. ——— 22.
7. ——— 38, 39.
3. —— xix. 27.
5. —— xx. 3.
7. ——— 23 (ap.)
5. ——— 24.
— —— xxii. 19, see M (of)
7. ——— 21 1st.
2. ——— 21 2nd, 28.
— ——— 29, see M (unto)
7. ——— 34.
4. ——— 37 1st.
2. ——— 37 2nd.
2. ——— 42.
6. ——— 53.
7. ——— 61.
5. ——— 68 (om. μοί ἢ ἀπολύσητε, me, nor let me go, T Trb Ab ℵ.)

— Luke xxiii. 14, see M (unto)
6. ——— 28.
3. ——— 42.
2. ——— 43.
7. —— xxiv. 39 1st.
6. ——— 39 2nd.
2. ——— 44.
3. John i. 15 3 times, 27 1st, 27 2nd (ap.), 30 3 times.
7. ——— 33 1st.
— ——— 33 2nd, see M (unto)
5. ——— 43.
7. ——— 48.
7. —— ii. 17.
5. —— iii. 28.
5. —— iv. 7.
2. ——— 9.
5. ——— 10, 15, 21, 29.
7. ——— 34.
5. ——— 39.
7. —— v. 7 1st.
2. ——— 7 2nd.
7. ——— 11 1st.
— ——— 11 2nd, see M (unto)
7. ——— 24, 30.
2. ——— 32 twice.
5. ——— 36 1st.
2. ——— 36 2nd.
7. ——— 36 3rd, 37 1st.
2. ——— 37 2nd, 39.
7. ——— 40, 43.
4. ——— 46 1st.
2. ——— 46 2nd.
7. —— vi. 26.
7. ——— 35 1st (No. 6, T Tr A ℵ.)
6. ——— 35 2nd.
7. ——— 36 (om. Lb ℵ.)
5. ——— 37 1st.
6. ——— 37 2nd.
7. ——— 37 3rd, 38, 39 1st.
5. ——— 39 2nd.
7. ——— 40 (τοῦ πατρός μου, *my Father*, instead of τοῦ πέμψαντός με, *him that sent me*, G ∾ L T Tr A ℵ.)
7. ——— 44 1st (No. 6, T Tr A.)
7. ——— 44 2nd.
7. ——— 45 (No. 6, T Tr.)
6. ——— 47 (om. εἰς ἐμὲ, *on me*, T Trb Ab ℵ.)
4. ——— 56.
7. ——— 57 1st & 2nd.
6. ——— 57 3rd.
7. ——— 65.
6. —— vii. 7.
7. ——— 16, 19.
— ——— 23, see M (at)
— ——— 28 1st, see M (both)
7. ——— 28 2nd, 29, 33, 34, 36, 37.
6. ——— 38.
4. —— viii. 12 (No. 5, L [Tr.)
7. ——— 16.
2. ——— 18 1st.
7. ——— 18 2nd.
6. ——— 19 twice.
7. ——— 21, 26, 28, 29 1st.
2. ——— 29 2nd.
7. ——— 29 3rd, 37, 40.
6. ——— 42 1st.
7. ——— 42 2nd.
5. ——— 45.
7. ——— 46 1st.
5. ——— 46 2nd.
7. ——— 49, 54.
7. —— ix. 4.
— ——— 11, see M (unto)
2. —— x. 8, 9.
7. ——— 15, 17.
2. ——— 18, 25.
5. ——— 27, 29.

7. John x. 32 (No. 6, T Tr A ℵ.)
5. ——— 37.
4. ——— 38 twice.
6. —— xi. 25, 26.
3. ——— 41, 42 1st.
7. ——— 42 2nd.
6. —— xii. 8.
4. ——— 26 3 times.
7. ——— 27.
6. ——— 30.
8. ——— 32.
6. ——— 44 1st & 2nd.
7. ——— 44 3rd.
6. ——— 45 1st.
7. ——— 45 2nd.
6. ——— 46, 48.
7. ——— 49 1st.
5. ——— 49 2nd.
— ——— 50, see M (unto)
2. —— xiii. 8.
7. ——— 13.
2. ——— 18 1st (No. 3, Tr A.)
6. ——— 18 2nd, 20 1st.
7. ——— 20 2nd.
6. ——— 20 3rd.
7. ——— 21.
7. ——— 33.
5. ——— 36 1st.
5. ——— 36 2nd (om. L T Tr A ℵ.)
7. ——— 38.
6. —— xiv. 1.
2. ——— 6.
7. ——— 7, 9 1st.
6. ——— 9 2nd.
4. ——— 10 twice.
5. ——— 11 1st.
4. ——— 11 2nd.
5. ——— 11 3rd (om. G → T Trb.)
6. ——— 12.
7. ——— 15, 19 twice.
4. ——— 20.
7. ——— 21 twice, 23, 24 twice 28.
4. ——— 30.
5. ——— 31.
4. —— xv. 2, 4 twice, 5 1st.
2. ——— 5 2nd.
4. ——— 6, 7.
7. ——— 9, 16.
6. ——— 18, 20.
7. ——— 21.
6. ——— 23, 24.
7. ——— 25.
2. ——— 26, 27.
6. —— xvi. 3.
7. ——— 5 twice.
6. ——— 9.
7. ——— 10.
6. ——— 14.
7. ——— 16 twice, 17 twice, 19 twice.
6. ——— 23, 27.
6. ——— 32 1st (κἀμέ, T Tr A ℵ.)
2. ——— 32 2nd.
4. ——— 33.
5. —— xvii. 4.
7. ——— 5.
5. ——— 6 1st.
4. ——— 6 2nd (κἀμοί, Tr.)
5. ——— 7, 8 1st.
7. ——— 8 2nd.
5. ——— 9, 11, 12.
6. ——— 18, 20.
4. ——— 21 1st.
7. ——— 21 2nd.
5. ——— 22.
4. ——— 23 1st.
7. ——— 23 2nd.
6. ——— 23 3rd.
5. ——— 24 1st.
2. ——— 24 2nd.
5. ——— 24 3rd.
7. ——— 24 4th.

7. John xvii. 25, 26.
6. —— xviii. 8.
5. ——— 9, 11.
7. ——— 21, 23.
2. ——— 34.
— ——— 35, } see M
— —— xix. 10, } (unto)
2. ——— 11 1st.
7. ——— 11 2nd.
5. —— xx. 15.
3. ——— 17.
7. ——— 21, 29.
7. —— xxi. 15, 16, 17 twice.
5. ——— 19, 22.
— Acts i. 4, see M (of)
— ——— 8, see M (unto)
— —— ii. 28 1st, see M (to)
7. ——— 28 2nd
6. —— iii. 22.
5. —— v. 8.
5. —— vii. 7.
7. ——— 28.
6. ——— 37, marg. *myself.*
— ——— 42, see M (to)
5. ——— 49.
— —— viii. 19, see M also.
2. ——— 24 1st.
6. ——— 24 2nd.
7. ——— 31, 36.
7. —— ix. 4, 6 (ap.)
— ——— 15, see M (unto)
7. ——— 17.
4. —— x. 28 (κἀμοί, L T Tr A ℵ.)
7. ——— 29.
3. ——— 30.
2. —— xi. 5.
— ——— 7, see M (unto)
5. ——— 9 (om. L T Tr A ℵ.)
7. ——— 11.
5. ——— 12 1st.
4. ——— 12 2nd.
5. —— xii. 8.
7. ——— 11.
5. —— xiii. 2.
6. ——— 25.
3. —— xv. 7.
— ——— 13, see M (unto)
3. ——— 17.
7. —— xvi. 15.
5. —— xx. 19, 22.
7. ——— 23.
2. ——— 34.
5. —— xxi. 39.
5. —— xxii. 5.
6. ——— 6.
— ——— 7 1st, see M (unto
7. ——— 7 2nd.
7. ——— 8 (No. 6, L Tr ℵ.)
4. ——— 9 1st.
— ——— 9 2nd, see M (to)
7. ——— 10.
5. ——— 11.
7. ——— 13 1st (No. 6, L Tr ℵ.)
— ——— 13 2nd, } see M
— ——— 18 1st, } (unto)
2. ——— 18 2nd.
7. ——— 21.
5. ——— 27.
7. —— xxiii. 3 twice.
2. ——— 11.
7. ——— 18.
5. ——— 19.
7. ——— 22.
5. ——— 30.
7. —— xxiv. 12.
3. ——— 13.
7. ——— 18.
7. ——— 19 (No. 6, L T ℵ.)
4. ——— 20 (om. ἐν ἐμοί, *in me*, L T Trb Ab ℵ.)
2. —— xxv. 6.
3. ——— 11 1st.
7. ——— 11 2nd.

5. Acts xxv. 24.
— ——— 27, see M (to)
3. —— xxvi. 3.
7. ——— 5, 13 1st.
4. ——— 13 2nd.
7. ——— 14 twice, 21, 28.
6. ——— 18.
7. ——— 21, 28.
3. ——— 29.
— —— xxvii. 21, see M (unto)
5. ——— 23, 25.
7. —— xxviii. 18 1st.
4. ——— 18 2nd.
— Rom. i. 12, see M (of)
6. ——— 15, and see M is (as much as)
4. —— vii. 8.
7. ——— 11.
— ——— 13 1st, see M (unto)
— ——— 13 2nd, see M (to)
4. ——— 17, 18 1st.
— ——— 18 2nd, see M (with)
4. ——— 20.
— ——— 21, see M (with)
7. ——— 23, 24.
7. —— viii. 2 (σε, *thee*, Lm T A* ℵ.)
5. —— ix. 1.
— ——— 19, see M (unto)
7. ——— 20.
6. —— x. 20 twice.
3. —— xii. 3, see M (unto)
— —— xiv. 11, see M (to)
6. —— xv. 3.
— ——— 15, see M (to)
2. ——— 18.
5. ——— 30 1st.
2. ——— 30 2nd.
2. —— xvi. 7.
— 1 Cor. i. 2, see M (unto)
7. ——— 17.
— —— iii. 10, see M (unto)
— —— iv. 3, see M (with)
7. ——— 4.
— ——— 16, see M (of)
— —— vi. 12 1st, see M (unto)
— ——— 12 2nd, see M (for)
— —— vii. 1, see M (unto)
6. —— ix. 3.
4. ——— 15 1st.
— ——— 15 2nd, see M (for)
5. ——— 16 1st.
— ——— 16 2nd.
— —— x. 23 twice, see M (for)
— —— xi. 1, see M (of)
3. ——— 2.
— ——— 24, 25, see M (of)
4. —— xiv. 11.
3. ——— 21.
— —— xv. 8, see M also (of)
6. ——— 10 1st.
4. ——— 10 2nd.
5. ——— 32.
4. —— xvi. 4.
7. ——— 6.
— ——— 9, see M (unto)
7. ——— 11 (No. 6, L A.)
4. 2 Cor. i. 17.
2. ——— 19.
7. —— ii. 2 1st.
2. ——— 2 2nd.
6. ——— 5.
— ——— 12, see M (unto)
2. —— vii. 7.
— —— ix. 1, see M (for)
4. ——— 4.
3. —— xi. 1 twice.
— ——— 9, see M (to)
4. ——— 10 1st.
6. ——— 10 2nd.
7. 2 Cor. xi. 16 twice.
3. ——— 28 (No. 5, L T Tr A ℵ.)
7. ——— 32.
— —— xii. 1, see M (for)
6. ——— 6 1st.
7. ——— 6 2nd.
2. ——— 6 3rd.
— ——— 7 1st, see M (to)
7. ——— 7 2nd.
2. ——— 8.
— ——— 9 1st, see M (unto)
6. ——— 9 2nd.
7. ——— 11.
5. ——— 13.
7. ——— 21 (*om.* St E G.)
4. —— xiii. 3.
5. ——— 10.
4. Gal. i. 2.
2. ——— 11.
7. ——— 15.
4. ——— 16.
2. ——— 17.
4. ——— 24.
4. —— ii. 3.
— ——— 6 twice, see M (to)
4. ——— 8 (καμοὶ, L T Tr.)
— ——— 9 1st, see M (unto)
— ——— 9 2nd, see M (to)
4. ——— 20 1st.
7. ——— 20 2nd.
2. ——— 20 3rd.
7. —— iv. 12, 14.
— ——— 15, see M (to)
5. ——— 21.
— —— vi. 14, see M (unto)
5. ——— 17.
5. Eph. iii. 2.
— ——— 3, 7, 8, see M (unto)
2. — — vi. 19 1st.
— ——— 19 2nd, see M (unto)
— Phil. i. 7, see M (for)
7. ——— 7, marg. (text, I.)
— ——— 12, see M (the things which happened unto)
— ——— 21, see M (to)
4. ——— 26, 30 twice.
5. —— ii. 18.
4. ——— 22.
— ——— 23, see M (how it will go with)
6. ——— 27.
7. ——— 30.
— —— iii. 1, 7, see M (to)
— ——— 17, see M (of)
5. —— iv. 3.
4. ——— 9.
2. ——— 10.
7. ——— 13.
— ——— 15, see M (with)
4. ——— 21.
— Col. i. 25, see M (to)
4. ——— 29.
— —— iv. 11, see M (unto)
— ——— 18, see M (of)
7. 1 Tim. i. 12 twice.
4. ——— 16.
6. 2 Tim. i. 8.
2. ——— 13.
7. ——— 15, 16, 17.
2. —— ii. 2.
— —— iii. 11 1st, see M (unto)
7. ——— 11 2nd.
— —— iv. 8 1st, see M (for)
5. ——— 8 2nd.
— ——— 8 3rd, see M (to)
7. ——— 9, 10.
2. ——— 11 1st.
— ——— 11 2nd, see M (to)
5. ——— 14.
5. ——— 16 1st.
7. ——— 16 2nd.
5. ——— 17 1st.
7. 2 Tim. iv. 17 2nd.
— ——— 17 3rd, see M (to)
7. ——— 18.
— Titus i. 3, see M (be committed unto)
7. —— iii. 12.
2. ——— 15.
— Philem. 11, see M (to)
8. ——— 13 1st.
— ——— 13 2nd, see M (unto)
6. ——— 17 (No. 7, G L T Tr ℵ.)
— ——— 19, see M (unto)
1. ——— 20.
5. ——— 22.
— Heb. i. 5, see M (to)
5. —— ii. 13.
7. —— iii. 9 1st (*om.* G ~ L T Tr A ℵ.)
7. ——— 9 2nd (*ap.*)
— —— viii. 10, see M (to)
7. ——— 11.
5. —— x. 5.
2. ——— 7.
— ——— 30, see M (unto)
7. —— xi. 32.
— ——— xiii. 6, see M (unto)
5. Jas. ii. 18.
5. 2 Pet. i. 14.
3. Rev. i. 10.
2. ——— 12.
6. ——— 17 1st.
— Rev. i. 17 2nd, see M (unto)
2. —— iii. 4, 18, 20, 21.
2. —— iv. 1.
— —— v. 5, } see M
— —— vii. 13, } (unto)
— ——— 14, see M (to)
— —— x. 4, see M (unto)
2. ——— 8.
5. ——— 9 1st.
— ——— 9 2nd, } see M
— ——— 11, } (unto)
5. —— xi. 1.
— —— xiv. 13, see M (unto)
2. —— xvii. 1 1st.
— ——— 1 2nd, see M (unto)
7. ——— 3.
— —— vii. 15, } see M
— —— xix. 9 twice, 10, } (unto)
— —— xxi. 5, 6, }
7. ——— 9 1st (*om.* πρὸς με, *unto me*, G L T Tr A ℵ.)
2. ——— 9 2nd.
7. ——— 10 1st.
5. ——— 10 2nd.
2. ——— 15.
5. —— xxii. 1.
— ——— 6, see M (unto)
5. ——— 8.
— ——— 9, 10, see M (unto)
2. ——— 12.

(The following combinations where there are not two separate words in the Greek.)

ME (AT)

5. John vii. 23.

ME (BOTH)

κἀμε, both me, me also.

John vii. 28.

ME (BE COMMITTED UNTO)

{ ἐπιστεύθην, I was intrusted.
{ ἐγὼ, I.

Tit. i. 3.

ME (FOR)

5. Matt. xx. 15.
5. 1 Cor. vi. 12.
5. —— ix. 15.
5. —— x. 23 twice (*om.* GLT Tr A ℵ.)
5. 2 Cor. ix. 1.
5. —— xii. 1 (*ap.*)
4. Phil. i. 7.
5. 2 Tim. iv. 8.

ME (HOW IT WILL GO WITH)

{ τὰ, the things, περὶ, about, concerning, ἐμέ, me, } *i.e.* [*whensoever I may look away from*] the things which concern me.

Phil. ii. 23.

ME (IN)

5. Rom. vii. 13.

ME ALSO.

κἀμοί, to me also, even to me.

Acts viii. 19.

ME (OF)

1. *ἐμοῦ*, *see* "ME," *No.* 2.
2. *μοῦ*, *see* "ME," *No.* 3.
3. *ἐμός*, my, mine; *more emphatic, denoting possession, power over, authorship, right, etc.*

2. Matt. x. 37 twice, 38.
3. Luke xxii. 19.
2. Acts i. 4.
1. Rom. i. 12.
2. 1 Cor. iv. 16.
2. —— xi. 1.
3. ——— 24, 25.
2. Phil. iii. 17.
3. Col. iv. 18.

ME ALSO (OF)

κἀμοί, even unto me.

1 Cor. xv. 8.

ME (THE THINGS WHICH HAPPENED UNTO)

{ *τὰ*, the *things*,
κατά, relating to,
ἐμέ, me.

Phil. i. 12.

ME (TO)

1. *ἐμοί*, *see* "ME," *No.* 4.
2. *μοί*, *see* "ME," *No.* 5.
3. *μοῦ*, *see* "ME," *No.* 3.

2. Matt. vii. 22.
2. —— xiv. 18.
2. —— xvii. 17.
1. —— xxv. 45.
2. Luke i. 43, 49
2. —— x. 22.
2. —— xviii. 13.
2. Acts ii. 28.
2. —— vii. 42.
2. —— xxii. 9.
2. —— xxv. 27.
1. Rom. xiv. 11.
3. 2 Cor. xi. 9.
2. 2 Cor. xii. 7.
2. Gal. ii. 6 1st.
1. ——— 6 2nd, 9.
2. —— iv. 15.
1. Phil i. 21.
1. —— iii. i.
2. ——— 7.
2. Col. i. 25.
2. 2 Tim. iv. 11.
1. Philem. 11, 16.
2. Heb. i. 5.
2. —— viii. 10.
2. Rev. vii. 14.

ME ALSO (TO)

κἀμοί, even unto me.

Luke i. 3.

ME (UNTO)

1. *ἐμοί*, *see* "ME," *No.* 4.
2. *μοί*, *see* "ME," *No.* 5.
3. *μοῦ*, *see* "ME," *No.* 3.

2. Matt. vii. 21.
2. —— xi. 27.
2. —— xv. 8 (*ap.*)
1. —— xvi. 23 (*ἐμοῦ*, *my*, L Tr A ℵ, i.e. *thou art my stumbling-block.*)
2. —— xxi. 2.
2. —— xxv. 20, 22.
1. ——— 40.
2. —— xxviii. 18.
2. Luke i. 38.
1. —— iv. 6.
2. ——— 23.
2. —— xxii. 29.
2. —— xxiii. 14.
2. John i. 33.
2. —— v. 11.
2. —— ix. 11.
2. —— xii. 50.
1. —— xviii. 35.
1. —— xix. 10.
2. Acts i. 8 (No. 3, L T Tr A ℵ.)
2. —— ix. 15.
2. —— xi. 7.
3. —— xv. 13.
2. —— xxii. 7, 13, 18.
2. —— xxvii. 21.
2. Rom. ix. 19.
2. —— xii. 3.
1. ——— 13.
2. 1 Cor. i. 11.
2. 1 Cor. iii. 10.
2. —— vi. 12.
2. —— vii. 1 (*om.* T Trᵇ [A ℵ.)
2. —— ix. 16.
2. —— xvi. 9.
2. 2 Cor. ii. 12.
2. —— xii. 9.
2. Gal. ii. 9.
1. —— vi. 14.
2. Eph. iii. 3, 7.
1. ——— 8.
2. —— vi. 19.
2. Col. iv. 11.
2. 2 Tim. iii. 11.
2. Philem. 13, 19.
1. Heb. x. 30.
2. —— xiii. 6.
2. Rev. i. 17 (*om.* G L T Tr A ℵ.)
2. —— v. 5.
2. —— vii. 13.
2. —— x. 4 (*om.* G L T Tr A ℵ.)
2. ——— 9, 11.
2. —— xiv. 13 (*om.* G L T Tr A ℵ.)
2. —— xvii. 1 (*om.* G L T Tr A ℵ.)
2. ——— 7, 15.
2. —— xix. 9 twice, 10.
2. —— xxi. 5 (*om.* G ⇉ L T Tr A.)
2. ——— 6.
2. Rev. xxii. 6, 9, 10.

ME (WITH)

1. *ἐμοί*, *see* "ME," *No.* 4.
2. *μοί*, *see* "ME," *No.* 5.

2. Luke i. 25.
2. Rom. vii. 18.
1. Rom. vii. 21.
1. 1 Cor. iv. 3.
2. Phil. iv. 15.

MEAL.

ἄλευρον, wheaten flour, fine meal, (*from ἀλέω*, to grind) (*non occ.*)

Matt. xiii. 33. | Luke xiii. 21.

MEAN [adj.]

ἄσημος, without mark: *of money*, unstamped; *then*, indistinct *to the senses;* unknown, unperceived, not recognised; *hence*, of persons, unknown, obscure, not recognised, (*non occ.*)

Acts xxi. 39.

MEAN THINGS [marg.]

{ *τοῖς*, the, *ταπεινοῖς*, lowly, } *here*, to the lowly.

Rom. xii. 16 twice (text, *men of low estate.*)

MEANWHILE.

μεταξύ, in the midst; *of time*, mean time, meanwhile.

John iv. 31. | Rom. ii. 15, marg. *between.*

MEAN [verb.]

(-ETH, -ING, MEANT, SHOULD MEAN.)

1. ἐστί, (*3rd pers. sing. pres. tense Indic. of* εἰμί, to be) he, she, *or* it is.
2. εἴη, (*3rd pers. sing. pres. tense Opt. of* εἰμί, to be) he, she, *or* it might be.
3. { θέλω, to will, wish, desire, / εἶναι, to be, } *lit.*, what would this mean, *or* what pleases this to be?
4. μέλλω, to be about to, to be on the point of. *Here, part.*, being about to, *or* on the point of.
5. ποιέω, to make *or* do, (*lit.*, here, what are ye doing weeping? etc.)

1. Matt. ix. 10, 13.
1. —— xii. 7.
2. Luke xvi. 26.
2. —— xviii. 36.
3. Acts ii. 12.
2. —— x. 17.
3. —— xvii. 20.
5. —— xxi. 13.
4. Acts xxvii. 2.

MEANING.

δύναμις, power, force; *of language*, the power *or* signification of a word.

1 Cor. xiv. 11.

MEANS.

(*For various combinations with other words, see below; see also* "SEEK," *and* "DESPAIR.")

MEANS (BY ALL)

1. πάντως, wholly, altogether, entirely.
2. { ἐν, in, / παντὶ, every, / τρόπῳ, turning, way, } [mode,] in every state, *or* at every turn.

1. Acts xviii. 21 (*ap.*)
1. 1 Cor. ix. 22.
2. 2 Thes. iii. 16, (τόπος, *place*, instead of τρόπον, *way*, G ∾ L.)

MEANS (BY ANY)

1. πως, in any way, at all, by any means.
2. { οὐ, no *or* not, / μή, no *or* not, } (*here, with another negative*) no not, assuredly not, not at all, by no means, in no wise (*see under* "No.")
3. { κατὰ, according to. / μηδένα, no. / τρόπον, manner. }

2. Luke x. 19.
1. Acts xvii. 12.
1. Rom. i. 10.
1. —— xi. 14.
1. 1 Cor. viii. 9.
1. 1 Cor. ix. 27.
1. 2 Cor. xi. 3.
1. Gal. ii. 2.
1. Phil. iii. 11.
3. 2 Thes. ii. 3.

MEANS (IF BY ANY)

{ εἰ, if, (*see* "IF," *No.* 4b.) / πως, in any way. }

Acts xxvii. 12.
Rom. i. 10.
Rom. xi. 14.
Phil. iii. 11.

MEANS (BY NO)

οὐ, μή, no not, in no wise.

Matt. v. 26.

MEANS OF DEATH (BY)

θανάτου γενομένου, a death taking place.

Heb. ix. 15.

MEANS (LEST BY ANY)

μήπως, lest in any way, peradventure that in no way.

1 Cor. viii. 9.
2 Cor. xi. 3.
Gal. ii. 2.

MEANS (LEST THAT BY ANY)

μήπως, *see above.*

1 Cor. ix. 27.

MEANS (LEST BY SOME)

μήπως, *see above.*

1 Thes. iii. 5

MEANS (BY SOME)

πως, in any way, at all, by any means.

1 Thes. iii. 5.

MEANS OF (BY THE)

ἐκ, out of, from *or* by.

2 Cor. i. 11.

MEANS (BY WHAT)

1. { ἐν, in, / τίνι, whom, *or* what, } in what, (*as the conditional element*), wherein.
2. πῶς, how? in what way or manner? by what means?

2. Luke viii. 36.
2. John ix. 21.
1. Acts iv. 9.

MEASURE [noun.]

(*For various combinations with other words, see below.*)

1. μέτρον, that by which any thing is measured, a measure *or* rule; *gen.*, a measure *or* standard; *esp.*, a measure of content, *whether solid or liquid*, (*non occ.*)

2. σάτον, satum, a measure, סאה, seah, *Aram.*, סאתא, satah; a Heb. measure for things dry = nearly 1½ peck Eng., (*non occ.*)

3. βάτος, *Heb.*, בת, bath, a measure for wine and oil, equal to the ephah for dry measure, = from 7½ to 9 galls. Eng., (*non occ.*)

4. κόρος, *Heb.*, כר cor, the largest Heb. dry measure, equal to the Homer, *i.e.* to 10 baths or ephahs (*No.* 3), = 14½ bushels Eng., (*non occ.*)

5. χοῖνιξ, a chœnix, an Attic measure for grain, and things dry, = nearly 1 quart Eng.

[A *chœnix* of grain was the daily allowance for one man, whether soldier or slave. A *denarius* was the usual price of a day's labour. The usual price of a chœnix of wheat was about ⅛ of a denarius; in the time of Cicero, 1/16; in the time of Trajan, 1/20. All this shows the severity of the famine predicted,] (*non occ.*)

1. Matt. vii. 2.
2. —— xiii. 33.
1. —— xxiii. 32.
1. Mark iv. 24.
1. Luke vi. 38 twice.
2. —— xiii. 21.
3. —— xvi. 6.
4. Luke xvi. 7
1. John iii. 34.
1. Rom. xii. 3.
1. 2 Cor. x. 13 twice.
1. Eph. iv. 7, 13, 16.
5. Rev. vi. 6 twice.
1. —— xxi. 17.

MEASURE (ABOVE)

ὑπερβαλλόντως, far beyond the mark, beyond measure, (*non occ.*)

2 Cor. xi. 23. | 2 Cor. xii. 7 twice, see Exalt.

MEASURE (BEYOND)

1. { ἐκ, out of, περισσός, over and above, more than enough, } beyond measure.

2. ὑπερπερισσῶς, over-superabundantly, beyond all measure, (*non occ.*)

3. { κατά, according to, ὑπερβολή, a throwing beyond, *Eng.*, hyperbole, } exceedingly super-eminently.

1. Mark vi. 51 (om. G → Tr[b] [ℵ.]) | —2 Cor. x. 14, see Stretch.
2. Mark vii. 37. | 3. Gal. i. 13.

MEASURE (OUT OF)

1. περισσῶς, exceedingly, abundantly.

2. { κατά, ὑπερβολή, } *see above, No.* 3.

1. Mark x. 26. | 2. 2 Cor. i. 8.

MEASURE (THINGS WITHOUT)

{ τὰ, the *things*. ἄμετρα, unmeasured. }

2 Cor. x. 13, 15.

MEASURE (-ED, ING.) [verb.]

μετρέω, to measure, *in any way*, *of space*, *number*, *capacity*, *length*, etc., (*elsewhere*, "mete.")

Mark iv. 24. | Rev. xi. 1, 2.
2 Cor. x. 12. | —— xxi. 15, 16, 17.

MEASURE AGAIN.

ἀντιμετρέω, to measure out again, *or* in turn, (*non occ.*)

Matt. vii. 2, (*μετρέω, to measure*, G L T Tr A ℵ.)
Luke vi. 38. (*μετρέω, to measure*, L[m].)

MEAT.

1. βρῶμα, whatever is eaten, solid food, *as opp.* to *milk, etc.*

2. βρῶσις, eating, the act of eating.

3. βρώσιμος, eatable.

4. τροφή, nourishment, sustenance, food, victuals.

5. φάγω, to eat, take food, take a meal, eat and drink, (*see* "EAT," *No.* 1.) *Here, inf.*

6. προσφάγιον, what is eaten thereto, *i.e.* along with *bread; hence*, meat, fish, etc., (*non occ.*)

7. τράπεζα, a table; *and as to set a table, is to make ready a meal, so* τράπεζα *is used for* a meal *or* banquet.

4. Matt. iii. 4.
4. —— vi. 25.
— —— ix. 10, see Sit.
4. —— x. 10.
— —— xiv. 9, see Sit.
— —— xv. 37, see Broken.
4. —— xxiv. 45.
5. —— xxv. 35, 42.
— Mark ii. 15, see Sit.
1. —— vii. 19.
— —— viii. 8, see Broken.
— —— xiv. 3, } see Sit.
— —— xvi. 14, } see Sit.
1. Luke iii. 11, pl.
— —— vii. 37, 49, see Sit.
5. —— viii. 55.
1. —— ix. 13, pl.
— —— xi. 37, see Sit.
4. —— xii. 23.
— ——— 42, see M (portion of)
— —— xiv. 10, 15, } see Sit.
— —— xvii. 7, } see Sit.
— —— xxii. 27 twice, } see Sit.
— —— xxiv. 30, } see Sit.
3. ——— 41.
4. John iv. 8.
2. ——— 32.
1. John iv. 34.
2. —— vi. 27 twice, 55.
6. —— xxi. 5,
4. Acts ii. 46.
4. —— ix. 19.
— —— xv. 29, see Idols.
7. —— xvi. 34.
4. —— xxvii. 33.
— ——— 34, 36, see M (portion of)
1. Rom. xiv. 15 twice.
2. ——— 17.
1. ——— 20.
— ——— 23 (marg.), see Doubt.
1. 1 Cor. iii. 2.
1. —— vi. 13 twice.
1. —— viii. 8.
— ——— 10, see Sit.
1. ——— 13.
1. —— x. 3.
2 Col. ii. 16, marg. *eating*.
1. 1 Tim. iv. 3.
4. Heb. v. 12, 14.
1. —— ix. 10.
— —— xii. 16, see M (morsel of)

1. Heb. xiii. 9.

MEAT (MORSEL OF)

2. Heb. xii. 16.

MEAT (PORTION OF)

σιτομέτριον, grain measured out, a measured allowance of corn, rations, (*non occ.*)

Luke xii. 42.

MEAT (SOME)

τροφή, *see above, No.* 4, (*here, Genitive case.*)

Acts xvii. 34, 36.

MEDIATOR.

μεσίτης, (*from* μέσος, middle, and εἶμι, to go) a go-between, a mediator, one who intervenes between two parties, one who mediates for peace and unites parties at variance. *A word that does not occur in profane Greek, for they had no higher words than* διαιτήτης διαλλακτήρ, διαλλακτής, the arbitrator. In the lxx. it only occurs once, Job ix. 33.

* [Gal. iii. 19, 20, seems to need further explanation. A mediator presupposes two differing parties. But God is one; therefore this disagreement cannot be in Him, which would be the case if the Law disannulled the promise—both being given by Him. Inasmuch as a mediator had been introduced, the relations between God and Israel had been disturbed, and Israel was no longer "the seed to whom the promise was made." The law was given, therefore, on account of Israel and their sin, they having rejected the promise, and there being yet no "seed" who might inherit those promises.]

* Gal. iii. 19, 20.
1 Tim. ii. 5.
Heb. viii. 6.
—— ix. 15.

Heb. xii. 24.

MEDITATE BEFORE.

προμελετάω, (μελετάω, (*see below*) *with* πρό, before, *prefixed.*)

Luke xxi. 14.

MEDITATE UPON.

μελετάω, to care for, take care for *anything*, so as to be able to perform it.

1 Tim. iv. 15.

MEEK.

1. πραΰς, (*an earlier but not better form of No.* 2) meek, gentle, enduring all things with an even temper, tender, free from haughty self-sufficiency, tender of spirit (ἤπιος *is rather* the exhibition of that tenderness in bearing with others. *See* "GENTLE.")

2. πρᾷος, (*a later form of No.* 1.)

1. Matt. v. 5.
2. —— xi. 29 (No. 1, L T Tr A ℵ.)
1. Matt. xxi. 5.
1. 1 Pet. iii. 4.

MEEKNESS.

1. πραότης, meekness, mildness, *see* "MEEK," *No.* 1, (*non occ.*)

2. πραΰτης, (*an earlier form of No.* 1.)

1. 1 Cor. iv. 21 (No. 2, L T Tr A ℵ.)
1. 2 Cor. x. 1 (No. 2, L T Tr A.)
1. Gal. v. 23 (No. 2, L T Tr A ℵ.)
1. —— vi. 1 (No. 2, T Tr A ℵ.)
1. Eph. iv. 2 (No. 2, T Tr A ℵ.)
1. Col. iii. 12 (No. 2, L T Tr A ℵ.)
1. 1 Tim. vi: 11 (*πραϋπάθεια, suffering meekly,* G~L T Tr ℵ.)
1. 2 Tim. ii. 25 (No. 2, L T Tr A ℵ.)
1. Tit. iii. 2 (No. 2, L T Tr A ℵ.)
2. Jas. i. 21.
2. —— iii. 13.
2. 1 Pet. iii. 15.

MEET. [adj.]

1. *ἄξιος*, worth, worthy; of equal value, of like worth; worthy of, deserving of.

2. *δίκαιος*, right, just, *see* "RIGHT."

3. *εὔθετος*, well adapted, well arranged, conveniently placed; convenient for use.

4. *ἱκανός*, coming to, reaching to; *hence,* sufficing, sufficient; *of persons,* adequate, competent.

5. *καλός*, beautiful, agreeable, (*see* "GOOD," *No.* 2.)

1. Matt. iii. 8, marg. *answerable.*
5. —— xv. 26 (*ἔξεστι, allowed,* L T A.)
5. Mark vii. 27.
1. Luke iii. 8, marg. (text, *worthy.*)
— —— xv. 32, see M (be)
1. Acts xxvi. 20.
— Rom. i. 27, see M (be)
4. 1 Cor. xv. 9.
1. —— xvi. 4.
2. Phil. i. 7.
— Col. i. 12, see M (make)
1. 2 Thes. i. 3.
— 2 Tim. ii. 21, see Use.
3. Heb. vi. 7.
2. 2 Pet. i. 13.

MEET (BE)

δεῖ, it needs, there is need of, it is necessary, *implying that* something is absent *or* wanting.

Luke xv. 32. | Rom. i. 27.

MEET (MAKE)

ἱκανόω, to make sufficient, render competent *or* adequate, (*occ.* 2 Cor. iii. 6.)

Col. i. 12.

MEET, MET. [verb.]

1. *ἀπαντάω*, to come *or* go from *a place* towards a person; *and* so to meet face to face from opposite directions; *esp.*, to meet and come back with the person met (*non occ.*)

2. { *εἰς*, unto, with a view to, *ἀπάντησις*, a meeting, (*subst. of No.* 1) (*non occ.*)

3. *συναντάω*, (*No.* 1, *with σύν*, in conjunction with, *instead of ἀπό*, from, *prefixed*) to come to meet together with any one, *i.e.* to fall in with, or meet one another, (*occ.* Acts xx. 22.

4. { *εἰς*, unto, with a view to, *συναπάντησις*, a meeting, (*subst. of No.* 3) (*non occ.*)

5. *ὑπαντάω*, to come or go to meet, *with the idea of stealth, unperceived, without noise or notice,* (*occ.* John xi. 20.)

6. { *εἰς*, unto, with a view to, *ὑπάντησις*, a meeting, (*subst. of No.* 5) (*non occ.*)

5. Matt. viii. 28.
4. —— 34 (No. 6, L T Tr A* ℵ.)
2. —— xxv. 1 (No. 6, T Tr A ℵ.)
2. —— 6.
1. —— xxviii. 9 (No. 5, T Tr A* ℵ.)
1. Mark v. 2 (No. 5, T Tr ℵ.)
— —— xi. 4, see Ways.
1. —— xiv. 13.
5. Luke viii. 27.
3. —— ix. 37.
1. —— xiv. 31 (No. 5, L T Tr A ℵ.)
1. —— xvii. 12.
3. Luke xxii. 10.
1. John iv. 51 (No. 5, L T Tr A ℵ.)
— —— xi. 20, see M (go and)
5. —— 30.
6. —— xii. 13.
5. —— 18.
3. Acts x. 25.
1. —— xvi. 16 (No. 5, T Tr A ℵ.)
— —— xvii. 17, } see M
— —— xx. 14, } with.
— —— xxvii. 41, see Seas.
2. —— xxviii. 15.
2. 1 Thes. iv. 17.
3. Heb. vii. 1, 10.

MEET (GO AND)

5. John xi. 20.

MEET WITH.

1. *παρατυγχάνω*, to happen to be near, to chance to be by, *i.e.* be the first comer, (*non occ.*)

2. *συμβάλλω*, to throw together; *of persons,* to throw one's self together with another, meet with.

1. Acts xvii. 17. | 2. Acts xx. 14.

MELODY (MAKE)

ψάλλω, to touch, twitch, pluck, *e.g. the hair or beard; but esp., a string,* to twang; *then,* to touch the lyre *or* harp, to play. *In* lxx. *and N.T.*, to sing, to chant accompanied by stringed instruments.

Eph. v. 19.

MELT.

1. λύω, to loose, to loosen, set loose.
2. τήκω, to melt, make liquid. *In N.T. pass.*, to be melted, melt.

1. 2 Pet. iii. 10, pass. | 2. 2 Pet. iii. 12, pass.

MEMBER (-s.)

μέλος, a limb *or* member of the body, (*non occ.*)

Matt. v. 29, 30.
Rom. vi. 13 twice, 19 twice.
—— vii. 5, 23 twice.
—— xii. 4 twice, 5.
1 Cor. vi. 15 3 times.
1 Cor. xii. 12, 14, 18, 19, 20, 22, 25, 26 4 times, [27.
Eph. iv. 25.
—— v. 30.
Col. iii. 5.
Jas. iii. 5, 6. Jas. iv. 1.

MEMORIAL (FOR A)

{ εἰς, with a view to,
μνημόσυνον, commemorative, a memorial *or* monument, (*non occ.*) }

Matt. xxvi. 13. | Mark xiv. 9.
Acts x. 4.

MEMORY.

See, KEEP.

MEN (AFTER THE MANNER OF)

1. ἀνθρώπινος, pertaining to man, human.
2. { κατά, according to,
ἄνθρωπον, man, (*i.e.* "MAN," *No.* 1.) }

1. Rom. vi. 19. | 2. 1 Cor. xv. 32.
2. Gal. iii. 15.

MEN (AS)

2. 1 Cor. iii. 3, marg. *according to man.*

MEN (QUIT YOU LIKE)

ἀνδρίζομαι, to make *or* render like a man, (ἀνήρ, *i.e.* "MAN," *No.* 2) *i.e.* make or render brave. *Here*, ἀνδρίζεσθε, (*mid.*) to acquit as, *or* show one's self a man.

1 Cor. xvi. 13.

See also, ALL, BAND, BUSYBODY, FAIL, GOOD, GREAT, LOW, MAN, THESE, THRUST, TWO, WAR.

MEND (-ING.)

καταρτίζω, to make fully ready, to put in full order.

Matt. iv. 21. | Mark i. 19.

MEN-PLEASER (-s.)

ἀνθρωπάρεσκος, desirous to please men, (*i.e.* "MAN," *No.* 1.)

Eph. vi. 6. | Col. iii. 22.

MEN-SERVANTS.

παῖς, a child, boy, servant, *pl.*, youths.

Luke xii. 45.

MEN-STEALER (-s.)

ἀνδραποδιστής, a man-stealer, kidnapper, *see* Exod. xxi. 61; Deut. xxiv. 7, (*non occ.*)

1 Tim. i. 10.

MENTION.

μνεία, recollection, remembrance, memory; mention.

Rom. i. 9.
Eph. i. 16.
1 Thes. i. 2.
Phil. i. 3, marg. (text, *remembrance.*)
Philem. 4.

MENTION (MAKE)

μνημονεύω, to remember, call to mind, bear in mind; to mention, speak of.

Heb. xi. 22, marg. (with περί, concerning) *remembrance.*

MERCHANDISE.

1. γόμος, a load, *esp.*, *of an animal; also, of a ship; hence*, merchandise, wares, (*occ.* Acts xxi. 3.)
2. ἐμπορία, a journey for traffic, *esp.*, *by sea; hence*, commerce by sea, traffic, trade, commerce; *then*, the goods trafficked in, merchandise, (*non occ.*)
3. ἐμπόριον, belonging to commerce *or* merchants; *esp.*, a factory, entrepôt of merchandise, (*Eng.*, emporium) mart, (*non occ.*)

2. Matt. xxii. 5. | 3. John ii. 16.
1. Rev. xviii. 11, 12.

MERCHANDISE OF (MAKE)

ἐμπορεύομαι, to go *or* travel in *or* to; to travel for traffic *or* business; *with acc.* of thing, to deal in, *esp.*, to import; with acc. of *person*, to make gain of, overreach, cheat, (*occ.* Jas. iv. 13.)

2 Pet. ii. 3.

MERCHANT.

ἔμπορος, one who goes on ship-board as a passenger; *hence*, a merchant, wholesale dealer, (*non occ.*)

Matt. xiii. 45. | Rev. xviii. 3, 11, 15, 23.

MERCIFUL.

1. ἐλεήμων, merciful, actively compassionate, *not merely unhappy for the ills of others*, (*which is No.* 3) *but* desirous of relieving them; *not merely pity, but* beneficent aid promptly applied, (*non occ.*)

2. ἵλεως, propitious. *Used of the gods in profane Greek, as signifying* that good-pleasure towards men, which does not originally dwell in them, but is secured by prayer and sacrifice. *Hence, as used of our God, it is a sentiment that* belongs indeed to Him, but which does not properly pertain to man, because he is not deserving of it; *hence*, gracious, *applied to God only*, (*occ.* Matt. xvi. 22.)

3. οἰκτίρμων, pitiful, compassionate for the ills of others, *and that is all*, merely pitiful, (*see No.* 1) (*occ.* Jas. v. 11.)

1. Matt. v. 7.
3. Luke vi. 36 twice.
— Luke xviii. 13, see M(be)
1. Heb. ii. 17.
2. Heb. viii. 12.

MERCIFUL (BE)

ἱλάσκομαι, to incline one's self towards any one. *Pass.*, to be reconciled, to be gracious.

[In profane Greek, it is to render propitious by prayer and sacrifice. But God is not of Himself alienated from man. His sentiment does not therefore need to be changed. But in order that He may not for righteousness' sake be necessitated to comport Himself otherwise, an expiation is necessary, which He, Himself, and His love institute and give. Man, exposed to wrath, could neither venture nor find an expiation. But God, in finding it, anticipates and meets His righteousness. Nothing happens to God as in the heathen view. Therefore, we never read in the Bible, ἱλάσκεσθαι τὸν θεόν. Rather something happens to man, who escapes the wrath to come, (*Cremer.*)] *Therefore, the cry for mercy, with this word, implies* a sense of guilt, *while with the sense of succour or pity it would have been* ἐλέησον, (*occ.* Heb. ii. 17.)

Luke xviii. 13.

MERCY (-IES.)

(*For various combinations with other words, see below.*)

1. ἔλεος, a feeling of sympathy with misery, active compassion, the desire of relieving the miserable. (*Hence*, ἐλεημοσύνη, *is put for* those benefits which are bestowed on the miserable; but οἰκτιρμός (*No.* 2) *is never so put; hence*, succour, *as distinguished from mere pity.* (*The cry for* ἔλεος *is prompted by* distress, *while with* ἵλεως, *there is a sense of guilt*), (*non occ.*)

2. οἰκτιρμός, mere subjective compassion *or* pity *as felt on witnessing misfortune or calamity*; a sense of unhappiness for the ills of others; pity, *as distinguished from succour.* [*See* Rom. ix. 15. ἐλεήσω ὃν ἂν ἐλεῶ καὶ οἰκτειρήσω ὃν ἂν οἰκτείρω. "I will succour whom I will succour, I will pity whom I pity."]

1. Matt. ix. 13.
1. — xii. 7.
1. — xxiii. 23.
1. Luke i. 50, 54, 58, 72, 78.
1. — x. 37.
— Acts xiii. 34, see M (sure)
1. Rom. ix. 23.
1. — xi. 31.
2. — xii. 1.
1. — xv. 9.
2. 2 Cor. i. 3.
1. Gal. vi. 16.
1. Eph. ii. 4.
2. Phil. ii. 1.
2. Col. iii. 12.
1. 1 Tim. i. 2.
1. 2 Tim. i. 2, 16, 18.
1. Tit. i. 4.
1. — iii. 5.
1. Heb. iv. 16.
2. — x. 28.
1. Jas. ii. 13 twice.
1. — iii. 17.
1. 1 Pet. i. 3.
1. 2 John 3.
1. Jude 2, 21.

MERCY ON (HAVE)

ἐλεέω, to have the desire of relieving the miserable, (ὁ ἐλεῶν, strives to relieve the distressed, and does if he is able, *while* he who limits himself to compassion only, is οἰκτείρει) to have pity upon any one by actually relieving them. *ἐλεέω, is not, to forgive, though forgiveness may be part of the succour which is bestowed.*

(a) *Passive*, to obtain *or* receive the succour *or* pity.

Matt. ix. 27. — xv. 22. — xvii. 15. — xx. 30, 31. Mark x. 47, 48. | Luke xvi. 24. — xvii. 13. — xviii. 38, 39. Rom. ix. 15 twice, 18. Phil. ii. 27.

MERCY UPON (HAVE)

Rom. xi. 32.

MERCY (OBTAIN)

a. Matt. v. 7. a. Rom. xi. 30, 31. | a. 1 Cor. vii. 25. a. 1 Tim. i. 13, 16. a. 1 Pet. ii. 10 twice.

MERCY (RECEIVE)

a. 2 Cor. iv. 1.

MERCY (OF TENDER)

οἰκτίρμων, *see* "MERCIFUL," *No.* 3, (*occ.* Luke vi. 36 twice.)

Jas. v. 11.

MERCY (SHOW)

ἐλεέω, *see* "MERCY ON (HAVE)"

Rom. ix. 16. | Rom. xii. 8.

MERCY (WITHOUT)

ἀνίλεως, (*the opposite of* "MERCIFUL," *No.* 2,) unpropitious, ungracious; with reference to guilt, without propitiation.

Jas. ii. 13 (ἀνέλεος, *without pity* or *succour*, *unmerciful*, G ∾ L T Tr A ℵ.)

MERCIES (THE SURE)

{ τὰ, the *things*, ὅσια, holy (*pl.*), τά, the *things*, πιστά, faithful (*pl.*), } [*i.e.* God will perform in Christ, David's son and heir, all the *holy* and *faithful* promises and favours that He gave to David, (Is. lv. 3,) *see* 2 Sam. vii. 8—17; Ps. lxxxix. 1—4, 20—37; Luke i. 31—33; Rev. iii. 7; v. 5; xxii. 16.]

Acts xvii. 34, marg. *holy or just things.*

MERCY-SEAT (THE)

{ τὸ, the, ἱλαστήριον, mercy- [seat, } the lid *or* cover of the Ark of the Covenant; so called because of the expiation made once a year on the great day of atonement, (*occ.* Rom. iii. 25.)

Heb. ix. 5.

MERRY (BE)

1. εὐφραίνω, to make glad-minded, cause to rejoice.
2. εὐθυμέω, to be of a cheerful mind, be of good cheer, (*occ.* Acts xxvii. 22, 25.)

1. Luke xii. 19. | 1. Luke xv. 23, 24. 2. Jas. v. 13.

MERRY (MAKE)

1. Luke xv. 29, 32. | 1. Rev. xi. 10.

MESSAGE.

1. ἀγγελία, message brought, proclamation, news, (*non occ.*)
2. ἐπαγγελία, message brought upon, announcement, (*elsewhere*, "promise.")
3. πρεσβεία, age, seniority, eldership; an embassy, embassage, the body of ambassadors; *Eng.* "the embassy," (*this sense arose from* elders *being usually chosen as ambassadors.*)

3. Luke xix. 14. | 2. 1 John i. 5 (G ∾) (No. 1, G L T Tr A) (ἀπαγγελία, *a message from, a report*, ℵ.)
1. 1 John iii. 11, marg. *commandment.*

MESSENGER.

1. ἄγγελος, *see under* "ANGEL."
2. ἀπόστολος, *see under* "APOSTLE."

1. Matt. xi. 10. 1. Mark i. 2. 1. Luke vii. 24, 27. 1. — ix. 52. | 2. 2 Cor. viii. 23. 1. — xii. 7. 2. Phil. ii. 25. 1. Jas. ii. 25.

METE.

μετρέω, to measure, *esp., of capacity, but also of length.*

Matt. vii. 2. | Mark iv. 24.
Luke vi. 38.

MID-DAY.

{ ἡμέρας, of the day, / μέση, the middle, } *here, Acc.*, at mid-day.

Acts xxvi. 13.

MIDDLE.

See, WALL.

MIDNIGHT.

μεσονύκτιον, midnight.

Acts xvi. 25. | Acts xx. 7.

MIDNIGHT (ABOUT)

{ κατὰ, down towards, / μέσον, middle, / τῆς, of the, / νυκτός, of the night, } about the middle of the night.

Acts xxvii. 27.

MIDNIGHT (AT)

1. μεσονύκτιον, midnight.
2. { μέσος, middle, / νυκτός, of the night.

2. Matt. xxv. 6. | 1. Mark xiii. 35, gen.
1. Luke xi. 5, gen.

MIDST.

μέσος, mid, middle, midst. *Generally with art. and preposition, as follows:*

(a) *with* ἐν, in.

(b) *with* εἰς, unto *or* into.

(c) *with* διά, through.

a. Matt. x. 16.
—— xiv. 24, see M (in the)
a. —— xviii. 2, 20.
a. Mark vi. 47.
—— vii. 31, see M (through the)
a. —— ix. 36.
b. —— xiv. 60.
a. Luke ii. 46.
—— iv. 30, 35.
b. —— v. 19.
b. —— vi. 8.
c. —— xvii. 11.
a. —— xxi. 21.
a. Luke xxii. 55.
—— xxiii. 45, see M (in the)
—— xxiv. 36.
— John vii. 14, see M (about the)
a. —— viii. 3 (*ap.*), 9 (*ap.*)
c. ——— 59.
—— xix. 18, see M (in the)
b. —— xx. 19, 26.
a. Acts i. 15.
——— 18, see M (in the)
a. —— ii. 22.
a. —— iv. 7.
a. Acts xvii. 22.
a. —— xxvii. 21.
a. Phil. ii. 15 (μέσον, G ~ L T Tr A ℵ.)
a. Heb. ii. 12.
a. Rev. i. 13 twice (μέσον, [ℵ.)
a. —— ii. 1 twice.
a. ——— 7 (*om.* μέσῳ, *the midst of*, G L T Tr A ℵ.)
a. Rev. iv. 6 twice.
a. —— v. 6 twice.
a. —— vi. 6 twice.
—— vii. 17, see M (in the)
—— viii. 13, } see Heaven.
—— xiv. 6, }
—— xix. 17, }
a. —— xxii. 2 twice.

MIDST OF THE FEAST (ABOUT THE)

{ τῆς, the, / ἑορτῆς, feast, / μεσούσης, being in the middle, } the feast being in the middle, *i.e.* at its height.

John vii. 14.

MIDST (IN THE)

1. μέσος, mid, middle, midst.
2. μέσον, (*neut. as subst.*) the middle, the midst.
3. { ἀνὰ, up in, / μέσον, the midst, } in the midst of, among.

2. Matt. xiv. 24 (*ap.*) | 2. John xix. 18.
2. Luke xxiii. 45. | 1. Acts i. 18.
3. Rev. vii. 17.

MIDST (THROUGH THE)

{ ἀνὰ, up in, / μέσον, the midst, } in the midst of, among.

Mark vii. 31.

MIGHT. [noun.]

1. δυναμις, the being able, *i.e.* ability, inherent power, natural capacity, moral as well as physical ability, miraculous energy, ability to effect all the purposes of rectitude and wisdom; a work, *with reference to the power required for its performance.*
2. ἰσχύς, physical strength, *Lat.*, vires, power naturally resident in the subject, ability brought into action.

1. Eph. i. 21. | 1. Col. i. 11.
1. —— iii. 16. | 1. 2 Pet. ii. 11.
2. —— vi. 10. | 2. Rev. vii. 12.

MIGHT. [verb.]

See, BE, MAY, THAT.

MIGHTIER.

ἰσχυρότερός, comp. of "MIGHTY," *No.* **1.**

Matt. iii. 11. | Mark i. 7. | Luke iii. 16.

MIGHTILY.

1. { ἐν, in, / δυναμις, *see* "MIGHT," *No.* 1, } with power.

2. εὐτόνως, (*from* εὔτονος, well stretched) *hence*, intensely, forcibly, with main strength, with fine force, (*occ.* Luke xxiii. 10.)

3. { ἐν, in, / ἰσχύς, *see* "MIGHT," [*No.* 2, } powerful, strong.

4. { κατὰ, down towards, according to, / κράτος, strength, might, power in effect, force, superiority, } with powerful effect.

1. Acts xviii. 28 | 1. Col. i. 29.
4. —— xix. 20. | 3. Rev. xviii. 2 (ap.)

MIGHTY.

(*For various combinations, see below.*)

1. ἰσχυρός, *physically* strong, *naturally* powerful.
2. ἰσχύς, *see* "MIGHT," *No.* 2.
3. δύνατος, able, strong; morally as well as physically powerful.
4. δύναμις, *see* "MIGHT," *No.* 1.
5. δυνάστης, one in power, one possessed of δύναμις, (*No.* 4), one in authority.
6. βίαιος, violent, vehement, *spoken of wind*, (*non occ.*)
7. κραταιός, strong, mighty, powerful in effect, forcible, (*non occ.*)
8. μέγας, great.

5. Luke i. 52.
1. —— iii. 16.
1. —— xv. 14.
3. —— xxiv. 19.
6. Acts ii. 2.
3. —— vii. 22.
3. —— xviii. 24.
4. Rom. xv. 19.
3. 1 Cor. i. 26.
1. —— i. 27.
3. 2 Cor. x. 4.
2. Eph. i. 9, marg. *of might.*
4. 2 Thes. i. 7, marg. *of power.*
7. 1 Pet. v. 6.
8. Rev. vi. 13.
1. —— x. 1.
1. —— xviii. 10, 21.
1. —— xix. 6, 18.

MIGHTY (BE)

δυνατέω, to be able, show one's self able *or* powerful, (*non occ.*)

2 Cor. xiii. 3.

MIGHTY IN (BE)

ἐνεργέω, to be in work, *i.e.* to work, be effective, be effectually operative, be powerful *or* energetic in action

Gal. ii. 8.

MIGHTY DEED.

δύναμις, (*see* "MIGHT," *No.* 1.)

2 Cor. xii. 12.

MIGHTY MAN.

δυνατός, (*see above*, *No.* 3.)

Rev. vi. 15 (No. 1, G L T Tr A ℵ.)

MIGHTY WORK.

δύναμις, (*see* "MIGHT," *No.* 1.)

Matt. xi. 20, 21, 23.
—— xiii. 54, 58.
—— xiv. 2.
Mark vi. 2, 5, 14.
Luke x. 13.
—— xix. 37.

MIGHTY POWER.

μεγαλειότης, greatness, majesty.

Luke ix. 43.

MIGHTY (SO)

τηλικοῦτος, so great.

Rev. xvi. 18.

MIGHTY (THAT IS)

δυνατός, (*see above*, *No.* 3.)

Luke i. 49.

MILE.

μίλιον, a mile, *i.e. the Roman* milliare *or* mile, of 1000 paces, *whence its name.*

[It is usually estimated at 1611 yards, while the Eng. mile is 1760 yards,] (*non occ.*)

Matt. v. 41.

MILK.

γάλα, milk, (γάλα, γά-λακ-τος, *is the same as Lat.*, lac, *akin also to* α-μέλγ-ω, to milk, *Lat.*, melgere, *Eng.*, milk): (*non occ.*)

1. Cor. iii. 2.
—— ix. 7.
Heb. v. 12, 13.
1 Pet. ii. 2.

MILL.

μύλων, mill-house, place where the *μύλος*, (a grinder, millstone) is, (*non occ.*)

Matt. xxiv. 41 (*μύλος, a grinder, millstone,* L T Tr A ℵ.)

MILLSTONE.

1. *μύλος*, a grinder, *hence*, a millstone.

[Eastern mills consisted of two stones; the lower one was fixed, the upper being turned round upon it, with a hole in the middle for receiving the grain. This was generally turned by women, the larger ones by an ass; *hence* called *ὀνικος*, (pertaining to an ass),] *see No.* 3.

2. { *λίθος*, a stone, / *μυλικός*, of *or* belonging to } [a mill, } *non occ.*

3. { *μύλος*, a millstone, / *ὀνικός*, pertaining to an ass, } a large millstone, (*non occ.*)

3. Matt. xviii. 6. [T Tr A ℵ.)
2. Mark ix. 42 (No. 3, G ~ L
3. Luke xvii. 2 (No. 2, G ~ L T Tr A ℵ.)
1. Rev. xviii. 21 (*μύλινος, like a millstone,* L Tr A) (ℵ *λίθος*, in error.)
1. —— 22.

MIND. [noun.]

(*For various combinations with other words, see below.*)

1. *νοῦς*, *Eng.*, nous, the organ of mental perception and apprehension, the organ of conscious life; the organ of the consciousness preceding the act, or recognising and judging the fact. *It is gen.*, the organ of thinking and knowledge, *i.e.* the understanding; *or esp.*, the organ of moral thinking, *i.e.* contemplation. In the *N.T.* (except Luke xxiv. 45, and Rev. xiii. 18; xvii. 9), *it occurs only in Paul's Epistles, and is used of* the reflective consciousness, *as distinct from the impulse of the spirit apart from such consciousness.*"

[The *νοῦς* takes cognizance of external objects, and denotes the reasoning faculty. Its chief material organ is the brain, but all the senses serve it actively or passively. *νοῦς* is the human side of God's Spirit in man; as to its source, it is Spirit; as to its action in man for intellectual purposes it is mind, *i.e.* the product of the Spirit.]

2. *διάνοια*, a thinking through, mature thought; activity of thinking, *then*, the faculty of thought; the reflective exercise of the heart, consciousness called into exercise by the moral affections.

3. *ἔννοια*, what is in the *νοῦς* (*No.* 1), idea, notion, thought, intent, (*occ.* Heb. iv. 12.)

4. *νόημα*, the product of the action of the *νοῦς* (*No.* 1), that which is thought out, excogitated; purpose, project, device, the thoughts.

5. *ψυχή*, the breath, breath of animal life; one of the manifestations of *ζωή*, *viz.* that which is manifested in animals; *hence*, life, animal life, the living individual as such. *Hence*, it is used of the mind, as being one of the manifestations of life (*ζωή*.)

6. *γνώμη*, the decision formed, mind made up, resolution.

7. *φρόνημα*, what one has in mind, what one thinks and feels; *hence*, mind, thought, feeling, will; knowledge *or* wisdom, as being the product of the mind, (*occ.* Rom. viii. 6 twice.)

2. Matt. xxii. 37.
2. Mark xii. 30.
2. Luke x. 27.
5. Acts xiv. 2.
1. Rom. i. 28.
1. —— vii. 23, 25.
7. —— viii. 7, marg. *minding.*
7. —— —— 27.
1. —— xi. 34.
1. —— xii. 2.
1. —— xiv. 5.
1. 1 Cor. i. 10.
1. —— ii. 16 twice.
4. 2 Cor. iii. 14.
4. —— iv. 4.
4. —— xi. 3.
2. Eph. ii. 3.
1. —— iv. 17, 23.
5. Phil. i. 27.
4. —— iv. 7.
2. Col. i. 21.
1. —— ii. 18.
1. 2 Thes. ii. 2.
1. Tit. i. 15.
6. Philem. 14.
2. Heb. viii. 10.
2. —— x. 16.
5. —— xii. 3.
2. 1 Pet. i. 13.
3. —— iv. 1.
2. 2 Pet. iii. 1.
1. Rev. xvii. 9.
6. —— —— 13.

MIND (BE OF ONE)

{ *τὸ*, the, / *αὐτὸ*, same thing, / *φρονεῖτε*, be regarding or minding. } To have the same mind; *not merely* not to differ in council, but to seek the same object, (*occ.* Rom. xv. 5; Phil. iii. 16.)

2 Cor. xiii. 11.

MIND (BE OF THE SAME)

Same as above.

Rom. xii. 16. | Phil. iv. 2.

MIND BE IN YOU (LET THIS)

τοῦτο, this.
φρονεῖσθω, let [this] be regarded, (φρονεῖτε, be ye regarding, G ∾ L T Tr A ℵ.)
ἐν, in, (*not among*.)
ὑμῖν, you.

Phil. ii. 5.

MIND (CALL TO)

ἀναμιμνήσκω, to call up to memory, cause to remember.

Mark xiv. 72.

MIND (IN ONE'S RIGHT)

σωφρονέω, to be of sound mind.

Mark v. 15, part. | Luke viii. 35, part.

MIND (OF ONE)

ὁμόφρων, of the same mind, like minded, (*non occ.*)

1 Pet. iii. 8.

MIND (PUT IN)

1. ἐπαναμιμνήσκω, to call up the memory upon, *i.e.* to remind of, put in mind upon, (*non occ.*)
2. ὑπομιμνήσκω, to recall to one's memory, *privately*, *silently*, *by hints* or *suggestions*; to suggest to one's memory.

1. Rom. xv. 15. | 2. Tit. iii. 1.

MIND ON (set one's) [marg.]

φρονέω, to have mind, intellect; to mind, be minded; regard, care for.

Col. iii. 2, text, *set one's affection on.*

MIND (SOUND)

σωφρονισμός, a making of sound mind; *hence*, making sober-minded, controlling all inordinate desires by self restraint, (*non occ.*)

2 Tim. i. 7.

MIND (WITH ONE)

ὁμοθυμαδόν, with the same mind, with one accord, all together.

Rom. xv. 6.

See also CAST, CHANGE, DOUBTFUL, FERVENT, FORWARDNESS, HOSTILE, HUMBLENESS, HUMILITY, LOWLINESS, READINESS, READY, TROUBLE, WILLING.

MIND (-ING.) [verb.]

(*For various combinations, see below.*)

1. φρονέω, to have mind, intellect; to mind, be minded; regard, care for.
2. μέλλω, to be about to do *any thing*, to be on the point of.

2. Acts xx. 13.
1. Rom. viii. 5.
1. Rom. xii. 16.
1. Phil. iii. 16 (*ap.*), 19.

MIND THE SAME THING.

το αὐτὸ φρονεῖτε, *see* "M (BE OF ONE)"

Phil. iii. 16 (*ap.*)

MINDED (BE)

1. φρονέω, *see* "MIND," [verb] *No.* 1.
2. φρόνημα, *see* "MIND," [noun] *No.* 7.
3. βούλομαι, to will, be willing, wish, desire; a passive desire, propensity, *or* willingness.
4. βουλεύομαι, to take counsel, consult, deliberate *with one's self, or with one another in council.*

3. Matt. i. 19.
4. Acts xxvii. 39.
2. Rom. viii. 6 twice, marg. *minding.*
— — xv. 5, see Like.
3. 2 Cor. i. 15.
4. — 17, part (No. 3, G ∾ L Tr A ℵ.)
1. Gal. v. 10.
— Phil. ii. 2, 20, see Like.
1. Phil. iii. 15 twice.

MINDFUL OF (BE)

1. μιμνήσκω, to think much of a thing, *and so* to remember, to recall to one's mind, to begin to remember, remind. *Here, mid.*, to begin to call to mind, recollect, remember, (*see No.* 3.)
2. μνημονεύω, *act.*, to call to *another's* mind; mention; *pass.*, to be remembered, have in memory.
3. μνάομαι, to woo to wife, court, sue for, solicit.

(*The tenses of No.* 1 *are derived from this word, and probably the meanings were originally the same, for there is not much distance between* thinking much of *a thing, and* trying to get it; *gradually, however, the ideas separated, and so, though in Epic and Ionic Greek No.* 3 *was used in both senses, yet, later, No.* 1 *was confined to the former, and No.* 3 *to the latter.*)

3. 2 Tim. i. 4.
1. Heb. ii. 6.
2. Heb. xi. 15.
3. 2 Pet. iii. 2.

MINE.

(*See also* "MY," *and combinations below.*)

1. μοῦ, (*Gen. case of* ἐγώ, I) of me, mine.
2. ἐμοῦ, *another form of No.* 1.
3. μοί, (*Dat. case of* ἐγώ, I) to *or* for me.
4. ἐμοί, *another form of the No.* 3.
5. ἐμός, mine, *much more emphatic than the above;* mine, *denoting possession, power over, authorship, right, etc. As the possessive adjective, it has a greater emphasis than the personal pronoun above.*

1. Mark ix. 24.
1. Luke i. 44.
1. —— ii. 30.
3. —— ix. 38.
1. —— xviii. 3.
1. —— xix. 27.
1. John ii. 4.
5. —— v. 30.
5. —— vii. 16.
1. —— ix. 11, 15, 30.
5. —— x. 14.
5. —— xvi. 14, 15.
5. John xvii. 10 twice.
1. Acts xxi. 13.
1. Rom. xi. 13.
4. —— xii. 19.
2. —— xvi. 13.
1. —— 23.
5. 1 Cor. ix. 2, 3.
1. 2 Cor. xi. 30.
1. —— xii. 5 (om. L T Tr Ab.)
1. Phil. i. 4.
1. Rev. xxii. 16.

MINE OWN.

1. ἐμός, *see above, No.* 5.
2. μοῦ, *see above, No.* 1.
3. ἐμαυτοῦ, of mine own self.

1. Matt. xx. 15.
1. —— xxv. 27.
1. John v. 30.
1. —— vi. 38.
2. —— viii. 50.
2. Acts xiii. 22.
2. —— xxvi. 4.
1. 1 Cor. i. 15.
3. —— x. 33.
1. —— xvi. 21.
2. Gal. i. 14.
1. —— vi. 11.
1. Phil. iii. 9.
1. 2 Thes. iii. 17.
1. Philem. 12, 19.

MINE OWN SELF.

ἐμαυτοῦ, of mine own self.

John v. 30. | 1 Cor. iv. 3.

MINE (OF)

μοῦ, (*Gen. case of* ἐγώ, I) of me, mine.

Matt. vii. 24, 26. | Luke xi. 6.

MINGLE (-ED.)

μίγνυμι, to mix, mix up, mingle.

Matt. xxvii. 34.
Mark xv. 23, see Myrrh.
Luke xiii. 1.
Rev. viii. 7.
Rev. xv. 2.

MINISTER (-S.) [noun.]

1. ἄγγελος, messenger, *see* "ANGEL."
2. ἀπόστολος, *see* "APOSTLE."
3. διάκονος, *see* "DEACON."
4. λειτουργός, a server in an office *or* ministry. *In the O.T. used only of the Levites and priests. In the N.T. the word is extended to apostles, prophets, pastors, and teachers in the Church. It denotes not merely one who serves, but* one who worships.
5. ὑπηρετης, an under-rower *or* common sailor, *as distinguished from* ναῦται, seamen, *and* ἐπιβάται, mariners. *Hence,* a hand, any subordinate acting under the direction of another. An attendant in the synagogue.

1. Matt. xi. 10.
3. —— xx. 26.
1. Mark i. 2.
3. —— x. 43.
5. Luke i. 2.
5. —— iv. 20.
5. —— vii. 24, 27.
5. —— ix. 52.
5. Acts xiii. 5.
5. —— xxvi. 16.
3. Rom. xiii. 4 twice.
4. —— 6.
3. —— xv. 8.
4. —— 16.
3. 1 Cor. iii. 5.
5. —— iv. 1.
3. 2 Cor. iii. 6.
3. —— vi. 4.
2. —— viii. 23.
3. —— xi. 15 twice, 23.
1. —— xii. 7.
3. Gal. ii. 17.
4. Eph. iii. 7.
3. —— vi 21.
2. Phil. ii. 25.
3. Col. i. 7, 23, 25.
3. —— iv. 7.
3. 1 Thes. iii. 2 (ap.)
3. 1 Tim. iv. 6.
4. Heb. i. 7.
4. —— viii. 2.
1. Jas. ii. 25.

MINISTER (-ED, -ETH, -ING.) [verb.]

1. διακονέω, to serve, to render service, to wait upon. *In its narrowest sense,* to wait at table; *gen.,* to do

any one a service, care for one's needs, (*not to be subject to, this is* δουλεύω*; in* διακονέω, *there is always a reference to the work done, as* service rendered.)

2. { εἰς, unto, with a view to, / διακονία, service, (*noun, from No.* 1.) }

3. λειτουργέω, to perform some public service, *esp.*, *publicly in religious worship;* but also to serve the public *at one's own expense, gen.;* to serve, minister, worship, (*non occ.*)

4. ὑπηρετέω, to do the service of an ὑπηρέτης (*see the noun, No.* 3, *above*); *hence, gen.*, to act for another, and under his direction, to subserve, (*occ.* Acts xiii. 36.)

5. δίδωμι, to give, *of one's own accord and with good will.*

6. ἱερουργέω, to perform sacred rites, *esp.*, to sacrifice, to officiate as a priest, do priestly service, (*non occ.*)

7. παρέχω, to hold near *to any one*, offer; to occasion.

8. χορηγέω, to be chorus-leader, to lead a chorus of singers; *then*, to lead out *or* furnish a chorus *on public occasions; hence, gen.*, to furnish, supply, (*occ.* 1 Pet. iv. 11.)

— Matt. iv. 11, }
— —— viii. 15, } see M unto.
— —— xx. 28 1st, }
1. —— 28 2nd.
— —— xxv. 44, }
— —— xxvii. 55, } see M unto.
— Mark i. 13, 31, }
— —— x. 45 1st, }
1. —— 45 2nd.
— —— xv. 41, see M unto.
— Luke iv. 39, } see M
— —— viii. 3, } unto.
3. Acts xiii. 2, part.
— —— xix. 22, see M unto.
4. —— xx. 34.
4. —— xxiv. 23.
— Rom. xii. 7, see Ministering.
6. —— xv. 16.
— —— 25, see M unto.
3. —— 27.
— 1 Cor. ix. 13, see M about.
1. 2 Cor. iii. 3.
— 2 Cor. viii. 4, } see Minis-
— —— ix. 1, } tering.
— —— 10 1st, see M to.
8. —— 10 2nd.
— Gal. iii. 5, see M to.
5. Eph. iv. 29.
— Phil. ii. 25, see M (he that)
— Col. ii. 19, see M (have nourishment)
7. 1 Tim. i. 4.
1. —— iii. 13, marg. (text, *use the office of a deacon.*)
— 2 Tim. i. 18, } see M
— Philem. 13, } unto.
— Heb. i. 14 1st, see Ministering.
2. —— 14 2nd.
— —— vi. 10 1st, see M to.
1. —— 10 2nd.
3. —— x. 11.
1. 1 Pet. i. 12.
1. —— iv. 10, 11.

MINISTER ABOUT.

ἐργάζομαι, *intrans.*, to work, labour; *trans.*, to work, perform, practice, conduct *certain works.*

1 Cor. ix. 13.

MINISTER TO.

1. διακονέω, *see above, No.* 1.

2. ἐπιχορηγέω, (*No.* 8, *above, with* ἐπὶ, upon, *prefixed*) to furnish upon, *i.e.* besides, in addition, supply further, superadd.

2. 2 Cor. ix. 10.
1. Heb. vi. 10.
2. Gal. iii. 5.

MINISTER UNTO.

1. διακονέω, *see above. No.* 1.

2. επιχορηγέω, *see above, No.* 2.

1. Matt. iv. 11.
1. —— viii. 15.
1. —— xx. 28.
1. —— xxv. 44.
1. —— xxvii. 55.
1. Mark i. 13, 31.
1. —— x. 45.
1. Mark xv. 41.
1. Luke iv. 39.
1. —— viii. 3.
1. Acts xix. 22.
1. Rom. xv. 25.
1. 2 Tim. i. 18.
1. Philem. 13.
2. 2 Pet. i. 11.

MINISTERED (HAVE NOURISHMENT)

ἐπιχορηγέω, *see* "MINISTER TO," *No.* 2.

Col. ii. 19, pass.

MINISTERED (HE THAT)

λειτουργός, *see the noun, No.* 2.

Phil. ii. 25.

MINISTERING.

1. διακονία, service, attendance; any ministerial office with reference to the labour pertaining thereto.

2. λειτουργικός, pertaining to the public service, *esp.*, *of* the temple; *hence*, worshipping. *Hence*, Heb. i. 14 *reads*, "Are they not all worshipping spirits sent forth to serve, *etc.*"

1. Rom. xii. 7.
1. 2 Cor. viii. 4.
1. 2 Cor. ix. 1.
2. Heb. i. 14.

MINISTRATION.

1. διακονία, *see No.* 1, *above.*

2. λειτουργία, public service, public office; *esp.*, the public ministrations of the Jewish priesthood, and of the temple service, (*hence, the Eng. word,* Liturgy.)

2. Luke i. 23.
1. Acts vi. 1.
1. 2 Cor. iii. 7, 8, 9 twice.
1. —— ix. 13.

MINISTRY.

1. διακονία, *see* "MINISTERING," *No.* 1.

2. λειτουργία, *see* "MINISTRATION," *No.* 2.

1. Acts i. 17, 25.
1. —— vi. 4.
1. —— xii. 25, marg. *charge.*
1. —— xx. 24.
1. —— xxi. 19.
1. Rom. xii. 7.
1. 1 Cor. xvi. 15.
1. 2 Cor. iv. 1.
1. —— v. 18.
1. —— vi. 3.
1. Eph. iv. 12.
1. Col. iv. 17.
1. 1 Tim. i. 12.
1. 2 Tim. iv. 5, 11.
2. Heb. viii. 6.
2. Heb. ix. 21.

MINSTREL (-s.)

αὐλητής, a flute-player; a player on a pipe *or* flute, (*occ.* Rev. xviii. 22.)

Matt. ix. 23.

MINT.

ἡδύοσμον, sweet-scented; *hence,* garden *or* spear mint. [*The Rabbins called it* מינתא, mintha, and it was strewed by the Jews on the floors of their houses and synagogues.] (*non occ.*)

Matt. xxiii. 23. | Luke xi. 42.

MIRACLE (-s.)

1. σημεῖον, a sign, a signal; an ensign, a standard, a sign by which any thing is designated, distinguished, *or* known; *hence,* used of the miracles of Christ, as being the signs by which it might be known that He was the Christ of God; a sign authenticating Christ's mission; a sign with reference to what it demonstrates.

2. δύναμις, capability, power *to do any thing; then,* power, might *in action. In pl. applied to* the miracles of Christ, as effects wherein divine power was in a special sense put forth, unfolded, and manifested. A miracle *as wrought by divine power;* a work, *with reference to the power required for its performance.*

[τέρας, *translated* "wonder," is used of Christ's miracles as wonderful acts, with special reference to their supernatural character, and to their excitement of surprise. τεκήρια, (Acts i. 3) are evidences derived from logical deduction.]

2. Mark ix. 39.
1. Luke xxiii. 8.
1. John ii. 11, 23.
1. —— iii. 2.
1. —— iv. 54.
1. —— vi. 2, 14, 26.
1. —— vii. 31.
1. —— ix. 16.
1. —— x. 41.
1. —— xi. 47.
1. —— xii. 18, 37.
2. Acts ii. 22.
1. —— iv. 16, 22.
1. Acts vi. 8.
1. —— viii. 6.
2. —— 13.
1. —— xv. 12.
2. —— xix. 11.
2. 1 Cor. xii. 10, 28.
— —— 29, see M (workers of)
2. Gal. iii. 5.
2. Heb. ii. 4.
1. Rev. xiii. 14.
1. —— xvi. 14.
1. —— xix. 20.

MIRACLES (WORKERS OF)

δύναμαι, mighty works, (*see above, No.* 1.) *Here, some words must be supplied, e.g.* "doers of," *or* "are all in possession of miraculous powers."

1 Cor. xii. 29, marg. *power.*

MIRE.

βόρβορος, slime, mud, mire, *such as accumulates where animals are kept, hence,* dung, (*non occ.*)

2. Pet. ii. 22.

MISCHIEF.

ῥᾳδιουργία, ease *or* lightness of doing, levity in doing; recklessness, (*non occ.*)

Acts xiii. 10.

MISERABLE.

ἐλεεινός, finding pity *that succours; hence,* pitiable, piteous, (*non occ.*)

Rev. iii. 17.

MISERABLE (MOST)

1 Cor. xv. 19, comparative.

MISERABLY.

κακῶς, badly, grievously, *denoting the badness or the ill quality of the word with which it is combined.*

Matt. xxi. 41.

MISERY

ταλαιπωρία, hard work, severe labour, great bodily exertion; *hence,* bodily pain, hardship, trouble, misery, distress, (*non occ.*)

Rom. iii. 16. | Jas. v. 1.

MIST.

1. ἀχλύς, a mist *which shrouds objects from view*, (*non occ.*)
2. ζόφος, the gloom of the outer world, murkiness, thick gloom, (*occ.* 2 Pet. ii. 4; Jude 6, 13.)

1. Acts xiii. 11. | 2. 2 Pet. ii. 17.

MITE.

λεπτόν, lepton. *The name of* the smallest Jewish coin, *in value about* one-fourth of our farthing, (*non occ.*)

Mark xii. 42. | Luke xii. 59.
Luke xxi. 2.

MIXED WITH (BE)

συγκεράννυμι, to mix together, to mingle with; to temper, blend, (*occ.* 1 Cor. xii. 24.)

Heb. iv. 2, part. (marg. *be united with.*)

MIXTURE.

μίγμα, a mixture, compound, (*non occ.*)

John xix. 39.

MIXTURE (WITHOUT)

ἄκρατον, unmixed, *i.e.* pure, undiluted, (*non occ.*)

Rev. xiv. 10.

MOCK (-ED, -ING.)

1. ἐμπαίζω, to sport in, with, *or* against *any one; Lat.*, illudere; *Eng.*, illude *or* mock, *i.e.* to deride. *Also*, to delude, trick, deceive.
2. μυκτηρίζω, to turn up one's nose at *in scorn; hence*, to mock, deride, (*non occ.*)
3. χλευάζω, to jest, joke, scoff; to jeer at, (*non occ.*)

1. Matt. ii. 16.
1. —— xx. 19.
1. —— xxvii. 29, 31, 41.
1. Mark x. 34.
1. —— xv. 20, 31.
1. Luke xiv. 29.
1. —— xviii. 32.
1. Luke xxii. 63.
1. —— xxiii. 11, 36.
3. Acts ii. 13 (διαχλευάζω, *to jeer greatly*, G L T Tr A ℵ.)
3. —— xvii. 32.
2. Gal. vi. 7.

MOCKER (-S.)

ἐμπαίκτης, a mocker, scoffer, *spoken of impostors, false prophets, etc.*, (*occ.* 2 Pet. iii. 3.)

Jude 18.

MOCKING (-S.)

ἐμπαιγμός, derision, scoffing, mocking, (*non occ.*)

Heb. xi. 36.

MODERATE [adj.] (marg.)

ἀνθρώπινος, pertaining to man, human.

1 Cor. x. 13 (text, *common to man.*)

MODERATE (-ING.) [verb.] [marg.]

ἀνίημι, to send up *or* forth; to let go, relax, loosen; *hence*, to cease from.

Eph. vi. 9 (text, *forbearing.*)

MODERATION.

ἐπιεικής, fitting upon, *i.e.* fit, suitable, proper; *hence, neut.*, τὸ ἐπιεικές, propriety, moderation, consideration, (*i.e.* not insisting on just rights), forbearance.

Phil. iv. 5.

MODEST.

κόσμιος, well ordered, orderly, *i.e.* well behaved, discreet, decorous, (*non occ.*)

1 Tim. ii. 9.
—— iii. 9, marg. (text, *of good behaviour.*)

MOISTURE.

ἰκμάς, moisture *of any kind*, dampness (*non occ.*)

Luke viii. 6.

MOMENT.

1. ἄτομος, uncut, undissected, not divisible. *Eng.*, atom. *Spoken of time*, it denotes the smallest possible portion, (*non occ.*)
2. στιγμή, a prick, a point. *Of time*, an instant, (*non occ.*)

2. Luke iv. 5. | 1. 1 Cor. xv. 52.

MOMENT (BUT FOR A)

παραυτίκα, at this very instant, momentary, the briefest duration, transient.

2 Cor. iv. 17.

MONEY.

1. ἀργύριον, silver; *then*, money *in general; also, for* a piece of silver, *i.e.* a silver coin.

2. χρῆμα, something usable, what one can use; *hence*, money. *Once*, (*) *in sing., denoting* the price; *elsewhere plural*, money.

3. χαλκός, ore, metal *of any kind. Generally*, copper, *especially as wrought and tempered for use; hence*, copper coin, money.

4. κέρμα, a small piece, bit; *hence*, small coin, change.

5. νόμισμα, anything acknowledged and sanctioned by custom or law; *hence*, current money, currency.

— Matt. xvii. 24, see Tribute.
— —— 27, see M (piece of)
5. —— xxii. 19.
1. —— xxv. 18, 27.
1. —— xxviii. 12, 15.
3. Mark vi. 8.
3. —— xii. 41.
1. —— xiv. 11.
1. Luke ix. 3.
1. —— xix. 15, 23.
1. Luke xxii. 5.
— John ii. 14, see M (changer of)
4. —— 15.
2*. Acts iv. 37.
1. —— vii. 16.
2. —— viii. 18.
1. —— 20 1st.
2. —— 20 2nd.
2. —— xxiv. 26.
— 1 Tim. vi. 10, see M (love of)

MONEY (CHANGER OF)

κερματιστής, a money-changer.

[NOTE.—The annual tribute of each Jew to the Temple was a Jewish half-shekel (Ex. xxx. 13), and this, the money-changer in the outer court furnished to the people as they came up, in exchange for their Greek and Roman coins.] (*non occ.*)

John ii. 14.

MONEY (LOVE OF)

φιλαργυρία, love of silver, *i.e.* love of money, covetousness, (*non occ.*)

1 Tim. vi. 10.

MONEY (PIECE OF)

στατήρ, any weight; *esp.*, a coin of a certain weight, a stater, an Attic silver coin equal to about 3s. 6d. Later (in Philip's *time*), a gold stater = 16s. 3d.

Matt. xvii. 27, marg. *stater*.

MONEY-CHANGER (-s.)

κολλυβιστής, a small coin, change; *also*, the premium of exchange; *hence*, a money-changer, broker, *see* "M (changer of)," *above*, (*occ.* John ii. 15.)

Matt. xxi. 12. | Mark xi. 15.

MONTH (-s.)

μήν, a month, (*from Sanscr.* mâ, to measure, *and from this*, μήνη, the moon, *and Eng.*, moon, moneth, *or* month; *Germ.*, mond; *Lat.*, mensis), (*non occ.*)

Luke i. 24, 26, 36, 56.
—— iv. 25.
John iv. 35, see M (four)
Acts vii. 20.
—— xviii. 11.
—— xix. 8.
—— xx. 3.
Acts xxviii. 11.
Gal. iv. 10.
Heb. xi. 23, see M (three)
Jas. v. 17.
Rev. ix. 5, 10, 15.
—— xi. 2.
—— xiii. 5.
Rev. xxii. 2.

MONTHS (FOUR,

τετράμηνος, of four months, (*non occ.*)

John iv. 35.

MONTHS (THREE,

τρίμηνος, of three months. *Here, neut.*, τὸ τρίμηνον, three months, trimestre, (*non occ.*)

Heb. xi. 23.

MOON.

σελνη, the moon, (*prob. akin to* σέλας, light, brightness) (*non occ.*)

Matt. xxiv. 29.
Mark xiii. 24.
Luke xxi. 25.
Acts ii. 20.
1 Cor. xv. 41.
Col. ii. 16, see M (new)
Rev. vi. 12.
—— viii. 12.
—— xii. 1.
—— xxi. 23.

MOON (NEW)

νουμηνία, new month, *i.e.* the time of the new month *or* moon, as a festival, (*non occ.*)

Col. ii. 16.

MORE [adj. and adv.]

(*For various combinations with other words, see below.*)

1. μᾶλλον, (*adv., comp. of* μάλα, very, very much, exceedingly), more, more strongly; *also denoting constant increase*, more and more, still more; rather.

2. ἔτι, (*adv.*) yet, still, longer, ***implying duration, as to time; or accession, addition***, etc., yet further, besides.

3. πλείων, (*adj.*) more, ***not only of number, but gen. of bulk, (comp. of*** πολύς, many much,) ****plural.***

4. περισσός, (*adj.*) over and above, more than enough, superabundant.

5. περισσότερος, (*adj., comp. of No.* 4) more abundant.

6. ἄλλος, (*pronominal adj.*) other, ***denoting numerical (not generic) distinction.***

7. μείζων, (*adj., comp. of* μέγας, great, large, *of physical magnitude*) greater, larger.

8. ὑπέρ, (*prep.*) over. *Used adverbially* over *or* beyond.

4. Matt. v. 37, 47.
3. —— vi. 25.
1. —— 30.
1. —— vii. 11.
1. —— x. 25.
5. —— xi. 9.
1. —— xviii. 13.
2. —— 16.
3. —— xx. 10.
3*. —— xxi. 36.
6. —— xxv. 20.
3*. —— xxvi. 53.
3. Mark xii. 33 (No. 5, T
3. —— 43. [Tr ℵ.)
3. Luke iii. 13.
3. —— ix. 13.
1. —— xi. 13.
5. —— xii. 4 (No. 4, L.)
3. —— 23.
1. —— 24, 28.
3. —— xxi. 3.
3*. John iv. 1, 41.
3*. —— vii. 31.
1. —— xii. 43.
3. —— xv. 2.
3. —— xxi. 15.
1. Acts iv. 19.
1. —— xx. 35.
3*. —— xxiii. 13, 21.
3*. —— xxv. 6.
1. —— xxvii. 11.
1. Rom. v. 9, 10, 15, 17.
1. —— xi. 12, 24.
1. 1 Cor. xii. 22.
1. —— xiv. 18.
1. 2 Cor. iii. 9, 11.
5. —— x. 8.
8. —— xi. 23.
1. Gal. iv. 27.
1. Phil. i. 9 twice.
1. —— ii. 12.
1. —— iii. 4.
3. 2 Tim. ii. 16.
1. —— iii. 4.
1. Philem. 16.
3. Heb. iii. 3 twice.
2. —— viii. 12.
1. —— ix. 14.
2. —— x. 2, 17.
2. —— xi. 32.
1. —— xii. 25.
7. Jas. iv. 6.
3*. Rev. ii. 19.
2. —— iii. 12.
2. —— vii. 16.
2. —— ix. 12.
2. —— xviii. 21, 22 twice, 23 twice.
2. —— xx. 3.
2. —— xxi. 1, 4.
2. —— xxii. 3 (ἐκεῖ, *there*, G∾) (*om.* ℵ.)

MORE (FAR)

5. Heb. vii. 15.

MORE (have the) [marg.]

See "BETTER."

MORE (MUCH)

5. Luke vii. 26. | 5. Phil. i. 14, adv.

MORE (SO MUCH THE)

1. μᾶλλον, *see above, No.* 1.

2. { πολλῷ, more, / μᾶλλον, much, } much more.

3. { μᾶλλον, *see No.* 1, / περισσότερος, *see No.* 5, } exceeding more abundantly.

3. Mark vii. 36. | 1. Luke v. 15.
2. Luke xviii. 39.

MORE THAN.

1. { εἰ, if, / μή, not, } *i.e.* except.

2. ἐπάνω, up above, above, over; *of number*, more than.

3. ἤ, (*a disjunctive or comparative particle*) or, than, rather than, (*see a similar use in* Luke xvii. 2, and 1 Cor. xiv. 19.)

4. παρά, beside.

(a) *with Gen.*, from beside, (*used of persons.*)

(b) *with Dat.*, beside and at, at the side of.

(c) *with Acc.*, to *or* along the side of, beside, compared with, *so as to be shown*, beyond *or* contrary to.

5. ὑπέρ, over.

(a) *with Gen.*, over and separate from.

(b) *with Acc.*, over and towards, beyond, above, *used in comparison.*

5b. Matt. x. 37 twice.
1. Mark viii. 14.
2. —— xiv. 5.
5b. Philem. 21.
3. Luke xv. 7.
4c. Rom. i. 25.
4c. —— xii. 3.

MORE (THE)

1. μᾶλλον, *see* "MORE," *No.* 1.

2. μείζων, *see* "MORE," *No.* 7.

3. περισσότερος, *see* "MORE," *No.* 5.

4. περισσῶς, abundantly, exceedingly, *i.e. vehemently.*

5. πολύς, many, much. **** Here, pl., with art.***, the many.

6. ὅσος, how much, how great.

2. Matt. xx. 31.
4. —— xxvii. 23.
6. Mark vii. 36.
1. —— xiv. 31 (*om.* G ⇉ L T Tr A ℵ.)
3. Luke xii. 48.
1. John v. 18.
1. John xix. 8.
1. Acts v. 14.
1. —— ix. 22.
1. —— xxii. 2.
5. 1 Cor. ix. 19.
1. 2 Cor. vii. 7, 13.
1. Heb. x. 25.

MORE PART (THE)

πολύς, *see above, No.* 5.*

Acts xix. 32. | Acts xxvii. 12.

See also, ABOUND, ABUNDANCE, ABUNDANT, ABUNDANTLY, ANY, BOLDLY, CAREFULLY, CHEERFULLY, CONQUEROR, EARNESTLY, EXCEEDING, EXCEEDINGLY, EXCELLENT, FIERCE, FREQUENT, GIVE, HEED, HENCEFORTH, HOW, INCREASE, MANIFOLD, MISERABLE, NO, SPEAK, SPEND, TWOFOLD, VALUE, YET.

MOREOVER.

1. ἔτι, yet, still, *implying duration or accession.*
2. καί, and, also.
3. { αλλὰ, but, / καὶ, and, also, } nay! even, but also.
4. { δὲ, but, / και, and, also, } but also.
5. { δὲ, but, *marking an antithesis,* / ὁμοίως, in like manner, likewise, } but ... in like manner.
6. ὅ λοιπόν, as to the rest, finally.

3. Luke xvi. 21.
1. Acts ii. 26.
2. —— xix. 26.
6. 1 Cor. iv. 2.
4. 1 Tim. iii. 7.
5. Heb. ix. 21.
1. —— xi. 36.
4. 2 Pet. i. 15.

MORNING.

1. πρωΐ, early, early in the day, at morn; *gen.*, betimes, early, in good time: (*from* πρό, before, *Germ.*, früh, early; *Sanscr.*, prâhua, forenoon.)
2. πρωΐος, early, early in the day, morning; *also*, early in the year.
3. πρωϊνος, a later form of *No.* 2, (*non occ.*) (πρôινός, T.)
4. ὀρθρινός, at daybreak, in the morning early, (*non occ.*)

1. Matt. xv. 1.
2. —— xxvii. 1.
2. John xxi. 4.
1. Acts xxviii. 23.
3. Rev. ii. 28. [T Tr A ℵ.)
4. —— xxii. 16 (No. 3, G L

MORNING (COME EARLY IN THE)

ὀρθρίζω, to rise early, wake early; to do anything early in the morning, *or* at daybreak, (*non occ.*)

Luke xxi. 38.

MORNING (EARLY IN THE)

1. { ἅμα, with, / πρωΐ, *the* morning. }
2. ὄρθρος, the time before *or* about day-break, dawn, cock-crow, (*non occ.*)

1. Matt. xx. 1. | 2. John viii. 2 (*ap.*)
2. Acts v. 21.

MORNING (IN THE)

1. πρωΐ, *see* "MORNING," *No.* 1.
2. πρωΐος, *see* "MORNING," *No.* 2.

1. Matt. xvi. 3.
2. —— xxi. 18 (No. 1, T Tr ℵ.)
1. Mark i. 35.
1. —— xi. 20.
1. —— xiii. 35.

MORNING (VERY EARLY IN THE)

1. { λίαν, very, exceedingly, / πρωΐ, early in the morning. }
2. { ὄρθρου, the time before daybreak, / βαθέος, deep, profound, } deep twilight, earliest dawn.

1. Mark xvi. 2. | 2. Luke xxiv. 1.

MORROW.

αὔριον, to-morrow, *with art.*, the morrow.

Matt. vi. 34 twice.
Luke x. 35.
Acts iv. 5.
Jas. iv. 14.

MORROW (ON THE)

1. { τῇ, on the, / ἐπαύριον, upon the morrow. }
2. { τῇ, on the, / ἑξῆς, the next in order, } on the following [*day*.]

Mark xi. 12.
Acts x. 9, 23.
—— xx. 7.
Acts xxii. 30.
—— xxiii. 32.
—— xxv. 17.
Acts xxv. 23.

MORROW AFTER (THE)

1. Acts x. 24.

MORSEL. [marg.]

John xiii. 26, see Sop. | Heb. xii. 16, see Meat.

MORTAL.

θνητός, liable, *or* subject to death, mortal, (*occ.* 2 Cor. v. 4.)

Rom. vi. 12.
—— viii. 11.
1 Cor. xv. 53, 54.
2 Cor. iv. 11.

MORTALITY.

τὸ, the, θνητόν, mortal, } that which is mortal.

2 Cor. v. 4.

MORTIFY.

1. θανατόω, to put to death, to take away ζωή, the vital principle, (the *aspect being towards the lifelessness and powerlessness of that from which the life has been taken away.*)

2. νεκρόω, to make a dead body *or* a corpse, to make dead, (*the aspect being towards the corpse, and the deed by which it became such.*)

1. Rom. viii. 13. | 2. Col. iii. 5.

MOSES.

Μωσῆς, Moses, (*Hebrew*, משה, drawn out, *i.e. from the water*) the proper name of the great Hebrew prophet and legislator.

In all passages, except

John viii. 5 (*ap.*)

MOST.

1. πλείων, more, (*comp. of* πολύς, many, much) *properly of number, but also of magnitude and in comparison.*

2. πλεῖστος, the most, (*superl. of* πολύς, many, much) the greatest, *in N.T., only of number.*

2. Matt. xi. 20.
1. Luke vii. 42, 43, with art.

MOST (AT THE)

2. 1 Cor. xiv. 27, with art.

MOST OF ALL.

μάλιστα, (*superl. of* μάλα, very) most, most of all, especially.

Acts xx. 38.

See also, BELIEVED, EXCELLENT, GLADLY, HIGH, NOBLE, STRAITEST.

MOTE.

κάρφος, something dry, i.e. *any small dry particle, as of chaff, wood, or dust*, (*non occ.*)

Matt. vii. 3, 4, 5. | Luke vi. 41, 42 twice.

MOTH.

σής, a moth, clothes-moth, *which* eats woollen stuff, (*non occ.*)

Matt. vi. 19, 20. | Luke xii. 33.

MOTH-EATEN.

σητόβρωτος, moth-eaten, eaten by moths, (*non occ.*)

Jas. v. 2.

MOTHER (-s.)

1. μήτηρ, a mother, (*so Lat.*, mater; *Sanscr.*, mâtri; *Germ.*, mutter, etc.) (*non occ.*)

2. ἡ, the, *followed by Gen.*, the...of. *Here the word* μήτηρ *is understood.*

1. Matt. i. 18.
1. — ii. 11, 13, 14, 20, 21.
— — viii. 14, see Wife.
1. — x. 35, 37.
1. — xii. 46, 47, 48, 49, 50.
1. — xiii. 55.
1. — xiv. 8, 11.
1. — xv. 4 twice, 5 1st, 5 2nd (*ap.*)
1. — xix. 5, 12, 19, 29 (*ap.*)
1. — xx. 20.
1. — xxvii. 56 twice.
— Mark i. 30, see Wife.
1. — iii. 31, 32, 33, 34, 35.
1. — v. 40.
1. — vi. 24, 28.
1. — vii. 10 twice, 11, 12.
1. — x. 7, 19, 29, 30.
1. — xv. 40.
2. — xvi. 1.
1. Luke i. 15, 43, 60.
1. — ii. 33, 34, 43 (*ap.*), 48, 51.
— — iv. 38, see Wife.
1. Luke vii. 12, 15.
1. — viii. 19, 20, 21, 51.
1. — xii. 53 twice.
1. — xiv. 26.
1. — xviii. 20.
1. John ii. 1, 3, 5, 12.
1. — iii. 4.
1. — vi. 42.
1. — xix. 25 twice, 26 twice, 27.
1. Acts i. 14.
1. — iii. 2.
1. — xii. 12.
1. — xiv. 8.
1. Rom. xvi. 13.
1. Gal. i. 15.
1. — iv. 26.
1. Eph. v. 31.
1. — vi. 2.
— 1 Tim. i. 9, see M (murderer of)
1. — v. 2.
1. 2 Tim. i. 5.
— Heb. vii. 3, see M (without)

1. Rev. xvii. 5.

MOTHER (MURDERER OF)

μητραλῴας, a smiter of his mother, (*non occ.*)

1. Tim. i. 9.

MOTHER (WITHOUT)

ἀμήτωρ, without mother, motherless. *Spoken of those who have* lost the mother, *or of those who, with whatever meaning can be said* not to have had father or mother, *whether literally as in classic writers, of the gods, or improperly, of one whose parents are unknown.*

[The description of Melchisedek can be literally true of none except the λόγος of God (*see under* "WORD,")

who in reference to His humanity was ἀπάτωρ (without father), and in reference to His divinity was ἀμήτωρ (without mother).]

Heb. vii. 3.

MOTHER-IN-LAW.

πενθερά, a mother-in-law.

Matt. x. 35.
Luke xii. 53 twice.

MOTION (-s.)

πάθημα, what is suffered, suffering; *then*, any passion *or* affection of mind, emotion.

Rom. vii. 5, marg. *passion*.

MOUNT.

ὄρος, anything rising, a mountain, hill, height, chain of hills, (*prob. from* ὄρνυμι, to stir up, make arise.)

Matt. xxi. 1.
— xxiv. 3.
— xxvi. 30.
Mark xi. 1.
— xiii. 3.
— xiv. 26.
Luke xix. 29, 37.
— xxi. 37.
— xxii. 39.
John viii. 1 (*ap.*)
Acts i. 12.
— vii. 30, 38.
Gal. iv. 24, 25.
Heb. viii. 5.
— xii. 18 (om. L T Tr A ℵ.)
— — 22.
2 Pet. i. 18.
Rev. xiv. 1.

MOUNTAIN.

ὄρος, *see* "MOUNT."

Matt. iv. 8.
— v. 1.
— viii. 1.
— xiv. 23.
— xv. 29.
— xvii. 1, 9, 20.
— xviii. 12.
— xxi. 21.
— xxiv. 16.
— xxviii. 16.
Mark iii. 13.
— v. 5.
— — 11 (om. G→ℵ.)
— vi. 46.
— ix. 2, 9.
— xi. 23.
— xiii. 14.
Luke iii. 5.
— iv. 5 (*ap.*)
— vi. 12.
— viii. 32.
— ix. 28.
— xxi. 21.
— xxiii. 30.
John iv. 20, 21.
— vi. 3, 15.
1 Cor. xiii. 2.
Heb. xi. 38.
— xii. 20.
Rev. vi. 14, 15, 16.
— viii. 8.
— xvi. 20.
— xvii. 9.
— xxi. 10.

MOURN (-ED.)

1. πενθέω, to bewail, lament, mourn for, *esp.*, *for one dead.*
2. θρηνέω, to sing a dirge, to wail.
3. κόπτω, to beat, to cut *by a blow; here, mid.*, to beat or cut one's self, *i.e. the breast, in loud expression of grief.*

1. Matt. v. 4.
1. — ix. 15.
3. — xxiv. 30.
2. Mark vi. 17. [(*ap.*)
1. — xvi. 10 part.
1. Luke vi. 25.
2. — vii. 32.
1. 1 Cor. v. 2.
1. Jas. iv. 9.
1. Rev. xviii. 11.

MOURNING.

1. ὀδυρμός, a complaining, lamenting.
2. πένθος, bewailing, grief, *esp.*, *for the dead.*

1. Matt. ii. 18.
1. 2 Cor. vii. 7.
2. Jas. iv. 9.
2. Rev. xviii. 8.

MOUTH (-s.)

1. στόμα, the mouth; *hence*, also, speech, speaking. *Applied also to* any opening in the shore or the earth, (*occ.* Luke xxi. 24; Heb. xi. 34; 2 John 12; 3 John 14.)
2. λόγος, the word *spoken, not written; then*, that which is spoken, etc.

1. Matt. iv. 4.
1. — v. 2.
1. — xii. 34.
1. — xiii. 35.
1. — xv. 8 (*ap.*), 11 twice, 17, 18.
1. — xvii. 27.
1. — xviii. 16.
1. — xxi. 16.
1. Luke i. 64, 70.
1. — iv. 22.
1. — vi. 45.
1. — xi. 54.
1. — xix. 22.
1. — xxi. 15.
1. — xxii. 71.
1. John xix. 29.
1. Acts i. 16.
1. — iii. 18, 21.
1. — iv. 25.
1. — viii. 32, 35.
1. — x. 34.
1. — xi. 8.
1. — xv. 7.
2. — — 27.
1. — xviii. 14.
1. — xxii. 14.
1. Acts xxiii. 2.
1. Rom. iii. 14, 19.
1. — x. 8, 9, 10.
1. — xv. 6.
1. 2 Cor. vi. 11.
1. — xiii. 1.
1. Eph. iv. 29.
1. — vi. 19.
1. Col. iii. 8.
1. 2 Thes. ii. 8.
1. 2 Tim. iv. 17.
— Tit. i. 11, see M of (stop the)
1. Heb. xi. 33.
1. Jas. iii. 3, 10.
1. 1 Pet. ii. 22.
1. Jude 16.
1. Rev. i. 16.
1. — ii. 16.
1. — iii. 16.
1. — ix. 17, 18, 19.
1. — x. 9, 10.
1. — xi. 5.
1. — xii. 15, 16 twice.
1. — xiii. 2, 5, 6.
1. — xiv. 5.
1. — xvi. 13 3 times.
1. Rev. xix. 15, 21.

MOUTH OF (STOP THE)

ἐπιστομίζω, to put upon the mouth, *i.e.* to stop the mouth *with a bit or curb; hence*, to check, to curb, (*non occ.*)

Titus i. 11.

MOVE (-ED.)

(*For various combinations with other words, see below.*)

1. κίνεω, to set in motion: *then, simply* to move. * *mid.*, to move one's self.
2. σείω, to move to and fro, shake, *with the idea of shock, concussion.*

3. *ἀνασείω*, (*No.* 2, *with ἀνά*, up *or* back, *prefixed*) to shake back, swing to and fro, brandish, *esp.*, to make threatening gestures, *and so*, stir up, persuade, (*occ.* Luke xxiii. 5.)

4. *σαλεύω*, to make to shake, rock, to put into a state of waving, rocking *or* vibratory motion, to agitate.

5. *σαίνω*, to wag the tail, fawn, flatter, to deceive through flattery, (*non occ.*) *The sense here is*, that no one should be deceived or deluded in the midst of the persecutions by the suggestions of seeming well-wishers.

6. *φέρω*, to bear, carry, bear along.

2. Matt. xxi. 10.
1. —— xxiii. 4.
3. Mark xv. 11.
4. Acts ii. 25.
1*.—— xvii. 28.
— —— xx. 24, see M me (none of these things)
1. Acts xxi. 30.
— Col. i. 23, see M away.
5. 1 Thes. iii. 3.
— Heb. xii. 28, see Moved (which cannot be)
6. 2 Pet. i. 21, part.
1. Rev. vi. 14.

MOVE AWAY.

μετακινέω, (*No.* 1, *with μετά*, *implying* change, *prefixed*) to move from one place to another, remove, (*non occ.*)

Col. i. 23.

MOVE ME (NONE OF THESE THINGS)

{ *οὐδείς*, not one, *λόγος*, a word, account, *ποιέω*, to make, } "I am making of no account," etc.; *or* "by no single word am I making," etc.

Acts xx. 24.

MOVED (WHICH CANNOT BE)

ἀσάλευτος, (*from No.* 4, *above*) that cannot shake, rock, *or* vibrate, unshakable, (*occ.* Acts xxvii. 41.)

Heb. xii. 28.

See also, COMPASSION, ENVY, FEAR, INDIGNATION.

MOVER OF.

κίνεω, *see* "MOVE," *No.* 1. *Here, participle.*

Acts xxiv. 5.

MOVING.

κίνησις, a moving, a being moved, *as opp. to repose*; a movement, disturbance, (*non occ.*)

John v. 3 (*ap.*)

MUCH. [adj. and adv.]

(*For various combinations with other words, see below.*)

1. *πολύς*, many, much, *of number, quantity, or amount.*

(a) *plural*, many. * *with art.*, the many.

2. *ἱκανός*, coming to, reaching to, *and hence*, sufficing; *of things*, enough; *of number or magnitude*, abundant, great, much.

1. Matt. vi. 30.
1. —— xiii. 5.
1. —— xxvi. 9.
1a. Mark i. 45.
1. —— iv. 5.
1a.—— v. 10.
1. ——— 21, 24.
1 —— vi. 34.
1. Luke vii. 11.
2. ——— 12.
1. ——— 47.
1. —— viii. 4.
1 —— ix. 37.
1. —— x. 40.
1a.—— xii. 19.
1. ——— 48 3 times.
1. —— xvi. 10 twice
1a. John iii. 23.
1. —— vi. 10.
1. —— vii. 12.
1. —— xii. 9, 12, 24.
1a.——xiv. 30.
1. —— xv. 5, 8.
2. Acts v. 37 (om. G→L Tr A ℵ.)
1a.—— x. 2.
2. —— xi. 24, 26.
1a.—— xiv. 22.
1. —— xv. 7.
1. —— xvi. 16.
1. —— xviii. 10, 27.
2. Acts xix. 26.
1a*—— xxvi. 24.
2. —— xxvii. 9.
1. ——— 10.
1. Rom. iii. 2.
1. —— v. 10, 15, 17.
1. —— ix. 22.
1a*—— xv. 22, marg. *many ways or oftentimes*; (*πολλάκις*, *many times*, L Trm.)
1a. —— xvi. 6, 12 (*ap.*)
1. 1 Cor. ii. 3.
1. —— xii. 22.
1a.—— xvi. 19.
1. 2 Cor. ii. 4.
1. —— iii. 9, 11.
1. —— vi. 4.
1. —— viii. 4, 15, 22.
1. Phil. ii. 12.
1. 1 Thes. i. 5, 6.
1. —— ii. 2.
1. 1 Tim. iii. 8.
1a. 2 Tim. iv. 14.
1. Tit. ii. 3.
1. Heb. xii. 9, 25.
1. Jas. v. 16.
1. 1 Pet. i. 7.
1a. Rev. v. 4 (*πολύ*, *much*, G∾L T Tr A ℵ.)
1a.—— viii. 3.
1. Rev. xix. 1.

MUCH AS.

{ *τὰ*, the, *ἴσα*, equivalent *things*. }

Luke vi. 34.

MUCH AS IN ME IS (AS)

{ *τὸ*, the, *κατὰ*, according to. *ἐμέ*, me. }

Rom. i. 15.

MUCH AS IN YOU IS (as) [marg.]

{ τὸ, the, / ἐν, in, among, / ὑμίν, you, } the...among you, *or* the...in you.

1 Pet. v. 2, text, *which is among you.*

MUCH AS LIETH IN YOU (AS)

{ τὸ, the. / ἐξ, out of, from. / ὑμῶν, of you. }

Rom. xii. 18.

MUCH AS (NOT SO)

1. οὐδέ, and not, also not, *denying absolutely and objectively;* not even.

2. { ἀλλά, but, / οὐδέ, not, } not even.

1. Luke vi. 3. | 2. Acts xix. 2.
1. 1 Cor. v. 1.

MUCH AS (NO...)

οὐδέ, *see above, No.* 1.

Mark vi. 31.

MUCH AS (NO, NOT SO)

μηδέ, not even.

Mark ii. 2.

MUCH (SO)

τοσοῦτος, so great, so much.

Matt. xv. 33.
Acts v. 8 twice.
Heb. i. 4.
Heb. vii. 22
—— x. 25.
Rev. xviii. 7.

MUCH AS (AND IF SO)

κἄν, and if.

Heb. xii. 20.

MUCH AS (SO)

μητέ, not even.

Mark iii. 20 (μηδέ, L Tr A.)

See also, ABOUND, BETTER, BOLD, DISPLEASED, EXHORTATION, GRACED, HOW, MORE, PERPLEXED, SO, SPEAKING, WANTONNESS, WORK.

MULTIPLY (-ED, -ING.)

πληθύνω, to make full; *hence,* to multiply, increase. * *Pass.,* to be multiplied, increased, (*occ.* Matt. xxiv. 12.)

Acts vi. 1, see M (be)
—— 7*.
—— vii. 17*.
—— ix. 31.
—— xii. 24*.
2 Cor. ix. 10.
Heb. vi. 14 twice.
1 Pet. i. 2.
2 Pet. i. 2.
Jude 2.

MULTIPLIED (BE)

Acts vi. 1, part.

MULTITUDE (-S.)

1. ὄχλος, a confused multitude, a throng of people, *esp.,* the populace, mob; *Lat.,* turba. *Opp. to* δῆμος, the people; *Lat.,* populus *or* plebs; (*hence,* the noise made by such a crowd, riot, tumult) a tumultuous multitude.

2. πλῆθος, fulness, a great number, a throng *or* crowd, (*the only reference being to its* numbers, *not to its character as No.* 1,) (*occ.* Luke xxiii. 27; Acts xxviii. 3.

1. Matt. iv. 25.
1. —— v. 1.
1. —— viii. 1, 18.
1. —— ix. 8, 33, 36.
1. —— xi. 7.
1. —— xii. 15 (*om.* L Tr[b] A[b] ℵ.)
1. —— xiii. 2 twice, 34, 36.
1. —— xiv. 5, 14, 15, 19 twice, 22, 23.
1. —— xv. 10, 30, 31, 32, 33, 35, 36, 39.
1. —— xvii. 14.
1. —— xix. 2.
1. —— xx. 29, 31.
1. —— xxi. 8, 9, 11, 46.
1. —— xxii. 33.
1. —— xxiii. 1.
1. —— xxvi. 47, 55.
1. —— xxvii. 20, 24.
1. Mark ii. 13.
2. —— iii. 7, 8.
1. ———— 9, 20, 32.
1. —— iv. 1 twice, 36.
1. —— v. 31.
1. —— vii. 33.
1. —— viii. 1, 2.
1. —— ix. 14, 17.
1. —— xiv. 43.
1. —— xv. 8.
2. Luke i. 10.
2. —— ii. 13.
1. —— iii. 7.
2. —— v. 6.
1. ———— 15, 19.
2. —— vi. 17.
1. ———— 19.
2. —— viii. 37.
1. ———— 45.
1. Luke ix. 12, 16.
— —— xii. 1, see M (an innumerable)
1. —— xiv. 25.
1. —— xviii. 36.
2. —— xix. 37.
1. ———— 39.
1. —— xxii. 6, marg. tu- [mult.
1. ———— 47.
2. —— xxiii. 1.
2. John v. 3.
1. ———— 13.
1. —— vi. 2.
2. —— xxi. 6.
2. Acts ii. 6.
2. —— iv. 32.
2. —— v. 14, 16.
2. —— vi. 2, 5.
1. —— xiii. 45.
2. —— xiv. 1, 4.
2. —— xv. 12, 30.
1. —— xvi. 22.
2. —— xvii. 4.
2. —— xix. 9.
1. ———— 33.
2. —— xxi. 22.
1. ———— 34.
2. ———— 36.
2. —— xxiii. 7.
1. —— xxiv. 18.
2. —— xxv. 24.
— Eph. iv. 8, see Captives.
2. Heb. xi. 12.
2. Jas. v. 20.
2. 1 Pet. iv. 8.
1. Rev. vii. 9.
1. —— xvii. 15.
1. —— xix. 6.

MULTITUDE (AN INNUMERABLE)

υριάς, a myriad, (*i.e.* ten thousand.) *Here, plural,* tens of thousands. *Put for any indefinitely large number.*

Luke xii. 1.

MURDER (-S.)

φόνος, a killing *of* men, murder, (*occ.* Acts ix. 1.)

Matt. xv. 19.
— xix. 18, see M [(do)
Mark vii. 21.
— xv. 7.
Luke xxiii. 19, 25.
Rom. i. 29.
Gal. v. 21 (*om.* Lb T Trb [AbＮ.)
Rev. ix. 21.

MURDER (DO)

φονεύω, to kill a person, to slay, to murder.

Matt. xix. 18.

MURDERER (-S.)

1. φονεύς, a murderer.

2. ἀνθρωποκτόνος, murdering men. *In No.* 1 *the emphasis is on* the killing; *in No.* 2 *upon the fact that it is* men, (*see* "MAN," *No.* 1) *who are killed,* (*non occ.*)

3. { ἀνήρ, a man, (*see* "MAN," *No.* 2,) φονεύς, a murderer, } a man, a murderer.

1. Matt. xxii. 7.
2. John viii. 44.
3. Acts iii. 14.
1. — vii. 52.
1. — xxviii. 4.
— 1 Tim. i. 9, see Father and Mother.
1. 1 Peter iv. 15.
2. 1 John iii. 15 twice.
1. Rev. xxi. 8.
1. Rev. xxii. 15.

MURDERER (THAT IS A)

σικάριος, a dagger-man, assassin, (*Lat.,* sicarius, *from* sica, a dagger) *non occ.*

Acts xxi 38.

MURMUR (-ED.)

1. γογγύζω, to murmur, prob. the murmuring sound of air in a shell, (κόγχη) to utter in a low voice, privately; *and because such murmurings are generally complaints, it denotes* to manifest discontent, (*non occ.*)

(a) *Trans.* (b) *Intrans.*

2. διαγογγυζω, (*No.* 1, *with* διά, through, *or* throughout, *prefixed*) to keep on murmuring, (*non occ.*)

1b. Matt. xx. 11.
— Mark xiv. 5, see M against.
1b. — v. 30.
2. Luke xv. 2.
2. Luke xix. 7.
1b. John vi. 41, 43, 61.
1a. — vii. 32.
1b. — 41, 43, 61.
1b. 1 Cor. x. 10 twice.

MURMUR AGAINST.

ἐμβριμάομαι, to express indignation against *any one,* admonish sternly, to threaten with one's indignation.

Mark xiv. 5.

MURMURER (-S.)

γογγυστής, a murmurer, (*see the verb No.* 1, *above*) (*non occ.*)

Jude 16.

MURMURING (-S.)

γογγυσμός, a murmuring, (*see the verb, No.* 1, *above*) (*occ.* 1 Pet. iv. 9.)

John vii. 12.
Acts vi. 1.
Phil. ii. 14.

MUSE (-ED.)

διαλογίζομαι, to reckon through.

Luke iii. 15, marg. *reason or debate.*

MUSIC.

συμφωνία, a sounding together, concert *of instruments.* Eng., symphony, (*non occ.*)

Luke xv. 25.

MUSICIAN (-S.)

μουσικός, devoted to the muses, *i.e.* to the liberal arts and sciences; learned. In *N.T.,* skilled in music a musician, (*non occ.*)

Rev. xviii. 22.

MUST.

1. δεῖ, it needs, there is need of *something absent or wanting;* it needs, it is necessary, one must, it ought.

2. ἵνα, in order that.

1. Matt. xvi. 21.
1. —— xvii. 10.
1. —— xxiv. 6.
1. —— xxvi. 54.
1. Mark viii. 31.
1. —— ix. 11.
1. —— xiii. 10.
2. —— xiv. 49.
1. Luke ii. 49.
1. —— iv. 43.
1. —— ix. 22.
1. —— xiii. 33.
1. —— xvii. 25.
1. —— xix. 5.
1. —— xxi. 9.
1. —— xxii. 7, imperf.
1. —— 37.
1. —— xxiv. 7, 44.
1. John iii. 7.
1. —— 14 (om. Lm.)
1. —— 30.
1. —— iv. 24.
1. —— ix. 4.
1. —— x. 16.
1. —— xii. 34.
1. —— xx. 9.
1. Acts i. 22.
1. —— iii. 21.
1. —— iv. 12.
1. —— ix. 6, 16.
1. —— xiv. 22.
1. —— xvi. 30.
1. —— xviii. 21 (ap.)
1. —— xix. 21.
1. —— xxiii. 11.
1. —— xxvii. 24, 26.
1. 1 Cor. xi. 19.
1. —— xv. 25, 53.
1. 2 Cor. v. 10.
1. 1 Tim. iii. 2, 7.
1. 2 Tim. ii. 6, 24.
1. Tit. i. 7, 11.
1. Heb. ix. 26, imperf.
1. —— xi. 6.
— 1 Pet. iv. 17, see M (that...)
1. Rev. i. 1.
1. —— iv. 1.
1. —— x. 11.
1. —— xi. 5.
1. —— xiii. 10.
1. —— xx. 3.

1. Rev. xxii. 6.

MUST (THAT...)

τοῦ, of the, ***with inf.**, **here***, "of the to begin, *i.e.* to begin *or* make a beginning.

1 Pet. iv. 17.

See also, NECESSITY, NEEDS, PUT.

MUSTARD-SEED.

σίναπι, sinapis orientalis, mustard, *a plant often growing in Palestine to a considerable size.* κόκκον σινάπεως, a grain of mustard, *is a proverbial phrase for* the smallest particle.

Matt. xiii. 31.
—— xvii. 20.
Mark iv. 31.
Luke xiii. 19.
Luke xvii. 6.

MUTUAL.

{ ἐν, in.
{ ἀλλήλων, each other, one another.

Rom. i. 12.

MUZZLE.

φιμόω, to muzzle.

1 Cor. ix. 9. | 1 Tim. v. 18.

MY.

1. **μοῦ**, *Gen. sing. of* ἐγώ, I; of me.

2. **ἐμοῦ**, *another form of No.* 1.

3. { **παρά**, from beside,
{ **ἐμοῦ**, me.

4. **μοί**, *Dat. sing. of* ἐγώ, I; to me.

5. **ἐμοί**, *another form of No.* 4.

6. **ἐμός**, mine, denoting possession, power over, authorship, right, etc. *As the possessive adjective it has a greater emphasis than the cases of the personal pronoun above.*

1. Matt. ii. 6, 15.
1. —— iii. 17.
2. —— v. 11.
1. —— vii. 21.
1. —— viii. 6, 8 twice, 9, 21.
1. —— ix. 18.
2. —— x. 18.
1. —— 22, 32, 33.
2. —— 39.
1. —— xi. 10, 27, 29, 30 twice.
1. —— xii. 18 4 times, 44, 48 twice, 49 twice, 50 twice.
1. —— xiii. 30, 35.
1. —— xv. 13, 22.
1. —— xvi. 17, 18.
2. —— 25.
1. —— xvii. 5, 15.
1. —— xviii. 5, 10, 19.
6. —— 20.
1. —— 21, 35.
1. —— xix. 20 (om. G→L T Tr A ℵ.)
1. —— 29.
1. —— xx. 21, 23 1st & 2nd.
1. —— 23 3rd (om. G⇄L T Tr A ℵ.)
1. —— 23 4th.
1. —— xxi. 13.
1. —— 28 (om. G⇄T Tr A ℵ.)
1. —— 37.
1. —— xxii. 4 twice.
1. —— xxiv. 5, 9, 35.
1. —— 36 (om. G L T Tr Ab ℵ.)
1. —— 48.
1. —— xxv. 27, 34.
1. —— 40 (om. Lb.)
1. —— xxvi. 12 1st.
— —— 12 2nd, see M burial.
1. —— 18 twice, 26, 28, 29.
1. —— 38.
1. —— 39 (om. T Trb.)
1. —— 42, 53.
1. —— xxvii. 35 twice (ap.)
1. —— 46 twice.
1. —— xxviii. 10.
1. Mark i. 2, 11.
1. —— iii. 33 1st.
1. —— 33 2nd (om. T Trb A.)
1. —— 34 twice, 35 1st.
1. —— 35 2nd (om. L T Tr A ℵ.)
4. —— v. 9.
1. —— 23, 30.
1. —— vi. 23.
2. —— viii. 35.
6. —— 38.
1. —— ix. 7, 17, 37, 39.
1. —— 41 (om. G L T Tr A.)
1. —— x. 20.
2. —— 29.
1. —— 40 1st.
1. —— 40 2nd (om. G L T Tr A ℵ.)
1. —— xi. 17.
1. —— xii. 6, 36 twice.
1. —— xiii. 6.
2. —— 9.
1. —— 13, 31.
1. Mark xiv. 8, 14, 22, 24, 34.
1. —— xv. 34 twice.
1. —— xvi. 17 (ap.)
1. Luke i. 18, 20, 25, 43, 44, 46, 47 twice.
1. —— ii. 49.
1. —— iii. 22.
1. —— vi. 47.
1. —— vii. 6, 7, 8, 27.
1. —— 44 1st (No. 4, T Tr A.)
1. —— 44 2nd, 45, 46 1st.
1. —— 46 2nd (om. G→)
1. —— viii. 21 twice.
2. —— ix. 24.
6. —— 26.
1. —— 35, 38, 48, 59, 61.
1. —— x. 22, 29, 40.
1. —— xi. 7, 24.
1. —— xii. 4, 13, 17, 18 1st.
1. —— 18 2nd (om. Tr Ab.)
1. —— 18 3rd, 19, 45.
1. —— xiv. 23, 24, 26, 27, 33.
1. —— xv. 6, 17, 18, 24, 29.
1. —— xvi. 3, 5, 24, 27.
1. —— xviii. 21 (om. T Trb A.)
1. —— xix. 8, 23, 46.
1. —— xx. 13, 42 twice.
1. —— xxi. 8, 12, 17, 33.
1. —— xxii. 11, 19, 20, 28, 29.
1. —— 30 twice, 42.
1. —— xxiii. 46.
1. —— xxiv. 39 twice, 49.
1. John ii. 16.
6. —— iii. 29.
6. —— iv. 34.
1. —— v. 17, 24, 31, 43.
6. —— 47.
1. —— vi. 32, 51, 54 twice, 55 twice, 56 twice.
1. —— 65 (om. G⇄L T Tr A ℵ.)
6. —— vii. 6, 8, 16.
1. —— viii. 14.
6. —— 16.
1. —— 19 twice.
1. —— 28 (om. L T Tr A ℵ.)
6. —— 31 1st.
1. —— 31 2nd.
6. —— 37.
1. —— 38 (om. G⇄L T Tr A.)
6. —— 43 twice.
1. —— 49.
6. —— 51.
1. —— 52, 54 twice.
6. —— 56.
6. —— x. 14.
1. —— 15, 16, 17, 18, 25.
6. —— 26, 27 1st.
1. —— 27 2nd, 28, 29 1st.
1. —— 29 2nd (om. T Trb A ℵ.)
1. —— 32 (om. Lb T Trb A ℵ.)
1. —— 37.
1. —— xi. 21, 32.
1. —— xii. 7.
6. —— 26.

1. John xii. 27, 47, 48.
1. —— xiii. 6, 8, 9.
6. —— 35.
1. —— 37.
2. —— 38.
1. —— xiv. 2, 7.
1. —— 12 (om. G ⇉ L T Tr A ℵ.)
1. —— 13, 14.
6. —— 15.
1. —— 20, 21 twice, 23 twice, 24, 26.
6. —— 27.
1. —— 28 (om. G → Lb T Tr A.)
1. —— xv. 1, 7, 8 1st.
6. —— 8 2nd, 9.
1. —— 10 1st & 2nd.
1. —— 10 3rd (om. L A.)
6. —— 11, 12.
1. —— 14, 15, 16, 20, 21, 23, 24.
1. —— xvi. 10 (om. G ⇉ T Tr Ab ℵ), 23, 24, 26.
6. —— xvii. 13, 24.
6. —— xviii. 36 4 times.
1. —— 37.
1. —— xix. 24 twice.
1. —— xx. 13.
1. —— 17 1st (om. Lb T Tr A.)
1. —— 17 2nd, 3rd, & 4th.
1. —— 25 twice, 27 twice, 28 twice.
1. —— xxi. 15, 16, 17.
1. Acts ii. 14, 17, 18 3 times, 25 twice, 26 3 times, 27, 34 twice.
1. —— vii. 34.
4. —— 49 1st.
1. —— 49 2nd & 3rd, 50, 59.
1. —— ix. 15, 16.
1. —— x. 30.
1. —— xi. 8.
1. —— xiii. 22, 33.
1. —— xv. 7, 17.
— —— 19, see Sentence.
1. —— xvi. 15.
1. —— xx. 24 1st (om. G ⇉ L T Tr A ℵ.)
1. —— 24 2nd, 25, 29, 34.
1. —— xxii. 1.
1. —— xxiv. 17.
1. —— xxvi. 4.
1. —— xxviii. 19.
1. Rom. i. 8, 9 3 times.
1. —— ii. 16.
6. —— iii. 7.
1. —— vii. 4, 18, 23 3 times.
1. —— ix. 1, 2, 3 twice, 17 twice, 25 twice, 26.
6. —— x. 1.
1. —— 21.
1. —— xi. 3, 14.
3. —— 27.
1. —— xv. 14, 31.
1. —— xvi. 3, 4, 5, 7 twice, 8, 9, 11, 21 twice, 25.
1. 1 Cor. i. 4, 11.
1. —— ii. 4 twice.
1. —— iv. 14, 17 twice.
6. —— v. 4.
6. —— vii. 40.
1. —— viii. 13 twice.
1. —— ix. 1. 15.
4. —— 18 1st (No. 1, T Tr A ℵ.)
1. —— 18 2nd, 27.
1. —— x. 14, 29.
1. —— xi. 24.
6. —— 25.
1. —— 33.
1. —— xiii. 3 twice.
1. —— xiv. 14 twice.
1. —— 18 (om. G L T Tr A ℵ.)
1. —— 19.
1. 1 Cor. xv. 58.
6. —— xvi. 18.
1. —— 24.
6. 2 Cor. i. 23.
6. —— ii. 3.
1. —— 13 twice.
4. —— vi. 16 (No. 1, L T Tr ℵ.)
4. —— 18.
4. —— vii. 4 twice.
6. —— viii. 23.
1. —— xii. 9 1st.
1. —— 9 2nd (om. G → L T A ℵ.)
1. —— 9 3rd, 21.
6. Gal. i. 13.
1. —— 14, 15.
1. —— iv. 14 1st (om. G ∾) (ὑμῶν, your, L T Tr A ℵ.)
1. —— 14 2nd, 19, 20.
1. —— vi. 17.
1. Eph. i. 16.
1. —— iii. 4, 13, 14.
1. —— vi. 10 (om. G → L T Tr A ℵ.)
1. —— 19.
— —— 21, see M affairs.
1. Phil. i. 3, 7 1st.
1. —— 7 2nd, marg. *with me.*
1. —— 8, 13, 14, 16.
4. —— 19.
1. —— 20 twice.
4. —— 22.
6. —— 26.
1. —— ii. 2, 12 3 times, 25 twice.
1. —— iii. 1.
1. —— 8 (ἡμῶν, our, Lm.)
1. —— iv. 1 twice, 3, 14.
4. —— 16.
1. —— 19.
1. Col. i. 24 1st (om. G L T Tr A ℵ.)
1. —— 24 2nd.
1. —— ii. 1.
— —— iv. 7, see M state.
1. —— 10, 18.
— 1 Tim i. 11, see M trust (committed to)
1. 2 Tim. i. 3, 6, 16.
1. —— ii. 1, 8.
1. —— iii. 10.
6. —— iv. 6 (No. 1, L Tr ℵ.)
1. —— 16.
1. Philem. 4 twice.
6. —— 10 1st.
1. —— 10 2nd (om. G ⇉ L T Tr A ℵ.)
1. —— 20, 23, 24.
1. Heb. i. 5, 13.
1. —— ii. 12.
1. —— iii. 9, 10, 11 twice.
1. —— iv. 3 twice, 5.
1. —— viii. 9, 10.
1. —— x. 16.
1. —— 34 (δέσμιος, *those in bonds*, instead of δεσμοῖς μοῦ, *me in my bonds*, G L T Tr A.)
1. —— 38.
1. —— xii. 5.
5. —— xiii. 6.
1. Jas. i. 2, 16, 19.
1. —— ii. 1, 3, 5, 14, 18 1st.
1. —— 18 2nd (om. G ⇉ T Tr A ℵ.)
1. —— iii. 1, 10, 12.
1. —— v. 10 (om. L Tr A.)
1. —— 12.
1. 1 Pet. v. 13.
1. 2 Pet. i. 14.
6. —— 15.
1. —— 17.
1. 1 John ii. 1.
1. —— iii. 13, } (om. G ⇉ L
1. —— 18, } T Tr A ℵ.)
6. 3 John 4.
1. Rev. i. 20.
1. —— ii. 3, 13 3 times, 16.
6. —— 20.
1. —— 26, 27.
4. Rev. xxi. 7.
1. Rev. iii. 5, 8 twice, 10, 12 5 times, 16, 20, 21 twice.
1. —— x. 10 twice.
1. —— xi. 3.
1. —— xviii. 4.
1. Rev. xxii. 12.

MY AFFAIRS.

τὰ, the *things*,
κατὰ, according to,
ἐμὲ, me,
— the things relating to me.

Eph. vi. 21.

MY BURIAL (FOR)

πρὸς, towards
το, the,
ἐνταφιάσαι, to make preparation for burial,
με, me,
— with a view to prepare me for burial.

Matt. xxvi. 12.

MY STATE.

τὰ, the *things*,
κατὰ, relating to,
ἐμὲ, me.

Col. iv. 7.

MY TRUST (BE COMMITTED TO)

ἐγώ, I,
πιστεύομαι, [trusted with, to be en-
— entrusted was I.

1 Tim. i. 11.

MYRRH.

σμύρνα, myrrh. *A substance exuding from a small thorny tree growing in Arabia and Abyssinia, hardening into a bitter aromatic gum, prized by the ancients for use in incense and perfumes.*

Matt. ii. 11. | John xix. 39.

MYRRH (MINGLE WITH)

σμυρνίζω, to myrrh, to mingle with myrrh.

Mark xv. 23.

MYSELF.

1. ἐμαυτοῦ, of myself, *a reflexive pron. often used with active verbs denoting spontaneous action.*
2. ἐμέ, (*acc. of* ἐγώ, I) me.
3. ἐγώ, I, αὐτός, self, — I myself.

1. Luke vii. 7.
1. John v. 31.
1. —— vii. 17, 28.
1. —— viii. 14, 18, 28, 42, [54.
1. —— x. 18.
1. —— xii. 49.
1. —— xiv. 3, 10, 21.
1. —— xvii. 19.
2. Acts vii. 37, marg. (text, ms.)
1. —— xx. 24.
1. —— xxiv. 10.
1. Acts xxvi. 2, 9.
3. Rom. ix. 3.
1. —— xi. 4.
— —— xvi. 2, see M (of)
1. 1 Cor. iv. 4, 6.
1. —— ix. 19.
1. 2 Cor. ii. 1.
1. —— xi. 7, 9.
1. —— xii. 5.
1. Gal. ii. 18.
1. Phil. iii. 13.
1. Philem. 17.

MYSELF (I)

1. *αὐτός*, self.
2. { *ἐγώ*, I, / *αὐτός*, self, } I myself.
3. *ἐμαυτοῦ*, (*see* "MYSELF," *No.* 1.)

2. Luke xxiv. 39.
2. Acts x. 26.
1. —— xxiv. 16.
1. —— xxv. 22.
2. Rom. vii. 25.
2. Rom. ix. 3.
3. 1 Cor. vii. 7.
1. —— ix. 27.
2. 2 Cor. x. 1.
2. —— xii. 13.
1. Phil. ii. 24.

MYSELF (OF)

{ *αὐτόυ*, of self, / *ἐμοῦ*, of me, } of me myself.

Rom. xvi. 2.

MYSTERY.

μυστήριον, a secret. [lxx. for רז Dan. ii. 18, 19, 27, 28, 29, 30, 47; iv. 9. In the Apoc. books used of *the secret* of a friend, of private life, of State, and of a king. Ecclus. xxii. 22; xxvii. 16, 17, 21. Tobit xii. 7, 11. Judith ii. 2. 2 Macc. xiii. 21. Wisd. ii. 22. Later, of *a secret symbol* Justin Mart. Apol. i. 27. Tryph. c. 40, c. 44, c. 68, as in Eph. v. 32, and Rev. xvii. 5, 7. The Latin "*Sacramentum*" must have had the same meaning. In the N.T. used especially of the "*great secret*" which is *Christ Mystical*. See Rom. xvi. 25, 26. Eph. iii. 1—11. Col. i. 25, 26. Compare also 1 Cor. ii. 1—iii. 1. 1 Tim. iii. 16, where the same "secret" is referred to; and see a pamphlet on the MYSTERY, by the same author.]

Matt. xiii. 11.
Mark iv. 11.
Luke viii. 10.
Rom. xi. 25.
—— xvi. 25.
1 Cor. ii. 7.
—— iv. 1.
—— xiii. 2.
—— xiv. 2.
—— xv. 51.
Eph. i. 9.
Eph. iii. 3, 4, 9.
—— v. 32.
—— vi. 19.
Col. i. 26, 27.
—— ii. 2.
—— iv. 3.
2 Thes. ii. 7.
1 Tim. iii. 9, 16.
Rev. i. 20.
—— x. 7.
—— xvii. 5, 7.

N

NAIL (-S.) [noun.]

ἧλος, a nail, *used by Homer only for ornament*, not *to fasten; hence*, nail heads, studs; *later*, a nail to fasten with, (*non occ.*)

John xx. 25 twice.

NAIL TO (-ING.)

προσηλόω, to nail to *any thing*, to affix with nails, nail up, (*non occ.*)

Col. ii. 14.

NAKED.

γυμνός, naked, unclad; *in common language*, lightly clad, *i.e.* in the under garment only (*χιτών*), *without the ἱμάτιον; and hence*, poorly clad, (*occ.* 1 Cor. xv. 37.)

Matt. xxv. 36, 38, 43, 44.
Mark xiv. 51, 52.
John xxi. 7.
Acts xix. 16.
2 Cor. v. 3.
Heb. iv. 13.
Jas. ii. 15.
Rev. iii. 17.
—— xvi. 15.
—— xvii. 16.

NAKED (BE)

γυμνητεύω, to be *γυμνός* (naked), (*non occ.*)

1 Cor. iv. 11.

NAKEDNESS.

γυμνότης, nakedness, want, (*non occ.*)

Rom. viii. 35.
2 Cor. xi. 27.
Rev. iii. 18.

NAME (-S.) [noun.]

ὄνομα, that by which one is known, the name by which a person or thing is called; *hence*, the proper name or appellation of a person. (*The ὀ in ὄνομα is for euphony; compare Lat.*, nomen; *Sanscr.*, nâma; *Eng.*, name, etc. *The common root being γνω-of γινώσκω*, to know; *Lat.*, nosco; *Eng.*, know, *and therefore, strictly*, that by which one is known.)

Matt. i. 21, 23, 25.
—— vi. 9.
—— vii. 22 3 times.
—— x. 2, 22, 41 twice, 42.
—— xii. 21.
—— xviii. 5, 20.
—— xix. 29.
—— xxi. 9.
—— xxiii. 39.
—— xxiv. 5, 9.
—— xxvii. 32.
—— xxviii. 19.
Mark v. 9 twice, 22 (*om.* G →)
—— vi. 14.
—— ix. 37, 38, 39, 41.
—— xi. 9, 10 (*ap.*)
—— xiii. 6, 13.
—— xvi. 17 (*ap.*)
Luke i. 5, 13, 27 twice, 31, 49, 59, 61, 63.
—— ii. 21, 25.
—— vi. 22.
—— viii. 30.
—— ix. 48, 49.
—— x. 17, 20.
—— xi. 2.
—— xiii. 35.
—— xix. 38.
—— xxi. 8, 12, 17.
—— xxiv. 18, 47.
John i. 6, 12.
—— ii. 23.
—— iii. 18.
—— v. 43 twice.
—— x. 3, 25.
—— xii. 13, 28.
—— xiv. 13, 14, 26.
—— xv. 16, 21.
—— xvi. 23, 24, 26.
—— xvii. 6, 11, 12, 26.
—— xviii. 10.
—— xx. 31.
Acts i. 15.
—— ii. 21, 38.
—— iii. 6, 16 twice.
—— iv. 7, 10, 12, 17, 18, 30.
—— v. 28, 40, 41.
—— viii. 12, 16.
—— ix. 14, 15, 16, 21, 27, 29.
—— x. 43, 48.
Acts xiii. 6, 8.
—— xv. 14, 17, 26.
—— xvi. 18.
—— xviii. 15.
—— xix. 5, 13, 17.
—— xxi. 13.
—— xxii. 16.
—— xxvi. 9.
—— xxviii. 7.
Rom. i. 5.
—— ii. 24.
—— ix. 17.
—— x. 13.
—— xv. 9.
1 Cor. i. 2, 10, 13, 15.
—— v. 4.
—— vi. 11.
Eph. i. 21.
—— v. 20.
Phil. ii. 9, 10.
—— iv. 3.
Col. iii. 17.
2 Thes. i. 12.
—— iii. 6.
1 Tim. vi. 1.
2 Tim. ii. 19.
Heb. i. 4.
—— ii. 12.
—— vi. 10.
—— xiii. 15.
Jas. ii. 7.
—— v. 10, 14.
1 Pet. iv. 14.
1 John ii. 12.
—— iii. 23.
—— v. 13 1st (*ap.*), 13 2nd.
3 John 7, 14.
Rev. ii. 3, 13, 17.
—— iii. 1, 4, 5 twice, 8, 12 3 times.
—— vi. 8.
—— viii. 11.
—— ix. 11 twice.
—— xi. 18.
—— xiii. 1, 6, 8, 17 twice.
—— xiv. 1, 11.
—— xv. 2, 4.
—— xvi. 9.
—— xvii. 3, 5, 8.
—— xix. 12, 13, 16.
—— xxi. 12, 14.

Rev. xxii. 4.

NAME (BE ONE'S)

καλέω, to call to *any one, so that he may come or go anywhere*, to call, to name. *Here, pass. part.* called.

Acts vii. 58.

NAME (-ED, -ETH.) [verb.]

1. **ὀνομάζω**, to name, call by name, to name the name *of any one*, to call *or* pronounce his name; to give a name *or* appellation, (*elsewhere*, "CALL.")

2. **λέγω**, to lay, lay together, collect; *hence*, to say, relate, discourse; to speak of as being called so and so; *hence, part.*, called, spoken of.

3. **καλέω**, *see* "N (BE ONE'S)."

2. Matt. ix. 9.
2. Mark xv. 7.
1. Luke vi. 13, 14.
3. —— xix. 2.
1. Rom. xv. 20.
1. 1 Cor. v. 1 (*om.* ὀνομάζεται, *so much as named*, G L T Tr A ℵ, substitute *even.*)
Eph. i. 21.

Eph. iii. 15. Eph. v. 3. 2 Tim. ii. 19.

NAMED (so)

{ **τὸ**, the, { which it was
{ **κληθὲν**, it was called, { called.

Luke ii. 21.

NAMED.

ὄνομα, name (*see the noun*). Here, *Dat.*, by name; or with αὐτῷ, to him; *or* οὗ, of which; *or* ᾧ, to which, *i.e.* by name; *or* the name to him or it, *etc.*

Matt. xxvii. 57.
Mark xiv. 32.
Luke i. 5, 26.
—— v. 27.
—— viii. 41.
—— x. 38.
—— xvi. 20.
—— xix. 2.
—— xxiii. 50.
John iii. 1.
Acts v. 1, 34.
—— ix. 10, 12, 33, 36.
—— xi. 28.
—— xii. 13.
—— xvi. 1, 14.
—— xvii. 34.
—— xviii. 2, 7, 24.
—— xix. 24.
—— xx. 9.
—— xxi. 10.

Acts xxvii. 1.

NAMELY

{ **ἐν**, in, { namely.
{ **τῷ**, the, {

Rom. xiii. 9 (Lb Trb Ab.)

NAPKIN.

σουδάριον, a sweat-cloth; a handkerchief *or* napkin, (*occ.* Acts xix. 12.)

Luke xix. 20. John xi. 44.
John xx. 7.

NARD (*liquid*) [margin.]

Mark xiv. 3, see Spikenard.

NARROW.

θλίβω, to press, press upon. *Here, pass. part.*, pressed, compressed.

Matt. vii. 14.

NATION (s.)

1. **ἔθνος**, a multitude; people, living under common institutions. *In pl.* the Gentile nations as distinct from Israel.

2. γένος, race, people having a common descent.

3. γενεά, progeny, offspring, generation.

All the occurrences of the word "NATION" *are the translation of No.* 1 (ἔθνος) *except—*

2. Mark vii. 26.
2. Gal. i. 14.
3. Phil. ii. 15.

NATION (ONE OF ANOTHER)

ἀλλόφυλος, of another tribe *or* nation, *i.e.* not a Jew, (*non occ.*)

Acts x. 28.

NATURAL.

1. φυσικός, physical, natural, *i.e.* from *or* by nature, according to nature, following the natural bent.

2. { κατὰ, according to, φύσις, nature. }

3. ψυχικός, breathing, animal, possessing animal life, swayed by the animal or natural mind and affections, *i.e.* not under the influences of the Holy Spirit.

4. γένεσις, birth; *here Gen.*, of [his] birth.

1. Rom. i. 26, 27.
— —— 31, see Affection.
2. —— xi. 21, 24.
3. 1 Cor. ii. 14.
3. —— xv. 44 twice.
— 1 Cor. xv. 46, see N (that which is)
— 2 Tim. iii. 3, see Affection.
4. Jas. i. 23.
3. —— iii. 15, marg. (text, *sensual.*)
1. 2 Pet. ii. 12.

NATURAL (THAT WHICH IS)

{ τὸ, the, ψυχικόν, *see No.* 3, [*above,*] } the animal.

1 Cor. xv. 46.

NATURALLY.

1. γνησίως, genuinely, really, truly, (*prop. spoken of children* legitimately *begotten*), (*non occ.*)

2. φυσικῶς, physically, naturally, *i.e.* from *or* by nature, (*non occ.*)

1. Phil. ii. 20. | 2. Jude 10.

NATURE.

1. φύσις, nature, generative and productive power, *viz. genetrix*, (*from* φύω; *like* natura, *from* nascor); *hence*, nature, *i.e.* the essence, inborn quality; nature, natural source *or* origin; a nature *as generated, i.e.* a genus, kind, (*occ.* Rom. xi. 21, 24; Jas. iii. 7.)

2. γένεσις, birth; (in Jas. iii. 6, τρόχος τῆς γ, the wheel of birth, i.e. *the natural life which is set in motion at birth and rolls on;* i.e. *course of life.*)

1. Rom. i. 26.
1. —— ii. 14, 27.
1. —— xi. 24 twice.
1. 1 Cor. xi. 14.
1. Gal. ii. 15.
1. —— iv. 8.
1. Eph. ii. 3.
1. 2 Pet. i. 4.
2. Jas. iii. 6.

NAUGHTINESS.

κακία, vice *generally, esp.*, malice, and the evil habit of it.

James i. 21.

NAY.

1. οὐ, no, not, *expressing full and direct negation, independently and absolutely,* (*see* "NO," *No.* 1.)

2. οὐχί, not, *a strengthened form of No.* 1.

3. ἀλλά, but, *always emphatic, marking opposition, interruption, or transition. Hence, often denoting in various connections,* nay, yea, yet.

1. Matt. v. 37 twice.
1. —— xiii. 29.
2. Luke xii. 51.
2. —— xiii. 3, 5.
2. —— xvi. 30.
1. John vii. 12.
1. Acts xvi. 37.
2. Rom. iii. 27.
3. —— vii. 7.
3. —— viii. 37.
— —— ix. 20, see N but.
3. 1 Cor. vi. 8.
3. —— xii. 22.
1. 2 Cor. i. 17 twice, 18, 19.
1. Jas. v. 12 twice.

NAY BUT.

μενοῦνγε, yea indeed, yea verily, nevertheless.

Rom. ix. 20 (G→)

NEAR.

(*See below for* "COME N., DRAW N., etc.")

1. ἐγγύς, near; *of place*, nigh at hand, hard by; *of time*, nigh at hand *of number*, nearly.

2. πλησίον, near, near by, (*hence*, ὁ πλ. *is* one's neighbour.)

3. ἀναγκαῖος, of, with, *or* by force; *pass.*, constrained; *hence, of friends*, very intimate, close, (*but see* "NECESSARY," *No.* 1.)

1. Matt. xxiv. 33.
1. Mark xiii. 28.
2. John iv. 5.
— Acts viii. 29, see Go.
3. —— x. 24.
1. Rom. xiii. 11.

NEAR (COME)

ἐγγίζω, to bring near, cause to approach; *also*, to draw near, approach.

Luke xviii. 40 past.
—— xix. 41.
Acts ix. 3.
—— xxi. 33.
Acts xxiii. 15.

NEAR (DRAW)

1. ἐγγίζω, *see above.*

2. προσέρχομαι, to come *or* go near to *any person or place*, to approach.

8 προσάγω, to lead *or* conduct to *any one*, to bring near, present before. *Here intrans.*, to come *or* draw near.

1. Matt. xxi. 34.
1. Luke xv. 1 part, with [εἰμὶ, to be.
1. —— xxi. 8.
1. —— xxii. 47.
1. Luke xxiv. 15.
2. Acts vii. 31 part.
3. Acts xxvii. 27.
2. Heb. x. 22.

NEAR TO.

ἐγγύς, *see* "NEAR," *No.* 1.

John iii. 23. | John xi. 54.

NEARER.

ἐγγυτέρον, *comp. of* "NEAR," *No.* 1.

Rom. xiii. 11.

NECESSARY.

1. ἀναγκαῖος, of, with, *or* by force; *act.*, constrainedly, applying force; *pass.*, forced, necessary.

2. ἀνάγκη, force, constraint, necessity; necessary that..., necessitv *arising from constraint.*

3. ἐπάναγκες, (*No.* 2, *with* ἐπί, upon, *prefixed*), (*non occ.*)

1. Acts xiii. 46.
3. —— xv. 18.
— —— xxviii. 10, see N (such things as are)
1. 1 Cor. xii. 22.
1. 2 Cor. ix. 5.
1. Phil. ii. 25.
1. Tit. iii. 14.
2. Heb. ix. 23.

NECESSARY (SUCH AS ARE)

{ τὰ, the *things*, πρὸς, towards, in consideration of, τὴν, the, χρείαν, need, (*see below, No.* 2,) } the things suited to *our* need, (L T Tr A ℵ, *have* τὰς χρείας, *pl.*, our *needs.*)

Acts xxviii. 10.

NECESSITY (-IES.)

1. ἀνάγκη, *see above, No.* 2.

2. χρεία, use; *as a property*, use, advantage, service; *as an action*, using, use; *hence*, requisiteness, need, necessity; *and then*, the result of such need, *viz.* want, poverty.

— Luke xxiii. 17, see N
2. Acts xx. 34. [must (of)
2. Rom. xii. 13.
1. 1 Cor. vii. 26, marg. (text, *distress.*)
1. —— 37.
1. —— ix. 16.
1. 2 Cor. vi. 4.
1. 2 Cor. ix. 7.
1. —— xii. 10.
2. Phil. iv. 16.
1. Philem. 14.
1. Heb. vii. 12.
— —— viii. 3, see N (of)
— —— ix. 16, see N (must of)

NECESSITY (MUST OF)

1. Heb. ix. 16.

NECESSITY MUST (OF)

{ ἀνάγκη, necessity, (*arising from con-* ἔχω, to have. [*straint.*)

Luke xxiii. 17 (ap.)

NECESSITY (OF)

ἀναγκαῖος, *see* "NECESSARY," *No.* 1.

Heb. viii. 3.

NECK.

τράχηλος, the throat, the neck.

Matt. xviii. 6.
Mark ix. 42.
Luke xv. 20.
Luke xvii. 2.
Acts xv. 10.
—— xx. 37.
Rom. xvi. 4.

NEED. [noun.]

(*See also* "NEEDS," *and the verb; and various combinations with other words below.*)

χρεία, *see* "NECESSITY," *No.* 2.

Matt. iii. 14.
— vi. 8.
— xxi. 3.
— xxvi. 65.
Mark ii. 17, 25.
— xi. 3.
Luke ix. 11.
— xix. 31, 34.
John xiii. 29.
Acts ii. 45.
Acts iv. 35.
1 Cor. xii. 21 twice, 24.
Phil. iv. 19.
1 Thes. v. 1.
Heb. iv. 16, see Time.
— v. 12 twice.
— vii. 11.
— x. 36.
1 John iii. 17.
Rev. iii. 17.
Rev. xxi. 23.

NEED BE.

{ δέον, necessary, proper, ἐστίν, it is, } *not moral necessity, but logical; from the circumstances or nature of the case.*

1 Pet. i. 6.

NEED OF (HAVE)

χρῄζω, to need, have need of, want.

Matt. vi. 32. | Luke xii. 30.
Rom. xvi. 2.

NEED SO REQUIRE.

{ οὕτως, thus, ὀφείλει, it ought, γίνεσθαι, to be brought about.

1 Cor. vii. 36.

NEED (SUFFER)

ὑστερέω, to be last, behind, inferior; to lack, to come short.

Phil. iv. 12.

NEED (-ED, -EST, -ETH.) [verb.]

1. { χρεία, *see* "NECESSITY," *No.* 2, ἔχω, to have, } to have need of, to want, *(the need arising from a want of what is requisite for use.)*

2. χρῄζω, to need, have need of, want.

3. { ἀνάγκη, necessity, *(the need arising from the pressure, constraint, or force of circumstances, etc.,)* ἔχω, to have, } to have necessity.

4. προσδέομαι, to need besides, need in addition, *(non occ.)*

1. Matt. ix. 12.
1. — xiv. 16.
1. Mark xiv. 63.
1. Luke v. 31.
2. — xi. 8.
1. — xv. 7.
1. — xxii. 71.
1. John ii. 25.
1. — xiii. 10.
1. — xvi. 30.
4. Acts xvii. 25 part.
2. 2 Cor. iii. 1.
1. Eph. iv. 28.
1. 1 Thes. i. 8.
1. — iv. 9.
— 2 Tim. ii. 15, see Ashamed.
3. Heb. vii. 27.
1. 1 John ii. 27. [ἔχω, G.)
1. Rev. xxii. 5 (G∾) (om

NEEDFUL.

1. χρεία, *see* "NECESSITY," *No.* 2.

2. ἀναγκαῖος, *see* "NECESSARY," *No.* 1.

1. Luke x. 42. | 2. Phil. i. 24.

NEEDFUL (BE)

1. { ἀνάγκη, ἔχω, } *see* "NEED," (verb) *No.* 3.

2. δεῖ, *impers. of* δέω, it needs *that;* it behoveth, *implying rather logical than moral necessity.*

2. Acts xv. 5. | 1. Jude 3.

NEEDFUL TO (THOSE THINGS WHICH ARE)

{ τὰ, the *things,* ἐπιτήδεια, apt, proper, } the things needful *(to the circumstances, etc., of the body), (non occ.)*

Jas. ii. 16.

NEEDLE.

ῥαφίς, a needle, *(non occ.)*

Matt. xix. 24.
Mark x. 25.
Luke xviii. 25 (βελόνη, *point of a weapon; hence, a needle,* G∾ L T Tr A ℵ.)

NEEDS (MUST)

1. δεῖ, *see* "NEEDFUL (BE)," *No.* 2.

2. { πάντως, at all events, surely. δεῖ, it needs.

3. { ἀνάγκη, ἔχω, } *see* "NEED" (verb), *No.* 3.

4. ὀφείλω, to owe, to be indebted; *hence,* to be obligated *to the performance of any duty;* I ought, I must.

— Matt. xviii. 7, see N be (it must)
1. Mark xiii. 7.
3. Luke xiv. 18.
1. John iv. 4, imperf.
1. Acts i. 16, imperf.
1. — xvii. 3, imperf.
2. Acts xxi. 22 (om. δεῖ πλῆθος συνελθεῖν—γαρ; *the multitude must needs come together, for they will,* [i.e. *they will surely hear that thou art come*] G∾Tr.)
— Rom. xiii. 5, *see below.*
4. 1 Cor. v. 10.
1. 2 Cor. xi. 30.

NEEDS BE (IT MUST)

{ ἀνάγκη, necessity, need, *arising from constraint*,
{ ἔστιν, it is, there is.

Matt. xviii. 7 (*om.* ἔστιν, L Tr A.)

NEEDS BE SUBJECT (MUST)

{ ἀνάγκη, necessity, need, *arising from constraint.*
{ ὑποτάσσεσθαι, to be submitting.

Rom. xiii. 5.

NEGLECT (-ED.) [verb.]

1. ἀμελέω, not to care for, be heedless, negligent.
2. παραθεωρέω, to look at *a thing* by the side of *another*, then to look by *or* beside *any thing*, to overlook, slight, (*non occ.*)

— Matt. xviii. 17 twice, see [Hear.
2. Acts vi. 1.
1. 1 Tim. iv. 14.
1. Heb. ii. 3 part.

NEGLECTING.

ἀφειδία, unsparingness, *i.e.* rigour, austerity, (*non occ.*)

Col. ii. 23, marg. *punishing, or not sparing.*

NEGLIGENT (BE)

ἀμελέω, not to care for, be heedless, negligent.

2 Pet. i. 12 (μελλήσω, *I shall be ever sure*, instead of οὐκ ἀμελήσω, *I will not be negligent*, G ∾ L T Tr A ℵ.)

NEIGHBOUR (-S.)

1. { ὁ, the, { πλησίον, near, } the *one* near, a neighbour; *also*, a fellow-man, *i.e. any other member of the human family*, (*occ.* John iv. 5.)
2. γείτων, a neighbour, *i.e.* one living in the same land or country, *or* in the same neighbourhood, a borderer, (*non occ.*)
3. περίοικος, dwelling round *or* near, (*non occ.*)

1. Matt. v. 43.
1. —— xix. 19.
1. —— xxii. 39.
1. Mark xii. 31, 33.
3. Luke i. 58.
1. —— x. 27, 29, 36.
2. —— xiv. 12.
2. —— xv. 6, 9.
2. John ix. 8.
1. Acts vii. 27.
1. Rom. xiii. 9, 10.
1. —— xv. 2.
1. Gal. v. 14.
1. Eph. iv. 25.
1. Heb. viii. 11, πολίτης, *townsman*, G L T Tr A ℵ.)
1. Jas. ii. 8.

NEITHER.

1. οὐ, no, not, *expressing full and direct negation, independently and absolutely*, (*see* "NO," *Nos.* 1, 2, *and note.*)
   (a) *with* δέ, but.
   (b) *with* καί, and, also.
2. μή, no, not, *expressing a dependent and conditional negation*, (*see* "NO," *No.* 2, *and note.*) **with imperative.*
3. { οὐ, *see No.* 1, { μή, *see No.* 2, } *a double negative, expressing a strong denial*, assuredly not, by no means, no wise.
4. οὐδέ, and not, also not; not even, neither, no not, (*see* "NO," *No.* 2, *and note.*)
5. μήδε, and not, also not; *hence*, neither, not even, (*see* "NO," *No.* 2 *and note.*)
6. οὔτε, and not, also not, neither, *a connative negative, referring usually to a part of a proposition or clause.*
   (a) *Followed by another* οὔτε, *and translated* neither...nor, * neither ... nor yet; † nor ... neither; ‡ neither...neither.
7. μήτε, and not, also not, (*differing from No.* 6, *as described under* "NO," *No.* 2.)
8. ἤ, or, *a disjunctive particle.*
9. { ἀλλά, but, { οὐδέ, (*see No.* 4,) } but, not even.
10. καί, and, also, (a) *with another* καί, *translated* * neither...nor; † and neither...nor.

4. Matt. v. 15.
7. —— 34, 35, 36.
4. —— vi. 15.
6a. —— 20.
4. —— 26, 28.
5. —— vii. 6.
4. —— 18.
4. —— ix. 17.
2*. —— x. 9.
5. —— 10 twice.
7. —— xi. 18.
4. —— 27.
4. —— xii. 4, 19.
4. —— xiii. 13.
4. —— xvi. 9, 10.
4. —— xxi. 27.
1b. —— xxii. 16.
6a. —— 30.
4. —— 46.
5. —— xxiii. 10.
1. —— 13 1st.
4. —— 13 2nd.
2*. —— xxiv. 18.
5. Matt. xxiv. 20.
1. —— xxv. 13.
4. Mark iv. 22.
— —— v. 4, see N any [man.
1b. —— viii. 14.
4. —— 17.
5. —— 26.
4. —— xi. 26 (*ap.*), 33.
4. —— xii. 21 (*ap.*)
5. —— 24.
6a. —— 25.
5. —— xiii. 11 (*om.* μηδὲ μελετᾶτε, *neither do ye premeditate*, G ⇉ Lb T Tr Ab ℵ.)
5. —— 15.
3. —— 19.
4. —— 32.
1b. —— xiv. 40.
4. —— 59.
4. —— 68 (No. 6, L T Tr A ℵ.)
4. —— xvi. 13 (*ap.*)

10a & 3. Luke i. 15 (i.e. *and* wine *and* strong drink, shall *by no means* drink.)
5. —— iii. 14.
4. —— vi. 45.
4. —— vii. 7.
7. ——— 33.
4. —— viii. 17.
1b.——— 27.
1. ——— 43.
7. —— ix. 3 4 times.
2*.—— x. 4.
4. —— xi. 33.
5. —— xii. 22.
1. ——— 24 1st (No. 6, T A ℵ.)
1. ——— 24 2nd.
2. ——— 29.
4. ——— 33.
5. ——— 47.
5. —— xiv. 12 (*ap.*)
6a*——— 35.
5. —— xvi. 26.
4. ——— 31.
4. —— xvii. 21.
2. —— xviii. 2.
1b.——— 34.
4. —— xx. 8.
1b.——— 21.
6a.——— 35.
6. ——— 36.
6a† John i. 25 (No. 4, L T Tr A ℵ.)
1b.—— iii. 20.
5. —— iv. 15.
6a*——— 21.
6a.—— v. 37.
4. —— vi. 24.
4. —— vii. 5.
4. —— viii. 11 (*ap.*)
6a.——— 19.
4. ——— 42.
6a.—— ix. 3.
1b.—— x. 28.
4. —— xiii. 16.
4. —— xiv. 17.
5. ——— 27.
1. —— xvii. 20.
4. Acts ii. 27.
4. ——— 31 (No. 6, G~L T Tr A ℵ.)
1b.—— iv. 12 (*ap.*)
4. ——— 32, 34.
1. —— viii. 21.
1. —— ix. 9.
6a.—— xv. 10.
4. —— xvi. 21.
4. —— xvii. 25.
6a*—— xix. 37.
4. —— xx. 24 (*om.* οὐδὲ ἔχω, i.e. *I count my life of no value*, instead of "*none of these move me, neither count I my life dear*," T Tr A ℵ.)
5. —— xxi. 21.
5. —— xxiii. 8 (No. 7, L T Tr A ℵ.)
7. ——— 12, 21.
7. —— xxiv. 12 1st.
8. ——— 12 2nd.
7. ——— 12 3rd, 13.
1. Acts xxiv. 18.
6. —— xxv. 8 twice.
7. —— xxvii. 20.
8. Rom. i. 21.
4. —— ii. 28.
2. —— iv. 21.
5. —— vi. 13.
6. —— viii. 38.
4. —— ix. 7.
5. ——— 11.
1b. 1 Cor. ii. 9, 14.
9. —— iii. 2.
6a‡——— 7 twice.
5. —— v. 8.
6. —— vi. 9.
6a‡—— viii. 8.
1a.—— ix. 15.
5. —— x. 7, 8, 9, 10.
10a.——— 32.
1b.—— xi. 9.
6a‡——— 11.
4. ——— 16.
4. —— xv. 50.
4. Gal. i. 1, 12 1st.
6. ——— 12 2nd.
4. ——— 17.
4. —— ii. 3.
1. —— iii. 28 3 times.
6a.—— v. 6.
4. —— vi. 13.
6a.——— 15.
7. —— iv. 27 (No. 5, L T Tr A ℵ.)
10.—— v. 4.
1b.—— vi. 9.
4. Phil. ii. 16.
1. Col. iii. 11.
6a. 1 Thes. ii. 5.
6. ——— 6.
7. 2 Thes. ii. 2.
4. ——— 22.
5. —— iii. 10.
5. 1 Tim. i. 4.
7. ——— 7.
5. ——— 22.
1b. Heb. iv. 13.
7. —— vii. 3.
4. —— ix. 12, 18.
4. —— x. 8.
8. Jas. i. 17.
7. —— v. 12 3 times.
4. 1 Pet. ii. 22.
5. —— iii. 14.
5. —— v. 3.
1. 2 Pet. i. 8.
5. 1 John ii. 15.
4. —— iii. 6.
5. ——— 18.
2. 2 John 10.
6. 3 John 10.
6a. Rev. iii. 15, 16.
6. —— v. 4.
4. ——— 3 twice.
7. —— vii. 3.
4. ——— 16 twice.
4. —— ix. 4 twice.
6. ——— 20.
1b.——— 21.
6. —— xii. 8 (No. 4, G L T Tr A ℵ.)
6. —— xx. 4 1st.
1b.——— 4 2nd.
6. —— xxi. 4.
4. ——— 23.

NEITHER...ANY MAN.

{ καί, and,
{ οὐδείς, no one.

Mark v. 4. | Jas. i. 13.

NEITHER INDEED.

4. Rom. viii. 7.

NEITHER ANY THING.

{ καί, and,
{ οὐδέν, no thing.

Mark xvi. 8.

NEITHER AT ANY TIME.

οὐδέποτε, not ever, never.

Luke xv. 29.

NEPHEWS.

ἔκγονα, sprung from, born of; *hence*, descendants, *as* sons, daughters, grandchildren, etc., (*non occ.*)

1 Tim. v. 4.

NEST (-s.)

κατασκηνωσις, the act of pitching a tent; *then*, a tent pitched; *hence*, a dwelling-place; *spoken of birds*, a haunt, (*non occ.*)

Matt. viii. 20. | Luke ix. 58.

NET.

1. δίκτυον, a net, a fishing-net, *any net in general*, (*non occ.*)

2. ἀμφίβληστρον, any thing thrown round, a large fishing-net *flung from the hand*, (*non occ.*)

3. σαγήνη, a drag-net, *used in fishing, and drawn to the shore*, (*non occ.*)

2. Matt. iv. 18.
1. ——— 20, 21.
3. —— xiii. 47.
2. Mark i. 16 (*om.* T Tr [A ℵ.)
1. Mark i. 18, 19.
1. Luke v. 2, 4, 5, 6.
1. John xxi. 6, 8, 11 twice.

NEVER.

(*For various combinations with other words, see below.*)

1. οὐ, no, not, *denying absolutely*, (*see* "NO," *Nos.* 1, 2, *and note.*)

2. μή, no, not *denying conditionally*, (*see* "NO," *No.* 2, *and note.*)

3. { οὐ, *see No.* 1, } by no means, *a very*
{ μή, *see No.* 2, } *strong denial*, in no wise, assuredly not.

4. οὐδέ, (οὐ, not, and δέ, but) and not, also not, not even.

5. οὐδέποτε, (οὐδέ, *No.* 4, and ποτέ, at any time, ever) not ever, not at any time, (*see* "NO," *No.* 2, *and note.*)

6. μηδέποτε, (μή, *No.* 2, δέ, but, *and* ποτέ, ever) not ever, not at any time, (*see* "NO," *No.* 2, *and note*) (*non occ.*)

7. { οὐ, μή, } by no means, (*see No.* 3,) εἰς, unto, τὸν, the, αἰῶν, age (*see* "ETERNAL," *No.* 1,) } for ever. } *The verb generally follows* οὐ, μή, e.g. *in* John xi. 26, *it is,* ...*shall* by no means *die* for ever, [*i.e.* he may die, but being united to Christ by faith, shall not die for ever, but has the hope of "the resurrection of the just."]

8. { οὐκ, not, (*denying absolutely*) εἰς, unto, τὸν, the, αἰῶνα, age (*see* "ETERNAL," *No.* 1,) } here ἔχει ἄφεσιν follows οὐκ, *i.e. hath* not *forgiveness*—for ever.

9. { οὐ, μή, } by no means, in no wise (*see No.* 3,) ποτέ, when, at any time, ever, } in no wise ... at any time.

10. { οὐ, μή, } *see No.* 3, πώποτε, yet ever, yet at any time, } in no wise ... not even at any time.

5. Matt. vii. 23.	2. John vii. 15.
5. —— ix. 33.	5. ——— 46.
5. —— xxi. 16, 42.	7. —— viii. 51.
4. —— xxvii. 14.	7. ——— 52 (εἰς τὸν αἰωνά, G →)
5. Mark ii. 12, 25.	7. —— x. 28.
8. —— iii. 29 (εἰς τὸν αἰωνά, G →)	7. —— xi. 26.
— —— ix. 43, 45, see Quenched.	7. —— xiii. 8.
1. —— xiv. 21.	5. Acts x. 14.
5. Luke xv. 29.	5. —— xiv. 8.
1. —— xxiii. 29 twice.	5. 1 Cor. xiii. 8.
7. John iv. 14 (*ap.*)	6. 2 Tim. iii. 7.
3. —— vi. 35 1st.	5. Heb. x. 1, 11.
10. —— 35 2nd.	3. —— xiii. 5.
	9. 2 Pet. i. 10.

NEVER BEFORE.

οὐδέπω, also not ever, not ever yet, not yet, never, (*with another neg., strengthening.*)

Luke xxiii. 53.

NEVER ANY MAN.

{ οὐδείς, no one, not one.
πώποτε, not yet ever at any time.

John viii. 33.

NEVER MAN.

{ οὐδείς, πώποτε, } *see above.*

Luke xix. 30.

NEVER MAN BEFORE.

{ οὐδέπω, also not ever, not ever yet, οὐδείς, no one, not one, } no one as yet.

Luke xxiii. 53.

NEVER MAN YET.

{ οὐδέπω, οὐδείς, } *see above.*

John xix. 41.

NEVER (YET)

οὐδέποτε, *see above, No.* 5.

Matt. xxvi. 33.

NEVERTHELESS.

1. ἀλλά, but, (*emphatic as contrasted with No.* 3) *marking opposition, interruption, and transition, indicating a reference to something else.*

2. πλήν, besides, moreover, except.

3. δέ, but, (*though less emphatic than No.* 1) *it marks an antithesis, however it may be concealed.*

4. καίτοιγε, (καί, and τοί, consequently, *and* γέ, indeed) and consequently indeed.

5. μέντοι, indeed therefore, indeed then; nevertheless.

6. { ὅμως, at the same time, μέντοι, *see No.* 5, } nevertheless indeed.

2. Matt. xxvi. 39, 64.	1. 1 Cor. ix. 12.
1. Mark xiv. 36.	2. —— xi. 11.
2. Luke xiii. 33.	1. 2 Cor. vii. 6.
2. —— xviii. 8.	1. —— xii. 16.
2. —— xxii. 42.	3. Gal. iv. 30.
1. John xi. 15.	2. Ephes. v. 33.
6. —— xii. 42.	2. Phil. iii. 16.
1. —— xvi. 7.	1. 2 Tim. i. 12.
4. Acts xiv. 17.	5. —— ii. 19.
1. Rom. v. 14.	1. Rev. ii. 4.

NEW

1. καινός, new, *i.e.* newly made; *not merely recent, but different from that which had been formerly;* new, *as coming in the place of a thing that was formerly, and as not yet used.*

2. νέος, young, new, *as that which has only lately originated, or only lately been established.*

[When the two words are used of the same thing there is always this difference: thus, the καινός ἀνθρώπος, (*No.* 1) "*the new man,*" is one who differs from the former; the νέος, (*No.* 2) is one who is "renewed after the image of Him that created him," (Col. iii. 10).]

3. ἄγναφος, not yet fulled, *or* dressed, (*from* γναφεύς, a fuller.)

4. πρόσφατος, slain thereto, *or* thereby, *i.e.* lately-slain, fresh-slaughtered, newly-killed, (*non occ.*)

3. Matt. ix. 16, marg. *raw or unwrought.*
2. —— ix. 17 1st & 2nd.
1. —— 17 3rd.
— —— xiii. 52, see N things.
1. —— xxvi. 28 (*om.* L T Tr A ℵ.)
1. —— 29.
1. —— xxvii. 60.
1. Mark i. 27.
3. —— ii. 21 1st.
1. —— 21 2nd.
2. —— 22 1st.
2. —— 22 2nd (*om.* G⇉L T Tr A ℵ.)
2. —— 22 3rd (*ap.*)
1. —— 22 4th (*ap.*)
1. —— xiv. 24 (*om.* G⇉T Tr A ℵ.)
1. —— 25.
1. —— xvi. 17 (*ap.*)
1. Luke v. 36 3 times.
2. —— 37 twice, 38 1st.
1. —— 38 2nd.
2. —— 39.
1. —— xxii. 20.
1. John xiii. 34.
1. —— xix. 41.
— Acts ii. 13, see Wine.
1. —— xvii. 19.
1. —— 21 (comparative.)
2. 1 Cor. v. 7.
1. —— xi. 25.
1. 2 Cor. iii. 6.
1. —— v. 17 twice.
1. Gal. vi. 15.
1. Eph. ii. 15.
1. —— iv. 24.
— Col. ii. 16, see Moon.
— —— iii.10, see N man.
1. Heb. viii. 8, 13.
1. —— ix. 15.
4. —— x. 10.
— —— 20, see *N(make.)*
2. —— xii. 24.
1. 2 Pet. iii. 13 twice.
1. 1 John ii. 7, 8.
1. 2 John 5.
1. Rev. ii. 17.
1. —— iii. 12 twice.
1. —— v. 9.
1. —— xiv. 3.

Rev. xxi. 1 twice, 2, 5.

NEW (*make*) [marg.]

Heb. x. 20, see "CONSECRATE."

NEW MAN.

(*Where not two separate words in the Greek.*)

2 Col. iii. 10.

NEW THINGS.

1. Matt. xiii. 52, neut. pl.

NEW BORN.

ἀρτιγέννητος, just now born, even now born, (*non occ.*)

1 Pet. ii. 2.

NEWLY COME TO THE FAITH. [marg.]

1 Tim. iii. 6, see "NOVICE."

NEWNESS.

καινότης, newness, (*see* "NEW," *No.* 1, *and the note after No.* 2), (*non occ.*)

Rom. vi. 4; vii. 6.

NEXT.

(*For* NEXT DAY, etc., *see below.*)

1. ἑξῆς, in order, successively, the following next in order.

2. μεταξύ, in the midst, *i.e.* betwixt, between, intervening.

3. ἔχω, to have and hold; *here, mid.*, to hold one's self upon *or* to, to be adjacent, contiguous; *here, part.*, adjacent, contiguous.

4. ἔπειμι, to go *or* come upon; *here, part.*, the coming, the following *or* succeeding.

5. ἔρχομαι, to go *or* come; *here, part.*, the coming, the approaching.

3. Mark i. 38.
1. Luke ix. 37.
4. Acts vii. 26.
2. Acts xiii. 42, marg. *between.*
5. —— 44 (G~), (No. 3, G L A.)

3. Acts xxi. 26.

NEXT DAY (THE)

1. αὔριον, (αὔρα, morning air, *from* ἄω, αὔω, to blow) to-morrow; *with art.*, *as here,* the morrow, the next day.

2. { ἡ, the, ἐπαύριον, (*No.* 1, *with* ἐπί, upon, *prefixed*) upon the morrow, } upon the morrow.

3. { τῇ, *on* the, ἐπιούσῃ, coming upon, } on the following ("*day*" *being understood.*)

4. ἕτερος, the other, (*denoting not numerical, but generic distinction*) different from.

5. δευτεραῖος, on the second day, (*non occ.*)

6. ἑξῆς, (*see* "NEXT," *No.* 1) *here, with art.*, the (*day*) next in order.

7. ἔχω, (*see* "NEXT," *No.* 3.)

2. Matt. xxvii. 62.	4. Acts xx. 15 2nd.
2. John i. 29.	7. —— 15 3rd.
1. Acts iv. 3.	2. —— xxi. 8.
2. —— xiv. 20.	2. —— xxv. 6.
3. —— xvi. 11.	4. —— xxvii. 3.
3. —— xx. 15 1st.	6. —— 18.

5. Acts xxviii. 13.

NEXT DAY (ON THE)

2. John xii. 12.

NEXT DAY AFTER (THE)

2. John i. 35.

NIGH.

ἐγγύς, near, *of place or time.*

Matt. xxiv. 32.	Acts xxvii. 18.
Mark xiii. 29.	Rom. x. 8.
John vi. 4.	Eph. ii. 13, 17.

NIGH AT HAND.

ἐγγύς, near, *of place or time.*

Luke xxi. 30, 31. | John xi. 55.

John xix. 42.

NIGH (BE)

ἐγγίζω, to bring near, cause to approach; *then*, to draw near, approach.

Luke xxi. 20. | Phil. ii. 30.

NIGH (COME)

ἐγγίζω, *see above.*

Mark ii. 4, see Come.	Luke x. 9, 11.
—— xi. 1.	—— xviii. 35.
Luke vii. 12.	—— xix. 29, 37 part.

Acts xxii. 6 part.

NIGH (DRAW)

ἐγγίζω, *see above.*

Matt. xv. 8 (ap.)	Acts vii. 17.
—— xxi. 1.	—— x. 9 part.
Luke xv. 25.	Heb. vii. 19.
—— xxi. 1.	Jas. iv. 8 twice.
—— xxiv. 28.	—— v. 8.

NIGH TO.

ἐγγύς, near, *of time or place.*

Luke xix. 1 | John xix. 20.

Acts ix. 38.

NIGH UNTO.

1. ἐγγύς, near, *of time or place.*

2. παρά, beside; *here, with Acc.*, to or alongside of, beside.

3. παραπλήσιον, near by, nigh unto, like, (*non occ.*)

4. πρός, towards; *here with Acc.*, hitherwards, towards.

2. Matt. xv. 29.	1. John vi. 19, 23.
4. Mark v. 11 (G →) (*with Dat., close by,* G L T Tr A ℵ.)	1. —— xi. 18.
	3. Phil. ii. 27.
	1. Heb. vi. 8.

NIGHT.

νύξ, night, (*Lat.*, nox) *both of* the night-season, *as opp. to day, and of* a night.

Matt. ii. 14, see N (by)	Acts ix. 24.
—— iv. 2.	—— 25, see N (by)
—— xii. 40 twice.	—— xii. 6.
—— xiv. 25.	—— xvi. 9, 33.
—— xxvi. 31, 34.	—— xvii. 10.
—— xxvii. 64, } see N	—— xviii. 9.
—— xxviii. 13, } (by)	—— xx. 31.
Mark iv. 27.	—— xxiii. 11, 23, 31.
—— v. 5.	—— xxvi. 7.
—— vi. 48.	—— xxvii, 23, 27.
—— xiv. 27 (*om.* ἐν τῇ νυκτὶ ταύτῃ, *this night,* G ≡ Lb T Tr A ℵ.)	Rom. xiii. 12.
	1 Cor. xi. 23.
—— 30.	2 Cor. xi. 25, see N and a day (a)
Luke ii. 8, see N (by), and Watch.	1 Thes. ii. 9.
	—— iii. 10.
—— 37.	—— v. 2, 5.
—— v. 5, see N (all the)	—— 7, see N (in the)
—— vi. 12, see Continue.	2 Thes. iii. 8.
—— xii. 20.	1 Tim. v. 5.
—— xvii. 34.	2 Tim. i. 3.
—— xviii. 7.	2 Pet. iii. 10 (*om.* ἐν νυκτί, *in the night,* G L T Tr A ℵ.)
—— xxi. 37.	
John iii. 2, } see N (by)	
—— vii. 50, }	Rev. iv. 8.
—— ix. 4.	—— vii. 15.
—— xi. 10.	—— viii. 12.
—— xiii. 30.	—— xii. 10.
—— xix. 39, see N (by)	—— xiv. 11.
—— xxi. 3.	—— xx. 10.
Acts v. 19.	—— xxi. 25.

Rev. xxii. 5.

NIGHT (ALL THE)

{ διὰ, throughout,
ὅλης, the whole,
τῆς, of the,
νυκτός, of the night.

Luke v. 5.

NIGHT AND A DAY (A)

νυχθήμερον, a day and night, *twenty-four hours,* (*non occ.*)

2 Cor. xi. 25.

NIGHT (BY)

νυκτός, (*Gen. of* νύξ, *see* "NIGHT.")

Matt. ii. 14.
— xxvii. 64 (*om.* νυκτός *by night*, G L T Tr A ℵ.)
— xxviii. 13.
Luke ii. 8.
John iii. 2.
— vii. 50 (πρότερον, *beforetime*, L T Tr A) (*om.* ℵ.)
— xix. 39.
Acts v. 19.
Acts ix. 25.

NIGHT (IN THE)

νυκτός, *see above.*

1 Thes. v. 7 twice.

NINE.

ἐννέα, nine.

Luke xvii. 17.

NINETY AND NINE.

ἐννενηκονταεννέα, ninety-nine.

Matt. xviii. 12, 13. | Luke xv. 4, 7.

NINEVE.

Νινευΐ, Nineveh, (*the city of Ninus.*)

Luke xi. 32 (Νινευῖται, *Ninevites*, G~L T Tr ℵ.)

NINTH.

ἔννατος, *or* ἔνατος, ninth.

Matt. xx. 5.
— xxvii. 45, 46.
Mark xv. 33, 34.
Luke xxiii. 44.
Acts iii. 1.
— x. 3, 30.
Rev. xxi. 20.

NO.

(*For various combinations with other words, see below.*)

1. οὐ, (*before a vowel*, οὐκ; *before an aspirated vowel*, οὐχ) not, no, *expressing full and direct negation, independently and absolutely; hence objective*, (*see below*, *No.* 2, *and note.*)

2. μή, not, no, *expressing a dependent and conditional negation*, i.e. *depending on the idea, conception, or thoughts of some subject, and therefore subjective.*

* *with the imperative mood.*

[NOTE.—οὐ denies absolutely and directly, μή, on some condition, expressed or implied; οὐ, denies what is a matter of fact, μή, denies what is matter of supposition or thought; οὐ, negatives an affirmation, μή, negatives a supposition, and prohibits or forbids; οὐ is used when an object is regarded independently in itself, μή, when it is regarded as depending on some thought, wish, or purpose; οὐ, implies non-existence absolutely, μή, implies non-existence, when that existence was probable or possible. οὐ is, therefore, generally used with the *Indicative Mood*, μή, with the other moods of the verb.

The spirit and meaning of many passages entirely depends on our preserving these important powers of the negative; *e.g.* οὐ, 1 Cor. ii. 14, ψυχικὸς δὲ ἄνθρωπος οὐ δέχεται, "but the natural man receiveth not (*No.* 1) the things of the Spirit of God"; John iii. 18, ὁ πιστεύων εἰς αὐτὸν οὐ κρίνεται, he that believeth on Him is not (*No.* 1) condemned (*an absolute fact is here stated*); *e.g.* μή, 1 Cor. ix. 31, μὴ ὢν ἄνομος Θεῷ, being not (*No.* 2, *in my opinion*) without law as regards God; John iii. 18, ὁ δὲ μὴ πιστεύων, but he that believeth not (*No.* 2, *supposing such a case*) is condemned already, ὅτι μὴ πεπιστευκεν, because he hath not (*No.* 2) believed, (*according to the supposition made above*).

The same distinction applies to all the compounds of οὐ and μή, below.]

3. οὐδείς, (οὐ, not; *and* εἷς, one) not one, no one, nothing, (*see note above.*)

* *with another negative, strengthening it.*

4. μηδείς, (μή, not; *and* εἷς, one) not one, no one, no person, no thing, (*see note above.*)

5. { οὐ, not (*see No.* 1, *and note*), πᾶς, all, every, } everything *is* not, *i.e.* nothing *is*, (*following a Hebrew idiom of combining the numeral*, etc., *with the subject, and the negative with the predicate.*)

6. { μή, not (*see No.* 2, *and note*), πᾶς, all, every, } *see No.* 5.

7. οὐδέ, and not, also not; not even, neither, no not, (*see note above.*)

8. μηκέτι, no more, no further, no longer, (*see note above.*)

9. { οὐ, no, not, *see No.* 1 *and* μή, no, not, *No.* 2, *and note* } *a double negative expressing a strong denial*, assuredly not, by no means, in no wise.

10. ἀλλά, but, *marking opposition, interruption, or transition. In transition it has sometimes the force of* yea. *In interruption it has the force of* nay, (*see* Matt. xi. 8, 9; Luke vii. 25.)

11. εἰ, if. *Here*, "if a sign shall be given," *a Hebraism for* "it shall in no wise be given."

1. Matt. vi. 1.
2*.—— 25, 31, 34.
2. —— ix. 36.
2*.—— x. 19.
1. —— xii. 39.
2. —— xiii. 5, 6.
1. —— xvi. 4, 7, 8.
1. —— xix. 18.
1. —— xx. 13.
2. —— xxii. 23, 24, 25.
2. —— xxiii. 9.
5. —— xxiv. 22.
1. —— xxv. 3, 42 twice.
1. —— xxvi. 55.
8. Mark ii. 2.
1. —— 17.
2. —— iv. 5.
1. —— 7, 17, 40 (*ap.*)
3*.—— vi. 5.
2. —— 8 8 times.
11.—— viii. 12.
1. —— 16, 17.
1. —— ix. 3.
2. —— xii. 18, 19.
1. —— 20, 22.
5. —— xiii. 20.
1. Luke i. 7, 33.
1. —— ii. 7.
4. —— iii. 13.
3. —— iv. 24.
1. —— vii. 44, 45.
1. —— viii. 13, 14, 27.
1. —— ix. 13.
1. —— xi. 29.
2*.—— xii. 11.
1. —— 17.
2*.—— 22.
1. —— 33.
2. —— xiii. 11.
1. —— xv. 7.
1. —— xvi. 2.
3. —— 13.
1. —— xx. 22, 31.
2. —— xxii. 36.
1. —— 53.
3. —— xxiii. 4, 14.
10.—— 15.
3. —— 22.
1. John i. 21, 47.
1. —— ii. 3.
1. —— iv. 9, 17 twice, 38, 44.
1. —— v. 7.
1. John vi. 53.
1. —— vii. 18, 52.
1. —— viii. 37, 44.
1. —— ix. 41.
3. —— x. 41.
1. —— xi. 10.
1. —— xiii. 8.
1. —— xv. 22.
3. —— xvi. 29.
3. —— xix. 4.
1. —— 6, 9, 15.
1. —— xxi. 5.
2. Acts i. 20.
4. —— iv. 17.
1. —— vii. 5, 11.
1. —— x. 34.
1. —— xii. 18.
4. —— xiii. 28.
1. —— 37.
1. —— xv. 2.
3. —— 9.
4. —— 28.
4. —— xvi. 28.
1. —— xviii. 15.
1. —— xix. 23, 24, 26.
4. —— 40.
4. —— xxi. 25 (*ap.*)
1. —— 39.
2. —— xxiii. 8.
3. —— 9.
3. —— xxv. 10.
1. —— 26.
1. —— xxvii. 20.
3. —— 22.
1. —— xxviii. 2.
3. —— 5.
4. —— 6, 18.
1. Rom. ii. 11.
1. —— iii. 9, 18.
5. —— 28.
1. —— 22.
1. —— iv. 15 1st.
7. —— 15 2nd.
2. —— v. 13.
2. —— vii. 3.
1. —— 18.
3. —— viii. 1.
1. —— x. 12, 19.
1. —— xiii. 1, 10.
4. 1 Cor. i. 7.
2. —— 10.
6. —— 29.
1. 1 Cor. vii. 25.
2. —— 37.
9. —— viii. 13.
1. —— x. 13.
4. —— 25, 27.
1. —— xi. 16.
1. —— xii. 21 twice, 24.
2. —— xiii. 2.
1. —— 5.
1. —— xv. 12, 13.
1. 2 Cor. ii. 13.
7. —— iii. 10 (G∾) (No. 1, G L T Tr A ℵ.)
2. —— v. 21.
4. —— vi. 3.
3. —— vii. 5.
1. —— viii. 15.
1. —— xi. 14, 15.
2 & 4. —— xiii. 7.
1. Gal. ii. 6.
5. —— 16.
2. —— iv. 8.
1. —— v. 23.
2. Eph. ii. 12.
6. —— iv. 29.
5. —— v. 5.
2*.—— 11.
1. Phil. iii. 3.
3. —— iv. 15.
1. Col. iii. 25.
2. 1 Thes. iv. 6, 13.
1. —— v. 1.
2. 2 Thes. iii. 14.
2. 1 Tim. i. 3.
2. 1 Tim. iii. 3.
3. 2 Tim. ii. 14.
1. —— iii. 9.
2. Titus i. 7.
1. Heb. viii. 7.
1. —— ix. 22.
4. —— x. 2.
1. —— 6, 38.
5. —— xii. 11.
1. —— 17.
1. —— xiii. 10, 14.
1. Jas. i. 17.
1. —— ii. 11.
2. —— 13.
3. —— iii. 12 (*ap.*)
1. 1 Pet. ii. 22.
2. —— iii. 10.
5. 2 Pet. i. 20.
1. 1 John i. 8.
1. —— ii. 7.
5. —— 21.
1. —— 27.
1. —— iii. 5.
5. —— 15.
1. —— iv. 18.
1. 3 John 4.
1. Rev. vii. 16.
1. —— x. 6.
1. —— xiv. 5, 11.
9. —— xviii. 7.
5. —— 22.
1. —— xx. 6, 11.
1. —— xxi. 1, 4, 22, 23, 25.
1. —— xxii. 3, 5 twice.

NO (IF...)

ἐάν, *with pres. subj. See* "IF," *No.* 1b*.

1 Cor. xiv. 28.

NO...AS YET.

οὔπω, not even yet, not yet.

Rev. xvii. 2.

NO...AT ALL.

1. μήποτε, not even, never, *in no supposable case*, (*see No.* 2, *note.*)

2. οὐδείς, not one, not even one; *here, fem., i.e.* not one αἰτίαν, fault.

3. { οὐ, no, not, (*see No.* 1) οὐδείς, *see No.* 2, } no, not even one.

2. John xviii. 38.
3. —— xix. 11.
1. Heb. ix. 17.
3. 1 John i. 5.

NO...HENCEFORWARD.

μηκέτι, *see* "NO," *No.* 8.

Matt. xxi. 19.

NO LONGER.

1. μηκέτι, *see* "NO," *No.* 8.

2. οὐκέτι, (*differing only from* No. 1, *as described in note after* "NO," *No.* 2.)

2. Gal. iii. 25.
1. 1 Thes. iii. 1, 5.
1. 1 Tim. v. 23.
1. 1 Pet. iv. 2.

NO MAN.

(*Where not two words in the Greek.*)

1. οὐδείς, *see* "NO...AT ALL," *No.* 2.
   * *with another negative strengthening it.*

2. μηδείς, not one, (*differing from No.* 1, *as described in note after* "NO," *No.* 2.)

3. μήτις, not any, (*see* "NO," *No.* 2, *note.*)

4. { οὐ, not,
   { τις, any.

5. οὐ, *see* "NO," *No.* 1.

6. μή, *see* "NO," *No.* 2, *and note.*

1. Matt. vi. 24.
2. —— viii. 4.
3. ——— 28.
1. —— ix. 16.
2. ——— 30.
1. —— xi. 27.
2. —— xvi. 20.
1. —— xvii. 8.
2. ——— 9.
1. —— xx. 7.
1. —— xxii. 46.
1. —— xxiv. 36.
1. Mark ii. 21, 22.
1*.—— iii. 27.
1. —— v. 3.
1*.——— 37.
2. ——— 43.
1. —— vii. 24.
2. ——— 36.
2. —— viii. 30.
1* —— ix. 8.
2. ——— 9.
1. ——— 39.
1. —— x. 18 (until A.D. 1660. In editions since then, *none.*)
1. ——— 29.
2. —— xi. 14.
1*.—— xii. 14, 34.
1. —— xiii. 32.
2. Luke iii. 14.
2. —— v. 14.
1. ——— 36, 37, 39.
1. —— viii. 16.
1*.——— 51 (*ap.*)
2. ——— 56.
2. —— ix. 21.
1. ——— 36, 62.
2. —— x. 4.
1. ——— 22.
1. —— xi. 33.
1. —— xv. 16.
1. —— xviii. 29.
1. John i. 18.
1. —— iii. 2, 13, 32.
1. —— iv. 27.
1. —— v. 22.
1. —— vi. 44, 65.
1. —— vii. 4, 13, 27, 30, 44.
1. —— viii. 10 (*ap.*), 11 [(*ap.*)
1*.——— 15.
1. ——— 20.
1. —— ix. 4.
1. —— x. 18, 29.
1. —— xiii. 28.
1. —— xiv. 6.
1. —— xv. 13.
1. John xvi. 22.
1. Acts v. 13, 23.
2. —— ix. 7.
1. ——— 8 (neut., L T Tr [ℵ.)
1. —— xviii. 10.
1. —— xx. 33.
2. —— xxiii. 22.
1. —— xxv. 11.
2. Rom. xii. 17.
2. —— xiii. 8.
1. —— xiv. 7.
6. ——— 13.
1. 1 Cor. ii. 11, 15.
1. —— iii. 11.
2. ——— 18, 21.
2. —— x. 24.
1. —— xii. 3 twice.
1. —— xiv. 2.
3. —— xvi. 11.
1. 2 Cor. v. 16.
1. —— vii. 2 3 times.
1. —— xi. 9 (οὐθείς, L T ℵ.)
5. ——— 10.
3. ——— 16.
1. Gal. iii. 11, 15.
2. —— vi. 17.
2. Eph. v. 6.
1. ——— 29.
1. Phil. ii. 20.
3. Col. ii. 16, with im- [perat.
2. 1 Thes. iii. 3.
2. —— iv. 12, marg. (text, *nothing.*)
3. 2 Thes. ii. 3.
2. 1 Tim. iv. 12.
2. —— v. 22.
1. —— vi. 16.
1. 2 Tim. ii. 4.
1. —— iv. 16.
2. Tit. ii. 15.
2. —— iii. 2.
4. Heb. v. 4.
1. —— vii. 13.
1. —— xii. 14.
2. Jas. i. 13.
1. —— iii. 8.
2. 1 John iii. 7.
1. —— iv. 12.
1. Rev. ii. 17.
1. —— iii. 7 twice, 8.
2. ——— 11.
1. —— v. 3, 4.
1. —— vii. 9.
1. —— xiv. 3.
1. —— xv. 8.
1*.—— xviii. 11.
1. —— xix. 12.

NO MAN (THAT)

1. { μή, no, not, } lest any one.
   { τις, any one, }

2. { ἵνα, in order that,
   { μή, no, not,
   { τις, any one.

1. Matt. xxiv. 4. | 1. 2 Cor. viii. 20.
2. Rev. xiii. 17.

NO MAN CAN APPROACH UNTO.

ἀπρόσιτος, unapproachable, inaccessible, (*non occ.*)

1 Tim. vi. 16.

NO MORE.

1. οὐκέτι, no longer, no further, no more, (*see* "NO," *No.* 2, *note.*)
   * *with another negative strengthening it.*

2. μηκέτι, (*differing from No.* 1 *only as described in* "NO," *No.* 2, *note.*)

3. { οὐ, no, not, *see* "NO," *No.* 1, / μή, no, not, *see* "NO," *No.* 2, } by no means, in no wise, (*see* "NO," *No.* 9,) / ἔτι, yet, still, (*implying duration or accession,*) } in no wise, ...any more.

4. { οὕτως, in this manner, or this wise, / οὐδέ, and not, not even, neither, } thus neither.

1. Matt. xix. 6.
2. Mark i. 45.
1. —— vii. 12.
2. —— ix. 25.
1. —— x. 8.
1*.—— xiv. 25.
1. Luke xv. 19, 21.
2. John v. 14.
1. —— vi. 66.
2. —— viii. 11 (*ap.*)
1. —— xi. 54.
1. —— xiv. 19.
4. —— xv. 4.
1. —— xvi. 10, 21, 25.
1. —— xvii. 11.
1*. Acts viii. 39.
2. Acts xiii. 34.
1. —— xx. 25, 38.
1. Rom. vi. 9 twice.
1. —— vii. 17, 20.
1. —— xi. 6 1st & 2nd.
1. ——— 6 3rd & 4th (*ap.*)
2. —— xv. 23.
1. 2 Cor. v. 16.
1. Gal. iii. 18.
1. —— iv. 7.
1. Eph. ii. 19.
2. —— iv. 28.
3. Heb. viii. 12.
3. —— x. 17.
1. ——— 18, 26.
3. Rev. iii. 12.

NO MORE (HENCEFORTH)

μηκέτι, no longer, no more (*see* "NO," *No.* 2, *note.*)

Eph. iv. 14.

NO MORE (NOW HENCEFORTH)

{ νῦν, now,
{ οὐκέτι, no longer, (*see* "NO," *No.* 2, *and note.*)

2 Cor. v. 16.

NO MORE AT ALL.

1. { οὐ, μη, ἔτι, } *see* "NO MORE," *No.* 3.

2. { οὐκέτι, no longer. { οὐ, μή, } by no means, in no wise, (*see* "NO," *No.* 9.

1. Rev. xviii. 14.
2. Rev. xviii. 21, 22 twice, 23 twice.

NO, NOR.

οὐδέ, and not, also not, not even, (*see* "NO," *No.* 2, *note.*)

Luke xxii. 15.

NO, NOR EVER.

{ οὐδέ, *see above,* οὐ μή, *see* "NO," *No.* 9, } no indeed, nor in any wise.

Matt. xxiv. 21.

NO, NOT.

1. οὐδέ, { and not, not ever,
2. μήδε, { also not, } (*differing according to* "NO," *No.* 2, *note.*)

3. οὔτε, and not, not ever, (*referring to a part of a proposition or clause.*)

1. Matt. viii. 10 (παρ' οὐδενί, *with no one,* L Tr [A.
1. —— xxiv. 36.
3. Mark v. 3 (No. 1, L T Tr A ℵ.)
1. —— xiii. 32.
1. Luke vii. 9.
1. Acts vii. 5.
1. Rom. iii. 10.
2. 1 Cor. v. 11.
1. —— vi. 5 (G→)
1. Gal. ii. 5 (G⇉)

NO, NOT ONE.

{ οὐκ, not, (*see* "NO," *No.* 1), ἔστιν, there is, ἕως, unto, as far as, ἑνός, one, } there is not so much as one.

Rom. iii. 12.

NO, NOT SO MUCH AS.

μηδέ, and not, not even, (*see* "NO," *No.* 2, *note.*)

Mark ii. 2.

NO ONE OF YOU.

μή, (*see* "NO," *No.* 2.)

1 Cor. iv. 6.

NO...SO MUCH AS.

οὐδέ, and not, not even.

Mark vi. 31.

NO SUCH.

οὐ, no, not, (*see No.* 1.)

Acts xv. 24.

NO THING.

μηδείς, *see* "NO," *No.* 4.

Tit. ii. 8.

NO WISE (IN)

1. { οὐ, no, not, μή, no, not, } (*see* "NO," *No.* 9.)

2. { μή, not, (*see* "NO," *No.* 2.) εἰς, unto, τὸ, the, παντελές, wholly ended, complete, always, } completely, } wholly [*unable.*]

3. { οὐ, not, (*see* "NO," *No.* 1) πάντως, wholly, altogether, } not at all.

1. Matt. v. 18.
1. —— x. 42.
2. Luke xiii. 11.
1. —— xviii. 17.
1. John vi. 37.
1. Acts xiii. 41.
3. Rom. iii. 9.
1. Rev. xxi. 27.

See also, BRAWLER, CASE, DOUBT, DWELLING, EFFECT, FORBIDDING, HENCEFORTH, JUDGMENT, LITTLE, LONGER, MATTER, MEANS, MUCH, REPUTATION, THAT.

NOBLE.

εὐγενής, well-born, of high birth, noble.

Acts xvii. 11. | 1 Cor. i. 26.

NOBLE (MOST)

κράτιστος, (superl. of κράτος, strength) most powerful, most excellent.

Acts xxiv. 3. | Acts xxvi. 25.

NOBLEMAN.

1. βασιλικός, belonging to a king, kingly, royal; *spoken of a person attached to a court,* a courtier.

2. { ἄνθρωπος, a man, (*see* "MAN," *No.* 1), εὐγενής, well-born, noble, } *a certain* man of noble birth.

2. Luke xix. 12. | 1. John iv. 46, marg. *courtier or ruler.*
1. John iv. 49.

NOISE. [noun.]

φωνή, a sound, tone, *as given forth or uttered.*

Rev. vi. 1.

NOISE (MAKE A)

θορυβέω, to make an uproar, clamour, *spoken of a multitude, as applauding, dissenting, or lamenting. Here, mid.*, to make a noise together *among themselves*, to wail together.

Matt. ix. 23.

NOISE (WITH A GREAT)

ῥοιζηδόν, with great noise, with a crash, (*adv. of* ῥοιζέω, ῥοῖζος, noise, rushing, *as of winds and waves*), (*non occ.*)

2 Pet. iii. 10.

NOISE ABROAD. [verb.]

διαλαλέω, to speak throughout, to tell everywhere, tell abroad, divulge, (*occ.* Luke vi. 11.)

Luke i. 65.

NOISED (BE)

ἀκούω, to hear; *pass.*, to be heard of, *i.e.* to be reported.

Mark ii. 1.

NOISED ABROAD (BE)

{ φωνή, sound, γίνομαι, to become, happen, } *this* sound occurring (*part.*)

Acts ii. 6 part. (marg. *noise be made.*)

NOISOME.

κακός, bad; *generically, embracing* every form of evil, *whether moral or physical;* baneful.

Rev. xvi. 2.

NONE.

1. οὐ, no, not, } (*see* "NO," *Nos.* 1 *and* 2, *and note.*)
2. μή, no, not, }

3. οὐδείς, (οὐ, not, *and* εἷς, one) not one, none, (*see* "NO," *Nos.* 3 *and* 2, *note.*)

* *with another negative, strengthening the negation.*

4. μηδείς, (μή, not, *and* εἷς, one) not one, none, (*see* "NO," *Nos.* 4 *and* 2, *note.*)

5. οὔτε, and not, not even, *referring to a part of a proposition or clause.*

(* *Thus differing from* οὐδέ, *which is more emphatic, and refers to whole clauses and propositions.*)

6. { μή, not, (*see* "NO," *No.* 2, *and note.*) τις, any one, any thing. }

1. Matt. xii. 43.
3. —— xix. 17 (*ap.*)
1. —— xxvi. 60 1st.
1. ——— 60 2nd (*om.* οὐκ εὗρον, *yet found they none,* G L[b] T Tr A ℵ.)
1. Mark xii. 31, 32.
1. —— xiv. 55.
3. Luke i. 61.
2. —— iii. 11.
3. —— iv. 26, 27.
2. —— xi. 24.
1. —— xiii. 6, 7.
3. —— xiv. 24.
3. —— xviii. 19, 34.
1. John vi. 22.
3. —— vii. 19.
4. —— viii. 10 (*ap.*)
3. —— xv. 24.
3. —— xvi. 5.
3. —— xvii. 12.
3*. —— xviii. 9.
3. —— xxi. 12.
1. Acts iii. 6.
5. —— iv. 12 (οὐδέ, see No. 5*, L T Tr A* ℵ.)
1. —— vii. 5.
3. —— viii. 16.
4. ——— 24.
4. Acts xi. 19.
3. —— xviii. 17.
— —— xx. 24 (see N of these things.)
4. —— xxiv. 23.
3. —— xxv. 11, 18.
3. —— xxvi. 22.
3*. ——— 26 (i.e. *that any of these things is escaping [the King] I am not persuaded.*)
1. Rom. iii. 10, 11 twice, 12.
1. —— viii. 9.
3. —— xiv. 7.
3. 1 Cor. i. 14.
3. —— ii. 8.
2. —— vii. 29.
3. —— viii. 4.
3. —— ix. 15.
3. —— xiv. 10.
1. 2 Cor. i. 13.
1. Gal. i. 19.
3. —— v. 10.
— 1 Thes. v. 15, see N (that)
4. 1 Tim. v. 14.
6. 1 Pet. iv. 15.
1. 1 John ii. 10.
4. Rev. ii. 10 (No. 2, G ~ L Tr A.)

NONE OF THESE THINGS.

3. Acts xx. 24.

NONE (THAT)

6. 1 Thes. v. 15.

See also, EFFECT, OFFENCE.

NOON.

μεσημβρία, mid-day, noon; *also used of* the mid-day quarter of the sun, *i.e.* the south, (*occ.* Acts viii. 26.)

Acts xxii. 6.

NOR.

(*For various combinations with other words, see below.*)

1. οὐδέ, and not, not even, (*see* "NO," *No.* 2, *and note) referring to the whole of a proposition or clause, and more emphatic than No.* 2, *below.*

2. οὔτε, and not, not even (*see* "NO," *No.* 2, *and note) referring to part of a proposition or clause, and less emphatic than No.* 1.)
   * *preceded by another* οὔτε, *translated* neither.
   † *followed by another* οὔτε, *translated* neither.

3. μήδε, and not, not even, (*for difference between this and No.* 1, *see* "NO," *No.* 2, *and note.*)

4. καί, and, also.

5. { οὐ, not, (*see* "NO," *No.* 1,) } also
   { καί, and, also, } not.

6. ἤ, (*a disjunctive particle,*) or.

7. οὐ, no, not, (*see* "NO," *No.* 1.)

8. μή, no, not, (*see* "NO," *No.* 2.)

2*. Matt. vi. 20 1st.
1. —— 20 2nd.
— —— 25, see N yet.
1. —— 26.
3. —— x. 9 twice, 14.
8. —— 10, with imperat.
1. —— 24.
1. —— xii. 19.
3. —— xxii. 29.
2*. —— 30.
1. —— xxiv. 21.
1. —— xxv. 13.
8. Mark vi. 11.
3. —— viii. 26.
2*. —— xii. 25.
1. Luke vi. 44.
8. —— x. 4 1st.
3. —— 4 2nd.
1. —— xii. 24 1st (No. 2, T A ℵ.)
1. —— 24 2nd.
8. —— xiv. 12 twice.
— —— 35, see Neither.
3. —— xvii. 23.
5. —— xviii. 4 (No. 1, L Tr ℵ.)
2*. —— xx. 35.
1. —— xxi. 15 (No. 6, G T Tr A ℵ.)
6. —— xxii. 68 (*om.* μοι ἢ ἀπολύσητε, *me, nor let me go,* T Tr[b] A[b] ℵ.)
1. John i. 13 twice.
2†. —— 25 (No. 1, L T Tr A ℵ.)
— —— iv. 21, see Neither.
2*. —— v. 37.
2* —— viii. 19.
2*. —— ix. 3.
1. —— xi. 50.
4. —— xii. 40.
1. —— xvi. 3.
3. Acts iv. 18.
1. Acts viii. 21.
1. —— ix. 9.
2*. —— xv. 10.
— —— xix. 37, see Neither
2. —— xxiv. 12.
1. —— 18.
2. Rom. viii. 38 6 times, 39 3 times.
1. —— ix. 16.
3. —— xiv. 21 twice.
1. 1 Cor. ii. 6.
5. —— 9.
2. —— vi. 9 4 times.
2. —— 10 1st & 2nd.
2. —— 10 3rd (No. 7, T A ℵ.)
7. —— 10 4th & 5th.
4. —— x. 32.
6. —— xii. 21.
3. 2 Cor. iv. 2.
1. —— vii. 12.
1. Gal. iii. 28 1st & 2nd.
4. —— 28 3rd.
1. —— iv. 14.
2*. —— v. 6.
2*. —— vi. 15.
4. Eph. v. 3.
6. —— 4, 5 twice.
1. 1 Thes. ii. 3 1st.
2. —— 3 2nd.
2*. —— 5.
1. —— v. 5.
1. 1 Tim. ii. 12.
1. —— vi. 16.
3. —— 17.
3. 2 Tim. i. 8.
3. Heb. xii. 5.
1. —— xiii. 5.
1. 2 Pet. i. 8.
2*. Rev. iii. 15, 16.
1. —— v. 3.
1. —— vii. 16.
2. —— ix. 20 twice, 21 3 times.
2. —— xxi. 4.

NOR YET.

3. Matt. vi. 25.
3. —— x. 10.
2. Acts. xxv. 8.
2. 1 Thes. ii. 6.
1. Heb. ix. 25.

NOR EVER (NO)

{ οὐδε, not even, nor.
{ οὐ, } by no means.
{ μή, } in no wise.

Matt. xxiv. 21.

NORTH.

βοῤῥᾶς, the north wind; *also,* the north.

Luke xiii. 29. | Rev. xxi. 13.

NORTH-WEST.

χῶρος, *Lat.,* corus, caurus, *the Latin name for* the north-west wind; *then,* the north-west.

Acts xxvii. 12.

NOT.

(*For various combinations with other words, see below.*)

1. οὐ, *see* "NO," *No.* 1, *and note.*
   * *used interrogatively.*
   † *with another negative, giving greater emphasis to the negation.*

2. μή, *see* "NO," *No.* 2, *and note.*

3. { οὐ, μή, } *see* "NO," *No.* 9.

4. οὐχί, not; *a strengthened form of* οὐ, (*No.* 1) by no means. *In negative questions,* is not? are not? *expecting an affirmative answer, except when marked* *.

5. οὐδέ, *see* "NO," *No.* 7.

6. μηδέ, and not, also not; *hence,* neither, not even, (*see* "NO," *No.* 7, *and* "*note*" *at No.* 2.)

7. μηδείς, *see* "NO," *No.* 4.

8. οὔτε, and not, also not, neither, *a continuative negative, referring usually to a part of a proposition or clause.*

9. οὐδαμῶς, in no wise, by no means.

10. { μή, no, not, (*see No.* 2,) οὐκ, no, not, (*see No.* 1,) } *an emphatic interrogative, which has lost its negative power, and*

expresses fear and anxiety. μή *is interrogative, and* οὐ *belongs to the following verb.* Yes indeed.

11. μήτι, not at all, not perhaps, if not perhaps, unless perhaps. *As interrog.*, whether at all, whether perhaps? is *or* has then perhaps?

12. εἰ, *see* "NO," *No.* 11.

2. Matt. i. 19, 20.
1. —— 25.
9. —— ii. 6.
2. —— 12.
1. —— 18 twice.
2. —— iii. 9, 10.
1. —— 11.
1. —— iv. 4, 7.
1. —— v. 14.
2. —— 17 1st.
1. —— 17 2nd, 21, 27.
2. —— 29, 30.
1. —— 33.
2. —— 34.
1. —— 36.
2. —— 39, 42.
4. —— 46, 47.
2. —— vi. 1, 2, 3.
1. —— 5.
2. —— 7, 8, 13, 16, 18, 19.
1. —— 20.
2. —— 25.
1. —— 26 1st.
1. —— 26 2nd*.
1. —— 28, 30*.
2. —— vii. 1.
1. —— 3.
2. —— 6.
1. —— 18.
2. —— 19.
1. —— 21, 22, 25.
2. —— 26.
1. —— 29.
1. —— viii. 8, 20.
1. —— ix. 12, 13, 14, 24.
2. —— x. 5 twice.
1. —— 20.
3. —— 23.
1. —— 24.
2. —— 26 1st.
1. —— 26 2nd & 3rd.
2. —— 28 twice.
4. —— 29 1st.
1. —— 29 2nd.
2. —— 31, 34 1st.
1. —— 34 2nd, 37 twice.
1. —— 38 1st (ἂν μή, Lm.)
1. —— 38 2nd.
1. —— xi. 11, 17 twice, 20.
1. —— xii. 2, 3*, 4, 5*, 7 twice.
4. —— 11.
1. —— 19, 20 twice.
11. —— 23 (from year 1638.)
1. —— 24, 25.
2. —— 30 twice.
1. —— 31, 32.
1. —— xiii. 5.
2. —— 6.
1. —— 12, 13 twice.
3. —— 14 twice.
1. —— 17.
2. —— 19.
1. —— 21.
4. —— 27.
1. —— 34 (No. 5, L T Tr A ℵ.)
1. —— 55* 1st.
4. —— 55 2nd (No. 1, L T Tr A ℵ.)

4. Matt. xiii. 56.
1. —— 57, 58.
1. —— xiv. 4, 16.
2. —— 27.
1. —— xv. 2.
3. —— 6.
1. —— 11, 13, 20, 23, 24, 26, 32.
1. —— xvi. 3, 11 twice, 12, 17, 18.
3. —— 22.
1. —— 23.
3. —— 28.
2. —— xvii. 7.
1. —— 12, 16, 19, 21 (ap.), [24*.
3. —— xviii. 3.
4. —— 12.
2. —— 13.
1. —— 14, 22.
2. —— 25.
1. —— 30, 33*.
1. —— xix. 4*.
2. —— 6.
1. —— 8, 10, 11.
2. —— 14.
1. —— 18 3 times.
4. —— xx. 13.
1. —— 15*, 22, 23, 26, 28.
2. —— xxi. 21 1st.
1. —— 21 2nd, 25, 27, 29, 30, 32 1st.
1. —— 32 2nd (No. 5, L Tr Ab.)
1. —— xxii. 3, 8, 11.
2. —— 12.
1. —— 16, 17.
2. —— 29.
1. —— 31*, 32.
2. —— xxiii. 3 1st.
1. —— 3 2nd, 4.
2. —— 8, 23.
1. —— 30, 37.
3. —— 39.
1. —— xxiv. 2* 1st (om. G⇉)
3. —— 2 2nd.
3. —— 2 3rd (No. 1, G L T Tr A ℵ.)
2. —— 17.
1. —— 21.
2. —— 23, 26 twice.
1. —— 29.
3. —— 34, 35.
1. —— 39, 42, 43, 44, 50 twice.
1. —— xxv. 9 (No. 3, G L T Tr A.)
1. —— 12, 24 twice, 26 twice, 43 3 times.
1. —— 44, 45 1st.
5. —— 45 2nd.
2. —— xxvi. 5.
1. —— 11, 24.
3. —— 29, 35.
1. —— 39, 40, 42, 53, 70, 72, 74.
1. —— xxvii. 6, 13*, 34, [42.
2. —— xxviii. 5.
1. —— 6.
2. —— 10.
1. Mark i. 7, 22, 34.

2. Mark ii. 4.
1. —— 17, 18, 19 (ap.), 24, 26, 27.
2. —— iii. 20.
1. —— 24, 25, 26.
1. —— iv. 5.
2. —— 12.
1. —— 13*, 21*, 25, 27, 34, 38*.
1. —— v. 19.
2. —— 36.
1. —— 39.
1. —— vi. 3* twice, 4.
2. —— 9, 11.
1. —— 18, 19, 26.
2. —— 34, 50.
1. —— 52.
1. —— vii. 3, 4, 5, 18* 1st, 18 2nd, 19, 24, 27.
1. —— viii. 18* 3 times.
1. —— 21 (οὔπω, [do you] not yet, instead of πῶς οὐ, how is it that ye do not, L T Tr [A* ℵ.)
1. —— 33.
3. —— ix. 1.
1. —— 6, 18, 28, 30, 37, 38 twice (ap.)
2. —— 39.
1. —— 40.
3. —— 41.
1. —— 44 twice (ap.), 46 twice (ap.), 48 twice.
2. —— x. 9, 14.
3. —— 15.
2. —— 19 1st.
2. —— 19 2nd (om. G→)
2. —— 19 3rd.
1. —— 27, 38, 40, 43, 45.
1. —— xi. 13, 16, 17*.
2. —— 23.
1. —— 26, 31, 33.
5. —— xii. 10.
1. —— 14 twice.
2. —— 15.
1. —— 24* 1st.
2. —— 24 2nd.
1. —— 26*, 27, 34.
3. —— xiii. 2 twice.
2. —— 7.
1. —— 11, 14.
2. —— 15, 16.
1. —— 19.
2. —— 21.
1. —— 24.
3. —— 30, 31.
1. —— 33, 35.
2. —— xiv. 2. [56.
1. —— 7, 29, 36, 37, 49,
1. —— 68 (No. 8, L T Tr A ℵ.)
1. —— 71.
1. —— xv. 23, 31.
2. —— xvi. 6 1st.
1. —— 6 2nd, 14 (ap.)
3. —— 18 (ap.)
2. Luke i. 13, 20 1st.
1. —— 20 2nd, 22.
2. —— 30.
1. —— 33, 34.
2. —— ii. 10, 26.
1. —— 37, 43.
2. —— 45.
1. —— 49*, 50.
2. —— iii. 8, 9.
1. —— 16.
2. —— iv. 2.
1. —— 4, 12, 22*.
7. —— 35.
1. —— 41.
2. —— v. 10, 19.
1. —— 31, 32, 36.
1. —— vi. 2, 4.
2. —— 29, 30, 37 1st.
3. —— 37 2nd (ἵνα μή, in order that...not, instead of καὶ οὐ μή, and...not, L.)

2. Luke vi. 37 3rd.
3. —— 37 4th.
4. —— 39.
1. —— 40, 41, 42, 43, 44, 46, 48.
2. —— 49.
1. —— vii. 6 1st.
2. —— 6 2nd.
1. —— 6 3rd.
2. —— 13, 30.
1. —— 32 twice, 45, 46.
2. —— viii. 10 twice.
1. —— 17 1st.
1. —— 17 2nd (No. 3, L T Tr A ℵ.)
2. —— 18.
1. —— 19.
2. —— 28.
1. —— 47.
2. —— 49 (μηκέτι, not any longer, L T Tr ℵ.)
2. —— 50, 52 1st.
1. —— 52 2nd.
2. —— ix. 5.
3. —— 27.
2. —— 33.
1. —— 40, 49.
2. —— 50 1st.
1. —— 50 2nd.
2. —— 52.
1. —— 53, 55* (ap.), 56 (ap.), 58.
2. —— x. 7, 10, 20.
1. —— 24 twice, 40*, 42.
2. —— xi. 4, 7 1st.
1. —— 7 2nd, 8.
2. —— 23 twice, 35.
1. —— 38, 40*.
2. —— 42.
1. —— 44, 46, 52.
1. —— xii. 2 twice.
2. —— 4.
4. —— 6 1st.
1. —— 6 2nd.
2. —— 7.
1. —— 10, 15.
4. —— 21.
8. —— 26 (No. 5, L Tr A ℵ.)
1. —— 27 1st (ap.)
5. —— 27 2nd (ap.), 27 3rd.
2. —— 29, 32, 33.
1. —— 39, 40, 46 twice.
2. —— 47, 48.
1. —— 56, 57.
3. —— 59.
2. —— xiii. 14.
1. —— 15*, 16*, 24, 25, 27, 33, 34.
3. —— 35.
1. —— xiv. 5*, 6.
2. —— 8, 12.
1. —— 14, 20, 26 twice, 27 twice.
4. —— 28.
2. —— 29.
1. —— 30.
4. —— 31.
1. —— 33 twice.
1. —— xv. 4*.
4. —— 8.
1. —— 13, 28.
1. —— xvi. 3, 11, 12, 13.
2. —— 26.
1. —— 31.
4. —— xvii. 8.
1. —— 9 (om. οὐ δοκῶ, I trow not, Lb T Tr A ℵ*.)
4. —— 17 (No. 1, L A.)
1. —— 18, 20, 22.
2. —— 23, 31 twice.
2. —— xviii. 1, 2.
1. —— 4 twice.
3. —— 7.
1. —— 11, 13†.
2. —— 16, 20 4 times.
3. —— 30.

1. Luke xix. 3, 14, 21 twice, 22 twice, 23.
2. —— 26, 27.
1. —— 44 twice, 48.
1. —— xx. 5.
2. —— 7.
1. —— 26, 38.
1. —— xxi. 6 twice.
2. —— 8, 9 1st.
1. —— 9 2nd.
2. —— 14.
1. —— 15.
3. —— 18.
2. —— 21.
3. —— 32, 33.
3. —— xxii. 16, 18.
1. —— 26.
4. —— 27.
3. —— 34 (No. 1, T Tr A ℵ.)
2. —— 40, 42.
1. —— 57, 58, 60.
3. —— 67, 68.
2. —— xxiii. 28.
1. —— 34 (ap.)
5. —— 40.
1. —— 51.
1. —— xxiv. 3, 6.
2. —— 16.
1. —— 18.
2. —— 23.
1. —— 24.
4. —— 26, 32.
1. —— 39.
5. John i. 3.
1. —— 5, 8, 10, 11, 13, 20 twice, 21, 25, 26, 27, 31, 33.
1. —— ii. 9, 12.
2. —— 16.
1. —— 24, 25.
1. —— iii. 3, 5.
2. —— 7.
1. —— 8, 10, 11, 12.
2. —— 16 (ap.)
1. —— 17, 18 1st.
2. —— 18 2nd & 3rd
1. —— 28, 34, 36.
1. —— iv. 2, 18, 22.
11. —— 29.
1. —— 32, 35*.
3. —— 48.
1. —— v. 10, 13, 18.
2. —— 23 1st.
1. —— 23 2nd, 24.
2. —— 28.
1. —— 30, 31, 34, 38 twice, 40, 41, 42, 43, 44.
2. —— 45.
1. —— 47.
1. —— vi. 7.
1. —— 17 (οὔπω, *not yet*, L T Tr A ℵ.)
2. —— 20.
1. —— 22, 24, 26.
2. —— 27.
1. —— 32, 36, 38, 42*.
2. —— 43.
1. —— 46, 58, 64 1st.
2. —— 64 2nd.
1. —— 70†.
1. —— vii. 1, 7, 10, 16, 19*, 22.
2. —— 24.
1. —— 25*, 28 twice, 34 twice, 35, 36 twice.
4. —— 42 (No. 1, L.)
1. —— 45.
2. —— 49.
2. —— viii. 6 (ap.)
3. —— 12.
1. —— 13, 14, 16, 21, 22, 23, 27, 29, 35, 40, 41, 43 twice, 44, 45, 46, 47 twice, 48*, 49, 55 twice.
1. —— ix. 8*, 12, 16 twice, 18, 21 twice, 25, 27, 29, 30, 31, 32.
2. John ix. 39.
2. —— x. 1.
3. —— 5 1st.
1. —— 5 2nd, 6, 8, 10, 12 twice, 13, 16, 21, 25, 26 twice, 33, 34*, 35, 37 1st.
2. —— 37 2nd, 38.
1. —— xi. 4.
4. —— 9 1st.
1. —— 9 2nd, 15, 21, 32, 37* 1st.
2. —— 37 2nd.
1. —— 40*.
2. —— 50.
1. —— 51, 52.
3. —— 56.
1. —— xii. 5, 6, 8, 9.
2. —— 15.
1. —— 16, 30, 35, 37, 39, 42, 44.
2. —— 47 1st (μὴ φυλάξῃ, *have not kept them*, instead of μὴ πιστεύσῃ, *believe not*, G∾L T Tr A ℵ.)
1. —— 47 2nd & 3rd
2. —— 48.
1. —— 49.
1. —— xiii. 7.
2. —— 9.
1. —— 10 1st.
4. —— 10* 2nd, 11*.
1. —— 16, 18, 33, 36, 37.
3. —— 38.
2. —— xiv. 1.
1. —— 5, 9, 10* 1st, 10 2nd, 17 twice, 18, 22 1st.
4. —— 22 2nd.
2. —— 24 1st.
1. —— 24 2nd & 3rd, 27 1st.
2. —— 27 2nd.
2. —— xv. 2.
1. —— 4, 15, 16, 19, 20, 21, 22, 24.
1. —— xvi. 3, 4.
1. —— 7 (No. 3, Tr.)
1. —— 9, 12, 13.
1. —— 16 (οὐκέτι, *no longer*, L T Tr A ℵ.)
1. —— 17, 18, 19, 26, 30, 32.
1. —— xvii. 9, 14 twice, 15, 16 twice, 25.
3. —— xviii. 11.
2. —— 17 1st.
1. —— 17 2nd.
2. —— 25 1st.
1. —— 25 2nd, 26*, 28, 30, 31†, 36 twice.
2. —— 40.
1. —— xix. 10* twice, 12.
2. —— 21, 24.
1. —— 33, 36.
1. —— xx. 2, 5, 7, 13, 14.
2. —— 17.
1. —— 24.
3. —— 25.
2. —— 27, 29.
1. —— 30.
1. —— xxi. 4, 8, 11, 18, 23 3 times.
2. Acts i. 4.
1. —— 5, 7.
1. —— ii. 7*, 15, 24, 27.
1. —— 31 (No. 8, G∾L T Tr A ℵ.)
1. —— 34.
2. —— iii. 23.
1. —— iv. 16.
2. —— 18.
1. —— 20.
4. —— v. 4 1st & 2nd.
1. —— 4 3rd.
2. —— 7.
1. —— 22.
1. Acts v. 28* 1st (*om.* G→L T Tr A ℵ, i.e. *We did*, instead of, *Did we not?*)
2. —— 28 2nd.
1. —— 39.
2. —— 40.
1. —— 42.
1. —— vi. 2, 10, 1
1. —— vii. 18.
2. —— 19.
1. —— 25, 32, 39, 40, 48.
4. —— 50.
1. —— 52, 53.
2. —— 60.
1. —— viii. 21, 32.
1. —— ix. 21*.
2. —— 26, 38.
2. —— x. 15.
7. —— 28.
1. —— 41.
2. —— 47.
2. —— xi. 9.
1. —— xii. 9, 14.
2. —— 19.
1. —— 22, 23.
1. —— xiii. 10*.
2. —— 11.
1. —— 25 twice, 35, 39.
1. —— xiv. 17.
2. —— 18.
1. —— xv. 1.
2. —— 19, 38 twice.
1. —— xvi. 7, 21.
1. —— xvii. 4.
2. —— 6.
1. —— 12, 24, 27, 29.
2. —— xviii. 9 twice.
1. —— 20.
1. —— xix. 26, 27, 30.
2. —— 31.
1. —— 32, 35.
2. —— xx. 10.
1. —— 12.
2. —— 16, 22.
1. —— 27.
2. —— 29.
1. —— 31.
2. —— xxi. 4, 12.
1. —— 13.
2. —— 14, 21, 34.
1. —— 38*.
1. —— xxii. 9, 11, 18, 22.
1. —— xxiii. 5 twice.
2. —— 9 (*om.* μὴ θεομαχῶμεν, *let us not fight against God*, G L T Tr A ℵ.)
2. —— 21.
1. —— xxv. 7, 11, 16.
2. —— 24, 27.
1. —— xxvi. 19, 25, 26, 29.
2. —— xxvii. 7.
1. —— 10, 14.
2. —— 15, 21, 24.
1. —— 31, 39.
1. —— xxviii. 4, 19.
3. —— 26 twice.
1. Rom. i. 13, 16, 21, [28 1st.
2. —— 28 2nd.
1. —— 32.
1. —— ii. 13.
2. —— 14 twice.
1. —— 21 1st.
2. —— 21 2nd, 22.
4. —— 26 (No. 1, L T Tr ℵ.)
1. —— 28, 29 twice.
2. —— iii. 8.
1. —— 17.
4. —— 29.
1. —— iv. 2, 4.
2. —— 5.
3. —— 8.
1. —— 10, 12, 13, 16.
2. —— 17, 19 1st.
1. —— 19 2nd (*om.* G⇄L T Tr Ab ℵ.)
1. Rom. iv. 20, 23.
1. —— v. 3, 5, 11, 13.
2. —— 14 (*om.* G→)
1. —— 15, 16.
2. —— vi. 12.
1. —— 14 twice, 15, 16*.
1. —— vii. 6, 7 3 times, 15 twice, 16, 18, 19 twice, 20.
2. —— viii. 1 (ap.), 4.
1. —— 7, 8, 9 twice, 12, 15, 18, 20, 23, 24, 25, 26, 32 1st.
4. —— 32 2nd.
1. —— ix. 1, 6 twice, 8, 10, 11, 16, 21*, 24, 25 twice, [26.
2. —— 30.
1. —— 31, 32, 33.
1. —— x. 2, 3.
2. —— 6.
1. —— 11, 14 twice, 16.
10. —— 18, 19.
2. —— 20 twice.
1. —— xi. 2 1st, 2* 2nd, 4, 7.
2. —— 8 twice, 10, 18 1st.
1. —— 18 2nd.
2. —— 20.
1. —— 21, 25.
2. —— xii. 2, 3.
1. —— 4.
2. —— 11, 14, 16, 19, 21.
1. —— xiii. 3 1st.
2. —— 3 2nd.
1. —— 4, 5, 9 1st, 2nd, & 3rd.
1. —— 9 4th (*om.* οὐ ψευδομαρτυρήσεις, *thou shalt not bear false witness*, G L T Tr A.)
1. —— 9 5th.
2. —— 13 3 times, 14.
2. —— xiv. 1, 3 4 times.
2. —— 6 1st (ap.)
1. —— 6 2nd (ap.), 6 3rd, 17, 23.
2. —— xv. 1.
1. —— 3, 18 twice, 20, 21 twice.
1. —— xvi. 4, 18.
1. 1 Cor. i. 16, 17 twice.
4. —— 20.
1. —— 21, 26 3 times.
2. —— 28.
1. —— ii. 1, 2, 4, 6, 8, 9, 12, 13, 14.
1. —— iii. 1, 2.
2. —— 3.
2. —— 4 (No. 1, L T Tr A ℵ.)
1. —— 16.
5. —— iv. 3.
1. —— 4, 7 1st.
2. —— 7 2nd.
1. —— 14, 15.
2. —— 18.
1. —— 19, 20.
4. —— v. 2.
1. —— 6 1st, 6* 2nd.
2. —— 8, 9.
1. —— 10.
2. —— 11.
4. —— 12.
4. —— vi. 1.
1. —— 2*, 3*, 5*.
4. —— 7 twice.
1. —— 9* 1st, 9 2nd.
2. —— 9 3rd.
1. —— 12 twice, 13, 15*, 16*, 19* 1st, 19 2nd.
2. —— vii. 1.
1. —— 4 twice.
2. —— 5.
1. —— 6, 9, 10 1st.
2. —— 10 2nd, 11.
1. —— 12 1st.
2. —— 12 2nd, 13.
1. —— 15.
2. —— 18 twice, 21, 23, 27 twice.

1. 1 Cor. vii. 28 twice.
2. ——— 30 3 times, 31.
1. ——— 35, 36.
2. ——— 38.
1. —— viii. 7, 8.
4. ——— 10.
1. —— ix. 1* 1st & 2nd.
4. ——— 1 3rd.
1. ——— 1 4th, 2.
10. ——— 4, 5.
1. ——— 6*, 7 1st, 7* 2nd.
4. ——— 8 (No. 1, G ~ L T Tr A ℵ.)
1. ——— 9, 12* 1st, 12 2nd, 13*.
2. ——— 18, 21.
1. ——— 24*, 26 twice.
1. —— x. 1, 5.
2. ——— 6.
1. ——— 13.
4. ——— 16 twice.
4. ——— 18 (No. 1, L T A ℵ.)
1. ——— 20 twice, 21 twice, 23 twice
2. ——— 28, 33.
1. —— xi. 6, 7, 8, 17 twice,
2. ——— 22 1st & 2nd. [20.
1. ——— 22 3rd.
2. ——— 29.
1. ——— 31.
1. —— xii. 1, 14, 15 3 times, 16 3 times, 21.
2. —— xiii. 1, 3.
1. ——— 4 3 times, 5 3 times,
1. —— xiv. 2, 16, 17. [6.
2. ——— 20.
5. ——— 21.
1. ——— 22 twice, 23*, 33, 34.
2. ——— 39.
1. —— xv. 9, 10 twice, 14, 15 twice, 16, 17, 29, 32.
2. ——— 33, 34.
1. ——— 36, 37, 39, 46, 50, 51 (ap.), 58.
1. —— xvi. 7, 12, 22.
1. 2 Cor. i. 8, 12, 18, 19, 24.
2. —— ii. 1.
1. ——— 4, 5, 11.
2. ——— 13.
1. ——— 17.
1. —— iii. 3 twice, 5, 6.
2. ——— 7.
1. ——— 13 1st.
2. ——— 13 2nd.
1. —— iv. 1.
2. ——— 2.
1. ——— 5.
2. ——— 8 twice.
1. ——— 9 twice, 16.
2. ——— 18 twice.
1. —— v. 3, 4, 7, 12 1st.
1. ——— 12 2nd (No. 2, L T Tr ℵ.)
2. ——— 19.
2. —— vi. 1, 9.
1. ——— 12.
2. ——— 14, 17.
1. —— vii. 3, 7, 8, 9, 12, 14.
1. —— viii. 5, 8, 10, 12, 13, 19, 21.
2. —— ix. 5, 7.
1. ——— 12.
2. —— x. 2.
1. ——— 3.
2. ——— 14.
1. ——— 16, 18.
1. —— xi. 4 3 times, 6, 11, 17, 29 twice, 31.
1. —— xii. 1, 2 twice.
1. ——— 3 (om. L.)
1. ——— 4, 5, 6, 13, 14 3 times, 16, 18 twice, 20 twice.
2. ——— 21.
1. —— xiii. 2, 3, 5*, 6, 7, 10.

1. Gal. i. 1, 7, 10, 11, 16, 19, 20.
1. —— ii. 14 twice, 15, 16 twice, 21.
2. —— iii. 1 (ap.)
1. ——— 10, 12, 16, 17, 20.
1. —— iv. 8, 14, 17.
2. ——— 18.
1. ——— 21, 27 twice.
3. ——— 30.
1. ——— 31.
2. —— v. 1, 7.
1. ——— 8.
2. ——— 13.
3. ——— 16.
1. ——— 18, 21.
2. ——— 26.
1. —— vi. 4.
2. ——— 7 1st.
1. ——— 7 2nd.
2. ——— 9 twice.
1. Eph. i. 16, 21.
1. —— ii. 8, 9.
1. —— iii. 5.
2. ——— 13.
1. —— iv. 20.
2. ——— 26 twice, 30.
1. —— v. 4.
2. ——— 7, 15, 17, 18, 27.
2. —— vi. 4, 6.
1. ——— 7, 12.
1. Phil. i. 16, 22, 29.
2. —— ii. 4.
1. ——— 6.
2. ——— 12.
1. ——— 16, 21, 27.
1. —— iii. 1.
2. ——— 9.
1. ——— 12.
1. ——— 13 (οὔπω, *not yet*, Lm T ℵ.)
1. —— iv. 11, 17.
1. Col. i. 9.
2. ——— 23.
1. —— ii. 1, 8.
2. ——— 18 (*om.* G ∺ Lb T Tr A ℵ.)
1. ——— 19.
2. ——— 21 1st.
6. ——— 21 2nd & 3rd.
1. ——— 23.
2. —— iii. 2, 9, 19, 21, 22.
1. ——— 23.
1. 1 Thes. i. 5, 8 1st.
2. ——— 8 2nd.
1. —— ii. 1, 3, 4, 8.
2. ——— 9.
1. ——— 13.
2. ——— 15.
1. ——— 17.
2. ——— 19.
2. —— iv. 5 twice.
1. ——— 7, 8, 9, 13.
3. ——— 15.
3. —— v. 3.
1. ——— 4, 5.
2. ——— 6.
1. ——— 9.
2. ——— 19, 20.
2. 2 Thes. i. 8.
2. —— ii. 2.
1. ——— 5, 10.
2. ——— 12.
1. —— iii. 2.
2. ——— 6.
1. ——— 7.
2. ——— 8.
1. ——— 9, 10.
2. ——— 13.
1. ——— 14.
2. ——— 15.
1. 1 Tim. i. 9.
2. ——— 20.
1. —— ii. 7.
2. ——— 9.
1. ——— 12, 14.
2. —— iii. 3 1st.

2. 1 Tim. iii. 3 2nd (*om.* μὴ αἰσχροκερδῆ, *not greedy of filthy lucre*, G L T Tr A ℵ.)
1. ——— 5.
2. ——— 6, 8 3 times, 11.
2. —— iv. 14.
2. —— v. 1.
1. ——— 8.
2. ——— 9.
1. ——— 13 1st.
2. ——— 13 2nd, 16.
1. ——— 18.
2. ——— 19.
1. ——— 25.
2. —— vi. 2, 3, 17.
1. 2 Tim. i. 7.
2. ——— 8.
1. ——— 9, 12, 16.
1. —— ii. 5, 9.
2. ——— 14.
1. ——— 20, 24.
1. —— iv. 3, 8.
2. Titus i. 6, 7 4 times, 11, 14.
2. —— ii. 3 twice, 9, 10.
1. —— iii. 5.
1. Heb. i. 12.
4. ——— 14.
1. —— ii. 5, 11, 16.
2. ——— 3, 8.
1. ——— 10.
12. ——— 11, with indicative (see If.)
2. ——— 15.
1. ——— 16.
4. ——— 17.
2. ——— 18.
1. ——— 19.
1. —— iv. 2 1st.
2. ——— 2 2nd.
1. ——— 6.
2. ——— 7.
1. ——— 8, 15 2nd.
2. ——— 15 3rd.
1. —— v. 4, 5, 12.
2. —— vi. 1.
1. ——— 10.
2. —— vii. 6.
1. ——— 11, 16, 20, 21, 27.
1. —— viii. 2.
2. ——— 4.
1. ——— 9 twice.
2. ——— 11.
1. —— ix. 5, 7.
2. ——— 9.
1. ——— 11 twice, 24.
1. —— x. 1.
1. ——— 2 (*om.* E), 5, 8.
2. ——— 25, 35.
1. ——— 37, 39.
1. —— xi. 1.
2. ——— 5 1st.
1. ——— 5 2nd.
2. ——— 8, 13.
1. ——— 16, 23.
2. ——— 27.
1. ——— 31, 35, 38, 39.
2. —— xii. 5.
1. ——— 7, 8, 9, 18.
2. ——— 19.
1. ——— 20, 25, 26.
2. ——— 27.
2. —— xiii. 2.
1. ——— 6.
2. ——— 9 1st.
1. ——— 9 2nd.
2. ——— 16, 17.
2. Jas. i. 5, 7, 16.
1. ——— 20.
2. ——— 22.
1. ——— 23, 25.
2. ——— 26.
2. —— ii. 1.
1. ——— 4*, 5*, 6*, 7*.
2. ——— 11 twice, 14, 16.
1. ——— 21*, 24, 25*.
2. —— iii. 1.

1. Jas. iii. 2, 10.
2. ——— 14.
1. ——— 15.
1. —— iv. 1*, 2 1st, 2nd, & 3rd.
2. ——— 2 4th.
1. ——— 3, 4*.
2. ——— 11 1st.
1. ——— 11 2nd, 14.
2. ——— 17.
1. —— v. 6.
2. ——— 9, 12, 17 1st.
1. ——— 17 2nd.
1. 1 Pet. i. 8 1st.
2. ——— 8 2nd.
1. ——— 12.
2. ——— 14.
1. ——— 18, 23.
2. —— ii. 6.
1. ——— 10 twice.
2. ——— 16.
1. ——— 18, 23 twice.
1. —— iii. 3.
2. ——— 6, 7, 9, 14.
1. ——— 21.
2. —— iv. 4, 12, 16.
1. 2 Pet. i. 12, (*om.* G ~ L T Tr A ℵ; i.e. *I shall be ever sure*, instead of, *I will not be negligent.*)
1. ——— 16, 21.
1. —— ii. 3 twice, 4, 5, 10, 11.
2. ——— 21.
2. —— iii. 8.
1. ——— 9 1st.
2. ——— 9 2nd.
1. 1 John i. 6, 8, 10 twice.
1. —— ii. 2.
2. ——— 4 1st.
1. ——— 4 2nd, 11.
2. ——— 15 1st.
1. ——— 15 2nd, 16 19 twice, 21 twice.
5. ——— 23.
1. ——— 27.
2. ——— 28.
1. —— iii. 1 twice, 6 twice, 9 twice.
1. ——— 10 1st.
1. ——— 10 2nd, 12.
2. ——— 13, 14, 18, 21.
2. —— iv. 1, 3 1st.
1. ——— 3 2nd, 6 twice.
2. ——— 8 1st.
1. ——— 8 2nd, 10, 18.
2. ——— 20 1st.
1. ——— 20 2nd.
1. —— v. 3, 6.
2. ——— 10 1st.
1. ——— 10 2nd.
2. ——— 12 1st.
1. ——— 12 2nd.
2. ——— 16 1st & 2nd.
1. ——— 16 3rd, 17, 18 twice.
1. 2 John 1, 5.
2. ——— 7, 9 1st.
1. ——— 9 2nd, 10 1st.
2. ——— 10 2nd.
1. ——— 12.
2. 3 John 5, 6.
1. ——— 9.
2. ——— 10, 11 1st.
1. ——— 11 2nd, 13.
2. Jude 5, 6.
1. ——— 9, 10.
2. ——— 19.
2. Rev. i. 17.
1. —— ii. 2 twice, 3 (*ap.*), 9.
2. ——— 11.
1. ——— 13, 21, 24 twice.
1. —— iii. 2.
2. ——— 3.
1. ——— 4.
2. ——— 5.
1. ——— 8, 9, 17.
2. ——— 18.
1. —— iv. 8.
2. —— v. 5.

2. Rev. vi. 6.
1. —— 10.
2. — vii. 3.
2. — viii. 12.
1. — ix. 4.
1. —— 6 (No. 3, G L T Tr A ℵ.)
1. —— 20.
2. — x. 4.
2. — xi. 2.
1. Rev. xi. 9.
1. — xii. 8, 11.
1. — xiii. 8.
2. —— 15.
1. — xiv. 4.
3. — xv. 4.
1. — xvi. 9, 11, 18, 20.
1. — xvii. 8 3 times, 11.
1. — xx. 4, 5, 15.
2. — xxii. 10.

NOT (ALSO)

οὐδέ, and not, also not, not even.

Rom. xi. 21.

NOT (AND IF)

{ **εἰ**, if, / **δε**, but, / **μήγε**, not indeed. } if otherwise, indeed, *annulling the preceding proposition.*

Luke xiii. 19, indic.

NOT (AS YET...)

οὐδέπω, also not ever, not ever yet, not yet.

John xx. 9.

NOT (EVEN)

οὐδέ, and not, not even.

Matt. vi. 29. | John xxi. 25.

NOT (HENCEFORTH)

1. **οὐκέτι**, and not, not even.
2. **μηκέτι**, no more, no further, no longer.

2. John xv. 15. | 1. Rom. vi. 6.
1. Eph. iv. 17.

NOT (HEREAFTER...)

οὐκέτι, no more, no longer, no further.

John xiv. 30.

NOT (HITHERTO)

οὔπω, not even yet, not yet.

1 Cor. iii. 2.

NOT (IF)

1. { **ἐάν**, if, (*see* "IF," *No.* 1,) / **μή**, not, (*see* "NO," *No.* 2,) } (a) *followed by subj., aor.*, (*see* "IF," *No.* 1b†.) (b) *followed by subj., present*, (*see* "IF," *No.* 1b*.)
2. { **εἰ**, if, (*see* "IF," *No.* 4.) / **μή**, not, (*see* "NO," *No.* 2.) }
3. { **εἰ**, if, (*see* "IF," *No.* 4,) / **δὲ**, but, / **μήγε**, not indeed, } *see* "NOT (AND IF)"

1a. Matt. vi. 15.
1b. — x. 13.
1a. — xviii. 16, 35.
3. Luke x. 6, *with indic.*
1a. John viii. 24.
2. — ix. 33.
1a. — xiii. 8.
3. — xiv. 3.
1a. — xv. 6.
2. —— 22, 24.
1a. John xvi. 7.
2. — xviii. 30.
2. Acts xxvi. 32.
1a. Rom. xi. 23.
1a. 1 Cor. viii. 8.
1b. — ix. 16.
1b. — xiv. 11.
1b. Jas. ii. 17.
1b. 1 John iii. 21.
1a. Rev. iii. 3.

NOT A.

οὐδείς, not one, (*see* "NO," *No.* 2, *note.*)

Luke vii. 23.

NOT ANY.

οὐδείς, *see above.*

Acts xxvii. 34.

NOT ANY AT ALL.

οὐδείς, *see above.*

Luke xx. 40.

NOT ANY MAN.

μηδείς, not one, (*see* "NO," *No.* 2, *note.*)

Acts x. 28.

NOT ANY MORE.

μηκέτι, no more, no further, no longer, (*see* "NO," *No.* 2, *note.*)

Rom. xiv. 13.

NOT AS YET.

1. **οὐκέτι**, no more, no longer, no further, (*see* "NO," *No.* 2, *note.*)
2. **μηδέπω**, even not yet, not even yet.

1. 2 Cor. i. 23. | 2. Heb. xi. 7.

NOT A WHIT.

μηδείς, not one, (*see* "NO," *No.* 2, *note.*)

2 Cor. xi. 5.

NOT AT ALL.

1. **οὐδείς**, not one *thing*,
2. **μηδείς**, not one *thing*,

} *see* "NO," *No.* 2, *and note.*

3. { οὐ, μή, } *see* "NO," *No.* 9.

1. Gal. iv. 12. | 2. 1 Thes. iii. 11.
3. Rev. xxi. 25.

NOT EVEN.

οὐδέ, and not, also not, not even.

1 Cor. xi. 14.

NOT HENCEFORTH.

μηκέτι, no more, no further, no longer.

2 Cor. v. 15.

NOT IN ANY WISE.

οὐ μή, *see* "NO," *No.* 9.

Mark xiv. 31.

NOT ONCE.

μηδέ, and not, not even.

Eph. v. 3.

NOT SO.

1. **μηδαμῶς**, by no means.
2. **οὐχί**, *see* "NOT," *No.* 4.

2. Luke i. 60. | 1. Acts x. 14.
1. Acts xi. 8.

NOT SO MUCH AS.

οὐδέ, not even.

Luke vi. 3. | Acts xix. 2.
1 Cor. v. 1.

NOT NOW.

οὐκέτι, no more, no further, no longer.

Philem. 16.

NOT (NOW)

οὐκέτι, *see above.*

John iv. 22. | John xxi. 6.
Rom. xiv. 15.

NOT (THEN)

οὐδέ, not even.

1 Cor. xv. 13.

NOT (THOU DO IT)

μή, *see* "NO," *No. 2, and note.*

Rev. xix. 10. | Rev. xxii. 9.

NOT YET.

1. **οὔπω**, not even yet, } *see* "NO," *No.* 2,
2. **μήπω**, not even yet, } *and note.*

3. **οὐδέπω**, also not even, not even yet.

1. Matt. xv. 17 (*οὐ*, *no*, L T Tr), i.e. *om. yet.*
1. —— xvi. 9.
1. —— xxiv. 6.
1. Mark viii. 17.
1. —— xiii. 7.
1. John ii. 4.
1. —— iii. 24.
1. —— vii. 6.
1. —— 8 1st (*οὐκ*, *not*, G T Tr A ℵ), i.e. *om. yet.*
1. —— 8 2nd, 30, 39 1st.
3. John vii. 39 2nd (No. 1, L Tr A ℵ.)
1. —— viii. 20, 57.
1. —— xi. 30.
1. —— xx. 17.
2. Rom. ix. 11.
1. Heb. ii. 8.
2. —— ix. 8.
1. —— xii. 4.
1. 1 John iii. 2.
1. Rev. xvii. 10 (*οὐκ*, *not*, L; *οὕτω*, *thus*, ℵ.)

NOT (WHETHER OR)

μήποτε, not even, never, *in no supposable case; also, in indirect inquiry*, whether perhaps, if perhaps.

Luke iii. 15.

NOT (YET)

1. **οὐτέ**, and not, not even.
2. **οὐκέτι**, no more, no further, no longer.

1. Acts xxv. 8. | 2. Gal. ii. 20.
1. 1 Thes. ii. 6.

See also, AGREE, AIM, ALBEIT, ALSO, ANY, APPEAR, ASHAMED, BELIEVE, BRAWLER, CAN, CEASE, CIRCUMCISED, COMMODIOUS, CONDEMNED, CORRUPTIBLE, COULD, FADETH, FAILETH, HAND, HENCEFORTH, KNOW, KNOWLEDGE, LIE, LUCRE, MANIFEST, MUCH, NO, OBEY, ONE, PASSING, POSSIBLE, PUT, REGARD, REPENT, SEE, SPARING, SPOKEN, SUFFER, TEMPTED, THAT, UNDERSTAND, UTTERED, YET.

NOTABLE.

1. **γνωστός**, known; capable of being known, knowable. *In an emphatic sense*, known *of all*, *i.e.* notable.
2. **ἐπίσημος**, having a mark upon; *of money*, stamped, coined. *In a good sense*, noted, distinguished, eminent; *in a bad sense*, notorious, (*occ.* Rom. xvi. 7.)

3. ἐπιφανής, appearing upon *or* to, visible, manifest; celebrated, distinguished, renowned, (*non occ.*)

2. Matt. xxvii. 16. | 3. Acts ii. 20.
1. Acts iv. 16.

NOTE (OF)

ἐπίσημος, *see above, No.* 2.

Rom. xvi. 7.

NOTE. [verb.]

σημειόω, to sign, to mark, note with marks. *In N.T. only mid.*, to mark for one's self, to note, set a mark on, (*non occ.*)

2 Thes. iii. 14, marg. *signify*.

NOTHING.

(*For various combinations with other words, see below.*)

1. οὐδείς, not one *thing*, *i.e.* none at all, not even one, (*for difference between No.* 1 *and No.* 2, *see* "NO," *No.* 2, *and note.*)

* *With another negative, strengthening the negation.*

2. μηδείς, (*same as above, with difference as described in* "NO," *No.* 2, *note.*)

3. οὐ, no, not, (*see* "NO," *No.* 1.)

4. μή, no, not, (*see* "NO," *No.* 2)

5. { οὐ, no, not, / τί, anything, }
6. { μή, no, not, / τι, anything, } *see note,* "NO," *No.*2, for the difference between *No.* 5 and *No.* 6.

7. οὐθείς, *a later form of No.* 1.

8. { ουδε, not even, / τι, anything, } *see note,* "NO," *No.* 2.

9. { οὐ, no, not, / πᾶν, every, / ῥῆμα, word, declaration, statement. } *In* Luke i. 37, every declaration of God *is not impossible*, *i.e.* no declaration *is impossible*, *cf.* Gen. xviii. 14.

1. Matt. v. 13.
1. —— x. 26.
5. —— xv. 32.
1. —— xvii. 20.
1. —— xxi. 19.
1. —— xxiii. 16, 18.
1. —— xxvi. 62.
1. —— xxvii. 12.
2. ——— 19, and see N to do with (have thou)
1. Matt. xxvii. 24.
2. Mark i. 44.
2. —— v. 26.
2. —— vi. 8.
5. ——— 36 (*om.* ἄρτους ... γαρ ... ουκ ἔχουσιν, *bread, for they have nothing*, (i.e. *by themselves something to eat*) (G ~ L^b Tr A.)
1. Mark vii. 15.
6. —— viii. 1.
5. ——— 2.
1. —— ix. 29.
1. —— xi. 13.
1*.—— xiv. 60.
1. ——— 61.
1. —— xv. 3 (*om.* S^t E A [א.)
1. ——— 4.
1*.——— 5.
9. Luke i. 37.
1*.—— iv. 2.
1. —— v. 5.
2. —— vi. 35.
4. —— vii. 42.
3. —— viii. 17.
2. —— ix. 3.
1*.—— x. 19.
3. —— xi. 6.
1. —— xii. 2.
1. —— xxii. 35.
1. —— xxiii. 9, 15, 41.
1. John iii. 27.
— —— iv. 11, see Draw.
1*.—— v. 19, 30.
— —— vi. 12, see N (that)
— ——— 39, see N of
1*.——— 63.
1. —— vii. 26.
1. —— viii. 28, 54.
1. —— ix. 33.
— —— xi. 49, see N at all.
1*.—— xii. 19.
1*.—— xiv. 30.
1*.—— xv. 5.
1*.—— xvi. 23, 24.
1. —— xviii. 20.
1. —— xxi. 3.
1. Acts iv. 14.
2. ——— 21.
2. —— x. 20.
— —— xi. 8, see N at any time.
2. ——— 12 (*om.* μηδὲν διακρινόμενον, *nothing doubting*, G→A.)
1. —— xvii. 21.
2. —— xix. 36.
1. —— xx. 20.
1. Acts xxi. 24.
2. —— xxiii. 14, 29.
2. —— xxv. 25.
1. —— xxvi. 31.
2. —— xxvii. 33.
1. —— xxviii. 17.
1. Rom. xiv. 14.
— 1 Cor. i. 19, see N (bring to)
1. —— iv. 4.
6. ——— 5.
1. —— vii. 19 twice.
1*.—— viii. 2 (*om.* G → L T Tr A א, i.e. *not*, instead of *nothing*.)
1. ——— 4.
3. —— ix. 16, and see Glory.
7. —— xiii. 2 (οὐδέν, No. 1, G.)
1. ——— 3.
2. 2 Cor. vi. 10.
2. —— vii. 9.
— —— viii. 15, see N over (have)
1. —— xii. 11 twice.
1. Gal. ii. 6.
1. —— iv. 1.
1. —— v. 2.
2. —— vi. 3.
1. Phil. i. 20.
2. ——— 28.
2. —— ii. 3.
2. —— iv. 6.
2. 1 Thes. iv. 12, marg. *no man.*
1. 1 Tim. iv. 4.
2. —— v. 21.
2. —— vi. 4.
1. ——— 7 1st.
8. ——— 7 2nd.
1. Tit. i. 15.
2. —— iii. 13.
1. Philem. 14.
1. Heb. ii. 8.
1. —— vii. 14, 19.
2. Jas. i. 4, 6.
2. 3 John 7.
1. Rev. iii. 17.

NOTHING (BRING TO)

ἀθετέω, to displace, *i.e.* to abrogate, abolish, get rid of; make void, render null.

1 Cor. i. 19.

NOTHING AT ALL.

1 & 3. John xi. 49.

NOTHING AT ANY TIME.

{ πᾶν, everything, / οὐδέποτε, not ever, } nothing ever.

Acts xi. 8 (*om.* πᾶν, G L T Tr A א.)

NOTHING OF.

{ μή, no *thing*. / ἐξ, out of. / αὐτου, of it. }

John vi. 39.

NOTHING OVER (HAVE)

οὐ, no *thing.*
πλεονάζω, to be more than enough.

2 Cor. viii. 15.

NOTHING (THAT)

ἵνα, in order that
μή, not
τι, anything.

John vi. 12.

NOTHING TO DO WITH (HAVE THOU)

μηδέν, nothing } *i.e.* [*let*] nothing [*arise*]
σοί, to thee, } between thee and [*that*
καί, and, } *righteous one.*]

Matt. xxvii. 19.

NOTICE BEFORE (WHEREOF YE HAD)

τήν, the, } your before
προκατηγγελμένην, before announced, } announced *blessing.*

2 Cor. ix. 5, marg. *which hath been so much spoken of before*, (προεπαγγέλλω, *before promised*, G ~ L T Tr A ℵ.)

NOTWITHSTANDING.

1. πλήν, more than, over and above; *hence*, besides, exceot, rather, but rather.
2. ἀλλά, but, *marking opposition, antithesis, or transition.*

1. Luke x. 11, 20. | 1. Phil. iv. 14.
1. Phil. i. 18. | 2. Rev. ii. 20.

NOUGHT.

οὐδείς, no *thing*, not one *thing*, (*see* "NO," *No.* 2, *note.*

Acts v. 36.

NOUGHT (AT)

εἰς, unto
ἀπελεγμός, confutation.

Acts xix. 27.

NOUGHT (BRING TO)

καταργέω, to render inactive, useless; *then*, to cause to cease do away, put an end to.

1 Cor. i. 28.

NOUGHT (COME TO)

1. καταργέω, (*see above*) *here, passive.*
2. καταλύω, to loosen down, dissolve, disunite the parts of anything; *hence, of buildings*, to throw down, destroy; to destroy, render vain. (*Here, passive.*)
3. ἐρημόω, to desolate, lay waste, make desert. (*Here, passive.*)

2. Acts v. 38. | 1. 1 Cor. ii. 6.
3. Rev. xviii. 17.

NOUGHT (FOR)

δωρεάν, gratis, gratuitously; freely, without requital; *also*, groundlessly, without cause.

2 Thes. iii. 8.

NOUGHT (SET AT)

1. ἐξουθενέω, to set at nought, despise, treat with despite.
2. ἐξουδενόω, to reject with contempt, treat with scorn.
3. ἐλθεῖν, to come,
εἰς, into,
ἀπελεγμὸν, confutation, refutation, *and by impl.* disrepute, ill-repute.

2. Mark ix. 12. | 1. Acts iv. 11.
1. Luke xxiii. 11. | 3. —— xix. 27.
1. Rom. xiv. 10.

NOURISH (-ED, -ETH.)

1. τρέφω, to make thick, *or* fat, *by feeding; hence*, to feed, nurse, nourish.
2. ἀνατρέφω, (*No.* 1, *with* ἀνά, up, *prefixed.*)
3. ἐκτρέφω, (*No.* 1, *with* ἐκ, out of, *prefixed,*) to nourish out, *i.e.* in full, bring up to maturity, (*occ.* Eph. vi. 4.)

— Acts vii. 20, see N up. | — 1 Tim. iv. 6, see N up in (be)
2. —— 21. | 1. Jas. v. 5.
1. —— xii. 20. | 1. Rev. xii. 14.
3. Eph. v. 29.

NOURISH UP.

2. Acts vii. 20.

NOURISHED UP IN (BE)

ἐντρέφομαι, to be nourished *or* brought up in *anything*, to be imbued with, (*non occ.*)

1 Tim. iv. 6.

NOURISHMENT.

See, MINISTERED.

NOVICE.

νεόφυτος, newly planted; *as subst.*, a neophyte, (*i.e.* a new plant,) (*non occ.*)

1 Tim. iii. 6, marg. *one newly come to the faith.*

NOW.

Adverbs:—

1. **νῦν**, now, (*Lat.*, nunc; *Germ.*, nun) *i.e.* the actually present time; now, *in relation to time past or future*, just now, even now, at this instant.

2. **ὁ, ἡ, τὸ, νῦν**, (*i.e. No.* 1, *with the article*) the now, the present, the now existing present, *more emphatic, therefore, than No.* 1.

3. **νῦνι**, (*No.* 1, *strengthened by the demonstr.* ἰ) now, at this moment · *used exclusively of the present.*

4. **ἤδη**, now, even now, already, *of time already past, and marking action as completed.*

5. **ἄρτι**, now, *of time just elapsed;* at present, at this moment.

6. { **ἀπό**, from, away from, / **ἄρτι**, *see No.* 5, } from now.

Conjunctions:—

7. **οὖν**, thereupon, therefore, then, *employed in arguing, etc., and denoting either an external or internal relation between two clauses,* (a) with **μέν**, indeed, truly.

8. **δέ**, but, now, moreover, *always implying antithesis, however concealed.*

9. **τὸ λοιπόν**, for the rest, henceforth, henceforward.

10. **δή**, indeed, then, now, (*giving certainty or reality to a sentence, in opp. to mere conjecture*), truly, really.

11. { **δέ**, but. / **καί**, and. }

8. Matt. i. 22.
4. —— iii. 10.
5. ——— 15.
— —— ix. 18, see N (even)
— —— xi. 12, see N (until)
4. —— xiv. 15, 24.
4. —— xv. 32.
9. —— xxvi. 45.
5. ——— 53.
1. ——— 65.
1. —— xxvii. 42, 43.
4. Mark iv. 37.
4. —— vi. 35 twice.
4. —— viii. 2.
1. —— x. 30.
4. —— xi. 11.
7. ——— 20 (E) (om. St) (om. G L T Tr A ℵ.)
9. —— xiv. 41.
1. —— xv. 32.
4. ——— 42.
10. Luke ii. 15.
1. ——— 29.
4. —— iii. 9.
1. —— vi. 21 twice, 25.
4. —— vii. 6.
7. —— x. 36 (om. Lᵇ T Trᵇ A ℵ.)
4. —— xi. 7.
1. ——— 39.
4. —— xiv. 17.
1. —— xvi. 25.
— —— xix. 37, see N (even)
1. ——— 42.
4. —— xxi. 30 twice.
1. —— xxii. 36.
1. John ii. 8.
——— 10, see N (until)
1. —— iv. 18, 23.
— ——— 42, see N...not.
4. ——— 51.
4. —— v. 6.
8. ——— 25.
4. —— vi. 10.
4. ——— 17.
4. —— vii. 14.
1. —— viii. 40, 52.
5. —— ix. 19.
1. ——— 21.
5. ——— 25.
1. ——— 41.
1. —— xi. 22.
4. —— xiii. 2.
5. ——— 7.
6. ——— 19, marg. *from henceforth.*
1. ——— 31.
5. ——— 33.
1. ——— 36.
5. ——— 37.
1. —— xiv. 29.
4. —— xv. 3.
1. ——— 22, 24.
1. —— xvi. 5.
5. ——— 12.
7. ——— 19 (om. G T Tr A ℵ.)
1. ——— 22, 29, 30.
5. ——— 31.
1. ——— 32 (om. G ≈ L T Tr A ℵ.)
1. —— xvii. 5, 7, 13.
7. —— xviii. 24 (om. St G.)
1. ——— 36.
8. —— xix. 23.
4. ——— 28.
7. ——— 29 (om. L Tr A ℵ.)
4. —— xxi. 4.
— ——— 6, see N...not.
7. ——— 7.
1. ——— 10.
4. ——— 14.
7a. Acts i. 18.
1. —— ii. 33 (om. G L T Tr A ℵ.)
1. —— iii. 17.
4. —— iv. 3.
2. Acts iv. 29.
2. —— v. 38.
1. —— vii. 4, 32, 52.
1. —— x. 5, 33.
7a.—— xi. 19.
1. —— xii. 11.
1. —— xiii. 11.
1. —— xv. 10.
1. —— xvi. 36, 37.
— —— xvii. 30, see N (but)
1. —— xx. 22, 25.
2. ——— 32.
— —— xxii. 1, see N (which I make)
1. ——— 16.
1. —— xxiii. 15, 21.
1. —— xxiv. 13 (No. 3, L T Tr A ℵ.)
7. —— xxv. 1.
1. —— xxvi. 6.
1. ——— 17 (G≈) (ἐγώ, *I* (emphatic) G L T Tr A ℵ.)
8. —— xxvii. 9 1st.
4. ——— 9 2nd.
— ——— 9 3rd, see N already.
2. ——— 22.
4. Rom. i. 10.
3. —— iii. 21.
4. —— iv. 19 (om. Lᵇ T Tr A ℵ.)
1. —— v. 9, 11.
3. —— vi. 22.
3. —— vii. 6, 17.
1. —— viii. 1, 22.
1. —— xi. 30, 31.
4. —— xiii. 11 1st.
1. ——— 11 2nd.
— —— xiv. 15, see N not.
8. —— xv. 8 (γάρ, *for*, G≈L T Tr A ℵ.)
3. ——— 23, 25.
1. —— xvi. 26.
1. 1 Cor. iii. 2.
11.—— iv. 7, and see N (if)
4. ——— 8 twice.
3. —— v. 11.
4. —— vi. 7.
1. —— vii. 14.
7a.—— ix. 25.
8. —— x. 11.
3. —— xii. 18.
1. ——— 20.
5. —— xiii. 12 twice.
3. ——— 13.
3. —— xiv. 6.
3. —— xv. 20.
8. ——— 50.
5. —— xvi. 7.
— 2 Cor. v. 16, see N henceforth no more.
— ——— 20, see N then.
1. —— vi. 2 twice.
1. —— vii. 9.
3. —— viii. 11.
— ——— 14, see N at this time.
3. ——— 22.
1. —— xiii. 2.
5. Gal. i. 9, 10.
8. ——— 20.
1. ——— 23.
1. —— ii. 20.
1. —— iii. 3.
8. —— iv. 1.
1. ——— 9.
5. ——— 20.
1. ——— 25, 29.
1. Eph. ii. 2.
3. ——— 13.
— ——— 19, see N therefore.
1. —— iii. 5, 10.
— —— iv. 9, see N that.
1. —— v. 8.
1. Phil. i. 5, 20, 30.

NOW (BUT)

2. Acts xvii. 30.

NOW (EVEN)

5. Matt. ix. 18. | 4. Luke xix. 37.

NOW (NOT)

ουκετι, no more, no longer, no further.

Philem. 16.

NOW ALREADY.

ἤδη, *see* "NOW," *No.* 4.

Acts xxvii. 9.

NOW AT THIS TIME.

{ *ἐν*, in,
{ *τὸ νῦν*, the present (*see No.* 2, *above,*)
{ *καιρῷ*, season.

2 Cor. viii. 14.

NOW HENCEFORTH NO MORE.

{ *νῦν*, now, (*see* "NOW," *No.* 1.)
{ *οὐκέτι*, no longer, no more.

2 Cor. v. 16.

NOW IF.

{ *εἰ*, if, }
{ *δέ*, but, } but and if.
{ *καὶ*, and, }

1 Cor. iv. 7.

NOW IS (THAT)

2. 1 Tim. iv. 8.

NOW...NOT.

οὐκέτι, no longer, no more, no further.

John iv. 42. | John xxi. 6.
Rom. xiv. 15.

NOW THAT.

{ *τὸ*, the, this, }
{ *δέ*, but, } but this.

Eph. iv. 9.

NOW THEN.

7. 2 Cor. v. 20.

NOW THEREFORE.

{ *ἄρα*, accordingly, } *οὖν*, *marking the*
{ *οὖν*, therefore, } *logical inference, and ἄρα, intimating the harmony between the premises and the conclusion.*

Eph. ii. 19.

NOW (UNTIL)

{ *ἕως*, }
{ *ἄρτι*, } *see* "NOW (EVEN UNTIL)."

Matt. xi. 12. | John ii. 10.

NOW (WHICH I MAKE)

2. Acts xxii. 1 (No. 3, G L T Tr A ℵ.)

NUMBER.

1. *ἀριθμός*, number, *spoken of a definite number*, (*non occ.*)
2. *ὄχλος*, a confused multitude, a crowd, a throng

NUMBER (MAKE OF THE)

ἐγκρίνω, to judge in, admit after trial, to reckon among, (*non occ.*)

2 Cor. x. 12.

NUMBER (TAKE INTO THE)

καταλέγω, to lay down to *or* among *others*, *i.e.* to enrol, to reckon under *or* to *a number*.

1 Tim. v. 9, marg. *choose into the number.*

NUMBER (-ED.) [verb.]

1. *ἀριθμέω*, to number.
2. *λογίζομαι*, to count, reckon, calculate, compute.

1. Matt. x. 30. | 1. Luke xii. 7.
2. Mark xv. 28 (ap.) | 1. Rev. vii. 9.

NUMBER WITH.

1. καταριθμέω, (*No.* 1, *with* κατά, down, *prefixed*) to number down, *i.e.* number under, *or* among, (*non occ.*)

2. συγκαταψηφίζω, to be allotted *or* voted with, to count down with, (*from* σύν, together with, κατά, down, *and* ψηφίζω, to count or reckon with pebbles (*from* ψῆφος, a small stone worn smooth by water) (*non occ.*)

1. Acts i. 17.	2. Acts i. 26.

NURSE. [noun.]

τροφός, a nurser, a nurse, (*from* τρέφω, *see* "NOURISH," *No.* 1.) (*non occ.*)

Acts xiii. 18, see Manners.	1 Thes. ii. 7.

NURTURE.

παιδεία, the training of a child, *including education and discipline; and consisting of teaching, admonition, rewards, and punishments.*

Eph. vi. 4.

O

O is generally represented in the Greek by the vocative case of the noun, and sometimes the definite article. When it is the translation of a separate Greek word, it is the interjection, ὦ, and is, of course, very emphatic—Oh!

Matt. xv. 28.	Acts xviii. 14.
—— xvii. 17.	Rom. ii. 1, 3.
Mark ix. 19.	—— ix. 20.
Luke ix. 41.	—— xi. 33.
—— xxiv. 25.	Gal. iii. 1.
Acts i. 1.	1 Tim. vi. 20.
—— xiii. 10.	Jas. ii. 20.

ὦ also occurs in Acts xxvii. 21, where it is not translated.

OATH (-s.)

1. ὅρκος, the object by which one swears, the witness of an oath; *then*, an oath, (ὅρκος *was orig. equiv. to* ἕρκος, a fence, *from* ἔργω, to shut in, restrain, *and so, strictly, it denotes*, that which restrains from doing *a thing; hence, Lat.*, orcus, "the bourne from whence no traveller returns.")

2. ὁρκωμοσία, asseverations on oath; the sacrifice on taking a solemn oath.

1. Matt. v. 33.	— Acts xxiii. 21, see O (bind with an)
1. —— xiv. 7, 9.	1. Heb. vi. 16, 17.
1. —— xxvi. 72.	2. —— vii. 20.
1. Mark vi. 26.	2. —— 21 1st, marg. *swearing of an oath.*
1. Luke i. 73.	2. —— 21 2nd, 28.
1. Acts ii. 30.	1. Jas. v. 12.
— —— xxiii. 12, see *Execration.*	

OATH (BIND WITH AN)

ἀναθεματίζω, to declare one to be ἀνάθεμα (devoted to destruction.)

Acts xxiii. 21.

OBEDIENCE.

1. ὑπακοή, a hearing attentively, or listening; *hence*, obedience, *as the result of attentive hearing.*

Rom. i. v.	2 Cor. vii. 15.
—— v. 19.	—— x. 5, 6.
—— vi. 16.	Philem. 21.
—— xvi. 19, 26. [under)	Heb. v. 8.
1 Cor. xiv. 34, see O (be	1 Pet. i. 2.

OBEDIENCE (BE UNDER)

ὑποτάσσω, to range *or* put under, to subordinate; *pass.*, to be subjected.

1 Cor. xiv. 34.

OBEDIENT.

1. ὑπήκοος, listening attentively, obedient, (*occ.* Acts vii. 39).

2. ὑπακοή, *see* "OBEDIENCE." *Here, Gen.*, of obedience.

1. 2. Cor. ii. 9.	1. Phil. i. 14.
2. 1 Pet. i. 14.	

OBEDIENT TO (BE)

1. ὑπακούω, to hear, (*with the idea of stealth, stillness or attention in order to answer*) to listen; *hence*, (*as the result of this*) to obey.
2. ὑποτάσσω, *see* "OBEDIENCE (BE UNDER)."

1. Acts vi. 7. | 1. Eph. vi. 5.
2. Tit. ii. 5, part.

OBEDIENT UNTO (BE)

ὑποτάσσω, *see No.* 2, *above.*

Tit. ii. 9.

OBEDIENT (MAKE THE GENTILES)

{ εἰς, unto.
ὑπακοή, *the* obedience.
ἐθνῶν, of *the* Gentiles. }

Rom. xv. 8.

OBEY (-ED, -ING.)

1. ὑπακούω, *see* "OBEDIENT TO (BE)," *No.* 1.
2. { εἰς, unto, ὑπακοή, obedience. }
3. { ὑπήκοος, listening attentively, γίνομαι, to become, } to become obedient.
4. πείθω, (a) *Act.*, to persuade, win by words, influence *or* gain any one, win for one's self.

   (b) *Medial Passive*, to suffer one's self to be persuaded *or* convinced, to be persuaded in favour of *any one*, yield assent to, obey *or* trust *him*.
5. πειθαρχέω, (*No.* 4 *applied to an* ἀρχή, a ruler,) to obey a ruler, obey one in authority, to obey or follow one's advice.

1. Matt. viii. 27.
1. Mark i. 27.
1. —— iv. 41.
1. Luke viii. 25.
1. —— xvii. 6.
5. Acts v. 29, 32.
4b.—— 36, marg *believe.*
4b.—— 37.
3. —— vii. 39.
4. Rom. ii. 8, and see O not.
1. —— vi. 12.
2. —— 16 1st.
1. —— 16 2nd.
1. —— x. 16.
— —— xi. 30, 31, see O not.
4. Gal. iii. 1 (*ap.*)
4. —— v. 7.
1. Eph. vi. 1.
1. Phil. ii. 12.
1. Col. iii. 20, 22.
1. 2 Thes. i. 8.
1. —— iii. 14.
— Tit. iii. 1, see O a magistrate.
1. Heb. v. 1.
1. —— xi. 8.
4. —— xiii. 17.
4. Jas. iii. 3.
— 1 Pet. iii. 1, see O not.
1. —— 6.
— —— iv. 17, see O not.

OBEY A MAGISTRATE.

5. Tit. iii. 1.

OBEY NOT.

ἀπειθέω, ("OBEY," *No.* 4, *with* α, *negative, prefixed, making it*) the opposite of "OBEY," *No.* 4.

Rom. ii. 8.
—— xi. 30, marg. (text, *believe not.*)
1 Pet. iii. 1.
—— iv. 17.

OBEYING.

ὑπακοή, (*see* "OBEDIENCE.")

1 Pet. i. 22.

OBJECT [verb.]

κατηγορέω, to speak against, *in public, before a* court; to accuse, complain of, *in a judicial sense.*

Acts xxiv. 19.

OBSERVATION.

παρατήρησις, an observing beside *or* near, close watching, accurate *or* constant observation. (*See the verb* "OBSERVE," *No.* 3.)

Luke xvii. 20, marg. *outward show.*

OBSERVE (-ED.)

1. τηρέω, to keep an eye upon, to watch; *hence*, to keep, to guard; to watch, observe attentively.
2. συντηρέω, (*No.* 1, *with* σύν, together with, *prefixed*) to have an eye upon in conjunction with *any one*, to watch *or* keep with *any one or* with *one's self.*
3. παρατηρέω, (*No.* 1, *with* παρά, beside, *prefixed*) to have an eye near, watch closely, *with superstitious or sinister intent.*
4. φυλάσσω, to watch, *not to sleep*, to keep watch *by night;* to guard, preserve.
5. ποιέω, to make; to do.
6. φρονέω, to have mind, think; *then*, to be minded, to have in mind; regard, care for.

1. Matt. xxiii. 3 1st (*om.* G→T Tr A ℵ.)
1. —— 3 2nd.
1. —— xxviii. 20.
2. Mark vi. 20, marg. *keep or save.*
4. Mark x. 20.
5. Acts xvi. 21.
1. —— xxi. 25 (*ap.*)
6. Rom. xiv. 6, marg. (text, *regard.*)
3. Gal. iv. 10.
4. 1 Tim. v. 21.

OBTAIN (-ED, -ING.)

1. τυγχάνω, to hit, to strike, to reacn *a mark or object. Trans.*, to attain unto, *i.e.* to obtain, gain; *Intrans.*, to fall out, to happen, to chance.

2. ἐπιτυγχάνω, (*No.* 1, *with* ἐπί, upon, *prefixed*) to light upon, attain one's aim, attain unto, acquire, (*non occ.*)

3. λαγχάνω, to obtain by lot, to have fall to one's self.

4. κτάομαι, to get for one's self, to acquire, to procure *by purchase or otherwise*, to possess.

5. κρατέω, to be strong, mighty, powerful; to have power over, become master of, attain to, (a) *with Gen.*, to take hold of a thing *or* to possess it, (b) *with Acc.*, to have and hold it in one's power.

6. λαμβάνω, to take, *as with the hand;* to lay hold of; to receive.

7. καταλαμβάνω, (*No.* 6, *with* κατά, down, *prefixed*) to take, to receive *with the idea of eagerness*, lay hold of, seize *with eagerness*, to grasp, seize upon.

8. εὑρίσκω, to find, (*without seeking*) to meet with, light upon; *also*, to find *by search or enquiry*, discover; *Mid.*, to find for one's self, obtain.

9. { εἰς, unto, περιποίησις, a making remain over, a laying up, acquisition, obtaining, } unto acquiring, for obtaining.

— Matt. v. 7, see Mercy.
1. Luke xx. 35.
3. Acts i. 17.
4. —— xxii. 28.
1. —— xxvi. 22.
5a. —— xxvii. 13.
2. Rom. xi. 7 twice.
— —— 30, 31, } see Mercy.
— 1 Cor. vii. 25, }
7. —— ix. 24.
— Eph. i. 11, see Inheritance.
9. 1 Thes. v. 9.
— 1 Tim. i. 13, 16, see Mercy.
1. 2 Tim. ii. 10.
— Heb. i. 4, see Inheritance.
2. —— vi. 15.
1. —— viii. 6.
8. —— ix. 12.
— —— xi. 2, see Report.
— —— 4, see Witness.
2. —— 33.
1. —— 35.
— —— 39, see Report.
2. Jas. iv. 2.
— 1 Pet. ii. 10 twice, see Mercy.
3. 2 Pet. i. 1.

OBTAINING.

περιποίησις, *see above, No.* 9.

2 Thes. ii. 14.

OCCASION.

αφορμή, that from which anything proceeds, a starting place, base of operations; means, material, apparatus *for beginning or accomplishing anything; hence*, occasion, opportunity, (*non occ.*)

Rom. vii. 8, 11.
—— xiv. 13, see Fall.
2 Cor. v. 12.
—— viii. 8, see O of (by)
Gal. v. 13.
1 Tim. v. 14.
1 John ii. 10, see Stumbling.

OCCASION OF (BY)

διά, *with the Gen.*, through, by means of, *in reference* to agency.

2 Cor. viii. 8.

OCCUPATION.

τέχνη, an art, trade, craft.

Acts xviii. 3 (*ap.*)

OCCUPATION (OF LIKE)

{ περί, about, τὰ, the things, τοιαῦτα, such things, } about such things.

Acts xix. 25.

OCCUPY (-ETH, -IED.)

1. πραγματεύομαι, to be doing, to be busy *or* occupied; *like Eng.*, to do business, *i.e.* to trade, traffic, (*non occ.*)

2. ἀναπληρόω, to fill up, *e.g. a chasm; hence, spoken of work*, to fulfil, perform

1. Luke xix. 13. | 2. 1 Cor. xiv. 16.

OCCUPIED (BE)

περιπατέω, to walk about, be walking.

Heb. xiii. 9.

ODOUR.

1. ὀσμη, a smell, odour; *in N.T.*, only of fragrant odour. By Hebr. ὀ. εὐωδίας, odour of fragrance, sweet odour, *as accompanying an acceptable sacrifice.*

2. θυμίαμα, incense *burnt in worship.*

1. John xii. 3.
1. Phil. iv. 18.
2. Rev. v. 8, marg. *incense.*
2. Rev. xviii. 13.

OF.

(*For list of combinations with other words, see below.*)

OF is frequently part of the translation of a Greek *verb* or some case of a noun, or a *part of some phrase.* References to most of these will be found below, or in the list of words at the foot.

OF is more frequently, however, the translation of the *Genitive case* of the noun: indeed, in most of the references not quoted below. The *Genitive* signifies *motion from*, and answers the question, *whence?*

[In interpreting the word OF as the translation of the *Genitive* case, great care will be necessary, as sometimes important conclusions may result. The interpretation will, as a rule, come under one of the following heads:

(i.) The Genitive of *Origin* ("*proceeding from,*" "bestowed by.")
ἔργον τῆς πίστεως, (1 Thes. i. 3) work of faith.
παραπλήσιον τῶν γραφῶν, (Rom. xv. 4) comfort of the Scriptures.

(ii.) Genitive of *Possession,* ("*of or belonging to*")
οικία Σίμωνος, (Mark i. 29) house of Simon.
εἰρήνη τοῦ θεοῦ, (Phil. iv. 7) the peace of God.
δοῦλος Ιησοῦ Χρ, (Rom. i. 1) servant of Jesus Christ.
This and other Genitives may denote either the *subject* or the *object, e.g.*
ἀγάπη τοῦ Θεοῦ, (1 John ii. 16, etc.) } Love of God, (to us) *sub.* / (our) Love of God, *obj.*
μαρτυρία τοῦ Ἰησοῦ, (Rev. xix. 10, etc.) the testimony of Jesus, *i.e.* } the testimony (borne to) Jesus, *obj.* / the testimony (borne by) Jesus, *sub.*

(iii.) Genitive of *Character or Quality,* ("*characterised by.*")
υἱοὶ τῆς ἀπειθείας, (Eph. ii. 2) children of disobedience.
οἰκονόμος τῆς ἀδικίας, (Luke xvi. 8) steward of unrighteousness.

(iv.) Genitive of *the Ruling Principle,* ("energizing.")
ὁμοιώματα σαρκὸς ἁμαρτίας, (Rom. viii. 3) the likeness of sinful flesh.

(v.) Genitive of *Relation,* ("in regard *or* respect to"; "pertaining to.")
βάπτισμα μετανοίας, (Mark i. 4) baptism of repentance.
ἀνάστασις νεκρῶν, resurrection of the dead, *i.e.* of dead persons. [This must be carefully distinguished from the use of the prep. ἐκ, "*out of,*" "*from among.*" Ἀνάστασις ἐκ νεκρῶν is the resurrection (not of "the dead") but of others out of, from among the dead. For further examples consult the references below.]

(vi.) Genitive of *Apposition,* ("consisting of"; "which is") σημεῖον περιτομῆς, (Rom. iv. 11) the sign of circumcision.
συνδέσμος της εἰρήνης, (Eph. iv. 3) the bond of peace.

(vii.) Genitive of *Partition* ("part of.")
τὰ ἡμίση τῶν ὑπαρχόντων, (Luke xix. 8) the half of my goods.
τὸ τρίτον τῆς γῆς, (Rev. viii. 7) the third of the land.

(viii.) Genitive of the *Contents,* ("*full of,*" "*consisting of.*")
ποτήριον ψυχροῦ, (Matt. x. 42) a cup of cold water.
τιμὴ ἀργυρίου, (Acts vii. 16) a sum of money.

The tracing out of the various meanings of the word "OF" as the translation of the Genitive case, will prove an unfailing and increasing source of interest to the Bible student.]

When "OF" is the translation of a separate Greek word, then it is one of these following:

1. ἐκ, out of, from among, (*a prep. governing only the Gen. case, and denoting* motion from the interior;* *opp. to No.* 9.)

2. περί, around.
   (a) *with Gen.*, around and separate from; about, concerning, on behalf of.
   (b) *with Acc.*, around and towards; around (*of place*), about (*of place*). Matt. iii. 4, about his loins.

3. ἀπό, away from, *denoting* motion from the exterior;* *hence, denoting cause or occasion;* from, on account of.

4. ὑπό, under.
   (a) *with Gen.*, under and separate from, *denoting that from which the fact, event, or action springs, and marking the agent; hence,* by, (*the agent or efficient cause.*)
   (b) *with Acc.*, under and towards; under, close upon.

5. παρά, beside.
   (a) *with Gen.*, beside and proceeding from;* from beside, from (*used of persons, as No.* 3 *is of places.*)
   (b) *with Dat.*, beside and at; at the side of, with, near.
   (c) *with Acc.*, to, *or* alongside of, beside.

6. ἐπί, upon.

(a) *with Gen.*, upon and proceeding from; on, upon; over; on, *as on a basis.*

(b) *with Dat.*, upon and resting upon, in addition to, on account of.

(c) *with Acc.*, upon, by direction towards; up to, upon (*with implied motion*); to (*implying intention.*)

7. ὑπέρ, over.

(a) *with Gen.*, over and separate from; of, on behalf of, (*as though bending over to protect, etc.*,) for the sake of, in reference to.

(b) *with Acc.*, over and towards; beyond, above.

8. ἐν, in, *of time, place, or element;* among; *the sphere in which the subject is concerned, as dwelling or acting* in.

9. εἰς, into, to, unto, with a view to; *with respect to a certain result,* in order to for, towards.

10. κατά, down.

(a) *with Gen.*, down from; against, in opposition to, (*opp. of No.* 7.)

(b) *with Acc.*, down towards; down upon *or* along; throughout, according to.

11. διά, through, (*with idea of separation.*)

(a) *with Gen.*, through, as proceeding from; through, by means of; *denoting the instrument of an action.*

(b) *with Acc.*, through, as tending towards; on account of, owing to; *denoting the reason or ground of an action.*

12. πρός, towards, in the direction of.

(a) *with Gen.*, hitherwards; in favour of, (*occ.* Acts xxvii. 34.)

(b) *with Dat.*, resting in a direction towards; at, close by.

(c) *with Acc.*, hitherwards, to wards, in reference to, in regard to

13. μετά, with, (*locally, implying association, and thus distinguished from σύν*, with, *which implies conjunction or co-operation.*)

(a) *with Gen.*, with and from; together with.

(b) *with Acc.*, after.

14. ἔμπροσθεν, before, in front, in presence of.

[* The difference between the meanings of *Nos.* 1 (ἐκ), 3 (ἀπό), and 5 (παρά), may be thus further illustrated :—

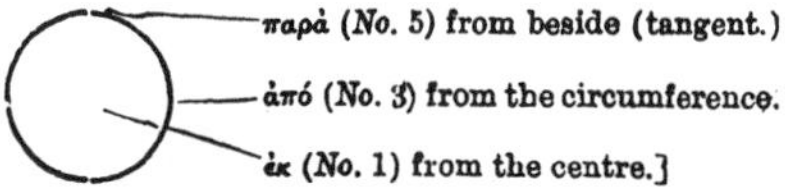

1. Matt. i. 3, 5 twice, 6 1st, 16 2nd, 18 2nd, 20 3rd.
4a.—— 22.
5a.—— ii. 4 2nd, 7.
4a.—— 15 2nd, 16 1st.
5a.—— 16 2nd.
3. —— iii. 4.
4a.—— 6.
1. —— 9.
4a —— 13, 14.
4a.—— iv. 1 twice.
4a.—— v. 13.
— —— 22 1st & 2nd, Dat. case.
9. —— 22 3rd.
1. —— 37.
3. —— 42.
— —— vi. 1 1st, Dat. case.
5b.—— 1 2nd, marg. *with.*
4a.—— 2.
1. —— 27.
1. —— vii. 9.
3. —— 15, 16 twice.
3. —— x. 17.
4a.—— 22.
1. —— 29.
2a.—— xi. 10.
3. —— 19 3rd.
4a.—— 27.
3. —— 29.
1. —— xiii. 47 2nd.
4a.—— xiv. 8.
3. —— xv. 1.
2a.—— 7.
3. —— 27.
3. —— xvi. 6 1st.
3. —— 11 1st, 12 1st & 2nd, 21.
4a.—— xvii. 12 2nd.
2a.—— 13.
3. —— 25 1st, 3rd, & 4th, 26.
1. —— xviii. 12.
6b.—— 13 twice.
14.—— 14 2nd.
5a.—— 19 2nd.
13a.—— 23 2nd.
4a.—— xix. 12 1st.
— —— xx. 20 1st, see Sake of (for the)
5a.—— 20 2nd (No. 3, L T Tr A*.)
4a.—— 23 2nd.
3. —— xxi. 11 1st.
1. —— 25 2nd, 26, 31 1st.
2a.—— 45.
1. Matt. xxii. 35.
2a.—— xxii. 42 1st.
4a.—— xxiii. 7.
1. —— 25 3rd (om. L Trb A.)
— —— 34 twice, see Of (some)
4a.—— xxiv. 9.
3. —— 32.
2a.—— 36 1st.
1. —— xxv. 2, 8.
1. —— xxvi. 21.
2a.—— 24 2nd.
1. —— 27, 29 1st.
— —— 73, see Of (some)
— —— xxvii. 9 3rd, see Of (they)
4a.—— 12.
3. —— 21, 24 1st.
1. —— 29 1st, 48.
3. —— 57.
4a. Mark i. 5 3rd, 9 2nd, 13.
2a.—— 30 2nd.
4a.—— ii. 3 2nd.
2b.—— iv. 19 3rd.
4a.—— v. 26.
2a.—— 27.
3. —— 29 2nd, 34.
3. —— vi. 43 2nd.
6b.—— 52.
2a.—— vii. 6, 25.
3. —— 28.
5a.—— viii. 11.
3. —— 15 1st.
2a.—— 30.
3. —— 31 2nd & 3rd (No. 4a, G ~ L T Tr A ℵ.)
6c.—— ix. 12 1st, 13.
1. —— 17.
2a.—— x. 10.
1. —— xi. 14, 30 2nd, 32.
3. —— xii. 2 1st, 38.
1. —— 44 twice.
4a.—— xiii. 13.
3. —— 28.
2a.—— 32.
1. —— xiv. 18.
1. —— 20 (*om.* Trb ℵ.)
2a.—— 21 2nd.
1. —— 23, 25 1st.
— —— 69, 70, see Of (one)
3. —— xv. 43 1st, 45.
4a.—— xvi. 11 (*ap.*)
1. —— 12 (*ap.*)
2a. Luke i. 1.
1. —— 5 3rd & 5th, 27 1st.

1. Luke i. 35 2nd (ἐκ σοῦ, B G ∾ Lb.)
8. —— 61.
1. —— ii. 4 1st, 35, 36 2nd.
4a. —— iii. 7 1st.
1. —— 8.
2a. —— 15.
3. —— iv. 2.
2a. —— 14 2nd.
3. —— 15.
6a. —— 25 1st.
— —— 29 1st, see Thrust.
2a. —— v. 15 1st.
3. —— 15 2nd.
3. —— vi. 13, 17 3rd, 30 2nd.
5a. —— 34.
1. —— 44 twice, 45 5th.
2a. —— vii. 3 1st, 17, 18 2nd.
3. —— 21 1st.
2a. —— 27.
4a. —— 30 2nd.
3. —— 35.
3. —— viii. 2 1st.
— —— 2 2nd, see O (out)
3. —— 3 2nd (No. 1, G ∾ L T Tr A ℵ.)
— —— 29 1st, see O (out)
4a. —— 29 2nd, 43.
4a. —— ix. 7 2nd, 8 1st.
2a. —— 9, 11 1st.
3. —— 22 2nd.
3. —— 38.
1. —— x. 11 1st.
4a. —— 22.
1. —— xi. 5, 15 1st.
5a. —— 16.
1. —— 27, 49 2nd.
3. —— 50 3rd, 51 3rd.
2a. —— 53.
3. —— xii. 1 3rd, 4.
1. —— 6, 13.
3. —— 15 1st, 20.
1. —— 25.
5a. —— 48 2nd.
3. —— 57.
2a. —— xiii. 1.
4a. —— xiv. 8 twice.
1. —— 28.
— —— 32, see Conditions.
1. —— 33.
1. —— xv. 4 twice.
2a. —— xvi. 2 1st.
1. —— 9 1st.
1. —— xvii. 7 (om. Trb), 15.
4a. —— 20 1st.
3. —— 25.
3. —— xviii. 3.
— —— 17, 25, see Of (one.)
1. —— xx. 4 2nd, 6.
3. —— 10 1st, 46.
1. —— xxi. 4 1st & 3rd.
2a. —— 5.
— —— 16, see Of (some)
4a. —— 17.
1. —— 18.
4a. —— 24 2nd.
3. —— 30.
1. —— xxii. 3 1st.
3. —— 18 1st.
1. —— 23, 50 1st, 58.
6a. —— 59 2nd.
3. —— 71.
1. —— xxiii. 8 1st.
2a. —— 8 2nd.
3. —— 51 2nd.
— —— 52, see Of (them)
1. —— xxiv. 13.
2a. —— 14.
1. —— 18, (om. ἐξ αὐτῶν, *of them*, St G Lb T Tr A ℵ.)
3. —— 42 2nd (ap.)
2a. John i. 7, 8.
1. —— 13 1st, 2nd, 4th, & 6th.
5a. —— 14 2nd.
2a. —— 15.
1. John i. 16.
2a. —— 22.
1. —— 24, 35, 40.
3. —— 44 twice.
2a. —— 47.
1. —— ii. 15 twice.
2a. —— 21 1st, 25.
1. —— iii. 1 1st, 5 1st & 2nd, 6 twice, 8, 31 twice.
1. —— iv. 7.
5a. —— 9 2nd.
1. —— 13, 14 1st, 22, 39 2nd.
5a. —— 52.
3. —— v. 19, 30 1st.
2a. —— 31, 32 twice, 36 2nd, 37, 39.
5a. —— 44.
2a. —— 46.
1. —— vi. 8, 11, 13, 26.
— —— 39, see Nothing.
5a. —— 45 2nd, 46.
1. —— 51 1st, 60, 64, 65, 70, 71 3rd.
2a. —— vii. 7, 13 1st, 17 1st.
1. —— 17 2nd.
3. —— 17 3rd, 18.
1. —— 19, 22 twice, 25 2nd.
3. —— 28.
1. —— 31.
2a. —— 39.
1. —— 40 1st, 42 1st, 44, 48 twice, 50, 52 twice.
2a. —— viii. 13, 14, 18 twice.
1. —— 23 twice.
2a. —— 26 1st.
5a. —— 26 2nd.
3. —— 28.
5a. —— 40.
1. —— 41 2nd.
3. —— 42.
1. —— 44 1st & 3rd, 46 1st.
2a. —— 46 2nd.
1. —— 47 twice.
1. —— ix. 6 1st, 16 1st.
5a. —— 16 2nd.
2a. —— 17.
— —— 18, see Of him.
5a. —— 33.
— —— 40, see Of (some)
4a. —— x. 14 (ap.)
1. —— 16.
3. —— 18 1st.
5a. —— 18 2nd.
1. —— 20.
2a. —— 25.
1. —— 26.
2a. —— 41.
3. —— xi. 1 1st.
2a. —— 13 twice.
1. —— 19, 37 1st & 2nd, 45, 46, 49.
3. —— 51.
1. —— xii. 4 (om. Tr.)
1. —— 9.
6b. —— 16.
3. —— 21 1st.
2a. —— 41.
1. —— 49.
2a. —— xiii. 18.
1. —— 21.
2a. —— 22, 24.
4a. —— xiv. 21.
3. —— xv. 4.
5a. —— 15.
1. —— 19 3 times.
2a. —— 26 2nd.
1. —— xvi. 5.
2a. —— 8 3 times, 9, 10, 11.
3. —— 13 2nd.
1. —— 14, 15.
— —— 17, see Of (some)
2a. —— 19, 25.
5a. —— xvii. 7.
1. —— 12 1st, 14 twice, 16 twice.
1. —— xviii. 9.
2a. —— 19 twice, 23.
1. John xviii. 26 1st.
3. —— 34 1st.
2a. —— 34 2nd.
1. —— 36 twice, 37.
1. —— xix. 2.
3. —— 38 1st.
1. —— xx. 24.
3. —— xxi. 2 1st.
1. —— 2 3rd.
3. —— 10.
2a. —— 24.
2a. Acts i. 1.
1. —— 24 2nd.
3. —— ii. 17, 18, 22 3rd.
4a. —— 24 2nd.
2a. —— 29.
1. —— 30 1st.
2a. —— 31 1st.
5a. —— 33 2nd.
5a. —— iii. 2 2nd, 5.
1. —— 22.
1. —— iv. 6 1st.
6b. —— 9.
4a. —— 11 1st.
6a. —— 27 1st.
3. —— v. 2, 3 1st.
2a. —— 24 2nd.
1. —— 38, 39.
1. —— vi. 9 1st.
3. —— 9 3rd & 4th.
5a. —— vii. 16 1st.
1. —— 37 2nd.
2a. —— 52 2nd.
3. —— viii. 22 1st.
2a. —— 34 3 times.
5a. —— ix. 2 1st.
2a. —— 13.
1. —— x. 1.
5a. —— 22 3rd.
4a. —— 33 (No. 3, L Tr A ℵ.)
6a. —— 34 1st.
3. —— 38 1st.
4a. —— 38 2nd, 41, 42 1st.
1. —— 45 1st.
1. —— xi. 2, 20 1st.
2a. —— 22 1st.
1. —— 28 1st.
3. —— xii. 1.
4a. —— 5.
1. —— xiii. 21 2nd.
3. —— 23.
2a. —— 29.
1. —— xv. 2.
4a. —— 4.
3. —— 5 1st.
2a. —— 6.
1. —— 21, 22, 23.
4a. —— xvi. 4, 6 2nd, 14 3rd.
1. —— xvii. 4 1st.
5a. —— 9 1st.
1. —— 12 1st.
3. —— 13 1st.
4a. —— 13 3rd.
1. —— 26 1st.
2a. —— 32 3rd.
2a. —— xviii. 15 1st, 25 2nd.
3. —— xix. 13 1st (καί, *also*, G ∾ L T Tr A ℵ.)
5a. —— xx. 24 2nd.
1. —— 30.
— —— xxi. 8 1st, see Company.
— —— 8 3rd, see Of (one)
3. —— 16 2nd.
2a. —— 21.
3. —— 27.
4a. —— 35 1st.
2a. —— xxii. 10.
4a. —— 11 2nd, 12.
1. —— 14 2nd.
5a. —— 30 (No. 4a, G ∾ L Tr A ℵ.)
2a. —— xxiii. 6 2nd.
4a. —— 10.
2a. —— 11 2nd, 20.
1. —— 21.
4a. —— 27 twice.
2a. Acts xxiii. 29 1st.
1. —— 34 1st.
3. —— 34 2nd.
5a. —— xxiv. 8 1st.
2a. —— 8 2nd.
1. —— 10.
2a. —— 22 1st, 25.
4a. —— 26.
2a. —— xxv. 9, 19 twice, 20 1st.
9. —— 20 2nd.
2a. —— 26.
4a. —— xxvi. 2, 6 2nd, 7.
5a. —— 22 (No. 3, L T Tr A ℵ.)
2a. —— 26 1st.
10b. —— xxvii. 2 2nd, 5 1st.
3. —— 44.
— —— xxviii. 21 1st, see Out of.
2a. —— 21 2nd.
5a. —— 22.
1. Rom. i. 3 1st.
8. —— ii. 17, 23.
1. —— 29 2nd & 3rd.
10b. —— iv. 4 twice.
1. —— 12, 14 1st, 16 1st, 2nd, & 3rd.
1. —— v. 16.
1. —— ix. 5, 6 2nd, 11 2nd & 3rd, 21, 24 twice, 30.
1. —— x. 5, 6.
8. —— xi. 2.
1. —— 6 1st, 6 2nd (ap.), 14, 36.
— —— xii. 16 1st, see Mind.
— —— 10 2nd, see Low estate.
4a. —— 21.
3. —— xiii. 1 1st (No. 4a, G ∾ L T Tr A* ℵ.)
4a. —— 1 2nd.
1. —— 3 2nd.
2a. —— xiv. 12 2nd.
11a. —— 14.
1. —— 23 twice.
2a. —— xv. 14 1st.
4a. —— 15 2nd.
2a. —— 21.
1. —— xvi. 10, 11 1st.
2a. 1 Cor. i. 11 1st.
1. —— 30 1st.
3. —— 30 2nd.
1. —— ii. 12 2nd.
4a. —— 12 3rd.
4a. —— iv. 3 twice.
3. —— 5 3rd.
4a. —— vi. 12.
3. —— 19 2nd.
10b. —— vii. 6.
1. —— 7.
4a. —— 25 2nd.
4a. —— viii. 3.
1. —— 6.
1. —— ix. 7 1st (om. L T Tr A ℵ.)
1. —— 7 2nd, 13 1st, 14.
1. —— x. 4.
4a. —— 9 2nd, 10 2nd.
1. —— 17.
4a. —— 29 2nd.
1. —— xi. 8 twice, 12 twice.
3. —— 23.
1. —— 28 twice.
4a. —— 32.
1. —— 15 twice, 16 twice.
4a. —— xiv. 24 twice.
1. —— xv. 6 2nd.
10a. —— 15 2nd.
1. —— 47.
6b. —— xvi. 17 1st.
4a. 2 Cor. i. 4.
7a. —— 7 1st.
7a. —— 8 1st (No. 2a, G ∾ L T Tr ℵ.)
— —— 16 1st, see Out of.
4a. —— 16 2nd.
3. —— ii. 3 1st.
4a. —— 6.

8. 2 Cor. ii. 12.
1. —— 17 2nd & 3rd.
4a.—— iii. 2.
3. —— 5 1st.
1. —— 5 2nd & 3rd.
3. —— 18 2nd.
1. —— iv. 7 3rd.
4a.—— v. 4.
1. —— 18 1st.
7a.—— vii. 4 2nd, 14.
4a.—— viii. 19 1st.
7a.—— ix. 2 2nd, 3.
1. —— 7.
3. —— x. 7.
2a.—— 8.
9. —— 13, 15 1st.
8. —— 15 2nd.
9. —— 16.
4a.—— xi. 24.
7a.—— xii. 5 twice.
9. —— 6 1st.
1. —— 6 2nd.
4a.—— 11.
6b.—— 21.
—— xiii. 11 1st, see Mind.
3. Gal. i. 1.
4a.—— 11.
5a.—— 12 1st.
3. —— ii. 6.
1. —— 12, 15.
3. —— iii. 2 1st.
1. —— 7 1st, 9, 10 1st, 12.
6a.—— 16 twice.
4a.—— 17 1st.
1. —— 18 twice.
1. —— iv. 4 2nd.
4a.—— 9.
8. —— 20, marg. *for*.
1. —— 23 twice.
1. —— v. 8.
4a.—— 15.
1. —— vi. 8 twice.
1. Eph. ii. 8 1st, 9.
1. —— iii. 15.
8. —— iv. 1 1st.
4a.—— v. 12 2nd.
1. —— 30 2nd & 3rd (*ap.*)
5a.—— vi. 8.
11a. Phil. i. 15 twice.
1. —— 16, 17 1st.
3. —— 28 3rd.
—— 29, see Behalf.
7a.—— ii. 13.
1. —— iii. 5 1st & 5th, 9 1st & 3rd.
4a.—— 12.
—— iv. 2, see Mind.
7a.—— 10.
5a.—— 18 1st.
1. —— 22.
3. Col. i. 7 1st.
3. —— iii. 24 1st.
1. —— iv. 11 1st.
4a. 1 Thes. i. 4.
2a.—— 9 1st.
1. —— ii. 8 twice.
4a.—— 4.
1. —— 6 1st.
3. —— 6 2nd & 3rd.
5a.—— 13 2nd.
4a.—— 14 2nd & 3rd.
5a.—— iv. 1.
2a.—— 6.
2a.—— v. 1.
4a. 2 Thes. ii. 13 1st.
5a.—— iii. 6 2nd.
3. 1 Tim. iii. 7 1st.
2a. 2 Tim. i. 3.
5a.—— 13 2nd, 18.
5a.—— ii. 2.
1. —— 8 1st.
1. —— iii. 6.
5a.—— 14 2nd.
1. Titus i. 10, 12 1st.
1. —— ii. 8 1st.
2a.—— 8 2nd.
3. —— iii. 5 1st.
10b. Philem. 14.
12c. Heb. i. 7 1st.
1. —— ii. 11.
1. —— iii. 13 1st.
1. —— iv. 1 2nd.
2a.—— 4, 8.
4a.—— v. 4, 10 1st.
2a.—— 11 1st.
2a.—— vi. 9.
3. —— vii. 2 1st.
1. —— 4, 5 1st.
4a.—— 7.
1. —— 12 1st.
6c.—— 13 1st.
3. —— 13 2nd.
—— 14 1st, see Out of.
9. —— 14 2nd.
6b.—— viii. 1 1st.
2a.—— ix. 5 2nd.
—— 20, see Of himself.
2a.—— x. 7 2nd.
1. —— xi. 3 2nd.
6b.—— 4.
2a.—— 7 2nd.
3. —— 13.
12c.—— 18, marg. *to*.
2a.—— 22 1st, marg. (with μνημονεύω, *remember*.)
4a.—— 23 1st.
2a.—— 32 1st.
4a.—— xii. 3, 5 2nd.
3. —— 15 1st, marg. *from*.
3. —— xiii. 24.
5a. Jas. i. 5 2nd, 7.
3. —— 13.
4a.—— 14.
4a.—— ii. 9.
1. —— 16.
4a.—— iii. 4, 6 3rd.
1. —— iv. 1.
3. —— v. 4 2nd.
8. —— 19.
2a. 1 Pet. i. 10 twice.
9. —— 11 2nd.
1. —— 23 1st.
4a.—— ii. 4 1st.
5b.—— 4 2nd.
2a.—— iii. 15.
1. —— iv. 11 2nd.
2a. 2 Pet. i. 12.
8. —— ii. 12.
2a.—— iii. 16.
2a. 1 John i. 1 1st.
3. —— 5.
1. —— ii. 16 4th & 5th, 19 3 times, 21.
3. —— 27 1st.
2a.—— 27 2nd.
1. —— 29.
1. —— iii. 8 1st, 9 twice, 10 3rd, 12, 19.
5a.—— 22 (No. 3, L T Tr A ℵ.)
1. —— iv. 1, 2 2nd, 3 1st, 4, 5 twice, 6 1st & 2nd, 7 twice, 13.
1. —— v. 1 twice, 4.
2a.—— 9 4th, 10 2nd.
5a.—— 15 (No. 3, L T Tr ℵ.)
1. —— 18 twice, 19.
1. 2 John 4.
1. 3 John 11.
4a.—— 12 1st.
2a. Jude 3.
4a.—— 12 2nd.
2a.—— 15 twice.
4a.—— 17 1st.
1. Rev. i. 5 1st (om. G L T Tr A ℵ.)
1. —— ii. 7 1st.
—— 10 1st, see Of (some)
1. —— 10 2nd, 11.
3. Rev. ii. 17 (*om.* φαγεῖν ἀπό, *to eat of*, G L T Tr A ℵ.)
1. —— 21, 22.
5a.—— 27 3rd.
—— iii. 9, see Of (them)
5a.—— 18 1st.
1. —— v. 5 1st & 2nd.
1. —— vi. 1 1st & 3rd.
4a.—— 13 2nd.
1. —— vii. 4 2nd, 5 1st, 3rd, & 5th, 6 1st, 3rd, & 5th, 7 1st, 3rd, & 5th, 8 1st, 3rd, & 5th, 9, 13.
1. —— viii. 11 3rd.
6a.—— 13 1st.
1. Rev. ix. 20 2nd, 21 4 times.
—— xi. 9, see Of (they)
3. —— xii. 6.
1. —— xiv. 8 1st, 10 1st.
1. —— xv. 7 1st.
1. —— xvi. 7 (*om.* ἄλλον ἐκ, *another out of*, G L T Tr A ℵ.)
1. —— 11 2nd.
3. —— 12 2nd.
1. —— 13 1st, 3rd, & 5th, see Out of.
1. —— xvii. 1 1st, 11.
1. —— xviii. 3 1st, 4 3rd, 12 4th.
1. —— xix. 15 1st, 21 2nd.
1. —— xxi. 6 1st, 21 1st.

OF HIM.

αὐτοῦ, of himself, (*emphatic.*)

John ix. 18.

OF HIMSELF.

αὐτοῦ, see above.

Heb. ix. 20.

OF THEM.

αὐτῶν, of them, (*emphatic.*)

Luke xxiii. 51.

OF (ONE)

ἐκ, of, from among, out of, (*see* "OF," *No.* 1.)

Matt. xxvi. 73. | John xviii. 17, 25.
Mark xiv. 69, 70. | Acts xxi. 8.
Col. iv. 9, 12.

OF (SOME)

ἐκ, see "OF," *No.* 1.

Matt. xxiii. 34 twice. | John ix. 40.
Luke xxi. 16. | —— xvi. 17.
Rev. ii. 10.

OF (THEM)

ἐκ, see "OF," *No.* 1.

Rev. iii. 9.

OF (THEY)

1. *ἐκ, see* "OF," *No.* 1.
2. *ἀπό, see* "OF," *No.* 3.

2. Matt. xxvii. 9. | 1. Rev. xi. 9.

See also, ACCOUNT, ASK, BECAUSE, BETWEEN, BEWARE, CHARGE, COMPASSION, DAYS, DEMAND, DRINK, EXAMPLE, FALL, FULL, GLORY,

GUILTY, HAVOC, IGNORANT, KNOW, MANNER, MEANS, NECESSITY, NOTHING, OCCASION, OUT, REASON, RESPECT, SHORT, SIGHT, SPACE, SPEAK, STOP, TELL, TIME

OFF.

ἐκ, *see* "OF," *No.* 1.

Mark xi. 8, (*in* A.V. 1611, "of.")

See also, AFAR, BREAK, CAST, CUT, FALL, FAR, PUT, PUTTING, REND, SEE, SHAKE, SMITE, TAKE, WAY, WIPE.

OFFENCE (-S.)

1. *σκάνδαλον*, a trap-stick, *i.e. a crooked stick on which a bait is fastened, which, being struck by the animal, springs the trap*, a trap, gin, snare; *hence*, anything which one strikes, or stumbles against, a stumbling-block; *esp.*, a cause of stumbling.
2. *παράπτωμα*, a mis-fall, mis-hap, a falling aside from right, truth, or duty, *through ignorance, inadvertence, or negligence.*

[*No.* 2 is the lapse towards sin, while *No.* 3 is the completed act of sin. *No.* 2 is sin rashly committed as by one who is unwilling to do it, while in *No.* 1 the act is expressed which he who does it does willingly, whether he errs from passion, or from improperly thinking that he is doing right.]

3. *ἁμαρτία*, aberration from prescribed laws, innate vice, *not merely the vicious act*, but, the very corruption of the soul itself. *Not the mere incitement to sin, but*, that which is in itself evil and vicious, the corruption which is by nature in us, (*see No.* 2, *and note.*)
4. *πρόσκομμα*, the thing struck against *by any one*, a stumbling-*block*.
5. *προσκοπή*, a stumbling, a being offended. *In N.T.*, offence, cause of stumbling.

1. Matt. xvi. 23.
1. —— xviii. 7 3 times.
1. Luke xvii. 1.
— Acts xxiv. 16, see O (void of)
2. Rom. iv. 25.
2. —— v. 15 twice, 16, 17, 18, 20.
1. —— ix. 33.
4. Rom. xiv. 20.
1. —— xvi. 17.
— 1 Cor. x. 32, see O (give none)
5. 2 Cor. vi. 3.
3. —— xi. 7.
1. Gal. v. 11.
— Phil. i. 10, see O (without)
1. 1 Pet. ii. 8.

OFFENCE (GIVE NONE)

{ *ἀπρόσκοπτος*, void of offence, (*see below.*)
{ *γίνομαι*, to become.

1 Cor. x. 32.

OFFENCE (VOID OF)

ἀπρόσκοπτος, not stumbling, not causing to stumble · *or Pass.*, not falling *into sin.*

Acts xxiv. 16.

OFFENCE (WITHOUT)

ἀπρόσκοπτος, *see above.*

Phil. i. 10.

OFFEND (-ED.)

1. *σκανδαλίζω*, to lay a snare for, set a trap for; *hence*, to cause to stumble *or* fall, to give offence or scandal *to anyone.*
2. *πταίω*, to stumble against, fall over; to strike the foot against and fall, trip.
3. *ἁμαρτάνω*, to miss the mark, err from, swerve from the truth; *gen.*, to sin.

1. Matt. v. 29, marg. *cause to offend.*
1. —— 30.
1. —— xi. 6.
1. —— xiii. 21.
— —— 41, see O (thing that)
1. —— 57.
1. —— xv. 12.
1. —— xvii. 27.
1. —— xviii. 6, 8, 9.
1. —— xxiv. 10.
1. —— xxvi. 31, 33 twice.
1. Mark iv. 17.
1. —— vi. 3.
1. —— ix. 42.
1. —— 43, marg. *cause to offend.*
1. —— 45.
1. Mark ix. 47, marg. *cause to offend.*
1. —— xiv. 27, 29.
1. Luke vii. 23.
1. —— xvii. 2.
1. John vi. 61.
1. —— xvi. 1.
3. Acts xxv. 8.
1. Rom. xiv. 21 (*om.* *ἢ σκανδαλίζεται ἢ ἀσθενεῖ*, *or is offended or is made weak*, G → T Trmb ℵ.)
— 1 Cor. viii. 13 twice, see O (make to)
1. 2 Cor. xi. 29.
2. Jas. ii. 10.
2. —— iii. 2 twice.

OFFEND (MAKE TO)

1. 1 Cor. viii. 13 twice.

OFFENDETH (THING THAT)

σκάνδαλον, *see* "OFFENCE," *No.* 1.

Matt. xiii. 41, marg. *scandal.*

OFFENDER (BE AN)

ἀδικέω, to violate right, act unjustly.

Acts xxv. 11.

OFFER (-ED, -ING.)

1. προσφέρω, to bear *or* bring to *or* towards *any place or person*, bring near to; *hence*, to offer, present.

2. ἀναφέρω, (*No.* 1, *with* ἄνα, up, *prefixed, instead of* πρός, towards) to bear upwards, carry up; *of sacrifices*, place upon the altar, *i.e.* to offer up.

3. δίδωμι, to give, bestow upon; render up, yield.

4. ἐπιδίδωμι, (*No.* 3, *with* ἐπί, upon, *prefixed*) to give upon, *i.e.* in addition to, to give over, deliver over *into another's hands*.

5. ἀνάγω, to lead up, conduct *or* bring up, *as a sacrifice to the altar, hence*, to offer sacrifice.

6. παρέχω, to hold near *to any one*, to hold out near *or* beside *any one, so as* to present *or* offer anything.

1. Matt. ii. 11, marg. *present unto.*	— Phil. ii. 17, see O (be)
1. —— v. 24.	— 2 Tim. iv. 6, see O (ready to be)
1. —— viii. 4.	1. Heb. v. 1, 3.
1. Mark i. 44.	— —— vi. 7, see O up.
3. Luke ii. 24.	— —— vii. 27, see O up.
1. —— v. 14.	1. —— viii. 3 twice, 4.
6. —— vi. 29.	1. —— ix. 7, 9, 14, 25, 28.
4. —— xi. 12.	1. —— x. 1, 2, 8, 11, 12 part.
1. —— xxiii. 36.	1. —— xi. 4.
5. Acts vii. 41.	— ——— 17, see O up.
1. ——— 42.	2. —— xiii. 15.
1. —— viii. 18.	2. Jas. ii. 21 part.
6. —— xvii. 31, marg. (text, *to give.*)	— 1 Pet. ii. 5, see O up.
1. —— xxi. 26.	3. Rev. viii. 3, marg. *add.*

OFFER UP.

1. Heb. vi. 7 part.	1. Heb. xi. 17 twice.
2. —— vii. 27 1st, 27 2nd part.	2. 1 Pet. ii. 5.

OFFERED (BE)

σπένδω, to pour out, to make a libation. *Here, mid.*, to pour out one's self, *i.e. one's blood*, to offer one's self.

Phil. ii. 17, marg. *poured forth.*

OFFERED (BE READY TO BE)

σπένδω, *see above.*

2 Tim. iv. 6.

See also, IDOL, WRONG.

OFFERING (-S.) [noun.]

1. προσφορά, an offering, oblation; (*strictly, without blood; opp. to* θυσία *and* ὁλοκαυτώμα.)

2. δῶρον, a gift, present, *esp., gifts dedicated to God.*

2. Luke xxi. 4.	— Rom. xv. 16, see O up.
1. Acts xxi. 26.	1. Eph. v. 2.
1. —— xxiv. 17.	1. Heb. x. 5, 8, 10, 14, 18.

OFFERING UP.

1. Rom. xv. 16.

OFFICE.

1. διακονία, service, serviceable labour, attendance, ministry; every labour that is a service benefiting others *is a* διακονία.

2. ἐπισκοπή, visitation, *implying inspection and tender guardianship; then, of* the duty *of visiting and inspecting*, the office of an ἐπίσκοπος.

3. πρᾶξις, a doing, action, *something done; also, something to be done*, business, office, function.

— Luke i. 8, 9, see Priest.	3. Rom. xii. 4.
2. Acts i. 20, marg. (text, *Bishoprick.*)	— 1 Tim. iii. 1, see Bishop.
1. Rom. xi. 13.	— ——— 10, 13, see Deacon.

— Heb. vii. 5, see Priesthood.

OFFICER (-S.)

1. ὑπηρέτης, an under-rower, a common sailor, (*as distinguished from* ναῦται, seamen.) *Hence, gen.*, one who does service under the direction of any one, *esp., of magistrates, e.g.* a lictor *or* officer, like *Eng.*, constable, beadle.

2. πράκτωρ, an exactor, collector, *i.e.* a public officer who collected debts, fines, or penalties, (*non occ.*)

1. Matt. v. 25.	1. John xviii. 3, 12, 18, 22.
2. Luke xii. 58 twice.	1. —— xix. 6.
1. John vii. 32, 45, 46.	1. Acts v. 22, 26.

OFFSCOURING.

περίψημα, scrapings from all round, (*from* περίψαω, to wipe *or* scrape all round) scum, filth, (*non occ.*)

1 Cor. iv. 13.

OFFSPRING.

γένος, genus, race, offspring, posterity.

Acts xvii. 28, 29. | Rev. xxii. 16.

OFT.

1. πολλάκις, many times, often.
2. πολλά, much.
3. πυγμῇ, with the fist, *i.e. rubbing with; hence*, diligently, sedulously, carefully.

[An ancient interpretation of Mark vii. 3, makes it as meaning *up to the elbow*.]

2. Matt. ix. 14 (*om.* L T ℵ.)
1. —— xvii. 15.
— —— xviii. 21, see O (how)
3. Mark vii. 3, marg. *diligently*.
1. Acts. xxvi. 11.
— 1 Cor. xi. 25, see O as (as)
1. 2 Cor. xi. 23.
1. 2 Tim. i. 16.
1. Heb. vi. 7.

OFT? (HOW)

ποσάκις, how many times? how often?

Matt. xviii. 21.

OFT AS (AS)

ὁσάκις, how many times? how often? *In N.T., with ἄν*, however often, so often as.

1 Cor. xi. 25.

OFTEN.

1. πολλάκις, many times, often.
2. πυκνός, *adj.*, thick, firm, solid, close together; *hence*, frequent, often.
3. πυκνά, *neut. pl.* of *No.* 2, frequently.

— Matt. xxiii. 37, see O (how)
1. Mark v. 4.
3. Luke v. 33.
— —— xiii. 34, see O (how)
— 1 Cor. xi. 26, see O as (as)
1. 2 Cor. xi. 26, 27 twice.
1. Phil. iii. 18.
2. 1 Tim. v. 23.
1. Heb. ix. 25, 26.

OFTEN (HOW)

ποσάκις, how many times?

Matt. xxiii. 37. | Luke xiii. 34.

OFTEN AS (AS)

ὁσάκις, *see* "OFT AS (AS)"

1 Cor. xi. 26. | Rev. xi. 6.

OFTENER (THE)

πυκνότερον, (*comp. of* "OFTEN," *No.* 2.)

Acts xxiv. 26.

OFTENTIMES.

1. πολλάκις, many times, often.
2. { τά, the, / πολλά, many, } these many [*times*.]
3. { πολλοῖς, many, / χρόνοις, times, } many times, (*emphatic*.)

3. Luke viii. 29.
1. Rom. i. 13.
2. Rom. xv. 22, marg. (text, *much*.)
1. 2 Cor. viii. 22.
1. Heb. x. 11.

OFTTIMES.

πολλάκις, many times, often.

Matt. xvii. 15. | Mark ix. 22.
John xviii. 2.

OIL.

ἔλαιον, olive oil, (*non occ.*)

Matt. xxv. 3, 4, 8.
Mark vi. 13.
Luke vii. 46.
—— x. 34.
Luke xvi. 6.
Heb. i. 9.
Jas. v. 14.
Rev. vi. 6.
Rev. xviii. 13.

OINTMENT (-S.)

μύρον, any aromatic balsam, *distilling itself from a tree or plant, esp.*, myrrh. *In N.T.*, ointment (*perfumed*), (*non occ.*)

Matt. xxvi. 7.
—— 9 (*om.* G L T Tr A ℵ.)
—— 12.
Mark xiv. 3, 4.
Luke vii. 37, 38, 46.
—— xxiii. 56.
John xi. 2.
—— xii. 3 twice, 5.
Rev. xviii. 13.

OLD.

(*For various combinations, see below.*)

1. παλαιός, old, *as having existed a long time; hence*, old, worn out, decayed, etc.
2. ἀρχαῖος, old, as having existed formerly, of former days, of old time.
3. πάλαι, long ago, of old, already long.
4. γέρων, an old man, (*non occ.*)

— Matt. ii. 16, see Year.
1. —— ix. 16, 17.
1. Mark ii. 21 twice, 22.
— Luke i. 36, see Age.
1. —— v. 36 twice, 37, 39.
2. —— ix. 8, 19.
4. —— John iii. 4.
— Acts vii. 23, see Forty.
2. —— xxi. 16.
— Rom. iv. 19, see Hundred.
1. Rom. vi. 6.
1. 1 Cor. v. 7, 8.
1. 2 Cor. iii. 14.
1. Eph. iv. 22.
1. Col. iii. 9.
3. 2 Pet. i. 9.
2. —— ii. 5.
1. 1 John ii. 7 twice.
2. Rev. xii. 9.
2. —— xx. 2.

OLD (BE)

1. γηράσκω, to grow *or* become old, (*occ.* Heb. viii. 13.)

2. ἔχω, to have, [*here*, to have so many years, *i.e.* to be so many years old.]

2. John viii. 57. | 1. John xxi. 18.

OLD TIME (IN THE)

ποτέ, when, whenever, *i.e.* at some time, once, formerly.

1 Pet. iii. 5.

OLD TIME (IN)

ποτέ, *see above.*

2 Pet. i. 21, marg. *at any time.*

OLD (MAKE)

παλαιόω, to let grow old, wax old, become old, become antiquated.

Heb. viii. 13.

OLD MAN.

1. πρεσβύτης, an old man, one aged.
2. πρεσβύτηρος, older, elder, an elder-man; *like Eng.*, alderman.

1. Luke i. 18. | 2. Acts ii. 17.

OLD (OF)

1. πάλαι, long ago, of old, already long.
2. ἔκπαλαι, (*No.* 1, *with* ἐκ, out of, *prefixed*), (*occ.* 2 Pet. ii. 3.)

2. 2 Pet. iii. 5. | 1. Jude 4.

OLD TIME (OF)

1. ἀρχαῖος, (*see* "OLD," *No.* 1.)
2. { ἐκ, out of, / γενεῶν, generations, / ἀρχαίων, ancient, } out of ancient generations.

1. Matt. v. 21.
1. —— 27 (om. τοῖς ἀρχαίος, *by them of old time*, G L T Tr A ℵ.)
1. Matt. v. 33.
2. Acts xv. 21.

OLD THINGS.

1. παλαιά, *neut. pl. of* "OLD," *No.* 1.
2. { τὰ, the, / ἀρχαῖα, old things, } (*see* "OLD," *No.* 2.)

1. Matt. xiii. 52. | 2. 2 Cor. v. 17.

OLD (WAX)

1. παλαιόω, *see* "OLD (MAKE)"
2. γηράσκω, *see* "OLD (BE)," *No.* 1, (*occ.* John xxi. 18.)

1. Luke xii. 33. | 2. Heb. viii. 13.

OLD WINE.

παλαιός, *see* "OLD," *No.* 1.

Luke v. 39.

OLD WIVES'.

γραώδης, old-womanish, (*non occ.*)

1 Tim. iv. 7.

OLDNESS.

παλαιότης, oldness, antiquatedness, (*non occ.*)

Rom. vii. 6.

OLIVE BERRIES.

ἐλαία, an olive, an olive tree, *also used of the* fruit.

Jas. iii. 12.

OLIVE TREE.

Rom. xi. 17, 24. | Rev. xi. 4.

OLIVE TREE (GOOD)

καλλιέλαιος, yielding fine oil, *and hence*, a good *or* beautiful olive tree, (*non occ.*)

Rom. xi. 24.

OLIVE TREE (WILD)

ἀγριέλαιος, a field *or* wild olive tree, oleaster, (*this tree bears no fruit.*)

Rom. xi. 17.

OLIVE TREE WHICH IS WILD.

ἀγριέλαιος, *see above.*

Rom. xi. 24.

OLIVES.

ἐλαία, an olive tree. Τὸ ὄρος τῶν ἐλαιῶν, the Mount of Olives, *i.e.* the hill on the east side of Jerusalem, and separated from it by the valley of the Kedron.

Matt. xxi. 1.
—— xxiv. 3.
—— xxvi. 30.
Mark xi. 1.
—— xiii. 3.
Mark xiv. 26.
Luke xix. 29, 37.
—— xxi. 37.
—— xxii. 39.
John viii. 1 (*ap.*)

OLIVET.

ἐλαιῶν, of olives, (*non occ.*)

Acts i. 12.

OMEGA.

Ω, omega, the last letter of the Greek alphabet.

Rev. i. 8, 11 (*ap.*)
Rev. xxi. 6.
Rev. xxii. 13.

OMIT.

ἀφίημι, to send forth *or* away from, to dismiss.

Matt. xxiii. 23.

OMNIPOTENT.

παντοκράτωρ, the Omnipotent, the Almighty.

Rev. xix. 6.

ON.

(*For various combinations with other words, see below.*)

1. ἐπί, upon.
   (a) *with Gen.*, upon, and proceeding from, (e.g. *as a pillar from the ground*) on, *as springing from.*
   (b) *with Dat.*, upon, *as resting on*, upon, *locally, with the idea of rest simply.*
   (c) *with Acc.*, upon, *by direction towards*, upon, *with motion implied*, (i.e. *downward pressure.*)
2. εἰς, into, (*motion to the interior*) to, unto.
3. ἐν, in, *of time, place, or element.*
4. ἐπάνω, above, upon.
5. ἀπό, from, *from the exterior*, (*see diagram under* "OF"); away from.
6. περί, around.
   (a) *with Gen.*, around *and separate from*, about, concerning.
   (b) *with Acc.*, around *and towards.*
7. κατά, down.
   (a) *with Gen.*, down from.
   (b) *with Acc.*, down upon, *or* along.
8. ἐκ, out of, from among.
9. μετά, with, in association with, (*as dist. from* σύν, *which implies conjunction and co-operation.*)
   (a) *with Gen.*, with. [In Luke x. 37, *the sense is*, "he that dealt mercifully with."]
   (b) *with Acc.*, after.

1c. Matt. iv. 5.
4. —— v. 14.
1c. ——— 15.
1c. ——— 39 (No. 2, L T Tr A ℵ.)
1c. ——— 45 twice.
1a. —— ix. 2, 6.
6a. ——— 36.
1c. —— x. 29 (om. G⇉)
1c. ——— 34.
1c. —— xiii. 2.
1c. —— xiv. 19 (No. 1a, L T Tr A* ℵ.)
1a. ——— 25 (No. 1c, L T Tr A ℵ.)
1c. ——— 26 (No. 1a, L T Tr A ℵ.)
1c. ——— 28, 29.
1c. —— xv. 32, 35.
1a. —— xvi. 19 twice.
1c. —— xvii. 6.
1a. —— xviii. 18 twice, 19.
4. —— xxi. 7.
8. ——— 19.
1c. ——— 44 twice (*ap.*)
3. —— xxii. 40.
1c. —— xxiii. 4.
1a. —— xxiv. 17.
3. ——— 20 (*om.* G L T Tr A ℵ.)
3. —— xxvi. 5.
1c. ——— 7 (No. 1a, L T Tr ℵ.)
1a. ——— 12.
1c. ——— 39, 50.
1a. —— xxvii. 19.
1c. ——— 25 twice.
2. ——— 30.
1a. Mark ii. 10.
1b. ——— 21 (No. 1c, L T Tr A ℵ.)
3. ——— 23.
3. ——— 24 (*om.* G⇉ L T Tr A ℵ.)
1a. —— iv. 1.
1c. ——— 5.
2. ——— 8.
1c. ——— 16, 20, 21, 38.
1a. —— vi. 47.
1c. —— viii. 2.
1a. ——— 6.
2. ——— 23.
1a. —— ix. 3, 20.
1c. ——— 22.
1a. —— xiii. 15.
3. —— xiv. 2.
7a. ——— 3 (*om.* L T Tr A ℵ.)
2. ——— 6 (No. 3, G L T Tr A ℵ.)
1a. ——— 35.
1c. ——— 46 (*om.* T Tr A ℵ.)
3. —— xvi. 5.
1c. ——— 18 (*ap.*)
3. Luke i. 59.
1c. ——— 65.
1a. Luke ii. 14.
1c. —— iv. 9.
3. ——— 16, 31.
1c. —— v. 12.
3. ——— 17.
3. —— vi. 1.
3. ——— 2 (*om.* L T Tr A ℵ.)
3. ——— 6, 7.
2. ——— 20.
1c. ——— 29, 49.
1b. —— vii. 13.
1c. —— viii. 8 (No. 2, G L T Tr A ℵ.)
1a. ——— 13.
3. ——— 15
1a. ——— 16.
3. ——— 22.
2. ——— 23.
3. ——— 32.
3. —— ix. 37 (*om.* Tr^b A ℵ.)
—— —— x. 11, see On us.
4. ——— 19.
1c. ——— 34, 35.
9. ——— 37.
1c. —— xi. 33.
2. —— xii. 49 (No. 1c, G∾L T Tr A* ℵ.)
3. ——— 51.
3. —— xiii. 7, 10.
3. —— xiv. 5 (*om.* L^b Tr.)
1c. —— xv. 5, 29.
2. ——— 22 twice.
1c. —— xvii. 16.
1a. —— xviii. 8.
3. —— xx. 1.
1c. ——— 18, 19.
1c. —— xxi. 12, 35 twice.
1a. —— xxii. 21, 30.
1c. —— xxiii. 30.
2. John i. 12.
1c. ——— 33.
2. —— ii. 11.
2. —— iii. 18, 33 1st.
1b. ——— 36 2nd.
1b. —— iv. 6.
2. ——— 39.
3. —— v. 9, 16.
1a. —— vi. 2, 19.
2. ——— 29, 35, 40.
2. ——— 47 (*om.* εἰς ἐμέ, *on me*, T Tr^b A ℵ.)
3. —— vii. 22 (*om.* L^b.)
3. ——— 23 twice.
1c. ——— 30.
2. ——— 31, 38, 39.
1c. ——— 44.
2. ——— 48.
2. —— viii. 6 (*ap.*), 8 (*ap.*), 30.
2. —— ix. 35, 36.
2. —— x. 42.
2. —— xi. 45, 48.
2. —— xii. 11.
1c. ——— 15.
2. ——— 37, 42, 44 3 times, 46.

2. John xiii. 22.
3. ——— 23.
1c.——— 25.
2. —— xiv. 12.
2. —— xvi. 9.
1a.—— xvii. 4.
2. ——— 20.
1a.—— xix. 19.
3. ——— 31.
2. ——— 37.
2. —— xxi. 4 (No. 1c, G ∾
2. ——— 6. [L T Trm ℵ.)
1c.——— 20.
1c. Acts ii. 18 twice.
1a.——— 30 (No. 1c, L T Tr A ℵ.)
1c.—— iv. 5, 22.
1c.—— v. 5.
1a.——— 15.
1c.——— 18.
1a.——— 30.
2. —— vi. 15.
1c.—— vii. 54.
1c.—— viii. 17.
7b.——— 36.
1c.—— ix. 17.
6a.—— x. 19.
1a.——— 39.
1c.——— 44, 45.
1c.—— xi. 15 twice, 17.
2. —— xiii. 9.
1c.——— 11.
1c.—— xiv. 10.
2. ——— 23.
1c.—— xvi. 31.
1c.—— xvii. 26 (No. 1a, L T Tr A ℵ.)
2. —— xix. 4.
1c.——— 6, 16, 17.
1c.—— xx. 37.
1c.—— xxi. 5.
1a.——— 23.
1c.——— 27.
1a.——— 40.
1c.—— xxii. 19.
1a.—— xxv. 17.
1b.—— xxvii. 44 1st.
1a.——— 44 2nd.
1c.—— xxviii. 3.
1c. Rom. iv. 5, 24.
1c.—— ix. 23.
1b.——— 33.
1b.—— x. 11.
1c.—— xi. 22.
3. —— xii. 7 twice, 8.
1c.——— 20.
1c.—— xv. 3.
2. —— xvi. 6.
1a. 1 Cor. xi. 10.
1c.—— xiv. 25.
3. 2 Cor. iv. 8.
3. —— vii. 5.
3. —— viii. 1.
2. —— xi. 20.
1a. Gal. iii. 13.
2. ——— 14.
1c.—— vi. 16.
1a. Eph. i. 10.
1a.—— vi. 3.
2. Phil. i. 29.
3. Col. iii. 1.
1a.——— 2.
1c.——— 6 (ap.)

1b. 1 Tim. i. 16.
1c.——— 18.
1c. Titus iii. 6.
3. Heb. i. 3.
3. —— viii. 1.
1a.——— 4.
3. —— x. 12.
6. —— xi. 13.
1a.—— xii. 25.
1a. Jas. v. 5, 17.
1b. 1 Pet. ii. 6.
1c.——— 24, marg. *to.*
3. —— iii. 22.
3. —— iv. 16.
2. 1 John v. 10, 13 1st, 13 2nd (*ap.*)
3. Rev. i. 10.
1c.—— iii. 3 (*om.* ἐπὶ σε, *on thee*, G → L T Trb A.)
1a.—— iv. 2 (No. 1c, L T Tr A ℵ.)
1c.——— 4.
1a.——— 9 (No. 1b, L T Tr A ℵ.)
1a.——— 10.
1a.—— v. 1, 10.
3. ——— 13 (No. 1c, G L T Tr A ℵ.)
1b.—— vi. 2, } (No. 1c, G L
1b.——— 5, } T Tr A ℵ.)
4. ——— 8.
5. ——— 10 1st (No. 8, G ∾ L T Tr A ℵ.)
1a.——— 10 2nd.
1c.——— 16 1st.
1a.——— 16 2nd (No. 1b, T Trm A ℵ.)
1c.—— vii. 1 1st.
1a.——— 1 2nd & 3rd.
1c.——— 1 4th, 11.
1a.——— 15.
1c.——— 16.
1c.—— ix. 7.
1a.——— 17.
1c.—— x. 2 (No. 1a, G L T Tr A ℵ.)
1a.—— xi. 10.
1c.——— 16.
2. —— xiii. 13.
1a.——— 14 twice.
1c.—— xiv. 1.
1a.——— 6.
1a.——— 14 (No. 1c, L.)
1a.——— 15.
1c.——— 16 1st (No. 1a, L T Tr A ℵ.)
1c.——— 16 2nd.
1c.—— xv. 2.
1a.—— xvii. 8, 9.
— ——— 11, see O which.
1c.—— xviii. 19.
8. ——— 20.
1a.—— xix. 4 (No. 1b, G ∾ L T Tr A ℵ.)
1c.——— 12, 16 twice.
1a.——— 18 (No. 1c, L Tr A), (No. 1b, ℵ.)
1a.——— 19.
1a.—— xx. 6.
1c.——— 9.
1a.——— 11 (No. 1c, G T Trm), (No. 4, Tr ℵ.)
5. —— xxi. 13 4 times.

ON THE LEFT HAND.

εὐώνυμος, of good name; *hence*, of good omen, *a word used instead of* ἀριστερός, the left, *which was a word of ill omen, since all omens on the left were regarded by the Greeks as unfortunate.*

Acts xxi. 3.

ON THE [*or* ON ONE'S] LEFT [HAND].

{ ἐξ, out of, from,
{ εὐωνύμων, the left, (*see above.*)

Matt. xx. 21, 23.
—— xxv. 33, 41.
—— xxvii. 38.
Mark x. 37 (ἀριστέρος, T Tr A.)
—— xv. 27.

ON US.

ἡμῖν, to us.

Luke x. 11.

ON WHICH.

{ ὅπου, where...[*the woman is sitting.*]
{ ἐπί, upon.
{ αὐτῶν, them.

Rev. xvii. 9.

See also, ACCOUNT, AFFECTION, BACKSIDE, BEHALF, BIND, BREATHE, BRING, CAST, COME, COMPASSION, DRAW, EITHER, FALL, FASHION, FASTEN, FIRE, FOOT, GO, ROUND, HAVE, HIGH, HOLD, IMPOSED, JOURNEY, LAY, LAYING, LEAP, LIE, LOOK, MORROW, PART, PAST, PUT, PUTTING, RAIL, RIGHT, SAY, SEIZE, SET, SEW, SLEEP, SPIT, TAKE, THINK, THIS, WANT.

ON [adv.]

See, SAY.

ONCE.

1. ἅπαξ, once, one time, once for all, (*non occ.*)

2. ἐφάπαξ, (*No.* 1, *with* ἐπί, upon, *prefixed*) upon once, *i.e.* once for all; once, not several times.

3. ποτέ, at some time, one time or other, once, *both of time past and future.*

— Luke xiii. 25, see When.
— —— xxiii. 18, see O (all at)
2. Rom. vi. 10.
3. —— vii. 9.
— 1 Cor. xv. 6, see O (at)
1. 2 Cor. xi. 25.
3. Gal. i. 23.
— Eph. v. 3, see Not.
1. Phil. iv. 16.
1. 1 Thes. ii. 18.
1. Heb. vi. 4.
2. —— vii. 27.

2. Heb. ix. 12.
1. ——— 7, 26, 27, 28.
1. —— x. 2.
— ——— 10, see O for all.
1. —— xii. 26, 27.
1. 1 Pet. iii. 18.
1. ——— 20 (ἀπεξεδέχετο [the longsuffering of God] *was waiting*, instead of ἅπαξ ἐξεδέχετο, *once* [the longsuffering of God] *waited*, G L T Tr A ℵ.)

1. Jude 3, 5.

ONCE (AT)

2. 1 Cor. xv. 6.

ONCE (ALL AT)

παμπληθεί, the whole multitude together.

Luke xxiii. 18.

ONCE FOR ALL.

2. Heb. x. 10.

ONE.

(*For* "ONE ANOTHER," *and various combinations with other words, see below.*)

1. εἷς, (*fem.*, μία, *neut.*, ἕν) one, *the first cardinal numeral; emphatic,* one, even one, one single.
2. μία, *fem. of No.* 1.
3. τις, (*neut.*, τι) one, some one, a certain one; any one.
4. ὅς, (*fem.*, ἥ; *neut.*, ὅ) this, that; who, which, what; *in distinctions,* this one, the one.

1. Matt. v. 18 1st.
2. —— 18 2nd, 19.
1. —— 29, 30.
2. —— 36.
1. —— vi. 24 twice, 27, 29.
1. —— x. 29, 42.
1. —— xii. 11.
3. —— 29, 47.
1. —— xiii. 46.
1. —— xvi. 14.
2. —— xvii. 4 4 times.
1. —— xviii. 5, 6, 10, 12, 14, 16, 24, 28.
2. —— xix. 5, 6.
1. —— 16, 17.
2. —— xx. 12.
1. —— 13.
1. —— xxi. 24.
1. —— xxii. 35.
1. —— xxiii. 8, 9, 10 (om. G∾)
1. —— 15.
1. —— xxv. 15, 17, 24, 40, [45.
1. —— xxvi. 14, 21.
2. —— 40.
1. —— 47, 51.
1. —— xxvii. 48.
1. Mark v. 22.
1. —— vi. 15, xxiv. 40, 41.
1. —— viii. 14, 28.
2. —— ix. 5 3 times.
1. —— 17, 37.
3. —— 38.
1. —— 42.
2. —— x. 8 twice.
1. —— 17, 18, 21.
1. —— xi. 29.
1. —— xii. 6, 28, 29, 32.
1. —— xiii. 1.
1. —— xiv. 10, 18, 20.
2. —— 37.
1. —— 43, 47.
2. —— 66.
1. —— xv. 6.
3. —— 21.
1. Mark xv. 36 (No. 3, T Tr A ℵ.)
1. Luke iv. 40.
1. —— v. 3.
3. —— vii. 36.
1. —— 41.
3. —— viii. 49.
1. —— ix. 8 (No. 3, T Tr A ℵ.)
3. —— 19.
2. —— 33 3 times.
3. —— 49.
3. —— xi. 1, 45.
1. —— 46.
1. —— xii. 6.
3. —— 13.
1. —— 25 (om. T Tr b A ℵ.)
1. —— 27.
2. —— xiii. 10.
3. —— 23.
1. —— xiv. 1, 15.
1. —— xv. 4, 7.
2. —— 8.
1. —— 10, 19, 26.
1. —— xvi. 5, 13 twice.
2. —— 17.
3. —— 30, 31.
1. —— xvii. 2, 15.
2. —— 22, 34 1st (om. L b.)
1. —— 34 2nd.
2. —— 35.
1. —— 36 (ap.)
1. —— xviii. 10, 19.
2. —— xx. 1.
1. —— 3 (om. G⇌L T Tr A ℵ.)
1. —— xxii. 47, 50.
2. —— 59.
1. —— xxiii. 17 (ap.)
3. —— 26.
1. —— 39.
1. —— xxiv. 18.
1. John i. 40.
1. —— vi. 8, 22, 70, 71.
1. John vii. 21, 50.
1. —— viii. 41.
2. —— x. 16 1st.
1. —— 16 2nd, 30.
1. —— xi. 49, 50, 52.
1. —— xii. 2, 4.
1. —— xiii. 21, 23.
1. —— xvii. 11, 21 1st.
1. —— 21 2nd (om. G⇌L b T Tr A ℵ.)
1. —— 22 twice, 23.
1. —— xviii. 14, 22, 26, 39.
1. —— xix. 34.
1. —— xx. 24.
1. Acts i. 22.
2. —— iv. 32.
3. —— v. 25, 34.
3. —— vii. 24.
3. —— ix. 43.
3. —— x. 6.
1. —— xi. 28.
2. —— xii. 10.
1. —— xvii. 26, 27.
3. —— xix. 9 (om. L T Tr A ℵ.)
2. —— 34.
1. —— xx. 31.
2. —— xxi. 7.
3. —— 16.
1. —— 26.
3. —— xxii. 12.
1. —— xxiii. 6, 17.
2. —— xxiv. 21.
3. —— xxv. 19.
2. —— xxviii. 13.
1. —— 25.
1. Rom. iii. 10, 12, 30.
3. —— v. 7.
1. —— 12, 15 twice, 16 twice.
1. —— 17, marg. (text, *one man.*)
1. —— 17 2nd & 3rd, 18 twice, 19 twice.
1. —— ix. 10.
1. —— xii. 4, 5.
4. —— xiv. 2.
1. —— xv. 6.
3. 1 Cor. iii. 4.
1. —— 8.
1. —— iv. 6 twice.
3. —— v. 1.
1. —— vi. 16 1st.
2. —— 16 2nd.
1. —— 17.
1. —— viii. 4, 6 twice.
1. —— ix. 24.
2. —— x. 8.
1. 1 Cor. x. 17 3 times.
1. —— xi. 5.
4. —— xii. 8.
1. —— 11, 12 1st.
1. —— 12 2nd (om. G⇌L T Tr A ℵ.)
1. —— 12 3rd, 13 3 times, 14, 18, 19, 20, 26 twice.
3. —— xiv. 24.
1. —— 27.
1. 2 Cor. v. 14.
1. —— xi. 2.
2. —— 24.
1. Gal. iii. 16, 20 twice, 28.
2. —— iv. 24.
1. —— v. 14.
1. Eph. ii. 14, 15, 16, 18.
1. —— iv. 4 1st & 2nd.
2. —— 4 3rd.
1. —— 5 1st.
2. —— 5 2nd.
1. —— 5 3rd.
1. —— 6, 7.
2. —— v. 31.
1. Phil. i. 27 1st.
2. —— 27 2nd.
1. —— ii. 2.
1. Col. iii. 15.
1. 1 Thes. ii. 11.
1. 2 Thes. i. 3.
1. 1 Tim. ii. 5 twice.
2. —— iii. 2, 12.
1. —— v. 9.
2. Tit. i. 6.
3. —— 12.
3. Heb. ii. 6.
1. —— 11.
2. —— x. 12, 14.
1. —— xi. 12.
2. —— xii. 16.
1. Jas. ii. 10.
3. —— 16.
1. —— 19.
1. —— iv. 12.
3. —— v. 19.
2. 2 Pet. iii. 8 twice.
1. 1 John v. 7 (ap.), 8.
1. Rev. v. 5.
2. —— vi. 1 1st.
1. —— 1 2nd.
1. —— vii. 13.
2. —— ix. 12.
2. —— xiii. 3.
1. —— xv. 7.
1. —— xvii. 1, 10.
2. —— 12, 13.
2. —— xviii. 8, 10, 17, 19.
1. —— xxi. 9, 21.

ONE ANOTHER.

1. ἀλλήλων, each other, one another.
2. ἑαυτοῖς, (*Dat., pl.*) to themselves, *i.e. each* to themselves, to one another.
3. ἑαυτούς, (*Acc., pl.*) themselves, one another.
4. ἑαυτῶν, (*Gen., pl.*) of themselves, of one another.
5. { εἷς, one, / τὸν, the, / ἕνα, one *or* other, } one, the other.

1. Matt. xxiv. 10 twice.
1. —— xxv. 32.
1. Mark iv. 41.
1. —— ix. 50.
1. Luke ii. 15.
1. Luke vi. 11.
1. —— vii. 32.
1. —— viii. 25.
1. —— xii. 1.
1. —— xxiv. 17, 32.

1. John iv. 33.
1. —— v. 44.
1. —— xiii. 14, 22, 34 twice.
1. —— xv. 12, 17.
1. Acts ii. 7 (*om.* πρὸς ἀλλήλους, *one to another*, L T Tr A ℵ.)
1. —— vii. 26.
1. —— xix. 38.
1. —— xxi. 6.
1. Rom. i. 27.
1. —— ii. 15, marg. *themselves.*
1. —— xii. 5, 10 twice, 16.
1. —— xiii. 8.
1. —— xiv. 13, 19.
1. —— xv. 5, 7.
1. —— 14 (ἄλλους, *others*, [G.)
1. —— xvi. 16.
4. 1 Cor. vi. 7.
1. —— xi. 33.
1. —— xii. 25.
1. —— xvi. 20.
1. 2 Cor. xiii. 12.
1. Gal. v. 13, 15 twice, 26 twice.
1. Gal. vi. 2.
1. Eph. iv. 2.
1. —— 25, 32 1st.
2. —— 32 2nd.
1. —— v. 21.
1. Col. iii. 9, 13 1st.
2. —— 13 2nd.
3. —— 16.
1. 1 Thes. iii. 12.
1. —— iv. 9, 18.
5. —— v. 11.
1. Tit. iii. 3.
3. Heb. iii. 13.
1. —— x. 24.
1. Jas. iv. 11.
1. —— v. 9, 16 twice.
1. 1 Pet. i. 22.
1. —— iv. 9.
3. —— 10.
1. —— v. 5, 14.
1. 1 John i. 7.
1. —— iii. 11, 23.
1. —— iv. 7, 11, 12.
1. 2 John 5.
1. Rev. vi. 4.
1. —— xi. 10.

ONE ANOTHER (EXHORT)

παρακαλέω, to call near, call beside, to call some one hither that he may do something; *hence*, to speak to *with the intention of producing a* particular effect; *hence*, to speak to *with the idea of* persuading, exhorting, admonishing, encouraging.

Heb. x. 25.

ONE...ANOTHER.

1. { ἄλλος...other, different, another, *marking numerical (not generic) distinction*, ἄλλος, (*same as above*) } one...another. * *with* μὲν and δε, *see No.* 2. † *with* δε and δε, *see No.* 3.

2. { ὃς, this, that, μὲν, truly, indeed, ὃς, this, that, δὲ, but, } this indeed...but that; this on the one hand...that on the other.

3. { ὃς, this, that, δὲ, but, ὃς, this, that, δέ, but, } but this...but that.

4. { εἷς, one, εἷς, one, } one...one.

5. { ἕτερος...another, μὲν, indeed, ἕτερος, another, δε, but, } (*marking generic distinction*) one indeed...but another.

3. Matt. xxi. 35.
3. —— xxii. 5.
3. —— xxv. 15.
4. —— xxvii. 38.
1. John iv. 37.
1. Acts ii. 12.
3. Rom. ix. 21.
2. —— xiv. 2.
2. 1 Cor. vii. 7 (ὁ, *the one*, instead of ὃς, *this one*, L T Tr A ℵ.)
2. —— xi. 21.
2. —— xii. 8.
1*. —— xv. 39 1st.
1†. —— 39 2nd.
5. —— 40.
1. 1 Cor. xv. 41.

ONE OF ANOTHER (*gallings*) [margin.]

1 Tim. vi. 5, *see* "PERVERSE DISPUTINGS."

ONE OF ANOTHER (HAVE COMPASSION)

συμπαθής, *pl.*, suffering together with another, mutually compassionate, having fellow feeling.

1 Pet. iii. 8.

ONE TO ANOTHER (*not passing*) [margin.]

Heb. vii. 24, *see* "UNCHANGEABLE."

ONE WITH ANOTHER (QUESTION)

συζητέω, to seek *any thing* with *another*, to seek together.

Mark ix. 10.

ONE STONE UPON ANOTHER.

{ λίθος, stone, ἐπὶ, upon, λίθῳ, stone.

Matt. xxiv. 2. | Luke xix. 44.
Mark xiii. 2. | —— xxi. 6.

ONE THE OTHER.

ἀλλήλων, each other, one another.

Acts xv. 39. | 1 Cor. vii. 5.
Gal. v. 17.

ONE...THE OTHER.

ὃς μὲν...ὃς δε, (*see* "ONE...ANOTHER," *No.* 2.)

Luke xxiii. 33.

ONE (THE)...[AND] THE OTHER.

ὃς μὲν...ὃς δε, *see above.*

2 Cor ii. 16. | Phil. i. 16, 17.

ONE...OTHER.

εἷς,.. εἷς, one...one (*or other.*)

Matt. xx. 21. | Mark xv. 27.
—— xxiv. 40. | John xx. 12.
Mark x. 37. | Gal. iv. 22.

ONE MAN...ANOTHER.

ὃς μὲν...ὃς δὲ (*see* "O...ANOTHER," *No.* 2.)

Rom. xiv. 5.

ONE (AT)

{ εἰς, unto,
{ εἰρήνη, peace.

Acts vii. 26.

ONE AS IF (EVEN ALL)

{ ἓν, one,
{ καὶ, and,
{ τὸ, the,
{ αὐτὸ, same.

1 Cor. xi. 5.

ONE (EVERY)

ἅπας, the whole, every one.

Acts v. 16.

ONE DEAD.

νεκρός, one dead, a dead person.

Mark ix. 26.

ONE HOUR AFTER (THE SPACE OF)

{ διαστάσης, departed, } one hour
{ ὥρας, hour, } having
{ μιᾶς, one, } elapsed.

Luke xxii. 59.

ONE PLACE (IN)

{ ἐπὶ, upon, } for the same object,
{ τὸ, the, } *or* to the same place.
{ αὐτὸ, same, }

Acts ii. 1.

ONE PLACE (INTO)

{ ἐπὶ, upon, } (*see above.*)
{ τὸ, the, }
{ αὐτὸ, same, }

1 Cor. xi. 20. | 1 Cor. xiv. 23.

ONE MAN.

εἷς, one, (*masc.*, one *man or person.*)

Rom. v. 17. marg. one.

ONE (NO, NOT)

{ οὐκ, not, } There is not
{ ἔστιν, there is, } even one.
{ ἕως, even, unto, }
{ ἑνός, one. }

Rom. iii. 12.

ONE THING.

1. ἓν, one, (*neut.*, one thing.)
2. τι, one, some thing, a certain thing.

2. Luke vi. 9 (E G~), (τί, *what*, St G), (εἰ, *if*, L T Tr A ℵ.)
1. —— x. 42.
1. Luke xviii. 22.
1. John ix. 25.
1. Phil. iii. 13.
1. 2 Pet. iii. 8.

ONE THING, SOME ANOTHER (SOME)

{ ἄλλοι, others, } others * [*therefore*
{ ἄλλοι, others, } *were crying aloud*],
{ τι, something, } *or* † [*were calling*
out] something else.

* Acts xix. 32. | † Acts xxi. 34.

ONE (UNTO)

τούτῳ, (*Dat.* of οὗτος, this, this same) unto this one.

Luke vii. 8.

See also, ACCORD, ANY, COMPASSION, CONSENT, EACH, EDIFY, END, EVERY, EXHORT, EYE, GATHER, GREAT, HOLY, LITTLE, MIND, NATION, NO, OF, SET, SUCH, WICKED.

ONLY.

1. μόνος, only, (*i.e.* alone, without others) alone, (*of many*, one out of many.)
   (a) *Neut.*, *as adv.*, only, alone.
2. μονογενής, the only begotten, *i.e.* only child.
3. εἷς, one.

1. Matt. iv. 10.
1a. —— v. 47.
1a. —— viii. 8.
1a. —— x. 42.
1. —— xii. 4.
1a. —— xiv. 36.
1. —— xvii. 8.
1a. —— xxi. 19, 21.
1. —— xxiv. 36.
3. Mark ii. 7.
1a. —— v. 36.
1a. —— vi. 8.
1. —— ix. 8.
1. Luke iv. 8.
2. Luke vii. 12.
2. —— viii. 42.
— —— ix. 38, see Child.
1a. —— 50.
1. —— xxiv. 18.
— John i. 14, 18, } see Be-
— —— iii. 16, 18, } gotten.
1a. —— v. 18.
1. —— 44.
1a. —— xi. 52.
1a. —— xii. 9.
1a. —— xiii. 9.
1. —— xvii. 3.
1a. Acts viii. 16.

1a. Acts xi. 19.
1a. —— xviii. 25.
1a. —— xix. 27.
1a. —— xxi. 13.
1a. —— xxvi. 29.
1a. —— xxvii. 10.
1a. Rom. i. 32.
1a. —— iii. 29.
1a. —— iv. 12, 16.
1a. —— v. 3, 11.
1a. —— viii. 23.
1a. —— ix. 10, 24.
1a. —— xiii. 5.
1. —— xvi. 4, 27.
1a. 1 Cor. vii. 39.
1. —— ix. 6.
1. —— xiv. 36.
1a. —— xv. 19.
1a. 2 Cor. vii. 7.
1a. —— viii. 10, 19, 21.
1a. —— ix. 12.
1a. Gal. i. 23.
1a. —— ii. 10.
1a. —— iii. 2.
1a. —— iv. 18.
1a. —— v. 13.
1a. —— vi. 12.
1a. Eph. i. 21.
1a. Phil. i. 27, 29.
1a. —— ii. 12, 27.
1. —— iv. 15.
1. Col. iv. 11.
1a. 1 Thes. i. 5, 8.
1a. —— ii. 8.
1a. 2 Thes. ii. 7.
1. 1 Tim. i. 17.
1a. —— v. 13.
1. —— vi. 15, 16.
1a. 2 Tim. ii. 20.
1a. —— iv. 8.
1a. —— —— 11.
1a. Heb. ix. 10.
— —— xi. 17, see Begotten.
1a. —— xii. 26.
1a. Jas. i. 22.
1a. —— ii. 24.
1a. 1 Pet. ii. 18.
1a. 1 John ii. 2.
— —— iv. 9, see Begotten.
1a. —— v. 6.
1. 2 John 1.
1. Jude 4, 25.
1. Rev. ix. 4 (*om.* G L T Tr A ℵ.)
1. —— xv. 4.

ONLY THAT (SAVE)

{ εἰ, if, / μὴ, not, } except.

Acts xxi. 25 (*ap.*)

OPEN. [adj.]

1. ἀνοίγω, to open. *Here, participle,* open.
2. ἀνακαλύπτω, to unveil. *Here, part. pass.,* unveiled.

1. John i. 51.
1. Acts xvi. 27.
1. Rom. iii. 13.
2. 2 Cor. iii. 18.
— Heb. vi. 6, see Shame.
1. Rev. iii. 8.
1. Rev. x. 2, 8.

OPEN (BE)

ἄγω, to lead, conduct; celebrate, hold.

Acts xix. 38, marg. *be kept,* (*i.e.* court days are held.)

OPEN BEFOREHAND.

πρόδηλος, manifest beforehand; manifest before all, well known.

1 Tim. v. 24.

OPEN (-ED, -ETH, -ING.) [verb.]

1. ἀνοίγω, to open, stand open, *spoken of doors, heaven, a book, the mouth, ears, and eyes.*
2. διανοίγω, (*No.* 1, *with* διά, through, *prefixed*) to open through, *of what before was closed,* to open fully, lay open.
3. ἀναπτύσσω, to fold back, unfold, *as a roll of a book,* (*non occ.*)
4. σχίζω, to split, to rend, to divide with violence, *prop., of wood.*
5. τραχηλίζω, to twist the neck, throttle, to bend back the neck, *e.g. of an animal for slaughter so as to expose the throat; hence,* to expose, lay bare, (*non occ.*)

1. Matt. ii. 11 part.
1. —— iii. 16.
1. —— v. 2.
1. —— vii. 7, 8.
1. —— ix. 30.
1. —— xiii. 35.
1. —— xvii. 27 part.
1. —— xx. 33.
1. —— xxv. 11.
1. —— xxvii. 52.
4. Mark i. 10, marg. *cleave or rend.*
2. —— vii. 34.
2. —— —— 35 (No. 1, L T Tr A ℵ.)
1. Luke i. 64.
2. —— ii. 23.
1. —— iii. 21.
3. —— iv. 17 part (No. 1, L Tr.)
1. —— xi. 9, 10.
1. —— xii. 36.
1. —— xiii. 25.
2. —— xxiv. 31, 32, 45.
1. John ix. 10, 14, 17, 21, 26, 30, 32.
1. —— x. 3, 21.
1. —— xi. 37.
1. Acts v. 19, 23 part.
1. —— vii. 56 (No. 2, L T Tr A ℵ.)
1. Acts viii. 32, 35.
1. —— ix. 8 part, 40.
1. —— x. 11, 34 part.
1. —— xii. 10, 14, 16 part.
1. —— xiv. 27.
2. —— xvi. 14.
1. —— —— 26.
2. —— xvii. 3.
1. —— xviii. 14.
1. —— xxvi. 18.
1. 1 Cor. xvi. 9.
1. 2 Cor. ii. 12 part.
1. —— vi. 11.
1. Col. iv. 3.
— Eph. vi. 19, see O (that may)
5. Heb. iv. 13.
1. Rev. iii. 7 twice, 20.
1. —— iv. 1.
1. —— v. 2, 3, 4, 5, 9.
1. —— vi. 1, 3, 5, 7, 9, 12.
1. —— viii. 1.
1. —— ix. 2 (*ap.*)
1. —— xi. 19.
1. —— xii. 16.
1. —— xiii. 6.
1. —— xv. 5.
1. —— xix. 11.
1. —— xx. 12 twice.

OPEN (THAT MAY)

{ ἐν, in, / ἄνοιξις, an opening. }

Eph. vi. 19.

OPENLY.

1. παρρησία, freedom *or* frankness in speaking: *the frankness under some circumstances amounts to* boldness *or* intrepidity; *hence,* fearless candour, the candid, confident boldness *of a joyous heart,* (*here, Dative case,*) with freedom or frankness, etc.
2. { ἐν, in, / παρρησια, *see No.* 1, } with boldness, etc.
3. φανερῶς, manifestly, *i.e.* clearly, evidently.
4. { ἐν, in, / τῷ, the, / φανερῷ, visible, manifest, } *the word* "place" *being understood.*
5. ἐμφανής, appearing in *anything; hence,* apparent, seen openly.

6. *δημοσίᾳ*, publicly, in public, before the people.

4. Matt. vi. 4 (*om.* G⇄L T Tr A ℵ.)
4. —— 6 (*om.* L T Tr A ℵ.)
4. —— 18 (*om.* G L T Tr A ℵ.)
3. Mark i. 45.
1. — viii. 32.
2. John vii. 4.
3. —— 10.
1. —— 13.
1. — xi. 54.
1. — xviii. 20.
5. Acts x. 40, and see "SHOW."
6. — xvi. 37.
2. Col. ii. 15.

OPERATION.

1. *ἐνέργεια*, the being in work, energy, efficiency, active power.

2. *ἐνέργημα*, what is wrought, *i.e.* effect produced.

2. 1 Cor. xii. 6. | 1. Col. ii. 12.

OPPORTUNITY.

1. *καιρός*, the right measure, the just proportion, *esp.* as regards time and place, *but most frequently of* time; *hence*, the right time, the convenient time.

2. *εὐκαιρία*, fit time, good opportunity.

2. Matt. xxvi. 16.
2. Luke xxii. 6.
1. Gal. vi. 10.
— Phil. iv. 10, see O (lack)
1. Heb. xi. 15.

OPPORTUNITY (LACK)

ἀκαιρέομαι, to lack opportunity.

Phil. iv. 10.

OPPOSE (-ED, -ETH.)

ἀντίκειμαι, to lie opposite; *hence*, to oppose, be adverse *or* repugnant to.

2 Thes. ii. 4.

OPPOSE ONE'S SELF.

1. *ἀντιτάσσομαι*, to arrange and set, *or* array one's self against, oppose, resist.

2. *ἀντιδιατίθεμαι*, to place *or* dispose one's self over against, to be adverse, (*non occ.*)

1. Acts xviii. 6 part. | 2. 2 Tim. ii. 25.

OPPOSITIONS.

ἀντίθεσις, (*here*, *pl.*) antitheses, contrary positions, opinions, or doctrines, (*non occ.*)

1 Tim. vi. 20.

OPPRESS.

1. *καταδυναστεύω*, to exercise power against *any one*; *hence*, to overpower, oppress, (*non occ.*)

2. *καταπονέω*, (*here*, *pass.*) to be worn down by labour, (*occ.* 2 Pet. ii. 7.)

3. *πλεονεκτέω*, to have more than another, have an advantage; *then*, to take advantage, defraud.

2. Acts vii. 24.
1. —— x. 38.
3. 1 Thes. ii. 6, marg. (text, *defraud.*)
1. Jas. ii. 6.

OR.

1. *ἤ*, *a particle, disjunctive*, or; *interrogative*, whether; *or comparative*, than.

(a) *preceded by another ἤ, and translated*...either...or.

(b) *preceded by ἤτοι*, (whether) *and implying that there is no other alternative.*

* *disjunctive.* † *in the latter clause of a double interrogation, also disjunctive.*

2. *εἴτε*, or, whether.

(a) *εἴτε...εἴτε*, whether...or.

3. *μήτε*, and not, also not, neither, not even.

4. *ἐάν, τε*, and if, (a) *repeated*, whether ...or.

1*.Matt. v. 17, 18, 36.
1a.—— vi. 24.
1†.—— 31 twice.
1†.——vii. 4, 9.
— —— 10, see O if.
1†.—— 16.
1†.—— ix. 5.
1*.—— x. 11, 14, 19, 37 twice.
1†.—— xi. 3.
1†.—— xii. 5.
— —— 29, see O else.
1a.—— 33.
1*.—— xiii. 21.
1*.—— xv. 4, 5, 6 (*ap.*)
1*.—— xvi. 14.
1†.—— 26.
1*.—— xvii. 25 1st.
1†.—— 25 2nd.
1*.—— xviii. 8 3 times, 16 twice, 20.
1*.—— xix. 29 1st & 2nd.
1*.—— 29 3rd & 4th (*ap.*)
1*.—— 29 5th (*om.* ἢ γυναῖκα, *or wife*, L T Tr A.)
1*.—— 29 6th & 7th.
1†.—— xxi. 25.
1†.—— xxii. 17.
1†.—— xxiii. 17, 19.
1*.—— xxiv. 23.
1†.—— xxv. 37, 38.
1*.—— 39, 44 5 times.
1†.—— xxvii. 17.
1†.Mark ii. 9.
1†.—— iii. 4 twice.
1†.—— 33 (*καὶ, and*, L T Tr A ℵ.)
1†.—— iv. 21, 30.
1*.—— vi. 15 (*om.* G L T Tr A ℵ.)
1*.—— 56 twice.
1*.—— vii. 10, 11, 12.
1†.—— viii. 37 (*γάρ, for*, T Tr A ℵ.)
1*.—— x. 29 1st, 2nd, 3rd & 4th.
1*.—— 29 5th (*om.* ἢ γυναῖκα, *or wife*, G∼L T Tr A ℵ.)
1*.—— 29 6th & 7th.
1†.—— xi. 30.
1†.—— xii. 14, 15.
1*.—— xiii. 21 (*om.* G→T A ℵ.)
1*.—— 35 3 times.
1*.Luke ii. 24.
— —— iii. 15, see O (whether)
1†.—— vi. 9 twice.
1†.—— vii. 19, 20.
1*.—— viii. 16.
1*.—— ix. 25.
— —— xi. 11, see O if.
1†.—— 12.
1†.—— xii. 11 1st. (*om.* ἢ τί, *or what*, Tr[b] A[b].)
1†.—— 11 2nd.

1*.Luke xii. 14.
1†.——— 29, *καί, and,* T Tr ℵ.)
1†.——— 41.
[illegible]—— xiii. 4.
1*.——— 15.
1*.—— xiv. 5, 12.
1†.——— 31.
— ——— 32, see O else.
1a.——xvi. 13.
1*.—— xvii. 7, 21.
1*.——— 23 (*om.* G⇉T Tr), (*καὶ, and,* ℵ.)
1*.—— xviii. 11, 29 4 times.
1†.—— xx. 2, 4, 22.
1†.—— xxii. 27.
1*.John ii. 6.
1†.—— iv. 27.
1*.—— vi. 19.
1†.—— vii. 17.
1*.——— 48.
1†.—— ix. 2.
1*.——— 21.
1*.—— xiii. 29.
— —— xiv. 11, see O else.
1†.—— xviii. 34.
1*.Acts i. 7.
1. —— iii. 12 twice.
1*.—— iv. 7, 34.
1*.—— v. 38.
1†.—— vii. 49.
1†.—— viii. 34.
1*.—— x. 14 (*καί, and,* L T Tr A ℵ.)
1*.——— 28 twice.
1*.—— xi. 8.
1*.—— xvii. 29 twice.
1*.—— xviii. 14.
1*.—— xix. 12.
1*.—— xx. 33 twice.
1*.—— xxiii. 9.
— ——— 15, see O ever.
1*.——— 29.
1*.—— xxiv. 20, see O else.
1*.——— 23 (*om.* ἢ προσέρχεσθαι, *or come,* G⇉L T Tr A ℵ.)
1*.—— xxvi. 31.
1*.—— xxviii. 6, 17, 21.
1†. Rom. ii. 4.
— ——— 15, see O else.
1†.—— iii. 1.
1†.—— iv. 9, 10.
1*.——— 13.
1b.—— vi. 16.
1†.—— viii. 35 6 times.
1*.—— x. 7.
1†.—— xi. 34, 35.
2. —— xii. 7 twice, 8.
1*.—— xiv. 4.
4. ——— 8.
1*.——— 10, 13.
1*.——— 21 twice (*om.* ἢ σκανδαλίζεται ἢ ἀσθενεῖ, *or is offended, or is made weak,* G→T Tr^mb ℵ.)
1†.1 Cor. i. 13.
1*.—— ii. 1.
2a.—— iii. 22 1st.
2. ——— 22 2nd, 3rd, 4th.
2. ——— 22 5th, 6th, & 7th.
1*.—— iv. 3.
1†.——— 21.
1*.—— v. 10 1st.
1*.——— 10 2nd (*καί, and,* G∾L T Tr A ℵ.)
1*.——— 10 3rd, 11 5 times.
1*.—— vii. 11, 15.
1†.——— 16.
2a.—— viii. 15.
1†.1 Cor. ix. 6.
1†.——— 7 (*om.* L Tr^b A.)
1†——— 8, 10.
1†.—— x. 19 (*ap.*)
2a.—— —— 31 1st.
2. ——— 31 2nd.
1*.—— xi. 4, 5, 6.
1†.——— 22.
2a.—— xii. 13 twice, 26.
1*.—— xiii. 1.
1a.—— xiv. 6.
2a.——— 7 1st.
1*.——— 7 2nd, 23, 24, 27, 29.
1†.——— 36.
1*.——— 37.
2a.—— xv. 11.
1*.——— 37.
1*. 2 Cor. i. 13.
1†.——— 17.
1†.—— iii. 1 1st (*εἰ μὴ, unless,* St G∾)
1†.——— 1 2nd.
2a.—— v. 9, 10.
1†.—— vi. 15.
2a.—— viii. 23.
1*.—— ix. 7.
1*.—— x. 12.
1*.—— xi. 4 twice.
2a.—— xii. 3.
1*.——— 6.
1*. Gal. i. 8.
1†.——— 10 twice.
1*.—— ii. 2.
1†.—— iii. 2, 5.
1*.——— 15.
— —— iv. 9, see O rather.
1*. Eph. iii. 20.
1*.—— v. 3, 27 twice.
2a.—— vi. 8.
2a. Phil. i. 18, 20, 27.
1*.—— ii. 3 (*μηδὲ κατά, nothing according to,* L T Tr A ℵ.)
2a. Col. i. 16 1st.
2. ——— 16 2nd & 3rd.
2a.——— 20.
1*.—— ii. 16 4 times.
1*.—— iii. 17.
1†. 1 Thes. ii. 19 twice.
2a.—— v. 10.
3. 2 Thes. ii. 2 (*μηδέ, and not,* L T Tr A ℵ.)
1*.——— 4.
2a.——— 15.
1*. 1 Tim. ii. 9 1st (*καί, and,* L)
1*.——— 9 2nd & 3rd.
1*.—— v. 4.
1*.——— 16, 19.
1*. Tit. i. 6.
1*.—— iii. 12.
1*. Philem. 18.
1*. Heb. ii. 6.
1*.—— x. 28.
1*.—— xii. 16, 20 (*ap.*)
1*. Jas. ii. 3, 15.
1*.—— iv. 15.
1*. 1 Pet. i. 11.
2a.—— ii. 13, 14.
1*.—— iii. 3, 9.
1*.—— iv. 15 3 times.
— Rev. ii. 5, 16, see O else.
1*.—— iii. 15.
1*.—— xiii. 16, 17 1st.
1*.——— 17 2nd (*om.* G L T Tr A.)
1*.——— 17 3rd.
1*.—— xiv. 9.

OR ELSE.

1. ἤ, *see* "OR," *No.* 1.
2. { ἤ, or, / καὶ, even.

3. { εἰ, if, / δὲ, but, / μὴ, not.
4. { εἰ, if, / δε, but, / μήγε, not by any means.

1. Matt. xii. 29.
4. Luke xiv. 32.
3. John xiv. 11.
1. Acts xxiv. 20.
2. Rom. ii. 15.
3. Rev. ii. 5, 16.

OR EVER.

πρό, before.

Acts xxiii. 15.

OR IF.

1. ἤ, or (*see* "OR," *No.* 1.)
2. { καὶ, and, / ἐάν, if.

2. Matt. vii. 10 (ἢ *καί, or also,* L T Tr A ℵ.)
1. Luke xi. 11.

OR NOT (WHETHER)

μήποτε, (*with opt.*) whether perhaps, lest perhaps.

Luke iii. 15.

OR RATHER.

{ μᾶλλον, more, rather. / δέ, but.

Gal. iv. 9.

OR WHETHER...(WHETHER)

εἴτε...εἴτε, (*see* "OR," *No.* 2.)

2 Cor. i. 6; v. 13; xii. 2.

ORACLE (-S.)

λόγιον, *something* uttered, utterance, sentence, declaration, (*esp. the sayings of the oracles of the gods.*)

Acts vii. 38.
Rom. iii. 2.
Heb. v. 12.
1 Pet. iv. 11.

ORATION (MAKE AN)

δημηγορέω, to address a public assembly, to harangue the people, (*non occ.*)

Acts xii. 21.

ORATOR.

ῥήτωρ, a speaker, orator, advocate.

Acts xxiv. 1.

ORDAIN (-ED.)

1. *τίθημι*, to set, to put, to place, to lay; *hence*, to place, (*see* "APPOINT," *No.* 1.)
2. *καθίστημι*, (*No.* 1, *with* *κατά*, down, *prefixed*) to set down, constitute.
3. *τάσσω*, to arrange, put in order *or* ranks, *esp. in a military sense*, to draw up *soldiers*, array; *then, mid.*, to order *anything* to be done, to appoint.
4. *διατάσσω*, (*No.* 3, *with* *διά*, throughout, *prefixed*) to arrange throughout, dispose fully in order.
5. *ὁρίζω*, to make *or* set a boundary, to bound; *then*, to mark out definitely, determine
6. *προορίζω*, (*No.* 5, *with* *πρό*, before, *prefixed*) to mark out before, predetermine.
7. *ποιέω*, to make, bring about, cause.
8. *κατασκευάζω*, to prepare fully, put in readiness.
9. *κρίνω*, to divide, separate, make a distinction, come to a decision.
10. *χειροτονέω*, to stretch out the hand, to hold up the hand as in voting; *hence*, to vote, give one's vote *by holding up the hand*.

7. Mark iii. 14.
1. John xv. 16.
— Acts i. 22, see O to be (be)
5. —— x. 42.
3. —— xiii. 48.
10. —— xiv. 23 part.
9. —— xvi. 4.
5. —— xvii. 31.
3. Rom. xiii. 1, marg. [order.
6. 1 Cor. ii. 17.
4. —— vii. 17, mid.
— Eph. ii. 10, see O before.
1. 1 Tim. ii. 7.
2. Tit. i. 5.
2. Heb. v. 1.
2. —— viii. 3.
8. —— ix. 6 part.
— Jude 4, see O before.

ORDAIN BEFORE.

1. *προγράφω*, to write before, to notify, set forth as in a public written tablet.
2. *προετιμάζω*, to prepare beforehand.

2. Eph. ii. 10, marg. (text, *prepare before.*)
1. Jude 4.

ORDAINED TO BE (BE)

γίνομαι, to become.

Acts i. 22.

ORDER [noun.]

1. *τάξις*, a setting in order, arrangement, disposition, series, (*non occ.*)
2. *τάγμα*, any thing arranged in order, an array, a body *of troops*, a band, a rank, (*non occ.*)

1. Luke i. 8.
1. 1 Cor. xiv. 40.
2. —— xv. 23.
1. Col. ii. 5.
1. Heb. v. 6, 10.
1. —— vi. 20.
1. Heb. vii. 11 twice, 17, 21 (*ap.*)

ORDER (BY)

καθεξῆς, according to the order *or* succession, consecutively, in connected order.

Acts xi. 4.

ORDER (GIVE)

διατάσσω, to arrange throughout, dispose fully in order.

1 Cor. xvi. 1.

ORDER (IN)

καθεξῆς, *see* "ORDER (BY)"

Luke i. 3. | Acts xviii. 23.

ORDER (SET FORTH IN)

1. *ἀνατάσσομαι*, to set *or* draw up in order, *or* to re-arrange, to go regularly through again.
2. *ἐπιδιορθόω*, to make straight upon, to put further to rights, arrange further, (*non occ.*)

1. 1 Cor. xi. 34, mid. | 2. Tit. i. 5, mid.

ORDER. [verb.]

Rom. xiii. 1, *see* "ORDAIN."

ORDERLY.

See, WALK.

ORDINANCE (-S.)

1. *δικαίωμα*, the product *or* result of justifying; *hence*, legal decision, statute of right *as the result of the settlement of the right;* legal statutes, ordinances.
2. *δόγμα*, that which seems true to one, an opinion, *esp. of philosophic dogmas;* a public resolution, decree, (*occ.* Luke ii. 1; Acts xvi. 4, xvii. 7.)

3. διαταγή, a disposing in order, arrangement, (*occ.* Acts vii. 53.)

4. παράδοσις, delivery, the act of delivering over from one to another, precept, ordinance, instruction.

5. κτίσις, a founding, creation.

1. Luke i. 6.
3. Rom. xiii. 2.
4. 1 Cor. xi. 2, marg. *tradition.*
2. Eph. ii. 15.
2. Col. ii. 14.
— Col. ii. 20, see O (be subject to)
1. Heb. ix. 1, marg. *ceremony.*
1. ——— 10, marg. *rite or ceremony.*
5. 1 Pet. ii. 13.

ORDINANCES (BE SUBJECT TO)

δογματίζομαι, to submit to opinions laid down, to suffer opinions to be laid down as laws for one's self.

Col. ii. 20.

ORDINARY [margin.]

Acts xix. 39, see "LAWFUL."

ORPHAN [margin.]

John xiv. 18, see "COMFORTLESS."

OTHER.

(*For various combinations with other words, see below.*)

1. ἄλλος, other, not the same, *i.e.* one besides what has been mentioned, denoting numerical distinction.

   (a) *with the article.*

2. ἕτερος, the other, *denoting generic distinction*, the other, different of two; *a stronger expression therefore than No.* 1.

   (a) *preceded by another* ἕτερος, *and translated* "some...other."

3. λοιπός, the remaining, the rest, what is left.

   (a) *with art.*, τὰ λοιπὰ, (*pl.*) the rest, *Lat.*, cetera.

4. εἷς, one, the one.

1. Matt. iv. 21.
1a.—— v. 39.
2. —— vi. 24 twice.
1a.—— xii. 13.
2. ——— 45.
1. —— xiii. 8.
2. —— xv. 30.
2. —— xvi. 14.
1. —— xx. 3, 6.
4. ——— 21.
1. —— xxi. 8, 36, 41.
1. —— xxii. 4.
— —— xxiv. 31, see End.
4. ——— 40.
1. Matt. xxv. 16, 17, 20, 22.
1. —— xxvii. 42.
1a.——— 61.
1a.—— xxviii. 1.
1a. Mark iii. 5 (*om.* ὑγιὴς ὡς ἡ ἄλλη, *whole as the other*, G L T Tr A ℵ.)
1. —— iv. 8, 36.
1. —— vi. 15 twice.
1. —— vii. 8 (*ap.*)
1. —— viii. 28.
4. —— x. 37.
1. —— xi. 8.
1. —— xii. 5, 9, 31, 32.
4. Mark xv. 27.
1. ——— 31, 41.
2. Luke iv. 43.
2. —— v. 7.
1. ——— 29.
1a.—— vi. 10 (*ap.*)
2. —— vii. 41.
2. —— viii. 3.
2a.——— 6, 7, 8.
1. —— ix. 8, 19.
2. —— x. 1.
— ——— 31, 32, see Pass.
2. —— xi. 16, 26.
2. —— xvi. 13 twice.
2. —— xvii. 34, 35, 36 (*ap.*)
2. —— xviii. 10.
1. —— xx. 16.
2. —— xxiii. 32.
— ——— 33, see One.
1. ——— 35.
2. ——— 40.
— —— xxiv. 1, see O (certain)
3. ——— 10.
1. John vi. 22, 23.
1. —— vii. 12, 41.
1. —— ix. 9, 16.
1. —— x. 16, 21.
1. —— xii. 29.
1a.—— xviii. 16.
1. ——— 34.
1. —— xix. 18.
1a.——— 32.
1a.—— xx. 2, 3, 4, 8.
4. ——— 12.
1a.——— 25.
1. ——— 30.
1. —— xxi. 2.
1a.——— 8.
2. Acts ii. 4, 13, 40.
1. —— iv. 12 1st.
2. ——— 12 2nd.
2. —— viii. 34.
1. Acts xv. 2.
2. —— xvii. 34.
2. —— xxiii. 6.
2. —— xxvii. 1.
3. Rom. i. 13.
2. —— viii. 39.
2. —— xiii. 9.
1. 1 Cor. i. 16.
1. —— iii. 11.
2. —— viii. 4 (om. G ⇉ L T Tr A ℵ.)
1. —— ix. 2.
3. ——— 5.
1. ——— 12, 27.
2. —— x. 29.
2. —— xiv. 17.
1. ——— 19.
2. ——— 21.
1a.——— 29.
3a.—— xv. 37.
— 2 Cor. ii. 16, see One.
2. —— viii. 8.
1. —— xi. 8.
3. —— xii. 13.
3. —— xiii. 2.
2. Gal. i. 9.
4. —— iv. 22.
2. Eph. iii. 5.
3a.—— iv. 17 (*om.* G ⇉ T Tr A ℵ.)
3. Phil. i. 13, marg. *others.*
— ——— 16, 17, see One.
2. —— ii. 4.
3. —— iv. 3.
1. 1 Thes. ii. 6.
2. 2 Tim. ii. 2.
1. Heb. xi. 35.
2. ——— 36.
1. Jas. v. 12.
— 1 Pet. iv. 15, see Busybody.
1. Rev. ii. 24.
1a.—— xvii. 10.

OTHER (EACH)

ἀλλήλων, each other, one another.

Phil. ii. 3. | 2 Thes. i. 3.

OTHER MAN.

1. John iv. 38.
1. —— xv. 24.
1. 2 Cor. viii. 13.
1. Phil. iii. 4.

OTHER MATTERS.

2. Acts xix. 39, (περαιτέρω, *further*, instead of, περὶ ἑτέρων, *concerning other matters*, L T Tr.)

OTHER SIDE (THE)

{ τὸ, the, πέραν, beyond, on the other side, } that beyond, the *region* on the other side.

Matt. viii. 18, 28.
—— xiv. 22.
—— xvi. 5.
Mark iv. 35.
Mark v. 1, 21.
—— vi. 45, marg. *over.*
—— viii. 13.
Luke viii. 22.

OTHER SIDE OF (ON THE)

πέραν, *see above.*

John vi. 22, 25.

OTHER (OF THE)

{ τὴν, the, / τοῦ, of the, / ἑτέρου, *see* "OTHER," *No.* 2. } the [*conscience*] of the other.

1 Cor. x. 29.

OTHER WAY (SOME)

ἀλλάχοθεν, from another place, (*non occ.*)

John x. 1.

OTHER THAN.

ἐκτός, out of, without, outside of.

Acts xxvi. 22.

OTHER (THE)

1. λοιπός, *see* "OTHER," *No.* 3.
2. ἐκεῖνος, that, that one there.

1. Matt. xxv. 11. | 2. Luke xviii. 14. | 1. Acts xvii. 9. | 1. Gal. ii. 13. | 1. 2 Pet. iii. 16. | 1. Rev. viii. 13.

OTHER (AND THE)

κἀκεῖνος, and that one there.

Matt. xxiii. 23. | Luke xi. 42.

OTHER THINGS.

1. ἄλλα, *see* "OTHER," *No.* 1. *Here, neut. pl.*
2. ἕτερος, *see* "OTHER," *No.* 2. *Here, neut. pl.*
3. τὰ λοιπά, *see* "OTHER," *No.* 3a.

3. Mark iv. 19. | 1. —— vii. 4. | 2. Luke iii. 18. | 2. Luke xxii. 65. | 1. John xxi. 25. | 1. 2 Cor. i. 13. | 2. 1 Tim. i. 10.

OTHERS.

1. λοιποί, *see* "OTHER," *No.* 3. *Here, pl.*
2. ἄλλοι, *see* "OTHER," *No.* 1. *Here, pl.*
3. οἱ, these.

1. Luke viii. 10. | 1. —— xviii. 9. | 2. John vii. 12. | 3. Acts xvii. 32. | 1. —— xxviii. 9. | 1. Eph. ii. 3. | 1. Phil. i. 13, marg. (text, *other.*) | 1. 1 Thes. iv. 13. | 1. —— v. 6. | 1. 1 Tim. v. 20. | 3. Jude 23.

OTHERS (CERTAIN)

τινες, some, certain *persons, or others.*

Luke xxiv. 1 (*ap.*)

OTHERS (OF)

ἀλλότριος, not one's own, another's, belonging to another *or* others.

Heb. ix. 25.

OTHERWISE.

1. ἐπεί, since, because, seeing that.
2. { εἰ, if, / δέ, but, / μήγε, not indeed, } but if, not indeed.
3. ἄλλος, *see* "OTHER," *No.* 1.
4. ἄλλως, otherwise, (*non occ.*)
5. ἑτέρως, otherwise, (*non occ.*)

} for the difference between *Nos.* 4 *and* 5, *see* "OTHER," *Nos.* 1 *and* 2.

2. Matt. vi. 1. | 1. Rom. xi. 6 1st. | 1. —— 6 2nd (*ap.*) | 1. —— 22. | 3. Gal. v. 10. | 5. Phil. iii. 15. | 4. 1 Tim. v. 25. | — —— vi. 3, *see* Teach. | 1. Heb. ix. 17.

OTHERWISE (IF)

2. Luke v. 36. | 2. 2 Cor. xi. 16.

OUGHT. [noun.]

See, AUGHT.

OUGHT (-EST.) [verb.]

1. δεῖ, it needs, there is need of *something that is absent or wanting*; it is necessary *from the nature of the case,* one must; it is right and proper, one ought. (*Commonly rendered by a change of construction,* e.g. "he *must* go," for "it *needs* that he go.") * *Imp. tense.*
2. { δέον, necessary, proper, (*part. of No.* 1) / ἐστί, it is, there is, } it is necessary, there is need, must needs.
3. ὀφείλω, to owe, to be indebted; *then,* to be bound to be obligated *to the performance of any duty.*
4. χράω, *impers.* χρή, there is use for it needs, it behoves, it is meet.

1. Matt. xxiii. 23*. | 1. —— xxv. 27*. | 1. Mark xiii. 14. | 1. Luke xi. 42*. | 1. —— xii. 12. | 1. —— xiii. 14, 16*. | 1. —— xviii. 1. | 1. —— xxiv. 26*. | 1. John iv. 20. | 3. —— xiii. 14. | 3. John xix. 7. | 1. Acts v. 29. | 1. —— x. 6 (*ap.*) | 3. —— xvii. 29. | 2. —— xix. 36. | 1. —— xx. 35. | 1. —— xxiv. 19*. | 1. —— xxv. 10, 24. | 1. —— xxvi. 9. | 1. Rom. viii. 26.

1. Rom. xii. 3.
3. —— xv. 1.
1. 1 Cor. viii. 2.
3. —— xi. 7, 10.
1. 2 Cor. ii. 3*.
3. —— xii. 11, 14.
3. Eph. v. 28.
1. —— vi. 20.
1. Col. iv. 4, 6.
1. 1 Thes. iv. 1.
1. 2 Thes. iii. 7.
1. 1 Tim. iii. 15.
— 1 Tim. v. 13, see O not (things which they)
1. Tit. i. 11.
1. Heb. ii. 1.
3. —— v. 3, 12 part.
4. Jas. iii. 10.
— —— iv. 15, see Say.
1. 2 Pet. iii. 11.
3. 1 John ii. 6.
3. —— iii. 16.
3. —— iv. 11.
3. 3 John 8.

OUGHT NOT (THINGS WHICH THEY)

{ τὰ, the *things*,
μὴ, not, (*see* "NO," *No.* 2, *and note*),
δέοντα, ought, (*part. of No.* 1), } the things that ought not.

1 Tim. v. 13.

OUR.

1. ἡμῶν, (*Gen. of* ἡμεῖς, we) of us.

2. { μετά, with,
ἡμῖν, us.

3. ἡμῖν, (*Dat. of* ἡμεῖς, we) to *or* for us.

4. ἡμέτερος, our, our own, (*more emphatic than the above.*)

5. ὑμέτερος, your, your own.

1. Matt. vi. 9, 11, 12 twice.
1. —— viii. 17.
1. —— xx. 33.
1. —— xxi. 42.
1. —— xxiii. 30.
1. —— xxv. 8.
1. —— xxvii. 25.
1. Mark ix. 40 (ὑμῶν, *your*, St G L.)
1. —— xi. 10.
— —— xii. 7, see Ours.
1. ——— 11, 29.
1. Luke i. 55, 71, 72, 73.
1. ——— 74 (*om.* Lb T Tr A ℵ.)
1. ——— 75 (*om.* τῆς ζωῆς, i.e. *our days*, instead of *the days of our life*, G L T Tr A.)
1. ——— 78, 79.
1. —— vii. 5.
1. —— xi. 2 (*ap.*), 3, 4.
1. —— xiii. 26.
3. —— xvii. 5.
— —— xx. 14, see Ours.
— —— xxiii. 41, see O deeds.
1. —— xxiv. 20.
— ——— 22, see O company.
1. ——— 32.
1. John iii. 11.
1. —— iv. 12, 20.
1. —— vi. 31.
1. —— vii. 51.
1. —— viii. 39, 53.
1. —— ix. 20.
1. —— xi. 11, 48.
1. —— xii. 38.
1. —— xix. 7 (*om.* G L T Tr A ℵ.)
1. Acts ii. 8.
4. ——— 11.
1. —— iii. 13, 25.
1. —— v. 30.
1. —— vii. 2, 11, 12, 15, 19 1st.
1. ——— 19 2nd (*om.* L T Tr A ℵ.)
1. ——— 38, 39, 44, 45 twice.
1. —— xiii. 17.
1. —— xiv. 17 (ὑμῶν, *your*, G L T Tr A ℵ.)
1. —— xv. 10, 25, 26.
1. ——— 36 (*om.* G L T Tr A ℵ.)
1. —— xvi. 20.
1. —— xvii. 20.
1. —— xix. 25 (No. 3, L T Tr A ℵ), (ὑμῶν, *your*, G∾)
3. ——— 27.
1. —— xx. 21.
1. —— xxii. 14.
4. —— xxiv. 6 (*ap.*)
1. ——— 7 (*ap.*)
4. —— xxvi. 5.
1. ——— 7.
1. —— xxvii. 10.
1. —— xxviii. 25 (ὑμῶν, *your*, L T Tr A ℵ.)
1. Rom. i. 3, 7.
1. —— iii. 5.
1. —— iv. 1, 12, 24, 25 twice.
1. —— v. 1, 5, 11, 21.
1. —— vi. 6.
1. ——— 11 (*om.* τῷ κυρίῳ ἡμῶν, *our Lord*, G L T Tr A.)
1. ——— 23.
1. —— vii. 5, 25.
1. Rom. viii. 16, 23, 26, 39.
1. —— ix. 10.
1. —— x. 16.
1. —— xiii. 11.
4. —— xv. 4.
1. ——— 6.
1. —— xvi. 1 (ὑμῶν, *your*, Lm.)
1. ——— 9, 18, 20, 24.
1. 1 Cor. i. 2 1st.
— ——— 2 2nd, see Ours.
1. ——— 3, 7, 8, 9, 10.
1. —— ii. 7.
1. —— v. 4 1st (*om.* Lb ℵ.)
1. ——— 4 2nd (*om.* Lb.)
1. —— vi. 11.
1. —— ix. 1.
— ——— 10 twice, see O sakes (for)
1. —— x. 1, 6, 11.
1. —— xii. 23, 24.
1. —— xv. 3, 14.
5. ——— 31 1st, marg. (text, *your*), (No. 4, St AVm G∾)
1. ——— 31 2nd, 57.
1. 2 Cor. i. 2, 3, 4, 5, 7, 8, 11, 12 twice.
— ——— 14, see Ours.
1. ——— 18, 22.
1. —— iii. 2, 5.
1. —— iv. 3, 6, 10, 11, 16, 17.
1. —— v. 1, 2.
1. ——— 12 ὑμῶν, *your*, Lm Trm ℵ.)
1. —— vi. 11 twice.
1. —— vii. 3, 4, 5.
— ——— 12 (ὑμῶν ὑπὲρ ἡμῶν, *your care for us*, instead of ἡμῶν ὑπὲρ ὑμῶν, *our care for you*, St L T Tr A ℵ.)
1. ——— 14 (ὑμῶν, *your*, L A.)
1. —— viii. 9, 22, 23, 24.
1. —— ix. 3.
1. —— x. 4, 8, 15.
1. —— xi. 31 (*om.* L T Tr A ℵ.)
1. Gal. i. 3, 4 twice.
1. —— ii. 4.
1. —— iii. 24.
1. —— vi. 14, 18.
1. Eph. i. 2, 3, 14, 17.
1. —— ii. 3, 14.
1. —— iii. 11, 14 (*ap.*)
1. —— v. 20.
1. —— vi. 22, 24.
1. Phil. i. 2.
1. —— iii. 20, 21.
1. —— iv. 20.
1. ——— 23 (*om.* G ⇉ L T Tr A ℵ.)
1. Col. i. 2, 3, 7.
1. —— iii. 4 (ὑμῶν, *your*, G ∾ Lm T Tr ℵ.)
1. 1 Thes. i. 1 (*ap.*), 2, 3 twice, 5.
1. —— ii. 1, 2, 3, 4.
— 1 Thes. ii. 8, see O own.
1. ——— 9, 19 twice, 20.
1. —— iii. 2 1st, 2 2nd (*ap.*), 5, 7, 9, 11 twice, 13 twice.
1. —— v. 9, 23, 28.
1. 2 Thes. i. 1.
1. ——— 2 (*om.* G → Lb T Trb A.)
1. ——— 8, 10, 11, 12 twice.
1. —— ii. 1 twice, 14 twice, 15, 16 twice.
1. —— iii. 6 (*om.* Lb T Trmb A.)
1. ——— 12 (*om.* G ∾ L T Tr A ℵ.)
1. ——— 14, 18.
1. 1 Tim. i. 1 twice.
1. ——— 2 (*om.* G ⇉ L T Tr A ℵ.)
1. ——— 12, 14.
1. —— ii. 3.
1. —— vi. 3, 4.
1. 2 Tim. i. 2, 8, 9, 10.
4. —— iv. 15.
1. Tit. i. 3, 4.
1. —— ii. 10 (ὑμῶν, *your*, St.)
1. ——— 13.
1. —— iii. 4, 6.
— ——— 14, see Ours.
1. Philem. 1, 2, 3, 25.
1. Heb. i. 3 (*om.* G ⇉ L T Tr A ℵ.)
1. —— iii. 1.
1. —— iv. 15.
1. —— vii. 14.
1. —— xii. 9, 29.
1. —— xiii. 20.
1. Jas. ii. 1, 21.
1. —— iii. 6.
1. 1 Pet. i. 3.
1. —— ii. 24.
1. 2 Pet. i. 1 (*ap.*), 2, 8, 11, 14, 16.
1. —— iii. 15 twice, 18.
1. 1 John i. 1 twice.
4. ——— 3.
1. —— ii. 2 1st.
— ——— 2 2nd, see Ours.
1. —— iii. 5 (*om.* G ⇉ L T Tr A.)
1. ——— 19, 20.
1. ——— 21 (*om.* L.)
1. —— iv. 10.
2. ——— 17, marg. *with us*.
1. —— v. 4.
1. 2 John 12 (ὑμῶν, *your*, G ∾ L Tr A.)
1. 3 John 12.
1. Jude 4 twice, 17, 21, 25.
1. Rev. i. 5.
1. —— v. 10.
1. —— vi. 10.
1. —— vii. 3, 10 (*ap.*), 12.
1. —— xi. 8 (αὐτῶν, *their*, G L T Tr A), (*om.* ℵ.)
1. ——— 15.
1. —— xii. 10 3 times.
1. —— xix. 1, 5.
1. —— xxii. 21 (*om.* G L T Tr A ℵ.)

OUR COMPANY.

1. Luke xxiv. 22.

OUR DEEDS.

{ ἅ, those things which
ἐπράξαμεν, we practised.

Luke xxiii. 41.

OUR OWN.

1. ἴδιος, own, one's own, *as pertaining to a private person, and not to the public.*
2. ἑαυτῶν, our own selves.

1. Acts ii. 8.
1. —— iii. 12.
1. 1 Cor. iv. 12.
2. 1 Thes. ii. 8.

OUR SAKES (FOR)

{ διὰ, on account of, for the sake of,
{ ἡμας, us.

1 Cor. ix. 10 twice.

OURS.

1. Mark xii. 7.
1. Luke xx. 14.
1. 1 Cor. i. 2.
1. 2 Cor. i. 14.
4. Tit. iii. 14.
4. 1 John ii. 2.

OURSELVES.

1. αὐτοί, (*pl.*) selves, *joined with each of the persons; here, 1st pl., we our*selves.
2. ἑαυτῶν, of *our*selves, *reflexive*, (*Gen. pl.*)
3. ἑαυτοῖς, to *or* for *our*selves, (*Dat. pl.*)
4. ἑαυτούς, ourselves, (*Acc. pl.*)

— Luke xxii. 71, } see O
— John iv. 42, } (we)
4. Acts xxiii. 14.
3. Rom. viii. 22.
1. —— 23 1st.
— —— 23 2nd, see O (we)
1. —— 28.
3. —— xv. 1.
— 2 Cor. i. 4, see O (we)
3. —— 9 twice.
4. —— iii. 1.
2. 2 Cor. iii. 5 1st.
2. —— 5 2nd (αὐτῶν, L.)
4. —— iv. 2, 5 twice.
4. —— v. 12.
4. —— vi. 4.
4. —— vii. 1.
4. —— x. 12, 14.
— Gal. ii. 17, see O (we)
1. 2 Thes. iii. 9.
— Tit. iii. 3, see O (we)
— Heb. x. 25, see O (of)
1. 1 John i. 8.

OURSELVES (OF)

2. Heb. x. 25.

OURSELVES (WE)

1. αὐτοί, *see No.* 1, *above.*
2. ἡμεῖς, we.
3. { ἡμεῖς, we,
{ αὐτοί, ourselves.

1. Luke xxii. 71.
1. John iv. 2.
3. Rom. viii. 23.
1. 2 Cor. i. 4.
1. Gal. ii. 7.
2. Tit. iii. 3.

OUT.

ἔξω, out, without, outside, out of doors.

Matt. v. 13.
—— xxvi. 75.
Mark xiv. 68.
Luke viii. 54 (*ap.*)
—— xiii. 28.
—— xiv. 35.
Luke xxii. 62.
—— xxiv. 50 (*om.* G→Lb Tr Ab ℵ.)
John vi. 37.
—— ix. 34, 35.
—— xii. 31.
Acts xvi. 30.
1 John iv. 18.
Rev. iii. 12.
—— xi. 2 (ἔξωθεν, *from without*, L T Tr), (ἔσω, *within*, ℵ.)

See also, BLOT, BRING, CARRY, CAST, CHASE, CRY, CUT, DEPART, DRAW, DRIVE, FALL, FETCH, FINDING, FOAM, GET, GIVE, GO, GOING, GUSH, LAUNCH, LEAD, LEAVE, LET, LIFT, LOOK, PLUCK, POUR, PULL, PURGE, PUT, RUN, SEND, SHOOT, SOUND, SPEAK, SPY, STREET, SWIM, TAKE, THRUST, TREAD, TURNED, WORK.

OUT OF.

(*For other words in connection, see below.*)

1. ἐκ, out of, from among, (*motion from the interior.*)
2. ἀπὸ, away from, (*motion from the exterior.*)
3. ἔξω, without, outside, out of doors.
4. ἐκτός, out of, without.
5. διά, through.
   (a) *with Gen.*, through, *as proceeding from;* through, by means of, (*in reference to agency, and denoting the instrument of action.*)
   (b) *with Acc.*, through, *as tending towards*, on account of, (*denoting the ground of action.*)
6. παρά, beside.
   (a) *with Gen.*, beside *and proceeding from, used with persons only, (as No. 2 is with* places); from, *implying that something is imparted.*
   (b) *with Dat.*, beside and at, near, with.
   (c) *with Acc.*, to *or* along the side of, beside.

1. Matt. ii. 6, 15.
2. —— iii. 16.
5a. —— iv. 4.
2. —— vii. 4 (No. 1, L T Tr ℵ.)
1. —— 5 twice.
1. —— viii. 28.
2. —— 34.
1. —— xii. 34, 35 twice.
2. Matt. xii. 43.
2. —— xiii. 1 (No. 1, L T ℵ), (*om.* Tr.)
1. —— 41, 52.
2. —— xiv. 13, 29.
1. —— xv. 11, 18, 19.
2. —— 22.
1. —— xvii. 5.
2. —— 18.

1. Matt. xxi. 16.
3. —— 17, 39.
1. —— xxiv. 17.
2. —— 27.
1. —— xxvii. 53.
2. Mark i. 10 (No. 1 G∾L T Tr A ℵ.)
1. —— 25.
1. —— 26 (No. 2, G∾L.)
1. —— 29.
1. —— v. 2 twice.
1. —— 8 (No. 2, Lm.)
3. —— 10.
2. —— 17.
1. —— 30.
2. —— vi. 33.
1. —— 54.
2. —— vii. 15 (No. 1, L T Tr A.)
1. —— 20, 21.
1. —— 26 (*om.* G⇉)
1. —— 29.
3. —— viii. 23.
1. —— ix. 7.
1. —— 25 (No. 2, L.)
2. —— x. 46 (ἐκεῖθεν, *from thence*, instead of ἀπὸ Ἱεριχώ, *from Jericho*, G∾)
3. —— xi. 19.
3. —— xii. 8.
1. —— xiii. 1, 15.
2. —— xv. 21.
1. —— 46.
2. —— xvi. 9 (No. 6, L Tr), (*ap.*)
1. Luke i. 74.
1. —— ii. 4.
1. —— iv. 22.
3. —— 29.
1. —— 35 1st (No. 2, G∾L T Tr A ℵ.)
— —— 35 2nd, see Come.
1. —— 38 (No. 2, G∾T Tr A ℵ.)
2. —— 41.
2. —— v. 2.
1. —— 3, 17.
2. —— 36.
2. —— vi. 17.
6a. —— 19.
1. —— 42, 45 twice.
2. —— viii. 2.
— —— 4, see O of every city.
2. —— 12.
1. —— 27.
2. —— 29, 33, 35, 38, 46.
2. —— ix. 5.
1. —— 35.
1. —— xi. 6, marg. (text, *in.*)
2. —— 24.
1. —— 54.
2. —— xii. 54.
3. —— xiii. 33.
1. —— xvii. 24.
2. —— 29.
1. —— xix. 22.
3. —— xx. 15.
2. —— xxiii. 26.
1. John i. 46.
1. —— ii. 15.
1. —— iv. 30, 47, 54.
1. —— vii. 38, 41.
2. —— 42.
1. —— 52.
1. —— viii. 59.
1. —— x. 28, 29, 39.
1. —— xi. 55.
1. —— xii. 17, 34.
1. —— xiii. 1.
1. —— xv. 19.
1. —— xvii. 6, 15.
1. —— xx. 2.
2. Acts i. 9.
2. —— ii. 5.
3. —— iv. 15.

1. Acts vii. 3, 4, 10, 40.
3. —— 58.
1. —— viii. 39.
1. —— xii. 11, 17.
1. —— xiii. 17, 42 (*ap.*), 50.
3. —— xiv. 19.
1. —— xv. 14.
3. —— xvi. 13.
2. —— 18.
1. —— 40 (No. 2, T ℵ.)
2. —— xvii. 2.
2. —— xix. 12 (*om.* ἀπ᾽ αὐτῶν, *of them*, G L T Tr A ℵ.)
1. —— 16, 33.
3. —— xxi. 5, 30.
1. —— xxiv. 7 (*ap.*)
1. —— xxvii. 29, 30 twice.
1. —— xxviii. 3 (No. 2, G ∾ L T Tr A ℵ.)
2. —— 21, 23.
1. Rom. ii. 18.
1. —— xi. 24, 26.
1. —— xiii. 11.
1. 1 Cor. v. 10.
2. 2 Cor. i. 16.
1. —— ii. 4.
1. —— iv. 6.
1. —— viii. 11.
4. —— xii. 2.
4. —— 3 (χωρίς, *separate from*, L T A.)
1. Eph. iv. 29.
1. Col. ii. 14.
1. —— iii. 8.
1. 2 Thes. ii. 7.
1. 1 Tim. i. 5.
1. 2 Tim. ii. 22, 26.
1. —— iii. 11.
1. —— iv. 17.
1. Heb. iii. 16.
1. —— vii. 5, 14.
1. —— viii. 9.
2. —— xi. 34.
1. Jas. iii. 10, 13.
1. 1 Pet. ii. 9.
1. 2 Pet. ii. 9.
1. —— iii. 5.
1. 3 John 10.
1. Jude 5, 23.
1. Rev. i. 16.
1. —— ii. 5.
1. —— iii. 5, 12, 16.
1. —— iv. 5.
1. —— v. 7, 9.
1. —— vi. 14.
1. —— vii. 14 (No. 2, L.)
1. —— viii. 4.
1. —— ix. 2, 3, 17, 18.
1. —— x. 10.
1. —— xi. 5, 7.
1. —— xii. 15, 16.
1. —— xiii. 1, 11.
1. —— xiv. 15 (*om.* G→)
1. —— 17, 20.
1. —— xv. 6 (*om.* ἐκ τοῦ ναοῦ, *out of the Temple*, G⇉Trb.)
1. —— xvi. 1 (*om.* ἐκ τοῦ ναοῦ, *out of the Temple*, G ⇉ Trb.)
1. —— 7 (*om.* ἀλλοῦ ἐκ, *another out of*, G L T Tr A ℵ.)
1. —— 13 twice.
2. —— 17 (No. 1, G∾L T Tr A ℵ.)
1. —— 21.
1. —— xvii. 8.
1. —— xviii. 4.
1. —— xix. 5 (No. 2, G∾L T Tr A.)
1. —— 15, 21.
1. —— xx. 7, 9, 12.
1. —— xxi. 2, 3, 10.
1. —— xxii. 1.
2. —— 19 1st.
1. —— 19 2nd.

OUT OF EVERY CITY.

{ κατὰ, throughout, / πόλιν, the city, } *distributively*, from every city.

Luke viii. 4.

See also, BORN, CAST, COME, DEPART, DRAW, FLEE, GET, GO, MEASURE, PUT, SEASON, SLEEP, VANISH, WAY.

OUTER.

ἐξώτερος, the outermost, most remote, (*non occ.*)

Matt. viii. 12. | Matt. xxv. 30. | Matt. xxii. 13.

OUTGO.

προέρχομαι, to go forward, go further, pass on, to go before in advance.

Mark vi. 33 (*ap.*)

OUTRUN.

{ προτρέχω, to run before in advance, / τάχιον, more swiftly. }

John xx. 4.

OUTSIDE.

1. ἔξωθεν, from without, *i.e.* outwardly, externally.

2. ἐκτός, out of, without, the outside.

1. Matt. xxiii. 25. | 1. Luke xi. 39. | 2. Matt. xxiii. 26.

OUTWARD.

1. ἔξω, out, without, external.

2. ἔξωθεν, from without, *i.e.* outwardly, externally.

3. { ἐν, in, / τῷ, the, / φανερῷ, open, manifest, [*place*, } openly, manifestedly.

2. Matt. xxiii. 27.
— Luke xvii. 20, see *Show.*
3. Rom. ii. 28.
1. 2 Cor. iv. 16.
— 2 Cor. x. 1, see *Appearance.*
— —— 7, see Appearance.
2. 1 Pet. iii. 3.

OUTWARDLY.

2. Matt. xxiii. 28. | 3. Rom. ii. 28.

OUTWENT.

See, OUTGO.

OVEN.

κλίβανος, an oven for baking bread. A large round earthen pot, first heated by a fire made within, and then the dough spread upon the sides to be baked into thin cakes, (*non occ.*)

Matt. vi. 30. | Luke xii. 28.

OVER.

1. ἐπί, upon, *superposition.*
   - (a) *with Gen.*, upon, (*as springing from*) upon and proceeding from; over, *of superintendence or government.*
   - (b) *with Dat.*, upon, (*as resting on*) *like the Gen., except that the point of view is different.*
   - (c) *with Acc.*, upon, (*by direction towards*) upon, *with motion implied;* over, *of authority in action.*
   - [Note.—1b is used when following a verb of existence.
     1c when the verb is transitive.]
2. ἐπάνω, up above, upon, over.
3. πέραν, beyond, over, on the other side.
   - (a) *with art.*, that beyond, the other side.
4. περί, around.
   - (a) *with Gen.*, around and separate from.
   - (b) *with Acc.*, around and towards, about, in reference to, concerning.
5. ἐκ, out of, from among, from.
6. ἐν, in.
7. ὑπέρ, over.
   - (a) *with Gen.*, over and separate from, on behalf of, *as though bending* over *to protect.*
   - (b) *with Acc.*, over and towards; beyond, above, *used in comparison.*
8. ὑπεράνω, up over, up above.

2. Matt. ii. 9.
— —— ix. 1, see Pass.
— —— x. 23, } see Go.
— —— xiv. 34, }
— —— xx. 25, see Dominion.
— —— xxi. 2, see Over against.
1a. Matt. xxiv. 45.
1b. —— 47.
1c. —— xxv. 21 1st.
1a. —— 21 2nd.
1c. —— 23 1st.
1a. —— 23 2nd.
2. —— xxvii. 37.
1c. —— 45.
— Matt. xxvii. 61, see O against
— Mark iv. 35, } see Pass.
— —— v. 21, }
3a. —— vi. 45, marg. (text, *the other side.*)
— —— 53, see Pass.
— —— x. 42 1st, see Rule.
— —— 42 2nd, see Lordship.
— —— xi. 2, } see O against.
— —— xii. 41, }
— —— xiii. 3, see Over against.
— —— xv. 26, see Write.
1c. —— 33.
— —— 39, see Over against.
1c. Luke i. 33.
1c. —— ii. 8.
4b. —— iv. 10.
2. —— 39.
— —— vi. 38, see Run.
— —— viii. 22, see Go.
— —— 26, see O against
1c. —— ix. 1.
1c. —— x. 19.
— —— xi. 42, see Pass.
2. —— 44.
1c. —— xii. 14.
1a. —— 42.
1b. —— 44.
1b. —— xv. 7 twice, 10.
1c. —— xix. 14.
2. —— 17, 19.
1c. —— 27.
— —— 30, see O against
1b. —— 41 (No. 1c, L T Tr A ℵ.)
— —— xxii. 25, see Lordship.
1c. —— xxiii. 23.
1b. —— 38.
1c. —— 44.
3. John vi. 1.
— —— 13, see Remain.
3. —— 17.
3. —— xviii. 1.
1a. Acts vi. 3.
1c. —— vii. 10, 11.
— —— 16, see Carry.
1c. —— 27 (No. 1a, L T Tr ℵ.)
1b. —— viii. 2.
— —— xvi. 9, see Come.
1c. Acts xix. 13.
— —— xx. 2, see Go.
— —— 15, see O against.
6. —— 28.
— —— xxi. 2, } see Sail.
— —— xxvii. 5, }
— —— 7 twice, see against.
— Rom. i. 28, see Give.
— —— iii. 25, see *Passing.*
1c. —— v. 14.
— —— 9, 14, } see Dominion.
— —— vii. 1, }
1a. —— ix. 5.
— —— xv. 12, see Reign.
4b. 1 Cor. vii. 37.
— 2 Cor. i, 24, see Dominion.
1c. —— iii. 13.
— —— viii. 15, see O (have nothing)
— —— xi. 2, see Jealous.
7b. Eph. i. 22.
— —— iv. 19, see Give.
— Col. iii. 15, see Triumph.
1b. 1 Thes. iii. 7.
— —— v. 12, see O (be)
1. Tim. ii. 12, see Authority.
1c. Heb. ii. 7 (*ap.*)
1c. —— iii. 6.
8. —— ix. 5.
1c. —— x. 21.
1c. Jas. v. 14.
1c. 1 Pet. iii. 12.
— —— v. 3, see Lord.
— Jude 7, see Fornication.
1a. Rev. ii. 26.
1c. —— vi. 8.
1a. —— ix. 11.
1a. —— xi. 6.
1b. —— 10.
1c. —— xiii. 7.
1a. —— xiv. 18.
5. —— xv. 2 1st, 2 2nd (*ap.*), 2 3rd & 4th.
1c. —— xvi. 9.
1a. —— xvii. 18.
1b. —— xviii. 11 (No. 1c, T Tr A ℵ.)
1c. —— 20 (No. 1b, G L T Tr A ℵ.)

OVER AGAINST.

1. κατέναντι, down over against, *i.e.* at *the point* over against.
2. ἀπέναντι, from over against, before, in the presence of.
3. { ἐξ, out of, from, ἐναντίας, over against, opposite, } over against.
4. ἀντικρύ, opposite to, (*non occ.*)
5. ἀντιπέραν, over against the other side, on the opposite shore, (*non occ.*)
6. κατά, down.
   - (a) *with Gen.*, down from, against.
   - (b) *with Acc.*, down towards, down upon *or* along, over against, (*locally.*)

7. πρός, towards.

(a) *with Gen.*, hitherwards.

(b) *with Dat.*, resting in the direction towards.

(c) *with Acc.*, hitherwards, towards, in reference to; to.

2. Matt. xxi. 2 (No. 1, L T Tr A* ℵ.)
2. — xxvii. 61.
7c. Mark vi. 45, marg. (text, *unto.*)
1. — xi. 2.
1. Mark xii. 41 (Trm)
1. — xiii. 3. [(No. 2, Tr.)
3. — xv. 39.
5. Luke viii. 26.
1. — xix. 30.
4. — xx. 15.
6b. Luke xxvii. 7 twice.

OVER (BE)

προΐστημι, to cause to stand before, to set over. *In N.T. only intrans.*, to be over, preside, rule.

1 Thes. v. 12.

OVER (HAVE NOTHING)

{ οὐ, no not, πλεονάζω, to be more than enough, } to have not more than enough.

2 Cor. viii. 5.

OVERCHARGE.

ἐπιβαρέω, to weigh down, press heavily upon, burden upon, be burdensome upon.

2 Cor. ii. 5.

OVERCHARGED (BE)

βαρύνομαι, to be heavy, be weighed down, be oppressed by weight, (*non occ.*)

Luke xxi. 34 (*Βαρέομαι*, G L T Tr A ℵ.)

OVERCOME.

1. νικάω, to be victorious, come off victor, conquer.
2. κατακυριεύω, to lord it against *or* over *any one;* have *or* exercise authority over, get the mastery over.
3. κατεργάζομαι, to work out, bring about, accomplish; to work down, make an end of.

1. Luke xi. 22.
1. John xvi. 33.
2. Acts xix. 16.
1. Rom. iii. 4.
1. Rom. xii. 21 twice.
3. Eph. vi. 13, marg. (text, do.)
1. 1 John ii. 13, 14.
1. 1 John iv. 4.
1. — v: 4 twice, 5.
— 2 Pet. ii. 19, 20, see O (be)
1. Rev. ii. 7, 11, 17, 26.
1. Rev. iii. 5, 12, 21 twice.
1. — xi. 7.
1. — xii. 11.
1. — xiii. 7 (*ap.*)
1. — xvii. 14.
1. Rev. xxi. 7.

OVERCOME (BE)

ἡττάομαι, to be inferior, to be subdued and vanquished; *hence*, enslaved.

2 Pet. ii. 19, 20.

OVERFLOW (-ED.)

κατακλύζω, to dash down upon; *hence*, to overflow, to flood, (*non occ.*)

2 Pet. iii. 6.

OVERLAY.

περικαλύπτω, to veil round, cover around; *hence*, overlay.

Heb. ix. 4.

OVERMUCH.

περισσότερος, (*comp. of* περισσός, over and above, more than enough) more abundant.

2 Cor. ii. 7.

OVERREACH. [margin.]

1 Thes. iv. 6, see "DEFRAUD."

OVERRULE. [margin.]

1 Pet. v. 3, see "LORD OVER (BE)"

OVERSEER.

ἐπίσκοπος, a watcher, overseer. (*In Athens it was the name given to the men sent into subdued states to conduct their affairs.*)

[In the *N.T.* it is used of presbyters, (Acts xx. 28), denoting the watchful care which they were to exercise, (*cf.* 1 Pet. v. 2). In Phil. i. 1, the ἐπίσκοποι, who elsewhere are called πρεσβύτεροι, are mentioned with the διακόνοι, (*cf.* 1 Tim. iii. 2, with v. 8; and Tit. i. 7, with verse 5.) While πρεσβύτερος therefore denotes the dignity of the office, ἐπίσκοπος denotes its duties.]

Acts xx. 28.

OVERSHADOW.

ἐπισκιάζω, to cast a shadow upon, to overshadow, (*non occ.*)

Matt. xvii. 5. | Luke i. 35.
Mark ix. 7. | —— ix. 34.
Acts v. 15.

OVERSIGHT OF (TAKE THE)

ἐπισκοπέω, to look upon, observe, to examine how it is concerning any thing. *Of the sick*, to visit and look after them; *in a military sense*, to review *or* muster, inspect.

1 Pet. v. 2.

OVERTAKE (-EN.)

1. καταλαμβάνω, to lay hold of, seize *suddenly*, come suddenly upon.

2. προλαμβάνω, to take before. *Here, Aor.* 1 *pass.*, to have been before taken, caught, (*either unexpectedly before he is aware, or able to offer resistance; or,* caught *before he can escape, thus implying an aggravation of the offence.*)

2. Gal. vi. 1. | 1. 1 Thes. v. 4.

OVERTHROW [noun.]

καταστροφή, (*Eng.*, catastrophe) a throwing down, an overturning, overthrow, destruction, *as of cities.*

2 Pet. ii. 6.

OVERTHROW (-N, -EW.) [verb.]

1. καταστρέφω, to turn down, turn under, *as with a plough;* to upset, overthrow.

2. ἀναστρέφω, to turn upside down, overturn.

3. ἀνατρέπω, to turn up *or* over, overturn, (Tit. i. 11.)

4. καταλύω, to loosen down, dissolve, disunite *the parts of anything; hence, of buildings,* to destroy, put an end to.

5. καταστρώννυμι, to spread *or* strew down; *of persons,* to strew *as corpses in the desert,* (*non occ.*)

1. Matt. xxi. 12. | 4. Acts v. 38.
1. Mark xi. 15. | 5. 1 Cor. x. 5.
2. John ii. 15. | 3. 2 Tim. ii. 8.

OWE (-ED, -EST, -ETH.)

ὀφείλω, to be indebted, *prop., in a pecuniary sense.*

Matt. xviii. 28 twice. | Acts xxi. 11 (A.V. 1611, see Owneth.)
Luke vii. 41. | Rom. xiii. 8.
—— xvi. 5, 7. |
Philem. 18.

OWETH (WHICH)

ὀφειλέτης, a debtor.

Matt. xviii. 24.

OWE BESIDES.

προσοφείλω, to owe in addition to.

Philem. 19.

OWN [adj.]

γνήσιος, genuine, legitimate, *prop., spoken of children. Also, by impl., sincere, faithful.*

1 Tim. i. 2. | Titus i. 4.

OWN (BE THINE)

{ μένω, to remain,
{ σοί, to thee.

Acts v. 4.

See also, ACCORD, BUSINESS, COMPANY, CONCEITS, COUNTRY, COUNTRYMEN, HAND, HER, HIS, HOME, LOVER, MINE, OUR, PLEASURE, THEIR, THINE, YOUR, WILL.

OWNETH. [verb.]

ἐστί, *with Gen.*, whose this is.

Acts xxi. 11 (in A.V. 1611, oweth.)

OWNER.

κύριος, (*from* κῦρος, might, power) lord, master, owner.

Luke xix. 33. | Acts xxvii. 11, see Ship.

OX (-EN.)

1. βοῦς, an ox *or* cow, *i.e.* an animal of the ox kind.

2. ταῦρος, a bull, bullock.

2. Matt. xxii. 4. | 1. John ii. 14, 15.
1. Luke xiii. 15. | 2. Acts xiv. 13.
1. —— xiv. 5, 19. | 1. 1 Cor. ix. 9 twice.
1. 1 Tim. v. 18.

P

PAIN (-S, -ED.)

1. πόνος, labour, travail; *hence,* sorrow, pain, anguish.
2. ὠδίν, a throe, pang, *as of a woman in travail.*

2. Acts ii. 24. [vail. — Rom. viii. 22, see Tra- | 1. Rev. xvi. 10, 11. 1. — xxi. 4.

PAIN (-ED.) [verb.]

βασανίζω, to apply a touch stone; to examine by words or torture; *hence,* to afflict with pain; *spoken of the pains of parturition and punishment.*

Rev. xii. 2.

PAINED (*be*) [margin.]

Luke xii. 50, see "STRAITENED (BE)."

PAINFULNESS.

μόχθος, wearisome labour, *including the idea of painful effect;* sorrow.

2 Cor. xi. 27.

PAIR.

ζεῦγος, a yoke; *hence, gen.,* a pair, a couple, (*occ.* Luke xiv. 19.)

Luke ii. 24.

PAIR OF BALANCES.

ζυγός, a yoke, *serving to couple any two things together; hence,* the beam *which unites two scales,* a balance.

Rev. vi. 5.

PALACE.

1. αὐλή, a court, a yard, *i.e.* any enclosed space in the open air exposed to winds and weather; *hence,* the courtyard of an oriental edifice, which served as a place of reception.
2. πραιτώριον, *Lat.,* prætorium, the general's tent in a camp; *then,* the residence of the governor of a province, *whether prætor or other officer;* a prætorian residence.

1. Matt. xxvi. 3, 58, 69. 1. Mark xiv. 54, 66. | 1. Luke xi. 21. 1. John xviii. 15. 2. Phil. i. 13, marg. *Cæsar's court.*

PALE.

χλωρός, pale-green, yellowish-green, like the *colour of the first shoots of grass, etc., which, though beautiful in a vegetable, is, in a living creature* livid, *and* plague-stricken. See Lev. xiii. 49; xiv. 37. *In* Rev. vi. 8, *The colour of the horse, whose rider's name is* "Pestilence," (*see* Matt. xxiv. 7).

Rev. vi. 8.

PALM.

Matt. xxvi. 67, see Smite. | John xviii. 22, see Strike.

PALM and PALM TREE.*

φοίνιξ, a palm-tree, the date-palm, *used also of* a bough carried in the hand.

John xii. 13.* | Rev. vii. 9.

PALSY (SICK OF THE)

1. παραλυτικός, paralytic, palsied.
2. παραλύω, to loosen at *or* from the side, to disjoin. *In N.T., pass. perf. part.,* relaxed, enfeebled.

1. Matt. viii. 6. 1. — ix. 2 twice, 6. 1. Mark ii. 3, 4, 5, 9, 10. | 2. Luke v. 24 (No. 1, G~ L ℵ.) 2. Acts ix. 33.

PALSY (TAKEN WITH A)

2. Luke v. 18. | 2. Acts viii. 7.

PALSY (THAT HATH THE)

1. Matt. iv. 24.

PAP (-S.)

μαστός, the breast, *esp. of a woman,* (μαζός, *of a man.*)

Luke xi. 27. — xxiii. 29. | Rev. i. 13 (*μαζός, the breast* (of a man), L.

PAPER.

χάρτης, *Lat.,* charta, a leaf of paper *made of the papyrus.*

2 John 12.

PARABLE (-s.)

1. *παραβολή*, a placing beside, *or* side by side for the purpose of comparison; an utterance which involves a comparison, and whose proper meaning is not that which is expressed by the words, but which must become clear by the intended application. A form, therefore, which conceals from the one what it reveals to the other.

[A PARABLE illustrates by what is wont or possible to happen, or by what either the speaker or hearers believe to be possible; AN EXAMPLE illustrates by what has happened; A FABLE transfers the case in point to a lower sphere in which it could not happen, and therefore the design and meaning are more easily discerned. It is not said whether Luke xvi. 19-31 is the former or latter of these; but in either case the teaching is not in the words, but in the comparison.]

2. *παροιμία*, something by *or* on the way, a wayside discourse, *or* a wayside illustration, lessons drawn from actions of ordinary life, and from objects and processes in nature; *also, an* out-of-the-way discourse; *hence*, an enigmatic speech, a dark saying, (*in opp. to παῤῥησίᾳ λαλεῖν*, to speak openly or plainly.)

1. **Matt. xiii. 3, 10, 13, 18, 24, 31, 33, 34 twice, 35, 36, 53.**
1. **—— xv. 15.**
1. **—— xxi. 33, 45.**
1. **—— xxii. 1.**
1. **—— xxiv. 32.**
1. **Mark iii. 23.**
1. **—— iv. 2, 10, 11, 13 twice, 33, 34.**
1. **—— vii. 17.**
1. **—— xii. 1, 12.**
1. **—— xiii. 28.**
1. **Luke v. 36.**
1. **Luke vi. 39.**
1. **—— viii. 4, 9, 10, 11.**
1. **—— xii. 16, 41.**
1. **—— xiii. 6.**
1. **—— xiv. 7.**
1. **—— xv. 3.**
1. **—— xviii. 1, 9.**
1. **—— xix. 11.**
1. **—— xx. 9, 19.**
1. **—— xxi. 29.**
2. **John x. 6.**
2. **—— xvi. 25 twice** } marg.
2. **—— —— 29,** } (text, *proverb.*)

PARADISE.

παράδεισος, *Eng.*, paradise. The lxx. *use it of* the garden in Eden, (Gen. ii. 8, etc.); *a word which the Greeks also use to describe* a large pleasure-garden with trees, *or* park of an Eastern monarch.

[The later Jewish teaching made Paradise that part of *ᾅδης* reserved for the blessed. But *ᾅδης* is gravedom, whither all go in death (*see* "HELL," *No.* 2, *and note*), and Paradise is the place of the risen saints. The Scripture teaches that Paradise was the dwelling-place of God with man in the first Heaven and Earth. It was barred from man at the Fall, and destroyed at the Flood. It will reappear again at the Regeneration, (Matt. xix. 28) when God shall fulfil His promise and make the new Heavens and Earth, (Is. li. 16; lxv. 17; lxvi. 22; 2 Pet. iii. 13; Rev. xxii.) of which the Millennial Earth will be at once the pledge and foretaste, (*see under* "HEAVEN"). Hence, the Scriptures relating to Paradise now, are all future, as the abode of *risen* saints, not of *dead* ones. (1) In Luke xxiii. 43, the Lord gives the dying robber a *present assurance*, instead of a *future remembrance*—"Verily I say unto thee to-day,"—the *future* fulfilment being required by the absence of *ὅτι*, (compare Luke xxii. 34, and Matt. xxi. 28, with Mark xiv. 30; Luke iv. 21, and xix. 9; and *see under* "TO-DAY.") (2) In 2 Cor. xii. 4 the verb is *ἁρπάζω*, "catch away," *not*, "up." (3) In Rev. ii. 7 the promise is clearly future, pointing to Rev. xxii.

Note also the expressions, "*the garden of the Lord*," (Gen. xiii. 10, and Isa. li. 3) the garden being viewed, in its relation to Jehovah, as what it was and what He had made it. Also, "*the garden of God*," (Ezek. xxviii. 13; xxxi. 8, 9; and Rev. ii. 7) the garden being viewed in its relation to man, as being the place where God (Elohim) did and yet would dwell with man—the latter being the *human* aspect, and the former the *Divine*. *See under* "WORD," *and note.*] (*non occ.*)

Luke xxiii. 43. | 2 Cor. xii. 4. | Rev. ii. 7.

PARCEL.

See, GROUND.

PARCHMENT (-s.)

μεμβράνα, *Lat.*, membrana, *i.e. Eng.*, membrane, skin, parchment, (*non occ.*)

2 Tim. iv. 13.

PARENT (-s.)

1. γονεύς, a parent. *In N.T. only pl.*
2. πρόγονος, earlier born, older. *In N.T. pl.*, progenitors, ancestors, forefathers.
3. πατήρ, a father. *Here, pl., i.e.* both father and mother.

1. Matt. x. 21.
1. Mark xiii. 12.
1. Luke ii. 27, 41.
1. —— viii. 56.
1. —— xviii. 29.
1. —— xxi. 16.
1. John ix. 2, 3, 18, 20, 22, 23.
1. Rom. 1. 30.
1. 2 Cor. xii. 14 twice.
1. Eph. vi. 1.
1. Col. iii. 20.
2. 1 Tim. v. 4.
1. 2 Tim. iii. 2.
3. Heb. xi. 23.

PART (-s.) [noun.]

(*For various combinations with other words, see below.*)

1. μέρος, a part, part *of a whole,* a portion.
2. μερίς, a part, division, part *assigned*, portion, share, (*occ.* Col. i. 12.)
3. κλῆρος, a lot, a die, anything used in determining chances; *hence*, a lot, *i.e.* a part *or* portion as assigned by lot, an heritage *so obtained.*
4. κλίμα, inclination, declivity; *then, from the apparent inclination of the heavens, the earth was divided into several* κλίματα, climates, *by lines drawn parallel to the sun's course; hence*, clime, region.
5. { οἱ, these, μὲν... indeed... οἱ, these, δὲ, but, } some indeed ... but some.

1. Matt. ii. 22.
1. Mark viii. 10.
2. Luke x. 42.
1. —— xi. 36.
1. John xiii. 8.
1. —— xix. 23 twice.
3. Acts i. 17.
3. —— 25 (τόπος, the place, G ∾ L T Tr A.)
1. —— ii. 10.
1. —— v. 2.
2. —— viii. 21.
5. —— xiv. 4.
2. Acts xvi. 12 (*om.* G→)
1. —— xx. 2.
1. —— xxiii. 6, 9 (*ap.*)
4. Rom. xv. 23.
2. 2 Cor. vi. 15.
1. Eph. iv. 9 (*om.* G⇉)
1. —— 16 (μέλος, member, G∾)
1. Col. ii. 16 marg. (text, respect.)
1. Rev. xvi. 19.
1. —— xx. 6.
1. —— xxi. 8.
1. —— xxii. 19.

PART (GIVE)

μερίζω, to part, divide into parts; *hence*, to assign, grant, bestow.

Heb. vii. 2.

PART (IN)

1. { ἀπὸ, away from, μέρους, a part, } partly, in some degree.
2. { ἐκ, from among, of, μέρους, a part, } *of things*, partially, imperfectly; *of persons*, individually.

1. Rom. xi. 25.
2. 1 Cor. xiii. 9 twice, 10, 12.
1. 2 Cor. i. 14.
1. —— ii. 5.

PART (ON ONE'S)

1. κατά, down.
   (a) *with Gen.*, down from.
   (b) *with Acc.*, down towards, down upon, according to.
2. ὑπέρ, over.
   (a) *with Gen.*, over and separate from, for, on behalf of.
   (b) *with Acc.*, over and towards, beyond, above.

2a. Mark ix. 40.
1b. 1 Pet. iv. 14 twice (*ap.*)

PART OF (TAKE)

μετέχω, to have with *another*, *i.e.* to partake of, share in.

Heb. ii. 14.

See also, FOURTH, GREATER, HINDER, INWARD, LACK, MORE, TENTH, THIRD, UTMOST, UTTERMOST, YOUR.

PART (-ED.) [verb.]

1. διαμερίζω, to dispart, separate into parts, divide out *to each person from a common source.*

Matt. xxvii. 35 1st, 35 2nd (*ap.*)
Mark xv. 24.
Luke xxiii. 34.
John xix. 24.
Acts ii. 45.

PARTED (BE)

διΐστημι, to place asunder, separate *one's self*, go away.

Luke xxiv. 51.

PARTAKE WITH (-EST.)

{ συγκοινωνός, a joint-partaker, co-
{ γίνομαι, to become. [partner.

Rom. xi. 17. | 1 Cor. ix. 23.

PARTAKER (-S.)

(*For various combinations with other words, see below.*)

1. κοινωνός, a sharer in common, (*from* κοινός, common to all) a partaker, partner, companion.
2. συγκοινωνός, (*No.* 1, *with* σύν, together with, *prefixed*) a sharer in common, in conjunction with others, a joint-partaker, co-partner.
3. μέτοχος, having in association with *another; as subst.*, a sharer with *another*.
4. συμμέτοχος, (*No.* 3, *with* σύν, together with, *prefixed*) a having in association together, in conjunction with *another*, a joint-sharer, (*occ.* Eph. v. 7.)
5. ἀντιλαμβάνομαι, to take hold of in one's turn; *hence*, to take part in, to interest one's self for. *Here, part.*, devoted to.

1. Matt. xxiii. 30.
3. 1 Cor. x. 30.
1. 2 Cor. i. 7.
4. Eph. iii. 6.
2. Phil. 1. 7.
5. 1 Tim. vi. 2.
— 2 Tim. i. 8, see Afflic- [tions.
3. Heb. iii. 1, 14.
3. — vi. 4.
3. — xii. 8.
1. 1 Pet. v. 1.
1. 2 Pet. i. 4.

PARTAKER (TO BE)

{ εἰς, unto, for the,
{ μερίς, part *assigned*, division, portion, share.

Col. i. 12.

PARTAKER OF (BE)

1. κοινωνέω, to share in common, to be a partaker of *or* in *anything* in common with others.
2. συγκοινωνέω, (*No.* 1, *with* σύν, together with, *prefixed*) to share *anything* in common in conjunction with others.
3. μετέχω, to have in association with another.
4. μεταλαμβάνω, to take a part *or* share of *anything* in association with *others*.

1. Rom. xv. 27.
3. 1 Cor. ix. 10, 12.
3. — x. 17, 21, 30.
1. 1 Tim. v. 22.
4. 2 Tim. ii. 6.
1. Heb. ii. 14.
4. — xii. 10.
1. 1 Pet. iv. 13.
1. 2 John 11.
2. Rev. xviii. 4.

PARTAKER WITH.

συμμέτοχος, (*see* "PARTAKER," *No.* 4.)

Eph. v. 7.

PARTAKER WITH (BE)

συμμερίζω, to divide in conjunction with *another*. *In N.T. mid.*, to divide in conjunction with, *so as to receive part to one's self*, (*non occ.*)

1 Cor. ix. 13.

PARTED. [verb.]

See, PART.

PARTIAL (BE)

διακρίνω, to separate throughout, make a distinction.

Jas. ii. 4.

PARTIALITY.

πρόσκλισις, a leaning against, inclination towards; *hence*, partiality, (*non occ.*)

1 Tim. v. 21 (*πρόσκλησις, summons, charge,* L Trm.)

PARTIALITY (WITHOUT)

ἀδιάκριτος, not making a distinction, (*non occ.*)

Jas. iii. 17, marg. *without wrangling.*

PARTICULAR (IN)

{ ἐκ, out of, } *i.e.* individually,
{ μερός, part, } *also*, imperfectly, *see* 1 Cor. xiii. 9, 12.

1 Cor. xii. 27.

PARTICULAR (EVERY ONE IN)

{ κατά, according } individually each
{ ἕνα, one, [to, } one *of you*,
{ ἕκαστος, each, } every one of *you*.

Eph. v. 33.

PARTICULARLY.

1. { κατὰ, according to, ἕν, one, ἕκαστον, each, } one by one, (*see also above.*)

2. { κατὰ, according to, μερός, part, } in detail.

1. Acts xxi. 19. | 2. Heb. ix. 5.

PARTITION.

φραγμός, a fence *or* hedge *as enclosing anything, i.e.* a thorn hedge round a vineyard, often in addition to a wall.

Eph. ii. 14.

PARTLY.

1. { μερός, part, τι, some, } in some part, in some measure.

2. { τοῦτο, this, μὲν...indeed, τοῦτο, this, δὲ, but, } on the one hand... and on the other.

1. 1 Cor. xi. 18. | 2. Heb. x. 33.

PARTNER (-s.)

1. κοινωνός, a sharer in common *with others.*

2. μέτοχος, having with *another; as subst.*, a partner.

2. Luke v. 7.
1. —— 10.
1. 2 Cor. viii. 23.
1. Philem. 17.

PASS (-ED, -ETH, -ING.)

(*For various combinations with other words, see below.*)

1. παρέρχομαι, to come beside *or* near *any person*, draw near; go *or* pass near, pass along by.

2. διέρχομαι, to come *or* go through, to pass through; *of water*, to pass over.

3. ἀπέρχομαι, to go away from *one place to another; hence*, go away, depart, pass away.

4. μεταβαίνω, to pass over from one place to another, *esp.*, to pass from one state to another.

5. διαβαίνω, to make a stride, walk, step across, pass over.

6. ἀναστρέφω, to turn up. *Here, mid.*, to turn one's self around, to be turned around; to move about in a place, sojourn, dwell in, live; to conduct one's self.

7. παράγω, to lead along near, to lead by or past. *Here, mid.*, pass along, pass away.

8. παραλέγω, to lay near. *Here, mid.*, to lie near *or* with *any one.* To lay one's course near, *i.e.* to sail near, by, *or* along *a place*, or coast.

9. παραπορεύομαι, to pass by the side or near *any one. Here followed by* διά, through, to journey through.

10. ὑπερβάλλω, to throw *or* cast over *or* beyond; *hence*, to surpass, exceed.

11. ὑπερέχω, to hold over; *then*, to hold over, *or* beyond, to jut out over *or* beyond, to be better, be superior to, surpass, excel.

1. Matt. v. 18 twice.
1. —— viii. 28.
1. —— xiv. 15.
1. —— xxiv. 34.
1. —— xxvi. 39.
9. Mark ix. 30 (πορεύομαι, *to pass*, L Tr), (παραπορεύομαι, *to pass near or by the side of*, A.)
1. —— xiii. 30.
1. —— xiv. 35.
1. Luke xvi. 17.
5. —— 26.
2. —— xix. 4.
4. John v 24.
2. Acts xii. 10 part.
2. —— xviii. 27.
8. Acts xxvii. 8.
1. —— 9.
2. Rom. v. 12.
— 1 Cor. vii. 36, see Flower.
— —— xv. 54, see Brought.
2. 2 Cor. i. 16 (No. 3, G ∾ L.)
10. Eph. iii. 19.
11. Phil. iv. 7.
2. Heb. iv. 14.
6. 1 Pet. i. 17.
7. 1 John ii. 8. 17.
4. —— iii. 14.
3. Rev. ix. 12.
3. —— xi. 14.

PASS AWAY.

1. Matt. xxiv. 35 twice.
1. —— xxvi. 42.
1. Mark xiii. 31 twice.
1. Luke xxi. 32, 33 twice.
7. 1 Cor. vii. 31.
1. 2 Cor. v. 17.
1. Jas. i. 10.
1. 2 Pet. iii. 10.
1. Rev. xxi. 1 (No. 3, G L T Tr A ℵ.)
3. Rev. xxi. 4.

PASS BY.

1. παράγω, *see* "PASS," *No.* 7.

2. διέρχομαι, *see* "PASS," *No.* 2.

3. ἔρχομαι, to come *or* go, *used of persons or things, denoting* the act of coming *or* going.

4. παρέρχομαι, *see* "PASS," *No.* 1.

5. παραπορεύομαι, *see* "PASS," *No.* 9.

6. **διαπορεύομαι**, to go *or* pass through *a place.*

1. Matt. xx. 30.	6. Mark xviii. 36.
5. —— xxvii. 39.	4. —— 37.
1. Mark ii. 14 part.	1. John viii. 59 (ap.)
4. —— vi. 48.	1. —— ix. 1 part.
5. —— xi. 20 part.	3. Acts v. 15.
1. —— xv. 21.	4. —— xvi. 8.
5. —— 29.	2. —— xvii. 23 part.

PASS BY ON THE OTHER SIDE.

ἀντιπαρέρχομαι, ("PASS," *No.* 1, *with* **ἀντί**, against, *prefixed*) to pass along over against, to pass by on the opposite side, (*non occ.*)

Luke x. 31, 32.

PASS (CAN)

διαπεράω, to pass through.

Luke xvi. 26.

PASS FORTH.

παράγω, *see* "PASS," *No.* 7.

Matt. ix. 9 part.

PASS ON.

προέρχομαι, to go forward, go further.

Acts xii. 10.

PASS OVER.

1. **διαπεράω**, to pass through; *of water*, to pass over.
2. **διέρχομαι**, *see* "PASS," *No.* 2.
3. **παρέρχομαι**, *see* "PASS," *No.* 1.

1. Matt. ix. 1.	1. Mark v. 21 part.
2. Mark iv. 35.	1. —— vi. 53 part.

3. Luke xi. 42.

PASS THROUGH.

1. **διέρχομαι**, *see* "PASS," *No.* 2.
2. **διαβαίνω**, *see* "PASS," *No.* 5.
3. **διοδεύω**, to travel through, to traverse, (*occ.* Luke viii. 1.)

1. Luke xix. 1.	3. Acts xvii. 1 part.
1. Acts viii. 40.	1. —— xix. 1, 21 part.
1. —— xv. 3.	1. 1 Cor. xvi. 5 twice.

2. Heb. xi. 29.

PASS THROUGHOUT.

διέρχομαι, *see* "PASS," *No.* 2.

Acts xiv. 24 part.

PASSED (FAR)

πολλή, much, of *time or hours*, late.

Mark vi. 35.

PASSING FROM ONE TO ANOTHER. [margin.]

Heb. vii. 24, see "UNCHANGEABLE."

See also, COME, PAST.

PASSING OVER. [margin.]

Rom. iii. 25, see "REMISSION."

PASSION.

1. **πάθημα**, what is suffered, affection *or* suffering of mind, emotion.
2. **πάσχω**, to suffer.

2. Acts i. 3.	1. Gal. v. 24 marg. (text, *affection.*)

PASSIONS (OF LIKE)

ὁμοιοπαθής, like affected, suffering like things, i.e. *of like nature, affections, or conditions.*

Jas. v. 17.

PASSOVER.

πάσχα, *the Greek spelling of the Aramaic* פַּסְחָא, the Passover, *i.e.* a sparing, immunity, *from Heb.*, פָּסַח, to pass over, to spare. *Hence, Eng.*, paschal, *i.e.* Paschal supper, *or* Paschal lamb, (*occ.* Acts xii. 4.)

Matt. xxvi. 2, 17, 18, 19.	John xi. 55 twice.
Mark xiv. 1, 12 twice, 14, 16.	—— xii. 1.
Luke ii. 41.	—— xiii. 1.
—— xxii. 1, 7, 8, 11, 13, 15.	—— xviii. 28, 39.
John ii. 13, 23.	—— xix. 14.
—— vi. 4.	1 Cor. v. 7.

Heb. xi. 28.

PAST.

1. **παρά**, beside.
   (a) *with Gen.*, beside and proceeding from, from.
   (b) *with Dat.*, beside and at, near, with.
   (c) *with Acc.*, to *or* along the side of, compared with, *so as to be shown* beyond, etc.; *hence*, beyond.

2. παρέρχομαι, to come near to *or* beside *any person or thing*, to go *or* pass near; *spoken of time*, to pass by, be past.

3. παροίχομαι, to be gone by, to have gone past, vanished, (*non occ.*)

3. Acts xiv. 16 part.
— Rom. xi. 33, see Finding.
— Gal. v. 21, see Time.
— Eph. iv. 19, see Feeling.
— Heb. i. 1, see Time.
1. —— xii. 11, *and see* Age.
2. 1 Pet. iv. 3 part.

PAST (BE)

1. γίνομαι, to begin to be; to become, come to pass.

2. διαγίνομαι, (*No.* 1, *with* διά, through, *prefixed*) to become throughout, to be through, *i.e.* be past, have elapsed.

3. προγίνομαι, (*No.* 1, *with* πρό, before, *prefixed*) to become before, to have previously committed, (*non occ.*)

2. Mark xvi. 1 part.
1. Luke ix. 36.
3. Rom. iii. 25.
1. 2 Tim. ii. 18.

PAST (IN TIME)

ποτέ, when, whenever, once, *both of time past and future; of the past*, once, formerly.

Gal. i. 13.
Eph. ii. 2, 11.
Philem. 11.
1 Pet. ii. 20.

PAST (IN TIMES)

ποτέ, *see above.*

Rom. xi. 30.
Eph. ii. 3.
Gal i. 23.

PASTOR (-S.)

ποιμήν, a shepherd, one who tends herds or flocks, *not merely one who feeds, but* one who tends, guides, nourishes, cherishes, and rules, etc.

Eph. iv. 11.

PASTURE.

νομή, pasture, the act of feeding; *also*, pasturage, (*non occ.*)

John x. 9.

PATH (-S.)

1. τρίβος, a beaten path, (*from* τρίβω, to rub, wear down), (*non occ.*)

2. τροχία, a wheel-track, rut, road-way, (*from* τροχός, a wheel), (*non occ.*)

1. Matt. iii. 3.
1. Mark i. 3.
1. Luke iii. 4.
2. Heb. xii. 13.

PATIENCE.

1. ὑπομονή, a remaining under, a bearing-up under; *hence*, patient endurance, holding out, enduring.

* ὑπομονή χριστοῦ, 2 Thes. iii. 5, is *the patience which waits for Christ.*

ὁ λόγος τῆς. ὑπ. μοῦ, Rev. iii. 10, *is* the word which treats of patient waiting for me, *i.e.* the word of prophecy.

‡ *Hence, Hope* being the grand basis of ὑπομονή, is put for it, *cf.* Rom. xv. 5, 13 with 4.

‖ *Also, cf.* the three graces of Tit. ii. 2 with 1 Cor. xiii. 13.

2. μακροθυμία, longanimity, slowness to anger, *i.e.* long-suffering, patient forbearance.

— Matt. xviii. 26, 29, see P (have)
1. Luke viii. 15.
1. —— xxi. 19.
1. Rom. v. 3, 4.
1. —— viii. 25.
1‡.—— xv. 4, 5.
1. 2 Cor. vi. 4.
1. —— xii. 12.
1. Col. i. 11.
1. 1 Thes. i. 3.
1. 2 Thes. i. 4.
1*.—— iii. 5, marg. (text, *patient waiting.*)
1. 1 Tim. vi. 11.
1. 2 Tim. iii. 10.
1‖.Tit. ii. 2.
2. Heb. vi. 12.
1. —— x. 36.
1. —— xii. 1.
1. Jas. i. 3, 4.
— —— v. 7, see P (have long)
2. —— 10.
1. —— 11.
1. 2 Pet. i. 6 twice.
1. Rev. i. 9.
1. —— ii. 2, 3, 19.
1†.—— iii. 10.
1. —— xiii. 10.
1. —— xiv. 12.

PATIENCE (HAVE)

μακροθυμέω, to be long-minded, *i.e.* slow to anger, passion, *etc.*; to be long-suffering, to be patiently forbearing.

Matt. xviii. 26, 29.

PATIENCE (HAVE LONG)

Jas. v. 7.

PATIENCE (suffer with long) [margin.]

Jas. v. 7 marg. See "PATIENT (BE)"

PATIENT.

1. ὑπομένω, to remain behind *when others have gone;* to remain under, to bear up under; *hence*, to endure patiently, (*here, participle.*)

2. ἐπιεικής, fitting upon, fitting, meet; *hence*, not insisting on just rights; *not only passively non-contentious, but actively* considerate, waiving just and legal redress, and tempering strict justice with gentle equity.

3. ἀνεξίκακος, patient holding up under evils and injuries.

— Rom. ii. 7, see Continuance.
1. — xii. 12 part.
— 1 Thes. v. 14, see P (be)
— 2 Thes. iii. 5, see Waiting.
2. 1 Tim. iii. 3.
3. 2 Tim. ii. 24.
— Jas. v. 7, 8, see P (be)

PATIENT (BE)

μακροθυμέω, *see* "PATIENCE (HAVE)"

1 Thes. v. 14.
Jas. v. 7, marg. *be long patient, or suffer with long patience.*
—— 8.

PATIENTLY.

μακροθύμως, patiently, *i.e.* with long-suffering, *or* with long forbearance, (*non occ.*)

Acts xxvi. 3. | Heb. vi. 15, see Endure.

PATIENTLY (TAKE)

ὑπομένω, *see* "PATIENT," *No.* 1.

1 Pet. ii. 20 twice.

PATRIARCH (-s.)

πατριάρχης, *Eng.*, patriarch, the father and founder of a family or tribe.

Acts ii. 29. | Acts vii. 8, 9.
Heb. vii. 4.

PATTERN (-s.)

1. τύπος, a mark or impress made by a hard substance on a softer one; *then*, model, pattern, exemplar *in its widest sense.*

2. ὑποτύπωσις, (*from* ὑποτυπόω, to form *or* copy slightly) delineation, outline, a primary draught *or* sketch to be afterwards filled in, *or* a subtracery to be afterwards painted over, (*occ.* 2 Tim. i. 13.)

3. ὑπόδειγμα, what is pointed out, *or* shown secretly or privately, what is given a glimpse of; *hence*, a representation.

2. 1 Tim. i. 16.
1. Tit. ii. 7.
1. Heb. viii. 5.
3. — ix. 23.

PAUL.

Παῦλος, Paul, the name of the great "Apostle of the Gentiles."

In all passages, except—

Acts xviii. 1 (*om.* L T Tr A ℵ.) [Tr A ℵ.)
— xxiii. 11 (*om.* G L T
— xxiv. 23 (αὐτός, *him*, G L T Tr A ℵ.)
Acts xxv. 7 (*ap.*)
— xxviii. 17 (αὐτός, *he*, G L T Tr A ℵ.)
—— 30 (*om.* G L T Tr A ℵ.)

PAVEMENT.

Λιθόστρωτον, stone-strewed, paved, *gen.*, a tesselated pavement of mosaic work.

John xix. 13.

PAY, PAID.

1. ἀποδίδωμι, to give away from *one's self*, deliver over, give up. *Spoken in ref. to obligation* to give in full, render, pay over *or* off *as debts or wages*, etc.

2. τελέω, to end, finish, complete; *of a law*, to fulfil it, execute it, accomplish it; *hence*, *of the law of paying tribute*, etc., to pay it.

1. Matt. v. 26.
2. — xvii. 24.
1. — xviii. 25, 26, 28, 29, 30, 34.
— Matt. xxiii. 23, see Tithe
1. Luke vii. 42.
1. — xii. 59.
2. Rom. xiii. 6.
— Heb. vii. 9, see Tithe.

PAYMENT BE MADE.

ἀποδίδωμι, *see above*, *No.* 1.

Matt. xviii. 25.

PEACE.

εἰρήνη, peace, rest; *in contrast with strife, and denoting* the absence *or* end of strife. *As influenced by the Heb.* שׁלום, a state of health *or* well-being, *it denotes* a state of untroubled, undisturbed well-being. *The Peace which is* the result of forgiveness enjoyed, must not be confounded with the Peace Christ has "made" by the blood of His cross.

[(a) "The Peace of God," in Phil iv. 7, is the Peace which God has, as being free from all anxiety and care, and arising from His perfectly knowing the future. In proportion, therefore, as we

"make our requests" unto Him, a measure of the peace which He has will "keep" us from being "careful" (= full of care), *see* Isa. xxvi. 3, 4.]

Matt. x. 13 twice, 34 twice.
—— xx. 31, ⎫
—— xxvi. 63, ⎬ see P (hold
Mark i. 25, ⎪ one's)
—— iii. 4, ⎭
—— v. 34.
—— ix. 34, see P (hold one's)
——— 50, see P (have)
—— x. 48, ⎫ see P (hold
—— xiv. 61, ⎭ one's)
Luke i. 79.
—— ii. 14, 29.
—— vii. 50.
—— viii. 48.
—— x. 5, 6 twice.
—— xi. 21.
—— xii. 51.
—— xiv. 4, see P (hold one's)
——— 32.
—— xviii. 39, see P (hold one's)
—— xix. 38.
——— 40, see P (hold one's)
——— 42.
—— xx. 26, see P (hold one's)
—— xxiv. 36 (*ap.*)
John xiv. 27 twice.
—— xvi. 33.
—— xx. 19, 21, 26.
Acts x. 36.
—— xi. 18, ⎫ see P (hold
—— xii. 17, ⎭ one's)
——— 20.
—— xv. 13, see P (hold
——— 33. [one's)
—— xvi. 36.
—— xviii. 9, see P (hold
Rom. i. 7. [one's)
—— ii. 10.
—— iii. 17.
—— v. 1.
—— viii. 6.
—— x. 15 (*om.* τῶν εὐαγγελιζομένων εἰρήνην, *preach the gospel of peace, and*, L T Tr^{mb} A^{b} ℵ.)

Rom. xiv. 17, 19.
—— xv. 13, 33.
—— xvi. 20.
1 Cor. i. 3.
—— vii. 15.
—— xiv. 30, see P (hold one's)
——— 33.
—— xvi. 11.
2 Cor. i. 2.
—— xiii. 11, and see P (live in)
Gal. i. 3.
—— v. 22.
—— vi. 16.
Eph. i. 2.
—— ii. 14, 15, 17.
—— iv. 3.
—— vi. 15, 23.
Phil. i. 2.
—— iv. 7 (a).
——— 9.
Col. i. 2.
——— 20, see P (make)
—— iii. 15.
1 Thes. i. 1.
—— v. 3, 23.
2 Thes. i. 2.
—— iii. 16.
—— v. 13, see P (be at)
1 Tim. i. 2.
2 Tim. i. 2.
—— ii. 22.
Tit. i. 4.
Philem. 3.
Heb. vii. 2.
—— xi. 31.
—— xii. 14.
—— xiii. 20.
Jas. ii. 16.
—— iii. 18 twice.
1 Pet. i. 2.
—— iii. 11.
—— v. 14.
2 Pet. i. 2.
—— iii. 14.
2 John 3.
3 John 14.
Jude 2.
Rev. i. 4.
—— vi. 4.

PEACE (BE AT)

εἰρηνεύω, to live in peace, to keep peace.

2 Thes. v. 13.

PEACE (HAVE)

Mark ix. 50.

PEACE (LIVE IN)

2 Cor. xiii. 11.

PEACE (HOLD ONE'S)

1. σιωπάω, to be silent, still, to keep silence, to keep secret; *also*, when silent not to speak.

2. σιγάω, to be silent or still. When speaking to cease to speak, (from σίζω, to say hush!)

3. ἡσυχάζω, to be at rest, be quiet or tranquil, rest *from further cavil or discussion*.

4. φιμόω, to muzzle. *Here Pass.*, to be muzzled, have the mouth stopped.

1. Matt. xx. 31.
1. —— xxvi. 63.
4. Mark i. 25.
1. —— iii. 4.
1. —— ix. 34.
1. —— x. 48.
1. —— xiv. 61.
3. Luke xiv. 4.

1. Luke xviii. 39 (No. 2, L T Tr A.)
1. —— xix. 40.
2. —— xx. 26.
3. Acts xi. 18.
2. —— xii. 17.
2. —— xv. 13.
1. —— xviii. 9.

2. 1 Cor. xiv. 30.

PEACE (MAKE)

εἰρηνοποιέω, to make peace, make reconciliation, (*non occ.*)

Col. i. 20.

PEACE.

σιωπάω, *see* "PEACE (HOLD ONE'S)," *No.* 1. *Here, imperative.*

Mark iv. 39.

PEACEABLE.

1. εἰρηνικός, relating to peace, peaceful, pacific, disposed to peace; *from the Heb.*, healthful, wholesome, (*non occ.*)

2. ἡσύχιος, quiet, tranquil, (*occ.* 1 Pet. iii. 4.)

2. 1 Tim. ii. 2. | 1. Heb. xii. 11.
1. Jas. iii. 17.

PEACEABLY (LIVE)

εἰρηνεύω, to live in peace, keep peace.

Rom. xii. 18.

PEACEMAKER (S.)

εἰρηνοποιός, a maker of peace, a peacemaker, (*non occ.*)

Matt. v. 9.

PEARL (-S.)

μαργαρίτης, a pearl.

Matt. vii. 6.
—— xiii. 45, 46.
1 Tim. ii. 9.

Rev. xvii. 4.
—— xviii. 12, 16.
—— xxi. 21 twice.

PECULIAR.

1. περιούσιος, what is over and above, property laid up. *Here, "a people* [*as*] an acquisition."

2. { εἰς, unto, for,
   { περιποίησις, acquisition.

1. Tit. ii. 14.
2. 1 Pet. ii. 9, marg. *purchased.*

PEDIGREE.

Heb. vii. 6, see "DESCENT."

PEN.

κάλαμος, a reed, *cut for various purposes; among others, for writing; Lat.,* calamus.

3 John 13.

PENNY.

δηνάριον, *a Greek word adapted from the Lat.,* denarius, *a Roman coin, equal to* 10 *asses, and afterwards to* 12 *and even* 16. *Reckoned as the same value as the Greek* δραχμή, *and equivalent to about* 9¾d.

Matt. xviii. 28.
—— xx. 2, 9, 10, 13.
—— xxii. 19.
Mark xii. 15.
—— xiv. 5.
Luke vii. 41.
—— x. 35.
—— xx. 24.
John xii. 5.
Rev. vi. 6 twice.

PENNYWORTH.

δηνάριον, *see above. Here, Gen. pl.,* of a denarius.

Mark vi. 37. | John vi. 7.

PENTECOST.

πεντηκοστή, a fiftieth *part.* The Feast of Pentecost, *so called because celebrated on* the fiftieth *day,* counting from the second day of the Feast of the Passover, (*non occ.*)

Acts ii. 1. | Acts xx. 16.
1 Cor. xvi. 8.

PENURY.

ὑστέρημα, that which is wanting, want, need, poverty.

Luke xxi. 4.

PEOPLE (-s.)

1. λαός, a people, the mass of any people, people collectively, *e.g.* the people of God, the people at large as a ruling power, (*opp. to No.* 3, *which is a community of free citizens*). * *plural.*

2. ὄχλος, a crowd, a throng, a confused multitude, (*opp. to No.* 3, which is a regular assembly) multitude.

3. δῆμος, the people as a municipality, free citizens enjoying a popular constitution.

4. ἔθνος, a people *or* race belonging and living together; *hence,* a nation, a people living under common institutions.

1. Matt. i. 21.
1. —— ii. 4, 6.
1. —— iv. 16, 23.
— ——— 24, see Sick.
2. —— vii. 28.
2. —— ix. 23, 25.
1. ——— 35 (*om.* ἐν τῷ λαῷ, *among the people,* G L T Tr A.)
2. —— xii. 23, 46.
1. —— xiii. 15.
2. —— xiv. 13.
1. —— xv. 8.
1. —— xxi. 23.
2. ——— 26.
1. —— xxvi. 3, 5, 47.
1. —— xxvii. 1.
2. ——— 15.
1. ——— 25, 64.
2. Mark v. 21, 24.
2. —— vi. 33 (εἶδον αὐτοὺς ὑπάγοντας, καὶ ἔγνωσαν πολλοί, *many saw them departing and knew them,* instead of εἶδον αὐτοὺς ὑπάγοντας οἱ ὄχλοι καὶ ἐπέγνωσαν αὐτὸν πολλοί, *the people saw him departing and many knew him,* G L T Tr A ℵ.)
2. ——— 34, 45.
1. —— vii. 6.
2. ——— 14, 17.
2. —— viii. 6 twice, 34.
2. —— ix. 15, 25.
2. —— x. 1.
— ——— 46, see P (number of)
2. —— xi. 18.
1. ——— 32.
2. —— xii. 12, 37, 41.
1. —— xiv. 2.
2. —— xv. 11, 15.
1. Luke i. 10, 17, 21, 68, [77.
1. —— ii. 10.
1*. ——— 31*.
1. ——— 32.
2. —— iii. 10.
1. ——— 15, 18, 21.
2. —— v. 1, 3.
1. —— vi. 17.
1. —— vii. 1.
2. ——— 9, 11, 12, 24.
1. ——— 29.
2. —— viii. 4, 40, 42.
1. ——— 47.
2. —— ix. 11.
1. Luke ix. 13.
2. ——— 18, 37.
2. —— xi. 14, 29.
2. —— xii. 1, 54.
2. —— xiii. 14, 17.
1. —— xviii. 43.
1. —— xix. 47, 48.
1. —— xx. 1, 6, 9, 19, 26, 45.
1. —— xxi. 23, 38.
1. —— xxii. 2, 66.
2. —— xxiii. 4.
1. ——— 5, 13, 14, 27, 35.
2. ——— 48.
1. —— xxiv. 19.
2. John vi. 22, 24.
2. —— vii. 12 twice, 20, 31, 32, 40, 43, 49.
1. —— viii. 2 (*ap.*)
2. —— xi. 42.
1. ——— 50.
2. —— xii. 9, 12, 17, 18, 29, 34.
1. —— xviii. 14.
1. Acts ii. 47.
1. —— iii. 9, 11, 12, 23.
1. —— iv. 1, 2, 8, 10, 17, 21.
1*. ——— 25, 27.
1. —— v. 12, 13, 20, 25, 26, 34, 37.
1. —— vi. 8, 12.
1. —— vii. 17, 34.
2. —— viii. 6.
4. ——— 9.
1. —— x. 2, 41, 42.
2. —— xi. 24, 26.
1. —— xii. 4, 11.
3. ——— 22.
1. —— xiii. 15, 17 twice, 24, 31.
2. —— xiv. 11, 13, 14, 18, 19.
1. —— xv. 14.
3. —— xvii. 5.
2. ——— 8, 13.
1. —— xviii. 10.
1. —— xix. 4.
2. ——— 26.
3. ——— 30, 33.
2. ——— 35.
2. —— xxi. 27.
1. ——— 28, 30.
2. ——— 35.
1. ——— 36, 39, 40.
1. —— xxiii. 5.
2. —— xxiv. 12, and see P (raise up the)

1. Acts xxvi. 17, 23.
1. —— xxviii. 17, 26, 27.
1. Rom. ix. 25 twice, 26.
4. —— x. 19.
1. ——— 21.
1. —— xi. 1, 2.
1. —— xv. 10.
1. ——— 11.
1. 1 Cor. x. 7.
1. —— xiv. 21.
1. 2 Cor. vi. 16.
1. Tit. ii. 14.
1. Heb. ii. 17.
1. —— iv. 9.
1. —— v. 3.
1. —— vii. 5, 11. [(the)
1. ——— 27, and see P's
1. Heb. viii. 10.
1. —— ix. 7, 19 twice.
1. —— x. 30.
1. —— xi. 25.
1. —— xiii. 12.
1. 1 Pet. ii. 9, 10 twice.
1. 2 Pet. ii. 1.
1. Jude 5.
1. Rev. v. 9.
1*.—— vii. 9.
1. —— x. 11.
1*.—— xi. 9.
1. —— xiv. 6.
1. —— xvii. 15.
1. —— xviii. 4.
2. —— xix. 1.
1*.—— xxi. 3.

PEOPLE (NUMBER OF)

2. Mark x. 46.

PEOPLE (RAISE UP THE)

ἐπισύστασις, a concourse, a tumultuous gathering, ποιέω, to make, ὄχλου, *see No.* 2, *above*,	causing a concourse of a multitude.

Acts xxiv. 12 (*ἐπίστασις, a stopping,* instead of *ἐπισύστασις, a concourse,* G∼L T Tr A ℵ.)

PEOPLE'S (THE)

τῶν, of the [*sins*], *i.e.* over those,
τοῦ, of the
λαοῦ, people, (*see No.* 1.)

Heb. vii. 27.

PERADVENTURE.

τάχα, quickly, speedily; *then,* readily, lightly; *hence,* perhaps, peradventure, (*occ.* Philem. 15.)

Rom. v. 7.

PERADVENTURE.

μήποτε, not even, never, in no supposable case. *As a conj.*, that not ever, lest ever, lest at some time or other.

2 Tim. ii. 25.

PERCEIVE (-ED, -EST, -ING.)

1. γινώσκω, to perceive, observe, obtain a knowledge of, or insight into, to know and be influenced by the personal relation between the person knowing and the object known, to have a knowledge which produces some emotion and affection of the mind.

2. ἐπιγινώσκω, (*No.* 1, *with* ἐπί, upon, *prefixed*) to know thereupon, *i.e.* by looking on the object; *hence,* to know fully, to gain and receive a full knowledge of, become fully acquainted with.

3. θεωρέω, to be a spectator of, to look on *or* at, behold, *denoting* the intention of mind with which one regards or contemplates an object, *expressing the desire of seeing;* to studiously and attentively consider, to see with regard and admiration, look diligently into, *and all this not being the mere act of an instant, but for a lengthened period.*

4. εἶδον, to see, *referring to the mind of him who sees.* εἶδον *is the Aor.* 2 *of* (*No.* 5) *in the sense of* I saw, (*trans.*) *implying, not* the mere act of seeing, (*like* βλέπω, *No.* 11) but the actual perception of some object.

5. ὁράω, to see, perceive with the eyes, to look at, *differing, like No.* 4, *from* βλέπω, (*No.* 11) *as implying* the actual perception of some object *or* thing seen and presented to the eye. *Also differing from No.* 4, in that it regards the object seen, (*while No.* 4 *must be referred to the subject, i.e. the mind of him who sees.*)

6. οἶδα, (2*nd perf. of* εἴδω, *No.* 4) to have seen, perceived, *or* apprehended; *hence,* it takes the *present signification,* to know, *and the pluperfect becomes an imperfect.*

7. νοέω, to see, perceive, observe, understand, comprehend, to have in mind, think of; *it denotes* conscious action of the mind, the mental correlative of sensational perception, the sensation accompanied with an act of the understanding following as an effect of *No.* 4; *hence,* to think, reflect, discern.

8. κατανοέω, (*No.* 7, *with* κατά, down, *prefixed*) to see *or* discern distinctly, perceive clearly, mind accurately.

9. *καταλαμβάνω*, to take, to receive *with the idea of eagerness*, to lay hold of, seize; *then*, to seize *with the mind, and mid., as here*, to comprehend for one's self, perceive, to find.

10. *αἰσθάνομαι*, to perceive with the external *senses*, apprehend *or* notice by the senses, (*non occ.*)

11. *βλέπω*, to use the eyes, *sometimes with desire, but not necessarily to see the thing looked at*, the act of seeing without any thought of the object presented to the sight, (*thus, βλέμμα denotes* the eye, *while ὅραμα* (from *No.* 5) *denotes* the vision that is seen by the eye, *ὅρασις*, the species *or* form of the thing that falls upon the eye, *and ὅρατον*, that which is submitted to the sight, *or* is visible.)

12. *εὑρίσκω*, to find *by perception, search, or inquiry*, find out, discover.

4. Matt. xiii. 14.
2. Mark ii. 8 part.
4. —— iv. 12.
7. —— vii. 18.
7. —— viii. 17. [Tr ℵ.)
6. —— xii. 28 (No. 4, L T
1. —— xvi. 8 part.
1. —— xxi. 45.
1. —— xxii. 18.
2. Luke i. 22.
2. —— v. 22 part.
8. —— vi. 41.
1. —— viii. 46.
10. —— ix. 45.
4. ——— 47.
1. —— xx. 19.
8. Luke xx. 23.
3. John iv. 19.
1. —— vi. 15 part.
3. —— xii. 19.
9. Acts iv. 13.
5. —— viii. 23.
9. —— x. 34.
4. —— xiv. 9.
3. —— xvii. 22.
1. —— xxiii. 6 part.
12. ——— 29.
3. —— xxvii. 10.
4. —— xxviii. 26.
11. 2 Cor. vii. 8.
1. Gal. ii. 9.
1. 1 John iii. 16.

PERDITION.

ἀπώλεια, loss, destruction, ruin; the end pronounced upon all who, having heard the summons to repentance and faith in Christ, have persisted in impenitence. The loss of all that such ever had, or might have had for ever; the destruction of such, in body, soul, and spirit; an utter and final ruin, which will not be reversed.

John xvii. 12.
Phil. i. 28.
2 Thes. ii. 3.
1 Tim. vi. 9.
Heb. x. 39.
2 Pet. iii. 7.
Rev. xvii. 8, 11.

PERFECT. [adj.]

(*For various combinations with other words, see below.*)

1. *τέλειος*, what has reached its end, term, *or* limit; *hence*, complete perfect, full, wanting nothing, *with special reference to the end for which it was intended.*

2. *ἀκριβῶς*, accurately, precisely, exactly, assiduously.

3. *ἄρτιος*, complete in all parts and proportions, *with special reference to the adaptation of the parts, and special aptitude for any given uses*, (*non occ.*)

4. *πληρόω*, to make full, fill up. *Here, pass. part.*, fulfilled, performed, accomplished.

1. Matt. v. 48 twice.
1. —— xix. 21.
2. Luke i. 3, and see Understanding.
2. —— xxiv. 22.
— Acts iii. 16, see Soundness.
1. Rom. xii. 2.
1. Eph. iv. 13.
1. Phil. iii. 15.
1. Col. i. 28.
1. Col. iv. 12.
2. 1 Thes. v. 2.
3. 2 Tim. iii. 17.
1. Heb. v. 14, marg. (text, *of full age.*)
1. —— ix. 11.
1. Jas. i. 4 twice, 17, 25.
1. —— iii. 2.
1. 1 John iv. 18.
4. Rev. iii. 2 part.

PERFECT (BE)

1. *τελειόω*, to complete, make perfect, *so as* to be full, wanting in nothing, to bring to a full end, consummate.

2. *καταρτίζω*, to make fully ready, put in full order, perfectly equip, prepare fully.

2. Luke vi. 40 marg. *be perfected.*
1. Phil. iii. 12.
2. 2 Cor. xiii. 11.

PERFECT (MAKE)

1. *τελειόω*, *see No.* 1, *above.*

2. *καταρτίζω*, *see No.* 2, *above.*

3. *ἐπιτελέω*, to bring through to an end.

1. John xvii. 23.
1. 2 Cor. xii. 9 (*τελέω, to make complete*, L T Tr A ℵ.)
3. Gal. iii. 3.
1. Heb. ii. 10.
1. —— v. 9.
1. —— vii. 19.
1. Heb. ix. 9.
1. —— x. 1.
1. —— xi. 40.
1. —— xii. 23.
2. —— xiii. 21.
1. Jas. ii. 22.
2. 1 Pet. v. 10.
1. 1 John iv. 17, 18.

PERFECT MANNER.

ἀκρίβεια, exactness, preciseness, extreme accuracy.

Act xxii. 3.

PERFECT (THAT WHICH IS)

τὸ, the, *τέλειος*, *see* "PERFECT," *No.* 1, } that which is complete *or* perfect.

1 Cor. xiii. 10.

PERFECT (THEY THAT ARE)

{ οἱ, the, those, τέλειος, *see* "PERFECT," *No.* 1, } the full-grown, the perfect.

1 Cor. ii. 6.

PERFECT (-ED, -ING.) [verb.]

1. τελειόω, *see* "P (BE)," *No.* 1.
2. καταρτίζω, *see* "P (BE)," *No.* 2.
3. ἐξαρτίζω, to equip out fully, perfectly prepared and fitted out.
4. ἐπιτελέω, to bring to a full end.

2. Matt. xxi. 16.
1. Luke xiii. 32.
4. 2 Cor. vii. 1.
— Eph. iv. 12, see Perfecting.
2. 1 Thes. iii. 10.
3. 2 Tim. iii. 17 marg. (text, *thoroughly furnished.*
1. Heb. x. 14.
1. 1 John ii. 5.
1. —— iv. 12.

PERFECTED (*be*) [margin.]

Luke vi. 40, see "PERFECT (BE)"

PERFECTION.

1. καταρτισις, the being made fully ready, the being perfectly equipped and prepared, (*non occ.*)
2. τελειότης, completeness, perfectness, *spoken of that which has reached its full and intended end,* (*occ.* Col. iii. 14.)
3. τελείωσις, completion, perfection, *spoken of that which has reached its full and intended end,* (*occ.* Luke i. 45.)
4. ἕξις, habitude, *as the result of long practice.*

1. 2 Cor. xiii. 9.
4. Heb. v. 14, marg. (text, use.)
2. Heb. vi. 1.
3. —— vii. 11.

PERFECTION (BRING FRUIT TO)

τελεσφορέω, to bring to perfection *or* maturity; *of fruit,* to ripen.

Luke viii. 14.

PERFECTING.

καταρτισμός, the act of making fully ready, the act of perfectly equipping and fully preparing, (*non occ.*)

Eph. iv. 12.

PERFECTLY.

ἀκρίβῶς, accurately, precisely, exactly, assiduously.

Matt. xiv. 36, see Whole.
Acts xviii. 26.
Acts xxiii. 15, 20.
1 Cor. i. 10, see Joined.
1 Thes. v. 2.

PERFECTNESS

τελειότης, completeness, *spoken of that which has reached its full and intended end.*

Col. iii. 14.

PERFORM (-ED.)

1. τελέω, to bring about, complete, fulfil, accomplish, *and generally,* to perform, do, finish.
2. ἐπιτελέω, (*No.* 1, *with* ἐπί, upon, *prefixed*) to bring through to an end.
3. ποιέω, to make, *i.e.* form, produce, cause; to do, *i.e. do repeatedly,* perform.
4. ἀποδίδωμι, to give away from *one's self, i.e.* deliver over; *spoken of obligation of any kind,* to give in full, render, pay over *or* off.
5. κατεργάζομαι, to work out, effect, produce.

4. Matt. v. 33.
3. Luke i. 72.
1. —— ii. 39.
3. Rom. iv. 21.
5. Rom. vii. 18.
2. —— xv. 28 part.
2. 2 Cor. viii. 11.
2. Phil. i. 6, marg. *finish.*

PERFORMED (BE)

γίνομαι, to begin to be, become, come to pass.

Luke i. 20.

PERFORMANCE.

1. ἐπιτελέω, to bring through to an end. *Here, inf.*
2. τελείωσις, completion, perfection; *of a prophecy,* fulfilment, (*occ.* Heb. vii. 11.)

2. Luke i. 45. | 1. 2 Cor. viii. 11.

PERHAPS.

1. πως, anyhow, in any way, in some way or other.
2. τάχα, quickly, speedily; readily, lightly; and *hence,* peradventure, perhaps, (*occ.* Rom. v. 7.)

1. 2 Cor. ii. 7. | 2. Philem. 15.

PERHAPS (IF)

{ εἰ, if, ἄρα, therefore, then, after all, } if perhaps, (*marking a result about which some uncertainty is felt.*)

Acts viii. 22.

PERHAPS (LEST)

μήπως, that in no way, lest in any way.

2 Cor. ii. 7.

PERIL (-S.)

κίνδυνος, danger, peril; risk, hazard, (*perhaps the orig. sense was* the risk of the dice-box, *from* κινέω, to agitate), (*non occ.*)

Rom. viii. 35. | 2 Cor. xi. 26 8 times.

PERILOUS.

χαλεπός, heavy, difficult, hard to bear; *connected with toil and suffering;* dangerous, (*occ.* Matt. viii. 28.)

2 Tim. iii. 1.

PERISH (-ED, -ETH.)

1. ἀπόλλυμι, to destroy, cause to perish. *Here, mid.*, (*which is peculiar to N.T. Greek*) *used of the eternal doom of the sinner,* (*chiefly by Paul and John*) to be utterly and finally ruined and destroyed, to be lost, brought to nought, put to death.

2. { εἴη, might it be, εἰς, for, ἀπώλειαν, destruction. }

3. ἀποθνήσκω, to die away, *used of the natural end of life, esp., as the wages of sin.*

4. ἀφανίζω, to cause to disappear, put out of sight. *Here, pass.*, to disappear, vanish.

5. διαφθείρω, to corrupt throughout, destroy. *Here, pass.*, to decay wholly, perish.

6. { εἰς, unto, for, φθορά, a spoiling, corruption, destruction, } for corruption, [*in the using up.*]

1. Matt. v. 29, 30.
1. —— viii. 25.
3, —— 32.
1. —— ix. 17.
1. —— xviii. 14.
1. —— xxvi. 52 (No. 3, G ~)
1. Mark iv. 38.
1. Luke v. 37.
1. —— viii. 24.
1. —— xi. 51.
1. —— xiii. 3, 5, 33.
1. —— xv. 17.
1. —— xxi. 18.
1. John iii. 15, 16 (ap.)
1. —— vi. 27.
1. —— x. 28.
1. —— xi. 50.
1. Acts v. 37.
2. —— viii. 20.
4. —— xiii. 41.
1. Rom. ii. 12.
1. 1 Cor. i. 18.
1. —— viii. 11.
1. —— xv. 18.
1. 2 Cor. ii. 15.
5. —— iv. 16.
6. Col. ii. 22.
1. 2 Thes. ii. 10.
1. Heb. i. 11.
— —— xi. 31, see P with.
1. Jas. i. 11.
1. 1 Pet. i. 7.
— 2 Pet. ii. 12, see P utterly.
1. —— iii. 6, 9.
1. Jude 11.

PERISH (UTTERLY)

καταφείρω, (*No.* 5, *with* κατά, down, *prefixed, instead of* διά, through) to spoil *or* corrupt utterly. *Here, pass.*, to perish completely, (*occ.* 2 Tim. iii. 8.)

2 Pet. ii. 12 (*καὶ φθείρω, even perish,* L T Tr A ℵ.)

PERISH WITH.

συναπόλλυμι, (*No.* 1, *with* σύν, together *or* in conjunction with, *prefixed*) *pass.*, to be destroyed with *any one*, to perish with *others*, (*non occ.*)

Heb. x. 31.

PERJURED PERSON.

ἐπίορκος, taking oath upon oath; *as this is generally a sign of false swearing, so the word comes to have this meaning, and as subst., denotes* a perjured person, one who has taken oath upon oath *lightly, and therefore breaking all,* (*non occ.*)

1 Tim. i. 10.

PERMISSION.

συγγνώμη, a knowing and thinking with *another; hence,* accordance; *then,* concession, (*non occ.*)

1 Cor. vii. 6.

PERMIT.

ἐπιτρέπω, to turn upon, direct upon; to give *or* entrust to *another; then,* give up, yield, permit, suffer.

Acts xxvi. 1.
1 Cor. xiv. 34.
1 Cor. xvi. 7.
Heb. vi. 3.

PERNICIOUS WAY.

ἀπώλεια, destruction, loss. *Here, Gen.*, of destruction, *i.e.* destructive.

2 Pet. ii. 2 (ἀσελγεία, *wanton*, AVm, G L T Tr A ℵ), marg. *lascivious way*.

PERPLEXED (BE)

1. ἀπορέομαι, to be without resource, to know not what to do.
2. διαπορέω, to be throughout in perplexity, be in much doubt, hesitate greatly. * *inf. pass.*

2. Luke ix. 7.
— — xxiv. P (be much)
1. 2 Cor. iv. 8.
1. Gal. iv. 20, marg. (text, *stand in doubt.*)

PERPLEXED (BE MUCH)

2*. Luke xxiv. 4 (No. 1, L T Tr A ℵ.)

PERPLEXITY.

ἀπορία, the state of one who has no way *or* resource, and who therefore knows not what to do, (*non occ.*)

Luke xxi. 25.

PERSECUTE (-ED, -EST, -ING.)

1. διώκω, to cause to flee; *hence, gen.*, to pursue after, *as flying enemies; then*, to pursue with malignity; *hence*, to persecute
2. ἐκδιώκω, (*No.* 1, *with* ἐκ, out of, *prefixed*) to pursue out, drive out of *or* from *a place*, (*non occ.*)

1. Matt. v. 10, 11, 12, 44.
1. — x. 23.
1. — xxiii. 34.
2. Luke xi. 49.
1. — xxi. 12.
1. John v. 16.
1. — xv. 20 twice.
1. Acts vii. 52.
1. — ix. 4, 5.
1. — xxii. 4, 7, 8.
1. Acts xxvi. 11, 14, 15.
1. Rom. xii. 14.
1. 1 Cor. iv. 12.
1. — xv. 9.
1. 2 Cor. iv. 9.
1. Gal. i. 13, 23.
1. — iv. 29.
1. Phil. iii. 6.
2. 1 Thes. ii. 15, marg. *chase out*.
1. Rev. xii. 13.

PERSECUTION.

1. διωγμός, pursuit, *as of enemies; hence*, persecution.
2. θλῖψις, pressure, compression. *In N.T., of evils, etc.*, trouble, distress, calamity.

1. Matt. xiii. 21.
1. Mark iv. 17.
1. — x. 30.
1. Acts viii. 1.
2. — xi. 19.
1. — xiii. 50.
1. Rom. viii. 35.
1. 2 Cor. xii. 10.
— Gal. v. 11, } see P
— — vi. 12, } (suffer)
1. 2 Thes. i. 4.
1. 2 Tim. iii. 11 twice.
— 2 Tim. iii. 12, see P (suffer)

PERSECUTION (SUFFER)

διώκω, *see* "PERSECUTE," *No.* 1.

Gal. v. 11. | Gal. vi. 12.
2 Tim. iii. 12.

PERSECUTOR.

διώκτης, a pursuer; *hence*, a persecutor, (*non occ.*)

1 Tim. i. 13.

PERSEVERANCE.

προσκαρτέρησις, strongness *or* firmness towards *anything*, endurance *or* perseverance in *or* with *anything*, (*non occ.*)

Eph. vi. 18.

PERSIS.

Περσίς, Persis, *a proper name of a female Christian.*

Rom. xvi. 12 (ap.)

PERSON (-S.)

(*For various combinations with other words, see below.*)

1. πρόσωπον, *the part* towards the eye, the part of anything which is presented to the eye, the front *of anything*, the face; *also*, a mask; *hence*, a dramatic part, character, person.
2. ὑπόστασις, what is set *or* stands under, a substructure, what really exists under *or* out of sight, the essence of a matter in contrast to its appearance. [Hence, Christ, as the λόγος, is the manifestation of Deity, the means by which we recognise the glory of God, and the manifestation of the Divine Essence, Heb. i. 3, *and see under* "WORD," *No.* 1.]

1. Matt. xxii. 16.
1. Mark xii. 14.
1. Luke xx. 21.
— Acts x. 34, see P (respecter of)
— Rom. ii. 11, see P (respect of)
1. 2 Cor. i. 11.
1. — ii. 10, marg. *sight*.
1. Gal. ii. 6.
— Eph. vi. 9, } see P (re-
— Col. iii. 25, } spect of)
2. Heb. i. 3.
— Jas. ii. 1, see P (respect of)
— — 9, see P (have respect to)
— 1 Pet. i. 17, see P (without respect of)
— Jude 16, see P (man's)

PERSONS (HAVE RESPECT TO)

προσωποληπτέω, to accept the person *of any one*, *i.e.* to show partiality, (*non occ.*)

Jas. ii. 9.

PERSON (MAN'S)

πρόσωπον, *see* "PERSON," *No.* 1.

Jude 16.

PERSONS (RESPECT OF)

προσωποληψία, acceptance of persons, *i.e.* partiality, (*non occ.*)

Rom. ii. 11. | Col. iii. 25.
Eph. vi. 9. | Jas. ii. 1.

PERSONS (RESPECTER OF)

προσωπολήπτης, an acceptor of persons, one who is partial, (*non occ.*)

Acts x. 34.

PERSONS (WITHOUT RESPECT OF)

ἀπροσωπολήπτως, without acceptance of persons, *i.e.* impartially, (*non occ.*)

1 Pet. i. 17.

See also, DEVOUT, PERJURED, PROFANE, WHAT, WICKED.

PERSUADE (-ED, -EST, -ETH, -ING.)

1. πείθω, (a) to persuade, win by words, influence, to speak with winning words. (b) *Mid. or pass.*, to suffer one's self to be persuaded *or* convinced, to be persuaded in favour of any one, be convinced of, to yield assent to, trust him, obey him.

2. ἀναπείθω, (*No.* 1, *with* ἀνα, back again, *prefixed*) to persuade over, *in a bad sense*, to seduce.

1a. Matt. xxvii. 20.
1a. —— xxviii. 14.
1a. Acts xiii. 43.
1a. —— xiv. 19.
1a. —— xviii. 4.
2. —— 13.
1a. Acts xix. 8, 26.
1a. —— xxvi. 28.
1a. —— xxviii. 23.
1a. —— 2 Cor. v. 11.
1a. Gal. i. 10.
1a. 1 John iii. 19, marg. (*text, assure.*)

PERSUADED (BE)

1b. Luke xvi. 31.
1b. —— xx. 6.
1b. Acts xxi. 14 part.
1b. —— xxvi. 26.
1b. Rom. viii. 38.
1b. —— xiv. 14.
1b. Rom. xv. 14.
1b. 2 Tim. i. 5, 12.
1b. Heb. vi. 9.
1b. —— xi. 13 (*om.* καὶ πεισθέντες, *and were persuaded of them*, G L T Tr A ℵ.)

PERSUADE FULLY.

πληροφορέω, to bear *or* bring fully; *hence*, to give full assurance. *Here, pass.*, to be fully assured.

Rom. iv. 21.
—— xiv. 5, marg. *be fully assured.*

PERSUASIBLE. [margin.]

1 Cor. ii. 4, see "ENTICING."

PERSUASION.

πεισμονή, the being easily persuaded, credulity, (*non occ.*)

Gal. v. 8.

PERTAIN TO.

(*For various combinations, see below.*)

μετέχω, to have in association with *another*, to partake of, share in, have part in.

1 Cor. vi. 3, see Life. | Heb. vii. 13.

PERTAIN TO (THOSE THINGS WHICH)

{ τὰ, the *things*, / πρός, towards, } the things pertaining to.

Rom. xv. 17.

PERTAIN UNTO (THINGS THAT)

{ τὰ, / πρός, } *see above.*

Heb. ii. 17. | Heb. v. 1.

PERTAINING TO (THE THINGS)

{ τὰ, the *things*, / περί, around, about, } the things concerning.

Acts i. 3.

PERVERSE.

διαστρέφω, to turn *or* twist throughout, *i.e.* distort, turn away, pervert. *Here, pass. part.*, perverted.

Matt. xvii. 17. | Acts xx. 30.
Luke ix. 41. | Phil. ii. 15.
1 Tim. vi. 5, see Disputings.

PERVERT (-ETH, -ING.)

1. διαστρέφω, *see* "PERVERSE."

2. ἀποστρέφω, to turn away from, to turn aside from.

3. *μεταστέφω*, to turn about; to turn into *something else*, to change.

1. Luke xxiii. 2.
2. —— 14.
1. Acts xiii. 10.
3. Gal. i. 7.

PESTILENCE (-s.)

λοιμός, pestilence, plague, any deadly infectious disorder, (*occ.* Acts xxiv. 5.)

Matt. xxiv. 7 (*om.* καὶ λοιμοί, *and pestilences*, L T Tr A ℵ)
Luke xxi. 11.

PESTILENT FELLOW.

λοιμός, *see above.* Used also of persons, as we say *in Eng.*, a plague, a pest.

Acts xxiv. 5.

PETER.

1. Πέτρος, a stone, a rolling stone, *in one place to-day and another to-morrow.*

In N.T. the proper name of Peter, (*Aram.*, כֵּיפָא, Κηφᾶς, Cephas) the surname of Simon, son of Jonas, and brother of Andrew, a fisherman of Bethsaida and apostle of Christ.

[*See* under "ROCK," for the difference between *πέτρος* and *πέτρα.*]

2. ἐκεῖνος, that, that one there, he, (*emphatic.*)

No. 1, in all passages, except—

1. Matt. xvii. 26 (*ap.*)
1. Luke xxii. 62 (*om.* G T Tr A[b] ℵ.)
1. —— xxiv. 12 (*ap.*)
2. John xiii. 6 [2nd] (*om.* L T Tr[b] A ℵ.)
1. Acts x. 23 (*ἀναστας, he rose up and*, G L T Tr A ℵ.)
1. Acts xii. 13 (*αὐτός, he himself*, G L T Tr A ℵ.)
1. Gal. i. 18 (Κηφᾶς G∾L T Tr A ℵ.)
1. Gal. ii. 11, } (Κηφᾶς, G∾L T Tr A ℵ.)
1. —— 14, }

PETITION (-s.)

αἴτημα, thing asked for, object sought.

1 John v. 15.

PHARISEE (-s.)

φαρισαῖος, a Pharisee, one of the sect of the Pharisees.

[In the time of our Saviour, the principal and most numerous of the Jewish sects; *Heb.*, פְּרוּשִׁים, *Perushim*, the separated. The fundamental principle (common to them with the "orthodox" modern Jews) is, that there was and is an *oral law* to complete and explain the written law. With this fatal error (like the Romish "*Tradition*") we cannot wonder at all their other errors. (1) They attributed all things to fate, but did not wholly exclude human free-will. (2) They held that every soul was imperishable, and consequently divided the eternal state, after resurrection, into happiness for the good, and torment for the wicked.]

In all passages, except—

Matt. xii. 38 (*om.* L.)
—— xxiii. 14 (*ap.*)
Mark ii. 16 (*τῶν φαρισαιῶν, of the Pharisees*, instead of καὶ οἱ φ. *and the Ph.* L[m] T Tr ℵ.)
—— 18 (οἱ φ. *the Pharisees*, instead of οἱ τῶν φ. *of the Ph*, G L T Tr A ℵ.)
Luke xi. 44 (*ap.*)
John viii. 3 (*ap.*)
Acts xxiii. 6 [3rd] (plural, G ∾ L T Tr A ℵ.)

PHILIP.

φίλιππος, Philip, *the proper name of several persons, viz.* one of the Twelve, John i. 44-47; the Evangelist,* Acts vi. 5; the Tetrarch of Batanea, etc., Luke iii. 1; Philip† Herod, Matt. xiv. 3; Mark vi. 17; and Luke iii. 19.

In all passages, except—

† Matt. xiv. 3 (*om.* T[b] A.)
† Luke iii. 19 (*om.* G ∾ L T Tr A ℵ.)
* Acts viii. 37 (*ap.*)

PHILOSOPHER (-s.)

φιλοσοφός, loving wisdom; *then, as subst.*, a philosopher, *i.e.* an inquirer after wisdom and knowledge, (*non occ.*)

Acts xvii. 18.

PHILOSOPHY.

φιλοσοφία, love of wisdom; *then, Eng.*, philosophy, (*non occ.*)

Col. ii. 8.

PHYLACTERY (-IES.)

φυλακτήριον, a watch post, guarded place; *then*, protection, safeguard; *hence*, an amulet, a prayer-fillet, *i.e.* a strip of parchment, on which were written various parts of the law, bound about the forehead or round the wrist, (*non occ.*)

Matt. xxiii. 5.

PHYSICIAN (-s.)

ἰατρός, a healer, (*from* ἰάομαι, to heal.)

Matt. ix. 12.
Mark ii. 17.
—— v. 26.
Luke iv. 23.
—— v. 31.
—— viii. 43.
Col. iv. 14.

PIECE (-s.)

1. ἐπίβλημα, anything put on, an addition; *hence*, a patch.

2. δραχμή, as much as one can hold in the hand, an Attic weight, a drachm, *about* 66 grs. avdp. A silver coin *worth* 6 obols, *i.e.* 9¾d.; *it nearly equalled the Roman* denarius, (*non occ.*)

3. μέρος, a part, part of a whole, piece of a whole.

1. Matt. ix. 16.
— —— xvii. 27, see Money
— —— xxvi. 6, 15, } see
— —— xxvii. 3, 5, 9, } Silver
1. Mark ii. 21, and see Fill.
— —— v. 4, see Break.
1. Luke v. 36 1st (*cutteth a piece off a new garment and putteth it*, inst. of, "*putteth a piece of a new garment*," T Tr A ℵ.)
1. Luke v. 36 2nd (om. G ~)
— —— xiv. 18, see Ground.
2. —— xv. 8, and see Silver
2. —— 9.
3. —— xxiv. 42.
— Acts xix. 19, see Silver.
— —— xxiii. 10, see Pull.
— —— xxvii. 44, see P (broken)

PIECES (BROKEN)

{ τι, certain *parts*,
{ τῶν, of the.

Acts xxvii. 44.

PIERCE (-ED, -ING.)

1. ἐκκεντέω, to pierce through, transfix, (*non occ.*)

2. διϊκνέομαι, to go *or* pass through, (*non occ.*)

3. νύσσω, to prick, to pierce, (*non occ.*)

— Luke ii. 35, see P through.
3. John xix. 34.
1. —— 37.
— 1 Tim. vi. 10, see P through.
2. Heb. iv. 12.
1. Rev. i. 7.

PIERCE THROUGH.

1. διέρχομαι, to come *or* go through, to pass through.
2. περιπείρω, to pierce about, *or* to pierce *so that the weapon is wholly* surrounded and covered, (*non occ.*)

1 Tim. vi. 10.

PIETY (*for one's*) [margin.]

Heb. v. 7, see "FEARETH."

PIETY (SHOW)

εὐσεβέω, to be pious, to act as in the fear of God, (*occ.* Acts xvii. 23.)

1 Tim. v. 4, marg. *kindness*.

PIGEON (-s.)

περιστερά, a dove *or* pigeon. [Two of these were the offerings of the poor, Lev. v. 7; xiv. 22.]

Luke ii. 24.

PILATE'S HOUSE. [margin.]

John xviii. 28, see "HALL OF JUDGMENT."

PILGRIM (-s.)

παρεπίδημος, a resident beside, a by-resident, a sojourner in a strange place, away from one's own people, (*occ.* 1 Pet. i. 1.)

Heb. xi. 13. | 1 Pet. ii. 11.

PILLAR (-s.)

στύλος, a column, pillar; *then, used of* any firm support, (*non occ.*)

Gal. ii. 9.
1 Tim. iii. 15.
Rev. iii. 12.
—— x. 1.

PILLOW.

προσκεφάλαιον, a cushion for the head, a pillow, (*non occ.*)

Mark iv. 38.

PINE AWAY.

ξηραίνω, to dry, make dry. *Here, pass.*, to be dried up, wither away.

Mark ix. 18.

PINNACLE.

πτερύγιον, a little wing, *used of* the feather of an arrow; *then, of any thing* like a wing running out to a point, a pinnacle, (*non occ.*)

Mark iv. 5. | Luke iv. 9.

PIPE. [noun.]

αὐλός, a pipe, *an instrument* blown with the mouth, *prob. like our flageolet*, (*non occ.*)

1 Cor. xiv. 7 1st.

PIPE (-ED.) [verb.]

αὐλέω, to play on the *αὐλός*, (*see above*); to pipe.

Matt. xi. 17. | 1 Cor. xiv. 7 2nd. | Luke vii. 32.

PIPER (-S.)

αὐλητής, a player on the *αὐλός*, (*see* "PIPE") a piper, a minstrel, (*occ.* Matt. ix. 23.)

Rev. xviii. 22.

PIT.

1. *φρέαρ*, a well, or pit *for water, dug in the earth*, (*thus dist. from πηγή*, a fountain.) *Then, used of any* pit *or* abyss, (*occ.* John iv. 11, 12.)

2. *βόθυνος*, a pit, a ditch; any hole *or* pit dug in the ground, (*occ.* Matt. xv. 14; Luke vi. 39.)

2. Matt. xii. 11.
1. Luke xiv. 5.
1. Rev. ix. 1, 2 1st (*ap.*)
1. —— 2 2nd & 3rd.
— Rev. ix. 11,
— — xi. 7,
— — xvii. 8,
— — xx. 1, 3, } see Bottomless

PITCH (-ED.) [verb.]

πήγνυμι, to fasten, make fast and firm, to fix *or* fasten together, construct, build; *of a tent*, to set up, pitch, (*non occ.*)

Heb. viii. 2.

PITCHER.

κεράμιον, an earthen vessel; a pot, a pitcher, (*non occ.*)

Mark xiv. 13. | Luke xxii. 10.

PITIFUL.

εὔσπλαγχνος, with good *or* healthy bowels; *then*, compassionate, having fellow-feeling, tender-hearted, (*occ.* Eph. iv. 32.)

1 Pet. iii. 8.

PITIFUL (VERY)

πολύσπλαγχνος, very compassionate, full of fellow-feeling, of great tender-heartedness.

Jas. v. 11 (*πολυεύσπλαγχνος*, more emphatic than *πολύσπλαγχνος*, G ∾)

PITY ON (HAVE)

ἐλεέω, *see* "MERCY ON (HAVE)"

Matt. xviii. 33. | Tit. iii. 4, see Man.

PLACE.

(*For various combinations, see below.*)

1. *τόπος*, a place, spot; *used either of* a particular place, place where one dwells, *or in a geographical or topographical sense*.

2. *ὀπή*, an opening, a hole; *e.g.* a fissure in the earth, *or* a well.

3. *περιοχή*, circumference, circuit; contents, *of a writing; hence*, the arguments or contents within certain limits, a section, chapter, or passage of a book, (*non occ.*)

4. *χωρίον*, a place, spot, country, region; *like Eng.*, place, *i.e.* a possession, of fields *or* farm.

1. Matt. xii. 43.
1. —— xiv. 13, 15, 35.
1. —— xxiv. 15.
4. —— xxvi. 36.
1. ——— 52.
1. —— xxvii. 33 twice.
1. —— xxviii. 6.
1. Mark i. 35, 45.
1. —— vi. 31, 32, 35.
4. —— xiv. 32.
1. —— xv. 22 twice.
1. —— xvi. 6.
1. Luke iv. 17, 37, 42.
1. —— ix. 10 (*ap.*), 12
1. —— x. 1, 32.
1. —— xi. 1, 24.
1. —— xiv. 9.
1. —— xvi. 28.
1. —— xix. 5.
1. —— xxii. 40.
1. —— xxiii. 33.
1. John iv. 20.
1. —— v. 13.
1. —— vi. 10, 23.
1. —— x. 40.
1. —— xi. 6, 30, 48.
1. —— xiv. 2, 3.
1. —— xviii. 2.
1. John xix. 13, 17, 20, 41.
1. —— xx. 7.
1. Acts i. 25.
1. —— iv. 31.
1. —— vi. 13, 14.
1. —— vii. 7, 33, 49.
3. —— viii. 32.
1. —— xii. 17.
1. —— xxi. 28 twice.
1. —— xxvii. 8, 41.
1. Rom. ix. 26.
1. —— xii. 19.
1. —— xv. 23.
1. 1 Cor. i. 2.
1. 2 Cor. ii. 14.
1. Eph. iv. 27.
1. 1 Thes. i. 8.
1. Heb. viii. 7.
1. —— xi. 8.
1. —— xii. 17, marg. *way*.
2. —— Jas. iii. 11, marg. *hole*.
1. 2 Pet. i. 19.
1. Rev. ii. 5.
1. —— vi. 14.
1. —— xii. 6, 8, 14.
1. —— xvi. 16.
1. —— xx. 11.

PLACE (FROM THAT)

ἐκεῖθεν, thence, from thence, from that place.

Mark vi. 10.

PLACE (GIVE)

1. *ἀναχωρέω*, to go back, recede, *spoken of those who flee*, Jer. iv. 29; Judges iv. 17.

2. *εἴκω*, give way, yield, (*non occ.*)

1. Matt. ix. 24. | 2. Gal. ii. 5.

PLACE (HAVE)

χωρέω, to give space, place, room; to make room for one's self, *and so,* to go forward, go on and on, be advancing; find entrance.

John viii. 37.

PLACE (IN A CERTAIN)

πού, somewhere, in some place or other, (*occ.* Rom. iv. 19.)

Heb. ii. 6. | Heb. iv. 4.

PLACE (IN THIS)

ὧδε, hither, here.

Matt. xii. 6.

PLACE SOEVER (IN WHAT)

{ ὅπου, where, in what } wherever-
{ ἐάν, soever, [place, } soever.

Mark vi. 10.

PLACE (OF THAT)

ἐντόπιος, in the place, (*spoken of one who belongs to any place*) a resident, inhabitant, (*non occ.*)

Acts xxi. 12.

PLACE (TO THIS)

ὧδε, hither, here.

Luke xxiii. 5.

PLACES (IN ALL)

πανταχοῦ, in all places, everywhere.

Acts xxiv. 3.

PLACES (IN DIVERS)

{ κατὰ, from one to an- } in various
{ τόπους, places, [other, } places.

Matt. xxiv. 7. | Mark xiii. 8.
Luke xxi. 11.

PLACE WHERE CUSTOM WAS RECEIVED. [margin.]

Mark ii. 14, see "RECEIPT OF CUSTOM."

See also, ANOTHER, DWELLING, EMINENT, GOOD, HEARING, HEAVENLY, HIGH, HOLY, MARKET, ONE, SECRET, SKULL, STEEP, STONY, THIS, WAY, YONDER.

PLAGUE (-s.)

1. πληγή, a stroke, a blow, *then, as inflicted by God.*
2. μάστιξ, a whip, a scourge; *then,* a scourge *from God.*

2. Mark iii. 10.
2. —— v. 29, 34.
2. Luke vii. 21.
1. Rev. ix. 20.
1. —— xi. 6.
1. Rev. xv. 1, 6, 8.
1. —— xvi. 9, 21 twice.
1. —— xviii. 4, 8.
1. —— xxi. 9.
1. —— xxii. 18.

PLAIN. [noun.]

{ τόπος, place, *see* "PLACE," *No.* 1, } a level
{ πεδινός, plain, level, } place, (*non occ.*)

Luke vi. 17.

PLAIN. [adj.]

ὀρθῶς, straight, right, erectly; *then,* rightly, correctly.

Mark vii. 35.

PLAINLY.

παῤῥησία, the speaking all one thinks, free-spokenness, frankness in speaking, the candid, confident boldness of a joyous heart. *Here, Dative.*

John x. 24.
—— xi. 14.
—— xvi. 25.
John xvi. 29 (*ἐν παρ. in, or with boldness, etc.,* L T Tr A ℵ.)

Heb. xi. 14, see Declare.

PLAINNESS OF SPEECH.

παῤῥησία, *see above.*

2 Cor. iii. 12, marg. *boldness.*

PLAIT.

See, PLAT.

PLAITED. [margin.]

1 Tim. ii. 9, see "BROIDED."

PLAITING.

ἐμπλοκή, a braiding, intertwining, *esp.,* of the *hair in ornament,* (*non occ.*)

1 Pet. iii. 3.

PLANT. [noun.]

φυτεία, a planting, the act of planting, (*non occ.*)

Matt. xv. 13.

PLANT (-ETH.) [verb.]

φυτεύω, to plant; *esp., of trees, etc.* (*non occ.*)

Matt. xv. 13.
—— xxi. 33.
Mark xii. 1.
Luke xiii. 6.
Luke xvii. 6, 28.
Rom. vi. 5, see P together.
1 Cor. iii. 6, 7, 8.
—— ix. 7.

PLANTED TOGETHER.

σύμφυτος, grown *or* growing in conjunction with, grown together, (*non occ.*)

Rom. vi. 5.

PLAT. [verb.]

πλέκω, to plait, to braid, to weave, *Lat.*, plico, plecto.

Matt. xxvii. 29 part. | Mark xv. 17.
John xix. 2.

PLATTER.

1. **παροψίς**, a side-dish in which dainties are served up, *entremet; then,* a dish on which such meats are served, (*non occ.*)
2. **πίναξ**, a board, table; *esp.*, a writing tablet *covered with wax; then,* any wooden plate *or* dish *covered with food.*

1. Matt. xxiii. 25.
1. —— 26 (*om.* καὶ τῆς παροψίδος, and the platter, G ∾ T A.)
2. Luke xi. 39.

PLAY.

παίζω, to play as a child; *then*, to dance. [A citation from Exod. xxxii. 6, where it is the lxx. for צחק, which, it is evident from verses 18, 19, includes the *shouting*, *singing*, and *dancing* in honour of their idol. It is also used by Homer in this sense, see Odys. viii. 51, and xxiii. 147.]

1 Cor. x. 7.

PLEASE (-ED, -ING.)

(*For various combinations with other words, see below.*)

1. **ἀρέσκω**, to please, to be pleasing and acceptable to; *also*, to seek to please *or* gratify.
2. { **εἰμί**, to be, **ἀρεστός**, pleasing, acceptable, grateful to.
3. **εὐαρεστέω**, to please well.
4. **δοκέω**, to appear, have the appearance. *Here, impersonally,* it seemed [*good*]; it appeared [*the right thing to do.*]
5. **εὐδοκέω**, (*No.* 4, *with* εὖ, well, *prefixed*). *Here, the good and right thing is not merely understood, as in No.* 4, *but actually asserted,* it seemed good, *where stress is laid on the resolve and its willingness and freedom, marking the design as something good, either in reality or intention.*
6. **θέλω**, to will, to wish, to desire, *implying active volition and purpose.*

1. Matt. xiv. 6.
1. Mark vi. 22.
1. Acts vi. 5.
2. —— xii. 3.
4. —— xv. 22, 34 (ap.)
1 Rom. viii. 8.
1. —— xv. 1, 2, 3.
5. —— 26, 27.
5. 1 Cor. i. 21.
1. —— vii. 32, 33, 34.
1. 1 Cor. x. 33.
6. —— xii. 18.
6. —— xv. 38.
1. Gal. i. 10 twice.
5. —— 15.
5. Col. i. 19.
1. 1 Thes. ii. 4, 15.
1. —— iv. 1.
1. 2 Tim. ii. 4.
3. Heb. xi. 5, 6.

PLEASE (THOSE THINGS THAT)

{ **τὰ**, the *things*, **ἀρεστά**, pleasing, acceptable, grateful to.

John viii. 29.

PLEASE WELL.

1. **εὐδοκέω**, *see* "PLEASE," *No.* 5.
2. { **εἰμί**, **ἀρεστός**, } *see* "PLEASE," *No.* 2.

1. Matt. iii. 17.
1. —— xii. 18.
1. —— xvii. 5.
1. Mark i. 11.
1. Luke iii. 22.
1. 1 Cor. x. 5.
2. Tit. ii. 9.
1. 2 Pet. i. 17.

PLEASED WITH (BE WELL)

εὐαρεστέω, *see* "PLEASE," *No.* 3.

Heb. xiii. 16, pass.

PLEASING (THOSE THINGS THAT ARE)

{ **τὰ**, the *things*, **ἀρεστά**, pleasing, acceptable, grateful to.

1 John iii. 22.

PLEASING.

ἀρέσκεια, desire of pleasing, very great complaisance, (*non occ.*)

Col. i. 10.

PLEASURE.

(*For various combinations with other words, see below.*)

1. ἡδονή, delight, enjoyment, pleasurable sensation; *Lat.*, voluptas; sensual pleasures, pleasures or lusts of the flesh.
2. θέλημα, will, (*the act of willing, active* volition.)
3. χάρις, a pleasing work, a favour, a kindness.

1. Luke viii. 14.
3. Acts xxiv. 27.
3. —— xxv. 9.
1. Tit. iii. 3.
— Heb. xi. 25, see Enjoy.
1. Jas. iv. 1, } marg. *lust.*
—— 3, } marg. *lust.*
1. 2 Pet. ii. 13.
2. Rev. iv. 11.

PLEASURE (GOOD)

εὐδοκία, a being well pleased, good pleasure, *including the idea of free and willing purpose with a good design.*

Eph. i. 5, 9. | Phil. ii. 13.
2 Thes. i. 11.

PLEASURE (BE ONE'S GOOD)

εὐδοκέω, *see* "PLEASE," *No.* 5.

Luke xii. 32.

PLEASURE (HAVE)

εὐδοκέω, *see* "PLEASE," *No.* 5.

2 Thes. ii. 12. | Heb. x. 6, 8, 38.

PLEASURE (TAKE)

εὐδοκέω, *see* "PLEASE," *No.* 5.

2 Cor. xii. 10.

PLEASURE IN (HAVE)

συνευδοκέω, to take pleasure in, in conjunction with *others.*

Rom. i. 32, marg. *consent with.*

PLEASURE (LIVE IN)

1. σπαταλάω, to live in luxury in eating and drinking, to indulge one's self, (*occ.* Jas. v. 6, *and translated,* "have been wanton.")
2. τρυφάω, to break down the mind and make it effeminate by luxury; *hence,* to live luxuriously.

1. 1 Tim. v. 6, marg. *live delicately.*
2. Jas. v. 5.

PLEASURE (THEIR OWN)

τὸ, that which
δοκοῦν, seemed *good,* appeared *right,*
αὐτοῖς, to them.

Heb. xii. 10 part.

PLEASURES (LOVER OF)

φιλήδονος, pleasure loving; *then, as subst.*, a lover of ἡδονή, (*see* "PLEASURE," *No.* 1), (*non occ.*)

2 Tim. iii. 4.

PLENTEOUS.

πολύς, much; *and with a noun implying number, multitude, or magnitude,* great, large, plenteous.

Matt. ix. 37.

PLENTIFULLY.

See, BRING.

PLOUGH, OR PLOW. [noun.]

ἄροτρον, a plough, *see below,* (*non occ.*)

Luke ix. 62.

PLOUGH (-ETH, -ING.)

ἀροτριάω, to plough.

[Language preserves a wonderful illustration of this, the oldest art, e.g. :—

TO PLOUGH, open the soil :—

AR, Sanscr.; ἀρουν, Gk.; a[illegible]re, Lat.; ar, Irish; arti, Lithuanian; orati, Russ.; arjan, Goth.; erjan, Ang. Sax.; ear, Old Eng., (Deut. xxi. 4.)

THE PLOUGH :—

ἄροτρον, Gk.; aratrum, Lat.; oradlo, Bohem.; arklas, Lith.; aradar, Cornish; arad, Welsh; ardhr, Old Norse.

THE ACT OF PLOUGHING :—

ἄροσις, Gk.; aratio, Lat.; aroma, Eng.

THE LAND FOR PLOUGHING :—

ἔρα, Gk.; ארץ (aretz), Heb.; ira, Sanscr.; ëra, Old High Germ.; ire, irionn, Gaelic; earth, Eng.; airtha, Gothic; eorthe, Ang. Sax.

OTHER RELATED WORDS :—

ἄρτος, bread, (the great earth product.)
ἄρουρα, Gk., (and Lat., aroum) a field.
armentum, (Lat.) any animal fit for ploughing.
arbeit, (Germ.) labour; and arbeitsam, industrious.

erfidhi, (Old Norse) ploughing, but afterwards (like A. Sax., earfod[illegible] or earfedni) it denoted labour.

art, (Old High Germ.) } was the oldest art, of
ars, artis, (Lat.) } ploughing.
arunti, (Old High Germ.) and œrend, is simply work; and so is Eng., errand and errand-boy.
aritra, (Sanscr.) } is the rudder that ploughs the
âr, (A. Sax.) } sea.
oar, (Eng.) }
ἐρετής, (Greek) is a rower.
τριηρης, is a three-oared ship.] (*non occ.*)

Luke xvii. 7. | 1 Cor. ix. 10.

PLUCK (-ED.) [verb.]

1. τίλλω, to pull, pluck, pull out *or* off, *as the hair,* (*non occ.*)
2. ἁρπάζω, to seize upon, snatch away, carry off, *spoken of beasts of prey.*

1. Matt. xii. 1.
1. Mark ii. 23.
1. Luke vi. 1.
— Luke xvii. 6, see Root.
2. John x. 28, 29.
— Jude 12, see Root.

PLUCK ASUNDER.

διασπάω, to pull asunder, tear in pieces, (*occ.* Acts xxiii. 10.)

Mark v. 4.

PLUCK OUT.

1. ἐκβάλλω, to cast out, throw out, *with the idea of force and impulse.*
2. ἐξαιρέω, to take out, (*i.e. as a city or camp, as in war*) pluck out, tear out.
3. ἐξορύσσω, to dig out, (*occ.* Mark ii. 4.)

2. Matt. v. 29.
2. —— xviii. 9.
1. Mark ix. 47.
3. Gal. iv. 15.

POET (-S.)

ποιητής, a maker *of anything,* inventor; *esp.*, the creator of a poem, *like Old Eng.*, maker; *cf. French,* trouvere, troubadour; *gen.*, the author of any mental production.

Acts xvii. 28 (*om.* G →)

POINT.

See, ALL, and DEATH.

POISON.

ἰός, something sent out, emitted; *hence,* a missile, weapon; rust as being emitted on metals; and poison, as emitted by serpents, (*occ.* Jas. v. 3.)

Rom. iii. 13. | Jas. iii. 8.

POLLUTE (-ED.)

κοινόω, to make common, to communicate *with others; hence, in a Levitical sense,* to render unclean, to defile *ceremonially.*

Acts xxi. 28.

POLLUTION (-S.)

1. ἀλίσγημα, pollution by unclean, *i.e.* by forbidden food, (*occ.* in lxx., Dan. i. 8; Mal. i. 7, 12; Ecclus. xl. 29.)

[What is called in Acts xv. 20, *pollutions of idols,* is in verse 29 called εἰδωλοθύτων, *meats offered to idols, i.e.* the parts of the victim not offered to the gods, sold for general food,] (*non occ.*)

2. μίασμα, (*Eng.*, miasma) a colouring, staining, dyeing; *then,* stain, defilement, *esp. by murder or foul crime, then any* taint of guilt, (*non occ.*)

1. Acts xv. 20. | 2. 2 Pet. ii. 20.

POMP.

φαντασία, (*Eng.*, phantasy) an appearing, appearance, show, (*non occ.*)

Acts xxv. 23.

PONDER (-ED.)

συμβάλλω, to throw together; *of thoughts in the mind,* to confer with one's self, ponder in mind.

Luke ii. 19.

POOL.

κολυμβήθρα, a swimming place, any reservoir for bathing and swimming.

John v. 2, 4 (ap.), 7.
—— ix. 7.
John ix. 11 (*om.* τὴν κολ. τοῦ, *the pool of,* G L T Tr A ℵ.)

POOR.

1. πτωχός, crouching, cringing *in the manner of beggars; hence,* begging, beggarly, poor; *then, as subst.,* a beggar, mendicant, living on the alms of others, having nothing at all.

2. *πένης*, working for a living, poor; *not in extreme want, but simply* having only what one earns, having nothing superfluous, living sparingly.

3. *πενιχρός*, poor, needy, (*like No.* 2.)

1. Matt. v. 3.
1. —— xi. 5.
1. —— xix. 21.
1. —— xxvi. 9, 11.
1. Mark x. 21.
1. —— xii. 42 (G →), 43.
1. —— xiv. 5, 7.
1. Luke iv. 18.
1. —— vi. 20.
1. —— vii. 22.
1. —— xiv. 13, 21.
1. —— xviii. 22.
1. —— xix. 8.
3. —— xxi. 2.
1. Luke xxi. 3.
1. John xii. 5, 6, 8.
1. —— xiii. 29.
1. Rom. xv. 26.
— 1 Cor. xi. 22, see P (be)
1. 2 Cor. vi. 10.
— —— viii. 9, see P (become)
2. —— ix. 9.
1. Gal. ii. 10.
— Jas. ii. 2, see P man.
1. ——— 3, 5, 6.
1. Rev. iii. 17.
1. —— xiii. 16.

POOR (*be*) [margin.]

1 Cor. xi. 22, see "HAVE NOT."

POOR (BECOME)

πτωχεύω, to become *πτωχός*, (*see* "POOR," *No.* 1.)

2 Cor. viii. 9.

POOR MAN.

1. Jas. ii. 2.

PORCH (-ES.)

1. *στοά*, a pillar, column; *then, any* portico *or* porch, (piazza) surrounded and supported by columns, (*non occ.*)

2. *πυλών*, a large door, a gate, *at the entrance of a building or city*, a gateway.

3. *προαύλιον*, the place before the *αὐλή*, (or interior court) the large gateway of an oriental house, the deep arch under which the *πυλών* (*No.* 2) opens.

2. Matt. xxvi. 71.
3. Mark xiv. 68.
1. John v. 2.
1. John x. 23.
1. Acts iii. 11.
1. —— v. 12.

PORTER.

θυρωρός, the keeper of a *θύρα*, (a door, a small door or wicket within a larger), (*occ.* John xviii. 16, 17.)

Mark xiii. 34. | John x. 3.

PORTION.

μέρος, a part *of a whole*, a portion, piece.

Matt. xxiv. 51.
Luke xii. 42, see Meat.
Luke xii. 46.
—— xv. 12.

POSSESS (-ED, -ING.)

(*For various combinations, see below.*)

1. *κτάομαι*, to get for one's self, acquire, procure, *by purchase or otherwise*, to possess.

2. *κατέχω*, to have and hold fast, hold firmly, to hold in secure and firm possession.

1. Luke xviii. 12.
1. —— xxi. 19.
2. 1 Cor. vii. 30.
2. 2 Cor. vi. 10.
1. 1 Thes. iv. 4.

POSSESSETH (THE THINGS WHICH ONE)

{ *τὰ*, the *things*, *ὑπάρχοντα*, being, existing, } the *things* which one possesseth, (*calling attention to the fact that they are what they were originally.*)

Luke xii. 15. | Acts iv. 32.

POSSESSED WITH (BE)

ἔχω, to have.

Acts viii. 7. | Acts xvi. 16.

See also, DEVIL.

POSSESSION (-S.)

1. *κτῆμα*, what is acquired *by purchase or otherwise;* acquisition, property, (*non occ.*)

2. *κατάσχεσις*, any thing held *or* possessed, *as a dwelling or land, etc.*, (*non occ.*)

1. Matt. xix. 22.
1. Mark x. 22.
1. Acts ii. 45.
1. —— v. 1.
2. Acts vii. 5, 45.
— —— xxviii. 7, see Possessions.
— Eph. i. 14, see Purchased.

POSSESSOR (-S.)

κτήτωρ, possessor of what has been acquired *by purchase or otherwise;* owner, (*non occ.*)

Acts iv. 34.

POSSIBLE.

δυνατός, *in an active sense*, strong, having inherent and moral power, able to effect; *in a passive sense*, possible, capable of being done; *here, neut.*, able to be done.

Matt. xix. 26. — xxvi. 39. Mark ix. 23. — x. 27 (ap.) | Mark xiv. 35, 36. Luke xviii. 27. Acts ii. 24. — xx. 16.

POSSIBLE (BE)

δύναμαι, to be able, to have inherent and moral power.

Acts xxvii. 39 (δυνατόν, see "POSSIBLE," G~)

POSSIBLE (IF IT BE)

{ **εἰ**, if,
{ **δυνατόν**, *see* "POSSIBLE."

Rom. xii. 18.

POSSIBLE (IF IT HAD BEEN)

εἰ δυνατόν, *see above.*

Gal. iv. 15.

POSSIBLE (IF IT WERE)

εἰ δυνατόν, *see above.*

Matt. xxiv. 24. | Mark xiii. 22.

POSSIBLE (*it is*) [margin.]

ἔξεστι, it is possible, one can, referring to moral propriety; it is lawful, it is right, it is permitted.

2 Cor. xii. 4, text, *it is lawful.*

POSSIBLE (NOT)

ἀδύνατον, impossible.

Heb. x. 4.

POT (-S.)

1. **ξέστης**, *Lat.*, sextus, *or* sextarius, a Roman measure, liquid *or* dry, *very nearly equal to an Eng.* pint, (*non occ.*)
2. **στάμνος**, an earthen jar, *or* jug, *for racking off wine.* (In Exod. xvi. 33, lxx. for צִנְצֶנֶת.)

1. Mark vii. 4, 8 (ap.) | 2. Heb. ix. 4.

POTENTATE.

δυνάστης, possessor of power, used of those who are in possession of authority, and occupying a high position.

1 Tim. vi. 15.

POTTER.

κεραμεύς, a potter, (*from* κέραμος, potter's clay), (*non occ.*)

Matt. xxvii. 7, 10. | Rom. ix. 21.

POTTER (OF A)

κεραμικός, of *or* made by a potter, (*Eng.*, ceramic), (*non occ.*)

Mark xiv. 13. | Luke xxii. 10.

POUND (-S.)

1. **λίτρα**, (*Lat.*, libra) a pound *in weight*, = 12 oz. avoirdupois, (*non occ.*)
2. **μνᾶ**, (*Lat.*, mina) *prop.*, a Greek weight = 100 drachmæ = 15 oz., 83¾ grs.; *also*, as a sum of money = 100 drachmæ = £4 1s. 3d. 60 μναῖ make a talent, (*prob. akin to Heb.* maneh, *perhaps also to our Eng.* money, etc.), (*non occ.*)

2. Luke xix. 13, 16 twice, 18 twice, 20, 24 twice, 25. | 1. John xii. 3. 1. — xix. 39.

POUR (-ED, -ETH, -ING.)

1. **βάλλω**, to throw, to cast *with a greater or less degree of force, as determined by the context; of liquids*, to pour.
2. **καταχέω**, to pour down upon, *and so gen.*, to pour upon, (*non occ.*)

2. Matt. xxvi. 7. 1. —— 12 part. | 2. Mark xiv. 3. 1. John xiii. 5.

POUR IN.

ἐπιχέω, to pour over, pour upon, (*non occ.*)

Luke x. 34.

POUR OUT.

1. **ἐκχέω**, to pour out.
2. **ἐκχύνω**, *another form of No.* 1.
3. **κεράννυμι**, to mix, mingle; *then*, to prepare a draught, to pour out *for drinking*, to fill *one's cup.*

1. John ii. 15.
1. Acts ii. 17, 18.
2. —— x. 45.
3. Rev. xiv. 10.
1. —— xvi. 1, 2, 3, 4, 8, 10, 12, 17.

POVERTY.

πτωχεία, begging, mendicancy; poverty, want.

2 Cor. viii. 2, 9.
Rev. ii. 9.

POWDER.

See, GRIND.

POWER (-s.)

1. δύναμις, natural capability, inherent power; capability of anything, ability to perform anything; *then, absolutely, not merely power capable of action, but*, power in action. The Power of *God*, *is* the power which manifests itself in all the modes, *esp.* in His redeeming work, where God is at work, revealing and carrying out the plan of salvation. (*As opp. to No.* 5, *it denotes* moral power.)

[In Rev. v. 12, we have δύναμις, inherent ability to effect all the Divine purposes; ἰσχύς, physical ability prevailing in action; πλοῦτος, the fulness of all good; τιμή, honour, intrinsic excellence; and εὐλογία, the utterance of blessing from a redeemed creation.]

2. { ὁ, the, δυνατός, *see* "POSSIBLE," } His power, *see No.* 1.

3. ἐξουσία, (*from* ἔξεστι, it is allowed, one can, it is permitted, *denying the presence of a hindrance*) delegated authority, liberty *or* authority to do anything; *combining the two ideas of right and might.* (*While No.* 1 *implies* the ability to make power felt, *No.* 3 affirms that free movement is ensured to the ability.)

4. κράτος, strength, *esp.* bodily strength; power in effect, force, superiority, strength as exerted.

5. ἰσχύς, strength, *as an endowment;* physical strength, (*Lat.*, vires.)

6. ἀρχή, beginning; *then, spoken of dignity, etc.*, the *first place, i.e.* the power, rule, dominion.

[*Another synonymous word, not translated power, is* ἐνέργεια, energy, power in action, effectual operation; ἐνέργημα, a work wrought in us and by us.]

1. Matt. vi. 13 (*ap.*)
3. —— ix. 6, 8.
3. —— x. 1.
1. —— xxii. 29.
1. —— xxiv. 29, 30.
1. —— xxvi. 64.
3. —— xxviii. 18.
3. Mark ii. 10.
3. —— iii. 15.
3. —— vi. 7.
1. —— ix. 1.
1. —— xii. 24.
1. —— xiii. 25, 26.
1. —— xiv. 62.
1. Luke i. 17, 35.
3. —— iv. 6.
1. —— 14.
3. —— 32.
1. —— 36.
1. —— v. 17.
3. —— 24.
1. —— ix. 1.
— —— 43, see Mighty.
3. —— x. 19 1st.
1. —— 19 2nd.
3. —— xii. 5, 11.
6. —— xx. 20.
1. —— xxi. 26, 27.
3. —— xxii. 53.
1. —— 69.
1. —— xxiv. 49.
3. John i. 12, marg. *right or privilege.*
3. —— x. 18.
3. —— xvii. 2.
3. —— xix. 10 twice, 11.
3. Acts i. 7.
1. —— 8.
1. —— iii. 12.
1. —— iv. 7, 33.
3. —— v. 4.
1. —— vi. 8.
1. —— viii. 10.
3. —— 19.
1. —— x. 38.
3. —— xxvi. 18.
1. Rom. i. 4, 16, 20.
1. —— viii. 38.
1. —— ix. 17.
3. —— 21.
2. —— 22.
3. —— xiii. 1 1st & 2nd.
3. —— 1 3rd (*om.* G L T Tr A ℵ [i.e. *those*].)
3. —— 2, 3.
1. —— xv. 13, 19.
— —— xvi. 25, see P (that is of)
1. 1 Cor. i. 18, 24.
1. —— ii. 4, 5.
1. —— iv. 19, 20.
1. —— v. 4.
— —— vi. 12, see P (bring under)
1. —— 14.
— —— vii. 4 twice, see P of (have)
3. —— 37.
3. —— viii. 9, marg. (text, *liberty.*)
3. 1 Cor. ix. 4, 5. 6, 12 twice, 18.
3. —— xi. 10, see margin.
1. —— xii. 29, margin (text, *worker of miracles.*)
1. —— xv. 24, 43.
1. 2 Cor. iv. 7.
1. —— vi. 7.
1. —— viii. 3 twice.
1. —— xii. 9.
1. —— xiii. 4.
3. —— 10.
1. Eph. i. 19 1st.
4. —— 19 2nd.
3. —— 21.
3. —— ii. 2.
1. —— iii. 7.
3. —— 10.
1. —— 20.
4. —— vi. 10.
3. —— 12.
4. Col. i. 11.
3. —— 13, 16.
3. —— ii. 10, 15.
1. Phil. iii. 10.
1. 1 Thes. i. 5.
5. 2 Thes. i. 9.
1. —— 11.
1. —— ii. 9.
3. —— iii. 9.
1. 1 Tim. i. 7, 8.
1. —— iii. 5.
4. —— vi. 16.
3. Tit. iii. 1.
1. Heb. i. 3.
4. —— ii. 14.
1. —— vi. 5.
1. —— vii. 16.
1. 1 Pet. i. 5.
1. —— iii. 22.
1. 2 Pet. i. 3, 16.
5. —— ii. 11.
3. Jude 25.
3. Rev. ii. 26.
1. —— iv. 11.
1. —— v. 12.
4. —— 13.
3. —— vi. 8.
1. —— vii. 12.
3. —— ix. 3 twice, 10, 19.
3. —— xi. 6 twice.
1. —— 17.
3. —— xii. 10.
1. —— xiii. 2.
3. —— 4, 5, 7, 12.
— —— 14, 15, see P (have)
3. —— xiv. 18.
1. —— xv. 8.
3. —— xvi. 9.
3. —— xvii. 12.
1. —— 13.
3. —— xviii. 1.
1. —— 3, marg. (text, *abundance.*)
1. —— xix. 1.
3. —— xx. 6.

POWER (BRING UNDER)

ἐξουσιάζω, to have *or* exercise authority.

1 Cor. vi. 12.

POWER (HAVE)

δίδωμι, to give to. *Here, with Dat. following,* "it was given to him."

Rev. xiii. 14, 15.

POWER OF (HAVE)

ἐξουσιάζω, to have *or* exercise authority.

1 Cor. vii. 4 twice.

POWER (THAT IS OF)

δύναμαι, to be able, have inherent and moral power. *Here, part.,* having power.

Rom. xvi. 25.

POWERFUL.

1. ἐνεργής, in work, *i.e.* working, energetic in exercise, powerful in action, effectual in operation, (*occ.* 1 Cor. xvi. 9; Philem. 6.)
2. ἰσχυρός, physically strong, mighty.

2. 2 Cor. x. 10. | 1. Heb. iv. 12.

PRACTICE.

See, COVETOUS.

PRÆTORIUM.

πραιτώριον, *Lat.,* prætorium, the general's tent in a camp; *then,* the residence of the governor of a province, the prætorian residence.

Mark xv. 16.

PRAISE (-S.) [noun.]

1. αἶνος, discourse, narration; *then, in N.T.,* praise, used only of praise to God, (*non occ.*)
2. ἔπαινος, (*No.* 1, *with* ἐπί, upon, *prefixed*) praise upon, applause, commendation, approbation.
3. δόξα, glory, (*see* "GLORY," *No.* 1.)
4. αἴνεσις, a praising, (*non occ.*)
5. ἀρετή, virtue, excellence *of any kind,* goodness of action, (*occ.* Phil. iv. 8; 2 Pet. i. 3, 5 twice.)

1. Matt. xxi. 16.
1. Luke xviii. 43.
3. John ix. 24.
3. —— xii. 43 twice.
— Acts xvi. 25, see P unto (sing)
2. Rom. ii. 29.
2. —— xiii. 3.
2. 1 Cor. iv. 5.
2. 2 Cor. viii. 18.
2. Eph. i. 6, 12, 14.
2. Phil. i. 11.
2. —— iv. 8.
— Heb. ii. 12, see P unto (sing)
4. —— xiii. 1
2. 1 Pet. i. 7.
5. —— ii. 9, marg. virtue.
2. —— 14.
3. —— iv. 11.

PRAISE UNTO (SING)

ὑμνεω, to hymn; sing hymns to *any one;* to praise in song.

Heb. ii. 12.

PRAISES UNTO (SING)

ὑμνέω, *see above.*

Acts xvi. 25.

PRAISE (-ED, -ING.) [verb.]

1. αἰνέω, to tell *or* speak of, to speak in praise of; bestow praise, celebrate, (*non occ.*)
2. ἐπαινέω, (*No.* 1, *with* ἐπί, upon, *prefixed*) to praise upon, applaud, commend, (*occ.* Luke xvi. 8; Rom. xv. 11.)
3. εὐλογέω, to speak well of, bless; with praise, gratitude, and thanksgiving to invoke blessing upon.

3. Luke i. 64.
1. —— ii. 13, 20.
1. —— xix. 37.
1. —— xxiv. 53 (ap.)
1. Acts ii. 47.
1. —— iii. 8, 9.
1. Rom. xv. 11.
2. 1 Cor. xi. 2, 17, 22 twice.
1. Rev. xix. 5.

PRATE AGAINST.

φλυαρέω, to overflow with talk; *hence,* to prate about, tattle, (*non occ.*)

3 John 10.

PRAY (-ED, -ETH, -EST, -ING.)

1. εὔχομαι, to speak out, utter aloud; *hence,* to pray, wish strongly.
2. προσεύχομαι, (*No.* 1, *with* πρός, towards, *prefixed*) to pray to *God,* offer prayer, (*restricted to* prayer towards *God.*)
3. ἐρωτάω, to interrogate, to ask, implying *familiarity, if not equality; hence,* never used of our prayers to God, while it is used of Christ's prayers to the Father, (John xiv. 16; xvi. 26; xvii. 9, 15, 20; and compare the two in John xvi. 23, and 1 John v. 16.)

[Martha unworthily ascribes αἰτέω, *to beg, to pray,* (the more submissive and suppliant word) to Him, which He never ascribes to Himself, John xi. 22, *see* under "ASK."]

4. δέομαι, to need, to want; *then,* to make known one's need, urgently request, supplicate, beseech.

5. παρακαλέω, to call beside, call near; to call *some one* hither, *that he may* do *something*; to call on any one, to call him near in order to say something to him, to use persuasion with him.

2. Matt. v. 44.
2. —— vi. 5 twice, 6 twice, 7 part., 9.
4. —— ix. 38.
2. —— xiv. 23.
2. —— xix. 13.
2. —— xxiv. 20.
2. —— xxvi. 36, 39, 41, 42, 44.
5. ——— 53.
2. Mark i. 35.
5. —— v. 17, 18.
2. —— vi. 46.
2. —— xi. 24 part., 25.
2. —— xiii. 18.
2. ——— 33 (*om.* καὶ προς., *and pray,* L T Tr[b] A.)
2. —— xiv. 32, 35, 38, 39.
2. Luke i. 10.
2. —— iii. 21.
3. —— v. 3.
2. ——— 16.
2. —— vi. 12, 28.
2. —— ix. 18, 28, 29.
4. —— x. 2.
2. —— xi. 1 twice, 2.
3. —— xiv. 18, 19.
3. —— xvi. 27.
2. —— xviii. 1, 10, 11.
4. —— xxi. 36.
4. —— xxii. 32.
2. ——— 40, 41, 44 (*ap.*), 46.
3. John iv. 31.
3. —— xiv. 16.
3. —— xvi. 26.
3. —— xvii. 9 twice, 15, 20.
2. Acts i. 24.
4. —— iv. 31 part.
2. —— vi. 6 part.
2. —— viii. 15.
4. ——— 22, 24, 34.
2. —— ix. 11, 40.
4. Acts x. 2.
2. ——— 9, 30.
3. ——— 48.
2. —— xi. 5.
2. —— xii. 12.
2. —— xiii. 3.
2. —— xiv. 23.
5. —— xvi. 9.
2. ——— 25.
2. —— xx. 36.
2. —— xxi. 5.
2. —— xxii. 17 part.
4. —— xxiii. 18.
5. —— xxiv. 4.
5. —— xxvii. 34.
2. —— xxviii. 8.
— Rom. viii. 26, see P for
2. 1 Cor. xi. 4, 5, 13.
2. —— xiv. 13, 14 twice, 15 twice.
4. 2 Cor. v. 20.
4. —— viii. 4.
1. —— xiii. 7.
2. Eph. vi. 18.
2. Phil. i. 9.
2. Col. i. 3, 9.
2. —— iv. 3.
4. 1 Thes. iii. 10.
2. —— v. 17, 25.
2. 2 Thes. i. 11.
2. —— iii. 1.
2. 1 Tim. ii. 8.
2. Heb. xiii. 18.
2. Jas. v. 13, 14.
1. ——— 16 (No. 2, L Tr[m].)
2. ——— 17, and see P earnestly.
2. ——— 18.
3. 1 John v. 16.
1. 3 John 2, marg. (text, *wish.*)
2. Jude 20.

PRAY FOR

2. Rom. viii. 26.

PRAYED EARNESTLY.

{ προσευχῇ, with prayer.
{ προσηύξατο, he prayed.

Jas. v. 17.

PRAYER (-s.)

1. εὐχή, a speaking out, uttering aloud; *then,* prayer, (*occ.* Acts xviii. 18; xxi. 23.)

2. προσευχή, (*No.* 1, *with* πρός, towards, *prefixed*) speaking out to, prayer towards, (*restricted to* prayer to God, *and marking the power of Him, whom we invoke*); *sometimes it denotes* a place of prayer, *a building below the synagogue in rank.*

3. δέησις, want, need; *then,* the expression of need; urgent request, supplication; *marking esp. our need and insufficiency;* seeking aid in special necessity (*a special form of No.* 1.)

4. ἔντευξις, a falling in with, meeting with, coming together, access, audience, petition, *esp.,* intercession *on behalf of others;* prayer in its most individual form; God sought in audience and drawn nigh to, (*occ.* 1 Tim. ii. 1.)

[Another synonymous word is προστροπή, *a turning to* any quarter for help, (*not used in N.T.*) *Here, No.* 2 marks our devotion, *No.* 4 our confidence, *No.* 3 our need.]

2. Matt. xvii. 21 (*ap.*)
2. —— xxi. 13, 22.
— —— xxiii. 14, see P (make long)
2. Mark ix. 29.
2. —— xi. 17.
— —— xii. 40, see P's (make long)
3. Luke i. 13.
3. —— ii. 37.
3. —— v. 33.
2. —— vi. 12.
2. —— xix. 46.
— —— xx. 47, see P's (make long)
2. —— xxii. 45.
2. Acts i. 14.
2. —— ii. 42.
2. —— iii. 1.
2. —— vi. 4.
2. —— x. 4, 31.
2. —— xii. 5.
2. —— xvi. 13, 16.
2. Rom. i. 9.
3. —— x. 1.
2. Rom. xii. 12.
2. —— xv. 30.
2. 1 Cor. vii. 5.
3. 2 Cor. i. 11.
3. —— ix. 14.
2. Eph. i. 16.
2. —— vi. 18.
3. Phil. i. 4, 19.
2. —— iv. 6.
2. Col. iv. 2, 12.
2. 1 Thes. i. 2.
2. 1 Tim. ii. 1.
4. —— iv. 5.
2. —— v. 5.
3. 2 Tim. i. 3.
2. Philem. 4, 22.
3. Heb. v. 7.
1. Jas. v. 15.
3. ——— 16.
— ——— 17, see Prayed earnestly.
2. 1 Pet. iii. 7.
3. ——— 12.
2. —— iv. 7.
2. Rev. v. 8.
2. —— viii. 3, 4.

PRAYER (MAKE LONG)

{ μακρά, long, προσευχόμαι, *see* "PRAY," *No.* 2, } make much prayer, *or* long in prayer.

Matt. xxiii. 14 (*ap.*)

PRAYERS (MAKE LONG)

Mark xii. 40. | Luke xx. 47.

PREACH (-ED, -EST, -ETH, -ING.)

(*For various combinations, see below. See also, under* "GOSPEL," *for* "Preach the Gospel.")

1. κηρύσσω, to be a herald, discharge an herald's office, to make proclamation, proclaim, announce publicly, publish announcements.

[*No.* 1 simply regards the making known, without any reference to *the contents*, which is done by *No.* 2, and not including the idea of *teaching*, which is done by διδάσκω. *See*, "TEACH."]

2. εὐαγγελίζω, to bring a joyful message. *Here, mid.*, to proclaim *something to somebody as* a divine glad-message of salvation; *then, simply* to proclaim the divine message of salvation, to bring some one into relation with it, to evangelize *him*.

3. καταγγελάω, to bring word down upon *any one*, to bring it home to *any one*, preach, set forth.

4. διαγγέλλω, to make known through *an intervening space*, report further, proclaim far and wide.

5. λαλέω, to use the voice *merely, without any reference to the words spoken;* to speak, talk.

6. διαλέγομαι, to speak to and fro, *i.e.* alternately, to converse with, discuss, reason, argue, (*see* "SPEAK," *No.* 1.)

1. Matt. iii. 1.
1. —— iv. 17, 23.
1. —— ix. 35.
1. —— x. 7, 27.
1. —— xi. 1.
1. —— xxiv. 14.
1. —— xxvi. 13.
1. Mark i. 4, 7, 14, 38.
1. ——— 39, with ἦν (ἦλθεν), *and he went making proclamation.*
5. —— ii. 2.
1. —— iii. 14.
1. —— vi. 12.
1. —— xiv. 9.
1. —— xvi. 15 (*ap.*), 20 (*ap.*)
1. Luke iii. 3.
— ——— 18, see P unto.
1. —— iv. 18, 19.
2. ——— 43.
1. ——— 44, with ἦν, *and he was proclaiming.*
1. —— viii. 1.
1. —— ix. 2.
4. ——— 60.
1. —— xxiv. 47.
— Acts iii. 20, see P before.
3. —— iv. 2.
2. —— v. 42.
2. —— viii. 4.
1. ——— 5.
2. ——— 12.
5. ——— 25.
2. Acts viii. 35, 40.
1. —— ix. 20.
— ——— 27, see Boldly.
2. —— x. 36.
1. ——— 37, 42.
5. —— xi. 19.
2. ——— 20.
3. —— xiii. 5.
— ——— 24, see P first.
3. ——— 38.
5. ——— 42.
— —— xiv. 15, see P unto.
5. ——— 25.
1. —— xv. 21.
2. ——— 35.
3. ——— 36.
5. —— xvi. 6.
3. —— xvii. 3, 13.
2. ——— 18 (*ap.*)
1. —— xix. 13.
6. —— xx. 7, 9 part.
1. ——— 25.
1. —— xxviii. 31.
1. Rom. ii. 21.
1. —— x. 8, 15.
— ——— 16, see Preaching.
— —— xv. 19, see Fully.
1. 1 Cor. i. 23.
3. —— ix. 14.
1. ——— 27 part.
2. —— xv. 1, 2.
1. ——— 11, 12.
1. 2 Cor. i. 19.
1. —— iv. 5.
1. 2 Cor. xi. 4 twice.
2. ——— 7.
2. Gal. i. 16, 23.
1. —— ii. 2.
1. —— v. 11.
2. Eph. ii. 17.
2. —— iii. 8.
1. Phil. i. 15.
2. ——— 16, 18.
1. Col. i. 23.
— ——— 25, see *Fully.*
3. ——— 28.
1. 1 Thes. ii. 9.
1. 1 Tim. iii. 16.
1. 2 Tim. iv. 2.
— Heb. iv. 2, see Preached.
1. 1 Pet. iii. 19.
— Rev. xiv. 6, see P unto.

PREACH BEFORE.

προκηρύσσω, (*No.* 1, *with* πρό, before, *prefixed*) to proclaim beforehand.

Acts iii. 20.

PREACH FIRST.

προκηρύσσω, *see above.*

Acts xiii. 24 part.

PREACH UNTO.

εὐαγγελίζω, (*see above, No.* 2.) (a) *Active, followed by* ἐπί, upon. (b) middle.

b. Luke iii. 18. | b. Acts xiv. 15.
a. Rev. xiv. 6.

PREACHED.

ἀκοή, hearing; *then*, that which is heard.

Heb. iv. 2, marg. *of hearing.*

PREACHING.

ἀκοή, *see above.*

Rom. x. 16, marg. (text, *report.*)

PREACHER.

1. κήρυξ, a herald; a public servant of the supreme power, both in peace and war; one who summons the ἐκκλησία, (*see* "CHURCH,") conveys messages; one who proclaims *or* communicates something.

[κηρυξ expresses the herald's work *as proclaimer;* ἀπόστολος, (APOSTLE) expresses his relation to him by whom he is *sent;* εὐαγγελίστης, (EVANGELIST) expresses the *glad message* with which he is entrusted; διδάσκαλος, (TEACHER) refers to the *continuous instruction* in that which has been already proclaimed.] (*non occ.*)

2. κηρύσσω, (*see* "PREACH," *No.* 1.) *Here, the participle.*

2. Rom. x. 14.
1. 1 Tim. ii. 7.
1. 2 Tim. i. 11.
1. 2 Pet. ii. 5.

PREACHING. [noun.]

1. κήρυγμα, that which is proclaimed *or* "cried" by the herald, the command, the communication, (*non occ.*)
2. ἀκοή, hearing; *then,* that which is heard.
3. λόγος, the word *spoken* (*not written*); the word *or* speech *as a means or instrument, and not as a product;* the word *as* that which is spoken; the expression, *both of single expressions and of longer speeches. Hence,* the word of the Gospel *denotes* all that God says or has caused to be said to men. *And as* the word manifests the inward and invisible thought, so this manifests God's will, and makes it known to men.

1. Matt. xii. 41.
1. Luke xi. 32.
2. Rom. x. 16, marg. (text, *report.*)
1. —— xvi. 25.
3. 1 Cor. i. 18.
2. 1 Cor. i. 21.
1. —— ii. 4.
1. —— xv. 14.
3. 2 Cor. i. 18, marg. (text, *report.*)
1. 2 Tim. iv. 17.
1. Titus i. 3.

PRECEPT.

ἐντολή, instruction, charge, direction; *elsewhere translated* commandment.

Mark x. 5. | Heb. ix. 19.

PRECIOUS.

1. τίμιος, held worth, estimated, honoured; *hence,* valued, prized, precious.
2. ἔντιμος, in honour; *hence, like No.* 1, honoured, estimable, dear.
3. τιμή, a holding worth, estimation; value, price; *then,* a thing of price, *and hence, collectively,* precious things.

— Matt. xxvi. 7, } see P
— Mark xiv. 3, } (very)
1. 1 Cor. iii. 12.
1. Jas. v. 7.
1. 1 Pet. i. 7 (πολυτιμότερος, *of very great value or price, very precious,* instead of πολὺ τιμιώτερος, *much more precious,* G L T Tr A ℵ.)
1. 1 Pet. i. 19.
2. —— ii. 4, 6.
3. —— 7, marg. *honour.*
— 2 Pet. i. 1, see P (like)
1. —— 4.
1. Rev. xvii. 4.
1. —— xviii. 12 twice, 16.
1. Rev. xxi. 11, 19.

PRECIOUS (LIKE)

ἰσότιμος, alike honoured, alike prized; *i.e.* of equal honour, of equal honour and estimation, (*non occ.*)

2 Pet. i. 1.

PRECIOUS (VERY)

1. βαρύτιμος, of heavy price.
2. πολυτελής, very expensive, very costly.

1. Matt. xxvi. 7 (πολύτιμος, *of great price,* L T Trm ℵ.)
2. Mark xiv. 3.

PREDESTINATE (-ED.)

προορίζω, to set bounds before, determine, decree *or* ordain beforehand.

[In Rom. viii. 30, it is simply a formal conception, and not (like προγινώσκω, in verse 29) an independent conception, complete in itself. When προορίζω is used, the question is not *who* are its objects, but *what* they are predestined to. προορίζω precedes history, and those who, in history, God "*foreknows.*" (προγίνωσκω) are the subjects of what He has before all history prepared and counselled for them.] (*non occ.*)

Rom. viii. 29, 30. | Eph. i. 5, 11.

PRE-EMINENCE (HAVE THE)

πρωτεύω, to be first, hold the first *place, or highest dignity,* (*non occ.*)

Col. i. 18.

PRE-EMINENCE (LOVE TO HAVE THE)

φιλοπρωτεύω, (*the above, with* φιλέω, to love, *prefixed.*)

3 John 9.

PREFER (-ING.)

προηγέομαι, to lead forward, go on before, take the lead. *Here,* "as to honour, each taking the lead in rendering it to the other," (*non occ.*)

Rom. xii. 10.

PREFERRED (BE)

γίνομαι, to become, come to pass, gotten; advance, take a place.

John i. 15, 27 (*ap.*), 30.

PREFERRING ONE BEFORE ANOTHER.

πρόκριμα, a fore-judging, prejudice.

1 Tim. v. 21, marg. *prejudice.*

PREJUDICE. [margin.]

1 Tim. v. 21, *see above.*

PREMEDITATE.

μελετάω, to care for, to take care for *any thing, i.e. so as to be able to perform it; hence*, to premeditate, (*occ.* Acts iv. 25; 1 Tim. iv. 15.)

Mark xiii. 11 (*om.* μηδὲ μελετᾶτε, *neither do ye premeditate*, G ⇉ L^b T Tr A^b ℵ.)

PREPARATION.

1. παρασκευή, a making ready at hand, *i.e.* preparation.

   [In the Jewish sense, *preparation, i.e.* the day or hours before the sabbath, or other festival when preparation was made for its celebration; *hence, the eve of the sabbath* or *feast.*] (*non occ.*)

2. ἑτοιμασία, preparation, *i.e.* readiness. *Here*, the preparedness *arising from* the gospel of peace, (*non occ.*)

1. Matt. xxvii. 62.
1. Mark xv. 42.
1. Luke xxiii. 54.
1. John xix. 14, 31, 42.
2. Eph. vi. 15.

PREPARE (-ED, -ING.)

1. ἑτοιμάζω, to make ready, prepare.
2. κατασκευάζω, to prepare fully.
3. καταρτίζω, to make fully ready, prepare, constitute.

1. Matt. iii. 3.
2. —— xi. 10.
1. —— xx. 23.
1. —— xxii. 4.
1. —— xxv. 34, 41.
1. —— xxvi. 17.
2. Mark i. 2.
1. —— —— 3.
1. —— x. 40.
1. —— xiv. 12.
— —— —— 15, see Prepared.
2. Luke i. 17.
1. —— —— 76.
1. —— ii. 31.
1. —— iii. 4.
2. —— vii. 27.
1. —— xii. 47.
1. —— xxii. 8, 9.
1. —— xxiii. 56.
1. —— xxiv. 1.
1. John xiv. 2, 3.
— Rom. ix. 23, see P afore.
1. 1 Cor. ii. 9.
— —— xiv. 8, see P one's self.
— Eph. ii. 10, see P *before.*
1. 2 Tim. ii. 21.
1. Philem. 22.
3. Heb. x. 5.
2. —— xi. 7.
1. —— —— 16.
— 1 Pet. iii. 20, see Preparing (be a)
1. Rev. viii. 6.
1. —— ix. 7, 15.
1. —— xii. 6.
1. —— xvi. 12.
1. —— xxi. 2.

PREPARE AFORE.

προετοιμάζω, (*No.* 1, *with* πρό, before, *prefixed*) to make ready beforehand, (*occ.* Eph. ii. 10.)

Rom. ix. 23.

PREPARED (*before*) [margin.]

Eph. ii. 10, see "ORDAIN."

PREPARE ONE'S SELF.

παρασκευάζω, (*No.* 2, *with* παρά, beside, *prefixed, instead of* κατά, down) to make ready near *or* for *any one*, to prepare at hand. *Here, mid.*, to prepare one's self, to be ready.

1 Cor. xiv. 8.

PREPARED.

ἕτοιμος, ready, prepared.

Mark xiv. 15 (*om.* G → L.)

PRESBYTERY.

πρεσβυτέριον, an assembly of aged men, council of elders, senate, (*occ. spoken of the Jewish Sanhedrim*, Luke xxii. 66; Acts xxii. 5.

1 Tim. iv. 14.

PRESENCE.

(*For various combinations with other words, see below.*)

1. πρόσωπον, *the part* towards the eye, the part of anything which is presented to the eye, the front of anything, the face; *hence, that which is in one's* presence, before one's eyes.
2. παρουσία, the being *or* becoming present; presence, arrival.

1. Acts iii. 13, 19.
1. —— v. 41.
1. 2 Cor. x. 1, marg. *outward appearance.*
2. 2 Cor. x. 10.
2. Phil. ii. 12.
1. 1 Thes. ii. 17.
1. 2 Thes. i. 9.
1. Heb. ix. 24.

PRESENCE OF (BEFORE THE)

κατενώπιον, down in the presence of, in the very presence of.

Jude 24.

PRESENCE (IN ONE'S)

ἐνώπιον, in the presence of, before.

Luke xiii. 26. | 1 Cor. i. 29.

PRESENCE OF (IN THE)

1. ἐνώπιον, *see above.*
2. ἔμπροσθεν, before; *hence,* in the presence of, in the sight of, God being witness.
3. ἀπέναντι, from over against, opposite to; *hence,* before, in the presence of.

1. Luke i. 19.
1. —— xiv. 10.
1. —— xv. 10.
1. John xx. 30.
3. Acts iii. 16.
1. —— xxvii. 35.
2. 1 Thes. ii. 19.
1. Rev. xiv. 10 twice.

PRESENT. [adj.]

(*For various combinations with other words, see below.*)

1. πάρειμι, to be near by, to be present, to have come; *hence,* having come—to be and remain present, (*here, participle.*)
2. ἐνίστημι, (*intrans.*) to stand in, instant, *i.e.* present, (*here, participle.*)
3. ἐφίστημι, (*trans.*) to place upon *or* over. *In N.T. only intrans. forms, and mid.*, to place one's self upon or near, to come upon. *Hence, of rain, as here,* to fall upon, set in, (*here, participle.*)
4. ἐνδημέω, to be among one's people, (*from* ἐν, in, *and* δῆμος, the people); present with them, (*here, participle.*)

3. Acts xxviii. 2.
1. 1 Cor. v. 3.
2. —— vii. 26.
4. 2 Cor. v. 9.
2. Gal. i. 4.
2. Heb. ix. 9.
1. —— xii. 11.
1. 2 Pet. i. 12.

PRESENT (BE)

1. πάρειμι, *see above, No.* 1.
2. ἐνδημέω, *see above, No.* 4.
3. μένω, to remain, continue.
4. παραγίνομαι, to become beside, become near *or* present. (*Here, only aor.*, were present, *i.e.* had come *or* arrived.)

1. Luke xiii. 1.
3. John xiv. 25.
2. Acts xxi. 18.
1. 1 Cor. v. 3 part.
2. 2 Cor. v. 8.
1. —— x. 2 part, 11 part.
1. —— xi. 9 part.
1. —— xiii. 2 part, 10.
1. Gal. iv. 18, 20.

PRESENT (BE HERE)

πάρειμι, *see* "PRESENT," *No.* 1, *above.*

Acts x. 33.

PRESENT WITH (BE)

παράκειμαι, to be beside *or* near, be ready at hand, (*non occ.*)

Rom. vii. 18, 21.

PRESENT WITH (BE HERE)

συμπάρειμι, to be present in conjunction with *any one,* (*non occ.*)

Acts xxv. 24.

PRESENT HOUR (EVEN UNTO THIS)

{ ἄχρι, continuedly until
τῆς, the,
ἄρτι, even now,
ὥρας, hour.

1 Cor. iv. 11.

PRESENT (UNTO THIS)

{ ἕως, until, as long as; until, unto.
ἄρτι, just now, even now.

1 Cor. xv. 6.

PRESENT WORLD (THIS)

{ ὁ, the
νῦν, now existing
αἰών, age, (*see* "AGES," *No.* 1), } the age or world that now is, 2 Pet. iii. 7, (*see note under* "HEAVEN."

2 Tim. iv. 10. | Tit. ii. 12.

PRESENT (THINGS)

ἐνεστῶτα, (*part of* ἐνίστημι, to stand in, in-stant, present) things present, *as opp.* to the things about to happen (μέλλοντα).

Rom. viii. 38. | 1 Cor. iii. 22.

PRESENT (-ED.) [verb.]

1. ἵστημι, *trans.*, to cause to stand, place; *intrans.*, to stand. (*Here, trans.*)
2. παρίστημι, (*No.* 1, *with* παρά, beside, *prefixed*) *trans.*, to cause to stand beside *or* near, place near by, present, exhibit; *intrans.*, to stand near, stand by. (*Here, trans.*)

— Matt. ii. 11, see P unto.
2. Luke ii. 22.
2. Acts ix. 41.
2. —— xxiii. 33.
2. Rom. xii. 1.
2. 2 Cor. iv. 14.
2. —— xi. 2.
2. Eph. v. 27.
2. Col. i. 22, 28.
1. Jude 24.

PRESENT UNTO.

προσφέρω, to bear *or* bring towards *or* to *any place or person*, to bring near to, present, offer.

Matt. ii. 11, marg. *offer*.

PRESENTLY.

1. ἐξαυτῆς, from this *time*, forthwith, immediately.
2. παραχρῆμα, with the thing itself, *i.e.* at the very moment, on the spot; directly *after something else has taken place.*

2. Matt. xxi. 19. | — Matt. xxvi. 53, see [Give.
1. Phil. ii. 23.

PRESERVE (-ED.)

1. τηρέω, to keep an eye upon, to watch; *and hence*, to keep, to guard, watch; *then*, to keep in safety, preserve, maintain.
2. συντηρέω, (*No.* 1, *with* σύν, together, *or* in conjunction with, *prefixed*) to be kept in safety together, *or* in conjunction with *each other.*
3. ζωογονέω, to bring forth alive; *and pass.*, to be born alive; *then*, to be preserved alive, (*occ.* Acts vii. 19.)
4. σώζω, to make sound, save, preserve, heal, restore; *hence*, to keep, to maintain intact what is established, (*see* "SAVE," *No.* 1.)

2. Matt. ix. 17.
2. Luke v. 38 (om. καὶ ἀμφότεροι συντηροῦνται, *and both are preserved*, G → T Tr[b] A ℵ.)
3. Luke xvii. 33.
1. 1 Thes. v. 23.
4. 2 Tim. iv. 18.
1. Jude 1.

PRESS. [noun.]

ὄχλος, a crowd, a throng, multitude; a confused multitude, (*as opp. to* δῆμος, a regular assembly.)

Mark ii. 4. | Luke viii. 19.
— v. 27, 30. | — xix. 3.

PRESS (-ED, -ETH.) [verb.]

1. ἀποθλίβω, to press from *every side*, to crowd, throng, (*non occ.*)
2. βιάζομαι, to use force, to force, use violence, force the way, (*occ.* Matt. xi. 12.)
3. συνέχω, to hold *or* press together; constrain, urge on.

[*Here, Paul was* urged on, *or* occupied earnestly with, in his discourse, *or* as to the word, *for the reading is* λόγῳ, *not* πνεύματι, (in spirit) G L T Tr A ℵ.]

1. Luke viii. 45. | 2. Luke xvi. 16.
3. Acts xviii. 5.

PRESS DOWN.

πιέζω, to press, press down *and make compact*, (*non occ.*)

Luke vi. 38.

PRESS TOWARD.

διώκω, to pursue after, follow earnestly.

Phil. iii. 14.

PRESS UPON.

1. ἐπίκειμαι, to lie upon; be laid upon, press heavily upon.
2. ἐπιπίπτω, to fall upon, to throw one's self upon.

2. Mark iii. 10. | 1. Luke v. 1.

PRESSED (BE)

βαρέομαι, to be heavy, be weighed down, be oppressed, borne down *as by evils or calamities.*

2 Cor. i. 8.

PRESUMPTUOUS.

τολμητής, one who is bold, a darer, enterpriser. *In N.T., in a bad sense*, one over-bold, audacious, presumptuous.

2 Pet. ii. 10.

PRETENCE.

πρόφασις, what is shown *or* appears before any one, *i.e.* show, pretence, pretext, *put forth to cover the real intent.*

Matt. xxiii. 14 (*ap.*) | Mark xii. 40.
Phil. i. 18.

PREVAIL (-ED.)

1. ἰσχύω, to be strong, have physical ability; be strong *in physical health and mental power*, have efficacy, prevail.

2. κατισχύω, (*No.* 1, *with* κατά, down, *prefixed*) to be strong against *any one*, to prevail against *or* over, *in a hostile sense*, overcome, vanquish, (*occ.* Matt. xvi. 18, *see below.*)

3. ὠφελέω, to further, profit, be of use, avail.

3. Matt. xxvii. 24.	1. Acts xix. 16, 20.
2. Luke xxiii. 23.	4. Rev. v. 5.
3. John xii. 19.	1. —— xii. 8.

PREVAIL AGAINST.

2. Matt. xvi. 18.

PREVENT (-ED.)

1. φθάνω, to come *or* do before, get first *in doing or being anything*, be beforehand with, anticipate, *in running, etc.; φθάνω with the part. of another verb may often be rendered adverbially*, sooner than.

2. προφθάνω, (*No.* 1, *with* πρό, before, *prefixed*) *more emphatic than No.* 1, to get first before another, anticipate, (*non occ.*)

2. Matt. xvii. 25.	1. 1 Thes. iv. 15.

PRICE (-S.)

τιμή, a holding worth, estimation; esteem, honour, respect; value, price.

Matt. xiii. 46, see P (of great)	Acts xix. 19.
—— xxvii. 6, 9.	1 Cor. vi. 20.
Acts iv. 34.	—— vii. 23.
—— v. 2, 3.	—— ix. 24, } in A.V.1611.
	Phil. iii. 14, } in A.V.1611.

PRICE (OF GREAT)

πολύτιμος, of great value *or* price, very costly.

Matt. xiii. 46.

PRICK (-S.) [noun.]

κέντρον, a point, a prick; *hence*, a sting, (*as of locusts or scorpions*, Rev. ix. 10); *also*, a goad, *i.e.* a rod *or* staff with an iron point for urging oxen on, etc.

Acts ix. 5 (ap.)	Acts xxvi. 14.

PRICK (-ED.) [verb.]

κατανύσσω, to pierce through; *hence*, to be greatly pained.

Acts ii. 37.

PRIDE.

1. ἀλαζονεία, the character of an ἀλαζών, (*i.e.* a wanderer about the country; *hence*, a false pretender, impostor, quack; *hence*, swaggering, boastful, braggart) false pretension, imposture, quackery; *and by implication*, ostentation, arrogance, pride, (*occ.* Jas. iv. 16.)

2. ὑπερηφανία, appearance over, conspicuousness above *other persons or things; hence*, pride, haughtiness, boasting, *and in N.T. with the accessory idea of impiety*, (*non occ.*)

2. Mark vii. 22.	— 1 Tim. iii. 6, *see below.*
1. 1 John ii. 16.	

PRIDE (BE LIFTED UP WITH)

τοφόω, to smoke, fume, surround with smoke; *hence*, to make inflated *or* conceited, *or* to becloud.

1 Tim. iii. 16.

PRIEST.

(*For* CHIEF PRIEST *and* HIGH PRIEST, *see below.*)

ἱερεύς, he who has the care of τὰ ἱερὰ, (the sacrifices); priest.

[Among the Greeks only a *calling*, not a *caste*, but in the Bible, being connected with *substitution*, it is also connected with the substitution of a priestly *caste* on behalf of the nation. As sacrifice is a rendering to God what is due to Him, so, too, the ἱερεύς is a servant of God, (Deut. xvii. 12.) What the whole people ought to be, the priests *are*, (Exod. xix. 3—6; Deut. vii. 6, with Num. iii. 12, 13, 45; Exod. xxviii. 1, 29; Num. xvi. *Hence*, Isa. lxi. 6; Rev. i. 6; xx. 6.) They undertake the offering of sacrifices which represent what man can neither do nor suffer before God, *i.e.* they represent man himself in his relation to God, (Heb. ii. 17; v. 1). This, however, they are only able to do on account of their own holiness, and this does not belong to them

as a personal quality, but they are considered so by God, being elected and separated by God to be His property, (Num. xvi. 5; Heb. v. 4). The Biblical priesthood and the Biblical sacrifice find their perfect consummation in the priesthood of Christ, (to which reference is made in Heb. v., vii., viii., ix., x.) and all who are "in Christ" become "priests unto God," (1 Pet. ii. 5, 9; Rev. i. 6; xx. 6).]

Matt. viii. 4.
— xii. 4, 5.
Mark i. 44.
— ii. 26.
Luke i. 5.
— 8, see P office (execute the)
— 9, see P office.
— v. 14.
— vi. 4.
— x. 31.
— xvii. 14.
John i. 19.
Acts iv. 1.
— vi. 7.
Acts xiv. 13.
— xix. 14, see P (chief of the)
Heb. v. 6.
— vii. 1, 3, 11, 15, 17, 21, 23.
— viii. 4 1st.
— 4 2nd (*om.* G ⇉ L T Tr A ℵ.)
— ix. 6.
— x. 11 (ἀρχιερεύς, *chief-priest,* (see below) L [Trm A.)
— 21.
Rev. i. 6.
— v. 10.
— xx. 6.

PRIEST (CHIEF)

ἀρχιερεύς, Chief-priest, High-priest, *a dignity unknown to the Greeks.*

[In the ἀρχιερεύς culminates the priesthood, so far as it was his duty to represent the whole people, (Lev. iv. 5, 16; xvi; Num. xvi. 10). In the *N.T.* it means the *O.T.* high-priest. Perhaps, in John xviii. 19, 22; Acts v. 17, 21, 27, a designation of the president of the Sanhedrim. In Acts iv. 5, 6; Matt. ii. 4; xvi. 21, the heads of the 24 courses or classes of the priests, 1 Chron. xxiv. 6; 2 Chron. xxvi. 14.]

Matt. ii. 4.
— xvi. 21.
— xx. 18.
— xxi. 15, 23, 45.
— xxvi. 3, 14, 47, 59.
— xxvii. 1, 3, 6, 12, 20, 41, 62.
— xxviii. 11.
Mark viii. 31.
— x. 33.
— xi. 18, 27.
— xiv. 1, 10, 43, 53, 55.
— xv. 1, 3, 10, 11, 31.
Luke ix. 22.
— xix. 47.
— xx. 1 (ἱερεύς, see "PRIEST," G ∾ T A.)
— 19.
Luke xxii. 2, 4, 52, 66.
— xxiii. 4, 10, 13.
— 23 (*om.* καὶ τῶν ἀρχιέρων, *and of the chief priests,* L^b T Tr^b A^b ℵ.)
— xxiv. 20.
John vii. 32, 45.
— xi. 47, 57.
— xii. 10.
— xviii. 3, 35.
— xix. 6, 15, 21.
Acts iv. 23.
— v. 24.
— ix. 14, 21.
— xxii. 30.
— xxiii. 14.
— xxv. 15.
Acts xxvi. 10, 12.

PRIESTS (CHIEF OF THE)

ἀρχιερεύς, *see above.*

Acts xix. 14.

PRIEST (HIGH)

ἀρχιερεύς, *see above.* * *said of Christ.*

Matt. xxvi. 3, 51, 57, 58, 62, 63, 65.
Mark ii. 26.
— xiv. 47, 53, 54, 60, 61, 63, 66.
Luke iii. 2.
— xxii. 50, 54.
John xi. 49, 51.
— xviii. 10, 13, 15 twice, 16, 19, 22, 24, 26.
Acts iv. 6.
— v. 17, 21.
— 24 (ἱερεύς, see "PRIEST," S^t G) (*om.* ἀρχιερεύς καὶ ὁ, *High priest and the,* L T Tr A ℵ.)
Acts v. 27.
— vii. 1.
— ix. 1.
— xxii. 5.
— xxiii. 2, 4, 5.
— xxiv. 1.
— xxv. 2.
Heb. ii. 17*.
— iii. 1*.
— iv. 14*.
— 15.
— v. 1, 5, 10*.
— vi. 20*.
— vii. 26*, 27, 28
— viii. 1*, 3.
— ix. 7, 11*, 25.
— xiii. 11.

PRIEST'S OFFICE.

ἱερατεία, priesthood, *i.e.* the priest's office and duties, (*occ.* Heb. vii. 5.)

Luke i. 9.

PRIEST'S OFFICE (EXECUTE THE)

ἱερατεύω, to be an ἱερεύς, (*see* "PRIEST") to officiate as a priest, (*non occ.*)

Luke i. 8.

PRIESTHOOD.

1. ἱεράτευμα, priesthood; the body of priests as composed of persons, (*non occ.*)
2. ἱερωσύνη, the office, quality, rank, and power of an ἱερεύς, (*see* "PRIEST,") (*non occ.*)

— Heb. vii. 5, see P (office of the)
2. — 11, 12.
2. Heb. vii. 14 (ἱερεύς, *priests,* G L T Tr A ℵ.)
2. — 24.
1. 1 Pet. ii. 5, 9.

PRIESTHOOD (OFFICE OF THE)

ἱερατεία, the service of the priest, (*occ.* Luke i. 9.)

Heb. vii. 5.

PRINCE (-S.)

1. ἄρχων, one first in power, authority, *or* dominion; *hence,* a ruler, lord, prince, chief person.
2. ἀρχηγός, one who makes a beginning, the author, source, cause of *anything.*

3. *ἡγεμών*, a leader, commander *of an army*.

[*In* Matt. ii. 6, quoted from Micah v. 1, where Heb., באלפי יהודה, *i.e. the families into which each tribe was divided*, the heads of which were called אלפים. Zech. xii. 5, 6, and Matthew puts ἡγεμονές, *heads of families*, for the families themselves. The lxx. also puts ἡγεμών for אלוף, Gen. xxxvi. 15, 16, but in Micah v. 1, puts ἐν χιλιάσιν Ἰουδα, the thousands of Judah.]

3. Matt. ii. 6.
1. —— ix. 34.
1. —— xii. 24.
1. —— xx. 25.
1. Mark iii. 22.
1. John xii. 31.
1. —— xiv. 30.
1. John xvi. 11.
2. Acts iii. 15, marg. *author*.
2. —— v. 31.
1. 1 Cor. ii. 6, 8.
1. Eph. ii. 2.
1. Rev. i. 5.

PRINCIPAL.

{ *κατά*, according to, *ἐξοχήν*, eminence, *ὤν*, being, } being of eminence, *or* distinction, (*non occ.*)

Acts xxv. 23.

PRINCIPALITY (-IES.)

ἀρχή, beginning; *of time*, the commencement; *of dignity*, the first place; government, the highest dignitaries *of the State; ἀρχή* relates to the dignity of the position; *ἐξουσία to its* executive authority and power.

[*Used of* supra-mundane powers, *prob.*, evil powers. In 1 Cor. xv. 26, we read of ἔσχατος ἐχθρός, the *last enemy*, which may imply that these names (Col. i. 16, etc.) designate the mutual rank of evil supra-mundane powers, so far as they relate to men.]

Rom. viii. 38.
Eph. i. 21.
—— iii. 10.
—— vi. 12.
Col. i. 16.
—— ii. 10, 15.
Tit. iii. 1.
Jude 6, marg. *first estate*.

PRINCIPLE (S.)

1. *στοιχεῖον*, (*from στοιχέω*, to stand *or* go in order, advance in steps *or* rows) *dim.*, of *στοῖχος* (a row, series, *as of* steps); a little step, a small upright rod *or* post, *esp.* the gnomon *of a sun-dial, or* the shadow *thrown by it; hence*, first beginning, first principle, element, *esp.* of learning; rudiments.

2. *ἀρχή*, beginning, (*see* "PRINCIPALITY.")

1. Heb. v. 12.
2. Heb. vi. 1, marg. *beginning*.

PRINT.

τύπος, a mark *or* impress *made by a hard substance on a soft;* mark, imprint, impression.

John xx. 25 1st, 25 2nd (*τόπος, place*, L T Trm.)

PRISON (-S.)

1. *φυλακή*, watch, guard, *i.e.* the act of keeping watch, guarding; *of persons*, the guards; *of the place*, watch-post, station, prison.

2. *δεσμωτήριον*, a prison, place of bonds, (*non occ.*)

3. *τήρησις*, a watching, keeping an eye upon, observing; *hence*, a guarding; *then*, a guard, place of guarding, prison, (*occ.* Acts iv. 3; 1 Cor. vii. 19.)

4. *οἴκημα*, a dwelling, a building; *of a prison*, the cell, (*non occ.*)

— Matt. iv. 2, see Cast.
1. —— v. 25.
2. —— xi. 2.
1. —— xiv. 3, 10.
1. —— xviii. 30.
1. —— xxv. 36, 39, 43, 44.
— Mark i. 14, see Put.
1. —— vi. 17, 28.
1. Luke iii. 20.
1. —— xii. 58.
1. —— xxi. 12.
1. —— xxii. 33.
1. —— xxiii. 19, 25.
3. Acts v. 18.
1. —— 19.
2. —— 21.
1. —— 22.
2. Acts v. 23.
1. —— 25.
1. —— viii. 3.
1. —— xii. 4, 5, 6.
4. —— 7.
1. —— 17.
1. —— xvi. 23, 24.
2. —— 26.
— —— 27 1st, see P (keeper of the)
1. —— 27 2nd, 37, 40.
1. —— xxii. 4.
1. —— xxvi. 10.
1. 2 Cor. xi. 23.
1. 1 Pet. iii. 19.
1. Rev. ii. 10.
1. —— xx. 7.

PRISON (KEEPER OF THE)

δεσμοφύλαξ, a prison-keeper, (*occ.* Acts xvi. 23.)

Acts xvi. 27, 36.

PRISONER.

1. *δέσμιος*, binding; *hence, pass.*, bound; a captive, a prisoner, (*occ.* Acts xxv. 14; Heb. xiii. 3.)

2. *δεσμώτης*, a prisoner, a captive, (*non occ.*)

1. Matt. xxvii. 15, 16.
1. Mark xv. 6.
1. Acts xvi. 25, 27.
1. —— xxiii. 18.
1. —— xxv. 27.
2. —— xxvii. 1, 42.
1. —— xxviii. 16 (ap.), 17.
— Rom. xvi. 7, see P (fellow)
1. Eph. iii. 1.
1. —— iv. 1.
— Col. iv. 10, see P (fellow)
1. 2 Tim. i. 8.
1. Philem. 1, 9.
— Philem. 23, see P (fellow)

PRISONER (FELLOW)

συναιχμάλωτος, taken prisoner in conjunction with *another, as in war,* (*lit., by the spear*) a fellow-prisoner of war, (*non occ.*)

Rom. xvi. 7. | Col. iv. 10.
Philem. 23.

PRIVATE.

ἴδιος, own, one's own, individual; [*i.e.* here no prophecy is to be interpreted *individually*, apart from reference to the other prophecies of God's word, but is to be understood as being in harmony with the whole of God's counsels, purposes, and plans, as revealed in the prophetic scriptures.]

2 Pet. i. 20.

PRIVATELY.

{ κατά, according to, ἰδίαν, one's own, } by one's self, apart from others, alone.

Matt. xxiv. 3.
Mark vi. 32.
—— ix. 28.
—— xiii. 3.
Luke ix. 10.
—— x. 23.
Acts xxiii. 19.
Gal. ii. 2, marg. *severally.*

PRIVILEGE.

John i. 12, see "POWER."

PRIVILY.

λάθρα, secretly, by stealth.

Matt. i. 19.
—— ii. 7.
Acts xvi. 37.
Gal. ii. 4, see Come.
2 Pet. ii. 1, see Bring.

PRIVY TO (BE)

σύνοιδα, to know in conjunction with another.

Acts v. 2.

PRIZE. (PRICE, A.V. 1611.)

βραβεῖον, a prize bestowed on the victors in the public games of the Greeks, such as a wreath, chaplet, *or* garland.

1 Cor. ix. 24. | Phil. iii. 14.

PROCEED (-ED, -ETH.)

1. ἐκπορεύομαι, to proceed out of, to lead *or* pass out of, *having regard to the end that is to be reached.*

2. ἐξέρχομαι, to come *or* go out of *any place,* to arrive out of.

3. προκόπτω, to cut down impediments that impede one's progress; *hence,* advance, move forward, increase.

1. Matt. iv. 4.
1. —— xv. 8.
2. —— 19.
1. Mark vii. 21.
1. Luke iv. 22.
— John viii. 42, see P forth.
1. —— xv. 26.
— Acts xii. 3, see P further.
1. Eph. iv. 29.
3. 2 Tim. iii. 9.
2. Jas. iii. 10.
1. Rev. iv. 5.
1. —— xi. 5.
1. —— xix. 21 (No. 2, G L T Tr A ℵ.)
1. Rev. xxii. 1.

PROCEED FORTH.

2. John viii. 42.

PROCEED FURTHER.

προστίθημι, to place beside, add unto.

Acts xii. 3.

PROCLAIM (-ED, -ING.)

κηρύσσω, *see* "PREACH," *No.* 1.)

Luke xii. 3. | Rev. v. 2.

PROFANE. [adj.]

βέβηλος, allowable to tread, (*from* βηλός, a threshold) *opposite to* ἱερός, (sacred) unhallowed, common, profane; *of persons,* profane, *i.e.* not initiated, (*non occ.*)

1 Tim. i. 9.
—— iv. 7.
1 Tim. vi. 20.
2 Tim. ii. 16.

PROFANE PERSON.

Heb. xii. 16.

PROFANE. [verb.]

βεβηλόω, to cross the threshold (*of what is holy*), to profane, pollute, violate, (*non occ.*)

Matt. xii. 5. | Acts xxiv. 6.

PROFESS (-ED, -ING.)

1. ὁμολογέω, to speak *or* say the same *with another,* to assent, accord, agree with, confess.

2. ἐπαγγέλλομαι, to announce one's self *as doing or about to do anything*, to promise, make profession of.

3. φάσκω, to assert, affirm, (*occ.* Acts xxiv. 19; xxv. 9; Rev. ii. 2.)

4. προΐστημι, to cause to stand before, propose, prefer; *then*, to care for anything, give attention to it, be diligent in it.

1. Matt. vii. 23.
3. Rom. i. 22.
— 2 Cor. ix. 13, see Professed.
2. 1 Tim. ii. 10.
1. —— vi. 12.
2. ——— 21.
1. Tit. i. 16.
4. Tit. iii. 14, marg. (text. *maintain.*)

PROFESSED.

ὁμολογία, saying the same thing with another; *hence*, assent, accord, agreement; *then*, confession. *Here*, *Gen.*, of [*your*] confession.

2 Cor. ix. 13.

PROFESSION.

ὁμολογία, *see* "PROFESSED."

1 Tim. vi. 12.
——— 13, marg. (text, *confession.*)
Heb. iii. 1.
—— iv. 14.
—— x. 23.

PROFIT. [noun.]

1. συμφέρω, to bear *or* bring together, *i.e. in conjunction with others*, to bring together for, contribute, conduce; *hence*, to be well, profitable. (*Here, participle.*)

2. χρήσιμος, fit for use, usable, useful, serviceable, profitable. *Here, neut.*, (*non occ.*)

3. ὠφέλεια, beneficial advantage, benefit, emolument; furthering, help, aid.

4. ὠφελέω, to confer benefit, further, help. *Here, mid. or pass.*, to be advantaged, benefited, *or* helped.

5. τό, the, that.

3. Rom. iii. 1.
1. 1 Cor. vii. 35.
1. —— x. 33 1st (τὸ σύμφερον, *the profitable thing*, L T Tr A ℵ.)
5. 1 Cor. x. 33 2nd.
2. 2 Tim. ii. 14.
1. Heb. xii. 10.
4. Heb. xiii. 9.

PROFIT (-ED, -ETH.) [verb.]

1. ὠφελέω, to further, help, benefit; be of service *to any one*. *Mid. or pass.*, to be helped *or* profited

2. ὄφελος, furtherance, advantage, assistance, (*occ.* 1 Cor. xv. 32.)

3. προκόπτω, to cut down impediments that impede one's progress; *hence*, advance, move forward, progress.

4. { εἰμί, to be, ὠφέλιμος, helping, aiding, } to be advantageous.

1. Matt. viii. 36.
— —— xv. 5, } see P (be)
— —— xvi. 26, }
— Mark vii. 11, }
1. John vi. 63.
1. Rom. ii. 25.
— 1 Cor. xii. 7, see P (to) withal
1. 1 Cor. xiii. 3.
1. —— xiv. 6.
3. Gal. i. 14.
1. —— v. 2.
4. 1 Tim. iv. 8.
1. Heb. iv. 2.
2. Jas. ii. 14, 16.

PROFIT WITHAL (TO)

{ πρός, towards, τὸ, the, συμφέρον, profitable *thing*, } with a view to what is profitable.

1 Cor. xii. 7.

PROFITED (BE)

1. Matt. xv. 5.
1. Matt. xvi. 26.
1. Mark vii. 11.

PROFITABLE.

1. ὠφέλιμος, helping, aiding; useful, serviceable, advantageous.

2. εὔχρηστος, very useful, very good of its kind; very beneficial.

— Matt. v. 29, 30, } see P (be)
— Acts xx. 20, }
— 1 Cor. vi. 12, }
1. 1 Tim. iv. 8.
1. 2 Tim. iii. 16.
2. —— iv. 11.
1. Titus iii. 8.
2. Philem. 11.

PROFITABLE (BE)

συμφέρω, *see* "PROFIT" (noun.) * *Intrans. and impersonal.*

Matt. v. 29*, 30*.
Acts xx. 20.
1 Cor. vi. 12, marg. (text, *be expedient.*)

PROFITABLY. [margin.]

Eph. iv. 29, see "USE."

PROFITING.

προκοπή, a cutting down of impediments that are in one's way; *hence*, progress, a going forward, advancement, (*occ.* Phil. i. 12, 25.)

1 Tim. iv. 15.

PROMISE (-s.) [noun.]

1. *ἐπαγγελία*, proclamation as the content of *ἐπαγγέλω*, (*see* "PROMISE," [verb] *No.* 1) *denoting both* the fact of the proclamation, *and* that which is proclaimed; declaration made on account of something; *hence*, a promise, offer, (*occ.* 1 John i. 5.)

2. *ἐπάγγελμα*, the thing promised, (*non occ.*)

1. Luke xxiv. 49.
1. Acts i. 4.
1. —— ii. 33, 39.
1. —— vii. 17.
1. —— xiii. 23, 32.
1. —— xxiii. 21.
1. —— xxvi. 6.
1. Rom. iv. 13, 14, 18, 20.
1. —— ix. 4, 8, 9.
1. —— xv. 8.
1. 2 Cor. i. 20.
1. —— vii. 1.
1. Gal. iii. 14, 16, 17, 18 twice.
— —— 19, see P is made.
1. —— 21, 22, 29.
1. —— iv. 23, 28.
1. Eph. i. 13.
1. —— ii. 12.
1. Eph. iii. 6.
1. —— vi. 2.
1. 1 Tim. iv. 8.
1. 2 Tim. i. 1.
1. Heb. iv. 1.
1. —— vi. 12.
— —— 13, see P (make)
1. —— 15, 17.
1. —— vii. 6.
1. —— viii. 6.
1. —— ix. 15.
1. —— x. 36.
1. —— xi. 9 twice, 13, 17, 33, 39.
2. 2 Pet. i. 4.
1. —— iii. 4, 9.
2. —— 13.
1. 1 John ii. 25.

PROMISE (MAKE)

ἐπαγγέλλομαι, (*see below, No.* 1.)

Heb. vi. 13 part.

PROMISE IS MADE.

ἐπαγγέλλομαι, (*see below, No.* 1.)

Gal. iii. 19, pass. impers.

PROMISE (-ED.) [verb.]

1. *ἐπαγγέλλομαι*, to proclaim, promulgate, *be it a message, a summons, or a promise;* to tell in consequence *of something; then, mid. and pass. perf.*, to announce concerning one's self, announce one's intentions, engage, hold out, promise.

2. *ὁμολογέω*, to say the same thing, agree, coincide with, grant, admit, confess.

3. *ἐξομολογέω*, (*No.* 2, *with ἐκ*, out of, *prefixed*) to speak out the same things *as another*, concede, acknowledge, confess fully.

2. Matt. xiv. 7.
1. Mark xiv. 11.
— Luke i. 72, see P to.
3. —— xxii. 6 (*om. καὶ ἐξωμολόγησεν, and he promised*, L ℵ.)
1. Acts vii. 5.
— Rom. i. 2, see P afore.
1. Rom. iv. 21.
1. Tit. i. 2.
1. Heb. x. 23.
1. —— xi. 11.
1. —— xii. 26.
1. Jas. i. 12.
1. —— ii. 5.
1. 2 Pet. ii. 19 part.
1. 1 John ii. 25.

PROMISE AFORE.

προεπαγγέλλομαι, (*No.* 1, *above, with πρό*, before, *prefixed*), (*non occ.*)

Rom. i. 2.

PROMISED TO.

μετά, with, in association with. *Here, to perform mercy* with *our fathers*, [*i.e.* to work, accomplish, *or* fulfil that which the fathers had lived on as promised to their faith.]

Luke i. 72.

PROOF.

1. *δοκιμή*, proof, trial; *the state of being tried*, a trying, (2 Cor. viii. 2); *the state of having been tried*, tried probity, approved integrity; proved true.

2. *ἔνδειξις*, a pointing out with the finger, indication, declaration, manifestation.

1. 2 Cor. ii. 9.
2. —— viii. 24.
1. 2 Cor. xiii. 3.
1. Phil. ii. 22.

PROOF (INFALLIBLE)

τεκμήριον, a fixed sign, certain token; a standard by which to ascertain the truth of a thing; criterion, (*non occ.*)

Acts i. 3.

PROOF OF (MAKE FULL)

πληροφορέω, to bear *or* bring fully; *hence*, give full assurance; *of persons*, to be fully assured; *of things*, to make fully assured, confirm fully, fulfil to the utmost.

2 Tim. iv. 5, marg. *fulfil*.

PROPER.

{ *ἀστεῖος*, elegant, fair, beautiful, *τῷ θεῷ*, to God, } *i.e.* exceedingly fair.

[For the beauty of Moses, *see* Exod. ii. 2; Josephus Ant. 2,9,6,7. And for the idiom, *see μεγάλη τῷ θεῷ*, lxx. for לֵאלֹהִים Jonah iii. 3.]

Heb. xi. 23.

PROPER (ONE'S)

ἴδιος, one's own, private, individual.

Acts i. 19. | 1 Cor. vii. 7.

PROPHECY (-IES.) [noun.]

προφητεία, a speaking forth, prophetic declarations, exhortations, warnings, uttered by the prophets while under divine influence, and referring either to the past, present, or future.

Matt. xiii. 14.
Rom. xii. 6.
1 Cor. xii. 10.
— xiii. 8.
1 Tim. i. 18.
1 Tim. iv. 14.
2 Pet. i. 20, 21.
Rev. i. 3.
— xi. 6.
— xix. 10.
Rev. xxii. 7, 10, 18, 19.

PROPHECY (OF)

προφετικός, relating *or* pertaining to prophecy, prophetic, (*occ.* Rom. xvi. 26.)

2 Pet. i. 19.

PROPHECY (THE GIFT OF)

προφητεία, a prophecy, that which is uttered forth by the prophet; *also*, the prophetic rank *or* work, the office *or* gift of a prophet.

1 Cor. xiii. 2.

PROPHESY (-IETH, -IED, -ING.) [verb.]

προφητεύω, to be a *προφήτης*, (*see* "PROPHET," *No.* 1) to hold the office of a prophet; to do the work of a prophet, *i.e.* to speak forth, in declaration, warning, or exhortation, as directed by the Spirit of God, (*non occ.*)

Matt. vii. 22.
— xi. 13.
— xv. 7.
— xxvi. 68.
Mark vii. 6.
— xiv. 65.
Luke i. 67.
— xxii. 64.
John xi. 51.
Acts ii. 17, 18.
Acts xix. 6.
— xxi. 9.
1 Cor. xi. 4, 5.
— xiii. 9.
— xiv. 1, 3, 4, 5 twice, 24, 31, 39.
1 Pet. i. 10.
Jude 14.
Rev. x. 11.
— xi. 3.

PROPHESYING (-s.) [noun.]

προφητεία, *see* "PROPHECY."

1 Cor. xiv. 6, 22. | 1 Thes. v. 20.

PROPHET (-s.)

1. *προφήτης*, one who speaks forth openly before any one, a proclaimer of a divine message; *among the heathen*, an interpreter of the oracle. In the lxx. *it is the translation of the earlier* ראה, seer, *showing that what really constituted the prophet, was* immediate intercourse with God; *it is the ordinary word for* נביא, *which means, either* one in whom the Divinity permits his word to spring forth, *or* one to whom anything is whispered. *The usage, however, of the word is clear; it signifies* one on whom the Spirit of God rested, (Numb. xi. 17, 25, 26, 29); one to whom and through whom God speaks, (Num. xii. 2); one to whom God makes known His mysteries, (Amos iii. 7, 8). *Hence, it means,* one to whom God reveals His truth, and through whom He speaks, (Gen. xx. 7, 17, 18). Prediction *was not part of the true conception of the prophet,* (*see* Deut. xviii. 15, 18—20; Numb. xii. 8) *but* a showing forth of God's will. Two things together go to make the *προφήτης*: (1) an insight granted by God into the divine secrets or mysteries, and (2) a communication of these to others, *which, from the very nature of the case, are* His purposes of grace, with the warnings and announcements of judgments that pertain thereto. *Hence, in the O.T. prophets* their preaching was a prophesying of a salvation and purposes of grace and glory yet to be accomplished, *while in the case of the N.T. prophets* their prophesying was a preaching of those purposes of grace already accomplished, *and also* a foretelling of the purposes of glory which were still future. It is used of the *O.T.* prophets (*gen., οἱ πρ., plural*) in all the references below, except—

(a) *denotes ὁ προφήτης*, the prophet, *as used of* Christ, *with obvious reference to* Deut. xviii. 18—20.

(b) *προφήτης*, (*without the article*) *also used of* Christ.

(c) *the word is used of* the *N.T.* prophets.

(d) *once in a general sense of* the Cretan poet, Epimenides.

(e) The two witnesses yet to be raised up for the special purposes of God. Whether Elijah be one of them it is not said. He is yet, however, to appear, (Matt. iv. 5, 6; xi. 14; xvii. 11—13). (For the *fem.*, *see* "PROPHETESS.") (*non occ.*)

2. ἀνήρ, a man, *see* "MAN," *No.* 2, προφήτης, a prophet, (*see above.*) — *Here, with* ὅς ἐγένετο, who became a man, a prophet.

1. Matt. i. 22.
1. —— ii. 5, 15, 17, 23.
1. —— iii. 3.
1. —— iv. 14.
1. —— v. 12, 17.
1. —— vii. 12.
— —— 15, see P (false)
1. —— viii. 17.
1. —— x. 41 3 times.
1. —— xi. 9 twice, 13.
1. —— xii. 17, 39.
1. —— xiii. 17, 35.
1b.—— 57.
1b.—— xiv. 5.
1. —— xvi. 4 (om. G → L T Tr A ℵ.)
1. —— 14.
1. —— xxi. 4.
1b.—— 11.
1. —— 26, 46.
1. —— xxii. 40.
1. —— xxiii. 29, 30, 31, 34, [37.
— —— xxiv. 11, see P (false)
1. —— 15.
— —— 24, see P (false)
1. —— xxvi. 56.
1. —— xxvii. 9, 35 (ap.)
1. Mark i. 2, (ἐν τῷ Ἡσαΐᾳ τῷ προφήτῃ, in Esaias the prophet, inst. of ἐν τοῖς προφήταις, in the prophets, G L T Tr A ℵ.)
1b.—— vi. 4, 15 twice.
1. —— viii. 28.
1. —— xi. 32.
1. —— xiii. 14 (ap.)
— —— 22, see P (false)
1. Luke i. 70, 76.
1. —— iii. 4.
1. —— iv. 17.
1b.—— 24.
1. —— 27.
1. —— vi. 23.
— —— 26, see P (false)
1b.—— vii. 16.
1. —— 26 twice.
1. —— 28 (om. G → L Tr^b A^b ℵ.)
1b.—— 39.
1. —— ix. 8, 19.
1. —— x. 24.
1. —— xi. 29 (om. G L T Tr A ℵ.)
1. —— 47, 49, 50.
1. —— xiii. 28.
1b.—— 33.
1. —— 34.
1. —— xvi. 16, 29, 31.
1. Luke xviii. 31.
1. —— xx. 6.
2. —— xxiv. 19.
1. —— 25, 27, 44.
1a. John i. 21.
1. —— 23, 25, 45.
1b.—— iv. 19, 44.
1a.—— vi. 14.
1. —— 45.
1a.—— vii. 40.
1. —— 52.
1. —— viii. 52, 53.
1b.—— ix. 17.
1. —— xii. 38.
1. Acts ii. 16, 30.
1. —— iii. 18, 21.
1a.—— 22.
1. —— 23, 24, 25.
1a.—— vii. 37.
1. —— 42, 48, 52.
1. —— viii. 28, 30, 34.
1. —— x. 43.
1c.—— xi. 27.
1c.—— xiii. 1.
— —— 6, see P (false)
1. —— 15, 20, 27, 40.
1. —— xv. 15.
1c.—— 32.
1c.—— xxi. 10.
1. —— xxiv. 14.
1. —— xxvi. 22, 27.
1. —— xxviii. 23, 25.
1. Rom. i. 2.
1. —— iii. 21.
1. —— xi. 3.
1. —— xvi. 26, see Prophets (of the)
1c. 1 Cor. xii. 28, 29.
1c.—— xiv. 29, 32 twice, 37.
1c. Eph. ii. 20.
1c.—— iii. 5.
1c.—— iv. 11.
1. 1 Thes. ii. 15.
1d. Tit. i. 12.
1. Heb. i. 1.
1. —— xi. 32.
1. Jas. v. 10.
1. 1 Pet. i. 10.
— 2 Pet. ii. 1, see P (false)
1. —— 16.
1. —— iii. 2.
— 1 John iv. 1, see P [(false)
1. Rev. x. 7.
1e.—— xi. 10, 18.
1. —— xvi. 6.
— —— 13, see P (false)
1. —— xviii. 20, 24.
— —— xix. 20, } see P
— —— xx. 10, } (false)
1. —— xxii. 6, 9.

PROPHET (FALSE)

ψευδοπροφήτης, a false hypocritical prophet, one falsely professing to come as a messenger, and with a message from God.

Matt. vii. 15.
—— xxiv. 11, 24.
Mark xiii. 22.
Luke vi. 26.
Acts xiii. 6.
2 Pet. ii. 1.
1 John iv. 1.
Rev. xvi. 13.
—— xix. 20.
—— xx. 10.

PROPHETS (OF THE)

προφητικός, relating to, uttered by, *or* belonging to the prophets; prophetic, (*occ.* 2 Pet. i. 19.)

Rom. xvi. 26.

PROPHETESS.

προφῆτις, *fem. of* προφήτης, (*see* "PROPHET," *No.* 1), (*non occ.*)

Luke ii. 36. | Rev. ii. 20.

PROPITIATION.

1. ἱλασμός, conciliation, expiation; *also*, all actions which have expiation for their object, *as sacrifices, etc. So Christ is called* ἱλασμός, *as it is* He by whom, as by a sacrifice, sin is expiated. The lxx. translate כפרים, (the covering of sin by means of sacrifice) by ἱλασμός, (Lev. xxv. 9; Numb. v. 8), (*non occ.*)

2. ἱλαστήριον, (*is not the neuter of* ἱλαστήριος, (*adj.*) expiatory, *but a substantive. Such an adj. never occurs in Greek, and only in eccles. Gk. very late and seldom,*) *it denotes*, the place of conciliation, *or* expiation. *The* lxx. *always use it, as the name of a place, as* כפרת, Ex. xxv. 18, 19, 20, 21, 22; xxxi. 7; xxxv. 12; xxxvii. 7, 8, 9; Lev. xvi. 2, 13, 14, 15; Num. vii. 89, etc. *Accordingly,* ἱλαστήριον *is used for* כפרת *not only in* Heb. ix. 5, *but also in* Rom. iii. 25. *In* Exod. xxv. 22, *and* Lev. xvi. 2, *the* Capporeth *is* the central seat of the saving presence and gracious revelations of God, *and was so far the principal part of the Holy of Holies that the latter is even called* "the House of the Capporeth," (1 Chron. xxviii. 11; *see* 1 Kings vi. 5), (*occ.* Heb. ix. 5.)

2. Rom. iii. 25. | 1. 1 John ii. 2.
1. 1 John iv. 10.

PROPORTION.

ἀναλογία, equality of ratios, proportion, *e.g.* a : b : : c : d ; *hence*, proportion, analogy, (*non occ.*)

Rom. xii. 6.

PROSELYTE (-s.)

προσήλυτος, come to, that has arrived at *a place*, stranger, sojourner; one who comes over to another; *hence*, a proselyte, (*non occ.*)

Matt. xxiii. 15.
Acts ii. 10.
Acts vi. 5.
— xiii. 43.

PROSPER (-ED, -ETH.)

εὐοδόομαι, to be led in a good way, have a prosperous journey, (*occ.* Rom. i. 10.)

1 Cor. xvi. 2.
3 John 2 twice.

PROSPEROUS.

See, JOURNEY.

PROTEST BY (I)

νή, *a particle of strong affirmation*, yea, (*non occ.*)

1 Cor. xv. 31.

PROUD.

ὑπερήφανος, appearing over, conspicuous above *other persons or things*; *hence, of persons*, haughty, arrogant.

Luke i. 51.
Rom. i. 30.
1 Tim. vi. 4, see P (be)
2 Tim. iii. 2.
Jas. iv. 6.
1 Pet. v. 5.

PROUD (BE)

τυφόω, to smoke, surround with smoke; *hence*, to becloud. *In N.T. only pass.*, to become beclouded.

1 Tim. vi. 4, marg. *be a fool.*

PROVE (-ED, -EST, -ING.)

1. δοκιμάζω, to assay, to make trial of, put to the proof, examine; *hence*, to examine and judge of; prove by test; approve on trial.
2. ἀποδείκνυμι, to point away from other objects at one, *and so*, point out, show; show by argument, demonstrate.
3. παρίστημι, (*trans.*) to cause to stand near, to place *or* set before any one, set forth, *as by argument*, etc.
4. πειράζω, to essay, to make a trial *or* an attempt; to tempt, try.
5. συμβιβάζω, to bring together (*in conjunction*), put together, *so as to compare; here*, to bring together *scriptures or proofs, so as to prove a thing.*

1. Luke xiv. 19.
4. John vi. 6.
5. Acts ix. 22.
3. — xxiv. 13.
2. — xxv. 7.
— Rom. iii. 9, see P before.
1. — xii. 2.
1. 2 Cor. viii. 8, 22.
1. — xiii. 5.
1. Gal. vi. 4.
1. Eph. v. 10.
1. 1 Thes. v. 21.
1. 1 Tim. iii. 10.
1. Heb. iii. 9 (*ap.*)

PROVE BEFORE.

προαιτιάομαι, to accuse beforehand. *Here, Aor.* 1, "we before accused," *or* brought a charge.

Rom. iii. 9, marg. *charge before.*

PROVERB (-s.)

1. παραβολή, *see* "PARABLE," *No.* 1.
2. παροιμία, *see* "PARABLE," *No.* 2, (*occ.* John x. 6.)

1. Luke iv. 23.
2. John xvi. 25 twice, marg. *parable.*
2. John xvi. 29, marg. *parable.*
2. 2 Pet. ii. 22.

PROVIDE (-ED, -ING.)

1. ἑτοιμάζω, to make ready, prepare.
2. κτάομαι, to get for one's self, acquire, procure, *by purchase or otherwise.*
3. παρίστημι, (*trans.*) to cause to stand beside *or* near, set before *any one*, place at hand, furnish.
4. ποιέω, to make.
5. προβλέπω, to foresee. *Here, mid.*, (*non occ.*)
6. προνοέω, to perceive beforehand, provide for, see to beforehand.
   (a) *Mid.*, to provide for on one's own behalf.

2. Matt. x. 9, marg. *get.*
1. Luke xii. 20.
4. — 33.
3. Acts xxiii. 24.
6. Rom. xii. 17.
— 2 Cor. viii. 21, } see P for.
— 1 Tim. v. 8, } see P for.
5. Heb. xi. 40, marg. *foresee*

PROVIDE FOR.

6a. 2 Cor. viii. 21.
6a. 1 Tim. v. 8.

PROVIDENCE.

πρόνοια, foresight, provision, (*occ.* Rom. xiii. 14.)

Acts xxiv. 2.

PROVINCE.

ἐπαρχία, the post *or* office of an ἔπαρχος, (governor of a country, *esp. a conquered one*) prefecture, (*non occ.*)

Acts xxiii. 34. | Acts xxv. 1.

PROVISION FOR.

πρόνοια, foresight, provision, (*occ.* Acts xxiv. 2.)

Rom. xiii. 14.

PROVOCATION.

παραπικρασμός, an embittering with *or* towards *any one;* lxx. for מְרִיבָה, Ps. xcv. 8, (*not found elsewhere or in the classics.*)

Heb. iii. 8, 15.

PROVOKE (-ED, -ING.)

(*For various combinations with other words, see below.*)

1. ἐρεθίζω, to rouse to anger, rouse to fight; *hence, gen.*, to excite, irritate, provoke, (*occ.* Col. iii. 21.)
2. παραπικραίνω, to make bitter with *or* towards *any one*, to treat with bitterness; *hence*, to embitter, provoke, (lxx. for מרה, to rebel. Ps. v. 12; lxxviii. 17, 40, 56; Ezek. xx. 13, 21), (*non occ.*)
3. προκαλέω, to call forth, invite to stand forth. *Here, mid.*, to call forth before one's self, to challenge, defy, (*non occ.*)

— Rom. x. 19, } see
— — xi. 11, } Jealousy.
— — — 14, see Emulation.
— 1 Cor. x. 22, see Jealousy.
1. 2 Cor. ix. 2.
3. Gal. v. 26.
— Eph. vi. 4, see Wrath.
2. Heb. iii. 16.

PROVOKE TO ANGER.

1. Col. iii. 21.

PROVOKE TO SPEAK.

ἀποστοματίζω, to repeat from the mouth, to repeat to pupils; cause pupils to repeat by heart; *hence*, to prepare questions to be answered off-hand, ensnare by questions, (*non occ.*)

Luke xi. 53.

PROVOKE UNTO (TO)

{ εἰς, unto, παροξυσμός, a sharpening, } unto an incitement [*of love, etc.*]

Heb. x. 24.

PROVOKED (BE EASILY)

παροξύνω, to sharpen *by rubbing* on *anything*, to whet; to sharpen, incite, exasperate.

1 Cor. xiii. 5.

PRUDENCE.

φρόνησις, a minding to do *so and so*, purpose, intention; thoughtfulness, good sense, practical wisdom, prudence, *esp. in the management of affairs*, (*occ.* Luke i. 17.)

Eph. i. 8.

PRUDENT.

συνετός, putting together in mind; discerning, sagacious, *esp. by nature*, (*non occ.*)

Matt. xi. 25. | Acts xiii. 7.
Luke x. 21. | 1 Cor. i. 19.

PSALM (S.)

1. ψαλμός, a touching, twang, *e.g.* of a bowstring; *of stringed instruments*, a playing, music; *in later usage*, a song *as accompanied by stringed instruments; hence, gen.*, a psalm *or* song *in commemoration of mercies received, rather than of praise to God* (*like No.* 2.)

   (a) *Esp. of* the Book of Psalms as part of the *O.T.*

2. ὑμνέω, to hymn, *i.e.* to sing a hymn *or* hymns, praise in song, *esp. in praise of a god or hero after death.* [*Hence*, the word was so connected with heathenism that it was not generally used till the 4th century. The word ᾠδή (*ode*) is used in the Rev. v. 9; xiv. 3; xv. 3.]

2. Matt. xxvi. 30, } marg.
2. —— xiv. 26, } (text, *sing a hymn.*)
— Luke xx. 42, see Psalms (the)
1. —— xxiv. 44.
— Acts i. 20, see Psalms [(the)
1. Acts xiii. 23.
— —— 35, see Another.
1. 1 Cor. xiv. 26.
1. Eph. v. 19.
1. Col. iii. 16.
1. Jas. v. 13.

PSALMS (THE)

1a. Luke xx. 42. | 1a. Acts i. 20.

PSALMS (SING)

ψάλλω, to touch, twitch, pluck, *esp. a string*, to twang; strike the chords; touch the lyre *or* other stringed instrument; play. In lxx. and *N.T.*, to sing, chant, accompanied by stringed instruments.

Jas. v. 13.

PUBLIC.

See, EXAMPLE.

PUBLICAN (-S.)

τελώνης, a farmer of the taxes *or* customs. One who paid to the government a certain sum for the privilege of collecting the taxes and customs of a district, (*Lat.*, publicanus) *consequently the object of bitter hatred among the Jews*, (*from* τέλος, tax, *and* ὠνέομαι, to purchase), (*non occ.*)

Matt. v. 46.
—— 47 (G ~) (*ἐθνικοί, heathen*, G L T Tr A ℵ.)
—— ix. 10, 11.
—— x. 3.
—— xi. 19.
—— xviii. 17.
Matt. xxi. 31, 32.
Mark ii. 15, 16.
Luke iii. 12.
—— v. 27, 29, 30.
—— vii. 29, 34.
—— xv. 1.
—— xviii. 10, 11, 13.

PUBLICANS (CHIEF AMONG THE)

ἀρχιτελώνης, a chief farmer *or* collector of taxes, (*non occ.*)

Luke xix. 2.

PUBLICLY.

δημοσίᾳ, in public, before the people.

Acts xviii. 28. | Acts xx. 20.

PUBLISH.

1. *κηρύσσω*, to be a herald, (*see* "PREACH," *No.* 1.)
2. *διαφέρω*, to bear *or* carry through *a place or country*. *Pass.*, to be published abroad.

1. Mark i. 45.
1. —— v. 20.
1. —— vii. 36.
1. Mark xiii. 10.
1. Luke viii. 39.
— Acts x. 37, see P (be)
2. Acts xiii. 49.

PUBLISHED (BE)

γίνομαι, to begin to be, come to pass, be done; *of a declaration*, to be *declared*, etc.

Acts x. 37.

PUFF UP (-ED.)

φυσιόω, to blow, puff, pant; puff up, inflate, (*non occ.*)

1 Cor. viii. 1.

PUFFED UP (BE)

φυσιόω, *see above*, (*here, pass. or mid.*)

1 Cor. iv. 6, 18, 19.
—— v. 2.
1 Cor. xiii. 4.
Col. ii. 18.

PULL (-ED, -ING.)

ἁρπάζω, to seize upon, snatch away, *spoken of beasts of prey*.

Jude 23.

PULL DOWN.

καθαιρέω, to take down, *as from a higher place; then, with violence implied*, to pull down, demolish.

Luke xii. 18.

PULL IN PIECES.

διασπάω, to pull in sunder, tear in pieces, (*occ.* Mark v. 4.)

Acts xxiii. 10.

PULL OUT.

1. *ἐκβάλλω*, to throw *or* cast out, *with or without violence, implied;* take out, extract.
2. *ἀνασπάω*, to draw up, pull up, (*occ.* Acts xi. 10.)

1. Matt. vii. 4. | 1. Luke vi. 42 twice.
2. Luke xiv. 5.

PULLING DOWN.

καθαίρεσις, a pulling down, demolition, *as of a fortress, etc.*, (*occ.* 2 Cor. x. 8; xiii. 10.)

2 Cor. x. 4.

PUNISH (-ED.)

1. κολάζω, to curtail, dock, prune, *but usually like Lat., castigare,* to keep within bounds, check, chastise; *pass.,* to be punished, *generally. (In N.T. the future punishment of sin is clearly defined as death and destruction.) (non occ.)*

2. τιμωρέω, to watch *or* protect the honour of any one, *i.e.* to help, aid, to assist by way of redressing injuries, to avenge. (It is from τιμωρός, watching one's honour, *i.e.* vindicating it, avenging it.) *(non occ.)*

1. Acts iv. 21.	2. Acts xxvi. 11.
2. —— xxii. 5.	1. 2 Pet. ii. 9.

PUNISHED (BE)

δίκη, right, *esp.* a judicial process, the name of the heathen Goddess of Justice, Nemesis, vengeance.
τίω, to hold worth, honour *by making compensation for;* to pay for *a wrong done.*

Here, "a penalty shall pay"—*or* shall give satisfaction.

2 Thes. i. 9.

PUNISHING. [margin.]

Col. ii. 23, see "NEGLECTING."

PUNISHMENT.

1. ἐκδίκησις, execution of right and justice; maintenance of right, avengement, vengeance.

2. ἐπιτιμία, the condition of an ἐπίτιμος, (in possession of the rights of citizenship) the enjoyment of all civil rights and privileges, (from ἐπιτιμάω, to put further honour upon, estimate higher) *hence, spoken of* the estimate fixed by *a judge on the infringement of civil rights and citizenship; then, gen.,* penalty, judicial infliction, *(non occ.)*

3. κόλασις, a pruning; *hence, gen.,* punishment.

[The nature of which must be looked for in *other parts* of the Scriptures as being there clearly defined as a result and not a process. "*Eternal punishment*" is an expression analogous to "eternal judgment," Heb. vi. 2, (not judging) "eternal redemption," Heb. ix. 12, (not redeeming) "eternal salvation," Heb. v. 9, (not saving) *i.e. the eternal effect of an act; here,* an act of punishment, described in Matt. iii. 10-12, and Luke iii. 17—"shall be *burned up* with unquenchable fire."]

4. τιμωρία, watching one's honour, vindication of it, avengement of it, *(non occ).*

3. Matt. xxv. 46. [*sure.*	4. Heb. x. 29.
2. 2 Cor. ii. 6, marg, *cen-*	1. 1 Pet. ii. 14.

PURCHASE (-ED.)

1. κτάομαι, to get for one's self, acquire, to procure *by purchase or otherwise.*

2. περιποιέω, to make over and above, *i.e.* to lay up, acquire, save up, lay by. *In mid., as here,* to get and keep for one's self, gain possession of.

1. Acts i. 18.	2. Acts xx. 28.
1. —— viii. 20.	2. 1 Tim. iii. 13.

PURCHASED [margin.]

1 Pet. ii. 9, see "PECULIAR."

PECULIAR POSSESSION.

περιποίησις, a making *over and above,* acquiring and keeping safe, laying up, acquired possession.

Eph. i. 14.

PURE.

1. καθαρός, pure from everything that would change or corrupt the nature of the subject with which it is combined, free from every foreign admixture, whether good or bad; clean, and free from every stain, odour, colour, or any useless thing whatever; free from every false adornment, (*see note at No.* 2), (*occ.* Mark xiv. 3.)

2. ἁγνός, pure, chaste, clean, not contaminated by anything in itself really evil (*though mixed with it*); pure from every defilement.

[Wine mixed with water may be *No.* 2, because it is not defiled or contaminated; but it cannot be *No.* 1, because there is a foreign admixture which, notwithstanding, may be good in itself. Water and wine may be *No.* 1 apart, but not when mixed, though the new mixture may be *No.* 2.]

3. εἰλικρινής, judged of in the sunlight, *and so found to be* genuine; *hence*, unmixed, pure, (*Lat.*, sincere), (*occ.* Phil. i. 10.)

[Other synonymous words, not occurring here, are—

ὅσιος, pure from crime or impious deed.

ἅγιος, the reverence due to such purity, holy.

ἱερός, pure, set apart for God, sacred.

ἀμίαντος, pure, unstained, unsoiled.]

1. Matt. v. 8.
— Mark xiv. 3, see *Nard.*
1. Acts xx. 26.
1. Rom. xiv. 20.
2. Phil. iv. 8.
1. 1 Tim. i. 5.
1. —— iii. 9.
2. —— v. 22.
1. 2 Tim. i. 3.
1. —— ii. 22.
1. Tit. i. 15 3 times.
1. Heb. x. 22.
1. Jas. i. 27.
2. —— iii. 17.
1. 1 Pet. i. 22 (*om.* L T Tr A.)
3. 2 Pet. iii. 1.
2. 1 John iii. 3.
1. Rev. xv. 6.
1. —— xxi. 18, 21.
1. —— xxii. 1 (*om.* G L T Tr A ℵ.)

PURENESS.

ἁγνότης, purity, the state of being ἁγνός, (*see* "PURE," *No.* 2), (*non occ.*)

2 Cor. vi. 6.

PURGE (-ED, -ETH, -ING.)

1. καθαίρω, to cleanse from filth; *as, e.g. grain, by winnowing*, (2 Sam. iv. 6); *a tree, by pruning*, (John xv. 2); *sin, by atonement or expiation*, (Heb. x. 2). (*An earlier form of No.* 3.) (*non occ.*)

2. ἐκκαθαίρω, (*No.* 1, *with* ἐκ, out of, *prefixed*) to purge out, cleanse thoroughly, (*occ.* 1 Cor. v. 7.)

3. καθαρίζω, to make καθαρός, (*see* "PURE," *No.* 1.)

4. { ποιέω, to make, (*here, part.*), καθαρισμός, a cleansing, ceremonial purification, } having made [*by himself*] the purification [*of our sins*].

— Matt. iii. 12, see P thoroughly.
3. Mark vii. 19.
— Luke iii. 17, see P thoroughly.
1. John xv. 2.
— 1 Cor. v. 7, see P out.
2. 2 Tim. ii. 21.
4. Heb. i. 3.
3. —— ix. 14, 22.
1. —— x. 2 (No. 3, L T Tr A ℵ.)
— 2 Pet. i. 9, see P (forget that one was.)

PURGE OUT.

2. 1 Cor. v. 7.

PURGE THOROUGHLY.

διακαθαρίζω, (*No.* 3, *with* διά, through, *prefixed*) to make καθαρός (*see* "PURE," *No.* 1) throughout, (*non occ.*)

Matt. iii. 12. | Luke iii. 17.

PURGED (FORGET THAT ONE WAS)

{ λήθην, a forgetfulness,
λαμβάνω, (*part.*) taking,
τοῦ, of the,
καθαρισμενôυ, purifying.

2 Pet. i. 9.

PURIFICATION.

1. καθαρισμός, a cleansing, purification, *esp.* the ceremonial washings *or* purification *of the Law.*

2. ἁγνισμός, lustration, *i.e.* a preparation of one's self for the sacred festivals, by visiting the Temple, offering prayers, abstinence, washings, etc. (lxx. for טהר and חטאת, Numb. viii. 7, 8; נזר, Numb. vi. 5; נזיר, Amos ii. 1.) (*non occ.*)

1. Luke ii. 22. | 2. Acts xxi. 26.

PURIFY (-IED, -IETH, -ING.)

1. ἁγνίζω, to make ἁγνός, (*see* "PURE," *No.* 2); to lustrate, prepare one's self by purification, etc., for a festival, (*non occ.*)

2. καθαρίζω, to make καθαρός, (*see* "PURE," *No.* 1) to make clean, and free from all admixture.

1. John xi. 55.
2. Acts xv. 9.
1. —— xxi. 24, 26.
1. —— xxiv. 18.
2. Tit. ii. 14.
— Heb. ix. 18, marg. (see Dedicate.)
2. —— 23.
1. Jas. iv. 8.
1. 1 Pet. i. 22.
1. 1 John iii. 3.

PURIFYING. [noun.]

1. καθαρισμός, a cleansing, purification, *esp.* the ceremonial washings and purification *of the Law.*
2. καθαρότης, cleanness, pureness *in the Levitical sense,* (*non occ.*)

1. John ii. 6. | 1. John iii. 25.
2. Heb. ix. 13.

PURITY.

ἁγνεία, purity, the state of being ἁγνός, (*see* "PURE," *No.* 2.)

1 Tim. iv. 12. | 1 Tim. v. 2.

PURLOIN (-ING.)

νοσθίζω, to put apart, separate. *In N.T., mid.,* to put aside for one's self, (*occ.* Acts v. 2, 3.)

Tit. ii. 10.

PURPLE.

1. πορφύρα, *Lat.* purpura, *i.e.* the purple mussel, *found on the Mediterranean coasts, which yields a reddish purple dye, much prized by the ancients. In N.T.,* purple, *i.e.* anything so dyed, purple clothes *or* robes worn by persons of rank and wealth.
2. πορφυρεος, (*adj. of No.* 1) purple, *i.e.* reddish purple.

1. Matt. xv. 17, 20.
1. Luke xvi. 19.
2. John xix. 2, 5.
— Acts xvi. 14, see P (seller of)
— Heb. ix. 19, marg. (see Scarlet.)
1. Rev. xvii. 4.
1. —— xviii. 12.
2. —— 16.

PURPLE (SELLER OF)

πορφυρόπωλις, a seller of purple cloth, (*see above.*)

Acts xvi. 14.

PURPOSE. [noun.]

1. πρόθεσις, a setting before *or* forth, a setting out; *then, of what one* sets before *his mind,* proposes *to himself,* purpose, deliberate resolution, (*non occ.*)
2. βούλημα, counsel; that which is decided *or* determined, (*occ.* Rom. ix. 19.)

— Matt. xxvi. 8, see P (to what)
1. Acts xi. 23.
1. —— xxvii. 13.
2. —— 43.
1. Rom. viii. 28.
1. —— ix. 11.
— Rom. ix. 17, see P (for this same)
1. Eph. i. 11.
1. —— iii. 11.
— —— vi. 22, } see P (for
— Col. iv. 8, } the same)
1. 2 Tim. i. 9.
1. 2 Tim. iii. 10.

PURPOSE (FOR THE SAME)

{ εἰς, unto, for, / αὐτὸ, very, same, / τοῦτο, this, } for this same *thing.*

Eph. vi. 22. | Col. iv. 8.

PURPOSE (FOR THIS SAME)

εἰς αὐτὸ τοῦτο, *see above.*

Rom. ix. 17.

PURPOSE? (TO WHAT)

{ εἰς, unto, / τί, what? } to what *end?*

Matt. xxvi. 8.

PURPOSE (-ED, -ETH.) [verb.]

1. τίθημι, to put, to set, to place; *and here, followed by* ἐν τῷ πνεύματι, *mid.,* to lay up in one's spirit, *i.e.* to revolve in mind, *also* to resolve in his spirit.
2. προτίθημι, (*No.* 1, *with* πρό, before, *prefixed*) to set *or* put before *any one,* to set before one's self, propose to one's self, *i.e.* to purpose.
3. βουλεύομαι, to resolve in council, to decree. *In N.T. only mid.,* to take counsel, consult, deliberate with one's self, determine; to determinedly resolve.
4. { γνώμη, opinion, / γίνομαι, to come to be, } [*he*] came to be of opinion.
5. ποιέω, to make.
6. προαιρέω, to take forth *out of any place,* to take one thing before another, prefer, choose. *In N.T. mid.,* to propose *or* prefer to one's self.

1. Acts xix. 21.
4. —— xx. 3.
2. Rom. i. 13.
3. 2 Cor. i. 17 twice.
6. —— ix. 7.
2. Eph. i. 9.
5. Eph. iii. 11.

PURSE.

1. *βαλάντιον*, a bag, pouch, or purse, (*prob. from βαλλεῖν ἐντός*, to cast within), (*occ.* Luke xii. 33.)
2. *ζώνη*, *Eng.*, zone · a belt *or* girdle; *often serving as* a purse for money.

2. Matt. x. 9.	1. Luke x. 4.
2. Mark vi. 8.	1. —— xxii. 35, 36.

PUT (-ETH, -ING.)

(*For various combinations with other words, see below.*)

1. *τίθημι*, to put, to set, to place.
2. *βάλλω*, to throw, to cast, *with a greater or less degree of force, as required by the context.*
3. *δίδωμι*, to give, (*of one's own accord and with good will*) give, bestow upon, commit to.
4. *ποιέω*, to make; to do. *Here*, to make [*the men go outside.*]

1. Matt. v. 15.	2. John xiii. 2.
2. —— ix. 17 twice.	1. —— xix. 19.
1. —— xii. 18.	2. —— xx. 25.
2. —— xxv. 27.	4. Acts v. 34.
2. —— xxvii. 6.	1. Rom. xiv. 13.
2. Mark ii. 22.	1. 1 Cor. xv. 25.
1. —— iv. 21.	1. 2 Cor. iii. 13.
2. —— vii. 33.	3. —— viii. 16.
1. —— x. 16.	3. Heb. viii. 10, marg. give.
2. Luke v. 37.	3. —— x. 16.
1. —— viii. 16.	2. Jas. iii. 3.
1. —— xi. 33.	2. Rev. ii. 24.
3. —— xv. 22.	1. —— xi. 9.
2. John v. 7.	3. —— xvii. 17.
2. —— xii. 6.	

PUT ABOUT

περιτίθημι, to put *or* place around *any person or thing.*

Mark xv. 17.

PUT ASUNDER.

χωρίζω, to put a space between, put apart, separate.

Matt. xix. 6.	Mark x. 9.

PUT AWAY.

1. *ἀπολύω*, to let loose from, loosen away from, let go free.
2. *αἴρω*, to take up, lift up, to raise; to take up and carry away, remove.
3. *ἐξαίρω*, (*No.* 2, *with ἐκ*, out of, *prefixed*) to take up out of *any place*, to take and remove out of, (*occ.* 1 Cor. v. 2.)
4. { *εἰς*, unto, for, *ἀθέτησιν*, a setting aside, (*occ.* Heb. vii. 18,) } for the setting aside, for the abolition.
5. *ἀποτίθεμαι*, to put off away from one's self, lay aside.
6. *ἀπωθέομαι*, to thrust away from one's self, cast off, repulse.
7. *ἀφίημι*, to send forth *or* away, to let go from one's self.
8. *καταργέω*, to render inactive, idle, useless; to spoil, cause to cease, put an end to.

1. Matt. i. 19.	7. 1 Cor. vii. 11, 12.
1. —— v. 31, 32.	8. —— xiii. 11.
1. —— xix. 3, 7, 8, 9 twice.	5. Eph. iv. 25.
1. Mark x. 2, 4, 11, 12.	2. —— 31.
1. Luke xvi. 18 twice.	6. 1 Tim. i. 19.
3. 1 Cor. v. 13.	4. Heb. ix. 26.

PUT DOWN.

1. *καθαιρέω*, to take down; *of buildings, with the idea of force*, to pull down, demolish; *of people*, to overthrow; *of princes, etc.*, to dethrone.
2. *καταργέω*, (*see* "P AWAY," *No.* 8.)

1. Luke i. 52.	2. 1 Cor. xv. 24.

PUT FORTH.

1. *ἐκβάλλω*, to throw out, cast out, put forth.
2. *ἐκτείνω*, to stretch out, extend, *as the hand, or the body.*
3. *ἐκφύω*, to generate out, produce, shoot forth *as leaves, etc.*, (*non occ.*)
4. *λέγω*, to lay, to lay before, relate; *hence*, to say, speak, *of significant discourse.*
5. *παρατίθημι*, to put *or* place beside *or* near *any one; of a teacher*, to lay before, propound.

2. Matt. viii. 3.	3. Mark xiii. 28.
1. —— ix. 25.	2. Luke v. 13.
5. —— xiii. 24, 31.	4. —— xiv. 7.
3. —— xxiv. 32.	1. John x. 4.
2. Mark i. 41.	1. Acts ix. 40.

PUT FORWARD.

προβάλλω, to cast *or* thrust forward, (*occ.* Luke xxi. 30.)

Acts xix. 33.

PUT FROM.

ἀπωθέομαι, *see* "PUT AWAY," *No.* 6.

Acts xiii. 46.

PUT IN.

ἀποστέλλω, to send away, send forth.

Mark iv. 29.

PUT IN PRISON

παραδίδωμι, to give near, with *or* to *any one*, give over, deliver up *into the possession or power of any one.*

Mark i. 14.

PUT OFF

1. *ἀποτίθεμαι*, to put off, away from one's self, lay aside.
2. *ἀπεκδύομαι*, to strip off, despoil, deprive of, *as spoil*, (*occ.* Col. ii. 15.)
3. *λύω*, to loose, to loosen *what is fast bound*, unbind, untie, *as a sandal, etc.*

3. Acts vii. 33.
1. Eph. iv. 22.
1. Col. iii. 8.
2. —— 9.

PUT OFF (MUST)

ἐστί, is,
ἀπόθεσις, the putting off.

2 Pet. i. 14.

PUT ON.

1. *ἐνδύω*, to go in, to envelope, to go into, *as into a garment*, *i.e.* to clothe, to dress.
2. *ἐπιτίθημι*, to place *or* put upon, lay upon.
   (a) *with ἐπανω*, above, over, upon.
3. *περιτίθημι*, to put *or* place around *any person or thing;* to bestow upon.
4. *περιβάλλω*, to cast *or* throw around.

2. Matt. xix. 13.
2a. —— xxi. 7.
3. —— xxvii. 28.
1. —— 31.
3. —— 48.
1. Mark xv. 20.
3. Mark xv. 36.
1. Luke xv. 22.
2. John xix. 2 1st.
4. —— 2 2nd.
2. Acts ix. 12.
3. 1 Cor. xii. 23, marg. (text, *bestow upon.*)

PUT OUT.

ἐκβαλλω, to cast out of, thrust out.

Mark v. 40 part. | Luke viii. 54 (*ap.*)

PUT OUT OF.

μεθίστημι, to place in another way, to substitute; to remove from one place to another, drive away from.

Luke xvi. 4.

PUT THEREIN.

ἐμβιβάζω, to cause to go in, to embark,
εἰς, unto, into,
αὐτὸ, the same.

Acts xxvii. 6.

PUT TO.

1. *ἐπιβάλλω*, to throw *or* cast upon *or* over; to lay *the hand* upon, *i.e.* to undertake.
2. *προσφέρω*, to bear *or* bring to *any person or place*, to bring near, put to.

1. Luke ix. 62, with *ἐπί*, *upon.*
2. John xix. 29.

PUT UNDER.

ὑποτάσσω, to range, subordinate, make subject to.

1 Cor. xv. 27 3 times, 28. | Eph. i. 22. | Heb. ii. 8.

PUT UNTO.

ἐπιβάλλω, *see above*, *No.* 1.

Matt. ix. 16, with *ἐπί*, *upon.*

PUT UP.

βάλλω, to throw, *or* cast, (*the degree of force must be modified by the context.*)

John xviii. 11.

PUT UP AGAIN.

ἀποστρέφω, to turn away from; turn back, return.

Matt. xxvi. 52.

PUT UPON.

1. ἐπιτίθημι, to place or put upon, lay upon.

2. περιτίθημι, to put around, place around *any person or thing*.

3. ἐπιβάλλω, to throw *or* cast upon, place upon.

1. Matt. xxvii. 29. | 3. Luke v. 36.
1. Mark viii. 25 (τίθημι, *to place*, Tr A.) | 1. John ix. 15.
2. —— xix. 29.
1. Acts xv. 10.

PUT (MUST BE)

βλητέος, that ought to be put, (*a verbal adj., implying obligation, propriety, or duty*), (*non occ.*)

Mark ii. 22 (*ap.*) | Luke v. 38.

PUT UNDER (THAT IS NOT)

ἀνυπότακτος, unsubjected, not made subject, *of persons and things*, (*occ.* 1 Tim. i. 9; Tit. i. 6, 10.)

Heb. ii. 8.

See also, ACCOUNT, DEATH, DIFFERENCE, FEAR, FILL, MIND, REMEMBRANCE, SHAME, SILENCE, SUBJECTION, SYNAGOGUE, TRUST.

PUTTING AWAY.

ἀπόθεσις, a putting away from, putting off, laying aside, (*occ.* 2 Pet. i. 14.)

1 Pet. iii. 21.

PUTTING OFF.

ἀπέκδυσις, a stripping off, despoiling, (*non occ.*)

Col. ii. 11.

PUTTING ON.

1. ἔνδυσις, the getting into, *as clothes*; *i.e.* the putting on, (*non occ.*)

2. ἐπίθεσις, the placing upon, laying upon, *as of hands*; the imposition *of hands*.

2. 2 Tim. i. 6. | 1. 1 Pet. iii. 3.

Q

QUAKE.

1. { εἰμί, I am, ἔντρομος, in trembling, *i.e.* trembling with fear.

2. σείω, to move to and fro, to shake *with the idea of shock or concussion, esp. of earthquakes.*

2. Matt. xxvii. 51, pass. | 2. Heb. xii. 21.

QUARREL.

1. μομφή, fault found, occasion of blame or censure, (*non occ.*)

2. ἐνέχω, to have in *anything*, to have in *one's self, implying a disposition of mind towards a person or thing; in N.T., unfavourable*; to entertain *a grudge, etc.*, against *another*.

2. Mark vi. 19, marg. *an inward grudge.* | 1. Col. iii. 13, marg. *complaint.*

QUARREL (*ready to*) [margin.]

1 Tim. iii. 3, see "WINE (GIVEN TO)"

QUARTER.

1. γωνία, an angle, a corner, *either an exterior projecting* corner, *or an interior* angle; a dark corner.

2. τόπος, a place, spot, space, room *occupied or filled by any person or thing.*

— Mark i. 45, see Every. | — Acts ix. 32, see All.
2. Acts xvi. 3. | 1. Rev. xx. 8.

QUARTERS (THE SAME)

{ τὸ, the, περὶ, around, τὸν, the, τόπον, place, ἐκεῖνου, that there, } the *parts* around that place.

Acts xxviii. 7.

QUATERNION (-s.)

τετράδιον, (*dim. of* τετράς, a tetrad, *the number* four) a detachment of four men, *the usual number of a Roman night-watch, relieved every three hours*, (*non occ.*)

Acts xii. 4.

QUEEN.

βασίλισσα, a queen, (lxx. 1 Kings x. 1; Esth. i. 9, 11, 12, 15, 16, 17), (*non occ.*)

Matt. xii. 42. | Luke xi. 31. | Acts viii. 27. | Rev. xviii. 7.

QUENCH (-ED.)

σβέννυμι, to quench, put out, extinguish, *as a light or fire;* to damp, hinder, repress.

Matt. xii. 20. | Mark ix. 44 (ap.), 46 (ap.), 48. | Eph. vi. 16. | 1 Thes. v. 19. | Heb. xi. 34.

QUENCHED (THAT NEVER SHALL BE)

ἄσβεστος, not extinguished, unquenched.

[Used in prof. Greek of prolonged laughter that cannot be suppressed; of fierce, obstinate battle; to the fire which burnt part of some ships; to indefatigable vigour. In lxx. Gen. xi. 3, for unslaked lime, and in the ancient ecclesiastical writers, for the fire which burnt up the martyrs. It occurs elsewhere only in Matt. iii. 12 and Luke iii. 17, where it is declared that those who are cast into it shall be "*burned up*," and have no power to quench it, and therefore no opportunity or hope of escape from the wages of sin, which is death. The reference in Mark ix. 43, etc., is to Is. lxvi. 24.]

Mark ix. 43 (*ap.*), 45 (*ap.*)

QUESTION (-s.) [noun.]

1. ζήτησις, the act of seeking, search; inquiry.
2. ζήτημα, the thing sought *or* inquired about, question; topic of inquiry, (*non occ.*)
3. λόγος, a word *spoken; hence*, an expression, statement, (*see* "ACCOUNT"); *here*, "*I will question you as to one* matter."

— Matt. xxii. 35, 46, see Ask.
3. Mark xi. 29, marg. *thing*.
— — xii. 34, see Ask.
— Luke ii. 46, see Ask.
— — xx. 40, see Ask.
1. John iii. 25.
2. Acts xv. 2.
2. — xviii. 15.
— Acts xxiii. 6, see Call.
2. — 29.
2. — xxv. 19.
— — 20, see Q (of such manner of)
2. — xxvi. 3.
1. 1 Tim. i. 4.
1. — vi. 4.
1. 2 Tim. ii. 23.
1. Tit. iii. 9.

QUESTIONS (OF SUCH MANNER OF)

εἰς, as to, (*om.* T Tr A[b] א.)
τὴν, the,
ζήτησιν, inquiry, (*see above, No.* 1.)
περὶ, concerning,
τούτου, this, (τούτῶν, these, G ~ L T Tr A א), [*i.e.* this person or this matter.]

Acts xxv. 20, marg. *how to enquire hereof.*

QUESTION (-ED, -ING.) [verb.]

συζητέω, to seek *anything* in conjunction with *another;* to seek together; *hence*, to inquire of one another, question with.

Mark i. 27. | Mark ix. 16.

QUESTION WITH.

1. συζητέω, *see above.*
2. ἐπερωτάω, to ask at *or* of *any one*, to inquire of; question, interrogate.

2 Mark viii. 11. | 2 Mark ix. 14. | 2 Luke xxiii. 9.

QUESTION ONE WITH ANOTHER.

1. Mark ix. 10.

QUICK.

ζάω, to live, to have life. *Here, the part.*, living.

Acts x. 42. | 2 Tim. iv. 1. | Heb. iv. 12. | 1 Pet. iv. 5.

QUICKEN (-ED, -ETH, -ING.)

ζωοποιέω, to make alive, give life, *esp. of that life which will last for ever*, to give eternal life.

John v. 21 twice.
— vi. 63.
Rom. iv. 17.
— viii. 11.
1 Cor. xv. 36, 45. [*give life.*]
2 Cor. iii. 6, marg. (text,
Eph. ii. 5, see Q together with.
Col. ii. 13, see Q together with.
1 Tim. vi. 13 (ζωογονέω, *endue with life*, G~L T Tr A.)
1 Pet. iii. 18.

QUICKEN TOGETHER WITH.

συζωοποιέω, to make alive in conjunction with another, (*non occ.*)

Eph. ii. 5. | Col. ii. 13.

QUICKLY.

1. **ταχύ,** (*neut. of* ταχύς, swift, *as adv.*) quickly, speedily, *with haste.*
2. **τάχος,** quickness, swiftness, speed. (*Here, Dative.*)
3. { **ἐν,** in, / **τάχει,** swiftness, } with speed.
4. **ταχέως,** quickly, speedily; soon, shortly.
5. **τάχιον,** (*comp. of* ταχύς, swift) more swiftly, more quickly *or* speedily. *Here, with art.*, the more speedily.

1. Matt. v. 25.	3. Acts xii. 7.
1. —— xxviii. 7, 8.	3. —— xxii. 18.
1. Mark xvi. 8 (*om.* G L T Tr A ℵ.)	2. Rev. ii. 5 (*om.* G⇉L T Tr A ℵ.)
4. Luke xiv. 21.	1. —— 16.
4. —— xvi. 6.	1. —— iii. 11.
1. John xi. 29.	1. —— xi. 14.
5. —— xiii. 27.	1. —— xxii. 7, 12, 20.

QUICKSANDS.

σύρτις, syrtis, *i.e.* a sand-bank, *so called because* drawn *together by currents,* (σύρω, to draw). [Two famous among the ancients: Syrtis major, between Cyrene and Leptis, and Syrtis minor, near Carthage.] (*non occ.*)

Acts xxvii. 17.

QUIET. [adj.]

1. **ἤρεμος,** free from all agitation *or* disturbance, not disturbed by others; tranquillity arising from without, (*non occ.*)
2. **ἡσύχιος,** making no agitation *or* disturbance, exciting no disturbance in others; tranquillity arising from within.

1. 1 Tim. ii. 2. | 2. 1 Pet. iii. 4.

QUIET (BE)

1. **ἡσυχάζω,** to be quiet, tranquil, *in contrast* to *excited and unquiet bustle.*
2. **καταστέλλω,** to put *or* let down; *then,* to put down, quell, assuage, pacify. *Here, pass. part.*, be calmed *or* calm, (*occ.* Acts xix. 35.)

2. Acts xix. 30. | 1. 1 Thes. iv. 11.

QUIETNESS.

1. **εἰρήνη,** peace; the state of repose and security.
2. **ἡσυχία,** quietness, tranquillity *arising from within, and exciting no disturbance in others.*

Acts xxiv. 2. | 2 Thes. iii. 12.

QUIT.

1 Cor. xvi. 13, see "MEN."

R

RABBI.

ῥαββί, Rabbi, (Heb. רַבִּי, one great, a chief, a master) *a title of honour in the Jewish schools,* my master.

Matt. xxiii. 7 1st.	John i. 38, 49.
—— 7 2nd (*om.* G → L T Tr A ℵ*.)	—— iii. 2, 26.
—— 8.	—— vi. 25.

RABBONI.

ῥαββονί, Rabboni, my great master, a title of the highest dignity in the Jewish schools, (*occ.* Mark x. 51.)

John xx. 16.

RACA.

ῥακά, raka, *a term of contempt in Heb. or Syr.;* רק, to be empty; so it denotes an empty, vain, worthless fellow.

In edition of 1611 *it was spelt* racha, *since the edition of* 1638 *it has been* raca.

Matt. v. 22.

RACE.

1. ἀγών, place of assembly *where games were often celebrated; hence*, a stadium, a course; *then*, the race *or* contest *itself.*
2. στάδιον, a stadium, *i.e.* the standard *of measure*, viz. *a distance of* 600 Greek feet or 625 Roman, *equivalent to* 604½ feet, or 201⅓ yards Eng. *The course for the Olympic games was a stadium in length; hence*, a stadium *came to be used of* any course where public games were exhibited.

2. 1 Cor. ix. 24. | 1. Heb. xii. 1.

RAGE. [verb.]

φρυάσσω, to neigh, whinny, prance, *of spirited, high-fed horses; of men*, to be haughty, insolent, (*quoted from* Ps. ii. 1, *where*, lxx. for רגשׁ), (*non occ.*)

Acts iv. 25.

RAGING.

1. ἄγριος, living in the fields, wild, savage, *of animals; then*, vehement, furious, *of the sea.*
2. κλύδιον, a dashing *of the sea*, surging, dashing, (*occ.* John i. 6.)

2. Luke viii. 24. | 1. Jude 13.

RAIL ON.

βλασφημέω, to drop evil *or* profane words, speak lightly *or* amiss of sacred things; *it is also* applied to rash, ill-advised, *or* wicked prayers; *hence*, to blaspheme, speak evil of *or* against any one, calumniate.

Mark xv. 29. | Luke xxiii. 39.

RAILER.

λοίδορος, railing, abusive; *as subst.*, a railer, reviler, abuser, (*occ.* 1 Cor. vi. 10.)

1 Cor. v. 11.

RAILING (-s.)

1. βλασφημία, calumniation, abuse, the very worst kind of slander; blasphemy, attacking sacred things; defamation, the speaking to a man's prejudice.
2. βλάσφημος, blasphemous, evil speaking against God and Divine things.
3. λοιδορία, railing, abuse, reviling *a man to his face*, abuse *of him personally.*

1. 1 Tim. vi. 4.
3. 1 Pet. iii. 9 twice.
2. 2 Pet. ii. 11.
1. Jude 9.

RAIMENT.

1. ἱμάτιον, a piece of dress, a garment; *esp.* the outer garment, (*as opp. to* χιτών, the inner vest) *then, gen.*, raiment *of any kind.*
2. ἱματισμός, clothing, apparel.
3. ἔνδυμα, anything put on, covering, (*occ.* Matt. vii. 15; xxii. 11, 12), (*spoken of prophet's garment*, 2 Kings i. 8; Zech. xiii. 4.)
4. ἐσθής, dress; *esp. what is ornate or splendid.*
5. σκέπασμα, covering, *i.e.* shelter *or* clothing.

3. Matt. iii. 4.
3. —— vi. 25, 28.
1. —— xi. 8 (*om.* L[b] T Tr [A ℵ.)
1. —— xvii. 2.
1. —— xxvii. 31.
3. —— xxviii. 3.
1. Mark ix. 3.
1. Luke vii. 25.
2. —— ix. 29.
3. Luke xii. 23.
1. —— xxiii. 34.
1. John xix. 24.
1. Acts xviii. 6.
1. —— xxii. 20.
5. 1 Tim. vi. 8.
4. Jas. ii. 2.
1. Rev. iii. 5, 18.
1. Rev. iv. 4.

RAIN. [noun.]

1. ὑετός, rain, *esp.* a heavy shower, (*opp. to* ὄμβρος, a lasting rain; *and* ψεκάς, a drizzling rain). *The word appears in Eng.*, wet, (*non occ.*)
2. βροχή, a wetting; *hence*, rain, *esp.* rain as *sent or caused*, (lxx. for גשׁם, Ps. lxviii. 10; cv. 32, plentiful rain), (*non occ.*)

— Matt. v. 45, see R (send)
2. —— vii. 25, 27.
1. Acts xiv. 17.
1. —— xxviii. 2.
1. Heb. vi. 7.
1. Jas. v. 7 (*om.* L T Tr A) (καρπός, *fruit*, ℵ.)
1. —— 18.

RAIN (SEND)

βρέχω, *see below.*

Matt. v. 45.

RAIN (-ED.) [verb.]

βρέχω, to moisten, wet, make wet; *then*, to rain, send rain, cause to rain. (a) *trans.* (b) *intrans.* (c) *with ὑετός*, (*see* "RAIN," *No.* 1.)

a. Luke xvii. 29.
b. Jas. v. 17[1st], inf.
b. Jas. v. 17[2nd].
c. Rev. xi. 6.

RAINBOW.

ἶρις, a rainbow; *Eng.*, iris. [*Here*, referring back to the covenant with Noah, Gen. ix. 14, 15. A cloud of judgment is about to burst upon the earth, but the bow is in the cloud, a token that of all the plagues not one was to be a flood of waters. For as the days of Noah, so is the presence of the Son of Man, Matt. xxiv. 37. In Noah's day the *bow* was in the cloud; in Moses's day Jehovah was in it. *Here*, both the bow and Jehovah are in the cloud. The book is concerning *judgment*; *hence*, the seven-fold mention and presence of *the cloud*, i. 7; x. 1; xi. 12; xiv. 14[twice], 15, 16.]

Rev. iv. 3.
Rev. x. 1.

RAISE (-ED, -ETH, -ING.)

(*For various combinations*, (*e.g.* Raise up, etc.) *see below.*)

1. *ἐγείρω*, to awaken, wake up, arouse, cause to rise up; *properly*, from sleep. *Pass.*, to wake, be awake.
2. *διεγείρω*, (*No.* 1, *with διά*, through, *prefixed*) to wake up fully, rouse.
3. *ἐπεγείρω*, (*No.* 1, *with ἐπί*, upon, *prefixed*) to rouse up upon, *i.e.* against *any one*, excite against, (*occ.* Acts xiv. 2.)
4. *ἀνίστημι*, *trans.*, to cause to stand, raise up; *intrans.*, to rise up, arise, stand up.

2. Matt. i. 24 (No. 1, L T Tr A.)
1. —— x. 8 (*om. νεκροὺς ἐγείρετε, raise the dead,* G → T Tr.)
1. Luke vii. 22.
1. —— ix. 22 (No. 4, G ~ L Trm A.)
1. —— xx. 37.
1. John xii. 1, 9, 17.
1. Acts iii. 15.
1. —— iv. 10.
1. —— xiii. 23 (*ἤγαγε, brought,* G L T Tr A ℵ.)
1. —— —— 30.
3. Acts xiii. 50.
4. —— xvii. 31.
1. —— xxvi. 8.
1. Rom. vi. 9.
1. —— vii. 4.
1. —— x. 9.
1. 1 Cor. xv. 16, 17, 42, 43[twice], 44.
1. —— —— 52 (No. 4, L.)
1. 2 Cor. i. 9.
1. Gal. i. 1.
1. Eph. i. 20 part.
1. Col. ii. 12.
1. 1 Thes. i. 10.
1. 2 Tim. ii. 8.

RAISE AGAIN.

1. Matt. xvi. 21.
1. —— xvii. 23 (No. 4, L.)
1. Acts xiii. 37.
1. Rom. iv. 25.

RAISE UP.

1. *ἐγείρω*, *see* "RAISE," *No.* 1.
2. *ἐξεγείρω*, (*No.* 1, *with ἐκ*, out of, *prefixed*) to wake up out of, arouse out of, (*non occ.*)
3. *ἀνίστημι*, *see* "RAISE," *No.* 4.
4. *ἐξανίστημι*, (*No.* 3, *with ἐκ*, out of, *prefixed*) to cause to stand *or* rise up out of, (*occ.* Acts xv. 5.)

1. Matt. iii. 9.
1. —— xi. 5.
3. —— xxii. 24.
4. Mark xii. 19.
1. Luke i. 69.
1. —— iii. 8.
4. —— xx. 28.
1. John ii. 19.
1. —— v. 21.
3. —— vi. 40, 44, 54.
3. Acts ii. 24, 30 (*ap.*), 32.
3. —— iii. 22, 26.
1. —— v. 30.
3. —— vii. 37.
1. Acts x. 40.
1. —— xii. 7.
1. —— xiii. 22.
3. —— —— 34.
1. Rom. iv. 24.
1. —— vi. 4.
1. —— viii. 11[twice].
2. —— ix. 17.
1. 1 Cor. vi. 14[1st].
2. —— —— 14[2nd].
1. —— xv. 15[twice], 35.
1. 2 Cor. iv. 14[twice].
1. Heb. xi. 19.
1. Jas. v. 15.
1. 1 Pet. i. 21.

RAISE UP AGAIN.

ἀνίστημι, *see* "RAISE," *No.* 4.

John vi. 39.
Acts xiii. 33.

RAISE UP THE PEOPLE.

{ *ἐπισύστασις*, a concourse, a tumultuous gathering,
ποιέω, to make,
ὄχλου, of the people, (*see* "PEOPLE," *No.* 2) } causing a concourse of the multitude.

Acts xxiv. 12 (*ἐπίστασις, a stopping,* instead of *ἐπισύστασις, a concourse,* G ~ L T Tr A ℵ.)

RAISE UP TOGETHER.

συνεγείρω, ("RAISE," *No.* 1, *with σύν*, together with, *prefixed*) to raise up together in conjunction with, (*occ.* Col. ii. 12; iii. 1.)

Eph. ii. 6.

RAISED TO LIFE AGAIN.

{ *ἐξ*, out of, by
ἀναστάσις, resurrection. }

Heb. xi. 35.

RANK WITH (be on the same) [margin.]

Gal. iv. 25, see "ANSWER TO."

RANKS (IN)

{ πρασιαὶ, a bed in a garden, πρασιαὶ, *ditto*, } squares—squares, *i.e.* in squares *like beds in a garden.*

Mark vi. 40.

RANSOM.

1. λύτρον, loosing-money, ransom; the price paid for letting loose, *or* setting free; *hence*, expiation, atonement, *with esp. reference to the result rather than to the means.* The ransom price is an expiation, or (Num. xxxv. 31) an equivalent for the punishment due, and therefore frees from the consequences of guilt.
2. ἀντίλυτρον, (*No.* 1, *with* ἀντί, instead of, *prefixed*) *occurs only in N.T.*, a ransom paid, instead of others having to pay it. (*The verbal form occurs in* Gal. i. 4.) (*non occ.*)

1. Matt. xx. 28. | 1. Mark x. 45.
2. 1 Tim. ii. 6.

RASH (be) [margin.]

1 Cor. xiii. 4, see "VAUNT ONE'S SELF."

RASHLY.

προπετής, falling forwards; precipitate, headlong, sudden, (*occ.* 2 Tim. iii. 4.)

Acts xix. 36.

RATHER.

(*For various combinations, see below.*)

μᾶλλον, (*adv. comp. of* μάλα, very, very much, exceedingly) more, more strongly; *also*, more and more; rather.

Matt. x. 6, 28.
—— xxv. 9.
—— xxvii. 24.
Mark v. 26.
—— xv. 11.
Luke x. 20 (om. G L T Tr [A ℵ.)
John iii. 19.
Acts v. 29.
Rom. viii. 34, see Yea.
—— xiv. 13.
1 Cor. v. 2.
—— vi. 7 twice.
—— vii. 21.
1 Cor. ix. 12.
2 Cor. ii. 7.
—— iii. 8.
—— v. 8.
—— xii. 9.
Gal. iv. 9.
Eph. v. 4.
Phil. i. 12.
1 Tim. i. 4.
—— vi. 2.
Philem. 9.
Heb. xi. 25.
—— xii. 9, 13.

RATHER (AND)

ἀλλά, but, on the contrary.

Luke xvii. 8.

RATHER (BUT)

1. { μᾶλλον, rather, (*see* "RATHER" *above*) δέ, but, } but rather.
2. { μᾶλλον, rather, δὲ, but, καί, even, } but rather even.
3. { ἀλλά, but, ἤ, rather than [*that*], } unless, except.
4. πλήν, more than, besides; but rather; notwithstanding.

4. Luke xi. 41.
4. —— xii. 31.
3. —— 51.
1. 1 Cor. xiv. 1, 5.
1. Eph. iv. 28.
2. —— v. 11.

RATHER (HAD)

θέλω, to will, to wish, desire, (*implying active volition and purpose.*)

1 Cor. xiv. 19.

RATHER (OR)

{ μᾶλλον, rather, δὲ, but, } but rather.

Gal. iv. 9.

RATHER (THAN)

ἤ, rather than.

Matt. xviii. 8, 9.
Luke xviii. 14 (ἤ γάρ, G T), (παρά, instead of L Tr [A ℵ.)

RATHER (THE)

1. μᾶλλον, *see* "RATHER," *above.*
2. περισσοτέρως, more abundantly, the more.

2. Heb. xiii. 19. | 1. 2 Pet. i. 10.

RAVEN (-S.)

κόραξ, a raven, (lxx. *for* ערב, Gen. viii. 7; Lev. xi. 15), (*non occ.*)

Luke xii. 24.

RAVENING.

1. ἁρπαγή, (*noun*) plundering, pillage, the act of snatching away, (*occ.* Matt. xxiii. 25; Heb. x. 34.)

2. ἅρπαξ, (*adj.*) ravenous, (*spoken of wild beasts, as No.* 1 *also is*) rapacious, (*occ.* Luke xviii. 11; 1 Cor. v. 10, 11; vi. 10.)

2. Matt. vii. 15. | 1. Luke xi. 39.

RAW. [margin.]

Matt. ix. 16, } see New.
Mark ii. 21, }

REACH (-ED, -ING.)

1. ἀκολουθέω, to follow.

1. Rev. xviii. 5, (κολλάομαι, *joined together* [*as in a heap and reaching up to*], G L T Tr A ℵ.)

REACH FORTH UNTO.

ἐπεκτείνομαι, to stretch *or* reach forth towards, (*non occ.*)

Phil. iii. 13.

REACH HITHER.

1. { φέρω, to bear, bear hither, reach, ὧδε, thus, so, in this way or manner; *or*, hither, here, to *or* in this place.

2. φέρω, to bear, bear hither, reach.

1. John xx. 27 1st. | 2. John xx. 27 2nd.

REACH UNTO.

ἐφικνέομαι, to come upon *or* to any one, to arrive at, (*non occ.*)

2 Cor. x. 13, with ἄχρι, *as far as.*
—— 14, with εἰς, *unto.*

READ (-EST, -ETH, -ING.)

ἀναγινώσκω, to know accurately, to distinguish; to know by reading, *and then simply*, to read, learn by reading, (*non occ.*)

Matt. xii. 3, 5.
—— xix. 4.
—— xxi. 16, 42.
—— xxii. 31.
—— xxiv. 15.
Mark ii. 25.
—— xii. 10, 26.
—— xiii. 14.
Luke iv. 16.
—— vi. 3.
—— x. 26.
John xix. 20.
Acts viii. 28, 30 twice, 32.
—— xiii. 15, see Reading.
Acts xiii. 27.
—— xv. 21, 31 part.
—— xxiii. 34 part.
2 Cor. i. 13.
—— iii. 2.
—— —— 14, see Reading.
—— —— 15.
Eph. iii. 4 part.
Col. iv. 16 3 times.
1 Thes. v. 27.
1 Tim. iv. 13, see Reading.
Rev. i. 3.
—— v. 4 (*om*, καὶ ἀναγνῶναι, *and to read*, G L T Tr A ℵ.)

READINESS.

1. ἕτοιμος, ready, prepared, (*see* "READY," *No.* 1.)

2. προθυμία, predisposition, willingness, eagerness, alacrity *of mind.*

1. 2 Cor. x. 6. | 2. 2 Cor. viii. 11.

READINESS OF MIND.

2. Acts xvii. 11.

READING.

ἀνάγνωσις, a knowing accurately, knowing by reading; *then simply*, reading.

Acts xiii. 15. | 2 Cor. iii. 14.
1 Tim. iv. 13.

READY.

(*For various combinations,* (*e.g.* "Be Ready," "Make Ready," etc.) *see below.*)

1. ἕτοιμος, at hand, ready, prepared; *of persons*, ready, active, zealous; *of the mind*, ready, bold; *of the future*, sure to come, certain; *of the past*, carried into effect, realized.

2. πρόθυμος, predisposed, willing, eager, zealous.

3. μέλλω, to be about to do *or suffer any thing*, to be on the point of. (*Here, part.*)

4. ἐγγύς, near, *of place or time.*

5. παρασκευάζω, to make ready near *or* for *any one*, to prepare at hand.

(a) *Mid.*, to prepare one's self, be ready.

1. Matt. xxii. 4, 8.
1. —— xxiv. 44.
1. —— xxv. 10.
2. Mark xiv. 38.
3. Luke vii. 2 part.
1. —— xii. 40.
1. —— xiv. 17.
1. —— xxii. 33.
1. John vii. 6.
3. Acts xx. 7 part.
1. —— xxiii. 15, 21.
2. Rom. i. 15.
5. 2 Cor. ix. 3 part.
1. —— —— 5.
— 1 Tim. iii. 3, see *Quarrel*, or Wine.
— —— vi. 18, see Distribute.
— 2 Tim. iv. 6, see Offend.
1. Tit. iii. 1.
4. Heb. viii. 13.
1. 1 Pet. i. 5.
1. —— iii. 15.

READY (BE)

1. { ἔχω, to have, ἕτοιμος, ready, (*see No.* 1, *above*) } to have in readiness, (*non occ.*)

2. *μέλλω, see above, No.* 3.

3. *παρασκευάζω, see above, No.* 5a.

2. Luke vii. 2. | 1. 2 Cor. xii. 14.
1. Acts xxi. 13. | 1. 1 Pet. iv. 5.
3. 2 Cor. ix. 2. | 2. Rev. iii. 2.
2. Rev. xii. 4.

READY (MAKE)

1. ἑτοιμάζω, to make or get ready, prepare, provide.

2. παρασκευάζω, to make ready near *or* for *any one*, prepare at hand, *as food*.

(a) *Mid.*, to prepare one's self, be ready, get ready.

1. Matt. xxvi. 19. | 1. Luke xvii. 8.
1. Mark xiv. 15, 16. | 1. —— xxii. 12, 13.
1. Luke i. 17. | 2. Acts x. 10 part.
1. —— ix. 52. | 1. —— xxiii. 23.
1. Rev. xix. 7.

READY MIND.

προθυμία, predisposition, willingness, eagerness, zeal, alacrity *of mind.*

2 Cor. viii. 19.
1 Pet. v. 2.

READY TO HAND (THINGS MADE)

{ τὰ, the *things*, } the things ready *or* { ἕτοιμα, ready, } prepared; *i.e.* what one has.

2 Cor. x. 16.

REAP (-ED, -ETH, -ING.)

θερίζω, (*from* θέρος, summer, harvest-time); *hence,* to pass the summer; *then,* to do the work of summer, to harvest; to mow and reap, and gather in the harvest.

Matt. vi. 26. | 1 Cor. ix. 11.
—— xxv. 24, 26. | 2 Cor. ix. 6 twice.
Luke xii. 24. | Gal. vi. 7, 8 twice, 9.
—— xix. 21, 22. | Jas. v. 4 1st, see R down.
John iv. 36 twice, 37, 38. | —— 4 2nd.
Rev. xiv. 15 twice, 16.

REAP DOWN.

ἀμάω, to collect, gather together, as a reaper does the stalks of corn; *hence*, to cut corn, to reap, gather the harvest, (*non occ.*)

Jas. v. 4.

REAPER (-S.)

θεριστής, a harvestman, (*see* "REAP.")

Matt. xiii. 30, 39.

REAR UP.

ἐγείρω, to wake, rouse up; cause to rise up; *then,* to set upright *from a recumbent posture.*

John ii. 20.

REASON. [noun.]

1. ἀρεστός, pleasing; *here,* pleasing *to God, and therefore,* proper, fitting, *in His sight.* (*Used arbitrarily of man:* טוב בעיני, Gen. xvi. 6, and Acts xii. 3.)

2. λόγος, an account which one gives, *a narrative or treatise spoken or written.*

1. Acts vi. 2. | 2. 1 Pet. iii. 15.

REASON OF (BY)

1. διὰ, through.

(a) *with Gen.*, through (*and proceeding from*), *denoting the instrument of an action,* by means of.

(b) *with Acc.*, through, (*as tending towards*) *denoting the ground or reason of the action,* on account of, because of.

(c) *with Art. and Inf. mood,* on account of, because of.

2. ἐκ, out of, from among; *then,* originating in, *as the source, cause, or occasion;* from, by, *marking* the origin or cause *rather than the reason or means.*

3. ἕνεκα, (ἕνεκεν, or εἵνεκεν) because of, by reason of, wherefore, *marking the end or object.*

1b. John xii. 11. | 1c. Heb. vii. 23.
1b. Rom. viii. 20. | 1b. 2 Pet. ii. 2.
3. 2 Cor. iii. 10. | 2. Rev. viii. 13.
1b. Heb. v. 14. | 2. —— ix. 2.
2. Rev. xviii. 19.

REASON HEREOF (BY)

{ διὰ, on account of, because of,
{ ταύτην, this.

Heb. v. 3 (δι' αὐτήν, *on account of it*, L T Tr A ℵ.)

REASON WOULD.

{ κατὰ, according to
{ λόγον, reason.

Acts xviii. 14.

REASON (-ED, -ING.) [verb.]

1. λογίζομαι, to occupy one's self with reckonings *or* with calculations; to reckon; reason, use the reason.

2. διαλογίζομαι, (*No.* 1, *with* διά, through, *prefixed*) to reckon through, consider thoroughly, reason out.

3. διαλέγομαι, to speak to and fro, *i.e.* *alternately*, to converse with, discuss, reason, argue.

4. συζητέω, to seek *any thing* in conjunction with *another*, to seek together, inquire of one another, question with.

2. Matt. xvi. 7, 8.
2. —— xxi. 25.
2. Mark ii. 6, 8 twice.
2. —— viii. 16, 17.
1. —— xi. 31 (No. 3, G∾L T Tr A), (προσλογίζομαι, *to reason in addition to*, ℵ.)
2. Luke iii. 15, marg. (text, *muse.*)
2. —— v. 21, 22.
2. —— xx. 14.
4. —— xxiv. 15.
3. Acts xviii. 4.
3. —— xxiv. 25 part.
1. 1 Cor. xiii. 5, 11, marg. (text, *think.*)

REASON TOGETHER.

4. Mark xii. 28.

REASON WITH.

1. διαλέγομαι, *see above, No.* 3.

2. συλλογίζομαι, (*No.* 1, *with* σύν, together with, *prefixed*) to occupy one's self with reckonings in conjunction with *another*, to reason together with *another*.

(a) *with* πρός, towards, *or*, in addition to.

2a. Luke xx. 5. | 1. Acts xvii. 2.
1. Acts xviii. 19.

REASONABLE.

λογικός, pertaining to the reason, rational, (*Eng.*, logical), (*occ.* Pet. ii. 2.)

Rom. xii. 1.

REASONABLY BEAR WITH. [margin.]

Heb. v. 2, see "COMPASSION ON (HAVE)"

REASONING. [noun.]

1. λογισμός, reckoning, the art of reckoning, *i.e.* arithmetic; computation, consideration, reasoning.

2. διαλογισμός, (*No.* 1, *with* διά, through, *prefixed*) reckoning through, computation, adjustment of accounts; *hence*, dispute.

3. συζήτησις, a seeker in conjunction with *another*, a questioner, reasoner.

2. Luke ix. 46. | 3. Acts xxviii. 29 (ap.)
1. 2 Cor. x. 5, marg. (text, *imagination.*)

REBUKE (WITHOUT)

ἀμώμητος, without blemish, spotless; one in whom there is nothing reprehensible; without shame, stain, *or* disgrace, not open to censure.

[Thus differing from ἄμεμπτος, *see* "Blameless," "Faultless," "Unblamable," which means that no fault can be found on account of any incompleteness.] (*occ.* 2 Pet. iii. 14.)

Phil. ii. 15.

REBUKE (-ED, -ING.) [verb.]

1. ἐπιτιμάω, to put further honour upon, estimate higher; *then, of judges*, to estimate the value *or* penalty on *a person; hence*, to object to one as blamable, find fault with, reprove, admonish strongly.

2. ἐλέγχω, to put to shame, convince, refute, confute, show to be wrong, prove guilty; to prove *anything that was disputed or denied (and therefore implying opposition)*; *hence*, to reprimand, blame.

3. ἐπιπλήσσω, to strike upon, give blows upon; *hence*, rebuke sharply, (*non occ.*)

1. Matt. viii. 26.
1. —— xvi. 22.
1. —— xvii. 18.
1. —— xix. 13.
1. —— xx. 31.
1. Mark i. 25.
1. —— iv. 39.
1. —— viii. 32, 33.
1. —— ix. 25.
1. —— x. 13.
1. Luke iv. 35, 39, 41.
1. —— viii. 24.
1. Luke ix. 42, 55.
1. —— xvii. 3.
1. —— xviii. 15, 39.
1. —— xix. 39.
1. —— xxiii. 40.
3. 1 Tim. v. 1.
2. —— 20.
1. 2 Tim. iv. 2.
2. Tit. i. 13.
2. —— ii. 15.
2. Heb. xii. 5 part.
1. Jude 9.
2. Rev. iii. 19 part.

REBUKED (BE)

ἔχω, to have, ἔλεγξις, conviction, reproof, } have a reproof, (*non occ.*)

2 Pet. ii. 16.

RECEIPT.

Matt. ix. 9, Mark ii. 14, } see "CUSTOM."

RECEIVE (-ED, -EST, -ETH, -ING.)

1. λαμβάνω, to take, take hold of, apprehend, to take *or receive from another; to take what is given; hence,* receive, *pointing to an objective reception, (see No. 7.)*

2. παραλαμβάνω, (*No.* 1, *with* παρά, beside, *prefixed*) to take near, with *or* to *one's self;* receive with *or* to *one's self;* receive *in charge what is delivered over.*

3. ἀπολαμβάνω, (*No.* 1, *with* ἀπό, from, *prefixed*) to take from *any one,* to receive *with idea of completeness,* to receive in full.

4. προσλαμβάνω, (*No.* 1, *with* πρός, towards, *prefixed*) to take thereto, *i.e. in addition,* to take besides. *In N.T. mid.,* to take *or* receive to *and* for one's self.

5. μεταλαμβάνω, (*No.* 1, *with* μετά, in association with, *prefixed*) to take in association with *others,* take a part with, to partake of, share.

6. ὑπολαμβάνω, (*No.* 1, *with* ὑπό, under, *prefixed*) to take under, *i.e.* to take up by placing one's self underneath; *hence,* to take up.

7. δέχομαι, to take to one's self what is presented *or* brought by another, to accept, embrace, receive *hospitably;* admit, approve, allow. *It implies a subjective reception, showing that a decision of the will has taken place with respect to the object presented, and that the acceptance manifests it.*

8. παραδέχομαι, (*No.* 7, *with* παρά, beside, *prefixed*) to receive *or* accept near *or* to one's self, from another, with approval, (lxx. for רצה, Prov. iii. 12), (*non occ.*)

9. προσδέχομαι, (*No.* 7, *with* πρός, towards, *prefixed*) to accept to one's self, admit, receive kindly, entertain *as a host.*

10. ὑποδέχομαι, (*No.* 7, *with* ὑπό, under, *prefixed*) to accept *or* receive to one's self *as if placing the arms* under *a person or thing; hence,* to receive to one's self with evident favour and kindness; to welcome, (*non occ.*)

11. ἀναδέχομαι, (*No.* 7, *with* ἀνά, up, *prefixed*) to accept, receive *or* take on one's self, *physically, or as a debt of responsibility;* to take up, appropriate, adopt, (*non occ.*)

12. ἀποδέχομαι, (*No.* 7, *with* ἀπό, from, *prefixed*) to accept *or* receive from another for one's self, accept with joy, to welcome. *Here, mid.*

13. εἰσδέχομαι, (*No.* 7, *with* εἰς, unto, *prefixed*) to receive unto one's self *or* one's house. lxx. *everywhere* for קבץ, where God is said to gather and bring again His own people into their own land, (*non occ.*)

14. ἐπιδέχομαι, (*No.* 7, *with* ἐπί, upon, *prefixed*) to receive upon *or* up to one's self, admit, (*non occ.*)

15 κομίζω, to take care of, provide for; *of one fallen in battle,* to take up and bear away; *hence, gen.,* to take up, carry off, so as to preserve. *Here, mid.,* to carry for one's self, bear *or* bring to one's self, *i.e.* acquire, obtain, receive *so as to preserve.*

16. ἀπέχω, to hold off from; to have off *or* out, *i.e.* to have all *that is one's due, so as* to cease from having *more;* to have received in full; *spoken of a person,* to have for good and all.

17. χωρέω, to give space, place, room; make place *or* room *so as* to take in *or* receive *any thing,* to hold contain.

18. { ἵνα, that
δῶσιν, they may give
αὐτοῖς, to them.

1. Matt. vii. 8.
1. —— x. 8.
7. ——— 14.
7. ——— 40 4 times.
7. ——— 41 1st.
1. ——— 41 2nd.
7. ——— 41 3rd.
1. ——— 41 4th.
— —— xi. 5, see Sight.
7. ——— 14.
— —— xiii. 19, 20 1st, see Seed.
1. ——— 20 2nd.
— ——— 23, see Seed.
1. —— xvii. 24.
7. —— xviii. 5 twice.
— —— xix. 11, see R (can)
17.——— 12 twice.
1. ——— 29.
1. —— xx. 7 (ap.), 9, 10 twice, 11 part.
— ——— 34, see Sight.
1. —— xxi. 22, 34.
1. —— xxiii. 14 (ap.)
1. —— xxv. 16.
— ——— 17, see R (he that had)
1. ——— 18, 20.
1. ——— 22 (om. G → L T Tr A.)
1. ——— 24.
15.——— 27.
— Mark ii. 2, see Room.
1. —— iv. 16.
8. ——— 20.
7. —— vi. 11.
2. —— vii. 4.
7. —— ix. 37 4 times.
7. —— x. 15.
1. ——— 30.
— ——— 51, 52, see Sight.
1. —— xi. 24.
1. —— xii. 2, 40.
1. —— xv. 23.
— —— xvi. 19, see R up.
— Luke v. 27, see Custom.
16.—— vi. 24.
3. ——— 34 1st (No. 1, T Tr A ℵ.)
— ——— 34 2nd, see R [(again)
7. —— viii. 13.
— ——— 40, see R (gladly)
7. —— ix. 5.
7. ——— 11 (No. 12, L T Tr A ℵ.)
7. ——— 48 4 times.
— ——— 51, see R up (that...should be)
7. ——— 53.
7. —— x. 8, 10.
10.——— 38.
1. —— xi. 10.
9. —— xv. 2.
3. ——— 27.
7. —— xvi. 4, 9.
3. ——— 25.
7. —— xviii. 17.
3. ——— 30 (No. 1, L.)
— ——— 41, 42, 43, see [Sight.
10.—— xix. 6.
1. ——— 12, 15.
1. —— xx. 47.
3. —— xxiii. 41.
2. John i. 11.
1. ——— 12, 16.
1. —— iii. 11.
1. ——— 27, marg. *take unto one's self.*
1. ——— 32, 33.
1. —— iv. 36.
7. ——— 45.
1. —— v. 34, 41, 43 twice, 44.
1. —— vi. 21.

1. John vii. 23, 39.
— —— ix. 11, 15, 18 twice, see Sight.
1. —— x. 18.
1. —— xii. 48.
1. —— xiii. 20 4 times, 30.
2. —— xiv. 3.
1. ——— 17.
1. —— xvi. 14, 24.
1. —— xvii. 8.
1. —— xviii. 3.
1. —— xix. 30.
1. —— xx. 22.
1. Acts i. 8.
6. ——— 9.
1. —— ii. 33, 38.
— ——— 41, see R (gladly)
1. —— iii. 5.
— ——— 7, see Strength.
7. ——— 21.
7. —— vii. 38.
1. ——— 53.
7. ——— 59.
7. —— viii. 14.
1. ——— 15, 17, 19.
— —— ix. 12, 17, 18, see Sight.
1. ——— 19 part.
— —— x. 16, see R up.
1. ——— 43, 47.
7. —— xi. 1.
— —— xv. 4, see R (be)
8. —— xvi. 21.
1. ——— 24.
10.—— xvii. 7.
7. ——— 11.
1. ——— 15.
12.—— xviii. 27.
1. —— xix. 2.
1. —— xx. 24, 35.
7. —— xxi. 17 (No. 12, G ∾ L T Tr A ℵ.)
7. —— xxii. 5.
— ——— 13, see Sight.
8. ——— 18.
1. —— xxvi. 10, 18.
4. —— xxviii. 2.
11.——— 7.
7. ——— 21.
12.——— 30.
1. Rom. i. 5.
3. ——— 27.
1. —— iv. 11.
1. —— v. 11, 17.
1. —— viii. 15 twice.
— —— ix. 15, see Receiving.
1. —— xiii. 2.
4. —— xiv. 1, 3.
4. —— xv. 7 twice.
9. —— xvi. 2.
1. 1 Cor. ii. 12.
7. ——— 14.
1. —— iii. 8, 14.
1. —— iv. 7 3 times.
1. —— ix. 24.
2. —— xi. 23.
1. —— xiv. 5.
2. —— xv. 1, 3.
— 2 Cor. iv. 1, see Mercy.
15.—— v. 10.
7. —— vi. 1.
13.——— 17.
17.—— vii. 2.
— ——— 9, see Damage.
7. ——— 15.
7. —— viii. 4 (om. δέξασθαι ἡμᾶς, G L T Tr A ℵ), i.e. *Praying of us with much entreaty the gift and, etc.*
1. —— xi. 4 twice.
7. ——— 16, marg. *suffer.*

1. 2 Cor. xi. 24.
2. Gal. i. 9, 12.
1. —— iii. 2, 14.
3. —— iv. 5.
7. ——— 14.
15. Eph. vi. 8.
9. Phil. ii. 29.
2. —— iv. 9.
— ——— 15, see Receiving.
7. ——— 18.
16.——— 18, marg. (text, *have.*)
2. Col. ii. 6.
3. —— iii. 24.
— ——— 25, see R for.
1. —— iv. 10 1st.
7. ——— 10 2nd.
2. ——— 17.
7. 1 Thes. i. 6.
2. ——— 13 1st part.
7. ——— 13 2nd.
2. —— iv. 1.
7. 2 Thes. ii. 10.
2. —— iii. 6.
— 1 Tim. iii. 16, see R up.
— —— iv. 3, see R (to be)
1. ——— 4 part.
8. —— v. 19.
4. Philem. 12 (om. L T Trmb A ℵ), the sense being completed in ver. 17.
16.——— 15.
4. ——— 17.
1. Heb. ii. 2.
5. —— vi. 7.
1. —— vii. 5.
— ——— 6, see Tithes.
1. ——— 8, 9.
— ——— 11, see Law.
1. —— ix. 15.
1. —— x. 26.

15. Heb. x. 36.
1. —— xi. 8, 11.
1. ——— 13 (No. 9, L), (No. 15, T Tr ℵ.)
11.——— 17.
15.——— 19.
7. ——— 31 part.
1. ——— 35.
15.——— 39.
8. —— xii. 6.
2. ——— 28.
1. Jas. i. 7, 12.
7. ——— 21.
10.—— ii. 25 part.
1. —— iii. 1.
1. —— iv. 3.
1. —— v. 7.
15. 1 Pet. i. 9.
— ——— 18, see Fathers.
1. —— iv. 10.
15.—— v. 4.
1. 2 Pet. i. 17.
15. —— ii. 13.
1. 1 John ii. 27.
1. —— iii. 22.
1. —— v. 9.
1. 2 John 4.
3. ——— 8.
1. ——— 10.
3. 3 John 8 (No. 6, G ∾ L T Tr A ℵ.)
14.——— 9, 10.
1. Rev. ii. 17, 27.
1. —— iii. 3.
1. —— iv. 11.
1. —— v. 12.
18.—— xiii. 16, marg. *give.*
1. —— xiv. 9, 11.
1. —— xvii. 12 twice.
1. —— xviii. 4.
1. —— xix. 20.
1. —— xx. 4.

RECEIVE AGAIN.

3. Luke vi. 34.

RECEIVE (CAN)

17. Matt. xix. 11.

RECEIVE FOR.

15. Col. iii. 25.

RECEIVE (GLADLY)

12. Luke viii. 40. | 12. Acts ii. 41.

RECEIVE UP.

ἀναλαμβάνω, (*No.* 1, *with* ἀνά, up *or* again, *prefixed.*)

Matt. xvi. 19 (ap.) | Acts x. 16.
1 Tim. iii. 16.

RECEIVED (BE)

12. Acts xv. 4 (No. 8, L T ℵ.)

RECEIVED (HE THAT HAD)

ὁ, the *one*, (*with an ellipsis in the construction.*)

Matt. xxv. 17.

RECEIVED UP (THAT...SHOULD BE)

τῆς ἀναλήψεως, of the taking [*Him*] up.

Luke ix. 51.

RECEIVED (TO BE)

{ εἰς, unto, with a view to, μετάληψις, reception, (*see above, No.* 5.) }

1 Tim. iv. 3.

RECEIVING.

1. λῆψις, a taking; a receiving, (*non occ.*)
2. πρόσληψις, (*No.* 1, *with* πρός, towards, *prefixed*) a taking to one's self, receiving, admission, (*non occ.*)

2. Rom. ix. 15. | 1. Phil. iv. 15.

RECKON (-ED, -ETH.)

1. λογίζομαι, to count, reckon, calculate, compute, (*strictly of numerical calculation*); *then*, to think, consider.
2. συναίρω, to take up together, to take up a *matter or account* together *for adjustment; hence*, to reckon together.
3. { συναίρω, *see No.* 2, *above*, λόγος, an account, a matter, } to take *or* make up the account with.

2. Matt. xviii. 24.
3. —— xxv. 19.
1. Luke xxii. 37.
1. Rom. iv. 4, 9, 10.
1. —— vi. 11.
1. —— viii. 18.
1. 2 Cor. x. 2, marg. (text, *think of.*)

RECOMMEND (-ED.)

παραδίδωμι, to give near, with, *or* to *any one;* give over, deliver over; commit, entrust, commend to.

Acts xiv. 26. | Acts xv. 40.

RECOMPENCE. [noun.]

1. ἀνταπόδομα, a giving back instead of *something received; or simply*, repayment, (*non occ.*)
2. ἀντιμισθία, wages, retribution; reward, compensation, (*non occ.*)

1. Luke xiv. 12.
2. Rom. i. 27.
1. Rom. xi. 9.
2. 2 Cor. vi. 13.

RECOMPENCE IN THE SAME (FOR A)

{ τὴν, the αὐτὴν, same ἀντιμισθίαν, recompence, } for a corresponding *or* answering recompence.

2 Cor. vi. 13.

RECOMPENCE OF REWARD.

μισθαποδοσία, full payment of wages, (*non occ.*)

Heb. ii. 2. | Heb. xi. 26. | Heb. x. 35.

RECOMPENSE (-ED.) [verb.]

1. ἀνταποδίδωμι, to give back instead of something received; to repay, requite.
2. ἀποδίδωμι, to give away from *one's self, i.e.* to deliver over, bestow, render, pay over, pay off.

1. Luke xiv. 14 twice.
2. Rom. xii. 17.
1. 2 Thes. i. 6.
1. Heb. x. 30.

RECOMPENSE AGAIN.

1. Rom. xi. 35.

RECONCILE.

1. καταλλάσσω, to change against *any thing*, to exchange; *then*, to change a person, reconcile to any one, (*thus differing from* διαλλάσσω, *which implies a* mutual change, and refers to many, *while No.* 1 *is said of* one only) so to act that the opposite party may lay aside his enmity, (*non occ.*)
2. ἀποκαταλλάσσω, (*No.* 1, *with* ἀπό, from, *prefixed, indicating that the thing intended by No.* 1 *is done altogether, absolutely, or in a greater degree*) to change from *one state into another*, to so put away all enmity that amity follows, and no impediment remains to unity and peace, (*non occ.*)

1. Rom. v. 10.
1. 1 Cor. vii. 11.
1. 2 Cor. v. 18, 19, 20.
2. Eph. ii. 16.
2. Col. i. 20, 21.

RECONCILED (BE)

διαλλάσσομαι, to change one's own feelings towards *another, so that* he

changes his; to be reconciled to each other, (*non occ.*)

Matt. v. 24.

RECONCILIATION.

καταλλαγή, change on the part of one party only, induced by some action on the part of another; the reconciliation of men by the love of God in the gift of His Son.

[The Ministry of Reconciliation is not the office of teaching the doctrine of remission or expiation; but it is the office of advising, exhorting, beseeching men to be reconciled to God. For it is not God who is the enemy of men, but men who are enemies to God. (Rom. v. 8-10; viii. 7.)]

2 Cor. v. 18, 19.

RECONCILIATION (MAKE)

ἱλάσκομαι, to incline one's self towards any one.

[In profane Greek, it is *to appease, propitiate the gods*, but Biblical Greek differs remarkably; only in Gen. xxxii. 20, and Zech. vii. 2, is the construction like profane Greek usage, *and here the Heb. is* נשא, *lift up*, be *gracious*, and חלה, *beseech*, *implore*. Elsewhere it is never joined with the *Acc.* or *Dat.* of the person whose goodwill is to be won, *i.e. God is never the object of the action denoted; it never means to conciliate God.* It is the equivalent for כפר, because it was the set expression for expiatory acts, though totally different from the heathen idea. For God is not of Himself alienated from man, but in order that He may not be necessitated to act otherwise, *i.e.* for righteousness' sake an expiation is necessary. This expiation is of God—His love anticipating and meeting His righteousness. Nothing happens to God as in the heathen view, rather, something happens to man, who escapes the wrath to come and remains in the covenant of grace.] (*occ.* Luke xviii. 13.)

Heb. ii. 17.

RECONCILING. [noun.]

καταλλαγή, *see* "RECONCILIATION."

Rom. xi. 15.

RECORD.

1. μάρτυς, a witness, (*not an eye-witness*) but one who has information or knowledge of a thing; *and hence*, one who can give information about, *or* confirm anything.

2. μαρτυρία, a bearing witness, certifying, witnessing to; *then*, that which any one witnesses, or states concerning any person or thing.

2. John i. 19.
2. —— viii. 13, 14.
2. —— xix. 35.
1. 2 Cor. i. 23.
1. Phil. i. 8.
2. 1 John v. 10, 11.
2. 3 John 12.

RECORD (BEAR)

μαρτυρέω, to be a witness, to bear witness, *i.e.* to attest anything that one knows, *and therefore* to state with a certain degree of authority, *usually* for *something*, *and hence*, to confirm *or* prove.

John i. 32, 34.
—— viii. 13, 14.
—— xii. 17.
—— xix. 35.
Rom. x. 2.
2 Cor. viii. 3.
Gal. iv. 15.
Col. iv. 13.
1 John v. 7.
3 John 12.
Rev. i. 2.

RECORD (TAKE TO)

μαρτύρομαι, to call to witness; *oftener*, to assert or attest anything, to make known or affirm a truth with emphasis; *also*, to conjure any one, to exhort earnestly, (*occ.* Gal. v. 3; Eph. iv. 17.)

Acts xx. 26.

RECOVER (-ING.)

{ ἔχω, to have, } to have one's self well,
{ καλῶς, well, } *i.e.* to be well, recover from sickness.

Mark xvi. 18 (*ap.*)

RECOVER ONE'S SELF.

ἀνανήφω, to become sober again, come to one's senses; recover sobriety, wake up to sobriety, (*non occ.*)

2 Tim. ii. 26, marg. *awake*.

RECOVERING.

Luke iv. 18, see Sight.

RED.

πυῤῥός, fire-coloured; *hence*, fiery red, red.

[It is also the colour of blood, ch. vi. 4, 12. When combined with fire, and applied to a being denotes him as bloodthirsty and cruel. So John describes the Devil in his Gospel and Epistle, (John viii. 44; 1 John iii. 12.) *Hence*, the Throne is set to judge him in accordance with Gen. ix. 5.]

Rev. xii. 3.

RED (BE)

πυῤῥάζω, to be fire-coloured *or* fire red, (*non occ.*)

Matt. xvi. 2, 3.

RED (THAT IS)

πυῤῥός, *see* "RED," *above.*

Rev. vi. 4.

RED SEA.

ἐρυθρός, red; *spoken of the colour of nectar and wine, also of copper and of blood*, (*answering to Eng.*, ruddy, red, *and Germ.*, roth; *also like Lat.*, rufus, ruber,) θάλασσα, sea,	the Erythræan Sea; *our* Red Sea *or* Indian Ocean, (*non occ.*)

Acts vii. 36. | Heb. xi. 29.

REDEEM (-ED, -ING.)

1. λυτρόω, to bring forward a ransom; *the Act. being used, not of him who gives, but of him who receives it; hence*, to release on receipt of a ransom, (*non occ.*)

   (a) *Mid.*, to release by payment of a ransom, to redeem.

2. ἀγοράζω, to be in the ἀγορά, (the assembly *or* place of assembly; *hence*, market) to do business there, *i.e.* buy and sell. *In N.T.*, to buy, to purchase, acquire for one's self by a price duly and freely paid.

3. ἐξαγοράζω, (*No.* 2, *with* ἐκ, out of, *prefixed*) to purchase out, buy up *from the power or possession* of any one; purchase from; *hence*, to redeem, release, set free *out of service or bondage*, (*non occ.*)

4.	ποιέω, to make, λύτρωσις, the act of freeing *or* releasing; ransom, redemption, deliverance, (*see below*)	work redemption, effect deliverance, (*occ.* Luke ii. 38; Heb. ix. 2.)

4. Luke i. 68.
1a. —— xxiv. 21.
3. Gal. iii. 13.
3. —— iv. 5.
3. Eph. v. 16.
3. Col. iv. 5.
1a. Tit. ii. 14.
1. 1 Pet. i. 18.
2. Rev. v. 9.
2. —— xiv. 3.
2. Rev. xiv. 4, marg. *buy.*

REDEMPTION.

1. λύτρωσις, the act of freeing *or* releasing; deliverance; redemption, *not with reference to the person delivering, but to the person delivered. Hence*, redemption for one from guilt and punishment, brought about by expiation.

2. ἀπολύτρωσις, (*No.* 1, *with* ἀπό, from, away from, *prefixed*) releasing on receipt of a ransom; redemption as the result of expiation; deliverance from the guilt and punishment of sin, *and, applying to the whole being*, deliverance of the soul from sin, and the body from the grave, (*occ.* Heb. xi. 35.)

1. Luke ii. 38.
2. —— xxi. 28.
2. Rom. iii. 24.
2. —— viii. 23.
2. 1 Cor. i. 30.
2. Eph. i. 7, 14.
2. —— iv. 30.
2. Col. i. 14.
1. Heb. ix. 12.
2. —— 15.

REDOUND.

περισσεύω, to be over and above, to exceed *in number, measure, or degree.*

2 Cor. iv. 15.

REED.

κάλαμος, a reed; a plant with jointed hollow stalk growing in wet grounds; the stalk as cut for use, a reed; *used for writing*, (*occ.* 3 John 13) a pen, *Lat.*, calamus.

Matt. xi. 7.
—— xii. 20.
—— xxvii. 29, 30, 48.
Mark xv. 19, 36.
Luke vii. 24.
Rev. xi. 1.
Rev. xxi. 15, 16.

REFORMATION.

διόρθωσις, a making straight, setting right, restoring to order, (*non occ.*)

Heb. ix. 10.

REFRAIN.

1. παύω, *Eng.*, to pause, to make pause, restrain; *here, mid.*, to pause, refrain from.

2. ἀφίστημι, to place away from, to separate, *i.e.* remove, withdraw.

2. Acts v. 38. | 1. 1 Pet. iii. 10.

REFRESH (-ED.)

1. ἀναπαύω, (*No.* 1, *above, with* ἀνά, again, *prefixed*) to cause to pause again, to cause to rest, to give rest *from labour or effort; hence*, to refresh.

2. ἀναψύχω, to draw breath again, to take breath; to revive by fresh air, be refreshed, *esp. with cooling*, (*non occ.*)

1. 1 Cor. xvi. 18.
1. 2 Cor. vii. 13.
2. 2 Tim. i. 16.
1. Philem. 7, 20.

REFRESH ONE'S SELF.

τυγχάνω, to obtain, receive, } *i.e.* to enjoy the kind attentions of his friends, (*see* 2 Macc. xi. 23.)
ἐπιμελεία, care for, attention, }

Acts xxvii. 3.

REFRESHED (BE)

συναναπαύω, (*No.* 1, *above, with* σύν, in conjunction with, *prefixed*) *mid.*, to refresh one's self, *or* be refreshed in conjunction with *any one, or* in his company.

Rom. xv. 32 (*ap.*)

REFRESHING.

ἀνάψυξις, drawing breath again, a relieving and recovering *from toil and all evils*, (*non occ.*)

Acts iii. 19.

REFUGE, Heb. vi. 18, see FLEE.

REFUSE. [verb.]

1. παραιτέομαι, to ask beside *or* aside, to beg off from, entreat *that something may* not *take place*, excuse one's self; *then*, to refuse.

2. ἀρνέομαι, to deny, renounce, reject.

[This rejection of Moses, Acts vii. 35, (quoted from Exod. ii. 14) takes its place with that of Joseph, Gen. xxxvii. 8, and Jesus, Luke xix. 14, and in each case the one rejected does afterwards bear the rule, in connection with a Gentile bride!]

2. Acts vii. 35.
1. —— xxv. 11.
1. 1 Tim. iv. 7.
1. 1 Tim. v. 11.
2. Heb. xi. 24.
1. —— xii. 25 twice.

REFUSED (TO BE)

ἀπόβλητος, what should be cast away, to be thrown away *as worthless*, (*non occ.*)

1 Tim. i. 4.

REGARD (-ED, -EST, -ETH, -ING.)

1. βλέπω, to use the eyes, to see, to look, (*see under* "SEE," *No.* 5) *here, followed by* εἰς, unto.

2. ἐπιβλέπω, (*No.* 1, *with* ἐπί, upon, *prefixed*) to use *or* fix the eyes upon, to look upon; *hence*, to have respect to. *Here, followed by* ἐπί, upon.

3. φρονέω, to have mind, to think, *i.e.* to understand; to mind, regard, care for.

4. ἐντρέπω, to invert, turn about, to turn one in *upon himself*, *i.e.* to bring to reflection, to affect, to move. *Here, mid.*, to feel *or* have respect *or* deference towards, to respect.

1. Matt. xxii. 16.
1. Mark xii. 14.
2. Luke i. 48.
4. —— xviii. 2, 4.
3. Rom. xiv. 6 1st, marg. *observe.*
3. Rom. xiv. 6 2nd.
3. —— 6 3rd & 4th (*ap.*)
— Phil. ii. 30, see R not.
— Heb. viii. 9, see R not.

REGARD (NOT)

1. παραβουλεύομαι, to misconsult.

2. ἀμελέω, not to care for, neglect, disregard.

1. Phil. ii. 30 (παραβολεύομαι, *to expose one's self to danger, hazarding*, G L T Tr A ℵ.)
2. Heb. viii. 9.

REGENERATION.

παλιγγενεσία, (πάλιν, again, back again; *and* γένεσις, creation) regeneration, *used of the new man, man in Christ*, (*compare* ἄνωθεν γεννεθῆναι, to be begotten from above, John iii. 6, 7; *and* γεννηθῆναι ἐκ θεοῦ, begotten *or* born of God, John i. 13; 1 John ii. 19; iii. 9; iv. 7; v. 1, 4, 18. *The verb* ἀναγεννάομαι, to be begotten *or* born again, 1 Pet. i. 3, 23. The noun ἀναγέννησις, *does not occur in N.T., but often in the Greek Fathers.*) παλιγγενεσία is also used of the new creation, the restoration *or* restitution of all things alluded to in Acts iii. 21; Rom. viii. 21, etc., (*non occ.*)

Matt. xix. 28. | Titus iii. 5.

REGION (-s.)

1. χώρα, space *which receives, contains, or surrounds anything; and so,* place, spot *where one is or anything takes place. Then used with the name of a town, etc., of* the district *or* the open country round it.

2. κλίμα, inclination, declivity; *then, from the apparent inclination of the heavens, the earth was divided into several* κλίματα, climates, *by lines drawn parallel to the sun's course; hence,* clime, region, (*occ.* Rom. xv. 23.)

1. Matt. iv. 16.
1. Luke iii. 1.
1. Acts viii. 1.
1. Acts xiii. 49.
1. —— xvi. 6.
2. 2 Cor. xi. 10.
2. Gal. i. 21.

REGION ROUND ABOUT.

περίχωρος, around a place, *i.e.* circumjacent, neighbouring. *Here, fem., with art., and* γῆ, land, *understood*, the country round about, the adjacent region.

Matt. iii. 5.
Mark i. 28.
Mark vi. 55 (χώρα, *region*,
Luke iv. 14. [LmTTrAℵ.)
Luke vii. 17.

REGION THAT LIETH ROUND ABOUT.

περίχωρος, *see above.*

Acts xiv. 6.

REGIONS BEYOND (THE)

{ τὰ, the (*neut. pl.*)...
{ ὑπερέκεινα, beyond those, (*non occ.*)

2 Cor. x. 16.

REHEARSE (-ED.)

ἀναγγέλλω, to bring a message back again, report back, used of the reports brought by persons returning from somewhere; *hence in a weaker sense*, to report.

Acts xiv. 27.

REHEARSE FROM THE BEGINNING.

ἄρχομαι, to begin, *intrans., and gen. followed by another verb. Here,* "beginning—*was setting forth.*"

Acts xi. 4.

REIGN. [noun.]

ἡγεμονία, leadership, supremacy, government.

Luke iii. 1.

REIGN (-ED, -ETH.) [verb.]

1. βασιλεύω, to be king, possess regal authority, to reign, (*occ.* 1 Tim. vi. 15 part.)

2. { ἔχω, to have,
{ βασιλεία, a kingdom.

1. Matt. ii. 22.
1. Luke i. 33.
1. —— xix. 14, 27.
1. Rom. v. 14, 17 twice, 21 twice.
1. —— vi. 12.
— —— xv. 12, see R over.
1. 1 Cor. iv. 8 1st & 2nd.
— ——— 8 3rd, see R with.
1. 1 Cor. xv. 25.
— 2 Tim. ii. 12, see R with.
1. Rev. v. 10.
1. —— xi. 15, 17.
1. —— xix. 6.
1. —— xx. 4, 6.
2. —— xvii. 18.
1. —— xxii. 5.

REIGN OVER.

ἄρχω, to begin, be first, in rank *or* dignity; *hence*, to rule, reign.

Rom. xv. 12.

REIGN WITH.

συμβασιλεύω, ("REIGN," *No.* 1, *with* σύν, in conjunction with, *prefixed*) to reign in conjunction with another, (*non occ.*)

1 Cor. iv. 8. | 2 Tim. ii. 12.

REINS.

νεφρός, kidney; *usually pl. οἱ νεφροί*, the kidneys, reins, loins; used of the seat of the desires and passions, (lxx. for כליות, Ps. vii. 10; Jer. xi. 20; xvii. 10; xx. 12), (*non occ.*)

Rev. ii. 23.

REJECT (-ED, -ETH.)

1. *ἀποδοκιμάζω*, to disapprove, to reject after making trial, (*occ.* 1 Pet. ii. 4, 7.)
2. *ἀθετέω*, to displace, set aside, cast off, get rid of.
3. *ἐκπτύω*, to spit out, to spit *in token of disgust*, (*non occ.*)
4. *παραιτέομαι*, to ask beside, ask aside, get rid of by asking, beg off from, to excuse one's self.

1. Matt. xxi. 42.
2. Mark vi. 26.
2. —— vii. 9, marg. *frustrate.*
1. —— viii. 31.
1. —— xii. 10.
2. Luke vii. 30, marg. frustrate.
1. —— ix. 22.
1. Luke xvii. 25.
1. —— xx. 17
2. John xii. 48.
3. Gal. iv. 14.
2. 1 Thes. ii. 8 twice, marg. (text, *despise.*)
4. Tit. iii. 10.
— Heb. vi. 8, see Rejected.
1. —— xii. 17.

REJECTED.

ἀδόκιμος, not approved, rejected after trial.

Heb. vi. 8.

REJOICE (-ED, -ETH, -ING.)

1. *χαίρω*, to rejoice, be delighted *or* pleased, to be glad.
2. *ἀγαλλιάω*, to leap *or* dance much, to rejoice with song and dance; *hence*, to exult, leap for joy.
3. *εὐφραίνω*, to make glad-minded, to cheer. *Here, mid. or Aor. pass.*, to make merry, enjoy one's self, *esp., as connected with feasting.*
4. *καυχάομαι*, to speak loud, be loud-tongued, boast *or* vaunt one's self, to glory *or* exult *both in a good and bad sense.*

1. Matt. ii. 10.
1. —— v. 12.
1. —— xviii. 13.
1. Luke i. 14.
1. —— 47.
2. —— 58, see R with.
—
1. Luke vi. 23.
1. —— x. 20 twice.
2. —— 21.
1. —— xiii. 17.
1. —— xv. 5.
— —— 6, 9, see R with.
1. Luke xix. 37.
1. John iii. 29.
1. —— iv. 36.
2. —— v. 35.
2. —— viii. 56.
1. —— xiv. 28.
1. —— xvi. 20, 22.
3. Acts ii. 26.
1. —— v. 41.
3. —— vii. 41.
1. —— viii. 39.
1. —— xv. 31.
2. —— xvi. 34.
4. Rom. v. 2.
1. —— xii. 12, 15 twice.
3. —— xv. 10.
1. 1 Cor. vii. 30 twice.
— —— xii. 26, see R with.
1. 1 Cor. xiii. 6 1st, with *ἐπί, upon.*
— —— 6 2nd, see R in.
1. 2 Cor. ii. 3.
1. —— vi. 10.
1. —— vii. 7, 9, 16.
3. Gal. iv. 27.
1. Phil. i. 18 twice.
— —— ii. 16, see R (that I may)
— —— 17, 18, see R with.
1. —— 28.
1. —— iii. 1.
4. —— 3.
1. —— iv. 4 twice, 10.
1. Col. i. 24.
1. 1 Thes. v. 16.
4. Jas. i. 9, marg. *glory.*
— —— ii. 13, see R against.
4. —— iv. 16.
— 1 Pet. i. 6, see R (greatly)
2. —— 8.
1. —— iv. 13.
1. 2 John 4.
1. 3 John 3.
1. Rev. xi. 10.
3. —— xii. 12.
3. —— xviii. 20.
2. —— xix. 7.

REJOICE AGAINST.

κατακαυχάομαι, (*No.* 4, *with κατά*, against, *prefixed*) to speak loud *or* be loud tongued against, boast *or* vaunt one's self against.

Jas. ii. 13, marg. *glory against.*

REJOICE (GREATLY)

2. 1 Pet. i. 6.

REJOICE (THAT I MAY)

εἰς, unto, for,
καύχημα, a matter *or* subject of boasting,
ἐμοί, to me.

Phil. ii. 16.

REJOICE IN.

συγχαίρω, (*No.* 1, *with σύν, in conjunction with, prefixed*) to rejoice in conjunction with.

1 Cor. xiii. 6, marg. *Rejoice with.*

REJOICE WITH.

συγχαίρω, *see above.*

Luke i. 58.
—— xv. 6, 9.
1 Cor. xii. 26.
1 Cor. xiii. 6, marg. (text, *rejoice in.*)
Phil. ii. 17, 18.

REJOICING.

1. *καύχημα*, the subject-matter *or* theme of glorying, a boasting *or* exulting, (*see* "REJOICE," *No.* 4.

2. *καύχησις*, the act of glorying *or* boasting, (*see* "REJOICE," *No.* 4.)

2. 1 Cor. xv. 31.
2. 2 Cor. i. 12.
1. —— 14.
1. Gal. vi. 4.
1. Phil. i. 26.
2. 1 Thes. ii. 19, marg. [*glorying.*
1. Heb. iii. 6.
2. Jas. iv. 16.

RELEASE (-ED.) [verb.]

ἀπολύω, to let loose from, loosen, unbind; free, relieve from; release, let go free.

Matt. xxvii. 15, 17, 21, 26.
Mark xv. 6, 9, 11, 15.
Luke xxiii. 16, 17 (ap.), 18, [20, 25.
John xviii. 39 twice.
John xix. 10, 12.

RELIEF.

διακονία, serviceable labour, service, ministry. *In the Christian church it denotes* any ministerial office with reference to the labour pertaining thereto.

Acts xi. 29.

RELIEVE (-ED.)

ἐπαρκέω, to ward off, keep off *something from one; hence*, to help, assist, succour, (*non occ.*)

1 Tim. v. 10, 16 twice.

RELIGION.

θρησκεία, religious observance, the outward ceremonial service of religion, the external form, (*as opp. to εὐσεβεία*, practical piety rightly directed; *θεοσεβεία*, the worship of God; *εὐλάβεια*, the devoutness arising from godly fear) *see* "RELIGIOUS," *No.* 1, (*occ.* Col. ii. 18.)

Acts xxvi. 5.
Gal. i. 13, 14, see Jews'.
Jas. i. 26, 27.

RELIGIOUS.

1. *θρῆσκος*, religious, *esp., in a bad sense*, superstitious; *as subst.*, the zealous and diligent performer of the outward service of God, (*either from θρῆξ, because of their* mysteries; *or from τρέω*, full of religious fear; *or from θρέω*, muttering forms of prayer), (*non occ.*)

2. *σέβω*, to stand in awe *or* fear *before God and man, and esp., when about to do something disgraceful*, to feel shame, be afraid; *hence*, God-fearing, to be God-fearing as to doing something. *In classical Greek only* the fear of wrong, *not the conscientious practice of right, but this is accounted for if we consider the nature of their gods. Used in N.T. only of proselytes. Here pass. part.*, devout, pious.

2. Acts xiii. 43.
1. Jas. i. 26.

REMAIN (-ED, -EST, -ETH, -ING.)

1. *μένω*, to remain, continue, abide; stay, dwell.

2. *διαμένω*, (*No.* 1, *with διά*, through, *prefixed*) to continue throughout, to remain through.

3. *ἀπολείπω*, to leave away from *one's self. Here, pass.*, to be left behind, remain, (lxx. for נשאר, Ex. xiv. 28.)

4. *περιλείπω*, to leave over. *Here pass.*, to be left over, be left remaining, to survive, (*non occ.*)

5. *περισσεύω*, to be over and above, to exceed *in number or measure;* be more than enough.

1. Matt. xi. 23.
5. —— xiv. 20.
2. Luke i. 22.
5. —— ix. 17.
1. —— x. 7.
1. John i. 33.
5. —— vi. 12.
1. —— ix. 41.
1. —— xv. 11 (ᾖ *may be*, G ~ L T Tr A.)
1. —— 16.
1. —— xix. 31.
1. Acts v. 4 part.
1. Acts xxvii. 41.
1. 1 Cor. vii. 11.
— —— 29, see R (it)
1. —— xv. 6.
1. 2 Cor. iii. 11, 14.
1. —— ix. 9.
4. 1 Thes. iv. 15, 17.
2. Heb. i. 11.
3. —— iv. 6, 9.
3. —— x. 26.
1. —— xii. 27.
1. 1 John ii. 24.
1. —— iii. 9.

REMAIN OVER AND ABOVE.

5. John vi. 13.

REMAIN (THE THINGS WHICH)

τὰ λοιπά, the rest, the remaining things.

Rev. iii. 2.

REMAINETH (IT)

τὸ λοιπόν, for the rest, as to the rest; *or, the time* that remains *is short; or* the opportunity is contracted for what remains.

1 Cor. vii. 29.

REMEMBER (-ED, -EST, -ETH.)

1. μνημονεύω, *act.*, to call to *another's* mind, mention; *then*, to call to one's own mind, to remember. *Pass.*, to be remembered, have in memory, (*occ.* Heb. xi. 15, 22.)

2. μιμνήσκω, to think much of *a thing, and so* to remember, to call to one's mind, begin to remember, remind.

   (a) *Mid.*, to begin to call to mind, recollect, remember, (*see* "MINDFUL OF (BE)," *No.* 3.)

3. ἀναμιμνήσκω, (*No.* 2, *with* ἀνά, up, *or* back, *prefixed*) to call up to mind, to recall to one's mind.

4. ὑπομιμνήσκω, (*No.* 2, *with* ὑπό, *implying* stealth, *prefixed*) to call to one's mind, *privately, silently, by hints or suggestions; hence,* to suggest to one's mind, put in mind of, bring to remembrance.

   (a) *Mid.*, to call to one's own mind *from something unobserved by others.*

2. Matt. v. 23.
1. —— xvi. 9.
2. —— xxvi. 75.
2. —— xxvii. 63.
1. Mark viii. 18.
2. Luke i. 72.
2. —— xvi. 25.
1. —— xvii. 32.
4a.—— xxii. 61.
2. —— xxiii. 42.
2. —— xxiv. 6, 8.
2. John ii. 17, 22.
2. —— xii. 16.
1. —— xv. 20.
1. —— xvi. 4, 21.
2. Acts xi. 16
1. —— xx. 31 35.
2. 1 Cor. xi. 2
3. 2 Cor. vii. 15.
2. Gal. ii. 10.
1. Col. iv. 18.
1. 1 Thes. i. 3.
1. —— ii. 9.
1. 2 Thes. ii. 5.
1. 2 Tim. ii. 8.
2. Heb. viii. 12.
2. —— x. 17.
1. —— xi. 22, marg. (text, *make mention.*)
2a.—— xiii. 3.
1. —— —— 7.
4. 3 John 10.
2. Jude 17.
1. Rev. ii. 5.
1. —— iii. 3.
1. —— xviii. 5.

REMEMBRANCE.

(*For various combinations with other words, see below.*)

1. ἀνάμνησις, a calling up to mind, a causing to remember, remembrance, (*occ.* Heb. x. 3.)

2. ὑπόμνησις, a putting in mind, *privately, or by hints or suggestions;* a suggesting to one's mind; a bringing to remembrance, (*non occ.*)

3. μνεία, remembrance memory, mention.

4. μνήμη, memory *as a power of the mind, esp. as distinguished from No. 1, which is the act of recollecting;* remembrance, record *of a thing,* (*non occ.*)

1. Luke xxii. 19.
1. 1 Cor. xi. 24, 25.
3. Phil. i. 3, marg. *mention.*
3. 1 Thes. iii. 6.
3. 2 Tim. i. 3.
2. —— 5.
2. 2 Pet. i. 13.
4. —— 15, and see R (have in)
2. 2 Pet. iii. 1.

REMEMBRANCE AGAIN.

1. Heb. x. 3.

REMEMBRANCE (BE HAD IN)

μιμνήσκω, *see* "REMEMBER," *No.* 2.

Acts x. 31, pass.

REMEMBRANCE (BRING INTO)

ἀναμιμνήσκω, *see* "REMEMBER," *No.* 3.

1 Cor. iv. 17.

REMEMBRANCE (BRING TO)

ὑπομιμνήσκω, *see* "REMEMBER," *No.* 4.

John xiv. 26.

REMEMBRANCE (CALL TO)

ἀναμιμνήσκω, *see* "REMEMBER," *No.* 3.

Mark xi. 21. | Heb. x. 32.

REMEMBRANCE (COME IN)

μιμνήσκω, *see* "REMEMBER," *No.* 2.

Rev. xvi. 19.

REMEMBRANCE (HAVE IN)

{ μνήμη, *see above, No.* 4, ποιέω, to make, } to make a remembrance, (*i.e. keep it up.*)

2 Pet. i. 15.

REMEMBRANCE OF (IN)

μιμνήσκω, *see* "REMEMBER," *No.* 2. (*Here,* 1 *aor. inf.*)

Luke i. 54.

REMEMBRANCE (PUT IN)

1. ἀναμιμνήσκω, *see* "REMEMBER," *No.* 3.
2. ὑπομιμνήσκω, *see* "REMEMBER," *No.* 4.

3. ὑποτίθημι, to set *or* put under, to lay under; *here, mid.*, to bring under *the mind or notice of any one*, to suggest, put in mind of *as a teacher or otherwise*, (*occ.* Rom. xvi. 4.)

3. 1 Tim. iv. 6 part.
1. 2 Tim. i. 6.
2. 2 Pet. i. 12.
2. Jude 5.

REMEMBRANCE OF (PUT IN)

ὑπομιμνήσκω, *see* "REMEMBER," *No.* 4.

2 Tim. ii. 14.

REMISSION.

1. ἄφεσις, dismission, discharge, setting free. *In* lxx. and *N.T.*, setting free, remission *of debt or* punishment; *hence*, the forgiveness of sins on the part of God, and with reference to the future judgment; total remission and forgiveness excluding all idea of punishment, (*see No.* 2, *below.*)

2. πάρεσις, a letting pass, overlooking, not punishing, suspension of punishment, tolerating without special intervention, *not like No.* 1, *which implies full pardon and forgiveness*, but, a passing by of sins for the present.

[*No.* 2 is the word which describes the *O.T. remission of punishment*, solely traceable to the Divine patience; while *No.* 1 is the *N.T. remission of sins* as characteristic of the *N.T.* salvation. Before the death of Christ, there was remission (*No.* 2) as a work of ἀνοχή (or *forbearance.*) After it there was remission (*No.* 1) as a work of χάρις (or *grace*),] (*non occ.*)

1. Matt. xxvi. 28.
1. Mark i. 4.
1. Luke i. 77.
1. —— iii. 3.
1. —— xxiv. 47.
1. Acts ii. 38.
1. —— x. 43.
2. Rom. iii. 25, marg. *passing over.*
1. Heb. ix. 22.
1. Heb. x. 18.

REMIT (-ED.)

ἀφίημι, to send away, dismiss, set free; *of sins*, to remit the penalty of, *i.e.* to pardon, forgive.

[Here, by proclaiming and promising forgiveness, as influenced by the Spirit, not as influencing the Spirit, for ministerial acts are not creative, but declarative of the preceding acts of the Holy Ghost. With the gift of the Holy Ghost to any disciple, comes the knowledge of "sin, righteousness, and judgment," and therefore a pre-eminent fitness for the discernment of sin and repentance in others, and an authority to declare the fulfilment of God's promises, or the contrary.]

John xx. 23 1st.
—— 23 2nd (ἀφέωνται, *have been remitted*, L T Tr ℵc.)

REMNANT.

1. λοιπός, left, remaining; the rest.

2. λεῖμμα, a remnant left; *esp.*, the less of two parts; remains, (*non occ.*)

3. κατάλειμμα, (*No.* 2, *with* κατά, down, *prefixed*) a remnant left behind, (*non occ.*)

1. Matt. xxii. 6.
3. Rom. ix. 27 (ὑπόλειμμα, *a secret remnant*, L T Tr A ℵ.)
2. Rom. xi. 5.
1. Rev. xi. 13.
1. —— xii. 17.
1. —— xix. 21.

REMORSE. [margin.]

Rom. xi. 8, see "SLUMBER."

REMOVE (-ED.)

1. αἴρω, to raise, raise *or* lift up; to take up, *to carry*; *and hence*, to carry; carry away.

2. κινέω, to move, put in motion, shake.

3. μεθίστημι, to set *or* move over *from one place to another*, to transfer, to remove.

4. μεταβαίνω, to go *or* pass over *from one place to another.*

5. μετατίθημι, place among, place differently, change, alter; *hence*, to transfer, transpose, transport.

6. παραφέρω, to bear beside *or* near, bear along by, bear away *as does a stream.*

(a) *Act.*, to let pass away, (*occ.* Mark xiv. 36.)

(b) *Pass.*, to be borne along by.

4. Matt. xvii. 20 twice.
1. —— xxi. 21.
1. Mark xi. 23.
6a. Luke xxii. 42.
— Acts vii. 4, see R into.
3. —— xiii. 22 part.
— 1 Cor. xiii. 2, see R (can)
5. Gal. i. 6.
2. Rev. ii. 5.

REMOVE (CAN)

3. 1 Cor. xiii. 2.

REMOVE INTO.

μετοικίζω, to lead to another abode, (*occ.* Acts vii. 43.)

Acts vii. 4.

REMOVING.

μετάθεσις, transposition. *Eng.*, metathesis, a removal from one place to another, change, (*occ.* Heb. vii. 12; xi. 5.)

Heb. xii. 27.

REND, RENT.

1. σχίζω, to split, cleave, rend; to divide with violence; *esp.*, *of wood, also of rocks, etc.*

2. ῥήγνυμι, to break, burst through, break asunder *or* in pieces; shiver, shatter.

3. διαῤῥήσσω, (*another form of No.* 2, *with* διά, through, *prefixed*) to tear through, rend asunder, *esp.*, *of the clothes*, (*occ.* Luke v. 6; viii. 29.)

4. σπαράσσω, to tear, lacerate, mangle, *esp.*, *of dogs or carnivorous animals; also*, to convulse, throw into spasms *or* convulsions.

2. Matt. vii. 6.
3. —— xxvi. 65.
1. —— xxvii. 51 twice.
1. Mark i. 10, marg. (text, open.)
4. —— ix. 26.
3. Mark xiv. 63.
1. —— xv. 38.
1. Luke xxiii. 45.
1. John xix. 24.
3. Acts xiv. 14.
— —— xvi. 22, see R off.

REND OFF.

περιῤῥήγνυμι, (*No.* 2, *with* περί, around, *prefixed*) to tear from around any one, *as fetters, or garments*, (*non occ.*)

Acts xvi. 22.

RENDER (-ING.)

1. ἀποδίδωμι, to give away from *one's self*, to deliver over, to give up, to bestow; *used in ref. to obligation*, to give in full, to render, pay over *or* off, *as vows or wages.*

2. ἀνταποδίδωμι, (*No.* 1, *with* ἀντί, in place of, *prefixed*) to give back instead of *something received*, recompense, to reward.

1. Matt. xxi. 41.
1. —— xxii. 21.
1. Mark xii. 17.
1. Luke xx. 25.
1. Rom. ii. 6.
1. Rom. xiii. 7.
1. 1 Cor. vii. 3.
2. 1 Thes. iii. 9.
1. —— v. 15.
1. 1 Pet. iii. 9.

RENEW (-ED.)

1. ἀνακαινόω, to renew, (*from* καινός, *not recent, but* different) to come in the place of what was formerly and has not yet been used. *Here*, to daily acquire new strength, which previously it had not, (*non occ.*), (*see under* "NEW.")

2. ἀνακαινίζω, (*differing from No.* 1 *only in the termination, denoting more activity in the making new*), (*non occ.*)

1. 2 Cor. iv. 16.
1. Col. iii. 10.
2. Heb. vi. 6.

RENEWED (BE)

ἀνανεόομαι, to be renewed, (*from* νέος, recent, *as well as different*, only lately originated) to be only lately originated or established; *denoting that* a new spirit should dwell in those who have put on the καινός *or* new man, (*non occ.*)

Eph. iv. 23.

RENEWING.

ἀνακαίνωσις, renewal, renovation, a making other and different from that which had been formerly, (*non occ.*)

Rom. xii. 2.
Tit. iii. 5.

RENOUNCE.

ἀπεῖπον, to speak out or off, *i.e. to the end. In N.T. only mid.*, to speak one's self off from *any thing, i.e.* renounce, disown, (*non occ.*)

2 Cor. iv. 2.

RENT. [noun.]

σχίσμα, that which is cloven *or* parted, *esp. by violence;* a cleft, division, rent.

Matt. ix. 16. | Mark ii. 21.

RENT (MAKE A)

σχίζω, *see* "REND," *No.* 1.

Luke v. 38.

REPAY.

1. ἀποδίδωμι, *see* "RENDER," *No.* 1.
2. ἀνταποδίδωμι, *see* "RENDER," *No.* 2.
3. ἀποτίω, to pay back, repay, pay in full; *esp.*, to avenge, take vengeance, (*non occ.*)

1. Luke x. 35. | 2. Rom. xii. 19.
3. Philem. 19.

REPENT (-ED.)

1. μετανοέω, to perceive afterwards, (*opp. to* προνοέω) *hence*, to change one's mind and purpose. *This change is always for the better, and denotes* a change of moral thought and reflection; *not merely to repent of, nor* to forsake sin, *but* to change one's mind and apprehensions regarding it; *hence*, to repent in a moral and religious sense, with the feeling of remorse and sorrow. (*Lat.*, resipisco, to recover one's senses, come to a right understanding; *and* resipiscentia, the growing wise.) μετανοέω *denotes* to reform, to have a genuine change of heart and life from worse to better.

   (a) *Followed by* ἐκ, *showing a complete change*, out of *a former mode of life, to a new and different life.*

2. μεταμέλομαι, to rue, regret; to have dissatisfaction with one's self for what one has done, to change *or* alter one's purpose, have anxiety consequent on a past transaction; to have pain of mind, *rather than change of mind;* and change of purpose, *rather than change of heart.*

[Godly sorrow works a reformation (*No.* 1) which brings no regrets, (*No.* 2) 2 Cor. vii. 10. Esau found no place for changing his father's mind, (*No.* 1) though his father might deeply regret it, (*No.* 2) Heb. xii. 17. Judas might have *No.* 2, but not *No.* 1, *see* Matt. xxvii. 3.]

1. Matt. iii. 2.
1. —— iv. 17.
1. —— xi. 20, 21.
1. —— xii. 41.
2. —— xxi. 29, 32.
— —— xxvii. 3, see R one's self.
1. Mark i. 15.
1. —— vi. 12.
1. Luke x. 13.
1. —— xi. 32.
1. —— xiii. 3, 5.
1. —— xv. 7, 10.
1. —— xvi. 30.
1. —— xvii. 3, 4.
1. Acts ii. 38.
1. Acts iii. 19.
1. —— viii. 22.
1. —— xvii. 30.
1. —— xxvi. 20.
2. 2 Cor. vii. 8 twice.
— —— 10, see R of (not to be)
1. —— xii. 21.
2. Heb. vii. 21.
1. Rev. ii. 5 twice, 16.
1a. —— 21 1st.
1. —— 21 2nd.
1a. —— 22.
1. —— iii. 3, 19.
1a. —— ix. 20, 21.
1. —— xvi. 9.
1a. Rev. xvi. 11.

REPENT ONE'S SELF.

2. Matt. xxvii. 3.

REPENTED OF (NOT TO BE)

ἀμεταμέλητος, (*verbal adj. of No.* 2, *above, with* a, *negative, prefixed*) not to be regretted; without change of purpose, (*occ.* Rom. xi. 29.)

2 Cor. vii. 10.

REPENTANCE.

μετάνοια, afterthought; *hence*, repentance, change of mind, (*the* νοῦς *being* the faculty of moral reflection); change of mind *from bad to good, not merely pain of mind;* reformation, (*see* "REPENT," *No.* 1, *of which it is the noun*), (*non occ.*)

Matt. iii. 8, marg. *amendment of life.*
—— 11.
—— ix. 13 (*om.* εἰς μετάνοιαν, *to repentance*, G L T Tr A ℵ.)
Mark i. 4.
—— ii. 17 (*om.* εἰς μετάνοιαν, *to repentance*, G L T Tr A ℵ.)
Luke iii. 3, 8.
—— v. 32.
—— xv. 7.
—— xxiv. 47.
Acts v. 31.
—— xi. 18.
—— xiii. 24.
—— xix. 4.
—— xx. 21.
—— xxvi. 20.
Rom. ii. 4.
—— xi. 29, see R (without)
2 Cor. vii. 9, 10.
2 Tim. ii. 25.
Heb. vi. i. 6.
—— xii. 17, marg. *to change one's mind.*
2 Pet. iii. 9.

REPENTANCE (WITHOUT)

ἀμεταμέλητος, *see* "REPENTED OF (NOT TO BE)."

Rom. xi. 29.

REPETITIONS (USE VAIN)

βαττολογέω, to babble, (compounded of λεγω, to speak, and *βάττος*, *prob. from* Heb. בטא, to prate, use many words, Lev. v. 4.) [Herod. (iv. 155) says *βάττος* was a king of Cyrene who stuttered. According to others, *βάττος* was a silly, loquacious poet, who made long hymns, full of repetitions, (*Suid.*) It is more probably onomatœpoetic, from a person who stutters and stammers; and thus] *βαττολογέω originally signified* to stammer; *then*, to babble, chatter; *so*, to use empty words, (*non occ.*)

Matt. vi. 7.

REPLY (-IEST) **AGAINST.**

ἀνταποκρίνομαι, to reply against, answer again.

Rom. ix. 20, marg. *answer again, or dispute with.*

REPORT. [noun.]

(*For various combinations, see below.*)

1. *ἀκοή*, hearing; *the sense or faculty of* hearing; *the instrument of hearing*, the ears; that which is heard, rumour, report.
2. *μαρτυρία*, witness, testimony *borne or* given.

1. John xii. 38.
1. Rom. x. 16, marg. *preaching or hearing.*
2. 1 Tim. iii. 7.

REPORT (EVIL)

δυσφημία, ill-omened language, malediction; evil speaking, (*non occ.*)

2 Cor. vi. 8.

REPORT (GOOD)

εὐφημία, words of good import *or* omen, acclamation; good report, (*non occ.*)

2 Cor. vi. 8.

REPORT (HAVE GOOD)

μαρτυρέω, to witness, be a witness; bear witness, testify. *Here, pass or mid.*, to be well testified of, have good witness borne in favour of.

Acts xxii. 12. | 3 John 12.

REPORT (OBTAIN GOOD)

μαρτυρέω, see above.

Heb. xi. 2, 39.

REPORT (OF GOOD)

1. *μαρτυρέω, see above.*
2. *εὔφημος*, well-spoken, well-worded; *hence*, of good import; of good report, (*non occ.*)

1. Acts x. 22 part. | 2. Phil. iv. 8.

REPORT (OF HONEST)

μαρτυρέω, see "REPORT (HAVE GOOD)"

Acts vi. 3 part.

REPORT (-ED.) [verb.]

(*For various combinations, see below.*)

1. *ἀπαγγέλλω*, to bring a message from *some place or person*, to report intelligence from.
2. *ἀναγγέλλω*, to bring a message back from; send news of, announce, proclaim.

1. Acts iv. 23.
— Rom. iii. 8, see Slanderously.
1. 1 Cor. xiv. 25.
2. 1 Pet. i. 12.

REPORT (COMMONLY)

διαφημίζω, to rumour abroad, divulge, spread abroad.

Matt. xxviii. 15.

REPORTED (BE)

ἀκούω, to hear; learn by hearing. *Here, pass*, to be heard of, *i.e.* to be reported, to be noised abroad.

1 Cor. v. 1.

REPORTED OF (BE WELL)

μαρτυρέω, see "R (HAVE GOOD)"

Acts xvi. 2. | 1 Tim. v. 10.

REPROACH (-ES.) [noun.]

1. *ὀνειδισμός*, defamation, reproach, reviling, contumely, (*see No.* 2), (*non occ.*)

2. ὄνειδος, fame; report, *good or bad. Usually and in N.T.*, reproach, blame, (*non occ.*)

3. ὕβρις, wanton violence, *arising from the pride of strength, passion, or lust;* wantonness, insolence, injurious treatment.

4. ἀτιμία, dishonour, disgrace, stigma.

2. Luke i. 25.
1. Rom. xv. 3.
4. 2 Cor. xi. 21.
3. —— xii. 10.
1. 1 Tim. iii. 7.
— —— 10, see R (suffer)
1. Heb. x. 33.
1. —— xi. 26.
1. Heb. xiii. 13.

REPROACH (SUFFER)

ὀνειδείζω, *see below. Here, pass.*

1 Tim. iv. 10 (ἀγωνίζομαι, *strive*, G ∾ L T Tr A* ℵ.)

REPROACH (-ED, -EST.) [verb.]

1. ὀνειδίζω, to defame, *i.e.* to disparage, reproach, cast in one's teeth, upbraid.

2. ὑβρίζω, to wax wanton, run riot, *esp. in the use of superior strength, or in the enjoyment of pleasure;* to outrage, personally insult.

1. Luke vi. 22.
2. —— xi. 45.
1. Rom. xv. 3.
1. 1 Pet. iv. 14.

REPROACHFULLY (SPEAK)

{ χάριν, in respect of, *implying the motive before the mind as an attraction, not as a cause,*
λοιδορία, railing, reviling, } in respect of reviling, [the enemy finding in the reproach that which produces an occasion to exercise his hostility, the reproach being a favoured or accepted motive to the adversary.]

1 Tim. v. 14, marg. *for railing.*

REPROBATE (-S.)

ἀδόκιμος, unapproved, unworthy; spurious, that will not stand proof, (*occ.* Heb. vi. 8; 1 Cor. ix. 27.)

Rom. i. 28, marg. *void of judgment.*
2 Cor. xiii. 5, 6, 7.
2 Tim. iii. 8, marg. *of no judgment.*
Tit. i. 16, marg. *void of judgment.*

REPROOF.

ἔλεγχος, proof, means of conviction *or* of proof, convincing argument, (*occ.* Heb. xi. 1.)

2 Tim. iii. 16 (ἐλεγμός, *conviction*, L T Tr A ℵ.)

REPROVE (-ED.)

ἐλέγχω, to shame, put to shame; to do so by proving one in the wrong.

Luke iii. 19.
John iii. 20, marg. *discover.*
—— xvi. 8, marg. *convince.*
Eph. v. 11.
—— 13, marg. *discover.*
2 Tim. iv. 2.

REPUTATION (BE OF)

δοκέω, to seem, to have the appearance, to seem to be something.

Gal. ii. 2.

REPUTATION (HAD IN)

τίμιος, held worth, estimated; valued, prized.

Acts v. 34.

REPUTATION (HOLD IN)

{ ἔντιμος, in honour,
{ ἔχω, to have *or* hold.

Phil. ii. 22, marg. *honour.*

REPUTATION (MAKE OF NO)

κενόω, to empty, make empty.

Phil. ii. 7.

REQUEST (-S.)

1. αἴτημα, thing asked for, object sought.

2. δέησις, want, need, the expression of need.

— Rom. i. 10, see R (make)
2. Phil. i. 4.
1. Phil. iv. 6.
— 1 Thes. iv. 1, marg. see *Beseech.*

REQUEST (MAKE)

δέομαι, to need, to want; to make known one's need.

Rom. i. 10.

REQUIRE (-ED, -ING.)

1. αἰτέω, to ask, ask for something, to beg, pray for; to ask *or* call for, require, demand.

2. αἴτημα, thing asked for; object sought.

3. ζητέω, to seek, seek after, look for, to strive to find; *also*, to seek for, inquire, require.

4. *ἐκζητέω*, (*No.* 3, *with ἐκ*, out of, *prefixed*) to seek out, search out, inquire diligently, scrutinise. *Here, by Hebraism*, to require, *i.e.* to demand, avenge (*like* lxx. בקש, Ez. iii. 18, 20; 2 Sam. iv. 11.; *and* דרש, Gen. ix. 5; xlii. 22.)

5. *πράσσω*, to do; *spoken in reference to a person*, to do to *or* in respect of *any one; also*, to do from *any one, i.e.* to exact *or* collect *money* from *any one*.

4. Luke xi. 50, 51.	1. Luke xxiii. 23.
— —— xii. 20, see R (be)	2. ——— 24.
3. ——— 48.	1. 1 Cor. i. 22.
5. —— xix. 23.	3. —— iv. 2.

— 1 Cor. vii. 36, see R (need so)

REQUIRETH (NEED SO)

οὕτως, thus *ὀφείλει*, it ought *γίνεσθαι*, to become,	thus it ought to be brought about; *or* so it must be.

1 Cor. vii. 36.

REQUIRED (BE)

ἀπαιτέω, (*No.* 1, *with ἀπό*, away from, *prefixed*) to demand back from *any one*. *Here, spoken of ψυχή*, "they shall require thy life," *i.e.* thy life shall be required by Him who gave it.

Luke xii. 20, marg. *do they require.*

REQUITE.

ἀποδίδωμι, to render, *ἀμοιβή*, change, requital, returns,	returns to be rendering; *or* to render in return, (*non occ.*)

1 Tim. v. 4.

RESCUE (-ED.)

ἐξαιρέω, to take out, pluck out; *hence, mid.*, to rescue out of *any one's power*.

Acts xxiii. 27 mid.

RESEMBLE.

ὁμοιόω, to make like, to liken, to make to resemble any other objects of the same kind.

Luke xiii. 18.

RESERVE (-ED.)

1. *τηρέω*, to keep an eye upon, to watch; *and hence*, to guard, keep; keep in safety, preserve, maintain.

2. *καταλείπω*, to leave down, *as to one's heirs;* to leave behind; to leave remaining.

1. Acts xxv. 21.	instead of *τηρουμένους, to be reserved,* L א.)
2. Rom. xi. 4.	1. 2 Pet. ii. 9, 17.
1. 1 Pet. i. 4.	1. —— iii. 7.
1. 2 Pet. ii. 4 (*κολαζόμενους τηρεῖν, to be reserved to be punished,*	1. Jude 6, 13.

RESIDUE (THE)

1.	*οἱ*, the *ones*, *λοιποί*, left, remaining,	those who were left, *i.e.* to the rest.
2.	*οἱ*, the *ones*, *κατάλειποι*, left behind, (*non occ.*)	the residue, (*quoted from* Amos ix. 12, *where* lxx. *for* שארית.

Also for שאר, Ez. iii. 8; *and* יתר, Deut. iii. 13.)

1. Mark xvi. 13 (*ap*). | 2. Acts xv. 17.

RESIST (-ED, -ETH.)

1. *ἀνθίστημι*, to stand against, to set one's self against, *i.e.* to withstand, oppose, resist, *either in words, or deeds, or both.*

2. *ἀντικαθίστημι*, to stand firm against, resist, (*non occ.*)

3. *ἀντιτάσσομαι*, to set one's self in battle array against; to set one's self in opposition to, (*occ.* Acts xviii. 6.)

4. *ἀντιπίπτω*, to fall against *or* upon *in a hostile* manner, to strive against, (lxx. *inf. for* מריבה, Numb. xxvii. 14), (*non occ.*)

1. Matt. v. 39.	1. 2 Tim. iii. 8.
1. Luke xxi. 15.	2. Heb. xii. 4.
1. Acts vi. 10.	3. Jas. iv. 6.
4. —— vii. 51.	1. ——— 7.
1. Rom. ix. 19.	3. —— v. 6.
3. —— xiii. 2 1st.	3. 1 Pet. v. 5.
1. ——— 2 2nd & 3rd.	1. ——— 9.

RESOLVED (BE)

γινώσκω, to know, perceive; to be influenced by our knowledge of the object and be determined thereby.

Luke xvi. 4.

RESORT (-ED.)

1. ἔρχομαι, to come *or* go, move *or* pass along.

2. συνέρχομαι, (*No.* 1, *with* σύν, in conjunction with, *prefixed*) to come *or* go together with *any one*, to come together, assemble.

3. συνάγω, to lead *or* bring together, gather, gather together.

4. συμπορεύομαι, to transport *or* betake one's self in conjunction with *another*, to pass from *one place* to *another* together.

1. Mark ii. 13.	3. John xviii. 2.
4. —— x. 1.	2. —— 20.
1. John x. 41.	2. Acts xvi. 13.

RESPECT.

See also, under "PERSONS."

μέρος, a part, particular.

2 Cor. iii. 10.	Col. ii. 16, marg. *part.*

RESPECT (HAVE)

ἀποβλέπω, to look away towards *any thing*, to fix the eyes intently upon; *hence*, to have regard to, (*non occ.*)

Heb. xi. 26.

RESPECT TO (HAVE)

ἐπιβλέπω, to look upon, to fix the eyes upon, have respect to, *with favour or partiality*.

Jas. ii. 3.

RESPECT OF (IN)

κατά, *with Acc.*, down upon, over against; *then, in reference to some standard of comparison*, according to, with regard to, as to.

Phil. iv. 11.

RESPECTER.

See, PERSONS.

REST. [noun.]

(*See below for* "THE REST," *and* "REST OF;" *also for the verb,* "TO REST.")

1. ἀνάπαυσις, a resting up, pause, cessation from labour; *the constant word in* lxx. *for* the rest of the Sabbath (Ex. xvi. 23; xxxi. 15; xxxv. 2, etc.), (*occ.* Rev. iv. 8.)

2. κατάπαυσις, a resting down, putting to rest, a resting; *hence*, a place of rest, fixed abode, *implying a final rest, as No.* 1 *does a temporary pause*, (*non occ.*)

3. ἄνεσις, a loosening, relaxing, *as of strings or chords that have been tightly stretched; also used of bonds or exertions. Not merely a rest from labour, but* a relaxation from endurance and expectation, (*occ.* Acts xxiv. 23; 2 Cor. viii. 13.)

4. εἰρήνη, peace, state of peace, tranquillity; *and the effect*, security.

5. σαββατισμός, a Sabbath-keeping, (*from* σαββατίζω, to keep Sabbath, Ex. xvi. 30), (*non occ.*)

— Matt. xi. 28, see R (give)	3. 2 Cor. ii. 13.
1. —— 29.	3. —— vii. 5.
1. —— xii. 43.	3. 2 Thes. i. 7.
— —— xxvi. 45, see R (take)	2. Heb. iii. 11, 18.
— Mark xiv. 41, see R (take)	2. —— iv. 1, 3 twice, 5.
1. Luke xi. 24.	— —— 8, see R (give)
— John xi. 13, see R (taking of)	5. —— 9, marg. *keeping of a Sabbath.*
2. Acts vii. 49.	2. —— 10, 11.
4. —— ix. 31.	1. Rev. xiv. 11.

REST (GIVE)

1. ἀναπαύω, to cause to rest up, cause to cease or desist from, give rest to *or* from.

2. καταπαύω, to put *or* lay to rest, quiet down, cause to rest, *implying a final rest.*

1. Matt. xi. 28.	2. Heb. iv. 8.

REST (TAKE)

ἀναπαύω, (*see above, No.* 1.) *Here, mid.*, to rest one's self, *i.e.* to take rest, enjoy rest, *the idea of previous toil or suffering being included.*

Matt. xxvi. 45.	Mark xiv. 41.

REST (TAKING OF)

κοίμησις, a sleeping, sleep, (*non occ.*)

John xi. 13.

REST (-ED, -EST, -ETH.) [verb.]

1. ἀναπαύω, *see* "REST (TAKE)"
2. { ἔχω, to have / ἀνάπαυσις, rest, (*see* "REST," *No.* 1.)
3. καταπαύω, *see* "REST (GIVE)," *No.* 2.
4. κατασκηνόω, to plant down a tent, *i.e.* to pitch a tent.
5. ἡσυχάζω, to be still *or* quiet, be at rest.

1. Mark vi. 31.
— Luke x. 6, see R upon.
5. —— xxiii. 56.
4. Acts ii. 26.
— Rom. ii. 17, see R in.
— 2 Cor. xii. 9, see R upon.
3. Heb. iv. 4.
1. 1 Pet. iv. 14.
2. Rev. iv. 8, marg. *have rest.*
1. —— vi. 11.
1. —— xiv. 13 (ἀναπαήσονται, *shall rest*, instead of ἀναπαύσωνται, *may rest*, L T Tr A ℵ.)

REST IN.

ἐπαναπαύομαι, to rest one's self upon, lean upon.

Rom. ii. 17.

REST UPON.

1. ἐπαναπαύομαι, to rest one's self upon. *Here, followed by* ἐπί, upon.
2. ἐπισκηνόω, to pitch a tent upon, to come and dwell upon *or* in, to descend and abide upon. *Here, followed by* ἐπί, upon.

1. Luke x. 6. | 2. 2 Cor. xii. 9.

REST (THE)

λοιπός, left, remaining.

(a) *Masc. or fem.*, οἱ λοιποί, *or* αἱ λοιπαί, the rest, the others.

(b) *Neut. pl.*, τὰ λοιπά, the remaining things.

a. Matt. xxvii. 49.
b. Luke xii. 26.
a. —— xxiv. 9.
a. Acts ii. 37.
a. —— v. 13.
a. —— xxvii. 44.
a. Rom. xi. 7.
a. 1 Cor. vii. 12.
b. —— xi. 34.
— 1 Pet. iv. 2, see R of.
a. Rev. ii. 24.
a. —— ix. 20.
a. Rev. xx. 5.

REST OF.

ἐπίλοιπος, remaining over.

1 Pet. iv. 2.

RESTITUTION.

ἀποκατάστασις, complete restoration, reëstablishment, restitution, (*non occ.*)

Acts iii. 21.

RESTORE (-ED, -ETH.)

1. ἀποκαθίστημι, to put back into a former state, reëstablish, reinstate.
2. ἀποδίδωμι, to give away from one's self, deliver over, give up; give back again, restore.
3. καταρτίζω, make fully ready, put in full order; *esp. of what is broken*, refit, repair, restore.

1. Matt. xii. 13.
1. —— xvii. 11.
1. Mark iii. 5.
1. —— viii. 25.
1. —— ix. 12.
1. Luke vi. 10.
2. —— xix. 8.
— Acts i. 6, see R again.
3. Gal. vi. 1.
1. Heb. xiii. 19.

RESTORE AGAIN.

ἀποκαθιστάνω, (*another form of* "RESTORE," *No.* 1), (*non c.*)

Acts i. 6.

RESTRAIN (-ED.)

καταπαύω, to quiet down, cause to cease, make desist, *and so*, to restrain.

Acts xiv. 18.

RESURRECTION.

1. ἀνάστασις, a standing up, rising up, *as from the dead; hence*, Resurrection.

[There are Three Resurrections, "Every man in his own order."

(1) Christ the first-fruits, 1 Cor. xv. 23; Acts xxvi. 23.

(2) "They that are Christ's at His coming," (1 Cor. xv. 23). This is ἀνάστασις ἐκ τῶν νεκρῶν, the resurrection out of or from among the dead, called "The first Resurrection," (Rev. xx. 5, 6.) The "better resurrection" (Heb. xi. 35.) The "Resurrection unto life," (John v. 29; Dan. xii. 2.) The "Resurrection of the just," (Acts xxiv. 15; Luke xiv. 14.) Those who partake of it are called "Children of God, being children of the resurrection," (Luke xx. 35, 36.) (It was this new doctrine of Resurrection from among (ἐκ) the dead that

excited such surprise among both Jews and Gentiles, and not merely *a* Resurrection.)

(3) The rest, (τὸ τέλος, 1 Cor. xv. 23, not "the end," but the last rank, the last of the three companies) "the rest of the dead," (Rev. xx. 5) and always ἀνάστασις τῶν νεκρῶν, the resurrection of the dead (*i.e.* dead people, not of others out from among them) called "the resurrection of the unjust," (Acts xxiv. 15) "the resurrection of damnation," (John v. 29) "to shame and everlasting contempt," (Dan. xii. 2),] (*occ.* Luke ii. 34; Acts xxvi. 23; Heb. xi. 35.)

2. ἐξανάστασις, (*No.* 1, *with* ἐκ, out of, *prefixed*) the out-resurrection. *Here followed by* ἐκ, *lit.* "the out-resurrection from among the dead."

3. ἔγερσις, a waking up *as from sleep*, a rousing up, a rising; *hence*, resurrection, *because death is a sleep.*

1. Matt. xxii. 23, 28, 30, [31.
3. —— xxvii. 53.
1. Mark xii. 18, 23.
1. Luke xiv. 14.
1. —— xx. 27, 33, 35, 36.
1. John v. 29 twice.
1. —— xi. 24, 25.
1. Acts i. 22.
1. —— ii. 31.
1. —— iv. 2, 33.
1. —— xvii. 18 (*ap.*), 32.
1. —— xxiii. 6, 8.
1. Acts xxiv. 15, 21.
1. Rom. i. 4.
1. —— vi. 5.
1. 1 Cor. xv. 12, 13, 21, 42.
1. Phil. iii. 10.
2. —— 11.
1. 2 Tim. ii. 18.
1. Heb. vi. 2.
1. —— xi. 35.
1. 1 Pet. i. 3.
1. —— iii. 21.
1. Rev. xx. 5, 6.

RETAIN (-ED.)

1. ἔχω, to have and hold; *spoken of temporary holding and of lasting possession.*

2. κατέχω, to hold down, to have and hold fast, hold firmly, retain.

3. κρατέω, to be strong, mighty, powerful; have power over, control; *spoken of sins*, to retain, not to remit, (*see under* "REMIT.")

3. John xx. 23 twice.
2. Philem. 13.
1. Rom. i. 28, marg. to [*acknowledge.*

RETURN (-ED, -ING.)

1. ὑποστρέφω, to turn behind, *i.e.* back; to turn back.

2. { μέλλω, to be on the point of, ὑποστρέφω, *see above*, } about to return.

3. ἐπιστρέφω, to turn upon *or* to, turn towards; *hence*, to turn back from.

4. ἀναστρέφω, to turn up, turn back, return, turn again.

5. ἀνακάμπτω, to bend *or* turn up back, (*occ.* Luke x. 6.)

6. ἀναλύω, to loosen again *with the idea of* coming back to the same place again, (*used of a ship returning home from a foreign part*); *hence*, to return, depart and return. *Used in* lxx. *of returning from a feast*, (*occ.* Phil. i. 23, where it is εἰς τὸ ἀναλῦσαι, unto the return, *viz.* of Christ, *for only then and thus* (οὕτω) *shall we be with Him*, 1 Thes. iv. 17.)

7. ἐπανέρχομαι, to come back upon *or* to *a place;* to return hither, thither, etc., (*occ.* Luke x. 35.)

8. ἐπανάγω, to lead up upon, lead back upon *or* to *a place*, to cause to return. *In N.T.*, *intrans.*, to return to.

5. Matt. ii. 12.
3. —— xii. 44.
1. —— xiv. 40 part (*ap.*)
8. —— xxi. 8 part.
3. —— xxiv. 18.
1. Luke i. 56.
3. —— ii. 20 (No. 1, G L T Tr A ℵ.)
1. —— 39, 43.
1. —— iv. 1, 14.
1. —— vii. 10.
— —— viii. 37, see R back again.
1. —— 39, 40.
1. —— ix. 10 part.
— —— x. 17, see R again.
1. —— xi. 24.
6. —— xii. 36.
1. —— xvii. 18.
3. —— 31.
1. Luke xix. 12.
7. —— 15.
1. —— xxiii. 48, 56.
1. —— xxiv. 9, 33, 52.
1. Acts i. 12.
4. —— v. 22.
1. —— xii. 25.
1. —— xiii. 13.
2. —— 34.
— —— xiv. 21, see R again.
4. —— xv. 16.
5. —— xviii. 21.
1. —— xx. 3.
— —— xxi. 6, see R again.
1. —— xxiii. 32.
— Gal i. 17, see R again.
— —— vi. 18, marg. see [Go up.
1. Heb. vii. 1.
5. —— xi. 15.

RETURN AGAIN.

1. Luke x. 17.
1. Acts xiv. 21.
1. Acts xxi. 6.
1. Gal. i. 17.

RETURN BACK AGAIN.

1. Luke viii. 37.

REVEAL (-ED.)

1. ἀποκαλύπτω, to remove th eil or covering away from, *and so* to expose to open view what was before hidden; *hence*, to reveal, make manifest, (*non occ.*)

2. χρηματιζω, to do or carry on business. *Then*, to be called *or* named, *since names were imposed on men from their business or office.* To speak to *or* treat with *another about some* business. To utter oracles, give divine directions *or* instructions, make divine communications.

1. Matt. x. 26.
1. — xi. 25.
1. —— 27 (ἀποκαλύψῃ, *may reveal*, instead of βούληται ἀποκαλύψαι, *may be pleased to reveal*, Lm.)
1. — xvi. 17.
2. Luke ii. 26.
1. —— 35.
1. — x. 21, 22.
1. — xii. 2.
1. — xvii. 30.
1. John xii. 38.
1. Rom. i. 17, 18.
1. Rom. viii. 18.
1. 1 Cor. ii. 10.
1. — iii. 13.
1. — xiv. 30.
1. Gal. i. 16.
1. — iii. 23.
1. Eph. iii. 5.
1. Phil. iii. 15.
— 2 Thes. i. 7, see R (when...shall be)
1. — ii. 3, 6, 8.
1. 1 Pet. i. 5, 12.
— — iv. 13, see R (when...shall be)
1. — v. 1.

REVEALED (WHEN...SHALL BE)

{ ἐν, in
ἀποκάλυψις, the unveiling, uncovering, manifestation, appearing.

2 Thes. i. 7. | 1 Pet. iv. 13.

REVELATION (-S.)

ἀποκάλυψις, unveiling, uncovering; *of facts and truths*, disclosure, revelation; *of persons*, appearing, manifestation.

[The book so called, relates all the facts and circumstances and judgments attending the Second coming, *or* revelation, *or* appearing of the Lord Jesus Christ.]

Rom. ii. 5.
— xvi. 25.
1 Cor. xiv. 6, 26.
2 Cor. xii. 1, 7.
Gal. i. 12.
Gal. ii. 2.
Eph. i. 17.
— iii. 3.
1 Pet. i. 13.
Rev. i. 1.

REVELLING (-S.)

κῶμος, a feasting, revel; *Lat.*, comissatio, a carousing or merrymaking after supper, *the guests often sallying into the streets with torches and music, etc., in honour of Bacchus*, (*occ.* Rom. xiii. 13.)

Gal. v. 21. | 1 Pet. iv. 3.

REVENGE. [noun.]

ἐκδίκησις, execution of right and justice, maintenance of right (*if necessary by vengeance or penal retribution.*)

2 Cor. vii. 11.

REVENGE. [verb.]

ἐκδικέω, to execute right and justice, maintain right (*if necessary by vengeance*); *hence*, to avenge.

2 Cor. x. 6.

REVENGER.

ἔκδικος, executing right and justice; *hence*, a retributer, avenger, (*occ.* 1 Thes. iv. 6.)

Rom. xiii. 4.

REVERENCE. [noun.]

αἰδώς, sense of shame, bashfulness, modesty; *then*, regard for others, respect, reverence, (*occ.* 1 Tim. ii. 9.)

Heb. xii. 28 (δεύς, *fear* or *awe*, G ~ L T Tr A ℵ.)
1 Pet. iii. 15, marg. see Fear.

REVERENCE (GIVE...)

ἐντρέπω, *see below*, *No.* 1.

Heb. xii. 9.

REVERENCE.

1. ἐντρέπω, to invert, to turn one in *upon himself*, bring to reflection; to affect, move; *here*, *mid.*, to shame one's self before *any one*, feel respect *or* deference towards, respect, reverence.

2. φοβέομαι, to fear, be afraid; *morally*, to fear, *i.e.* to honour.

1. Matt. xxi. 37.
1. Mark xii. 6.
1. Luke xx. 13.
2. Eph. v. 33.

REVILE (-ED, -EST.)

1. λοιδορέω, to rail at, abuse, revile, (*non occ.*)

2. ὀνειδίζω, to defame, assail with opprobrious words, cast in one's teeth, reproach with *any thing*

3. βλασφημέω, to drop evil *or* profane words, speak lightly *or* amiss of sacred things; to speak ill *or* to the prejudice of *one*; *hence*, to slander.

2. Matt. v. 11.
3. — xxvii. 39.
2. Mark xv. 32.
1. John ix. 28.
1. Acts xxiii. 4.
1. 1 Cor. iv. 12.
1. 1 Pet. ii. 23 1st.
— — 23 2nd, see R again

REVILE AGAIN.

ἀντιλοιδορέω, (*No.* 1, *with* ἀντί, back, *prefixed*) to rail at back, revile in turn.

1 Pet. ii. 23.

REVILER.

λοίδορος, a railer, abuser, reviler, (*occ.* 1 Cor. v. ii.)

1 Cor. vi. 10.

REVIVE (-ED.)

ἀναζάω, to live again, return to life.

Rom. vii. 9.
—— xiv. 9 (ἔζησεν, *lived*, instead of ἀνέστη καὶ ἀνέζησεν, *rose and revived*, G L T Tr A ℵ.)
Phil. iv. 10, marg. see Flourish again.

REWARD. [noun.]

1. μισθός, hire, wages, pay.
2. ἀνταπόδοσις, giving back in turn, a rendering, requiting, recompense, (*non occ.*)

1. Matt. v. 12, 46.
1. —— vi. 1, 2, 5, 16.
1. —— x. 41 twice, 42.
1. Mark ix. 41.
1. Luke vi. 23, 35.
— —— xxiii. 41, see R (due)
1. Acts i. 18.
1. Rom. iv. 4.
1. 1 Cor. iii. 8, 14.
1. —— ix. 17, 18.
— Col. ii. 18, see R (beguile of one's)
2. —— iii. 24.
1. 1 Tim. v. 18.
— Heb. ii. 2, } see Recompense.
— —— x. 35, }
— —— xi. 26, }
1. 2 Pet. ii. 13.
1. 2 John 8.
1. Jude 11.
1. Rev. xi. 18.
1. Rev. xxii. 12.

REWARD (BEGUILE OF ONE'S)

καταβραβεύω, to give the prize against *any one*, to deprive of the palm.

Col. ii. 18, marg. *judge against*.

REWARD (DUE)

ἄξιος, worthy; of equal worth; *hence*, suitable, congruent. *Here, neut. pl.*

Luke xxiii. 41.

REWARD (-ED.) [verb.]

ἀποδίδωμι, to give away from *one's self*, bestow; *spoken in reference to obligation of any kind*, to give in full, pay over *or* off, render.

Matt. vi. 4, 6, 18.
—— xvi. 27.
2. Tim. iv. 14.
Rev. xviii. 6.

REWARDER.

μισθαποδότης, a payer in full of wages; *hence*, requiter, rewarder, (*non occ.*)

Heb. xi. 6.

RICH.

(*For various combinations with other words, see below.*)

1. πλούσιος, rich, having *or* abounding in riches, (*prob. akin to* πολύς, much; πλέων, more.)
2. πλουτέω, to be rich *or* wealthy.

1. Matt. xxvii. 57.
1. Mark xii. 41.
2. Luke i. 53 part.
1. —— vi. 24.
1. —— xii. 16.
1. —— xiv. 12.
1. —— xvi. 1, 19.
1. —— xviii. 23.
1. Luke xix. 2.
1. 2 Cor. viii. 9.
1. Eph. ii. 4.
1. 1 Tim. vi. 17.
1. Jas. i. 10.
1. —— ii. 5.
1. Rev. ii. 9.
1. —— iii. 17.
1. Rev. xiii. 16.

RICH (BE)

2. Luke xii. 21.
2. Rom. x. 12.
2. 1 Cor. iv. 8.
2. 2 Cor. viii. 9.
2. 1 Tim. vi. 9, 18.
2. Rev. iii. 16.

RICH (BE MADE)

2. Rev. xiii. 15, 19.

RICH (WAX)

2. Rev. xviii. 3.

RICH (MAKE)

πλουτίζω, to make rich, enrich; bestow richly.

2 Cor. vi. 10.

RICH MAN.

1. Matt. xix. 23, 24.
1. Mark x. 25.
1. Luke xvi. 21, 22.
1. —— xxi. 1.
1. Jas. i. 11.
1. —— ii. 6.
1. —— v. 1.
1. Rev. vi. 15.

RICHES.

1. πλοῦτος, riches, wealth, (*see* "RICH," *No.* 1), (*non occ.*)
2. χρῆμα, something useful, useful, what one can use *or* needs; *hence*, goods, property, money. *Here, pl.*

1. Matt. xiii. 22.
1. Mark iv. 19.
2. —— x. 23, 24.
1. Luke viii. 14.
— —— xvi. 9, 11, marg. see Mammon.
2. Luke xviii. 24.
1. Rom. ii. 4.
1. —— ix. 23.
1. —— xi. 12 twice, 33.
1. 2 Cor. viii. 2.
1. Eph. i. 7, 18.

1. Eph. ii. 7.
1. —— iii. 8, 16.
1. Phil. iv. 19.
1. Col. i. 27.
1. —— ii. 2.
1. 1 Tim. vi. 17.
1. Heb. xi. 26.
1. Jas. v. 2.
1. Rev. v. 12.
1. —— xviii. 17.

RICHLY.

πλουσίως, richly, *i.e.* abundantly, largely.

Col. iii. 16. | 1 Tim. vi. 17.

RIGHT. [not "left."]

(*For* "RIGHT HAND," *and other combinations, see below.*)

δεξιός, right, *as opposed to left; Lat.*, dexter, on the right hand side.

Matt. v. 29, 30, 39
Luke vi. 6.
—— xxii. 50.
John xviii. 10.
John xxi. 6.
Acts iii. 7.
Rev. i. 16, 17.
—— x. 2.
Rev. xiii. 16.

RIGHT HAND.

Matt. vi. 3.
—— xxvii. 29.
Acts ii. 33.
—— v. 31.
Rom. viii. 34.
Gal. ii. 9.
Eph. i. 20.
Col. iii. 1.
Heb. i. 3.
—— viii. 1.
—— x. 12.
—— xii. 2.
1 Pet. iii. 22.
Rev. i. 20.
—— ii. 1.
—— v. 1, 7.

RIGHT HAND (ON THE)

1. δεξιός, *see above.*

2. { ἐκ, out of, from, / δεξιῶν, *see above,* } off from the right hand parts.

2. Matt. xx. 21, 23.
2. —— xxii. 44.
2. —— xxv. 33, 34.
2. —— xxvi. 64.
2. —— xxvii. 38.
2. Mark x. 37, 40.
2. —— xii. 36.
2. —— xiv. 62.
2. Mark xv. 27.
2. —— xvi. 19 (*ap.*)
2. Luke xx. 42.
2. —— xxii. 69.
2. —— xxiii. 33.
2. Acts ii. 25, 34.
2. —— vii. 55, 56.
1. 2 Cor. vi. 7.
2. Heb. i. 13.

RIGHT SIDE (ON THE)

1. { ἐκ, / δεξιῶν, } *see above, No.* 2.

2. { ἐν, in / τοῖς, the / δεξιοῖς, right, } on the right.

3. { τὰ, the / δεξιὰ, right / μέρη, part. }

2. Mark xvi. 5. | 1. Luke i. 11.
3. John xxi. 6.

RIGHT. [not "wrong."]

1. δίκαιος, *see* "RIGHTEOUS."

2. εὐθύς, straight; *hence, metaph.*, right, true.

3. ὀρθῶς, straight up, uprightly, (*Lat.*, rectè) really, truly.

1. Matt. xx. 4, 7 (*ap.*)
— Mark v. 15, part, } see Mind.
— Luke viii. 35, [part, } see Mind.
3. —— x. 28.
1. Luke xii. 57.
1. Acts iv. 19.
2. —— viii. 21.
2. —— xiii. 10.
1. Eph. vi. 1.
2. 2 Pet. ii. 15.

RIGHT. [noun.]

ἐξουσία, authority, the power *or* right to do anything; *esp.*, power, *as entrusted.*

John i. 12, marg. (text, *power*) | Heb. xiii. 10.
Rev. xxii. 14.

RIGHTEOUS.

δίκαιος, right, just, *i.e.* fulfilling all claims which are right and becoming; just as it should be; a right state, *of which God is the standard. Used of God, it denotes* the perfect agreement subsisting between His nature (*which is the standard for all*) and His acts.

Matt. ix. 13.
—— x. 41 3 times.
—— xiii. 17, 43.
—— xxiii. 28, 29, 35 twice.
—— xxv. 37, 46.
Mark ii. 17.
Luke i. 6.
—— v. 32.
—— xviii. 9.
—— xxiii. 47.
John vii. 24.
—— xvii. 25.
Rom. ii. 5, marg. see "Judgment."
—— iii. 10.
Rom. v. 7, 19.
2 Thes. i. 5, 6.
1 Tim. i. 9.
2 Tim. iv. 8.
Heb. xi. 4.
Jas. v. 16.
1 Pet. iii. 12.
—— iv. 18.
2 Pet. ii. 8 twice.
1 John ii. 1, 29.
—— iii. 7, 12.
Rev. xvi. 5, 7.
—— xix. 2.
—— xxii. 11 1st.
—— 11 2nd, see R (be)

RIGHTEOUS (BE)

δικαιόω, to justify, to make and regard as δίκαιος (*see above*). *Here, pass.*, to present *or* show one's self as righteous.

Rev. xxii. 11 (*δικαιοσύνην ποιησάτω, do righteousness, instead of δικαιωθήτω, be righteous,* G L T Tr A ℵ.)

RIGHTEOUSLY.

δικαίως, *adv. of* δίκαιος, (*see* "RIGHTEOUS") justly, rightly, with strict justice and righteousness.

Tit. ii. 12. | 1 Pet. ii. 23.

RIGHTEOUSNESS.

1. δικαιοσύνη, the doing *or* being what is just and right; the character and acts of a man commanded by and approved of God, in virtue of which the man corresponds with Him and His will as His ideal and His standard; *it signifies* the sum total of all that God commands and approves. *As such it is* not only what God demands, *but* what He gives to man, and which is appropriated by faith; *and hence it is* a state called forth by God's act of justification, *viz.* by judicial deliverance from all that stands in the way of being δίκαιος, (*see* "RIGHTEOUS.")

2. δικαίωμα, the product or result of δικαιόω, (*see* "RIGHTEOUS (BE)") marking the action relating to the recognition or determining *or* setting forth of a δίκαιος *or* a man as righteous; the act of justification accomplished in and for the sinner.

3. εὐθύτης, straightness. *Trop.* rectitude.

1. Matt. iii. 15.
1. —— v. 6, 10, 20.
1. —— vi. 33.
1. —— xxi. 32.
1. Luke i. 75.
1. John xvi. 8, 10.
1. Acts x. 35.
1. —— xiii. 10.
1. —— xvii. 31.
1. —— xxiv. 25.
1. Rom. i. 17.
2. —— [illegible] 36.
1. —— [illegible] 5, 21, 22, 25, 26.
1. —— iv. [illegible] 5, 6, 9, 11 twice, 1[illegible], 22.
1. —— v. 17.
2. ——— 18.
1. ——— 21.
1. —— vi. 13, 16, 18, 19, [20.
2. —— viii. 4.
1. ——— 10.
1. —— ix. 28 (*ap.*)
1. ——— 30 3 times, 31 1st.
1. ——— 31 2nd (*om.* δικαιοσύνης, *of righteousness*, G→L T Tr A ℵ.)
1. —— x. 3 1st.
1. ——— 3 2nd (*om.* G L Tr A b.)
1. ——— 3 3rd, 4, 5, 6, 10.
1. —— xiv. 17.
1. 1 Cor. i. 30.
— —— xv. 34, see R (to)
1. 2 Cor. iii. 9.
1. —— v. 21.
1. 2 Cor. vi. 7, 14.
1. —— ix. 9, 10.
1. —— xi. 15.
1. Gal. ii. 21.
1. —— iii. 6, 21.
1. —— v. 5.
1. Eph. iv. 24.
1. —— v. 9.
1. —— vi. 14.
1. Phil. i. 11.
1. —— iii. 6, 9 twice.
1. 1 Tim. vi. 11.
1. 2 Tim. ii. 22.
1. —— iii. 16.
1. —— iv. 8.
1. Tit. iii. 5.
3. Heb. i. 8, marg. *rightness or straightness.*
1. ——— 9.
1. —— v. 13.
1. —— vii. 2.
1. —— xi. 7, 33.
1. —— xii. 11.
1. Jas. i. 20.
1. —— ii. 23.
1. —— iii. 18.
1. 1 Pet. ii. 24.
1. —— iii. 14.
1. 2 Pet. i. 1.
1. —— ii. 5, 21.
1. —— iii. 13.
1. 1 John ii. 29.
1. —— iii. 7, 10 (*ap.*)
2. Rev. xix. 8.
1. ——— 11.

RIGHTEOUSNESS (TO)

δικαίως, *see* "RIGHTEOUSLY."

1 Cor. xv. 34.

RIGHTLY.

ὀρθῶς, (*adv. of* ὀρθός, straight, upright) uprightly, really, truly.

Luke vii. 43. | Luke xx. 21.
2 Tim. ii. 15, see Divide.

RING.

δακτύλιος, a finger-ring, lxx. for טַבַּעַת, Gen. xli. 43; Est. viii. 2.

Luke xv. 22. | Jas. ii. 2, see Gold.

RINGLEADER.

πρωτοστάτης, who stands first; *trop.*, a leader, (*non occ.*)

Acts xxiv. 5.

RIOT. [noun.]

ἀσωτία, the life and character of an ἄσωτος, (one who is unsaveable, incorrigible, past hope); dissoluteness, profligacy, (*occ.* Eph. v. 18.)

Tit. i. 6. | 1 Pet. iv. 4.

RIOT (TO) [verb.]

ἡ, the τρυφή, a breaking down, *esp., of the mind*, and making effeminate; *hence*, luxury, indulgence, *i.e.* "*esteeming* the *daytime*, luxury, a pleasure"; *or* "*a pleasure accounting* the indulgence *by day*" (prob. in allusion to 1 Thes. v. 7, *and marking a greater degeneracy.*)

2 Pet. ii. 13.

RIOTING.

κῶμος, *see* "REVELLING."

Rom. xiii. 13.

RIOTOUS.

ἀσώτως, *adv. of* ἄσωτος, (not saveable, abandoned) dissolutely (*here, lit.*, "living abandonedly, dissolutely, *or* in riotous excess."

Luke xv. 13.

RIPE (BE)

ξηραίνω, *here, pass.*, to be dried up, become fully dry; *more than* "*to be-*

come ripe"; and indicative of something evil, (*see* Matt. xxi. 19.)

Mark iv. 29, marg. see Brought forth (be)
Rev. xiv. 15.

RIPE (BE FULLY)

ἀκμάζω, to flourish, be in one's prime, be in full blow, full harvest, (*non occ.*)

Rev. xiv. 18.

RISE (-EN, -ETH, -ING, ROSE.)

(*For various combinations with other words, see below.*)

1. ἐγείρω, to wake, arouse, rouse up *from sleep;* to wake up from the sleep of death. (*Here, mid., and pass. Aor.*)
2. ἀνίστημι, *trans.*, to cause to stand up; *intrans.*, to stand up.
3. ἀνατέλλω, *trans.*, to make rise up, *as water, light,* etc.; *intrans.*, to rise up, *esp., of the sun and moon,* (ἐπιτέλλω is more usual of the stars) *used also of rivers and events.*

1. Matt. xi. 11.
2. —— xii. 41.
1. —— xiv. 2.
1. —— xxiv. 7, 11.
1. —— xxvi. 46.
1. —— xxvii. 64.
1. —— xxviii. 6, 7,
1. Mark iv. 27.
1. —— vi. 14, 16.
2. —— ix. 9, 31.
1. —— x. 49 (*active*, G L T Tr A ℵ.)
2 ——— 50 (ἀναπηδήσας, *leaped up*, L T Tr A ℵ.)
2. —— xii. 23 (*om.* ὅταν ἀναστῶσι, *when then they shall rise*, G⇉L^b Tr ℵ.)
2. ——— 25.
1. ——— 26.
1. —— xiii. 8, 22.
1. —— xiv. 28.
1. —— xvi. 6.
2. ——— 9 part (*ap.*)
1. ——— 14 (*ap.*)
1. Luke ix. 7.
1. —— xi. 7.
2. Luke xi. 8 1st.
1. ——— 8 2nd.
3. —— xii. 54.
2. —— xvi. 31.
1. —— xxi. 10.
2. —— xxii. 46.
1. —— xxiv. 6, 34.
2. ——— 46.
1. John ii. 22.
1. —— v. 8 (*active*, L T Tr A ℵ.)
1. —— xiii. 4.
1. —— xxi. 14 part.
2. Acts x. 13, 41.
2. —— xxvi. 16.
2. Rom. xiv. 9 (ἔζησεν, *lived*, inst. of ἀνέστη καὶ ἀνέζησεν, *rose and revived*, G L T Tr A ℵ.)
2. —— xv. 12.
1. 1 Cor. xv. 12, 13, 14, 15, 16, 20, 29, 32.
2. 1 Thes. iv. 16.
2. Heb. vii. 11.
3. Jas. i. 11.
1. Rev. xi. 1 (*active*, L T Tr A ℵ.)

RISE AGAIN.

2. Matt. xvii. 9 (No. 1, L T Tr A.)
2. —— xx. 19 (No. 1, T Tr ℵ.)
1. —— xxvi. 32.
1. —— xxvii. 63.
2. Mark viii. 31.
2. —— x. 34.
2. Luke ix. 8, 19.
2. Luke xviii. 33.
2. —— xxiv. 7.
2. John xi. 23, 24.
2. —— xx. 9.
2. Acts xvii. 3.
1. Rom. viii. 34.
1. 1 Cor. xv. 4.
1. 2 Cor. v. 15.
2. 1 Thes. iv. 14.

RISE (MAKE TO)

3. Matt. v. 45.

RISE (THE FIRST THAT SHOULD)

πρῶτος, the first,
ἐξ, out of, from,
ἀναστάσεως, the standing up, the resurrection.

Acts xxvi. 23.

RISE UP.

1. ἐγείρω, *see above, No.* 1.
2. ἀνίστημι, *see above, No.* 2.
3. ἐξανίστημι, (*No*, 2, *with* ἐκ, out of, *prefixed*) to stand up out of.
4. ἀναβαίνω, to go up, ascend *from a lower to a higher place.*

1. Matt. xii. 42.
2. Mark i. 35.
2. —— iii. 26.
1. —— xiv. 42.
2. Luke iv. 29.
1. —— v. 23 (*active*, G L T Tr A ℵ.)
2. ——— 25, 28.
1. —— vi. 8 (*active*, G L T Tr A ℵ.)
2. —— vii. 16.
1. —— xi. 31.
2. ——— 32.
1. —— xiii. 25.
2. Luke xxii. 45 part.
1. —— xxiv. 33.
2. John xi. 31.
1. Acts iii. 6 (*active*, L T), (*om.* ἔγειραι καὶ *rise up and*, Tr^b A^b ℵ.)
2. —— v. 17, 36, 37.
2. —— xiv. 20.
3. —— xv. 5.
2. ——— 7.
2. —— xxvi. 30.
2. 1 Cor. x. 7.
4. Rev. xiii. 1.
4. —— xix. 3.

RISE UP TOGETHER.

συνεφίστημι, to stand upon in conjunction with others, to assail together.

Acts xvi. 22.

RISE WITH.

συνεγείρω, (*No.* 1, *with* σύν, in conjunction with, *prefixed*) to wake up, rouse up, in conjunction with another.

Col. ii. 12.
Col. iii. 1.

RISING.

1. ἀνατέλλω, *see* "RISE," *No.* 3. *Here, part.*
2. τὸ, the, ἀνιστῆναι, to arise, (*inf. of* "RISE," *No.* 2), — the arising [*from among dead ones.*]

2. Mark ix. 10
1. Mark xvi. 2.

RITE.

Acts vi. 14. marg. see "CUSTOM."
Heb. ix. 10, marg. see "ORDINANCE."

RIVER (-s.)

ποταμός, a river, a stream.

Mark i. 5.
John vii. 38.
Acts xvi. 10.
Rev. viii. 10.
— ix. 14.
— xvi. 4, 12.
Rev. xxii. 1, 2.

ROAR (-ETH, -ING.) [verb.]

1. ἠχέω, to sound, resound, (*occ.* 1 Cor. xiii. 1.)

2. μυκάομαι, to moo, to low, *as an ox or cow;* to bellow. *Transferred to other animals; of a lion,* to roar, (*non occ.*)

3. ὠρύομαι, to roar *or* howl, *as beasts of prey, from rage or hunger.* lxx. for שָׁאַג, Judg. xiv. 5; Ps. xxii. 4, (*non occ.*)

1. Luke xxi. 25 (G ∾), (ἤχους, *at the noise [of the sea and the waves]*, instead of ἠχούσης, *the sea and the waves roaring*, G L T Tr A ℵ.)
3. 1 Pet. v. 8.
2. Rev. x. 3.

ROB (-ED.)

συλάω, to spoil, plunder, rob, (*non occ.*)

2 Cor. xi. 8.

ROBBER (-s.)

λῃστής, a plunderer, a robber, one who plunders by violence and open force, (*thus differing from* κλέπτης, the thief who steals by fraud secretly.)

John x. 1, 8.
John xviii. 40.
2 Cor. xi. 26.

ROBBER OF CHURCHES.

ἱερόσυλος, robbing temples; *as subst.*, temple-robber, (*non occ.*)

Acts xix. 37.

ROBBERY.

ἁρπαγμός, object of rapine, something to be eagerly seized upon.

Phil. ii. 6.

ROBE (-s.)

1. στολή, a fitting out, *i.e.* apparatus; *then*, apparel, attire. *In N.T., like Lat.*, stola, a long flowing robe, reaching to the feet, *and worn by kings, priests, and persons of rank and distinction.*

2. χλαμύς, chlamys, a wide and coarse cloak, worn sometimes by kings, military officers, and soldiers. *In N.T., spoken prob. of the Roman* paludamentum, *or* officer's cloak, *usually of scarlet*, (*non occ.*)

3. ἱμάτιον, a garment, *esp.*, an outer garment, "pallium," (*as opp. to* χιτών, the inner vest, "tunica.")

4. ἐσθής, apparel, raiment, *esp., what is ornate or splendid.*

2. Matt. xxvii. 28, 31.
1. Luke xv. 22.
— — xx. 46, see R (long)
4. Luke xxiii. 11.
3. John xix. 2, 5.
1. Rev. vi. 11.
1. Rev. vii. 9, 13, 14.

ROBE (LONG)

1. Luke xx. 46.

ROCK (-s.)

1. πέτρα, a rock, a projecting rock, a cliff; *geologically*, "a rock *in situ*," *as distinguished from* πέτρος, a stone, a rolling stone, a loose stone, *that might be thrown by the hand, etc.*

[Hence the name of the apostle—Πέτρος, Peter, who was so called, not because of firmness of character, but for the very opposite reason. Peter was like a πέτρος, a rolling stone—in one place to-day and in another to-morrow, restless and changeable. Not one of the Twelve was so vacillating or so failing (except Judas.) Christ is "that Rock," (Matt. xvi. 18; 1 Cor. x. 4) and "other foundation can no man lay," (1 Cor. iii. 11.) Saints now, as "living stones," are built upon Christ, the "Rock of Ages." Peter, "who was also an elder," (1 Pet. v. 1) is *the* apostle who, of all others, teaches so clearly

that Christ is the Rock on which His Church is built. *See further, under* "STONE."]

2. { τραχεῖς, rough, / τόποι, places, } *i.e.* rocks, reefs, *or* breakers.

1. Matt. vii. 24, 25.
1. —— xvi. 18, see Note, above.
1. —— xxvii. 51, 60.
1. Mark xv. 46. [(ap.)
1. Luke vi. 48 1st, 48 2nd
1. Luke viii. 6, 13.
2. Acts xxvii. 29.
1. Rom. ix. 33.
1. 1 Cor. x. 4 twice.
1. 1 Pet. ii. 8.
1. Rev. vi. 15, 16.

ROD.

ῥάβδος, a rod, wand, staff, *for chastising,* walking; *or* a sceptre *of authority and office.*

Matt. xxvi. 67, marg. see Smite.
John xviii. 22, marg. see Strike.
1 Cor. iv. 21.
2 Cor. xi. 25, see Beat.
Heb. ix. 4.
Rev. ii. 27.
—— xi. 1.
—— xii. 5.
Rev. xix. 15.

ROLL AWAY.

ἀποκυλίω, to roll off *or* away, (*non occ.*)

Mark xvi. 3.
—— 4 (*ἀνακυλίω, roll back,* T Tr A ℵ.)
Luke xxiv. 2.

ROLL BACK.

Matt. xxviii. 2.

ROLL TO.

προσκυλίω, to roll towards *or* to, (*non occ.*)

Matt. xxvii. 60 (with *ἐπί, upon,* L.)

ROLL TOGETHER.

εἱλίσσω, to turn round *or* about, *as a chariot round the doubling post; of a scroll,* to roll up *or* together.

Rev. vi. 24 part.

ROLL UNTO.

προσκυλίω, to roll towards *or* to.

Mark xv. 46, *with ἐπί, upon.*

ROOF.

στέγη, a covering, roof, (*non occ.*)

Matt. viii. 8. | Mark ii. 4.
Luke vii. 6.

ROOM (-S.)

τόπος, place, locus, spot, space, room.

Luke ii. 7. | Luke xiv. 9, 10, 22.
1 Cor. xiv. 16.

ROOM TO RECEIVE (BE)

χωρέω, to give space, place, room; to make space to take in, contain *or* hold.

Mark ii. 2.

ROOM (CHIEF)

πρωτοκλισία, the first place of reclining *at table,* the chief place at a banquet, (*usually the middle place on the middle triclinium.*)

Luke xiv. 7. | Luke xx. 46.

ROOM (HIGHEST)

πρωτοκλισία, *see above.*

Luke xiv. 8.

ROOM OF (IN THE)

ἀντί, in place of, instead of.

Matt. ii. 22.

ROOM (UPPER)

1. ἀνώγεον, a room above the ground, upper room, chamber *over the porch, on or connected with the roof, where meals were generally taken, and privacy sought.*

2. ὑπερῷος, upper, over; *then,* the part of the house so situated, an upper room, (*here, neut., with art.*)

1. Mark xiv. 15.
1. Luke xxii. 12.
2. Acts i. 13.
— —— xxiv. 27, see Come.

ROOT.

ῥίζα, a root, (*non occ.*)

Matt. iii. 10.
—— xiii. 6, 21.
Mark iv. 6, 17.
—— xi. 20.
Luke iii. 9.
—— viii. 13.
Rom. xi. 16, 17, 18 twice.
—— xv. 12.
1 Tim. vi. 10.
Heb. xii. 15.
Rev. v. 5.
—— xxii. 16.

ROOT (PLUCK UP BY THE)

ἐκριζόω, to root out *or* up.

Luke xvii. 6. | Jude 12.

ROOT UP.

ἐκριζόω, to root out *or* up.

Matt. xiii. 29. | Matt. xv. 13.

ROOTED (BE)

ῥιζόω, to root. *Here, pass. or mid.*, to be *or* become rooted, to take root.

Eph. iii. 17. | Col. ii. 7.

ROPE (-S.)

σχοινίον, a cord made of bulrushes; *hence, gen.*, a cord *or* rope, (*occ.* John ii. 15.)

Acts xxvii. 32.

ROUGH.

τραχύς, rough, uneven, (*occ.* Acts xxvii. 29.)

Luke iii. 5.

ROUND.

See, COMPASS, SHINE.

ROUND ABOUT.

1. *κύκλος*, a circle. *In N.T. only Dat. κύκλῳ, as adv.*, in a circle, round, around, round about.
2. *κυκλόθεν*, from around.
3. *πάντοθεν*, from every side *or* quarter; *and hence*, on every side, round about, (*occ.* Luke xix. 43.)
4. *περίξ*, about, surrounding, circumjacent, (*non occ.*)

1. Mark iii. 34.
1. —— vi. 6, 36.
1. Luke ix. 12.
4. Acts v. 16.
1. Rom. xv. 19.
3. Heb. ix. 4.
2. Rev. iv. 3, 4.
1. —— 6.
2. —— v. 11 (No. 1, G L T
1. —— vii. 11. [Tr A ℵ.)

ROUND ABOUT (COME)

κυκλόω, to encircle, to surround.

John x. 24.

See also, COUNTRY, DWELL, GO, HEDGE, LOOK, REGION, SHINE, STAND.

ROW (-ED, -ING.) [verb.]

ἐλαύνω, to drive, impel, urge on; *used of ships* driven *by winds or oars; hence*, to row.

Mark vi. 48. | John vi. 19 part.

ROYAL.

1. *βασίλειος*, royal, like a king, destined *or* suitable for a king, (*occ.* Luke vii. 25.)
2. *βασιλικός*, royal, belonging to a king.

2. Acts xii. 21. | 2. Jas. ii. 8.
1. 1 Pet. ii. 9.

RUB (-ING.)

ψώχω, to rub in pieces, (*non occ.*)

Luke vi. 1.

RUDDER.

πηδάλιον, a helm, a rudder.

Acts xxvii. 40.

RUDE.

ἰδιώτης, a private citizen, *opp. to one in a public station;* an individual, *opp. to the many;* one who has no professional knowledge, *whether of politics or any other subject, as we say*, a layman. *Then gen.*, uninformed, ignorant.

2 Cor. xi. 6.

RUDIMENT (-S.)

στοιχεῖον, a little step, a pin, a peg *standing upright* (*as the gnomon of a dial*); *then*, the elements *or* rudiments *of instruction.*

Col. ii. 8, 20, marg. *element.*
Gal. iv. 3, 9, marg. (text, *element.*)

RUE. [noun.]

πήγανον, rue, *a plant*, (*non occ.*)

Luke xi. 42.

RUIN.

ῥῆγμα, a rending, breach, ruin, (*non occ.*)

Luke vi. 49.

RUINS.

κατεσκαμμένα, the things overthrown, digged down *or* raised; *hence*, ruins *of cities or buildings*, (*occ.* Rom. xi. 3.)

Acts xv. 16.

RULE. [noun.]

1. *ἀρχή*, beginning; *spoken of dignity*, the first place, *i.e.* power, dominion, pre-eminence, precedence.

2. κανών, a reed, staff *or* rod; a measuring rod *or* line; *then*, a standard *or* rule; *hence*, *Eng.*, canon, (*non occ.*)

1. 1 Cor. xv. 24.
2. 2 Cor. x. 13.
2. —— 15.
2. 2 Cor. 16, marg. (text, [*line.*)
2. Gal. vi. 16.
2. Phil. iii. 16.

RULE OVER (HAVE THE)

ἡγέομαι, to lead, lead the way, go first; be leader, chief.

Heb. xiii. 7, 17, marg. *be the guide.*
—— 24, marg. *guide.*

RULE (-ETH, -ING.) [verb.]

1. προΐστημι, *trans.*, to cause to stand before, to set over. *In N.T. only intrans.*, to stand before, be over, preside, rule *as with care and diligence.*

* *2nd Aorist.* † *Mid.*

2. ποιμαίνω, to tend a flock *or* herd; *i.e.* to provide for, lead, cherish, and defend, *as well as* to feed a flock.

3. βραβεύω, to be an arbiter in the public games; sit and act as umpire, be enthroned as decider *of everything*, (*non occ.*)

2. Matt. ii. 6, marg. *feed.*
— Mark x. 42, see R over.
1†. Rom. xii. 8.
3. Col. iii. 15.
1†. 1 Tim. iii. 4.
1*. 1 Tim. iii. 5.
1†. —— 12.
1*. —— v. 17.
2. Rev. ii. 27.
2. —— xii. 5.
2. Rev. xix. 15.

RULE OVER.

ἄρχω, to begin, be first *in any thing;* to be first *in rank, dignity, etc.;* *hence*, to rule.

Mark x. 42.

RULER (-S.)

1. ἄρχων, one first in power, authority, or dominion; *hence*, a ruler, lord, prince, *or* chief person.

2. ἡγεμών, a leader, guide; commander *of an army; hence*, governor, president, prefect.

3. κοσμοκράτωρ, lord of the world. *Here, pl.*, the world holders [*of this darkness.*]

1. Matt. ix. 18, 23.
— Mark v. 22, 35, 36, 38, see Synagogue.
2. —— xiii. 9.
1. Luke viii. 41.
— —— 49, } see Synagogue.
— —— xiii. 14, }
1. —— xviii. 18.
2. —— xxi. 12.
1. —— xxiii. 13, 35.
1. —— xxiv. 20.
— John ii. 9, see R of the feast.
1. —— iii. 1.
— —— iv. 46, marg. see Nobleman.
1. —— vii. 26, 48.
— John xii. 42, see R (chief)
1. Acts iii. 17.
— —— iv. 1, see Captain.
1. —— 5, 8, 26.
1. —— vii. 27, 35 twice.
— —— xiii. 15, see Synagogue.
1. —— 27.
1. —— xiv. 5.
1. —— xvi. 19.
— —— xvii. 6, 8, see R of the City.
— —— xviii. 8, 17, see Synagogue.
1. —— xxiii. 5.
1. Rom. xiii. 3.
3. Eph. vi. 12.

RULER (CHIEF)

1. John xii. 42.

RULER OF THE CITY.

πολιτάρχης, a city ruler, prefect, magistrate, (*non occ.*)

Acts xvii. 6, 8.

RULER OF THE FEAST.

ἀρχιτρίκλινος, the master of a feast, "master of the ceremonies."

John ii. 9.

RUMOUR (-S.)

1. ἀκοή, hearing; *then*, that which is heard, report, rumour.

2. λόγος, word *as spoken*, account *which one* gives, (*see* "ACCOUNT.")

1. Matt. xxiv. 6.
1. Mark xiii. 7.
2. Luke vii. 17.

RUN (-ETH, -ING, -RAN.)

(*For various combinations with other words, see below.*)

1. τρέχω, to run, hasten, hurry, (*occ.* 2 Thes. iii. 1.)

2. προστρέχω, (*No.* 1, *with* πρός, towards, *prefixed*) to run towards *or* to *any one.*

3. συντρέχω, (*No.* 1, *with* σύν, in conjunction with, *prefixed*) to run together in conjunction with *another or others*, run in company.

4. ὁρμάω, *trans.*, to set in motion, urge, prick, spur on; *intrans.*, to put one's self in violent motion, to rush.

1. Matt. xxvii. 48.
1. —— xxviii. 8.
1. Mark v. 6 (in A.V. 1611 to 1687 printed *come*, prob. a misprint.)
3. —— vi. 33.
2. —— x. 17.
1. —— xv. 36.
1. Luke xv. 20.
1. Luke xxiv. 12 (*ap.*)
1. John xx. 2, 4.
4. Acts vii. 57.
1. Rom. ix. 16.
1. 1 Cor. ix. 24 twice, 26.
1. Gal. ii. 2 twice.
1. Phil. ii. 16.
— Heb. xiii. 1.
— Rev. ix. 9.

RUN AGROUND.

ἐποκέλλω, to drive *or* force upon, *as a* ship *upon a shoal*, (*non occ.*)

Acts xxvii. 41.

RUN BEFORE.

προτρέχω, (*No.* 1, *with* πρό, before, *prefixed*), (*occ.* John xx. 4.)

Luke xix. 4.

RUN GREEDILY.

ἐκχύνω, to pour out; pour forth, rush tumultuously; *spoken of a passion*, to rush into, give one's self up to.

Jude 11.

RUN IN.

1. εἰστρέχω, (*No.* 1, *with* εἰς, into, *prefixed*), (*non occ.*)
2. εἰσπηδάω, to leap into, spring in, (*occ.* Acts xvi. 29.)

Acts xii. 14.
—— xiv. 14 (ἐκπηδάω, *to leap out, rush forth*, G L T Tr A ℵ.)

RUN OUT.

ἐκχέω, *see* "RUN GREEDILY."

Matt. ix. 17.

RUN OVER.

ὑπερεκχύνω, *here, pass*, to be poured out over, *as from a vessel;* to run over, overflow, (*non occ.*)

Luke vi. 38.

RUN TO.

προστρέχω, *see* "RUN," *No.* 2.

Mark ix. 15.

RUN THITHER TO.

προστρέχω, *see* "RUN," *No.* 2.

Acts viii. 30.

RUN THROUGH.

περιτρέχω, ("RUN," *No.* 1, *with* περί, around, *prefixed*) to run around, *or* about, (*non occ.*)

Mark vi. 55.

RUN TOGETHER.

1. { γίνομαι, to become, συνδρομή, a running together, concourse, } *i.e.* there took place a concourse, *or* a running together.
2. συντρέχω, *see* "RUN," *No.* 3.

2. Acts iii. 11. | 1. Acts xxi. 30.

RUN UNDER.

ὑποτρέχω, ("RUN," *No.* 1, *with* ὑπό, under, *prefixed*), (*non occ.*)

Acts xxvii. 16.

RUN VIOLENTLY.

ὁρμάω, *see* "RUN," *No.* 4.

Matt. viii. 32. | Mark v. 13.
Luke viii. 33.

RUN WITH.

συντρέχω, *see* "RUN," *No.* 3.

1 Pet. iv. 4 part.

RUNNING TOGETHER (COME)

ἐπισυντρέχω, ("RUN," *No.* 3, *with* ἐπί, upon, *prefixed*) to run together upon.

Mark ix. 25.

RUSH (-ED, -ING.)

1. ὁρμάω, *see* "RUN," *No.* 4.
2. φέρω, to bear, bear along. *Here, mid.*, to bear one's self along, move along, *as the wind*, rush.

— Mark iii. 10, see Press. | 2. Acts ii. 2.
1. Acts xix. 29.

RUST.

1. βρῶσις, eating, the act of eating; *also*, erosion, corrosion.
2. ἰός, something sent out, emitted, *as a missile;* venom, *as* emitted *from serpents; also* rust, *as* emitted on metals, (*occ.* Rom. iii. 13; Jas. iii. 8.)

1. Matt. vi. 19, 20. | 2. Jas. v. 3.

S

SABACHTHANI.

σαβαχθανί, the Greek spelling of the Chald. שבקתני, sabachthani, thou hast forsaken me (*from root* שבק, to leave, forsake) *quoted from* Psalm xxii. 2, *where Chald. for Heb.* עזבתני, *from root* עזב.

Matt. xxvii. 46. | Mark xv. 34.

SABAOTH.

σαβαώθ, the Greek spelling of the Heb. צבאות, hosts, armies, (*pl. of* צבא, host) *quoted from* Is. i. 9.

Rom. ix. 29. | Jas. v. 4.

SABBATH.

(*See below for* "SABBATH DAY.")

σάββατον, Sabbath; *Heb.*, שבת, rest, a lying by from labour.

* *denotes that the plural is translated by the singular.*

† *indicates the Dat. pl. σάββασι.*

‡ *denotes that the Gen. of the noun is used as an adjective.*

Matt. xii. 5.
—— xxviii. 1*.
Mark ii. 27 twice, 28.
—— xv. 42, see S (day before the)
—— xvi. 1.
Luke iv. 16‡.
—— vi. 1, 5, 6.
—— xiii. 10†, 14‡, 15, 16‡.
Luke xiv. 5‡.
—— xxiii. 54.
John v. 9, 18.
—— xix. 31‡.
Acts xiii. 14‡.
—— —— 42, marg. week.
—— xvi. 13, see S (on the)
—— xviii. 4.
Col. ii. 16‡.
Heb. iv. 9, marg. see Rest.

SABBATH DAY.

Matt. xii. 1*†, 2, 5†, 8, 10†, 11*†, 12†.
—— xxiv. 20.
Mark i. 21*†.
—— ii. 23*†, 24*†.
—— iii. 2*†, 4†.
—— vi. 2.
Luke iv. 31†.
—— vi. 2†, 7, 9†.
Luke xiv. 1, 3.
—— xxiii. 56.
John v. 10, 16.
—— vii. 22, 23 twice.
—— ix. 14, 16.
—— xix. 31.
Acts i. 12.
—— xiii. 27, 44.
—— xv. 21.
Acts xvii. 2.

SABBATH (DAY BEFORE THE)

προσάββατον, (*the above, with πρό, before, prefixed*) fore-sabbath, eve of the sabbath, (*non occ.*)

Mark xv. 42 (*πρὸς σάββατον, for the Sabbath,* L Tr.)

KEEPING OF A SABBATH. [margin.]

Heb. iv. 9, see "REST."

SABBATH (ON THE)

τῇ, on the
ἡμέρᾳ, day
τῶν, of the
σαββάτων, sabbaths.

Acts xvi. 13.

SACKCLOTH.

σάκκος, *Heb.*, שק, sack-*ing*, sack-cloth; a coarse black cloth, commonly made of hair, (*non occ.*)

Matt. xi. 21.
Luke x. 13.
Rev. vi. 12.
—— xi. 3.

SACRIFICE (-S.) [noun.]

θυσία, sacrifice; the act of killing and offering in sacrifice; *also* used of the thing sacrificed, the flesh of the victim, *part of which was burned on the altar, and part given to the priests,* (*non occ.*)

Matt. ix. 13.
—— xii. 7.
Mark ix. 49.
—— xii. 33.
Luke ii. 24.
—— xiii. 1.
Acts vii. 41, 42.
—— xiv. 13, 18, see S (do)
Rom. viii. 3, see Sin
—— xii. 1.
1 Cor. x. 18.
1 Cor. x. 19, 28, see Idols.
Eph. v. 2.
Phil. ii. 17.
—— iv. 18.
Heb. v. 1.
—— vii. 27.
—— viii. 3.
—— ix. 9, 23, 26.
—— x. 1, 5, 8, 11, 12, 26.
—— xi. 4.
—— xiii. 15, 16.
1 Pet. ii. 5.

SACRIFICE FOR (*by a*) [margin.]

Rom. viii. 3, see "FOR."

SACRIFICE (DO)

θύω, see below.

Acts xiv. 13, 18.

SACRIFICE (-ED.) [verb.]

θύω, to kill and offer in sacrifice, sacrifice, immolate.

Mark xiv. 12, marg. (text, kill.)
1 Cor. v. 7, marg. slay.
1 Cor. viii. 4, see Idol.
—— x. 20 twice.
—— —— 19, 28, see Idol.
Rev. ii. 14, 20, see Idol.

SACRIFICING. [margin.]

Rom. xv. 16, see "OFFERING UP."

SACRILEGE (COMMIT)

ἱεροσυλέω, to rob temples, commit sacrilege, (*non occ.*)

Rom. ii. 22.

SAD.

1. σκυθρωπός, grim-visaged, of angry *or* sullen countenance, (*occ.* Matt. vi. 16.)
2. στυγνάζω, to be *or* become *outwardly* hateful, gloomy, *or* sad, to look so, (*occ.* Matt. xvi. 3.)

— Matt. vi. 16, see Countenance. | 2. Mark x. 22. | 1. Luke xxiv. 17.

SAFE.

ἀσφαλής, not falling, *i.e.* firm, fixed, immoveable; *hence,* affording safety *and* support.

Phil. iii. 1.

SAFE AND SOUND.

ὑγιαίνω, to be sound, healthy, well.

Luke xv. 27 part.

SAFE (BRING)

διασώζω, to save through *or* throughout, *i.e.* to bring safely through.

Acts xxiii. 24.

SAFE (ESCAPE)

διασώζω, *see above.*

Acts xxvii. 44, pass.

SAFELY.

ἀσφαλῶς, firmly, without falling; *hence,* safely, securely, (*occ.* Acts ii. 36.)

Mark xiv. 44. | Acts xvi. 23.

SAFETY.

ἀσφάλεια, firmness, fixedness, security *from falling, rupture, etc.,* (*occ.* Luke i. 4.)

Acts v. 23. | 1 Thes. v. 3.

SAID.

See, SAY.

SAID (THE)

αὐτός, the same.

Mark vi. 22.

SAIL. [noun.]

σκεῦος, a vessel, utensil; *in respect to use,* an implement, instrument; *of a ship or sailing,* the chief instrument, the mast, *or* sail, (ancient ships having only one.) τὰ σκεύη, the implements of a ship, *i.e.* the tackle.

Acts xxvii. 17.

SAIL (-ED, -ING.) [verb.]

(*For various combinations with other words, see below.*)

1. πλέω, to sail, go by water, [the root being πλε-, or πλυ-; Sanscr. plu., *to swim; cf.* Lat., flu-ere; Eng., flow, flood, plunge, etc. etc.]
2. ἀποπλέω, (*No.* 1, *with* ἀπό, away from, *prefixed*) to sail away from *one place to another,* depart by ship, (*non occ.*)
3. ἐκπλέω, (*No.* 1, *with* ἐκ, out of, *prefixed*) to sail out of *a port or harbour,* (*here followed by* εἰς, unto.)
4. ἀνάγω, to lead *or* conduct up; *hence, of a ship,* to conduct it up *or* out upon the sea.

1. Luke viii. 23 part.
2. Acts xiii. 4.
2. — xiv. 26.
3. — xv. 39.
4. — xviii. 21,
4. — xx. 3, 13.
2. Acts xx. 15.
1. — xxi. 3.
2. — xxvii. 1.
1. — 6.
— — 9, see Sailing.
1. — 24.

SAIL AWAY.

3. Acts xx. 6.

SAIL BY.

1. παραλέγω, to lay near; *Mid., to lie near; hence,* to lay one's course near, *i.e.* to sail near, by *or* along a place *or* coast, (*occ.* Acts xxvii. 8.)
2. πλέω, *see above, No.* 1.
3. παραπλέω, (*No.* 2, *with* παρά, beside, *prefixed*) to sail near *or* beside *a place,* (*non occ.*)

3. Acts xx. 16. | 2. Acts xxvii. 2. | 1. Acts xxvii. 13.

SAIL OVER.

1. διαπλέω, ("SAIL," *No.* 1, *with* διά, through, *prefixed*) to sail throughout, (*non occ.*)
2. διαπεράω, to pass through *or* over.

2. Acts xxi. 2. | 1. Acts xxvii. 5 part.

SAIL SLOWLY.

βραδυπλοέω, ("SAIL," *No.* 1, *with* βραδύς, slow, not hasty, *prefixed*) to sail leisurely *or* slowly, (*non occ.*)

Acts xxvii. 7 part.

SAIL THENCE.

ἐκπλέω, *see* "SAIL," *No.* 3.

Acts xxviii. 18.

SAIL UNDER.

ὑποπλέω, ("SAIL," *No.* 1, *with* ὑπό, under, *prefixed*) to sail under, *i.e.* under the lee shore, *or shelter of land.*

Acts xxvii. 4, 7.

SAILING [noun.]

πλόος, sailing, navigation.

Acts xxvii. 9.

SAILOR (-s.)

ναύτης, a ship-man, sailor, seaman, (*occ.* Acts xxvii. 27, 30.)

Rev. xviii. 17.

SAINT.

ἅγιος, reverence, *and* the object thereof; *hence,* holy, sacred; an attribute belonging to the God of Revelation and Redemption. Also used of men and things in that relation to God required by His revealed character. *The Spirit of God, as the organ by which He reveals Himself, is for this reason called* ἅγιον, *at every stage of revelation. Then, it is used substantively of* angels, *or* holy ones, and of things which stand in peculiar relation to God; also of men who have, as the ground of their life, Christ as ὁ ἅγιος τοῦ θεοῦ, (Mark i. 24; Luke iv. 34, etc.) and πνεῦμα ἅγιον.

Phil. iv. 21.

SAINTS.

ἅγιοι, (*pl. of above*) holy ones, *used either of angels or of men, according to the context and parallel scriptures.*

[Care must be taken to distinguish the Old Test. "saints," used of God's earthly people (Dan. vii. 18, 22, etc.); New Test. "saints," God's heavenly people; and the Holy Angels.

* In some places "angels" are meant, where the translation is "saints." *See* 1 Thes. iii. 13, and Jude 14, and compare Matt. xxv. 31; also, Deut. xxxiii. 2, and Zech. xiv. 5. In some passages it is doubtful which are meant, as, 1 Cor. vi. 2; Col. i. 12, etc.]

Matt. xxvii. 52 [*"Saints which slept,"* i. e. *sleeping saints.*]
Acts ix. 13, 32, 41.
— xxvi. 10.
Rom. i. 7.
— viii. 27.
— xii. 13.
— xv. 25, 26, 31.
— xvi. 2, 15.
1 Cor. i. 2.
— vi. 1, 2.
— xiv. 33.
— xvi. 1. 15.
2 Cor. i. 1.
— viii. 4.
— ix. 12.
— xiii. 13.
Eph. i. 1, 15, 18.
— ii. 19.
— iii. 8 (om. G →)
— 18.
— iv. 12.
— v. 3.
Eph. vi. 18.
Phil. i. 1.
— iv. 22.
Col. i. 2, 4, 12, 26.
1 Thes. iii. 13*.
2 Thes. i. 10.
1 Tim. v. 10.
Philem. 5, 7.
Heb. vi. 10.
— xiii. 24.
Jude 3, 14*.
Rev. v. 8.
— viii. 3, 4.
— xi. 18.
— xiii. 7 (ap.), 10.
— xiv. 12.
— xv. 3 (ἐθνῶν, *the nations,* G L T Tr A); (αἰώνιων, *the ages,* G→ℵ.)
— xvi. 6.
— xvii. 6.
— xviii. 24.
— xix. 8.
Rev. xx. 9.

SAKE.

See, FOR.

SALT. [noun.]

1. ἅλας, (*a common form of No.* 2) salt, (*non occ.*)
2. ἅλς, (*Lat.,* sal; *Eng.,* salt) *in sing.,* a grain *or* lump of salt; *in pl.,* salt, as prepared for use, (*non occ.*)

1. Matt. v. 13 1st & 2nd.
— — 13 3rd, see the verb.
2. Mark ix. 49 (ap.)
1. Mark ix. 50 3 times.
1. Luke xiv. 34 twice.
1. Col. iv. 6.
— Jas. iii. 12, see the adj.

SALT. [adj.]

ἁλυκός, of the sea; *hence,* salt.

Jas. iii. 12.

SALT (-ED.) [verb.]

ἁλίζω, to sprinkle with salt.

["Every oblation of the meat-offering shalt thou season with salt," Lev. ii. 13. Why? Salt is the emblem of *perpetuity, and esp.* of *friendliness perpetually preserved. Hence,* the covenant of priesthood made with Aaron, (Numb. xviii. 19) and of kingship with David, (2 Chron. xiii. 5) are each called "*a covenant of salt.*" The salt with the meat-offering betokened the reconciliation of man and the friendliness of God. All who have now "made a covenant with Him by sacrifice" are reconciled to Him. But "every one," *i.e.* all, (viz. those referred to in verse 48, who are finally cast into the "unquenchable fire") all these have no sacrifice, and therefore no salt. They are not reconciled to God; they bear their own punishment; they themselves are the victims, and the fire itself is the salt.

With this, harmonises the next verse, "Have salt in yourselves, and have peace one with another," *i.e.* have reconciliation with God, then you will have friendliness one with another, and you will not dispute, as in verse 33.

The salt did not preserve the sacrifice from being consumed, nor prolong the process of combustion. The offering was consumed by the fire, but the salt was the token that the atonement was accepted and the *friendliness* preserved.

The impossibility of giving *or* restoring the salt its flavour, showed the impossibility of making any other atonement.]

Matt. v. 13. | Mark ix. 49 1st, 49 2nd (ap.)

SALTNESS (LOSE)

{ γίνομαι, to become,
{ ἄναλος, not salt.

Mark ix. 50.

SALUTATION.

ἀσπασμός, a drawing to one's self, an embracing; *hence,* salutation, greeting.

Mark xii. 38.
Luke i. 29, 41, 44.
1 Cor. xvi. 21.
Col. iv. 18.
2 Thes. iii. 17.

SALUTE (-ED, -ETH.)

ἀσπάζομαι, to draw to one's self; *hence,* to embrace, salute, greet.

Matt. v. 47.
— x. 12.
Mark ix. 15.
— xv. 18.
Luke i. 40.
— x. 4.
Acts xviii. 22, part.
— xxi. 7, 19 part.
— xxv. 13.
Rom. xvi. 5, 7, 9, 10 twice, 11, 12 1st, 12 2nd (ap.), 13, 14, 15, 16 twice, 21, 22, 23 twice.
1 Cor. xvi. 19 twice.
2 Cor. xiii. 13.
Phil. iv. 21, 22.
Col. iv. 10, 12, 15.
2 Tim. iv. 19.
Tit. iii. 15.
Philem. 23.
Heb. xiii. 24 twice.
1 Pet. v. 13.
3 John 14.

SALVATION.

1. σωτηρία, safety, preservation *from danger or destruction. Only in a Christian sense,* salvation. *Contrasted with θάνατος,* (death) 2 Cor. vii. 10; ἀπώλεια, (destruction) Phil. i. 28; ὀργή, (wrath) 1 Thes. v. 9; John iv. 22. *In its full sense it is still future,* (1 Thes. v. 8; 2 Thes. ii. 13; 1 Pet. i. 5) *for salvation will not be complete till we are redeemed by power and glory from the grave, as we are now by blood from sin. Hence the expression* ἐλπίδα σωτηρίας, (the hope of salvation) 1 Thes. v. 8; *cf.* Heb. i. 14; ix. 28; 1 Pet. i. 5.

2. σωτήριος, saving, delivering, bringing salvation, (*but rarely used as an adj.; gen. as a neuter subst.*)

1. Luke i. 69, 77.
2. — ii. 30.
2. — iii. 6.
1. — xix. 9.
1. John iv. 22.
1. Acts iv. 12 (ap.)
1. — xiii. 26, 47.
1. — xvi. 17.
2. — xxviii. 28.
1. Rom. i. 16.
1. — x. 10.
1. — xi. 11.
1. — xiii. 11.
1. 2 Cor. i. 6 twice.
1. — vi. 2 twice.
1. — vii. 10.
1. Eph. i. 13.
2. — vi. 17.
1. Phil. i. 19, 28.
1. — ii. 12.
1. 1 Thes. v. 8, 9.
1. 2 Thes. ii. 13.
1. 2 Tim. ii. 10.
1. — iii. 15.
— Tit. ii. 11, see S (that bringeth)
1. Heb. i. 14.
1. — ii. 3, 10.
1. — v. 9.
1. — vi. 9.
1. — ix. 28.
1. 1 Pet. i. 5, 9, 10.
1. 2 Pet. iii. 15.
1. Jude 3.
1. Rev. vii. 10.
1. — xii. 10.
1. Rev. xix. 1.

SALVATION (THAT BRINGETH)

2. Tit. ii. 11.

SALVE.

See, EYE.

SAME.

(*See below for* "THE SAME," *and other combinations.*)

1. ἐκεῖνος, that, that one there; *used of the more remote person,* (*the* 3*rd*) *as No.* 3 *is of the nearer,* (*the* 2*nd person.*)

2. αὐτός, very, self, selfsame. *With the article,* the same, the selfsame.

* *without the article.*

3. οὗτος, this, *the nearer, used of the* 2*nd person,* (*see No.* 1.)

4. καί, also, and.

1. Matt. xiii. 1.
1. —— xv. 22.
1. —— xviii. 1.
1. ——— 28 (*om.* L)
1. —— xxii. 23.
1. Mark iv. 35.
2*. Luke x. 7.
1. John i. 33.
1. —— iv. 53.
1. —— v. 9, 11.
1. —— x. 1.
1. John xii. 48.
1. —— xx. 19.
1. Acts ii. 41.
3. —— viii. 35.
1. —— xii. 6.
1. —— xvi. 33.
1. —— xix. 23.
1. —— xxviii. 7.
1. 2 Cor. vii. 8.
2. —— viii. 19 (*om.* G→L Tr A.)
1. Rev. xi. 13.

SAME (THE)

2*. Matt. iii. 4.
3. —— v. 19.
2. ——— 46 (οὕτως, *thus, or so,* L T Tr A.)
2*. —— xii. 50.
3. —— xiii. 20.
3. —— xviii. 4.
3. —— xxi. 42.
3. —— xxiv. 13.
2. —— xxv. 16, Dat. pl.
3. —— xxvi. 23.
2. ——— 44.
2. —— xxvii. 44.
3. Mark iii. 35.
3. —— viii. 35 (*om.* G L T Tr A ℵ.)
3. —— xiii. 13.
2. —— xiv. 39.
2. Luke ii. 8.
3. ——— 25.
2. —— vi. 33.
2. ——— 38 (ᾧ, *what,* L T Tr A ℵ.)
3. —— ix. 24, 48.
2. —— x. 10, Gen. fem.
3. —— xvi. 1.
3. —— xx. 17.
3. ——— 47, masc. pl.
2. —— xxiii. 40.
3. ——— 51 1st.
3. John i. 2, 7.
3. John i. 33 (No. 2, Lm.)
3. —— iii. 2, 26.
3. —— vii. 18.
3. —— xii. 21, masc. pl.
3. —— xv. 5.
3. Acts vii. 19.
3. ——— 35, Acc. masc.
3. —— xiii. 33, Acc. fem.
3. —— xiv. 9.
3. —— xvi. 17, fem. sing.
3. —— xxi. 9, Dat. sing.
2. Rom. ix. 21.
2. —— x. 12.
2. —— xii. 4.
— 1 Cor. i. 10 1st, see SAME THING (THE)
2. ——— 10 2nd & 3rd.
3. —— vii. 20, fem. sing. Dat.
3. —— viii. 3.
3. —— ix. 8, neut. pl.
2. —— x. 3, 4.
2. —— xii. 4, 5, 6, 8, 9 1st.
2. ——— 9 2nd (ἑνὶ *one,* L T Tr A.)
2. —— xv. 39.
2. 2 Cor. i. 6.
2. —— iii. 14, 18.
2. —— iv. 13.
3. —— viii. 6, Acc. fem.
2. ——— 16.
3. —— ix. 5, Acc. fem.
2. 2 Cor. xii. 18 twice.
4. Gal. ii. 8.
2. ——— 10, Acc., with τοῦτο.
3. —— iii. 7, masc. pl.
2*. Eph. iv. 10.
3. —— vi. 8, neut. sing.
2. Phil. i. 30.
2. —— ii. 2.
2. —— iii. 16.
3. 2 Tim. ii. 2, neut. pl.
2. Heb. i. 12.
2. —— ii. 14.
2. —— iv. 11.
2. —— vi. 11.
2. Heb. x. 11.
2. —— xi. 9.
2. —— xiii. 8.
3. Jas. iii. 2.
2. ——— 10, 11.
3. 1 Pet. ii. 7.
2. —— iv. 1, 4.
2. —— v. 9.
3. 2 Pet. ii. 19, sing. Dat., "*of the same.*"
2. 1 John ii. 27 (αὐτοῦ, *his,* G~T Tr A ℵ.)
3. Rev. iii. 5 (οὕτως, *thus,* L T Tr A* ℵ.)
2*. —— xiv. 10.

SAME (THAT)

1. Matt. x. 19 (*ap.*)
2*. —— xxvi. 48.
1. ——— 55.
2*. Mark xiv. 44.
— Luke vii. 21, see Hour.
— —— xxiv. 13, see Day.
1. John xi. 49.
1. —— xviii. 13.
3. Acts ii. 36, acc.

SAME THAT (THE)

ὅστις, whatever.

John viii. 25.

SAME MATTER (THE)

2. Mark x. 10.

SAME THING (THE)

2. Acts xv. 27, pl.
2. Rom. ii. 1, pl.
2. 1 Cor. i. 10.
2. Eph. vi. 9, pl.
2. Phil. iii. 1, pl.

SAME (THESE)

2. Acts xxiv. 20, pl. masc.

SAME HERE (THESE)

{ αὐτοί, same, / αὗτοι, these, } these themselves.

Acts xxiv. 20.

SAME (THIS)

1. { αὐτόν, same, / τοῦτο, this, } this very *thing.*

2. οὗτος, *see* "SAME," *No.* 3.

2. Acts i. 11.
1. 2 Cor. ii. 3.
— Rom. ix. 17, see Purpose.

See also, BODY, CARE, CAUSE, CRAFT, DAY, HOUR, MANNER, MIND, PURPOSE, QUARTER, RANK.

SANCTIFICATION.

ἁγιασμός, sanctification, essential purity; the accomplishment of what is expressed in ἁγιάζω,

(*see below*) and the result of this action, in that it is contemplated as effected. (Elsewhere, "HOLINESS.")

1 Cor. i. 30.
1 Thes. iv. 3, 4.
2 Thes. ii. 13.
1 Pet. i. 2.

SANCTIFY (-IED, -ETH.)

ἁγιάζω, to make ἅγιος, (*see* "HOLY," *No.* 1) to set in a state opposed to κοινόν, (common, unclean); *or* to deliver from that state, if already κοινόν, and put into a state corresponding to the nature of God.

Matt. xxiii. 17, 19.
John x. 36.
—— xvii. 17, 19 twice.
Acts xx. 32.
—— xxvi. 18.
Rom. xv. 16.
1 Cor. i. 2.
—— vi. 11.
—— vii. 14 twice.
Eph. v. 26.
1 Thes. v. 23.
1 Tim. iv. 5.
2 Tim. ii. 21.
Heb. ii. 11 twice.
—— ix. 13.
Heb. x. 10, 14, 29.
—— xiii. 12.
1 Pet. iii. 15.
Jude 1 (ἠγαπημένοις, *beloved*, instead of ἡγιασμένοις, *sanctified*, G ~ L T Tr A ℵ.)

SANCTUARY.

ἅγιον, neut., (*see* "HOLY," *No.* 1.)

Heb. viii. 2, pl., marg. *holy things.*
—— ix. 1.
—— —— 2, pl., marg. *holy* (ἁγία, *holy*, fem. sing., as agreeing with σκηνή (tabernacle), St. Mill., etc.) (ἅγια, *holies*, B E T Tr) (ἅγια, *the holy place*, A) (ἅγια ἁγίων, *holy of holies*, L.)
Heb. xiii. 11, pl.

SAND.

ἄμμος, sand, *also*, sandy ground, (*non occ.*)

Matt. vii. 26.
Rom. ix. 27.
Heb. xi. 12.
Rev. xiii. 1.
Rev. xx. 8.

SANDAL (-S.)

σανδάλιον, *dim. of* σάνδαλον, a wooden sole firmly bound on by straps round the instep and ankle, a sandal, (*non occ.*)

Mark vi. 9.
Acts xii. 8.

SAPPHIRE.

σαπφειρος, sapphire, a precious stone, next in hardness to the diamond, in various shades of blue, (lxx. for Heb. ספיר, Ex. xxiv. 10; xxviii. 18, *from* ספר, to shine.)

Rev. xxi. 19.

SARDINE.

σάρδινος, the sardine, (σάρδιος, G L T Tr A ℵ, sardius, the Sardian stone, *used esp. for seal-rings. It was of two kinds, the transparent or blood-red being our* carnelian; *the brownish*, our sardine, lxx. for אדם, Ex. xxviii. 7; Ezek. xxviii. 13.) Here it denotes the indignation of Him who sits on the throne, *cf.* Ezek. xxxviii. 18, (*non occ.*)

Rev. iv. 3.

SARDIUS.

σάρδιος, *see above*, (*non occ.*)

Rev. xxi. 20.

SARDONYX.

σαρδόνυξ, sardonyx, *a kind of onyx, or chalcedony. Called* onyx *when the dark ground was regularly* spotted *or* striped *with white; called* sardonyx *when the diff. colours were* disposed in layers, (*non occ.*)

Rev. xxi. 20.

SATAN.

Σατανᾶς, the Greek form of the Heb. שטן, Satan, adversary, lxx. for שטן, (1 Kings xi. 14, 23, 25, *cf.* 2 Sam. xix. 23, where lxx.=ἐπιβολους.) *In N.T. gen. with art.*, the adversary, the Heb. proper name for the devil, (Greek, ὁ διαβόλος, the accuser.)

[Satan seems to be the great adversary of the Word, (the living and the written word) the second person in the Blessed Trinity; as the World is said to be the great adversary of the Father (1 John ii. 15-17); and the Flesh, of the Spirit, (Gal. v. 17.)]

In all passages, except—
Luke iv. 8 (ap.)
2 Cor. xii. 7, Σατᾶν (the Heb. word with Greek letters.)

SATISFY.

χορτάζω, to feed with grass, hay, etc., to fodder, *prop. of beasts;* to feed, fill with food.

Mark viii. 4.

SATISFYING.

πλησμονή, a filling *as with food; hence*, a satisfying.

Col. ii. 23.

SAUL.

Σαῦλος, Saul, (lxx. *for the Hebrew name of the first king of Israel*) the Jewish name of Paul, who, like his namesake, (of the same tribe of Benjamin) 1 Sam. ix. 2, towered above all in pride, (Phil. iii. 4) yet afterwards became Paul, (*Lat.*, "paulus," "little") "less than the least of all saints," 1 Cor. xv. 9; Eph. iii. 8.

In all passages, except—
Acts ix. 19, } (om. G L T Tr A ℵ.)
—— 26, }

SAVE [preposition.]

1. { εἰ, if / μή, not, (*see* "NO," *No.* 2, *and note*,) } except.

2. ἀλλά, but.

3. ἤ, than, more than.

4. πλήν, more than, over and above; *hence*, besides, except.

5. παρά, *with Acc.*, to or along the side of, near. *Here, it denotes the approximation to an extreme point*, until to, until upon. (*The reference is to* Deut. xxv. 3.)

1. Matt. xi. 27.
1. —— xiii. 57.
1. —— xvii. 8.
2. —— xix. 11.
1. Mark v. 37.
— —— vi. 5, see S that.
1. ——— 8.
2. —— ix. 8 (No. 1, L ℵ.)
1. Luke iv. 26.
1. —— viii. 51.
1. —— xvii. 18.
1. Luke xviii. 19.
1. John vi. 22, 46.
3. —— xiii. 10 (No. 1, L Tr A) (om. G → ℵ.)
5. Acts xx. 23.
— —— xxi. 25, see S only [that.
1. 1 Cor. ii. 2, 11.
4. 2 Cor. xi. 24.
1. Gal. i. 19.
1. —— vi. 14.
1. Rev. xiii. 17.

SAVE THAT.

1. Mark vi. 5.

SAVE ONLY THAT.

1. Acts xxi. 25 (*ap.*)

SAVE (-ED.) [verb.]

1. σώζω, to make sound, to save, preserve safe *from danger, loss, or destruction. In a Christian sense*, to save from death and judgment, (as the consequences of sin) and to bring in all positive blessing in the place of condemnation. To save from the penalty of death and destruction, (not merely to make happy) but to bestow everlasting life as the result of resurrection.

2. διασώζω, (*No.* 1, *with* διά, through, *prefixed*) to save through, bring safely through.

3. φυλάσσω, to watch, not to sleep, to keep watch *by night*; to guard, keep.

1. Matt. i. 21.
1. —— viii. 25.
1. —— x. 22.
1. —— xiv. 30.
1. —— xvi. 25.
1. —— xviii. 11 (*ap.*)
1. —— xix. 25.
1. —— xxiv. 13, 22.
1. —— xxvii. 40, 42 twice, 49.
1. Mark iii. 4.
— —— vi. 20, marg. see Observe.
1. —— viii. 35 twice.
1. —— x. 26.
1. ——— 52, marg. (text, *make whole.*)
1. —— xiii. 13, 20.
1. —— xv. 30, 31 twice.
1. —— xvi. 16 (*ap.*)
— Luke i. 71, see S (that we should be)
1. —— vi. 9.
1. —— vii. 50.
1. —— viii. 12.
1. —— ix. 24 twice, 56 (*ap.*)
1. —— xiii. 23.
1. —— xvii. 33 (περιποιέομαι, *to lay up, or acquire*, T Tr A.)
1. —— xviii. 26, 42.
1. —— xix. 10.
1. —— xxiii. 35 twice, 37, 39.
1. John iii. 17.
1. —— v. 34.
1. —— x. 9.
1. —— xii. 27, 47.
1. Acts ii. 21.
— ——— 40, see S one's self.
— ——— 47, see S (such as should be)
1. Acts iv. 12.
1. —— xi. 14.
1. —— xv. 1, 11.
1. —— xvi. 30, 31.
1. —— xxvii. 20, 31.
2. ——— 43.
1. Rom. v. 9, 10.
1. —— viii. 24.
1. —— ix. 27.
1. —— x. 9, 10.
1. —— xi. 14, 26.
1. 1 Cor. i. 18, 21.
1. —— iii. 15.
1. —— v. 5.
1. —— vii. 16 twice.
1. —— ix. 22.
1. —— x. 33.
1. —— xv. 2.
1. 2 Cor. ii. 15.
1. Eph. ii. 5, 8.
1. 1 Thes. ii. 16.
1. 2 Thes. ii. 10.
1. 1 Tim. i. 15.
1. —— ii. 4, 15.
1. —— iv. 16.
1. 2 Tim. i. 9.
1. Tit. iii. 5.
1. Heb. v. 7.
1. —— vii. 25.
1. Jas. i. 21.
1. —— ii. 14.
1. —— iv. 12.
1. —— v. 15, 20.
2. 1 Pet. iii. 20.
1. ——— 21.
1. —— iv. 18.
3. 2 Pet. ii. 5.
1. Jude 5, 23.
1. Rev. xxi. 24 (*om.* τῶν σωζομένων, *of them which are saved*, G L T Tr A ℵ.)

SAVE ONE'S SELF.

1. Acts ii. 40, pass.

SAVED (THAT WE SHOULD BE)

σωτηρία, safety, deliverance, preservation from danger or destruction; salvation.

Luke i. 71.

SAVED (SUCH AS SHOULD BE)

οἱ, those σωζόμενοι, being saved, — *denoting the class, not the state, or the fact of saving.*

Acts ii. 47.

SAVING. [noun.]

1. σωτηρία, safety, deliverance, preservation from danger or destruction.
2. περιποίησις, a making remain over, a laying up; acquisition, obtaining. (*Here referring to the* ψυχή, the life.)

2. Heb. x. 39. | 1. Heb. xi. 7.

SAVING. [prep.]

1. εἰ, if μή, not, — except.
2. παρεκτός, near by without, out near; out of, without, besides.

2. Matt. v. 32. | 1. Luke iv. 27.
1. Rev. ii. 17.

SAVIOUR.

σωτήρ, saviour, deliverer, preserver. *Used of* God, as the author of all help, of every salvation, and above all of salvation by, and life in, Christ. *Also of* Christ Himself as the accomplisher of salvation, (*non occ.*)

Luke i. 47.	1 Tim. iv. 10.
—— ii. 11.	2 Tim. i. 10.
John iv. 42.	Tit. i. 3, 4.
Acts v. 31.	—— ii. 10, 13.
—— xiii. 23.	—— iii. 4, 6.
Eph. v. 23.	2 Pet. i. 1, 11.
Phil. iii. 20.	—— ii. 20.
1 Tim. i. 1.	—— iii. 2, 18.
—— ii. 3.	1 John iv. 14.

Jude 25.

SAVOUR. [noun.]

ὀσμή, a smell, odour. *In N.T. only of* fragrant odour, (lxx. for ריח, Song i. 3, 12; ii. 13.) Used of the sweet odour as accompanying an acceptable sacrifice, (*see* Lev. i. 9, 13, 17; ii. 2, 9; Gen. viii. 21.)

2 Cor. ii. 14, 16 twice. | Eph. v. 2.

SAVOUR (LOSE)

μωραίνω, to make dull, not acute; *e.g.* of *impressions on the taste,* to become insipid, tasteless, to lose its savour. *Here, pass.*

Matt. v. 13. | Luke xiv. 34.

SAVOUR (SWEET)

εὐωδία, good odour, fragrance, Ecclus. xxiv. 15.

2 Cor. ii. 15.

SAVOUR (-EST.) [verb.]

φρονέω, to have mind; to think, be minded; to regard, care for.

Matt. xvi. 23. | Mark viii. 33.

SAW ASUNDER.

πρίζω *or* πρίω, to saw, to saw asunder, (*see* 1 Sam. xv. 33; 2 Sam. xii. 31; 1 Ch. xx. 3; Dan. ii. 5; iii. 29) lxx. for חרש, Am. i. 3, (*non occ.*)

Heb. xi. 37.

SAY (-ING, -EST; SAID, -ST; SAITH.)

1. λέγω, to lay, lay together, to collect; *then,* to lay before, relate, *differing from the words below in that it refers to the* purport *or* sentiment of what is said *and* the connection of the words; *it denotes* the collecting of words in a sentence *or* oration; *in reference to the scripture it denotes* the statement of the scriptures, (while *No.* 5 *is the utterance or speaking of that statement.*) *When* λέγω *seems to be put for No.* 2, *it has reference, not to the meaning of speaking but of* thinking, feeling, commanding. *When used in connection with No.* 2 *the speaking is an additional notion,* (*when used alone the idea of speaking already exists.*)

* *When joined with* ἀποκρίνομαι, (to answer) *or* ἐρωτάω, (to ask) *or Nos.* 2, 3, 4, *and* 5, *it is marked with an asterisk.*

2. εἶπον, (*Aor.* 2 *of obs. root,* ἔπω) to utter definite words, to enunciate words and things to auditors and commune respecting them, to speak *or* utter words successively, communicate by words.

When used with ἀποκρίνομαι, (to take occasion to speak, answer) *this is to be referred to* the mind and thought, *while No.* 2 *refers to* the actual words.

(a) ἀποκριθεὶς, (*nom. sing. masc. part. Aor.* 1 *pass.*)...εἶπε, He answering ...said.

(b) ἀπεκρίθη, (*3rd pers. sing. Aor.* 1 *mid. pass.*)...εἶπε, He answered (*the action being regarded as complete*) and said.

3. φημί, to bring to light by speech, declare, make known, *and so*, to say, speak, make known *or* show by speaking, (*occ.* Rom. iii. 8.)

4. ἐρῶ, (*fut. from* εἴρω) I will say, I will tell, (*relating, not to the words only of the speaker, as No.* 2, *nor to the sentiment or speech* only, but) relating to the mind and will of the speaker; *hence it has the force of* denouncing, affirming, objecting, commanding, *or some other thing* which involves the mind and will of the speaker; *hence,* to enunciate *or* give forth thought.

5. λαλέω, to speak, to employ the organ of utterance, to utter words of any language, independently of any reason why they are uttered, (not, *to speak inconsiderately or imprudently*, but) to use the human voice with words; *hence,* to talk; *and with another,* to hold colloquy.

6. ῥέω, (*an obs. form, whence*) ἐῤῥήθην, *and* ἐῤῥέθην, (*Aor.* 1 *pass.*) to say, to speak, speak of, direct, command, prescribe, to address *one* as *anything*, to call, name, (*similar to No.* 4.)

7. φάσκω, to say, *esp.*, to say yes, to affirm, assert, allege, *with the collative notion of* alleging what is untrue, to pretend, (*occ.* Acts xxv. 19; Rom. i. 22.)

8. ἀποφθέγγομαι, to speak one's opinion plainly, to speak out, utter aloud, to utter solemn, weighty, *or* pithy sayings, to utter an apophthegm.

1. Matt. i. 20, 22*.
1. —— ii. 2.
2. —— 5, 8.
1. —— 13, 15*, 17*, 20.
1. —— iii. 2, 3, 9 twice, 14.
2a. —— 15.
1. —— 17.
2. —— iv. 3.
2a. —— 4.
1. —— 6 (No. 2 L.)
3. Matt. iv. 7.
1. —— 9 (No. 2, L T Tr A ℵ.)
1. —— 10, 14*, 17, 19.
1. —— v. 2.
2. —— 11.
1. —— 18, 20.
6. —— 21.
1. —— 22* 1st.
2. —— 22 2nd & 3rd.
1. Matt. v. 26.
6. —— 27.
1. —— 28*.
6. —— 31.
1. —— 32*.
6. —— 33.
1. —— 34*.
6. —— 38.
1. —— 39*.
6. —— 43.
1. —— 44*.
1. —— vi. 2, 5, 16, 25, 29, [31.
4. —— vii. 4.
1. —— 21.
4. —— 22.
1. —— viii. 2, 3, 4*, 6, 7.
3. —— 8.
1. —— 9.
2. —— 10 1st.
1. —— 10 2nd, 11.
2. —— 13.
1. —— 17*.
2. —— 19.
1. —— 20.
2. —— 21.
2. —— 22 (No. 1, L T Tr A ℵ.)
1. —— 25, 26, 27, 29, 31.
2. —— 32.
2. —— ix. 2, 3, 4, 5 twice.
1. —— 6, 9.
2. —— 11 (No. 1, L Tr A* ℵ.)
2. —— 12.
1. —— 14.
2. —— 15.
1. —— 18*, 21.
2. —— 22.
1. —— 24, 27, 28 twice, 29, 30, 33, 34, 37.
1. —— x. 5, 7, 15, 23, 42.
2. —— xi. 3.
2a. —— 4.
1. —— 7, 9, 11, 17, 18, 19, 22, 24.
2a. —— 25.
2. —— xii. 2, 3.
1. —— 6, 10*.
2. —— 11.
1. —— 13, 17*, 23.
2. —— 24, 25.
1. —— 31, 36, 38.
2a. —— 39.
1. —— 44.
2. —— 47.
2a. —— 48.
2a. —— 49.
1. —— xiii. 3.
2. —— 10.
2a. —— 11.
1. —— 14, 17, 24.
2. —— 27.
3. —— 28 1st.
2. —— 28 2nd (No. 1, L T Tr A ℵ.)
3. —— 29.
4. —— 30.
1. —— 31, 35, 36.
2a. —— 37.
1. —— 51 1st (*ap.*), 51 2nd.
2. —— 52 (No. 1, L.)
1. —— 54.
2. —— 57.
2. —— xiv. 2.
1. —— 4.
3. —— 8.
1. —— 15.
2. —— 16.
1. —— 17.
2. —— 18.
1. —— 26, 27*.
2a. —— 28.
2. —— 29.
1. —— 30, 31, 33.
1. —— xv. 1.
2a. —— 3.
1. —— 4 (No. 2, G ~ L Tr ℵ.)
1. Matt. xv. 5* 1st.
2. —— 5 2nd.
1. —— 7.
2. —— 10.
2. —— 12 (No. 1, L T Tr A.)
2a. —— 13, 15.
2. —— 16.
1. —— 22, 23.
2a. —— 24.
1. —— 25.
2a. —— 26.
2. —— 27.
2a. —— 28.
2. —— 32.
1. —— 33, 34 1st.
2. —— 34 2nd.
2a. —— xvi. 2 1st.
1. —— 2 2nd.
2. —— 6.
1. —— 7.
2. —— 8.
1. —— 13* 1st, 13 2nd.
2. —— 14.
1. —— 15 twice.
2a. —— 16, 17.
1. —— 18, 22.
2. —— 23, 24.
1. —— 28.
2a. —— xvii. 4.
1. —— 5.
2. —— 7.
1. —— 9*, 10 twice
2a. —— 11.
1. —— 12.
2. —— 13.
1. —— 14.
2a. —— 17.
2. —— 19.
2. —— 20 1st (No. 1, L T Tr A ℵ.)
1. —— 20 2nd.
4. —— 20 3rd.
2. —— 22, 24.
1. —— 25* 1st, 25 2nd, 26 1st (*ap.*)
3. —— 26 2nd.
1. —— xviii. 1.
2. —— 3 1st.
1. —— 3* 2nd, 10, 13, 18, 19.
2. —— 21.
1. —— 22 twice, 26, 28, 29, 32.
1. —— xix. 3.
2a. —— 4.
2. —— 5.
1. —— 8, 9, 10.
2. —— 11, 14, 16, 17.
1. —— 18 1st (No. 3, L ℵ.)
2. —— 18 2nd.
1. —— 20.
2. —— 23 1st.
1. —— 23* 2nd, 24, 25.
2. —— 26.
2a. —— 27.
2. —— 28 1st.
1. —— 28 2nd.
2. —— xx. 4.
1. —— 6, 7 twice, 8, 12.
2a. —— 13, 17.
2. —— 21 1st.
1. —— 21 2nd.
2a. —— 22 1st.
1. —— 22 2nd, 23.
2. —— 25.
1. —— 30, 31.
2. —— 32.
1. —— 33.
1. —— xxi. 2.
2. —— 3 1st.
4. —— 3 2nd.
1. —— 4*, 9, 10, 11, 13, 15.
2. —— 16 1st.
1. —— 16 2nd & 3rd, 19, 20.
2a. —— 21 1st.

1. Matt. xxi. 21 2nd.
2. —— 21 3rd.
1. —— 23.
2a. —— 24.
1. —— 25 1st.
2. —— 25 2nd.
2. —— 26.
2a. —— 27 1st.
3. —— 27 2nd.
2. —— 28.
2a. —— 29, 30 1st.
2. —— 30 2nd.
1. —— 31 3 times, 37.
2. —— 38.
1. —— 41, 42, 43.
1. —— xxii. 1*, 4*, 8, 12.
2. —— 13.
1. —— 16.
2. —— 18.
1. —— 20, 21 twice, 23, 24 1st.
2. —— 24 2nd.
2a. —— 29.
1. —— 31*.
1. —— 35*, (om. καὶ λέγων, and saying, L T Tr ℵ.)
2. —— 37 (No. 3, G L T Tr A ℵ.)
1. —— 42* 1st, 42 2nd, [43 twice.
2. —— 44.
1. —— xxiii. 2*, 3, 16, 30, 36, 39 1st.
2. —— 39 2nd.
2. —— xxiv. 2 1st.
1. —— 2* 2nd, 3*.
2. —— 4.
1. —— 5.
2. —— 23, 26.
1. —— 34, 47.
2. —— 48.
2. —— xxv. 8.
1. —— 9*, 11.
2a. —— 12 1st.
1. —— 12* 2nd, 20.
3. —— 21.
2. —— 22.
3. —— 23.
2. —— 24.
2a. —— 26.
4. —— 34.
1. —— 37*.
4. —— 40 1st.
1. —— 40* 2nd.
4. —— 41.
1. —— 44*, 45* 1st, 45 2nd.
2. —— xxvi. 1.
1. —— 5, 8.
2. —— 10.
1. —— 13.
2. —— 15.
1. —— 17.
2. —— 18 1st & 2nd.
1. —— 18* 3rd.
2. —— 21 1st.
1. —— 21* 2nd, 22.
2a. —— 23.
2a. —— 25 1st.
2. —— 25 2nd.
1. —— 25* 3rd.
2. —— 26.
1. —— 27, 29, 31.
2a. —— 33.
3. —— 34 1st.
1. —— 34* 2nd.
1. —— 35 1st.
2. —— 35 2nd.
1. —— 36, 38, 39, 40, 42.
2. —— 44.
1. —— 45, 48.
2. —— 49, 50.
1. —— 52.
2. —— 55, 61 1st.
3. —— 61 2nd.
2. —— 62.
2a. —— 63.
1. —— 64* 1st.
2. —— 64 2nd.

1. Matt. xxvi. 64 3rd, 65.
2. —— 66.
1. —— 68, 69, 70 twice, 71.
2. —— 73.
4. —— 75.
1. —— xxvii. 4 1st.
2. —— 4 2nd, 6.
1. —— 9*, 11* 1st.
3. —— 11 2nd.
1. —— 11 3rd, 13.
2. —— 17.
1. —— 19.
2a. —— 21 1st.
?. —— 21 2nd.
1. —— 22* 1st, 22 2nd.
3. —— 23 1st.
1. —— 23 2nd, 24.
2a. —— 25.
1. —— 29.
1. —— 33, pass. part. (om. G→)
1. —— 40, 41.
2. —— 43.
1. —— 46 1st.
— —— 46 2nd, see S (that is to)
1. —— 47.
1. —— 49 (No. 2, L Tr.)
1. —— 54, 63 1st.
2. —— 63 2nd, 64.
2a. —— xxviii. 5.
2. —— 6, 7.
1. —— 9, 10, 13* 1st.
2. —— 13 2nd.
1. —— 18*.
1. Mark i. 7, 15.
2. —— 17.
1. —— 24, 25, 27.
5. —— 34, marg. (text, speak.)
1. —— 37, 38, 40, 41, 44 1st.
2. —— 44 2nd.
1. —— ii. 5.
2. —— 8 (No. 1, T Tr ℵ.)
2. —— 9 twice.
1. —— 10, 11.
1. —— 12 (om. Lb.)
1. —— 14, 16, 18.
2. —— 19.
1. —— 24, 25, 27.
1. —— iii. 3, 4, 5.
2. —— 9.
1. —— 11, 21, 22, 23, 28, 30.
2. —— 32 (No. 1, L T Tr A ℵ.)
1. —— 33*, 34.
1. —— iv. 2, 9, 11, 13, 21, 24, 26, 30, 35, 38.
2. —— 39, 40.
1. —— 41.
2. —— v. 7 (No. 1, G∾L T Tr A ℵ.)
1. —— 8, 9, 12, 19, 23, 28, 30, 31 twice.
2. —— 34.
1. —— 35*, 36*, 39, 41 twice.
1. —— vi. 2, 4, 10, 11 (ap.), 14, 15 twice.
2. —— 16 (No. 1, T Tr A ℵ.)
1. —— 18.
— —— 22 1st, see S (the)
2. —— 22 2nd, 24 twice.
1. —— 25.
2. —— 31 (No. 1, T Tr A ℵ.)
1. —— 35.
2a. —— 37 1st.
1. —— 37 2nd.
1. —— 38 twice, 50*.
2a. —— vii. 6.
1. —— 9.
2. —— 10.
1. —— 11* 1st.

2. Mark vii. 11 2nd.
— —— 11 3rd, see S (that is to)
1. —— 14, 18, 20.
2. —— 27 (No. 1, L T Tr [A ℵ.)
1. —— 28.
2. —— 29.
1. —— 34, 37.
1. —— viii. 1.
2. —— 5.
1. —— 12 twice, 15.
1. —— 16 (ὅτι ἄρτους οὐκ ἔχουσιν, because they had no bread, instead of λέγοντες, ὅτι, ἄρτους οὐκ ἔχομεν, saying it is because we have no bread, L T Tr A ℵ.)
1. —— 17, 19.
2. —— 20 (No. 1, T Trm A ℵ.)
1. —— 21*.
1. —— 24 (No.2, Lm ℵ.)
1. —— 26, 27* 1st, 27 2nd.
1. —— 29 1st (ἐπηρώτα, he asked, G ∾ L T Tr A ℵ.)
1. —— 29 2nd & 3rd, 33.
2. —— 34.
1. —— ix. 1 twice, 5*.
5. —— 6 (ἀποκρίνομαι, to answer, Tr A ℵ.)
1. —— 7 (om. G T Tr A ℵ.)
1. —— 11* 1st, 11 2nd, 13.
2a. —— 17 (ἀπεκρίθη αὐτῷ, answered him, instead of ἀποκριθεὶς εἶπε, answered and said, L T Tr A ℵ.)
1. —— 19*.
2. —— 21, 23.
1. —— 24, 25, 26.
2. —— 29.
1. —— 31, 35.
2. —— 36.
1. —— 38.
2. —— 39.
1. —— 41.
2a. —— x. 3.
2. —— 4.
2a. —— 5.
1. —— 11.
2. —— 14.
1. —— 15.
2. —— 18.
2. —— 20 (No. 3, Tr A ℵ.)
2. —— 21.
1. —— 23, 24*, 26, 27, 28.
2a. —— 29 1st (No. 3, ἔφη ὁ Ἰησοῦς, Jesus said, instead of ἀποκριθεὶς δὲ ὁ Ἰησοῦς εἶπεν, and Jesus answered and said, T Trm A ℵ.)
1. —— 29 2nd, 35.
2. —— 36, 37, 38, 39 twice.
1. —— 42, 47, 49.
1. —— 51* 1st (No. 2, T Tr A ℵ.)
2. —— 51 2nd, 52.
1. —— xi. 2.
2. —— 3 twice.
1. —— 5.
2. —— 6.
1. —— 9 (om. G → Lb T Tr A ℵ.)
2a. —— 14.
1. —— 17, 21, 22*, 23* 1st.
2. —— 23 2nd.
1. —— 23 3rd (No. 5, L T Tr A ℵ.)
2. —— 23 4th (om. ὃ ἐὰν εἴπῃ, whatsoever he saith, G⇉T Tr Ab ℵ.)

1. Mark xi. 24, 28.
2a. —— 29.
1. —— 31* 1st.
2. —— 31 2nd.
4. —— 31 3rd.
2. —— 32.
1. —— 33* 1st, 33 2nd.
1. —— xii. 6.
2. —— 7.
1. —— 14.
2. —— 15.
1. —— 16* 1st.
2. —— 16 2nd (No. 1, [Lm.)
2a. —— 17.
1. —— 18 1st, 18* 2nd.
2. —— 24 (No. 3, T Tr A ℵ.)
1. —— 26*.
2. —— 32 twice, 34.
1. —— 35* 1st, 35 2nd.
2. —— 36 1st.
2. —— 36 2nd (G ∾), (No. 1, G T Tr.)
1. —— 38.
1. —— 43* 1st (G ∾), (No. 2, G L T Tr ℵ.)
1. —— 43 2nd.
1. —— xiii. 1.
2a. —— 2.
1. —— 5*, 6.
2. —— 21.
1. —— 30, 37 twice.
1. —— xiv. 2.
1. —— 4 (om. καὶ λέγοντες, and said, T Trb A ℵ.)
2. —— 6.
1. —— 9*, 12, 13.
2. —— 14 1st.
1. —— 14* 2nd.
2. —— 16, 18 1st.
1. —— 18* 2nd, 19.
2a. —— 20, 22, 24.
1. —— 25, 27.
3. —— 29.
1. —— 30 twice, 31, 32, 34, 36, 37, 41, 44, 45.
2a. —— 48.
1. —— 57, 58, 60*, 61*.
2. —— 62.
1. —— 63, 65, 67, 68 twice, 69, 70.
2. —— 72.
2a. —— xv. 2 1st (No. 1, T Tr A ℵ.)
1. —— 2 2nd, 4*, 9*. [A.)
2a. —— 12 (No. 1, T Tr
1. —— 14, 28 (ap.), 29, 31. [ℵ.)
1. —— 34 (om. T Tr A
1. —— 35, 36.
2. —— 39.
1. —— xvi. 3, 6.
2. —— 7, 8, 15 (ap.)
2. Luke i. 13, 18.
2a. —— 19.
1. —— 24.
2. —— 28, 30, 34.
2a. —— 35.
2. —— 38, 42, 46.
2a. —— 60.
2. —— 61.
1. —— 63, 66, 67.
2. —— ii. 10.
1. —— 13.
2. —— 15 (No. 5, Lm ℵ.)
4. —— 24.
2. —— 28, 34, 48, 49.
1. —— iii. 4 (om. G ⇉ L T Tr A ℵ.)
1. —— 7, 8 twice, 10*, 11.
2. —— 12, 13.
1. —— 14* 1st.
2. —— 14 2nd.
1. —— 16*.
1. —— 22 (om. λεγοῦσαν, which said, G⇉L T Tr A ℵ.)

2. Luke iv. 3.
1. —— 4* (om. T Tr A ℵ.)
2. —— 6.
2a. —— 8.
2. —— 9.
2a. —— 12 1st.
4. —— 12 2nd.
1. —— 21, 22*.
2. —— 23 1st.
4. —— 23 2nd.
2. —— 24 1st.
1. —— 24* 2nd.
1. —— 34 (om. T Tr^b A ℵ.)
1. —— 35, 36, 41.
2. —— 43.
2a. —— v. 5.
1. —— 8.
2. —— 10.
1. —— 12.
2. —— 13 (No. 1, L Tr ℵ.)
2. —— 20.
1. —— 21*.
2a. —— 22.
2. —— 23 twice.
2. —— 24 1st.
1. —— 24* 2nd, 26.
2. —— 27.
1. —— 30.
2a. —— 31.
2. —— 33, 34.
1. —— 39.
2. —— vi. 2.
2a. —— 3.
1. —— 5.
2. —— 8, 9, 10.
1. —— 20, 27, 42, 46.
1. —— vii. 4, 6.
2. —— 7.
1. —— 8.
2. —— 9 1st.
1. —— 9* 2nd.
2. —— 13, 14 1st.
1. —— 14* 2nd, 16, 19.
2. —— 20 1st.
1. —— 20* 2nd.
2a. —— 22.
1. —— 26, 28.
2. —— 31 (ap.)
1. —— 32, 33, 34, 39.
2a. —— 40 1st.
2. —— 40 2nd.
3. —— 40 3rd. [on.
— —— 40 4th, see Say
2a. —— 43 1st.
2. —— 43 2nd.
1. —— 47.
2. —— 48.
1. —— 49.
2. —— 50.
1. —— viii. 8 part.
1. —— 9* (om. G → L T Tr A^b ℵ.)
2. —— 10.
1. —— 20 (om. λεγόντων, *by certain which said*, L T Tr A^b ℵ.)
2. —— 21, 22.
1. —— 24.
2. —— 25 1st.
1. —— 25* 2nd.
2. —— 28.
1. —— 30* 1st (om. L ℵ.)
2. —— 30 2nd.
1. —— 38.
2. —— 45 1st & 2nd.
1. —— 45* 3rd (ap.)
2. —— 46, 48.
1. —— 49*.
1. —— 50 (om. L T Tr A^b ℵ.)
2. —— 52.
1. —— 54.
2. —— ix. 3.
1. —— 7.
2. —— 9, 12, 13 twice, 14.

1. Luke ix. 18.
2a. —— 19.
2. —— 20 1st.
1. —— 20 2nd.
2a. —— 20 3rd.
2. —— 22.
1. —— 23.
2. —— 33 1st.
1. —— 33 2nd, 35, 38.
2. —— 41, 43, 48.
2a. —— 49.
2. —— 50, 54, 55 (ap.), 57, 58, 59 twice, 60, 61, 62.
1. —— x. 2, 5, 9.
2. —— 10.
1. —— 12, 17.
2. —— 18, 21, 23.
1. —— 25.
2. —— 26.
2a. —— 27.
2. —— 28, 29, 30, 35, 37 twice, 40.
2a. —— 41.
2. —— xi. 1, 2 1st.
1. —— 2* 2nd.
2. —— 5 1st.
2. —— 5 2nd (No. 4, L.)
2a. —— 7.
1. —— 8, 9.
2. —— 15, 17.
1. —— 18, 24.
2. —— 27, 28.
1. —— 29.
2. —— 39.
1. —— 45* 1st, 45 2nd.
2. —— 46, 49.
1. —— 53 part. (ap.)
1. —— xii. 1, 4, 5, 8.
2. —— 11, 12, 13, 14, 15.
1. —— 16*, 17.
2. —— 18.
4. —— 19.
2. —— 20, 22 1st.
1. —— 22* 2nd, 27, 37.
2. —— 41, 42.
1. —— 44.
2. —— 45.
1. —— 54 twice, 55.
2a. —— xiii. 2.
2. —— 7.
1. —— 8.
2. —— 12.
1. —— 14*.
2a. —— 15.
1. —— 17 part., 18.
2. —— 20, 23 twice.
1. —— 24, 25* 1st.
4. —— 25 2nd.
1. —— 26.
4. —— 27.
1. —— 31.
2. —— 32.
1. —— 35* 1st.
2. —— 35 2nd.
1. —— xiv. 3* (om. L^b.)
2a. —— 5.
1. —— 7.
4. —— 9.
2. —— 10 (No. 4, T Tr
1. —— 12. [ℵ.)
2. —— 15, 16, 17, 18, 19, 20, 21, 22, 23.
1. —— 24.
2. —— 25.
1. —— 30
1. —— xv. 2, 3, 6, 7, 9, 10.
2. —— 11, 12.
2. —— 17 (No. 3, T Tr^m
4. —— 18. [ℵ.)
2. —— 21, 22, 27.
2a. —— 29.
2. —— 31.
1. —— xvi. 1.
2. —— 2, 3.
1. —— 5*.
2. —— 6 twice, 7 1st & 2nd.
1. —— 7 3rd, 9.

2. Luke xvi. 15, 24, 25, 27.
1. —— 29.
2. —— 30, 31.
2. —— xvii. 1.
1. —— 4.
2. —— 5, 6 1st.
1. —— 6 2nd.
4. —— 7, 8.
1. —— 10, 13.
2. —— 14.
2a. —— 17.
2. —— 19.
2a. —— 20.
4. —— 21.
2. —— 22.
4. —— 23.
1. —— 37 1st.
2. —— 37 2nd.
1. —— xviii. 2, 3.
2. —— 4, 6 1st.
1. —— 6 2nd, 13.
2. —— 16.
1. —— 17, 18.
2. —— 19.
2. —— 21, 22, 24, 26, 27, 28, 29 1st.
1. —— 29* 2nd.
2. —— 31.
1. —— 38.
1. —— 41 1st (om. T Tr^b A ℵ.)
2. —— 41 2nd, 42.
2. —— xix. 5.
1. —— 7.
2. —— 8, 9, 12, 13.
1. —— 14, 16.
2. —— 17.
1. —— 18.
2. —— 19.
1. —— 20, 22.
2. —— 24, 25.
1. —— 26.
2. —— 30 (No. 1, L Tr A* ℵ.)
4. —— 31.
2. —— 32, 33, 34.
1. —— 38.
2. —— 39.
2a. —— 40.
1. —— 42, 46.
1. —— xx. 2* (om. Tr A.)
2a. —— 3.
1. —— 5 1st.
2. —— 5 2nd.
4. —— 5 3rd.
2. —— 6, 8, 13.
1. —— 14.
2. —— 16, 17.
1. —— 21* 1st, 21 2nd.
2. —— 23.
2a. —— 24.
2. —— 25.
1. —— 28*.
2a. —— 34, 39 1st.
2. —— 39 2nd, 41 1st.
1. —— 41 2nd, 42* 1st.
2. —— 42 2nd, 45.
2. —— xxi. 3 1st.
1. —— 3* 2nd.
2. —— 5.
1. —— 7*.
2. —— 8 1st.
1. —— 8 2nd, 10, 32.
2. —— xxii. 8, 9, 10.
4. —— 11 1st.
1. —— 11 2nd.
4. —— 13.
2. —— 15.
1. —— 16.
2. —— 17.
1. —— 18, 19, 20.
2. —— 25, 31 (ap.), 33, 34, 35 twice, 36.
1. —— 37.
2. —— 38 twice, 40.
1. —— 42.
2. —— 46, 48, 49.
2a. —— 51.

2. Luke xxii. 52, 56.
1. —— 57.
3. —— 58 1st.
2. —— 58 2nd.
1. —— 59.
2. —— 60 1st.
1. —— 60 2nd.
2. —— 61.
1. —— 64, 66*.
2. —— 67, 70 1st.
3. —— 70 2nd.
1. —— 70* 3rd.
2. —— 71.
1. —— xxiii. 2 twice, 3 1st.
3. —— 3 2nd.
1. —— 3 3rd.
2. —— 4.
1. —— 5.
2. —— 14.
1. —— 18, 21.
2. —— 22, 28.
4. —— 29.
1. —— 30, 34 (ap.), 35, 37.
1. —— 39 (om. T Tr^b A.)
1. —— 40 (No. 3, T Tr A ℵ.)
1. —— 42.
2. —— 43 1st.
1. —— 43* 2nd.
2. —— 46 twice.
1. —— 47.
2. —— xxiv. 5.
1. —— 7*.
2. —— 17.
2a. —— 18.
2. —— 19 twice.
1. —— 23 twice.
2. —— 24, 25.
1. —— 29, 34, 36* (ap.)
2. —— 38, 41, 44, 46.
1. John i. 15*, 21.
2. —— 22 1st.
1. —— 22 2nd.
3. —— 23 1st.
2. —— 23 2nd, 25.
1. —— 26*, 29.
2. —— 30.
1. —— 32.
2. —— 33.
1. —— 36, 38 1st.
2. —— 38 2nd.
— —— 38 3rd, see S (is to)
1. —— 39, 41.
2. —— 42.
1. —— 45.
2. —— 46 1st.
1. —— 46* 2nd, 47, 48* 1st.
2b. —— 48 2nd.
1. —— 49* (om. καὶ λέγει αὐτῷ, *and saith unto him*, L^b T Tr A), (No. 2, ℵ.)
2b. —— 50 1st.
2. —— 50 2nd.
1. —— 51 twice.
1. —— ii. 3, 4, 5 twice, 7, 8, 10.
2. —— 16.
2b. —— 18, 19.
2. —— 20.
1. —— 22* 1st.
2. —— 22 2nd.
2. —— iii. 2.
2b. —— 3 1st.
1. —— 3* 2nd, 4, 5.
2. —— 7.
2b. —— 9, 10.
1. —— 11*.
2. —— 26.
2b. —— 27.
2. —— 28.
1. —— iv. 7, 9.
2b. —— 10 1st.
1. —— 10* 2nd, 11.
2b. —— 13.
1. —— 15, 16*.

2b. John iv. 17 1st.
1. —— 17* 2nd.
2. —— 17 3rd.
4. —— 18.
1. —— 19, 20, 21, 25, 26*.
2. —— 27.
1. —— 28*, 31*.
2. —— 32.
1. —— 33, 34, 35 twice, 42.
2. —— 48.
1. —— 49, 50, 51.
2. —— 52, 53.
1. —— v. 6, 8, 10.
2. —— 11, 12, 14.
1. —— 18.
2b. —— 19 1st.
1. —— 19* 2nd, 24, 25, 34.
1. —— vi. 5, 6, 8.
2. —— 10.
1. —— 12, 14, 20.
2. —— 25.
2b. —— 26 1st.
1. —— 26* 2nd.
2. —— 28.
2b. —— 29.
2. —— 30.
2. —— 32 1st.
1. —— 32* 2nd.
2. —— 34, 35, 36, 41.
1. —— 42 twice.
2b. —— 43.
1. —— 47, 52.
2. —— 53 1st.
1. —— 53* 2nd.
2. —— 59, 60, 61.
1. —— 65* 1st.
4. —— 65 2nd.
2. —— 67.
2. —— vii. 3.
1. —— 6.
2. —— 9 part.
1. —— 11, 12 twice, 15.
2b. —— 16 (*om.* in eds. of A.V. 1611—1701 by error.)
2b. —— 20 (*om.* καὶ εἶπε, *and said*, L T Tr A ℵ.)
2b. —— 21.
1. —— 25, 26, 28, 31.
2. —— 33, 35, 36.
1. —— 37.
2. —— 38.
1. —— 40, 41 twice.
2. —— 42, 45.
1. —— 50.
2b. —— 52.
1. —— viii. 4 (*ap.*), 5 (*ap.*), 6 (*ap.*)
2. —— 7 (*ap.*), 10 (*ap.*), 11 twice (*ap.*)
1. —— 12.
2. —— 13.
2b. —— 14.
1. —— 19.
2. —— 21.
1. —— 22 twice.
2. —— 23 (No. 1, L T Tr A ℵ.)
2. —— 24.
1. —— 25 1st.
2. —— 25 2nd.
5. —— 25 3rd, 26.
2. —— 28.
2b. —— 29.
1. —— 31, 33, 34, 39*.
2. —— 41, 42.
1. —— 46.
2b. —— 48 1st.
1. —— 48* 2nd, 51.
2. —— 52 1st.
1. —— 52* 2nd, 54.
2. —— 55, 57, 58 1st.
1. —— 58* 2nd.
1. —— ix. 2.
2. —— 7.

1. John ix. 8, 9 twice, 10.
2b. —— 11 1st (*om.* καὶ εἶπε, *and said*, Lb T Tr A ℵ.)
2. —— 11 2nd, 12 1st.
1. —— 12* 2nd.
2. —— 15.
1. —— 16 twice, 17 1st & 2nd.
2. —— 17 3rd.
1. —— 19 twice.
2b. —— 20.
2. —— 23, 24.
2b. —— 25 (*om.* καὶ εἶπε, *and said*, L T Tr A ℵ.)
2. —— 26, 28.
2b. —— 30, 34.
2. —— 35.
2b. —— 36.
2. —— 37.
3. —— 38.
2. —— 39, 40, 41 1st.
1. —— 41* 2nd.
1. —— x. 1.
2. —— 7 1st.
1. —— 7* 2nd, 20, 21, 24.
2. —— 26 (*ap.*)
1. —— 33 (*om.* G ∺ L T Tr A ℵ.)
2. —— 34.
1. —— 36* 1st.
2. —— 36 2nd.
1. —— 41*.
1. —— xi. 3.
2. —— 4.
1. —— 7, 8.
2. —— 11 1st.
1. —— 11 2nd.
2. —— 12, 14, 16, 21.
1. —— 23, 24.
2. —— 25.
1. —— 27.
2. —— 28 1st part, 28 2nd.
1. —— 31 (δόξαντες [from δοκέω], *supposing*, G ~ T Tr A ℵ.)
1. —— 32.
2. —— 34 1st.
1. —— 34* 2nd.
1. —— 36.
2. —— 37.
1. —— 39 twice, 40* 1st.
2. —— 40 2nd, 41, 42.
1. —— 44, 47.
2. —— 49.
1. —— xii. 4.
2. —— 6, 7, 19.
1. —— 21, 23, 24.
2. —— 27.
1. —— 29 1st, 29* 2nd.
2b. —— 30.
1. —— 33, 34.
2. —— 35, 39, 41, 44, 49.
4. —— 50.
1. —— xiii. 6.
2b. —— 7.
1. —— 9, 10.
2. —— 11, 12.
1. —— 13, 16, 20.
2. —— 21 1st part, 21 2nd.
1. —— 21* 3rd, 25, 27, 29, 31.
2. —— 33 1st.
1. —— 33* 2nd, 36, 37, 38.
1. —— xiv. 5, 6, 8, 9 twice, 12, 22.
2b. —— 23.
2. —— 26, 28 1st.
2. —— 28 2nd (*om.* εἶπον, *I said*, G L T Tr A ℵ.)
2. —— xv. 20.
2. —— xvi. 4.
5. —— 6.
1. —— 12.
2. —— 15.
2. —— 17 1st.
1. —— 17 2nd.

1. John xvi. 18* 1st, 18 2nd.
5. —— 18 3rd.
2. —— 19 twice.
1. —— 20, 23, 26*, 29.
2. —— xvii. 1.
2. —— xviii. 4 (No. 1, L T Tr A.)
1. —— 5.
2. —— 6, 7, 11.
1. —— 17 twice.
5. —— 20, 21 1st.
2. —— 21 2nd, 22, 25 twice.
1. —— 26.
2. —— 29 (No. 3, T Tr A ℵ.)
2b. —— 30.
2. —— 31 twice, 32, 33.
1. —— 34*.
2. —— 37 1st.
1. —— 37 2nd, 38 1st.
2. —— 38 2nd part.
1. —— 38 3rd, 40.
1. —— xix. 3, 4, 5, 6 twice, 9, 10, 12, 14, 15, 21* 1st.
2. —— 21 2nd, 24 1st.
1. —— 24 2nd (*om.* ἡ λέγουσα, *which saith*, L T ℵ.)
1. —— 26, 27, 28.
2. —— 30.
1. —— 35, 37.
1. —— xx. 2, 13 twice.
2. —— 14 part.
1. —— 15 twice, 16 1st & 2nd
— —— 16 3rd, see S (is to)
1. —— 17 1st.
2. —— 17 2nd (No. 1, Lm.)
1. —— 19.
2. —— 20 part, 21, 22 1st part.
1. —— 22 2nd.
1. —— 25 1st.
2. —— 25 2nd, 26.
1. —— 27*.
2b. —— 28.
1. —— 29.
1. —— xxi. 3 twice, 5.
2. —— 6.
1. —— 7, 10, 12, 15 3 times, 16 3 times, 17* 1st.
2. —— 17 2nd & 3rd.
1. —— 17 4th, 18, 19*.
2. —— 20.
1. —— 21, 22.
2. —— 23.
1. Acts i. 6*.
2. —— 7, 11, 15.
— —— 19, see S (that is to)
2. —— 24.
1. —— ii. 7, 12, 13.
3. —— 14.
1. —— 17, 34* 1st.
2. —— 34 2nd, 37.
3. —— 38 (*om.* L Tr A ℵ, but the word, in English, must be understood.)
1. —— 40.
2. —— iii. 4, 6, 22 1st.
5. —— 22 2nd.
1. —— 25.
2. —— iv. 8.
— —— 14, see S against.
1. —— 16.
2. —— 19, 23, 24, 25.
1. —— 32.
2. —— v. 3, 8.
2. —— 9 (*om.* L T Tr A ℵ, see above, ii. 38.)
2. —— 19.
1. —— 23.
1. —— 25 (*om.* G L T Tr A ℵ.)
1. —— 28.
2a. —— 29, 35.

1. Acts v. 38.
2. —— vi. 2.
1. —— 11, 13, 14.
2. —— vii. 1.
3. —— 2.
2. —— 3, 7, 26, 27, 33, 35, 37, 40.
1. —— 48, 49.
2. —— 56.
1. —— 59.
2. —— 60 part.
1. —— viii. 10, 19.
2. —— 20.
2a. —— 24.
1. —— 26*.
2. —— 29, 30, 31.
2a. —— 34.
3. —— 36.
2a. —— 37 1st (*ap.*), 37 2nd (*ap.*)
1. —— ix. 4.
2. —— 5 1st.
2. —— 5 2nd (*om.* Κύριος εἶπε, G ∺ L T Tr A, i.e. *and he* [answered].)
2. —— 6 (*ap.*), 10 twice, 15, 17.
1. —— 21.
2. —— 34, 40.
2. —— x. 3, 4 twice, 14, 19, 21, 22.
1. —— 26.
3. —— 28, 30, 31.
2. —— 34.
1. —— xi. 3, 4, 7.
2. —— 8, 13.
1. —— 16, 18.
1. —— xii. 7.
2. —— 8 1st.
1. —— 8* 2nd.
2. —— 11, 15 1st.
1. —— 15* 2nd (No. 2, L Tr A.)
2. —— 17.
2. —— xiii. 2, 10.
1. —— 15 1st.
— —— 15 2nd, see S on.
2. —— 16, 22.
1. —— 25.
4. —— 34.
2. —— 46.
2. —— xiv. 10.
1. —— 11, 15.
1. —— xv. 5.
2. —— 7.
1. —— 13*, 17, 24 (*ap.*)
2. —— 36.
1. —— xvi. 9, 15, 17.
2. —— 18, 20.
1. —— 28.
3. —— 30.
2. —— 31.
1. —— 35.
3. —— 37.
1. —— xvii. 7, 18 twice, 19.
3. —— 22.
4. —— 28.
2. —— 32.
2. —— xviii. 6.
1. —— 13.
2. —— 14, 21.
2. —— xix. 2 1st.
2. —— 2 2nd (*om.* G ∺ L T Tr A ℵ, i.e. *they* [answered].)
2. —— 3 twice, 4 1st.
1. —— 4* 2nd, 13.
2a. —— 15, 21, 25.
1. —— 26, 28.
3. —— 35.
2. —— xx. 10, 18.
1. —— 23.
1. —— xxi. 4.
2. —— 11 1st.
1. —— 11 2nd.
2. —— 14, 20.
1. —— 21, 23, 37 1st.
3. —— 37* 2nd.

2. Acts xxi. 39.
1. ——— 40.
3. —— xxii. 2.
1. ——— 7.
2. ——— 8, 10 twice, 13, 14.
1. ——— 18.
2. ——— 19, 21.
1. ——— 22.
2. ——— 25.
1. ——— 26.
2. ——— 27 1st.
3. ——— 27 2nd, 28.
2. —— xxiii. 1, 3, 4.
3. ——— 5.
5. ——— 7 part (No. 2, L Tr ℵ.)
1. ——— 8, 9.
2. ——— 11.
1. ——— 12.
2. ——— 14.
3. ——— 17.
3. ——— 18 1st.
5. ——— 18 2nd.
2. ——— 20, 23.
1. ——— 30.
3. ——— 35.
1. —— xxiv. 2.
7. ——— 9.
2. ——— 20, 22.
3. —— xxv. 5.
2a. ——— 9.
2. ——— 10.
1. ——— 14.
2. ——— 22 1st (*om.* L T Tr A ℵ.)
2. ——— 22 2nd, 24.
3. —— xxvi. 1.
1*. ——— 14 (*om.* καὶ λέγουσιν, *and saying*, G ∾ L T Tr A ℵ.)
2. ——— 15 twice.
1. ——— 22* 1st.
5. ——— 22 2nd.
3. ——— 24, 25.
3. ——— 28 (*om.* G ⇉ L T Tr A ℵ.)
2. ——— 29 (*om.* G ⇉ L T Tr A ℵ.)
1. ——— 31*.
3. ——— 32.
1. —— xxvii. 10.
2. ——— 21.
1. ——— 24.
2. ——— 31.
1. ——— 33.
1. —— xxviii. 4, 6, 17.
2. ——— 21.
1. ——— 26* 1st.
2. ——— 26 2nd, 29 part (*ap.*)
1. Rom. ii. 22.
4. —— iii. 5.
1. ——— 8*, 19* 1st.
5. ——— 19 2nd.
4. —— iv. 1.
1. ——— 3, 9.
4. —— vi. 1.
4. —— vii. 7 1st.
1. ——— 7* 2nd.
4. —— viii. 31.
1. —— ix. 1.
6. ——— 12.
4. ——— 14.
1. ——— 15, 17.
4. ——— 19, 20.
1. ——— 25.
6. ——— 26.
— ——— 29, see S before.
4. ——— 30.
2. —— x. 6.
1. ——— 8, 11, 16, 18, 19 twice, 20, 21.
1. —— xi. 1, 2 1st.
1. ——— 2 2nd (*om.* G L T Tr A.)
1. ——— 4, 9, 11.
4. ——— 19.
1. —— xii. 3, 19.

1. Rom. xiv. 11.
1. —— xv. 3, 10, 12.
1. 1 Cor. i. 12 twice.
2. ——— 15.
1. —— iii. 4.
3. —— vi. 16 (*om.* Lb.)
1. —— vii. 8.
3. ——— 29.
5. —— ix. 8 1st.
1. ——— 8* 2nd, 10.
3. —— x. 15, 19.
2. ——— 28.
1. ——— 29.
2. —— xi. 22, 24.
1. ——— 25.
2. —— xii. 3, 15, 16, 21.
4. —— xiv. 16 1st.
1. ——— 16* 2nd, 21*.
2. ——— 23.
1. ——— 34*.
1. —— xv. 12.
2. ——— 27.
4. ——— 35.
3. ——— 50.
1. 2 Cor. vi. 2.
2. ——— 16.
1. ——— 17, 18.
— —— vii. 3, see S before.
1. —— ix. 3, 4.
3. —— x. 10.
1. —— xi. 16.
4. —— xii. 6, 9.
— Gal. i. 9 1st, see S before.
1. ——— 9 2nd.
2. —— ii. 14.
1. —— iii. 16*, 17.
1. —— iv. 1, 30.
1. —— v. 2, 16.
1. Eph. iv. 8, 17.
1. —— v. 14.
1. Col. ii. 4.
2. —— iv. 17.
1. 1 Thes. iv. 15.
1. —— v. 3.
1. 1 Tim. i. 7.
1. —— v. 18.
1. 2 Tim. ii. 7, 18.
2. Tit. i. 12.
1. —— ii. 8.
1. Philem. 19, 21.
2. Heb. i. 5.
1. ——— 6, 7.
4. ——— 13.
1. —— ii. 6, 12.
1. —— iii. 7.
2. ——— 10.
1. ——— 15.
4. —— iv. 3.
1. ——— 7* 1st.
4. ——— 7 2nd (προείρηται, *has been said before*, instead of εἴρηται, *it is said*, G ∾ L T Tr A ℵ.)
5. —— v. 5.
1. ——— 6.
— ——— 11, see S (things to)
1. —— vi. 14.
— —— vii. 9 1st, see S (as I may so)
2. ——— 9 2nd.
1. ——— 21.
3. —— viii. 5.
1. ——— 8 twice, 9, 10, 11, 13.
— —— ix. 11, see S (that is to)
1. ——— 20.
1. —— x. 5.
2. ——— 7.
1. ——— 8 part.
4. ——— 9.
— ——— 15, see Say before.
1. ——— 16.
— ——— 20, see S (that is to)

2. Heb. x. 30 1st.
1. ——— 30 2nd (*om.* λέγει Κύριος, *saith the Lord*, G ⇉ T Tr ℵ.)
1. —— xi. 14.
5. ——— 18.
1. ——— 32.
2. —— xii. 21.
1. ——— 26.
4. —— xiii. 5.
1. ——— 6.
1. Jas. i. 13.
2. —— ii. 3 twice, 11 twice.
1. ——— 14.
2. ——— 16.
4. ——— 18.
1. ——— 23.
1. —— iv. 5, 6, 13.
1. ——— 15, and see Say (for that one ought to)
1. 2 Pet. iii. 4.
2. 1 John i. 6, 8, 10.
1. —— ii. 4, 6, 9.
2. —— iv. 20.
1. —— v. 16.
2. Jude 9.
1. ——— 14.
1. Rev. i. 8, 11, 17.
1. —— ii. 1.
2. ——— 2 (*ap.*)
1. ——— 7, 8, 9, 11, 12, 17, 18, 24, 29.
1. —— iii. 1, 6, 7, 9, 13, 14, 17, 22.
1. —— iv. 1*, 8, 10.

1. Rev. v. 5, 9, 12, 13, 14.
1. —— vi. 1, 3, 5, 6, 7, 10.
6. ——— 11.
1. ——— 16.
1. —— vii. 3, 10, 12, 13*.
4. ——— 14 1st.
2. ——— 14 2nd.
1. —— viii. 13.
1. —— ix. 14.
1. —— x. 4*, 8*, 9 twice, 11.
1. —— xi. 1, 12, 15, 17.
1. —— xii. 10.
1. —— xiii. 4, 14.
1. —— xiv. 7, 8, 9, 13 twice, 18.
1. —— xv. 3.
1. —— xvi. 1, 5, 7, 17.
1. —— xvii. 1*.
2. ——— 7.
1. ——— 15 (No. 2, L.)
1. —— xviii. 2, 4, 7, 10, 16, 18, 19, 21.
1. —— xix. 1.
4. ——— 3.
1. ——— 4, 5, 6, 9 twice, 10, 17.
1. —— xxi. 3.
2. ——— 5 1st.
1. ——— 5 2nd.
2. ——— 6.
1. ——— 9*.
2. —— xxii. 6 (No. 1, G ∾)
1. ——— 9.
1. ——— 10, 17* 1st.
2. ——— 17 2nd.
1. ——— 20.

SAY (AS I MAY SO)

{ ὡς, *as*, ἔπος, *a word*, εἰπεῖν, *to say*, (*see above, No.* 2,) } so to say a word, so to speak, (*non occ.*)

Heb. vii. 9.

SAY (FOR THAT ONE OUGHT TO)

{ ἀντὶ, *instead of*, τοῦ, *of the*, λέγειν, *to say*, } instead of your saying, [verse 14 being parenthetical, and the sense being taken up from verse 13.]

Jas. iv. 15.

SAY (THAT [OR WHICH] IS TO)

1. { τοῦτ', *that* ἐστί, *is*, } *like Eng.*, i.e.

2. { ὅ, *which* λέγεται, *is said*, (*pass. of* "SAY," *No.* 1.) }

1. Matt. xxvii. 46.
1. Mark vii. 11.
2. John i. 38.
2. John xx. 16.
1. Acts i. 19.
1. Heb. ix. 11.
1. Heb. x. 20.

SAY (THINGS TO)

{ ὁ, *the* [*of us*] λόγος, *word*, *discourse*, } *i.e.* ["*concerning whom great, or much, is*] *our* discourse."

Heb. v. 11.

SAY BEFORE.

προεῖπον, "SAY," *No.* 2, *with* πρό, before, *prefixed.*

Rom. ix. 29.
2 Cor. vii. 3.
Gal. i. 9.
Heb. x. 15 (εἰρηκέναι, *having said*, G ∾ L T Tr A ℵ.)

SAY AGAINST.

ἀντεῖπον, "SAY," *No.* 2, *with* ἀντί, against, *prefixed,* (*occ.* Luke xxi. 15.)

Acts iv. 14.

SAY ON.

1. λέγω, *see* "SAY," *No.* 1.
2. εἶπον, *see* "SAY," *No.* 2.

2. Luke vii. 40. | 1. Acts xiii. 15.

SAID (THE)

αὐτῆς, of this very.

Mark vi. 22.

SAYING (-S.) [noun.]

1. λόγος, the word *spoken, and as* connected with the inward thought; the word (*not as a part of speech, but*) as part of what is uttered; *hence,* that which is spoken, an exposition, *or* account which is given, *as expressive of the speaker's thoughts.*
2. ῥῆμα, that which is spoken, a word, *as uttered by the living voice.* (*No.* 1 *is* the subject matter of spoken words, *No.* 2 *is* the word pronounced and considered in itself.)
3. λαλία, utterance, talk, discourse; prattle.

1. Matt. vii. 24, 26, 28.
1. —— xv. 12.
1. —— xix. 1, 11, 22.
1. —— xxvi. 1.
1. —— xxviii. 15.
1. Mark vii. 29.
1. —— viii. 32.
1. —— ix. 10.
2. —— —— 32.
1. —— x. 22.
1. Luke i. 29 (om. G ∾)
2. —— —— 65, marg. *thing.*
2. —— ii. 17, 50, 51.
1. —— vi. 47.
2. —— vii. 1.
1. —— ix. 28, marg. *thing.*
1. —— —— 44.
2. —— —— 45 twice.
2. —— xviii. 34.
1. John iv. 37, 39.
3. —— —— 42.
1. —— vi. 60.
1. —— vii. 36, 40.
1. John viii. 51, 52, 55.
1. —— x. 19.
1. —— xii. 38.
1. —— xiv. 24.
1. —— xv. 20.
1. —— xviii. 9, 32.
1. —— xix. 8, 13.
1. —— xxi. 23.
1. Acts vi. 5.
1. —— vii. 29.
1. —— xiv. 18, see S (with these)
1. —— xvi. 36.
1. Rom. iii. 4.
1. —— xiii. 9, and see Namely.
1. 1 Cor. xv. 54.
1. 1 Tim. i. 15.
1. —— iii. 1.
1. —— iv. 9.
1. 2 Tim. ii. 11.
1. Tit. iii. 8.
1. Rev. xix. 9.
1. Rev. xxii. 6, 7, 9, 10.

SAYINGS (WITH THESE)

{ ταῦτα, these *things* λέγοντες, saying, (*see* "SAY," *No.* 1,) } these things saying.

Acts xiv. 18.

SCALE.

λεπίς, a scale, rind, husk; *used coll.,* scales, *as of fish,* (*non occ.*)

Acts ix. 18.

SCARCE.

μόλις, with labour, with pains; *hence,* with difficulty, hardly, scarcely.

Acts xiv. 18. | Acts xxvii. 7.

SCARCELY.

μόλις, *see above.*

Rom. v. 7. | 1. Pet. iv. 18.

SCANDAL. [margin.]

Matt. xiii. 41, see "OFFENDETH (THING THAT)"

SCARLET.

κόκκινος, (*adj. from* κόκκος, grain, kernel; *also, the* coccus ilicis or kermes, a small insect found adhering to trees, and used by the ancients for dyeing crimson or deep scarlet) *hence,* coccus-dyed, crimson, (lxx. *for* תּוֹלַעַת, Ex. xxv. 4; xxviii. 5; שָׁנִי, Jos. ii. 18, 21.)

Matt. xxvii. 28. | Heb. ix. 19, marg. *purple.*
Rev. xviii. 12, 16, neut.

SCARLET COLOUR.

Rev. xvii. 4, neut.

SCARLET COLOURED.

Rev. xvii. 3.

SCATTER (-ED, ETH.)

1. σκορπίζω, to scatter, disperse.
2. διασκορπίζω, (*No.* 1, *with* διά, through, *prefixed*) to scatter throughout, scatter abroad.
3. διαλύω, to dissolve; *of a collection of people,* to break up, disperse. (*non occ.*)

4. διασπείρω, to sow hither and thither, to scatter as seed.

2. Matt. xiv. 27. | 1. John xi. 12.
2. Luke i. 51. | 1. — xvi. 32.
1. — xi. 23. | 3. Acts v. 36.

SCATTER ABROAD.

1. Matt. xii. 30. | 2. John xi. 52.
2. — xxvi. 31. | 4. Acts viii. 1, 4.
4. Acts xi. 19.

SCATTERED.

διασπορά, a sowing hither and thither, a scattering, *as* of seed.

1 Pet. i. 1.

SCATTERED ABROAD (BE)

ῥίπτω, to throw *or* cast, hurl, jerk *with a sudden motion. Here, pass. part. perf.*, cast forth, thrown down.

Matt. ix. 36.

SCATTERED ABROAD (WHICH ARE)

{ ἐν, in, διασπορά, *see* "SCATTERED" } in the scattering *as of seed.*

Jas. i. 1.

SCEPTRE.

ῥάβδος, a rod, wand, *or* staff; a sceptre. (*Here quoted from* Ps. xlv. 7, *where* lxx. *for* שבט, *comp.* Rev. ii. 27; xi. 1; xii. 5; xix. 15. *Also for* מטה, Ps. cx. 2.)

Heb. i. 8 twice.

SCHISM.

σχίσμα, a rent, a split.

1 Cor. i. 10, 18, marg. (text, *division.*) | 1 Cor. xii. 25, marg. *division.*

SCHOOL.

σχολή, leisure, rest, freedom from business *or* labour, vacation. *Then,* leisure as applied to anything, *as* study; *hence,* a place of learned leisure, *where a teacher and his disciples came together and held discussions and disputations,* (*non occ.*)

Acts xix. 9.

SCHOOLMASTER.

παιδαγωγός, *Eng.*, pedagogue, *i.e.* a slave *or* freedman to whose care the boys of a family were committed, who trained them up, instructed them at home, and accompanied them to the public schools.

[In this passage Christ is not alluded to as a Teacher to whom the children were brought. The law is the teacher and controller, and Christ is the ἐλευθερία, (liberty) of the *sons,* (v. 26) in which there is no more bondage of the law.] (*occ.* 1 Cor. iv. 15.)

Gal. iii. 24, 25.

SCIENCE.

γνῶσις, knowledge. [*Hence,* what *man* calls γνῶσις is falsely so called, because it is mostly hypothesis, conjecture, (*e.g.* astronomy and geology.) The result of man's "so-called" γνῶσις can only, therefore, be "oppositious," (ἀντίθεσις, opposite positions),] (*elsewhere translated* "KNOWLEDGE.")

1 Tim. vi. 20.

SCOFFER.

ἐμπαίκτης, a sporter with; one who sports with *or* against *another;* a mocker, (*occ.* Jude 18.)

2 Pet. iii. 3.

SCORCH (-ED.)

καυματίζω, to burn.

Matt. xiii. 6. | Rev. xvi. 8.
Mark iv. 6. | — 9, marg. *burn.*

SCORN.

See, LAUGH.

SCORPION.

σκορπίος, a scorpion; a large insect found only in hot countries, having a venomous sting which produces swelling and inflammation. lxx. for עקרב, Deut. viii. 15; 1 Kings xii. 11, 14, (*non occ.*)

Luke x. 19. | Luke xi. 12.
Rev. ix. 3, 5, 10.

SCOURGE. [noun.]

φραγέλλιον, *Lat.*, flagellum, *i.e.* a whip, (*non occ.*)

John ii. 15.

SCOURGE (ED, -ETH.) [verb.]

1. μαστιγόω, to scourge, flog, (lxx. *for* הכה, Ex. v. 14; Deut. xxv. 3), (*non occ.*)
2. μαστίζω, to whip, whip forward, (lxx. *for* הכה, Numb. xxii. 5), (*non occ.*)
3. φραγελλόω, *Lat.*, flagello, *i.e.* to flagellate, (*non occ.*)

1. Matt. x. 17.
1. —— xx. 19.
1. —— xxiii. 34.
3. —— xxvii. 26, part.
1. Mark x. 34.
3. Mark xv. 15.
1. Luke xviii. 33.
1. John xix. 1.
2. Acts xxii. 25.
1. Heb. xii. 6.

SCOURGING (-s.) [noun.]

μαστιξ, a whip, a scourge, (lxx. for שוט, 1 Kings xii. 11, 14; Prov. xxvi. 3.)

Acts xxii. 24. | Heb. xi. 36.

SCRIBE (-s.)

γραμματεύς, a writer, a scribe (lat.) lxx. for ספר, the king's scribe, Sec. of State, 2 Sam. viii. 17; xx. 25. Military clerk, 2 Kings xxv. 19; 2 Chron. xxvi. 11. *Later, in* lxx. *and N.T.* a scribe, *i.e.* one skilled in the Jewish law, an interpreter of the Scriptures, a lawyer. *They are also called* νομικοί, νομοδιδασκάλοι. *Comp.* Mark xii. 28 *with* Matt. xxii. 35. *So*, lxx. *for* סופרים, 1 Chron. xxvii. 32; Ezra vii. 6; Neh. viii. 1. *Hence*, one instructed, a scholar, a learned teacher, (*occ.* Acts xix. 35.)

Matt. ii. 4.
—— v. 20.
—— vii. 29.
—— viii. 19.
—— ix. 3.
—— xii. 38.
—— xiii. 52.
—— xv. 1.
—— xvi. 21.
—— xvii. 10.
—— xx. 18.
—— xxi. 15.
—— xxiii. 2, 13, 14 (*ap.*), 15, 23, 25, 27, 29, 34.
—— xxvi. 3, (*om.* καὶ οἱ γραμματεῖς, *and the scribes*, G → L T Tr A ℵ.)
—— 57.
Matt. xxvii. 41.
Mark i. 22.
—— ii. 6, 16.
—— iii. 22.
—— vii. 1, 5.
—— viii. 31.
—— ix. 11, 14.
—— 16 (G∾), (αὐτούς, *them*, G L T Tr A ℵ.)
—— x. 33.
—— xi. 18, 27.
—— xii. 28, 32, 35, 38.
—— xiv. 1, 43, 53.
—— xv. 1, 31.
Luke v. 21, 30.
—— vi. 7.
—— ix. 22.
—— xi. 44 (*ap.*), 43.
—— xv. 2.
Luke xix. 47.
—— xx. 1, 19, 39, 46.
—— xxii. 2, 66.
—— xxiii. 10.
John viii. 3 (*ap.*)
Acts iv. 5.
—— vi. 12.
—— xxiii. 9 (*ap.*)
1 Cor. i. 20.

SCRIP.

πήρα, a bag, sack, wallet; *Lat.*, pera, *of leather, used by shepherds and travellers*, (*non occ.*)

Matt. x. 10.
Mark vi. 8.
Luke ix. 3.
—— x. 4.
Luke xxii. 35, 36.

SCRIPTURE (-s.)

1. γραφή, that which is written, the writing. *The N.T. use of* ἡ γραφή *to denote* the collection of the γραφαὶ ἁγίαι, the holy writings, Rom. i. 2, θεόπνευστοι, God-breathed, 2 Tim. iii. 16, (*one part of which are called* προφητικαί, prophetical, Rom. xvi. 26, τῶν προφητῶν, of the prophets, Matt. xxvi. 56) *implies a reference to* the authoritative character of the Scriptures as a whole.

   Used of a single *text*, Mark xii. 10; Luke iv. 21; John xiii. 18; xix. 24, 36, 37; xx. 9, 6; Acts i. 16; viii. 35. *Used also of* Him who speaks in the Scripture, Rom. ix. 17; Gal. iii. 8, 22; iv. 30, (*non occ.*)

2. γράμμα, that which is written, a letter of the alphabet, a book, letter, bond, etc. τὰ ἱερὰ γράμματα, the Holy Scriptures, *is a name distinct from No.* 1, *describing them as* the object of study or knowlege; *whereas No.* 1 *describes them as an* authority.

1. Matt. xxi. 42.
1. —— xxii. 29.
1. —— xxvi. 54, 56.
1. Mark xii. 10, 24.
1. —— xiv. 49.
1. —— xv. 28 (*ap.*)
1. Luke iv. 21.
1. —— xxiv. 27, 32, 45.
1. John ii. 22.
1. —— v. 39.
1. —— vii. 38, 42.
1. —— x. 35.
1. —— xiii. 18.
1. —— xvii. 12.
1. —— xix. 24, 28, 36, 37.
1. —— xx. 9.
1. Acts i. 6.
1. —— viii. 32, 35.
1. —— xvii. 2, 11.
1. Acts xviii. 24, 28.
1. Rom. i. 2.
1. —— iv. 3.
1. —— ix. 17.
1. —— x. 11.
1. —— xi. 2.
1. —— xv. 4.
1. —— xvi. 26.
1. 1 Cor. xv. 3, 4.
1. Gal. iii. 8, 22.
1. —— iv. 30.
1. 1 Tim. v. 18.
2. 2 Tim. iii. 15.
1. —— 16.
1. Jas. ii. 8, 23.
1. —— iv. 5.
1. 1 Pet. ii. 6.
1. 2 Pet. i. 20.
1. —— iii. 16.

SCROLL.

βιβλίον, (*dim.* of βίβλος, the inner rind of the papyrus, *anciently used for writing*) a roll, volume, scroll, *the ancient form of a book.*

Rev. vi. 14.

SEA (-s.)

1. θάλασσα, the sea; a sea, *as the Mediterranean, the Red Sea; Hebraïstically for* the lake of Genesaret; *also of* "the molten sea" of Solomon, (1 Kings vii. 23; 2 Kings xxv. 13) *answering to* the laver of Moses, (Ex. xxxviii. 8.)

[The Temple scene in Rev. may have reference to this, and its crystal form and use to Ex. xxiv. 10, (*non occ.*)]

2. πέλαγος, the high sea, the open sea, the deep, the main, *remote from land,* (*occ.* Matt. xviii. 6.)

1. Matt. iv. 15, 18 twice.
1. —— viii. 24, 26, 27, 32.
1. —— xiii. 1, 47.
1. —— xiv. 24 (ap.), 25, 26.
1. —— xv. 19.
1. —— xvii. 27.
1. —— xviii. 6.
1. —— xxi. 21.
1. —— xxiii. 15.
1. Mark i. 16 twice.
1. —— ii. 13.
1. —— iii. 7.
1. —— iv. 1 3 times, 39, 41.
1. —— v. 1, 13 twice, 21,
1. —— vi. 47, 48, 49.
1. —— vii. 31.
1. —— ix. 42.
1. —— xi. 23.
1. Luke xvii. 2, 6.
1. —— xxi. 25.
1. John vi. 1, 16, 17, 18, 19, 22, 25.
1. —— xxi. 1, 7.
1. Acts iv. 24.
1. —— vii. 36.
1. —— x. 6, 32.
1. Acts xiv. 15.
1. —— xvii. 14.
2. —— xxvii. 5.
1. —— —— 30, 38, 40.
— —— —— 41, see S meet (where two)
1. —— xxviii. 4.
1. Rom. ix. 27.
1. 1 Cor. x. 1, 2.
1. 2 Cor. xi. 26.
1. Heb. xi. 12.
1. Jas. i. 6.
— —— iii. 7, see S (things in)
1. Jude 13.
1. Rev. iv. 6.
1. —— v. 13.
1. —— vii. 1, 2, 3.
1. —— viii. 8 twice, 9.
1. —— x. 2, 5, 6 (ap.), 8.
1. —— xii. 12.
1. —— xiii. 1 twice.
1. —— xiv. 7.
1. —— xv. 2 twice.
1. —— xvi. 3 twice.
1. —— xviii. 17, 19, 21.
1. —— xx. 8, 13.
1. Rev. xxi. 1.

SEA (THINGS IN)

ἐνάλιος, belonging to the salt water *or* sea; marine, (*non occ.*)

Jas. iii. 7.

SEAS MEET (WHERE TWO)

διθάλασσης, between two seas; *prob.* at the confluence of two opposite currents, (*non occ.*)

Acts xxvii. 41.

SEA COAST.

παράλιος, by *or* near the salt water *or* sea, (*non occ.*)

Luke vi. 17.

SEA COAST (WHICH IS UPON)

{ ὁ, the, that,
{ παραθαλάσσιος, beside *or* near the sea, (*non occ.*)

Matt. iv. 13.

SEAL (-s.) [noun.]

σφραγίς, a seal with which any thing is fastened up *or* marked; an instrument for sealing, (lxx. for חותם, 1 Kings xxi. 8; Song viii. 6); a seal, *as impressed for privacy or secrecy,* (1 Kings xxi. 8; Is. xxix. 11; Jer. xxii. 24; Dan. ix. 24); *for security,* (Dan. vi. 17); *and authority,* (Est. iii. 12; viii. 8, 10.)

[(a) Prob. all these implied in Rev. v. and vi. Veiling in mystery seen in the book being fully sealed; the unveiling of mystery in the breaking of them.

(b) In Rev. vii. it is the sealing of those who are to escape the coming judgment. "The Lord knoweth them that are His," (2 Cor. i. 22; Eph. i. 13; iv. 30; 2 Tim. ii. 19; Rev. ii. 17.)

The Lord's sealing always visible—1, circumcision; 2, the fruits of the Spirit; 3, Rev. vii. 2, 3; xxii. 4.]

— John iii. 33, see S (set to one's)
— Rom. iv. 11.
— 1 Cor. ix. 2.
— 2 Tim. ii. 19.
a. Rev. v. 1, 2, 5, 9.
a. Rev. vi. 1, 3, 5, 7, 9, 12.
b. —— vii. 2.
a. —— viii. 1.
b. —— ix. 4.
— —— xx. 3, see S (set a)

SEAL (SET A)

σφραγίζω, *see below.*

Rev. xx. 3.

SEAL (SET TO ONE'S)

σφραγίζω, *see below.*

John iii. 33.

SEAL (-ED, -ING.) [verb.]

1. *σφραγίζω*, to seal, seal up, make fast with seal *or* signet, *e.g. letters, writings, etc., that they may not be read*, (lxx. for חתם, 1 Kings xxi. 8; Is. xxix. 11; Dan. xii. 4.) *Also*, to seal for security, (*see under* "SEAL.")

* *Omit* ἐσφραγισαμένοι, were sealed, G÷L T Tr[b] A ℵ.

2. *κατασφραγίζω*, (*No.* 1, *with* κατά, down, *prefixed*) to seal down, (lxx. for חתם, Job. ix. 7; Wisd. ii. 5), (*non occ.*)

1. Matt. xxvii. 66.
1. John vi. 27.
1. Rom. xv. 28.
1. 2 Cor. i. 22.
1. Eph. i. 13.
1. —— iv. 30.
2. Rev. v. 1.
1. —— vii. 3, 4 twice, 5* twice, 6* 3 times, 7* 3 times, 8* twice.
— —— x. 4, see S up.
1. —— xxii. 10.

SEAL UP.

1. Rev. x. 4.

SEAM (WITHOUT)

ἄρραφος, not sewn; *hence*, having no seam, (*non occ.*)

John xix. 23.

SEAR WITH A HOT IRON.

καυτηριάζω, to cauterise, to brand with a hot iron, (*non occ.*)

1 Tim. iv. 2.

SEARCH (-ED, -ETH, -ING.)

1. *ἐρευνάω*, to seek out, trace; used *of a lion who "scours the plains and* traces the footsteps of the man who had robbed him," Hom. Il. xviii. 321; *used of dogs* tracing *their game* by the foot, Hom. Odyss. xix. 436. *Hence*, to track, trace, investigate, (lxx. for חפש, to search by uncovering, Gen. xliv. 12; 1 Kings xx. 6; 2 Kings x. 24; Prov. xx. 27; חקר, to search minutely, explore, Judges xviii. 2; 2 Sam. x. 3; חשף, to strip, Joel i. 7; *and for* משש, to feel, search by feeling, Gen. xxxi. 35, 36.)

[(a) In John v. 39, *ἐρευνᾶτε is 2nd pers. imperative*, not indicative; for the 2nd pers. pl. indicative is never used at the beginning of a sentence without the pronoun, (ὑμεῖς, you) or some other word, (such as οὐ, not) while the imperative is frequently so used, *see* John xiv. 11; xv. 20. The Jews *read*, but did not *search.*] (*non occ.*)

2. *ἀνακρίνω*, (κρίνω, to divide, separate, make a distinction, come to a decision, *and* ἀνά, up, *prefixed*) to separate *or* divide up; *hence*, to estimate carefully, judge of, sift.

3. *ἐξετάζω*, to verify out, to search the truth of *a thing* out; to examine whether a thing is true or not.

3. Matt. ii. 8.
1a. John v. 39.
1. —— vii. 52.
2. Acts xvii. 11.
1. Rom. viii. 27.
1. 1 Cor. ii. 10.
— 1 Pet. i. 10, see S diligently.
1. —— 11.
1. Rev. ii. 23.

SEARCH DILIGENTLY.

ἐξερευνάω, (*No.* 1, *with* ἐξ, out of, *prefixed*) to trace out, (lxx. for נצר, to observe, Ps. cxix. 2, 34, 69, 115, 129; חפש, to search by uncovering, Ps. lxiii. 6; Prov. ii. 4; Zeph. i. 13; חקר, to search minutely, 1 Ch. xix. 3), (*non occ.*)

1. Pet. i. 10.

SEASON (-S.) [noun.]

(*For various combinations with other words, see below.*)

1. *καιρός*, the right measure and relation, *esp.* as regards time and place, (*gen. of time.*) *Hence*, the right time, suitable *or* convenient time; the opportune point of time at which a thing SHOULD BE done, (a certain limited and definite portion of *No.* 2.)

2. *χρόνος*, time, duration, time in general, any time, (while *No.* 1 is *the* time) the time in which anything IS done.

3. *ὥρα*, a portion of time, (*Lat.*, hora; *Eng.*, hour) season, time of blossoming, (ὡραῖος, blossoming, ἄωρος, unseasonable.) *Orig.*, the season

of the year; *then*, the time of the day, *and when reckoning by hours was practised*, the hour; *hence*, A definite, limited, and determined time, (*thus differing from No.* 1, *which is* THE definite time.)

[That which endures for *No.* 3 is conceived to last no longer, while what is said to be done in *No.* 1 is conceived as being done up to another point of time.]

1. Matt. xxi. 41.
1. Mark xii. 2.
1. Luke i. 20.
1. —— iv. 13.
1. —— xiii. 1.
1. —— xx. 10.
3. John v. 35.
1. Acts i. 7.
1. —— xiii. 11.
1. Acts xiv. 17.
2. —— xix. 22.
2. —— xx. 18.
3. 2 Cor. vii. 8.
1. Gal. vi. 9.
1. 1 Thes. v. 1.
3. Philem. 15.
2. Rev. vi. 11.
2. —— xx. 3.

SEASON (AT A CERTAIN)

{ κατὰ, according to, καίρον, *see No.* 1, } opportunely, in the needful time *to do it.*

John v. 4 (*ap.*)

SEASON (CONVENIENT)

1. Acts xxiv. 25.

SEASON (DUE)

1. Matt. xxiv. 45. | 1. Luke xii. 42.

SEASON (FOR A)

1. ὀλίγον, little, *opp. of* πολύς, much; *of time*, little, brief, short. *Here, neut.*, ὀλίγον *as adv.*, *spoken of time*, for a little.

2. πρόσκαιρος, for a καιρός, (*see* "SEASON," *No.* 1) *not necessarily for a short time*, but until and up to another point of time.

2. Heb. xi. 25. | 1. 1 Pet. i. 6.

SEASON (IN)

εὐκαίρως, (*adv. of* "SEASON," *No.* 1, *with* εὖ., well, *prefixed*) in good season.

2 Tim. iv. 2.

SEASON (OUT OF)

ἀκαίρως, (*adv. of* "SEASON," *No.* 1) unseasonably, out of season, (*not out of* GOOD *season, as above.*)

2 Tim. iv. 2.

SEASON (OF A LONG)

{ ἐξ, out of, of, ἱκανοῦ, sufficing, abundant, great, much, } for a long [*time.*]

Luke xxiii. 8 (ἐξ ἱκανῶν χρόνων, *for a sufficient number of times*, L Tr A ℵ.)

SEASON (-ED.) [verb.]

ἀρτύω, to prepare fitly, *used of all things requiring art and cunning*, to dress savoury *meat*, to season.

Mark ix. 50. | Luke xiv. 34.
Col. iv. 6.

SEAT (-S.)

1. θρόνος, a seat; prop. a high seat with a footstool. *Later, and in N.T.*, a throne, *as the emblem of regal authority*, (lxx. *for* כסא, 1 Kings x. 18; Job xxxvi. 7; Ps. xlvii. 9; ciii. 19.

2. καθέδρα, a seat, any seat, a chair, (*non occ.*)

2. Matt. xxi. 12.
2. —— xxiii. 2.
— —— 6, see S (chief)
— —— xxvii. 19, see Judgment-seat.
2. Mark xi. 15.
1. Luke i. 52.
— —— xi. 43, see S (uppermost)
— —— xx. 46, see S (highest)
— John xix. 13, } see Judgment-seat.
— Acts xviii. 12, 16, 17, [17, } see Judgment-seat.
— —— xxv. 6, 10, } see Judgment-seat.
— Rom. iv. 10, } see Judgment-seat.
— 2 Cor. v. 10, } see Judgment-seat.
— Jas. ii. 6, } see Judgment-seat.
1. Rev. ii. 13.
1. —— iv. 4 twice.
1. —— xi. 16.
1. —— xiii. 2.
1. Rev. xvi. 10.

SEAT (CHIEF)

πρωτοκαθεδρία, (*No.* 2, *with* πρῶτος, first, *prefixed*) the first seat, the chief seat.

Matt. xxiii. 6.

SEAT (HIGHEST)

πρωτοκαθεδρία, *see above.*

Luke xx. 46.

SEAT (UPPERMOST)

πρωτοκαθεδρία, *see above.*

Luke xi. 43.

SECOND.

δεύτερος, second, *of number, order, place, or time.*

Matt. xxi. 30 (G∾) (ἕτερος, *the other*, G T A ℵ.)
—— xxii. 26, 39.
—— xxvi. 42, see S time (the)
Mark xii. 21, 31.
—— xiv. 72, see S time (the)
Luke vi. 1, see S after the first.

Luke xii. 38.
— xix. 18.
— xx. 30.
John iii. 4, see S time (the)
— iv. 54.
— xxi. 16, see S time (the)
Acts vii. 13.
— x. 15, see S time(the)
— xii. 10.
— xiii. 33 (G∾) (πρῶτος, *the first*, G L T TrA*.) [The 1st and 2nd Psalms were orig. *one*, beginning and ending with a Beatitude (i. 1; ii. 12) and forming a theological and prophetical prologue to the whole book.]
1 Cor. xv. 47.
2 Cor. i. 15.
— xiii. 2, see S time (the)
Tit. iii. 10.
Heb. viii. 7.
— ix. 3, 7.
— — 28, see S time(the)
— x. 9.
2 Pet. iii. 1.
Rev. ii. 11.
— iv. 7.
— vi. 3 twice.
— viii. 8.
— xi. 14.
— xvi. 3.
— xx. 6, 14.
Rev. xxi. 8, 19.

SECOND AFTER THE FIRST (THE)

δευτεροπρώτος, the second-first; *prob.* the first Sabbath of the second year of the week of years, (*non occ.*)

Luke vi. 1 (*om.* L^b Tr^b A^b ℵ) i.e. *a sabbath.*

SECOND TIME (THE)

1. δευτέρον, *neut. of* δεύτερος, second, *used either with or without the art.*, the second time, again.
2. { ἐκ, out of / δεύτερον, the second, } for the second time.

2. Matt. xxvi. 42.
2. Mark xiv. 72.
1. John iii. 4.
1. John xxi. 16.
2. Acts x. 15.
1. 2 Cor. xiii. 2.
2. Heb. ix. 28.

SECONDARILY.

δευτέρος, *see* "SECOND"

1 Cor. xii. 28.

SECRET (-S.) [noun and adj.*]

κρυπτός, hidden, concealed, *and therefore* secret.

Matt. xxiv. 26, see Chamber.
Luke viii. 17*.
Rom. ii. 16.
1 Cor. xiv. 25.

SECRET (IN)

1. κρυφῆ, secretly, (*non occ.*)
2. { ἐν, in, / κρυπτός, *see above*, } in the hidden or secret [*place.*]

2. Matt. vi. 4 twice, 6 twice.
2. — 18 twice (κρυφαῖος, *adj.*, G∾L T Tr A ℵ.)
2. John vii. 4, 10.
2. — xviii. 20.
1. Eph. v. 12.

SECRET PLACE (IN A)

{ εἰς, into / κρυπτήν, a covered place.

Luke xi. 33.

SECRET (KEEP)

1. κρύπτω, to hide, conceal.
2. σιγάω, to be silent *or* still; when speaking to cease to speak, (*from* σίζω, to say hush!)

1. Matt. xiii. 35. | 2. Rom. xvi. 25.

SECRET (KEPT)

ἀπόκρυφος, hidden away, concealed.

Mark iv. 22.

SECRETLY.

1. κρύπτω, to hide, conceal. *Here, part.* κεκρυμμένος, having been a secret one.
2. λάθρα, secretly, by stealth.

2. John xi. 28. | 1. John xix. 38.

SECT.

αἵρεσις, a choice, (lxx. Lev. xxii. 11, 21) *hence*, an opinion, *then*, a party. [Used only by St. Paul in 1 Cor. xi. 19, (heresies) and in Gal. v. 20, as one of the works of the flesh. In Tit. iii. 10, αἱρέτικος denotes one who occasions divisions in the Church by turning aside from sound doctrine) *comp.* 2 Pet. ii. 1.] *It seems to denote* a division (arising from opinions) without any formal separation; *while the* σχίσματα (*Eng.*, schisms) *were* cliques separated from each other by social distinctions and petty alienations of feeling. The later ecclesiastical use of the words is very different.]

Acts v. 17.
— xv. 5.
— xxiv. 5.
Acts xxvi. 5.
— xxviii. 22.
1 Cor. xi. 19, marg. (text, *heresy.*)

SECURE (TO)

{ ποιέω, to make, / ἀμέριμνος, without anxiety, (*occ.* 1 Cor. vii. 32.)

Matt. xxviii. 14.

SECURITY.

{ τὸ, the, ἱκανόν, sufficient, } satisfaction, *i.e* security.

Acts xvii. 9.

SEDITION (-s.)

1. στάσις, a setting up; an upstand, uproar; *hence*, insurrection.
2. διχοστασία, a standing apart; *hence*, dissension.

1. Luke xxiii. 19, 25. | 1. Acts xxiv. 5. 2. Gal. v. 20.

SEDUCE.

1. πλανάω, to make to wander, to lead astray.
2. ἀποπλανάω, (*No.* 1, *with* ἀπό, away from, *prefixed*) to make to wander away from, to lead astray from.

2. Mark xiii. 22. | 1. 1 John ii. 26. 1. Rev. ii. 20.

SEDUCED (*be*) [margin.]

1 Tim. vi. 10, see "ERR."

SEDUCER (-s.)

γόης, a wizard, juggler, a juggling imposter, (*from* γοάω, to wail, *because such people chanted their spells in a* sort of howl), (*non occ.*)

2 Tim. iii. 13.

SEDUCING.

πλάνος, wandering about.

1 Tim. iv. 1.

SEE (-EST, -ETH, -ING; SEEN; SAW, -EST.)

1. εἶδον, to see; *implying not the mere act of seeing, but* the actual perception of the object, *thus differing from No.* 5; *and referring to* the mind and thought of him who sees, *thus differing from No.* 8, *in that it refers to the subject, while No.* 8 *refers to the object.*
2. ἰδού, (*imperative aor. mid. of No.* 1) see! behold! *calling attention to something external to one's self.*
3. ἴδε, (*imperat. of aor.* 2 *of No.* 1) see! lo! behold! *as calling attention to something present.*
4. οἶδα, to have seen, perceived, *or* apprehended; *hence*, to know.
5. βλέπω, to use the eyes; to see, look; *used of* the act of seeing, *even though nothing is seen;* to observe accurately with desire; *hence*, of mental vision, *implying more contemplation than No.* 8.
6. ἀναβλέπω, (*No.* 5, *with* ἀνά, up, *prefixed*) to look up.
7. ἐμβλέπω, (*No.* 5, *with* ἐν, in, *prefixed*) to look in *or* into, fix the eyes upon, regard intently.
8. ὁράω, to perceive with the eyes, see something, used of bodily sight; *never used without a reference in thought to the object which is looked at. Differing from No.* 5 *in the same way as No.* 1 *does; and differing from No.* 1 *in that* it refers in thought to the object, while *No.* 1 refers to *the subject.* (*No.* 8 *may be the act of an instant, thus differing from Nos.* 12 *and* 13.)

   (a) ὄψομαι, (*used as the future and passive*) *is referred to the object presented to the eye, and to the subject which perceives at the same time. It denotes, not the action of seeing,* (*like Nos.* 5 *and* 8) *but* the state of him, and the affection of the mind of him to whose eye or mind the object is presented, to truly comprehend and know.

9. ἀφοράω, (*No.* 8, *with* ἀπό, away from, *prefixed*) to look away from one thing so as to see another, to look off from one thing unto another, (*occ.* Heb. xii. 2.)
10. ὀπτάνω, (*a rare form of the present, formed from* ὄψομαι, *which is used as the future of No.* 8) *see No.* 8a, (*non occ.*)
11. θεωρέω, to be a spectator of, to view with attention, (*denoting* the intention of mind with which one regards or contemplates an object) to studiously and attentively

consider. θεωρέω *is used of bodily sight, and assumes that the object is actually present. It is used moreover of* a continued and lengthened looking, (*while No.* 8 *may be the act of an instant.*)

12. θεάομαι, (*in meaning, like No.* 11, *but differing from it, in that No.* 11 *refers to* the object beheld, *while No.* 12 *refers to* the subject, the person beholding) to gaze upon, look at with a purpose, regard; to see with desire, regard, *or* admiration.

13. ἱστορέω, to inquire into *or* about, to learn *or* know by inquiry, to ascertain by personal examination; *hence*, to see *or* visit *a person* in order to make his acquaintance, (*non occ.*)

1. Matt. ii. 2, 9, 10 part.
1. —— (εὑρίσκω, *to find*, St E.)
1. —— 16 part.
1. —— iii. 7 part., 16.
1. —— iv. 16, 18, 21.
1. —— v. 1.
8a. —— 8.
1. —— 16.
— —— vi. 1, see Seen (be)
5. —— 4.
— —— 5, see Seen (be)
5. —— 6, 18.
— —— vii. 5, see S clearly
8. —— viii. 4.
1. —— 14, 18 part.
1. —— 34 part.
1. —— ix. 2, 8 part., 9, 11 part., 22 part., 23.
8. —— 30.
— —— 33, see Seen (be)
1. —— 36 part.
5. —— xi. 4.
12. —— 7.
1. —— 8, 9.
1. —— xii. 2 part.
5. —— 22.
1. —— 38.
5. —— xiii. 13 twice, 14 twice
1. —— 15.
5. —— 16.
1. —— 17 1st.
5. —— 17 2nd.
1. —— 17 3rd.
1. —— xiv. 14, 26 twice.
5. —— 30 part.
5. —— xv. 31 1st part., 31 2nd.
1. —— xvi. 28.
1. —— xvii. 8.
1. —— xviii. 31 part.
1. —— xx. 3.
1. —— xxi. 15 part., 19 part., 20 part., 32 part., 38 part.
12. —— xxii. 11 1st.
1. —— 11 2nd.
— —— xxiii. 5, see Seen (be)
1. —— 39.
5. —— xxiv. 2.
8. —— 6.
1. —— 15.

8a. Matt. xxiv. 30.
1. —— 33.
1. —— xxv. 37, 38, 39, 44.
1. —— xxvi. 8 part., 58.
8a. —— 64.
1. —— 71.
1. —— xxvii. 3 part.
— —— 4, see S to.
1. —— 24 part., 49, 54.
11. —— xxviii. 1.
1. —— 6.
8a. —— 7, 10.
1. —— 17 part.
1. Mark i. 10, 16, 19.
8. —— 44.
1. —— ii. 5 part., 12, 14, 16 part.
11. —— iii. 11.
5. —— iv. 12.
1. —— v. 6 part., 14.
11. —— 15.
1. —— 16, 22 part.
5. —— 31.
1. —— 32.
11. —— 38.
1. —— vi. 33, 34, 38, 48, 49 part., 50.
1. —— vii. 2.
5. —— viii. 18, 23, 24.
7. —— 25.
1. —— ix. 1, 8, 9, 14, 20 part., 25 part., 38
1. —— x. 14 part.
1. —— xi. 13, 20.
1. —— xii. 15, 34 part.
3. —— xiii. 1.
5. —— 2.
1. —— 14.
8a. —— 26.
1. —— 29.
8a. —— xiv. 62.
1. —— 67 part., 69.
1. —— xv. 32, 36, 39 part.
11. —— xvi. 4.
1. —— 5.
8a. —— 7.
— —— 11, see Seen (be)
12. —— 14.
1. Luke i. 12 part.
8. —— 22.
1. —— 29 part. (*om.* ἰδοῦσα, *when she saw him*, G T Tr A ℵ.)

1. Luke ii. 15, 17 part., 20, 26 twice, 30, 48 part.
8a. —— iii. 6.
1. —— v. 2, 8 twice, 12, 20 part., 26.
12. —— 27 (No. 1, Lm.)
— —— vi. 42, see S clearly.
1. —— vii. 13 part., 22 1st.
6. —— 22 2nd.
12. —— 24.
1. —— 25, 26, 39 part.
5. —— 44.
5. —— viii. 10 twice, 16.
1. —— 20, 28 part., 34 part., 35, 36, 47 part.
1. —— ix. 9, 27, 32.
8. —— 36.
1. —— 49, 54 part.
5. —— x. 23 twice.
1. —— 24 1st.
5. —— 24 2nd.
1. —— 24 3rd, 31 part., 33 part.
5. —— xi. 33.
1. —— 38 part.
1. —— xii. 54.
1. —— xiii. 12 part., 35.
8a. —— 28.
1. —— xiv. 18.
1. —— xv. 20.
8. —— xvi. 23.
1. —— xvii. 14 part., 15 part., 22 1st.
8a. —— 22 2nd.
1. —— 23 twice.
1. —— xviii. 15 part., 24 part., 43 part.
1. —— xix. 3, 4.
1. —— 5 (*om*, εἰδόν αὐτόν, καὶ, *looked up and saw him and*, T Tr Ab ℵ.)
1. —— 7 part., 37.
1. —— xx. 13 part. (*om.* ἰδοντες, *when they see him*, G ⇉ L T Tr Ab ℵ.)
1. —— 14 part.
1. —— xxi. 1, 2, 20.
8a. —— 27.
5. —— 30.
1. —— 31.
1. —— xxii. 49 part., 58.
1. —— xxiii. 8 1st part., 8 2nd & 3rd, 47 part.
8. —— xxiv. 23.
1. —— 24.
— —— 31, see Cease.
11. —— 37.
1. —— 39 1st.
11. —— 39 2nd.
8. John i. 18.
5. —— 29.
12. —— 32.
1. —— 33.
8. —— 34.
12. —— 38.
1. —— 39 1st (No. 8, G ∾ T Tr A.)
1. —— 39 2nd, 46, 47, 48, 50 1st.
8a. —— 50 2nd, 51.
11. —— ii. 23 part.
1. —— iii. 3.
8. —— 11, 32.
8a. —— 36.
1. —— iv. 29.
8. —— 45.
1. —— 48.
1. —— v. 6 part.
5. —— 19.
8. —— 37.
8. —— vi. 2 (No. 11, L Tr A.)
12. —— 5.
1. —— 14 part.
11. —— 19.

1. John vi. 22 part., 24, 26, 30.
8. —— 36.
11. —— 40.
8. —— 46 twice.
11. —— 62.
11. —— vii. 3.
12. —— viii. 10 (*ap.*)
8. —— 38 1st.
8. —— 38 2nd (ἠκούσατε παρὰ, *heard from*, instead of ἑωράκατε παρὰ, *seen with*, G ∾ L T Tr A.)
11. —— 51.
1. —— 56 twice.
8. —— 57.
1. —— ix. 1.
5. —— 7.
11. —— 8.
5. —— 15, 19, 21, 25.
8. —— 37.
5. —— 39 twice, 41.
11. —— x. 12.
5. —— xi. 9.
1. —— 31 part., 32, 33, 34.
8a. —— 40.
12. —— 45.
1. —— xii. 9, 21, 40, 41.
11. —— 45 twice.
8. —— xiv. 7, 9 twice.
11. —— 17, 19.
8. —— xv. 24.
11. —— xvi. 10, 16 1st.
8a. —— 16 2nd.
11. —— 17 1st.
8a. —— 17 2nd.
11. —— 19 1st.
8a. —— 19 2nd, 22.
1. —— xviii. 26.
1. —— xix. 6, 26 part., 33.
8. —— 35.
5. —— xx. 1, 5.
11. —— 6.
1. —— 8.
11. —— 12, 14.
8. —— 18.
1. —— 20 part.
8. —— 25 1st.
1. —— 25 2nd.
8. —— 29 1st.
1. —— 29 2nd.
5. —— xxi. 9 (No. 1, Lm.)
5. —— 20.
1. —— 21.
10. Acts i. 3.
12. —— 11.
8a. —— ii. 17.
1. —— 27.
— —— 31 1st, see S before.
1. —— 31 2nd.
5. —— 33.
1. —— iii. 3.
11. —— 6.
1. —— 9, 12 part.
11. —— iv. 13 part.
1. —— 20.
1. —— vi. 15.
1. —— vii. 24, 31 part., 34 twice, 35.
8. —— 44.
11. —— 56.
5. —— viii. 6.
12. —— 18 part. (No. 1, G L T Tr A ℵ.)
2. —— 36.
1. —— 39.
11. —— ix. 7.
5. —— 8.
1. —— 12, 27, 35, 40 part.
1. —— x. 3.
11. —— 11.
1. —— 17.
1. —— xi. 5, 6, 13, 23 part.

1. Acts xii. 3 part.
5. ——— 9.
1. ——— 16.
5. —— xiii. 11.
1. ——— 12 part.
8a.——— 31.
1. ——— 35, 36, 37, 45 part.
1. —— xiv. 11.
1. —— xvi. 10, 19 part., 27, 40 part.
11.—— xvii. 6 part.
1. —— xix. 21.
11.——— 26.
8a.—— xx. 25.
11.——— 38.
11.—— xxi. 20.
12.——— 27 part.
— ——— 29, see S before.
1. ——— 32 part.
12.—— xxii. 9.
— ——— 11, see S before.
1. ——— 14.
8. ——— 15.
1. ——— 18.
11.—— xxv. 24.
1. —— xxvi. 13, 16.
1. —— xxviii. 4.
11.——— 6.
1. ——— 15 part., 20.
5. ——— 26 twice.
1. ——— 27.
1. Rom. i. 11.
— ——— 20, see S (clearly)
5. —— vii. 23.
5. —— viii. 24 twice, 25.
5. —— xi. 8 inf., 10.
8a.—— xv. 21.
12.——— 24.
5. 1 Cor. i. 26.
1. —— ii. 9.
1. —— viii. 10.
8. —— ix. 1.
5. —— xiii. 12.
8a.—— xv. 5, 6, 7, 8.
5. —— xvi. 10.
1. ——— 7.
5. 2 Cor. iv. 18 4 times.
5. ——— xii. 6.
13. Gal. i. 18.
1. ——— 19.
1. —— ii. 7 part., 14.
1. —— vi. 11.
— Eph. iii. 9, see S (make)
5. —— v. 15.
1. Phil. i. 27, 30.
9. —— ii. 23.
1. ——— 28 part.
1. —— iv. 9.
8. Col. ii. 1, 18.
1. 1 Thes. ii. 17.
1. —— iii. 6, 10.
8. —— v. 15.
8. 2 Thes. iii. 16.
8a. 1 Tim. iii. 16.
1. —— vi. 16 twice.
1. 2 Tim. i. 4.
8. Heb. ii. 8.
5. ——— 9.
1. —— iii. 9.
5. ——— 10.
8. —— viii. 5.
5. —— x. 25.
5. —— xi. 1, 3.
1. ——— 5.
5. Heb. xi. 7.
1. ——— 13, 23.
8. ——— 27.
8a.—— xii. 14.
5. ——— 25.
8a.—— xiii. 23.
5. Jas. ii. 22.
8. ——— 24.
1. —— v. 11.
4. 1 Pet. i. 8 1st (No. 1, L T Tr A ℵ.)
8. ——— 8 2nd part.
1. —— iii. 10.
— 2 Pet. i. 9, see S afar off (that cannot)
8. 1 John i. 1, 2, 3.
8a.—— iii. 2.
8. ——— 6.
11.——— 17.
12.—— iv. 12, 14.
8. ——— 20 twice.
1. —— v. 16.
8. 3 John 11.
1. ——— 14.
1. Rev. i. 2.
8a.——— 7.
5. ——— 11.
5. ——— 12 1st.
1. ——— 12 2nd, 17, 19, 21 1st.
1. ——— 20 2nd, (*om.* ἃς εἶδες, *which thou sawest*, G L T Tr A ℵ.)
5. —— iii. 18.
1. —— iv. 4 (*om.* εἶδον, *I saw*, G L T Tr A ℵ.)
1. —— v. 1, 2.
1. —— vi. 1 1st.
5. ——— 1 2nd (No. 3, G ℵ), (*om.* G→L T Tr A.)
1. ——— 2 (*om.* καὶ εἶδον, *and I saw*, G ⇉)
5. ——— 3 (No. 3, ℵ), (*om.* G L T Tr A.)
5. ——— 5 (No. 3, G ℵ), (*om.* L T Tr A.)
5. ——— 7 (No. 3, G ℵ), (*om.* G → L T Tr A.)
1. ——— 9.
1. —— vii. 1, 2.
1. —— viii. 2.
1. —— ix. 1, 17.
5. ——— 20.
1. —— x. 1, 5.
5. —— xi. 9.
11.——— 11.
8. ——— 19.
1. —— xii. 13.
1. —— xiii. 1, 2.
1. ——— 3 (*om.* G L T Tr A ℵ.)
1. —— xiv. 6.
1. —— xv. 1, 2.
1. —— xvi. 13.
5. ——— 15.
1. —— xvii. 3, 6 1st, 6 2nd part., 8, 12, 15, 16, 18.
1. —— xviii. 1, 7.
5. ——— 9.
8. ——— 18 part. (No. 5, G L T Tr A ℵ.)
8. —— xix. 10.
1. ——— 11, 17, 19.
1. —— xx. 1, 4, 11, 12.
1. —— xxi. 1, 2, 22.
8a.—— xxii. 4.
5. ——— 8 1st, 8 2nd.
8. ——— 9.

SEE BEFORE.

1. προεῖδον, (*No.* 1, *with* πρό, before, *prefixed*), (*occ.* Gal. iii. 8.)
2. προοράω, (*No.* 8, *with* πρό, before, *prefixed*), (*occ.* Acts ii. 25.)

1. Acts ii. 31. | 2. Acts xxi. 29.

SEE (CAN)

7. Acts xxii. 11.

SEE FAR OFF (CAN NOT)

μυωπάζω, to shut the eyes, *i.e.* to contract the eyelids, *like one who cannot see clearly; hence*, to be near-sighted, (*non occ.*)

2 Pet. i. 9.

SEE CLEARLY.

1. διαβλέπω, (*No.* 5, *with* διά, through *or* throughout, *prefixed*), (*non occ.*)
2. καθοράω, (*No.* 8, *with* κατά, down, *prefixed*) to look down upon, (lxx. ראה, Num. xxiv. 2) to perceive clearly, (*non occ.*)

Matt. vii. 5. | Luke vi. 42.

SEE (MAKE)

φωτίζω, to light, lighten; *intrans.*, to give light, shine; *trans.*, to give light to, shine upon, enlighten.

Eph. iii. 9.

SEE TO.

8. Matt. xxvii. 4, 24.

SEEN (BE)

1. θεάομαι, *see above*, *No.* 12.
2. φαίνω, to shine.

1. Matt. vi. 1. | 2. Matt. ix. 33.
2. ——— 5. | 1. —— xxiii. 5.
1. Mark xvi. 11 (*ap.*)

SEED (-S.)

1. σπέρμα, that which is sown, the seed *or* germ *of anything; then*, children, offspring, posterity; *also*, a remnant, a few survivors, *like seed kept over from a former year*.

* Rom. ix. 29 is quoted from Is. i. 9, where lxx. for שריד, (*occ.* Matt. xxii. 25.)

2. σπόρος, a sowing, seed-time; seed, produce, (lxx. for חריש, Ex. xxxiv. 21; זרע, Deut. xi. 10), (*occ.* 2 Cor. ix. 10.)

3. *σπορά*, a sowing, a begetting of children; the seed sown, (lxx. for זרע, 2 Kings xix. 29), (*non occ.*)

— Matt. xiii. 19, 20, 22, 23, see S (receive)
1. —— 24, 27.
— —— 31, see Mustard.
1. —— 32, 37, 38.
— —— xvii. 20, see Mustard.
1. —— xxii. 24.
2. Mark iv. 26, 27.
— —— 31 1st, see Mustard.
1. —— 31 2nd.
1. —— xii. 19, 20, 21, 22.
1. Luke i. 55.
2. —— viii. 5, 11.
— —— xiii. 19, } see Mustard.
— —— xvii. 6, }
1. —— xx. 28.
1. John vii. 42.
1. —— viii. 33, 37.
1. Acts iii. 25.
1. —— vii. 5, 6
1. —— xiii. 23.
1. Rom. i. 3.
1. —— iv. 13, 16, 18.
1. —— ix. 7 twice, 8.
1* —— 29.
1. —— xi. 1.
1. 1 Cor. xv. 38.
1. 2 Cor. ix. 10 1st (No. 2, L)
— —— 10 2nd, see S sown.
1. —— xi. 22.
1. Gal. iii. 16 3 times, 19, 29.
1. 2 Tim. ii. 8.
1. Heb. ii. 16.
1. —— xi. 11, 18.
3. 1 Pet. i. 23.
1. 1 John iii. 9.
1. Rev. xii. 17.

SEED (RECEIVE)

σπείρω, to sow, to scatter seed, (lxx. *gen.* for זרע); *here, pass.*

Matt. xiii. 19, 20, 22, 23.

SEED SOWN.

2. 2 Cor. ix. 10.

SEEING. [noun.]

βλεμμα, seeing, the act of seeing, (*noun, from* "SEE," *No.* 5), (*non occ.*)

2 Pet. ii. 8.

SEEING. [conj.]

1. *ἐπεί*, as; *of time*, as, when, after that, (lxx. *for* אחרי, Gen. xlvi. 30; Josh. vii. 8); *of ground or motive*, as, since, because, inasmuch as.

2. *ἐπειδή*, (*No.* 1, *with* *δή*, indeed, truly, *suffixed*) as indeed, since, truly.

3. *ἐπείπερ*, (*No.* 1, *with* *περ* (*from* *περί*, *adv.*, very) very, wholly, ever, *adding increased strength and emphasis* to *No.* 1) since indeed, (*more emphatic than No.* 1), (*non occ.*)

4. { *εἰ*, if, *περ*, very, wholly, ever, } if at least. [Here looking back in thought to verse 5, and putting the case that the thing is. (*εἴγε* would have put the possibility that it was not.)]

5. *γάρ*, truly then, (*for* *γε ἄρα*) verily then; *hence*, in fact, *and when the fact is given as a reason or explanation*, for.

1. Luke i. 34.
5. Acts ii. 15.
2. —— xiii. 46.
3. Rom. iii. 30.
2. 1 Cor. xiv. 16.
— 2 Cor. xi. 18, see S that.
— 2 Cor. xi. 19, see S...are.
4. 2 Thes. i. 6.
1. Heb. iv. 6.
1. —— v. 11.
— —— viii. 4, see S that there are.

SEEING THAT.

1. 2 Cor. xi. 18.

SEEING THAT THERE ARE.

ὤν, οὖσα ὄν, (*part of* *εἰμί*, to be) there being.

Heb. viii. 4 (om. *τῶν ἱερέων*, *priests*, after *ὄντων*, G⇉L T Tr A ℵ.)

SEEING...ARE

ὤν, οὖσα ὄν, (*see above*) being.

2 Cor. xi. 19.

SEEK (-EST; -ETH, -ING; SOUGHT.)

1. *ζητέω*, to seek, seek after, look for, strive to find, (lxx. *for* בקש, Gen. xxxvii. 15; Ex. xxiii. 7; 1 Sam. x. 2, 14; Deut. xiii. 10; 1 Sam. xix. 10; שאל, Is. lxv. 1, quoted in Acts xvii. 27 and Rom. x. 20) to seek, *in the sense of* to endeavour, to try.

2. *ἀναζητέω*, (*No.* 1, *with* *ἀνά*, up, upward, back again, *prefixed*) to seek diligently, look back for, seek again for, (lxx. *for* דרש, Job iii. 4; בקש, Job x. 6), (*non occ.*)

1. Matt. ii. 13, 20.
— —— vi. 32, see S after.
1. —— 33.
1. —— vii. 7, 8.
— —— xii. 39, see S after.
1. —— 43.
1. —— xiii. 45.
— —— xvi. 4, see S after.
1. —— xviii. 12.
1. —— xxi. 46 part.
1. —— xxvi. 16, 59.
1. —— xxviii. 5.
— Mark i. 37, } see S for.
— —— iii. 32, }
1. —— viii. 11.
— —— 12, see S after.
1. —— xi. 18.
1. —— xii. 12.
1. —— xiv. 1, 11.
— —— 55, see S for.
1. —— xvi. 6.
2. Luke ii. 44.
1. —— 45 (No. 2, G⇉L T Tr A.)
1. —— 48, 49
1. Luke iv. 42 (*ἐπιζητέω*, see "S AFTER," No. 2, G L T Tr A ℵ.)
— —— v. 18, see S means.
1. —— vi. 19.
1. —— xi. 9, 10, 16, 24.
1. —— 54 (*om.* *καὶ ζητοῦντες*, *and seeking*, G⇉L T Tr[b] A ℵ.)
1. —— xii. 29.
— —— 30, see S after.
1. —— 31.
1. —— xiii. 6, 7, 24.
1. —— xv. 8.
1. —— xvii. 33.
1. —— xix. 3, 10, 47.
1. —— xx. 19.
1. —— xxii. 2, 6.
1. —— xxiv. 5.
1. John i. 38.
1. —— iv. 23, 27.
1. —— v. 16 (*ap.*), 18, 30, 44.
— —— vi. 24, see S for.
1. —— 26.

1. John vii. 1, 4, 11, 18 twice, 25, 30, 34, 36.
1. —— viii. 21, 37, 40, 50 twice.
1. —— x. 39.
1. —— xi. 8, 56.
1. —— xiii. 33.
1. —— xviii. 4, 7, 8.
1. —— xix. 12.
1. —— xx. 15.
1. Acts x. 19, 21.
2. —— xi. 25.
— —— xii. 19, see S for.
1. —— xiii. 8, 11.
— —— xv. 17, see S after.
1. —— xvii. 5, 27.
— Rom. ii. 7, see S for.
— —— iii. 11, see S after.
1. —— x. 20.
1. —— xi. 3.
— —— 7, see S for.
— 1 Cor. i. 22, see S after.
1. —— vii. 27 twice.
1. —— x. 24, 33.
1. —— xiii. 5.
1. —— xiv. 12.
1. 2 Cor. xii. 14
1. —— xiii. 3.
1. Gal. i. 10.
1. —— ii. 17 part
1. Phil. ii. 21.
1. Col. iii. 1.
1. 1 Thes. ii. 6
1. 2 Tim. i. 17.
— Heb. viii. 7, see S for.
— —— xi. 6, see S diligently.
— —— xii. 17, see S carefully.
1. 1 Pet. iii. 11.
1. —— v. 8.
1. Rev. ix. 6.

SEEK AFTER.

1. ζητέω, *see above*, *No.* 1.

2. ἐπιζητέω, (*No.* 1, *with* ἐπί, upon, *prefixed*) to seek upon *or* for, *i.e.* to seek earnestly *or* continuedly.

3. ἐκζητέω, (*No.* 1, *with* ἐκ, out of, *prefixed*) to seek out of, seek out, search out, (lxx. *for* דרש, Ez. xxxiv. 11; בקר, Ez. xxxiv. 12.

2. Matt. vi. 32.
2. —— xii. 39.
2. —— xvi. 4. [Tr A ℵ.)
2. Mark viii. 12 (No. 1, LT
2. Luke xii. 30.
3. Acts xv. 17.
3. Rom. iii. 11.
1. 1 Cor. i. 22.

SEEK CAREFULLY.

3. Heb. xii. 17.

SEEK DILIGENTLY.

3. Heb. xi. 6.

SEEK FOR.

1. ζητέω, *see above*, *No.* 1.

2. ἐπιζητέω, *see above*, *No.* 2.

1. Mark i. 37.
1. —— iii. 32.
1. —— xiv. 55.
1. John vi. 24.
2. Acts xii. 19 part.
1. Rom. ii. 7.
2. —— xi. 7.
1. Heb. viii. 7.

SEEK MEANS.

1. Luke v. 18.

SEEM (-ED, -ETH.)

1. δοκέω, to seem, to have the appearance; *hence*, to be of opinion, to hold for, suppose, (lxx. *for* חשב, Gen. xxxviii. 15.)

2. φαίνω, to shine; *hence*, to appear, appear in the eyes of any one.

— Matt. xi. 26, } see S
— Luke i. 3, } good (it)
1. —— viii. 18, marg. *think.*
— —— x. 21, see S good (it)
2. —— xxiv. 11.
— Acts xv. 25, 28, see S good (it)
1. Acts xvii. 18.
1. 1 Cor. iii. 18.
1. —— xi. 16.
1. —— xii. 22.
1. 2 Cor. x. 9.
1. Gal. ii. 6 twice, 9.
1. Heb. iv. 1.
1. —— xii. 11.
1. Jas. i. 26.

SEEM (-ED, -ETH) GOOD (IT)

1. δοκεῖ, (*3rd pers. sing. of No.* 1, *impers.*)

2. { ἐγένετο, it became,
εὐδοκία, the deeming good, good pleasure, gracious purpose. }

2. Matt. xi. 26.
1. Luke i. 3.
2. Luke x. 21.
1. Acts xv. 25, 28.

SEEMLY. [margin.]

Jas. ii. 3, see "GOOD PLACE (IN A)"

SEIZE ON.

κατέχω, to have and hold down fast, hold firmly; *hence*, retain, detain.

Matt. xxi. 38 (ἔχω, *to have*, G∾L T Tr A ℵ.)

SELF (OF ONE'S)

αὐτόματος, (αὐτός, self, *and* μέμαα, to strive for, *from obs.* μάω) existing *or* acting of one's self, spontaneous, (lxx. *for* ספיח, Lev. xxv. 5, 11), (*occ.* Acts xii. 10.)

Mark iv. 28.

See also, HIS, MY, IT, etc.

SELFSAME.

ἐκεῖνος, that, that one there, that same, that very.

Matt. viii. 13.

SELFSAME (THE)

{ ὁ, the,
αὐτός, same, self, selfsame }

1 Cor. xii. 11.

SELFSAME THING (FOR THE)

{ αὐτὸ, same thing,
τοῦτο, this, } this very thing.

2 Cor. vii. 11.

SELFSAME THING (FOR THIS)

{ *εἰς*, unto, with a view to,
{ *αὐτὸ*, selfsame thing,
{ *τοῦτο*, this.

2 Cor. v. 5.

SELFWILLED.

αὐθάδης, (*αὐτός*, self, *and ἥδομαι*, to satisfy) self-complacent; *and hence*, assuming, presumptuous, self-willed, (lxx. *for* עז, Gen. xlix. 3, 7; יהיר, Prov. xxi. 24.)

Tit. i. 7. | 2 Pet. ii. 10.

SELL (-ETH, SOLD.)

1. *πωλέω*, to trade away *wares*, to barter; *hence*, to sell, (lxx. *for* מכר, Neh. v. 8; Joel iii. 3; Ez. vii. 3.)

2. *πιπράσκω*, to traffick away *beyond the seas in other lands; hence*, to sell. *Pass.*, to be sold, *esp. for exportation; hence*, to be sold into slavery, (lxx. *for* מכר, Gen. xxxi. 15; Lev. xxvii. 27), (*non occ.*)

3. *ἀποδίδωμι*, to give away from *one's self*, deliver over, give up. *Mid.*, *as here*, to deliver over for one's self, *i.e.* to dispose of, *as by sale*, to sell, (lxx. *for* חשביר, Deut. ii. 8; מכר, Gen. xxv. 33; xxxvii. 27, 35; Amos ii. 6.)

1. Matt. x. 29.
1. —— xiii. 44.
2. ——— 46.
2. —— xviii. 25.
1. —— xix. 21.
1. —— xxi. 12 twice.
1. —— xxv. 9.
2. —— xxvi. 9
1. Mark x. 21.
1. —— xi. 15 twice.
2. —— xiv. 5.
1. Luke xii. 6, 33.
1. —— xvii. 28.
1. —— xviii. 22.
1. —— xix. 45.
1. —— xxii. 36.
1. John ii. 14, 16.
— —— iv. 13, see Buy.
2. —— xii. 5.
2. Acts ii. 45.
1. —— iv. 34 1st.
2. ——— 34 2nd.
1. ——— 37.
1. —— v. 1.
2. ——— 4 part.
3. ——— 8.
3. —— vii. 9.
2. Rom. vii. 14.
— 1 Cor. x. 25, see S (whatsoever is)
3. Heb. xii. 16.
1. Rev. xiii. 17.

SOLD (WHATSOEVER IS)

1. 1 Cor. x. 25, pass. part., with art.

SELLER.

See, PURPLE.

SELVES.

See, OUR, YOUR, THEIR, THEM, etc.

SENATE.

γερουσία, a council of elders, (lxx. for זקנים, Ex. iii. 16, 18; Deut. xxvii. 1; xix. 12.)

Acts v. 21.

SEND (-ETH, SENT.)

1. *ἀποστέλλω*, to send away, send off, send forth, equip and despatch upon a certain mission, commission. *When any one is thus sent it implies the mission which he has to fulfil, and the authority which backs him.* (*Hence the noun, ἀπόστολος*, Apostle, one sent.)

2. *ἐξαποστέλλω*, (*No.* 1, *with ἐκ*, out of, *prefixed*) to send away out of *the place where one is, implying the same mission and authority as No.* 1.

3. *πέμπω*, to send, *simply* let go, *as well of persons or things;* to send forth *or* away, *esp.* to send home; to send *or* transmit, *as presents.* (*No.* 3 *lacks the importance of mission and authority which is found in No.* 1), (*occ.* Rev. xiv. 15, 18.)

4. *ἀναπέμπω*, (*No.* 3, *with ἀνά*, up *or* back, *prefixed*) to send up, as before a judge or tribunal; to send back, remit; to send again, (*occ.* Luke xxiii. 11; Philem. 12.)

5. *βάλλω*, to throw, to cast, *with a greater or less degree of force, as required by the context.*

3. Matt. ii. 8.
— ——— 16, see S forth.
— —— v. 45, see Rain.
— —— ix. 38, } see S
— —— x. 5, 16, } forth.
5. ——— 34 twice.
1. ——— 40.
3. —— xi. 2.
1. ——— 10.
— —— xii. 20, see S forth.
— —— xiii. 36, see S away.
— ——— 41, see S forth.
3. —— xiv. 10.
3. ——— 15, 22, 23, see S away.
— ——— 35, see S out.
— —— xv. 23, see S away.
1. ——— 24.
— ——— 32, 39, see S away.
1. —— xx. 2.
1. —— xxi. 1, 3, 34, 36, 37.
— —— xxii. 3, 4, see S forth.
3. ——— 7.
— ——— 16, see S out.
1. —— xxiii. 34, 37.
1. —— xxiv. 31.
1. —— xxvii. 19.
1. Mark i. 2.
— ——— 43, see S away.
— —— iii. 14, see S forth.
1. ——— 31.
— —— iv. 36, see S away.
1. —— v. 10.
3. ——— 12.
— —— vi. 7, 17, see S forth.
1. ——— 27.
— ——— 36, 45, 46, see S away.
3. —— viii. 3, 9, } see S
— ——— 26, } away.
1. —— ix. 37.
— —— xi. 1, see S forth.
1. ——— 3.
1. —— xii. 2.
— ——— 3, see S away.
1. ——— 4, 5, 6, 13.
1. —— xiii. 27.
— —— xiv. 13, see S forth.
1. Luke i. 19, 26.
— ——— 53, see S away.
1. —— iv. 18.
3. ——— 26.
1. ——— 43.
1. —— vii. 3.
3. ——— 6, 10, 19.

1. Luke vii. 20, 27.
— —— viii. 38, see S away.
1. —— ix. 2.
— —— 12, see S away.
1. —— 48, 52.
1. —— x. 1.
— —— 2, 3, see S forth.
1. —— 16.
1. —— xi. 49.
5. —— xii. 49.
1. —— xiii. 34.
1. —— xiv. 17, 32.
3. —— xv. 15.
3. —— xvi. 24, 27.
1. —— xix. 14, 29, 32.
1. —— xx. 10 1st
— —— 10 2nd, see S away.
3. —— 11 1st.
— —— 11 2nd, see S away.
3. —— 12, 13.
— —— 20, see S forth.
1. —— xxii. 8, 35.
4. —— xxiii. 7.
— —— 11, see S again.
4. —— 15.
1. —— xxiv. 49 (No 2, T Tr A.)
1. John i. 6, 19, 24.
3. —— 22, 33.
1. —— iii. 17, 28, 34.
3. —— iv. 34.
1. —— 38.
3. —— v. 23, 24, 30.
1. —— 33, 36.
3. —— 37.
1. —— 38.
1. —— vi. 29.
3. —— 38, 39.
3. —— 40 part. (τοῦ πατρός μου, *my father*, instead of τοῦ πέμψαντος με, *him that sent me*, G ~ L T Tr A ℵ.)
3. —— 44.
1. —— 57.
3. —— vii. 16, 18, 28.
1. —— 29, 32.
3. —— 33.
3. —— viii. 16, 18, 26, 29.
1. —— 42.
3. —— ix. 4.
1. —— 7.
1. —— x. 36.
1. —— xi. 3, 42.
3. —— xii. 44, 45, 49.
— —— xiii. 16 1st, see S (he that is)
3. —— 16 2nd, 20 twice.
3. —— xiv. 24, 26.
3. —— xv. 21, 26.
3. —— xvi. 5, 7.
1. —— xvii. 3, 8, 18 twice, 21, 23, 35.
1. —— xviii. 24.
1. —— xx. 21 1st.
3. —— 21 2nd.
1. Acts iii. 20, 26.
1. —— v. 21.
1. —— vii. 14, 34, 35.
— —— viii. 12, see S out.
1. —— 14.
1. —— ix. 17.
— Acts ix. 30, see S forth.
1. —— 38.
3. —— x. 5.
1. —— 8, 17, 20, 21 (ap.)
— —— 22, 29 twice, see S for.
3. —— 32, 33.
1. —— 36.
1. —— xi. 11, 13, 20.
— —— 22, see S forth.
3. —— 29.
2. —— xii. 11.
— —— xiii. 3, see S away.
— —— 4, see S forth.
1. —— 15.
1. —— 26 (No. 2, L T ℵ.)
3. —— xv. 22.
— —— 23, see Greeting.
3. —— 25.
1. —— 27.
1. —— xvi. 35, 36.
— —— xvii. 10, 14, see S away.
1. —— xix. 22 part.
3. —— 31.
3. —— xx. 17.
2. —— xxii. 21.
— —— xxiii. 26, see Greeting.
3. —— 30.
— —— xxiv. 24, 26, } see S for.
— —— xxv. 3, }
3. —— 21 (No. 4, L T Tr A ℵ.)
3. —— 25, 27.
1. —— xxvi. 17.
1. —— xxviii. 28.
3. Rom. viii. 3.
1. —— x. 15.
1. 1 Cor. 1, 17.
3. —— iv. 17.
3. —— xvi. 3.
— 2 Cor. viii. 18, 22, see S with.
3. —— ix. 3.
1. —— xii. 17.
— —— 18, see S with.
— Gal. iv. 4, 6, see S forth.
3. Eph. vi. 22.
3. Phil. ii. 19, 23, 25, 28.
3. —— iv. 16.
3. Col. iv. 8.
3. 1 Thes. iii. 2, 5.
3. 2 Thes. ii. 11.
1. 2 Tim. iv. 12.
3. —— iii. 12.
— Philem. 12, see S again.
— Heb. i. 14, see S forth.
— Jas. ii. 25, see S out.
— —— iii. 14, see S forth.
1. 1 Pet. i. 12.
3. —— ii. 14.
1. 1 John iv. 9, 10, 14.
1. Rev. i. 1.
3. —— 11.
— —— v. 6, see S forth.
3. —— xi. 10 (δίδωμι, *give*, G ~)
1. —— xxii. 6.
3. —— 16.

SEND AGAIN.

4. Luke xxiii. 11.
4. Philem. 12 (No. 1, G ~)

SEND AWAY.

1. ἀποστέλλω, *see above*, *No.* 1.
2. ἐξαποστέλλω, *see above*, *No.* 2.
3. ἀπολύω, to loosen from, let loose from, release, let go away.
4. ἀφίημι, to send forth *or* away, let go from *one's self*, dismiss.
5. ἀποτάσσομαι, to arrange one's self off, separate one's self from, *i.e.* take leave off, bid farewell.
6. ἐκβάλλω, to throw out, cast out, drive *or* thrust out of.
7. ἐκπέμπω, ("SEND," *No.* 1, *with* ἐκ, out of, *prefixed*), (*occ.* Acts xiii. 4.)

4. Matt. xiii. 36.
3. —— xiv. 15, 22, 23 part.
3. —— xv. 23, 32, 39.
6. Mark i. 43.
4. —— iv. 36 part.
3. —— vi. 36, 45.
5. —— 46 part.
3. —— viii. 3, 9.
1. —— 26.
1. —— xii. 3 (ἠτίμησαν, *treated him shamefully*, instead of ἀπέστειλαν, ἠτιμωμένον, *sent him away shamefully handled*, L T Tr [A ℵ.)
2. Luke i. 53.
3. —— viii. 38.
3. —— ix. 12.
2. —— xx. 10, 11.
3. Acts xiii. 3.
2. —— xvii. 4.
7. —— 10.

SEND FOR.

μεταπέμπω, ("SEND," *No.* 3, *with* μετά, with *or* after) to send after, send for, (*occ.* Acts. x. 5; xi. 13.)

Acts x. 22, 29 1st part, 29 2nd.
Acts xxiv. 24, 26.
—— xxv. 3.

SEND FORTH.

1. ἀποστέλλω, *see* "SEND," *No.* 1.
2. ἐξαποστέλλω, *see* "SEND," *No.* 2.
3. ἐκβάλλω, *see* "SEND AWAY," *No.* 6.
4. ἐκπέμπω, *see* "SEND AWAY," *No.* 7, (*occ.* Acts xvii. 10.)
5. βρύω, to be full, to overflow; *hence*, to emit largely, pour forth, (*non occ.*)

1. Matt. ii. 16.
3. —— ix. 38.
1. —— x. 5, 16.
3. —— xii. 20.
1. —— xiii. 41.
1. —— xxii. 3, 4.
1. Mark iii. 14.
1. —— vi. 7, 17.
1. —— xi. i.
1. —— xiv. 13.
2. Luke x. 2.
1. —— 3.
1. —— xx. 20.
2. Acts ix. 30.
2. —— xi. 22.
4. —— xiii. 4.
2. Gal. iv. 4, 6.
1. Heb. i. 14.
5. Jas. iii. 14.
1. Rev. v. 6.

SEND OUT.

1. ἀποστέλλω, *see* "SEND," *No.* 1.
2. ἐξαποστέλλω, *see* "SEND," *No.* 2.
3. ἐκβάλλω, *see* "SEND AWAY," *No.* 6.

1. Matt. xiv. 35.
1. —— xxii. 16.
2. Acts vii. 12.
3. Jas. ii. 25.

SEND WITH.

1. συναποστέλλω, "SEND," No. 1, } with σύν, in conjunction with, prefixed.
2. συνπέμπω, "SEND," No. 3, } with σύν, in conjunction with, prefixed.

2. 2 Cor. viii. 18, 22. | 1. 2 Cor. xii. 18.

SENT (HE THAT IS)

ἀπόστολος, one sent forth, (*noun, from* "SEND," *No.* 1), (*see under* "APOSTLE.")

John xiii. 16.

SENSE. [margin.]

Phil. i. 9, see Judgment.

SENSES.

αἰσθητήριον, the seat of the senses; the faculty of perception, (*non occ.*)

Heb. v. 14.

SENSUAL.

ψυχικός, what pertains to the ψυχή, (animal life, *see* "SOUL,") animal, natural, of the nature of ψυχή; *it denotes* man as he is by nature, *i.e.* a stranger to what is of the Spirit; *and hence,* man as a sinner estranged from the divine principle of eternal life.

[In Jas. iii. 15 the three predicates express a logical sequence, ἐπίγειος, (*belonging to the earth*) fit antithesis of ἄνωθεν, (*from above*); but, because ἐπίγειος, therefore ψυχικός, destitute of the Spirit of God, (*see* 1 Cor. xv. 48) and because thus destitute of the Spirit, therefore actually opposed thereto, *i.e.* δαιμονιώδης, (*belonging to demons*).]

Jas. iii. 15, marg. *natural.* | Jude 19.

SENTENCE.

ἀπόκριμα, the judicial sentence, as the result *or* issue of κρίνειν, (*see* "JUDGE," verb, *No.* 1) condemnation, (*non occ.*)

2 Cor. i. 9, marg. *answer.*

SENTENCE (GIVE)

ἐπικρίνω, to judge upon, confirm by a like judgment, give judgment upon, adjudge, (*non occ.*)

Luke xxiii. 24, marg. *assent.*

SENTENCE IS (MY)

{ ἐγώ, I, (*emphatic*)
κρίνω, to judge, (*see* "JUDGE," verb, *No.* 1,) } I judge.

Acts xv. 19.

SEPARATE. [adj.]

χωρίζω, *see below, No.* 2.

Heb. vii. 26, pass. part.

SEPARATE (BE)

ἀφορίζω, *see below, No.* 1.

2 Cor. vi. 17, pass.

SEPARATE (-ED.) [verb.]

1. ἀφορίζω, to set off by bounds, to limit off, (lxx. *for* הִבְדִּיל, Ex. xix. 12, 23; Lev. xx. 25); to set off apart, separate.
2. χωρίζω, to put apart, separate, sunder, (lxx. *for* נִבְדַּל, Neh. ix. 2.)
3. ἀποδιορίζω, to set off by drawing a boundary through, make a complete separation, (*non occ.*)

1. Matt. xxv. 32.
1. Luke vi. 22.
1. Acts xiii. 2.
1. —— xix. 9.
1. Rom. i. 1.
2. Rom. viii. 35, 39.
— —— ix. 3, marg. (*see accursed.*)
1. Gal. i. 15.
1. —— ii. 12.
3. Jude 19.

SEPULCHRE.

1. μνῆμα, a memorial, monument, any object dedicated to preserve the recollection of a deceased person, (lxx. *for* קֶבֶר, Ex. xiv. 11; Ez. xxxvii. 12; קְבוּרָה, Ez. xxxii. 23.)
2. μνημεῖον, anything said, written, or done to preserve the memory of things or persons, an inscription, a monument, memorial, (lxx. *for* קֶבֶר, Gen. xxiii. 6, 9; xlix. 30; קְבוּרָה, Gen. xxxv. 20.)

3. τάφος, burial, sepulchre; *hence*, a burial-place, (lxx. *for* קבר, Gen. xxiii. 4, 20; 2 Sam. ii. 31; Ps. v. 10), (*occ.* Matt. xxiii. 9.)

3. Matt. xxiii. 27.
2. —— 29.
2. —— xxvii. 60.
3. —— 61, 64, 66.
3. —— xxviii. 1.
2. —— 8.
2. Mark xv. 46 twice.
2. —— xvi. 2, 3, 5, 8.
2. Luke xi. 47.
2. —— 48 (*om.* αὐτῶν τὰ μνημεῖα, *their sepulchres*, G⇄L[b] T Tr [A ℵ.)
1. Luke xxiii. 53.
2. —— 55.
1. —— xxiv. 1. [(*ap.*)
2. —— 2, 9, 12, 22, 24
2. John xix. 41, 42.
2. —— xx. 1 twice, 2, 3, 4, 6, 8, 11 twice.
1. Acts ii. 29.
1. —— vii. 16.
2. —— xiii. 29.
3. Rom. iii. 13.

SERJEANT (-s.)

ῥαβδοῦχος, a rod-holder; *i.e.* a lictor, *so called from* bearing the Roman fasces *or* bundle of rods, (*non occ.*)

Acts xvi. 35, 38.

SERPENT.

1. ὄφις, a serpent; lxx. *for* נחש, Gen iii. 15; Ex. iv. 3. *Hence*, symbolically used of the devil. ὄφις *is prob. from* ὄπτομαι, to see, (*as* δράκων, a species of serpent, *is from* δέρκω, to behold; *and the Heb.* נחש, a serpent, *is from* נחש, to eye, view acutely.) ("A serpent's eye" *was a Greek and Roman proverb.*) (*non occ.*)

2. ἑρπετόν, a creeping animal, a reptile; lxx. *for* רמש, Gen. i. 24; vi. 7; שרץ, Gen. i. 20; Lev. xi. 41.

1. Matt. vii. 10.
1. —— x. 16.
1. —— xxiii. 33.
1. Mark xvi. 18 (*ap.*)
1. Luke x. 19.
1. —— xi. 11
1. John iii. 14.
1. 1 Cor. x. 9.
1. 2 Cor. xi. 3.
2. Jas. iii. 7.
1. Rev. xi. 19.
1. —— xii. 9, 14, 15.
1. Rev. xx. 2.

SERVANT (-s.)

1. δοῦλος, a slave, one bound to serve, (*from* δέω, to bind) one whose will and capacities are wholly at the service of another, (*opp.* to ἐλεύθερος, free). δοῦλος *is used of* the lowest scale of servitude, *but when transferred to Christian service* it expresses the highest devotion of one who is bound by love.

(a) *with* Θεοῦ, of God, *or* χριστοῦ, of Christ, etc.

(b) *Adj.*, serving, bound to serve, in bondage.

2. παῖς, a child, *male or female*, a boy or girl, a child in legal relation. *Then, like Eng.*, boy (*Lat.*, puer; *Fr.*, garçon) put for a servant; (lxx. *for* עבד, Gen. ix. 26, 27; xxiv. 2; xxvi. 15, etc. *Also for* minister, Gen. xli. 38; Jer. xxxvi. 24; *and for* the servant of God, Is. xli. 8, 9; xliv. 1, 2; xlv. 4; *and hence of* the Messiah, Matt. xii. 18, *in allusion* to Is. xlii. 1, where lxx. עבד. So, Acts iii. 13, 26; iv. 27, 30; from Is. xlix. 6 l. 10; and lii. 13.)

3. διάκονος, servant, hasty messenger, (*prob. from* διάκω *or* διήκω, to hasten, *whence*, διώκω, to pursue) lxx. *for* משרת, Est. i. 10; ii. 2; vi. 3; a servant, *with special reference to the person whom the service benefits*, (*while in No.* 1 *the reference is to the master's benefit, and in No.* 5 *it is to subservience to another's will.*)

4. οἰκέτης, house-companion, one living in the same house; *hence*, a domestic, household servant; lxx. *for* עבד, Gen. ix. 25; xxvii. 37, (*occ.* Acts x. 7.)

5. ὑπηρέτες, an under-rower, a common sailor, a hand, agent, one who does service under the immediate direction of any one.

6. θεράπων, ministering servant, attendant, guardian, care-taker, (*hence, the verb* θεραπεύω, to cherish, care for, *as applied to the sick, gave rise to the Eng. medical term* "therapeutics.") *It differs from No.* 1, *in that it is always used of* free and honourable service; lxx. *for* עבד, Exod. xiv. 31; Num. xii. 7, 8; Job i. 8; ii. 3, (*non occ.*)

2. Matt. viii. 6, 8.
1. —— 9.
2. —— 13.
1. —— x. 24, 25.
1. —— xii. 18.
1. —— xiii. 27, 28.
2. —— xiv. 2.
1. —— xviii. 23, 26, 27, 28 1st.
— —— 28 2nd, 29, 31, see S (fellow)
1. —— 32.
— Matt. xviii. 33, see S (fellow)
1. —— xx. 27.
1. —— xxi. 34, 35, 36.
1. —— xxii. 3, 4. 6, 8, 10.
3. —— 13.
3. —— xxiii. 11.
1. —— xxiv. 45, 46, 48.
— —— 49, see S (fellow)
1. —— 50.
1. —— xxv. 14, 19, 21, 23, 26, 30.

1. Matt. xxvi. 51.
5. —— 58.
— Mark i. 20, see Hired.
3. —— ix. 35.
1. —— x. 44.
1. —— xii. 2, 4.
1. —— xiii. 34.
1. —— xiv. 47.
5. —— 54, 65.
2. Luke i. 54, 69.
1a. —— ii. 29.
1. —— vii. 2, 3.
2. —— 7.
1. —— 8, 10.
1. —— xii. 37.
1. —— 38 (*om.* οἱ δοῦλοι, *those servants*, G → T Tr^{b}A^{b}ℵ, i.e. "blessed are they.")
1. —— 43, 45 1st.
— —— 45 2nd, see Man-servant.
1. —— 46, 47.
1. —— xiv. 17, 21 twice, 22, 23.
— —— xv. 17, 19, see Hired.
1. —— 22.
2. —— 26.
4. —— xvi. 13.
1. —— xvii. 7, 9, 10.
1. —— xix. 13, 15, 17, 22.
1. —— xx. 10, 11.
1. —— xxii. 50.
3. John ii. 5, 9.
1. —— iv. 51.
1. —— viii. 34, 35.
3. —— xii. 26.
1. —— xiii. 16.
1. —— xv. 15 twice, 20.
1. —— xviii. 10 twice, 18, 26.
5. —— 36.
1a. Acts ii. 18.
2. —— iv. 25.
1a. —— 29.
— —— x. 7, see Household.
1a. —— xvi. 17.
1a. Rom. i. 1.
1. Rom. vi. 16 twice, 17.
— —— 18, see S (become)
1b. —— 19 twice.
1. —— 20.
— —— 22, see S (become)
4. —— xiv. 4.
3. —— xvi. 1.
1. 1 Cor. vii. 21, 22 1st.
1a. —— 22 2nd.
1. —— 23.
— —— ix. 19, see S (make)
1. 2 Cor. iv. 5.
1a. Gal. i. 10.
1. —— iv. 1, 7.
1. Eph. vi. 5.
1a. —— 6.
1a. Phil. i. 1.
1. —— ii. 7.
— Col. i. 7, see S (fellow)
1. —— iii. 22.
1. —— iv. 1.
— —— 7, see S (fellow)
1a. —— 12.
1. 1 Tim. vi. 1.
1a. 2 Tim. ii. 24
1a. Tit. i. 1.
1. —— ii. 9.
1. Philem. 16 twice.
6. Heb. iii. 5.
1a. Jas. i. 1.
1a. 1 Pet. ii. 16.
4. —— 18.
1a. 2 Pet. i. 1.
1. —— ii. 19.
1a. Jude 1.
1a. Rev. i. 1 twice.
1a. —— ii. 20.
— —— vi. 11, see S (fellow)
1a. —— vii. 3.
1a. —— x. 7.
1a. —— xi. 18.
1a. —— xv. 3.
1a. —— xix. 2, 5.
— —— 10, see S (fellow)
1a. —— xxii. 3, 6.
— —— 9, see S (fellow)

SERVANT (BECOME)

δουλόω, to make a slave of, bring into bondage, enslave, (*differing from* δουλεύω, to serve as a slave, *see* "SERVE," *No.* 1.)

(a) *pass.*, to be enslaved, to be *or* become a slave of.

a. Rom. vi. 18, 22.

SERVANT (FELLOW)

συνδουλος, (*No.* 1, *with* σύν, together *or* in conjunction with, *prefixed*) a fellow-slave, (*non occ.*)

Matt. xviii. 28, 29, 31, 33.
—— xxiv. 49.
Col. i. 7.
Col. iv. 7.
Rev. vi. 11.
—— xix. 10.
Rev. xxii. 9.

SERVANT (MAKE)

δουλόω, *see* "SERVANT (BECOME)"

1 Cor. ix. 19.

SERVE (-ED, -ETH, -ING.)

1. δουλεύω, to serve as a slave, to be in the position of a δοῦλος, (*see* "SERVANT," *No.* 1) and to act accordingly, *i.e. both* to be subject, *and* to serve in subjection, *used of actions which are directed by others.*

2. λατρεύω, to serve, *esp. for hire, but also of service with or without pay.* To render service to God, *esp. with reference to sacrifice; hence,* to worship.

3. διακονέω, to serve, render service, wait upon, (*a department of No.* 1) to do any one a service, to help, to minister to any one in anything.

4. ὑπηρετέω, to do the service of an ὑπηρέτης, (*see* "SERVANT," *No.* 5); *hence*, to act in subservience to another's will, to subserve, (*occ.* Acts xx. 34; xxiv. 23.)

2. Matt. iv. 10.
1. —— vi. 24 twice.
2. Luke i. 74.
2. —— ii. 37.
2. —— iv. 8.
3. —— x. 40.
3. —— xii. 37.
1. —— xv. 29.
1. —— xvi. 13 twice.
3. —— xvii. 8.
3. —— xxii. 26, 27 twice.
3. John xii. 2, 26 twice.
3. Acts vi. 2.
2. —— vii. 7.
4. —— xiii. 36 part.
1. —— xx. 19.
2. —— xxvi. 7.
2. —— xxvii. 23.
2. Rom. i. 9, 25.
1. —— vi. 6.
1. —— vii. 6, 25.
1. —— ix. 12.
1. —— xii. 11.
1. —— xiv. 18.
1. —— xvi. 18.
1. Gal. v. 13.
1. Phil. ii. 22.
1. Col. iii. 24.
1. 1 Thes. i. 9.
2. 2 Tim. i. 3.
1. Tit. iii. 3.
2. Heb. viii. 5.
2. —— ix. 14.
2. —— xii. 28.
2. —— xiii. 10.
2. Rev. vii. 15.
2. Rev. xxii. 3.

SERVICE.

1. λατρεία, service, divine service, (*see above, No.* 2); obedience and adoration rendered to God, (lxx. for עבדה, Ex. xii. 25, 26; Josh. xxii. 27), (*occ.* Heb. ix. 1.)

2. διακονία, serviceable labour, service rendered, *esp.* as benefitting others, ministry *in every form.*

3. λειτουργία, public service, *esp.* solemn and stated office and ministry, *as of the Jewish priesthood.*

[*No.* 1 is used of the duties of all men, *No.* 2 of the duties of special

officials on behalf of others. Every *No.* 3 is a *No.* 1, though every *No.* 1 is not a *No.* 3.]

1. John xvi. 2.
1. Rom. ix. 4.
1. —— xii. 1.
2. —— xv. 31. (δωροφορία, *a bringing of presents*, L Tr[m].)
3. 2 Cor. ix. 12.
— Eph. vi. 12, see Eye.
3. Phil. ii. 17, 30.
— Col. iii. 22, see Eye.
2. Rev. ii. 19.

SERVICE (DIVINE)

1. Heb. ix. 1.

SERVICE (DO)

1. δουλεύω, *see* "SERVE," *No.* 1.

2. λατρεύω, *see* "SERVE," *No.* 2.

3. { πρός, towards, διακονία, *see No.* 2, *above*, } with a view to the ministering.

3. 2 Cor. xi. 8.
1. Gal. iv. 8.
1. Eph. vi. 7.
1. 1 Tim. vi. 2.
2. Heb. ix. 9.

SERVING. [noun.]

διακονία, *see* "SERVICE," *No.* 2.

Luke x. 40.

SET (-ETH, -ING.)

(*For various combinations with other words, see below.*)

1. ἵστημι, (a) *trans.*, to cause to stand, to set, to place. (b) *intrans.*, to stand.

2. καθίστημι, (*No.* 1, *with* κατά, down, *prefixed.*) *In N.T. only trans.*, *pass.*, *or mid.*, to set, constitute.

3. τίθημι, to set, to put, to place, to lay.

4. καθίζω, *trans.*, to cause to sit down, to seat; *intrans.*, to sit down, sit, be seated.

5. ἀποστέλλω, to send away, send forth, send off, (*see* "SEND," *No.* 1.)

6. δίδωμι, to give, bestow upon.

7. τάσσω, to rank, to order, set in order, arrange, *esp.* of soldiers in ranks, etc.

8. δύνω, to sink, to go down, (lxx. for בּוֹא, Gen. xxviii. 11; 2 Ch. xviii. 34.)

9. τακτός, (*part. of No.* 7) set in order, arranged, set, fixed, appointed, (lxx. Job xii. 5), (*non occ.*)

1a. Matt. iv. 5.
1a. —— xviii. 2.
1a. —— xxv. 33.
8. Mark i. 32.
1a. —— ix. 36.
1a. Luke iv. 9.
5. —— 18.
7. —— vii. 8.
1a. —— ix. 47.
1a. John viii. 3 part. (*ap.*)
1a. Acts iv. 7 part.
1a. —— v. 27.
1a. —— vi. 6.
9. —— xii. 21.
3. —— xiii. 47.
1a. —— xxii. 30.
4. 1 Cor. vi. 4.
4. Eph. i. 20.
2. Heb. ii. 7 (*ap.*)
6. Rev. iii. 8.
3. Rev. x. 2.

SET ABOUT.

περιτίθημι, (*No.* 3, *with* περί, around, *prefixed*) to put around, place around.

Mark xii. 1.

SET AT ONE AGAIN.

{ συνελαύνω, to drive together, unite, (*here Aor. tense*) εἰς, unto, εἰρήνην, peace, } he united *them* into peace, (*non occ.*)

Acts vii. 26 (συνήλασσεν, imperf. tense, instead of aorist, συνήλασεν) *he was reconciling*, or *attempted to reconcile* them *into peace*, G ∾ L T Tr ℵ.)

SET BEFORE.

παρατίθημι, (*No.* 3, *with* παρά, beside, *prefixed*) to put *or* place near *any one*, to set *or* lay before.

Mark vi. 41.
—— viii. 6 twice, 7.
Luke ix. 16.
—— x. 8, see S before (such things as are)
Luke xi. 6.
Acts xvi. 34.
1 Cor. x. 27.

SET FORTH.

1. τίθημι, to set, to put, to place, to lay.

2. προτίθημι, (*No.* 1, *with* πρό, before, *prefixed.*) *Here*, *mid.*, to set before one's self *or* on one's own part.

3. ἀνάγω, to lead up, conduct *or* bring up, *as from a lower to a higher place. In navigation*, to lead a ship up *or* out upon the sea, to put to sea.

4. **ἀποδείκνυμι**, to point out, show, exhibit.

1. John ii. 10. | 2. Rom. iii. 25, *marg. foreordain.*
3. Acts xxi. 2. | 4. 1 Cor. iv. 9.

SET FORTH EVIDENTLY.

προγράφω, to write before, *in ref. to time past; also, in reference to present or future*, to pourtray.

Gal. iii. 1.

SET ON.

1. **ἐπιβιβάζω**, to cause to mount, *as an animal for riding*, (lxx. for הרכיב, 1 Kings i. 33; 2 Kings ix. 28), (*non occ.*)

2. { **ἐπικαθίζω**, to cause to sit upon, to seat upon, **ἐπάνω**, upon, } *Here*, they set [*him*] upon *them*.

3. **ἐπιτίθημι**, to set, put, place *or* lay upon.

2. Matt. xxi. 7 (*ἐπεκάθισεν, he set upon* them, S[t] G L T Tr A), (*καθίζω*, ℵ.) | 1. Luke x. 34. 1. —— xix. 35. 3. Acts xviii. 10. 1. —— xxiii. 24.

SET ONE'S EYES.

ἀτενίζω, to fix the eyes intently upon, gaze upon intently.

Acts xiii. 9 part.

SET ONE'S FOOT ON.

{ **βῆμα**, a pace, **ποδός**, of a foot, } a foot-breadth, (lxx. for מדרך כף־רגל, Deut. ii. 5.)

Acts vii. 5.

SET STEADFASTLY.

στηρίζω, to set fast *or* steadfast, to fix firmly.

Luke ix. 51.

SET UP.

1. **ἵστημι**, *see* "SET," *No.* 1a.

2. **ἐπιτίθημι**, to set, place, put *or* lay upon.

3. **ἀνορθόω**, to set upright, to erect; to erect again, rebuild: *quoted from* Amos. ix. 11, *where* Heb. בנה, and lxx. *ἀνοικοδομέω*, to rebuild; *in* Acts xv. 16, build again.

2. Matt. xxvii. 37. | 1. Acts vi. 13.
3. Acts xv. 16.

SET (BE)

1. **κεῖμαι**, to lie: to be laid, set, *or* placed.

[(a) Rev. iv. 2 doubtless refers to Dan. vii. 9, *where* Chald. רמה, and lxx. *τίθημι*, (*see* "SET," *No.* 3.) רמה is akin to ירה, *to place*, Job xxxviii. 6, and Gen. xxxi. 51.]

2. **καθιζω**, *trans.*, to cause to sit down, to seat; *intrans.*, to seat one's self, to sit down.

2. Matt. v. 1 part. | 1. John xix. 29.
1. —— 14. | 1. Phil. i. 17.
1. Luke ii. 34. | 2. Heb. viii. 1.
1. John ii. 6. | 1a. Rev. iv. 2.

SET BEFORE (BE)

πρόκειμαι, (*No.* 1, *above, with πρό*, before, *prefixed*) to lie before, to be laid *or* set forth *or* before any one.

Heb. vi. 18. | Heb. xii. 1, 2.

SET DOWN (BE)

1. **ἀνάκειμαι**, (*No.* 1, *above, with ἀνά*, up, *prefixed*) to be laid up, *as at a meal.*

2. **ἀναπίπτω**, to fall up, *as at table; hence*, to recline, *as at meals.*

3. **κάθημαι**, to sit down, *esp. in state, or as a judge.*

4. **καθίζω**, *trans.*, to cause to sit, to seat; *intrans.*, to seat one's self, to sit down.

3. Matt. xxvii. 19 part. | 2. John xiii. 12 part.
1. John vi. 11. | 4. Heb. xii. 2.
4. Rev. iii. 21.

SET DOWN TOGETHER (BE)

συγκαθίζω, (*No.* 4, *above, with σύν*, together *or* in conjunction with), (*occ.* Eph. ii. 6.)

Luke xxii. 55 (*περικαθίζω, to sit down around*, L.)

SET FORTH (BE)

πρόκειμαι, *see* "SET BEFORE (BE)."
Jude 7.

SET BEFORE (SUCH THINGS AS ARE)

{ τὰ, the *things*
{ παρατιθέμενα, being set before.
Luke x. 8.

See also, AFFECTION, FIRE, FOOT, LIBERTY, MIND, NOUGHT, ORDER, SEAL, UPROAR, VARIANCE.

SETTING (AND)

μετά, with; *here*, "with the guard," *or* with the guard (*or* watch) besides.
Matt. xxvii. 66.

SETTING (BE)

δύνω, *see* "SET," *No.* 8.
Luke iv. 40 part.

SETTER FORTH.

καταγγελεύς, an announcer, declarer, proclaimer, (*non occ.*)
Acts xvii. 18.

SETTLE.

1. τίθημι, to set, to put, to place, to lay. *Here, mid.*, to set *or* put for one's self.
2. θεμελιόω, to lay the foundation *of anything*, to found; *hence*, ground *or* establish.

1. Luke xxi. 14 (active, L T Tr A ℵ.)
2. 1 Pet. v. 10 (*om.* G ⇉ L.)

SETTLED.

ἑδραῖος, seated; *hence*, firm, steadfast, (*occ.* 1 Cor. vii. 37; xv. 58.)
Col. i. 23.

SEVEN.

ἑπτά, seven, (*occ.* Matt. xxii. 26.)

[As a symbolical number, its signification is indicated by the meaning of the Heb. שבע, *to be* or *become satisfied, satiated*, or *filled*, the primary idea being that of *abundance*. Probably "seven," so called because it satisfies so many things in nature and revelation, *e.g.* the seven notes of music and the seven colours, each note having its correlative colour, (determined by the proportions of the vibrations of air and light respectively) viz. C = red, D = orange, E = yellow, F = green, G = blue, A = indigo, B = violet, so that discords and harmonies correspond in sound and colour. In Revelation we have the number "seven," beginning with the "days" of Gen. i., and ending with the flowering of the number in the Apocalypse; running through the Levitical ceremonial as satisfying the requirements of God's righteousness; and ruling the principle of the Dispensational reckoning of *Time*, in the 7 of days, 7 of weeks, 7 of years, and 7 × 7 of years (Jubilee), and finally in the 7 × 7 × 10, or the 70 weeks (or hebdomads) of years. See notes on pages 390 and 391.]

Matt. xii. 45.
—— xv. 34, 36, 37.
—— xvi. 10.
—— xviii. 21.
—— —— 22 1st, see S times.
—— —— 22 2nd.
—— xxii. 25, 28.
Mark viii. 5, 6, 8, 20 twice.
—— xii. 20, 22, 23.
—— xvi. 9 (*ap.*)
Luke ii. 36.
—— viii. 2.
—— xi. 26.
—— xvii. 4 twice, see S times.
—— xx. 29, 31, 33.
Acts vi. 3.
—— xiii. 19.
—— xix. 14.
—— xx. 6.
—— xxi. 4, 8, 27.
—— xxviii. 14.
Rom. xi. 4, see Thousand.
Heb. xi. 30.
Rev. i. 4 twice.
—— —— 11 (*om.* St.)
—— —— 12.
—— —— 13 (*om.* G ⇉ L T Tr Ab.)
—— —— 16, 20 6 times.
—— ii. 1 twice.
—— iii. 1 1st (*om.* St), 1 2nd.
—— iv. 5 twice.
—— v. 1, 5, 6 1st & 2nd.
—— —— 6 3rd (*om.* L.)
—— viii. 2 twice, 6 twice.
—— x. 3, 4 1st.
—— —— 4 2nd (*om.* Tr.)
—— xi. 13.
—— xii. 3 twice.
—— xiii. 1.
—— xv. 1 twice, 6 twice, 7 twice, 8 twice.
—— xvi. 1.
—— xvii. 1 twice, 3, 7, 9 twice, 10, 11.
—— xxi. 9 3 times.

SEVEN TIMES.

ἑπτάκις, seven times, (*non occ.*)
Matt. xviii. 21, 22. | Luke xvii. 4 twice.

SEVENTH.

1. ἕβδομος, seventh, (*non occ.*)
2. ἑπτά, seven.

2. Matt. xxii. 26.
1. John iv. 52.
1. Heb. iv. 4 twice.
1. Rev. viii. 1.
1. Rev. x. 7.
1. —— xi. 15.
1. —— xvi. 17.
1. —— xxi. 20.

SEVENTY.

ἑβδομήκοντα, seventy.

Luke x. 1, 17.

SEVENTY TIMES.

ἑβδομηκοντάκις, seventy times, (*non occ.*)

Matt. xviii. 22.

SEVER.

ἀφορίζω, to set off by bounds, to limit off, (lxx. for הגביל, Ex. xix. 12, 33; to set off apart, separate, lxx. for הבדיל, Lev. xx. 25; Is. lvi. 3.)

Matt. xiii. 49.

SEVERED FROM. [margin.]

John xv. 5, see "WITHOUT."

SEVERAL (ONE'S)

ἴδιος, own, one's own, private, particular, individual.

Matt. xxv. 15. | Rev. xxi. 21, see Every.

SEVERALLY.

ἰδίᾳ, (*the above, adverbially*) individually, privately, particularly.

1 Cor. xii. 11. | Gal. ii. 2, see Privately.

SEVERITY.

ἀποτομία, a cutting off, (*non occ.*)

Rom. xi. 22 twice.

SEW ON.

{ ἐπιρράπτω, to sew upon,
{ ἐπί, upon.

Mark ii. 21.

SHADOW. [noun.]

1. σκιά, shadow, shade, (*non occ.*)

2. ἀποσκίασμα, the dark mark of the shadow. *Here,* the shadow *arising from the turning of any body,* (*non occ.*)

1. Matt. iv. 16.
1. Mark iv. 32.
1. Luke i. 79.
1. Acts v. 15.
1. Col. ii. 17.
1. Heb. viii. 5.
1. —— x. 1.
2. Jas. i. 17.

SHADOW (-ING.) [verb.]

κατασκιάζω, to shadow down upon, to overshadow, (*non occ*

Heb. ix. 5.

SHAKE (-EN, SHOOK.)

1. σαλεύω, to move to and fro, to shake, (lxx. for נגש, Ps. xviii. 18; מוט 1 Ch. xvi. 30; Ps. lxxxii. 5.)

2. σείω, to move to and fro with a shock *or* concussion.

   (a) *Passive,* to be shaken.

3. ἐκτινάσσω, to shake out *or* off violently.

1. Matt. xi. 7.
1. —— xxiv. 29.
2a.—— xxviii. 4.
1. Mark xiii. 25.
1. Luke vi. 48.
1. —— vii. 24.
1. —— xxi. 26.
1. Acts iv. 31.
1. —— xvi. 26.
3. —— xviii. 6.
1. 2 Thes. ii. 2.
1. Heb. xii. 26 1st.
2. —— 26 2nd.
2. Rev. vi. 13.

SHAKE OFF.

1. ἀποτινάσσω, to shake off, beat off, (*non occ.*)

2. ἐκτινάσσω, to shake out *or* off.

2. Matt. x. 14.
2. Mark vi. 11.
1. Luke ix. 5.
2. Acts xiii. 51.
1. Acts xxviii. 5.

SHAKE TOGETHER.

σαλεύω, *see* "SHAKE," *No.* 1.

Luke vi. 38.

SHAKEN (THOSE THINGS WHICH ARE)

{ τὰ, the *things,*
{ σαλευόμενα, (*part. of* "SHAKE," *No.* 1) being shaken,
} what is *or* can be shaken.

Heb. xii. 27.

SHAKEN (THOSE THINGS WHICH CANNOT BE)

{ τὰ, the *things,*
{ μὴ, not,
{ σαλευόμενα, *see above,*
} what is not, *or* cannot be, shaken.

Heb. xii. 27.

SHALL, SHALT.

SHALL is frequently part of the translation of *the future tense* of a verb.

When it is the translation of a separate Greek word, it is here shown.

For "SHALL BE," *see below.*

μέλλω, to be about to *do or suffer anything*, to be on the point of, to be about to do *of one's own free will*, to intend *or* purpose doing.

Matt. xvi. 27 1st.
—— xvii. 12, 22.
—— xx. 22.
—— xxiv. 6.
Mark xiii. 4 3rd.
Luke ix. 44.
—— xxi. 7 2nd, 36.
Acts xxiii. 3.
—— xxiv. 15.
—— xxvi. 2 part.
Rom. iv. 24.
—— viii. 13 1st, 18.
2 Tim. iv. 1.
Heb. i. 14.
—— x. 27.
Jas. ii. 12.
1 Pet. v. 1.
Rev. i. 19.
—— ii. 10 1st & 2nd.
—— iii. 10.
Rev. xvii. 8 1st.

SHALL BE.

ἔσομαι, etc., the future tense of εἰμί, to be.

Matt. v. 21, 22 3 times.
—— vi. 5, 22, 23.
—— viii. 12 2nd.
—— x. 15, 22.
—— xi. 22, 24.
—— xii. 11 (*om.* ἔσται, *shall there be*, T Tr A.)
—— 27, 40, 45.
—— xiii. 40, 42, 49, 50.
—— xvi. 19 twice, 22.
—— xvii. 17.
—— xviii. 18 twice.
—— xix. 5.
—— 27, see S have.
—— 30 1st.
—— xx. 16.
—— 26 (ἐστίν, *is*, L Tr.)
—— xxii. 13, 28.
—— xxiii. 11.
—— xxiv. 3 1st, 7, 9, 21 1st, 27, 37, 39, 40 1st, 51.
—— xxv. 30.
—— xxvii. 64.
Mark vi. 11 (*ap.*)
—— ix. 19, 35.
—— x. 8, 31.
—— 43 1st (ἐστίν, *is it not, instead of* ἔσται, *shall it not be*, L T Tr A ℵ.)
—— 43 2nd, 44.
—— xi. 23, 24, see S have.
—— xii. 7, 23.
—— xiii. 4 1st, 8 twice, 13 1st, 19 1st.
Luke i. 14, see S have, 15 1st, 20 1st, 32 1st, 33, 34, 45, 66.
—— ii. 10.
—— iii. 5 3rd, see S be made.
—— iv. 7.
—— vi. 35 twice, 40.
—— ix. 41.
—— 48 (ἐστίν, *is*, G ~ L T Tr A ℵ.)
—— x. 12, 14.
—— xi. 19, 30, 36.
—— xii. 20 2nd, 52
—— xiii. 28, 30 t
—— xiv. 14 1st.
—— xv. 7.
Luke xvii. 24, 26, 30, 31, 34 1st, 35 1st, 36 1st (*ap.*)
—— xxi. 7, 11 twice, 17, 23, 24 3rd, 25.
—— xxiii. 43.
John vi. 45.
—— viii. 36, 55.
—— xii. 26.
—— xiv. 17 (ἐστίν, *is*, L Tr A.)
—— xix. 24.
Acts i. 8.
—— ii. 17, 21.
—— iii. 23.
—— xiii. 11.
—— xxii. 15.
—— xxiv. 15, see S be (that there)
—— xxvii. 22, 25.
Rom. iv. 18.
—— vi. 5.
—— ix. 9, see S have.
—— 26, see S come to [pass.
—— xv. 12.
1 Cor. vi. 16.
—— xi. 27.
—— xiv. 11 1st.
2 Cor. iii. 8.
—— vi. 16, 18.
—— xi. 15.
—— xii. 6.
—— xiii. 11.
Eph. v. 31 2nd.
Phil. iv. 9.
1 Thes. iv. 17 2nd.
1 Tim. iv. 6.
2 Tim. ii. 2, 21.
—— iii. 2, 9.
Heb. i. 5.
—— viii. 10.
Jas. i. 25.
—— v. 3.
2 Pet. ii. 1.
1 John iii. 2 twice.
2 John 2.
Rev. x. 9.
—— xvi. 5, see S be (which)
—— xx. 6.
—— xxi. 3 twice, 4 twice, 7, 25 2nd.
—— xxii. 3 twice, 4 2nd, 5.
Rev. xxii. 12 (ἐστιν, *is*, L T Tr), (*om.* G→

SHALL BE MADE

Luke iii. 5 3rd & 4th.

SHALL COME TO PASS.

Acts ii. 17, 21.
Rom. ix. 26.
Acts iii. 23.

SHALL HAVE.

ἔσομαι, with Dat., there shall be to it, *i.e.* it shall have.

Matt. xix. 27.
Mark xi. 23, 24.
Rom. ix. 9.
Luke i. 14.
—— xiv. 10.

SHALL BE (THAT THERE)

{ *μέλλειν*, there is about
{ *ἔσεσθαι*, to be.

Acts xxiv. 15.

SHALT BE (WHICH)

{ ὁ, the *one who*
{ ἐσόμενος, shall be.

Rev. xvi. 5, ὁ ὅσιος, *the holy one* (E G L T Tr A ℵ.)

SHAMBLES.

μάκελλον, *from Lat.*, macellum, a meat market.

1 Cor. x. 25.

SHAME. [noun.]

1. *αἰσχύνη*, the sense of disgrace, the feeling of shame which attends the performance of a dishonourable deed; a shame *that may restrain a bad man*, (αἰδώς *being* the shame *or* inner grace that will restrain a good man.) lxx. for בשת, Job. viii. 22; כלמה, Is. l. 6; חרפה, Ps. lxix. 20, (*occ.* 2 Cor. iv. 2.)

2. *αἰσχρός*, deformed, (*opp. to* καλός. *see* "GOOD," *No.* 2), ugly, *whether of mind or body; hence, spoken of what is offensive to modesty or purity*, indecorous, indecent, shameful. lxx. for רע, Gen. xli. 3, 4, (*occ.* Tit. i. 11.)

3. *ἀσχημοσύνη*, deformity, unseemliness. lxx. for ערוה, Ex. xx. 26; Lev. xviii. 6, 7, (*occ.* Rom. i. 27.)

4. *ἐντροπή*, a turning in upon one's self, causing a recoil from what is unseemly *or* impure, a putting to shame. lxx. for כלמה, Ps. xxxv. 26; lxix. 8, 20, (*non occ.*)

5. *ἀτιμία*, dishonour, disgrace; (lxx. *for* נקלה, Prov. xii. 9; בוז, Job. xii. 21; כלמוו, Jer. xxiii. 4), vileness.

1. Luke xiv ^.
— Acts v. 41, see S (suffer)
4. 1 Cor. vi. 5.
2. —— xi. 6.
5. —— 14.
2. —— xiv. 35.
4. —— xv. 34.
2. Eph. v. 12.
1. Phil. iii. 19.
— Heb. vi. 6, see S (put to an open)
1. —— xii. 2.
1. Jude 13.
1. Rev. iii. 18.
3. —— xvi. 15.

SHAME (PUT TO AN OPEN)

παραδειγματίζω, to make an example of, make a show of, expose to public pointing at, (*occ.* Matt. i. 19.)

Heb. vi. 6.

SHAME (SUFFER)

ἀτιμάζω, not to hold in honour, esteem lightly; to dishonour, *whether persons or things, by word or deed*; (lxx. נבל, Mic. vii. 6; קלל, Gen. xvi. 4, 5.) *Here, pass.*, to suffer dishonour *or* insult; (lxx. *for* בוז, Prov. xiv. 21; דכא, Prov. xxii. 22.)

Acts v. 41.

SHAME. [verb.]

1. *ἐντρέπω*, to invert, to turn one in *upon himself*, bring to reflection, to affect, to move; (lxx. *for* חפר, Ps. xxxv. 26; xl. 15; lxxxiii. 18; נכלו, Is. xli. 11; Ez. xxxvi. 32.)

2. *καταισχύνω*, to bring down shame upon, put to shame; (lxx. *for* הביש, 2 Sam. xix. 5.)

1. 1 Cor. iv. 14. | 2. 1 Cor. xi. 22.

SHAMEFACEDNESS.

αἰδώς, the inner grace which recoils from any thing unseemly *or* impure, an innate moral repugnance to the doing of a dishonourable act, shamfastness, modesty, (*occ.* Heb. xii. 28.

1 Tim. ii. 9.

SHAMEFULLY (ENTREAT)

1. *ἀτιμάζω, see* "SHAME (SUFFER)"

2. *ὑβρίζω*, to wax wanton, to act with insolence, *esp. in the use of superior strength*; to treat despitefully, outrage, ill-treat, injure, abuse; (lxx. הקל, 2 Sam. xix. 43.)

1. Luke xx. 11. | 2. 1 Thes. ii. 2.

SHAMEFULLY HANDLED.

ἀτιμόω, to dishonour, to affect with disgrace.

Mark xii. 4 (*ἠτίμησαν*, *treated* him *shamefully*, instead of *ἀπέστειλαν ἠτιμωμένον*, *sent* him *away shamefully handled*, L T Tr A ℵ), (*ἠτίμασαν*, ℵ.)

SHAPE.

1. **εἶδος**, the thing seen, external appearance, form, shape.

2. *ὁμοίωμα*, something made like, a likeness; shape, *implying resemblance to other objects*.

1. Luke iii. 22. | 1. John v. 37.
2. Rev. ix. 7.

SHARP.

ὀξύς, sharp, keen, having a sharp edge; (lxx. *for* חדה, Is. xlix. 2; Ez. v. 1), (*occ.* Rom. iii. 15.)

Rev. i. 16.
—— ii. 12.
Rev. xiv. 14, 17, 18 twice.
—— xix. 5.

SHARPER.

τομώτερος, more cutting, (*non occ.*)

Heb. iv. 12.

SHARPLY.

ἀποτόμως, (*adv. of ἀπότομος*, cut off, abrupt; *then*, severe, harsh) severely, absolutely; *Lat.*, præcisé, (*occ.* 2 Cor. xiii. 10.)

Tit. i. 13.

SHARPNESS.

ἀποτόμως, *see above*, (*occ.* Tit. i. 13.)

2 Cor. xiii. 10.

SHAVE (-EN.)

ξυράω, to shave, to shear; lxx. *for* גלח, Gen. xli. 14; Num. vi. 9, 19.

* *Mid.*, to shave one's self.

Acts xxi. 24*. | 1 Cor. xi. 5 part., 6.

SHE.

SHE, is generally part of the translation of a verb.

When it is represented by a separate Greek word it is always emphatic.

αὐτός, as a simple pronoun, is generally rendered he, she, it, they, etc., in the oblique cases, and occurs too frequently for reference here.

When SHE is not included in the above, it is the translation of one of these following:

1. αὕτη, *fem. of* οὗτος, this, (the nearer, *connected with the 2nd person.*)

2. ἐκεῖνος, that, that one there, (the more remote, *connected with the 3rd person.*)

3. ἥδε, this, this here, (*marking a closer relation than No.* 1, *and connected with the* 1*st person.*)

1. Matt. xxvi. 12 1st.
— Mark v. 26, see S had (that)
1. —— xii. 44 1st.
1. —— xiv. 8 1st (om. Lb T Trb A ℵ.)
1. ——— 9.
2. —— xvi. 10.
1. Luke ii. 36.
1. ——— 37 (*αὐτή, she*, T Tr A.)
1. Luke ii. 38 (om. L Tr ℵ.)
1. —— vii. 12 (St), (*αὐτή, she*, T Tr A.)
1. ——— 44.
1. —— viii. 42.
3. —— x. 39.
1. —— xxi. 4 1st.
2. John xi. 29.
2. —— xx. 15, 16.
1. Rom. xvi. 2 2nd (G∾), (*αὐτή, she*, G L T Tr A.)

SHE HAD (THAT)

{ τὰ, the *things*
{ παρὰ, beside *or* with [A.)
{ ἑαυτῆς, herself, (αὐτῆς, *her*. G L T Tr

Mark v. 26.

SHEAR.

κείρω, to wear away, eat away *by rubbing*, gnawing, *or* cutting; *hence*, to shear, *as* a sheep; (lxx. *for* גזז, Is. liii. 7. *Esp. of the head*, to cut off the hair, גזז, Job i. 20; Jer. vii. 28; גלח, 2 Sam. xiv. 26), (*non occ.*)

Acts xviii. 18. | 1 Cor. xi. 6 twice.

SHEARER.

κείρω, see above. Here, part.

Acts viii. 32 part.

SHEATH.

θήκη, a place to put *or* set anything, repository, receptacle, *e.g. a sword.*

John xviii. 11.

SHED.

1. ἐκχέω, to pour out. *αἷμα ἐκχέω*, to pour out blood, to shed blood, to kill.

2. ἐκχύνω, *a later form of No.* 1.

2. Matt. xxiii. 35.
2. —— xxvi. 28.
2. Mark xiv. 24.
2. Luke xi. 50.
2. —— xxii. 20.
— Acts ii. 33, see S forth.
1. Acts xxii. 20 (No. 2, L T Tr A ℵ.)
1. Rom. iii. 15.
— —— v. 5, see S abroad.
1. Tit. iii. 6.
1. Rev. xvi. 6.

SHED ABROAD

2. Rom. v. 5.

SHED FORTH.

1. Acts ii. 33.

SHEDDING.

See, BLOOD.

SHEEP.

πρόβατον, whatever goes forwards, *i.e. moves its limbs forwards in going; hence*, quadrupeds, *as distinguished from things creeping, flying, or swimming: esp. tame* animals; *hence, gen.*, beasts, cattle. *In Attic and N.T usage, only of* sheep, (*non occ.*)

Matt. vii. 15.
—— ix. 36.
—— x. 6, 16.
—— xii. 11, 12.
—— xv. 24.
—— xviii. 12.
—— xxv. 32, 33.
—— xxvi. 31.
Mark vi. 34.
—— xiv. 27.
Luke xv. 4, 6.
John ii. 14, 15.
—— x. 2, 3 twice.
——— 4 1st (*τὰ ἴδια πάντα, all his own*, instead of *τὰ ἴδια πρόβατα, his own sheep*, L T Tr A), (*om. πρόβατα, sheep*, ℵ.)
John x. 4 2nd, 7, 8, 11, 12 1st & 2nd, 12 3rd (ap.) 13, 15, 16, 26, 27.
—— xxi. 16 (*προβάτιον, a little sheep*, T.)
——— 17, (*προβάτιον, a little sheep*, T Tr A.)
Acts viii. 32.
Rom. viii. 36.
Heb. xiii. 20.
1 Pet. ii. 25.
Rev. xviii. 13.

SHEEP-*MARKET.*

προβατικός, pertaining to sheep. *Here*, the sheep gate; (*so* lxx. *for* שער הצאן, Neh. iii. 1, 32; xii. 39.)

[This gate was near the Temple, and probably so called as the place where sheep were sold for the sacrifices of the Temple.]

John v. 2, marg. *gate*.

SHEEP-FOLD.

αὐλή, an inclosed ·urt open to the air,
τῶν, of the
προβάτων, sheep.

John x. 1.

SHEEPSKIN (-S.)

μηλωτή, a sheepskin, any rough, woolly skin *as used for clothing;* (lxx. *for* אדרת, *spoken of* a prophet's mantle, 1 Kings xix. 13, 19; 2 Kings ii. 8, 13), (*non occ.*)

Heb. xi. 37.

SHEPHERD (-S.)

1. ποιμήν, one who tends, feeds, leads, cherishes, guides, and protects a flock, (*not merely a feeder*); *hence*, a shepherd, (*occ.* Eph. iv. 11.)

   (a) *used of Christ.*

2. οἱ, the
ἀνθρῶποι, men,
οἱ, the
ποιμένες, shepherds, *see above.*

1. Matt. ix. 36.
1. —— xxv. 32.
1. —— xxvi. 31.
1. Mark vi. 34.
1. —— xiv. 27.
1. Luke ii. 8.
2. Luke ii. 15 (*om.* οἱ ἀνθρώποι, *the men*, Lb Trb Ab ℵ.)
2. —— 18, 20. [14, 16.
2. John x. 2, 11 twice, 12,
1a. Heb. xiii. 20.
1a. 1 Pet. ii. 25.

SHEPHERD (CHIEF)

ἀρχιποίμην, (*No.* 1, *above, with* ἀρχή, beginning, chief, *in pre-eminence or precedence.*)

1 Pet. v. 4.

SHEET.

ὀθόνη, fine white linen, a linen cloth, (*non occ.*)

Acts x. 11. | Acts xi. 5.

SHEW.

See, SHOW.

SHEW-BREAD.

See, SHOW-BREAD.

SHEWING.

See, SHOWING.

SHIELD.

θυρεός, a door, *i.e. a stone for closing the entrance of a cave. In later Greek, and N.T.*, a shield (*large and oblong, in shape like* a door); (lxx. *for* מגן, 2 Sam. i. 21; צנה, 1 Sam. xvii. 42; 2 Ch. ix. 15), (*non occ.*)

Eph. vi. 16.

SHINE (-ED, -ETH, -ING, SHONE.)

1. φαίνω, to lighten, give light, illuminate; shine forth; (lxx. *for* האיר, Gen. i. 17; Ex. xiii. 22.)

   (a) *Pass. or mid.*, to come to light, appear, be *or* become visible.

2. λάμπω, to shine, (*as a torch*) to beam, be bright *or* radiant; (lxx. *for* נגה, Prov. iv. 18; הזהיר, Dan. xii. 3), (*occ.* Matt. v. 5.)

3. ἀστράπτω, to lighten *as lightning;* (lxx. *for* ברק, Ps. cxliv. 6), (*occ.* Luke xvii. 24.)

4. αὐγάζω, to view in the clearest light, see distinctly, discern; *of the sun*, to beam upon. *Here, prob.*, "should not be discerned by them;" (lxx. *for* בהרת, Lev. xiii. 24, 25, 26, 28), (*non occ.*)

5. στίλβω, to glitter, glisten, *of polished or bright surfaces*, (*non occ.*)

2. Matt. v. 16.
— —— xiii. 43, see S forth.
2. —— xvii. 2.
1a. —— xxiv. 27.
5. Mark ix. 3.
— Luke ii. 9, see S round about.
2. xvii. 24.
3. xxiv. 4.
1. John i. 5.
1. —— v. 35.
— Acts ix. 3, see S round about.
2. —— xii. 7.
— Acts xxii. 6, see S round.
— —— xxvi. 13, see S round about.
4. 2 Cor. iv. 4 (καταυγάζω, *shine clearly upon*, Lm Trm.)
2. —— 6 twice.
1a. Phil. ii. 15.
1. 2 Pet. i. 19.
1. 1 John ii. 8.
1. Rev. i. 16.
1. —— viii. 12.
1a. —— xviii. 23.
1. —— xxi. 23.

SHINE FORTH.

ἐκλάμπω, (*No.* 2, *with* ἐκ, out of, *prefixed.*)

Matt. xiii. 43.

SHINE ROUND.

περιαστράπτω, (*No.* 3, *with* περί, around, *prefixed.*)

Acts xxii. 6.

SHINE ROUND ABOUT.

1. **περιαστράπτω**, *see above.*
2. **περιλάμπω**, (*No.* 2, *with* **περί**, around, *prefixed.*)

2. Luke ii. 9. | 1. Acts ix. 3.
2. Acts xxvi. 13.

SHINING (BRIGHT)

ἀστραπή, lightning; (lxx. *for* ברק, Ex. xix. 16; Jer. x. 12.)

Luke xi. 36.

SHIP.

1. **πλοῖον**, a floating vessel, a ship for merchandise *or* transport, (*No.* 2 being *a ship of war*); (lxx. *for* אניה, Gen. xlix. 13; Deut. xxviii. 68; Jonah i. 3-5), (*occ.* John vi. 24.)
2. **ναῦς**, a ship, a vessel; (lxx. *for* אני, 1 Kings ix. 26; אניה, Job ix. 26), (*non occ.*)

1. Matt. iv. 21, 22.
1. —— viii. 23, 24.
1. —— ix. 1.
1. —— xiii. 2.
1. —— xiv. 13, 22, 24, 29, 32, 33.
1. —— xv. 39.
1. Mark i. 19, 20.
— —— iii. 9, see S (small)
1. —— iv. 36 1st.
— ——— 36 2nd, see S (little)
1. ——— 37.
— ——— 38, see Hinder part.
1. —— v. 2, 18, 21.
1. —— vi. 32, 45, 47, 51, 54.
1. —— viii. 10.
1. ——— 13 (*om.* G⇉T Trb A ℵ, i.e. *going aboard*, instead of *entering into the ship.*)
1. ——— 14.
1. Luke v. 2 (*πλοιάριον, a small vessel, boat*, Lm T Trm A.)
1. ——— 3 twice, 7 twice, 11.
1. —— viii. 22, 37.
1. John vi. 17, 19, 21 twice.
1. —— xxi. 3, 6.
— ——— 8, see S (little)
1. Acts xx. 13, 38.
1. —— xxi. 2, 3.
— ——— 6, see S (take)
1. —— xxvii. 2, 6, 10.
— ——— 11, see S (owner of the)
1. ——— 15, 17.
— ——— 18, see Lighten.
1. ——— 19, 22, 30, 31, 37, 38, 39.
2. ——— 41.
1. ——— 44.
1. —— xxviii. 11.
1. Jas. iii. 4.
1. Rev. viii. 9.
1. —— xviii. 17 (*ap.*), 19.

SHIP (LITTLE)

πλοιάριον, a small vessel, a boat.

Mark iv. 36 (No. 1, G L T Tr A ℵ.)
John xxi. 8.

SHIP (SMALL)

πλοιάριον, *see above.*

Mark iii. 9.

SHIP (OWNER OF THE)

ναύκληρος, ship-owner, *i.e.* the master *or* owner of a trading vessel who took passengers and freight for hire.

Acts xxvii. 11.

SHIP (TAKE)

ἐπιβαίνω, to go upon, (**ἐμβαίνω**, to go in, L Tr.) **ἀναβαίνω**, to go up, (T Aℵ.)
εἰς, into
τὸ, the
πλοῖον, ship.

Acts xxi. 6.

SHIPMAN (-MEN.)

ναύτης, a shipman, sailor, seaman, (*occ.* Rev. xviii. 17.)

Acts xxvii. 27, 30.

SHIPMASTER.

κυβερνήτης, governor of a ship, *i.e.* the steersman *or* pilot; (lxx. *for* חבל, Ex. xxvii. 8, 27, 28.)

Rev. xviii. 17.

SHIPPING.

πλοῖον, *pl. of* "SHIP," *No.* 1.

John iii. 24 (**πλοιάριον**, *pl.* of "SHIP (LITTLE)," L T Tr A.)

SHIPWRECK (MAKE)

ναυαγέω, to make shipwreck; suffer shipwreck, (*non occ.*)

1 Tim. i. 19.

SHIPWRECK (SUFFER)

2 Cor. xi. 25.

SHIVERS.

See, BREAK.

SHOD (HAVE...)

ὑποδέω, to bind under, *as sandals under the* feet; *hence*, to put on sandals. *In N.T. only mid.*, to bind under *or* put on one's own sandals.

Eph. vi. 15.

SHOD WITH (BE)

Mark vi. 9.

SHOE (-S.)

ὑπόδημα, what is bound under, *as the foot; hence*, a sandal, a sole of

wood *or* leather bound on to the foot with thongs, (*non occ.*)

Matt. iii. 11.	Luke xv. 22.
—— x. 10.	—— xxii. 35.
Mark i. 7.	John i. 27.
Luke iii. 16.	Acts vii. 33.
—— x. 4.	—— xiii. 25.

SHOOT FORTH.

προβάλλω, to cast *or* thrust forward; *of plants or trees*, to put forth *leaves, blossoms*, *or* fruit, (*occ.* Acts xix. 33.)

Luke xxi. 30.

SHOOT OUT.

ποιέω, to make, *i.e.* to form, produce.

Mark iv. 32.

SHORE.

1. αἰγιαλός, that on which the sea breaks; *hence,* the coast, the shore of the sea.

2. χεῖλος, a lip; *hence,* the lip *of the sea, i.e.* the brink, bank, or shore; (lxx. *for* שׂפה, Gen. xxii. 17; Ex. xiv. 31.)

1. Matt. xiii. 2, 48.	1. Acts xxi. 5.
— Mark vi. 53, see Draw.	1. —— xxvii. 39, 40.
1. John xxi. 4.	° Heb. xi. 12.

SHORT.

1. ὀλίγος, little, (*opp. of* πολύς, much) *used of number, magnitude, amount, and time.*

2. συντέμνω, to cut together, contract by cutting; *of words or discourse, etc.*, to make concise; *hence, here pass. part.*, concise. Rom. ix. 28 *is quoted from* Is. x. 22, 23, *where Heb. reads,* "destruction is decreed, bringing in justice as a flood; for destruction and a decree (*i.e.* decreed destruction) doth Jehovah of Hosts execute." *Here,* (*see ap.*) "For the Lord will perform His word upon the earth, finishing it and cutting it short"; *or* "for a complete and concise account (*or* a matter cut short) will the Lord make (*or* do) on the earth." (*occ.* Rom. ix. 28.)

3. συστέλλω, to draw together, to straighten, contract. *Here, pass. part.*, straitened *or* contracted, "the opportunity is contracted," (*occ.* Acts v. 6.)

4. ὥρα, an hour, (*see under* "HOUR.") *Here,* καιρὸν ὥρας, a season of an hour, *or* an opportunity of a specific period.

— Rom. iii. 23, see S of (come)	3. 1 Cor. vii. 29.
— —— ix. 28 1st, see Cut.	4. 1 Thes. ii. 17.
2. —— 28 2nd.	1. Rev. xii. 12. [(a)
	— —— xvii. 10, see S space

SHORT SPACE (A)

ὀλίγον, *adv. of No.* 1, *above.*

Rev. xvii. 10.

SHORT OF (COME)

ὑστερέω, to be last; *hence,* to lack, to fail of *any thing*, to come short of, miss, not to reach; *hence,* to lack, to need, suffer need.

Rom. iii. 23.

SHORTEN (-ED.)

κολοβόω, to mutilate; (lxx. 2 Sam. iv. 12). *In N.T.*, *of time*, to cut off a portion. *So,* Heb. קצר, Prov. x. 27; (lxx. ὀλιγόω, to lessen, diminish), (*non occ.*)

Matt. xxiv. 22 twice. | Mark xiii. 20 twice.

SHORTLY.

1. ταχέως, quickly, speedily; *of time,* soon, shortly; lxx. *for* מהר, Judg. ix. 48; Is. viii. 3.

2. { ἐν, in
{ ταχει, quickness, swiftness, speed.

3. τάχιον, more quickly, more swiftly, more speedily.

4. ταχινός, quick, swift, speedy, *i.e* near at hand, impending, (*occ.* 2 Pet. ii. 1.)

5. εὐθέως, straightway, immediately, forthwith.

2. Acts xxv. 4.	1. 2 Tim. iv. 9.
2. Rom. xvi. 20.	3. Heb. xiii. 23.
1. 1 Cor. iv. 19.	4. 2 Pet. i. 14.
1. Phil. ii. 19, 24.	5. 3 John 14.
3. 1 Tim. iii. 14 (No. 2, L Tr.)	2. Rev. i. 1.
	2. —— xxii. 6.

SHOULD (-EST.)

SHOULD, is very frequently part of the translation of the tense and mood of a verb.

Where it is the translation of a separate Greek word it is one of these following.

(*For* "SHOULD BE," *etc., and various combinations with other words, see below.*)

1. μέλλω, to be about to *do or suffer* any thing, to be on the point of; *then, as implying necessity arising from the nature of things or with the divine appointment, and therefore certain and destined to take place*, ought, should, must.
2. δεῖ, it needs, there is need of, it is necessary; *then, as implying necessity arising from prescribed law or duty*, it is right *or* proper, one must, it ought, it should, *etc.*
   a) *imperfect tense.*
3. ὀφείλω, to owe, to be indebted; *hence*, I ought, he is obligated, *or* obliged to *the performance of any duty*.

2a. Matt. xviii. 33.
2. —— xxvii. 35.
2. Mark xiv. 31.
1. Luke xix. 11.
1. —— xxii. 23.
1. —— xxiv. 21.
1. John vi. 71.
1. —— vii. 39.
1. —— xi. 51.
1. —— xii. 4, 33.
1. —— xviii. 32.
— Acts ii. 47, see Saved.
1. —— xi. 28.
1. —— xix. 27.
1. —— xx. 38.
1. Acts xxiii. 27.
1. —— xxvi. 22, 23.
2a. —— xxvii. 21.
1. —— xxviii. 6.
3. 1 Cor. ix. 10.
— —— x. 6, see Intent.
— 2 Cor. iv. 4, see Lest.
— Gal. iii. 23, see Afterwards.
1. 1 Thes. iii. 4.
— 1 Tim. i. 16, see Hereafter.
— Heb. xi. 8, see After.
— 2 Pet. ii. 6, see After.
1. Rev. vi. 11.

SHOULD BE.

1. ᾧ, ῃ̂ς, ῃ̂, *etc.* (*subj. of* εἰμί, to be) may be, *asserting conditionally.*
2. εἴην, εἴης, εἴη, *etc.* (*opt. of* εἰμί, to be) might be, *implying the wish.*
3. ἦν, *etc.* (*indic. imperf. of* εἰμί, to be) was.
4. ἔσομαι, *etc.* (*indic. fut. of* εἰμί, to be) shall be.

1. Mark iii. 14.
2. Luke i. 29.
2. —— ix. 46.
2. John xiii. 24 (*ap.*)
1. Rom. xi. 25.
1. 1 Cor. xii. 25
1. 2 Cor. i. 17.
1. Eph. v. 27.
1. Philem. 14.
3. Heb. viii. 4.
4. Jude 18 (ἐλεύσονται, *shall come*, G ∾)
4. Rev. x. 6.

SHOULD BE (THAT...)

1. εἶναι, (*inf. of* εἰμί, to be) to be.
2. { εἰς, unto, with a view to, / τὸ, the, / εἶναι, to be, } to the end I might be.
3. ὁ, *the art. with the inf.*, that...may *or* might be

3. Acts xiii. 47.
1. Rom. iv. 13.
2. —— xv. 16.
1. Eph. i. 4.
2. —— 12.
1. —— iii. 6.
2. Jas. i. 18.

SHOULD (THAT)

1. { εἰς, unto, with a view to, / τὸ, the, / *with the inf. of a verb*, } with a view to the..., to the end that.., (*denoting purpose, not result.*
2. { τὸ, the, / *with the inf. of a verb*, } the... (*substantivizing the verb.*)

2. Luke i. 57.
2. —— ii. 6.
2. —— iv. 42.
2. —— v. 7.
2. —— xxiv. 16.
2. Acts x. 47.
2. —— xxvii. 1, 20.
1. Rom. vi. 12.
1. Rom. vii. 4.
2. —— xi. 8 twice.
1. —— xv. 16.
1. Gal. iii. 17.
1. Eph. i. 12.
1. 2 Thes. ii. 11.
2. Heb. xi. 5.
1. Jas. i. 18.
1. 1 Pet. iv. 2.

SHOULD BE (THAT THERE)

{ μέλλειν, to be about to be, / ἔσεσθαι, about to be. }

Acts xi. 28.

SHOULD NOT BE (I)

{ οὐκ, not, / ἤμην, I should have been, } I indeed were not, I should not have been, (*here, with* ἄν, *indicating that he did not seek to please men, and therefore he was the servant of Christ.*)

Gal. i. 10.

SHOULD HAVE BEEN.

ἦν, was, should have been, (*here, with* ἄν, *implying that the law could not give life, and therefore righteousness was not by the law.*)

Gal. iii. 21.

SHOULD MEAN.

εἴην, *etc.* (*opt. of* εἰμί, to be) might be.

Acts x. 17.

SHOULD STAND.

ᾦ, *etc.*, (*subj. of* εἰμί, to be) may be.

1 Cor. ii. 5.

SHOULD (TO THE INTENT THAT...)

εἰς τὸ εἶναι, (*see* "SHOULD BE (THAT)," *No.* 2.)

1 Cor. x. 6.

SHOULD (WHAT THINGS)

{ τὰ, the *things*,
{ μέλλοντα, about to be.

Mark x. 32.

SHOULDER (-S.)

ὦμος, a shoulder, (*the place of strength and safety*); (lxx. *for* שְׁכֶם, Gen. xxi. 14; Is. ix. 6; כָּתֵף, Numb. vii. 9; Is. xlix. 22), (*non occ.*)

Matt. xxiii. 4. | Luke xv. 5.

SHOUT.

κέλευσμα, (*from* κελεύω, to put in motion by word of command) cry *of incitement or of urging on*, a call, summons; a shout *which assembles*; *used of* the shout *which gave the time to the rowers that they might row all together*, (Æsch. Pers. 403). (*Hence*, ἀφ ἑνὸς κελεύσματος, all at once, Thuc. 2, 92) *used of* the call *of a huntsman to his dogs that they might all assemble*, (Xen. Ven. 6, 20); *hence, any* signal shout that summons and assembles all at once, (*non occ.*)

1 Thes. i. 16.

SHOUT (GIVE A)

ἐπιφωνέω, to cry out upon, *i.e.* thereupon, to make an outcry for *or* against *a person.*

Acts xxii. 22.

SHOW. [noun.]

1. πρόφασις, what is shown or appears before any one, *i.e.* show, pretence, pretext.
2. λόγος, the word, *spoken, not written*, an exposition *or* account *which one gives*, a representation in words; *hence, with* ἔχω, to have, *as here*, to have the repute of, *implying that there was* something to allege, something to say for it, *that it* had the repute without the reality.

1. Luke xx. 47. | 2. Col. ii. 23.

SHOW (MAKE A FAIR)

εὐπροσωπέω, to be well-faced, be specious, make a fair appearance, show a fair face, (*non occ*

Gal. vi. 12.

SHOW OF (MAKE A)

δειγματίζω, to make an example of, make a specimen *or* sample, (*non occ.*)

Col. ii. 15.

SHOW (*outward*) [margin.]

Luke xvii. 20, see "OBSERVATION."

SHOW (-ED, -EST, -ETH, -ING.) [verb.]

1. δείκνυμι, *and* δεικνύω, to point out, as with the finger, (*hence, Eng.*, indicate, *and Greek*, δάκτυλος, the finger) to point out, to show; *then also*, to show by words, explain, teach, (*like Lat.*, dic-*ere*, doc-*ere*), (*non occ.*)
2. ἀναδείκνυμι, (*No.* 1, *with* ἀνά, up, *prefixed*) to show up, lift up and show, to show by raising aloft; *hence*, to make public, notify, *esp.* to proclaim any one as elected to an office, (Xen. Hell. 3. 5, 16; Polyb. 4. 48, 3.)
3. ἀποδείκνυμι, (*No.* 1, *with* ἀπό, away from, *prefixed*) to point away from *other objects at one, and so*, to point out, show forth, display, make known *by word or deed.*
4. ἐνδείκνυμι, (*No.* 1, *with* ἐν, in, *prefixed*) to point out in *anything. Here, only mid.*, to show forth one's self *or* what is one's own, display one's self to.
5. ἐπιδείκνυμι, (*No.* 1, *with* ἐπί, upon, *prefixed*) to show upon, show up,

to, towards, *or* before *any one; hence,* to exhibit, *esp.* as a specimen, show off.

(a) *Mid.*, to display one's self, show one's self off, (*non occ.*)

6. ὑποδείκνυμι, (*No.* 1, *with* ὑπό, under, *implying secrecy, prefixed*) to show *or* point out privately *or* secretly, give a sight *or* glimpse of; show by tracing out; signify.

7. ἀπαγγέλλω, to give up intelligence, announce *or* report from *some place or person;* to publish *something that has happened, been experienced, or heard.*

8. ἀναγγέλλω, to report back, send news back; *hence,* to report, notify, announce.

9. καταγγέλλω, to bring word down to *any one, i.e.* bring it home to him; *hence,* to proclaim somewhither. *The word may contain a hint at the unknown contents of the proclamation, as well as an increased emphasis of the verb.*

10. ποιέω, to make, form, produce, cause to be; to do, *expressing an action begun and continued, or not yet completed.*

11 φανερόω, to make open to sight, make manifest *or* apparent, to show openly.

12. μηνύω, to disclose what is secret, reveal, betray.

13. παρίστημι, *here, trans.*, to cause to stand near, to place *or* set before *any one*, present.

14. δηλόω, to make visible *or* clear, make known, reveal, bring to light.

15. δίδωμι, to give.

16. διηγέομαι, to lead *or* conduct through *to the end; hence,* to go through with, set out in detail.

17. ἐμφανίζω, to make apparent, cause to be seen.

18. κατατίθημι, to put *or* lay down, deposit, lay up for future use; *here, with* χάριν, to lay up favour with *any one.*

19. λέγω, to lay; lay before *in words,* relate, tell, (*see* "SAY," *No.* 1.)

20. παρέχω, to hold near *or* beside *any one*, offer, present.

1. Matt. iv. 8.
1. —— viii. 4.
— —— xi. 4, see S again.
7. —— xii. 18.
— —— xiv. 2, see S forth one's self.
5. —— xvi. 1.
1. —— 21.
5. —— xxii. 19.
5. —— xxiv. 1.
7. —— xxviii. 11.
1. Mark i. 44.
— —— vi. 14, see S forth one's self.
15. —— xiii. 22 (No. 10, T A.)
1. —— xiv. 15.
— Luke i. 19, see Tidings.
10. —— 51.
— —— 58, see Great.
— —— 80, see Showing.
1. —— iv. 5.
1. —— v. 14.
6. —— vi. 47.
7. —— vii. 18.
16. —— viii. 39.
10. —— x. 37.
7. —— xiv. 21.
5. —— xvii. 14.
5. —— xx. 24 (No. 1, G L T Tr A ℵ.)
12. —— 37.
1. —— xxii. 12.
5. —— xxiv. 40 (*ap.*)
1. John ii. 18.
1. —— v. 20 twice.
10. —— vi. 30.
11. —— vii. 4.
1. —— x. 32.
12. —— xi. 57.
1. —— xiv. 8, 9.
8. —— xvi. 13, 14.
8. —— 15 (No. 7, L T Tr ℵ.)
1. —— xx. 20.
— —— xxi. 1 twice, 14, see S one's self.
13. Acts i. 3.
2. —— 24.
— —— iii. 18, see S again.
— —— iv. 22, see Showed (be)
1. —— vii. 3.
— Acts vii. 26, see S one's self.
10. —— 36 part.
— —— 52, see S again.
6. —— ix. 35.
5a. —— 39.
1. —— x. 28.
— —— 40, see S openly.
7. —— xi. 13.
7. —— xii. 17.
9. —— xvi. 17.
8. —— xix. 18.
8. —— xx. 20.
17. —— xxiii. 22.
18. —— xxiv. 27.
7. —— xxvi. 20.
9. —— 23.
20. —— xxviii. 2.
7. —— 21.
5. —— 28.
11. Rom. i. 19.
4. —— ii. 15.
— —— ix. 16, see Mercy.
4. —— 17, 22.
— —— xii. 8, see Mercy.
12. 1 Cor. x. 28.
9. —— xi. 26.
1. —— xii. 31.
19. —— xv. 51.
4. 2 Cor. viii. 24.
4. Eph. ii. 9.
7. 1 Thes. i. 9.
3. 2 Thes. ii. 4.
— 1 Tim. i. 16, see S forth.
— —— v. 4, see Piety.
1. —— vi. 15.
13. 2 Tim. ii. 15.
4. Tit. ii. 10.
4. —— iii. 2.
4. Heb. vi. 10, 11.
5. —— 17.
1. —— viii. 5.
10. Jas. ii. 13.
1. —— 18 twice.
1. —— iii. 13.
— 1 Pet. ii. 9, see S forth.
14. 2 Pet. i. 14.
7. 1 John i. 2.
1. Rev. i. 1.
1. —— iv. 1.
1. —— xvii. 1.
1. —— xxi. 9, 10.
1. —— xxii. 1, 6, 8.

SHOW AGAIN.

8. Matt. xi. 4.

SHOW BEFORE.

προκαταγγέλλω, (*No.* 8, *with* πρό, before *or* forth, *prefixed.*)

Acts iii. 18. | Acts vii. 52.

SHOW FORTH.

1. ἐνδείκνυμι, *see above, No.* 4.

2. ἐξαγγέλλω, bring word out, give out intelligence, *from one place to another;* (lxx. *for* ספר, Ps. ix. 15; lxxix. 13), (*non occ.*)

1. 1 Tim. i. 16. | 2. 1 Pet. ii. 9.

SHOW FORTH ONE'S SELF.

ἐνεργέω, to be in work, *i.e.* to work, be effective, operate, produce effect.

Matt. xiv. 2. | Mark vi. 14.

SHOW ONE'S SELF.

1. ὁράω, to see with the eyes, (*pass. of* "SEE," *No.* 8) to be seen, be beheld.
2. φανερόω, to make apparent, manifest, known. *Mid., as here,* to manifest one's self, show one's self openly, to appear.

2. John xxi. 1, 14. | 1. Acts vii. 26.

SHOW OPENLY.

{ δίδωμι, to give, ἐμφανῆ, manifest, γενέσθαι, to become, } *here,* gave [*him*] to become manifest, *or* openly seen.

Acts x. 40.

SHOWED (BE)

γίνομαι, to become, take place, happen.

Acts iv. 22.

SHOW-BREAD.

1. { οἱ, the ἄρτοι, loaves τῆς, of the, προθέσεως, of setting forth, arrangement, exposure, *or* exhibition, } the loaves of the setting forth, (*see the note, below.*)
2. { ἡ, the πρόθεσις, setting forth *or* arrangement τῶν, of the ἄρτων, loaves, } the arrangement *or* setting forth of the loaves, (*the writer having the loaves themselves arranged in view.*)

[In Heb. לחם חפנים, *bread of the face* or *faces,* Ex. xxv. 30; xxxv. 13; xxxix. 36, *etc.* לחם אפים *or* לחם המערכת, *bread set in order,* 1 Ch. ix. 32; xxiii. 29; 2 Ch. xxix. 18; Neh. x. 34. In Num. iv. 7, we find לחם התמיד, *the perpetual bread,* and in 1 Sam. xxi. 4-6, לחם קדש, *holy bread.* In the lxx. we have ἄρτοι ἐνώπιοι, *the bread in front of,* Ex. xxv. 30; and ἄρτοι τῆς προσφορᾶς, *the bread of the offering,* 1 Kings vii. 48.

The Heb. *bread of the face* or *faces, i.e. of the presence,* must refer to the presence of God, from the expressions above in the lxx. and 1 Sam. xxi. 6. Compare the expression, מלאך פנים, the angel of God's presence, (Is. lxiii. 9, compared with Ex. xxxiii. 14, 15, and Deut. iv. 37.) God's "name is in him," Ex. xxiii. 20. The "*bread of the face*" is therefore symbolical of that heavenly bread, through eating of which that life is given and nourished, by and in which alone God's presence shall be enjoyed. The "show-bread" was "taken from the children of Israel by an everlasting covenant" (Lev. xxiv. 8.) Christ (who is God Himself) took flesh of "the children of Israel by an everlasting covenant," that by partaking of Him who is "the bread of life" set before us, we may enjoy the presence of God. (*See also,* Ps. xxiii. 5; Luke xxii. 30.)]

1. Matt. xii. 4. | 1. Luke vi. 4.
1. Mark ii. 26. | 2. Heb. ix. 2.

SHOWER.

ὄμβρος, a heavy shower, violent rain *with thunder and tempest. Lat.,* imber; (lxx. *for* שעירים, Deut. xxxii. 2), (*non occ.*)

Luke xii. 54.

SHOWING.

ἀνάδειξις, a showing up, a lifting up and showing; *hence,* a showing forth, (*non occ.*)

Luke i. 80.

SHRINE.

ναός, dwelling; *hence,* the most sacred part of a temple, *where the image of the god was set up.*

Acts xix. 24.

SHUN (-ED.)

1. περιΐστημι, *trans.,* to cause to stand around; *intrans.,* to stand around; *here, mid.,* to place one's self around, *i.e.* so as not to come near; *hence,* to stand aloof from.

2. *ὑποστέλλω*, to send or draw under. *In N.T.*, *mid.*, to draw one's self back under cover *or* out of sight; *hence*, to shrink from; to draw or keep back anything, suppress it.

2. Acts xx. 27.
1. 2 Tim. ii. 16.

SHUT (-ETH.)

1. *κλείω*, to shut, to close; shut up; (lxx. *for* סגר, Gen. vii. 16; Josh. ii. 7), (*non occ.*)

2. *ἀποκλείω*, (*No.* 1, *with ἀπό*, away from, *prefixed*) to shut up away from, shut away, shut to, make quite fast; (lxx. *for* סגר, Gen. xix. 10; Judg. iii. 23; נעל, 2 Sam. xiii. 17), (*non occ.*)

1. Matt. vi. 6 part.
1. —— xxv. 10.
1. Luke xi. 7.
2. —— xiii. 25.
1. John xx. 19 part., 26.
1. Acts. v. 23.
1. —— xxi. 30.
1. Rev. iii. 7 twice, 8.
1. —— xi. 6.
1. —— xxi. 25.

SHUT UP.

1. *κλείω*, *see above*, *No.* 1.

2. *κατακλείω*, (*No.* 1, *with κατά*, down, *prefixed*) to shut down, *as in a subterranean prison, and then gen.*, to shut up, confine; (lxx. *for* כלא, Jer. xxxii. 3), (*non occ.*)

3. *συγκλείω*, (*No.* 1, *with σύν*, in conjunction with, *prefixed*) to shut up together; (lxx. *for* הסגיר ביד, Ps. xxxi. 9; Josh. xx. 5.)

1. Matt. xxiii. 13.
2. Luke iii. 20.
1. —— iv. 25.
2. Acts xxvi. 10.
— Gal. iii. 22, marg.; see Conclude.
3. —— 23.
1. 1 John iii. 17.
1. Rev. xx. 3.

SICK.

(*For* "BE SICK," *and other combinations, see below.*)

1. *ἀσθενέω*, to want strength, to be *ασθενής*, (*see No.* 2) be infirm, weak, feeble.

(*a*) *Participle*, wanting strength, being weak or infirm.

2. *ἀσθενής*, without strength, infirm, imbecile; to have (naturally) no strength, impotent, one whose strength has gone.

3. *ἄρρωστος*, one whose strength has failed through disease, languid, sick. (*Hence, No.* 3 *is applied to* one sick at heart, sick in spirit; *while No.* 2 *would apply to* one weak in mind.)

4. *κάμνω*, to be weary, faint, *as from* labour, faint or weary in mind, distressed with *labour or anything else.*

(*a*) *Participle*, one whose strength gives way in consequence of excessive labour, (*whence*, *κάμοντες* and *κεκμηκότες* (*but not κάμνοντες*) are the dead, whose labours are ended.)

[Here used of such sick as may recover; *hence*, no ground is afforded for "*extreme unction*," which is never administered till all hope of recovery has vanished.]

5. *νοσέω*, to have a sickly longing for *anything*, to pine after, dote about, (*non occ.*)

— Matt. viii. 6, see Palsy.
— —— 14, see Fever.
— —— ix. 2 twice, 6, see Palsy.
1a. —— x. 8.
3. —— xiv. 14.
2. —— xxv. 39 (No. 1a, L T Tr A.)
2. —— 43, 44.
— Mark i. 30, see Fever.
— —— ii. 3, 4, 5, 9, 10, see Palsy.
1a. —— vi. 56.
3. —— xvi. 18 (ap.)
1a. Luke iv. 40.
— —— v. 24, see Palsy.
1a. —— ix. 2 (No. 2, L Tr[b] א), (om. *τοὺς ασθενοῦντας, the sick*, T A.)
2. —— x. 9.
4a. Jas. v. 15.
1a. John xi. 1.
2. Acts v. 15.
— —— ix. 33, see Palsy.
1a. —— xix. 12.
5. 1 Tim. vi. 4, marg. (text, *dote.*)
1a. 2 Tim. iv. 20.

SICK (BE)

1. *ασθενέω*,

2. { *ἔχω*, to have, / *κακῶς*, ill, evil, } to be ill.

2. Matt. viii. 16.
2. —— ix. 12.
1. —— xxv. 36.
2. Mark i. 34.
2. —— ii. 17.
2. —— vi. 55.
2. Luke v. 31.
2. —— vii. 2.
1. Luke vii. 10 (om. *ἀσθενοῦντα, was sick*, L T Tr א), (A[b].)
1. John iv. 46.
1. —— xi. 2, 3, 6.
1. Acts ix. 37.
1. Phil. ii. 26, 27.
1. Jas. v. 14.

SICK FOLK.

1. *ἀσθενής*, *see* "SICK," *No.* 2. *Here, pl.*

2. *ἄρρωστος*, *see* "SICK," *No.* 3. *Here, pl.*

2. Mark vi. 5.
1. Acts v. 16.

SICK OF (LIE)

συνέχω, to hold *or* press together. *Here, pass.*, to be held fast.

Acts xxviii. 8.

SICK PEOPLE.

{ οἱ, the [*people*]
{ ἔχων, having
{ κακῶς, ill, evil.

Matt. iv. 24.

SICK (THAT IS)

ἄρρωστος, *see* "SICK," *No.* 3.

Mark iv. 13.

SICKLE.

δρέπανον, a sickle *or crooked knife*, to pluck off *the harvest and vintage;* (lxx. *for* מגל, Joel. iii. 13), (*non occ.*)

Mark iv. 29.
Rev. xiv. 14, 15, 16, 17, 18 twice, 19.

SICKLY.

ἄρρωστος, *see* "SICK," *No.* 3.

1 Cor. xi. 30.

SICKNESS (-ES.)

1. νόσος, sickness, confirmed disease; (lxx. *for* חלי, 2 Ch. xxi. 19; מחלה, Ex. xv. 26.)

   (a) Matt. viii. 17 *is quoted from* Is. liii. 4, where it is lxx. *for* מכאבינו.

2. ἀσθενεία, want of strength, infirmity.

1. Matt. iv. 23.
1a. —— viii. 17.
1. —— ix. 35.
1. —— x. 1.
1. Mark iii. 15 (*om.* θεραπεύειν τὰς νόσους, καὶ, *to heal sicknesses and*, T Tr A ℵ.)
2. John xi. 4.

SIDE.

πλευρά, the side of the body, *Eng.*, pleura; (lxx. *for* צלע, rib, Gen. ii. 21; צד, Numb. xxxiii. 55; 2 Sam. ii. 16.)

John xix. 34.
John xx. 20, 25, 27.
Acts xii. 7.

See also, BY, EITHER, EVERY, FARTHER, HIGHWAY, OTHER, PASS, RIGHT, WAY.

SIDON.

Σιδών, Sidon. Heb. צידון, (fishing, fishery) Zidon, *now called* Saide.

[Josephus derives it from the eldest son of Canaan, Gen. x. 15; Jos. Ant. i. 6, 2. Mentioned as early as Gen. x. 19; xliv. 13. Assigned by Joshua to the tribe of Asher, but never subdued by them, Judg. i. 31; x. 12.]

In all passages, except

Mark vii. 24 (*om.* καὶ Σιδῶνος, *and Sidon*, G → T A.)
Luke iv. 26 (Σιδώνιος, *Sidonian*, G ∾ L T Tr A ℵ.)

SIFT.

σινιάζω, to sift, as grain in a sieve, (*non occ.*)

Luke xxii. 31.

SIGH (-ED.)

στενάζω, to groan, to sigh; (lxx. *for* נאנח, Is. xxiv. 7; Lam. i. 22.)

Mark vii. 34.

SIGH DEEPLY.

ἀναστενάζω, (*the above, with* ἀνά, up, *prefixed*) to fetch up a deep-drawn sigh; (lxx. *for* נאנח, Lam. i. 4), (*non occ.*)

Mark viii. 12.

SIGHT.

(*For various combinations with other words, see below.*)

1. εἶδος, the thing looked at and *actually* seen, (*subjective*) external appearance, (*subst. of* "SEE," *No.* 1.)
2. θεωρία, a sight, a spectacle, (*subst. of* "SEE," *No.* 11), (*non occ.*)
3. ὀφθαλμος, an eye. *Here,* ἀπὸ τῶν ὀφθαλμῶν αὐτῶν, away from their eyes.
4. ὅραμα, the thing seen, (*objective*); that which is presented to the vision; *hence*, a vision; (lxx. *for* מראה, Ex. iii. 3; Deut. xxviii. 34; Gen. xlvi. 2. חזון, Dan. viii. 2. מחזה, Gen. xv. 1), (*subst. of* "SEE," *No.* 8.)
5. ὅρασις, the sight, sense of seeing; *then*, aspect.
6. πρόσωπον, *the part presented* towards the eye; *hence*, presence, person.
7. φαντάζω, to make appear, make visible. *In N.T.*, *pass. and part.*, τὸ φαινόμενον, the phenomenon, *i.e.* the sight, (*non occ.*)

8. βλέπω, to use the eyes, look at, (*see* "SEE," *No.* 5.) *Here, inf.*

8. Luke vii. 21.
— — xxi. 11, see Fearful.
2. — xxiii. 48.
— — xxiv. 31, see Vanish.
3. Acts i. 9.
4. — vii. 31.
6. 2 Cor. ii. 10, marg. (text, *person.*)
1. — v. 7.
7. Heb. xii. 21.
5. Rev. iv. 3.

SIGHT (IN ONE'S)

1. ἐνώπιον, in the sight *or* presence of.
2. κατενώπίον, (*No.* 1, *with* κατά, down, *prefixed*) down, in the sight *or* presence of, in the very presence of.
3. ἔμπροσθεν, before.

3. Matt. xi. 26.
3. Luke x. 21.
1. — xv. 21.
1. Rom. iii. 20.
2. Col. i. 22.
1. Heb. iv. 13.
1. — xiii. 21.
1. 1 John iii. 22.

SIGHT OF (IN THE)

1. ἐνώπιον, in the sight *or* presence of, (*No.* 1, *above.*)
2. κατενώπιον, *see No.* 2, *above.*
3. ἔμπροσθεν, before.
4. ἐναντίον, over against, in the presence of, *but as being* opposite to.
5. παρά, *with Dat.*, beside and at, at the side of, near, with.

1. Luke i. 15.
1. — xvi. 15.
1. Acts iv. 19.
4. — vii. 10.
1. — viii. 21 (ἔναντι, *over against*, G L T Tr A ℵ.)
1. — x. 31.
1. Rom. xii. 17.
2. 2 Cor. ii. 17 (κατέναντι, *down over against*, G ∾ L T Tr A ℵ.)
1. 2 Cor. iv. 2.
1. — vii. 12.
1. — viii. 21 twice.
5. Gal. iii. 11.
3. 1 Thes. i. 3.
1. 1 Tim. ii. 3.
1. — vi. 13.
1. Jas. iv. 10.
1. 1 Pet. iii. 4.
1. Rev. xiii. 13, 14.

SIGHT (RECEIVE)

ἀναβλέπω, to look up, (*see* "SEE," *Nos.* 5 *and* 6.)

Matt. xi. 5.
— xx. 34.
Mark x. 51, 52.
Luke xviii. 41, 42, 43.
John ix. 11, 15, 18 twice.
Acts ix. 12, 17, 18.
Acts xxii. 13.

SIGHT (RECOVERING OF)

ἀνάβλεψις, a looking up, recovery of sight, (*non occ.*)

Luke iv. 18.

SIGHT (WITHOUT)

{ μὴ, not βλέπων, seeing, (*see* "SEE," *No.* 5), } not using *his* eyes.

Acts ix. 9.

SIGN (-S.)

σημεῖον, a sign, a signal; an ensign, a standard; a sign by which any thing is designated, distinguished, *or* known; *hence, used of* the miracles of Christ *as being* the signs by which He might be known as the Christ of God: a sign authenticating His mission; a sign with reference to what it demonstrates.

Matt. xii. 38, 39 3 times.
— xvi. 1, 3, 4 3 times.
— xxiv. 3, 24, 30.
— xxvi. 48.
Mark viii. 11, 12 twice.
— xiii. 4, 22.
— xvi. 17 (*ap.*), 20 (*ap.*)
Luke i. 62, see S to (make)
— ii. 12, 34.
— xi. 16, 29 3 times, 30.
— xxi. 7, 11, 25.
John ii. 18.
— iv. 48.
— vi. 30.
— xx. 30.
Acts ii. 19, 22, 43.
Acts v. 12.
— vii. 36.
— viii. 13.
— xiv. 3.
— xxviii. 11, see S was (whose)
Rom. iv. 11.
— xv. 19.
1 Cor. i. 22.
— xiv. 22.
2 Cor. xii. 12 twice.
2 Thes. ii. 9.
Heb. ii. 4.
Rev. xii. 1, 3, marg. (text, *wonder.*)
— xv. 1.

SIGN WAS (WHOSE)

παράσημος, marked on the side, (*non occ.*)

Acts xxviii. 11.

SIGNS TO (MAKE)

ἐννεύω, to nod *or* wink to *any one*, to make signs with *the head or eyes, etc.*; (lxx. *for* קרץ, Prov. vi. 13; x. 10.)

Luke i. 62.

SIGNIFICATION (WITHOUT)

ἄφωνος, without sound *or* tone, without voice *or* cry.

1 Cor. xiv. 10.

SIGNIFY (-ED, -ETH, -ING.)

1. σημαίνω, give a (*public*) sign *or* signal; (lxx. *for* הריע, Num. x. 9.) In *N.T.*, to signify, make known, *like* lxx. *for* הגיד, Est. ii. 22, (*non occ.*)

2. δηλόω, to make manifest; *of things past*, to tell, relate; *of things future*, to reveal, show, bring to light; (lxx. *for* נראה, 1 Sam. iii. 21. הודיע, Ex. vi. 3; Dan. iv. 15); *of words*, to imply, signify.

3. διαγγέλλω, to make known through *an intervening space*, to convey a message *or* tidings; *then*, report further, proclaim far and wide; (lxx. *for* ספר, Ex. ix. 16; Ps. ii. 7; אמר, Josh. vi. 10.)

4. ἐμφανίζω, to make apparent, cause to appear, to make known; (lxx. *for* אמר, Est. ii. 22.)

1. John xii. 33.
1. —— xviii. 32.
1. —— xxi. 19.
1. Acts xi. 28.
3. —— xxi. 26.
4. —— xxiii. 15.
1. Acts xxv. 27.
1. 2 Thes. iii. 14, marg. (text, *note*.)
2. Heb. ix. 8.
2. —— xii. 27.
2. 1 Pet. i. 11.
1. Rev. i. 1.

SILAS.

Σίλας, Silas, *contr. of* Σιλουανός, Silvanus.

In all passages, except
Acts xv. 34 (*ap.*)

SILENCE.

1. σιγή, silence, *implying a previous speaking*, (*non occ.*)

2. ἡσυχία, quiet, tranquillity, stillness, (*occ.* 2 Thes. iii. 12.)

1. Acts xxi. 40.
2. —— xxii. 2.
2. 1 Tim. ii. 11, 12.
1. Rev. viii. 1.

SILENCE (KEEP)

σιγάω, to be silent, when speaking, to cease to speak (*from* σίζω, to say hush!)

Acts xv. 12. | **1 Cor. xiv. 28, 34.**

SILENCE (PUT TO)

φιμόω, to muzzle, stop the mouth.

Matt. xxii. 34. | **1 Pet. ii. 15.**

SILK.

σηρικός, silken, of silk, (*from* σήρ, silk-worm); *here*, neut., τὸ σηρικόν, *subst.*, silk, silk-stuffs.

Rev. xviii. 12.

SILLY.

See, WOMAN.

SILVER. [noun and adj.]

1. ἄργυρος, (*from* ἀργός, white) silver; *then*, silver-work, *as images, plate, vessels, or money.*

2. ἀργύριον, silver, *used of money in general.*

2. ἀργύρεος, made of silver; (lxx. *for* כסף, Gen. xxiv. 53; Ex. iii. 22.)

4. δραχμή, as much as one can hold in the hand; an *Attic weight*, a drachma, *or* dram, *about* 66 grains avdp.; a silver coin *worth* 6 obols, *i.e.* nearly 9¾d.

1. Matt. x. 9.
2. Acts iii. 6.
1. —— xvii. 29.
3. —— xix. 24.
2. Acts xx. 33.
1. 1 Cor. iii. 22.
1. Jas. v. 3.
2. 1 Pet. i. 18.
1. Rev. xviii. 12.

SILVER (OF)

3. 2 Tim. ii. 20. | **3. Rev. ix. 20.**

SILVER (PIECE OF)

2. Matt. xxvi. 15.
2. —— xxvii. 3, 5, 9.
4. Luke xv. 8. [*pieces.*
2. Acts xix. 19, marg.

SILVER PIECE.

2. Matt. xxvii. 6.

SILVERSMITH.

ἀργυροκόπος, a labourer in silver, silver-smith; (lxx. *for* צרוף, Jer. vi. 29), (*non occ.*)

Acts xix. 24.

SIMILITUDE.

1. ὁμοιότης, likeness, resemblance; (lxx. *for* מין, Gen. i. 11, 12), (*occ.* Heb. iv. 15.)

2. ὁμοίωμα, something made like, a likeness, resemblance.

3. ὁμοίωσις, a likening, comparison; (lxx. *for* דמות, Gen. i. 26), (*non occ.*)

2. Rom. v. 14. | **1. Heb. vii. 15.**
3. Jas. iii. 9.

SIMON.

Σίμων, Simon, (Heb. שמעון, a hearing) a proper name of several persons in *O.* and *N.T.*

In all passages, except
2 Pet. i. 1, Συμεών, Simeon (St G T Tr A ℵ.)

SIMPLE.

1. ἄκακος, void of evil; (lxx. *for* תם, Job. ii. 3; viii. 20; פתי, Prov. i. 4; xiv. 15), (*occ.* Heb. vii. 26.)

2. ἀκέραιος, unmixed; *hence*, without guile, artless, (*occ.* Matt. x. 16; Phil. i. 15.)

2. Matt. x. 16 marg. (text, *harmless.*)
1. Rom. xvi. 18.
2. —— 19.

SIMPLICITY.

ἁπλότης, singleness, simplicity, plainness; *always opp. to duplicity.*

Rom. xii. 8, with ἐν, in (marg. *liberally.*)
2 Cor. i. 12 (ἁγιότης, *holiness*, L T Tr A ℵ.)
—— xi. 3 (add καὶ τῆς ἁγνότητος, *and your chastity*, L Tr A ℵ), i.e. "*your singleness and your chastity towards* (εἰς, not ἐν) *Christ.*"

SIN (-s.) [noun.]

1. ἁμαρτία, miss, failure, aberration from prescribed law or duty; *hence*, sin, *considered not as an action, but as the* quality of action, the evil principle, (*from which No.* 2 *springs*) *i.e.* sin *generically*, all forms, phases, and movements of sin, whether entertained in thought or consummated in act. *In the singular*, (*only once in the first three Gospels*, Matt. xii. 31, *but frequently in the Epistles*) *it denotes* the generic idea of sin, *or* a single sinful action. *With the art.*, it refers to the entire contents, *not merely the representation of the idea.* Sin *is not merely*, *however*, *the quality of an action*, *but* a principle manifesting itself in the activity of the subject. The "man of sin," 2 Thes. ii. 3, *being* the personal embodiment of sin.

Also used of the sin offering, Heb. x. 6, 8, 18; xiii. 11; (lxx. *for* חטאת, Ps. xl. 7; *cf.* Lev. v. 8.)

[If ἁμαρτία is from ἀμαρα, a duct *or* canal by which water flows down to any place, then it is akin to אמר, to speak *or* put forth, and חמר, which implies an evil influence, and to all the cognate dialects, (Chald., Syr., Arab., Eth.) in which it has the idea of turpidity and excitement, muddy confusion in water, acetous fermentation in wine, bitumen arising from hot natural springs, collection of mud brought down by tumultuous waters, bitter and brackish waters, etc.; *and hence*, we have the *Lat.* amarus, and the *French* amère. ἁμαρτία then, is the defiling influence and bitter principle of disturbance which has flowed down upon the creation of God.]

2. ἁμάρτημα *is always used for* the actual transgression, the result of the evil principle in action; *hence*, sinful action, sinful deed; (lxx. *for* חטאת, Gen. xxxi. 36, etc.; עון, Ex xxviii. 38, etc.; פשע, Is. lviii. 1, etc.)

3. παράπτωμα, a falling when one should have stood upright, a misfall, mishap; *hence*, a falling aside from right, truth, *or* duty, the particular and special act of sin from ignorance, inadvertence, or negligence; sin rashly committed by one unwilling to do an injury.

[In Rom. v. 12, *No.* 1 is said to have entered the world. The disobedience of Adam is called *No.* 3, (Rom. v. 15, 17, 18); and then, in verse 20, it says, "The law entered that *No.* 3 might abound," and that which before was the result of imprudence or error might become criminal in the knowledge of the sinner. And then, after this, where *No.* 1 abounded, there grace did much more abound.]

1. Matt. i. 21.
1. —— iii. 6.
1. —— ix. 2, 5, 6.
1. —— xii. 31.
1. —— xxvi. 28.
1. Mark i. 4, 5.
1. —— ii. 5, 7, 9, 10.
2. —— iii. 28.
2. —— iv. 12 (om. τὰ ἁμαρτήματα, *their sins*, G ⇉ Lᵇ T Tr A ℵ), i.e. *it.*
1. Luke i. 77.
1. —— iii. 3.
1. —— v. 20, 21, 23, 24.
1. —— vii. 47, 48, 49.
1. —— xi. 4.
1. —— xxiv. 47.
1. John i. 29.
— —— viii. 7, see S (without)
1. John viii. 21, 24 twice, 34 1st. [46.
— —— 34 2nd (om. G ⇉),
1. —— ix. 34, 41 twice.
1. —— xv. 22 twice, 24.
1. —— xvi. 8, 9.
1. —— xix. 11.
1. —— xx. 23.
1. Acts ii. 38.
1. —— iii. 19.
1. —— v. 31.
1. —— vii. 60.
1. —— x. 43.
1. —— xiii. 38.
1. —— xxii. 16.
1. —— xxvi. 18.
1. Rom. iii. 9, 20.
2. —— 25.
1. —— iv. 7, 8. [20, 21.
1. —— v. 12 twice, 13 twice,

1. Rom. vi. 1, 2, 6 twice, 7, 10, 11, 12, 13, 14, 16, 17, 18, 20, 22, 23.
1. —— vii. 5, 7 twice, 8 twice, 9, 11, 13 3 times, 14, 17, 20, 23, 25.
1. —— viii. 2.
1. —— 3 1st, marg. *sacrifice for sin.*
1. —— 3 2nd, 10.
1. —— xi. 27.
1. —— xiv. 23.
2. 1 Cor. vi. 18.
1. —— xv. 3, 17, 56 twice.
1. 2 Cor. v. 21 twice.
1. Gal. i. 4.
1. —— ii. 17.
1. —— iii. 22.
3. Eph. i. 7.
1. —— ii. 1.
3. —— 5.
1. Col. i. 14.
1. —— ii. 11 (*om.* τῶν ἁμαρτιῶν, *of the sins,* G L T Tr A ℵ.)
3. —— 13.
1. 1 Thes. ii. 16.
1. 2 Thes. ii. 3.
1. 1 Tim. v. 22, 24.
1. 2 Tim. iii. 6.
1. Heb. i. 3.
1. —— ii. 17.
1. Heb. iii. 13.
1. —— iv. 15.
1. —— v. 1, 3.
1. —— vii. 27.
1. —— viii. 12.
1. —— ix. 26, 28 twice.
1. —— x. 2, 3, 4, 6, 8, 11, 12, 17, 18, 26.
1. —— xi. 25.
1. —— xii. i. 4.
1. —— xiii. 11.
1. Jas. i. 15 twice.
1. —— ii. 9.
1. —— iv. 17.
1. —— v. 15, 20.
1. 1 Pet. ii. 22, 24 twice.
1. —— iii. 18.
1. —— iv. 1, 8.
1. 2 Pet. i. 9 (G ∾), (No. 2, G T Tr ℵ.)
1. —— ii. 14.
1. 1 John 1, 7, 8, 9 twice.
1. —— ii. 2 1st.
— —— 2 2nd, see S of (for the)
1. —— 12.
1. —— iii. 4 twice, 5 twice 8, 9.
1. —— iv. 10.
1. —— v. 16 twice, 17 twice.
1. Rev. i. 5.
1. —— xviii. 4, 5.

SIN (WITHOUT)

ἀναμάρτητος, without missing *or* failing; unfailing, unerring; *esp. in a moral sense,* faultless, blameless.

John viii. 7 (*ap.*)

SINS OF (FOR THE)

περί, around. *Here, with Gen.,* concerning, on behalf of.

1 John ii. 2.

SIN (-ED, -ETH.) [verb.]

ἁμαρτάνω, to miss the mark, swerve from, err; *hence,* to sin; (lxx. *for* חטא, Ex. ix. 28, 35, etc.)

Matt. xviii. 21.
—— xxvii. 4.
Luke xv. 18, 21.
John v. 14.
—— viii. 11 (*ap.*)
—— ix. 2, 3.
Rom. ii. 12 twice.
—— iii. 23.
—— v. 12, 14.
—— 16 part. (ἁμαρτήματος, gen. of "SIN," No. 2, G ∾)
—— vi. 15.
1 Cor. vi. 18.
—— vii. 28 twice, 36.
1 Cor. viii. 12 twice.
—— xv. 34.
2 Cor. xii. 21, see S already.
—— xiii. 2, see S heretofore.
Eph. iv. 26.
1 Tim. v. 20.
Tit. iii. 11.
Heb. iii. 17.
—— x. 26.
2 Pet. ii. 4.
1 John i. 10.
—— ii. 1 twice.
—— iii. 6 twice, 8, 9.
—— v. 16 twice, 18.

SIN ALREADY.

προαμαρτάνω, *here perf.,* to have sinned before *or* previously.

2 Cor. xii. 21.

SIN HERETOFORE.

προαμαρτάνω, *see above.*

2 Cor. xiii. 2.

SINCE.

1. ἀπό, from, away from.
2. { ἀπό, from / οὗ, which.
3. ἐπεί, since, because, in as much as.
4. ἐπειδή, (*No.* 3, *with* δή, indeed, *affixed*) since indeed, because truly, in as much as really.
5. μετά, with, in association with; *here, with Acc.,* after.
6. ὡς, as, in what way; *in a clause referring to time,* when, from when, since.

1. Matt. xxiv. 21.
6. Mark ix. 21.
— Luke i. 70, see World.
— —— vii. 45, see S the time.
— —— xvi. 16, see Time.
2. —— xxiv. 21.
— John ix. 32, } see World.
— Acts iii. 21, } see World.
— Rom. xvi. 25, } see World.
4. 1 Cor. xv. 21.
3. 2 Cor. xiii. 3.
1. Col. i. 6, 9.
5. Heb. vii. 28.
1. Heb. ix. 26.

SINCE THE TIME.

{ ἀπό, from, away from, / ἧς, which, } (*the word* day *or* time *being understood.*)

Luke vii. 45.

SINCERE.

1. ἄδολος, without guile *or* deceit, unadulterated, pure, (*non occ.*)
2. εἰλικρινής, judged of in the sunlight, *and so* found genuine; *hence,* pure, distinct, sheer, (*occ.* 2 Pet. iii. 1.)

2. Phil. i. 10.
— Phil. ii. 15, marg. see [*Harmless.*
1. 1 Pet. ii. 2.

SINCERELY.

ἁγνῶς, (*adv. of* "PURE," *No.* 2) sincerely, purely, with pure intention, (*non occ.*)

Phil. i. 16.

SINCERITY.

1. εἰλικρίνεια, clearness, pureness, genuineness, *as found so by being judged of in the sunlight,* (*non occ.*)

2. ἀφθαρσία, incorruption, incapacity of decay; *of things*, perpetuity.

3. { τὸ, the γνήσιον, legitimate, genuine, } genuineness, reality.

1. 1 Cor. v. 8.
1. 2 Cor. i. 12.
1. — ii. 17.
3. — viii. 8.
2. Eph. vi. 24, marg. *incorruption.*
2. Tit. ii. 7 (*om.* G L T Tr A ℵ.)

SINFUL.

1. ἁμαρτωλός, erring from the way or mark, erring from the divine law, sinful.

2. ἁμαρτία, *see* "SIN," *No.* 1. *Here, gen.*, of sin.

1. Mark viii. 38.
1. Luke v. 8.
1. Luke xxiv. 7.
1. Rom. vii. 13.
2. Rom. viii. 3.

SING (-ING, SANG, SUNG.)

1. ᾄδω, to sing, *used of all kinds of sounds made by the voice both of men and animals: of man as distinct from animals*, to sing, to chant; *then*, to sing in praise or honour, celebrate in song; (lxx. *for* שׁוּר, Ex. xiv. 32; xv. 21; Numb. xxi. 17; 1 Ch. xvi. 23), (*non occ.*)

2. ψάλλω, to touch, twitch, pluck, *as a string*, to twang; *hence*, to touch the lyre, play. In lxx. and *N.T.*, to sing as accompanied by stringed instruments; (lxx. נָגַן, 1 Sam. xvi. 23; xviii. 10; xix. 9.)

— Matt. xxvi. 30, } see
— Mark xiv. 26, } Hymn.
— Acts xvi. 25, see Praise.
2. Rom. xv. 9.
2. 1 Cor. xiv. 15 twice.
1. Eph. v. 19.
1. Col. iii. 16.
— Heb. ii. 12, see Praise.
— Jas. v. 13, see Psalm.
1. Rev. v. 9.
1. — xiv. 3.
1. — xv. 3.

SINGLE.

ἁπλόος, *like Lat.*, simplex, *opp. to* διπλόος, *Lat.*, duplex, two-fold; *and so*, single, in one way; *hence*, simple, (*non occ.*)

Matt. vi. 22. | Luke xi. 34.

SINGLENESS.

1. ἁπλότης, singleness, simplicity; *always opp. to duplicity.*

2. ἀφελότες, (from ἀφελής, not stony, level) simplicity, neatness, plainness, (*non occ.*)

2. Acts ii. 46.
1. Eph. vi. 5.
1. Col. iii. 22.

SINK, SUNK.

καταποντίζω, to sink down in the sea. *In N.T.*, *pass or mid.*, to sink, be sunk, drowned.

Matt. xiv. 30.

SINK (BEGIN TO)

βυθίζω, to sink in the deep. *Here pass.*, to sink, (*occ.* 1 Tim. vi. 9.)

Luke v. 7.

SINK DOWN.

καταφέρω, to bear *or* carry down *from a higher to a lower place*, to bear down. *Here pass.*, to be borne *or* thrown down.

Acts xx. 9.

SINK DOWN (LET)

τίθημι, to set, put, place, lay. *Here mid.*, to set or put for one's self, *i.e. on one's own part or behalf.*

Luke ix. 44.

SINNER (-S.)

1. ἁμαρτωλός, erring from the way or mark, erring from the divine law, sinful; *also, as subst.*, one who thus errs, a sinner, transgressor. *Among the Jews*, Gentiles were called ἁμαρτωλοί, Matt. xxvi. 45; Mark xiv. 41, *compared with* Luke xviii. 32; Matt. xx. 19; Mark x. 33. *So*, lxx. and רָשָׁע, Is. xiv. 5.

2. ὀφειλέτης, a debtor, one morally bound to the performance of any duty; *then*, one who fails in that performance, a delinquent.

1. Matt. ix. 10, 11, 13.
1. — xi. 19.
1. — xxvi. 45.
1. Mark ii. 15, 16 twice, 17.
1. — xiv. 41.
1. Luke v. 30, 32.
1. — vi. 32, 33, 34 twice.
1. — vii. 34, 37, 39.
1. — xiii. 2.
2. — — 4.
1. — xv. 1, 2, 7, 10.
1. — xviii. 13.
1. Luke xix. 7.
1. John ix. 16, 24, 25, 31.
1. Rom. iii. 7.
1. — v. 8, 19.
1. Gal. ii. 15, 17.
1. 1 Tim. i. 9, 15.
1. Heb. vii. 26.
1. — xii. 3.
1. Jas. iv. 8.
1. — v. 20.
1. 1 Pet. iv. 18.
1. Jude 15.

SIR (-S.)

1. κύριος, lord, master, owner, (*see* "LORD," *No.* 1*.)

2. ἀνήρ, a man; *Lat.* vir., *i.e.* an adult male person, a man *in sex and age*, (*see* "MAN," *Nos.* 1 *and* 2.)

3. παιδίον, a little child, *either male or female; an endearing appellation when used of adults.*

1. Matt. xiii. 27.
1. —— xxi. 30.
1. —— xxvii. 63.
1. Luke xiv. 21.
1. John iv. 11, 15, 19, 49.
1. —— v. 7.
1. —— xii. 21.
1. —— xx. 15.
3. John xxi. 5 marg. (text, *child.*)
2. Acts vii. 26.
2. —— xiv. 15.
1. —— xvi. 30.
2. —— xix. 25.
2. —— xxvii. 10, 21, 25.
1. Rev. vii. 14.

SISTER (-s.)

ἀδελφή, a sister, (*fem. of* ἀδελφός, *being* α, *indicating unity, and* δελφυς, uterus, (*non occ.*)

Matt. xii. 50.
—— xiii. 56.
—— xix. 29.
Mark iii. 35.
—— vi. 3.
—— x. 29, 30.
Luke x. 39, 40.
—— xiv. 26.
John xi. 1, 3, 5, 28, 39.
John xix. 25.
Acts xxiii. 16.
Rom. xvi. 1, 15.
1 Cor. vii. 15.
—— ix. 5.
Col. iv. 10, see Sister's [Son.
1 Tim. v. 2.
Jas. ii. 15.
2 John 13.

SISTER'S SON.

ἀνεψιός, a nephew; lxx. *for* בן דוד, Numb. xxxvi. 11, (*non. occ.*)

Col. iv. 10.

SIT (-EST, -ETH, -ING; SAT, SET.)

(*For various combinations with other words, see below.*)

1. κάθημαι, to sit down, *but more usually*, to sit; (lxx. *for* ישב, Gen. xxi. 16, etc.) *In the sense of* to abide, dwell, *as in* Matt. iv. 16, *quoted from* Is. ix. 1, *where* lxx. *is* κατοικέω, *for* ישב, Luke i. 79; Acts xiv. 8.

2. καθίζω, *trans.*, to cause to sit down, to seat; *intrans.*, to sit down, to sit.

3. ἀνάκειμαι, to be laid up (*as offerings in the temples of the gods*, etc.); to be laid out (*as a dead body*, Mark v. 40); *in later usage*, to be laid up at a meal on a triclinium, to recline at table, sit at meat.

1. Matt. iv. 16 twice.
1. —— ix. 9.
1. —— xi. 16.
1. —— xiii. 1, 2.
2. —— xix. 28.
2. —— xx. 21, 23.
1. —— 30.
1. —— xxii. 44.
2. —— xxiii. 2.
1. —— 22.
1. Matt. xxiv. 3 part.
2. —— xxv. 31.
3. —— xxvi. 7 part.
2. —— 36.
1. —— 58, 64, 69.
1. —— xxvii. 61.
1. —— xxviii. 2.
1. Mark ii. 6, 14.
1. —— iii. 32, 34.
1. —— iv. 1.
1. Mark v. 15.
2. —— x. 37, 40.
1. —— 46.
2. —— xi. 2, 7.
1. —— xiii. 36 (No. 2, T Tr A.)
2. —— 41.
1. —— xiii. 3 part.
3. —— xiv. 18 part.
2. —— 32.
1. —— 62.
1. —— xvi. 5.
2. —— 19 (*ap.*)
1. Luke i. 79.
1. —— v. 27.
1. —— vii. 32.
1. —— viii. 35.
1. —— x. 13.
1. —— xviii. 35.
2. —— xix. 30.
1. —— xx. 42.
2. —— xxii. 30.
1. —— 56 part.
1. —— 69 (with εἰμί, *to be.*)
1. John ii. 14.
1. —— vi. 3.
1. —— ix. 8.
2. —— xii. 14.
1. —— 15.
1. Acts ii. 2 (καθέζομαι, *to set one's self down, sit down, sit still*, L.)
2. Acts ii. 3, 30.
1. —— 34.
1. —— iii. 10.
1. —— viii. 28.
2. —— 31.
2. —— xii. 21.
1. —— xiv. 8.
1. —— xx. 9 (καθέζομαι, *to set one's self down, sit down, sit still*, L T Tr A ℵ.)
1. —— xxiii. 3.
2. —— xxv. 6, 17.
1. Col. iii. 1 (with εἰμί, *to be.*)
2. 2 Thes. ii. 4.
1. Heb. i. 13.
1. Jas. ii. 3 twice.
2. Rev. iii. 21.
1. —— iv. 2, 3 (*ap.*), 4, 9, 10.
1. —— v. 1, 7, 13.
1. —— vi. 2, 4, 5, 8, 16.
1. —— vii. 10, 15.
1. —— ix. 17.
1. —— xi. 16.
1. —— xiv. 14, 15, 16.
1. —— xvii. 1, 3, 9, 15.
1. —— xviii. 7.
1. —— xix. 4, 11, 18, 19, [21.
2. —— xx. 4.
1. —— 11.
1. —— xxi. 5.

SIT AT.

παρακαθίζω, to sit down near, seat one's self near, παρά, beside, (*non occ.*)

Luke x. 39.

SIT AT MEAT.

1. ἀνάκειμαι, *see above, No.* 3.

2. κατάκειμαι, to lie down, to lie, be recumbent; *then*, to recline *as at table, in the oriental manner.*

3. κατακλίνω, to make incline, *i.e.* to make lie down. *In N.T., only of the oriental posture at meals*, to make recline *as at a meal.*

1. Matt. ix. 10 part.
2. Mark ii. 15.
2. —— xiv. 3.
1. —— xvi. 14 part., marg. *sit together* (*ap.*)
1. Luke vii. 37 (No. 2, L T Tr A ℵ.)
1. —— xxii. 27 twice.
3. —— xxiv. 30.
1. 1 Cor. viii. 10.

SIT AT MEAT WITH.

συνανάκειμαι, (*No.* 1, *above, with* σύν, in conjunction together with, *prefixed.*)

Matt. xiv. 9.
Luke xiv. 10, 15.
Luke vii. 49.

SIT AT THE TABLE WITH.

συνανάκειμαι, *see above.*

John xii. 2 (ἀνάκειμαι, see "SIT," No. 1, G L T Tr A ℵ.)

SIT BY.

κάθημαι, see "SIT," *No.* 1.

uke v. 17. | 1 Cor. xiv. 30.

SIT DOWN.

1. *καθίζω, see* "SIT," *No.* 2.
2. *ἀναπίπτω*, to fall upon *or* towards, *i.e.* to fall down, lie down; (lxx. *for* כרע, Gen. xlix. 9.) *In N.T.*, to recline *as at meals*, etc.
3. *ἀνάκλινω*, to cause to lie upon, to cause to recline *in order to take a meal. Here mid.*, to recline *as at a meal.*
4. *κάθημαι, see* "SIT," *No.* 1.
5. *ἀνάκειμαι, see* "SIT," *No.* 3.
6. *κατάκειμαι*, to lie down, be recumbent; *then*, to recline *as at meals.*
7. *καταλίνω, see* "SIT AT MEAT," *No.* 3.

3. Matt. viii. 11.
1. —— xiii. 48.
3. —— xiv. 19.
4. —— xv. 29.
2. ——— 35.
5. —— xxvi. 20.
4. —— xxvii. 36.
2. Mark vi. 40.
2. —— viii. 6.
1. —— ix. 35.
1. Luke iv. 20.
1. —— v. 3.
6. ——— 29.
3. —— vii. 36 (No. 7, L T Tr A), (No. 6, ℵ.)
3. Luke xiii. 20.
7. —— xiv. 8.
2. ——— 10.
1. ——— 28, 31.
1. —— xvi. 6.
2. —— xxii. 14.
4. ——— 55.
2. John vi. 10 twice.
1. —— viii. 2 (*ap.*)
1. —— xix. 13.
1. Acts xiii. 14.
1. —— xvi. 13.
1. 1 Cor. x. 7.
1. Heb. i. 3.
1. —— x. 12.

SIT DOWN (MAKE)

1. *ἀνακλίνω, see above, No.* 3.
2. *κατακλίνω, see* "SIT AT MEAT," *No.* 3.

1. Mark vi. 39 (mid., L ℵ.)
2. Luke ix. 14.
1. Luke ix. 15 (No. 2, T Tr A* ℵ.)
2. Luke xii. 37.

SIT DOWN TO MEAT.

ἀναπίπτω, see "SIT DOWN," *No.* 2.

Luke xi. 37. | Luke xvii. 7.

SIT DOWN WITH.

συνανάκειμαι, to recline with *any one, as at table*, to eat with, etc.

Matt. ix. 10.

SIT TOGETHER (MAKE)

συγκαθίζω, ("SIT," *No.* 2, *with σύν*, together *or* in conjunction with, *prefixed.*)

Eph. ii. 6.

SIT TOGETHER. [margin.]

Mark xvi. 14, see "SIT AT MEAT."

SIT TOGETHER WITH.

συνανάκειμαι, see "SIT DOWN WITH."

Mark ii. 15.

SIT UP.

ἀνακαθίζω, "SIT," *No.* 2, *with ἀνά*, up, *prefixed; trans.*, to set up. *In N.T.*, *intrans.*, to sit up, (*non occ.*)

Luke vii. 15 (*καθίζω*, "SIT," No. 2, Lm.)
Acts ix. 40.

SIT UPON.

ἐπιβαίνω, to go upon, tread upon; to set foot upon; go up upon, to mount. *Here perfect, followed* by *ἐπί*, upon.

Matt. xxi. 5.

SIT WITH.

1. *συνανάκειμαι*, ("SIT," *No.* 3, *with σύν*, together in conjunction with, *prefixed.*)
2. *συνκάθημαι*, ("SIT," *No.* 1, *with σύν*, together in conjunction with, *prefixed*), (*non occ.*)

Mark vi. 22.
——— 26 ("SIT," No. 3, T Tr A.)
Mark xiv. 54 part., with *ἦν*, was.
Acts xxvi. 30.

SIX.

ἕξ, six.

[As a symbolical number it denotes *imperfection, non-completeness*, falling as it does just short of seven, which denotes perfection. See Job v. 19; Prov. vi. 16; John ii. 6. *See further under* "HUNDRED THREESCORE AND SIX (SIX,)" page 391.]

Matt. xvii. 1.
Mark ix. 1.
Luke iv. 25.
—— xiii. 14.
John ii. 6, 20.
—— xii. 1.
Acts xi. 12.
Acts xviii. 11.
Jas. v. 17.
Rev. iv. 8.
—— xiii. 18, see "Hundred threescore and six (six)"
—— xiv. 20, see "Hundred [(six)"

SIXTEEN (THREESCORE AND)

{ *ἑβδομήκοντα*, seventy
{ *ἕξ*, six.

Acts xxvii. 37.

SIXTH.

ἕκτος, the sixth, (*see note above*), (*non occ.*)

Matt. xx. 5.
— xxvii. 45.
Mark xv. 33.
Luke i. 26, 36.
— xxiii. 44.
John iv. 6.
John xix. 14 (τρίτος, *third*, [G ∾)
Acts x. 9.
Rev. vi. 12.
— ix. 13, 14.
— xvi. 12.
— xxi. 20.

SIXTY.

ἑξήκοντα, sixty.

Matt. xiii. 23. | Mark iv. 8, 20.

SIXTY-FOLD.

Matt. xiii. 8.

SKIN.

Heb. xi. 37, see "GOAT-SKIN."

SKIN (OF A)

δερμάτινος, made of skin, leathern; (lxx. *for* עור, 2 Kings i. 8; Zech. xiii. 4), (*occ.* Matt. iii. 4.)

Mark i. 6.

SKULL.

κρανίον, a skull; *Lat.*, cranium; (lxx. *for* גלגלת, Judg. ix. 53; 2 Kings ix. 35), (*non occ.*)

Matt. xxvii. 33. | Mark xv. 22.
John xix. 17.

SKULL (*the place of a*) [margin.]

Luke xxiii. 33, text, *Calvary*.

SKY.

οὐρανός, heaven; *spoken of* the expanse of the sky above, *as well as the regions above.*

Matt. xvi. 2, 3 twice. | Luke xii. 56.
Heb. xi. 12.

SLACK (BE)

βραδύνω, to be slow, to delay; (lxx. *for* אחר, Deut. vii. 10; Is. xlvi. 13), (*occ.* 1 Tim. iii. 15.)

2 Pet. iii. 9.

SLACKNESS.

βραδυτής, slowness, tardiness; delay.

2 Pet. iii. 9.

SLANDERER (-S.)

διάβολος, a calumniator, slanderer, accuser; (lxx. *of* Haman, צר, Est. vii. 4; צורר, Est. viii. 1), (*with art.*, the Devil, the accuser *by way of eminence.*)

1 Tim. iii. 11.

SLANDEROUSLY REPORT.

βλασφημέω, to blaspheme, speak evil of, slander, defame.

Rom. iii. 8.

SLAUGHTER.

1. σφαγή, slaughter, as of animals *for food or in sacrifice.*
   (a) *quoted from* Is. liii. 7, *where* lxx. *for* טבח.
   (b) *quoted from* Ps. xliv. 23, *where* lxx. *for* צאן טבחה, (*cf.* lxx. *for* הרגה, Zech. xi. 4.)
   (c) *quoted from* Jer. xii. 3, *where* lxx. *for* ליום הרגה, (*non occ.*)
2. κοπή, cutting down, carnage. *Here, in allusion to* Gen. xiv. 17, *where* lxx. *for Inf.* הכות; (lxx. *for* מכה, Josh. x. 20), (*non oc*
3. φόνος, a killing *of men*, murder.

1a. Acts viii. 32. | 1b. Rom. viii. 36.
3. — ix. 1. | 2. Heb. vii. 1.
1c. Jas. v. 5.

SLAVE.

σῶμα, a body, *as an organised whole made up of parts and members.*

Rev. xviii. 13, marg. *body*.

SLAY (SLAIN, SLEW.)

1. ἀποκτείνω, to kill outright, put to death.
2. ἀναιρέω, to take up, lift up, take away, remove, put out of the way.
3. σφαζω, (σφάττω) to slaughter, to slay, *as animals for food or in sacrifice; hence, of persons*, to slay.
4. κατασφάζω, (*No.* 3, *with* κατά, down, *prefixed*) to slaughter down, *i.e.* to slay, *as a butcher;* (lxx. *for* חרג, Zech. xi. 5), (*non occ.*)
5. θύω, to kill and offer in sacrifice, to immolate; *also*, to kill for a feast.

6. *διαχειρίζομαι*, to have pass through one's hands, to administer. *Here mid.*, to get into one's hands, (*occ.* Acts xxvi. 21.)

7. *φονεύω*, to murder.

2. Matt. ii. 16.
1. —— xxi. 39.
1. —— xxii. 6.
7. —— xxiii. 35.
1. Luke ix. 22.
1. —— xi. 49.
1. —— xiii. 4.
4. —— xix. 27.
1. John v. 16 (*ap.*)
2. Acts ii. 23.
6. —— v. 30.
2. —— 33, 36.
— —— vii. 42, see S beast.
1. —— 52.
2. —— ix. 29.
2. —— x. 39.
5. —— xi. 7.
2. —— xiii. 28.
2. Acts xxii. 20.
1. —— xxiii. 14.
1. Rom. vii. 11.
5. 1 Cor. v. 7, marg. (text, *sacrifice.*)
1. Eph. ii. 16.
— Heb. xi. 37, see S (be)
3. 1 John iii. 12 twice.
1. Rev. ii. 13.
3. —— v. 6, 9, 12.
3. —— vi. 4, marg. (text, *wound.*)
3. —— 9.
1. —— ix. 15.
1. —— xi. 13.
3. —— xiii. 8.
3. —— xviii. 24.
1. —— xix. 21.

SLAIN (BE)

{ *ἐν*, by
{ *φόνῳ*, murder,
{ *αποθνήσκω*, died.

Heb. xi. 37.

SLAIN BEAST.

σφάγιον, a victim, *as slaughtered in sacrifice; here, quoted from* Amos v. 5, *where* lxx. *for* זבח, (*non occ.*)

Acts vii. 42.

SLEEP. [noun.]

ὕπνος, sleep; (lxx. *for* שנה, Gen. xxviii. 16; Ecc. v. 11.)

Matt. i. 24.
Luke ix. 32.
John xi. 13.
Acts xx. 9 twice.
Rom. xiii. 11

SLEEP (AWAKE OUT OF)

1. *ἐξυπνίζω*, to wake out of sleep; (lxx. *for* יקץ, 1 Kings iii. 15; עור, Job xiv. 12.)

2. { *γίνομαι*, to become,
{ *ἔξυπνος*, out of sleep, wakened.

1. John xi. 11.
2. Acts xvi. 27.

SLEEP (FALL ON)

κοιμάω, *see below.*

Acts xiii. 36.

SLEEP (-EST, -ETH, -ING; SLEPT.) [verb.]

1. *καθεύδω*, to lie down to sleep; to sleep, go to sleep; (lxx. *for* ישן, Dan. xii. 2.)

2. *κοιμάω*, to make sleep, put to sleep; *hence, in N.T., pass. and fut. mid.*, to fall asleep, sleep. *Spoken generally of* the sleep of death, *and affirmed of man as man, not spoken of his body, or any part of man,* (*see* Job. vii. 21; Deut. xxxi. 16) *because death is an unbroken slumber till the Resurrection morn, when the sleepers shall wake,* (Dan. xii. 2.)

[1 Thes. iv. 15 assures us that those who are alive and remain to the Lord's coming shall not get before those who "are asleep." Paul does not write nonsense and mean "before those who have been before us in glory for centuries." Neither the quick nor the dead shall get before the other, but the changed "quick" and wakened "sleepers" shall "be caught up together," and so (*οὕτω*, thus, in this manner) shall we ever be with the Lord, 1 Thes. iv. 15-17.]

1. Matt. ix. 24.
1. —— xiii. 25.
1. —— xxv. 5.
1. —— xxvi. 45.
2. —— xxvii. 52.
2. —— xxviii. 13 part.
1. Mark iv. 27.
1. —— v. 39.
1. —— xiii. 36.
1. —— xiv. 37 twice, 41.
1. Luke viii. 56.
2. —— xxii. 45.
1. —— 46.
2. John xi. 11, 12.
2. Acts xii. 6.
2. 1 Cor. xi. 30.
2. —— xv. 20, 51.
1. Eph. v. 14.
2. 1 Thes. iv. 14.
1. 1 Thes. v. 6, 7 twice, 10.

SLEIGHT.

κυβεία, dice playing, (*from* *κύβος*, a cube *or* die.) *In N.T.*, game, gambling; *hence*, entrapping by deceit, (*non occ.*)

Eph. iv. 14.

SLIP (LET)

παραῤῥέω, to flow near, flow by; glide away. *Here, the* 2 *Aor. pass.*, carried away beside *or* with; *referring, not like the active, to the act of floating away, but to* the being carried away beside *or* floating away past any thing with the

stream, [*the marginal reading is quite wrong, and follows the Vulgate pereffluamus.*]

Heb. ii. 1, marg. *run out, as leaking vessels.*

SLOTHFUL.

1. ὀκνηρός, slow, tardy, slothful, *of persons*; (lxx. *for* עָצֵל, Prov. vi. 6, 9), (*occ.* Phil. iii. 1.)
2. νωθρός, slow, dull, stupid, (*occ.* Heb. v. 11.)

1. Matt. xxv. 26. | 1. Rom. xii. 11.
2. Heb. vi. 12.

SLOW.

1. βραδύς, slow, heavy, *of the mind*, (*non occ.*)
2. ἀργός, not labouring, unemployed, inactive, idle.

1. Luke xxiv. 25. | 2. Tit. i. 12.
1. Jas. i. 19 *twice*.

SLOWLY.

See, SAIL.

SLUMBER. [noun.]

κατάνυξις, a piercing through, vehement pain, grief. *Here, quoted from* Is. xxix. 10, *where* lxx. *for* תרדמה, deep sleep, stupor, *in which case it must be derived, not from* κατανύσσω, to prick through, *but from* καταννυστάζω, to nod, fall asleep, (*see below.*)

Rom. xi. 8, marg. *remorse.*

SLUMBER (-ED, -ETH.) [verb.]

νυστάζω, to nod; *hence*, to slumber, drowse; (lxx. *for* נוּם, Ps. cxxi. 3; Nah. iii. 18), (*non occ.*)

Matt. xxv. 5. | 2 Pet. ii. 3.

SMALL.

1. μικρός, small, *of magnitude, stature, age, quantity, space*, etc.
2. ὀλίγος, little; *opp. of* πολύς, much, *of number, amount, time*, etc.

— Mark iii. 9, see Ship.
— —— viii. 7, see Fish.
— John ii. 15, see Cord.
— —— vi. 9, see Fish.
2. Acts xii. 18.
2. —— xv. 2.
2. Acts xix. 23, 24.
1. —— xxvi. 22.
2. —— xxvii. 20.
1. Rev. xi. 18.
1. —— xiii. 16.
1. —— xix. 5, 18.
1. Rev. xx. 12.

SMALL (VERY)

ἐλάχιστος, the least, (*superl. of old epic* ἐλαχύς, *but used as superl. of No.* 1, *above.*)

Jas. iii. 4.

SMALL THING (VERY)

ἐλάχιστος, *see above.*

1 Cor. iv. 3.

SMALLEST.

ἐλάχιστος, *see above.*

1 Cor. vi. 2.

SMELL.

εὐωδία, good odour, sweet savour, fragrance.

1 Cor. vi. 2.

SMELL (SWEET)

Phil. iv. 18.

SMELLING.

ὄσφρησις, the smell, the sense of smell, (*non occ.*)

1 Cor. xii. 17.

SMITE (-EST, -ETH, -TEN; SMOTE.)

1. πατάσσω, to beat, knock; *later*, to strike, smite, *so as to kill*; *also*, to smite, inflict evil, (*occ.* Matt. xxvi. 51.)

   * *quoted from* Zech. xiii. 7, *where* lxx. *for* הכה, *as also* Ex. xii. 12; 2 Ch. xxxiii. 25.
2. τύπτω, to beat, strike, smite, *strictly with a stick, or with repeated strokes.*
3. παίω, to strike, smite, *whether with the hand, rod, or weapon*, (*occ.* Rev. ix. 5.)
4. δέρω, to skin, flay; *then, like the slang words*, to tan, hide; to scourge, beat.
5. πλήσσω, to strike, *esp. of a direct blow;* to afflict; *hence, Eng.*, plague, *so*, lxx. *for* הכה, Ex. ix. 32, 33, (*non occ.*)

6. ῥαπίζω, to rap *or* strike with a stick, to beat with rods, scourge; *then*, to slap in the face, box on the ears, cuff, (*occ.* Matt. xxvi. 67.)

6. Matt. v. 39.
2. —— xxiv. 49.
1* —— xxvi. 31.
— —— 51, see S off.
— —— 67, see S with the palm of one's hand.
3. —— 68.
2. —— xxvii. 30.
1* Mark xiv. 27.
3. —— 47.
2. —— xv. 19.
2. Luke vi. 29.
2. —— xviii. 13.
1. Luke xxii. 49, 50.
4. —— 63.
3. —— 64.
2. —— xxiii. 48.
3. John xviii. 10.
4. —— 23.
— —— xix. 3, see S with one's hand.
1. Acts vii. 24.
1. —— xii. 7, 23.
2. —— xxiii. 2, 3 twice.
4. 2 Cor. xi. 20.
5. Rev. viii. 12.
1. —— xi. 6.
1. Rev. xix. 15.

SMITE OFF.

ἀφαιρέω, to take away, take off; *so*, lxx. *for* כרת, 1 Sam. xvii. 51; Is. ix. 14; xviii. 5.

Matt. xxvi. 51.

SMITE WITH ONE'S HAND.

{ δίδωμι, to give
{ ῥάπισμα, a rap, slap, box, cuff.

John xix. 3.

SMITE WITH THE PALM OF ONE'S HAND.

ῥαπίζω, *see above, No.* 6.

Matt. xxvi. 67, marg. ...rods.

SMOKE. [noun.]

καπνός, smoke; (lxx. *for* עשן, Ex. xix. 18; Josh. viii. 20), (*non occ.*)

Acts ii. 19.
Rev. viii. 4.
—— ix. 2 3 times, 3, 17, 18.
Rev. xiv. 11.
—— xv. 8.
—— xviii. 9, 18.
Rev. xix. 3.

SMOKE (-ING.) [verb.]

τύφω, to make a smoke. *In N.T. pass.*, to smoke, *i.e. of a wick burning faintly, and so*, making a smoke; *quoted from* Is. xlii. 3, *where* lxx. *for* כהה, (*non occ.*)

Matt. xii. 20.

SMOOTH.

λεῖος, smooth, level, plain, (*opp. to* τραχύς); *quoted from* Is. xl. 4, *where Heb.* לבקעה, lxx. εἰς πέδια, (*non occ.*)

Luke iii. 5.

SNARE.

1. παγίς, whatever makes or holds fast; *hence*, a snare, trap, gin, (*non occ.*)

* *quoted from* Ps. lxix. 23, *where* lxx. *for* פח.

2. βρόχος, a noose *or* slip knot for hanging or strangling; *later*, a snare, the mesh *of a net*, (*non occ.*)

1. Luke xxi. 35.
1* Rom. xi. 9.
2. 1 Cor. vii. 35.
1. 1 Tim. iii. 7.
1. —— vi. 9.
1. 2 Tim. ii. 26.

SNOW.

χιών, snow; (lxx. *for* שלג, Job. xxxvii. 6; Is. i. 18; lv. 10.)

Matt. xxviii. 3.
Mark ix. 3 (om. ὡς χιών, *as snow*, G ⇉ T Tr A ℵ.)
Rev. i. 14.

SO.

(*For various combinations with other words, see below.*)

1. οὔτω, (*before a vowel*, οὔτως) in this manner, on this wise, thus, so.

2. καί, also.

   (a) *preceded by* ὧς, (*No.* 6) *or* καθὼς, according as.

3. οὖν, thereupon, *i.e.* now, then, therefore.

4. οὗτος, this, that, this same

   (a) τοῦτο, *neut. sing.*, this.

   (b) ταῦτα, *neut. plural*, these *things*.

5. ὁμοίως, in like manner, likewise.

6. ὧς, in which way, in what way; *and hence, gen.*, as, so as, how.

8. Matt. i. 17.
1. —— v. 12, 16, 19.
1. —— 47 (τὸ αὐτὸ, *the same*, L T Tr A ℵ.)
1. —— vi. 30.
1. —— vii. 12.
1. —— ix. 33.
1. —— xi. 26.
1. —— xii. 40.
1. —— xiii. 40, 49.
1. —— xviii. 35.
1. —— xix. 8, 10, 12.
1. —— xx. 16, 26.
1. —— xxiv. 27, 33, 37, 39, 46.
2. —— xxvii. 64.
1. Mark ii. 8 (*om.* L.)
1. —— iv. 26, 40 (*ap.*)
1. —— vii. 18.
1. —— x. 43.
1. —— xiv. 59.
1. —— xv. 39.
5. Luke v. 10.
1. —— vi. 10 (*om.* G T Tr A ℵ.)
1. —— ix. 15.
1. —— x. 21.
2. —— xi. 2 (*ap.*)
1. —— 30.
1. —— xii. 21, 28, 38, 43, 54.
1. —— xvii. 10, 24, 26.
1. —— xxi. 31.
1. —— xxii. 26.
1. —— xxiv. 24.
1. John iii. 8, 16.
3. —— iv. 40, 46, 53.
1. —— v. 21, 26.
3. —— vi. 10 (*om.* G ⇉)
1a. —— 57.
1. —— viii. 59 (*ap.*)
4b. —— xi. 28.
1. —— xii. 50.
2a. —— xiii. 33.

2a. John xv. 9.
1. —— xviii. 22.
4a. —— xxi. 20.
1. Acts i. 11.
1. —— iii. 18.
1. —— vii. 1, 8.
2a. ——— 51.
1. —— viii. 32.
1. —— xii. 8.
3. —— xiii. 4.
1. ——— 8, 47.
1. —— xiv. 1.
3. —— xv. 30.
1. —— xvii. 11, 33.
4a. —— xix. 14.
1. ——— 20.
1. —— xx. 11, 13, 35.
1. —— xxi. 11.
1. —— xxii. 24.
4a. —— xxiii. 7.
1. ——— 11.
3. ——— 18, 22.
1. —— xxiv. 9, 14.
1. —— xxvii. 17, 44.
3. —— xxviii. 9 (*δέ, but,* L T Tr A ℵ.)
1. ——— 14.
1. Rom. i. 15.
1. —— iv. 18.
1. —— v. 12, 15, 18.
1 & 2. ——— 19.
1. ——— 21.
1. —— xi. 5.
2. ——— 16.
1. ——— 26.
1. —— xii. 5.
4a. ——— 20.
1. —— xv. 20.
1. 1 Cor. ii. 11.
1. —— iii. 15.
1. —— iv. 1.
1. —— v. 3.
1. —— vi. 5.
1. —— vii. 17 twice, 26, 36.
4a. ——— 37.
1. ——— 40.
1. —— viii. 12.
1. —— ix. 14, 15, 24, 26 twice.
1. 1 Cor. xi. 28.
1. —— xii. 12.
1. —— xiv. 9, 12, 25.
1. —— xv. 11 twice, 22, 42, 45.
1. —— xvi. 1.
1. 2 Cor. i. 5, 7
1. —— vii. 14.
1. —— viii. 6, 11.
1. —— x. 7.
1. —— xi. 3 (*om.* G → L T Tr A ℵ.)
1. Gal. i. 6.
2a. ——— 9.
1. —— iii. 3.
1. —— iv. 3, 29.
1. —— vi. 2.
1. Eph. iv. 20.
1 & 2. —— v. 24.
1. ——— 28, 33.
2a. Phil. i. 20.
1. —— iv. 1.
1. Col. iii. 13.
1. 1 Thes. ii. 8.
1. —— iv. 17.
1. —— v. 2.
1. 2 Thes. iii. 17.
1. 2 Tim. iii. 8.
6. Heb. iii. 11.
1. —— iv. 3, 5.
1. —— vi. 15.
1. —— ix. 28.
1. —— x. 33.
1. —— xii. 21.
1. Jas. i. 11.
1. —— ii. 12 twice, 17, 26.
1. —— iii. 5.
1. ——— 6 (*om.* G ⇉ L T Tr A ℵ.)
1. ——— 10, 12 (*ap.*)
2. 1 Pet. i. 15.
1. —— ii. 15.
1. 2 Pet. i. 11.
1. 1 John ii. 6 (*om.* L.)
1. —— iv. 11.
2a. ——— 17.
1. Rev. ii. 15.
1. —— iii. 16.
1. —— xvi. 18.

SO AS.

1. *ἵνα*, that, in order that, to the end that.
2. *οἷα*, of what kind *or* sort, such as.

2. Mark ix. 3. | 1. Rev. viii. 12.

SO BE...DONE.

γίνομαι, to begin to be; become, come to pass.

Matt. viii. 13.

SO I.

κἀγω, and I; I also.

John xv. 9. | 2 Cor. xi. 22 3 times.

SO IT WAS.

συμβαίνω, to go with the feet close together, come together; *of events*, to happen together, fall out. *Here*, *συνέβη*, it befell *him to be borne along, etc.*

Acts xxi. 35.

SO LIKEWISE.

{ *οὕτως*, thus, in this way.
{ *οὖν*, then.

Luke xiv. 33.

SO MANY AS.

ὅσος, how great, how many; as great as, as much as.

Rom. vi. 3.

SO MUCH AS (NOT)

οὐδέ, and not, also not, not even.

Luke xviii. 13.

SO THAT.

1. *ὥστε*, so as that, so that, *expressing result or consequence.*
2. *τοῦ*, of the. *With inf., marking design or purpose,* to the end that.
3. *ἵνα*, that, in order that, to the end that.
4. *ὅπως*, in what manner; in such manner, and then, so that, that.
5. *ὥς*, *see* "SO," *No.* 6.

1. Matt. viii. 28.
1. —— xiii. 2, 32.
1. Mark iii. 20.
1. —— iv. 1, 32, 37.
1. —— xv. 5.
1. Luke v. 7.
4. —— xvi. 26.
2. Acts vii. 19.
1. —— xvi. 26.
1. —— xix. 10, 12, 16.
5. —— xx. 24.
2. Rom. vii. 3.
1. Rom. xv. 19.
1. 1 Cor. i. 7.
1. —— xiii. 2.
1. 2 Cor. ii. 7.
1. —— iii. 7.
1. —— vii. 7.
1. Phil. i. 13.
1. 1 Thes. i. 7, 8.
1. 2 Thes. i. 4.
1. —— ii. 4.
1. Heb. xiii. 6.
3. Rev. xiii. 18.

SO THAT NOT.

{ *ἵνα*, in order that,
{ *μή*, not, (*see* "NO," *No.* 2.)

Gal. v. 17.

SO THEN.

1. *ὥστε*, so as that, so that, *expressing result or consequence.*
2. *οὖν*, thereupon, *i.e.* now, then, therefore.
3. { *ἄρα*, therefore, thence, since, / *οὖν*, therefore, then, } so therefore. (*οὖν marking the logical inference*, and *ἄρα intimating the harmony between the premises and conclusion.*)

1. Mark x. 8.
2. —— xvi. 19 (*ap.*)
3. Rom. vii. 3, 25.
3. —— ix. 16.
3. Rom. xiv. 12 (*om.* οὖν, [L Tr A^b.)
1. 1 Cor. iii. 7.
1. —— vii. 38.
1. 2 Cor. iv. 12.
1. Gal. iii. 9.

SO (AND)

οὖν, therefore, then.

Acts xvi. 5.

SO (BE)

1. *ἔστω*, (*imperat. of* *εἰμί*, to be) let it be.
2. *θέλω*, to will, to wish, desire. *Here*, *θέλοι*, it pleases, wills it.

1. 2 Cor. xii. 16. | 2. 1 Pet. iii. 17.

SO BE (IF)

εἴπερ, if indeed, if so be, *assuming the supposition as true, whether justly or not.*

1 Pet. ii. 3 (*εἰ*, if, L T Tr ℵ.)

SO BE THAT (IF)

1. *εἴπερ*, *see above.*
2. *εἴγε*, if at least, if indeed.
3. { *εἴγε*, if at least, if indeed, *καὶ*, also.

1. 1 Cor. xv. 15. | 3. 2 Cor. v. 3 (No. 1, L T Tr.)
2. Eph. iv. 21.

SO I (EVEN)

κἀγω, I also, even I.

John x. 15. | John xx. 21.

SO I ALSO (EVEN)

κἀγω, *see above.*

John xvii. 18.

SO MIGHT (THAT...)

{ *εἰς*, unto, with a view to, *τὸ*, the, *with inf.* } with the view of, etc.; to the end that *they* might, etc.

Luke xx. 20 (*ὥστε*, *so that* (see "SO THAT," No. 1), L T Tr A ℵ.)

SO MUCH SPOKEN OF BEFORE (*which hath been*) [margin.]

2 Cor. ix. 5, see "NOTICE."

See also, BESET, DONE, EVEN, FALSELY, GREAT, IF, LONG, MANY, MIGHTY, MORE, MUCH, NAME, NOT, REQUIRE, SAY, SUFFER, THEN.

SOBER.

1. *νήφω*, to be sober, temperate, abstinent, *esp. in respect to wine. Here part.*, sober-minded, watchful, circumspect.
2. *νηφάλιος*, sober, temperate, abstinent, *esp. in respect to wine*, (*occ.* 1 Tim. iii. 2.)
3. *σώφρων*, of sound mind, sane; *used of* one who follows sound reason, and restrains his passions.

3. 1 Tim. iii. 2. | 2. Tit. ii. 2, marg. *vigilant.*
2. —— 11. | 1. 1 Pet. i. 13
3. Tit. i. 8.

SOBER (BE)

1. *νήφω*, *see above, No.* 1.
2. *σωφρονέω*, to be of sound mind; think and act discreetly, to use sound judgment and moderation.

2. 2 Cor. v. 13. | 2. 1 Pet. iv. 7.
1. 1 Thes. v. 6, 8. | 1. —— v. 8.

SOBER (TEACH TO BE)

σωφρονίζω, to make of sound mind; to make, think, and act soberly, discreetly, *or* prudently.

Tit. ii. 4, marg. *wise.*

SOBERLY.

1. *σωφρόνως*, with sound mind, prudently, discreetly.
2. { *εἰς*, unto, *τὸ*, the, *σωφρονεῖν*, *see* "SOBER (BE)" *No.* 2, } so as to have a sound judgment *or* estimate.

2. Rom. xii. 3, marg. *to sobriety.*
1. Tit. ii. 12.

SOBER MINDED (BE)

σωφρονέω, *see* "SOBER (BE)," *No.* 2.

Tit. ii. 6, marg. *be discreet.*

SOBERNESS.

σωφροσύνη, soundness of mind, discretion, prudence, *which controls all inordinate desires, and exercises a dignified restraint on all the actions*, (*occ.* 1 Tim. ii. 9, 15.)

Acts xxvi. 25.

SOBRIETY.

σωφροσύνη, *see above.*

1 Tim. ii. 9, 15.

SOCIABLE. [margin.]

1 Tim. vi. 18, see "COMMUNICATE (WILLING TO)"

SODOM.

Σόδομα, Sodom; *Heb.*, סדם, burning.

In all passages, except—
Mark vi. 11 (*ap*)

SOEVER.

See, PLACE, WHAT, WHERE, WITH.

SOFT.

μαλακός, soft *as to the touch*, spoken of raiment made of soft materials.

Matt. xi. 8[1st]. | Luke vii. 25.

SOFT CLOTHING.

{ τὰ, the
{ μαλακά, soft things.

Matt. xi. 8.

SOFTLY.

See, BLOW.

SOJOURN (-ED.)

1. παροικέω, to dwell beside *or* near; *hence*, to sojourn, dwell as a stranger; (lxx. *for* גור, Gen. xx. 1; xxvi. 3; ישב, Gen. xxiv. 37.)

{ εἰμί, to be
{ πάροικος, dwelling beside *or* near, neighbouring; (lxx. *for* גר, Gen. xv. 13; Ex. ii. 22.)

2. Acts vii. 6. | 1. Heb. xi. 9.

SOJOURNING HERE.

παροικία, a dwelling beside *or* near; *esp. residence in a foreign land without the rights of citizenship.*

1 Pet. i. 17.

SOLDIER (-s.)

1. στρατιώτης, a citizen bound to *or* performing military service; *then, gen.*, one serving as a soldier; *later*, a soldier by profession, (*non occ.*)

2. στράτευμα, an expedition; an armament, army, host, company, band.

3. στρατεύω, to serve as a soldier, do military service, take the field. *Here part., those who were* serving as soldiers.

1. Matt. viii. 9.
1. —— xxvii. 27.
1. —— xxviii. 12.
1. Mark xv. 16.
3. Luke iii. 14.
1. —— vii. 8.
1. —— xxiii. 36. [32, 34.
1. John xix. 2, 23 twice, 24,
1. Acts x. 7.
1. —— xii. 4, 6, 18.
1. —— xxi. 32 twice, 35.
2. —— xxiii. 10.
1. —— —— 23, 31.
1. —— xxvii. 31, 32, 42.
1. —— xxviii. 16.
1. 2 Tim. ii. 3.

SOLDIER (CHOOSE...TO BE)

στρατολογέω, to collect *or* levy an army, enlist soldiers, (*non occ.*)

2 Tim. ii. 4.

SOLDIER (FELLOW)

συστρατιώτης, a στρατιώτης, (*see No.* 1, *above*) together *or* in conjunction with another; a fellow-soldier.

Phil. ii. 25. | Philem. 2.

SOLITARY.

ἔρημος, solitary, desert.

Mark i. 35.

SOME.

(*For various combinations with other words, see below.*)

1. τις, one, some one, a certain one; *pl.*, some.
2. ἄλλος, other, not the same; *denoting numerical, not generic distinction like No.* 7.
3. { ἄλλοι, others, / δὲ, but, } but others.
4. { ἄλλο, *nom. sing. neut. of No.* 2, / δὲ, but.
5. { ἄλλα, *nom. pl. neut. of No.* 2, / δὲ, but.
6. ἓν, one, (*neut. of* εἷς.)
7. ἕτερος, the other, other, *denoting generic, not numerical distinction like No.* 2.
8. { ἕτεροι, *pl. of No.* 7, / δὲ, but, } but others.
9. { ὃ, the, / μὲν, indeed, } the [*seed*] indeed; *or* some.

10. { ὃ, the, / δὲ, but, however, } but some, some however.

11. { οἱ, the, (*pl.*) / μὲν, indeed, } some indeed.

12. { οἱ, the, (*pl.*) / δὲ, but, however, } but some (*pl.*); some (*pl.*) however.

13. { οὓς, these, (*Acc. pl.*) / μὲν, indeed, } these (*pl.*) indeed.

14. { οὓς, these, (*Acc. masc. pl.*) / δὲ, but, however, } but these; some (*pl.*) however.

15. { ἃ, the, (*neut. pl.*) / μὲν, indeed, } some (*neut. pl.*) indeed.

16. { ἃ, the, (*neut. pl.*) / δὲ, but, how-[ever, } but some (*neut. pl.*); some however.

17. { τοὺς, the, (*Acc. pl.*) / μὲν, indeed, } some (*pl.*) indeed.

18. { τοὺς, the, (*Acc. pl.*) / δὲ, but, how-[ever, } but some (*pl.*); some (*pl.*) however.

15. Matt. xiii. 4.
5. —— 5 1st.
2. —— 5 2nd, 7.
9. —— 8 1st.
10. —— 8 2nd & 3rd.
9. —— 23 1st.
10. —— 23 2nd & 3rd.
11. —— xvi. 14 1st.
3. —— 14 2nd ("others" [=No. 8.)
1. —— 28.
1. —— xxvii. 47.
1. —— xxviii. 11
9. Mark iv. 4.
4. —— 5.
2. —— 7.
6. —— 8 3 times (ἐν, *in*, G ∾), (εἰς, *unto*, T Tr ℵ), (εἷς, *one* (masc.) A.)
6. —— 20 3 times, (ἐν, *in*, G ∾ T Tr.)
1. —— vii. 2.
2. —— viii. 28.
1. —— ix. 1.
17. —— xii. 5 1st.
18. —— 5 2nd.
1. —— xiv. 4, 65.
1. —— xv. 35.
9. Luke viii. 5.
7. —— 6, 7, 8.
1. —— ix. 7, 8.
2. —— 19.
1. —— 27.
1. —— xi. 15.
1. —— xiii. 1.
1. —— xix. 39.
1. —— xxi. 5.
1. —— xxiii. 8.
1. John vi. 64.
11. —— vii. 12.
1. —— 25.
2. —— 41 (No. 12, L Tr A), (οἳ δὲ, *but these*, T.)
1. —— 44.
2. —— ix. 9.
1. —— 16.
1. —— xi. 37, 46.
1. —— xiii. 29.
1. Acts v. 15.
1. —— viii. 34.
1. —— xi. 20.
1. —— xv. 36.
1. —— xvii. 4, 18, 21.
11. —— 32.
1. —— xviii. 23.
1. —— xxvii. 27.
13. —— 44 1st.
14. —— 44 2nd.
11. —— xxviii. 24 1st.
12. —— 24 2nd.
1. Rom. i. 11, 13.
1. —— iii. 3, 8.
1. —— v. 7.
1. —— xi. 14.
1. 1 Cor. iv. 18.
1. —— vi. 11.
1. —— viii. 7.
1. —— ix. 22.
1. —— x. 7, 8, 9, 10.
1. —— xv. 6, 12, 34, 37.
1. 2 Cor. iii. 1.
1. —— x. 2, 12.
1. Gal. i. 7.
17. Eph. iv. 11 1st.
18. —— 11 2nd & 3rd.
1. Phil. i. 15 twice.
1. 2 Thes. iii. 11.
1. 1 Tim. i. 3, 6, 19.
1. —— iv. 1.
1. —— v. 15, 24 twice.
1. —— vi. 10, 21.
1. 2 Tim. ii. 18.
15. —— 20 1st.
16. —— 20 2nd.
1. Heb. iii. 4.
1. —— 16 (τίνες, *who?* G L T Tr A, *i.e. who? ...was it not all?* instead of τινές, *for some ...but not all.*)
1. —— iv. 6.
1. —— x. 25.
1. —— xi. 40.
1. —— xiii. 2.
1. 2 Pet. iii. 9.
13. Jude 22.

SOME ONE THING, SOME ANOTHER.

{ ἄλλοι, others, [*were crying aloud*] / ἄλλο, another / τι, thing. }

Acts xix. 32. | Acts xxi. 34.

SOME (IF)

{ εἰ, if / τινές, some. }

Rom. xi. 17.

SOME SORT (IN)

{ ἀπὸ, from / μέρος, a part, } in part, partly.

Rom. xv. 15.

SOME MAN.

τις, *see* "SOME," *No.* 1.

Acts viii. 31. | 1 Cor. xv. 35.

SOME THINGS.

τινα, *neut. pl. of* "SOME," *No.* 1.

2 Pet. iii. 16.

SOME TIME.

ποτέ, when, whenever; at some time; once, formerly.

Col. iii. 7.

See also, BETWEEN, HAND, MEANS, MEAT, OF, OTHER, TIME.

SOMEBODY.

τις, *see* "SOME," *No.* 1.

Luke viii. 46. | Acts v. 36.

SOMETHING.

τι, *neut. of* "SOME," *No.* 1.

Luke xi. 54.
John xiii. 29.
Acts iii. 5.
—— xxiii. 18.
Gal. vi. 3.

SOMETIME, SOMETIMES.*

ποτέ, when, whenever; at some time; once, formerly.

Eph. ii. 13*.
—— v. 8*.
Col. i. 21.
Tit. iii. 3*.
1 Pet. iii. 20.

SOMEWHAT.

1. τις, *see* "SOME," *No.* 1. *Here, neut. sing.*, some thing, a certain thing.

2. { ἀπὸ, from / μέρος, a part, } in part, partly, in a measure.

1. Luke vii. 40.
1. Acts xxiii. 20.
1. —— xxv. 26.
2. Rom. xv. 24.
1. 2 Cor. x. 8.
1. Gal. ii. 6.
1. Heb. viii. 3.

SON.

1. υἱός, a son.

[This word is used as the *Heb.* בן *or* בני, to characterise any one as to his *origin* and *nature*, the points which determine his *character* and *idiosyncracy*. Thus *men* are not simply ἄνθρωποι, but υἱοὶ τῶν ἀνθρώπων, *sons of men*, as denoting their origin and nature. *Hence*, in the *O.T.*, we have υἱοὶ παρανόμων, *sons of lawlessness*, (Belial) Judg. xix. 22; υἱὸς θανάτου, *son of death*, 1 Sam. xx. 31, (*Heb.* "shall surely die"); υἱοὶ δυνάμεως, *sons of valour*, 2 Sam. ii. 7; xiii. 28, (*Heb.* "be valiant"); υἱοὶ τῆς ἀποικίας, *sons of the transportation*, Ezra iv. 1; vi. 19, (*Heb.* "of captivity.") Also in the *N.T.* we have, υἱοὶ προφητῶν, *of the prophets*, Acts iii. 25; διαθήκης, *of the covenant*, Acts iii. 25; σοφίας, *of wisdom*, Matt. xi. 19; ἀναστάσεως, *of the resurrection*, Luke xx. 36; φονυσάντων, *of murderers*, Matt. xxiii. 31; νυμφῶνος, *of the bride-chamber*, Matt. ix. 15; Mark ii. 19; Luke v. 34; βασιλείας, *of the kingdom*, Matt. viii. 12; xiii. 38; πονηροῦ, *of the wicked one*, Matt. xiii. 38; γεέννης, *of Gehenna*, Matt. xxiii. 15; εἰρήνης, *of peace*, Luke x. 6; ἀπωλείας, *of perdition*, John xvii. 12; 2 Thes. ii. 3; παρακλήσεως, *of consolation*, Acts iv. 30; διαβόλου, *of the devil*, Acts xiii. 10; τοῦ αἰῶνος, *of this age*, Luke xvi. 8; xx. 34; φωτός, *of light*, Luke xvi. 8; John xii. 36; 1 Thes. v. 5; ἀπειθείας, *of disobedience*, Eph. ii. 2; v. 6; Col. iii. 6; Luke vi. 35.

In all these expressions reference is made to the origin or starting-point of the persons named, and to the relation in which they stand; or to their characters, idiosyncracies, and associations.

Hence, in υἱός θεοῦ, *a son or child of God*, is declared the relationship of the person and his characteristics.]

(a) ὁ υἱὸς, the Son, *is used of Christ*.

[But the following combinations deserve the greatest discrimination.

(b) υἱός θεοῦ, (*without the article*) son, *or* a son of God, *denoting* the relationship as the result of the elective love of God, and as resting upon God's own act. *It is thus used of men as well as of Christ, as denoting* a kinship to God, a partaking of what appertains to Him from whom the whole life is derived, and according to whom it is moulded. *When used of Christ, the reference is to* the act of God, placing Him in this relationship; *hence, used of* His birth, (Luke i. 35; Acts xiii. 33; Rom. i. 4; *cf.* Acts ii. 32, 36.) υἱὸς θεοῦ, *is therefore* the man Christ Jesus as the elect and chosen of God.

(c) ὁ υἱὸς (*or* υἱός) τοῦ θεοῦ, (*with the article*) the son of the God, *indicates, not only His election or choosing, but* His especial and distinctive relationship, by which He is raised above the rank of the more general υἱοὶ θεοῦ, (*see under* b.) *This title indicates Him as* the Messiah, upon whom the relation of all others as "sons of God" depends. *Hence, this title is never used of His supernatural birth, because it was not by birth that this relation was brought about. It is* a relation in virtue of which the humanity of Jesus possesses its special significance.

(d) ὁ υἱὸς τοῦ ἀνθρώπου, the son of (*the*) man, signifies humanity itself; not what merely resembles, but what essentially belongs to man. *Hence, it is never used by the disciples*, (*and not until Jesus is exalted in glory is it used by Stephen*, Acts vii. 56.) *By this*

title Jesus is raised above the general υἱοὶ ἀνθρώπων, sons of men, and as given to Jesus by Himself it becomes a Messianic name, adopted by Him on account of the relation in which He stands as the promised "seed of the woman" to His brethren. (*No.* 1c thus indicates the divine side, referring to His personal and divine glory, *while No.* 1d is the human side of this title, as denoting not merely His need and rejection, but in this connection, as yet securing blessing and righteous rule over the earth as "the second man," "the last Adam," (*see under* "HEIR.")

(e) ὁ υἱὸς τοῦ πατρὸς, the Son of the Father, a complete and solemn setting forth of the union of Jesus with the Father in the essence of the Godhead.

(f) υἱὸς ὑψίστου, son of the Highest; a theocratic title, pointing to the anointed king, so fully referred to in 2 Sam. vii. 14; Ps. ii. 7; lxxxix. 28.

(g) ὁ υἱὸς τοῦ εὐλογητοῦ, the son of the blessed. This was a hypocritical expression of reverence, in refraining from using the name of God, intending to designate Christ's declaration blasphemy of God, of the Blessed.

(h) υἱὸς Δαβίδ, son of David, pointing to Jesus as the son and successor of David, and heir of the promises given to him, Luke i. 32, etc.

2. τέκνον, that which is born, (*from* τίκτω, to bear; *like Ang.-Sax.*, bearn; *Scot.*, bairn, *from* beran, to bear) a child, *whether son or daughter; often used as a term of endearment*, dear child.

3. παῖς, *in relation to descent*, a child, (*whether son or daughter*); *in relation to age*, a boy *or* girl; *in relation to condition*, (*like Lat.*, puer) a slave, servant.

4. ὁ, the; *when followed by the Genitive of a person, it denotes* the of, *i.e.* the son of. *Sometimes these words are given in italics* in A.V., (*as in* Mark iii. 17, 18, *and* Luke iv.) *which are not quoted below.*

1. Matt. i. 1 twice, 20, 21, 23, 25.
1. —— ii. 15.
1a. —— iii. 17.
1c. —— iv. 3, 6.
4. —— 21.
1. —— vii. 9.
1d. —— viii. 20.
1c. —— 29.
2. —— ix. 2.
1d. —— 6.
1h. —— 27.
4. —— x. 2, 3.
1d. —— 23.
1. —— 37.
1d. —— xi. 19.
1a. —— 27 3 times.
1d. —— xii. 8.
1h. —— 23.
1d. —— 32, 40.
1d. —— xiii. 37, 41.
1. —— 55.
1b. —— xiv. 33.
1h. —— xv. 22.
1d. —— xvi. 13.
1c. —— 16.
1d. —— 27, 28.
1a. —— xvii. 5.
1d. —— 9, 12.
1. —— 15.
1d. —— 22.
1d. —— xviii. 11 (*ap.*)
1d. —— xix. 28.
1d. —— xx. 18.
1. —— 20, 21.
1d. —— 28.
1h. —— 30, 31.
1h. —— xxi. 9, 15.
2. —— 28 twice.
1. —— 37 twice, 38.
1. —— xxii. 2.
1h. —— 42.
1. —— 45.
1. —— xxiii. 35.
1d. —— xxiv. 27, 30 twice, 37, 39, 44.
1d. —— xxv. 13 (*ap.*), 31.
1d. —— xxvi. 2, 24 twice.
1. —— 37.
1d. —— 45.
1c. —— 63.
1d. —— 64.
1c. —— xxvii. 40.
1b. —— 43, 54.
1a. —— xxviii. 19.
1c. Mark i. 1.
1a. —— 11.
4. —— 19.
2. —— ii. 5.
1d. —— 10.
4. —— 14.
1d. —— 28.
1c. —— iii. 11.
1. —— 17, 28.
1c. —— v. 7.
1. —— vi. 3.
1d. —— viii. 31, 38.
1a. —— ix. 7.
1d. —— 9, 12.
1. —— 17.
1d. —— 31.
1d. —— x. 33.
1. —— 35.
1d. —— 45.
1. —— 46.
1h. —— 47, 48.
1. —— xii. 6 twice.
1h. —— 35.
1. —— 37.
2. —— xiii. 12.
1d. —— 26.
1a. Mark xiii. 32.
1d. —— xiv. 21 twice, 41.
1g. —— 61.
1d. —— 62.
1b. —— xv. 39.
1. Luke i. 13, 31.
1f. —— 32.
1b. —— 35.
1. —— 36, 57.
1. —— ii. 7.
2. —— 48.
1. —— iii. 2.
1a. —— 22.
1. —— 23.
1c. —— iv. 3, 9.
1. —— 22.
1c. —— 41.
1. —— v. 10.
1d. —— 24.
1d. —— vi. 5.
4. —— 15.
1d. —— 22.
1. —— vii. 12.
1d. —— 34.
1c. —— viii. 28.
1d. —— ix. 22, 26.
1a. —— 35.
1. —— 38, 41.
1d. —— 44, 56 (*ap.*), 58.
1. —— x. 6.
1a. —— 22 3 times.
1. —— xi. 11, 19.
1d. —— 30.
1d. —— xii. 8, 10, 40.
1. —— 53 twice.
1. —— xv. 11, 13, 19, 21 twice, 24, 25, 30.
2. —— 31.
2. —— xvi. 25.
1d. —— xvii. 22, 24, 26, 30.
1d. —— xviii. 8, 31.
1h. —— 38, 39.
1. —— xix. 9.
1d. —— 10.
1. —— xx. 13, 41, 44.
1d. —— xxi. 27, 36.
1d. —— xxii. 22, 48, 69.
1c. —— 70.
1d. —— xxiv. 7.
2. John i. 12.
1a. —— 18, (Θεός, *God*, L^m TrA ℵ), (*om.* G→)
1c. —— 34.
1. —— 42, 45.
1c. —— 49, 51.
1d. —— iii. 13, 14.
1a. —— 16, 17.
1c. —— 18.
1a. —— 35, 36 twice.
1. —— iv. 5, 46, 47, 50.
3. —— 51.
1. —— 53.
1a. —— v. 19 twice, 20, 21, 22, 23 twice.
1c. —— 25.
1a. —— 26.
1d. —— 27.
1d. —— vi. 27.
1a. —— 40.
1. —— 42.
1d. —— 53, 62.
1c. —— 69 (*ap.*)
1d. —— viii. 28.
1a. —— 35, 36.
1. —— ix. 19, 20
1c. —— 35.
1c. —— x. 36.
1c. —— xi. 4, 27.
1d. —— xii. 23, 34 twice.
1d. —— xiii. 31.
1a. —— xiv. 13.

1a. John xvii. 1 twice.
1. —— 12.
1a. —— xix. 7 (No. 1c, B, E.)
1. —— 26.
1c. —— xx. 31.
4. —— xxi. 2.
1. Acts ii. 17.
3. —— iii. 13, 26.
1. —— iv. 36.
1. —— vii. 16, 21, 29.
1d. —— 56.
1c. —— viii. 37 (*ap.*)
1c. —— ix. 20.
1. —— xiii. 21.
4. —— 22.
1a. —— 33.
1. —— xvi. 1.
1. —— xix. 14.
1. —— xxiii. 6, 16.
1a. Rom. i. 3.
1b. —— 4.
1a. —— 9.
1a. —— v. 10.
1a. —— viii. 3.
1. —— 14, 19.
1a. —— 29, 32.
1. —— ix. 9.
1a. 1 Cor. i. 9.
2. —— iv. 14, 17.
1a. —— xv. 28.
1c. 2 Cor. i. 19.
1. —— vi. 18.
1a. Gal. i. 16.
1c. —— ii. 20 (*ap.*)
1a. —— iv. 4.
— —— 5, see Adoption.
1. —— 6 1st.
1a. —— 6 2nd.
1. —— 7 twice, 22, 30 3 times
1. Eph. iii. 5.
1c. —— iv. 13.
2. Phil. ii. 15, 22.
1a. Col. i. 13.
— —— iv. 10, see Sister's [ten.
1a. 1 Thes. i. 10.
1. 2 Thes. ii. 3.
2. 1 Tim. i. 2, 18.
2. 2 Tim. i. 2.
2. —— ii. 1.
2. Tit. i. 4.
2. Philem. 10.
1a. Heb. i, 2, 5 twice, 8.
1. —— ii. 6, 10.
1. —— iii. 6.
1c. —— iv. 14.
1a. —— v. 5, 8.
1c. —— vi. 6.
1c. —— vii. 3.
1. —— 5 (*om.* υἱῶν, *of the sons*, L.)
1a. —— 28.
1c. —— x. 29.
— —— xi. 17, see Begot-
1. —— 21, 24.
1. —— xii. 5, 6, 7 twice, 8.
1. Jas. ii. 21.
1. 1 Pet. v. 13.
1a. 2 Pet. i. 17.
1a. 1 John i. 3, 7.
1a. —— ii. 22, 23, 24.
2. —— iii. 1, 2.
1c. —— 10 1st.
1a. —— 10 2nd, 11, 12 1st.
1c. —— 12 2nd, 13 1st (*ap.*), 13 2nd.
1c. —— 20 1st.
1a. —— 20 2nd
1c. 2 John 3.
1a. —— 9.
1d. Rev. i. 13.
1c. —— ii. 18.
1d. —— xiv. 14.
1. —— xxi. 7.

SONG.

ῳδή, (*from* ᾄδω, to sing) an ode, *or* song; (lxx. *for* שיר, Judg. v. 12; 1 Kings iv. 32; Ps. xlii. 9); any kind of song, of battle *or* harvest, festal or hymeneal.

* *With the adj.* πνευματική, spiritual, *probably implying that* the songs were composed by spiritual men; *or that* they related to spiritual things, (*non occ.*)

Eph. v. 19*.
Col. iii. 16*.
Rev. v. 9.
—— xiv. 3 twice.
Rev. xv. 3 twice.

SOON.

1. ταχέως, quickly, speedily.
2. παραχρῆμα, with the thing itself, at the very moment, on the spot; forthwith, immediately *after something else has taken place.*

2. Matt. xxi. 20.
1. Gal. i. 6.
1. 2 Thes. ii. 2.
— Tit. i. 7, see Angry.

SOON AS (AS)

1. ὡς, in which way, in what way; *hence*, as, so as, how, when.
2. { ὡς, *see above,* / ἄν, perhaps, } whensoever.
3. ὅτε, when.
4. ὅταν, whensoever, if ever, in case that.
5. εὐθέως. straightway, immediately, forthwith.

5. Mark v. 36 (*om.* εὐθέως, G→L[b] T Tr A ℵ, and παρακούσας, instead of ἀκούσας, T A ℵ), i.e. *but Jesus overhearing,* instead of *"as soon as Jesus had heard."*
5. —— xi. 2 (εὐθύς, *straight,* T Tr A ℵ.)
1. Luke i. 23, 44.
3. —— xv. 30.
1. —— xxii. 66.
1. John xi. 20, 29.
4. —— xvi. 21.
1. —— xviii. 6.
1. —— xxi. 9.
2. Phil. ii. 23.
3. Rev. x. 10.
4. —— xii. 4.

SOONER (THE)

τάχιον, more quickly, more speedily.

Heb. xiii. 19.

SOOTHSAYING (BY)

μαντεύομαι, to utter responses *as from an oracle,* to divine, foretell; (lxx. *for* קסם, Deut. xviii. 10; 1 Sam. xxviii. 8.) *Here, participle,* (*non occ.*)

Acts xvi. 16.

SOP.

ψωμίον, a little bit, a morsel, a mouthful, (*non occ.*)

John xiii. 26 1st, marg. *morsel.*
John xiii. 26 2nd.
—— 27, 30.

SORCERER (-S.)

1. μάγος, great, powerful (*Heb.* מג, and *Grk.*, μέγας; *Lat.*, magis, magnus). A magus, a magian, *the name for* priests and wise men among the Medes and Babylonians; *cf.* Jer. xxxix. 3.

[Their learning was connected with astronomy and enchantment; *hence*, lxx. for Chald. אשף, *enchanter, magician,* Dan. i. 20; ii. 2, 27; v. 7. Also Chald. חכים, lxx. σοφός, Dan. ii. 12, 18, 24, 27; v. 7, 8; *cf.* v. 11, 12, (*occ.* Matt. ii. 1, 7, 16 twice.)

2. φαρμακεύς, one who prepares, administers, *or* deals in medicines, drugs, or poison, (*hence, Eng.*,

pharmacy); *then*, one who uses enchantments or practises sorcery *or* poisoning, (*non occ.*)

3. φαρμακός, one who uses any artificial means for producing physical effects; *hence*, one who uses drugs, enchanted potions as a charm or spell; *hence*, a poisoner, sorcerer, enchanter; (lxx. *for* חרטום, Ex. ix. 12; מכשף, Ex. vii. 11; Deut. xviii. 10; Dan. ii. 2), (*non occ.*)

1. Acts xiii. 6, 8. | 2. Rev. xxi. 8 (No. 3, G L T Tr A ℵ.)
3. Rev. xxii. 15.

SORCERY (-IES.)

1. φαρμακεία, the preparing or using of medicine, (*Eng.*, pharmacy); *then*, the using of any kind of drugs, potions, or spells; (lxx. *for* לחטים לטים, Ex. vii. 11, 22; כשפים, Is. xlvii. 9, 12.)

2. μαγεία, the theology of the Magians, (*see* "SORCERER," *No.* 1) *pl.*, magic arts.

2. Acts viii. 11.
1. Rev. ix. 21 (φαρμακός (*see above*, No. 3), ℵ.)
1. Rev. xviii. 23.

SORCERY (USE)

μαγεύω, to be a magus *or* skilled in Magian lore; to use incantations; *trans.*, to enchant.

Acts viii. 9.

SORE (-s.) [noun.]

ἕλκος, a wound. *In N.T. and later*, an ulcer, a sore; (lxx. *for* שחין, Ex. ix. 9; Job ii. 7.)

Luke xvi. 21. | Rev. xvi. 2, 11.

SORES (FULL OF)

ἑλκόω, to ulcerate, *trans. Here, pass. part.*, full of ulcers.

Luke xvi. 20.

SORE. [adj.]

ἱκανός, coming to, reaching to; *hence*, sufficing, sufficient; *then*, abundant, great, much.

Acts xx. 37.

SORE. [adverb.]

1. κακῶς, badly, evilly.
2. λίαν, very, exceedingly.
3. { φόβον, fear, / μέγαν, great, } lit., [*they feared*] a great fear.
4. πολλα; *as adv.*, much, greatly; *also*, many times, often.
5. σφόδρα, vehemently, very much.

5. Matt. xvii. 6.
1. —— 15. [pleased.
— —— xxi. 15, *see* Dis-
2. Mark vi. 51 (om. G→)
— Mark ix. 6, *see* Afraid.
4. —— 26.
— —— xiv. 33, *see* Amazed.
3. Luke ii. 9.

SORER.

χείρων, worse, more severe.

Heb. x. 29.

SORROW (s.) [noun.]

1. λύπη, grief, sorrow; (lxx. *for* יגון, Gen. xlii. 38; רעה, Jonah iv. 1.)
2. ὀδύνη, pain *of body; then*, pain *of mind*, distress; (lxx. *for* און, Gen. xxxv. 18; יגון, Jer. viii. 18; עמל, Job vii. 3), (*non occ.*)
3. πένθος, mourning, bewailing, lamenting; (lxx. *for* אבל, Lam. v. 15: תוגה, Prov. xiv. 13.)
4. ὠδίν, a throe, a pain, a pang, *esp. of a woman in travail;* (lxx. *for* חבל, Is. xxii. 23; Job xxi. 17; חיל, Ez. xv. 14.)

4. Matt. xxiv. 8.
4. Mark xiii. 8, marg. *pain of a woman in travail.*
1. Luke xxii. 45.
1. John xvi. 6, 20, 21, 22.
2. Rom. ix. 2.
1. 2 Cor. ii. 3, 7.
1. —— vii. 10 twice.
1. Phil. ii. 27 twice.
2. 1 Tim. vi. 10.
3. Rev. xviii. 7 twice.
3. Rev. xxi. 4

SORROW (-ED, -ING.) [verb.]

1. λυπέω, to grieve. *Here, pass. or mid.*, to be grieved, be sad, be sorrowful; (lxx. *for* ירע, Deut. xv. 10; Jon. iv. 1; עצב, 2 Sam. xix. 2.)
2. ὀδυνάω, to cause pain *or* suffering. *Here, pass. or mid.*, to feel pain, to suffer; (lxx. *for* החיל, Zech. ix. 5; חמר, Zech. xii. 10.)

2. Luke ii. 48.
2. Acts xx. 38.
1. 2 Cor. vii. 9, 11.
1. 1 Thes. iv. 13.

SORROWFUL.

λυπέω, *see above, No.* 1.

Matt. xix. 22. | 2 Cor. vi. 10.

SORROWFUL (BE)

Matt. xxvi. 22, 37. | Mark xiv. 19.
John xvi. 20.

SORROWFUL (EXCEEDING)

περίλυπος, environed with grief, wholly grieved, very sorrowful; (lxx. *for* השתוחח, Ps. xlii. 6, 12; xliii. 5.)

Matt. xxvi. 38. | Mark xiv. 34.

SORROWFUL (LESS)

ἄλυπος, free from sorrow. *Here, comp.*, more free from sorrow, less sorrowful, (*non occ.*)

Phil. ii. 28.

SORROWFUL (VERY)

περίλυπος, *see* "SORROWFUL (EXCEEDING)"

Luke xviii. 23.
—— 24 (*om.* περίλυπον γενόμενον, *that he was very sorrowful*, T Trᵇ A ℵ), i.e. *him.*

SORRY.

λυπέω, *see* "SORROW," *No.* 1, (verb.)

Matt. xiv. 9. | Matt. xvii. 23.
Matt. xviii. 31.

SORRY (EXCEEDING)

περίλυπος, *see* "SORROWFUL (EXCEEDING)"

Mark vi. 26.

SORRY (MAKE)

λυπέω, *see* "SORROW," *No.* 1, (verb.)

2 Cor. ii. 2. | 2 Cor. vii. 8 twice.

SORT.

See, BASER, GODLY, SOME, THIS, WHAT.

SOUL (-S.)

ψυχή, one of the manifestations of ζωή (life), *viz.* that which is manifested in animals, animal life; *hence*, breath, (*not breath as mere air, but* as the sign of life.) *Once applied to* vegetable life, Is. x. 18.

In O.T. everywhere lxx. *for* נפש, nephesh) *and is said to be* possessed by all the lower creatures, Gen. i. 20, 21, 24, 30; ii. 7, 19; ix. 10, 12, 15, 16; Lev. xi. 10, 46; Numb. xxxi. 28; Prov. vii. 23; xii. 10; Ezek. xlvii. 9. *So also*, Rev. viii. 9; xvi. 3.

It denotes the vital principle in animal bodies, 2 Ch. i. 11; 1 Sam. xxii. 23; 1 Kings i. 12; 2 Ch. i. 11; Est. vii. 3; Prov. i. 19; vi. 26; xii. 10; Lam. ii. 19. *Also*, Matt. xvi. 25, 26; xx. 28; Luke xii. 19-23; 1 John iii. 16.

It is used of the person as possessed of such life, Gen. xii. 5; xiv. 21; xvii. 14; xix. 17, 19, 20; xlvi. 18; Ex. xii. 15; Lev. iv. 2; v. 15; vii. 27; Est. ix. 31; Is. xlvii. 14, (*cf.* Rev. vi. 9.) *Also of* a dead person, (with the adj.) Lev. xxi. 11. *And of* those raised, Rev. xx. 4, *as contrasted with those yet unraised*, Rev. xx. 5.

It can die *or* be killed, Lev. xxiv. 17, 18; Judg. xvi. 30; Numb. xxiii. 10; xxxi. 19; Deut. xix. 6; xxii. 26; xxvii. 25; Prov. vii. 23; Ecc. iii. 19. *So of* persons, Josh. x. 28, 30, 39; Lev. xxiii. 30. *Also*, Matt. x. 28; Mark iii. 4; Luke ix. 54-56; Rev. xvi. 3.

It goes to the grave, Job xxxiii. 22, and can be hazarded by danger, Acts xv. 26; Rom. xi. 3.

It is identified with the blood, (*as the Spirit never is*) Gen. ix. 4, 5; Lev. xvii. 11, 14; Ps. lxxii. 14; xciv. 21; Prov. xxviii. 17.

The Greek ψυχή is identified with Heb. נפש, by comparing Acts ii. 27 with Ps. xvi. 10; Rom. xi. 3 with 1 Kings xix. 10; 1 Cor. xv. 45 with Gen. ii. 7; Matt. xx. 28 with Is. liii. 10.

"My soul" *is the same as* "me," *or* "myself," Numb. xxiii. 10; Judg. xvi. 30; 1 Kings xx. 32; Ps. lix. 3; xxxv. 13; cxxxi. 2; Jer. xviii. 20, (*cf.* xxxviii. 6.)

"His soul" is the same as "him" *or* "himself," Gen. xxxvii. 21; Job xviii. 4; Ps. xx. 29; cv. 17, 18.

[The Hebrew word נפש (nephesh) occurs 752 times, and is translated in 44 different ways, which may be thus grouped in four great classes.

I. "CREATURE," (9) Gen. i. 21, 24; ii. 19; ix. 10, 12, 15, 16; Lev. xi. 46. "Beast," (2) Lev. xxiv. 18. "Thing," (2) Lev. xi. 10; Ezek. xlvii. 9. "Fish," (1) Is. xix. 10.

II. "PERSON," (30) Gen. xiv. 21; xxxvi. 6; Ex. xvi. 16; Lev. xxvii. 2; Numb. v. 6; xix. 18; xxxi. 19, 35, 40, 46; xxxv. 11, 15, 30; Deut. x. 22; xxvii. 25; Josh. xx. 3, 9; 1 Sam. xxii. 22; 2 Sam. xiv. 14; Prov. xxviii. 17; Jer. xliii. 6; lii. 29, 30; Ezek. xvi. 5; xvii. 17; xxvii. 13; xxxiii. 6. "Man," (4) Ex. xii. 16; Lev. xxiv. 17; 2 Kings xii. 4; Is. xlix. 7. "Men," (1) 1 Ch. v. 21. "Him," (4) Gen. xxxvii. 21; Deut. xix. 6; xxii. 26; Prov. vi. 16. "Me," (3) Numb. xxiii. 10; Judg. xvi. 30; 1 Kings xx. 32. "Yourselves," (6) Lev. xi. 43, 44; Deut. iv. 15; Josh. xxiii. 11; Jer. xvii. 21; xxxvii. 9. "Himself," (8) 1 Kings xix. 4; Job xviii. 4; xxxii. 2; Jer. li. 14; Amos ii. 14, 15; vi. 8; Jonah iv. 8. "We," (1) Ps. xxxv. 25. "He," (2) Ps. cv. 18; Prov. xvi. 26. "Myself," (1) Ps. cxxxi. 2. "Her," (1) Jer. ii. 24. "Thee," (2) Jer. xl. 14, 15. "Herself," (2) Is. v. 14; Jer. iii. 11. "Thyself," (1) Est. iv. 13. "Themselves," (3) Est. ix. 31; Is. xlvi. 2; xlvii. 14. "Dead," (5) Lev. xix. 28; xxi. 1; xxii. 4; Numb. v. 2; vi. 11. "Body," (7) Lev. xxi. 11; Numb. vi. 6; ix. 6, 7, 10; xix. 13; Hag. ii. 13. "One," (1) Lev. iv. 27. "Any," (3) Lev. ii. 1; Numb. xix. 11; Deut. xxiv. 7. "They," (1) Job xxxvi. 14. "Own," (1) Prov. xiv. 10. "Fellow," (1) Judg. xviii. 25. "Deadly," (1) Ps. xvii. 9. "Mortally," (1) Deut. xix. 11. "Tablets," (1) Is. iii. 20. "Soul," (475 *times, everywhere except* Job xxx. 15, *where it is* נדיבה, (nobility) *and* נשמה (breath) Is. lvii. 16.

III. "LIFE" *and* "LIVES," (120) Gen. i. 20, 30; ix. 4, 5; xix. 17, 19; xxxii. 30; xliv. 30; Ex. iv. 19; xxi. 23, 30; Lev. xvii. 11, 14; Numb. xxxv. 31; Deut. xii. 23; xix. 21; xxiv. 6; Josh. ii. 13, 14; ix. 24; Judg. v. 18; ix. 17; xii. 3; xviii. 25; Ruth iv. 15; 1 Sam. xix. 5, 11; xx. 1; xxii. 23; xxiii. 15; xxvi. 24; xxviii. 9, 21; 2 Sam. i. 9; iv. 8; xiv. 7; xvi. 11; xviii. 13; xix. 5; xxiii. 17; 1 Kings i. 12; ii. 23; iii. 11; xix. 2, 3, 4, 10, 14; xx. 31, 39, 42; 2 Kings i. 13, 14; vii. 7; x. 24; 1 Ch. xi. 19; 2 Ch. i. 11; Est. vii. 3, 7; viii. 11; ix. 16; Job ii. 4, 6; vi. 11; xiii. 14; xxxi. 39; Ps. xxxi. 13; xxxviii. 12; Prov. i. 18, 19; vi. 26; vii. 23; xii. 10; xiii. 3, 8; Is. xv. 4; xliii. 4; Jer. iv. 30; xi. 21; xix. 7, 9; xxi. 7, 9; xxii. 25; xxxiv. 20, 21; xxxviii. 2, 16; xxxix. 18; xliv. 30; xlv. 5; xlvi. 26; xlviii. 6; xlix. 37; Lam. ii. 19; v. 9; Ezek. xxxii. 10; Jonah i. 14; iv. 3. "Ghost," (2) Job xi. 20; Jer. xv. 9. "Breath," (1) Job xli. 21.

IV. "DESIRE," (5) Ecc. vi. 9; Jer. xxii. 27; xliv. 14; Micah vii. 3; Hab. ii. 5. "Mind," (15) Gen. xxiii. 8; Deut. xviii. 6; xxviii. 65; 1 Sam. ii. 35; 2 Sam. xvii. 8; 2 Kings ix. 15; 1 Ch. xxviii. 9; Jer. xv. 1; Ezek. xxiii. 17, 18, 22, 28; xxiv. 25; xxxvi. 5. "Heart," (15) Ex. xxiii. 9; Lev. xxvi. 16; Deut. xxiv. 15; 1 Sam. ii. 23; 2 Sam. iii. 21; Ps. x. 3; Prov. xxiii. 7; xxviii. 25; xxxi. 6; Jer. xlii. 20; Lam. iii. 51; Ezek. xxv. 6, 15; xxvii. 31; Hos. iv. 8. "Lust," (2) Ex. xv. 9; Ps. lxxviii. 18. "She will," (1) Deut. xxi. 14. "Pleasure," (3) Deut. xxiii. 24; Ps. cv. 22; Jer. xxxiv. 16. "Discontented," (1) 1 Sam. xxii. 2. "Will," (3) Ps. xxvii. 12; xli. 2; Ez. xvi. 27. "Greedy," (1) Is. lv. 11. "Hearty," (1) Prov. xxvii. 9. "Appetite," (2) Prov. xxiii. 2; Ecc. vi. 7.

In the N.T. ψυχή (the equivalent of the Heb. נפש) occurs 105 times, and is translated as follows:— "Life" and "Lives," (40 times); "Soul," (58); "Mind," (3); "You," (1); "Heart," (1); "Us," (1); "Heartily," (1). See under each word for the occurrences.]

Matt. x. 28 twice.
—— xi. 29.
—— xii. 18.
—— xvi. 26 twice.
—— xxii. 37.
—— xxvi. 38.
Mark viii. 36, 37.
—— xii. 30, 33 (ap.)
—— xiv. 34.
Luke i. 46.
—— ii. 35.
—— x. 27.
—— xii. 19 twice, 20.
—— xxi. 19.
John xii. 27.
Acts ii. 27.
—— 31 (om. ἡ ψυχὴ αὐτοῦ, *his soul*, G L T Tr A ℵ), i.e. *he*.
—— 41, 43.
—— iii. 23.
—— iv. 32.
—— vii. 14.
—— xiv. 22.
Acts xv. 24.
—— xxvii. 37.
Rom. ii. 9.
—— xiii. 1.
1 Cor. xv. 45.
2 Cor. i. 23.
1 Thes. ii. 8.
—— v. 23.
Heb. iv. 12
—— vi. 19.
—— x. 38, 39.
—— xiii. 17.
Jas. i. 21.
—— v. 20.
1 Pet. i. 9, 22.
—— ii. 11, 25.
—— iii. 20.
—— iv. 19.
2 Pet. ii. 8, 14.
3 John 2.
Rev. vi. 9.
—— xvi. 3.
—— xviii. 13, 14.
—— xx. 4.

SOUND (-s.) [noun.]

1. φωνή, a sound, a tone, *as given forth or uttered;* a voice, a cry.

2. ἦχος, a sound *of any sort, esp. of* a confused noise, *as of a crowd, or in the ears, of trees, the sea, etc.,* (*occ.* Luke iv. 37.)

3. φθόγγος, a sound, *esp. of a musical instrument,* the voice; loud and clear utterance, (*non occ.*)

(a) *Quoted from* Ps. xix. 5, *where* lxx. *for* קו.

1. Matt. xxiv. 31, marg. [voice.
1. John iii. 8.
2. Acts ii. 2
1. 1 Cor. xiv. 7 1st.
3. —— 7 2nd.
1. 1 Cor. xiv. 8.
2. Heb. xii. 19.
1. Rev. i. 15.
1. —— ix. 9 twice.
1. —— xviii. 22.

SOUND. [adj.]

1. ὑγιαίνω, to be sound, healthy, well be in good health.

2. ὑγιής, sound, healthy, well.

1. 1 Tim. i. 10.
— 2 Tim. i. 7, see Mind.
1. —— 13 part.
1. 2 Tim. iv. 3 part.
1. Tit. i. 9 part.
1. —— ii. 1 part., 2 part.
2. Tit. ii. 8.

SOUND (BE)

1. Tit. i. 13.

SOUND (SAFE AND)

1. Luke xv. 27 part.

SOUND (-ED, -ING.) [verb.]

1. σαλπίζω, to trumpet, to sound a trumpet; (lxx. *for* תקע, Numb. x. 3, etc.; Is. xxvii. 13; Joel. ii. 1.)

2. *ἠχέω*, to sound, resound, *of a confused noise*, (*occ.* Luke xxi. 25.)

3. *βολίζω*, to heave the lead, to sound. (*Pass.*, to sink in water), (*non occ.*)

4. *γίνομαι*, to become. *Here, lit.*, came *into mine ears.*

— Matt. vi. 2, see Trumpet.
4. Luke i. 44.
3. Acts xxvii. 28 twice.
2. 1 Cor. xiii. 1.
— — xv. 52, see Trumpet.
1. Rev. viii. 6, 7, 8, 10, 12, 13.
1. — ix. 1, 13.
1. — x. 7.
1. — xi. 15.

SOUND OUT.

ἐξηχέομαι, (*No.* 2, *with ἐκ*, out of, *prefixed*) to sound out, sound abroad; (lxx. *for* המון, Joel iii. 14), (*non occ.*)

1 Thes. i. 8.

SOUNDNESS (PERFECT)

ὁλοκληρία, wholeness in every part; (lxx. *for* מתם, Is. i. 6.)

Acts iii. 16.

SOUTH.

1. *νότος*, the south wind, *or strictly*, the south-west wind; *Lat.*, notus. *Then*, the southern quarter of the heavens and earth.

2. *μεσημβρία*, mid-day, noon; (lxx. צהר ים, Gen. xliii. 16, 25.) *Then*, the mid-day quarter, *i.e.* the south, (*occ.* Acts xxii. 6.)

1. Matt. xii. 42.
1. Luke xi. 31.
1. Luke xiii. 29.
2. Acts viii. 26.
1. Rev. xxi. 13.

SOUTH WIND.

1. Luke xii. 55.
1. Acts xxvii. 13.
1. Acts xxviii. 13.

SOUTH WEST.

λίψ, the south *or* south-west wind; (lxx. *for* חימן, Ps. lxxviii. 26.) *Then*, the south, the southern quarter; (lxx. *for* נגב, Gen. xiii. 14; חימן, Numb. ii. 10.)

Acts xxvii. 12.

SOW. [noun.]

ὗς, a swine; (lxx. *for* חזיר, Deut. xiv. 8.)

2 Pet. ii. 22.

SOW (-ED, -EST, -ETH; SOWN.) [verb.]

σπείρω, to scatter *seed*, to sow *seed*; (lxx. *gen. for* זרע, Ecc. xi. 4; Gen. xxvi. 12, etc.)

Matt. vi. 26.
— xiii. 3, 4, 19, 24.
—— 25 (*ἐπισπείρω*, *to sow over*, L T Tr A ℵ.)
—— 27, 31, 37, 39.
— xxv. 24, 26.
Mark iv. 3, 4, 14, 15 twice, 16, 18, 20, 31, 32.
Luke viii. 5 twice.
Luke xii. 24.
— xix. 21, 22.
John iv. 36, 37.
1 Cor. ix. 11.
— xv. 36, 37 twice, 42, 43 twice, 44.
2 Cor. ix. 6 twice.
—— 10, see Seed.
Gal. vi. 7, 8.
Jas. iii. 18.

SOWER.

σπείρω, *see above. Here, participle, i.e.* one who scatters seed, one who sows.

Matt. xiii. 3, 18.
Mark iv. 3, 14.
Luke viii. 5.
2 Cor. ix. 10.

SOWN.

See, SEED.

SPACE.

1. *χρόνος*, time during which anything occurs.

2. *διάστημα*, distance, interval *of time or place*, (*non occ.*)

— Luke xxii. 59, see S of one hour after (the)
2. Acts v. 7.
— —— 34, see Little.
— — xv. 33, see Tarry.
— — xix. 8, see S of (for the)
— Acts xix. 10, see S of (by the)
— —— 34, see S of (the)
— — xx. 31, see Years.
1. Rev. ii. 21.
— — viii. 1, see Hour.
— — xvii. 10, see Short.

SPACE OF (THE)

ἐπί, upon. *With the Acc.*, up to, as long as.

Acts xix. 34.

SPACE OF (BY THE)

Acts xix. 10.

SPACE OF (FOR THE)

Acts xix. 8.

SPACE OF ONE HOUR AFTER (THE)

{ *διαστάσης*, having elapsed,
{ *ὥρας*, hour,
{ *μιᾶς*, one.

Luke xxii. 59.

SPAKE.

See, SPEAK.

SPARE (-ED, -ING.)

φείδομαι, to spare, *e.g.* to abstain from using *or* doing *any thing*, (*occ.* 2 Cor. xii. 6.

Acts xx. 29.
Rom. viii. 32.
—— xi. 21 twice.
1 Cor. vii. 28.
2 Cor i. 23.
—— xiii. 2.
2 Pet. ii. 4, 5.

SPARE (HAVE ENOUGH AND TO)

περισσεύω, to be over and above, to exceed in number *or* measure, to be left over, to superabound, have more than enough.

Luke xv. 17.

SPARING (not) [margin.]

Col. ii. 23, see "NEGLECTING."

SPARINGLY.

φειδομένως, sparingly, *i.e.* frugally, not bountifully, (*non occ.*)

2 Cor. ix. 6 twice.

SPARROW (-S.)

στρουθίον, any small bird, *esp.* a sparrow; (lxx. *for* צִפּוֹר, Ps. xi. 1; Lam. iii. 51), (*non occ.*)

Matt. x. 29, 31. | Luke xii. 6, 7.

SPEAK (-EST, -ETH, -ING; SPAKE; SPOKEN.)

1. λαλέω, *see* "SAY," *No.* 5.
2. λέγω, *see* "SAY," *No.* 1.
   * *see No.* 1*.
3. διαλέγομαι, (*No.* 2, *with* διά, through *or* throughout, *prefixed.*)
4. εἶπον, *see* "SAY," *No.* 2.
   * *see No.* 2b.
5. ἐρῶ, *see* "SAY," *No.* 4.
6. φθέγγομαι, to sound, emit a sound.
7. χρηματίζω, to do business, be engaged in business *private or public. Of kings, etc.*, to do business *publicly*, *i.e.* give audience and answer *to ambassadors, etc.*; give response.

— Matt. i. 22, — —— ii. 15, 17, 23, see Spoken of (which were)
— —— iii. 3, see Spoken of (he that was)
— —— iv. 14, see Spoken of (was)
4. —— viii. 8.
— ——— 17, see Spoken of (which was)
1. —— ix. 18 part., 33.
1. —— x. 19 1st, 19 2nd (*ap.*), 20 twice.
4. ——— 27.
— —— xii. 17, see Spoken of (which was)
1. ——— 22.
4. ——— 32 twice.
1. ——— 34 twice, 36.
— ——— 46, 47, see S with.
1. —— xiii. 3, 10, 13, 33, 34 twice.
— ——— 35, see Spoken of (which was)
1. —— xiv. 27.
1. —— xv. 31.
4. —— xvi. 11.
1. —— xvii. 5 part.
4. ——— 13.
— —— xxi. 4, see Spoken of (which was)
2. ——— 45.
4* —— xxii. 1.
— ——— 31, see Spoken of (which was)
1. —— xxiii. 1.
— —— xxiv. 15, see Spoken of.
1. —— xxvi. 47 part.
— ——— 65, see Blasphemy.
— —— xxvii. 9, 35, see Spoken (which was)
1. —— xxviii. 18.
1. Mark i. 34, marg. *say.*
4. ——— 42 (*om.* εἰπόντος αὐτοῦ, *as soon as He had spoken*, G → L T Tr A ℵ.)
1. —— ii. 7.
4. —— iii. 9.
1. —— iv. 33, 34.
1. —— v. 35 part., 36.
1. —— vii. 35, 37.
1. —— viii. 32.
4. —— ix. 18.
— ——— 39, see S evil of.
2. —— xii. 1 (No. 1, L T Tr A ℵ.)
4. ——— 12, 26.
1. —— xiii. 11 3 times.
— ——— 14, — —— xiv. 9, see Spoken of
2. ——— 31 (No. 1, L T Tr A ℵ.)
4. ——— 39.
1. ——— 43.
2. ——— 71.
1. —— xvi. 17 (*ap.*), 19 (*ap.*)
1. Luke i. 19, 20, 22.
— ——— 42, see S out.
1. ——— 55, 64, 70.
1. —— ii. 33.
— ——— 34, see S against.
1. ——— 38, 50.
— —— iv. 36, see S among.
1. ——— 41, marg. *say.*
1. —— v. 4, 21.
2. ——— 36.
4. —— vi. 26, 39.
1. ——— 45.
1. —— vii. 15.
2. ——— 24.
4. ——— 39.
4. Luke vii. 4.
4. ——— 49.
1. —— ix. 11.
2. ——— 31, 34 part.
1. —— xi. 14.
2* ——— 27.
1. ——— 37.
— ——— 53, see Provoke.
4. —— xii. 3 1st.
1. ——— 3 2nd.
5. ——— 10.
4. ——— 13, 16.
2* ——— 41.
2. —— xiii. 6.
4* —— xiv. 3.
4. —— xv. 3.
2. —— xviii. 1.
4. ——— 9.
— ——— 34, see Spoken (the things which were)
4. —— xix. 11, 28 part.
4. —— xx. 2.
2. ——— 9.
4. ——— 19.
2* —— xxi. 5 part.
4. ——— 29.
1. —— xxii. 47, 60.
2. ——— 65.
— —— xxiii. 20, see Spoken to.
1. —— xxiv. 6, 25, 36.
4. ——— 40 part. (*ap.*)
1. ——— 44.
— John i. 15, see Spoken of.
1. ——— 37.
— ——— 40, 41, see S (hear one)
2. —— ii. 21.
1. —— iii. 11, 31, 34.
1. —— iv. 26.
4. ——— 50.
1. —— vi. 63.
— ——— 71, see Spoken of.
1. —— vii. 13, 17, 18, 26.
4. ——— 39.
1. ——— 46.
1. —— viii. 12, 20.
2. ——— 26 (No. 1, G ~ L T Tr A ℵ.)
2. ——— 27.
1. ——— 28, 30 part., 38, 44 twice.
1. —— ix. 6 part.
1. ——— 21.
4. ——— 22.
1. ——— 29.
4. —— x. 6 1st.
1. ——— 6 2nd.
4. ——— 41.
5. —— xi. 13 1st.
2* ——— 13 2nd.
4. ——— 43 part., 51.
2* ——— 56.
1. —— xii. 29, 36.
4. ——— 38.
1. ——— 41, 48, 49 twice, 50 twice.
2. —— xiii. 18, 22, 24.
4. ——— 28.
1. —— xiv. 10 1st (No. 2, T Tr A.)
1. ——— 10 2nd, 25.
1. —— xv. 3, 11, 22.
1. —— xvi. 13 twice, 25 twice, 29 1st.
2. ——— 29 2nd.
1. ——— 33.
1. —— xvii. i. 13.
4. —— xviii. 1 part., 9, 16.
1. ——— 20.
4. ——— 22.
1. ——— 23.
4. ——— 32.
1. —— xix. 10.
— ——— 12, see S against.

4. John xx. 18.
4. —— xxi. 19 1st, 19 2nd part.
2. Acts i. 3.
4. —— 9 part.
—— 16, see S before.
1. —— ii. 4, 6, 7, 11.
5. —— 16.
2. —— 25.
4. —— 29.
1. —— 31.
1. —— iii. 21, 24.
1. —— iv. 1 part., 17.
6. —— 18.
1. —— 20, 29, 31.
1. —— v. 20, 40.
1. —— vi. 10, 11, 13.
1. —— vii. 6, 38, 44.
—— viii. 6, see Spake (those things which...)
1. —— 26.
5. —— 24.
2* —— 34.
1. —— ix. 27, 29.
1. —— x. 7, 32 (ap.), 44, 46.
1. —— xi. 15, 20.
—— xiii. 40, see S of.
—— 43, see S to.
—— 45 1st, see S against.
—— 45 2nd, see Spoken (those things which were)
1. —— 46.
1. —— xiv. 1.
—— 3, see Boldly.
1. —— 9.
1. —— xvi. 13, 14, 32.
1. —— xvii. 19, and see Speakest (whereof thou)
4. —— xviii. 9 1st.
1. —— 9 2nd, 25.
—— 26, see Boldly.
1. —— xix. 6.
—— 8, see Boldly.
—— 9, see S evil of.
—— 36, see S against (cannot be)
4. —— 41 part.
1. —— xx. 30.
4. —— 36 part.
5 —— 38.
4. —— xxi. 37 1st.
—— 37 2nd, see S Greek (can)
1. —— 39.
—— 40, see S unto.
—— xxii. 2, see S to.
1. —— 9.
—— xxiii. 5, see S of.
1. —— 9.
2. —— xxvi. 1.
1. —— 14 (No. 2, L T Tr A א.)
—— 24, see S for one's self.
—— 25, see S forth.
1. —— 26.
4. —— 30 part. (ap.)
—— xxvii. 11, see Spoken (those things which were)
4. —— 35 part.
—— xxviii. 19, see S against.
—— 20, see S with.
1. —— 21.
—— 22, see S against.
—— 24, see Spoken (the things which were)
4. —— 25 1st part.
1. —— 25 2nd.
—— Rom. i. 8, see S of.
2. —— iii. 5.
5. —— iv. 18.

2. Rom. vi. 19.
1. —— vii. 1.
2* —— x. 6.
2. —— xi. 13.
—— xiv. 16, } see S
—— xv. 18, 21, } evil of.
2. 1 Cor. i. 10.
1. —— ii. 6, 7, 13.
1. —— iii. 1.
2. —— vi. 5 (No. 1, L Trm.)
2. —— vii. 6, 12, 35.
2* —— x. 15.
—— 30, see S evil of.
1. —— xii. 3, 30.
1. —— xiii. 1, 11.
1. —— xiv. 2 3 times, 3, 4, 5 twice, 6 twice, 9 1st, 9 2nd (with εἰμί, to be), 11 twice, 13, 18, 19, 21, 23, 27, 28, 29, 34, 35, 39.
2. —— xv. 34 (No. 1, L T Tr A א.)
2. 2 Cor. ii. 17.
1. —— iv. 13 twice.
2. —— vi. 13.
2. —— vii. 3.
1. —— 14.
2. —— viii. 8.
1. —— xi. 17 twice
2. —— 21 twice.
1. —— 23.
1. —— xii. 19.
1. —— xiii. 3.
2. Gal. iii. 15.
—— iv. 15, see S of (ye)
—— Eph. iv. 15, see Truth.
1. —— 25.
2. —— v. 12.
1. —— 19.
2. —— 32.
—— vi. 20 1st, see Boldly.
1. —— 20 2nd.
1. Phil. i. 14.
2. —— iv. 11.
1. Col. iv. 3, 4.
1. 1 Thes. i. 8.
1. —— ii. 2, 4, 16.
2. 1 Tim. ii. 7.
1. —— iv. 1.
1. —— 1.
—— 2, see Lies.
1. —— v. 13.
—— 14, see Reproachfully.
1. Tit. ii. 1, 15.
—— iii. 2, see S evil of.
1. Heb. i. 1, 2.
1. —— ii. 2, 3, 5.
—— iii. 5, see S after (to be)
5. —— iv. 4.
1. —— 8.
2. —— vi. 9.
2. —— vii. 13.
1. —— 14.
2. —— viii. 1, and see S (the things which... have)
2. —— ix. 9.
1. —— 19.
1. —— xi. 4 (pass. St A Vm G ~), marg. be spoken of.
3. —— xii. 5.
—— 19, see S any more.
1. —— 24, 25 1st.
7. —— 25 2nd.
1. —— xiii. 7.
1. Jas. i. 19.
1. —— ii. 12.
—— iv. 11 3 times, see S evil of.
1. —— v. 10.

1. 1 Pet. iii. 10.
—— 16, } see S evil
—— iv. 4, } of.
1. —— 11.
—— 14, see S evil of.
1. 2 Pet. i. 21.
—— ii. 2, 10, 12, see S evil of.
6. —— 16, 18 part.
—— iii. 2, see S before.
1. —— 16.

SPEAK AGAINST.

1. *ἀντιλέγω*, (*No.* 2, *with ἀντί*, against, in opposition, *prefixed.*)

2. *καταλαλέω*, (*No.* 1, *with κατά*, downwards, against, in a hostile sense, *prefixed.*)

1. Luke ii. 34. 1. Acts xxviii. 19 part.,
1. John xix. 12. [א.] 22.
1. Acts xiii. 45 (om. G→L 2. 1 Pet. ii. 12.

SPEAK AMONG.

συλλαλέω, ("SPEAK," *No.* 1, *with σύν*, together with, *prefixed*) *πρός*, towards, } conversing with.

SPEAK ANY MORE.

προστίθημι, to set, put, lay unto *or* with *any thing*, to add unto.

Heb. xii. 19.

SPEAK BEFORE.

προεῖπον, (*No.* 4, *with πρό*, before, *prefixed.*)

Acts i. 16. | 2 Pet. iii. 2.
 Jude 17.

SPEAK EVIL OF.

1. *βλασφημέω*, to blaspheme, speak evil of, slander, defame, revile; (lxx. *for* נדף, 2 Kings xix. 6, 22; התנאץ, Is. lii. 5.)

2. *καταλαλέω*, (*see* "SPEAK AGAINST," *No.* 2) to speak against, *in a hostile sense*, (lxx. *for* נדף, Ps. xliv. 17; דבר, Ps. lxxviii. 19.)

3. *κακολογέω*, to speak evilly *or* viciously of, (lxx. *for* קלל, to curse, Ex. xxi. 17; Prov. xxii. 20; Ez. xxii. 7.)

3. Mark ix. 39. 2. Jas. iv. 11 3 times.
3. Acts xix. 9. 2. 1 Pet. iii. 16.
1. Rom. xiv. 16. 1. —— iv. 4, 14 (ap.)
1. 1 Cor. x. 30. 1. 2 Pet. ii. 2, 10, 12.
1. Tit. iii. 2. 1. Jude 8, 10.

1. 1 John iv. 5.
1. 2 John 12.
1. 3 John 14.
—— Jude 8, 10, see S evil of.
1. —— 15, 16.
—— 17, see S before.
1. Rev. i. 12.
2. —— ii. 24.
2. —— viii. 11.
1. —— x. 8.
1. —— xiii. 5, 11, 15.

SPEAK FOR ONE'S SELF.

ἀπολογέομαι, to speak one's self off, (*hence, Eng.*, apologise); to plead for, *or* defend one's self before a tribunal, (lxx. *for* הריב, Jer. xii. 1.)

Acts xxvi. 24 part.

SPEAK FORTH.

ἀποφθέγγομαι, ("SPEAK," *No.* 6, *with* ἀπό, from, *prefixed*) to sound forth, sound out; (lxx. *for* נבא, 1 Ch. xxv. 1; קסם, Ez. xiii. 9.)

Acts xxvi. 25.

SPEAK OF.

1. ἀναγγέλλω, to bring word back again, report back; *then, gen.*, to report, notify, announce, proclaim, make known.
2. καταγγέλλω, to bring word down, proclaim somewhither, announce.
3. εἶπον, *see* "SPEAK," *No.* 4.
4. ἐρῶ, *see* "SPEAK," *No.* 5.
5. λαλέω, *see* "SPEAK," *No.* 1.
6. λέγω, *see* "SPEAK," *No.* 2.

4. Mark xiv. 9.
2. John i. 15.
5. —— vi. 71.
3. Acts xiii. 40.
3. Acts xxiii. 5.
2. Rom i. 8.
4. —— xv. 18.
1. —— 21.

SPEAK OUT.

ἀναφωνέω, to lift up the voice, exclaim, cry out; (lxx. *for* השמיע, 1 Ch. xv. 28; 2 Ch. v. 13), (*non occ.*)

Luke i. 42.

SPEAK TO.

1. προσφωνέω, to utter sounds towards *any one*, to address *any one*.
2. προσλαλέω, ("SPEAK," *No.* 1, *with* προς, towards *or* to, *prefixed.*)

1. Luke xxiii. 20. | 2. Acts xiii. 43.
1. Acts xxii. 2.

SPEAK UNTO.

προσφωνέω, *see above*, *No.* 1.

Acts xxi. 40.

SPEAK WITH.

1. λαλέω, *see* "SPEAK," *No.* 1.
2. προσλαλέω, (*No.* 1, *with* πρός, to *or* towards, *prefixed.*)

1. Matt. xii. 46, 47. | 2. Acts xxviii. 20.

SPAKE OF (YE)

ὑμῶν, your.

Gal. iv. 15 (*you*, in A.V. 1611.)

SPEAK GREEK (CAN)

{ Ἑλληνιστὶ, with Greek, γινώσκεις, art thou becoming acquainted, } [it being notorious that an Egyptian (whom the chief captain supposed Paul to be) was unable to speak Greek.]

Acts xxi. 37.

SPEAK (HEAR ONE)

{ ἀκούω, to hear, παρά, from beside. }

John i. 40, 41.

SPEAKEST (WHEREOF THOU)

{ ὑπὸ, [*that*] by σοῦ, thee λαλουμένη, is being spoken. }

Acts xvii. 19.

SPOKEN AFTER (TO BE)

λαλέω, *here, fut. pass. part. of* "SPEAK," *No.* 1, to be afterwards spoken.

Heb. iii. 5.

SPOKEN AGAINST (CANNOT BE)

{ αναντίῤῥητος, not to be contradicted, εἰμί, to be, } are not to be contradicted.

Acts xix. 36.

SPOKEN OF.

ῥέω, *an obs. verb. from which is formed some of the tenses of* ειπον, (*see* "SPEAK," *Nos.* 4 *and* 5.)

Matt. xxiv. 15. | Mark xiii. 14 (ap.)

SPOKEN OF (*be*) [margin.]

Heb. xi. 4, see "SPEAK."

SPOKEN OF (HE THAT WAS)

ὁ, he [*who*]
ῥηθέν, was spoken of, (*see* "SPEAK," *Nos.* 4 *and* 5.)

Matt. iii. 3.

SPOKEN OF BEFORE (*which hath been so much*) [margin.]

2 Cor. ix. 5, see "NOTICE."

SPOKEN (THAT *or* IT WHICH WAS)

τὸ, the [*thing or matter*] *which*
ῥηθέν, was spoken of, (*see* "SAY," *No.*6.)

Matt. i. —.
— ii. 15, 17, 23.
— iv. 14.
— viii. 17.
Matt. xii. 17.
— xiii. 35.
— xxi. 4.
— xxii. 31.
Matt. xxvii. 9, 35 (*ap.*)

SPOKEN (THE *or* THOSE THINGS WHICH WERE)

τὰ, the *things* [*which were*]
λεγόμενα, spoken, (*see* "SAY," *No.* 1.)

Luke xviii. 34.
Acts xiii. 45.
Acts xxvii. 11.
— xxviii. 24.

SPAKE (THOSE THINGS WHICH...)

τὰ λεγομένα, *see above.*

Acts viii. 6.

SPOKEN (THE THINGS WHICH...HAVE)

τὰ λεγομένα, *see above.*

Heb. viii. 1.

SPEAKER (CHIEF)

ἡγούμενος, *the* leader
τοῦ, of the
λόγου, discourse.

Acts xiv. 12.

SPEAKING (EVIL)

1. βλασφημία, blasphemy, slander, reviling; (lxx. *for* נאצה, Ezek. xxxv. 12.)
2. καταλαλία, speaking against, (*implying hostility.*)

1. Eph. iv. 31. | 2. 1 Pet. ii. 1.

SPEAKING (MUCH)

πολυλογία, much speaking, loquacity; (lxx. *for* רב דברים, Prov. x. 19.)

Matt. vi. 7.

SPEAR.

λόγχη, the triangular iron head of a lance *or* javelin; *hence,* lance, spear; (lxx. *for* רמח, Judg. v. 8; Neh. iv. 13, 16), (*non occ.*)

John xix. 34.

SPEARMAN.

δεξιολάβος, one who takes the right hand; *hence, prob.,* a guard, body-guard. *A word unknown to classic writers. Prob.* some kind of light armed soldiers. *Vulg. has* lancearii, (*non occ.*)

Acts xxiii. 23.

SPECIAL.

οὐ, not
τυγχάνω, the ordinary, casual, common,
} no ordinary, uncommon.

Acts xix. 11.

SPECIALLY.

μάλιστα, most, most of all, especially.

Acts xxv. 26.
Phil. iv. 22.
1 Tim. iv. 10.
1 Tim. v. 8.
Tit. i. 10.
Philem. 16

SPECTACLE.

θέατρον, theatre, a public show, (*occ.* Acts xix. 19, 31.)

1 Cor. iv. 9, marg. *theatre.*

SPEECH.

1. λόγος, the word *spoken, not in its outward form, but as* connected with the thought expressed, as a part of what is uttered. *Hence,* the word *or* speech, exposition, account; the word *as* a means or instrument, (*not like No.* 2, *as a product, i.e. not the mere act of speaking.*)
2. λαλιά, the mere act of speaking, prattle, talk, brogue; (lxx. *for* מדבר, Song, iv. 3; דבר, Job xxxiii. 1.)

2. Matt. xxvi. 73.
— Mark vii. 32, see Impediment.
2. —— xiv. 70.
2. John viii. 43.
— Acts xiv. 11, see S of Lycaonia (in the)
1. —— xx. 7.
— Rom. xvi. 18, see Ss (fair)
1. 1 Cor. i. 17, marg. (text, *words*)
1. 1 Cor. ii. 1, 4.
1. —— iv. 19.
— —— xv. 2, marg. see What.
— 2 Cor. iii. 12, see Plainness.
— —— vii. 4, see Boldness.
1. —— x. 10.
1. —— xi. 6.
1. Col. iv. 6.
1. Tit. ii. 8.

SPEECH OF LYCAONIA.

Λυκαονιστί, *adv.* Lycaonicè, in the Lycaonic dialect.

Acts xiv. 11.

SPEECHES (FAIR)

εὐλογία, eulogy, commendation; *then, because with man such is often false, it comes to mean here* fair speech, adulation.

Rom. xvi. 18.

SPEECHLESS.

1. ἐννέος, (*prob.* the same word, except in pronunciation, as ἄνεως, from ἄω, αὔω, speechless, dumb, *with amazement*) dumb, speechless, (*cf. Germ.*, dumm); (lxx. *for* אלם, Is. lvi. 10.)
2. κωφός, blunted, dull, lame; *as to the tongue or speech*, dumb; (lxx. *for* אלם, Hab. ii. 18.)

2. Luke i. 22. | 1. Acts ix. 7.

SPEECHLESS (BE)

φιμόω, to muzzle; *hence*, put to silence. *Here, pass.*, to be silenced.

Matt. xxii. 12.

SPEED.

2 John 10, 11, see "GOD."

SPEED (WITH ALL)

{ ὡς, as, τάχιστα, most speedily, } as quickly as possible.

Acts xvii. 15.

SPEEDILY.

{ ἐν, in
ταχῷς, quickness, speed.

Luke xviii. 8.

SPEND (-EST, SPENT.)

1. δαπανάω, to spend, be at expense; *esp.*, to consume, use up, waste.
2. προσαναλίσκω, to consume besides, expend further, (*non occ.*)

1. Mark v. 26.
2. Luke viii. 43.
1. —— xv. 14 part.
— Acts xvii. 21, } see
— —— xviii. 23, } Time.
— —— xx. 16, }
1. 2 Cor. xii. 15.

SPEND MORE.

προσδαπανάω, (*No.* 1, *above, with* πρός, towards, *prefixed*) to spend more, in addition to, (*non occ.*)

Luke x. 35.

SPENT (BE)

1. ἐκδαπανάομαι, (*No.* 1, *above, with* ἐκ, out of, *prefixed*) to spend out, spend entirely, (*non occ.*)
2. διαγίνομαι, to be throughout, to be always; *of time*, to be through, to have elapsed, be past.

2. Acts xxvii. 9 part. | 1. 2 Cor. xii. 15.

SPENT (BE FAR)

1. προκόπτω, to beat *or* drive forwards *as if with repeated strokes.*
2. { κλίνω, to bend, incline, ἡ, the, ἡμέρα, day, } the day is declining; (lxx. *for* ירד, Judg. xix. 11; נטה, Judg. xix. 8; פנה, Jer. vi. 4.)

2. Luke xxiv. 29. | 1. Rom. xiii. 12.

SPENT (WHEN THE DAY WAS

{ ὥρας, hours,
πολλῆς, many,
γενομένης, having occurred.

Mark vi. 35.

SPICES.

ἄρωμα, aromatics, spicery, (*e.g. myrrh and aloe*); (lxx. *for* בשם, 2 Kings xx. 13; 2 Ch. ix. 1, 9; Song iv. 10, 16.)

Luke xxiii. 56. | Luke xxiv. 1.
John xix. 40.

SPICES (SWEET)

Mark xvi. 1.

SPIES.

See, SPY.

SPIKENARD.

{ νάρδος, nard, spikenard, (Heb. נרד)
πιστικός, true, genuine, pure, *i.e. the most precious*

Mark xiv. 3, marg. *pure nard or liquid nard.*
John xii. 3.

SPILL (-ED.)

1. ἐκχέω, to pour out.
2. ἐκχύνω, (*a later form of No.* 1.)

1. Mark ii. 22 (ὁ οἶ ἀπόλλυται καὶ οἱ ἀσκοί, *is lost and the bottles*, instead of ὁ οἶνος ἐκχεῖται καὶ οἱ ἀσκοὶ ἀπολοῦνται, *is spilled and the bottles will be marred*, T Tr A.)
2. Luke v. 37.

SPIN.

νήθω, to spin; (lxx. *for* טוה, Ex. xxxv. 25, *comp.* xxvi. 31; xxxviii. 18), (*non occ.*)

Matt. vi. 28. | Luke xii. 27.

SPIRIT (-s.)

1. πνεῦμα, (*from* πνέω, to blow, breathe; to draw breath, breathe, *and so* to live); *hence*, breathing *as the sign and condition of life*, breath. That which cannot be apprehended by the senses, but is recognised only by its operations or manifestations, as it is seen in life. *In the O.T.*, πνεῦμα *is everywhere the translation of* רוח (Ruach) *and is* the life principle springing from God, *and is said to be* possessed by all the lower creatures, Gen. vi. 17; vii. 22; Ps. civ. 29, 30; Ecc. iii. 19, 20; Is. xlii. 5.

Its usages may be thus distinguished:

1. GOD, (John iv. 24; 1 Cor. iii. 16,) as the source of life in all its manifestations.
2. CHRIST, (1 Cor. vi. 17; 2 Cor. iii. 17, 18.)
3. THE HOLY SPIRIT. Generally with the article, but not always or necessarily so.
4. THE OPERATIONS OF THE HOLY SPIRIT. Spiritual gifts, (1 Cor. xiv. 32.) Passages marked with asterisk (4*) are *pneuma hagion.* No. 14.
5. THE NEW NATURE, as the greatest of His gifts. This is the Pauline usage: *spirit* as opposed to flesh, (John iii. 6; Rom. viii. 4.)
6. MAN, (Psychologically.) Spirit as imparted to man, making him "a living soul," (Gen. ii. 7; Ps. civ. 29, 30; Ecc. xii. 7.) When taken back to and by God, man becomes "a dead soul." (The Heb. Nephesh (soul) is translated "body" in Lev. xxi. 11; Num. vi. 6; xix. 11, 13. "Dead body," Num. ix. 6, 7, 10; Hag. ii. 13. And, "the dead," Lev. xix. 28; xxi. 1; xxii. 4; Num. v. 2; vi. 11.)
7. CHARACTER, as invisible, and manifested only in one's actions, (2 Tim. i. 7; Rom. viii. 15, etc.)
8. OTHER INVISIBLE CHARACTERISTICS, (by *Metonymy*,) such as *feelings* or *desires*, (Matt. xxvi. 41, etc.): or for that which is supernatural.
9. THE WHOLE PERSON, (by *Synecdoche*,) a part being put for the whole, (Luke i. 47.)
10. ADVERBIALLY, either in the Dative case, or with a Preposition, as ἐν δόλῳ, craftily, (2 Cor. xi. 16.)
11. ANGELS, or SPIRIT-BEINGS, (Heb. i. 7, 14; Acts viii. 29; Rev. i. 4, etc.) As to 1 Pet. iii. 19, the following should be noted:

πνεύματα, *spirits*, when standing alone, (without any qualifying words, as it does here,) is never used of men in any form, state or condition. These are spiritual beings. He "maketh His angels spirits," Heb. i. 7, 14; Ps. civ. 4. The angels who sinned in Gen. vi. 2, 4, see 2 Pet. ii. 4—9 and Jude 6, 7. The term "Sons of God," Gen. vi. 2, 4, is always used of angels, see Job ii. 1; xxxviii. 7; Ps. xxix. 1; lxxxix. 6; Dan. iii. 25, (Codex A of the lxx. in Gen. vi. 2 reads "ἄγγελοι τοῦ Θεοῦ *angels of God.*) They left their own "habitation," (οἰκητήριον occurs only here and 2 Cor. v. 2, where it is used of a *spiritual body!*) For their sin they were "cast down to Tartarus," "delivered unto chains of darkness"; in other words, put "in prison" and reserved unto the judgment of the great day. Christ's triumph was so complete that the proclamation (see "PREACH," No. 1) of it reached even to Tartarus. See a pamphlet by the same author on *The Spirits in Prison*, (Eyre & Spottiswoode, 33, Paternoster Row, E.C.) The passage is introduced for the purpose of proving that "it is better, if the will of God be so, that ye suffer for well doing than for evil doing, FOR Christ also once suffered," etc. He had a glorious triumph, (Eph. iv. 8; Col. ii. 15; 1 Pet. i. 21); so will you in like manner. Even when angels were put in prison men (Noah and Lot) were delivered (see "SAVE," No. 2);—You will likewise be delivered from your tribulation.

12. DEMONS, or EVIL SPIRIT-BEINGS.
13. THE RESURRECTION BODY, 1 Cor. xv. 45; 1 Pet. iii. 18. As to 1 Pet. iv. 6, note that

In the A.V. and R.V. the particle μεν, *though*, is left untranslated. It does not say that the Gospel was preached to them "that they might be judged," but, that "*though* (μέν) they might

be judged." They might be judged indeed (μέν) by man's tribunal, (κατὰ ἀνθρώπους, *according to* the will of *men*, see Rom. viii. 27; xv. 5; 1 Cor. xii. 8; xv. 32; 2 Cor. vii. 9, 10, 11; xi. 17; Gal. i. 11; Eph. ii. 2; Col. ii. 8; 1 Pet. iv. 14.) They might be put to death indeed (μέν) as regards the flesh, (σαρκί, the Dat. of reference,) yet (δὲ) they shall live according to the will of God, (κατὰ θεόν, see the refs. above.) For this cause—to give them this hope—was the Gospel preached to them as is described in 1 Pet. i. 12, 25. The hope of glory was set over against their sufferings, see 1 Pet. i. 11; iv. 13.

In Heb. xii. 23 the spirits of just men (returned to God) will not be "perfected" till united to the risen body in resurrection.

14. Pneuma Hagion. This expression, (which occurs fifty times) without articles, is never used of the Giver, (the Holy Spirit,) but of His Gift. "The promise of the Father" is (in Acts i. 4, 5) called *pneuma hagion*, (holy spirit,) and (in Luke xxiv. 49) it is called "power from on high." This "power" includes whatever spiritual gifts the Holy Spirit may be pleased to bestow.

Pneuma hagion is usually translated "the Holy Spirit," the article being inserted, and capital letters used. But then we have no stronger expression by which to translate "*to pneuma, to hagion*," (the Spirit, the holy [Spirit].)

Whenever spirit is said to *fall*, or to be *given*, or to *fill*, or be baptized with, it is always *pneuma* without the article, or *pneuma hagion*

15. *Φάντασμα*, *a phantasm, phantom*, (*occ.* Matt. xiv. 26; Mark vi. 49.)

4*. Matt. i. 18, 20.
4*.—— iii. 11.
3. —— 16.
3. —— iv. 1.
7. —— v. 8.
12. —— viii. 16.
12. —— x. 1.
8. —— 20.
4. —— xii. 18.
3. —— 28, 31, 32.
12. —— 43, 45.
15. —— xiv. 26.
3. —— xxii. 43.
8. —— xxvi. 41.
6. —— xxvii. 50.
3. —— xxviii. 19.
4*. Mark i. 8.
3. —— 10.
3. —— 12.
12. —— 23, 26, 27.
9. —— ii. 8.
12. —— iii. 11.
3. —— 29.
12. —— 30.
12. —— v. 2, 8, 13.
12. —— vi. 7.
15. Mark vi. 49.
12. —— vii. 25.
9. —— viii. 12.
12. —— ix. 17, 20, 25 twice.
3. —— xii. 36.
3. —— xiii. 11.
8. —— xiv. 38.
6. —— xv. 39.
4*. Luke i. 15.
4. —— 17.
4*.—— 35, 41.
9. —— 47.
4*.—— 67.
6. —— 80.
4*.—— ii. 25.
3. —— 26, 27.
6. —— 40, (*om.* All.)
4*.—— iii. 16.
4*.—— iv. 1 1st.
3. —— 1 2nd, 14.
4. —— 18.
12. —— 33, 36.
12. —— vi. 18.
12. —— vii. 21.
12. —— viii. 2, 29.
6. —— 55.
12. Luke ix. 39, 42.
7. —— 55.
12. —— x. 20.
3. —— 21 (*add* ἐν, *by*, and τῷ ἁγίῳ, *the holy*.)
4*.—— xi. 13.
12. —— 24, 26.
8. —— xii. 10.
12. —— xiii. 11.
6. —— xxiii. 46.
11. —— xxiv. 37, 39.
3. John i. 32, 33 1st.
4*.—— 33 2nd.
4. —— iii. 5.
3. —— 6 1st.
4. —— 6 2nd.
3. —— 8 twice, 34 (*om.* ὁ θεὸς, L Tr[b] T A W H and RV.)
4. —— iv. 23.
1. —— 24 1st.
4. —— 24 2nd.
6. —— vi. 63 twice.
4. —— vii. 39 twice.
9. —— xi. 33.
9. —— xiii. 21.
3. —— xiv. 17, 26.
3. —— xv. 26.
3. —— xvi. 13.
6. —— xix. 30.
4*.—— xx. 22.
4*. Acts i. 2, 5, 8.
3. —— 16.
4*.—— ii. 4 1st.
3. —— 4 2nd.
4. —— 17, 18.
4*.—— 33.
4*.—— iv. 8.
4*.—— 25, (*add*, All,) 31.
3. —— v. 3, 9
12. —— 16.
4. —— 32†.
4*.—— vi. 3, 5, 10.
3. —— vii. 51.
4*.—— 55.
6. —— 59.
12. —— viii. 7.
4*.—— 15, 17, 18, (*om.* τὸ ἅγιον, L T Tr[b] A and RV,) 19.
11. —— 29, 39.
4*.—— ix. 17.
3. —— 31.
11. —— x. 19.
4*.—— 38.
4. —— 44.
4*.—— 45.
4. —— 47.
11. —— xi. 12.
4 —— 15.
4*.—— 16, 24.
3. —— 28.
3. —— xiii. 2, 4.
4*.—— 9, 52.
4. —— xv. 8.
3. —— 28.
3. —— xvi. 6, 7 (*add* Ἰησοῦ, *Jesus*, All & RV.)
12. —— 16, 18.
8. —— xvii. 16.
8. —— xviii. 5, (λόγῳ, *engrossed in the Word*, All.)
10. —— 25.
4*.—— xix. 2 twice, 6.
12. —— 12, 13, 15, 16.
10. —— 21.
10. —— xx. 22.
11 or 12. —— xxiii. 8, 9.
3. —— xxviii. 25.
13. Rom. i. 4.
10. —— 9.
10. —— ii. 29.
4*.—— v. 5.
10. —— vii. 6.
5. —— viii. 1, (*om.* All,) 2, 4, 5 twice, 6, 9 3 times, 10, 11 twice, 13, 14.
7. Rom. viii. 15 twice.
3. —— 16 1st.
5. —— 16 2nd, 23.
3. —— 26 twice, 27.
4*.—— ix. 1.
10. —— xii. 11.
4*.—— xiv. 17.
4. —— xv. 13.
3. —— 16.
4. —— 19.
1. —— 30.
4. 1 Cor. ii. 4.
6. —— 11 1st.
3. —— 11 2nd.
6. —— 12 1st.
5. —— 12 2nd.
4. —— 13 (*om.* ἅγιον, *holy*, All.)
3. —— 14.
1. —— iii. 16.
7. —— iv. 21.
10. —— v. 3.
8. —— 4.
6. —— 5.
3. —— vi. 11.
2. —— 17.
4*.—— 19.
6. —— 20 (*om.* All.)
6. —— 34 (*add* Art., All.)
4. —— 40.
5. —— xii. 3 1st.
4*.—— 3 2nd.
3. —— 4, 7, 8 twice.
12. —— 10.
3. —— 11.
4. —— 13 twice.
4. —— xiv. 2, 32.
9. —— 14.
13. —— xv. 45.
9. —— xvi. 18.
4. 2 Cor. i. 22.
9. —— ii. 13.
4. —— iii. 3.
6. —— 6 twice, 8.
2. —— 17 twice, 18.
4. —— iv. 13.
4. —— v. 5.
4*.—— vi. 6.
9. —— vii. 1, 13.
12. —— xi. 4n.
8. —— xii. 18.
3. —— xiii. 14.
5. Gal. iii. 2, 3, 5.
3 —— 14.
5. —— iv. 6. 29.
4. —— v. 5.
5. —— 16, 17 twice, 18.
3. —— 22.
5. —— 25 twice.
7. —— vi. 1.
5. —— 8 1st.
3. —— 8 2nd.
9. —— 18.
3 or 4. Eph. i. 13.
4. —— 17.
12. —— ii. 2.
3. —— iii. 5, 16.
3. —— iv. 3, 4.
5. —— 23.
3. —— 30.
3. —— v. 9 (φωτός, *of light*, All.)
3. —— 18 (see under Fill.)
3. —— vi. 17, 18.
8. Phil. i. 27.
8. —— ii. 1.
10. —— iii. 3.
9. —— iv. 23, (*add* instead of "on all," All.)
10. Col. i. 8.
10. —— ii. 5.
4*. 1 Thess. i. 5, 6.
4. —— iv. 8.
4. —— v. 19.
6. —— 23.
12. 2 Thess. ii. 2.

8. 2 Thess. ii. 3.
3. —— 13.
13. 1 Tim. iii. 16.
3. —— iv. 1 1st
12. —— 1 2nd.
7. —— 12 (*om.* All.)
7. 2 Tim. i. 7.
4*. —— 14.
9. —— iv. 22.
4*. Titus iii. 5.
9. Philem. 25.
4*. Heb. ii. 4.
3. —— iii. 7.
6. —— iv. 12.
4*. —— vi. 4.
3. —— ix. 8, 14.
3. —— x. 15, 29.
6 & 12. —— xii. 23 (see above, under No. 12.)
6. Jas. ii. 23.
6. —— iv. 5.
3. 1 Pet. i. 2, 11.
4. —— 12.
3. —— 22, (*om.* All.)
13. —— iii. 18 (see above.)
13. —— iv. 6 (see above.)
4*. 2 Pet. i. 21.
4 & 5. 1 John iii. 24.
12. —— iv. 1 twice.
3. 1 John iv. 2.
12. —— 3.
11. —— 6 1st.
12. —— 6 2nd.
4. —— 13.
3. —— v. 6 twice, 7, (*ap.,*) 8
5. Jude 19.
4*. —— 20.
11. Rev. i. 4.
3. —— 10.
3. —— ii. 7, 11, 17, 29.
11. —— iii. 1.
3. —— 6, 13, 22.
3. —— iv. 2.
11. —— 5.
11. —— v. 6.
6. —— xi. 11.
6. —— xiii. 15.
3. —— xiv. 13.
12. —— xvi. 13, 14.
3. —— xvii. 3.
12. —— xviii. 2.
7. —— xix. 10.
3. —— xxi. 10.
4*. —— xxii. 6 (*add πνευμάτων τῶν, spirits of the,* All.)
3. —— 17.

SPIRITUAL.

1. πνευματικός, belonging to the Spirit, *or* determined by the πνεῦμα; influenced by it, *or* proceeding from it.

[(a) In 1 Cor. x. 4, the spiritual rock was the rock pointed out by Him who made the water to spring from it, Himself being the source, (*see* Deut. viii. 15; Ex. xvii. 6, *and* Deut. xxxii. 4; xv. 18.) And as that Rock when once "smitten" was afterwards only to be "spoken to," so now with Christ, who, once *smitten* for us, now when *spoken to* in prayer refreshes our souls.]

2. πνεῦμα, (*see* "SPIRIT," *No.* 1.) *Here Gen. pl.*, of spirits, *i.e.* demons, of the actings of which the Gentile Corinthians seemed to be "envious," confounding them with the Holy Ghost (*cf.* xii. 10.)

1. Rom. i. 11.
1. —— vii. 14, } see S things.
— Rom. xv. 27, } see S things.
— 1 Cor. ii. 13 1st, } see S things.
1. —— 13 2nd.
— —— 15, see S (he that is)
1. —— iii. 1.
1. —— ix. 11, see S things.
1. —— x. 3, 4 1st.
1a. —— 4 2nd.
1. —— xii. 1.
— —— xiv. 1, see S gifts.
2. 1 Cor. xiv. 12.
1. —— 37.
1. —— xv. 44 twice.
— —— 46 twice, see S (that which is)
— Gal. vi. 1, see S (ye which are)
1. Eph. i. 3.
1. —— v. 19 (*om.* Lb.)
1. —— vi. 12, marg. *spirit.*
1. Col. i. 9.
1. —— iii. 16.
1. 1 Pet. ii. 5 twice.

SPIRITUAL GIFTS.

1 Cor. xiv. 1.

SPIRITUAL THINGS.

Rom. xv. 27. | 1 Cor. ii. 13.
1 Cor. ix. 11.

SPIRITUAL (HE THAT IS)

No. 1, *with art.*

1 Cor. ii. 15.

SPIRITUAL (THAT WHICH IS)

No. 1, *with art.*

1 Cor. xv. 46 twice.

SPIRITUAL (YE WHICH ARE)

ὑμεῖς, you,
οἱ, the
πνευματικοί, spiritual.

Gal. vi. 1.

SPIRITUALLY.

1. πνευματικῶς, (*adv. of No.* 1, *above*) spiritually, *i.e.* in accordance with *or* through the Spirit.

2. πνεῦμα, (*Gen. of* "SPIRIT," *No.* 1) of the Spirit, *i.e.* "[*the mind*] of the Spirit [*is life and peace.*]"

2. Rom. viii. 6. | 1. 1 Cor. ii. 14.
1. Rev. xi. 8.

SPIT (-ED, SPAT.)

πτύω, to spit, spit out, (*same as Lat.* spuo, sputo; *and Eng.* spew, spit); lxx. *for* ירק, Numb. xii. 4, (*non occ.*)

Mark vii. 33. | Mark viii. 23 part.
John ix. 6.

SPIT IN.

ἐμπτύω, (*the above, with* ἐν, in, *prefixed*) (a) *followed by* εἰς, into.

a. Matt. xxvi. 67.

SPIT ON.

Mark xiv. 65. | Luke xviii. 32.

SPIT UPON.

a. Matt. xxvii. 30. | Mark x. 34.
Mark xv. 19.

SPITEFULLY (ENTREAT)

ὑβρίζω, to wax wanton, run riot, *esp. in the use of superior strength; hence, in dealing with other persons,* to treat despitefully, outrage, insult insolently, abuse; (lxx. *for* הקל, 2 Sam. xix. 43.)

Matt. xxii. 6. | Luke xviii. 32.

SPITTLE.

πτύσμα, what is spit out, spittle, (*see* "SPIT"), (*non occ.*)

John ix. 6.

SPOIL (-s.) [noun.]

1. σκῦλον, skin *as stripped off*, hide; *then*, spoil, booty *as stripped from an enemy;* (lxx. *for* שׁלל, Zech. xiv. 1; Is. liii. 12), (*non occ.*)
2. ἀκροθίνιον, the topmost *or* best part of a heap; *hence*, the choice part, the first-fruits of the field, booty, (*non occ.*)

1. Luke xi. 22. | 2. Heb. vii. 4.

SPOIL (-ED.) [verb.]

1. διαρπάζω, to snatch asunder, pillage, plunder; (lxx. *for* בזז, Gen. xxxiv. 27, 29; Nah. ii. 9; גזל, Deut. xxviii. 29; שסה, 1 Sam. xxiii. 1; Is. xlii. 22), (*non occ.*)
2. ἀπεκδύομαι, to strip off from one's self, to put off, divest one's self of; *then*, to strip off for one's self, despoil.

[*Here*, it must mean either the spoiling of the powers of darkness, (*cf.* i. 16; ii. 10; Eph. ii. 2; vi. 11, 12), or, the putting off the law, the handwriting of ordinances which was against us, which had been given by heavenly and angelic powers, (Gal. iii. 19; Heb. ii. 2) and triumphed over them, rendering them powerless for His people.] (*occ.* Col. iii. 9.)

3. { ἔσται, there shall be, ὁ, who, [is] συλαγωγῶν, leading [*you*] off as a prey. } [*Here, lit.*, "lest someone there shall be who is, etc." The "*you*" is emphatic, and the verb in the future implies present danger more than mere possibility.] (*non occ.*)

1. Matt. xii. 29 1st (ἁρπάζω, *seize upon*, L T Tr A.) | 1. Mark iii. 27 twice.
1. —— 29 2nd (ἁρπάζω, L.) | 3. Col. ii. 8.
| 2. —— 15.

SPOILING.

ἁρπαγή, plundering, pillage; (lxx. *for* גזל, Ecc. v. 7.)

Heb. x. 34.

SPOKE, SPOKEN.

See, SPEAK.

SPONGE.

σπόγγος, a sponge, (*non occ.*)

Matt. xxvii. 48. | Mark xv. 36.
John xix. 29.

SPORT ONE'S SELF.

ἐντρυφάω, to live delicately *or* luxuriously, (*see* "DECEIVINGS"), (*non occ.*)

2 Pet. ii. 13.

SPOT (-s.) [noun.]

1. σπῖλος, a spot, a stain; mark, stain, *in a moral sense*, (*non occ.*)
2. σπιλάς, a cliff, breaker, *on which vessels are wrecked*, craggy rocks, (*non occ.*)

1. Eph. v. 27. | 1. 2 Pet. ii. 13.
2. Jude 12

SPOT (WITHOUT)

1. ἄσπιλος, (*No.* 1, *with* α, without, *prefixed.*)
2. ἄμωμος, without blemish, without bodily defect.

1. 1 Tim. vi. 14. [*out fault*. | 1. 1 Pet. i. 19.
2. Heb. ix. 14, *marg. with-* | 1. 2 Pet. iii. 14.

SPOT (-TED.) [verb.]

σπιλόω, to spot, to stain, to defile, (*occ.* Jas. iii. 6.)

Jude 23.

SPREAD.

1. στρώννυμι, to strow, to spread; (lxx. *for* יצע, Est. iv. 3; Is. xiv. 11.)
2. ὑποστρώννυμι, to strow *or* spread underneath; (lxx. *for* הציע, Ps. lviii. 6), (*non occ.*)
3. διανέμω, to cut through, distribute throughout, spread abroad.

— Matt. ix. 31, see Fame. | 1. Mark xi. 8 (*ap.*)
1. —— xxi. 8. | 2. Luke xix. 36.

SPREAD ABROAD.

ἐξέρχομαι, to go *or* come out of *any place*, proceed; (lxx. *everywhere for* יצא.)

Mark i. 28. | 1 Thes. i. 8.

SPREAD UPON. [margin.]

John ix. 6, see "ANOINT."

SPREAD ABROAD (BE)

{ γίνομαι, to become φανερόν, conspicuous, famous, } *lit.*, famous became [*his name*]

Mark vi. 14.

SPRING.

1. ἀνατέλλω, *trans.*, to cause to rise up; *intrans.*, to rise up; *spoken of the sun or light, the stars or clouds; comp.* Luke i. 78; Numb. xxiv. 17.

2. γεννάω, to beget, *spoken of men; to bear, spoken of women; pass.*, to be begotten *or* born.

1. Heb. vii. 14. | 2. Heb. xi. 19.

SPRING IN.

εἰσπηδάω, to leap into; (lxx. *for* בוא, Amos v. 19.)

Acts xvi. 29.

SPRING UP.

1. ἅλλομαι, to leap, jump, spring; (lxx. *for* סלד, Job vi. 10; אלה, 1 Sam. x. 10), (*occ.* Acts iii. 8; xiv. 10.)

2. ἀνατέλλω, *see* "SPRING," *No.* 1.

3. βλαστάνω, to germinate, put forth; (*so*, lxx. *for* פרח, Numb. xvii. 23; דשא, Joel ii. 22), (*occ.* Heb. ix. 4; Jas. v. 18.)

4. ἐξανατέλλω, (*No.* 2, *with* ἐξ, out of, *prefixed*) to rise up out of, (*non occ.*)

5. φύω, to generate, produce, bring forth, (*non occ.*)

6. ἀναβαίνω, to cause to ascend, ascend, come up, *as thoughts, plants, etc.*

2. Matt. iv. 16.
4. —— xiii. 5.
6. —— 7.
3. —— 26.
4. Mark iv. 5.
6. Mark iv. 8.
3. —— 27.
5. Luke viii. 6 part., 8.
1. John iv. 14.
5. Heb. xii. 15.

SPRING UP WITH.

συμφύω, (*No.* 5, *above, with* σύν, together with *or* in conjunction with, *prefixed.*)

Luke viii. 7 pass.

SPRINKLE (-ED, -ING.)

ῥαντίζω, to sprinkle, besprinkle; (lxx. *for* נזה, Lev. vi. 27; 2 Kings ix. 33; *also for* חטא, Ps. li. 9), (*non occ.*)

Heb. ix. 13, 19, 21. | Heb. x. 22.

SPRINKLING.

1. ῥαντισμός, a sprinkling; (lxx. *for* נדה, Numb. xix. 9; xiii. 20, 21), (*non occ.*)

2. πρόσχυσις, a pouring out towards or upon; (lxx. Ex. xii. 7, 22), (*non occ.*)

2. Heb. xi. 28. | 1. Heb. xii. 24.
1. 1 Pet. i. 2.

SPUE.

ἐμέω, to spue out, vomit forth; (lxx. *for* קיא, Is. xix. 14), (*non occ.*)

Rev. iii. 16.

SPUNGE.

See, SPONGE.

SPY, SPIES.

1. ἐγκάθετος, a sitting in ambush, lying in wait; (lxx. *for* ערב, Job xxxi. 9), (*non occ.*)

2. κατάσκοπος, one who views accurately, a scout, reconnoiterer; (lxx. *for* מרגל, Gen. xlii. 9, 11.)

1. Luke xx. 20. | 2. Heb. xi. 21.

SPY OUT.

κατασκοπέω, to view accurately, reconnoitre, spy out, explore; (lxx. *for* רגל, 2 Sam. x. 3; 1 Ch. xix. 3), (*non occ.*)

Gal. ii. 4.

STABLISH (-ED, -ETH.)

1. στηρίζω, to set fast, fix firmly, make steadfast, establish; (lxx. *for* סמך, Ps. li. 14; cxii. 8.)

2. *βεβαιόω*, to make steadfast, confirm; (lxx. *for* קים, Ps. cxix. 28; הציב, Ps. xli. 13); *spoken of things*, to corroborate, ratify.

1. Rom. xvi. 25.
2. 2 Cor. i. 21.
2. Col. ii. 7.
1. 1 Thes. iii. 13.
1. 2 Thes. ii. 17.
1. —— iii. 1.
1. Jas. v. 8.
1. 1 Pet. v. 10.

STAFF, STAVES.

1. *ῥάβδος*, a rod, wand, staff.

(a) Heb. xi. 21, *ἐπὶ*, (Heb. אל, upon) *τὸ ἄκρον τῆς ῥάβδου*, upon the top of his rod, *in allusion to* Gen. xlvii. 31.

2. *ξύλον*, wood; *then*, anything made of wood, *as* a staff, club.

1. Matt. x. 10.
2. —— xxvi. 47, 55.
1. Mark vi. 8.
2. Mark xiv. 43, 48.
1. Luke ix. 3.
2. —— xxii. 52.
1a. Heb. xi. 21.

STAGGER (-ED.)

διακρίνω, to separate throughout, *i.e. wholly, completely. Here, mid.*, to separate one's self from; be in strife with one's self, *i.e.* to doubt, hesitate, waver.

Rom. iv. 20.

STAIR (-S.)

ἀναβαθμός, act of ascending; *then*, means of ascent, *as* steps, stairs; (lxx. *for* מעלה, 1 Kings x. 19, 20), (*non occ.*)

Acts xxi. 35, 40.

STALL.

φάτνη, a crib, a manger; (lxx *for* אבום, Job. xxxix. 9; Is. i. 3.)

Luke xiii. 15.

STANCH (-ED.)

ἵστημι, (a) *trans.*, to cause to stand, to place.

(b) *intrans.*, to stand; *then*, to stand still, stop.

b. Luke viii. 44.

STAND (-EST, -ETH, -ING; STOOD.)

(*For various combinations with other words, see below.*)

1 *ἵστημι*, (a) *trans., in the present, imp. and Aor.* 1 *of the act.*, to cause to stand, to set, to place; (b) *Aor. and fut. pass., and fut. mid.; and* (c) *intrans., perf., plup., and Aor.* 2, to stand, *as opp. to falling;* stand fast, stand still.

2. *ἐφίστημι*, (*No.* 1, *with ἐπί*, upon, *prefixed*) *trans.*, to place upon *or* over, set over. *In N.T. only intrans.*, to place one's self upon *or* near, stand upon *or* over.

3. *παρίστημι*, (*No.* 1, *with παρά*, beside, *prefixed*); (a) *trans.*, to cause to stand near, to place beside *or* near by.

(b) *intrans.*, to stand near, stand by.

4. *συνίστημι*, (*No.* 1, *with σύν*, together in conjunction with *prefixed*); (a) *trans.*, to make stand with *or* together, to place together.

(b) *intrans.*, to stand with, place together, set together.

5. *στήκω*, (*a late form found only in the present, from ἕστηκα*, I stand, *the perf. of No.* 1) to stand, stand firm; (lxx. *for* התיצב, Ex. xiv. 13.)

6. *μένω*, to remain, continue, abide.

1c. Matt. ii. 9 (1b, G ~ L T Tr A ℵ.)
1c. —— vi. 5.
1b. —— xii. 25, 26.
1c. —— 46, 47.
1c. —— xiii. 2.
1c. —— xvi. 28.
1c. —— xx. 3, 6 twice.
1c. —— xxiv. 15.
1c. —— xxvii. 11, 47.
1b. Mark iii. 24, 25.
1b. —— 26 (1c, L T Tr A ℵ.)
1c. —— 31.
1c. —— ix. 1.
1c. —— xi. 5.
5. —— 25.
1c. —— xiii. 14.
3b. —— xv. 39.
1c. Luke i. 11.
3b. —— 19.
2. —— iv. 39.
1c. —— v. i, 2.
1c. —— vi. 17.
1c. —— vii. 38.
1c. —— viii. 20.
1c. —— ix. 27.
1b. —— xi. 18.
1c. —— xiii. 25.
1c. —— xvii. 12.
1b. —— xviii. 11.
1c. —— 13.
1b. —— 40.
1b. —— xix. 8.
1b. —— xxi. 36.
1c. —— xxiii. 10, 35, 49.
1c. —— xxiv. 36.
1c. John i. 26, 35.
1c. —— iii. 29.
1c. —— vi. 22.
1c. —— vii. 37
1c. John viii. 9 (ap.)
1c. —— xi. 56 part.
1c. —— xviii. 5, 16, 18 twice, 25.
1c. —— xix. 25.
1c. —— xx. 11, 14, 19, 26.
1e. —— xxi. 4.
1c. Acts i. 11.
1c. —— iii. 8.
1c. —— iv. 14.
1b. —— v. 20.
1c. —— 23, 25.
1c. —— vii. 33, 55, 56.
1c. —— ix. 7.
1c. —— x. 30.
1b. —— xi. 13.
1c. —— xvi. 9.
1b. —— xvii. 22.
1c. —— xxi. 40.
2. —— xxii. 13.
1c. —— xxiv. 20 part., 21.
1c. —— xxv. 10.
1c. —— xxvi. 6, 16.
1c. Rom. v. 2.
6. —— ix. 11.
1c. —— xi. 20.
5. —— xiv. 4.
1c. 1 Cor. vii. 37.
— —— viii. 13, see World.
1c. —— x. 12.
1c. —— xv. 1.
— —— 30, see Jeopardy
1c. 2 Cor. i. 24.
— Gal. iv. 20, see Doubt.
1c. Eph. vi. 11, 13, 14.
1c. Col. iv. 12.
1c. 1 Tim. ii. 19.
1c. Heb. x. 11.
1c. Jas. ii. 3.
1c. —— v. 9.

1c. 1 Pet. v. 12.
4b. 2 Pet. iii. 5.
1c. Rev. iii. 20.
1c. —— v. 6.
1b. —— vi. 17.
1c. —— vii. 1, 9, 11.
1c. —— viii. 2.
1b. —— 3.
1c. —— x. 5, 8.
1c. —— xi. 1 (ap.), 4, 11.
1c. —— xii. 4.
1b. Rev. xiii. 1 (ἐστάθη, *it or he stood;* instead of ἐστάθην, *I stood,* L Tr A ℵ.)
1c. —— xiv. 1.
1c. —— xv. 2.
1c. —— xviii. 10.
1b. —— 1[5].
1c. —— 17.
1c. —— xix. 17.
1c. —— xx. 12.

STAND BEFORE.

2. Acts x. 17. | 3. Rom. xiv. 10 (mid.)

STAND BY.

1. παρίστημι, *see above, No.* 3b.
2. ἵστημι, *see above, No.* 1c.
3. ἐφίστημι, *see above, No.* 2.
4. περιΐστημι, ("STAND," *No.* 1, *with* περί, around, *prefixed*) *trans.,* to cause to stand around, place around; *intrans.,* to stand around; (lxx. *for* נצב, 2 Sam. xiii. 31.)

2. Matt. xxvi. 73.
1. Mark xiv. 47, 69, 70.
1. —— xv. 35.
1. Luke xix. 24.
3. —— xxiv. 4.
4. John xi. 42.
2. —— xii. 29.
1. John xviii. 22.
1. —— xix. 26.
1. Acts i. 10.
1. —— ix. 39.
2. —— xxii. 25.
1. —— xxiii. 2, 4.
3. —— 11.
1. Acts xxvii. 23.

STAND FAST.

5. 1 Cor. xvi. 13.
5. Gal. v. 1.
5. Phil. i. 27.
5. Phil. iv. 1.
5. 1 Thes. iii. 8.
5. 2 Thes. ii. 15.

STAND FORTH.

1. ἵστημι, *see* "STAND," *No.* 1c.
2. { ἔγειραι, rise up [*and come*] *under-* / εἰς, into, [*stood,* / τὸ, the, / μέσον, midst. }

Mark iii. 3 (ἔγειρε, *stand forth* (active), G L T Tr A ℵ.)
Luke vi. 8 twice.

STAND HERE.

παρίστημι, *see* "STAND," *No.* 3b.

Acts iv. 10.

STAND (MAKE)

ἵστημι, *see* "STAND," *No.* 1a.

Rom. xiv. 4.

STAND (SHOULD)

ὦ, might be, (*subj. of* εἰμί, to be.)

1 Cor. ii. 5.

STAND ROUND ABOUT.

1. περιΐστημι, *see* "STAND BY," *No.* 4.
2. κυκλόω, to encircle, surround; (lxx. *for* סבב, 1 Kings vii. 15; 1 Sam. vii. 16; *and* חנה, Is. xxix. 3.)

2. Acts xiv. 20 part. | 1. Acts xxv. 7.

STAND STILL.

ἵστημι, *see* "STAND," *No.* 1c.

Matt. xx. 32.
Mark x. 49.
Luke vii. 14.
Acts viii. 38.

STAND UP.

1. ἀνίστημι, ("STAND," *No.* 1, *with* ἀνά, up, *prefixed*) *trans.,* to cause to stand *or* rise up, to raise up; *intrans.,* to rise up, arise.
2. ἵστημι, *see* "STAND," *No.* 1b.
3. παρίστημι, *see* "STAND," *No.* 3b.

1. Mark xiv. 60.
1. Luke iv. 16.
1. —— x. 25.
1. Acts i. 15.
2. —— ii. 14.
3. Acts iv. 26.
1. —— v. 34 part.
1. —— x. 26.
1. —— xi. 28.
1. —— xiii. 16 part.
2. Acts xxv. 18 part.

STAND UPRIGHT.

ἀνίστημι, *see above, No.* 1.

Acts xiv. 10.

STAND WITH.

1. παρίστημι, *see* "STAND," *No.* 3b.
2. συνίστημι, *see* "STAND," *No.* 4b.
3. συμπαραγίνομαι, to come in at the same time, to come in to assist, *and so* to stand by another; (lxx. *for* נלוה, Ps. lxxxiii. 9.)

2. Luke ix. 32.
3. 2 Tim. iv. 16 (παραγίνομαι, *to be at hand or near,* L T Tr ℵ.)
1. —— iv. 16.

STANDING (BE)

{ ἔχω, to have, (*here,* has a, *or* has its) / στάσις, a standing. }

Heb. ix. 8.

STAR (-S.)

1. ἀστήρ, a star, a single star; spoken of fixed stars, planets, *or* meteors; (lxx. *for* כוכב, Gen. i. 16; Is. xiii. 10; Joel iii. 15.)

(a) ὁ ἀστὴρ ὁ πρωϊνός, the morning star.

[Spoken of Christ as the coming one, seen by His bride, the Church, just before the dawn, seen by those who watch through the night, before He rises as "the Sun of Righteousness" upon Israel.]

2. ἄστρον, a constellation; *gen. in pl.*, the stars; *seldom used of a single star, as No.* 1 is.

1. Matt. ii. 2, 7, 9, 10.
1. — xxiv. 29.
1. Mark xiii. 35.
2. Luke xx. 25.
2. Acts vii. 43.
2. — xxvii. 20.
1. 1 Cor. xv. 41 3 times.
2. Heb. xi. 12.
— 2 Pet. i. 19, see Day-star.
1. Rev. i. 16, 20 twice.
1. — ii. 1.
1a. — 28.
1. — iii. 1.
1. — vi. 13.
1. — viii. 10, 11, 12.
1. — ix. 1.
1. — xii. 1, 4.
1a. — xxii. 16.

STATE (YOUR)

τά, the *things*
περὶ, concerning
ὑμῶν, you.

Phil. ii. 19, 20.

See also, LAST, MY, YOUR.

STATER. [margin.]

Matt. xvii. 27, see "PIECE OF MONEY."

STATURE.

ἡλικία, adultness, maturity *of life, mind, age, or person;* (lxx. *for* קוֹמָה, Ez. xiii. 18.)

Matt. vi. 27.
Luke ii. 52, marg. *age.*
Luke xii. 25.
— xix. 3.
Eph. iv. 13, marg. *age.*

STAVES.

See, STAFF.

STAY. [margin.]

1 Tim. iii. 15, see "GROUND."

STAY (-ED.) [verb.]

1. κατέχω, to have and hold fast down; to detain; (lxx. *for* אחר, Gen. xxiv. 56; אסר, Gen. xlii. 19.)

2. ἐπέχω, to have *or* hold upon; to hold on, *i.e.* remain; (lxx. *for* יחל, Gen. viii. 10; חדל, 2 Chron. 5, 14.)

1. Luke iv. 42. | 2. Acts xix. 22.

STEAD.

See, IN.

STEDFAST.

See, STEADFAST.

STEADFAST.

1. βέβαιος, firm, steady; *hence, of persons,* steadfast, steady, sure.

2. ἑδραῖος, seated, sedentary; *then,* sitting fast, fixed, settled, (*occ.* Col. i. 23.)

3. στερεός, stiff and stark, hard, firm, solid; firm, immoveable.

2. 1 Cor. vii. 37 (*om.* G→)
2. — xv. 58.
1. 2 Cor. i. 7.
1. Heb. ii. 2.
1. — iii. 14.
1. — vi. 19.
3. 1 Pet. v. 9.

STEADFASTLY (BEHOLD)

ἀτενίζω, to fix the eyes intently upon, gaze upon intently; stretch and strain the eyes to be able to see.

Acts xiv. 9. | 2 Cor. iii. 7 (with εἰς, *unto.*)

STEADFASTLY (LOOK)

Acts i. 10, with εἰμί, lit., *were gazing.*
Acts vi. 15.
2 Cor. iii. 13.

STEADFASTLY (LOOK UP)

Acts vii. 55.

See also, CONTINUE, SET.

STEADFASTNESS.

1. στηριγμός, a setting fast, fixedness, (*non occ.*)

2. στερέωμα, anything firm, solid; (the firmament, lxx. *for* רקיע, Gen. i. 6; Ez. i. 22); *hence,* stability, solidity, (*non occ.*)

2. Col. ii. 5. | 1. 2 Pet. iii. 17.

STEADY. [margin.]

2 Tim. ii. 19, see "SURE."

STEAL, STOLE.

κλέπτω, to steal, take by stealth, (*not to rob by violence.*)

Matt. vi. 19, 20.
— xix. 18.
— xxvii. 64.
— xxviii. 13.
Mark x. 19.
Luke xviii. 20.
John x. 10.
Rom. ii. 21 twice.
— xiii. 9.
Eph. iv. 28 twice.

STEEP PLACE.

κρημνός, an overhanging steep, a beetling crag *or* cliff, a precipice; (lxx., סלע, 2 Chron. xxv. 12), (*non occ.*)

Matt. viii. 32. | Mark v. 13. Luke viii. 33.

STEP (-s.) [noun.]

ἴχνος, a footstep.

Rom. iv. 12. | 2 Cor. xii. 18. 1 Pet. ii. 21.

STEP DOWN.

καταβαίνω, to step down.

John v. 7.

STEP IN.

ἐμβαίνω, to step in, enter.

John v. 4 part. (*ap.*)

STERN.

πρύμνα, (*fem. of* *πρυμνός*, last, hindmost) the hindmost part; *of a ship*, the stern.

Acts xxvii. 29.

STEWARD (s.)

1. *οἰκονόμος*, a house-manager, one who had authority over the servants of a family, assigning their tasks, etc., and generally managing all the affairs and accounts. These persons were generally slaves, but also free-men, (Eliezer, Gen. xv. 2; xxiv. 2; Joseph, Gen. xxxix. 4.) The *οἰκονόμοι* also had charge of the pecuniary affairs of the sons, thus differing from the *ἐπίτροποι*, *or* tutors (*No.* 2), (*occ.* Rom. xvi. 23; Gal. iv. 2.)
2. *ἐπίτροπος*, one to whom a charge is committed, *i.e.* a steward, manager, agent, tutor, (*occ.* Gal. iv. 2.)

2. Matt. xx. 8.
2. Luke viii. 3.
1. —— xii. 42. [(be)
—— —— xvi. 2, see Steward
1. Luke xvi. 1, 3, 8.
1. 1 Cor. iv. 1, 2.
1. Tit. i. 7.
1. 1 Pet. iv. 10.

STEWARD (BE)

οἰκονομέω, to be an *οἰκονομός*, (*see above, No.* 1) be manager of a household; *gen.*, be manager *or* steward, (*non occ.*)

Luke xvi. 2.

STEWARDSHIP.

οἰκονομία, management of a household *or* of household affairs; stewardship, administration.

Luke xvi. 2, 3, 4.

STICK (-s.) [noun.]

φρύγανον, a dry stick *or* twig, dry brushwood; (lxx. *for* קש, Is. xl. 24; xlvii. 14), (*non occ.*)

Acts xxviii. 3.

STICK FAST.

ἐρείδω, *trans.*, to fix firmly. *In N.T.*, *intrans.*, to become fixed, stick fast, (*non occ.*)

Acts xxvii. 41.

STIFF-NECKED.

σκληροτράχηλος, hard-necked, stiff-necked, *i.e.* obstinate; (lxx. *for* קשה־ערף, Ex. xxxiii. 3, 5; Deut. ix. 6, 13), (*non occ.*)

Acts vii. 51.

STILL (BE)

φιμόω, to muzzle. *Here, pass.*, to be hushed, be quiet.

Mark iv. 39.

See also, ABIDE, STAND.

STILL. [adv.]

ἔτι, *of the future*, any more, any longer; *of the present*, yet, still, hitherto; *implying accession or addition*, besides; *of the present, in allusion to the past*, yet, still, even now.

Rev. xxii. 11 4 times.

STING (-s.)

κέντρον, a prick, a point; *hence, gen.*, a sting, a thing of venom *or* poison.

1 Cor. xv. 55, 56, *probably referring to* Hos. xiii. 4, *where Heb.* קטב, plague; *comp.* Hos. v. 12; (*also for* רקב, rottenness.)

1 Cor. xv. 55, 56. | Rev. ix. 10.

STINK (-ETH.)

ὄζω, to smell, emit a scent; (lxx. *for* באש, Ex. viii. 14.)

John xi. 39.

STIR. [noun.]

τάραχος, stir, commotion, agitation, disturbance, (*non occ.*)

Acts xii. 18. | Acts xix. 23.

STIR UP (-ED, -ETH.)

1. διεγείρω, to wake up fully, to rouse; excite, incite.
2. ἐπεγείρω, to rouse upon, *i.e.* to wake up, rouse up *as from sleep. Then,* to rouse upon *or* against *any one,* to excite against; (lxx. *for* העיר, 2 Chron. xxi. 16; הקים, 1 Sam. xxii. 8; Am. vi. 14), (*occ.* Acts xiii. 50.)
3. ἀναζωπυρέω, to rekindle up, light up again; (lxx. *for* חיה, Gen. xlv. 27), (*non occ.*)
4. ἀνασείω, to shake up, *or* to and fro, *with the idea of shock or concussion; hence,* to stir up *with idea of vigour and force,* instigate; (lxx. *for* הסית, Job. ii. 3), (*occ.* Mark xv. 11.)
5. παροτρύνω, to urge on by *or* along with *something else,* to stir up, incite *thereby or therewith,* (*non occ.*)
6. σαλεύω, to move to and fro, put into a state of waving, vibration; to sway to and fro, agitate.
7. συγκινέω, to move with; to move together, excite together *or* at the same time, (*non occ.*)
8. συγχέω, to pour together; *hence,* to confuse, throw into confusion, put in perplexity *or* uproar.

4. Luke xxiii. 5.
7. Acts vi. 12.
5. — xiii. 50.
2. — xiv. 2.
6. — xvii. 13.
— Luke xvii. 16, see Stirred (be)
8. — xxi. 27.
3. 2 Tim. i. 6.
1. 2 Pet. i. 13.
1. — iii. 1.

STIRRED (BE)

παροξύνω, to sharpen by *or* on anything, *as by rubbing,* to whet. *In N.T. only mid. or pass.; hence,* to be spurred on, *or* painfully excited, (*occ.* 1 Cor. xiii. 5.)

Acts xvii. 16.

STOCK.

γένος, genus, race; family, lineage, stock; (lxx. *for* זרע, Jer. xli. 1.)

Acts xiii. 26. | Phil. iii. 5.

STOCKS.

ξύλον, wood; *then,* anything made of wood, *as* stocks, (*Lat.,* nervus); (lxx. *for* סד, Job. xxxiii. 11.)

Acts xvi. 24.

STOMACH.

στόμαχος, a mouth, an opening; *then, used of* the throat, the gullet; *then,* of the orifice of the stomach; *and later,* of the stomach itself, (*non occ.*)

1 Tim. v. 23.

STONE. [noun.]

1. λίθος, a stone, stone *as opp. to wood, flesh, etc.; then,* stones of various kinds.
2. πέτρος, a piece of rock; [*not* πέτρα, the rock itself, which is Christ. Peter was a piece of a rock, a stone, here to-day and gone to-morrow, shifting, changing, vacillating. Peter, not so-called because of firmness of character, but the reverse.]
3. ψῆφος, a small stone worn smooth by water, a pebble; *hence,* any polished stone, a gem, stone of a ring. *Also,* of the black and white stones used anciently in voting, *viz.* the black for condemnation, the white for approval *or* acquittal, (*occ.* Acts xxvi. 10.)

1. Matt. iii. 9.
1. — iv. 3, 6.
1. — vii. 9.
1. — xxi. 42, 44 (ap.)
— — xxiv. 2, see S upon another (one)
1. — xxvii. 60, 66.
1. — xxviii. 2.
1. Mark v. 5.
— — xii. 4, see S (cast)
1. — 10.
1. — xiii. 1.
— — 2, see S upon another (one)
1. — xv. 46.
1. — xvi. 3, 4.
1. Luke iii. 8.
1. — iv. 3, 11.
1. — xi. 11.
1. Luke xix. 40.
— — 44, see S upon another (one)
1. — xx. 17, 18.
1. — xxi. 5.
— — 6, see S upon another (one)
1. — xxii. 41. [Hewn.
— — xxiii. 53, see
1. — xxiv. 2.
2. John i. 42, marg. Peter.
— — ii. 6, see S (of)
1. — viii. 7 (ap.), 59.
1. — x. 31.
1. — xi. 38, 39, 41.
1. — xx. 1.
1. Acts iv. 11.
1. — xvii. 29.
— Rom. ix. 32, 33, see Stumbling.

1. 1 Cor. iii. 12.
— 2 Cor. iii. 3, see S (of)
1. —— 7.
1. 1 Pet. ii. 4, 5, 6, 7, 8.
3. Rev. ii. 17 twice.
1. Rev. iv. 3.
— —— ix. 20, see S (of)
1. —— xvii. 4.
1. —— xviii. 12, 16, 21.
1. —— xxi. 11 twice, 19.

STONE (OF)

λίθινος, made of stone; (lxx. *for* אבן, Gen. xxxv. 14; Ezek. xxxi. 17.)

John. ii. 6. | Rev. ix. 20. | 2 Cor. iii. 3.

STONES (CAST)

λιθοβολέω, to throw stones at *any one*, to stone in order to wound or kill. A Mosaic punishment, John viii. 5, *cf.* Lev. xx. 10, and Deut. xxii. 22; *cf.* ver. 21, where, lxx. *for* סקל; Heb. xii. 20, *cf.* Ex. xix. 13, where lxx. *for* סקל; *also*, lxx. *for* רגם, Lev. xx. 27; xxiv. 14, 16.

Mark xii. 4 (*om.* G ⇉ L T Tr A ℵ, i.e. *him they wounded*, instead of *at him they cast stones and wounded him.*)

STONE UPON ANOTHER (ONE)

1. { λίθος, stone
ἐπί, resting upon (*of simple rest*)
λίθῳ, stone.

2. { λίθος, stone
ἐπί, resting on (*of the downward pressure*)
λίθον, stone.

2. Matt. xxiv. 2.
1. Mark xiii. 2.
1. Luke xix. 44.
1. —— xxi. 6.

STONE. [verb.]

1. λιθοβολέω, *see* "STONES (CAST)," (*occ.* Mark xii. 4.)

2. λιθάζω, to stone, (*the emphasis being upon the stones rather than the casting, as in No.* 1), (*non occ*

3. καταλιθάζω, (*No.* 2, *with* κατά, down, *prefixed*) to stone down, (*stronger than No.* 2) to stone to death, (*non occ.*)

1. Matt. xxi. 35.
1. —— xxiii. 37.
1. Luke xiii. 34.
3. —— xx. 6.
1. John viii. 5 (ap.)
2. —— x. 31, 32, 33.
2. —— xi. 8.
2. Acts v. 26.
1. —— vii. 58, 59.
1. —— xiv. 5.
2. —— 19.
2. 2 Cor. xi. 25.
2. Heb. xi. 37.
1. —— xii. 20.

STONY GROUND.

1. { τὸ, the *place or ground*,
πετρώδες, like rock, (*Acc. sing. neut.*)

2. { τὰ, the,
πετρώδη, rocky places, (*Acc. pl. neut.*)

1. Mark iv. 5. | 2. Mark iv. 16.

STONY PLACES.

2. Matt. xiii. 5, 20.

STOOP (-ED, -ING.)

κύπτω, to stoop, bow one's self; (lxx. *for* קדד, 1 Sam. xxiv. 9; 1 Kings i. 16, 31.)

John viii. 6 (ap.), 8 (ap.)

STOOP DOWN.

1. κύπτω, *see above.*

2. παρακύπτω, (*No.* 1, *with* παρά, beside, *prefixed*) to stoop down near by *anything*, to bend forward beside *or* near anything *in order to look at it more closely.*

1. Mark i. 7. | 2. John xx. 5, 11. | 2. Luke xxiv. 12 (ap.)

STOP (-ED.)

1. φράσσω, to enclose with a fence *for protection*, to fence round, hedge in; (lxx. *for* שוך, Hos. ii. 6); *of a city with walls*, to fortify; *of a defile with troops*, to shut up; *of* the *ears with wax*, to stop; (lxx. *for* אטם, Prov. xxi. 13), *hence, gen.*, to stop.

2. συνέχω, to hold together, to press together, to shut up.

2. Acts vii. 57.
— Tit. i. 11, see Mouth.
1. Rom. iii. 19.
1. Heb. xi. 33.

SHALL STOP ME OF.

{ φραγήσεται, shall not be stopped *or* silenced,
εἰς, unto,
ἐμέ, me.

2 Cor. xi. 10.

STORE (IN)

θησαυρίζω, to treasure up, lay up in store.

1 Cor. xvi. 2 part.

STORE (keep in)

2 Pet. iii. 7.

STORE (lay up in)

ἀποθησαυρίζω, to treasure up away, lay up away in store, (*non occ.*)

1 Tim. vi. 19.

STORE-HOUSE

ταμεῖον, a store-chamber, store-house, (lxx. *for* אסם, Deut. xxviii 8, Prov. iii. 10; חדר, Prov. xxiv 4.)

Luke xii. 24.

STORM.

λαῖλαψ, a tempest *of wind with rain*, whirlwind, hurricane; (lxx. *for* סער, Jer. xxxv. 32; סערה, Job xxxviii. 1; סופה, Job xxi. 18) (*occ.* 2 Pet. ii. 17.)

Mark iv. 37. | Luke viii. 23.

STRAIGHT.

1. εὐθύς, straight, (a) *quoted from* Is. xl. 3, *where* lxx. *for* ישר; (b) *quoted from* Is. xl. 4, *where* lxx. *for* מישור.

2. ὀρθός, upright; (lxx. *for* ישר, Prov. xii. 16; xvi. 25.)

1a. Matt. iii. 3.
1a. Mark i. 3.
1b. Luke iii. 4, 5.
1. Acts ix. 11.
2. Heb. xii. 13, marg. *even*.

STRAIGHT COURSE (come with a)

εὐθυδρομέω, to run straight; *of a ship*, to sail with a straight course.

Acts xvi. 11.

STRAIGHT COURSE (with a)

Acts xxi. 11 part.

STRAIGHT (make)

1. εὐθύνω, to make straight *and level*, (*occ.* John iii. 4.)

2. ἀνορθόω, to set upright, to stand erect.

2. Luke xiii. 13. | 1. John i. 23.

STRAIGHTWAY.

1. εὐθέως, straightway, immediately.

   * *In these passages most of the critical editors prefer No.* 2.

2. εὐθύς, straight; *of time*, straight, *i.e.* forthwith.

3. παραχρῆμα, with the thing itself, at the very moment, on the spot.

4. ἐξαυτῆς, from this *time*, *i.e.* immediately.

2. Matt. iii. 16.
1. —— iv. 20.
1. —— xiv. 22.
1. ——— 27*.
1. —— xxi. 2, 3*
1. —— xxv. 15.
1. —— xxvii. 48.
1. Mark i. 10*, 18, 20*, 21.
1. —— ii. 2 (*om.* L^b T Tr^b ℵ.)
1. —— iii. 6*.
1. —— v. 29*, 42*.
1. —— vi. 25* (*om.* G→)
1. ——— 45*, 54*.
1. —— vii. 35 (*om.* L^b Tr A ℵ.)
1. —— viii. 10*.
1. —— ix. 15*, 20*, 24*.
1. —— xi. 3*.
1. —— xiv. 45*.
1. Mark xv. 1*.
1. Luke v. 39 (*om.* T Tr A ℵ.)
3. —— viii. 55.
1. —— xii. 54.
1. —— xiv. 5.
2. John xiii. 32.
3. Acts v. 10.
1. —— ix. 20.
3. —— xvi. 33.
1. —— xxii. 29.
4. —— xxiii. 30 (ἐξ αὐτῶν, *by them*, L T Tr ℵ, *i.e.* and when *it was disclosed to me a plot against the man which was to be* [carried out] by them, I sent [him] to thee.)
1. Jas. i. 24.

STRAIN AT.

διϋλίζω, to filter *or* strain through, *as through a sieve or strainer; hence*, to strain out, (*non occ.*)

Matt. xxiii. 24.

STRAIT (be in a)

συνέχω, to hold together, press together. *Here, pres. pass.*, I am being pressed.

[The verse (Phil. i. 23) requires the following translation:—

συνέχομαι, *I am being pressed.*

ἐκ, *out of*, (ἐκ is translated "*betwixt*" only once, but "*out of*," 165 times.) This does not require the verb to have had ἐκ instead of σύν, because ἔχω does not contain the idea of pressure without the σύν.

τῶν, *the* } *viz.* the living and dying
δύο, *two*, } as mentioned in ver. 21.

ἔχων, *having*, [a third thing, which causes the pressure.]

τὴν, *the.*

ἐπιθυμίαν, *earnest desire or* longing, inordinate desire, lust.

εἰς, *unto*,

τὸ, *the*,

ἀναλῦσαι, *to loosen back again*, (as the fastenings of a ship) so as to depart and return. This is the invariable meaning of the verb in the lxx., see every occurrence, Tobit. ii. 9; Judith xiii. 1; 1 Esdras iii. 3; Wisd. ii. 1; v. 12; xvi. 14; Ecclus. iii. 15; 2 Mac. viii. 25; ix. 1; xii. 7; xv. 28; 3 Macc. v. 40; vii. 13; and Josephus, Ant. vi. 4, 1; and in N.T. only Luke xii. 36. In all these places it is used of *returning* after a feast or war, or from the grave, etc., etc.

The art. with the aor. inf. substantivizing the verb, and representing the verb as a single action; hence, here, *unto the return*.

καὶ, *and*,

σὺν, *together in conjunction with*,

χριστῷ, *with Christ*.

εἶναι, *to be*,

There being no other way of being "with Christ," *see* John xiv. 3, and 1 Thes. iv. 17. *οὕτω*, thus, in this manner, shall we ever be *σὺν κυρίῳ*, with the Lord. The Apostle does not contradict himself.

[*which is*]
πολλῷ, *much*.
μᾶλλον, *more*, rather.
κρεῖσσον, better, (thus, if he *lived*, Christ would be "magnified," v. 20, and they would be profited, v. 24. If he *died*, Christ would still be "magnified," v. 20; it would be "gain" to Christ. But, if Christ should "*return*," it would be "far better" than either.)]

Phil. i. 23.

STRAIT. [adj.]

στενός, strait, narrow, (*non occ.*)

Matt. vii. 13, 14. | Luke xiii. 24.

STRAITEN (-ED.)

στενοχωρέω, to crowd into a narrow space, to straiten as to room, to be pressed for room, (*occ.* 2 Cor. iv. 8.)

2 Cor. vi. 12 twice.

STRAITENED (BE)

συνέχω, to hold together, press together. *Here, pass.*, to be pressed, pressed together.

Luke xii. 50, marg. pained.

STRAITEST (MOST)

ἀκριβής, exact, accurate, precise. *Here, superl.*, the most exact, (*non occ.*)

Acts xxvi. 5.

STRAITLY.

1. *πολλά*, much, *of quantity or amount*.
2. *ἀπειλή*, threat. *Here, with the verb, ἀπειλέω, i.e.* to threaten with a threat.
3. *παραγγελία*, announcement, declaration; charge, precept. *Here, with the verb, παραγγελέω*, to charge with a charge.

— Matt. ix. 30, } see
— Mark i. 43, } Charge.
1. —— iii. 12.
1. —— v. 43.
— Luke ix. 21, see Charge
2. Acts iv. 17 (*om.* L T Tr A[b] ℵ.)
3. —— v. 28.

STRANGE.

1. *ξένος*, not of one's family; *as adj.*, strange, *i.e.* foreign, unknown, *as coming from another country*.
2. *ἀλλότριος*, alien, not one's own; another's, belonging to another, different; *then*, strange.
3. *ἔξω*, out, without; outside.
4. *ἕτερος*, the other, other, *denoting generic (not numerical) distinction*, different.

2. Acts vii. 6.
1. —— xvii. 18.
3. —— xxvi. 11.
2. Heb. xi. 9.
1. —— xiii. 9.
4. Jude 7, marg. *other*.

STRANGE THINGS.

1. *ξένος*, *see above, No.* 1.
2. *ξενίζω*, to receive as a guest. *Pass.*, to be received as one. *Then*, to appear strange to *any one*. *Here, part.*, strange things, *i.e.* novel, surprising.

3. παράδοξος, aside from received opinion; *hence*, paradoxical, strange, incredible, (*non occ.*)

3. Luke v. 26. | 2. Acts xvii. 20.
1. 1 Pet. iv. 12.

STRANGE (THINK)

ξενίζω, *see* "STRANGE THINGS," *No.* 2. *Here, mid.*, to be surprised, think strange of.

1 Pet. iv. 4.

STRANGE CONCERNING (THINK)

ξενίζω, *see above.*

1 Pet. iv. 12.

STRANGER (-S.)

1. ξένος, not of one's own family, stranger; a guest, a stranger; a friend who lived in a different city or country, allied with another for the purpose of affording mutual entertainment when travelling.
2. ἀλλότριος, *see* "STRANGE," *No.* 2.
3. πάροικος, dwelling near, neighbouring; *hence*, a by-dweller, sojourner, (*without the rights of citizenship.*)
4. ἀλλογενής, of another race *or* nation, (*non occ.*)
5. ἐπιδημέω, to be among one's own people, to be at home. *Here, part.*, "[the Romans] sojourning [*here*]," (*occ.* Acts xvii. 21.)
6. παρεπίδημος, a by-resident, sojourner *among a people not one's own;* (lxx. *for* תושב, Gen. xxiii. 4; Ps. xxxix. 13), (*occ.* Heb. xi. 13; 1 Pet. ii. 11.)

1. Matt. xxv. 35, 38, 43, 44.
1. —— xxvii. 7.
2. —— 25, 26.
4. Luke xvii. 18.
2. John x. 5 twice.
5. Acts ii. 10 part.
3. Acts vii. 29.
1. —— xvii. 21.
1. Eph. ii. 12, 19.
1. Heb. xi. 13.
6. 1 Pet. i. 1.
3. —— ii. 11.
1. 3 John 5.

STRANGER (BE A)

παροικέω, to dwell near, dwell as a sojourner; (lxx. *for* גור, Gen. xx. 1; xxvi. 3, ישב; Gen. xxiv. 37.)

Luke xxiv. 18.

STRANGERS (WHEN THEY DWELT AS)

ἐν, in
τῇ, the (*i.e. their*)
παροικίᾳ, sojourn.

Acts xiii. 17.

STRANGERS (ENTERTAIN)

φιλοξενία, love to strangers, hospitality.

Heb. xiii. 2.

STRANGERS (LODGE)

ξενοδοχέω, to receive and entertain strangers, to show *or* practise hospitality, (*non occ.*)

1 Tim. v. 10.

STRANGLED.

πνικτός, strangled. *In N.T.*, τὸ πνικτόν, strangled meat, *i.e.* the flesh of animals killed by being strangled, without shedding their blood. *This was forbidden to the Jews in* Lev. xvii. 13, 14; *cf.* vii. 26, 27, and Deut. xii. 16, 23.

Acts xxi. 25. (*om.* G →)

STRANGLED (THINGS)

Acts xv. 20 (*om.* G →)
—— 29 (*pl.* L T Tr A ℵ), (*om.* G →)

STRAWED.

See, STREW.

STREAM.

ποταμός, a river, a stream.

Luke vi. 48, 49.

STREET (-S.)

1. πλατεῖα, a broad way, wide street in a city; (lxx. *for* רחב, Judg. xix. 15, 20; Zech. viii. 4, 5; חוץ, Is. xv. 3), (*non occ.*)
2. ῥύμη, a narrow street, a lane, alley; (lxx. *for* רחב, Is. xv. 3), (*occ.* Luke xiv. 21.)
3. ἀγορά, any place of public resort in the towns and cities where the people came together; market-place.

2. Matt. vi. 2.
1. —— 5.
1. —— xii. 19.
3. Mark vi. 56.
1. Luke x. 10.
1. —— xiii. 26.
1. —— xiv. 21.
1. Acts v. 15, marg. pl. with κατά, *in every street.*
2. —— ix. 11.
2. —— xii. 10.
1. Rev. xi. 8.
1. —— xxi. 21.
1. —— xxii. 2.

STRENGTH.

1. δύναμις, *see* "POWER," *No.* 1.
2. ἰσχύς, *see* "POWER," *No.* 5.
3. ἐξοοσία, *see* "POWER," *No* 3.
4. κράτος, *see* "POWER," *No.* 4.

2. Mark xii. 30, 33.
4. Luke i. 51.
2. —— x. 27.
1. 1 Cor. xv. 56.
1. 2 Cor. i. 8.
1. —— xii. 9.
1. Heb. xi. 11.
1. Rev. i. 16.
1. —— iii. 8.
2. —— v. 12.
1. —— xii. 10.
3. —— xvii. 13.

STRENGTH (BE OF)

ἰσχύω, to be strong, to have strength, ability, power both physical and moral; to be strong, have efficacy.

Heb. ix. 17.

STRENGTH (INCREASE OF)

ἐνδυναμόω, to strengthen in, *i.e.* to render strong, impart strength to. *Here mid. or pass.*, to acquire strength; (lxx. *for* עז, Ps. lii. 9.)

Acts ix. 22.

STRENGTH (RECEIVE)

στερεόω, to make stable, firm, strong; to confirm, settle.

Acts iii. 7, pass.

STRENGTH (WITHOUT)

ἀσθενής, without strength, infirm, weak, feeble, impotent, sick.

Rom. v. 6.

STRENGTHEN (-ED, -ETH, -ING.)

1. δυναμόω, to strengthen; (lxx. *for* עז, Ps. lxviii. 29; גבר, Ecc. x. 10; Dan. ix. 27), (*non occ.*)
2. ἐνδυναμόω, (*No.* 1, *with* ἐν, in, *prefixed*) to strengthen in, *i.e.* to render strong, impart strength to.
3. ἐνισχύω, to be strong in *any thing*, to in-strengthen; *intrans.*, to be invigorated, become strong; *trans.*, to invigorate, cause to be strong.
4. στηρίζω, to set fast, fix firmly; make steadfast.
5. ἐπιστηρίζω, (*No.* 4, *with* ἐπί, upon, *prefixed*) to set fast upon, place *or* fix firmly upon; to establish.
6. κραταιόω, to make powerful, make powerful in effect.
7. σθενόω, to strengthen, (*of bodily health and strength*), (*non occ.*)

4. Luke xxii. 32.
3. —— 43 (*ap.*)
— Acts ix. 19, see S (be)
5. —— xviii. 23 (No. 4, L T Tr A ℵ.)
6. Eph. iii. 16.
2. Phil. iv. 13.
1. Col. i. 11.
2. 2 Tim. iv. 17.
7. 1 Pet. v. 10.
4. Rev. iii. 2.

STRENGTHENED (BE)

3. Acts ix. 19.

STRETCH (-ED, -ING.)

STRETCH BEYOND ONE'S MEASURE.

ὑπερεκτείνω, ("STRETCH FORTH," *No.* 1, *with* ὑπέρ, over, beyond, *prefixed*) to stretch out unduly *or* overmuch, *i.e.* beyond measure.

2 Cor. x. 14.

STRETCH FORTH.

1. ἐκτείνω, to stretch out, extend; *of the hands*, to stretch forth.
2. ἐκπετάννυμι, to spread out, expand. *Quoted here from* Is. lv. 2, *where* lxx. *for* פרש, *as also* Ex. ix. 30, (*non occ.*)
3. ἐπιβάλλω, to throw *or* cast upon; *of the hands*, to lay hands upon, seize, do violence to.

1. Matt. xii. 13 twice, 49.
1. —— xiv. 31.
1. Mark iii. 5.
1. Luke vi. 10.
1. —— xxii. 53.
1. John xxi. 18.
1. Acts iv. 30.
3. —— xii. 1, marg. *begin.*
1. —— xxvi. 1.
2. Rom. x. 21.

STRETCH OUT.

1. Matt. xxvi. 51. | 1. Mark iii. 5.

STREW, STRAWED.

1. στρώννυμι, to strow, to spread, *esp. of a bed or couch, or of a table; hence*, to furnish, prepare.
2. διασκορπίζω, to scatter throughout, disperse abroad.

1. Matt. xxi. 8.
2. Matt. xxv. 24, 26.
1. Mark xi. 8 (*ap.*)

STRICKEN IN YEARS (WELL)

προβεβηκὼς, advanced ἐν, in ταῖς, the ἡμέραις, days αὐτῆς, of her, (verse 18) αὐτῶν, of them, (v. 7)	advanced in her (*or* their) days.

Luke i. 7, 18.

STRIFE (-s.)

1. ἔρις, rivalry, contention; strife, quarrel.
2. ἐριθεία, labour for wages; *hence*, canvassing, intriguing; *gen.*, party-spirit, faction.
3. ἀντιλογία, contradiction, controversy; (lxx. *for* דבר, Ex. xviii. 16; ריב, Deut. xxv. 1; 2 Sam. xv. 4.)
4. μάχη, a fight, battle, contest; (lxx. *for* ריב, Gen. xiii. 7; מדון, Prov. xv. 18.)
5. φιλονεικία, love of quarrel, eager of contention, (*non occ.*)

5. Luke xxii. 24.
1. Rom. xiii. 13.
1. 1 Cor. iii. 3.
2. 2 Cor. xii. 20.
2. Gal. v. 20.
1. Phil. i. 15.
2. Phil. ii. 3.
— 1 Tim. vi. 4 1st, see S of words.
1. ——— 4 2nd.
4. 2 Tim. ii. 23.
3. Heb. vi. 16.
2. Jas. iii. 14, 16.

STRIFE OF WORDS.

λογομαχία, word-battles, war about words, (*non occ.*)

1 Tim. vi. 4.

STRIKE (-ETH, STRAKE, STRUCK.)

1. παίω, to strike, to smite, *as with the fist, a rod or sword.*
2. πατάσσω, to strike, to beat.
3. τύπτω, to beat *with repeated strokes.*
4. χαλάω, to let go, to relax, to loosen; (lxx. *for* פרש, Is. xxxiii. 23; שלח, Jer. xxxviii. 6.)

2. Matt. xxvi. 51.
— ——— 67, } see S with the palm of
— Mark xiv. 65, } one's hand.
3. Luke xxii. 64 (*ap.*)
4. Acts xxvii. 17.
1. Rev. ix. 5.

STRIKE WITH THE PALM OF ONE'S HAND.

1. ῥαπίζω, to beat with rods, to scourge; *later*, to smite with the open hand, rap, slap, cuff, box, *esp. the face, cheek, or ears.*
2. ῥάπισμα, a rap, slap, cuff, box; a blow, βάλλω, to throw *or* cast, — *lit.*, they threw him smart blows.

1. Matt. xxvi. 67.
2. Mark xiv. 65 (λαμβάνω, *to take*, i.e. *with smart blows they took him*, G ~ L T Tr A ℵ.)

STRIKER.

πλήκτης, a striker, *esp.*, one apt to strike, (*non occ.*)

1 Tim. iii. 3. | Tit. i. 7.

STRING.

δεσμός, band, bond, ligament; (lxx. *for* אסור, Judg. xv. 13; Dan. iv. 12.)

Mark vii. 35.

STRIP (-ED.)

ἐκδύω, to go *or* come out of; *of clothes*, to put off, strip *one of his clothes*, unclothe; (lxx. *for* פשט, Gen. xxxvii. 22; Numb. xx. 28.)

Matt. xxvii. 28 (ἐνδύω, *to clothe*, L.)
Luke x. 30.

STRIPE (-s.)

πληγή, a stroke, stripe, blow.

Luke xii. 47, see Many.
——— 48 1st.
——— 48 2nd, see Few.
Acts xvi. 23, 33.
2 Cor. vi. 5.
—— xi. 23.

STRIPES.

μώλωψ, mark of a stripe *or* blow; a stripe, a weal. *Quoted from* Is. liii. 5, *where* lxx. *for* חבורה.

1 Pet. ii. 24.

STRIVE (-ED, -ETH, -ING, STROVE.)

1. ἀγωνίζομαι, to be a competitor in a contest; *hence*, to contend, exert one's self, strive very earnestly.
2. μάχομαι, to fight *in war or battle;* oppose, (*occ.* Jas. iv. 2.)

3. διαμάχομαι, (*No.* 2, *with* διά, through, *prefixed*) to fight throughout, strive with, struggle against *in opposition*, fight it out, contend obstinately, (*non occ.*)

4. ἀθλέω, to contend, contend for the mastery in the public games, *e.g. boxing, throwing, wrestling, etc.*, (*non occ.*)

5. ἐρίζω, to strive, (*gen. of wordy contests*); *hence*, to wrangle, quarrel, cry out, be vociferous like wranglers. *Quoted from* Is. xlii. 2, *where Heb.* לא יצעק ולא ישא; lxx. οὐ κεκράζεται, οὐδὲ ἀνήσει, *i.e.* "he shall not cry, nor lift up," (*i.e.* his voice), (*non occ.*)

6. φιλοτιμέομαι, to love, honour, esteem *or* respect, to be ambitious, to make it a point of honour.

5. Matt. xii. 19.
1. Luke xiii. 24.
2. John vi. 52.
2. Acts vii. 26 part.
3. —— xxiii. 9.
6. Rom. xv. 20.
1. 1 Cor. ix. 29.
1. Col. i. 29.
1. —— iv. 12, marg. (text, *labour fervently*.)
4. 2 Tim. ii. 5 twice.
2. —— 24.

STRIVE ABOUT WORDS.

λογομαχέω, to contend with words, (*non occ.*)

2 Tim. ii. 14.

STRIVE AGAINST.

ἀνταγωνίζομαι, (*No.* 1, *with* ἀντί, against, *prefixed.*)

Heb. xii. 4.

STRIVE TOGETHER FOR.

συναθλέω, (*No.* 4, *with* σύν, together in conjunction with, *prefixed*), (*occ.* Phil. iv. 3.)

Phil. i. 27.

STRIVE TOGETHER WITH.

συναγωνίζομαι, (*No.* 1, *with* σύν, together in conjunction with, *prefixed*), (*non occ.*)

Rom. xv. 30.

STRIVING. [noun.]

μάχη, a fight, a battle; *then*, contest, controversy.

Tit. iii. 9.

STRONG, STRONGER.

1. ἰσχυρός, physically strong, mighty, powerful.

2. δυνατός, *in an active sense*, strong, having (inherent and moral) power; *in a passive sense*, possible, capable of being done.

3. ἐνέργεια, the being in work, *i.e.* operation, energy, power in action, effectual operation.

4. μέγας, great.

5. στερεός, stable, firm, solid.

1. Matt. xiv. 30, marg. (text, *boisterous*.)
— Luke i. 15, see Drink.
1. —— xi. 22.
2. Rom. xv. 1.
1. 1 Cor. i. 25.
1. —— iv. 10.
1. —— x. 22.
2. 2 Cor. xii. 10.
2. 2 Cor. xiii. 9.
3. 2 Thes. ii. 11.
1. Heb. v. 7.
5. —— 12, 14.
1. —— vi. 18.
1. 1 John ii. 14.
1. Rev. v. 2.
4. —— xviii. 2 (*ap.*)
1. —— 8.

STRONG (BE)

1. ἐνδυναμόω, to strengthen in, *i.e.* to render strong, to impart strength. *Trans., pass. or mid.*, to acquire strength, to be strong.

2. κραταιόω, to make κράτος (bodily strength) to make powerful in effect. *In N.T. only pass.*, to be strong, grow strong.

1. Rom. iv. 20.
2. 1 Cor. xvi. 13.
1. Eph. vi. 10.
1. 2 Tim. ii. 1.

STRONG (BE MADE)

ἐνδυναμόω, *see above, No.* 1.

Heb. xi. 34 (δυναμόω, *to make strong*, L ℵ.)

STRONG (MAKE)

στερεόω, to make stable, firm, strong, establish.

Acts iii. 16.

STRONG MAN.

ἰσχυρός, *see* "STRONG," *No.* 1.

Matt. xii. 29 twice. | Mark iii. 27 twice. | Luke xi. 21.

STRONG (WAX)

κραταιόω, *see* "STRONG (BE)" *No.* 2.

Luke i. 80. | Luke ii. 40.

STRONGHOLD.

ὀχύρωμα, a fastness, fortress, stronghold; (lxx. *for* מבצר, Josh. xix. 29; Is. xxxiv. 13; מצודה, 2 Kings xxii. 2), (*non occ.*)

2 Cor. x. 4.

STUBBLE.

καλάμη, the stalk *of grain; hence*, stubble, straw *after the ears are removed;* (lxx. קש, Ex. xv. 7; Joel ii. 5), (*non occ.*)

1 Cor. iii. 12.

STUCK.

See, STICK.

STUDY. [verb.]

1. σπουδάζω, to speed, make haste, (*as manifested in diligence, earnestness, zeal, etc.*)
2. φιλοτιμέομαι, to love honour; to exert one's self from a love and sense of honour, to make it a point of honour.

2. 1 Thes. iv. 11. | 1. 2 Tim. ii. 15.

STUFF.

σκεῦος, a vessel, utensil, implement; *here, pl.*, τὰ σκεύη, household stuff, goods, furniture.

Luke xvii. 31.

STUMBLE (-ED, -ETH, -ING.)

1. προσκόπτω, to beat towards *or* against anything; *esp.* to strike the foot against *anything*, to stumble.
2. πταίω, to stumble, to fall; (lxx. *for* נגף, 1 Sam. iv. 2; 2 Sam. xviii. 7) to fail, offend.

1. John xi. 9, 10. | 2. Rom. xi. 11.
1. Rom. xiv. 21.

STUMBLE AT.

1. Rom. ix. 32. | 1. 1 Pet. ii. 8.

STUMBLING.

πρόσκομμα, a stumbling.

1 Pet. ii. 8.

STUMBLING (OCCASION OF)

σκάνδαλον, a trap-stick, a crooked stick on which the bait is fastened, which the animal strikes against and so springs the trap; that against which any one strikes or stumbles; (lxx. *for* מכשול, Lev. xix. 14.)

1 John ii. 10.

STUMBLING-BLOCK.

1. σκάνδαλον, *see above.*
2. πρόσκομμα, a stumbling.

1. Rom. xi. 9. | 1. 1 Cor. i. 23.
2. — xiv. 13. | 2. — viii. 9.
1. Rev. ii. 14.

STUMBLING-STONE.

λίθος, a stone
προσκόμματος, of stumbling.

Rom. ix. 32, 33.

SUBDUE (-ED.)

καταγωνίζομαι, to contend against, prevail in contest, (*non occ.*)

Heb. xi. 33.

SUBDUE UNTO.

ὑποτάσσω, to range *or* put under, to subordinate, to make subject.

Phil. iii. 21.

SUBDUED UNTO (BE)

ὑποτάσσω, *see above. Here, mid. or pass.*, to submit one's self, be subordinate, be subject.

1 Cor. xv. 28.

SUBJECT (BE)

ὑποτάσσω, *see above.*

Rom. xiii. 5.

SUBJECT TO (BE)

Rom. viii. 7. | Tit. iii. 1.
1 Cor. xiv. 32. | 1 Pet. ii. 18.
1 Pet. v. 5 (*om.* G → L T Tr A ℵ.)

SUBJECT UNTO (BE)

Rom. xiii. 1. | 1 Cor. xv. 28.
Eph. v. 24.

SUBJECT TO (BE MADE)

Rom. viii. 20.

SUBJECT UNTO (BE MADE)

1 Pet. iii. 22.

SUBJECT TO.

ἔνοχος, held in, bound by, contained in; *hence,* liable, liable to.

Heb. ii. 15.

SUBJECT UNTO.

ὑποτάσσω, *see* "SUBDUED UNTO (BE)"

Luke ii. 15 part. | Luke x. 17, 20.

See also, JUDGMENT, ORDINANCES, PASSIONS.

SUBJECT (-ED.) [verb.]

ὑποτάσσω, *see* "SUBDUE UNTO."

Rom. viii. 20.

SUBJECTION.

ὑποταγή, subordination, submission, subjection, (*non occ.*)

2 Cor. ix. 13. | 1 Tim. ii. 11.
Gal. ii. 5. | —— iii. 4.

SUBJECTION TO (BE IN)

ὑποτάσσω, *see* "SUBDUED UNTO (BE)"

1 Pet. iii. 1.

SUBJECTION UNTO (BE IN)

Heb. xii. 9. | 1 Pet. iii. 5.

SUBJECTION (BRING INTO)

δουλαγωγέω, to lead as a slave, make a slave of.

1 Cor. ix. 27.

SUBJECTION (PUT IN)

ὑποτάσσω, *see* "SUBDUE UNTO."

Heb. ii. 8.

SUBJECTION UNDER (PUT IN)

Heb. ii 8.

SUBJECTION UNTO (PUT IN)

Heb. ii. 5.

SUBMIT (-ED, -ING.)

SUBMIT ONE'S SELF.

ὑπείκω, to cease fighting, to give way under, to give under, yield, (*non occ.*)

Heb. xiii. 17.

SUBMIT ONE'S SELF TO.

ὑποτάσσω, *see* "SUBDUED UNTO (BE)"

Eph. v. 21. | Jas. iv. 7.
1 Pet. ii. 13.

SUBMIT ONE'S SELF UNTO.

Rom. x. 3. | Eph. v. 22 (*om.* ὑποτάσσεσθε, *submit yourselves,* [G ≠ T A.)
1 Cor. xvi. 16. | Col. iii. 18.

SUBORN (-ED.)

ὑποβάλλω, to cast *or* throw under; to thrust under, instigate, put forward by collusion.

Acts vi. 11.

SUBSTANCE.

1. οὐσία, what is to *any one,* what he has, *i.e.* substance, property.
2. ὕπαρξις, being, existence; possession, substance.
3. { τὰ, the (*of them, i.e.* their) ὑπαρχοντα, property, goods.
4 ὑπόστασις, what is set *or* stands under; underlayer, prop, foundation; that which lies at the foundation of a matter; confidence; (lxx. *for* תוחלת, Ps. xxxix. 8, תקוה, Ruth i. 12; Ezek. xix. 5.)

3. Luke viii. 3. | 2. Heb. x. 34. [*or confidence.*
1. —— xv. 13. | 4. —— xi. 1, marg. *ground*

SUBTILELY WITH (DEAL)

κατασοφίζομαι, to be wise against *any one,* deal craftily, insidiously, *or* deceitfully with. *In allusion to* Ex. i. 10, *where* lxx. *for* התחכם, (*non occ.*)

Acts vii. 19.

SUBTILTY.

1. δόλος, bait; *hence*, guile, deceit; (lxx. *for* מרמה, Gen. xxvii. 35; Is. liii. 9; רמיה, Job. xiii. 7; Ps. xxxii. 2.)

2. πανουργία, unscrupulous conduct, knavery, villany; *in pl.*, knavish tricks.

1. Matt. xxvi. 4. | 1. Acts xiii. 10.
2. 2 Cor. xi. 3.

SUBVERT (-ED, -ING.)

1. ἀνατρέπω, to overturn, overthrow; (lxx. *for* הדף, Prov. x. 3), (*occ.* 2 Tim. ii. 18.)

2. ἀνασκευάζω, to pack up baggage, dismantle; *hence*, upset, (*non occ.*)

3. ἐκστρέφω, to turn out of *a place*, (*as a tree or post*) turn inside out, (*as a garment*); *of a person*, to change for the worse; (lxx. *for* הפך, Am. vi. 12; *pass. for* תהפכה, Deut. xxxii. 20), (*non occ.*)

2. Acts xv. 24. | 1. Tit. i. 11.
3. Tit. iii. 1.

SUBVERTING.

καταστροφή, catastrophe, *i.e.* overthrow, destruction; (lxx. *for* הפכה, Gen. xix. 29; שוד, Job. xv. 21), (*occ.* 2 Pet. ii. 6.)

2 Tim. ii. 14.

SUCCOUR (-ED.)

βοηθέω, to run up at a cry for help, to advance in aid of *any one*; *gen.*, to succour, help, aid.

2 Cor. vi. 2. | Heb. ii. 18.

SUCCOURER.

προστάτις, *fem. of* προστάτης, (a presider, prefect, magistrate,) (lxx. 2 Chron. viii. 10) a curator, guardian, patron); *hence, the fem.*, a patroness, helper, succourer, (*non occ.*)

Rom. xvi. 2.

SUCH.

(*For various combinations with other words, see below.*)

1. τοιοῦτος, of this kind, of this sort, such.

2. τοιόσδε, of this kind *or* sort, such, (*non occ.*)

3. τούτους, (*Acc. pl. of* οὗτος, this, this here) these, these here, such as these.

4. ταῦτα, (*neut. pl. of* οὗτος, *see above*) these *things*.

5. τούτων, (*Gen. pl. of* οὗτος, *see above*) of these.

6. ἥδε, this here, this one here.

1. Matt. ix. 8.	4. 1 Cor. vi. 11.
1. —— xviii. 5.	1. —— vii. 15, 28.
1. —— xix. 14.	1. —— xi. 16.
1. Mark iv. 33.	1. —— xv. 48 twice.
1. —— vi. 2.	1. —— xvi. 16, 18.
1. —— vii. 8 (*ap.*), 13.	1. 2 Cor. iii. 4, 12.
1. —— ix. 37.	1. —— x. 11.
— —— x. 7, see Give.	1. —— xi. 13.
— ——— 8, see Set.	1. —— xii. 3.
1. ——— 14.	1. Phil. ii. 29.
1. —— xiii. 19.	5. 1 Thes. iv. 6.
1. Luke xviii. 16.	1. 2 Thes. iii. 12.
1. John iv. 23.	1. 1 Tim. vi. 5 (*ap.*)
1. —— viii. 5 (*ap.*)	3. 2 Tim. iii. 5.
1. —— ix. 16.	1. Tit. iii. 11.
— Acts xv. 24, see No.	1. Heb. vii. 26.
1. —— xvi. 24.	1. —— viii. 1.
— —— xxv. 20, see Manner.	1. —— xii. 3.
— —— xxviii. 10, see Necessary.	1. —— xiii. 6.
1. Rom. xvi. 18.	6. Jas. iv. 13.
1. 1 Cor. v. 1.	1. ——— 16.
	2. 2 Pet. i. 17.
	1. 3 John 8.

5. Rev. xx. 6.

SUCH AS

1. οἷος, of what kind *or* sort, what, such as.

2. { τοιοῦτος, of this kind, such as, ὁποῖος, of what kind *or* sort, } such as this, what sort.

3. ὅστις, any one who, some one who, whoever, whatever.

1. Matt. xxiv. 21.	3. 1 Cor. v. 1.
3. Mark iv. 20.	1. 2 Cor. x. 11.
1. —— xiii. 29.	1. —— xii. 20 twice.
2. Acts xxvi. 29.	1. Rev. xvi. 18.

SUCH AS SHOULD BE SAVED.

{ οἱ, the, *i.e.* those, σωζόμενοι, being saved, } those being saved, (*marking the character and class of persons God was then saving, rather than the fact of their being saved.*)

Acts ii. 47.

SUCH A FELLOW.

τοιοῦτος, of this kind, of this sort, such *an one*.

Acts xxii. 22.

SUCH A MAN.

1. τοιοῦτος, (*see above*) such an one, (*whom one does know.*)

2. δεῖνα, some one, such an one, (*spoken of a person whom one does not know, or does not wish to name.*)

2. Matt. xxvi. 18. | 1. 2 Cor. ii. 6.

SUCH A [AN] ONE.

τοιοῦτος, *see* "SUCH," *No.* 1.

1 Cor. v. 5, 11.
2 Cor. ii. 7.
— x. 11.
2 Cor. xii. 2, 5.
Gal. vi. 1.
Philem. 9.

SUCH MATTERS (OF)

τούτων, of these things, of these matters here.

Acts xviii. 15.

SUCH THINGS.

ταῦτα, these things.

John vii. 32. | 2 Pet. iii. 14.

SUCH THING.

τοιοῦτος, *see* "SUCH," *No.* 1.

Luke ix. 9.
— xiii. 2 (ταῦτα, *these things*, T Tr A ℵ.)
Acts xxi. 25 (*ap.*)
Rom. i. 32.
— ii. 2, 3.
Gal. v. 21.
Eph. v. 27.
Heb. xi. 14.

SUCH THINGS AS ONE HATH.

{ τὰ, the
{ πάροντα, present *things.*

Heb. xiii. 5.

SUCH THINGS AS YE HAVE.

{ τὰ, the
{ ἐνόντα, things within.

Luke xi. 41, marg. *as ye are able.*

SUCK (GIVE)

θηλάζω, to suckle, give suck; *also,* to suck at the breast.

Matt. xxiv. 19.
Mark xiii. 17.
Luke xxi. 23.
— xxiii. 29 (τρέφω, *to nourish*, L T Tr ℵ.)

SUCK (-ED.) [verb.]

θηλάζω, *see above.*

Luke xi. 27.

SUCKLING (s.)

θηλάζω, *see above. Here part.,* θηλάζων, suckling, *quoted from* Ps. viii. 3, *where* lxx. *for* יונק.

Matt. xxi. 16.

SUDDEN.

αἰφνίδιος, unforeseen; sudden, (*occ.* Luke xxi. 34.)

1 Thes. v. 3.

SUDDENLY.

1. ἐξαίφνης, suddenly, unexpectedly; (lxx. *for* פתאם, Prov. xxiv. 2; Jer. vi. 26; רגע, Is. xlvii. 9), (*non occ.*)

2. ἄφνω, unawares, of a sudden; (lxx. *for* פתאם, Josh. x. 9; Ecc. ix. 12), (*non occ.*)

3. ἐξάπινα, *another and softer form of No.* 1, (*non occ.*)

4. ταχέως, quickly, speedily; (lxx. *for* מהר, Prov. xxv. 8.)

3. Mark ix. 8.
1. — xiii. 36.
1. Luke ii. 13.
1. — ix. 39.
2. Acts ii. 2.
1. Acts ix. 3.
2. — xvi. 26.
1. — xxii. 6.
2. — xxviii. 6.
4. 1 Tim. v. 22.

SUE.

See, LAW.

SUFFER (-ED, -EST, -ETH, -ING.)

1. πάσχω, to be affected by *anything from without,* to be acted on, to experience *either good or evil; of good,* to experience; *of evil,* to suffer, be subjected to evil, receive it, suffer from it.

2. ἀφίημι, to send forth *or* away, let go from *one's self,* dismiss; to let go, *i.e.* let pass, permit, to suffer.

3. ἐάω, to let, let be; permit, suffer, not to hinder.

4. ἐπιτρέπω, to turn upon, direct upon; to commit *or* entrust to *any one,* to entrust; give up, yield, allow, suffer.

5. ἀνέχομαι, to hold one's self upright, bear up, hold out; *hence,* endure, bear patiently, have patience with, put up with.

6. δίδωμι, to give; give over, deliver over.

7. δέχομαι, to take to one's self *what is brought or presented by another*, to receive.

8. προσεάω, (*No.* 3, *with* πρός, towards, *prefixed*) to permit *or* suffer further.

9. στέγω, to cover, cover over, conceal, not to make known.

10. ὑπέχω, to hold under; to undergo, *as punishment or sentence, (non occ.)*

11. ὑπομένω, to remain under, to bear up under, be patient under, endure; (lxx. *for* כלכל, Mal. iii. 2; חכה, Dan. xii. 12.)

— Matt. iii. 15 1st, see S it to be so now.
2. —— 15 2nd.
4. —— viii. 21.
4. —— 31 (ἀπόστειλον ἡμᾶς, *send us*, instead of ἐπίτρεψον ἡμῖν ἀπελθεῖν, *suffer us to go away*. G L T Tr A ℵ.)
— —— xi. 12, see Violence.
1. —— xvi. 21.
1. —— xvii. 12.
5. —— 17.
4. —— xix. 8.
2. —— 14.
2. —— xxiii. 13.
3. —— xxiv. 43.
1. —— xxvii. 19.
2. Mark i. 34.
2. —— v. 19.
1. —— 26.
2. —— 37.
2. —— vii. 12.
1. —— viii. 31.
1. —— ix. 12.
5. —— 19.
4. —— x. 4.
2. —— 14.
2. —— xi. 16.
3. Luke iv. 41.
4. —— viii. 32 twice.
2. —— 51.
1. —— ix. 22.
5. —— 41.
4. —— 59.
2. —— xii. 39.
1. —— xiii. 2.
1. —— xvii. 25.
2. —— xviii. 16.
1. —— xxii. 15.
3. —— 51.
1. —— xxiv. 26, 46.
6. Acts ii. 17.
1. —— iii. 18.
— —— v. 41, see Shame.
— —— vii. 24, see Wrong.
1. —— ix. 16.
— —— xiii. 8, see Manners.
6. —— 35.
3. —— xiv. 16.
3. —— xvi. 7.
1. —— xvii. 3.
3. —— xix. 30.
4. —— xxi. 39.
— —— xxvi. 23, see S (should)
8. —— xxvii. 7.
3. —— xxviii. 4.
4. —— 16.
— Rom. viii. 17, see S with.
5. 1 Cor. iv. 12.
9. —— ix. 12.
3. —— x. 13.
1. —— xii. 26 1st.
— —— 26 2nd, see S with.
— —— xiii. 4, see S long.
— —— 15, see Loss.
1. 2 Cor. i. 6.
— —— vii. 12, see Wrong.
7. —— xi. 16, marg. (text, *receive.*)
5. —— 19, 20.
— —— 25, see Shipwreck.
1. Gal. iii. 4.
— —— v. 11, } see Persecution.
— —— vi. 12, }
1. Phil. i. 29.
— —— iii. 8, see Loss.
— —— iv. 12, see Need.
— 1 Thes. ii. 2, see S before.
1. —— 14.
— —— iii. 4, see Tribulation.
1. 2 Thes. i. 5.
4. 1 Tim. ii. 12.
— —— iv. 10, see Reproach.
1. 2 Tim. i. 12.
— —— ii. 9, see S trouble.
11. —— 12.
— —— iii. 12, see Persecution.
1. Heb. ii. 18.
1. —— v. 8.
— —— vii. 23, see S not.
1. —— ix. 26.
— —— xiii. 2, see Adversity.
1. —— 12.
5. —— 22.
— Jas. v. 8, see *Patience.*
— —— 10, see Affliction.
1. 1 Pet. ii. 9, 20, 21, 23.
1. —— iii. 14, 17.
1. —— 18 (ἀπέθανε, *died*, G ∾ L ℵ.)
1. —— iv. 1 1st part., 1 2nd, 15, 19.
1. —— v. 10 part.
10. Jude 7.
1. Rev. ii. 10.
3. —— 20 (No. 2, G L T Tr A ℵ.)
2. —— xi. 9.

SUFFER BEFORE.

προπάσχω, (*No.* 1, *with* πρό, before, *prefixed*) to be affected beforehand, to experience before. *in N.T. part. aor.*, to have suffered before, *i.e.* previously, (*non occ.*)

1 Thes. ii. 2.

SUFFER IT TO BE SO.

2. Matt. iii. 15.

SUFFER LONG.

μακροθυμέω, to be long-minded, *i.e.* slow to anger; to be long-suffering.

1 Cor. xiii. 4.

SUFFER NOT.

κωλύω, to hinder, prevent, restrain.

Heb. vii. 23.

SUFFER (SHOULD)

παθητός, subject to suffering, passible; *or perhaps* destined to suffer; *comp.* Luke xxiv. 26.

Acts xxvi. 23.

SUFFER TROUBLE.

κακοπαθέω, to suffer evil, be afflicted, endure hardships; (lxx. *for* עמל, Jon. iv. 10.)

2 Tim. ii. 9.

SUFFER WITH.

συμπάσχω, ("SUFFER," *No.* 1, *with* σύν, together in conjunction with, *prefixed*), (*non occ.*)

Rom. viii. 17. | 1 Cor. xii. 26.

SUFFERING.

πάθημα, what is suffered; evil suffered, affliction, Heb. ii. 9. *Elsewhere only pl.*, sufferings, calamities.

Rom. viii. 18.
2 Cor. i. 5, 6, 7.
Phil. iii. 10.
Col. i. 24.
Heb. ii. 9, 10.
1 Pet. i. 11.
—— iv. 13.
—— v. 1.

See also, LONG.

SUFFERING AFFLICTION.

κακοπάθεια, suffering of evil; (lxx. *for* תלאה, Mal. i. 13.)

Jas. v. 10.

SUFFICE (-ETH.)

1. ἀρκέω, to ward off, keep off; *hence*, to be of use, avail, suffice, be strong enough.

2. { εἰμί, to be
   ἀρκετός, sufficient.

1. John xiv. 8. | 2. 1 Pet. iv. 3.

SUFFICIENCY.

1. αὐτάρκεια, self-sufficiency, (*in a good sense*) *i.e.* sufficiency within one's self, (*occ.* 1 Tim. vi. 6.)

2. ἱκανότης, sufficiency, fitness, competency, ability.

2. 2 Cor. iii. 5. | 1. 2 Cor. ix. 8.

SUFFICIENT.

1. ἱκανός, coming to, reaching to; *hence*, sufficing, *i.e.* sufficient.

2. ἀρκετός, sufficient, *i.e.* availing, enough.

2. Matt. vi. 34.
— Luke xiv. 28, see Have.
1. 2 Cor. ii. 6, 16.
1. — iii. 5.

SUFFICIENT (BE)

ἀρκέω, *see* "SUFFICE," *No.* 1.

John vi. 7. | 2 Cor. xii. 9.

SUM.

1. κεφάλαιον, the head; *hence*, the chief thing, the main point, (*non occ.*)

2. τιμή, a holding worth, estimation; *hence*, value, price.

2. Acts vii. 16. | 1. Acts xxii. 28.
1. Heb. viii. 1.

SUMMER.

θέρος, the warm season, *i.e.* summer, summer-time; (lxx. *for* קציר, Prov. xxvi. 1), (*non occ.*)

Matt. xxiv. 32. | Mark xiii. 28.
Luke xxi. 30.

SUMPTUOUSLY.

λαμπρῶς, radiantly, splendidly, sumptuously, (*non occ.*)

Luke xvi. 19.

SUN.

ἥλιος, the sun; (lxx. *for* שמש, Gen. xv. 12, 17.)

Matt. v. 45.
— xiii. 6, 43.
— xvii. 2.
— xxiv. 29.
Mark i. 32.
— iv. 6.
— xiii. 24.
— xvi. 2.
Luke iv. 40.
— xxi. 25.
— xxiii. 45.
Acts ii. 20.
— xiii. 11.
— xxvi. 13.
Acts xxvii. 20.
1 Cor. xv. 41.
Eph. iv. 26.
Jas. i. 11.
Rev. i. 16.
— vi. 12.
— vii. 16.
— viii. 12.
— ix. 2.
— x. 1.
— xii. 1.
— xvi. 8.
— xix. 17.
— xxi. 23.
Rev. xxii. 5.

SUNDER.

See, CUT.

SUNDRY.

See, TIMES.

SUN-RISING. [margin.]

Luke i. 78, see "DAY-SPRING."

SUP.

δειπνέω, to make a meal, to take the chief meal, to dine; (lxx. *for* לחם, Prov. xxiii. 1), (*occ.* Luke xxii. 20.)

Luke xvii. 8. | 1 Cor. xi. 25.
Rev. iii. 20.

SUPERFLUITY.

περισσεία, more than enough, superabundance.

Jas. i. 21.

SUPERFLUOUS.

περισσός, over and above, more than enough, superabundant.

2 Cor. ix. 1.

SUPERSCRIPTION.

ἐπιγραφή, a writing upon *or* over, superscription, (*non occ.*)

Matt. xxii. 20, marg. *inscription.*
Mark xii. 16.
Mark xv. 26.
Luke xx. 24.
— xxiii. 38.

SUPERSTITION.

δεισιδαιμονία, fear of the gods, *i.e. in a good sense*, religiousness, religion.

Acts xxv. 19.

SUPERSTITIOUS (TOO)

δεισιδαίμων, fearing the gods, *i.e. in a good sense*, religiously disposed. *Here, comparative, i.e. more so than others.*

Acts xvii. 22.

SUPPER.

1. δεῖπνον, a meal; the principal meal *whenever taken, but gen. towards evening.*
2. δειπνέω, (*see* "SUP") *here part.*, supping.

1. Mark vi. 21.	1. John xiii. 2, 4.
1. Luke xiv. 12, 16, 17, 24.	1. —— xxi. 20.
2. —— xxii. 20.	1. 1 Cor. xi. 20, 21.
1. John xii. 2.	1. Rev. xix. 9, 17.

SUPPLICATION.

1. δέησις, want, need; *then*, prayer, *as the* expression of need, supplication.
2. ἱκετηρία, the olive-branch, *i.e.* the suppliant-branch which suppliants held in the hand; *hence*, petition, (*non occ.*)

1. Acts i. 14 (*om.* καὶ τῇ δεήσει, *and supplication*, G L T Tr A ℵ.)	1. Phil. iv. 6.
1. Eph. vi. 18 twice.	1. 1 Tim. ii. 1.
	1. —— v. 5.
	2. Heb. v. 7.

SUPPLY. [noun.]

ἐπιχορηγία, a furnishing upon, further supply, super-addition; *hence*, aid, help.

Phil. i. 19.

SUPPLY (-ED, -ETH.) [verb.]

1. πληρόω, to make full, to fill.
2. ἀναπληρόω, (*No.* 1, with ἀνά, up, *prefixed*) to fill up, fulfil, complete.
3. προσαναπληρόω, (*No.* 2, *with* πρός, towards, *prefixed*) to fill up thereto, *as by adding*, to supply *or* complete fully.
4. ἐπιχορηγία, (*see the noun* "SUPPLY") *here*, "[*by every point of*] the supply."

2. 1 Cor. xvi. 17.	4. Eph. iv. 16.
3. 2 Cor. ix. 12.	2. Phil. ii. 30.
3. —— xi. 9.	1. —— iv. 19.

SUPPORT. [verb.]

1. ἀντιλαμβάνομαι, to take hold of in one's turn, to take part in, to interest one's self for.
2. ἀντέχομαι, to hold fast to, cleave to, faithfully to care for.

1. Acts xx. 35.	2. 1 Thes. v. 14.

SUPPOSE (-ED, -ING.)

1. νομίζω, to regard *or* acknowledge as custom, to have and hold as customary; *hence, gen.*, to assume, suppose.
2. δοκέω, *intrans.*, to appear, have the appearance; *trans.*, to hold for, be of opinion, believe.
3. λογίζομαι, to count, reckon, calculate, compute; *then*, to reckon, reason out.
4. ὑπολαμβάνω, to take under *any person or thing;* to take up by placing one's self underneath; *hence*, to take up *in thought*, to suppose, think; "*like Eng.*, "I take it."
5. οἴομαι, to suppose, (*always of something as yet doubtful*), to deem, conceive, imagine, (*with the idea of wrong judgment or conceit*), (*occ.* Jas. i. 7.)
6. ἡγέομαι, to lead, go before, to go first, lead the way; *then*, to lead out *the mind, i.e.* to view, regard *as being so and so.*
7. ὑπονοέω, to perceive under, suspect, surmise; conjecture.

1. Matt. xx. 10.	1. Acts xiv. 19.
2. Mark vi. 49.	1. —— xvi. 27.
1. Luke ii. 44.	1. —— xxi. 29.
1. —— iii. 23.	7. —— xxv. 18.
4. —— vii. 43.	2. —— xxvii. 13.
2. —— xii. 51.	1. 1 Cor. vii. 26.
2. —— xiii. 2.	3. 2 Cor. xi. 5.
2. —— xxiv. 37.	5. Phil. i. 16.
2. John xx. 15.	6. —— ii. 25.
5. —— xxi. 25.	1. 1 Tim. vi. 5.
4. Acts ii. 15.	2. Heb. x. 29.
1. —— vii. 25.	3. 1 Pet. v. 12.

SUPREME.

ὑπερέχω, to hold over; *intrans.*, to hold over *any one* for protection; to be over, be prominent, jut out over *or* beyond; *hence*, to be superior; *here part.*, protecting, superior.

1 Pet. ii. 13.

SURE.

1. ἀσφαλής, not falling, immoveable; safe, secure.
2. βέβαιος, firm, sure, steady; *hence*, steadfast.
3. πιστός, worthy of belief, trustworthy, sure, certain.
4. στερεός, solid, firm, stable; immoveable.

3. Acts xiii. 34. | 4. 2 Tim. ii. 19.
2. Rom. iv. 16. | 1. Heb. vi. 19.
2. 2 Pet. i. 10, 19.

SURE (BE)

1. οἶδα, to have seen, perceived, apprehended; to know.
2. γινώσκω, to perceive, observe, obtain a knowledge of; to be influenced by one's knowledge of the object and to suffer one's self to be determined thereby.

2. John vi. 69. | 1. Rom. ii. 2.
1. —— xvi. 30. | 1. —— xv. 29.

SURE OF (BE)

γινώσκω, *see above, No.* 2.

Luke x. 11.

SURE (MAKE)

ἀσφαλίζω, to make firm, make fast; *then*, to make safe.

Matt. xxvii. 65, 66.

SURELY.

1. ἀληθῶς, truly, really, in truth, in very deed.
2. ναί, yea, yes, certainly.
3. πάντως, wholly, altogether, entirely; by all means, at all events.
4. { ἦ, truly, certainly, / μήν, yea, assuredly, } most certainly, most surely.

1. Matt. xxvi. 73. | 1. John xvii. 8.
1. Mark xiv. 70. | 4. Heb. vi. 14 (εἰ μήν, *truly if*, instead of ἦ μήν, *most surely*, L T Tr A ℵ.)
— Luke i. 1, see Believed.
3. —— iv. 23.
3. Rev. xxii. 20.

SURETY.

ἔγγυος, yielding a pledge. *In N.T. masc.*, a surety, bondsman, (*non occ.*)

Heb. vii. 22.

SURETY (OF A)

ἀληθῶς, truly, really; in truth, in very deed.

Acts xii. 11.

SURFEITING.

κραιπάλη, seizure *of the head; and hence*, intoxication *and its consequences, giddiness, headache, etc.*, (*non occ.*)

Luke xxi. 34.

SURMISING.

ὑπόνοια, under-thought, *i.e.* suspicion, surmise, (*non occ.*)

1. Tim. vi. 4.

SURNAME (BE ONE'S)

1. καλέω, to call, to call to *any one in order that he may come or go anywhere; hence*, to call, to name, to give a name to *any person or thing. Here pass.*, to be called *or* named.
2. ἐπικαλέω, (*No.* 1, *with* ἐπί, upon, *prefixed*) to call upon; to call a name upon, *i.e.* to name in addition, to surname. *Here pass.*, to be surnamed.

2. Matt. x. 3 (om. ὁ ἐπικληθεὶς Θαδδαῖος, *whose surname was Thadæus*, G → L T Tr A ℵ.)
1. Acts xv. 37.

SURNAME (-ED.) [verb.]

{ ἐπιτίθημι, to place *or* put upon, / ὄνομα, a name, } to impose a name upon.

Mark iii. 16, 17.

SURNAMED (BE)

ἐπικαλέω, *see* "SURNAME (BE ONE'S)" *No.* 2.

Luke xxii. 3 (καλεόμαι, *to be named*, T Tr A ℵ.)
Acts i. 23.
— iv. 36.
Acts x. 18.
— xv. 22 (καλεόμαι, *to be named*, L T Tr A ℵ.)

SUSPENSE (*be in*) [margin.]

Luke iii. 15, see "EXPECTATION (BE IN)"

SUSPENSE (*hold in*) [margin.]

John x. 24, see "DOUBT (MAKE TO)"

SUSPENSE (*live in careful*) [margin.]

Luke xii. 29, see "DOUBTFUL MIND (BE OF)"

SUSTENANCE.

χόρτασμα, fodder, *green or dry, for animals;* (lxx. *for* מִסְפּוֹא, Gen. xxiv. 25, 32); *hence, gen.*, food, sustenance *for persons*, (*non occ.*)

Acts vii. 11.

SWADDLING CLOTHES (WRAP IN)

σπαργανόω, to swathe, wrap in swaddling clothes; (lxx. *pass., for* חתל, Ezek. xvi. 4.)

Luke ii. 7, 12.

SWALLOW. [verb.]

καταπίνω, to drink down, swallow down *as in drinking; or, as in Eng.*, to swallow up, (*non occ.*)

Matt. xxiii. 24.

SWALLOW UP.

1 Cor. xv. 54.
2 Cor. ii. 7.
2 Cor. v. 4.
Rev. xii. 16.

SWEAR (-ETH, SWARE, SWORN.)

ὄμνυμι, *or* ὀμνύω, to swear, *i.e.* to take *or* make an oath; to declare with an oath, promise with an oath.

Matt. v. 34, 36.
— xxiii. 16 twice, 18 twice, 20 twice, 21 twice, 22 twice.
— xxvi. 74.
Mark vi. 23.
— xiv. 71.
Luke i. 73.
Acts ii. 30.
Acts vii. 17 (ὁμολογέω, *engage, or agree*, G ~ L T Tr A ℵ.)
Heb. iii. 11, 18.
— iv. 3.
— vi. 13 twice, 16.
— vii. 21.
Jas. v. 12.
Rev. x. 6.

SWEARING OF AN OATH. [margin.]

Heb. vii. 21, see "OATH."

SWEAT.

ἱδρώς, sweat; (lxx. *for* זֵעָה, Gen. iii. 19), (*non occ.*)

Luke xxii. 24 (ap.)

SWEEP, SWEPT.

σαρόω, to sweep, to cleanse with a broom, (*non occ.*)

Matt. xii. 44.
Luke xv. 8.
Luke xi. 25.

SWEET.

γλυκύς, sweet; (lxx. *for* מָתוֹק, Judg. xiv. 14; Is. v. 20), (*occ.* Jas. iii. 12.)

Jas. iii. 11.
Rev. x. 9, 10.
Rev. xviii. 12, marg. (text, *thyme.*)

See also, SAVOUR, SMELL, SPICES.

SWEET SMELLING.

εὐωδία, good odour, sweet savour, fragrance. *Used of persons and things well pleasing* to God; (lxx. *for* רֵיחַ נִיחוֹחַ, Lev. i. 9, 13, 17; Numb. xxviii. 13.)

Eph. iv. 1.

SWELL, SWOLLEN.

πίμπρημι, to set on fire, to burn; *hence*, to be inflamed, swell, become swollen, (*non occ.*)

Acts xxvii. 6.

SWELLING. [noun.]

φυσίωσις, a puffing up, inflation, (*non occ.*)

2 Cor. xii. 20.

SWELLING WORDS (GREAT)

ὑπέρογκος, over-swollen, much swollen, *here, neut. pl.*, pompous things, boastful, highflown things, (*non occ.*) (lxx. *for* גָּדוֹל, Ex. xviii. 22: קָשֶׁה, Ex. xviii. 26: נִפְלָאוֹת, Dan. xi. 36.)

2 Pet. ii. 18.
Jude 16.

SWERVE (-ED) FROM.

ἀστοχέω, to miss the mark; to turn aside.

1 Tim. i. 6, marg. *not aim at.*

SWIFT.

1. ὀξύς, sharp, keen; *and since the idea of sharpness and keenness implies eagerness and vehemence,* quick, swift; (lxx. *for* קַל, Amos ii. 15; מָהִיר, Prov. xxii. 28.)
2. ταχύς, quick, swift, nimble; fast, fleet.
3. ταχινός, (*a poetical form of No.* 2) quick, swift, speedy, (*occ.* 2 Pet. i. 14.)

1. Rom. iii. 15. | 2. Jas. i. 19.
3. 2 Pet. ii. 1.

SWIM.

κολυμβάω, to dive; to jump into the sea and swim, (*non occ.*)

Acts xxvii. 43.

SWIM OUT.

ἐκκολυμβάω, (*the above, with* ἐκ, out of, *prefixed*) to swim out.

Acts xxvii. 42.

SWINE.

χοῖρος,, a young swine, pig, *like Lat.,* porcus, (*non occ.*)

Matt. vii. 6.
— viii. 30, 31, 32 1st.
— 32 2nd (om. τῶν χοίρων, *of the swine,* G L T Tr A^b ℵ.)
Mark v. 11, 12, 13.
— 14 (αὐτους, *them,* G L T Tr A ℵ.)
— 16.
Luke viii. 32, 33.
Luke xv. 15, 16.

SWORD (-s.)

1. μάχαιρα, a knife, slaughter-knife *worn with the sword; hence, later,* a sword *for cutting,* (*non occ.*)
2. ῥομφαία, a sword, a sabre, a long and broad sword used esp. by the Thracians, and carried on the right shoulder; (lxx. *for* חֶרֶב, Ex. xxxii. 26; Ezek. v. 1), (*non occ.*)

1. Matt. x. 34.
1. — xxvi. 47, 51, 52 3 times, 55.
1. Mark xiv. 43, 47, 48.
2. Luke ii. 35.
1. — xxi. 24.
1. — xxii. 36, 38, 49, 52.
1. John xviii. 10, 11.
1. Acts xii. 2.
1. — xvi. 27.
1. Rom. viii. 35.
1. — xiii. 4.
1. Eph. vi. 17.
1. Heb. iv. 12.
1. — xi. 34, 37.
2. Rev. i. 16.
2. — ii. 12, 16.
1. — vi. 4.
2. — 8.
1. — xiii. 10 twice, 14.
2. Rev. xix. 15, 21.

SYCAMINE TREE.

συκάμινος, a sycamine tree, *called also* the sycamore, (*Heb. pl.,* שִׁקְמִים, 1 Kings x. 27; 1 Ch. xxvii. 28; Is. ix. 9), (*non occ.*)

Luke xvii. 6.

SYCAMORE TREE.

συκομοραία, the fig-mulberry, a sycamore-tree, (*with the leaves like the mulberry-tree, and fruit like the fig.*)

Luke xix. 4.

SYNAGOGUE.

συναγωγή, a collecting, gathering, as *of fruits, cattle, etc.;* a mass, a multitude *as collected. Hence,* an assembly, congregation; (lxx. *for* עֵדָה, *which is never rendered* ἐκκλησία, a term confined to the Christian Church.) *Then,* a synagogue, בית כנסת, house of assembly.

[Synagogues appear to have been first introduced during the captivity in Babylon, when, deprived of the Temple worship, they assembled on the Sabbath to hear portions of the law read. The practice afterwards continued in Palestine, Neh. viii. 1, etc.]

Matt. iv. 23.
— vi. 2, 5.
— ix. 35.
— x. 17.
— xii. 9.
— xiii. 54.
— xxiii. 6, 34.
Mark i. 21, 23, 29, 39.
— iii. 1.
— vi. 2.
— xii. 39.
— xiii. 9.
Luke iv. 15, 16, 20, 28, 33, 38, 44.
— vi. 6.
— vii. 5.
— viii. 41.
— xi. 43.
Luke xii. 11.
— xiii. 10.
— xx. 46.
— xxi. 12.
John vi. 59.
— xviii. 20.
Acts vi. 9.
— ix. 2, 20.
— xiii. 5, 14, 42 (*ap.*)
— xiv. 1.
— xv. 21.
— xvii. 1, 10, 17.
— xviii. 4, 7, 19, 26.
— xix. 8.
— xxiv. 12.
Jas. ii. 2, marg. (text, *assembly.*)
Rev. ii. 9.
Rev. iii. 9.

SYNAGOGUE (IN EVERY)

{ κατὰ, *distributive,* τὰς, the, συναγωγάς, } from one synagogue to another, at different synagogues.

Acts xxii. 19. | Acts xxvi. 11.

SYNAGOGUE (PUT OUT OF THE)

ἀποσυνάγωγος, excommunicant from the synagogue,
ποιέω, to make.

John xvi. 2.

SYNAGOGUE (BE PUT OUT OF THE)

ἀποσυνάγωγος, excommunicant from the synagogue,
γίνομαι, to become, be made.

John ix. 22. | John xii. 42.

SYNAGOGUE (RULER OF THE)

ἀρχισυνάγωγος, a ruler *or* moderator of the synagogue. The presiding elder of the synagogue, whose duty it was to preserve order and select and invite persons to read or speak in the assembly.

Mark v. 22, 35, 36, 38. | Luke xiii. 14.
Luke viii. 49. | Acts xiii. 15.

SYNAGOGUE (CHIEF RULER OF THE)

ἀρχισυνάγωγος, *see above.*

Acts xviii. 8, 17.

T

TABERNACLE (-s.)

1. σκηνή, any covered sheltered place; *esp.* a tent; *as of green boughs,* a booth; *of skins,* a tent; (lxx. *for* סכה.) *Esp.*, The Tabernacle.

   (a) *quoted from* Amos ix. 11, *where* lxx. *for* סכה, *used of the throne and house and line of David.*

   (b) *quoted from* Amos v. 26, *where* lxx. *for* סכות.

2. σκῆνος, a booth, tent, tabernacle, (*non occ.*)

3. σκήνωμα, a booth or tent pitched, a dwelling-place; (lxx. *for* משכן, Ps. cxxxii. 5; xlvi. 4; אהל, 1 Kings ii. 28; viii. 4), (*non occ.*)

1. Matt. xvii. 4.
1. Mark ix. 5.
1. Luke ix. 33.
— John vii. 2, see T (of)
1b. Acts vii. 43.
1. —— 44.
3. —— 46.
1a. —— xv. 16.
2. 2 Cor. v. 1, 4.
1. Heb. viii. 2, 5.
1. —— ix. 2, 3, 6, 8, 11, 21.
1. —— xi. 9.
1. —— xiii. 10.
3. 2 Pet. i. 13, 14.
1. Rev. xiii. 6.
1. —— xv. 5.
1. Rev. xxi. 3.

TABERNACLES (OF)

σκηνοπηγία, a booth-pitching, tent-pitching, *i.e.* the festival of booths *or* tabernacles, the third of the great annual feasts of the Jews; *see* Deut. xvi. 16, etc.; John vii. 2; partly as a memorial of the forty years' wandering, (Lev. xxiii. 42, 43), partly as a harvest thanksgiving, (Ex. xxiii. 16; xxxiv. 22); *see also* Deut. xxxi. 10, etc.; Neh. viii. 18, (*non occ.*)

John vii. 2.

TABLE (-s.)

1. τράπεζα, a piece of furniture with four feet; *hence,* a table.

2. πλάξ, any broad and flat surface, *hence,* a tablet, table *of wood or stone;* (lxx. *for* לוחות, Ex. xxxi. 18; xxxii. 15; xxxiv. 1, 4; לוח, Prov. iii. 3; Jer. xvii. 1), (*non occ.*)

3. κλίνη, any thing on which one reclines, a bed, a couch.

1. Matt. xv. 27.
1. —— xxi. 12.
3. Mark vii. 4.
1. —— 28.
1. —— xi. 15.
— Luke i. 63, see Writing.
1. —— xvi. 21.
1. —— xxii. 21, 30.
1. John ii. 15.
— —— xii. 2, see Sit.
— —— xiii. 28, see T (at the)
1. Acts vi. 2.
1. Rom. xi. 9.
1. 1 Cor. x. 21 twice.
2. 2 Cor. iii. 3 twice.
1. Heb. ix. 2.
2. —— 4.

TABLE (AT THE)

ἀνάκειμαι, to be laid up *as at table or as at* a meal. *Here part.*, reclining at the table.

John xiii. 28.

TACKLING.

σκευή, apparatus, equipment, implements; *of a ship,* the rigging, the tackling, (*non occ.*)

Acts xxvii. 19.

TAIL.

οὐρά, the tail *of an animal*; (lxx. *for* זָנָב, Deut. xxviii 13; Job xl. 12.)

Rev. ix. 10 twice, 19 (*ap.*) | Rev. xii. 4.

TAKE (-EN -ETH, TOOK.)

(*For various combinations with other words, see below.*)

1. *λαμβάνω*, to take, take hold of, apprehend; take *with the hand.*

2. *ἀναλαμβάνω*, (*No.* 1, *with ἀνά*, up, *prefixed*) to take up, to take up *or* with, take along.

3. *ἀπολαμβάνω*, (*No.* 1, *with ἀπό*, away from, *prefixed*) to take one away from *another or from others.*

4. *ἐπιλαμβάνομαι*, (*No.* 1, *with ἐπί*, upon, *prefixed*) to take hold upon, lay hold of *in order to hold or detain for one's self.*

5. *καταλαμβάνω*, (*No.* 1, *with κατά*, down, *prefixed*) to take down, to take, lay hold of, (*more intensive than No.* 1, *and perhaps more hostile.*)

6. *μεταλαμβάνω*, (*No.* 1, *with μετά*, with, in association with, *prefixed*) to take a part, take a share of *anything in association with others.*

7. *παραλαμβάνω*, (*No.* 1, *with παρά*, from beside, *prefixed*) to take near, with, *or* to *one's self;* take from beside another, *i.e.* from him; take to one's self.

8. *προσλαμβάνω*, (*No.* 1, *with πρός*, towards, *prefixed*) to take thereto, *i.e.* in addition, take besides. *In N.T.*, *mid.*, to take to one's self, *i.e.* take by the hand and draw aside.

9. *συλλαμβάνω*, (*No.* 1, *with σύν*, together with, in conjunction with, *prefixed*) to take together, to enclose in the hands; to take or seize altogether, enclose and take.

10. *αἴρω*, to take up, lift up, raise; to take up and carry away, take away.

11. *ἀπαίρω*, (*No.* 10, *with ἀπό*, away from, *prefixed*) *trans.*, to take away from, remove; *intrans.*, to go away, depart. *In N.T.*, *only aor.* 1, *pass.*, to be taken away from.

12. *συναίρω*, (*No.* 10, *with σύν*, together in conjunction with, *prefixed*) to take up together, take up *one* in conjunction with *others.*

13. *δέχομαι*, to take to one's self what is presented or brought by another; *hence*, to accept, receive; receive into one's hands.

14. *προσδέχομαι*, (*No.* 13, *with πρός*, towards, *prefixed*) to receive towards one's self, to accept, allow.

15. *κρατέω*, to be strong, mighty, powerful; to have power over, be master of, take hold of and have and hold in one's power.

16. *πιάζω*, to press, to hold fast; to take, arrest, to catch.

17. *ἐμβαίνω*, to go in, to enter; *of a ship*, to go on board, embark.

18. *δίδωμι*, to give, bestow upon.

19. *δράσσομαι*, to grasp *with the hand*, to seize, take.

20. *ἐπιφέρω*, to bear upon, to bring upon *or* against *in a judicial sense, spoken of accusation, sentence, wrath or punishment.*

21. *κατέχω*, to have and hold down, hold fast *or* firmly; *hence*, to possess, to occupy, *implying that what is occupied is held in retained possession.*

22. *ποιέω*, to make; to do; *here, with συμβούλιον*, to make a consultation, *i.e.* to consult together.

7. Matt. ii. 13, 14, 21, 29.
7. —— iv. 5, 8.
1. —— viii. 17.
11. —— ix. 15.
10. ——— 16.
5. ——— 18.
1. —— x. 38 (No. 10, Lm.)
— —— xi. 12, see Force.
10. ——— 29.
1. —— xii. 14, marg. (text, *take hold.*)
7. ——— 45.
1. —— xiii. 31, 33.
1. —— xiv. 19.
1. —— xv. 26, 36.
17. Matt. xv. 39 (*ἀναβαίνω, go up*, G T Tr A.)
1. —— xvi. 5, 7.
8. ——— 22.
7. —— xvii. 1.
1. ——— 25, 27.
7. —— xviii. 16.
12. ——— 23.
— ——— 28, see Throat.
10. —— xx. 14.
7. ——— 17.
1. —— xxi. 35.
10. ——— 43.
15. —— xxii. 6.
1. ——— 15.
10. —— xxiv. 17, 18.

7. Matt. xxiv. 40, 41.
1. —— xxv. 1, 3 1st part., 3 2nd, 4.
10.—— 28.
15.—— xxvi. 4.
1. —— 26 twice, 27.
— —— 45, see Rest.
15.—— 50.
1. —— 52.
9. —— 55.
1. —— xxvii. 1, 6, 7, 9, 24.
7. —— 27.
1. —— 30, 48, 59 part.
1. —— xxviii. 12, 15.
22. Mark iii. 6 (No. 18, Tr A.)
10.—— iv. 25.
7. —— 36.
7. —— v. 40.
10.—— vi. 8.
1. —— 41 part.
1. —— vii. 27.
3. —— 33.
1. —— viii. 6, 14.
8. —— 32.
7. —— ix. 2.
1. —— 36 1st.
— —— 36 2nd, } see
— —— x. 16, } Arms.
7. —— 32.
1. —— xii. 8, 19, 20, 21.
10.—— xiii. 15.
15.—— xiv. 1.
1. —— 22 twice, 23.
7. —— 33.
— —— 41, see Rest.
15.—— 44, 46.
9. —— 48.
15.—— 49.
10.—— xv. 24.
— Luke i. 1, see Hand.
13.—— ii. 28.
1. —— v. 5.
9. —— 9.
— —— 18, see Palsy.
1. —— vi. 4 (om. G → ℵ.)
10.—— viii. 18.
10.—— ix. 3.
7. —— 10.
1. —— 16.
7. —— 28.
1. —— 39.
4. —— 47.
— —— x. 34, 35, see Care.
10.—— xi. 22.
7. —— 26.
— —— xii. 19, see Ease.
1. —— xiii. 19, 21.
4. —— xiv. 4.
21.—— 9.
13.—— xvi. 6, 7.
7. —— xvii. 34, 35, 36 (ap.)
7. —— xviii. 31.
— —— xix. 8, see Accusation.
10.—— 24.
1. —— xx. 28, 29, 30 (ap.), [31.
13.—— xxii. 17 1st.
1. —— 17 2nd, 19.
10.—— 36.
9. —— 54.
1. —— xxiv. 30, 43.
10. John ii. 16.
1. —— vi. 7, 11.
— —— 15, see Force.
17.—— 24.
16.—— vii. 30, 32, 44.
5. —— viii. 3 (ap.), 4 (ap.)
1. —— x. 17.
10.—— 18 1st.
1. —— 18 2nd.
16.—— 39.
— —— xi. 13, see Rest.
— —— 53, see Counsel.
16.—— 57.
1. —— xii. 3, 13.
1. —— xiii. 4, 12.
1. —— xvi. 15.
10. John xvi. 22.
10.—— xvii. 15.
9. —— xviii. 12.
1. —— 31.
1. —— xix. 1, 6.
7. —— 16 (ap.)
1. —— 23, 27.
10.—— 38.
1. —— 40.
1. —— xxi. 13.
9. Acts i. 16.
1. —— 20, 25.
1. —— ii. 23 (διὰ χειρός, *by hand of wicked men,* instead of λαβόντες διὰ χειρῶν, *have taken and by wicked hands,* G ⇉ L T Tr. A ℵ.)
16.—— iii. 7.
— —— iv. 13, see Knowledge.
— —— v. 33, see Counsel.
— —— viii. 7, see Palsy.
10.—— 33.
— —— ix. 23, see Counsel.
1. —— 25.
4. —— 27.
9. —— xii. 3.
1. —— xv. 14.
7. —— 39.
1. —— xvi. 3.
7. —— 33.
1. —— xvii. 9 part.
4. —— 19.
4. —— xviii. 17.
— —— 18, see Leave.
— —— xx. 26, see Record.
— —— xxi. 6 1st, see Leave.
— —— 6 2nd, see Ship.
10.—— 11.
7. —— 24, 26.
4. —— 30.
7. —— 32 (No. 1, L.)
4. —— 33.
— —— xxiii. 10, see Force.
7. —— 18.
9. —— 27.
2. —— 31.
15.—— xxiv. 6.
— —— 8, see Knowledge.
6. —— xxvii. 33 1st.
8. —— 33 2nd.
8. —— 34 (No. 5, G L T ℵ.)
1. —— 35.
8. —— 36.
20. Rom. iii. 5.
1. —— vii. 8, 11.
— —— ix. 6, see Effect.
19. 1 Cor. iii. 19.
— —— vi. 7, see Wrong.
10.—— 15.
— —— ix. 9, see Care.
1. —— x. 13.
1. —— xi. 23.
1. —— 24 (om. λάβετε, φάγετε, *take, eat,* G L T Tr A ℵ.)
— 2 Cor. ii. 13, see Leave.
1. —— xi. 8, 20.
— —— xii. 10, see Pleasure.
2. Eph. vi. 16.
13.—— 17 (om. G →)
10. Col. ii. 14.
18. 2 Thes. i. 8, marg. *yield.*
— 1 Tim. iii. 5, see Care.
— —— v. 9, see Number.
— 2 Tim. ii. 26, see Captive.
2. —— iv. 11.
— Heb. ii. 14, see Part.
1. —— v. 1, 4.
— —— vii. 5, see Tithe.
1. Heb. ix. 19.
14.—— x. 34.
1. Jas. v. 10.
— 1 Pet. ii. 20, see Patiently.
— —— v. 2, see Oversight.
1. 3 John 7.
1. Rev. iii. 11.
1. —— v. 7, 8, 9.
1. —— vi. 4.
1. —— viii. 5.
1. —— x. 8, 9, 10.
16.—— xix. 20.
1. —— xxii. 17.

TAKE AWAY.

1. αἴρω, *see* "TAKE," *No.* 10.

2. ἀπαίρω, *see* "TAKE," *No.* 11.

3. ἐξαίρω, (*No.* 1, *with* ἐκ, from out of, *prefixed*) to take up out of *any place,* to lift up from; to take away from out of.

4. ἀφαιρέω, to take away from, to remove from, deprive of.

5. ἀναιρέω, to take up, lift up; to take up to one's self, adopt; to take away, remove, put out of the way.

6. περιαιρέω, to take away *what is* round about, to take away wholly, *i.e.* all around.

7. ἀπάγω, to lead away, conduct away.

8. λαμβάνω, *see* "TAKE," *No.* 1.

9. παραφέρω, to bear from beside, bear away *as does a stream,* pass away.

8. Matt. v. 40.
1. —— xiii. 12.
1. —— xxii. 13 (om. ἄρατε αὐτὸν καὶ, *and take him away,* G ⇉ L T Tr A ℵ.)
1. —— xxiv. 39.
1. —— xxv. 29.
2. Mark ii. 20.
1. —— 21.
1. —— iv. 15.
2. —— v. 35.
9. —— xiv. 36.
4. Luke i. 25.
1. —— vi. 29, 30.
1. —— viii. 12.
4. —— x. 42.
1. —— xi. 52.
4. —— xvi. 3.
1. Luke xvii. 31.
1. —— xix. 26.
1. John i. 29, marg. *bear.*
1. —— xi. 39, 41, 48.
1. —— xv. 2.
1. —— xix. 31, 38.
1. —— xx. 1, 2, 13, 15.
1. Acts viii. 33.
7. —— xxiv. 7 (ap.)
6. —— xxvii. 20.
4. Rom. xi. 27.
3. 1 Cor. v. 2 (No. 1, G L T Tr A ℵ.)
6. 2 Cor. iii. 16.
4. Heb. x. 4.
5. —— 9.
6. —— 11.
1. 1 John iii. 5.
4. Rev. xxii. 19 twice.

TAKE BEFORE.

προλαμβάνω, ("TAKE," *No.* 1, *with* πρό, before, *prefixed.*)

1 Cor. xi. 21.

TAKE BY.

1. κρατέω, *see* "TAKE," *No.* 15.

2. ἐπιλαμβάνομαι, to take hold upon, lay hold of in order to hold *or* detain.

1. Matt. ix. 25.	1. Mark ix. 27.
1. Mark i. 31.	1. Luke viii. 54.
1. —— v. 41.	2. Acts xxiii. 19.
2. —— viii. 23.	2. Heb. viii. 9 part.

TAKE DOWN.

καθαιρέω, to take down *from a higher place*, pull down.

Mark xv. 36, 46. | Luke xxiii. 53. Acts xiii. 29.

TAKE FOR.

ἔχω, to have and hold; *then, by impl.*, to hold for *or* as, to regard.

Matt. xxi. 46.

TAKE HOLD OF.

ἐπιλαμβάνομαι, *see* "TAKE BY," *No.* 2.

Luke xx. 20, 26.

TAKE IN.

1. **ἀναλαμβάνω**, *see* "TAKE," *No.* 2.
2. **συνάγω**, to lead *or* bring together, gather together, to lead *or* take together with one's self, *i.e.* to receive to one's hospitality; (*so*, lxx. *for* אסף אל, Deut. xxii. 2; Josh. ii. 18; Judg. xix. 15. 18.)

2. Matt. xxv. 35, 38, 43. | 1. Acts xx. 13, 14.

TAKE OFF FROM.

ἐκδύω, to go *or* come out of; to put off, strip one *of his clothes*, to unclothe.

Matt. xxvii. 21. | Mark xv. 20.

TAKE ON.

ἐπιλαμβάνομαι, *see* "TAKE BY," *No.* 2.

Heb. ii. 16 twice, marg. *take hold of.*

TAKE OUT.

ἐκβάλλω, to throw *or* cast out; *then*, to take out, extract.

Luke x. 35.

TAKE TO ONE'S SELF.

λαμβάνω, *see* "TAKE," *No.* 1.

Rev. xi. 17.

TAKE UNTO.

1. **ἀναλάμβανω**, *see* "TAKE," *No.* 2.
2. **παραλάμβανω**, *see* "TAKE," *No.* 7.

2. Matt. i. 20, 24. | 1. Eph. vi. 13.

TAKE UNTO ONE.

προσλαμβάνω, (*see* "TAKE," *No.* 8.) *Here, mid.*

Acts xvii. 5. | Acts xviii. 26.

TAKE UNTO ONE'S SELF. [margin.]

John iii. 27, see "RECEIVE."

TAKE UP.

1. **αἴρω**, *see* "TAKE," *No.* 10.
2. **ἐπαίρω**, (*No.* 1, *with* ἐπί, upon, *prefixed*) to take up, to raise up.
3. **ἀναιρέω**, to take up, lift up; to take up to one's self, to adopt, bring up.
4. **περιαιρέω**, to take away *what is* round about.
5. **λαμβάνω**, *see* "TAKE," *No.* 1.
6. **ἀναλαμβάνω**, *see* "TAKE," *No.* 2.
7. **ἀνάγω**, to lead *or* conduct up *from a lower to a higher place*.
8. **βαστάζω**, to raise upon a basis; to lift up, to take up and hold, to bear *or* carry about.
9. **ἐγείρω**, to rouse up, cause to rise up, set upright.

1. Matt. ix. 6.	1. Luke v. 24, 25.
1. —— xiv. 12, 20.	1. —— ix. 17, 23 (*ap.*)
1. —— xv. 37.	1. —— xix. 21, 22.
5. —— xvi. 9, 10.	1. John v. 8, 9, 11, 12.
1. —— —— 24.	1. —— viii. 59.
1. —— xvii. 27.	8. —— x. 31.
1. Mark ii. 9, 11, 12.	6. Acts i. 2.
1. —— vi. 29, 43.	2. —— —— 9.
1. —— viii. 8, 19, 20, 34.	6. —— —— 11, 22.
1. —— x. 21 (*om.* ἄρας τὸν σταυρόν, *take up the cross and*, G ⇉ Lb T Tr ℵ.)	3. —— vii. 21.
	6. —— —— 43.
	9. —— x. 26.
	1. —— xx. 9.
1. —— xiii. 16.	1. —— xxvii. 17.
1. —— xvi. 18 (*ap.*)	4. —— —— 40 part.
7. Luke iv. 5.	1. Rev. xviii. 21.

TAKE UP ONE'S CARRIAGE.

ἀποσκευάζομαι, to divest one's self of baggage, putting aside impediments.

Acts xxi. 15 (*ἐπισκευάζομαι, to make or get one's effects ready, to pack up*, G ∾ L T Tr A ℵ.)

[NOTE.
"Carriages" in AV. is used as in Judg. xviii. 21, where it answers to *baggage*, i.e. *things carried*, not vehicles.]

TAKE UPON.

ἐπιχειρέω, to lay hands upon; *hence*, to take in hand, undertake.

Acts xix. 13.

TAKE UPON ONE'S SELF.

λαμβάνω, *see* "TAKE," *No.* 1.

Phil. ii. 7.

TAKE WITH.

1. παραλαμβάνω, *see* "TAKE," *No.* 7.
2. συμπαραλαμβάνω, (*No.* 1, *with* σύν, together *or* in conjunction with, *prefixed*) to take along with *one's self, as a companion*, to take *another to walk* together beside one's self.

1. Matt. xxvi. 37. | 2. Acts xv. 37, 38.
2. Acts xii. 25. | 2. Gal. ii. 1.

TAKEN (BE)

γίνομαι, to become, begin to be, arise or be [*revealed*]. *Here, with* ἐκ μέσου, arise out of the midst, repeating the word "*revealed*" from *v.* 3 and 6, and referring to the Antichrist.

2 Thes. ii. 7.

TAKEN FROM (BE)

ἀπορφανίζομαι, to bereave of. *In N.T. pass.*, to be bereaved of.

1 Thes. ii. 17.

TAKEN (TO BE)

{ εἰς, unto, for,
{ ἅλωσις, capture.

2 Pet. ii. 12.

TAKEN WITH (BE)

συνέχω, to hold together, press together. *Here, pass.*, to be seized, be affected, pressed, distressed.

Matt. iv. 24. | Luke iv. 38.
Luke viii. 37.

See also, NEED, JOURNEY, THOUGHT.

TALENT (-S.)

τάλαντον, scale *of a balance*, (*pl.*, scales); *then*, something weighed, a weight; *hence*, a certain fixed weight. The Jewish talent, ככר, contained 3,000 shekels of the sanctuary, (Ex. xxxviii. 25, 26), and probably was equal to 113 lbs. 10 oz. 1 dwt. $2\frac{2}{7}$ grs. troy. *Further, the talent was also used for* money, *which was anciently reckoned by weight, and in proportion to which its value varied*, the Attic talent being about £243 15s. *It also denoted* anything which is weighed out, apportioned *or* allotted to one; *hence our Eng. word* talent, *i.e.* a gift, as what is apportioned to one for use, (*non occ.*)

Matt. xviii. 24. | Matt. 20 1st.
—— xxv. 15, 16 1st. | —— 20 2nd (*om.* Trb.)
—— 16 2nd (*om.* G → L Tr Ab.) | —— 20 3rd & 4th.
| —— 22 3 times.
Matt. xxv. 24, 25, 28 twice.

TALENT (THE WEIGHT OF A)

ταλαντιαῖος, weighing a talent, a talent in weight, (*see above*), (*non occ.*)

Rev. xvi. 21.

TALES.

See, IDLE.

TALITHA.

ταλιθά, *Aram. fem.* טליתא, talitha, *i.e.* a damsel, maiden, (*non occ.*)

Mark v. 41.

TALK. [noun.]

λόγος, word *as spoken*, anything spoken, a speaking, discourse.

Mark xxii. 15.

TALK (-ED, -EST, -ETH, -ING.) [verb.]

1. λαλέω, to speak, to talk, to use the voice without any necessary reference to the words spoken, (*see* "SAY," *No.* 5, *and cf. No.* 1, *etc.*)
2. ὁμιλέω, to be together in a crowd *or* company, to come into company with; *hence*, to talk as with companions, have intercourse with.

1. Matt. xii. 46 part.
1. Mark vi. 50.
2. Luke xxiv. 14.
1. John iv. 27 twice.
1. —— ix. 37.
1. —— xiv. 30.
1. John xvi. 4.
2. Acts xx. 11.
1. —— xxvi. 31.
1. Rev. iv. 1.
1. —— xvii. 1.
1. —— xxi. 9, 15.

TALK WITH.

1. *λαλέω, see above, No.* 1.

2. *συλλαλέω*, (*No.* 1, *with σύν*, together in conjunction with, *prefixed*) to speak *or* talk with, confer with.

3. *συνομιλέω*, ("TALK," *No.* 2, *with σύν*, together in conjunction with, *prefixed*) to come into company together with another, (*non occ.*)

2. Matt. xvii. 3.
2. Mark ix. 4.
2. Luke ix. 30.
1. —— xxiv. 32.
3. Acts x. 27 part.

TALKER (VAIN)

ματαιολόγος, given to vain talking; *subst.*, vain talker, empty speakers, (*non occ.*)

Tit. i. 10.

TALKING.

See, FOOLISH.

TAME (-ED.)

δαμάζω, to overpower, to subdue; (LXX. *for* Chald. חשל *and* רעע, Dan. ii. 40), (*non occ.*)

Mark v. 4. | Jas. iii. 7 twice, 8.

TANNER.

βυρσεύς, a leather-dresser, tanner, (*from βύρσα*, hide), (*non occ.*)

Acts ix. 43. | Acts x. 6, 32.

TARES.

ζιζάνιον, zizanium, *a general name for* weeds in grain, *like Eng.*, cockle, darnel.

[In *N.T.* spoken of a plant common in Palestine which infests fields of grain and resembles wheat in appearance. Called by the Rabbins זונין, *bastard.*] (*non occ.*)

Matt. xiii. 25, 26, 27, 29, 30, 36, 38, 40.

TARRY (-ED, -EST.)

1. *μένω*, to remain, continue, abide, (*Lat., maneo.*)

2. *ἐπιμένω*, (*No.* 1, *with ἐπί*, upon, *prefixed*) to remain upon, *i.e.* in addition, longer.

3. *χρονίζω*, to make out the time, spend time, tarry, linger, delay, be long in *doing anything.*

4. *διατρίβω*, to rub in pieces, to wear away, consume *as by rubbing; of time*, to wear away the time, pass the time.

5. *βραδύνω*, to be slow, delay, be slack *or* tardy, (*occ.* 2 Pet. iii. 9.)

6. *καθίζω*, *trans.*, to cause to sit down, to seat; *here, intrans.*, to sit down, to sit, be seated.

7. *μέλλω*, to be about to, to be on the point of; *here*, "what art thou about to [*do*]?"

8. *προσδοκάω*, to watch toward *or* for *any thing*, to wait in expectation *or* suspense.

3. Matt. xxv. 5 part.
1. —— xxvi. 38.
1. Mark xiv. 34.
3. Luke i. 21.
— —— ii. 43, see T behind.
1. —— xxiv. 29.
6. ——— 49.
4. John iii. 22.
1. —— iv. 40.
1. —— xxi. 22, 23.
1. Acts ix. 43.
2. —— x. 48.
— —— xv. 33, see T there a space.
— Acts xviii. 18, see T there.
1. ——— 20.
— —— xx. 5, see T for.
1. ——— 15 part.
2. —— xxi. 4, 10 part.
7. —— xxii. 16.
4. —— xxv. 6 part.
8. —— xxvii. 33.
2. —— xxviii. 12, 14.
— 1 Cor. xi. 33, see T for.
2. —— xvi. 7, 8.
5. 1 Tim. iii. 15.
3. Heb. x. 37.

TARRY BEHIND.

ὑπομένω, (*No.* 1, *above, with ὑπό*, under, *prefixed*) to remain behind *after others are gone, unperceived, without noise or notice, implying stealth.*

Luke ii. 43.

TARRY FOR.

1. *μένω, see* "TARRY," *No.* 1.

2. *ἐκδέχομαι*, to receive *from another*, to succeed, follow *another*, come next.

1. Acts xx. 5. | 2. 1 Cor. xi. 33.

TARRY THERE.

προσμένω, to remain at *a place* with *a person*, remain there; continue with.

Acts xviii. 18.

TARRY THERE A SPACE.

{ ποιέω, to make } *i.e.* made
{ χρόνος, time, } a delay.

Acts xv. 33 part.

TASTE (-ED.)

γεύομαι, to taste; *metaph.*, experience, partake of, (*occ.* Acts x. 10; xx. 11; xxiii. 14.)

Matt. xvi. 28.
—— xxvii. 34 part.
Mark ix. 1.
Luke ix. 27.
—— xiv. 24.
John ii. 9.
—— viii. 52.
Col. ii. 21.
Heb. ii. 9.
—— vi. 4, 5.
1 Pet. ii. 3.

TATTLER (-S.)

φλύαρος, overflowing with talk; *hence*, a prater, trifler, (*non occ.*)

1 Tim. v. 13.

TAVERNS (THE THREE)

{ τρεῖς, three } the proper name
{ ταβέρναι, taverns, } of a small place on the Appian way, 33 Rom. miles from Rome towards Brundusium.

Acts xxviii. 15.

TAXED (BE)

ἀπογράφω, to write off; enrol *as in a* register; *here, mid.*, to cause one's self to be enrolled, give one's name to the census.

Luke ii. 1.

TAXING.

ἀπογραφή, registry, enrolment. A register *or* catalogue *of those capable of military duty, or of citizens, their names, property, etc.*, (*non occ.*)

Luke ii. 2. | Acts v. 37.

TEACH (-EST, -ETH, -ING, TAUGHT.)

1. διδάσκω, to teach, to give instruction *or* direction.

   (a) *Part., with* εἰμί, to be; *i.e.* was teaching, *etc.*

2. παιδεύω, to train up a child; *not merely to instruct him; but* to educate, *i.e.* discipline, correct, admonish, train, etc.

3. μαθητεύω, to disciple; *with a Dative*, to be the disciple of *any one*, (Matt. xxvii. 57); *with an Accusative, as here*, to make a disciple, to train as a disciple.

4. κατηχέω, to sound forth towards, to sound a thing in one's ears, impress it *upon one* by word of mouth.

5. καταγγέλλω, to bring word down upon *any one; hence*, announce, publish.

1. Matt. iv. 23.
1. —— v. 2, 19 twice.
1a. —— vii. 29.
1. —— ix. 35.
1. —— xi. 1.
1. —— xiii. 54.
1. —— xv. 9.
1. —— xxi. 23 part.
1. —— xxii. 16.
1. —— xxvi. 55 (*om.* G → ℵ*.)
1. —— xxviii. 15.
3. —— 19.
1. Mark i. 21.
1a. —— 22.
1. —— ii. 13.
1. —— iv. 1, 2.
1. —— vi. 2, 6, 30, 34.
1. —— vii. 7.
1. —— viii. 31.
1. —— ix. 31.
1. —— x. 1.
1. —— xi. 17.
1. —— xii. 14, 35.
1. —— xiv. 49.
1. Luke iv. 15.
1a. —— 31.
1. —— v. 3, 17.
1. —— vi. 6.
1. —— xi. 1 twice.
1. —— xii. 12.
1. —— xiii. 10, 22, 26
1a. —— xix. 47.
1. —— xx. 1 part., 21 twice.
1. —— xxi. 37.
1. —— xxiii. 5.
— John vi. 45, see Taught.
1. —— 59 part.
1. —— vii. 14, 28 part., 35.
1. —— viii. 2 (*ap.*), 20, 28.
1. —— ix. 34.
1. —— xiv. 26.
1. —— xviii. 20.
1. Acts i. 1.
1. —— iv. 2, 18.
1. Acts v. 21, 25, 28, 42.
1. —— xi. 26.
3. —— xiv. 21.
1. —— xv. 1. 35.
5. —— xvi. 21.
1. —— xviii. 11, 25.
1. —— xx. 20.
1. —— xxi. 21, 28.
2. —— xxii. 3.
1. —— xxviii. 31.
1. Rom. ii. 21 twice.
1. —— xii. 7.
— 1 Cor. ii. 13 twice, see T (which one)
1. —— iv. 17.
1. —— xi. 14.
4. —— xiv. 19.
1. Gal. i. 12.
4. —— vi. 6.
1. Eph. iv. 21.
1. Col. i. 28.
1. —— ii. 7.
1. —— iii. 16.
— 1 Thes. iv. 9, see T of God.
1. 2 Thes. ii. 15.
— 1 Tim. i. 3, see T another doctrine.
1. —— ii. 12.
— —— iii. 2, see T (apt to)
1. —— iv. 11.
1. —— vi. 2.
— —— 3, see T otherwise.
1. 2 Tim. ii. 2.
— —— 24, see T (apt to)
— Tit. i. 9, T (as he hath been)
1. —— 11.
— —— ii. 4, see Sober.
— —— 4, see *Wise.*
2. —— 12.
1. Heb v. 12.
1. —— viii. 11.
1. 1 John ii. 27 3 times.
1. Rev. ii. 14, 20.

TEACH ANOTHER DOCTRINE.

ἑτεροδιδασκαλέω, (*No.* 1, *with* ἑτερός, another, *prefixed*) to teach another thing, *i.e.* different, teach another and different doctrine, (*occ.* 1 Tim. vi. 3.)

1 Tim. i. 3.

TEACH OTHERWISE.

ἑτεροδιδασκαλέω, *see above.*

1 Tim. vi. 3.

TEACH (APT TO)

διδακτικός, didactic; apt to teach, skilled in teaching.

1 Tim. iii. 2. | 2 Tim. ii. 24.

TAUGHT.

διδακτός, taught, instructed. *Here,* ἔσονται πάντες διδακτοὶ θεοῦ, they shall all be God's taught ones.

John vi. 45.

TEACHETH (WHICH ONE)

διδακτός, taught, instructed, (*occ.* John vi. 45.)

1 Cor. ii. 13 twice.

TAUGHT (AS HE HATH BEEN)

{ κατὰ, according to
{ διδαχή, the teaching.

Tit. i. 9, marg. *in teaching.*

TAUGHT OF GOD.

Θεοδίδακτος, God-taught, (*non occ.*)

1 Thes. iv. 9.

TEACHER (-S.)

διδάσκαλος, a teacher, instructor, master. *A term distinct from* κῆρυξ, herald, *and* εὐαγγελιστής, evangelist.

John iii. 2.
Acts xiii. 1.
Rom. ii. 20.
1 Cor. xii. 28, 29.
Eph. ii. 11.
1 Tim. i. 7, see Law.
1 Tim. ii. 7.
2 Tim. i. 11.
— iv. 3.
Tit. ii. 3, see T of good [things.
Heb. v. 12.
2 Pet. ii. 1, see T (false)

TEACHER OF GOOD THINGS.

καλοδιδάσκαλος, teaching that which is beautiful or good, (*see* "GOOD," *No.* 2); *as subst.*, teacher of good.

Tit. ii. 3.

TEACHERS (FALSE)

ψευδοδιδάσκαλος, a false teacher; *here, pl.*

2 Pet. ii. 1.

TEACHING.

διδασκαλία, teaching, instruction, (lxx. *for* מלמדה, Is. xxix. 13, and אלוף, Prov. ii. 17.

Rom. xii. 7. | Tit. i. 9 marg., see Taught (as he hath been)

TEAR (-S.) [noun.]

δάκρυ *or* δάκρυον, a tear; *pl.* τὰ δάκρυα, tears; (lxx. *for* בדמעה, 2 Kings xx. 5.)

Mark ix. 24 (*om.* μετὰ δακρύων, *with tears,* L T Tr A ℵ.)
Luke vii. 38, 44.
Acts xx. 19, 31.
2 Cor. ii. 4.
2 Tim. i. 4.
Heb. v. 7.
— xii. 17.
Rev. vii. 17.
Rev. xxi. 4.

TEAR (-ETH, TARE, TORN.)

1. σπαράσσω, to tear, rend; lacerate, (*occ.* Mark ix. 26.)
2. ῥήγνυμι, to rend, tear, break, burst.
3. συσπαράσσω, (*No.* 1, *with* σύν, together with, *prefixed*) to tear *or* lacerate altogether, tear violently, (*non occ.*)

1. Mark i. 26 part.
2. — ix. 18, marg. *dash.*
Mark ix. 20 (No. 3, L T [Tr^m ℵ.)
1. Luke ix. 39.
3. Luke ix. 42.

TEDIOUS UNTO (BE)

ἐγκόπτω, to strike in, cut in; *hence,* to impede, hinder, weary.

Acts xxiv. 4.

TELL, TOLD.

1. εἶπον, (*aor.* 2 *of obs. root* ἔπω) to utter definite words, to enunciate words and things to auditors, and commune respecting them, to speak *or* utter words successively, communicate by words.
   (a) ἀποκριθεὶς...εἶπε. He answering, said.
2. λέγω, *see* "SAY," *No.* 1.
3. ἀπαγγέλλω, to give intelligence, bring word from *any person or place,* to relate, inform of, to tell *what had occurred.*
4. ἀναγγέλλω, to give up intelligence, announce, make known, declare.
5. λαλέω, *see* "SAY," *No.* 5.
6. ἐκλαλέω, to speak out, tell, disclose.
7. ἐρῶ, *see* "SAY," *No.* 4.
8. διηγέομαι, to lead *or* conduct through *to the end; hence,* to go through with, recount.

9. ἐξηγέομαι, to lead *or* conduct out; to lead *or* bring out, bring out *in conversation*, make known.

10. διασαφέω, to make clear, make fully manifest; (lxx. *for* באר, Deut. i. 5.)

11. μηνύω, to disclose *something before unknown*, to reveal *a secret*.

1. Matt. viii. 4.
3. —— 33.
2. —— x. 27.
1. —— xii. 48 (No. 2, L T Tr A ℵ.)
3. —— xiv. 12.
1. —— xvi. 20.
1. —— xvii. 9.
— —— xviii. 15, see Fault.
1. —— 17.
10. —— 31.
1. —— xxi. 5, 24 1st.
7. —— 24 2nd.
— —— 27 1st, see Can.
2. —— 27 2nd.
1. —— xxii. 4, 17.
1. —— xxiv. 3.
— —— 25, see T before.
5. —— xxvi. 13.
1. —— 63.
1. —— xxviii. 7 twice.
3. —— 9 (ap.), 10.
2. Mark i. 30.
4. —— v. 14 (No. 3, G L T Tr A ℵ.)
8. —— 16.
4. —— 19 (No. 3, L T Tr A ℵ.)
1. —— 33.
3. —— vi. 30.
1. —— vii. 36 (No. 2, T Tr A ℵ.)
2. —— viii. 30 (No. 1, L.)
1. —— 26.
8. —— ix. 9.
1a. —— 12.
2. —— x. 32.
7. —— xi. 29.
— —— 33 1st, see Can.
2. —— 33 2nd.
1. —— xiii. 4. [(ap.)
3. —— xvi. 10 (ap.), 13
1. —— 7.
5. Luke i. 45.
5. —— ii. 17 18, 20.
2. —— iv. 25.
1. —— v. 14.
8. —— vii. 22.
1. —— 42 (om. εἰπὲ tell me, G → L T Tr A^b ℵ.)
3. —— viii. 20, 34, 36.
1. —— 56.
8. —— ix. 10.
2. —— 27.
3. —— 36.
2. —— x. 24.
2. —— xii. 51, 59.
3. —— xiii. 1.
2. —— 3, 5, 27.
1. —— 32.
2. —— xvii. 34.
2. —— xviii. 8, 14.
3. —— 37.
2. —— xix. 40.
1. —— xx. 2.
— Luke. xx. 7.
2. —— 8.
2. —— xxii. 34.
1. —— 67 twice.
3. —— xxiv. 9.
2. —— 10.
9. —— 35.
— John iii. 8.
1. —— 12 1st.
— —— 12 2nd, see T of.
4. —— iv. 25.
1. —— 29, 39.
3. —— 51 (ἀγγέλλω, *bring word*, T Tr^b A^b ℵ.)
4. —— v. 15 (No. 1, L^m ℵ.)
— —— viii. 14, see Can.
5. —— 40.
2. —— 45.
1. —— ix. 27.
1. —— x. 24, 25.
1. —— xi. 46.
2. —— xii. 22 twice.
2. —— xiii. 19.
1. —— xiv. 2.
7. —— 29.
1. —— xvi. 4.
2. —— 7.
— —— 18, see Can.
1. —— xviii. 8, 34.
1. —— xx. 15.
3. —— 18 (ἀγγέλλω, *bring word*, L T Tr A ℵ.)
1. Acts v. 8.
3. —— 22, 25.
5. —— ix. 6.
5. —— x. 6 (ap.)
5. —— xi. 14.
3. —— xii. 14.
3. —— xv. 27.
3. —— xvi. 36.
4. —— 38 (No. 3, L T Tr A ℵ.)
2. —— xvii. 21.
5. —— xxii. 10.
3. —— 26.
2. —— 27.
3. —— xxiii. 16, 17, 19.
6. —— 22.
11. —— 30 part.
5. —— xxvii. 25.
— 1 Cor. xiii. 3, see T before.
4. 2 Cor. vii. 7 part.
— —— xii. 2 twice, 3, see Can.
— Gal. iv. 16, see Truth.
2. —— 21.
— —— v. 21, see T in times past.
2. Phil. iii. 18 twice.
2. 2 Thes. ii. 5.
8. Heb. xi. 32.
2. Jude 18.
7. Rev. xvii. 7.

TELL BEFORE.

προεῖπον, *No.* 1, *with* πρό, before, *prefixed.*

Matt. xxiv. 25. | 2 Cor. xiii. 3.

TELL IN TIMES PAST.

προεῖπον, *see above.*

Gal. v. 21.

TELL OF.

2 John iii. 12.

TEMPER TOGETHER.

συγκεράννυμι, to mix together, to intermingle with, to join together, to temper.

1 Cor. xii. 24
Heb. iv. 2.

TEMPERANCE.

ἐγκράτεια, mastery *or* dominion over; self-command, self-control, (*opp. to self-indulgence*) the grace by which the flesh is controlled, (*non occ.*)

Acts xxiv. 25. | Gal. v. 23.
2 Pet. i. 6 twice.

TEMPERATE.

1. ἐγκρατής, having power over, being master of *one's self*, having self-control, (*non occ.*)

2. σώφρων, of sound mind; sanæ mentis; *hence*, discreet, prudent; *esp.*, free from sensual desires, temperate.

1. Tit. i. 8. | 2. Tit. ii. 2.

TEMPERATE (BE)

ἐγκρατεύομαι, to exercise power *or* mastery over; *hence*, to exercise self-control; (lxx. *for* התאפק, Gen. xliii. 31), (*occ.* 1 Cor. vii. 9.)

1 Cor. ix. 25.

TEMPEST.

1. θύελλα, a tempest, whirlwind; (lxx. *for* ערפל, Deut. iv. 11; v. 22), (*non occ.*)

2. λαῖλαψ, a tempest *of wind with rain;* (lxx. *for* סער, Jer. xxxv. 32; סערה, Job xxxviii. 1; סופה, Job xxi. 18.)

3. σεισμός, motion, a shaking, concussion; (lxx. *for* סערה שערה, Jer. xxiii. 19; Neh. i. 3.)

4. χειμών, rain, storm with rain, foul weather, wintry weather.

3. Matt. viii. 24.
— Acts xxvii. 18, see T (be tossed with)
4. Acts xxvii. 20.
1. Heb. xii. 18.
2. 2 Pet. ii. 17.

TEMPEST (BE TOSSED WITH)

χειμάζω, to storm, to raise a storm. *Here, pass.*, to be storm-beaten, to be tempest-tossed.

Acts xxvii. 18.

TEMPESTUOUS.

τυφωνικός, like a typhoon, *i.e.* like a whirlwind, tempestuous, (*non occ.*)

Acts xxvii. 14.

TEMPLE (-s.)

1. ἱερόν, a place consecrated *or* sacred as given *or* devoted to God, a place that subserves a sacred purpose, *as* the Temple, *and as* the sacred things themselves; (*e.g.* τά ἱερά *are* the sacrifices; ἱερεύς *is* the person who offers them; τὸ ἱερὸν *is* the place where they are offered). ἱερὸν *is used of* the whole compass of the sacred enclosure, including the outer courts, porches, and all the other subordinate buildings appertaining to the Temple. (*This word must be carefully distinguished in every passage from No.* 2.) (*non occ.*)

2. ναός, dwelling, habitation (*of God*); the interior and most sacred part of *No.* 1, where the presence of God was manifested; the Holy place, *or* the Holy of Holies.

[NOTE.

There are seven buildings mentioned in Scripture:—1st, *The Mosaic Tabernacle* (translated "*Temple*," 1 Sam. i. 9; iii. 3); lasted 500 years, and was superseded by the 2nd, *Solomon's Temple*, 1 Kings vi. 7; lasted 400 years, and destroyed by Nebuchadnezzar. 3rd, *Zerubbabel's Temple*, Ezra iv. 1, 2; lasted 500 years, and destroyed by Antiochus Epiphanes. 4th, *Herod's Temple*, John ii. 9; 46 years in building, lasted 85 years, destroyed by Titus. 5th, "*The Temple of God*," 2 Thes. ii. 4, yet to be built and indwelt by "the man of sin," the anti-Christ. 6th, *The Millenial Temple*, Ezek. xli.—xliv. 7th, *The Heavenly Temple*, Rev. xxi. 3, 22.] (*occ.* Acts xix. 24.)

3. { ὁ, the / οἶκος, house. } [The whole "saying" in Luke xi. 51 is a reference to 2 Chron xxiv. 18-22, verse 19 being amplified to show the purpose and counsel of God in the historical notice of the facts.]

1. Matt. iv. 5.
1. — xii. 5, 6.
1. — xxi. 12 twice, 14, 15, 23.
2. — xxiii. 16 twice, 17, 21, 35.
1. — xxiv. 1 twice.
1. — xxvi. 55.
2. —— 61.
2. — xxvii. 5, 40, 51.
1. Mark xi. 11, 15 twice, 16, 27.
1. — xii. 35.
1. — xiii. 1, 3.
1. — xiv. 49.
2. —— 58.
2. — xv. 29, 38.
2. Luke i. 9, 21, 22.
1. — ii. 27, 37, 46.
1. — iv. 9.
3. — xi. 51.
1. — xviii. 10.
1. — xix. 45, 47.
1. — xx. 1.
1. — xxi. 5, 37, 38.
1. — xxii. 52, 53.
2. — xxiii. 45.
1. — xxiv. 53.
1. John ii. 14, 15.
2. —— 19, 20, 21.
1. — v. 14.
1. — vii. 14, 28.
1. — viii. 2 (*ap.*), 20, 59.
1. — x. 23.
1. — xi. 56.
1. — xviii. 20.
1. Acts ii. 46.
1. Acts iii. 1, 2 twice, 3, 8, 10.
1. — iv. 1.
1. — v. 20, 21, 24, 25, 42.
2. — vii. 48 (*om.* G L T Tr A ℵ, i.e. *in hand-wrought places.*)
2. — xvii. 24.
1. — xix. 27.
1. — xxi. 26, 27, 28, 29, 30.
1. — xxii. 17.
1. — xxiv. 6, 12, 18.
1. — xxv. 8.
1. — xxvi. 21.
2. 1 Cor. iii. 16, 17 twice.
2. — vi. 19.
— — viii. 10, see Idols.
1. — ix. 13.
2. 2 Cor. vi. 16 twice.
2. Eph. ii. 21.
2. 2 Thes. ii. 4.
2. Rev. iii. 12.
2. — vii. 15.
2. — xi. 1, 2, 19 twice.
2. — xiv. 15 (*om.* G →)
2. —— 17.
2. — xv. 5.
2. —— 6 (*om.* ἐκ τοῦ ναοῦ, *out of the temple*, G → Trb.)
2. —— 8 twice.
2. — xvi. 1 (*om.* ἐκ τοῦ ναοῦ, *out of the temple*, G ⇉ Trb.)
2. —— 17.
2. — xxi. 22 twice.

TEMPORAL.

πρόσκαιρος, for a season.

2 Cor. iv. 18.

TEMPT (-ED, -ETH, -ING.)

1. πειράζω, to make trial of, to try; to put to the test, (*gen. in a good sense, in order to ascertain the character, views, or feelings of any one*); *also, in a bad sense, with ill intent*, to tempt.

2. ἐκπειράζω, (*No.* 1, *with* ἐκ, out, *prefixed*) to try out, try thoroughly.

and in a bad sense; (lxx. *for* נסה, Deut. vi. 16; viii. 16; Ps. lxxviii. 18), (*non occ.*)

1. Matt. iv. 1.
2. —— 7.
1. —— xvi. 1.
1. —— xix. 3.
1. —— xxii. 18, 35.
1. Mark i. 13.
1. —— viii. 11.
1. —— x. 2.
1. —— xii. 15.
1. Luke iv. 2.
2. —— 12.
2. —— x. 25.
1. —— xi. 16.
1. —— xx. 23 (*ap.*)
1. John viii. 6 (*ap.*)
1. Acts v. 9.
1. —— xv. 10.
1. 1 Cor. vii. 5.
2. —— x. 9 1st.
1. —— 9 2nd (No. 2, Lm [א.)
1. —— 13.
1. Gal. vi. 1.
1. 1 Thes. iii. 5.
1. Heb. ii. 18 twice.
1. —— iii. 9.
1. —— iv. 15 (πειράω, *to try*, Sᵗ G [illegible])
1. —— xi. 37.
1. Jas. i. 13 1st.
1. —— 13 2nd.
— —— 13 3rd, see T (cannot be)
1. —— 13 4th.
1. —— 14.

TEMPTED (CANNOT BE)

{ εἰμί, to be / ἀπείραστος, incapable of being tempted, temptation-proof, (*non occ.*) } *lit.* is not to be tempted

Jas. i. 13.

TEMPTATION (-s.)

πειρασμός, a putting to the test, proof, trial; ***also, in a bad sense,*** temptation, (*occ.* 1 Pet. iv. 12.)

Matt. vi. 13.
—— xxvi. 41.
Mark xiv. 38.
Luke iv. 13.
—— viii. 13.
—— xi. 4.
—— xxii. 28, 40, 46.
Acts xx. 19.
1 Cor. x. 13 twice.
Gal. iv. 14.
1 Tim. vi. 2.
Heb. iii. 8.
Jas. i. 2, 12.
1 Pet. i. 6.
2 Pet. ii. 9.
Rev. iii. 10.

TEMPTER.

{ ὁ, the / πειράζων, tempting / *one*, } the one who tempts, the tempter.

Matt. iv. 3. | 1 Thes. iii. 5.

TEN.

δέκα, ten.

[As a typical number it stands connected with God's testimony to man, by command *or* by judgment. It is also expressive of man's responsibility to God. In each case a part is put for and denotes the whole, *e.g.* ten generations of antediluvians; ten plagues on Egypt; ten nations of Canaan (Gen. xv. 18); ten burdens laid on Isaiah to the nations grouped around Babylon; Jeremiah's prophecies fall into ten against the Gentiles; the toes of Nebuchadnezzar's image; the ten virgins; and so with the tithes. ***See further under*** "THREE."]

Matt. xviii. 24, see Thousand.
—— xx. 24.
—— xxv. 1, 28.
Mark x. 41.
Luke xiv. 31.
—— xv. 8.
—— xvii. 12, 17.
—— xix. 13 twice, 16, 17, 24, 25.
Acts xxiii. 23, see T (three score and)
—— xxv. 6.
1 Cor. iv. 15, } see Thousand.
—— xiv. 19, }
Jude 14, }
Rev. ii. 10.
—— v. 11, see Thousand.
—— xii. 3.
—— xiii. 1 twice.
Rev. xvii. 3, 7, 12 twice, 16.

TEN (THREE SCORE AND)

ἑβδομήκοντα, seventy.

Acts xxiii. 23.

TENDER.

1. ἁπαλός, soft, tender, ***spoken of the shoot of a tree, also of flesh;*** (lxx. *for* רך, Gen. xviii. 7), (*non occ.*)

2. σπλάγχνα, bowels; ***hence,*** yearning; ***here,*** yearning ***compassion.***

1. Matt. xxiv. 32.
1. Mark. xiii. 28.
2. Luke i. 78, marg. bowels.
— Jas. v. 11, see Mercy.

TENDER-HEARTED.

εὔσπλαγχνος, tenderly *or* yearningly affectionate, (*occ.* 1 Pet. iii. 8.)

Eph. iv. 32.

TENT MAKER (-s.)

σκηνοποιός, a tent-maker, (*non occ.*)

Acts xviii. 3 (*ap.*)

TENTH.

1. δέκατος, the tenth.

2. δεκάτη, a tenth part, a tithe.

1. John i. 39.
2. Heb. vii. 4.
1. Rev. xi. 13.
1. —— xxi. 20.

TENTH PART.

2. Heb. vii. 2.

TERRESTRIAL.

ἐπίγειος, upon earth, *i.e.* earthly, terrestrial, belonging to the earth, (i.e. ***to earth as opposed to heaven, or land as opposed to water.***)

1 Cor. xv. 40 twice.

TERRIBLE.

φοβερός, fearful, terrible, frightful; (lxx. *for* נורא, Gen. xxviii. 17; Deut. x. 17.)

Heb. xii. 21.

TERRIFY (-IED.)

1. πτυέω, to terrify, put in trepidation; (lxx. *for* חרד, Ex. xix. 16; חתת, 1 Ch. xxviii. 30; Jer. i. 17), (*non occ.*)

2. πτύρω, to frighten, scare; *esp. of horses*, to shy, start, (*non occ.*)

3. ἐκφοβέω, to frighten outright, terrify greatly; (lxx. *for* החריד, Lev. xxvi. 6; Zeph. iii. 14; חתת, Job vii. 14), (*non occ.*)

1. Luke xxi. 9.
1. — xxiv. 37.
3. 2 Cor. x. 9.
2. Phil. i. 28.

TERROR.

φόβος, fear, terror, affright.

Rom. xiii. 3.
1 Pet. iii. 14.
2 Cor. v. 11.

TESTAMENT.

διαθήκη, *in classical Greek it denotes* a last will and testament, *but in the Scriptures it is used always of the Heb.* ברית, *to which the word* "*testament*" *has no correspondence.* ברית *is* a covenant, agreement, *from* ברה, to cut, *because* the victims were cut in two, *or* divided, in making covenants, (Gen. xv. 9; Jer. xxxiv. 18, 19); *hence, it denotes* a covenant made either conditionally between two parties, *or* unconditionally by one, (*as by God with Abraham and David.*)

* *For the use of the translation,* "covenant," with that of "testator," *see below, under* "TESTATOR."

Matt. xxvi. 28.
Mark xiv. 24.
Luke xxii. 20.
Rom. ix. 4, marg. (text, *covenant.*)
1 Cor. xi. 25.
2 Cor. iii. 6, 14.
Gal. iii. 15, marg. (text, *covenant.*)
Gal. iv. 24, marg. (text, *covenant.*)
Heb. vii. 22.
— viii. 6, marg. (text, *covenant.*)
— ix. 15 twice, 16*, 17*, 20.
— xii. 24, } marg. (text
— xiii. 20, } *covenant.*)
Rev. xi. 19.

TESTATOR.

{ ὁ, the *one* διαθεμένος, making a covenant, } that which makes the covenant, (*see above.*)

[Here, the context (Heb. ix. 16, 17) must be read as follows:—

γάρ, for.
ὅπου, where.
διαθήκη, a covenant [*is*].
θάνατον, a death [*is*].
ἀνάγκη, necessary.
φέρεσθαι, to be brought in.
τοῦ, of him *or* that.
διαθεμένου, that makes the covenant.
γάρ, for.
διαθήκη, a covenant.
ἐπί, over.
νεκροῖς, dead *ones or victims* [*is*].
βεβαία, sure.
ἐπεί, since.
μήποτε, at no time.
ἰσχύει, has it force.
ὅτε, when.
ζῇ, he is living.
ὁ, the *one who is.*
διαθέμενος, making the covenant.

Thus it is all clear, when we remember that He who makes the covenant of which the apostle speaks, is Himself the victim, and hence must of necessity die.]

Heb. ix. 16, 17.

TESTIFY (-ED, -ETH, -ING.)

1. μαρτυρέω, to be a witness, bear witness; to be able and ready to attest anything that one knows, *and therefore*, to state with a certain degree of authority, (*usually* for *something*); *and hence*, to confirm *or* prove, to witness in favour.

2. ἐπιμαρτυρέω, (*No.* 1, *with* ἐπί, upon, *prefixed*) to bear witness upon, testify emphatically, to appear as a witness decidedly for *anything*, (*non occ.*)

3. μαρτύρομαι, to witness for one's self, to call to witness, invoke as witness, to attest and ratify as truth, (*occ.* Acts xx. 26.)

4. διαμαρτύρομαι, (*No.* 3, *with* διά, through, *prefixed*) to call throughout to witness, (*viz. God and men and all beings*); to affirm with solemn protestations; to testify through and through, bear full and complete witness; to conjure any one, exhort earnestly.

4. Luke xvi. 28.
1. John ii. 25.
1. —— iii. 11, 32.
1. —— iv. 39, 44.
1. —— v. 39.
1. —— vii. 7.
1. —— xiii. 21.
1. —— xv. 26.
1. —— xxi. 24.
4. Acts ii. 40.
4. —— viii. 25 part.
4. —— x. 42.
4. —— xviii. 5.
4. —— xx. 21, 24.
4. —— xxiii. 11.
1. —— xxvi. 5.
4. —— xxviii. 23.
1. 1 Cor. xv. 15.
3. Gal. v. 3.
3. Eph. iv. 17.
4. 1 Thes. iv. 6.
— 1 Tim. ii. 16, see T (to be)
4. Heb. ii. 6.
1. —— vii. 17.
1. —— xi. 4.
— 1 Pet. i. 11, see T beforehand.
2. —— v. 12.
1. 1 John iv. 14.
1. —— v. 9.
1. 3 John 3.
1. Rev. xxii. 16.
— —— 18, see T unto.
1. Rev. xxii. 20.

TESTIFY BEFOREHAND.

προμαρτύρομαι, (*No.* 3, *with* πρό, before, *prefixed*) to call to witness beforehand, *etc.*, (*non occ.*)

1 Pet. i. 11 part.

TESTIFY UNTO.

συμμαρτυρέω, (*No.* 1, *with* σύν, together with, *prefixed*) to witness with, bear witness together with others, *i.e. at the same time and* to the same effect. (*Here, mid.*)

Rev. xxii. 18 (No. 1, G L T Tr A ℵ.)

TESTIFIED (TO BE)

μαρτύριον, witness *as borne*, (*see below, No.* 1) that which was to be testified. *Here,* the testimony *in its own seasons,* (*i.e. in its own appointed seasons*) *or* the testimony *to be rendered, etc.*

1 Tim. ii. 6 (om. L T), marg. *testimony.*

TESTIMONY.

1. μαρτύριον, witness, testimony *as borne;* the declaration which confirms *or* makes known any thing.

2. μαρτυρία, a bearing witness, certifying; a testimony that informs as well as corroborates; that which any one witnesses *or* states concerning *any person or thing.*

1. Matt. viii. 4.
1. —— x. 18.
1. Mark i. 44.
1. —— vi. 11.
1. —— xiii. 9
1. Luke v. 14.
1. —— ix. 5.
1. —— xxi. 13.
2. John iii. 32, 33.
2. —— v. 34.
2. —— vii. 17.
2. —— xxi. 24.
2. Acts xxii. 18.
1. 1 Cor. i. 6.
1. 1 Cor. ii. 1. (μυστήριον, *mystery,* G~ℵ)
1. 2 Cor. i. 12.
1. 2 Thes. i. 10.
1. 1 Tim. ii. 6, marg. *to be testified.*
1. 2 Tim. i. 8.
1. Heb. iii. 5.
— —— xi. 5, see T (have)
2. Rev. i. 2, 9.
2. —— vi. 9.
2. —— xi. 7.
2. —— xii. 11, 17.
1. —— xv. 5.
2. Rev. xix. 10 twice.

TESTIMONY (HAVE)

μαρτύρεω, *see* "TESTIFY," *No.* 1.

Heb. xi. 5

TETRARCH.

1. τετράρχης, a tetrarch, the ruler of the fourth part of a district or province. *Later, it became* a common title for those who governed a province or kingdom, subject to the Roman emperor.

2. τετραρχέω, to be a τετράρχης, (*see No.* 1) *here part.*, being tetrarch.

1. Matt. xiv. 1.
— Luke iii. 1 1st, see T (be.)
2. Luke iii. 1 2nd & 3rd.
1. —— iii. 19.
1. —— ix. 7
1. Acts xiii. 1.

TETRARCH (BE)

2. Luke iii. 1 1st.

THADDEUS.

Θαδδαῖος, Thaddeus; a surname of the Apostle Jude, also called Lebbeus the brother of James the less.

Matt. x. 3 (om. ὁ ἐπικληθεὶς Θαδδαῖος, *whose surname was Thaddeus,* G→T A), (om. Λεββαῖος ὁ ἐπικληθεὶς, *Lebbæus, whose surname was,* L Tr.)
Mark iii. 18.

THAN.

THAN is frequently the translation of the Genitive case of a noun when it follows an adjective of the comparative degree, *e.g.* μείζων τοῦ κυρίου, *greater than his lord,* (John xiii. 16); μείζων τούτων (1 Cor. xiii. 13); πλεῖον τούτων, *more than these* (John xxi. 15); χείρων ἀπίστου, *worse than an unbeliever* (1 Tim. v. 8.)

When THAN is the translation of a separate Greek word it is one of these following:—

1. ἤ, *after a comparative,* than; *after a positive,* rather than, more than.

2. { ἀλλὰ, but, / ἤ, than, } unless, except.

3. παρά, beside.

(a) *with Gen.*, beside and proceeding from, from beside.

(b) *with Dat.*, beside and at; at the side of.

(c) *with Acc.*, to *or* along the side of; beside *with the idea of comparison* (*instituting the comparison but leaving the superiority to be inferred*); above, rather than, better than, than.

4. ὑπέρ, over.

(a) *with Gen.*, over and separate from; above, on behalf.

(b) *with Acc.*, over and towards; beyond, above, (*asserting superiority*.)

5. πλήν, more than, over and above; *hence*, besides, expect.

6. ἤπερ, than perhaps, than indeed.

— Matt. v. 37, see T these.
1. —— x. 15.
1. —— xi. 22, 24.
— —— xviii. 8, 9, see Rather.
1. ——— 13.
1. —— xix. 24.
1. —— xxvi. 53.
1. Mark vi. 11 (*ap.*)
1. —— ix. 43, 45, 47.
1. —— x. 25.
— —— xii. 31, see T these.
3c. Luke iii. 13.
1. —— x. 12, 14.
4b. —— xvi. 8.
1. ——— 17.
1. —— xvii. 2.
— —— xviii. 14, see Rather.
1. ——— 25.
— John i. 50, see T these.
1. —— iii. 19.
1. —— iv. 1.
— —— v. 20, } see
— —— vii. 31, } T these.
6. —— xii. 43.
— —— xiv. 12, } see
— —— xxi. 15, } T these.
1. Acts iv. 19.
1. —— v. 29.
5. —— xv. 28.
1. —— xx. 35.
1. Acts xxv. 6 (ἡμέρας οὐ πλείους ὀκτὼ ἢ δέκα, *not more than eight or ten days*, instead of ἡμέρας πλείους ἢ δέκα, *more than ten days*, A V[m] G L T Tr A ℵ.)
— —— xxvi. 22, see Other.
1. —— xxvii. 11.
— Rom. viii. 37, see Conqueror.
1. —— xiii. 11.
3c. 1 Cor. iii. 11.
1. —— vii. 9.
1. —— ix. 15.
1. —— xiv. 5, 19.
2. 2 Cor. 1, 13, *om.* ἀλλὰ, L[b].)
3c. Gal. i. 8, 9.
1. —— iv. 27.
— Eph. iii. 8, see Least.
1. 1 Tim. i. 4.
1. 2 Tim. iii. 4.
3c. Heb. i. 4.
3c. —— ii. 7, marg. *to*.
3c. ——— 9.
3c. —— iii. 3.
4b. —— iv. 12.
3c. —— ix. 23.
3c. —— xi. 4.
1. ——— 25.
3c. —— xii. 24.
1. 1 Pet. iii. 17.
1. 2 Pet. ii. 21.
1. 1 John iv. 4.

THAN THESE.

τούτων, of these; *here, following a comparative*, than these.

Matt. v. 37.
Mark xii. 31.
John i. 50.
—— v. 20.
John vii. 31 (*om.* G → L T Tr A ℵ.)
—— xiv. 12.
—— xxi. 15.

THANK (-s.) [noun.]

1. χάρις, that which causes joy; *objectively*, personal gracefulness, a pleasing work; *subjectively*, an inclining towards, courteous *or* graceful disposition; *on the part of the giver*, kindness, favour, grace; *on the part of the receiver*, thanks, respect, homage.

2. εὐχαριστία, thankfulness, gratitude; a giving of thanks, expression of gratitude.

Luke vi. 32, 33, 34.
1 Cor. xv. 57.
2 Cor. ii. 14.
—— viii. 16.
2 Cor. ix. 15.
1 Thes. iii. 9.
1 Pet. ii. 20, marg. (text, *acceptable*.)
Rev. iv. 19.

THANKS (GIVE)

1. εὐχαριστέω, to show one's self grateful; give thanks.

2. ὁμολογέω, to speak *or* say the same *with another; hence*, to agree, coincide with, to grant, admit, confess; to expressly acknowledge, to make known one's profession, to confess.

3. ἀνθομολογέομαι, to mutually utter the same things. *In N.T., mid.*, to profess publicly *with others, i.e.* to praise, celebrate *alternately* (*as in the temple worship*), (*non occ.*)

1. Matt. xv. 36.
1. —— xxvi. 27.
1. Mark viii. 6.
1. —— xiv. 23 part.
3. Luke ii. 38.
1. —— xvii. 16.
1. —— xxii. 17, 19.
1. John vi. 11 part.
1. ——— 23 part (*om.* G→)
1. Acts xxvii. 35.
1. Rom. xiv. 6 twice.
1. —— xvi. 4.
1. 1 Cor. x. 30.
1. —— xi. 24 part.
1. —— xiv. 17.
1. Eph. i. 16.
1. —— v. 20.
1. Col. i. 3, 12.
1. —— iii. 17.
1. 1 Thes. i. 2.
1. —— v. 18.
1. 2 Thes. ii. 13.
2. Heb. xiii. 15, marg. *confess*.
1. Rev. xi. 17.

THANKS ARE GIVEN.

1. 2 Cor. i. 11 (passive.)

THANKS (GIVING OF)

1. 1 Cor. xiv. 16.
1. Eph. v. 4.
1. 1 Tim. ii. 1.

THANK (-ED.) [verb.]

1. εὐχαριστέω, *see above, No.* 1.

2. ἐξομολογέω, to speak out the same things as another; *hence*, to confess fully; make acknowledgements *as for benefits, i.e.* to give thanks, praise.

3. { χάρις, *see* "THANKS," *No.* 1, ἔχω, to have, } to have gratitude.

2. Matt. xi. 25.
2. Luke x. 21.
3. —— xvii. 9.
1. —— xviii. 11.
1. John xi. 41.
1. Acts xxviii. 15.
1. Rom. i. 8.
— —— vi. 17, see T (God be)
1. —— vii. 25 (χάρις, *thanks to*, instead of εὐχαριστῶ, *I thank*, G∾L T Tr A.)
1. 1 Cor. i. 4, 14.
1. —— xiv. 18.
1. Phil. i. 3.
1. 1 Thes. ii. 13.
1. 2 Thes. i. 3.
3. 1 Tim. i. 12.
3. 2 Tim. i. 3.
1. Philem. 4.

THANKED (GOD BE)

χάρις, thanks [be] / τῷ, to *the*, / Θεῷ, to God, — thanks be to God.

Rom. vi. 17.

THANKFUL (BE)

1. εὐχαριστέω, *see* "THANK," *No.* 1.
2. εὐχάριστος, grateful, pleasing, / γίνομαι, to become.

1. Rom. i. 21. | 2. Col. iii. 15.

THANKFULNESS.

εὐχαριστία, thankfulness, gratitude, a giving of thanks.

Acts xxiv. 3.

THANKSGIVING.

1. εὐχαριστία, *see above.*
2. χάρις, *see* "THANKS," *No.* 1.

2. 1 Cor. x. 30, marg. (text, *grace.*)
1. 2 Cor. iv. 15.
1. —— ix. 11, 12.
1. Phil. iv. 6.
1. Col. ii. 7.
1. —— iv. 2.
1. 1 Tim. iv. 3, 4.
1. Rev. vii. 12.

THANKWORTHY.

χάρις, *see* "THANKS," *No.* 1.

1 Pet. ii. 19.

THAT. [conj.; demonstr. pron.; and relat. pron.]

"THAT" is frequently the translation of the Accusative of the noun with inf. of the verb; also of the article with participle, *he who, he that, that which, etc.*, of which there are at least 1,200 occurrences; sometimes the article with an adjective is rendered "*he that is* [*good*]," *etc.*

(*For various combinations with other words, see below, the list of references.*)

When "THAT" is the translation of a separate word in the Greek, it is one of these following.

Conjunctions :—

1. ἵνα, that, in order that, to the end that, *with the emphasis on the purpose, design, and result,* (*not on the manner or method as with No.* 3.) *It must also be distinguished from No.* 2, *which is objective, and introduces the matter, while No.* 1 specifies the purpose. *Thus* "*hope*" *is followed by No.* 2, *which presents the object of the hope, while* "prayer" is *followed by No.* 1, *showing* the purpose and design *of the prayer.*

Then, as to the degrees of the result, No. 1 *marks* the primary result, *while No.* 3 *marks the secondary.*

This final *significance of* ἵνα *is always present, if not always discernible.*

ἵνα *is generally followed by the subjunctive mood, to signify the objective possibility or intention,* in order that it might be.

But in passages marked

(a) *it is followed by the indicative, pointing to* the fact *rather than the possibility.*

(b) *it is followed by the optative, denoting* a wish *rather than possibility.*

2. ὅτι, that, because, *with emphasis on the cause, and expressive of the reason or matter of a communication, etc.* ὅτι *is objective, having reference not to the design, but to the* cause, (*see further, under No.* 1.)

3. ὅπως, in order that, *with emphasis on the manner and method;* in such manner that, to the end that; so that ὅπως *has* an eventual aspect, and (*unlike* ἵνα) *is used with the future, and*

(a) *occasionally associated with* ἄν, (*which implies the condition of uncertainty.*) *See further, under No.* 1.)

4. ὡς, *in comparative sentences,* as; *in objective,* that; *in final,* in order to; *in causal,* for on the ground that.

5. ὥστε, so as that, so that, so as to, (*expressive of event, result, or consequence.*)

6. τοῦ, of the, *before the infinitive*, of *or* from *whatever is the subject of the verb*, "of returning," "from doing sacrifice," etc.

7. εἰς τὸ, *with the infinitive*, to the end that, *expressing purpose.*

8. ἐν τὸ, *with the infinitive*, in that; *esp. relating to time*, during, while.

9. εἰ, if, (*see* "IF," *No.* 1.)

10. { ἀφ', from / ᾗς, which. }

11. διὰ τὸ, *with the inf.*, on account of. *Here*, "*of* [*their teaching.*]"

12. ὅτε, when, (*relating to an actual event, something actually taking place.*)

13. ὅταν, whensoever, (*followed by the subj. mood; hence, with the accessory idea of uncertainty*) whensoever, if ever, in case that.

14. πῶς, how, in what way *or* manner.

14a. καί, also, even.

Demonstr. pronouns:—

15. ἐκεῖνος, that, that one there, (*referring to the more remote*) emphatic.

16. τοῦτο, (*neut. sing. of* οὗτος) this, this here.

17. τοῦτον, (*Acc. of* οὗτος) this, this here.

18. ταύτην, (*Acc. fem. of* οὗτος) this, this here.

19. τούτου, (*masc. sing. Gen. of* οὗτος) of this, of this here.

20. ταύτῃ, (*Dat. sing. of* οὗτος) to this, to this here.

21. αὐτῷ, (*Dat. of* αὐτός) in the same, at the same.

22. καί, also, even.

Relative pronouns:—

23. { ὅς, who, which, that, ἐάν, if, (*implying a condition which experience must determine, i.e. an objective, future possibility*) } which if, whosoever, whatsoever.

24. ὅσος, how great, how much, how many; as much as, as many as.

25. ὅστις, who, one who; whoever, whatever.

1. Matt. i. 22.
25.—— ii. 6
3. ——— 8.
1. ——— 15.
2. ——— 16 1st, 22.
3. ——— 23.
1. —— iii. 9.
1. —— iv. 3.
2. ——— 12.
1. ——— 14.
3. —— v. 16.
2. ——— 17, 20, 21, 22, 23, 27, 28.
1. ——— 29 1st, 30 1st.
2. ——— 32 1st, 33, 38, 43.
3. ——— 45.
3. —— vi. 2, 4.
3a.——— 5 (*om.* ἄν, L T Tr A ℵ.)
2. ——— 7.
3. ——— 16, 18.
2. ——— 29, 32.
1. —— vii. 12.
15.——— 22, 25, 27.
1. —— viii. 8.
2. ——— 11.
3. ——— 17.
2. ——— 27.
5. ——— 28 1st.
15.——— 28 2nd.
3. ——— 34 (No. 1, L.)
1. —— ix. 6 1st.
2. ——— 6 2nd.
15.——— 22, 26.
2. ——— 28.
15.——— 31.
3. ——— 38.
15.—— x. 14, 15.
1. ——— 25.
2. ——— 34.
2. —— xi. 24.
15.——— 25.
15.—— xii. 1.
2. ——— 6.
1. ——— 10.
3. ——— 17 (No. 1, L T Tr A ℵ.)
2. ——— 36 1st.
23.——— 36 2nd (*om.* ἐάν, L T Tr A ℵ.)
15.——— 45.
2. —— xiii. 17.
3. ——— 35.
24.——— 44 1st.
15.——— 44 2nd.
24.——— 46.
15.—— xiv. 1.
1. ——— 15.
15.——— 35 1st & 2nd.
1. ——— 36.
2. —— xv. 12, 17.
2. —— xvi. 11 1st, 18.
1. ——— 20 1st.
2. ——— 20 2nd.
2. —— xvii. 10, 12, 13.
15.——— 27 2nd.
1. Matt. xviii. 6 1st.
15.——— 7 2nd (*om.* L T Tr ℵ, i.e. *the man.*)
2. ——— 10 2nd.
1. ——— 14, 16.
2. ——— 19 1st.
23.——— 19 2nd.
24.——— 25.
15.——— 27 (*om.* L.)
25.——— 28.
15.——— 32 2nd.
2. —— xix. 4.
1. ——— 13, 16.
2. ——— 23, 28.
2. —— xx. 10.
1. ——— 21.
2. ——— 25 1st, 30.
1. ——— 33.
1. —— xxi. 4.
2. ——— 31.
2. ——— 45.
2. —— xxii. 16, 34.
15.——— 46.
1. —— xxiii. 26 2nd.
2. ——— 31.
3. ——— 35.
2. —— xxiv. 32, 33.
15.——— 36.
2. ——— 43.
15.——— 46.
2. ——— 47.
15.——— 48, 50 1st.
2. —— xxv. 24, 26.
2. —— xxvi. 2.
1. ——— 4.
2. ——— 21.
15.——— 24 twice, 29.
2. ——— 34, 53.
1. ——— 56, 63.
2. —— xxvii. 3.
15.——— 8.
2. ——— 18.
15.——— 19.
1. ——— 20.
2. ——— 24.
1. ——— 35 (*ap.*)
25.——— 62.
2. ——— 63 1st.
15.——— 63 2nd.
2. —— xxviii. 5, 7.
1. ——— 10.
2. Mark ii. 1, 8.
1. ——— 10 1st.
2. ——— 10 2nd, 16.
1. ——— 38.
1. —— iii. 2, 9, 14 twice.
15.——— 24, 25.
1. —— iv. 12, 22.
2. ——— 38, 41.
1. —— v. 12, 18 2nd.
3. ——— 23 (No. 1, G ∾ L T Tr A ℵ.)
2. ——— 29 1st.
1. ——— 43 1st.
2. —— vi. 2 (*om.* G L T Tr A ℵ.)

1. Mark vi. 8.
15.—— 11 (ap.)
1. —— 12.
2. —— 14, 15 twice.
12.—— 21.
1. —— 25, 36, 56.
1. —— vii. 9.
2. —— 18.
15.—— 20 2nd.
1. —— 26, 36.
1. —— viii. 30.
2. —— 31.
2. —— ix. 1 1st.
1. —— 9.
2. —— 11.
1. —— 12.
2. —— 13.
1. —— 18.
2. —— 25.
1. —— 30.
9. —— 42 2nd.
1. —— x. 13 1st, 17, 35, 37.
2. —— 42, 47.
1. —— 48, 51 2nd.
2. —— xi. 3 (*om.* L T Tr A.)
1. —— 16.
2. —— 23 twice, 24.
1. —— 25.
2. —— 32.
1. —— xii. 2.
2. —— 12, 14.
1. —— 15, 19.
2. —— 26, 28, 34 1st, 35, 43.
24.—— 44.
15.—— xiii. 11 1st.
16.—— 11 2nd.
15.—— 24.
2. —— 28, 29, 30.
15.—— 32 1st.
1. —— xiv. 12 2nd.
15.—— 21 twice, 25 1st.
13.—— 25 2nd.
2. —— 30.
1. —— 35.
2. —— xv. 10.
1. —— 11, 32 1st.
2. —— 39.
1. —— xvi. 1.
2. —— 4, 7, 11 (ap.)
1. Luke i. 4.
8. —— 21.
2. —— 22.
1. —— 43.
2. —— 45, marg. (text, *for.*)
3a.—— ii. 35.
2. —— 49 twice.
2. —— iii. 8.
1. —— iv. 3.
2. —— 4.
24.—— 40.
2. —— 41, marg. (text, *for.*)
1. —— v. 24 1st.
2. —— 24 2nd.
2. —— vi. 5 (*om.* Tr^b ℵ.)
1. —— 7.
15.—— 23.
1. —— 31.
15.—— 48, 49 3rd.
3. —— vii. 3.
2. —— 4.
1. —— 6.
2. —— 16 twice.
1. —— 36.
2. —— 37.
25.—— 39.
2. —— 43.
1. —— viii. 16, 32.
2. —— 47, 53.
15.—— ix. 5.
2. —— 7 3rd, 8 twice.
1. —— 12.
2. —— 19.
19.—— 45.
3. —— x. 2.

2. Luke x. 11, 12 1st.
15.—— 12 2nd & 3rd.
2. —— 20, 21 2nd, 24.
15.—— 31.
14a.—— 38.
2. —— 40 1st.
1. —— 40 2nd.
15.—— xi. 26.
1. —— 33.
2. —— 38.
1. —— 50, 54 (ap.)
2. —— xii. 30.
1. —— 36 2nd.
2. —— 37, 39.
15.—— 43.
2. —— 44 1st.
15.—— 45, 46, 47.
2. —— 51.
21.—— xiii. 1 1st.
2. —— 2, 4 1st.
20.—— 32.
14a.—— xiv. 1.
1. —— 10 1st.
15.—— 21 (*om.* G → L T Tr A ℵ.)
1. —— 23.
2. —— 24.
2. —— xv. 7 1st.
15.—— 14, 15.
1. —— 29.
4. —— xvi. 1.
1. —— 4, 9, 24.
2. —— 25.
1. —— 27.
3. —— 28.
14a.—— xvii. 1.
9. —— 2 1st.
1. —— 2 2nd.
15.—— 9 1st (*om.* L T Tr A ℵ.)
2. —— 15.
15.—— 31 1st.
20.—— 34.
15.—— xviii. 3.
2. —— 8.
2. —— 9, marg. (with *εἰσί*) *as being.*
2. —— 11.
24.—— 12.
1. —— 15.
24.—— 22.
2. —— 37.
1. —— 39, 41 2nd.
15.—— xix. 4.
2. —— 7 1st.
1. —— 15 2nd.
2. —— 22 1st, 26 1st.
2. —— 40 (*om.* Tr^b.)
14a.—— 43.
1. —— xx. 10, 14.
15.—— 18.
2. —— 19.
1. —— 20 1st.
2. —— 21.
1. —— 28.
15.—— 35.
2. —— 37.
2. —— xxi. 3, 20, 30, 31.
15.—— 34.
1. —— 36 1st.
1. —— xxii. 8.
15.—— 22.
1. —— 30.
2. —— 37 1st, 70.
2. —— xxiii. 7 1st.
18.—— 48 2nd.
2. —— xxiv. 21, 39, 44.
1. John i. 7, 22 1st, 31.
2. —— 34.
15.—— 39.
2. —— ii. 17, 18, 22.
1. —— 25.
2. —— iii. 2 1st, 7.
5. —— 16 1st.
1. —— 16 2nd.
1. —— 17.
2. —— 19.
1. —— 21 2nd.

2. John iii. 21 3rd, 28 twice.
16.—— 32 (*om.* G ⇄ ℵ.)
2. —— 33 2nd.
2. —— iv. 1.
16.—— 18.
2. —— 19, 20, 25, 27.
1. —— 36 2nd.
15.—— 39 1st.
2. —— 42, 44, 47 1st.
1. —— 47 2nd.
2. —— 53.
2. —— v. 6 1st, 15.
1. —— 20 2nd, 23 1st.
2. —— 32 2nd.
1. —— 34.
2. —— 36 3rd.
1. —— 40.
2. —— 42, 45 1st.
1. —— vi. 5, 7.
2. —— 15, 22 1st.
15.—— 22 2nd (ap.)
2. —— 22 3rd, 24.
1. —— 28, 29, 30.
2. —— 36.
1. —— 40 2nd.
2. —— 46.
1. —— 50.
2. —— 61, 65, 69.
1. —— vii. 3.
2. —— 26, 35, 42.
1. —— viii. 6 (ap.)
1. —— 17, 24 twice, 27, 28 1st, 37, 48, 52, 54.
1. —— ix. 2, 3.
2. —— 8 1st, 17, 18 1st, 20 twice.
1. —— 22 1st.
2. —— 24 2nd, 25, 29, 30, 31, 32 1st, 35.
1. —— 36, 39 1st.
1. —— x. 10 1st, 17, 38 1st.
2. —— 38 2nd.
24.—— 41.
1. —— xi. 4 2nd.
2. —— 6.
16.—— 7, 11 1st.
1. —— 11 2nd.
2. —— 13, 15.
1. —— 16.
2. —— 20, 22, 24, 27, 31, 40, 41, 42 1st.
1. —— 42 2nd.
2. —— 42 3rd, 50 1st.
1. —— 50 2nd.
15.—— 51 1st.
2. —— 51 2nd.
1. —— 52 2nd.
15.—— 53.
2. —— 56.
1. —— 57 1st.
3. —— 57 2nd.
2. —— xii. 9 1st.
1. —— 9 2nd, 10.
2. —— 12, 16 1st.
1. —— 23.
2. —— 34.
1. —— 36, 38, 46.
2. —— 50.
2. —— xiii. 1 1st.
1. —— 1 2nd.
2. —— 3 twice.
1. —— 15, 18 1st, 19 1st.
2. —— 19 2nd, 21, 29 1st.
1. —— 29 3rd, 34 twice.
2. —— 35.
1. —— xiv. 3.
2. —— 10 1st, 11.
16.—— 13 1st.
1. —— 13 2nd, 16.
15.—— 20 1st.
2. —— 20 2nd, 22.
1. —— 29, 31 1st.
2. —— 31 2nd.
1. —— xv. 2 2nd, 8, 11 1st, 12, 13, 16 1st & 3rd, 17.
2. —— 18.
1. —— 25 1st.
1. —— xvi. 2 1st, 4 1st.

2. John xvi. 4 2nd.
1. —— 7.
24.—— 15 1st.
2. —— 15 2nd, 19 1st.
19.—— 19 2nd.
2. —— 20, 21.
15.—— 23.
1. —— 24.
15.—— 26 1st.
2. —— 26 2nd, 27, 30 1st.
1. —— 30 2nd.
2. —— 30 3rd.
1. —— 32, 33.
1. —— xvii. 1.
1. —— 2 (No. 1a, *δώσει, he shall give,* A.) (*δώσω, I shall give,* ℵ.)
1. —— 3.
2. —— 7, 8 twice.
1. —— 11, 12 2nd, 13, 15 twice, 19.
1. —— 21 1st, 2nd, & 3rd.
2. —— 21 4th.
1. —— 22, 23 1st & 2nd.
2. —— 23 3rd.
1. —— 24 2nd.
2. —— 25.
1. —— 26.
2. —— xviii. 8.
1. —— 9.
2. —— 14 2nd.
15.—— 15.
1. —— 28 (*om.* L T Tr A ℵ.)
1. —— 32.
2. —— 37 1st.
1. —— 37 2nd, 39 1st.
1. —— xix. 4 1st.
2. —— 4 2nd.
17.—— 8.
2. —— 10.
17 —— 13 1st (*τῶν λόγων τούτων, these words,* instead of *τοῦτον τὸν λόγον, that saying,* G ∾ L T Tr A ℵ.)
2. —— 21.
1. —— 24.
15.—— 27 1st.
2. —— 28 1st.
1. —— 28 2nd, 31 1st.
15.—— 31 2nd.
1. —— 31 3rd.
2. —— 35 2nd.
1. —— 35 3rd, 36, 38.
2. —— xx. 9, 14, 18 2nd.
1. —— 31 1st.
2. —— 31 2nd.
1. —— 31 3rd.
15.—— xxi. 3.
2. —— 4.
15.—— 7 1st.
2. —— 7 2nd, 12, 15, 16, 17, 23 1st.
15.—— 23 2nd.
2. —— 24.
15. Acts i. 19 1st.
2. —— ii. 29, 30 1st, 31, 36 1st.
17.—— 36 2nd.
2. —— iii. 10 1st, 17.
15.—— 23 2nd.
11.—— iv. 2.
2. —— 10, 13 twice, 16 1st.
2. —— v. 9.
1. —— 15 2nd.
2. —— 41.
2. —— vi. 14.
2. —— vii. 6 1st.
15.—— viii. 1, 8.
2. —— 14.
3. —— 15.
2. —— 18.
1. —— 19.
3. —— 24.
3. —— ix. 2, 12, 17 2nd.
2. —— 20.

1. Acts ix. 21 4th.
2. —— 22, 26, 27, 38 1st.
2. —— x. 34, 42.
2. —— xi. 1 2nd.
15. —— xii. 1.
2. —— 9, 11.
2. —— xiii. 38.
5. —— xiv. 1 2nd.
2. —— 9.
6. —— 18.
15. —— 21.
2. —— 22.
2. —— xv. 5.
3a. —— 17.
6. —— 20 2nd.
2. —— 24.
5. —— 39.
2. —— xvi. 3, 10.
20. —— 12 2nd.
2. —— 19, 38.
2. —— xvii. 3 twice, 13.
4. —— 22.
4. —— xix. 4 1st.
15. —— 16 2nd.
2. —— 25, 26 twice, 34.
10. —— xx. 18.
2. —— 23 twice, 25, 26, 29, 31, 34 1st, 38.
2. —— xxi. 21, 22.
1. —— 24 1st.
2. —— 24 2nd, 29, 31.
2. —— xxii. 2.
15. —— 11 1st.
2. —— 19 1st.
1. —— 24 2nd.
2. —— 29.
2. —— xxiii. 5, 6.
3. —— 15, 20.
2. —— 22.
1. —— 24.
2. —— 27, 34.
2. —— xxiv. 11 1st, 14, 26 1st.
3. —— 26 2nd (ap.)
3. —— xxv. 3, 26.
2. —— xxvi. 5.
9. —— 8, 23 1st & 2nd.
2. —— 27.
2. —— xxvii. 10, 25.
2. —— xxviii. 1.
4. —— 19.
2. —— 22, 28 1st.
2. Rom. i. 8.
4. —— 9.
1. —— 11.
16. —— 12 1st.
2. —— 13 1st.
1. —— 13 2nd.
2. —— 32.
2. —— ii. 2, 3 2nd, 4.
2. —— iii. 2.
3a. —— 4.
1. —— 8 2nd.
2. —— 19 1st.
1. —— 19 2nd.
2. —— iv. 9 (*om.* Lb T Tr ℵ.)
1. —— 16 1st.
2. —— 21, 23.
2. —— v. 3.
1. —— 20, 21.
1. —— vi. 1.
25. —— 2.
2. —— 3.
1. —— 4.
2. —— 6 1st.
1. —— 6 2nd.
2. —— 8, 9, 16, 17 1st.
7. —— vii. 4 1st.
1. —— 4 2nd, 13 twice.
2. —— 14.
16. —— 15 1st (*om.* G→)
16. —— 15 2nd.
16. —— 16 1st.
2. —— 16 2nd, 18 1st.
16. —— 19 2nd, 20 1st.
2. —— 21.
1. —— viii. 4.
2. Rom. viii. 16.
1. —— 17 2nd.
2. —— 18, 22.
2. —— 27, marg. (text, *because.*)
2. —— 28 1st, 38.
2. —— ix. 2.
1. —— 11 1st.
3. —— 17 twice.
1. —— 23.
2. —— 30.
2. —— x. 2, 5, 9 twice.
19. —— xi. 7 (No. 16, G L T Tr A ℵ.)
1. —— 11, 19.
2. —— 25 2nd.
1. —— 31, 32.
16. —— xiii. 11 1st.
2. —— 11 2nd.
1. —— xiv. 9.
2. —— 14 1st.
1. —— xv. 4, 6.
2. —— 14.
7. —— 16 1st.
1. —— 16 2nd.
2. —— 29.
1. —— 31 1st.
1. —— 31 3rd (*om.* G∾L T Tr A ℵ.)
1. —— 32.
1. —— xvi. 2 1st.
2. 1 Cor. i. 5.
1. —— 10 1st.
2. —— 11, 12, 14, 15.
3. —— 29.
1. —— 31 1st.
1. —— ii. 12 1st.
2. —— iii. 16 1st.
1. —— 18.
2. —— 20.
1. —— iv. 2, 3, 6 1st, 8.
2. —— 9 (*om.* G ⇉ L T Tr A ℵ.)
1. —— v. 2 1st, 5.
2. —— 6.
1. —— 7.
2. —— vi. 2, 3 1st.
16. —— 6.
2. —— 9, 15, 16.
23. —— 18 1st.
2. —— 19.
1. —— vii. 5 1st.
2. —— 26 2nd.
1. —— 29 1st, 34 1st, 35 1st.
2. —— viii. 1, 4 2nd & 3rd.
1. —— ix. 3.
2. —— 10 1st, 13.
1. —— 15 1st.
1. —— 15 2nd (οὐδείς, *no one*, instead of ἵνα τις, *that any man*, L T Tr A* ℵ.)
1. —— 18 1st.
7. —— 18 2nd.
1. —— 19, 20 twice, 21 2nd, 22 twice, 23.
2. —— 24 1st.
1. —— 24 2nd.
2. —— x. 19 twice (ap.), 20 1st.
1. —— 33.
2. —— xi. 2, 3.
2. —— 14.
1. —— 16.
2. —— 17 2nd.
1. —— 19.
2. —— 23 2nd.
2. —— xii. 2, 3 1st.
1. —— 9.
1. —— xiv. 1, 5 2nd & 5th, 12, 13 2nd, 19.
2. —— 23 2nd, 25.
1. —— 31.
2. —— 37 1st.
2. —— xv. 4 twice, 5, 12 twice, 15 1st, 27.
1. —— 28 2nd.
2. 1 Cor. xv. 50, 58.
1. —— xvi. 2.
6. —— 4.
1. —— 6 2nd, 10, 11.
2. —— 15 1st.
1. —— 16 1st.
2. 2 Cor. i. 7, 8 1st.
2. —— 10 (*om.* Lb Trb.)
1. —— 11.
2. —— 12, 14.
1. —— 15.
1. —— 17 2nd.
2. —— 23.
2. —— ii. 3.
1. —— 4 twice, 9.
2. —— iii. 5.
1. —— iv. 7, 10, 11.
2. —— 14.
1. —— 15.
2. —— v. 1.
1. —— 5.
2. —— 6.
1. —— 10 1st, 12.
2. —— 14.
1. —— 15 2nd, 21.
2. —— vii. 3, 8, 9 1st & 2nd.
1. —— 9 3rd, 14.
2. —— 16.
1. —— viii. 6 2nd, 7.
2. —— 9 1st.
1. —— 9 2nd.
3. —— 11 1st.
1. —— 13, 14 1st.
3. —— 14 2nd.
2. —— ix. 2.
1. —— 3, 5 1st, 8.
2. —— x. 7 2nd, 11.
1. —— xi. 7.
14a. —— 12 1st.
1. —— 12 2nd & 3rd, 16.
2. —— 31.
1. —— xii. 8, 9.
2. —— 13, 19.
2. —— xiii. 2, 6 twice.
1. —— 7 2nd & 3rd.
3. Gal. i. 4.
2. —— 6 1st, 11.
1. —— 16.
2. —— 23.
1. —— ii. 4 2nd (No. 1b, L T Tr A ℵ.)
1. —— 5.
2. —— 7.
1. —— 9 2nd, 10.
2. —— 14, 16 1st.
1. —— 16 2nd, 19.
2. —— iii. 7, 8, 11.
1. —— 14 twice, 22 1st, 24.
1. —— iv. 5 2nd.
2. —— 15.
1a. —— 17.
2. —— 22.
2. —— v. 2, 3 1st, 10 1st.
23. —— 17 2nd.
2. —— 21.
16. —— vi. 7.
1. —— 13.
1b. Eph. i. 17.
1. —— ii. 7.
16. —— 8.
1. —— 10.
2. —— 11 1st, 12 1st.
15. —— 12 2nd.
1b. —— iii. 16 (No. 1, L.)
1b. —— 17 2nd, 19.
2. —— iv. 9 2nd.
1. —— 10 3rd, 14, 28 2nd, 29 2nd.
2. —— v. 5.
14. —— 15.
1. —— 26, 27 twice, 33.
1. —— vi. 3 (2nd verb, indic. mood.)
2. —— 8, 9.
1. —— 13, 19 1st, 20, 21, 22 1st.
2. Phil. i. 6.
1. Phil. i. 9.
7. —— 10 1st.
1. —— 10 3rd.
2. —— 12, 17, 19, 20 1st, 25.
1. —— 26, 27 1st.
2. —— 27 2nd.
16. —— 28.
1. —— ii. 2, 10.
2. —— 11 2nd.
1. —— 15.
2. —— 16 2nd.
1. —— 19.
2. —— 22, 24, 26 2nd.
1. —— 28 1st.
1. —— iii. 8.
2. —— iv. 10, 11, 15.
1. Col. i. 9, 18, 28.
1. —— ii. 2.
2. —— iii. 24.
2. —— iv. 1 2nd.
1. —— 3, 4, 8, 12.
2. —— 13 1st.
1. —— 16 twice, 17.
2. 1 Thes. ii. 1.
1. —— 16.
2. —— iii. 3 2nd, 4, 6.
1. —— iv. 1, 12 1st.
2. —— 14, 15.
2. —— v. 2.
1. —— 4 1st, 10.
15. 2 Thes. i. 10 2nd.
1. —— 11.
3. —— 12.
7. —— ii. 2 1st.
2. —— 2 2nd, 4 4th, 5.
1. —— 12.
1. —— iii. 1, 2.
2. —— 4, 10.
1. —— 12 2nd, 14 2nd.
1. 1 Tim. i. 3 1st.
2. —— 8, 9, 15.
1. —— 16, 18, 20.
1. —— ii. 2 2nd.
1. —— iii. 15.
2. —— iv. 1.
1. —— 15.
16. —— v. 4.
1. —— 7, 16 2nd, 20 2nd, 21.
1. —— vi. 19.
4. 2 Tim. i. 3.
1. —— 4.
2. —— 5 2nd.
2. —— 12 1st.
— —— 12 2nd, see Committed.
15. —— 12 3rd.
2. —— 15.
15. —— 18 2nd.
1. —— ii. 4 2nd, 10.
2. —— 23.
2. —— iii. 1, 15.
1. —— 17.
15. —— iv. 8 1st.
1. —— 17 1st.
1. Titus i. 5 1st, 9, 13.
1. —— ii. 4, 8 2nd, 10, 12, 14.
1. —— iii. 7, 8 2nd.
2. —— 11 1st.
1. —— 13.
3. Philem. 6.
1. —— 13, 15.
16. —— 18.
2. —— 21, 22.
2. Heb. ii. 6 twice.
3. —— 9.
1. —— 14 1st, 17.
17. —— iii. 10.
2. —— 19.
17. —— iv. 11.
1. —— 16.
1. —— v. 1.
6. —— 12.
1. —— vi. 18.
2. —— vii. 8 2nd, 14.
17. —— viii. 7.

3. Heb. ix. 15 1st.
1. ——— 25.
1. —— x. 9, 36.
2. —— xi. 6 1st, 13, 14 2nd.
17. ——— 15.
2. ——— 18, 19.
1. ——— 35.
1. —— xii. 27 3rd.
1. —— xiii. 12.
1. ——— 17 3rd.
16. ——— 17 4th.
1. ——— 19.
2. Jas. i. 3.
1. ——— 4.
15. ——— 7 1st.
2. ——— 7 2nd.
2. —— ii. 19, 20.
2. —— iii. 1.
1. —— iv. 3.
2. ——— 4, 5 1st.
17. ——— 15 3rd.
2. —— v. 11.
3. ——— 16.
1. 1 Pet. i. 7 1st.
2. ——— 12 1st, 18.
1. —— ii. 2.
2. ——— 3.
1. ——— 12, 21, 24.
1. —— iii. 1 (No. 1a, G~ L T Tr A ℵ.)
7. ——— 7.
2. ——— 9 1st.
1. ——— 9 2nd.
6. ——— 10 2nd.
1. ——— 16 1st, 18.
1. —— iv. 6 2nd, 11, 13.
1. —— v. 6.
1. 2 Pet. i. 4 1st.
2. ——— 14, 20.
2. —— iii. 3, 5, 8.
1. 1 John i. 3 2nd, 4.
2. ——— 5, 6, 8, 10.
2. —— ii. 3, 5, 18 twice.
1. ——— 19 1st.
2. ——— 19 2nd, 21, 22 2nd.
1. ——— 27, 28.
2. ——— 29 twice.
1. —— iii. 1.
2. ——— 2, 5.
1. ——— 8 2nd, 11 2nd.
2. ——— 14 1st, 15, 19.
1. ——— 23.
2. ——— 24 2nd.
2. —— iv. 3 3rd.
1. ——— 9 3rd.
2. 1 John iv. 10 twice, 13, 14, 15.
1. ——— 17, 21.
2. —— v. 1 1st, 2.
1. ——— 3.
2. ——— 5 3rd, 11.
— ——— 13 1st (*ap.*)
1. ——— 13 2nd.
2. ——— 13 3rd.
1. ——— 13 4th (οἱ πιστεύοντες, *you that believe*, instead of καὶ ἵνα πιστεύητε, *and that ye may believe*, G L T Tr A ℵ.)
2. ——— 14 2nd, 15 1st & 2nd.
1. ——— 16.
2. ——— 18 1st, 19, 20 1st.
1. ——— 20 2nd.
2. 2 John 4.
1. ——— 5 2nd, 6 twice, 12.
1. 3 John 8.
2. ——— 12.
25. Rev. i. 12.
2. —— ii. 6.
1. ——— 10.
2. ——— 23.
2. —— iii. 1 2nd & 3rd, 9.
1. ——— 11 2nd.
2. ——— 15, 17.
1. ——— 18 1st, 2nd, & 4th.
1. —— vi. 4 3rd (No. 1a, L T Tr A.)
1. ——— 11 1st.
1. —— viii. 3 (No. 1a, L T A ℵ.)
1. —— ix. 5 1st (No. 1a, L T Tr A ℵ.)
2. —— x. 6 3rd.
1. —— xii. 6 1st.
2. ——— 12 2nd, 13.
1. ——— 14, 15.
1. —— xiii. 15 1st.
1. ——— 15 2nd (*om.* T A ℵ.)
1. —— xiv. 13 (No. 1a, L T Tr A ℵ.)
1. —— xvi. 12.
15. ——— 14 (*om.* G→L T Tr[b] A ℵ.)
25. —— xvii. 8 3rd (No. 2, G L T Tr A ℵ.)
1. —— xviii. 4 1st.
1. —— xix. 8, 15, 18 1st.
1a. —— xxii. 14 2nd.

THAT...COULD.

πρὸς τό, *with the inf.*, in order to, in order that.

2 Cor. iii. 13.

THAT...EVER.

24. John iv. 29 (ἅ, *which*, T Tr[m] A ℵ.)
24. ——— 39 (Tr[m]), (ἅ, *which*, T Tr A ℵ.)
24. —— x. 8.

THAT I MAY REJOICE.

{ εἰς, unto, for
{ καυχῆμα, a subject *or* theme of rejoicing,
{ ἐμοί, to me.

Phil. ii. 16.

THAT IS.

{ τοῦτο, this *thing* (*this here*)
{ ἐστί, is.

Acts xix. 4.
Rom. vii. 18.
—— ix. 8.
—— x. 6, 7, 8.
Philem. 12.
Heb. ii. 14.
—— vii. 5.
—— xi. 16.
—— xiii. 15.
1 Pet. iii. 20.

THAT IS AFAR OFF.

{ οἱ, those
{ εἰς, unto
{ μακραν, a distance.

Acts ii. 39.

THAT IS OF POWER.

δύναμαι, to be able, to have power. *Here, part.*

Rom. xvi. 25.

THAT IS TO SAY.

{ τοῦτο, this *thing* (*this here*)
{ ἐστί, is.

Matt. xxvii. 46.
Mark vii. 11.
Acts i. 19.
Heb. ix. 11.
Heb. x. 20.

THAT MAN.

οὗτος, this, this one here.

2 Thes. iii. 14.

THAT MAY OPEN.

{ ἐν, in
{ ἄνοιξις, an opening.

Eph. vi. 19.

THAT...MAY.

1. εἰς τὸ, *with inf.*, *see* "THAT," *No. 7.*

2. τοῦ, *with inf.*, *see* "THAT," *No. 6.*

3. πρὸς τό, *with inf.*, in order to, in order that.

6. Luke xxi. 22.
6. —— xxii. 31.
7. Acts iii. 19.
6. —— xxvi. 18. [*so that.*)
7. Rom. i. 20 marg. (text,
6. —— vi. 10.
7. —— xii. 2.
7. —— xv. 13.
6. 1 Cor. x. 13.
7. 2 Cor. i. 4.
7. Eph. i. 18.
3. —— vi. 11.
7. Phil. i. 10.
6. —— iii. 10.
7. ——— 21.
7. 2 Thes. i. 5.
3. Jas. iii. 3 (No. 7, L T Tr A ℵ.)

THAT WHICH IS COMELY, AND THAT ONE MAY ATTEND UPON.

{ πρὸς, with a view to,
τὸ, the thing,
εὔσχημων, comely, seemly,
καὶ, and,
ευπροσεδρος, devotedness, (εὐπάρεδρος, setting diligently by, *i.e.* assiduous, devoted, G L T Tr A ℵ) } with a view to what is seemly and devoted to, (*or* waiting on) [*the Lord.*]

1 Cor. vii. 35.

THAT MIGHT.

1. εἰς τό, *with the inf.*, *see* "THAT," *No.* 7.
2. τοῦ, *with the inf.*, *see* "THAT," *No.* 6.
3. πρὸς τό, *with the inf.*, in order to, in order that.
4. ἕνεκα, *with inf.*, for the sake of.
5. ὥστε, *with inf.*, so that, so as that, (*expressive of event, result, or consequence.*)

2. Matt. xxi. 32.
1. Luke iv. 29 (No. 5, G L T Tr A ℵ.)
2. —— xxiv. 45.
1. Rom. iii. 26.
1. —— iv. 11 twice, 18.
2. —— vi. 6.
1. Rom. viii. 29.
4. 2 Cor. vii. 12.
1. 1 Thes. iii. 10.
1. 2 Thes. ii. 6, 10.
3. —— iii. 8.
1. Heb. xii. 10.
2. Jas. v. 17.
5. 1 Pet. i. 21.

THAT...MIGHT BE.

1. εἰς, unto, for. (*Here*, εἰς σωτηρίαν, for salvation.)
2. { ὥστε, so that...,
εἶναι, to be, } so that...might be, so that...are [*turned*], that...should be.

1. Rom. x. 1. | 2. 2 Pet. i. 21.

THAT MUST.

τοῦ, *with inf.*, (*see* "THAT" *No.* 6) for...to.

1 Pet. iv. 17.

THAT...NO.

{ ἵνα, in order that, (*see* "THAT," *No.* 1)
μή, no, not, (*see* "NO," *No.* [2.]) } in order that... not.

Acts iv. 17.
1 Cor. iv. 6.
1 Cor. xii. 25.
—— xvi. 2.
Rev. xx. 3.

THAT NONE.

{ μή, not, lest
τις, any. }

1 Thes. v. 15.

THAT NOT.

ἵνα μη, *see* "THAT NO."

Matt. vii. 1.
—— xii. 16.
—— xviii. 10.
—— xxiv. 6, 20.
—— xxvi. 41.
Mark iii. 12.
—— v. 7, 10.
—— xiii. 18.
Luke viii. 10, 31.
—— ix. 45.
—— xxi. 8.
—— xxii. 32.
John iii. 15, 16.
—— iv. 15.
—— vi. 50.
—— vii. 23, marg. *without.*
—— xi. 37.
—— xii. 40, 46.
—— xvi. 1.
—— xviii. 36.
Acts ii. 25.
—— xxiv. 4.
1 Cor. ii. 5.
1 Cor. vii. 5.
—— xi. 32, 34.
2 Cor. i. 9.
—— ii. 5.
—— vi. 3.
—— ix. 3.
—— x. 9.
Gal. v. 15.
1 Thes. iv. 13.
2 Thes. iv. 16.
1 Tim. vi. 1.
Tit. ii. 5.
—— iii. 14.
Philem. 14.
Heb. vi. 12.
—— xi. 40.
—— xii. 25.
1 John ii. 1.
2 John 8.
Rev. vii. 1.
—— ix. 4, 20.
—— xi. 6.
—— xviii. 4 twice.

THAT NO MAN.

1. { ἵνα, in order that, (*see* "THAT" *No.* 1)
μή, not (*see* "NO," *No.* 2)
τίς, any one. }
2. ἵνα μή, *see* "THAT NO."

2. Matt. xxiv. 4. | 2. 2 Cor. viii. 20.
1. Rev. xiii. 17.

THAT NOTHING.

1. { ἵνα, in order that
μή, not
τι, anything. }
2. ἵνα μή, in order that not.

1. John vi. 12. | 2 John vi. 39.

THAT SHOULD.

1. εἰς τὸ, *with inf.*, *see* "THAT," *No.* 7.
2. τοῦ, *with inf.*, *see* "THAT," *No.* 6.
3. ὥστε, *with inf.*, *see* "THAT," *No.* 5.
4. { οὗτος, this one, this same,
ἤμελλεν, was about to be. }

2. Luke i. 57.
2. —— ii. 6.
2. —— iv. 42.
2. —— v. 7.
2. —— xxiv. 16.
4. John vi. 71.
2. Acts x. 47.
2. —— xiii. 47.
2. —— xxvii. 1, 20.
1. Rom. vi. 12.

1. Rom. vii. 4. | 1. Gal. iii. 17.
3. —— 6. | 1. Eph. i. 12.
2. —— xi. 8 twice. | 1. 2 Thes. ii. 11.
1. —— xv. 16. | 1. Jas. i. 18.
3. 1 Cor. v. 1. | 2. Heb. xi. 5.
1. 1 Pet. iv. 2.

THAT...SHOULD BE RECEIVED UP.

{ τῆς, of the [up, } of [*his*] re-
{ ἀναλήψεως, taking [*him*] } ceiving up.

Luke ix. 51.

THAT...SHOULD BE SAVED.

σωτηρία, salvation, deliverance.

Luke i. 71.

THAT SAME.

1. ἐκεῖνος, that one, that one there.

2. οὗτος, this one, this one here.

1. Matt. x. 19 (*ap.*) | 1. John xi. 49.
1. —— xxvi. 55. | 1. —— xviii. 13.
2. Acts ii. 36.

THAT SAME DAY.

{ ἐν, in
{ αὐτῇ, the same, } in the self-same day.
{ τῇ, the
{ ἡμέρᾳ, day,

Luke xxiv. 13.

THAT SO...MIGHT.

εἰς τό, *with the inf.*, *see* "THAT," *No.* 7.

Luke xx. 20 (ὥστε, *so that*, L T Tr A ℵ.)

THAT THING.

τοῦτο, that *thing*.

Luke ix. 21.

THAT GOOD THING WHICH IS COMMITTED UNTO ME.

{ ὁ, the
{ κάλος, good, (*see* "GOOD," *No.* 2)
{ παρακαταθήκη, something delivered down to one's charge. (παραθήκη, something committed to one's charge, G L T Tr A ℵ),
} the good, goodly, *or* noble deposit.

2 Tim. i. 14.

THAT VERY.

ἐκεῖνος, *see* "THAT," *No.* 15.

Matt. xv. 28. | Matt. xvii. 18.

THAT WAY.

1. { δία, through *or* by
{ ἐκεῖκος, that [*way.*]

2. { ἐν, in
{ τῇ, the
{ ὁδῷ, way, road.

2. Luke x. 31. | 1. Luke xix. 4.

THAT WHICH IS COMMITTED TO ONE'S TRUST.

παρακαθήκη, something delivered down to one's charge.

1 Tim. vi. 20 (G ∾), (παραθήκη, *something committed to one's charge, deposit*, G L T Tr A ℵ.)

THAT WHICH IS EVIL.

{ ὁ, the
{ πονηρός, evil.

Luke vi. 45. | Rom. xii. 9.

THAT WHICH IS EQUAL.

{ ὁ, the
{ ἰσότης, equal *thing*.

Col. iv. 1.

THAT WICKED ONE.

{ ὁ, the
{ πονηρός, evil *one*.

1 Cor. v. 13.

THAT...WILL.

τοῦ, *with inf.*, *see* "THAT," *No.* 6.

Luke xvii. 1.

THAT WOULD.

τοῦ, *with inf.*, *see* "THAT," *No.* 6.

Acts xxiii. 20.

THAT (AND)

καί, and.

1 Cor. xiv. 27.

THAT IS WITH (HE, THEY, etc.)

1. { ὁ, the, / μετά, with, (*in association with*) } the one, (*or in pl.*, those *who are*) with.

2. ὅς, he who.

2. Matt. x. 38.
1. —— xii. 3, 30.
1. Mark i. 36.
1. —— v. 40.
2. —— ix. 40.
1. Luke vi. 4.
1. —— viii. 45 (*σύν, in conjunction with, instead of μετά, in association with*, G L T Tr A א.)
1. Tit. iii. 15.

THAT (NOW)

{ τὸ, this, / δέ, but. } but this.

Eph. iv. 9.

THAT (SAVE)

{ εἰ, if / μή, not, } except.

Mark vi. 5.

THAT (SAVE ONLY THAT)

εἰ μή, see above.

Acts xxi. 25 (*ap.*)

THAT (THE SAME)

ὅστις, whatever.

John viii. 25.

THAT (TO WIT)

{ ὡς, as, so as, how, / ὅτι, that, (*see* "THAT," *No.* 2) } how that.

2 Cor. v. 19.

See also, ACCORDING, AFTER, BECAUSE, BEFORE, CONCERNING, FOAM, FOR, HOW, IF, IN, INSOMUCH, LEST, MUST, PLACE, SEEING, SO, TIME, WAY.

THE.

The English word "THE" is generally the translation of the definite article (ὁ, ἡ, τό) in the Greek. But not necessarily so. Frequently (partly arising from difference of idiom) the word "THE" has no equivalent in the Greek.

1. Indicates the absence of the article in the Greek in the few selected passages given. (*The English word is that which the word* "THE" *precedes. In each case such English word should have* a *or* an *prefixed, or be left indefinite.*)

2. ταύτην, (*Acc. fem. sing. of* οὗτος) this, this here.

3. αὐτῶν, (*Gen. pl. of* αὐτοῦ) their.

4. ταῦτα, (*neut. pl. of* οὗτος) these, *or* these *things here.*

5. ἐκεῖνος, that, that there.

1. Matt. i. 20, } angel.
1. —— ii. 13, } angel.
1. —— iii. 3, voice.
1. —— viii. 8, word.
1. —— xv. 9, commandments.
5. —— xxii. 7 (*om.* G ~ Tr A.)
1. —— 30, angels.
1. —— xxviii. 2, angel.
1. Mark i. 45, city.
1. —— ii. 1, house.
1. —— vii. 7, commandments.
1. —— xii. 25, angels.
1. Luke i. 78, dayspring.
1. —— ii. 9, angel.
1. —— 12, babe.
1. —— vii. 3, elders.
1. —— xxii. 17, cup (insert art. L.)
1. —— 37, transgressors.
2. —— xxiv. 21.
1. Acts v. 19, } angel.
1. —— vii. 35, } angel.
1. —— 38, lively oracles.
3. —— 54, heart.
1. —— viii. 26, angel.
1. —— ix. 5, pricks (*ap.*)
1. —— x. 22, centurion.
1. —— xii. 7, 23, } angel.
1. —— xxvii. 23, } angel.
1. Rom. ii, 12 twice, law.
1. —— 14 4 times, gentiles, law 1st, law 3rd, law 4th.
1. Rom. iii. 20 twice, deeds, law.
1. —— 21, without...law.
1. —— 27, by...law.
1. —— 28 twice, Jews, Gentiles.
1. —— 31, void...law.
1. —— iv. 13, righteousness.
1. —— 14, of...law.
1. —— ix. 22, vessels.
1. —— 23, vessels.
1. —— xi. 5, election.
1. —— xiii. 4, minister.
1. 1 Cor. ii. 14, natural.
1. —— iii. 16, temple.
1. —— vi. 15 twice, members, member.
1. —— 19, temple.
1. —— x. 4, that rock (lit. *a spiritual, following rock.*)
1. —— 16 twice, communion.
1. —— xii. 15 twice, hand, eye.
1. —— xv. 47, earth.
1. 2 Cor. iii. 3, epistle.
1. —— vi. 16 twice, temple.
1. —— 17, unclean.
1. —— xi. 13, apostles.
1. —— 15, ministers.
4. Gal. ii. 18, things.
4. —— v. 17, things.
1. 1 Tim. v. 11, younger.
1. Heb. i. 6, angels.
1. 3 John 3, brethren.

The Greek article is sometimes translated by A or AN (which, see.) Generally it is translated by THE or some other word. Frequently it is untranslated. It was intended to present in the Appendix a list of these passages (as mentioned on page 17), but the use of Rotherham's *New Testament Critically Emphasised* (Bagster's) or Newberry's *New Testament* (Bagster's) will indicate every such occurrence by special sign used in the text.

See also, HEART, SAME, etc., SELFSAME, SAID.

THEATRE.

θέατρον, place of public spectacles; *hence*, theatre, the place where dramatic performances took place, and where the public assembled on other occasions to hear har-

angues and hold public consultations, (*occ.* 1 Cor. iv. 9.)

Acts xix. 19, 31.

THEE.

(*For various combinations with other words, see below.*)

1. σοῦ, (*Gen. of* σύ, thou) of thee, *but translated* thee, (*the Gen. case being governed by some verb or preposition.*)

2. σοί, (*Dat. of* σύ, thou) to *or* for thee, (*see above.*)

3. σέ, (*Acc. of* σύ, thee) thee, (*see under No.* 1.) *Followed by inf.*, thee...that those.

4. σεαυτοῦ, thyself.

1. Matt. ii. 6.
2. —— 13.
1. —— iii. 14.
1. —— iv. 6 1st.
3. —— 6 2nd.
2. —— 9.
1. —— v. 23.
3. —— 25 1st.
3. —— 25 2nd (om. σε παραδῷ, deliver thee, L T Trb ℵ.)
3. —— 29 1st.
1. —— 29 2nd.
2. —— 29 3rd.
3. —— 30 1st.
1. —— 30 2nd.
2. —— 30 3rd.
3. —— 39.
2. —— 40.
3. —— 41, 42 1st.
1. —— 42 2nd.
1. —— vi. 2.
2. —— 4, 6, 18, 23.
2. —— viii. 19.
2. —— ix. 2 (om. G L T Tr A ℵ.)
2. —— 5 (No. 1, G L T Tr A ℵ.)
3. —— 22.
1. —— xi. 10.
2. —— 23, 25.
1. —— xii. 38.
2. —— 47.
3. —— xiv. 28.
1. —— xvii. 27.
3. —— xviii. 8 1st.
1. —— 8 2nd.
2. —— 8 3rd.
3. —— 9 1st.
1. —— 9 2nd.
2. —— 9 3rd.
3. —— 15 1st (om. εἰς σε, against thee, L T Trmb Ab ℵ.)
1. —— 15 2nd & 3rd.
1. —— 16 (No. 4, T.)
2. —— 26, 29, 32.
3. —— 33.
2. —— xix. 27.
3. —— xx. 13.
1. —— xxi. 19.
2. —— 23.
3. —— xxv. 21, 23, 24, 37, 38, 39 twice, 44.
2. —— xxvi. 33, 35 1st.
3. —— 35 2nd.
1. Matt. xxvi. 62.
3. —— 63, 68, 73.
1. —— xxvii. 13.
1 Mark i. 2 (om. ἔμπροσθέν σου, before thee, G L T Tr A ℵ.)
2. —— 24 1st, and see T (what have we to do with)
3. —— 24 2nd, 37.
2. —— ii. 5 (G ~), (om. G T Tr A ℵ.)
2. —— 9 (No. 1, G T Tr A ℵ.)
3. —— iii. 32.
3. —— v. 7, 19, 31, 34.
2. —— vi. 22, 23.
3. —— ix. 17.
2. —— 25.
3. —— 43, 45, 47.
2. —— x. 28.
3. —— 49, 52.
1. —— xi. 14.
2. —— 28.
3. —— xiv. 31 1st.
3. —— 31 2nd.
1. —— 60.
1. —— xv. 4.
2. Luke i. 13.
3. —— 19 1st.
2. —— 19 2nd.
1. —— 28.
3. —— 35 1st.
2. —— 35 2nd.
1. —— 35 3rd (G⇔Lb), (om. ἐκ σου, of thee, St T Tr A ℵ.)
3. —— ii. 48.
3. —— iii. 22.
2. —— iv. 6.
1. —— 10 1st.
3. —— 10 2nd, 11, 34.
2. —— v. 20, 23.
3. —— vi. 29, 30.
3. —— vii. 7, 20.
1. —— 27.
3. —— 50.
3. —— viii. 20.
1. —— 28.
3. —— 45, 48.
1. —— ix. 38.
2. —— 57, 61.
2. —— x. 21, 35.
2. —— xi. 7.
3. —— 27.
2. —— 35.
3. Luke xi. 36.
1. —— xii. 20.
3. —— 58 3 times.
2. —— 59.
2. —— xiii. 31.
3. —— xiv. 9, 10 1st.
2. —— 10 2nd.
3. —— 12 1st.
2. —— 12 2nd, 14.
3. —— 18, 19.
1. —— xv. 18.
2. —— 29.
1. —— xvi. 2.
3. —— 27.
3. —— xvii. 3 (om. εἰς σε, against thee, G → L T Tr A ℵ.)
3. —— 4 1st.
3. —— 4 2nd (om. ἐπὶ σε, to thee, G), (πρὸς σε, towards thee, T Tr A.)
3. —— 18.
2. —— xviii. 11, 28.
3. —— 42.
3. —— xix. 2, 22, 43 1st.
2. —— 43 2nd.
3. —— 43 3rd & 4th, 44 1st.
2. —— 44 2nd.
2. —— xx. 2.
1. —— xxii. 32, 33.
2. —— 34.
3. —— 64.
3. John i. 48 twice, 50 twice.
1. —— iii. 26.
2. —— iv. 10.
2. —— vi. 30.
3. —— vii. 20.
3. —— viii. 10 (ap.), 11 (ap.)
1. —— ix. 37.
3. —— x. 33.
3. —— xi. 8.
2. —— 22.
3. —— 28.
2. —— 41.
3. —— xiii. 8.
2. —— 37.
3. —— xvi. 30.
3. —— xvii. 1, 3, 4.
2. —— 5.
1. —— 7, 8.
3. —— 11, 13.
2. —— 21.
3. —— 25 twice.
3. —— xviii. 26.
2. —— 34.
3. —— 35.
3. —— xix. 10 twice.
2. —— 11.
2. —— xxi. 3.
3. —— 15, 16, 17, 18, 20, 22, 23.
2. Acts iii. 6.
3. —— v. 9.
3. —— vi. 27, 34, 35.
2. —— vii. 3.
2. —— viii. 20, 22.
1. —— 34.
2. —— ix. 6.
3. —— 34.
2. —— x. 6 (ap.)
3. —— 19, 22 1st.
1. —— 22 2nd.
3. —— 33 1st.
2. —— 33 2nd.
3. —— xi. 14.
3. —— xiii. 11, 33, 47.
2. —— xvi. 18.
1. —— xvii. 32.
1. —— xviii. 10 1st.
2. —— 10 2nd.
3. —— 10 3rd.
1. —— xxi. 21, 24.
3. —— 37.
1. —— 39.
2. —— xxii. 10
3a. —— 14.
3. Acts xxii. 19, 21.
3. —— xxiii. 18, 20.
1. —— 21.
3. —— 30 1st.
1. —— 30 2nd, 35.
1. —— xxiv. 2.
3a. —— 4.
3. —— 8 (ap.)
1. —— 19.
3. —— 25.
1. —— xxv. 26.
1. —— xxvi. 2.
3. —— 3 1st.
1. —— 3 2nd (om. G⇄L T Tr A ℵ.)
3. —— 16, 17 twice, 24.
2. —— xxvii. 24 1st.
1. —— 24 2nd.
1. —— xxviii. 21, 22.
3. Rom. ii. 4, 27.
3. —— iv. 17.
3. —— ix. 17 1st.
2. —— 17 2nd.
1. —— x. 8.
3. —— xi. 18.
1. —— 21.
3. —— 22.
3. —— xv. 3.
3. 1 Cor. iv. 7.
3. —— viii. 10 (om. Lb.)
1. 2 Cor. vi. 2 1st.
2. —— 2 2nd.
2. Gal. iii. 8.
2. Eph. v. 14.
2. —— vi. 3.
3. Phil. iv. 3.
3. 1 Tim. i. 3, 18.
3. —— iii. 14.
2. —— iv. 14.
1. —— 16.
2. —— vi. 13.
1. —— 21 (ὑμῶν, you, L T Tr ℵ.)
1. 2 Tim. i. 3.
3. —— 4.
2. —— 5 twice.
3. —— 6 1st.
2. —— 6 2nd.
2. —— ii. 7.
3. —— iii. 15.
4. —— iv. 11.
3. —— 21.
3. Tit. i. 5 1st.
2. —— 5 2nd.
1. —— ii. 15.
3. —— iii. 12, 15.
1. Philem. 7.
2. —— 8.
3. —— 10, 18, 23.
3. Heb. i. 5, 9.
3. —— ii. 12.
3. —— v. 5.
3. —— vi. 14 twice.
3. —— xiii. 5 twice.
2. Jas. ii. 18.
3. 2 John 5, 13.
1. 3 John 3.
3. —— 14 twice.
2. Jude 9.
1. Rev. ii. 4.
2. —— 10.
1. —— 14, 20.
3. —— iii. 3 1st (om. ἐπὶ σε, on thee, G → L T Trb A.)
3. —— 3 2nd.
1. —— 8.
3. —— 9, 10, 16.
2. —— 18.
2. —— iv. 1.
2. —— xii. 17.
3. —— xv. 4 1st (om. G⇄L T Tr A.)
1. —— 4 2nd.
2. —— xvii. 7.
1. —— xviii. 14.
2. —— 22 3 times, 23 twice.
2. —— xxi. 9.

THEE (BE IT FAR FROM)

ἵλεως, propitious, merciful, pitiful, σοι, to thee, } ἔστω (*or* εἴη) ὁ θεός, may God be, *must be understood* [in accordance with the Heb. idiom; (lxx. *for* חלילה ל, 2 Sam. xx. 20; xxiii. 17; 1 Chron. xi. 19.) God be *pitiful to thee*, God forbid.]

Matt. xvi. 22.

THEE (FOR)

σοί, (*Dat. of* σύ, thee) to *or* for thee.

(*In passages not quoted,* "FOR" *is the translation of a preposition in the Greek.*)

Matt. v. 29, 30.
— xi. 24.
— xiv. 4.
— xvii. 4.
— xviii. 8. 9.
— xxvi. 17.
Mark v. 19.
— vi. 18.
— ix. 5.
— 43 (σε (Acc.), thee, L T Tr A ℵ.)
Mark ix. 45 (σε (Acc.), thee, L T Tr A ℵ.)
— 47 (σε, thee, T Tr A ℵ.)
Luke ix. 33.
John v. 10.
Acts ix. 5 (ap.)
— xxii. 10.
— xxvi. 14.
2 Cor. xii. 9.
Rev. xiv. 15 (om. G L T Tr A ℵ.)

THEE (OF)

σοῦ, (*Gen. of* σύ, thee) of thee.

1 Cor. xii. 21. | Philem. 20.

THEE (TO)

σοί, (*Dat. of* σύ, thee) to *or* for thee,

(*in passages not quoted,* "TO" (*or* "UNTO" *is the translation of a preposition in the Greek.*)

Luke xiv. 9.
John iv. 10.
— ix. 26.
Acts xxi. 23.
Rom. xiii. 4.
— xv. 9.
Philem. 11 twice, 19.
Heb. viii. 5.
3 John 14.

THEE (UNTO)

σοί, *see above.*

Matt. v. 26.
— viii. 13.
— xi. 21 twice.
— xv. 18.
— xvi. 17, 18, 19, 22.
— xviii. 17, 22.
— xx. 14.
— xxi. 5.
— xxv. 44.
— xxvi. 34.
Mark ii. 11.
— v. 41.
— x. 51.
— xiv. 30, 36.
Luke i. 3.
— v. 24.
— vii. 14, 40, 47.
— viii. 39.
— x. 13 twice.
— xviii. 41.
— xxii. 11.
Luke xxiii. 43, see To-day.
John i. 50.
— iii. 3, 5, 7, 11.
— iv. 26.
— v. 12, 14.
— xi. 40.
— xiii. 38.
— xviii. 30.
— xix. 11.
— xxi. 18.
Acts ix. 17.
— x. 32 (ap.)
— xxiii. 18.
— xxiv. 14.
— xxvi. 16 twice.
1 Tim. i. 18.
— iii. 14.
Philem. 16, 21.
2 John 5.
3 John 13.
Rev. ii. 5, 16.
Rev. xvii. 1.

THEE (WHAT HAVE I TO DO WITH)

τί, what
ἐμοὶ, to me
καὶ, and
σοί, to thee.

Mark v. 7. | Luke viii. 28.
John ii. 4.

THEE (WHAT HAVE WE TO DO WITH)

τί, what
ἡμῖν, to us
καὶ, and
σοί, to thee.

Matt. viii. 29. | Mark i. 24.
Luke iv. 34.

THEFT (-S.)

1. κλοπή, theft, *by stealth, (as distinguished from force)*; (lxx. *for inf.* of גנב, Gen. xl. 15), (*non occ.*)
2. κλέμμα, the thing stolen; a theft, (*non occ.*)

1. Matt. xv. 19. | 1. Mark vii. 22.
2. Rev. ix. 21.

THEIR, THEIRS.

"THEIR" is generally the translation of αὐτός in those passages not given below.

1. ἑαυτῶν, of *or* belonging to themselves.
2. ἴδιος, own, one's own, private, particular.
3. τούτων, (*Gen. pl. of* οὗτος) of *or* belonging to these, (of these here).
4. ἐκείνων, (*Gen. pl. of* ἐκεῖνος) of *or* belonging to those, (*of those there*).

1. Matt. viii. 22.
1. — xxi. 8.
1. — xxv. 3 (αὐτῶν, *their*, G L T Tr A), (om. ℵ.)
1. Luke ix. 60.
1. — xii. 36.
1. — xvi. 8.
1. — xix. 35 (αὐτῶν, *their*, L Tr A ℵ.)
1. — xxii. 66 (αὐτῶν, *their*, G ∾ Tr A ℵ.)
1. — xxiii. 48 (om. G ⇉ T Tr A ℵ.)
3. Rom. xi. 30.
2. 1 Cor. xiv. 35.
4. 2 Cor. viii. 14 twice.
1. Eph. v. 28.
1. 1 Pet. iv. 19 (αὐτῶν, *their*, G ∾ L T Tr A ℵ.)
2. 1 Tim. iv. 2.
4. 2 Tim. iii. 9.
1. Jude 6.
1. Rev. x. 3.
1. — 4 (om. τὰς φωνὰς ἑαυτῶν, *uttered their voices*, G L T Tr A ℵ), i.e. *sounded*.
1. — xvii. 13 (αὐτῶν, *their*, G ∾ L T Tr A ℵ.)

THEIR OWN.

1. αὐτῶν, of them their.
2. ἑαυτῶν, of *or* belonging to themselves.

1. Matt. ii. 12.
1. — xvii. 25.
1. Mark viii. 3.
1. Luke ii. 39.
1. Acts vii. 41.
1. — xiv. 16.

2. Rom. xvi. 4, 18.
2. Eph. v. 28.
2. Phil. ii. 21.
2. 2 Thes. iii. 12.
1. Heb. xii. 10.
1. 2 Pet. ii. 12, 13.
2. Jude 13.
1. —— 16.
2. Jude 18.

THEIR OWN PLEASURE.

{ τὸ, the, δοκοῦν, to seem αὐτοῖς, to them, } that which seemed [*good*] to them.

Heb. xii. 10.

THEIR OWN SELVES.

ἑαυτοὺς, themselves.

2 Cor. viii. 5.

THEIR OWN HOME (UNTO)

{ πρὸς, towards, ἑαυτούς, themselves, } unto their own [*lodging*.]

John xx. 10 (πρὸς αὐτούς, *unto them*, T Tr ℵ.)

THEIR WAYS (WENT)

ἀπέρχομαι, to go away from *one place to another*, to go away, depart. *Here*, ἀπῆλθον, went off.

Matt. xxii. 5.

THEM.

"THEM" is generally the translation of αὐτός, (and is always emphatic) in those passages which are not quoted below.

1. ἐκεῖνος, that, that one *Here*, *pl*. those, those there.
2. ἑαυτῶν, themselves.
3. τούτους, (*Acc. pl. of* οὗτος) these, these (*persons*) here.
4. ταῦτα, (*neut. pl. of* οὗτος) these, these (*things*) here.
5. τούτοις, (*masc. and neut. Dat. pl. of* οὗτος) to *or* for these, these here.
6. ταύταις, (*fem. Dat. pl. of* οὗτος) to *or* for *or* in these, these here.

1. Matt. xiii. 11.
2. —— xv. 30.
1. —— xx. 4.
2. —— xxv. 3.
2. Mark ii. 19 (*ap.*)
1. —— iv. 11.
2. —— viii. 14.
1. —— xvi. 13.
1. Luke x. 35.
6. —— xiii. 14 (αὐταῖς, *in these*, L T Tr A ℵ.)
4. John x. 25.
1. —— 35.
1. Acts xviii. 19.
2. —— xxi. 23.
3. —— 24.
3. Rom. viii. 30 3 times.
3. 1 Cor. vi. 4.
4. —— 13.
1. —— x. 11.
3. —— xvi. 3.
5. 1 Tim. iv. 15.
3. Heb. ii. 15.
1. —— iv. 2 twice.
1. —— vi. 7.
4. Rev. x. 4 (αὐτά, *these*, L T Tr A ℵ.)

THEM ALSO.

2 John x. 16.

THEM (AMONG)

ἑαυτοῖς, among themselves.

Matt. xxvii. 35 (*ap.*) | John xix. 24.

THEMSELVES.

(*For various combinations with other words, see below.*)

1. ἑαυτοὺς, (*Acc. pl.*) themselves, their own selves.
2. ἑαυτῶν, (*pl. Gen.*) themselves, their own selves.
3. ἑαυτοῖς, (*pl. Dat.*) to *or* for themselves.
4. ἀλλήλων, each other, one another.
5. αὐτοί, (*pl.*) them.
6. αὐτά, (*Acc. sing.*) them.
7. αὐτοῖς, (*Dat. pl.*) to *or* for them.
8. αὐτούς, (*Acc. pl.*) them.

3. Matt. ix. 3.
3. —— xiv. 15.
3. —— xvi. 7.
1. —— xix. 12.
3. —— xxi. 25, 38.
3. Mark ii. 8.
3. —— iv. 17.
—— —— vi. 30, see Gather.
3. —— 36, 51.
4. —— viii. 16.
2. —— ix. 8.
1. —— 10.
8. —— 16, marg. (text, *them*.)
4. —— 34.
1. —— x. 26.
1. —— xi. 31.
1. —— xii. 7.
1. —— xiv. 4.
4. —— xv. 31.
1. —— xvi. 3.
4. Luke iv. 36.
1. —— vii. 30.
3. —— 49.
3. —— xviii. 9.
1. —— xx. 5.
1. —— 14 (No. 4, T Tr A ℵ.)
1. —— 20.
1. —— xxii. 23.
1. —— xxiii. 12 (No. 8, T Tr A ℵ.)
4. John vi. 52.
1. —— vii. 35.
1. —— xi. 55.
4. John xi. 56.
1. —— xii. 19.
4. —— xvi. 17.
7. —— xvii. 13.
4. —— xix. 24.
4. Acts iv. 15.
—— —— xi. 26, see Assemble.
5. —— xv. 32.
5. —— xvi. 37.
1. —— xxiii. 12, 21.
4. —— xxvi. 31.
4. —— xxviii. 4, 25.
3. —— 29.
3. Rom. i. 24 (No. 7, L T Tr A.)
3. —— 27.
4. —— ii. 15, marg. (text, *one another*.)
3. 1 Cor. x. 12.
1. —— xvi. 15.
1. 2 Cor. x. 12 3 times.
1. Eph. iv. 19.
2. Phil. ii. 3.
1. 1 Tim. ii. 9.
1. —— vi. 10.
6. Heb. ix. 23.
1. 1 Pet. iii. 5.
1. Jude 12.
1. —— 19 (*om.* S[t] G ⇉ L T Tr A ℵ.)
1. Rev. vi. 15.
1. —— viii. 6 (No. 8, L T ℵ.)
—— —— xix. 17, see Gather

THEY THEMSELVES.

1. αὐτοί, they, them.
2. { αὐτοί, them, οὗτοι, these, these here, } these themselves.

1. John xviii. 28.
2. Acts xxiv. 15.
1. Gal. vi. 13.
1. 1 Thes. i. 9.
1. 2 Pet. ii. 19.

THEMSELVES (AMONG)

ἑαυτοῖς, (*Dat. pl.*) to, for, unto, among *or* upon, themselves.

2 Cor. x. 12.

THEMSELVES (FOR)

1 Tim. vi. 19.

THEMSELVES (TO)

Rom. xiii. 2.
1 Tim. iii. 13.
2 Tim. iv. 3.
Heb. vi. 6.

THEMSELVES (UNTO)

Rom. ii. 14.
1 Pet. i. 12.
2 Cor. v. 15.

THEMSELVES (UPON)

Pet. ii. 1.

THEN. [adv. and conj.]

Adverbs :—

1. τότε, then, at that time.
2. εἶτα, then, afterwards, after that.
3. ἔπειτα, (*No.* 2, *with* ἐπί, upon, *prefixed*) thereupon, afterwards, next.

Conjunctions :—

4. οὖν, therefore, then, *marking the formal or logical inference; used in arguing, exhortation, interrogation, to resume an interrupted subject, and to indicate mere transition from one thing to another.*

    (a) *with* μέν, (indeed); therefore indeed, then truly.

5. ἄρα, accordingly, therefore, consequently thence, since, (according to nature and custom) *marking a correspondence in point of fact* (ergo); *and a transition to what naturally follows from the words preceding;* still further, beyond that.
6. ἄραγε, (*No.* 5, *with* γε, indeed, *suffixed*) accordingly indeed (*more emphatic than No.* 5); since at least, well then; [γε strengthens the assertion, while ἄρα sums up the premisses on which it is made.]
7. καί, and, also, even.
8. { τε, and, both, (*simply annexing*) / καί, and, also, even, (*uniting*) } and...also.
9. τε, and, (*simply annexing.*)
10. δέ, but; *although* δέ *may be sometimes translated* and, then, now, *or* so, *yet there is always a degree of opposition and interruption.*
11. λοιπόν, henceforward, finally.
12. οὐκοῦν, not so then, therefore then. *Here, "and* yet *thou* (*emph.*) *art* not *a King?" or "thou art* then *a King?"* (*non occ.*)
13. τοίνυν, indeed now, (*drawing an inference, and used where one proceeds with an inference.*)

1. Matt. i. 7, 16, 17.
1. —— iii. 5, 13, 15.
1. —— iv. 1, 5, 10, 11.
1. —— v. 24.
1. —— vii. 5.
4. ——— 11.
1. ——— 23.
1. —— viii. 26.
1. —— ix. 6, 14, 15, 29, 37.
1. —— xi. 20.
4. —— xii. 12.
1. ——— 13, 22.
4. ——— 26.
5. ——— 28.
1. ——— 29, 38, 44, 45.
1. —— xiii. 26.
4. ——— 27, 28.
1. ——— 36, 43.
— ——— 52, see T he.
4. ——— 56.
1. —— xv. 1, 12, 28.
1. —— xvi. 12, 20, 24, 27.
4. —— xvii. 10.
1. ——— 13, 19.
6. ——— 26.
1. —— xviii. 21, 32.
4. —— xix. 7.
1. ——— 13.
5. ——— 25.
1. ——— 27.
1. —— xx. 20.
1. —— xxi. 1.
4. ——— 25.
1. —— xxii. 8, 13, 15, 21.
4. ——— 43, 45.
1. —— xxiii. 1.
1. —— xxiv. 9, 10, 14, 16, 21, 23, 30 twice, 40.
5. ——— 45.
1. —— xxv. 1, 7.
8. ——— 24.
1. ——— 31, 34, 37, 41, 44, 45.
1. —— xxvi. 3, 14, 31, 36, 38, 45, 50, 52.
4. ——— 54.
1. ——— 56, 65, 67, 74.
1. —— xxvii. 3, 9, 13, 16.
4. ——— 22.
1. ——— 26, 27, 38, 58.
1. —— xxviii. 10.
1. Mark ii. 20.
1. —— iii. 27.
4. ——— 31 (No. 7, L T Tr A ℵ.)
2. —— iv. 28.
3. —— vii. 5 (No. 7, G∾L T Tr A ℵ.)
— —— x. 8, see So.
4. —— xi. 31 (om. L T Tr A.)
1. —— xiv. 14, 21, 26, 27.
4. —— xv. 12.
— —— xvi. 19, see So.
4. Luke iii. 7, 10.
1. —— v. 35.
4. —— vi. 9 (No. 10, L T Tr ℵ.)
1. ——— 42.
4. —— vii. 31.
2. —— viii. 12.
4. —— x. 37 (G∾), (No. 10, G L T Tr A ℵ.)
4. —— xi. 13.
1. ——— 26.
4. —— xii. 26.
5. ——— 42.
4. —— xiii. 15 (No. 10, L T Tr A ℵ.)
1. ——— 26.
1. —— xiv. 10, 21.
3. —— xvi. 7.
7. —— xix. 15.
4. —— xx. 5 (*om.* G → L^b T Tr A ℵ.)
4. ——— 17.
1. —— xxi. 10, 20, 21, 27.
4. —— xxii. 36 (No. 10, T Tr ℵ.)
4. ——— 70.
1. —— xxiii. 30.
1. —— xxiv. 45.
4. John i. 21.
4. ——— 22 (*om.* L.)
4. ——— 25.
1. —— ii. 10 (*om.* L^b T Tr^b A^b ℵ.)
4. ——— 18, 20.
4. —— iii. 25.
4. —— iv. 5, 9, 11, 28.
4. ——— 30 (*om.* G L T Tr A.)
— ——— 35, see T (and)

4. John iv. 45, 48, 52.
4. —— v. 4 (ap.)
4. ——— 12 (om. G→Lb T Trb A ℵ.)
4. ——— 19.
4. —— vi. 5, 14, 21, 28, 30.
4. ——— 32 (om. G ⇉)
4. ——— 34, 41.
4. ——— 42 (νῦν, *now*, T Tr A), i.e. *that he now*, instead of *then that he*.
4. ——— 53, 67.
4. ——— 68 (om. G L T Tr A ℵ.)
4. —— vii. 6 (om. G ⇉ ℵ.)
1. ——— 10.
4. ——— 11, 25, 28, 30, 33, 35, 45.
4. ——— 47 (om. T A ℵ.)
4. ——— viii. 12, 19, 21, 22, 25, 28 1st.
1. ——— 28 2nd.
4. ——— 31.
4. ——— 41 (om. G → L T Tr A ℵ.)
4. ——— 48 (om. G L T Tr A ℵ.)
4. ——— 52 (om. L T Tr A ℵ.)
4. ——— 57, 59.
4. —— ix. 12 (om. L T Tr A ℵ.)
4. ——— 15, 19, 24.
4. ——— 28 (om. G L Tr A ℵ.)
4. —— x. 7, 24.
4. ——— 31 (om. T Trb [ℵ.)
1. —— xi. 7.
4. ——— 12.
1 & 4. ——— 14 (om. Lb.)
4. ——— 16, 17, 20, 21, 31, 32, 36, 41, 45, 47, 53, 56.
4. —— xii. 1, 3, 4, 7.
1. ——— 16.
4. ——— 28, 35.
4. —— xiii. 6, 14.
4. ——— 22 (om. G ⇉ T Trb A.)
4. ——— 27, 30.
4. —— xvi. 17.
4. —— xviii. 3, 6, 7, 10, 11, 12, 16, 17, 19, 27.
4. ——— 28 (om. G ⇉)
4. ——— 29.
4. ——— 31 (om. Lb.)
4. ——— 33.
12. ——— 37.
4. ——— 40.
1. —— xix. 1.
4. ——— 5.
4. ——— 10 (om. G ⇉ T Ab ℵ.)
1. ——— 16.
4. ——— 20, 21, 23.
2. ——— 27.
4. ——— 32, 40.
4. —— xx. 2, 6.
1. ——— 8.
4. ——— 10, 19, 20, 21.
2. ——— 27.
4. —— xxi. 5, 9.
4. ——— 13 (om. G L T Tr ℵ.)
4. ——— 23.
1. Acts i. 12.
4a. —— ii. 41.
1. —— iv. 8.
1. —— v. 26.
1. —— vi. 11.
1. —— vii. 4.
1. —— viii. 17.
4a. —— ix. 31.
4. —— x. 23.
1. ——— 46, 48.
4. —— xi. 17.
6. ——— 18 (No. 5, L T Tr ℵ), (ἄρα [γε] A.)
10. Acts xii. 3.
1. —— xiii. 12.
1. —— xv. 22.
1. —— xvii. 14.
4. ——— 29.
4. —— xix. 3, 36.
1. —— xxi. 26, 33.
4. —— xxii. 29.
1. —— xxiii. 3.
9. ——— 5.
4a. ——— 31.
1. —— xxv. 12.
1. —— xxvi. 1.
11. —— xxvii. 20.
9. ——— 29.
1. ——— 32.
1. —— xxviii. 1.
4. Rom. iii. 1, 9, 27, 31.
4. —— iv. 1, 9, 10.
4. —— v. 9.
4. —— vi. 1, 15.
4 & 1. ——— 21.
— —— vii. 3, see So.
4. ——— 7, 13.
5. ——— 21.
— ——— 25, see So.
7. —— viii. 17.
4. ——— 31.
4. —— ix. 14, 19, 30.
4. —— x. 14.
— ——— 17, see So.
4. —— xi. 1, 5, 7, 11, 19.
4. —— xiv. 16.
4. 1 Cor. iii. 5.
— ——— 7, see So.
1. —— iv. 5.
— —— v. 10, see For.
4a. —— vi. 4.
4. ——— 15.
— —— vii. 38, see So.
4. —— ix. 18.
4. —— x. 19.
2. —— xii. 28 (No. 3, L T Tr A ℵ.)
1. —— xiii. 10 (om. G ⇉ L T Tr A ℵ.)
4. —— xiv. 15, 26.
2. —— xv. 5.
2. ——— 7 (No. 3, Lm T Tr A ℵ.)
— ——— 13, see Not.
5. ——— 14.
— ——— 16, see Not.
5. ——— 18.
2. ——— 24.
1. ——— 28.
7. ——— 29.
1. ——— 54.
4. 2 Cor. iii. 12.
— —— iv. 12, see So.
5. —— v. 14.
— ——— 20, see Now.
8. —— vi. 1.
1. —— xii. 10.
3. Gal. i. 18.
3. —— ii. 1.
5. ——— 21.
— —— iii. 9, see So.
4. ——— 19, 21.
5. ——— 29.
7. —— iv. 7.
1. ——— 8.
4. ——— 15.
1. ——— 29.
— ——— 31, see So.
3. —— v. 11.
1. —— vi. 4.
4. Eph. v. 15.
— Phil. i. 18, see What.
4. Col. iii. 1.
1. ——— 4.
4. 1 Thes. iv. 1.
3. ——— 17.
1. —— v. 3.
1. 2 Thes. ii. 8.
2. 1 Tim. ii. 13.
1. —— iii. 2.
2. ——— 10.
4. Heb. ii. 14.
4. —— iv. 14.
3. —— vii. 27.
4a. —— ix. 1.
1. —— x. 7, 9.
5. —— xii. 8.
1. ——— 26.
2. Jas. i. 15.
13. —— ii. 2.
7. Jas. ii. 4 (om. G ⇉ L T Tr A ℵ.)
13. ——— 24 (om. G L T Tr A ℵ.)
3. —— iii. 17.
3. —— iv. 14.
4. 1 Pet. iv. 1.
— 2 Pet. iii. 6, see T was (that)
4. ——— 11.

THEN HE.

{ ὁ, he, / δέ, but, } but he.

Matt. xiii. 52.

THEN WAS (THAT)

{ ὁ, the, / τότε, then.

2 Pet. iii. 6.

THEN (AND)

καί, and.

John iv. 35.

THENCE.

ἐκεῖθεν, thence, from that place.

Matt. v. 26.
—— ix. 27.
—— xi. 1.
—— xii. 9.
—— xiii. 53.
—— xiv. 13.
—— xv. 21.
—— xix. 15. [Tr A.)
Mark i. 19 (om. G ⇉ Lb T
Mark vi. 11.
—— ix. 30.
—— x. 11, see Go.
Luke ix. 4.
—— xii. 59.
John iv. 43.
—— xi. 54.
Acts xviii. 7.
——— 18, see Sail.

THENCE (AND)

κἀκεῖθεν, and thence, from that place also.

Acts xiv. 26.
Acts xx. 15.

THENCE (AND FROM)

κἀκεῖθεν, *see above*.

Mark x. 1.
Acts vii. 4.
Acts xxi. 1.
—— xxvii. 4.
Acts xxviii. 15.

THENCE ALSO.

κἀκεῖθεν, *see above*.

Acts xxvii. 12 (ἐκεῖθεν, *thence*, L T Tr A ℵ.)

THENCE (FROM)

1. ἐκεῖθεν, *see* "THENCE."
2. ὅθεν, whence.

1. Matt. iv. 21.
1. —— ix. 9.
1. —— xii. 15.
1. —— xv. 29.
1. Mark vi. 1.
1. Mark vii. 24.
1. Luke xvi. 26.
1. Acts xiii. 4.
1. —— xvi. 12.
2. —— xxviii. 13.

THENCE FORTH.

ἔτι, yet, still : any longer.

Matt. v. 13.

THENCEFORTH (FROM)

{ ἐκ, from
{ τούτου, this.

John xix. 12.

THERE.

1. ἐκεῖ, there, in that place.
2. ἐκεῖσε, thither, to that place, (*non occ.*)
3. ἐκεῖθεν, thence, from that place.
4. ἐν, in, in *it*, therein.
5. ἐνθάδε, here, in this place.
6. αὐτοῦ, (*adv. of place*) here, t ere, in this or that place; (lxx. *for* בּמה, Ex. xxiv. 14; Numb. xxii. 19, פּה, Numb. xxxii. 6; Deut. v. 31; 2 Sam. xx. 4), (*occ.* Matt. xxvi. 36.)
7. κεῖμαι, to lie, to be laid. *Here part.*, laid.
8. ὧδε, hither, here, in this place.

1. Matt. ii. 13, 15.
— —— v. 23, see T (and)
1. ——— 24.
1. —— vi. 21.
1. —— viii. 12.
1. —— xii. 45.
1. —— xiii. 42, 50, 58.
1. —— xiv. 23.
1. —— xv. 29.
1. —— xviii. 20.
1. —— xix. 2.
1. —— xxi. 17.
1. —— xxii. 11, 13.
8. —— xxiv. 23.
1. ——— 28, 51.
1. —— xxv. 30.
1. —— xxvi. 71.
1. —— xxvii. 36, 47, 55, 61.
1. —— xxviii. 7.
— ——— 10, see T (and)
1. Mark i. 13 (*om.* G L T Tr A ℵ.)
— ——— 35, see T (and)
— ——— 38, see T also.
1. —— ii. 6.
1. —— iii. 1.
1. —— v. 11.
1. —— vi. 5, 10.
1. —— xi. 5.
1. —— xiii. 21.
1. —— xiv. 15.
1. —— xvi. 7.
1. Luke ii. 6.
1. —— vi. 6.
1. —— viii. 32.
1. —— ix. 4.
1. —— x. 6.
1. —— xi. 26.
1. —— xii. 18, 34.
1. Luke xiii. 28.
1. —— xv. 13.
1. —— xvii. 21, 23.
1. —— xxii. 12.
1. —— xxiii. 33.
4. —— xxiv. 18.
1. John ii. 1, 6, 12.
1. —— iii. 22, 23.
1. —— iv. 6, 40.
1. —— v. 5.
1. —— vi. 3, 22, 24.
1. —— x. 40, 42.
1. —— xi. 15, 31.
— ——— 54, see T (and)
1. —— xii. 2, 9, 26.
1. —— xix. 42.
7. —— xxi. 9.
1. Acts ix. 33.
4. ——— 38.
5. —— x. 18.
— —— xii. 13, marg. see Hearken.
— —— xiv. 7, see T (and)
1. ——— 28 (*om.* G L T Tr A ℵ.)
— —— xv. 33, see Tarry.
6. ——— 34.
1. —— xvi. 1.
1. —— xvii. 14.
— ——— 21, see T (be)
6. —— xviii. 19 (No. 1, L Tr[m] ℵ.)
— ——— 23, see Time.
1. —— xix. 21.
3. —— xx. 13.
4. ——— 22.
2. —— xxi. 3.
6. ——— 4.
2. —— xxii. 5.
— ——— 10, see T (and)
1. Acts xxv. 9, 14.
— ——— 20, } see T
— —— xxvii. 6, } (and)
1. Rom. ix. 26.
1. 2 Cor. iii. 17 (*om.* G ⇉ L T Tr A ℵ.)
— Gal. iii. 28 3 times, } see
— Col. iii. 11, } T is.
1. Tit. iii. 12.
1. Heb. vii. 8.
1. Jas. ii. 3.
1. —— iii. 16.
1. —— iv. 13.
1. Rev. ii. 14.
1. —— xii. 6.
1. —— xxi. 25.
1. —— xxii. 5 (ἔτι, G L T Tr[b] A ℵ, i.e. *more night*, instead of, *night there.*)

THERE (AND)

κἀκεῖ, and there, there also.

Matt. v. 23.
—— xxviii. 10.
Mark i. 35.
John xi. 54.
Acts xiv. 7.
—— xxii. 10.
—— xxv. 20.
—— xxvii. 6.

THERE ALSO.

κἀκεῖ, *see above.*

Mark i. 38.

THERE (BE)

ἐπιδημέω, to be among one's own people, to be at home. *Here*, sojourning *foreigners*, *or strangers* sojourning there.

Acts xvii. 21.

THERE IS.

ἔνι, (*for* ἔνεστι, *impers.* of ἔνειμι, to be in *any place*) there is in, among *or* with.

Gal. iii. 28 3 times. | Col. iii. 11.

THEREABOUT.

{ περὶ, concerning
{ τούτου, this.

Luke xxiv. 4.

THEREAT.

{ διὰ, through
{ αὐτῆς, it.

Matt. vii. 13.

THEREBY.

1. { διὰ, through
   { αὐτῆς, it.
2. { διὰ, through
   { ταύτης, this.
3. { ἐν, in *or* by
   { αὐτῷ, it.

1. John xi. 4.
3. Eph. ii 16, marg. *in himself.*
1. Heb. xii. 11.
2. —— 15.
2. —— xiii. 2.
3. 1 Pet. ii. 2.

THEREFORE.

1. οὖν, therefore, then, (*marking the logical or formal inference.*) *See* "THEN," *No.* 4.

   (a) *with* μέν, indeed.

2. { διὰ, on account of, τοῦτο, this, this here, } on this account, because of, for the sake of, (*marking the reason of an action, not the instrument.*)

3. διό, on which account, wherefore.

4. διότι, on account of this or that, for this reason that.

5. ἄρα, accordingly, therefore, by consequence, consequently, thence, since, *i.e.* according to nature and custom, (*marking a correspondence in point of fact, and a transition to what naturally follows from the words preceding*) still further, beyond that.

   (a) ἆρα, (*interrogative.*)

6. { ἄρα, *see No.* 5, οὖν, *see No.* 1, } so, therefore, (*οὖν marking the logical inference, and ἄρα the harmony that exists between the premisses and conclusion.*)

7. ὥστε, so that, *expressing the result.*

8. { εἰς, unto, with respect to a certain result, τοῦτο, this, } in order to this; with a view to this result.

9. { παρὰ, to or along the side of, (*with idea of comparison*) τοῦτο, this, } therefore (*with the notion of consequence.*)

10. τοίνυν, surely now, indeed now, (*drawing an inference, and used where one proceeds with an inference.*)

11. τοιγαροῦν, consequently, therefore, by certain consequence, wherefore then.

12. ἀλλά, other, otherwise, but; but on the contrary, but still, yet.

13. { ἀνθ', instead of, for, ὧν, which, } in return for which things, because.

14. γάρ, (*contr. of* γὲ ἄρα, verily, therefore); *hence*, the fact is, in fact; *and when the fact is given as an explanation*, as the case stands; (*expressing more than the Eng.* for, *inasmuch as it includes the cause, reason, motive, principle, occasion, or inducement of what has been previously affirmed.*)

15. δέ, but, (*see* "THEN," *No.* 10.)

16. δή, truly, indeed, by all means.

17. { τε, and, both, (*simply annexing*) καί, and, also, even, (*uniting*) } and...also.

1. Matt. iii. 8, 10.
1. —— v. 19, 23, 48.
1. —— vi. 2, 8, 9, 22, 23.
2. ——— 25.
1. ——— 31, 34.
1. —— vii. 12, 24.
1. —— ix. 38.
1. —— x. 16, 26, 31, 32.
2. —— xii. 27.
2. —— xiii. 13.
1. ——— 18, 40.
2. ——— 52.
2. —— xiv. 2.
1. —— xviii. 4.
2. ——— 23.
1. ——— 26.
1. —— xix. 6.
5. ——— 27.
1. —— xxi. 40.
2. ——— 43.
1. —— xxii. 9, 17, 21, 28.
1. —— xxiii. 3.
2. ——— 14 (*ap.*)
1. ——— 20.
1. —— xxiv. 15, 42.
2. ——— 44.
1. —— xxv. 13, 27, 28.
1. —— xxvii. 17, 64.
1. —— xxviii. 19 (*om.* G → L^b T Tr^b A ℵ.)
8. Mark i. 38.
7. —— ii. 28.
3. —— vi. 14.
14. —— viii. 38.
1. —— x. 9.
2. —— xi. 24.
1. —— xii. 6 (*om.* L^b T Tr A ℵ.)
1. ——— 9 (*om.* T A.)
1. ——— 23 (*om.* G → T Tr A ℵ.)
2. ——— 24.
1. ——— 27 (*om.* T Tr^b A ℵ.)
1. ——— 37 (*om.* G → L^b T Tr A ℵ.)
1. —— xiii. 35.
3. Luke i. 35.
1. —— iii. 8, 9.
1. —— iv. 7.
8. ——— 43 (ἐπὶ τοῦτο, *for this*, L T Tr A ℵ.)
1. —— vi. 36 (*om.* G ⇄ L T Tr A ℵ.)
1. —— vii. 42.
1. —— viii. 18.
1. —— x. 2 1st (No. 15, G ∼ L T Tr A ℵ.)
1. ——— 2 2nd, 40.
2. —— xi. 19.
1. ——— 34 (*om.* G → L T Tr A ℵ.)
1. Mark xi. 35, 36.
2. ——— 49.
13. —— xii. 3.
1. ——— 7 (*om.* L^b T Tr A.)
2. ——— 22.
1. ——— 40 (*om.* L T Tr A ℵ.)
1. —— xiii. 14.
2. —— xiv. 20.
1. —— xv. 28 (No. 15, L T Tr A ℵ.)
1. —— xvi. 11, 27.
1. —— xix. 12.
1. —— xx. 15.
10. ——— 25.
1. ——— 29, 33, 44.
1. —— xxi. 8 (*om.* L T Tr A ℵ*.)
1. ——— 14.
1. ——— 36 (No. 15, L T Tr A ℵ.)
1. —— xxiii. 16.
1. ——— 20 (No. 15, L Tr A ℵ.)
1. ——— 22.
2. John i. 31.
1. —— ii. 22.
1. —— iii. 29.
1. —— iv. 1, 6, 33.
1. —— v. 10.
2. ——— 16, 18.
1. —— vi. 13, 15, 24, 30.
1. ——— 43 (*om.* G L^b T Tr A.)
1. ——— 45 (*om.* G L T Tr A ℵ.)
1. ——— 52, 60.
2. ——— 65.
1. —— vii. 3.
2. ——— 22.
1. ——— 40.
1. —— viii. 13, 24, 36.
2. ——— 47.
1. —— ix. 7, 8, 10, 16.
2. ——— 23.
1. ——— 41 (*om.* G ⇄ L^b T Tr A ℵ.)
2. —— x. 17.
1. ——— 19 (*om.* G → L T Tr A ℵ.)
1. ——— 39 (*om.* Tr^b A^b.)
1. —— xi. 3, 6, 33, 38, 54.
1. —— xii. 9, 17, 19, 21.
1. ——— 29 (*om.* L^b Tr^b.)
2. ——— 39.
1. ——— 50.
2. —— xiii. 11.
1. ——— 24, 31 (*om.* St G.)
1. —— xv. 18.

2. John xv. 19.
1. —— 22.
2. —— xvi. 15.
1. —— xviii. 4, 8, 25.
1. —— 31 (*om.* L T Tr A.)
1. —— 37, 39.
1. —— xix. 1.
1. —— 4 (*om.* G L T Tr A ℵ.)
1. —— 6.
2. —— 11.
1. —— 13, 16, 24 1st.
1a. —— 24 2nd.
1. —— 26, 30, 31, 38, 42.
1. —— xx. 8, 25.
1. —— xxi. 6, 7.
1a. Acts i. 6.
2. —— ii. 26.
1. —— 30, 33, 36.
1. —— iii. 19.
1a. —— viii. 4.
1. —— 22.
12. —— x. 20.
3. —— 29 1st.
1. —— 29 2nd, 32, 33 twice.
1a. —— xii. 5.
1. —— xiii. 38, 40.
1a. —— xiv. 3.
1. —— xv. 2 (No. 15, T Tr ℵ.)
1. —— 10, 27.
1. —— xvi. 11 (No. 15, T A ℵ.)
1. —— 36.
1a. —— xvii. 12, 17.
1. —— 20, 23.
1a. —— xix. 32.
1. —— xx. 28 (*om.* Lb T Tr ℵ.)
3. —— 31.
1. —— xxi. 22, 23.
1. —— xxiii. 15.
1. —— xxv. 5, 17.
1. —— xxvi. 22.
1. —— xxviii. 20, 28
3. Rom. ii. 1.
1. —— 21, 26.
4. —— iii. 20.
1. —— 28 (No. 14, G L T Tr A* ℵ.)
2. —— iv. 16.
3. —— 22.
1. —— v. 1.
6. —— 18.
1. —— vi. 4, 12.
5. —— viii. 1.
6. —— 12.
6. —— ix. 18.
1. —— xi. 22.
1. —— xii. 1.
1. —— 20 (G ∾), (No. 12, L T Tr A ℵ.)
7. —— xiii. 2.
1. —— 7, 10, 12.
1. —— xiv. 8, 13.
6. —— 19.
1. —— xv. 17, 28.
1. —— xvi. 19.
7. 1 Cor. iii. 21.
7. —— iv. 5.
1. —— v. 7 (*om.* G L T Tr A ℵ.)
7. —— 8.
1a. —— vi. 7.
16. —— 20.
15. —— vii. 8.
1. —— 26.
1. —— viii. 4.
10. —— ix. 26.
1. —— x. 31.
1. —— xi. 20.
9. —— xii. 15, 16.
1. —— xiv. 11, 23.
1. —— xv. 11.
7. —— 58.
1. —— xvi. 11, 18.
1. 2 Cor. i. 17.
2. —— iv. 1.
— —— 13 1st, see T (and)
3. —— 13 2nd.
1. —— v. 6, 11.
7. —— 17.
1. —— vii. 1.
2. —— 13.
1. —— 16 (*om.* St L T Tr A ℵ.)
12. —— viii. 7.
17. —— 11.
1. —— ix. 5.
1. —— xi. 15.
1. —— xii. 9.
3. —— 10.
2. —— xiii. 10.
5a. Gal. ii. 17 (No. 5, L.)
1. —— iii. 5.
5. —— 7.
7. —— iv. 16.
1. —— v. 1 (*ap.*)
6. —— vi. 10.
— Eph. ii. 19, see T (now)
1. —— iv. 1, 17.
1. —— v. 1, 17.
1. —— vi. 14.
12. —— 24.
1. Phil. ii. 1.
1a. —— 23.
1. —— 28, 29.
1. —— iii. 15.
7. —— iv. 1.
1. Col. ii. 6, 16.
1. —— iii. 5, 12.
2. 1 Thes. iii. 7.
11. —— iv. 8.
6. —— v. 6.
6. 2 Thes. ii. 15.
1. 1 Tim. ii. 1, 8.
8. —— iv. 10.
1. —— v. 14.
1. 2 Tim. i. 8.
1. —— ii. 1.
1. —— 3 (συγκακοπάθησον, *take thy share in suffering hardship, instead of* σὺ οὖν κακοπάθησον, *thou therefore endure hardness,* G ∾ L T Tr A ℵ.)
2. —— 10.
1. —— 21.
1. —— iv. 1 (*om.* G L T Tr A ℵ.)
2. Philem. 15.
1. —— 17.
2. Heb. i. 9.
2. —— ii. 1.
1. —— iv. 1, 6.
5. —— 9.
1. —— 11, 16.
3. —— vi. 1.
1a. —— vii. 11.
1. —— ix. 23.
1. —— x. 19, 35.
3. —— xi. 12.
10. —— xiii. 13.
1. —— 15.
1. Jas. iv. 4, 7, 17.
1. —— v. 7.
1. 1 Pet. ii. 7.
1. —— iv. 7.
1. —— v. 6.
1. 2 Pet. iii. 17.
1. 1 John ii. 24 (*om.* G ⇄ L T Tr A ℵ.)
2. —— iii. 1.
2. —— iv. 5.
1. 3 John 8.
1. Rev. ii. 5.
1. —— iii. 3 twice, 19.
2. —— vii. 15.
2. —— xii. 12.
2. —— xviii. 8.

THEREFORE (AND)

3. 2 Cor. iv. 13.

THEREFORE (NOW)

6. Eph. ii. 19.

THEREIN.

1. { ἐν, in
   { αὐτῷ, it.

2. { εἰς, unto, into,
   { αὐτήν (αὐτό) it.

3. { ἐν, in
   { τούτῳ, this, this here.

4. τούτοις, in these.

2. Mark x. 15.
1. Luke x. 9.
2. —— xviii. 17.
1. —— xix. 45 (*ap.*)
1. Acts i. 20.
1. —— xiv. 15.
1. —— xvii. 24.
2. —— xxvii. 6, and see T (put)
1. Rom. i. 17.
1. —— vi. 2.
3. 1 Cor. vii. 24.
1. Eph. vi. 20, marg. *thereof.*
3. Phil. i. 18.
1. Col. ii. 7 (*om.* G → T Tr Ab ℵ.)
2. Heb. iv. 6.
4. 2 Pet. ii. 20.
1. —— iii. 10.
1. Rev. i. 3.
1. —— x. 6 3 times.
1. —— xi. 1.
1. —— xii. 12.
1. Rev. xxi. 22.

THEREIN (PUT)

{ ἐπιβιβάζω, to make go [upon, } to make go on board.
{ εἰς, into
{ αὐτό, it,

Acts xxvii. 6.

THEREINTO.

εἰς αὐτήν, into it.

Luke xxi. 21.

THEREOF.

1. { ἐν, in
   { αὐτῳ, it.

2. { περὶ, about, concerning,
   { αὐτοῦ, it.

3. { ἐξ, out of
   { αὐτοῦ, it.

2. Matt. xii. 36.
3. Luke xxii. 16.
3. John iv. 12.
3. —— vi. 50.
1. Eph. vi. 20, marg. (text, *therein.*)

THEREON.

1. { ἐπὶ, upon } (a) *with the Dat.*, thereon, (*with idea of simple rest.*)
   { αὐτός it, }

(b) *with the Acc.*, thereon, (*with idea of downward pressure.*)

2. { ἐπάνω, above, upon,
αὐτοῦ, it.

3. { ἐν, in
αὐτῷ, it.

2. Matt. xxi. 7.
3. —— 19.
2. —— xxiii. 20, 22.
3. Mark xi. 23.
3. Luke xiii. 6.
1b. John xii. 14.
1a. Rev. vi. 4 (No. 1b, G L T Tr A ℵ.)

See also, BUILD, LAID, LOOK, THINK, WRITE.

THEREOUT.

See, COME.

THERETO.

See, ADD, AGREE.

THEREUNTO.

1. { εἰς, unto, for,
αὐτὸ, it,
τοῦτο, this (*om.* G≓L T Tr A ℵ.)

2. { εἰς, unto
τοῦτο, this, this *here*.

1. Eph. vi. 18.
2. 1 Thes. iii. 3.
— Heb. x. 1, see Comers.
2. 1 Pet. iii. 9.

THEREUPON.

See, BUILD.

THEREWITH.

1. { ἐν, in *or* with
αὐτῷ, it.

2. { ἐπὶ, on, upon,
τούτοις, these.

3. τούτοις, with these, with these *here*.

3. 1 Tim. vi. 8.
1. Jas. iii. 9 twice.
2. 3 John 10.

THESE.

(*For various combinations with other words, see below.*)

1. οὗτοι, (*masc. pl. of* οὗτος) these persons, these here, (*the nearer.*)

2. αὗται, (*fem. pl. of* οὗτος) these, these here.

3. ταῦτα, (*neut. pl. of* οὗτος) these things, these things here.

4. τούτων, (*Gen. pl. of* οὗτος) of these, of these here.

5. τούτοις, (*Dat. pl. of* οὗτος) to *or* for these, (these here.)

6. ταύταις, (*Dat. pl. fem. of* οὗτος) to *or* for these.

7. τούτους, (*Acc. pl. of* οὗτος) these, these here.

8. ταύτας, (*Acc. pl. fem. of* οὗτος) these, these here.

4. Matt. iii. 9.
1. —— iv. 3.
4. —— v. 19.
7. —— vii. 24 (*om.* Lb Trb A.)
7. —— 26, 28.
3. —— x. 2.
7. —— 5.
4. —— 42.
8. —— xiii. 53.
3. —— xv. 20.
4. —— xviii. 6, 10, 14.
7. —— xix. 1.
1. —— xx. 12.
1. —— 21 (*om.* Lb.)
1. —— xxi. 16.
6. —— xxii. 40.
3. —— xxiii. 23.
3. —— xxiv. 8.
1. —— xxv. 46.
7. —— xxvi. 1.
1. —— 62.
1. Mark iv. 15, 16.
1. —— 18 (ἄλλοι, G L T Tr A ℵ, i.e. *there are others*, instead of *these are they.*)
1. —— 20 (ἐκεῖνοι, *those*, T Tr A ℵ.)
3. —— vii. 23.
3. —— x. 20.
1. —— xii. 40.
8. —— xiii. 2.
3. —— 8.
1. —— xiv. 60.
3. —— xvi. 17 (*ap.*)
3. Luke i. 19, 65.
3. —— ii. 19.
3. —— 51 (*om.* Lb T Trmb Ab ℵ.)
4. —— iii. 8.
1. —— viii. 13, 21.
7. —— ix. 28, 44.
3. —— xi. 42.
1. —— xiii. 2.
4. —— xvii. 2.
3. —— xviii. 21.
7. —— xix. 15.
1. —— 40.
1. —— xxi. 4.
4. —— 12.
2. —— 22.
1. —— xxiv. 17.
6. —— 18.
1. —— 44.
3. John iii. 2
6. —— v. 3.
3. —— 19.
1. —— vi. 5.
3. —— vii. 9.
3. —— viii. 20, 30.
7. —— x. 19.
3. —— 21.
1. —— xvii. 11.
4. —— 20.
1. John xvii. 25.
7. —— xviii. 8.
3. —— xx. 31.
1. Acts i. 14.
4. —— 21.
1. —— ii. 7, 15.
7. —— 22.
8. —— iii. 24.
5. —— iv. 16.
7. —— v. 5, 24.
4. —— 32.
5. —— 35.
4. —— 36, 38.
3. —— x. 44.
7. —— 47.
1. —— xi. 12.
6. —— 27.
3. —— xiii. 42 (*om.* G→)
4. —— xiv. 15.
4. —— xv. 28 (*om.* G⇉)
1. —— xvi. 17, 20.
3. —— 38.
1. —— xvii. 6, 7, 11.
3. —— xix. 37.
1. —— xx. 5.
2. —— 34.
4. —— xxi. 38.
1. —— xxv. 11.
4. —— xxvi. 29.
1. —— xxvii. 31.
1. Rom. ii. 14 (οἱ τοιοῦτοι, *such*, Lm.)
3. —— ix. 8.
1. —— xi. 24, 31.
5. —— xv. 23.
3. 1 Cor. xii. 11.
3. —— xiii. 13.
8. 2 Cor. vii. 1.
2. Gal. iv. 24.
3. —— v. 17.
1. Col. iv. 11.
6. 1 Thes. iii. 3.
5. —— iv. 18.
1. 1 Tim. iii. 10.
4. 2 Tim. ii. 21.
1. —— iii. 8.
4. Heb. i. 2.
8. —— ix. 23.
1. —— xi. 13, 39.
4. 2 Pet. i. 4.
1. —— ii. 12, 17.
1. 1 John v. 7.
1. Jude 8, 10, 12.
5. —— 14.
1. —— 16, 19.
1. Rev. vii. 13, 14.
4. —— ix. 18.
6. —— 20.
1. —— xi. 4, 6, 10.
1. —— xiv. 4 3 times.
8. —— xvi. 9.
1. —— xviii. 13, 14, 16.
1. —— xix. 9.
1. —— xxi. 5.
1. —— xxii. 6.

THESE MANY.

τοσοῦτος, so great, so much. *Here, pl.*, so many.

Luke xv. 29.

THESE MATTERS (OF)

{ περὶ, concerning
{ τούτων, these things.

Acts xxv. 20.

THESE MEN.

7. Mark viii. 4.

THESE THINGS.

1. ταῦτα, (*neut. pl. of* οὗτος) these things, (these here.)

2. τούτων, (*Gen. pl. of* οὗτος) of these things.

3. τούτοις, (*Dat. pl. of* οὗτος) to *or* for these things.

4. τάδε, this, this here, (*marking a closer relation than either of the above.*)

1. Matt. i. 20.
1. —— iv. 9.
1. —— vi. 32, 33.
1. —— ix. 18.
1. —— xi. 25.
1. —— xiii. 34, 51, 56.
1. —— xxiv. 2, 3, 33, 34.
1. Mark ii. 8.
1. —— vi. 2.
1. —— xi. 28 twice, 29, 33.
1. —— xiii. 4 twice, 29, 30.
1. —— xvi. 17 (*ap.*)
1. Luke i. 20.
1. —— iv. 28.
1. —— v. 27.
1. —— vii. 9.
2. ——— 18.
1. —— viii. 8.
1. —— x. 1, 21.
1. —— xi. 25, 53 (*ap.*)
1. —— xii. 30, 31.
1. —— xiii. 17.
1. —— xiv. 6, 15, 21.
1. —— xv. 26.
1. —— xvi. 14.
1. —— xviii. 22 (*om.* L T Tr A ℵ.)
1. —— xix. 11.
1. —— xx. 2, 8.
1. —— xxi. 6, 7 twice, 9.
2. ——— 28.
1. ——— 31, 36.
1. —— xxiii. 31, 49.
1. —— xxiv. 9, 10.
2. ——— 14.
1. ——— 21, 26.
1. John i. 28.
1. —— ii. 16, 18.
1. —— iii. 9, 10, 22.
1. —— v. 16, 34.
1. —— vi. 1, 59.
1. —— vii. 1, 4.
1. —— viii. 28.
1. —— xi. 11.
1. —— xii. 16 3 times, 26, 41.
1. —— xiii. 17.
1. —— xiv. 25.
1. —— xv. 11, 17, 21.
1. —— xvi. 1, 3, 4 twice, 6, 25, 33.
1. —— xvii. 13.
1. —— xix. 24, 36.
1. —— xx. 18.
1. —— xxi. 1, 24.
1. Acts i. 9.
1. —— v. 5 (*om.* G ⇉ L T Tr A ℵ.)
1. ——— 11.
1. —— vii. 1, 50, 54.
1. —— xi. 18.
1. —— xii. 17.
1. —— xiv. 15.
1. —— xv. 17.
1. —— xvii. 8, 20.
1. —— xviii. 1.
1. —— xix. 21.
2. ——— 36.
1. —— xxi. 12.
1. —— xxiii. 22.
2. —— xxiv. 8.
1. ——— 9.
1. ——— 22 (*om.* ἀκούσας ταῦτα, *heard these things*, G L T Tr A ℵ.)
2. —— xxv. 9.
2. —— xxvi. 26.
1. Rom. viii. 31.
3. ——— 37.
3. —— xiv. 18 (τούτῳ, *this thing*, G L T Tr A ℵ.)
1. 1 Cor. iv. 6, 14.
1. —— ix. 8, 15.
1. —— x. 6, 11.
1. 2 Cor. ii. 16.
1. —— xiii. 10.
1. Eph. v. 6.
1. Phil. iv. 8.
3. Col. iii. 14.
1. 2 Thes. ii. 5.
1. 1 Tim. iii. 14.
1. —— iv. 6, 11, 15.
1. —— v. 7, 21.
1. —— vi. 2, 11.
1. 2 Tim. i. 12.
1. —— ii. 14.
1. Tit. ii. 15.
2. —— iii. 8 1st.
1. ——— 8 2nd.
1. Heb. vii. 13.
2. —— ix. 6.
1. Jas. iii. 10.
1. 2 Pet. i. 8, 9, 10.
2. ——— 12, 15.
2. —— iii. 11, 16.
1. 1 John i. 4.
1. —— ii. 1, 26.
1. —— v. 13.
4. Rev. ii. 1, 8, 12, 18.
4. Rev. iii. 1, 7, 14.
1. —— vii. 1 (τοῦτο, *this*, G ∾ L T Tr A ℵ.)
1. —— xviii. 1.
1. —— xix. 1.
1. Rev. xxii. 8 twice, 16.
1. ——— 18 (αὐτά, *them*, G L T Tr A), (αυτόν, *this*, ℵ.)
1. ——— 20.

THESE THINGS (OF)

τούτων, of these things, of these things here.

Matt. vi. 32.
Luke xii. 30.
—— xviii. 34.
Luke xxiv. 48.
Acts xxvi. 26.
1 Cor. ix. 15.
Rev. xviii. 15.

THESE WORDS.

ταῦτα, these things.

John ix. 22, 40.
—— xvii. 1.
John xviii. 1.
Acts xxviii. 29 (*ap.*)

THESE CAUSES (FOR)

{ ἕνεκα, because of, by reason of, on account of, for the sake of,
{ τούτων, these *things*.

Acts xxvi. 21.

THESE (OF)

τούτων, of these, of these here.

Matt. vi. 29.
—— xxv. 40, 45.
Luke x. 36.
Luke xii. 27.
Acts i. 24.
1 Cor. xiii. 13.
Heb. x. 18.

THESE (THAN)

τούτων, (*after a comparative*) than these things, than these here.

Matt. v. 37.
Mark xii. 31.
John i. 50.
—— v. 20.
John vii. 31 (*om.* G → L T Tr A ℵ.)
—— xiv. 12.
—— xxi. 15.

THESE (UPON)

τούτοις, to, for, *or* on these.

1 Cor. xii. 23.

THESE (WITH)

τούτοις, to, for, *or* with these.

Heb. ix. 23.

See also, NONE, SAME, SAYINGS.

THEY.

"THEY" is frequently part of the translation of the 3rd pers. pl. of the verb.

Also of the plural of αὐτός, or of the article ὁ, ἡ, τό.

In all other passages it is the translation of one of these words following.

1. ἐκεῖνος, that, that one there. *In pl.*, those, those there.
2. κἀκεῖνος, (*No.* 1, *with* καί, and, also, *prefixed*) and those, even those, those also.
3. οὗτοι, (*masc. pl.*) these, these here.
4. ταῦτα, (*neut. pl.*) these things, these things here.
5. τούτων, (*Gen. pl.*) of these; of these here.
6. ἑαυτούς (ἑαυτάς), (*pl. Acc.*) they themselves.
7. ὅστις, any one who, some one who. *Pl.*, every one who, all who, whosoever, whatsoever.

5. Matt. xi. 7.
1. Mark xvi. 20 (*ap.*)
3. Luke viii. 14, 15.
1. —— ix. 34 2nd (αὐτοί, *they*, G T Tr ℵ.)
3. —— xiii. 4 (αὐτοί, *they*, L T Tr A ℵ.)
1. John v. 39 1st.
4. —— vi. 9.
4. —— x. 25.
1. —— 6 1st.
1. —— xi. 13.
3. —— xviii. 21.
7. Acts v. 16. [G ∾ ℵ.)
1. —— x. 9 (αὐτοί, *they*,
1. —— 10 (αὐτοί, *they*, G ∾ L T Tr A ℵ.)
3. Acts xiii. 4 1st (αὐτοί, *they*, L T Tr A ℵ.)
2. —— xv. 11.
1. —— xxi. 6.
7. —— xxiii. 14.
3. Rom. viii. 14.
3. —— ix. 6.
1. —— xi. 23 1st.
1. 1 Cor. ix. 25.
1. —— xv. 11.
3. —— xvi. 17 (αὐτοί, *they*, L T Tr A.)
3. Gal. vi. 12 1st.
1. Heb. xii. 25.
6. Rev. ii. 9.
6. —— iii. 9.

THEY OF.

1. ἀπό, from, (*here, lit., whom they valued* from *Israel's sons.*)
2. ἐκ, from among.

1. Matt. xxvii. 9. | 2. Rev. xi. 9.

THEY THAT.

αἵτινες, *nom. pl. fem. of No.* 7, *above.*

Matt. xxv. 3 (αἵ δε, *but the* L), (αἵ γαρ, *for the*, T Tr A ℵ.)

THEY THEMSELVES.

1. αὐτοί, they.
2. { αὐτοὶ, they, / οὗτοι, these, } even these, these themselves.

1. John xviii. 28.
2. Acts xxiv. 15.
1. Gal. vi. 13.
1. 1 Thes. i. 9.
1. 2 Pet. ii. 19.

THEY (AND)

1. κἀκεῖνοι, and those (those there); those also.
2. αἵτινες, *pl. fem. nom. of* "THEY," *No.* 7.

1. Matt. xv. 18.
1. Mark xvi. 11 (*ap.*), 13 (*ap.*)
1. John xvii. 24.
2. Acts v. 16.
2. —— xxiii. 14.
1. 1 Cor. x. 6.

THEY (IN THAT)

αιτινες, *see* "THEY," *No.* 7.

Acts xvii. 11.

THICK.

See, GATHERED.

THIEF.

1. κλεπτης, a thief, one who steals by fraud *or* in secret, (*Lat.*, fur.)
2. λῃστής, a robber, one who robs openly and by violence, a plunderer, (*Lat.*, latro.)

1. Matt. vi. 19, 20.
2. —— xxi. 13.
1. —— xxiv. 43.
2. —— xxvi. 55.
2. —— xxvii. 38, 44.
2. Mark xi. 17.
2. —— xiv. 48.
2. —— xv. 27.
2. Luke x. 30, 36.
1. —— xii. 33, 39.
2. Luke xix. 46.
2. —— xxii. 52.
1. John x. 1, 8, 10.
1. —— xii. 6.
1. 1 Cor. vi. 10.
1. 1 Thes. v. 2, 4.
1. 1 Pet. iv. 15.
1. 2 Pet. iii. 10.
1. Rev. iii. 3.
1. —— xvi. 15.

THIGH.

μηρος, the thigh; (LXX. *for* ירך, Gen. xxiv. 2, 9), (*non occ.*)

Rev. xix. 16.

THINE.

See, THY.

THING, THINGS.

THING is frequently the translation of the neuter gender of the article ὁ (τό.)

THINGS generally represents the neuter pl. of adjectives without nouns, (most of which are referred to in list of words below.)

When THING is represented by a separate word in the Greek, it is one of these following.

1. *πρᾶγμα*, a thing done *or* to be done; deed, act, fact, matter.

2. *λόγος*, a word (*spoken, not written*); the thing spoken; a word, a saying, an account, (*with reference to what is in the speaker's mind.*)

3. *ῥῆμα*, that which is spoken, a word *as uttered by the living voice and considered by itself; including more than No.* 2, the matter, the whole transaction, discourse, saying.

4. *τι*, a certain thing, some thing.

1. Matt. xviii. 19.
2. —— xxi. 24 2nd.
1. Luke i. 1.
2. —— 4. [saying.)
3. —— 65, marg. text,
3. —— ii. 15, 19.
2. —— ix. 28, marg. (text, *saying.*)
2. Luke xx. 3.
1. Acts v. 4.
2. —— 24.
3. —— 32.
1. —— xxv. 26.
1. Heb. vi. 18.
1. —— x. 1 2nd.
1. —— xi. 1.

THINGS (THE)

1. *ταῦτα*, these *things*, these *things here*.

2. *αὐτά*, them.

1. Gal. v. 17. | 2. 1 Pet. i. 12. | 1. Gal. ii. 18.

THINGS THAT BE (THE)

τά, the *things*.

Matt. xvi. 23. | Mark viii. 33 twice.

THINGS THAT BELONG TO (THE)

τά, the *things*.

1 Cor. vii. 32.

THINGS THAT BE (THOSE)

τά, the *things*.

Matt. xvi. 23.

THINGS WHICH ARE (THE)

τά, the *things*.

Matt. xxii. 21.
Mark xii. 17 twice.
1 Cor. vii. 33.
Phil. ii. 21.

THINGS WHICH ARE CONTAINED IN (THE)

τά, the *things*.

Rom. ii. 14.

THINGS WHICH BE (THE)

τά, the *things*.

Luke xx. 25 twice.

THINGS WHICH CONCERN (THE)

τά, the *things*, (*lit.*, the things *of my weakness.*)

2 Cor. xi. 30.

THINGS WHICH MAKE FOR (THE)

τά, the *things*, (*lit.*, the things of peace.)

Rom. xiv. 19.

See also, ALL, ANY, APPEAR, BASE, BEFALL, BEHIND, BELONG, BETTER, BOAST, CARNAL, CERTAIN, CHARGE, COME, CONCERN, CONCERNING, CONTAINED, CONVENIENT, CORRUPTIBLE, CREEPING, DEADLY, DEEP, EARTHLY, EDIFY, EVERY, EVIL, EXCELLENT, FEARFUL, FEW, FOOLISH, FORMED, GIVE, GIVEN, GOOD, GREAT, GREATER, GREEN, HAPPEN, HAVE, HEAVENLY, HIDDEN, HIGH, HOLY, HONEST, HOPED, IDOL, INCREDIBLE, INVISIBLE, LEAST, LIFE, LIKE, MADE, MAKE, MANY, MARVELLOUS, MEAN, MEASURE, NECESSARY, NEEDFUL, NEITHER, NEW, NO, NONE, OFFEND, OLD, ONE, OTHER, OUGHT, PERTAIN, PERTAINING, PLEASE, PLEASING, POSSESS, PRESENT, READY, REMAIN, SAME, SAY, SEA, SELFSAME, SHAKEN, SMALL, SOME, SPIRITUAL, SPOKEN, STRANGE, STRANGLED, SUCH, THAT, THESE, THIS, THOSE, UNHOLY, UNLAWFUL, VAIN, VERY, WEAK, WHAT, WHATSOEVER, WHICH, WONDERFUL, WORSE, YOUR.

THINK (-EST, ETH, THOUGHT.)

1. *δοκέω*, to seem, to appear, to have the appearance; *then*, to seem to one's self, be of opinion, to hold for, believe; to form an estimate *or* opinion, *which may be right*, (John v. 39; Acts xv. 28; 1 Cor.

iv. 9; vii. 40) *but which may be wrong*, (Matt. vi. 7; Mark vi. 49; John xvi. 2.)

(a) *See* "SEARCH," *No.* 1a.

2. κρίνω, to divide, separate; make a distinction, come to a decision, to judge.

3. νομίζω, to regard *or* acknowledge as custom, to have *or* hold as customary; to regard *or* acknowledge as *anything, i.e. in its customary character, or in its customary* manner; *hence, gen.*, to regard, think, suppose.

4. φρονέω, to have mind, have intellect, to think, think out; to mind, be minded, have in mind.

5. ἡγέομαι, to lead, to go before, go first, lead the way; *then*, to lead out *before the mind*, to view, regard *as being so and so*, to esteem, account, reckon.

6. λογίζομαι, to occupy one's self with reckonings *or* calculations; *hence*, to reckon *or* count, to reason, (use the reason) to think, consider, conclude.

7. διαλογίζομαι, (*No.* 6, *with* διά, through *prefixed*) to reckon through, compute; deliberate, debate.

8. ἐνθυμέομαι, to have in one's emotions, to revolve in one's mind, think upon, (*occ.* Mark i. 20.)

9. νοέω, to perceive, observe, (*the mental correlative of sensational perception, the conscious action of the mind*); *hence*, to perceive, observe, *as distinct from mere sensation or feeling;* to understand, apprehend, discern.

10. ὑπονοέω, (*No.* 9, *with* ὑπό, under, *prefixed*) to suspect, surmise, conjecture.

11. οἴομαι, to suppose, (*always of something yet doubtful.*)

12. φαίνομαι, to appear, (*expressive of how a matter phenomenally shows and presents itself*) to show one's self, to show itself, to appear to be. *Here, lit.*, "How does it appear to you?"

— Matt. i. 20, see T on.
1. —— iii. 9.
3. —— v. 17.
1. —— vi. 7.
8. —— ix. 4.
3. —— x. 34.
1. —— xxiv. 44.
1. —— xxvi. 53.
— Mark x. 42, see T good.
12. —— xiv. 64.
— —— 72, see T thereon.
— Luke vii. 7, see Worthy.
1. —— viii. 18, marg. (text, *seem.*)
7. —— xii. 17.
1. —— 40.
1. —— xiii. 4.
1. —— xix. 11.
1a. John v. 39.
1. —— 45.
1. —— xi. 13.
1. —— xiii. 29.
1. —— xvi. 2.
3. Acts viii. 20.
8. —— x. 19, part, (διενθυμέομαι, *to ponder through*, G L T Tr A ℵ.)
1. —— xii. 9.
10. —— xiii. 25.
— —— xv. 38, see T good.
3. —— xvii. 29.
5. —— xxvi. 2.
2. —— 8.
1. —— 9.
4. —— xxviii. 22.
2. Rom. ii. 3.
— —— xii. 3 1st, see T highly.
4. Rom. xii. 3 2nd & 3rd.
4. 1 Cor. iv. 6 (*om.* φρονεῖν, *to think of men above*, L T Tr A ℵ, i.e. "*learn in us the motto*," or *lesson*—"*Not above what things have been written.*")
1. —— 9.
3. —— vii. 36.
1. —— 40.
1. —— viii. 2.
1. —— x. 12.
1. —— xii. 23.
2. —— xiii. 5.
4. —— 11.
2. —— 11, marg. (text, *reason.*
1. —— xiv. 37.
2. 2 Cor. iii. 5.
5. —— ix. 5.
2. —— x. 2 1st.
— —— 2 2nd, see T of.
2. —— 7, 11.
1. —— xi. 16.
6. —— xii. 6.
1. —— 19.
1. Gal. vi. 3.
9. Eph. iii. 20.
4. Phil. i. 7.
5. —— ii. 6.
1. —— iii. 4.
— —— iv. 8, see T on.
— 1 Thes. iii. 1, see T good.
— Heb. x. 29, see Worthy.
11. Jas. i. 7.
1. —— iv. 5.
— 1 Pet. iv. 4, 12, see Strange.
5. 2 Pet. i. 13.

THINK GOOD.

1. δοκεω, *see above, No.* 1.

2. εὐδοκέω, (*No.* 1, *with* εὐ, well *or* good, *prefixed.*)

3. ἀξιόω, to regard as deserving, hold worthy of; deem proper, regard as suitable, think good.

1. Mark x. 42, marg. (text, *be accounted.*)
3. Acts xv. 38.
2. 1 Thes. iii. 1.

THINK HIGHLY.

ὑπερφρονέω, ("THINK," *No.* 4, *with* ὑπέρ, over, *prefixed*) to think over much of one's self, be high-minded, (*non occ.*)

Rom. xii. 3.

THINK OF.

λογίζομαι, *see* "THINK," *No.* 6.

2 Cor. x. 2.

THINK ON.

1. λογίζομαι, *see* "THINK," *No.* 6.
2. ἐνθυμέομαι, *see* "THINK," *No.* 8.

2. Matt. i. 20 part. | 1. Phil. iv. 8.

THINK THEREON.

ἐπιβάλλω, to cast upon, cast over, *as in the mind. Here (part.) referring to Peter,* casting the matter over in his mind, going over the past step by step.

Mark xiv. 72 part.

THIRD.

τρίτος, the third. (*For typical meaning, see under* "THREE.")

[(a) The expression "*the third day,*" used of Christ's being in the grave "three days and three nights," is explained by a Jewish idiom *or* custom, of which there are two examples in the *O.T.*, viz. Esth. iv. 16, comp. with v. 1; and 1 Sam. xxx. 12, comp. with verse 13.

(b) The expression "the third heaven" is explained under the words "PARADISE" and "HEAVEN."]

a. Matt. xvi. 21.
a. —— xvii. 23.
— —— xx. 3.
a. ——— 19.
— —— xxii. 26.
a. —— xxvii. 64.
a. Mark ix. 31, } μετὰ τρεῖς
— —— x. 34, } ἡμέρας, *after three days,* instead of τῇ τρίτῃ ἡμέρα, *the third day,* G ∾ L T Tr A ℵ.)
— —— xii. 21.
— —— xv. 25.
a. Luke ix. 22.
— —— xii. 38.
a. —— xviii. 33.
— —— xx. 12, 31.
a. Luke xxiv. 7.
— ——— 21.
a. ——— 46.
— John ii. 1.
— Acts ii. 15.
a. —— x. 40.
— —— xx. 9, see Loft.
— —— xxiii. 23.
a. 1 Cor. xv. 4.
b. 2 Cor. xii. 2.
— Rev. iv. 7.
— —— vi. 5 twice.
— —— viii. 10 1st.
— ——— 10 2nd, see T past [(the)
— —— xi. 14.
— —— xiv. 9 (*om.* G → [ℵ*.)
— —— xvi. 4.
— —— xxi. 19.

THIRD DAY (THE)

(*When not separate words in the Greek.*)

τῇ τρίτῃ, on the third.

Luke xiii. 32. | Acts xxvii. 19.

THIRD PART (THE)

τὸ τρίτον, the third *of a whole,* the third part.

Rev. viii. 7 twice, 8, 9 twice, 10, 11, 12 5 times. | Rev. ix. 15, 18. —— xii. 4.

THIRD TIME (THE)

τὸ τρίτον, (*as adv.*) the third.

Mark xiv. 41.
Luke xxiii. 22.
John xxi. 14, 17 twice.
2 Cor. xii. 14.
2 Cor. xiii. 1.

THIRDLY.

τὸ τρίτον (*as adv.*), the third.

1 Cor. xii. 28.

THIRST. [noun.]

δίψος, thirst; (lxx. *for* צמא, Ex. xvii. 3.)

2 Cor. xi. 27.

THIRST. [verb.]

διψάω, to thirst, to be athirst; (lxx. *for* צמא, Judg. xv. 18; Prov. xxv. 22) metaph. to thirst after, long for.

Matt. v. 6.
John iv. 13, 14 (ap.)
—— vi. 35.
—— vii. 37.
John xix. 28.
Rom. xii. 20.
1 Cor. iv. 11.
Rev. vii. 16.

THIRSTY (BE)

Matt. xxv. 35. 37 part., 42.

THIRTY.

τριάκοντα, thirty.

Matt. xiii. 23.
—— xxvi. 15.
—— xxvii. 3, 9.
Mark iv. 8.
Luke iii. 23.
John v. 5.
—— vi. 19.
Gal. iii. 17.

THIRTY-FOLD.

Matt. xiii. 8. | Mark iv. 20.

THIS.

(*For various combinations with other words, see below.*)

1. οὗτος, (*nom. sing. masc.*) this, this here, this one here, (*the nearer, connected with the 2nd pers.*)
2. αὕτη, *nom. sing. fem. of No.* 1.
3. τοῦτο, *nom. and Acc. sing. neut. of No.* 1.
4. τούτου, *Gen. sing. masc. and neut. of No.* 1.
5. ταύτης, *Gen. sing. fem. of No.* 1.
6. τούτῳ, *Dat. sing. masc. and neut. of No.* 1.
7. ταύτῃ, *Dat. sing. fem. of No.* 1.

8. τούτοις, *Dat. pl. masc. and fem. of No.* 1.

9. τοῦτον, *Acc. sing. masc. of No.* 1.

10. ταύτην, *Acc. sing. fem. of No.* 1.

11. τούτους, *Acc. masc. pl. of No.* 1.

12. ταῦτα, *nom. and Acc. pl. masc. of No.* 1.

13. ὁ, ἡ, τό, the, (*see under* "A.")

14. ἐκεῖνος, that, that there, that one *or* that thing there, (*the more remote, connected with the 3rd person.*)

15. αὐτός, self, very; he, she, it; himself, herself, itself.

3. Matt. i. 22.
1. —— iii. 3, 17.
1. —— vii. 12 (οὕτω, *thus*, G ~)
3. —— viii. 9.
1. —— 27.
7. —— ix. 26, marg. (text, *hereof.*)
3. —— 28.
7. —— x. 23.
1. —— xi. 10.
15. —— 14.
10. —— 16.
1. —— xii. 23, 24.
6. —— 32.
5. —— 41, 42.
7. —— 45.
4. —— xiii. 15.
1. —— 19.
4. —— 22 (*om.* L T Tr A ℵ, i.e. *the.*)
3. —— 28.
4. —— 40 (*om.* G→ L T Tr Ab ℵ, i.e. *the.*)
2. —— 54.
1. —— 55.
1. —— xiv. 2.
1. —— xv. 8.
3. —— 11.
10. —— 15 (*om.* L T Tr A ℵ, i.e. *the.*)
7. —— xvi. 18.
3. —— 22.
1. —— xvii. 5.
6. —— 20.
3. —— 21 (*ap.*)
3. —— xviii. 4.
9. —— xix. 11 (*om.* Lb.)
3. —— 26.
3. —— xxi. 4.
1. —— 10, 11.
13. —— 21 1st.
6. —— 21 2nd.
10. —— 23.
1. —— 38.
2. —— 42.
9. —— 44 (*ap.*)
2. —— xxii. 20, 38.
10. —— xxiii. 36.
3. —— xxiv. 14.
2. —— 34.
14. —— 43.
2. —— xxvi. 8.
3. —— 9, 12, 13.
1. —— 21.
3. —— 26, 28.
4. —— 29.
7. —— 31, 34.
3. —— 39, 42, 56.
4. —— xxvii. 24.
1. —— 37, 54.
3. —— xxviii. 14.

1. Matt. xxviii. 15.
3. Mark i. 27 1st (*ap.*)
2. —— 27 2nd (*ap.*)
10. —— iv. 13.
4. —— 19 (*om.* G L T Tr A ℵ, i.e. *the.*)
1. —— 41.
1. —— vi. 3.
1. —— vii. 6.
9. —— 29.
2. —— viii. 12 1st.
7. —— 12 2nd, 38.
1. —— ix. 7.
3. —— 21, 29.
10. —— x. 5.
6. —— 30.
3. —— xi. 3 (*ap.*)
10. —— 28.
6. —— 33.
1. —— xii. 7.
10. —— 10.
2. —— 11, 16, 30 (*ap.*)
2. —— 31 (No. 15, G~L Tr.)
2. —— 43.
2. —— xiii. 30.
2. —— xiv. 4.
3. —— 9 1st (*om.* Lb T Tr A ℵ, i.e. *the.*)
13. —— 9 2nd.
3. —— 22, 24.
7. —— 27 (*om.* ἐν τῇ νυκτὶ ταύτῃ, *this night*, G ~ Lb T Tr A ℵ.)
7. —— 30.
3. —— 36.
9. —— 58.
1. —— 69.
9. —— 71.
3. Luke i. 18.
1. —— 29.
3. —— 34.
1. —— 36.
3. —— 43.
6. —— 61.
3. —— 66.
2. —— ii. 2.
3. —— 12, 15.
4. —— 17.
3. —— iii. 20.
6. —— iv. 3.
10. —— 6.
2. —— 21.
1. —— 22.
10. —— 23.
1. —— 36.
3. —— v. 6.
1. —— 21.
3. —— vi. 3.
3. —— vii. 4, 8.
1. —— 17, 27.
5. —— 31.

10. Luke vii. 44.
1. —— 49.
2. —— viii. 9, 11.
1. —— 25.
1. —— ix. 9.
9. —— 13.
1. —— 35.
3. —— 45, 48.
6. —— x. 5.
3. —— 11.
6. —— 20.
3. —— 28.
2. —— xi. 29.
7. —— 30.
5. —— 31, 32, 50, 51.
3. —— xii. 18.
7. —— 20.
3. —— 39.
10. —— 41.
9. —— 56.
10. —— xiii. 6.
7. —— 7.
3. —— 8.
4. —— 16.
10. —— xv. 3.
1. —— 24, 30, 32.
3. —— xvi. 2.
4. —— 8.
7. —— 24.
8. —— 26.
9. —— 28.
7. —— xvii. 6.
1. —— 18.
5. —— 25.
3. —— xviii. 5, 9.
1. —— 11.
12. —— 23.
6. —— 30.
3. —— 34.
6. —— xix. 9.
7. —— 42.
10. —— xx. 2, 9.
1. —— 14.
3. —— 17.
10. —— 19.
4. —— 34.
2. —— xxi. 3.
6. —— 23.
2. —— 32.
3. —— xxii. 15, 17, 19 twice, 20, 37, 42.
2. —— 53.
6. —— xxiii. 4.
9. —— 14 1st.
6. —— 14 2nd.
1. —— 38 (*ap.*)
8. —— xxiv. 21.
1. John i. 15.
2. —— 19.
1. —— 30, 34.
10. —— ii. 11.
3. —— 12.
9. —— 19.
1. —— 20.
3. —— 22.
2. —— iii. 19, 20.
4. —— iv. 13.
3. —— 15.
6. —— 20, 21, 27.
1. —— 29, 42.
3. —— 54.
12. —— v. 1.
3. —— 28.
1. —— vi. 14
3. —— 29.
9. —— 34.
3. —— 39, 40.
1. —— 42, 50.
4. —— 51.
1. —— 58 1st.
9. —— 58 2nd, 60.
3. —— 61.
10. —— vii. 8 1st (*om.* G⇉L T Tr A, i.e. *the.*)
10. —— 8 2nd.
1. —— 25, 26, 36.
3. —— 39. [49.
1. —— 40, 41, 46 (*ap.*),

2. John viii. 4 (*ap.*)
3. —— 6 (*ap.*)
4. —— 23 twice.
3. —— 40.
1. —— ix. 8, 9, 16, 19, 20, 24.
9. —— 39.
10. —— x. 6.
5. —— 16.
10. —— 18.
2. —— xi. 4.
4. —— 9.
3. —— 26.
1. —— 47.
3. —— 51.
3. —— xii. 5, 6.
15. —— 7.
3. —— 18.
6. —— 25.
5. —— 27 1st.
10. —— 27 2nd.
2. —— 30.
4. —— 31 1st (*om.* G⇉)
4. —— 31 2nd.
3. —— 33.
1. —— 34.
4. —— xiii. 1.
3. —— 28.
6. —— 35.
4. —— xiv. 30 (*om.* G L T Tr A ℵ, i.e. *the.*)
4. —— xv. 11.
3. —— 17, 18.
6. —— 30.
2. —— xvii. 2, 3.
4. —— xviii. 17, 29, 36 twice.
3. —— 38.
9. —— xix. 20.
3. —— 28.
12. —— 38.
3. —— xx. 22.
6. —— 30.
3. —— xxi. 14, 19 twice.
1. —— 23, 24.
6. Acts i. 6.
10. —— 16 (*om.* G→L T Tr Ab ℵ, i.e. *the.*)
5. —— 17, 25.
5. —— ii. 6.
3. —— 12, 14, 16.
6. —— 29.
9. —— 32.
3. —— 33.
5. —— 40.
6. —— iii. 12.
10. —— 16.
3. —— iv. 7.
1. —— 11.
6. —— 17.
3. —— 22.
3. —— v. 4.
5. —— 20.
3. —— 24.
6. —— 28 1st.
4. —— 28 2nd.
2. —— 38 1st (*om.* G.)
3. —— 38 2nd.
3. —— vi. 3.
1. —— 13 1st.
4. —— 13 2nd (*om.* G L T Tr A ℵ, i.e. *the.*)
1. —— 14 1st.
9. —— 14 2nd.
10. —— vii. 4.
6. —— 7, 29.
9. —— 35.
1. —— 37, 38, 40.
10. —— 60 1st.
3. —— 60 2nd.
10. —— viii. 19.
6. —— 21.
5. —— 22.
6. —— 29.
2. —— 32.
3. —— 34.
4. —— ix. 13.
1. —— 21 1st.

3. Acts ix. 21 2nd.
1. ——— 22.
3. —— x. 16.
5. ——— 30.
3. —— xi. 10.
4. —— xiii. 17.
5. ——— 26.
4. —— xv. 2, 6.
12.——— 16.
3. —— xvi. 18.
11.——— 36 (*om.* L Tr.)
1. ——— xvii. 3, 18.
2. ——— 19.
7. —— xviii. 10.
3. —— xix. 10, 17.
1. ——— 26.
5. ——— 25.
3. ——— 27.
5. ——— 40.
3. —— xx. 29 (*om.* G ⇉ L T Tr A ℵ, i.e. *the.*)
2. —— xxi. 11.
3. ——— 23.
1. ——— 28 1st.
4. ——— 28 2nd.
9. ——— 28 3rd.
7. —— xxii. 3.
10.——— 4.
4. ——— 22.
1. ——— 26.
10.——— 28.
5. —— xxiii. 1.
6. ——— 9.
10.——— 13.
9. ——— 17, 18, 25, 27.
6. —— xxiv. 2.
9. ——— 5.
6. ——— 10.
3. ——— 14.
5. ——— 21.
5. —— xxvi. 22.
1. ——— 31, 32.
10.—— xxvii. 21.
7. ——— 23.
3. ——— 34.
1. —— xxviii. 4.
4. ——— 9.
10.——— 20 twice.
5. ——— 22.
9. ——— 26.
4. ——— 27.
3. Rom. ii. 3.
1. —— iv. 9.
10.—— v. 2.
3. —— vi. 6.
4. —— vii. 24.
1. —— ix. 9 1st.
9. ——— 9 2nd.
3. —— xi. 25.
2. ——— 27.
6. —— xii. 2.
13.—— xiii. 9 1st.
6. ——— 9 2nd.
3. —— xiv. 13.
3. —— xv. 28 1st.
9. ——— 28 2nd
3. 1 Cor. i. 12.
4. ——— 20 1st.
4. ——— 20 2nd (*om.* G ⇉ L T Tr A ℵ, i.e. *the.*)
4. —— ii. 6 twice, 8.
9. —— iii. 12 (*om.* G → L T Tr Ab ℵ, i.e. *the.*)
6. ——— 18.
4. ——— 19.
3. —— v. 2.
4. ——— 10.
3. —— vii. 6, 26, 29.
4. ——— 31 1st.
6. ——— 31 2nd (τὸν κόσμον, *the world,* instead of τῷ κόσμῳ τούτῳ, *this world,* L T Tr A ℵ.)
3. ——— 35.
2. —— viii. 9.
2. —— ix. 3.
7. ——— 12.

3. 1 Cor. ix. 23 (πάντα, *all things,* G ∾ L T Tr A ℵ.)
3. —— x. 28.
2. —— xi. 10.
3. ——— 17.
6. ——— 22.
3. ——— 24 twice, 25 twice.
9. ——— 26 1st.
3. ——— 26 2nd (*om.* G ⇉ L T Tr A ℵ, i.e. *the.*)
9. ——— 27 (*om.* G L T Tr A ℵ, i.e. *the.*)
6. —— xiv. 21.
7. —— xv. 19.
3. ——— 50, 53 twice, 54 twice.
2. 2 Cor. i. 12.
7. ——— 15.
3. —— ii. 1.
2. ——— 6.
6. —— iii. 10.
10.—— iv. 1.
4. ——— 4.
9. ——— 7.
6. —— v. 2.
7. —— viii. 7.
3. ——— 10.
7. ——— 19.
3. ——— 20 1st.
7. ——— 20 2nd.
6. —— ix. 3.
3. ——— 6.
5. ——— 12, 13.
3. —— x. 7, 11.
7. —— xi. 17.
10.—— xii. 13.
3. —— xiii. 1, 9.
3. Gal. iii. 2, 17.
13.—— v. 14
6. —— vi. 16.
6. Eph. i. 21.
4. —— ii. 2.
2. —— iii. 8.
3. —— iv. 17.
3. —— v. 33.
3. —— vi. 1.
4. ——— 12.
3. Phil. i. 7, 9, 19, 22, 25.
3. —— ii. 5.
3. —— iii. 15.
4. Col. i. 27.
3. —— ii. 4.
3. —— iii. 20.
3. 1 Thes. iv. 3, 15.
3. —— v. 18.
2. 2 Thes. iii. 10.
3. 1 Tim. i. 9.
10.——— 18.
3. —— ii. 3.
3. —— iv. 16.
3. 2 Tim. i. 15.
10.—— ii. 19.
3. —— iii. 1.
2. Tit. i. 13.
1. Heb. iii. 3.
3. —— vi. 3.
1. —— vii. 1.
13.——— 21.
3. ——— 27.
2. —— viii. 10.
3. —— ix. 8.
5. ——— 11.
3. ——— 20, 27.
2. —— x. 16.
13.—— xii. 27.
3. —— xiii. 19.
2. Jas. i. 27.
4. —— ii. 5 (τῷ κόσμῳ, *as regards the world,* instead of τοῦ κόσμου τούτου, *of this world,* G L T Tr A ℵ.)
2. —— iii. 15.
3. —— iv. 15.
3. 1 Pet. i. 25.
3. —— ii. 19, 20.
6. —— iv. 16.

10. 1 Pet. v. 12.
6. 2 Pet. i. 13.
1. ——— 17.
10.——— 18.
3. ——— 20.
10.—— iii. 1.
3. ——— 5, 8.
2. 1 John i. 5.
2. —— ii. 25.
10.—— iii. 3.
6. ——— 10.
2. ——— 11, 23.
3. —— iv. 3.
6. ——— 9, 1.
10.——— 21.
6. —— v. 2.
2. ——— 3, 4.
1. ——— 6.
2. ——— 9, 11 twice, 14.

1. 1 John v. 20.
1. 2 John 7.
10.——— 10.
2. 3 John 6 twice.
3. Jude 4.
3. ——— 5 (πάντα, *all things,* L T Tr A ℵ), (*om.* G∾)
3. Rev. ii. 6.
10.——— 24.
12.—— iv. 1.
12.—— vii. 9.
2. —— xx. 5.
1. ——— 14.
4. —— xxii. 7, 9, 10.
4. ——— 18 1st.
6. ——— 18 2nd.
5. ——— 19 1st.
6. ——— 19 2nd.

THIS CHILD.

1. Luke ii. 34.

THIS DEED.

3. 1 Cor. v. 3.

THIS FELLOW.

9. Luke xxiii. 2.
9. John ix. 29.

THIS MAN.

1. Matt. ix. 3
6. —— xiii. 54, 56.
1. —— xxvii. 47.
1. Mark ii. 7.
6. —— vi. 2.
1. —— xv. 39.
1. Luke vii. 39.
6. —— xiv. 9.
1. ——— 30.
1. —— xv. 2.
1. —— xviii. 14.
9. —— xix. 14.
1. —— xxii. 56.
9. —— xxiii. 18.
1. ——— 41, 52.
1. John vi. 52.
1. —— vii. 15.
9. ——— 27.
1. ——— 31.

1. John ix. 2, 3, 33.
4. —— x. 41.
1. —— xi. 37 twice.
9. —— xviii. 40.
9. —— xix. 12.
1. —— xxi. 21.
1. Acts i. 18.
9. —— iii. 16.
1. —— iv. 10.
9. —— v. 37.
1. —— viii. 10.
15.—— xiii. 12.
4. ——— 38.
1. —— xviii. 25.
9. —— xxv. 24.
1. Heb. vii. 4.
9. —— viii. 3.
15.—— x. 12 (No. 1, AV., G∾L T Tr A ℵ.)

1. Jas. i. 25.

THIS MAN'S.

4. Acts xiii. 23.
4. Jas. i. 26.

THIS MATTER.

4. Acts xvii. 32.

THIS PLACE.

6. Heb. iv. 5.

THIS SELF-SAME THING.

{ αὐτὸ, very, self, } this same,
{ τοῦτο, this, } this very.

2 Cor. vii. 11.

THIS SORT.

οὕτων, *Gen. pl. masc. and neut. of No.* 1.

2 Tim. iii. 6.

THIS THING.

3. Mark v. 32.
3. Luke xxii. 23.
3. John xviii. 34.
3. Acts xxvi. 26.
3. 1 Cor. ix. 17.
4. 2 Cor. xii. 8.

THIS VERY THING.

{ αὐτὸ, self, very, / τοῦτο, this, } this very thing.

Philem. 16.

THIS VERY THING (UPON)

{ εἰς, unto, / αὐτὸ, self, very, / τοῦτο, this, } unto this very thing.

Rom. xiii. 6.

THIS WISE (ON)

οὕτως, in this manner, so, thus, on this wise.

Matt. i. 18.
John xxi. 1.
Acts vii. 6.
Acts xiii. 34.
Rom. x. 6.
Heb. iv. 4.

THIS WOMAN.

15. Matt. xxvi. 13.
15. Luke vii. 45, 46.
10. Luke xiii. 16.
15. Acts ix. 36.

See also, CAUSE, DAY, DEED, END, FASHION, HOUR, INSCRIPTION, LIFE, MANNER, MIND, NAMELY, PLACE, PRESENT, SAME, TIME, WORLD.

THISTLE.

τρίβολος, three-pointed, three-pronged. *In N.T.* tribulus, land-caltrop, a low, thorny shrub, *so called from its resemblance to the* ὁ τρίβολος, *or* military caltrop, *i.e.* an instrument composed of three or more spikes or prongs, and thrown on the ground to impede cavalry.

[τὰ τρίβολα is *a threshing-machine*, so the Lat., *tribulum;* whence, Eng., *tribulation*, which is a divine threshing to winnow the chaff from the wheat.]

(lxx. *for* דרדר, Gen. iii. 18; צנים, Prov. xxii. 5), (*occ.* Heb. vi. 8.)

Matt. vii. 16.

THITHER.

ἐκεῖ, there, in that place.

Matt. ii. 22.
Mark vi. 33.
Luke xvii. 37.
Luke xxi. 2.
John xi. 8.
—— xviii. 2, 3.

THITHER ALSO.

κἀκεῖ, and there, there also.

Acts xvii. 13.

THITHER (WHERE...)

ὅπου, where, in which *or* what place.

John vii. 34, 36.

See also, COME, RUN.

THITHERWARD

ἐκεῖ, there, in that place.

Rom. xv. 24.

THOMAS.

Θωμᾶς, Thomas, (Heb. תאם, twin) one of the twelve apostles.

In all passages, except—
John xx. 29 (*om.* G L T Tr A), (καί, even א.)

THONG.

ἱμάς, a thong *or* strap *of leather.*

Acts xxii. 25.

THORN (-S.)

1. ἄκανθα, (*from* ἀκή, a point) thorn; (lxx. *for* קוץ, Gen. iii. 18; Is. xxxii. 13; Jer. iv. 3; חוח, Song ii. 2), (*non occ.*)
2. σκόλοψ, anything pointed or sharp, *esp.* a pale *or* stake *for fixing heads on, or for impaling; then*, a thorn, splinter, *which when in the flesh excites severe pain;* (lxx. *for* סיר, Hos. ii. 6), (*non occ.*)

[Prob. Paul's "thorn in the flesh" was some infirmity of the eyes, *see* Acts ix. 9; xxiii. 1-5, (and *see under* "EARNESTLY BEHOLD"); Gal. iv. 14, 15, and vi. 11, (*see* "HOW LARGE," page 388.)]

1. Matt. vii. 16.
1. —— xiii. 7 twice, 22.
1. —— xxvii. 29.
1. Mark iv. 7 twice, 18.
—— —— xv. 17, see T (of)
1. Luke vi. 44.
1. —— viii. 7 twice, 14.
1. John xix. 2.
—— —— 5, see T (of)
2. 2 Cor. xii. 7.
— Heb. vi. 8, see T (of)

THORNS (OF)

ἀκάνθινος, made of *or* with thorns, (*non occ.*)

Mark xv. 17. | John xix. 5.

THOROUGHLY.

See, THROUGHLY.

THOSE.

(*For various combinations with other words, see below.*)

1. ἐκεῖνος, that, that there. *Here, pl.*, those, those there.
2. ταύτα, (*neut. pl. of* οὗτος) these things, these here.
3. τούτων, (*Gen. pl. of* οὗτος) of these, of these here.
4. ταύταις, (*Dat. pl. of* οὗτος) to *or* for those here.
5. ταύτας, (*Acc. pl. of* οὗτος) these, these here.
6. αὐτοι, they.
7. οἱ, (*masc. pl.*) the.

1. Matt. iii. 1.
6. —— xxi. 41.
1. —— xxii. 7, 10.
1. —— xxiv. 19, 22 twice, 29.
1. —— xxv. 7, 19.
1. Mark i. 9.
1. —— ii. 20.
1. —— vii. 15 (*om.* Trb ℵ.)
1. —— viii. 1.
1. —— xii. 7.
1. —— xiii. 17, 19, 24 1st.
5. Luke i. 24.
4. —— —— 39.
1. —— ii. 1.
1. —— iv. 2.
1. —— v. 35.
4. —— vi. 12.
1. —— ix. 36.
1. —— xii. 37, 38.
1. —— xiii. 4, 24.
1. Luke xx. 1 (*om.* G ⇉ L T Tr A ℵ.)
1. —— xxi. 23.
1. John i. 39.
1. —— viii. 10 (*ap.*)
6. —— xvii. 11.
4. Acts i. 15.
1. —— ii. 18.
4. —— vi. 1.
1. —— vii. 41.
1. —— ix. 37.
1. —— xvi. 3, 35.
1. —— xx. 2.
5. —— xxi. 15.
1. Rom. vi. 21.
2. Phil. iii. 7.
7. Heb. vii. 21.
1. —— viii. 10.
6. —— x. 1.
1. —— —— 16.
3. —— xiii. 11.
1. Rev. ix. 6.

THOSE BY...SIDE.

{ οἱ, the *persons*
{ παρά, beside *or* near.

Luke viii. 12.

THOSE THINGS.

1. ταύτα, these *things*, these things here.
2. τούτοις, *Dat. pl. of above.*
3. { τὰ, the *things*
   { μεν, indeed.
4. { τοὶς, the *things*
   { δὲ, but.

1. John viii. 26.
1. Acts xvii. 11.
3. Phil. iii. 13 1st.
4. Phil. iii. 13 2nd.
1. —— iv. 9.
2. Jude 10 2nd.

THOSE THINGS WHICH.

{ ὅσα, as many things
{ μεν, indeed.

Jude 10 1st.

THOSE THINGS WHICH ARE COMING ON.

{ τᾶ, the *things*
{ ἐπερχομένα, coming upon, overtaking.

Luke xxi. 26.

THOSE THINGS (OF)

τούτων, of these *things*, (*these here.*)

Acts xviii. 17.

See also, BEHIND, BELIEVED, CONCERN, PLEASE, SHAKEN.

THOU.

THOU is very frequently part of the inflection of the verb; and sometimes is represented by the article, as in Matt. xxvii. 40.

For "THOU ART" and "ART THOU," *see under* "ART."

1. σύ, thou, (*always emphatic, never used unless for marked emphasis.*)
2. σοί, *Dat. sing. of No.* 1.
3. σέ, *Acc. sing. of No.* 1.

1. Matt. ii. 6.
1. —— iii. 14.
1. —— vi. 3, 6 1st, 17 1st.
1. —— xi. 3, 23.
1. —— xiv. 28.
1. —— xvi. 16, 18.
2. —— xvii. 25.
3. —— xviii. 33.
1. —— xix. 21 2nd.
2. —— xxii. 16 2nd, 17.
3. —— xxv. 27.
1. —— xxvi. 25, 39, 63 2nd, 64, 69, 73.
1. —— xxvii. 4, 11 twice.
1. Mark i. 11.
1. —— iii. 11.
2. —— iv. 38.
1. —— viii. 29.
2. —— x. 21 1st (No. 3, T A ℵ.)
1. —— xiv. 30 (G L T Tr A.)
1. —— —— 36, 61, 67, 68.
1. —— xv. 2 twice.
2. Luke i. 14.
1. —— —— 28 2nd (*ap.*), 42, [76 1st.
1. Luke iii. 22.
1. —— iv. 7, 41.
— —— vi. 42 2nd, see T thyself.
1. —— vii. 19, 20.
1. —— ix. 60.
1. —— x. 15.
2. —— —— 36.
1. —— —— 37.
2. —— —— 40.
1. —— xiv. 8 2nd.
2. —— —— 10 2nd, 14 2nd.
1. —— xv. 31.
1. —— xvi. 7.
1. —— —— 25 1st (*om.* G T Tr A ℵ.)
1. —— —— 25 2nd.
1. —— xvii. 8.
2. —— xviii. 22 1st.
1. —— xix. 19, 42 1st.
1. —— xxii. 32, 58, 67, 70.
1. —— xxiii. 3 twice, 37, 39, 40 1st.
1. —— xxiv. 18.
1. John i. 19, 21 twice, 25, 42 twice, 49 twice.

1. John ii. 10, 20.
1. —— iii. 2 2nd, 10, 26.
1. —— iv. 9, 10, 12, 19.
1. —— vi. 30 1st, 69.
2. —— vii. 3.
1. ——— 52.
1. —— viii. 5 (*ap.*), 13, 25, 33, 48, 52 2nd, 53 1st.
1. ——— 53 2nd (*om.* G L T Tr A ℵ.)
1. —— ix. 17, 28, 34 twice, 35.
1. —— x. 24 2nd, 33.
1. —— xi. 27, 42 2nd.
1. —— xii. 34.
1. —— xiii. 6, 7 1st.
1. —— xiv. 9 2nd.
1. —— xvii. 5, 8 2nd, 2 twice, 23 twice, 25.
1. —— xviii. 17, 25, 33, 34, 37 twice.
1. —— xix. 9.
1. —— xx. 15 3rd.
1. —— xxi. 12, 15 2nd, 16 2nd, 17 twice, 22.
1. Acts i. 24 1st.
1. —— iv. 24.
1. —— vii. 28 1st.
2. —— viii. 21.
3. ——— 23.
1. —— ix. 5 2nd.
3. ——— 6 2nd.
3. —— x. 6 (*ap.*)
1. ——— 15, 33 1st.
1. —— xi. 9, 14.
1. —— xiii. 33.
3. ——— 11.
1. —— xvi. 31.
2. —— xvii. 19.
— —— xxi. 24, see T thyself.
1. ——— 38.
1. —— xxii. 8 2nd, 27.
1. —— xxiii. 3 2nd.
3. ——— 11 2nd.
1. ——— 21.
3. —— xxiv. 4, 10.
1. ——— 11.
1. Acts xxv. 10.
2. —— xxvi. 1.
1. ——— 15.
3. ——— 29.
3. —— xxvii. 24.
1. Rom. ii. 3 2nd.
3. ——— 4.
1. ——— 17.
— ——— 19, see T thyself.
1. —— ix. 20 1st.
1. —— xi. 17, 18 2nd, 20, 22 2nd, 24.
1. —— xiv. 4, 10 twice, 22 1st.
1. 1 Cor. xiv. 17.
1. —— xv. 36 2nd.
1. Gal. ii. 14 1st.
1. —— vi. 1.
1. 1 Tim. vi. 11.
3. ——— 14.
1. 2 Tim. i. 18.
1. —— ii. 1.
1. ——— 3 (*συγκακοπάθησον, share in evils or hardness, instead of σὺ οὖν κακοπάθησον, thou therefore endure hardness,* G ~ L T Tr A ℵ.)
1. —— iii. 10, 14 1st.
1. —— iv. 5, 15.
1. Tit. ii. 1.
3. —— iii. 8.
1. Philem. 12 (No. 2, L T Tr A ℵ.)
1. Heb. i. 5, 10, 11, 12 2nd.
1. —— v. 5, 6.
1. —— vii. 17, 21.
1. Jas. ii. 3 twice, 18, 19 1st.
1. —— iv. 12.
3. 3 John 3.
1. ——— 3.
1. Rev. ii. 15.
1. —— iii. 17 2nd.
1. —— iv. 11 2nd.
1. —— vii. 14.
3. —— x. 11.

THOU THYSELF.

1. αὐτός, self, very, he, she, it; *with 2nd pers.*, thou.

2. σεαυτοῦ, thou thyself.

1. Luke vi. 42. | 1. Acts xxi. 24.
2. Rom. ii. 19.

THOUGH.

1. ἐάν, if haply, if so be that, (*see* "IF," *No.* 1 and *No.* 1b.)
   (a) *subj. pres.*, (*see* "IF," *No.* 1b*.)
   (b) *subj. aor.*, (*see* "IF," *No.* 1b†.)

2. { καὶ, even / ἐάν, if haply, } (*see No.* 1a.)

3. { ἐάν, if perchance, / τε, and (*om.* L^b Tr A^b), } and if perchance, (*see No.* 1b.)

4. κἄν, (*No.* 1, *with* καί, and, also, even, *prefixed*) and if, if also.

5. εἰ, if, (*simply putting the condition*) (*see* "IF," *No.* 2a.)

6. { εἰ, if / καί, even, } *with emphasis on the fact referred to*, if even, (*not* "though.")

7. { καὶ, even / εἰ, if, } *with emphasis on the hypothetical* "if," even if.

8. { εἰ, if / περ, indeed, } *assuming the supposition to be true, whether justly or not.*

9. καί, and, also, even.

10. καίπερ, even indeed, (*occ.* Rev. xvii. 8.)

11. καίτοιγε, though indeed.

6. Matt. xxvi. 33 (*om.* καί, *even,* G L T Tr A), (*om.* εἰ, *if* ℵ.)
4. ——— 35.
6. Luke xi. 8.
1b. —— xvi. 31.
6. —— xviii. 4.
9. ——— 7.
11. John iv. 2.
4. —— viii. 14.
4. —— x. 38.
4. —— xi. 25.
1a. Acts xiii. 41.
11. —— xvii. 27 (*καίγε, and at least* (not that He is distant, but we are ignorant), (G ~ L T Tr A.)
— Rom. iv. 11, see Circumcised.
— ——— 17, see T they were (as)
— —— ix. 6, see As.
1a. ——— 27.
1a. 1 Cor. iv. 15.
8. —— viii. 5.
1a. —— ix. 16.
— ——— 19, see T...be.
1a. —— xiii. 1, 2 twice.
1b. 1 Cor. xiii. 3 twice.
6. 2 Cor. iv. 16.
6. —— v. 16.
6. —— vii. 8 3 times.
— ——— 9, see T it was.
6. ——— 12.
3. —— x. 8.
6. —— xi. 6.
— ——— 21, see As.
1b. —— xii. 6.
6. ——— 11.
6. ——— 15 (*om.* καί, *even,* L T Tr A ℵ.)
7. —— xiii. 4 (No. 6, Tr), (*om.* L^b ℵ), (*om.* εἰ, *if,* T A.)
2. Gal. i. 8.
— —— iii. 15, see T it be but.
— —— iv. 1, see T...be.
10. Phil. iii. 4.
— ——— 12, see As.
6. Col. ii. 5.
10. Heb. v. 8, and see T...were.
10. —— vii. 5.
10. —— xii. 17.
1a. Jas. ii. 14.
— —— iii. 4, see T...be.
10. 2 Pet. i. 12.

THOUGH...BE.

ὤν, (*part. of* εἰμί, to be) being.

1 Cor. ix. 19. | Gal. iv. 1.
Jas. iii. 4.

THOUGH IT BE BUT.

ὅμως, at the same time, nevertheless, notwithstanding.

Gal. iii. 15.

THOUGH THEY WERE (AS)

{ ὡς, as, / ὄντα, things that are, (*neut. pl. part. of* εἰμί, to be.) }

Rom. iv. 17.

THOUGH...WAS.

ὤν, being.

2 Cor. viii. 9.

THOUGH...WERE.

{ καίπερ, even indeed, ὤν, being, } even though [*he was*] indeed.

Heb. v. 8.

THOUGHT (-s.)

1. λογισμός, reckoning, (*i.e. the art of* arithmetic); *hence*, reasonings *of the mind*, (*occ.* 2 Cor. x. 5.)

2. διαλογισμός, (*No.* 1, *with* διά, through, *prefixed*) reckoning through *or* throughout, computation; *hence*, cogitations, reflections.

3. ἐνθύμησις, a revolving of the mind, (*as regards the emotions*); revolvings of mind, *thought, as being the result of a commotion of the mind*, secret motives, (*occ.* Acts xvii. 29.)

4. νόημα, what is thought out *or* excogitated; *hence*, purpose, design, project, device.

5. διανόημα, (*No.* 4, *with* διά, through *or* throughout, *prefixed*) excogitating through, a thinking through, (*non occ.*)

6. ἐπίνοια, thought upon, serious purpose *or* intent, (*not necessarily executed afterwards*), (*non occ.*)

3. Matt. ix. 4.
3. —— xii. 25.
2. —— xv. 19.
2. Mark vii. 21.
2. Luke ii. 35.
2. —— v. 22.
2. —— vi. 8.
2. —— ix. 47.
5. Luke xi. 17.
2. —— xxiv. 38.
6. Acts viii. 22.
1. Rom. ii. 15.
2. —— xiv. 1, marg. (text doubtful.)
2. 1 Cor. iii. 20.
4. 2 Cor. x. 5.
3. Heb. iv. 12.
2. Jas. ii. 4.

THOUGHT (TAKE)

μεριμνάω, to be full of anxiety *which divides up and distracts the mind*, to be full of cares, anxious; be full of anxious or distracting care.

Matt. vi. 25, 27, 28, 31, 34 twice.
Matt. x. 19.
Luke xii. 11, 22, 26.

THOUGHT (WITH TAKING)

Luke xii. 25.

THOUGHT BEFOREHAND (TAKE)

προμεριμνάω, (*the above, with* πρό, before, *prefixed*) to be full of care or distracting thought beforehand, (*non occ.*)

Mark xiii. 11.

THOUSAND (-s.)

1. χίλιοι, (*num. adj.*) a thousand.

2. χιλιάς, (*subst.*) a thousand in number. (a) *plural.*

3. μυριάς, a myriad, *i.e.* ten thousand. (*Here, plural.*)

[As a symbolical number it probably denotes the perfection of God's testimony to man in grace and judgment, and of man's responsibility to God. *See under* "TEN" and "THREE."]

2. Luke xiv. 31 twice.
2. Acts iv. 4.
3. —— xxi. 20.
2. 1 Cor. x. 8.
1. 2 Pet. iii. 8 twice.
2a. Rev. v. 11 twice.
2. —— vii. 4, 5 3 times, 6 3 times.
2. Rev. vii. 7 3 times, 8 3 times.
1. —— xi. 3.
2. —— 13.
1. —— xii. 6.
2. —— xiv. 1, 3.
1. —— 20.
1. —— xx. 2, 3, 4, 5, 6, 7.
2. —— 16.

THOUSAND (FIFTY)

{ μυριάδες, (*pl. of No.* 3) tens of thousands, πέντε, five. }

Acts xix. 19.

THOUSAND (FIVE)

πεντακισχίλιοι, five times one thousand

Matt. xiv. 21.
—— xvi. 9.
Mark vi. 44.
Mark viii. 19.
Luke ix. 14.
John vi. 10.

THOUSAND (FOUR)

τετρακισχίλιοι, four times one thousand.

Matt. xv. 38.
—— xvi. 10.
Mark viii. 9, 20.
Acts xxi. 38.

THOUSAND (SEVEN)

ἑπτακισχίλιοι, seven thousand, (*quoted from* 1 Kings xix. 18, *where* lxx. ἑπτὰ χιλιάδες *for Heb.*, שבעת אלפים.)

Rom. xi. 4.

THOUSAND (TEN)

1. μυριάς, a myriad, *i.e.* ten thousand.

2. { μύριοι, μυρίοι, } (*pl. of* μυρίος, numberless) an indefinite number.

2. Matt. xviii. 24.
2. 1 Cor. iv. 15.
2. 1 Cor. xiv. 19.
1. Jude 14.

THOUSAND (TEN THOUSAND TIMES TEN)

μυριάδες, (*pl. of No.* 1, *above*) myriads
μυριάδων, (*Gen. pl. of No* 1, *above*) of myriads.

Rev. v. 11 (ap.)

THOUSAND (THREE)

τρισχίλιοι, three thousand.

Acts ii. 41.

THOUSAND (TWO)

δισχίλιοι, two thousand.

Mark v. 13.

THOUSAND (TWO HUNDRED THOUSAND)

δύο, two
μυριάδες, myriads
μυριάδων, of myriads.

Rev. ix. 16.

THREATEN (-ED.)

ἀπελέω, to hold out promises *or* threats; to threaten, to menace.

1 Pet. ii. 23.

THREATEN (FURTHER)

προσαπειλέω, to threaten further. *Here part.*

Acts iv. 21.

THREATEN (STRAITLY)

ἀπειλῇ, with a threat, ἀπειλέω, to threaten, } to threaten with a threat.

Acts iv. 17.

THREATENING.

ἀπειλή, threatening, a threatening.

Acts iv. 29. | Eph. vi. 9. | Acts ix, 1.

THREE.

τρεῖς, (*neut.*, τρία) three.

[THREE, as a symbolical number, represents *heavenly things*, as Four does the things relating to the earth, (*see under* "FOUR.")

ONE is *unity*, and shows us the unity of God (Deut. vi. 4; Mark xii. 32); of His *attributes*, (1 Kings vi. 25); of Christ and His Church (1 Cor. xii. 12, 13); of divine things upon earth, (Eph. iv. 4-6); and of millenial glory and blessing, (Ezek. xxxiv. 23; John x. 16; xvii. 23; Eph. i. 10.) It is also the expression of the Church's worship of God now, (Rom. xv. 6) and of the divine work on which we rest for salvation, (Heb. x. 12, 14, etc.)

Two is symbolical of the *fulness of Testimony*, whether divine or human, (*see* Deut. xvii. 6; Matt. xviii. 19; xxii. 40; Mark vi. 7; xi. 1; Luke x. 35; John viii. 17; 1 Cor. xiv. 27; Gal. iv. 24; 1 Tim. v. 19; Heb. vi. 18; x. 28; Rev. xi. 3, 4.)

THREE represents *Trinity, the divine and heavenly things* in nature and grace, (*see* Gen. xviii. 2; xlviii. 15, 16; Numb. vi. 23-27; Is. vi. 3; Matt. xxviii. 19; 1 Cor. xiii. 13; Rev. i. 4, etc.)

FOUR is (3+1) unity and Trinity, "Let us make;" *hence*, the number of creation, of *earth and earthly things*, (*see under* "FOUR.")

FIVE is (4+1), and is therefore symbolical of *human weakness*, but perfected by divine strength. God brought Israel out of Egypt in fives, (Ex. xiii. 18, marg.) while the enemy who pursued were 600 chariots, (Ex. xiv. 7.) Faithful Israel, though small, should prevail, (Lev. xxvi. 8; Is. xxx. 17.) David's five stones were in harmony with his faith, but victorious through divine strength, (1 Sam. xvii. 40.) The feeding of the multitudes with five loaves was likewise symbolical, (Matt. xiv. 19, etc.) as were St. Paul's five words, (1 Cor. xiv. 19.)

SIX is (7—1) the number of *Imperfection*, Gen. i.; Job v. 19; Prov. vi. 16; John ii. 6.) It was the day of the crucifixion. (*See under* "SIX"), and note the six thousand years and the 7th chiliad.

SEVEN is the *combination of the divine* (the Trinity) *with creation*, the application *or* addition (3+4) of the one to the other in nature

and grace, God's connection with the world in mercy; *hence*, the number of *perfection* in earthly things, (*see under* "SEVEN.")

EIGHT is (7+1) symbolical of *a new commencement*. It was the day on which *Circumcision* was to take place, (Lev. xii. 3); the leper cleansed, (Lev. xiv. 10); the sacrifice accepted, (Lev. xxii. 27); the sheaf of first-fruits presented, (Lev. xxiii. 11); feast of tabernacles held, (Lev. xxiii. 36—39). And as the eighth day of the Feasts of the Lord pointed to a new future millenial feast; so, the *eighth* day, at the Resurrection became the *first*, and hence the connection of this number with *Resurrection*, (comp. Lev. xiv. 23; xxv. 22; Matt. xxviii. 1; Luke ii. 21; John vii. 37; 1 Pet. iii. 20.)

NINE is (3×3), and is the product of or *perfection in divine things*, (Matt. xxvii. 45, 46; Mark xv. 33, 34; Numb. xxix. 26; Lev. xxv. 22; Luke xvii. 17; Acts iii. 1; x. 3, 30.)

TEN, the number of *divine testimony* in grace and judgment, and of human responsibility, (*see under* "TEN.")

ELEVEN is (12−1) symbolical of *Incompleteness*, (as six is of imperfection), (*see* Gen. xxxii. 22; Exod. xxvi. 7, 8; xxxvi. 14, 15; Matt. xxviii. 16; Mark xvi. 14; Acts i. 26; ii. 14.) Also the eve of perfection, (*see under* "TWELVE"), (Matt. xx. 6, 9.)

TWELVE is (3×4), three times four, and symbolises a multiplication, *or product*, as it were, of the divine and human. It expresses the perfection and universality of *Administration*. Twelve patriarchs head the *O.T.* and twelve apostles the *N.T.* Combined in the millenium, (Matt. xix. 28). The number of the sealed election of the Jewish Remnant, (Rev. vii. compare with Numb. xxxi. See also Lev. xxiv. 5; Numb. i. 44; vii. 84; xvii. 2; 1 Kings vii. 25, 44; Luke xxii. 30; John vi. 9.)

FORTY is the number of *Probation*, etc., (*see under* "FORTY.")

COMBINATIONS of numbers have a corresponding value, (addition implying union *or* connection, and multiplication product or intensity) *e.g.*

TWENTY-FOUR, (2×12) expresses the product of testimony and administration, (*see under* "ELDERS.")

ONE HUNDRED AND FORTY-FOUR, (12×12) the product of administrative fulness.

SIX HUNDRED AND SIXTY-SIX, (6+60+600) the combined *perfection of imperfection*. It was the sum of *the world's riches*, (1 Kings x. 14-29.) The power of Egypt was 600, (Ex. xiv. 7) in pursuit of Israel, who went out by fives, (*i.e.* in weakness) led by God, (Ex. xiii. 18, margin.) It has relation to Nebuchadnezzar's image, (Dan. iii. 1.) (*See* p. 391.)

FIFTY seems to be a new commencement from 7×7, (*i.e.* from the perfection of perfection) as the Pentecost and Jubilee were.

ONE HUNDRED AND FIFTY AND THREE. 150 was a great number, "yet for all there were so many, yet was not the net broken." "All that the Father giveth me shall come to me." "This is the Father's will which hath sent me, that of all which He hath given me, I should lose nothing," not one will be overlooked, "not a hoof shall be left behind." Down to the THREE which exceed, the numbering proceeds.

SEVENTY HEBDOMADS, (7×70) the product of divine perfection and testimony as applied to earthly things, as in the 70 Hebdomads, (490 years). (*See* pp. 390 and 687.)

So with other numbers. In each case the symbolism arises from the fitness of divine things; not from any virtue in the numbers themselves, but from the simple fact that when they are used by the Spirit they are used with design, purpose, and harmony.]

Matt. xii. 40[4 times].
—— xiii. 33.
—— xv. 32.
—— xvii. 4.
—— xviii. 16, 20.
—— xxvi. 61.
—— xxvii. 40, 63.
Mark viii. 2, 31.
—— ix. 5.
—— xiv. 5, see Hundred.
——— 58.
—— xv. 29.
Luke i. 56.
—— ii. 46.
—— iv. 25.
—— ix. 33.
—— x. 36.
—— xi. 5.
—— xii. 52.
—— xiii. 7, 21.
John ii. 6, 19, 20.
—— xii. 5, see Hundred.
—— xxi. 11.
Acts ii. 41, see Thousand.
—— v. 7.
—— vii. 20.
—— ix. 9.
Acts x. 19 (*om.* G ⇉ T Trmb A.)
—— xi. 10, see T times.
——— 11.
—— xvii. 2.
—— xix. 8.
—— xx. 3.
——— 31, see Years.
—— xxv. 1.
—— xxviii. 7, 11, 12.
——— 15, see Taverns.
——— 17.
1 Cor. x. 8.
—— xiii. 13.
—— xiv. 27, 29.
2 Cor. xiii. 1.
Gal. i. 18.
1 Tim. v. 19.
Heb. x. 28.
—— xi. 23, see Months.
Jas. v. 17.
1 John v. 7[1st], 7[2nd] (*ap.*), 8[twice].
Rev. vi. 6.
—— viii. 13.
—— ix. 18.
—— xi. 9, 11.
—— xvi. 13, 19.
Rev. xxi. 13[4 times].

THREE TIMES.

{ ἐπὶ, upon, up to
{ τρίς, thrice, three times.

Acts xi. 10.

THREESCORE

ἑξήκοντα, six tens, sixty.

Luke xxiv. 13.
Acts vii. 14, see "FIFTEEN" (and note, p. 283.)
—— xxiii. 23, see "TEN."
—— xxvii. 37, see "SIXTEEN."
1 Tim. v. 9.
Rev. xi. 3.
—— xii. 6.
—— xiii. 18, see "SIX HUNDRED THREESCORE AND SIX."

THRESH.

ἀλοάω, to beat, to thresh; *hence*, to drive round in a circle, *esp. oxen, etc.*, upon grain, in order to thresh it; (lxx. *for* דוש, Is. xli. 15; דיש, Deut. xxv. 4; דרך, Jer. li. 53.)

1 Cor. ix. 10.

THRICE.

1. τρίς, thrice, three times.

2. { ἐπὶ, upon, up to,
   { τρίς, three times.

1. Matt. xxvi. 34, 75.
1. Mark xiv. 30, 72.
1. Luke xxii. 34, 61.
1. John xiii. 38.
2. Acts x. 16.
1. 2 Cor. xi. 25[twice].
1. 2 Cor. xii. 8.

THROAT.

λάρυγξ, larynx, the throat, (*quoted from* Ps. v. 10, *where* lxx. *for* גרון), (*non occ.*)

Rom. iii. 13.

THROAT (TAKE BY THE)

πνίγω, to choke, strangle *by stopping the breath*, (*occ.* Mark v. 13.)

Matt. xviii. 28.

THRONE (-s.)

1. θρόνος, a seat, (*prop.* a high seat with a footstool); *later, and in N.T.*, a throne *as the emblem of regal authority*.

2. βῆμα, a pace, a footstep; *then*, any elevated place approached by steps; *hence*, a tribunal, *seat of a judge or magistrate*.

1. Matt. v. 34.
1. —— xix. 28[twice].
1. —— xxiii. 22.
1. —— xxv. 31.
1. Luke i. 32.
1. —— xxii. 30.
1. Acts ii. 30.
1. —— vii. 49.
2. —— xii. 21.
1. Col. i. 16.
1. Heb. i. 8.
1. —— iv. 16.
1. —— viii. 1.
1. —— xii. 2.
1. Rev. i. 4.
1. Rev. iii. 21[twice].
1. —— iv. 2[twice], 3, 5[twice], 6[3 times], 9, 10[twice].
1. —— v. 1, 6, 7, 11, 13.
1. —— vi. 16.
1. —— vii. 9, 10 (*ap.*), 11[twice], 15[twice], 17.
1. —— viii. 3.
1. —— xii. 5.
1. —— xiv. 3, 5 (*ap.*)
1. —— xvi. 17.
1. —— xix. 4, 5.
1. —— xx. 4, 11.
1. —— xxi. 5.
1. —— xxii. 1, 3.

THRONG (-ED, -ING.)

1. θλίβω, to press, press upon, compress; oppress, distress.

2. συνθλίβω, (*No.* 1, *with* σύν, together with, *prefixed*) to press together, press closely *on all sides, as a crowd upon a person*.

3. συμπνίγνω, to choke together, to throttle; suffocate; *then*, to suffocate *as by crowding*.

4. συνέχω, to hold together, press together, hold fast, shut up.

1. Mark iii. 9.
2. —— v. 24, 31.
3. Luke viii. 42.
4. ——— 45.

THROUGH.

(***For words used with it in various connections, see below.***)

1. διά, through.

   (a) *with Gen.*, through, (*as proceeding from*) through, by means of *marking the agency or instrument of an action*.

   (b) *with Acc.*, through, (*as tending towards*) through, owing to, on

account of, because of, for the sake of, *marking the reason or motive of an action.*

2. ἐν, in; *in the power of*, by *or* through; with.

3. ἐκ, out of, from; *then, of anything originating in and proceeding out of, as source, cause, or occasion,* from, by, of.

4. ἐπί, upon.

(a) *with Gen.*, upon *and proceeding from.*

(b) *with Dat.*, upon *and resting upon;* on, *as the groundwork of any* fact, occasion, cause, *or* circumstance.

(c) *with Acc.*, upon, *direction towards.*

2. Matt. ix. 34.
1a.—— xii. 1, 43.
1a.—— xix. 24.
1a. Mark ii. 23.
1a.—— ix. 30.
1a.—— x. 25.
1a.—— xi. 16.
1b. Luke i. 78.
1a.—— iv. 30.
1a.—— v. 19.
1a.—— vi. 1.
2. —— x. 17.
2. —— xi. 15, 18.
1a.——— 24.
1a.—— xvii. 1, 11.
1a.—— xviii. 25.
1a. John i. 7.
1a.—— iii. 17.
1a.—— iv. 4.
1a.—— viii. 59.
1b.—— xv. 3.
2. —— xvii. 11, 17.
2. ——— 19, marg. *truly*, (with ἀλήθεια, *truth.*)
1a.——— 20.
2. —— xx. 31.
1a. Acts i. 2.
4b.—— iii. 16.
2. —— iv. 2.
1a.—— viii. 18.
1a.—— x. 43.
1a.—— xiii. 38.
1a.—— xiv. 22.
1a.—— xv. 11.
1a.—— xviii. 27.
1a.—— xx. 3.
1a.—— xxi. 4.
1a. Rom. i. 8.
2. ——— 24.
1a.—— ii. 23.
1b.——— 24.
2. —— iii. 7.
1a. ——— 24, 25 [1st].
2. ——— 25 [2nd].
1a.——— 30, 31.
1a.—— iv. 13 [twice].
1a.—— v. 1, 9, 11, 21.
2. —— vi. 11, 23.
1a.—— vii. 25.
1a.—— viii. 3, 37.
1a.—— xi. 36.
1a.—— xii. 3.
1a.—— xv. 4.
2. ——— 13, 17, 19.
1a.—— xvi. 27.
1a. 1 Cor. i. 1.
1a. 1 Cor. iv. 15.
4b.—— viii. 11, ἀπόλλυται ὁ ἀσθενῶν ἐν τῇ σῇ γνώσει, ὁ ἀδελφός, *is the weak one perishing, with your knowledge, the brother,* instead of ἀπολεῖται ὁ ἀσθενῶν ἀδελφὸς ἐπὶ τῇ σῇ γνώσει, *through thy knowledge shall the weak brother perish,* G∾L T Tr A ℵ.)
1a.—— x. 1.
1a.—— xiii. 12.
1a.—— xv. 57.
1a. 2 Cor. iii. 4.
3. ——— 8.
2. ——— 14 [1st].
1a.——— 14 [2nd].
1a.—— iv. 7 (*ap.*)
1b.——— 13.
2. —— v. 10.
1a. Eph. i. 7.
2. —— ii. 7.
1a.——— 8, 18.
2. ——— 22.
1a.—— iv. 6.
1b.——— 18.
1a. Phil. i. 19.
1a. —— iii. 9.
2. —— iv. 7, 13.
1a. Col. i. 14 (*ap.*), 20, 22.
1a.—— ii. 8, 12.
2. 2 Thes. ii. 13, 16.
1a. 2 Tim. i. 10.
1a.—— iii. 15.
2. Tit. i. 3.
1a.—— iii. 6.
1a. Philem. 22.
1a. Heb. ii. 10, 14.
1a.—— vi. 12.
1a.—— ix. 14.
1a.—— x. 10, 20.
1a.—— xi. 33, 39.
2. —— xiii. 20.
1a.——— 21.
2. 1 Pet. i. 2.
1a.——— 5.
2. ——— 6.
1a.——— 22 (*om.* διὰ πνεύματος, *through the Spirit,* G ⇉ L T Tr A ℵ.)
1a.—— iv. 11.
2. 2 Pet. i. 1, 2.
1a. 2 Pet. i. 3.
2. ——— 4.
2. —— ii. 3.
2. ——— 18 (*om.* G ℵ.)
2. 2 Pet. ii. 20.
1a. 1 John iv. 9.
2. Rev. viii. 13.
3. —— xviii. 3.

See also, BREAK, CARRY, GO, MIDST, PASS, PIERCE, RUN, THRUST, WALK.

THROUGHLY.

{ ἐν, in
{ παντί, every [*way*].

2 Cor. xi. 6.

See also, FURNISH, PURGE.

THROUGHOUT.

1. εἰς, unto, into.

2. ἐν, in.

3. διά, through.

(a) *with Gen.*, through, *as proceeding from.*

(b) *with Acc.*, through, *as tending towards.*

4. { διὰ, through
{ ὅλου, the whole.

5. κατά, down,

(a) *with Gen.*, down from.

(b) *with Acc.*, down along, through, throughout.

6. ἐπί, upon.

(a) *with Gen.*, upon, *and proceeding from.*

(b) *with Dat.*, upon, *and resting on.*

(c) *with Acc.*, upon, *by direction towards,* (*marking* motion *or* activity.)

1. Matt. iv. 24.
1. Mark i. 28, 39.
1. —— xiv. 9.
2. Luke i. 65.
6c.—— iv. 25.
2. —— vii. 17 [1st].
2. ——— 17 [2nd] (*om.* L[b] Tr[b] ℵ.)
5b.—— viii. 39.
3a. John xix. 23.
5b. Acts viii. 1.
3a. Acts ix. 32, and see Throughout all quarters.
6c.—— xi. 28.
3a.—— xiii. 49.
5b.—— xxiv. 5.
1. —— xxvi. 20 (Tr[mb]), (*om.* L T Tr A[b] ℵ.)
2. Rom. i. 8.
2. —— ix. 17.
3a. 2 Cor. viii. 18.
1. Eph. iii. 21.

THROUGHOUT ALL QUARTERS.

{ διὰ, through
{ πάντων, all, (*places, or* all *the churches.*)

Acts ix. 32.

See also, GO, PASS.

THROW (THREW, THROWN.)

1. βάλλω, to throw, to cast; throw down.
2. ῥίπτω, to throw *or* cast *with a sudden motion*, to hurl, jerk.

1. Mark xii. 42. | 2. Luke iv. 35 part. 1. Acts xxii. 23 part.

THROW DOWN.

1. καταλύω, to loosen down, disunite *the parts of anything; hence, of buildings*, to throw down, destroy.
2. βάλλω, *see No.* 1, *above.*

1. Matt. xxiv. 2. 1. Mark xiii. 2. | 1. Luke xxi. 6. 2. Rev. xviii. 21.

THRUST.

βάλλω, to throw, to cast.

John xx. 25, 27. | Acts xvi. 24. Rev. xiv. 16, 19.

THRUST AWAY.

ἀπωθέομαι, to repulse, reject. *In N.T. mid.*, to thrust away from one's self.

Acts vii. 27.

THRUST DOWN.

καταβιβάζω, to cause to descend, bring down, (*occ.* Matt. xi. 23.)

Luke x. 15.

THRUST FROM.

ἀπωθέομαι, *see* "THRUST AWAY."

Acts vii. 39.

THRUST IN.

1. ἐξωθέω, to thrust out, drive out from. *Here, to* thrust out from *the water, and drive the ship ashore.*
2. πέμπω, to send, (*esp. as messengers or agents.*)

1. Acts xxvii. 39. | 2. Rev. xiv. 15, 18.

THRUST OUT.

1. ἐκβάλλω, to throw or cast out.
   (a) *with* ἔξω, without.
2. ἐπανάγω, to lead up upon, *as a ship* up or out upon *the* sea; *hence*, to put to sea.

2. Luke v. 3. | 1a. Luke xiii. 28. 1. Acts xvi. 37.

THRUST OUT OF.

{ ἐκβάλλω, to throw or cast out.
{ ἔξω, without.

Luke iv. 29.

THRUST OUT MEN (*they that*) [margin.]

Matt. xi. 12, see "VIOLENT."

THRUST THROUGH.

κατατοξεύω, to shoot down with an arrow *or* dart; (lxx. *for* ירה, Ex. xix. 13), (*non occ.*)

Heb. xii. 20 (*ap.*)

THUNDER. [noun.]

βροντή, thunder; (lxx. *for* רעם, Job xxvi. 14; Ps. lxxvii. 19.)

Mark iii. 17. Rev. vi. 1. | Rev. x. 3, 4 twice. — xiv. 2. Rev. xvi. 18.

THUNDER (-ED.) [verb.]

{ γίνομαι, to bring about, cause, βροντή, thunder, } *lit.*, thunder had been caused, *or* there was thunder.

John xii. 29.

THUNDERING (-S.)

βροντή, *see* "THUNDER."

Rev. iv. 5. — viii. 5. | Rev. xi. 19. — xix. 6.

THUS.

1. οὕτω, in this manner, on this wise, *i.e.* so, thus.
2. ταῦτα, (*neut. pl. of* οὗτος) these *things*, these here.
3. τοῦτο, (*neut. sing. of* οὗτος) this, this here.
4. ὅδε, this, this here, (*more emphatic than Nos.* 2 *and* 3.)

1. Matt. ii. 5.
1. —— iii. 15.
1. —— xxvi. 54.
1. Mark ii. 7.
1. Luke i. 25.
1. —— ii. 48.
2. —— ix. 34.
2. —— xi. 45.
— —— xvii. 30, see T (even)
2. —— xviii. 11.
2. —— xix. 28.
1. ———— 31.
— —— xxii. 51, see T far.
2. —— xxiii. 46.
2. —— xxiv. 36.
1. ———— 46 1st.
1. ———— 46 2nd (*om.* καὶ οὕτως ἔδει, G → Lb T Tr A ℵ, i.e. *that the Christ should suffer,* instead of "*and thus it behoved Christ to suffer.*")
1. John iv. 6.
2. —— ix. 6.
2. —— xi. 43.
1. ———— 48.
2. —— xiii. 21.
2. —— xviii. 22.
2. —— xx. 14.
2. Acts xix. 41.
2. —— xx. 36.
4. —— xxi. 11.
2. —— xxvi. 24, 30 (*ap.*)
2. —— xxvii. 35.
1. Rom. ix. 20.
1. 1 Cor. xiv. 25 (*om.* καὶ οὕτω, *and thus,* G L T Tr A ℵ.)
3. 2 Cor. i. 17.
3. —— v. 14.
3. Phil. iii. 15.
1. Heb. vi. 9.
1. —— ix. 6.
1. Rev. ix. 17.
2. —— xvi. 5.
1. —— xviii. 21.

THUS (EVEN)

{ κατὰ, according to
{ ταῦτα, these things.

Luke xvii. 30.

THUS FAR.

{ ἕως, as long as
{ τούτου, this.

Luke xxii. 51.

THY, THINE.

1. σοῦ, (*Gen. sing. of* σύ, thou) of thee, *i.e.* thine, (*but not so emphatic as No.* 3.)

2. σοί, (*Dat. sing. of* σύ, thou) to thee, *i.e.* to *or* belonging to thee.

3. σός, (*poss. pron.*) thy, thine, (*more emphatic than Nos.* 1 and 2, *and denoting actual possession, power over, authorship, right, etc.*)

4. σεαυτοῦ, of thyself.

1. Matt. i. 20.
1. —— iv. 6, 7, 10.
1. —— v. 23 twice, 24 3 times, 25, 29 3 times, 30 3 times, 33, 36, 39, 40, 43 twice.
1. —— vi. 3 twice, 4 twice, 6 4 times, 9, 10 twice, 13 (*ap.*), 17 twice, 18 twice, 22 twice, 23 twice.
1. —— vii. 3 1st.
— ———— 3 2nd, see T own.
1. ———— 4 1st & 2nd.
— ———— 4 3rd, } see T
— ———— 5 1st, } own.
1. ———— 5 2nd.
3. ———— 22 3 times.
1. —— ix. 2, 6 twice, 14, 18, 22.
1. —— xi. 10 twice, 26.
1. —— xii. 2, 13, 37 twice, 47 twice.
3. —— xiii. 27.
1. Matt. xv. 2.
1. ———— 4 (*om.* G L T Tr A ℵ.)
1. ———— 19.
— —— xx. 14, see T (that is)
1. ———— 15.
1. ———— 21 1st (*om.* L ℵ.)
1. ———— 21 2nd.
1. —— xxi. 5.
1. —— xxii. 37 4 times, 39, 44 twice.
1. —— xxiii. 37.
3. —— xxiv. 3.
1. —— xxv. 21, 23, 25 1st.
— ———— 25 2nd, see T (that is)
— —— xxvi. 18, see T house.
1. ———— 42, 52, 73.
1. Mark i. 2 twice, 44.
1. —— ii. 5 (*om.* Lb.)
1. Mark ii. 9, 11 twice.
3. ———— 18.
1. —— iii. 5 (*om.* T Trb A.)
1. ———— 32 twice.
2. —— v. 9.
1. ———— 19, and see T friends.
1. ———— 34 twice, 35.
1. —— vi. 18.
1. —— vii. 5, 10 twice, 29.
1. —— ix. 18, 38, 43, 45, 47.
1. —— x. 19, 37 1st.
1. ———— 37 2nd (*om.* Lb T Tr A.)
1. ———— 37 3rd, 52.
1. —— xii. 30 5 times, 31, 36 twice.
1. —— xiv. 70 (*ap.*)
1. Luke i. 13 twice, 36, 38, 42, 44, 61.
1. —— ii. 29 twice, 30, 32, 35, 48.
1. —— iv. 7, 8, 11, 12, 23.
1. —— v. 5, 14, 20, 23, 24 twice.
3. ———— 33.
1. —— vi. 10, 29.
— ———— 30, see T goods.
1. ———— 41, 42 1st & 2nd.
— ———— 42 3rd, see T own.
1. —— vii. 27 twice, 44, 48, 50.
1. —— viii. 20 twice.
2. ———— 30.
— ———— 39, see T own.
1. ———— 48, 49.
1. —— ix. 40, 41, 49.
1. —— x. 17, 21, 27 6 times.
1. —— xi. 2 1st & 2nd, 2 3rd (*ap.*), 34 twice, 36.
1. —— xii. 20, 58.
1. —— xiii. 12, 26, 34.
1. —— xiv. 12 1st & 2nd, 12 3rd (*ap.*)
1. —— xv. 19 twice, 21 twice, 27 twice, 29, 30 twice.
3. ———— 31.
1. ———— 32.
1. —— xvi. 2 (*om.* G ⇄), 6, 7, 25 twice.
1. —— xvii. 3, 19.
1. —— xviii. 20 1st.
1. ———— 20 2nd (*om.* G ⇄ L Tr A.)
1. ———— 42.
1. —— xix. 5, 16, 18, 20.
— ———— 22, see T own.
1. ———— 39.
1. ———— 42 1st (*om.* G → L Tr Ab ℵ.)
1. ———— 42 2nd (*om.* Lb Trb Ab ℵ.)
1. ———— 42 3rd, 43, 44 twice.
1. —— xx. 43 twice.
1. —— xxii. 32 twice.
3. ———— 42.
1. —— xxiii. 42, 46.
1. John ii. 17.
1. —— iv. 16, 18.
3. ———— 42.
1. ———— 50.
1. ———— 51 (αὐτοῦ, *his,* L T Tr A ℵ.)
1. ———— 53.
1. —— v. 8, 11.
1. ———— 12 (*om.* τὸν κραβατόν σου, *thy bed,* T Trb A ℵ.)
1. —— vii. 3.
1. —— viii. 10 (*ap.*), 13, 19.
1. —— ix. 10 (No. 2, Lm), 17, 26.
1. —— xi. 23.
1. —— xii. 15, 28.
1. —— xiii. 37, 38.
1. John xvii. 1 1st.
1. ———— 1 2nd (*om.* T Tr A ℵ.)
— ———— 5, see T own self.
1. ———— 6 1st.
2. ———— 6 2nd.
1. ———— 6 3rd.
2. ———— 9.
3. ———— 10 twice.
— ———— 11, see T own.
1. ———— 12, 14.
1. ———— 17 1st (*om.* G ⇄ L Tr A ℵ*, i.e. *the truth.*)
3. ———— 17 2nd.
1. ———— 26.
1. —— xviii. 11 (*om.* G L T Tr A ℵ, i.e. *the.*)
— ———— 35, see T own.
1. —— xix. 26, 27.
1. —— xx. 27 twice.
1. —— xxi. 18.
1. Acts ii. 27, 28, 35 twice.
1. —— iii. 25.
1. —— iv. 25, 27, 28 1st.
1. ———— 28 2nd (*om.* L Trb.)
1. ———— 29 twice.
1. ———— 30 1st (*om.* L T Ab.)
1. ———— 30 2nd.
1. —— v. 3.
— ———— 4 1st, see T own (be)
— ———— 4 2nd, see T own.
1. ———— 4 3rd, 9.
1. —— vii. 3 twice, 32, 33.
1. —— viii. 20, 21, 22 twice.
1. —— ix. 13, 14.
4. ———— 34.
1. —— x. 4 twice, 31 twice.
1. —— xi. 14.
1. —— xii. 8 twice.
1. —— xiii. 35.
1. —— xiv. 10.
1. —— xvi. 31.
1. —— xxii. 16, 18, 20.
1. —— xxiii. 5, 35.
3. —— xxiv. 2, 4.
1. —— xxvi. 16.
1. Rom. ii. 5, 25.
1. —— iii. 4.
1. —— iv. 18.
1. —— viii. 36.
2. —— ix. 7.
1. —— x. 6, 8 twice, 9 twice.
1. —— xi. 3 twice.
1. —— xii. 20.
1. —— xiii. 9.
1. —— xiv. 10 twice, 15 twice, 21.
1. —— xv. 9.
3. 1 Cor. viii. 11.
— —— x. 29, see T own.
3. —— xiv. 16.
1. —— xv. 55 twice.
1. Gal. iii. 16.
1. —— v. 14.
1. Eph. vi. 2.
1. 1 Tim. iv. 12, 15.
1. —— v. 23 1st (*om.* L T Tr A ℵ.)
1. ———— 23 2nd.
1. 2 Tim. i. 4, 5 twice.
1. —— iv. 5, 22.
1. Philem. 2, 5, 6, 7, 13.
3. ———— 14 1st.
1. ———— 14 2nd.
— ———— 19, see T own self.
1. ———— 21.
1. Heb. i. 8 twice, 9 twice, 10, 12, 13 twice.
1. —— ii. 7 (*ap.*), 12.
1. —— x. 7, 9.
2. —— xi. 18.
1. Jas. ii. 8, 18 1st.
1. ———— 18 2nd (*om.* G ⇄ L T Tr A ℵ, i.e. *the.*)

1. 2 John 4, 13.
1. 3 John 2, 6.
1. Rev. ii. 2 1st.
1. —— 2 2nd (*om.* G⇉L T Tr A.)
1. —— 2 3rd, 4, 9, 13 (*ap.*), 19 3 times.
1. —— iii. 1, 2, 8, 9, 11, 15, 18 twice.
1. —— iv. 11.
1. Rev. v. 9.
1. —— x. 9 twice.
1. —— xi. 17, 18 3 times.
1. —— xiv. 15, 18.
1. —— xv. 3 twice, 4 twice.
1. —— xvi. 7.
1. —— xviii. 10, 14, 23 twice.
1. —— xix. 10 twice.
1. —— xxii. 9 twice.

THINE OWN.

1. σοῦ; *see No.* 1, *above.*
2. σός, *see No.* 3, *above.*
3. { ὁ, the, / ἑαυτοῦ, of thyself.

2. Matt. vii. 3.
1. —— 4, 5.
1. Luke vi. 42 twice.
1. —— viii. 39.
1. Luke xix. 22.
1. John xvii. 11.
2. —— xviii. 35.
2. Acts v. 4 2nd.
3. 1 Cor. x. 29.

THINE OWN (BE)

{ μένω, to remain / σοί, to thee.

Acts v. 4 1st.

THINE OWN SELF.

σεαυτοῦ, *see* "THY," *No.* 4.

John xvii. 5. | Philem. 19.

THINE (THAT IS)

{ τὸ, the *thing*, / σόν, thy, (*see* "THY," *No.* 3.)

Matt. xx. 14. | Matt. xxv. 25.

THY FRIENDS.

{ οἱ, the, (*masc. pl.*) / σοί, to thee, *belonging* to thee.

Mark v. 19.

THY GOODS.

{ τὰ, the *things*, / σα, thy, thine, (*see* "THY," *No.* 3.)

Luke vi. 30.

THY HOUSE.

{ πρὸς, toward, hither, with / σέ, thee.

Matt. xxvi. 18.

THYINE.

θύϊνος, thyine, an evergreen African tree of aromatic wood.

Rev. xviii. 12, marg. *sweet.*

THYSELF.

THYSELF is the translation of αὐτὸς, self, in all passages not quoted below. (See "THOU" for "THOU THYSELF.")

1. σεαυτοῦ, of thyself.
2. ἑαυτοῦ, of one's self.
3. ἑαυτόν, (*Acc.*) himself, herself, itself.

1. Matt. iv. 6.
1. —— viii. 4.
1. —— xix. 19.
1. —— xxii. 39 (No. 2, G ~)
1. —— xxvii. 40.
1. Mark i. 44.
1. —— xii. 31.
1. —— xv. 30.
1. Luke iv. 9, 23.
1. —— v. 14.
1. —— x. 27.
1. —— xxiii. 37, 39.
1. John i. 22.
1. —— vii. 4.
1. —— viii. 13, 53.
1. —— x. 33.
1. John xiv. 22.
2. —— xviii. 34 (No. 1, L Tr A ℵ.)
1. —— xxi. 18.
1. Acts xvi. 28.
1. —— xxvi. 1.
1. Rom. ii. 1, 21.
3. —— xiii. 9 (No. 1, L T Tr A ℵ.)
1. —— xiv. 22.
3. Gal. v. 14 (No. 1, G L T Tr A ℵ.)
1. —— vi. 1.
1. 1 Tim. iv. 7, 16.
1. —— v. 22.
1. 2 Tim. ii. 15.
1. Tit. ii. 7.
1. Jas. ii. 8.

See also, THOU.

TIDINGS.

(*For various combinations with other words, see below.*)

1. λόγος, the word (*spoken, not written*); that which is spoken *or* told; an exposition *or* account which one gives *by word of mouth.*
2. φάσις, report, information, light shed on *anything* by speech (*non occ.*)

1. Acts xi. 22. | 2. Acts xxi. 31.

TIDINGS OF (BRING GLAD)

εὐαγγελίζω, to bring a joyful message, *or* good news. *Here, mid.*, to proclaim *something to somebody*, as a divine message of salvation, to proclaim the divine message of salvation; bring some one into relation to it, to evangelise *him.*

Rom. x. 15.

TIDINGS UNTO (DECLARE GLAD)

Acts xiii. 32.

TIDINGS (SHOW GLAD)

Luke i. 19.
—— viii. 1.

TIDINGS OF (BRING GOOD)

Luke ii. 10. | 1 Thes. iii. 6.

TIE, TIED.

δέω, to bind, tie, fasten.

Matt. xxi. 2. | Mark xi. 2, 4.
Luke xix. 30.

TILING.

κέραμος, potters' clay; *then*, any earthen vessel *or* tile, *etc.*, made of clay. *Here*, *pl.*, (*whence Eng. word*, ceramic), (*non occ.*)

Luke v. 19.

TILL.

1. ἕως, *as adv.*, until, as long as, *marking the continuance* of an action up to the time of another action.

 (a) *with* ἄν (*and sub. aor.*), *where the later action is only probable.*

 (b) *with* οὗ, until what *time.*

 (c) *with* ὅτου, until when.

 (d) *with the Gen.*, (*as a prep.*) until, unto, *marking the "terminus ad quem," and spoken both of time and place.*

2. ἄχρι, *of time*, continuedly, *marking duration*, continuedly until, during, (*see No.* 3.)

 (a) *with* οὗ, (*with a noun*) until *the time* when; (*with a verb in the present*) so long as, while, } (*without implying the cessation of the duration then.*)

 (b) ἄχρις οὗ ἄν, until the time whensoever.

3. μέχρι, until, *referring solely to the limit, implying that the action there terminates, while No. 2 fixes the attention upon the whole duration up to the limit, but leaving the further continuance undetermined.*

 (a) *with* οὗ, until what time, (*implying that the action then terminates.*)

4. { εἰ, if, / μή, not, } except, / ὅταν, when, whensoever.

5. εἰς, unto, *when referring to time, denoting either the interval up to a certain point*, during; *or the point itself as the object or aim of some purpose*, up to, for.

1b. Matt. i. 25.
1. —— ii. 9.
1a. —— v. 18 twice, 26.
1a. —— x. 11, 23.
1a. —— xii. 20.
1b. —— xiii. 33.
1a. —— xvi. 28.
1. —— xviii. 21.
1b. —— 30 (No. 1, L T Tr A ℵ.)
1b. —— 34 (No. 1, L.)
1a. —— xxii. 44.
1a. —— xxiii. 39.
1a. —— xxiv. 34.
1a. Mark vi. 10.
1a. —— ix. 1.
4. —— 9.
1b. —— xii. 36.
3a. —— xiii. 30.
1d. Luke i. 80.
1a. —— ix. 27.
1b. —— xii. 50, 59.
1c. —— xiii. 8.
1b. —— 21.
1c. —— xv. 8.
1. —— xvii. 8.
1. Luke xix. 13 (ἐν ᾧ, *in which while*, G ~ L T Tr A ℵ, *i.e. while I go and return.*)
1a. —— xx. 43.
1a. —— xxi. 32.
1b. John xiii. 38.
1. —— xxi. 22, 23.
2a. Acts vii. 18.
1a. —— viii. 40, with inf.
2. —— xx. 11.
1. —— xxi. 5.
1b. —— xxiii. 12, 21.
1b. —— xxv. 21.
1d. —— xxviii. 23.
2a. 1 Cor. xi. 26. [Tr A ℵ.)
2b. —— xv. 25 (No. 2, A L T
2a. Gal. iii. 19.
3. Eph iv. 13.
5. Phil. i. 10.
1. 1 Tim. iv. 13.
1. Heb. x. 13.
2b. Rev. ii. 25. [Tr A ℵ.)
2a. —— vii. 3 (No. 2, L T
2. —— xv. 8.
2. —— xx. 3.

TILLAGE. [margin.]

1 Cor. iii. 9, see "HUSBANDRY."

TIME (-s.)

(*For various combinations with other words, see below.*)

1. καιρός, the right measure and relation, *esp. as regards time and place*, (*gen. of time*); *hence*, the right time, suitable *or* convenient time; the opportune point of time at which a thing SHOULD BE done, (a certain limited portion of *No.* 2.)

2. χρόνος, time, duration, time in general, any time, (*while No.* 1 *is* THE time); the time in which anything IS done.

3. ὥρα, a portion of time, (*Lat.*, hora; *Eng.*, hour) season, time of blossoming, (ὡραῖος, blossoming; ἄωρος, unseasonable). *Orig.*, the season of the year; *then*, the time of the day, and when *reckoning by hours was practised*, the hour; *hence*, a definite, limited, and determined time, (*thus differing from No.* 1, *which is* THE definite opportune time), (*see* "SEASON," *No.* 3.)

4. ἡμέρα, day, *i.e.* the time from one sunrise *or* sunset to another; *also*, day, *i.e.* daylight, from sunrise to

sunset; *then, sometimes,* time in general; *in sing.*, a period *or* point of time; *in pl.*, days, *i.e.* time.

5. γενεά, a generation, the period of time occupied by a generation.

2. Matt. ii. 7, 16.
— — iv. 17, see T (from that)
1. — viii. 29.
1. — xi. 25.
1. — xii. 1.
1. — xiii. 30.
1. — xiv. 1.
3. — — 15.
1. — xvi. 3.
— — — 21, see T (from that)
3. — xviii. 1 (No. 4, G∾L.)
1. — xxi. 34.
— — xxiv. 21, see T (to this)
2. — xxv. 19.
— — xxvi. 16, see T (from that)
1. — — 18.
1. Mark i. 15.
— — iv. 17, see T (endureth but for a)
3. — vi. 35.
1. — x. 30.
1. — xi. 13.
— — xiii. 19, see T (unto this)
1. — — 33.
3. Luke i. 10.
2. — — 57, and see T come (full)
2. — iv. 5.
— — — 27, see T of (in the)
1. — viii. 13.
— — — 27, see T (long)
4. — ix. 51, pl.
1. — xii. 56.
3. — xiv. 17.
— — xv. 29, see T (neither at any)
— — xvi. 16, see T (since that)
1. — xviii. 30.
1. — xix. 44.
— — xx. 9, see T (for a long)
1. — xxi. 8, 24.
— — xxiii. 7, see T (at that)
— John i. 18, see T (at any)
2. — v. 6.
— — — 37, see T (at any)
— — vi. 66, see T (from that)
1. — vii. 6 twice, 8.
— — xi. 39, see T (by this)
2. — xiv. 9.
3. — xvi. 2, 4, 25.
2. Acts i. 6, 7.
— — — 21, see T that (all the)
1. — iii. 19.
2. — — 21.
2. — vii. 17.
1. — — 20.
4. — viii. 1.
— — — 11, see T (of long)
— — xi. 8, see T (nothing at any)
1. — xii. 1.
2. — xiii. 18.
— — xiv. 3, see T (long)
5. Acts xiv. 16.
2. — — 28.
5. — xv. 21, pl.
— — xvii. 21, see T (spend one's)
1. — — 26.
2. — — 30.
2. — xviii. 20.
— — — 23, see T there (spend some)
1. — xix. 23.
— — xx. 16, see T (spend the)
— — xxiv. 25, see T (for this)
2. — xxvii. 9.
1. Rom. iii. 26, and see T (this)
1. — v. 6, marg. (text, *due time.*)
1. — viii. 18, and see T (this present)
1. — ix. 9.
1. — xi. 5.
1. — xiii. 11 1st.
— — — 11 2nd, see T (high)
1. 1 Cor. iv. 5.
1. — vii. 5, 29.
— — xvi. 12, see T (at this)
1. 2 Cor. vi. 2 twice.
1. — viii. 14, and see T (now at this present)
2. Gal. iv. 4.
1. — — 10.
— — v. 21, see T past (tell in)
1. Eph. i. 10.
1. — ii. 12.
1. — v. 16.
1. Col. iv. 5.
1. 1 Thes. ii. 17.
2. — v. 1.
1. 2 Thes. ii. 6.
1. 1 Tim. ii. 6, pl.
1. — iv. 1.
1. — vi. 15.
— — — 19, see T to come (against the)
1. 2 Tim. iii. 1.
1. — iv. 3, 6.
1. Tit. i. 3.
— Heb. i. 1 1st, see T (at sundry)
— — — 2 2nd, see T past (in)
2. — iv. 7.
— — — 16, see T of need (in)
2. — v. 12.
1. — ix. 9, 10.
2. — xi. 32.
1. 1 Pet. i. 5, 11.
2. — — 17, 20.
2. — iv. 2, 3.
1. — — 17.
— — v. 6, see T (due)
3. 1 John ii. 18 twice.
— — iv. 12, see T (at any)
2. Jude 18.
1. Rev. i. 3.
2. — x. 6.
1. — xi. 18.
1. — xii. 12, 14 3 times.
3. — xiv. 15.
1. — xxii. 10.

TIME TO COME (AGAINST THE)

εἰς, unto, with a view to
τὸ, the
μέλλον, impending future.

1 Tim. vi. 19.

TIME THAT (ALL THE)

ἐν, in, during
παντὶ, all
χρόνῳ, [*the*] time
ἐν, in
ᾧ, which.

Acts i. 21.

TIME (AT ANY)

πώποτε, yet, ever, at any time. *In N.T. only after a negative,* not yet ever, not at any time, never.

John i. 18. | 1 John iv. 12. | John v. 37.

TIME (AT THAT)

ἐν, in; ταύταις, these; ταῖς, the; ἡμέραις, days — in these days.

Luke xxiii. 7.

TIME (AT THIS)

1. νῦν, now, just now, even now, the present.

2. ἐν, in; τῷ, the; νῦν, present; καιρῷ, season — in the now existing present season (*see* "TIME," *No.* 1)

2. Rom. iii. 26. | 1. 1 Cor. xvi. 12.

TIMES (AT SUNDRY)

πολυμερῶς, consisting of many parts, manifold, in many portions; by many fragments *in and through many persons, and therefore necessarily imperfect compared with the Son, by whom God has now spoken.*

Heb. i. 1.

TIME (BY THIS)

ἤδη, even now, already.

John xi. 39.

TIME (DUE)

καιρός, *see* "TIME," *No.* 1.

Rom. v. 6 marg. *time.* | 1 Pet. v. 6.

TIME (ENDURE BUT FOR A)

ἀλλὰ, but
πρόσκαιροί, for a season
εἰσιν, are,
} are but for a season.

Mark iv. 17.

TIME (FOR A LONG)

χρόνοι, times,
ἱκανοὶ, coming to, reaching to; *hence*, sufficing, sufficient,
} a sufficient *or* long time.

Luke xx. 9.

TIME (FOR THIS)

τὸ, the
νῦν, present,
ἔχον, having.

Acts xxiv. 25.

TIME (FROM THAT)

1. ἀπὸ, from, away from, [time,
τότε, then, at that
} from then, from that time.

2. ἐκ, out of, from,
τούτου, of this [*circumstance or time*]
} because of this.

1. Matt. iv. 17. | 1. Matt. xxvi. 16.
1. —— xvi. 21. | 2. John vi. 66.

TIME COME (FULL)

πίμπλημι, to fill, fulfil,
ὁ, the
χρονος, time, (*see* "TIME," *No.* 2)
} *lit.* [*to Elisabeth*] the time was fulfilled.

Luke i. 57.

TIME (HIGH)

ὥρα, (*see* "TIME," *No.* 3) an hour.

Rom. xiii. 11.

TIME OF (IN THE)

ἐπί, upon. *Here, with Gen.*, in the time of, at the time of.

Luke iv. 27.

TIME OF NEED (IN)

εἰς, for
εὔκαιρον, well timed, opportune *help or succour.*

Heb. iv. 16.

TIME PAST (IN)

πάλαι, of old, formerly.

Heb. i. 1.

TIME (LONG)

1. ἐκ, out of, from,
χρονῶν, times,
ἱκανῶν, sufficient [*-ly long*]

2. ἱκανὸν, sufficient
χρόνον, time.

1. Luke viii. 27. | 2. Acts xiv. 3.

TIME (NOTHING AT ANY)

οὐδέποτε, not ever,
πᾶν, everything, anything,
} at no time.

Acts xi. 8 (*om.* πᾶν, G L T Tr A ℵ.)

TIME (NEITHER AT ANY)

οὐδέποτε, not ever, at no time.

Luke xv. 29.

TIME (NOW AT THIS)

ἐν, in
τῷ, the
νῦν, now present
καιρῷ, season, (*see* "TIME," *No.* 1.)

2 Cor. viii. 14.

TIME (OF LONG)

διὰ, through
τῷ, the
ἱκανῷ, sufficient
χρόνῳ, time, (*see No.* 2.)

Acts viii. 11.

TIME (SINCE THAT)

ἀπὸ, from
τότε, then.

Luke xvi. 16.

TIME (SPEND ONE'S)

εὐκαιρέω, to have a good season, to have and enjoy the opportunity, ("TIME," *No.* 1, *and* εὖ, good, *prefixed.*)

Acts xvii. 21.

TIME (SPEND THE)

χρονοτριβέω, to wear away the time, (*No.* 2) spend the time, delay, (*non occ.*)

Acts xx. 16.

TIME THERE (SPEND SOME)

{ ποιέω, to make } to spend *or* stay
{ χρόνος, time, } some time.

Acts xviii. 23 part.

TIME PAST (TELL IN)

προεῖπον, to tell before, (*see* "SAY," *No.* 2, *with* πρό, before, *prefixed.*)

Gal. v. 21.

TIME (THIS PRESENT)

{ ὁ, the
{ νῦν, present, now,
{ καιρός, season, opportunity.

Rom. viii. 18.

TIME (TO THIS)

{ ἕως, until, unto,
{ τοῦ, the,
{ νῦν, now, present.

Matt. xxiv. 21.

TIME (UNTO THIS)

{ ἕως, until, unto,
{ τοῦ, the,
{ νῦν, now, present.

Mark xiii. 19.

See also, ABOUT, ANY, APPOINTED, BORN, CONVENIENT, GIVE, LIFE, NEITHER, OLD, PAST, SECOND, SEVEN, SEVENTY, SINCE, SOME, THIRD, THOUSAND, THREE, UNTIL.

TINKLE.

ἀλαλάζω, to raise the cry of battle; (lxx. *for* Josh. vi. 20.) *Hence,* to make a loud cry *or* shout, (lxx. *for* הריע, Ps. xlvii. 2; lxvi. 1); to wail, (lxx. *for* הילִיל, Jer. xxv. 34; xlvii. 2.) *Of cymbals,* to clang, to give a clanging sound.

1 Cor. xiii. 1.

TIP.

ἄκρον, pointed; *hence, neut., with art.* τὸ ἄκρον, *as subst.*, a point, end, extremity.

Luke xvi. 24.

TIRED (*be*) [margin.]

Matt. ix. 36, see "FAINT (TO)"

TITHE (-S.) [noun.]

δεκάτη, a tenth part. *Here, see* Gen. xiv. 20, *where* lxx. *for* מַעֲשֵׂר; *and* Lev. xxvii. 30, 31, 32.

Heb. vii. 8, 9.

TITHES (GIVE)

ἀποδεκατόω, to tithe off; levy tithes; (*so* lxx. *for* עשר, 1 Sam. viii. 15, 17; *also,* to pay *or* give tithes of; *so also* lxx. *for* עִשֵּׂר, Gen. xxviii. 22; Deut. xiv. 22.)

Luke xviii. 12.

TITHES (PAY)

1. ἀποδεκατόω, *see above.*
2. δεκατόω, to tithe. *Here, pass.*, to be tithed; *hence,* to pay tithes; (*here,* lxx. *for* עִשֵּׂר, Neh. x. 38.)

1. Matt. xxiii. 23. | 2. Heb. vii. 9.

TITHES OF (RECEIVE)

δεκατόω, to tithe; *trans.*, to receive tithes from.

Heb. vii. 6.

TITHES (TAKE)

ἀποδεκατόω, *see* "TITHES (GIVE)"

Heb. vii. 5.

TITHE. [verb.]

ἀποδεκατόω, *see* "TITHES (GIVE)"

Luke xi. 42.

TITLE.

τίτλος, (*Lat.*, titulus, *i.e.*) a title, superscription.

John xix. 19, 20.

TITTLE.

κεραια, a little horn, apex *or* point *of a letter*, (*i e* the differences between ד and ר, ב and כ, etc.)

Matt. v. 18. | Luke xvi. 17.

TO

"To" is frequently either the translation of the infinitive of the verb, *or* of the Dative case of the noun. It forms also sometimes part of a phrase.

A list of words will be found at the foot, in connection with which it is also found.

When it is the translation of a separate Greek word, it is one of these following.

1. **εἰς**, unto, (*implying motion to the interior*); into, towards, with a view to; *implying immediate purpose.*

2. **εἰς τὸ**, *with the inf.*, to the end that, with a view to *doing, being, or suffering whatever the verb may mean.*

3. **πρός**, towards, in the direction of.

   (a) *with Gen.*, hitherwards, in favour of, in consideration of, *as a motive.*

   (b) *with Dat.*, resting in a direction towards, at, close by, in addition to, *as an act.*

   (c) *with Acc.*, hitherwards, towards, to, with a view to, *as an end, implying ultimate purpose.*

4. **ἵνα**, that, in order that, to the end that, *with* the emphasis on the purpose, design, and result. *Here, followed by the inf. mood, (and consequently often represented by two "to's.")*

5. **ἐπί**, upon.

   (a) *with Gen.*, upon and proceeding from, on, upon, before.

   (b) *with Dat.*, upon and resting on, on *or* at, *as the groundwork of any fact or circumstance. Here, we must understand the words* "but practised," *retaining the force of* ἐπί, upon, *the ruin being the necessary consequence of that which was the groundwork of it.*

   (c) *with Acc.*, upon, (*by direction towards*); (*with motion implied*) up to; to, (*implying intention*); for.

6. **ἐν**, in; *of place*, within, among; in *or* with; in, *i.e. the sphere in which the subject is contained or concerned.*

7. **ἕως**, (*as prep.*) until, unto, *marking the "terminus ad quem," and spoken both of time and place.*

8. **κατά**, down.

   (a) *with Gen.*, down from.

   (b) *with Acc.*, down towards, down to, *implying destination.*

9. **ὅπως**, in order that, (*with emphasis on the manner and method*); in such manner that, to the end that, so that.

10. **ὥστε**, so as that, so that, so as to, (*expressing event, result, or consequence.*)

11. **διά**, through.

   (a) *with Gen.*, through and proceeding from, through, by means of, (*marking the instrument of an action.*)

   (b) *with Acc., through and tending towards*, because of, for the sake of, (*marking the ground of an action.*)

12. **ἐνώπιον**, in the sight of, in the presence of.

13. **μέχρι**, until, (*referring solely to the limit, end, or close of the time or space within which any thing is done, and implying that what is spoken of then terminates.*)

14. **ὑπέρ**, over.

   (a) *with Gen.*, over and separate from.

   (b) *with Acc.*, over and towards, beyond.

15. παρά, beside.

(a) *with Gen.*, beside and proceeding from, from beside.

(b) *with Dat.*, beside and at, at the side of, near, with.

(c) *with Acc.*, to *or* along the side of, beside, in comparison with.

7. Matt. i. 17.
1. —— ii. 1, 8.
3c. —— 12.
3c. —— iii. 5.
5c. —— 7 1st, 13 1st.
3c. —— 14 2nd.
5c. —— v. 23.
1. —— vii. 13.
3c. —— 15.
1. —— viii. 28.
1. —— ix. 7.
1. —— 13 (*om.* εἰς μετάνοιαν, *to repentance*, G L T Tr A ℵ.)
10. —— x. 1 1st.
3c. —— 6, 13.
1. —— 17, 21 1st, 22.
7. —— xi. 23.
5c. —— xiii. 48.
1. —— xiv. 19.
3c. —— 29.
1. —— xvi. 5 1st.
3c. —— xvii. 14 1st.
1. —— 24 1st, 27.
1. —— xx. 17, 18 1st.
2. —— 19 2nd.
1. —— xxi. 1.
5c. —— 19.
3c. —— 34.
1. —— xxii. 3 2nd, 5 1st.
1. —— 5 2nd (No. 5c, G∾L T Tr A ℵ.)
1. —— 9.
1. —— xxiii. 34.
7. —— xxiv. 31.
3c. —— xxv. 9.
1. —— 10 2nd.
2. —— xxvi. 2.
4. —— 16.
3c. —— 18 1st, 45, 57.
9. —— 59 1st.
10. —— xxvii. 1 1st.
3c. —— 4 1st, 14.
4. —— 26.
2. —— 31.
4. —— 32.
3c. Mark i. 40 1st, 45 3rd.
1. —— ii. 17 2nd (*om.* εἰς μετάνοιαν, *to repentance*, G L T Tr A ℵ.)
3c. —— iii. 7 (No. 1, G L T.)
4. —— iv. 21 twice.
3c. —— 41.
3c. —— v. 15, 19.
1. —— 38.
1. —— vi. 41 1st.
4. —— 41 3rd.
1. —— 45 1st.
1. —— vii. 30.
4. —— 32.
1. —— 34.
1. —— viii. 3.
4. —— 6 3rd.
1. —— 13, 22 1st.
4. —— 22 2nd.
1. —— 26 1st.
3c. —— ix. 14.
4. —— 22.
1. —— 33.
3c. —— x. 7 (*om.* L ℵ.)
1. —— 32 1st, 33 1st, 46.
3c. —— 50.
1. —— xi. 1.
3c. —— 7.
5c. —— 13.
1. —— 15 1st, 27 1st.
3c. Mark xi. 27 2nd.
4. —— 28.
3c. —— xii. 2.
4. —— 13.
1. —— xiii. 9, 12 1st, 14.
7. —— 27.
4. —— 34 3rd.
1. —— xiv. 8 2nd.
4. —— 10.
1. —— 32 1st.
3c. —— 53.
2. —— 55 1st.
4. —— xv. 15 2nd, 20, 21.
5c. Luke i. 16, 17 2nd.
6. —— 17 3rd, marg. *by*.
1. —— 23 1st.
3c. —— 27 1st, 43 2nd, 55 1st.
1. —— 56.
3c. —— 73.
3c. —— ii. 15 1st.
1. —— 22 2nd, 39 2nd, 41.
1. —— 42 (*om.* εἰς Ἱεροσόλυμα, *to Jerusalem*, G ⇄ T Trb A ℵ.)
1. —— 45, 51.
1. —— iv. 9, 16, 31.
5c. —— v. 11.
2. —— 17 2nd.
1. —— 25, 32 2nd.
4. —— vi. 34 4th.
3c. —— 47 1st.
3c. —— vii. 4, 6.
1. —— 10.
3c. —— 19, 44, 50.
3c. —— viii. 19, 25.
5c. —— 27.
3c. —— 35 2nd.
1. —— 39.
3c. —— ix. 14.
1. —— 16 1st.
3c. —— 23.
4. —— 40.
1. —— 51 3rd.
10. —— 52 (ὡς, *as if*, Lm ℵ.)
1. —— 53.
—— 56 1st & 2nd (*ap.*)
1. —— 56 3rd.
5c. —— 62.
5c. —— x. 6.
1. —— 7.
7. —— 15 twice.
1. —— 30, 34 2nd.
3c. —— xi. 6 1st.
9. —— 37.
5c. —— xii. 25.
3c. —— 41.
5c. —— 58 1st.
3c. —— 58 2nd.
3c. —— xiv. 6, 7.
1. —— 8.
3c. —— 26.
1. —— xv. 17 1st.
3c. —— 18, 20, 22.
3c. —— xvi. 26 twice.
1. —— 27.
5c. —— xvii. 4 (No. 3c, L T Tr A ℵ), (*om*, G.)
1. —— 11.
1. —— xviii. 14, 31.
4. —— xix. 4 1st.
5c. —— 5 1st.
1. —— 28, 29 2nd.
3c. —— 35.
3c. —— xx. 9 2nd, 10.
1. —— xxi. 12, 21.
3c. —— 38 1st.
1. Luke xxii. 33 2nd, 39.
5c. —— 44 (*ap.*)
3c. —— 45.
5c. —— 52.
3c. —— xxiii. 4 1st, 7, 15.
5c. —— 33, 48.
1. —— xxiv. 5.
12. —— 11.
1. —— 13.
3c. —— 17.
5c. —— 24.
1. —— 33.
1. —— 50 (No. 3c, L T Tr A ℵ.)
1. —— 52.
4. John i. 7, 8, 19.
2. —— 27.
3c. —— 42, 47.
1. —— ii. 2, 12, 13.
3c. —— iii. 2.
1. —— 13.
4. —— 17.
3c. —— 20, 21, 26.
1. —— iv. 5 1st.
4. —— 8.
3c. —— 33.
4. —— 34 1st.
3c. —— 35.
1. —— v. 1.
4. —— 7, 36.
3c. —— 40, 45.
4. —— vi. 15.
3c. —— 17.
1. —— 24.
3c. —— 35, 37 twice.
4. —— 38.
3c. —— 44, 68.
4. —— vii. 32.
3c. —— 45, 50.
1. —— viii. 26 3rd.
3c. —— 31.
4. —— 56, 59.
1. —— ix. 11.
3c. —— 13.
4. —— x. 31.
3. —— xi. 19 1st.
4. —— 19 2nd, 31.
1. —— 38.
3c. —— 45, 46.
1. —— 55 1st.
4. —— 55 2nd.
1. —— 56.
1. —— xii. 1, 12 twice.
4. —— 20, 47 1st.
4. —— xiii. 2.
3c. —— 3, 6.
6. —— 35.
3c. —— xiv. 18.
3c. —— xvi. 5, 10, 16 (*ap.*), 17, 28.
1. —— 32.
1. —— xvii. 1.
4. —— 4.
3c. —— 11, 13.
3c. —— xviii. 13 1st.
4. —— xix. 16.
5c. —— 33.
3c. —— 39.
3c. —— xx. 2 twice.
1. —— 3, 4, 8.
3c. —— 17 twice.
1. —— xxi. 9.
5a. —— 11 (No. 1, L T Tr A ℵ.)
3c. —— 22, 23.
1. Acts i. 25.
3c. —— ii. 7 (*om.* πρὸς ἀλλήλους, *one to another*, L T Tr A ℵ.)
3c. —— 12.
3c. —— iv. 23, 24.
1. —— v. 21 1st, 36 3rd.
1. —— vi. 12.
1. —— viii. 3, 5.
7. —— 10 2nd.
3c. —— 24.
1. —— 25, 27 1st.
5c. —— 32.
1. Acts viii. 40.
1. —— ix. 2 1st.
3c. —— 2 2nd.
5c. —— 4.
3c. —— 10.
9. —— 24.
1. —— 26 1st (No. 6, G∾L.)
3c. —— 27 1st.
1. —— 30 twice.
3c. —— 32 2nd.
5c. —— 35.
7. —— 38 3rd.
3c. —— 40.
3c. —— x. 3.
1. —— 5, 8.
5a. —— 11.
3c. —— 13, 21.
1. —— 32.
3c. —— 33 1st.
1. —— xi. 2.
3c. —— 3.
—— 5, see T (even)
1. —— 13, 20, 25.
3c. —— 30.
6. —— xii. 11.
5c. —— 12.
1. —— 19 2nd.
3c. —— 20.
1. —— xiii. 4, 13 twice, 14, 31, 34 2nd, 46 2nd, 48.
3c. —— xiv. 11.
1. —— 20, 21 2nd, 24, 26 1st.
1. —— xv. 2, 4.
5c. —— 19.
1. —— 22 2nd, 30, 38 2nd.
1. —— xvi. 1.
8b. —— 7 1st.
1. —— 8, 11 twice, 12, 16.
4. —— 30.
3. —— 36 1st.
4. —— 36 2nd.
1. —— xvii. 1, 5 2nd.
5c. —— 14 2nd.
4. —— 15 1st.
3c. —— 15 2nd.
1. —— 20.
1. —— xviii. 1.
5c. —— 12.
1. —— 19, 22, 24.
1. —— xix. 1, 21 2nd.
1. —— xx. 6.
5c. —— 13 1st.
1. —— 14, 15, 17.
3c. —— 18.
1. —— xxi. 4 2nd, 7, 12 2nd, 15, 17.
1. —— xxii. 5 1st, 17 2nd.
3c. —— xxiii. 18 1st, 22.
9. —— 23 1st.
7. —— 23 2nd.
3c. —— 30 1st.
1. —— 31, 32 2nd, 33 1st.
1. —— xxiv. 17 2nd.
1. —— xxv. 1, 3 1st, 9 2nd.
3c. —— 16 1st, 21 3rd.
3c. —— xxvi. 9 2nd.
1. —— 12, 14 1st, 18 3rd.
5c. —— 20 2nd.
1. —— xxvii. 5.
3c. —— 12 1st.
1. —— 12 3rd.
4. —— 42.
5c. —— 43 2nd, 44 2nd.
1. —— xxviii. 6.
3c. —— 8 2nd.
1. —— 13 twice, 16 1st.
3c. —— 23 1st.
1. Rom. i. 5, marg. (text, *for*.)
1. —— 17.
6. —— 19, marg. (text, *in*.)
1. —— 24, 28 2nd
1. —— ii. 4.
13. —— v. 14.
1. —— 16, 18.

2. Rom. vii. 5.
1. —— 10 1st.
1. —— viii. 15.
3c.—— 31.
1. —— ix. 22 3rd, 31.
3c.—— x. 1, 21.
1. —— xi. 36 1st.
1. —— xii. 10.
1. —— xiii. 4 2nd (lit. εἰς ὀργήν, *unto wrath.*)
1. —— 14.
1. —— xiv. 1.
8b.—— 22.
3c.—— xv. 2.
1. —— 7.
2. —— 8.
1. —— 16.
2. —— 18 2nd.
3c.—— 22, 24 1st (*ap.*), 30.
1. —— xvi. 26 2nd.
4. 1 Cor. i. 27 1st (*ap.*), 27 2nd, 28 1st.
3c.—— ii. 1.
1. —— iv. 6 1st.
3c.—— 18, 19.
3c. —— vi. 5 1st.
6. —— vii. 15, marg. *in.*
2. —— viii. 10 2nd.
4. —— ix. 25.
1. —— x. 31.
2. —— xi. 22 1st, 33.
4. —— xiii. 3 2nd.
3c.—— 12.
1. —— xiv. 8.
3c.—— 12.
3c.—— xv. 34 2nd
4. —— xvi. 12 twice.
1. —— 15.
— 2 Cor. i. 12, see T...-ward.
7. —— 13.
3c.—— ii. 1.
1. —— 12 twice.
3c.—— iii. 1 2nd.
— —— 4, see T...-ward.
1. —— 13.
3c.—— 16.
1. —— 18.
3c.—— iv. 2.
6. —— 3.
1. —— 15.
2. —— vii. 3 2nd.
1. —— 9, 10 1st.
8b.—— viii. 3.
1. —— 4.
6. —— 7.
3c.—— 19 2nd.
1. —— 24.
1. —— ix. 1 1st, 8, 11.
3c.—— x. 4.
1. —— 5.
— —— 14, see T (as far as)
1. —— xi. 1.
7. —— xii. 2.
4. —— 7 2nd.
14b.—— 13 1st.
3c.—— 14 2nd.
3c.—— xiii. 1, 7.
1. —— 10 twice.
1. Gal. i. 17 1st.
3. —— 17 2nd.
1. —— 18 1st.
1. —— ii. 1, 8, 11 1st.
8b.—— 11 2nd.
4. —— iv. 5.
5c.—— 9 1st.
1. —— 24.
1. —— vi. 8 twice.
1. Eph. i. 5 1st, 6, 12.
3c.—— iv. 29.
1. —— 32.
1. Phil. i. 19.
2. —— 23 1st, see Note under "Strait (be in a)"
3c.—— 26.

1. Phil. ii. 11.
3c.—— 25 2nd.
4. —— 30.
1. —— iv. 17.
1. Col. i. 4.
6. —— 23.
1. —— ii. 2.
3c.—— 23.
1. —— iii. 9, 15.
— 1 Thes. i. 8 1st, see T...-ward.
3c.—— 9 1st.
2. —— ii. 16 3rd.
2. —— iii. 2 1st, 5.
1. —— v. 9 1st, 15.
1. 2 Thes. ii. 13 3rd, 14.
4. —— iii. 9 1st.
2. —— 9 2nd.
3c. 1 Tim. i. 16 1st.
1. —— 16 2nd.
1. —— v. 24.
1. 2 Tim. ii. 14 1st (No. 5c, L T Tr A ℵ.)
1. —— 20 twice, 25.
1. —— iii. 7 2nd.
1. —— iv. 10, 12.
3c. Tit. iii. 1 5th.
1. —— 12 2nd.
3c. Heb. i. 13.
15c.—— ii. 7, marg. (text, *than.*)
2. —— 17 2nd.
— —— iv. 12, see T(even)
3c.—— vi. 11.
2. —— vii. 25 2nd.
2. —— viii. 3 1st.
7. —— 11.
3c.—— ix. 13.
2. —— 14 2nd, 28.
1. —— x. 39.
1. —— xi. 7.
3c.—— 18, marg. (text, *of.*)
2. —— xiii. 21 1st.
2. Jas. i. 19 1st & 2nd.
1. —— 19 3rd.
5c.—— ii. 3 1st.
3c.—— iv. 5, marg. with φθόνος, *enviously.*
1. —— 9 twice.
1. 1 Pet. i. 4.
3c.—— ii. 4.
5c.—— 24, marg. (text, *on.*)
1. —— iv. 4, 9, 10.
11a. 2 Pet. i. 3, marg. *by* (ἰδίᾳ δόξῃ καὶ ἀρετῇ *by his own glory and virtue*, instead of διὰ δόξης καὶ ἀρετῆς, *to glory and virtue*, G ∾ L T Tr A ℵ.)
5c.—— ii. 22 2nd
1. —— 22 3rd.
1. —— iii. 9 2nd.
4. 1 John i. 9 1st.
4. —— iii. 5.
6. —— iv. 16.
3c. 2 John 12 3rd.
4. 3 John 4.
1. —— 5 1st.
1. —— 5 2nd (τοῦτο, *that too when*, instead of, εἰς τούς, *to*, G ∾ L T Tr A ℵ.)
3c.—— 14 1st.
1. Jude 4.
4. Rev. ii. 21.
4. —— iii. 9 1st.
3c.—— 20.
4. —— vi. 2.
4. —— viii. 6.
1. —— ix. 9.
1. —— x. 5.
1. —— xi. 6 3rd, 12.
1. —— xii. 4 1st.
4. —— 4 3rd.
1. —— xiii. 3.

4. Rev. xiii. 12, 16.
1. —— xvi. 14 2nd.
1. —— xx. 8 3rd.
5c. Rev. xxi. 10.
4. —— 15, 23.
5c.—— xxii. 14.

TO...-WARD.

3c. 2 Cor. i. 12. | 3c. 2 Cor. iii. 4.
3c. 1 Thes. i. 8.

TO (AS FAR AS)

ἄχρι, *of time*, continuedly, *marking duration*, continuedly, until, during, (*without implying the cessation when a certain point may be reached.*)

2 Cor. x. 14.

TO (EVEN)

ἄχρι, *see above.*

Acts xi. 5. | Heb. iv. 12.

See also, ACCORDING, ANSWER, APPEAL, AS, ATTAIN, ATTENDANCE, BOTTOM, BRING, CALL, CARRY, CHARGE, CHARGEABLE, CLEAVE, COME, CONDESCEND, CONFORMED, CONSENT, CONTRARY, END, FALL, FOR, FROM, GENERATION, GIVE, GIVEN, GO, GRIND, GROUND, HEARKEN, HEED, HOME, INTENT, JOIN, KNEEL, LAUGH, LAW, LOOK, MINISTER, NEAR, OBEDIENT, PERTAIN, PLACE, PRIVY, PROMISED, PURPOSE, PUT, READY, REGARD, RESPECT, ROLL, RUN, SEE, SPEAK, SUBJECT, SUBJECTION, SUBMIT, SUFFICIENT, TAKE, TOSSING, TRY, TURN, UTTERMOST.

TO AND FRO.

See, TOSS.

TO-DAY.

σήμερον, to-day, this day.

[When it comes after a verb, it belongs to that verb, unless it is separated from it and thrown into the next clause by the presence of ὅτι, (*that*) *e.g.*

With ὅτι.

Luke xix. 9. "Εἶπε δὲ πρὸς αὐτὸν ὁ Ἰησοῦς ὅτι σήμερον." "But Jesus said unto him, that to-day" (*or* this day is salvation come, etc.)

Luke IV. 21. "ἤρξατο δὲ λέγειν. πρὸς αὐτοὺς ὅτι"...σήμερον. "But He began to say unto them that this day," (or to-day is this scripture fulfilled, etc.)

Mark xiv. 30. "καὶ λέγει αὐτῷ ὁ Ἰησους Ἀμὴν λέγω σοι ὅτι σήμερον," etc. "And Jesus saith unto him, Verily I say unto thee, that this day," (*i.e.* to-day before the cock crow, etc.)

Without ὅτι.

Matt. xxi. 28. "καὶ, προσελθὼν τῷ πρώτῳ εἶπε, τέκνον, ὕπαγε σήμερον ἐργαζου ἐν τῷ ἀμπελῶνι μου," etc. "And coming to the first He said, Son, *go to-day*, work in my vineyard."

Luke xxii. 34. "λέγω σοι, Πέτρε, οὐ μὴ φωνήσει σήμερον ἀλέκτωρ," etc. "I tell thee, Peter, the cock shall not *crow this day*, before," etc.

Luke xxiii. 43. "καὶ εἶπεν αὐτῷ ὁ Ἰησοῦς, Αμην σοι λέγω * σήμερον, μετ' ἐμοῦ ἔσῃ ἐν τῷ παραδείσῳ." "And Jesus said to him, Verily, to thee I *say this day*, with Me shalt thou be in the Paradise." The words *to-day* being made solemn and emphatic. Thus, instead of *a remembrance*, when He shall come in (ἐν, ver. 22) His kingdom, He promises *a presence* then in association (μετά) with Himself. And this promise He makes on that very day when He was dying, but when the faith of the dying robber read aright the inscription above Him and the signs around Him.

Thus we are saved (1) the trouble of explaining why Jesus did not answer the question in its own terms; and (2) the inconvenience of endorsing the punctuation of the Auth. Vers. as inspired; and we also place this passage in harmony with numberless passages in the *O.T.*, such as "Verily I say unto you, this day," etc.; "I testify unto you this day," etc. Deut. vi. 6; vii. 11; viii. 1; x. 13; xi. 8, 13, 28; xiii. 18; xix. 9; xxvii. 4; xxxi. 2, etc., where the Septuagint corresponds to Luke xxiii. 43.]

* T Tr A prefer σοι λέγω, to thee I say, with emphasis on the pronoun, "to thee I say this day" (instead of λέγω σοι, "I say to thee," as in the AV.)

Matt. vi. 30.
— xvi. 3.
— xxi. 28.
Luke v. 26.
— xii. 28.
— xiii. 32.
— 33.
— xix. 5.
Luke xxiii. 43, see NOTE above. [Ab ℵ.)
— xxiv. 21 (om. T Trb
Heb. iii. 7, 13, 15.
— iv. 7 twice.
— v. 5.
— xiii. 8.
Jas. iv. 13.

See also, under DAY.

TOGETHER.

1. { ἐπί, upon, τὸ, the, αὐτό, same } (*spoken of place, object. or time.*)

2. { κατὰ, down upon, at τὸ, the αὐτό, same, (*time or place.*)

3. ὁμοῦ, (*Gen. neut. of* ὁμος, one and the same) at one and the same *place or time*, together, at once

4. ἅμα, at once, uniting two different actions, persons, or things.

(a) *Here uniting* two different sets of persons, *viz. those who* "are alive and remain," *and* "the dead in Christ," raised first, (*i.e. not merely before* "the rest of the dead," *but before the living are changed,*) *in order that we may not* "prevent" *or get before them,* and that they may not get before us, but that both, both parties,* united in one, *may be caught up* "together," (ἅμα)

5. { μετὰ, with, in association with, ἀλλήλων, each other, one another.

6. { πρὸς, towards, to ἀλλήλων, each other, one another.

1. Matt. xxii. 34.
1. Luke xvii. 35.
5. — xxiii. 12.
6. — xxiv. 14.
3. John iv. 36.
3. — xx. 4.
3. — xxi. 2.
1. Acts i. 15.
1. Acts ii. 44.
1. — iii. 1.
1. — iv. 26.
2. — xiv. 1.
4. Rom. iii. 12.
1. 1 Cor. vii. 5.
4a. 1 Thes. iv. 17.
4. — v. 10.

* How could the living possibly get to glory before those who, many say, have been there for centuries! And yet this was written that we should not be "ignorant" (1 Thes. iv. 13.)

See also, AGREE, ASSEMBLE, ASSEMBLING, BAND, BOWED, BRING, BUILD, CALL, COME, COMFORTED, COMMUNE, COUNSEL, EAT, ELECTED, FOLLOWER, FRAME, GATHER, GATHERING, GLORIFY, GROAN, GROW, HEIR, HELP, JOIN, KNIT, LABOURER, PLANTED, QUICKEN, RAISE, REASON, RISE, ROLL, RUN, SHAKE, SHUT, SIT, STRIVE, TEMPER, TRAVAIL, TREASURE, WORK, WORKER, WRAP, YOKED, YOURSELVES.

TOIL (-ED, -ING.)

1. κοπιάω, to beat out, *i.e.* to be weary. *Then*, to weary one's self, beat one's self out *as with* labour.

2. βασανίζω, to apply a touchstone; *metaph.*, to examine, test, scrutinise, *either by words or torture; then, pass., as here*, to be afflicted with pain, be tortured *or* tormented, be vexed *or* harassed.

1. Matt. vi. 28.
2. —— 48.
1. Luke v. 5.
1. —— xii. 27 (ap.)

TOKEN.

1. σημεῖον, a sign, signal, (*see under* "SIGN.")

2. σύσσημον, a concerted sign, a sign *or* signal agreed upon in conjunction with others, (*non occ.*)

2. Mark xiv. 44.
1. 2 Thes. iii. 17.

TOKEN (EVIDENT)

ἔνδειξις, a pointing out *with the finger*, an indicating.

Phil. i. 28.

TOKEN (MANIFEST)

ἔνδειγμα, the thing pointed out *with the finger*, a proof, an instance, (*non occ.*)

2 Thes. i. 5.

TOLERABLE.

ἀνεκτός, bearable, endurable, supportable. *In N.T., only in the comparative*, more endurable, *etc.*, (*non occ.*)

Matt. x. 15.
—— xi. 22, 24.
Mark vi. 11 (ap.)
Luke x. 12, 14.

TOMB (-S.)

1. μνημεῖον, a memorial, a monument; *hence*, a sepulchral monument.

2. μνῆμα, a memorial, memory, remembrance *or* record *of a person or thing; esp.* a memorial *of one dead*, tribute of respect; a mound or building in honour of the dead, a monument.

3. τάφος, a burial, sepulture; *esp.*, a funeral-feast; *then*, the grave itself, (lxx. *for* קבר, (*the word for* a single grave, as שאול *is for* gravedom) Gen. xxiii. 4, 20 · 2 Sam. ii. 31.)

1. Matt. viii. 28.
3. —— xxiii. 29.
1. —— xxvii. 60.
1. Mark v. 2.
1. Mark v. 3 (No. 2, G L T Tr A ℵ.)
2. —— 5.
1. —— 29.
2. Luke viii. 27.

TO-MORROW.

αὔριον, to-morrow, (*from* αὔρα, morning-air, *from* ἄω, αὔω); (lxx. *for* מחר, Ex. viii. 10, 23; ix. 5, 19; 2 Sam. xi. 12, etc.)

Matt. vi. 30.
Luke xii. 28.
—— xiii. 32, 33. [Tr A ℵ.)
Acts xxiii. 15 (*om.* G L T
Acts xxiii. 20.
—— xxv. 22.
1 Cor. xv. 32.
Jas. iv. 32.

TONGUE (-S.)

1. γλῶσσα, the tongue, *as part of the body; also, personified,* (*as in* Phil. ii. 11) πᾶσα γλῶσσα, *i.e.* every person; *comp.* Is. xlv. 23, *where* lxx. *for* לשון, (*non occ.*); *and also*, a tongue, a language, a gift of language.

2. διάλεκτος, a speaking through, *or* to and fro; *hence*, language spoken by a people or province, *esp.*, a dialect, peculiar idiom, (*occ.* Acts ii. 6.)

1. Mark vii. 33, 35.
1. —— xvi. 17 (ap.)
1. Luke i. 64.
1. —— xvi. 24.
— John ix. 11, see Hebrew.
2. Acts i. 19.
1. —— ii. 3, 4.
2. —— 8.
1. —— 11, 26.
1. —— x. 46.
1. —— xix. 6.
2. —— xxi. 40.
2. —— xxii. 2.
2. —— xxvi. 14.
1. Rom. iii. 13.
1. —— xiv. 11. [30.
1. 1 Cor. xii. 10 twice, 28,
1. —— xiii. 1, 8.
1. —— xiv. 2, 4, 5 twice, 6, 9, 13, 14, 18, 19.
— 1 Cor. xiv. 21, see T (of another)
1. —— 22, 23, 26, 27, 39.
1. Phil. ii. 11, see note above.
1. Jas. i. 26.
1. —— iii. 5, 6 twice, 8.
1. 1 Pet. iii. 10.
1. 1 John iii. 18.
1. Rev. v. 9.
1. —— vii. 9.
— —— ix. 11, see Hebrew.
1. —— x. 11.
1. —— xi. 9.
1. —— xiii. 7.
1. —— xiv. 6.
1. —— xvi. 10.
— —— 16, see Hebrew.
1. —— xvii. 15.

TONGUE (of another)

ἑτερόγλωσσος, other-tongued, of another (*i.e.* a different) language, (*non occ.*)

1 Cor. xiv. 21.

TOO.

See, SUPERSTITIOUS.

TOOTH, TEETH.

ὀδούς, a tooth; (lxx. *for* שֵׁן, Lev. xxiv. 30; Job. xvi. 9.)

Matt. v. 38.
— viii. 12.
— xiii. 42, 50.
— xxii. 13.
— xxiv. 51.
Matt. xxv. 30.
— xxvii. 44, see Cast.
Mark ix. 18.
Luke xiii. 28.
Acts vii. 54.
Rev. ix. 8.

TOP.

ἄκρον, pointed; *hence, neut. as subst.*, τὸ ἄκρον, a point, end, extremity.

Heb. xi. 21.

TOP (from the)

1. { ἀπὸ, from, away from, ἄνωθεν, from above.

2. { ἐκ, out of, from, τῶν, the (*pl.*) ἄνωθεν, from above.

1. Matt. xxvii. 51. | 1. Mark xv. 38.
2. John xix. 23.

TOPAZ.

τοπάζιον, the topaz, a transparent gem of a golden or orange colour; (lxx. *for* פִּטְדָה, Ex. xxviii. 17; Ezek. xxviii. 13), (*non occ.*)

Rev. xxi. 20.

TORCH.

λαμπάς, a torch, (*see* "LIGHT," *No.* 6, *and* "LAMP.")

John xviii. 3.

TORMENT (-s.) [noun.]

1. βασανισμός, examination, *as by a touchstone;* scrutiny, *either by words or torture; hence*, torture, torment, (*non occ.*)

(a) Spoken of those who worship the Beast and his image, and who receive the mark of his name.

(b) Spoken of the future punishment of Babylon.

2. βάσανος, a touchstone, *the ancient lapis Lydius for trying metals, etc.*, (*on which when gold is rubbed it leaves a peculiar mark*); *hence*, examination, trial, enquiry by torture; *also*, torture, pain; (lxx. *for* רִנּוּת, Ezek. xii. 18.) Spoken of the pains of parturition, (Anthol. Gr. ed. Jac. ii., p. 205) *and* of the pains of disease, (Matt. iv. 24), (*non occ.*)

3. κόλασις, a pruning; *hence, in N.T.* punishment, *i.e.* a cutting off, *the double result of which is*, (*like that of pruning a plant*) *viz.* that he who is so cut off *or* punished, is destroyed, and those who are saved are the better for the absence of those who are so cut off, (*occ.* Matt. xxv. 46.)

2. Matt. iv. 24.
2. Luke xvi. 23, 28.
3. 1 John iv. 18.
1. Rev. ix. 5.
1a.— xiv. 11.
1b.— xviii. 7, 10, 15.

TORMENT (-ed.) [verb.]

βασανίζω, to rub upon the βάσανος, *or* touchstone, (*see No.* 2, *above*); *hence*, to put to the test, prove, to examine closely, cross-question; *later*, to question by applying torture, to torture, rack.

(*) Spoken of those who worship the Beast and his image, and who receive the mark of his name.

(†) Spoken of the future punishment of the Devil.

Matt. viii. 6, 29.
Mark v. 7.
Luke viii. 28.
Rev. ix. 5.
— xi. 10.
— xiv. 10*.
Rev. xx. 10†.

TORMENTED (be)

1. κακουχέω, to hold *or* treat ill, to maltreat. *In N.T. only pass. part.*, evilly entreated; (lxx. *for* עָנָה, 1 Kings ii. 26; xi. 39), (*occ.* Heb. xiii. 3.)

2. ὀδυνάω, to pain, distress. *In N.T. only mid. or pass.*, to be pained *or* distressed; (lxx. *for* הָחִיל, Zech. ix. 5; הָמַר, Zech. xii. 10), (*occ.* Luke ii. 48; Acts xx. 38.)

2. Luke xvi. 24, 25. | 1. Heb. xi. 37.

TORMENTOR (-s.)

βασανιστής, an examiner, an inquisitor; *hence*, one who applies the torture; a prison keeper, gaoler, (*non occ.*)

Matt. xviii. 34.

TORTURE (-ED.)

1. *τυμπανίζω*, to beat on a *τύμπανον*, (a tympanum, which was either a drum or an instrument of torture, being a wooden frame resembling a drum, on which criminals were bound to be beaten to death. (*See* 2 Macc. vi. 19, 28, 30; vii. 9.) *Hence*, to tympanize, to beat the drum; *or* to scourge upon a tympanum *or* rack, to torture, drum to death.

2. *ἀνετάζω*, to examine thoroughly, to enquire strictly; (lxx. *for* דרשׁ, Judg. vi. 29.)

2. Acts xxii. 29, marg. (text, *examine*.)
1. Heb. xi. 35.

TOSS.

1. *βασανίζω*, *see the verb* "TORMENT."

2. *ῥιπίζω*, to fan, to blow, (*as a fire or fuel*); *hence*, to move to and fro, to toss, agitate, (*non occ.*)

1. Matt. xiv. 24.
2. Jas. i. 6.
— Acts xxvii. 18, see Tempest.

TOSSED TO AND FRO (BE)

κλυδωνίζομαι, to surge, to be tossed in billows; (lxx. *for* נגרשׁ, Is. lvii. 20), (*non occ.*)

Eph. iv. 14.

TOSSING TO AND FRO. [margin.]

2 Cor. vi. 5, see "TUMULT."

TOUCH (-ED, -ETH.)

1. *ἅπτομαι*, to apply one's self to, *i.e.* to touch, *so in the sense of* to eat in a Levitical sense, Lev. v. 2, 3, *where* lxx. *for* נגע, and Lev. vii. 18-21.)

2. *θιγγάνω*, to touch lightly, just touch, (*less emphatic than No.* 1.)

3. *κατάγω*, to lead down, bring *or* conduct down; *of a ship*, to bring down to land, to come to land.

4. *προσψαύω*, to touch to *or* upon, touch, handle, feel upon, (*non occ.*)

1. Matt. viii. 3, 15.
1. —— ix. 20, 21, 29,
1. —— xiv. 36 twice.
1. —— xvii. 7.
1. —— xx. 34.
1. Mark i. 41.
1. —— iii. 10.
1. —— v. 27, 28, 30, 31.
1. —— vi. 56 twice.
1. —— vii. 33.
1. —— viii. 22.
1. —— x. 13.
1. Luke v. 13.
1. —— vi. 19.
1. —— vii. 14, 39.
1. Luke viii. 44, 45 1st, 45 2nd (ap.), 46, 47.
4. —— xi. 46.
1. —— xviii. 15.
1. —— xxii. 51.
1. John xx. 17.
3. Acts xxvii. 3.
1. 1 Cor. vii. 1.
1. 2 Cor. vi. 17.
1. Col. ii. 21.
— Heb. iv. 15, see Feeling.
2. —— xi. 28.
— —— xii. 18, see T (that might be)
2. Heb. xii. 20.

TOUCHED (THAT MIGHT BE)

ψηλαφάω, to touch, to feel, to handle. *Here, pass.*

Heb. xii. 18.

TOUCHING.

1. *περί*, around.
   (a) *with Gen.*, around and separate from, about, concerning.
   (b) *with Acc.*, around and towards, about, in reference to.

2. *ἐπί*, upon.
   (a) *with Gen.*, upon and springing from, on, upon.
   (b) *with Dat.*, upon, on, resting on, on account of.
   (c) *with Acc.*, upon by direction towards, upon, *with motion implied*, in the direction of.

3. *κατά*, down.
   (a) *with Gen.*, down from.
   (b) *with Acc.*, down towards, according to, as to.

1a. Acts xxiv. 21.
1a. —— xxvi. 2.
3b. Phil. iii. 16.
1a. Col. iv. 10.
2c. 2 Thes. iii. 4.

TOUCHING (AS)

1a. Matt. xviii. 19.
1a. —— xxii. 31.
1a. Mark xii. 26.
2b. Acts v. 35.
1a. —— xxi. 25.
3b. Rom. xi. 28.
1a. 1 Cor. viii. 1.
1a. —— xvi. 12.
1a. 2 Cor. ix. 1.
3b. Phil. iii. 5.
1a. 1 Thes. iv. 9.

TOWARD (-s.)

1. *εἰς*, unto, to, towards.
2. *πρός*, towards, in the direction of.
   * *translated* to...-ward.

(a) *with Gen.*, hitherwards.

(b) *with Dat.*, resting in a direction towards, at, close by.

(c) *with Acc.*, hitherwards, to, towards.

3. ἐπί, *see* "TOUCHING," *No.* 2.

(a), (b), and (c), *see* "TOUCHING," *No.* 2, (a), (b), and (c.)

4. ἐν, in, *denoting the sphere in which the subject is concerned as dwelling or acting in.*

5. κατά, *see* "TOUCHING," *No.* 3.

(a), (b), and (c.) *see* "TOUCHING," *No.* 2, (a), (b), and (c.)

6. ὑπέρ, over.

(a) *with Gen.*, over, on behalf of, for the sake of, in reference to.

(b) *with Acc.*, over and towards.

3c. Matt. xii. 49.
3c. —— xiv. 14 (No. 3b, G L T Tr A ℵ.)
1. —— xxviii. 1.
3b. Mark vi. 34 (No. 3c, L T Tr A ℵ.)
4. Luke ii. 14.
1. —— xii. 21.
1. —— xiii. 22.
2c. —— xxiv. 29.
1. John vi. 17.
1. Acts i. 10.
5b. —— viii. 26.
1. —— xx. 21.
1. —— xxiv. 15.
2c. —— 16.
5b. —— xxvii. 12.
1. —— xxviii. 14.
1. Rom. i. 27.
1. —— v. 8.
3c. —— xi. 22.
1. —— xii. 16.
1. —— xiv. 19.
4. —— xv. 5.
3c. 1 Cor. vii. 36.
2c. 2 Cor. i. 12*
1. —— 16.
2c. —— 18.
1. —— ii. 8.
2c. —— iii. 4*
2c. 2 Cor. vii. 4.
6a. —— 7.
1. —— 15.
1. —— ix. 8.
1. —— x. 1.
1. —— xiii. 3, 4.
1. Gal. ii. 8.
1. Eph. i. 8, 19.
3c. —— ii. 7.
1. —— iii. 2.
2c. Phil. ii. 30.
5b. —— iii. 14.
2c. Col. iv. 5.
2c. 1 Thes. i. 8*.
1. —— iii. 12 3 times.
1. —— iv. 10.
2c. —— 12.
2c. —— v. 14.
1. 2 Thes. i. 3.
2c. Philem. 5 1st (No. 1, L Tr A.)
1. —— 5 2nd
3b. Heb. vi. 1.
1. —— 10.
1. 1 Pet. iii. 21.
1. 2 Pet. iii. 9 (G∼), (διά, *through*, G L Trm ℵ.)
2c. 1 John iii. 21.
4. —— iv. 9.

See also, MAKE, MAN, PRESS.

TOWEL.

λέντιον, (*Lat.*, lenteum) a linen cloth, *e.g.* a towel, apron *worn by servants and persons in waiting.*

John xiii. 4, 5.

TOWER.

πύργος, a tower, *esp.* the watchtower *or* turret of a vineyard; (*so*, lxx. *for* מגדל, Is. v. 2.)

Matt. xxi. 33.
Mark xii. 1.
Luke xiii. 4.
—— xiv. 28.

TOWN (-S.)

1. κώμη, a village, hamlet, *in the country and without walls;* (lxx. *for* כפר, 1 Ch. xxvii. 25; Song vii. 12; בנות, Josh. xv. 45; xvii. 11; חצר, Josh. xv. 31, etc.; xix. 6, etc.)

2. κωμόπολις, a village city, *i.e.* a large village *or* town like a city, but without walls, (*non occ.*)

1. Matt. ix. 35.
1. —— xiv. 15.
1. —— xxi. 2.
2. Mark i. 38.
1. Mark viii. 23, 26 twice, 27.
1. Luke v. 17.
1. —— ix. 6, 12.
1. John vii. 42.
1. John xi. 1, 30.

TOWN-CLERK.

γραμματεύς, a writer, a scribe. *In the Greek sense,* a public officer in the cities of Asia Minor who presided in the senate, had charge of the laws and decrees, and read what was to be made known to the people, a public clerk, (*elsewhere translated,* in Jewish Church, "SCRIBE.")

Acts xix. 35.

TRADE. [margin.]

Tit. iii. 14, see "WORK."

TRADE (-ED.) [verb.]

ἐργάζομαι, to work, to labour.

Matt. xxv. 16.

TRADE BY.

Rev. xviii. 17.

TRADING (GAIN BY)

διαπραγματεύομαι, to work through *or* out, to go through with; to do *or* effect in business, to accomplish by traffick, gain by trade, (*non occ.*)

Luke xix. 15.

TRADITION.

παράδοσις, delivery, *i.e.* the act of delivering over from one to another.

Matt. xv. 2, 3, 6.
Mark vii. 3, 5, 8, 9, 13.
1 Cor. xi. 2, marg. (text, *ordinance.*)
Gal. i. 14.
Col. ii. 8.
2 Thes. ii. 15.
—— iii. 6.
1 Pet. i. 18, see Fathers.

TRAITOR (-s.)

προδότης, a betrayer, a traitor.

Luke vi. 16. | 2 Tim. iii. 4.

TRAMPLE

καταπατέω, to tread down, to trample down; (lxx. *for* רמס, 2 Chron. xxv. 18; Ezek. xxxiv 18.)

Matt. vii. 6.

TRANCE.

ἔκστασις, a standing out of, removal, a standing out of one's usual mind; the state of a person out of his senses, ecstasy.

Acts x. 10. | Acts xi. 5.
Acts xxii. 17.

TRANSFER IN A FIGURE.

μετασχηματίζω, to change the outward figure; to transfer a thing in its application, to transfer the thoughts as to one object to another which is an image of it.

1 Cor. iv. 6.

TRANSFIGURED (BE)

μεταμορφόομαι, to change one's form, fashion, *or* appearance, to transform, alter one's form; (*hence the Eng.*, metamorphosis.)

[Used here of the Transfiguration of Christ; which seems to have been the inauguration of His office as *Priest*, as the Baptism was of His office as *Prophet*, (the same form of words being used by the Father from heaven, Matt. iii. 17; xvii. 5, on both occasions; as similar words will yet be used at His inauguration as *King*, Ps. ii. 7.) It seems to be connected with His approaching priestly work, from the following considerations.

(1) It is dated by all three Evangelists, from circumstances connected with the *first mention* of His sufferings.

(2) Those sufferings formed the subject of the conversation with Moses and Elijah, and also immediately afterwards again with His disciples.

(3) Peter tells us (2 Pet. i. 17) that it was on "the Holy Mount" that Jesus received from the Father "honour and glory;" while Heb. ii. 9 tells us that He was crowned with "glory and honour," "on account of (διά, *with Acc., see* 'FOR') *the suffering of death.*"

(4) In Rom. xii. 1, 2, *we* are exhorted to be "transformed" (the same word) in our minds, by presenting *our* "bodies as a living sacrifice, (as Jesus did His, when He was transfigured) holy, acceptable unto God."

The Transfiguration was also a showing of "the power and coming of our Lord Jesus Christ," (2 Pet. i. 16) an event which shows that though about to suffer and die, He will yet come "with power and great glory," and that until He does so come, His church will try in vain to heal a demoniac world, (Matt. xvii. 14-21; Mark ix. 14-29; Luke ix. 37-45]. (*occ.* Rom. xii. 2; 2 Cor. iii. 18, *and the event recorded also in* Luke ix. 28-36.)

Matt. xvii. 2. | Mark ix. 20.

TRANSFORM ONE'S SELF.

μετασχηματίζω, (*here, mid.*) to change the outward figure, alter the shape *or* mien, alter one's bearing, look, *or* air.

2 Cor. xi. 13.

TRANSFORMED (BE)

1. μεταμορφόομαι, *see* "TRANSFIGURED (BE)" *and note* (4.)
2. μετασχηματίζω, *see* "TRANSFORM ONE'S SELF."

1. Rom. xii. 2. | 2. 2 Cor. xi. 14, 15.

TRANSGRESS (-ED, -ETH.)

1. παραβαίνω, to step on one side, go aside from, transgress; (lxx. *for* סור מן, Ex. xxxii. 8; עבר, Numb.

xiv. 41; Josh vii. 11, 15), (*occ.* Acts i. 25.)

2. *παρέρχομαι*, to come *or* go by, to pass beside *or* by, pass over, transgress; (*so*, lxx. *for* עבר, Deut. xxvi. 13; Jer. xxxiv. 18.)

1. Matt. xv. 2, 3.
2. Luke xv. 29.
— Rom. ii. 27, see T (who doth)
— 1 John iii. 4, see Law.
1. 2 John 9 (*προάγω*, *to lead forward*, *to go in advance*, L T Tr A ℵ.)

TRANSGRESS (WHO DOTH)

παραβάτης, one who steps aside, a transgressor; (lxx. *for* פריץ, Ps. xvii. 4; Ezek. xviii. 10.)

Rom. ii. 27.

TRANSGRESSION (-S.)

παράβασις, a stepping aside, *as from right*; *hence*, transgression; (lxx. *for* סטים, Ps. ci. 3.)

Acts i. 25, see T (fall by)
Rom. iv. 15.
—— v. 14.
Gal. iii. 19.
1 Tim. ii. 14.
Heb. ii. 2.
—— ix. 15.
1 John iii. 4, see Law.

TRANSGRESSION (FALL BY)

παραβαίνω, *see* "TRANSGRESS," *No.* 1.

Acts i. 25.

TRANSGRESSOR (-S.)

1. *παραβάτης*, *see* "TRANSGRESS (WHO DOTH)"

2. *ἄνομος*, without law, lawless, not subject to law; a violator of the divine law.

2. Mark xv. 28.
2. Luke xxii. 37.
1. Gal. ii. 18.
1. Jas ii. 9, 11.

TRANSLATE (-ED.)

1. *μεθίστημι*, to stand or set in another place, to transfer.

2. *μετατίθημι*, to put or place in another place, to transport.

1. Col. i. 13.
2. Heb. xi. 5 twice.

TRANSLATION.

μετάθεσις, metathesis, a standing, setting in another place.

Heb. xi. 5.

TRANSPARENT.

διαφανής, diaphanous, transparent, able to be seen through; (lxx. *for* זך, Ex. xxx. 34), (*non occ.*)

Rev. xxi. 21 (*διαυγής*, *shining through*, G L T Tr A ℵ.)

TRAP

θήρα, hunting, the chase; *hence*, cause of destruction, (*non occ.*)

Rom. xi. 9.

TRAVAIL. [noun.]

1. *μόχθος*, wearisome labour, travail, *including the idea of painful effort*, sorrow; (lxx. *for* עמל, Deut. xxvi. 7; Ecc. ii. 18), (*occ.* 2 Cor. xi. 27.)

2. *ὠδίν*, a throe, a pang, *as of a woman in travail*; (*so*, lxx. *for* חבל, Is. xxii. 23; Hos. xiii. 3, *cf.* Is. xxxvii. 3.)

1. 1 Thes. ii. 9.
2. 1 Thes. v. 3.
1. 2 Thes. iii. 8.

TRAVAIL (BE IN)

τίκτω, to bring forth, to bear.

John xvi. 21.

TRAVAIL (EST, -ETH, -ING.) [verb.]

ὠδίνω, to be in the throes, to travail *in child-birth*, (*non occ.*)

Gal. iv. 27.

TRAVAIL IN BIRTH.

Rev. xii. 2.

TRAVAIL IN BIRTH OF.

Gal. iv. 19.

TRAVAIL IN BIRTH TOGETHER.

συνωδίνω, to jointly travail in the throes of birth, (*non occ.*)

Rom. viii. 22.

TRAVEL (COMPANION IN)

συνέκδημος, absent together from one's people, (*occ.* 2 Cor. viii. 19.)

Acts xix. 29.

TRAVEL (-ED, -ING.) [verb.]

διέρχομαι, to come, go, *or* pass through *any country or place; hence*, to travel through.

Acts xi. 19.

TRAVEL WITH.

συνέκδημος, absent together from one's people.

2 Cor. viii. 19.

See also, COUNTRY.

TREAD (-ETH, TRODE, TRODDEN.) [verb.]

1. *πατέω*, to tread *with the feet*, trample on, press by treading, (*non occ.*)
2. *καταπατέω*, (*No.* 1, *with κατά*, down, *prefixed*) to tread down, trample down, (*occ.* Matt. vii. 6.)

1. Luke x. 19. | 1. Rev. xiv. 20.
2. —— xii. 1. | — —— xvi. 20, marg. see [Bruise.
1. Rev. xix. 15.

TREAD DOWN.

2. Luke viii. 5. | 1. Luke xxi. 24.

TREAD UNDER FOOT.

2. Matt. v. 13. | 2. Heb. x. 29.
1. Rev. xi. 2.

TREAD OUT THE CORN.

ἀλοάω, to beat, to thresh; *then*, to drive round in a circle, *esp. oxen upon grain* to thresh it, to thresh with oxen; (lxx. *for* דוש, Is. xli. 15; דיש, Deut. xxv. 4; דרך, Jer. li. 53), (*occ.* 1 Cor. ix. 10.)

1 Cor. ix. 9. | 1 Tim. v. 18.

TREASURE (-S.) [noun.]

1. *θησαυρός*, anything laid up in store; *hence*, treasure, wealth; (lxx. *for* מטמון, mammon, Gen. xliii. 23; Prov. ii. 4; אוצר, 1 Kings xiv. 26; Prov. xv. 17), (*non occ.*)
2. *γάζα*, the royal treasure; *then, as in Lat.*, gaza, riches; (*a word of Persian origin*); (lxx. *for* גנז, Ezra v. 17; vi. 1; Esth. iv. 7), (*non occ.*)

1. Matt. ii. 11.
1. —— vi. 19, 20, 21.
1. —— xii. 35 twice.
1. —— xiii. 44, 52.
1. —— xix. 21.
1. Mark x. 21. [(ap.)
1. Luke vi. 45 1st, 45 2nd
— —— xii. 21, see T (lay up)
1. Luke xii. 33, 34.
1. —— xviii. 22.
2. Acts viii. 27.
— Rom. ii. 5, see T up.
1. 2 Cor. iv. 7.
1. Col. ii. 3.
1. Heb. xi. 26.
— Jas. v. 3, (see T together (heap)

TREASURE TOGETHER (HEAP)

θησαυρίζω, to lay up in store, treasure; (lxx. *for* אצר, 2 Kings xx. 17; Am. iii. 10; צבר, Zech. ix. 3.)

Jas. v. 3.

TREASURE (LAY UP)

Luke xii. 21.

TREASURE UP (-EST.) [verb.]

θησαυρίζω, see above.

Rom. ii. 5.

TREASURY.

1. *γαζοφυλάκιον*, a place for keeping under guard the public treasure. *Among the Jews*, the sacred treasury in one of the courts of the Temple; *see* Neh. xiii. 7; x. 37, 38; xiii. 4, 5, 8, *where* lxx. *for* לשכה, *and for* גנז, Esth. iii. 9, (*non occ.*)
2. *κορβανᾶς*, *the Heb.*, קרבן, *i.e.* a gift, offering *or* oblation to God, (Lev. ii. 1, 4, 12, 13); *then*, something devoted to God, (*κορβᾶν*, *occ.* Mark vii. 11); *then*, spoken of money offered to God in the Temple, the sacred treasure.

2. Matt. xxvii. 6. | 1. Luke xxi. 1.
1. Mark xii. 41 twice, 43. | 1. John viii. 20.

TREATISE.

λόγος, a word, *as forming part of* what is spoken, an exposition or account which one gives, (*see the noun*, "ACCOUNT," p. 25.)

Acts i. 1.

TREE (-S.)

1. *δένδρον*, a tree, a living, growing tree; (lxx. *for* עץ, Gen. xviii. 4, 8.)
2. *ξύλον*, wood, *i.e.* for fuel, timber; *then*, anything made of wood; *here*, a piece of timber, a wooden stake

(a) [*Used here for the σταυρός* on which Jesus was crucified. Both words disagree with the modern idea of a cross, with which we have become familiarised by pictures. The σταυρός was simply *an upright pale or stake* to which the Romans nailed those who were thus said to be crucified, Σταυρόω, *merely means to drive stakes.* It never means two pieces of wood joining each other at any angle. Even the Latin word *crux* means a mere stake. The initial letter X, (chi) of Χριστός, (Christ) was anciently used for His name,* until it was displaced by the T, the initial of the Pagan God Tammuz, about the end of cent. iv.]

* Just so I H̄ Σ (the first three letters of the word JESus) were used for that name until made by the Romish Church (which repudiates the knowledge of the sacred languages) into I h S, the long mark over the Greek H̄ (being turned into a cross running through the h); and made to stand as the initials of three Latin words.

1 Matt. iii. 10 twice.
1. —— vii.17 twice, 18 twice, 19.
1. —— xii. 33 3 times.
1. —— xiii. 32.
1. —— xxi. 8.
1. Mark viii. 24.
1. —— xi. 8 (ἀγρῶν, *out of the fields*, instead of δένδρων, *off the trees*, T Tr A ℵ.)
1. Luke iii. 9 twice.
1. —— vi. 43 twice, 44.
1. Luke xiii. 19.
1. —— xxi. 29.
2. —— xxiii. 31.
2a. Acts v. 30.
2a. —— x. 39.
2a. —— xiii. 29.
2a. Gal. iii. 13.
2a. 1 Pet. ii. 24.
1. Jude 12.
2. Rev. ii. 7.
1. —— vii. 1, 3.
1. —— viii. 7.
1. —— ix. 4.
2. Rev. xxii. 2 twice, 14.

See also, FIG, OLIVE, PALM, SYCAMINE, SYCAMORE.

TREMBLE (-ED, -ING.)

1. τρέμω, to tremble, quake, quiver, flutter; *then*, to tremble at, *as from fear*, (*occ.* 2 Pet. ii. 10.)

2. { ἔχω, to have
{ τρόμος, a trembling.

3. { γίνομαι, to become
{ ἔντρομος, in a tremble.

4. { γίνομαι, to become
{ ἔμφοβος, in fear.

5. φρίσσω, to be rough, uneven, jagged *as with bristling points*, to bristle, stand on end; to shudder *so that the skin becomes rough and pimpled and the hair stands on end;* (lxx. Dan. vii. 15; Judith xvi. 8.)

1. Mark v. 33.
2. —— xvi. 8.
1. Luke viii. 47.
3. Acts vii. 32.
1. —— ix. 6 (ap.)
4. —— xxiv. 25.
5. Jas. ii. 19.

TREMBLING.

1. τρόμος, a trembling, quaking, *shivering with fear.*

2. ἔντρομος, (*No.* 1, *with* ἐν, in, *prefixed*) in trembling.

2. Acts xvi. 29.
1. 1 Cor. ii. 3.
1. 2 Cor. vii. 15.
1. Eph. vi. 5.
1. Phil. ii. 12.

TRENCH.

χάραξ, a pointed stake *or* pale; a palisade; (*Lat.*, vallus, *in fortification*); a place paled in, a palisaded camp, (*non occ.*)

Luke xix. 43.

TRESPASS (-ES.) [noun.]

παράπτωμα, a falling aside from *right truth or duty*, lapse.

Matt. vi. 14.
—— 15 1st (*om.* παραπτώματα αὐτῶν, *their trespasses*, G ⇉ T ℵ.)
—— 15 2nd.
—— xviii. 35 (*om* τὰ παραπτώματα αὐτῶν, *their trespasses*, G L T Tr A ℵ.)
Mark xi. 25, 26 (*ap.*)
2 Cor. v. 19.
Eph. ii. 1.
Col. ii. 13.

TRESPASS. [verb.]

ἁμαρτάνω, to miss, err from, *as from a mark*, to err, swerve from *truth and right*, go wrong; to sin.

Matt. xviii. 15.
Luke xvii. 3, 4.

TRIAL.

1. δοκιμή, proof, test, trial, assay, a putting to the proof, *as metals, etc., by fire;* the state of being tried, a trying, the state of having been tried.

2. δοκίμιον, a proof, a test; (lxx. *for* מצרף, a crucible, Prov. xxvii. 21.)

3. πεῖρα, a making trial, attempt, essay; *then, a receiving of trial*, an attempt on *or* against *one*, an assault, attack, an attempt on *one's life or property.*

1. 2 Cor. viii. 2.
3. Heb. xi. 36.
2. 1 Pet. i. 7.
—— —— iv. 12, see Fiery.

TRIBE.

φυλή, a union of individuals into a community *or* state; a union *of men* according to ties of blood *and* descent; a clan, a tribe; (lxx. *for* מטה, Ex. xxxi. 2, 6; שבט, Ex. xxiv. 4; Deut. i. 13, etc.)

Matt. xix. 28.	Phil. iii. 5.
— xxiv. 30.	Heb. vii. 13, 14.
Luke ii. 36.	Jas. i. 1.
— xxii. 30.	Rev. v. 5.
Acts xiii. 21.	— vii. 4, 5 3 times, 6 3 times, 7 3 times, 8 3 times.
Rom. xi. 1.	

Rev. xxi. 12.

TRIBES (TWELVE)

δωδεκάφυλον, the twelve tribes *as of Israel*, (*non occ.*)

Acts xxvi. 7.

TRIBULATION (-s.)

θλῖψις, pressure, compression, straitness; *hence*, pressure *from evils*, affliction, distress; (lxx. *for* צר, Deut. iv. 30; Ps. cxix. 143; צרה, Neh. ix. 37; 1 Sam. x. 19; Is. viii. 22.)

Matt. xiii. 21.	Rom. xii. 12.
— xxiv. 21, 29.	2 Cor. i. 4.
Mark xiii. 24.	— vii. 4.
John xvi. 33.	Eph. iii. 13.
Acts xiv. 22.	2 Thes. i. 4, 6.
Rom. ii. 9.	Rev. i. 9.
— v. 3 twice.	— ii. 9, 10, 22.
— viii. 35.	— vii. 14.

TRIBULATION (SUFFER)

θλίβω, to press, press upon; *hence*, *pass.*, *as here.*, to be oppressed *with evils*, to be distressed.

1 Thes. iii. 4.

TRIBUTE. [noun.]

1. φόρος, what is borne, brought; *hence*, a tax *or* tribute brought *by persons as imposed on their persons and property*, (*as distinct from* τέλος, the toll *levied on merchandise*, *etc.*); lxx. *for* מס, Judg. i. 30; 2 Sam. xx. 24; מדה, Ezra iv. 20), (*non occ.*)
2. κῆσος, (*Lat.*, census) an enumeration of the people and valuation of property; *hence*, a poll-tax *paid by each person whose name was taken in the census*, (*occ.* Matt. xxxiii. 19.)
3. δίδραχμον, a didrachm, a double drachma, a silver coin equal to the Jewish half-shekel, the yearly tribute paid by every Jew to the Temple treasury at Jerusalem; (*see* Exod. xxx. 13; xxxviii. 26); (lxx. *everywhere for* שקל, Gen. xxiii. 15, 16; Neh. x. 32), (*occ.* Matt. xvii. 24, *pl.*)

3. Matt. xvii. 24, pl.	2. Mark xii. 14.
2. — 25.	1. Luke xx. 22.
2. — xxii. 17.	1. — xxiii. 2.

1. Rom. xiii. 6, 7 twice.

TRIBUTE. [adj.]

κῆνσος, *see No.* 2, *above; here the Genitive.*

Matt. xxii. 19.

TRIBUTE-MONEY.

δίδραχμον, *see the noun*, "TRIBUTE," *No.* 3.

Matt. xvii. 24, pl.

TRIM (-ED.)

κοσμέω, to put in order, adjust.

Matt. xxv. 7.

TRIUMPH (CAUSE TO)

θριαμβεύω, to triumph, to hold a triumph; to make to triumph; to lead in triumph, *esp. with triumphal hymns*, (*non occ.*)

2 Cor. ii. 14.

TRIUMPH OVER.

Col. ii. 15.

TROGYLLIUM.

Τρωγύλλιον, Trogyllium, the proper name of a town and promontory on the W. coast of Asia Minor, opp. Samos, at the foot of Mount Mycale.

Acts xx. 15 (ap.)

TROUBLE. [noun.]

1. θλῖψις, *see* "TRIBULATION."
2. ταραχή, a stirring up, agitation, *as of water or people*, commotion, tumult, (*occ.* John v. 1 (*ap.*).)

2. Mark xiii. 8 (om. καὶ ταραχαί, G → L T Tr Ab N°.)	1. 1 Cor. vii. 28.
	1. 2 Cor. i. 4, 8.
	— 2 Tim. ii. 9, see Suffer.

TROUBLE (-ED, -EST, -ETH.) [verb.]

(*For various combinations with other words, see below.*)

1. ταράσσω, to stir up, to agitate, *as water in a pool; of the mind*, to stir up, trouble, disturb *with various emotions.*

2. διαταράσσω, (*No.* 1, *with* διά, throughout, *prefixed*) to stir up throughout; *spoken of the mind, etc.*, to disturb, agitate, (*non occ.*)

3. { κόπος, a beating, (*as of the breast*); *hence*, wailing; *also*, the being beat out, weariness, παρέχω, to hold out, present, offer, } offer trouble, give trouble.

4. θλίβω, to press, press upon; *hence*, to oppress *as with evils*, distress.

5. ἐνοχλέω, to excite tumult in; *hence*, to disturb, annoy, (*non occ.*)

6. παρενοχλέω, (*No.* 5, *with* παρά, beside, *prefixed*) to disturb alongside *of something else*, to trouble besides, (*non occ.*)

7. σκύλλω, to strip off the skin, to flay, lacerate; to harass, wound, rend.

8. ἀναστατόω, to unsettle, stir to sedition, throw into confusion.

1. Matt. ii. 3.
1. —— xiv. 26.
3. —— xxvi. 10.
7. Mark v. 35.
1. —— vi. 50.
3. —— xiv. 6.
1. Luke i. 12.
2. ——— 29.
7. —— viii. 49.
3. —— xi. 7.
3. —— xviii. 5.
1. —— xxiv. 38.
1. John v. 4 (*ap.*), 7.
1. —— xii. 27.
1. John xiii. 21.
1. —— xiv. 1, 27.
6. Acts xv. 19.
1. ——— 24.
1. —— xvii. 8.
4. 2 Cor. iv. 8.
4. —— vii. 5.
1. Gal. i. 7.
3. —— iii. 17.
1. —— v. 10.
8. ——— 12.
4. 2 Thes. i. 6, 7.
5. Heb. xii. 15.
1. 1 Pet. iii. 14.

TROUBLE EXCEEDINGLY.

ἐκταράσσω, (*No.* 1, *with* ἐκ, out of, *prefixed, intensifying it*) to stir up wholly, disturb greatly, (*non occ.*)

Acts xvi. 20.

TROUBLE IN MIND. [margin.]

Acts ii. 6, see "CONFOUND."

TROUBLE ONE'S SELF.

1. σκύλλω, (*see No.* 7, *above. Here, mid.*)

2. θορυβέω, to make a noise, uproar, clamour. *Here, mid.*, to make a noise together, wail together.

1. Luke vii. 6. | 2. Acts xx. 10.

TROUBLED (BE)

1. θροέω, to cry aloud, to make a clamour. *Here, pass.*, to be frightened so as to be made to cry aloud or make a clamour, (*non occ.*)

2. τυρβάζω, to make turbid. *Pass. as here*, to be in disorder, jumbled *or* crowded together, *as of the mind with cares, etc.*, (*non occ.*)

3. { ἐτάραξεν, he troubled
ἑαυτόν, himself.

1. Matt. xxiv. 6.
1. Mark xiii. 7.
2. Luke x. 41 (θορυβάζω, *to confuse by noise*, L T Tr A ℵ.)
3. John xi. 33, marg. *troubled himself.*
1. 2 Thes. ii. 2.

TROUBLING.

ταραχή, *see the noun*, "TROUBLE."

John v. 4 (*ap.*)

TROW.

δοκέω, *see* "THINK," *No.* 1.

Luke xvii. 9 (*om.* οὐ δοκῶ, *I trow not*, L^b T Tr A ℵ.)

TRUCE-BREAKER.

ἄσπονδος, without treaty, libation, league, *or* compact, (*occ.* Rom. i. 31.)

2 Tim. iii. 3.

TRUE.

1. ἀληθής, (true), unconcealed, manifest, open; *hence*, real, actual; *that is* ἀληθής, whose appearance is not mere show, but is the reality it appears to be; *that is* ἀληθής, whose utterance agrees with the reality and does not conceal it. True, *as opposed to what is false; thus*, "*God is* ἀληθής, (John iii. 33) *inasmuch as*

He cannot lie—as He is ἀψευδής," (Tit. i. 2), (*occ.* John iv. 18; 1 John ii. 27.)

2. ἀληθινός, (very), (*the ending, -ινός, denoting that the quality as a fundamental idea exists in abundance*) ; *hence ἀληθινός is* that which has truth for its base, is all which it pretends to be; genuine, real; true *as opposed to what is apparent or fictitious; thus,* "God is ἀληθινός, (1 Thes. i. 9) *inasmuch as other gods are no gods.*" "Very" *God, as distinguished from idols and all false gods. Hence the expression* "the true vine," etc., *all others being inferior and subordinate realisations, only what the shadow is to the substance,* (*non occ.*)

3. γνήσιος, legitimate, genuine, (*spoken of children.*)

4. πιστός, (*prob. a verbal adj., from* πείθειν, to persuade, win by words, influence; *hence it may be taken either actively or passively, as the verb is.*) *Pass.*, faithful, trusty, worthy of confidence; *of persons,* on whom we may rely; *of things,* trustworthy, sure, firm, certain. *Act.*, trusting, believing.

1. Matt. xxii. 16.
1. Mark xii. 14.
2. Luke xvi. 11.
2. John i. 9.
1. —— iii. 33.
2. —— iv. 23, 37.
1. —— v. 31, 32.
2. —— vi. 32.
1. —— vii. 18.
2. —— 28.
1. —— viii. 13, 14.
1. —— 16 (No. 2, L T Tr A.)
1. —— 17, 26.
1. —— x. 41.
2. —— xv. 1.
2. —— xvii. 3.
2. —— xix. 35 1st.
1. —— 35 2nd.
1. —— xxi. 24.
1. Acts xii. 9.
1. Rom. iii. 4.
4. 2 Cor. i. 18.
1. —— vi. 8.
3. Phil. iv. 3.
1. —— 8.
2. 1 Thes. i. 9.
4. 1 Tim. iii. 1.
1. Tit. i. 13.
2. Heb. viii. 2.
2. —— ix. 24.
2. —— x. 22.
1. 1 Pet. v. 12.
1. 2 Pet. ii. 22.
1. 1 John ii. 8 1st.
2. —— 8 2nd.
2. —— v. 20 3 times.
1. 3 John 12.
2. Rev. iii. 7, 14.
2. —— vi. 10.
2. —— xv. 3.
2. —— xvi. 7.
2. —— xix. 2, 9, 11.
2. —— xxi. 5.
2. Rev. xxii. 6.

TRULY.

1. μέν, indeed, truly, *implying affirmation or concession, and at the same time pointing forward to something antithetic,* (*which gen. takes the particle* δὲ, but.)

(a) *with* οὖν, therefore, then.

2. ἀληθῶς, truly, really; *i.e.* in truth, in very deed, certainly, (*adv. of* ἀληθής, *see* "TRUE," *No.* 1.)

3. { ἐν, in, ἀλήθεια, truth, (*see* "TRUTH," *No.* 1.) }

4. { ἐπί, upon, (*as the basis on which the truth rested.*) ἀλήθεια, truth. }

5. ἄρα, accordingly.

6. δὲ, but.

1. Matt. ix. 37.
1. —— xvii. 11.
2. —— xxvii. 54.
1. Mark xiv. 38.
2. —— xv. 39.
1. Luke x. 2.
5. —— xi. 48. [*truth.*
4. —— xx. 21, marg. *of a*
1. —— xxii. 22.
3. John xvii. 19, marg. (text, *truth.*)
1a. John xx. 30.
1. Acts i. 5.
1. —— iii. 22.
1. —— v. 23 (*om.* L T Tr A א.)
1. 2 Cor. xii. 12.
1. Heb. vii. 23.
1. —— xi. 15.
6. 1 John i. 3.
3. 3 John 1, marg. (text, *truth.*)

TRUMP.

σάλπιγξ, a trump, trumpet; (lxx. *for* שׁופר, 1 Sam. xiii. 3; חצצרה, 2 Kings xii. 14.)

1. Cor. xv. 52. | 1 Thes. iv. 16.

TRUMPET.

σάλπιγξ, *see above.* * *See under* "VIAL."

Matt. xxiv. 31.
1 Cor. xiv. 8.
Heb. xii. 19.
Rev. i. 10.
—— iv. 1.
—— viii. 2*, 6*, 13*.
Rev. ix. 14*.

TRUMPET TO BE SOUNDED

(*cause a*) [margin.]

Matt. vi. 2, see "TRUMPET (SOUND A)"

TRUMPET (SOUND A)

σαλπίζω, to trumpet, sound a trumpet; (lxx. *for* תקע, Numb. x. 3, etc.; Is. xxvii. 13; Joel ii. 1.)

Matt. vi. 2.

TRUMPET SOUNDETH (A)

σαλπίζω, *see above.*

1 Cor. xv. 52.

TRUMPETER (-S.)

σαλπιστής, a trumpeter, (*non occ.*)

Rev. xviii. 22.

TRUST. [noun.]

πεποίθησις, confidence, trust, boldness; (lxx. בִּטָּחוֹן, 2 Kings xviii. 20.)

2 Cor. iii. 4.

TRUST (COMMIT TO ONE'S)

πιστεύω, to rely upon, to trust; to have a fully convinced persuasion of *a thing as true.* *With the Dat of person and Acc. of the thing*, to entrust *anything* to *anyone.*

Luke xvi. 11.

TRUST (BE COMMITTED TO MY)

{ ὅ, *with* which / ἐπιστεύθην, was en-[trusted, / ἐγώ, I. } with which entrusted was I.

1 Tim. i. 11.

TRUST WITH (BE PUT IN)

πιστεύω, *see* "TRUST (COMMIT TO ONE'S)" (*Here, pass.*)

1 Thes. ii. 4.

TRUST (PUT ONE'S)

πείθω, *see the verb below,* "TRUST," *No.* 2a.

Heb. ii. 13.

See also, COMMITTED.

TRUST (-ED.) [verb.]

1. ἐλπιζω, to expect, to hope. *With an object*, to long for and expect a thing *with real or fancied probability; without an object*, to set one's hope upon something.

2. πείθω, (a) *trans.*, to persuade, win by words, to influence.

(b) *intrans.*, to suffer one's self to be persuaded or convinced; to be persuaded in favour of any one, to yield assent to, obey *him or* trust *him;* to be convinced of, to have an assurance concerning, to confide or trust to.

1. Matt. xii. 21.
2b.—— xxvii. 43.
2b.Mark x. 24.
2b.Luke xi. 22.
2b.—— xviii. 9.
1. —— xxiv. 21.
1. John v. 45.
1. Rom. xv. 12, 24.
1. 1 Cor. xvi. 7.
2b.2 Cor. i. 9.
1. —— 10, 13.
1. —— v. 11.
2b.—— x. 7.
1. —— xiii. 6.
— Eph. i. 12, see T (first)
1. Phil. ii. 19.
2b.—— 24.
— —— iii. 4, see T (have whereof one might)
1. 1 Tim. iv. 10.
1. —— v. 5.
1. 1 Tim. vi. 17.
— 2 Tim. i. 12, marg. see Believe.
1. Philem. 22.
2b.Heb. xiii. 18.
1. 1 Pet. iii. 5.
1. 2 John 12.
1. 3 John 14.

TRUST (FIRST)

προελπίζω, *No.* 1, *above, with* πρό, before, *prefixed,* (*non occ.*)

Eph. i. 12, marg. *hope first.*

TRUST (HAVE WHEREOF ONE MIGHT)

πείθω, *see above, No.* 2b.

Phil. iii. 4.

TRUTH.

1. ἀλήθεια, truth, *as the revealed reality lying at the basis of, and agreeing with, an appearance;* the manifested, veritable essence of a matter; *hence,* the reality *appertaining to an appearance or manifestation*, truth.

2. { ἐπὶ, upon, (*as a basis and groundwork.*) / ἀλήθεια, truth. }

3. ἀληθής, *see* "TRUTH," *No.* 1.

4. ναι, yea, yes, certainly, (*in assent and strong affirmation.*)

— Matt. xiv. 33, see T (of a)
4. —— xv. 27.
1. —— xxii. 16.
1. Mark v. 33.
1. —— xii. 14, 32.
1. Luke iv. 25.
— —— ix. 27, see T (of a)
— —— xii. 44, see T (of a)
2. —— xx. 21, marg. (text, *truly.*)
1. —— xxi. 3, see T (of a)
1. —— xxii. 59.
1. John i. 14, 17.
1. —— iii. 21.
1. —— iv. 23, 24.
1. —— v. 33.
— —— vi. 14, see T (of a)
— —— vii. 40, see T (of a)
1. —— viii. 32 twice, 40, 44 twice, 45, 46.
1. —— xiv. 6, 17.
1. —— xv. 26.
1. —— xvi. 7, 13 twice.
1. —— xvii. 17 twice.
1. —— 19 (with ἐν, in), (marg. *truly.*)
1. —— xviii. 37 twice, 38.
1. Acts iv. 27.
1. —— x. 34.
1. —— xxvi. 25.
1. Rom. i. 18, 25.
1. —— ii. 2, 8, 20.
1. —— iii. 7.
1. —— ix. 1.
1. —— xv. 8.
1. 1 Cor. v. 8.
1. —— xiii. 6.
— —— xiv. 25, see T (of a)
1. 2 Cor. iv. 2.
1. —— vi. 7.
1. —— vii. 14 twice.
1. —— xi. 10.
1. —— xii. 6.
1. —— xiii. 8 twice.
1. Gal. ii. 5, 14.
1. —— iii. 1 (ap.)
— —— iv. 16, see T (tell the)
1. —— v. 7.
1. Eph. i. 13.
— —— iv. 15, see T (speak the)
1. —— 21.
1. —— 24, marg. (text, *true.*)
1. —— 25.
1. —— v. 9.
1. —— vi. 14.
1. Phil. i. 18.
1. Col. i. 5, 6.
— 1 Thes. ii. 13, see T (in)
1. 2 Thes. ii. 10, 12, 13.
1. 1 Tim. ii. 4, 7.
1. —— iii. 15.
1. —— iv. 3.
1. —— vi. 5.
1. 2 Tim. ii. 15, 18, 25.
1. —— iii. 7, 8.
1. —— iv. 4.
1. Tit. i. 1, 14.
1. Heb. x. 26.

1. Jas. i. 18.
1. —— iii. 14.
1. —— v. 19.
1. 1 Pet. i. 22.
1. 2 Pet. i. 12.
1. —— ii. 2.
1. 1 John i. 6, 8.
1. —— ii. 4, 21 twice.
2. 1 John ii. 27.
1. —— iii. 18, 19.
1. —— iv. 6.
1. —— v. 6.
1. 2 John 1 twice, 2, 3, 4.
1. 3 John 1 (with ἐν, *in*), (marg. *truly*.)
1. ——— 3 twice, 4, 8, 12.

TRUTH (IN)

ἀληθῶς, *see* "TRULY," *No.* 2.

1 Thes. ii. 13.

TRUTH (OF A)

1. ἀληθῶς, *see* "TRULY," *No.* 2.

2. ὄντως, really, truly, in very deed, as being so.

1. Matt. xiv. 33.
1. Luke ix. 27.
1. —— xii. 44.
— —— xx. 21, marg. see [Truly.
1. Luke xxi. 3.
1. John vi. 14.
1. —— vii. 40.
2. 1 Cor. xiv. 25.

TRUTH (SPEAK THE)

ἀληθεύω, to be ἀληθής, (*see* "TRUE," *No.* 1) *and being so*, to act truly, to speak *or* tell the truth.

Eph. iv. 15.

TRUTH (TELL THE)

Gal. iv. 16 part.

TRY (-IED, -ETH.)

1. δοκιμάζω, assay, to make trial of, put to the proof, examine, *as metals by fire, etc.*, to prove, try.

2. πειράζω, essay, to make an attempt; make proof *or* trial of; *of actions*, to attempt; *of persons*, to tempt, to put to the test.

3. { πρὸς, for, in order to, πειρασμός, putting to the test, trial, proof.

— Rom. ii. 18, marg. see Approve.
1. 1 Cor. iii. 13.
— Phil. i. 10, marg. see Approve.
1. 1 Thes. ii. 4.
2. Heb. xi. 17 part.
— Jas. i. 12, see Tried.
1. 1 Pet. i. 7 part.
3. —— iv. 12.
1. 1 John iv. 1.
2. Rev. ii. 2, 10.
2. —— iii. 10.
— ——— 18, see T (be)

TRIED.

δόκιμος, assayed, tried, proved, approved.

Jas. i. 12.

TRIED (BE)

πυρόω, to set on fire; *here*, *pass.*, be fired, be burned; *hence*, *of metals*, to be tried by fire, be purified; (lxx. *for* בחר, Prov. x. 20; צרף, Zech. xiii. 9; Ps. xi. 7.)

Rev. iii. 18.

TRYING.

δοκίμιον, a proof, a test; (lxx. *for* מצרף, a crucible, Prov. xxvii. 21), (*occ.* 1 Pet. i. 7.)

Jas. i. 3.

TUMULT (-S.)

1. θορυβος, noise, uproar, clamour *as of a multitude; then*, a popular commotion, tumult.

2. ἀκαταστασία, instability; *hence*, disorder, sedition.

1. Matt. xxvii. 24.
— Luke xxii. 6, marg. see Multitude.
1. Mark v. 38.
1. Acts xxi. 34.
1. —— xxiv. 18.
2. 2 Cor. vi. 5, marg. *tossing to and fro.*
2. 2 Cor. xii. 20.

TUNE. [margin.]

1 Cor. xiv. 7, see "SOUND."

TURN (-ED, -ING.)

(*For various combinations with other words, see below.*)

1. στρέφω, to turn, turn about.
   (a) *mid.*, to turn one's self, change, to turn to.

2. ἐπιστρέφω, (*No.* 1, *with* ἐπί, upon, *prefixed*) to turn upon, turn towards; *hence*, to turn back again upon.
   (a) *Mid.*, to turn one's self back upon.

3. μεταστρέφω, (*No.* 1, *with* μετά, in association with, *prefixed*) to turn into *something* else, to change.

4. ἀποβαίνω, to step away from, step off; to go away, depart; *hence, of events*, to issue *or* result from, to turn out, end *or* issue *in a certain way*.

5. μετατίθημι, to put in another place; *hence*, to transfer, to change.

1. Matt. v. 39.	2. Acts xi. 21.
1a.—— xvi. 23.	1a.—— xiii. 46.
2. Luke i. 16, 17.	2. —— xv. 19.
1a.—— vii. 44.	2. —— xvi. 18.
1a.—— ix. 55.	2. —— xxvi. 18, 20.
1a.—— xiv. 25.	2. 2 Cor. iii. 16.
4. —— xxi. 13.	1a. Phil. i. 19.
1a.—— xxii. 61.	2. 1 Thes. i. 9.
1a.—— xxiii. 28.	3. Jas. iv. 9.
1a. John i. 38.	— 2 Pet. ii. 6, see Ashes.
3. Acts ii. 20.	2. ——— 21 (ap.)
1. —— vii. 42.	3. Jude 4.
2. —— ix. 35, 40.	2. Rev. i. 12 twice.

1. Rev. xi. 6.

TURN ABOUT.

1. ἐπιστρέφω, *see No.* 2a, *above.*

2. μετάγω, to lead over from one place to another; to move about from one side to another, (*non occ.*)

1. Matt. ix. 22 (No. 1, L T Tr A ℵ.)	1. Mark viii. 33, part.
1. Mark v. 30.	1. John xxi. 20.
	2. Jas. iii. 3, 4.

TURN ONE ABOUT.

στρέφω, *see* "TURN," *No.* 1a.

Luke vii. 9.

TURN AGAIN.

1. ἐπιστρέφω, *see* "TURN," *No.* 2.

2. στρέφω, *see* "TURN," *No.* 1a.

3. ἀνακάμπτω, to bend *or* turn up *or* back, turn back, return.

2. Matt. vii. 6.	1. Luke xvii. 4.
1. Mark xiii. 16.	1. Gal. iv. 9, marg. turn back.
3. Luke x. 6.	1. 2 Pet. ii. 22.

TURN ASIDE.

1. ἐκτρέπομαι, to turn out of, *as out of a way or course,* to turn aside from.

2. ἀναχωρέω, to give place, go back, retire, withdraw, *spoken of those who flee.*

2. Matt. ii. 22.	1. 1 Tim. i. 6.

1. 1 Tim. v. 15.

TURN AWAY.

1. ἀποστρέφω, to turn away from, turn right away.

   (a) *Mid. or pass.,* to turn one's self away from.

2. διαστρέφω, to turn throughout, to distort, turn away, seduce, pervert.

3. ἀποτρέπομαι, to turn right away from. *In N.T., mid.,* to turn one's self away from, avoid, shun.

4. μεθίστημι, to stand *or* set over *from one place to another,* to transfer, remove.

1a. Matt. v. 42.	1a. 2 Tim. i. 15.
2. Acts xiii. 8.	1a. —— iii. 5.
4. —— xix. 26.	1a. Tit. i. 14.

1a. Heb. xii. 25 part.

TURN AWAY FROM.

1a. Matt. v. 42.	1a. Tit. i. 14.
1a. 2 Tim. i. 15.	1a. Heb. xii. 25 part.

TURN BACK.

ὑποστρέφω, to turn under, turn behind, *implying stealth, without noise or notice.*

Luke xvii. 15.

TURN BACK AGAIN.

1. ὑποστρέφω, *see above.*

2. στρέφω, (*see* "TURN," *No.* 1a.)

1. Luke ii. 45.	2. Acts vii. 39.

TURN ONE.

στρέφω, *here, mid. of* "TURN," *No.* 1.

Luke x. 23 (ap.)

TURN ONE'S SELF.

John xx. 14, 16.

TURN TO FLIGHT.

κλίνω, to incline, bend anything down. *In military language, like Lat.,* inclinare aciem, to make give way, rout.

Heb. xi. 34.

TURN UPSIDE DOWN.

ἀναστατόω, to unsettle, stir to sedition, put in commotion.

Acts xvii. 6.

TURNED (BE)

1. γίνομαι, to become.

2. ἐκτρέπομαι, to be turned out of *the way to somewhere else.*

1. John xvi. 20.	2. 2 Tim. iv. 4.

BE TURNED OUT OF THE WAY.

2. Heb. xii. 13.

TURNING.

τροπή, a turning, a turning back, *as of the heavenly bodies in their courses;* (lxx. Job xxxviii. 33; Deut. xxxiii. 14), (*non occ.*)

Jas. i. 17.

TURTLE-DOVE (-s.)

τρυγών, a turtle-dove, (*from* τρύζω, to murmur, to coo); (lxx. *for* תֹּר, Lev. v. 7, 11), (*non occ.*)

Luke ii. 24.

TUTOR (-s.)

ἐπίτροπος, one to whom a charge is committed, a steward, manager, agent; a tutor, guardian, curator, (*see* "STEWARD.")

Gal. iv. 2.

TWAIN.

δύο, two.

Matt. v. 41.
—— xix. 5, 6.
—— xxi. 31.
Matt. xxvii. 21, 51.
Mark x. 8 twice.
—— xv. 38.
Eph. ii. 15.

TWELFTH.

δωδέκατος, the twelfth.

Rev. xxi. 20.

TWELVE.

1. **δώδεκα**, twelve; *for symbolical significance, see under* "THREE."

(a) οἱ δώδεκα, the twelve, *i.e.* the twelve apostles.

2. **δεκαδύο**, *a less usual form of No.* 1.

1. Matt. ix. 20.
1a. —— x. 1, 2, 5.
1a. —— xi. 1.
1. —— xiv. 20.
1. —— xix. 28 twice.
1a. —— xx. 17.
1a. —— xxvi. 14, 20, 47.
1. ——— 53.
1a. Mark iii. 14.
1a. —— iv. 10.
1. —— v. 25, 42.
1a. —— vi. 7.
1. ——— 43.
1. —— viii. 19.
1a. —— ix. 35.
1a. —— x. 32.
1a. —— xi. 11.
1a. —— xiv. 10, 17, 20, 43.
1. Luke ii. 42.
1a. —— vi. 13.
1a. —— viii. 1.
1. ——— 42; 43.
1a. —— ix. 1, 12.
1. ——— 17.
1a. —— xviii. 31.
1a. Luke xxii. 3.
1a. ——— 14 (*om.* L T Tr A א.)
1. ——— 30.
1a. ——— 47.
1. John vi. 13.
1a. ——— 67, 70, 71.
1. —— xi. 9.
1a. —— xx. 24.
1a. Acts vi. 2.
1. —— vii. 8.
2. —— xix. 7 } (No. 1, L
2. —— xxiv. 11 } TTrA*א)
— —— xxvi. 7, see Tribes.
1a. 1 Cor. xv. 5.
1. Jas. i. 1.
1. Rev. vii. 5 3 times, 6 3 times, 7 3 times, 8 3 times.
1. —— xii. 1.
1. —— xxi. 12 1st, 12 2nd (*ap.*), 12 3rd.
1. ——— 14 1st.
1a. ——— 14 2nd.
1. ——— 16, 21.
1. —— xxii. 2.

TWENTY.

εἴκοσι, twenty, (*as a symbolical number it would denote* an intensity of divine testimony and of human responsibility. *See* NOTE *under* "THREE," "TEN," and "TWO.")

Luke xiv. 31.
John vi. 19.
Acts i. 15.
—— xxvii. 28.
1 Cor. x. 8.
Rev. iv. 4 twice, 10.
Rev. v. 8.
——— 14 (*om.* εικοσιτέσσαρες, *four and twenty,* G L T Tr A א.)
—— xi. 16.
—— xix. 4.

TWICE.

δίς, twice.

Mark xiv. 30, 72.
Luke xviii. 12.
Jude 12.

TWINKLING.

ῥιπή, a throw, jerk, cast, *as of a stone or weapon; of the wind,* a gust; *of the eye,* a wink, a movement of the eyelid.

1 Cor. xv. 52 (ῥοπή, *a sinking, a falling,* Lm.)

TWO.

δύο, two, (*as a symbolical number, see note under* "THREE.")

Matt. iv. 18, 21.
—— vi. 24.
—— viii. 28.
—— ix. 27.
—— x. 10, 29.
—— xi. 2 (διά, *through,* instead of δύο, *two of,* G~L T Tr A א.)
—— xiv. 17, 19.
—— xviii. 8 twice, 9, 16 twice, 19, 20.
—— xx. 21, 24, 30.
—— xxi. 1, 28.
—— xxii. 40.
—— xxiv. 40, 41.
—— xxv. 15, 17 twice.
——— 22 3 times.
—— xxvi. 2, 37, 60.
—— xxvii. 38.
Mark vi. 9, 38, 41 twice.
—— ix. 43, 45, 47.
—— xi. 1.
—— xii. 42.
—— xiv. 1, 13.
—— xv. 27.
—— xvi. 12 (*ap.*)
Luke ii. 24.
—— iii. 11.
—— v. 2.
—— vii. 19, 41.
—— ix. 13, 16, 30, 32.
—— x. 35.
—— xii. 6, 52 twice.
—— xv. 11.
—— xvi. 13.
—— xvii. 34.
Luke xviii. 10.
—— xix. 29.
—— xxi. 2.
—— xxii. 38.
—— xxiii. 32.
—— xxiv. 4, 13.
John i. 35, 37, 40.
—— iv. 40, 43.
—— vi. 9.
—— viii. 17.
—— xi. 6.
—— xix. 18.
—— xx. 12.
—— xxi. 2.
Acts i. 10, 23, 24.
—— vii. 29.
—— ix. 38 (*om.* G→)
—— x. 7.
—— xii. 6 twice.
—— xix. 10, 22, 34.
—— xxi. 33.
—— xxiii. 23.
1 Cor. vi. 16.
—— xiv. 27, 29.
2 Cor. xiii. 1.
Gal. iv. 22, 24.
Eph. v. 31.
Phil. i. 23.
1 Tim. v. 19.
Heb. vi. 18.
—— x. 28.
Rev. ix. 12.
——— 16.
—— xi. 2, 3, 4 twice, 10.
—— xii. 14.
—— xiii. 5, 11.

TWO AND TWO.

ἀνὰ δυο, by twos.

Luke x. 1.

TWO AND TWO (BY)

{ δύο, two [*and*]
{ δύο, two.

Mark vi. 7.

TWO APIECE.

ἀνὰ δύο, by twos.

Luke ix. 3. | John ii. 6.

TWO MEN.

δύο, two.

Luke xvii. 36 (ap.)

TWO WOMEN.

δύο, two.

Luke xvii. 35.

See also, EDGE, HUNDRED, SEAS, THOUSAND, WAYS, YEARS

TWO-EDGED.

δίστομος, double-mouthed, (*of a river*); *of a sword*, two-edged.

Heb. iv. 12. | Rev. i. 16.

TWOFOLD MORE.

διπλοῦς, twofold, double. *Here, comparative*, διπλότερον *as adv.*, twofold more.

Matt. xxiii. 15.

TYPE. [margin.]

1 Cor. x. 11, see "ENSAMPLE."

U

UNAWARES.

1. αἰφνίδιος, unforeseen, sudden.
2. λανθάνω, to lie hid, be concealed, be unkown. *When joined with the participle of another verb it has the force of an adverb,* unknowingly, unawares.

1. Luke xxi. 34. | 2. Heb. xiii. 2.

See also, BROUGHT, CREEP.

UNBELIEF.

1. ἀπιστία, faithlessness, untrustiness; distrust, unbelief, *applying to all, without regard to their circumstances, or opportunities of knowing the truth.*
2. ἀπείθεια, unwillingness to be persuaded, wilful unbelief which opposes itself; *hence,* unbelief in action, disobedience, *restricted to those who have heard and know the truth, (a stronger term, therefore, than No.* 1, *and denoting an actual manifestation* of it.)

1. Matt. xiii. 58.
1. —— xvii. 20 (ὀλιγοπιστία, *little faith*, L T Tr A* ℵ.)
1. Mark vi. 6.
1. —— ix. 24.
1. —— xvi. 14 (ap.)
1. Rom. iii. 3.
1. Rom. iv. 20.
1. —— xi. 20, 23.
2. —— 30, 32.
2. Eph. v. 6 (ap.), marg. *disobedience.*
1. 1 Tim. i. 13.
1. Heb. iii. 12, 19.
2. —— iv. 6, 11.

UNBELIEVER.

ἄπιστος, disbelieving, distrustful, faithless.

Luke xii. 46.
1 Cor. vi. 6.
1 Cor. xiv. 23.
2 Cor. vi. 14.

UNBELIEVING.

1. ἄπιστος, (*see above*) unbelieving, *simply*, (*without reference to opportunities of hearing and knowing.*)
2. ἀπειθέω, (*here part.*) unbelieving in the active opposition of disobedience. *Used of those* who will not be *persuaded.*

2. Acts xiv. 2.
1. 1 Cor. vii. 14 twice, 15.
1. Tit. i. 15.
1. Rev. xxi. 8.

UNBLAMEABLE.

1. ἄμεμπτος, not blamed, without reproach.
2. ἄμωμος, spotless, without stain *or* blemish, (*the Levitical requirement for all victims*); (lxx. *for* תמים, Lev. i. 10; xxii. 19-22.)

2. Col. i. 22. | 1. 1 Thes. iii. 13.

UNBLAMEABLY.

ἀμέμπτως, (*adv. of No.* 1, *above*) blamelessly, faultlessly, so as to merit no blame, so that nothing can be said against, (*occ.* 1 Thes. v. 23.)

1 Thes. ii. 10.

UNCERTAIN.

1. ἄδηλος, *to the eye*, not manifest, not obvious; *to the ear*, not distinct, (*occ.* Luke xi. 44.)

2. ἀδηλότης, non-evidentness, indistinctness.

[Here, ἐπὶ πλούτου ἀδηλότητι, *upon*, (*i.e.* counting on, reckoning on, leaning on) *riches' uncertainty*, (not "the uncertainty of riches," but "resting upon that which to the eye is non-evident and to the ear indistinct," *i.e.* uncertainty.] (*non occ.*)

1. 1 Cor. xiv. 8.
2. 1 Tim. vi. 17, marg. *uncertainty*.

UNCERTAINLY.

ἀδήλως, not openly; *of mind or will*, irresolutely, (*non occ.*)

1 Cor. ix. 26.

UNCERTAINTY. [margin.]

1 Tim. vi. 17, see "UNCERTAIN."

UNCHANGEABLE.

ἀπαράβατος, not passing from beside, *i.e.* not passing away; *hence*, unchangeable, (*non occ.*)

Heb. vii. 24, marg. *not passing from one to another.*

UNCIRCUMCISED.

1. { ἔχω, to have, ἀκροβυστία, the prepuce, the foreskin, (*from* ἄκρον *and* βύω.) }

2. { ἐν, in ἀκροβυστία, the prepuce, the foreskin, (*see above.*) }

3. ἀπερίτμητος, not circumcised; (lxx. *for* ערל, Gen. xvii. 14; Ex. xii. 48.)

3. Acts vii. 51. | 1. Acts xi. 3.
2. Rom. iv. 11, 12.

UNCIRCUMCISED (BECOME)

ἐπισπάομαι, to draw upon, draw over, *as the prepuce*, [an allusion to the mode of removing the mark of circumcision practised by Jews who apostatized, 1 Macc. i. 15; Josephus, Ant. xii. 5, 1], (*non occ.*)

1. Cor. vii. 18.

UNCIRCUMCISION.

ἀκροβυστία, the prepuce, the foreskin, (*from* ἄκρον *and* βύω); (lxx. *for* ערלה, Gen. xvii. 11, 14; Lev. xii. 13); *hence*, the state of uncircumcision.

Rom. ii. 25, 26 twice, 27.
—— iii. 30.
—— iv. 9, 10 twice.
1 Cor. vii. 18, 19.
Gal. ii. 7.
Gal. v. 6.
—— vi. 15.
Eph. ii. 11.
Col. ii. 13.
—— iii. 11.

UNCLEAN.

1. ἀκάθαρτος, unpurified; *in a Levitical sense*, unatoned; *then, as transferred to the moral sphere*, impure, *embracing impurity of all kinds*, (*occ.* Mark ix. 13; xviii. 2.)

2. κοινός, common, pertaining to all, what comes into contact with everything, unholy, unsanctified; *hence, the opposite of* ἅγιος, ("HOLY," *No.* 1.)

3. κοινόω, to make κοινός (*No.* 2), make common; *hence*, to render unholy, unlawful; to defile. *Here, pass. part. pl.*, the profaned, the defiled.

1. Matt. x. 1.
1. —— xii. 43.
1. Mark i. 23, 26, 27.
1. —— iii. 11, 30.
1. —— v. 2, 8, 13.
1. —— vi. 7.
1. —— vii. 25.
1. Luke iv. 33, 36.
1. —— vi. 18.
1. —— viii. 29.
1. —— ix. 42.
1. —— xi. 24.
1. Acts v. 16.
1. —— viii. 7.
1. —— x. 14, 28.
1. —— xi. 8.
1. 1 Cor. vii. 14.
1. 2 Cor. vi. 17.
1. Eph. v. 5.
3. Heb. ix. 13.
2. Rev. xiv. 14 1st & 2nd, marg. *common*.
1. —— xvi. 13.
1. —— xviii. 2.

UNCLEANNESS.

1. ἀκαθαρσία, *in a ritual sense*, impurity; *also in an ethical sense*, impurity in general, *as opposed to* ἁγιασμός, (*see* "HOLINESS.") ἀκαθαρσία is comprehensive; *hence, it is the genus, of which* πορνεία, (lewdness) *and* ἀσέλγεια, (dissoluteness) *etc., are only species*, (*non occ.*)

2. μιασμός, a dyeing; *hence*, pollution, stain, taint, *in a moral sense*, (*non occ.*)

1. Matt. xxiii. 27.
1. Rom. i. 24.
1. —— vi. 19.
1. 2 Cor. xii. 21.
1. Gal. v. 19.
1. Eph. iv. 19.
1. —— v. 3.
1. Col. iii. 5.
1. 1 Thes. ii. 3.
1. —— iv. 7.
2. 2 Pet. ii. 10.

UNCLOTHED (BE)

ἐκδύω, to go *or* come out of; *hence*, of clothes, to get out of them, to put off, strip *one of his clothes*, to unclothe. *Here*, *mid.*, to strip or put off one's clothes from one's self.

[Here, prob. referring to the *state of death*, of the *body in the grave*, which is emphatically the "*naked*" state, *see* Job i. 21 and Ecc. v. 15. In 2 Cor. v. our present state is characterised by "our earthly house" or body, (ver. 1) in which we "groan," (ver. 2 and 4.) But we "groan" for two reasons. (1) We "groan," (ver. 4) because we do not wish to die, to be "unclothed," (Job i. 21; Ecc. v. 15) and lie naked in the grave, while mortality is swallowed up of death. (2) We also "groan," (ver. 2) because we "earnestly desire" the Lord's coming, when He shall "change" our bodies of humiliation and make them like His own body of glory, (Phil. iii. 21) when we shall be "clothed upon with our house which is from heaven," (ver. 1, 2) "that mortality might be swallowed up of life" (ver. 4). We earnestly desire this, because, being thus clothed, we shall not be found naked, *i.e.* shall not die, for "we shall not all sleep, but we shall all be changed," (1 Cor. xv. 51) "for this mortal must put on immortality" (1 Cor. xv. 53). Therefore we dread the "being unclothed," and we long for the "putting on," (1 Cor. xv. 53, 54) and "clothing upon," (2 Cor. v. 2, 4). The whole passage is founded on, treats of, and is written in the spirit of "Resurrection," with which it begins in 2 Cor. iv. 14. To be "absent" from the Lord is to be here, or in the grave; to be "present" with Him, is to be "raised" or "changed." For this latter we are "willing rather."] (*occ.* Matt. xxvii. 28, 31; Mark xv. 20; Luke x. 30.)

2 Cor. v. 4.

UNCOMELY.

ἀσχήμων, uncomely in outward figure, shape, and mien; *hence*, unseemly, (*non occ.*)

1 Cor. xii. 23.

UNCOMELY (BEHAVE ONE'S SELF)

ἀσχημονέω, to be ἀσχήμων, (*see above*) to behave in unseemly guise; (lxx. *for* עריה, Ezek. xvi. 7, 22; and also נקלה, Deut. xxv. 3), (*occ.* 1 Cor. xiii. 5.)

1 Cor. vii. 36.

UNCONDEMNED.

ἀκατάκριτος, not under condemnation, (*non occ.*)

Acts xvi. 37. | Acts xxii. 25.

UNCORRUPTIBLE.

ἄφθαρτος, not liable to corruption, incapable of decay. *Spoken of God only, and of the future bodies of the saints "risen" or "changed,"* (*occ.* 1 Cor. ix. 25; xv. 52; 1 Tim. i. 17; 1 Pet. i. 4, 23; iii. 4.)

Rom. i. 23.

UNCORRUPTNESS.

ἀδιαφθορία, incorruptibleness; *then*, incorruption, purity.

Tit. ii. 7 (ἀφθορία, *incorruptness, integrity*, G ~ L T Tr A ℵ.)

UNCOVER (-ED.)

ἀποστεγάζω, to remove the roof, (*non occ.*)

Mark ii. 4.

UNCOVERED.

ἀκατακάλυπτος, without the veil down, unveiled, (*non occ.*)

1 Cor. xi. 5, 13.

UNCTION.

χρίσμα, something rubbed in, an anointing; (lxx. *for* משחה, Ex. xxix. 7; xxx. 25.) *Spoken of the anointing of saints now, as holy and royal priests*, (1 Pet. ii. 9), (*occ.* 1 John ii. 27.)

1 John ii. 20.

UNDEFILED.

ἀμίαντος, unstained, unsoiled, (*non occ.*)

Heb. vii. 26.
—— xiii. 4.
Jas. i. 27.
1 Pet. i. 4.

UNDER.

(*For list of words with which it is elsewhere combined, see below.*)

1. ὑπό, under.
   (a) *with Gen.*, beneath and separate from, by.
   (b) *with Acc.*, under and towards, under, (*actually or figuratively*); in the power of, close upon, (*occ.* Acts v. 21; Jas. v. 12.)
2. ὑποκάτω, down under, underneath.
3. ἐπί, upon.
   (a) *with Gen.*, upon and springing from.
   (b) *with Dat.*, upon or resting on; on, *as the groundwork of any fact or circumstance.*
   (c) *with Acc.*, upon by direction towards.
4. ἐν, in, *of time, place, or element;* with; in, *of the sphere in which a subject is concerned.*
5. κατωτέρω, lower.
6. ἐλάσσων, less, minor; *of quality*, inferior; *of age*, younger. *Here*, *neut.*, *as adv.*, less than.

5. Matt. ii. 16.
1b.—— v. 15.
4. —— vii. 6.
1b.—— viii. 8, 9 twice.
1b.—— xxiii. 37.
1b.Mark iv. 21 twice, 32.
2. —— vi. 11.
2. —— vii. 28.
1b.Luke vii. 6, 8 twice.
2. —— viii. 16.
1b.—— xi. 33.
1b.—— xiii. 34.
1b.—— xvii. 24 twice.
1b.John i. 48.
2. —— 50.
1b.Acts ii. 5.
1b.—— iv. 12.
1b.Rom. iii. 9, 13.
4. —— 19.
1b.—— vi. 14 twice, 15 twice.
1b.—— vii. 14.
1b.—— xvi. 20.
1b.1 Cor. ix. 20 3 times.
1b.—— x. 1.
1b.—— xv. 25, 27.
1b.Gal. iii. 10, 22, 23, 25.
1b.—— iv. 2, 3, 4, 5, 21.
1b.—— v. 18.
1b.Eph. i. 22.
1b.Col. i. 23.
6. 1 Tim. v. 9.
3a.—— 19, marg. (text, *before.*)
1b.—— vi. 1.
2. Heb. ii. 8.
3b.—— vii. 11 (No. 3a, G ∾ L T Tr A ℵ.)
3b.—— ix. 15.
3b.—— x. 28.
1b.Jas. ii. 3.
1b.1 Pet. v. 6.
1b.Jude 6.
2. Rev. v. 3, 13.
2. —— vi. 9.
2. Rev. xii. 1.

See also, BONDAGE, CURSE, EARTH, KEEP, LAW, OBEDIENCE, POWER, PUT, RUN, SAIL, SUBJECTION, TREAD.

UNDERGIRD (-ING.)

ὑποζώννυμι, to put a girdle under, to undergird. *Here*, to put chains or cables right under and so around the ship, (*non occ.*)

Acts xxvii. 17.

UNDERSTAND.

(*For various combinations with other words, see below.*)

1. συνίημι, to bring together, *as foes in battle;* to collect together the single features of an object into a whole; *hence*, to collect, apprehend, grasp, comprehend, understand, to be earnestly occupied with the object, to reflect morally, ponder, lay to heart, (*implying mental activity, knowledge acquired by reflection and consideration, while No.* 3 *implies an immediate knowledge.*)
2. νοέω, to perceive, observe, the mental correlative of perception by the senses; to perceive, observe, *as distinct from mere sensation or feeling.* νοέω *refers to* the object of knowledge, *while No.* 3 *emphasises* the fact of knowing.
3. γινώσκω, to perceive, obtain a knowledge of *or* insight into; *hence*, to know, (*spoken of immediate or actual knowledge*) to know so as to be influenced by one's knowledge, (*see* "KNOW," *No.* 2.)
4. οἶδα, I have perceived *or* seen, (*see* "KNOW," *No.* 1.)
5. ἐπίσταμαι, to fix one's mind upon, *i.e.* to understand, to know how to do *anything*, to know well, to have knowledge.
6. μανθάνω, to learn, *esp.*, by enquiry, *also*, to learn by experience.
7. πυνθάνομαι, to ask, enquire; to enquire out, to find out *by enquiry;* to learn, to hear.
8. φρονέω, to have mind, intellect, to think; to mind, be minded, have in mind.

1. Matt. xiii. 13, 14, 15, 19, 23, 51.
1. —— xv. 10.
2. —— 17.
2. —— xvi. 9, 11.
1. —— 12.
1. —— xvii. 13.
2. —— xxiv. 15.
3. —— xxvi. 10 part.
1. Mark iv. 12.
1. —— vii. 14.
1. —— viii. 17, 21.
2. —— xiii. 14.
5. —— xiv. 68.
1. Luke ii. 50.
1. —— viii. 10.
1. —— xviii. 34.
1. —— xxiv. 45.
3. John viii. 27, 43.
3. —— x. 6.
3. —— xii. 16.
2. —— 40.
1. Acts vii. 25 twice.
3. —— viii. 30.
6. —— xxiii. 27.
7. —— 34 part.
3. —— xxiv. 11 (ἐπιγινώσκω, *to understand fully*, L T Tr A ℵ.)
1. —— xxviii. 26, 27.
2. Rom. i. 20.
1. —— iii. 11.
1. —— xv. 21.
4. 1 Cor. xiii. 2.
8. —— 11.
9. —— xiv. 2, marg. *hear.*
4. —— 16.
1. 2 Cor. x. 12, marg. (text, *be wise.*)
2. Eph. iii. 4.
1. —— v. 17.
3. Phil. i. 12.
2. 1 Tim. i. 7.
2. Heb. xi. 3.

UNDERSTAND (GIVE TO)

γνωρίζω, to make known, declare, reveal.

1 Cor. xii. 3.

UNDERSTOOD NOT.

ἀγνοέω, (*No.* 2, *with* α, not, *prefixed*) not to know, to be ignorant of, unacquainted with.

Mark ix. 32. | Luke ix. 45. | 2 Pet. ii. 12.

UNDERSTOOD (EASY TO BE)

εὔσημος, well marked, distinguishable *by distinct marks; of speech*, easy to be understood, (*non occ.*)

1 Cor. xiv. 9, marg. *significant.*

UNDERSTOOD (HARD TO BE)

δυσνόητος, (νοητός, *from No.* 2, *with* δυς, *a participle implying* difficulty, *etc., prefixed*) hard to be understood.

2 Pet. iii. 16.

UNDERSTANDING.

1. συνεσις, intelligence, insight into *anything*, understanding, cleverness *as shown in* quickness of apprehension; acuteness, the intelligent penetrating consideration which precedes decision and action. συνεσις *is used of* reflective thought, σοφία, (wisdom) of productive thought.

2. νοῦς, the organ of mental perception and apprehension, the organ of reflective consciousness preceding the act, *or* recognising and judging the fact; the organ of thinking and knowledge; the understanding, *esp. of* moral thinking *or* contemplation.

3. διάνοια, a thinking through, meditation *or* musing upon; the faculty of moral reflection, consciousness called into exercise by the moral affections.

4. φρήν, the diaphragm, midriff, præcordia; *hence, as the supposed seat of all mental emotions and faculties*, the mind, *including* the intellect, disposition, feelings, *etc.*

— Matt. xv. 16 } see U (without)
— Mark vii. 18 }
1. —— xii. 33.
— Luke i. 3, see U of (have perfect)
1. —— ii. 47.
2. —— xxiv. 45.
— Rom. i. 31, see U (without)
1. 1 Cor. i. 19.
2. 1 Cor. xiv. 14, 15 twice, 19.
4. —— 20 twice (pl.)
3. Eph. i. 18 (καρδία, *heart*, G L T Tr A ℵ.)
3. —— iv. 18.
2. Phil. iv. 7.
1. Col. i. 9.
1. —— ii. 2.
1. 2 Tim. ii. 7.
3. 1 John v. 20.
2. Rev. xiii. 18.

UNDERSTANDING OF (HAVE PERFECT)

παρακολουθέω, to accompany side by side, to follow closely; *then*, to follow out closely *in mind*, trace out, examine.

Luke i. 3.

UNDERSTANDING (WITHOUT)

ἀσύνετος, void of understanding, dull of apprehension, foolish; (lxx. *for* כסיל, Ps. xcii. 7.)

Matt. xv. 16. | Mark vii. 18. | Rom. i. 31.

UNDONE (*be left*) [margin.]

Tit. i. 5, see "WANTING (BE)"

UNEQUALLY.

See, YOKED.

UNFEIGNED.

ἀνυπόκριτος, without dissimulation, not playing a part.

2 Cor. vi. 6. | 2 Tim. i. 5.
1 Tim. i. 5. | 1 Pet. i. 22.

UNFRUITFUL.

ἄκαρπος, without fruit, yielding no fruit, (*occ.* Jude 12.)

Matt. xiii. 22.
Mark iv. 19.
1 Cor. xiv. 14.
Eph. v. 11.
Tit. iii. 14.
2 Pet. i. 8.

UNGODLINESS.

ἀσέβεια, impiety directed against what should be held sacred; *hence*, godlessness, practical impiety. (*The only word in* lxx. *for* פשע, *see* Jer. v. 6; Ezek. xxi. 24. *Also used for* זמה, Ezek. xvi. 57; רשע, Prov. iv. 17; Ecc. viii. 8), (*occ.* Jude 15, 18.)

Rom. i. 18.
— xi. 26.
2 Tim. ii. 16.
Tit. ii. 12.

UNGODLY. [adj.]

1. **ἀσέβεια**, *see above.*
2. **ἀσεβής**, one who has no reverence for sacred things, godless, without fear and reverence before God; *not merely irreligious, but* he who actually practises the opposite of what God demands.

2. Rom. iv. 5.
2. — v. 6.
2. 1 Tim. i. 9.
2. 1 Pet. iv. 18.
2. 2 Pet. ii. 5.
2. — iii. 7.
2. Jude 15 1st (*om.* αὐτῶν, *among them,* G ⇉ L T Tr A.)
1. — 15 2nd, (om. G→ℵ.)
Jude 18.

UNGODLY MAN.

2. Jude 4.

UNGODLY (THAT IS)

2. Jude 15, with art.

UNGODLY COMMIT.

ἀσεβέω, to act impiously concerning what we should account sacred; (lxx. *for* פשע, Zeph. iii. 12; רשע, Dan. ix. 5), (*non occ.*)

Jude 15.

UNGODLY (LIVE)

ἀσεβέω, *see above.*

2 Pet. ii. 6.

UNHOLY.

ἀνόσιος, unholy, (*the opp. of* "HOLY," *No.* 2), (*non occ.*)

1 Tim. i. 9.
2 Tim. iii. 2.

UNHOLY THING.

κοινόν, a common thing.

Heb. x. 29.

UNITED WITH (*be*) [margin.]

Heb. iv. 2, see "MIXED (BE)"

UNITY.

ἑνότης, oneness, unity, (*non occ.*)

Eph. iv. 3, 13.

UNJUST.

1. **ἄδικος**, not in conformity with δίκη (right); not as it should and ought to be; *hence,* unjust, unrighteous.
2. **ἀδικία**, what is not conformable with δικη (right); what ought not to be, wrong; *here, lit.*, of injustice, of unrighteousness.

1. Matt. v. 45.
2. Luke xvi. 8.
1. — 10 twice.
2. — xviii. 6.
1. Luke xviii. 11.
1. Acts xxiv. 15.
1. 1 Cor. vi. 1.
1. 1 Pet. iii. 18.
1. 2 Pet. ii. 9.

UNJUST (BE)

ἀδικέω, to be an ἄδικος, (*see No.* 1, *above*) and to act as one, to be and do wrong, to be and act unrighteously.

Rev. xxii. 11 twice.

UNKNOWN.

1. **ἀγνοέω**, (*the opp. of* "UNDERSTAND," *No.* 2) not to know, to be ignorant of, unacquainted with, (*referring to the absence of the object of knowledge.*)
2. **ἄγνωστος**, what is unknown, what withdraws itself from being known, (*referring to the absence of actual knowledge*), (*non occ.*)

2. Acts xvii. 23.
1. 2 Cor. vi. 9.
1. Gal. i. 22.

UNLADE.

ἀποφορτίζομαι, to unlade, *spoken only of a ship,* (*non occ.*)

Acts xxi. 3.

UNLAWFUL.

ἄνομος, without law, lawless; what is not in harmony with law, what

contradicts the law. (ἄνομος *is negative, while* παράνομος *is positive lawlessness.*)

2 Pet. ii. 8.

UNLAWFUL THING.

ἀθέμιτος, lawless, without law *or* government, godless. *Lat.*, nefarious; forbidden by law, criminal, (*occ.* 1 Pet. iv. 3.)

Acts x. 28.

UNLEARNED.

1. ἰδιώτης, a private citizen *as opposed to one in a public station;* an individual opp. to the many; *then,* one who has no professional knowledge, *whether of politics, law, or any other subject, as we say,* a layman; *then, gen.,* an ill-informed *as opp. to a trained and learned man,* (*occ.* Acts iv. 13; 2 Cor. xi. 6.)
2. ἀγράμματος, unlettered, illiterate, (*non occ.*)
3. ἀμαθής, untaught, uninstructed, (*non occ.*)
4. ἀπαίδευτος, untrained, undisciplined, uneducated; *hence,* ignorant, stupid, foolish; (lxx. *for* נבל, Prov. xvii. 22; כסיל, Prov. viii. 5; xv. 15), (*non occ.*)

2. Acts iv. 13.
1. 1 Cor. xiv. 16, 23, 24.
4. 2 Tim. ii. 23.
3. 2 Pet. iii. 16.

UNLEAVENED.

ἄζυμος, without leaven, unleavened; *hence,* unmixed, unadulterated, uncorrupted. *Spoken of bread,* unleavened bread.

1 Cor. v. 7.

UNLEAVENED BREAD.

Matt. xxvi. 17.
Mark xiv. 1, 12.
Luke xxii. 1, 7.
Acts xii. 3.
—— xx. 6.
1 Cor. v. 8.

UNLESS.

ἐκτὸς, out of, without, | εἰ, if, | μή, not, } unless, except, } nevertheless except.

1 Cor. xv. 2.

UNLOOSE.

λύω, to loose, to loosen *what is fast bound;* to unbind, untie.

Mark i. 7. | John i. 27. | Luke iii. 16.

UNMARRIED.

ἄγαμος, without nuptials, *i.e.* unmarried.

1 Cor. vii. 8, 11, 32, 34.

UNMERCIFUL.

ἀνελεήμων, not actively compassionate, not desirous of relieving the ills of others, not applying beneficent aid; *then,* uncompassionate, cruel; (lxx. *for* אכזר, Prov. v. 9; xi. 17), (*non occ.*)

Rom. i. 31.

UNMOVEABLE.

1. ἀσάλευτος, without vibration, unshaken, immoveable, (*occ.* Heb. xii. 28.)
2. ἀμετακίνητος, without moving from one place to another, not moving away; unmoved, firm, (*non occ.*)

1. Acts xxvii. 41. | 2. 1 Cor. xv. 58.

UNPREPARED.

ἀπαρασκεύαστος, not made ready *or* prepared for, unprepared, (*non occ.*)

2 Cor. ix. 4.

UNPROFITABLE.

1. ἀχρεῖος, of no use, no use for, useless; not needed, not wanted, (*non occ.*)
2. ἄχρηστος, not well disposed; *hence,* not useful, not fit *or* good for *any thing,* (*non occ.*)
3. ἀλυσιτελής, not paying *or* making good the expense incurred, yielding no gain, unprofitable, (*non occ.*)
4. ἀνωφελές, no help, serving no purpose, no furtherance, no advantage, (*occ.* Heb. vii. 18.)

1. Matt. xxv. 30.
1. Luke xvii. 10. [come)
— Rom. iii. 12, see U (be-
4. Tit. iii. 9.
2. Philem. 11.
3. Heb. xiii. 17.

UNPROFITABLE (BECOME)

ἀχρειόομαι, to become ἀχρεῖος, (*see No.* 1, *above*) to become of no use, etc., (*non occ.*)

Rom. iii. 12.

UNPROFITABLENESS.

ἀνωφελής, *see above, No.* 4. *Here, with art.*

Heb. vii. 18.

UNQUENCHABLE.

ἄσβεστος, unquenched; used of fire, that which cannot be put out, *not necessarily that which will never go out.*

[In Homer the word is applied to undying fame, prolonged laughter, the incessant roar of the ocean, and indefatigable strength. So in the Prophets, it is used of a fire that has gone out, but which could not be put out until it had consumed all that on which it fed, thus denoting the inevitable destruction and the eternal result of such an awful punishment. *See* 2 Kings xxii. 17; Is. xxxiv. 8-10; Jer. vii. 20; xvii. 27; Ezek. xx. 47, 48; and Jude 7. With this agrees the solemn declaration of the Lord Jesus here (Matt. iii. 12; Luke iii. 17) that "He will BURN UP the chaff with unquenchable fire."] (*occ.* Mark ix. 43, 45.)

Matt. iii. 12. | Luke iii. 17.

UNREASONABLE.

1. ἄλογος, unreasonable, *as manifesting itself in a speech or address*, irrational.
2. ἄτοπος, out of place, out of the way; *hence*, strange; *then*, unnatural, monstrous; (lxx. *for* און, Job iv. 8; xi. 11.)

1. Acts xxv. 27.
2. 2 Thes. iii. 2, marg. *absurd.*

UNREBUKABLE.

ἀνεπίληπτος, not open to be attacked, taken, *or* apprehended, *i.e.* irreprehensible.

1 Tim. vi. 14.

UNREPROVEABLE.

ἀνέγκλητος, not accused, with nothing laid to one's charge (*as the result of public investigation*); though blamed, yet undeserving of blame.

Col. i. 22.

UNRIGHTEOUS.

ἄδικος, not in conformity with δίκη (right), not as one should and ought to be; *hence*, unrighteous.

Luke xvi. 11.
Rom. iii. 5.
1 Cor. vi. 9.
Heb. vi. 10.

UNRIGHTEOUSNESS.

1. ἀδικία, what is not conformable to δίκη (right), what ought not to be; that which ought not to be *because of revealed truth; hence*, wrong, unrighteousness.
2. ἀνομία, lawlessness, contempt of law; *hence*, sin in relation to God's will and law.

1. Luke xvi. 9.
1. John vii. 18.
1. Rom. i. 18 twice, 29.
1. —— ii. 8.
1. —— iii. 5.
1. —— vi. 13.
1. Rom ix. 14.
2. 2 Cor. vi. 14.
1. 2 Thes. ii. 10, 12.
1. Heb. viii. 12.
1. 2 Pet. ii. 13, 15.
1. 1 John i. 9.
1. 1 John v. 17.

UNRULY.

1. ἄτακτος, out of rank, not keeping the ranks, (*as soldiers do*); *hence*, irregular, out of order, disorderly.
2. ἀνυπότακτος, not ranged or put in order, not subordinated, unsubjected; *hence*, insubordinate, refractory.
3. ἀκατάσχετος, not coercible, untameable, not to be restrained, (*non occ.*)

1. 1 Thes. v. 14, marg. *disorderly.*
2. Tit. i. 6, 10.
3. Jas. iii. 8 (ἀκατάστατος, *restless or inconstant,* L T Tr A ℵ.)

UNSEARCHABLE.

1. ἀνεξερεύνητος, which cannot be traced *or* searched out, inscrutable, (*the opp. of* "SEARCH," *No.* 1), (*non occ.*)
2. ἀνεξιχνίαστος, which cannot be explored, which cannot be tracked or

followed out; (lxx. *for* אין חקר, Job v. 9; ix. 10; xxxiv. 24), (*occ.* Rom. xi. 33.)

1. Rom. xi. 33. | 2. Eph. iii. 8.

UNSEEMLY (THAT WHICH IS)

ἀσχημοσύνη, without fashion, figure, mien, *or* deportment *of body or person; hence*, deformity, *then, of* moral deformity, indecency, (*occ.* Rev. xvi. 15.)

Rom. i. 27.

UNSEEMLY (BEHAVE ONE'S SELF)

ἀσχημονέω, to be ἀσχήμων, *i.e.* to behave in unseemly guise, be void of proper deportment, to act with moral deformity; (lxx. *for* ערוה, Ezek. xvi. 7, 22; and also נקלה, Deut. xxv. 3), (*occ.* 1 Cor. vii. 36.)

1 Cor. xiii. 5.

UNSKILFUL.

ἄπειρος, without making trial or attempt; without experience, inexperienced; (lxx. *for* אויל, Zech. xi. 15; לא נסה, 1 Sam. xvii. 39), (*non occ.*)

Heb. v. 13, marg. *having no experience.*

UNSOCIABLE.

Rom. i. 31, see "AFFECTION (WITHOUT NATURAL)"

UNSPEAKABLE.

1. ἀνεκδιήγητος, what cannot be told out to the end; what cannot be told in detail, *or* related, (*non occ.*)
2. ἀνεκλάλητος, what cannot be spoken out, what cannot be divulged, unspeakable, (*non occ.*)
3. ἄρρητος, what cannot be specified *or* enunciated in express words. (*In profane Greek it is used* for unspoken, wrong to be spoken, secret), (*non occ.*)

1. 2 Cor. ix. 15. | 3. 2 Cor. xii. 4.
2. 1 Pet. i. 8.

UNSPOTTED.

ἄσπιλος, without spot, stain, *or* blemish.

Jas. i. 27.

UNSTABLE.

1. ἀστήρικτος, not set fast, not firmly set *or* fixed, not established, (*non occ.*)
2. ἀκατάστατος, not settled, not standing fixed, not steady, inconstant; (lxx. *for* סער, Is. liv. 11), (*non occ.*)

2. Jas. i. 8. | 1. 2 Pet. ii. 14.
1. 2 Pet. iii. 16.

UNTAKEN AWAY.

{ μὴ, not ἀνακαλυπτάμενον, unveiled, } the veil not removed.

2 Cor. iii. 14.

UNTHANKFUL.

ἀχάριστος, unpleasant, unpleasing, without grace *or* charms; *hence*, ungracious, ungrateful, (*non occ.*)

Luke vi. 35. | 2 Tim. iii. 2.

UNTIL.

1. ἕως, until, as long as, *marking* the continuance of an action up to the time of another action.
   (a) *with* ἄν, perhaps, perchance, *implying uncertainty, and indicating a dependence on circumstances, used where the later action is only probable.*
   (b) *with the Gen.*, until, unto, *marking the* terminus ad quem, *and spoken both of time and place.*
   (c) *with* οὗ, until what *time.*
   (d) *with* ὅτου, until when.
2. ἄχρι, continuedly, continuedly until, *fixing the attention on* the whole duration up to a certain time, *but* leaving the further continuance undetermined.
   (a) *with* οὗ, continuedly until what *time.*
3. μέχρι, until, *referring to the limit, and implying that the action there terminates*, enduring up to a certain point of time and then having an end.
4. εἰς, unto; *implying purpose*, to the end that; *when referring to time, marking either* the interval, during; *or the point itself as the object of the aim or purpose*, up to, for.

1b. Matt. i. 17.
1a. —— ii. 13.
1b. —— 15.
1. —— xi. 12.
1b. —— 13.
3. —— xiii. 30 (No. 1, Tr A), (No. 2, ℵ.)
1c. —— xvii. 9.
1. —— xviii. 22 twice.
2. —— xxiv. 38.
1. —— 39.
1b. —— xxvi. 29.
1b. —— xxvii. 64.
3. —— xxviii. 15.
1b. Mark xiv. 25.
1b. —— xv. 33.
2. Luke i. 20.
1. —— xv. 4.
1b. —— xvi. 16 (No. 3, T Tr A ℵ.)
2. —— xvii. 27.
2. —— xxi. 24.
1d. —— xxii. 16, 18.
1b. —— xxiii. 44.
1c. —— xxiv. 49.
1. John ii. 10.
1d. —— ix. 18.
2. Acts i. 2.
1a. Acts ii. 35.
2. —— iii. 21.
3. —— x. 30.
1b. —— xiii. 20.
3. —— xx. 7.
1c. —— xxi. 26.
2. —— xxiii. 1.
1c. —— 14.
2. Rom. v. 13.
2. —— viii. 22.
2a. —— xi. 25.
1a. 1 Cor. iv. 5.
1b. —— xvi. 8.
2. 2 Cor. iii. 14.
2. Gal. iv. 2.
3a. —— 19.
4. Eph. i. 14.
2. Phil. i. 5, 6.
1. 2 Thes. ii. 7.
3. 1 Tim. vi. 14.
1a. Heb. i. 13.
3. —— ix. 10.
1. Jas. v. 7 (No. 1a, T.)
1c. 2 Pet. i. 19.
1. Rev. vi. 11 (No. 1c, St.)
2. —— xvii. 17.
1. —— xx. 5 (No. 2, G L Tr A), (*om.* ℵ*.)

UNTIL THE TIME.

1a. Luke xiii. 35.

See also, NOW (UNTIL)

UNTIMELY.

See, FIG.

UNTO.

UNTO is frequently the translation of the Dative case of nouns, pronouns, etc., and is often part of a phrase, or is combined in translation with other words, a list of which will be found below.

When UNTIL is represented by a separate Greek word, it is one of the following:

1. πρός, towards, in the direction of.
   (a) *with Gen.*, hitherwards, in favour of, (*only in* Acts xxvii. 34) in consideration of, *as a motive.*
   (b) *with Dat.*, resting in the direction towards, at, close by, in addition to, *as an act.*
   (c) *with Acc.*, towards, *of literal and mental direction*, in reference to, in order to, with a view to, *as an end*, (*marking the ultimate purpose*).
2. εἰς, unto; *implying purpose*, to the end that; *when referring to time it marks either* the interval during; *or the point itself as an object of the aim or purpose*, up to, for, (*marking the immediate purpose.*)
3. ἐπί, upon,
   (a) *with Gen.*, upon as springing from.
   (b) *with Dat.*, upon and resting on, (*of rest simply*) in addition to, on account of.
   (c) *with Acc.*, upon and resting on, (*of the downward pressure*) upon, by direction towards, up to, to, (*implying intention.*)
4. ἕως, until, as long as, *marking* the continuance of an action up to the time of another action. *Here, followed by the Gen.*, until, unto, *marking* the terminus ad quem, *and spoken both of time and place.*
5. ἄχρι, continuedly, continuedly until, *fixing the attention on* the whole duration up to a certain point, *but* leaving the further duration undetermined.
6. μέχρι, until, *referring to the limit, and implying that the action there terminates;* enduring up to a certain point of time and then having an end.
7. ἐν, in, within, upon, at, *of place;* in, *of the sphere in which the subject is* concerned; *of persons*, with or by, (*like* Heb. ב.)
8. μετά, with, in association with.
   (a) *with Gen.*, with, together with.
9. ὡς, as, like as.
10. ἐκ, out of, from, of.

4. Matt. i. 17.
1c. —— iii. 10.
2. —— 11.
1c. —— 13, 15 (*om.* L.)
3c. —— vi. 27.
2. —— vii. 14.
2. —— viii. 4 2nd, 18.
2. —— ix. 6.
3b. —— 16.
4. —— xi. 23.
1c. —— 28.
2. —— xii. 20.
3c. —— 28.
1c. —— xiii. 2.
2. —— 52 2nd (No. 7, L), *τῇ βασιλείᾳ, for the kingdom,* instead of *εἰς τὴν βασιλείαν, unto the kingdom,* G T Tr A ℵ.)
2. Matt. xiv. 22.
1c. —— 25, 28.
2. —— xv. 24.
2. —— xvi. 21 2nd.
7. —— xvii. 12 2nd.
1c. —— xix. 14.
4. —— xx. 8 2nd.
2. —— xxi. 1 1st.
1c. —— 1 2nd (No. 2, L T Tr A.)
1c. —— 32, 37.
2. —— xxii. 4.
4. —— 26.
1c. —— xxiii. 34.
4. —— 35.
1c. —— 37.
2. —— xxiv. 13.
— —— 27, see U (even)
1c. —— xxv. 36, 39.
2. —— xxvi. 3.

1c. Matt. xxvi. 14, 36 1st.
— —— 38 2nd, see U (even)
1c.—— 40 1st.
4. —— 58.
1c.—— xxvii. 19.
3c.—— 27.
2. —— 33.
4. —— 45.
1c.—— 62.
4. —— xxviii. 20.
2. Mark i. 4, marg. (text, *for*.)
1c.—— 5, 32.
1c.—— ii. 3, 13.
1c.—— iii. 8, 13 2nd, 31.
1c.—— iv. 1.
2. —— 35 2nd.
2. —— v. 1, 21 1st.
3c.—— 21 2nd.
4. —— vi. 23 2nd.
1c.—— 25, 30, 33.
1c.—— 45, marg. *over against*.
1c.—— 48 2nd, 51.
1c.—— vii. 1.
1c.—— 31 (No. 2, G L T Tr A ℵ.)
1c.—— ix. 17, 19, 20.
1c.—— x. 1, 14 2nd.
2. —— xi. 1, 11.
1c.—— xii. 4, 6, 13, 18.
2. —— xiii. 13.
1c.—— xiv. 10 1st.
4. —— 34 2nd.
3c.—— xv. 22.
2. —— 41 2nd.
1c.—— 43.
3c.—— 46.
3c.—— xvi. 2.
1c. Luke i. 13, 18, 19 2nd.
2. —— 26.
1c.—— 28, 34, 61, 80.
2. —— ii. 4.
4. —— 15 1st.
1c.—— 20, 34, 48, 49.
3c.—— iii. 2.
1c.—— 9, 12, 13.
1c.—— 14 (*om*. L T Tr A.)
1c.—— iv. 21, 23 1st, 26 1st.
2. —— 26 2nd.
1c.—— 26 3rd.
4. —— 29.
1c.—— 40.
4. —— 42.
1c.—— 43.
1c.—— v. 4, 10, 22.
2. —— 24 3rd.
1c.—— 31, 33, 34, 36.
1c.—— vi. 9.
3c.—— 35.
1c.—— vii. 3, 7, 20 twice, 24, 40 1st.
1c.—— viii. 21 (*om*. L.)
1c.—— 22 1st.
2. —— 22 2nd.
1c.—— ix. 3, 13, 33, 43, 50, 57, 59, 62.
1c.—— x. 2.
3c.—— 9 2nd.
3c.—— 11 (*om*. ἐφ' ὑμᾶς, *unto you*, G L T Tr A ℵ.)
1c.—— 23, 26, 29.
1c.—— xi. 1, 5 1st & 2nd.
2. —— 24.
1c.—— 39.
4. —— 51 1st.
1c.—— 53 (*ap*.)
1c.—— xii. 1.
3c.—— 11 1st.
1c.—— 15, 16, 22 1st, 41 2nd.
1c.—— xiii. 7, 23 2nd, 34.
1c.—— xiv. 3, 7, 23, 25.
1c.—— xv. 3.
1c.—— xvi. 1 1st, 30.

1c. Luke xvii. 1 1st, 22.
2. —— 24.
1c.—— xviii. 3.
1c.—— 7 (*om*. T Tr ℵ.)
1c.—— 9.
2. —— 13.
1c.—— 31 2nd.
2. —— 35.
1c.—— 40.
1c.—— xix. 5, 8, 9, 13, 33, 39.
1c.—— xx. 2, 3, 23, 41.
1c.—— xxii. 15, 52, 70.
3c.—— xxiii. 1.
1c.—— 7.
1c.—— 14 1st, 22, 28.
3c.—— xxiv. 1.
1c.—— 5, 10.
3c.—— 12 (*ap*.)
1c.—— 17, 18, 25.
2. —— 28.
1c.—— 44 2nd.
2. John i. 11.
1c.—— 29.
1c.—— ii. 3.
1c.—— iii. 4, 26 1st.
2. —— iv. 8.
1c.—— 15, 30.
2. —— 36.
1c.—— 40.
2. —— 45, 47, 48, 49.
2. —— v. 24, 29 twice.
1c.—— 33 1st.
1c.—— vi. 5 twice.
3c.—— 16.
2. —— 27 1st.
1c.—— 28, 34, 45, 65 2nd.
1c.—— vii. 3.
2. —— 8 twice, 10.
1c.—— 33 2nd.
2. —— 35.
1c.—— 37, 50.
2. —— 53 (*ap*.)
2. —— viii. 1.
1c.—— 2 (*ap*.), 3 (*ap*.), 7 (*ap*.)
4. —— 9 (*ap*.)
1c.—— 57.
1c.—— x. 35, 41.
1c.—— xi. 3, 4, 15, 21, 29.
2. —— 31, 54.
2. —— xii. 25, 27.
1c.—— xiii. 1 1st.
2. —— 1 2nd.
1c.—— xiv. 3, 6 2nd, 12 2nd, 23 2nd, 23 2nd & 3rd.
1c.—— xvi. 7 twice.
1c.—— xviii. 24.
2. —— 28.
1c.—— 29, 38 2nd.
2. —— xix. 27.
2. —— xx. 1.
1c.—— 10, 17 3rd.
1c. Acts i. 7.
4. —— 8 2nd.
2. —— 12.
4. —— 22.
1c.—— ii. 29 1st.
5. —— 29 2nd.
1c.—— 37, 38.
1c.—— iii. 11, 12, 22 1st (*ap*), 22 3rd, 25.
1c.—— iv. 1.
2. —— 3.
1c.—— 8, 19 1st, 23.
1c.—— v. 9.
2. —— 16 (*om*. G→L T Tr A ℵ.)
1c.—— 35.
1c.—— vii. 3.
1c.—— 31 (*om*. πρός αὐτόν, *unto him*, G⇄L T Tr A ℵ.)
4. —— 45.
1c.—— viii. 14, 20, 26 1st.
3c.—— 26 2nd.
2. —— 26 3rd.
3c.—— 36.

2. Acts ix. 2.
1c.—— 6 (*ap*.), 11, 15.
3c.—— 21.
1c.—— 38.
3c.—— x. 11 (*om*. ἐπ' αὐτόν, *unto him*, G L T Tr A ℵ.)
1c.—— 15, 21 (*ap*.), 28.
3c.—— xi. 11 1st.
1c.—— 11 2nd.
2. —— 18.
1c.—— 20.
3c.—— 21.
2. —— 22, 26, 27.
1c.—— xii. 5, 8 1st.
3c.—— 10 1st.
2. —— 10 2nd.
1c.—— 15, 21.
2. —— xiii. 4.
5. —— 6.
1c.—— 15, 31, 32 2nd, 36.
4. —— 47.
2. —— 51.
2. —— xiv. 6.
3c.—— 13, 15 2nd.
1c.—— xv. 2, 7, 25 2nd, 33, 36.
2. —— 39.
3c.—— xvi. 19.
1c.—— 37.
1c.—— xvii. 2.
3c.—— 6.
2. —— 10.
4. —— 15 1st.
1c.—— 15 2nd.
3c.—— 19.
1c.—— xviii. 6 1st.
2. —— 6 2nd, 14, 21.
1c.—— xix. 2 twice.
1c.—— 3 1st (*om*. πρὸς αὐτούς, G ⇄ L T Tr A ℵ.)
2. —— 3 2nd & 3rd.
3c.—— 12.
1c.—— 31.
1c.—— xx. 6.
2. —— 13 (No. 3c, L T Tr A ℵ.)
2. —— 22, 38.
2. —— xxi. 1 3 times, 2, 8.
1c.—— 11, 18.
3c.—— 32.
1c.—— 37 2nd, 39.
1c.—— xxii. 1.
5. —— 4.
1c.—— 5 1st.
2. —— 5 2nd.
2. —— 7 1st.
1c.—— 8, 10, 13 1st, 15, 21 1st.
2. —— 21 2nd.
5. —— 22.
1c.—— 25.
1c.—— xxiii. 3.
1c.—— 15 (No. 2, L T Tr A ℵ.)
1c.—— 17 2nd, 18 2nd, 21.
3c.—— xxiv. 8 (*ap*.)
2. —— xxv. 6.
3c.—— 12 2nd.
2. —— 13, 21.
1c.—— xxvi. 1.
1c.—— 6 (No. 2, G ~ L T Tr A ℵ.)
2. —— 7.
— —— 11, see U (even)
1c.—— 14.
2. —— 17.
3c.—— 18.
7. —— 20.
5. —— 22.
1c.—— 28.
1c.—— xxvii. 3.
2. —— 8, 40.
1c.—— xxviii. 17, 21, 25, 26, 30.
2. Rom. i. 1.
1c.—— 10, 13.

2. Rom. i. 16, 26.
2. —— iii. 7, 22.
2. —— v. 15, 16, 18.
7. —— 21 1st.
2. —— 21 2nd.
2. —— vi. 16 1st (*om*. G⇄)
2. —— 16 2nd, 19 twice, 22.
2. —— vii. 10.
2. —— ix. 21 twice, 23.
9. —— 29.
2. —— x. 10 twice, 12, 18.
1c.—— 21.
4. —— xi. 8.
6. —— xv. 19.
1c.—— 23.
3. —— 25 1st.
1c.—— 29, 32.
2. —— xvi. 5, 19 1st.
4. 1 Cor. i. 8.
2. —— 9.
2. —— ii. 7.
5. —— iv. 11.
1c.—— 21.
7. —— ix. 15.
2. —— x. 2.
2. —— xi. 34.
1c.—— xii. 2.
1c.—— xiv. 6.
7. —— 11.
1c.—— 26.
2. —— 36.
2. —— xvi. 3.
1c.—— 5, 11, 12.
1c. 2 Cor. i. 15, 16, 20.
2. —— 23.
2. —— ii. 4 2nd, 16 twice.
2. —— iv. 11.
7. —— v. 19 3rd, marg. ἐν.
1c.—— vi. 11.
1c.—— vii. 12 2nd.
2. —— viii. 2.
1c.—— 17.
2. —— ix. 5, 13 3 times.
5. —— x. 13.
2. —— 14.
1c.—— xii. 17.
2. Gal. i. 6, 17.
2. —— ii. 9 2nd & 3rd.
2. —— iii. 23, 24.
3b.—— v. 13.
1c.—— vi. 10 twice.
2. Eph. i. 5, 14, 15.
3b.—— ii. 10.
1c.—— 18.
2. —— 21.
1c.—— iii. 14.
2. —— iv. 13 twice, 16, 30.
1c.—— v. 31 (*om*. L T Tr ℵ.)
1c.—— vi. 9, 22.
2. Phil. i. 2, 12 2nd.
6. —— ii. 8, 30.
2. —— iii. 11.
1c.—— iv. 6.
2. —— 16 (*om*. Lb.)
2. Col. i. 6, 10, 11, 20.
2. —— ii. 2.
1c.—— iv. 8, 10.
2. —— 11 1st.
2. 1 Thes. i. 5 (No. 1, G~L.)
1c.—— 9.
1c.—— ii. 1, 2.
2. —— 9 2nd, 12.
1c.—— 18.
1c.—— iii. 6, 11.
3b.—— iv. 7 1st.
7. —— 7 2nd.
2. —— 8, 15 2nd.
7. —— v. 23.
3c. 2 Thes. ii. 1.
2. 1 Tim. i. 6.
2. —— ii. 4.
1c.—— iii. 14 2nd.
7. —— 16.
1c.—— iv. 7, 8.
6. 2 Tim. ii. 9.

3c. 2 Tim. ii. 16.
2. —— 21 twice.
1c. —— 24.
2. —— iii. 15.
1c. —— 17.
3c. —— iv. 4.
1c. —— 9.
2. —— 10 twice, 18.
1c. Tit. i. 16.
1c. —— iii. 2, 12 twice.
1c. Heb. i. 8.
2. —— ii. 3, 10.
6. —— iii. 6 (*ap.*), 14.
1c. —— v. 5, 7.
3c. —— vi. 1.
2. —— 6.
5. —— 11.
1c. —— vii. 21.
1c. —— ix. 20.
2. —— 28 2nd.
2. —— x. 39.
2. —— xi. 26.
2. —— xii. 2.
6. —— 4.
1c. —— xiii. 13.
2. Jas. ii. 2.
4. —— v. 7.
2. 1 Pet. i. 2 1st, 3, 5, 7, 10, 22, 25.
3c. —— ii. 25.
2. 1 Pet. iii. 12.
2. —— iv. 7.
2. 2 Pet. ii. 4, 9.
1c. —— iii. 16.
2. 1 John iii. 14.
1c. —— v. 16 3 times, 17.
1c. 2 John 10, 12 2nd.
2. Jude 6, 21.
2. Rev. i. 11 2nd, 3rd, 4th.
2. —— 11 5th, 6th, 7th.
5. —— iii. 10, 26.
2. —— vi. 13.
3c. —— vii. 17.
2. —— ix. 1, 7 2nd.
8a. —— x. 8.
1c. —— 9 1st.
1c. —— xii. 5.
5. —— 11.
1c. —— 12.
2. —— 13.
5. —— xiv. 20.
3c. —— xvi. 14.
5. —— xviii. 5.
2. —— xix. 9 2nd, 17.
1c. —— xxi. 9 (*om.* πρὸς με, *unto me*, G L T Tr A ℵ.)
1c. —— xxii. 18 1st (No. 3c, G L T Tr A ℵ.)
3c. Rev. xxii. 18 2nd.

UNTO (EVEN)

1. ἕως, *see above, No.* 4.

2. { ἕως, (*see above, No.* 4) as far as.
κaὶ, even
εἰς, into.

1. Matt. xxiv. 27. | 1. Matt. xxvi. 38.
2. Acts xxvi. 11.

See also, ADD, APPEAL, APPROACH, ATTAIN, ATTEND, AUTHORITY, BECKON, BELONG, BRING, CALL, CHARGEABLE, CLEAVE, COME, COMMIT, COMMITTED, CONFORMABLE, CONSENT, DAY, DESPITE, FALL, FASHIONED, GIRD, GO, GOSPEL, HAPPEN, HASTE, HEARKEN, HEED, HOUR, IN, JOINED, LAY, LIKE, LOOK, ME, MINISTER, NIGH, OBEDIENT, PERTAIN, PREACH, PRESENT, PROVOKE, PUT, REACH, ROLL, SPEAK, SUBDUE, SUBJECT, SUBJECTION, SUBMIT, TAKE, TEDIOUS, TESTIMONY, THEM, THESE, THIS, THOSE, TURN, US, WRITE.

UNTOWARD.

σκολιός, crooked, bent *from dryness.*

Acts ii. 40.

UNWASHEN.

ἄνιπτος, unwashed, (*spoken only of the hands, face, feet, or of a part of the body only.*)

Matt. xv. 20. | Mark vii. 2.
Mark vii. 5 (κοίνος, *defiled*, G L T Tr A ℵ.)

UNWISE.

1. ἀνόητος, one who does not think *or* reflect, unintelligent.

2. ἄφρων, without mind, simple, ignorant.

1. Rom. i. 14. | 2. Eph. v. 17.

UNWORTHILY.

ἀναξίως, not suitably, improperly. *As an adverb, it properly refers, not to condition, but to manner,* not in a becoming manner, in an improper manner, a manner not corresponding to.

1 Cor. xi. 27.
—— 29 (*om.* G⇉ L T Tr A ℵ.)

UNWROUGHT. [margin.]

Matt. ix. 16, and Mark ii. 21, see "NEW."

UP.

ἄνω, up, above.

John xi. 41. | Heb. xii. 15.

UP (BE)

ἀνατέλλω, to cause to rise up; to rise up; *of a cloud, the morning star, the sun, etc.; here, part.,* arising.

Matt. xiii. 6. | Mark iv. 6.

See also, ARISE, ASCEND, BEAR, BIND, BREAK, BRIM, BRING, BROUGHT, BUILD, BURN, CARRY, CATCH, CHILD, CLIMB, COME, DELIVER, DEVOUR, DRAW, DRIVE, DRY, EAT, FILL, FOLD, FROM, GATHER, GAZE, GIRD, GIVE, GO, GROW, HOISE, HOLDEN, LAID, LAY, LEAD, LEAP, LIFT, LOOK, MAKE, NOURISH, OFFER, OFFERING, PUFF, PUT, RAISE, REAR, RECEIVE, RISE, ROOT, SEAL, SET, SHUT, SIT, SPRING, STAND, STEADFASTLY, STIR, STORE, SWALLOW, TAKE, TREASURE, WIND, YIELD.

UPBRAID (-ED, -ETH.)

ὀνειδίζω, to reproach, to reproach with *anything*, upbraid, chide.

Matt. xi. 20. | Mark xvi. 14 (*ap.*)
Jas. i. 5.

UPHOLD (-ING.)

φέρω, to bear, bear up, *as a burden*, bear up and along.

Heb. i. 3.

UPON

(*For list of words used with* "UPON," *in various connections, see below.*)

UPON is sometimes the translation of the case of a noun, pronoun, *or* adjective; sometimes also part of a verb. When it is the translation of a separate Greek word, it is one of these following.

1. ἐπί, upon.

(a) *with Gen.*, upon and proceeding from, upon and springing from.

(b) *with Dat.*, upon and resting on, resting upon, (*of rest simply*) rest upon, *as hope or faith*, upon *a fact*, (*see* 2 Cor. i. 9, *and* 1 Tim. iv. 10.)

(c) *with Acc.*, upon by direction towards, upon, *with motion implied*, rest upon, (*marking the downward pressure*); *placed* upon, *as by an act*, (*see* 2 Cor. ii. 3; 1 Tim. v. 5.)

2. εἰς, unto, into, *implying* motion to an object; unto, *implying object. and purpose*; into, *union and communion with.*

3. ἐν, in, with.

4. ἐπάνω, above, upon.

5. ἀπό, from, away from, *implying separation from a certain source or point.*

6. κατά, down.

(a) *with Gen.*, down upon, *marking the object to which the object is directed.*

(b) *with Acc.*, down along, *marking the course along which it proceeds.*

7. μετά, with, association with.

(a) *with Gen.*, together with.

(b) *with Acc.*, after.

1c.Matt. iii. 16.
1a.—— vi. 19.
1c.—— vii. 24, 25 2nd, 26.
1c.—— ix. 18.
1c.—— x. 13.
1a.——— 27.
1c.—— xi. 29.
3. —— xii. 2.
1c.——— 18.
1c.—— xiii. 5.
1b.—— xvi. 18.
1c.—— xix. 28.
1c.—— xxi. 5.
4. —— xxiii. 18.
1a.——— 9.
1c.——— 35 1st.
1a.——— 35 2nd.
1c.——— 36.
1c.—— xxiv. 2.
1a.——— 3.
1a.—— xxv. 31.
2. —— xxvi. 10.
1c.—— xxvii. 29 (No. 1a, T Tr G ℵ.)
2. ——— 30.
1c.——— 35 (*ap.*)
4. —— xxviii. 2.
1c.Mark i. 10 (No. 2, L T Tr A.)
1b.—— vi. 39.
1a.——— 48, 49.
1a.—— vii. 30 (No. 1c, L T Tr A ℵ.)
1c.—— viii. 25.
1c.—— x. 16.
1b.—— xi. 7 (No. 1c, G∾L T Tr A ℵ.)
1b.—— xiii. 2 (No. 1c, Tr ℵ.)
1c.—— xv. 24.
1c.Luke i. 12, 35.
7a.——— 58.
1c.—— ii. 25, 40.
1c.—— iii. 22.
1c.—— iv. 18.
1c.—— v. 19.
5. ——— 24.
1c.——— 36.
1c.—— vi. 48 2nd, 49 (*ap.*)
1c.—— viii. 6.
2. ——— 43 (*om.* G L T Tr A ℵ.)
1c.—— ix. 38.
1c.—— x. 6.
1c.—— xi. 20.
1a.—— xii. 3.
1c.—— xiii. 4.
1a.—— xvii. 31.
2. —— xviii. 13 (*om.* G⇉L T Tr A^b ℵ.)
1c.—— xix. 35, 43.
1b.——— 44 (No. 1c, T Tr A ℵ.)
1c.—— xx. 18.
1b.—— xxi. 6.
3. ——— 23 (*om.* G L T Tr A ℵ.)
1a.——— 25.
1c.——— 34.
1c.—— xxiv. 49.
1c.John i. 32, 33, 51.
1b.—— iv. 27.
1c.—— ix. 15.
1b.—— xi. 38.
1c.—— xviii. 4.
1a.—— xix. 31.
1c.Acts i. 8, 26.
1c.—— ii. 3, 17.
2. —— iii. 4.
1c.—— iv. 33.
1c.—— v. 11 twice, 28.
1c.—— vii. 57.
1b.—— viii. 16.
1c.——— 24.
1c.—— x. 9.
2. —— xi. 6.
5. ——— 19.
1a.—— xii. 21 2nd.
1c.Acts xiii. 11.
1c.——— 40 (*om.* ἐφ' ὑμᾶς, *upon you*, L T Tr A^b ℵ.)
1c.—— xv. 10.
1c.—— xviii. 6.
3. —— xx. 7.
1c.—— xxi. 35.
2. —— xxii. 13.
1c.—— xxvi. 16.
2. —— xxvii. 26.
2. ——— 29 (No. 6b, G⇉L T Tr A ℵ.)
1c.Rom. ii. 9.
1c.—— iii. 22 (*ap.*)
1c.—— iv. 9 twice.
2. —— v. 12, 18 twice.
1a.—— ix. 28.
2. —— xiii. 6.
1c.—— xv. 20.
1c.1 Cor. iii. 12.
2. —— x. 11.
2. —— xv. 10.
6b.—— xvi. 2.
2. 2 Cor. i. 11.
1c.——— 23.
1c.—— iii. 15.
1c.—— xii. 9.
2. Gal. iv. 11.
1c.—— vi. 16.
1b.Eph. ii. 20.
1b.—— iv. 26.
1c.—— v. 6.
1b.Phil. i. 3.
1b.—— ii. 17.
1b.——— 27 (No. 1c, G L T Tr A ℵ.)
1a.Col. iii. 5.
1c.1 Thes. ii. 16.
1a.Heb. vi. 7.
1b.—— viii. 6. [*in.*)
1a.——— 10, marg. (text,
1c.—— xi. 21.
1c.Jas. ii. 21.
3. —— iv. 3.
1c.1 Pet. iv. 14.
1c.—— v. 7.
6a.Jude 15.
1c.Rev. i. 17.
1c.—— ii. 24.
1c.—— iii. 3.
1a.——— 10 twice.
1c.——— 12 1st.
1c.—— iv. 4.
1a.—— v. 7.
1a.——— 13 (No. 1b, L T Tr A.)
1a.—— vii. 10 (No. 1b, G∾L T Tr A ℵ.)
1c.—— viii. 3.
2. ——— 7.
1c.——— 10 twice.
2. —— ix. 3.
1a.—— x. 1 (No. 1c, L T Tr A.)
1c.——— 2 (No. 1a, G L T Tr A ℵ.)
1a.——— 5 twice, 8 twice.
1a.—— xi. 10.
1c.——— 11 twice, 16.
1a.—— xii. 1.
1c.——— 3.
1c.—— xiii. 1 1st.
1a.——— 1 2nd.
1c.——— 1 3rd.
1a.——— 8.
1c.—— xiv. 14.
2. —— xvi. 1.
1c.——— 2 1st (No. 2, G∾L T Tr A ℵ.)
2. ——— 2 2nd (No. 1c, G→L T Tr A ℵ.)
2. ——— 3, 4.
1c.——— 8, 10, 12.
1a.——— 18.
1c.——— 21.
1a.—— xvii. 1.
1c.——— 3, 5.

1c. Rev. xvii. 16 (*καί, and,* G L T Tr A ℵ.)
1a. —— xviii. 24.
1c. —— xix. 11.
1b. —— 14.
1a. Rev. xix. 21.
4. —— xx. 3.
1c. —— 4 twice.
1a. —— xxi. 5 (No. 1b, G L T Tr A ℵ.)

See also, ATTEND, AUTHORITY, BEAT, BESTOW, BRING, BUILD, CALL, CAST, CLOTHED, COME, EARNESTLY, FALL, GO, HOLD, LAID, LIE, LOOK, MEDITATE, MERCY, PRESS, PUT, REST, SEA, SIT, SPIT, SPREAD, STONE, TAKE, US.

UPPER.

ἀνωτερικός, upper, higher, (*non occ.*)

Acts xix. 1.

See also, CHAMBER, ROOM.

UPRIGHT.

ὀρθός, *vertically*, upright, erect; *but also, horizontally*, straight, right; (*so* lxx. *for* ישר, Prov. xii. 16; xvi. 25), (*occ.* Heb. xii. 13.)

Acts xiv. 10.

See also, STAND.

UPRIGHTLY.

See, WALK.

UPROAR.

1. **θόρυβος**, noise, uproar, clamour, *as of a multitude; hence*, popular commotion, tumult.

2. **στάσις**, a setting up, a standing; an upstand, an upstanding.

1. Matt. xxvi. 5.
1. Mark xiv. 2.
2. Acts xix. 40.
1. —— xx. 1.

UPROAR (BE IN AN)

συγχέω, to pour together; *hence*, confuse. *Here, pass.*, to be thrown into confusion.

Acts xxi. 31.

UPROAR (MAKE AN)

ἀναστατόω, to unsettle, agitate, stir to sedition; (*Aquila and Symmachus for* Heb. נוד, Ps. xi. 1; *and* הניע, Ps. lix. 12; *and in the sense of* devastate, destroy, *as cities, by Josephus, Ant.* viii. 12, 2, *and* x. 6, 2.)

Acts xxi. 28.

UPROAR (SET ON AN)

θορυβέω, to make a noise, clamour *or* uproar, *spoken of a multitude as applauding or dissenting.*

Acts xvii. 5.

UPSIDE DOWN.

See, TURN.

URGE.

ἐνέχω, to have in *anything*, to hold *or* keep fast within; to entangle, hem in.

Luke xi. 53.

US.

(*For* "OF US," "TO US," "UNTO US," etc., etc., *see below.*)

1. **ἡμεῖς**, (*nom. pl. of* ἐγώ, I) we, (*always emphatic.*)

2. **ἡμῶν**, (*Gen. pl. of No.* 1) of us, *or simply,* us, (*the* "of" *being frequently the consequence of a preceding verb or preposition.*)

3. **ἡμῖν**, (*Dat. pl. of No.* 1) to, for, unto, on *or* upon us, (*or simply,* us; *see note after No.* 2.)

4. **ἡμᾶς**, (*Acc. pl. of No.* 1) us.

5. { **ψυχὴν**, the soul, (*see* "SOUL") **ἡμῶν**, of us, } our selves.

2. Matt. i. 23.
3. —— iii. 15.
3. —— vi. 11, 12.
4. —— 13 twice.
4. —— viii. 25 (*om.* L T Tr A ℵ.)
4. —— 29, 31 1st.
3. —— 31 2nd (G∾)(No. 4, G L T Tr A ℵ.)
4. —— ix. 27.
4. —— xiii. 56.
2. —— xv. 23.
4. —— xvii. 4 1st.
4. —— xx. 7, 30, 31.
3. —— xxii. 17, 25.
3. —— xxiv. 3.
3. —— xxv. 8.
3. —— xxvi. 63.
4. —— xxvii. 4, 25.
4. Mark i. 24 2nd.
4. —— v. 12.
4. —— vi. 3.
4. —— ix. 5 1st, 22 1st. {(ap.)
3. —— 22 2nd, 38 twice
2. Mark ix. 40 (*ὑμῶν, you,* St G L.)
3. —— xiii. 4.
3. —— xvi. 3.
3. Luke i. 1.
4. —— 71, 78.
4. —— iv. 34 2nd.
3. —— vii. 5, 16.
4. —— 20.
4. —— ix. 33 1st.
2. —— 49.
2. —— 50 twice (*ὑμῶν, you,* G L T Tr A ℵ.)
4. —— xi. 1.
3. —— 3, 4 1st & 2nd.
4. —— 4 3rd, 4 4th (ap.)
4. —— xii. 41.
2. —— xvi. 26 1st.
4. —— 26 2nd.
4. —— xvii. 13.
4. —— xix. 14.
3. —— xx. 2.
4. —— 6.
3. —— xxii. 8, 67.

4. Luke xxiii. 30 twice, 39.
4. —— xxiv. 22.
3. ——— 24.
2. ——— 29.
3. ——— 32 1st (om. ἐν ἡμῖν, within us, Tr[b] A[b].)
3. ——— 32 2nd.
3. John i. 14.
4. ——— 22.
3. —— iv. 12, 25.
3. —— vi. 34, 52.
3. —— viii. 5 (ap.)
4. —— ix. 34.
5. —— x. 24 1st, and see "DOUBT."
3. ——— 24 2nd.
1. —— xi. 16.
3. —— xiv. 8 twice, 9.
3. —— xvii. 21.
3. Acts i. 17, 21 1st
4. ——— 21 2nd.
2. ——— 22 1st.
3. ——— 22 2nd.
3. —— ii. 29.
4. —— iii. 4.
3. ——— 12.
4 —— v. 28.
4. —— vii. 27 (No. 2, L T Tr ℵ.)
3. ——— 40 1st.
2. ——— 40 2nd.
4. ——— 40 3rd.
3. —— x. 42.
3. —— xi. 13.
4. ——— 15.
3. —— xiii. 47.
4. —— xiv. 11.
3. ——— 17 (ὑμῶν, you, G L T Tr A ℵ.)
3. —— xv. 7.
2. ——— 9, 24.
3. —— xvi. 9.
4. ——— 10, 15 2nd.
3. ——— 16, 17 1st.
4. ——— 37 3 times.
4. —— xx. 5.
3. ——— 14.
4. —— xxi. 5, 11.
3. ——— 16.
4. ——— 17.
3. ——— 18.
2. —— xxiv. 4.
3. —— xxv. 24.
3. —— xxvii. 2.
4. ——— 6, 7.
3. —— xxviii. 2 1st.
4. ——— 2 2nd, 7 1st, 10 1st.
2. ——— 15 1st.
3. ——— 15 2nd.
4. Rom. iv. 24.
4. —— v. 8 1st.
2. ——— 8 2nd.
3. —— viii. 4.
4. ——— 18.
2. ——— 26 (om. ὑπὲρ ἡμῶν, for us, G → L T Tr A ℵ.)
2. ——— 31 twice, 32 1st.
3. ——— 32 2nd.
2. ——— 34.
4. ——— 35, 37, 39
4. —— ix. 24.
3. ——— 29.
4. —— xv. 7 (ὑμᾶς, you, G L T Tr A ℵ.)
4. —— xvi. 6 (ὑμᾶς, you, G∾L T Tr A ℵ.)
4. 1 Cor. iv. 1.
3. ——— 6.
2. ——— 8.
4. ——— 9.
2. —— v. 7 (om. ὑπὲρ ἡμῶν, for us, G⇉L T Tr A ℵ.)
4. —— vi. 14.
4. —— vii. 15 (ὑμᾶς, you, T ℵ.)
4. 1 Cor. viii. 8.
3. —— xv. 57.
4. 2 Cor. i. 4, 5, 10 1st.
2. ——— 11 1st.
4. ——— 11 2nd, 14.
2. ——— 19, 20.
4. ——— 21 twice, 22.
4. —— ii. 14 1st.
2. ——— 14 2nd.
2. —— iii. 3.
4. ——— 6.
2. —— iv. 7.
3. ——— 12.
4. ——— 14 1st.
4. —— v. 5 1st, 14, 18 1st.
3. ——— 19.
2. ——— 20.
3. —— vi. 12.
4. —— vii. 2, 6.
3. ——— 7.
2. ——— 9.
2. —— viii. 4 1st.
3. ——— 7.
2. ——— 19 twice.
4. ——— 20 1st.
2. ——— 20 2nd.
2. —— ix. 11.
4. —— x. 2.
3. ——— 8 (om. L T Tr A ℵ.)
4. Gal. i. 4, 23.
4. —— ii. 4.
4. —— iii. 13 1st.
2. ——— 13 2nd.
—— —— iv. 17, marg. (see "YOU.")
4. —— v. 1.
4. Eph. i. 3, 4, 5, 6, 18, 19.
4. —— ii. 4, 7.
3. —— iii. 20.
4. —— v. 2 1st (ὑμᾶς, you, T Tr A ℵ.)
2. ——— 2 2nd (ὑμῶν, you, T A.)
4. Phil. iii. 17.
4. Col. i. 12, 13 1st.
2. —— ii. 14 1st.
2. —— iv. 3 1st.
2. 1 Thes. i. 9.
4. ——— 10.
2. —— ii. 13.
4. ——— 15 (ὑμᾶς, you, St.)
4. ——— 16, 18.
2. —— iii. 6 1st.
4. ——— 6 2nd & 3rd.
2. —— iv. 1.
4. ——— 7.
4. ——— 8 (ὑμᾶς, you, G∾L T Tr A ℵ.)
1. —— v. 8.
4. ——— 9.
2. ——— 10.
2. 2 Thes. i. 7.
2. —— ii. 2.
4. ——— 16 1st.
2. —— iii. 1, 6.
4. ——— 7, 9.
3. 1 Tim. vi. 17.
3. 2 Tim. i. 7, 9 1st.
4. ——— 9 2nd.
3. ——— 14.
4. —— ii. 12.
4. Tit. ii. 12.
2. ——— 14 1st.
4. ——— 14 2nd.
4. —— iii. 5, 6, 15.
4. Heb. ii. 3.
2. —— vi. 20.
3. —— vii. 26.
2. —— ix. 24.
2. —— xi. 40 twice.
3. —— xii. 1 4th.
2. —— xiii. 18.
4. Jas. i. 18.
3. —— iii. 3.
2. —— iv. 5.
4. 1 Pet. i. 3. ["YOU."
—— —— 4, marg. (see
2. 1 Pet. ii. 21 1st. (ὑμῶν, you, A V[m] G L T Tr A ℵ.)
3. ——— 21 2nd (ὑμῖν, you, G L T Tr A ℵ.)
4. —— iii. 18.
4. ——— 21 (ὑμᾶς, you, L T Tr A ℵ.)
2. —— iv. 1 (om. ὑπὲρ ἡμῶν, for us, G→L T Tr A), (ὑπὲρ ὑμῶν, for you, ℵ.)
3. ——— 3 (om. G→L T Tr A), (ὑμῖν, you, ℵ.)
2. ——— 17.
4. —— v. 10 (ὑμᾶς, you, G∾L T Tr A ℵ.)
4. 2 Pet. i. 3 2nd.
4. —— iii. 9 (ὑμᾶς, you, G∾L T Tr A ℵ.)
2. 1 John i. 3.
4. ——— 7.
3. ——— 8.
2. ——— 9 1st.
4. 1 John i. 9 2nd.
3. ——— 10.
2. —— ii. 19 5 times.
3. ——— 25.
4. —— iii. 1 1st.
2. ——— 16, 20, 21.
3. ——— 23, 24 twice.
2. —— iv. 6 twice.
3. ——— 9.
4. ——— 10, 11. [16.
3. ——— 12 twice, 13 twice,
4. ——— 19.
2. —— v. 14, 15.
3. ——— 20.
3. 2 John 2 1st.
2. ——— 2 2nd.
4. 3 John 9, 10.
4. Rev. i. 5 twice.
4. ——— 6 (No. 2, L.)
4. —— v. 9 (om. G→L T A.)
4. ——— 10 (αὐτοὺς, them, G L T Tr A ℵ.)
4. —— vi. 16 twice.

(The following combinations are in the Greek only one word; in other passages there is a preposition in the original.)

US (FOR)

3. Matt. xxv. 9. ["we."
4. Mark ix. 5, ℵt. "that
3. —— x. 35.
3. —— xiv. 15.
3. Luke i. 69. [A ℵ.)
3. —— xx. 22 (No. 4, T Tr
3. John xi. 50 (ὑμῖν, you, T Tr A), (om. ἡμῖν, for
3. —— xviii. 31. [us, ℵ.)
3. Acts xvi. 21.
3. 2 Cor. iv. 17.
3. Heb. x. 20.

US (OF)

2. Acts xvii. 27.
2. Rom. iv. 16.
2. —— xiv. 7, 12.
2. —— xv. 2.
2. Gal. iv. 26.
2. Eph. iv. 7.
2. 1 Thes. i. 6.
2. —— iii. 6.
2. 2 Pet. iii. 2 (ὑμῶν, of you, L T Tr A ℵ, i.e. your apostles, that, instead of us the apostles)

US (ON)

3. Luke x. 11.

US (TO)

3. Matt. xxv. 11.
3. Luke xi. 4.
3. —— xxiv. 32.
3. Acts x. 41.
3. —— xv. 28.
3. Rom. xii. 6.
3. 1 Cor. ii. 12.
3. 1 Cor. viii. 6.
3. 2 Cor. i. 8 (om. G⇉L T Tr A ℵ.)
3. —— v. 18.
3. —— x. 13.
3. Col. ii. 14.
3. Heb. x. 15.
3. 1 John v. 11.

US (UNTO)

3. Matt. xiii. 36.
3. —— xv. 15.
3. —— xx. 12.
3. —— xxi. 25.
3. —— xxvi. 68.
3. Mark x. 37.
3. —— xii. 19.
3. Luke i. 2, 74.
3. —— ii. 15.
3. —— x. 17.
3. —— xiii. 25.
3. —— xx. 28.
3. —— xxiii. 18.
3. John ii. 18.
3. —— xiv. 22.
3. —— xvi. 17.
3. Acts vi. 14.
3. —— vii. 38.
3. —— xi. 17.
3. —— xiii. 33 (ἡμῶν, for our, instead of αὐτῶν ἡμῖν, unto us their, L T Tr A* ℵ.)
3. —— xv. 8, 25.
3. —— xvi. 17 (ὑμῖν, unto you, B E T Tr ℵ.)

3. Rom. v. 5.
3. 1 Cor. i. 18, 30.
3. — ii. 10.
3. 2 Cor. v. 5.
3. — viii. 5.
3. Eph. i. 9.
3. Col. i. 8.
3. Col. iv. 3
3. 1 Thes. ii. 8.
3. Heb. i. 2.
3. 1 Pet. i. 12 (G ~), (ὑμῖν, you, G L T Tr A ℵ.)
3. 2 Pet. i. 3, 4.
3. 1 John i. 2.

US (UPON)

3. 1 John iii. 1.

US (WITH)

3. Luke xxiv. 32. | 3. 2 Pet. i. 1.

USE [noun.]

1. χρεία, use, usage, employment, *i.e.* the act of using; use, advantage, service; *hence*, need, necessity, want.

   (a) *lit.*, for the edification *or* building up of the need.

2. χρῆσις, a using, use *made of a thing*, power *or* means of using, usefulness, (*non occ.*)

3. ἕξις, a having possession; a being in a certain state, *esp. as produced by practice*, a habit; skill, *as the result of practice*, (*non occ.*)

1. Rom. i. 26, 27.
2a. Eph. iv. 29, marg. *profitably* πιστεως. *of the faith*, [G ~]
1. Tit. iii. 14.
3. Heb. v. 14, marg. *habit or perfection.*

USE (MEET FOR)

εὔχρηστος, very useful.

2. Tim. ii. 21.

USE (-ED, -ETH, -ING.) [verb.]

1. χράω, to furnish what is needful; *hence*, to give the needful answer. *Here, mid., and from the sense of* consulting *or* using an oracle *comes the common signification of simply* to use, *always* to use *for a purpose*, to use means *to an end.*

2. πράσσω, to do, *expressing an action as continued or not yet completed; hence*, to practise, carry on.

3. μετέχω, to have with another, to partake of, share in, partake of *as food.*

4. ἔχω, to have and hold.

5. { γίνομαι, to become, ἐν, in }

1. Acts xix. 19.
1. — xxvii. 17.
1. 1 Cor. vii. 21, 31.
1. — ix. 12, 15.
1. 2 Cor. i. 17.
1. — iii. 12.
1. — xiii. 10.
5. 1 Thes. ii. 5.
1. 1 Tim. i. 8.
1. — v. 23.
3. Heb. v. 13.
— — x. 33, see U (be)
4. 1 Pet. ii. 16, marg. *have.*

USED (BE)

ἀναστρέφω, to turn up. *Here, mid.*, to turn one's self, move about in *a place*, sojourn, dwell, live in. *Here, lit.*, "were *thus* living."

Heb. x. 33.

See also, AUTHORITY, DEACON, DECEIT, DESPITEFULLY, FAST, HOSPITABLY, REPETITIONS, SORCERY.

USING.

ἀπόχρησις, a using up, consumption by use, (*non occ.*)

Col. ii. 22.

USURP.

See, AUTHORITY.

USURY.

τόκος, a bringing forth *as children*, offspring; *metaph.*, the produce *or* offspring of money lent out; *hence*, interest, (*non occ.*)

Matt. xxv. 27. | Luke xix. 23.

UTMOST PART.

πέρας, end, extremity, *as of the earth;* (*so* lxx. *for* אפסי־ארץ, Ps. ii. 8; מקצה הארץ, Ps. lxi. 3; xix. 5.)

Luke xi. 31.

UTTER (-ED.)

1. λέγω, to lay, lay together, collect; *then*, to lay before, relate, *referring to the* purport or sentiment of what is said, *and* the connection of the words; (*see further under* "SAY," *No.* 1.)

2. λαλέω, to speak, employ the organ of utterance, to utter words in any language, *independently of any reason why they are uttered;* to talk.

3. ἐρεύγομαι, to eject through the mouth, to vomit; *hence, in N.T. and Alexandrine usage, of the voice and words*, to bring up, to speak forth; (lxx. *for* הביע, Ps. xix. 2; cxix. 171; cxlv. 7.)

4. δίδωμι, to give.

3. Matt. xiii. 35.
— Rom. viii. 26, see U (which cannot be)
4. 1 Cor. xiv. 9.
2. 2 Cor. xii. 4.
1. Heb. v. 11, and see U (hard to be)
2. Rev. x. 3, 4 twice.

UTTERED (HARD TO BE)

{ δυσερμηνεύτος, of difficult interpretation,
{ λέγειν, to relate, (*see No.* 1)

Heb. v. 11.

UTTERED (WHICH CANNOT BE)

ἀλάλητος, unutterable, not to be expressed in words, (*non occ.*)

Rom. viii. 26.

UTTERANCE.

1. λόγος, the word *spoken, and connected with the thought expressed.*
2. ἀπόφθεγγομαι, to speak one's opinion plainly, to speak out, utter aloud, to utter solemn, weighty, *or* pithy sayings, to utter an apothegm.

2. Acts ii. 4.
1. 1 Cor. i. 5.
1. 2 Cor. viii. 7.
1. Eph. vi. 19.
1. Col. iv. 3.

UTTERLY.

ὅλως, wholly, altogether, *in every part or sense.*

1 Cor. vi. 7.

See also, BURN, PERISH.

UTTERMOST.

ἔσχατος, the last, the extreme, uttermost.

Matt. v. 26.

UTTERMOST PART.

1. πέρας, *see* "UTMOST PART."
2. ἔσχατος, the last, the extreme *or* remotest part.
3. ἄκρον, the point, end *or* extremity.

1. Matt. xii. 42.
2. Acts i. 8.
3. Mark xiii. 27 twice.

UTTERMOST OF YOUR MATTER (I WILL KNOW THE)

{ διαγνώσομαι, I will know through
{ τὰ, the things
{ κατά, as to
{ ὑμᾶς, you.

Acts xxiv. 22.

UTTERMOST (TO THE)

1. { εἰς, unto
{ τὸ, the,
{ παντελές, *the* very end; *adv.*, wholly, entirely, } to the uttermost portion of time.

2. { εἰς, unto, with a view to,
{ τέλος, a fulfilment *or* accomplishment, end.

2. 1 Thes. ii. 16.
1. Heb. vii. 25, marg. *evermore.*

V

VAGABOND.

περιέρχομαι, to go about, wander around. *Here, part.*, wandering.

Acts xix. 13.

VAIL.

See, VEIL.

VAIN.

1. κενός, empty, *referring to the contents of anything*, (*opp. of* πλήρης, full.)
2. μάταιος, foolish, idle, useless, empty, *referring to results*, (*occ.* Acts xiv. 15.)

2. 1 Cor. iii. 20.
1. —— xv. 14 twice.
2. —— 17.
1. Eph. v. 6.
1. Col. ii. 8.
2. Tit. iii. 9.
1. Jas. i. 20.
2. —— 26.
2. 1 Pet. i. 18.

VAIN (BE IN)

κενόω, *here*, *pass.*, to be empty, *as to contents.*

2 Cor. ix. 3.

VAIN (BECOME)

ματαιόω, *here*, *pass.*, to become foolish, useless, empty, *as to results.*

Rom. i. 21.

VAIN (IN)

1. *κενός*, empty, (*as to contents.*)
2. *εἰς κενόν*, in vain.
3. *εἰκῆ*, without purpose, to no purpose.
4. *μάτην*, foolishly, *i.e.* fruitlessly, idly.
5. *δωρεάν*, gratuitously; *hence*, without just cause, groundlessly.

4. Matt. xv. 9.
4. Mark vii. 7.
3. Rom. xiii. 4.
3. 1 Cor. xv. 2.
1. —— 10.
1. —— 58.
2. 2 Cor. vi. 1.
2. Gal. ii. 2.
5. Gal. ii. 21.
3. —— iii. 4 twice.
3. —— iv. 11.
2. Phil. ii. 16 twice.
1. 1 Thes. ii. 1.
2. —— iii. 5.

—1 Tim. vi. 20 } see V
—2 Tim. ii. 16 } babblings

VAIN BABBLINGS.

κενοφωνία, empty sounds, sounds containing nothing.

1 Tim. vi. 20. | 2 Tim. ii. 16.

VAIN THINGS.

κενός, *here*, *neut. pl.*, empty things, (*as to their contents.*)

Acts iv. 25.

See also, GLORY, JANGLING, REPETITIONS, TALKER.

VAINGLORY.

κενοδοξία, empty glory, empty as to glory, (*marking the contents.*)

Phil. ii. 3.

VAINLY.

εἰκῆ, without purpose, to no purpose.

Col. ii. 18.

VALIANT.

ἰσχυρός, strong, mighty, powerful, *of persons and things.*

Heb. xi. 34.

VALLEY.

φάραγξ, a gorge, ravine, a narrow and deep pass between high rocks. *Here, quoted from* Is. xl. 4, *where* lxx. *for* גיא; *as also* xxii. 1; Josh. xv. 8. lxx. *also for* אפיק, Is. viii. 7; נחל, Gen. xxvi. 17; Deut. ii. 24, (*non occ.*)

Luke iii. 5.

VALUE (BE OF MORE)

διαφέρω, to bear or carry through; to bear apart; *hence*, to differ, be different from, be other than.

Matt. x. 31. | Luke xii. 7.

VALUE (-ED.) [verb.]

τιμάω, to hold worth, to estimate; to price, fix a value *or* price upon *anything.*

Matt. xxvii. 9 1st.
—— 9 2nd, marg. *buy.*

VANISH AWAY (-ED, -ETH.)

1. *ἀφανίζω*, become unseen; to put out of sight. *Here*, *pass.*, to disappear, to be out of sight, to vanish away.
2. *καταργέω*, to render inactive; make useless, make void, abolish, put an end to. *Here*, *pass*, to cease, to be done away.

2. 1 Cor. xiii. 8.
1. Jas. iv. 14.

— Heb. viii. 13, see V (ready to)

VANISH AWAY (READY TO)

{ *ἐγγὺς*, near,
{ *ἀφανισμοῦ*, a disappearing.

Heb. viii. 13.

VANISH OUT OF SIGHT.

{ *γίνομαι*, to become
{ *ἄφαντος*, invisible, not seen.

Luke xxiv. 31.

VANITY (-IES.)

1. *ματαιότης*, folly, vanity, emptiness *as to results*, (*non occ.*)

2. *μάταιος*, vain, empty *as to results*, fruitless; *here*, *τὰ μάταια*, *these empty* things, *or* these meaningless things.

2. Acts xiv. 15. | 1. Eph. iv. 17.
1. Rom. viii. 20. | 1. 2 Pet. ii. 18.

VAPOUR.

ατμίς, vapour, *i.e.* an exhalation; (lxx. *for* תמרות, Joel ii. 30; ענן, Lev. xvi. 13; Ezek. viii. 11; קיטור, Gen. xix. 28), (*non occ.*)

Acts ii. 19. | Jas. iv. 14.

VARIABLENESS.

παραλλαγή, a passing from side to side, vicissitude, alternation, variation, (*non occ.*)

Jas. i. 17.

VARIANCE.

ἔρις, strife, quarrel, *esp.*, rivalry, contention, wrangling.

Gal. v. 20.

VARIANCE (SET AT)

διχάζω, to divide in two, part asunder, disunite, (*non occ.*)

Matt. x. 35.

VAUNT ONE'S SELF.

περπερεύομαι, to show one's self a boaster *or* braggart, (*non occ.*)

1 Cor. xiii. 4, marg. *be rash.*

VEHEMENT.

See, DESIRE.

VEHEMENTLY.

1. *δεινῶς*, unusually, terribly, (*like Eng. slang*, "awfully)," (*occ.* Matt. viii. 6.)

2. *εὐτόνως*, intensely, with main strength, violently, zealously, (*occ.* Acts xxviii. 28.)

3. { *ἐκ*, out of, *περισσοῦ*, over and above, more than enough, abundant, } so much the more.

3. Mark xiv. 31 (*ἐκπερισσῶς, very abundantly*, G∾L T Tr A ℵ.) | — Luke vi. 48, 49, see [Beat. 1. — xi. 53. 2. — xxiii. 10.

VEIL.

1. *καταπέτασμα*, a covering *which hangs down or spreads out over*, a curtain; (lxx. *for* the outer covering, מסך, Ex. xxvi. 37; xl. 6; *and*, for the inner veil, פרכת, Ex. xxvi. 31; xxvii. 21; xl. 3), (*non occ.*)

2. *κάλυμμα*, a covering, *esp.* the head covering *of women*, a hood *or* veil, *hiding all the face, except the eyes*, and falling upon *the shoulders*; (lxx. *for* מסוה, Ex. xxxiv. 33, etc.), (*non occ.*)

3. *περιβόλαιον*, something thrown around, a covering *or* garment; (lxx. *for* לבוש, Ps. cii. 27, etc.) *then, by impl.*, a covering for the head, a head-dress, etc.

1. Matt. xxvii. 51. | 2. 2 Cor. iii. 13, 14 1st.
1. Mark xv. 38. | — — 14 2nd, see V [(which)
1. Luke xxiii. 45. | 2. — 15, 16.
3. 1 Cor. xi. 15, marg. (text, *covering.*) | 1. Heb. vi. 19.
| 1. — ix. 3.
1. Heb. x. 20.

VEIL (WHICH)

{ *ὅ*, which
{ *τι*, one.

2 Cor. iii. 14 (*ὅτι, because*, G L T Tr A.)

VENGEANCE.

1. *ἐκδίκησις*, execution of right and justice, maintenance of right.

2. *δίκη*, right, justice; *hence*, judgment, sentence.

3. *ὀργή*, wrath, *the active outgo of* wrath, (*not the affection itself, which is θυμός*); indignation, anger *conjoined with the desire of* revenge.

1. Luke xxi. 22. | 1. 2 Thes. i. 8.
3. Rom. iii. 5. | 1. Heb. x. 30.
1. — xii. 19. | 2. Jude 7.

VENERABLE.

Phil. iv. 8, see "HONEST."

VENOMOUS.

See, BEAST.

VERILY.

1. *ἀμήν*, amen. *Heb.* אמן, *strictly adj.*, true, certain, faithful; *but also as adv.*, truly, certainly, surely. *At*

the beginning of a sentence, truly, assuredly, certainly, verily; *at the end*, so be it, amen.

* *In John's Gospel always twice*, verily, verily.

2. μέν, indeed, truly, *implying affirmation or concession, and at the same time pointing forward to something antithetic, which is then commonly*
   (a) *subjoined with* δέ, but, *or*
   (b) *with* οὖν, therefore, *i.e.* indeed therefore.
3. γάρ, (*composed of* γε, verily, *and* ἄρα, accordingly) the fact is, in fact, as the case stands.
4. ἀληθῶς, in truth, truly.
5. δήπου, *a particle equivalent to* I wot, and you allow; δή *giving the assertion, decision, and confidence;* που *generalizing this decision, and implying the success of an appeal for the truth of what is said*, indeed, truly, verily.
6. ναί, yea, yes, certainly.
7. ὄντως, really, in very deed; (lxx. *for* אמנם, Numb. xxii. 37.)

1. Matt. v. 18, 26.
1. —— vi. 2, 5, 16.
1. —— viii. 10.
1. —— x. 15, 23, 42.
1. —— xi. 11.
1. —— xiii. 17.
1. —— xvi. 28.
1. —— xvii. 20.
1. —— xviii. 3, 13, 18.
1. —— xix. 23, 28.
1. —— xxi. 21, 31.
1. —— xxiii. 36.
1. —— xxiv. 2, 34, 47.
1. —— xxv. 12, 40, 45.
1. —— xxvi. 13, 21, 34.
1. Mark iii. 28.
1. —— vi. 11 (*ap.*)
1. —— viii. 12.
1. —— ix. 1.
2a. —— 12 (*om.* T Tr^{b}.)
1. —— 41.
1. —— x. 15, 29.
1. —— xi. 23.
1. —— xii. 43.
1. —— xiii. 30.
1. —— xiv. 9, 18, 25, 30.
1. Luke iv. 24.
6. —— xi. 51.
1. —— xii. 37.
1. —— xiii. 35 (*om.* G L T Tr A ℵ.)
1. —— xviii. 17, 29.
1. —— xxi. 32.
1. Luke xxiii. 43.
1* John i. 51 twice.
1* —— iii. 3, 5, 11.
1* —— v. 19, 24, 25.
1* —— vi. 26, 32, 47, 53.
1* —— viii. 34, 51, 58.
1* —— x. 1, 7.
1* —— xii. 24.
1* —— xiii. 16, 20, 21, 38.
1* —— xiv. 12.
1* —— xvi. 20, 23.
1* —— xxi. 18.
3. Acts xvi. 37.
2a. —— xix. 4 (*om.* G L T Tr A ℵ.)
2. —— xxii. 3 (*om.* G ⇉ L T Tr A ℵ.)
2ab. —— xxvi. 9.
2. Rom. ii. 25.
— —— x. 18, see Yes.
3. —— xv. 27.
2. 1 Cor. v. 3.
2. —— xiv. 17.
7. Gal. iii. 21.
4. 1 Tim. ii. 5.
5. Heb. ii. 16.
2. —— iii. 5.
2a. —— vi. 16 (*om.* L T Tr A^{b} ℵ.)
2. —— vii. 5, 18.
2b. —— ix. 1.
2. —— xii. 10.
2. 1 Pet. i. 1, 20.

VERITY.

ἀλήθεια, truth *as* the revealed reality lying at the basis of, and agreeing with an appearance; truth *as* the representation of what is *and* the realisation of what ought to be.

1 Tim. ii. 7.

VERY.

(*For list of other words used in various connections with it, see below.*)

1. σφόδρα, very, very much, exceedingly, excessively.
2. αὐτός, self, same.
3. αὐτήν, (*Acc. fem. sing. of No.* 2.)
4. αὐτά, (*Acc. neut. pl. of No.* 2.)
5. καί, and, also, even.
6. ἀληθῶς, (*adv. of* ἀλήθεια, *see* "VERITY") in truth, truly, really.

5. Matt. x. 30.
1. —— xviii. 31.
5. —— xxiv. 24.
1. Mark xvi. 4.
5. Luke ix. 5 (*om.* L^{b} Tr A ℵ.)
5. —— xii. 59.
1. —— xviii. 23.
6. John vii. 26 (*om.* G L T Tr A ℵ.)
3. —— xiv. 11.
— Rom. xiii. 6, see V thing (upon this)
— Phil. i. 6, see V thing (this)
2. 1 Thes. v. 23.
4. Heb. xi. 1.

VERY THING (THIS)

{ αὐτὸ, same, / τοῦτο, this, } this same *thing*, *or* this very *thing*.

Phil. i. 6.

VERY THING (UPON THIS)

{ εἰς, unto, / αὐτὸ, same, / τοῦτο, this, } unto this same, *or* very *thing*, (*this one that we are speaking of.*)

Rom. xiii. 6.

See also, ACT, ATTENTIVE, BOLD, CHIEFEST, COSTLY, DILIGENTLY, EARLY, EVEN, FIRST, GLADLY, GREAT, HEAVY, HIGHLY, HUNGRY, LITTLE, MANY, MORNING, PITIFUL, PRECIOUS, SMALL, SORROWFUL, THAT, WORTHY, WELL.

VESSEL (-s.)

1. σκεῦος, a vessel, or implement of any kind, utensil, instrument; (*hence, in pl. it denotes* all that belongs to a complete outfit; moveables *as opp. to fixtures.*)

2. ἀγγεῖον, (*dim. of* ἄγγος) a small vessel, reservoir, receptacle, (*e.g.* a blood-vessel); *esp.* a small vessel *in which oil was carried to replenish torches and lamps*. (*so* lxx. *for* כְּלִי, (Numb. iv. 9), (*non occ.*) *See* "LIGHT," *No.* 6.

2. Matt. xiii. 48 (ἄγγος, *a larger vessel, a jar, pan, pail,* T Tr A ℵ.)
2. —— xxv. 4.
— Mark vii. 4, see Brazen.
1. —— xi. 16.
1. Luke viii. 16.
1. John xix. 29.
1. Acts ix. 15.
1. Acts x. 11, 16.
1. —— xi. 5.
1. Rom. ix. 21, 22, 23.
1. 2 Cor. iv. 7.
1. 1 Thes. iv. 4.
1. 2 Tim. ii. 20, 21.
1. Heb. ix. 21.
1. 1 Pet. iii. 7.
1. Rev. ii. 27.
1. Rev. xviii. 12 twice.

VESTURE.

1. ἱματισμός, clothing, raiment, garments; *here, quoted from* Ps. xxii. 19, *where* lxx. *for* לְבוּשׁ; *also for* בְּגָדִים, 1 Kings xxii. 30; 2 Kings vii. 8.)

2. ἱμάτιον, a garment, *esp.* the outer garment *or* mantle, (*as opp. to* χιτών, the inner vest.)

3. περιβόλαιον, *something* thrown around, *i.e.* a covering. *Here, in allusion to* Ps. cii. 27, *where* lxx. *for* לְבוּשׁ; *so for* כְּסוּת, Ex. xxii. 27; מְכַסֶּה, Ezek. xxvii. 7.

1. Matt. xxvii. 35 (ap.)
1. John xix. 24.
3. Heb. i. 12.
2. Rev. xix. 13, 16.

VEX (-ED.)

1. ὀχλέω, to harass, with crowds *or* tumults; *then, gen.*, to trouble, or importune. *In N.T., only pass.*, to harass, (*non occ.*)

2. βασανίζω, to apply a touchstone, to examine *or* scrutinise *by words or by torture*; *then, gen.*, to torture, afflict with pain.

3. κακόω, to affect with evil; to do evil to *any one, esp. physically*, to maltreat, harm.

4. καταπονέω, to wear down by hard labour. *Here, pass.*, to get worn out, (Acts vii. 24.)

— Matt. xv. 22, see Devil.
— —— xvii. 15, see V (be)
1. Luke vi. 18 (ἐνοχλέω, *to excite tumult in,* G∾L T Tr A ℵ.)
1. Acts v. 16.
3. —— xii. 1.
4. 2 Pet. ii. 7.
2. 2 Pet. ii. 8.

VEXED (BE)

πάσχω, to suffer, to be subjected to evil *or* calamity.

Matt. xvii. 15 (ἔχω, *to have,* L Tr A* ℵ, i.e. lit. *is in a grievous condition.*)

VIAL (-S.)

φιάλη, a bowl, goblet *having more breadth than depth;* (lxx. *for* מִזְרָק, Ex. xxvii. 3; Numb. vii. 13, etc.)

[Here, the "vials" are the drink-offering belonging to the sacrifice, Lev. xxiii. 13; Numb. xv. 1-11; xxviii. 11-14.) The seven Seals had unfolded the mystery; the seven Trumpets proclaim and open the war; now seven "Vials" prepare the sacrifice for the last great slaughter, and are significant of plagues which cannot be escaped. Men cannot reach the height from whence they are poured, nor slay those who pour them.

It is submitted that in *the seven seals* we have the comprehensive aspect of the history of Daniel's last week, (yet future) a summary rehearsal of judgment, covering the whole period in broad outline, while in *the seven trumpets* we have the woes that relate specially to the apostate Jews, and in *the seven vials* the woes that are to come upon their oppressors, the Gentiles, (Deut. xxxii. 43; Is. li. 21-23; Jer. xxv. 28, 29; Rom. ii. 5-10.) The seals are thus parallel to the two series, of *trumpets* and *vials* combined. At the seventh seal there is silence, (viii. 1) a turning-point, while we go back again to begin the other parallel (but two-fold series). The seventh trumpet celebrates the accomplishment of God's purposes regarding His own people, (x. 7; xi. 15) while it initiates the seven vials, the anger of the "*nations*," and proclaims that for them, "*Thy wrath is come.*" Whereas in the seventh vial, there is no transition, but instead, the

angel who pours it declares "It is done," (xvi. 17-21).] (*non occ.*)

Rev. v. 8. | Rev. xvi. 1, 2, 3, 4, 8, 10, [12, 17.
— xv. 7. | — xvii. 1.
Rev. xxi. 9.

VICTORY.

1. *νίκη*, conquest, victory, *esp.* victory in battle, (*non occ.*)

2. *νῖκος*, *a later form of No.* 1, (*non occ.*)

2. Matt. xii. 20. | 2. 1 Cor. xv. 54, 55, 57.
1. 1 John v. 4.

VICTORY (GET THE)

νικάω, to conquer, get the upper hand, prevail, be victorious.

Rev. xv. 2.

VICTUALS.

1. *βρῶμα*, that which is eaten, food, *i.e.* solid food, *as opp. to liquid; hence*, sustenance, nourishment, (*here, pl.*)

2. *ἐπισιτισμός*, a furnishing one's self with provisions, a stock *or* store of provisions, (*non occ.*)

1. Matt. xiv. 15. | 2. Luke ix. 12.

VIGILANT.

νηφάλιος, sober, temperate, *esp. in respect to wine*, abstinent; *hence*, sober *in mind*, watchful, circumspect, (*occ.* 1 Tim. iii. 11.)

1 Tim. iii. 2.
Tit. ii. 2, marg. (text, sober.)

VIGILANT (BE)

γρηγορέω, to wake, keep awake, watch; (lxx. *for* עמד, Neh. vii. 3; שקד, Jer. i. 12; v. 6.)

1 Pet. v. 8.

VILE.

1. *ἀτιμία*, dishonour; *here, gen.*, of dishonour, of vileness.

2. *ῥυπαρός*, filthy, dirty, foul; (lxx. *for* צוֹא, Zech. iii. 3, 4), (*non occ.*)

3. *ταπείνωσις*, humiliation; *here, gen.*, of humiliation.

1. Rom. i. 26. | 3. Phil. iii. 21.
2. Jas. ii. 2.

VILLAGE (-S.)

κώμη, a village *or* hamlet *in the open country and without walls.*

Matt. ix. 35.
— xiv. 15.
— xxi. 2.
Mark vi. 6, 36, 56.
— xi. 2.
Luke viii. 1.
Luke ix. 52, 56.
— x. 38.
— xiii. 22.
— xvii. 12.
— xix. 30.
— xxiv. 13, 28.
Acts viii. 25.

VINE.

ἄμπελος, a vine, (*non occ.*)

Matt. xxvi. 29.
Mark xiv. 25.
Luke xxii. 18.
John xv. 1, 4, 5.
Jas. iii. 12.
Rev. xiv. 18, 19.

VINEGAR.

ὄξος, sharp wine, sour wine, a cheap, common kind of wine, *which, mixed with water, constituted the common drink of the poorer classes and soldiers.*

Matt. xxvii. 34 (*οἶνος, wine,* G∾L T Tr ℵ.)
— 48.
Mark xv. 36.
Luke xxiii. 36.
John xix. 29 twice, 30.

VINEYARD.

ἀμπελών, a vine-yard, (*non occ.*)

Matt. xx. 1, 2, 4, 7, 8.
— xxi. 28, 33, 39, 40, 41.
Mark xii. 1, 2, 8, 9 twice.
Luke xiii. 6.
— xx. 9, 10, 13, 15 twice, [16.
1. Cor. ix. 7.

VINEYARD (DRESSER OF ONE'S)

ἀμπελουργός, a worker in a vineyard, a vine-dresser; (lxx. *for* כרם, 2 Ch. xxvi. 10; Is. lxi. 5), (*non occ.*)

Luke xiii. 7.

VIOLENCE.

1. *βία*, strength, *esp.*, a violent *or* unjust exertion of strength *or* power, compulsion, constraint.

2. *δύναμις*, the being able, *i.e.* ability, the inherent or natural power *or* capacity.

3. *ὅρμημα*, impetus, a rush, main force, (*non occ.*)

— Matt. xi. 12, see V (suffer) [(do)
— Luke iii. 14, see V to
1. Acts v. 26.
1. Acts xxi. 35.
1. — xxiv. 7 (ap.)
1. — xxvii. 41.
2. Heb. xi. 34.
3. Rev. xviii. 21.

VIOLENCE TO (DO)

διασείω, to shake throughout, shake vehemently; *hence*, to inspire terror, (*non occ.*)

Luke iii. 14, marg. *put in fear*.

VIOLENCE (SUFFER)

βιάζομαι, to force, compel, to use force, to carry a point by obstinate perseverance, (*occ.* Luke xvi. 16.)

Matt. xi. 12, marg. *begotten by force*.

VIOLENT.

βιαστής, one who commits violence, one who unjustly exerts strength *or* power; *here, pl.*

Matt. xi. 12.

VIOLENTLY.

See, RUN.

VIPER.

ἔχιδνα, a viper, (*non occ.*)

Matt. iii. 7.
— xii. 34.
Matt. xxiii. 33.
Luke iii. 7.
Acts xxviii. 3.

VIRGIN (-S.)

παρθένος, (adj.) virgin, (*fem. as subst.*) a virgin.

* *masc.*, chaste, pure, *or* unmarried, *as for the sake of greater devotedness for Christ.*

† *quoted from* Is. vii., *where* lxx. *for* עלמה, *cf.* Is. viii. 3, 4; vii. 3; x. 21; *thus fulfilling in a strict and literal sense that which the Prophet spoke in a wider sense, and on a different occasion.*

Matt. i. 23†.
— xxv. 1, 7, 11.
Luke i. 27 twice.
Acts xxi. 9.
1 Cor. vii. 25, 28.
—— 34 (om. G∾L.)
—— 36, 37.
2 Cor. xi. 2.
Rev. xiv. 4*.

VIRGINITY.

παρθενία, virginity, virgin age; (lxx. *for* נעורים, Jer. iii. 4), (*non occ.*)

Luke ii. 36.

VIRTUE.

1. **ἀρετή**, superiority *in every respect; thus, spoken of God;* (*and* lxx. *for* תהלה, Is. xlii. 8, 12; xliii. 21; lxiii. 7; *and* הוד, Hab. iii. 3); *then, in a moral sense,* that which gives man his worth, his efficiency, his moral excellence; *hence,* good quality, excellence *of any kind,* (*non occ.*)

2. **δύναμις**, the being able, *i.e.* ability, inherent power, natural capacity, moral as well as physical ability.

2. Mark v. 30.
2. Luke vi. 19.
2. — viii. 46.
1. Phil. iv. 8.
1. 1 Pet. ii. 9, marg. (text, *praise*.)
1. 2 Pet. i. 3, 5 twice.

VISIBLE.

ὁρατός, seen, visible; (lxx. Job xxxiv. 26; xxxvii. 21), (*non occ.*)

Col. i. 16.

VISION (-S.)

1. **ὅραμα**, thing seen, a sight, spectacle; (lxx. *for* מראה, Gen. xlvi. 2; Ex. iii. 3; Deut. xxviii. 34; חזון, Dan. viii. 2; מחזה, Gen. xv. 1), (*occ.* Acts vii. 31.)

2. **ὀπτασία**; a sight, an appearance; (lxx. *for* מראה, Dan. ix. 23; x. 1, 7, 8), (*non occ.*)

3. **ὅρασις**, seeing, the sense of sight; *then,* that which is seen.

(a) *quoted from* Joel ii. 28, 29, *where* lxx. *for* חזיון; *and for* חזון, Is. i. 1; Jer. xiv. 14.

1. Matt. xvii. 9.
2. Luke i. 22.
2. — xxiv. 23.
3a. Acts ii. 17.
1. — ix. 10.
1. —— 12 (om. *ἐν ὁράματι, in a vision,* L T Tr^b A ℵ.)
1. Acts x. 3, 17, 19.
1. — xi. 5.
1. — xii. 9.
1. — xvi. 9, 10.
1. — xviii. 9.
2. — xxvi. 19.
2. 2 Cor. xii. 1.
3. Rev. ix. 17.

VISIT (-ED, -EST.)

ἐπισκέπτομαι, to look upon, to look at view; to go to see, go to look after; *hence,* to visit, *with a view to help, relieve, or deliver; but also with a* view to punish; (*so* lxx *for* פקד, Ps. lxxxix. 33; Jer. xiv. 10), (*occ.* Acts vi. 3.)

* *here quoted from* Ps. viii. 5, *where* lxx. *for* פקד, as also Gen. l. 24, 25 Ps. cvi. 4.

Matt. xxv. 36, 43.
Luke i. 68, 78.
— vii. 16.
Acts vii. 23.
— xv. 14, 36.
Heb. ii. 6*.
Jas. i. 27.

VISITATION.

ἐπισκοπή, a looking upon, *for help, relief, deliverance, or punishment; hence*, visitation.

Luke xix. 44. | 1 Pet. ii. 12.

VOCATION.

κλῆσις, a call, a summons, invitation, a calling.

Eph. iv. 1.

VOICE (-s.)

1. φωνή, a sound, a tone, *as given forth or uttered; hence*, a voice, a cry.

2. ψῆφος, a small stone *worn smooth by water*, a pebble, (*Lat.*, calculus); *then, because small black and white pebbles were anciently used in voting* (*viz. the white for approval, the black for disapproval*), a vote.

1. Matt. ii. 18.
1. —— iii. 3, 17.
1. —— xii. 19.
1. —— xvii. 5.
1. —— xxiv. 31, marg. (text, *sound*.)
1. —— xxvii. 46, 50.
1. Mark i. 3, 11, 26.
1. —— v. 7.
1. —— ix. 7.
1. —— xv. 34, 37.
1. Luke i. 42 (κραυγή, *exclamation*, L Tr A.)
1. —— 44.
1. —— iii. 4, 22.
1. —— iv. 33.
1. —— viii. 28.
1. —— ix. 35, 36.
1. —— xi. 27.
1. —— xvii. 13 pl., 15.
1. —— xix. 37.
1. —— xxiii. 23 twice, 46.
1. John i. 23.
1. —— iii. 29.
1. —— v. 25, 28, 37.
1. —— x. 3, 4, 5, 16, 27.
1. —— xi. 43.
1. —— xii. 28, 30.
1. —— xviii. 37.
1. Acts ii. 14.
1. —— iv. 24.
1. —— vii. 31, 57, 60.
1. —— viii. 7.
1. —— ix. 4, 7.
1. —— x. 13, 15.
1. —— xi. 7, 9.
1. —— xii. 14, 22.
1. —— xiii. 27.
1. —— xiv. 10, 11, pl.
1. —— xvi. 28.
— Acts xix. 34, see V cried out (all with one)
1. —— xxii. 7, 9, 14, 22, pl.
1. —— xxiv. 21.
2. —— xxvi. 10.
1. —— 14, 24.
1. 1 Cor. xiv. 10, 11.
1. Gal. iv. 20.
1. 1 Thes. iv. 16.
1. Heb. iii. 7, 15.
1. —— iv. 7.
1. —— xii. 19, 26.
1. 2 Pet. i. 17, 18.
1. —— ii. 16.
1. Rev. i. 10, 12, 15.
1. —— iii. 20.
1. —— iv. 1, 5.
1. —— v. 2, 11, 12.
1. —— vi. 6.
1. —— 7 (om. φωνήν, *the voice of*, G.)
1. —— 10.
1. —— vii. 2, 10.
1. —— viii. 5, 13 twice.
1. —— ix. 13.
1. —— x. 3 twice.
1. —— 4 1st (om. τὰς φωνὰς ἑαυτῶν, *their voices*, G L T Tr A ℵ.)
1. —— 4 2nd, 7, 8.
1. —— xi. 12, 15, 19.
1. —— xii. 10.
1. —— xiv. 2 4 times, 7, 9, 13, 15.
1. —— xvi. 1, 17, 18.
1. —— xviii. 2 (ap.), 4, 22, 23.
1. —— xix. 1, 5, 6 3 times, [17.
1. —— xxi. 3.

VOICE CRIED OUT (ALL WITH ONE)

φωνή, voice, μία, one, ἐγένετο, became, ἐκ, out of, πάντων, all,	one voice arose out of all.

Acts xix. 34.

VOID (MAKE)

1. κενόω, to empty, to make empty, *as to the contents*, make in vain.

2. καταργέω, to render useless, put an end to, do away with, abolish.

2. Rom. iii. 31. | 1. Rom. iv. 14.
1. 1 Cor. ix. 15.

See also, JUDGMENT, OFFENCE.

VOLUME.

κεφαλίς, a little head, (*Lat.* capitulum) chapter, the summary *or* contents of a chapter; *here, lit.*, "in the heading of a scroll," *and quoted from* Ps. xl. 8, *where* lxx. *for* מגלת־ספר, (*non occ.*)

Heb. x. 7.

VOLUNTARY.

θέλω, to will, to wish, to desire, *implying active volition and purpose;* to purpose, intend; *here part., lit.*, "let no one fraudulently defraud you of your prize, though doing it of purpose in humility," etc.

Col. ii. 18, marg. *being a voluntary.*

VOMIT.

ἐξέραμα, that which is vomited out, vomit, (*non occ.*)

2 Pet. ii. 22.

VOUCHSAFE. [margin.]

2 Thes. i. 11, see "WORTHY (COUNT)"

VOW.

εὐχή, prayer, prayer *to God; then*, a vow made in prayer; *esp.* the vow of the Nazarite; (*so* lxx. *for* נדר, Numb. vi. 2, 21), (*occ.* Jas. v. 15.)

Acts xviii. 18. | Acts xxi. 23.

VOYAGE.

πλόος, sailing, navigation, voyage, (*occ.* Acts xxi. 7; xxvii. 9.)

Acts xxvii. 10.

W

WAG (-ING.) [verb.]

κινέω, to move, put in motion, *esp. of the head*, to shake; (lxx. *for* הניע ראש, 2 Kings xix. 21; Job xvi. 4; Ps. xxii. 8.)

Matt. xxvii. 39. | Mark xv. 29.

WAGES.

1. ὀψώνιον, whatever is bought to be eaten with bread, *as meat, fish, etc. Hired soldiers were paid partly in meat, fruit, etc.; hence,* a stipend, wages, *esp., of soldiers,* (*occ.* 1 Cor. ix. 7.)
   (a) *plural.*
2. μισθός, hire; wages, pay; recompense, reward.

1a. Luke iii. 14, marg. *allowance.*
2. John iv. 36.
1a. Rom. vi. 23.
1. 2 Cor. xi. 8.
2. 2 Pet. ii. 15.

WAIL (-ED, -ING.) [verb.]

1. ἀλαλάζω, to utter a loud cry; *of mournful cries,* to lament aloud, wail; (*so* lxx. *for* הילִיל, Jer. xxv. 34; xlvii. 2), (*occ.* 1 Cor. xiii. 1.)
2. κόπτω, to beat, to cut, *as by a blow. Here, mid.,* to beat *or* cut one's self, *e.g. the breast in loud expression of grief; hence, put for* to wail, bewail; (lxx. *for* ספד, 2 Sam. i. 12.)
3. πενθέω, to mourn, lament, to grieve, mourn for.

1. Mark v. 38. | 2. Rev. i. 7.
3. Rev. xviii. 15, 19.

WAILING.

κλαυθμός, weeping, *implying not only* tears, but every outward expression of grief.

Matt. xiii. 42, 50.

WAIT. [noun.]

See, LAY, LIE, LYING.

WAIT (-ED, -ETH, ING.) [verb.]

ἐκδέχομαι, to receive from *any quarter,* to be about to receive from *any quarter, i.e.* to wait for, look for, expect.

1 Pet. iii. 20 (ἀπεκδέχετο, instead of ἅπαξ ἐξεδέχετο, i.e. *the longsuffering of God was waiting long for,* instead of *once the longsuffering of God waited,* G L T Tr A ℵ.)

WAIT AT.

προσεδρεύω, to sit towards, sit by; *hence,* to wait near, to attend, (*non occ.*)

1 Cor. ix. 13 (παρεδρεύω, *sit beside, wait near,* G ∾ L T Tr A ℵ.)

WAIT FOR.

1. ἐκδέχομαι, *see* "WAIT."
2. ἀπεκδέχομαι, (*No.* 1, *with* ἀπό, from, *prefixed*) to wait out, wait long for, await ardently.
3. προσδέχομαι, to receive to *one's self,* admit; to wait for, await, expect.
4. προσδοκάω, to watch toward *or* for *anything,* to look for.
5. ἀναμένω, to remain firm, hold out, to wait for *as the coming of the morn, etc.,* (*non occ.*)
6. περιμένω, to wait around *or* about anything, to remain for, (*non occ.*)

3. Mark xv. 43.
4. Luke i. 21.
3. —— ii. 25.
4. —— viii. 40.
3. —— xii. 36.
3. —— xxiii. 51.
1. John v. 3 (ap.)
6. Acts i. 4.
6. Acts x. 7, see Continually.
4. —— 24.
1. —— xvii. 16 part.
2. Rom. viii. 19, 23, 25.
2. 1 Cor. i. 7.
2. Gal. v. 5.
5. 1 Thes. i. 10.

WAIT ON.

προσκαρτερέω, to be strong *or* firm towards *anything,* to endure *or* persevere in *or* with, to be continually with *any person or thing.*

Mark iii. 9.

WAITING (PATIENT)

ὑπομονή, a remaining under, a bearing up under; patient endurance *of evils, etc., while* remaining *or* waiting.

2 Thes. iii. 5, marg. *patience.*

WAKE.

γρηγορέω, to keep awake; (*spoken of being alive, as "to sleep" is of death.*)

1 Thes. v. 10.

WALK (-ED, -EDST, -EST, -ETH, -ING.) [verb.]

1. περιπατέω, to tread about, walk about, *and gen.*, to walk, to be walking.
2. πορεύω, to cause to pass over *by land or water*, to transport; to pass, to go, *having regard, not to the point of departure, but to the end to be reached.*
3. στοιχέω, to stand *or* go in order, advance in rows *or* ranks; *hence*, to walk orderly, walk according to any rule *or* order, (*non occ.*)

1. Matt. iv. 18
1. —— ix. 5.
1. —— xi. 5.
— —— xii. 43, see W through.
1. —— xiv. 25, 26, 29.
1. —— xv. 31.
1. Mark i. 16 part. (*παράγω, to pass near,* G ~ L T Tr A ℵ.)
1. —— ii. 9.
1. —— v. 42.
1. —— vi. 48, 49.
1. —— vii. 5.
1. —— viii. 24.
— —— xi. 27, see Walking (be)
1. —— xvi. 12 part. (*ap.*)
2. Luke i. 6.
1. —— v. 23.
1. —— vii. 22.
— —— xi. 24, see W through.
1. ——— 41.
2. —— xiii. 33.
1. —— xx. 46.
1. —— xxiv. 17 part.
1. John i. 36 part.
1. —— v. 8, 9, 11, 12.
1. —— vi. 19, 66.
1. —— vii. 1 twice.
1. —— viii. 12.
1. —— x. 23.
1. —— xi. 9, 10, 54.
1. —— xii. 35 twice.
1. —— xxi. 18.
1. Acts iii. 6, 8 twice, 9, 12.
2. —— ix. 31.
1. —— xiv. 8, 10.
2. ——— 16.
1. —— xxi. 21.
— ——— 24, see W orderly.
3. Rom. iv. 12.
1. —— vi. 4.
1. —— viii. 1 (*ap.*), 4.
1. —— xiii. 13.
1. —— xiv. 15.
1. 1 Cor. iii. 3.
1. —— vii. 17.
1. 2 Cor. iv. 2.
1. —— v. 7.
— —— vi. 16, see W in.
1. —— x. 2 part., 3 part.
1. —— xii. 18.
— Gal. ii. 14, see W uprightly.
1. —— v. 16.
3. ——— 25.
3. —— vi. 16.
1. Eph. ii. 2, 10.
1. —— iv. 1, 17 twice.
1. —— v. 2, 8, 15.
3. Phil. iii. 16.
1. ——— 17, 18.
1. Col. i. 10.
1. —— ii. 6.
1. —— iii. 7.
1. —— iv. 5.
1. 1 Thes. ii. 12.
1. —— iv. 1, 12.
1. 2 Thes. iii. 6, 11.
2. 1 Pet. iv. 3 part.
— —— v. 8, see W about.
2. 2 Pet. ii. 10.
2. —— iii. 3.
1. 1 John i. 6, 7.
1. —— ii. 6 twice, 11.
1. 2 John 4, 6 twice.
1. 3 John 3, 4.
2. Jude 16, 18.
1. Rev. ii. 1.
1. —— iii. 4.
1. —— ix. 20.
1. —— xvi. 15.
1. —— xxi. 24.

WALK ABOUT.

1. 1 Pet. v. 8.

WALK IN.

ἐμπεριπατέω, (*No.* 1, *with* ἐν, in, *prefixed*) to walk about in, (*non occ.*)

2 Cor. vi. 16.

WALK ORDERLY.

3. Acts xxi. 24.

WALK THROUGH.

διέρχομαι, to come *or* go through, to pass through.

Matt. xii. 43. | Luke xi. 24.

WALK UPRIGHTLY.

ὀρθοποδέω, to foot it straight, to walk straight, *i.e.* in a straight course; *metaph.*, to walk *or* live uprightly, (*non occ.*)

Gal. ii. 14.

WALKING (BE)

1. Mark xi. 27 part.

WALL (-S.)

1. τεῖχος, a city wall, fortification; (lxx. *for* חוֹמָה, Deut. iii. 5; Josh. vi. 5, 20), (*non occ.*)
2. τοῖχος, the wall of a house *or* court, the inside wall of a dwelling, a partition; (lxx. *for* קִיר, Ex. xxx. 3; Lev. xiv. 37), (*non occ.*)

1. Acts ix. 25.
2. —— xxiii. 3.
1. 2 Cor. xi. 33.
— Eph. ii. 14, see W between (middle)
1. Heb. xi. 30.
1. Rev. xxi. 12, 14, 15, 17, 18, 19.

WALL BETWEEN (MIDDLE)

μεσότοιχον, a middle partition.

Eph. ii. 14.

WALLOW (-ED, ING.)

κυλίω, to roll, roll on *or* along. *Here, mid.*, to roll one's self, wallow; (lxx. *for* גלל, Josh. x. 18), (*non occ.*)

Mark ix. 20.

WALLOWING. [noun.]

κύλισμα, *something* rolled, a wheel; *then*, a rolling *or* wallowing, (*non occ.*)

2 Pet. ii. 22.

WANDER.

πλανάω, to make wander, lead astray; *here*, *pass.*, to wander, go astray; (lxx. *for* תעה, 2 Kings xxi. 9; Ezek. xliv. 10, 15.)

Heb. xi. 38.

WANDER ABOUT.

περιέρχομαι, to go *or* come around, *or* up and down; *hence*, to wander about.

1 Tim. v. 13. | Heb. xi. 37.

WANDERING. [adj.]

πλανήτης, one wandering about, a wanderer, *whence Eng.*, planet, *for a star, which, as opp. to the fixed stars, wanders or moves in a course of its own*, (*non occ.*)

Jude 13.

WANT. [noun.]

1. ὑστέρησις, the being last, the coming short; *hence*, the being in want, (*non occ.*)
2. ὑστέρημα, that which comes short, that which is wanting, lack, deficiency, want.
3. χρεία, use, advantage, service; *then*, what is needed for use *or* service; want, need.

1. Mark xii. 44. | 2. 2 Cor. ix. 12, pl.
2. 2 Cor. viii. 14 twice. | 3. Phil. ii. 25.
1. Phil. iv. 11.

WANT (BE IN)

ὑστερέω, to be last, behind; to lack, come short of; to be without, to want, suffer need.

Luke xv. 14, pass.

WANT (-ED, -ING.) [verb.]

1. ὑστερέω, *see above*.
2. λείπω, to leave, forsake.
   (a) *pass.*, to be left, forsaken of *any thing*, to be destitute of, to lack.

1. John ii. 3 part. | 2a. Jas. i. 4.

WANTING (BE)

2. Tit. i. 5, marg. *be left undone.*

WANTON AGAINST (BEGIN TO WAX)

καταστρηνιάω, (κατά, against, *and* στρηνιάω, to live strenuously, rudely, *as Eng.*, "to live hard," revel, run riot); to run riot against, lead a life of luxury and gaiety, *to the neglect of another or in opposition to him.*

1 Tim. v. 11.

WANTONNESS.

ἀσέλγεια, excess, licentiousness; *later*, lasciviousness, lewdness.

Rom. xiii. 13.

WANTONNESS (MUCH)

2 Pet. ii. 18, plural.

WAR (-S.) [noun.]

πόλεμος, the agitation and tumult of battle, (*Lat.*, pello, bellum); *hence*, fight, battle, war; (lxx. *for* מלחמה, Ex. i. 10; 2 Kings iii. 7.)

Matt. xxiv. 6 twice. | Jas. iv. 1.
Mark xiii. 7 twice. | Rev. xi. 7.
Luke xiv. 31. | —— xii. 7, 17.
—— xxi. 9. | —— xiii. 7 (ap.)
Rev. xix. 19.

WAR WITH (*intend*) [margin.]

Acts xii. 20, see "DISPLEASED WITH (BE HIGHLY)"

WAR (MAKE)

πολεμέω, to war, make war, to fight.

Rev. xiii. 4. | Rev. xvii. 14.
—— 5, marg. see Con-[tinue. | —— xix. 11.

WAR (MEN OF)

στράτευμα, an army, forces, troops, soldiery.

Luke xxiii. 11, plural.

WAR (-ETH, -ING.) [verb.]

1. στρατεύω, to serve in war; *then*, to wage war. *In N.T. only mid.*, to serve in war, to war, be a soldier.
2. πολεμέω, to war, make war, fight.

1. 2 Cor. x. 3. | 1. Jas. iv. 1.
1. 1 Tim. i. 18. | 2. —— 2.
1. 2 Tim. ii. 4. | 1. 1 Pet. ii. 11.

WAR AGAINST.

ἀντιστρατεύομαι, to lead out an army against, to oppose, war against, (*non occ.*)

Rom. vii. 23.

WARD.

φυλακή, the act of keeping watch; *then*, the watch itself, watch, guard.

Acts xii. 10.

WARE OF (BE)

1. γινώσκω, to perceive, observe, obtain a knowledge of *or* insight into, to learn, recognise, to be influenced by one's knowledge of the object, to suffer one's self to be determined thereby.

2. συνεῖδον, to see into *or* understand with *one's self*, *or* with one's senses, to be aware

3. φυλάσσω, to watch, *not to sleep*, to keep watch *by night; here, mid.*, to keep one's self from *or* as to *anything*, to be ware of, avoid.

1. Matt. xxiv. 50, } in AV. 1611, but altered in edition
1. Luke xii. 46, } of 1762, to "*be aware.*"
2. Acts xiv. 6.
3. 2 Tim. iv. 15.

WARFARE.

στρατεία, military service, warfare; a military expedition, campaign, (*non occ.*)

2 Cor. x. 4. | 1 Tim. i. 18.

WARFARE (GO A)

στρατεύω, to serve in war, to be a soldier; *here, mid.*, to serve in war, take the field, go on active service.

1 Cor. ix. 7.

WARM ONE'S SELF (-ED, -ING.)

θερμαίνω, to warm, heat; *here, mid.*, to warm one's self, *as by a fire;* (lxx. *for* חמם, Is. xliv. 15, 16; 1 Kings i. 1, 2), (*non occ.*)

Mark xiv. 54, 67. | John xviii. 18 twice, 25.

WARMED (BE)

Jas. ii. 16.

WARN (-ED, -ING.)

1. νουθετέο, to put in mind; *hence*, to warn, admonish, exhort; (lxx. *for* יסר, Job iv. 3.)

2. ὑποδείκνυμι, to point out *privately with the finger*, to give to understand *as it were by stealth*, to signify, let be known; (lxx. *for* הגיד, Est. ii. 20.)

2. Matt. iii. 7.
2. Luke iii. 7.
1. Acts xx. 31.
1. 1 Cor. iv. 14.
1. Col. i. 28.
1. 1 Thes. v. 14.

WARNED OF [OR FROM] GOD (BE)

χρηματίζω, to do *or* carry on business, have dealings, *esp. in money matters*, to negotiate, transact business; *of kings and magistrates*, to do business publicly, *i.e.* to give audience and answer *as to ambassadors or petitioners*, to give response *or* decision. *Then, spoken of a divine response*, to give response, to speak as an oracle, speak *or* warn from God; (*so* lxx. *for* דבר, Jer. xxvi. 2; xxx. 2; xxxvi. 4.)

Matt. ii. 12, 22. | Heb. xi. 7. | Acts x. 22.

WARY (be)

Heb. xi. 7, see "MOVED WITH FEAR (BE)"

WAS (HE, SHE, IT, THERE)

AS, AS SOON AS, FORASMUCH AS, SO, THAT, THOUGH, WHEN, WHEREAS, WHICH, WHILE, WHO.

When not part of another verb, or phrase, it is the translation of one of these following.

1. εἰμι, I am, (*the ordinary state of existence.*)

* *with pronoun* ἔγω, I.

(a) ἐστί, he, she, *or* it is, (*3rd pers. sing. pres. ind.*)

(b) *Optative*, εἴη, *etc.*, might be.

(c) εἶναι, to be, (*inf.*)

* *with Acc. of noun*, that is, *etc.*, ("that" *being sometimes understood.*)

† *with* διὰ τὸ, on account of, for the sake of, because of...being.

‡ *with* ἐν τῷ, in the being, *etc.*

(d) ὤν οὖσα, ὄν, being, (*participle*).

* *with Acc. before it*, that...is, *etc.*

(e) ἦν or ἤμην, he, she, *or* it was.

2. γίνομαι, to come into being, to begin to be, to become, to arise, to happen.

3. ὑπάρχω, to begin, to start; to begin to be, (*referring to original state or existence.*)

4. ἔχω, to have.

5. ἀπέχω, to keep off *or* away from.

6. μέλλω, to delay, to be on the point of, to be about to.

7. συμβαίνω, to stand with the feet together; *hence*, to stand with *or* beside (*so as to assist*); to come together, meet.

8. κατά, (*with Acc. as here*) according to, (*in reference to some standard of comparison implied or expressed.*)

1e. Matt. i. 18 1st.
1e.— ii. 9, 15 1st.
1e.— iii. 4.
1e.— vii. 27.
2. — viii. 26.
1e.— 30.
6. — xi. 14.
1e.— xii. 4.
1e.— 10 (om. G→L T Tr A ℵ.)
1e.— xii. 40.
2. — xiv. 15, when...W.
1e.— 23.
1e.— 24 1st (ap.)
1e.— 24 2nd.
1a.— xvi. 20.
2. — xvii. 2 2nd.
2. — xix. 8.
1e.— xxi. 25, 33.
2. — xxiv. 21.
2. — xxvi. 6, when...W.
1e.— 71 2nd.
2. — xxvii. 45.
1e.— 54, 56, 61.
2. — xxviii. 2.
1e.— 3. [33.
1e. Mark i. 6, 13 twice, 23,
1e.— 45 (om. Lb.)
1a.— ii. 1.
1e.— 4.
1e.— iii. 1 (om. L Trb.)
1e.— iv. 1 2nd.
2. — 10.
1e.— 38.
2. — 39.
1e.— v. 5, 11.
1a.— 14.
1e.— 21 2nd, 40, 42.
2. — vi. 26.
2. — 35, when...W.
1e.— 47, 48, 52.
1a.— 55.
1e.— vii. 26.
2. — ix. 7, 26.

1a. Mark x. 47.
1e.— xi. 13, 30, 32.
2. — xiii. 19.
1e.— xiv. 1.
1d.— 66, as...W.
1e.— xv. 7, 25, 26.
2. — 33, was come.
1e.— 39.
1e.— 40 (om. Trb ℵ.)
1c.— 41, 42, 46.
1e.— xvi. 4.
2. Luke i. 5.
1e.— 7, 66, 80.
2. — ii. 2.
1c†— 4.
2. — 6.
1e.— 7.
2. — 13. [40.
1e.— 25 twice, 26, 36 1st,
2. — 42.
1e.— 51.
1e.— iv. 17.
2. — 25.
1e.— 32, 33, 38.
1c*— 41.
2. — 42, when...W.
1e.— v. 3, 17 twice, 18, 29.
1e.— vi. 6 twice.
2. — 13, 16, 49.
1e.— vii. 2 2nd.
1a.— 4.
5. — 6, when...W.
1e.— 12 2nd (om. G T.)
1e.— 12 3rd (om. St G ⇄ T Trb A.)
1e.— 37, 39.
2. — viii. 24.
1e.— 32.
3. — 41.
1c‡— ix. 18, as...W.
2. — 29 twice, not in Greek.
1e.— 45, 53.

2. Luke x. 32, when...W (om. Tr.)
2. — 36.
1c‡— xi. 1, when...W.
1e.— 14 twice.
2. — 30.
1e.— xiii. 10.
1e.— 11 1st (om. L T
1e.— 11 2nd. [Tr.)
1e.— xiv. 2.
5. — xv. 20, when...W.
1e.— 24 1st.
1e.— 24 2nd (om. G→ℵ)
1e.— 25, 32 2nd.
1e.— 32 3rd (om. G ⇄ L T Tr A.)
1e.— xvi. 1 1st, 19.
1e.— 20 (om. Lb T Tr
1e.— xvii. 16. [ℵ.)
2. — 26.
1e.— xviii. 2, 3.
2. — 23 1st.
1e.— 23 2nd.
2. — 24 (om. T Trb A ℵ.)
1e.— 34.
1e.— xix. 2 2nd.
1e.— 2 3rd (om. Lb Tr.)
1a.— 3 1st.
1e.— 3 2nd.
6. — 4.
1c†— 11.
1*— 22.
1e.— xx. 4.
1c*— 6.
1e.— xxi. 37.
1b.— xxii. 23.
2. — 24, 40, when...W.
2. — 44 (ap.)
1d.— 53, when...W.
1e.— 56, 59.
2. — 66.
1d†— xxiii. 7, who...W.
1e.— 8 2nd, 19, 38, 44 1st.
2. — 44 2nd.
1e.— 47 2nd, 53, 54.
1d.— xxiv. 6, when...W.
1e.— 10 (ἦν, *it was*, for ἦσαν, *they were*, G∾T), (om. ἦσαν, *they were*, G∾Trb.)
5. — 13.
2. — 19.
1e. John i. 1 3 times, 2.
1e.— 4 1st (No. 1a, L ℵ.)
1e.— 4 2nd.
2. — 6.
1e.— 8, 9, 10, 15 twice, 28, 30, 40, 44.
2. — ii. 1 1st.
1e.— 1 2nd.
1a.— 9.
1e.— 13.
1a.— 17.
1e.— 23, 25. [26.
1e.— iii. 1, 23 twice, 24,
1e.— iv. 6 twice, 46 1st.
1e.— v. 1, 5, 9.
1a.— 13, 15.
1e.— 35.
1e.— vi. 4, 10.
2. — 17, 21.
1e.— 22.
1a.— 24.
1e.— 62.
6. — 71.
1e.— vii. 2, 12, 39, 42.
2. — 43.
1e.— viii. 44.
2. — 58.
1e.— ix. 8, 14, 16, 24.
1d.— 25, whereas...W.
2. — x. 19, 22 1st.
1e.— 22 2nd.
1e.— xi. 1, 2, 6 2nd, 18, 30, 32, 38.

1e. John xi. 41 (ap.)
1e.— 55.
1e.— xii. 1, 2, 6.
1a.— 9.
1d*— 17, that...W.
1e.— xiii. 5, 23, 30.
1c*— xvii. 5.
1e.— xviii. 1, 10, 13 twice, 14, 15, 16, 18, 40.
1e.— xix. 14, 19, 20 twice, 23, 31 twice, 41, 42.
1d.— xx. 1, when...W.
1e.— 7.
1a.— 14.
1e.— 24.
1a.— xxi. 4.
1a.— 7 1st.
1e.— 7 2nd.
1a.— 12.
2. Acts i. 16, which...W.
1e.— 17.
2. — 19.
2. — 26, when...W.
1e.— ii. 24.
1e.— iii. 10.
1e.— iv. 3.
2. — 4.
1e.— 22.
1c*— 32.
1e.— 33.
3. — 34 (No. 1e, L ℵ.)
3. — v. 4.
2. — 7 1st.
1d.— vii. 2, when...W.
1e.— 9.
1d*— 12.
1e.— 20 2nd, 22.
2. — 29, 38.
1e.— viii. 1 1st.
2. — 1 2nd.
2. — 8.
1c*— 9 2nd.
1e.— 16, 28, 32.
1e.— ix. 9, 10.
2. — 19.
1a.— 26.
1e.— 28, 33, 36 2nd.
1d.— 38 1st, forasmuch as...W.
1a.— 38 2nd.
1d.— 39 2nd, while...
2. — ix. 42. [W.
1c.— x. 1 (om. All.)
2. — 4, 25.
1e.— 38.
1e.— xi. 21, 24.
1e.— xii. 5, 6.
1a.— 9 1st.
2. — 9 2nd, Was done.
4. — 15.
2. — 18 1st, as soon as it W.
1e.— 18 2nd, 20.
2. — 23.
1d*— xiii. 1 1st (with κατά), lit. *in Antioch, throughout the existing Church.*
1e.— 7, 46.
1e.— xiv. 12.
1d*.— 13, which...W.
2. — xv. 39.
1e.— xvi. 1.
3. — 3.
2. — 26.
2. — 35, when...W.
1e.— xvii. 1.
1c†— xviii. 3.
1e.— 25.
1c*— 28.
1c‡— xix. 1, while...W.
1e.— 16.
2. — 17.
1e.— 32.
1a.— 34.
1e.— xxi. 3.
1b.— 33.
7. — 35, so it W.

6. Acts xxi. 37.
8. —— xxii. 3.
2. ——— 17.
1a.——— 29 2nd.
1a.—— xxiii. 5.
2. ——— 12, when...W.
1a.——— 27, 34.
1d*—— xxiv. 24, which ...W.
2. —— xxv. 15, when...W.
2. —— xxvi. 4, when...W.
2. ——— 19.
1a.——— 26.
1e.—— xxvii. 8.
1d.——— 9 2nd, when...W.
3. ——— 12, because...W (lit. *being*.)
2. ——— 39, 42.
1c*—— xxviii. 6.
1d. Rom. iv. 10, when...W.
3. ——— 19.
1a.——— 21.
1e.——— 13.
2. —— xv. 8.
2. 1 Cor. ii. 3.
1e.—— x. 4.
2. —— xv. 10.
1e.—— xvi. 12.
2. 2 Cor. i. 18 (No. 1a, G∾L T Tr A ℵ.)
2. ——— 19 1st & 2nd.
2. —— iii. 7 1st.
1e.—— v. 19.
1d.—— viii. 9, though ...W.
1e. Gal. ii. 11 2nd.
2. —— iii. 17, which W.
2. ——— 24.
8. —— iv. 28, as...W.
2. 1 Thes. ii. 1.
1d. 2 Thes. ii. 5, when ...W.
1d* 1 Tim. i. 13, who...W.
2. —— ii. 14.
2. 2 Tim. i. 17, when...W.
2. —— iii. 9.
2. Heb. ii. 2.
1d* —— iii. 2 1st.
— ——— 2 2nd (*καί, also*.)
1c*—— xi. 4.
1e.——— 38.
1e.—— xii. 21.
1e. Jas. i. 24.
1e.—— v. 17.
1e. 1 John i. 1, 2.
1e.—— iii. 12.
1e. Rev. i. 4, 8.
2. ——— 9, 10, 18.
2. —— iv. 2 1st.
1e.——— 3 (*ap.*)
1e.——— 8.
1e.—— v. 11.
2. —— vi. 12, there...W.
2. —— viii. 1.
1e.—— x. 10 1st.
2. —— xi. 13.
1e.——— 17.
6. —— xii. 5.
2. ——— 7.
1e.—— xiii. 2.
2. —— xvi. 10.
2. ——— 18 1st (*om.* G→)
2. ——— 18 2nd.
1a.——— 21.
1e.—— xvii. 8 twice, 11.
1a.—— xxi. 1.
1e.——— 18 (*om.* L A.)
1e.——— 21.

WASH (-ED, -ING.)

1. *νίπτω*, to wash some part of the body, *as the face, hands, or feet*; (*so* lxx. *for* רחץ, Gen. xviii. 4; xliii. 31; Ex. xxx. 20; Deut. xxi. 6; 1 Sam. xxv. 41), (*see under No.* 5.)

2. *ἀπονίπτω*, (*No.* 1, *with ἀπό*, away from, *prefixed*) to wash off. *In N.T., mid.*, to wash off from and for one's self, (*a symbolical action of innocence. See* Deut. xxi. 6, 7; and Josephus, Ant. iv. 8, 16), (*non occ.*)

3. *λούω*, to bathe, *used only of* the whole body; (lxx. *for* רחץ, Lev. viii. 7; Ruth iii. 3); *hence*, to cleanse, purify; (lxx. *for* רחץ, Is. i. 16), (*see under No.* 5.)

4. *ἀπολούω*, (*No.* 5, *with ἀπό*, away from, *prefixed*) to wash off by bathing. *In N.T., mid.*, to wash off *or* from one's self by bathing, cleanse from, wash away; (lxx. *for* התרחץ, Job ix. 30; *cf.* Ps. li. 2, 7; Is. i. 16; Jer. iv. 14.)

5. *πλύνω*, to wash inanimate things, *as nets, but esp. clothes*, to rinse; (lxx. *for* כבס, Gen. xlix. 11; Ex. xix. 10; Lev. xiv. 9; Numb. xix. 7, 10.)

[These words are to be carefully distinguished, *esp. in* John xiii. 10, where the Lord's teaching entirely turns upon their meanings. One verse (in lxx.) Lev. xv. 11, gives, and contains, all three words. "And whomsoever he toucheth that hath the issue, and hath not *rinsed* (*No.* 1) his hands in water, he shall *wash* (*No.* 5) his clothes, and *bathe* (*No.* 3) himself in water and be unclean until the even." So John xiii. 10, "He that is *washed* (*No.* 3) needeth not save to wash (*No.* 1) his feet"; *i.e.* he that is bathed, needs only the washing of his feet, and so in the spiritual truths Jesus was teaching, he that has tasted the enjoyment of the provision of the atonement of the brazen altar, needs only the sanctification of the brazen laver, which was "for the priests to wash in." In other words, our *atonement* can never be repeated, our *cleansing* must be a daily work, as the feet (our "walk") need a constant washing.]

6. *ἀποπλύνω*, (*No.* 5, *with ἀπό*, away from, *prefixed*) to wash off or out, *spoken only of washing inanimate things*, to wash thoroughly; (lxx. *for* כבס, 1 Sam. xix. 24; שטף, Ezek. xvi. 9), (*non occ.*)

7. *βαπτίζω*, to dip *or* immerse, *spoken of ships, etc.*; to wash, cleanse by washing. *Mid. and aor. pass., as here*, to wash one's self, perform ablution; (lxx. *for* טבל, 2 Kings v. 14, *cf.* verse 10, where it is רחץ, and *λούω*, (*No.* 3) *cf.* also Lev. xi. 25, 28, 40; Numb. xix. 18.)

8. *βρέχω*, *trans.*, to wet, wet on the surface, to moisten; *hence, intrans.*, to rain; (lxx. *for* המסה, Ps. vi. 7; מסס, Is. xxxiv. 3; טהר, Ezek. xxii. 24.)

1. Matt. vi. 17.
1. —— xv. 2.
2. —— xxvii. 24.
1. Mark vii. 3.
7. —— 4.
6. Luke v. 2 (No. 3, G ~ L T Tr A ℵ.)
8. —— vii. 38, 44.
7. —— xi. 38.
1. John ix. 7 1st (om. Lb.)
1. —— 7 2nd, 11 twice, 15.
1. —— xiii. 5, 6, 8 twice.
3. —— 10 1st.
1. John xiii. 10 2nd.
— —— 12,
— —— 14, twice.
3. Acts ix. 37 part.
3. —— xvi. 33
— —— xxii. 16, see W away.
4. 1 Cor. vi. 11.
1. 1 Tim. v. 10.
3. Heb. x. 22.
3. 2 Pet. ii. 22.
3. Rev. i. 5.
5. —— vii. 14.

WASH AWAY.

4. Acts xxii. 16.

WASHING.

1. *βαπτισμός*, the act of washing, ablution, *with special reference to purification.*

2. *λουτρόν*, a bath; a vessel *or* water for bathing; (lxx. *for* רחצה, Song iv. 2), (*non occ.*)

1. Mark vii. 4, 8 (ap.)
2. Eph. v. 26.
2. Tit. iii. 5.
1. Heb. ix. 10.

WAST.

When not part of another verb or phrase, it is the translation of

1. *ἦς, or ἦσθα*, thou wast, (*2nd pers. sing. pres. ind. of εἰμί, the ordinary verb of existence*);

* *with personal pronoun σύ*, thou.

2. *ἦν, imperfect*, he, she, *or* it was;

* *with article*, the *one who* was.

3. *ὤν, etc., part.*, being.

1* Matt. xxvi. 69.
1* Mark xiv. 67.
3. John i. 48.
1. John xxi. 18.
2* Rev. xi. 17.
2* —— xvi. 5.

WASTE. [noun.]

ἀπώλεια, trans., the losing *or* loss; *intrans.*, destruction, ruin.

Matt. xxvi. 8. | Mark xiv. 4.

WASTE (-ED.) [verb.]

1. *διασκορπίζω*, to scatter throughout, scatter abroad, disperse.

2. *πορθέω*, to lay waste, ravage, destroy, *as a city or country.*

1. Luke xv. 13.
2. Gal. i. 13.
1. Luke xvi. 1.

WATCH. [noun.]

1. *φυλακή*, the act of keeping watch; watch, guards; the place of keeping guard; *also*, the time of a watch. *Gen., among the Hebrews, a division of the night into three watches of four hours each;* (lxx. *for* אשמרה, Judg. vii. 19; Ps. xc. 6); *among the Romans, into four watches of three hours each, and either numbered* 1st, 2nd, 3rd, *and* 4th, *or called ὀψέ* (evening), *μεσονύκτιον* (midnight), *ἀλεκτοροφωνία* (cock-crowing), *πρωΐ* (morning).

(a) Prob. the 1st watch not named because the marriage itself occurs on it; and the 4th not named because the return not likely to be so long delayed.

2. *κουστωδία*, custody, (*the Latin military word* "custodia," guard.)

1. Matt. xiv. 25.
1. —— xxiv. 43.
2. —— xxvii. 65, 66.
2. —— xxviii. 11.
1. Luke ii. 8, pl., marg. *night watches.*
1. —— xii. 38 1st (*κἂν ἐν τῇ δευτέρᾳ κἂν, and if in the second and if,* instead of *καὶ ἐὰν ἔλθῃ ἐν τῇ δευτέρᾳ φυλακῇ, καί, and if he shall come in the second watch, or,* T Tr A ℵ.)
1. Luke xii. 38 2nd.

WATCH (-ED, -ETH, -ING.) [verb.]

1. *γρηγορέω*, to keep awake, to watch; (lxx. *for* עמד, Neh. vii. 3; שקד, Jer. v. 6.)

2. *τηρέω*, to keep an eye upon, to watch *or* observe attentively, keep the eyes fixed upon.

3. *παρατηρέω*, (*No. 2, with παρά*, beside, *prefixed*) to have an eye near, watch closely, *esp. with sinister intent*, (*occ.* Gal. iv. 10.)

4. *ἀγρυπνέω*, to be sleepless, lie awake, (*through care or anxiety*); *hence*, to be watchful of *or* very intent upon *a thing*, (*non occ.*)

5. *νήφω*, to be sober, abstinent, *esp. as to wine.*

1. Matt. xxiv. 42, 43.
1. —— xxv. 13.
1. —— xxvi. 38, 40, 41.
2. —— xxvii. 36, 54.
3. Mark iii. 2.
4. —— xiii. 33.
1. —— 34, 35, 37.
1. —— xiv. 34, 37, 38.
3. Luke vi. 7.
1. —— xii. 37, 39.
3. —— xiv. 1.
3. —— xx. 20.
4. Luke xxi. 36.
3. Acts ix. 24.
1. —— xx. 31.
1. 1 Cor. xvi. 13.
4. Eph. vi. 18.
1. Col. iv. 2.
1. 1 Thes. v. 6.
5. 2 Tim. iv. 5.
4. Heb. xiii. 17.
5. 1 Pet. iv. 7.
1. Rev. iii. 3.
1. —— xvi. 15.

WATCHFUL.

γρηγορέω, see above, No. 1. *Here, part.*, watching.

Rev. iii. 2.

WATCHING (-s.)

ἀγρυπνία, sleeplessness, watching, *implying care and anxiety*, (*non occ.*)

2 Cor. vi. 5. | 2 Cor. xi. 27.

WATER. [noun.]

1. ὕδωρ, water, *used of standing or flowing water.*
   - (a) ὕδωρ ζῶν, living water, *i.e.* springing water.
   - (b) ὕδατα πολλά, many waters, (*pl.*)
   - (c) *Used of the* watery fluid *found in the pericardium.*
2. ποταμός, a river, a stream.

1. Matt. iii. 11, 16.
1. —— viii. 32.
— —— x. 42, see Cold.
1. —— xiv. 28, 29.
1. —— xvii. 15.
1. —— xxvii. 24.
1. Mark i. 8, 10.
1. —— ix. 22, 41.
1. —— xiv. 13.
1. Luke iii. 16.
1. —— vii. 44.
1. —— viii. 24, 25.
1. —— xvi. 24.
1. —— xxii. 10.
1. John i. 26, 31, 33.
1. —— ii. 7, 9 twice.
1. —— iii. 5.
1b. ——— 23.
1. —— iv. 7.
1a. ——— 10, 11.
1. ——— 13, 14 1st, 14 2nd (*ap.*), 14 3rd, 15, 46.
1. —— v. 3 (*ap.*), 4 twice (*ap.*), 7.
1a. —— vii. 38.
1. —— xiii. 5.
1c. —— xix. 34.
1. Acts i. 5.
1. —— viii. 36 twice, 38, 39.
1. —— x. 47.
1. —— xi. 16.
2. 2 Cor. xi. 26.
1. Eph. v. 26.
— 1 Tim. v. 23, see W (drink)
1. Heb. ix. 19.
1. —— x. 22.
1. Jas. iii. 12.
1. 1 Pet. iii. 20.
— 2 Pet. ii. 17, see W (without)
1. —— iii. 5 twice, 6.
1. 1 John v. 6 3 times, 8.
— Jude 12, see W (without)
1. Rev. i. 15.
1. —— vii. 17.
1. —— viii. 11 twice.
1. —— xi. 6.
1. —— xii. 15.
1. —— xiv. 2, 7.
1. —— xvi. 4, 5, 12.
1. —— xvii. 1, 15.
1. —— xix. 6.
1. —— xxi. 6.
1. Rev. xxii. 1, 17.

WATER (DRINK)

ὑδροποτέω, to drink water, be a water-drinker, (*non occ.*)

1 Tim. v. 23.

WATER (WITHOUT)

ἄνυδρος, waterless, dry

2 Pet. ii. 17. | Jude 12.

WATER (-ED, -ETH.) [verb.]

1. ποτίζω, to let drink, to give to drink; *of plants, etc.*, to water, irrigate.

1 Cor. iii. 6, 7, 8.

WATERING (LEAD AWAY TO)

{ ἀπαγαγὼ, to lead *or* conduct away, ποτίζω, to give to drink, } *here, lit.*, leading [*it*] away, give [*it*] drink.

Luke xiii. 15.

WATER-POT (-s.)

ὑδρία, a water-pot, *i.e.* a vessel for drawing, carrying, *or* containing water; (lxx. *for* כד, Gen. xxiv. 14, *etc.*; Judg. vii. 16, 19), (*non occ.*)

John ii. 6, 7. | John iv. 28.

WAVE (-s.)

1. κῦμα, a wave, a billow; (lxx. *for* גל, Job xxxviii. 11; Is. xlviii. 18), (*non occ.*)
2. κλύδων, a dashing *of the sea*, surge; (lxx. *for* סער, Josh, i. 4, 11, 12.)
3. σάλος, motion to and fro, tossing; the rolling sea; (lxx. *for* זעף, Jonah i. 15; מוט, Is. xxiv. 20), (*non occ.*)

1. Matt. viii. 24.
1. —— xiv. 24.
1. Mark iv. 37.
3. Luke xxi. 25.
1. Acts xxvii. 41 (*om.* τῶν κυμάτων, *of the waves*, L T Tr Ab ℵ.)
2. Jas. i. 6.
1. Jude 13.

WAVER (-ETH, -ING.)

διακρίνω, to separate throughout; *here, mid.*, to separate one's self entirely; *also*, to be in separation within one's self, be in strife with one's self, hesitate, waver.

Jas. i. 6 twice.

WAVERING (WITHOUT)

ἀκλινής, not inclining, without bending, not giving way.

Heb. x. 23.

WAX (-ED.) [verb.]

1. γίνομαι, to begin to be, to become.
2. προκόπτω, to drive forwards *as if with repeated strokes*, beat forward, beat ahead, push forward, advance.

1. Luke xiii. 19. | 2. 2 Tim. iii. 13.
1. Heb. xi. 34.

See also, BOLD, COLD, CONFIDENT, GROSS, OLD, RICH, STRONG, WANTON.

WAY (-S.)

(*For various combinations with other words, see below.*)

1. ὁδός, a way, highway, road ; a going, progress ; *metaph.*, manner of action, method of proceeding ; access.
2. πάροδος, (No. 1, *with* παρά, beside, *prefixed*), a way beside, a by-way, a passing by, (*non occ.*)
3. τρόπος, a turning, turn ; *hence*, manner, mode.
4. πορεία, a going, way, journey ; (lxx. *for* מהלך, Jonah iii. 3, 4) ; *hence*, goings, ways, journey of life ; (lxx. *for* הלך, Prov. ii. 7), (*occ.* Luke xiii. 22.)
5. τόπος, place, spot, space ; *also metaph.*, place, *i.e.* opportunity, occasion.

1. Matt. ii. 12, and see W (another)
1. —— iii. 3.
1. —— iv. 15.
1. —— v. 25.
1. —— vii. 13, 14.
1. —— viii. 28.
— —— 30, see W off (a good)
1. —— x. 5.
1. —— xi. 10.
— —— xiii. 4, 19, see W side (by the)
1. —— xv. 32.
1. —— xx. 17.
— —— 30, see W side (by the)
1. —— xxi. 8 twice, 19, 32.
1. —— xxii. 16.
1. Mark i. 2, 3.
— —— iv. 4, 15, see W side (by the)
1. —— viii. 3, 27.
1. —— ix. 33.
1. —— 34 (*om.* Lb.)
1. —— x. 17, 32, 52.
— —— xi. 4, see W meet (in a place where two)
1. —— 8 1st, 8 2nd (*ap.*)
1. —— xii. 14.
1. Luke i. 76, 79.
1. —— iii. 4, 5.
1. —— vii. 27.
— —— viii. 5, 12, see W side (by the)
1. —— ix. 57.
1. —— x. 4.
— —— 31, see W (that)
1. —— xi. 6, marg. (text, *journey.*)
1. —— xii. 58.
— —— xiv. 32, } see W off
— —— xv. 20, } (a great)
— —— xviii. 35, see W side (by the)
— Luke xix. 4, see W (that)
1. —— 36.
1. —— xx. 21.
1. —— xxiv. 32, 35.
1. John i. 23.
1. —— xiv. 4, 5, 6.
1. Acts ii. 28.
1. —— viii. 26, 36, 39.
1. —— ix. 2, 17, 27.
1. —— xiii. 10.
1. —— xiv. 16.
1. —— xvi. 17.
1. —— xviii. 25, 26.
1. —— xix. 9, 23.
1. —— xxii. 4.
1. —— xxiv. 14, 22.
1. —— xxv. 3.
1. —— xxvi. 13.
3. Rom. iii. 2.
1. —— 16, 17.
1. —— xi. 33.
1. 1 Cor. iv. 17.
1. —— xii. 31.
2. —— xvi. 7.
3. Phil. i, 18.
— Col. ii. 14, see W (out of the)
1. 1 Thes. iii. 11.
— 2 Thes. ii. 7, see W (out of the)
1. Heb. iii. 10.
— —— v. 2, see W (be out of the)
1. —— ix. 8.
1. —— x. 20.
5. —— xii. 17 marg. (text, *place.*)
1. Jas. i. 8.
4. —— 11.
1. —— ii. 25.
1. —— v. 20.
1. 2 Pet. ii. 2, 15 twice, 21.
1. Jude 11.
1. Rev. xv. 3.
1. —— xvi. 12.

WAY OFF (A GOOD)

μακράν, long, (*strictly, for* μακρὰν ὁδόν, a long way, a great way, far, far off ; (lxx. *for* רחוק ; Josh. ix. 22 ; Judg. xviii. 7.)

Matt. viii. 30.

WAY OFF (A GREAT)

1. μακράν, *see above.*
2. πόρρω, forwards, far forwards.

2. Luke xiv. 32. | 1. Luke xv. 20.

WAY (ANOTHER)

{ διὰ, through
{ ἄλλης, another
{ ὁδοῦ, way.

Matt. ii. 12.

WAY (BE OUT OF THE)

πλανάω, *here, pass.*, to wander, go astray ; *here, part. with art.*, οἱ πλανώμενοι, those led astray.

Heb. v. 2.

WAY (OUT OF THE)

{ ἐκ, from out of, away out of,
{ μέσου, the midst.

Col. ii. 14. | 2 Thes. ii. 7.

WAY SIDE (BY THE)

{ παρά, along the side of
{ τὴν, the
{ ὁδόν, way.

Matt. xiii. 4, 19. | Mark iv. 4, 15.
—— xx. 30. | Luke viii. 5, 12.
Luke xviii. 35.

WAYS MEET (IN A PLACE WHERE TWO)

{ ἐπὶ, upon
{ τοῦ, the
{ ἄμφοδον, bivium, an open place where two or more ways meet, (*non occ.*) } at the cross-way.

Mark xi. 4.

WAY (THAT)

1. { διὰ, through
{ ἐκείνης, that [*way.*]

2. { ἐν, in / τῇ, the / ὁδῷ, way, } on his way.

2. Luke x. 31.
1. —— xix. 4 (*om.* διά, *through*, G L T Tr A ℵ.)

See also, BRING, BY, ESCAPE, GO, LASCIVIOUS, MANY, OTHER, PERNICIOUS, THAT, TURNED, WHAT.

WE.

WE, is frequently part of the translation of a verb or of a phrase.

When it is represented by a separate word in the Greek it is always emphatic, and is one of these following.

(*For* "WE ARE," "ARE WE," *and various combinations, see below.*)

1. ἡμεῖς, we.
2. ἡμῶν, (*Gen.*) of *or* from us, (*translated* "we" *by being in the* "*genitive absolute.*")
3. ἡμῖν, (*Dat.*) to *or* for us, (*generally after a verb of possession*, "there is to us," *etc.*, *i.e.* we have, *etc.*)
4. ἡμᾶς, (*Acc.*) us, (*generally before an infinitive*, "that we," *or governed by another verb.*)

1. Matt. vi. 12.
1. —— ix. 14.
3. —— xv. 33.
1. —— xvii. 19.
1. —— xix. 27 1st.
3. ——— 27 3rd.
2. —— xxviii. 13.
1. ——— 14.
1. Mark ix. 28.
1. —— x. 28.
1. —— xiv. 58.
1. Luke iii. 14.
3. —— ix. 13 1st.
1. ——— 13 2nd.
1. —— xviii. 28.
1. —— xxiii. 41 1st.
1. —— xxiv. 21.
1. John i. 16.
1. —— iv. 22 1st.
1. —— vi. 42, 69.
1. —— vii. 35.
1. —— viii. 41 1st, 48.
1. —— ix. 21 2nd, 24, 28, 29 1st, 40.
1. —— xii. 34.
1. —— xvii. 11, 22.
1. —— xix. 7.
1. —— xxi. 3.
1. Acts ii. 8 1st, 32.
1. —— iii. 15.
1. —— iv. 9.
4. ——— 12.
1. ——— 20 2nd.
1. —— v. 32.
4. —— vi. 2.
1. ——— 4.
1. —— x. 33, 39, 47.
1. Acts xiii. 32.
1. —— xiv. 15.
4. ——— 22.
1. —— xv. 10.
2. —— xvi. 16.
1. —— xx. 6 1st, 13.
4. —— xxi. 1 1st, 5 2nd.
1. ——— 7 1st.
2. ——— 10 (*om.* L T Tr A), (αὐτῶν, *they*, ℵ.)
1. ——— 12 2nd.
2. ——— 17.
3. ——— 23 2nd.
1. ——— 25.
1. —— xxiii. 15.
1. —— xxiv. 8.
2. —— xxvi. 14.
4. —— xxvii. 1.
2. ——— 18.
4. ——— 20, 26.
2. ——— 27.
1. —— xxviii. 21.
3. ——— 22.
4. Rom. iii. 8 2nd.
2. —— v. 6, 8.
1. —— vi. 4 2nd.
4. ——— 6.
4. —— vii. 6 3rd (*om.* Lb Trb.)
1. —— viii. 23 (*om.* L Tr ℵ.)
1. —— xv. 1.
1. 1 Cor. i. 23.
1. —— ii. 12 1st, 16.
1. —— iv. 8, 10 3 times.
1. —— viii. 6 twice.
1. —— ix. 11 twice, 12 1st, 25.
4. 1 Cor. x. 6.
1. —— xi. 16.
1. —— xii. 13 1st.
1. —— xv. 30, 52.
4. 2 Cor. i. 4 1st.
1. ——— 6 2nd.
4. ——— 8 3rd.
1. —— iii. 18.
1. —— iv. 11, 13 2nd.
2. ——— 18.
4. —— v. 10.
1. ——— 16 1st, 21.
2. —— vii. 5 1st.
4. —— viii. 4 (*om.* δέξασθαι ἡμᾶς, G L T Tr A ℵ, i.e. *of us with much intreaty the gift and, instead of us with much intreaty that we would receive the gift and take upon us.*)
4. ——— 6.
1. —— ix. 4 1st.
1. —— x. 7, 13.
1. —— xi. 12, 21.
1. —— xiii. 4 1st, 6, 7 twice, 9 2nd.
1. Gal. i. 8 1st.
1. —— ii. 9, 15, 16 1st.
1. —— iv. 3 1st.
1. ——— 28 (ὑμεῖς, *you*, L T Tr A.)
1. Gal. v. 5.
4. Eph. i. 4, 12.
1. —— ii. 3.
4. ——— 5.
3. —— vi. 12 (ὑμῖν, *you*, L Trm A*.)
1. Phil. iii. 3.
1. Col. i. 9 1st, 28 1st.
4. 1 Thes. i. 8.
1. —— ii. 13, 17.
1. —— iii. 6, 12.
1. —— iv. 15 2nd, 17 1st.
4. 2 Thes. i. 4.
1. —— ii. 13.
1. Tit. iii. 5.
4. Heb. ii. 1 1st.
1. ——— 3 1st.
1. —— iii. 6 1st.
3. —— iv. 13.
3. —— v. 11.
2. —— x. 26 1st.
1. ——— 39.
3. —— xii. 1.
1. ——— 25 1st.
4. —— xiii. 6.
4. Jas. i. 18.
3. —— v. 17.
1. 2 Pet. i. 18 1st.
1. 1 John iii. 14 1st, 16 2nd.
1. —— iv. 6 1st, 10, 11, 14, 16, 17 2nd, 19.
1. 3 John 8, 12.

WE...ARE and ARE WE.

ἐσμέν, (*1st pers. pl. pres. ind. of* εἰμί, to be) we are, are we.

* *with the pronoun* ἡμεῖς, we, (*emph.*)

Mark v. 9.
Luke ix. 12.
—— xvii. 10.
John ix. 28, 40*.
—— xvii. 22* (*om.* ἐσμέν, *are*, T Tr A ℵ.)
Acts ii. 32*.
—— iii. 15*.
—— v. 32*.
—— x. 39* (*om.* ἐσμέν, *are*, G L T Tr A ℵ.)
—— xiv. 15*.
—— xvi. 28.
—— xvii. 28.
—— xxiii. 15*.
Rom. vi. 15.
—— viii. 12, 16.
—— xii. 5.
—— xiv. 8.
1 Cor. iii. 9.
—— x. 17 1st, 22.
1 Cor. xv. 19.
2 Cor. i. 14, 24.
—— ii. 15, 17.
—— iii. 5.
—— x. 11 1st.
—— xiii. 6*.
Gal. iii. 25.
—— iv. 28* (ἐστέ, *ye are*, L T Tr A.)
——— 31.
Eph. ii. 10.
—— iv. 25.
—— v. 30.
Phil. iii. 3*.
1 Thes. v. 5.
Heb. iii. 6*.
—— x. 10, 39*.
1 John ii. 5.
—— iii. 2, 19.
—— iv. 6*, 17*.
—— v. 19, 20.

WE BE.

ἐσμέν, we are, (*see above.*)

John viii. 33.

WE CAN NOT.

{ οὐκ, not, / ἐστί, it is, } it is not [*needful, etc.*]

Heb. ix. 5.

WE HAVE OUR BEING.

ἐσμέν, we are.

Acts xvii. 28.

WE HAVE TO DO.

{ ἡμῖν, to us, / ὁ, the, / λόγος, account, } *is* our account.

Heb. iv. 13.

WE KNOW.

{ γνωστόν, known / ἐστίν, it is / ἡμῖν, to us.

Acts xxviii. 22.

WE OURSELVES.

1. αὐτοί, selves, our selves.
2. ἡμεῖς, we.
3. { αὐτοί, (*No.* 1) / ἡμεῖς, (*No.* 2) } we ourselves.

1. Luke xxii. 71. | 1. 2 Cor. i. 4.
1. John iv. 42. | 1. Gal. ii. 17.
3. Rom. viii. 28. | 2. Tit. iii. 3.

WE TO DO WITH THEE (WHAT HAVE)

{ τί, what / ἡμῖν, to us / καὶ, and / σοί, to thee.

Matt. viii. 29. | Mark i. 24.
Luke iv. 34.

WEAK.

1. ἀσθενής, without strength, infirm, feeble, weak; *hence*, sick, wanting strength *or* power.
2. ἀσθενέω, to be weak *or* ill, *i.e.* be usually so, to be feeble.
3. ἀδύνατος, not able, not powerful, not strong; deficient in strength *or* power.

1. Matt. xxvi. 41. | 2. 1 Cor. viii. 12 part.
1. Mark xiv. 38. | 1. — ix. 22 3 times.
2. Acts xx. 35 part. | 1. — xi. 30.
3. Rom. xv. 1. | 1. 2 Cor. x. 10.
1. 1 Cor. iv. 10. | 1. Gal. iv. 9.
1. — viii. 7, 10. | 1. 1 Thes. v. 14.
2. — 11 part. | 1. 1 Pet. iii. 7.

WEAK (BE)

2. Rom. iv. 19. | 2. 2 Cor. xi. 21.
2. — viii. 3. | 2. — 29 twice.
2. — xiv. 1, 2. [G~LTℵ) | 2. — xii. 10.
2. 1 Cor. viii. 9 part. (No. 1, | 2. — xiii. 3, 4, 9.

WEAK (BE MADE)

2. Rom. xiv. 21 (*om.* ἢ σκανδαλίζεται ἢ ἀσθενεῖ, *or is offended, or is made weak,* G→T Trmb ℵ.)

WEAK THINGS.

{ τὰ, the *things,* / ἀσθενῆ, *see No.* 1, *above,* } the weak things.

1 Cor. i. 27 (*ap.*)

WEAKER.

ἀσθενεστέρος, *comp. of No.* 1, *above.*

1 Pet. iii. 7.

WEAKNESS.

1. ἀσθένεια, want of strength, infirmity, weakness, feebleness.
2. { τὸ, the / ἀσθενές, weak, } that which *is* weak.

2. 1 Cor. i. 25. | 1. 2 Cor. xii. 9.
1. — ii. 3. | 1. — xiii. 4.
1. — xv. 43. | 2. Heb. vii. 18.
1. Heb. xi. 34.

WEALTH.

εὐπορία, prosperity, well-living, (*from* εὐπορέω, to live well, be prosperous), (*non occ.*)

Acts xix. 25.

WEALTH (ANOTHER'S)

{ τὸ, the *thing* / τοῦ, of the / ἑτέρου, other, (*different*) } which *is* the other's.

1 Cor. x. 24.

WEAPON (-S.)

ὅπλον, an instrument, implement *of an artisan. In N.T. only pl.,* τὰ ὅπλα, *and used of a soldier,* instruments, etc., of war, weapons, arms, armour, (*occ.* Rom. xiii. 12; 2 Cor. vi. 7.)

John xviii. 3. | Rom. vi. 13, marg. (text, *instrument.*)
2 Cor. x. 4.

WEAR (-ETH, -ING; WARE.)

1. φορέω, (*a frequentative form of* φέρω, to bear, *implying the repetition and continuance of the simple action of bearing*) to bear about *as with or on one's self; hence,* to wear.

2. *ἐνδιδύσκω*, to clothe in *a garment*, *here*, *mid.*, to clothe one's self in.

1. Matt. xi. 8. | 1. John xix. 5.
2. Luke viii. 27. | 1. Jas. ii. 3.
— 1 Pet. iii. 3, see Wearing.

WEAR AWAY.

κλίνω, to incline, bend down; *spoken of the day, or the sun*, to decline; (*so* lxx. *for* ירד, Judg. xix. 11; נטה, Judg. xix. 8; פנה, Jer. vi. 4.)

Luke ix. 12.

WEARINESS.

κόπος, a beating; the being beat out, weariness.

2 Cor. xi. 27.

WEARING.

περίθεσις, a putting round, *as of ornaments, chains, etc.*, (*non occ.*)

1 Pet. iii. 3.

WEARY (-IED.)

ὑπωπιάζω, to give a blow under the eyes, to beat the face black and blue; *hence*, to beat out, make succumb, make give in through being beaten, (*occ.* 1 Cor. ix. 27.)

Luke xviii. 5.

WEARY (BE)

ἐκκακέω, to turn out a coward, *i.e.* to lose one's courage; to despond, lose heart *in view of trial or evils.*

Gal. vi. 9. [L T Tr A א.)
2 Thes. iii. 13, marg. *faint* (*ἐγκακέω, to act as a coward,*

WEARIED (BE)

1. *κοπιάω*, to be beat out; *here, perf.*, having become beaten out.

2. *κάμνω*, to work one's self weary, be weary (*or even* sick), (*occ.* Jas. v. 15; Rev. ii. 3.)

2. Heb. xii. 3. | 1. John iv. 6.

WEATHER (FAIR)

εὐδία, serene sky, fair in the heavens, fine weather, (*non occ.*)

Matt. xvi. 2.

WEATHER (FOUL)

χειμών, rain; storm with rain; rainy weather.

Matt. xvi. 3.

WEDDING.

γάμος, a wedding, nuptials, *i.e.* the nuptial solemnities; (lxx. *for* משתה, Gen. xxix. 22; Esth. ii. 18.)

Matt. xxii. 3, 8, 10, 11, 12. | Luke xii. 36.
Luke xiv. 8.

WEEK.

σάββατον, rest, a lying by from labour. Heb. שבת, Sabbath. "The first of the sabbath" is the first day after the sabbath, (*the title for "Sunday" in most languages*) *i.e.* the first day of the week; "twice in the week," (Luke xviii. 12) *is* twice of the sabbath, *i.e.* twice *in the days* after the sabbath.

* *denotes the pl. rendered by the singular.*

Matt. xxviii. 1*. | Luke xxiv. 1*.
Mark xvi. 2*, 9 (ap.) | John xx. 1*, 19*.
Luke xviii. 12. | Acts xx. 7*.
1 Cor. xvi. 2*.

WEEP (-EST, -ING; WEPT.)

1. *κλαίω*, to lament, *not only by shedding tears, but also by every outward expression of grief*, bewail, mourn for, (*occ.* Rev. xviii. 9.)

2. *δακρύω*, to shed tears, weep, (*non occ.*)

3. { *γίνομαι*, to become, arise, *κλαυθμός*, *see below*, } *lit.*, wailing arose.

1. Matt. ii. 18. | 1. John xi. 31, 33 twice.
1. — xxvi. 75. | 2. — 35.
1. Mark v. 38, 39. | 1. — xvi. 20.
1. — xiv. 72, marg. (with *ἐπιβάλλω*, *weep abundantly, or begin to weep.* | 1. — xx. 11 twice, 13, 15.
| 1. Acts ix. 39.
| 3. — xx. 37.
| 1. — xxi. 13.
1. — xvi. 10 (ap.) | 1. Rom. xii. 15 twice.
1. Luke vi. 21, 25. | 1. 1 Cor. vii. 30 twice.
1. — vii. 13, 32, 38. | 1. Phil. iii. 18.
1. — viii. 52 twice. | 1. Jas. iv. 9.
1. — xix. 41. | 1. — v. 1.
1. — xxii. 62. | 1. Rev. v. 4, 5.
1. — xxiii. 28 twice. | 1. — xviii. 11, 15, 19.

WEEPING.

κλαυθμός, a wailing, *not merely with tears, but with every outward expression of grief.*

Matt. ii. 18. | Matt. xxiv. 51.
— viii. 12. | — xxv. 30.
— xxii. 13. | Luke xiii. 28.

WEIGHT.

1. βάρος, weight, *in reference to its pressure; not the load that has to be borne*, but *the* weight, *in reference to its cause, i.e.* greatness, fulness, abundance.

2. ὄγκος, a prominence, protuberance, swelling; *hence*, incumbrance, (*non occ.*)

1. 2 Cor. iv. 17. | 2. Heb. xii. 1.
Rev. xvi. 21, see Talent.

WEIGHTIER MATTER.

βαρύτερα, weightier, more weighty; *hence*, more important.

Matt. xxiii. 33.

WEIGHTY.

βορύς, heavy, weighty; *hence*, important.

2 Cor. x. 10.

WELL (-s.) [noun.]

1. πηγή, a fountain, source, spring.

2. φρέαρ, a well *or* pit *dug in the earth*.

[*No.* 1 need not be *No.* 2, and *No.* 2 may be *No.* 1. Though both are distinct, they may be combined.]

1. John iv. 6 twice. | 1. John iv. 14.
2. —— 11, 12. | 1. 2 Pet. ii. 17.

WELL. [adverb.]

(*For various combinations with other words, see below.*)

1. καλῶς, (*adv. of* καλός, beautiful, *see* "GOOD," *No.* 2) handsomely, beautifully; *as to manner*, well, *i.e.* becomingly, suitably, properly; *as to duty*, well, *i.e.* excellently; *as to effect, etc.*, aptly.

2. καλός, beautiful, becoming, well-suited, (*see* "GOOD," *No.* 2.)

3. εὖ, well, (*opp. to* κακῶς, evilly); happily, fortunately, well off; *with care and diligence implied*, properly, cleverly, rightly.

4. ἀγαθός, worthy of admiration, admirable; *hence*, good, good of its kind, (*see* "GOOD," *No.* 1)

1. Matt. xii. 12.
1. —— xv. 7.
1. Mark vii. 6, 37.
1. —— xii. 28, 32.
1. Luke vi. 26.
3. —— xix. 17 (εὖγε, *good! or well done!* L T Tr A.)
1. —— xx. 39.
1. John iv. 17.
1. —— viii. 48.
1. —— xiii. 13.
1. —— xviii. 23.
1. Acts x. 33.
3. —— xv. 29.
1. —— xxviii. 25.
4. Rom. ii. 7.
1. Rom. xi. 20.
1. 1 Cor. vii. 37, 38.
1. —— xiv. 17.
1. 2 Cor. xi. 4.
1. Gal. iv. 17.
1. —— v. 7.
2. —— vi. 9.
3. Eph. vi. 3.
1. Phil. iv. 14.
1. 1 Tim. iii. 4, 12, 13.
1. —— v. 17.
1. Jas. ii. 8.
1. —— 13 marg. (text, *in a good place.*)
1. —— 19.
1. 2 Pet. i. 19.
1. 3 John 6.

WELL (DO)

1. ἀγαθοποιέω, to do good, (*see* "GOOD," *No.* 1) *not merely to work good, but actually* to do and perform some good thing *or* work.

2. σώζω, (*here, pass.*) to be safe, be safe *from danger, loss, or destruction.*

2. John xi. 12. 1. 1 Pet. ii. 20 part.
1. 1 Pet. iii. 6 part.

WELL (THAT DOETH)

ἀγαθοποιός, doing good, beneficent, (*non occ.*)

1 Pet. ii. 14.

WELL DOING.

ἀγαθοποιΐα, well doing, (*non occ.*)

1 Pet. iv. 19.

WELL DOING (FOR)

ἀγαθοποιέω, (*see* "WELL (DO)," *No.* 1) *here part., lit., as* doers of good.

1 Pet. iii. 17.

WELL DOING (IN)

καλοποιέω, to do well, do excellently, *i.e.* properly, aptly, thoroughly, etc., (*non occ.*)

2 Thes. iii. 13 part.

WELL DOING (WITH)

ἀγαθοποιέω, *see* "WELL DOING (FOR)"

1 Pet. ii. 15 part.

WELL DONE.

εὖ, *see* "WELL," *No.* 3.

Matt. xxv. 21, 23.

WELL (FULL)

καλῶς, *see* "WELL," *No.* 1.

Mark vii. 9.

WELL (VERY)

1. κάλλιων, better, *i.e.* more excellently, (*comp. of* "WELL," *No.* 1.)
2. βελτίων, better, *comp. of* ἀγαθός, (*see* "WELL," *No.* 4), (*non occ.*)

1. Acts xxv. 10. | 2. 2 Tim. i. 18.

See also, DRUNK, KNOW, PLEASE, REPORT, STRICKEN.

WELL BELOVED.

ἀγαπητός, beloved, dear; dearly-beloved.

Mark xii. 6. | 3 John 1. | Rom. xvi. 5.

WELL PLEASING.

εὐάρεστος, well-pleasing, acceptable.

Phil. iv. 18. | Col. iii. 20.

WELL PLEASING (THAT WHICH IS)

{ τὸ, the thing,
{ εὐάρεστον, well-pleasing.

Heb. xiii. 21.

WENT, WENTEST.

See, GO.

WERE.

(FOR ALL THERE W., THAT W., THEN W., WHICH W., WHILE...W., WHO W., ALMOST (W).)

When not part of another word or phrase it is the translation of one of these following.

1. εἰμί, I am, (*the ordinary state of existence.*)
   (a) ἐστί, he, she, it, is, (*3rd pers. sing. pres. ind.*)
   (b) εἰσί, they are, (*3rd pers. pl. pres. ind.*)
   (c) *subjunctive*, may be.
   (d) *optative*, might be.
   (e) *infinitive*, εἶναι, to be.
   * *with Acc.*, that...is, *etc.*
   † *with* ἐν τῳ, in the...being, *etc.*
   ‡ *with* διὰ τὸ, on account of the ...being, *etc.*
   (f) ὤν, οὖσα, ὄν, being, (*participle.*)
   (g) *imperfect*, ἦσαν, *etc.*, they were, *etc.*
2. γίνομαι, to come into being, to be born, to become, to arise, to happen.
3. ὑπάρχω, to begin, to start; to begin to be, (*referring to original state or existence.*)
4. ἔχω, to have.
5. μέλλω, to be on the point of, to be about to.
6. σύνειμι, to be with, be joined *or* linked with; *of persons*, to live with, have intercourse with.
7. οὔτω, so, thus, under these circumstances *or* conditions.

1g. Matt. iv. 18.
1g. —— xiv. 21.
1g. —— xv. 38.
1g. —— xxii. 8 2nd, 25.
1g. —— xxiv. 38 1st.
1g. —— xxv. 2 1st.
1g. —— xxvi. 43.
1g. Mark i. 16.
1g. —— ii. 15.
1f. —— —— 26, which W.
1g. —— iv. 36.
1g. —— v. 13 1st (*om.* G ⇉ T Tr A ℵ.)
1g. —— vi. 31, 34, 44.
1g. —— viii. 9.
1g. —— ix. 4.
1g. —— —— 6 (No. 2, G ~ L T Tr A ℵ.)
1g. —— x. 32 1st.
1g. —— xii. 20.
1g. —— xiv. 4.
1g. —— —— 21 (*om.* Lb T Trb A.)
1g. —— —— 40.
1g. —— xv. 40.
2. Luke i. 2, which W.
1g. —— —— 6, 7.
1e† —— ii. 6 1st, while W.
1g. —— —— 8.
1d. —— iii. 15.
1g. —— iv. 20 2nd, 25, 27.
2. —— —— 36.
1g. —— v. 10, 17 twice.
1f. —— vi. 3, which W (*om.* L Tr ℵ.)
1g. —— vii. 39.
1g. —— viii. 40.
1g. —— ix. 14.
6. —— —— 18.
1g. —— —— 30, 32 2nd.
2. —— xiii. 2, 4.
3. —— xvi. 14, who W.
1b. —— xviii. 9 (*marg. as being.*)
1g. Luke xx. 29.
2. —— xxiv. 5, 22, 37.
1g. —— —— 53.
1g. John i. 24 2nd.
1g. —— ii. 6.
1g. —— iii. 19.
1b. —— vi. 64.
1c. —— —— 65.
1g. —— viii. 39 (ἐστέ, *ye are*, G L Tr A ℵ.)
1g. —— —— 42.
1g. —— ix. 33.
1f. —— —— 40, which W.
1g. —— —— 41.
1g. —— x. 6 (ἦ, *it may be*, Tr.)
1g. —— —— 41.
1f. —— xi. 31, which W.
1g. —— xii. 16, 20.
1g. —— xv. 19.
1g. —— xvii. 6.
1g. —— xviii. 30, 36.
1g. —— xix. 11.
1g. —— xx. 19, 26.
1g. —— xxi. 2, 8 1st.
1f. —— —— 11, for all there [W.
1g. Acts i. 15.
1g. —— ii. 1, 2, 5, 44.
1g. —— iv. 6 1st.
1b. —— —— 13.
1g. —— —— 31 1st*, 32.
3. —— —— 34.
2. —— v. 12 1st.
1g. —— —— 12 2nd.
3. —— viii. 16.
3. —— x. 12.
1f. —— xi. 1, that.
1g. —— —— 20 1st.
1g. —— xii. 3, 12.
1g. —— xiii. 1.
2. —— —— 5.
1g. —— —— 48 2nd.
1f. —— xvi. 3, which W.
1g. —— —— 12.

1b. Acts xvi. 38.
1g.—— xvii. 11 1st.
4. ——— 11 2nd.
1g.—— xviii. 3 (*ap.*), 14.
1g.—— xix. 7, 14.
2. ——— 28.
1f.——— 31, which W.
1. —— xx. 8 twice.
1g.——— 16 (*εἴη*, *it might be*, L Tr A ℵ.)
1f.——— 34.
1f.—— xxi. 8.
5. ——— 27, almost (W)
1f.—— xxii. 5, which W.
1f.——— 9 1st, that W.
2. ——— 9 2nd (*om.* "*and were afraid*," G⇉L T Tr Ab ℵ.)
6. ——— 11.
1a.—— xxiii. 6.
1g.——— 13.
4. —— xxiv. 9.
2. —— xxvi. 29.
1e‡—— xxvii. 4.
2. ——— 36, then W.
1g.——— 37 (*ἤμεθα*, *we were*, L T Tr A ℵ.)
3. —— xxviii. 7.
1f. Rom. iv. 17 (*ὡς ὄντα*, *as though they were.*)
1f.—— v. 6, 8, 10 1st.
1g.—— vi. 17, 20 twice.
1g.—— vii. 5 1st.
1e*—— ix. 3, that W.
2. —— xvi. 7.
1g. 1 Cor. vi. 11.
1e*—— vii. 7, that W.
1a.—— vi. 14 (neut. pl.)
1g. 1 Cor. x. 1.
2. ——— 6.
1g.—— xii. 2 1st, 19 1st.
1g. Gal. ii. 6.
1g.—— iv. 3 twice.
1f. Eph. ii. 1, who W.
1g.——— 3, 12.
1f.——— 13, who W.
1g.—— v. 8.
1g. Phil. iii. 7.
1f. Col. i. 21.
2. 1 Thes. i. 5, 7.
2. —— ii. 7, 8 2nd.
1g.—— iii. 4.
1g. 2 Thes. iii. 10.
1g. Tit. iii. 3.
1g. Heb. ii. 15.
1g —— vii. 11.
1b. ——— 21.
1b & 2.——— 23, lit. *are* [*made.*
1g.—— viii. 4.
1b.—— xi. 13 2nd.
1g. 1 Pet. ii. 25.
2. 2 Pet. i. 16.
1f.——— 18.
2. —— ii. 1.
7. —— iii. 4.
1g.——— 5.
1g. 1 John ii. 19 1st.
1b.——— 19 2nd.
1g.—— iii. 12.
2. Rev. viii. 5.
1g.—— ix. 8, 10 (*κάι*, *and*, L T Tr A ℵ), (*om.* G∾)
2. —— xi. 13 1st, 15, 19.
2. —— xvi. 13 twice.
1g.—— xviii. 23 1st.

See also, AS, BE.

WERT.

When not part of another verb or phrase, it is the translation of

εἴης, thou mightest be, (*2nd pers. sing. pres. opt. of εἰμί*, to be.)

Rev. iii. 15 (*ἦς*, *thou mayest be*, G L T Tr A ℵ.)

WEST.

δυσμή, (*usually only pl.*) the going down, the setting *as of the sun;* (lxx. *for* בוא, Gen. xv. 12, etc.; מבוא, Deut. xi. 30.) *Hence, used of* the west; (*so*, lxx. *for* מערב, Ps. lxxv. 6; Is. xliii. 4; lix. 19; מבור, Ps. l. 2; cxiii. 3; Mal. i. 11), (*non occ.*)

Matt. viii. 11.
—— xxiv. 27.
Luke xii. 54.
—— xiii. 29.
Rev. xxi. 13.

See also, NORTH, SOUTH.

WHALE.

κῆτος, any large fish; *hence, Eng.*, cetacea; (lxx. *for* דג גדול, Jon. ii. 1), (*non occ.*)

Matt. xii. 40.

WHAT, WHAT?

"WHAT" is frequently part of some phrase, and very generally the translation of the relative pronoun, *ὅς, ἥ, ὅ*, who, which, what, that, etc.

In all other cases, WHAT is the translation of one of these words following.

(*For various combinations with other words and phrases, see below.*)

1. *τίς, τί*, who? which? what? (*Lat.*, quis, quæ, quid?); (lxx. *τίς for* מי, *τί for* מה.)
   (a) *with the Indicative mood, relating to some actual matter of fact.*
   (b) *with the Subjunctive, expressing something objectively possible, something which may or should take place.*
   (c) *with the Optative, expressing something subjectively possible, something simply conceived in the mind.*
   (d) *with ἄρα*, what then?
2. *οἷος*, of what kind *or* sort. what, such as.
3. *ποῖος*, what? of what kind *or* sort?
4. *ὅσος*, how great, how much, how many; as great as, as much as.
5. *πόσος*, how great? how much?
6. { *τίνι*, with what / *λόγῳ*, discourse.
7. *οὕτω*, in this manner, on this wise; so! thus!
8. *ποταπός*, of what kind, sort, *or* manner? *a later corruption of ποδαπός*, from what country? whence?
9. *ἤ*, or.
10. *γάρ*, for.

1. Matt. v. 46, 47.
1a.—— vi. 3.
1b.——— 25 1st.
1b.——— 25 2nd (*om.* G⇉ℵ)
1b.——— 25 3rd, 31 twice.
1. —— vii. 9.
1. —— viii. 29.
1a.—— ix. 13.
1b.—— x. 19 1st.
1a.——— 19 2nd (*ap.*)
1. —— xi. 7, 8, 9.
1a.—— xii. 3, 7.
1. ——— 11.
1. Matt. xvi. 26 twice.
1. —— xvii. 25.
1. —— xix. 16, 20, 27.
1. —— xx. 21.
1a.——— 22.
1. ——— 32.
1a.—— xxi. 16.
3. ——— 23, 24, 27.
1. ——— 28, 40.
1. —— xxii. 17, 42.
1. —— xxiv. 3.
3. ——— 42, 43.
1. —— xxvi. 15.

7. Matt. xxvi. 40.
1. —— 65, 66.
1a.—— 70.
1. —— xxvii. 4, 22, 23.
1. Mark i. 24. [thing.
—— 27 1st, see W
1. —— 27 2nd (ap.)
1a.—— ii. 25.
1a.—— iv. 24 1st.
3. —— 30 (No. 1b, L T Tr A ℵ.)
1. —— v. 7, 9.
1a.—— 14.
1. —— vi. 2, 24.
4. —— 30 twice.
1. —— viii. 36, 37.
1b.—— ix. 6.
1a.—— 10.
1. —— 16, 33.
1. —— x. 3, 17, 36.
1a.—— 38.
1. —— 51.
1. —— xi. 5.
3. —— 28, 29, 33.
1. —— xii. 9.
—— xiii. 1 1st, see W manner of.
8. —— 1 2nd.
1. —— 4.
1b.—— 11.
1a.—— xiv. 36 twice.
1b.—— 40.
1. —— 63, 64.
1a.—— 68.
1. —— xv. 12, 14.
1. Luke iii. 10, 12, 14.
1. —— iv. 34, 36.
1. —— v. 22.
1c.—— vi. 11.
3. —— 32, 33, 34.
1. —— vii. 24, 25, 26, 31.
1c.—— viii. 9.
1. —— 28, 30.
1. —— ix. 25.
1. —— x. 25, 26.
—— xii. 11 1st, see W thing.
1b.—— 11 2nd, 22 twice, [29 twice.
3. —— 39.
1. —— 49.
1. —— xiii. 18.
1. —— xiv. 31.
1. —— xv. 4, 8.
1c.—— 26.
1. —— xvi. 3.
1b.—— 4.
1a. —— xviii. 6.
1. —— 18.
1c.—— 36.
1. —— 41.
1b.—— xix. 48.
3. —— xx. 2, 8.
1. —— 13, 15, 17.
1. —— xxi. 7.
1. —— xxii. 71.
1. —— xxiii. 22.
1b.—— 31.
1a.—— 34 (ap.)
1. John i. 21, 22, 38.
1. —— ii. 4, 18, 25.
1. —— iv. 27.
1. —— v. 12.
1. —— vi. 6, 9.
1b.—— 28.
1. —— 30 twice.
1a.—— vii. 51.
1. —— viii. 5 (ap.)
1. —— ix. 17, 26.
1. —— xi. 47, 56.
1b.—— xii. 27.
3. —— 33.
1b.—— 49 twice.
1a.—— xiii. 12.
1a.—— xv. 15.
1. —— xvi. 17, 18 1st.
1a.—— 18 2nd.
1a.—— xviii. 21.
1. —— 29.

3. John xviii. 32.
1. —— 35, 38.
3. —— xxi. 19.
1. —— 21.
1c. Acts ii. 12.
1. —— 37.
3. —— iv. 7 twice.
1. —— 16.
1a.—— v. 35.
1. —— vii. 40.
3. —— 49 1st.
1. —— 49 2nd.
1. —— viii. 36.
1. —— ix. 6 1st (ap.)
1a.—— 6 2nd (ὅστις, *whatsoever*, G∾L T Tr A [ℵ.)
1. —— x. 4, 6 (ap.)
1c.—— 17.
1. —— 21, 29.
1. —— xi. 17.
1ad.—— xii. 18.
4. —— xv. 12.
1. —— xvi. 30.
1c.—— xvii. 18.
1a.—— 19.
1c —— 20.
1. —— xix. 3, 35.
1. —— xxi. 13, 22, 33.
1. —— xxii. 10, 26.
1. —— xxiii. 19.
3. —— 34.
1. Rom. iii. 1 twice, 3, 5, 9
3. —— 27.
1. —— iv. 1, 3.
1. —— vi. 1, 15, 21.
1. —— vii. 7.
1b.—— viii. 26.
1a.—— 27.
1. —— 31.
1. —— ix. 14, 30.
1. —— x. 8.
1a.—— xi. 2.
1. —— 4, 7, 15.
1a.—— xii. 2.
1. 1 Cor. ii. 11.
1. —— iv. 7, 21.
1. —— v. 12.
9. —— vi. 16, 19.
1. —— vii. 16.
1. —— ix. 18.
1. —— x. 19.
10.—— xi. 22 1st.
1b.—— 22 2nd.
1. —— xiv. 6, 15.
1a.—— 16.
9. —— 36.
6. —— xv. 2, marg. by *what speech.*
1. —— 29, 32.
3. —— 35.
1. 2 Cor. vi. 14 twice, 15 twice, [16.
5. —— vii. 11 1st.
1. —— xii. 13.
1. Gal. iv. 15, marg. (text, [*when.*)
1. —— 30.
1a. Eph. i. 18 twice, 19.
1. —— iii. 9.
1a.—— 18.
1. —— iv. 9.
1a.—— v. 10, 17.
1. Phil. i. 18, 22.
1a. Col. i. 27.
1. 1 Thes. ii. 19.
1. —— iii. 9.
1. —— iv. 2.
2. 2 Tim. iii. 11.
1. Heb. ii. 6.
1. —— vii. 11.
1. —— xi. 32.
1. —— xii. 7.
1. —— xiii. 6.
1. Jas. ii. 14, 16.
3. —— iv. 14.
1. 1 Pet. i. 11 1st.
—— 11 2nd, see W manner of.
3. —— ii. 20.
1. —— iv. 17.

1a. 1 John iii. 2.
1a. Rev. ii. 7, 11, 17, 29.
3. —— iii. 3.
1a. Rev. iii. 6, 13, 22.
1. —— vii. 13.
1. —— xviii. 18.

WHAT (BUT)

1. { ἐάν, if / μή, not / τι, anything } except perchance.

2. { ὅσα, as many things, / δέ, but, howbeit.

1. John v. 19. | 2. Jude 10.

WHAT EVERY MAN.

{ τίς, who, / τί, what, } who [*should take*] what (*or* anything); *followed here by indicative. See No.* 1a.

Mark xv. 24.

WHAT MANNER.

οἷος, *see* "WHAT," *No.* 2.

Luke ix. 55 (ap.)

WHAT MANNER OF.

1. ποταπός, *see* "WHAT," *No.* 8.

2. ποῖος, *see* "WHAT," *No.* 3.

3. ὁποῖος, what, of what kind *or* sort.

4. { τίς, what / ἄρα, then, therefore, *or* now.

1. Matt. viii. 27.
1. Mark xiii. 1.
1. Luke i. 29.
4. —— 66.
1. Luke vii. 39.
3. 1 Thes. i. 9.
2. Jas. i. 24.
2. 1 Pet. i. 11.
1. 1 John iii. 1.

WHAT MANNER OF MAN.

1. { τίς, / ἄρα, } *see above, No.* 4.

2. οἷος, *see* "WHAT," *No.* 2.

1. Mark iv. 41. | 2. 1 Thes. i. 5.

WHAT MANNER OF PERSON.

ποταπός, *see* "WHAT," *No.* 8.

2 Pet. iii. 11.

WHAT SORT (OF)

ὁποῖος, what, of what kind *or* sort.

1 Cor. iii. 13.

WHAT THINGS.

1. ὅστις, (*here, neut. pl.*) whatsoever things.

2. ποῖος, (*here, neut. pl.*) what things?

2. Luke xxiv. 19. | 1. Phil. iii. 7.

WHAT THINGS SOEVER.

1. { ἅ, what things, ἄν, perchance.

2. ὅσα, as many things as.

3. { ὅσα, as many things as, ἄν, perchance.

3. Mark xi. 24 (om. ἄν, G∺L T Tr A ℵ.) | 1. John v. 19 (om. ἄν, L [Trb.) 2. Rom. iii. 19.

WHAT WAS BEFALLEN TO.

τὰ, the things, (*lit.* the things *of* [*i.e. relating to*] *the demonized men.*)

Matt. viii. 33.

WHAT WAY.

ποῖος, what? of what kind or sort? what way? *i.e.* by what means.

Luke v. 19.

WHAT IS IT WHICH?

τί, what?

Matt. xxvi. 62. | Mark xiv. 60.

WHAT IS THAT?

τί, what?

John xxi. 22, 23.

WHAT MANNER OF?

τί, what?

Luke xxiv. 17. | John vii. 36.

WHAT THEN?

{ τί, what? γάρ, for, because, } what for? what then?

Phil. i. 18.

WHAT THING?

τί, what?

Mark i. 27. | Luke xii. 11, sub. (Trb.) John x. 6, ind.

WHAT HAVE I TO DO WITH THEE?

{ τί, what
ἐμοὶ, to me
καὶ, and
σοί, to thee.

Mark v. 7. | Luke viii. 28. John ii. 4.

WHAT HAVE WE TO DO WITH THEE?

{ τί, what
ἡμῖν, to us
καὶ, and
σοί, thee.

Matt. viii. 29. | Mark i. 24. Luke iv. 34.

See also, BEFALLEN, GREAT, INTENT? MANNER, MEANS, PLACE, PURPOSE? WHY?

WHATSOEVER.

1. ὅς, who, which, what, that, *introducing a dependent clause, and marking its close relation to the leading preposition.*

   (a) *with* ἄν, perhaps, perchance, *giving the stamp of uncertainty and mere possibility, and indicating a dependence on circumstances; hence,* ὅς ἄν, what...perchance, *i.e.* whatsoever.

   (b) *with* ἐάν, *implying objective possibility, and expressing the prospect of decision, or a condition which experience must determine.*

2. ὅσος, how great, how much, how many; as great as, as much as, as many as. *Here, neut. pl.,* ὅσα, how many and great things.

   (a) *with* ἄν, perhaps, perchance, (*see* (a) *above.*)

   (b) *with* ἐάν, *implying a condition which experience must decide, i.e. an objective future possibility,* (*see* (b) *above.*)

3. πᾶς, all, the whole, every kind of; *neut.*, every thing, (*see* "ALL," *No.* 1.)

   (a) *with* ὅς, who, which.

4. { ὅστις, (*here, neut.*) anything which, whatever.
ἄν, perchance, perhaps, *implying a dependence on circumstances.* }

5. τι, something, a certain thing, anything.

6. { ὁποῖος, of what kind or sort,
πότε, at one time, some time or other, } whatever at one time.

7. { ὅς, which, what,
δήποτε, in fine, in short. }

2a. Matt. vii. 12.
1a. — x. 11.
1b. — xiv. 7 (No. 1a, L Tr A.)
1b. — xv. 5.
3. —— 17.
1b. — xvi. 19 1st (No. 1a, L Tr A), (No. 2, Lm.)
1b. —— 19 2nd (No. 1a, Tr.)
2. — xvii. 12.
2b. — xviii. 18 1st (No. 2a, L Tr A.)
2b. —— 18 2nd.
1b. — xx. 4, 7 (*ap.*)
2a. — xxi. 22 (No. 2b, T Tr.)
2a. — xxiii. 3 (No. 2b, T ℵ.)
2. — xxviii. 20.
1b. Mark vi. 22, 23.
1b. — vii. 12.
— —— 18, see W thing.
2. — ix. 13.
2. — x. 21.
1b. —— 35.
1b. — xi. 23 (*om.* ὅ ἐάν εἴπῃ, *whatsoever he saith,* G ⇉ T Tr Ab ℵ.)
1b. — xiii. 11.
2. Luke iv. 23.
1a. — ix. 4.
1a. — x. 5, 8, 10.
4. Luke x. 35.
2. — xii. 3.
4. John ii. 5.
7. — v. 4 (*ap.*)
2a. — xi. 22.
4. — xiv. 13.
2. — xv. 14 (ἅ, *what things,* L T Tr A ℵ.)
4. —— 16.
2a. — xvi. 13 (*om.* ἄν, L T Tr A ℵ.)
2a. —— 23 (ἄν τι, *perchance anything,* L T Tr A), (ὅ τι ἄν, Lm), (ὅ ἄν ℵ.)
2. — xvii. 7.
2a. Acts iii. 22.
2. — iv. 28.
3a. Rom. xiv. 23.
— — xv. 4, see W things
1a. — xvi. 2.
3. 1 Cor. x. 25.
3. —— 27.
5. —— 31.
6. Gal. ii. 6.
1b. — vi. 7 (No. 1a, L Tr.)
3. Eph. v. 13.
— — vi. 8, see W good things, etc.
— Phil. iv. 8, see W things.
1b. 1 John iii. 22.
3. — v. 4.
1a. —— 15 (No. 1b, T ℵ.)
1b. 3 John 5.
3. Rev. xviii. 22.

WHATSOEVER...THING.

1. ὅ ἐάν τι, *here, lit.,* whatsoever [*good*] thing [*each man shall have done*]. (*Received text.*)

but,

ὅ ἄν, whatsoever [*good each man,* etc.] G~Tr.

ἐάν τι, if, [*he shall have done*] any [*good thing*] Lm T A.

ἐάν, if, [*he shall have done any good*] ℵ.

2. ὅσα, how great *things,* as many *things* as.

3. Mark vii. 18.
2. Rom. xv. 4.
1. Eph. vi. 8.
2. Phil. iv. 8 6 times.

WHEAT.

σῖτος, wheat; *and gen. for* grain, corn; (lxx. *for* בר, Gen. xli. 49; xlii. 3; דגן, Gen. xxvii. 28, 37; Is. xxxvi. 17), (*occ.* Mark iv. 28; Acts vii. 12.)

Matt. iii. 12.
— xiii. 25, 29, 30.
Luke iii. 17.
— xvi. 7.
— xxii. 31.
John xii. 24.
Acts xxvii. 38.
1 Cor. xv. 37.
Rev. vi. 6.
— xviii. 13.

WHEN (or WHEN?)

When is frequently part of the translation of a participle or of a phrase. When it is the translation of a separate Greek word it is one of those below.

(*For various combinations, such as* "when...was," *etc., see below.*)

1. ὅταν, when, *with the accessory idea of uncertainty or possibility, i.e.* whensoever, if ever, in case that; *gen. with the subjunctive, referring to an oft-repeated or possible action in the present or future time.*

   (a) *with the indicative, in narration of an actual event, past or future.*

2. ὅτε, when, *relating to an actual event, to something actually taking place,* (*correlative with No.* 6.)

3. ὡς, in which way, in what way; *and hence,* as, so as, how; *before a clause implying time,* in which time, at what time, when.

4. { ἐν, in,
τῷ, the,
with the inf. } during, while.

5. { ἐν, in
ᾧ, which, } in which *time.*

6. ποτέ, when, whenever, at some time, once, *of time past or future.*

7. πότε, when? at what time? *used in direct questions.*

   (a) *in an indirect question.*

8. ἐάν, if, *implying a condition which experience must determine, i.e. an objective possibility, and referring therefore always to something future; here, with subj. pres., implying probability, which the future will show whether it is really so or not.*

9. ἐπάν, whenever, so soon as.

10. ἐπεί, as, *spoken of time and motive; of time*, as, when, after that; *of motive*, as, since.

11. ἡνίκα, when, whenever; *here, with* ἄν, perchance, *i.e.* at whatever time *the thing may happen*.

12. καθώς, according as.

13. { καὶ, even / ὅταν, when, (*see No.* 1) } even when.

14. μετά, with; *here, with Acc.*, after.

15. οὗ, (*Gen. of* ὅς, *used as adv.*) where.

16. τότε, then, at that time.

17. ὁπότε, when, at what time, (*used of what actually took place at a certain time*, (*non occ.*)

9. Matt. ii. 8.
1. —— v. 11.
1. —— vi. 2, 5, 6, 16.
2. —— vii. 28.
1. —— ix. 15.
2. ——— 25.
1. —— x. 19, 23.
2. —— xi. 1.
2. —— xii. 3.
1. ——— 43.
4. —— xiii. 4.
2. ——— 26.
1. ——— 32.
2. ——— 48, 53.
1. —— xv. 2.
2. —— xvii. 25 (ἐλθόντα εἰς, *coming into*, instead of ὅτε εἰσῆλθεν, *when he was come*, L T Tr A ℵ.)
2. —— xix. 1.
1. ——— 28.
2. —— xxi. 1, 34.
1. ——— 40.
1. —— xxiii. 15.
7a. —— xxiv. 3.
1. ——— 15, 32, 33.
1. —— xxv. 31.
7. ——— 37, 38, 39, 44.
2. —— xxvi. 1.
1. ——— 29.
4. —— xxvii. 12.
2. Mark i. 32.
1. —— ii. 20.
2. ——— 25.
1a. —— iii. 11.
2. —— iv. 10.
1. ——— 15, 16, 29, 31, 32.
2. —— vii. 17.
2. —— viii. 19, 20.
1. ——— 38.
2. —— xi. 1.
2. ——— 19 (No. 1, T Tr ℵ.)
1. ——— 25.
1. —— xii. 23 (om. ὅταν ἀναστῶσι, *when they shall rise*, G⇄Lᵇ Tr ℵ.)
1. ——— 25.
7. —— xiii. 4 1st.
1. ——— 4 2nd, 7, 11.
2. ——— 12.
1. ——— 14, 28, 29.
7a. ——— 33, 35.
2. —— xv. 20, 41.

3. Luke i. 41.
2. —— ii. 21, 22.
4. ——— 27.
3. ——— 39.
2. ——— 42.
4. —— iii. 21.
2. —— iv. 25 1st.
3. ——— 25 2nd.
3. —— v. 4.
4. ——— 12.
13. ——— 35.
17. —— vi. 3 (No. 2, L Tr ℵ.)
2. ——— 13.
1. ——— 22 twice, 26.
10. —— vii. 1 (ἐπειδή, *because now*, instead of ἐπεί δέ, *now when*, L T Tr A.)
3. ——— 12.
1. —— viii. 13.
4. ——— 40.
1. —— ix. 26.
4. ——— 36, 51.
4. —— x. 35.
3. —— xi. 1.
1. ——— 2, 21.
9. ——— 22.
1. ——— 24, 34 1st.
9. ——— 34 2nd.
1. ——— 36.
1. —— xii. 11.
7a. ——— 36 2nd.
1. ——— 54, 55.
3. ——— 58.
1. —— xiii. 28.
2. ——— 35 (om. ἥξει ὅτε, *the time come when*, Trᵇ Aᵇ ℵ.)
1. —— xiv. 8, 10 twice, 12, 13.
1. —— xvi. 4, 9.
1. —— xvii. 10.
7a. ——— 20 2nd.
2. ——— 22.
3. —— xix. 5.
4. ——— 15.
3. ——— 29, 41.
3. —— xx. 37.
7. —— xxi. 7 1st.
1. ——— 7 2nd, 9, 20, 30, 31.
5. —— xxii. 7.
2. ——— 14.
6. ——— 32.
2. ——— 35.
2. —— xxiii. 33.
1. ——— 42.

2. John i. 19.
3. —— ii. 9.
1. ——— 10.
2. ——— 22.
3. ——— 23.
3. —— iv. 1.
2. ——— 21, 23.
1. ——— 25.
3. ——— 40.
2. ——— 45.
5. ——— 52.
1. —— v. 7.
2. ——— 25.
3. —— vi. 12, 16.
2. ——— 24.
7. ——— 25 2nd.
3. —— vii. 10.
1. ——— 27, 31.
3. —— viii. 7 (ap.)
1. ——— 28, 44.
2. —— ix. 4.
2. ——— 14 (ἐν ᾗ ἡμέρᾳ, *on the day when*, instead of ὅτε, *day when*, L T Tr A ℵ.)
1. —— x. 4.
3. —— xi. 6, 32, 33.
2. —— xii. 16.
2. ——— 17 (ὅτι, *because*, G L T Trᵐ.)
2. ——— 41 (ὅτι, *because*, L T Tr A ℵ.)
1. —— xiii. 19.
2. ——— 31.
1. —— xiv. 29.
1. —— xv. 26.
1. —— xvi. 4, 13, 21.
2. ——— 25.
2. —— xix. 6, 8, 23, 30.
3. ——— 33.
2. —— xx. 24.
2. —— xxi. 15, 18 1st.
1. ——— 18 2nd.
2. Acts i. 13.
4. —— ii. 1.
4. —— iii. 19.
3. —— v. 24.
14. —— vii. 4.
12. ——— 17.
3. ——— 23.
2. —— viii. 12, 39.
3. —— x. 7.
2. —— xi. 2.
2. —— xii. 6.
16. —— xiii. 3.
3. ——— 29.
3. —— xiv. 5.
3. —— xvi. 15.
3. —— xvii. 13.
3. —— xviii. 5.
3. —— xix. 9.
3. —— xx. 14, 18.
2. —— xxi. 5.
3. ——— 12, 27.
2. ——— 35.
3. —— xxii. 11.
2. ——— 20.
1. —— xxiii. 35.
1. —— xxiv. 22 2nd.
3. —— xxv. 14.

3. Acts xxvii. 1, 27.
2. ——— 39.
3. —— xxviii. 4.
2. ——— 16.
1. Rom. ii. 14.
2. ——— 16 (ᾗ, *in which*, L Trᵐ A.)
4. —— iii. 4.
2. —— vi. 20.
2. —— vii. 5.
1. —— xi. 27.
2. —— xiii. 11.
14. 1 Cor. xi. 25.
1. —— xiii. 10.
2. ——— 11 twice.
8. —— xiv. 16.
1. ——— 26.
1. —— xv. 24 twice, 27, 28, 54.
1. —— xvi. 2, 3, 5, 12.
11. 2 Cor. iii. 15, 16.
1. —— x. 6.
1. —— xii. 10.
1. —— xiii. 9.
2. Gal. i. 15.
2. —— ii. 11, 12, 14.
2. —— iv. 3, 4.
4. ——— 18.
2. Phil. iv. 15.
1. Col. iii. 4.
2. ——— 7.
1. —— iv. 16.
2. 1 Thes. iii. 4.
1. —— v. 3.
— 2 Thes. i. 7, see W the Lord Jesus shall be revealed.
1. ——— 10.
2. —— iii. 10.
1. 1 Tim. v. 11.
2. 2 Tim. iv. 3.
1. Tit. iii. 12.
1. Heb. i. 6.
15. —— iii. 9.
3. —— vii. 10.
1. Jas. i. 2.
2. 1 Pet. iii. 20.
1. 1 John ii. 28 (No. 8, L T Tr A ℵ.)
8. —— iii. 2.
1. —— v. 2.
2. Jude 9 (No. 16, L.)
2. Rev. i. 17.
1a. —— iv. 9.
2. —— v. 8.
2. —— vi. 1, 3, 5, 7, 9, 12.
2. —— viii. 1 (No. 1, L T Tr A.)
1. —— ix. 5.
2. —— x. 3 2nd, 4.
1. ——— 7.
1. —— xi. 7.
2. —— xii. 13.
1. —— xvii. 10.
1. —— xviii. 9.
1. —— xx. 7 (μετά, *after*, inst. of ὅταν τελεσθῇ, *when ... are expired*, G∾)
2. —— xxii. 8.

WHEN AS YET HE HAD NO...

{ οὐκ, not / ὄντος, being / αὐτῷ, to him, } [*there*] not being to him, *i.e.* he not having.

Acts vii. 5.

WHEN...IS.

ὤν, being,

John iii. 4. | Gal. vi. 3. | Rom. v. 13.

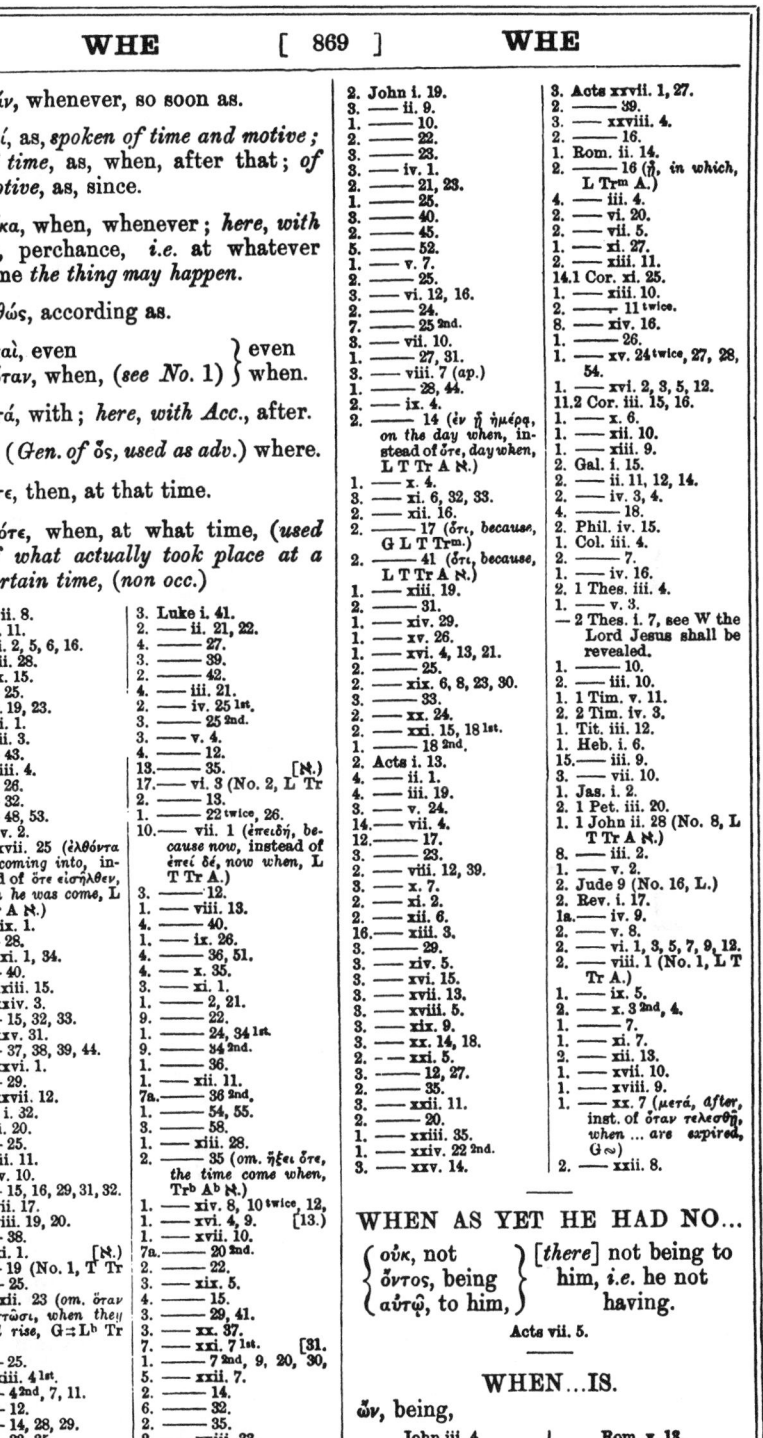

WHEN ONCE.

1. { ἀφ', from
οὐ, } whatsoever [*time.*]
ἄν, }

2. { ποτέ, when,
ἅπαξ, one time.

1. Luke xiii. 25.
2. 1 Pet. iii. 20, see Once.

WHEN THE DAY WAS FAR SPENT.

{ ὥρας, hours,
πολλῆς, many,
γενομένης, having taken place, *i.e.* arrived, elapsed.

Mark vi. 35.

WHEN THE LORD JESUS SHALL BE REVEALED.

{ ἐν, in
τῇ, the
ἀποκαλύψει, unveiling, appearing, revelation,
τοῦ, of the
Κυρίου, Lord
Ἰησοῦ, Jesus.

2 Thes. i. 7.

WHEN THEY DWELT AS STRANGERS.

{ ἐν, in [*their*]
παροικίᾳ, sojourning.

Acts xiii. 17.

WHEN...WAS (or WERE)

ὤν, being.

Luke xxii. 53.
—— xxiv. 6.
John i. 48.
—— xx. 1.
Acts vii. 2.
Acts xxvii. 9.
Rom. iv. 10.
—— v. 6, 10.
Eph. ii. 5.
2 Thes. ii. 5.
2 Pet. i. 18.

See also, ALONE, DEAD, LOOK.

WHENCE.

1. πόθεν, (*interrog. adv.*) whence? from whence? (*of place, source, author, cause, or manner.*)

2. ὅθεν, *whence,* (*relat. adv.*) whence, from whence, (*of place, source, ground, motive, etc.*)

3. { ἐξ, out of
οὗ, which [*place.*]

1. Matt. xiii. 54, 56.
1. —— xv. 33.
1. —— xxi. 25.
1. Mark xii. 37.
1. Luke i. 43.
2. —— xi. 24.
1. —— xiii. 25, 27.
1. —— xx. 7.
1. John i. 48.
1. —— ii. 9.
1. —— iii. 8.
1. —— vi. 5.
1. —— vii. 25 twice, 28.
1. —— viii. 14 twice.
1. —— xix. 9.
1. Rev. vii. 13.

WHENCE (FROM)

2. Matt. xii. 44.
1. —— xiii. 27.
1. Mark vi. 2.
1. —— viii. 4.
1. John iv. 11.
1. John ix. 29, 30.
2. Acts xiv. 26.
3. Phil. iii. 20.
2 Heb. xi. 19.
1. Jas. iv. 1.
1. Rev. ii. 5.

WHENSOEVER.

1. ὅταν, when, (*see* "WHEN," *No.* 1.)

2. { ὡς, as, (*see* "WHEN," *No.* 3)
ἐάν, if, (*see* "WHEN," *No.* 8) } whenever (*implying possibility and intention.*)

1. Mark xiv. 7.
2. Rom. xv. 24 (ὡς ἄν, *when perchance,* L T Tr A ℵ.)

WHERE (or WHERE?)

1. ὅπου, where, in which *or* what place.

2. οὗ, (*Gen. of* ὅς, *used as adv.*) where.

3. ποῦ? where? in what place? *gen. in a direct question.*

(a) *in an indirect question.*

4. { ἐν, in
ᾧ, which.

5. { ὅπου, where,
ἐκεῖ, there.

(a) *lit.*, where *they were hearing*—"There *He is.*"

(b) *lit.* where *she is to be nourished,* there, *etc.*

6. ὅθεν, whence, from whence.

7. τίς, what?

3. Matt. ii. 2.
3a.—— 4.
2. —— 9.
1. —— vi. 19 twice, 20 twice, [21.
3a.—— viii. 20.
1. —— xiii. 5.
2. —— xviii. 20.
1. —— xxv. 24 1st.
6. —— 24 2nd.
1. —— 26 1st.
6. —— 26 2nd.
3. —— xxvi. 17.
1. Matt. xxvi. 57.
1. —— xxviii. 6.
2. —— 16.
1. Mark ii. 4.
1. —— iv. 5, 15.
1. —— v. 40.
5a.—— vi. 55 (*om.* ἐκεῖ, *there,* L T Tr[b] ℵ.)
1. —— ix. 44 (*ap.*), 46 (*ap.*), 48.
1. —— xiii. 14.
3. —— xiv. 12, 14 1st.

1. Mark xiv. 14 2nd.
3a. —— 47.
1. —— xvi. 6.
2. Luke iv. 16, 17.
3. —— viii. 25.
3a. —— ix. 58.
3a. —— xii. 17.
1. —— 33, 34.
3. —— xvii. 17, 37.
3. —— xxii. 9.
2. —— 10 (*εἰς ἣν, into which*, L T Tr A ℵ.)
3. —— 11 1st.
1. —— 11 2nd.
1. John i. 28.
3. —— 38, 39.
1. —— iii. 8.
1. —— iv. 20, 46.
1. —— vi. 23, 62.
3. —— vii. 11.
1. —— 42.
1. —— viii. 10 (*ap.*), 19.
3. —— ix. 12.
1. —— x. 40.
1. —— xi. 30, 32.
3. —— 34.
2. —— 41 (*ap.*)
3a. —— 57.
1. —— xii. 1, 26.
1. —— xvii. 24.
1. —— xviii. 1.
1. —— xix. 18, 20, 41.
3a. —— xx. 2.
1. —— 12.
3a. —— 13, 15.
1. —— 19.
2. Acts i. 13.
2. —— ii. 2.
2. Acts vii. 29.
4. —— 33 (*ἐπὶ ᾧ, upon which*, L T Tr A ℵ.)
4. —— xi. 11.
2. —— xii. 12.
4. —— xv. 36.
2. —— xvi. 13.
1. —— xvii. 1.
4. —— xx. 6, 8.
2. —— xxv. 10.
2. —— xxviii. 14.
3. Rom. iii. 27.
2. —— iv. 15.
2. —— v. 20.
2. —— ix. 26.
1. —— xv. 20.
3. 1 Cor. i. 20 3 times.
3. —— xii. 17 twice, 19.
3. —— xv. 55 twice.
2. 2 Cor. iii. 17.
7. Gal. iv. 15, marg. *what?* (No. 3, L T Tr A ℵ.)
2. Col. iii. 1.
1. —— 11.
1. Heb. ix. 16.
1. —— x. 18.
1. Jas. iii. 16.
3. 1 Pet. iv. 18.
3. 2 Pet. iii. 4.
3. Rev. ii. 13 1st.
1. —— 13 2nd & 3rd.
1. —— xi. 8.
1. —— xii. 6.
5b. —— 14 (*ὅπως, so that*, instead of *ὅπου, where*, G∾)
2. —— xvii. 15.
1. —— xx. 10.

See also, EVERY, SEAS, WAYS.

WHEREAS.

1. { ἐν, in
ᾧ, which.
2. ὅπου, where, in which *or* what place.

2. 1 Cor. iii. 3. [*wherein*.
1. 1 Pet. ii. 12, marg.
1. 1 Pet. iii. 16.
2. 2 Pet. ii. 11.

WHEREAS...WAS.

ὤν, being.

John ix. 25.

WHEREAS YE KNOW NOT WHAT SHALL BE ON THE MORROW.

{ οἵτινες, who *are* such as
οὐκ, not, }
ἐπίστασθε, } have not knowledge of
τὸ, the *thing*
τῆς, of the
αὔριον, morrow.

Jas. iv. 14.

WHEREBY.

1. { ἐν, in *or* by
ᾧ which.
2. { διά, through, by means of,
οὗ, of which.
3. { περὶ, concerning
οὗ, which.
4. { πρὸς, respecting } *lit.*, respecting
ὅ, which, } which *ye are able* [*by*] *reading to perceive, etc.*
5. { κατὰ, according to
τί, which.
6. ὅθεν, whence, from whence.
7. τοῦ, of the. *Here, lit.*, "*according to the working* (*or energy*) of the *power which He has* also," etc

7. Luke i. 18.
1. —— 78.
1. Acts iv. 12.
1. —— xi. 14.
3. —— xix. 40.
1. Rom. viii. 15.
1. —— xiv. 21.
2. Gal. vi. 14, marg. (text, *by*.)
4. Eph. iii. 4.
— —— iv. 14, see W one lieth in wait.
1. —— 30.
7. Phil. iii. 21.
2. Heb. xii. 28.
6. 1 John ii. 18.
2. 2 Pet. i. 4.
2. —— iii. 6.

WHEREBY ONE LIETH IN WAIT TO DECEIVE.

{ πρὸς, towards, suited to,
τὴν, the
μεθοδείαν, artifice
τῆς, of
πλάνης, error.

Eph. iv. 14.

WHEREFORE (or WHEREFORE?)

1. διό, on which account, wherefore.
2. ὥστε, so as that, *marking the result; with the indicative, representing the result as a fact; with the inf.*, representing it as a necessary and logical consequence.
3. { διὰ, through } for the sake of this,
τοῦτο, this, } on this account.
4. { διὰ, through } for the sake of which,
ἣν, which, } on which account.
5. { διὰ, for the sake of
ἣν, which
αἰτίαν, cause, *i.e.* reason, motive, *or* ground.
6. οὖν, thereupon, *i.e.* now, then, therefore, *not implying a logical inference, like Nos.* 15 *and* 16, *but merely confirming what has gone before.*

(a) *with μέν*, indeed; the οὖν *looking back to the line of reasoning, the μέν looking forward to the completion of the statement or argument.*

7. ὅθεν, thence, from thence.

8. διατί, wherefore? on what account? why?

9. διόπερ, (*No.* 1, *with* περ, very, *affixed*) on which very account; wherefore, *more emphatic than No.* 1.)

10. τί, (*Acc.*) which? what? *also*, for what cause? why?

11. { τίνος, of what? ἕνεκεν, on account of, } on account of what? for what cause?

12. { χάριν, in favour of, in behalf of, τίνος, of what?

13. { εἰς, unto, for, τί, what? } why? for what reason?

14. { εἰς, unto, for, ὅ, which, } for which, in order to which.

15. ἄρα, therefore, then, consequently; still further, beyond that, (*drawing a logical conclusion.*)

16. ἄραγε, (*No.* 15, *with* γε, at least, *suffixed*) therefore indeed, consequently then.

17. ἐπί, upon.

(a) *with Gen.*, upon and springing from.

(b) *with Dat.*, upon and resting on, on account of, (*marking the ground of the act.*)

(c) *with Acc.*, upon by direction towards, to, for, (*marking the intention of the act.*)

18. ἱνατί, in order that what, to what end, (*marking the final end or purpose.*)

19. { οὗ, of which, χάριν, in favour of, in behalf of, } for which cause.

20. τοιγαροῦν, by certain consequence, consequently.

16. Matt. vii. 20.
18. —— ix. 4.
2. —— xii. 12.
3. —— —— 21.
13. —— xiv. 31.
2. —— xix. 6.
2. —— xxiii. 31.
3. —— —— 34.
6. —— xxiv. 26.
17b. —— xxvi. 50 (No. 17c, G L T Tr A ℵ.)
1. —— xxvii. 8.
1. Luke vii. 7.
19. —— —— 47.
8. —— xix. 23.
10. John ix. 27.
6. Acts i. 21.
6. —— vi. 3 (δή, *indeed*, L), (δέ, *but*, or *now*, T Trm ℵ.)
4. —— x. 21.
1. —— xiii. 35 No. 8, L T Tr A ℵ.)
1. —— xv. 19.
11. —— xix. 32.
6a. —— —— 38.
1. —— xx. 26.
4. —— xxii. 24.
10. —— —— 30.
4. —— xxiii. 28.
1. —— xxiv. 26.
1. —— xxv. 26.
1. —— xxvii. 25, 34.
1. Rom. i. 24.
3. —— v. 12.
2. —— vii. 4, 12.
8. —— ix. 32.
1. —— xiii. 5.
1. —— xv. 7.
6. 1 Cor. iv. 16.
9. —— viii. 13.
2. —— x. 12.
9. —— —— 14.
2. —— xi. 27, 33.
1. —— xii. 3.
9. —— xiv. 13 (No. 1, L T Tr A ℵ.)
2. —— —— 22, 39.
1. 2 Cor. ii. 8.
1. —— v. 9.
2. —— —— 16.
1. —— vi. 17.
15. 2 Cor. vii. 12.
6. —— viii. 24.
8. —— xi. 11.
10. Gal. iii. 19.
2. —— —— 24.
2. —— iv. 7.
3. Eph. i. 15.
1. —— ii. 11.
1. —— iii. 13.
1. —— iv. 8, 25.
1. —— v. 14.
3. —— —— 17.
3. —— vi. 13.
1. Phil. ii. 9.
2. —— —— 12.
6. Col. ii. 20 (*om.* G L T Tr A.)
1. 1 Thes. ii. 18 (No. 8, G∾L T Tr A ℵ.)
1. —— iii. 1.
2. —— iv. 18.
1. —— v. 11.
14. 2 Thes. i. 11.
5. 2 Tim. i. 6 1st.
5. Tit. i. 13.
1. Philem. 8.
7. Heb. ii. 17.
7. —— iii. 1.
1. —— —— 7, 10.
7. —— vii. 25.
7. —— viii. 3.
1. —— x. 5.
1. —— xi. 16.
20. —— xii. 1.
1. —— —— 12, 28.
1. —— xiii. 12.
2. Jas. i. 19 (ἴστε, *ye know*, instead of ὥστε, *wherefore*, G∾L T Tr A), (ἴστω, *know ye*, ℵ.)
1. —— —— 21.
1. —— iv. 6.
1. 1 Pet. i. 13.
6. —— ii. 1.
1. —— —— 6 (No. 8, AV. 1611, G∾L T Tr A ℵ.)
2. —— iv. 19.
1. 2 Pet. i. 10, 12.
1. —— iii. 14.
12. 1 John iii. 12.
3. 3 John 10.
8. Rev. xvii. 7.

WHEREIN.

1. { ἐν, in, ᾧ, (ᾗ, οἷς *or* αἷς) which, (*or* whom).

2. { ἐπὶ, upon ᾧ, which.

3. { εἰς, into, and in, ἥ, which.

4. { διὰ, through, on account of, ἥν, which.

5. { περὶ, about, concerning, οὗ, which.

6. οὗ, where.

1. Matt. xi. 20.
1. —— xxv. 13 (*ap.*)
2. Mark ii. 4 (ὅπου, *where*, G∾L T Tr A ℵ.)
5. Luke i. 4.
2. —— xi. 22.
6. —— xxiii. 53.
1. John xix. 41.
1. Acts ii. 8.
1. —— x. 12.
1. Rom. ii. 1.
1. —— v. 2.
1. —— vii. 6.
1. 1 Cor. vii. 20, 24.
1. —— xv. 1.
1. 2 Cor. xi. 12.

1. Eph. i. 6 (ᾗς, wherewith, G ~ L T Tr A ℵ.)
1. —— ii. 2.
1. —— v. 18.
2. Phil. iv. 10. [in.)
1. Col. ii. 3, marg. (text,
1. —— 12.
1. 2 Tim. ii. 9.
1. Heb. vi. 17.
1. Heb. ix. 2, 4.
1. 1 Pet. i. 6.
1. —— ii. 12, marg. (text, whereas.)
1. —— iv. 4.
1. 2 Pet. iii. 13.
1. Rev. ii. 13 (om. G ⇉ L T Tr A^b,) i.e. in the days of Antipas.
1. —— xviii. 19.

WHEREINSOEVER.

{ ἐν, in
{ ᾧ, what
{ ἄν, perchance.

2 Cor. xi. 21.

WHEREINTO.

{ εἰς, into
{ ὅ, which.

John vi. 22.

WHEREOF.

1. { περὶ, about, concerning,
{ οὗ, which.

2. { ἐξ, out of
{ οὗ, which.

3. { ἐπὶ, upon
{ ᾧ, which.

4. { περὶ, about, concerning,
{ τίνων, what.

5. οὗ, of which.

5. Acts ii. 32.
5. —— iii. 15.
— —— xvii. 19, see W thou speakest.
1. —— xxiv. 13.
3. Rom. vi. 21.
— —— xv. 17, see Glory.
1. 1 Cor. vii. 1.
— 2 Cor. ix. 5, see Notice.
— Phil. iii. 4, see Trust.
4. 1 Tim. i. 7.
2. —— vi. 4.
1. Heb. ii. 5.
2. —— xiii. 10.

WHEREOF THOU SPEAKEST.

{ ὑπὸ, [that] by
{ σοῦ, thee
{ λαλουμένη, is being spoken.

Acts xvii. 19.

WHEREON.

1. { ἐπὶ, upon } (Gen.) *marking the*
{ οὗ, which, } *basis, or local situation.*

2. { ἐπὶ, upon } (Dat.) *marking the*
{ ᾧ, which, } *simple act of rest.*

3. { ἐπὶ, upon } (Acc.) *marking the*
{ ὅν, which, } *downward pressure.*

3. Mark xi. 2.
1. Luke iv. 29.
2. Luke v. 25 (No. 3, G ~ T Tr A ℵ.)
3. Luke xix. 30.

WHERESOEVER.

ὅπου, where.

* *with* ἄν, perchance, *implying uncertainty and dependence on circumstances.*

† *with* ἐάν, if, *implying an objective hypothetical possibility.*

Matt. xxiv. 28†.
—— xxvi. 13†.
Mark ix. 18*.
Mark xiv. 9* (†, T A ℵ.)
—— 14† (*, L Tr A.)
Luke xvii. 37.

WHERETO.

{ εἰς, unto
{ ὅ, what.

Phil. iii. 16.

WHEREUNTO.

1. { εἰς, unto
{ ἣν, which *or* what.

2. ᾧ, to which.

John vi. 22 (ap.)
Acts xiii. 2, see Call.
Col. i. 29.
2 Thes. ii. 14.
1 Tim. ii. 7.
1 Tim. iv. 6, see Attain.
—— vi. 12.
2 Tim. i. 11.
1 Pet. ii. 8.
2 Pet. i. 19.

WHEREUNTO THIS WOULD GROW.

{ τί, what ?
{ ἂν, perchance
{ γινομαι, to become
{ τοῦτο, this, (*opt.*)

} *lit.*, what perchance this might come to.

Acts v. 24.

WHEREUNTO.

τίνι, to what ?

Matt. xi. 16. [L^m T Tr A ℵ.)
Mark iv. 30 (πῶς, *how?* G ~)
Luke vii. 31.
—— xiii. 18, 20.

WHEREUPON.

1. ὅθεν, whence, from whence ; *also, as referring to a cause*, wherefore, whereupon.

2. { ἐν, in, among,
{ οἷς, which *things*.

1. Matt. xiv. 7.
2. Acts xxiv. 18.
2. Acts xxvi. 12.
1. —— 19.
1. Heb. ix. 18.

WHEREWITH.

1. { ἐν, in, *or* with,
{ ᾧ, which.

2. { ἐν, in, *or* with,
τίνι, what.

2. Matt. v. 13.
2. Mark ix. 50.
2. Luke xiv. 34.
— Rom. xiv. 19, see Edify.
1. Eph. vi. 16.
1. Heb. x. 29.

WHEREWITH SOEVER.

{ ὅσα, as many
ἄν, perchance, } as many soever.

Mark iii. 28 (ἐάν, implying less uncertainty, T Tr A.)

WHEREWITH?

τι, something [*on which.*]

Luke xvii. 8.

WHEREWITHAL

See, CLOTHED.

WHETHER.

1. εἴτε, whether; *gen. followed by another εἴτε, which is translated* or, *or* or whether.

(a) *with indicative,*
(b) *with subjunctive,*
(c) *with optative,* } *see No.* 2.

2. εἰ, if, *expressing a merely hypothetical condition apart from all experience.*

(a) *with the indicative, implying a condition or contingency as to which there is no doubt.*

(b) *with the subjunctive, where an action, etc., depends on something future,* if so be, supposing that.

(c) *with the optative, implying that the thing, though assumed as probable, is uncertain and problematical.*

3. τίς, τί, who? which? what?

4. ἐάν, if, *expressing a condition which experience must determine,* i.e. *an objective possibility.*

(a) *with subj., implying uncertainty, with prospect of decision.*

(b) *with indicative, used of a thing certain as if it were uncertain.*

Here, with τε, if it be, if perchance.

5. ὅς, who, which

6. ἤτοι, whether indeed.

7. πότερος, which of two, whether *of two.*

8. { τε, and
καὶ, also, } *here lit., men* and also *women.*

3. Matt. ix. 5.
3. —— xxi. 31.
3. —— xxiii. 17, 19.
2a.—— xxvi. 63.
3. —— xxvii. 21.
2a.——— 49.
3. Mark ii. 9.
2a.—— iii. 2.
2a.—— xv. 36.
— Luke iii. 15, see W or not.
3. —— v. 23.
2a.—— vi. 7.
2a.—— xiv. 28, 31.
3. —— xxii. 27.
2a.—— xxiii. 6.
7. John vii. 17.
2a.—— ix. 25.
5. Acts i. 24.
2a.—— iv. 19.
2a.—— v. 8.
8. —— ix. 2.
2a.—— x. 18.
2c.—— xvii. 11.
2a.—— xix. 2.
2c.—— xxv. 20.
6. Rom. vi. 16.
1a.—— xii. 6, 7, 8.
4a. Rom. xiv. 8 1st.
4a.——— 8 2nd (No. 4b, L.)
4a.——— 8 3rd.
1a. 1 Cor. iii. 22.
2a.—— vii. 16 twice.
2a.—— viii. 5.
2a.—— x. 31.
2a.—— xii. 13 twice.
1a.—— xiii. 8 3 times.
1a.—— xiv. 7.
1a.—— xv. 11.
— 2 Cor. i. 6, see W... or W.
2a.—— ii. 11.
1a.—— v. 9, 10.
— ——— 13, see W...or W.
1a.—— viii. 23.
— —— xii. 2, see W... or W.
1a.——— 3.
2a.—— xiii. 5.
1a. Eph. vi. 8.
1a. Phil. i. 18, 20, 27.
1a. Col. i. 16, 20.
1b. 1 Thes. v. 10.
1a. 2 Thes. ii. 15.
1a. 1 Pet. ii. 13, 14.
2a. 1 John iv. 1.

WHETHER...OR WHETHER.

1a. 2 Cor. i. 6. | 1a. 2 Cor. xii. 2. | 1a. 2 Cor. v. 13.

WHETHER OR NOT.

μήποτε, lest perhaps, whether perhaps.

Luke iii. 15.

WHICH, WHICH?

WHICH is frequently the translation of the article with nouns, adjectives, numerals, *or* participles, "he which, etc.," "that which."

It is also the translation of the relative ὅς, "who" or "which," relating to nouns, sentences, *or* clauses. The occurrences are not given below.

(*For various combinations with other words, see at the end of the first body of references.*)

1. ὅστις, any one who, some one who, whoever; (*differing from* ὅς, *in referring to a subject only generally, not definitely, as one of a class.*)

2. τίς, τί, who? which? what?

(a) *with the indicative mood, relating to some actual matter of fact.*

(b) *with the subjunctive, expressing something objectively possible, something which may or should take place.*

(c) *with the optative, expressing something subjectively possible, something simply conceived in the mind.*

* *with ἄρα*, what then? which then?

3. οἷος, of what kind *or* sort, what, such as.

4. ποῖος, what? of what kind *or* sort? which?

5. ὅσος, how great, how much, how many; as great as, as much as, as many as.

6. { καὶ, and
   αὐτός, he.

7. αὕτη, the same.

2. Matt. vi. 27.
1. —— vii. 15, 24, 26.
1. —— xiii. 52 2nd.
1. —— xvi. 28.
6. —— xix. 2.
1. ——— 12 3 times.
4. ——— 18.
1. —— xx. 1.
1. —— xxi. 33, 41.
1. —— xxii. 2.
4. ——— 36.
1. —— xxiii. 27.
1. —— xxv. 1.
1. —— xxvii. 55.
1. Mark ix. 1.
1. —— xii. 18.
4. ——— 28.
1. Luke i. 20.
1. —— ii. 4, 10.
1. —— vii. 37.
2. ——— 42.
1. —— viii. 3, 15, 26, 43.
1. —— ix. 30.
2c. ——— 46.
2. —— x. 36.
1. ——— 42.
2. —— xi. 5.
1. —— xii. 1.
2. ——— 25.
2. —— xiv. 5, 28.
1. —— xv. 7.
2. —— xvii. 7.
2c* —— xxii. 23.
2a. ——— 24.
1. —— xxiii. 55.
2. John viii. 46.
1. ——— 53.
4. —— x. 32.
2. —— xxi. 20 2nd.
5. ——— 25 1st.
2. Acts vii. 52 1st.
7. —— viii. 26.
5. —— ix. 39.
1. —— x. 47.
1. Acts xi. 20, 28.
1. —— xii. 10.
1. —— xvi. 12, 16, 17.
1. —— xxiii. 21.
1. Rom. ii. 15.
1. —— xvi. 12 (*ap.*)
1. 1 Cor. iii. 17.
1. —— vi. 20 (*ap.*)
1. —— vii. 13.
— 2 Cor. iii. 14, see Veil.
1. —— ix. 11.
1. Gal. iv. 24 twice, 26 2nd.
1. —— v. 19.
1. Eph. i. 23.
1. —— iii. 13.
1. —— vi. 2.
1. Phil. i. 28.
3. ——— 30.
1. —— iv. 3.
1. Col. iii. 5 (ὅ, *which*, G∾L T Tr A ℵ.)
1. —— iv. 11 2nd.
1. 1 Tim. i. 4.
1. —— iii. 15.
1. —— vi. 9.
1. 2 Tim. i. 5.
3. —— iii. 11.
2. Heb. i. 5, 13.
1. —— ii. 3.
2a. —— v. 12.
1. —— viii. 6.
1. —— ix. 2, 9 1st.
1. —— x. 8, 11, 35.
1. —— xii. 5.
1. —— xiii. 7.
1. 1 Pet. ii. 11.
1. 1 John i. 2.
1. Rev. ii. 24.
1. —— ix. 4.
1. —— xi. 8.
1. —— xii. 13.
1. —— xvii. 12 2nd.
1. —— xix. 2.
1. —— xx. 4.

WHICH AM, ART, ETC.

(*Generally the translation of the participle* (ὤν) *of* εἰμί, to be.)

WHICH ARE [or BE] OF ONE'S HOUSEHOLD (THEY)

{ οἱ, the *one's*
  ἐκ, out of,
  τῶν, of the, } those of the.

Rom. xvi. 10, 11.

WHICH ARE [or BE] (THE THINGS)

τά, the things, *lit.*, the things *of Cæsar, etc.; of Jesus, etc.*

Matt. xxii. 21. | Luke xx. 25.
Phil. ii. 21.

WHICH ART, AND WAST, AND ART TO COME.

ὁ, the one
ὤν, being,
καὶ, and
ὁ, the one [*who*]
ἦν, wast,
καὶ, and
ὁ, the
ἐρχόμενος, coming one,
} who art, and who wast, and the coming one.

Rev. xi. 17 (*om.* καὶ ὁ ἐρχόμενος, *and the coming one*, G L T Tr A ℵ.)

WHICH ART, AND WAST, AND SHALT BE.

ὁ, the one
ὤν, being,
καὶ, and
ὁ, the one [*who*]
ἦν, wast,
καὶ, and
ὁ, the
ὅσιος, *the* holy one,
} who art, and who wast, and the holy one.

Rev. xvi. 5 (*om.* καὶ ὁ, *and the* before "holy," G L T Tr A ℵ, i.e. *who art and wast the holy one.*)

WHICH CAUSE (FOR)

διό, wherefore.

Rev. xv. 22. | 2 Cor. iv. 16.

WHICH CONCERN (THE THINGS)

τὰ, the *things; here, with Gen., following, lit.*, the things of.

2 Cor. xi. 30.

WHICH (EVERY...)

{ πᾶς, every [*soul*],
  ὅστις, whatsoever,
  ἄν, perchance.

Acts iii. 23.

WHICH IS, AND WHICH WAS, AND WHICH IS TO COME.

ὁ, the *one*
ὤν, being,
καὶ, and
ὁ, the one [*who*]
ἦν, was,
καὶ, and
ὁ, the
ἐρχόμενος, coming *one*,
— who art, and who wast, and the coming one.

Rev. i. 4, 8.

WHICH IS SPOKEN.

τὸ, the *thing*
ῥηθέν, spoken.

Matt. ii. 17. | Matt. xxii. 31.

WHICH IS TO TRY.

πρὸς, for, with a view to,
πειρασμόν, trying.

1 Pet. iv. 12.

WHICH IS WITH (HE)

ὁ, the *one*
μετὰ, with, in association with.

Matt. xii. 4. | Matt. xxvi. 51.

WHICH MAKE FOR (THE THINGS)

τὰ, the things; *lit.*, the things *of or belonging to.*

Rom. xiv. 19.

WHICH (ON)

ὅπου, where,...
ἐπὶ, upon
αὐτῶν, them.

Rev. xvii. 9.

WHICH (THAT)

εἰ, if
τίς, τί, anything.

Eph. iv. 29.

WHICH (THE LIFE)

ὅ, which; *lit.*, in what respect.

Gal. ii. 20.

WHICH (THE)

1. John xxi. 25.

WHICH (THEY)

1. Rev. i. 7, pl.

WHICH (THOSE THINGS)

ὅσα, as many things
μέν, indeed.

Jude 10.

WHICH THING (-S.)

1. ἅτινα, which, (*pl., see No.* 1, *above.*)
2. ὅ or ἅ, which things.

2. Acts xxvi. 10. | 1. Col. ii. 23.

WHICH WAS, AND IS, AND IS TO COME.

ὁ, the one [*who*]
ἦν, was,
καὶ, and
ὤν, being,
καὶ, and
ὁ, the
ἐρχόμενος, coming *one*,
— which was, and art, and art the coming one.

Rev. iv. 8.

WHICH? (WHAT IS IT)

τί, what?

Matt. xxvi. 62. | Mark xiv. 60.

WHILE.

(*For various combinations with other words, see below.*)

1. ἐν, in / τῷ, the, / *with inf.* — in, during, while (*what the verb relates to is going on.*)
2. ἕως, until, as long as, *marking the continuance of an action up to the time of another action.*
   (a) *with* οὗ, until what time, until when.
3. ὡς, in which way, in what way; *and hence, gen.*, as, so as, how.
4. ἀχρίς, continuedly until, marking the duration *but not determining it.*
   (a) *with* οὗ, so long as, while.
5. ἐν, in / ᾧ, which [*time.*]
6. χρόνος, time, *i.e. in the abstract,* time *as measured by the succession of objects and events.*

(a) χρόνον τινά, some time, a certain time.

7. καιρός, a season, opportunity, occasion.

8. ὅταν, when, whensoever, so often as, *with the accessory idea of uncertainty or possibility.*

9. ὅτε, when, *as relating to an actual event, to something actually taking place.*

10. ὀλίγον, little, (*opp. of* πολύς, much.)

11. μικρόν, little, (*opp. of* μέγας, great.)

1. Matt. xiii. 25.
2. —— xiv. 22.
2a.—— xxvi. 36.
11.—— 73.
5. Mark ii. 19.
10.—— vi. 31.
2. —— 45.
2. —— xiv. 32.
1. Luke i. 8.
1. —— ii. 6.
5. —— v. 34.
7. —— viii. 13.
6. —— xviii. 4.
1. —— xxiv. 15.
3. —— 32 twice.
1. —— 15, 51.
5. John v. 7.
6. —— vii. 33.
2. John ix. 4.
6. —— xii. 35 1st.
2. —— 35 2nd (No. 3, L T Tr A.)
2. —— 36 (No. 3, L T Tr A ℵ.)
9. —— xvii. 12.
3. Acts i. 10.
3. —— x. 17.
1. —— xix. 1.
4a.—— xxvii. 33.
8. 1 Cor. iii. 4.
6a.—— xvi. 7.
4a. Heb. iii. 13.
1. —— 15.
9. —— ix. 17.
10. 1 Pet. v. 10. [Clean.
— 2 Pet. ii. 18, marg. see

WHILES.

{ ἕως, until / ὅτου, when, } whilst.

Matt. v. 25.

WHILE (A GOOD)

{ ἡμέρας, days, / ἱκανάς, sufficient.

Acts xviii. 18.

WHILE (A GREAT)

{ ἐπὶ, upon, / πολύς, much, } for long, *lit., were* long *looking.*

Acts xxviii. 6.

WHILE BEFORE DAY (A GREAT)

{ ἔννυχον, in the night, / λίαν, very, exceedingly.

Mark i. 35.

WHILE (ANY)

πάλαι, long ago.

Mark xv. 44 (ἤδη, *already,* L Tr A.)

WHILE (DURE FOR A)

{ εἰμί, to be / πρόσκαιρος, for a season.

Matt. xiii. 21.

WHILE...IS.

ὤν, being.

Luke xiv. 32.

WHILE...WAS.

ὤν, being.

Luke xxiv. 44. | Acts ix. 39.

WHILE...WERE.

ὤν, being.

Rom. v. 8.

See also, AGO, LITTLE, LONG, MEAN, WORLD.

WHISPERER.

ψιθυριστής, a whisperer; *hence,* a slanderer, (*non occ.*)

Rom. i. 19.

WHISPERING.

ψιθυρισμός, a whispering, (from ψιθυρίζω, to whisper, say in the ear, *esp.,* to whisper what one dares not speak out); *hence,* a secret slandering, (*non occ.*)

2 Cor. xii. 20.

WHIT.

See, EVERY, NOT A.

WHITE. [adj.]

1. λευκός, light, *i.e.* emitting light, bright, brilliant, shining, glittering; *and hence,* radiant white; (lxx. *for* חוּר, Dan. vii. 9; *and* לָבָן, Lev. xiii. 3, 4), (*non occ.*)

2. λαμπρός, radiant, splendid; *of raiment,* sumptuous, magnificent.

1. Matt. v. 36.
1. —— xvii. 2.
— —— xxiii. 27, see the verb, below.
1. —— xxviii. 3.
1. Mark ix. 3 1st.
— —— 3 2nd, see the verb, below.
1. Mark xvi. 5.
1. Luke ix. 29.
1. John iv. 35.
1. —— xx. 12.
1. Acts i. 10.
— —— xxiii. 3, see the verb, below.
1. Rev. i. 14 twice.

1. Rev. ii. 17.
1. — iii. 4, 5, 18.
1. — iv. 4.
1. — vi. 2, 11.
1. — vii. 9, 13.
— Rev. vii. 14, see W [(make)
1. — xiv. 14.
2. — xv. 6.
2. — xix. 8.
1. —— 11, 14 twice.
1. Rev. xx. 11.

WHITE (MAKE)

λευκαίνω, to make white, whiten, bleach; (lxx. *for* הלבין, Ps. li. 9; Is. i. 18.)

Rev. vii. 14.

WHITE (-ED.) [verb.]

1. κονιάω, to whitewash, to wash with slacked lime, (*implying fairness without, but foulness within*); (lxx. *for* שׂיד, Deut. xxvii. 2, 4), (*non occ.*)

2. λευκαίνω, *see* "WHITE (MAKE)"

1. Matt. xxiii. 27. | 2. Mark ix. 3.
1. Acts xxiii. 3.

WHITHER, or WHITHER?

1. ποῦ, where? in what place? *after verbs of motion*, where? to what place? whither?
   (a) *in a direct question followed by the indicative.*

2. ὅπου, (*correl. of No.* 1) where, in which *or* what place; *after verbs of motion*, whither.

3. οὗ, (*Gen. of* ὅς) where; *after verbs of motion*, whither.

4. { εἰς, unto / ἥν, which.

3. Luke x. 1.
3. — xxiv. 28.
1a. John iii. 8.
4. — vi. 21.
1. — vii. 35.
1a.— viii. 14 twice.
2. —— 21, 22.
1a.— xii. 35.
2. — xiii. 33.
1a.John xiii. 36 1st.
2. —— 36 2nd.
2. — xiv. 4.
1a.—— 5.
1. — xvi. 5.
2. — xviii. 20.
2. — xxi. 18 twice.
2. Heb. vi. 20.
1a.— xi. 8.
1a. 1 John ii. 11.

WHITHERSOEVER.

1. ὅπου, where, in which *or* what place.
   (a) *with* ἄν, perhaps, perchance, *giving a stamp of uncertainty, and implying a dependence on circumstances.*
   (b) *with* ἐάν, if, *expressing a possible condition which experience or results will decide.*

2. { οὗ, where / ἐάν, if (*see No.*1b) } wheresoever, whithersoever.

1b.Matt. viii. 19.
1a.Mark vi. 56. [T Tr A.)
1a.Luke ix. 57 (No. 1b, L
2. 1 Cor. xvi. 6.
1a.Jas. iii. 4.
1a.Rev. xiv. 4.

WHO, or WHO? (WHOSE? WHOM?)

"WHO," etc., is generally the translation of the relative ὅς, who, which.

It is also frequently the translation of the article with nouns, adjectives, etc., and of participles, "he who," "they who," etc.

It is often (in 792 instances) the translation of the article repeated after nouns with defining words following, and rendered "who is," etc.

The following are exceptions to the above:—

1. τίς, τί, who? which? what? (*Lat.*, quis, quæ, quid; lxx. τίς *for* מִי; τί *for* מָה.)
   (a) *with the indicative mood, relating to some actual matter of fact.*
   (b) *with the subjunctive, expressing something objectively possible, something which may or should take place.*
   (c) *with the optative, expressing something subjectively possible, but something simply conceived in the mind.*
   (d) *with* ἄρα, who then?

2. ὅστις, any one who, some one who, whoever, (*differing from* ὅς, *in referring to a subject only generally, as one of a class, and not definitely.*)

3. ὅσος, how many, as many as.

4. οὗτος, this, this one, this one here.

1. Matt. iii. 7.
1a.— x. 11.
1. — xii. 27, 48 twice.
1. — xvi. 13, 15.
1. — xvii. 25.
1d.— xviii. 1.
1. — xix. 25.
1. — xxi. 10, 23.
1. — xxii. 20, 28, 42.
1. — xxiv. 45 1st.
1. — xxvi. 68.
1. — xxvii. 17.
1a.Mark i. 24.
1. — ii. 7.
1. Mark iii. 33.
1. — v. 30, 31.
1. — viii. 27, 29.
1a.—— 34.
1. — x. 26.
1. — xi. 28.
1. — xii. 16, 23.
2. — xv. 7.
1. — xvi. 3.
1. Luke iii. 7.
1a.— iv. 34.
1. — v. 21 twice.
1a.— vi. 47.
1a.— vii. 39.

1. Luke vii. 49.
1. —— viii. 45 1st, 45 2nd (ap.)
1. —— ix. 9, 18, 20.
1a.—— x. 22 twice.
1. ——— 29.
1. —— xi. 19.
1b.—— xii. 5.
1. ——— 14, 20, 42 1st.
1. —— xvi. 11, 12.
1. —— xviii. 26.
1a.—— xix. 3.
1. —— xx. 2, 24, 33.
1. —— xxii. 64.
2. —— xxiii. 19.
1. John i. 19, 22.
1a.—— iv. 10.
1a.—— v. 13.
1. —— vi. 60.
1a.——— 64 twice, 68.
1. —— vii. 20.
1. —— viii. 25, 53.
1. —— ix. 2.
1a.——— 21.
1. ——— 36.
1. —— xii. 34, 38 twice.
1a.—— xiii. 22.
1c.——— 24.
1. ——— 25.
1. —— xviii. 4, 7.
1a.—— xix. 24.
1. —— xx. 15.
1. —— xxi. 12.
1. Acts vii. 27, 35.
2. ——— 53.
2. —— viii. 15.
1. ——— 33, 34.
1. —— ix. 5.
2. —— x. 41.
4. —— xiii. 7.
1. ——— 25.
2. ——— 31, 43.
2. —— xvii. 10.
1. —— xix. 15.
2. —— xxi. 4.
1c.——— 33.
1. —— xxii. 8 1st.
2. —— xxiii. 33.

2. Acts xxiv. 1.
1. —— xxvi. 15 1st.
2. —— xxviii. 18.
2. Rom. i. 25 1st, 32.
— —— v. 12, see *W* (*in*)
1. —— vii. 24.
1. —— viii. 31, 33, 34 1st, 35.
2. —— ix. 4 1st.
1. ——— 19, 20.
1. —— x. 6, 7, 16.
2. —— xi. 4.
1. ——— 34 twice, 35.
— —— xiii. 7 4 times, see W (to)
1. —— xiv. 4.
2. —— xvi. 4 1st, 6, 7 1st.
1. 1 Cor. ii. 16.
1. —— iii. 5 1st.
1. —— iv. 7.
1. —— ix. 7 3 times.
1. —— xiv. 8.
1. 2 Cor. ii. 2, 16.
2. —— viii. 10.
1. —— xi. 29 twice
2. Gal. ii. 4.
1. —— iii. 1.
1. —— v. 7.
2. Eph. iv. 19.
2. Phil. ii. 20.
2. 2 Thes. i. 9.
2. 2 Tim. ii. 2, 18.
1a.—— iii. 14.
2. Tit. i. 11.
3. Heb. ii. 15.
1. —— iii. 17, 18.
2. —— viii. 5.
1. Jas. iii. 13.
1. —— iv. 12 2nd.
1. 1 Pet. iii. 13.
1a.—— v. 8.
2. 2 Pet. ii. 1.
1. 1 John ii. 22.
1. —— v. 5.
1. Rev. v. 2.
1. —— vi. 17.
1. —— xiii. 4 twice.
1b —— xv. 4.

WHOM (*in*) [margin.]

{ ἐπὶ, upon } on ground of, on condition that, (*implying close juxtaposition, the argument resting upon it.*)
{ ᾧ, which, }

Rom. v. 12 (text, *for that.*)

WHOM (TO)

τῷ, to whom.

Rom. xiii. 7 4 times.

WHOLE.

(*For various combinations with other words, see below.*)

1. ὅλος, the whole, all, *including every part.*
2. πᾶς, all; *of one only*, all of him; *of one in a number*, any; *of several*, every; *in pl.*, all. *Sing. with art.*, the whole.
3. ἅπας, quite all, all together, all. (*No.* 1, *strengthened by* ἅμα, at once, at the same time.
4. ὁλόκληρος, whole in every part *or* portion, (*No.* 1, *with* κλῆρος, a lot *or* portion), complete, entire
5. ὑγιής, sound, healthy, well, in good health, (*occ.* Tit. ii. 8.)
6. ὑγιαίνω, to be sound, healthy, well, be in good health. *Here, participle.*

1. Matt. v. 29, 30.
1. —— vi. 22, 23.
2. —— viii. 32, 34.
5. —— xii. 13.
3. —— xiii. 2.
1 ——— 33.
5. —— xv. 31.
1. —— xvi. 26.
1. —— xxvi. 13.
1. —— xxvii. 27.
5. Mark iii. 5 (*om.* ὑγιης ὡς ἡ ἄλλη, *whole as the other*, G L T Tr A ℵ.)
2. —— iv. 1.
5. —— v. 34.
1. —— vi. 55.
1. —— viii. 36.
— —— xii. 33, see Burnt offering.
1. —— xiv. 9.
1. —— xv. 1, 16, 33.
2. Luke i. 10.
5. —— vi. 10 (ap.)
2. ——— 19.
6. —— vii. 10 part
3. —— viii. 37.
1. ——— 39.
1. —— ix. 25.
1. —— xi. 34, 36 twice.
1. —— xiii. 21.
3. —— xix. 37.

2. Luke xxi. 35.
3. —— xxiii. 1.
1. John iv. 53.
5. —— v. 4 (*ap.*), 6, 9, 11, 14, 15.
5. —— vii. 23.
1. —— xi. 50.
5. Acts iv. 10.
2. —— vi. 5.
1. —— xi. 26.
2. —— xiii. 44.
1. —— xv. 22.
1. —— xix. 29 (*om.* L T Tr A ℵ.)
1. —— xxviii. 30.
1. Rom. i. 8.
2. —— viii. 22, marg. *every*
1. —— xvi. 23.
1. 1 Cor. v. 6.
1. —— xii. 17 twice
1. —— xiv. 23.
1. Gal. v. 3, 9.
2. Eph. iii. 15.
2. —— iv. 16.
4. 1 Thes. v. 23.
1. Tit. i. 11.
1. Jas. ii. 10.
1. —— iii. 2, 3, 6.
1. 1 John ii. 2.
1. —— v. 19.
1. Rev. xii. 9.
1. —— xvi. 14.

WHOLE (BE)

1. ἰσχύω, to be strong, robust.
2. σώζω, *here, pass.*, to be saved, delivered, *or* preserved *from danger, loss, or destruction*, be healed, recover *from sickness to health.*
3. ὑγιαίνω, to be sound, healthy, *or* well, to be in good health.

1. Matt. ix. 12.
2. ——— 21.
1. Mark ii. 17.
2. —— v. 28.
3. Luke v. 31.

WHOLE (MAKE)

1. σώζω, to save, deliver, *or* preserve safe from danger, loss, *or* destruction.
2. ἰάομαι, to heal, to cure.

1. Matt. ix. 22 twice.
2. —— xv. 28.
1. Mark v. 34.
1. —— vi. 56.
1. Mark x. 52, marg. *save.*
1. Luke viii. 48, 50.
1. —— xvii. 10.
1. Acts iv. 9.
2. Acts ix. 34.

WHOLE (MAKE PERFECTLY)

διασώζω, (*No.* 1, *above, with* διά, through, *prefixed*) to save through, to bring safely through, (*of danger, sickness, etc.*)

Matt. xiv. 36.

See also, ARMOUR, BURNT-OFFERING.

WHOLESOME.

ὑγιαίνω, *see* "WHOLE," *No.* 6.

1 Tim. vi. 3 part.

WHOLLY.

ὁλοτελής, whole to the end, wholly complete, (*non occ.*)

1 Thes. v. 23.

See also, GIVE, IDOLATRY.

WHOM.

See, WHO.

WHOMSOEVER.

See, WHOSOEVER.

WHORE.

πόρνη, (*fem. of* πόρνος, *from* περνάω, to sell, *because among the Greeks these were usually* bought slaves) a harlot *or* whore, (*elsewhere translated* "harlot.")

Rev. xvii. 1, 15, 16. | Rev. xix. 2.

WHOREMONGER (-s.)

πόρνος, a sodomite, a catamite.

Eph. v. 5. | Heb. xiii. 4.
1 Tim. i. 10. | Rev xxi. 8.
Rev. xxii. 15.

WHOSE.

See, WHO.

WHOSO.

ὅς, who, which.

* *with* ἄν, perhaps, perchance, (*see below, No.* 1a.)

† *with* ἐάν, if, *expressing an objective possibility, and implying a condition which experience or results must determine.*

Matt. xviii. 5† (*L Tr.) | 1 John ii. 5*.
—— 6*. | —— iii. 17.

WHOSOEVER, WHOMSOEVER.

1. ὅς, who, which.

   (a) *with* ἄν, perchance, perhaps, *giving a stamp of uncertainty, and implying a dependence on circumstances.*

   (b) *with* ἐάν, if, *expressing an objective possibility, and implying a condition which experience or results must determine.*

2. πᾶς, all; *of one only,* all of him; *of one in a number,* any; *of several,* every; *in pl.,* all.

   (a) *with* ὅς, (*No.* 1) all who, every one who.

3. { πᾶς, all, every one, / ὅς, who } / ἄν, perchance, } (*see No.*1a) } every one whosoever.

4. ὅστις, any one who, some one who, whoever, (*referring to a subject only generally, as one of a class, and not definitely, like No.* 1.)

   (a) *with* ἄν, perchance, (*see No.* 1a.)

   (b) *with* ἐάν, if, (*see No.* 1b.)

5. { ὅσοι, as many as / ἄν, perchance, (*see No.* 1a.) }

6. ὅσπερ, (*No.* 1, *strengthened by* περ, indeed) who indeed, who namely, (*non occ.*)

7. { εἰ, if (*expressing a hypothetical condition*) / τις, any. }

8. { ἐάν, if (*expressing a possible condition which experience must determine*) / τις, any. }

9. { ἄν, perhaps, perchance, (*implying uncertainty, or a dependence on circumstances*) / τις, any. }

1b. Matt. v. 19 1st.
1a. ——— 19 2nd, 21.
2. ——— 22 1st.
1a. ——— 22 2nd & 3rd.
2. ——— 28.
1a. ——— 31.
1a. ——— 32 1st (No. 2, G∾L T Tr A ℵ.)
1b. ——— 32 2nd.
4. ——— 39, 41.
4. —— vii. 24.
1b. —— x. 14 (No. 1a, L T Tr A ℵ.)
4. ——— 32.
4a. ——— 33 (*om.* ἄν, L Tr A.)
1b. ——— 42 (No. 1a, L Tr A* ℵ.)
1b. —— xi. 6 (No. 1a, L Tr.)
1b. ——— 27.
1a. —— xii. 32 1st (No. 1b, L T Tr A ℵ.)
1a. ——— 32 2nd.
4a. ——— 50.
4. —— xiii. 12 twice.
1a. —— xv. 5.
1a. —— xvi. 25 1st (No. 1b, L T Tr A.)
1a. ——— 25 2nd.
4. —— xviii. 4.
1a. —— xix. 9.
1b. —— xx. 26 (No. 1a, L T Tr.)
1b. ——— 27 (No. 1a, L T Tr A ℵ.)
1a. —— xxi. 44.
4. —— xxiii. 12.
1a. ——— 16 twice.
1b. ——— 18 1st (No. 1a, L T Tr A ℵ.)
1a. ——— 18 2nd.
1a. —— xxvi. 48 (No. 1b, T A ℵ.)
1a. Mark iii. 35.
6. —— vi. 11 (*ap.*)
4. —— viii. 34 (No. 7, G∾L Tr ℵ.)
1a. ——— 35 1st (No. 1b, T Tr A ℵ.)
1a. ——— 35 2nd.
1a. ——— 38 (No. 1b, L T Tr A.)
1b. —— ix. 37 1st (No. 1a, L T Tr A ℵ.)
1b. ——— 37 2nd (No. 1a, L T Tr A.)
1a. ——— 41, 42.
1b. —— x. 11, } (No. 1a, L
1b. ——— 15, } T Tr A ℵ.)
1b. ——— 43 (No. 1a, L T Tr ℵ.)
1a. ——— 44 (No. 1b, G T Tr A.)
1a. —— xi. 23.
1a. —— xiv. 44.
6. —— xv. 6.

1b. Luke iv. 6 (No. 1a, L Tr A.)
2. —— vi. 47.
1b. —— vii. 23.
1a. —— viii. 18.
5. —— ix. 5. [T ℵ.)
1a. ——— 24 1st (No. 1b,
1a. ——— 24 2nd, 26.
1b. ——— 48 1st (No. 1a, L.)
1b. ——— 48 2nd.
3. —— xii. 8.
2a. ——— 10.
2. ——— 48.
2. —— xiv. 11.
4. ——— 27.
2a. ——— 33.
2. —— xvi. 18 1st.
2. ——— 18 2nd (ὁ, with part., i.e. *he who*, instead of No. 2, G⇉L T Tr A.)
1b. —— xvii. 33 twice.
1b. —— xviii. 17 (No. 1a, L T Tr A ℵ.)
2. —— xx. 18 1st.
1a. ——— 18 2nd.
2. John iii. 15, 16.
2. —— iv. 13.
1a. ——— 14.
2. —— viii. 34.
2. —— xi. 26.
2. —— xii. 46.
8. —— xiii. 20 (No. 9, L T Tr A ℵ.)
2. —— xvi. 2.
2. —— xix. 12.
9. —— xx. 23 1st (No. 8, L.)
9. ——— 23 2nd (No. 8, L ℵ.)
3. Acts ii. 21.
1a. —— viii. 19 (No. 1b, G L T Tr A ℵ.)
2. —— x. 43.
2. Rom. ii. 1.
2. —— ix. 33 (ὁ, with part., i.e. *he that*, instead of No. 2, G⇉L T Tr A ℵ.)
2. —— x. 11.
3. ——— 13.
1a. 1 Cor. xi. 27.
1b. —— xvi. 3 (No. 1a, L.)
4. Gal. v. 4.
4a. ——— 10 (No. 4b, T Tr A ℵ.)
4. Jas. ii. 10.
2. 1 John ii. 23.
2. —— iii. 4, 6 twice, 9, 10, 15.
1a. —— iv. 15.
2. —— v. 1, 18.
2. 2 John 9.
7. Rev. xiv. 11.
7. —— xx. 15.
2. —— xxii. 15.

WHY, WHY?

1. τί, (*neut. of* τίς, who? what? *as adv.*) wherefore? why?

2. διατί, on account of what? for the sake of what?

3. ἱνατί, in order to what? for what purpose? (*occ.* Mark ix. 4.)

4. { εἰς, unto } to what end?
   { τί, what, } with a view to what?

5. ὅτι, because; *after a pronoun, as interrog.*, for what cause, for what reason.

6. γάρ, verily then, in fact; *in questions*, γάρ is used with reference to the words *or* thoughts of the other party.

1. Matt. vi. 28.
1. —— vii. 3.
1. —— viii. 26.
2. —— ix. 11, 14.
2. —— xiii. 10.
2. —— xv. 2, 3.
1. —— xvi. 8.
1. —— xvii. 10.
2. ——— 19.
1. —— xix. 7, 17
1. —— xx. 6.
2. —— xxi. 25.
1. —— xxii. 18.
1. —— xxvi. 10.
— —— xxvii. 23, see W what?
3. ——— 46.
1. Mark ii. 7, 8.
2. ——— 18.
1. ——— 24.
1. —— iv. 40.
1. —— v. 35, 39.
2. —— vii. 5.
1. —— viii. 12, 17.
5. —— ix. 11, 28.
1. —— x. 18.
1. —— xi. 3.
2. ——— 31.
1. —— xii. 15.
4. —— xiv. 4.
1. ——— 6.
— —— xv. 14, see W what?
4. ——— 34.
1. Luke ii. 48.
2. —— v. 30.
2. ——— 33 (*om.* διατί, *why do*, T Tr[b] A.)
1. —— vi. 2, 41, 46.
1. —— xii. 26, 57.
3. —— xiii. 7.
1. —— xviii. 19.
2. —— xix. 31.

1. Luke xix. 33.
2. —— xx. 5.
1. ——— 23 (*ap.*)
1. —— xxii. 46.
— —— xxiii. 22, see W what?
1. —— xxiv. 5, 38 1st.
2. ——— 38 2nd.
1. John i. 25.
1. —— iv. 27.
1. —— vii. 19.
2. ——— 45.
2. —— viii. 43, 46.
6. —— ix. 20.
1. —— x. 20.
2. —— xii. 5.
2. —— xiii. 37.
1. —— xviii. 21, 23.
1. —— xx. 13, 15.
1. Acts i. 11.
1. —— iii. 12 twice.
3. —— iv. 25.
2. —— v. 3.
1. ——— 4.
3. —— vii. 26.
1. —— ix. 4.
1. —— xiv. 15.
1. —— xv. 10.
1. —— xxii. 7, 16.
1. —— xxvi. 8, 14.
1. Rom. iii. 7.
1. —— viii. 24.
1. —— ix. 19, 20.
1. —— xiv. 10 twice.
1. 1 Cor. iv. 7.
2. —— vi. 7 twice.
3. —— x. 29.
1. ——— 30.
1. —— xv. 29, 30.
1. Gal. ii. 14 (πῶς, *how?* G L T Tr A ℵ.)
1. —— v. 11.
1. Col. ii. 20.

WHY WHAT?

{ τί, what } *lit.*, what
{ γάρ, for, then, in fact, } [*evil*] in fact.

Matt. xxvii. 23. | Mark xv. 14.
Luke xxiii. 22.

WICKED.

1. πονηρός, causing *or* having labour, sorrow, pain; *hence gen., actively, as causing evil to others*, evil-disposed, malignant, malevolent; *or passively, as made evil*, evil in nature *or* quality, bad, ill, vicious.

   (a) *with the article*, the evil *one*, the malignant *one*.

2. ἄνομος, without law, not subject to law, lawless; *then*, a violator of the divine law.

3. ἄθεσμος, a violator of established ordinances, rules, *or* institutions, (*divine or human*), (*non occ.*)

4. κακός, bad, (*generically*) worthless, including every form of evil, physical and moral.

1. Matt. xii. 45 1st.
1. —— 45 2nd (comparative.)
1. —— xiii. 49.
1. —— xvi. 4.
1. —— xviii. 32.
4. —— xxi. 41.
1. —— xxv. 26.
1. Luke xi. 26.
1. Luke xix. 22.
2. Acts ii. 23.
1. —— xviii. 14.
— Eph. vi. 12, marg. see Wickedness.
1. Col. i. 21.
2. 2 Thes. ii. 8.
1. —— iii. 2.
3. 2 Pet. ii. 7.
3. 2 Pet. iii. 17.

WICKED (THE)

1a. Eph. vi. 16.

WICKED ONE (THAT)

1a. 1 John v. 18.

WICKED ONE (THE)

1a. Matt. iii. 19, 38.
1a. 1 John ii. 13, 14.
1a. 1 John iii. 12.

WICKED PERSON (THAT)

1a. 1 Cor. v. 13.

WICKEDNESS.

1. πονηρία, evil nature, delight in evil, malignity, malevolence, the wicked act of the mind, (*occ.* Acts iii. 26.)

2. πονηρός, *see No.* 1a, *above.*

3. κακία, badness, the evil habit, malice.

4. τούτῳ, in this, *lit.*, *if there be any thing* in this *man.*

1. Matt. xxii. 18.
1. Mark vii. 22, pl.
1. Luke xi. 39.
3. Acts viii. 22.
4. —— xxv. 5 (ἄτοπος, out *of place*, St L T Tr A), (*om.* G.)
1. Rom. i. 29.
1. 1 Cor. v. 8.
1. Eph. vi. 12, marg. *wickedness.*
2. 1 John v. 19.

WIDE.

πλατύς, broad, wide; (lxx. *for* רחב, Judg. xix. 15, 20; Neh. ix. 35; Zech. viii. 4, 5; חוץ, Is. xv. 3), (*non occ.*)

Matt. vii. 13.

WIDOW (-S.)

χήρα, bereaved; *then*, bereaved *of one's husband*, a widow; (lxx. *for* אלמנה, Gen. xxxviii. 11; Ex. xx. 22, etc.; 2 Sam. xiv. 5; 1 Kings vii. 14), (*non occ.*)

Matt. xxiii. 14 (*ap.*)
Mark xii. 40, 42, 43.
Luke ii. 37.
—— iv. 25.
—— vii. 12.
—— xviii. 3, 5.
—— xx. 47.
Luke xxi. 2, 3.
Acts vi. 1.
—— ix. 39, 41.
1 Cor. vii. 8.
1 Tim. v. 3 twice, 4, 5, 9, 11, 16 twice.
Jas. i. 27.
Rev. xviii. 7.

WIDOW (THAT WAS A)

Luke iv. 26.

WIFE, WIVES.

1. γυνή, a woman, *one of the female sex;* used of a maiden; (lxx. *for* נערה, Esth. ii. 4) *and of an adult; also, with a Genitive, or* ἔχειν (to have), *or the adj.*, ὕπανδρος, (under a husband) *it implies* betrothed, a bride, *but not yet married; also used of* a married woman, a wife; (*so* lxx. *for* אשה, Gen. xxiv. 3, etc.)

2. γυναικεῖος, womanly, womanish, female; *here, Dat. with art.*, the female, (*non occ.*)

3. ἡ, the. *Here, with Gen. following*, the of, *i.e.* the *wife of.*

— Matt. i. 6, see W (her ...the)
1. —— 20, 24.
1. —— v. 31, 32.
— —— viii. 14, see W's mother.
1. —— xiv. 3.
1. —— xviii. 25.
1. —— xix. 3, 5, 8, 9, 10.
1. —— 29 (*om.* ἢ γυναῖκα, *or wife*, L T Tr A.)
1. —— xxii. 24, 25, 28.
1. —— xxvii. 19.
— Mark i. 30, see W's mother.
1. —— vi. 17, 18.
1. —— x. 2, 7, 11.
1. —— 29 (*om.* ἢ γυναῖκα, *or wife*, G→L T Tr A ℵ.)
1. —— xii. 19 twice, 20, 23 twice.
1. Luke i. 5, 13, 18, 24.
1. —— ii. 5 (*om.* L T Tr A ℵ.)
1. —— iii. 19.
— —— iv. 38, see W's mother.
1. Luke viii. 3.
1. —— xiv. 20, 26.
1. —— xvi. 18.
1. —— xvii. 32.
1. —— xviii. 29.
3. —— xix. 25.
1. —— xx. 28 twice, 29, 30 (*ap.*), 33 twice.
1. Acts v. 1, 2, 7.
1. —— xviii. 2.
1. —— xxi. 5.
1. —— xxiv. 24.
1. 1 Cor. v. 1.
1. —— vii. 2, 3 twice, 4 twice, 10, 11, 12, 14 twice, 16 twice, 27 3 times, 29, 33, 34, 39.
1. —— ix. 5, marg. *woman.*
1. Eph. v. 22, 23, 24, 25, 28 twice, 31, 33 twice.
1. Col. iii. 18, 19.
1. 1 Tim. iii. 2, 11, 12.
1. —— v. 9.
1. Tit. i. 6.
1. 1 Pet. iii. 1 twice.
2. —— 7.
1. Rev. xix. 7.
1. —— xxi. 9.

WIFE (HER...THE)

3. Matt. i. 6.

WIFE'S MOTHER.

πενθερά, a mother-in-law, *e.g.* a wife's mother; (also the husband's

mother, Matt. x. 35; Luke xii. 53); (lxx. *for* חמות, Ruth i. 14; ii. 11; iii. 1.)

Matt. viii. 14. | Mark i. 30. | Luke iv. 38.

WILD.

ἄγριος, living in the fields, living wild; *hence, used of animals, trees, etc.,* wild, and *of things having* the qualities incident to a wild *or* natural state, (*occ.* Jude 13.)

Matt. iii. 4. | Mark i. 6.

See also, BEAST, OLIVE-TREE.

WILDERNESS.

1. ἔρημος, (*adj.*) lonely, desolate, solitary, desert, *used of persons, etc.; also as subst.*, a lonely *place*, a desert *place*, a place *or* region uninhabited and uncultivated.

2. ἐρημία, (*subst.*) a solitude, a desert, a wilderness, (*occ.* Heb. xi. 38.)

1. Matt, iii. 1, 3.
1. —— iv. 1.
1. —— xi. 7.
2. —— xv. 33.
1. Mark i. 3, 4, 12, 13.
2. —— viii. 4.
1. Luke iii. 2, 4.
1. —— iv. 1.
1. —— v. 16.
1. —— vii. 24.
1. —— viii. 29.
1. —— xv. 4.
1. John i. 23.
1. —— iii. 14.
1. —— vi. 49.
1. —— xi. 54.
1. Acts vii. 30, 36, 38, 42, [44.
1. —— xiii. 18.
1. —— xxi. 38.
1. 1 Cor. x. 5.
2. 2 Cor. xi. 26.
1. Heb. iii. 8, 17.
1. Rev. xii. 6, 14.
1. —— xvii. 3.

WILE (-s.)

μεθοδεία, (μετά, with, *and* ὅδος, a way) method, art, artifice, cunning device, contrivance, craft, wiles, (*occ.* Eph. iv. 14.)

Eph. vi. 11.

WILFULLY.

ἑκουσίως, willingly, of free-will, voluntarily; (lxx. *for* בנדבה, Neh. xv. 3), (*occ.* 1 Pet. v. 2.)

Heb. x. 26.

WILL. [noun.]

(*For the verb* "TO WILL," *see below; also for various combinations with other words.*)

1. θέλημα, will, active volition, wish, desire.

2. θέλησις, a willing, a wishing, (*non occ.*)

3. γνώμη, a means of knowing; that by which one knows, the mind; *and then the various ways in which the mind exerts itself, as* opinion, judgment, consent, inclination, desire, etc.

4. βουλή, determination, decision, decree, counsel.

5. βουλημα, deliberate intention, that which is purposed, designed, planned *or* intended, (*occ.* Acts xxvii. 43.)

1. Matt. vi. 10.
1. —— vii. 21.
1. —— xii. 50.
1. —— xviii. 14.
1. —— xxi. 31.
1. —— xxvi. 42.
1. —— xxvii. 43.
1. Mark iii. 35.
1. Luke xi. 2 (*ap.*)
1. —— xii. 47 twice.
1. —— xxii. 42.
1. —— xxiii. 35.
1. John i. 13 twice.
1. —— iv. 34.
1. —— v. 30 twice.
1. —— vi. 38 twice, 39, 40.
1. —— vii. 17.
1. —— ix. 31.
1. Acts xiii. 22, pl.
4. —— 36.
1. —— xxi. 14.
1. Rom. i. 10.
1. —— ii. 18.
5. —— ix. 19.
1. —— xii. 2.
1. —— xv. 32.
1. 1 Cor. i. 1.
1. 1 Cor. vii. 37.
1. —— xvi. 12.
1. 2 Cor. i. 1.
1. —— viii. 5.
1. Gal. i. 4.
1. Eph. i. 1, 5, 9, 11.
1. —— ii. 3 marg. (text, [*desire.*)
1. —— v. 17.
1. —— vi. 6.
1. Col. i. 1, 9.
1. —— iv. 12.
1. 1 Thes. iv. 3.
1. —— v. 18.
1. 2 Tim. i. 1
1. —— ii. 26
2. Heb. ii. 4.
1. —— x. 7, 9, 10, 36.
1. —— xiii. 21.
1. 1 Pet. ii. 15.
1. —— iii. 17.
1. —— iv. 2.
1. —— 3 (No. 5, G ~ L T [Tr A ℵ.)
1. —— 19.
1. 2 Pet. i. 21.
1. 1 John ii. 17.
1. —— v. 14.
3. Rev. xvii. 17.

WILL (AGAINST ONE'S)

ἄκων, unwilling, against one's will, perforce, (*non occ.*)

1 Cor. ix. 17.

WILL (GOOD)

1. εὐδοκία, the deeming good, a free-willing pleasure whose object is something good, good pleasure, gracious purpose; *not* "*good will*" *in a moral sense, nor a purpose morally good, but* a resolve, with emphasis on the willingness or freedom with which it is taken, at the same time denoting that it is good.

2. εὔνοια, willing mind, good will, (*occ* 1 Cor. viii. 3.)

1. Luke ii. 14 (εὐδοκίας (*gen.*), i.e. *among men of* [God's] *good pleasure, instead of good will toward men,* L T Tr A ℵ.)
2. Eph. vi. 7.
1. Phil. i. 15.

WILL (OF ONE'S OWN)

βούλομαι, to purpose, to will. *Here, part.*

Jas. i. 18.

WILL WORSHIP.

ἐθελοθρησκεία, a self-devised external form of ceremonial service, a mode of ceremonial worship chosen for one's self, (*non occ.*)

Col. ii. 23.

WILL (-ETH, -ING, WILT.) [verb]

WILL is frequently part of the translation of the future tense of verbs. When it is the translation of a separate Greek work it is one of these following.

1. θέλω, to will, to wish, to desire, *implying the simple act of volition;* to have a natural impulse or desire, *without regard to the deliberation or consideration;* (*No.* 1 *may thus be stronger in some sense than No.* 2, *because a natural impulse is more violent than a reasonable resolve*). *θέλω is therefore used of cases where the wisdom and iustice, etc., are not apparent, but where the will is arbitrary or absolute.*

2. βούλομαι, to wish, to desire, to have *that* desire *from which No.* 1 *sometimes springs,* to have a wish, intention, *or* purpose, formed after mature deliberation; to deliberately purpose after careful consideration. (*For the difference between Nos.* 1 and 2, *compare* Mark xv. 9 and 12, (*No.* 1) *with* 15, (*No.* 2.)

3. μέλλω, to be about to, to be on the point of; *used of some act or event in the future as the result of present determination,* to be going to *do anything.*

1. Matt. i. 19.
3. —— ii. 13.
1. —— v. 40.
1. —— viii. 2, 3.
— —— ix. 13, see W have.
1. —— xi. 14.
2. —— 27 (ἀποκαλυψη, *may reveal*, instead of βούληται ἀποκαλύψαι, *purposes to reveal*, Lm.)
— Matt. xii. 7, see W have.
1. —— xiii. 28.
1. —— xv. 28, 32.
1. —— xvi. 24, 25 1st.
1. —— xvii. 4.
1. —— xix. 17, 21.
1. —— xx. 14, 15, 21, 26, 27, 32.
1. —— xxi. 29.
1. —— xxiii. 4.
1. Matt. xxvi. 15 1st, 17, 39 1st (2nd not in Greek.)
1. —— xxvii. 17, 21.
— —— 43, see W have.
1. Mark i. 40, 41.
1. —— vi. 22 1st.
1. —— viii. 34, 35.
1. —— x. 43, 44, 51.
1. —— xiv. 7, 12, 36 1st (2nd not in Greek.)
1. —— xv. 9.
1. —— 12 (*om.* θέλετε, *will ye that,* Tr^b ℵ.)
2. —— 15.
1. Luke iv. 6 2nd.
1. —— v. 12, 13.
1. —— ix. 23, 24 1st, 54.
2. —— x. 22.
1. —— 29.
1. —— xii. 49.
1. —— xiii. 31.
1. —— xviii. 41.
1. —— xix. 14.
1. —— xxii. 9.
1. —— xxiii. 20.
1. John v. 6, 21, 40.
1. —— vi. 67.
1. —— vii. 17 1st.
3. —— 35 twice.
1. —— viii. 44.
3. —— xiv. 22.
1. —— xv. 7.
1. —— xvii. 24.
2. —— xviii. 39.
1. —— xxi. 22, 23.
1. Acts vii. 28.
— —— ix. 6, see W have.
1. Acts xvii. 18.
3. —— 31.
2. —— xviii. 15.
1. —— 21 2nd part.
3. —— xxiii. 20 part.
1. —— xxiv. 27.
1. —— xxv. 9 twice.
3. —— xxvii. 10.
2. —— 43.
1. Rom. ix. 16, 18 twice, 22.
1. —— xiii. 3.
1. 1 Cor. iv. 19 2nd, 21.
1. —— vii. 36, 39.
1. —— x. 20.
2. —— xii. 11.
1. —— xiv. 35.
1. —— xvi. 7.
1. 2 Cor. viii. 11.
1. Phil. ii. 13.
— 1 Tim. ii. 4, see W have.
2. —— 8.
1. —— v. 11.
2. —— 14.
2. —— vi. 9.
1. 2 Tim. iii. 12.
2. Tit. iii. 8.
2. Heb. vi. 17.
1. —— xiii. 18.
1. Jas. ii. 20.
2. —— iv. 4.
1. —— 15.
1. 1 Pet. iii. 10.
2. 2 Pet. iii. 9.
1. 3 John 13.
2. Jude 5.
3. Rev. iii. 16.
1. —— xi. 5 twice, 6.
1. —— xxii. 17.

WILL HAVE.

1. Matt. ix. 13.
1. —— xii. 7.
1. Matt. xxvii. 43.
1. Acts ix. 6 (ap.)
1. 1 Tim. ii. 4.

WILLING.

πρόθυμος, predisposed, having a mind (*as regards the passions*) beforehand; (lxx. *for* נדיב, 1 Ch. xxviii. 21; 2 Ch. xxix. 31.)

Matt. xxvi. 41.

WILLING (BE)

1. θέλω, *see above, No.* 1.
2. βούλομαι, *see above, No.* 2.
3. εὐδοκέω, to deem good, to take pleasure in; *when followed by inf.,* to determine, to will, *with stress on the willingness of the cause and the goodness of the purpose.*

2. Luke xxii. 42.
1. John v. 35.
3. 2 Cor. v. 8.
3. 1 Thes. ii. 8.
— 1 Tim. vi. 18, see Communicate.

WILLING MIND.

προθυμία, predisposition, the having a mind (*as regards the passions*) beforehand.

2 Cor. viii. 12.

WILLING OF ONE'S SELF.

αὐθαίρετος, self chosen for one's self, spontaneously acting from one's own choice.

2 Cor. viii. 3.

WILLINGLY.

1. **ἑκών**, out of free will, willing, voluntary; wittingly, purposely.
2. { **κατὰ**, according to, **ἑκούσιον**, free-will, voluntary, } (lxx. *for* בנדבה, Neh. xv. 3), (*non occ.*)
3. **ἑκουσίως**, willingly, of free-will, voluntarily; (lxx. *for* בנדבה, Ps. liv. 8), (*occ.* Heb. x. 26.)
4. **θέλω**, *see* "WILL," *No.* 1.
   (a) *lit.*, willed to.
   (b) *participle, lit.*, this is unknown to them, wishing it, *i.e.* they are naturally desirous of ignorance on the subject.

4a. John vi. 21.
1. Rom. viii. 20.
1. 1 Cor. ix. 17.
2. Philem. 14.
3. 1 Pet. v. 2.
4b. 2 Pet. iii. 5.

WIN, WON.

κερδαίνω, to gain, acquire *as gain*, win.

Phil. iii. 8. | 1 Pet. iii. 1.

WIND (-s.) [noun.]

1. **ἄνεμος**, a stream of air, air in motion, (*from* ἄω, ἄημι, to breathe, to blow); (lxx. *for* רוח, Job xxi. 18; Is. xli. 16, etc.; *and* ארבע רוחות, 1 Ch. ix. 24; Jer. xlix. 36; Dan. xi. 4), (*non occ.*)
2. **πνέω**, to blow, breathe, (*of the wind or air*); to breathe, send forth an odour; *gen., of men, etc.*, to draw breath, breathe; *of the air*, to blow. *Here, part.*, blowing.
3. **πνοή**, a blowing, blast; (lxx. *for* נשמה, Job xxxvii. 10), (*occ.* Acts xvii. 25.)
4. **πνεῦμα**, the air we breathe, wind, (*see* "SPIRIT.")

1. Matt. vii. 25, 27.
1. —— viii. 26, 27.
1. —— xi. 7.
1. —— xiv. 24, 30, 32.
1. —— xxiv. 31.
1. Mark iv. 37, 39 twice, 41.
1. —— vi. 48, 51.
1. —— xiii. 27.
1. Luke vii. 24.
1. —— viii. 23, 24, 25.
— —— xii. 55, see South.
4. John iii. 8.
1. —— vi. 18.
3. Acts ii. 2.
1. —— xxvii. 4, 7.
— —— 13, see South.
1. Acts xxvii. 14, 15.
2. —— 40.
— —— xxviii. 13, see South.
1. Eph. iv. 14.
— Jas. i. 6, see W (be driven with the)
1. —— iii. 4.
1. Jude 12.
1. Rev. vi. 13.
1. Rev. vii. 1 twice.

WIND (BE DRIVEN WITH THE)

ἀνεμίζομαι, to be driven by the wind, (*No.* 1); (*a verb, not occurring in the* lxx., *nor in classic writers.*)

Jas. i. 6.

WIND, WOUND. [verb.]

δέω, to bind, fasten.

John xix. 40.

WIND UP.

συστέλλω, to wrap together, to envelope, to wind *in a garment*, (*occ.* 1 Cor. vii. 29.)

Acts v. 6.

WINDOW.

θυρίς, a little door, an aperture. *In N.T.*, a window; (lxx. *for* חלון, Josh. ii. 15, 18, 21; Judg. v. 28), (*non occ.*)

Acts xx. 9. | 2 Cor. xi. 33.

WINE.

οἶνος, wine, the fermented juice of the grape; (lxx. *for* יין, Gen. ix. 21, 24; xiv. 18; תירוש, Gen. xxvii. 28; Judg. ix. 13; Joel i. 10.)

Matt. ix. 17 3 times.
Mark ii. 22 3 times, 22 (*ap.*)
—— xv. 23.
Luke i. 15.
—— v. 37 twice, 38.
—— 39, see Old.
—— vii. 33 (*om.* G→)
—— x. 34.
John ii. 3 twice, 9, 10 twice.
—— iv. 46.
Acts ii. 13, see W (new)
Rom. xiv. 21.
Eph. v. 18.
1 Tim. iii. 3, see W (given to)
—— 8.
—— v. 23.
Tit. ii. 3.
1 Pet. iv. 3, see W (excess of)
Rev. vi. 6.
—— xiv. 8, 10.
—— xvi. 19.
—— xvii. 2.
—— xviii. 3 (*om.* τοῦ οἴνου, *of the wine*, L Tr A.)
—— 13.
Rev. xix. 15, see W press.

WINE (EXCESS OF)

οἰνοφλυγία, overflowing with wine, (*non occ.*)

1 Pet. iv. 3.

WINE (GIVEN TO)

πάροινος, beside wine, *sitting long* beside wine: *also implying that* which goes on or takes place beside *or* over wine, (*occ.* Tit. i. 3.)

1 Tim. iii. 3.

WINE (NEW)

γλεῦκος, must, sweet *or* new wine, (*non occ.*)

Acts ii. 13.

WINE-BIBBER.

οἰνοπότης, a wine-drinker; (lxx. *for* סבא יין, Prov. xxiii. 20), (*non occ.*)

Matt. xi. 19. | Luke vii. 34.

WINE-FAT.

ὑπολήνιον, the under-vat *of a wine-press, into which the juice of the grapes flowed, gen. dug in the rock,* (*not that in which the grapes were pressed, which was the upper vat or press, see below*); lxx. *for* יקב, Is. xvi. 10; Joel iii. 13; Hag. ii. 17), (*non occ.*)

Mark xii. 1.

WINE-PRESS.

1. **ληνός**, a trough *for drinking or watering;* (lxx. *for* רהט, Gen. xxx. 39, 42.) *Hence*, a wine trough *or* wine vat; the upper vat *or* press *into which the grapes were cast or trodden;* (lxx. *for* גת, Neh. xiii. 15; Is. lxiii. 2), (*non occ.*)
2. { **οἶνος**, wine / **ληνός**, press, (*see above.*) }

1. Matt. xxi. 33. | 1. Rev. xiv. 19, 20 twice.
2. Rev. xix. 15.

WING (-S.)

πτέρυξ, a pinion, a wing; (lxx. *for* אבר, Ps. lv. 7; כנף, Ex. xix. 4), (*non occ.*)

Matt. xxiii. 37. | Rev. iv. 8.
Luke xiii. 34. | —— ix. 9.
Rev. xii. 14.

WINK AT.

ὑπερεῖδον, to see *or* look out over, to overlook, not to regard; (lxx. *for* העלים, Lev. xx. 4), (*non occ.*)

Acts xvii. 30.

WINTER. [noun.]

χειμών, rain, storm, tempest; *then, used of* the season of rains and storms, the rainy season.

Matt. xxiv. 20. | John x. 22.
Mark xiii. 18. | 2 Tim. iv. 21.

WINTER (-ED.) [verb.]

παραχειμάζω, to winter near *or* at *a place*, (*non occ.*)

Acts xxvii. 12. | 1 Cor. xvi. 6.
—— xxviii. 11. | Tit. iii. 12.

WINTER IN.

{ **πρὸς**, for, / **παραχειμασία**, a wintering near *or* at, (*non occ.*) }

Acts xxvii. 12.

WIPE (-ED.)

ἐκμάσσω, to wipe out, *i.e.* to wipe dry, (*non occ.*)

Luke vii. 38, 44. | John xii. 3.
John xi. 2. | —— xiii. 5.

WIPE AWAY.

ἐξαλείφω, to smear out, blot out, obliterate.

Rev. vii. 17. | Rev. xxi. 4.

WIPE OFF.

ἀπομασσομαι, to wipe away from off one's self, (*non occ.*)

Luke x. 11.

WIS.

See, WIST.

WISDOM.

1. **σοφία**, wisdom, cleverness, skill, etc.; a right application of (γνῶσις) knowledge; wisdom regarded as residing in the mind, (*non occ.*)
2. **φρόνησις**, a fruit of *No.* 1; *No.* 1 in action; the faculty which applies the principles of wisdom; a minding to do *so and so*, purpose, intention, practical wisdom, prudence, (*occ.* Eph. i. 8.)

1. Matt. xi. 19.
1. —— xii. 42.
1. —— xiii. 54.
1. Mark vi. 2.
2. Luke i. 17.
1. —— ii. 40, 52.
1. —— vii. 35.
1. —— xii. 31, 49.
1. —— xxi. 15.
1. Acts vi. 3, 10.
1. —— vii. 10, 22.
1. Rom. xi. 33.
1. 1 Cor. i. 17, 19, 20, 21 twice, 22, 24, 30. [13.
1. —— ii. 1, 4, 5, 6 twice, 7,
1. 1 Cor. iii. 19.
1. —— xii. 8.
1. 2 Cor. i. 12.
1. Eph. i. 8, 17.
1. —— iii. 10.
1. Col. i. 9, 28.
1. —— ii. 3, 23.
1. —— iii. 16.
1. —— iv. 5.
1. Jas. i. 5.
1. —— iii. 13, 15, 17.
1. 2 Pet. iii. 15.
1. Rev. v. 12.
1. —— vii. 12.
1. —— xiii. 18.
1. Rev. xvii. 9.

WISE. [adj.]

(*For various combinations with other words, see below.*)

1. σοφός, wise, *i.e.* clever, skilled, skilful, *esp.*, one who has natural abilities, (*as opp. to* ὁ μαθών, *one who owes all to teaching.*)

2. φρόνιμος, understanding, thoughtful, practically wise, sensible, prudent, (*occ.* 1 Cor. x. 19.)

2. Matt. vii. 24.
2. —— x. 16.
1. —— xi. 25.
2. —— xxiv. 45.
2. —— xxv. 2, 4, 8, 9.
1. Luke x. 21.
2. —— xii. 42.
2. —— xvi. 8.
1. Rom. i. 14, 22.
2. —— xi. 25.
2. —— xii. 16.
1. Rom xvi. 19, 27.
1. 1 Cor. i. 19, 20, 25, 26, 27 (*ap.*)
1. —— iii. 10, 18 twice, 19, [20.
2. —— iv. 10.
2. 2 Cor. xi. 19.
1. Eph. v. 15.
1. 1 Tim. i. 17 (*om.* G L Tr A ℵ.)
1. Jude 25 (*om.* G L T Tr A ℵ.)

WISE (BE)

συνίημι, to send *or* bring together; bring or put together *in the mind; hence*, to discern, perceive, understand, comprehend.

2 Cor. x. 12, marg. *understand.* | Tit. ii. 4, marg., see Sober.

WISE (MAKE)

σοφίζω, to make wise, *i.e.* skilful, expert; (lxx. *for* חכּים, Ps. xix. 8; cv. 22), (*occ.* 2 Pet. i. 16.)

2 Tim. iii. 15.

WISE MAN.

1. σοφός, *see above, No.* 1.

2. φρόνιμος, *see above, No.* 2.

3. μάγος, great, powerful; magus, *pl.* magi, *the name for priests and wise men among the Medes, Persians, and Babylonians, whose learning was chiefly astrology and enchantment;* lxx. *for Chald.* אָשַׁף, enchanter, magician, Dan. i. 20; ii. 2, 27; v. 7), (*occ.* Acts xiii. 6, 8.)

3. Matt. ii. 1, 7, 16 twice.
1. —— xxiii. 34.
1. 1 Cor. vi. 5.
2. —— x. 15.
1. Jas. iii. 13.

WISE (TEACH TO BE) [margin.]

Tit. ii. 4, see "SOBER (TEACH TO BE)"

WISE.

See, ANY, NO, THIS.

WISELY.

φρονίμως, with mind, thinkingly, *i.e.* prudently, (*non occ.*)

Luke xvi. 8.

WISER.

Included in "WISE."

WISH (ED.) [verb.]

εὔχομαι, to speak out, to utter aloud; *hence*, to pray, pray for.

Acts xxvii. 29. | 2 Cor. xiii. 9.
3 John 2, marg. *pray.*

WISH (CAN)

Rom. ix. 3.

WIST, WIS.

οἶδα, *see* "KNOW," *No.* 1.

Mark ix. 6.
—— xiv. 40.
Luke ii. 49.
John v. 13.
Acts xii. 9.
—— xxiii. 5.

WIT (DO TO)

γνωρίζω, to make known, declare, reveal.

2 Cor. viii. 1.

WIT, THAT (TO)

ὡς, in which way, as, so as, how, *indicating that the proposition following it, introduced by* ὅτι, that, *is matter of indirect reference,* } how that.

2 Cor. v. 19.

See also, WOT.

WITCHCRAFT.

φαρμακεία, *see* "SORCERY," *No.* 1.

Gal. v. 20.

WITH.

"WITH" is frequently the translation of a case of a noun, or part of some phrase in combination with other words; for a list of the latter, see below.

When WITH is represented by a separate word (preposition) in the Greek, it is one of these following.

1. μετά, with, in association with, in proximity with. *Here, with Gen.*, with, together with, in company with. (*Hence, with the Acc.*, together *or near, so as to be* after.)

2. σύν, with, in conjunction with, united with, together *in, something common to both, implying* fellowship, union, *or* agreement with.

3. ἐν, in; *then, it is used of what accompanies or characterises*, with, in the power of, (*not marking the origin or source of the power, but only the character of it.*) *When it refers to an action, it is not* (*like No.* 7) *the effective instrument of it, but that which characterises it.*

4. παρά, beside, by the side of.
   (a) *with Gen.*, from beside, beside and proceeding from.
   (b) *with Dat.*, beside and at, with *or* near a person; with, *i.e. in the estimation or power of.*
   (c) *with Acc.*, to *or* along the side of, beyond, outside of.

5. πρός, towards.
   (a) *with Gen.*, hitherwards, *gen.*, *with the idea of something imparted, in favour of, as a motive.*
   (b) *with Dat.*, at the side of, at, with, near, *of persons only.*
   (c) *with Acc.*, towards, *implying an object*, up to, with a view to, *as an object to be attained; then*, with, *but as distinct from*, over against, in direction towards; *not like* παρά, (along with) *but* directed towards, *implying intimate and closest intercommunion, together with distinct independence.*

6. ἐκ, out of, from, (*calling attention to the source, origin, or principle.*)

7. διά, through.
   (a) *with Gen.*, through *as proceeding from, denoting the means or instrument of an action*, by means of, by, the effective instrument of activity.
   (b) *with Acc.*, through, on account of, because of, for the sake of, *denoting the reason or motive of the action*, by reason of.

8. ὑπό, under.
   (a) *with Gen.*, motion from beneath, *as denoting that from which the fact, event, or action springs, and marking the agent or efficient cause; hence*, with, by.

9. ἐπί, upon.
   (a) *with Gen.*, upon, *as springing from.*
   (b) *with Dat.*, resting upon, *marking the condition, occasion, cause, or circumstance by reason of which the act takes place.*
   (c) *with Acc.*, upon, *by direction towards, marking the mental direction with a view to the act.*

10. ἀπό, from, away from, *marking the point of departure; hence*, from, on account of, occasioned by.

11. κατά, down.
   (a) *with Gen.*, down from.
   (b) *with Acc.*, down along, over against; *hence, in reference to some standard of comparison expressed or implied*, according to, corresponding to.

12. ἅμα, at the same time with, together with, in company with.

13. εἰς, into, *implying either motion to a place, or arrival at a place by motion;* up to, *as the object of some aim or purpose.*

14. περί, around.

(a) *with Gen.*, about, concerning, *as the object of thought, emotion, etc.*

(b) *with Acc.*, about, round about.

15. ἔχω, to have; *here, participle*, having.

1. Matt. i. 23 2nd.
1. —— ii. 3, 11.
3. —— iii. 11 twice.
1. —— iv. 21.
1. —— v. 25 2nd, 41.
4b.—— vi. 1, marg. (text, *of.*)
3. —— vii. 2 twice.
1. —— viii. 11.
8a.—— 24.
—— 29, see W thee (what have we to do)
1. —— ix. 11, 15.
8a.—— xi. 7.
1. —— xii. 3, 4, 30 twice, 41, 42, 45.
1. —— xiii. 20.
12.—— 29.
5c.—— 56.
1. —— xiv. 7.
8a.—— 24.
1. —— xv. 30.
1. —— xvi. 27.
1. —— xvii. 3, 17.
1. —— xviii. 16.
9b.—— 26 (No. 9c, Tr.)
9b.—— 29 (No. 9c, L Tr A*.)
1. —— xix. 10.
4b.—— 26 twice.
1. —— xx. 2.
3. —— 15.
1. —— 20.
1. —— xxi. 2.
4b.—— 25 (No. 3, L Tr.)
1. —— xxii. 16.
4b.—— 25.
3. —— 37 3 times.
1. —— xxiv. 30, 31, 49, 51.
1. —— xxv. 3, 4, 10.
3. —— 16.
1. —— 19.
2. —— 27.
1. —— 31.
1. —— xxvi. 11, 18, 20, 23, 29.
2. —— 35.
1. —— 36, 38, 40, 47 twice, 51.
3. —— 52.
1. —— 55 1st.
5c.—— 55 2nd (*om.* πρὸς ὑμᾶς, *with you*, G→Trb A ℵ.)
1. —— 58, 69, 71, 72.
6. —— xxvii. 7.
1. —— 34.
2. —— 38.
1. —— 41, 54.
1. —— xxviii. 8, 12, 20.
3. Mark i. 8 1st (*om.* T Trb A ℵ.)
3. —— 8 2nd (*om.* Lb T T Trb A.)
1. —— 13, 20.
3. —— 23.
—— 24, see W thee (what have we to do)
11c.—— 27.
1. —— 29, 36.
1. —— ii. 16 twice 19 1st, 19 2nd (*ap.*), 25.
2. —— 26.
1. —— iii. 5, 6, 7, 14.
2. Mark iv. 10.
1. —— 16.
3. —— 24, 30.
1. —— 36.
3. —— v. 2.
—— 7 2nd, see W thee (what have I to do with)
1. —— 18 2nd, 24, 40.
5c.—— vi. 3.
1. —— 25, 50.
1. —— viii. 10, 14.
2. —— 34.
1. —— 38.
3. —— ix. 1.
2. —— 4.
1. —— 8.
5c.—— 10.
5c.—— 16 marg. *among.*
5c.—— 19.
1. —— 24 (*om.* μετὰ δακρύων, *with tears*, L T Tr A ℵ.)
3. —— 50.
4b.—— x. 27 1st & 2nd, 27 3rd (*ap.*)
1. —— 30.
1. —— xi. 11.
5c.—— 31.
6. —— xii. 30 4 times, 33 1st & 2nd, 33 3rd (*ap.*), 33 4th.
1. —— xiii. 26.
1. —— xiv. 7, 14, 17, 18, 20, 33, 43 twice, 48 1st.
5c.—— 49.
1. —— 54, 67.
1. —— xv. 1, 7 1st.
2. —— 27.
1. —— 28 (*ap.*), 31.
1. —— xvi. 10 (*ap.*)
7a.—— 20 2nd (*ap.*)
1. Luke i. 28.
4b.—— 30.
4b.—— 37 (No. 4a, Lm T Tr A ℵ.)
1. —— 39.
3. —— 51.
2. —— 56.
1. —— 66.
2. —— ii. 5 1st, 13.
1. —— 36, 51.
4b.—— 52.
3. —— iii. 16 2nd.
3. —— iv. 32.
—— 34, see W thee (what have we to do)
3. —— 36.
2. —— v. 19.
1. —— 29, 30, 34.
1. —— vi. 3, 4.
5c.—— 11 2nd.
1. —— 17.
8a.—— 18 (No. 10, G L T Tr A ℵ.)
2. —— vii. 6, 12.
8a.—— 24.
1. —— 36.
2. —— viii. 1.
1. —— 13.
8a.—— 14.
3. —— 15.
—— 28 2nd, see W thee (what have I to do)
2. —— 38.
1. Luke viii. 45.
2. —— ix. 32 1st.
5c.—— 41.
1. —— 49.
1. —— x. 17.
6. —— 27 1st.
6. —— 27 2nd, 3rd, & 4th (No. 3, L T Tr ℵ.)
1. —— xi. 7.
3. —— 20.
1. —— 23 twice, 31, 32.
4b.—— 37.
1. —— xii. 13, 46, 58.
1. —— xiii. 1.
1. —— xiv. 9.
3. —— 31 1st.
1. —— 31 2nd.
10.—— xv. 16.
1. —— 29, 30, 31.
10.—— xvi. 21.
1. —— xvii. 15, 20.
9b.—— xviii. 7.
5c.—— 11.
4b.—— 27 twice.
4b.—— xix. 7.
2. —— 23.
2. —— xx. 1.
5c.—— 5.
8a.—— xxi. 20.
3. —— 25.
1. —— 27.
3. —— 34.
1. —— xxii. 11.
2. —— 14.
1. —— 15 2nd, 21, 28, 33.
3. —— 49.
1. —— 52, 53.
2. —— 56.
1. —— 59.
2. —— xxiii. 11, 32.
2. —— 35 (*om.* σὺν αὐτοῖς, *with them*, G→Lb T Tr A ℵ.)
1. —— 43.
2. —— xxiv. 1 (*ap.*), 10, 24.
1. —— 29 1st.
2. —— 29 2nd.
1. —— 30.
2. —— 33, 44.
1. —— 52.
5c. John i. 1, 2.
3. —— 26, 31, 33 twice.
4b.—— 39.
—— ii. 4, see W thee (what have I to do)
1. —— iii. 2, 22, 26.
6. —— iv. 6.
1. —— 27 twice.
4b.—— 40.
1. —— vi. 3, 66.
1. —— vii. 33.
1. —— viii. 29.
4b.—— 38 1st.
4b.—— 38 2nd (No. 4a, L T Tr A ℵ.)
1. —— ix. 37, 40.
1. —— xi. 16, 31, 54.
6. —— xii. 3 2nd.
1. —— 8, 17.
1. —— 35 (No. 3, G L T Tr A ℵ.)
1. —— xiii. 8.
1. —— 18 (*om.* Tr A.)
1. —— 33.
1. —— xiv. 9, 16.
4b.—— 17, 23, 25.
—— 27, see You.
1. —— 30.
1. —— xv. 27.
1. —— xvi. 4, 32.
4b.—— xvii. 5 1st & 3rd.
1. —— 12, 24.
2. —— xviii. 1.
1. —— 2, 3, 5, 18, 26.
1. —— xix. 18, 40.
1. —— xx. 7, 24, 26.
2. —— xxi. 3.
1. Acts i. 4 (Beza), (*om.* G L T Tr A ℵ.)
3. —— 5 2nd.
—— 14 1st, see Accord.
2. —— 14 2nd.
2. —— 14 3rd (*om.* G⇄L Trb A ℵ.)
2. —— 17 (No. 3, G L T Tr A ℵ.)
6. —— 18.
2. —— 22.
1. —— 26.
2. —— ii. 14.
1. —— 28.
3. —— 29, 46 2nd.
5c.—— 47.
2. —— iii. 4, 8.
5c.—— 25.
2. —— iv. 13, 14, 27.
1. —— 29, 31 2nd.
2. —— v. 1.
8a.—— 16.
2. —— 17 1st.
3. —— 23.
2. —— 26.
1. —— vii. 9 2nd, 38 1st, 45
2. —— viii. 20 1st.
7a.—— 20 2nd.
6. —— 37 (*ap.*)
1. —— ix. 19, 28, 39 2nd.
4b.—— 43.
2. —— x. 2.
4b.—— 6.
2. —— 20, 23.
5c.—— xi. 2.
3. —— 16 2nd.
1. —— 21.
3. —— 26, marg. *in.*
2. —— xiii. 7.
1. —— 17.
2. —— xiv. 4 twice, 5, 13.
—— 15, see You.
—— 18, see Saying.
2. —— 20.
1. —— 23, 27.
2. —— 28.
5c.—— xv. 2.
1. —— 4.
2. —— 22 twice, 25 2nd.
7a.—— 32.
1. —— 35.
2. —— xvi. 3.
1. —— xvii. 11.
5c.—— 17 3rd.
8a.—— 25.
2. —— 34.
4b.—— xviii. 3.
2. —— 8.
1. —— 10.
2. —— 18.
4b.—— 20 (*om.* παρ' αὐτοῖς, *with them*, L T Tr A ℵ.)
7a.—— xix. 26.
—— 34, see Voice.
2. —— 38.
10.—— xx. 9.
1. —— 18, 19 1st.
1. —— 24 (*om.* μετὰ χαρᾶς, *with joy*, G⇄L T Tr A ℵ.)
7a.—— 28.
1. —— 31, 34.
2. —— 36.
2. —— xxi. 5.
4b.—— 7, 8.
2. —— 16 2nd.
4b.—— 16 3rd.
2. —— 18, 24 1st.
9b.—— 24 2nd.
2. —— 26, 29.
2. —— xxii. 9.
2. —— xxiii. 15, 27, 32.
1. —— xxiv. 1 1st, 3, 7 (*ap.*)
5c.—— 12.
1. —— 18 twice.
2. —— 24.

1. Acts xxv. 12, 23 1st.
2. —— 23 2nd.
4b.— xxvi. 8.
1. —— 12.
2. —— 13.
2. — xxvii. 2.
1. —— 10, 24.
15.—— 39.
8a.—— 41.
9b.— xxviii. 14 (No. 4b, L T Tr A ℵ.)
2. —— 16.
1. —— 31.
3. Rom. i. 4.
3. —— 9, } marg. in.
3. —— 12, }
3. —— 27.
4b.— ii. 11.
5c.— v. 1.
2. — vi. 8 1st.
— — vii. 21, see Me.
7a.— viii. 25.
2. —— 32.
4b.— ix. 14.
3. —— 22.
3. — x. 9.
3. — xii. 8 3 times.
1. —— 18.
3. —— 21.
7b.— xiv. 15 1st.
7a.—— 20.
1. — xv. 10.
3. —— 32 1st.
1. —— 33.
2. — xvi. 14.
3. —— 16.
1. —— 20, 24 (ap.)
2. 1 Cor. i. 2.
3. —— 17.
11c.— ii. 1.
5c.—— 3.
3. —— 4.
4b.— iii. 19.
— — iv. 3, see Me.
2. —— 4.
3. —— 21.
2. — v. 4.
3. —— 8 3 times.
1. — vi. 6, 7.
6. — vii. 5.
1. —— 12, 13.
4b.—— 24.
3. — x. 5.
2. —— 13.
2. — xi. 32. [Tr A ℵ.)
7a.— xiv. 19 (om. G→L
3. —— 21 twice.
2. — xvi. 4.
5c.—— 6, 7, 10.
1. —— 11, 12.
3. —— 14.
2. —— 19.
3. —— 20.
1. —— 23, 24.
2. 2 Cor. i. 1.
3. —— 12.
4b.—— 17.
2. —— 21.
7a.— ii. 4.
2. — iv. 14.
5c.— v. 8.
5c.— vi. 14 3rd, 15 1st.
1. —— 15 2nd, 16.
3. — vii. 8.
1. —— 15.
1. — viii. 4, 18.
2. —— 19 2nd (No. 3, G∾L T Tr A.)
2. — ix. 4.
5c.— xi. 9.
2. — xiii. 4.
1. —— 11.
3. —— 12.
1. —— 14.
2. Gal. i. 2.
5c.—— 18.
5c.—— ii. 5.
2. — iii. 9.
5c. Gal. iv. 18, 20.
1. —— 25, 30.
2. — v. 24.
1. — vi. 18.
3. Eph. i. 3.
3. — iii. 12.
2. —— 18.
13.—— 19.
1. — iv. 2 twice.
3. —— 19.
1. —— 25.
2. —— 31.
3. — v. 18 2nd.
3. — vi. 2.
1. —— 5.
11c.—— 6.
1. —— 7.
4b.—— 9.
3. —— 14, 15.
7a.—— 18 1st.
3. —— 18 2nd.
1. —— 23, 24.
3. —— 24, marg. (text, [in.)
2. Phil. i. 1.
1. —— 4.
— —— 7, marg. see Me.
3. —— 20.
1. — ii. 12.
2. —— 22 2nd.
— —— 23, see Go.
1. —— 29.
1. — iv. 3 2nd, 6, 9, 23.
2. —— 21.
3. Col. i. 11 1st.
1. —— 11 2nd.
3. — ii. 4.
2. —— 5.
3. —— 7.
2. —— 13, 20.
2. — iii. 3, 4, 9.
3. —— 16, 22.
3. — iv. 2, 6 1st.
2. —— 9.
1. —— 18.
1. 1 Thes. i. 6.
3. — ii. 2, 17.
5c.— iii. 4.
1. —— 13.
2. — iv. 14.
3. —— 16 3 times.
2. —— 17 twice.
3. —— 18.
2. — v. 10.
3. —— 26.
1. —— 28.
4b. 2 Thes. i. 6.
1. —— 7 twice.
3. —— 11.
5c.— ii. 5.
3. —— 9, 10.
5c.— iii. 1.
3. —— 8.
5c.—— 10.
1. —— 16, 18.
1. 1 Tim. i. 14.
1. — ii. 9 1st.
3. —— 9 2nd.
7a.—— 10.
3. —— 11.
1. —— 15.
1. — iii. 4.
1. — iv. 3, 4, 14.
8. — v. 2.
1. — — vi. 6, 21.
3. 2 Tim. i. 3.
1. — ii. 10, 22.
3. — iv. 2.
1. —— 11 twice.
4b.—— 13.
1. —— 21 1st, 22 2nd (ap.)
1. Tit. ii. 15.
1. — iii. 15 twice.
5c. Philem. 13.
1. —— 25.
5c. Heb. iv. 13.
1. — v. 7.
1. — vii. 21.
9c.— viii. 8 2nd & 3rd.
1. Heb. ix. 19.
3. —— 22, 25.
5c.— x. 16.
1. —— 22 1st.
1. — xi. 9 1st, 31 2nd.
3. —— 37.
7a.— xii. 1 2nd.
1. —— 14, 17, 28.
7a.— xiii. 12.
1. —— 17 1st, 23, 25.
2. Jas. i. 11.
4b.—— 17.
3. —— 21.
3. — ii. 1.
8a.— iii. 4.
3. —— 13 2nd.
7a. 1 Pet. i. 7. [Tr. A.)
3. —— 12 (om. G→L T
6. —— 22.
3. — ii. 18.
4b.—— 20.
3. — iii. 2.
3. — v. 14 1st.
2. 2 Pet. i. 18.
3. — ii. 7.
8a.—— 8.
3. —— 13 1st, 16.
8a.—— 17.
4b.— iii. 8.
5c. 1 John i. 2.
5c.— ii. 1.
1. 2 John 2, 3.
7a.—— 12.
7a. 3 John 13.
3. Jude 14, 23, 24.
1. Rev. i. 7, 12.
3. — ii. 16.
1. —— 22.
3. —— 23, 27.
1. Rev. iii. 4, 20 twice.
1. — iv. 1. [ℵ.)
1. — vi. 8 1st (om. G∾
3. —— 8 2nd, 3rd, 4th.
8a.—— 8 5th.
6. — viii. 5.
3. — ix. 19.
3. — xii. 5.
1. —— 9.
9b.—— 17 1st (om. L.)
1. —— 17 2nd.
1. — xiii. 4, 7 (ap.)
3. —— 10 twice.
1. — xiv. 1.
3. —— 2.
1. —— 4.
3. —— 7 (om. L.)
3. —— 9, 10, 15.
3. — xvi. 8.
1. — xvii. 1, 2 1st.
6. —— 2 2nd, 6 twice.
1. —— 12, 14 twice.
3. —— 16.
6. — xviii. 1.
1. —— 3.
3. —— 8.
1. —— 9. [Trb Ab.)
3. —— 16 (om. G≕L
3. — xix. 2, 15 twice.
1. —— 20 1st.
3. —— 20 2nd & 3rd, 21 1st.
6. —— 21 2nd.
1. — xx. 4.
1. —— 6 (μετὰ ταῦτα, *after these things*, instead of μετ' αὐτοῦ, *with him*, G∾)
1. — xxi. 3 3 times, 9, 15.
1. — xxii. 12, 21.

See also, ACCORD, AFFLICTION, AGREE, ASSEMBLE, AWAY, BE, BEAR, BEAT, BIND, BOUND, BROUGHT, BURY, CARRY, CHILD, CLOTHE, COME, COMMUNE, COMMUNICATE, COMPANY, COMPARE, COMPASS, COMPASSION, CONFER, CONSENT, CONSORT, CONTENTED, CONTINUE, COVENANT, CRUCIFY, DEAD, DEAL, DEALINGS, DEVIL, DIE, DISPUTE, DISSEMBLE, DRAW, DRINK, DWELL, EAT, ELECTED, ENDURED, ENTANGLE, FEAR, FEAST, FEED, FEELING, FELLOWSHIP, FILL, GNASH, GO, GRIEF, GRIEVE, HAND, HASTE, HAVE, HEIR, HELP, INSCRIPTION, INSURRECTION, JOURNEY, LABOUR, LABOURER, LADE, LEAD, LIVE, ME, MEET, MIND, MIXED, NOISE, NUMBER, PARTAKE, PARTAKER, PERISH, PLEASE, POSSESS, PRESENT, QUESTION, QUICKEN, RANK, REASON, REIGN, REJOICE, RISE, RUN, SEAR, SEND, SHOD, SIT, SMITE, SPEAK, SPEED, SPRING, STAND, STRIKE, STRIVE, SUBTILELY, SUFFER, TAKE, TAKEN, TALK, TEMPEST, THEE, TRAVEL, TRUST, UNITED, US, VOICE, WHAT, WIND, WITNESS, WORK.

WITHAL.

1. ἅμα, together with, at the same time.

2. καί, and, also, even.

1. Acts xxv. 27.
— 1 Cor. xii. 7, see Profit.
— 1 Tim. v. 13, see W(and)
1. Philem. 22.

WITHAL (AND)

ἅμα, at the same time, δὲ, but καί, also, } but at the same time also.

1 Tim. v. 17.

WITHDRAW (-DREW, -DRAWN.)

1. ἀποσπάω, to draw away from, to draw away from others.

2. ὑποστέλλω, to send *or* draw under. *In N.T., mid.*, to draw one's self back, *i.e. under cover, out of sight, privately or by stealth.*

1. Luke xxii. 41. | 2. Gal. ii. 12.

WITHDRAW ONE'S SELF.

1. ἀναχωρέω, to give place, give way, recede, retire.

2. ὑποχωρέω, to give place covertly, to recede *or* retire under *cover, without noise or notice.*

3. ἀφίστημι, to place away from, separate, remove, cause to depart. *Here, mid.*, to separate one's self.

4. στέλλω, to set, to place, make stand in order; *hence, with the idea of motion comes the usual signification,* to send, despatch, *implying a previous fitting out. Pass. or mid.*, to be sent, to *go. Then, from the idea of motion back to a former place,* to draw in, contract, to repress *or* restrain one's self, (*occ.* 2 Cor. viii. 20.)

1. Matt. xii. 15.
1. Mark iii. 7.
2. Luke v. 16, here part., with εἰμί, *to be*, lit., *was retiring.*
3. 1 Tim. vi. 5 (*ap.*)
4. 2 Thes. iii. 6.

WITHER (-ED, -ETH.)

ξηραίνω, to dry, make dry. *Here, pass.*, to be dried up, become dry, wither away.

1 Pet. i. 24.

WITHER AWAY.

Matt. xiii. 6.
— xxi. 19, 20.
Mark iv. 6.
— xi. 21.
Luke viii. 6.

WITHERETH (WHOSE FRUIT)

φθινοπωρινός, autumnal failing, pertaining to the decay of autumn, (*from* φθίνω, to fail, *and* ὀπώρα, autumnal.)

Jude 12.

WITHERED.

ξηρός, dry, withered.

Matt. xii. 10. | Luke vi. 6, 8.
John v. 3.

WITHERED (BE)

ξηραίνω, *see* "WITHER."

Mark iii. 1.
— 3 part. (ξηρός, *dry*, L T Tr A.)
John xv. 6.

WITHHOLD.

κατέχω, to have and hold down, hold fast, restrain.

[Here prob. it refers to the presence of the Holy Ghost in the Church, as the restraining influence, hindering the manifestation of "the man of sin," the Antichrist, until He is removed with the Church when she is caught up to meet the Lord in the air.]

2 Thes. ii. 6, marg. *hold.*

WITHIN.

1. ἐν, in, *of place, time, or element; also of the sphere or element in which the subject is concerned as dwelling or acting.*

2. ἔσωθεν, from within.

3. ἔσω, within.

4. ἐντός, within.

[*Here*, with ὑμῶν, *within you*, i.e. *within* your midst, *within* your borders *or* country. Certainly the Kingdom of God was not within the Pharisees individually, but within their midst, as shown by the presence of Jesus, the King, if they would have Him to reign over them.]

5. πρός, towards; *here, with Acc.*, in reference to, towards, against.

6. διά, through; *here, with Gen., in reference to time, marking the passage through an interval*, during, *or* after the lapse of.

2. Matt. xxiii. 25.
4. —— 26.
2. —— 27, 28.
5. Mark xiv. 4.
6. —— 58.
— Luke vii. 30, marg. see Against.
4. Luke xvii. 21, marg. *among.*
3. John xx. 26.
3. Acts v. 23.
3. 1 Cor. v. 12.
2. 2 Cor. vii. 5.
2. Rev. iv. 8.
2. Rev. v. 1.

WITHIN (FROM)

2. Mark vii. 21, 23 | 2. Luke xi. 7.

WITHIN (THAT)

{ ὁ, the
{ ἐσώτερος, inner, interior.

Heb. vi. 19.

WITHIN (THAT WHICH IS)

{ ὁ, the, *that,*
{ ἔσωθεν, from within.

Luke xi. 40.

WITHOUT. [adv, and prep.]

(*For various combinations, and list of other words used in connection, see below.*)

1. χωρίς, apart, asunder, apart from.
2. ἔξω, out of, without, outside, out of doors.
3. ἔξωθεν, from without, *i.e.* outwardly, externally.
4. ἄνευ, without, apart from, far from, (*the opp. of* σύν, together, in conjunction with, *and denoting distance*); without, *i.e.* without *the aid of the will or consent of, the instigation of, etc.*, (*non occ.*)
5. ἄτερ, without, *i.e.* not with, *either*, not having, *or* in the absence of, (*non occ.*)
6. ἐκτός, out of, without, outside.
7. { οὐ, not, (*see* "NO," *No.* 1) / μετά, with, (*see* "WITH," *No.* 1) } not with.

2. Matt. vii. 28, marg. see That not.
4. —— x. 29.
2. —— xii. 46, 47.
1. —— xiii. 34.
2. —— xxvi. 69.
2. Mark i. 45.
2. —— iii. 31, 32.
1. —— iv. 34.
2. —— xi. 4.
2. Luke i. 10.
1. —— vi. 49.
2. —— viii. 20.
2. —— xiii. 25.
5. —— xxii. 6 marg. (text, *in the absence of.*)
5. —— 35.
1. John i. 3.
1. —— xv. 5, marg. *severed from.*
2. —— xviii. 16.
2. —— xx. 11 (*om.* L ℵ.)
2. Acts v. 23 (*om.* G L T Tr A ℵ.)
7. —— 26.
1. Rom. iii. 21, 28.
1. Rom. iv. 6.
1. —— vii. 8, 9.
1. —— x. 14.
1. 1 Cor. iv. 8.
6. —— vi. 18.
1. —— xi. 11 twice.
3. 2 Cor. vii. 5.
1. Eph. ii. 12.
1. Phil. ii. 14.
1. 1 Tim. ii. 8.
1. —— v. 21.
1. Philem. 14.
1. Heb. iv. 15.
1. —— vii. 7, 20, 21.
1. —— ix. 7, 18, 22, 28.
1. —— x. 28.
1. —— xi. 6, 40.
1. —— xii. 8, 14.
2. —— xiii. 11, 12, 13.
1. Jas. ii. 18 (ἐκ, *out of*, St AVm E, marg. *by.*)
1. —— 20, 26 twice.
4. 1 Pet. iii. 1.
4. —— iv. 9.
2. Rev. xiv. 20 (No. 3, G L T Tr.)
2. Rev. xxii. 15.

WITHOUT (FROM)

3. Mark. vii. 15, 18.

WITHOUT (ONE THAT [OR WHICH] IS)

1. { ὁ, the *one* / ἔξωθεν, from without, (*see No.* 3, *above.*)
2. { ὁ, the *one* / ἔξω, out of, without, (*see No.* 2, *above.*)

2. Mark iv. 11.
1. Luke xi. 40.
2. 1 Cor. v. 12, 13.
2. Col. iv. 5.
2. 1 Thes. iv. 12.
1. 1 Tim. iii. 7.
1. Rev. xi. 2 (ὁ ἔσωθεν, *which is within*, St ℵ.)

WITHOUT (THOSE THINGS THAT ARE)

{ τὰ, the *things*
{ παρεκτός, near by without, out near.

2 Cor. xi. 28.

WITHOUT ANY.

{ μηδεμίαν, not even one, not any,
{ ποιησάμενος, making.

Acts xxv. 17.

See also, AFFECTION, BLAME, BLEMISH, CAREFULNESS, CAUSE, CEASING, CHARGE, CHILDREN, CONTROVERSY, COVETOUSNESS, DESCENT, DISSIMULATION, DISTRACTION, EFFECT, EXCUSE, FATHER, FAULT, FEAR, FRUIT, GAINSAYING, GOD, HANDS, HELP, HONOUR, HYPOCRISY, LAW, LIFE, MEASURE, MERCY, MIXTURE, MOTHER, OFFENCE, PARTIALITY, PER-

SONS, REBUKE, REPENTANCE, SEAM, SIGHT, SIGNIFICATION, SIN, SPOT, STRENGTH, UNDERSTANDING, WATER, WAVERING, WITNESS, WORLD, WRANGLING.

WITHSTAND, WITHSTOOD.

1. ἀνθίστημι, to stand against. *In N.T. only mid.*, to set one's self against, *i.e.* to withstand, oppose, resist.
2. κωλύω, to cut off; *hence,* to impede, hinder, prevent, restrain.

2. Acts xi. 17.
1. —— xiii. 8.
1. Gal. ii. 11.
1. Eph. vi. 13.
1. 2 Tim. iii. 8.
1. —— iv. 15.

WITNESS (-ES.) [noun.]

(*For the verb, and for various combinations with other words, see below.*)

1. μάρτυς, (*from the Sanscr. root,* smri, smarami, to remember; smrtis, remembrance; *Lat.*, memor); *hence, lit.* one who remembers, *i.e.* one who has information *or* knowledge of a thing, and can therefore give information concerning, bring to light *or* confirm anything. *Also, it sometimes implies that* the witness avers something and supports his statement on the strength of his own authority. *And afterwards was applied to* one who bore witness to the truth *by his death, for such is the Eng. word* martyr.
2. μαρτυρία, a bearing witness, certifying, witnessing to.
3. μαρτύριον, testimony, *as borne or given;* the declaration which confirms *or* makes known anything; witness, *or* testimony stated from direct knowledge and as an actual declaration of facts.

1. Matt. xviii. 16.
3. —— xxiv. 14.
1. —— xxvi. 65.
2. Mark xiv. 55, 56, 59.
1. —— 63.
— Luke i. 2, see Eye.
2. —— xxii. 71.
1. —— xxiv. 48.
2. John i. 7.
2. —— iii. 11.
2. —— v. 31, 32, 36.
1. Acts i. 8, 22.
1. —— ii. 32.
1. —— iii. 15.
3. —— iv. 33.
1. Acts v. 32.
1. —— vi. 13.
3. —— vii. 44.
1. —— 58.
1. —— x. 39, 41.
1. —— xiii. 31.
1. —— xxii. 15.
1. —— xxvi. 16.
1. Rom. i. 9.
1. 2 Cor. xiii. 1.
1. 1 Thes. ii. 5, 10.
1. 1 Tim. v. 19.
1. —— vi. 12.
1. 2 Tim. ii. 2.
2. Tit. i. 13.
1. Heb. x. 28.
1. —— xii. 1.
3. Jas. v. 3.
1. 1 Pet. v. 1.
— 2 Pet. i. 16, see Eye.
2. 1 John v. 9 3 times, 10.
1. Rev. i. 5.
1. —— iii. 14.
1. —— xi. 3.
2. —— xx. 4.

WITNESS (BE)

μαρτυρέω, to be a μάρτυς, (*see No.* 1, *above*), to be a witness, bear witness, *i.e.* to attest anything that one knows, *and therefore* to state with a certain degree of authority, *usually* for *something; and hence,* to confirm *or* prove.

Matt. xxiii. 31. | Heb. x. 15.

WITNESS (BEAR)

1. μαρτυρέω, *see above.*
2. συμμαρτυρέω, (*No.* 1, *with* σύν, together with, in conjunction with, *prefixed*) to bear witness with *another, i.e. to the same end or purpose.*

1. Luke iv. 22.
1. —— xi. 48 (*μάρτυρές ἐστε, witnesses are ye,* instead of *μαρτυρεῖτε,* T Tr A ℵ.)
1. John i. 7, 8, 15.
1. —— iii. 26, 28.
1. —— v. 31, 32, 33, 36, 37.
1. —— viii. 18 twice.
1. John x. 25.
1. —— xv. 27.
1. —— xviii. 23, 37.
1. Acts xv. 8.
1. —— xxii. 5.
1. —— xxiii. 11.
2. Rom. ix. 1.
1. 1 John i. 2.
1. —— v. 6, 8 (*ap.*)
1. 3 John 6.

WITNESS ALSO (BEAR)

1. συμμαρτυρέω, *see No.* 2, *above.*
2. συνεπιμαρτυρέω, (*No.* 1, *with* ἐπί, upon, *prefixed after the* σύν) to bear conjoint additional decided witness, to bear further *or* emphatic witness with, (*non occ.*)

1. Rom. ii. 15, marg. *witness with.*
2. Heb. ii. 4.

WITNESS WITH (BEAR)

συμμαρτυρέω, *see* "WITNESS (BEAR)" *No.* 2.

Rom. viii. 16.

WITNESS (BEAR FALSE)

ψευδομαρτυρέω, ("WITNESS (BE)" *with* ψευδής, false, *prefixed.*)

Matt. xix. 18.
Mark x. 19.
—— xiv. 56, 57.
Luke xviii. 20.
Rom. xiii. 9 (*om.* οὐ ψευδομαρτυρήσεις, *thou shalt not bear false witness,* G L T Tr A.)

WITNESS (-ES) (FALSE)

1. ψευδομάρτυρ, ("WITNESS," *No.* 1, *with* ψευδής, false, *prefixed.*)

2. ψευδομαρτυρία, ("WITNESS," *No.* 2, *with* ψευδής, false, *prefixed.*)

2. Matt. xv. 19.
2. —— xxvi. 59.
1. —— 60 1st (*ap.*)
1. Matt. xxvi. 60 2nd (*om.* G L T Tr A.)
1. 1 Cor. xv. 15.

WITNESS (GIVE)

μαρτυρέω, *see* "WITNESS (BE)"

Acts x. 43.

WITNESS (OBTAIN)

μαρτυρέω, *see* "WITNESS (BE)" *Here, pass.*, to be witnessed to, to have good witness, to obtain attestation.

Heb. xi. 4.

WITNESS (WITHOUT)

ἀμάρτυρος, without testimony, (*non occ.*)

Acts xiv. 17.

WITNESS (-ED, -ETH, -ING.) [verb.]

1. μαρτυρέω, *see* "WITNESS (BE)"

2. διαμαρτύρομαι, to witness throughout, to call throughout to witness; to assert, attest, or affirm *a truth with emphasis*, testify through and through, bear full and complete witness.

1. John v. 32.
2. Acts xx. 23.
1. Rom. iii. 21.
1. 1 Tim. vi. 13.
1. Heb. vii. 8.

WITNESS AGAINST.

καταμαρτυρέω, ("WITNESS (BE)" *with* κατά, against, *prefixed*), (*non occ.*)

Matt. xxvi. 62.
—— xxvii. 13.
Mark xiv. 60.
Mark xv. 4 (κατηγορέω, *lay a charge against*, L T Tr A ℵ.)

WITNESS WITH. [margin.]

Rom. ii. 15, see "WITNESS ALSO (BEAR)"

WIVES.

See, OLD.

WOE (-S.)

οὐαί, wo! alas! (Heb. אוֹי, *or* הוֹי) *uttered in grief or indignation,* (*occ.* Rev. xviii. 10, 16, 19.)

Matt. x. 21 twice.
—— xviii. 7 twice.
—— xxiii. 13, 14 (*ap.*), 15, 16, 23, 25, 27, 29.
—— xxiv. 19.
—— xxvi. 24.
Mark xiii. 17.
—— xiv. 21.
Luke vi. 24, 25 twice, 26.
—— x. 13 twice.
Luke xi. 42, 43, 44, 46, 47, [52.
—— xvii. 1.
—— xxi. 23.
—— xxii. 22.
1 Cor. ix. 16.
Jude 11.
Rev. viii. 13 3 times.
—— ix. 12 twice.
—— xi. 14 twice.
—— xii. 12.

WOLF, WOLVES.

λύκος, a wolf; (lxx. *for* זְאֵב, Is. xi. 6) *metaph. used of* a rapacious, violent, *or* wolf-like person; (*so* lxx. *for* זְאֵב, Zeph. iii. 4), (*non occ.*)

Matt. vii. 15.
—— x. 16.
Luke x. 3.
John x. 12 twice.
Acts xx. 29.

WOMAN, WOMEN.

(*For words used in various combinations, see below.*)

1. γυνή, a woman, (lxx. *for* אִשָּׁה, Gen. ii. 22, 23); *used also of a* maiden, damsel, (lxx. *for* נַעֲרָה, Esth. ii. 4), (*non occ.*)

2. θήλεια, a female; (lxx. *for* נְקֵבָה, Gen. i. 27; vi. 19; Lev. xxvii. 4, *etc.*)

1. Matt. v. 28.
1. —— ix. 20, 22.
1. —— xi. 11.
1. —— xiii. 33.
1. —— xiv. 21.
1. —— xv. 22, 28, 38.
1. —— xxii. 27.
1. —— xxvi. 7, 10.
— —— 13, see This.
1. —— xxvii. 55.
1. —— xxviii. 5.
1. Mark v. 25, 33.
1. —— vii. 25, 26.
1. —— x. 12 (αὐτή, *she*, T Tr A ℵ.)
1. —— xii. 22.
1. —— xiv. 3.
1. —— xv. 40.
1. Luke i. 28 (*ap.*), 42.
1. —— iv. 26. [44 twice.
1. —— vii. 28, 37, 39,
— —— 45, 46, see This.
1. —— 50.
1. —— viii. 2, 43, 47.
1. —— x. 38.
1. —— xi. 27.
1. —— xiii. 11, 12, 21.
1. —— xv. 8.
1. —— xx. 32.
1. —— xxii. 57.
1. —— xxiii. 27, 49, 55.
1. —— xxiv. 22, 24.
1. John ii. 4.
1. —— iv. 7, 9 twice, 11, 15, 17, 19, 21, 25, 27, 28, 39, 42.
1. John viii. 3 (*ap.*), 4 (*ap.*), 9 (*ap.*), 10 twice (*ap.*)
1. —— xvi. 21.
1. —— xix. 26.
1. —— xx. 13, 15.
1. Acts i. 14.
1. —— v. 14.
1. —— viii. 3, 12.
1. —— ix. 2.
— —— 36, see This.
1. —— xiii. 50.
1. —— xvi. 1, 13, 14.
1. —— xvii. 4, 12, 34.
1. —— xxii. 4.
2. Rom. i. 26, 27.
1. —— vii. 2.
1. 1 Cor. vii. 1.
— —— 2, see Every.
1. —— 13.
1. —— xi. 3, 5, 6 twice, 7, 8 twice, 9 twice, 10, 11 twice, 12 twice, 13, 15.
1. —— xiv. 34, 35.
1. Gal. iv. 4. [14.
1. 1 Tim. ii. 9, 10, 11, 12,
— 2 Tim. iii. 6, see W (silly)
1. Heb. xi. 35.
1. 1 Pet. iii. 5.
1. Rev. ii. 20.
1. —— ix. 8.
1. —— xii. 1, 4, 6, 13, 14, 15, 16, 17.
1. —— xiv. 4. [18.
1. —— xvii. 3, 4, 6, 7, 9,

WOMAN (SILLY)

γυναικάριον, a little woman; *then, in contempt*, a weak, silly woman, (*non occ.*)

2 Tim. iii. 6.

See also, AGED, ELDER, EVERY, FREE, HOLY, THIS, TWO, YOUNG.

WOMB (-s.)

1. κοιλία, (*from* κοῖλος, hollow) the belly, the bowels, *as the receptacle of food, put as often in Eng. for* the stomach, *either in men or animals. Then, from the Heb., put for* the womb, *and, as personified, put for the woman herself*, Lev. xi. 27; xxiii. 29; (*so* lxx. *for* בטן, Gen. xxv. 24; Is. xliv. 2; מעים, Gen. xxv. 23; Ruth i. 11; *for* רחם, Job iii. 11; x. 18.)

2. μήτρα, matrix, womb; (lxx. *for* רחם, Numb. iii. 12; 1 Sam. i. 5, 6; Jer. i. 5), (*non occ.*)

3. γαστήρ, the belly; *also* the womb; (lxx. *for* בטן, Gen. xxv. 23; Numb. v. 22; Ps. lviii. 4.)

1. Matt. xix. 12.
1. Luke i. 15.
3. —— 31.
1. —— 41, 42, 44.
1. —— ii. 21.
2. —— 23.
1. Luke xi. 27.
1. —— xxiii. 29.
1. John iii. 4.
1. Acts iii. 2.
1. —— xiv. 8.
2. Rom. iv. 19.
1. Gal. i. 15.

WON.

See, WIN.

WONDER (-s.) [noun.]

1. τέρας, a supernatural prodigy, a wonder, *with ref. to the excitement of surprise, esp. as portending something future rather than as arising from anything in the past. As used of Christ's miracles it has special reference to their* supernatural *character.*

2. σημεῖον, a sign *or* token *by which anything is designated, distinguished, or known. As used of Christ's miracles it has special reference to their object as the credentials of His mission and of His fulfilment of the O.T. prophecies.*

3. θάμβος, astonishment, amazement; awe, surprise *at a strange or unusual deed or occurrence.*

1. Matt. xxiv. 24.
1. Mark xiii. 22.
1. John iv. 48.
1. Acts ii. 19, 22, 43.
3. —— iii. 10.
1. —— iv. 30.
1. —— v. 12.
1. —— vi. 8.
1. —— vii. 36.
1. Acts xiv. 3.
1. —— xv. 12.
1. Rom. xv. 19.
1. 2 Cor. xii. 12.
1. 2 Thes. ii. 9.
1. Heb. ii. 4.
2. Rev. xii. 1, } marg.
2. —— 3, } *sign.*
2. —— xiii. 13.

WONDER (-ED, -ING.) [verb.]

1. θαυμάζω, to wonder, marvel, be astonished *or* amazed; to wonder at; *hence*, to admire.

2. ἐξίστημι, to put out of place. *In the 2 aor. and mid., as here*, to be beside one's self, be confused, filled with astonishment.

1. Matt. xv. 31.
1. Mark vi. 51 (*om.* καὶ ἐθαύμαζον, *and wondered*, G L[b] T Tr A ℵ.)
1. Luke ii. 18.
1. —— iv. 22.
1. —— viii. 25.
1. Luke ix. 43.
1. —— xi. 14.
1. —— xxiv. 12 (*ap.*), 41.
2. Acts viii. 13.
1. —— xiii. 41.
1. Rev. xiii. 3.
1. —— xvii. 6.
1. —— 8, mid.

WONDER AT.

1. Acts vii. 31.

WONDERING (GREATLY)

ἔκθαμβος, ("WONDER," (noun) *No.* 3, *with* ἐκ, out of, *prefixed*) greatly amazed, awe-struck, (*non occ.*)

Acts iii. 11.

WONDERFUL THING.

{ τὸ, the,
{ θαυμάσιον, a wonderful, admirable *thing*, (*non occ.*)

Matt. xxi. 15.

WONDERFUL WORK.

1. δύναμις, the being able, ability, power. *As used of Christ's miracles it has special reference to the* divine power *by which they were wrought; hence*, a work *with reference to* the power *required for its performance.*

2. μεγαλεῖος, great, grand, magnificent; (lxx. *for* גדלות, Ps. lxxi. 19), (*occ.* Luke i. 49.)

1. Matt. vii. 22.
2. Acts ii. 11.

WONT (AS ONE IS)

κατὰ, according to
τὸ, the
ἔθος, custom, usage.

Luke xxii. 39.

WONT (BE)

1. ἔθω, to be accustomed, to be wont.
2. νομίζω, to regard *or* acknowledge as custom, to have and hold as customary. *Here, pass.*, to be accustomed, be wont.

1. Matt. xxvii. 15. | 1. Mark x. 1.
2. Acts xvi. 13.

WOOD.

1. ξύλον, wood, timber; wood *for fuel or any other use.*
2. ὕλη, a wood, a forest, (*non occ.*)

1. 1 Cor. iii. 5. | 2. Jas. iii. 5, marg. matter.
1. Rev. xviii. 12 twice.

WOOL.

ἔριον, wool; (lxx. *for* צֶמֶר, Is. i. 18; Prov. xxxi. 13), (*non occ.*)

Heb. ix. 19. | Rev. i. 14.

WORD (-S.)

(*For various combinations with other words, see below.*)

1. λόγος, the word, (*not in the grammatical sense like No.* 2, but) the spoken word; the word, *not in its outward form, but as connected with the inward thought;* the word, *not written, but spoken;* the word, *not as a part of speech, but as part of what is uttered.*

(a) *Hence, used of* the 2nd person of the blessed Trinity, *because as* the word spoken *manifests the invisible thought, so* He manifests *to us* the invisible Deity and Godhead.

[As λόγος is the embodiment and outward expression of the invisible thought, so the 2nd person manifests the invisible Deity, and is said to be "God manifest in the flesh," (1 Tim. iii. 16); "the express image of His person," (Heb. i. 3); "the image of the invisible God," (Col. i. 15.)

The Godhead is "Spirit," (John iv. 24) and as spirit has no likeness to matter, God himself took some *creature form*, (not human) before He created anything, in order that creation might have a mediator, or a means of communion with Deity. Hence, Christ is said to have been, "In the beginning," (John i. 1); "before all things," (Col. i. 17.) "The first-born of every creature," (Col. i. 15) "the beginning of the creation of God," (Rev. iii. 14); and hence, "In Him dwelleth all the fulness of the Godhead bodily," (Col. ii. 9.)

The λόγος is therefore God, *i.e.* אלהים, Elohim. The work of creation is predicated of both, (Gen. i. 1; John i. 3 Col. i. 16; Heb. i. 2.) Elohim is not the title of Deity, but the title of God as the Creator, and always has reference to creation, power, and glory, (while the title "Jehovah" sets forth the self-existent one, and His covenant relationships.)

Elohim is the one who was set apart by Deity (so to speak) by an oath for His office in relation to creation. For Alah means to take an oath, and thus the term Elohim is not the title of Deity, but is applied to any who are set apart with the solemnity of an oath to be the representative of another, to carry out certain acts; hence, it is applied not only to the 2nd person of the Trinity, but also to magistrates, (Ex. xxi. 6; xxii. 8, 9, 28, quoted Acts xxiii. 5), to Moses (Ex. vii. 1), and even to Idols, (Ex. xii. 12; Numb. xxv. 2; Gen. xxxi. 30, *cf.* 19) because they were used for representing God. Plural, because Elohim *represents* the Godhead.

Elohim, therefore, is the λόγος or "WORD," who took creaturehood, to create, (as He afterwards took humanity, to redeem.) As such

He is the Father's "Servant," "Angel," or "Messenger," (*Elohim*, denotes His being set apart to the office with an oath; *Messiah*, or Christ, His anointing to the work of Redemption; *Angel, or Messenger*, referring to His actual dispatch; *Servant*, with reference to the service actually to be done). He appeared to Adam and the Patriarchs, (Gen. xvi., xvii., xviii., xxi., xxii., xxxii.; Ex. iii., vi.; Josh. v. 13-15 (*cf.* Ex. xxiii. 23); Judg. xiii., etc., etc.). This view only makes permanent that which most commentators assume as being only temporary.

His mission in connection with creation was to manifest Deity to His creatures, (Prov. viii. 22-31.) His work was begun with Adam (made in His likeness and image), but the fall interrupted that mission, and it was necessarily suspended. Then "the Word (λόγος) was made flesh," (John i. 14) in order that He might redeem the creation from the curse. Made flesh in order that He might suffer and die, (*see* Heb. x. 5; Ps. xl. 6; Is. xlii. 1; Phil. ii. 7.)

As the λόγος, He was "the everlasting Son of the Father," "the only-begotten Son," who was GIVEN. Given to become a human child. Hence, He was "the Son" before He was "a gift," but could not be a human "child" before He was "born."

"God of the substance of His Father, begotten before the worlds," but "Man of the substance of His mother, born in the world."*

But further, inasmuch as the λόγος, as the Living Word, became so to manifest and reveal Deity to us, so "the written Word" was given with the same object and for the same purpose. Hence, it is sometimes difficult to know which is intended, as the same things are predicated of each. Both are "*the truth*," (John xiv. 6; xvii. 17.) Both are "*everlasting*," (Ps. cxix. 89; Matt. xxiv. 34, 35; 1 Pet. i. 25.) Both are "*life*," (John xi. 25; xiv. 6; 1 Pet. i. 22; 1 John i. 1.) Both "*save*," (Acts xvi. 31; 1 Cor. xv. 2.) Both "*purify*," (Tit. ii. 14; 1 Pet. i. 22.) Both "*sanctify*," (John xvii. 17.) Both "*beget to new life*," (1 Pet. i. 23; Jas. i. 18.) Both "*shall judge*," (John vi. 26, 27; xii. 48.) Both are "*glorified*," (Rom. xv. 9; Acts xiii. 48.)]

(b) *Plural, or translated by the plural*, discourse, the word *as spoken*, and *as forming* the subject matter of discourse.

2. ῥῆμα, that which is spoken, a sentence; saying, speech, discourse, a declaration, command, *or* promise. *Then*, the thing spoken of, the matter, affair, thing. (*As distinguished from No.* 1 *it is a part of what is spoken*, a word *as part of a sentence*, a sentence *as part of a discourse, a portion as part of a whole.*)

— Matt. ii. 8, see W again (bring)
— —— 13, see W (bring)
2. —— iv. 4.
1. —— viii. 8, 16.
1. —— x. 14.
1. —— xii. 32.
2. —— 36.
1. —— 37 twice.
1. —— xiii. 19, 20, 21, 22 twice, 23.
1. —— xv. 23.
2. —— xviii. 16.
1. —— xxii. 46.
1. —— xxiv. 35.
1b. —— xxvi. 44.
2. —— 75.
2. —— xxvii. 14.
— —— xxviii. 8, see W (bring)
1. Mark ii. 2.
1. —— iv. 14, 15 twice, 16, 17, 18, 19, 20, 33.
1. —— v. 36.
1. —— vii. 13.
1. —— viii. 38.
1. —— x. 24.
1b. —— xii. 13.
1. —— xiii. 31.
1b. —— xiv. 39.
2. —— 72.
1. —— xvi. 20 (*ap.*)
1. Luke i. 2, 20.
2. —— 38.
2. —— ii. 29.
2. —— iii. 2.
1. —— 4.
2. —— iv. 4 (*ap.*)
1. —— 22, 32, 36.
1. Luke v. 1.
2. —— 5.
1. —— vii. 7.
1. —— viii. 11, 12, 13, 15, 21.
1. —— ix. 26.
1. —— x. 39.
1. —— xi. 28.
1. —— xii. 10.
1b. —— xx. 20.
2. —— 26.
1. —— xxi. 33.
1. —— xxii. 61.
1. —— xxiii. 9.
2. —— xxiv. 8, 11.
1. —— 19, 44.
1a. John i. 1 3 times, 14.
1. —— ii. 22.
2. —— iii. 34.
1. —— iv. 41, 50.
1. —— v. 24, 38.
2. —— 47.
2. —— vi. 63, 68.
2. —— viii. 20.
1. —— 31, 37, 43.
2. —— 47.
2. —— x. 21.
1. —— 35.
2. —— xii. 47, 48 1st.
1. —— 48 2nd.
2. —— xiv. 10.
1b. —— 23.
1. —— 24.
1. —— xv. 3.
2. —— 7.
1. —— 20, 25.
1. —— xvii. 6.
2. —— 8.
1. —— 14, 17, 20.

* The author is indebted to his friend the Rev. H. S. Warleigh, Rector of Ashchurch, for most of the ideas developed above.

2. Acts ii. 14.
1. ——— 23, 40, 41.
1. —— iv. 4, 29, 31.
1. —— v. 5.
2. ——— 20.
1. —— vi. 2, 4, 7.
2. ——— 11, 13.
1. —— vii. 22.
1. —— viii. 4, 14, 25.
2. —— x. 22.
1. ——— 36.
2. ——— 37, 44 1st.
1. ——— 44 2nd.
1. —— xi. 1.
2. ——— 14, 16.
1. ——— 19.
1. —— xii. 24.
1. —— xiii. 5, 7, 15, 26.
2. ——— 42.
1. ——— 44, 46, 48, 49.
1. —— xiv. 3, 25.
1. —— xv. 7, 15, 24.
— ——— 32, see W (with many)
1. ——— 35, 36.
1. —— xvi. 6, 32.
2. ——— 38.
1. —— xvii. 11, 13.
1. —— xviii. 11.
1b.——— 15.
1. —— xix. 10, 20.
1. —— xx. 32, 35.
1b.——— 38.
1. —— xxii. 22.
2. —— xxvi. 25.
2. —— xxviii. 25.
1. Rom. ix. 6, 9.
2. —— x. 8 twice, 17, 18.
1. —— xv. 18.
— —— xvi. 18, see W (good)
1b.1 Cor. i. 17, marg. *speech.*
1. —— ii. 4 (*om.* G∾), 13.
1. —— iv. 20.
1. —— xii. 8 twice.
1b.—— xiv. 9.
1. ——— 19 twice, 36.
1. 2 Cor. i. 18, marg. *preaching.*
1. —— ii. 17.
1. —— iv. 2.
1. —— v. 19.
1. —— vi. 7.
1. —— x. 11.
2. —— xii. 4.
2. —— xiii. 1.
1. Gal. v. 14.
1. —— vi. 6.
1. Eph. i. 13.
1. Eph. v. 6.
2. ——— 26.
2. —— vi. 17.
1. Phil. i. 14.
1. —— ii. 16.
1. Col. i. 5, 25.
1. —— iii. 16, 17.
1. 1 Thes. i. 5, 6, 8.
1b.—— ii. 5.
1. ——— 13 twice.
1. —— iv. 15, 18.
1. 2 Thes. ii. 2, 15, 17.
1. —— iii. 1, 14.
1. 1 Tim. iv. 5, 6, 12.
1. —— v. 17.
1. —— vi. 3.
1. 2 Tim. i. 13.
1. —— ii. 9, 15, 17.
1. —— iv. 2. [ing.
1. ——— 15, marg. *preach-*
1. Tit. i. 3, 9.
1. —— ii. 5.
2. Heb. i. 3.
1. —— ii. 2.
1. —— iv. 2, 12.
1. —— v. 13.
1. —— vi. 1, marg. (text, *doctrine.*)
2. ——— 5.
1. —— vii. 28.
2. —— xi. 3, 19 1st.
1. —— xii. 19 2nd.
1. —— xiii. 7, 22.
1. Jas. i. 18, 21, 22, 23.
1. —— iii. 2.
1. 1 Pet. i. 23.
2. ——— 25.
1. —— ii. 8.
1. —— iii. 1 twice.
1. 2 Pet. i. 19.
1. —— ii. 3.
2. —— iii. 2.
1. ——— 5, 7.
1a.1 John i. 1.
1. ——— 10.
1. —— ii. 5. 7, 14.
1. —— iii. 18.
1a.—— v. 7 (*ap.*)
1. 3 John 10.
2. Jude 17.
1. Rev. i. 2, 3, 9.
1. —— iii. 8, 10.
1. —— vi. 9.
1. —— xii. 11.
2. —— xvii. 17 (No. 1b. G L T Tr A ℵ.)
1b.—— xix. 13.
1. —— xx. 4.
1. —— xxi. 5.
1. —— xxii. 18, 19.

WORD (BRING)

1. ἀπαγγέλλω, to announce *or* report from *some place or person; then, gen.*, to announce, report, *or* publish *something that has happened, been experienced, or heard.*

2. εἶπον, to utter definite words, to enunciate words and things to auditors and commune respecting them, to speak *or* utter words successively, communicate by words.

2. Matt. ii. 13. | 1. Matt. xxviii. 8.

WORD AGAIN (BRING)

ἀπαγγέλλω, *see above, No.* 1.

Matt. ii. 13.

WORD (OF THE)

λογικός, pertaining to speech, pertaining to reason; reasonable, united to the rational faculties *with an allusion to the word* λόγος, (*see* "WORD," *No.* 1) gifted with reason, *i.e.* milk to be found in the Word of God.

1 Pet. ii. 2.

WORDS (GOOD)

χρηστολογία, useful *or* profitable discourse, good-natured *or* kind words, (*non occ.*)

Rom. xvi. 18.

WORDS (WITH MANY)

διὰ, through, by means of, λόγου, discourse, πολλοῦ, much,	by means of much discourse.

Acts xv. 32.

See also, ENTICING, FEW, STRIFE, STRIVE, SWELLING, THESE.

WORK (-s.) [noun.]

1. ἔργον, work, deed, *the result or object of employment*; work as a single act; *then*, that which is brought into being or accomplished by labour, the thing wrought.

2. λόγος, the word, (*spoken, not written, see* "WORD," *No.* 1). *In a formal sense*, a word *as forming part of what is spoken; as a means or instrument* (*not as a product*) the speaking. *In a material sense*, the word *as that which is spoken*, an exposition *or* account *which one gives; hence*, an account, a reckoning.

3. πρᾶγμα, the thing done *or* to be done, any deed, act, fact, matter; business, affair.

4. *πρᾶξις*, a doing, action; practice; conduct.

1. Matt. v. 16.
1. —— xi. 2.
4. —— xvi. 27.
1. —— xxiii. 3, 5.
1. —— xxvi. 10.
1. Mark xiii. 34.
1. —— xiv. 6.
1. John iv. 34.
1. —— v. 20, 36 twice.
1. —— vi. 28, 29.
1. —— vii. 3, 7, 21.
1. —— viii. 39.
1. —— ix. 3, 4. [37, 38.
1. —— x. 25, 32 twice, 33,
1. —— xiv. 10, 11, 12.
1. —— xv. 24.
1. —— xvii. 4.
1. Acts v. 38.
1. —— vii. 41.
1. —— ix. 36.
1. —— xiii. 2, 41 1st.
1. ——— 41 2nd (*om.* G→)
1. —— xiv. 26.
1. —— xv. 18 (*ap.*), 38.
1. —— xxvi. 20.
— —— xxvii. 16, see W (have much)
1. Rom. ii. 15.
1. —— iii. 27.
1. —— iv. 2, 6.
1. —— ix. 11.
2 ——— 28 1st, } account, marg.
2. ——— 28 2nd, (*ap.*) } account, marg.
1. ——— 32.
1. —— xi. 6 1st, 6 2nd.
1. ——— 6 3rd & 4th (*ap.*)
1. —— xiii. 3, 12.
1. —— xiv. 20. [15.
1. 1 Cor. iii. 13 twice, 14,
1. —— ix. 1.
1. —— xv. 58.
1. —— xvi. 10.
1. 2 Cor. ix. 8.
1. —— xi. 15.
1. Gal. ii. 16 3 times.
1. —— iii. 2, 5, 10.
1. —— v. 19.
1. —— vi. 4.
1. Eph. ii. 9, 10.
1. —— iv. 12.
1. —— v. 11.
1. Phil. i. 6.
1. —— ii. 30.
1. Col. i. 10, 21.
1. 1 Thes. i. 3.
1. —— v. 13.
1. 2 Thes. i. 11.
1. —— ii. 17.
1. 1 Tim. ii. 10.
1. —— iii. 1.
1. —— v. 10 twice, 25.
1. —— vi. 18.
1. 2 Tim. i. 9.
1. —— ii. 21.
1. —— iii. 17.
1. —— iv. 5, 14, 18.
1. Tit. i. 16 twice.
1. —— ii. 7, 14.
1. —— iii. 1, 5, 8.
1. ——— 14, marg. *trade.*
1. Heb. i. 10.
1. —— ii. 7 (*ap.*)
1. —— iii. 9.
1. —— iv. 3, 4, 10.
1. —— vi. 1, 10.
1. —— ix. 14.
1. —— x. 24.
1. —— xiii. 21.
1. Jas. i. 4, 25.
1. —— ii. 14, 17. 18 3 times, 20, 21, 22 twice, 24, 25,
1. —— iii. 13. [26.
3. ——— 16.
1. 1 Pet. i. 17.
1. —— ii. 12.
1. 2 Pet. iii. 10.
1. 1 John iii. 8, 12.
1. Rev. ii. 2, 5.
1. ——— 9 (*om.* ἔργα καί, *works and*, G⇉L T Tr A.)
1. ——— 13 (*ap.*)
1. ——— 19 1st (*om.* τὰ ἔργα καί, *thy works and*, G→)
1. ——— 19 2nd, 23, 26.
1. —— iii. 1, 2, 8, 15.
1. —— ix. 20.
1. —— xiv. 13.
1. —— xv. 3.
1. —— xviii. 6.
1. —— xx. 12, 13.
1. —— xxii. 12.

WORK (HAVE MUCH)

{ *μόλις*, with difficulty, hardly, } *lit.*, we were scarcely able;
{ *ἰσχύω*, to be able, prevail, } *or* we prevailed with difficulty.

Acts xxvii. 16.

See also, GREATER, MIGHTY, WONDERFUL.

WORK (-ETH, -ING, WROUGHT.) [verb.]

1. *ἐργάζομαι*, to work, to labour; to form by labour, produce, bring to pass.

2. *κατεργάζομαι*, (*No.* 1, *with* κατά, down, *prefixed*) to work down, effect, achieve.

3. *ἐνεργέω*, to be in work, to be effective, active, operative. to energize *or* be energized.

4. *ποιέω*, to make, *i.e.* to form, bring about, cause; *also*, to do, *i.e. of actions continued and not yet completed*, to do.

5. { *εἰς*, unto, with a view to, *ἐργασία*, work, labour; practice, performance; occupation, trade, craft, } unto making a trade of.

1. Matt. vii. 23.
4. —— xx. 12, marg. *continue.*
1. —— xxi. 28.
1. —— xxvi. 10.
— Mark vi. 2, see Wrought [(be)
1. —— xiv. 6.
— —— xvi. 20, see W with.
1. Luke xiii. 14.
— John iii. 21, see Wrought (be)
1. John v. 17 twice.
1. —— vi. 28, 30.
1. —— ix. 4 twice.
— —— xix. 23, marg. see Woven.
— Acts v. 12, see Wrought [(be)
1. —— x. 35.
1. —— xiii. 41.
4. —— xv. 12.
1. —— xviii. 3.
4. —— xix. 11.
4. —— xxi. 19.
2. Rom. i. 27.
1. —— ii. 10.
1. —— iv. 4, 5.
2. ——— 15.
2. —— v. 3.
2. —— vii. 8, 13.
— —— viii. 28, see W together.
1. —— xiii. 10.
2. Rom. xv. 18.
1. 1 Cor. iv. 12.
3. —— xii. 6, 11.
1. —— xvi. 10.
3. 2 Cor. iv. 12.
2. ——— 17.
2. —— v. 5.
2. —— vii. 10 1st (No. 1, L T Tr A ℵ.)
2. ——— 10 2nd, 11.
— —— xii. 12, see Wrought [(be)
3. Gal. iii. 5.
3. —— v. 6.
3. Eph. i. 11, 20.
3. —— ii. 2.
5. —— iv. 19.
1. ——— 28.
— Phil. ii. 12, see W out.
3. ——— 13.
1. 1 Thes. iv. 11.
1. 2 Thes. iii. 8, 10, 11, 12.
1. Heb. xi. 23.
4. —— xiii. 21, marg. *do.*
2. Jas. i. 3.
2. ——— 20 (No. 1, L T Tr A ℵ.)
— —— ii. 22, see W with.
2. 1 Pet. iv. 3.
1. 2 John 8, marg. *gain.*
4. Rev. xvi. 14.
4. —— xix. 20.
4. —— xxi. 27.

WORK EFFECTUALLY.

3. 1 Thes. ii. 13, mid.

WORK EFFECTUALLY IN.

3. Gal. ii. 8.

WORK OUT.

2. Phil. ii. 12.

WORK TOGETHER.

συνεργέω, (*No.* 3, *with* σύν, together in conjunction with, *prefixed.*)

Rom. viii. 28.

WORK WITH.

συνεργέω, *see above.*

Mark xvi. 20 (*ap.*) | Jas. ii. 22.

WROUGHT (BE)

1. ἐργάζομαι, *see No.* 1, *above. Here, pass.*

2. κατεργάζομαι, *see No.* 2, *above.*

3. γίνομαι, to begin to be, to become, come to pass, arise; *of works*, to be wrought *or* performed.

3. Mark vi. 2.
1. John iii. 21.
3. Acts v. 12.
— 2 Cor. i. 6, marg. see Effectual (be)
2. 2 Cor. xii. 12.

WORKER (-S.)

ἐργάτης, a worker, a labourer; a worker *or* doer *of anything.*

Luke xiii. 27.
1 Cor. xii. 29, see Miracles.
2 Cor. xi. 13.
Phil. iii. 2.

WORKER (FELLOW)

συνεργός, a working together with, *i.e. with the same motives and objects*, co-operating, fellow-helper.

Col. iv. 11.

WORKER TOGETHER.

συνεργέω, *see* "WORK TOGETHER." *Here, participle.*

2 Cor. vi. 1.

WORK-FELLOW.

συνεργός, *see* "WORKER (FELLOW)"

Rom. xvi. 21.

WORKING. [noun.]

1. ἐνέργεια, the being in work, energy, power in action, *i.e.* effectual operation, efficiency, active power.

2. ἐνέργημα, what is wrought, *i.e.* effect produced; a work wrought *by us and in us,* (*occ.* 1 Cor. xii. 6.)

2. 1 Cor. xii. 10.
1. Eph. i. 19.
1. Phil. iii. 21.
1. Col. i. 29.
1. 2 Thes. ii. 9.

WORKING (EFFECTUAL)

1. Eph. iii. 7. | 1. Eph. iv. 16.

WORKING (FORBEAR)

{ μὴ, not, (*see* "NO," *No.* 2)
ἐργάζομαι, to work, (*see* "WORK," *No.* 1) } not to work, to forbear working.

1 Cor. ix. 6.

WORKMAN (-MEN.)

ἐργάτης, *see* "WORKER."

Matt. x. 10. | 2 Tim. ii. 15. | Acts xix. 25.

WORKMANSHIP.

ποίημα, a thing made, a thing produced, *as with effort, object, and design,* (*occ.* Rom. i. 20.)

Eph. ii. 10.

WORLD (-S.)

1. κόσμος, order, *i.e.* regular disposition and arrangement; *hence,* ornament, decoration; (lxx. *for* עדי, Ex. xxxiii. 4, 5, 6; Is. xlix. 18; Jer. iv. 30; Ezek. vii. 20; *and* תפארת, Prov. xx. 29; Is. iii. 18), (*prob. from the root* καδ, *as it occurs e.g. in* καίνυμαι, to polish. *The same is found in the Heb. word* ברא, create, *which means lit.* to cut, cut out, carve, to cut *or* pare down, to plane and polish. *All which implies that the creation was* a perfect work, in perfect and beautiful order. *Not a chaos as is usually conceived.* Gen. i. 1 *says,* בראשית, in former times, of old, God created (*in perfect order*) the heavens and the earth. "And the earth became (היה *being very frequently so translated*) confusion and emptiness." *See* the expression in Is. xxxiv. 11, *and* Jer. iv. 23; *but how and when it became so prior to fitting it up for man is not revealed. The* lxx. *never use* κόσμος *to denote* the world: *it is first used in the apocryphal books of Wisdom and 2 Macc. to denote* the universe; *and in the N.T. is used with a new force.*

Thus, κόσμος denotes the order of the world, the ordered universe, the ordered entirety of God's creation, *but considered as separated from God. Then,* the abode of humanity, *or* that order of things in which humanity moves *or* of which man is the centre; *then,* mankind as it manifests itself in and through such an order; *then,*

that order of things which, in consequence of and since the Fall, is alienated from God, as manifested in and through the human race.

[The Scriptures are taken up with the histories and destinies of *three worlds:*

I. "The world that then was," 2 Pet. iii. 5, 6, *i.e.* before the flood.

II. "The heavens and the earth which now are," 2 Pet. iii. 7; *and*

III. "The new heavens and the new earth," 2 Pet. iii. 13; Rev. xxi. 1; Is. li. 16; lxv. 17; lxvi. 22. See also under "HEAVEN," (*occ.* 1 Pet. iii. 3.)

(a) *with* οὗτος, this; *i.e.* this world—the world that now is, *as distinguished "from the world that then was," or the "new earth" that is yet to be.*

2. αἰών, (*from* ἄω, ἄημι, to blow, to breathe). *αἰών denoted originally* the life which hastes away in the breathing of our breath, life *as transitory; then,* the course of life, time of life, life in its temporal form. *Then,* the space of a human life, an age, *or* generation *in respect of duration,* (*as γένεα is* a generation in respect of race). The time lived *or* to be lived by men, time as moving, historical time *as well as eternity.* Ἀιών *always includes a reference to* the filling of time, (*as the Lat.* seculum *does* to the time in which life passes). *Accordingly,* αἰών denotes the unbounded time, past or future, in which the history of the world is accomplished.

Hence, an age, end, *or* dispensation, designed, adjusted, and fitted out by God, (Heb. xi. 3) *according to what is called in* Eph. iii. 11 πρόθεσις τῶν αἰώνιων, the purpose of the ages *or* dispensations.

(a) *plural,* ages.

3. οἰκουμένη, (*the pres. part. of* οἰκέω, to inhabit; *hence*) the inhabited world. *In a more restricted sense* used by the Greeks and Romans to designate their portions of the world, in contrast with barbarian lands, (*occ.* Luke xxi. 26.)

4. γῆ, the earth, the dry land, (*as opp. to water or the sea*); the earth, *as contrasted with heaven, naturally and morally.*

1. Matt. iv. 8.
1. —— v. 14.
2. —— xii. 32.
2. —— xiii. 22.
1. —— 35 (*om.* τοῦ κόσμου, *of the world,* L T Tr A.)
1. —— 38.
2. —— 39, 40, 49.
1. —— xvi. 26.
1. —— xviii. 7.
2. —— xxiv. 3.
3. —— 14.
1. —— 21.
1. —— xxv. 34.
1. —— xxvi. 13.
2. —— xxviii. 20.
2. Mark iv. 19.
1. —— viii. 36.
2. —— x. 30.
1. —— xiv. 9.
1. —— xvi. 15 (*ap.*)
3. Luke ii. 1.
3. —— iv. 5.
1. —— ix. 25.
1. —— xi. 50.
1. —— xii. 30.
2. —— xvi. 8.
2. —— xviii. 30.
2. —— xx. 34, 35.
1. John i. 9, 10[3 times], 29.
1. —— iii. 16, 17[3 times], 19.
1. —— iv. 42.
1. —— vi. 14, 33, 51.
1. —— vii. 4, 7.
1. —— viii. 12.
1a. —— 23[twice].
1. —— 26.
1. —— ix. 5[twice].
1a. —— 39.
1. —— x. 36.
1a. —— xi. 9.
1. —— 27.
1. —— xii. 19.
1a. —— 25, 31[twice].
1. —— 46, 47[twice].
1a. —— xiii. 1[1st].
1. —— 1[2nd].
1. —— xiv. 17, 19, 22, 27.
1a. —— 30 (*om.* οὗτος, *this,* G L T Tr A ℵ), i.e. *the.*
1. —— 31.
1. —— xv. 18, 19,[5 times].
1. —— xvi. 8.
1a. —— 11.
1. —— 20, 21, 28[twice], 33[twice].
1. —— xvii. 5, 6, 9, 11[twice].
1. —— 12 (*om.* ἐν τῷ κόσμῳ, *in the world,* G→L T Tr A ℵ.)
1. —— 13, 14[3 times], 15, 16[twice], 18[twice], 21, 23, 24, 25.
1. —— xviii. 20.
1a. —— 36[twice], 37.
1. —— xxi. 25.
3. Acts xi. 28.
3. —— xvii. 6.
1. —— 24.
3. —— 31.
3. —— xix. 27.
3. —— xxiv. 5.
1. Rom. i. 8, 20.
1. —— iii. 6, 19.
1. Rom. iv. 13.
1. —— v. 12, 13.
3. —— x. 18.
1. —— xi. 12, 15.
2. —— xii. 2.
2. 1 Cor. i. 20[1st].
1a. —— 20[2nd].
1. —— 21, 27[1st], 27[2nd] (*ap.*), 28.
2. —— ii. 6[twice].
2a. —— 7.
2. —— 8.
1. —— 12.
2. —— iii. 18.
1a. —— 19.
1. —— 22.
1. —— iv. 9, 13.
1a. —— v. 10[1st].
1. —— 10[2nd].
1. —— vi. 2[twice].
1a. —— vii. 31[twice].
1. —— 33, 34.
1. —— viii. 4.
2a. —— x. 11.
1. —— xi. 32.
1. —— xiv. 10.
1. 2 Cor. i. 12.
2. —— iv. 4.
1. —— v. 19.
1. —— vii. 10.
2. Gal. i. 4.
1. —— iv. 3.
1. —— vi. 14[twice].
1. Eph. i. 4.
2. —— 21.
1a. —— ii. 2.
1. —— 12.
2. —— vi. 12 (*om.* τοῦ αἰῶνος, i.e. *world-rulers of this darkness,* instead of *rulers of the darkness of this world,* G L T Tr A ℵ.)
1. Phil. ii. 15.
1. Col. i. 6.
1. —— ii. 8, 20[twice].
1. 1 Tim. i. 15.
1. —— iii. 16.
1. —— vi. 7.
2. —— 17, }
2. 2 Tim. iv. 10, } with ὁ νῦν, i.e. *the now, actually present age.*
2. Tit. ii. 12, }
2. Heb. i. 2.
3. —— 6.
3. —— ii. 5.
1. —— iv. 3.
2. —— vi. 5.
1. —— ix. 26[1st].
2a. —— 26[2nd].
1. —— x. 5.
2a. —— xi. 3.
1. —— 7, 38.
1. Jas. i. 27.
1a. —— ii. 5 (τῷ κόσμῳ, *as regards the world,* instead of τοῦ κόσμου τούτου, *of this world,* G L T Tr A ℵ.)
1. —— iii. 6.
1. —— iv. 4[twice].
1. 1 Pet. i. 20.
1. —— v. 9.

1. 2 Pet. i. 4.
1. —— ii. 5 twice, 20.
1. —— iii. 6.
1. 1 John ii. 2, 15 3 times, 16 twice, 17.
1. —— iii. 1, 13, 17.
1. —— iv. 1, 3, 4, 5 3 times, 9, 14.
1a. —— 17.
1. 1 John v. 4 twice, 5, 19.
1. 2 John 7.
3. Rev. iii. 10.
1. —— xi. 15.
3. —— xii. 9.
4. —— xiii. 3.
1. —— —— 8.
3. —— xvi. 14.
1. —— xvii. 8.

WORLD BEGAN (BEFORE THE)

{ πρὸ, before
{ χρόνων, the times
{ αἰωνίων, of the ages, (*see No.* 2a, *above.*)

2 Tim. i. 9. | Tit. i. 2.

WORLD (FROM THE BEGINNING OF THE)

{ ἀπὸ, from, away from,
{ αἰῶνος, *see No.* 2, *above.*
} from antiquity, from the age, from eternity.

* *plural*, from the ages.

Acts xv. 18. | Eph. iii. 9*.

WORLD BEGAN (SINCE THE)

1. { ἀπὸ, αἰῶνος, } *see above.*

2. { ἐκ, out of, τοῦ, the, αἰῶνος, age, } out of antiquity, since the beginning of the age, (*see No.* 2, *above.*)

3. { χρόνοις, in times, αἰωνίοις, in the ages, } in the times of the ages, (*see No.* 2, *above.*)

1. Luke i. 70.
2. John ix. 32.
1. Acts iii. 21 (*om.* G⇉)
3. Rom. xvi. 25.

WORLD STANDETH (WHILE THE)

{ εἰς, unto
{ τὸν, the
{ αἰῶνα, age,
} for ever.

1 Cor. viii. 13.

WORLD WITHOUT END.

{ τοῦ, of the
{ αἰῶνος, age } (*om.* G→)
{ τῶν, of the (*pl.*)
{ αἰώνων, ages,
} of the age of the ages.

Eph. iii. 21.

WORLDLY.

κοσμικός, relating to the κόσμος, (*see No.* 1, *above*); what belong to this present order of things, (*non occ.*)

Tit. ii. 12. | Heb. ix. 1.

WORM.

σκώληξ, a worm.

[lxx. for תולע Isa. lxvi. 24, from the root *to lick up, swallow up, consume*, hence used of the worm which feeds upon the carcases or dead bodies. *See* Deut. xxviii. 31; Job v. 7, vii. 5, xvii. 14, xix. 26, xxi. 26, xxiv. 20; Isa. xiv. 11; Ecclus. x. 13. There is no need to take the word figuratively in the N.T., while in the O.T. it is used literally. The natural meaning of the word is to exclude all hope of restoration, and to declare that the punishment is eternal and without hope.] (*non occ.*)

Mark ix. 44 (ap.), 46 (ap.), 48.

WORMS (EATEN OF)

σκωληκόβρωτος, worm-eaten, devoured by worms, *spoken of* the disease φθειρίασις, (*non occ.*)

Acts xii. 23.

WORMWOOD.

ἄψινθος, *Lat.*, artemisia absinthium, *i.e.* wormwood, as the emblem of poisonous bitterness; (Heb. לענה, Prov. v. 4, *where* lxx. χολή, bile, gall), (*non occ.*)

Rev. viii. 11.

WORSE.

1. χείρων, worse, *spoken of state, condition, or quality.*

2. { εἰς, into, τὸ, the, χεῖρον, worse, } *lit.*, into the worse *state* [*came.*]

1. Matt. ix. 16.
1. —— xii. 45.
1. —— xxvii. 64.
1. Mark ii. 21.
2. Mark. v. 26.
1. Luke xi. 26.
1. 1 Tim. v. 8.
1. 2 Pet. ii. 20.

WORSE (BE THE)

ὑστερέω, to get behind; to come short, suffer need. *Here, pass.*

1 Cor. viii. 8 (*ap.*), marg. *have the less.*

WORSE (THE)

{ τὸ, the
{ ἧττον, inferior, worse.

1 Cor. xi. 17.

WORSE AND WORSE.

{ ἐπὶ, upon (*implying motion or direction*)
{ τὸ, the
{ χεῖρον, worse,
} upon the road to the worse; *or* in the direction of the worse.

2 Tim. iii. 13.

WORSE THING (A)

{ χειρόν, a worse,
{ τι, a certain thing.

John v. 14.

WORSHIP. [noun.]

δόξα, opinion; a seeming, an appearance; reputation.

Luke xiv. 10.

See also, WILL.

WORSHIP (-ED, -ETH, -ING.) [verb.]

1. προσκυνέω, to crouch, crawl, *or* fawn, *like a dog at his master's feet; hence,* to prostrate one's self, *after the eastern custom,* to do reverence *or* homage to *any one, by kneeling or prostrating one's self before him;* (lxx. *everywhere for* השתחוה, to bow down, to prostrate one's self *in reverence.*) *Used therefore of* the act of worship.

   (a) *with* ἐνώπιον, in the presence of, before.

2. σέβομαι, to be shy *or* timid, to shame one's self, be abashed; *hence,* to cherish *or* to pay devotion, *and used of the religious feeling,* (*as No.* 1 *is of the act.*)

3. σεβάζομαι, to be shy *of doing any thing;* to stand in awe of *any one, i.e.* to reverence *or* venerate, (*non occ.*)

4. λατρεύω, to serve, *esp. for hire; hence, spoken in respect to God,* to serve Him, *esp. with external or official service.*

5. εὐσεβέω, to be pious or devout towards *any one,* to be *or* act religiously towards, respect, honour.

6. θεραπεύω, to wait upon, minister unto, *i.e.* to render voluntary service and attendance; *hence,* to take care of, tend, etc.

1. Matt. ii. 2, 8, 11.
1. —— iv. 9, 10.
1. —— viii. 2.
1. —— ix. 18.
1. —— xiv. 33.
2. —— xv. 9.
1. —— —— 25.
1. —— xviii. 26, marg. *beseech.*
1. —— xx. 20.
1. —— xxviii. 9, 17.
1. Mark v. 6.
2. —— vii. 7.
1. —— xv. 19.
1a. Luke iv. 7, marg. *fall down before.*
1. —— —— 8.
1. —— xxiv. 52 (*ap.*)
1. John iv. 20 twice, 21, 22 twice, 23 twice, 24 twice.
1. —— ix. 38.
1. —— xii. 20.
4. Acts vii. 42.
1. —— —— 43.
1. —— viii. 27.
1. —— x. 25.
2. —— xvi. 14.
— —— xvii. 23, marg., see *devotion.*
5. Acts xvii. 23.
6. —— —— 25.
2. —— xviii. 7, 13.
2. —— xix. 27.
1. —— xxiv. 11.
4. —— —— 14.
3. Rom. i. 25.
1. 1 Cor. xiv. 25.
4. Phil. iii. 3.
— Col. ii. 18, see Worshipping.
— 2 Thes. ii. 4, see W (that is)
1. Heb. i. 6.
1. —— xi. 21.
1. Rev. iii. 9.
1. —— iv. 10.
1. —— v. 14.
1. —— vii. 11.
1. —— ix. 20.
1. —— xi. 1, 16.
1. —— xiii. 4 twice, 8, 12, 15.
1. —— xiv. 7, 9, 11.
1. —— xv. 4.
1. —— xvi. 2.
1. —— xix. 4, 10 twice, 20.
1. —— xx. 4.
1. —— xxii. 8, 9.

WORSHIPPED (THAT IS)

σέβασμα, an object of veneration, (*occ.* Acts xvii. 23.)

2 Thes. ii. 4.

WORSHIPPER (-S.)

1. προσκυνητής, a worshipper, (*the noun from* "WORSHIP," *No.* 1), (*non occ.*)

2. λατρεύω, (*see No.* 4, *above.*) *Here, part., those who are* rendering divine service.

3. *νεωκόρος*, temple-sweeper; *hence*, temple-keeper, (*non occ.*)

1. John iv. 23. | 2. Heb. x. 2. | 3. Acts xix. 35, marg. *temple-keeper*.

WORSHIPPER OF GOD.

θεοσεβής, reverencing God; (LXX. *for* ירא אלהים, Ex. xviii. 21; Job i. 1, 8.)

John ix. 31.

WORSHIPPING.

θρησκεία, the ceremonial *or* external service of religion, the external form of worship.

Col. ii. 18.

WORTHY.

1. *ἄξιος*, worth, worthy; of equal value *or* like worth; *then*, worthy of.
2. *ἀξίως*, (*adv. of No.* 1) suitably, in a becoming manner; in a manner of equal value with *the thing referred to.*
3. *ἱκανος*, coming to, reaching to; *hence*, sufficing, sufficient; adequate, competent.
4. *καλός*, beautiful, excellent, noble, (*see* "GOOD," *No.* 2.)

3. Matt. iii. 11.
3. —— viii. 8.
1. —— x. 10, 11, 13 twice, 37 twice, 38.
1. —— xxii. 8.
3. Mark i. 7.
1. Luke iii. 8, marg. *meet*.
3. —— 16.
1. —— vii. 4.
3. —— 6.
1. —— x. 7.
1. —— xii. 48.
1. —— xv. 19, 21.
1. —— xxiii. 15.
1. John i. 27.
1. Acts xiii. 25.
1. —— xxiii. 29.
1. Acts xxv. 11, 25.
1. —— xxvi. 31.
1. Rom. i. 32.
1. —— viii. 18.
2. Eph. iv. 1.
2. Col. i. 10.
2. 1 Thes. ii. 12.
1. 1 Tim. i. 15.
1. —— iv. 9.
1. —— v. 18.
1. —— vi. 1.
1. Heb. xi. 38.
4. Jas. ii. 7.
1. Rev. iii. 4.
1. —— iv. 11.
1. —— v. 2, 4, 9, 12.
1. —— xvi. 6.

WORTHY (ACCOUNT)

καταξιόω, to count *ἄξιος*, (*see No.* 1, *above.*) *In N.T. only pass.*, to be accounted worthy.

Luke xx. 35.
—— xxi. 36 (*κατισχύω, to be in full vigour*, T Tr A ℵ.)

WORTHY (COUNT)

1. *ἀξιόω*, to regard as deserving, hold worthy of, regard as suitable *or* proper.
2. *καταξιόω*, (*No.* 1, *with κατά*, down, *prefixed*) *see* "WORTHY (ACCOUNT)"

2. Acts v. 41.
2. 2 Thes. i. 5.
1. 2 Thes. i. 11, marg.
1. 1 Tim. v. 17. [*vouchsafe*.
1. Heb. iii. 3.

WORTHY (THINK)

ἀξιόω, *see No.* 1, *above.*

Luke vii. 7. | Heb. x. 29.

WORTHY DEED (VERY)

κατόρθωμα, (*from κατορθόω*, to set upright, establish; (LXX., 2 Ch. xxiii. 16; 1 Ch. xxviii. 7, to direct successfully, achieve prosperously); *hence, in N.T.*, anything happily achieved; *here, such as* national reforms, excellent measures, (*non occ.*)

Acts xxiv. 2.

WOT.

1. *οἶδα*, I have perceived *or* seen; *hence*, to have knowledge of, to know, (*see* "KNOW," *No.* 1.)
2. *γνωρίζω*, to make known; declare, reveal.

1. Acts iii. 17.
1. —— vii. 40.
1. Rom. xi. 2.
2. Phil. i. 22.

WOULD.

"WOULD" is very frequently the translation of various inflections of the Greek verb.

When it is the translation of a separate word it is always emphatic, and is one of these following.

1. *θέλω*, to will, to wish, to desire, *implying the simple act of volition*, (*see* "WILL," *No.* 1.)
2. *βούλομαι*, to have a wish, intention, *or* purpose, *formed after mature deliberation*, (*see* "WILL," *No.* 2.)
3. *μέλλω*, to be about to, to be on the point of, *used of some act or event in the future as the result of present determination*, to be going to *do anything*.

1. Matt. ii. 18.
1. —— v. 42.
1. —— vii. 12.
1. —— xii. 38.
1. —— xiv. 5 part.
1. —— xviii. 23, 30.
1. Matt. xxii. 3.
1. —— xxiii. 37 twice.
1. —— xxvii. 15, 34.
1. Mark iii. 13.
1. —— vi. 19 (*ζητέω, to seek*, L.)

1. Mark vi. 26, 48.
1. —— vii. 24.
1. —— ix. 30.
1. —— x. 35, 36.
1. Luke i. 62.
1. —— vi. 31.
3. —— x. 1.
1. —— xiii. 34 twice.
1. —— xv. 28.
1. —— xvi. 26 1st.
1. —— xviii. 4, 13.
1. —— xix. 27.
1. John i. 43.
3. —— vi. 6.
1. ——— 11.
3. ——— 15.
1. —— vii. 1, 44.
1. —— ix. 27.
1. —— xii. 21.
1. —— xxi. 18 twice.
1. Acts vii. 39.
1. —— x. 10.
3. —— xii. 6.
1. —— xiv. 13.
— —— xvi. 3, see W have.
3. ——— 27.
2. —— xvii. 20.
2. —— xix. 30 part.
1. ——— 33.
2. —— xxii. 30 part.
3. —— xxiii. 15 part.
3. ——— 28 part.
1. —— xxiv. 6.
3. —— xxv. 4.
2. ——— 20, 22.
1. —— xxvi. 5.
— Acts xxvi. 29, see W (I)
3. —— xxvii. 30 part.
2. —— xxviii. 18.
— Rom. i. 13, see W have.
1. —— vii. 15, 16, 19 twice, 20, 21 part.
1. —— xi. 25.
1. —— xvi. 19. [God (I)
— 1 Cor. iv. 8, see W to
1. —— vii. 7, 32.
1. —— x. 1.
— —— xi. 3, } see W
— —— xii. 1, } have.
1. —— xiv. 5.
1. 2 Cor. i. 8.
1. —— v. 4.
— —— xi. 1, see W to God.
1. —— xii. 20 twice.
1. Gal. i. 7.
1. —— iii. 2.
1. —— iv. 17.
— —— v. 12, see W (I)
1. ——— 17.
2. Phil. i. 12.
1. Col. i. 27.
1. —— ii. 1.
1. 1 Thes. ii. 18.
— —— iv. 13, see W have.
1. 2 Thes. iii. 10.
2. Philem. 13.
1. ——— 14.
1. Heb. x. 5, 8.
1. —— xii. 17 part.
2. 2 John 12.
2. 3 John 10.
— Rev. iii. 15, see W (I)

WOULD HAVE.

1. Acts xvi. 3. | 1. Rom. i. 13. | 1. 1 Cor. xi. 3. | 1. —— xii. 1. | 1. 1 Thes. iv. 13.

WOULD (I)

1. ὄφελον, (*aor.* 2 *of* ὀφείλω, to owe) I ought, *but used only in the implied sense of wishing*, O that! would that!

2. { εὔχομαι, to speak aloud, pray for, earnestly desire, ἄν, perchance, perhaps, } *here*, εὐξαίμην, *lit.*, I might perchance pray [*to God.*]

2. Acts xxvi. 29. | 1. Gal. v. 12. | 1. Rev. iii. 15.

WOULD TO GOD.

ὄφελον, *see No.* 1, *above.*

2 Cor. xi. 1.

WOULD TO GOD (I)

1 Cor. iv. 8.

See also, BECAUSE, FAIN, REASON, WILL.

WOUND. [noun.]

1. πλεγή, a stroke, a stripe, a blow; *then*, a wound *caused by a stripe or blow.*

2. τραῦμα, a wound, a hurt, a damage, (*non occ.*)

2. Luke x. 34. | 1. Rev. xiii. 3, 12, 14.

WOUND (-ED.) [verb.]

1. τραυματίζω, to wound, hurt, damage, (*non occ.*)

2. σφάζω, to slaughter, slay, *as animals in sacrifice, but of persons also*

3. { ἐπιτίθημι, to place, put, *or* lay upon, πληγή, a stroke, a stripe, a blow, } to inflict wounds, *esp. by blows.*

— Mark xii. 4, see Head. | 3. Luke x. 30. | 1. Luke xx. 12. | 1. Acts xix. 16. | 2. Rev. xiii. 3, marg. *slay.*

WOVEN.

ὑφαντός, woven; (lxx. *for* ארג, Ex. xxxix. 21, 26; חשב, Ex. xxvi. 32; xxviii. 6), (*non occ.*)

John xix. 23, marg. *wrought.*

WRANGLING (*without*) [margin.]

Jas. iii. 17, see "PARTIALITY (WITHOUT)"

WRAP (-ED) IN.

1. ἐντυλίττω, to roll up in, to inwrap; *also* to roll up *or* wrap together, (*non occ.*)

2. ἐνειλέω, to roll in, involve in, inwrap, (*non occ.*)

1. Matt. xxvii. 59. | 2. Mark. xv. 46. | — Luke ii. 7, 12, see Swaddling. | 1. —— xxiii. 53.

WRAP TOGETHER.

1. John xx. 7.

WRATH (-S).

1. ὀργή, the native character, disposition, temper of mind; anger *together with* the desire for revenge, (*from Heb.* הרג, to kill, and all the tumults of passion which terminate in killing. *This is traced in the German*, kreig, war; *French*, orgueil; *and Eng.*, rage.) *The idea of* sanguinary revenge *belongs etymologically* to ὀργή, (*see note, below.*)

2. θυμός, the mind, the spirit that is breathed out, an intense passion of

the mind. *θυμός is from* חמה, *and is* the animus, the working and fermenting of the mind, the demonstration of strong passion, *which may issue in anger or revenge, though it does not necessarily include it.*

[NOTE.—*No.* 1 is the abiding, settled habit of mind, the settled purpose of wrath. *No.* 2 is the turbulent commotion of the mind, rage. *No.* 1 is, as it were, the heat of the fire; *No.* 2 the bursting forth of the flame. *No.* 1 is less sudden in its rise, but more lasting.]

3. *παροργισμός*, the provocation of anger, chafing, exasperation, the working into a passion.

1. Matt. iii. 7.
1. Luke iii. 7.
2. —— iv. 28.
1. —— xxi. 23.
1. John iii. 36.
2. Acts xix. 28.
1. Rom. i. 18.
1. —— ii. 5 twice, 8.
1. —— iv. 15.
1. —— v. 9.
1. —— ix. 22 twice.
1. —— xii. 19.
1. —— xiii. 4 (*om.* G →), 5.
2. 2 Cor. xii. 20.
2. Gal. v. 20, pl.
1. Eph. ii. 3.
3. —— iv. 26.
2. —— —— 31.
1. —— v. 6.
— —— vi. 4, see W (provoke to)
1. Col. iii. 6.
2. —— —— 8.
1. 1 Thes. i. 10.
1. —— ii. 16.
1. —— v. 9.
1. 1 Tim. ii. 8.
1. Heb. iii. 11.
1. —— iv. 3.
2. —— xi. 27.
1. Jas. i. 19, 20.
1. Rev. vi. 16, 17.
1. —— xi. 18.
2. —— xii. 12.
2. —— xiv. 8 (*om.* G → ℵ*)
2. —— —— 10, 19.
2. —— xv. 1, 7.
2. —— xvi. 1.
1. —— —— 19.
2. —— xviii. 3.
1. —— xix. 15.

WRATH (PROVOKE TO)

παροργίζω, to chafe, to work into a passion, exasperate.

Eph. vi. 4.

WREST.

στρεβλόω, (*from στρεβλή*, a windlass, winch, *or* instrument of torture); to wrench, torture *by twisting or turning; hence* to wrest, pervert, (*non occ.*)

2 Pet. iii. 16.

WRESTLE NOT (WE)

οὐκ, not, (*see* "NO," *No.* 1,) *ἔστιν*, is, *ἡμῖν*, to us, *ἡ*, the, *πάλη*, a wrestling, (*from πάλλω*, to vibrate) a struggling,	the wrestling (*or* struggling) for us is not.

Eph. vi. 12.

WRETCHED.

ταλαίπωρος, enduring toil and hardship, *as from severe bodily effort; then, the state arising from this*, wretched, miserable, (*non occ.*)

Rom. vii. 24. | Rev. iii. 17.

WRINKLE.

ῥυτίς, a fold which draws together, a wrinkle, *esp. in the face*, (*non occ.*)

Eph. v. 27.

WRITE, WRITTEN, WROTE.

1. *γράφω*, to grave, *or* cut in; (lxx. *for* קלע, 1 Kings vi. 28) to sketch, to picture. *In N.T.*, to form letters with a stylus in the ancient manner, so that the letters were cut *or* graven upon the material; *hence, gen.*, to write.

2. *προγράφω*, (*No.* 1, *with πρό*, before *prefixed*) to write before. *In ref to time past*, to have written before at a former time. *In ref. to time future*, to write beforehand, announce.

3. *ἐπιστέλλω*, to send upon, *i.e.* to send word to any one *verbally or by letter*.

1. Matt. ii. 5.
1. —— iv. 4, 6, 7, 10.
1. —— xi. 10.
1. —— xxi. 13.
1. —— xxvi. 24, 31.
1. —— xxvii. 31.
1. Mark i. 2.
1. —— vii. 6.
1. —— ix. 12, 13.
1. —— x. 4, 6.
1. —— xi. 17.
1. —— xii. 19.
1. —— xiv. 21, 27.
— —— xv. 26, see W over.
1. Luke i. 3, 63.
1. —— ii. 23.
1. —— iii. 4.
1. —— iv. 4, 8, 10, 17.
1. —— vii. 27.
1. —— x. 20 (*ἐγγεγράπται, have been inscribed, instead of ἐγράφη, are written*, T Tr A ℵ.)
1. —— —— 26.
1. —— xvi. 6, 7.
1. —— xviii. 31.
1. —— xix. 46.
1. —— xx. 17, 28.
1. —— xxi. 22.
1. —— xxii. 37.
1. Luke xxiii. 38 (*om.* T A ℵ), (*ἐπιγράφω, to write over*, L Tr[b].)
1. —— xxiv. 44, 46.
1. John i. 45.
1. —— ii. 17.
1. —— v. 46.
1. —— vi. 31, 35.
1. —— viii. 6 (*ap.*), 8 (*ap.*). 17.
1. —— x. 34.
1. —— xii. 14, 16.
1. —— xv. 25.
1. —— xix. 19, 20, 21, 22.
1. —— xx. 30, 31.
1. —— xxi. 24, 25 twice.
1. Acts i. 20.
1. —— vii. 42.
1. —— xiii. 29, 33.
1. —— xv. 15.
— —— —— 20, see W unto.
1. —— —— 23.
1. —— xviii. 27.
3. —— xxi. 25 (*ἀποστέλλω, to send off*, L Tr.)
1. —— xxiii. 5, 25.
1. —— xxiv. 14.
1. —— xxv. 26 twice.
1. Rom. i. 17.

— Rom. ii. 15, see Written.
1. —— 24.
1. —— iii. 4, 10.
1. —— iv. 17, 23.
1. —— viii. 36.
1. —— ix. 13, 33.
1. —— x. 15.
1. —— xi. 8, 26.
1. —— xii. 19.
1. —— xiv. 11.
— —— xv. 4 1st, see W aforetime.
2. —— 4 2nd (No. 1, G~L T Tr A ℵ.)
1. —— 15, 21.
1. —— xvi. 22.
1. 1 Cor. i. 19, 31.
1. —— ii. 9.
1. —— iii. 19.
1. —— iv. 6, 14.
1. —— v. 9, 11.
1. —— vii. 1.
1. —— ix. 9, 10, 15.
1. —— x. 7, 11.
1. —— xiv. 21, 37.
1. —— xv. 45, 54.
1. 2 Cor. i. 13.
1. —— ii. 3, 4, 9.
— —— iii. 2, 3, see W in.
— —— 7, see Written.
— —— iv. 13, see W (according as it is)
1. —— vii. 12.
1. —— viii. 15.
1. —— ix. 1, 9.
1. — xiii. 2 (om. γράφω, *I write*, G L T Tr A ℵ.)
1. —— 10.
1. Gal. i. 20.
1. —— iii. 10 twice, 13.
1. Gal. iv. 22, 27.
1. —— vi. 11.
1. Phil. iii. 1.
1. 1 Thes. iv. 9.
1. —— v. 1.
1. 2 Thes. iii. 17.
1. 1 Tim. iii. 14.
1. Philem. 19, 21.
— Heb. viii. 10, see W in.
1. —— x. 7.
— —— 16, see W in.
— —— xii. 23, see W (be)
— —— xiii. 22, see W a letter unto.
1. 1 Pet. i. 16.
1. —— v. 12.
1. 2 Pet. iii. 1, 15.
1. 1 John i. 4.
1. —— ii. 1, 7, 8, 12, 13 3 times, 14 twice, 21, 26.
1. 2 John 5, 12.
1. 3 John 9, 13 twice.
1. Jude 3 twice.
1. Rev. i. 3, 11, 19.
1. —— ii. 1, 8, 12, 17, 18.
1. —— iii. 1, 7, 12, 14.
1. —— v. 1.
1. —— x. 4 twice.
1. —— xiii. 8.
1. —— xiv. 1, 13.
1. —— xvii. 5, 8.
1. —— xix. 9, 12, 16.
1. —— xx. 12, 15.
1. —— xxi. 5.
— —— 12, see W thereon.
1. —— 27.
1. —— xxii. 18, 19.

WRITE AFORETIME.

2. Rom. xv. 4 (No. 1, Lm.)

WRITE IN.

1. ἐπιγράφω, *No.* 1, *with* ἐπί, upon, *prefixed.*

2. ἐγγράφω, *No.* 1, *with* ἐν, in, *prefixed.* (*non occ.*)

2. 2 Cor. iii. 2, 3. | 1. Heb. viii. 10.
1. Heb. x. 16.

WRITE OVER.

ἐπιγράφω, *see No.* 1, *above.*

Mark xv. 26.

WRITE THEREON.

ἐπιγράφω, *see above.*

Rev. xxi. 12.

WRITE UNTO.

ἐπιστέλλω, *see No.* 3, *above.*

Acts xv. 20.

WRITE A LETTER UNTO.

ἐπιστέλλω, *see No.* 3, *above.*

Heb. xiii. 22.

WRITTEN.

1. γραπτός; written, (*non occ.*)

2. { ἐν, in / γράμμασιν, written characters, } in writing, in manuscript.

1. Rom. ii. 15. | 2. 2 Cor. iii. 7.

WRITTEN (ACCORDING AS IT IS)

{ κατὰ, according to / τὸ, the *thing* / γεγραμμένον, written, } according to that which has been written.

2 Cor. iv. 13.

WRITTEN (BE)

ἀπογράφω, to write off, copy; *hence,* to enrol, inscribe *as in a register. Here, pass.*

Heb. xii. 23, marg. *enrolled.*

WRITING.

1. βιβλίον, a roll, a volume, a scroll, *such being the form of ancient books.*

2. γράμμα, the written, *i.e.* something written *or* cut in with the stylus in the ancient manner of writing; *then,* anything written.

— Matt. v. 31, see Divorcement.
1. —— xix. 7.
2. John v. 47.
— —— xix. 19, see W was (the)

WRITING WAS (THE)

{ ἦν, it was / γεγραμμένον, written, } it had been written.

John xix. 19.

WRITING-TABLE.

πινακίδιον, a small tablet, writing table, (*non occ.*)

Luke i. 63.

WRONG. [noun.]

ἀδικία, what is not in conformity with δίκη, right; what it ought not to be, *i.e.* wrong.

2 Cor. xii. 13.

WRONG (DO)

ἀδικέω, to do wrong, to act not in conformity with δίκη, right; to be an ἄδικος, and act like one.

Matt. xx. 13.
Acts vii. 26, 27.
—— xxv. 10.
1 Cor. vi. 8.
2 Cor. vii. 12.
Col. iii. 25 twice.

WRONG (MATTER OF)

ἀδίκημα, wrong, the wrong done.

Acts xviii. 14.

WRONG AS ONE IN WINE

(*ready to quarrel and offer*) [margin.]

1 Tim. iii. 3, see "WINE (GIVEN TO)"

WRONG (SUFFER)

ἀδικέω, *see* "WRONG (DO)"; *here, pass.*

Acts vii. 24.
2 Cor. vii. 12.

WRONG (TAKE)

ἀδικέω, *see* "WRONG (DO)"; *here, mid.*

1 Cor. vi. 7.

WRONG (-ED.) [verb.]

ἀδικέω, *see* "WRONG (DO)"

2 Cor. vii. 2.
Philem. 18.

WRONGFULLY.

ἀδίκως, wrongly, unjustly.

1 Pet. ii. 19.

WROTH (BE)

1. **ὀργίζω**, to make ὀργή, (*see* "WRATH," *No.* 1) to be *or* become wroth.
2. **θυμόω**, to make θυμός, (*see* "WRATH," *No.* 2) to provoke. *Here, pass.*, to be stirred up into a tumultuous state of mind, (*non occ.*)

2. Matt. ii. 16.
1. —— xviii. 34.
1. Matt. xxii. 7.
1. Rev. xii. 17.

WROUGHT.

See, WORK, and WOVEN.

Y

YE.

YE is generally the translation of various inflections of the Greek verb, (2nd pers. pl.)

It is also sometimes the translation of the article before a nominative used as a vocative.

When it is the translation of a separate pronoun in the Greek, it is always emphatic, and is one of these following.

(*For* "YE ARE" *and* "ARE YE," *see below.*)

1. **ὑμεῖς**, (*nom. pl. of* σύ, thou) ye, you. *It is generally omitted, except where a special emphasis is required.*
   (a) *In the edition of* A.D. 1611, *it was translated* you *in passages thus marked.*
2. **ὑμῶν**, (*Gen. pl. of* σύ, thou) of ye, of you,
   (a) "you," *in edition of* A.D. 1611.
3. **ὑμῖν**, (*Dat. pl. of* σύ, thou) to you, to ye,
   (a) "you," *in edition of* A.D. 1611.

When translated you, *these cases are simply the result of government, or required by construction.*

4. **ὑμᾶς**, (*Acc. pl. of* σύ, thou) you, ye,
   (a) "you," *in edition of* A.D. 1611.

1. Matt. v. 13, 14, 48.
4. —— vi. 8 3rd.
1. —— 9, 26.
1. —— vii. 11, 12 2nd.
1. —— ix. 4 (*om.* L T Tr A ℵ.)
1. —— x. 20, and see Y (it is not)
1. —— 31 2nd.
1. —— xiii. 18.
1. —— xiv. 16.
1a. —— xv. 3.
1. —— 5, 16.
1. —— xvi. 15.
3. —— xviii. 12.
1. Matt. xix. 28 1st.
1. —— 28 2nd (*αὐτοί, yourselves,* T Tr ℵ.)
1. —— xx. 4, 7 1st.
1. —— xxi. 13.
3a. —— 28.
1. —— 32 2nd.
3. —— xxii. 42.
1. —— xxiii. 8 twice, 13 2nd, 28 1st, 32.
1. —— xxiv. 33 1st, 44 1st.
1. —— xxvi. 31.
3. —— 66.
1. —— xxvii. 24.
1. —— xxviii. 5 1st.

1. Mark vi. 31, 37.
1. —— vii. 11, 18 1st.
1. —— viii. 29.
— —— ix. 41, see Ye belong to.
1. —— xi. 17.
1a.——— 26 (ap.)
3. ——— 24 4th.
1. —— xii. 27 (om. ὑμεῖς οὖν, ye therefore, T Tr A ℵ.)
1. —— xiii. 11 4th, and see Ye (it is not)
1. ——— 23, 29 1st.
3. —— xiv. 64 2nd.
1. Luke vi. 31 2nd (om. Lb.)
3. ——— 32 2nd, 33 2nd, 34 3rd.
1. —— ix. 13, 20, 55 2nd
1. —— x. 23, 24 1st. [(ap.)
1. —— xi. 13.
1. ——— 39.
— ——— 46 3rd, see Ye yourselves.
1. ——— 48 3rd.
— ——— 52 2nd, see Ye yourselves.
1. —— xii. 24, 29.
— ——— 36, see Ye yourselves.
1. ——— 40 1st.
1. —— xvi. 15.
1. —— xvii. 10 1st.
1. —— xix. 46.
1. —— xxi. 31 1st.
2. —— xxii. 10.
1. ——— 26, 28, 70.
1. —— xxiv. 48, 49.
1. John i. 26.
4. —— iii. 7.
1. ——— 28.
1. —— iv. 20, 22 1st, 32, 35, 38 twice.
1. —— v. 20, 33, 34, 35, 38 2nd, 39 1st, 44, 45.
1. —— vi. 67.
1. —— vii. 8, 28 3rd, 34, 36 2nd, 47.
1. —— viii. 14, 15, 21 2nd, 22, 23 twice, 31 1st, 38 1st, 41, 44, 46, 47, 49, 54.
1. —— ix. 19, 27 2nd, 30.
1. —— x. 26 1st, 36.
1. —— xi. 49.
3. ——— 56.
1. —— xiii. 10, 13 1st, 14, 15, 33, 34 2nd.
1. —— xiv. 3, 17, 19 twice.
1. ——— 20 1st (om. Lb.)
1a.——— 20 2nd.
1. —— xv. 3, 4 1st, 5 1st, 14, 16 1st.
1a.——— 16 2nd.
1. ——— 27 1st.
— ——— 27 2nd, see Ye have been.
1. —— xvi. 20 twice, 22, 27.
1. —— xviii. 31.
3. ——— 39 1st.
1. —— xix. 6, 35.
1. Acts i. 5.
1. —— ii. 15.
— ——— 22 2nd, see Ye yourselves.
1. ——— 33, 36.
1. —— iii. 13, 14, 25.
1. —— iv. 7, 10.
3. —— v. 9.
1. ——— 30.
1. —— vii. 4.
1. ——— 26 1st (om. G~L T Tr Ab ℵ.)
1. ——— 51 twice, 52.
1. —— viii. 24 1st.
1. —— x. 28.
1a.——— 37.
1. —— xi. 16.
3. Acts xiii. 15 2nd.
1. —— xv. 7.
4. —— xvii. 22 2nd.
1. —— xix. 15.
4. ——— 36.
1. —— xx. 18, 25.
1. —— xxii. 3.
1. —— xxiii. 15 1st.
1. —— xxvii. 31.
1. Rom. i. 6.
4a.——— 11.
1. —— vi. 11.
1. —— vii. 4 1st.
4. ——— 4 2nd.
1. —— viii. 9.
1. —— ix. 26.
4. —— xi. 25 1st.
1. ——— 30.
4. —— xii. 2 2nd.
4. —— xv. 13.
1. —— xvi. 17.
4. 1 Cor. i. 7.
1. —— iii. 17, 23.
1. —— iv. 10 3 times.
1. —— v. 2.
2. ——— 4.
1. ——— 12.
1a.—— vi. 8.
1a.—— ix. 1.
1. ——— 2.
4. —— x. 1.
4 ——— 13 2nd (om. G L T Tr A ℵ.)
1. ——— 15.
4. ——— 20.
4. —— xi. 18, 20.
1. —— xii. 27.
4. —— xiv. 5 1st.
1a.——— 9 1st, 12 1st.
2a.——— 18.
1. —— xvi. 1, 6, 16.
2a. 2 Cor. i. 11.
1. ——— 14 2nd.
4. —— ii. 7.
— ——— 9, see Y be.
1. —— iii. 2.
4. —— vi. 1.
1. ——— 13.
1. ——— 16 (ἡμεῖς, we, L T Tr ℵ.)
1. ——— 18.
4. —— vii. 11 1st (om. G→L T Tr Ab ℵ.)
1. —— viii. 9 2nd.
3a.——— 13.
1a.—— ix. 4.
1a.—— xi. 7.
1. —— xii. 11.
— ——— xiii. 5, see Y be.
4. ——— 7 1st.
1. ——— 7 2nd, 9.
1. Gal. iii. 28, 29 1st.
1. —— iv. 12 1st.
— ——— 15 1st, see Ye spake of.
1. —— v. 13.
1. —— vi. 1.
1. Eph. i. 13 1st.
4. ——— 18.
1. —— ii. 11, 13.
1a.——— 22.
4. —— iv. 17.
1. ——— 20.
4. ——— 22.
— —— v. 5, see Ye know.
4. —— vi. 11.
1. ——— 21.
4. Phil. i. 7, 10 1st, 12.
1. —— ii. 18.
1. —— iv. 15 twice.
4. Col. i. 10 (om. G L T Tr A ℵ.)
4. —— ii. 1.
1. —— iii. 4, 7 1st.
1a.——— 8.
1. ——— 13.
1. —— iv. 1.
4a.——— 6.
1. Col. iv. 16.
1. 1 Thes. i. 6.
4. ——— 7.
1. —— ii. 10.
4. ——— 12.
1. ——— 14 twice, 19, 20.
1. —— iii. 8.
4. —— iv. 1 1st, 3.
— ——— 9 2nd, see Y yourselves.
1. —— v. 4, 5.
4. 2 Thes. i. 5 1st.
1. ——— 12.
4. —— ii. 2.
4. —— iii. 6.
1. ——— 13.
— Heb. xii. 8 1st, see Ye be.
1. Jas. ii. 6.
4. ——— 7.
4. —— iv. 2 5th.
— ——— 14, see Ye (whereas)
4. ——— 15.
1. —— v. 8.
1. 1 Pet. ii. 9 1st.
2a.—— iv. 4.
4a. 2 Pet. i. 15.
4. —— iii. 11.
1. ——— 17 1st.
1. 1 John i. 3.
1. —— ii. 20, 24 1st, 24 3rd, 27 1st.
1. —— iv. 4.
4. Jude 5 (om. G~L T Tr [A.
1. ——— 17, 20.

YE...ARE, and ARE YE.

ἐστέ, (*2nd pers. pl. ind. of* εἰμί, to be) ye are, are ye.

* *with the pronoun* ὑμᾶς, ye (*very emphatic.*)

Matt. v. 11, 13*, 14*.
—— viii. 26.
—— xv. 16*.
—— xxiii. 8*, 28, 31.
Mark iv. 40.
—— vii. 18*.
Luke vi. 22.
—— ix. 55*, (ap.)
—— xi. 44.
—— xiii. 25, 27.
—— xvi. 15*.
—— xxii. 28.
—— xxiv. 17 (ἐστάθησαν, *they came to a stand,* L T Trb Ab ℵ.)
——— 38.
——— 48* (om. ἐστέ, *are,* T Trb A.)
John viii. 23* 1st, 23 2nd, 31, 37, 44, 47.
—— x. 26, 34.
—— xiii. 10, 11, 17, 35.
—— xv. 3*, 14*, 19.
Acts iii. 25*.
—— vii. 26*.
—— xix. 15.
—— xxii. 3*.
Rom. i. 6*.
—— vi. 14, 16.
—— viii. 9*.
Rom. xv. 14,
1 Cor. i. 30*.
—— iii. 3 twice, 4.
——— 9, lit., *God's husbandry, God's building are ye.*
——— 16, 17*.
—— iv. 8 1st.
—— v. 2, 7.
—— vi. 2. 19.
—— ix. 1*, 2*.
—— xii. 27*.
—— xiv. 12.
—— xv. 17.
2 Cor. i. 7.
—— iii. 2*.
—— vi. 16* (ἐσμέν (with ἡμεῖς) *we are,* L T Tr ℵ.)
—— vii. 3.
Gal. iii. 3 1st, 26, 28*, 29.
—— iv. 6.
—— v. 18.
Eph. ii. 5, 8, 19.
Col. ii. 10.
1 Thes. ii. 20*.
—— iv. 9.
—— v. 4, 5*.
Heb. xii. 8.
1 John ii. 14.
1 John iv. 4.

YE BE.

ἐστέ, ye are, (*see above.*)

2 Cor. ii. 9. | 2 Cor. xiii. 5 twice.
Heb. xii. 8.

YE BELONG TO.

ἐστέ, ye are, (*see above*). *Here, with Gen. case,* ye are *of.*

Mark ix. 41.

YE HAVE BEEN.

ἐστέ, ye are, (*see above.*)

John xv. 27.

YE (IT IS NOT)

οὐ, not (*see* "NO," *No.* 1)
ὑμεῖς, ye, (*emphatic*)
ἐστέ, ye are,
} ye are not, it is not ye.

Matt. x. 20. | Mark xiii. 11.

YE KNOW.

ἐστέ, ye are [ἴστε, ye know, (*of internal conscious knowledge*) G L T Tr A ℵ.]
γινώσκοντες, knowing, (*implying objective acquaintance*) taking note.

Eph. v. 5, lit., "*ye know—taking note*," or "*ye are well informed*."

YE SPAKE OF.

ὑμῶν, of you, your, ("YOU," *in edition of* A.D. 1611.)

Gal. iv. 15.

YE (WHEREAS)

ὅστις, whoever, *i.e.* ye who, who indeed, *lit.*, ye who *do not know, etc.*

Jas. iv. 14.

YE YOURSELVES.

1. ὑμεῖς, ye, you, (*emphatic*)
   αὐτοί, selves.

2. αὐτοί, *your* selves.

1. Mark vi. 31.
1. Luke xi. 36.
2. —— 46, 52.
1. John iii. 28.
2. Acts ii. 22.
1. 1 Thes. iv. 9.

YEA.

1. ναί, yea, yes, certainly, *expressing assent* and affirmation.

2. ἀλλά, but, *indicating a reference to something else, either in direct antithesis, or, as here, continuative,* but, *i.e.* but further, moreover.

3. καί, and, also, even.

1. Matt. v. 37 twice.
1. —— ix. 28.
1. —— xi. 9.
1. —— xiii. 51.
1. —— xxi. 16.
3. —— xxvi. 60 (*om.* G L T Tr A ℵ.)
— Luke ii. 35, see Y...also
1. —— vii. 26.
— —— xi. 28, see Y rather.
1. —— xii. 5.
— —— xxiv. 22, see Y... and.
1. John xi. 27.
2. —— xvi. 2.
3. John xvi. 32.
1. —— xxi. 15, 16.
1. Acts v. 8.
3. —— vii. 43.
1. —— xxii. 27.
2. Rom. iii. 31.
— —— viii. 34, see Y rather.
3. 1 Cor. ii. 10.
2. —— iv. 3.
— —— xv. 15, } see Y...
— —— xvi. 6, } and.
1. 2 Cor. i. 17 twice, 18, 19 twice, 20.
— 2 Cor. v. 16, see Y though.
2. —— vii. 11 6 times.
— —— viii. 3, see Y...and
2 Gal. iv. 17.
— Phil. i. 18, } see Y...
— —— ii. 17, } and.
2. Phil. iii. 8 (*om.* L^b.)
1. Philem. 20.
2. Jas. ii. 18.
1. —— v. 12 twice.
— 3 John 12, see Y... and.
1. Rev. xiv. 13.

YEA...ALSO.

καὶ, also,
δέ, but,
} but also (*om.* δέ, but, L^b Tr^b.)

Luke ii. 35.

YEA...AND.

1. καί, and, also, even.

2. τὲ, and,
   καί, and, also, even,
   } and even.

3. ἀλλὰ, but
   καί, also, even,
   } but even, moreover.

4. ἤ, or,
   καί, also, even,
   } or even.

3. Luke xxiv. 22.
2. 1 Cor. xv. 15.
4. —— xvi. 6.
1. 2 Cor. viii. 3.
3. Phil. i. 18.
3. —— ii. 17.
2. 3 John 12.

YEA RATHER.

1. μενοῦνγε, yea indeed, yea verily.

2. μᾶλλον, more, rather,
   δὲ, but,
   καί, and, also, even,
   } but rather even.

1. Luke xi. 28. | 2. Rom. viii. 34.

YEA THOUGH.

εἰ, if,
δὲ, but,
καί, and, also, even,
} but if even.

2 Cor. v. 16.

YEAR (-s.)

(*For various combinations with other words, see below.*)

1. ἔτος, a year; (lxx. *for* שָׁנָה, 1 Kings xv. 1; Jer. i. 2, 3, etc.); (*like* ἕνος, it is connected with the *Lat.*, vetus, old), (*non occ.*)

2. ἐνιαυτός, a year, *so called because* ἐν ἑαυτῷ εἶσι, it goes *or* returns upon itself; (lxx. *for* שָׁנָה, *meaning* to iterate, to repeat), (*non occ.*)

— Matt. ii. 16, see Y old (two)
1. —— ix. 20.
1. Mark v. 25, 42.
— Luke i. 7, 18, see Stricken.
1. —— ii. 36, 37.
1. ——— 41, and see Y (every)
1. ——— 42.
1. —— iii. 1, 23.
2. —— iv. 19.
1. ——— 25.
1. —— viii. 42, 43.
1. —— xii. 19.
1. —— xiii. 7, 8, 11, 16.
1. —— xv. 29.
1. John ii. 20.
1. —— v. 5.
1. —— viii. 57.
2. —— xi. 49, 51.
2. —— xviii. 13.
1. Acts iv. 22.
1. —— vii. 6, 30, 36, 42.
1. —— ix. 33.
2. —— xi. 26.
1. —— xiii. 20, 21.
2. —— xviii. 11.
1. —— xix. 10.
— —— xx. 31, see Y (space of three)
1. Acts xxiv. 10, 17.
— ——— 27, } see Y (two)
— —— xxviii. 30, } see Y (two)
1. Rom. xv. 23.
— 2 Cor. viii. 10, } see Y ago (a)
— —— ix. 2, } see Y ago (a)
1. —— xii. 2.
1. Gal. i. 18.
1. —— ii. 1.
1. —— iii. 17, and see Hundred and thirty years (from)
2. —— iv. 10.
1. 1 Tim. v. 9.
1. Heb. i. 12.
1. —— iii. 9, 17.
1. —— ix. 7.
1. ——— 25, and see Y (every)
1. —— x. 1, and see Y by Y.
1. ——— 3, and see Y (every)
— —— xi. 24, see Y (come to)
2. Jas. iv. 13.
1. —— v. 17.
1. 2 Pet. iii. 8 twice.
2. Rev. ix. 15.
1. —— xx. 2, 3, 4, 5, 6, 7.

YEAR BY YEAR.

{ κατὰ, according to, (*here distributively*)
{ ἐνιαυτός, a year, (*see No. 2, above*)
} year by year, each year.

Heb. x. 1.

YEAR AGO (A)

{ ἀπὸ, from,
{ πέρυσι, the past, the past year,
} since a year ago.

2 Cor. viii. 10. | 2 Cor. ix. 2.

YEARS (COME TO)

{ γίνομαι, to become
{ μέγας, great,
} when he had become great, *or* being grown up.

Heb. xi. 24.

YEAR (EVERY)

1. { κατὰ, according to, (*here distributively*)
{ ἔτος, a year, (*see No. 1, above*)
} year by year, each year.

2. { κατὰ, according to, (*here distributively*)
{ ἐνιαυτός, a year, (*see No. 2, above*)
} year by year, each year.

1. Luke ii. 41. | 2. Heb. ix. 25. | 2. Heb. x. 3.

YEARS (SPACE OF THREE)

τριετία, the space of three years, (*non occ.*)

Acts xx. 31.

YEARS (TWO)

διετία, the space of two years, (*non occ.*)

Acts xxiv. 27. | Acts xxviii. 30.

YEARS OLD (TWO)

διετής, of two years, *i.e.* two years old, (*non occ.*)

Matt. ii. 16.

See also, FORTY, HUNDRED.

YES.

ναί, yea, yes, certainly, *expressing assent or affirmation.*

Matt. xvii. 25. | Mark vii. 28. | Rom. iii. 29.

YES VERILY.

μενοῦνγε, yes indeed, yea verily.

Rom. x. 18.

YESTERDAY.

χθές, yesterday; (lxx. *for* חמול, Gen. xxxi. 2; 2 Sam. iii. 17), (*non occ.*)

John iv. 52. | Acts vii. 28. | Heb. xiii. 8.

YET.

(*For various combinations with other words, see below.*)

1. ἔτι, yet, still, *implying duration,* hitherto; *also as implying accession or addition, etc.,* yet, further, besides.
2. ἀλλά, but, *marking an antithesis; also as marking a transition,* but, but now, but further, moreover.
3. καί, and, even, also.
4. { καὶ, and, even, also, { γάρ, for, } for even.
5. κἄν, (*for* καὶ ἐάν) and if, also if, even if, although.
6. μέντοι, indeed, truly, certainly, forsooth; though, yet, nevertheless.

7. γέ, at least, indeed, even.

8. ἀκμήν, (*prop., Acc. of* ἀκμή, a point, *as of a weapon; Eng.*, acme.) *In later writers and in N.T., for* κατ' ἀκμήν χρόνου, at this point of time, yet still, even now, to this moment, (*non occ.*)

9. οὐκέτι, (*No.* 1, *with* οὐκ, not, *prefixed*) no more, no further, no longer.

10. οὐδέπω, also not ever, not ever yet, not yet.

11. ἤδη, now, even now, already.

1. Matt. xii. 46.
8. —— xv. 16.
4. —— 27.
1. —— xvii. 5.
1. —— xix. 20.
11. —— xxiv. 32.
1. —— xxvi. 47.
1. —— xxvii. 63.
1. Mark v. 35.
4. —— vii. 28 (*om* γάρ, *for*, L[b] T Tr ℵ.)
1. —— viii. 17 (*om.* G→L T Tr A ℵ.)
1. —— xii. 6.
11. —— xiii. 28.
2. —— xiv. 29.
1. —— 43.
9. —— xv. 5.
3. Luke iii. 20.
1. —— viii. 49.
1. —— ix. 42.
7. —— xi. 8.
1. —— xiv. 22, 32.
1. —— xv. 20.
7. —— xvii. 5.
1. —— xviii. 22.
1. —— xxii. 37 (*om.* G→L T Tr A ℵ.)
1. —— 47, 60.
1. —— xxiv. 6, 41, 44.
6. John iv. 27.
1. —— 35 (*om.* G→)
1. —— vii. 33.
3. —— viii. 16.
1. —— xii. 35.
1. —— xiii. 33.
1. John xiv. 19.
1. —— xvi. 12.
1. —— xx. 1.
6. —— 5.
1. Acts ix. 1.
1. —— x. 44.
1. —— xviii. 18.
1. Rom. iii. 7.
1. —— v. 6, 8.
1. —— ix. 19.
1. 1 Cor. iii. 2 (*om.* L[b].)
1. —— 3.
2. —— iv. 4, 15.
10. —— viii. 2 (οὔπω, *not even yet*, L T Tr A ℵ.)
2. —— ix. 2.
1. —— xii. 31.
2. —— xiv. 19.
1. —— xv. 17.
1. 2 Cor. i. 10 (*om.* L[m].)
2. —— iv. 8, 16.
2. —— v. 16.
2. —— xi. 6.
5. —— 16.
2. —— xiii. 4.
1. Gal. i. 10.
3. —— iii. 4.
1. —— v. 11 twice.
1. Phil. i. 9.
2. Col. ii. 5.
1. 2 Thes. ii. 5.
1. Heb. vii. 10, 15.
1. —— ix. 8.
1. —— x. 37.
1. —— xi. 4.
1. Rev. vi. 11.

YET (AND)

{ καὶ, and also, even, / δέ, but, } but even.

John viii. 16.

YET...NOT (AS)

10. John xx. 9.

YET (EVER)

ποτέ, at any time.

Eph. v. 29.

YET (IF)

{ εἴγε, if at least, if even, / καί, and also, even, } if indeed also, since, although.

Gal. iii. 4.

YET (NEVER)

10. John xix. 41.

YET (NOT)

10. John vii. 39 (οὔπω, *not yet*, L Tr A ℵ.)

YET (NOT AS)

9. 2 Cor. i. 23.

YET NEVER.

1. οὐδέποτε, not ever, not at any time.

2. { οὐδεὶς, no one, / πώποτε, at any time, not yet even, } *lit.*, no one [*of men*] at any time, *or* even yet.

1. Matt. xxvi. 33. | 2. Luke xix. 30.

YET BUT.

{ οὐ, not / πλείους, more / ἤ, than. }

Acts xxiv. 11 (*om.* ἤ, *than*, G L T Tr A ℵ.)

YET DOUBTLESS.

{ ἀλλά, but, moreover, / γε, at least, } certainly, at least, at any rate.

1 Cor. ix. 2.

YET MORE.

ἔτι, *see* "YET," *No.* 1.

Heb. xii. 26, 27.

YET NOT.

1. οὐκέτι, *see No.* 9, *above*.

2. οὔτε, and not, not even.

1. Gal. ii. 20.
2. Rev. ix. 20 (οὐ, *not*, G T Tr A), (οὐδέ, ℵ.)

See also, AND, AS, BE, NEVER, NOR, NOT.

YIELD (-ED, -ETH.)

1. διδωμι, to give; to give forth, render, yield.

2. ἀποδίδωμι, (*No.* 1, *with* ἀπό, from, *prefixed*) to give away from, to deliver over, bestow, to give in full, render; *of trees*, to yield.

3. *παρίστημι, here, trans.*, to cause to stand near, to place near by; *hence*, to place *or* present before, to place at hand, to furnish.

4. *παριστάνω, a later form used as the present of No.* 3.

5. *ποιέω*, to make, to produce.

1. Mark iv. 7, 8.
4. Rom. vi. 13 1st.
3. —— 13 2nd, 19 twice.
— Acts v. 10, see Ghost.
1. 1 Thes. i. 8, marg. (text, take.)
2. Heb. xii. 11.
5. Jas. iii. 12.
2. Rev. xxii. 2.

YIELD UNTO.

πείθω, trans., to persuade; *here, intrans.*, to be persuaded, to be won by words, to suffer one's self to be convinced.

Acts xxiii. 21.

YIELD UP.

ἀφίημι, to send forth *or* away, to let go from *one's self*, dismiss, let escape.

Matt. xxvii. 50.

YOKE. [noun.]

1. *ζυγός*, a yoke, *serving to couple any two things together, as cattle or scales, etc.*, (*occ.* Rev. vi. 5.)

2. *ζεῦγος*, a yoke, *i.e.* two or more animals yoked or working together; *hence*, a pair, a couple, (*occ.* Luke ii. 24.)

1. Matt. xi. 29, 30.
2. Luke xiv. 19.
1. Acts xv. 10.
1. Gal. v. 1.
1. 1 Tim. vi. 1.

YOKE-FELLOW.

σύζυγος, adj., yoked together; *as subst.*, a yoke-fellow, a fellow-labourer, a colleague, (*non occ.*)

Phil. iv. 3.

YOKED TOGETHER WITH (BE NOT UNEQUALLY)

μὴ, not (*see* "NO," *No.* 2) *γίνεσθε*, become *ἑτεροζυγοῦντες*, diversely yoked, *i.e.* yoked with another who is different, (*not merely another, numerically; nor, unequally, which is only a consequence of being so yoked*), } do not become diversely yoked; (lxx. *for* כִּלְאַיִם, Lev. xix. 19, *which is here referred to*), (*non occ.*)

2 Cor. vi. 14.

YONDER.

ἐκεῖ, there, in that place.

Matt. xxvi. 36.

YONDER PLACE (TO)

Matt. xvii. 20.

YOU.

"You," is very frequently the translation of the inflection of the Greek verb.

When it is represented by a separate pronoun in the Greek it is always emphatic, and is one of these following.

(*See below for* YOU (OF), YOU (FOR), YOU (TO), *etc.*)

1. *ὑμῶν*, (*Gen. pl. of σύ*, thou) of you,
2. *ὑμῖν*, (*Dat. pl. of σύ*, thou) to, unto, for, in, *or* with you,

} *when translated* "YOU" *it is the result of government or construction.*

3. *ὑμᾶς*, (*Acc. pl. of σύ*, thou) you.

4. { *τῶν*, of the / *ψυχῶν*, souls, (*see* "SOUL") / *ὑμῶν*, of you, } of your souls, *i.e. according to the Heb. idiom*, yourselves, (*see* Numb. xxiii. 10; Judg. xvi. 30; 1 Kings xx. 32; Ps. lix. 3; xxxv. 13; cxxxi. 2; Jer. xviii. 20, and *cf.* xxxviii. 6.)

5. *ἑαυτῶν*, yourselves.

6. *ἑαυτοῖς, masc.*, (*ἑαυταῖς, fem.*) to, unto, for, in, *or* with yourselves.

2. Matt. iii. 7.
3. —— 11 twice.
3. —— iv. 19.
3. —— v. 11 1st.
1. —— 11 3rd, 12.
— —— 44 1st, see Y (unto)
3. —— 44 2nd, 3rd & 4th
3. —— 44 5th, 46. (ap.)
2. —— vi. 14.
1. —— 27.
3. —— 30.
3. —— vii. 6.
2. —— 7 1st.
1. —— 7 2nd, see U (unto)
1. —— 9.
3. —— 15, 23.
3. —— x. 13, 14, 16, 17 twice, 19 1st.
2. —— 19 2nd, 20.
3. —— 23 1st.
— —— 23 2nd, see Y (unto)
2. —— 27.
3. —— 40.
2. —— xi. 21.
3. Matt. xi. 28, 29.
1. —— xii. 11.
3. —— 28.
1. —— xv. 7.
1. —— xvii. 17 twice.
2. —— xix. 8.
2. —— xx. 4, 26 twice, 27.
1. —— xxi. 2.
3. —— 24 1st.
2. —— 24 2nd, 27.
3. —— 32.
— —— 43 1st, see Y (unto)
1. —— 43 2nd.
2. —— xxiii. 3.
1. —— 11.
3. —— 34, 35.
3. —— xxiv. 4, 9 twice.
2. —— 25.
— —— xxv. 12 1st, see Y (unto)
3. —— 12 2nd.
5. —— xxvi. 11.
— —— 21 1st, see Y (unto)
1. —— 21 2nd.

— Matt. xxvi. 29 1st, see Y (unto)
1. —— 29 2nd.
3. —— 32.
3. —— 55 (om. πρὸς ὑμᾶς, *with you*, G→T Tr^b A ℵ.)
3. —— xxviii. 7 1st.
2. —— 7 2nd.
3. —— 14.
2. —— 20 1st.
1. —— 20 2nd.
3. Mark i. 8 twice, 17.
3. —— vi. 11 1st.
1. —— 11 2nd.
— —— 11 3rd, see Y (unto)
1. —— vii. 6.
3. —— ix. 19 1st.
1. —— 19 2nd.
3. —— 41 1st.
— —— 41 2nd, see Y (unto)
2. —— x. 3, 5, 43 twice.
1. —— xi. 2.
2. —— 25.
3. —— 29 1st.
2. —— 29 2nd, 33.
3. —— xiii. 5, 9, 11 1st.
2 —— 11 3rd, 23.
3. —— 36.
5. —— xiv. 7.
2. —— 13, 15.
— —— 18 1st, see Y (unto)
1. —— 18 2nd.
3. —— 28, 49.
3. —— xvi. 7 1st.
— —— 7 2nd, see Y (unto)
2. Luke ii. 10.
2. —— iii. 7, 13.
3. —— 16 twice.
2. —— iv. 25.
3. —— vi. 9, 22 1st & 2nd, 26 2nd, 27 2nd.
2. —— 28 1st (No. 3, G L T Tr A ℵ.)
3. —— 28 2nd, 32, 33.
2. —— 47.
3. —— ix. 5.
2. —— 27.
3. —— 41 1st.
1. —— 41 2nd.
2. —— 48.
3. —— x. 3, 6, 8 1st.
2. —— 8 2nd.
3. —— 9, 10.
— —— 11 1st, see Y (against)
3. —— 11 2nd (om. ἐφ' ὑμᾶς, *unto you*, G L T Tr A ℵ.)
2. —— 13.
1. —— 16 1st.
3. —— 16 2nd, 19 2nd.
2. —— 24.
1. —— xi. 5.
2. —— 9 2nd.
3. —— 20.
2. —— xii. 5 1st.
3. —— 11, 12, 14.
1. —— 25.
3. —— 28.
2. —— 32, 51.
2. —— xiii. 3, 5.
3. —— 25 2nd.
2. —— 27 1st.
3. —— 27 2nd (om. L^b T Tr A.)
3. —— 28.
1. —— xiv. 28, 33.
1. —— xv. 4.
3. —— xvi. 9 2nd.
2. —— 12.
1. —— 26 1st.
3. —— 26 2nd.
2. —— xvii. 6.
1. —— 7.
2. Luke xvii. 10.
1. —— 21.
2. —— 34.
2. —— xviii. 8, 14.
3. —— xix. 31.
2. —— 40.
3. —— xx. 3.
2. —— 8.
3. —— xxi. 12 1st.
2. —— 15.
1. —— 16.
3. —— 34.
2. —— xxii. 10, 12.
1. —— 15, 19, 20.
2. —— 26.
1. —— 27.
3. —— 31 1st, 35.
1. —— 53.
2. —— 67.
1. —— xxiii. 14.
3. —— 15 (ap.)
3. —— xxiv. 44 1st.
2. —— 44 2nd.
3. —— 49.
1. John i. 26.
2. —— iii. 12 twice.
3. —— iv. 38.
2. —— v. 38.
3. —— 42 1st.
6. —— 42 2nd.
1. —— 45 twice.
2. —— vi. 32 2nd & 3rd.
6. —— 53 2nd.
3. —— 61.
1. —— 64.
3. —— 70 1st.
1. —— 70 2nd.
3. —— vii. 7.
2. —— 19 1st.
1. —— 19 2nd, 33.
1. —— viii. 7 (ap.), 26.
3. —— 32, 36.
3. —— 37, 40.
1. —— 46.
1. —— 55 (No. 2, L Tr A*)
2. —— ix. 27.
2. —— x. 25, 32.
5. —— xii. 8.
1. —— 35 1st (ἐν ὑμῖν, *in or among you*, instead of μεθ' ὑμῶν, *with you*, G L T Tr A ℵ.)
3. —— 35 2nd.
2. —— xiii. 15 1st.
1. —— 18.
2. —— 19.
1. —— 21 1st, 33 1st.
3. —— 34 2nd.
2. —— xiv. 2 1st.
— —— 2 2nd, } see Y
— —— 3 1st, } (for)
3. —— 3 2nd.
1. —— 9.
2. —— 16 1st.
1. —— 16 2nd.
2. —— 17 twice.
3. —— 18 twice.
2. —— 20, 25 2nd.
3. —— 26 1st, 28 2nd.
2. —— 29.
1. —— 30.
2. —— xv. 4, 7 1st.
3. —— 9.
2. —— 11 2nd.
3. —— 12.
2. —— 14.
3. —— 15 1st & 2nd.
3. —— 16 1st & 2nd.
2. —— 16 3rd, 17.
3. —— 18 1st.
1. —— 18 2nd.
3. —— 19 twice, 20 2nd.
3. —— xvi. 2 twice.
2. —— 4 1st, 2nd, & 3rd.
1. —— 4 4th, 5.
2. —— 7 1st.
— —— 7 2nd, see Y (for)
3. John xvi. 7 3rd & 4th, [13 1st.
2. —— 13 2nd.
3. —— 22 1st.
1. —— 22 2nd.
2. —— 23 2nd, 25 3rd, 26 1st.
1. —— 26 2nd.
3. —— 27.
2. —— xviii. 8.
3. —— xx. 21 2nd.
1. Acts i. 7.
3. —— 8.
1. —— 11.
3. —— ii. 22 1st, 29.
1. —— iii. 16.
3. —— 22 2nd.
3. —— 26 2nd (lit., *from your iniquities.*)
1. —— iv. 10 2nd, 11, 19.
9. —— v. 28.
1. —— vi. 3.
3. —— vii. 43.
2. —— xiii. 26 1st.
3. —— 32.
2. —— 34.
3. —— 40 (om. ἐφ' ὑμᾶς, *upon you*, L T Tr A^b [ℵ.)
3. —— xv. 24, 25.
2. —— 28.
1. —— xviii. 14.
3. —— 21.
3. —— xix. 13.
1. —— xx. 18.
2. —— 20 1st.
3. —— 20 2nd.
2. —— 26.
3. —— 28, 29.
3. —— 32 1st.
2. —— 32 2nd (om. L T Tr A ℵ.)
2. —— 35.
3. —— xxii. 1.
3. —— xxiii. 15.
1. —— xxiv. 21.
2. —— xxv. 5.
1. —— 26.
2. —— xxvi. 8.
3. —— xxvii. 22 1st.
1. —— 22 2nd.
3. —— 34 1st.
3. —— xxviii. 20 2nd.
1. Rom. i. 8.
3. —— 10, 11 1st.
2. —— 12 1st.
3. —— 13 1st & 2nd.
2. —— 13 3rd.
3. —— ii. 24.
1. —— vi. 14.
2. —— viii. 9, 10, 11 twice.
3. —— x. 19 twice.
3. —— xii. 1.
2. —— 3.
3. —— 14.
1. —— 18.
2. —— xv. 5.
3. —— 13.
1. —— 14.
3. —— 15 2nd, 22, 23, 24 1st (ap.)
3. —— 24 2nd.
1. —— 24 3rd, 28.
3. —— 29, 30, 32 1st.
2. —— 32 2nd (ap.)
1. —— 33.
1. —— xvi. 2.
3. —— 16, 17, 19.
1. —— 20.
3. —— 21, 22, 23 twice.
1. —— 24 (ap.)
3. —— 25.
2. 1 Cor. i. 4, 6.
3. —— 10 1st.
2. —— 10 2nd.
1. —— 11 1st.
2. —— 11 2nd.
1. —— 13.
3. —— ii. 1 1st.
2. —— 2.
3. 1 Cor. ii. 3.
3. —— iii. 2.
2. —— 3, 16, 18.
2. —— iv. 3, 8.
3. —— 14 1st, 15, 16, 17 2nd, 18, 19, 21.
2. —— v. 1.
1. —— 2.
2. —— vi. 2, 5, 7, 19.
3. —— vii. 5.
1. —— 28.
3. —— 32.
2. —— 35.
1. —— ix. 12.
3. —— x. 13 twice, 27 1st.
2. —— 27 2nd.
3. —— xi. 2 1st, 3, 14.
2. —— 18, 19 twice.
3. —— 22 2nd.
1. —— 24.
2. —— 30.
3. —— xii. 1.
2. —— 3.
3. —— xiv. 6 1st & 2nd.
2. —— 25.
1. —— 36 1st.
3. —— 36 2nd.
2. —— xv. 12, 51.
3. —— xvi. 5, 6, 7 twice, 10, 12, 15, 19 twice, 20.
1. —— 23, 24.
1. 2 Cor. i. 7.
3. —— 8, 12, 15.
1. —— 16 1st.
3. —— 16 2nd.
1. —— 16 3rd.
3. —— 18.
2. —— 19, 21.
1. —— 23.
3. —— ii. 1, 2, 3 2nd, 4 3rd, 5, 8.
3. —— iii. 1 1st.
1. —— 1 2nd.
2. —— iv. 12, 14.
3. —— vi. 11, 17.
3. —— vii. 4 1st.
1. —— 4 2nd.
2. —— 7.
3. —— 8 twice.
2. —— 11.
— —— 12 1st, see Y (unto)
1. —— 12 2nd (ὑμῶν ὑπὲρ ἡμῶν *your care for us*, instead of ἡμῶν ὑπὲρ ὑμῶν, *our care for you*, St L T Tr A.)
3. —— 12 3rd.
1. —— 13, 14 1st.
3. —— 15 1st.
2. —— 16.
2. —— viii. 1.
3. —— 6.
1. —— 16.
3. —— 17, 22, 23.
1. —— ix. 2, 3.
3. —— 4, 5, 8.
1. —— 14 1st.
3. —— 14 2nd.
2. —— 14 3rd.
3. —— x. 1 1st.
2. —— 1 2nd.
3. —— 1 3rd, 9.
1. —— 13.
3. —— 14 1st.
1. —— 14 2nd.
2. —— 15.
1. —— 16.
3. —— xi. 2 2nd & 3rd, 6.
1. —— 8.
3. —— 9 1st, 11, 20 1st & 4th.
1. —— xii. 11.
2. —— 12.
1. —— 13.
3. —— 14 1st.
1. —— 14 2nd.
3. —— 14 3rd.
4. —— 15 1st, marg. *your souls.*

3. 2 Cor. xii. 15 2nd, 16 twice, 17 twice, 18, 20 1st, 21.
3. —— xiii. 1.
— ——— 3 1st, see Y-ward.
2. ——— 3 2nd.
3. ——— 4.
2. ——— 5.
1. ——— 11.
3. ——— 13.
1. ——— 14.
3. Gal. i. 6, 7, 9.
2. ——— 11.
3. —— ii. 5.
3. —— iii. 1 1st.
2. ——— 1 2nd (om. ἐν ὑμῖν, among you, G ⇉ L T Tr A ℵ.)
1. ——— 2.
3. —— iv. 11 twice.
1. ——— 12.
2. ——— 15, 16.
3. ——— 17 1st.
3. ——— 17 2nd (ἡμᾶς, us, E and margin.)
3. ——— 18.
2. ——— 19.
3. ——— 20 1st.
2. ——— 20 2nd.
3. —— v. 2 2nd, 7, 8, 10 twice, 12.
2. ——— 21 1st.
3. —— vi. 12, 13.
1. Eph. i. 16 1st.
3. —— ii. 1.
1. —— iii. 1.
3. ——— 2.
1. ——— 13.
2. ——— 16.
3. —— iv. 1.
2. ——— 6 (om. G ⇉ L T Tr A ℵ), (ἡμῖν, us, G.)
1. ——— 31.
2. ——— 32 (ἡμῖν, us, G∾L Trm A*)
2. —— v. 3.
3. ——— 6.
3. —— vi. 22.
1. Phil. i. 4.
2. ——— 6.
1. ——— 7 1st.
3. ——— 7 2nd, 8, 24.
2. ——— 25.
3. ——— 26, 27.
2. —— ii. 5, 13, 17.
3. ——— 25, 26.
2. —— iii. 18 1st.
1. —— iv. 9, 18.
3. ——— 21, 22.
1. ——— 23.
1. Col. i. 3.
3. ——— 6 1st.
2. ——— 6 2nd.
1. ——— 7 (ἡμῶν, us, G∾L Tr A ℵ.)
1. ——— 9.
3. ——— 21, 22.
1. ——— 24.
3. ——— 25.
2. ——— 27.
1. —— ii. 1.
3. ——— 4.
2. ——— 5.
3. ——— 8, 13 1st.
2. ——— 13 2nd (ἡμῖν, us, St G L T Tr A ℵ.)
3. ——— 16, 18.
2. —— iii. 13, 16.
3. —— iv. 8.
1. ——— 9 1st.
3. ——— 10 twice.
1. ——— 12 1st.
3. ——— 12 2nd.
1. ——— 12 3rd, 13.
3. ——— 14.
2. ——— 16.
1. ——— 18.
2. 1 Thes. i. 1.
1. ——— 2 1st.
3. 1 Thes. i. 5 1st.
2. ——— 5 2nd.
1. ——— 8.
3. ——— 9.
3. —— ii. 1, 2.
1. ——— 6, 7, 8 1st.
3. ——— 9 2nd.
2. ——— 10.
3. ——— 11, 12.
2. ——— 13.
1. ——— 17.
3. ——— 18.
3. —— iii. 2 1st.
3. ——— 2 2nd (om. G→L T Tr A ℵ.)
3. ——— 4 1st.
2. ——— 4 2nd.
3. ——— 5.
1. ——— 6 1st.
3. ——— 6 2nd.
2. ——— 7.
1. ——— 9.
3. ——— 11, 12 twice.
3. —— iv. 1 1st.
2. ——— 2, 6.
3. ——— 10.
2. ——— 11.
3. ——— 13.
3. —— v. 4, 12 1st.
2. ——— 12 2nd.
1. ——— 12 3rd. [24, 27.
3. ——— 12 4th, 14, 18, 23,
1. ——— 28.
1. 2 Thes. i. 3 1st.
2. ——— 4.
3. ——— 6, 10.
1. ——— 11 1st.
3. ——— 11 2nd.
2. ——— 12.
3. —— ii. 1, 3, 5 1st.
2. ——— 5 2nd.
1. ——— 13 1st.
3. ——— 13 2nd.
3. ——— 14 (ἡμᾶς, us, L Trm.)
3. ——— 17 (om. G ⇉ L T Tr A ℵ.)
3. —— iii. 1, 3 1st, 4 1st.
2. ——— 4 2nd, 6, 7.
3. ——— 10 1st.
2. ——— 10 2nd, 11, 16 1st.
1. ——— 16 2nd, 18.
1. 2 Tim. iv. 22 (ap.)
1. Titus ii. 8 (ἡμῶν, of us, G L T Tr A ℵ.)
1. —— iii. 15.
2. Philem. 6 (G∾), (ἡμῖν, us, G L T Tr A ℵ.)
1. Heb. iii. 13.
1. —— iv. 1.
3. —— v. 12.
1. —— vi. 9.
3. —— ix. 20.
3. —— xii. 7.
1. —— xiii. 7 1st, 17 1st.
3. ——— 21 1st.
2. ——— 21 2nd.
3. ——— 22 1st, 23.
1. ——— 24 1st.
3. ——— 24 2nd.
1. ——— 25.
2. Jas. i. 26 (G∾), (om. ἐν ὑμῖν, among you, G L T Tr A ℵ.)
1. —— ii. 6 1st.
3. ——— 6 2nd.
1. ——— 16.
2. —— iii. 13.
2. —— iv. 1.
1. ——— 7.
3. ——— 10.
2. —— v. 3.
1. ——— 4.
2. ——— 6, 13, 14, 19.
3. 1 Pet. i. 4, marg. us (ἡμᾶς, us, St.)
3. ——— 10, 12 1st, 15, 20, 25.
3. 1 Pet. ii. 9.
1. ——— 12.
3. —— iii. 13, 15 1st.
2. ——— 15 2nd.
1. ——— 16 (ap.)
2. —— iv. 12 1st.
3. ——— 14.
2. —— v. 1, 2.
3. ——— 6.
1. ——— 7.
3. ——— 10 1st (om. G→L T Tr A ℵ.)
3. ——— 13 2nd.
2. ——— 14.
2. 2 Pet. i. 8 1st.
3. ——— 12, 13 1st.
2. —— ii. 1.
3. ——— 3.
2. ——— 13.
2. 1 John ii. 8 2nd, 12 2nd, 14 2nd, 24 twice.
3. ——— 26 2nd.
2. ——— 27 1st.
3. ——— 27 2nd, 3rd, & 4th.
3. 1 John iii. 7, 13.
2. —— iv. 4.
1. 2 John 3 (ἡμῶν, us, St ℵ.)
3. ——— 10, 12 2nd.
3. Jude 5.
2. ——— 12 (om. St ℵ.)
2. ——— 18.
3. ——— 24 1st (αὐτούς, them, St.)
1. Rev. ii. 10.
2. ——— 13.
3. ——— 24 2nd.
3. —— xii. 12.
2. —— xviii. 6 (om. G L T Tr A ℵ.)
1. ——— 20.
1. —— xxii. 21 (πάντων τῶν ἁγίων, all the saints, instead of πάντων ὑμῶν ἀμήν, you all amen, G Tr A ℵ), (om. G→L T, i.e. with all.)

YOU (AGAINST)

2. Luke x. 11.

YOU (FOR)

2. Matt. xi. 22.
2. —— xxv. 9, 34.
2. Mark x. 36.
2. Luke x. 14.
2. John xiv. 2, 3.
2. John xvi. 7.
2. Acts xxii. 25.
2. 2 Cor. viii. 10.
2. Phil. iii. 1.
2. Col. i. 5.
2. Heb. xiii. 17.

YOU (NO ONE OF)

μή, not; *lit.*, that ye might not be puffing yourselves up, etc.

1 Cor. iv. 6.

YOU (OF)

1. ὑμῶν, *see No.* 1, *above.*

2. ὑμῖν, *see No.* 2, *above.*

3. ὑμεῖς, (*nom. pl. of* σύ, thou) you.

1. Matt. xviii. 19.
1. Mark x. 44 (ἐν ὑμῖν, among you, L ℵ.)
1. Luke xi. 11.
1. —— xiii. 15.
1. —— xiv. 5.
1. Acts ii. 22, 38.
1. —— iii. 26 (αὐτῶν, of them, L.)
1. —— xxvii. 34.
1. Rom. i. 9, 12.
1. 1 Cor. i. 12, 14.
1. —— vi. 1.
1. —— xii. 21.
1. —— xiv. 26 (om. L T Tr Ab ℵ.)
1. —— xvi. 2.
1. 2 Cor. ii. 3, 9.
1. —— vii. 15.
1. Eph. i. 16 (om. L T Tr A ℵ.)
3. —— v. 33.
1. Phil. i. 3.
1. 1 Thes. i. 2 (om. L T Tr Ab ℵ.)
1. —— ii. 9, 11.
1. —— iv. 4.
1. 2 Thes. i. 3.
1. —— iii. 8.
1. Heb. iii. 12.
1. —— vi. 11.
1. Jas. i. 5.
1. 1 Pet. iv. 15.
2. Rev. ii. 23.

YOU (TO)

ὑμῖν, (*Dat. pl. of* σύ, thou) to, unto, *or* for you.

Matt. vii. 2, 12.
—— xvi. 11.
Mark iv. 24.
—— xiii. 21.
Luke vi. 31, 38.
—— vii. 32 (*om.* T Tr ℵ.)
—— xvii. 23.
—— xxi. 13.
John xiii. 12, 15, 33.
—— xix. 4.
Acts xiii. 26, 46.
Rom. i. 7, 15.
—— xi. 13.
1 Cor. ix. 2.
—— xi. 2, 22.
—— xiv. 6.

2 Cor. i. 2.
—— vii. 14.
—— ix. 1.
—— xi. 7.
Gal. i. 3.
—— iii. 5.
Eph. i. 2.
—— ii. 17.
—— vi. 21.
Phil. i. 28 (ὑμῶν, *of you, i.e. of your salvation,* G∾L T Tr ℵ.)
—— iii. 1.
2 Thes. i. 7.
Philem. 3.
Heb. xiii. 19.

Jas. iv. 8.

Gal. vi. 11.
Eph. i. 17.
Phil. i. 2, 29.
—— ii. 19.
—— iii. 15.
Col. i. 2.
—— iv. 7, 9.
1 Thes. i. 1.
—— ii. 8.
—— iv. 9, 15.
—— v. 1.
2 Thes. i. 2.
—— iii. 9.
Philem. 22.
Heb. xii. 5.
—— xiii. 7, 22.
1 Pet. i. 2, 12 2nd, 13.

1 Pet. ii. 7.
—— iv. 12.
—— v. 12.
2 Pet. i. 2, 11, 16.
—— iii. 1, 15.
1 John i. 2, 3.
——— 4 (ἡμεῖς, *we,* St L T Tr A ℵ; i.e. *we write.*)
——— 5.
—— ii. 1, 7, 8, 12, 13 3 times, 14 twice, 21, 26.
—— v. 13.
2 John 12 1st.
Jude 2, 3 twice.
Rev. i. 4.
—— ii. 24.
—— xxii. 16.

YOU (UNTO)

ὑμῖν, (*Dat. pl. of* σύ, thou) to, unto, *or* for you.

Matt. iii. 9.
—— v. 18, 20, 22, 28, 32, 34, 39, 44.
—— vi. 2, 5, 16, 25, 29, 33.
—— vii. 7.
—— viii. 10 11.
—— ix. 29.
—— x. 15, 23, 42.
—— xi. 9, 11, 17 1st.
——— 17 2nd (*om.* L T Tr A ℵ.)
——— 22, 24.
—— xii. 6, 31, 36.
—— xiii. 11, 17.
—— xvi. 28.
—— xvii. 12, 20 twice.
—— xviii. 3, 10, 13, 18, 19, 35.
—— xix. 9, 23, 24, 28.
—— xx. 32.
—— xxi. 3, 21, 31, 43.
—— xxii. 31.
—— xxiii. 13, 14 (*ap.*), 15, 16, 23, 25, 27, 29, 36, 38, 39.
—— xxiv. 2, 23, 26, 34, 47.
—— xxv. 12, 40, 45.
—— xxvi. 13, 15, 21, 29,
—— xxvii. 17, 21. [64.
Mark iii. 28.
—— iv. 11, 24 (*ap.*)
—— vi. 11 (*ap.*)
—— viii. 12.
—— ix. 1, 13, 41.
—— x. 15, 29.
—— xi. 3, 23, 24.
—— xii. 43.
—— xiii. 30, 37.
—— xiv. 9, 18, 25.
—— xv. 9.
—— xvi. 7.
Luke ii. 11, 12.
—— iii. 8.
—— iv. 24.
—— vi. 24, 25 1st.
——— 25 2nd (*om.* G→T Tr A ℵ, i.e. *ye who are laughing.*)
——— 26 (*om.* G L T Tr A ℵ.)
——— 27, 38.
—— vii. 9, 26, 28, 32.
—— viii. 10.
—— x. 12, 19, 20.
—— xi. 8, 9 twice, 41, 42, 43, 44, 46, 47, 51, 52.
—— xii. 4, 5, 8, 22, 27, 31, 37, 44.
—— xiii. 24, 25, 35 twice.
—— xiv. 24.
—— xv. 7, 10.
—— xvi. 9.

Luke xviii. 17, 29.
—— xix. 26.
—— xxi. 3, 32.
—— xxii. 16, 18, 29, 37.
—— xxiv. 6, 36 (*ap.*)
John i. 51.
—— ii. 5.
—— iv. 35.
—— v. 19, 24, 25.
—— vi. 26, 27, 32, 36, 47, 53, 63, 65.
—— vii. 22.
—— viii. 24, 25, 34, 51, 58.
—— x. 1, 7, 26 (*ap.*)
—— xii. 24.
—— xiii. 16, 20, 21, 34.
—— xiv. 10, 12, 25, 26, 27 twice, 28 1st.
—— xv. 3, 7, 11, 15, 20.
——— 21 (εἰς ὑμᾶς, *unto you,* G∾L T Tr), (*om.*
——— 26. [ℵ.)
—— xvi. 1.
——— 3 (*om.* G L T Tr A.)
——— 4, 6, 12, 14, 15, 20, 23, 25 twice, 26, 33.
—— xviii. 39 twice.
—— xx. 19, 21, 26.
Acts ii. 14, 39.
—— iii. 14, 20, 22 1st, 26.
—— iv. 10.
—— v. 38.
—— vii. 37.
—— xiii. 38 twice, 41.
—— xvii. 3, 23.
—— xx. 27.
—— xxviii. 28.
Rom. i. 11.
—— xv. 15.
—— xvi. 1.
1 Cor. i. 3.
—— ii. 1.
—— iii. 1.
—— iv. 17.
—— v. 9, 11.
—— ix. 11.
—— x. 28.
—— xi. 23.
—— xii. 31.
—— xiv. 37.
—— xv. 1 twice, 2, 6.
2 Cor. i. 13.
—— ii. 3 (*om.* G⇉L T Tr
——— 4 1st. [A ℵ.)
—— v. 12.
—— vi. 18.
—— vii. 12 1st.
—— xi. 9.
—— xii. 19, 20.
Gal. i. 8 twice, 20.
—— iv. 18.
—— v. 2.

YOU (WITH)

ὑμῖν, (*Dat. pl. of* σύ, thou) to, unto, for, *or* with you.

John xiv. 27. | Acts xiv. 15.

YOU...YE.

ὑμᾶς, (*Acc. pl. of* σύ, thou) you, *lit.*, you to be turning, etc.

Acts xiv. 15.

YOU-WARD (TO)

{ εἰς, unto, towards,
{ ὑμᾶς, you.

2 Cor. xiii. 3.

YOU YOURSELVES.

αὐτοί, *your*selves.

Acts xx. 34.

YOUNG.

1. νεώτερος, (*comp. of* νέος, new, recent, young) younger, *of two or more;* (lxx. *for* קטן, Gen. ix. 24; xxvii. 15; xlii. 13.)

2. νεοσσός, youngling, *the young of animals, but esp. of birds;* (lxx. *for* בן, Lev. v. 7; Prov. xxx. 17; *and* אפרחים, Deut. xxii. 6), (*non occ.*)

2. Luke ii. 24. | 1 John xxi. 18.

YOUNG MAN (MEN)

1. νεανίσκος, a youth, a young man until forty, (*often in Greek prose, for* a soldier); (lxx. *for* נער, 1 Sam. xvii. 55; Is. iii. 3; ילד, Ezra x. 1.)

2. *νεανίας*, a youth, a young man; *esp.* a youth *in character, either as brave or active, wilful or headstrong;* (lxx. *for* נער, Judg. xvi. 26; בחור, 2 Sam. vi. 1; 1 Ch. xix. 10.)

3. *νεώτερος, see* "YOUNG," *No.* 1.

4. *παῖς*, a child, *male or female*, a boy, a youth; a girl, a maiden; (lxx. *gen. for* ילד, 2 Kings ii. 24; בֵּן, Prov. iv. 1; נער, Ruth ii. 6; נערה, Gen. xxiv. 28, 57; xxxiv. 12.)

1. Matt. xix. 20, 22.
1. Mark xiv. 51 1st.
— —— 51 2nd (*om. οἱ νεανίσκοι, the young men,* G⇉L T Tr A ℵ,
1. —— xvi. 5. [i.e. *they.*)
1. Luke vii. 14.
1. Acts ii. 17.
3. —— v. 6.
1. Acts v. 10.
2. —— vii. 58.
2. —— xx. 9.
4. —— 12.
2. —— xxiii. 17.
2. —— 18, } (No. 1, L T
2. —— 22, } Tr A ℵ.)
3. Tit. ii. 6.
1. 1 John ii. 13, 14.

YOUNG WOMAN (-EN.)

νεός, new, recent, young. *Here, fem.*

Tit. ii. 4.

See also, ASS, CHILD, DAUGHTER.

YOUNGER.

1. *νεώτερος, see* "YOUNG," *No.* 1.

2. *ἐλάσσων*, less, minor; *in quality*, inferior; *in age*, younger; (lxx. *for* צעיר, Gen. xxv. 23.)

1. Luke xv. 12, 13.
1. —— xxii. 26.
2. Rom. ix. 12, marg.
1. 1 Tim. v. 2, 11, 14. [*lesser.*
1. 1 Pet. v. 5.

YOUNGER MAN.

1. 1 Tim. v. 1.

YOUR.

(*For* "YOURS," *and various combinations with other words, see below.*)

1. *ὑμῶν*, (*Gen. pl. of σύ*, thou) of you, yours; (*not so emphatic as No.* 6.)

2. { *ἐκ*, of, / *ὑμῶν*, of you, } of or belonging to you.

3. *ὑμῖν*, (*Dat. pl. of σύ*, thou) to, unto, for, *or* with you.

4. *ὑμᾶς*, (*Acc. pl. of σύ*, thou) you; *here lit.*, put you in mind.

5. { *κατὰ*, in accordance with, according to, / *ὑμᾶς*, you, } which ye have.

6. *ὑμέτερος*, your, *as belonging to or proceeding from, more emphatic than any of the above.*

1. Matt. v. 12, 16 3 times, 20, 37, 44, 45, 47, 48.
1. —— vi. 1 twice, 8, 14, 15 twice.
1. —— 21 twice (*σοῦ, thy,* G∼L T Tr A ℵ.)
1. —— 25 twice, 26, 32.
1. —— vii. 6, 11 twice.
1. —— ix. 4, 11, 29.
1. —— x. 9, 13 twice, 14 twice, 20, 29, 30.
1. —— xi. 29.
1. —— xii. 27 twice.
1. —— xiii. 16 1st.
1. —— 16 2nd (*om.* L Tr b A b.)
1. —— xv. 3, 6.
1. —— xvii. 20, 24.
1. —— xviii. 14 (*μοῦ, my,* L Tr.)
1. —— 35.
1. —— xix. 8 twice.
1. —— xx. 26, 27.
1. —— xxiii. 8, 9 twice, 10 (*om.* G∼), 11, 32, 34, 38.
1. —— xxiv. 20, 42.
1. —— xxv. 8.
1. Mark ii. 8.
1. —— vi. 11.
1. —— vii. 13.
1. —— viii. 17.
1. —— x. 5, 43.
1. —— xi. 25 twice, 26 twice (*ap.*)
1. —— xiii. 18 (*om. ἡ φυγὴ ὑμῶν, your flight,* G⇉L T Tr A ℵ; i.e. *it.*)
1. Luke iii. 14.
1. —— iv. 21.
1. —— v. 4, 22.
1. —— vi. 22, 23, 24, 27, 35 twice, 36, 38.
1. —— viii. 25.
1. —— ix. 5, 44.
1. —— x. 6, 11, 20.
1. —— xi. 13, 19 twice, 39, 46, 47, 48.
1. —— xii. 7.
1. —— 22 (*om.* G⇉L T Tr A ℵ.)
1. —— 30, 32, 34 twice, 35.
1. —— xiii. 35.
3. —— xvi. 11.
1. —— 15.
1. —— xxi. 14.
3. —— 15.
1. —— 18, 19 twice, 28 twice, 34.
1. —— xxii. 53.
1. —— xxiii. 28.
1. —— xxiv. 38.
1. John iv. 35.
1. —— vi. 49.
1. —— 58 (*om.* G⇉L T Tr A ℵ, i.e. *the.*)
6. —— vii. 6.
6. —— viii. 17.
1. —— 21, 24 twice.
1. —— 38 (*om.* G⇉L T Tr A, i.e. *the father, their father.*)
1. —— 41, 42, 44.
1. —— 54 (*ἡμῶν, our,* G∼T Tr A.)
1. —— 56.
1. —— ix. 19, 41.
1. —— x. 34.
1. —— xiii. 14.
1. —— xiv. 1.
5. —— 26.
1. —— 27.
1. John xv. 11, 16.
1. —— xvi. 6, 20, 22 twice, 24.
1. —— xviii. 31.
1. —— xix. 14, 15.
1. —— xx. 17 twice.
1. Acts ii. 17 4 times, 39.
1. —— iii. 17, 19, 22 twice.
1. —— v. 28.
1. —— vii. 37 1st (*om.* Κύριος, and ὑμῶν, i.e. God, instead of *the Lord your God,* G L T Tr A ℵ.)
1. —— 37 2nd.
1. —— 43 (*om.* L T Tr A, i.e. *the.*)
1. —— 51, 52.
1. —— xiii. 41.
1. —— xv. 24.
1. —— xvii. 23.
1. —— xviii. 6.
4. —— 15.
1. —— xix. 37.
6. —— xxvii. 34.
1. Rom. i. 8.
1. —— vi. 12, 13 twice, 19 3 times, 22.
1. —— viii. 11.
6. —— xi. 31.
1. —— xii. 1 twice.
1. —— 2 (*om.* G⇉L T Tr A, i.e. *the.*)
1. —— xiv. 16.
1. —— xv. 24, marg. *you.*
1. —— xvi. 19, 20.
1. 1 Cor. i. 4, 26.
1. —— ii. 5.
1. —— v. 6.
3. —— vi. 5.
1. —— 15, 19, 20 1st, 2 2nd (*ap.*)
1. —— vii. 5, 14.
1. —— ix. 11.
1. —— xiv. 34 (*om.* G→L T Tr A ℵ, i.e. *the.*)
1. —— xv. 14, 17.
6. —— 31 (*ἡμέτερος, our,* St AVm G∼), marg. *our.*
3. —— 34.
1. —— 58.
1. —— xvi. 3.
1. 2 Cor. i. 6 twice, 14, 24 twice.
1. —— iv. 5.
1. —— v. 11.
1. —— vii. 7 3 times.
1. —— 13 (*δὲ τῇ παρακλήσει ἡμῶν...δε, and on our comfort,* instead of *τῇ παρακλήσει ὑμῶν, in your comfort yea and,* L T Tr A ℵ.)
2. —— viii. 7.
6. —— 8.
1. —— 14 twice.
1. —— 19 (G∼), (*ἡμῶν, our,* G L T Tr A ℵ.)
1. —— 24 twice.
1. —— ix. 2 1st.
2. —— 2 2nd (*om. ἐκ,* L T Tr A b ℵ.)
1. —— 5, 10 twice, 13.
1. —— x. 6, 8, 15.
1. —— xi. 8.
1. —— xii. 19.
1. —— xiii. 9.
1. Gal. iv. 6 (G∼), (*ἡμῶν, our,* G L T Tr A ℵ.)
1. —— 15, 16.
6. —— vi. 13.
1. —— 18.

1. Eph. i. 13.
4. ——— 15.
1. ——— 18.
1. —— iii. 13, 17.
1. —— iv. 4, 23, 26, 29.
1. —— v. 19. [14, 22.
1. —— vi. 1, 4, 5, 9 (*ap.*),
1. Phil. i. 5, 9, 19, 25, 26.
1. —— ii. 17, 25, 30.
1. —— iv. 5, 6, 7 twice, 17,
1. Col. i. 4, 8. [19.
1. —— ii. 5 twice, 13.
1. —— iii. 3, 5, 8, 15, 16.
1. —— iv. 6, 8.
1. 1 Thes. i. 3, 4, 8.
1. —— ii. 17.
1. —— iii. 2, 5, 6, 7, 10 twice, 13.
1. —— iv. 3, 11.
1. —— v. 23.
1. 2 Thes. i. 3, 4 twice.
1. —— ii. 17.
1. —— iii. 5.
1. Philem. 22, 25.
1. Heb. iii. 8, 9, 15.
1. —— iv. 7.
1. Heb. vi. 10.
1. —— ix. 14 (ἡμῶν, G∾L Trm A.)
1. —— x. 34, 35.
1. —— xii. 3, 13.
1. —— xiii. 17.
1. Jas. i. 3, 21.
1. —— ii. 2.
1. —— iii. 14. [16.
1. —— iv. 1 twice, 3, 9, 14,
1. —— v. 1, 2 twice, 3 twice, 4, 5, 8, 12.
1. 1 Pet. i. 7, 9, 13, 14, 17, 18, 21, 22.
1. —— ii. 12.
— ——— 20, see Faulty.
1. ——— 25.
1. —— iii. 2, 7, 15, 16.
1. —— v. 7, 8, 9.
1. 2 Pet. 1, 5, 10, 19.
1. —— iii. 1.
1. 1 John i. 4 (ἡμῶν, *our*, St L T Tr A ℵ.)
1. Jude 12, 20.
1. Rev. i. 9.
1. —— ii. 23.

YOUR AFFAIRS.

{ τὰ, the *things*
{ περὶ, around *or* concerning
{ ὑμῶν, you.

Phil. i. 27.

YOUR BEHALF (ON)

{ τὸ, the *matter* }
{ ἐπὶ, upon } over you.
{ ὑμῖν, you, }

Rom. xvi. 19.

YOUR CAUSE (FOR)

ὑμῖν, for you.

2 Cor. v. 13.

YOUR ESTATE.

{ τὰ, the *things*
{ περὶ, around *or* concerning
{ ὑμῶν, you.

Col. iv. 8 (τὰ περὶ ἡμῶν, *the things concerning us*, G∾L T Tr.)

YOUR MATTER (THE UTTERMOST OF)

{ τὰ, the *affair or matter* }
{ κατὰ, in accordance with } in accordance with, according to, *or* as to, your affair.
{ ὑμᾶς, you, }

Acts xxiv. 22.

YOUR OWN.

1. ὑμῶν, of you, your.

2. { ὑμῶν, of you, your
{ αὐτῶν, selves.

3. { κατὰ, amongst
{ υμᾶς, you.

4. ἑαυτῶν, of *or* belonging to yourselves.

1. Mark vii. 9.
3. Acts xvii. 28.
1. —— xviii. 6.
4. 1 Cor. vi. 19.
2. ——— 35.
1. 2 Cor. vi. 12.
4. Phil. ii. 12.

YOUR OWN CONCEITS (IN)

{ παρὰ, beside, with, among
{ ἑαυτοῖς, yourselves,
{ φρονιμοι, prudent.

Rom. xi. 25. | Rom. xii. 16.

YOUR OWN SELVES.

1. ἑαυτῶν, yourselves, (*Gen.*)

2. ἑαυτοῖς, yourselves, (*Dat.*)

3. { ὑμῶν, of you your
{ αὐτῶν, selves.

1. Luke xxi. 30.
3. Acts xx. 30.
2. 2 Cor. xiii. 5 twice.
2. Jas. i. 22.

YOUR OWN (THAT WHICH IS)

{ τὸ, the *thing*
{ ὑμέτερων, yours, your own, (*emphatic.*)

Luke xvi. 12.

YOUR PART (ON)

1. ὑμῶν, of you, your.

2. { ἐπὶ, upon
{ ὑμᾶς, you.

1. 1 Cor. xvi. 17 (ὑμετερόν, *your* (emphatic), L T Tr A.)
2. 1 Pet. iv. 14 (*ap.*)

YOUR SAKE (-S.)

{ διὰ, through, for the sake of, on account of,
{ ὑμᾶς, you.

John xi. 15.
—— xii. 30.
Rom. xi. 28.
1 Cor. iv. 6.
2 Cor. ii. 10.
—— iv. 15.
—— viii. 9.
1 Thes. i. 5.
1 Thes. iii. 9.

YOUR STATE.

τὰ, the *things*
περὶ, around *or* concerning
ὑμῶν, you.

Phil. ii. 19, 20.

YOUR THINGS.

ὑμῶν, of you, your.

1 Cor. xvi. 14.

YOURS.

1. ὑμῶν, of you, yours.
2. ὑμέτερος, yours, of *or* belonging to you, (*more emphatic than No.* 1 *or No.* 3.)
3. ὁ, the [*spirit*] ὑμῶν, of you.

2. Luke vi. 20.
2. John xv. 20.
1. 1 Cor. iii. 21, 22.
3. —— xvi. 18.
3. 2 Cor. xii. 14.

YOURS (OF)

ὑμῶν, of you, yours.

1 Cor. viii. 9.

YOURSELVES.

(*For various combinations with other words, see below.*)

1. ἑαυτῶν, (*Gen. pl.*) yourselves.
2. ἑαυτοῖς, (*Dat. pl.*) yourselves.
3. ἑαυτοὺς, (*Acc. pl.*) yourselves.
4. αὐτοί, selves, *your*selves.
5. ὑμῶν, of you, your αὐτῶν, -selves.
6. ὑμῖν, to *or* for you, αυτοῖς, -selves, to yourselves.
7. ὑμῶν, of you, your.
8. ἀλλήλων, each other, one another.

2. Matt. iii. 9.
2. —— xvi. 8.
7. —— xxiii. 15.
3. Mark ix. 33 (*om.* πρὸς ἑαυτοὺς, *among yourselves*, G⇄L T Tr A ℵ.)
2. —— 50.
2. Luke iii. 8.
2. —— xii. 33.
1. —— 57.
3. —— xvi. 15.
2. Luke xvii. 3.
3. —— 14.
2. —— xxi. 34.
3. —— xxiii. 28.
8. John vi. 43.
8. —— xvi. 19.
2. Acts v. 35.
3. —— xiii. 46.
3. —— xv. 29.
3. —— xx. 28.
3. Rom. vi. 11, 13, 16.
3. —— xii. 19.
5. 1 Cor. v. 13.
3. —— vii. 11.
6. —— xi. 13.
3. —— xiii. 5.
3. 2 Cor. vii. 11.
3. —— xiii. 5.
7. Eph. ii. 8.
4. 1 Thes. ii. 1.
4. —— iii. 3.
4. —— v. 2.
2. 1 Thes. v. 13 (αὐτοῖς, *yourselves*, G∾T Tr ℵ.)
8. —— 15.
4. 2 Thes. iii. 7.
2. Heb. x. 34.
4. —— xiii. 3.
2. Jas. ii. 4.
3. 1 Pet. iv. 8.
3. 1 John v. 21
3. 2 John 8.
3. Jude 20, 21.

YOURSELVES (AMONG)

2. Luke xxii. 17 (εἰς ἑαυτοὺς, *unto* or *for yourselves*, L T Tr A), (ἀλλήλοις, *with each other*; No. 8, ℵ.)

YOURSELVES (FOR)

1. ἑαυτοῖς, (*No.* 2, *above*) to *or* for yourselves.
2. ὑμῖν, to *or* for you.

2. Matt. vi. 19, 20. | 1. Matt. xxv. 9.

YOURSELVES (TO)

ἑαυτοῖς, to *or* for yourselves.

Luke xvi. 9. | Eph. v. 19

YOURSELVES TOGETHER.

8. 1 Thes. v. 11.

YOURSELVES (UNTO)

ἑαυτοῖς, to *or* for yourselves.

Matt. xxiii. 31.

YOURSELVES (YE)

See, YE.

YOURSELVES (YOU)

αὐτοί, *your*-selves.

Acts xx. 34.

YOUTH.

νεότης, newness, recentness; *hence*, youth, youthful age; (lxx. *for* נעורים, Gen. viii. 21; Num. xxx. 17; ילדות, Ecc. xi. 9, 10), (*non occ.*)

Matt. xix. 20 (*om.* ἐκ νεότητός μου, *from my youth up*, G→L T Tr A ℵ.)
Mark x. 20.
Luke xviii. 21.
Acts xxvi. 4.
1 Tim. iv. 12.

YOUTHFUL.

νεωτερικός, pertaining *or* belonging to youth, (*non occ.*)

2 Tim. ii. 22.

Z

ZEAL.

ζῆλος, zeal, (*from* ζέω, to boil, seethe) *gen.*, any eager, vehement passion; *esp.* jealousy.

John ii. 17.	Phil. iii. 6.
Rom. x. 2.	Col. iv. 13 (πόνος, labour
2 Cor. vii. 11.	or toil, G L T Tr A
— ix. 2.	א.)

ZEALOUS.

ζηλωτής, one zealous for *anything*, a zealot, *esp. from jealousy*, (*non occ.*)

Acts xxi. 20.	1 Cor. xiv. 12.
— xxii. 3.	Gal. i. 14.
	Tit. ii. 14.

ZEALOUS (BE)

ζηλόω, to make zealous towards, *i.e.* for *or* against *any person or thing;* to rival, vie with.

Rev. iii. 19 (ζηλεύω, to be zealous, G א L T Tr A.)

ZEALOUSLY AFFECT.

ζηλόω, *see* "ZEALOUS (BE)"

Gal. iv. 17, 18.

INDEX.

GREEK AND ENGLISH.

As one Greek word is found under several English words in the body of the work, this Index is designed to enable the student to trace out for himself any particular Greek word, through all its renderings, and in all its occurrences.

This Index, therefore, combined with the work itself, contains all the elements of a Greek and English Concordance.

For example, the student is referring to the word "HOLY" to ascertain the meaning of the word in a particular passage; he finds there three Greek words, ἅγιος, ὅσιος, and ἱερός; if now he wishes to see how these words are translated elsewhere he has only to refer to them in this Index, and there he will find under each a list of English words with a figure against each showing the number of times such word occurs. These may again be referred to, and traced back to see what other Greek words are used to represent them. Thus the full Scripture use of any word may easily be found, a matter ofttimes of no small importance when we are dealing with "words which the Holy Ghost speaketh."

The following observations are necessary for a full explanation of the plan and design of this Index:—

1. Each Greek word is placed in its alphabetical order.

2. Greek words not occurring in the "Received Text," (*i.e.* the text from which the Authorized Version was made, 1611—see the Preface), but inserted or substituted for others in MS. and other critical authorities, have an asterisk (*) prefixed to them.

3. After each Greek word is placed every English word which is used as the translation of it, with a figure showing the number of times such a translation is found.

The arrangement of the English words is determined by the order in which they *most correctly* represent the Greek word. This will materially help

the student in tracing any particular word, and almost serve the purpose of a Lexicon.

4. In the case of Greek words not occurring in the "Received Text," (*see above, No.* 2), the Greek word is given, for which it is proposed to be substituted, with the passage where it occurs; and also the English word of which it is the translation. On referring to this word in the body of the work, full particulars as to the meaning of the word and the editorial authorities for it will be found.

5. English renderings occurring as marginal readings in the Authorized Version are printed in *italic* type, and placed immediately after the word for which they are the alternative renderings in the margin.

6. No reference is given to pages, as the words themselves can readily be found in their alphabetical order in the body of the work. Where the translation consists of more than one word, each will generally be found in its place, or referred to by a cross reference from the other. In the case of phrases, however, the more important word should be referred to.

7. Besides the Greek word itself, every *combination* with it, of other Greek words, is given where an important or peculiar translation is the result. For an example of what is meant, see below under ἅγιος.

Α,
Alpha, 4.

ἀβαρής,
from being burdensome, 1.

ἀββᾶ,
abba, 3.

ἄβυσσος,
bottomless pit, 5.
bottomless, 2.
deep, 2.

ἀγαθοεργέω,
do good, 1.

ἀγαθοποιέω,
do good, 7.
do well, 2.
with well doing, 1.
for well doing, 1.

ἀγαθοποιΐα,
well doing, 1.

ἀγαθοποιός,
that doeth well, 1.

ἀγαθος,
good, 63.
good, 12 (*subst.*)
good thing, 14.
goods, 2.
benefit, 1.
well, 1.
— *with art.*,
that which is good, 9.
the thing which is good, 1.

ἀγαθουργέω, *see* ἀγαθοεργέω.

ἀγαθωσύνη,
goodness, 4.

ἀγαλλίασις,
gladness, 3.
joy, 1.
exceeding joy, 1.

ἀγαλλιάω,
be glad, 1.
be exceeding glad, 1.
rejoice, 7.
greatly rejoice, 1.
with exceeding joy, 1.

ἄγαμος,
unmarried, 4.

ἀγανακτέω,
have indignation, 2.
with indignation, 1.
be moved with indignation, 1.
be much displeased, 2.
be sore displeased, 1.

ἀγανάκτησις,
indignation, 1.

ἀγαπάω,
to love, 135.
beloved, 7.

ἀγάπη,
love, 86.
charity, 27.
feast of charity, 1.
dear, 1.
— *with* κατά,
charitably, 1.

ἀγαπητός,
beloved, 47.
dearly beloved, 9.
well beloved, 3.
dear, 3.

ἀγγαρεύω,
compel to go, 1.
compel, 2.

ἀγγεῖον,
vessel, 2.

ἀγγελία,
message, 1.
commandment, 1.

* ἀγγέλλω,
[*for* ἀπαγγέλλω, John xx. 18, *see* Tell.]

ἄγγελος,
messenger, 7.
angel, 181.

* ἄγγος,
[*for* ἀγγεῖον, Matt. xiii. 48, *see* Vessel.]

ἄγε, (*imperative of* ἄγω),
go to, 2.

ἀγέλη,
herd, 8.

ἀγενεαλόγητος,
without descent, 1.
without pedigree, 1.

ἀγενής,
base thing, 1.

ἁγιάζω,
sanctify, 26.
hallow, 2.
— *passive*,
be holy, 1.

ἁγιασμός,
holiness, 5.
sanctification, 5.

ἅγιος,
holy, 68.
Holy One, 4.
saint, 1.
— *neuter*,
holy thing, 1.
holy place, 3.
sanctuary, 3.
holy things, 1.
holy, 1.
— ἅγια,
holiest, 1.
holiest of all, 1.
— ἅγια ἁγίων,
Holiest of all, 1.
— *with* πνεῦμα,
Holy Ghost, 89.
Holy Spirit, 4.
— *plural*,
saints, 61.

ἁγιότης,
holiness, 1.

ἁγιωσύνη,
holiness, 3.

ἀγκάλαι,
arms, 1.

ἄγκιστρον,
hook, 1.

ἄγκυρα,
anchor, 4.

ἄγναφος,
new, 2.
raw or unwrought, 2.

ἁγνεία,
purity, 2.

ἁγνίζω,
purify, 7.

ἁγνισμός,
purification, 1.

ἀγνοέω,
know not, 4.
unknown, 2.
understand not, 3.
be ignorant, 7.
ignorant, 4.
ignorantly, 2.

ἀγνόημα,
error, 1.

ἄγνοια,
ignorance, 4.

ἁγνός,
pure, 4.
clear, 1.
chaste, 3.

ἁγνότης,
pureness, 1.

ἁγνῶς,
sincerely, 1.

ἀγνωσία,
not knowledge
ignorance, 1.

ἄγνωστος,
unknown, 1.

ἀγορά,
market, 6.
market-place, 4.
court, 1.
street, 1.

ἀγοράζω,
buy, 28.
redeem, 3.

ἀγοραῖος,
baser sort (of the), 1.
law, 1.
court-days, 1.

ἄγρα,
draught, 2.

ἀγράμματος,
unlearned, 1.

ἀγραυλέω,
abide in the field, 1.

ἀγρεύω,
catch, 1.

ἀγριέλαιος,
wild olive tree, 1.
olive tree which is wild, 1.

ἄγριος,
wild, 2.
raging, 1

ἀγρός,
country, 8.
field, 22.
farm, 1.
land, 4.
piece of ground, 1.

ἀγρυπνέω,
to watch, 4.

ἀγρυπνία,
watching, 2.

ἄγω,
lead, 12.
lead away, 1.
bring, 45.
bring forth, 2.
carry, 1.
go, 7 (*mid.*)
be, 1.
keep, 1.
be open, 1
be kept, 1.

ἀγωγή,
manner of life, 1.

ἀγών,
conflict, 2.
fear or care, 1.
contention, 1.
fight, 2.
race, 1.

ἀγωνία,
agony, 1.

ἀγωνίζομαι,
strive, 3.
fight, 3.
labour fervently, 1.
strive, 1.

ἀδάπανος,
without charge, 1.

ἀδελφή,
sister, 24.

ἀδελφός,
brother, brethren (*pl.*) } 352.

ἀδελφότης,
brotherhood, 1.
brethren, 1.

ἄδηλος,
which appears not, 1.
uncertain, 1.

ἀδηλότης,
uncertain, 1.
uncertainty, 1.

ἀδήλως,
uncertainly, 1.

ἀδημονέω,
be very heavy, 2.
be full of heaviness, 1.

ᾅδης,
grave, 1.
hell, 1.
hell, 10.
grave, 1.

ἀδιάκριτος,
without partiality, 1.
without wrangling, 1.

ἀδιάλειπτος,
without ceasing, 1.
continual, 1.

ἀδιαλείπτως,
without ceasing,

ἀδιαφθορία,
uncorruptness, 1.

ἀδικέω,
wrong, 2.
do wrong, 8.
suffer wrong, 2 (*pass.*)
take wrong, 1 (*mid.*)
be unjust, 2.
be an offender, 1.
injure, 1.
hurt, 10.

ἀδίκημα,
matter of wrong, 1.
evil doing, 1.
iniquity, 1.

ἀδικία,
wrong, 1.
unjust, 2.
unrighteousness, 16.
iniquity, 6.

ἄδικος,
unjust, 8.
unrighteous, 4.

ἀδίκως,
wrongfully, 1.

ἀδόκιμος,
reprobate, 6.
void of judgment, 2.
of no judgment, 1.
rejected, 1.
castaway, 1.

ἄδολος,
sincere, 1.

ἁδρότης,
abundance, 1.

ἀδυνατέω,
be impossible, 2.

ἀδύνατος,
weak, 1.
impotent, 1.
not possible, 1.
impossible, 6.
what...could not do, 1 (*see* Law.)

ᾄδω,
sing, 5.

ἀεί,
ever, 1.
alway, 4.
always, 3.

ἀετός,
eagle, 4.

ἄζυμος,
unleavened, 1.
unleavened bread, 8.

ἀήρ,
air, 7.

ἀθανασία,
immortality, 3.

ἀθέμιτος,
unlawful thing, 1.
abominable, 1.

ἄθεος,
without God, 1.

ἄθεσμος,
wicked, 2.

ἀθετέω,
reject, 4.
frustrate, 3.
cast off, 1.
despise, 8.
reject, 1.
bring to nothing, 1.
disannul, 1.
frustrate, 1.

ἀθέτησις,
put away, 1.
disannulling, 1.

ἀθλέω,
strive, 2.

ἄθλησις,
fight, 1.

* ἀθροίζω,
[*for* συναθροίζω, Luke xxiv. 33, *see* Gather together.]

ἀθυμέω,
be discouraged, 1.

ἀθῷος,
innocent, 2.

αἴγειος,
goat, 1.

αἰγιαλός,
shore, 6.

ἀΐδιος,
everlasting, 1.
eternal, 1.

αἰδώς,
shamefacedness, 1.
reverence, 1.

αἷμα,
blood, 99.

αἱματεκχυσία,
shedding of blood, 1.

αἱμορροέω,
diseased with an issue of blood, 1.

αἴνεσις,
praise, 1.

αἰνέω,
to praise, 9.

αἴνιγμα, with ἐν,
darkly, 1,
in a riddle, 1.

αἶνος,
praise, 2.

αἱρέομαι,
choose, 3.

αἵρεσις,
sect, 5.
heresy, 4.
sect, 1.

αἱρετίζω,
choose, 1.

αἱρετικός,
that is an heretic, 1.

αἴρω,
take up, 32.
lift up, 4.
bear, 3.
bear up, 3.
carry, 1.
take away, 25.
bear, 1.
away with, 5.
put away, 1.
remove, 2.
take, 25.
loose, 1.
— *with ψυχή*,
make to doubt, 1.
hold in suspense, 1.

αἰσθάνομαι,
perceive, 1.

αἴσθησις,
judgment, 1.
sense, 1.

αἰσθητήριον,
senses, 1.

αἰσχροκερδής,
greedy of filthy lucre, 2.
given to lucre, 1.

αἰσχροκερδῶς,
for filthy lucre, 1.

αἰσχρολογία,
filthy communication, 1.

αἰσχρός,
shame, 3.
filthy, 1.

αἰσχρότης,
filthiness, 1.

αἰσχύνη,
shame, 5.
dishonesty, 1.
shame, 1.

αἰσχύνομαι,
be ashamed, 5.

αἰτέω,
ask, 48.
crave, 1.
beg, 2.
desire, 17.
call for, 1.
require, 2.

αἴτημα,
request, 1.
require, 1.
petition, 1.

αἰτία,
cause, 9.
case, 1.
accusation, 3.
crime, 1.
fault, 3.
— *with δι' ἥν*,
wherefore, 3.

αἰτίαμα,
complaint, 1.

αἴτιον,
cause, 2.
fault, 2.

αἴτιος,
author, 1.

αἰτίωμα, *see* αἰτίαμα.

αἰφνίδιος,
sudden, 1.
unawares, 1.

αἰχμαλωσία,
captivity, 3.
multitude of captives, 1.

αἰχμαλωτεύω,
lead captive, 2.

αἰχμαλωτίζω,
lead away captive, 1.
bring into captivity, 2.

αἰχμάλωτος,
captive, 1.

αἰών,
age, 2.
course, 1.
world, 32.
eternal, 2.
— *with ἀπό*,
since the world began, 2.
from the beginning of the world, 2.
— *with ἐκ*,
since the world began, 1.
— *with εἰς*,
for ever, 27.
for evermore, 2.
ever, 1.
while the world standeth, 1.
— *εἰς τὸν αἰῶνα τοῦ αἰῶνος*,
for ever and ever, 1.
— *εἰς αἰῶνας αἰώνων*,
for ever and ever, 1.
— *εἰς τοὺς αἰῶνας τῶν αἰώνων*,
for ever and ever, 19.
for evermore, 1.
— *τοῦ αἰῶνος τῶν αἰώνων*,
world without end, 1.
— *εἰς πάντας τοὺς αἰῶνας*,
ever, 1.
— *εἰς ἡμέραν αἰῶνος*,
for ever, 1.
— *with οὐκ εἰς*,
never, 1.
— *with οὐ μή εἰς*,
never, 6.

αἰώνιος,
everlasting, 11.
eternal, 12.
for ever, 1.
— *with ζωή*,
everlasting life, 10.
life everlasting, 4.
eternal life, 26.
life eternal, 4.
— *χρόνοις αἰωνίος*,
since the world began, 1.
— *πρὸ χρόνων αἰωνίων*,
before the world began, 2.

ἀκαθαρσία,
uncleanness, 10.

ἀκαθάρτης,
filthiness, 1.

ἀκάθαρτος,
unclean, 28.
foul, 2.

ἀκαιρέομαι,
lack opportunity, 1.

ἀκαίρως,
out of season, 1.

ἄκακος,
harmless, 1.
simple, 1.

ἄκανθα,
thorns, 14.

ἀκάνθινος,
of thorns, 2.

ἄκαρπος,
unfruitful, 6.
without fruit, 1.

ἀκατάγνωστος,
that cannot be condemned, 1.

ἀκατακάλυπτος,
uncovered, 2.

ἀκατάκριτος,
uncondemned, 2.

ἀκατάλυπτος,
endless, 1.

* ἀκατάπαστος,
[*for* ἀκατάπαυστος, 2 Pet. ii. 14, *see* that cannot Cease.]

ἀκατάπαυστος,
that cannot cease, 1.

ἀκαταστασία,
commotion, 1.
tumult, 2.
tossing to and fro, 1.
confusion, 2.
tumult or unquietness, 2.

ἀκατάστατος,
unstable, 1.

ἀκατάσχετος,
unruly, 1.

ἀκέραιος,
simple, 1.
harmless, 1.
harmless, 2.
simple, 1.
sincere, 1.

ἀκλινής,
without wavering, 1.

ἀκμάζω,
be fully ripe, 1.

ἀκμήν,
yet, 1.

ἀκοή,
hearing, 9.
hearing, 1 (*participle*).
which…hear, 1.
audience, 1.
ears, 4.
preached, 1.
of hearing, 1.
report, 1.
preaching, 1.
hearing, 1.
rumour, 1.
fame, 3.

ἀκολουθέω,
follow, 90.
go with, 1.
reach, 1.

ἀκούω,
hear, 415.
hearer, 2.
hearken, 6.
give audience, 3.
in the audience of, 1.
understand, 1.
hear, 1.
— *Passive*,
be noised, 1.
be reported, 1.
come to…ears, 1.
— *with λόγος*,
tidings come, 1.
— *with βαρέως*,
be dull of hearing, 1.

ἀκρασία,
incontinency, 1.
excess, 1.

ἀκρατής,
incontinent, 1.

ἄκρατον,
without mixture, 1.

ἀκρίβεια,
perfect manner, 1.

ἀκριβής,
most straitest, 1.

ἀκριβόω,
inquire diligently, 2.

ἀκριβῶς,
perfectly, 4.
perfect, 2.
diligently, 2.
circumspectly, 1.

ἀκρίς,
locusts, 4.

ἀκροατήριον,
place of hearing, 1.

ἀκροατής,
hearer, 4.

ἀκροβυστία,
uncircumcision, 16.
— *with ἔχω*,
uncircumcised, 1.
— *with ἐν*,
uncircumcised, 1.
— *with διά*,
though not circumcised, 1.

ἀκρογωνιαῖος,
chief corner, 2.

ἀκροθίνιον,
spoils, 1.

ἄκρον,
top, 1.
tip, 1.
uttermost part, 2.
— *ἀπ' ἄκρων ἕως ἄκρων*,
from one end to the other, 1.

ἀκυρόω,
make of none effect, 2.
disannul, 1.

ἀκωλύτως,
no man forbidding, 1.

ἄκων,
against one's will, 1.

ἀλάβαστρον,
alabaster box, 3
box, 1.

ἀμφίβληστρον,
net, 2.

ἀμφιέννυμι,
clothe, 4.

ἄμφοδον,
place where two ways meet, 1.

ἀμφότεροι,
both, 14.

ἀμώμητος,
without rebuke, 1.
blameless, 1.

* ἄμωμον,
[*add after* κινάμωμον, cinnamon, Rev. xviii. 13, "and amomum," G L T Tr A ℵ.]

ἄμωμος,
without blemish, 2.
without spot, 1.
without fault, 1.
without fault, 1.
faultless, 1.
without blame, 1.
unblameable, 1.

ἄν,
[*not apparent in translation, used gen. in the apodosis of conditional sentences.*]

ἀνά,
— *with* μέρος,
by course, 1.
— *with* μέσον,
through the midst, 1.
in the midst, 1.
among, 1.
between, 1.
— *used distributively*,
apiece, 2.
each, 1.
every man, 2.
— ἀνὰ εἰς ἕκαστος,
every, several, 1.
— ἀνὰ δύο,
two and two, 1.
— ἀνὰ πεντήκοντα,
by fifties, 2.
— ἀνὰ ἑκατόν.
by hundreds, 1.

ἀναβαθμός,
stair, 2.

ἀναβαίνω,
go up, 37.
arise, 2.
rise up, 2.
come up, 10.
come up again, 1.
ascend, 10.
ascend up, 8.
climb up, 2.
grow up, 2.
spring up, 2.
enter, 1.
come, 2.
— *with* ἐπὶ,
go upon, 1.

ἀναβάλλομαι,
defer, 1.

ἀναβιβάζω,
draw, 1.

ἀναβλέπω,
look up, 9.
look, 1.
see, 1.
receive sight, 15.

ἀνάβλεψις,
recovering of sight, 1.

ἀναβοάω,
cry aloud, 1.
cry out, 1.
cry, 1.

ἀναβολή,
delay, 1.

ἀνάγειον, *see* ἀνώγεον.

ἀναγγέλλω,
tell, 6.
rehearse, 1.
report, 1.
declare, 3.
show, 4.
speak of, 1.

ἀναγεννάω,
beget again, 1.
— *passive*,
be born again, 1.

ἀναγινώσκω,
read, 33.

ἀναγκάζω,
compel, 5.
constrain, 4.

ἀναγκαῖος,
necessary, 5.
of necessity, 1.
needful, 1.
near, 1.

ἀναγκαστῶς,
by constraint, 1.

ἀναγκή,
necessity, 7.
must of necessity, 1.
necessary, 1.
distress, 3.
necessity, 1.
— *with* ἐστίν,
it must needs be, 1.
— *with* ἔχω,
must needs, 1.
must of necessity, 1.
to need, 1.
be needful, 1.
— ἀναγκή ὑποτάσσεσθαι,
must needs be subject, 1.

ἀναγνωρίζομαι,
be made known, 1.

ἀνάγνωσις,
reading, 3.

ἀνάγω,
lead up, 1.
bring again, 1.
bring up again, 1.
bring forth, 1.
take up, 1.
lead, 1.
bring, 3.
offer, 1.
— *mid. or pass.*
launch forth, 1.
launch, 3.
set forth, 1.
depart, 3.
loose, 3.
sail, 3.

ἀναδείκνυμι,
show, 1.
appoint, 1.

ἀνάδειξις,
showing, 1.

ἀναδέχομαι,
receive, 2.

ἀναδίδωμι,
deliver, 1.

ἀναζάω,
live again, 1.
be alive again, 2.
revive, 2.

ἀναζητέω,
seek, 2.

ἀναζώννυμι,
gird up, 1 (*mid.*)

ἀναζωπυρέω,
stir up, 1.

ἀναθάλλω,
flourish again, 1.
be revived, 1.

ἀνάθεμα,
accursed, 4.
separated, 1.
anathema, 2.
anathema, 1.
— *with* ἀναθεματίζω,
bind under a great curse, 1.

ἀναθεματίζω,
to curse, 1.
bind under a curse, 1.
bind with an oath, 1.
bind with an oath of execration, 1.
— *with* ἀνάθεμα,
bind under a great curse, 1.

ἀναθεωρέω,
behold, 1.
consider, 1.

ἀνάθημα,
gift, 1.

ἀναίδεια,
importunity, 1.

ἀναίρεσις,
death, 2.

ἀναιρέω,
take up, 1.
take away, 1.
put to death, 2.
slay, 8.
kill, 11.

ἀναίτιος,
guiltless, 1.
blameless, 1.

ἀνακαθίζω,
sit up, 2.

ἀνακαινίζω,
renew, 1.

ἀνακαινόω,
renew, 2.

ἀνακαίνωσις,
renewing, 2.

ἀνακαλύπτω (*pass.*),
open, 1.
— *with* μή,
untaken away,

ἀνακάμπτω,
to return, 3.
turn again, 1.

ἀνάκειμαι,
lie, 1.
lean, 1.
sit down, 1.
be set down, 1.
sit, 2.
sit at meat, 5.
sit together, 1.
at the table, 1.
guest, 1.

ἀνακεφαλαιόομαι,
be briefly comprehended, 1,
— *middle*,
gather together in one, 1.

ἀνακλίνω,
make sit down, 3.
lay, 1.
— *middle*,
sit down, 4.

ἀνακόπτω,
hinder, 1.
drive back, 1.

ἀνακράζω,
cry out, 5.

ἀνακρίνω,
examine, 6.
search, 1.
ask question, 2.
discern, 1.
judge, 6.
discern, 1.

ἀνάκρισις,
examination, 1.

* ἀνακυλίω,
[*for* ἀποκυλίω, Mark xvi. 4, *see* Roll away.]

ἀνακύπτω,
lift up one's self, 3.
look up, 1.

ἀναλαμβάνω,
take up, 4.
receive up, 3.
take, 3.
take unto, 1.
take in, 2.

ἀνάληψις,
that...should be received up, 1.

ἀναλίσκω,
consume, 3.

ἀναλογία,
proportion, 1.

ἀναλογίζομαι,
consider, 1.

ἄναλος, *with* γίνομαι,
lose saltness, 1.

ἀνάλυσις,
departure, 1.

ἀναλύω,
return, 1.
depart, 1.

ἀναμάρτητος,
without sin, 1.

ἀναμένω,
wait for, 1.

ἀναμιμνήσκω,
bring into remembrance, 1.
put in remembrance, 1.
call to remembrance, 1.
call to mind, 1.
remember, 1.

ἀνάμνησις,
remembrance, 3.
remembrance again, 1.

ἀνανεόομαι,
be renewed, 1.

ἀνανήφω,
recover one's self, 1.
awake, 1.

ἀναντίρρητος, *with* **εἰμί,**
cannot be spoken against, 1.

ἀναντιρρήτως,
without gainsaying, 1.

ἀνάξιος,
unworthy, 1.

ἀναξίως,
unworthily, 2.

ἀνάπαυσις,
rest, 4.
— *with* ἔχω,
to rest, 1.
have rest, 1.

ἀναπαύω,
give rest, 1.
refresh, 4.
— *middle,*
take rest, 2.
rest, 4.
take ease, 1.

ἀναπείθω,
persuade, 1.

ἀνάπειρος, *see* **ἀνάπηρος.**

ἀναπέμπω,
send again, 2.
send, 2.

* **ἀναπηδάω,**
[*for* ἀνίστημι, Mark x. 50, *see* Rise.]

ἀνάπηρος,
maimed, 2.

ἀναπίπτω,
sit down, 7.
sit down to meat, 2
be set down, 1.
lean, 1.

ἀναπληρόω,
fill up, 1.
fulfil, 2.
supply, 2.
occupy, 1.

ἀναπολόγητος,
without excuse, 1.
inexcusable, 1.

ἀναπτύσσω,
open, 1.

ἀνάπτω,
kindle, 3.

ἀναρίθμητος,
innumerable, 1.

ἀνασείω,
stir up, 1.
move, 1.

ἀνασκευάζω,
subvert, 1.

ἀνασπάω,
draw up, 1.
pull out, 1.

ἀνάστασις,
resurrection, 39.
rising again, 1.
— *with* ἐκ,
raised to life again, 1.
— πρῶτος ἐξ ἀναστάσεως,
the first that should rise, 1.

ἀναστατόω,
turn upside down, 1.
make an uproar, 1.
trouble, 1.

ἀνασταυρόω,
crucify afresh, 1.

ἀναστενάζω,
sigh deeply, 1.

ἀναστρέφω,
overthrow, 1.
return, 2.
— *pass. or mid.,*
be used, 1.
have one's conversation, 2.
behave one's self, 1.
live, 2.
abide, 1.
pass, 1.

ἀναστροφή,
conversation, 13.

ἀνατάσσομαι,
set forth in order, 1.

ἀνατέλλω,
make to rise, 1.
rise, 2.
rising, 1.
arise, 1.
be up, 2.
spring up, 1.
spring, 1.

ἀνατίθεμαι,
declare, 1.
communicate, 1.

ἀνατολή,
dayspring, 1.
sun-rising or branch, 1.
east, 7.
— *with* ἡλίου,
east, 2.

ἀνατρέπω,
overthrow, 1.
subvert, 1.

ἀνατρέφω,
nourish up, 1.
nourish, 1.
bring up, 1.

ἀναφαίνομαι,
appear, 1.
discover, 1.

ἀναφέρω,
carry up, 1.
bring up, 1.
lead up, 1.
bear, 2.
offer up, 3.
offer, 2.

ἀναφωνέω,
speak out, 1.

ἀνάχυσις,
excess, 1.

ἀναχωρέω,
give place, 1.
withdraw one's self, 2.
depart, 8.
go aside, 2.
turn aside, 1.

ἀνάψυξις,
refreshing, 1.

ἀναψύχω,
refresh, 1.

ἀνδραποδιστής,
menstealer, 1.

ἀνδρίζομαι,
quit you like men, 1
(ἀνδρίζεσθε.)

ἀνδροφόνος,
manslayer, 1.

ἀνέγκλητος,
unreprovable, 1.
blameless, 4.

ἀνεκδιήγητος,
unspeakable, 1.

ἀνεκλάλητος,
unspeakable, 1.

ἀνέκλειπτος,
that faileth not, 1.

ἀνεκτός,
tolerable, 6.

ἀνελεήμων,
unmerciful, 1.

ἀνέλεος, *see* **ἀνίλεως.**

ἀνεμίζομαι,
be driven with the wind, 1.

ἄνεμος,
wind, 31.

ἀνένδεκτος,
impossible, 1.

ἀνεξερεύνητος,
unsearchable, 1.

ἀνεξίκακος,
patient, 1.
forbearing, 1.

ἀνεξιχνίαστος,
unsearchable, 1.
past finding out, 1.

ἀνεπαίσχυντος,
that needeth not to be ashamed, 1.

ἀνεπίληπτος,
unrebukable, 1.
blameless, 2.

ἀνέρχομαι,
go up, 3.
return, 1.

ἄνεσις,
rest, 3.
liberty, 1.
be eased, 1.

ἀνετάζω,
examine, 2.
torture, 1.

ἄνευ,
without, 3.

ἀνεύθετος,
not commodious, 1.

ἀνευρίσκω,
find, 2.

ἀνέχομαι,
forbear, 2.
bear with, 4.
suffer, 7.
endure, 2.

ἀνεψιός,
sister's son, 1.

ἄνηθον,
anise, 1.

ἀνήκω,
be fit, 1.
be convenient, 2.

ἀνήμερος,
fierce, 1.

ἀνήρ,
man, 156.
husband, 50.
sir, 6.
fellow, 1.
— ἀνὴρ προφήτης,
a prophet, 1.
— ἀνὴρ φονεύς,
a murderer, 1.

ἀνθίστημι,
resist, 9.
withstand, 5.

ἀνθομολογέομαι,
give thanks, 1.

ἄνθος,
flower, 4.

ἀνθρακιά,
fire of coals, 2.

ἄνθραξ,
coal, 1.

ἀνθρωπάρεσκος,
menpleasers, 2.

ἀνθρώπινος,
man's, 3.
of man, 1.
after the manner of men, 1.
common to man, 1.
moderate, 1.
— *with* φύσις,
mankind, 1.
nature, 1.

ἀνθρωποκτόνος,
murderer, 3.

ἄνθρωπος,
man, 457.
—— *with υἱός,*
Son of man, 88.
—— ἄνθρωπος βασιλεύς,
a certain king, 2.
—— ἄνθρωπος εὐγενής,
nobleman, 1.
—— ἐχθρὸς ἄνθρωπος,
an enemy, 1.
—— ἄνθρωπος οἰκοδεσπότης,
a certain householder, 1.
—— οἱ ἄνθρωποι οἱ ποιμένης,
the shepherds, 1.
—— ἄνθρωποι, Ῥωμαῖοι,
Romans, 1.
—— κατὰ ἄνθρωπον,
after man, 1.
after the manner of men, 2.
as a man, 2.
as men, 1.
according to man, 2.

ἀνθυπατεύω,
be deputy, 1.

ἀνθύπατος,
deputy, 4.

ἀνίημι,
to loose, 2.
leave, 1.
forbear, 1.
moderate, 1.

ἀνίλεως,
without mercy, 1.

ἄνιπτος,
unwashed, 3.

ἀνίστημι,
raise, 1.
raise up, 11.
raise up again, 2.
lift up, 1.
stand up, 8.
stand upright, 1.
rise, 19.
rising, 1.
rise up, 15.
rise again, 13.
arise, 38.
arise up, 1.

ἀνόητος,
unwise, 1.
foolish, 4.
fool, 1.

ἄνοια,
folly, 1.
madness, 1.

ἀνοίγω,
to open, 70.
open, 6.

ἀνοικοδομέω,
build again, 2.

ἄνοιξις, *with* ἐν,
that...may open, 1.

ἀνομία,
transgression of the law, 1.
iniquity, 12.
unrighteousness, 1.
—— *with ποιέω,*
transgress the law, 1.

ἄνομος,
without law, 4.
unlawful, 1.
lawless, 1.
transgressor, 2.
wicked, 2.

ἀνόμως,
without law, 2.

ἀνορθόω,
make straight, 1.
set up, 1.
lift up, 1.

ἀνόσιος,
unholy, 2.

ἀνοχή,
forbearance, 2.

ἀνταγωνίζομαι,
strive against, 1.

ἀντάλλαγμα,
in exchange, 2.

ἀνταναπληρόω,
fill up, 1.

ἀνταποδίδωμι,
repay, 1.
recompense, 4.
recompense again, 1.
render, 1.

ἀνταπόδομα,
recompense, 2.

ἀνταπόδοσις,
reward, 1.

ἀνταποκρίνομαι,
answer again, 1.
reply against, 1.
answer again or dispute with, 1.

ἀντεῖπον,
say against, 1.
gainsay, 1.

ἀντέχομαι,
hold to, 2.
hold fast, 1.
support, 1.

ἀντί,
in the room of, 1.
for, 14.
—— ἀντὶ τούτου,
for this cause, 1.
—— ἀνθ' ὧν,
because, 4.
therefore, 1.
—— ἀντὶ τοῦ λέγειν,
for that...ought to say, 1.

ἀντιβάλλω,
have, 1.

ἀντιδιατίθεμαι,
oppose one's self, 1.

ἀντίδικος,
adversary, 5.

ἀντίθεσις,
opposition, 1.

ἀντικαθίστημι,
resist, 1.

ἀντικαλέω,
bid again, 1.

ἀντίκειμαι,
be contrary, 2.
oppose, 1.
adversary, 5.

ἀντικρύ,
over against, 1.

ἀντιλαμβάνομαι,
to support, 1.
help, 1.
partaker, 1.

ἀντιλέγω,
speak against, 5.
gainsay, 1.
gainsayer, 1.
answer again, 1.
gainsay, 1.
contradict, 1.
—— *with μή,*
deny, 1.

ἀντίληψις,
help, 1.

ἀντιλογία,
gainsaying, 1.
contradiction, 2.
strife, 1.

ἀντιλοιδορέω,
revile again, 1.

ἀντίλυτρον,
ransom, 1.

ἀντιμετρεω,
measure again, 2.

ἀντιμισθία,
recompense, 2.

ἀντιπαρέρχομαι,
pass by on the other side, 2.

ἀντιπέραν,
over against, 1.

ἀντιπίπτω,
resist, 1.

ἀντιστρατεύομαι,
war against, 1.

ἀντιτάσσομαι,
oppose one's self, 1.
resist, 4.

ἀντίτυπον,
like figure, 1.
figure, 1.

ἀντίχριστος,
antichrist, 5.

ἀντλέω,
draw out, 1.
draw, 3.

ἄντλημα, *with* οὔτε,
nothing to draw with, 1.

ἀντοφθαλμέω,
bear up into, 1.

ἄνυδρος,
without water, 2.
dry, 2.

ἀνυπόκριτος,
without hypocrisy, 1.
without dissimulation, 1.
unfeigned, 4.

ἀνυπότακτος,
that is not put under, 1.
disobedient, 1.
unruly, 1.

ἄνω,
up, 2.
above, 5.
high, 1.
—— *with ἕως,*
up to the brim, 1.

ἀνώγεον,
upper room, 2.

ἄνωθεν,
from above, 5.
from the beginning, 1.
from the very first, 1.
again, 1.
from above, 1.
—— ἀπὸ ἄνωθεν,
from the top, 2.
—— ἐκ τῶν ἄνωθεν,
from the top, 1.
—— πάλιν ἄνωθεν,
again, 1.

ἀνωτερικός,
upper, 1.

ἀνώτερον,
higher, 1.
above, 1.

ἀνωφελής,
unprofitable, 1.
—— *with art.,*
unprofitableness, 1.

ἀξίνη,
axe, 2.

ἄξιος,
worthy, 35.
meet, 1.
meet, 4.
answerable, 1.
—— *neut. pl.,*
due reward, 1.
—— *with οὐ,*
unworthy, 1.

ἀξιόω,
count worthy, 3.
vouchsafe, 1.
think worthy
think good, 1.
desire, 1.

ἀξίως,
as becometh, 2.
worthy, 3.
—— ἀξίως τοῦ θεοῦ,
after a godly sort, 1.

ἀόρατος,
invisible, 4.
—— τὰ ἀόρατα,
the invisible things, 1.

ἀπαγγέλλω,
bring word, 1.
bring word again, 1.
report, 2.
tell, 26.
declare, 3.
show, 10.
show again, 1.

ἀπάγχομαι,
hang one's self, 1.

ἀπάγω,
lead away, 10.
lead, 2.
take away, 1.
put to death, 1.
carry away, 1.
bring, 1.

ἀπαίδευτος,
unlearned, 1.

ἀπαίρω,
take away, 2.
take, 1.

ἀπαιτέω,
be required, 1.
do they require, 1.
ask again, 1.

ἀπαλγέω,
be past feeling, 1.

ἀπαλλάσσω,
deliver, 2.
depart, 1 (*mid.*)

ἀπολλοτριόομαι,
alienated, 1.
— *with* εἰμί,
be alienated, 1.
be an alien, 1.

ἀπαλός,
tender, 2.

ἀπαντάω,
to meet, 7.

ἀπάντησις, *with* εἰς,
to meet, 4.

ἅπαξ,
once, 15.

ἀπαράβατος,
unchangeable, 1.
not passing from one to another, 1.

ἀπαρασκεύαστος,
unprepared, 1.

ἀπαρνέομαι,
deny, 12.
— *with* μή,
deny, 1.

ἀπάρτι,
from henceforth, 1.

ἀπαρτισμός, *with* εἰς,
to finish, 1.

ἀπαρχή,
first fruit, 1.
first fruits, 7.

ἅπας,
every man, 1.
every one, 1.
all, 4.
whole, 3.
— plural,
all, 31.
all things, 4.

* ἀπασπάζομαι,
[*for* ἀσπάζομαι, Acts xxi. 6, *see* Take leave of.]

ἀπατάω,
deceive, 4.

ἀπάτη,
deceit, 1.
deceiving, 1.
deceitfulness, 3.
deceitful, 1.
deceivableness, 1.

ἀπάτωρ,
without father, 1.

ἀπαύγασμα,
brightness, 1.

ἀπείθεια,
unbelief, 4.
disobedience, 1.
disobedience, 3.
unbelief, 1.

ἀπειθέω,
believe not, 8.
obey not, 1,
be disobedient, 2.
unbelieving, 1.
obey not, 3.
be disobedient, 3.
disobedient, 1.

ἀπειθής,
disobedient, 6.

ἀπειλέω,
threaten, 2.

ἀπειλή,
threatening, 3.
straitly, 1.

ἄπειμι,
be absent, 6.
absent, 1.

ἄπειμι,
go, 1.

ἀπεῖπον,
renounce, 1.

ἀπείραστος, *with* εἰμί,
can not be tempted, 1.

ἄπειρος,
unskilful, 1.
having no experience, 1.

ἀπεκδέχομαι,
wait for, 5.
look for, 2.

ἀπεκδύομαι,
put off, 1.
spoil, 1.

ἀπέκδυσις,
putting off, 1.

ἀπελαύνω,
drive, 1.

ἀπελεγμός, *with* εἰς,
at naught, 1.

ἀπελεύθερος,
freeman, 1.
made free, 1.

ἀπελπίζω,
hope for again, 1.

ἀπέναντι,
over against, 2.
before, 2.
in the presence of, 1.
contrary to, 1.

ἀπέραντος,
endless, 1.

ἀπερισπάστως,
without distraction, 1.

ἀπερίτμητος,
uncircumcised, 1.

ἀπέρχομαι,
go away, 14.
go one's way, 16.
go, 54.
depart, 27.
go aside, 1.
go out, 1.
pass away, 1.
pass, 1.
come, 4.

ἀπέχω,
have, 4.
have received, 1.
receive, 2,
be, 5.
— *impers.*,
it is enough, 1.
— *middle*,
abstain, 6.

ἀπιστέω,
believe not, 7.

ἀπιστία,
unbelief, 12.

ἄπιστος,
unbelieving, 5.
that believeth not, 6.
which believeth not, 1.
unbeliever, 4.
faithless, 4.
infidel, 2.
thing incredible, 1.

ἁπλόος,
single, 2.

ἁπλότης,
singleness, 2.
simplicity, 3.
liberally, 1 (*with* ἐν).
liberality, 1.
liberal, 1.
bountifulness, 1.

ἁπλῶς,
liberally, 1.

ἀπό,
from, 370.
of, 128.
from, 1.
from among, 1.
they of, 1.
out of, 47.
because of, 1.
for, 10.
by, 9.
of, 1.
with, 3.
in, 1.
at, 10.
before, 2.
on, 5.
upon, 1.
since, 4.
— ἀφ' ἧς,
since the time, 1.
since, 2.
that, 1.

ἀποβαίνω,
go out, 1.
turn, 2.
come, 1.

ἀποβάλλω,
cast away, 2.

ἀποβλέπω,
have respect, 1.

ἀπόβλητος,
to be refused, 1.

ἀποβολή,
casting away, 1.
loss, 1.

ἀπογίνομαι,
be dead, 1.

ἀπογραφή,
taxing, 2.

ἀπογράφω, (*pass.*)
be written, 1.
enrolled, 1.
be taxed, 3.
be enrolled, 1.

ἀποδείκνυμι,
show, 1.
set forth, 1.
prove, 1.
approve, 1.

ἀπόδειξις,
demonstration, 1.

ἀποδεκατόω,
pay tithe, 1.
give tithes, 1.
tithe, 1.
take tithes, 1.

ἀπόδεκτος,
acceptable, 2.

ἀποδέχομαι,
be received, 1.
— *middle*,
gladly receive, 2.
receive, 2.
accept, 1.

ἀποδημέω,
go into a far country, 3.
travel into a far country, 1.
take one's journey, 2.

ἀπόδημος,
taking a far journey, 1.

ἀποδίδωμι,
give, 9.
give again, 1.
deliver, 1.
deliver again, 1.
sell, 3.
pay, 9.
payment be made, 1.
repay, 1.
recompense, 1.
reward, 6.
restore, 1.
render, 9.
yield, 2.
perform, 1.
— *with* ὁμοιβάς,
requite, 1.

ἀποδιορίζω,
to separate, 1.

ἀποδοκιμάζω,
disallow, 2.
reject, 7.

ἀποδοχή,
acceptation, 2.

ἀπόθεσις,
putting away, 1.
— *with* ἐστί,
must put off, 1.

ἀποθήκη,
garner, 2.
barn, 4.

ἀποθησαυρίζω,
lay up in store, 1.

ἀποθνήσκω,
die, 76.
be a dying, 1.
lie a dying, 1.
be dead, 27.
dead, 1.
perish, 1.
— *with* μέλλω,
be at the point of death, 1.
— *with* φόνῳ,
be slain, 1.
— μετὰ τὸ ἀποθανεῖν,
when...was dead, 1.

ἀποκαθιστάνω,
restore again, 1.

ἀποκαθίστημι,
restore, 7.

ἀποκαλύπτω,
reveal, 26.

ἀποκάλυψις,
revelation, 12.
manifestation, 1.
appearing, 1.
coming, 1.
revelation, 1.
— *with* εἰς,
to enlighten, 1.
— *with* ἐν,
when...shall be revealed, 2.

ἀποκαραδοκία,
earnest expectation, 2.

ἀποκαταλλάττω,
reconcile, 3.

ἀποκατάστασις,
restitution, 1.

ἀπόκειμει,
be laid up, 3.
be appointed, 1.

ἀποκεφαλίζω,
behead, 4.

ἀποκλείω,
shut, 1.

ἀποκόπτω,
cut off, 6.

ἀπόκριμα,
sentence, 1.
answer, 1.

ἀποκρίνομαι,
to answer, 250.

ἀπόκρισις,
answer, 4.

ἀποκρύπτω,
hide, 6.

ἀπόκρυφος,
hid, 2.
kept secret, 1.

ἀποκτείνω,
kill, 55.
slay, 14.
put to death, 5.
— θέλων...ἀποκτεῖναι,
when he would have put...to death, 1.

ἀποκυέω,
bring forth, 1.
beget, 1.

ἀποκυλίω,
roll away, 3.
roll back, 1.

ἀπολαμβάνω,
receive, 10.
receive again, 1.
take, 1.

ἀπόλαυσις, *with* εἰς,
to enjoy, 1.
— *with* ἔχω,
enjoy the pleasure, 1.

ἀπολείπω,
to leave, 3.
remain, 3 (*pass.*)

ἀπολείχω,
lick, 1.

ἀπόλλυμι,
destroy, 23.
lose, 28.
— *mid.*,
be destroyed, 3.
perish, 33.
die, 1.
be lost, 3.
be marred, 1.

ἀπολλύων,
Apollyon, 1.
destroyer, 1.

ἀπολογέομαι,
speak for one's self, 1.
answer for one's self, 3.
answer, 3.
excuse one's self, 1.
excuse, 1.
make defence, 1.

ἀπολογία,
answer for one's self, 1.
answer, 1.
clearing of one's self, 1.
defence, 3.

ἀπολούω,
wash away, 1.
wash, 1.

ἀπολύτρωσις,
redemption, 9.
deliverance, 1.

ἀπολύω,
loose, 2.
release, 17.
forgive, 2.
let go, 13.
let depart, 2.
set at liberty, 2.
send away, 13.
dismiss, 2.
put away, 14.
divorce, 1.
— *middle*,
depart, 1.

ἀπομάσσομαι,
wipe off, 1.

ἀπονέμω,
give, 1.

ἀπονίπτομαι,
wash, 1.

ἀποπίπτω,
fall from, 1.

ἀποπλανάω,
seduce, 1.
— *passive*,
err, 1.
be seduced, 1.

ἀποπλέω,
to sail, 4.

ἀποπλύνω,
wash, 1.

ἀποπνίγω,
choke, 3.

ἀπορέομαι,
be perplexed, 1.
stand in doubt, 1.
be perplexed, 1.
doubt, 2.
be doubtful, 1.

ἀπορία,
perplexity, 1.

ἀπορρίπτω,
cast one's self, 1.

ἀπορφανίζομαι,
be taken from, 1.

ἀποσκευάζομαι,
take up one's carriage, 1.

ἀποσκίασμα,
shadow, 1.

ἀποσπάω,
draw away, 1.
withdraw, 1.
draw, 1.
— *passive*,
be gotten from, 1.

ἀποστασία,
falling away, 1.
— *with* ἀπό,
to forsake, 1.

ἀποστάσιον,
divorcement, 2.
writing of divorcement, 1.

ἀποστεγάζω,
uncover, 1.

ἀποστέλλω,
send away, 3.
send forth, 15.
send out, 2.
send, 111.
put in, 1.
set, 1.

ἀποστερέω,
defraud, 4.
keep back by fraud, 1.
— *passive*,
destitute, 1.

ἀποστολή,
apostleship, 4

ἀπόστολος,
he that is sent, 1.
messenger, 2.
apostle, 78.

ἀποστοματίζω,
provoke to speak, 1.

ἀποστρέφω,
turn away, 3.
pervert, 1.
put up again, 1.
bring again, 1.
— *mid. and pass. aor.*
turn away from, 4.

ἀποστυγέω,
abhor, 1.

ἀποσυνάγωγος, *with* ποιέω,
put out of the synagogue, 1.
— γίνομαι,
be put out of the synagogue, 2.

ἀποτάσσομαι,
take leave of, 2.
bid farewell, 2.
forsake, 1.
send away, 1.

ἀποτελέω,
finish, 1.

ἀποτίθεμαι,
put off, 2.
put away, 1.
cast off, 1.
lay aside, 2.
lay apart, 1.
lay down, 1.

ἀποτινάσσω,
shake off, 2.

ἀποτίω,
repay, 1.

ἀποτολμάι,
be very bold, 1.

ἀποτομία,
severity, 2.

ἀποτόμως,
sharply, 1.
sharpness, 1.

ἀποτρέπομαι,
turn away, 1.

ἀπουσία,
absence, 1.

ἀποφέρω,
carry away, 3.
carry, 1.
bring, 1.

ἀποφεύγω,
to escape, 3.

ἀποφθέγγομαι,
speak forth, 1.
utterance, 1.
say, 1.

ἀποφορτίζομαι,
unlade, 1.

ἀπόχρησις,
using, 1.

ἀποχωρέω,
depart, 3.

ἀποχωρίζομαι,
depart, 1.
depart asunder, 1.

ἀποψύχω, *with* ἀνθρώπων,
men's hearts failing them, 1.

ἀπρόσιτος,
which no man can approach unto, 1.

ἀπρόσκοτος,
without offence, 1.
void of offence, 1.
— *with* γίνομαι,
give none offence, 1.

ἀπροσωπολήπτως,
without respect of persons, 1.

ἄπταιστος, *with* φυλάσσω,
keep from falling, 1.

ἅπτω,
kindle, 1.
light, 3.
— *mid.*,
touch, 36.

ἀπωθέομαι,
thrust from, 1.
thrust away, 1.
put from, 1.
put away, 1.
cast away, 2.

ἀπώλεια,
destruction, 5.
perdition, 8.
waste, 2.
pernicious way, 1.
lascivious way, 1.
damnation, 1.
damnable, 1.
— *with* εἰς,
to die, 1.
— *with* εἰμί εἰς,
perish, 1.

ἀρά,
cursing, 1.

ἄρα,
then, 12.
so then, 2.
therefore, 4.
wherefore, 1.
no doubt, 1.
truly, 1.
— ἄραγε,
then, 2.
wherefore, 1.
— ἄρα οὖν,
so then, 4.
now therefore, 1.
therefore, 7.
— ἐπεὶ ἄρα,
for then, 1.
else, 1.
— εἰ ἄρα,
if haply, 1.
if perhaps, 1.
— εἰ ἄραγε,
if haply, 1.
— εἴπερ ἄρα,
if so be, 1.
— τίς ἄρα,
what manner of man, 2.
what manner of, 1.

ἆρα, (*interrogative*)
therefore, 1.
— *with* εὑρίσκω, Luke xviii. 8.
— ἆραγέ *with* γινώσκω, Acts viii. 30.

ἀραβών, *see* ἀρραβών.

ἄραφος, *see* ἄρραφος.

ἀργέω,
linger, 1.

ἀργός,
idle, 6.
slow, 1.
barren, 1.

ἀργύριον,
silver, 3.
silver piece, 1.
piece of silver, 5
money, 11.

ἀργυροκόπος,
silversmith, 1.

ἄργυρος,
silver, 5.

ἀργυροῦς,
of silver, 2.
silver, 1.

ἀρέσκεια,
pleasing, 1.

ἀρέσκω,
please, 17.

ἀρεστός, *with art.*
those things that are pleasing, 1.
those things that please, 1.
reason, 1.
— *with* εἰμι,
please, 1.

ἀρετή,
virtue, 4.
praise, 1.
virtue, 1.

ἀρήν,
lamb, 1 (*gen.* ἀρνός).

ἀριθμέω,
to number, 3.

ἀριθμός,
number, 18.

ἀριστάω,
dine, 3.

ἀριστερός,
left, 2.
on the left, 1.

ἄριστον,
dinner, 3.

ἀρκετός,
enough, 1.
sufficient, 1.
suffice, 1 (*with* εἰμί, *understood.*)

ἀρκέω,
be enough, 1.
suffice, 1.
be sufficient, 2.

— *middle*,
be content, 3.
content, 1.

ἄρκτος,
bear, 1.

ἅρμα,
chariot, 4.

ἁρμόζομαι,
espouse, 1.

ἁρμός,
joint, 1.

ἀρνέομαι,
deny, 28.
refuse, 2.

ἀρνίον,
lamb, 1.
Lamb, 29 (*said of Christ in Rev.*)

ἀρνός, *see* ἀρήν.

ἀροτριάω,
to plow, 2.

ἄροτρον,
plow, 1.

ἁρπαγή,
spoiling, 1.
ravening, 1.
extortion, 1.

ἁρπαγμός,
robbery, 1.

ἁρπάζω,
take by force, 3.
catch away, 2.
catch, 1.
catch up, 4.
pluck, 2.
pull, 1.

ἅρπαξ,
ravening, 1.
extortioner, 4.

ἀρραβών,
earnest, 3.

ἄρραφος,
without seam, 1.

ἄρρην,
man, 2.
man child, 1.

ἄρρητος,
unspeakable, 1.

ἄρρωστος,
sick, 2.
that is sick, 1.
sickly, 1.
sick folk, 1 (*pl.*)

ἀρσενοκοίτης,
abuser of one's self with mankind, 1.
that defileth one's self with mankind, 1.

ἄρσην,
male, 4.
man, 2.

ἀρτέμων,
mainsail, 1.

ἄρτι,
even now, 1.
now, 20.
— *with* ἀπό,
henceforth, 2.
from henceforth, 2.
hereafter, 2.
now, 1.
from henceforth, 1.
— *with* ἕως,
until now, 2.
even until now, 1.
unto this present, 1.
unto this day, 1.
unto this hour, 1.
hitherto, 2.
— ἄχρι τῆς ἄρτι ὥρας,
even unto this present hour, 1.

ἀρτιγέννητος,
new-born, 1.

ἄρτιος,
perfect, 1.

ἄρτος,
bread, 72.
loaf, 23.
— ἄρτοι τῆς προθέσεως,
show-bread, 3.
— πρόθεσις τῶν ἄρτων,
show-bread, 1.

ἀρτύω,
to season, 3.

ἀρχάγγελος,
archangel, 2.

ἀρχαῖος,
of old time, 2.
old, 6.
— *with art.*,
old things, 1.
— ἀφ' ἡμερῶν ἀρχαίων,
a good while ago, 1.
— ἐκ γενεῶν ἀρχαίων,
of old time, 1.

ἀρχή,
beginning, 40.
first, 1.
corner, 2,
first estate, 1.
principality, 1.
principles, 1.
beginning, 1.
principality, 8.
rule, 1.
power, 1.
magistrate, 1.
— *with* ἀπό,
at the first, 1.
— *with* λαμβάνω,
begin at the first, 1.

ἀρχηγός,
Prince, 1.
author, 1.
captain, 1.
author, 1.
beginner, 1.

ἀρχιερακτικός,
high priest, 1.

ἀρχιερεύς,
chief priest, 64.
chief of the priests, 1.
high priest, 59.

ἀρχιποίμην,
chief shepherd, 1.

ἀρχισυνάγωγος,
ruler of the synagogue, 7.
chief ruler of the synagogue, 2.

ἀρχιτέκτων,
master builder, 1.

ἀρχιτελώνης,
chief among the publicans, 1.

ἀρχιτρίκλινος,
governor of the feast, 2.
ruler of the feast, 1.

ἄρχω,
rule over, 1.
reign over, 1.
— *middle,*
begin, 82.
— *with εἰμί,*
begin, 1.
rehearse from the beginning, 1.

ἄρχων,
prince, 11,
chief, 2.
ruler, 22.
chief ruler, 1.
magistrate, 1.

ἄρωμα,
spices, 3.
sweet spices, 1.

ἀσαίνομαι, *see* **σαίνομαι.**

ἀσάλευτος,
unmoveable, 1.
which can not be moved, 1.

ἄσβεστος,
unquenchable, 2.
that never shall be quenched, 2.

ἀσέβεια,
ungodliness, 4.
ungodly, 2.

ἀσεβέω,
live ungodly, 1.
commit ungodly, 1.

ἀσεβής,
ungodly, 7.
ungodly man, 1.
— *with art.,*
that is ungodly, 1.

ἀσέλγεια,
lasciviousness, 6.
wantonness, 1.
filthy, 1.
— *plural,*
much wantonness, 1.

ἄσημος,
mean, 1.

ἀσθένεια,
weakness, 5.
infirmity, 17.
sickness, 1.
disease, 1.

ἀσθενέω,
be weak, 12.
be made weak, 1.
weak, 3.
impotent man, 1.
impotent folk, 1 (pl.)
be sick, 10.
sick, 7.
diseased, 1.

ἀσθένημα,
infirmity, 1.

ἀσθενής,
without strength, 1.
weak, 13.
feeble, 1.
impotent, 1.
sick, 5.
sick folks, 1.
— *with art.,*
weakness, 2.
weak things, 1.

ἀσιτία,
abstinence, 1.

ἄσιτος,
fasting, 1.

ἀσκέω,
to exercise, 1.

ἀσκός,
bottle, 12.

ἀσμένως,
gladly, 2.

ἄσοφος,
fool, 1.

ἀσπάζομαι,
greet, 15.
salute, 42.
embrace, 2.
take leave of, 1.

ἀσπασμός,
greeting, 3.
salutation, 7.

ἄσπιλος,
without spot, 3.
unspotted, 1.

ἀσπίς,
asp, 1.

ἄσπονδος,
implacable, 1.
truce-bearer, 1.

ἀσσάριον,
farthing, 2.

ἆσσον,
close by, 1.

ἀστατέω,
have no certain dwelling-place, 1.

ἀστεῖος,
fair, 1.
proper, 1.

ἀστήρ,
star, 24.

ἀστήρικτος,
unstable, 2.

ἄστοργος,
without natural affection, 2.
unsociable, 1.

ἀστοχέω,
swerve from, 1.
not aim at, 1.
err, 2.

ἀστραπή,
lightning, 8.
bright-shining, 1.

ἀστράπτω,
lighten, 1.
shine, 1.

ἄστρον,
star, 4.

ἀσύμφωνος, *with* **εἰμί.**
agree not, 1.

ἀσύνετος,
without understanding, 3.
foolish, 2.

ἀσύνθετος,
covenant breaker, 1.

ἀσφάλεια,
safety, 2.
certainty, 1.

ἀσφαλής,
safe, 1.
sure, 1.
certain, 1.
— *with art.,*
certainty, 2.

ἀσφαλίζω,
make sure, 1.
— *middle,*
make fast, 1.
make sure, 2.

ἀσφαλῶς,
safely, 2.
assuredly, 1.

ἀσχημονέω,
behave one's self unseemly, 1.
behave one's self uncomely, 1.

ἀσχημοσύνη,
unseemly, 1.
shame, 1.

ἀσχήμων,
uncomely, 1.

ἀσωτία,
riot, 2.
excess, 1.

ἀσώτως,
riotous, 1.

ἀτακτέω,
behave one's self disorderly, 1.

ἄτακτος,
unruly, 1.
disorderly, 1.

ἀτάκτως,
disorderly, 1.

ἄτεκνος,
without children, 2.
childless, 1.

ἀτενίζω,
look steadfastly, 3 (*with* εἰμί).
look up steadfastly, 1.
look earnestly on, 1.
look earnestly upon, 1.
look on, 1.
behold steadfastly, 2 (*with* εἰς).
behold earnestly, 1.
fasten one's eyes, 2.
be fastened on, 1 (*with* εἰμί).
set one's eyes, 1.

ἄτερ,
without, 1.
in the absence of, 1.
without, 1.

ἀτιμάζω,
to dishonour, 2.
despise, 1.
entreat shamefully, 1.
— *middle,*
dishonour, 1.
— *passive,*
suffer shame, 1.

ἀτιμάω, *see* **ἀτιμόω.**

ἀτιμία,
dishonour, 4.
reproach, 1.
shame, 1.
vile, 1.

ἄτιμος,
without honour, 2.
less honourable, 1.
despised, 1.

ἀτιμόω,
handle shamefully, 1.

ἀτμίς,
vapour, 2.

ἄτομος,
moment, 1.

ἄτοπος,
amiss, 1.
harm, 1.
unreasonable, 1.
absurd, 1.
wickedness, 1.

αὐγάζω,
shine, 1.

αὐγή,
break of day, 1.

αὐθάδης,
self-willed, 2.

αὐθαίρετος,
willing of one's self, 1.
of one's own accord, 1.

αὐθεντέω,
usurp authority over, 1.

αὐλέω,
to pipe, 3.

αὐλή,
fold, 1.
court, 1.
hall, 2.
palace, 7.
— *with* τῶν προβάτων,
sheepfold, 1.

αὐλητής,
piper, 1.
minstrel, 1.

αὐλίζομαι,
to lodge, 1.
abide, 1.

αὐλός,
pipe, 1.

αὐξάνω, or αὔξω.
— *transitive,*
increase, 1.
give the increase, 2.
— *intrans.,*
grow, 10.
grow up, 1.
increase, 3.
— *passive,*
grow, 2.
increase, 3.

αὔξησις,
increase, 2.

αὔριον,
to-morrow, 9.
morrow, 5.
next day, 1,

αὐστηρός,
austere, 2.

αὗται, see οὗτος.

αὐτάρκεια,
sufficiency, 1.
contentment, 1.

αὐτάρκης,
content, 1.

αὕτη, see οὗτος.

αὐτοκατάκριτος,
condemned of one's self, 1.

αὐτόματος,
of one's self, 1.
of one's own accord, 1.

αὐτόπτης,
eye-witness, 1.

αὐτός,
— *nom. sing. masc., αὐτός,*
I myself, 4.
thou thyself, 2.
thyself, 1,
he himself, 13.
his own self, 1.
himself, 27.
he, 101.
this, 1.
this man, 1.
the same, 5.
that same, 2.
very, 1.
it, 1.
— *with ἐγώ,*
I myself, 7.
— *with καί,*
which, 1.
— *nom. pl., αὐτοί,*
we ourselves, 1.
ourselves, 1.
ye yourselves, 3.
you yourselves, 1.
yourselves, 5.
they themselves (in italics, Matt. xxiii. 4).
themselves, 2.
they, 48.
these same, 1.
— *with ἡμεῖς,*
we ourselves, 1.
— *with ὑμεῖς,*
ye yourselves, 3.
— *with οὗτοι,*
they themselves, 1.
— *nom. sing. fem., αὐτή,*
herself, 1.
she, 3.
itself, 2.
— *nom. sing. neut., αὐτό,*
itself, 2.
it, 1.
the same, 1 (pl.)
— *Acc. sing. masc., αὐτόν,*
himself, 3.
him, 2.
itself, 2.
— *Acc. pl. masc.,*
them, 1.
themselves, 1.
— *Acc. sing. fem., αὐτήν,*
very, 1.
thee, 1.
— *Acc. sing. neut., αὐτό.*
[*not rendered*, Heb. ix. 18, *after* book.]
— *with τοῦτο,*
this very thing, 1.
this selfsame thing, 1.
this same, 1.
the same, 1.
besides this, 1.
— *εἰς αὐτό τοῦτο,*
upon this very thing, 1.
for the selfsame thing, 1.
even for this same purpose, 1.
for the same purpose, 2.
thereunto, 1.
— *Acc. pl. neut., αὐτά*
very, 1.
themselves, 1.
them, 1.
— *Gen. sing. masc., αὐτοῦ,*
of himself, 1.
of him, 1.
his, 1,
same, 1.
his own, 23.
— *with τούτου,*
he himself, 1.
— *Gen. pl., αὐτῶν,*
their own, 11.
— *Gen. sing. fem., αὐτῆς,*
itself, 1.
the said, 1.
— *Dat. sing. masc., αὐτῷ,*
himself, 1.
even him, 1.
that, 1.
— *Dat. pl., αὐτοῖς,*
themselves, 1.
them, 2 (*see* Mark xvi. 14, ap.)
— *Dat. sing. fem., αὐτῇ,*
her, 1.
same, 1.
— *ἐν αὐτῇ τῇ ἡμέρᾳ,*
that same day, 1.
the same day, 2.
— *ἐν αὐτῇ τῇ ὥρᾳ,*
in that same hour, 1.
in that hour, 1.
in the same hour, 1.
the same hour, 1.
— *αὐτῇ τῇ ὥρᾳ,*
the same hour, 2.
in that instant, 1.
— *with the art., ὁ αὐτός,* etc.
the same, 45.
the selfsame, 1.
the same thing, 5.
the same matter, 1.
for the same cause, 1.
those, 1.
— *ταὐτά,*
like things, 1.
— *ἐπὶ τὸ αὐτό,*
in one place, 1.
together, 7.
— *κατὰ τὸ αὐτό,*
together, 1.
— *τὴν αὐτὴν ἀντιμισθίαν,*
for a recompense in the same, 1.
— *with ἐν καί,*
even all one as if, 1.
— *with μεριμνάω,*
have the same care, 1.
— *with φρονέω,*
mind the same thing, 1.
be of the same mind, 2.
be of one mind, 1.
be likeminded, 2.
— *as a simple pronoun* (in the *oblique cases*),
he / she / it / they } *and their inflected forms.*
— *with διά,*
thereat, 1.
thereby, 2.
— *with εἰς,*
therein, 2.
thereinto, 1.
— *with ἐν,*
therein, 15.
thereof, 1.
thereon, 2.
thereby, 1.
therewith, 2.
— *with ἐπί,*
thereupon, 2.
— *with περί,*
thereof, 1.
— *Redundant*, 37.

αὐτοῦ,
there, 3.
here, 1.

αὐτόφωρος, see ἐπαυτοφώρῳ.

αὐτόχειρ,
with one's own hand, 1.

αὐχέω, see μεγαλαυχέω.

αὐχμηρός,
dark, 1.

ἀφαιρέω,
take away, 7.
cut off, 2.
smite off, 1.

ἀφανής,
that is not manifest, 1.

ἀφανίζω,
disfigure, 1.
corrupt, 2.
— *passive,*
vanish away, 1.
perish, 1.

ἀφανισμός,
to vanish away, 1.

ἄφαντος, with γίνομαι,
vanish out of sight, 1.
cease to be seen, 1.

ἀφεδρών,
draught, 2.

ἀφειδία,
neglecting, 1.
punishing or not sparing, 1.

ἀφελότης,
singleness, 1.

ἄφεσις,
deliverance, 1.
liberty, 1.
remission, 9.
forgiveness, 6.

ἁφή,
joint, 2.

ἀφθαρσία,
incorruption, 4.
immortality, 2.
sincerity, 1.
incorruption, 1.

ἄφθαρτος,
not corruptible, 1.
incorruptible, 4.
uncorruptible, 1.
immortal, 1.

*** ἀφθορσία,**
[*for* ἀδιαφθορία, Tit. ii. 7, *see* Uncorruptness.]

ἀφίημι, ἀφέω, or ἀφίω,
send away, 2.
put away, 2.
lay aside, 1.
let go, 1.
let be, 1.
let alone, 6.
let have, 1.
yield up, 1.
leave, 52.
forsake, 6.
forgive, 47.
remit, 2.
omit, 1,
let, 8.
suffer, 13.
suffer it to be so now, 1.

ἀφικνέομαι,
come abroad, 1.

ἀφιλάγαθος,
despiser of those that are good, 1.

ἀφιλάργυρος,
without covetousness, 1.
not greedy of filthy lucre, 1.

ἄφιξις,
departing, 1.

ἀφίστημι,
draw away, 1.
depart from, 8.
refrain from, 1.
fall away, 1.
— *middle,*
depart from, 3.
withdraw one's self, 1.

ἄφνω,
suddenly, 3.

ἀφόβως,
without fear, 4.

ἀφομοιόομαι,
be made like, 1.

ἀφοράω, or ἀπεῖδον,
look, 1.
see, 1.

ἀφορίζω,
to separate, 7.
divide, 1.
sever, 1.
—— *passive*,
be separate, 1.

ἀφορμή,
occasion, 7.

ἀφρίζω,
to foam, 2.

ἀφρός, *with* μετά,
that one foameth again, 1.

ἀφροσύνη,
foolishness, 1.
—— *with* ἐν,
foolishly, 2.
folly, 1.

ἄφρων,
unwise, 1.
foolish, 2.
fool, 8.

ἀφυπνόω,
fall asleep, 1.

ἄφωνος,
dumb, 3.
without signification, 1.

ἀχάριστος,
unthankful, 2.

ἀχειροποίητος,
made without hands, 2.
not made with hands, 1.

ἀχλύς,
mist, 1.

ἀχρειόομαι,
become unprofitable, 1.

ἀχρεῖος,
unprofitable, 2.

ἄχρηστος,
unprofitable, 1.

ἄχρι, *or* ἄχρις,
until, 14.
till, 3.
as far as, 1.
as far as to, 1.
unto, 13.
even to, 2.
into, 1.
in, 1.
for, 2.
—— ἄχρις οὗ ἄν,
till, 2.
—— ἄχρι τοῦ δεῦρο,
hitherto, 1.

ἄχυρον,
chaff, 2.

ἀψευδής,
that cannot lie, 1.

ἄψινθος,
wormwood, 1.

ἄψυχος, *with art.*,
things without life, 1.

* βαθέως,
[*for* ὄρθρου βαθεος, Luke xxiv. 1, *see* Morning (very early in the).]

βαθμός,
degree, 1.

βάθος,
depth, 5.
deepness, 1.
deep, 1 (*subst.*)
deep things, 1 (*pl.*)
—— *with* κατὰ,
deep, 1.

* βαθύνω,
[*for* σκάπτω καὶ βαθύνω, Luke vi. 48, *see* Dig.]

βαθύς,
deep, 2.
—— ὄρθρου βαθεος,
very early in morning, 1.

βάϊον,
branch, 1.

βαλάντιον,
bag, 1.
purse, 3.

βάλλω,
cast, 86.
throw, 2.
cast out, 4.
throw down, 1.
send, 3.
thrust, 5.
strike, 1.
put, 13.
put up, 1.
pour, 2.
lay, 3.
arise, 1.
beat, 1.
—— *passive*,
lie, 2.
—— *with* κόπρια,
dung, 1.

βαπτίζω,
baptize, 74.
Baptist, 1.
—— *mid. and pass. aorist*,
wash, 2.
be baptized, 2.

βάπτισμα,
baptism, 22.

βαπτισμός,
washing, 3.
baptism, 1.

βαπτιστής,
Baptist, 14.

βάπτω,
dip, 3.

βάρ,
Bar, 1.

βάρβαρος,
barbarian, 5.
barbarous, 1.

βαρέομαι,
heavy, 3.
be burdened, 1.
be pressed, 1.
be charged, 1.

βαρέως, *with* ἀκούω,
be dull of hearing, 2.

βάρος,
weight, 1.
burden, 4.
—— ἐν βάρει εἶναι,
be burdensome, 1.
use authority, 1.

βαρύνομαι,
overcharged, 1.

βαρύς,
heavy, 1.
weighty, 1.
grievous, 1.
—— *comparative*,
weightier matter,

βαρύτιμος,
very precious, 1.

βασανίζω,
to torment, 8.
pain, 1.
vex, 1.
toss, 1.
—— *passive*,
toil, 1.

βασανισμός,
torment, 5.

βασανιστής,
tormentor, 1.

βάσανος,
torment, 3.

βασιλεία,
kingdom, 57.
—— *with* τοῦ Θεοῦ,
kingdom of God, 72.
—— *with* τῶν οὐρανῶν,
kingdom of heaven, 32.
—— *with* ἔχω,
to reign, 1.

βασίλειος,
royal, 1.
—— *with art.*,
king's court, 1.

βασιλεύς,
king, 118.

βασιλεύω,
to reign, 20.
king, 1.

βασιλικός,
royal, 2.
nobleman, 2.
courtier or ruler, 1.
—— *with art.*,
king's country, 1.

βασίλισσα,
queen, 4.

βάσις,
foot, 1.

βασκαίνω,
bewitch, 1.

βαστάζω,
bear, 22.
carry, 3.
take up, 1.

βάτος, (*fem.*)
bramble bush, 1.
bush, 4.

βάτος, (*masc.*)
measure, 1.

βάτραχος,
frog, 1.

βαττολογέω,
use vain repetitions, 1

βδέλυγμα,
abomination, 6

βδελυκτός,
abhor, 1.
abominable, 1.

βέβαιος,
steadfast, 4.
firm, 1.
sure, 3.
of force, 1.

βεβαιόω,
establish, 1.
stablish, 2.
confirm, 5.

βεβαίωσις,
confirmation, 2.

βέβηλος,
profane, 4.
profane person, 1.

βεβηλόω,
profane, 2.

* βελόνη,
[*for* ῥάφις, Luke xviii. 25 *see* Needle.]

βέλος,
dart, 1.

βελτίων, (*neut.*)
very well, 1.

βῆμα,
throne, 1.
judgment seat, 10.
—— βῆμα ποδός,
to set one's foot on, 1.

βήρυλλος,
beryl, 1.

βία,
violence, 4.

βιάζομαι,
suffer violence, 1.
be gotten by force, 1.
press, 1.

βίαιος,
mighty, 1.

βιαστής,
violent, 1.
they that thrust men, 1.

βιβλαρίδιον,
little book, 4.

βιβλίον,
scroll, 1.
book, 29.
bill, 1.
writing, 1.

βίβλος,
book, 13.

βιβρώσκω,
eat, 1.

βίος,
life, 5.
living, 5.
good, 1 (*subst.*)

βιόω,
live, 1.

βίωσις,
manner of life, 1.

βιωτικός,
of this life, 1.
of things pertaining to this life, 1.
things that pertain to this life, 1.

βλαβερός,
hurtful, 1.

βλάπτω,
to hurt, 2.

βλαστάνω,
to bud, 1.
spring up, 2.
bring forth, 1.

βλασφημέω,
speak evil of, 10.
revile, 1.
rail on, 2.
report slanderously, 1.
defame, 1.
blaspheme, 17.
speak blasphemy, 1.
blasphemously, 1.
blasphemer, 1.

βλασφημία,
evil speaking, 1.
railing, 2.
blasphemy, 16.

βλάσφημος,
railing, 1.
blasphemous, 2.
blasphemer, 2.

βλέμμα,
seeing, 1.

βλέπω,
look, 3.
look on, 4.
look to, 1.
lie, 1.
behold, 10.
take heed, 12.
take heed to, 2.
beware, 4.
beware of, 3.
see, 90.
sight, 1.
perceive, 1.
—— *with εἰς,*
regard, 2.
—— *μὴ βλέπων,*
without sight, 1.

βλητέος, (with εἰμί understood)
must be put, 2.

βοάω,
to cry, 11.

βοή,
cry, 1.

βοήθεια,
help, 1.
—— *with εἰς,*
to help, 1.

βοηθέω,
to help, 6.
succour, 2.

βοηθός,
helper, 1.

βόθυνος,
pit, 1.
ditch, 2.

βολή,
cast, 1.

βολίζω,
to sound, 2.

βολίς,
dart, 1.

βόρβορος,
mire, 1.

βορρᾶς,
north, 2.

βόσκω,
feed, 5.
keep, 1.
—— *middle,*
feed, 3.

βοτάνη,
herbs, 1.

βότρυς,
cluster, 1.

βουλεύομαι,
take counsel, 1.
consult, 2.
be minded, 2.
determine, 1.
purpose, 2.

βουλευτής,
counsellor, 2.

βουλή,
counsel, 10.
will, 1.
—— *with τίθεμαι,*
advise, 1.

βούλημα,
purpose, 1.
will, 1.

βούλομαι,
would, 11.
will, 15.
of one's own will, 1.
be willing, 1.
be minded, 2.
be disposed, 1.
intend, 2.
list, 1.

βουνός,
hill, 2.

βοῦς,
ox, 8.

βραβεῖον,
prize, 2.

βραβεύω,
to rule, 1.

βραδύνω,
tarry, 1.
be slack, 1.

βραδυπλοέω,
sail slowly, 1.

βραδύς,
slow, 3.

βραδυτής,
slackness, 1.

βραχίων,
arm, 3.

βραχύς,
—— *neut.,*
a little while, 1.
—— *βραχύ τι,*
a little, 3.
a little while, 1.
a little space, 1.
—— *βραχύ διΐστημι,*
go a little further, 1.
—— *διὰ βραχέων,*
in few words, 1.

βρέφος,
babe, 5.
infant, 1.
young child, 1.
child, 1.

βρέχω,
send rain, 1.
rain, 1 (*trans.*)
rain, 2 (*intrans.*)
wash, 2.
—— *with ὑετός,*
rain, 1 (*intrans.*)

βροντή,
thunder, 7.
thundering, 4.
—— *with γίνομαι,*
to thunder, 1.

βροχή,
rain, 2.

βρόχος,
snare, 1.

βρυγμός,
gnashing, 7.

βρύχω,
gnash, 1.

βρύω,
send forth, 1.

βρῶμα,
meat, 16.
victuals, 1.

βρώσιμος, (neut.)
meat, 1.

βρῶσις,
eating, 1.
rust, 2.
food, 1.
meat, 6.
eating, 1.
morsel of meat, 1.

βρώσκω, see βιβρώσκω.

βυθίζω,
drown, 1.
—— *passive,*
begin to sink, 1.

βυθός,
deep, 1 (*subst.*)

βυρσεύς,
tanner, 3.

βύσσινος,
fine linen, 4.

βύσσος,
fine linen, 2.

βωμός,
altar, 1.

γάγγραινα,
canker, 1.
gangrene, 1.

γάζα,
treasure, 1.

γαζοφυλάκιον,
treasury, 5.

γάλα,
milk, 5.

γαλήνη,
calm, 3.

γαμέω, or γάμω,
marry a wife, 2.
marry, 26.
married, 1.

* *γαμίζω,*
[*for ἐγγαμίζω,*
Matt. xxii. 30, Lu. xvii. 27, —— xx. 35 } *see* Marriage (give in)
for γαμίσκω, Mark xii. 25, *see* Marriage.]

γαμίσκω,
give in marriage, 1 (*see above*).

γάμος,
wedding, 7.
marriage, 9.

γάρ,
for, 992.
because, 3.
because that, 2.
therefore, 1.
seeing, 1.
indeed, 1.
verily, 2.
no doubt, 1.
and, 3.
even, 1.
but, 2.
yet, 1.
why, 1.
what? 1.
—— *καὶ γάρ,*
for, 23.
for also, 7.
for even, 5.
for indeed, 1.
for verily, 1.
and indeed, 1.
yet, 2.
—— *γὰρ ὅτι,*
because that, 1.
—— *τί γάρ,*
why, what? 3.
what then? 1.

γαστήρ,
belly, 1.
womb, 1.
—— *ἐν γαστρὶ ἔχω,*
be with child, 5.
with child, 2.

γέ,
(*used with other words to add emphasis.*)
yet, 2.
— ἀλλά γὲ,
yet doubtless, 1.
— ἀλλά γὲ σύν,
and beside, 1.
— καὶ γέ,
at least, 1.
and, 1.

γέεννα,
hell, 9.
— γέεννα τοῦ πυρός,
hell fire, 3.

γείτων,
neighbour, 4.

γελάω,
to laugh, 2.

γέλως,
laughter, 1.

γεμίζω,
fill, 7.
fill full, 1.
— *passive*,
be full, 1.

γέμω,
be full of, 5.
full of, 6.

γενεά,
generation, 34.
nation, 1.
age, 2.
time, 2.
— εἰς γενέας γενεῶν,
from generation to generation, 1.

γενεαλογέομαι,
one's descent is counted, 1.
one's *pedigree* is counted, 1.

γενεαλογία,
genealogy, 2.

γενέσια,
birthday, 2.

γένεσις,
generation, 1.
nature, 1.
natural, 1.

γενετή,
birth.

* γένημα,
[*instead of* γέννημα *by most critical editors, see* Fruit.]

γεννάω,
beget, 49.
gender, 2.
conceive, 1.
delivered of, 1.
bring forth, 1.
bear, 2.
— *passive*,
be born, 39.
spring, 1.
be made, 1.

γέννημα,
generation, 4.
fruit, 5.

γέννησις,
birth, 2.

γεννητός,
that is born, 2.

γένος,
offspring, 3.
generation, 1.
stock, 2.
kindred, 3.
one's own countrymen, 1.
of the country, 1.
born in, 1.
born at, 1.
nation, 2.
kind, 5.
diversity, 1.
kind, 1.

γερουσία,
senate, 1.

γέρων,
old, 1.

γεύομαι,
to taste, 12.
eat, 3.

γεωργέομαι,
be dressed, 1.

γεώργιον,
husbandry, 1.
tillage, 1.

γεωργός,
husbandman, 19.

γῆ,
earth, 188.
land, 1.
ground, 18.
land, 42.
country, 2.
world, 1.
— *with* ἐκ,
earthly, 1.

γῆρας,
old age, 1.

γηράσκω,
wax old, 1.
be old, 1.

γίνομαι,
become, 42.
be made, 69.
grow, 2.
wax, 2.
draw, 1.
arise, 16.
come, 53.
come to pass, 82.
be brought to pass, 1.
fall, 1.
befall, 1.
happen, 1.
follow, 1.
be wrought, 2.
be performed, 1.
be done, 62.
so be done, 1.
be one's doing, 2.
be fulfilled, 3.
be finished, 1.
be ended, 1.
be past, 2.
be had, 1.
be kept, 1.
be found, 1.
be brought, 1.
be showed, 1.
be published, 1.
be ordained to be, 1.
be preferred, 3.
be turned, 1.
be divided, 1.
be taken, 1.
be assembled, 1.
be, 248.
so be, 1.
have, 3 (*lit.* belong to).
be married, 3.
behave one's self, 1.
continue, 1.
— *with* εἰς,
become, 5.
be made, 1.
wax, 1.
— *with* εἰμί,
be, 1.
— μὴ γένοιτο,
God forbid, 15 (*lit.* may it not be).
— ὅπως μὴ γένεται αὐτῷ,
because he would not, 1.
— *with* ἐν,
to use, 1.
— *with* βαπτίζω,
baptize, 1.

γινώσκω,
know, 196.
have knowledge, 1.
perceive, 9.
be aware of, 1. } ("ware," *edition of* 1611).
be aware, 1. }
be sure of, 1.
be sure, 1.
understand, 8.
can, 1 (*lit.* know how).
allow, 1.
know, 1.
feel, 1.
be resolved, 1.
can speak, 1.

γλεῦκος,
new wine, 1.

γλυκύς,
sweet, 3.
fresh, 1.

γλῶσσα,
tongue, 50.

γλωσσόκομον,
bag, 2.

γναφεύς,
fuller, 1.

γνήσιος,
own, 2.
true, 1.
— *with art.*,
sincerity, 1.

γνησίως,
naturally, 1.

γνόφος,
blackness, 1.

γνώμη,
mind, 2.
judgment, 3.
advice, 1.
will, 1.
— *with* γίνομαι,
to purpose, 1.
— ποιῆσαι γνώμην μίαν,
agree, 1.

γνωρίζω,
make known, 16.
do to wit, 1.
give to understand, 1.
declare, 4.
certify, 1.
wot, 1.

γνῶσις,
knowledge, 28.
science, 1.

γνώστης,
expert, 1.

γνωστός,
known, 10.
notable, 1.
— *with art.*,
acquaintance, 2 (*pl.*)
that which may be known, 1.
— γνωστόν ἐστιν ἡμίν,
we know, 1.

γογγύζω,
murmur, 1, *trans.*; 7, *intrans.*

γογγυσμός,
murmuring, 3.
grudging, 1.

γογγυστής,
murmurer, 1.

γόης,
seducer, 1.

γόμος,
burden, 1.
merchandise, 2.

γονεύς, (*plural*)
parents, 19.

γόνυ,
knee, 7.
— τίθημι τὰ γόνατα,
kneel, 5.

γονυπετέω,
kneel down to, 2.
kneel to, 1.
bow the knee, 1.

γράμμα,
letter, 9.
learning, 1.
writing, 1.
scripture, 1.
bill, 1.
learning, 1.

γραμματεύς,
scribe, 66.
town-clerk, 1.

γραπτός,
written, 1,

γραφή,
scripture, 51.

γράφω,
write, 89.
describe, 1.
— ἦν γεγραμμένον,
the writing was, 1.
— κατὰ τὸ γεγραμμένον,
according as it is written, 1.

γραώδης,
old wives', 1.

γρηγορέω,
watch, 20.
watchful, 1.
be vigilant, 1.
wake, 1.

γυμνάζω,
to exercise, 4.

γυμνασία,
exercise, 1.

γυμνητεύω,
be naked, 1.

γυμνός,
naked, 14.
bare, 1.

γυμνότης,
nakedness, 3.

γυναικάριον,
silly woman, 1.

γυναικεῖος,
wife, 1 (lit. of woman).

γυνή,
woman, 129.
wife, 92.
woman, 1.

γωνία,
corner, 8.
quarter, 1.

δαιμονίζομαι,
be possessed with devil, 5.
he that hath a devil, 1.
be possessed with devils, 4.
be possessed of the devils, 2.
be vexed with a devil, 1.

δαιμόνιον,
devil, 59.
god, 1.

δαιμονιώδης,
devilish, 1.

δαίμων,
devil, 5.

δάκνω,
bite, 1.

δάκρυ, or δάκρυον,
tear, 11.

δακρύω,
weep, 1.

δακτύλιος,
ring, 1.

δάκτυλος,
finger, 8.

δαμάζω,
to tame, 4

δάμαλις,
heifer, 1.

δανείζω,
lend, 3.
— middle,
borrow, 1.

δάνειον,
debt, 1.

δανειστής,
creditor, 1.

δαπανάω,
spend, 3.
be at charges, 1.
consume, 1.

δαπάνη,
cost, 1.

δέ,
(a particle of constant occurrence, too frequent for enumeration, and translated
but.
and.
now.
further.
nevertheless.
then.
therefore.
for.
even,
howbeit.
etc.)

δέησις,
request, 1.
supplication, 6.
prayer, 12.

δεῖ,
be needful, 1.
must needs, 6.
must, 58.
should, 4.
ought, 30.
be meet, 2.
behove, 1.
— δέον ἐστίν,
be need, 1.
ought, 1.
— τὰ μὴ δέοντα,
things which they ought not, 1.

δεῖγμα,
example, 1.

δειγματίζω,
make a show of, 1.

δείκνυμι,
show, 31.

δειλία,
fear, 1.

δειλιάω,
be afraid, 1.

δειλός,
fearful, 3.

δεῖνα,
such a man, 1.

δεινῶς,
vehemently, 1.
grievously, 1.

δειπνέω,
sup, 3.
supper, 1.

δεῖπνον,
supper, 13.
feast, 3.

δεισιδαιμονία,
superstition, 1.

δεισιδαίμων,
too superstitious, 1.

δέκα,
ten, 24.
— δέκα καὶ ὀκτώ,
eighteen, 3.

* δεκαέξ,
[ἑξακόσιοι δεκα ἕξ, for χξϛ, Rev. xiii. 18, see "Hundred."]

δεκαδύο,
twelve, 2.

δεκαπέντε,
fifteen, 3.

δεκατέσσαρες,
fourteen, 5.

δεκάτη,
tenth part, 1.
tenth, 1.
tithe, 2.

δέκατος,
tenth, 3.

δεκατόω,
receive tithes of, 1.
pay tithes, 1 (pass.)

δεκτός,
accepted, 3.
acceptable, 2.

δελεάζω,
entice, 1.
beguile, 1.
allure, 1.

δένδρον,
tree, 26.

δεξιολάβος,
spearman, 1.

δεξιός,
right, 12.
on the right hand, 1.
right hand, 16.
— plural,
right side, 1.
on the right side, 1.
— ἐκ δεξιῶν,
on the right hand, 21.

δέομαι,
make request, 1.
beseech, 9.
pray, 12.

* δέος,
[for αἰδώς, Heb. xii. 28, see Reverence.]

δέρμα, with αἴγειος,
goatskin, 1.

δερμάτινος,
of a skin, 1.
leathern, 1.

δέρω,
beat, 12.
smite, 3.

δεσμεύω,
bind, 2.

δεσμέω,
bind, 1.

δέσμη,
bundle, 1.

δέσμιος,
in bonds, 1.
that is in bonds, 1.
prisoner, 13.

δεσμός,
band, 3 (neut.)
string, 1.
bond, 15.
chain, 1.

δεσμοφύλαξ,
keeper of the prison, 2.
jailor, 1.

δεσμωτήριον,
prison, 4.

δεσμώτης,
prisoner, 2.

δεσπότης,
master, 5.
Lord, 5.

δεῦρο,
come hither, 2.
come, 6.
— ἄχρι τοῦ δεῦρο,
hitherto, 1.

δεῦτε,
come, 12.
— with ὀπίσω,
follow, 1.

δευτεραῖος,
the next day, 1.

δευτερόπρωτος,
second after the first, 1.

δεύτερος,
second, 31.
— neuter,
the second time, 3.
secondarily, 1.
again, 1.
afterward, 1.
— ἐκ δευτέρου,
the second time, 4.
again, 2.

δέχομαι,
receive, 52.
suffer, 1.
accept, 2.
take, 5.

δέω,
bind, 37.
tie, 4.
wind, 1.
knit, 1.
— perf. pass.,
be in bonds, 1.

δή,
doubtless, 1.
now, 1.
therefore, 1.
also, 1.

δῆλος,
manifest, 1.
evident, 1.
certain, 1.
— with ποιέω,
bewray, 1.

δηλόω,
declare, 3.
show, 1.
signify, 3.

δημηγορέω,
make an oration, 1.

δημιουργός,
maker, 1.

δῆμος,
people, 4.

δημόσιος,
common, 1.
—— δημοσίᾳ,
publicly, 2.
openly, 1.

δηνάριον,
penny, 14.
—— *Gen. pl.*,
pennyworth, 2.

δήποτε or δή ποτε, *with* ᾧ (*from* ὅς),
whatsoever, 1.

δήπου or δή που,
verily, 1.

διά,
—— *with Genitive*,
through, 87.
throughout, 4.
after, 2.
after some, 1.
by, 235.
because of, 1.
whereby, 1.
for, 1.
for...sake, 1.
from, 1.
of, 1.
out of, 1.
by occasion of, 1.
with, 16.
to, 1.
by, 1.
at, 2.
in, 8.
within, 1.
among, 1.
by, 1.
—— διὰ παντὸς τοῦ ζῆν,
all their life time, 1.
—— δι' ὅλης τῆς νυκτός,
all the night, 1.
—— δι' ἡμερῶν τεσσ.,
forty days, 1.
—— *with* αὐτός,
thereby, 2.
thereat, 1.
—— *with* οὗτος,
thereby, 2.
—— *with* ὅς,
whereby, 3.
—— δι' ἄλλης ὁδοῦ,
another way, 1.
—— δι' ἐκείνης,
that way, 1.
—— *with Accusative*,
because of, 29.
by reason of, 4.
to avoid, 1.
for, 58.
by, 1.
for...sake, 45.
through, 6.
of, 2.
by, 8.
for, 1.
with, 1.
—— *with an infinitive*,
because, 23.
because that, 2.
that, 1.
by reason of, 1.

—— διὰ τοῦτο,
for this cause, 14.
therefore, 44.
wherefore, 8.
—— δι' ἣν αἰτίαν,
wherefore, 1.
—— δι' ἥν,
wherefore, 3.
wherein, 1.
—— διὰ ταύτην,
by reason hereof.

διαβαίνω,
pass through, 1.
pass, 1.
come over, 1.

διαβάλλω,
accuse, 1.

διαβεβαιόομαι,
affirm constantly, 1.
affirm, 1.

διαβλέπω,
see clearly, 2.

διάβολος,
false accuser, 2.
makebate, 1.
slanderer, 1.
devil, 35.

*** διάγε,**
[*for* διά γε, Luke xi.8,G.]

διαγγέλλω,
declare, 1.
preach, 1.
signify, 1.

διαγίνομαι,
be past, 1.
be spent, 1.
—— ἡμερῶν διαγενομένων τινῶν,
after certain days, 1.

διαγινώσκω,
know the uttermost, 1.
inquire, 1.

διαγνωρίζω,
make known abroad, 1.

διάγνωσις,
hearing, 1.
judgment, 1.

διαγογγύζω,
murmur, 2.

διαγρηγορέω,
be awake, 1.

διάγω,
lead a life, 1.
live, 1.

διαδέχομαι,
come after, 1.

διάδημα,
crown, 3.

διαδίδωμι,
distribute, 2.
make distribution, 1.
divide, 1.
give, 1.

διάδοχος, *with* λαμβάνω,
come into one's room, 1.

διαζώννυμι,
gird unto one's self, 1.
gird, 2.

διαθήκη,
covenant, 20.
testament, 6.
testament, 13.

διαίρεσις,
difference, 1.
diversity, 2.

διαιρέω,
divide, 2.

διακαθαρίζω,
thoroughly purge, 2.

διακατελέγχομαι,
convince, 1.

διακονέω,
minister unto, 15.
minister to, 1.
minister, 7.
administer, 2.
serve, 10.
use the office of deacon, 2.
minister, 1.

διακονία,
ministering, 3.
ministration, 6.
serving, 1.
service, 2.
relief, 1.
administration, 2.
ministry, 16.
charge, 1.
office, 1.
—— *with* εἰς,
to minister, 1.
—— *with* πρός,
to do service, 1.

διάκονος,
minister, 20.
servant, 7.
deacon, 3.

διακόσια,
two hundred, 8.

διακούω,
hear, 1.

διακρίνω,
make to differ, 1.
distinguish, 1.
put a difference, 1.
discern, 2.
judge, 3.
—— *mid. and pass. aor.*,
make a difference, 1.
be partial, 1.
contend, 2.
doubt, 5.
discern, and put a difference between meats, 1.
waver, 2.
stagger, 1.

διάκρισις,
discerning, 1.
disputation, 1.
to judge, 1 (*with* εἰς).
—— *with* πρός,
discern, 1.

διακωλύω,
forbid, 1.

διαλαλέω,
commune, 1.
noise abroad, 1.

διαλέγομαι,
reason with, 2.
reason, 2.
dispute, 6.
speak, 1.
preach, 2.

διαλείπω,
cease, 1.

διάλεκτος,
language, 1.
tongue, 5.

διαλλάσσομαι,
be reconciled, 1.

διαλογίζομαι,
to reason, 11.
consider, 1.
think, 1.
muse, 1.
reason or debate, 1.
cast in one's mind 1.
dispute, 1.

διαλογισμός,
reasoning, 1.
thought, 9.
imagination, 1.
doubting, 1.
doubtful, 1.
doubtful thoughts, 1.
disputing, 1.

διαλύω,
scatter, 1.

διαμαρτύρομαι,
witness, 1.
testify, 11.
charge, 3.

διαμάχομαι,
strive, 1.

διαμένω,
remain, 2.
continue, 3.

διαμερίζω,
divide, 5.
part, 6.
—— *passive*,
cloven, 1.

διαμερισμός,
division, 1.

διανέμω, (*pass.*)
spread, 1.

διανεύω, *with* εἰμί,
beckon, 1.

διανόημα,
thought, 1.

διάνοια,
mind, 9.
understanding, 3.
imagination, 1.

διανοίγω,
to open, 8.

διανυκτερεύω,
continue all night, 1.

διανύω,
finish, 1.

διαπαντός,
always *or* alway, 5.
continually, 2.

*** διαπαρατριβή,**
[*for* παραδιατριβή, 1 Tim. vi. 5, *see* Perverse disputings.]

διαπεράω,
pass over, 3.
can pass, 1.
go over, 1.
sail over, 1.

διαπλέω,
sail over, 1.

διαπονέομαι,
be grieved, 2.

διαπορεύομαι,
go through, 3.
pass by, 1.
in one's journey, 1.

διαπορέω,
be perplexed, 1.
be in doubt, 1.
doubt, 2.
— *passive*,
be much perplexed, 1.

διαπραγματεύομαι,
gain by trading, 1.

διαπρίομαι,
be cut to heart, 1.
be cut, 1.

διαρπάζω,
to spoil, 4.

διαρρήσσω, *or* διαρρήγνυμι,
rend, 3.
break, 1.
— *middle*,
break, 1.

διασαφέω,
tell, 1.

διασείω,
do violence to, 1.
put in fear, 1.

διασκορπίζω,
scatter abroad, 2.
scatter, 2.
disperse, 1.
waste, 2.
strew, 2.

διασπάω,
pluck asunder, 1.
pull in pieces, 1.

διασπείρω,
scatter abroad, 3.

διασπορά,
scattered, 1.
dispersed, 1.
— *with* ἐν,
which are scattered abroad, 1.

διαστέλλομαι,
— *middle*,
charge, 6.
give commandment, 1.
— *passive*,
be commanded, 1.

διάστημι,
space, 1.

διαστολή,
distinction, 1.
difference, 2.

διαστρέφω,
turn away, 1.
pervert, 2.
— *pass. part.*,
perverse, 4.

διασώζω,
bring safe, 1.
save, 2.
make perfectly whole, 1.
heal, 1.
— *passive*,
escape safe, 1.
escape, 2.

διαταγή,
disposition, 1.
ordinance, 1.

διάταγμα,
commandment, 1.

διαταράσσω, *or* -ττω,
trouble, 1.

διατάσσω,
give order, 1.
ordain, 2.
appoint, 2.
command, 6.
— *middle*,
set in order, 1.
appoint, 2.
command, 1.

διατελέω,
continue, 1.

διατηρέω,
keep, 2.

διατί,
wherefore? 4.
why? 23.

διατίθεμαι,
appoint, 2.
make, 3.
testator, 2.

διατρίβω,
be, 1.
tarry, 2.
continue, 2.
abide, 5.

διατροφή,
food, 1.

διαυγάζω,
to dawn, 1.

* διαυγής,
[*for* διαφανής, Rev. xxi. 21, *see* Transparent.]

διαφανής,
transparent, 1.

διαφέρω,
drive up and down, 1.
publish, 1.
differ from, 2.
be better, 3.
be of more value, 2.
— *impers., with* οὐδέν,
it maketh no matter, 1.
— *with* διά,
carry through, 1.
— τὰ διαφέροντα,
things that are excellent, 1.
differ, 1.
the things that are more excellent, 1.
the things that differ, 1.

διαφεύγω,
to escape, 1.

διαφημίζω,
spread abroad one's fame, 1.
blaze abroad, 1.
commonly report, 1.

διαφθείρω,
destroy, 3.
corrupt, 1.
corrupt, 1.
— *passive*,
perish, 1.
corrupt, 1 (*adj.*)

διαφθορά,
corruption, 6.

διάφορος,
diverse, 1.
differing, 1.
— *comparative*,
more excellent, 2.

διαφυλάσσω, *or* -ττω,
keep, 1.

διαχειρίζομαι,
slay, 1.
kill, 1.

* διαχλευάζω,
[*for* χλευάζω, Acts ii. 13, *see* Mock.]

διαχωρίζομαι,
depart, 1.

διδακτικός,
apt to teach, 2.

διδακτός,
taught, 1.
which one teacheth, 2.

διδασκαλία,
teaching, 1.
learning, 1.
doctrine, 19.

διδάσκαλος,
teacher, 10.
doctor, 1.
master, 6.
Master, 41.

διδάσκω,
teach, 93.
— *with* εἰμί,
teach, 4.

διδαχή,
doctrine, 29.
— *with* κατὰ,
as he hath been taught, 1.
in teaching, 1.

δίδραχμον, (*plural*)
tribute money, 1.
tribute, 1.

δίδωμι,
give, 367.
give up, 1.
give forth, 1.
grant, 10.
bestow, 2.
minister, 1.
yield, 2.
bring forth, 1.
offer, 2.
add, 1.
suffer, 2.
adventure, 1.
deliver, 1.
deliver up, 1.
commit, 1.
utter, 1.
show, 1.
set, 1.
put, 5.
make, 2.
take, 2.
yield, 1.
— ἵνα δῶσιν αὐτοῖς,
to receive, 1.
give, 1.
— *pass. with Dat.*,
have power, 2.

διεγείρω,
to awake, 2.
stir up, 2.
raise, 1.
— *passive*,
arise, 2.

* διενθυμέομαι,
[*for* ἐνθυμέομαι, Acts x. 19, *see* Think.]

* διεξέρχομαι,
[*for* ἔρχομαι, Acts xxviii. 3, *see* Come.]

διέξοδος, *with* τῶν ὁδῶν,
highway, 1.

* διερμηνεία,
[*for* ἑρμηνεία, 1 Cor. xii. 10, *see* Interpretation.]

διερμηνευτής,
interpreter, 1.

διερμηνεύω,
interpret, 4.
expound, 1.
— *passive*,
by interpretation, 1.

διέρχομαι,
go through, 2.
go throughout, 1.
go over, 2.
go over all, 1.
go everywhere, 1.
go about, 1.
go abroad, 1.
go, 3.
pass through, 7.
pass throughout, 1.
pass over, 1.
pass by, 1.
pass, 6.
pierce through, 1.
come, 1.
depart, 1.
travel, 1.
— *with* κατά,
go through, 1.
— *with* διά,
go through, 3.
pass through, 3.
pass throughout, 1.
walk through, 2.

διερωτάω,
make enquiry for, 1.

διετής,
two years old, 1.

διετία,
two years, 2.

διηγέομαι,
tell, 4.
declare, 3.
show, 1.

διήγησις,
declaration, 1.

διηνεκής, *with* εἰς τὸ,
continually, 2.
for ever, 2.

διθάλασσος,
where two seas meet, 1.

διΐκνεομαι,
pierce, 1.

διΐστημι,
be parted, 1.
go further, 1.
—— διαστάσης ὥρας μιᾶς,
the space of one hour after, 1.

διϊσχυρίζομαι,
constantly affirm, 1.
confidently affirm, 1.

δικαιοκρισία,
righteous judgment, 1.

δίκαιος,
right, 5.
meet, 2.
just, 33.
righteous, 41.

δικαιοσύνη,
righteousness, 94.

δικαιόω,
justify, 37.
justifier, 1.
free, 1.
justify, 1.
—— *passive*,
be righteous, 1.

δικαίωμα,
judgment, 2.
ordinance, 3.
ceremony, 1.
rite or ceremony, 1.
righteousness, 4.
justification, 1.

δικαίως,
justly, 2.
righteously, 2.
to righteousness, 1.

δικαίωσις,
justification, 2.

δικαστής,
judge, 3.

δίκη,
judgment, 2.
vengeance, 2.
—— *with* τίω,
be punished, 1.

δίκτυον,
net, 12.

δίλογος,
double-tongued, 1.

διό,
for which cause, 2.
wherefore, 40.
and therefore, 1.
therefore, 9.

διοδεύω,
pass through, 1.
go throughout, 1.

διόπερ,
wherefore, 3.

Διοπετής,
which fell down from Jupiter, 1.

* διόρθωμα,
[*for* κατόρθωμα, Acts xxiv. 3, *see* Deed.]

διόρθωσις,
reformation, 1.

διορύσσω,
break through, 3.
break up, 1.

διότι,
because that, 3.
because, 10.
for, 8.
for that, 1.
therefore, 1.

διπλοῦς,
double, 3.
twofold more, 1.

διπλόω,
to double, 1.

δίς,
twice, 4.
again, 2.

δισμυριάδες, *see* μυριάς.

διστάζω,
to doubt, 2.

δίστομος,
two-edged, 2.
with two edges, 1.

δισχίλιοι,
two thousand, 1.

διϋλίζω,
strain at, 1.

διχάζω,
set at variance, 1.

διχοστασία,
division, 2.
faction, 1.
sedition, 1.

διχοτομέω,
cut asunder, 1.
cut in sunder, 1.
cut off, 2.

διψάω,
to thirst, 10.
be thirsty, 3.
be athirst, 3.

δίψος,
thirst, 1.

δίψυχος,
double-minded, 2.

διωγμός,
persecuti u, 10.

διώκτης,
persecutor, 1.

διώκω,
persecute, 28.
follow after, 6.
follow, 4.
ensue, 1.
press forward, 1.
given to, 1.
—— *passive*,
suffer persecution, 3.

δόγμα,
decree, 3.
ordinance, 2.

δογματίζομαι,
be subject to ordinances, 1.

δοκέω,
think, 25.
suppose, 7.
trow, 1.
seem, 12.
think, 1.
be accounted, 2.
think good, 1.
be of reputation, 1.
—— *impersonal*,
it seemeth, 1.
it seemeth good, 3.
it pleaseth, 2.
think, 8 (*with Dat.*)
—— τὸ δοκοῦν αὐτοῖς,
their own pleasure, 1.

δοκιμάζω,
try, 4.
prove, 10.
examine, 1.
discern, 2.
approve, 3.
try, 2.
allow, 2.
like, 1.

* δοκιμασια,
[*see ap.*, Heb. iii. 9.]

δοκιμή,
trial, 1.
experiment, 1.
experience, 2.
proof, 3.

δοκίμιον,
trial, 1.
trying, 1.

δόκιμος,
tried, 1.
approved, 5.
which is approved, 1.

δοκός,
beam, 6.

δόλιος,
deceitful, 1.

δολιόω,
use deceit, 1.

δόλος,
guile, 7.
deceit, 2.
craft, 1.
subtilty, 2.

δολόω,
handle deceitfully, 1.

δόμα,
gift, 4.

δόξα,
glory, 144.
glorious, 6.
praise, 4.
honour, 6.
worship, 1.
dignity, 2.
—— *with* διά,
glorious, 1.
—— *with* ἐν,
glorious, 3.

δοξάζω,
glorify, 54.
honour, 3.
magnify, 1.
—— *passive*,
be made glorious, 1.
have glory, 2.
full of glory, 1.

δόσις,
giving, 1.
gift, 1.

δότης,
giver, 1.

δουλαγωγέω,
bring into subjection, 1.

δουλεία,
bondage, 5.

δουλεύω,
be in bondage, 4.
serve, 18.
do service, 3.

δούλη,
handmaid, 1.
handmaiden, 2.

δοῦλος, (*adj.*)
servant, 2.

δοῦλος, (*subst.*)
bondman, 1.
bond, 6.
servant, 81.
—— *with* Θεοῦ, Χριστοῦ, *etc.*,
servant, 27.

δουλόω,
bring into bondage, 1.
make servant, 1.
—— *passive*,
be brought in bondage, 1.
in bondage, 1.
be under bondage, 1.
become servant, 2.
given to, 1.

δοχή,
feast, 2.

δράκων,
dragon, 13.

δράσσομαι,
take, 1.

δραχμή,
piece of silver, 1.
piece, 2.

δρεμω, *see* τρέχω.

δρέπανον,
sickle, 8.

δρόμος.
course, 3.

δῦμι, *see* δύνω.

δύναμαι,
can, 147.
can do, 2.
be able, 37.
able, 3.
be able to do, 1.
that is of power, 1.
be possible, 1.
may, 18.

δύναμις,
power, 77.
ability, 1.
strength, 7.
might, 4.
mighty, 2.
of power, 1.
mighty work, 11.
mighty deed, 1.
wonderful work, 1.
miracle, 8.
worker of miracles, 1.
power, 1.
abundance, 1.
power, 1.
violence, 1.
virtue, 3.
meaning, 1.
— *with ἐν*,
mightily, 1.

δυναμόω,
strengthen, 1.

δυνάστης,
Potentate, 1.
mighty, 1.
of great authority, 1.

δυνατέω,
be mighty, 1.

δυνατός,
able, 10.
that I could, 1.
strong, 3.
mighty, 5.
that is mighty, 1.
mighty man, 1.
— *neuter*,
possible, 9.
power, 1 (*with art.*)
— *εἰ δυνατόν*,
if it be possible, 1.
if it were possible, 2.
if it had been possible, 1.

δύνω, *or* δῦμι,
set, 1.
be setting, 1.

δύο,
two, 116.
two men, 1.
two women, 1.
twain, 10.
both, 2.
— *δύο δύο*,
by two and two, 1.
— *ἀνά δύο*,
two and two, 1.
two apiece, 2.

δυσβάστικος,
grievous to be borne, 2.

δυσεντερία,
bloody flux, 1.

δυσερμήνευτος,
hard to be uttered, 1.

δύσκολος,
hard, 1.

δυσκόλως,
hardly, 3.

δυσμή,
west, 5 (pl.)

δυσμυριάδες, *see* μυριάς.

δυσνόητος,
hard to be understood, 1.

*** δυσφημέω,**
[*for* βλασφημέω, 1 Cor. iv. 13, *see* Defame.]

δυσφημία,
evil report, 1.

δώδεκα,
twelve, 77 (spoken of the Apostles, 39).

δωδέκατος,
twelfth, 1.

δωδεκάφυλον,
twelve tribes, 1.

δῶμα,
house-top, 7.

δωρεά,
gift, 11.

δωρεάν,
freely, 6.
for naught, 1.
without a cause, 1.
in vain, 1.

δωρέω,
give, 3.

δώρημα,
gift, 2.

δῶρον,
gift, 18.
offering, 1.

*** δωροφορία,**
[*for* διακονία, Rom. xv. 31, *see* Service.]

ἔα, (*imperat. of* ἐάω)
let alone, 2.
away, 1.

ἐάν,
— *with indicative*,
if, 1.
— *with subj. present*,
if, 73.
and if, 1.
though, 8.
— *with subj. aor.*,
if, 119.
though, 4.
when, 2.
— *καὶ ἐάν*,
though, 1.
— *ἐάν καί*,
if, 1.
although, 1.
— *ἐάν δὲ καί*,
but and if, 2.
— *ἐάν δέ*,
but and if, 3.
— *ἐάνπερ*,
if, 3.
— *ἐάν τε*,
whether, 3.
or, 3.
though, 1.
— *ἐάν μή*,
if not, 15.
if no, 1.
except, 33.
but, 3.
— *ἐάν μὴ πρότερον*,
before, 1.
former, 2.
first, 2.
at the first, 1.

ἑαυτοῦ,
— *masc. sing.*, ἑαυτοῦ,
his own, 7.
his, 19.
himself, 15.
him, 1.
of itself, 1.
itself, 2.
thine own, 1.
thyself, 1.
— *fem.*, ἑαυτῆς,
her own, 1.
her, 4.
of itself, 1.
itself, 2.
that she had, 1 (*with* τὰ παρά).
— *plural*, ἑαυτῶν,
their own, 7.
his own, 1.
their, 14.
themselves, 2.
them, 5.
our own, 1.
of ourselves, 1.
ourselves, 2.
your own, 2.
your, 1.
your own selves, 1.
yourselves, 1.
you, 3.
one another, 1.
— *Dat. sing.*, ἑαυτῷ,
to himself, 7.
unto himself, 4.
for himself, 2.
himself, 16.
him, 2.
— *Dat. fem.*, ἑαυτῇ,
for her own, 1.
herself, 1.
— *Dat. pl.*, ἑαυτοῖς, ἑαυταῖς,
to themselves, 4.
unto themselves, 3.
upon themselves, 1.
for themselves, 1.
among themselves, 1.
themselves, 15.
among them, 2.
ourselves, 4.
to yourselves, 2.
unto yourselves, 1.
for yourselves, 1.
among yourselves, 1.
yourselves, 11.
you, 2.
one another, 2.
— *with παρά*,
in your own conceits, 2.
— *Acc. masc.*,
himself, 65.
he himself, 2.
thyself, 2.
— *Acc. fem.*, ἑαυτήν,
herself, 4.
itself, 3.
— *with κατά*,
alone, 1.
by itself, 1.
— *neut.*, ἐν καθ' ἑαυτό,
each of them, 1.
— *Acc. pl.*, ἑαυτούς, ἑαυτάς,
their own selves, 1.
themselves, 30.
they, 2.
ourselves, 13.
your own selves, 3.
yourselves, 19.
one another, 3.
— *with πρός*,
unto their own home, 1.

ἐάω,
let, 1.
suffer, 9.
let alone, 1.
leave, 1.
commit, 1.
leave, 1.

ἑβδομήκοντα,
seventy, 2.
three score and ten, 1.
— *with πέντε*,
three score and fifteen, 1.
— *with ἕξ*,
three score and sixteen, 1.

ἑβδομηκοντάκις,
seventy times, 1.

ἕβδομος,
seventh, 9.

Ἑβραΐστι,
in Hebrew, 1.
in the Hebrew, 2.
in the Hebrew tongue, 3.

ἐγγίζω,
draw near, 5.
draw nigh, 12.
come near, 5.
come nigh, 8.
approach, 2.
be nigh, 2.
be at hand, 9.

ἐγγράφω,
write in, 2.

ἔγγυος,
surety, 1.

ἐγγύς,
near, 3.
near to, 2.
nigh, 7.
nigh to, 3.
nigh unto, 4.
from, 1.
at hand, 6.
nigh at hand, 4.
ready, 1.

ἐγείρω,
awake, 1.
raise, 28.
raise up, 23.
raise again, 4.
rear up, 1.
lift up, 3.
lift out, 1.
take up, 1.
— *mid. and pass. aor.*
awake, 2.
arise, 27.
rise, 36.
rise up, 8.
rise again, 5.
— *ἔγειραι εἰς τὸ μέσον*,
stand forth, 1.

ἔγερσις,
resurrection, 1.

ἐγκάθετος,
spy, 1.

ἐγκαίνια,
feast of the dedication, 1.

ἐγκαινίζω,
consecrate, 1.
make new, 1.
dedicate, 1.
purify, 1.

* ἐγκακέω,
[*for* ἐκκακέω, Luke xviii. 1, *see* Faint.]

ἐγκαλέω,
call in question, 1.
implead, 1.
accuse, 4.
— *with* κατά,
lay a thing to the charge of, 1.

ἐγκαταλείπω,
leave, 2.
forsake, 7.

* ἐγκαυχάομαι,
[*for* καυχάομαι, 2 Thes. i. 4, *see* Glory.]

ἐγκατοικέω,
dwell among, 1.

ἐγκεντρίζω,
graff in, 4.
graff into, 2.

ἔγκλημα,
crime laid against one, 1.
laid to one's charge, 1.

ἐγκομβόομαι,
be clothed with, 1.

ἐγκοπή, *with* δίδωμι,
hinder, 1.

ἐγκόπτω,
hinder, 2.
be tedious unto, 1.

ἐγκράτεια,
temperance, 4.

ἐγκρατεύομαι,
can contain, 1.
be temperate, 1.

ἐγκρατής,
temperate, 1.

ἐγκρίνω,
make of the number, 1.

ἐγκρύπτω,
hide, 2.

ἔγκυος,
great with child, 1.

ἐγχρίω,
anoint, 1.

ἐγώ,
— *nominative*, ἐγώ,
I, 364.
me, 1.
— *with* αὐτός,
myself, 1.
— *with* καί = κἀγώ,
and I, 34.
I also, 15.
also I, 1.
even I, 3.
even I also, 2.
even so I, 2.
so I, 4.
even so I also, 1.
I in like wise, 1.
I, 4.
— *Genitive* (a), ἐμοῦ,
of me, 1.
my, 9.
mine, 1.
me, 96.
— *with* αὐτός,
of myself, 1.
— *with* παρά,
my, 1.
— (b) μοῦ,
of me, 7.
with me, 1.
my, 502.
mine, 16.
mine own, 4.
of mine, 3.
me, 43.
to me, 1.
unto me, 2.
I, 11.
— *Dative* (a), ἐμοί,
to me, 9.
unto me, 8.
for me, 1.
with me, 2.
at me, 1.
me, 65.
my, 1.
mine, 1.
I, 2.
— κἀμοί,
to me also, 1.
of me also, 1.
me also, 1.
— τί ἐμοὶ καὶ σοί,
what have I to do with thee, 3.
— (b) μοί,
to me, 21.
unto me, 60.
for me, 8.
with me, 3.
in me, 1.
me, 127.
my, 11.
mine, 1.
I, 9.
— *Accusative* (a) ἐμέ,
myself, 1.
me, 81.
myself, 1.
I, 2.
— κἀμέ,
both me, 1.
I also, 1.
— τὰ κατ' ἐμέ,
my affairs, 1.
my state, 1.
the things which happened unto me, 1.
— τὰ περὶ ἐμέ,
how it will go with me, 1.
— (b) μέ,
me, 262.
I, 38.
me, 1.
— κἀμέ,
both me, 1.
I also, 1.

ἐδαφίζω,
lay even with the ground, 1.

ἔδαφος,
ground, 1.

ἑδραῖος,
steadfast, 2.
settled, 1.

ἑδραίωμα,
ground, 1.
stay, 1.

ἐθελοθρησκεία,
will worship, 1.

ἐθέλω, *see* θέλω.

ἐθίζω, (*pass.*)
custom, 1.

ἐθνάρχης,
governor, 1.

ἐθνικός,
heathen man, 1.
— *with art.* (*pl.*)
the heathen, 1.

ἐθνικῶς,
after the manner of Gentiles, 1.

ἔθνος,
nation, 64.
people, 2.
— *plural*,
Gentiles, 93.
heathen, 5.

ἔθος,
custom, 7.
rite, 1.
manner, 4.
— κατὰ τὸ ἔθος,
as one is wont, 1.

ἔθω, εἴωθα,
be wont, 2.
— κατὰ τὸ εἰωθός.
as his custom was, 1.
as his manner was, 1.

εἶ, *see* εἰμί.

εἰ,
(*with indicative* *; *with optative* †; *with subjunctive* ‡).
if, 237*, 3†.
whether, 2†.
that, 5*.
for that, 1*.
forasmuch as, 1*.
though, 1*.
not, 1*.
if, 1*.
no, 1*.
whether? 18*.
if? 2*.
— εἴγε, *or* εἰ γε,
if so be that, 2*.
if, 2*.
— εἴγε καί,
if yet, 1*.
— εἰ δὲ μή,
or else, 3*.
else, 2*.
— εἰ δὲ μήγε,
and if not, 1*.
if not, 2*.
if otherwise, 2*.
otherwise, 1*.
or else, 1*.
else, 2*.
— εἰ καί,
if also, 1*.
now if, 1*.
if that, 1‡.
though, 11*.
— εἰ δὲ καί,
if also, 1*.
but if, 1*.
yea though, 1*.
but though, 1*.
— αλλ' εἰ καί,
but if, 1*.
but and if, 1*.
yea and if, 1*.
but though, 1*
— καὶ εἰ,
although, 1*
— εἰ μή,
if not, 5*.
except, 6*.
except that, 1*.
but, 53*.
save, 16*.
saving, 2*.
save that, 1*.
save only that, 1*.
more than, 1*.
— εἰ μὴ ὅταν,
till, 1*.
— εἰ μή τι,
except, 1‡, 2*.
— ἐκτὸς εἰ μή,
unless, 1*.
except, 1*
but, 1*.
— εἴ περ, *or* εἴπερ,
if so be that, 3*
if so be, 1*.
seeing, 1*.
though, 1*.
— εἴ πως, *or* εἴπως,
if by any means, 3*, 1†.
— εἴ τε (*or* εἴτε)...εἴτε,
whether, 1*.
or, 11*.
whether...or, 21*, 1‡.
whether...or whether, 3*.
whether, 3*.
if, 1*.
— εἴ τις (*neut.* εἴ τι),
if any, 20*.
if some, 1 (*pl.*)
if any man, 33*, 2‡.
if a man, 8*.
if any thing, 5*.
if aught, 2*, 1†.
whether any, 1*.
whosoever, 2*.
he that, 2*.
that which, 1*.

εἰδέα, *see* ἰδέα.

εἶδον *and* οἶδα.
(a) εἶδον, (*for pres. tense, see* ὁράω)
see, 316.
perceive, 5.
behold, 16.
look, 6.
look on, 2.
consider, 1.
know, 1.
(b) οἶδα,
know, 291.
know of, 1.
have knowledge, 1.
wis [*imp.* wist], 6.
wot, 3.
understand, 2.
perceive, 1.
see, 1.
be aware, 1.
be sure, 3.
can tell, 9.
can, 2.

εἶδος,
sight, 1.
appearance, 1.
shape, 2.
fashion, 1.

εἴδω, *see* εἶδον,

εἰδωλεῖον,
idol's temple, 1.

εἰδωλόθυτον,
thing sacrificed unto idols, 2.
offered in sacrifice unto idols, 1.
that which is offered in sacrifice to idols, 1.
thing that is offered in sacrifice unto idols, 1.
thing offered unto an idol, 1.
thing offered to idols, 1.
thing offered unto idols, 1.
thing which is offered to idols, 1.
meat offered to idols, 1.

εἰδωλολατρεία,
idolatry, 4.

εἰδωλολάτρης,
idolator, 7.

εἴδωλον,
idol, 11.

εἴην, *etc., see* εἰμί.

εἰκῆ,
without a cause, 1.
in vain, 5.
vainly, 1.

εἰκόναν,
image, 1.

εἴκοσι,
twenty, 13.

εἴκω,
give place, 1.

εἴκω, ἔοικα,
be like, 2.

εἰκών,
image, 23.

εἰλικρίνεια,
sincerity, 3.

εἰλικρινής,
sincere, 1.
pure, 1.

εἱλίσσω,
roll together, 1.

εἰ μή, *see under* εἰ.

εἰμί,
[*In all the tenses, with pronouns marked* *
PRESENT:
Indicative, εἰμι, (*1st person sing.*)]
I am, or am I, 58, 71*.
it is I, 6*.
have I been? 1.
I was, 1*.
— *with conj.,*
if I be, 1.
though I be, 1.
— εἶ (*2nd pers. sing.*),
thou art, or art thou, 49, 33*.
— *with* εἰ,
if thou be, 5, 4*.
if it be thou, 1*.
whether thou be, 1*.
— ἐστί, ἐστίν (*3rd pers. sing.*),
is, 752.
can, 1.
be, 1 (*imperat.*)
be, 1 (*pl.*)
was, 30.
had been, 1.
are, 4.
were, 1.
is to say, 1.
meaneth, 2.
should mean, 1.
consisteth, 1.
make, 1.
cometh, 1.
belongeth to, 1.
— *with conj.,*
be, 18.
were, 3.
— *with* ὅτι,
to be, 1.
— *with* ἐκ,
belonged unto, 1.
— *with* ἐν,
have, 1.
— *with neut. pl.*
are, 47.
be, 1.
were, 1.
— ὅ ἐστι,
called, 1.
— οὐκ ἐστί,
we can not, 1.
— τοῦτ' ἔστι,
that is, 12.
that is to say, 5.
— *with genitive,*
owneth, 1 (AV. 1611, oweth).
have, 1.
— *with Dative,*
have, 9.
— ἐσμέν (*1st pers. pl. pres. ind.*),
we are (are we), 31, 15*.
are, 1.
we be, 1.
we have our being, 1.
— ἐστέ (*2nd pers. pl. pres. ind.*),
ye are (are ye), 55, 27*.
it is ye, 2.
ye have been, 1.
— *with conjunctive,*
ye be, 4.
— *with Genitive,*
ye belong to, 1.
— *with* γινώσκω (*part.*),
ye know, 1.
— ὅτι ἐστέ,
to be, 1.
— εἰσί, εἰσίν (*3rd pers. pl. pres. ind.*),
are, 135.
be, 14.
were, 8.
— *with* εἰς,
agree in, 1.
— *with Dative,*
have, 2.
— ὦ, ἦς, ᾖ, *etc.* (*pres. subj.*)
be, 23.
may be, 22.
might be, 2.
should be, 6.
were, 1.
am, 1.
is, 5.
are, 1.
should stand, 1.
— εἴην, εἴης, εἴη, *etc.* (*pres. opt.*)
might be, 1.
should be, 3.
wert, 1.
were, 1.
was, 2.
meant, 2.
— ἴσθι (*imp. 2nd pers. sing.*)
be thou, 1.
be, 1.
— ἴσθι ἐν,
give thyself wholly to, 1.
— ἔστω, ἔστωσαν (*imp. 3rd pers. sing. and pl.*)
be, 4.
let be, 10.
be so, 1.
— ἤτω (*imp. 3rd pers. sing.*)
let be, 2.
— εἶναι (*pres. infinit.*)
to be, 33.
be, 12.
to have been, 1.
have been, 1.
that...am (art, is, are, be), 27.
that...was (were), 10.
had been, 1.
that ... may (might, should) be, 6.
to be made, 1.
come, 1.
— τοῦ εἶναι,
that shouldest be, 1.
— *with* διά,
because...is(was, were), 5.
— *with* εἰς,
that ... might (should) be, 7.
so that...are, 1.
so *that...may be,* 1.
— *with* ἐν,
as...was, 2.
when...was, 1.
while...was (were), 2.
— *with* ὥστε,
that...might be, 1.
— ὤν, οὖσα, ὄν (*pres. part.*),
being, 36.
to be, 1.
that...art (is, was, hast been), 4.
who (which, that), am (art, etc.), 43.
who (etc.), was (etc.), 21.
as...was, 1.
for all there were, 1.
forasmuch as...was, 1.
inasmuch as...are, 1.
seeing . are, 1.
seeing that there are, 1.
though...be, 3.
though...was, 1.
though...were, 1.
when...is, 3.
when...was, 12.
whereas...was, 1.
while...is, 1.
while, was (were), 3.
and was come, 1.
— οὔσης ὀψίας,
at evening, 1.
— ὢν ὄντα,
as though they were, 1.
— οὐκ ὄντος αὐτῷ,
when as yet he had no, 1.
— οὖσα ἐν,
having, 1.
which had, 1.
— ὁ ὢν καὶ ὁ ἦν καὶ ὁ ἐρχόμενος,
which is, and which was, and which is to come, Rev. i. 4, 8.
which art, and wast, and art to come, Rev. xi. 17.
— ὁ ἦν καὶ ὁ ὢν καὶ ὁ ἐρχόμενος,
which was, and is, and is to come, Rev. iv. 8.
— ὁ ὢν καὶ ὁ ἦν καὶ ὁ ἐσόμενος,
which art, and wast, and shalt be, Rev. xvi. 5.

IMPERFECT:
— ἦν, ἦς (ἦσθα), ἦν, ἦμεν, ἦτε, ἦσαν,
was (wast, were), 381, 1*.
hast been, 2.
had (hadst) been, 12.
is, 1.
began to be, 1.
held, 1.
— *with* ἄν,
would have been, 1.
should have been, 1.
should be, 1.
— *with* ἀκούω (*part.*),
had heard, 1.
— *with* ἀτενίζω (*part.*),
looked steadfastly, 1.
— *with* βαπτίζω (*part.*),
baptized.
— *with* δέω (*part.*),
had bound, 1.
— *with* διανυκτερεύω (*part.*),
continued all night, 1.
— *with* ἐγγίζω (*part.*),
drew near, 1.
— ἤμην, (*imp. ind. 1st sing.*),
I was, 13, 2*.
— ἂν ἤμην,
I should be, 1.

FUTURE:
— ἔσομαι, ἔσῃ, ἔσται, ἐσόμεθα, ἔσεσθε, ἔσονται,
shall be, 153.
should be, 2.
will be, 9.
be, 4.
shall come to pass, 4.
will come, 1.
— *with* εἰς,
shall be made, 1.
— *with Genitive,*
may have, 1.
— *with Dative,*
shall have, 6.
— ἔσεσθαι (*future infinitive*), *with* μέλλειν,
that there shall be, 1.
that there should be, 1.
that...will be, 1.
— μέλλοντος ἔσεσθαι,
to come, 1.
— ἐσόμενος (*future part.*), *with art.,*
which shalt be, 1.
what would follow, 1.

εἵνεκεν, *see* ἕνεκα.

εἴπερ, *see* εἰ.

εἶπον,
say, 765 (*of these 85 are* ἀποκριθεὶς εἶπε, *and 32* ἀπεκρίθη καὶ εἶπε, *the latter all in John's Gospel*).
say on, 1.
speak, 55.
speak of, 1.
tell, 40.
tell of, 1.
bring word, 1.
answer, 1.
call, 1.
bid, 5.
command, 8.
grant, 1.

ἐκγαμίζω,
give in marriage, 5.

ἐκγαμίσκω,
give in marriage, 2.

ἔκγονα,
nephews, 1.

ἐκδαπανάομαι,
be spent, 1.

ἐκδέχομαι,
wait for, 3.
wait, 1.
expect, 1.
tarry for, 1.
look for, 2.

ἔκδηλος,
manifest, 1.

ἐκδημέω,
be absent, 2.
absent, 1.

ἐκδίδωμι,
let out, 3.
let forth, 1.

ἐκδιηγέομαι,
declare, 2.

ἐκδικέω,
avenge, 5.
revenge, 1.

ἐκδίκησις,
vengeance, 4.
revenge, 1.
punishment, 1.
— with ποιέω,
revenge, 3.

ἔκδικος,
avenger, 1.
revenger, 1.

ἐκδιώκω,
persecute, 2.
chase out, 1.

ἔκδοτος,
being delivered, 1.

ἐκδοχή,
looking for, 1.

ἐκδύω,
take off from, 2.
strip, 2.
— middle,
be unclothed, 1.

ἐκεῖ,
there, 36.
thither, 7.
thitherward, 1.
yonder, 1.
to yonder place, 1.
— κἀκεῖ,
and there, 9.
there also, 1.
thither also, 1.
— ὅπου ἐκεῖ,
where, 2.

ἐκεῖθεν,
thence, 16.
from thence, 9.
from that place, 1.
there, 1.
— κἀκεῖθεν,
and thence, 2.
thence also, 1.
and from thence, 5.
and afterward, 1.

ἐκεῖνος,
that (or those), 137.
he (she, it, they, etc.),
81.
that very, 2.
that way, 1.
that same, 4.
same, 19.
self-same, 1.
the other, 1.
this, 1.
Peter, 1 (John xiii. 6).
— κἀκεῖνος,
and he (etc.), 11.
he (etc.) also, 7.
even he, 1.
they, 1.
them, 1.
and the other, 2.

ἐκεῖσε,
there, 2.

ἐκζητέω,
seek after, 2.
seek diligently, 1.
seek carefully, 1.
inquire diligently, 1.
require, 2.

ἐκθαμβέομαι,
be greatly amazed, 1.
be sore amazed, 1.
be affrighted, 2.

ἔκθαμβος,
greatly wondering, 1.

ἔκθετος, with ποιέω,
cast out, 1.

ἐκκαθαίρω,
purge out, 1.
purge, 1.

ἐκκαίω, ἐκκαίομαι,
burn, 1.

ἐκκακέω,
to faint, 4.
be weary, 2.
faint, 1.

ἐκκεντέω,
pierce, 2.

ἐκκλάω, ἐκκλάζω,
break off, 3.

ἐκκλείω,
exclude, 2.

ἐκκλησία,
assembly, 3.
church, 112.

ἐκκλίνω,
go out of the way, 1.
avoid, 1.
eschew, 1.

ἐκκολυμβάω,
swim out, 1.

ἐκκομίζω,
carry out, 1.

ἐκκόπτω,
cut out, 1.
cut off, 4.
cut down, 2.
hew down, 3.
hinder, 1.

* ἐκκράζω,
[for κράζω, Acts xxiv.
21, see Cry.]

ἐκκρέμαμαι,
be very attentive, 1.
hang on, 1.

ἐκλαλέω,
tell, 1.

ἐκλάμπω,
shine forth, 1.

ἐκλανθάνομαι,
forget, 1.

ἐκλέγω,
choose, 2.
— middle,
choose, 17.
choose out, 1.
make choice, 1.

ἐκλείπω,
fail, 3.

ἐκλεκτός,
chosen, 7.
elect, 16.

ἐκλογή,
election, 6.
chosen, 1.

ἐκλύω, (pass.)
to faint, 4.
— with εἰμί,
to faint, 1.
be tired and his down, 1.

ἐκμάσσω,
wipe, 5.

ἐκμυκτηρίζω,
deride, 2.

ἐκνεύω,
convey one's self away,
1.

ἐκνήφω,
awake, 1.

ἑκούσιος, (neut. with
κατά)
willingly, 1.

ἑκουσίως,
willingly, 1.
wilfully, 1.

ἔκπαλαι,
of old, 1.
of a long time, 1.

ἐκπειράζω,
tempt, 4.

ἐκπέμπω,
send forth, 1.
send away, 1.

* ἐκπερισσῶς,
[for ἐκ περισσοῦ, Mark
xiv. 31, see Vehe-
mently.]

ἐκπετάννυμι,
stretch forth, 1.

* ἐκπηδάω,
[for εἰσπηδάω, Acts
xiv. 14, see Run in.]

ἐκπίπτω,
fall from, 2.
fall off, 2.
fall away, 1.

fall, 4.
be cast, 1.
fail, 1.
take none effect, 1.
— with εἰμί,
fall, 1.

ἐκπλέω,
sail away, 1.
sail thence, 1.
sail, 1.

ἐκπληρόω,
fulfil, 1.

ἐκπλήρωσις,
accomplishment, 1.

ἐκπλήσσω,
astonish, 10.
amaze, 3.

ἐκπνέω,
give up the ghost, 3.

ἐκπορεύομαι,
go out, 6.
go forth, 2.
proceed, 10.
depart, 3.
issue, 1.
come forth, 2.
— with ἀπό,
go out of, 1.
come out of, 1.
— with ἐξ,
go out of, 2.
come out of, 2.
— with ἔσωθεν,
come from within, 1.

ἐκπορνεύω,
give one's self over to
fornication, 1.

ἐκπτύω,
reject, 1.

ἐκριζόω,
root up, 2.
pluck up by the root, 2.

ἔκστασις,
astonishment, 1.
amazement, 1.
trance, 3.
— with ἔχω,
be amazed, 1.
— with λαμβάνω,
be amazed, 1.

ἐκστρέφω,
subvert, 1.

ἐκταράσσω,
trouble exceedingly, 1.

ἐκτείνω,
stretch out, 2.
stretch forth, 10.
put forth, 3.
cast out, 1.

ἐκτελέω,
finish, 2.

ἐκτένεια, with ἐν,
instantly, 1.

ἐκτενέστερον,
more earnestly, 1

ἐκτενής,
fervent, 1.
without ceasing, 1.
instant and earnest, 1.

ἐνισχύω,
be strengthened, 1.
strengthen, 1.

ἐνκακέω, *see* **ἐγκακέω.**

ἔννατος, *or* **ἔνατος,**
ninth, 10.

ἐννέα,
nine, 1.

ἐννενηκονταεννέα,
ninety and nine, 4.

ἐννεός,
speechless, 1.

ἐννεύω,
make signs to, 1.

ἔννοια,
intent, 1.
mind, 1.

ἔννομος,
lawful, 1.
ordinary, 1.
under the law, 1.

ἔννυχον,
great while before day, 1.

ἐνοικέω,
dwell in, 5.

ἐνόντα, *see* **ἔνειμι.**

ἐνότης,
unity, 2.

* **ἐνορκίζω,**
[*for* ὁρκίζω, 1 Thes. v. 27, *see* Charge.]

ἐνοχλέω,
to trouble, 1

ἔνοχος,
subject to, 1.
in danger of, 5.
guilty of, 4.

ἔνταλμα,
commandment, 3.

ἐνταφιάζω,
bury, 1.
— *infinitive*,
burial, 1.

ἐνταφιασμός,
burying, 2.

ἐντέλλομαι,
to command, 10.
give commandment, 3.
charge, 1.
give charge, 2.
enjoin, 1.

ἐντεῦθεν,
hence, 6.
from hence, 3.
— ἐντεῦθεν καὶ ἐντεῦθεν,
on either side, 1.
of either side, 1 (on either side, *ed.* 1762, *etc.*)

ἔντευξις,
intercession, 1.
prayer, 1.

ἔντιμος,
honourable, 1.
dear, 1.
precious, 2.
— *with* ἔχω,
hold in reputation, 1.
honour, 1.

ἐντολή,
commandment, 69.
precept, 2.

ἐντόπιος,
of that place, 1.

ἐντός,
within, 2.
among, 1.

ἐντρέπω,
to shame, 1.
— *passive*,
be ashamed, 2.
— *middle*,
regard, 2.
reverence, 4.

ἐντρέφομαι,
be nourished up in, 1.

ἔντρομος,
trembling, 1.
— *with* γίνομαι,
tremble, 1.
— *with* εἰμί,
quake, 1.

ἐντροπή,
shame, 2.

ἐντρυφάω,
to sport one's self, 1.

ἐντυγχάνω,
deal with, 1.
make intercession, 4.

ἐντυλίττω,
wrap in, 2.
wrap together, 1.

ἐντυπόω,
engrave, 1.

ἐνυβρίζω,
do despite unto, 1.

ἐνυπνιάζομαι,
to dream, 1.
filthy dreamer, 1.

ἐνύπνιον,
dream, 1.

ἐνώπιον,
in the presence of, 7.
in one's presence, 2.
in the sight of, 16.
in one's sight, 5.
before, 63.
to, 1.

ἐνωτίζομαι,
hearken to, 1.

ἐξ, *see* **ἐκ.**

ἕξ,
six, 12.

ἐξαγγέλλω,
shew forth, 1.

ἐξαγοράζω,
redeem, 4.

ἐξάγω,
lead out, 6.
bring out, 5.
bring forth, 1.
fetch out, 1.

ἐξαιρέω,
pluck out, 2.
— *middle*,
rescue, 1.
deliver, 5.

ἐξαίρω,
take away, 1.
put away, 1.

ἐξαιτέομαι,
to desire, 1.

ἐξαίφνης,
suddenly, 5.

ἐξακολουθέω,
follow, 3.

ἐξακόσιοι,
six hundred, 2.

ἐξαλείφω,
blot out, 3.
wipe away, 2.

ἐξάλλομαι,
leap up, 1.

ἐξανάστασις,
resurrection, 1.

ἐξανατέλλω,
spring up, 2.

ἐξανίστημι,
raise up, 2.
rise up, 1.

ἐξαπατάω,
deceive, 4.
beguile, 1.

ἐξάπινα,
suddenly, 1.

ἐξαπορέομαι,
in despair, 1.
altogether without help of means, 1.
to despair, 1.

ἐξαποστέλλω,
send out, 1.
send forth, 4.
send away, 4.
send, 2.

ἐξαρτίζω,
furnish throughly, 1.
perfect, 1.
— *with* γίνομαι,
accomplish, 1.

ἐξαστράπτω,
to glister, 1.

ἐξαυτῆς,
immediately, 3.
straightway, 1.
presently, 1.
by and by, 1.

ἐξεγείρω,
raise up, 2.

ἔξειμι,
go out, 1.
depart, 2.
get, 1.

ἐξελέγχω,
convince, 1.

ἐξέλκομαι,
be drawn away, 1.

ἐξέλω, *see* **ἐξαιρέω.**

ἐξέραμα,
vomit, 1.

ἐξερευνάω,
search diligently, 1.

ἐξέρχομαι,
go out, 64.
go forth, 25.
go abroad, 2.
go away, 1.
go, 7.
proceed, 2.
proceed forth, 1.
spread abroad, 2.
depart, 27.
depart out of, 2.
get out, 1.
escape, 1.
come out, 21.
come thereout, 1.
come out of, 1.
come forth, 9.
come, 4.
— *with* ἀπό,
go out of, 9.
depart out of, 1.
come out of, 8.
— *with* ἐκ,
go out of, 6.
get out of, 2.
come out of, 21.
— *with* ἔξω,
go out of, 2.
come forth, 1.
— *with* παρά,
go out of, 1.

ἔξεστι,
it is lawful, 19.
it is possible, 1.
is (are) lawful, 9.
may, 2.
— *part.* ἐξόν,
lawful, 1.
let, 1.
may, 1.

ἐξετάζω,
to search, 1.
ask, 1.
inquire, 1.

ἐξηγέομαι,
declare, 5.
tell, 1.

ἑξήκοντα,
sixty, 3.
sixty-fold, 1.
three-score, 5.

ἑξῆς,
next, 1.
— *with* τῇ,
the next day, 1.
the day following, 1.
the day after, 1.
on the morrow, 1.

ἐξηχέομαι,
sound out, 1.

ἕξις,
use, 1.
habit or perfection, 1.

ἐξίστημι,
make astonished, 1.
bewitch, 2.
— *2nd aor. and mid.*,
be beside one's self, 2.
wonder, 1.
be astonished, 5.
be amazed, 6.

ἐξισχύω,
be able, 1.

ἔξοδος,
departing, 1.
decease, 2.

ἐξολοθρεύω,
destroy, 1.

ἐξομολογέω,
to promise, 1.
— *middle*,
confess, 8.
thank, 2.

ἐξόν, *see* ἔξεστι.

ἐξορκίζω,
adjure, 1.

ἐξορκιστής,
exorcist, 1.

ἐξορύσσω,
pluck out, 1.
break up, 1.

* ἐξουδενέω,
[*for* ἐξουδενόω, Mark ix. 12, *see* Naught.
for ἐξουθενέω, 2 Cor. x. 10, *see* Contemptible.]

ἐξουδενόω,
set at nought, 1.

ἐξουθενέω,
set at nought, 3.
despise, 6.
— *passive*,
be least esteemed, 1.
contemptible, 1.

ἐξουσία,
authority, 29.
power, 69.
right or privilege, 1.
strength, 1.
liberty, 1.
power, 1.
right, 2.
jurisdiction, 1.

ἐξουσιάζω,
exercise authority upon, 1.
have power of, 2.
bring under power, 1.

ἐξοχή,
— κατ' ἐξοχὴν ὤν,
principle, 1 (Acts xxv. 23).

ἐξυπνίζω,
awake out of sleep, 1.

ἔξυπνος, *with* γίνομαι,
awake out of sleep, 1.

ἔξω,
without, 18.
out, 16.
outward, 1.
strange, 1.
out of, 15.
forth, 8.
away, 1.
— *with art.*,
one that is without, 5.

ἔξωθεν,
from without, 2.
without, 1.
outward, 2.
outwardly, 1.
— *with art.*,
one that (which) is without, 3.
the outside, 2.

ἐξωθέω,
drive out, 1.
thrust in, 1.

ἐξώτερος,
outer, 3.

ἑορτάζω,
keep the feast, 1.
holiday, 1

ἑορτή,
feast, 24.
feast-day, 2.
holyday, 1.

ἐπαγγελία,
message, 1.
promise, 52.

ἐπαγγέλλομαι,
— *mid. and pass. perf.*,
to promise, 11.
make promise, 1.
profess, 2.
— *pass. impers.*,
promise is made, 1.

ἐπάγγελμα,
promise, 2.

ἐπάγω,
bring upon, 2.
bring in upon, 1.

ἐπαγωνίζομαι,
earnestly contend for, 1.

ἐπαθροίζομαι,
be gathered thick together, 1.

ἐπαινέω,
to praise, 4.
laud, 1.
commend, 1.

ἔπαινος,
praise, 11.

ἐπαίρω,
take up, 1.
lift up, 15.
hoise up, 1.
— *middle*,
exalt one's self, 2.

ἐπαισχύνομαι,
be ashamed of, 8.
be ashamed, 3.

ἐπαιτέω,
beg, 1.

ἐπακολουθέω,
follow after, 1.
follow, 3.

ἐπακούω,
hear, 1.

ἐπακροάομαι,
hear, 1.

ἐπάν,
when, 3.

ἐπάναγκες,
necessary, 1.

ἐπανάγω,
to return, 1.
thrust out, 1.
launch out, 1.

ἐπαναμιμνήσκω,
put in mind, 1.

ἐπαναπαύομαι,
rest in, 1.
— *with* ἐπί,
rest upon, 1.

ἐπανέρχομαι,
come again, 1.
return, 1.

ἐπανίσταμαι,
rise up against, 2.

ἐπανόρθωσις,
correction, 1.

ἐπάνω,
above, 3.
more than, 1.
over, 6.
upon, 3.
on, 4.
— ἐπ' αὐτοῦ,
thereon, 3.

* ἐπάρατος,
[*for* ἐπικατάρατος, John vii. 49, *see* Cursed.]

ἐπαρκέω,
relieve, 3.

ἐπαρχία,
province, 2.

ἔπαυλις,
habitation, 1.

ἐπαύριον, *with art.*
on the morrow, 7.
the morrow after, 1.
on the next day, 1.
the next day, 5.
the next day after, 1.
the day following, 2.

ἐπαυτοφώρω,
in the very act, 1.

ἐπαφρίζω,
foam out, 1.

ἐπεγείρω,
stir up, 1.
raise, 1.

ἐπεί,
since, 1.
seeing, 3.
seeing that, 1.
for then, 4.
when, 1.
for that, 1.
forasmuch as, 2.
because, 7.
otherwise, 4.
else, 3.

ἐπειδή,
since, 1.
seeing, 2.
after that, 1.
for that, 1.
forasmuch as, 1.
for, 3.
because, 2.

ἐπειδήπερ,
forasmuch as, 1.

ἐπεῖδον,
look on, 1.
— *with* ἐπί,
behold, 1.

ἔπειμι, (*part.*, ἐπιών, ἐπιοῦσα)
following, 1.
next, 1.
— *with art.* (τῇ),
the day following, 1.
the next day, 1.

ἐπείπερ,
seeing, 1.

ἐπεισαγωγή,
bringing in, 1.

* ἐπεισέρχομαι,
[*for* ἐπέρχομαι, Luke xxi. 35, *see* Come on.]

ἔπειτα,
afterward, 2.
afterwards, 1.
after that, 4.
then, 9.

ἐπέκεινα,
beyond, 1.

ἐπεκτείνομαι,
reach forth unto, 1.

ἐπενδύομαι,
be clothed upon, 2.

ἐπενδύτης,
fisher's coat, 1.

ἐπέρχομαι,
come upon, 6.
come on, 1.
come thither, 1.
come, 1.
— *with art.*,
those things which are coming on, 1.

ἐπερωτάω,
ask of, 2.
ask, 47.
ask a question, 3.
ask questions, 2.
question with, 1.
ask after, 1.
desire, 1.
demand of, 1.
demand, 1.

ἐπερώτημα,
answer, 1.

ἐπέχω,
hold forth, 1.
take heed unto, 1.
give heed unto, 1.
mark, 1.
stay, 1.

ἐπηρεάζω,
use despitefully,
accuse falsely, 1.

ἐπί,
— *with the Genitive,*
upon, 37.
on, 71.
over, 11.
above, 1.
before, 14.
under, 1.
about, 2.
at, 6.
in, 50.
upon, 1.
in the time of, 1.
in the days of, 2.
to, 2.
into, 2.
of, 8.
— ἐφ' οὗ,
whereon, 1.
— *with* εἰμί,
have the charge of, 1.
— ἐπὶ τοῦ ἀμφόδου,
in a place where two ways meet, 1.
— ἐπὶ ἀρχιερέως Ἄννα καὶ Καϊάφα,
Annas and Caiaphas being the high priests, 1.
— *with the Dative,*
upon, 16.
on, 10.
over, 11.
above, 3.
beside, 3.
at, 29.
unto, 4.
to, 1.
toward, 1.
against, 6.
before, 1.
in, 52.
for, 1.
by, 8.
with, 6.
through, 2.
under, 3.
after, 2.
about, 1.
as touching, 1.
for, 19.
on one's behalf, 1.
of, 9.
— ἐπ' αὐτῷ,
thereon, 1.
— ἐφ' ᾧ (ᾗ, οἷς),
whereon, 1.
wherein, 3.
wherefore, 1.
for that, 1.
in whom, 1.
whereof, 1.
— ἐπὶ τούτοις,
therewith, 1.
— *with the Accusative,*
upon, 105.
on, 114.
to, 1.
over, 27.
above, 1.
unto, 41.
to, 38.
toward, 6.
after, 1.
against, 33.
upon, 1.
at, 9.
into, 13.
in, 13.
among, 4.
before, 3.
about, 1.
with, 2.
touching, 1.
of, 3.
because of, 1.
for, 9.
throughout, 2.
for the space of, 1.
by the space of, 1.
the space of, 1.
— ἐπ' αὐτό,
thereon, 1.
— ἐφ' ὅν,
whereon, 2.
— ἐπί τὸ αὐτό,
into one place, 2.

ἐπιβαίνω,
come into, 2.
enter into, 1.
go aboard, 1.
take ship, 1.
— *perf., with* εἰμί,
sit upon, 1.

ἐπιβάλλω,
cast upon, 1.
cast, 1.
lay on, 1.
stretch forth, 1.
begin, 1 (*marg. with* χείρ).
fall to, 1.
think thereon, 1.
— *with* ἐπί,
put upon, 1.
put unto, 1.
put to, 1.
lay on, 8.
— *with* εἰς,
beat into, 1.

ἐπιβαρέω,
be chargeable unto, 1.
be chargeable to, 1.
overcharge, 1.

ἐπιβιβάζω,
set on, 3.

ἐπιβλέπω, *with* ἐπί,
look upon, 1.
have respect to, 1.
regard, 1.

ἐπίβλημα,
piece, 4.

ἐπιβοάω,
to cry, 1.

ἐπιβουλή,
laying await, 1.
lying in wait, 1.
— *with* γίνομαι,
lay wait for, 1.
— *with* μέλλειν ἔσεσθαι,
lay wait, 1.

ἐπιγαμβρεύω,
marry, 1.

ἐπίγειος,
in earth, 1.
earthy, 2.
terrestrial, 2.
— *plural, with art.*,
earthly things, 2.

ἐπιγίνομαι,
to blow, 1.

ἐπιγινώσκω,
know well, 1.
know, 30.
perceive, 3.
take knowledge of, 2.
have knowledge of, 1.
acknowledge, 5.

ἐπίγνωσις,
knowledge, 16.
acknowledge, 1.
acknowledgment, 1.
acknowledging, 3.
acknowledgment, 1.

ἐπιγραφή,
superscription, 5.
inscription, 1.

ἐπιγράφω,
write thereon, 1.
write over, 1.
write in, 2.
— ἐν ᾧ ἐπεγέγραπτο,
with this inscription, 1.

ἐπιδείκνυμι,
to show, 8.
— *middle,*
show, 1.

ἐπιδέχομαι,
receive, 2.

ἐπιδημέω,
be there, 1.
stranger, 1.

ἐπιδιατάσσομαι,
add thereto, 1.

ἐπιδίδωμι,
deliver, 2.
give, 7.
offer, 1.
— *part., with* φέρω (*pass.*),
let drive, 1.

ἐπιδιορθόω, (*mid.*)
set in order, 1.

ἐπιδύω, *with* ἐπί,
go down upon, 1.

ἐπιείκεια,
gentleness, 1.
clemency, 1.

ἐπιεικής,
gentle, 3.
patient, 1.
— *with art.*,
moderation, 1.

ἐπιζητέω,
seek after, 5.
seek for, 2.
seek, 3.
desire, 3.
inquire, 1.

ἐπιθανάτιος,
appointed (approved, *ed.* 1611, *in error*) to death, 1.

ἐπίθεσις,
putting on, 1.
laying on, 3.

ἐπιθυμέω,
to desire, 8,
would fain, 1.
covet, 3.
lust after, 1.
lust, 3.

ἐπιθυμητής, *with* εἰμί,
lust after, 1.

ἐπιθυμία,
desire, 3.
heartily, 1 (*Dat.*)
lust, 31.
concupiscence, 1.
that...lusteth after, 1.
concupiscence, 3.

ἐπικαθίζω, *with* ἐπάνω,
set on, 1.

ἐπικαλέω,
— *middle,*
call upon, 4.
call on, 7.
call, 1.
appeal unto, 4.
appeal to, 1.
appeal, 1.
— *passive,*
be called upon, 1.
be called by, 1.
be called, 1.
be surnamed, 5.
be one's surname, 6.

ἐπικάλυμμα,
cloak, 1.

ἐπικαλύπτω,
to cover, 1.

ἐπικατάρατος,
cursed, 2.

ἐπίκειμαι,
lie upon, 1.
lie on, 1.
be laid upon, 1.
be laid thereon, 1.
be imposed on, 1.
press upon, 1.
be instant, 1.

*** ἐπικέλλω,**
[*for* ἐποκέλλω, Acts xxvii. 41, *see* Run aground].

ἐπικουρία,
help, 1.

ἐπικρίνω,
give sentence, 1.
assent, 1.

ἐπιλαμβάνομαι,
take hold of, 2.
take on, 2.
take hold of, 2.
take by, 3.
take, 7.
lay hold upon, 1.
lay hold on, 2.
catch, 2.

ἐπιλανθάνομαι,
forget, 7.
be forgetful, 1.

ἐπιλέγω,
to call, 1.
choose, 1 (*mid.*)

ἐπιλείπω,
fail, 1.

*** ἐπιλείχω,**
[*for* ἀπολείχω, Luke xvi. 21, *see* Lick.]

ἐπιλησμονή,
forgetful, 1.

ἐπίλοιπος,
rest of, 1.

ἐπίλυσις,
interpretation, 1.

ἐπιλύω,
expound, 1.
determine, 1.

ἐπιμαρτυρέω,
testify, 1.

ἐπιμέλεια, *with* τυγχάνω,
refresh one's self, 1.

ἐπιμελέομαι,
take care of, 3.

ἐπιμελῶς,
diligently, 1.

ἐπιμένω,
abide in, 1.
abide still in, 1.
abide still, 1.
abide, 1.
tarry, 7.
continue in, 5.
continue, 2.

ἐπινεύω,
to consent, 1.

ἐπίνοια,
thought. 1.

ἐπιορκέω,
forswear one's self, 1.

ἐπίορκος,
perjured person, 1.

ἐπιοῦσα, *see* ἔπειμι.

ἐπιούσιος,
daily, 2.

ἐπιπίπτω,
fall on, 1.
press upon, 1.
rush upon, 1.
— *with* ἐπί,
fall upon, 2.
fall on, 7.
fall into, 1.
lie on, 1.

ἐπιπλήσσω,
to rebuke, 1.

ἐπιποθέω,
desire earnestly, 1.
desire greatly, 2.
desire, 1.
long after, 2.
long after greatly, 1.
long, 1.
lust, 1.

ἐπιπόθησις,
earnest desire, 1.
vehement desire, 1.

ἐπιπόθητος,
longed for, 1.

ἐπιποθία,
great desire, 1.

ἐπιπορεύομαι, *with* πρός,
come to, 1.

ἐπιρράπτω, *with* ἐπί,
sew on, 1.

ἐπιρρίπτω, *with* ἐπί,
cast upon, 2.

ἐπίσημος,
of note, 1.
notable, 1.

ἐπισιτισμός,
victuals, 1.

ἐπισκέπτομαι,
look out, 1.
visit, 10.

*** ἐπισκευάζομαι,**
[*for* ἀποσκευάζομαι, Acts xxi. 15, *see* Carriage (take up one's).]

ἐπισκηνόω, *with* ἐπί,
rest upon, 1.

ἐπισκιάζω,
overshadow, 5.

ἐπισκοπέω,
take the oversight, 1.
look diligently, 1.

ἐπισκοπή,
visitation, 2.
office of bishop, 1.
bishopric, 1.
office or charge, 1.

ἐπίσκοπος,
overseer, 1.
bishop, 4.

ἐπισπάομαι,
become uncircumcised, 1.

*** ἐπισπείρω,**
[*for* σπείρω, Matt. xiii. 25, *see* Sow.]

ἐπίσταμαι,
understand, 1.
know, 13.

*** ἐπίστασις,**
[*for* ἐπισύστασις, Acts xxiv. 12, *see* People (raise up the); *and* 2 Cor. xi. 28, *see* Cometh upon (that which).]

ἐπιστάτης,
Master, 7.

ἐπιστέλλω,
write a letter unto, 1.
write unto, 1.
write, 1.

ἐπιστήμων,
endued with knowledge, 1.

ἐπιστηρίζω,
confirm, 3.
strengthen, 1.

ἐπιστολή,
epistle, 15.
letter, 9.

ἐπιστομίζω,
stop the mouth of, 1.

ἐπιστρέφω,
turn again, 4.
turn back, 1.
return, 4.
turn, 4.
convert, 2.
be converted, 5.
come again, 1.
go again, 1.
— *with* ἐπί,
turn unto, 2.
turn to, 5.
— *with* εἰς,
turn to, 1.
— *with* πρός,
turn to, 3.
— *mid. and pass. aor.*,
turn about, 4.
return, 2.
be converted, 1.

ἐπιστροφή,
conversion, 1.

ἐπισυνάγω,
gather together, 6.
gather, 1.

ἐπισυναγωγή,
gathering together, 1.
assembling together, 1.

ἐπισυντρέχω,
come running together, 1.

ἐπισύστασις,
that which cometh upon, 1.
— ἐπισύστασις ποιέω ὄχλον,
raise up the people, 1.

ἐπισφαλής,
dangerous, 1.

ἐπισχύω,
be the more fierce, 1.

ἐπισωρεύω,
to heap, 1.

ἐπιταγή,
commandment, 6.
authority, 1.

ἐπιτάσσω,
enjoin, 1.
charge, 1.
command, 8.

ἐπιτελέω,
finish, 1.
accomplish, 2.
perfect, 1.
make perfect, 1.
perform, 3.
finish, 1.
do, 1.
make, 1.
— *infinitive*,
performance, 1.

ἐπιτήδειος,
— *pl., with art.*,
those things which are needful to, 1.

ἐπιτίθημι,
put upon, 2.
put on, 3.
set on, 1.
set up, 1.
lay upon, 4.
lay on, 12.
— *with* ἐπί,
put upon, 4.
put on, 1.
set on, 2.
lay upon, 2.
lay on, 4.
add unto, 2.
— *with* ἐπάνω,
put on, 1.
— *with* ὄνομα,
surname, 2.
— *with* πληγή,
wound, 1.
— *middle*,
lade with, 1.

ἐπιτιμάω,
to rebuke, 24.
charge straitly, 1.
charge, 4.

ἐπιτιμία,
punishment, 1.
censure, 1.

ἐπιτοαυτό, *see* ἐπὶ τὸ αὐτό.

ἐπιτρέπω,
permit, 4.
give leave, 2.
give liberty, 1.
give license, 1.
let, 1.
suffer, 10.

ἐπιτροπή,
commission, 1.

ἐπίτροπος,
steward, 2.
tutor, 1.

ἐπιτυγχάνω,
obtain, 5.

ἐπιφαίνω,
give light to, 1.
appear, 1.
— *passive*,
appear, 2.

ἐπιφάνεια,
appearing, 5.
brightness, 1.

ἐπιφανής,
notable, 1.

ἐπιφαύω, -αύσκω,
give light, 1.

ἐπιφέρω,
bring against, 1.
bring, 2.
add, 1.
take, 1.

ἐπιφωνέω,
cry against, 1.
cry, 1.
give a shout, 1.

ἐπιφώσκω,
begin to dawn, 1.
draw on, 1.

ἐπιχειρέω,
take in hand, 1.
take upon, 1.
go about, 1.

ἐπιχέω,
pour in, 1.

ἐπιχορηγέω,
minister unto, 1.
minister to, 2.
add, 1.
— *passive*,
have nourishment ministered, 1.

ἐπιχορηγία,
supply, 1.
to supply, 1.

ἐπιχρίω, *with* ἐπί,
anoint, 1.
spread upon, 1.

ἐποικοδομέω,
build thereupon, 2.
build thereon, 1.
build up on, 1.
build up, 1.
— *with* ἐπί,
build upon, 2.

ἐποκέλλω,
run aground, 1.

ἐπονομάζω,
to call, 1.

ἐποπτεύω,
behold, 2.

ἐπόπτης,
eye-witness, 1.

ἔπος,
— ὡς ἔπος εἰπεῖν,
as I may so say, 1.

ἐπουράνιος,
in heaven, 1.
heavenly, 9.
celestial, 2.
— *pl. masc., with art.,*
they that are heavenly, 1.
— *pl. neut., with art.,*
heavenly things, 3.
heavenly places, 3.
heavenly things, 1.
high places, 1,
heavenly places, 1.

ἑπτά,
seven, 86.
seventh, 1.

ἑπτάκις,
seven times, 4.

ἑπτακισχίλιοι,
seven thousand, 1.

ἔπω, *see* εἶπον.

ἐραυνάω, *see* ἐρευνάω.

ἐργάζομαι,
to work, 28.
gain, 1.
labour, 1.
labour for, 1.
do, 3.
commit, 1.
trade by, 1.
trade, 1.
minister about, 1.
— *with* μή,
forbear working, 1.

ἐργασία,
diligence, 1.
craft, 1.
gain, 2.
gains, 1.
— *with* εἰς,
to work, 1.

ἐργάτης,
worker, 3.
workman, 3.
labourer, 9.

ἔργον,
work, 152.
trade, 1,
deed, 22.
doing, 1.
labour, 1.

ἐρεθίζω,
provoke, 1.
provoke to anger, 1.

ἐρείδω,
stick fast, 1.

ἐρεύγομαι,
utter, 1.

ἐρευνάω,
to search, 6.

ἐρέω, *see* ἐρῶ.

ἐρημία,
desert, 1.
wilderness, 3.

ἔρημος, (*adj.*)
desert, 10.
desolate, 4.
solitary, 1.

ἔρημος, (*subst.*)
desert, 3.
wilderness, 32.

ἐρημόω,
bring to desolation, 2.
make desolate, 1.
desolate, 1.
— *passive*,
come to naught, 1.

ἐρήμωσις,
desolation, 3.

ἐρίζω,
strive, 1.

ἐριθεία,
strife, 5.
contention, 1.
— οἱ ἐξ ἐριθείας,
they that are contentious, 1.

ἔριον,
wool, 2.

ἔρις,
strife, 4.
contention, 2.
debate, 2.
variance, 1.

ἐρίφων,
goat, 1.

ἔριφος,
kid, 1.
goat, 1.

ἑρμηνεία,
interpretation, 2.

*** ἑρμηνευτής,**
[*for* διερμηνευτής, 1 Cor. xiv. 28, *see* Interpreter.]

ἑρμηνεύω,
interpret, 1.
— *passive*,
be by interpretation, 3.

ἑρπετόν,
creeping thing, 3.
serpent, 1.

ἐρυθρός, *with* θάλασσα,
Red sea, 2.

ἔρχομαι,
come, 582.
be coming, 7.
coming, 6.
light, 1.
be brought, 1.
go, 13.
resort, 2.
pass by, 1.
fall out, 1.
grow, 1.
appear, 1.
next, 1.
— ὁ ἐρχόμενος (*said of Christ*).
that cometh, 2.
he that cometh, 6.
who coming, 1.
he that shall come, 1.
that should come, 1.
which should come, 1.
he that should come, 3.
he which should come, 1.
which is to come, 3.
which art to come, 1.
— ὁ ἐλθών,
he that came, 1.
— *with* εἰς,
enter into, 2.
— *with* σύν,
accompany, 1.

ἐρῶ, εἴρηκα,
say, 57.
speak, 7.
speak of, 2.
tell, 4.
call, 1.

ἐρωτάω,
ask, 23.
desire, 6.
pray, 14.
beseech, 14.
entreat, 1.

ἔσεσθαι, *see* εἰμί.

ἐσθής,
robe, 1.
raiment, 1.
clothing, 2.
apparel, 3.

ἔσθησις,
garment, 1.

ἐσθίω,
eat, 61.
be eating, 1.
live, 1.
feed of, 1.
devour, 1.

ἐσμέν, ἔσομαι, ἐσόμενος, } *see* εἰμί.

ἔσοπτρον,
glass, 2.

ἑσπέρα,
evening, 2.
eventide, 1.

ἐστέ, ἐστί, ἔστω, } *see* εἰμί.

ἔσχατος,
last, 46.
uttermost, 1.
uttermost part, 1.
ends, 1.
lowest, 2.
— τὰ ἔσχατα,
the last state, 2.
the latter end, 1.

ἐσχάτως, *with* ἔχω,
lie at the point of death, 1.

ἔσω,
into, 2.
in, 1.
within, 3.
inward, 1.
inner, 1.

ἔσωθεν,
from within, 3.
within, 6.
inwardly, 1.
— *with art.*,
the inward man, 1.
that which is within, 1.
inward part, 1.

ἐσώτερος,
inner, 1.
— *with art.*,
that within, 1.

ἑταῖρος,
fellow, 1.
friend, 3.

ἑτερόγλωσσος,
of another tongue, 1.

ἑτεροδιδασκαλέω,
teach otherwise, 1.
teach another doctrine, 1.

ἑτεροζυγέω, *with* γίνομαι,
be unequally yoked together with, 1.

ἕτερος,
other, 41.
other thing, 3.
other matter, 1.
strange, 1.
other, 1.
else, 1.
another, 42.
another place, 1.
another psalm, 1.
next day, 2.
— ἕτερος...ἕτερος,
some...other, 3.
one...another, 1.
— *with* γίνομαι,
be altered, 1.

ἑτέρως,
otherwise, 1.

ἔτι,
yet, 51.
still, 4.
longer, 1.
any longer, 1.
more, 17.
yet more, 2.
any more, 5.
moreover, 2.
further, 3.
any further, 3.
thenceforth, 1.
also, 1.
even, 1.

ἑτοιμάζω,
make ready, 10.
prepare, 29.
provide, 1.

ἑτοιμασία,
preparation, 1.

ἕτοιμασια,
ready, 14.
readiness, 1.
prepared, 1.
— τὰ ἕτοιμα,
things made ready to our hand, 1.

ἑτοίμως, *with* ἔχω,
be ready, 3.

ἔτος,
year, 49.

εὖ,
well, 3.
well done, 2.
good, 1.

εὐαγγελίζω,
— *active*,
declare to, 1.
preach unto, 1.
— *middle*,
bring good tidings of, 2.
bring glad tidings of, 1.
declare glad tidings unto, 1.
show glad tidings, 1.
show the glad tidings of, 1.
preach the gospel, 11.
preach...gospel, 2.
preach the gospel of, 1.
preach the gospel to, 2.
preach the gospel unto, 2.
preach the gospel in, 1.
preach, 17.
preach unto, 2.
— *passive*,
be preached by the gospel, 1.
the gospel is preached, 1.
have the gospel preached to one's self, 1.
the gospel is preached to, 1.
it is preached to, 1.
the gospel is preached unto, 1.
be preached, 2.

εὐαγγέλιον,
gospel, 76.

εὐαγγελιστής,
evangelist, 3.

εὐαρεστέω,
please, 2.
— *passive*,
be well pleased with, 1.

εὐάρεστος.
well-pleasing, 2.
acceptable, 4.
— *with art.*,
that which is well-pleasing, 1.
— *with* εἰμί,
please well, 1.
be accepted of, 1.

εὐαρέστως,
acceptably, 1.

* εὖγε,
[*for* εὖ, Luke xix. 17, *see* Well.]

εὐγενής,
noble, 2.
— *with* ἄνθρωπος,
nobleman, 1.

εὐδία,
fair weather, 1.

εὐδοκέω,
be well pleased, 7.
have pleasure, 4.
take pleasure, 1.
it pleaseth, 5.
be one's good pleasure, 1.
think good, 1.
be willing, 2.

εὐδοκία,
good-will, 2.
good pleasure, 4.
desire, 1.
— *with* γίνομαι,
seem good, 2.

εὐεργεσία,
good deed done to, benefit, 1.

εὐεργετέω,
do good, 1.

εὐεργέτης,
benefactor, 1.

εὔθετος,
fit, 2.
meet, 1.

εὐθέως,
straightway, 32.
immediately, 35.
forthwith, 7.
as soon as, 2.
anon, 1.
by and by, 2.
shortly, 1.

εὐθυδρομέω,
come with a straight course, 1.
with a straight course, 1.

εὐθυμέω,
be of good cheer, 2.
be merry, 1.

εὔθυμος,
of good cheer, 1.

εὐθυμότερον,
more cheerfully, 1.

* εὐθύμως,
[*for* εὐθυμότερον, Acts xxiv. 10, *see* Cheerfully (more).]

εὐθύνω,
make straight, 1.
governor, 1.

εὐθύς, (*adj.*)
straight, 5.
right, 3.

εὐθύς, (*adv.*)
straightway, 2.
immediately, 3.
forthwith, 1.
anon, 1.
by and by, 1.

εὐθύτης,
righteousness, 1.
rightness or straightness, 1.

εὐκαιρέω,
have convenient time, 1.
have leisure, 1.
spend one's time, 1,

εὐκαιρία,
opportunity, 2.

εὔκαιρος,
in time of need, 1.
convenient, 1.

εὐκαίρως,
in season, 1.
conveniently, 1.

εὐκοπώτερος,
easier, 7.

εὐλάβεια,
godly fear, 1.
— *with* ἀπό,
in that he feareth, 1.
for one's piety, 1.

εὐλαβέομαι,
be moved with fear, 1.
be wary, 1.
fear. 1.

εὐλαβής,
devout, 3.

εὐλογέω,
bless, 43.
praise, 1.

εὐλογητός,
blessed, 8,

εὐλογία,
fair speeches, 1.
blessing, 11.
bounty, 1.
blessing, 1.
matter of bounty, 1.
— *pl., with* ἐπί,
bountifully, 2.

εὐμετάδοτος,
ready to distribute, 1.

εὐνοέω,
agree, 1.

εὔνοια,
good will, 1.
benevolence, 1.

εὐνουχίζω,
make eunuch, 2.

εὐνοῦχος,
eunuch, 8.

εὐοδόομαι,
have a prosperous journey, 1.
prosper, 3.

* εὐπάρεδρος,
[*for* εὐπρόσεδρος, 1 Cor. vii. 35, *see* Attend.]

εὐπειθής,
easy to be entreated, 1.

εὐπερίστατος,
which doth so easily beset us, 1.

εὐποιΐα,
to do good, 1.

εὐπορέομαι, *with* καθώς,
according to one's ability, 1.

εὐπορία,
wealth, 1.

εὐπρέπεια,
grace, 1.

εὐπρόσδεκτος,
acceptable, 2.
accepted, 3.

εὐπρόσεδρος,
that one may attend upon, 1.

εὐπροσωπέω,
make a fair show, 1.

εὑρίσκω,
find, 174.
can find, 1.
obtain, 1.
get, 1.

εὐρύχωρος,
broad, 1.

εὐσέβεια,
godliness, 14.
holiness, 1.

εὐσεβέω,
show piety at, 1.
show kindness at, 1.
worship, 1.

εὐσεβής,
devout, 3.
godly, 1.

εὐσεβῶς,
godly, 2.

εὔσημος,
easy to be understood, 1.
significant, 1.

εὔσπλαγχνος,
tender-hearted, 1.
pitiful, 1.

εὐσχημόνως,
decently, 1.
honestly, 2.
decently, 1.

εὐσχημοσύνη,
comeliness, 1.

εὐσχήμων,
comely, 1.
honourable,
— *with art.*,
that which is comely, 1.

εὐτόνως,
mightily, 1.
vehemently, 1.

εὐτραπελία,
jesting, 1.

εὐφημία,
good report, 1.

εὔφημος,
of good report, 1.

εὐφορεω,
bring forth plentifully, 1.

εὐφραίνω,
make glad, 1.
— *mid. and pass. aor.*,
rejoice, 6.
be merry, 3.
make merry, 3.
fare, 1.

εὐφροσύνη,
gladness, 1.
joy, 1.

εὐχαριστέω,
give thanks, 25.
thank, 12.
be thankful, 1.
— *passive*,
thanks are given, 1.

εὐχαριστία,
thankfulness, 1.
thanksgiving, 9.
giving of thanks, 3.
thanks, 2.

εὐχάριστος,
thankful, 1.

εὐχή,
prayer, 1.
vow, 2.

εὔχομαι,
pray, 2.
wish, 3.
pray, 1.
can wish, 1.
— εὐξαίμην ἄν,
I would, 1.

εὔχρηστος,
meet for use, 1.
profitable, 2.

εὐψυχέω,
be of good comfort, 1.

εὐωδία,
sweet smell, 1.
sweet smelling, 1.
sweet savour, 1.

εὐώνυμος,
on the left hand, 1.
left foot, 1.
— ἐξ εὐωνύμων,
on the (one's) left, 5.
on the (one's) left hand, 3.

ἐφάλλομαι, *with* ἐπί,
leap on, 1.

ἐφάπαξ,
once for all, 1.
at once, 1.
once, 3.

ἐφεῖδον, *see* ἐπεῖδον.

ἐφευρετής,
inventor, 1.

ἐφημερία,
course, 2.

ἐφήμερος,
daily, 1.

ἔφιδε, *see* ἐπεῖδον.

ἐφικνέομαι,
reach unto, 2.

ἐφίστημι,
stand by, 3.
stand over, 1 (*with* ἐπάνω).
stand before, 1 (*with* ἐπί).
stand, 1.
come upon, 7.
come unto, 1 (*with* ἐπί).
come to, 1.
come in, 1.
come, 1.
assault, 1.
be instant, 1.
be at hand, 1.
present, 1.

ἐφοράω, *see* ἐπεῖδον.

ἐφφαθά,
ephphatha, 1.

ἐχθές, *see* χθές.

ἔχθρα,
enmity, 5.
hatred, 1.

ἐχθρός,
enemy, 30.
foe, 2.

ἔχιδνα,
viper, 5.

ἔχω,
have, 607.
have sufficient, 1.
can have, 1.
can, 4.
be able, 1.
be possessed with, 2.
be in that case, 1.
hold, 5.
hold fast, 1.
keep, 1.
retain, 1.
with, 1.
count, 4.
take for, 1.
use, 1.
have, 1.
do, 1.
lie, 1.
be, 6.
be old, 1.
— *middle*,
accompany, 1.
next, 2.
next day, 1.
day following, 1.
— μὴ ἔχω,
have not, 1.
be poor, 1.
lack, 1.

ἕως,
— *with a verb*,
till, 7.
until, 5.
while, 6.
— *with* ἄν,
till, 15.
until, 6.
until the time, 1.
— *with* οὗ,
till, 11.
until, 5.
while, 1.
— *with* ὅτου,
till, 2.
until, 3.
whiles, 1.
— *with a Genitive*,
till, 3.
until, 11.
to, 12.
unto, 23.
even unto, 2.
as far as, 2.
— ἕως καὶ εἰς,
even unto, 1.
— ἕως τούτου,
thus far, 1.
— οὐκ ἔστιν ἕως ἑνός,
no, not one, 1.
— *with other particles*,
till, 2.
until, 4.
unto, 1.
even unto, 1.
as far as, 1.
— ἕως ἔσω εἰς,
even into, 1.
— ἕως τοῦ νῦν,
to this time, 1.
unto this time, 1.
— ἕως πότε;
how long? 7.
— ἕως ὧδε,
to this place, 1.

ζάω,
to live, 117.
be alive, 9.
— *participle*,
alive, 7.
lively, 3.
quick, 4.
— *infinitive*,
life, 1.
life-time, 1.
— ζῶν ἀσώτως,
with riotous living, 1.

ζβέννυμι, *see* σβέννυμι.

ζεστός,
hot, 3.

ζεῦγος,
yoke, 1.
pair, 1.

ζευκτηρία,
band, 1.

ζέω,
be fervent, 1.
fervent, 1.

*** ζηλεύω,**
[*for* ζηλόω, Rev. iii. 19, *see* Be zealous.]

ζῆλος,
zeal, 6.
fervent mind, 1.
emulation, 1.
envy, 1.
envying, 5.
jealousy, 1.
indignation, 2.
envy, 1.

ζηλόω,
be zealous, 1.
zealously affect, 2.
affect, 1.
desire, 1.
desire to have, 1.
covet earnestly, 1.
covet, 1.
be jealous over, 1.
envy, 1.
be moved with envy, 1.

ζηλωτής,
zealous, 5.

ζημία,
loss, 3.
damage, 1.

ζημιόω, (*mid. or pass.*)
lose, 2.
suffer loss, 1.
suffer the loss of, 1.
receive damage, 1.
be cast away, 1.

ζητέω,
seek, 98.
seek for, 6.
seek after, 1.
seek means, 1.
go about, 4.
be about, 1.
endeavour, 1.
desire, 3.
inquire for, 1.
inquire, 1.
require, 2.

ζήτημα,
question, 5.

ζήτησις,
question, 5.
— εἰς τὴν περὶ τούτου ζήτησιν,
of such manner of questions, 1.
how to inquire hereof, 1.

ζιζάνιον, (*pl.*)
tares, 8.

ζόφος,
darkness, 2.
blackness, 1.
mist, 1.

ζυγός,
yoke, 5.
pair of balances, 1.

ζύμη,
leaven, 13.

ζυμόω,
to leaven, 4.

ζωγρέω,
take captive, 1.
take alive, 1.
catch, 1.

ζωή,
life, 90.
life-time, 1.

ζώνη,
girdle, 6.
purse, 2.

ζώννυμι, ζωννύω,
gird, 2.

ζωογονέω,
preserve, 1.
— *passive*,
live, 1.

ζῶον,
beast, 23.

ζωοποιέω,
make alive, 1.
give life, 2.
quicken, 1.
quicken, 9.

—— *disjunctive*,
or, 173.
or else, 1.
either, 1.
and, 3.
except it be, 1.
neither, 3.
nor, 5.
—— in contrast repeated, ἤ...ἤ,
either...or else, 3.
either...or, 1.
—— ἤ καί,
or else, 1.
yea and, 1.
—— ἤτοι...ἤ,
whether...or, 1.
—— *interrogative*,
or, 82.
or else, 1.
or of, 1.
what ? 3.
either, 3.
—— *comparative*,
than, 35.
more than, 1.
rather than, 3.
but either, 1.
but, 1.
save, 1.
—— ἤπερ,
than, 1.
—— ἀλλ' ἤ,
but rather, 1.
but, 1.
than, 1.
—— οὐ πλείους ἤ,
yet but, 1.

* ἦ μήν,
[*for* εἰ μήν, Heb. vi. 14, *see* Surely.]

ἡγεμονεύω,
be governour, 2.

ἡγεμονία,
reign, 1.

ἡγεμών,
governour, 19.
ruler, 2.
prince, 1.

ἡγέομαι, ἡγοῦμαι,
be chief, 1.
chief, 1.
governour, 2.
have the rule over, 3.
be the guide, 1.
guide, 1.
count, 10.
account, 1.
judge, 1.
esteem, 3.
think, 4.
suppose, 1.
—— ἡγούμενος τοῦ λόγου,
chief speaker, 1.

ἡδέως,
gladly, 3.
—— ἥδιστα,
most gladly, 1.
very gladly, 1.

ἤδη,
now, 37.
even now, 1.
already, 17.
by this time, 1.
yet, 2.
—— καὶ ἤδη,
now already, 1.

ἥδιστα, *see* ἡδέως.

ἡδονή,
pleasure, 3.
lust, 2.
pleasure, 2.

ἡδύοσμον,
mint, 2.

ἦθος,
manner, 1.

ἥκω,
come, 27.

Ἡλί,
Eli, 2.

ἡλικία,
age, 1.
stature, 5.
age, 2.
—— *with* ἔχω,
be of age, 2.

ἡλίκος,
how great, 1.
what great, 1.

ἥλιος,
sun, 30.

ἧλος,
nail, 2.

ἡμεῖς,
—— *nominative*,
we, 123.
we ourselves, 1.
us, 2.
—— *Genitive*, ἡμῶν,
of us, 10.
our, 304.
ours, 4.
our company, 1.
us, 72.
we, 12.
—— μεθ' ἡμῶν,
our, 1.
with us, 1.
—— ψυχὴν ἡμῶν,
us, 1.
—— *Dative*, ἡμῖν,
to us, 14.
unto us, 39.
for us, 10.
on us, 1.
upon us, 1.
with us, 2.
us, 94.
our, 2.
we, 10.
—— τί ἡμῖν κα σοί,
what have we to do with thee, 3.
—— *Accusative*, ἡμᾶς,
us, 151.
we, 25.
—— *with* διά,
for our sakes, 2.

ἡμέρα,
day, 350.
time, 2.
judgment, 1.
day, 1.
—— μία τῶν ἡμερῶν,
a certain day, 2.
—— ἡμέρᾳ καὶ ἡμέρα,
day by day, 1.
—— ἡμέραν ἐξ ἡμέρας,
from day to day, 1.
—— καθ' ἡμέραν,
daily, 15.
day by day, 1.
for this day, 1.
every day, 1.
—— καθ' ἑκάστην ἡμέραν,
daily, 1.
—— καθ' πᾶσαν ἡμέραν,
daily, 1.
—— ἡμέρας μέσης,
at mid-day, 1.
—— τὰς ἡμέρας,
in the day time, 1.
—— ἐνταύταις ταῖς ἡμέραις,
at that time, 1.
—— ἡμέρας ἱκανάς,
a good while, 1.
—— πᾶσαν ἡμέραν,
daily,
—— πάσας τὰς ἡμέρας,
alway, 1.
—— τῇ ἡμέρα τῶν σαββάτων,
on the sabbath, 1.

ἡμέτερος,
our, 6.
—— *pl., with art.*
ours, 2.

ἤμην, *see* εἰμί.

ἡμιθανής,
half dead, 1.

ἥμισυ,
half, 5.

ἡμιώριον,
the space of half an hour, 1.

ἦν, ἦς, ἦσθα, *see* εἰμί.

ἡνίκα, *with* ἄν,
when, 2.

ἤπερ, *see* ἤ.

ἤπιος,
gentle, 2.

ἤρεμος,
quiet, 1.

ἡσυχάζω,
be quiet, 1.
rest, 1.
hold one's peace, 2.
cease, 1.

ἡσυχία,
quietness, 1.
silence, 3.

ἡσύχιος,
quiet, 1.
peaceable, 1.

ἤτοι, *see* ἤ.

ἡττάομαι, -ῶμαι,
be inferior, 1.
be overcome, 2.

ἥττημα,
diminishing, 1.
decay or loss, 1.
fault, 1.

ἥττων, ἥσσων,
the worse, 1 (*neut., with art.*),
the less, 1 (*adv.*)

ἤτω, *see* εἰμί.

ἠχέω,
to sound, 1.
roar, 1.

ἦχος,
sound, 2.
fame, 1.

* ἦχος,
[*for* ἠχέω, Luke xxi. 25, *see* Roar.]

θάλασσα,
sea, 91.

θάλπω,
cherish, 2.

θαμβέω,
be astonished, 1.
—— *passive*,
be astonished, 1.
be amazed, 2.

θάμβος,
wonder, 1.
—— *with* περιέχω,
be astonished, 1.
—— *with* γίνομαι ἐπί,
be amazed, 1.

θανάσιμος,
deadly thing, 1.

θανατηφόρος,
deadly, 1.

θάνατος,
death, 115.
Death, 1.
deadly, 2.
—— θανάτου γενομένου,
by means of death, 1.

θανατόω,
put to death, 4.
cause to be put t death, 3.
mortify, 1.
kill, 2.
—— *passive*,
become dead, 1.

θάπτω,
bury, 11.

θαρρέω,
be bold, 2.
boldly, 1.
be confident, 1.
confident, 1.
have confidence, 1.

θαρσέω,
be of good cheer, 5.
be of good comfort, 3,

θάρσος,
courage, 1.

θαῦμα,
admiration, 1.

θαυμάζω,
to wonder, 12.
wonder at, 1.
marvel, 28.
marvel at, 2.
admire, 1.
have in admiration, 1.
— *middle,*
wonder, 1.

θαυμάσιος,
wonderful thing, 1.

θαυμαστός,
marvellous, 5.
— *neuter,*
marvellous thing, 1.
marvel, 1.

θεά,
goddess, 3.

θεάομαι,
see, 17.
behold, 2.
look on, 1.
look upon, 1.
— *passive,*
be seen, 3.

θεατρίζω,
make a gazing stock, 1.

θέατρον,
theatre, 1.
spectacle, 1.
theatre, 1.

θεῖον,
brimstone, 7.

θεῖος,
divine, 2.
— *neut., with art.,*
the godhead, 1.

θειότης,
godhead, 1.

θειώδης,
of brimstone, 1.

θέλημα,
well, 61.
pleasure, 1.
desire, 1.
will, 1.
— *plural,*
will, 1.

θέλησις,
will, 1.

θέλω,
will, 98.
would, 70.
be willing, 1.
willingly, 2.
voluntary, 1.
being a voluntary, 1.
will have, 5.
would have, 5.
list, 3.
be disposed, 1.
desire, 13.
be desirous, 1.
desirous, 2.
be forward, 1.
be willing, 1.
please, 2.
had rather, 1.
intend, 1.
so be, 1.
love, 1.
— *with εἶναι,*
mean, 2.

θεμέλιος, θεμέλιον,
foundation, 15.

θεμελιόω,
lay the foundation of, 1.
found, 2.
ground, 2.
settle, 1.

θεοδίδακτος,
taught of God, 1.

θεομαχέω,
fight against God, 1.

θεομάχος,
to fight against God, 1.

θεόπνευστος,
given by inspiration of God, 1.

Θεος,
God, 1326.
god, 12.
— *Genitive,*
godly, 3.
— *Dative,*
exceeding, 1.
to God, 1.
— *κατὰ Θεόν,*
after a godly manner, 1.
according to God, 1.
after a godly sort, 1.
godly, 1.
— *ἀξίως τοῦ Θεοῦ,*
after a godly sort, 1.

θεοσέβεια,
godliness, 1.

θεοσεβής,
worshipper of God, 1.

θεοστυγής,
hater of God, 1.

θεότης,
Godhead, 1.

θεραπεία,
healing, 2.
household, 2.

θεραπεύω,
to worship, 1.
cure, 5.
heal, 38.

θεράπων,
servant, 1.

θερίζω,
reap, 21.

θερισμός,
harvest, 13.

θεριστής,
reaper, 2.

θερμαίνω, (*mid.*)
warm one's self, 5.
be warmed, 1.

θέρμη,
heat, 1.

θέρος,
summer, 3.

θεωρέω,
look on, 1.
behold, 11.
consider, 1.
see, 40.
perceive, 4.

θεωρία,
sight, 1.

θήκη,
sheath, 1.

θηλάζω,
to suck, 1.
suckling, 1.
give suck, 4.

θῆλυς, θήλεια*, θῆλυ†,
woman, 2*.
female, 3†.

θήρα,
trap, 1.

θηρεύω,
to catch, 1.

θηριομαχέω,
fight with beasts, 1.

θηρίον,
wild beast, 3.
venomous beast, 1.
beast, 42.

θησαυρίζω,
treasure up, 1.
lay up treasure, 1.
heap treasure together, 1.
lay up, 3.
keep in store, 1.
in store, 1.

θησαυρός,
treasure, 18.

θιγγάνω,
to touch, 2.
handle, 1.

θλίβω,
narrow, 1.
suffer tribulation, 1.
throng, 1.
afflict, 3.
trouble, 4.

θλῖψις,
burdened, 1.
anguish, 1.
affliction, 17.
tribulation, 21.
persecution, 1.
trouble, 3.
— *with εἰς,*
to be afflicted, 1.

θνήσκω,
to die, 1.
be dead, 9.
dead, 3.

θνητός,
mortal, 5.
— *with art.,*
mortality, 1.

*** θορυβάζω,**
[*for* τυρβάζω, Luke x. 41, *see* Troubled (be).]

θορυβέω,
set on an uproar, 1.
— *middle,*
make a noise, 1.
make this ado, 1.
trouble one's self, 1.

θόρυβος,
uproar, 3.
tumult, 4.

θραύω,
to bruise, 1.

θρέμμα,
cattle, 1.

θρηνέω,
mourn, 2.
lament, 2.

θρῆνος,
lamentation, 1.

θρησκεία,
worshipping, 1.
religion, 3.

θρῆσκος,
religious, 1.

θριαμβεύω,
triumph over, 1.
cause to triumph, 1.

θρίξ, τρίχος,
hair, 15.

θροέω, (*pass.*)
be troubled, 3.

θρόμβος,
great drop, 1.

θρόνος,
seat, 7.
throne, 54.

θυγάτηρ,
daughter, 29.

θυγάτριον,
little daughter, 1.
young daughter, 1.

θύελλα,
tempest, 1.

θύϊνος,
thyme, 1.
sweet, 1.

θυμίαμα,
incense, 4.
odour, 2.
incense, 1.

θυμιατήριον,
censer, 1.

θυμιάω,
burn incense, 1.

θυμομαχέω, *with* εἰμί,
be highly displeased with, 1.
bear an hostile mind, intending war with, 1.

θυμόω, (*pass.*)
be wroth, 1.

θυμός,
wrath, 15.
indignation, 1.
fierceness, 2.

θύρα,
door, 38.
gate, 1.

θυρεός,
shield, 1.

θυρίς,
window, 2.

θυρωρός,
porter, 2.
— *with art.*,
that keepeth the door, 2.

θυσία,
sacrifice, 29.

θυσιαστήριον,
altar, 23.

θύω,
to sacrifice, 3.
slay, 1.
do sacrifice, 2.
kill, 8.
sacrifice, 1.
slay, 1.

θώραξ,
breastplate, 5.

ἴαμα,
healing, 3.

ἰάομαι,
heal, 26.
make whole, 2.

ἴασις,
healing, 1.
cure, 1.
— *with* εἰς,
to heal, 1.

ἴασπις,
jasper, 4.

ἰατρός,
physician, 7.

ἴδε, (*imperat. of* εἶδον)
see, 1.
look, 1.
lo, 3.
behold, 23.

ἰδέα,
countenance, 1.

ἴδιος,
one's own, 72.
his, 5.
there, 2.
private, 1.
his several, 1.
one's proper, 2.
due, 3.
— *plural*,
one's own company, 1.
one's acquaintance, 1.
— τὰ ἴδια,
one's own, 2.
one's own home, 1.
one's own home, 1.
one's own business, 1.
— εἰς τὰ ἴδια,
home, 1.
— ὁ ἴδιος οἶκος,
home, 1.
— κατ' ἰδίαν,
privately, 8.
severally, 1.
apart, 7.
aside, 1.
when they were alone, 1.
— ἰδίᾳ,
severally, 1.

ἰδιώτης,
unlearned, 3.
ignorant, 1.
rude, 1.

ἰδού, (*imper. of* εἶδον, *aor. mid.*)
see, 3.
lo, 29.
behold, 181.

ἱδρώς,
sweat, 1.

ἱερατεία,
priest's office, 1.
office of the priesthood, 1.

ἱεράτευμα,
priesthood, 2.

ἱερατεύω,
execute the priest's office, 1.

ἱερεύς,
priest, 31.

* ἱερόθυτος,
[*for* εἰδωλόθυτος, 1 Cor. x. 28, *see* "Offered in sacrifice to idols."]

ἱερόν,
temple, 71.

ἱεροπρεπής,
as becometh holiness, 1.
as becometh holy women, 1.

ἱερός,
holy, 1.
— τὰ ἱερά,
holy things, 1.

ἱεροσυλέω,
commit sacrilege, 1.

ἱερόσυλος,
robber of churches, 1.

ἱερουργέω,
to minister, 1.

ἱερωσύνη,
priesthood, 4.

ἱκανός,
enough, 1.
sufficient, 3.
able, 1.
meet, 1.
worthy, 5.
large, 1.
sore, 1.
great, 1.
great number of, 1.
much, 6.
— *plural*,
many, 10.
many of, 1.
— τὸ ἱκανόν,
security, 1.
— τὸ ἱκανὸν ποιέω,
to content, 1.
— ἐξ ἱκανοῦ,
of a long season, 1.
— ἐφ' ἱκανόν,
a long while, 1.

ἱκανότης,
sufficiency, 1.

ἱκανόω,
make able, 1.
make meet, 1.

ἱκετηρία,
supplication, 1.

ἰκμάς,
moisture, 1.

ἱλαρός,
cheerful, 1.

ἱλαρότης,
cheerfulness, 1.

ἱλάσκομαι,
make reconciliation for, 1.
— *passive*,
be merciful, 1.

ἱλασμός,
propitiation, 2.

ἱλαστήριον, (*neut.*)
propitiation, 1.
mercy-seat, 1.

ἵλεως,
merciful, 1.
— ἱλεώς σοι,
be it far from thee, 1.

ἱμάς,
latchet, 3.
thong, 1.

ἱματίζω,
clothe, 2.

ἱμάτιον,
garment, 31.
clothes, 1.
vesture, 2.
cloak, 2.
robe, 2.
— *plural*,
clothes, 11.
raiment, 12.
apparel, 1.

ἱματισμός,
raiment, 1.
vesture, 2.
apparel, 1.
array, 1.
— οἱ ἐν ἱματισμῷ ἐνδόξῳ,
they which are gorgeously apparelled, 1.

ἱμείρω, -ομαι,
be affectionately desirous of, 1.

ἵνα,
to the intent that, 1.
to the intent, 1.
that, 484.
to, 70 (*with inf.*)
for to, 8 (*with inf.*)
so as, 1.
so that, 1.
because, 1.
must, 1.
— ἵνα μή,
that not, 50.
that no, 5.
that nothing, 1.
albeit not, 1.
lest, 43.
so that not, 1.
— ἵνα μή τις,
that no man, 1.
— ἵνα μή τι,
that nothing, 1.

ἱνατί, *or* ἵνα τί,
wherefore? 1.
why? 5.

ἰός,
rust, 1.
poison, 2.

Ἰουδαΐζω,
to live as do the Jews, 1.

Ἰουδαϊσμός,
Jews' religion, 2.

ἱππεύς,
horseman, 2.

ἱππικόν,
horsemen, 1.

ἵππος,
horse, 16.

ἶρις,
rainbow, 2.

ἰσάγγελος,
equal to the angels, 1.

ἴσημι, ἴστε, ἴσασι, *see* εἶδον, οἶδα.

ἴσθι, *see* εἰμί.

ἴσος, *or* ἶσος,
equal, 4.
like, 1.
— τὰ ἴσα,
as much, 1.
— *with* εἰμί,
agree, 2.

ἰσότης,
equality, 2.
— *with art.*,
that which is equal, 1.

ἰσότιμος,
like precious, 1.

ἰσόψυχος,
like-minded, 1.
so dear to me, 1.

ἵστημι,
— *trans.* (*pres.* 1 *aor. fut.*),
make stand, 1.
set, 11.
set up, 1.
establish, 3.
present, 1.
appoint, 2.
covenant with for, 1.
lay to one's charge, 1.
— (*pass., aor., and fut., mid. fut.*),
stand, 17.
stand up, 2.
stand forth, 1.
be holden up, 1.
be established, 2.
be brought, 1.
— *intrans.* (*perf., plup., and* 2 *aor.*),
stand, 99.
stand forth, 2.
stand by, 3.
stand still, 4.
abide, 1.
continue, 1.
stanch, 1.

ἱστορέω,
to see, 1.

ἰσχυρός,
strong, 9.
strong man, 5.
mighty, 10.
powerful, 1.
valiant, 1.
boisterous, 1.
strong, 1.

sore, 1.
miserably, 1.
— *with ἔχω*,
be diseased, 2.
be sick, 7.
sick people, 1.

κάκωσις,
affliction, 1.

καλάμη,
stubble, 1.

κάλαμος,
reed, 11.
pen, 1.

καλέω,
to call, 126.
call forth, 1.
bid, 16.
name, 1.
so name, 1.
— *passive*,
be one's name, 1.
be one's surname, 1.

καλλιέλαιος,
good olive tree, 1.

κάλλιον, *see* **καλῶς.**

καλοδιδάσκαλος,
teacher of good things, 1.

καλοποιέω,
in well doing, 1.

καλός,
goodly, 2.
good, 76.
better, 7.
well, 1.
honest, 2.
meet, 2.
worthy, 1.
— *neuter*,
honest thing, 2.
good thing, 2.
good, 3.
— τὸ καλόν,
that which is honest, 1.
that which is good, 2.

κάλυμμα,
veil, 4.

καλύπτω,
to cover, 5.
hide, 3.

καλῶς,
well, 30.
full well, 1.
good, 2.
in a good place, 1.
well or seemly, 1.
honestly, 1.
— *comp.* κάλλιον,
very well, 1.
— *with ἔχω*,
recover, 1.

κἀμέ, *see* **κἀγώ.**

κάμηλος,
camel, 6.

κάμινος,
furnace, 4.

καμμύω,
to close, 2.

κάμνω,
be wearied, 1.
faint, 1.
sick, 1.

κἀμοί, *see* **κἀγώ.**

κάμπτω,
to bow, 4.

κἄν,
and if, 3.
and if so much as, 1.
also if, 1.
if but, 2.
though, 4.
yet, 1.
at the least, 1.

κανών,
rule, 1.
line, 1.
line, 1.
rule, 1.

καπηλεύω,
to corrupt, 1.
deal deceitfully with, 1.

καπνός,
smoke, 13.

καρδία,
heart, 158.

καρδιογνώστης,
which knoweth the hearts, 2.

καρπός,
fruit, 66.

καρποφορέω,
bear fruit, 1.
bring forth fruit, 5.
be fruitful, 1.
— *mid., with εἰμί*,
bring forth fruit, 1.

καρποφόρος,
fruitful, 1.

καρτερέω,
endure, 1.

κάρφος,
mote, 6.

* **καρχηδών,**
[*for* χαλκηδών, Rev. xxi. 19, *see* "Chalcedony."]

κατά,
— *with Genitive*,
down, 3.
on, 1.
upon, 1.
covered, 1.
against, 58.
of, 1.
through, 1.
throughout, 4.
by, 4.
— *with Accusative*,
through, 4.
throughout, 3.
over against, 2.
before, 2.
toward, 3.
to, 4.
into, 2.
among, 2.
about, 3.
at, 7.
in, 35.
according to, 2.
upon, 1.
on, 1.
according to, 102.
after, 59.
after the manner of, 1.
with, 3.
by, 25.
of, 6.
in respect of, 1.
concerning, 2.
as concerning, 3.
as pertaining to, 2.
touching, 1.
as touching, 2.
on one's part, 2.
for, 1.
— κατ' αὐτόν,
where he was, 1.
— κατὰ πόλιν,
in every city, 3.
throughout every city, 1.
out of every city, 1.
— κατ' ἐκκλησίαν,
in every church, 1.
— κατὰ τόπους,
in divers places, 3.
— κατ' ἐνιαυτόν,
year by year, 1.
every year, 2.
— κατ' ἔτος,
every year, 1.
— κατὰ ταῦτα,
in the like manner, 1.
so, 1.
even thus, 1.
— κατὰ τὸ διατεταγμένον,
as it was commanded, 1.
— κατὰ τὸν καλέσαντα,
as he which hath called, 1.
— κατὰ Ἰσαάκ,
as Isaac was, 1.
— τὸ κατ' ἐμέ,
as much as in me is, 1.
— κατὰ λόγον,
reason would, 1.
— κατὰ τί,
whereby? 1.
— τὰ κατὰ τὸν Παῦλον,
Paul's cause, 1.

καταβαίνω,
go down, 17.
came down, 41.
step down, 1.
descend, 18.
get down, 1.
fall down, 1.
fall, 1.

καταβάλλω,
cast down, 2.
— *middle*,
lay, 1.

καταβαρέω,
to burden, 1.

* **καταβαρύνω,**
[*for* βαρέω, Mark xiv. 40, *see* Heavy.]

κατάβασις,
descent, 1.

καταβιβάζω,
bring down, 1.
thrust down, 1.

καταβολή,
foundation, 10.
— *with εἰς*,
to conceive, 1.

καταβραβεύω,
beguile of one's reward, 1.
judge against, 1.

καταγγελεύς,
setter forth, 1.

καταγγέλλω,
declare, 2.
show, 3.
speak of, 1.
preach, 10.
teach, 1.

καταγελάω,
laugh to scorn, 3.

καταγινώσκω,
condemn, 2.
— *passive*,
to be blamed, 1.

κατάγνυμι,
to break, 4.

κατάγω,
bring down, 5.
bring forth, 1.
bring, 1.
— *passive*,
land, 2.
touch, 1.

καταγωνίζομαι,
subdue, 1.

καταδέω,
bind up, 1.

κατάδηλος,
evident, 1.

καταδικάζω,
condemn, 5.

* **καταδίκη,**
[*for* δίκη, Acts xxv. 15, *see* "Judgment."]

καταδιώκω,
follow after, 1.

καταδουλόω,
bring into bondage, 2.

καταδρέμω, *see* **κατατρέχω.**

καταδυναστεω,
oppress, 2.

* **κατάθεμα,**
[*for* κατανάθεμα, Rev. xxii. 3, *see* "Curse."]

* **καταθεματίζω,**
[*for* καταναθεματίζω, Matt. xxvi. 74, *see* "Curse (to)."]

καταισχύνω,
to shame, 1.
make ashamed, 1.
— *passive*,
be ashamed, 16.
be confounded, 1.
confound, 3.
dishonour, 2.

κατακαίω,
burn up, 4.
burn utterly, 1.
burn, 7.

κατακαλύπτω,
— *middle,*
be covered, 2.
cover, 1.

κατακαυχάομαι,
boast against, 1.
boast, 1.
rejoice against, 1.
glory against, 1.
glory, 1.

κατάκειμαι,
to lie, 6.
sit down, 1.
sit at meat, 3.
— *with* ἐπί,
keep, 1.

κατακλάω, *or* κατακλάζω,
to break, 2.

κατακλείω,
shut up, 2.

κατακληροδοτέω,
divide by lot, 1.

* κατακληρονομέω,
[*for* κατακληροδοτέω, Acts xiii. 19, *see* Divide by lot.]

κατακλίνω,
make sit down, 1.
— *middle,*
sit down, 1.
sit at meat, 1.

κατακλύζω,
overflow, 1.

κατακλυσμός,
flood, 4.

κατακολουθέω,
follow after, 1.
follow, 1.

κατακόπτω,
to cut, 1.

κατακρημνίζω,
cast down headlong, 1.

κατάκριμα,
condemnation, 3.

κατακρίνω,
condemn, 17.
damn, 2.

κατάκρισις,
condemnation, 1.
— *with* πρός,
to condemn, 1.

κατακυριεύω,
exercise lordship over, 1.
be lord over, 1.
overrule, 1.
exercise dominion over, 1.
overcome, 1.

καταλαλέω,
speak against, 1.
speak evil of, 4.

καταλαλία,
evil speaking, 1.
backbiting, 1.

κατάλαλος,
backbiter, 1.

καταλαμβάνω,
overtake, 1.
take, 3.
apprehend, 3.
attain to, 1.
obtain, 1.
come upon, 1.
comprehend, 1.
— *middle,*
comprehend, 1.
perceive, 2.
find, 1.

καταλέγω,
take into the number, 1.
choose, &c., 1.

κατάλειμμα,
remnant, 1.

καταλείπω,
to leave, 22.
forsake, 2.
reserve, 1.

καταλιθάζω,
to stone, 1.

καταλλαγή,
reconciliation, 2.
reconciling, 1.
atonement, 1.

καταλλάσσω,
reconcile, 6.

κατάλοιπος, (*pl.*)
residue, 1.

κατάλυμα,
inn, 1.
guest-chamber, 2.

καταλύω,
dissolve, 1.
throw down, 3.
overthrow, 1.
destroy, 9.
lodge, 1.
be guest, 1.
— *passive,*
come to nought, 1.

καταμανθάνω,
consider, 1.

καταμαρτυρέω,
witness against, 4.

καταμένω, *with* εἰμί,
abide, 1.

καταμόνας,
alone, 2.

καταναθεμα,
curse, 1.

καταναθεματίζω,
to curse, 1.

καταναλίσκω,
consume, 1.

καταναρκάω,
be burdensome to, 2.
be chargeable to, 1.

κατανεύω,
beckon unto, 1.

κατανοέω,
perceive, 2.
discover, 1.
behold, 4.
consider, 7.

καταντάω,
— *with* εἰς,
attain to, 1.
attain unto, 1.
come to, 5.
come unto, 4.
come upon, 1.
— *with* ἀντικρύ,
come over against, 1.

κατάνυξις,
slumber, 1.
remorse, 1.

κατανύσσω,
to prick, 1.

καταξιόω,
count worthy, 2.
account worthy, 2.

καταπατέω,
tread down, 1.
tread under foot, 2.
tread, 1.
trample, 1.

κατάπαυσις,
rest, 9.

καταπαύω,
give rest, 1.
restrain, 1.
rest, 1.
cease, 1.

καταπέτασμα,
veil, 6.

καταπίνω,
swallow up, 4.
swallow, 1.
drown, 1.
devour, 1.

καταπίπτω,
fall down, 1.
fall, 1.

καταπλέω,
arrive, 1.

καταπονέω,
oppress, 1.
vex, 1.

καταποντίζω, (*mid. or pass.*)
sink, 1.
be drowned, 1.

κατάρα,
cursing, 2.
curse, 3.
— *Genitive,*
cursed, 1.

καταράομαι,
to curse, 5.
— *passive,*
be cursed, 1.

καταργέω,
make without effect, 1.
make of none effect, 2.
make void, 1.
cumber, 1.
deliver, 1.
loose, 1.
do away, 3.
put away, 1.
put down, 1.
abolish, 3.
destroy, 5.
bring to nought, 1.
— *passive,*
become of none effect, 1.
come to nought, 1.
be done away, 4.
fail, 1.
cease, 1.
vanish away, 1.

καταριθμέω, *with* ἐν,
number with, 1.

καταρτίζω,
mend, 2.
restore, 1.
make perfect, 2.
perfect, 2.
fit, 1.
make up, 1.
prepare, 1.
fit, 1.
frame, 1.
— *passive,*
be perfect, 1.
be perfected, 1.
be perfectly joined together, 1.

κατάρτισις,
perfection, 1.

καταρτισμός,
perfecting, 1.

κατασείω,
beckon, 4.

κατασκάπτω,
dig down, 1.
— κατεσκαμμένα,
ruins, 1.

κατασκευάζω,
prepare, 5.
build, 3.
make, 1.
ordain, 1.
— *passive,*
be a preparing, 1.

κατασκηνόω,
to lodge, 3.
rest, 1.

κατασκήνωσις,
nest, 2.

κατασκιάζω,
to shadow, 1.

κατασκοπέω,
spy out, 1.

κατάσκοπος,
spy, 1.

κατασοφίζομαι,
deal subtilely with, 1.

καταστέλλω,
appease, 1.
— *passive,*
quiet, 1.

κατάστημα,
behaviour, 1.

καταστολή,
apparel, 1.

καταστρέφω,
to overthrow, 2.

καταστρηνιάω,
begin to wax wanton against, 1.

καταστροφή,
overthrow, 1.
subverting, 1.

καταστρώννυμι,
to overthrow, 1.

κατασύρω,
to hale, 1.

κατασφάζω,
slay, 1.

κατασφραγίζω,
to seal, 1.

κατάσχεσις,
possession, 2.

κατατίθημι,
lay, 1.
do, 1.
show, 1.

κατατομή,
concision, 1.

κατατοξεύω,
thrust through, 1.

κατατρέχω,
run down, 1.

* καταυγάζω,
[*for* αὐγάζω, 2 Cor. iv. 4, *see* "Shine."]

καταφάγω, *see* κατεσθίω.

καταφέρω,
give against, 1.
— passive,
sink down, 1.
fall, 1.

καταφεύγω,
flee, 2.

καταφθείρω, (*pass.*)
perish utterly, 1.
corrupt, 1.

καταφιλέω,
to kiss, 6.

καταφρονέω,
despise, 9.

καταφρονητής,
despiser, 1.

καταχέω,
pour, 2.

καταχθόνιος,
under the earth, 1.

καταχράομαι,
to abuse, 2.

καταψύχω,
to cool, 1.

κατείδωλος,
wholly given to idolatry, 1.
full of idols, 1.

κατέναντι,
over against, 4.
before, 1.
like unto, 1.

κατενώπιον,
in the sight of, 1.
in one's sight, 1.
before the presence of, 1.
before, 2.

κατεξουσιάζω,
exercise authority upon, 2.

κατεργάζομαι,
work out, 1.
work, 14.
be wrought, 1.
perform, 1.
do, 5.
overcome, 1.
cause, 1.
— *with* τοῦτο,
do this deed, 1.

κατέρχομαι,
come down, 5.
go down, 2.
come, 3.
descend, 1.
depart, 1.
land, 1.

κατεσθίω, (2*nd aor.*, κατέφαγον)
eat up, 3.
devour up, 2.
devour, 10.

κατευθύνω,
to direct, 2.
guide, 1.

* κατευλογέω,
[*for* εὐλογέω, Mark x. 16, *see* "Bless."]

κατεφίστημι,
make insurrection against, 1.

κατέχω,
hold fast, 3.
withhold, 1.
hold, 1.
hold, 3.
retain, 1.
stay, 1.
let, 1.
keep, 2.
keep in memory, 1.
hold fast, 1.
take, 1.
seize on, 1.
possess, 2.
make toward, 1.
— *passive*,
have, 1.

κατηγορέω,
accuse, 21.
object, 1.

κατηγορία,
accusation, 3.
— *with* ἐν,
accused, 1.

κατήγορος,
accuser, 7.

* κατήγωρ,
[*for* κατήγορος, Rev. xii. 10, *see* "Accuser."]

κατήφεια,
heaviness, 1.

κατηχέω,
teach, 3.
instruct, 3.
inform, 2.

κατ' ἰδίαν, *see* ἴδιος

κατιόω,
to canker, 1.

κατισχύω,
prevail against, 1.
prevail, 1.

κατοικέω,
dwell in, 4.
dweller in, 1.
dwell at, 4.
dweller at, 1.
dwell, 35.
inhabiter of, 1.
inhabitant, 1.
inhabiter, 1.

κατοίκησις,
dwelling, 1.

κατοικητήριον,
habitation, 2.

κατοικία,
habitation, 1.

* κατοικίζω,
[*for* κατοικέω, Jas. iv. 5, *see* "Dwell."]

κατοπτρίζω, (*mid.*)
behold as in a glass, 1.

κατόρθωμα,
very worthy deed, 1.

κάτω,
down, 5.
beneath, 2.
— ἕως κάτω,
to the bottom, 2.
— τὰ κάτω,
beneath, 1.

κατώτερος,
lower, 1.

καῦμα,
heat, 2.

καυματίζω,
scorch, 4.
burn, 1.

καῦσις, (*with* εἰς)
to be burned, 1.

καυσόω, (*pass.*)
with fervent heat, 2.

καύσων,
burning heat, 1.
heat, 2.

καυτηριάζω,
sear with a hot iron, 1.

καυχάομαι,
to boast, 7.
boast one's self, 2.
glory, 22.
in glorying, 1.
rejoice, 4.
glory, 1.
joy, 1.

καύχημα,
boasting, 1.
glorying, 2.
to glory, 2.
rejoicing, 4.
— *with* οὐ,
nothing to glory of, 1.
— εἰς καύχημα ἐμοί,
that I may rejoice, 1.

καύχησις,
boasting, 6.
glorying, 1.
whereof I may glory, 1.
rejoicing, 4.
glorying, 1.

κεῖμαι,
to lie, 9.
there, 1.
be laid, 6.
be laid up, 1.
be set, 6.
be appointed, 1.
be made, 1.
be, 1.

κειρίαι,
grave-clothes, 1.

κείρω,
to shear, 3.
shearer, 1.

κέλευσμα,
shout, 1.

κελεύω,
to command, 24.
give commandment, 1.
at one's commandment, 1.
bid, 1.

κενοδοξία,
vain-glory, 1.

κενόδοξος,
desirous of vain glory, 1.

κενός,
empty, 4.
vain, 5.
in vain, 3.
— *neut. pl.*,
vain things, 1.
— εἰς κενόν,
in vain, 5.

κενοφωνία, (*Gen.*)
vain, 2.

κενόω,
make void, 2.
make of none effect, 1.
make of no reputation, 1.
— *passive*,
be in vain, 1.

κέντρον,
prick, 2.
sting, 3.

κεντυρίων,
centurion, 3.

κενῶς,
in vain, 1.

κεραία,
tittle, 2.

κεραμεύς,
potter, 3.

κεραμικός,
of a potter, 1.

κεράμιον,
pitcher, 2.

κέραμος,
tiling, 1.

κεράννυμι, κεραννύω,
pour out, 1.
fill, 2.

κέρας,
horn, 11.

κεράτιον,
husk, 1.

κερδαίνω,
to gain, 13.
get gain, 1.
win, 2.

κέρδος,
gain, 2.
lucre, 1.

κέρμα,
money, 1.

κερματιστής,
changer of money, 1.

κεφάλαιον,
sum, 2.

κεφαλαιόω,
to wound in the head, 1.

κεφαλή,
head, 75.
Head, 1.

κεφαλίς,
volume, 1.

* κημόω,
[*for* φιμόω, 1 Cor. ix. 9, *see* "Muzzle."]

κῆνσος,
tribute, 3.
— *Genitive*,
tribute, 1.

κῆπος,
garden, 5.

κηπουρός,
gardener, 1.

κηρίον, *with* μελίσσιος,
honey-comb, 1.

κήρυγμα,
preaching, 8.

κήρυξ,
preacher, 3.

κηρύσσω,
proclaim, 2.
publish, 5.
preach, 53.
preacher, 1.

κῆτος,
whale, 1.

κιβωτός,
ark, 6.

κιθάρα,
harp, 4.

κιθαρίζω,
to harp, 2.

κιθαρῳδός,
harper, 2.

κινάμωμον,
cinnamon, 1.

κινδυνεύω,
be in danger, 2.
be in jeopardy, 1.
stand in jeopardy, 1.

κίνδυνος,
peril, 9.

κινέω,
move, 3.
mover of, 1.
remove, 1.
wag, 2.
— *middle*,
move, 1.

κίνησις,
moving, 1.

κίχρημι, *see* χράω.

κλάδος,
branch, 11.

κλάζω, *see* κλάω.

κλαίω,
weep, 39.
weep abundantly, 1, } *with* ἐπιβάλλω.
begin to weep, 1 }
bewail, 1.

κλάσις,
breaking, 2.

κλάσμα,
fragment, 7.
— *plural*,
broken meat, 2.

κλαυθμός,
weeping, 6.
wailing, 2.
— *with* γίνομαι,
weep, 1.

κλάω,
break, 15.

κλείς,
key, 6.

κλείω,
shut, 12.
shut up, 4.

κλέμμα,
theft, 1.

κλέος,
glory, 1.

κλέπτης,
thief, 16.

κλέπτω,
steal, 13.

κλῆμα,
branch, 4.

κληρονομέω,
inherit, 15.
obtain by inheritance, 1.
be heir of, 1.
be heir, 1.

κληρονομία,
inheritance, 14.

κληρονόμος,
heir, 15.

κλῆρος,
lot, 3.
lots, 5.
part, 2.
inheritance, 2.
heritage, 1.

κληρόω, (*pass.*)
obtain an inheritance, 1.

κλῆσις,
calling, 10.
vocation, 1.

κλητός,
called, 10.
which is called, 1.

καλίβανος,
oven, 2.

κλίμα,
region, 2.
part, 1.

* κλινάριον,
[*for* κλίνη, Acts v. 15, *see* Bed.]

κλίνη,
bed, 9.
table, 1.
bed, 1.

κλινίδιον,
couch, 2.

κλίνω,
to bow, 1.
bow down, 1.
lay, 2.
turn to flight, 1.
— *with* ἡμέρα,
wear away, 1.
be far spent, 1.

κλισία, (*Acc. pl.*)
in a company, 1.

κλοπή,
theft, 2.

κλύδων,
wave, 1.
raging, 1.

κλυδωνίζομαι,
be tossed to and fro, 1.

κνήθω, (*pass.*, *with* τὴν ἀκοήν)
have itching ears, 1.

κοδράντης,
farthing, 2.

κοιλία,
belly, 11.
womb, 12.

κοιμάω,
fall asleep, 4.
fall on sleep, 1.
sleep, 10.
be asleep, 2.
be dead, 1.

κοίμησις,
taking of rest, 1.

κοινός,
common, 7.
unclean, 2.
defiled, 1.
unholy thing, 1.

κοινόω,
call common, 2.
defile, 11.
pollute, 1.
— *passive*,
unclean, 1.

κοινωνέω,
be partaker of, 5.
communicate, 2.
distribute, 1.

κοινωνία,
communion, 4.
communication, 1.
to communicate, 1.
fellowship, 12.
contribution, 1.
distribution, 1.

κοινωνικός,
willing to communicate, 1.
sociable, 1.

κοινωνός,
partaker, 5.
partner, 3.
companion, 1.
— *with* γίνομαι,
have fellowship with, 1.

κοίτη,
bed, 2.
— *with* ἔχω,
conceive, 1.
— *plural*,
chambering, 1.

κοιτών,
— *with* ἐπί,
chamberlain, 1.

κόκκινος,
scarlet coloured, 1.
scarlet, 2.
— *neuter*,
scarlet colour, 1.
scarlet, 2.

κόκκος,
grain, 6.
corn, 1.

κολάζω,
punish, 2.

κολακεία,
flattering, 1.

κόλασις,
punishment, 1.
torment, 1.

κολαφίζω,
buffet, 5.

κολλάω,
cleave, 3.
join one's self, 4.
be joined, 2.
keep company, 1.

κολλούριον,
eye-slave, 1.

κολλυβιστής,
money-changer, 2.
changer, 1.

κολοβόω,
shorten, 4.

κόλπος,
bosom, 5.
creek, 1.

κολυμβάω,
swim, 1.

κολυμβήθρα,
pool, 5.

κολωνία,
colony, 1.

κομάω,
have long hair, 2.

κόμη,
hair, 1.

κομίζω,
bring, 1.
— *middle,*
receive, 9.
receive for, 1.

κομψότερον,
— *with ἔχω,*
begin to amend, 1.

κονιάω,
to white, 2.

κονιορτός,
dust, 5.

κοπάζω,
cease, 3.

κοπετός,
lamentation, 1.

κοπή,
slaughter, 1.

κοπιάω,
be wearied, 1.
toil, 3.
labour, 16.
bestow labour, 3.
bestow labour on, 1.

κόπος,
weariness, 1.
— *pl. with παρέχω,*
to trouble, 5.
labour, 13.

κοπρία,
dunghill, 1.
— *with βάλλω,*
to dung, 1.

* **κόπριος,**
[*for* κοπρία, Luke xiii. 8, *see* "to dung."]

κόπτω,
cut down, 2.
— *middle,*
lament, 2.
wail, 1.
bewail, 2.
mourn, 1.

κόραξ,
raven, 1.

κοράσιον,
damsel, 6.
maid, 2.

κορβᾶν, κορβανᾶς,
Corban, 1.
treasury, 1.

κορέννυμι, (*pass. or mid.*)
eat enough, 1.
full, 1.

κόρος,
measure, 1.

κοσμέω,
to trim, 1.
adorn, 5.
garnish, 4.

κοσμικός,
worldly, 2.

κόσμιος,
of good behaviour, 1.
modest, 1.
modest, 1.

κοσμοκράτωρ,
ruler, 1.

κόσμος,
adorning, 1.
world, 187.

κοῦμι,
cumi, 1.

κουστωδία,
watch, 3.

κουφίζω,
lighten, 1.

κόφινος,
basket, 6.

κράββατος,
couch, 1.
bed, 11.

κράζω,
to cry, 40.

κραιπάλη,
surfeiting, 1.

κρανίον,
skull, 3.
Calvary, 1.
the place of a skull, 1.

κράσπεδον,
border, 3.
hem, 2.

κραταιός,
mighty, 1.

κραταιόω,
strengthen, 1.
— *passive,*
wax strong, 2.
be strong, 1.

κρατέω,
lay hold on, 8.
lay hold upon, 2.
lay hands on, 2.
take, 8.
take by, 5.
obtain, 1.
hold, 12.
hold fast, 5.
hold by, 1.
keep, 1.
retain, 2.

κράτιστος,
most excellent, 2.
most noble, 2.

κράτος,
strength, 1.
power, 6.
dominion, 4.
— *with κατά,*
mightily, 1.

κραυγάζω,
to cry, 4.
cry out, 3.

κραυγή,
cry, 3.
crying, 2.
clamour, 1.

κρέας,
flesh, 2.

κρείσσων,
better, 14.
better country, 1.
best, 1.
— *neuter,*
better thing, 1.

κρεμάννυμι,
hang, 4.
— *middle,*
hang, 3.

κρημνός,
steep place, 3.

κριθή,
barley, 1.

κρίθινος,
barley, 2.

κρίμα,
judgment, 13.
condemnation, 5.
judgment, 2.
damnation, 7.
judgment, 1.
— *pl., with ἔχω,*
go to law, 1.
— *with κρίνω,*
avenge, 1.
— *with εἰς,*
to be condemned, 1.

κρίνον,
lily, 2.

κρίνω,
to esteem, 2.
think, 1.
determine, 7.
conclude, 1.
judge, 87.
determine, 1.
decree, 1.
ordain, 1.
condemn, 5.
damn, 1.
call in question, 2.
— *ἐγὼ κρίνω,*
my sentence is, 1.
— *with κρίμα,*
avenge, 1.
— *mid. or pass.,*
sue at the law, 1.
go to law, 2.

κρίσις,
judgment, 41.
condemnation, 3.
damnation, 3.
accusation, 2.

κριτήριον,
judgment-seat, 1.
judgment, 1.
— *Genitive,*
to judge, 1.

κριτής,
judge, 17.

κριτικός,
discerner, 1.

κρούω,
to knock, 9.

κρυπτός,
hid, 3.
hidden, 1.
secret, 1 (*adj.*)
secret, 2 (*subst.*)
— *neuter,*
hidden thing, 2.
— *with ἐν,*
in secret, 9.
inwardly, 1.
— *εἰς κρυπτήν,*
in a secret place, 1.

κρύπτω,
to hide, 12.
keep secret, 1.
secretly, 1.
— *passive,*
hide one's self, 2.

κρυσταλλίζω,
clear as crystal, 1.

κρύσταλλος,
crystal, 2.

* **κρυφαῖος,**
[*for* κρυπτός, Matt. vi. 18, *see* "in secret."]

κρυφῆ,
in secret, 1.

κτάομαι,
obtain, 1.
provide, 1.
get, 1.
purchase, 2.
possess, 3.

κτῆμα,
possession, 4.

κτῆνος,
beast, 4.

κτήτωρ,
possessor, 1.

κτίζω,
create, 12.
Creator, 1.
make, 1.

κτίσις,
creation, 6.
creature, 11.
building, 1.
ordinance, 1.

κτίσμα,
creature, 4.

κτίστης,
Creator, 1.

κυβεία,
sleight, 1.

κυβέρνησις,
government, 1.

κυβερνήτης,
ship-master, 1.
master, 1.

* **κυκλεύω,**
[*for* κυκλόω, Rev. xx. 9, *see* "Compass about."]

κυκλόθεν,
round about, 3.
about, 1.

κύκλος, (*Dat.*)
round about, 7.

κυκλόω,
to compass, 1.
compass about, 2.
come round about, 1.
stand round about, 1.

κύλισμα,
wallowing, 1.

κυλίω, (*mid.*)
wallow, 1.

κυλλός,
maimed, 4.

κῦμα,
wave, 5.

κύμβαλον,
cymbal, 1.

κύμινον,
cumin, 1.

κυνάριον,
dog, 4.

κύπτω,
stoop down, 1.
stoop, 2.

κυρία,
lady, 1.

κυριακός,
Lord's, 2.

κυριεύω,
be lord of, 1.
lord, 1.
exercise lordship over, 1.
have dominion over, 4.

κύριος,
lord, 56.
master, 12.
owner, 1.
sir, 13.
Lord, 663.
Master, 2.

κυριότης,
dominion, 3.
government, 1.
dominion, 1.

κυρόω,
confirm, 2.

κύων,
dog, 5.

κῶλον,
carcass, 1.

κωλύω,
to hinder, 2.
forbid, 1.
let, 1.
keep from, 1.
withstand, 1.
suffer not, 1.
forbid, 16.
—— *with* ἀπό,
forbid to take, 1.

κώμη,
village, 17.
town, 12.

κωμόπολις,
town, 38.

κῶμος,
revelling, 2.
rioting, 1.

κώνωψ,
gnat, 1.

κωφός,
dumb, 8.
speechless, 1.
deaf, 5.

λαγχάνω,
be one's lot, 1.
cast lots, 1.
obtain, 2.

λάθρα,
secretly, 1.
privily, 3.

λαῖλαψ,
storm, 2.
tempest, 1.

λακέω, *see* **λάσκω.**

λακτίζω,
to kick, 2.

λαλέω,
speak, 241.
say, 2.
be spoken of, 1.
speak of, 2,
speak with, 2.
talk, 12.
talk with, 1.
say, 15.
tell, 11.
utter, 4.
preach, 6.

λαλιά,
speech, 3.
saying, 1.

λαμά,
lama, 2.

λαμβάνω,
take, 104.
take to one's self, 1.
take upon one's self, 1.
take up, 2.
take away, 1.
catch, 3.
come on, 1.
receive, 133.
take unto one's self, 1.
obtain, 2.
attain, 1.
accept, 2.
have, 3.
hold, 1.
take, 1.
bring, 1.
call to, 1.

λᾶμμα, *see* **λαμά.**

λαμπάς,
torch, 1.
light, 1.
lamp, 7.

λαμπρός,
bright, 2.
white, 2.
clear, 1.
gorgeous, 1.
gay, 1.
goodly, 2.

λαμπρότης,
brightness, 1.

λαμπρῶς,
sumptuously, 1.

λάμπω,
shine, 6.
give light, 1.

λανθάνω,
be hid, 3.
unawares, 1.
be ignorant of, 2.

λαξευτός,
hewn in stone, 1.

λαός,
people, 143.

λάρυγξ,
throat, 1.

λάσκω,
burst asunder, 1.

λατομέω,
hew, 2.

λατρεία,
service, 4.
divine service, 1.

λατρεύω,
serve, 16.
do service, 1,
worship, 3.
worshipper, 1.

λάχανον,
herb, 4.

λεγεών,
legion, 2.
Legion, 2.

λέγω,
put forth, 1
give out, 1.
show, 1.
describe, 1.
tell, 33.
utter, 1.
say, 1180.
say on, 1.
speak, 56.
speak of, 1.
boast, 1.
ask, 1.
bid, 2.
call, 47.
name, 2.
—— *with* ταῦτα,
with these sayings, 1.
—— *passive,*
be to say, 2.
to say, 1.
—— τὰ λεγομένα,
the things which were spoken, 2.
those things which were spoken, 2.
those things which... spake, 1.
the things which...hath spoken, 1.

λεῖμμα,
remnant, 1.

λεῖος,
smooth, 1.

λείπω,
to lack, 1.
be wanting, 2.
be left undone, 1.
—— *passive,*
destitute, 1.
lack, 1.
—— *with* ἐν,
want, 1.

λειτουργέω,
to minister, 3.

λειτουργία,
service, 3.
ministration, 1.
ministry, 2.

λειτουργικός,
ministering, 1.

λειτουργός,
minister, 4.
he that ministereth, 1.

λέντιον,
towel, 2.

λεπίς,
scale, 1.

λέπρα,
leprosy, 4.

λεπρός,
leper, 9.

λεπτόν,
mite, 3.

λευκαίνω,
to white, 1.
make white, 1.

λευκός,
white, 25.

λέων,
lion, 8.
Lion, 1.

λήθη, *with* **λαμβάνω,**
forget, 1.

ληκέω, *see* **λάσκω.**

ληνός,
wine-press, 5.

λῆρος,
idle tales, 1.

λῃστής,
robber, 4.
thief, 11.

λῆψις,
receiving, 1.

λίαν,
greatly, 4.
sore, 1.
exceeding, 5.
—— ὑπὲρ λίαν,
very chiefest, 2.

λίβανος,
frankincense, 2.

λιβανωτός,
censer, 2.

λιθάζω,
to stone, 8.

λίθινος,
of stone, 3.

λιθοβολέω,
cast stones, 1.
stone, 8.

λίθος,
stone, 49.
—— λίθος ἐπὶ λίθῳ,
one stone upon another, 3.
—— λίθος ἐπὶ λίθον,
one stone upon another, 1.
—— λίθος μυλικός,
mill-stone, 1.
—— λίθος προσκόμματος,
stumbling-stone, 2.

λικμάω,
grind to powder, 2.

λιμήν,
haven, 2.
—— καλοὶ λιμένες,
the fair havens, 1.

λίμνη,
lake, 10.

λιμός,
hunger, 3.
famine, 7.
dearth, 2.

λίνον,
flax, 1.
linen, 1.

λιπαρός,
dainty, 1.

λίτρα,
pound, 2.

λίψ,
south-west, 1.

λογία,
gathering, 1.
collection, 1.

λογίζομαι,
—— *mid. and pass.*,
to number, 1.
account, 3.
impute, 1.
account of, 1.
count, 5.
lay to one's charge, 1.
reckon, 6.
impute, 8.
reason, 1.
think, 8.
reason, 1.
think of, 1.
reckon, 1.
think on, 1.
suppose, 2.
esteem, 1.
conclude, 1.
—— *with* εἰς οὐδέν,
despise, 1.

λογικός,
of the word, 1.
reasonable, 1.

λόγιον,
oracle, 4.

λόγιος,
eloquent, 1.

λογισμός,
thought, 1.
imagination, 1.
reasoning, 1.

λογομαχέω,
strive about words, 1.

λογομαχία,
strife of words, 1.

λόγος,
word, 208.
preaching, 2.
words, 11.
speech, 1.
Word, 7.
saying, 50.
thing, 1.
things to say, 1.
speech, 8.
talk, 1.
utterance, 4.
mouth, 1.
show, 1.
tidings, 1.
preaching, 1.
rumour, 1.
fame, 1.
communication, 8.
treatise, 1.
question, 1.
thing, 1.
account, 8.
work, 2.
account, 2.
thing, 4.
matter, 4.
doctrine, 1.
word, 1.
reason, 1.
intent, 1.
cause, 1.
—— τίνι λόγῳ,
what, 1.
by what speech, 1.
—— *with* συναίρω,
reckon, 1.
—— *with* εἰς,
as concerning, 1.
—— ὑμῖν ὁ λόγος,
we have to do, 1.
—— *with* κατά,
reason would, 1.

λόγχη,
spear, 1.

λοιδορέω,
revile, 4.

λοιδορία,
railing, 2.
—— λοιδορία χάριν,
to speak reproachfully, 1.
for railing, 1.

λοίδορος,
railer, 1.
reviler, 1.

λοιμός,
pestilence, 2.
pestilent fellow, 1.

λοιπός,
the remnant, 4.
the residue, 1.
the rest, 10.
the other, 5.
others, 7.
other, 7.
others, 1.
—— τὰ λοιπά (*neut. pl.*),
the things which remain, 1.
the rest, 2.
other things, 1.
other, 2.
—— τὸ λοιπόν, *etc.*,
besides, 1.
moreover, 1.
furthermore, 1.
henceforth, 1.
from henceforth, 1.
finally, 5.
now, 2.
then, 1.
—— *with* ἐστί,
it remaineth, 1.
—— *Genitive*,
from henceforth, 1.

λουτρόν,
washing, 2.

λούω,
wash, 6.

λύκος,
wolf, 6.

λυμαίνομαι,
make havoc of, 1.

λυπέω,
grieve, 2.
cause grief, 1.
make sorry, 3.
—— *mid. or pass.*,
be grieved, 4.
be made sorry, 3.
be sorry, 3.
sorrow, 3.
be sorrowful, 4.
sorrowful, 2.
be in heaviness, 1.

λύπη,
grief, 1.
sorrow, 11.
heaviness, 2.
—— *Genitive*,
grievous.
—— *with* ἐκ,
grudgingly.

λύσις,
to be loosed, 1.

λυσιτελέω, (*impers.*)
it is better, 1.

λύτρον,
ransom, 2.

λυτρόω,
redeem, 1,
—— *middle*,
redeem, 2.

λύτρωσις,
redemption, 2.
—— *with* ποιέω,
redeem, 1.

λυτρωτής,
deliverer, 1.

λυχνία,
candlestick, 12.

λύχνος,
light, 6.
candle, 8.

λύω,
to loose, 26.
be loosing, 1.
unloose, 3.
put off, 1.
dissolve, 2.
break, 6.
break up, 1.
destroy, 2.
—— *passive*,
melt, 1.

μαγεία,
sorcery, 1.

μαγεύω,
use sorcery, 1.

μάγος,
wise man, 4.
sorcerer, 2.

* μαζός,
[*for* μαστός, Rev. i. 13, *see* "Pap."]

μαθητεύω,
be a disciple, 1.
teach, 2.
make disciples or Christians of, 1.
instruct, 1.

μαθητής,
disciple, 269.

μαθητρία,
disciple, 1.

μαίνομαι,
be mad, 4.
be beside one's self, 1.

μακαρίζω,
count happy, 1.
call blessed, 1.

μακάριος,
happy, 6.
blessed, 43.

μακαρισμός,
blessedness, 3.

μάκελλον,
shambles, 1.

μακράν,
a great way off, 1.
a good way off, 1.
far off, 1.
far, 4.
far hence, 1.
—— *with art.*,
that is afar off, 1.
which is afar off, 1.

μακρόθεν,
from far, 1.
afar off, 4.
—— *with* ἀπό,
afar off, 9.

μακροθυμέω,
be long suffering, 1.
bear long, 1.
suffer long, 1.
have long patience, 1.
have patience, 2.
be patient, 3.
be long patient or suffer with long patience, 1.
endure patiently, 1.

μακροθυμία,
long-suffering, 11.
patience, 2.

μακροθύμως,
patiently, 1.

μακρός,
far, 2.

μακροχρόνιος, *with* εἰμί,
live long, 1.

μαλακία,
disease, 3.

μαλακός,
soft, 2.
effeminate, 1.
—— τὰ μαλακά,
soft clothing, 1.

μάλιστα,
most of all, 1.
chiefly, 2.
specially, 6.
especially, 4.

μᾶλλον,
more, 30.
the more, 8.
so much the more, 1.
rather, 28.
the rather, 1.
—— πολλῷ μᾶλλον,
the more a great deal, 1.
so much the more, 1.
far, 1.
—— *with* διαφέρω,
be much better, 1.
—— μᾶλλον δέ,
but rather, 2.
yea rather, 1.
or rather, 1.
and the more, 1.
—— μᾶλλον δὲ καί,
but rather, 1.

μάμμη,
grandmother, 1.

μαμμωνᾶς,
mammon, 4.
riches, 2.

μανθάνω,
learn, 24.
understand, 1.

μανία, *with* περιτρέπω,
make mad, 1.

μάννα,
manna, 5.

μαντεύομαι,
by soothsaying, 1.

μαραίνω, (*pass.*)
fade away, 1.

μαρὰν ἀθά,
Maran-atha, 1.

μαργαρίτης,
pearl, 9.

μάρμαρος,
marble, 1.

μάρτυρ, *see* μαρτυς.

μαρτυρέω,
be witness, 2.
witness, 4.
give witness, 1.
bear witness, 25.
testify, 19.
give testimony, 2.
bear record, 13.
give, 1.
—— *pass.* or *mid.*,
obtain witness, 1.
have testimony, 1.
have good report, 2.
of good report, 1.
be well reported of, 2.
obtain good report, 2.
of honest report, 1.
witness, 1.
charge, 1.

μαρτυρία,
witness, 15.
testimony, 14.
record, 7.
report, 1.

μαρτύριον,
witness, 4.
testimony, 15.
to be testified, 1.
testimony, 1.

μαρτύρομαι,
take to record, 1.
testify, 2.

μάρτυς,
witness, 29.
martyr, 3.
record, 2.

μασσάομαι,
gnaw, 1.

μαστιγόω,
to scourge, 7.

μαστίζω,
to scourge, 1.

μάστιξ,
scourging, 2.
plague, 4.

μαστός,
pap, 3.

ματαιολογία,
vain jangling, 1.

ματαιολόγος,
vain talker, 1.

μάταιος,
vain, 5.
—— *neuter*,
vanity, 1.

ματαιότης,
vanity, 3.

ματαιόω, (*pass.*)
become vain, 1.

μάτην,
in vain, 2.

μάχαιρα,
sword, 29.

μάχη,
fighting, 2.
brawling, 1.
strife, 1.
striving, 1.

μάχομαι,
to fight, 1.
strive, 3.

μέ, *see* ἐγώ.

μεγαλαυχέω,
boast great things, 1.

μεγαλεῖος, (*neut.*)
great thing, 1.
wonderful work, 1.

μεγαλειότης,
magnificence, 1.
majesty, 1.
mighty power, 1.

μεγαλοπρεπής,
excellent, 1.

μεγαλύνω,
enlarge, 2.
magnify, 1.
magnify, 5.
show great, 1.

μεγάλως,
greatly, 1.

μεγαλωσύνη,
majesty, 1.
Majesty, 2.

μέγας,
great, 145.
greatest, 2.
large, 2.
mighty, 1.
strong, 1.
loud, 33.
high, 2.
to years, 1.
—— οἱ μεγάλοι,
they that are great, 1.
great ones, 1.
—— *neuter*,
great thing, 3.
—— φόβον μέγαν,
exceedingly, 1.
sore, 1.
—— *comp.* (μείζων),
greater, 32.
greatest, 9.
more, 1.
elder, 1.
greater, 1.
—— *neuter*,
greater thing, 1.
greater work, 1.
—— *adverb*,
the more, 1.
—— *superl.* (μέγιστος),
exceeding great, 1.

μέγεθος,
greatness, 1.

μεγιστᾶνες,
great men, 2.
lords, 1.

μέγιστος, *see* μέγας.

μεθερμηνεύω,
interpret, 5.
—— *passive*,
be by interpretation, 2.

μέθη,
drunkenness, 3.

μεθίστημι, μεθιστάνω,
remove, 1.
can remove, 1.
translate, 1.
put out of, 1.
turn away, 1.

μεθοδεία,
wile, 1.
—— *with* πρός,
whereby one lieth in wait, 1.

μεθόριος, (*neut.*)
border, 1.

μεθύσκω, (*mid.*)
be drunk, 1.
be drunken, 2.

μέθυσος,
drunkard, 2.

μεθύω,
be drunken,
—— *middle*,
have well drunk, 1.
be made drunk, 1.

μεῖζων, *see* μέγας.

μέλαν,
ink, 3.

μέλας,
black, 3.

μέλει, *see* μέλω.

μελετάω,
meditate upon, 1.
premeditate, 1.
imagine, 1.

μέλι,
honey, 4.

μελίσσιος, *with* κηρίον,
honey-comb, 1.

μέλλω,
be about, 4.
about, 1.
be yet, 1.
tarry, 1.
be ready, 3.
ready, 2.
intend, 2.
mean, 1.
mind, 1.
be almost, 1.
be, 4.
be to come, 3.
begin, 1.
should hereafter, 1.
should afterwards, 1.
should after, 2.
shall, 25.
should, 20.
will, 8.
would, 8.
—— *participle*,
to come, 9.
thing to come, 4.
time to come, 1.
—— *with* γίνεσθαι,
be coming on, 1.
—— εἰς τὸ μέλλον,
after that, 1.
—— τὰ μέλλοντα,
what things should, 1.

μέλος,
member, 34.

μέλω, (*impers.*, *with a Dat.*)
to care, 9.
take care, 1.

μεμβράνα,
parchment, 1.

μέμφομαι,
find fault, 3.

μεμψίμοιρος,
complainer, 1.

μέν,
indeed, 22.
truly, 12.
verily, 14.
even, 1.
— οἱ μέν,
some, 1.
— ὁ μὲν...ὁ δέ.
— ὃς μὲν...ὃς δέ.
— ἄλλος μὲν...ἄλλος δέ,
the one...the other, 3.
one...the other, 1.
one...another, 10.
one man...another, 1.
some...others, 4.
some...some, 15.
part...part, 1.
he(they,etc.)...he(etc.), 6.
those...this, 1.
those things ... these things, 1.
— τοῦτο μὲν...τοῦτο δέ,
partly...partly, 1.
— ὅσα μὲν...ὅσα δέ,
those things which... but what, 1.

μενοῦνγε,
yea rather, 1.
yea doubtless, 1.
yes verily, 1.
nay but, 1.

μέντοι,
yet, 2.
nevertheless, 1.
howbeit, 1.
but, 1.
— ὅμως μέντοι,
nevertheless, 1.
— μέντοι καί,
also, 1.

μένω,
remain, 17.
abide, 59.
dwell, 15.
tarry, 9.
tarry for, 1.
be present, 1.
continue, 11.
endure, 3.
stand, 1.
— μένω σοί,
be thine own, 1.

μερίζω,
divide, 8.
give part, 1.
distribute, 2.
deal, 1.
— *middle,*
divide,
— *passive,*
be difference between, 1.

μέριμνα,
care, 6.

μεριμνάω,
be careful, 2.
have care, 1.
care, 5.
take thought, 10.
with taking thought, 1.

μερίς,
part, 4.
— *with* εἰς,
to be partaker, 1.

μερισμός,
dividing asunder, 1.
gift, 1.
distribution, 1.

μεριστής,
divider, 1.

μέρος,
part, 17.
piece, 1.
portion, 3.
coast, 3.
craft, 1.
behalf, 2.
respect, 2.
part, 1.
— *with* ἀπό,
in part, 3.
in some sort, 1.
somewhat, 1.
— *with* ἐκ,
in part, 4.
in particular, 1.
— *with* ἀνά,
by course, 1.
— *with* κατά,
particularly, 1.
— μέρος τι,
partly, 1.
— τὰ δεξιὰ μέρη,
on the right side, 1.

μεσημβρία,
noon, 1.
south, 1.

μεσιτεύω,
confirm, 1.
interpose one's self, 1.

μεσίτης,
mediator, 6.

μεσονύκτιον,
midnight, 2.
— *Genitive,*
at midnight, 2.

μέσος,
in the midst, 1.
among, 1.
— μέσον,
in the midst, 3.
— ἀνὰ μέσον,
through the midst, 1.
in the midst, 1.
among, 1.
between, 1.
— ἐν μέσῳ,
among, 5.
before, 1.
— ἐκ μέσου,
from among, 5.
out of the way, 2.
— *with* διά, εἰς, *or* ἐν,
...midst, 35.

μεσότοιχον,
middle wall between, 1.

μεσουράνημα,
midst of heaven, 3.

μεσόω,
about the midst, 1.

μεστός,
full, 8.

μεστόω, (*pass.*)
full, 1.

μετά,
— *with a Genitive,*
with, 337.
among, 5.
in, 2.
on, 1.
upon, 1.
unto, 1.
against, 4.
promised to, 1.
of, 1.
and setting, 1.
— ἐκ τῶν...μετά,
between some of...and, 1.
— *with art.,*
he that is with, 6.
he which is with, 2.
that is with, 1.
— οὐ μετά,
without, 1.
— *with an Accusative,*
after, 87.
since, 1.
hence, 1.
when, 2.
— *with* ταῦτα,
hereafter, 4.
afterward, 4.
that should follow, 1.
— *with* εἰμί,
follow, 1.

μεταβαίνω,
remove, 2.
pass, 2.
depart, 7.
go, 1.

μεταβάλλω, (*mid.*)
change one's mind, 1.

μετάγω,
turn about, 2.

μεταδίδωμι,
impart, 3.
give, 2.
impart, 1.
distribute, 1.

μετάθεσις,
removing, 1.
translation, 1.
change, 1.

μεταίρω,
depart, 2.

μετακαλέω, (*mid.*)
call for, 1.
call to one's self, 1.
call hither, 1.
call, 1.

μετακινέω,
move away, 1.

μεταλαμβάνω,
be partaker of, 2.
receive, 1.
take, 1.
eat, 1.
have, 1.

μετάληψις, *with* εἰς.
to be received, 1.

μεταλλάσσω,
to change, 2.

μεταμέλομαι,
repent, 5.
repent one's self, 1.

μεταμορφόω, (*mid.*)
be transformed, 1.
be transfigured, 2.
be changed, 1.

μετανοέω,
repent, 34.

μετάνοια,
repentance, 24.
amendment of life, 1.
to change one's mind, 1.

μεταξύ,
between, 6.
meanwhile, 2.
next, 1.
between, 2.

μεταπέμπω,
send for, 6.
call for, 2.

μεταστρέφω,
turn, 2.
pervert, 1.

μετασχηματίζω,
— *middle,*
transform one's self, 1.
be transformed, 2.
transfer in a figure, 1.
change, 1.

μετατίθημι,
translate, 2.
carry over, 1.
remove, 1.
change, 1.
turn, 1.

μετέπειτα,
afterward, 1.

μετέχω,
take part of, 1.
be partaker of, 5.
pertain to, 1.
use, 1.

μετεωρίζω, (*mid. or pass.*)
be of doubtful mind, 1.
live in careful suspense, 1.

μετοικεσία,
carrying away into, 2.
— *with* ἐπί,
about the time they were carried away to, 1.
— *with* μετά,
after they were brought to, 1.

μετοικίζω,
carry away, 1.
remove into, 1.

μετοχή,
fellowship, 1.

μέτοχος,
partaker, 4.
partner, 1.
fellow, 1.

μετρέω,
to measure, 7.
mete, 3.

μετρητής,
firkin, 1.

μετριοπαθέω,
have compassion on, 1.
reasonably bear with, 1.

μετρίως,
a little, 1.

μέτρον,
measure, 13.

μέτωπον,
forehead, 8.

μέχρι, μέχρις,
unto, 8.
to, 1.
until, 7.
till, 1.
— μέχρις οὗ,
till, 1.

μή,
not, 502.
thou do it not, 2.
no, 41.
neither, 7.
nor, 2.
that not, 2.
no man, 1.
no one of you, 1.
none, 3.
nothing, 1.
never, 1.
but, 3.
any, 1.
— εἰς τὸ μή,
lest, 1.
— μή τις,
none, 1.
no man, 5.
— μή τι,
nothing, 1.
no, 2.
— μή τί,
nothing, 1.
— μὴ οὐκ,
not? 5.
— οὐ μή,
not in any wise, 1.
in no wise, 6.
in no case, 1.
by no means, 1.
by any means, 1.
not at all, 1.
at all, 1.
not, 57.
no, 2.
neither, 2.
never, 2.
— οὐ μὴ ἔτι,
no more at all, 5.
no more, 1.
— πᾶς οὐ μὴ ἔτι,
no more, 1.
— οὐδ' οὐ μή,
no, nor ever, 1.
— *as a conjunction*,
that not, 6.
lest, 15.
— μή τις,
that none, 1.
that no man, 2.

μήτις, or μή τις,
any man? 1.
any? 3.

μήτι, or μή τι,
not? 2.
— *with* γε,
how much more? 1.

μήγε, see εἰ δὲ μήγε.

μηδαμῶς,
not so, 2.

μηδέ,
neither, 32.
nor, 17.
nor yet, 2.
no, not, 1.
not, 3.
not once, 1.
no, not so much as, 1.

μηδείς, *etc.*
no man, 32.
not any man, 1.
any man, 1.
none, 5.
no, 16.
any, 2.
no thing, 1.
nothing, 27.
no man, 1.
any thing, 2.
not, 2.
not a whit, 1.
not at all, 1.
— μηδεμίαν ποιησάμενος,
without any, 1.

μηδέποτε,
never, 1.

μηδέπω,
not as yet, 1.

μηκέτι,
no longer, 4.
any longer, 1.
no more, 7.
not any more, 1.
not henceforth, 1.
henceforth not, 2.
henceforth no more, 1.
henceforth, 1.
hereafter, 1.
no henceforward, 1.
no, 1.

μῆκος,
length, 3.

μηκύνω, (*mid.*)
grow up, 1.

μηλωτή,
sheepskin, 1.

μήν, (*adv.*) see ἦ.

μήν, (*subst.*)
month, 17.

μηνύω,
show, 3.
tell, 1.

μήποτε,
lest at any time, 7.
lest haply, 2.
lest, 12.
if peradventure, 1.
no...at all, 1.
whether or not, 1.

* μήπου,
[*for* μήπως, Acts xxvii. 29, *see* "Lest."]

μήπω,
not yet, 2.

μήπως,
lest by any means, 3.
lest that by any means, 1.
lest by some means, 1.
lest perhaps, 1.
lest haply, 1.
lest, 5.

μηρός,
thigh, 1.

μήτε,
neither, 20.
nor, 14.
or, 1.
so much as, 1.

μήτηρ,
mother, 85.

μήτις, see under μή.

μήτρα,
womb, 2.

μητραλῴας,
murderer of a mother, 1.

μία, see εἷς.
defile, 5.

μίασμα,
pollution, 1.

μιασμός,
uncleanness, 1.

μίγμα,
mixture, 1.

μίγνυμι,
mingle, 4.

μικρός,
little, 10.
little one, 6.
little one, 6.
less, 1.
least, 2.
small, 6.
— *comp.*, μικρότερος,
less, 1.
least, 4.
— *adv.*, μικρόν,
a little, 5.
a little while, 10.
a while, 1.

μίλιον,
mite, 1.

μιμέομαι,
follow, 4.

μιμητής,
follower, 7.

μιμνήσκω, (*mid.*)
be mindful of, 1.
remember, 1.
— ἐμνήσθην (1st aor.),
be mindful of, 2.
remember, 16.
in remembrance, 1.
— *passive*,
come in remembrance, 1.
be had in remembrance, 1.

μισέω,
to hate, 40.
— *pass. part.*,
hateful, 1.

μισθαποδοσία,
recompense of reward, 3.

μισθαποδότης,
rewarder, 1.

μίσθιος,
hired servant, 2.

μισθός,
hire, 3.
wages, 2.
reward, 24.

μισθόω, (*mid.*)
to hire, 2.

μίσθωμα,
hired house, 1.

μισθωτός,
hired servant, 1.
hireling, 3.

μνᾶ,
pound, 9.

μνάομαι, see μιμνήσκω.

μνεία,
remembrance, 3.
mention, 1.
mention, 4.

μνῆμα,
tomb, 2.
sepulchre, 4.
grave, 1.

μνημεῖον,
tomb, 5.
sepulchre, 29.
grave, 8.

μνήμη,
remembrance, 1.

μνημονεύω,
remember, 19.
be mindful of, 1.
make mention, 1.
remember, 1.

μνημόσυνον,
memorial, 3.

μνηστεύω, (*pass.*)
be espoused, 3.

* μογγιλάλος,
[*for* μογιλάλος, Mark vii. 32, *see* "Having an impediment in one's speech."]

μογιλάλος,
having an impediment in one's speech, 1.

μόγις,
hardly, 1.

μόδιος,
bushel, 3.

μοί, see ἐγώ.

μοιχαλίς,
adulteress, 3.
adulterous, 3.
adultery, 1.
adulteress, 1.

μοιχάω, (*mid.*)
commit adultery, 6.

μοιχεία,
adultery, 4.

μοιχεύω,
commit adultery, 12.
commit adultery with, 1.
— *pass. as mid.*,
in adultery, 1.

μοιχός,
adulterer, 4.

μόλις,
hardly, 1.
scarcely, 2.
scarce, 2.

μολύνω,
defile, 3.

μολυσμός,
filthiness, 1.

μομφή,
quarrel, 1.
complaint, 1.

μονή,
abode, 1.
mansion, 1.

μονογενής,
Only begotten, 5.
only begotten son, 1.
only child, 1.
only, 2.

μόνος,
only, 24.
alone, 21.
by one's self, 2.
— *adv.*, μόνον,
only, 62.
alone, 3.
but, 1.

μονόφθαλμος,
with one eye, 2.

μονόω, (*pass.*)
desolate, 1.

μορφή,
form, 3.

μορφόω,
to form, 1.

μόρφωσις,
form, 2.

μοσχοποιέω,
make a calf, 1.

μόσχος,
calf, 6.

μοῦ, *see* ἐγώ.

μουσικός,
musician, 1.

μόχθος,
travail, 2.
painfulness, 1.

μυελός,
marrow, 1.

μυέω,
instruct, 1.

μῦθος,
fable, 5.

μυκάομαι,
to roar, 1.

μυκτηρίζω,
to mock, 1.

μυλικός, *with* λίθος,
millstone, 1.

* μύλινος,
[*for* μύλος, Rev. xviii. 21, *see* "Millstone."]

μύλος,
millstone, 4.

μύλων,
mill, 1.

μυριάς,
ten thousand, 1.
— μυριάδες μυριάδων,
ten thousand times ten thousand, 1.
— μυριάδες πέντε,
fifty thousand, 1.
— δυομυριάδες μυριάδων,
two hundred thousand thousand, 1.
— *plural*,
thousands, 1.
an innumerable multitude, 1.
an innumerable company, 1.

μυρίζω,
anoint, 1.

μύριοι, μυρίοι,
ten thousand, 3.

μύρον,
ointment, 14.

μυστήριον,
mystery, 27.

μυωπάζω,
can not see afar off, 1.

μώλωψ,
stripes, 1.

μωμάομαι, μωμέομαι,
to blame, 2.

μῶμος,
blemish, 1.

μωραίνω,
make foolish, 1.
— *passive*,
lose savour, 2.
become a fool, 1.

μωρία,
foolishness, 5.

μωρολογία,
foolish talking, 1.

μωρός,
foolish, 6.
fool, 5.
— *neuter*,
foolish thing, 1.
foolishness, 1.

ναί,
yea, 23.
yes, 3.
even so, 5.
surely, 1.
verily, 1.
truth, 1.

ναός,
temple, 45.
shrine, 1.

νάρδος,
spikenard, 2.
pure nard or liquid nard, 1.

ναυαγέω,
suffer shipwreck, 1.
make shipwreck, 1.

ναύκληρος,
owner of a ship, 1.

ναῦς,
ship, 1.

ναύτης,
shipman, 2.
sailor, 1.

νεανίας,
young man, 5.

νεανίσκος,
young man, 10.

νεκρός,
dead, 105 (*subst.*)
one dead, 1.
dead man, 3.
he that is dead, 2.
dead, 21 (*adj.*)
— ἐπὶ νεκροῖς,
after men are dead, 1.

νεκρόω,
mortify, 1.
— *passive*,
dead, 2.

νέκρωσις,
dying, 1.
deadness, 1.

νεομηνία, *see* νουμηνία.

νέος,
new, 11.
new man, 1.
— *feminine*,
young woman, 1.
— *comp.*, νεώτερος,
younger, 7.
younger man, 1.
young, 1.
young man, 2.

νεοσσός,
young, 1.

νεότης,
youth, 5.

νεόφυτος,
novice, 1.
one newly come to the faith, 1.

νεύω,
beckon, 2.

νεφέλη,
cloud, 26.

νέφος,
cloud, 1.

νεφρός, (*pl.*)
reins, 1.

νεωκόρος,
worshipper, 1.
temple-keeper, 1.

νεωτερικός,
youthful, 1.

νεώτερος, *see* νέος.

νή,
I protest by, 1.

νήθω,
spin, 2.

νηπιάζω,
be a child, 1.

νήπιος,
babe, 6.
child, 7.
— *Genitive*,
childish, 1.

νησίον,
island, 1.

νῆσος,
island, 6.
isle, 3.

νηστεία,
fasting, 7.
fast, 1.

νηστεύω,
to fast, 20.
— *with* ἦν,
used to fast, 1.

νῆστις,
fasting, 2.

νηφάλιος, νηφάλεος,
sober, 2.
vigilant, 1.
vigilant, 1.

νήφω,
be sober, 3.
sober, 1.
watch, 2.

νικάω,
get the victory, 1.
prevail, 1.
overcome, 24
conquer, 2.

νίκη,
victory, 1.

νῖκος,
victory, 4.

νιπτήρ,
basin, 1.

νίπτω,
to wash, 17.

νοέω,
perceive, 2.
understand, 10.
think, 1.
consider, 1.

νόημα,
thought, 1.
device, 1.
mind, 4.

νόθος,
bastard, 1.

νομή,
pasture, 1.
— *with* ἔχω,
eat, 1.

νομίζω,
think, 5.
suppose, 9.
—— *passive,*
be wont, 1.

νομικός,
about the law, 1.
lawyer, 8.

νομίμως,
lawfully, 2.

νόμισμα,
money, 1.

νομοδιδάσκαλος,
teacher of the law, 1.
doctor of the law, 2.

νομοθεσία,
giving of the law, 1.

νομοθετέω,
establish, 1.
—— *passive,*
receive the law, 1.

νομοθέτης,
lawgiver, 1.

νόμος,
law, 195.

νοσέω,
dote, 1.
sick, 1.

νόσημα,
disease, 1.

νόσος,
sickness, 5.
disease, 6.
infirmity, 1.

νοσσιά,
brood, 1.

νοσσίον,
chicken, 1.

νοσσός, see νεοσσός.

νοσφίζω,
—— *middle,*
keep back, 2.
purloin, 1.

νότος,
south wind, 3.
south, 4.

νουθεσία,
admonition, 3.

νουθετέω,
admonish, 4.
warn, 4.

νουμηνία,
new moon, 1.

νουνεχῶς,
discreetly, 1.

νοῦς,
mind, 15.
minds, 2.
understanding, 7.

νύμφη,
bride, 5.
daughter-in-law, 3.

νυμφίος,
bridegroom, 16.

νυμφών,
bride-chamber, 3.

νῦν,
now, 116.
at this time, 1.
this time, 2.
of late, 1.
—— *with art.,*
that now is, 1.
which I make now, 1.
—— *τὸ νῦν ἔχον,*
for this time, 1.
—— *ὁ νῦν καιρός,*
this time, 1.
this present time, 1.
—— *with ἐν,*
now at this time, 1.
—— *ὁ νῦν αἰών,*
this world, 1.
this present world, 2.
—— *ἀπό τοῦ νῦν,*
from henceforth, 4.
henceforth, 1.
hereafter, 1.
—— *νῦν οὐκέτι,*
now henceforth no more, 1.
—— *τὰ νῦν,*
now, 4.
but now, 1.

νυνί,
now, 21.

νύξ,
night, 52.
—— *Genitive,*
by night, 9.
in the night, 2.
—— *μέσης νυκτός,*
at midnight, 1.
—— *μέσον τῆς νυκτός,*
about midnight, 1.

νύσσω,
pierce, 1.

νυστάζω,
to slumber, 2.

νυχθήμερον,
a night and a day, 1.

νωθρός,
slothful, 1.
dull, 1.

νῶτος,
back, 1.

ξενία,
lodging, 2.

ξενίζω,
entertain, 1.
lodge, 4.
strange thing, 1.
—— *passive,*
lodge, 2.
—— *middle,*
think strange concerning, 1.
think strange, 1.

ξενοδοχέω,
lodge strangers, 1.

ξένος,
stranger, 10.
strange, 2.
strange thing, 1.
host, 1.

ξέστης,
pot, 2.

ξηραίνω,
dry up, 3.
wither, 1.
—— *passive,*
be ripe, 1.
be dried, 1.
be withered, 3.
wither, 1.
wither away, 6.
pine away, 1.

ξηρός,
dry, 1.
dry land, 1.
land, 1.
withered, 4.

ξύλινος,
of wood, 2.

ξύλον,
wood, 3.
staff, 5.
stocks, 1.
tree, 10.

ξυράω,
shave, 2.
—— *middle,*
shave, 1.

ὁ, ἡ, το,
[*the def. art., frequently untranslated, generally translated* the, *and often in various ways, e.g. before nouns, etc.,* "he that."]

ὅ, see ὅς.

ὀγδοήκοντα,
fourscore, 2.

ὄγδοος,
eighth, 5.

ὄγκος,
weight, 1.

ὅδε,
he, 1.
—— *ἥδε,*
she, 1.
such, 1.
—— *τάδε,*
these things, 7.
thus, 1.
after this manner, 1.

ὁδεύω,
to journey, 1.

ὁδηγέω,
to lead, 3.
guide, 2.

ὁδηγός,
leader, 1.
guide, 4.

ὁδοιπορέω,
go on one's journey, 1.

ὁδοιπορία,
journeying, 1.
journey, 1.

* *ὁδοποιέω,*
[*for* ὁδὸν ποιέω, Mark ii. 23, *see* "Go."]

ὁδός,
way, 82.
highway, 3.
journey, 6.
way, 1.
—— *ἐν τῇ ὁδῷ*
that way, 1.
—— *with παρά,*
by the way-side, 8.
by the highway-side, 1.
—— *with ποιέω,*
go, 1.

ὀδούς,
tooth, 11.

ὀδυνάω, (mid.)
be tormented, 2.
sorrow, 2.

ὀδύνη,
sorrow 2.

ὀδυρμός,
mourning, 2.

ὄζω,
stink, 1.

ὅθεν,
whence, 1.
from thence, 1.
from whence, 3.
where, 2.
wherefore, 4.
whereby, 1.
whereupon, 3.

ὀθόνη,
sheet, 2.

ὀθόνιον,
linen cloth, 5.

οἶδα, see εἶδον.

οἰκεῖος,
of the household, 2.
of one's own home, 1.
kindred, 1.

* *οἰκετία,*
[*for* θεραπεία, Matt. xxiv. 45, *see* "Household."]

οἰκέτης,
household servant, 1.
servant, 3.

οἰκέω,
dwell, 9.

οἴκημα,
prison, 1.

οἰκητήριον,
habitation, 1.
house, 1.

οἰκία,
house, 92.
household, 1.
—— *τὰς οἰκίας,*
from house to house,
—— *with ἐν,*
at home, 1.

οἰκιακός,
of one's household, 2.

οἰκοδεσποτέω,
guide the house, 1.

οἰκοδεσπότης,
master of the house, 3.
householder, 4.
goodman of the house, 4.
goodman, 1.

οἰκοδομέω,
build, 24.
builder, 5.
build up, 1.
edify, 7.
embolden, 1.
edify, 1.
— *passive*,
be in building, 1.

οἰκοδομή,
building, 6.
edifying, 7.
edify, 1.
edification, 4.
— τὰ τῆς οἰκοδομῆς,
the things wherewith one may edify, 1.

οἰκοδομία,
edifying, 1.

* οἰκοδόμος,
[*for* οἰκοδομέω, Acts iv. 11, *see* "Builder."]

οἰκονομέω,
be steward, 1.

οἰκονομία,
stewardship, 3.
dispensation, 4.

οἰκονόμος,
steward, 8.
chamberlain, 1.
governour 1.

οἶκος,
house, 101.
household, 3.
temple, 1.
— *with* κατά,
from house to house, 1.
at home, 1.
in every house, 1.
into every house, 1.
— *with* εἰς,
home, 2.
— *with* ἐν,
at home, 2.
— *with* ἴδιος,
home, 1.

οἰκουμένη,
earth, 1.
world, 14.

* οἰκουργός,
[*for* οἰκουρός, Tit. ii. 5, *see* "Home (keeper at)."]

οἰκουρός,
keeper at home, 1.

οἰκτείρω,
have compassion on, 2.

οἰκτίρμων,
merciful, 2.
of tender mercy, 1.

οἶμαι, *see* οἴομαι.

οἰνοπότης,
wine-bibber, 2.

οἶνος,
wine, 32.
— *with* ληνός,
wine-press, 1.

οἰνοφλυγία,
excess of wine, 1.

οἴομαι,
suppose, 2.
think, 1.

οἷος,
what manner, 1.
what manner of man, 1.
what, 1.
which, 2.
such as, 6.
as, 2.
— οἷα,
so as, 1.
— οἷον ὅτι,
as though, 1.

οἴω, *see* φέρω.

ὀκνέω,
to delay, 1.
be grieved, 1.

ὀκνηρός,
slothful, 2.
grievous, 1.

ὀκταήμερος,
the eighth day

ὀκτώ,
eight, 6.

ὀλεθρεύω, *see* ὀλοθρεύω.

* ὀλέθριος,
[*for* ὄλεθρος, 2 Thes. i. 9, *see* "Destruction."]

ὄλεθρος,
destruction, 4.

* ὀλιγοπιστία,
[*for* ἀπιστία, Matt. xvii. 20, *see* "Unbelief."]

ὀλιγόπιστος,
of little faith, 5.

ὀλίγος,
little, 4.
small, 5.
short, 1.
— *with* ἐν,
almost, 2.
in few words, 1.
a little, 1.
— *with* οὐ,
long, 1.
— *with* πρός,
for a little time, 1.
little, 1.
for a little time, 1.
— *plural*,
few, 14.
few stripes, 1.
— *neut. pl.*,
a few things, 4.
— δι' ὀλίγων
briefly, 1.
— ὀλίγον *as adv.*,
a little, 3.
little, 1.
a short space, 1.
for a season, 1.
a while, 2.

ὀλιγόψυχος,
feeble-minded, 1.

ὀλιγωρέω,
despise, 1.

* ὀλίγως,
[*for* ὄντως, 2 Pet. ii. 18, *see* "Clean."]

ὀλοθρευτής,
destroyer, 1.

ὀλοθρεύω,
destroy, 1.

ὁλοκαύτωμα,
whole burnt-offering, 1.
burnt-offering, 1.

ὁλοκληρία,
perfect soundness, 1.

ὁλόκληρος,
whole, 1.
entire, 1.

ὀλολύζω,
to howl, 1.

ὅλος,
whole, 43.
all, 63.
all...long, 2.
altogether, 1.
every whit, 2.
— *with* διά,
throughout, 1.

ὁλοτελής.
wholly, 1.

ὄλυνθος,
untimely fig
green fig, 1.

ὅλως,
utterly, 1.
at all, 2.
commonly, 1.

ὄμβρος,
shower, 1.

* ὁμείρομαι,
[*for* ἱμείρομαι, 1 Thes. ii. 8, *see* "Affectionately desirous of (be)."]

ὁμιλέω,
commune together, 1.
commune with, 1.
talk, 2.

ὁμιλία,
communication, 1.

ὅμιλος,
company, 1.

* ὁμίχλη,
[*for* νεφέλη, 2 Pet. ii. 17, *see* "Cloud."]

ὄμμα,
eye, 1.

ὄμνυμι, ὀμνύω,
swear, 27.

ὁμοθυμαδόν,
with one accord, 11.
with one mind, 1.

ὁμιάζω,
agree thereto, 1.

ὁμοιοπαθης,
of like passions, 1.
subject to like passions, 1.

ὅμοιος,
like, 47

ὁμοιότης,
similitude, 1.
— *with* κατά,
like as, 1.

ὁμοιόω,
liken, 9.
made like, 2.
resemble, 1.
— *passive*,
be like, 2.
in the likeness of, 1.

ὁμοίωμα,
likeness, 3.
made like to, 1.
similitude, 1.
shape, 1.

ὁμοίως,
likewise, 18.
so, 1.
— καὶ...ὁμοίως,
moreover, 1.

ὁμοίωσις,
similitude, 1.

ὁμολογέω,
confess, 13.
give thanks, 1.
confess, 1.
profess, 3.
promise, 1.
— *with* ἐν,
confess, 4.
— *passive*,
confession is made, 1.

ὁμολογία,
confession, 1.
profession, 1.
profession, 4.
— *Genitive*,
professed, 1.

ὁμολογουμένως,
without controversy, 1.

ὁμότεχνος,
of the same craft, 1.

ὁμοῦ,
together, 3.

ὁμόφρων,
of one mind, 1.

ὀμόω, *see* ὄμνυμι.

ὅμως,
and even, 1.
though it be but, 1.
— ὅμως μέντοι,
nevertheless, 1.

ὄναρ,
dream, 6.

ὀνάριον,
young ass, 1

ὀνειδίζω,
revile, 2.
upbraid, 3.
cast in one's teeth, 1.
reproach, 3.
— *passive,*
suffer reproach, 1.

ὀνειδισμός,
reproach, 5.

ὄνειδος,
reproach, 1.

ὄνημι, *see* ὀνίνημι.

ὀνικός, *with* μύλος,
millstone, 2.

ὀνίνημι, (*mid.*)
have joy, 1.

ὄνομα,
name, 193.
— *Dat., or with* αὐτῷ, *or* οὗ, *or* ᾧ,
named, 28.
called, 4.
— τοὔνομα *for* τὸ ὄνομα,
named, 1.

ὀνομάζω,
to name, 8.
call, 2.

ὄνος,
ass, 6.

ὄντως,
indeed, 6.
certainly, 1.
verily, 1.
of a truth, 1.
clean, 1.

ὄξος,
vinegar, 7.

ὀξύς,
sharp, 7.
swift, 1.

ὀπή,
cave, 1.
place, 1.
hole, 1.

ὄπισθεν,
behind, 4.
on the backside, 1.
after, 2.

ὀπίσω,
behind, 5.
back, 1.
after, 22.
— τὰ ὀπίσω,
those things which are behind, 1
— εἰς τὰ ὀπίσω,
backward, 1
back, 5.

ὁπλίζω, (*mid.*)
arm one's self with, 1.

ὅπλον,
instrument, 2.
arms or weapons, 1.
weapon, 2.
— *plural,*
armour, 2.

ὁποῖος,
of what sort, 1.
what manner of, 2.
such as, 1.
— *with* πότε,
whatsoever, 1.

ὁπότε,
when, 1.

ὅπου,
where, 53.
wheresoever, 1.
where...there, 1.
where...thither, 2.
whither, 9.
whereas, 2.
— ὅπου...ἐκεῖ,
where, 2.
— ὅπου...ἐπ' αὐτῶν,
on which, 1.
— *with* ἄν,
wheresoever, 2.
whithersoever, 4.
— *with* ἐάν,
wheresoever, 3.
whithersoever, 1.
in what place soever, 1.

ὀπτάνω,
see, 1.

ὀπτασία,
vision, 4.

ὀπτός,
broiled, 1.

ὄπτω, ὄψομαι, ὤφθην, *see* ὁράω.

ὀπώρα,
fruits, 1.

ὅπως,
that, 41.
so that, 1.
to, 4.
because, 1.
how, 4.
— *with* ἄν,
that, 4.
when, 1.

ὅραμα,
sight, 1.
vision, 11.

ὅρασις,
sight, 1.
to look upon, 1.
vision, 2.

ὁρατός,
visible, 1.

ὁράω,
see, 86.
see to, 2.
perceive, 1.
look to, 1.
look, 1.
behold, 1.
take heed, 5.
— *passive,*
appear, 17.
show one's self, 1.

ὀργή,
anger, 3.
indignation, 1.
wrath, 31.
vengeance, 1.

ὀργίζω, (*pass. or mid.*)
be angry, 5.
be wroth, 3.

ὀργίλος,
soon angry, 1.

ὀργυιά,
fathom, 2.

ὀρέγω,
to desire, 2.
covet after, 1.

ὀρεινός, (*adj.*)
hill, 2.

ὄρεξις,
lust, 1.

ὀρθοποδέω,
walk uprightly, 1.

ὀρθός,
straight, 1.
even, 1.
upright, 1.

ὀρθοτομέω,
divide rightly, 1.

ὀρθρίζω,
come early in the morning, 1.

ὀρθρινός,
morning, 1.

ὄρθριος,
early, 1.

ὄρθρος, (*Gen. or Acc.*)
early in the morning, 2.

ὀρθῶς,
rightly, 2.
right, 1.
plain, 1.

ὁρίζω,
to limit, 1.
determine, 3.
ordain, 2.
declare, 1.
determine, 1.
— *pass. part.,*
determinate, 1.

ὅριον,
border, 1.
coast, 10.

ὁρκίζω,
adjure, 2.
charge, 1.
adjure, 1.

ὅρκος,
oath, 10.

ὁρκωμοσία,
oath, 4.
swearing of an oath, 1.

ὁρμάω,
to rush, 1.
run violently, 3.
run, 1.

ὁρμή,
assault, 1.

ὅρμημα,
violence, 1.

ὄρνεον,
bird, 1.
fowl, 2.

ὁροθεσία,
bound, 1.

ὄρος,
mountain, 41.
mount, 21.
hill, 3.

ὀρύσσω,
dig, 3.

ὀρφανός,
fatherless, 1.
comfortless, 1.
orphan, 1.

ὀρχέω, (*mid.*)
to dance, 4.

ὅς, ἥ, ὅ,
[*the relative pronoun, translated* who, which, that, *etc.; with* δὲ μέν, *etc.,* the one, some, *etc.; with* ἄν *or* ἐάν, whosoever, whoso, whatsoever, *etc.*]

ὁσάκις,
— *with* ἄν,
as often as, 1.
as oft as, 1.
— *with* ἐάν,
as often as, 1.

ὅσγε,
he that, 1.

ὅσιος,
holy, 4.
Holy One, 2.
— τὰ ὅσια,
mercies, 1.
holy or just things, 1.

ὁσιότης,
holiness, 2.

ὁσίως,
holily, 1.

ὀσμή,
odour, 2.
savour, 4.

ὅσος,
how much, 3.
as much as, 1.
as large as, 1.
as, 2.
the more, 1.
as many as, 24.
so many as, 1.
who, 1.
how great things, 5.
how many things, 1.
what great things, 1.
whatsoever, 9.
whatsoever things, 7.
what things soever, 1.
all that, 3.
all things that, 2.
that ever, 3.
all, 1.
that, 9.
what, 3.
which, 2.
— ἐφ' ὅσον,
inasmuch as, 3.

the same, 1.
which, 1.
—— ταύτην (*Acc. fem. sing.*),
this, 48.
this woman, 1.
her, 1.
it, 1.
the, 1.
the same, 3.
that, 1.
—— αὗται (*nom. fem. pl.*),
these, 3.
—— ταύτας (*Acc. fem. pl.*),
these, 6.
those, 2.
—— μετὰ πολλὰς ταύτας ἡμέρας,
many days hence, 1.
—— τοῦτο (*nom. neut. sing.*),
this, 180.
this thing, 5.
this deed, 1.
it, 5.
the same, 1.
that, 20.
that thing, 1.
thus, 4.
so, 5.
—— ταῦτα (*neut. pl., Acc. and nom.*),
these, 28.
these things, 158.
these words, 5.
this, 6.
they, 1.
them, 3.
him, 1.
such, 1.
such things, 2.
the things, 2.
the same, 2.
those, 1.
those things, 3.
that, 7.
thus, 17.
so, 1.
—— τούτου (*Gen. sing., masc. and neut.*),
this, 53.
this man's, 2.
this man, 2.
this thing, 1.
this matter, 1.
him, 2.
it, 1.
that, 2.
—— *with* ἕνεκα,
for this cause, 2.
—— αὐτοῦ τούτου,
he himself, 1.
—— ταύτης (*Gen. sing. fem.*),
this, 31.
same, 1.
—— *with* διά,
hereby, 1.
—— τούτων (*Gen. plural, masc. and neut.*),
of these, 8.
of these things, 7.
than these, 7.
these, 22.
these things, 14.
these matters, 1.
this sort, 1.
their, 1.
they, 1.
those, 1.
of those things, 1.
such, 2.
of such matters, 1.
—— *with* ἕνεκα,
for these causes, 1.
—— τούτῳ (*Dat. sing., masc. and neut.*),
this, 1.
unto this, 1.
this, 50.
to this man, 1.
this man, 4.
this place, 1.
of the same, 1.
the same, 1.
to him, 4.
him, 5.
unto one, 1.
—— τούτοις (*Dat. pl., masc. and neut.*),
upon these, 1.
with these, 1.
these, 4.
these things, 3.
this, 2.
them, 1.
therewith, 1.
therein, 1.
those things, 1.
such, 1.
—— ταύτῃ (*Dat. sing.fem.*),
this, 25.
this same, 1.
the same, 1.
it, 1.
that, 3.
—— ταύταις (*Dat. pl. fem.*),
these, 6.
them, 1.
those, 4.
that, 1.

οὕτω, οὕτως,
thus, 17.
in this manner, 1.
so, 158.
even so, 13.
even, 1.
after this manner, 2.
in like manner, 1.
on this fashion, 1.
on this wise, 6.
likewise, 4.
as they were, 1.
for all that, 1.
what, 1.
—— οὕτως...οὕτως,
after this manner... after that, 1.
—— οὕτως ὡς,
like, 1.

οὐχ, *see* οὐ.

οὐχί,
not, 50.
not so, 1.
nay, 5.

ὀφειλέτης,
debtor, 5.
which oweth, 1.
sinner, 1.
debtor, 1.

ὀφειλή,
debt, 1.
due, 1.

ὀφείλημα,
debt, 2.

ὀφείλω,
be indebted, 1.
be a debtor, 1.
owe, 7.
ought, 15.
should, 1.
be one's duty, 2.
must needs, 1.
it behoveth one, 1.
be bound, 2.
be guilty, 1.
a debtor or bound, 1.
—— *with* γίνεσθαι,
need so requireth, 1.
—— *passive*,
be due, 1.
due, 1.
debt, 1.

ὄφελον,
I would, 2.
I would to God, 1.
would to God, 1.

ὄφελος,
it profiteth, 2.
it advantageth, 1.

ὀφθαλμοδουλεία,
eye-service, 2.

ὀφθαλμός,
eye, 100.
—— *plural*,
sight, 1.

ὄφις,
serpent, 14.

ὀφρύς,
brow, 1.
edge, 1.

ὀχλέω,
vex, 1.

ὀχλοποιέω,
gather a company, 1.

ὄχλος,
press, 5.
multitude, 79.
company, 7.
people, 82.
number of people, 1.
number, 1.

ὀχύρωμα,
stronghold, 1.

ὀψάριον,
fish, 4.
small fish, 1.

ὀψέ,
at even, 1.
even, 1.
in the end, 1.

ὄψιμος,
later, 1.

ὄψιος, *with* ὥρα,
eventide, 1.
—— ὀψία (*subst.*),
evening, 3.
even, 8.
—— *with* γίνομαι,
in the evening, 1.
at even, 1.

ὄψις,
face, 1.
countenance, 1.
appearance, 1.

ὀψώνιον,
wages, 3.
allowance, 1.
charges, 1.

παγιδεύω,
entangle, 1.

παγίς,
snare, 5.

πάγος, *with* Ἄρειος,
Areopagus, 1.
Mars' hill, 1.
Mars' hill, 1.
Court of the Areopagites, 1.

πάθημα,
suffering, 11.
affliction, 3.
affection, 1.
motion, 1.
passion, 1.

παθητός,
should suffer, 1.

πάθος,
affection, 1.
inordinate affection, 1.
lust, 1.

παιδαγωγός,
schoolmaster, 2.
instructor, 1.

παιδάριον,
lad, 1.
child, 1.

παιδεία,
nurture, 1.
instruction, 1.
chastening, 3.
chastisement, 1.

παιδευτής,
instructor, 1.
which correcteth, 1.

παιδεύω,
instruct, 1.
teach, 2.
chasten, 6.
chastise, 2.
—— *passive*,
learn, 1.
be learned, 1.

παιδιόθεν,
of a child, 1.

παιδίον,
little child, 12.
young child, 10.
child, 25.
damsel, 4.

παιδίσκη,
damsel, 4.
maiden, 1.
maid, 3.
bondmaid, 1.
bondwoman, 4.

παίζω,
to play, 1.

παῖς,
child, 7.
son, 1.
Son, 2.
young man, 1.
maiden, 1.
maid, 1.
servant, 10.
manservant, 1.

παίω,
smite, 4.
strike, 1.

πάλαι,
of old, 1.
old, 1.
long ago, 1.
a great while ago, 1.
in time past, 1.
any while, 1.

παλαιός,
old, 17.
old wine, 1.
— παλαιά,
old things, 1.

παλαιότης,
oldness, 1.

παλαιόω,
make old, 1.
— *passive*,
wax old, 2.
decay, 1.

πάλη,
wrestle, 1.

παλιγγενεσία,
regeneration, 2.

πάλιν,
again, 140.
back, 1.
— εἰς τὸ παλιν
again, 1.
— πάλιν ἄνωθεν,
again, 1.

παμπληθεί,
all at once, 1.

πάμπολυς,
very great, 1.

πανδοχεῖον,
inn, 1.

πανδοχεύς,
host, 1.

πανήγυρις,
general assembly, 1.

πανοικί,
with all one's house, 1.

πανοπλία,
whole armour, 2.
all...armour, 1.

πανουργία,
craftiness, 3.
cunning craftiness, 1.
subtilty, 1.

πανοῦργος,
crafty, 1.

* πανταχῇ,
[*for* πανταχοῦ, Acts xxi. 28, *see* "Everywhere."]

πανταχόθεν,
from every quarter, 1.

πανταχοῦ,
everywhere, 6.
in all places. 1.

παντελής,
— εἰς τὸ παντελές,
to the uttermost, 1.
evermore, 1.
— μὴ εἰς τὸ παντελές,
in no wise, 1.

πάντη,
always, 1.

πάντοθεν,
on every side, 1.
round about, 1.

παντοκράτωρ,
Almighty, 9.
omnipotent, 1.

πάντοτε,
always, 29.
alway, 5.
ever, 6.
evermore, 2.

πάντως,
altogether, 2.
by all means, 2.
at all, 1.
surely, 1.
no doubt, 1.
— οὐ πάντως,
in no wise, 1.
— *with* δεῖ,
needs, 1.

παρά,
— *with Genitive*,
from, 24.
of, 50.
out of, 1.
— *with art.*,
one's friends, 1.
kinsmen, 1.
that one hath, 1.
such things as one giveth, 1.
— παρ' ἐμοῦ,
my, 1.
— παρὰ Κυρίου.
the Lord's, 2.
— παρά τινος,
any man's, 1.
— *with* ἀκούω,
hear one speak, 1.
— *with the Dative*,
by, 3.
with, 42.
before, 3.
in the sight of, 1.
among, 3.
of, 2.
with, 1.
— *with the Accusative*,
by...side, 14.
by 5.
at, 12.
nigh unto, 2.
above, 4.
past, 1.
more than, 2.
than, 11.
contrary to, 3.
against, 2.
save, 1.
— *with art.*,
those by...side, 1.
— παρὰ τοῦτο,
therefore, 2.

παραβαίνω,
transgress, 3,
fall by transgression, 1.

παραβάλλω,
compare, 1.

παράβασις,
transgression, 6.
breaking, 1.

παραβάτης,
transgressor, 3.
who doth transgress, 1.
breaker, 1.

παραβιάζομαι,
constrain, 2.

* παραβολεύομαι,
[*for* παραβουλεύομαι, Phil. ii. 30, *see* "Regard not."]

παραβολή,
comparison, 1.
parable, 46.
figure, 2.
proverb, 1.

παραβουλεύομαι,
regard not, 1.

παραγγελία,
commandment, 2.
charge, 2.
— *Dative*,
straitly, 1.

παραγγέλλω,
declare, 1.
command, 20.
give commandment, 1.
charge, 6.
give charge, 1.
give in charge, 1

παραγίνομαι,
come, 34.
come thither, 1.
go, 1.
— *aorist*,
be present, 1.

παράγω,
pass by, 5.
pass away, 1.
pass forth, 1.
depart, 1.
— *middle*,
pass, 1.
pass away, 1.

παραδειγματίζω,
make a public example, 1.
put to an open shame, 1.

παράδεισος,
paradise, 3.

παραδέχομαι,
receive, 5.

παραδιατριβή, (*pl.*)
perverse disputings, 1.
gallings one of another, 1.

παραδίδωμι,
give up, 4.
give over, 2.
give, 4.
be brought forth, 1.
be ripe, 1.
deliver, 54.
deliver up, 9.
cast into prison, 1.
deliver up, 1.
put in prison, 1.
commit, 1.
betray, 40.
hazard, 1.
recommend, 2.
— *mid. or pass.*,
commit one's self, 1.
commit one's cause, 1.

παράδοξος, (*neut.*)
strange thing, 1.

παράδοσις,
tradition, 12,
ordinance, 1.
tradition, 1.

παραζηλόω,
provoke to jealousy, 3.
provoke to emulation, 1.

παραθαλάσσιος,
— *with art.*,
which is upon the sea coast, 1.

παραθεωρέω,
to neglect, 1.

παραθήκη,
— ἡ π. μοῦ,
that which I have committed unto him, 1.

παραινέω,
exhort, 1.
admonish, 1.

παραιτέομαι,
— *middle*,
entreat, 1.
make excuse, 1.
refuse, 5.
reject, 1.
avoid, 1.
— *passive*,
be excused, 2.

παρακαθίζω,
— *with* παρά,
sit at, 1.

παρακαλέω,
call for, 1.
entreat, 3.
beseech, 43.
desire, 8.
pray, 6.
exhort, 19.
beseech, 1.
desire, 1.
exhort one another, 1.
in one's exhortation, 1.
comfort, 23.
exhort, 1.
— *with* λόγῳ πολλῷ,
give much exhortation, 1.
— *passive*,
be of good comfort, 1.

παρακαλύπτω,
to hide, 1.

παρακαταθήκη,
that thing which is committed unto one, 1.
that which is committed to one's trust, 1.

παράκειμαι,
be present with, 2.

παράκλησις,
entreaty, 1.
exhortation, 8.
comfort, 6.
consolation, 14.

παράκλητος,
advocate, 1.
Comforter, 4.

παρακοή,
disobedience, 3.

παρακολουθέω,
follow, 1.
know fully, 1.
be a diligent follower of, 1.
have perfect understanding of, 1.
— *with ἤ*,
attain whereunto, 1.

παρακούω,
neglect to hear, 2.

παρακύπτω,
stoop down, 3.
— *with εἰς*,
look into, 2.

παραλαμβάνω,
take with, 1.
take unto, 2.
take, 32.
receive, 15.

παραλέγω, (*mid.*)
sail by, 1.
pass, 1.

παράλιος,
sea coast, 1.

παραλλαγή,
variableness, 1.

παραλογίζομαι,
beguile, 1.
deceive, 1.

παραλύω,
— *pass. perf. part.*,
taken with a palsy, 2.
sick of a palsy, 2.
feeble, 1.

παραλυτικός,
that hath the palsy, 1.
sick of the palsy, 9.

παραμένω,
abide, 1.
continue, 2.

παραμυθέομαι,
to comfort, 4.

παραμυθία,
comfort, 1.

παραμύθιον,
comfort, 1.

παρανομέω,
contrary to the law, 1.

παρανομία,
iniquity, 1.

παραπικραίνω,
provoke, 1.

παραπικρασμός,
provocation, 2.

παραπίπτω,
fall away, 1.

παραπλέω,
sail by, 1.

παραπλήσιον,
nigh unto, 1.

παραπλησίως,
likewise, 1.

παραπορεύομαι,
pass by, 3.
pass, 1.
go, 1.

παράπτωμα,
fall, 2.
fault, 2.
offence, 7.
trespass, 9.
sin, 3.

παραῤῥέω,
let slip, 1.
run out as leaking vessels, 1.

παράσημος,
whose sign was, 1.

παρασκευάζω,
make ready, 1.
— *middle*,
prepare one's self, 1.
be ready, 1.
ready, 1.

παρασκευή,
preparation, 6.

παρατείνω,
continue, 1.

παρατηρέω,
observe, 1.
watch, 5.

παρατήρησις,
observation, 1.
outward show, 1.

παρατίθημι,
set before, 8.
put forth, 2.
allege, 1.
— *τὰ παρατιθέμενα*,
such things as are set before, 1.
— *middle*,
commit, 3.
commit the keeping of, 1.
commend, 3.

παρατυγχάνω,
meet with, 1.

παραυτίκα,
but for a moment, 1.

παραφέρω,
take away, 1.
remove, 1.

παραφρονέω,
as a fool, 1.

παραφρονία,
madness, 1.

παραχειμάζω,
to winter, 4.

παραχειμασία, *with* πρός,
to winter in, 1.

παραχρῆμα,
immediately, 13.
forthwith, 1.
straightway, 3.
presently, 1.
soon, 1.

πάρδαλις,
leopard, 1.

* **παρεδρεύω,**
[*for* προσεδρεύω, 1 Cor. ix. 13, *see* "Wait at."]

πάρειμι,
be present, 9.
present, 3.
be here present, 1.
be here, 1.
come, 10.
— *τὰ πάροντα*,
such things as one hath, 1.
— *ᾧ μὴ πάρεστι*,
he that lacketh, 1.

παρεισάγω,
bring in privily, 1.

παρείσακτος,
brought in unawares, 1.

παρεισδύνω,
creep in unawares, 1.

παρεισέρχομαι,
come in privily, 1
enter, 1.

παρεισφέρω,
give, 1.

παρεκτός,
except, 1.
saving, 1.
— *with art.*,
those things that are without, 1.

παρεμβολή,
army, 1.
camp, 3.
castle, 6.

παρενοχλέω,
to trouble, 1.

παρεπίδημος,
pilgrim, 2.
stranger, 1.

παρέρχομαι,
pass by, 3.
pass over, 1.
transgress, 1.
pass away, 12.
pass, 10.
past, 1.
go, 1.
come forth, 1.
come, 1.

πάρεσις,
remission, 1.
passing over, 1.

παρέχω,
offer, 1.
minister, 1.
give, 2.
offer, 1.
do for, 1.
bring, 1.
show, 1.
keep, 1.
— *middle*,
give, 1.
bring, 1.
show, 1.

παρηγορία,
comfort, 1.

παρθενία,
virginity, 1.

παρθένος,
virgin, 14.

παρίημι, (*pass.*)
hang down, 1.

παριστάνω,
yield, 2.

παρίστημι,
— *trans.* (*pres., aor.* 1, *and fut.*),
to present, 9.
give presently, 1.
yield, 3.
provide, 1.
commend, 1.
show, 2.
prove, 1.
— *intrans.* (*perf., plup., and aor.* 2),
stand by, 12.
assist, 1.
stand with, 1.
stand here, 1.
stand up, 1.
stand, 2.
be brought before, 1.
come, 1.
— *mid.* (*fut.*),
stand before, 1.

πάροδος,
way, 1.

παροικέω,
to sojourn, 1.
be a sojourner, 1.

παροικία,
sojourning here,
— *with ἐν*,
when they dwelt as strangers, 1.

πάροικος,
stranger, 2.
foreigner, 1.
— *with εἰμί*,
to sojourn, 1.

παροιμία,
proverb, 4.
parable, 1.
parable, 1.

πάροινος,
given to wine, 2.
ready to quarrel and offer wrong as one in wine, 1.

παροίχομαι,
past, 1.

παρομοιάζω,
be like unto, 1.

παρόμοιος (*neut. pl.*)
like things, 2.

παροξύνω, (*mid. or pass.*)
be stirred, 1.
be easily provoked, 1.

παροξυσμός,
contention, 1.
— *with εἰς*,
to provoke unto, 1.

παροργίζω,
to anger, 1.
provoke to wrath, 1.

παροργισμός,
wrath, 1.

against, 2.
over, 2.
above, 1.
— περὶ τούτου,
thereabout, 1.
— περὶ αὐτοῦ,
thereof, 1.
— περὶ τίνων,
whereof, 1.
— περὶ οὗ (ἧς or ὧν),
whereof, 3.
whereby, 1.
wherein, 1.
— *with art.*,
the things concerning, 4.
those things which concern, 1.
concerning, 1.
the things pertaining to, 1.
one's affairs, 2.
one's state, 2.
one's estate, 1.
for, 1.
of, 1.
— *with Accusative*,
about, 23.
concerning, 4.
in, 1.
of, 1.
— *with art.*,
they about, 1.
they that were about, 1.
they which were about, 1.
how it will go with, 1.
— οἱ περὶ τὸν Παῦλον,
we that were of Paul's company, 1.
Paul and his company, 1.

περιάγω,
lead about, 1.
go about, 3.
go round about, 1.
compass, 1.

περαιρέω,
take away, 3.
take up, 1.
cut, 1.

* **περιάπτω,**
[*for* ἅπτω, Luke xxii. 55, *see* "Kindle."]

περιαστράπτω,
shine round, 1.
shine round about, 1.

περιβάλλω,
cast about, 1.
put on, 1.
clothe, 3.
array in, 1.
— *mid. and pass.*,
cast about, 1.
have...cast about, 1.
be clothed, 3.
be clothed in, 3.
be clothed with, 4.
be arrayed, 3.
be arrayed in, 2.
— *with* τί,
be clothed (wherewithal), 1.

περιβλέπω, (*mid.*)
look round about, 3.
look about on, 1.
look round about on, 1.
look round about upon, 2.

περιβόλαιον,
vesture, 1.
covering, 1.
veil, 1.

περιδέω,
bind about, 1.

περιδρέμω, *see* περιτρέχω.

περιεργάζομαι,
be a busy-body, 1.

περίεργος,
busy-body, 1.
— τὰ περίεργα,
curious arts, 1.

περιέρχομαι,
wander about, 2.
vagabond, 1.
fetch a compass, 1.

περιέχω,
be contained, 1.
after, 1.

περιζώννυμι,
— *mid. or pass.*,
gird one's self, 3.
have...girt about, 1.
be girded about, 1.
be girt, 1.
— *with* περί,
have...girded, 1.

περίθεσις,
wearing, 1.

περιΐστημι,
stand round about, 1.
stand by, 1.
— *middle*,
avoid, 1.
shun, 1.

περικάθαρμα,
filth, 1.

* **περικαθίζω,**
[*for* συγκαθίζω, Luke xxii. 55, *see* "Be set down together."]

περικαλύπτω,
to cover, 1.
overlay, 1.
blindfold, 1.

περίκειμαι,
be hanged about, 2.
be compassed with, 1.
be bound with, 1.
— *with* ἔχω,
be compassed about with, 1.

περικεφαλαία,
helmet, 2.

περικρατής, *with* γίνομαι,
to come by, 1.

περικρύπτω,
hide, 1.

περικυκλόω,
compass round, 1.

περιλάμπω,
shine round about, 2.

περιλείπω, (*pass.*)
remain, 2.

περίλυπος,
exceeding sorrowful, 2,
exceeding sorry, 1.
very sorrowful, 2.

περιμένω,
wait for, 1.

πέριξ,
round about, 1.

περιοικέω,
dwell round about, 1.

περίοικος,
neighbour.

περιούσιος,
peculiar, 1,

περιοχή,
place, 1.

περιπατέω,
walk about, 1.
walk, 92.
be walking, 1.
be occupied, 1.
go, 1.

περιπείρω,
pierce through, 1.

περιπίπτω,
fall into, 2.
fall among, 1.

περιποιέω, (*mid.*)
purchase, 2.

περιποίησις,
obtaining, 1.
purchased possession, 1.
saving, 1.
— with εἰς,
to obtain, 1.
peculiar, 1.
purchased, 1.

περιῤῥήγνυμι,
rend off, 1.

περισπάω,
cumber, 1.

περισσεία,
superfluity, 1.
abundance, 2.
— εἰς περισσεία,
abundantly, 1.

περίσσευμα,
abundance, 4.
that was left, 1.

περισσεύω,
remain over and above, 1.
remain, 3.
be left, 1.
redound, 1.
exceed, 2.
excel, 1.
be the better, 1.
have the more, 1.
abound, 15.
abound more, 1.
abundant, 1.
abundance, 3.
be more abundant, 1.
increase, 1.
make abound, 2.
have enough and to spare, 1.
— *passive*,
have abundance, 1.
have more abundance 1.
— *with* μᾶλλον,
abound more and more, 1.
increase more and more. 1.

περισσός,
superfluous, 1.
more, 2.
more abundantly, 1.
advantage, 1.
— *with* ἐκ,
beyond measure, 1.
vehemently, 1.
— ὑπὲρ ἐκ περισσοῦ,
exceeding abundantly above, 1.
exceedingly, 1.
very highly, 1.
— περισσότερος (*comp.*),
more abundant, 3.
more abundantly, 2.
far more, 1.
much more, 1.
the more, 1.
more, 3.
overmuch, 1.
greater, 3.
— μᾶλλον πεσισσότερος
so much the more a great deal, 1.

περισσῶς,
exceedingly, 1.
out of measure, 1.
the more, 1.
— περισσοτέρως (*comp.*),
the more exceedingly, 1.
more exceedingly, 1.
exceedingly, 1.
the more abundantly, 2.
more abundant, 2.
much more, 1.
the rather, 1.
more frequent, 1.
— *with* προσέχω,
give the more earnest heed to, 1.

περιστερά,
dove, 9.
pigeon, 1.

περιτέμνω,
circumcise, 16.
— *passive*,
have...circumcised, 1.
— *infinitive*,
circumcising, 1.

περιτίθημι,
set about, 1.
put about, 1.
put on, 3.
put upon, 1.
bestow upon, 1.
put on, 1.

περιτομή,
circumcision, 35.
— *Dative*,
circumcised, 1.

περιτρέπω, *with* εἰς μανίαν,
make mad, 1.

περιτρέχω,
run through, 1.

περιφέρω,
bear about, 1.
carry about, 4.

περιφρονέω,
despise, 1.

περίχωρος,
region that lieth round about, 1.
region round about, 5.
country about, 1.
country round about, 3.

περίψημα,
offscouring, 1.

περπερεύομαι,
vaunt one's self, 1.
be rash, 1.

πέρυσι, with ἀπό,
a year ago, 2.

πετάομαι,
to fly, 4.

πετεινόν,
bird, 5.
fowl, 9.

πέτομαι,
to fly, 1.

πέτρα,
rock, 14.
Rock, 2.

Πέτρος,
stone, 1.
Peter, 1.

πετρώδης,
— *τὰ πετ.*,
stony places, 2.
stony ground, 1.
— *τὸ πετ.*,
stony ground, 1.

πήγανον,
rue, 1.

πηγή,
fountain, 8.
well, 4.

πήγνυμι,
to pitch, 1.

πηδάλιον,
helm, 1.
rudder, 1.

πηλίκος,
how great, 1.
how large, 1.

πηλός,
clay, 6.

πήρα,
scrip, 6.

πῆχυς,
cubit, 4.

πιάζω,
take, 7.
lay hands on, 1.
apprehend, 2.
catch, 2.

πιέζω,
press down, 1.

πιθανολογία,
enticing words, 1.

πικραίνω,
make bitter, 2.
— *passive*,
be bitter, 2.

πικρία,
bitterness, 4.

πικρός,
bitter, 2.

πικρῶς,
bitterly,

πίμπλημι, (πλήθω)
fill, 18.
accomplish, 4.
furnish, 1.
— *pass., with χρόνος*,
full time cometh, 1.

πίμπρημι, (pass.)
swell, 1.

πινακίδιον,
writing table, 1.

πίναξ,
platter, 1.
charger, 4.

πίνω,
to drink, 68.
drink of, 7.

πιότης,
fatness, 1.

πιπράσκω,
sell, 9.

πίπτω,
to fall, 68.
fall down, 19.
light, 1.
fail, 1.

πιστεύω,
believe, 233.
trust, 1.
believer, 1.
commit to one's trust, 1.
commit unto, 4.
— *with εἰς* (1 John v. 10),
believe, 1.
— *with ἐν* (Mark i. 15),
believe, 1.
— *with ἐπί* (Luke xxiv. 25),
believe, 1.
— *infinitive*,
believing, 1.
— *passive*,
be put in trust with, 1.
— *with ἐγώ*,
be committed to my trust, 1.
be committed unto me, 1.

πιστικός, see νάρδος.

πίστις,
faith, 239.
belief, 1.
fidelity, 1.
assurance, 1.
faith, 1.
— *Genitive*,
of them that believe, 1.
— *ὁ ἐκ πίστεως*,
he which believeth, 1.

πιστός,
faithful, 52.
believing, 1.
Faithful, 1.
believing, 2.
that believeth, 3.
which believeth, 3.
believer, 1.
sure, 1.
true, 2.
— *neuter*,
faithfully, 1.

πιστόω, (pass.)
be assured of, 1.

πλανάω, (pass.)
wander, 1.
go astray, 5.
be out of the way, 1.
err, 6.
seduce, 2.
deceive, 24.

πλάνη,
error, 7.
delusion, 1.
deceit, 1.
— *Genitive*,
to deceive, 1.

πλανήτης,
wandering, 1.

πλάνος,
seducing, 1.
deceiver, 4.

πλάξ,
table, 3.

πλάσμα,
thing formed, 1.

πλάσσω,
to form, 2.

πλαστός,
feigned, 1.

πλατεῖα,
street, 9.
— *pl., with κατά*,
in every street, 1.

πλάτος,
breadth, 4.

πλατύνω,
make broad, 1.
enlarge, 2.

πλατύς,
wide, 1.

πλέγμα,
braided hair, 1.
plaited hair, 1.

πλείων, πλεῖον,
more, 13.
more excellent, 1.
most, 1.
longer, 1.
greater, 5.
— *with art.*,
most, 1.
very many, 1.
— *with ἐπί*,
further, 3.
long, 1.
— *plural*,
more, 9.
many, 7.
many things, 1.
— *with οὐ*,
yet ut, 1.
— *pl., with art.*,
the more, 1.
the more part, 2.
many, 5.
very many, 1.
the greater part, 1.
— *πλεῖστος (superl., with art.)*,
at the most, 1.
very great, 1.
— *plural*,
most, 1.

πλέκω,
to plait, 3.

πλεονάζω,
abound, 6.
abundant, 1.
make to increase, 1.
— *with οὐ*,
have nothing over, 1.

πλεονεκτέω,
get an advantage of, 1.
make a gain of, 2.
defraud, 2.
oppress or overreach, 1.

πλεονέκτης,
covetous man, 1.
covetous, 3.

πλεονεξία,
covetousness, 8.
covetous practice, 1.
greediness, 1.

πλευρά,
side, 5.

πλέω,
to sail, 4.
sail by, 1.

πληγή,
stripe, 5.
wound, 3.
plague, 12.
— *with ἐπιτίθημι*,
to wound, 1.

πλῆθος,
multitude, 30.
company, 1.
bundle, 1.

πληθύνω,
multiply, 7.
be multiplied, 1.
— *passive*,
multiply, 3.
abound, 1.

πληθω, see πίμπλημι,

πλήκτης,
striker, 2.

πλήμμυρα,
flood, 1.

πλήν,
than, 1.
except, 1.
save, 1.
but, 14.
but rather, 2.
nevertheless, 8.
notwithstanding, 4.

πλήρης,
full, 17.

πληροφορέω,
make full proof of, 1.
fulfil, 1.
— *passive*,
be fully persuaded, 2.
be fully assured, 1.
— *part., with art.*,
those things which are most surely believed, 1.
be fully known, 1.

πληροφορία,
full assurance, 3.
assurance, 1.

πληρόω,
make full, 1.
fill, 17.
fulfil, 1.
fill up, 1.
preach fully, 1.
supply, 1.
fulfil, 51.
preach fully, 1.
accomplish, 1.
end, 2.
— *passive*,
be full, 3.
full, 3.
be filled with, 1.
fill, 1.
be full come, 1.
expire, 1.
after, 1.
complete, 2.
filled, 1.
perfect, 1.

πλήρωμα,
fulness, 13.
fulfilling, 1.
full, 1.
which is put in to fill up, 1.
piece that filleth up, 1.

πλησίον,
near, 1.
— *with art.*,
neighbour, 16.

πλησμονή,
satisfying, 1.

πλήσσω,
smite, 1.

πλοιάριον,
small ship, 1.
little ship, 2.
boat, 3.

πλοῖον,
ship, 66.
— *plural*,
shipping, 1.

πλόος,
sailing, 1.
voyage, 1.
course, 1.

πλούσιος,
rich, 17.
rich man, 11

πλουσίως,
richly, 2.
abundantly, 2
richly, 1.

πλουτέω,
be rich, 7.
rich, 1.
wax rich, 1.
be made rich, 2.
be increased with goods, 1.

πλουτίζω,
make rich, 1.
enrich, 2.

πλοῦτος,
riches, 22.

πλύνω,
to wash, 1.

πνεῦμα,
wind, 1.
life, 1.
breath, 1.
spirit, 151.
breath, 1.
spiritual, 1.
spirit, 1.
ghost, 2.
Spirit, 133.
— *Genitive*,
spiritually, 1.
of the spirit, 1.
— *with ἅγιος*,
Holy Ghost, 89.
Holy Spirit, 4.

πνευματικός,
spiritual, 18.
spirit, 1.
— *with art.*,
he that is spiritual, 1.
he which is spiritual, 1.
that which is spiritual, 2.
— *neut. pl.*,
spiritual things, 3.
spiritual gifts, 1.

πνευματικῶς,
spiritually, 2.

πνέω,
to blow, 6.

πνίγω,
choke, 1.
take by the throat, 1.

πνικτός,
strangled, 1.
things strangled, 1.

πνοή,
breath, 1.
wind, 1.

ποδήρης,
garment down to the foot, 1.

πόθεν,
whence, 20.
from whence, 8.

ποιέω,
to make, 102.
cause, 8.
cause to be, 1.
bring forth, 14.
bring, 1.
shoot out, 1.
bear, 4.
yield, 1.
give, 1.
put, 1.
show, 5.
purpose, 1.
mean, 1.
appoint, 1.
make, 1.
ordain, 1.
gain, 1.
provide, 1.
work, 8.
continue, 1.
do, 1.
do, 353.
in doing, 2.
can do, 1.
commit, 9.
execute, 2.
exercise, 1.
perform, 2.
fulfil, 3.
keep, 4.
observe, 1.
hold, 1.
take, 1.
abide, 1.
continue, 2.
be, 1.
— *middle*,
make, 12.
give, 1.
— *with μνήμη*,
have in remembrance, 1.
— *with λόγος*,
move, 1.
— *infinitive*,
doing, 1.
— *with a Dative*,
deal with, 2.

ποίημα,
thing that is made, 1.
workmanship, 1.

ποίησις,
deed, 1.
doing, 1.

ποιητής,
doer, 5.
poet, 1.

ποικίλος,
divers, 8.
manifold, 2.

ποιμαίνω,
feed cattle, 1.
feed, 6.
rule, 4.
feed, 1.

ποιμήν,
shepherd, 15.
Shepherd, 2.
pastor, 1.

ποίμνη,
flock, 4.
fold, 1.

ποίμνιον,
flock, 5.

ποῖος,
what manner of, 1.
what, 27.
what way, 1.
which, 4.
— *ποῖα*,
what things, 1.

πολεμέω,
make war, 3.
war, 1.
fight, 3.

πόλεμος,
war, 12.
battle, 5.
fight, 1.

πόλις,
city, 159.

πολιτάρχης,
ruler of the city, 2.

πολιτεία,
freedom, 1.
commonwealth, 1.

πολίτευμα,
conversation, 1.

πολιτεύω, (mid.)
one's conversation is, 1.
live, 1.

πολίτης,
citizen, 3.

πολλά, *see* πολύς.

πολλάκις,
often, 7.
oft, 4.
oftentimes, 3.
ofttimes, 3.

πολυπλασίων,
manifold more, 1.

* **πολυεύσπλαγχνος,**
[*for* πολύσπλαγχνος, Jas. v. 11, *see* "Very pitiful."]

πολυλογία,
much speaking, 1.

πολυμερῶς,
at sundry times, 1.

πολυποίκιλος,
manifold, 10.

πολύς,
much, 54.
plenteous, 1.
many, 2.
far passed, 1.
long, 3.
great, 47.
greatly, 1.
— *with art.*,
abundant, 1.
much, 1.
the common, 1.
great, 1.
— *ὥρας πολλῆς γενομένης*
when the day was far spent, 1.
— *μετὰ πολύ*,
long after, 1.
— *ἐπὶ πολύ*,
a great while, 1.
— *ἐν πολλῷ*,
altogether, 1.
— *plural*,
many, 173.
many things, 23.
many stripes, 15.
much, 15.
great, 11.
greatly, 3.
sore, 1.
straitly, 2.
oft, 1.
— *with art.*,
many, 10.
much, 2.
many ways, or oftentimes, 1.

πολύσπλαγχνος,
very pitiful, 1.

πολυτελής,
of great price, 1.
very precious, 1.
costly, 1.

πολύτιμος,
of great price, 1.
very costly, 1.

πολυτρόπως,
in divers manners, 1.

πόμα,
drink, 2.

πονηρία,
wickedness, 6.
wicked, 1.
iniquity, 1.

πονηρός,
evil, 38 (*adj.*)
evil, 4 (*subst.*)
bad, 1.
harm, 1.
grievous, 1.
malicious, 1.
wicked, 11.
—— *with art.*,
that which is evil, 2.
the evil, 1.
evil, 5 (*subst.*)
that wicked person, 1
the wicked one, 5.
the wicked, 1.
that wicked one, 1.
wickedness, 1.
—— πονηρὸν ῥῆμα,
evil, 1.
—— *neut. pl.*,
evil things, 2.

πόνος,
pain, 3.

πορεία,
way, 1.
—— *with* ποιέω (*mid.*),
to journey, 1.

πορεύομαι,
go away, 1.
go one's way, 8.
go forth, 1.
go, 119.
be going, 1.
go up, 1.
depart, 11.
journey, 2.
make one's journey, 1.
take one's journey, 1.
walk, 9.

πορθέω,
to waste, 1.
destroy, 2.

πορισμός,
gain, 2.

πορνεία,
fornication, 26.

πορνεύω,
commit fornication, 7.
commit, 1.

πόρνη,
harlot, 8.
fornication, 1.
whore, 4.

πόρνος,
fornicator, 5.
whoremonger, 5.

πόρρω,
far, 2.
a great way off, 1.
—— *comparative*,
further, 1.

πόρρωθεν,
afar off, 2.

πορφύρα,
purple, 5.

πορφύρεος,
purple, 2 (*adj.*)
purple, 1 (*subst.*)

πορφυρόπωλις,
seller of purple, 1.

ποσάκις,
how often? 2.
how oft? 1.

πόσις,
drink, 3.
drinking, 1.

πόσος,
how great? 1.
how much? 13.
what? 1.
—— *plural*,
how many? 9.
—— *neuter*,
how many things? 2.
—— πόσος χρόνος,
how long ago? 1

ποταμός,
river, 9.
stream, 2.
flood, 4.
water, 1.

ποταμοφόρητος,
carried away of the flood, 1.

ποταπός,
what manner of? 5.
what manner of person, 1.
what, 1.

ποτέ,
when, 1.
sometime, 2.
sometimes, 3.
some time, 1.
once, 2.
in time past, 5.
in times past, 3.
aforetime, 1.
in old time, 1.
at any time, 1.
in the old time, 1.
at length, 1.
at the last, 1.
at any time, 4.
any time, 1.
ever yet, 1.
—— οὐ μή ποτέ,
never, 1.

πότε,
when? 12.
—— ἕως πότε,
how long? 7.

πότερος, (*neut.*)
whether, 1.

ποτήριον,
cup, 33.

ποτίζω,
give to drink, 4.
give drink, 4.
make...drink, 1.
make to drink, 1.
water, 3.
feed with, 1.
—— ἀπαγαγὼν ποτίζω,
lead away to watering, 1.

πότος,
banqueting, 1.

που,
in a certain place, 2.
about, 1.

ποῦ,
where? 37.
whither? 10.

πούς,
foot, 85.
—— ὑποπόδιον των ποδῶν,
footstool, 8.

πρᾶγμα,
business, 1.
work, 1.
matter, 3.
thing, 6.

πραγματεία,
affair, 1.

πραγματεύομαι,
occupy, 1.

πραιτώριον,
Prætorium, 1.
palace, 1.
Cæsar's court, 1.
common hall, 1.
Pilate's house, 1.
judgment hall, 4.

πράκτωρ,
officer, 2.

πρᾶξις,
deed, 4.
works, 1.
office, 1.

πρᾷος,
meek, 1.

πρᾳότης,
meekness, 9.

πρασία,
—— πρασιαὶ πρασιαί,
in ranks, 1.

πράσσω,
do, 28.
commit, 5.
use, 1.
keep, 1.
require, 1.
exact, 1.
—— ἃ ἐπράξαμεν,
our deeds, 1.

* πραϋπάθεια,
[*for* πρᾳότης, 1 Tim. vi. 11, *see* "Meekness."]

πραΰς,
meek, 3.

πραΰτης,
meekness, 3.

πρέπω,
become, 3.
—— *impers.*,
it becometh, 2.
becometh, 1.
it is comely, 1.

πρεσβεία,
ambassage, 1.
message, 1.

πρεσβεύω,
be an ambassador, 2.

πρεσβυτέριον,
estate of elders, 1.
elders, 1.
presbytery, 1.

πρεσβύτερος,
elder, 2 (*adj.*)
eldest, 1.
old man, 1.
elder woman, 1.
elder, 62 (*subst.*)

πρεσβύτης,
old man, 1.
aged man, 1.
aged, 1.

πρεσβῦτις,
aged woman, 1.

πρηνής, *with* γίνομαι,
fall headlong, 1.

πρίζω, πρίω,
saw asunder, 1.

πρίν,
before, 6.
—— πρὶν ἤ,
before that, 2.
before, 5.
ere, 1.

πρό,
before, 36.
before, 9 (*adv.*)
or ever, 1.
above, 1.
above...ago, 1.

προάγω,
bring forth, 2.
bring out, 1.
go before, 15.

προαιρέω, (*mid.*)
to purpose, 1.

προαιτιάομαι,
prove before, 1.
charge, 1.

προακούω,
hear before, 1.

προαμαρτάνω,
sin heretofore, 1.
sin already, 1.

προαύλιον,
porch, 1.

προβαίνω,
go on, 1.
go farther, 1.
—— προβεβηκὼς ἐν ταῖς ἡμέραις αὐτοῦ,
well stricken in years, 2.
—— προβεβηκὼς ἐν ἡμέραις πολλαῖς,
of a great age, 1.

προβάλλω,
put forward, 1.
shoot forth, 1.

προβατικός,
sheep [*market*], 1.
sheep gate, 1.

* προβάτιον,
[*for* πρόβατον, John xxi. 16, 17, *see* "Sheep."]

πρόβατον,
sheep, 40.

προβιβάζω,
instruct before, 1.
— *with ἐκ,*
draw out of, 1.

προβλέπω, (*mid.*)
provide, 1.
foresee, 1.

προγίνομαι,
be past, 1.

προγινώσκω,
know before, 1.
foreknow, 2.
know, 1.
foreordain, 1.

πρόγνωσις,
foreknowledge, 2.

πρόγονος, (*pl.*)
forefathers, 1.
parents, 1.

προγράφω,
write aforetime, 1.
write afore, 1.
write, 1.
set forth evidently, 1.
ordain before, 1.

πρόδηλος,
manifest beforehand, 1.
open beforehand, 1.
evident, 1.

προδίδωμι,
give first, 1.

προδότης,
betrayer, 1.
traitor, 2.

προδρέμω, *see* προτρέχω.

πρόδρομος,
forerunner, 1.

προεῖδον,
see before, 1.
foresee, 1.

προειπον, προερῶ, προείρηκα,
speak before, 3.
say before, 4.
tell before, 2.
foretell, 1.
tell in time past, 1.
forewarn, 1.

προελπίζω,
trust first, 1.
hope, 1.

προενάρχομαι,
begin before, 1.
begin, 1.

προεπαγγέλλω,
— *middle,*
promise afore, 1.

προέπω, -ερῶ, *see* προεῖπον.

προέρχομαι,
go before, 5.
go forward, 1.
go farther, 1.
outgo, 1.
pass on, 1.

προετοιμάζω,
prepare afore, 1.
ordain, 1.
prepare before, 1.

προευαγγελίζομαι,
preach the gospel before, 1.

προέχω, (*mid.*)
be better, 1.

προηγέομαι,
prefer, 1.

πρόθεσις, (*see also* ἄρτος)
purpose, 8.

προθέσμιος, (*fem.*)
time appointed, 1.

προθυμία,
forwardness of mind, 1.
readiness of mind, 1.
readiness, 1.
ready mind, 1.
willing mind, 1.

πρόθυμος,
ready, 2.
willing, 1.

προθύμως,
of a ready mind, 1.

προΐμος, *see* πρώϊμος.

προϊνος, *see* πρωϊνός.

προΐστημι,
be over, 1.
rule, 5.
maintain, 1.
profess, 1.

προκαλέω, (*mid.*)
provoke, 1.

προκαταγγέλλω,
foretell, 1.
show before, 2.
— *pass. part., with art.,*
whereof ye had notice before, 1.
which hath been so much spoken of before, 1.

προκαταρτίζω,
make up beforehand, 1.

πρόκειμαι,
be set before, 3.
be set forth, 1.
be first, 1.

προκηρύσσω,
preach before, 1.
preach first, 1.

προκοπή,
furtherance, 2.
profiting, 1.

προκόπτω,
proceed, 1.
increase, 2.
wax, 1.
profit, 1.
be far spent, 1.

πρόκριμα,
preferring one before another, 1.
prejudice, 1.

προκυρόω,
confirm before, 1.

προλαμβάνω,
take before, 1.
overtake, 1.
come aforehand, 1.

προλέγω,
tell before, 2.
foretell, 1.

προμαρτύρομαι,
testify beforehand, 1.

προμελετάω,
meditate before, 1.

προμεριμνάω,
take thought beforehand, 1.

προνοέω,
provide for, 1.
— *middle,*
provide, 1.
provide for, 1.

πρόνοια,
providence, 1.
provision for, 1.

προοράω,
see before, 1.
— *middle,*
foresee, 1.

προορίζω,
determine before, 1.
predestinate, 4.
ordain, 1.

προπάσχω,
suffer before, 1.

* **προπάτωρ,**
[*for* πατήρ, Rom. iv. 1, *see* "Father."]

προπέμπω,
conduct forth, 1.
bring forward on one's journey, 1.
bring on one's journey, 2.
bring on one's way, 4.
accompany, 1.

προπετής,
heady, 1.
rashly, 1.

προπορεύομαι,
go before, 2.

πρός,
— *with Gen.,*
for, 1.
— *with Dat.,*
at, 4.
about, 1.
— *with Acc.,*
toward, 10.
to...ward, 3.
to, 174.
to do, 1.
to give, 1.
to answer, 1 (*in italics,* 2 Cor. v. 12).
unto, 338.
over against, 1.
nigh unto, 1.
at, 11.
against, 24.
before, 2.
by, 4.
with, 42.
among, 1.
to be compared with, 1.
within, 1.
in, 3.
concerning, 1.
between, 2.
among, 20.
according to, 3.
for, 23.
because of, 1.
of, 2.
to, 1.
— πρὸς πειρασμὸν,
which is to try, 1.
— πρὸς τό, *with inf.,*
to, 4.
for to, 1.
to this end, that, 1.
that may, 2.
that might, 1
that...could, 1
because...would, 1.
— πρὸς ὅ,
whereby, 1.
— τὰ πρός,
the things which belong unto, 1.
those things which pertain to, 1.
things that *pertain* unto, 1.
in things pertaining to, 1.
in things *pertaining* to, 1.
about, 1.
conditions of, 1.
sufficient to, 1.
what one hath against, 1.
— πρὸς τί,
for what intent, 1.

προσάββατον,
the day before the sabbath, 1.

προσαγορεύω,
to call, 1.

προσάγω,
bring, 3.
draw near, 1.

προσαγωγή,
access, 3.

προσαιτέω,
beg, 3.

* **προσαίτης,**
[*for* προσαιτέω, Mark x. 46, *see* "Beg." *for* τυφλος, John ix. 8, *see* "Blind."]

προσαναβαίνω,
go up, 1.

προσαναλίσκω,
spend, 1.

προσαναπληρόω,
to supply, 2.

προσανατίθημι,
— *middle,*
add in conference, 1.
confer, 1.

προσαπειλέω, (*mid.*)
threaten further, 1.

προσδαπανάω,
spend more, 1.

προσδέομαι,
to need, 1.

προσδέχομαι,
receive, 3.
accept, 1.
take, 1.
allow, 1.
look for, 4.
wait for, 4.

προσδοκάω,
look for, 8.
look when, 1.
look, 1.
expect, 1.
be in expectation, 1.
be in suspense, 1.
wait for, 3.
tarry, 1.

προσδοκία,
looking after, 1.
expectation, 1.

προσδρέμω, see
προστρέχω.

προσεάω,
suffer, 1.

προσεγγίζω,
come nigh unto, 1.

προσεδρεύω,
wait at, 1.

προσεργάζομαι,
to gain, 1.

προσέρχομαι,
come to, 24.
come unto, 19.
come thereunto, 1.
come, 32.
be a coming, 1.
go to, 2.
go unto, 2.
go, 1.
go near, 1.
draw near, 2.
consent to, 1.

προσευχή,
prayer, 36.
— Dative,
earnestly, 1.
in his prayer, 1.

προσεύχομαι,
pray, 83.
pray for, 1.
— with μακρά,
make long prayer, 1.
make long prayers, 2.

προσέχω,
give heed unto, 1.
give heed to, 4.
take heed unto, 1.
take heed to, 3.
take heed, 1.
beware, 7.
attend unto, 1.
give attendance to, 1.
give attendance at, 1.
have reward to, 1.
be given to, 1.
— with ῷ,
take heed whereunto, 1.

προσηλόω,
nail to, 1.

προσήλυτος,
proselyte, 4.

πρόσκαιρος,
for a season, 1.
temporal, 1.
— with εἰμί,
dure for a while, 1.
endure but for a time, 1.

προσκαλέω, (mid.)
call unto one, 20.
call to one, 1.
call for, 2.
call, 6.
— with ὅ,
call whereunto, 1.

προσκαρτερέω,
continue steadfastly in, 1.
continue instant in, 1.
continue in, 3.
continue with, 1.
attend continually upon, 1.
give one's self continually to, 1.
wait on continually, 1.
wait on, 1.

προσκαρτέρησις,
perseverance, 1.

προσκεφάλαιον,
pillow, 1.

προσκληρόω, (pass.)
consort with, 1.

* πρόσκλησις,
[for πρόσκλισις, 1 Tim.
v. 21, see "Partiality."]

* προσκλίνω,
[for προσκολλάω, Acts
v. 36, see "Join one's
self to."]

πρόσκλισις,
partiality, 1.

προσκολλάω, (pass.)
be joined unto, 1.
join one's self to, 1.
cleave to, 2.

πρόσκομμα,
stumbling, 1.
stumbling-block, 2.
offence, 1.

προσκοπή,
offence, 1.

προσκόπτω,
beat upon, 1.
stumble at, 2.
stumble, 3.
— with πρός,
dash against, 2.

προσκυλίω,
roll to, 1.
roll unto, 1.

προσκυνέω,
worship, 59.
beseech, 1.
— with ἐνώπιον,
to worship, 1.
fall down before, 1.

προσκυνητής,
worshipper, 1.

προσλαλέω,
speak to, 1.
speak with, 1.

προσλαμβάνω,
— middle,
take unto one, 2.
take, 5.
receive, 7.

πρόσληψις,
receiving, 1.

προσμένω,
continue with, 1
continue in, 1.
abide still, 1.
tarry there, 1.
cleave unto, 1.
be with, 1.

προσορμίζω, (mid.)
draw to the shore, 1.

προσοφείλω,
owe besides, 1.

προσοχθίζω,
be grieved with, 2.

* προσπαίω,
[for προσπίπτω, Matt.
vii. 25, see "Beat
upon."]

πρόσπεινος,
very hungry, 1.

προσπήγνυμι,
crucify, 1.

προσπίπτω,
fall at, 1.
fall down at, 1.
fall down before, 5.
beat upon, 1.

προσποιέω, (mid.)
make as though, 1.
— with μή,
as though he heard
them not, 1.

προσπορεύομαι,
come unto, 1.

προσρήγνυμι,
beat vehemently upon,
1.
beat vehemently
against, 1.

προστάσσω,
to command, 6.
bid, 1.

προστάτις,
succourer, 1.

προστίθημι,
lay unto, 1.
add, 11.
again, 2.
give more, 1.
increase, 1.
speak any more, 1.
proceed further, 1.

προστρέχω,
run to, 1.
run thither to, 1.
run, 1.

προσφάγιον,
meat, 1.

πρόσφυτος,
new, 1.

προσφάτως,
lately, 1.

προσφέρω,
bring unto, 10.
bring to, 5.
bring, 2.
put to, 1.
present unto, 1.
offer, 1.
offer, 24.
offer up, 3.
do, 1.
deal with, 1.

προσφιλής,
lovely, 1.

προσφορά,
offering up, 1.
sacrificing, 1.
offering, 6.

προσφωνέω,
speak unto, 1.
speak to, 2.
call unto, 1.
call to, 1.
call unto one, 1.
call to one, 1.

πρόσχυσις,
sprinkling, 1.

προσψαύω,
to touch, 1.

προσωπληπτέω,
have respect to persons, 1.

προσωπολήπτης,
respecter of persons, 1.

προσωπολημψία,
respect of persons, 4.

πρόσωπον,
face, 54.
countenance, 3.
appearance, 1.
the face, 1.
outward appearance, 1.
fashion, 1.
presence, 7.
outward appearance, 1.
person, 6.
sight, 1.
man's person, 1.
— κατὰ πρόσωπον,
face to face, 1.
— πρὸ προσώπου,
before, 1.
— εἰς πρόσωπον,
before, 1.

προτάσσω,
appoint before, 1.

προτείνω,
bind, 1.

πρότερος,
former, 1.
— πρότερον, or τὸ πρότ.
(adv.),
before, 4.
— ἐὰν μὴ πρότερον,
before, 1.
former, 1.
first, 2.
at the first, 1.

προτίθημι, (*mid.*)
set forth, 1.
foreordain, 1.
purpose, 2.

προτρέπω, (*mid.*)
exhort,

προτρέχω,
run before, 1.
—— *with* τάχιον,
outrun, 1.

προϋπάρχω,
be before, 1.
be...beforetime, 1.

πρόφασις,
show, 1.
pretence, 3.
cloak, 2.
excuse, 1.
colour, 1.

προφέρω,
bring forth, 2.

προφητεία,
prophecy, 15.
the gift of prophecy, 1.
prophesying, 3.

προφητεύω,
to prophesy, 28.

προφήτης,
prophet, 149.

προφητικός,
of the prophets, 1.
of prophecy, 1.

προφῆτις,
prophetess, 2.

προφθάνω,
prevent, 1.

προχειρίζομαι,
make, 1.
choose, 1.

προχειροτονέω,
choose before, 1.

πρύμνα,
hinder part of a ship, 1.
hinder part, 1.
stern, 1.

πρωΐ,
early, 2.
in the morning, 4.
morning, 2.
—— ἅμα πρωΐ,
early in the morning, 1.
—— λίαν πρωΐ,
very early in the morning, 1.

πρώϊμος,
early, 1.

πρωϊνός,
morning, 1.

πρωΐος,
early, 1.
in the morning, 1.
morning, 2.

πρῴρα,
foreship, 1.
forepart, 1.

πρωτεύω,
have the pre-eminence, 1.

πρωτοκαθεδρία,
chief seat, 2.
highest seat, 1.
uppermost seats, 1.

πρωτοκλισία,
chief room, 2.
highest room, 1.
uppermost room, 1.
uppermost rooms, 1.

πρῶτος,
—— *adjective*,
first, 78.
that are first, 1 (*pl.*)
first day, 2.
former, 2.
before, 2.
beginning, 1.
chief, 7.
first, 1.
chief man, 2.
chief estate, 1.
chiefest, 1.
best, 1.
—— ἐν πρώτοις,
first of all, 1.
—— *adverb*,
first, 51.
at first, 1.
at the first, 3.
first of all, 2.
it first beginneth, 1.
at the beginning, 1.
before, 1.
chiefly, 1.

πρωτοστάτης,
ringleader, 1.

πρωτοτόκια,
birthright, 1.

πρωτότοκος,
firstborn, 7.
first-begotten, 2.

πταίω,
stumble, 1.
fall, 1.
offend, 3.

πτέρνα,
heel, 1.

πτερύγιον,
pinnacle, 2.

πτέρυξ,
wing, 5.

πτηνόν,
bird, 1.

πτοέω,
terrify, 2.

πτόησις,
amazement, 1.

πτύον,
fan, 2.

πτύρω,
terrify, 1.

πτύσμα,
spittle, 1.

πτύσσω,
to close, 1.

πτύω,
spit, 3.

πτῶμα,
dead body, 3.
carcase, 1.
corpse, 1.

πτῶσις,
fall, 2.

πτωχεία,
poverty, 3.

πτωχεύω,
become poor, 3.

πτωχός,
poor, 30.
poor man, 1.
beggarly, 1.
beggar, 2.

πυγμῇ,
oft, 1.
diligently, 1.
with the fist, 1.
up to the elbow, 1.

πυκνός,
often, 1.
—— πυκνά,
often, 1.
—— πυκνότερον,
the oftener, 1.

πυκτεύω,
to fight, 1.

πύλη,
gate, 10.

πυλών,
gate, 17.
porch, 1.

πυνθάνομαι,
inquire, 2.
ask, 7.
demand, 2.
understand, 1.

πῦρ,
fire, 73.
—— *Genitive*,
fiery, 1.

πυρά,
fire, 2.

πύργος,
tower, 4.

πυρέσσω,
sick of a fever, 2.

πυρετός,
fever, 6.

πύρινος,
of fire, 1.

πυρόω, (*pass.*)
be on fire, 1.
fiery, 1.
burn, 3.
be tried, 1.

πυρράζω,
be red, 2.

πυῤῥός,
red, 1.
that is red, 1.

πύρωσις,
burning, 2.
fiery trial, 1.

πω, *see* μήπω, μηδέπω, οὔπω, οὐδέπω.

πωλέω,
sell, 21.
—— *pass. part., with art.*,
whatsoever is sold, 1.

πῶλος,
colt, 12.

πώποτε,
at any time, 3.
—— *with* οὐ μή,
never, 1.
—— *with* οὐδείς,
never, 2.

πωρόω,
harden, 3.
blind, 2.
harden, 1.

πώρωσις,
hardness, 1.
blindness, 1.
blindness, 2.
hardness, 2.

πως,
by any means, 8.
by some means, 1.
haply, 1.
perhaps, 1.

πῶς,
how? 49.
how is it that? 6.
how, 25.
after what manner, 1.
by what means, 2.
that, 1.
how! 6.
—— *with subj.*,
how? 2.
how, 7.
—— *with opt.*,
how? 1.

Ῥαββί,
Rabbi, 8.
master, 9.

ῥαββονί, ῥαββουνί,
Rabboni, 2.
lord, 1.

ῥαβδίζω,
beat with rods, 1.
beat, 1.

ῥάβδος,
rod, 6.
staff, 4.
sceptre, 2.

ῥαβδοῦχος,
serjeant, 2.

ῥᾳδιούργημα,
lewdness, 1.

ῥᾳδιουργία,
mischief, 1.

ῥακά,
racha, 1 (*ed.* 1611).
raca, 1 (*ed.* 1638).

ῥάκος,
cloth, 2.

ῥαντίζω,
sprinkle, 4.

ῥαντισμός,
sprinkling, 2.

ῥαπίζω,
smite with the palm of one's hand, 1.
...a rod, 1.
smite, 1.

ῥάπισμα,
— *with βαλλω,*
strike with the palm of one's hand, 1.
— *with δίδωμι,*
strike with the palm of one's hand, 1.
...a rod, 1.
smite with one's hand, 1.

ῥαφίς,
needle, 3.

ῥέδα,
chariot, 1.

ῥέω,
to flow, 1.

ῥέω, ἐρρήθην, ἐρρέθην,
say, 9.
command, 1.
make, 1.
— τὸ ῥηθέν,
that (*or* it) which was spoken, 12.
spoken of, 2.
— ὁ ῥηθέν,
he that was spoken of, 1.

ῥῆγμα,
ruin, 1

ῥήγνυμι, ῥήσσω,
rend, 1.
break forth, 1.
burst, 2.
tear, 2.
dash, 1.
— *passive,*
break, 1.

ῥῆμα,
word, 56.
saying, 9.
thing, 1.
thing, 3.

ῥήσσω, see ῥήγνυμι.

ῥήτωρ,
orator, 1.

ῥητῶς,
expressly, 1.

ῥίζα,
root, 16.
Root, 1.

ῥιζόω, (*pass. or mid.*)
be rooted, 2.

ῥιπή,
twinkling, 1.

ῥιπίζω,
toss, 1.

ῥιπτέω,
cast off, 1.

ῥίπτω,
throw, 1.
cast, 2.
cast down, 2.
cast out, 1.
— *passive,*
be scattered abroad, 1.
lie down, 1.

ῥοιζηδόν,
with a great noise, 1.

ῥομφαία,
sword, 7.

* **ῥοπή,**
[*for* ῥιπή, 1 Cor. xv. 52, *see* "Twinkling."]

ῥύμη,
street, 3.
lane, 1.

ῥύομαι,
deliver, 13.
Deliverer, 1.
— ἐρρύσθην (*aor.*),
be delivered, 4.

* **ῥυπαίνω,**
[*for* ῥυπόω, Rev. xxii. 11, *see* "be Filthy."]

* **ῥυπαρεύομαι,**
[*for* ῥυπόω, Rev. xxii. 11, *see* "be Filthy."]

ῥυπαρία,
filthiness, 1.

ῥυπαρός,
vile, 1.

ῥύπος,
filth, 1.

ῥυπόω,
be filthy, 2.

ῥύσις,
issue, 3.

ῥυτίς,
wrinkle, 1.

ῥώννυμι,
— *pass. imper.,*
farewell, 2.

σαβαχθανί,
sabachthani, 2.

σαβαώθ,
Sabaoth, 1.
sabaoth, 1.

σαββατισμός,
rest, 1.
keeping of a sabbath, 1.

σάββατον,
sabbath, 16.
sabbath day, 34.
week, 9.
— *Gen.* (*as adj.*)
sabbath, 7.

σαγήνη,
net, 1.

σαίνω,
move, 1.

σάκκος,
sackcloth, 4.

σαλεύω,
shake, 10.
shake together, 1.
stir up, 1.
move, 1.
— τα σαλευομενα,
those things that are shaken, 1.
...may be..., 1.
— τὰ μὴ σαλευόμενα,
those things which cannot be shaken, 1.

σάλος,
waves, 1.

σάλπιγξ,
trump, 2.
trumpet, 9.

σαλπίζω,
sound a trumpet, 1.
cause a trumpet to be sounded, 1.
a trumpet soundeth, 1.
sound, 10.

σαλπιστής,
trumpeter, 1.

σανδάλιον,
sandal, 2.

σανίς,
board, 1.

σαπρός,
corrupt, 7.
bad, 1.

σάπφειρος,
sapphire, 1.

σαργάνη,
basket, 1.

σάρδινος,
sardine, 1.

σάρδιος,
sardius, 3.

σαρδόνυξ,
sardonyx, 1.

σαρκικός,
fleshly, 2.
carnal, 7.
— τὰ σαρκικά,
carnal things, 2.

σάρκινος,
fleshy, 1.

σάρξ,
flesh, 147.
— *Genitive,*
fleshly, 1.
carnal, 2.
carnally, 1.
of the flesh, 1.

σαρόω,
sweep, 3.

σάτον,
measure, 2.

σαυτοῦ, see σεαυτοῦ.

σβέννυμι
quench, 7.
— *passive,*
go out, 1.
be going out, 1.

σέ, see σύ.

σεαυτοῦ, etc.
thyself, 33.
thine own self, 2.
thou thyself, 1.
thy, 1.
unto thyself, 2.
thee, 1.

σεβάζομαι,
to worship, 1.

σέβασμα.
that is worshipped, 1.
devotion, 1.
god that one worshippeth, 1.

σεβαστός, (*adj.*)
Augustus's, 1.

σέβω, (*pass.*)
to worship, 6.
devout, 2.
devout person, 1.
religious, 1.

σειρά,
chain, 1.

* **σειρός,**
[*for* σειρά, 2 Pet. ii. 4, *see* "Chain."]

σεισμός,
tempest, 1.
earthquake, 13.

σείω,
shake, 2.
move, 1.
— *passive,*
shake, 1.
quake, 1.

σελήνη,
moon, 9.

σεληνιάζομαι,
be lunatic, 2.

σεμίδαλις,
fine flour, 1.

σεμνός,
honest, 1.
venerable, 1.
grave, 3.

σεμνότης,
honesty, 1.
gravity, 2.

σημαίνω,
signify, 6.

σημεῖον,
sign, 51.
token, 1.
wonder, 3.
sign, 2.
miracle, 22.

σημειόω, (*mid.*)
note, 1.
signify, 1.

σήμερον,
to-day, 18.
this day, 22.
— σήμερον ἡμέρα,
this day, 1.

σήπω,
to corrupt, 1.

σηρικός, (*neut.*)
silk, 1.

σής,
moth, 3.

σητόβρωτος,
moth-eaten, 1.

σθενόω,
strengthen, 1.

σιαγών,
cheek, 2.

σιγάω,
keep silence, 3.
hold one's peace, 4.
keep secret, 1.
keep close, 1.

σιγή,
silence, 2.

σιδήρεος,
of iron, 4.
iron, 1 (*adj.*)

σίδηρος,
iron, 1.

σικάριος,
that is a murderer, 1.

σίκερα,
strong drink, 1.

σιμικίνθιον,
apron, 1.

σίναπι,
mustard seed, 5.

σινδών,
fine linen, 1.
linen, 2.
linen cloth, 3.

σινιάζω,
sift, 1.

σιρικός, *see* σηρικός.

σιτευτός,
fatted, 3.

* σιτίον,
[*for* σῖτος, Acts vii. 12, *see* "Corn."]

σιτιστός, (*neut.*)
fatling, 1.

σιτομέτριον,
portion of meat, 1.

σῖτος,
wheat, 12.
corn, 2.

σιωπάω,
hold one's peace, 9.
dumb, 1.
— *impers.*,
peace, 1.

σκανδαλίζω,
offend, 28.
cause to offend, 2.
make to offend, 2.

σκάνδαλον,
occasion of stumbling, 1.
stumbling block, 3.
occasion to fall, 1.
thing that offendeth, 1.
scandal, 2.
offence, 9.

σκάπτω,
dig, 3.

σκάφη,
boat, 3.

σκέλος,
leg, 3.

σκέπασμα, (*pl.*)
raiment, 1.

σκευή,
tackling, 1.

σκεῦος,
vessel, 19.
sail, 1.
— *plural*,
stuff, 1.
goods, 2.

σκηνή,
tabernacle, 19.
habitation, 1.

σκηνοπηγία,
of tabernacles, 1.

σκηνοποιός,
tent-maker, 1.

σκῆνος,
tabernacle, 1.

σκηνόω,
dwell, 5.

σκήνωμα,
tabernacle, 3.

σκία,
shadow, 7.

σκιρτάω,
leap, 2.
leap for joy, 1.

σκληροκαρδία,
hardness of heart, 3.

σκληρός,
hard, 5.
fierce, 1.

σκληρότης,
hardness, 1.

σκληροτράχηλος,
stiff-necked, 1.

σκληρύνω,
harden, 4.
— *pass. or mid.*,
be hardened, 2.

σκολιός,
crooked, 2.
untoward, 1.
froward, 1.

σκόλοψ,
thorn, 1.

σκοπέω,
look at, 1.
look on, 1.
mark, 2.
take heed, 1.
consider, 1.

σκοπός,
mark, 1.

σκορπίζω,
scatter, 3.
scatter abroad, 1.
disperse abroad, 1.

σκορπίος,
scorpion, 5.

σκοτεινός,
dark, 1.
full of darkness, 2.

σκοτία,
darkness, 14.
dark, 2.

σκοτίζω,
darken, 8.

σκότος,
darkness, 32.

σκοτόω, (*pass.*)
full of darkness, 1.

σκύβαλον, (*pl.*)
dung, 1.

σκυθρωπός,
of a sad countenance, 1.
sad, 1.

σκύλλω,
to trouble, 2.
— *middle*,
trouble one's self, 1.

σκῦλον,
spoil, 1.

σκωληκόβρωτος,
eaten of worms, 1.

σκώληξ,
worm, 3.

σμαράγδινος,
emerald, 1.

σμάραγδος,
emerald, 1.

σμύρνα,
myrrh, 2.

σμυρνίζω,
mingle with myrrh, 1.

σοί, *see* σύ.

σορός,
bier, 1.
coffin, 1.

σός,
thy *or* thine, 18.
thine own, 3.
— τὸ σόν,
that is thine, 2.
— οἱ σοί,
thy friends, 1.
— τὰ σοί,
thy goods, 1.

σοῦ, *see* σύ.

σουδάριον,
handkerchief, 1.
napkin, 3.

σοφία,
wisdom, 51.

σοφίζω,
make wise, 1.
— *middle*,
devise cunningly, 1.

σοφός,
wise, 19.
wise man, 3.

σπαράσσω,
to tear, 3.
rend, 1.

σπαργανόω,
wrap in swaddling clothes, 2.

σπάω, (*mid.*)
draw out, 1.
draw, 1.

σπαταλάω,
live in pleasure, 1.
live delicately, 1.

σπεῖρα,
band, 6.
band of men, 1.

σπείρω,
to sow, 43.
sower, 6.
— *passive*,
receive seed, 4.

σπεκουλάτωρ,
executioner, 1.
one of his guard, 1.

σπένδω, (*mid.*)
be offered, 1.
poured forth, 1.
be ready to be offered, 1.

σπέρμα,
seed, 43.
issue, 1.

σπερμολόγος,
babbler, 1.
base fellow, 1.

σπεύδω,
haste unto, 1.
haste, 1.
haste, 1.
make haste, 3.
with haste, 1.

σπήλαιον,
cave, 1.
den, 5.

σπιλάς,
spot, 1.

σπῖλος,
spot, 2.

σπιλόω,
to spot, 1.
defile, 1.

σπλάγχνα,
bowels, 7.
bowels of compassion, 1.

inward affection, 1.
tender, 1.
bowels, 2.

σπλαγχνίζομαι,
be moved with compassion, 5.
have compassion, 7.

σπόγγος,
sponge, 3.

σποδός,
ashes, 3.

σπορά,
seed, 1.

σπόριμος, (*neut. pl.*)
corn fields, 2.
corn, 1.

σπόρος,
seed, 4.
seed sown, 1.

σπουδάζω,
be forward, 1.
be diligent, 2.
do diligence, 2.
give diligence, 1.
endeavour, 3.
labour, 1.
study, 1.

σπουδαῖος,
forward, 1.
diligent, 2.

σπουδαίως,
diligently, 1.
instantly, 1.
— *comparative*,
the more carefully, 1.
very diligently, 1.

σπουδή,
haste, 2.
forwardness, 1.
diligence, 5.
business, 1.
earnest care, 1.
care, 1.
carefulness, 1.

σπυρίς,
basket, 5.

στάδιος,
furlong, 5.
race, 1.

στάμνος,
pot, 1.

* στασιαστής,
[*for* συστασιαστής, Mk. xv. 7, *see* "That had made insurrection with."]

στάσις,
insurrection, 1.
sedition, 3.
uproar, 1.
dissension, 3.
— *with* ἔχω,
be standing, 1.

στατήρ,
piece of money, 1.
stater, 1.

σταυρός,
cross, 28.

σταυρόω,
crucify, 46.

σταφυλή,
grapes, 3.

στάχυς,
ear of corn, 3.
ear, 1.

στέγη,
roof, 3.

στέγω,
suffer, 1.
bear, 1.
can forbear, 2.

στεῖρος,
barren, 4.

στέλλω,
— *mid. or pass.*,
withdraw one's self, 1.
avoid, 1.

στέμμα,
garland, 1.

στεναγμός,
groaning, 2.

στενάζω,
to sigh, 1.
groan, 3.
with grief, 1.
grudge, 1.
groan or grieve, 1.

στενός,
strait, 3.

στενοχωρέω,
straiten, 2.
distress, 1.

στενοχωρία,
distress, 3.
anguish, 1.

στερεός,
steadfast, 1.
sure, 1.
steady, 1.
strong, 2.

στερεόω,
establish, 1.
make strong, 1.
— *passive*,
receive strength, 1.

στερέωμα,
steadfastness, 1.

στέφανος,
crown, 18.

στεφανόω,
to crown, 4.

στῆθος,
breast, 5.

στήκω,
to stand, 2.
stand fast, 6.

στηριγμός,
steadfastness, 1.

στηρίζω,
set steadfastly, 1.
fix, 1.
establish, 3.
stablish, 6.
strengthen, 2.

* στιβάς,
[*for* στοιβάς, Mark xi. 8, *see* "Branch."]

στίγμα,
mark, 1.

στιγμή,
moment, 1.

στίλβω,
shine, 1.

στοά,
porch, 4.

στοιβάς,
branch, 1.

στοιχεῖον,
element, 4.
rudiment, 2.
rudiment, 2.
element, 1.
principle, 1.

στοιχέω,
walk orderly, 1.
walk, 4.

στολή,
robe, 5.
long robe, 1.
long garment, 1.
long clothing, 1.

στόμα,
mouth, 72.
edge, 2.
— στ. πρὸς στ.,
face to face, 2.
mouth to mouth, 1.

στόμαχος,
stomach, 1.

στρατεία,
warfare, 2.

στράτευμα,
army, 6.
men of war, 1.
soldiers, 1.

στρατεύω, (*mid.*)
go a warfare, 1.
war, 5.
soldier, 1.

στρατηγός,
captain, 5.
ruler, 1.
magistrate, 5.

στρατιά,
host, 2.

στρατιώτης,
soldier, 26.

στρατολογέω,
choose...to be a soldier, 1.

στρατοπεδάρχης,
captain of the guard, 1.

στρατόπεδον,
army, 1.

στρεβλόω,
wrest, 1.

στρέφω,
to turn, 3.
— *middle*,
turn one's self, 2.
turn one, 1.
turn, 8.
turn again, 1.
turn back again, 1.
turn one about, 1.
— *with* γίνομαι,
be converted, 1.

στρηνιάω,
live deliciously, 2.

στρῆνος,
delicacy, 1.

στρουθίον,
sparrow, 4.

στρώννυμι, στρωννύω,
strew, 2.
spread, 2.
furnish, 2.
— *with* σεαυτῷ,
make thy bed, 1.

στυγητός,
hateful, 1.

στυγνάζω,
be sad, 1.
lower, 1.

στύλος,
pillar, 4.

σύ,
thou, 178.
— σοῦ (*Gen.*),
of thee, 2.
thy *or* thine, 407.
thine own, 7.
thee, 74.
thou, 4.
— τὰ σοῦ,
that thou doest, 1.
— ὑπὸ σοῦ λαλουμένη,
whereof thou speakest, 1.
— σοί (*Dat.*),
to thee, 11.
unto thee, 59.
for thee, 21.
thee, 103.
thy, 4.
thine, 2.
thine own, 4.
thou, 13.
— μηδὲν σοὶ καί,
have thou nothing to do with, 1.
— σέ (*Acc.*),
thee, 176.
thee...thou, 2.
thou, 16.
— πρὸς σέ,
at thy house, 1.

συγγένεια,
kindred, 3.

συγγενής,
kin, 1.
kinsman, 7.
cousin, 2.
— *plural*,
kinsfolk, 1.
kinsfolks, 1.

* συγγενίς,
[*for* συγγενής, Luke i. 36, *see* "Cousin."]

συγγνώμη,
permission, 1.

συγκάθημαι,
sit with, 2.

συγκαθίζω,
make sit together, 1.
be set down together, 1.

συγκακοπαθέω,
be partaker of afflictions, 1.

συγκακουχέω,
— *passive*,
suffer affliction with, 1.

συγκαλέω,
call together, 2.
— *middle*,
call together, 6.

συγκαλύπτω,
to cover, 1.

συγκάμπτω,
bow down, 1.

συγκαταβαίνω,
go down with, 1.

συγκατάθεσις,
agreement, 1.

συγκατατίθεμαι, *with* εἰμί,
consent to, 1.

συγκαταψηφίζω,
number with, 1.

συγκεράννυμι,
temper together, 1.
— *passive*,
be mixed with, 1.
...*united*..., 1.

συγκινέω,
stir up, 1.

συγκλείω,
conclude, 2.
shut up together, 1.
shut up, 1.
inclose, 1.

συγκληρονόμος,
heir with, 1.
heir together, 1.
joint heir, 1.
fellow heir, 1.

συγκοινωνέω,
communicate with, 1.
have fellowship with, 1.
be partaker of, 1.

συγκοινωνός,
partaker, 1.
companion, 1.
— *with* γίνομαι,
partake with, 1.

συγκομίζω,
carry *to one's burial*, 1.

συγκρίνω,
compare with, 2.
compare among, 1.

συγκύπτω,
be bowed together, 1.

συγκυρία,
chance, 1.

συγχαίρω,
rejoice with, 6.
rejoice in, 1.
...with, 1.

συγχέω, συγχύνω,
confuse, 1.
confound, 2.
trouble in mind, 1.
stir up, 1.
— *passive*,
be in an uproar, 1.

συγχράομαι,
have dealings with, 1.

συγχύνω, *see* συγχέω.

σύγχυσις,
confusion, 1.

συζάω,
live with, 3.

συζεύγνυμι, συζευγνύω,
join together, 2.

συζητέω,
question with, 2.
question one with another, 1.
question, 2.
inquire, 1.
dispute with, 1.
dispute, 1.
reason together, 1.
reason, 1.

συζήτησις,
disputation, 1.
disputing, 1.
reasoning, 1.

συζητητής,
disputer, 1.

σύζυγος,
yoke fellow, 1.

συζωοποιέω,
quicken together with, 2.

συκάμινος,
sycamine tree, 1.

συκέα, συκῆ,
fig-tree, 16.

συκομωραία,
sycamore tree, 1.

σῦκον,
fig, 4.

συκοφαντέω,
accuse falsely, 1.
take by false accusation, 1.

συλαγωγέω, *with* εἰμί,
to spoil, 1.

συλάω,
rob, 1.

συλλαλέω,
talk with, 3.
commune with, 1.
confer with, 1.
— *with* πρός,
speak among, 1.

συλλαμβάνω,
catch, 1.
take, 8.
conceive, 5.
— *middle*,
help, 2.

συλλέγω,
gather together, 1.
gather up, 2.
gather, 5.

συλλογίζομαι, *with* πρός,
season with, 1.

συλλυπέω,
grieve, 1.

συμβαίνω,
happen, 6.
befal, 1.
— συνέβη,
so it was, 1.

συμβάλλω,
confer, 1.
ponder, 1.
meet with, 1.
encounter, 1.
— *middle*,
help, 1.
— *with* εἰς,
make, 1.

συμβασιλεύω,
reign with, 2.

συμβιβάζω,
knit together, 1.
gather assuredly, 1.
prove, 1.
instruct, 1.
— *passive*,
be compacted, 1.

συμβουλεύω,
to counsel, 1.
give counsel, 1.
— *middle*,
take counsel together, 1.
take counsel, 1.
consult, 1.

συμβούλιον,
council, 2.
counsel, 5.
consultation, 1.

σύμβουλος,
counsellor, 1.

συμμαθητής,
fellow disciple, 1.

συμμαρτυρέω,
bear witness with, 1.
bear witness also, 1.
witness with, 1.
bear witness, 1.
— *middle*,
testify unto, 1.

συμμερίζω, (*mid.*)
be partaker with, 1.

συμμέτοχος,
partaker with, 1.
partaker, 1.

συμμιμητής,
follow together, 1.

* συμμορφίζω,
[*for* συμμορφόω, Phil. iii. 10, *see* "Make conformable unto."]

σύμμορφος,
conformed to, 1.
fashioned like unto, 1.

συμμορφόω,
make conformable unto, 1.

συμπαθέω,
have compassion of, 1.
be touched with the feeling of, 1.

συμπαθής, (*pl.*)
having compassion one of another, 1.

συμπαραγίνομαι,
come together, 1.
stand with, 1.

συμπαρακαλέω,
— *passive*,
be comforted together, 1.

συμπαραλαμβάνω,
take with one, 4.

συμπαραμένω,
continue with, 1.

συμπάρειμι,
be here present with, 1.

συμπάσχω,
suffer with, 2.

συμπέμπω,
send with, 2.

συμπεριλαμβάνω,
to embrace, 1.

συμπίνω,
drink with, 1.

* συμπίπτω,
[*for* πίπτω, Luke vi. 49, *see* "to Fall."]

συμπληρόω,
fill, 1.
— *passive*,
be fully come, 1.
come, 1.

συμπνίγω,
choke, 4.
throng, 1.

συμπολίτης,
fellow-citizen, 1.

συμπορεύομαι,
go with, 3.
resort, 1.

συμπόσιον,
— συμπόσια συμπόσια,
by companies, 1.

συμπρεσβύτερος,
also an elder, 1.

συμφάγω, *see* συνεσθίω.

συμφέρω,
bring together, 1.
— *intransitive*,
be profitable, 1.
be expedient, 2.
be profitable, 1.
— *participle*,
profit, 2.
— *impersonal*,
be profitable, 2.
be expedient, 5.
be good, 1.
be better, 1.
— πρὸς τὸ σ.,
to profit withal, 1.

σύμφημι,
consent unto, 1.

* συμφορος,
[*for* συμφέρω, 1 Cor. vii. 35, *and* x. 33, *see* "Profit."]

συμφυλέτης,
countryman, 1.

σύμφυτος,
planted together, 1.

συμφύω, (*pass.*)
spring up with, 1.

συμφωνέω,
agree with, 2.
agree together, 1.
agree, 3.

συμφώνησις,
concord, 1.

συμφωνία,
music, 1.

σύμφωνος, *with* ἐκ,
with consent, 1.

συμψηφίζω,
to count, 1.

σύμψυχος,
of one accord, 1.

σύν,
with, 10?.
beside, 1.
— ὁ σύν,
who was with, 1.
which was with, 1.
— οἱ σύν,
they that / they which / or that which } are with, 12.

συνάγω,
lead into, 1.
gather together, 8.
gather up, 1.
gather, 15.
bestow, 2.
take in, 3.
— *pass. or mid.*,
be gathered together, 12.
be gathered, 4.
gather, 1.
gather...selves together, 2.
be assembled together, 1.
be assembled, 3.
assemble together, 1.
assemble themselves, 1.
come together, 6.
resort, 1.

συναγωγή,
assembly, 1.
synagogue, 1.
congregation, 1.
synagogue, 53.
— *pl., with* κατά,
in every synagogue, 2.

συναγωνίζομαι,
strive together with, 1.

συναθλέω,
strive together for, 1.
labour with, 1.

συναθροίζω,
gather together, 2.
call together, 1.

συναίρω,
take, 1.
reckon, 1.
— *with* λόγος,
reckon, 1.

συναιχμάλωτος,
fellow prisoner, 3.

συνακολουθέω,
follow, 2.

συναλίζω,
— *pass. or mid.*,
be assembled together with, 1.
eat..., 1.

* συναλλάσσω,
[*for* συνελαύνω, Acts vii. 26, *see* "Set at one again."]

συναναβαίνω,
come up with, 2.

συνανάκειμαι,
sit at the table with, 1.
sit down with, 1.
sit together with, 1.
sit with, 2.
sit at meat with, 4.

συναναμίγνυμι
— *pass. or mid.*,
have company with, 1.
company with, 1.
keep company, 1.

συναναπαύω, (*mid.*)
be refreshed, 1.

συναντάω,
to meet, 5.
— τὰ συναντήσοντα,
the things that shall befal, 1.

συνάντησις, *with* εἰς,
to meet, 1.

συναντιλαμβάνω,
— *middle*,
to help, 2.

συναπάγω,
lead away with, 1.
carry away with, 1.
— *passive*,
condescend to, 1.
be contented with, 1.

συναποθνήσκω,
die with, 2.
— *aorist*,
be dead with, 1.

συναπόλλυμι,
— *mid. or pass.*,
perish with, 1.

συναποστέλλω,
send with, 1.

συναρμολογέω,
join fitly together, 1.
frame fitly together, 1.

συναρπάζω,
catch, 4.

συναυξάνω, (*mid.*)
grow together, 1.

σύνδεσμος,
band, 1.
bond, 3.

συνδέω,
bind with, 1.

σύνδοξάζω,
glorify together, 1.

σύνδουλος,
fellow-servant, 10.

συνδρομή, *with* γίνομαι,
run together, 1.

συνεγείρω,
raise up together, 1.
— *passive*,
rise with, 2.

συνέδριον,
council, 22.

συνείδησις,
conscience, 32.

συνεῖδον,
be ware of, 1.
consider, 1.
— σύνοιδα,
know by, 1.
be privy to, 1.

σύνειμι,
be with, 2.

σύνειμι,
be gathered together, 1.

συνεισέρχομαι,
go into with, 1.
go in with, 1.

συνέκδημος,
companion in travel, 1.
to travel with, 1.

συνεκλεκτός,
elected together with, 1.

συνελαύνω, *with* εἰς εἰρήνην,
set at one again, 1.

συνεπιμαρτυρέω,
bear witness also, 1.

* συνεπιτίθημι,
[*for* συντίθημι, Acts xxiv. 9, *see* "Assent."]

συνέπομαι,
accompany, 1.

συνεργέω,
work with, 2.
work together, 1.
worker together, 1.
help with, 1.

συνεργός,
fellow worker, 1.
work fellow, 1.
fellow labourer, 3.
labourer together with, 1.
companion in labour, 1.
fellow helper, 2.
helper, 3.

συνέρχομαι,
come with, 5.
come together, 18.
come, 2.
company with, 1.
accompany, 1.
assemble with, 1.
go with, 4.
resort, 2.

συνεσθίω,
eat with, 5.

σύνεσις,
understanding, 6.
knowledge, 1.

συνετός,
prudent, 4.

συνευδοκέω,
have pleasure in, 1.
consent with, 1.
be pleased, 2.
consent unto, 2.
allow, 1.

συνευωχέω, (*mid.*)
feast with, 2.

συνεφίστημι,
rise up together, 1.

συνέχω,
keep in, 1.
man that holdeth, 1.
stop, 1.
constrain, 1.
press, 1.
throng, 1.
— *passive*,
be straitened, 1.
pained, 1.
be in a strait, 1.
be taken with, 3.
lie sick of, 1.

συνήδομαι,
delight in, 1.

συνήθεια,
custom, 2.

συνηλικιώτης,
equal, 1.
equal in years, 1.

συνθάπτω,
bury with, 2.

συνθλάω,
break, 2.

συνθλίβω,
to throng, 2.

συνθρύπτω,
break, 1.

συνίημι,
consider, 1.
understand, 24.
be wise, 1.
understand, 1.

συνίστημι,-άω, -άνω,
— *transitive*,
make, 1.
commend, 10.
approve, 2.
commend, 1.
— *intransitive*,
stand with, 1.
stand, 1.
consist, 1.
consist, 1.

συνοδεύω,
journey with, 1.

συνοδία,
company, 1.

συνοικέω,
dwell with, 1.

συνοικοδομέω,
build together, 1.

συνομιλέω,
talk with, 1.

συνομορέω, with εἰμί,
join hard to, 1.

συνοχή,
distress, 1.
anguish, 1.

συντάσσω,
appoint, 2.

συντέλεια,
end, 6.

συντελέω,
to end, 4.
finish, 1.
fulfil, 1.
make, 1.

συντέμνω,
cut short, 1.
— *pass. part.*,
short, 1.

συντηρέω,
keep, 1.
observe, 1.
keep or save, 1.
preserve, 2.

συντίθημι, (*mid.*)
to covenant, 1.
agree, 2.
assent, 1.

συντόμως,
a few words, 1.

συντρέχω,
run with, 1.
run together, 1.
run, 1.

συντρίβω,
break in pieces, 1.
break to shivers, 1.
break, 2.
bruise, 3.
tread, 1.
— συντετριμμένοσ τὴν καρδίαν,
broken-hearted, 1.

σύντριμμα,
destruction, 1.

σύντροφος,
which had been brought up with, 1.
foster-brother, 1.

συντυγχάνω,
come at, 1.

συνυποκρίνομαι,
dissemble with. 1.

συνυπουργέω,
help together, 1.

συνωδίνω,
travail in pain together, 1.

συνωμοσία,
conspiracy, 1.

σύρτις,
quicksands, 1.

σύρω,
drag, 1.
to draw, 3.
hale, 1.

συσπαράσσω,
to bear, 1.

σύσσημον,
token, 1,

σύσσωμος,
of the same body, 1.

συστασιαστής,
that had made insurrection with, 1.

συστατικός,
of commendation, 2.

συσταυρόω,
crucify with, 5.

συστέλλω,
wind up, 1.
— *pass. part.*,
short, 1.

συστενάζω,
groan together, 1.

συστοιχέω,
answer to, 1.
be in the same rank with, 1.

συστρατιώτης,
fellow-soldier, 2.

συστρέφω,
gather, 1.

συστροφή,
concourse, 1.
— *with ποιέω*,
band together, 1.

συσχηματίζω,
— *mid. or pass.*,
fashion one's self according to, 1.
be conformed to, 1.

σφαγή,
slaughter, 3.

σφάγιον,
slain beast, 1.

σφάζω, φ άττω,
slay, 8.
kill, 1.
wound, 1.
slay, 1.

σφόδρα,
greatly, 2.
very, 3.
sore, 1.
exceedingly, 1.
exceeding, 4.

σφοδρῶς,
exceedingly, 1.

σφραγίζω,
seal up, 1.
set a seal, 1.
set to one's seal, 1.
seal, 22.

σφραγίς,
seal, 16.

σφυρίς, *see* σπυρίς.

σφυρόν,
ankle-bone,

σχεδόν,
almost, 3.

σχῆμα,
fashion, 2.

σχίζω,
rend, 5.
make a rent, 1.
divide, 2.
open, 1.
cleave or rend, 1.
break, 1.

σχίσμα,
rent, 2.
division, 5.
schism, 1.
schism, 1.
division, 1.

σχοινίον,
small cord, 1.
rope, 1.

σχολάζω,
give one's self to, 1.
empty, 1.

σχολή,
school, 1.

σώζω,
to save, 92.
preserve, 1.
make whole, 9.
save, 1.
heal, 3.
— *passive*,
save one's self, 1.
be whole, 2.
do well, 1.
— οἱ σωζόμενοι,
such as should be saved, 1.

σῶμα,
body, 145.
slave, 1.
body, 1.
— *Genitive*,
bodily, 1.

σωματικός,
bodily, 2.

σωματικῶς,
bodily, 1.

σωρεύω,
to heap, 1.
lade, 1.

σωτήρ,
saviour, 1.
Saviour, 23.

σωτηρία,
saving, 1.
that we should be saved, 1.
salvation, 40.
health, 1.
— *with εἰς*,
that they might be saved, 1.
— *with δίδωμι*,
deliver, 1.

σωτήριος,
that bringeth salvation, 1.
— *neuter*,
salvation, 4.

σωφρονέω,
in one's right mind, 2.
be sober minded, 1.
be discreet, 1.
be sober, 2.
— εἰς τὸ σωφρονεῖν,
soberly, 1.
to sobriety, 1.

σωφρονίζω,
teach to be sober, 1.
...*wise*, 1.

σωφρονισμός,
sound mind, 1.

σωφρόνως,
soberly, 1.

σωφροσύνη,
soberness, 1.
sobriety, 2.

σώφρων,
sober, 2,
temperate, 1.
discreet, 1.

ταβέρναι, *see* τρεῖς.

τάγμα,
order, 1.

τακτός,
set, 1.

ταλαιπωρέω,
be afflicted, 1.

ταλαιπωρία,
misery, 2.

ταλαίπωρος,
wretched, 2.

ταλαντιαῖος,
the weight of a talent, 1.

τάλαντον,
talent, 15.

ταλιθά,
talitha, 1.

ταμεῖον,
store house, 1.
secret chamber, 1.
closet, 2.

τανῦν, *see* νῦν.

τάξις,
order, 10.

ταπεινός,
lowly, 1.
of low degree, 2.
humble, 2.
base, 1.
cast down, 1.
— *pl., with art.,*
men of low estate, 1.
mean things, 1.

ταπεινοφροσύνη,
lowliness of mind, 1.
lowliness, 1.
humbleness of mind, 1.
humility of mind, 1.
humility, 3.

* ταπεινόφρον,
[*for* φιλόφρων, 1 Pet. iii. 8, *see* "Courteous."]

ταπεινόω,
bring low, 1.
abase, 5.
humble, 6.
— *middle,*
humble one's self, 2.

ταπείνωσις,
low estate, 1.
humiliation, 1,
— *Genitive,*
vile, 1.
— ἐν τῇ ταπεινώσει,
in that he is made low, 1.

ταράσσω,
to trouble, 16.
— ἐτάραξεν ἑαυτόν,
was troubled, 1.
troubled himself, 1.

ταραχή,
troubling, 1.
trouble, 1.

τάραχος,
stir, 2.

ταρταρόω,
cast down to hell, 1.

τάσσω,
ordain, 2.
order, 1.
set, 1.
appoint, 1.
determine, 1.
addict, 1.
— *middle,*
appoint, 2.

ταῦρος,
bull, 2.
ox, 2.

ταὐτά, *see* αὐτός.

ταῦτα, *see* οὗτος.

ταφή, *with* εἰς,
to bury in, 1.

τάφος,
sepulchre, 6.
tomb, 1.

τάχα,
peradventure, 1.
perhaps, 1.

ταχέως,
quickly, 2.
shortly, 4.
soon, 2.
hastily, 1.
suddenly, 1.

ταχινός,
swift, 1.
shortly, 1.

τάχιον, τάχιστα, *see* ταχύς.

τάχος,
— *Dative,*
quickly, 1.
— *with* ἐν,
quickly, 2.
speedily, 4.

ταχύς,
swift, 1.
— ταχύ (*as adv.*),
quickly, 11.
lightly, 1.
— τάχιον,
the sooner, 1.
quickly, 1.
shortly, 2.
— ὡς τάχιστα,
with all speed, 1.

τε,
and, 128.
both, 1.
then, 2.
— *with* καί,
and, 30.
also, 1.
both, 35.
whether...or, 1.
— *with* δέ,
and, 3.
both, 1.
— *with* γάρ,
even, 1.
— ἐάν τε...ἐάν τε,
whether...and whether, 1.
whether...or, 1.

τεῖχος,
wall, 9.

τεκμήριον,
infallible proof, 1.

τεκνίον,
little child, 9.

τεκνογονέω,
bear children, 1.

τεκνογονία,
child-bearing, 1.

τέκνον,
child, 77.
son, 21.
daughter, 1.
child, 1.

τεκνοτροφέω,
bring up children, 1.

τέκτων,
carpenter, 2.

τέλειος,
perfect, 15.
of full age, 1.
perfect, 1.
man, 1.
perfect, or of a ripe age, 1.
— οἱ τελ.,
they that are perfect, 1.
— τὸ τελ.,
that which is perfect, 1.

τελειότης,
perfectness, 1.
perfection, 1.

τελειόω,
finish, 4.
fulfil, 2.
make perfect, 12.
perfect, 4.
consecrate, 1.
perfect, 1.
— *passive,*
be perfect, 1.

τελείως,
to the end, 1.
perfectly, 1.

τελείωσις,
performance, 1.
perfection, 1.

τελειωτής,
finisher, 1.

τελεσφορέω,
bring fruit to perfection, 1.

τελευτάω,
to die, 8.
be dead, 3.
decease, 1.

τελευτή,
death, 1.

τελέω,
make an end, 1.
finish, 8.
fulfil, 7.
fill up, 1.
accomplish, 4.
perform, 1.
pay, 2.
— *passive,*
expire, 1.
go over, 1.
end or finish, 1.

τέλος,
end, 35.
ending, 1.
finally, 1.
custom, 3.
— *with* εἰς,
to the uttermost, 1.
continual, 1.

τελώνης,
publican, 21.

τελώνιον,
receipt of custom, 3.
place where custom was received, 1.

τέρας,
wonder, 16.

τεσσαράκοντα,
forty, 21.

τεσσαρακονταετής,
of forty years, 1.
— ἐπληροῦτο αὐτῷ τεσσ. χρόνος,
he was full forty years old, 1.

τέσσαρες,
four, 43.

τεσσαρεσκαιδέκατος
fourteenth, 2.

τεσσεράκοντα, *see* τεσσαράκοντα.

τέσσερες, *see* τέσσαρες.

τεταρταῖος, *with* ἐστί,
hath been dead four days, 1.

τέταρτος,
fourth, 8.
fourth part, 1.
— ἀπὸ τετάρτης ἡμέρας,
four days ago, 1.

τετράγωνος,
foursquare, 1.

τετράδιον,
quaternion, 1.

τετρακισχίλιοι,
four thousand, 5.

τετρακόσιοι,
four hundred, 4.

τετράμηνος,
four months, 1.

τετραπλόος,
fourfold, 1.

τετράπους, (*neut.*)
four-footed beast, 3.

τετράρχης,
tetrarch, 4.

τετραρχέω,
tetrarch, 2.
be tetrarch, 1.

τεφρόω,
turn into ashes, 1.

τέχνη,
art, 1.
craft, 1.
occupation, 1.

τεχνίτης,
craftsman, 3.
builder, 1.

τήκω, (*pass.*)
melt, 1.

τηλαυγῶς,
clearly, 1.

τηλικοῦτος,
so great, 3.
so mighty, 1.

τηρέω,
to watch, 2.
observe, 4.
keep, 57.
keeper, 1.
hold fast, 1.
preserve, 2.
reserve, 8.

τήρησις,
keeping, 1.
hold, 1.
prison, 1.

τίθημι,
to set, 2.
put, 11.
lay, 28.
lay down, 12.
lay aside, 1.
bow, 1.
set forth, 1.
give, 1.
appoint, 5.
ordain, 2.
make, 10.
— *middle*,
set, 2.
put, 7.
lay up, 1.
let sink down, 1.
settle, 1.
commit, 1.
put, 1.
appoint, 1.
purpose, 1.
conceive, 1.

τίκτω,
bring forth, 9.
be delivered, 4.
be delivered of, 1.
bear, 1.
be born, 1.
be in travail, 1.
— *passive*,
be born, 2.

τίλλω,
to pluck, 3.

τιμάω,
to honour, 19.
esteem, 1.
value, 2.
buy, 1.

τιμή,
honour, 32.
price, 8.
precious, 1.
honour, 1.
sum, 1.

τίμιος,
honourable, 1.
had in reputation, 1.
precious, 11.
dear, 1.

τιμιότης,
costliness, 1.

τιμωρέω,
punish, 2.

τιμωρία,
punishment, 1.

τίνω, *see* τίω.

τις, τι,
one, 34.
one thing, 1.
a, 11.
a kind of, 1.
a man, 30.
a certain man, 7.
a certain thing, 2.
certain, 104.
certain others, 1.
divers, 2.
some man, 2.
somebody, 2.
some, 74.
something, 5.
somewhat, 6.
any man, 55.
any, 39.
anything, 24.
anything at all, 1.
thing, 1.
aught, 5.
whatsoever, 1.
he, 2.
his, 1.
— *with* οὐ,
no man, 1.
none, 1.
nothing, 2.
— *with* οὐδέ,
nothing, 1.
— τις μέγας,
some great one, 1.
— ἄν τις,
whosoever, 2.
every man, 1.
— ἐάν τις,
whosoever, 1.
— ἐάν μή τι,
but what, 1.
— τι τῶν,
broken piece, 1.

τίσ, τί,
who? whose? or whom? 135.
what? 253.
what is it which? 2.
what is that? 2.
what thing? 3.
what manner of, 2.
which? 17.
whether? 8.
any, 1.
where? 1.
what? 1.
— τίς τί,
what every man, 1.
how much every man, 1.
— *with* οὐ,
nothing, 4.
— τί γίνομαι,
grow whereunto, 1.
— *Dative*,
whereunto? 4.
— *Accusative*,
wherefore? 3.
why? 66.
how is it that? 1.
how is it? 4.
how, 5.
wherewith? 1.

τίτλος,
title, 2.

τίω, *see* δίκη.

τοι, τοίγε,
[*see* καιτοίγε, μέντοι, τοιγαροῦν, τοίνυν.]

τοιγαροῦν,
therefore, 1.
wherefore, 1.

τοίνυν,
therefore, 3.
then, 1.

τοιόσδε,
such, 1.

τοιοῦτος,
such, 41.
such an one, 8.
such a man, 1.
such a fellow, 1.
such thing, 9.
— περὶ τὰ τοιαῦτα,
of like occupation, 1.

τοῖχος,
wall, 1.

τόκος,
usury, 2.

τολμάω,
be bold, 4.
boldly, 1.
dare, 11.

τολμηρότερον,
the more boldly, 1.

τολμητής,
presumptuous, 1.

τομώτερος,
sharper, 1.

τόξον,
bow, 1.

τοπάζιον,
topaz, 1.

τόπος,
place, 77.
quarter, 1.
coast, 1.
room, 5.
license, 1.
— ἐν παντὶ τόπῳ,
every where, 1.
— τὰ περὶ τὸν τόπον ἐκεῖνον,
the same quarters, 1.

τοσοῦτος,
so great, 5.
so much, 7.
as large, 1.
so long, 2.
— *plural*,
so many, 4.
so many things, 1.
...*great*..., 1.
these many, 1.

τότε,
then, 148.
when, 1.
— ὁ τότε,
that then was, 1.
— ἀπὸ τότε,
from that time, 3.
since that time, 1.

τοὐναντίον,
contrariwise, 3.

τοὔνομα, *see* ὄνομα.

τουτέστι, *see* ἐστί.

τοῦτο, *etc.*, *see* οὗτος.

τράγος,
goat, 4.

τράπεζα,
table, 13.
meat, 1.
bank, 1.

τραπεζίτης
exchanger, 1.

τραῦμα,
wound, 1.

τραυματίζω,
to wound, 2.

τραχηλίζω,
to open, 1.

τράχηλος,
neck, 7.

τραχύς,
rough, 1.
— τραχεῖς τόποι,
rocks, 1.

τρεῖς, τρία,
three, 67.
— Τρεῖς Ταβέρναι,
The Three Taverns, 1.

τρέμω,
tremble, 3.
be afraid, 1.

τρέφω,
to feed, 4.
nourish, 3.
bring up, 1.

τρέχω,
to run, 18.
have course, 1.
run, 1.

* τρῆμα,
[*for* τρυμαλιά, Luke xviii. 25, *see* "Eye."]

τριάκοντα,
thirty, 9.
thirty-fold, 2.

τριακόσιοι,
three hundred, 2.

τρίβολος,
thistle, 1.
brier, 1.

τρίβος,
path, 3.

τριετία,
space of three years, 1.

τρίζω,
gnash with, 1.

τρίμηνος, (*neut.*)
three months, 1.

τρίς,
thrice, 10.
— ἐπὶ τρίς,
thrice, 1.
three times, 1.

τρίστεγος, (*neut.*)
third loft, 1.

τρισχίλιοι,
three thousand, 1.

τρίτος,
third, 32.
— τῇ τρίτῃ,
the third day, 2.
— τὸ τρίτον,
the third part, 15.
— ἐκ τρίτου,
the third time, 1.
— (τό) τρίτον (*as adv.*),
the third time, 7.
thirdly, 1.

τρίχινος,
of hair, 1.

τρόμος,
trembling, 4.
— *with* ἔχω,
tremble, 1.

τροπή,
turning, 1.

τρόπος,
manner, 1.
way, 2.
means, 2.

conversation, 1.
— ὃν τρόπον,
in like manner as, 1.
as, 3.
even as, 1.
— *with* κατά,
even as, 2.

τροποφορέω,
suffer one's manners, 1.
bear, or feed one, as a nurse beareth or feedeth her child, 1.

τροφή,
food, 2.
meat, 11.
— *Genitive,*
some meat, 2.

τροφός,
nurse, 1.

* **τροφοφορέω,**
[*for* τροποφορέω, Acts xiii. 18, *see* "Suffer one's manners."]

τροχιά,
path, 1.

τροχός,
course, 1.

τρύβλιον,
dish, 2.

τρυγάω,
gather, 3.

τρυγών,
turtle-dove, 1.

τρυμαλιά,
eye, 2.

τρύπημα,
eye, 1.

τρυφάω,
live in pleasure, 1.

τρυφή,
to riot, 1.
— *with* ἐν,
delicately, 1.

τρώγω,
eat, 6.

τυγχάνω,
obtain, 5.
enjoy, 1.
— εἰ τύχοι,
it may chance, 1.
it may be, 1.
— τυχόν,
it may be, 1.
— *part., with* οὐ,
no little, 1.
special, 1.

τυμπανίζω,
to torture, 1.

* **τυπικῶς,**
[*for* τύπος, 1 Cor. x. 11, *see* "Ensample."]

τύπος,
print, 2.
figure, 2.
form, 1.
fashion, 1.
manner, 1.
pattern, 2.
ensample, 5.
type, 1.
example, 2.
figure, 1.

τύπτω,
to beat, 3.
strike, 1.
smite, 9.
wound, 1.

τυρβάζω,
— *pass. or mid.,*
be troubled, 1.

τυφλός,
blind, 40.
which was blind, 1.
blind man, 10.
— *with art.,*
he that was blind, 1.
that was blind, 1.

τυφλόω,
to blind, 3.

τυφόω, (*pass.*)
be lifted up with pride, 1.
be proud, 1.
be a fool, 1.
be high-minded, 1.

τύφω, (*pass.*)
to smoke, 1.

τυφωνικός,
tempestuous, 1.

τυχόν, *see* τυγχάνω.

ὑακίνθινος,
of jacinth, 1.

ὑάκινθος,
jacinth, 1.

ὑάλινος,
of glass, 3.

ὕαλος,
glass, 2.

ὑβρίζω,
entreat spitefully, 2.
use despitefully, 1.
entreat shamefully, 1.
reproach, 1.

ὕβρις,
reproach, 1.
hurt, 1.
injury, 1.
harm, 1.

ὑβριστής,
despiteful, 1.
injurious, 1.

ὑγιαίνω,
be in health, 1.
be whole, 1.
whole, 1.
wholesome, 1.
be sound, 1.
sound, 6.
safe and sound, 1.

ὑγιής,
whole, 13.
sound, 1.

ὑγρός,
green, 1.

ὑδρία,
water-pot, 3.

ὑδροποτέω,
drink water, 1.

ὑδρωπικός,
which had the dropsy, 1.

ὕδωρ,
water, 74.

ὑετός,
rain, 5.

υἱοθεσία,
adoption of sons, 1.
adoption of children, 1.
adoption, 3.

υἱός,
son, 120.
Son, 210.
child, 50.
foal, 1.

ὕλη,
matter, 1.
wood, 1.

ὑμεῖς,
ye, 242.
ye yourselves, 1.
of you, 1.
— ὑμῶν (*Gen.*),
of you, 32.
your, 350.
your own, 3.
yours, 4.
of yours, 1.
your things, 1.
on your part, 1.
yourselves, 2.
you, 171.
ye, 7.
ye spake of, 1.
— *with* ἐκ,
your, 2.
— τὰ περὶ ὑμῶν,
your affairs, 1.
your state, 2.
your estate, 1
— ὑμῶν αὐτῶν,
your own selves, 1.
yourselves, 1.
your own, 1.
— τῶν ψυχῶν ὑμῶν,
you, 1.
your souls, 1.
— ὑμῖν (*Dat.*),
to you, 38.
unto you, 318.
for you, 13.
for yourselves, 2.
for your cause, 1.
against you, 1.
with you, 2.
of you, 1.
you, 224.
your, 4.
ye, 14.
— τὸ ἐφ' ὑμῖν,
on your behalf, 1.
— ὑμῖν αὐτοῖς,
yourselves, 1.
— ὑμᾶς (*Acc.*),
you, 379.
your, 1.
you...ye, 1.
ye, 41.
— δι' ὑμᾶς,
for your sake, 1.
for your sakes, 8.
— ἐφ' ὑμᾶς,
on your part, 1.
— καθ ὑμᾶς,
your, 2.
your own, 1.
— τὸ καθ' ὑμας,
the uttermost of your matter, 1.

ὑμέτερος,
your, 7.
yours, 2.
— τὸ ὑμέτερον,
that which is your own, 1.

ὑμνέω,
sing an hymn, 2.
...*psalm,* 2.
sing praise unto, 1.
sing praises unto, 1.

ὕμνος,
hymn, 2.

ὑπάγω,
go away, 3.
go one's way, 17.
go, 55.
depart, 2.
— ὕπαγε,
get thee hence, 1.
get thee, 3.

ὑπακοή,
obedience, 11.
obeying, 1.
— *with* εἰς,
to obey, 1.
to make obedient, 1.
— *Genitive,*
obedient, 1.

ὑπακούω,
hearken, 1.
ask who was there, 1.
obey, 18.
be obedient to, 2.

ὕπανδρος,
which hath an husband, 1.

ὑπαντάω,
to meet, 4.
go and meet, 1.

ὑπάντησις, *with* εἰς,
to meet, 1.

ὕπαρξις,
substance, 1.
goods, 1.

ὑπάρχω,
to be, 42.
after, 1.
live, 1.
have, 2.
— τὰ ὑπάρχοντα,
the things which one possesseth, 2.
that one hath, 4.
substance, 1.
goods, 7.

ὑπείκω,
submit one's self, 1.

ὑπεναντίος,
contrary, 1.
adversary, 1.

ὑπέρ,
— *with Gen.,*
for, 105.
on one's behalf, 3.
in the behalf of, 1.
on one's part, 1.
for one's sake, 8.
in one's stead, 2.
concerning, 1.

of, 11.
toward, 1.
by, 1.
— *with Acc.*,
over, 1.
above, 12.
beyond, 1.
more than, 3.
than, 2.
to, 1.
— *as adv.*,
more, 1.

ὑπεραίρω, (*mid.*)
exalt one's self, 1.
be exalted above measure, 2.

ὑπέρακμος, *with* εἰμί,
pass the flower of one's age, 1.

ὑπεράνω,
far above, 2.
over, 1.

ὑπεραυξάνω,
grow exceedingly, 1.

ὑπερβαίνω,
go beyond, 1.

ὑπερβαλλόντως,
above measure, 1.

ὑπερβάλλω,
exceed, 3.
excel, 1.
pass, 1.

ὑπερβολή,
excellency, 1.
abundance, 1.
— *with* κατά,
exceeding, 1.
far more exceeding, 1.
beyond measure, 1.
out of measure, 1.
more excellent, 1.

ὑπερεῖδον,
wink at, 1.

ὑπερέκεινα, *with* τὰ,
the regions beyond, 1.

ὑπερεκτείνω,
stretch beyond one's measure, 1.

ὑπερεκχύνω, (*pass.*)
run over, 1.

ὑπερεντυγχάνω,
make intercession for, 1.

ὑπερέχω,
pass, 1.
— *participle*,
higher, 1.
supreme, 1.
better, 1.

ὑπερηφανία,
pride, 1.

ὑπερήφανος,
proud, 5.

ὑπερλίαν, *see* λίαν.

ὑπερνικάω,
be more than conqueror, 1.

ὑπέρογκος,
— *neut. pl.*,
great swelling words, 2.

ὑπεροχή,
excellency, 1.
authority, 1.
eminent place, 1.

ὑπερπερισσεύω,
abound much more, 1.
— *pass., with* τῇ χαρᾷ,
be exceeding joyful, 1.

ὑπερπερισσῶς,
beyond measure, 1.

ὑπερπλεονάζω,
be exceeding abundant, 1.

ὑπερυψόω,
exalt highly, 1.

ὑπερφρονέω,
think highly, 1.

ὑπερῷος, (*neut.*)
upper room, 1.
upper chamber, 3.

ὑπέχω,
suffer, 1.

ὑπήκοος,
obedient, 2.
— *with* γίνομαι,
obey, 1.

ὑπηρετέω,
serve, 1.
minister, 2.

ὑπηρέτης,
servant, 4.
minister, 5.
officer, 11.

ὕπνος,
sleep, 6.

ὑπό,
— *with Gen.*,
by, 42.
with, 14.
from, 2.
among, 1.
of, 116.
— *with Acc.*,
under, 48.
into, 1.
in, 1.

ὑποβάλλω,
suborn, 1.

ὑπογραμμός,
example, 1.

ὑπόδειγμα,
pattern, 1.
ensample, 1.
example, 4.

ὑποδείκνυμι,
to show, 3.
warn, 2.
forewarn, 1.

ὑποδέχομαι,
receive, 4.

ὑποδέω, (*mid.*)
bind on, 1.
be shod with, 1
have...shod, 1.

ὑπόδημα,
shoe, 10.

ὑπόδικος,
guilty, 1.
subject to judgment, 1.

ὑποζύγιον,
ass, 2.

ὑποζώννυμι,
undergird, 1.

ὑποκάτω,
under, 9.

ὑποκρίνομαι,
to feign, 1.

ὑπόκρισις,
dissimulation, 1.
hypocrisy, 5.

ὑποκριτής,
hypocrite, 20.

ὑπολαμβάνω,
receive, 1.
answer, 1.
suppose, 2.

* ὑπ λειμμα,
[*for* κατάλειμμα, Rom. ix. 27, *see* "Remnant."]

ὑπολείπω,
to leave, 1.

ὑπολήνιον,
wine-fat, 1.

ὑπολιμπάνω,
to leave, 1.

ὑπομένω,
abide, 1.
tarry behind, 1.
endure, 11.
take patiently, 2.
patient, 1.
suffer, 1.

ὑπομιμνήσκω,
put in remembrance, 2.
put in remembrance of, 1.
bring to remembrance, 1.
put in mind, 1.
remember, 1.
— *middle*,
remember, 1.

ὑπόμνησις,
remembrance, 3.

ὑπομονή,
enduring, 1.
patient waiting, 1.
patience, 1.
patient continuance, 1.
patience, 29.

ὑπονοέω,
suppose, 1.
deem, 1.
think, 1.

ὑπόνοια,
surmising, 1.

ὑποπιάζω, *see* ὑπωπιάζω.

ὑποπλέω,
sail under, 2.

ὑποπνέω,
blow softly, 1.

ὑποπόδιον,
footstool, 9.

ὑπόστασις,
substance, 1.
ground or confidence, 1.
person, 1.
confidence, 2.
confident, 1.

ὑποστέλλω,
withdraw, 1.
— *middle*,
draw back, 1.
shun, 1.
keep back, 1.

ὑποστολή, (*Gen.*)
of them who draw back, 1.

ὑποστρέφω,
turn back, 1.
turn back again, 1.
return, 27.
return again, 4.
return back again, 1.
come again, 1.

ὑποστρωννύμι, -νύω,
spread, 1.

ὑποταγή,
subjection, 4.

ὑποτάσσω,
put under, 6.
put in subjection, 1.
put in subjection under, 1.
put in subjection unto, 1.
subject, 1.
subdue unto, 1.
— *mid. or pass.*,
submit one's self to, 3.
submit one's self unto, 5.
be subject, 1.
be subject to, 5.
be subject unto, 6.
be in subjection to, 1.
be in subjection unto, 2.
be made subject to, 1.
be made subject unto, 1.
obedient to, 1.
be obedient unto, 1.
be under obedience, 1.
be subdued unto, 1.

ὑποτίθημι,
lay down, 1.
— *middle*,
put in remembrance, 1.

ὑποτρέχω,
run under, 1.

ὑποτύπωσις,
pattern, 1.
form, 1.

ὑποφερω,
to bear, 1.
endure, 2.

ὑποχωρέω,
withdraw one's self, 1
go aside, 1.

ὑπωπιάζω,
keep under, 1.
weary, 1.

ὗς,
sow, 1.

ὕσσωπος,
hyssop, 2.

ὑστερέω,
be behind, 2.
come short of, 1.
lack, 3.
part which lacked, 1.
want, 1.
— *with ἀπό,*
fail of, 1.
fall from, 1.
— *passive,*
come behind, 1.
come short of, 1.
be destitute, 1.
be in want, 1.
want, 1.
suffer need, 1.
be the worse, 1.
have the less, 1.

ὑστέρημα,
which is behind, 1.
which is lacking, 3.
lack, 1.
want, 3.
penury, 1.

ὑστέρησις,
want, 2.

ὕστερος,
latter, 1.
— ὕστερον (*adv.*),
afterward, 7
afterwards, 1.
at the last, 1.
last, 2.
last of all, 1.

* **ὑφαίνω,**
[*see* Luke xii. 27 (*ap.*)]

ὑφαντός,
woven, 1.
wrought, 1.

ὑψηλός,
high, 8.
— τὰ ὑψηλα,
high things, 1.
— ἐν ὑψηλοῖς,
on high, 1.
— τὸ ὑψηλόν,
that which is highly esteemed, 1.

ὑψηλοφορέω,
be high-minded, 2.

ὕψιστος,
most high, 4.
Most High, 1.
Highest, 4.
— ἐν (τοῖς) ὑψίστοις,
in the highest, 4.

ὕψος,
height, 2.
— εἰς ὕψος,
on high, 1.
— ἐξ ὕψους,
from on high, 2.
— ἐν τῷ ὕψει αὐτοῦ,
in that he is exalted, 1.

ὑψόω,
exalt, 14.
lift up, 6.

ὕψωμα,
high thing, 1.
height, 1.

φάγω,
eat, 92.
— *infinitive,*
eating, 1.
aught to eat, 1.
meat, 3.

φαιλόνης,
cloak, 1.

φαίνω,
shine, 7.
— *pass. or mid.,*
shine, 3.
be seen, 2.
appear, 16.
seem, 1.
think, 1.
— φαινόμενα,
things which do appear, 1.

φανερός,
manifest, 9.
known, 3.
— ἐν τῷ φανερῷ,
openly, 2.
outwardly, 1.
outward, 1.
— *with εἰμί,*
appear, 1.
— *with εἰς,*
abroad, 2.
— *with γίνομαι,*
be spread abroad, 1.

φανερόω,
make manifest, 19.
manifest, 9.
manifest forth, 1.
declare manifestly, 1.
show, 3.
— *pass. or mid.,*
be manifest, 2.
show one's self, 2.
appear, 12.

φανερῶς,
evidently, 1.
openly, 2.

φανέρωσις,
manifestation, 2.

φανός,
lantern, 1.

φαντάζω,
— *pass. part.,*
sight, 1.

φαντασία,
pomp, 1.

φάντασμα,
spirit, 2.

φάραγξ,
valley, 1.

φαρμακεία,
sorcery, 2.
witchcraft, 1.

φαρμακεύς,
sorcerer, 1.

φαρμακός,
sorcerer, 1.

φάσις,
tidings, 1.

φάσκω,
affirm, 1.
say, 2.
profess, 1.

φάτνη,
manger, 3.
stall, 1.

φαῦλος,
evil, 1 (*adj.*)
evil, 2 (*subst.*)
— *neuter,*
evil thing, 1.

φέγγος,
light, 3.

φείδομαι,
to spare,
forbear, 1.

φειδομένως,
sparingly, 2.

φέρω,
to bear, 8.
endure, 2.
uphold, 1.
carry, 1.
move, 1.
bring, 33.
reach, 1.
reach hither, 1.
lead, 1.
lay, 1.
bring forth, 5.
— *passive,*
be to be brought, 1.
come, 3.
be, 1.
be brought in, 1.
let drive, 1.
be driven, 1.
— *middle,*
go on, 1.
rush, 1.

φεύγω,
flee, 26.
flee away, 2.
escape, 2.
can escape, 1.

φήμη,
fame, 2.

φημί,
say, 57.
affirm, 1.

φθάνω,
prevent, 1.
attain, 1.
come, 4.
— *aorist,*
attain already, 1.

φθαρτός,
corruptible, 5.
— *neut. pl.,*
corruptible things, 1.

φθέγγομαι,
speak, 3.

φθείρω,
to corrupt, 4.
destroy, 1.
defile, 1.
destroy, 1.
— *middle,*
corrupt one's self, 1.
— *passive,*
be corrupt, 1,

φθινοπωρινός,
whose fruit withereth, 1.

φθόγγος,
sound, 2.
time, 1.

φθονέω,
to envy, 1.

φθονός,
envy, 8.
enviously, 1.
envying, 1.

φθορά,
corruption, 7.
— *with εἰς,*
to perish, 1.
to be destroyed, 1.

φιάλη,
vial, 12.

φιλάγαθος,
lover of good men, 1.
...*things*, 1.

φιλαδελφία,
brotherly love, 3.
love of the brethren, 1.
love of the brethren, 1.
brotherly kindness, 2.

φιλάδελφος,
— *pl., with εἰμί, understood,*
love as brethren, 1.
loving to the brethren, 1.

φίλανδρος,
— *with εἰμί,*
love one's husband, 1.

φιλανθρωπία,
love toward man, 1.
pity..., 1.
kindness, 1.

φιλανθρώπως,
courteously, 1.

φιλαργυρία,
love of money, 1.

φιλάργυρος,
covetous, 2.

φίλαυτος,
lover of one's own self, 1.

φιλέω,
to love, 22.
kiss, 3.

φίλη, (*fem.*)
friend, 1.

φιλήδονος,
lover of pleasures, 1.

φίλημα,
kiss, 7.

φιλία,
friendship, 1.

φιλόθεος,
lover of God, 1.

φιλονεικία,
strife, 1.

φιλόνεικος,
contentious, 1.

all hail! 1.
farewell, 1.
— *infinitive*,
greeting, 1.
send greeting, 2.
God speed, 2.

χάλαζα,
hail, 4.

χαλάω,
let down, 5.
strike, 1.

χαλεπός,
perilous, 1.
fierce, 1.

χαλιναγωγέω,
to bridle, 2.

χαλινός,
bit, 1.
bridle, 1.

χάλκεος, χαλκοῦς,
of brass, 1.

χαλκεύς,
coppersmith, 1.

χαλκηδών,
chalcedony, 1.

χαλκίον,
brazen vessel, 1.

χαλκολίβανον,
fine brass, 2.

χαλκός,
brass, 3.
money, 2.

χαμαί,
to the ground, 1.
on the ground, 1.

χαρά,
joy, 53.
joyfulness, 1.
gladness, 3.
— *Genitive*,
joyous, 1.
— *Dative*,
greatly, 1.
— μετὰ χαρᾶς,
joyfully, 1.

χάραγμα,
mark, 8.
— *Dative*,
graven, 1.

χαρακτήρ,
express image, 1.

χάραξ,
trench, 1.

χαρίζομαι,
give freely, 1.
give, 6.
grant, 1.
deliver, 2.
forgive frankly, 1.
forgive, 11.
— τὰ χαρισθέντα,
the things that are freely given, 1.

χάρις,
grace, 129.
thanksgiving, 1.
favour, 6.
pleasure, 2.
liberality, 1.
gift, 1.
benefit, 1.
grace, 1.
thanks, 4.
thank, 3.
thankworthy, 1.
acceptable, 1.
thank, 1.
— *Genitive*,
gracious, 1.
— *with* ἔχω,
to thank, 3.
— χάρις τῷ Θεῷ,
God be thanked, 1.
— *Acc.* (χάριν),
for...sake, 1.
because of, 2.
— τουτο χάριν,
for this cause, 2.
— οὐ χάριν,
wherefore, 1.
— χάριν τίνος,
wherefore? 1.

χάρισμα,
free gift, 2.
gift, 15.

χαριτόω,
make accepted, 1.
— *pass. part.*,
highly favoured, 1.
graciously accepted or much graced, 1.

χάρτης,
paper, 1.

χάσμα,
gulf, 1.

χεῖλος,
lip, 6.
shore, 1.

χειμάζω, (*pass.*)
be tossed with a tempest, 1.

χείμαρρος,
brook, 1.

χειμών,
tempest, 1.
foul weather, 1.
winter, 4.

χείρ,
hand, 178.

χειραγωγέω,
lead by the hand, 2.

χειραγωγός, (*pl.*)
some to lead by the hand, 1.

χειρόγραφον,
handwriting, 1.

χειροποίητος,
made with hands, 4.
made by hands, 1.
— *with art.*,
that is made with hands, 1.

χειροτονέω,
choose, 1.
ordain, 1.

χείρων, χεῖρον,
worse, 7.
sorer, 1.
— εἰς τὸ χεῖρον,
worse, 1.
— ἐπὶ τὸ χεῖρον,
worse and worse, 1.
— χεῖρον τι,
a worse thing, 1.

χήρα,
widow, 26.
that was a widow, 1.

χθές,
yesterday, 3.

χιλίαρχος,
chief captain, 19.
high captain, 1.
captain, 2.

χιλιάς, (*pl.*)
thousands, 2.
thousand, 21.

χίλιοι,
thousand, 11.

χιτών,
coat, 9.
garment, 1.
— *plural*,
clothes, 1.

χιών,
snow, 3.

χλαμύς,
robe, 2.

χλευάζω,
mock, 2.

χλιαρός,
lukewarm, 1.

χλωρός,
pale, 1.
green, 2.
— *neuter*,
green thing, 1.

χξς´,
six hundred threescore and six, 1.

χοϊκός,
earthy, 3.
— οἱ χοϊκοί,
they that are earthy, 1.

χοῖνιξ,
measure, 1.

χοῖρος,
swine, 14.

χολάω,
be angry, 1.

χολή,
gall, 1.

χόος, χοῦς,
dust, 2.

χορηγέω,
to minister, 1.
give, 1.

χορός,
dancing, 1.

χορτάζω,
to feed, 1.
fill, 13.
satisfy, 1.

χόρτασμα,
sustenance, 1.

χόρτος,
grass, 12.
blade, 2.
hay, 1.

χράω,
— κίχρημι,
lend, 1.
— χράομαι (*mid.*),
use, 10.
entreat, 1.
— χρή (*impers.*),
ought, 1.

χρεία,
use, 2.
profitably, 1.
business, 1.
need, 25.
needful, 1.
necessity, 3.
want, 1.
lack, 1.
— *with* ἔχω,
to need, 14.
— τὰ πρὸς τὴν χρ.,
such things as are necessary, 1.

χρεωφειλέτης,
debtor, 2.

χρή, *see* χράω.

χρῄζω,
to need, 2.
have need of, 3.

χρῆμα,
money, 1.
— *plural*,
riches, 3.
money, 3.

χρηματίζω,
reveal, 1.
call, 2.
speak, 1.
— *passive*,
be warned of (*or* from) God, 4.

χρηματισμός,
answer of God, 1.

χρήσιμος, (*neut.*)
profit, 1.

χρῆσις,
use, 2.

χρηστεύομαι,
be kind, 1.

χρηστολογία,
good words, 1.

χρηστός,
good, 1.
kind, 2.
gracious, 1.
easy, 1.
— *neuter*,
goodness, 1.
— *comparative*,
better, 1.

χρηστότης,
goodness, 4.
good, 1 (*subst.*),
kindness, 4.
gentleness, 1.

χρίσμα,
anointing, 2
unction, 1.

χρίω,
anoint, 5.

χρονίζω,
delay, 2.
tarry, 3.

χρόνος,
time, 17.
while, 3.
season, 4.
space, 1.
— *with ἱκανός,*
long time, 1.
of long time, 1.
— *plural,*
for a long time, 1.
— with ἐκ,
long time, 1.
— πολλοῖς χρ.,
oftentimes, 1.
— ἐν παντὶ χρόνῳ ἐν ᾧ,
all the time that, 1.
— *with ποιέω,*
spend some time there, 1.
tarry there a space, 1.
— ὅσον χρόνον,
as long as, 1.
— *with ἐπί,*
as long as, 3.

χρονοτριβέω,
spend the time, 1.

χρύσεος, χρυσοῦς,
of gold, 3.
golden, 15.

χρυσίον,
gold, 9.

χρυσοδακτύλιος,
with a gold ring, 1.

χρυσόλιθος,
chrysolite, 1.

χρυσόπρασος,
chrysoprasus, 1.

χρυσός,
gold, 13.

χρυσόω,
to deck, 2.
gild, 1.

χρώς,
body, 1.

χωλός,
lame, 7.
that is lame, 1.
lame man, 1.
being a cripple, 1.
halt, 4.
— τὸ χω.,
that which is lame, 1.

χώρα,
country, 14.
region, 5.
lands, 3.
coasts, 1.
field, 2.
ground, 1.

χωρέω,
be room to receive, 1.
can receive, 1.
receive, 3.
can contain, 1.
contain, 1.
have place, 1.
go, 1.
come, 1.

χωρίζω,
put asunder, 2.
separate, 1.
— *pass. part.,*
separate, 1.
— *middle,*
depart, 8.

χωρίον,
place, 2.
field, 2.
parcel of ground, 1.
land, 3.
possessions, 1.

χωρίς,
by itself, 1.
without, 36.
severed from, 1.
beside, 3.

χῶρος,
north-west, 1.

ψάλλω,
sing, 3.
sing psalms, 1.
make melody, 1.

ψαλμός,
psalm, 5.
— *plural,*
Psalms, 2.

ψευδάδελφος, (*pl.*)
false brethren, 2.

ψευδαπόστολος,
— *plural,*
false apostles, 1.

ψευδής,
false, 1.
liar, 2.

ψευδοδιδάσκαλος,
— *plural,*
false teachers, 1.

ψευδολόγος,
speaking lies, 1.

ψεύδομαι, *see* ψεύδω.

ψευδομάρτυρ,
false witness, 3.

ψευδομαρτυρέω,
bear false witness, 6.

ψευδομαρτυρία,
false witness, 2.

ψευδοπροφήτης,
false prophet, 11.

ψεῦδος,
lie, 7.
lying, 1.
— *Gen.* (*adj.*),
lying, 1.

ψευδόχριστος, (*pl.*)
false Christs, 1.

ψεύδω, (*mid.*)
to lie, 10.
to lie to, 1.
falsely, 1.
lying, 1.

ψευδώνυμος,
falsely so called, 1.

ψεῦσμα,
lie, 1.

ψεύστης,
liar, 10.

ψηλαφάω,
handle, 2.
feel after, 1.
— *pass. part.,*
that might be touched, 1.

ψηφίζω,
to count, 2.

ψῆφος,
stone, 2.
voice, 1.

ψιθυρισμός,
whispering, 1.

ψιθυριστής,
whisperer, 1.

ψιχίον,
crumb, 3.

ψυχή,
life, 40.
soul, 58.
heart, 1.
mind, 3.
— *with ἐκ,*
heartily, 1.

ψυχικός,
natural, 3.
sensual, 1.
natural, 1.
— τὸ ψυχικόν,
that which is natural, 1.

ψῦχος,
cold, 3.

ψυχρός,
cold, 3.
cold water, 1.

ψύχω, (*pass.*)
wax cold, 1.

ψωμίζω,
bestow to feed, 1.
feed, 1.

ψωμίον,
sop, 4.
morsel, 1.

ψώχω,
to rub, 1.

Ω,
Omega, 4.

ὦ,
O, 15.

ὦ, ᾖς, ᾖ, *see* εἰμί.

ὧδε,
hither, 13.
here, 44.
in this place, 1.
— ὧδε...ὧδε,
here...there, 1.
— ἕως ὧδε,
to this place, 1.

ᾠδή,
song, 7.

ὠδίν,
travail, 1.
pain, 1.
sorrow, 2.
pain of a woman in travail, 1.

ὠδίνω,
to travail in birth, 1.
to travail in birth of, 1.
travail, 1.

ὦμος,
shoulder, 2.

ὤν, οὖσα, ὄν, *see* εἰμί.

ᾠόν,
egg, 1.

ὥρα,
hour, 89.
time, 11.
high time, 1.
season, 3.
instant, 1.
— *Genitive,*
short, 1.

ὡραῖος,
beautiful, 2.
Beautiful, 2.

ὠρύομαι,
to roar, 1.

ὡς,
as, 342.
as...as, 1.
according as, 3.
even as, 6.
like as, 1.
like, 7.
even like, 1.
like unto, 3.
as, 1.
unto, 1.
for, 2.
as it were (or had been), 22.
as soon as, 7.
when, 41.
while, 4.
after, 3.
after that, 1.
since, 1.
about, 14.
how, 19.
so, 1.
so that, 1.
that, 5.
— ὡς ἄν,
even as, 1.
as, 2.
as soon as, 1.
when, 1.
— ὡς ἐάν,
whensoever, 1.

ὡσαννά,
Hosanna, 6.

ὡσαύτως,
after the same manner, 1.
even so, 1.
in like manner, 2.
likewise, 12.

ὡσεί,
as it were (or had been), 3.
as, 7.
like as, 1.
like, 4.
about, 18.

ὥσπερ,
even as, 2.
as, 38.
like as, 1.
as when, 1.

ὡσπερεί,
as, 1.

ὥστε,
so that, 25.
insomuch that, 16.
insomuch as, 1.
that, 3.
so then, 5.
therefore, 9.
wherefore, 17.
— *with infinitive,*
to, 3.
as to, 1.
that...might, 1.
that...should, 2.

*** ὠτάριον,**
[*for* ὠτίον, Mark xiv. 47, *see* "Ear."]

ὠτίον,
ear, 5.

ὠφέλεια,
profit, 1.
advantage, 1

ὠφελέω,
to profit, 7.
prevail, 2.
— *mid. or pass.,*
be profited, 3.
profit, 1.
be advantaged, 1.
be bettered, 1.

ὠφέλιμος,
profitable, 3.
— *with* εἰμί,
to profit, 1.

APPENDIX

(A)

OF

VARIOUS READINGS, WHERE WORDS IN THE BODY OF THE WORK ARE INVOLVED IN LARGER CLAUSES,

REFERRED TO IN THE WORK BY *(Ap.)*

MATTHEW:

v. 44. Bless them that curse you, do good to them that hate you—*omit*, G⇉ L T Tr A א.

Despitefully use you and—*omit*, G→ L T Tr A א.

vi. 13. For thine is the kingdom, the power, and the glory, for ever and ever. Amen—*omit*, All.

x. 19. It shall be given you in that same hour what ye shall speak—G→ L^{b}.

xiii. 51. Jesus saith unto them—*omit*, G⇉ L T Tr A א.

xiv. 24. Was now in the midst of the sea—*substitute*, was now many stadii distant from the land—Tr.

xv. 5. Or his mother—*omit*, L א.

8. Draweth nigh unto me with their mouth, and—*omit*, All.

xvii. 21. *Omit the verse*—Tr^{b} א.

26. Peter saith unto Him—*substitute*, now when he said—L Tr; now he said—א; *omit*, Peter—G⇉ L A.

xviii. 11. *Omit the verse*—G⇉ L T Tr א.

xix. 9. Except it be for fornication, (*εἰ μὴ ἐπὶ πορνείᾳ*)—*substitute*, (*παρεκτὸς λόγου πορνείας*)—*substitute*, except on the ground of fornication—G L T Tr A א; (except, *instead of* not—L.)

And whoso marrieth her which is put away doth commit adultery—*omit*, Tr^{b} א.

Matthew:

xix. 17. Why callest thou me good? There is none good but one, that is God—*substitute,* Why askest thou me concerning that which is good? He who is good is One—G L T Tr A א; *add,* God—G~.

29. Or wife—*omit,* T Tr A.

xx. 7. And whatsoever is right that shall ye receive—*omit,* G⇉ L T Tr A א.

16. For many be called but few chosen—*omit,* T Tr^{b} א.

22. And to be baptized with the baptism that I am baptized with—*omit,* All.

23. And be baptized with the baptism that I am baptized with—*omit,* All.

xxi. 44. *Omit the verse*—G→ L^{b} T Tr^{m}.

xxiii. 14. *Omit the verse*—G⇉ L T Tr A א.

xxiv. 36. *After* of heaven—*add,* nor the Son—L T א.

xxv. 13. Wherein the Son of man cometh—*omit,* All.

41. Prepared—*substitute,* which my Father hath prepared—G~.

xxvi. 60. Yea, though many false witnesses came—*omit,* G→.

Yet found they none—*omit,* G L T A א.

xxvii. 35. That it might be fulfilled which was spoken by the prophet, they parted my garments among them, and upon my vesture did they cast lots—*omit,* G L T Tr A א.

xxviii. 9. As they went to tell His disciples—*omit,* G⇉ L T Tr A א.

Mark:

i. 27. What is this?—*omit,* G~.

What new doctrine is this? for with authority commandeth He—*substitute,* a new doctrine! with authority He commandeth—L Tr; a new doctrine with authority! He commandeth—T A א.

ii. 19. As long as they have the bridegroom with them they cannot fast—*omit,* G→.

22. But new wine must be put into new bottles—*omit,* T Tr^{b} A; must be put—*omit,* א.

iii. 12. *After* known, *add,* because they knew that He was the Christ—L^{b}.

32. *After* brethren, *add,* and thy sisters—G⇸ L T Tr^{bm} A.

iv. 15. In their hearts—*substitute,* in them (ἐν αὐτοῖς)—G~ L א; in them (εἰς αὐτοὺς, into them)—T Tr A.

24. And unto you that hear shall more be given—*omit,* G; that hear—*omit,* G L T Tr A א.

31. That be upon the earth—L^{b}.

40. Why are ye so fearful? How is it that ye have no faith?—*substitute,* Why are ye fearful? Have ye yet no faith—G~ L Tr א.

vi. 11. And whosoever shall not receive you—*substitute,* and what place soever shall not receive you—T Tr A א.

Verily I say unto you, it shall be more tolerable for Sodom and Gomorrha in the day of judgment than for that city—*omit,* G L^{b} T Tr A א.

33. *After* afoot, *and before* thither, *insert* and came—G~; and outwent them—*omit,* G A; and came together unto Him—*omit,* G L Tr A א.

54. They knew Him—*substitute,* the men of that place knew Him—L^{b}.

MARK:

vii. 8. As the washing of pots and cups: and many other such like things they do—*omit,* T Tr א.

16. *Omit the verse*—Tr^b A^b א.

viii. 24. I see men as trees walking—*substitute,* I see men, for I see them walking as it were trees—S^t G∼ L T Tr A א.

ix. 38. And he followeth not us—*omit,* G א; because he followeth not us—G⇉ T Tr^b.

43. Into the fire that never shall be quenched—*omit,* G→.

44. *Omit the verse*—G→ T Tr^b א.

45. Into the fire that never shall be quenched—*omit,* G⇉ L^b T Tr A^b א.

46. *Omit the verse*—G→ T Tr^b א.

49. And every sacrifice shall be salted with salt—*omit,* T Tr^b א.

x. 27. For with God all things are possible—*omit,* G→.

xi. 3. Why do ye this—*substitute,* why loose ye the colt—L^m.

8. And strawed them in the way—*omit,* T Tr A א.

10. In the name of the Lord—*omit,* All.

26. *Omit the verse*—T Tr א.

xii. 14. *Before* is it lawful, *insert,* tell me therefore—L.

21. For, neither left he (οὐδὲ αὐτὸς ἀφῆκε)—*substitute,* not leaving behind (μὴ καταλιπὼν)—L^m Tr A א.

29. The first of all the commandments is—*substitute,* the first is—G∼ T Tr A א; the first commandment of all—G; the first of all—G∼; the first commandment is—L^b.

30. This is the first commandment—*omit,* T A S.

33. And with all the soul—*omit,* L^b T Tr^{mb} א.

xiii. 14. Spoken of by Daniel the prophet—*omit,* G L^b T Tr A א.

xiv. 19. And another said, Is it I?—*omit,* G→ T Tr א.

40. And when He returned He found them asleep again—*substitute,* and again He came and found them asleep—L Tr A א; *omit,* again—G⇉ Tr.

70. And thy speech agreeth thereto—*omit,* G⇉ L T Tr A א.

xv. 28. *Omit the verse*—G⇉ T Tr^b A א.

xvi. 9-20. *Omit all these verses*—G⇉ T Tr^b A^b א* and B (The Vatican, MS. cent. iv.)

They are not cited by Justin Martyr (A.D. 140), Clement of Alexandria (A.D. 194), or by Origen the critic of his time (A.D. 230). Spoken of as wanting by Victor of Antioch (A.D. 401), Severus of Antioch (A.D. 513), Eusebius (A.D. 318), and Jerome (A.D. 392). Its absence in all the more accurate copies asserted by Eusebius and Gregory Nyssen (A.D. 371), nor is it reckoned in "the sections" of Ammonius (A.D. 220), or Eusebius.

The verses are retained by G L and in most of the ancient MSS. now extant, including A (the Alexandrian, cent. v.), C (Ephræmi, cent. v.), and D (Bezæ, or Cantabrigiensis, cent. vi.) They are also cited as *genuine* by Irenæus (A.D. 167), Hippolytus (A.D. 220), Cyril of Jerusalem (A.D. 350), Ambrose (A.D. 374), Augustine (A.D. 396), and Nestorius (A.D. 428.)

MARK:

Modern critics are likewise divided:—It is *retained* by Simon, Mill, Bengel, Matthæi, Storr, Eichorn, Kuinoel, Gueriche, Scholz, Feilmoser, Knapp, Vater, Rinck, Olshausen, Ebrard, De Wette, Bloomfield, Schrivener, Stuart, and others.

I. D. Michaelis and Hug regard it as a later addition by Mark himself.

Tregelles thinks it *canonical* (*i.e.* inspired), but not written by Mark.

It is *omitted* also by Rosenmüller, Bertholdt, Gratz, Schott, Schulz, Fritzsche, Credner, Wieseler, Neudecker, Theile, Reuss, Meyer, Davidson, Green, Norton, and others.

xvi. 14. *After* He was risen, *add*, from the dead—L.

18. *Between* take up *and* serpents, *insert* also, in their hands—Tr.

LUKE:

i. 28. Blessed art thou among women—*omit*, G→ T Tr^{b} A ℵ.

ii. 43. Joseph and his mother knew not of it—*substitute*, the parents knew not of it—G∾ L T Tr A ℵ.

iii. 16. *After* baptize you, *add*, unto repentance—L.

iv. 4. But by every word of God—*omit*, T Tr^{b} A ℵ.

5. Into an high mountain—*omit*, L^{b} T Tr A ℵ.

8. Get thee behind me Satan—*omit*, G⇄ L^{b} T Tr A ℵ.

18. To heal the broken-hearted—*omit*, G L^{b} T Tr A ℵ.

vi. 10. As the other—*omit*, G∾ L^{b} T Tr A ℵ.

35. *After* great, *add*, in the heavens—L^{b}.

45. Evil treasure of his heart—*omit*, treasure of his heart—G⇄ L^{b} T Tr A ℵ.

48. For it was founded upon a rock—*substitute*, because it was well built—T Tr A ℵ.

vii. 31. And the Lord said—*omit*, All.

viii. 42. But as He went (ἐν δὲ τῷ ὑπάγειν)—*substitute*, and it came to pass as He departed (καὶ ἐγένετο ἐν τῷ πορεύεσθαι)—L A.

45. And Jesus said, who touched me—*omit*, G→ T Tr^{b} ℵ.

51. *After* go in, *add*, with Him—L T Tr A.

54. Put them all out and—*omit*, G→ L T Tr A ℵ.

ix. 10. Into a desert place belonging to the city—*substitute*, to a city—G∾ T Tr A ℵ.

23. And take up his cross—*omit*, G→.

Daily—*omit*, G⇄ L.

54. Even as Elias did—*omit*, G→ T Tr A^{b} ℵ.

55. And said, ye know not what manner of spirit ye are of—*omit*, G⇄ L T Tr A ℵ.

56. For the son of man is not come to destroy men's lives, but to save them—*omit*, G L T Tr A^{b} ℵ.

x. 11. *After* on us, *add*, to our feet—L T Tr A ℵ.

Unto you—*omit*, G L T Tr A.

22. *Before* all things, *insert*, and turning to His disciples He said—S^{t} AV^{m} L T A.

LUKE:

xi. 2. Our Father which art in heaven—*substitute,* Father—G T Tr A א.

Thy will be done—*omit,* G T Tr A.

As in heaven so in earth—*omit,* G L T Tr A.

4. But deliver us from evil—*omit,* G T Tr A א.

43. *After* markets, *add,* and the chief couches at feasts—L^b.

44. Scribes and Pharisees, hypocrites—*omit,* G L^b T Tr A א.

53. Said these things unto them—*substitute,* went out from thence—T Tr A א.

54. That they might accuse Him—*omit,* G⇉ T Tr^b A א.

xii. 27. They grow, they toil not, they spin not—*substitute,* they spin not, they weave not—T A.

xiv. 12. Neither thy kinsmen—*omit,* G→.

xvii. 24. In his day—*omit,* L.

36. *Omit the verse* — St G L T Tr A א.

xix. 45. Therein, and them that bought — *omit,* G⇉ T Tr A א.

xx. 23. Why tempt ye me—*omit,* G⇉ T Tr A א.

24. *After* a penny, *add,* and they showed it (to Him א) and He said—L^b א.

30. Took her to wife, and he died childless—*omit,* G~ T Tr A א.

45. To His disciple (τοῖς μαθηταῖς αὐτοῦ)—*substitute,* to them (πρὸς αὐτοὺς) — T A.

xxii. 31. And the Lord said—*omit,* T Tr^b A.

43, 44. *Omit the verses*—L^b א2* Vatican and Alexandrian MSS.

64. Struck Him on the face, and—*omit,* L^b T Tr A א.

xxiii. 15. For I sent you to him —*substitute,* for he sent him to us—G ~ א and Vatican MS.

17. *Omit the verse*—G⇉ L^b T Tr.

34. And Jesus said, Father, forgive them, for they know not what they do — *omit,* L^b א2* and Vatican MS.

38. Written—*omit,* T Tr^b A א.

In letters of Greek, and Latin, and Hebrew—*omit,* L^b T Tr A^b

xxiv. 1. And certain others with them—*omit,* G→ L T Tr A א.

12. *Omit the verse*—L^b T Tr.

Laid by themselves—*omit,* Tr א.

36. And saith unto them, peace be unto you—*omit,* T; *add,* I am he, fear not—L^b

40. *Omit the verse*—T Tr^b.

42. And of an honeycomb—*omit,* G→ L T Tr^b א.

51. And carried up into heaven—*omit,* G→ T א.

52. Worshipping Him—*omit,* G→ T.

53. Praising and—*omit,* Tr^b א.

And blessing—*omit,* T.

* *i.e.* corrected by an ancient Copyist.

JOHN :

i. 27. He it is who coming after me, is preferred before me—*substitute*, who comes after me—G L^b T Tr A ℵ.

36. *After* God, *add*, which taketh away the sin of the world—L^b.

iii. 13. Which is in heaven—*omit*, G→ ℵ.

15. Not perish, but—*omit*, G⇉ L^b T Tr A ℵ.

31, 32. Is above all and—*omit*, G⇉ T ℵ.

iv. 14. Shall never thirst, but the water that I shall give him—*omit* L^b.

v. 3. Waiting for the moving of the water—*omit*, $G⇉^b$ T Tr A ℵ.

4. *Omit the verse*—$G⇉^b$ T Tr A ℵ.

16. And sought to slay Him—*omit*, G L^b T Tr A ℵ.

vi. 11. To the disciples, and the disciples—*omit*, G⇉ L T Tr A ℵ.

22. That one whereunto His (Jesu's ℵ) disciples were entered—*substitute*, one—G L T Tr A.

51. Which I will give—*omit*, G→ L T Tr ℵ.

69. The Christ the Son of—*substitute*, the holy One of—All.

vii. 46. Like this man—*substitute*, thus—G→ L Tr^b.

53 to viii. 11. *Omit the whole passage*, G⇉ L T Tr A ℵ. *Also omitted by* MSS. A (Alexandrian, cent. v.), B (Vatican, cent. iv.), C (Ephræmi, cent. v.), T (Borgianus, cent. v.), L (Regius, cent. ix.), X (Monacenses, cent. x.), Δ (Sangallensis, cent. ix.), *and by more than fifty cursives. Also by the following versions*, Old Latin, Peshito, and Harclean Syriac, the good MSS. of the Memphitic, and the Thebaic, Gothic, and Armenian. *Also by the following in their commentaries*, Origen and Chrysostom (A.D. 398), Theodore of Mopsuestia (A.D. 407), Theophylact (A.D. 1077), Nonnus (A.D. 400) in his paraphrase, Apollinaris and Basil (A.D. 370), Cyril of Alexandria (A.D. 412), and Cosmas (A.D. 535.) It is not used by Tertullian (A.D. 200), Cyprian (A.D. 248), and Juvencus (A.D. 330.) *Also by the following modern critics it is questioned or omitted*, Erasmus, Beza, Calvin, Grotius, Wetstein, Lemler, Paulus, Tittmann, De Wette, Brückner, Knapp, Theile, Lücke, Tholuck, Baumgarten, Bleek, Olshausen, Hitzig, Baur, Luthardt, Ewald, Hengstenberg, Meyer, Porter, Davidson, Scrivener, Green, Norton, and others.

It is retained by Griesbach and Scholtz, *also in the uncials*, D (Bezæ, cent. vi.), F (Boreelii, cent. x.), G (Seidelii I., cent. x.), H (Seidelii II., cent. ix.), K (Cyprius, cent. ix.), U (Nanianus, cent. x.), and in more than three hundred cursives. Of Versions, *it is also found in some copies of* the old Latin, the Vulgate, Ethiopic, Jerusalem Syriac Lectionary, and the Arabic. *It is cited of the Fathers*, by Euthymus (A.D. 1116), but with the remark that accurate copies omit it or mark it as doubtful. *It is recognised by the Latin Fathers*, Ambrose, Jerome, and Augustine, with note of its omission in some early copies. And by others since cent. iv. *It is also retained by the modern critics* Mill, Whitby, Lampe, Michaelis, Herrmann, Ständlin, Storr, Kuinoel, Hug, Halin, Maier, Ebrard, Hilgenfeld, Stier, Lange, Bloomfield, Stuart, and others.

Marked as doubtful by uncials E (Basileenis, cent. viii.), M (Campianus, cent. x.), and by about sixty cursives. More than fifteen cursives place it at the end of the gospel; one after vii. 36, and four after

JOHN :

Luke xxi. In D (Bezæ, cent. vi.) it differs widely from the received text and other MSS. vary from this and from each other.

Dr. Tregelles regards it as a true narrative, but not as a genuine part of St. John, nor as a Divine record.

viii. 59. Going through the midst of them and so passed by—*omit*, All.

x. 13. The hireling fleeth—*omit*, G⇄ L^b T Tr א.

14. And am known of mine (γινώσκομαι ὑπὸ τῶν ἐμῶν)—*substitute*, And mine know me (γινώσκουσίν με τὰ ἐμά)—L T Tr א.

26. As I said unto you—*omit*, G→ L^b T Tr א.

xi. 41. From the place where the dead was laid—*omit*, All.

xiii. 24. That he should ask, who it should be of whom He spake—*substitute*, and says to him, Tell, who is it of whom He speaks—L T Tr A.

32. If God be glorified in him—*omit*, L^b Tr א.

xvi. 16. Because I (*om.* ἐγώ, I—G L), go to the Father—*omit*, G→ L^b T Tr A א.

xix. 2. *After the word* robe, *add*, and came to Him—L T Tr A א.

16. And led Him away—*omit*, L T Tr A.

29. And they filled a sponge with vinegar, and put it upon hyssop, and put it to His mouth—*substitute*, having then put a sponge full of vinegar upon hyssop, they put it to His mouth—L T Tr A א.

ACTS :

ii. 30. According to the flesh that He would raise up Christ to sit—*substitute*, that He would seat—All.

iii. 22. For (*om.* G), unto the Fathers—*omit*, G⇄ L T Tr A א.

iv. 12. Neither is there salvation in any other—*omit*, G→.

25. Mouth of Thy servant David—*substitute*, Holy Ghost by the mouth of David our Father—L T Tr A א.

27. *After* together, *add*, in this city—All.

viii. 37. *Omit the verse*—All.

ix. 5, 6. It is hard for thee to kick against the pricks. And he trembling and astonished, said, Lord, what wilt Thou have me to do? And the Lord said unto him—*omit*, All.

x. 6. He shall tell thee what thou oughtest to do—*omit*, All.

21. Which were sent unto him from Cornelius—*omit*, All.

32. Who when he cometh shall speak unto thee—*omit*, G→ L T Tr א.

xiii. 20. And after that He gave unto them judges about the space of four hundred and fifty years (G A)—*substitute*, about the space of four hundred and fifty years. And after that He gave them judges—G↘ L T Tr א.

42. And when the Jews were gone out of the synagogue the Gentiles besought—*substitute*, and as they went out they besought—All.

xiv. 10. *After* voice, *add*, I say unto thee in the name of the Lord Jesus Christ—L.

xv. 17, 18. Doeth all these things. Known unto God are all His works, from the beginning of the world—*substitute*, maketh things known from the beginning—G T Tr A א; Known from the beginning to the Lord is His work—L.

24. Saying, ye must be circumcised and keep the law—*omit*, G⇄ L T Tr A א.

34. *Omit the verse*—G⇄ L T Tr A א.

Acts:

xvii. 18. Because he preached to them (*om.* to them—T Tr $A^{b'}$ ℵ), Jesus and the resurrection—G→ (and only MS. D (Bezæ, cent. vi.))

xviii. 3. For by trade they were tentmakers—*omit*, G→ and only MS. D (Bezæ, cent. vi.)

21. I must by all means keep this feast that cometh in Jerusalem—*omit*, G= L T Tr A ℵ.

xx. 15. And tarried at Trogyllium—*omit*, G∾ L T Tr ℵ.

18. *Between* him *and* he said, *insert*, and they were together—L (and only MS. A (Alexandrian, cent. v.)

xxi. 8. That were of Paul's company—*omit*, All.

25. That they observe no such thing, save only—*omit*, G∾ L T Tr ℵ.

xxiii. 9. *Before* the scribes, *insert* certain of—G∾ L T Tr A ℵ; *omit*, the scribes—L.

xxiv. 6. And would have judged according to our law—*omit*, G= L T Tr A^b ℵ.

7. *Omit the verse*—G= L T Tr A^b ℵ.

8. Commanding his accusers to come unto thee—*omit*, G= L T Tr A^b ℵ.

26. That he might loose him—*omit*, G= L Tr A ℵ.

xxv. 6. More than ten days—*substitute*, not more than eight or ten days—All.

7. Laid ... complaints (*αἰτιάματα φέροντες*—L T ℵ), (*αἰτιώματα καταφέροντες*—G Tr A.)

Against Paul—*omit*, G= L T Tr A ℵ.

xxvi. 30. And when he (G∾) had thus spoken—*omit*, All.

xxviii. 16. The Centurion delivered the prisoners to the Captain of the Guard; but—*omit*, G∾ L T Tr A ℵ.

29. *Omit the verse*—G= L T Tr A^b ℵ.

Romans:

iii. 22. And upon all—*omit*, G= L Tr A ℵ.

vi. 12. It in—*omit*, All.

In the lusts thereof—*omit*, G.

viii. 1. Who walk not after the flesh, but after the Spirit—*omit*, All.

ix. 28. In righteousness, because a short work—*omit*, L T Tr A^b ℵ (*substitute for verse* 28, For the Lord will perform *His* word upon the earth, finishing *it* and cutting it short—L Tr A^b ℵ.)

x. 1. For Israel—*substitute*, for them—All.

xi. 6. But if it be of works, then is it no more grace; otherwise work is no more work—*omit*, G L T Tr A^b ℵ.

17. *Between* honest *and* in, *insert*, in the sight of God and—L^b.

xv. 24. I will come to you—*omit*, G L T Tr A ℵ.

32. And may with you be refreshed—*omit*, G→ L A^b.

xvi. 12. Salute the beloved Persis which laboured much in the Lord—*omit*, L^b.

24. *Omit the verse*—L T Tr A^b ℵ.

1 Corinthians:

i. 27. To confound the wise; and God hath chosen the weak things of the world—*omit*, L^b.

vi. 20. And in your Spirit, which are God's—*omit*, All.

1 CORINTHIANS :

vii. 38. Giveth *her* in marriage (ἐκγαμίζων)—*substitute,* giveth his virgin in marriage (γαμίζων, G~ L T Tr A)—L Tr A[b] ℵ.

viii. 8. Neither, if we eat are we the better; neither, if we eat not are we the worse—*substitute,* neither, if we eat not are we the worse; neither, if we eat are we the better—Tr A. Neither if we eat not are we the better, neither if we eat are we the worse—L.

ix. 10. And he that thresheth in hope, should be partaker of his hope—*substitute,* and he that thresheth [should thresh] in hope of partaking—All.

20. *After* as under the law, *add,* not being really under law—All.

x. 19. That the idol is anything, or—*omit,* G= ℵ.

28. For the earth is the Lord's and the fulness thereof—*omit,* All.

xv. 51. Not all sleep—*substitute,* all sleep, but not—G~ L ℵ.

2 CORINTHIANS :

i. 20. And in him—*substitute,* wherefore through him too is the—G~ L T Tr A ℵ.

xii. 1. It is not expedient for me doubtless to glory. I will come—*substitute,* boast I must. It is no advantage, but I will also come—L. It is not expedient, indeed, to glory, but I will come—ℵ.

7. Lest I should be exalted above measure—*omit the second* (*after* buffet me)—G→ L[b] Tr A[b] ℵ.

GALATIANS :

ii. 20. Son of God—*substitute,* God and of Christ—L Tr.

iii. 1. That you should not obey the truth—*omit,* All.

iv. 7. Of God through Christ—*substitute,* through God*—L T Tr A ℵ.

v. 1. Therefore—*omit,* G T Tr A.

Wherewith—*omit,* L Tr A ℵ. †

vi. 15. In Christ Jesus—*omit,* G~ T Tr A.

EPHESIANS :

iii. 9. By Jesus Christ—*omit,* All.

14. Of our Lord Jesus Christ—*omit,* G= L T Tr A ℵ.

v. 30. Of His flesh and of His bones—*omit,* G→ L T Tr A[b] ℵ.

vi. 9. Your—*substitute,* both their and your—Rec[m] G~ L T Tr A ℵ.

PHILIPPIANS :

iii. 16. Rule, let us mind the same thing—*omit,* All.

21. That it may be—*omit,* All.

COLOSSIANS :

i. 2. And the Lord Jesus Christ—*omit,* G L[b] T Tr A.

14. Through His blood—*omit,* All.

ii. 2. And of the Father, and of—*omit,* G T Tr A.

* "Through God" combines on behalf of our race, the whole before-mentioned agency of the Blessed Trinity; the Father has sent the Son and the Spirit; the Son has freed us from the law, the Spirit has completed our sonship; and thus the redeemed are heirs through the Triune God Himself, not through the law, nor through fleshly descent.—(Windischmann, quoted by Alford.)

† For freedom Christ made us free; stand, ye then, and not again with the yoke of bondage be held fast.

Colossians:

ii. 2. And of the Father, and of Christ—*omit*, G A*; God *which is* Christ—L T Tr; the Father of Christ—ℵ.

iii. 6. On the children of disobedience—*omit*, L^b T Tr A.

17. The Lord Jesus—*substitute*, Jesus Christ—L; the Lord Jesus Christ—ℵ; *omit*, Lord—G=.

1 Thessalonians:

i. 1. From God our Father and the Lord Jesus Christ—*omit*, G− L^b T Tr A.

iii. 2. And our fellow labourer—*omit*, All.

iv. 1. *After* God. *add*, as also ye are walking—G∼ L T Tr A ℵ.

2 Thessalonians:

iii. 4. That ye both do and will do—*substitute*, that ye will do, and do—L^b A.

1 Timothy:

vi. 5. From such withdraw thyself—*omit*, G= L T Tr A ℵ.

2 Timothy:

iv. 22. Grace be with you—*omit*, G−.

Hebrews:

ii. 7. And didst set Him over the works of Thy hands—*omit*, G L^b T Tr^b A.

iii. 6. Firm unto the end—*omit*, A.

9. Proved me—*substitute*, by way of trial—G∼ L T Tr A ℵ.

vii. 21. After the order of Melchisedec—*omit*, G→ T Tr A ℵ*.

xii. 20. Or thrust through with a dart—*omit*, All.

James:

iii. 12. So can no fountain both yield salt water and fresh—*substitute*, neither can salt water produce sweet—All.

1 Peter:

iii. 16. They speak evil of you, as of evil doers—*substitute*, ye are spoken evil of—T A.

iv. 14. On their part he is evil spoken of, but on your part he is glorified—*omit*, G= L T Tr A ℵ.

2 Peter:

i. 1. ἡμῶν, our, *not rendered with* θεὸν, God, in A.V. *But* Beza *and* Elzevir *add it after* σωτῆρος, Saviour.

10. *After* give diligence, *add*, by your (*om.* your ℵ) good works—L ℵ (and A (Alexandrian, cent. v.), the only other uncial MS.)

ii. 21. To turn from (ἐπιστρέψαι ἐκ)—*substitute*, to turn back from (ὑποστρέψαι ἀπο)—L; to turn back out of (ὑποστρέψαι ἐκ)—Tr A; to bend backwards from (εἰς τὰ ὀπίσω ἀνακάμψαι ἀπὸ)—ℵ.

1 John:

ii. 23. [*But*] *he that acknowledgeth the Son hath the Father also.* These words though given as doubtful (in italics) in the A.V. and omitted in some MSS., are restored to the text by G L T Tr A ℵ, and are also contained in A (the Alexandrian, cent. v.), B (the Vatican, cent. iv.), and C (Ephræmi, cent. v.), (omitted in G and K, cents. ix. and x., but the omission plainly arose from the similar ending of the previous clause.)

* A correction of ℵ in the margin.

1 JOHN:

iii. 10. Doeth not righteousness (ποιῶν δικαιοσύνη)—*substitute*, is not righteous (ὢν δίκαιος)—L.

v. 7, 8. In heaven, the Father, the Word, and the Holy Ghost, and these three are one. And there are three that bear witness in earth—*omit*, All. (These words are found in no Greek Manuscript before the xv. or xvi. cents., and in no ancient Version.)

13. That believe on the name of the Son of God—*omit*, All.

JUDE:

22. Of some* have compassion (ἐλεῖτε)—*substitute*, some convict (ἐλέγχετε)—G~ L T Tr A.

Making a difference—*substitute*, when they are disputing—G~ L T Tr A ℵ.

23. And others save with fear, pulling them out of the fire—*substitute*, and others save snatching them from the fire—G L T Tr A ℵ. †

25. *After* Saviour, *add*, by Jesus Christ our Lord—G~ L T Tr A ℵ.

After power, *add*, before all time—G~ L T Tr A ℵ.

REVELATION:

i. 11. I am Alpha and Omega, the first and the last—*omit*, All.

ii. 2. Which say (φάσκοντας, assert, boast) that they are apostles—*substitute*, calling themselves apostles—All.

3. Hast borne, and hast patience and—*substitute*, thou hast patience, and barest—All.

13. Thy works, and—*omit*, G- L T Tr A ℵ.

21. *After* space to repent, *add*, and she will not (would not L^{m}) repent of her fornication (of this fornication ℵ)—All.

And she repented not—*omit*, ℵ.

iii. 3. And heard, and hold fast—*omit*, G=.

iv. 3. And He that sat—*omit*, G= Tr^{b}.

8. Each of them (ἐν καθ' ἑαυτό)—*substitute*, one by one of them (ἐν καθ' αὐτῶν)—G L T Tr A ℵ. (ℵ = ἐν ἕκαστον αὐτῶν, each one of them)—(*omit*, αὐτῶν, of them—G~.)

11. O Lord—*substitute*, O Lord and our God—L T Tr A ℵ.

v. 9. Us—*omit*, G- L T A.

10. Us—*substitute*, them—All.

Unto our God—*omit*, G L Tr A ℵ.

11. *After* elders, *add*, and the number of them was ten thousand times ten thousand. *These words are omitted in the Greek of the Received Text*, (Stephens), *but are inserted by* B E G L T Tr A ℵ.

14. Him that liveth for ever and ever—*omit*, All.

vii. 10. Salvation to our God which sitteth upon the throne. *The Greek of the Received Text reads*, Salvation to Him that sitteth upon the throne of our God.

viii. 7. *After* earth, *add*, and the third of the earth was burnt up—All.

ix. 2. And he opened the bottomless pit—*omit*, G- Tr^{b} ℵ.

* Some who waver ℵ.

† ℵ *add*, and of others have compassion with fear.

Revelation:

ix. 19. *Received Text has* ἐξουσίαι, powers, *for* ἐξουσία, power, *and omits,* and in their tails, *which is inserted by* B G T Tr A א.

Their power—*substitute,* the power of the horses—All.

x. 6. And the sea and the things which are therein—*omit,* L^b Tr^b א.

xi. 1. And the angel stood—*omit,* All (including S^t.)

xiii. 7. And it was given unto him to make war with the saints and to overcome them—*omit,* L.

xiv. 1. *After* having, *add,* his name, and—All.

5. Before the throne of God—*omit,* All.

xvii. 17. And to agree—*omit,* L A^b.

xviii. 2. Mightily, with a strong voice—*substitute,* with a mighty voice—All.

17. And all the company in ships—*substitute,* and every passenger*—All.

xix. 12. *After* He had, *add,* names written, and—T Tr A^b.

xx. 14. *After* second death, *add,* the lake of fire—G~ L T Tr A א.

xxi. 12. And at the gates twelve angels—*omit,* L.

xxii. 14. Do his commandments—*substitute,* wash their robes—G~ L T Tr A א.

* "Every one who saileth any whither."—Alford.

APPENDIX

B.

THE GREEK ALPHABET.

Characters.		Roman Letters.	Names.	Pronunciation (English method.)
Α	α	a	Al'pha	as in English
Β	β	b	Beta	as in English
Γ	γ	g	Gamma	always hard; before γ, κ, or χ like *ng* in *song*
Δ	δ	d	Delta	as in English
Ε	ε	ĕ	Epsilon	like *e* in *net*: final, like *e* in *be*
Ζ	ζ	z	Zeta	as in English
Η	η	ē	Eta	like *e* in *me*
Θ	θ	th	Theta	like *th* in *thin*
Ι	ι	i	Iöta	as in English: final, like *i* long
Κ	κ	k	Kappa	always hard
Λ	λ	l	Lambda	as in English
Μ	μ	m	Mu	as in English
Ν	ν	n	Nu	as in English
Ξ	ξ	x	Xi	at the beginning of a word as *z*, elsewhere as in English
Ο	ο	ŏ	Omicron	like *o* in *not*: final, like *o* in *go*
Π	π	p	Pi	as in English
Ρ	ρ	r	Rho	as in English
Σ	σ (ς final)	s	Sigma	as in English
Τ	τ	t	Tau	as in English
Υ	υ	uy	Upsilon	like *u* in *cube*: before ι, like *y*
Φ	φ	ph	Phi	as in English
Χ	χ	ch	Chi	always hard
Ψ	ψ	ps	Psi	as in English
Ω	ω	ō	Omega	like *o* in *note*.

DIPHTHONGS.

Character.	Roman.	Pronunciation.
αι	ai	like our affirmative *ay*
αυ	au	like *au* in *aught*
ευ and ηυ	eu	like *eu* in *Europe*
οι	oi	like *oi* in *toil*
ου and ωυ	ou	like *ou* in *thou*
υι	ui	like *ui* in *quiet*
υἱ	hui	like *whi* in *while.*

The rough breathing, ‘, has the power of *h.*

The smooth breathing, ’, has no sound.

Every word beginning with a vowel has one of these.

Final α, ε, ι, and ο, in prepositions and some other particles, are dropped before a word commencing with a vowel, thus for ἀπὸ ἐμοῦ, we have ἀπ' ἐμοῦ.

And π, κ, and τ, thus brought before a rough breathing, are changed, π to φ, κ to χ, τ to θ, thus, ἀφ' ὁυ.

PRONUNCIATION OF WORDS.

Two syllables, *accent* on first syllable.

More than two, *accent* on last syllable but one if long vowel.

" " " on last but two if short.

VERBS

Formed from *Nouns* or *Adjectives*, imply *to be* or *to have* that which the noun or adjective signifies, and may be thus classified. On referring a verb to this table, a shade of meaning may be discovered, which it may be difficult or impossible to express in translation.

STATE OR ACTION.

The having, being, or becoming that which the noun denotes.

Endings.	Examples.	Root Noun.
-άω	τολμάω, to have daring	τόλμη, daring.
-έω	πολεμεω, to be at war	πόλεμος, war.
-εύω	δουλεύω, to be a slave (of another)	δοῦλος, a slave.
"	μαθητεύω, to be a disciple*	μαθητής, a disciple.
-άζω	νηπιάζω, to be childish, play like a child	νήπιος, a child.
-ίζω	'Ιουδαΐζω, to be or act the Jew (Gal. ii. 14)	'Ιουδαῖος, a Jew.

* This is with a Dative following. But where an Accusative follows, it is transitive and therefore expresses some *action* implied in, or consequent upon the state or quality. Compare μαθητεύω with Dative, Matt. xxvii. 57 (be a disciple); and with Accusative, Matt. xxviii. 19 (make a disciple.)

CAUSATIVE.

Carrying out the act which is proper to the noun.

Endings.	Examples.	Root Noun.
-όω	δουλόω, to make a slave (of another), enslave	δοῦλος, a slave.
„	πολεμόω, to make hostile	πόλεμος, war.
-ίζω	πολεμίζω, to make war	„ „
-ύνω	πληθύνω, to make full, multiply	πλῆθος, a great number.
-αίνω	λευκαίνω, to make white, whiten	λευκός, white.
„	ποιμαίνω, to tend as a shepherd	ποιμήν, a shepherd.

Verbs from simpler verbal stems, are

FREQUENTATIVE.*

-άζω	στενάζω, to groan frequently	στένω, to groan.
-έω	φορέω, to bear frequently, *i.e.*, to wear	φέρω, to bear.

INCHOATIVE.

i.e., denoting the beginning or progress of an action.

-σκω	ἡβάσκω, to grow young	ἡβάω, to be young.
„	μεθύσκω, to grow tipsy	μεθύω, to be drunken.
„	γαμίσκω, to give in marriage	γαμέω, to marry.

DESIDERATIVE.

-είω	πολεμησείω, to desire to be at war	πολεμέω, to be at war.
„	γελασείω, to desire to laugh	γελάω, to laugh.

SUBSTANTIVES

are to a large extent derived from or connected with *verbs*, and may be classified according to their *endings or affixes*, to each of which a particular meaning is attached.

THE MALE AGENT OR DOER.

Nom.	Gen.	Examples.
-τήρ	-τῆρος	σωτήρ, Saviour.
-τής	-τοῦ	κριτής, Judge
-τωρ	-τωρος	ῥήτωρ, orator.
-εύς	-έως	βασιλεύς, King.
-ός	-οῦ	τροφος, nurturer.
-μήν	-μενος	ποιμήν, shepherd.
-ων	-όνος	ἡγεμών, leader.

FEMALE AGENT OR DOER.

-τειρα	-ας	σώτειρα, she that saves.
-εία	-ας	βασιλεία, kingdom.
-ισσα	-ης	βασίλισσα, Queen.

* Sometimes in -ίζω only *emphatic* as βαπτίζω.

ACTION

as incomplete and in progress.

Nom.	Gen.	Examples.
-σία	-ας	θυσία, sacrifice.
,,	,,	δοκιμασία, scrutiny.
-σις	-εως	τάξις, arranging; πρᾶξις, doing.

ACTION

of the verb proceeding from the subject, the action and its result.

-μός*	-μοῦ	διωγμός, pursuing, or being pursuing.
		σεισμός, shaking, earthquake.
		σταθμος, standing, station.
-σις†	-σεως	δόσις, giving, gift (*compare Eng.* "dose.")
		κρίσις, the act or time of pronouncing sentence.
		καύχησις, the act of glorying.
		βρῶσις, the act of eating.

RESULT,

the thing done, or the passive object; the result or product of an act.

-μα	-ματος	πρᾶγμα, thing done.
		βρωμα, the substance eaten, food.
		σπέρμα, thing sown.
		κρίμα, the sentence pronounced.
		καύχημα, the subject matter *or* theme of glorying.
-ος	-ους	κῆδος, sorrow.
		πένθος, grief.

ACTION

of the root, actively or passively.

-μή } -η }	-ῆς	μνήμη, memory, that which remembers.
		γραμμή, line (which has been drawn.)
		διδαχή, process of teaching; thing taught.

QUALITY.

These are derived from adjectives, and correspond to our Eng. terminations -dom, -hood, -ness.

-ία	-ίας	ἀλήθεια, truthfulness.
-οσύνη,	-οσύνης	δικαιοσύνη, righteousness.
		σωφροσύνη, sound-mindedness.
		ἁγιωσύνη,‡ sanctity (the condition.)
-της	-τητος	ἁγιότης, holiness (the abstract quality.)
		ἰσότης, equality.
		ταχυτής, (habitual) speed.
-ος	-εος	τάχος, (temporary) swiftness.

* Frequently θμος and σμος. † Some Nouns.

‡ ἁγιωσύνη differs from ἁγιότης, the former marking the condition, the latter the *abstract quality.* ἁγιωσύνη = the state or holy frame of mind in which the action of the verb is evidenced and exemplified.—(See 1 Thes. iv. 3, 4; 1 Pet. i. 2.)

INSTRUMENT

with which the agent acts, or place of action.

Nom.	Gen.	Examples.
-τρον	-τρου	ἄροτρον, plough.
,,	,,	λύτρον, ransom.
-τήριον	-τηρίου	ποτήριον, cup.
,,	,,	ἱλαστήριον, means or place of propitiation.
-ρα	-ας	καλύπτρα, veil.
-εῖον	-είου	τελωνεῖον, toll-house.
		εἰδωλεῖον, seat of an idol.
-ιον	-ιου	γυμνάσιον, school for exercise.

DIMINUTIVES

belong to the class of Gentile nouns, or Patronymics.

-ίον*	-ίου	παιδίον, a little child (from παῖς).
-ισκος	-ου	παιδίσκος, a youth (fem. παιδίσκη, a young girl).

Many of these forms are used without any Diminutive meaning, as βιβλίον, a book; φορτίον, a burden; just as *puella* is the only Latin word for *girl*.

ADJECTIVES

are of two or three terminations, masc., fem., and neuter; and like the nouns, their endings (in nom., sing., masc.,) indicate particular shades of meaning.

ATTRIBUTE or LOCALITY.

ENDINGS. Mas.	Fem.	Neut.	EXAMPLES.
-ιος	-ια†	-ιον	οὐράνιος, of or belonging to heaven, heavenly.
			δίκαιος, of or belonging to δίκη (justice), just.
			Ἐφέσιος, Ephesian, (and so gen., of cities or countries).

PROPERTY,

marking ability or fitness.

-ικός	-ική	-ικόν	διδακτικός, apt to teach, skilled in teaching.
			κριτκός, capable of judging.
			σαρκικός,‡ fleshly, of the nature of *flesh*, the bent of the mind.

* To ιον- is sometimes prefixed αρ-, or ιδ- as παιδάριον, (from παῖς) and κλινίδιον, a little bed, (from κλίνη, a couch.)

† Some of these are of two terminations.

‡ See σάρκινος, below.

MATERIAL.

ENDINGS. Mas.	Fem.	Neut.	EXAMPLES.
-εος	-εα	-εον	χάλκεος, made of bronze or copper.
			ἀργύρεος, of silver.
-ινος	-ινη	-ινον	ἀληθινός, of genuine or true materials.*
			σάρκινος, fleshy, made of flesh, indicates the nature of the *person.*
			λίθινος, of stone.

QUALITY,

the full expression and complete possession, expressed in English by the terminations -ful and -able.

-ρός	-ρα	-ρόν	ἰσχυρός, powerful (from ἰσχύς, strength.)
			φθονερός, full of envy.
-εις	-εσσα	-εν	χαρίεις, graceful.
-άλεος	-άλια	-άλεον	θαρσάλεος, full of confidence.

FITNESS,

expressing suitableness or capability for the action of the verb.

-ιμος†	-ιμον	δόκιμος, receivable (of current coin), (from δέχομαι, to receive.)
		χρήσιμος, useful (from χράομαι, to use.)
		ἐδώδιμος, eatable.

ATTRIBUTE,

making the action of the verb the prominent attribute of the person.

-μων	-μον	ἐλεήμων, compassionate (from ἐλεέω, to pity.)

TEMPORAL AND LOCAL.

-ινος	-ινον	ὀρθινός, at the dawn.
		ὀρεινός, in the mountain.
		θερινος, in the summer.
		πρωινός, early.

POSSIBILITY.

Gerundial adjectives formed from second Aorist tense of the verb convey the idea of capability or adaptation, both actively and passively.

-τός	-τή	-τόν	λυτός,‡ capable of being loosened (from λύω, to loose.)
			αἱρετός, an eligible man, adapted for choice, and one actually chosen.
			μεμπτός, capable of blaming, and deserving blame.

* Compare John xv. 1 and 1 Thes. i. 9 (ἀλήθης, true as opposed to false.)

† Sometimes σιμος.

‡ See λυτέος, below.

OBLIGATION.

Verbal adjectives conveying the idea of necessity or duty.

ENDINGS.			EXAMPLES.
Mas.	Fem.	Neut.	
-τέος	-τέα	τέον	λυτέος, that ought to be loosened (from λύω, to loose.)
			βλητέος, that ought to be put (from βάλλω, to cast.)

PREPOSITIONS.

The various meanings of these have been given more or less fully wherever they occur in the body of the work. But the following scheme may be presented of their primary significations, and also of their force in composition, *i.e.*, when pre fixed to a verb or noun.

"Prepositions represent primarily the local relation of one object to another."

The Geometrical parts of an object are three, *a solid*, *a superficies*, and *a line*. Examine first, the six Geometrical parts of

A SOLID OR CUBE.

The upper plane ... ὑπέρ, over.
The under plane ... ὑπό, under.
The front ... ἀντί, over against, opposite.
The side ... παρά, beside.
Both sides ... ἀμφί,* about.
The rear (out of sight) ... ὄπισθεν, behind.

THE SUPERFICIES.

The plane on which it stands ... ἐπί, upon.
The boundary line round it ... περί, around.
Inside of it ... ἐν, in.
Outside of it ... ἐκ, from, out of.

A VERTICAL LINE.

The top ... ἀνά, up.
The bottom ... κατά, down.

A HORIZONTAL LINE.

The front ... πρό, in front of, before.
The hinder extremity ... ἐπί, upon, or ὑπό, under.
The middle (if of *the same* substance as the extremities) ... μετά, with, after (implying association).
The middle (if *a different* substance from the extremities, as when a rope connects two trees) ... σύν, with (implying co-operation).
If the line is imaginary (as that which connects two stars) ... ἀπό, from.

* Not used in New Testament.

If the particle σε be added to πρό, before, it becomes πρός towards, to the point of an object.

If σε be added to ἐν, in, it becomes εἰς, into.

The Preposition does not really govern a case in the sense of determining it; it only adds a more precise geometrical view of the relation in which two objects stand to one another.*

The Cases are determined not by the preposition, but by the idea to be expressed.

The Genitive, implies *motion from*, whence?

The Dative, *rest in*, or *connection with*, where?

The Accusative, *motion towards*, whither?

PREPOSITIONS AS USED IN COMPOSITION.

ἀμφι-, round about.

ἀνά-, up, back again.

ἀντί-, instead of, against, in return for.

ἀπό-, away from, dismission, completeness.

δια-, through, thorough, between.

εἰς, into.

ἐκ, out of, forth, utterly.

ἐν, in, upon, intrinsically.

ἐπι-, upon, to, in addition.

κατα-, down, downright, against.

μετα-, with, implying association or participation, change.

παρα-, beside, beyond, along.

περι-, around, over and above, excess.

προ-, before, forward.

προς-, towards, in addition to.

συν-, with, implying co-operation, compression.

ὑπερ-, above, excess.

ὑπο-, under, concealment, repression.

COMPOUND WORDS.

It will be seen from the body of the work that the two languages do not exactly answer to each other, word for word; one Greek word may often require several English words to express it and vice versa. The words do not run in equal parallel lines, thus:—(each stroke representing a word)

Greek —— — ———— —— — ——— — ———— ——

English —— — ———— —— — ——— — ———— ——

* See Quarterly Review, January, 1863.

This would have made the work much more simple both in its preparation and in its use.

Rather do the languages run thus—

Greek ——— — ——— — — — ——— — — — — ——— —

English —— — — — — — ——— — ——— ——— — ———

There are many other particles used in composition besides the Prepositions above given: *e.g.*,

ADVERBS.

ἀ-, (from ἅμα) together, *as* ἅπας, all together.

ἀρτι-, lately, (*only in* 1 Pet. ii. 2, ἀρτιγέννητος, new-born.)

εὐ-, well, *prosperously.*

παλιν-, again, (*only in* Matt. xix. 28 and Titus iii. 5, παλιγγενεσία, regeneration.)

παν-, all, (from neuter of πᾶς.)

τηλε-, afar off, (*only in* Mark viii. 25, τηλαυγῶς, shining afar, or to a distance, clearly, distinctly.)

OTHER PARTICLES.

ἀ *or* ἀν, not, *usually called* ἀ *privitive, like our* un-.

ἀ, (*from* ἀνά, up,) *intensive.*

δυς-, hardly, *answering to English* dis-, mis-, or un-.

ἡμι-, half, (*like Latin,* semi), *only in* ἡμιώριον, half an hour, *and,* ἡμιθανής, half dead.

As a rule the prepositions* are used with verbs, and the above with nouns and adjectives.

Compounds may be of two kinds—

Parathetic, (παράθεσις, juxta-position) where the several parts of a word may exist distinct from each other; the former part of the word being always a preposition, adverb, or particle (never a verb.)

Synthetic, (συνθεσις, set together, or composed) where the former word is a noun or verb (never a particle.)

Illustration, showing how, in the New Testament † one word may be varied, by being compounded with a number of other verbs.

κρίνω, to separate, *hence,* to judge.

I.—SUBSTANTIVES (ACCORDING TO THE TABLE GIVEN ABOVE.)

(-σις) κρίσις, judgment, *the process of separation,* the act or time of judgment.

(-μα) κρίμα, sentence pronounced, *the result or product of judgment.*

(-τηριον) κριτήριον, tribunal, *the instrument or place of judgment.*

(-της) κριτής, a judge, *the male agent.*

II.—ADJECTIVE.

(-ικος) κριτικός, able *or* fit to judge *or* separate, (occ. Heb. iv. 12.)

* Sometimes two are used, each with their characteristic force.

† There are many other compounds of this verb existing in Greek literature, but not in the New Testament.

III.—VERB AND PREPOSITIONS.

ἀνα-κρίνω, separate up, investigate.

δια-κρίνω, separate throughout, distinguish. *In middle* to separate oneself.

ἐγ-κρίνω, to reckon in or among, admit, (2 Cor. x. 12.)

ἐπι κρίνω, to judge upon, to confirm by a like judgment, adjudge, (Luke xxiii. 24.)

κατα-κρίνω, to give judgment against, condemn.

συγ-κρίνω, (to separate distinct things and then bring them near unto one) *hence,* to judge together, compare (opposite to δια-κρίνω.)

ἀπο-κρίνομαι, (*in Middle*) to give a judicial answer, *hence, gen.*, to answer, respond.

ἀντ-απο-κρίνομαι, *to do the above again,* to answer again, *or* to answer against.

ὑπο-κρίνομαι,* to give judgment under *a cause or matter, gen.*, to answer, reply; then to answer *upon the stage,* to play a part; to represent another person by acting under *a mask,* to personate; to be thought *somebody different by being under a mask; hence,* to dissemble, (Luke xx. 20.)

συν-υπο-κρίνομαι, to do the above with any one, (Gal. ii. 13.)

IV.—SUBSTANTIVES AND PREPOSITIONS.†

ἀνά-κρισις, examination, (occ. Acts xxv. 26.)

ἀπό-κρισις, answer, reply.

διά-κρισις, the act of distinguishing, discernment.

κατά-κρισις, condemnation, censure.

ὑπό-κρισις, the act of stage playing or personating under *a mask, hence,* dissimulation, (*whence the word,* hypocrisy), (occ. Matt. xxiii. 28; Mark xii. 15; Luke xii. 1; Gal. ii. 13; 1 Tim. iv. 2; 1 Pet. ii. 1.)

ἀπό-κριμα, the result of judicial response; sentence of death, *and the result of it,* fear and exposure to death, despair of life.

κατά-κριμα, sentence against, condemnation.

πρό-κριμα, fore-judging, pre-judging, *i.e.*, prejudice, prepossession, (occ. 1 Tim. v. 21.)

ὑπο-κριτής, a stage player, one who personates under *a mask; hence,* a hypocrite.

V.—NEGATIVE COMPOUNDS.

ἀ διά-κριτος, not capable of separating, impartial or sincere, (James iii. 17.)

ἀ-κατά-κριτος, not subject to condemnation, uncondemned.

ἀν-υπό-κριτος, not capable of dissimulation, unfeigned.

VI.—WITH NOUNS AND PRONOUNS.

αὐτο-κατά-κριτος, self condemned, (occ. Titus iii. 12.)

εἰλι-κρινής, judged of in the sunlight, *then, by implication* clear as light, manifest, sincere, (occ. Phil. i. 10; 2 Pet. iii. 1), from εἵλη, sunshine, cognate with ἥλιος, the sun.)

εἰλι-κρίνεια, having the quality of the above,—clearness; *hence,* pureness, sincerity.

* Anciently synonymous with ἀποκρίνομαι.

† Compare these with the corresponding verbs given above.

APPENDIX

C

VARIATIONS IN THE READINGS

OF THE

CODEX SINAITICUS (א).

According to Professor Tischendorf the Codex Sinaiticus has been corrected (or rather, altered) by various copyists, whose variations he classifies as having been made respectively by Scribe A,* Scribe B,† and Scribe C. ‡ §

In the body of this work and in the appendix of longer clauses, *only* the readings of *the Original Manuscript* have been given, and these are complete. In the following list all the corrections of the different Scribes that are of any importance and likely to be referred to or required by the Student, are noticed. Scribe A, is quoted as $א^a$; Scribe B, as $א^b$; and Scribe C, as $א^c$; the original MS. is always quoted as א. Where these corrections accord with the Authorised Version, the signs are placed in the column so headed; and where they differ, but agree with the Critical Readings they are placed in the column headed "Critical Readings."

When the reading of the original MS. is doubtful it is expressed thus (א).

* Found through all the New Testament except the Revelation.

† Found in the Gospels only.

‡ Found throughout the whole of the New Testament.

§ There are further subdivisions made by Prof. Tischendorf, which in a work for popular use like this are not specified.

References.	AUTHORIZED VERSION.		CRITICAL READINGS.	
Matthew:				
v. 22.	Without cause	$\aleph^c$	*Omit*	$\aleph$
vi. 12.	We forgive	$\aleph^c$	We forgave	$\aleph$
vii. 14.	Because strait	$\aleph$	How strait	$\aleph^c$
viii. 15.	Them	$\aleph^b$	Him	$\aleph$
28.	Gergesenes	$\aleph^c$	Gadarenes	[1]
ix. 35.	Among the people	$\aleph$	*Omit*	$\aleph^b$
xvi. 20.	Jesus	$\aleph^c$	*Omit*	$\aleph$
xviii. 29.	All	$\aleph^c$	*Omit*	$\aleph$
xix. 20.	From my youth up	$\aleph^c$	*Omit*	$\aleph$
xx. 26.	Let him be	$\aleph^c$	Shall be	$\aleph$
xxii. 23.	Which say	$\aleph^c$	Saying	$\aleph$
xxiii. 3.	Bid you observe, that observe and do	[2]	Bid you, do and observe	$\aleph^c$
xxiv. 17.	Anything	[3]	The things	$\aleph^c$
Mark:				
i. 5.	And they of Jerusalem, and were all baptised	[4]	And all they of Jerusalem, and were baptised	$\aleph^c$
19.	Thence	$\aleph$	*Omit*	$\aleph^c$
24.	Let us alone	$\aleph^c$	*Omit*	$\aleph$
vii. 5.	Unwashen	$\aleph^c$	Defiled	$\aleph$
viii. 22.	He cometh	$\aleph$	They come	$\aleph^c$
xiii. 18.	Your flight be not	$\aleph^c$	It be not	$\aleph$
xv. 8.	Crying aloud	$\aleph^c$	Having gone up	$\aleph$
Luke:				
iv. 5.	Into an high mountain	$\aleph^a$	*Omit*	$\aleph$
viii. 37.	Gadarenes	$\aleph^c$	Gerasenes	[5]
ix. 10.	Into a desert place belonging to the city	[6]	To a city	$\aleph^c$
50.	Against us is for us	[7]	Against you is for you	$\aleph^c$(?)
xi. 34.	The eye	$\aleph^c$	Thine eye	$\aleph$
xii. 31.	All	$\aleph^a$	*Omit*	$\aleph$
xvi. 21.	The crumbs which	$\aleph^c$	That which	$\aleph$
xvii. 9.	I trow not	[8]		[8]
36.	*The verse*	$\aleph^a$	*Omit*	$\aleph$

[1] $\aleph$ reads literally "Gazerenes," which seems like a mistake for Gadarenes.
[2] $\aleph$ omits "and observe."
[3] $\aleph$ reads "that which."
[4] $\aleph$ reads "and they of Jerusalem all were baptized."
[5] The original reading of $\aleph$ is "Gergesenes."
[6] $\aleph$ omits "of a city called Bethsaida."
[7] $\aleph$ reads "against you is for us."
[8] $\aleph$ is defective here, omitting from "commanded him," to "commanded you."

References.	AUTHORIZED VERSION.		CRITICAL READINGS.	
LUKE:				
xviii. 28.	Have left all, and followed	ℵ	Having left all our own, have followed	ℵ^c
xix. 26.	From him 2nd time	ℵ^c	*Omit*	ℵ
46.	My house is the house	ℵ	And my house shall be a house	ℵ^c
xxi. 8.	Therefore	[1]	*Omit*	ℵ^c
xxii. 14.	Twelve	ℵ^c	*Omit*	ℵ
xxiv. 51.	And carried up into heaven	ℵ^c	*Omit*	ℵ
JOHN:				
iii. 25.	The Jews	ℵ	A Jew	ℵ^c
vi. 11.	To the disciples and the disciples	ℵ^c	*Omit*	ℵ
55.	Meat indeed...drink indeed	[2]	True meat...true drink	[3]
vii. 50.	By night	[4]	Formerly	ℵ^c
viii. 38.	Ye have seen with	ℵ	Ye have heard from	ℵ^c
59.	Going through the midst of them and so passed by	ℵ^c	*Omit*	ℵ
ix. 26.	Again	ℵ^c	*Omit*	ℵ
x. 4.	His own sheep		All his own	[5]
32.	My Father	ℵ^c	The Father	ℵ
xii. 22.	Again Andrew and Philip		Andrew and Philip came and	[6]
xiii. 24.	That he should ask, who it should be of whom He spake		And says to him; tell who it is of whom He speaks	[6]
25.	Lying	ℵ	Sitting at meat	ℵ^c
32.	If God be glorified in him	ℵ^c	*Omit*	ℵ
xvii. 12.	In Thy name: those that	[7]	In Thy name which	ℵ^c
17.	Thy truth	ℵ^c	The truth	[8]
xx. 19.	Assembled	ℵ^c	*Omit*	[9]
ACTS:				
ii. 23.	Have taken, and	ℵ^c	*Omit*	ℵ
v. 28.	Did not we straitly command	ℵ^c	We straitly commanded	ℵ
vii. 43.	Remphan		Rephan	[10]
ix. 29.	Jesus	ℵ^b	*Omit*	ℵ
x. 36.	The word which *God* sent	ℵ	He sent the word	ℵ^a

[1] ℵ is defective from "I am," to "go ye not."
[2] ℵ is defective.
[3] ℵc reads "my flesh is true meat, and my blood is truly drink."
[4] ℵ *omits* "that came to him formerly."
[5] ℵ reads "his own."
[6] ℵ combines the two readings.
[7] ℵ omits "that Thou hast given me."
[8] ℵ omits from "truth," to "truth."
[9] ℵ "into his hand."
[10] ℵ reads Romphan, ℵc Raiphan.

References.	AUTHORIZED VERSION.		CRITICAL READINGS.	
ACTS:				
xi. 20.	Grecians	1	Greeks[2]	א[c]
xiv. 17.	Our	א[c]	Your	א
xv. 23.	After this manner	א[c]	*Omit*	א
	Elders and brethren	א[c]	Elders, brethren	א
xviii. 21.	And he sailed	(א)	*Omit*	א[c]
ROMANS:				
i. 31.	Implacable	א[c]	*Omit*	א
iii. 22.	And upon all	א[c]	*Omit*	א
v. 1.	We have	א[a]	Let us have	א
viii. 1.	Who walk not after the flesh but after the Spirit	א[c]	*Omit*	א
26.	For us	א[c]	*Omit*	א
ix. 28.	He will finish the work, and cut it short in righteousness: because a short work will the Lord make upon the earth	א[c]	For the Lord will finally and promptly execute *His* work upon the earth	א
31.	Of righteousness [2nd time]	א[c]	*Omit*	א
32.	The works of the law	א[c]	Works	א
	For	א[c]	*Omit*	א
x. 15.	Preach the gospel of peace, and	א[c]	*Omit*	א
xi. 2.	Saying	א	*Omit*	א[c]
3.	And [1st]	א[c]	*Omit*	א
6.	But if *it be* of works, then is it no more grace: otherwise work is no more work	א[c]	*Omit*	א
xii. 2.	Be not conformed—be ye transformed		Not to be conformed—to be transformed	3
xiii. 7.	Therefore	א[c]	*Omit*	א
xiv. 9.	Both died	א[c]	Died (*omit* "both")	א
	Rose and revived	4	Lived	א
10.	Christ	א[c]	God	א
18.	These things	א[c]	This	א
xv. 24.	I will come to you	א[c]	*Omit*	א
29.	Of the Gospel	א[c]	*Omit*	א
32.	And may with you be refreshed	א[c]	*Omit*	5

[1] א reads "evangelists," which is evidently a mistake.

[2] *i.e.*, Gentile converts, not Jewish Proselytes of Greek extraction.

[3] א reads "and be ye not conformed, but to be transformed."

[4] א[c] reads "rose."

[5] א reads "that coming to you with joy by the will of Jesus Christ, I may be refreshed with you."

References.	AUTHORISED VERSION.		CRITICAL READINGS.	
1 CORINTHIANS:				
i. 20.	This world	ℵ[c]	The world	ℵ
28.	*Yea*, and things	ℵ[c]	*Omit*	ℵ
ii. 4.	Man's	ℵ[c]	*Omit*	ℵ
10.	His	ℵ[c]	The	ℵ
iii. 4.	Carnal	ℵ[c]	As men	ℵ
12.	This	ℵ[c]	The	ℵ
iv. 2.	Moreover		Moreover here	[1]
6.	To think *of men*	ℵ[c]	*Omit*	ℵ
v. 1.	So much as named	ℵ[c]	*Omit*	ℵ
4.	Christ—Christ		*Omit both*	[2]
7.	Therefore	ℵ[c]	*Omit*	ℵ
v. 7.	For us	ℵ[c]	*Omit*	ℵ
10.	Yet	ℵ[c]	*Omit*	ℵ
	Or extortioners	ℵ[c]	And[3] extortioners	ℵ
vii. 5.	Fasting and	ℵ[c]	*Omit*	ℵ
13.	Him	[4]	Her husband	ℵ[c]
14.	By the husband	ℵ[c]	By the brother	ℵ
38.	But	ℵ[c]	And	ℵ
39.	By the law	ℵ[c]	*Omit*	ℵ
viii. 4.	None other	ℵ[c]	No	ℵ
ix. 10.	And he that thresheth in hope should be partaker of his hope	ℵ[c]	And he that thresheth *should thresh* in hope of partaking	ℵ
16.	Yea woe	ℵ[c]	For woe	ℵ
22.	As	ℵ[c]	*Omit*	ℵ
x. 1.	Moreover	ℵ[c]	For	ℵ
23.	For me [twice]	ℵ[c]	*Omit both times*	ℵ
xi. 24.	Broken	ℵ[c]	*Omit*	ℵ
26.	This cup	ℵ[c]	The cup	ℵ
29.	Unworthily	ℵ[c]	*Omit*	ℵ
	Lord's	ℵ[c]	*Omit*	ℵ
34.	And if	ℵ[c]	If, *omit* "and"	ℵ
xii. 12.	That one body	ℵ[c]	The body	ℵ
xiii. 11.	But	ℵ[c]	*Omit*	ℵ
xiv. 35.	Women	ℵ[c]	A woman	ℵ
xv. 14.	Then *is*	ℵ[c]	Then *is* both	ℵ

[1] ℵ reads simply "here."
[2] ℵ omits the second only.
[3] "Covetous and extortioners," are joined by "and" as belonging to the same category.—*Alford.*
[4] ℵ combines both readings.

References.	AUTHORIZED VERSION.		CRITICAL READINGS.	
1 CORINTHIANS:				
xv. 47.	The Lord	$\aleph^c$	*Omit*	$\aleph$
55.	Grave	[1]	Death	$\aleph$
xvi. 22.	Jesus Christ	$\aleph^c$	*Omit*	$\aleph$
2 CORINTHIANS:				
i. 6, 7.	Or whether we be comforted, *it is* for your consolation and salvation, and our hope of you is steadfast knowing that		And our hope *is* steadfast on your behalf; or whether we be comforted, *it is* for your consolation and salvation knowing that	[2]
12.	Simplicity	$\aleph^c$	Holiness	$\aleph$
18.	Was	$\aleph^c$	Is	$\aleph$
ii. 3.	Unto you	$\aleph^c$	*Omit*	$\aleph$
iii. 17.	There	$\aleph^c$	*Omit*	$\aleph$
v. 5.	Also	$\aleph^c$	*Omit*	$\aleph$
14.	If	$\aleph^c$	*Omit* [3]	$\aleph$
21.	For 1st.	$\aleph^c$	*Omit*	$\aleph$
vii. 12.	Our care for you		Your care for us	[4]
ix. 4.	In this same confident boasting	$\aleph^c$	Of this confidence	$\aleph$
10.	Minister, multiply, increase	$\aleph^c$	Shall minister, shall multiply, shall increase	$\aleph$
x. 8.	Us	$\aleph^c$	*Omit*	$\aleph$
xi. 3.	Simplicity	[5]	Simplicity and chastity	$\aleph$
6.	We have been throughly made manifest among you in all things	$\aleph^c$	To every matter we made *things* manifest before all men unto you	$\aleph$
xii. 1.	It is not expedient for me doubtless to glory	($\aleph$)	Boast I must. It is no advantage	[6]
9.	My strength	$\aleph^c$	*Omit*, my	$\aleph$
19.	Again, think ye that we excuse ourselves unto you?	$\aleph^c$	Ye have been sometime thinking that we are excusing ourselves unto you	$\aleph$
xiii. 14.	Amen	$\aleph^c$	*Omit*	$\aleph$
GALATIANS:				
i. 18.	Peter	$\aleph^c$	Kephas	$\aleph$
iv. 7.	Of God through Christ	$\aleph^c$	Through God	$\aleph$
14.	My temptation	[7]	Your trial	$\aleph$

[1] $\aleph$ omits the verse.

[2] $\aleph$ reads, "whether we be comforted, it is for your consolation which is effectual by the enduring of the same sufferings which we also suffer, and our hope of you," etc.

[3] Denotes "that one died for all, therefore all died."

[4] $\aleph$ reads, "your care for yourselves."

[5] $\aleph^c$ "and chastity" only.

[6] $\aleph^c$ reads, "if it is not expedient."

[7] $\aleph^c$ reads, "the trial" (*i.e.*, omits the pronoun.)

References.	AUTHORIZED VERSION.		CRITICAL READINGS.	
GALATIANS :				
iv. 24.	The two	א	*Omit*	א^c
26.	All	א^c	*Omit*	א
v. 19.	Adultery	א^c	*Omit*	א
vi. 15.	Circumcision availeth	א^c	Is circumcision	א
EPHESIANS :				
i. 1.	Which are at Ephesus and to the faithful	א^c	Who are also faithful	א
10.	Both	א^c	*Omit*	א
18.	And	א^c	*Omit*	א
iii. 14.	Of our Lord Jesus Christ	א^c	*Omit*	א
iv. 9.	First	א^c	*Omit*	א
17.	Other	א^c	*Omit*	א
v. 22.	Submit yourselves		*Omit*	1
23.	And He is	א^c	Himself	א
30.	Of His flesh and of His bones	א^c	*Omit*	א
vi. 10.	My brethren	א^c	*Omit*	א
PHILIPPIANS :				
i. 23.	Which is far	א	For it is far	א^a
iii. 3.	Worship God in the Spirit	א^c	Worship by the Spirit of God	א
16.	Let us walk by the same rule	א^c	Let us walk uniformly	א
	Let us mind the same thing	א^c	*Omit*	א
iv. 13.	Christ	א^c	Him	א
23.	You all	א^c	Your spirit	א
COLOSSIANS :				
i. 7.	For you	א^c	For us	א
10.	In the knowledge	א^c	By the knowledge	א
28.	Jesus	א^c	*Omit*	א
ii. 2.	And of the Father and of Christ	2	*Omit*	
11.	The sins of	א^c	*Omit*	א
13.	Flesh	א^c	*Add*, even you	א
18.	Not	א^c	*Omit*	א
20.	Wherefore	א	*Omit*	א^a
iii. 13.	Christ	א^c	The Lord	3
22.	God	א^c	The Lord	א
iv. 18.	Amen	א^c	*Omit*	א
1 THESSALONIANS :				
ii. 7.	Gentle	א^c	Simple [4]	א
iv. 8.	Hath also given	א^c	Gives	א

[1] א reads "Let the wives be in subjection."
[2] א reads "The Father of Christ;" א^c "God and Father."
[3] א reads "God."
[4] With this reading a *comma* should be placed after "children," and a *colon* after "you."

References.	AUTHORIZED VERSION.		CRITICAL READINGS.	
1 Thessalonians:				
iv. 9.	Ye need not that I	$\aleph$	We have no need to	$\aleph^c$
v. 3.	For	[1]	*Omit*	$\aleph$
21.	Prove	$\aleph$	But prove	$\aleph^c$
27.	Holy	$\aleph^c$	*Omit*	$\aleph$
2 Thessalonians:				
iii. 18.	Amen	$\aleph^c$	*Omit*	$\aleph$
1 Timothy:				
i. 2.	Our Father	$\aleph^c$	The Father	$\aleph$
17.	Wise	$\aleph^c$	*Omit*	$\aleph$
ii. 7.	In Christ	$\aleph$	*Omit*	$\aleph^c$
14.	Being deceived	$\aleph^c$	Having been seduced by deceit	$\aleph$
iii. 16.	God	$\aleph^c$	Who	$\aleph$
iv. 10.	Suffer reproach	$\aleph^c$	Strive	$\aleph$
vi. 7.	*And it is* certain	$\aleph^c$	Because neither	$\aleph$
2 Timothy:				
ii. 12.	We deny	$\aleph^c$	We shall deny	$\aleph$
13.	He cannot	$\aleph^c$	For He cannot	$\aleph$
25.	Will give	$\aleph^c$	May give	$\aleph$
iv. 1.	At	$\aleph^c$	Both by	$\aleph$
22.	Christ	$\aleph^c$	*Omit*	[2]
	Amen	$\aleph^c$	*Omit*	$\aleph$
Titus:				
ij. 5.	Keepers at home	$\aleph^c$	Workers at home	$\aleph$
iii. 15.	Amen	$\aleph^c$	*Omit*	$\aleph$
Philemon:				
10.	My bonds	$\aleph^c$	*Omit*, my	$\aleph$
12.	Again: thou	$\aleph^c$	Again to thee	$\aleph$
	Receive	$\aleph^c$	*Omit* [3]	$\aleph$
Hebrews:				
iii. 9.	Tempted me	$\aleph^c$	*Omit*, me	$\aleph$
	Proved me	$\aleph^c$	By way of trial	$\aleph$
viii. 12.	And their iniquities	$\aleph^c$	*Omit*	$\aleph$
ix. 10.	Washings and	$\aleph^c$	*Omit*, and	$\aleph$
x. 9.	O God	$\aleph^c$	*Omit*	$\aleph$
34.	In yourselves		For yourselves	[4]
	In heaven	$\aleph^c$	*Omit*	$\aleph$
xi. 5.	His translation	$\aleph^c$	The translation	$\aleph$
11.	And was delivered of a child	$\aleph^c$	Even	$\aleph$

[1] $\aleph^c$ reads "ye received."
[2] $\aleph$ reads "the Lord."
[3] The sense is completed in verse 17, "Receive him as myself."
[4] $\aleph$ reads "yourselves" only.

References.	AUTHORIZED VERSION.		CRITICAL READINGS.	
Hebrews:				
xi. 15.	Came out	$\aleph^c$	Went out	$\aleph$
xiii. 18.	We trust	$\aleph^c$	We are persuaded	1
James:				
iii. 12.	So can no fountain both yield salt water and fresh		Neither can salt water produce sweet	2
iv. 4.	Adulterers	$\aleph^c$	*Omit*	$\aleph$
14.	It is		Ye are	3
v. 5.	As	$\aleph^c$	*Omit*	$\aleph$
1 Peter:				
i. 24.	The glory of man	$\aleph^c$	Its glory	4
iii. 21.	The like figure whereunto	5	Which[6] the antitype [of that]	$\aleph^c$
iv. 1.	For us	$\aleph^c$	*Omit*	$\aleph$
19.	*To him* in well doing as unto	7	In well-doings unto	$\aleph^c$
v. 8.	Because	$\aleph^c$	*Omit*	$\aleph$
2 Peter:				
ii. 18.	Clean	$\aleph$	In some degree	$\aleph^c$
22.	But	$\aleph^c$	*Omit*	$\aleph$
1 John:				
ii. 27.	The same anointing	8	His anointing	$\aleph^c$
3 John:				
9.	I wrote	$\aleph^c$	I wrote something	$\aleph$
Jude:				
15.	Among them		*Omit*	9
Revelation:				
i. 9.	Testimony of Jesus Christ *	$\aleph^c$	*Omit*, Christ	$\aleph$
18.	Amen	$\aleph^c$	*Omit*	$\aleph$
ii. 7.	The midst of	$\aleph^c$	*Omit*	$\aleph$
10.	Shall have	($\aleph$)	May have	
13.	Wherein	$\aleph^c$	*Omit*	10
20.	A few things		*Omit*	11
21.	Of her fornication; and she repented not	12	And she willeth not to repent of her fornication	$\aleph^c$
iii. 5.	The same shall	$\aleph^c$	Shall thus	$\aleph$

1 $\aleph$ is defective here.
2 $\aleph$ reads "so neither," etc., as Critical Readings.
3 $\aleph$ omits from "life," to "that."
4 $\aleph$ reads "his glory."
5 $\aleph$ omits the pronoun.
6 *i.e.*, water, not baptism (*Alford.*)
7 $\aleph$ reads "in well doing unto."
8 $\aleph$ reads "spirit" for "anointing."
9 $\aleph$ reads "every soul" for "all that are ungodly among them."
10 $\aleph$ has a manifest mistake here.
11 $\aleph$ reads "much."
12 $\aleph$ reads "this fornication," and omits "and she repented not."

References.	AUTHORIZED VERSION.		CRITICAL READINGS.	
REVELATION:				
iv. 2.	And	($\aleph^{c}$)	*Omit*	ℵ
vi. 1.	And see	(ℵ)	*Omit*	
3.	And see	(ℵ)	*Omit*	
5.	And see	(ℵ)	*Omit*	
7.	And see	(ℵ)	*Omit*	
15.	Every free man	$\aleph^{c}$	*Omit*, every	[1]
vii. 5-8.	Were sealed [10 times]	[2]	*Omit each time*	ℵ
ix. 18.	Three	[3]	Three plagues	ℵ
xi. 1.	And the angel stood	$\aleph^{c}$	*Omit*	ℵ
8.	Our	[4]	Their	$\aleph^{c}$
xii. 17.	Christ	[5]	*Omit*	$\aleph^{c}$
xiii. 6.	And them	$\aleph^{c}$	Those	ℵ
17.	And that	$\aleph^{c}$	*Omit*, and	ℵ
xiv. 8.		[6]		
9.	And the third angel	[7]	And another, a third angel	
xv. 3.	Saints	[8]	The nations	$\aleph^{c}$
xvi. 2.	Upon the earth	[9]	Into the earth	$\aleph^{c}$
3.	Angel	[10]	*Omit*	$\aleph^{c}$
	Died in the sea	(ℵ)	Died—*as respects* the things in the sea	
5.	And shalt be		Holy	[11]
6.	For they are	(ℵ)	*Omit*, for	
17.	Angel	$\aleph^{c}$	*Omit*	ℵ
	Of heaven	[12]	*Omit*	
xvii. 4.	Her fornication		The fornication of the earth	[13]
8.	And yet is	[14]	And shall be present	$\aleph^{c}$
xviii. 13.	Cinnamon	$\aleph^{c}$	Cinnamon and amonium [15]	ℵ
xix. 1.	Salvation, and glory, and honour, and power, unto the Lord our God		The salvation, and glory, and power of our God [16]	$\aleph^{c}$
xx. 9.	From God	$\aleph^{c}$	*Omit*	[17]
xxi. 6.	It is done		They are done	[18]
19.	And the foundations	ℵ	*Omit*, and	$\aleph^{c}$
xxii. 2.	On either side	$\aleph^{c}$	On this side and on that	[19]

[1] ℵ omits "and every free man."
[2] ℵ omits "of the tribe of Gad," "of the tribe of Simeon."
[3] ℵ omits "three."
[4] ℵ omits the pronoun.
[5] ℵ reads "God."
[6] ℵ omits the whole verse.
[7] ℵ reads "another, a second."
[8] ℵ reads "of ages."
[9] ℵ omits from "the first," to "the earth."
[10] ℵ omits "and the second angel poured out."
[11] ℵ reads "the holy one."
[12] ℵ reads "God" for "heaven."
[13] ℵ combines both readings.
[14] ℵ reads "and again shall be present."
[15] A precious ointment used for the hair, and made from an Asiatic Shrub.
[16] ℵ omits "and the glory."
[17] ℵ omits from "fire" to "of fire" in v. 10.
[18] ℵ reads "I have done, I am the Alpha."
[19] ℵ is defective here.